From Cyrus to Alexander

From Cyrus to Alexander

A History of the Persian Empire

PIERRE BRIANT

Translated
by
PETER T. DANIELS

Winona Lake, Indiana
Eisenbrauns
2002

Cataloging in Publication Data

Briant, Pierre.
   [Histoire de l'Empire perse. English]
   From Cyrus to Alexander : a history of the Persian Empire / Pierre
Briant ; translated by Peter T. Daniels.
      p.   cm.
   Includes bibliographical references and index.
   ISBN 1-57506-031-0 (cloth : alk. paper)
   1. Achaemenid dynasty, 559–330 B.C.   2. Iran—History—To 640.
I. Title.

DS281.B7513   2002
935′.01—dc21
                                        2001055736

Et même si ce n'est pas vrai,
Il faut croire à l'histoire ancienne.

> [And even if it is not true,
> you need to believe in ancient history.]

LÉO FERRÉ

Il est difficile de savoir si une interprétation
donnée est vraie, il est en revanche plus facile de
reconnaître les mauvaises.

> [It is difficult to know whether any particular
> interpretation is correct—the bad ones are so
> much easier to identify.]

UMBERTO ECO

for Charles and Marguerite

Contents

PART 1
THE EMPIRE-BUILDERS: FROM CYRUS TO DARIUS

PART 4
FROM XERXES TO DARIUS III: AN EMPIRE IN TURMOIL

List of Illustrations

Preface to the English Translation

The text of the book that is presented here to English-speaking readers differs very little from the French edition published by Éditions Fayard in June, 1996. Yet during the first stage in the process of translation, in the late 1996 and early 1997, I had hoped to make systematic modifications and additions to the original text in a way that took account of publications which had appeared after the latest revisions to the French manuscript, in September 1995.[1] A succession of delays in the preparation of the American translation dissuaded me from carrying out this enterprise, and here I would like to explain my decision to my readers.[2]

I have chosen to present updates and very detailed assessments of research in another form, the *Bulletin d'Histoire Achéménide* (*BHAch*), organized in a way that follows the thematic structure of my book. Its aim is to give scholars periodic opportunities not only to become acquainted with recent bibliography, but also to have a critical analysis of it. The first number (*BHAch* I) took the form of a long article published in Supplément 1 to the journal *Topoi* (1997, pp. 5–127).[3] In it, I analyzed about 450 titles (articles and books) published between October 1995 and October 1997. The second *Bulletin* (*BHAch* II) appeared in 2001, in book form.[4] Following the same plan, I analyzed more than 800 titles published between October 1997 and October 2000. To make it easier to use, *BHAch* II is accompanied by indexes which also cover the material in *BHAch* I. One of those indexes (pp. 327–30) makes it possible for readers to find the pages in my 1996 book that need to be revised in the light of new publications. Furthermore, the recent creation of a website specifically devoted to Achaemenid research

---

1. I point out that Ursula Weber and Josef Wiesehöfer have brought out an enormous Achaemenid bibliography,exhaustive and minutely classified (*Das Reich der Achaimeniden: Eine Bibliographie* (AMI, Ergänzungsband 15; Berlin: Dietrich Reimer, 1996).

2. A single significant addition has been made in the part of Chapter 9 devoted to customs and exchange: I have introduced an extraordinary document dealing with customs in Egypt, drawing on the main expositions and conclusions of the study by myself and R. Descat, "Un registre douanier de la satrapie d'Égypte," in N. Grimal and B. Menu, eds., *La commerce en Égypte ancienne* (IFAO Bibliothèque d'Études 121; Cairo, 1998) 59–104. Subsequently, I decided to stop introducing new material and discussion.

3. Supplément 1 to *Topoi* (distributed by Boccard, in Paris) included papers from a meeting organized at the Maison de l'Orient (Lyon), March 31–April 1, 1997, published under the title *Recherches récentes sur l'empire achéménide*. Almost twenty colleagues from various countries responded to an invitation from Jean-François Salles and Marie-Françoise Boussac to discuss my book, at that time newly published by Fayard.

4. *Bulletin d'Histoire Achéménide* II (Paris: Éditions Thotm, 2001), 334 pp. (see http://www.thotm-editions.com/editions/bhachII02.htm). This volume inaugurates a new series, *Persika*, undertaken on the initiative of the "Chaire d'histoire et de civilisation du monde achéménide et de l'empire d'Alexandre" with the cooperation of the Collège de France.

(www.achemenet.com) also gives scholars access to documentary and bibliographic resources on a continuing basis.[5]

I have discussed one of the methodological questions raised by a systematic update, a question that is not limited to Achaemenid studies, in the "Noruz Lecture" presented at the Foundation for Iranian Studies (Washington, D.C., March 23, 2001) under the title "New Trends in Achaemenid History."[6] There, with reference to the updates in *BHAch* I and II, I stated:

> When one strives to follow and evaluate research and publication on a day-to-day basis and in an exhaustive manner, one unavoidably develops a permanent habit of painful epistemological questioning of the real results of the research. This question is particularly difficult to resolve in the Humanities, where accumulated erudition and bibliographic tautology sometimes take the place of evidence that is accepted but misleading for scientific innovation. To speak bluntly: what is really *new* in what is published *recently*? In our domain, what are the signs that permit us to assert that this or that study marks *progress* in the order of knowledge? The answer may seem easy as long as one is dealing with publications of documents, but it is quite a different matter when one considers interpretive publications. And even among publications of documents one has to make distinctions: some of them add only one unpublished document in a series that is already known, without modifying the general sense by much; others, on the other hand, call attention to documentation that in itself may suggest wholly new lines of interpretation.

Then, after presenting results from excavations at Ayn Manâwir in Egypt, I concluded:

> In this respect, the discoveries and publications on Achaemenid Egypt that I have presented in brief are not just *recent*, they are really *new*, and they open prospects of fundamental new growth in the near future.

My point is that a thorough updating cannot be brought about in a satisfactory manner only with hundreds of bibliographic additions, heaped up one on the other. As publications accumulate, so the risk increases of burdening the text and the bibliographic notes with updates superimposed over one another, and of making the text more difficult to consult rather than more useful. Furthermore, in such a case the appearance of exhaustiveness would be largely an illusion, for two reasons. First, any book, however up-to-date its bibliography may be, is subject to some bibliographic lapse by the time it has appeared.[7] Furthermore, as I have indicated, many added references really add

---

5. The creation of this web site also responds to purposes specific to the overall framework of Achaemenid history, that is, an aim to transform what has been a virtual scientific community into an actual scientific community: see my "Call for Collaboration" (Paris, 2000), available for downloading at http://www.achement.com/pdf/call.pdf, as well as the proceedings of a colloquium that I organized at the Collège de France, Dec. 15–16, 2000, "Achaemenid History and Data Bases on the Internet: an Assessment of Work in Progress and Prospects for Future Developments," available at http://www. achemenet.com/pdf/colloque/resumes.pdf. With the agreement of the editors of *Topoi*, the entire text of *BHAch* I can be found on the site at http://www.achemenet.com/bibliographies/bhach1.htm.

6. An English version is available at http://www.fis-iran.org/achemenid.htm; the French text is available at http://ww.achemenet.com/ressources/enligne/jasr/jasr01/htm under the title "L'histoire de l'empire achéménide aujourd'hui: nouvelles tendances, nouvelles perspectives."

7. By way of example, I may mention that as I write this preface, in early July, 2001, the provisional bibliographic list for *BHAch* III (which is intended to appear in 2003) already includes more than 150 titles, including some important books and articles.

nothing new, so it would be necessary to introduce a clear hierarchical distinction between "recent" and "new," and to justify in detail the criteria for selection—precisely as I tried to do in my *Bulletins* of 1997 and 2001.

All this being so, I freely admit that taking into account the most innovative publications that appeared between 1995 and 2000 would make it possible to amend and detail many of the discussions in this book and to enrich significantly the iconographic documentation. If I have chosen nonetheless to present the American version practically in the same form as the initial French book, it is also because I have judged—whether rightly or wrongly the reader may decide—that the general image of the Achaemenid Empire that I expounded in 1996 has not been fundamentally modified.

Consider a particularly significant example, Chapter 16, in which I present a regional analysis of the empire and attempt an interpretation of relations between center and periphery, in the form of a prospective assessment (pp. 693ff.). The point of view that I adopt and defend there is that the documents discovered between about 1970 and 1995 put in serious doubt the "(pseudo-)statistical hypothesis of a scanty Persian presence and an inconsequential imperial occupation, based on bodies of evidence that are obsolete or reduced to a regional perspective" (p. 764). For this purpose, in the corresponding documentary notes (pp. 1029–1031) I present an assessment of recent discoveries, region by region. On the face of it, this section should be rewritten, since many new discoveries made available since 1995 ought to be included. But even if some discoveries treated in the 1996 version of the text remain under discussion,[8] I believe that overall the documents published between 1995 and 2000 tend rather to confirm the historical interpretation that I presented in the book, whether in the matter of the maintenance of organic links between central authority and the provinces,[9] or in the matter of the policy adopted toward local or national sanctuaries, or in the matter of the spread and adaptation of Persian imagery in various countries,[10] or even in the matter of the economic condition of the empire at the arrival of Alexander.[11] At the same time, wherever one or another interpretation has given rise to reservations and/or polemics, the reader can easily come to grips with it by consulting *BHAch* I and II and the indexes of *BHAch* II.[12]

---

8. For example, concerning the interpretation of the Elamite tablets found in Armenia (French edition, pp. 962–63; below p. 938), see the treatments discussed in *BHAch* I, 25 and *BHAch* II, 44. The discussion is obviously not closed.

9. To take only one example, the discovery of settlements, qanats, and hundreds of demotic documents dated to the reigns of Artaxerxes I and Darius II at the site of Ayn Manâwir is particularly striking (see most recently *BIFAO* 100 [2000], 469–79, as well as the description of the work by Michel Wuttmann at http://www.achemenet.com/recherche/sites/aynmanawir/aynmanawir.htm, and my remarks in *BHAch* I, 32–34 and 88–90, and II, 62, and in *Annales* 1999/5, 1130–35). The new discoveries tend to support the position that I took on pp. 520 and 1006–08 on the maintenance of links between the center and the Egyptian province throughout the fifth century B.C.

10. On these topics, to which I return at various points in the book, see now the specific treatments in *BHAch* I, 94–97, II, 176–184 (on religious policy), and I, 98–104, II, 911–206 (on the spread of images).

11. The discovery of a network of qanats at Ayn Manâwir also contributes to the discussion on pp. 000–000 about the relationship between the levying of tribute and investments in production, that is, about the economic rationality of the Achaemenid imperial system; see the studies collected in Pierre Briant, ed., *Irrigation et drainage dans l'Antiquité: qanats et canalisations souterraines en Iran, en Égypte et en Grèce* (Collection Persika 2; Paris: Éditions Thotm, 2001).

12. See especially *BHAch* II , 327–31: "Index des discussions."

In short, in order to be full and effective, a revision would have to be carried out on a strategy that is both selective and synthetic. But to do so would involve no more or less than writing a new book, or at least a fundamentally altered book.[13] That is not the purpose of the American translation made available today. The purpose is simply to put before English-speaking readers a book that was published in French five years ago. My book of 1996 represents a state-of-the-question , valid at a given moment, of the work carried out by many scholars, as well as a the state of my own historical reflections. Readers of the French edition and of the American edition can easily avail themselves of the several reviews published since the appearance of the *Histoire de l'empire perse* in 1996.[14] And if they want to know about the development of the author's thought, including his *pentimenti*, they can also consult the bibliographic tools that I have made available, as well as the updates that I have published, both on primary documents[15] and on problems of historiography and method.[16] I have no doubt that readers will be able to dispute the theses and interpretations of this book on the basis of their own thinking, but also in the light of publications that are recent and sometimes even publications that are new.

Paris, July 7, 2001

---

13. This is the consideration that eventually dissuaded me from introducing new and important iconographic documents that can be found with reproductions and commentaries in *BHAch* I (pp. 11, 16, 18, 21f., 26f., 34, 41, 67, 69, 74, 101) and *BHAch* II (pp. 34, 36, 40f., 43, 45, 47f., 58, 60l, 64, 69, 76, 110f., 116, 192, 195f., 198f., 202f., 205), though it would be technically simple to do so. The main and indispensable correction to illustrations in the French publication consists of adding to the list of illustrations (pp. xiff.) an indication of the source of the drawings reproduced here, unfortunately forgotten in the page proofs of the 1996 French version.

14. A list can be found in *BHAch* II, 9 n. 8. As usual, some are merely descriptive, while others present a deeper consideration of Achaemenid history today (see especially Matthew Stolper, "Une 'vision dure' de l'histoire achéménide (Note critique)," *Annales* 1999/5: 1109–26).

15. In particular, I have published drastic revisions of some Greek inscriptions pertinent to Achaemenid history, namely the inscription of Droaphernes and the Xanthus Trilingual in two articles published in 1998 ("Droaphernès et la statue de Sardes," in M. Brosius and A. Kuhrt, eds., *Studies in Persian History: Essays in Memory of David M. Lewis*, Achaemenid History, 11 (Leiden), 205–26; "Cités et satrapes dan l'Empire achéménide: Pixôdaros et Xanthos," *CRAI*: 305–40) and the letter of Darius to Gadatas in a study in press (available in pre-publication form at http://www.achemenet.com/ressources/souspresse/manuscrits01.htm). In the latter article I concluded that the document is a falsification, of Roman date, and I therefore propose that it should be eliminated from discussions of Achaemenid history. Given that this is one of the most celebrated documents in Achaemenid historiography, it is also one of the texts most frequently cited in my book (see the index, p. 000, s.v. ML 12). This last example shows clearly how difficult it would have been to patch up the original text in a satisfactory manner.

16. For example: "The Achaemenid Empire," in K. Raaflaub and N. Rosenstein, eds., *Soldiers, Society and War in the Ancient and Medieval Worlds* (Cambridge: Harvard University Press, 1998) 105–28; "L'histoire de l'empire achéménide aujourd'hui: l'historien et ses documents," *Annales* 1999/5, 1127–36; "Inscriptions multilingues d'époque achéménide: le texte et l'image," in D. Valbelle and J. Leclant, eds., *Le décret de Memphis* (Actes du Colloque de la Fondation Singer-Polignac, Paris 1er Juin 1999) (Paris: de Boccard, 2000), 91–115; "Histoire impériale et histoire régionale. À propos de l'histoire de Juda dans l'Empire achéménide,"in A. Lemaire and N. Saboe, eds., *Congress Volume Oslo 1998* (VT Suppl. 80; 2000) 235–45; "Darius III face à Alexandre: mythe, histoire, légende," *Annuaire du Collège de France, Résumé des cours et conférences 1999–2000* (Paris, 2000) 781–92 (also available at http://www.college-de-france.fr/college/annuaire-scientifique/cours99–2000/briant/briant.pdf); *Leçon inaugurale au Collège de France* (Paris, 2000).

Translator's Preface

What stretches before the reader is an almost exact equivalent of the 1996 French edition. This is not according to the original plan; the American edition was to incorporate the author's corrections, revisions, and additions reflecting subsequent Achaemenid research. With one exception, however, no supplementary material was received (for reasons described by the author above)—the exception being the discussion of the Aramaic customs document from Egypt discussed in chap. 9/3 (pp. 385–387). The author's bracketed added passages in the Research Notes, which were to be revised into the text, are marked with ⟦double brackets⟧. Numbering of figures and maps in the original was somewhat erratic, so it diverges here.

This is not to say there is *no* difference; hundreds of Classical references have been corrected. Given worlds enough and time, many corrections could also have been made to the citations of the contemporary literature. In order to avoid as much as possible the pitfalls of indirect renderings, quotations from ancient sources have, when possible, been taken from published English translations (the mark ✧ appears in the reference for each such passage), rather than translated from the author's French renderings (forms of names in published translations have not been regularized. Only in a few cases, where the two versions are completely irreconcilable (or where the citation could not be matched with published translations), has a translation of the author's version been made.

The sources used are the following:

Classical

Aelian, *Historical Miscellany*, trans. N. G. Wilson (Loeb Classical Library [LCL], 1997)

Aristotle, *The Complete Works*, the Oxford translations revised by Jonathan Barnes (Bollingen edition, 1984)

Arrian, *Anabasis of Alexander* and *Indica*, trans. P. A. Blunt (LCL, 1976–83)

Athenaeus, *The Deipnosophists*, trans. Charles Burton Gulick (LCL, 1928–33)

Demosthenes, trans. unnamed, intro. by John Harrington (Everyman, [1954])

Diodorus Siculus, *Library of History*, trans. C. H. Oldfather, Charles L. Sherman, C. Bradford Welles, Russel M. Geer, and F. R. Walton (LCL, 1933–67)

Herodotus, *The Histories*, trans. Aubrey de Sélincourt (Penguin, 1954; rev. ed. John Marincola, 1996)

Isocrates, trans. George Norton (LCL, 1928)

Josephus, *The Life: Against Apion*, trans. H. St. J. Thackeray; *The Jewish War*, trans. H. St. J. Thackeray; *Jewish Antiquities*, trans. H. St. J. Thackeray et al. (LCL, 1926–65 [13 vols.])

C. Nepos, trans. John C. Rolfe (LCL, 1984)

Pausanius, *Description of Greece*, trans. W. H. S. Jones, H. A. Ormered, and (arranged by) R. E. Wycherley (LCL, 1918–35 [5 vols.])

Plato, *Complete Works*, various translators, ed. John M. Cooper (Hackett edition, 1997)

Plutarch: *Lives*, trans. John Dryden, rev. Arthur Hugh Clough (Modern Library, undated repr. of 1864 ed.); *Moralia*, trans. Frank Cole Babbitt (LCL, 1931–36 [vols. 3–4])

Polyaenus, *Stratagems of War*, trans. R. Shepherd (Chicago: Ares, 1974).

Polybius, *The Histories*, trans. W. R. Paton (LCL, 1922–27) [6 vols.])

Quintus Curtius, *History of Alexander*, trans. John C. Rolfe (LCL, 1946)

Strabo, *The Geography*, trans. Horace Leonard Jones (LCL, 1928–30 [vols. 5–7])

Thucydides, *The Peleponnesian War*, trans. Crawley (Modern Library, 1951 repr. of undated trans.)

Xenophon, *Hellenica* and *Anabasis*, trans. Carleton L. Brownson; *Oeconomicus* and *Scripta Minora*, trans. E. C. Marchant; *Cyropaedia*, trans. Walter Miller [some citations, trans. H. G. Dakyns (Everyman, 1992 repr. of 1914 ed.)] (LCL, 1914–25)

The principal ancient sources for which no English edition was available to me are Ctesias and Justin.

Oriental

Aramaic from Egypt: A. Cowley, *Aramaic Papyri of the 5th Century* B.C. (1923) [AP]; G. R. Driver, *Aramaic Documents of the Fifth Century* B.C. (2d ed., 1957) [AD]; Emil G. Kraeling, *The Brooklyn Museum Aramaic Papyri* (1953) [BMAP]

Berossus: S. A. Burstein, *The Babyloniaca of Berossus* (1978)

Old Persian, Roland G. Kent, *Old Persian: Grammar Texts Lexicon* (2d ed., 1953)

Biblical

Jerusalem Bible

I would like to express my gratitude to Larissa Bonfante, Professor of Classics at New York University, who provided access to many of the editions listed above; to Maureen Gallery Kovacs and Matthew W. Stolper for help with technical terminology, especially in numismatics and ancient economy and society respectively; and to sundry contributors to the newsgroup sci.lang for discussing some obscure French terminology. I have scrupulously maintained the author's distinctions between *ville* and *cité* ('town' and 'city'; see p. 377), and between *sanctuaire* and *temple*, at his request.

I am also especially grateful to my friend and publisher Jim Eisenbraun for commissioning this project in July 1996; after the French publisher's approval of the submitted specimen, translating began at the very end of that year and proceed during, roughly, the first halves of 1997, 1998, 2000, and 2001. Jim and his editorial staff made many improvements in the English style and French renderings; and Jim as book designer has as usual created a look that is both elegant and practical.

After not too many pages, the reader will discover that this is not a connected narrative history of the Persian Empire. Moreover, the reader is expected to be familiar with the narrative sequence of Achaemenid history, with the career of Alexander the Great, and with the entire Greek and Latin literature from which such histories have hitherto been drawn. The reader might find it useful to first turn to Joseph Wiesehöfer, *Ancient Persia* (English translation, 1996) 1–101, for an overview that is thematically and conceptually remarkably similar to this work, and to the Chronological Chart therein for the sequence of events, as far as they can be determined. Only then, I think, can this book (whose aim, superbly realized, is to show just how a historian must evaluate and extrapolate from the available sources) be used with profit.

Clearly, this massive work represents only the first monument along the new highway through the crossroads of the ancient world.

Peter T. Daniels
New York City, March 2002

Introduction

On the Trail of an Empire

1. Was There an Achaemenid Empire?

The Achaemenid Empire: created by the conquests of Cyrus (ca. 559–530) and Cambyses (530–522) on the rubble and the fertile ground of the various kingdoms of the Near East, then expanded and reorganized by Darius I (522–486), for more than two centuries it extended from the Indus Valley to the Aegean Sea, from the Syr Darya to the Persian Gulf and the first cataract of the Nile—until the moment Darius III perished in a conspiracy, when his nemesis Alexander had already completed his conquest (330). The ordinary word *Empire*, as is well known, has no exact correspondence in any ancient language: the inscriptions of the Great Kings refer both to the land (Old Persian *būmi*) and to the peoples (Old Persian *dahyu/dahyāva*), and the Greek authors speak of 'royal territories' (*khōra basileōs*), of the 'power' (*arkhē*) of the Great King and his satraps, or again of "kings, dynasties, cities, and peoples." The term *Empire* implies a territorial authority. This is in fact the basic problem posed by the origin and construction of the Achaemenid Empire. Marked by extraordinary ethnocultural diversity and by a thriving variety of forms of local organization, it evokes two interpretations: one that sees it as a sort of loose federation of autonomous countries under the distant aegis of a Great King, a federation that is evident solely from the perspective of tribute levies and military conscriptions; and another that without rejecting the evidence of diversity emphasizes the organizational dynamic of the many sorts of intervention by the central authority and the intense processes of acculturation. The direction in which my own preferences tend can be discerned even from this formulation of the problem—I will explain myself along the way. This in a nutshell is the aim of this book, which I now offer for the appraisal of my readers.

2. From Alexander to Cyrus and Back Again:
Fragments of ego-histoire

This book was imprudently announced in a 1979 article but written between spring 1990 and spring 1993. I made limited revisions to the text and revised the Research Notes substantially in 1994 and 1995. But the conception and realization of the book, if only in a preliminary and preparatory form, goes back at least fifteen years, since it was in about 1982–83 that I began to jot down for myself the initial drafts, sketches, and plans that are now relegated to dead files. By way of a contribution to a genre that is fashionable (at least in France), *ego-histoire*, and coming straight out of the introduction I wrote in 1982 for my collection of articles (*RTP*), I would like to explain this book's origins in a personal way.

Nothing predisposed me to devoting the greater part of my life to researching and teaching Achaemenid history. When I was a historian-in-training, stirred by ancient history during my studies at Poitiers, it was almost by chance, or more exactly because of a comment by H. Bengtson, that I began to take an interest in one of the successors of Al-exander, the former satrap of Greater Phrygia, Antigonus the One-Eyed. That interest took shape as a thesis prepared under the supervision of Pierre Lévêque. A well-known passage in *Life of Eumenes* (5.9–10) regarding the machinations of Antigonus's oppo-nent in the environs of Celaenae, capital of Greater Phrygia, led me to ask questions about the status of the land and the peasants at the very beginning of the Hellenistic pe-riod—investigations that I developed into an article about these peasants (*laoi*) of Asia Minor (1972). The first step had been taken: I had settled on the Near East (Asia, as I called it then, following the Greek authors), but a Near East revisited by Greco-Mace-donian armies and by ancient and modern colonial historiography.

The preparation of a long article on Eumenes of Cardia (1972–73) and of a small book on Alexander (1st ed., 1974) quickly convinced me of the need to go further back in time. Just what was this Achaemenid Empire, which was perennially accused of deca-dence without being put in its historical context? I had always been struck by the fact that certain overeager epigones, following Droysen (who deserved less dogmatic disciples), insisted unequivocally that the Macedonian conquest had shaken up the political, eco-nomic, and cultural structures of "Asia" from top to bottom; but, at the same time, what came before Alexander was never defined except as a foil to what came after. These in-quiries led me to take as my first object of study the populations of the Zagros, whom the ancient authors presented as brigands who were unconcerned with agriculture and therefore "naturally" aggressive (1976). I came to realize with more and more conviction that our entire view of the Achaemenid Empire and its populations was corrupted by the distortions perpetrated by the ancient historians of Alexander. At the same time, it seemed to me equally evident that the historian could not avoid recourse to these same sources. I continued to plow this furrow for several years, and to some extent this book is intended as a contribution toward answering an ancient question: why did the Achaeme-nid Empire fall to the blow of Macedonian aggression?

But the chosen title is not simply a reflection of this veritable obsession or, if I may say so, of this long "quest for the Holy Grail." It is also meant to express a long-held and long-nourished conviction: Alexander and his successors took over much of the Achaemenid system, a conclusion that I have often expressed with the formula "Alexander, last of the Achaemenids." Like any formula, this one has its limits and gives rise to contradictions of its own. Yet when all is said and done, it seems to me all the same to express the ex-traordinary continuities that characterize the history of the Near East between the con-quests of Cyrus and the death of Alexander. Heinz Kreissig, from whom I have learned a great deal, used the phrase "orientalischer hellenistischer Staaten" to describe this con-tinuity. The Seleucid kingdom was in his eyes an obvious manifestation of it. The word *continuity* should not be misleading: it is not meant to deny the accommodations and adaptations brought about by the Macedonian conquest. But, at the same time, recent research makes it ever clearer, for example, that the Seleucid empire, in its origin and its constituent elements, was a branch grafted directly onto Achaemenid stock.

During the 1970s, and still more at the beginning of the 1980s, the realization dawned on me more and more clearly that, however indispensible the Classical sources were, they could not by themselves answer the questions I was asking. I needed to pene-trate the Achaemenid essence more intimately, a task for which I was not at all prepared. Luckily, I had already had some decisive encounters. First, Roman Ghirshman, who around 1972 had strongly encouraged me to plow my Achaemenid furrow: I could never forget the generous concern he showed me without fail until his death in 1979. Around 1977 (if I remember correctly), I made contact with Clarisse Herrenschmidt, who, if I may say so, "initiated" me into the royal Achaemenid inscriptions. During the 1970s, I also struck up contacts that have continued uninterrupted ever since with the Italian group led by Mario Liverani and sustained by his work and the work of his students: Mario Fales, Lucio Milano, and Carlo Zaccagnini, with whom I shared and still share thematic interests and conceptual approaches. The conversations that I have continued to have with them, as lively as they are frequent, have helped me put the Achaemenid case in the broader context of first-millennium Near Eastern history, and thus better to take into account the Assyro-Babylonian heritage in the structures of the Achaemenid Empire.

It was around 1977–78 that Jean-Claude Gardin, who was then leading explorations around the Hellenistic town of Ai-Khanūm in Afghanistan, invited me to join his team. He had invited me to participate in their discussions as a historian and to contrast the textual record and the archaeological record. Though I was not able to take part in the fieldwork (soon interrupted for reasons known to everyone), I learned about the tremendous contribution of archaeology and also about the interpretive challenges that it poses for the historian more familiar with a text of Arrian than with the "trash cans" full of sherds. This collaboration led me to publish a book in 1984 on the relationship between Central Asia and the kingdoms of the Near East, situated first and foremost in the context of Achaemenid history. The debate, which I was able to pursue thereafter, was extremely rich in ensuing discussions. The reader will observe in due course that disagreements among us persist. The methodological problem remains: how can we reconcile the archaeological picture and the textual picture, which seem to engender two different conceptualizations of the Achaemenid Empire? It will also be seen that this debate is not limited to the local context of Bactria.

During the second half of the 1970s, when I had finished my study of the "brigands" of the ancient Zagros, I also had frequent exchanges with anthropologists who specialized in pastoral nomadism, in particular with Jean-Pierre Digard, whose Bakhtiaris were contiguous with "my" Uxians. This collaboration, pursued over several years, led to the writing of a book on the anthropology and history of the pastoral peoples of the Near East (1982b). It also touched on the problem of relations between center and periphery both in the Achaemenid Empire and in its Assyro-Babylonian predecessors and its Hellenistic successors.

In my intellectual history, the year 1983 is marked with a gold star. It was then that I participated for the first time in an Achaemenid Workshop at Groningen, at the invitation of Heleen Sancisi-Weerdenburg, who, soon joined by Amélie Kuhrt, had launched a series that was to continue until 1990 in Ann Arbor (there in collaboration with Margaret Root). For the first time, I felt that I was not working alone, self-taught concerning the subject matter of my main objective. Now I could join the "Achaemenidist community," which, small in number, offers the inestimable advantage of being international and linked by bonds of friendship. I could then carry on discussions more systematically on a historical problem clearly posed by the organizers and on a corpus of evidence as varied as were the components of the Empire. The numerous relationships that I was able to form during and outside these meetings were crucial for me. The initiative of

Heleen Sancisi-Weerdenburg and Amélie Kuhrt gave a radically new impetus to Achaemenid research. On the model of the Achaemenid Workshops, Clarisse Herrenschmidt and I organized a conference on tribute in the Persian Empire; Pierre Debord, Raymond Descat, and the administration of the Centre Georges-Radet of Bordeaux set up two meetings, one on Asia Minor and one on monetary problems; Jean Kellens organized a colloquium at Liège dedicated to Persian religion; Josette Elayi and Jean Sapin organized three meetings on Syria–Palestine under the dominion of the Great Kings; and I organized a conference at Toulouse on the *Anabasis* of Xenophon, the proceedings of which have now been published (1995b). In short, the Groningen initiative set in motion intense scholarly activity and a sizable output of first-rate articles, whose regular publication in the series *Achaemenid History* as well as in many journals fostered and stimulated discussion and debate periodically—to such an extent that the exponential growth of the bibliography sometimes gave me a feeling of powerlessness and discouragement. As much as this book may be very personal work, it also reflects (or is meant to reflect) the richness and productivity of a field of research that had long remained partially fallow. In using this expression, I do not mean to minimize the importance or the scope of the work that the history of ancient Iran evoked over a long period and that I have carefully taken into account. What I want to say is simply that, taken in its entirety and not reduced to the study of a few major sites (Susa, Persepolis, Pasargadae), and despite the attempt at synthesis by Olmstead in 1948 that continues to deserve our respect, the history of the Achaemenid Empire remained largely *terrra incognita*. It had been abandoned both by Assyriologists (for whom the fall of Babylon to Cyrus in 539 long marked the end of history) and by Classicists (who "kidnapped" Near Eastern history as of Alexander's landing in Asia in 334). In a way, squeezed between "eternal Greece" and "the millennial Orient," tossed between Hellenocentrism (from Aeschylus to Alexander) and Judeocentrism (Cyrus refracted through the prism of the Return from the Exile), Achaemenid history did not exist as a distinct field of study. The initiative of Heleen Sancisi-Weerdenburg and Amélie Kuhrt thus brought Achaemenid studies securely back within the field of history, the way marked out by a set of problems whose terms and stakes I recognized all the more easily because I had begun to try to define them on my own.

There remains one aspect of my *ego-histoire* that I would like to broach quite frankly, as I have done on several occasions now and then in the last few years in publications and private conversations with colleagues and with students. The written sources for Achaemenid history are found in an extraordinary variety of languages: Old Persian, Elamite, Babylonian, Egyptian, Aramaic, Hebrew, Phoenician, Greek, and Latin, not to mention Lydian, Lycian, Phrygian, Carian, or any other yet-to-be-deciphered language. I must state at the outset that in no way am I a specialist in any of these languages. I can barely claim competence in Greek and Latin. This might be thought an insurmountable handicap. But though the term *handicap* expresses a reality that is beyond question, I do not think that the adjective *insurmountable* should be taken literally. To justify this position, I need to explain my working method. First of all, there are accessible translations of the basic texts, whether the royal inscriptions, selected Elamite tablets, Aramaic documents from Egypt or elsewhere, a certain number of Babylonian tablets, or hieroglyphic inscriptions—to give only a sampling of the available resources. But to use the texts in translation is not enough. It is necessary to turn to the original texts, at least the most important of them. Many documents that have been published in transliteration can be put to this use. There even a self-taught historian is able to identify what I will call the landmark words or the key words that give the text its sense. At this point one must turn to an exhaustive study of the philological literature, however difficult it may be. This is what I have tried to do, as systematically as I could. That is why, here and there, I have allowed myself to enter discussions and debates that in principle my linguistic and philological ignorance should prohibit me from approaching. From time to time I may propose that the historian's suggestions provide independent confirmation of a philological interpretation. And then, when a problem appeared that I found insoluble, I often have had recourse to the advice and counsel of friends and colleagues, who have not been stingy with their wisdom. How many e-mail messages have I exchanged with Matt Stolper, for example, about Babylonian tablets of the Achaemenid era? It should be clearly understood that I am obviously not endorsing ignorance. I cannot fail to recognize the limits of self-instruction. It would be a miracle to possess simultaneously a historian's training and immediate access to all the languages of the Empire. Unfortunately, as far as I know, such a rare bird does not exist—at any rate, neither my warble nor my plumage permits me to claim such a distinction!

In spite of all the precautions I have deployed, I still recognize the risks I have assumed in offering a book that—legitimately or not—claims to be exhaustive. As a result of my own failings, of unequal access to the corpora of documents, of the persistent and increasing breadth of the debates, or even of the uneven progress of thematic and regional studies, the word *exhaustive* can provoke confusion or laughter. The problem is that, from the moment I began this undertaking, I was stuck with a sort of encyclopedism, with all the risks and illusions that go with such an approach. I did not have the liberty of sidestepping some discussion or other, out of my own interest in this or that question, or out of my own limited familiarity with this or that corpus. A work of synthesis of this kind necessarily requires that the author tackle every aspect and component, whether political, ideological, socioeconomic, religious, cultural, etc., and attempt to integrate them, insofar as it is possible, into a general interpretation. I have thus had to consult all the dossiers of evidence, but I have also had to leave them only half-explored. In some areas, the breadth and complexity (not to mention the contradictions) of the discussions among specialists in this or that corpus has not resulted in well-defined positions on my part (I have in mind, inter alia, the exegetical and historical disputes about Ezra and Nehemiah). On the other hand, the reader will find, at least in the Research Notes, a "state-of-the-art"—that is, not just a bibliography but also and especially the reasons for the differing interpretations. In other cases, I have taken a firmer position and proposed my own interpretations. I hope that this book will thus give rise to new specialized investigations, which will, without doubt, reopen discussion on many interpretations that I have often presented in the explicit form of alternative suggestions.

3. *The Historian and His Evidence*

One of the most remarkable peculiarities of Achaemenid history is that, unlike most conquering peoples, the Persians left no written testaments of their own history, in the *narrative* sense of the word. It is noteworthy that unlike the Assyrian kings, the Great Kings had no Annals prepared where the memory of their mighty deeds on the battlefield or in the hunt could be made heroic and preserved. We have no chronicle prepared by a court scholar at the command of the Great Kings. To be sure, according to Diodorus (II.32.4), Ctesias—a Greek physician in the court of Artaxerxes II, author of a *Persica*—boasted of having had access to "the royal records (*basilikai diphtherai*), in which the Persians in accordance with a certain law (*nomos*) of theirs kept an account of their ancient affairs." However, there is not another shred of evidence of such Persian historical archives, aside from a late and suspect tradition that attributes their destruction to Alexander. The archives referred to by the editor of Ezra (6:1–2), for example, were, rather, administrative. In these satrapal and/or royal archives (*basilikai graphai*; *karammaru ša šarri*) is preserved the written record of the most important decisions (land grants and reassignments, for example, and also fiscal documents). It is perhaps to such documents (found in several satrapal and/or imperial capitals) that Herodotus had access in composing his well-known tribute list, but it is not out of the question that the historian from Halicarnassus collected his administrative data himself in interviews, a method mentioned on many occasions in his work. It is far more likely that at least in the *Persica* Ctesias relied on oral testimony, as explained by his epitomizer, Photius (*Persica*, §1). This is certainly how Herodotus, Ctesias, and several other Greek authors heard and retransmitted the different versions of the legend of the founder, Cyrus. The edifying tales of royal virtues were diffused throughout the Empire from the point of view of "educated people" (cf. Diodorus II.4.2); hence the interest that attaches, for example, to the Achaemenid tales told by a late author, Aelian, who clearly takes his information from Herodotus himself or from courtiers like Ctesias. From this point of view, the most striking example is a passage in which Polybius (X.28) transmits in writing an Achaemenid administrative datum of the greatest interest that the Hyrcanian peasants had preserved in their collective memory for generations. By a series of extraordinary coincidences, a royal archivist or memoirist happened to be present when, at the demand of Antiochus III, the heads of the Hyrcanian communities recounted the privileges they had enjoyed since the time "when the Persians were the masters of Asia." It must be stressed that the information would have been totally lost if it had not had immediate relevance in the course of a military expedition mounted by the Seleucid king in Central Asia. Polybius found the report in a work that is now lost.

We dare not underestimate the importance of oral tradition in the lands of the Near East. It was in oral form, in songs and recitations, mediated by the "masters of truth," the *magi*, that the Persians themselves transmitted the deeds of their kings and the memory of mythic heroes from generation to generation, and the young in their turn became the repositories of these oral traditions. In the collective imagination of the Persian people, history was conflated with its mythic expression and, in the royal pronouncements, with the genealogy of the dynasty. With the partial exception of the monumental trilingual inscription that Darius had engraved on the cliff at Behistun, the royal inscriptions are not narrative accounts: there is not a single direct reference to conquests or military expeditions in them. Rather, they celebrate the omnipotence of the great god Ahura-Mazda, the transhistoric permanence of the dynastic principle, and the incomparable brilliance of the royal virtues. The Book of Benefactors, to which Herodotus (III.140; VIII.85–86) and the composer of the book of Esther (6:1) allude, is no exception. It was a compilation of the names of persons who had rendered conspicuous services to the Great King and who (as such) could expect a royal gift; it therefore also had a place in the exaltation of the sovereign power. Achaemenid court art itself did not have a narrative purpose. Power and the King were represented in timeless attitudes, not a particular king in a historical situation; this holds true for royal images found on stone, coins, and seals as well. Written in the immovable and infinite time of the King, the history of the Persians was never situated in the measured time of History by the Persians themselves.

The Great Kings and the Persians thus left the control of their historical memory to others. Here is an extraordinary situation: one must reconstruct the narrative thread of Achaemenid history from the writings of their subjects and their enemies—hence the power and authority long ascribed to the Greek authors. It is readily understandable that most of them wrote books devoted to memorializing the Greeks; and in the Athens of the fifth and fourth centuries, this memorial was constructed to a great extent on the carefully laid foundation of remembrances of confrontations with the Persians and victories won over the "barbarians of Asia." Among these authors, there is one who holds a special, preeminent place: Herodotus. In contrast to most of his contemporaries, he shows no evidence of systematic hostility to the Persians—hence the accusation directed against him by Plutarch of being a 'friend of the barbarians' (*philobarbaros*). The object of his *Histories* is to understand and explain the origins, however distant, of the Persian Wars. This gives us the advantage of lengthy digressions in the form of flashbacks on the history and institutions of many peoples and kingdoms of the Near East, Egypt in particular. It also gives us the advantage of interesting chapters on events in Persian history: the conquests of Cyrus, the seizure of Egypt by Cambyses, the accession of Darius, the reforms he introduced in tribute organization, as well as a digression on the internal organization of the Persian people and their principal social customs, and, of course, very long accounts of the Ionian Revolt (ca. 500–493) and the Persian Wars (490–479). In spite of its gaps and deficiencies, the abrupt end of the *Histories* in 479 leaves the historian of the Achaemenid Empire something of an orphan. Among Herodotus's successors, Thucydides has only a very peripheral interest in the Achaemenid Empire; as for Xenophon and Diodorus Siculus, their unbalanced approach tends to lend disproportionate weight to the Mediterranean side. Aside from the *Anabasis* of Xenophon, it was not until Alexander's expedition that the ancient historians penetrated the depths of the imperial territories, following in the footsteps of the conqueror.

Finally, many ancient authors devoted works specifically to Persia, which are called the *Persicas*. But most are lost and known only from fragments (quotations in later authors). The longest preserved fragment is the patriarch Photius's summary of the *Persica* of Ctesias. It is disappointing to read. The author, who lived some fifteen years at the court of Artaxerxes II, transmitted nothing but a slanted view dominated by the tortuous machinations of wicked princesses and the murky conspiracies of crafty eunuchs. He is undoubtedly one of the chief culprits in the success of a very incomplete and ideologized approach to the Achaemenid world. His *Persica* is not without some adumbration of the "Orientalism" of the modern period, which analyzes the courts of the Near East through a haze of very debatable readings, permeated mostly by observations on the murmurs of the harems and the decadence of the sultans. As for Xenophon, he wrote a long historical romance, the *Cyropaedia*, dedicated, as indicated by the title, to the education of the young Cyrus. The "Cyrus" he presents is certainly not the historical Cyrus; but he is a sort of paradigmatic embodiment of royal virtues. It is necessary, then, at each step, to distinguish the kernel of Achaemenid facts from the Greek interpretation—not always an easy task. It comes as no surprise that, generally speaking, the Greek authors transmitted a very Hellenocentric vision of Persian history and customs, just as certain books of the Bible, namely Nehemiah, Ezra, Esther, and Judith, provide a uniformly Judeocentric approach. But historians cannot choose their sources: given the available evidence, we have no choice but overwhelming reliance on Greek historiography to reconstruct a narrative thread. However much one may rail, not to say become frustrated, at the nature of their works, the situation becomes even more awkward when one must do without them! What is more, one must not throw out the baby with the bathwater: some late authors (Athenaeus, Aelian) have preserved a great deal of information about the person of the Great King and court life which, once it has been decoded, allows the historian to decipher what was also an *Empire of signs* (cf. chapters 5–7). From a methodological point of view, this book and the interpretations in it are thus largely the result of a labor of deconstruction of the Classical texts through which I have tried to show that, however partisan and ideological a Greek text may be, when it is located in the web of its associations, it can provide a stimulating Achaemenid reading. Futhermore, the historical and historiographical status of royal pronouncements and images requires exactly the same approach.

Fortunately, we also have records from the central authority: the royal inscriptions truly mirror the vision the Great Kings had of their power, their virtues, and their imperial reach; they also furnish information of the greatest importance on their building activities. But without doubt the most important find has been large groups of archives written on clay known as the Persepolis tablets, written in cuneiform in an Elamite that is riddled with Persian words. They provide a bureaucratic and "paper-shuffling" picture of the imperial administration that could scarcely be guessed from the Greek sources but would scarcely come as a surprise to the heirs of Assyro-Babylonian tradition. It is the same picture that the many Aramaic documents found in Egypt convey. Some royal and satrapal decrees are also known from translations into various languages of the Empire: these include a letter copied in Greek from Darius to Gadatas, one of his administrators in Asia Minor, and the correspondence in Demotic between Pharandates, satrap of Egypt, and the administrators of the sanctuary of the god Khnūm at Elephantine. As a whole, this documentation shows both the many ways in which the central authority intervened in local affairs and the persistent multilingualism of the Empire, tempered by the widespread use of Aramaic. To these written documents must be added the considerable evidence from archaeology, iconography, and numismatics, from the Aegean to the Indus, that has been discovered and published.

When the iconographic evidence, whether monuments or minor arts, in the royal residences or from the provinces, is added to the written sources (royal inscriptions; Elamite and Babylonian tablets; inscriptions in Phoenician, Aramaic, or Egyptian, Lydian and Lycian, or more than one language; Aramaic papyri; Classical authors, etc.), the historian has access to documentation that is both impressive and varied. But even when these varied corpora are brought together, they suffer from a dual handicap: they are very unevenly distributed in space and time. Some portions of the Empire, especially the satrapies of the Iranian Plateau, Central Asia, and the Indus Valley, are virtually devoid of any written documentation. It is not until the conquest of Alexander that we have even minimal literary information; hence the overpowering weight of archaeological evidence, which poses its own considerable interpretive difficulty. Some regions, on the other hand, are extraordinarily well documented: aside from Persia itself (the Elamite tablets), we may specifically mention Susiana (both textual and archaeological evidence for royal building projects), Egypt (Aramaic documents from Elephantine and Saqqara, Demotic papyri, hieroglyphic inscriptions), Babylonia (thousands of tablets), and, obviously, Asia Minor (not only the Greek historians, but also late evidence in Greek, Aramaic, or Greek and Aramaic of the imperial Persian diaspora in Anatolia). Furthermore, the information from some provincial sites assumes special importance. This is true of Xanthus in Lycia, where the dynasts continued to build monuments of a different kind that regularly display both inscriptions in Lycian and Greek and court scenes whose iconographic repertoire testifies to Achaemenid influence. A written document of the greatest importance was discovered there in 1973: a stela with a text in three versions—Aramaic, Lycian, and Greek—that immediately became famous. It is now securely dated to the first year of Artaxerxes IV (338–336), a Great King of whom virtually nothing was known until then, apart from the name (Arses) regularly given him by the Classical sources (Aršu in Babylonian). For all of these reasons, I will frequently tarry at Xanthus, which appears to the historian as a sort of microcosm of Persian power in a regional subdivision of the Empire for the entire time from Cyrus to Alexander. At the same time, the example shows the interpretive difficulties that arise from the dominance of archaeological and iconographic sources.

The evidence is distributed as unevenly in time as it is in space: the documents from the central authority are concentrated to a striking degree within the period from the conquest of Babylon by Cyrus to the middle of the fifth century, the date of the last Persepolis documents; we can hardly expect to derive a complete history from the evidence of this single period. The reigns of Artaxerxes I (465–425/424) and Darius II (425/424–405/404) remain fairly well documented, thanks to late documents from Persepolis, the Murašû archives in Babylonia, and Aramaic documents in Egypt. Otherwise, from Artaxerxes II (405/404–359/358) on, the historian must resort, at least for the basic facts, to the reports of the Greek authors. But, as we have said, their attention is focused on the Aegean coast, military-diplomatic matters, and court intrigue. Not until Darius III (335–330) do we find more abundant documentation, namely the Alexander historians who constitute, as I shall show (chapters 16–18), an "Achaemenid" source of exceptional interest, once they have been decoded.

4. Space and Time

The above observations immediately reveal the great difficulty faced by anyone who intends to write an analytical synthesis of the Achaemenid Empire. It must embrace a diachronic approach, a synchronic vision, and regional distinctions all at the same time. Though a single entity, the Empire had multiple manifestations because of its longevity and because of the great variety of the lands and cultures it comprised. Thus the tyranny of the document reemerges. How can one compose a global history of the *longue durée*, when the most significant evidence is limited to a few decades and/or a few areas? For the same reasons, where, how, and with what justification can we establish chronological divisions that express an endogenous, ascertainable, and verifiable development? There is no reason to overlook the breaks marked by the death of a king and the accession of his successor, but one cannot attribute to them a determinative explanatory value because, whatever the recognized central position of the Great King, the pulse and breath of the history of the Empire over the *longue durée* cannot be reduced to incidents of dynastic history. Consequently, it is necessary to interrupt the chronological thread with thematic chapters.

Despite the inauspicious distribution of the evidence, I have taken the risk of writing a general history in all of the aspects that I have listed. *Risk* is a bit pretentious because I have defined the several parts of the book mostly according to the distribution in time and space of all of the different kinds of evidence. What I am trying to say is that I have attempted to restore a full measure of importance to the fourth century, whose development is too often misunderstood and treated superficially at the expense of surrendering the power of memory to the Greek polemicists and so rendering the end of the story unintelligible. I do not claim that the history in the chapters below (particularly chapter 15) is not primarily political, military, and diplomatic. It might be considered hard, even tedious, reading. But, on the one hand, to reprise a formula that I will repeat many times, historians cannot choose their sources. On the other hand, I hold as do others that there are no minor genres of history: in a history of a state built and destroyed by conquest, it would be unreasonable not to devote sustained attention to armies and military expeditions. In the end, the study of war cannot be reduced to the caricature sometimes made of it with the pejorative label "battle-history." War is especially revealing of the workings of a state, even if it only reveals, for example, the scale of mobilization of human, material, and technological means of production that it both presupposes and imposes.

In order to highlight diachronic development more clearly, I have periodically provided an overview of the Empire, taken in its regional or even microregional components (chapters 13/6–7; 14/8; 15/7). I have also drawn up some more general assessments at three key points. The first is at the death of Cambyses (522), to distinguish what is attributed to the first two kings from what must be attributed to Darius (chapter 2). I have also made an assessment, which is meant to be exhaustive, at the end of the reign of Darius. Several long chapters (6–12) will perhaps provoke some criticism because of the use of later sources for the early fifth century, but I try to explain on several occasions the reasons for my choice. The third general assessment occurs toward the beginning of the reign of Darius III, and it includes the entire fourth century. Its purpose is to take stock before the appearance of Alexander and better to assess what we have fallen into the unfortunate habit of calling "Achaemenid decadence (decline)." The reader will find there an overview of the peoples and countries of the Empire that is as complete as possible, without claiming to have exhausted the literature. This inventory is not confined to an analysis of the administrative organization; the longest passages are devoted to the analysis of intercultural relations (chapter 16). The assessment is filled out by a dynamic analysis of the central state apparatus (chapter 17). For reasons I will set forth in the proper place, in the introduction to part 4, such an assessment allows us to approach the last phase of Achaemenid history on a more solid basis: strictly speaking, the last chapter (18) is not about the conquest of Alexander but about the wars waged by Darius and the Empire against Macedonian aggression and about the response of the imperial elite to the general challenge of the Macedonian conquest. Conquest, resistance, and defection in turn eloquently reveal the state of the Empire when Darius perished in a conspiracy in the summer of 330.

To the Reader

Whatever the origin and nature of the evidence at hand, history is simultaneously both explanation and interpretation. It is thus appropriate that the reader be informed about the sources that justify the author's interpretive choice. As a guide at each step of the way, I attempt to provide an inventory under the title "Sources and Problems." For the same reasons of clarity and rigor, I give frequent and sometimes lengthy quotations of ancient texts. By way of support for the explanation and the argument, I have also included archaeological and iconographic evidence. In this way, I hope, readers will be clear about the path I have followed, the evidence that justifies and upports it, the arguments I bring into play, and the worth of the interpretations I propose. They will have before their eyes all the elements that will permit them to conceive and/or propose alternative solutions. However much references to ancient sources may seem to burden the main text, I have found it necessary to provide them in parentheses, so that readers may look them up immediately, if they wish to examine, verify, or dispute them on the spot. I have also provided many subheadings—informative ones, I hope—so that readers can find their way easily through this substantial tome. And finally, I have deliberately banished the reference and explanatory notes to the back of the book, not only because some are very long and very detailed but also and especially because I hope that in this way the book will be more easily accessible to students and nonspecialists, who are rightly put off by the display of a sometimes over-erudite critical apparatus. Those who are interested are free to turn to the research appendix, like the specialists.

Acknowledgments

I must first express my deepest gratitude to all those who have supported and stimulated me through these years and lifted my spirits when I became discouraged. I do not know whether I would have begun without their stimulation or whether I would have persevered with such an ambitious undertaking.

I thank all those who have been so kind as to provide me with advance copies of manuscripts that were in the course of publication.* Nor can I forget the exceptional access provided by Bernard Delavault and Alban Dussau, *chargés* of the Semitic and Assyriological libraries of the Collège de France, respectively, whose Egyptological collection I consulted just as diligently. I recall that the Conseil scientifique of my university kindly granted me a sabbatical year. I also extend a tip of the hat to all of the students at Toulouse who for years have listened to my musings aloud in front of them and whose questions have often helped me clarify my thought. I think also of Sandra Péré (Toulouse) and Wouter Henkelman (Utrecht), who were of indescribable help in preparing the indexes; I took care of the subject index and general coordination, and obviously I take final responsibility for them all.

My friends Amélie Kuhrt (London), Heleen Sancisi-Weerdenburg (Utrecht), Matt Stolper (Chicago), and Carlo Zaccagnini (Naples) read all or part of the manuscript and kindly shared their criticisms, always relevant and often extensive: I thank them from the bottom of my heart.

I have amassed a special debt to Heleen Sancisi-Weerdenburg, beginning with our first meeting in Groningen in 1983. Even when all the French publishers I had contacted exhibited great timidity, she offered to publish my book in the series she had founded and which she directs with Amélie Kuhrt. When Fayard and its editorial director Denis Maraval expressed a desire to publish the manuscript, which was then in the course of word-processing in Utrecht, under the care of Mme L. Van Rosmalen, Heleen Sancisi-Weerdenburg and the directors of the Netherlands Institute for the Near East (Leiden) accepted this proposal with great grace, for which I am especially grateful to them.

Toulouse, October 1995

---

* L. Bregstein (Philadelphia), M. Brosius (Oxford), P. Debord (Bordeaux), L. Depuydt (Providence), R. Descat (Bordeaux), D. Devauchelle (Paris), M. Garrison (San Antonio), L. L. Grabbe (Hull), L. A. Heidorn (Chicago), W. Henkelman (Utrecht), C. Herrenschmidt (Paris), F. Israel (Rome), F. Joannès (Paris), A. G. Keen (Belfast), H. Koch (Marburg), A. Kuhrt (London), A. Lemaire (Paris), G. Le Rider (Paris), B. Menu (Paris), M. C. Miller (Toronto), B. Porten (Jerusalem), M. C. Root (Ann Arbor), J. F. Salles (Lyon), H. Sancisi-Weerdenburg (Utrecht), S. Sherwin-White (London), M. Stolper (Chicago), F. Vallat (Paris), R. J. van der Spek (Amsterdam), W. Vogelsang (Leiden), H. Wallinga (Utrecht), A. Yardeni (Jerusalem).

Prologue

The Persians before the Empire

1. Why Cyrus?

Discontinuous Documentation and the Longue Durée

The violent collapse of the mighty Assyrian Empire after the fall of Nineveh in 612 to a coalition of the Medes and Babylonians has sometimes been called a "scandal of history." The sudden appearance of the Persians in Near Eastern history and the lightning campaigns of Cyrus II, the Great, pose questions for the historian that are urgent both in their breadth and in their complexity. In two decades (550–530), the Persian armies led by Cyrus II conquered the Median, Lydian, and Neo-Babylonian kingdoms in succession and prepared the ground for Persian domination of the Iranian Plateau and Central Asia. How can we explain this sudden outburst into history by a people and a state hitherto practically unknown? How can we explain not only that this people could forge military forces sufficient to achieve conquests as impressive as they were rapid but also that, as early as the reign of Cyrus, it had available the technological and intellectual equipment that made the planning and building of Pasargadae possible?

The historian who works on the *longue durée* is well aware that an illustrious reign and a decisive event are consistent only with a history whose roots delve deep into a fruitful past. The Hellenistic historian Polybius was fully aware of this when he explained to his readers in the introduction to his *History* the need to reach far back in time, to understand how "the Roman state was able without precedent to extend its dominion over nearly all the inhabited world, and that in less than fifty-three years"; and he continued, "In this manner, when we come to the heart of my subject, we will have no trouble understanding how the Romans made their plans, what the military means and the material resources available to them were when they engaged in this enterprise that permitted them to impose their law on sea as well as on land and in all our regions."

The same goes for the beginnings of Persian history: it is agreed that the victories of Cyrus could not be conceived without the prior existence of a structured state, an organized and trained army, a well-established royal authority, and numerous contacts with the Mesopotamian and Aegean kingdoms. Such great victories cannot be explained simply by a one-sided insistence on the decadence of the states conquered by Cyrus—a "decadence" whose rhythms and modalities it is convenient to avoid specifying. Nor can it be explained by recourse to the convenient but reductive supposition of the intrinsic superiority of nomads over settled peoples. In short, every historical reflection leads us to suggest that the accession of Cyrus II was not only the point of departure for the first territorial empire that brought political unification to the immense area from the Aegean to the Indus; it was at the same time the outcome of a long process for which we have only fragmentary, elliptical, and discontinuous information.

13

Persian History and Greek Representations

Persian history, indeed, was never treated in antiquity by a historian of the stature of a Polybius. The "theoretical model" of the Greek authors of histories of Persia is desperately schematic and poor. Generally speaking, they are content to emphasize that the Persian Empire was nothing but the continuation of the Median kingdom conquered by Cyrus in 550. Take the case of Strabo. He is not satisfied to note that Ecbatana retained its prestige after the victory of Cyrus (XI.13.5). With the aid of the most dubious arguments from climate, he states that the Persians borrowed from the Medes

> their "Persian" stole, as it is now called, and their zeal for archery and horsemanship, and the court they pay to their kings, and their ornaments, and the divine reverence paid by subjects to kings. . . . The customs even of the conquered looked to the conquerors so august and appropriate to royal pomp that they submitted to wear feminine robes instead of going naked or lightly clad, and to cover their bodies all over with clothes. (XI.13.9❖)

He also refers to the opinion of other authors: "Some say that Medeia introduced this kind of dress when she, along with Jason, held dominion in this region" (XI.13.10❖): how history and mythology are intertwined here! Still later (XI.13.11❖), he notes that Median customs are identical to Persian customs "because of the conquest of the Persians," and he concludes: "I shall discuss them in my account of the latter." But there (XV.3.20), he merely notes that Persian customs are identical to those of the Medes and other peoples.

It must always be stressed that, aside from the obvious chronological imprecision of Strabo's arguments, they are built on a series of cultural stereotypes such as can be found in many other Greek authors who claim cavalierly to recount the history of the Persian people: the Persian conquest brought Median wealth and luxury to the conquerors, symbolized especially by garments that in themselves demonstrated the "feminization" of the *nouveaux riches*. Similarly, it was from the Medes that Cyrus's Persians copied their court ceremonial altogether. The Persian conquest is fully explained by "the allure of riches." This is also the underpinning of Plato's version in the *Laws* (694c–695a): "Persian decadence," beginning with Cambyses, is explained by the fact that "Cyrus's own sons received a Median-style education, an education corrupted by so-called ease, in the hands of educators who were women and eunuchs"! Herodotus (I.126) reverts to the same sort of interpretation to explain to his readers why the Persians enlisted in great numbers under the banner of Cyrus: poverty-stricken, the Persians were consumed by the desire to lay their hands on Median riches.

In keeping with the perverse logic of this "theoretical" model, the evolution of a society could not be explained in any way other than by external stimuli and challenges. Therefore, the victors (the Persians) could only be characterized as a less developed people, with everything to learn from the peoples they were to conquer; they had no alternative but to assume the customs and institutions found among the earlier powers. In short, the Persians before Cyrus have no history. In other words, the authors regularly assume a priori the problem that excites and divides modern-day historians; or, more precisely, neither Herodotus nor Xenophon nor Strabo has the slightest idea that their presentation raises such a problem.

2. The Founder Legends

On the period before Cyrus, then, the Classical sources are virtually worthless, at least to those who would reconstruct the main stages in the formation of the Persian kingdom. In addition to recitation of military expeditions, Herodotus devotes a long passage (I.107–130) to the origins of the Persian people, in the context of his report of Cyrus's victory over the Median king Astyages. He himself justifies his long excursus with these concluding words: "That, then, is the story of the birth and upbringing of Cyrus, and of how he seized the throne" (I.130⬦).

Cyrus (II) is presented there as born to the Persian Cambyses, son of Cyrus I, and Princess Mandane, daughter of the Median king Astyages. Disturbed by omens that portended an uncommon destiny for the child to be born to his daughter, Astyages had wanted to choose as son-in-law "a man of good lineage and character, but one whom he judged to be below a Mede even of middling character." Another dream and the *magi's* interpretation of it convinced him that the child who was about to be born "would become king in his place." Even though he was "aged and without male offspring," the king then decided to dispose of his grandson. He charged Harpagus, "a relative of his, the Mede who was most devoted to him, to whom he had entrusted all his affairs," with this task. Because Harpagus was somewhat anxious about appearing to be the murderer in the end, he passed the task on to Mithradates, one of the royal shepherds, "who, as he knew, would graze his herds in pastures that were most convenient for his plan and in mountains that teemed with wild animals." Mithradates, in turn, decided not to expose the baby to the wild animals at all, but instead to raise him as his own, taking into account that his wife, who had just given birth to a stillborn child, was still grieving. To fool the royal constabulary, "he took his stillborn child, placed it in the basket in which he had brought the other, adorned it with all the trappings of the other, brought it to the most deserted mountain, and set it there." The ruse worked. From that moment, "he who would later be called Cyrus was raised by the wife of the shepherd who had adopted him."

Then Herodotus tells how at the age of ten Cyrus enjoyed great prestige in the eyes of his playmates, who chose him to play the king in their games. Cyrus played his role so well that he severely punished "the son of Artembares, a respected man of the Median community." Mithradates and Cyrus were denounced by Artembares' father and called before Astyages, who soon realized that Mithradates' son was none other than his own grandson. He punished Harpagus cruelly by serving him the flesh of his own son mixed with mutton at a banquet. Then, reassured by the *magi*, Astyages sent Cyrus to Persia, where he rejoined his family. Herodotus then tells how when Cyrus grew to manhood he was able to depose Astyages, with the aid of Harpagus, and give power to the Persians (I.123–130).

Herodotus (I.95⬦) claims to have this story from Persian informants, "from those who seem to tell the simple truth about him without trying to exaggerate his exploits." He adds that he knows three other versions of the origins of Cyrus. In one, reported by Justin (I.4.10), the suckling child, abandoned in the forest by the shepherd, survived thanks "to a female dog who gave suck to the child and protected him from the wild beasts and the birds of prey." A third version, preserved by Nicolaus of Damascus, who doubtless got it from Ctesias, has as Cyrus's father Atradates, a Mardian, a member of one of the most abject tribes of the Persian people. Cyrus's father practiced banditry and his mother, Argoste, raised goats. According to "the Median custom," the young Cyrus was "given" to a rich and exalted personage, Artembares, to take care of. This Artembares held the enviable position of royal cupbearer in the court of Astyages. Weakened by age and infirmity, Artembares, with the consent of the king, passed his title to Cyrus, whom he had adopted. Cyrus summoned his parents to court. Having become still more powerful, he made Atradates "the satrap of the Persians" and his mother the richest woman in Persia. Then came the revolt. . . .

What facts can the historian extract from these stories? The identity of certain folk-loric themes with themes in the legend of Sargon King of Akkad, as it may be reconstructed from the tablets, shows that the various versions are constructed on a very ancient Near Eastern framework, filled out both by the inspiration of popular storytellers and by the goals of political propaganda (cf. Diodorus II.4.3). There is scarcely any doubt that the legend incorporates typical Iranian features as well. All these tales are intended primarily to exalt the memory of a charismatic founder, marked from his birth by signs of uncommon destiny. For this reason, it was piously passed on to young Persians from generation to generation. Each of the various versions places the origins of Cyrus in the context of relations between the powerful Medes and their Persian vassals. They are all equally at home within the story of the overthrow of Median power by the Persians. But, of course, in turning Cyrus into the creator of the Persian kingdom that was to rise up against Ecbatana, the various versions of the founder legends become useless for discussing Persia before Cyrus.

3. *The Kings of Anšan*

The Persians, however, left no literary record of their own history. The only form of official historiography in this period is the genealogies recorded by the kings themselves. In his famous inscription carved into the cliff at Behistun, Darius provides details of his Achaemenid background:

> I am Darius the Great King, King of Kings, King in Persia, King of countries, son of Hystaspes, grandson of Arsames, an Achaemenian. Saith Darius the king: my father was Hystaspes; Hystaspes' father was Arsames; Arsames' father was Ariaramnes; Ariaramnes' father was Teispes; Teispes' father was Achaemenes. Saith Darius the King: For this reason we are called Achaemenians. From long ago we have been noble. From long ago our family had been kings. Saith Darius the king: VIII of our family (there are) who were kings afore; I am the ninth; IX in succession we have been kings. (DB I §§1–4◇)

A genealogy of this sort thus allows us in principle to reach far back in time, to the very beginnings of Achaemenid history, when Persia was still in Persis. We might add that Herodotus (VII.11) offers a royal genealogy that does not correspond exactly with that given by Darius, since the succession is thus presented by Xerxes: Achaemenes–Teispes–Cambyses–Cyrus–Teispes–Ariaramnes–Arsames–Hystaspes–Darius.

We have two other inscriptions in the names of Ariaramnes and Arsames, whom Darius gives as his great-grandfather and grandfather respectively. They contain the following text: "Ariaramnes [Arsames], the Great King, King of Kings, King in Persia . . . this country Persia which I hold, which is possessed of good horses, of good men, upon me the Great God Ahura-Mazda bestowed (it). . . ." (AmH; AsH). But these documents are something less than certain. For one thing, there are serious doubts about their authenticity. For another, the assertions of Darius are themselves highly suspect—not, of course, that their authenticity may be doubted for a moment, but simply because the primary intention of the text is to justify all of Darius's actions after the death of Cambyses and to establish what he asserts as his family's rights—a rather dubious claim, as we shall see. A past revised and corrected by Darius hardly allows historians to sharpen their knowledge of the epoch of the early kings.

To do this, it is much better to rely on a Babylonian text, the *Cyrus Cylinder*, which gives the oldest genealogy. Cyrus is there called the "king of Anšan," and the family line is presented as follows: "Son of Cambyses, Great King, king of Anšan, great-grandson (or "descendant") of Teispes, Great King, king of Anšan, from a family [that has] always [exercised] kingship." The dynastic succession is thus established in the form Teispes–Cyrus I–Cambyses I–Cyrus II. As for the domain of the kings, it consisted of Anšan, as shown by a seal engraved with the legend "Kuraš of Anšan, son of Teispes" (PFS *93), a person usually identified with Cyrus I (fig. 7). The country is now identified with certainty: it is the plain of Marv Dasht, in Fārs. It is thus in this region—which would later take the name Persis—that the first Persian kingdom was established.

4. *Anšan and Susa*

The country the Persians conquered and peopled was in no way a political backwater. As early as the beginning of the second millennium, the Elamite kings bore the title "king of Anšan and Susa." The Elamite kingdom thus occupied both the plain (Susa) and the High Country (Anšan). At the site of Anšan itself (Tall-i Malyan), Elamite tablets dated to the end of the second millennium have been discovered. These texts attest to the existence of an Elamite administration in the region, and considerable building activity (temples, palace) testifies to the authority of the "kings of Anšan and Susa" in the southern Zagros during the second millennium.

But after this time, the Elamite kingdom, in the chronological phase called Neo-Elamite II (ca. 750–653), weakened considerably. The dynasty was ravaged by continual internecine struggles. It is possible that several "kings" coexisted from the beginning of the seventh century on. At this date, the center of gravity of the kingdom was no longer in the highlands, but on the plain, where the texts reveal three "royal towns": Susa, Madaktu (a stronghold situated on the Duwairij River), and Hidalu (in the first foothills of the Zagros). In 691, the Elamite and Babylonian armies waged a brutal war against the Assyrian forces, with both sides claiming victory.

It seems that the dependence of Anšan on Susa became increasingly remote and merely formal, with the Neo-Elamite kings unable to assert their authority there in any concrete way. In particular, they had to do battle many times with the Neo-Assyrian kings, who mounted frequent expeditions against Elam, forcing the king to "flee to the mountain." The Elamites, for their part, attempted several times to support Babylonian revolts against Assyria, without much success. The battle of Halule (691) was nothing more than a respite. In 646, Aššurbanipal launched a broad, victorious offensive, which resulted in the capture and sack of Susa and the (temporary) disappearance of the Elamite kingdom. It is perhaps in this context that Teispes, Cyrus II's great-grandfather, arrogated to himself the title "king of Anšan," thus proclaiming himself successor to the Elamite kings in the highland that was to take the name *Persis*.

The problem of absolute chronology is more difficult. An inscription of the Assyrian king Aššurbanipal (669–ca. 630) mentions the submission of Kuraš, king of Parsumaš, who shortly after 646 sent tribute to Nineveh and sent his oldest son, Arukku, as a hostage. It has long been held that this Kuraš was none other than Cyrus I himself, king of Persia (Parsumaš). But this interpretation is now being questioned. The proposed equivalence between Parsumaš and Persia is uncertain, and Parsumaš is probably distinct from Anšan (though this point is still under discussion). Since the chronology of Cyrus

II is securely established (559–530), it would be necessary under this hypothesis to lower the chronology of the first Persian kings, whose approximate dates would otherwise be: Teispes (ca. 635–610), Cyrus I (ca. 610–585), Cambyses I (ca. 585–559). Moreover, the settlement of this Iranian population in the region of Anšan was certainly much earlier. It is generally agreed that, having come from the northern Zagros, rather than directly from the Iranian Plateau, the Iranians moved gradually into Anšan toward the end of the second millennium.

5. Persian Society before the Conquests: Herodotus and Archaeology

Herodotus and Persian Society

We know nothing, or nearly nothing, of the kingdom of Anšan before the offensive launched by Cyrus II against the Medes in the late 550s. In the account he gives of the revolt of Cyrus against the Medes, Herodotus reports that the young king assembled his people, and he describes their organization in the following terms:

> The Persian nation contains a number of tribes (*genea*), and the ones which Cyrus assembled and persuaded to revolt were the Pasargadae, Maraphii, and Maspii, upon which all the other tribes are dependent. Of these the Pasargadae are the most distinguished (*aristoi*); they contain the clan (*phrētrē*) of the Achaemenidae from which spring the Perseid kings. Other tribes are the Panthialaei, Derusiaei, Germanii, all of which are attached to the soil (*arotēres*), the remainder—Dai, Mardi, Dropici, Sagartii—being nomadic. (I, 125◊)

Persian society as understood by Herodotus was thus a tribal society. Herodotus obviously used Greek terms to designate the groupings and subgroupings. But the social division that can be recognized there is comparable to what is also known from Iranian terminology. The basic level of organization is the patrilineal family (Old Persian *māna*); a group of families constitutes a clan (Old Persian *viθ*); the clans are grouped into a tribe (Old Iranian **zantu*). The tribe is simultaneously a genealogical reality and a spatial reality: Maraphii and Pasargadae are both ethnonyms and toponyms. Each tribe and clan had a territory of its own, the former being led by a tribal chieftain (**zantupati*). This was a situation that was to obtain until the very end of the Achaemenid period, as seen from the example of Orxines, described in this way by Quintus Curtius at the time of Alexander:

> From there they came to Pasargadae; that is a Persian race (*gens*), whose satrap [= tribal chieftain] was Orsines, prominent among all the barbarians for high birth and wealth. He traced his descent from Cyrus, formerly king of the Persians; he had wealth, both what he had inherited from his forefathers and what he himself had amassed during long possession of sovereignty. (X.1.22–23◊)

Among the tribes, Herodotus makes a major distinction between farmers and nomads. This opposition is found in every Classical author who deals with "barbarian" peoples. It is based on a assumption that treats nomads, often likened to robbers, as backward populations in the same way that, for the Greeks in particular, farmers represent a superior level of civilization. We have seen, for example, how for Ctesias the father of Cyrus was a Mardian who practiced banditry while his mother raised goats. Throughout history, the Mardians kept the reputation of being a fierce population, warlike and aggressive. As for the Sagartians, Herodotus portrays them elsewhere as "a nomadic tribe . . . a people who speak Persian and dress in a manner half Persian" but who, although they were incorporated with the Persians into the army of Xerxes, retained weapons—lassos—and styles of combat all their own (VII.85◊).

The distinction between nomads and farmers correlates with another distinction, a political distinction. Herodotus assigns special prestige to the Pasargadae, the Maraphii, and the Maspii, "to whom all the other Persians are subject." The term used by Herodotus implies a relationship of subordination, linked to the antiquity of certain tribes. Within the dominant group, the Pasargadae are considered "the noblest." One gets the sense that intense struggles took place between tribal chieftains. Herodotus specifies that Cyrus convened "an assembly (*aliē*) of the Persians," which seems to indicate that in order to declare war on the Medes the king had to take the advice of the tribal chieftains, especially of the chiefs of the Maraphii and the Maspii. On the basis of this mention, one is tempted to suggest that in the army each chieftain retained the command of his own contingent, under the supreme authority of the king, who was the chief (Greek *karanos*) of the 'people in arms' (Old Persian *kāra*). All the evidence agrees, in any case, that one of the Achaemenid king's ideological justifications was his aptitude for war and for leading armies. However, the conditions that brought three tribes to preeminence, or how the Pasargadae themselves became *aristoi*, or, for that matter, how and when the Achaemenid clan within the Pasargadae arrogated to itself the royal power are impossible to determine. All we can do is observe that Herodotus wrote toward the middle of the fifth century, at a time when the antiquity of the rights of the Achaemenids had become the official version. But we will see that this quite doubtful version owes much to Darius I. In other words, there is nothing to prove that the Achaemenids (in the clan sense) had held any special place of any antiquity in Persian society.

Limits on the Use of Classical Sources

In a more general way, some limits should be set on the use of the information provided by Herodotus and other Classical authors. Reading uncritically, we are tempted to conclude that Cyrus's conquests can be compared to raids by "nomads" in search of booty from the settled kingdoms. This is clearly not so. Cyrus would soon show that his objectives were much more ambitious: he intended not to raid but to conquer permanently. This observation implies that Cyrus's army was something more than an ad hoc assembly of tribal contingents fighting in loose order, each retaining its own style of combat. Rather, we must assume that before starting a war the Persian king had an army that had no want of arms or training in comparison with those against which he launched his offensive. It is also likely that when he led his army against the Medes Cyrus was much more than the most important of the tribal chieftains, a *primus inter pares*. It is much more likely that, ever since his predecessors had assumed the royal title, they were able to exert their power. This is indicated by the regularity in dynastic succession, at least as it is reported by Cyrus himself in his Babylonian proclamation of 539.

It is true that Xenophon attributed vast military reforms to the Cyrus he described: modification of the Persian armament (breastplate, wicker shield, swords, and battle-axes rather than simple spears and bows; *Cyropaedia* II.1.9–10; 16–17), organization of the command on the decimal system (II, II.1.22–24), and establishment of a cavalry (IV.3.4–23; VI.4.1) and a chariotry (VI.1.27–30; 50–54). But, here as elsewhere, Xenophon's reports must be read with caution. However different the inspiration of Herodotus and Xenophon, both agree in making Cyrus the creator ex nihilo of a Persian state. Despite what Xenophon claims (I.3.3), it is particularly difficult to accept that before contact with the Medes the Persians did not raise or ride horses. Whatever the established reputation of Median horsebreeding and cavalry, the victories achieved by Cyrus imply that at that date he already had a powerful cavalry. How can it be denied that the army raised by Cyrus against Astyages was made up of troops perfectly capable of taking on the Median army? After all, does not the seal of Kuraš of Anšan show a mounted warrior trampling his enemies beneath the feet of his steed (fig. 7)? The victories of Cyrus over the Medes of Astyages do not represent chance or luck. They cannot be explained solely in terms of the treason of those close to Astyages, on which Herodotus places such emphasis.

The Findings of Archaeology

It is also true that recent archaeological work appears to be consistent with Herodotus. As a result of surveys of the Marv Dasht, the plain of Persepolis, it has been possible to determine that the number of occupation sites decreased drastically from the end of the second millennium on (or before), and that it was not until the reigns of Cyrus and Cambyses that important permanent sites reappear, at Pasargadae and on the plain of Persepolis. From these observations we can infer generally that the loss of sedentary settlements in the region must be directly related to an internal development of the Elamite populations in the second half of the second millennium and to the arrival of Iranian populations at the beginning of the first millennium, from which those whom we call the Persians would eventually arise. During the first half of the first millennium, the country would thus have been populated essentially by nomadic tribes who, by definition, leave no archaeological traces.

Nonetheless, this reconstruction is still problematic. First of all, if the Persians devoted most of their time to activities related to nomadism and stockbreeding, it is difficult to understand why the names of their months show the existence of a calendar organized primarily around agricultural activities. Furthermore, the agreement between archaeology and Herodotus is more apparent than real. Herodotus was writing in the fifth century, on the basis of unidentifiable sources. As has already been stressed, there is no reason to suppose that his information applies specifically or exclusively to central Fārs in the first half of the first millennium. Yet again, his analysis of Persian society remains very general and atemporal. One reason is doubtless that the Persian society of his time was still organized by clans and tribes (cf. IV.167). It also allows us to surmise that even in his time Persian tribes practiced nomadism (whatever the changing and varied reality hidden beneath that term). Archaeology seems to confirm this, when we consider that at the time of Darius and Xerxes, the number of urban sites remained very low.

As for archaeological results per se, let us first note that they come from explorations conducted in a single region of Fārs; this is certainly a central region, since it is there that the first Persian kingdom was established. But where and how the ancestors of the Persians lived in the first centuries of the first millennium remains totally unknown. Moreover, the reconstruction leaves an essential problem completely in shadow. From the time of their arrival in Fārs, the Persians lived in permanent contact, even symbiosis, with the Elamite population. The fruitfulness of the Elamite heritage in Achaemenid civilization known from Cyrus onward in itself attests to the breadth and depth of the acculturation processes at work between the two groups. This Elamite influence can already be seen in the seal attributed to Cyrus I: stylistically, it belongs to a Neo-Elamite type. When we consider further that this seal was still used in Persepolis through the closing years of the sixth century (503–501), it speaks volumes for the permanence and fruitfulness of Elamite influence. There is even an obvious relationship between the

Susa tablets and the Persepolis tablets. So it must be admitted that the break was not to-tal and that the picture of discontinuity gleaned from the archaeology of central Fārs provides only a partial explanation.

Perhaps the error lies in suggesting that all of the ancestors of Cyrus lived like nomads in the Marv Dasht. The archaeological picture obtained from several sectors of eastern Khūzestān, in the lowland, is quite different. There, in fact, a remarkably continuity of urban settlement can be observed. A built tomb, discovered at Arjan, some 10 km from Behbehan (probably Hidalu), allows us to recognize that very elaborate processes of acculturation had been at work in Elamite, Iranian, and Assyro-Babylonian traditions. Neo-Elamite tablets attest to the presence of Iranians at Hidalu in the course of the seventh century. Some of these tablets are part of a group called the Acropolis Tablets, which represents part of the administrative archives of the palace of Susa in the period now called Neo-Elamite III B (approximately the first half of the sixth century; but the dating is uncertain). In general, these texts refer to deliveries to the palace of a very wide array of products: wool, textiles, different colored clothing, wood, furniture, tools, weapons, and so on. One-tenth of the personal names can be identified as Iranian; nine-tenths are Elamite. Among the craftsmen are men with Iranian names, sometimes labeled "Persian." One of the clothing suppliers is a certain Kurluš, who has a son with the Persian name Parsirra. One of the Masters of the palace (*rab ekalli*) is called Harina (Iranian Aryaina); someone of the same name is designated son of Mardunuš (Mardonius), etc. The tablets also show that Iranian terms were introduced into the technical vocabulary in the areas of textiles and of weapons. One garment is called *sarpi*, a word in which we recognize Greek *sarapis*, which ancient grammarians (Pollux, Hesychius citing Ctesias) list sometimes as Median, sometimes as Persian; some arms (quivers, spears) have Persian names.

Overall, this evidence lets the historian flesh out the succinct analysis of Herodotus and refine the archaeological picture obtained from explorations in central Fārs. Repeating an observation of R. Ghirshman: "The idea that was advanced long ago and that views [Persians] as nomads moving about with their herds in search of pasture must be reconsidered." In any case, through contact with the Elamites, in particular in Khūzistān, the Persians acquired technology and know-how, observable most especially in metalwork, that complemented the Iranian traditions. Elsewhere, Persians assumed important posts at the courts of the last Elamite rulers, some of them being provided with 'domains' (*irmatam*) in several regions of the lowlands and the plateau. If it is added that the presence of Iranians and Persians can be detected in Babylon from the beginning of the sixth century, it will be correct to conclude that the kingdom of Cyrus did not constitute a peripheral, isolated region, mired in an "archaic" way of life. On the contrary, if the Persians under Cyrus were able to assume hegemony, it is because they were well able to reap the fruit of the close and prolonged contacts they had struck up in different forms with the Elamites, the Medes, and the Babylonians.

6. *Anšan, Ecbatana, Babylon, and Susa*

The Consequences of the Fall of the Assyrian Empire

Fortunately, the absence of written sources bearing on Anšan is counterbalanced, so to speak, by Babylonian chronicles that allow us to reconstruct the international context within which the first Persian kingdom rose to power. The fall of the Assyrian Empire is plainly the crucial event in that context, an event from which the victors, the Median and Neo-Babylonian kingdoms, were able to profit. Assyrian power was at its height during the reign of Aššurbanipal (669–ca. 630) but fell into decline after his death. Military defeats came on top of problems of dynastic succession. In 626, Nabopolassar was recognized in Babylon; this was the beginning of the Neo-Babylonian kingdom, which was to last until the conquest of Cyrus in 539. To the north and east, the Medes launched offensives against Assyrian territory, seizing the province of Arrapḫa in 615. In 614, the Median king Cyaxares took Aššur, which he sacked. This feat was followed by an alliance between the Medes and the Babylonians. Two years later (612), the allied Median and Babylonian armies took Nineveh. Assyria's attempts at resistance soon failed (612–610), despite the attack on the Babylonian positions led by Pharaoh Necho. The Assyrian Empire had perished in the storm. When the survivors of the Ten Thousand traversed the region two centuries later, Xenophon described the Assyrian capitals Kalaḫ and Nineveh (under the names Larissa and Mespila), which he saw as abandoned cities where nothing survived but miserable remnants (*Anab.* III.4.6–12).

We do not know for sure how the two conquerors divided the spoils of the Assyrian Empire. While the Babylonians retained control of the strategic site of Ḥarran, there is no doubt that the Medes not only seized much Assyrian territory but also carried on their conquests in other directions. In 585, King Astyages, successor of Cyaxares, signed a treaty with the Lydian King Alyattes. According to Herodotus (I.74), the treaty was brought about through the mediation of the Cilician and Neo-Babylonian kings. Astyages and Alyattes undertook to respect a border on the Halys River. The treaty was sealed with dynastic marriages that made Alyattes the brother-in-law of Astyages. It is perhaps also from this time that Median dominion over several Central Asian peoples dates—distant dominion to be sure, having more to do with alliances with local chieftains than with setting up imperial structures.

The Assyrian rout left two great powers face to face: the Medes and the Neo-Babylonian kingdom. During the reigns of Nebuchadnezzar II (604–562) and his successors, the Neo-Babylonian kingdom regained the Assyrian legacy in Syria–Palestine and annexed part of Cilicia. The campaigns against Egypt, however, met with defeat. Another region escaped Neo-Babylonian dominion, in part at least: Elam, which had disappeared from the scene after being defeated by Aššurbanipal. It seems clear that the destruction of Susa (646) was not as complete as the Assyrian annals would have us believe. A series of converging indications shows rather that, toward 625 at the latest, an Elamite kingdom was rebuilt around Susa, even if Babylon maintained its grasp on one or several Elamite principalities. This Neo-Elamite kingdom extended east to the foothills of the Zagros, which thus constituted a frontier zone between the Elamite kings of Susa and their old possession, Anšan, therafter in the hands of Cyrus. There is no indication that this Elamite kingdom of Susa was required to recognize Median hegemony at the beginning of the sixth century.

The fact remains that the international situation prevailing at the beginning of the reign of Cyrus (around 559) was quite different from the context in which the first "king of Anšan" arose, about a century earlier. In 559, the Near East was divided into several competing kingdoms: Media (Ecbatana/Astyages), Lydia (Sardis/Croesus), Babylonia (Babylon/Nabonidus), Elam (Susa/Ummaniš?), and Egypt (Saïs/Amasis). Two powers faced off: (1) the Neo-Babylonian kingdom, which continued to amass conquests in the west to the point of dominating the entire Fertile Crescent beginning with Nebuchadnezzar's victory at Carchemish on the Euphrates in 605 until, a few years after the accession of Cyrus (559), Nabonidus took supreme power in Babylon (556); and (2) the Median kingdom, which imposed its dominion to the west as far as the Halys under the direction of Astyages (king since 585–584) and seems to have succeeded in extending its influence over several local princes of the Iranian Plateau, apparently as far as Bactria.

Anšan on the World Stage

On the other hand, we know nothing of the kings of Anšan during this long period or of the consequences the military operations might have had for them. Were the kings of Anšan able to participate more directly in international relations thereafter? It would be most interesting to be able to consider this to the point of being able to assess the importance achieved by the kingdom governed by the grandfather, then the father of Cyrus II. It must be admitted that it is impossible to know, given that before 553 not one Babylonian source alludes explicitly to the leaders of Anšan.

We must show great caution in confronting the Classical texts dealing with the fall of the Assyrian Empire. According to Ctesias (used by Diodorus, II.23–28), the "moral decadence" displayed by Sardanapalus (Aššurbanipal) was what drove the Mede Arbaces to raise the banner of revolt and to organize a four-power coalition within which figured, alongside the Medes and Babylonians (under the command of Belesys), not only the king of the Arabs (Upper Mesopotamian populations), but also the Persians, "whom he summoned to liberty." Aside from the fact that an Arbaces is otherwise unknown, we must underscore the surprising nature of the declaration made by the ruler of Ecbatana, who all the sources agree held sway over the Persians. Here, in contrast, the Persians, on an equal footing with the Medes, the Babylonians, and the Arabs (of Mesopotamia), are subject to the unbearable yoke of the Assyrians! The same sources were probably responsible for the report of a Hellenistic author, Amyntas (cited by Athenaeus XII.529e–f), according to which the walls of Nineveh (attributed to Sardanapalus) were demolished by Cyrus during the siege. These tales of the Assyrian defeat point to a vision that is Medocentric (the leading role of Arbaces) and Persocentric (the role of the Persians and Cyrus), in the face of which the historian is forced to express strong reservations on principle. It is not out of the question, on the other hand, to imagine that at the request of the Medes, the Persians were able to send a contingent to the Medo-Babylonian army that then united against the Assyrian armies.

Median Dominion

Beyond this observation, we must return once more to the matter of Persian subjection to the Medes. According to Herodotus's story of Cyrus's revolt, "The Persians had long resented their subjection to the Medes" (I.127◊). Nonetheless, we must admit that we know neither the origins nor the precise nature of the subjugation of the Persians by the Medes. Herodotus attributes the conquest of the Persians by the Medes to King Phraortes: "He carried his military operations further afield, and the first country he attacked and brought into subjection was Persia. By the combination of these two powerful peoples he proceeded to the systematic conquest of Asia, and finally attacked the Assyrians" (I.102◊). Owing to the annalistic framework of Herodotus's Median episodes, we can date the reign of Phraortes to 647/646–625/624. If we adopt the dynastic chronology proposed for Persia, this official subjugation must be located in the reign of Teispes (ca. 635–610?). However it may have happened, the event must be situated in a much broader wave of conquest, which undoubtedly allowed Phraortes and his successors to seize many other princedoms that held the Zagros range. But we are simply unable to analyze further a situation whose exact nature is inaccessible to us, apart from proposing some plausible but vague hypotheses to explain why the Persians, like other peoples subject to the Medes, were required to send tribute and troops to Ecbatana.

Dynastic Marriages?

In other respects, the ancient authors liked to stress the continuity between the two kingdoms, Media and Persia. Herodotus (I.107), Justin (I.4.4), and Xenophon (I.2.1) make Cyrus the son of Cambyses (I) and Mandane. They portray Mandane as the daughter of Astyages and the Lydian princess Aryenis, daughter of Alyattes and thus sister (or half-sister) of Croesus. In this scenario, Cyrus was a second-generation offspring of the diplomatic marriage concluded in 585 between Media and Lydia, under the auspices of the *syennesis* of Cilicia and the Neo-Babylonian king. Indeed, interdynastic marriages were common in the ancient Near East until the Hellenistic era. In a way, this justifies the relevance of Herodotus's remark about the Medo-Lydian marriage in 585: "knowing that treaties seldom remain intact without powerful sanctions" (I.74◊). But it must be agreed that any information in the Classical authors is suspect. Moreover, they do not agree among themselves on the tradition of the Persian-Median marriages. Ctesias (§2) even asserts straightforwardly, "Cyrus did not have the slightest degree of kinship with Astyages." According to him, Amytis was married in 550 to the Mede Spitamas, and she was later wed to Cyrus after the execution of her husband. Berossus (*FGrH* 680 F7d) states that, after the fall of the Assyrian Empire, Astyages married his daughter Amytis to Nebuchadnezzar, son of Nabopolassar—all assertions that are virtually incomprehensible in view of both chronology and history. The evidentiary confusion is such that doubts exist as to the reality of the Median marriage of Cambyses, father of Cyrus, inasmuch as it could offer a convenient ideological justification for the power of Cyrus in Media and even in Lydia. This is a motif found elsewhere in Herodotus, used to explain the first contacts between Cyrus and Amasis of Egypt and then the conquests led by Cambyses (III.1–3). It seems clear that in most cases it is actually a dynastic justification invented *post eventum*.

7. From the Medes to the Persians

Borrowing and Inheritance

On the basis of the Greek reports, at least in part (it is generally thought, though with less and less agreement), that Median influence was decisive in the creation and organization of the Persian kingdom. The examination of Achaemenid administrative and palace vocabulary has led some historians to conclude that Median loanwords were particularly frequent in the areas of royal titulature and bureaucracy. This interpretation is based on a belief in the existence of a Median language different from Old Persian. At the same time, it is founded, explicitly or implicitly, on the hypothesis that the Persians themselves had no state tradition of their own and that the Median kingdom was the only available model, that the Medes also indirectly transmitted Assyro-Babylonian and Urartian traditions to the Persians in these areas. This interpretation is likewise based on the observation that, after the conquest of Ecbatana, the Greeks and the peoples of the

Near East frequently referred to the Persians under the name of Medes (thus, for example, the French term "Guerres Médiques" for what in English are the "Persian Wars," or ancient Greek characterization of political collaboration with the Achaemenid Empire and its representatives as "Medizing"). It is inferred that Cyrus slipped into the mold of Median traditions, lock, stock, and barrel—all the more so in that Media already exercised powerful influence during the period of Ecbatana's political supremacy.

This kind of explanation raises a series of historical problems, whose details we would do well to specify. The ethnocultural connection between the Medes and Persians is undeniable: both are Iranian peoples, springing from the same Indo-Iranian stock, albeit at considerable remove. But this observation is not in itself determinative. For this reason, the theory of linguistic borrowings remains quite disputable. It proceeds from an underlying hypothesis—the assumption that the dialect words found in the vocabulary of the Old Persian inscriptions come from a Median language. The problem is that we know virtually nothing of Median, for the plain and simple reason that we do not have a single inscription in that language. By reasoning that might be considered circular, Median has been reconstructed on the basis of Persian borrowings, themselves reconstructed. Given this fact, and not without solid arguments, the very existence of a Median language has itself been called into question. Some contend instead that the language of the Achaemenid inscriptions is a common language (*koinē*) used by the Medes as well as the Persians. According to this hypothesis, the theory of linguistic borrowings is considerably weakened, and it is not supported by the historical interpretations proposed by the Classical authors.

The Structure of the Median Kingdom

To be sure, the possible refutation of the theory that Old Persian borrowed political and ideological terms from a Median dialect used by a Median precursor state itself entails historical inferences of the greatest magnitude. In part at least, it is actually on the basis of these supposed borrowings that the picture of a strongly unified Median kingdom administered in the style of its Urartian and Assyro-Babylonian neighbors has been reconstructed. The interpretation is even more tempting when it seems at first sight to find agreement with the long discussion Herodotus gives in his *Mēdikos Logos* (I.95–106) of the origin and history of the Median kingdom. The essential role in this is attributed to Deioces, son of Phraortes (I), who, through a series of measures as brutal as they were effective, transformed a tribal society into a unified state dominated by an omnipotent king. The consolidation of royal power is illustrated and made concrete by the construction of a royal city, Ecbatana, a royal guard, and the creation of a very strict court protocol, in such a way that the heads of the great Median families whom he had stripped of their prerogatives "took him for a being of a different nature from themselves." Moreover, to exercise his power, Deioces' "spies were busy watching and listening in every corner of his dominions" (I.95–101◈). His successor, Phraortes (II), inherited such power that he was able to subjugate the Persians and begin the war against the Assyrians, but he perished in the war (I.102). After his death, his son Cyaxares continued the march of conquest. To this end, he reorganized his army in an effort to make the diverse contingents more unified. He marched against Nineveh, but he was thrown back by bands of Scythians. After a twenty-eight-year Scythian interregnum, he regained power: the Medes "recovered their former power and dominion. . . . They

captured Nineveh."❖ Shortly thereafter, his son Astyages succeeded him: this is exactly
where the legend of the origins of Cyrus commences, into which the *Mēdikos Logos* is
integrated.

But for many reasons Herodotus's Median tale is itself highly suspect. To be sure, the
historicity of the kings depicted is hard to deny, and there is no compelling reason to
doubt their chronology, but the story of the reforms imposed by Deioces resembles an
existing model of the "founding father" too closely for us to place blind confidence in it.
Furthermore, the institutions set up by Deioces (capital, personal guard, audience ritual, Eyes and Ears of the king) are strangely similar to the Achaemenid institutions frequently described by the Greek authors, so much so that we are tempted to think that
Herodotus (just like Strabo later on; XI.13.9) applied (or could have applied) what he
knew of the Persian court practices of his own day as a veneer over an entirely imaginary
Media. The question remains: Was the Media of the time of Astyages really a powerfully
integrated monarchic state, whose organization Cyrus could copy in Persia?

The Medes are also known from the Assyrian annals, to the extent that, beginning in
the ninth century in particular, the Assyrian kings attempted to impose their control on
the principalities of the Zagros. But the correspondences drawn from comparing Herodotus and the Assyrian sources remain hypothetical. It is clear, for example, that the
identifications proposed between the personal names cited by Herodotus and those in
the Assyrian annals cannot be taken on the probative value that is often attributed to
them. Furthermore, at the time of the first confrontation (835), the Medes encountered
by Šalmaneser III are described as a fragmented society, within which twenty-seven kings
(*šarrāni*) exercised power independently of each other. There is no indication that the
Median peoples underwent a rapid evolution toward the unification of the tribes around
a supreme chief who might be called king of the Medes before the seventh century.

The results of archaeological explorations, however, must still be taken cautiously:
no artifact can be called "Median" with absolute certainty, and the appropriateness of
the term "Median art" has frequently been questioned. Three sites have been excavated
within Median territory: Godin Tepe, Tepe Nūš-i Jān, and Bābā Jān. Fairly imposing
residential structures have been uncovered there, some of which (hypostyle halls) are
generally considered characteristic of Achaemenid architecture. But their precise dating
continues to be questioned as does, consequently, the dating of the relationships that
can be established between these constructions and the activities of the Median kings
described by Herodotus.

Appraisal of the Discussion

The conclusion of the discussion is necessarily a bit disappointing but mirrors the
corpus of evidence: historians cannot choose their sources. To a certain extent, in dealing with Median history, historians are faced with an evidentiary situation comparable
with the situation that faces them in dealing with Persian history before Cyrus. In the absence of inscriptions and irrefutable archaeological records, they are led on the one
hand to lengthy discussions of the credibility of Herodotus, while on the other hand,
they must at the same time conform their reflections to a theoretical model of the evolution of tribal states. The difference is that the Medes appear frequently in the annals
of Mesopotamian kingdoms, both Assyrian and Neo-Babylonian. But to which Medes
do these texts refer? Must they necessarily be identified with the Medes of Deioces,
Phraortes, Cyaxares, and Astyages? Nothing could be less certain.

All we can say is that the intervention of the Medes in international relations and their direct participation in the fall of the Assyrian Empire imply that the "Median kings" of the last third of the seventh century had succeeded in raising an army worthy of the name and thus that they possessed significant resources, amassed through tribute and through the profit on long-range trade with Central Asia—hence doubtless, for whatever reason, the interest in Herodotus's mention of military reforms carried out by Cyaxares. It is still appropriate to assess the respective contributions of the Medes and the Babylonians to the fall of Assyria. To be sure—notwithstanding the claims of Ctesias and Amyntas—the participation of the Medes (and the Persians!) seems to have had a considerably smaller effect than did the Babylonian armies, and it seems doubtful that this impression is due to a later rewriting of history by Babylonian authors anxious to emphasize the decisive role of the Babylonian armies.

Despite the absence of irrefutable evidence, in the end we must stress the limits of an argument based on the ethnocultural links between the Persians and the Medes. In fact, after their joint arrival in the Zagros, Medes and Persians underwent varied and distinct evolutions. After arriving in Fārs, those whom we call Persians were particularly prone to Elamite influence, to the point that we now tend to think that the Persians of the time of Cyrus comprised a population descended from a blending of Iranians and Elamites. What is more, the permanence of Elamite borrowings in every aspect of social and political life leads us to believe that the organization of the kingdom of Cyrus and his successors owes more to the Elamite legacy, which can be identified precisely, than to Median borrowings, which are very difficult to isolate. Certain indications lead us to suppose that, far from being a "nomadic and primitive" state, the kingdom of Cyrus, based on the Elamite model, was forged with administrative devices that evoke and presage the organization seen fully in operation in Fārs at the time of Darius.

8. Conclusion

For now, the question raised at the beginning of this chapter ("Why Cyrus?") has no satisfactory answer. All we can do is collect fragmentary and conflicting information and draw an impression from it that can be no more than probable. To be sure, examination of the stages of conquest undertaken by Cyrus will be able to shed some new light, but there is the risk of prophesying after the fact, in the manner of Diodorus Siculus:

> Cyrus, the son of Cambyses and Mandane, the daughter of Astyages who was king of the Medes, was pre-eminent among the men of his time in bravery and sagacity and the other virtues; for his father had reared him after the manner of kings and had made him zealous to emulate the highest achievements. And it was clear that he would take hold of great affairs, since he revealed an excellence (*aretē*) beyond his years. (IX.22✧)

Now, without wishing to get ahead of the story, we must always keep in mind that we have no specific idea of the plans Cyrus might have made at his accession. We are equally uninformed about his reign up to the moment when he confronted Astyages, not quite ten years after taking power. Was he even in control of events? We cannot say for sure, since several documents imply or assert on the contrary that the initiative came from Astyages in the late 550s, and from Croesus some years later. Were his conquests preceded by a mature, preestablished, overall plan? or did the successive stages actually follow one another as consequences of initial success and of decisions of his opponents? This problem cannot be solved, as is fully recognized by those historians who, equipped with more substantial tools for dealing with the evidence, are concerned with the origins and primary objectives of the conquests of Alexander or with the development of Roman imperialism.

PART ONE

The Empire-Builders: From Cyrus to Darius

Chapter 1

The Land-Collectors:
Cyrus the Great and Cambyses (559–522)

1. Medo-Persian Hostilities, the Defeat of Astyages, and the Fall of Ecbatana (553–550)

Sources and Problems

Aside from the factual elements in the founder legends recorded by Herodotus and Ctesias (via Nicolaus of Damascus) and a few isolated passages in Diodorus and Justin, the only information we have about the Medo-Persian hostilities comes from Babylonian records of the reign of Nabonidus (556/5–539). The Neo-Babylonian king claims that during the first year of his reign Marduk gave him assurance in a dream that the Median threat in the region of Ḥarran would soon be eliminated:

> [And in truth], when the third year [553] arrived, Marduk raised up Cyrus, king of Anšan, his young servant (*ardu*); Cyrus scattered the great armies of Umman-Manda with his small army and he seized Astyages, king of the Medes, and he led him captive to his own country.

Another Babylonian text, the *Nabonidus Chronicle* (II.1–4), refers directly to Cyrus's victory. The paragraph preceding the entry for Nabonidus's year 7 (549) includes the following:

> [Astyages] mobilized [his army] and he marched against Cyrus, king of Anšan, to conquer. . . . the army rebelled against Astyages and he was taken prisoner. [They handed him over] to Cyrus [. . .]. Cyrus marched toward Ecbatana, the royal city. Silver, gold, goods, property, [. . .] which he seized as booty [from] Ecbatana, he conveyed to Anšan. The goods [and] property of the army of [. . .].

These texts corroborate some points and clarify others in the material provided by the Classical authors. One of the questions that faces the historian is whether the operations Cyrus directed against Astyages were part of an overall strategy intended from the beginning to confront the Medes, the Lydians, and the Babylonians in succession and thus to create a unified empire of a kind new to the Near East. This is the impression the reader gets from the Classical texts dealing with the exploits of Cyrus. But as a general rule one must challenge interpretations that reduce History to matters of fate and exigency. And in this particular case, even though Herodotus presents the march on Ecbatana as the deliberate initiative of Cyrus alone, a Babylonian text, the *Nabonidus Chronicle*, says the contrary—that it was Astyages who launched the offensive.

What is more, within the "founder legend" that he presents in detail (I.95–130), Herodotus (I.108–29) dwells specifically on the treachery of a faction of the Median nobility toward Astyages. At the news of the approach of the Persian army raised by Cyrus, it is said, Astyages placed the Median army under the command of Harpagus—that is, the very person he had recently humiliated and severely punished for saving the infant

31

Cyrus from death. Harpagus quickly made contact with Cyrus, who was back in Persia with his father Cambyses (I); he even spurred him on in his revolt against the Medes. He also gathered around himself a group of Median nobles exasperated by the "severity" of Astyages: "Harpagus worked at persuading them to place Cyrus at their head and depose Astyages" (I.123◊). The prior understanding between Harpagus and Cyrus greatly favored Persian plans: "The Medes took to the field and engaged the Persian army; a few who were not in the plot did their duty, but of the remainder some deserted to the Persians and the greater number deliberately shirked fighting and took to their heels. The Median army collapsed disgracefully" (I.127–28◊). Thereupon, the Persians replaced the Medes as masters of Asia (I.130).

But by reducing the Medo-Persian war to a lucky battle and by presenting the conquest of Media as desired by the Medes themselves, Herodotus is obviously simplifying greatly. The Babylonian texts suggest that the decisive battle and the capture of Ecbatana were only the climax of open hostilities that had lasted at least three years (553–550). Indeed, the *Nabonidus Chronicle* confirms (II.2) that "the army rebelled against Astyages and he was taken prisoner." But it also states, as we have seen, that it was Astyages himself who had taken the offensive (II.1), perhaps in order to put down a Persian rebellion that threatened his strategic positions and furthered the designs of his principal rival, the Neo-Babylonian king Nabonidus. On the other hand, it is not out of the question that Nabonidus, without necessarily going so far as to enter into a formal alliance with Cyrus, did nothing to thwart the undertakings of the Persian king against the Medes of Astyages. In fact, the same year (553), Nabonidus left Babylonia to take up residence at the oasis of Teima in Arabia: before leaving, he had to ensure the power bases of his son Belshazzar, whom he left in charge in Babylon.

Offensives and Counteroffensives

Several Classical authors confirm that the victory of Cyrus was difficult and was long in coming. The undeniable treason of Harpagus did not suddenly turn the tide of the war. According to Ctesias (cited by Diodorus IX.23), Astyages then took draconian measures: he dismissed the commanders of the army and appointed trustworthy men; in short, he ruled by terror. Justin (probably depending on the same source) states that after the defeat and the treason of Harpagus, Astyages himself took command of the army and marched against the Persians (I.6.8–17). Nicolaus of Damascus and Polyaenus (VII.6.9) state emphatically that fierce combat was seen in Persia itself, near the site of Pasargadae. The latter writes (VII.6.1):

> Cyrus fought three times against the Medes, and he was defeated as many times. He did battle a fourth time at Pasargadae, where the women and children of the Persians were. They, the Persians, took flight yet again. . . . But then they returned to the charge, fell upon the Medes who had scattered in pursuit of them, and achieved a victory so complete that Cyrus had no need to fight again.

He even states that after the first defeats "many Persians defected to the Medes." The violence and turmoil of the hostilities that developed in Persia are likewise emphasized by Nicolaus of Damascus (*FGrH* 90 F66.16–45). Both Polyaenus and Nicolaus celebrate the valorous conduct of the women who took refuge on a height and exhorted their fathers, brothers, and husbands to refuse defeat—which is the reason why the Great King granted favors to the women every time he visited Persia (Nicolaus of Damascus, *FGrH* 90 F66.43; cf. Plutarch, *Alex.* 69.1 and *Mor.* 246a–b). When this victory was accomplished, Cyrus resumed the offensive against Media and seized Ecbatana, where Astyages had taken refuge. We might imagine that Astyages was counting on the town's fortifications to put up a lengthy resistance: according to Ctesias, he was taken prisoner while hiding in the attic of the royal palace along with his daughter and his son-in-law Spitamas (*Persica*, §2); according to Nicolaus of Damascus, Astyages actually managed to escape; he was taken prisoner only as the result of another battle (*FGrH* 90 F66.45–46).

The New Master of Ecbatana

Now that he was Master of Ecbatana, Cyrus displayed by formal, symbolic acts that dominion had passed to the Persians, who have become "masters of the Medes though they were once their slaves" (Herodotus I.129✧). Wholly surrounded by official ceremony, he entered the royal tent of Astyages, took his place on the throne of the vanquished monarch, and grasped his scepter. His lieutenant Oibaras placed on his head the upright tiara (*kidaris*), a symbol of royalty. The capture of the Median royal treasure also represented a striking sign of his new-found power; Oibaras was entrusted with conveying them to Persia. This booty was certainly of great practical importance; as far as we can tell, it was the first time Cyrus had inexhaustible resources at his disposal for the campaigns to come.

At the same time, Cyrus took care to conduct himself as Astyages' successor. He spared his life and granted him a princely style of life. Cyrus even married Amytis, the daughter of Astyages, say Ctesias and Xenophon. According to Nicolaus of Damascus, it was to the successor of Astyages that several Central Asian peoples (Parthians, Saka, and Bactrians) came to do homage. According to Ctesias, the Bactrians, who had recently revolted, "spontaneously submitted to Amytis and Cyrus" when they learned "that Astyages had become the father of Cyrus and Amytis . . . his wife." This tradition is suspect, in that it fulfills the wish of Cyrus to present himself as a "chivalrous" conqueror under whose authority the vanquished placed themselves of their own free will. Obviously, the entire Median aristocracy did not take gladly to being deprived of the profits drawn from the dominion exercised by Astyages. But at the same time the tradition agrees that the new master of Media was willing to connect himself with the dynasty he had just overthrown. A strategic center of the greatest importance to whoever wanted to control Central Asia, Ecbatana remained one of the regular residences of the Great Kings. Was it not in Ecbatana, after all, that at the time of Darius a copy of the edict of Cyrus regarding the return of the Judahites to Jerusalem was found? At least as early as 537, the Babylonian House of Egibi did business in the capital of Media, where the court of Cyrus was in residence for several months of the year. Furthermore, there is no doubt that once the defeat was an accomplished fact, some members of the Median elite agreed to cooperate with the new king.

2. The New International Situation and Cyrus's Projects

The Median Territorial and Diplomatic Heritage

For reasons already given, Cyrus's initial conquest must not be reduced to the Median packaging given it, particularly by the Classical sources. It is clear that supremacy over Ecbatana brought about a profound upheaval in the geopolitical situation through-out the Near East. Cyrus's self-presentation as the heir of Astyages—with Astyages' ap-parent assent, no less—in fact meant that the new master also assumed the territorial ambitions of his predecessor. This continuity required Cyrus sooner or later to clash with formidable powers, Lydia and the Neo-Babylonian kingdom. When Herodotus writes (I.130◊) that after the fall of Astyages the Persians were "masters of Asia," he is as-serting a programmatic objective more than analyzing a fully realized accomplishment. Even if Nabonidus had seen nothing but benefits in the Medo-Persian conflict, Cyrus's victory plunged him into a situation full of danger. Henceforth, Cyrus's Medo-Persian kingdom and the Neo-Babylonian kingdom were situated as rivals rather than allies.

The assumption of the Median heritage also brought Cyrus the problem of the west-ern front. Ever since 585 there had been a treaty between Astyages and the Lydian king Alyattes, according to which the Halys was the boundary between the Median and Ly-dian domains (I.74). At the time of the fall of Astyages, the king of Lydia was Croesus, celebrated throughout the Near East and Greece for his wealth and his military power. He controlled the Greek coastal cities, which sent him tribute. He also held all of Ana-tolia in his grasp, except for Lycia, Cilicia, and Tabal (Cappadocia).

Chronological Problems and Cyrus's Strategy

Analyzing the strategy of Cyrus, however, requires at the very least that we know its stages, which is far from the case. On the contrary, the chronology of the reign of Cyrus remains uncertain, to say the least. Bearing in mind that the date of the capture of Ec-batana continues to be problematic (within a year or two), only two events are precisely dated: the capture of Babylon (539) and the death of Cyrus in Central Asia (530). The chronology of the capture of Sardis remains disputed. In the *Nabonidus Chronicle* (II.13), a paragraph dated Year 9 (547–546) first mentions the death of the mother of Na-bonidus at Dūr-karāšu, "which is on the bank of the Euphrates above Sippar." In May of the same year, the *Chronicle* says, Cyrus gathered his army and crossed the Tigris below Arbela. Another expedition led by Cyrus against a country whose name is unreadable is mentioned next: "Cyrus killed its king, took his possessions, and stationed his own garri-son there; the king and the garrison resided there."

Contrary to what has long been believed, this text does not appear to refer to Cyrus's campaign against Lydia. Thus, the capture of Sardis is dated either to 546 or to 542–541. The first date assumes that the Lydian-Persian war followed the Medo-Persian hostilities almost immediately; the second date results from supposing that Cyrus led a series of campaigns in Central Asia and on the Iranian Plateau between the capture of Ecbatana and the capture of Sardis. The problem is that the chronology in Herodotus is highly un-certain. Following convention, we will here adopt the first proposal (the more widely fa-vored), while agreeing that between 546 and 540 Cyrus carried out operations in Central Asia and that the operations against Babylonian positions probably began well before 540.

Furthermore, Herodotus says, the initiative was not Cyrus's at all. He draws the oppo-site conclusion from the entire story—that the war was instigated by Croesus, who was uneasy because Cyrus "had destroyed the empire of Astyages, and the power of Persia was steadily increasing" (I.46◊). Desirous of expanding his domains to the east and fol-lowing the example of his predecessors, Croesus managed to present the operations that ensued as an expedition intended to avenge his brother-in-law Astyages: "Croesus had a craving to extend his territories. . . . He prepared an expedition in Cappadocia, sure of success in bringing down the power of Cyrus and the Persians" (I.71; I.73✧). In short, Croesus intended to profit from the new international situation by abrogating the treaty of 585 that had set the Halys as the limit of Lydian expansion.

3. The Defeat of Croesus and the Establishment of a Mediterranean Front

The Successful Counterattack by Cyrus (547–546)

Whatever Cyrus's strategic intentions may have been, the offensive by Croesus left him no choice. He now found himself at the head of an army considerably reinforced by the troops raised in Media and by the contingents brought to him by the Central Asian chieftains who had submitted after the fall of Ecbatana. As he advanced, he also mobilized the men of the regions he was crossing so successfully that, according to Herodotus (I.77), the Persian conqueror possessed an undeniable numerical superiority over Croesus. He likewise possessed powerful siege engines that served him well at Sardis and elsewhere. He intended once and for all to settle the quarrels between Media and Lydia. As Diodorus of Sicily tells it (IX.32.3), upon his arrival in Cappadocia, Cyrus sent an envoy to Croesus to let him know that he could remain in Lydia but as no more than satrap of the region. He was in effect proposing that his adversary recognize Persian dominion without a fight. One can imagine the response of the master of Sardis.

Croesus was clearly very confident facing Cyrus. He had concluded a "treaty of hospitality and alliance" with Sparta, from which he could count on fresh reinforcements. He had also sent many embassies and sumptuous gifts to the sanctuary at Delphi. Questioned at his behest, the oracle had responded ambiguously, as usual, reported thus by Herodotus (I.53✧): "If Croesus attacked the Persians, he would destroy a great empire": history was to show Croesus that it was the Lydian kingdom that would vanish. Elsewhere, there were treaties with the Neo-Babylonian kingdom and with Pharaoh Amasis. It appears that the latter sent troops, who would play an important part in various offensives against the Persians. Babylon, on the other hand, did not intervene. We may imagine that Nabonidus (still in Arabia) and Belshazzar (his son and regent in Babylon) did not take an unhappy view of the conflict between their two main rivals. Cyrus attempted to instigate defections among his enemy's allies: upon notification of the offensive by Croesus and "before starting he had sent representatives to the Ionians in an attempt to detach them from Croesus, but without success" (Herodotus I.76✧). The Ionians would soon pay heavily for their error in judgment.

The rash offensive of Croesus beyond the Halys ran into the army of Cyrus. The battle that unfolded in Cappadocia at Pteria (Boghazköy?) was not decisive. Croesus soon decided to retreat and take advantage of the winter to gather a powerful army, counting on receiving reinforcements from his nominal allies. He dispersed the army he had led in Cappadocia to its winter quarters. Imprudently, but also unexpectedly, Cyrus attacked in the dead of winter and took the Lydian army by surprise, just when it was about to be demobilized.

This bold attack was the result of keen logistic and political analysis. Cyrus had everything to fear from a reinforced Lydian army, whose valor and courage Herodotus extols (I.79–80). The decisions made by Croesus after Pteria provided Cyrus an opportunity to overcome an enemy who was in theory superior. The Persian king also understood well that a defeat would have raised hopes among yesterday's vanquished of throwing off a dominion that was as fragile as it was recent. Nor did he disregard the fact that at this time the lands of Central Asia were uneasy. Finally, he intended to profit immediately from the conflicts that the partial defeat of Croesus had provoked in the Greek cities of the Anatolian coast. It also seems likely that the Greeks sent no reinforcements to Sardis after Cyrus's arrival in Lydia was confirmed. After the battle of of Pteria, Miletus, a traditionally "Medizing" city, had let Cyrus know that it was ready for terms. In other Greek cities, the struggles between "Medizing" and "Lydianizing" factions had flared up, the former hoping to profit from the victory of Cyrus that they desired. An Ephesian, Eurybates, whom Croesus had commissioned to recruit mercenaries in the Peloponnesus, had already defected to Cyrus. His story was probably not unique: it is perhaps on this occasion that Pytharcus of Cyzicus received from Cyrus the revenues of seven cities of Asia Minor.

It would have been a grave political and strategic error on Cyrus's part to allow Croesus the time to regain undivided dominion over the Greeks of Asia Minor. The Persian's calculations proved to be precise. In the face of a tactical situation that was not entirely in his favor, Cyrus staged a battle close to Sardis, which forced Croesus to take refuge in the citadel, which was thought to be impregnable. The Lydian king sent desperate pleas to his allies. But, as the result of a strategem, the city fell on the fourteenth day of the siege, and the news reached Sparta just as relief was setting out for Asia Minor. The fall of Sardis sent a shock wave throughout the Near East nearly as great as that which had attended the fall of Nineveh in 612.

Takeover of the Lydian Kingdom

So Cyrus entered Sardis, where Croesus gave himself up. Thereafter, he remained in the entourage of Cyrus, who gave him a Median city as a grant, the revenue from which allowed the defeated king to maintain his accustomed lifestyle. The contents of the treasure-houses of Sardis were sent to Cyrus, who had them transported toward the center of his empire-in-the-making. The town of Sardis was provided with a garrison entrusted to Tabalus, a Persian.

The taking of Sardis nonetheless did not completely settle the question. Cities and dynasts of Asia Minor remained to be subjugated. Only one city, Miletus, had surrendered prior to the fall of Sardis, in consideration of which it "obtained the same terms from Cyrus as from Croesus" (I.141✧) that sheltered it from the Persian offensive (I.143): "It enjoyed tranquility" (I.169). According to Herodotus (I.141✧), "The Ionians and Aeolians immediately after the Persian conquest of Lydia sent representatives to Cyrus at Sardis, to try to obtain from him the same terms as they had had under Croesus." The king returned a refusal: he insisted that the Greek cities surrender unconditionally. They had to choose between bowing to Cyrus's will or organizing resistance. They chose the second solution, and "began to erect defences" (I.141✧). They also sent an embassy to Sparta requesting aid against the Persians. The Spartans rejected the request of the Ionians but sent observers, and when Cyrus received them at Sardis, they presumed to forbid the king "to destroy a single city in Greek lands." This was scarcely a realistic demand, if indeed it was ever made. Cyrus rejected it haughtily and not without a measure of contempt (I.152–53). The Greek cities thus faced the Persian conqueror on their own.

Despite their isolation and the Lydian defeat, the leaders of the Greek cities were probably counting on one element in their favor. Herodotus (I.153◊) specifies that Cyrus "himself started eastward on his march to Ecbatana [quite rapidly]. . . . He did not think the Ionians important enough to constitute a pirimary objective, for his mind was on Babylon and the Bactrians and the Saka and the Egyptians, against whom he intended to lead an expedition in person. Some other commander would suffice to tackle the Ionians." In other words, beginning in the spring of 546, Cyrus had to conduct operations on several fronts at once.

The Revolt of Pactyes

As soon as Cyrus left, "seeing the king occupied with other wars, the Lydians revolted," as Justin puts it (I.7.11). This late author is clearly referring to the revolt led by the Lydian Pactyes, whom Cyrus had assigned to gather tribute. Provided with these resources, "Pactyes induced the Lydians to rise against their Persian governor, and going down to the coast was enabled by his possession of the Sardian gold to hire soldiers and persuade the men from the coastal districts to support him. He then marched against Sardis and laid siege to Tabalus, who was shut up in the inner fortress of the city" (Herodotus, I.154◊). Thus was formed a very dangerous coalition against the Persians, between Lydians who had not accepted the defeat and the Greek cities that had refused to submit to Cyrus. To explain how the Persians succeeded is also to understand (at least in part) the methods that the Persians used to establish their sovereignty in the conquered countries.

Advised about the revolt on the way to Ecbatana, Cyrus sent the Mede Mazares back, entrusting him with some of his troops, and issued an order "to sell into slavery everybody who had joined in the Lydian attack on Sardis. Pactyes himself was at all costs to be taken alive and brought beforte him."◊ Pactyes chose to leave Sardis and take refuge in Cyme, a Greek city of Aeolis. Pressed by Mazares to hand over the rebel, the Cymeans queried the oracle of the sanctuary of Branchidae, near Miletus. Twice, the oracle told the Cymeans to obey the Persian order. To avoid reprisals, the Cymeans sent Pactyes away to Mytilene, on Lesbos; then, learning that the Mytilenians were negotiating the price of their hostage, they sent the rebel to Chios. The Chians handed him over to the Persians in return for the grant of a tract on the mainland, at Atarnaeus.

This episode elicits some comments. For all that remains unknown of the background of Pactyes, it seems clear that he was an important man in the time of Croesus, and it therefore seems that at Sardis Cyrus did not hesitate to call on local officials to stabilize the period of transition. This was not without risk, as was soon bitterly evident. Similarly, another of the missions entrusted to Mazares was to demobilize all the Lydians in a manner that would prevent any new armed revolt against Persian dominion. This picturesque language must surely be understood to mean that he intended the army to be placed entirely under the command of Medes and Persians. Furthermore, the reaction of the Greek cities to the demands of Mazares must be accounted for. One of them, Cyme, refused to join the armed resistance because its inhabitants could not "survive a siege." If Mytilene and Chios harbored the fugitive, it is because they were offshore cities that, in Herodotus's words (I.143◊), "had nothing to fear," for the Persians did not yet have a trained navy, whereas "the Ionians attained to great naval strength" (Thucydides I.13.6◊). Moreover, neither Mytilene nor Chios wished to test themselves against the Persians; instead they sought commercial advantage from the situation. In other words, there was neither cooperation nor enough community of interest between insular and continental cities to oppose the Persian conquerors.

It is also important to emphasize the reaction of the oracle of Branchidae, who twice urged the Cymeans to obey Mazares. This oracle worked in the sanctuary of Apollo of Didyma, near Miletus, named by Herodotus for the family, the Branchidae, who were traditionally responsible for its maintenance. Its good neighborly relations with Croesus are abundantly illustrated by the gifts offered on several occasions by the Lydian sovereign. It appears that Cyrus did the same, which doubtless resulted in the oracle's interference in the Mazares affair. Good relations between Cyrus and another sanctuary of Apollo, Aulai near Magnesia on the Meander, are evidenced in a document from the time of Darius, who reports the benefactions of his ancestors to the sanctuary (ML 12). Cyrus also maintained the sanctuary of Apollo at Claros, near Ephesus. These examples indicate that from the outset Cyrus felt the need to seek the good will of the local sanctuaries—a policy that he followed at Babylon and that his successors were later to extend throughout their empire.

Harpagus in Asia Minor

After the capture of Pactyes, Mazares began to reduce the cities that had collaborated with the rebel one by one: Priene and Magnesia were ravaged. After the death of Mazares, Cyrus sent another Mede, Harpagus, the same man who had deserted Astyages for Cyrus, to Asia Minor. Diodorus (IX.35◇) gives him the title "commander on the sea." No doubt he commanded other generals, Hystaspes and Adousios, both named by Xenophon (*Cyr.* VII.4.1–7; VIII.6.7). Knowing themselves unable to resist a siege, several communities (Phocaea, Teos) chose the path of exile. The other cities were conquered one by one, and Persian garrisons were stationed there. The Ionians had to provide contingents to Harpagus, who advanced toward Caria and Lycia: "The Carians were reduced to slavery by Harpagus, and in the fighting neither they nor any of the Greeks who lived in this part of the country managed to distinguish themselves" (Herodotus I.174◇). As for the inhabitants of Xanthus and Caunus in Lycia, they preferred death to submission (at least in the rather stereotyped version recorded by the historian of Halicarnassus; Herodotus I.175–76).

Despite the impression given by Herodotus's story, the Persian conquests were neither rapid nor easy, since it took at least four years for Cyrus's generals to establish their superiority. "In this way Ionia was once more reduced to subjection," concludes Herodotus (I.169◇), alluding to the previous Lydian dominion. We still must point out that, contrary to what the Halicarnassian historian supposes, the Ionians of the islands remained largely outside the reach of Achaemenid expansion.

4. Cyrus in Central Asia

"While Harpagus was turning upside-down the lower, or western, part of Asia, Cyrus was engaged with the north and east, bringing into subjection every nation without exception," writes Herodotus (I.177◇). We have seen how in the spring of 546 the king had left Asia Minor, called back by more pressing dangers: Babylon, the Saka and Bactrians, and Egypt, according to Herodotus (I.153). Unfortunately, the chronology, the timing, and the methods of the expeditions in Central Asia are very poorly known. The main reason is that Herodotus breathes not a word of the marches against the Saka and the Bactrians, passing directly (I.178–200) to the final offensive against Babylon, which took place beginning in 540, and then to the king's combat with the Massagetae, where Cyrus met his death in 530 (I.206–7). Herodotus does not conceal, though, that he made a deliberate choice from the information available to him: "Most of his minor conquests I will say nothing about, but mention only those of his campaigns which gave him the greatest trouble and are in themselves the most interesting."◊ As a result of selection criteria that are not necessarily the same as ours, Herodotus preferred to devote long digressions to the description of Babylon and Babylonian customs (I.178–88; 192–200) and to the manners and customs of the Massagetae of Central Asia (I.201–4; 215–16), rather than offering his readers a chronologically continuous tale of the expeditions of Cyrus. In the absence of Herodotus, we must resort to fragmentary, confused, and late sources: Ctesias (summarized by Photius) and the court historians of Alexander, who were ready and willing to identify the footprints of Cyrus beneath the steps of the Macedonian. In short, the available materials do not allow us to establish securely the chronology of the Persian expeditions in Central Asia, and they are silent on the likely occurrence of simultaneous military operations on the Babylonian and Central Asian fronts.

The reference in Herodotus to Saka and Bactrians among the dangers facing Cyrus after the capture of Sardis indicates at least that the submission that the Central Asian peoples (Hyrcanians, Parthians, Saka, Bactrians) had been willing to tender to Cyrus after the capture of Ecbatana had been no more than circumstantial and formal. Justin confirms this by writing (1.7.2): "When power changed hands, the states that until then were tributary to the Medes believed their situation also to be changed and revolted against Cyrus, and this defection was for Cyrus the cause and origin of numerous wars." To impose his own authority, it was not enough, then, for the Achaemenid to identify with Astyages; he had to appear in person at the head of his armies.

The geopolitics of the countries of the Iranian Plateau and Central Asia in the period preceding the Achaemenid conquest (first part of the first millennium) is very poorly known mainly because of the absence of credible and indisputable written sources. Bactria in the broader sense—from the Hindu Kush to the Syr Darya—probably represented the region's most important center, although we cannot say with certainty what its political structures may have been. At any rate, this whole region of northern Afghanistan was celebrated as far back as the third millennium for material culture and artistic achievement that in our eyes rival those of the great Mesopotamian centers. There had always been fruitful exchanges between Central Asia and Mesopotamia along the great routes through the south and north (called the Khorasan Road in later times), along which men and merchandise traveled, especially the lapis lazuli from Badakhshan in Bactria that was so prized in Mesopotamia. The agricultural wealth of the great oases of pre-Achaemenid Bactria is thrown into high relief by the gigantic irrigation works that served them and that surveys have revealed in the basin of the Upper Oxus (Amu Darya). Bactria was also a military power that could mobilize armies of renowned cavalry (30,000 at the time of Darius III, according to Quintus Curtius VII.4.30). This Bactria was in close contact with the Iranian-speaking Saka people ("Saka" in Old Persian, "Scythians" in Greek), some of whom were nomadic, others of whom lived not only on stockbreeding but also on agriculture and on commerce beyond the Syr Darya as far as Siberia. They were very powerful peoples in their own right, organized in confederations of tribes, clans, and kingdoms, and the qualities of their horsemen and bowmen are revealed in striking fashion as much by the figural representations in the art of the steppes as by the place they were to take in the Achaemenid armies and in the tales of Alexander's companions. The close relations between the Saka and the Bactrians made a military expedition in Central Asia even more difficult and risky.

It would be illusory and pointless to try to reconstruct the campaigns of Cyrus. We must be satisfied with a few details found by chance in the ancient texts. We know in particular that Cyrus established several garrison towns on the northern frontier, especially the famous Cyropolis, which would be destroyed and then rebuilt by Alexander. Cyrus's passage to the south of the Iranian Plateau is discernible in Seistan (the valley of the Helmand), where a local population, the Ariaspi, provided fresh supplies just when his army was in distress after leaving the desert. Late texts also seem to indicate that Cyrus, during the same expedition or on another occasion, crossed the region of the river of Kabul (the Gandhara of the royal inscriptions), as well as Gedrosia and Carmania. It is perhaps also from this period that the fortress of Old Kandahār, the Achaemenid capital of Arachosia, dates. It is tempting to suppose that Cyrus had subdued (or crossed) the Iranian countries that Darius, at the beginning of his reign, portrays as already conquered: Parthia, Drangiana, Aria, Chorasmia, Bactria, Sogdiana, Gandhara, Scythia, Sattagydia, Arachosia, and Makran. On the other hand, it is certain that he never penetrated the Indus Valley.

5. *The Capture of Babylon* (539)

Sources and Problems

The Neo-Babylonian kingdom now remained Cyrus's most formidable adversary and rival in the Near East. There is no lack of information on this part of the conquest, but the sources are both fragmentary and one-sided. They are first and foremost cuneiform texts: the Cyrus Cylinder (*Cylinder*), the Nabonidus Chronicle (*Chronicle*), and the Cyrus Panegyric [commonly known as *Verse Account of Nabonidus*]. The victory of Cyrus is also "foreseen" in a dynastic prophecy of the Hellenistic era: Cyrus, who is identifiable under the name "king of Elam," takes the throne of a king (Nabonidus) who had reigned seventeen years. In often similar terms, the Babylonian texts—especially the first three—express the point of view of the conqueror. In these texts a conventional interpretation that systematically contrasts the behavior of Cyrus and Nabonidus can be recognized. This is not the viewpoint of the *Dynastic Prophecy*, in which the policy of Cyrus is denounced as aggressive (II.22–24).

The *Chronicle* stresses the fact that during the absence of Nabonidus (then in Teima in Arabia until his seventeenth year), the Babylonian New Year's festival (*Akītu*) was not celebrated with all of the traditional pomp. In the *Cylinder*, Nabonidus is presented as an impious king: he deported the divine statues, "the worship of Marduk, the king of the gods, he made it fall into oblivion" (?), he imposed "a cult that was not proper to them." He was an unjust king in the treatment of his subjects as well: "He did evil toward his city without ceasing. Each day . . . [he tormented his people]. Under a pitiless yoke he crushed them all." An equally severe portrayal is found in the *Verse Account*: there Nabonidus is accused of all evil, in particular of having interrupted the Babylonian New Year in favor of the cult observed at Ḥarran in honor of the god Sîn. Similarly, in the *Dynastic Prophecy*, Nabonidus is the creator of a dynasty centered on Ḥarran; he suppressed the New Year ritual, and he oppressed Akkad.

Let us return to the *Cylinder*. In this context, the "people of Sumer and Akkad" turned away from Nabonidus and appealed to Marduk, who took pity on the Babylonians: "He then found a just prince, according to his heart, and took him by the hand. He pronounced the name of Cyrus, king of Anšan; he then called his name to sovereignty over all." Satisfied with Cyrus (whom his aid permitted to seize the country of Gutium and to conquer the Medes), Marduk "commanded him to turn toward Babylon, his city, and made him take the way to Babylon. As a friend and companion, he marched at his side." It is thus as the chosen of the great Babylonian deity that Cyrus entered Babylon at the head of his army "without combat or battle"; thus Marduk "saved his city of Babylon from distress; he delivered to him Nabonidus, the king who did not worship him. The people of Babylon, all of them, the whole country of Sumer and Akkad, lords and governors, all bowed before his royalty, their visage shone." In the second part of the *Cylinder*, Cyrus speaks in the first person: after presenting his titulature, he twice states that he and his army entered "Babylon peacefully," and he recounts his many pious actions, in particular the return of the divine statues that Nabonidus had deported. The *Chronicle* also specifies that the first Persian detachment (led by Gūbaru/Ugbaru) penetrated Babylon "without a battle" and that with Cyrus's arrival "peace reigned."

From these texts a canonical image of Cyrus has been derived, one that corresponds very closely to that found in the Jewish literature (see p. 46 below). It is also found in the Greek tradition, especially in Xenophon, who represents his power as accepted by the vanquished "with their consent" (*Cyr.* 1.1.4; cf. Diodorus IX.24). Unhappy with Nabonidus's impiety, the Babylonians, led by their priests, supposedly opened the gates voluntarily to the "just king," Cyrus, who from that moment on was received as a "liberator." This traditional interpretation evokes suspicion to the extent that it agrees with the image that Persian propaganda itself would have portrayed.

The Military Conquest

It appears prima facie unlikely that Babylonia could have fallen without resistance. Besides, the *Chronicle* (III.12–13) refers directly to an initial battle won by Cyrus at Opis on the Tigris, dated 10 October 539. This victory was followed by an immense haul of booty and the massacre of those who attempted to resist (III.14). The *Chronicle* continues: "The fourteenth day, Sippar was taken without a fight; Nabonidus took flight" (III.14–15). Then, "Ugbaru, governor of the district of Gutium, and the army of Cyrus entered Babylon without a battle. Then, after his retreat, Nabonidus was captured in Babylon." The capture of Babylon is dated 12 October.

Before returning to the capture of Babylon specifically, we must stress that direct hostilities between the Persians and Nabonidus's troops had perhaps (or probably?) begun before 540. The *Chronicle* (III.9–12) specifies that the cult statues of several Babylonian sanctuaries were brought to Babylon, a sign that Nabonidus had taken measures designed to prevent the Persians from capturing these divine statues. There is no doubt that the Persian threat had become serious. Moreover, one text may allude to hostilities in the Uruk region in the winter of 540–539.

As far as it can be reconstructed, the story of Ugbaru—the first of Cyrus's officers to enter Babylon—itself seems to indicate that the offensive against the Neo-Babylonian possessions had begun at a still earlier period. Ugbaru is referred to in the *Chronicle* with the title "governor of the country of Gutium." According to the *Cylinder* (§13), Cyrus achieved his first victories, under the protection of Marduk, over "the country of Gutium and over all the troops of Manda [Medes]." This Ugbaru is probably the Gobryas who, according to Xenophon, left the Babylonian side and switched to Cyrus. He commanded a vast region (*Cyr.* IV.6.1–11) at whose frontiers the Neo-Babylonian territory began (V.3.1). It was from the territory of Gobryas that Cyrus launched the attack on Babylon (V.2.1–21); it was Gobryas who guided Cyrus's army (V.2.22); he also was the one who took Babylon (VII.5.26–30). As fictionalized as it is, Xenophon's tale seems nonetheless to be based on oral transmission of Ugbaru's story. Ugbaru must have been the Babylonian governor of a territory situated in the foothills of the Diyala that, some years before 540, had seceded and was taking orders from Cyrus. Herodotus (I.189) states further that after his offensive against Babylon Cyrus passed through this region of the Diyala on a road that led to Opis. We thus realize that Nabonidus had massed his troops in this town in a manner that prevented passage over the Tigris by the army of Cyrus. The massacres perpetrated by Cyrus's troops after the battle attest to the vigor of the resistance of the Neo-Babylonian army. It is probably then (or a little before or after) that Susa fell into Cyrus's hands, and the last Neo-Elamite kingdom disappeared once and for all.

The capture of Sippar and the retreat of Nabonidus to Babylon suggest that the Neo-Babylonian king had decided to lead the resistance in the capital. According to Herodotus (I.190✧), at the approach of Cyrus, "the Babylonians had taken the field and were awaiting his approach. As soon as he was within striking distance of the city they attacked him but were defeated and forced to retire inside their defenses." According to Berossus, the Babylonian army was led by Nabonidus himself, who fled to Borsippa after the defeat (Josephus, *Ag. Ap.* I.150–53). However, Cyrus had not yet succeeded completely. Herodotus notes that the Babylonians had stockpiled provisions that would allow them to hold out for several years. Like Xenophon (*Cyr.* VII.5.1ff.), he describes the problems faced by Cyrus, who was unable to take a powerfully fortified town defended by troops resolutely determined to resist. Diverting the waters of the Euphrates enabled him to infiltrate a small company led by Ugbaru, who took advantage of the fact that the Babylonians were then celebrating a major festival. He surrounded the sanctuary of Esagila and took the strong points. A few days later, Cyrus was able to make his entrance into Babylon in the traditional ceremony. Nabonidus was taken prisoner but his life was spared. Beginning in the middle of October 539, tablets are dated by Cyrus's first regnal year.

The first conclusion drawn from this analysis is that the rapidity of the conquest is a distortion introduced by the methods of composition employed by the author of the *Chronicle*, whose object was not to describe military campaigns in detail. He thus left out information that the modern historian considers fundamental. Composed from the point of view of a Babylonian chronicler, the text mentions the Persians only to the extent that their actions concern the history of Babylonia or at least allow Babylonian events proper to be dated in a synchronic perspective (the fall of Astyages to Cyrus [II.1–4], Cyrus's first campaign against an unknown land [II.15–18], the victories of Cyrus in 539); hence the total silence regarding the activities of Cyrus between 547 and 539. Because of this, we know nothing of Persian-Babylonian relations during the long period that covers both Nabonidus's residence in Teima and the conquests achieved by Cyrus from 547 to 539. These gaps in the record necessarily shrink the Persian-Babylonian war to a very short period in autumn 539. But we have good reason to believe that Cyrus's progress did not go unnoticed by the Babylonian court. In other words, the war of 540–

539 was probably just the last stage of hostilities for which we unfortunately have few details. This implies that the suddenness of the conquest of 539 is also probably illusory.

From Nabonidus to Cyrus

The systematic contrast drawn between the impious behavior of Nabonidus and the pious attitude of Cyrus should not be taken at face value. It is doubtful that even before the fall of the town Cyrus was impatiently awaited by a population desperate for a "liberator." In particular, there is no sure proof that Cyrus forged amicable relations with the Babylonian clergy. Just as is true for Media or Lydia, the Persian victory over Babylon cannot be explained solely in terms of betrayals that made it considerably easier. The "triumphal" entry of the Persian king into Babylon does not imply unreserved submission by the Babylonians. In its style and method—very like those of Alexander in 331—the entry simply symbolized the obligations laid on a conquered town to demonstrate its allegiance to the new master.

Nevertheless, the *Cylinder* also allows us to understand what kind of propaganda the new regime put out in order to attract the cooperation of the local elite. Literary analysis of the text leads at once to the observation that Cyrus portrays himself as restoring the divine and earthly order that was set awry by the actions of Nabonidus. Here, as well as in the *Verse Account*, the Babylonian king is denounced for promoting the cult of the moon-god Sîn at the expense of the cult of Marduk. We do know that from the beginning of his reign Nabonidus had intended to restore the sanctuary (Eḫulḫul) of Sîn in the Syrian city of Ḥarran, but it was not until his return from Teima that he began to execute his plan. The motivations of Nabonidus remain in the realm of theory, but in any case, there is no sure proof that in doing this the king would have lost the support of the Babylonian social elite.

Nevertheless, Cyrus represents himself as the restorer of destroyed or abandoned civil and cult structures, beginning at Babylon, as a fragment of the *Cylinder* suggests. Cyrus claims to have rebuilt the fortifications and other structures at Babylon, but also at many other sites of Nabonidus's former kingdom:

> Of Nin[eveh], Aššur, and also of Susa, of Agade, of Ešnunna, of Zamban, of Meturnu and of Der, up to the borders of Gutium, the cult centers beyond the Tigris, whose [cult] structures had long remained in ruins, I returned to their place the gods who lived there and reestablished them for eternity. I gathered all their people and returned their habitations. And the gods of Sumer and Akkad whom Nabonidus, to the wrath of the lord of the gods [Marduk], had transported to Babylon, I had them, on the order of Marduk, the great lord, joyfully installed in their cella, in a dwelling for the joy of the heart. . . .

Several foundation documents from Uruk temples in fact bear the signature of Cyrus: "Cyrus, king of the lands, who loves Esagila and Ezida, son of Cambyses, powerful king, me." It is the same in other centers. But these statements must be put in perspective. Whether it is the sanctuary of Agade, the walls of Babylon, a gate of Uruk, or even the ziggurat of Ur, all these structures had already been restored by Nabonidus, whose activity as an archaeologist-restorer is abundantly documented. The building records of the last Neo-Babylonian king are no fewer than those that mention Cyrus.

By means of the geographic variety of the structures listed, Cyrus was primarily proclaiming his intention of taking over all the territories of the vanquished kingdom. His statement also allowed him to relegate the reign of Nabonidus to the forgotten pages of history. In a fragment of the *Cylinder,* Cyrus states that during the work carried out on a gate of the city he discovered the name of the great Assyrian king, Aššurbanipal, whom he presents as one of his predecessors. This passage is still more interesting because even before the discovery of the fragment, it had been shown that the text of the *Cyrus Cylinder* was composed on the model of inscriptions of Aššurbanipal. He also claims that at the beginning of his reign he had brought the statue of Marduk back to Babylon and made financial arrangements for regular sacrifices.

Nabonidus himself in several inscriptions had not hesitated to associate himself with illustrious predecessors of the dynasty, particularly Nebuchadnezzar II and Neriglissar; naming them was likewise an attempt to justify the power he usurped in a coup d'etat. He too cited Aššurbanipal as a model for his actions. But his later decrees diminishing the importance of Marduk had weakened his position. It became easy for Cyrus to publish counterpropaganda. It is likely that, in recalling the figure of Aššurbanipal, the Babylonian ruling classes expressed their longing for a period that in image and imagination was considered the apogee of Babylonian history. For his part, Cyrus offered himself not as a conquering outsider but as a legitimate king, coming to mend the thread of ancient Babylonian history. In the same spirit, he took up a traditional titulature. While he recalled that he was "son of the great king Cambyses, king of the city of Anšan, grandson of the great king Cyrus, king of the city of Anšan, great-grandson of the great king Teispes, king of Anšan," he also presented himself in the following way: "I am Cyrus, king of the world, great king, powerful king, king of Babylon, king of the country of Sumer and Akkad, king of the four corners of the earth."

Fidelity to the model of Aššurbanipal and the assumption of his titulature constituted a display of Cyrus's imperial program after his entry into Babylon. Without in the least breaking with his Persian heritage (the construction of Pasargadae illustrates this continuity), the conqueror intended to situate himself as the heir of ancient Assyrian power. The successive defeats of Astyages, Croesus, and Nabonidus enabled him to be considered "king of the world." To a certain extent, it may be thought that the capture of Babylon in 539 brought to a close a period of simultaneous equilibrium and uncertainty that began with the fall of the Assyrian Empire in 612–610. For several decades, the Neo-Babylonian and Median kingdoms had fought over the Assyrian heritage. The victory of Cyrus over both settled the question in his favor.

From the point of view of the Babylonians, Cyrus's victory could signify the reconstruction of the old empire. Crown prince Cambyses was recognized for several months as "king of Babylon"; perhaps he presided over the New Year's festival. But, for the victorious king, the fall of Babylon marked the consecration of a new empire that already extended from the Aegean to Central Asia. In this sense, the *Cylinder* does more than represent the opinion of the Babylonian elites; it also transmits the imperial program of Cyrus. The agreement between the two could not be founded on anything but ambiguities and second thoughts, for the Babylonians faced the problem of the integration of their country into an infinitely vaster whole; they risked losing their individuality, which had been restored with such apparent solemnity.

6. Cyrus, Trans-Euphrates, and Egypt

Trans-Euphrates after the Capture of Babylon

Once he was master of Babylon, Cyrus could in principle have claimed the Neo-Babylonian inheritance in the Syro-Palestinian territories, which were traditionally disputed between the masters of Babylon and the masters of Egypt, and where populations exhibiting very great ethnocultural diversity lived side by side: Phoenicians in their great port centers (Tyre, Sidon), Arameans, Hebrews, Palestinians, Arabs, and even Greeks settled in several coastal enclaves. The Neo-Babylonian kings had pursued a consistent and ambitious policy toward these territories with the specific intent of opening an outlet on the Mediterranean and profiting from Mediterranean and Arab trade. Thus they wished to dominate the Phoenician and Palestinian cities, in particular Gaza, which was largely Arabized and was the principal outlet for the trade in aromatics from South Arabia dominated by the kingdom of Saba. Moreover, in these regions the Mesopotamian sovereigns found the raw materials they lacked, such as wood from Lebanon and iron from Cilicia. This is why numerous expeditions were launched to subdue independent kingdoms (Damascus, Israel, Phoenician cities) and to hold in check the peoples of the northern Arabian Peninsula. During his reign, Nabonidus had waged many wars in Cilicia, Syria, Transjordan, and Arabia. His long stay at Teima can be explained in large part by a desire for control of the region.

Among the ancient civilizations of these territories was Judah. Judah had always maintained complex and often hostile relations with Assyro-Babylonian power, frequently attempting to maintain a dangerous policy of swinging in allegiance between Egypt and Babylonia. Let us review the immediately preceding events, which will help make sense of Cyrus's actions in the situation. After Pharaoh Necho II's victory at Megiddo in 609, Judah was incorporated into the Egyptian sphere of influence. At the same time, the ruin of the Neo-Assyrian Empire and the appearance of the Neo-Babylonian kingdom placed the Judahite leaders in an uncomfortable situation: they had to choose between Egypt and Babylonia, without in reality having the means of exerting any influence in the struggle between the two powers. In 605, Pharaoh Necho, who had just been defeated at Carchemish by the Babylonian king Nebuchadnezzar II, deposed the king of Judah, Jehoahaz, and replaced him with Jehoiakim. Jehoiakim saw an opportunity to take advantage of the Babylonian setback by revolting (about 600). In 598–597, when Jehoiachin had succeeded his father, Nebuchadnezzar in person marched against Jerusalem, which fell in March 597. A significant portion of the Judahite elite (royal family, military chiefs, nobles, landowners, priests) were taken captive to Babylonia, and a new king, Zedekiah, was installed by Nebuchadnezzar. Seduced by the promises of the pharaoh, Zedekiah tried to form an anti-Babylonian coalition around Judah. But circumstances were hardly favorable to him. Weakened and impoverished after the disaster of 597, the kingdom of Judah was also torn by internal quarrels, the faction favoring insurrection bitterly opposed by the advocates of submission, the most famous of whom is the prophet Jeremiah, who portrayed the Babylonian victory as a punishment sent by Yahweh against his unfaithful people. It should be added that the pharaoh was not inclined to support Zedekiah unconditionally. The offensive launched by the powerful Babylonian armies breached the Judahite defenses; in the summer of 587 Jerusalem fell, King Zedekiah was imprisoned and his sons massacred before his eyes, the town, the Temple, and other urban centers were razed, and another deportation ensued. A Judahite governor was installed by the Babylonians, but this governor took his orders from Babylon and the population under his authority was reduced in number and impoverished. The kingdom of Judah had ceased to exist; it had become an integral part of the Neo-Babylonian kingdom.

Cyrus and Jerusalem

The figure of Cyrus is unreservedly praised in the Jewish sources. It is possible that, as early as his arrival in Babylon, Cyrus had cemented relations with the leaders of the Jewish community in exile, in whose hands the traditions of the mother country were being maintained, despite significant integration into Babylonian society. It was at Babylon that the prophet Ezekiel had begun to preach in 593. He led his hearers to hope for a return to Jerusalem, the rebuilding of the Temple and the resumption of worship, as well as the renewal of the unified kingdom of Israel and Judah.

The terms used by the author of Second Isaiah are reminiscent of certain passages in the *Cyrus Cylinder*:

> Who roused from the east him that victory hails at every step? Who presents him with nations, subdues kings to him? His sword makes dust of them and his bow scatters them like straw. He pursues them and advances unhindered, his feet scarcely touching the road. Who is the author of this deed if not he who calls the generations from the beginning? I, Yahweh, who am the first and shall be with the last. (Isa 41:2–4)

Then the alliance between Cyrus and Yahweh is made explicit:

> Thus says Yahweh to his anointed, to Cyrus, whom he has taken by his right hand to subdue nations before him and strip the loins of kings, to force gateways before him that their gates be closed no more: I will go before you levelling the heights. I will shatter the bronze gateways, smash the iron bars. I will give you the hidden treasures, the secret hoards, that you may know that I am Yahweh. (Isa 45:1–3])

Chosen and directed by Yahweh—as he was by Marduk at Babylon—the Cyrus of the biblical sources no longer belongs to History; he becomes an ornament and a mythic figure of a Judeocentric history. But historians cannot choose their sources, here any more than elsewhere. In the absence of any other viewpoint, every attempt to understand the intentions and objectives of Cyrus's policy toward the Jewish community must be based on the Jewish literature.

The facts are known entirely from quotations and references to documents purporting to be official documents of the Achaemenid chancellery. These quotations are found in the book of Ezra. The first passage presents a proclamation attributed to Cyrus, inspired by Yahweh: the king is said to authorize the rebuilding of the Temple in Jerusalem and to permit the exiled Judahites to return to their homeland. The order is said to be given to the treasurer Mithradāta to return the sacred vessels, originally brought to Babylon by Nebuchadnezzar, to Sheshbazzar, "prince of Judah." Tyrians and Sidonians were to be conscripted to transport the wood needed for the project from Lebanon to Jerusalem (Ezra 1:1–4, 3:6). Furthermore, at the time of Darius, the text of Cyrus's memorandum was found in the royal archives of Ecbatana, and it is quoted cited in the following words:

> In the first year of Cyrus the king, King Cyrus decreed: Temple of God in Jerusalem. The Temple will be rebuilt as a place at which sacrifices are offered and to which offerings are brought to be burnt. Its height is to be sixty cubits, its width sixty cubits. There are to be three thicknesses of stone blocks and one of wood. The expense is to be met by the king's household. Furthermore, the vessels of gold and silver from the Temple of God which Nebuchadnezzar took from the sanctuary in Jerusalem and brought to Babylon are to be restored so that everything may be restored to the sanctuary in Jerusalem and be put back in the Temple of God. (Ezra 6:2–5)

Doubts persist about the authenticity of these quotations. They certainly do not show formal legal precision. It is also true that the Chronicler was interested entirely in stressing the preferential benevolence Cyrus showed toward the Jews. It is obvious as well that he has collapsed events that took place over a longer period than is indicated. In particular, it is possible that many of the events dated by the Chronicler to the beginning of the reign of Cyrus actually took place during the reign of Cambyses or even later. In sum, while the measures ascribed to Cyrus appear legitimate as a whole, contradictions and uncertainties regarding certain details of the royal decrees and their exact chronology still remain.

According to the editor of the book of Ezra, a first contingent left Babylonia under the joint leadership of two exalted personages, Sheshbazzar and Zerubbabel. Much remains obscure about their origins and their functional relationship. One of them, Sheshbazzar, who has the poorly understood title 'prince' (*tiršata*), may have been a descendant of the illustrious line of David. As for Zerubbabel, it is not absolutely certain that he was even in the first returning caravan. Upon their arrival in Jerusalem, the Jews set about restoring worship. They raised an altar on the old foundations to offer sacrifices, and they began again to honor the traditional festivals. However, this initial restoration remained fragile. A relatively small number of Jews had taken the road to Judah (some 50,000 according to the calculations of the Chronicler). The country had been considerably impoverished since the defeats by the Babylonians, and opposition to the restoration of the Temple arose among the neighbors, so that the work of reconstruction did not really commence during the reign of Cyrus. The Jews proceeded nonetheless with the official "foundation" ceremonies—that is, with the laying of the cornerstone, an act that connoted politico-religious symbolism more than actual construction work. The ancient monarchic institutions were obviously not restored by Cyrus. It appears rather that Judah became a province (*medinah*) controlled by a governor (*peḥā*) appointed by the Great King from among the Jews themselves—namely, Sheshbazzar.

One gets the impression from reading the Jewish texts that the favors and privileges granted by Cyrus were exceptional compared with normal relations between a Near Eastern sovereign and an ethnoreligious community. Along with the Babylonized Cyrus of the *Cylinder,* this portrayal has played no small part in creating an image of the Achaemenid conqueror as a pacific and tolerant king, making a final break with the "barbarous and cruel" practices of the Assyro-Babylonians. Even today, Cyrus is presented by his modern acolytes as the inventor of "human rights." Some have gone so far as to consider the demeanor of Cyrus to be that of a devotee of a religion, Zoroastrianism, that by its rejection of idols actually resembles the religion of the Judeo-Israelites, and that these Achaemenid–Jewish connections were part of a much broader reform of the "polytheistic chaos."

In truth, the issue was never posed in these terms either for Cyrus or even for the Jewish leaders. Because religion and politics were closely linked in ancient Near Eastern society, it is reasonable that the Jewish sources present History in religious terms. But any "religious" decision also had political implications and objectives. Since any city or people had protective deities, it was normal for them to dedicate a cult to these deities and to build sanctuaries for them that constituted both cult places and symbols of an independent or autonomous political entity. It is no less understandable that a conqueror would carry off the gods (that is, the cult statues and objects) along with the royal family and the political and military elites, thus dashing all hope of future revolt against his dominion. This is exactly what Nebuchadnezzar did after the capture of Jerusalem. Conversely, the political and religious restoration of a city or community was accompanied by the return—absolutely essential to the repatriated people—of the statues of the gods that had previously been deported to the former conqueror's capital. It was exactly this that Cyrus did in Babylon. The "exceptional" character of the actions taken by Cyrus on behalf of Jerusalem thus arises only from the narrowly Judeocentric perspective of our sources. Resituated in the ideological and political context of the Near East, they again become what they had been originally: certainly an important episode for the Jews themselves, but a banal and typical event that many Near Eastern peoples would already have experienced in the course of Assyrian and Babylonian dominion.

Cyrus and the Trans-Euphrates

If we deny the existence of special relationships between Cyrus and the Jewish leaders in Babylonia, how are we to interpret his directives? We are reduced to hypothesizing. Let us recall that, according to Herodotus (I.153), Egypt took the side of the enemies who feared Cyrus when he left the Lydian front in 546. For such reasons as this it is generally recognized that the creation of a province of Jerusalem entirely faithful to Persian interests took place in a wider strategic context, with the ultimate goal, sooner or later, of conquering Egypt. But we are very poorly informed about Cyrus's policy in the regions beyond the Euphrates. A passage of the *Cylinder* contains, at first sight, a record of the territorial ambitions of the new master of Babylon. After narrating his entry into Babylon and recalling Marduk's blessing of Cyrus, Cambyses, and the entire Persian army, the text states: "All the kings of the entire world from the Upper [Mediterranean] Sea to the Lower Sea [Persian Gulf], those who are seated in throne rooms, all the kings of Amurru living in tents, brought their heavy tribute and kissed my feet in Babylon." These "kings of Amurru" are probably the kings of the Arab populations of the northern Arabian Peninsula, traditionally called "Scenites" by the Greek authors, that is, those "who live in tents." But the expression used by the compiler of the *Cylinder* is too conventional to allow firm conclusions regarding the degree of these peoples' subjugation.

In his desire to make Cyrus the creator of the empire at its greatest extent, Xenophon assigns Cyrus numerous conquests in these regions. According to him (*Cyr.* I.1.4; VII.4.16), Cyrus subjugated the Arabs and placed a satrap over them (VIII.6.16). Cyprus surrendered voluntarily and sent contingents to the Great King after the conquest of Babylon (VIII.6.8); still according to Xenophon (VIII.8.1), Cyprus and Egypt represented the western edge of Cyrus's empire. It is indeed to Cyrus himself that Xenophon attributes the military expeditions that resulted in the conquest of Egypt (VIII, VIII.6.20). But Xenophon's information is hardly acceptable. Cyrus certainly did not lead a campaign against the Arabs of Arabia; he merely subjugated the "Arab" populations living in Mesopotamia. Just as certainly, he was not the one who conquered Egypt. As for Cyprus, far from having been conquered by the Persians, it seems on the contrary to have been a tributary of Pharaoh Amasis in 539. Nor do we know anything of the situation of in the Phoenician cities at this date. Ezra (3:7) states that, after the return of the Judahites, "to the Sidonians and Tyrians they gave food, drink and oil, so that they would bring cedar wood from Lebanon by sea to Jaffa, for which Cyrus king of Persia had given permission." But, even if such a decision had been made, it does not necessarily imply that political submission of the Phoenician cities to the new Persian power had already been secured. Even if the Phoenicians were subject to the Persians, we know nothing of the concrete forms Persian dominion took. The decisive actions more likely date to the reign of Cambyses, as a remark of Herodotus implies (II.19).

In reality, the only verifiable act of Cyrus was the creation of an immense satrapal administration uniting Babylonia and the countries of Ebir Nāri (literally, 'across the River', that is, Trans-Euphrates) four years after the capture of Babylon. In Herodotus's day, Trans-Euphrates extended "from the town of Posideium [Ras-el Bassit] . . . as far as Egypt. . . . This province (*nomos*) contains the whole of Phoenicia and that part of Syria which is called Palestine, and Cyprus" III.91◇). But it must be added that, before Cambyses, we know practically nothing of the conditions in the countries of Ebir Nāri and their relations with the Achaemenid authorities. It is possible that the province of Judah was not created until the time of Cambyses, since it seems clear that its governor received his instructions from the satrap of Babylonia via his subordinate in Trans-Euphrates.

Cyrus and Egypt

Did Pharaoh Amasis make contact with Cyrus after the capture of Babylon? We know nothing about this, apart from some contradictory information reported by Herodotus (III.1◇) and repeated by later authors. To explain to his readers the reasons for Cambyses' invasion" of Egypt, Herodotus highlights a matrimonial squabble that arose between the courts of Persia and Amasis. He provides the Persian version (III.1) and the version heard from the Egyptians (III.2–3), whose truthfulness he questions. Cyrus supposedly asked Amasis to send him the finest Egyptian oculist. At the urging of this specialist, Cambyses (Persian version) or Cyrus (Egyptian version) supposedly demanded that Amasis send one of his daughters to the Persian court. In the Persian version, she was to marry Cambyses; the Egyptians claimed that she was married to Cyrus and that Cambyses was born of this union. In yet another version, the young Cambyses supposedly swore to avenge his mother Cassandane, who had been humiliated by seeing Cyrus replace her with the Egyptian girl. The only point of agreement among all the versions collected by Herodotus is that Amasis deliberately tricked the Persian king: instead of his own daughter, he supposedly sent Nitetis, the daughter of the previous pharaoh, Apries. That Amasis hoodwinked him in this fashion infuriated Cambyses. To all appearances, this tradition seems to reflect later Persian propaganda, and the historian would do well not to take it into consideration.

7. From Cyrus to Cambyses

If, as seems likely, an Egyptian campaign was in the planning stages, Cyrus ended up unable to lead it himself. The last ten years of his reign are poorly known. All we know is that in 530 the king launched an expedition against the Massagetae of Central Asia. We have no certain evidence regarding the causes and the stages of the military operations, and even the circumstances of the death of Cyrus were very quickly surrounded with a halo of legend, so forcefully did the conflict between the glorious conqueror and Queen Tomyris strike people's imagination. This new expedition in Central Asia attests at least to the difficulties faced by Persian power in maintaining its dominion there.

Before departing, Cyrus took steps to ensure the succession. He sent back to Persia his oldest son Cambyses, "whom he had named as his successor." This note from Herodotus (I.208◇) is confirmed by a passage in Ctesias (*Persica*, §8). In a fictionalized context, Xenophon (*Cyr.* VIII.7.6–28) gives his version of the death of Cyrus in Persia and records the last words of the dying king in the presence of his two sons, the elder Cambyses and the younger Tanaoxares. This Tanaoxares (Ctesias has Tanyoxarces) is the person called Bardiya in the Behistun inscription and several Babylonian documents and called Smerdis by Herodotus. Cyrus then supposedly proceeded to divide duties and powers. Cambyses was made heir. As for Bardiya, he received an immense territory in Central Asia, to which was attached the privilege of not passing on tribute collected in the district to the central authority—a sort of grant, as it were, intended to soothe the anticipated resentment of the one who had not been awarded supreme power. After the death of Cyrus in Central Asia, Cambyses succeeded him with no evident difficulty, and he had his father's body transported to Pasargadae for burial in the tomb that he had prepared beforehand (cf. Ctesias §8).

Apart from scattered information in Babylonian tablets, the reign of the new Great King is known only from the story given by Herodotus about Cambyses' campaign in Egypt between 525 and 522, after which he died in Syria. In Herodotus and among the Classical authors in general, the figure of Cambyses is burdened with strongly negative judgments. The primary reason is that he is strongly contrasted with "good king Cyrus." This is certainly the case for Xenophon, who writes: "As soon as Cyrus was dead, his children at once fell into dissension, states and nations began to revolt, and everything began to deteriorate" (*Cyr.* VIII, 8.2◊). A long passage follows in which Xenophon illustrates his favorite thesis of "Persian decadence." The same version is found in Plato (*Laws*, III.693ff.), in whose eyes the perfect balance achieved under Cyrus deteriorated rapidly with Cambyses. He finds the reason for this in the effete education of the son of the founder of the empire. As proof of this "decadence," he refers to the revolt of Bardiya against Cambyses. It is unnecessary to dwell further on the polemical aspect of these analyses, which are built on a conventional view of the supposed relationship between the wealth of kings and their military incompetence.

For his part and following his Persian sources, Herodotus (III.89◊) also contrasts Cyrus with his successors: "The Persians have a saying that Darius was a tradesman, Cambyses a tyrant, and Cyrus a father." In the course of the story of the Egyptian campaign, Herodotus returns several times to the topic. He repeats the opinion of the Egyptians, according to whom "Cambyses went mad, but even before this he had been far from sound in his mind. . . . They say that from birth Cambyses suffered from a serious illness, which some call the sacred sickness" (III.30.33◊). In support of his reports, Herodotus describes in detail the "heinous crimes" perpetrated by the king both against the Egyptians and against well-born Persians, including his sister-wife. And Herodotus concludes: "In view of all this, I have no doubt whatever that Cambyses was completely out of his mind" (III.38◊). It is clear that here Herodotus was depending closely on the oral sources he used in his reconstruction of the Egyptian campaign and the bloody succession to Cambyses. It is thus important to place his judgments in historical context, so as to gain the necessary perspective and thus to award Cambyses proper credit for his part in the construction of the Achaemenid Empire.

8. *The Egyptian Campaign* (525–522)

The Egypt of Amasis

Herodotus (III.1–2), as we have seen, explains Cambyses' decision to march against Egypt by reasons that will scarcely satisfy the historian, for the interpretations he provides of an Egyptian–Persian dynastic marriage at the time of Cyrus primarily reflect the viewpoint of Persian propaganda. Instead, an examination of the general strategic situation can allow us to understand the conditions that led Cambyses to start so important a military campaign.

Having become master of Cyrus's empire, Cambyses had both to maintain dominion over the conquered countries and to extend the conquest toward the only remaining power of consequence in the Near East, the Egyptian kingdom. This must not be seen as a more or less irrational and uncontrollable desire to take over the entire inhabited world. Cambyses' strategy was instead predetermined by the decision made by his father to annex Trans-Euphrates to Babylonia. This would sooner or later require the subjugation of the countries located between the Euphrates and the Nile and thus necessitated conflict with Egypt, which in the past, and quite recently as well, had exhibited ambitions in this region.

The Egyptian campaign proper was thus certainly preceded by a series of conquests. Our ignorance in these areas is profound. We know in any case that Phoenicia and Cyprus were dependencies of Cambyses in 525. We know neither when nor how the conquest took place. According to Herodotus (III.19◊), "the Phoenicians had taken service under him of their own free will. . . . The Cyprians, too, had given their services to Persia." Both were included in the naval forces mustered by Cambyses for his campaign against Egypt. The conquest of Cyprus was a heavy blow to Pharaoh Amasis because, according to Herodotus (II.182◊), this king "was also the first man to take Cyprus and compel it to pay tribute."

Since 664, Egypt had been governed by the Saite dynasty, whose first members accomplished the difficult task of reuniting the country. Traditionally included in the "Late Period" by Egyptologists, the Saite period seems to have been a true renaissance for Egypt. Since 570, Egypt had been ruled by Amasis, who died in 526. According to Herodotus, "it is said that the reign of Amasis was a time of unexampled material prosperity for Egypt; the earth gave its riches to the people as the river gave its riches to the earth. The total number of inhabited towns at this period was twenty thousand" (II.177◊). Amasis also had powerful armed forces: a fleet that his predecessor, Necho II (610–595), had left him and an army considerably reinforced by contingents of mercenaries from all over the Near East, including Caria and Ionia.

Despite the assets he enjoyed, it can hardly be doubted that Amasis considered Cyrus's conquest of Babylonia a serious danger. He actively pursued a policy aimed at gaining allies for the struggle with the Persians, which was bound to break out in a short time. The Saite pharaohs had long since been fostering relations with numerous Greek states in Europe and Asia Minor. Herodotus (II.178) labels Amasis a "Philhellene." Among the proofs of his philhellenism, he cites the case of Naucratis, a trading post in the Delta established by cities of Asia Minor with the assent of the pharaoh, doubtless during the reign of Psammetichus I. This trade profited not only the Greeks and the Phoenicians (also represented in Egypt), but also the pharaoh, for Amasis maintained strict controls over imports and exports. Customs houses had been erected in the east of the Delta at the Pelusiac mouth and in the west, on the Canopic branch. Taxes were levied there on goods coming from the "northern foreign countries" (Phoenicia, Syria–Palestine) and "foreign countries of the Great Green" (Aegean, i.e., Greek countries), respectively.

Numerous Greek sanctuaries received offerings from the pharaoh: the temple of Delphi and, in Asia Minor, the temple of Athena at Lindos on Rhodes, the temple of Hera at Samos, and the temple of the Branchidae at Didyma, as well as the sanctuary of Athena at Cyrene. The interest of the Saite kings in the cities of Asia Minor was long-standing: traditionally, it was from these cities that they recruited auxiliary troops, who were granted land in Egypt, to reinforce the Egyptian army. According to Herodotus (II.163), Carians and Ionians under the command of Apries numbered 30,000 when he was defeated by Amasis. The author from Halicarnassus also states (II.154◊) that Amasis settled the Ionians and Carians in Memphis "to protect him from his own people." In spite of the discontent provoked in the Egyptian soldiers by these favors granted to the soldiers from Asia Minor, Amasis was following the policy of his predecessors.

Amasis could count among his allies Polycrates, who had established a tyranny on the island of Samos after a coup d'etat. "Once master of it, he concluded a pact of friendship with Amasis, king of Egypt, sealing it by a mutual exchange of presents," writes Herodotus (III.39◊). It was to strengthen this alliance, established with an exchange gifts, that Amasis dedicated "two likenesses of himself, in wood" in the Heraion of Samos (II.182◊). Herodotus emphasizes the power that Polycrates soon acquired: "It was not long before the rapid increase of his power became the talk of Ionia and the rest of Greece. All his campaigns were victorious, his every venture a success."◊ He extended his power as far as the Cyclades, including Rhenaea, near Delos. He soon represented a real threat to the Persian dominion over the Greek cities on the coast of Asia Minor after Cyrus. This is what Herodotus indicates, noting that Polycrates achieved a naval victory over the Mytilenians of Lesbos, allies of Miletus: but Miletus was a subject of the Persians. The raids launched by the tyrant against the islands and the mainland towns imperiled the Achaemenid positions. Herodotus himself emphatically notes that, in his opinion, Polycrates "had high hopes of making himself master of Ionia and the islands" (III.122◊). These were perhaps the circumstances in which Cyrus made Oroetes "governor of Sardis." Without doubt, Oroetes' main assignment was the defense of Achaemenid territories against the actions of the tyrant. In relation to the Persians, Polycrates to some extent played the same role as Croesus when he entered into alliance with the Egyptian pharaoh.

In discussing the concerns of Oroetes, Herodotus writes of Polycrates that he "was the first Greek we know of to plan the dominion of the sea" (III.122◊). He was able to nurture these ambitions thanks to his naval power. According to Herodotus (III.39◊), he had 100 penteconters (fifty-oared galleys). This was a naval force beyond the means of a Greek city, even one as rich as Samos. It is thus not out of the question that it was partially as a result of the aid of Amasis that Polycrates was able to build and maintain such a naval force. According to Herodotus (III.44), in 525 Polycrates even had 40 triremes (galley with three banks of oars). The trireme was a great technological and military innovation that appeared in the Aegean world between 550 and 525. This may be the type of warship that Egypt had as well; it enabled Amasis to take Cyprus.

The Conquest of the Nile Valley and Its Approaches

In 525, however, Egypt's situation had recently taken a turn for the worse. First of all, Amasis had died the year before; he was succeeded by his son Psammetichus III. The loss of Amasis, which occurred when Cambyses was preparing to march against Egypt, had serious consequences. In a long account in the form of a story, Herodotus describes the break between Amasis and Polycrates (III.40–43). According to Herodotus, the treaty of friendship was abrogated on the initiative of Amasis, who was uneasy about the prosperity and unbridled ambition of Polycrates. In reality, Polycrates had himself established contact with Cambyses, who had urged him to send him a squadron of ships. Polycrates dispatched a force of 40 triremes, which he was careful to man with "carefully selected crews, every man of which he had particular reason to suspect of disloyalty to himself . . . with instructions to Cambyses never to allow them to return to Samos."✧ The episode poses several difficulties of interpretation, but the essence is clear: Polycrates forsook the Egyptian alliance and made overtures to the Persian king. No doubt he was uneasy about the dangers mounting against him (Sparta was preparing to send a fleet against Samos) and about the increasing opposition of a faction of the Samian elites who favored cooperation with Egypt. The tyrant's sudden shift of strategy can be understood even better if we assume that it happened after the death of Amasis. Well informed about Cambyses' preparations, he had decided to seek safety in what he judged to be an inevitable Persian victory.

The pharaoh suffered another defection, that of Phanes of Halicarnassus, "a brave and intelligent soldier," in the words of his compatriot Herodotus (III.4✧). He was one of the officers of the Carian troops serving close to the pharaoh, who harbored a strong fear of him, "as he was a person of consequence in the army and had very precise knowledge of the internal condition of Egypt." Escaping the vigilance of the men sent in pursuit of him, Phanes reached Cambyses when he "was anxious to launch his attack on Egypt." He was able to provide the Great King with firsthand information on both the state of Egyptian forces and access routes to the Delta.

Meanwhile, Cambyses had made considerable military preparations. Herodotus notes that, after the conquest of Asia Minor by Cyrus's troops, "the islanders had nothing to fear, because the Phoenicians were not yet subject to Persia and Persia herself was not a sea power" (I.143✧). The subjugation of Cyprus and Phoenicia allowed Cambyses to shift the course of things. In 525, the Phoenicians "were entirely dependent on the strength of their navy (*nautikos stratos*)." This force also included Cypriots, as well as Greeks from Ionia and Aeolis, including a contingent from Mytilene. We may say that Cambyses was the real creator of the Persian Navy, which was built with men and materials levied from both Phoenicia and Asia Minor. This was the compliment that the Persians of Cambyses' entourage paid him when he asked them about his accomplishments: "They had answered that he was better than his father, because he had kept all Cyrus' possession and acquired Egypt and the command of the sea into the bargain" (III.34✧). It does in fact seem that Cambyses created the royal Persian navy in its entirety, and it was indispensable to his hopes of victorious engagement with the pharaoh, who had an imposing fleet of his own.

The military operations are not known in great detail. While telling the story of Phanes, Herodotus dwells at length (III.4–9) on the relations established by Cambyses with the "king of the Arabs," who controlled the desert region between Gaza and the Egyptian border. A formal treaty permitted the Persian king access to enough water to reach the Nile Valley. It was certainly this approach route that allowed Cambyses to impose his direct rule over Trans-Euphratian peoples and cities who before then had surely never seen a Persian soldier. This is the state of affairs that Polybius (XVI.22a) later reports, praising the fidelity of the inhabitants of Gaza to their allies: "When the Persians invaded, for example, when elsewhere all were terrified by the power of the adversary, when all to the last man surrendered to the adversary, they confronted the danger on their own and together withstood the siege." Gaza was an important commercial center—whose prosperity Herodotus compares to that of Sardis—and from that time onward it constituted an essential support for the Persian occupation of Palestine and a bridgehead for any expedition to Egypt.

Psammetichus headed an army comprising Egyptian soldiers and Carian and Greek auxiliaries and was positioned at the Pelusiac mouth of the Nile, where he awaited Cambyses. But Herodotus gives hardly any information about the fighting, being more interested in the terrible vengeance prepared by the pharaoh's Carian and Greek auxiliaries against Phanes (III.11) and in a picturesque comparison of the relative toughness of Egyptian skulls versus Persian skulls (III.12). He mentions simply that the battle ended badly for Psammetichus, whose Egyptian troops sought refuge in the citadel of Memphis. "Cambyses laid seige to the town, and after a time it was surrendered" (III.13◊). Psammetichus was taken prisoner.

The choices made by Herodotus from the information available to him led him to pass over in silence both the strength of the resistance and the role of Psammetichus's navy. A late author, Polyaenus (VII.9), instead emphasizes that Cambyses had to besiege Pelusium and that the Egyptians were able to use catapults and other machines to block Cambyses in front of the town, which ipso facto closed off his entry to Egypt, since Egypt could not be entered without taking the town or having naval superiority. We know that an Egyptian, Udjahorresnet, commanded the sea-going fleet for Amasis and then for Psammetichus III. Because he presents himself as a favorite of Cambyses, we might guess that Udjahorresnet had abandoned Amasis, thus considerably facilitating Cambyses' victory at Pelusium; but the hypothesis remains weak. Once Pelusium was taken, the troops and the Persian navy were able to penetrate the Nile Valley and lay siege to Memphis, which was linked to the sea by various waterways. One of these was traversed by Cambyses' boat, which carried a herald instructed to demand the surrender of the defenders. The herald was killed, along with his retinue. Psammetichus and his troops were in fact able to mount a long resistance in the shadow of the "White Wall," which could not be taken without the support of the fleet. At the end of the siege (whose length Herodotus does not give), Cambyses was able to make his triumphal entry into the town, and a Persian-Egyptian garrison was stationed in the "White Wall."

Once he had conquered Egypt, Cambyses intended to reassert on his own behalf the ambitions of the last pharaohs toward the west (Libya and Cyrenaica) and south (Nubia = Herodotus's Ethiopia). The Libyans, soon followed by the Greeks of Cyrene and Barca, sent gifts to Cambyses as tokens of surrender; as proof of his good will, Cambyses returned the Greek woman whom Amasis had wed when he made an alliance with the Greek town of Cyrene. Then, still following Herodotus (III.17), "he planned a threefold expedition: against the Carthaginians, against the Ammonians, against the Long-Lived Ethiopians who live in Libya on the edge of the southern sea." The expedition against Carthage was canceled because the Phoenicians were unwilling to make war on a Phoenician colony. Although the possibility of an expedition against Carthage seems unlikely, the same cannot be said for royal designs on the south. Cambyses dedicated his efforts to the realization of a great "African project," which consisted in part of acquiring the kingdom of Meroë and in part of seizing strategic positions in the western oases. In this strategy, Cambyses was clearly following the policy of the Saites, who since Psammetichus I had regularly sent expeditions to the south in order to put an end to the Cushite threat and to solidify their dominion at least as far as the First Cataract. A garrison was established at Elephantine. The garrison, already consisting partly of Jewish contingents, was there throughout the time of Cambyses, as we know because, in their petition dating to the reign of Darius II, the Jews recalled that their sanctuary had been built "in the days of the kings of Egypt" and was standing "when Cambyses came into Egypt," and they implied that Cambyses protected it (*DAE* 102 [*AP* 30–31*]).

According to Herodotus, the expeditions, one against the oasis of Ammon, the other against Ethiopia, were repaid with utter disaster. Herodotus blames the "madness" of Cambyses, who "at once began his march against Ethiopia, without any orders for the provision of supplies, and without for a moment considering the fact that he was to take his men to the ends of the earth" (III.26*). But the deliberate bias against Cambyses raises doubts about the accuracy of Herodotus's version. Other evidence indicates that the expedition did not founder in a military catastrophe, even if the difficulties of the undertaking perhaps obliged the Great King to retreat. Specific evidence of this are the latest results of excavations on the site of the fortress of Dorginarti, established in the Saite period at the same latitude as the Second Cataract. The pottery and an Aramaic text show that the fortress, which was doubtless part of an extended network, remained in use throughout the Achaemenid period.

9. *Cambyses and the Egyptian Traditions*

The "Madness" of Cambyses: Sources and Problems

According to Herodotus, up to this time, Cambyses behaved with a certain moderation. He even "felt a touch of pity" and ordered that the son of Psammetichus be spared (III.14*). On the other hand, in the eyes of the same Herodotus, the king "lost his wits completely and, like the madman he was," launched his expedition against the Ethiopians (III.25*). Madness completely possessed the spirit of the king after his return to Memphis. He was seized with fury toward the gods, the cults, the temples, and the priests of Egypt. Herodotus lays particular stress on the murder of the sacred bull Apis and his caretakers. He thinks that Cambyses considered the feasts held in honor of Apis to be celebrations saluting his Ethiopian (Nubian) defeat:

> Cambyses ordered the priests to be whipped by the men whose business it was to carry out such punishments, and any Egyptian who was found still keeping holiday to be put to death. In this way the festival was broken up, the priests punished, and Apis, who lay in the temple for a time wasting away from the wound in his thigh, finally died and was buried by the priests without the knowledge of Cambyses. Even before this Cambyses had been far from sound in his mind; but the Egyptians are convinced that the complete loss of his reason was the direct result of this crime. (III.29*)

There follows the tale of his "murderous madness" against highly placed Persians, against his brother Smerdis (III.30), his sister-wife (III.31–33), and against the Lydian Croesus (III.36–37). Then Herodotus brings grave accusations against the king who "broke open ancient tombs and examined the bodies, and even entered the temple of Hephaestus [Ptah] and jeered at the god's statue" (III.37*). And Herodotus concludes: "In view of all this, I have no doubt whatever that Cambyses was completely out of his mind; it is the only possible explanation of his assault upon, and mockery of, everything which ancient law and custom have made sacred in Egypt" (III.38*).

Following Herodotus, all of the Classical authors repeat the theme of the madness and impiety of Cambyses. "Shocked by Egyptian religious practices, he had the temples of Apis and other gods demolished," writes Justin (I.9.2). Strabo offers the same explanations to explain the destruction of the temples of Heliopolis and Thebes (XVII.1.27, 46). This hostile tradition is also found in Diodorus Siculus (I.46.4✧; 49.5✧):

> The silver and gold and costly works of ivory and rare stone [that the temples of Thebes contained] were carried off by the Persians when Cambyses burned the temples of Egypt; and it was at this time, they say, that the Persians, by transferring all this wealth to Asia and taking artisans along from Egypt, constructed their famous palaces in Persepolis and Susa and throughout Media. . . . [The circle of gold crowning the tomb of Ozymandias], they said, had been plundered by Cambyses and the Persians when he conquered Egypt.

A late tradition recorded by St. Jerome (*Comm. Dan.* I.7.9) even suggests that Cambyses deported 2500 Egyptian cult images. In short, Cambyses, we are led to believe, is supposed to have done everything he possibly could to alienate the Egyptian population as a whole, especially the great families who administered the temples, whose leading position in Egyptian society he certainly could not have been unaware of. Nor could he have been unaware of the role played by the pharaoh or the crown prince in the funeral rites that were intended to mark the earthly death of an Apis. We know for example that Psammetichus III, shortly before Cambyses' invasion, had himself gone through the especially trying ritual fast (total lack of nourishment for four days, and exclusively vegetarian diet for seventy days) and that he had participated in the exhausting ceremonies that played out over the seventy days it took to embalm the sacred bull. Lastly, Cambyses could not have been unaware of the enormous popularity of Apis among the common folk of Egypt, who joined in the mourning. These people made up the towns and nomes of the provinces who, on the demand of the authorities in Memphis, furnished the enormous quantities of materials needed for the mummification of the sacred animal (silver, gold, royal linen, myrrh, precious stones, and all sorts of "good things"). Even less could Cambyses have been unaware that, at the time of his return to Memphis, ceremonies marking the "revelation" of Apis were to be going on, which, according to Herodotus (III.27✧), were celebrated by Egyptians wearing "their best clothes." In conclusion, in the version presented by Herodotus, Cambyses' Egyptian policy (which he contrasts with that of Darius; III.38) shows a strong break with the policy of his father, Cyrus, in conquered countries. Unable to offer a political explanation, Herodotus had no option but to resort to the "madness" of the king (III.38). But modern historians are obliged to show much greater rigor.

Some of the deeds ascribed to the Persians cannot be denied, but they do not necessarily carry the significance that the ancient authors attribute to them. A man as favorable toward the new master as the Egyptian Udjahorresnet (who will be discussed at greater length shortly) himself speaks of the "trouble that arose in this nome [of Sais], when the very great trouble arose in the entire land [of Egypt]." And exalting his good deeds, he writes: "I saved its [my city of Sais's] inhabitants from the very great trouble that arose in the entire land [of Egypt], the likes of which had never existed in this world." This trouble coincides with the settlement of the "foreigners" in Egypt, which led to a temporary state of anarchy. The disorders were not limited to the Delta, since the destruction of Egyptian temples is also recorded on the southern frontier, at Elephantine. We can imagine that many other instances of outrage against both goods and persons were perpetrated by the troops. But it would be an error to see this as the manifestation of an anti-Egyptian policy laid down and enforced by Cambyses; it was simply the prerogative of the victors. Let us note also that sending Egyptian treasures (including the wealth of certain temples) to Persia was nothing out of the ordinary. It was exactly what Cyrus had done at Ecbatana and Sardis.

Moreover, the tradition of the murder of the Apis by Cambyses must be completely reinterpreted in light of discoveries made at the Serapeum of Memphis, where the deceased and embalmed Apises were laid to rest in sarcophagi. The epitaph of the Apis interred at the time of Cambyses, in 524, has actually been found. The king, garbed as an Egyptian and on his knees, is there called "the Horus [. . .], king of Upper and Lower Egypt [. . .]," and the inscription says:

> [Year] 6, third month of the season Shemou, day 10 (?), under the Majesty of the king of Upper and Lower Egypt [. . .] endowed with eternal life, the god was brought in [peace toward the good West and laid to rest in the necropolis in] his [place] which is the place which his Majesty had made for him, [after] all [the ceremonies had been done for him] in the embalming hall [. . .]. It was done according to everything his Majesty had said [. . .]. (Posener no. 3)

The inscription on the sarcophagus is equally eloquent on the role Cambyses played in the events:

> [Cambyses], the king of Upper and Lower Egypt . . . made as his monument to his father Apis-Osiris a large sarcophagus of granite, dedicated by the king [. . .], endowed with all life, with all perpetuity and prosperity (?), with all health, with all joy, appearing eternally as king of Upper and Lower Egypt. (Posener no. 4)

The conclusion seems undeniable: Herodotus recorded spurious information. Far from having killed the young Apis, Cambyses participated in the embalming and funeral rites of an Apis, following the regulations and the ceremony that were well known, particularly in the Saite period. The inscriptions also make it clear that it was in his capacity as "king of Upper and Lower Egypt," as "son of Rā"—in short, as pharaoh—that Cambyses led the funeral ceremonies. From this emerges an image of Cambyses quite different from that which Herodotus wished to convey. Cambyses was a conqueror seeking to take his place and his rank in the rites and rituals of the Egyptians; he was an Achaemenid king who wished to comply, as pharaoh, with the practices and beliefs that had become inscribed in the Egyptian *longue durée*. Confirmation of this wish is found in the inscription on the Egyptian seal of the new pharaoh:

> The king of Upper and Lower Egypt, Cambyses, beloved of [the goddess] Wajet, sovereign of [the town of] Imet, great, Eye of the Sun, sovereign of the Sky, mistress of the gods, to whom is given life, as to the Sun.

Udjahorresnet and Cambyses

Conclusions of the same kind can be drawn from the analysis of another, even better-known hieroglyphic text, namely, the inscriptions on a statuette that shows Udjahorresnet, whom we have already met, carrying a small, portable shrine (fig. 44, p. 473). This statue and its inscriptions, probably erected in the temple of Osiris at Saïs, were intended to ensure divine benevolence in the hereafter for the person represented, as is shown by the final appeal to the gods, who were asked to "recall all the meritorious deeds" of the dedicator. They were also intended to preserve his memory and his acts for future generations of pilgrims. Needless to say, the autobiographical character of the texts invites the historian to submit the texts to a critical reading.

Udjahorresnet presents himself as a benefactor: he restored the splendor of the temple of Neith at Saïs, he was "a good man" in the good town of Saïs, he "defended the weak against the powerful," he was "a good son and a good brother, filling those near to him with favors and privileges." On the other hand, he is much more discreet about the manner in which he passed from the service of Amasis and Psammetichus III to the service of Cambyses and then Darius. However it may have happened, there is no doubt that he turned to the new power. In detailing, with a touch of vanity, the titles bestowed on him by Amasis, Psammetichus, Cambyses, and Darius, he presents himself as a man very close to all of the kings, both Saite and Persian: "I was a (man) honored by all his masters. . . . They gave me gold ornaments and made for me all useful things" (Posener no. 1F). Udjahorresnet, a figure of the transition, was firmly devoted to situating his career and his actions in the service of purely Egyptian dynastic and ideological continuity.

It is true that Udjahorresnet, as we have seen, alludes directly to the Persian invasion that caused "great trouble," not only in Saïs but in all of Egypt. This reference permits him first and foremost to emphasize the relief he himself had brought to the temple of Neith, to his family, and more generally to the inhabitants of the Saite nome. However, it is also in this context that he established a special relationship with Cambyses. He had come before the king to complain about the presence of Achaemenid soldiers (the "foreigners") within the precinct of the sanctuary of Neith. The king ordered the evacuation of the troops and the purification of the temple. Throughout the text, Cambyses is presented as the restorer of order: expressions such as "as it was before," "as any king would do," "as any beneficent king would do," or "as any previous king would do" are used in regard to him several times. Cambyses "restored" landed estates to the goddess Neith; in the sanctuary he "replaced" people expelled by the soldiers. . . . In this way, Udjahorresnet absolves the king of all responsibility for the extortions that were committed. Cambyses is added to the long series of "beneficent kings" who took care of the temples and cults. He went in person to Saïs, prostrated himself before the goddess, and presented his offerings, "as any beneficent king would do." He "established the presentation of libations to the lord of Eternity (Osiris) within the temple of Neith, as any previous king would do."

Cambyses, the conqueror of Egypt, is thus clearly presented by Udjahorresnet as a pharaoh, in the full sense of the term. The Egyptian consistently names the Persian king "king of Upper and Lower Egypt"—a title he also bears in the inscriptions of the Serapeum. In reality, after the victory Cambyses played a sort of double role. He was "the great king of the foreign countries" who came to Egypt with "the foreigners of all the foreign countries." But, "as soon as he took possession of this entire land [. . .], he was great sovereign of Egypt, great king of all the foreign countries." Through his titulature and his privileged relationship with the gods, Cambyses acquired in the eyes of Udjahorresnet the status of pharaoh, which clothed him with all of the attributes and endowed him with all of the traditional virtues. Thus, ideological bases were put in place on which the collaboration between Cambyses (later Darius) and Udjahorresnet was founded. From this point of view, the Egyptian's statements are not inconsistent with the *Cyrus Cylinder*: in the same way that Cyrus was Babylonized, Cambyses in Egypt was Egyptianized by the Egyptians who wished to collaborate with the new power. For both of them it was the best way to present the image of a solicitous conqueror, graciously bending to the polit-ico-religious traditions of the conquered countries. It was, in a way, acquiescing to Baby-lonian and Egyptian continuity in order to highlight the Achaemenid discontinuity.

There can be no doubt that this policy was defined by Cambyses himself. Udjahorres-net even states that it was on the orders of the sovereign that he composed his titulature, namely "king of Upper and Lower Egypt." But it seems likely that Persian propaganda must have taken extra pains to justify the power of Cambyses in Egypt. Among the "im-pious" crimes perpetrated by Cambyses at Saïs, Herodotus (III.16◊) lists the violation of the sepulchre of Amasis: "He gave orders for his body to be taken from the tomb where it lay. This done, he proceeded to have it treated with every possible indignity, such as lashing with whips, pricking with goads, and the plucking of its hairs. . . . Cambyses ordered it to be burnt. This was a wicked thing to do. . . ." A priori, this behavior seems absolutely contrary to the express intention of Cambyses to act as the successor of the legitimate pharaohs. But other acts and accounts also tell of his desire to be linked di-rectly with Pharaoh Hophra (Apries), whom Amasis had deposed in order to seize power. This is also the sense of one of the accounts of Cambyses that describes him as a son of Cyrus and a daughter of Apries. Amasis fell victim to a veritable *damnatio memoriae* in the Persian period.

Collaboration and Resistance

It remains for us to inquire into the origin of Herodotus's presentation of the policy of Cambyses. If it is so contrary to the facts and to the statements of Udjahorresnet, it is be-cause, at the time of his investigation in Egypt two generations later, the historian from Halicarnassus encountered informants hostile to the memory of the conqueror of Egypt—namely, Egyptian informants whom he cites numerous times. Now, at the time of Herodotus, relations between Egyptians and Persians were strained and difficult, the Egyptians having revolted several times after 525. It is this context that gave rise to leg-ends and popular stories that presented Cambyses as the prototypical conqueror—bru-tal, impious, and bloody. It should be added that Herodotus also gathered information and opinion from Persian circles that were very hostile to Cambyses.

Nevertheless, it would also be excessive and misleading to suggest that the opinion and behavior of Udjahorresnet should be generalized. That the "legitimizing" propa-ganda of Cambyses would have been ubiquitous and clever is one thing; that it would have aroused unanimous adherance and sympathy is another. The allegiance of Udjahor-resnet himself was won conditionally: he would not have recognized Cambyses' power unless Cambyses had adopted the rules and precepts of traditional pharaonic royalty.

Moreover, several indications suggest that not all Egyptians were ready to submit to the Persian king. Herodotus (III.14◊) describes the punishment incurred by the Egyp-tians who massacred the herald sent by Cambyses to Memphis: 2000 young Egyptians, "their mouths bridled and a rope round their necks," were led to execution, the royal judges having decided that "for each man [massacred by the Egyptians] ten Egyptian noblemen should die." The staging of the "spectacle" is equally significant: the con-demned were paraded before the conquered pharaoh, who was surrounded by the fa-thers of the victims. Anxious above all to throw into relief the dignity of Psammetichus, Herodotus states that the pharaoh remained stone-faced upon seeing his son, unlike his companions, who dissolved in grief. Similarly, a few minutes earlier, Psammetichus had said nothing when his daughter was paraded, clothed as a slave, along with young aristocratic ladies, similarly dressed. Through his demeanor, the pharaoh expressed his refusal to accede to the new power.

Indeed, Herodotus reports that Cambyses, who "felt a touch of pity," ordered the son of Psammetichus to be spared. In reality, he was the first to be put to death! He adds that Psammetichus "lived at court from that time onward. Here he was well treated," and he even thinks that "if he had only had the sense to keep out of mischief, he might have recovered Egypt and ruled it as governor" (III.15◊). He explains the supposed behavior of Cambyses by a rule of the Persian kings, "who are in the habit of treating the sons of kings with honour, and even of restoring to their sons the thrones of those who have rebelled against them." But the Egyptian examples Herodotus cites are quite unconvincing. As for the behavior ascribed to the Persian kings, it is at least nuanced by Isocrates, who says kings "as a rule . . . do not reconcile with those who rebel before they have taken them prisoner" (*Evag.* 63). It is clear that Cambyses never dreamed of returning the government of Egypt to Psammetichus. It should be emphasized above all that Psammetichus was not content merely with intrigue: "He was caught in *flagrante delicto* inciting the Egyptians to revolt; and when he was discovered by Cambyses, he was forced to drink bull's blood; and he died on the spot. Thus was his end!" So it seems clear that the pharaoh had never agreed to recognize the one who claimed to be his successor.

Another social group—again closely linked to the Egyptian aristocracy—could with good reason claim to be unhappy with Cambyses' activities—namely, the administrators of the Egyptian temples. It is true that Udjahorresnet emphasizes that, at his request, the new pharaoh restored to the goddess the revenues of the landed estates, "as it had been previously." But his exaltation of the new pharaoh's piety toward Neith of Saïs must be placed in the context of a statement that was intended primarily to stress the amount of benefactions the sanctuary at Saïs realized from the cooperation between Udjahorresnet and Cambyses. It appears that not all of the temples would have been so happy about Cambyses' policy. The stelas marking royal generosity to the temples, so numerous before 525, disappeared in the time of Cambyses. This observation has been linked to a royal decree attributed to Cambyses. The text, unfortunately quite difficult to read, is preserved in a Demotic document on the verso of the *Demotic Chronicle.* Cambyses is accused of having set drastic limitations on the revenues in kind that the Egyptian temples collected in the time of Amasis. Only three temples were exempt from this regulation.

Many obscurities continue to surround the scope and objectives of the measure taken by Cambyses. The compilers contrast his conduct with that of Darius, who collected the Egyptian jurisprudential traditions, including those relating to "rights of the temples." Let us simply recall that the problem of relations between the temples and the king persisted throughout Egyptian history, with the pharaohs attempting simultaneously to recognize the rights of the temples and to limit their financial power. The gifts of land to the temples were not disinterested: the pharaoh, who retained a right of eminent domain, thus developed a policy "intended less to enrich the temples than to keep active the economy of which they were the center" (D. Meeks). The Saites acted no differently. In this area, the discontinuity introduced by Cambyses is perhaps more apparent than real. To evaluate it, this measure must be placed in the framework of an overall study of tribute administration in Egypt—a difficult task in view of the scarcity of documentation. Moreover, converging indications attest to the increase of tribute appropriations under his reign. The Egyptian temples no doubt did not avoid them.

It is thus quite likely that the negative image of Cambyses goes back in part to the moment of the conquest and administrative organization of Egypt. On this hypothesis, we might think that the fiscal measures enacted by Cambyses were reprisals against the sanctuaries that had little inclination to legitimate the installation of a foreign power. Whatever it was, the royal decision need not be considered a contradiction of the general policy applied to the Egyptians. As for the powerful Egyptian temples, the new pharaoh could not pursue a policy of unlimited generosity. He had to control them or risk reducing the conquest to a short-lived pretense. It was the same in Babylonia, where the proclamations of devotion to Cyrus and Cambyses went hand in hand with increased fiscal pressure (pp. 73f.). It was not only the financial power of the new pharaoh that was at stake but also the reality of his power, so recent and fragile and threatened by opposition. Perhaps this is also why Egypt was converted to a satrapy whose government Cambyses, before departing, turned over to the Persian Aryandes.

Called back by news of a rebellion in Persia, Cambyses left Egypt hastily in the spring of 522. While crossing Syria, he was wounded in the thigh; gangrene set in, and the son of Cyrus died at the beginning of summer, 522. Before returning at greater length to the events of 522, we should pause to draw up the initial balance sheet of the conquests.

Chapter 2

The Conquest and After:
An Interim Summary

1. *From Cyrus to Darius: Sources and Problems*

By the time of Cambyses' death in 522, an impresssive amount of territory had been conquered in the span of thirty years. The Achaemenid dynasty, which around 550 ruled a narrow territory of the southern Zagros, had engulfed every kingdom and empire that shared the Near East and Central Asia. The range of its dominion extended thenceforth from Cyrenaica to the Hindu Kush, from the Syr Darya to the Persian Gulf. The earlier political structures were officially dissolved, and their titulature had vanished or else had been assumed by the conquerors. From this point of view alone, the reigns of Cyrus and Cambyses would appear to be a high point on the scale of the ancient history of the Near East. For the first time, a state had been formed with a single purpose, and what is more, a state that was based not merely on continental possessions; it also had wide access to the sea via the Persian Gulf, the Mediterranean, and the Black Sea. With Cambyses, the new state had forged a naval power that allowed it to control a vast maritime front. This is in striking contrast to the geopolitical situation prevailing toward the middle of the sixth century.

Traditionally, the organizational work is attributed almost exclusively to Darius. But there is no a priori reason to distinguish sharply between a phase of military conquests (Cyrus and Cambyses) and a phase of organization (Darius). Obviously no one would dream of depriving Darius of his justified renown in this area. Nonetheless, it must also be recognized that Darius and his advisers built on preexisting structures, which emerged both from local traditions and from the initial adaptations introduced by Cyrus and his son. That said, it must be admitted that we do not have the sort of abundant and varied documentation for Cyrus and Cambyses that is available from the reign of Darius. Marked by the theme of "good king Cyrus," the Classical sources are of scant help. This remark holds true especially for Xenophon, who in the *Cyropaedia* assigns his hero an essential role in the organization of the empire: Cyrus, conqueror without peer (Xenophon even credits him with the conquest of Egypt) and creator of the Persian army and cavalry, would have been the first, after the conquest of Babylon, ever to have a global vision for the administrative organization of the Empire-in-the-making. He appointed the high officials of the central court (VIII.1.9–12), organized the finances (1.13–14), required nobles to attend the royal court (1.5–6, 17–22), etc. — everything is listed under the name of Cyrus. The same goes for the institution of satraps (VIII.6.1–15) and of the inspectors' service for the satrapies and the express postal service (VIII.6.16–18). And Xenophon insists repeatedly on the durability of decisions made by Cyrus: "And the institutions which Cyrus inaugurated as a means of securing the kingdom permanently to himself and the Persians, as has been set forth in the following narrative, these the succeeding kings have preserved unchanged even to this day" (VIII.1.7✧). But none of this presentation has any diachronic value. Xenophon instead paints a timeless tableau of the Achaemenid Empire. Sufficient proof may be found in a comparison of the identical portraits of Cyrus the Elder in the *Cyropaedia* and Cyrus the Younger in the *Anabasis*. To be sure, many of the institutions portrayed in the *Cyropaedia* are known and confirmed by many other texts, but nothing requires us to attribute them to Cyrus alone.

In fact, the strictly Persian written evidence is bafflingly sparse. Cyrus is never mentioned by Darius in the Behistun inscription other than as father of Cambyses and Bardiya. Darius, whose legitimacy as monarch was not entirely above suspicion, was not afraid to write about his predecessors: "Those who were the former kings, as long as they lived, by them was not done thus as by the favor of Ahuramazda was done by me in one and the same year" (*DB* §§50–52✧). It would be going too far, however, to attribute to Darius a desire to inflict a *damnatio memoriae* on the founder of the empire. Besides, we know that the memory of Cyrus was preserved with special fervor by the Persians. Cyrus was certainly one of the "great men" whose heroic deeds were passed on to the younger generation. "Cyrus—with whom nobody in Persia has ever dreamt of comparing himself," Herodotus remarks (III.160✧), claiming to represent Darius's views. Wishing above all to legitimate his newly won power, Darius quite naturally dedicated the Behistun inscription to exaltation of his own accomplishments, which he intended to be preserved for posterity. The Behistun inscription is not a textbook of Persian history! There are several copies of three trilingual inscriptions (in Old Persian, Akkadian, Elamite) in the name of Cyrus, found at Pasargadae. They are very short: "I am Cyrus the King, an Achaemenian" (*CMa*✧), or "Cyrus the Great King, an Achaemenian" (*CMc*✧). Another (*CMb*✧) reads: "Cyrus the Great King, son of Cambyses the King, an Achaemenian. He says: When . . . made . . ." But these documents must be excluded from the discussion, because their authenticity is now widely contested, not without excellent reasons. They most certainly derive from Darius, taking the role of forger that is attributed to him, who wished in this particular case to draw on the prestige of Cyrus to his own advantage.

On the other hand, we can turn to archaeological records discovered in Persis, as well as to written records of non-Persian origin. The many Akkadian tablets provide indirect but valuable indications of the administration of Babylonia at the time of the founders of the Empire. Information that is drawn from texts and iconography from Judah, Egypt, and western Asia Minor may be added.

Precisely because of the nature of the available documentation, the picture of the Empire around 522 cannot be more than partial. But it is well to attempt to paint it, in order better to comprehend not just the specifics of the reforms put in place by Darius after he seized power but also the breadth and limitations of the modifications and adaptations Cyrus and Cambyses made to the organization of the countries they had just subjugated.

2. Satraps and Satrapies

The Satraps of Cyrus and Cambyses

The long passage Herodotus dedicates to the reforms set in motion by Darius after his victory over his opponents begins with this phrase (III.89✧): Darius "proceded to set up twenty provincial governorships (*nomoi*), called satrapies." It would be venturing well beyond the evidence to conclude from this text that the first satrapies were inaugurated at the beginning of Darius's reign (which is not what Herodotus says, in any case). The term *satrap* is in fact firmly attested from the time of Cyrus and Cambyses. First of all, this is what the situation existing in 522 shows: in his Behistun inscription, Darius himself refers to Dādarši, "satrap in Bactria" (*DB* §§10–19), and Vivāna, "satrap in Arachosia" (*DB* §§54–64). We also learn that at this date Hystaspes, the father of Darius, held a high military post in Parthia-Hyrcania (and not the post of satrap of Persia, as Herodotus has it; III, III.70). In Asia Minor, the Persian Oroetes was named "governor of Sardis" by Cyrus (Herodotus III.120◊). There, as elsewhere, Herodotus does not use the term *satrap*, but the much less specific term *hyparch*. With the expression *Sardiōn hyparkhos*, Herodotus seems to refer to a vast district in Asia Minor, including both Lydia and Ionia (III.127). The residence of Oroetes is sometimes Sardis (III.126), sometimes Magnesia on the Meander (III.121). Oroetes was still in office at the accession of Darius. The satrapy of Hellespontine Phrygia is also known, held at the time of Cambyses by Mitrobates (*hyparkhos*), who resided at Dascylium (III.126). Shortly after the death of Cambyses, Oroetes put Mitrobates and his son Cranaspes to death and brought Hellespontine Phrygia under his authority. It is also known that, beginning in the fourth regnal year of Cyrus (535), a certain Gubāru was given the title "governor (*piḫatu*) of Babylonia and Trans-Euphrates." He was thus theoretically in charge of an immense satrapy that included nearly all of the countries previously under the control of the Neo-Babylonian king, from the Tigris to the approaches to the Nile. In an unclear context, he is mentioned together with a scribe-chancellor (*bēl ṭēmi*) of Media, which could lead one to suspect the presence of an imperial adminstration at Ecbatana (cf. also Ezra 6:2). As for Egypt, Cambyses provided it with a "governor/satrap" (*hyparkhos*), the Persian Aryandes (Herodotus IV.166).

It might be supposed that within the most extensive satrapies there were sub-governors, but we have no indisputable attestations for this period, except perhaps in Babylon. Otherwise, it is quite clear that the creation of satrapies did not cause the preexisting political entities to disappear. The Greek and Phoenician cities and the Babylonian towns retained considerable autonomy, as long as they fulfilled the obligations placed on them, especially the financial and military obligations. The same was true for the province of Judah within the satrapy of Babylonia and Trans-Euphrates. Xenophon (VII.4.2◊) states, with regard to Cilicia and Cyprus, that Cyrus "had never sent a Persian as satrap to govern either the Cilicians or the Cyprians, but was always satisfied with their native princes. Tribute, however, he did receive from them, and whenever he needed forces he made a requisition upon them for troops" (cf. also VIII.6.7). Herodotus says (I.28) that Cilicia had not been conquered by Croesus. It was still ruled at the time of Cyrus and Cambyses by a local dynast who bore the title *syennesis* (I.74), described as "king of the Cilicians" by Herodotus (V.118). In spite of the conquest of Xanthus by the Mede Harpagus on the orders of Cyrus, Lycia also continued under the rule of petty local dynasts, who nonetheless were required to recognize Persian power at least nominally. This situation does not necessarily imply that the Persians had no territorial base there, but we cannot verify this with a firsthand document as of this date. We are too poorly informed about the situation before Cyrus within Cilicia, Lycia, or even Caria to be able reasonably to discuss the modifications that may have come about in reaction to the Persian conquest.

The Duties of the Satrap

It is more difficult to determine the precise duties of Cyrus's and Cambyses' satraps. The actual word in Old Persian means 'protector of the realm [kingdom]'. In general, the Greek and Babylonian texts do not use the Old Persian word, preferring to render it with the more vague term 'governor' (*hyparkhos/pihatu*), and when it does appear, it generally does not convey any more specific meaning. At Behistun, when Darius names his two satraps, Vivāna in Arachosia and Dādarši in Bactria, he qualifies both as *bandaka*, a Persian term referring to a personal connection between the sovereign and the Persian aristocrats. In itself, the term connotes first and foremost the total loyalty to the king of the person described by it. In other words, the duty of a satrap was not necessarily connected to a territory. Moreover, the term *satrapy* (attributed to the Persians by Herodotus I.192) does not occur at Behistun: Vivāna and Dādarši are satraps *in* Arachosia and *in* Bactria, respectively. A satrap was first and foremost the personal representative of the king. At the same time, the examples known from the time of Cyrus and Cambyses indicate that their satraps were charged with missions in a specific territory.

A satrap was appointed by the king and had to adhere closely to the orders received from the central authority and remain accountable. Oroetes had already been a rebel in the time of Cambyses (who, according to Herodotus, wanted to dismiss him), and he clearly displayed his desire for independence when he killed the messenger of Darius. The messenger, it seems, had come to inform him of an order to appear at court (Herodotus III.126). This is confirmed by a story (probably fictionalized) of relations between Cambyses and his brother Bardiya (called Tanyoxarces by Ctesias), who had been given a major district in eastern Iran by Cyrus. An intimate of Cambyses counseled him to summon his brother: "To prove the infidelity of Tanyoxarces, he saw to it that if he were ordered to come, he would not come." Tanyoxarces did not defer to the royal command until the third summons and, says Ctesias, he was then put to death (§*Persica*, §10).

One of the primary tasks of the satrap must have been to maintain order and to extend Persian power. According to Herodotus (III.120), Oroetes fell out with Mitrobates when the latter reproached him for not having managed "to add the island of Samos to the domains of the king." After he had come over to Cambyses, the tyrant Polycrates of Samos, it seems, schemed incessantly against the Persian possessions on the mainland and showed himself to be an overt rival of the satrapal court in Sardis. He tried at the same time to gain the support of certain Lydian aristocrats who were unhappy with the government of Oroetes (Diodorus X.16.4). According to Herodotus (III.120◊), who places the event "about the time of Cambyses' last sickness," the satrap decided to put an end to the power of Polycrates. To this end, he sent his principal adviser, the Lydian Myrsos, son of Gyges, to the tyrant. Myrsos succeeded in persuading the tyrant to come and visit Oroetes, who for his part claimed to be threatened by Cambyses. Under these circumstances, Oroetes put Polycrates to death. Maeandrius then succeeded Polycrates. Although it does not imply direct submission to the Persian authorities, the death of Polycrates does attest to the desire of the satrap to expand the domains of the king.

The military duty of the satraps is also evident in the role played by Dādarši and Vivāna in 522–521 in the north and south of the Iranian Plateau, respectively. For these tasks, the satraps were definitely able to count on a standing army. We know that Oroetes "was a powerful man, being governor of Phrygia, Lydia, and Ionia, with a thousand

Persians in his bodyguard" (III.127✧). He thus had to be able to draft contingents from the conquered peoples. It is also likely that the system of assigning land in the conquered countries to Persian families began during the reigns of Cyrus and Cambyses. This was described by Xenophon as follows: "In times past it was their national custom that those who held lands should furnish cavalrymen from their possessions and that these, in case of war, should also take the field" (*Cyr.* VIII.8.20✧). In exchange for land grants, Persian nobles of the imperial diaspora thus had to lead mounted contingents if any satrap demanded it. Since the system was seen in operation around 500 in western Asia Minor, it can reasonably be supposed that it went back to the time of the conquest.

The satraps must have been able to rely on garrisons as well. A Persian garrison was stationed at Babylon. It is possible that the rebuilding of the fortress of Old Kandahār dates to the reign of Cyrus. In Egypt, the Elephantine garrison continued, as in the past, to guard the southern frontier of the country at the First Cataract; another watched over the White Wall at Memphis. Others are known to have been at Migdol (near Pelusium in the Delta) and other Delta sites. According to Herodotus (II.30✧), the Persians retained the Saite installations, not only at Elephantine, but also "in Daphne at Pelusium against the Arabs and Assyrians, and a third at Marea to keep a watch on Libya." It is likely that the granting of land to garrison soldiers, especially well attested at Elephantine, was also inherited by the Persians from the Saites (cf. II.152). In Asia Minor, we know of the fortress of Sardis, where Croesus took refuge and was promptly besieged by Cyrus's troops. The fortress was situated on a formidable height, as is stressed by all of the ancient authors from Herodotus to Polybius. The taking of existing fortresses is presented by Xenophon as one of the goals of *his* Cyrus in the course of his conquests. He did this especially in the various regions of Asia Minor, particularly Caria and Phrygia, where his generals placed garrisons in the numerous citadels that had already been fortified by the Carians or the Phrygians (cf. *Cyr.* VII.4.1–11). Finally, the tale of the struggles of 522–520 recorded in the Behistun inscription reveals the existence of numerous citadels (Old Persian *didā*; Elamite *halmarriš*) in the Iranian countries: Sikayauvatiš in Media (§*DB* §13), Tigra and Uyama in Armenia (§§27–28), and Kapišākaniš and Aršādā in Arachosia (§§45, 47).

The internal organization of these districts is very poorly known. We know of the existence of the treasurer Mithradāta at Babylon in the time of Cyrus, but he was a royal, not a satrapal, treasurer. We know that there was a 'royal secretary' (*grammatistes basileios*) with Oroetes, obviously in charge of the exchange of couriers with the central court. In this regard, Herodotus (III.128✧) adds an explanatory aside: "an officer who forms part of every governor's establishment." The best-known example, the administration of Gubāru, shows that the satrap exchanged extensive correspondence not just with the central authority but also with all of his underlings and perhaps also with officials of other provinces. He thus had under his command a chancellery made up of a large number of secretaries and scribes (*sipīru*). With this in mind, we can surely assume that, from this period on, archives must have existed in every satrapal capital, organized according to imperial instructions and according to the local traditions of each conquered country.

After his victory, Cyrus entrusted the guarding of the citadel of Sardis to a Persian named Tabalus. It thus appears that he was responsible directly to the king and not to the satrap. Let us recall in this regard what Xenophon wrote about the measures he attributes to Cyrus, stressing their permanence, as usual: "And as Cyrus then effected his organization, even so unto this day all the garrisons under the king (*hai hypo basilei phylakai*) are kept up" (*Cyr.* VIII.6.14◊). According to Xenophon (VI.1.1), the king considered this measure to be a precaution against revolts by the satraps. At the same time, it seems clear that, in a general way, the commanders of the citadels also had to function as subordinates to the satrap, to the extent that he had received orders from the king.

3. *Tributes and Gifts*

Revenues and Fiscal Administration

After mentioning the twenty districts (*nomoi*/satrapies) organized by Darius, Herodotus writes (III.89◊): "Darius had "each nation assessed for taxes (*pharoi*). . . . During the reigns of Cyrus and Cambyses there was no fixed tribute at all, the revenue coming from gifts (*dōra*) only." We will return below (chap. 10) to the extent of the modifications to the tribute system made by Darius. But at this point it is useful to introduce the subject in order to determine, as best we can, what revenues were paid to Cyrus and Cambyses in these regions. This means first and foremost understanding what Herodotus wrote and what he intended to tell his Greek readers.

First of all, it is self-evident that neither Cyrus nor Cambyses neglected fiscal administration. Both of them needed considerable resources to maintain their armies and to succeed in their expeditions. After each victory, Cyrus had the treasures of the conquered kings sent to his capitals: the treasure of Astyages was sent to Pasargadae. The same was true for the treasures of Croesus. It is likely that Cambyses gave similar orders in Egypt, as well as in Babylon. We know in fact that, when the Jews returned to Jerusalem, Cyrus ordered the treasurer Mithradāta to return the sacred vessels that Nebuchadnezzar had taken to Babylon after the fall of Jerusalem to the heads of the community (Ezra 1:7–11, 5:14–15). This is how the accumulation of royal wealth that later so impressed the Greeks began. Each imperial treasury was directed by a royal treasurer (**ganzabara*), such as Mithradāta in Babylon in Cyrus's time. He was charged less with literally guarding the treasure than with its management: management, the income and expenditure of capital by order of the king.

Both tribute and gifts accumulated in these treasuries. The existence of tribute levies in the time of Cyrus and Cambyses cannot be doubted. This is apparent not only in the *Cyropaedia*—which is always a priori under suspicion of anachronism—but also in Herodotus. It seems clear that the Greek cities of Ionia had to pay tribute, just as they had in the period of Lydian dominion (I.27). The principle is simple: whether in the form of "gifts" or "tribute," all peoples who acknowledged Persian supremacy were required to pay contributions in kind or in precious metal to the central authority, not to mention the military contingents or oarsmen they had to furnish in compliance with any royal requisition.

This state of affairs is expressed by Herodotus himself, who also says that one of the first measures taken by the usurper Smerdis/Bardiya in his struggle with Cambyses was "to every nation within his dominion he proclaimed, directly he came to the throne, a three years' remission of taxes and military service (*phorou . . . ateleia*)" (III.67◊; cf. Justin I.9.12). Furthermore, only the assumption of regular tribute can explain the regular and permanent exemptions known from this era. Such was the case for a people of the Helmand Valley, the Ariaspi, who, for having rescued Cyrus's army from the brink of

famine, received from the king the title *Euergetes* ('Benefactors') and thenceforth enjoyed an exemption (*ateleia*). The same was true for Bardiya, who, at the death of Cyrus,
had received a major district in Central Asia: "Cyrus had prescribed that he would hold
these countries while enjoying an exemption (*ateleis*)" (Ctesias, *Persica* §8).

Tribute-Paying Peoples and Gift-Giving Peoples

What, then, are the basic characteristics by which Herodotus distinguishes those he
calls gift-givers from those he calls tribute-payers? Let us note from the start that this distinction is not an Achaemenid innovation; it can be found in many states of the Near
East, from Mesopotamia to Egypt. It is thus likely that to a certain extent Herodotus
gives a Greek cast to Near Eastern phenomena. The problem is that the vocabulary he
uses manages to obscure the facts more than it lights the lamp for the modern historian.
In fact, he implicitly analyzes Achaemenid tribute in terms of the tribute (*phoros*) levied
by the Athenians on the membership of the Delian League, beginning in 478. But,
whatever the similarities that can be established between the two organizations, we
know that in reality the Achaemenid system was far more complex; tribute properly
speaking was just one of the constituent sub-parts of the revenue system (chap. 10). Consequently, it would be pointless to try to determine the Near Eastern terminology concealed under Herodotus's vocabulary. Rather, we should look to Herodotus's method of
literary development to bring to light his text's internal logic.

Indeed, it rapidly becomes clear that neither Herodotus's approach nor his objective
is that of a specialist in fiscal practice. The discussion in III.88–117 is dedicated primarily to highlighting the political power of Darius. The introductory phrase gives the key
to Herodotus's perspective: "In this way Darius became king of Persia. Following the
conquests of Cyrus and Cambyses, his dominion extended over the whole of Asia, with
the exception of Arabia" (III.88❖). From the first, he stresses that after the accession of
the new king, "power was felt in every corner of his dominions."❖ The first act of Darius
was to erect an equestrian statue to glorify himself (III.88). "He then proceeded to set up
twenty provincial governorships (*arkhoi*), called satrapies . . . and each nation [was] assessed for taxes" (III.89❖).

Herodotus is trying to place Darius in both continuity and discontinuity with his predecessors, whose conquests he had described. He intends first to show his readers that
Darius enlarged the Achaemenid possessions (III.117) and that his Empire thereafter extended far in all directions (III.98, 102, 106–7, 114–15). It is according to this logic that
the numerical listing of levies that the king assessed on the conquered peoples proceeds
from tribute proper to taxes imposed "over and above the regular tax" (III.91, 117❖) to
gifts (which are also added to the tribute in the calculation of royal revenues: III.97).
The parenthesis on tribute (III.89–98)—if we may venture this paradoxical formulation—is subordinate to an exposition of a political character and to a consideration of
territorial strength.

It is by this same logic that at the end of his story he states that even under Darius a
few "peoples upon whom no regular tax was imposed made a contribution in the form
of gifts."❖ These donors were first the Colchians and the Ethiopians, who even in Herodotus's day brought "presents for their taxes." The Colchians sent "a hundred boys and
a hundred girls," the Ethiopians "about two quarts of unrefined gold, two hundred logs
of ebony, [five Ethiopian boys,] and twenty elephant tusks. . . . Lastly, the Arabians
brought a thousand talents . . . of frankincense every year. This, then, was the revenue

which the king received over and above what was produced by regular taxation" (III.97✧). Let us attempt to explain the apparent paradox created by Herodotus's citation of the peoples who donated to Darius after peremptorily asserting that in the transition from Cyrus to Darius they passed from a system of gifts to a system of tribute.

Let us stress from the start the expression used by Herodotus: these people taxed *themselves*. The terminology explains what was in principle the voluntary nature of the gift. A similar formula is found with regard to the Libyans, the Cyrenians, and the Barcaeans, who were stunned by the victory of Cambyses in Egypt: "The neighbouring Libyans were alarmed by the fate of Egypt and gave themselves up without striking a blow, agreeing to pay tribute (*phoros*) and sending presents (*dōra*). A similar fear caused the people of Cyrene and Barca to follow their example" (III.13✧). It seems clear that from Herodotus's point of view people who sent donations were less dependent on the Great King than people who paid tribute because they were taxed. We may note also that these peoples were located at the extremities (*ta eskhata*) of the imperial territory of Darius (III.97, 106–7, 115–16), at the edge of the "inhabited world" (III.106–7✧). We may remark further that the periodicity of the gifts was not the same as that of tribute. While the Arabs' obligation was on an annual cycle, the Ethiopians paid only every two years and the Colchians every four years. But Herodotus himself expresses the limits of the very distinction that he posed as an absolute rule. On the one hand, both tributaries and donors were situated in the imperial realm, as he says very clearly regarding the Colchians (III.97). On the other hand, he states that the Libyans, the Cyrenians, and the Barcaeans did not just bring gifts to Cambyses; they also sent a tribute (*phoros*) "which they had set themselves" (III.13). Finally, he reports why Cambyses refused the gifts sent by the Cyrenians. In his opinion, the king "objected to the smallness of the amount—it was only 500 *minae* of silver."✧ In other words, however "voluntary" it may have been considered, the gift had to be of a certain value. All this leads us to believe that this amount was negotiated in advance with the king whose sovereignty was to be recognized. The Cyrenians probably "forgot" to do this; hence Cambyses' refusal of what quite reasonably appeared to him to be thinly veiled contempt.

From Cyrus to Darius

Let us return to Herodotus's contrast between Cyrus and Cambyses on the one hand and Darius on the other. In reality, Herodotus did not, strictly speaking, claim that Darius was the first to impose tribute; he intended primarily to stress that he was the first to *fix* the basis of the levies as well as their exact amounts. This is why the term *fix* recurs in his narrative several times, in different forms. This is probably the reason why, in Herodotus's eyes, Darius was the "creator" of tribute in the sense it would naturally have for an Athenian of the fifth century: a system where each subject entity was taxed by the ruling power for a determined amount, evaluated in precious metal and calculated on objective criteria. Thus the final remark on the Ethiopians, the Colchians, and the Arabs. After the reforms instituted by the king, the category of "donor" peoples (in the sense understood by Herodotus) did not disappear. But henceforth, in the eyes of Herodotus it represented more a surviving peripheral element than a constituent element of the Achaemenid tribute system.

From Cyrus to Darius, it was not the institution of tribute itself that was created from nothing; it was instead the conditions under which it was levied that were profoundly altered. This more technical point of view also explains Herodotus (III.89) when he draws the portrait of Cyrus, considered by the Persians themselves as a "father," in contrast to Cambyses, the "despot" and Darius the "shopkeeper" (*kapēlos*), in fact "driving a bargain in all things." Cambyses "was harsh and reckless"; Cyrus, on the contrary, "was gentle and he had procured for the Persians all sorts of benefits." This is Herodotus's own interpretation, and it is quite difficult to find any factual justification for it. In the Greek portrait of Cyrus, he was a chivalrous conqueror to whom people submitted of their own free will, as Xenophon especially puts it (*Cyr.* I.1). From this perspective, assessments are considered a "gift" in the political sense used by Herodotus. One can suppose that, from Cyrus to Cambyses, the initial modification occurred when Cyrus's successor strongly increased the fiscal pressure on his subjects (whether in the form of gifts or tributes) to finance the Persian fleet needed to conquer Egypt, and thus arose his reputation for "severity." Darius was the first to set a value on land and to establish fixed numbers in proportion to this valuation and in this way perhaps earned the qualification *kapēlos* 'retail trader' that Herodotus assigns to him. But this is nothing but conjecture.

Tribute and Coinage

It is likely that at the time of the first two kings the Persian administrators generally continued to profit from the fiscal practices already in effect in the conquered countries—at Sardis, where the Lydian Pactyes was entrusted with levying tribute, as well as at Ecbatana, Babylon, or Egypt. We can also theorize that, at the time of Cyrus and Cambyses, in certain regions where there were no tribute

rolls (eventually to be established by Darius), it was the satraps who negotiated with the local leaders, with all the risks of arbitrariness that such a procedure presupposes.

It also appears clear that the levying of tribute under Cyrus and Cambyses in no way implies the existence of coinage. When the peoples furnished their tribute in precious metal, a standard of weight served as the basis for calculation: thus, for example, the "gift" of 500 minas of silver from the Cyrenians to Cambyses. If we accept that these were Babylonian minas, then the gift from the Cyrenians amounted to about 252 kg of silver. In any case, there was no specifically Persian coinage before Darius. In western Asia Minor, it seems that the gold and silver Lydian coins called "croesids" continued to be struck and used by the royal Achaemenid administration at Sardis. It is even possible that the silver "croesids" circulated only after the conquest of Sardis by Cyrus, thus virtually playing the role of royal coinage. It is quite certainly in terms of the "light" croesid that the tribute from the Greek cities to the Achaemenid administration was measured.

4. Continuities and Adaptations: The Case of Babylonia

Changes and Integration

The question remains whether the conquest resulted in real changes for the conquered populations. Where the reigns of Cyrus and Cambyses are concerned, the response can only be qualified, because the work of empire-building had just begun. It is clear that neither Cyrus nor his son wished (would they even have been able?) to bring about a total disruption of existing conditions. Many institutions known from their time find their antecedents in the Mesopotamian imperial structures of the previous centuries. In other words, the transformations did not necessarily result from suppression or destruction of the existing institutions, but more often and doubtless more efficaciously came about by gradually adapting these institutions to the new structure outlined by the conquerors.

We have seen that Cyrus himself, beginning with the conquest of Babylon, wished to put the accent more on the continuities than on the discontinuities, at least in his propagandistic assertions. He was recognized in October 539 as 'king of Babylon' and 'king of the countries' (*šar Babili/šar mātāti*), in one instance even bearing the title 'king of the countries, king of the kings' (*šar šarrāni*). The title "king of Babylon" passed very soon to his son Cambyses, who kept it for about a year (early 538 to early 537). Cambyses thus bore the title "king of Babylon" in association with his father, Cyrus ("king of the countries"), as is seen in the dual titulature found on some tablets: "Year 1 of Cambyses, king of Babylon, son of Cyrus, king of the countries." What is more, the internal administration of Babylon does not seem to have been severely damaged. For the first three years of Persian dominion, the highest administrator of the region was a certain Nabū-aḫḫē-bulliṭ, who under Nabonidus already held the rank of *šakin ṭēmi*, the highest position in the administration after the *šakin māti* ('governor of the countries'). This system does not reflect the re-creation of the old kingdom at all, since the delegated authority of Cambyses was exercised only over northern Babylonia. Furthermore, the disappearance of the double titulature (early 537) and the creation of a satrapy under the conrol of the Persian Gubāru (535) indicate that after this period of transition Cyrus considered it useful to assert his direct supervision of the country. We know neither the reasons nor the circumstances that led the king to make these decisions, but the fact is clear: Babylonia was transformed at once into a full-blown satrapy. But what did this mean in practice?

At first sight, the Babylonian documentation exhibits great continuity. In the absence of any satrapal archives, the Akkadian tablets we have basically come from private archives or temple archives. They do not refer explicitly to political upheavals. In the private archives in particular, the major historical events, such as the conquest of Cyrus, would not even be noticeable if the notaries did not date their documents according to the regnal year of the sovereign in power. Several documents from the time of Cyrus and Cambyses indicate that the temple adminstrators continued to refer to regulations issued in the time of Nebuchadnezzar II, Neriglissar, and Nabonidus. Given these factors, it is not always easy to distinguish between the maintenance of Babylonian institutions and the assumption of power by the Persian conquerors. Thus, in a document like the *Craftsmen's Charter*, from the Eanna during the reign of Cyrus (535–534), the artisans of the sanctuary pledge themselves before the authorities (the *šatammu* and the royal Commissioner) to work exclusively on the projects of construction and restoration at the Eanna and take their oath in the name of "Bēl, Nabū, and the majesty of Cyrus, king of Babylon." If he does not keep his word, the guilty craftsman "will receive the punishment of the gods and the king." Should we see this document simply as an indication of strong continuity with prior practice? Or, rather, should it be considered *also* to be evidence of a policy of Cyrus, who was seeking to ensure the cooperation of the temple craftsmen in view of the restoration work he was then undertaking at Babylon, Uruk, and Ur?

Otherwise, many individuals continued to pursue their own careers, not in the least affected by the political changes. We may mention, for example, a certain scribe at Sippar who is attested without interruption from 545 to 500. The careers of higher officials also continued uninterrupted. Among other examples, we may cite the case of Ṣirikti-Ninurta, who held the highest position (*šandabakku*) at Nippur from year 17 of Nabonidus to year 7 of Cambyses. The title *šandabakku* itself continues to be attested at Nippur until (and beyond) the beginning of the reign of Darius (521) and intermittently as late as 73 B.C. We can make the same observation with regard to a major business firm like that of the Egibis, which is known from the beginning of the seventh century and which continued to operate under the reigns of Cyrus, Cambyses, and their immediate successors.

However, these formal continuities can conceal adaptations to the new conditions. The reference to prior regulations might also indicate that the regulations had undergone modification. For instance, the Egibi archives also bear witness to the integration of the Babylonian ruling class into the new imperial context. A tablet dated 537 states that the principal representative of the firm, Itti-Marduk-balāṭu, did business at Ecbatana, with the debt payable (in Babylon) in dates at the Babylonian rate. Four years later, the same person is found operating the same way at a place in Iran, with the debt payable at Ecbatana. Furthermore, several tablets dated to the reign of Cambyses (another is dated to the reign of Bardiya/Vahyazdāta?) show that the Egibis also did business in Persia, specifically at Ḫumadēšu, which is identified with Matezziš, very close to the site of Persepolis. The same Itti-Marduk-balāṭu entered into contracts there four times and also bought slaves with Iranian names there, whom he sold in Babylon, before selling them back again to his original business partner in Matezziš. Among other things, these documents show that the Egibis were able to adapt very quickly to the new conditions that derived from the Persian conquest, at the same time that the conquerors were perfectly able to exploit the possibilities opened by the Babylonian institutions and hierarchies.

Temple Lands and Royal Administration

The existing documentation also permits us to determine that the satrap Gubāru was involved in numerous matters. Given the fact that the majority of relevant tablets come from temple archives, his relations with the authorities of these temples are particularly well attested. This is particularly true of the Eanna of Uruk, which is dedicated to the goddess Inanna-Ištar, the "Lady of Uruk." The Eanna was in control of vast agricultural areas irrigated by a sophisticated system of canals in a network along the Euphrates and dedicated primarily to growing cereals (barley in particular) as well as dates. Some of the land remained more or less fallow and was used to pasture sizable herds of livestock that were branded with the star of the goddess. It was from these lands that the temple drew its most clearly visible revenues. This is why the assessment of the standing crops (*imittu emēdu*) was so important in the agricultural calendar. In the beginning, it is likely that this operation was linked to the calculation of the tithe that everyone, including the king, had to pay to the Babylonian temples.

In principle, the temple administration was autonomous and controlled by the free citizens (*mār banē*) of the city of Uruk, who gathered in assembly (*puḫru*) to adjudicate differences that might arise, for example, between the temple authorities and their subordinates or the ordinary farmers. The supreme authority over temple affairs consisted of the director (*qīpu*) and the administrator (*šatammu*) of the Eanna. The administrator was in charge of the lands, management of temple personnel, and activities relating to religious service. From the eighth year of his reign (553) on, however, Nabonidus, assisted by his son Bēlshazzar, introduced modifications that in general were not rescinded by Cyrus and Cambyses. In order to gain tighter control over such strategic financial powers and to improve agricultural profitability, the royal authority decided to play a direct role in the economic activities of the Babylonian temples under its control. Henceforth, the administrator of the temple of the goddess of Uruk was flanked by a "royal commissioner, overseer of the Eanna," who acted simultaneously as royal official and administrator of the Eanna. The Eanna also had a "head of the royal cash box," clearly a manager and protector of royal interests.

The most important of the modifications introduced by the son of Nabonidus, in the name of his father, was the creation of what is now called the *ferme générale*. The system "consists, as far as we are able to recreate the main features, of putting under the authority of a man or a small staff a certain amount of land and a certain number of men, on condition that the *fermier général* ('chief farmer') deliver a quantity of grain or dates fixed in advance" (F. Joannès). The farms (barley or dates) were allocated to the highest bidder. The royal commissioner was present at every stage: the conclusion of the contract with the *fermier général*, assessment of the harvest, transportation of the harvest, and so on. After the Persian conquest, a man named Kalba was *fermier général* of barley. He kept his post during the first two years of Cyrus, but thereafter the position was associated with Nergal-epuš for barley and Ardiya for dates. Beginning with the third year of Cyrus, Ardiya was in full control of the date farm. Beginning with Cambyses, this same concession was assigned jointly to four farmers, Ardiya retaining the most important farm until the end of Cambyses' reign. The same fragmentation is recorded for the barley farm. At the initiative of Gubāru in 528, ten temple oblates were summoned to Babylon, and a *ferme générale* was then created, with several heads. The situation at the end of the reign of Cambyses was rather different from the situation under Nabonidus. This change results in part from the tension that existed between the temple and royal power. After a short reestablishment of the *ferme générale* at the beginning of the reign of Darius for an oblate named Gimillu, the end of the development led to the reclaiming of the organization by the temple authorities. In view of intentions generally attributed to Nabonidus and his sons, this was to some extent a check on royal authority, but a check the nature and extent of which is difficult to measure because of the loss (or nonpublication) of the temple archives from Darius.

The Fiscal Obligations of the Babylonian Temples

There is no doubt whatever that the Great Kings drew considerable revenues from the Babylonian temples. Perhaps the fiscal pressure even increased in the time of Cyrus and Cambyses, especially if we recognize that, in contrast to their predecessors, the Persian kings no longer tithed to the Babylonian temples. But a recent study of the Ebabbar of Sippar seems to contradict such a clear-cut theory. In any case, the examples of royal appropriations are many and varied. Under orders received from the satrap, the authorities of the Eanna of Uruk frequently had to offer all sorts of payments. The temple repeatedly had to send laborers to do construction work at the royal palaces or furnish raw materials (wood, bricks) for buildings. Each order includes the following threat addressed to the person responsible for the delivery: "If not, he will incur the punishment of Gubāru." The temple also had to deliver foodstuffs to the court, as several documents from the time of Cyrus and Cambyses indicate. For instance, in 531 the Eanna had to deliver spices to the royal palace at Abanu. To fill this order, it had to borrow considerable amounts of silver. In 528, over a short period, the Eanna had to deliver successively 200 suckling lambs and kids, then 80 fatted oxen; several weeks earlier, the temple authorities had received an order to transport 200 casks of sweet date beer to Abanu for the provisioning of the court. Perhaps these were unusual requisitions, owing to the presence of the king and the court in residence near the Eanna. But other obligations also weighed permanently on the temples. At the Eanna, for example, we know of the existence of royal herds that obviously were fed and maintained at the expense of the temple.

The Eanna also had to furnish soldiers to the royal administration, at least under certain special conditions. A series of tablets dating to the Neo-Babylonian period (reigns of Nebuchadnezzar II and Nabonidus) and to the reigns of Cyrus and Cambyses shows, for example, that the temple herds were sent to distant pastures on the bank of the Tigris. To maintain security, the Eanna levied and equipped archers to keep guard in the lookouts. Indeed, some of these archers who answered to the Eanna were regularly attached to the royal army, even under Cyrus.

The temples were subject to levies and assessments that also applied to the Babylonian towns and their inhabitants. In particular, all those who owned land (whether individuals or organizations) had 'corvée' (*urāšu*) obligations. This duty was required by the royal administrators so that they could maintain the canals. The Eanna of Uruk was no exception to the rule: the administrators were answerable to the king for the proper functioning of the waterways that irrigated the lands of the sanctuary. In short, the Babylonian temples did not enjoy any more or any less right of extraterritoriality under Cyrus or Cambyses than under their Neo-Babylonian predecessors.

The Jurisdiction of Gubāru

Even the organization of the *ferme générale* implied frequent interference from the satrap Gubāru, who sometimes acted directly, sometimes through the royal commissioner at the Eanna. As the authority responsible for the farming contracts that were drawn up in the presence of the "royal commissioner, overseer of the Eanna," Gubāru had to see to the strict fulfillment of the obligations laid on the *fermiers généraux*. Violaters of any sort were generally summoned to Uruk by the royal commissioner. In 526, it was the satrap himself who sent the following summons to Ardiya, the date farmer:

> Before the end of the month of Kislimu of year 4 of Cambyses, king of Babylon, king of the countries, Ardiya, son of Nabû-bān-aḫi, descendant of Rēmūt-Ea, the *fermier général* of dates of Ištar of Uruk, will bring 5,000 loads of palm fronds and give them to the palace of the king that is appointed over the Eanna, to Nabû-aḫ-iddin, royal commissioner, overseer of the Eanna. If he does not bring them, he will incur the punishment of Gubāru, the governor of Babylon and Trans-Euphrates. (*YBT* 7.168)

In the same way, he was involved in disputes regarding the irrigation work:

> Aqrīya, son of Nabû-dala', will muster ten pioneers among the laborers who, divided into groups of six, are under his orders and give them for the canal Ḫarri-kippi. If Nabû-balaṭ-šarri-iqbi, *fermier général* of the Piqūdu canal, sends (different orders) to these pioneers and does not give them (for this work), he will incur the punishment of Gubāru, the governor of Babylon and Trans-Euphrates. (*TCL* 13.150)

Once Gubāru even intervened to settle a dispute that arose between the authority of the Eanna and the authorities of the city of Uruk, who were refusing to see to guarding the Eanna. A decision was made by the temple administrator and the royal commissioner: the offenders were threatened with an appearance before Gubāru. And one tablet seems to imply that the punishments ordered by Gubāru and his subordinates were applied without stinting (*YOS* 7.128).

These examples permit us to gauge the extent to which the overlapping interests of the cities, temples, farmers, and royal administration forced the satrap to intervene judicially, at the expense of the city assembly (*puḫru*). More precisely, in many cases Gubāru's administration served as an appeals tribunal. The most striking example is the case brought by the temple authorities against the oblate Gimillu in September 538, a little less than a year after Cyrus's entry into Babylon. A crafty man with few scruples about his methods, he has already been mentioned (p. 73) in connection with his job, "in charge of livestock revenues of the Eanna." He was hauled before a tribunal at Uruk and convicted of livestock theft and sentenced. However, he continued to perform various tasks at the Eanna and to enrich himself dishonestly, apparently thanks to protection from higher-ups. He even had the nerve to appeal to the jurisdiction of the satrap. The Uruk tribunal promptly decided to send him before the royal tribunal in Babylon. Suits and sentences apparently did not keep Gimillu from regaining his position in Cambyses' time, when he was again in charge of livestock at the Eanna. At the beginning of the reign of Darius, he even acquired the date concession, as well as a barley concession. In this capacity, we find him writing to the "accountant of Babylon" to complain of the conditions laid on him. Exasperated by his chicaneries, the leaders of the Eanna summoned him in 520. He lost the *ferme générale* and then disappeared from the scene.

Administration of Land

Finally, it is likely that one consequence of the Persian conquest was redistribution of some of the land for the profit of the king and the Persian conquerors. Despite the scarcity of evidence, there is hardly any doubt that land was allotted to the crown in the first place. A good illustration of this is found in documents that required the Eanna to send labor to assist in the creation of several "paradises," royal residences par excellence. In Babylonia, as elsewhere, land was also allotted to high officials. A tablet dated 529 refers to Silā, Gubāru's superintendent (*rab bīti*)—apparently the person charged with running the satrap's estates (*bītu*: 'house'). The use of "the canal of Gubāru," which is mentioned in this text, was conceded to communities located in the region of Ḫandid, which was apparently situated not far from Sippar. Two other estates near Uruk allotted to Persians are known from Cambyses' time.

But the greatest novelty seems to have been the institution of the *ḫaṭru*. This is well documented from the second half of the fifth century because of the archives of the house of Murašû. The term refers to a community that was alloted an area that it cultivated in family plots. These plots had various names: 'hand estate' (*bīt ritti*), 'bow estate' (*bīt qašti*), 'horse estate' (*bīt sisî*), 'chariot estate' (*bīt narkabti*). The last three terms indicate that the original function of these plots was to supply soldiers for the king. Some texts (unfortunately, difficult to interpret) indicate that these plots, or some of them at least, existed at the time of Cyrus and Cambyses. One of them, dated to the first year of Cambyses king of Babylon (538), refers to a group of Egyptians represented by "the Assembly of the Elders," which, it seems, had carried out the division of plots within a bow estate. Other documents from the time of Cambyses refer to a "town of the Carians." These people seem to have settled on the king's land and to have been required to furnish soldiers. Bow estates are also mentioned in the Babylonian version of the Behistun inscription. The passage seems to provide adequate confirmation that the institution was prevalent even before the accession of Darius, or at least that it was in the process of being organized (see p. 104).

To be sure, precedents for the institution can easily be identified in pre-Achaemenid Babylonia. But, as far as we can determine, Cyrus and Cambyses gave impetus and new significance to a system that simultaneously favored the territorial establishment of the new authority and the increase of agricultural production and royal revenues. Setting up communities of allotment-holders fully devoted to the new masters showed clearly that the conquest could not be reduced to a violent, transitory raid. Instead, the Great Kings demonstrated their intention to register their authority in space and time. The temple lands themselves were not treated any differently, because we know of the existence of *bīt ritti* 'hand estates' at the Eanna during the reign of Cyrus. The holder of the estate had to pay taxes (*ilku*) to the king. We may assume that these estates allowed for the maintenance of men whose service was owed to the king by the temple. It appears that even the inhabitants of Nippur were not excluded from this system that, from the time of the first kings, permitted the conquerors to control the lands that had previously been administered directly by the governor (*šandabakku*) for the profit of the city and the temple of Enlil. To be sure, the available evidence does not allow us to speak of a general reallocation of the land of Babylonia in the time of Cyrus and Cambyses, but it must be observed that the allotment of land to individuals or groups presupposes prior confiscation and/or the opening of previously unworked land. In any case, we get the impression that the kings and their counselors did not operate either from crisis to crisis or for the short term.

5. From Bactra to Sardis

Bactrian Polity and Achaemenid Power

The extant evidence does not permit us to draw up an indisputable accounting of the innovations introduced by the conquerors. This is particularly true of certain regions, such as Central Asia, known only from archaeological data that, although plentiful, are nevertheless ambiguous. The archaeologists have revealed that Bactria was developed well before the Achaemenid period, and they infer from this the existence of state structures in Bactria from the end of the second millennium. It is this state that initiated the great hydraulic works that surveys have brought to light, particularly in the valley of the Upper Oxus (Amu Darya). The Achaemenid military conquest does not seem to have made any detectable material impact on the region, where we find a surprising stability of local traditions (especially in the pottery and the hydraulic technology). Given these factors, the conclusion has been drawn that in these countries the Achaemenid conquest at the time of Cyrus and later was no more than a kind of politico-military epiphenomenon: the introduction of a satrap, garrisons, tribute and military levies, and so on. The hydraulic works that were carried out during the period of Persian dominion thus would not need to be credited to the satrapal administration. On the contrary, the archaeological continuities tend rather to imply the upholding of strong local political traditions, on which the Persians had no effect. In short, any impact of Cyrus's conquest is undetectable in the field.

Central Authority and Cultural Polycentrism

These fundamental discoveries most opportunely remind the historian that the ways and means of imperial conquest/administration must be evaluated in the light of ethnogeographic diversity. The heterogeneity of the Achaemenid political continuum is indeed striking. The societies existing before the conquest surely had not all reached the same stage of development. What, for example, did the master of the immense Neo-Babylonian kingdom, a Phoenician city, a small Anatolian principality, and a nomadic cthnic group of the Iranian Plateau have in common? There is nothing to suggest a priori that the conquest had the same impact on every country. We must recognize instead that the innovations took root in different ways, the conquerors adapting to the specific sociopolitical and cultural frameworks of the conquered peoples.

The best-known examples show indisputably that the conquerors never tried to unify the territories culturally. On the contrary, as we have seen, it was by building on the local hierarchy and traditions that Cyrus and Cambyses attempted to impose a new authority. The Persians, for example, did not try to spread either their language or their religion. Instead, they exhibited great reverence for the local religions and sanctuaries. Each people continued to speak its own language and use its own writing system. In Babylonia, the proclamations of Cyrus were made in Akkadian and written in cuneiform, and at least beginning with Darius the royal inscriptions were composed in three languages, Persian, Akkadian, and Elamite. When Cyrus promulgated his edict on the Jews' return to Jerusalem, it was proclaimed in Hebrew and recorded in Aramaic. With only a few exceptions, only the Persians spoke Persian, worshiped the Persian gods, and maintained the cultural traditions of the ruling socioethnic class.

Thus—can anyone reasonably doubt it?—neither Cyrus nor Cambyses had the simple aim of ruling in name only over some sort of loose federation of states that would have retained the essence of their sovereign prerogatives. Imperial multilingualism did not in itself present any obstacle to the exercise of Persian authority. It was kept under control by the Achaemenid administration's regular use of a form of Aramaic known as Imperial Aramaic. And if one observes that somewhat later the Persepolis tablets are written in Elamite, it is an Elamite laced with Persian technical terms.

The appointment of satraps in Media, Anatolia, Babylonia, Egypt, or Central Asia does not imply the systematic, formal extinction of local political entities. The administrative jurisdictions were probably modeled on preexisting politico-territorial institutions. The Great King continued to address himself to "peoples, cities, kings, and dynasts." On the one hand, the conquest led to the complete obliteration of the hegemonic kingdoms (Media, Lydia, Babylonia, Egypt) within a unified Empire. On the other hand, the institution of the satrapy perfectly illustrates the conqueror's intention of creating a new state whose unity cannot be reduced to the symbolic. The local political entities (peoples, cities, kings, dynasts) were integrated into the state, in different ways to be sure, but undeniably integrated nevertheless. All the same, the settling of a veritable imperial Persian diaspora in the provinces demonstrates the royal intent to create conditions for effective authority over the conquered territories and populations. The respect shown for the local sanctuaries by the kings went hand in hand (with the rarest exceptions) with very strict oversight of their material resources and with the obligation laid on them not to challenge Persian dominion in any way.

The means Cambyses adopted to create an *Achaemenid* navy are also instructive. The navy was not simply a haphazard conglomeration of regional contingents whose command was left to the local leaders, but rather a royal fleet constructed on the initiative of the central government and commanded by Persian officers. In this process, the subject peoples were required to pay taxes in silver or in kind and to furnish oarsmen. A final example is especially enlightening: the buildings built by Cyrus at Pasargadae. The activity of Lydian and Mesopotamian craftsmen there is indisputably attested, even apart from the stylistic and architectural borrowings from the Anatolian and Assyro-Babylonian areas, not to mention Phoenician and Egyptian. Consider the tomb of Cyrus or the familiar "winged genius." Moreover, the result of Cyrus's building activities cannot be explained simply as a collage of incompatible styles in which one might find confirmation of the permanence of the earlier artistic traditions. Thus, the introduction of irrigated gardens in Cyrus's new capital does not simply attest to the continuation of a technology well known particularly among the Neo-Assyrian kings. A more careful study shows that his landscape architects adapted the preexisting model by making the garden an integral part of the palace and one of the highlights of court life.

Thus it was not the foreign artisans (Lydian, Babylonian, Elamite, Egyptian, etc.) who worked out the plan and defined the function of Pasargadae. Just like Persepolis later on, Pasargadae was conceived in its entirety by the king and his counselors as a function of a dynastic and imperial program within which the stylistic diversity fed the political unity of the palace as a whole, rather than damaging it. The stylistic syncretism also expresses the fact that the cultural diversity of the empire went hand in hand with the exaltation of the sovereign who assured its political unity. In every case, it is better to speak of adaptations of local sociopolitical structures within an imperial framework defined by the kings and their counselors, rather than of continuities pure and simple. These adaptations do not imply the disappearance of local traditions, nor do they imply continuity of all their constituent elements. At this point, an initial methodological observation may be made: there is no *necessary* contradiction between imposition of Persian authority and maintenance/partial adaptation of regional and local conditions.

Text and Image

To return to the Bactrian example, it is important to realize that the problem it poses is unique: the history of this country, particularly during the reign of Cyrus and Cambyses, is known essentially from archaeological evidence. In fact, the Classical authors are hardly even interested in these regions before the conquest of Alexander. In the Greek imagination, these regions are located "at the extremities of the *oikoumenē*," on which they had no real information anyway. The countries of the Iranian Plateau remain largely terra incognita. It will suffice to recall here that before the time of Alexander no ancient author saw fit to offer his readers any description of Pasargadae or Persepolis.

There is no reason to infer from this gap in the evidence that in the eyes of the Great Kings themselves the eastern Iranian countries were distant—not just geographically, but politically. On the contrary, the appointment of Bardiya, the younger son of Cyrus, to Bactra leads us to think that the Great Kings attached great importance to Bactria. And in 522, Dādarši, the satrap of Bactra, made it possible for Darius to put down the rebellions that had broken out in the northern regions of the Iranian Plateau. In the eyes of Strabo (XI.11.4), the Syr Darya itself was the "boundary" of the Persian Empire bordering on the Saka of Central Asia, and Cyrus situated several garrison towns there. In short, the silence of the Classical authors cannot be used as an indication, one way or the other.

The case of Bactria is unique because of the importance of the gap in textual evidence. On the other hand, the methodological problems it poses turn up time and again in Achaemenid countries. Susa and Elam appear to have continued to exist as if nothing had happened; not a trace of Persian presence can be found in the archaeological record before Darius; the archaeological evidence shows the perseverance of Elamite traditions there. And we have hardly any archaeological evidence of Persian dominion in Egypt in the time of Cambyses.

Thus, the interpretations of "Bactrian" archaeologists throw a rather different light on the process of taking control in the countries conquered by Cyrus and Cambyses, then administered by the Persians for more than two centuries. Although the evidence from Bactria supports the notion that the conquest had only a superficial effect on already developed regional organization, consideration of other evidence permits a different view of the effects of the conquest on other developed regions of the empire. Consequently, the Bactrian case calls upon the historian to propose a general characterization of the question of imperial coherence, and this must await a later discussion (chap. 16).

6. Persians and Conquered Populations

Military Conquest and Ideological Strategy

The analysis of the regional cases leads the historian to inquire into the relationships between conquering and conquered populations. This is a basic problem to which we will return several times, because in large part it frames the discussion just mentioned about the very coherence of the imperial structure. Despite the gaps in evidence, it is imperative that we analyze the solutions adopted by Cyrus and Cambyses, insofar as these solutions also unavoidably concerned their successors.

The problem facing the conquerors can be presented in relatively simple terms. First and foremost, they needed to control the territories and populations as efficiently as possible. But considering the relatively small number of Persians, the military occupation of the territories constituted only a partial response to the problem facing the conquerors. They not only had to be able to quash whatever revolts might arise, but they also, and most importantly, had to be able to take steps to prevent revolts from arising in the first place. To this end, Cyrus and Cambyses followed an ideological strategy meant to create conditions for cooperation with the local elites, a most urgent need. This is why, rather than appearing to be outsiders bent on overturning the existing kingdoms and societies, the Great Kings endeavored to appropriate local traditions to their advantage over the long run and to present themselves as protectors of the sanctuaries. At the same time, this strategy required allowing the elites of the conquered countries to participate in the functioning of the new imperial power. But experience would soon show that the process of putting this policy in force was full of pitfalls and ambiguities.

In fact, while the adoption of this strategy seems well established in its broad outlines, we must not allow ourselves to be confused by it. The actual cooperation of the local elites presupposes that they agreed beforehand to serve the new authority loyally. We must also dispel the illusions created by the dominant view of the ancient sources. Herodotus and philo-Persian [or Persian-leaning] Babylonian and Egyptian sources tend to deny or discount the vigor of the resistance put forth by the states and kingdoms that the Great Kings coveted for themselves. In reality, no military victory was easy or immediate. The relatively humane fate that was accorded the vanquished monarchs is not evidence of Persian respect for the fallen kingdom. Rather, it was the first stage of their political strategy of "continuity," a strategy aimed at the same time at encouraging the ruling classes to ally with them. But putting this policy into effect presupposed the elites' allegiance to Persian imperial objectives—which obviously was not always the case. Cyrus

realized this quickly in Lydia: careful to cultivate the cooperation of the Lydian aristocracy, he conferred on one of them, Pactyes, the job of raising tribute, a function that he
may already have been responsible for under Croesus. Pactyes turned this to his advantage by inciting the Lydians against the Persians. Of course, on the other hand, Pactyes
was not representative of the entire aristocracy of the country. In Lydia, as elsewhere,
representatives of the local dominant class surely collaborated and probably did not participate in the revolt. This was certainly the case with "Myrsos, son of Gyges," who held
an important position in the bureaucracy of the satrap of Sardis from Cyrus to Darius.
The example of Pactyes could only make the Persians reluctant to award imperial command positions to local aristocrats in the future.

The origins of these resistance movements are not easy to analyze. The example of
the great rebellions of 522–520 (to which we will return in the next chapter) demonstrates that the strength and permanence of the local dynastic-political traditions are
only a partial explanation. It is also true that, initially, the aristocrats legitimately feared
for their socioeconomic status. The temporary concessions of the kings did not always
suffice to calm their uneasiness, especially because, in the face of resistance, Cyrus and
Cambyses sometimes had to retaliate. Consider for example an Egyptian noble who,
after the Persian victory, "fell from great wealth to poverty . . . , had nothing but what a
beggar has." He was a close companion of the pharaoh, to whose table he had access,
and his economic status was intimately linked to the fate of his master, whose destiny he
shared. In some sense, he was the antithesis of someone like Udjahorresnet, who had
had the forethought to choose the side of the victor. The will to resist expressed by someone like Pharaoh Psammetichus could only have weakened the position of the nobles
who had remained faithful to him. Hence the extreme vigor of Cambyses' reaction
against the great families. It was a very clear warning aimed at the local nobility: the
maintenance of their socioeconomic privileges depended on their unreserved allegiance to the victors and accepting the reality of the newly imposed imperial structures.
Otherwise, their property would be confiscated and their prestige would be abrogated.

The Political Personnel of Cyrus and Cambyses

In any event, an analysis of the political staff of Cyrus and Cambyses clearly shows the
limits of relying on local administrators. They are of course frequently mentioned in the
most important corpus of documents, the Babylonian tablets. But—without exception—after the first years of occupation, local officials were awarded subservient jobs,
not positions that involved setting policy at the highest level. Any attempt at statistical
analysis of personal names is doomed from the start. In fact, the basic data of personal
names come from private archives or temple archives, in which the proportion of Babylonians is necessarily overwhelming. Furthermore, the transmission of titles and professional qualifications was a matter of privilege, passed down along family lines. By
contrast, we do not have a single official (satrapal) archive that could provide comparable data on the ethnic origin of the highest officials of the satrapy.

Generally speaking, the Egyptian records reveal more continuity of lifestyle from before the conquest than novelties that may have been introduced by the Persians. This is
especially true of a very interesting Demotic text known as the "Petition of Peteisis." This
curious text tells of the quarrels of a family of priests serving the temple of Amon of Teuzoi (El-Hibeh) from year 4 of Psammetichus I (660) to year 4 of Cambyses. Provided

with a benefice at Teuzoi, Peteisis (I) passed on his position to his son Esemteu, despite some problems, and then to his grandson Peteisis (II). While he was away on a military expedition with Pharaoh Psammetichus II (594–589), Peteisis (II) was stripped of his property and privileges. The family's troubles continued for a long time, under Amasis (570–525) and then Cambyses and Darius. The document gives the impression that, apart from references to regnal years of Cambyses and Darius, the Persian conquest was only hazily perceived. In particular, the names are all Egyptian. The reason is simple: in this text it is "ordinary" Egyptians who speak, not the officials of the satrapy. A "governor" appears, before whom the members of the family come to seek redress. But, during the reign of Cambyses, was he Persian (the satrap), or was he Egyptian? At this time, no certain solution has been found.

Let us note simply that the Persian conquest did not bring a sudden end to the careers of the high bureaucrats (Khnemibre, Ahmose) who surrounded the last pharaohs. But it appears at the same time that their place in the administrative hierarchy was relatively modest, despite the sonorous titles they gave themselves, which say more about their prestige in Egyptian society than about political parity with the Persians of the satrapy. In any event, some titles disappeared with the conquest, in particular those of "elder before the king," "elder before his master," and "known to the king." Only a man like Udjahorresnet could boast of being "known to the king (Cambyses)."

Besides, if we examine Udjahorresnet's titulature before and after the conquest, we find that he retained many traditional titles. But this is more a question of honorary titles than political functions per se. We also see that he lost the only responsible position he held before the arrival of Cambyses, that of admiral of the fleet. Under Cambyses (then Darius) he held the position of chief medical officer. This was hardly an innovation, because Egyptian physicians were famous and were used at the Persian court in the time of Cyrus (cf. Herodotus III.1). To be sure, it was an honorary position, which gave its incumbent undeniable prestige. Udjahorresnet with pride specified that Cambyses "assigned him the position of chief medical officer, [he] placed [him] beside [him] as companion and director of the palace." He decked himself out with pompous titles like "pasha, royal chancellor, sole companion, true friend of the king who loves him," traditional Egyptian titles that had already been bestowed on him under Amasis and Psammetichus. This accumulation of titles does not obscure the fact that, despite his defection to Cambyses, Udjahorresnet did not receive a single position of political influence, either from the king or in Egypt itself.

The Medes were apparently the only conquered peoples who acquired positions of the highest rank. At the news of the revolt of the Lydian Pactyes, Cyrus assigned the Mede Mazares to lead the operation of reconquest and suppression. On his death, the command passed to another Mede, Harpagus—the same man who had switched allegiance to Cyrus at the time of the conquest of Media. It was he who completed the conquest of the coast of Asia Minor. Among the generals who were with Darius at the beginning of his reign, we know another Mede, Takhmaspada. We may also cite the case of Datis "the Mede," who held a military post of the first rank at the end of the 490s and who perhaps had begun his career under Cambyses.

The position of the Medes is certainly remarkable. It is likely that after the conquest of Ecbatana Media retained special prestige among the conquered countries, perhaps because of ancient political and cultural links between Persians and Medes. But at the same time it is clear that our perspective is somewhat skewed because of propaganda. For example, the marriage between Cyrus and Amytis, daughter of Astyages, recorded by Ctesias, is not a verified fact. It would thus be excessive to speak of a Persian-Median joint sovereignty. All of the ancient authors acclaim Cyrus as the one who uprooted ruling power from the Medes in order to transfer it to the Persians. The former are the vanquished, the latter the victors. Culturally, however, Medes and Persians were close cousins. In spite of these facts, the importance of the Median heritage in the state organization of Cyrus and Cambyses must be evaluated with detachment and moderation. The Elamite influence was far greater. In the Persian lists of known countries, starting from the time of Darius, Media is always listed after Persia. Media was also transformed into a satrapy and, unlike Persia, had to pay tribute like any other provincial government. Furthermore, no satrap of Median origin is known with certainty. Medes seem to have held only military posts. In this function they were subordinate to the orders of the king. In Asia Minor, for example, the Median generals had to cooperate (at least) with the Persian satraps, with the Persian generals, and with the commander of the citadel of Sardis, Tabalus, who also was a Persian.

It is quite remarkable that the satraps of Cyrus and Cambyses came without exception from Persian families: Gubāru in Babylonia–Trans-Euphrates, Aryandes in Egypt, Oroetes in Sardis, Mitrobates in Dascylium, Dādarši in Bactria, and Vivāna in Arachosia. The same was true for the imperial treasurer in Babylon, Mithradāta. As Herodotus says (III.64), Cambyses' entourage in Egypt also was made up only of Persians. It was "the most distinguished" Persians that the dying king called before him to exhort not to let the Medes take control. Among these aristocrats, Herodotus particularly distinguishes the Achaemenids themselves. For example, the future king, Darius, enjoyed a high position at the court of Cyrus and Cambyses (Aelian, *VH* XII.43; Herodotus III.139), and his father Hystaspes governed Parthia-Hyrcania or at least occupied a very important military position there (*DB* §35). It was also Persians who held trusted positions around the king, such as, under Cambyses, the "message-bearer" Prexaspes (whose son served as royal cupbearer) as well as the royal judges—for example, Sisamnes, who was put to death by Cambyses (Herodotus III.34; V.25).

Considered as a whole, the composition of the political staff under the first kings demonstrates the grip on power held by the representatives of the Persian aristocracy in the government of the Empire. It was exclusively Persians who held the command and policy positions. This simple observation strikingly confirms that the Empire-in-the-making was not simply the juxtaposition of preexisting state structures; it was an entirely new empire, where the conquerors, grouped around their king, kept for themselves positions, prebends, and benefices. The local political and social structures and elites were not appropriated, except to the extent they could be integrated into the new state-information. Local dignitaries were associated with the government of the Empire as auxiliaries to a new ethnically and socially homogenous ruling group. This group would henceforth become the dominant socioethnic class, consisting for the most part of representatives of the great aristocratic families of Persia.

Contacts and Acculturation

This observation obviously is not meant to imply that the Persians did not establish close relationships with the local ruling classes. Some examples and simple logic suggest the opposite. In some regions, particularly in Fārs and Elam, as we have seen, the contacts and exchanges predate the conquest of Cyrus. In Babylonia, for example, during the first quarter of the sixth century, there were Babylonians with Iranian patronymics. In a document from the reign of Cambyses, issued in Persia to Matezziš, the descendant of a Babylonian has an Iranian name (Bagapada). But we know nothing more about possible marriages between Persians and members of other peoples. We might almost suppose that during this period some of the Persian kings' concubines might have been Babylonian in origin. On the other hand, in Asia Minor, marriages between the Sardian aristocracy and families of the Greek cities, so abundantly attested from the Mermnad period, are completely absent from the documentation of the early Achaemenid period.

Among local princes who were fascinated by Persian luxury and ways of life, Polycrates, the tyrant of Samos, stands out. Herodotus (III.125◇) states that "apart from the lords of Syracuse, no other petty king in the Greek world can be compared with Polycrates for magnificence (*megaloprepeiē*)." And numerous ancient authors like to cite the example of the tyrant of Samos, since one of their favorite topics was the relationship between power, wealth, and decadence. In their eyes, Polycrates epitomized the characteristics they commonly imputed to oriental kings, especially their love of luxury (*tryphē*). At Samos he re-created a genuine court, to which he brought celebrated poets (such as Anacreon) and also craftsmen recruited at high price (cf. Aelian, *VH* IX.4). He established workshops to produce sumptuous fabrics and celebrated drinking vessels. The opulence of the furnishings of the men's hall (*andrōn*) was well known, not to mention the pomp of the banquets held there. Among the creations that the ancient authors underscore was a neighborhood in Samos reserved for prostitution. Clearchus states that this quarter was modeled on one at Sardis and was in competition with it. There can hardly be any doubt that it was a sort of park, a "paradise." It is also said that Polycrates brought fabled animals from everywhere: dogs from Aegina and Laconia, goats from Scyros and Naxos, sheep from Miletus and Attica, hogs from Sicily (cf. Athenaeus XII.540e–f). This constitutes one of the traditional functions of oriental paradises, which were also gardens for acclimatizing exotic species. In Polycrates, then, we have an example of a Greek tyrant fascinated by the luxury of the oriental courts, in whose eyes political rivalry was also expressed in the sumptuousness of court life. According to Herodotus (III.122◇), "he had high hopes of making himself master of Ionia and the islands." In Polycrates' view, contending with Sardis for power entailed copying and equalling the luxury of the Lydian kings and, later, of the Persian satrap of Sardis, who in a certain sense succeeded the Lydian kings.

The case of Polycrates is all the more interesting because a number of his innovations antedate the Persian conquest. The same authors who liked to extol the luxury of the Lydians in every aspect of life also condemned their love of luxury. The rivalry between the courts of Polycrates and Oroetes takes place in an ongoing history. Thus, on arriving at Sardis, the Persians adopted some of the Lydian royal practices to their advantage. Paradises are attested in Lydia before Cyrus, not just at Sardis but also at Dascylium; likewise, royal hunts (cf. Strabo XIII.1.17). This is not to say that Cyrus got the idea for the paradise at Pasargadae from Sardis. Such parks were known in Assyria and elsewhere well before. Rather, the Persians probably spread the model of the paradise still more widely in Asia Minor. Xenophon (*Cyr.* VIII.6.12◇) reports that "Cyrus" enjoined his satraps to "have parks, too, and keep wild animals in them." We might say, then, that social intercourse between the Lydian and Persian aristocracies ensured that their social behavior would not diverge very much from each other.

In Asia Minor we have further evidence of cultural exchange from this period. But the traces of Iranian influence are rare. One of the most frequently cited examples is the pyramidal tomb of Sardis (fig. 1, p. 87), which is so similar to the tomb of Cyrus at Pasargadae in Fārs that it is believed to have been built by a Persian aristocrat of the satrapal court shortly after the conquest of Cyrus. The tomb at Buzpar in Fārs also has obvious similarities to that of the founder of the Empire. Another tomb discovered near Phocaea, at Taš-Kule, shows principles of construction that appear to relate more to Persian traditions than to Lydian-Anatolian heritage. Unfortunately, the debate over the dating of the monument (either 540 or during the fifth century) is not settled. It thus cannot be said with certainty to represent the first generation of the imperial Persian diaspora.

In any event, in Asia Minor, the Persians encountered more than the local aristocracies. They also underwent strong Greek influence, just as the Lydian court of the Mermnads did. Striking evidence is found in the paintings on the four sides of a tomb found in Lycia at Kizilbel, near Elmali. The paintings essentially represent mythological scenes belonging to the Greek iconographic tradition. Other scenes probably allude to incidents from the life of the local prince who was buried there: a sailing scene and hunting scenes (wild boar, stag, and lion). To be sure, the scenes of the hunt and the funerary banquet would later be incorporated into the style traditionally known as "Greco-Persian." But they belong just as much to the local repertoire and do not presuppose Persian influence, to which, however, later Lycian materials bear witness. Dated around 525, the Elmali paintings, for instance, dramatically attest to Greek cultural influence in a small Lycian dynastic court.

7. *The Seats of Power*

The Old Royal Residences

After the conquest, the Achaemenids retained the royal residences of the conquered states for themselves: Ecbatana, Sardis, Bactra, Babylon, Susa, Saïs, and Memphis. Even after the foundation of Pasargadae in Persia, all of these capitals retained an eminent place in the new Empire, but with different roles. Some, such as Memphis, were reduced to the rank of satrapal capital or subsatrapal capital (e.g., Damascus); others, like Sardis in the west or Bactra in the east, represented centers of Persian authority over wider regions; still others—Ecbatana, Babylon, and probably Susa—were promoted to royal residences in the full sense, while maintaining their position as satrapal capitals. In Ecbatana and Babylon there were not only royal archives and treasury but also one or more palaces where the king and his retinue could stay.

In the absence of systematic excavations, we know nothing of the royal palaces of Ecbatana except for the description given by Herodotus (I.98) and the late information from Polybius (X.27). Herodotus assigns the construction of the town to King Deioces, whom he presents as the founder of the Median kingdom. The building of a capital is understood as the act that founds a new state. According to Herodotus, the town developed around the palace and the treasuries and was surrounded by seven walls of different colors: white, black, purple, blue, and red-orange. The blue wall had silver battlements; the red-orange had golden battlements. On the other hand, in a description from the Hellenistic period, Polybius holds that Ecbatana was at this date "without fortifications."

He stresses instead the splendor of the royal palace, enhanced by the gleam of the columns sheathed with plates of silver and gold and with tiles that "were all silver." But it is not possible to determine what in a late text goes back to the Median period and what is the result of Achaemenid and (even later) Hellenistic alterations. What is certain is that Ecbatana continued to be one of the royal residences, with its palaces, treasuries, and archives. The town, moreover, constituted a strategic site for a power that was reaching toward Central Asia.

It is true that, beyond the proclamations of Cyrus himself, we do not know much of anything about the palaces of Babylon at the time of the conqueror and his son. We know, however, that several secondary residences provided with paradises were built in Babylon and that the king or his son stayed in them on occasion. In the *Cyropaedia*, Xenophon assigns a central position to Babylon in the organization of the imperial space. This is where he places the principal decisions made by the conqueror regarding imperial administration (VII.5.37–86; VIII.1–7). He even says (VIII.6.22) that the king spent seven months of the year at Babylon, which was deliberately chosen because of its location at the center of the Empire. There is little doubt in fact that the practice of periodically relocating the Achaemenid court was inaugurated during the reign of Cyrus. Finally, the excavations at Susa show that the Great Kings did not undertake any architectural or urbanization projects before the reign of Darius. Until that time, the remains at Susa reflect only the maintenance of Neo-Elamite cultural traditions. This observation implies not that Susa was not a residence under Cyrus and Cambyses but that at this time Susa had not yet achieved the place it would hold beginning with Darius.

Palace and Gardens of Pasargadae

In truth, Persia, cradle and nursery of the Persian people, continued to occupy a central place under Cyrus and Cambyses, especially on the ideological plane. It was in Persia that Cyrus decided to erect a new capital, Pasargadae, situated at a height of about 1900 m in the Zagros, some 40 km as the crow flies from the site of Persepolis. Strabo (XV.3.8✧) describes the conditions of the foundation of the town in these terms:

> Cyrus held Pasargadae in honour, because he there conquered Astyages the Mede in his last battle, transferred to himself the empire of Asia, founded a city, and constructed a palace as a memorial of his victory.

In reality, the link of cause and effect asserted by Strabo is dubious, for the battles won at Pasargadae against the Medes were not the last ones; far from it. At any rate, numerous archaeological arguments favor a date after the conquest of Sardis for the founding of Pasargadae.

It is well to recall that, according to Herodotus (I.125✧), of the three tribes most important to the Persians, the Pasargadae were "the most distinguished; they contain the clan of the Achaemenidae from which sprung the Perseid kings." The choice of site is thus explained most naturally by its location in the tribal territory of the Pasargadae (which was both ethnonym and toponym). Throughout Achaemenid history, Pasargadae was considered the town of Cyrus. Nevertheless, it is established that Darius furthered the work of Cyrus so well that the dating of the various monuments remains cloaked in considerable uncertainty. Two palaces, which the archaeologists call P and R, have been cleared. The date of the first, a residential building in the full sense of the term, remains debated, the tendency being to attribute it to the reign of Darius. However, Palace R without doubt goes back to Cyrus. First, it fills the function of a monumental gateway providing access to the palace complex proper. It is also to the reign of Cyrus that the Zendan-i Sulaiman ("Prison of Solomon") dates; it is a tower of squared stone, entered by a stairway, and its precise purpose has not been determined. Alexander the Great, sometimes called *philokyros* ('friend of Cyrus'), stayed at Pasargadae twice, at the beginning of 330 and after his return from India. He took special care of the monumental tomb in which the founder of the Empire had been buried; his political acumen led him to demonstrate public admiration for Cyrus's memory. This leaves us contradictory descriptions by several Hellenistic authors (pp. 205–208). Archaeological work now reveals that the funerary chamber proper (topped by a roof with two sloping sides) was erected on top of a monumental podium with six tiers, the entirety rising originally nearly eleven meters (fig. 2).

The Classical authors emphasize the abundance of trees planted within the funerary area. Aristobulus, cited by Arrian (VI.29.4✧), states that the tomb was located "in the royal park; a grove had been planted round it with all sorts of trees and irrigated, and deep grass had grown in the meadow." The excavations carried out on the site have shown that this is true of all the buildings of Pasargadae, which all opened on gardens. A "royal garden" has been discovered there, with stone channels running through it and marked by basins fed by the Pulvar River, which waters the plain. There can be little doubt that the original plans for these gardens go back to the time of Cyrus, even if they were completed in the time of Darius and scrupulously maintained during the entire Achaemenid period. All of the royal palaces were so furnished, as several Babylonian documents from the time of Cambyses show unambiguously. The paradises, integrated into the Achaemenid palace space (cf. Esther 1:5, Vulg.), were always considered one of the most striking external manifestations of Persian wealth and luxury by the Greek authors.

The Beginnings of Persepolis

It is not only at Pasargadae that the continuity between Cyrus and Darius is visible. It can also be seen at Persepolis, which has traditionally been considered an entirely new project of Darius's. In one of his inscriptions, Darius proclaimed that he had constructed a fortress there where none had existed before (*DPf*), a legitimate assertion, for he inaugurated the work on the terrace. However, numerous remains of buildings have been discovered on the plain, indicating that a vast area of nearly 200 hectares was in the process of urbanization well before Darius. Analysis has shown that there were in fact several palaces and monumental gates and that the techniques used in their construction resemble those of Pasargadae more than those of Persepolis. We may add that some of the palatial ruins are located close to an unfinished monument, the Takht-i Rustam ('the throne of Rustam'), which seems to have been a nearly exact replica of the tomb of Cyrus at Pasargadae. It is sometimes interpreted as having been intended as a tomb for Cambyses. It is thus reasonable to conclude that these structures go back to the reigns of Cyrus and Cambyses. It is nearly certain that the site is the one that is called Matezziš (Uvādaicaya in Persian) in the Persepolis tablets from the time of Darius. Several Babylonian tablets make it perfectly clear that Matezziš was a very active urban center during the reign of Cambyses (see p. 72).

These recent discoveries and analyses do not call into question Darius's role in conceiving the Persepolitan palace complex; on the contrary, they help us situate it within

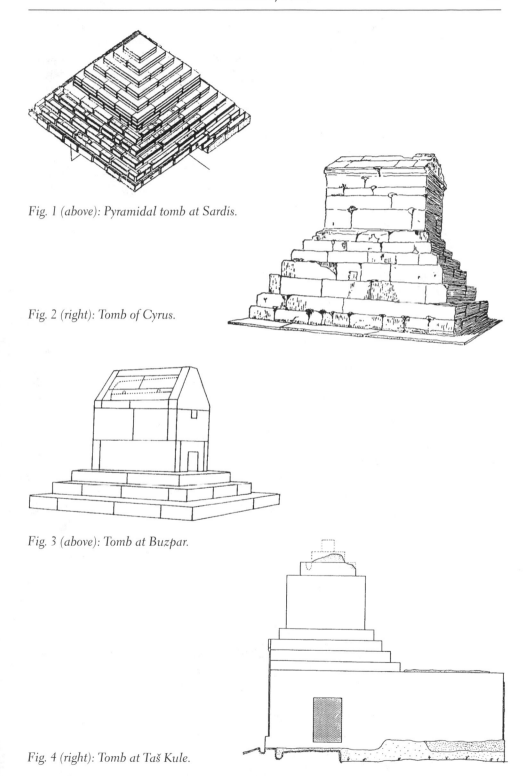

Fig. 1 (above): Pyramidal tomb at Sardis.

Fig. 2 (right): Tomb of Cyrus.

Fig. 3 (above): Tomb at Buzpar.

Fig. 4 (right): Tomb at Taš Kule.

the continuum of Achaemenid history. When Darius chose the site of Persepolis, it was not only to distinguish himself from Cyrus, whose work he actually carried on at Pasargadae. Nor was it simply because it was at Matezziš that he had his principal opponent of Persian origin, Vahyazdāta, executed (if the public execution was carried out there, it was rather because the city had already acquired some prestige by that time). The choice of Persepolis is explained by prior developments, which had made the region a vital, populous palace and urban center in contact with the Babylonian centers. It was also a center capable of providing the basic resources (particularly food staples) needed for the enormous works the king and his counselors had planned for the terrace. We know that, like Darius and Xerxes at Persepolis, Cyrus and Cambyses summoned workers from different parts of the Empire (especially Lydia), and we know that a ration system had been in place since the time of Cyrus (see p. 95 below). Considering these facts, it seems likely that, before the date of the first currently known Elamite tablet (509), an already well-organized "royal economy" of the Elamite type existed in Persia and that it was revised and improved by Darius and his son.

Persian Society and Empire

These regional policies imply profound modifications of the Persian way of life, which is usually thought (in a rather schematic way) to have been seminomadic or agropastoral before the conquests of Cyrus. Beginning with Cyrus and Cambyses *at the latest*, part of the population settled around the royal residences and thereafter turned to agricultural activity. However, the entire Persian population did not abandon the nomadic or seminomadic way of life. Even later, the Classical sources make it possible to identify several subgroups belonging to the Persian *ethnos* who practiced short-range nomadism along with subsistence agriculture in the valleys. Nevertheless, the general direction of the development can hardly be doubted—development that was the result of a conscious policy enacted by the kings and made possible by the influx of wealth to Persia from the military conquests.

Several Babylonian tablets from the time of Cambyses and Bardiya also explain the development of commercial activities at Matezziš. Six tablets refer to the purchase of slaves and three to contracts entered into in the city by the representative of the Babylonian business firm Egibi. They attest to the vigor of trade between Babylon and the royal residences and to the presence of Babylonian communities in Persia at this date. They also show that the Persians were fully integrated into these commercial networks, since in one tablet a Persian is called 'head merchant' (*tamkāru*). Finally, several slaves and their owners had Iranian names. If the names given to slaves were their own, they indicate that lower-class Persians could be enslaved; if they were names assigned by their Persian owners, we must conclude that prisoners of war were deported to Persia as early as the time of Cyrus and Cambyses.

In each case, the complex image of Persian society extracted from these documents is quite different from that supplied by Herodotus (I.125), who simply distinguishes agricultural and nomadic tribes. These same documents also allow us to clarify the claim of numerous Greek authors who say that the Persians "were completely unfamiliar with the concept of markets and did not use them at all," or "did not set foot in a market (*agora*), since they had nothing either to buy or sell." Herodotus also mentions a prohibition on going into debt as one of the Persian social rules (I.138). These brusque for-

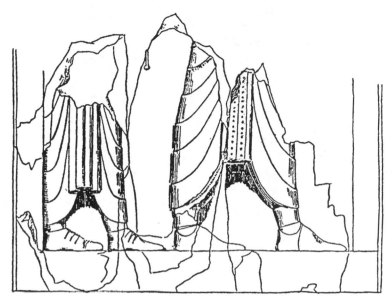

Fig. 5. Relief from Palace P at Pasargadae.

mulations may find their explanation in the aristocratic ethic of which some Greek admirers of Sparta were particularly enamored. But they express only part of the truth, which the Babylonian documents will be able to enrich substantially.

8. *Royalty and Authority*

Royal Representations and Titles at Pasargadae

If everything suggests that the construction of Pasargadae was striking evidence of a dynastic policy, it is also true that direct links between Cyrus and his new capital are not very clearly visible in the available archaeological and epigraphic evidence. An incomplete relief found at Palace P shows a king accompanied by two servants, one of whom seems to hold a fly-whisk (or parasol?). But this image (fig. 5), similar to some reliefs at Persepolis, may date only from the reign of Darius.

There remains the famous "winged genius" carved on Gate R (fig. 6). It shows a bearded man, garbed in an "Elamite" robe, wearing a complex Egyptian-type crown, and possessing four wings. The stone formerly bore inscriptions above the "winged genius," with the very simple text "I am Cyrus the King, an Achaemenian."✧ Hypotheses about the exact meaning of this atypical and in many ways mysterious image have come fast and furious. Influences from Egypt (the crown), Assyria (winged geniuses), and Phoenicia may be found in it. But does it relate to Cyrus himself, as is often supposed? Nothing could be less certain. Sometimes the relief is compared with a passage in Herodotus (I.209✧) about one of Cyrus's dreams, which he reported to Hystaspes, father of Darius: "I saw your eldest son with a pair of wings on his shoulders, shadowing Asia with one of them and Europe with the other." It is rather tempting to imagine that this is a metaphorical representation of Persian authority over regions of great cultural diversity.

The syncretistic originality of the monument continues to pose problems that, in the absence of comparable iconography, risk remaining insoluble.

The only "royal" Persian image dated before Darius is a seal that was still in use in the time of Darius at Persepolis but clearly goes back to a much earlier period. In fact, it has the legend "Kuraš of Anšan, son of Teispes," the person generally identified as Cyrus I, grandfather of Cyrus the Great, even though he is not explicitly identified as king. The scene engraved on it is a war scene, which, though Elamite in origin, became very popular in Achaemenid glyptic: a horseman jumps over two warriors, who lie fallen on the ground, and rushes in pursuit of a footsoldier (fig. 7). Whoever this figure may be (and he may be intentionally anonymous), there can scarcely be any doubt that at this time one of the justifications of royal authority was physical strength and bravery in war. It is around this theme that Herodotus also organizes his tale of the first confrontation between Cambyses and his brother Smerdis/Bardiya, who alone among the entire royal entourage succeeded in drawing the bow sent by the king of the Ethiopians (III.30). Beginning with the first kings, the bow appears as a symbol of royal power; this is why Cyrus was buried with his weapons (Quintus Curtius X.1.31).

The construction of the tomb of Cyrus at Pasargadae, which has an exact parallel near Persepolis (Takht-i Rustam), in itself also implies an exceptional position for the king in Persian society. The descriptions of the contents of the tomb of Cyrus confirm this. Here, for example, is what Arrian writes (*Anab.* VI.29.5–6✧):

> A Babylonian tapestry served as a coverlet and purple rugs as a carpet. There was placed on it a sleeved mantle and other garments of Babylonian workmanship. According to Aristobulus, Median trousers and robes dyed blue lay there, some dark, some of other varying shades, with necklaces, scimitars and earrings of stones set in gold, and a table stood there. It was between the table and the couch that the sarcophagus containing Cyrus' body was placed.

This text shows how luxurious the court of Cyrus must have been—the richness of his garments and the abundance of jewelry—characteristics of kingship that were to endure throughout Achaemenid history.

Unfortunately, doubts about the date of the inscriptions found in Cyrus's town make reconstruction of the royal titulature problematic (*CMa–b–c*). In some of them, Cyrus is simply called "Achaemenid king"; in others, he bears the more prestigious title "Great King," which is regularly borne by Darius and his successors. But several of these inscriptions have been ascribed to Darius himself, which makes it very difficult to distinguish precisely between Cyrus's original titulature and that which was later awarded him by Darius. The only indisputable title is the simple "king." But what exactly did this title mean in Persia at the beginning of the second half of the sixth century? We do not have a single undisputed relief or inscription at Pasargadae that allows us to discuss the themes of monarchic authority and ideology during the time of Cyrus. This statement does not imply that there was no discernible development in this area during the time of Cyrus, especially after his conquests. In all likelihood, some sort of development must be assumed. But historians cannot choose their sources. Care must thus be taken in putting forth interpretive hypotheses.

It is to the Babylonian documents that we must give preference instead. The Assyro-Babylonian titulature assumed by Cyrus and Cambyses should not be taken into account here any more than the Egyptian titulature adopted by Cambyses in Egypt, because they have nothing to do with the titulature belonging to the dynasty that ruled in Fārs. On the other hand, a passage in the *Cyrus Cylinder* is most interesting. Speaking in the first person, Cyrus appears as the son, grandson, and great-grandson of Cambyses [I], Cyrus [I], and Teispes, all of them called "king of Anšan." It is also by this title that the Babylonian writers refer to Cyrus in the *Dream of Nabonidus* and the *Nabonidus Chronicle*. If we assume that the writers followed explicit instructions from the king, we infer from this that Cyrus, like his predecessors, was concerned to announce clearly his position as heir of the Elamite kings in the high country of Anšan. Anšan was already named Persia (Parsu), but a considerable population of Elamite origin also lived among the native Persians. Use of the title "King of Anšan" does not mean that in Persia itself the kings did not also bear the title "King of Persia," because a few Babylonian documents in fact use this latter title. To be sure, no document from Pasargadae mentions this title, but later on it was occasionally used by Darius. Note also that in the Babylonian version of the Behistun inscription, Gaumata is accused of having fraudulently presented himself as such: "I am Barziya, the son of Cyrus, [himself] king of Parsu, younger brother of Cambyses" (*DB* Bab. §10).

Fig. 6. Winged genius at Pasargadae.

Royal Protocol

In 522, after the execution of Smerdis/Bardiya, the seven aristocrats who led the plot made an agreement, recorded by Herodotus (III.84✧) in the following terms: "Permission, namely, for any of the seven to enter the palace unannounced (*esaggeleos*), except when the king was in bed with a woman." It is often supposed that in reality these privileges already existed for some families under Cyrus and Cambyses. Nevertheless, the very conditions of the execution of Smerdis seem to suggest

Fig. 7. Seal of Kuraš of Anšan (PFS 93*).

that the Great Ones were not strictly bound by the rules of protocol. The guards of the outer gates (*phylakoi*) admitted men who counted as *prōtoi* and they did not "suspect that from them could come anything of [like a murder plot]"; but it was the "eunuch messengers" who intercepted the plotters in the courtyard (*aulē*) and who accused the guards at the gate of negligence. To get as far as the royal quarters, the Seven had to kill the eunuchs on the spot (Herodotus III.77). According to Ctesias (*Persica*, §14), the Seven succeeded in their undertaking only because of the complicity of Bagapates, "who held all of the keys to the palace." This episode thus seems to indicate that, at the time of the first kings, all of the aristocrats were subject to the usual rules of royal protocol that were meant to control access to the interior of the palace.

This passage in Herodotus and the existence of an official called "messenger" (III.34) indicate that the rules of protocol known in greater detail from a later period (cf. chap. 7) were in force at the time of Cambyses. But at what date did the king become "un-approachable," to use the word used by several Greek authors? Herodotus (I.99✧) pushes its origin back to the Median king Deioces:

> He introduced for the first time the ceremonial of royalty: admission to the king's presence was forbidden, and all communication had to be through messengers (*aggeloi*). Nobody was allowed to see the king. . . . This solemn ceremonial was designed as a safeguard against his contemporaries, men as good as himself in birth and personal quality, with whom he had been brought up in earlier years. There was a risk that if they saw him habitually, it might lead to jealousy and resentment, and plots would follow; but if nobody saw him, the legend would grow that he was a being of a different order from mere men.

In the *Cyropaedia*, Xenophon introduces the cupbearer Sacas, who at Astyages' court "had the office of introducing to Astyages those who had business with him and of keeping out those whom he thought it not expedient to admit" (I.3.8✧). And it is to Cyrus that he attributes the introduction of court protocol, in particular, the protocol that regulated the precedence and conditions of royal audiences.

Indeed, the Herodotean chronological framework must be treated with caution. He could have transferred regulations that he knew from the courts of Darius and Xerxes to the court of a mythical Deioces. The same goes for Xenophon, who is always inclined to attribute to Cyrus the creation of a state ex nihilo. Still, the construction of the royal palace and residences at Pasargadae and elsewhere implies that regulations were issued under Cyrus and that these regulations organized the king's life and fixed the courtiers' obligations. Otherwise, in this area as in so many others, the first Persian kings no doubt borrowed from the ceremonial of the Assyro-Babylonian courts.

From One King to the Next

According to Herodotus (I.125✧), the royal family itself came from a wider subcategory that he calls the *phratry* of the Achaemenids, a Greek term usually rendered 'clan'. These clans in turn made up "tribes," among which Herodotus especially notes three: the Pasargadae, the Maraphii, and the Maspii: "Of these the Pasargadae are the most distinguished; they contain the clan of the Achaemenidae from which spring the Perseid kings." It is just such a circumstance that is also represented in inscriptions from Pasargadae, where Cyrus is called Achaemenid (*CMa–b–c*). Aside from some information that has now been confirmed (the name *Maraphii* has been found in Persepolis tablets), Herodotus's presentation raises serious doubts. Because of suspicions that weigh heavily on the authorship (Darius!) of the inscriptions at Pasargadae [*DMa–b–c!*], it now appears that it is only with Darius that the term *Achaemenid* received all of its political value (see p. 111 below). It would be better to eliminate the term *Achaemenid* from the discussion and to depend on a more trustworthy document, the *Cylinder*, in which Cyrus carries his genealogy back to his great-grandfather Teispes, who is called "king of Anšan." There we have the simple but meaningful expression of dynastic justification by right of blood.

The circumstances of the accession of Cambyses also indicate that, to assure dynastic and familial continuity, the reigning king prepared for the succession during his lifetime. By delegating to Cambyses the title "King of Babylon," Cyrus had already clearly designated his choice. However, we should not *in any way* consider this decree to represent a co-regency, since Cambyses held the title for only a few months after the conquest of Babylon (p. 71). The Classical texts formally state that Cambyses had been designated crown prince by his father, whom he succeeded with no apparent difficulty. Nevertheless, the problem of younger siblings emerged at that very moment. The younger brother of Cambyses, Smerdis/Bardiya, had been "compensated" by the grant of a vast district in Central Asia. He was soon to show that he did not intend to settle for second place.

There is no indication that an obligation to take a wife from among the members of certain great aristocratic families was ever recognized by Cyrus or Cambyses. We know that, "born of the same father and the same mother," Cambyses and Bardiya were the fruit of the union of Cyrus and Cassandane, daughter of Pharnaspes (Herodotus II.1; III.3). Cambyses, like his father and his successors, had several wives. He wed Phaidime, a daughter of Otanes, who certainly was a high aristocrat, since Herodotus (III.68✧) calls him "one of the wealthiest members of the Persian nobility." But in the context of royal polygamy, Phaidime was only one of the king's wives. It is quite significant that Cambyses also married his sister Atossa, Cyrus's daughter (III.88), and a bit later another of his sisters "by father and by mother" (III.31). In these instances we can see the institution of a policy of endogamy that was applied consistently by the Achaemenids throughout their history and that permitted them to wipe out the royal ambitions of any other great aristocratic family.

9. The King and the Gods

Persian Religion and Iranian Traditions

Our information on Persian religious beliefs and practices at the time of Cyrus and Cambyses is extraordinarily thin and contradictory. The existence of sacred sites can scarcely be doubted. Darius in fact accuses the usurper Gaumata of destroying the *āyadanā* (DB §14). But there is no agreement among historians on the identification of these *āyadanā*. Were they clan sanctuaries, royal sanctuaries, or something quite different? We have no royal statement that might clarify the problem. Even the archaeological findings at Pasargadae are subject to caution. The interpretation of the tower called Zendan-i Sulaiman as a fire temple has hardly any supporters today, any more than the view that considers it the tomb of Cassandane. There are also two stone plinths that are sometimes considered a ritual site, where the king could sacrifice to the sacred fire; but this is a hypothesis that currently lacks any empirical confirmation.

The problem is that we do not know very much of Iranian religion—or religions—in the first half of the sixth century. The historical existence of Zarathustra, under the name Zoroaster, is frequently recorded by Classical sources (but not Herodotus). But many uncertainties remain regarding the period and the regions where the "prophet" is supposed to have carried out his reforms, and there is even more uncertainty about the actual content of these reforms. The only available written sources, aside from the inscriptions of Darius and his successors, are the various books of the *Avesta*, the sacred book of the Iranians, which the efforts of Anquetil Duperron brought to the attention of Western scholarship in the second half of the eighteenth century. Put in writing between the fifth and seventh centuries A.D., the *Avesta* is traditionally divided into three major parts: the *Yasna* (rituals of sacrifice), the *Yashts* (hymns to various divinities), and the *Vidēvdat* ('law of separation from the demons'). The most recent philological studies have shown that within the *Yasna* a subgroup, the *Gāthā* ('Songs'), goes back to a very ancient origin. Zarathustra is mentioned in the *Gāthā*, and his privileged relationship with the divinity Ahura-Mazda is stressed. From the linguistic point of view, the *Gāthā* are in what is now conventionally called Old Avestan, which could go back at least to the year 1000 B.C. From the history of religions point of view, this text allows us in principle to reconstruct Mazdaism in its pre-Achaemenid phase.

Beginning with a comparison of the Achaemenid written sources and the *Avesta*, historians have strived to answer the question of whether the Achaemenids were "Zoroastrians" or, more accurately, Mazdians—that is, initiates in the religion dominated by Mazda. The problem is that the Persian evidence for the reigns of Cyrus and Cambyses hardly permits access to their beliefs in the Mazdian religion, such as it can be reconstructed from the *Gatha*. The testimony of Herodotus remains unclear: on the one hand, he Hellenizes whatever information he receives; on the other, he is writing a century after the death of Cyrus. Beginning with such poor information, it seems quite reckless to try to reconstruct what the religion of Cyrus might have been. Some think that Darius's later insistence on the preeminence of Ahura-Mazda above all other gods (*baga*) indicates that he had broken with the tradition of Cyrus, for whom Mithra was the most important god. Exactly the opposite hypothesis makes Cyrus a Zoroastrian zealot. According to this hypothesis, the great "Zoroastrian" (Mazdian) continuity of the dynasty must be stressed, rather than any break between Cyrus and Darius.

But all of these interpretations seem to be built on sand. How in fact can we contrast the beliefs of Cyrus and Darius, when the former never "spoke" and the latter left conflicting messages for his contemporaries and the generations to come? The only indication in favor of a privileged cult in honor of Mithra is the institution of horse sacrifices around the tomb of Cyrus; in Iranian tradition, these sacrifices are often associated with the cult of Mithra.

The Tomb of Cyrus and Persian Funerary Practices

There is in fact just one aspect of the religion of Cyrus and Cambyses that is documented: the funerary customs. Cyrus was buried in the tomb he had had built during his lifetime at Pasargadae. Arrian (*Anab.* VI.29.5–6◇) gives a precise description of the burial chamber. According to his informants, Cyrus was placed in a gold sarcophagus; "a couch stood by its side with feet of wrought gold . . . and a table stood there." According to Quintus Curtius (X.1.31◇), the king was buried with his weapons. Alexander in fact discovered "the king's moldering shield, two Scythian bows, and a scimitar [*akinakēs*]."

Note first of all that the style of burial of Cyrus (and his successors) does not conform to the rules of the *Avesta*. The weeping and wailing that according to Herodotus (III.66) accompanied the death of Cambyses or Persian aristocrats (cf. IX.24) also flies in the face of the traditions called "Zoroastrian." Persian practices also differ from the customs that are well attested in eastern Iran until the end of the Achaemenid period (and well after), which required exposure of the corpses to animals who would scavenge the flesh, leaving the bones to be deposited in an ossuary. Herodotus, speaking of secret rites, states that "a male Persian is never buried until the body has been torn by a bird or a dog" (I.140◇). But the reservations expressed by the author himself and the continuation of the statement, as well as a passage in Strabo, show that only the corpses of the *magi* "were never interred without first being stripped by the birds or the dogs" (Strabo XV.3.20). Passages in Plutarch (*Art.* 18.7) and Herodotus (VII.10) also provide evidence that only inhumation, not the scavenging of the corpse, was considered normal among the Persians. The degrading character of the practice is well illustrated by the punishment inflicted on anyone who made an attempt on the life of the king: He "has his head and arms cut off and his body cast forth [to the beasts]" (Strabo XV.3.17✧). Furthermore, a passage in Ctesias indicates that cremation was contrary to established practice among the Persians (*para ton nomon*; *Persica* §57); this prohibition is confirmed by Strabo (XV.3.18).

Many texts, moreover, attest to the practice of inhumation. After the battle of Issus, "Alexander authorized the mother of Darius to bury whom she wished according to the custom of her country (*patrio more*). She interred (*humari*) a small number of very close relatives," while avoiding in her current situation "the pomp of the funerals with which the Persians celebrate the last rites to the dead . . . , when the [Macedonian] victors were cremated in no costly manner" (Quintus Curtius III.12.14✧). After the death of Artachaees, who had been in charge of digging the canal at Athos, "Xerxes had him carried out and buried with all pomp and ceremony. The whole army helped to raise a mound over his grave" (Herodotus VII.117✧). This repeats a practice already attested by Herodotus among another Iranian people, the Scythians: after royal obsequies, "everyone with great enthusiasm sets about raising a great mound, each competing with his neighbour to make it as big as possible" (IV.71✧). Furthermore, the archaeological evidence is also unambiguous. At Susa, an Achaemenid burial that dates to the beginning of the fourth century has been discovered. The body of a woman had been placed in a bronze casket along with much jewelry belonging to the deceased, as well as various Egyptian alabaster vases. A cemetery has also been discovered in Syria, a short distance from Carchemish (Deve Hüyük), in which the earliest tombs go back to the eighth century. In this cemetery we can witness the change in practice from cremation to burial in the Achaemenid period.

The Sacrifices around the Tomb of Cyrus

Ctesias writes that "immediately after his death, Cambyses returned the body of his father to Persia (*eis Persas*) in the care of the eunuch Bagapates for burial (*taphenai*), and he issued orders according to his father's last wishes" (§9). Although the phrasing is very general, it is tempting to connect it with what Arrian writes of the sacrifices instituted around the tomb "from the time of the reign of Cambyses":

> Within the enclosure and by the ascent to the tomb itself there was a small building put up for the Magians who used to guard Cyrus' tomb, from as long ago as Cambyses, son of Cyrus, an office transmitted from father to son. The king used to give them a sheep a day, a fixed amount of meal and wine, and a horse each month to sacrifice to Cyrus. (VI.29.7✧)

Arrian's text is fully understandable only if it is explicated in light of some types of tablets from Persepolis. One of these, called Category E (about 40 published tablets), includes quantitative information on the materials delivered to the caretakers of different religions (Iranian, Elamite, Babylonian). These materials were intended for the sacrifices themselves. Another, Category K1 (35 published tablets), includes the amount of rations (*gal*) delivered by the royal administration to the caretakers as payment for their services. Even though the Persepolis tablets are later than Cambyses, it is clear that the information given by Arrian corresponds quite closely to what can be determined from the tablets. The priests entrusted with the sacrifices at the tomb of Cyrus received rations for themselves (a sheep per day, wine, and flour) and a horse each month for the sacrifice.

In the Persepolis tablets, the rations provided by the administration consist of the following items: flour (12 times), beer (11), wine (6), grain (4), dates (1), figs (1). We find more or less the same items intended for the sacrifices themselves: grain (23), wine (14), flour (2), beer (1), sheep (1). We may note that the caretakers never receive meat in their monthly or daily rations. In this regard, the priests of Cyrus's tomb are favored. The quantities, too, are quite extraordinary: more than 360 sheep each year. Of course, we do not know how many *magi* were involved in these sacrifices.

Horse sacrifice is not recorded at all in the tablets, and it obviously was an exceptional practice. In a passage of the *Cyropaedia*, Xenophon states that horses were sacrificed to the Sun during the feasts periodically held by the king in Persia (VIII.3.12, 24) and that a chariot was dedicated to the Sun. Here, as often, the Sun is very likely Mithra. According to Strabo (XI.14.9), the satrap of Armenia had to send the king 20,000 colts for the feasts of Mithra (*Mithrakāna*) each year. The *magi* immolated white horses in 480 in the Strymon to obtain favorable omens (Herodotus VII.113). The link between the king and the white horses, often called "sacred horses," from the Median stud farms on the Plain of Nisaea is frequently attested. Recall that, according to Herodotus (I.189), after Cyrus marched against Babylon "one of the sacred horses, the white horses, bolted, went into the river and tried to cross it, but the river engulfed it in its waves and carried it away." Cyrus "took vengeance on the river by dividing it into 360 canals." We may then suppose that it was one of these horses that the *magi* were instructed to immolate each month in front of the tomb of Cyrus.

Finally, the guarding of the tomb and the performance of sacrifices were entrusted to the *magi*. Few institutions have given rise to as much discussion as that of the *magi*. The reason is that the evidence, basically the Classical sources, is extremely confused. The term, according to Herodotus (I.101), refers originally to one of the Median tribes. It is in this sense that Herodotus (III.73) and Darius (at least in the Babylonian version) call Smerdis/Gaumata a Median *magus* (DB Bab. §10). But, in the Persian context, the *magus* was primarily a ritual attendant (cf. Herodotus I.132). Arrian's text also shows that the status of *magus* was transmitted from father to son. Besides, it is certain that from the reigns of Cyrus and Cambyses on some of these *magi* were permanently in the entourage of the kings. According to Pliny (VI.116), it was the *magi* who advised that the tomb of Cyrus be oriented toward the east. Among their prerogatives, divination (*manteia*) was well known to the Greek authors. Their task of interpreting royal dreams is attested from this period on (Ctesias §12; cf. Aelian, *VH* II.17 [Artaxerxes III]).

To conclude, the funerary sacrifices practiced regularly at the tomb of Cyrus offer the only indisputable example of state religion established prior to Darius. It is obvious that, in the eyes of Cyrus himself, the construction of a tomb in the town he had just founded represented an important element of his dynastic policy. When his successors committed to maintaining these sacrifices intact, it was because they wished to profit from the renown of Cyrus. The case of Cambyses continues to be problematic. Cyrus is the only representative of the dynasty who can be said with certainty to have been buried in a tomb built above ground. Beginning with Darius, the kings chose tombs dug into the cliff of Naqš-i Rustam.

10. Bardiya's Usurpation (522)

The Reputation of Cambyses

The time has come to consider the circumstances of Cambyses' death. On this topic, it is important to stress right from the start that we depend heavily on the Classical sources, particularly Herodotus, who paints an exclusively negative portrait of Cambyses. The contrast between Cyrus and Cambyses is a veritable *topos* among the Classical authors. We must return to Herodotus's account; he explains that in the course of the campaign in Egypt, tensions arose between Cambyses and his entourage. The Egyptians were not the only victims of the king's "madness"; according to Herodotus (III.30), it also caused the death of his brother, Smerdis. Then, seized by a fit of rage, Cambyses caused the death of his sister-wife while she was pregnant (III.31–32). His "closest relatives" were not the only victims. He also put to death the son of Prexaspes, his cupbearer, with an arrow (III.34–35). "On another occasion he arrested twelve Persians of the highest rank (*prōtoi*) on some trifling charge and buried them alive, head downwards" (III.35✧). Croesus also was to suffer from the madness of the king (III.36), and Herodotus adds (III.37✧), without details: "All this may pass for a sample of the maniacal savagery with which Cambyses treated the Persians and his allies during his stay in Memphis." Perhaps this is a reference to the especially cruel execution of the royal judge Sisamnes:

> He had him flayed; all his skin was torn off and cut into strips, and the strips stretched across the seat of the chair which he used to sit on in court. Cambyses then appointed his son [Otanes] to be judge in his place, and told him not to forget what his chair was made of, when he gave his judgments. (V.25✧)

The information given by Herodotus need not necessarily be taken literally, and still less the "moralizing" interpretation he gives to the facts he reports. He himself stands back, hiding behind his informants ("they say"). He is quite willing to give several versions (Greek and Egyptian) of the death of the king's sister. Furthermore, it seems nearly certain that the story of the murder of Smerdis is an invention. Then again, the story of the torture inflicted on twelve Persian aristocrats is not in itself unbelievable. Elsewhere (VII.114✧) Herodotus states that, in 480 at a place called Nine Roads in Thrace, the Persians "took the same number of young men and young women of the country to bury them alive in this place," and Herodotus adds: "Burying people alive is a Persian custom; I understand that Xerxes' wife Amestris in her old age did it to fourteen Persian boys of distinguished family (*epiphaneis*), by way of a present which she hoped the supposed god of the underworld would accept instead of herself." If we reject the "moralizing" explanation of the behavior of Cambyses ("cruelty," "madness"), we may surmise that he was actually taking reprisals against the great families that had expressed opposition to some of his decrees.

According to Herodotus, Cambyses died in Syria shortly after receiving a messenger sent by the usurper who had taken power in Persia in the name of his brother Smerdis (III.62–65). Whatever the facts may be, it must be stressed that Herodotus at this point is once again highlighting some serious differences between the king and "the most esteemed of the Persians," whom he had summoned to his tent. The Persian aristocrats did not grant any credence to the version of the events presented by Cambyses: "They believed it was Smerdis, son of Cyrus, who had made himself king" (III.66). It thus appears clear that the anecdotes relating to the Persians and Smerdis were collected by Herodotus from people in Persian aristocratic circles who faithfully preserved the traditions hostile to Cambyses. Herodotus states elsewhere (III.89✧) that the Persians considered Cambyses "harsh and careless of his subjects," and he records the opinion of Otanes, one of the conspirators of 522, who condemned Cambyses' "pride of power" (III.80✧).

Smerdis, Tanyoxarces, Mergis, Mardos

In his narrative about Cambyses, Herodotus returns several times to the case of Smerdis, brother of the king, "born of the same father and the same mother" (cf. DB §10). This individual is given a variety of different names in the Greek sources (Tanyoxarces, Tanoxares, Mergis, Mardos). The Behistun inscription and the Babylonian tablets tell us that his name was Bardiya (Barziya in the tablets). Few events in Achaemenid history raise as many questions or rouse as much debate as the short period between the demise of Cambyses and the accession of Darius. An analysis of it is all the more necessary because it allows us to evaluate more carefully the strengths and weaknesses of the Empire at the end of the reign of Cambyses.

In the version recorded by Herodotus, Prexaspes put Smerdis to death on the orders of Cambyses. After the return of his brother from Egypt to Persia, Cambyses in fact was worried, having dreamed of Smerdis "sitting on the royal throne" (III.30✧). Later, two *magi* who were brothers took advantage of the fact that the execution of Smerdis had been kept secret and that "the majority of Persians believed Smerdis was still alive." They rose up against Cambyses. One of them, Patizeithes, entrusted by Cambyses with "the care of his house," placed his brother on the throne. This brother not only was named Smerdis but also resembled him feature for feature! From then on, he ruled under the name and in the place of Cambyses' brother until a conspiracy of aristocrats overthrew him and brought Darius to power (III.61–87).

Several other Classical authors devote discussions to these events. In addition to the brief allusion to Mardos in Aeschylus (*Persians*, 770–75), two authors give more or less circumstantial accounts of the usurpation. For Ctesias (*Persica* §10–13), the break between Cambyses and his brother Tanyoxarces/Bardiya arose as the result of a dispute between Tanyoxarces and a *magus* named Sphendadates, who denounced his master. After several fruitless summons, Cambyses succeeded in bringing Tanyoxarces to court and had him executed. The *magus* Sphendadates took the place of the king's brother, profiting from an extraordinary physical resemblance, and for nearly five years occupied the position of satrap of Bactria, a position that Tanyoxarces had previously held. Among the king's confidants were the eunuchs Artasyras, Bagapates, and Izabates. The first two put Sphendadates on the throne. But Izabates, who was entrusted with transporting Cambyses' body to Persia, denounced the fraud and was put to death.

Justin's version (I.9.4–11) agrees closely with Herodotus's, but there are some differences. It too takes into account the dream of Cambyses in Egypt, recounting that Cambyses ordered Cometes, who was a "*magus* among his friends," to execute Mergis/Smerdis. Without waiting for the death of Cambyses to become known, Cometes assassinated Mergis and substituted his brother Oropastes, who became king. The fraud succeeded so well because "in the conformation of his face and body, Oropastes strongly resembled Mergis."

From this comparison, we can see that all the versions agree on one or several common motifs: the murder of Smerdis (Tanyoxarces/Mergis/Bardiya) by order of his brother

Cambyses, his replacement by a *magus* (Smerdis/Sphendadates/Oropastes), and the physical resemblance between the *magus* and Bardiya that made it possible to keep the murder a secret from everyone. But the contradictions in the details are significant. Some violate the logic of the story. In Ctesias, for example, the role of Prexaspes is taken by the eunuch Izabates, and there is no involvement of two *magi*. The plot took place at the initiative of two highly placed individuals at court, the eunuchs Bagapates and Artasyras, who decided to bring the *magus* Sphendadates to power. The chronological differences are more significant: Ctesias locates the execution of Bardiya five years before the usurpation; Herodotus places the death of Bardiya and then the usurpation of Smerdis during the expedition to Egypt; Justin states that both took place after the death of Cambyses.

Darius, Bardiya, and Gaumata

After his victories over the usurper and the rebels, Darius had a long proclamation carved on the cliff at Behistun; in it he recounted the events that led to his triumph, from his own perspective:

> A son of Cyrus, Cambyses by name, of our family—he was king here. Of that Cambyses there was a brother, Bardiya by name, having the same mother and the same father as Cambyses. Afterwards, Cambyses slew that Bardiya. [This murder] did not become known to the people. Afterwards, Cambyses went to Egypt. When Cambyses had gone off to Egypt, after that the people became evil. After that the Lie (*drauga*) waxed great in the country, both in Persia and in Media and in the other provinces. . . . Afterwards there was one man, a Magian, Gaumata by name; he rose up from Paišiyauvādā. A mountain by name Arakadri— from there XIV days of the month of Viyakhna were past when he rose up. He lied to the people thus: "I am Bardiya, the son of Cyrus, brother of Cambyses." After that, all the people became rebellious from Cambyses, (and) went over to him, both Persia and Media and the other provinces. He seized the kingdom; of the month Garmapada IX days were past, then he seized the kingdom. After that, Cambyses died of natural causes. (*DB* §§10–11❖ [Kent writes "Smerdis" for Bardiya and writes "by his own hand" for "of natural causes"])

Darius also dwells on the illegitimacy of the usurper who had seized the kingdom "that belonged from the beginning to our line" and on the lack of reaction of the inhabitants:

> There was not a man, neither a Persian nor a Mede nor anyone of our family, who might make that Gaumata the Magian deprived of the kingdom. The people feared him greatly, (thinking that) he would slay in numbers the people who previously had known Bardiya; for this reason he would slay people, "lest they know me, that I am not Bardiya the son of Cyrus." Not anyone dared say anything about Gaumata the Magian, until I came. . . . (*DB* §13❖ [Kent writes "Smerdis" for Bardiya])

We see immediately that the version of Herodotus agrees with the statements of Darius on the most important points, in particular that the rebel was a *magus* who had assumed the identity of Bardiya/Smerdis, brother of Cambyses; that Cambyses was responsible for the death of his brother; and that the death of Bardiya was kept secret. The Behistun inscription also supplies precise information on the chronology: Gaumata's insurrection is dated March 11, 522. Starting in the month of April, the Babylonian tablets in fact begin to be dated to the reign of Bardiya (Barziya), who is called "king of the lands" and "king of Babylon, king of the lands." On July 1, Gaumata "seized power," shortly before the death of Cambyses. But we must emphasize that Darius is careful not to specify the date of the king's death, even though other events are quite consistently fixed to the month and the day throughout his narrative.

Bardiya/Smerdis and Gaumata

We can see that many obscurities about the identity of the rebel and the circumstances of his appearance persist. The general agreement between Herodotus and Darius does not in itself guarantee certainty. We know in fact that the Behistun text, on the orders of none other than Darius (*DB* §70), was proclaimed throughout every province of the Empire. Did a Greek version, which could have been consulted by Herodotus, exist? It is possible, but again we must note that if this be the case, Herodotus exercised his full freedom of interpretation. In fact, the points on which Herodotus differs from the text of Darius are also notable, including the role of Darius himself in the plot against the usurper (see chap. 3/2, pp. 114ff.). Herodotus also does not agree with Darius on the date of Bardiya's execution. He attributes it to Prexaspes (on the orders of Cambyses) and places it during the Egyptian expedition, whereas Darius states that Cambyses gave the order before departing for the Nile Valley. It is also noteworthy that Herodotus gives the usurper the name Smerdis—a "faithful" Greek transcription of the Iranian personal name Bardiya—while noting that, surprisingly, the *magus* had the same name as the son of Cyrus! The name Gaumata is found only in Justin, but the *magus* by this name (Cometes) was assigned by Cambyses himself to put to death the real Smerdis and was the one who put his brother Oropastes on the throne! It seems clear that Herodotus and his successors have mingled several oral versions that, at the time of his inquiry, were in circulation in Asia Minor and Greece and among the great Persian aristocratic families.

In any case, the agreements between Herodotus and Darius do not prove anything for the plain and simple reason that Darius's autobiography is itself highly suspect. Anxious to appear to be a legitimate king descended from the family of Achaemenes (*DB* §§1–4) and to be the restorer of dynastic legitimacy (*DB* §14), Darius had a serious interest in insisting on the death of Cambyses' brother and the deception of the man called Gaumata. The new king carefully highlighted the restrained character of his narrative (§58) and his love of truth (§63), but his assurances will not fully convince the reader who has been forewarned about the stereotypical character of these statements. It will also be noted that the information is not entirely consistent among the versions. The Babylonian version (§10) is the only one to call Gaumata a Mede. But what does this mean? Could it not simply be that for a Babylonian (as for a Greek or an Egyptian) the generic ethnic term *Mede* also included the Persians?

For all of these reasons, generations of historians have been asking the question: Was Gaumata really the usurper called *"magus"* by Darius, or was he just an invention of Darius, because he was anxious to conceal that it was really he who had overthrown Bardiya, the true son of Cyrus? The question may seem to be purely rhetorical, to the extent that the sources agree on the execution of Bardiya. But the rest of the story seems entirely too strange, not to say unbelievable. For Ctesias, Tanyoxarces' own chief eunuch was taken in by the scene imagined by Cambyses, "so that the *magus* deceived them by his resemblance"! How to explain, furthermore, that the execution of so important a person could be kept secret for four or five years—even, according to Herodotus (III.68–69), from his wives Atossa and Phaidime? Phaidime's discovery of the deception, as it is told by Herodotus, is more fairy tale than history.

Apparently aware of how difficult it would be to believe in a feature-for-feature resemblance between Bardiya and the usurper, Justin (I.9.11) tries to forestall the objections of his readers (or to respond to his own) by remarking: "The secret was so well guarded because, among the Persians, the kings do not show themselves." Justin is obviously referring to the royal protocol that kept the king isolated within the royal palace. But can we be expected to believe that the king (or his substitute) would not have granted a single audience during the course of several years? In any event, Herodotus himself reports that Otanes, Phaidime's father, had doubted the official story for some time. The same was true for Otanes' companions, Aspathines and Gobryas (III.70), as well as Darius (III.71). Herodotus (III.66✧) also acknowledges the skepticism of the nobles who surrounded Cambyses on his deathbed: "They were covinced that it was Smerdis the son of Cyrus who was on the throne." It is thus obvious that the version published by Darius was not universally accepted.

When, with good reason, the modern historian casts doubt on the reality of the execution of Bardiya, the entire structure collapses like a house of cards. But it must also be remembered that nothing has been established with certainty at the present time, given the available evidence. The historian is reduced to arguing for probabilities and choosing the option that appears the least uncertain. To explore the problem, we must now entertain the hypothesis, these days generally accepted, of a deception devised by Darius himself.

Cambyses and Bardiya

To explore the theory of Darius's ploy, we need to return to the succession of Cyrus, who, as we have seen, made the decision to transfer authority before his death to his older son Cambyses rather than to Bardiya, "born of the same father and the same mother." This is the first known case of a father's choosing the crown prince; many others are known afterward. The younger son, Bardiya, received a major district in Central Asia as compensation. The reasons for Cyrus's choice elude us completely. Preference for the older son, often presented as a rule by the Classical authors, did not obligate the reigning king, who always retained total freedom of choice based on his own preference and/or analysis (cf. pp. 518–522, below). It is sufficient to recall that Cyrus's preference was expressed early, since in 539 Cambyses had already received the title "king of Babylon." Reading the address placed by Xenophon on Cyrus's dying lips leaves the impression that the king nursed some fear for the future (VIII.7.11–28). It proves in any case that Bardiya had never really accepted his father's decision. Although mollified by an exemption from paying tribute to the central court, as a satrap he remained dependent on his brother, the king. This is made quite clear by Ctesias, who states that several times Cambyses summoned his brother to the court, and twice Bardiya refused, "detained by other obligations."

One can guess that relations between the two brothers could only deteriorate. This is the import of an anecdote Herodotus (III.30) locates in Egypt. The king of the Ethiopians gave the ambassador-spies sent by Cambyses a bow, along with the following message: "The king of Ethiopia has some advice to give him: when the Persians can draw a bow of this size thus easily, then let him raise an army of superior strength and invade the country of the long-lived Ethiopians" (III.21✧), an insolent challenge that could not be met by any Persian in Cambyses' entourage. Smerdis/Bardiya, on the other hand, was "the only Persian to succeed in drawing—though only a very little way, about two fingers' breadth—the bow" (III.29✧), thus providing occasion for the "jealousy" of

Cambyses, who sent his brother back to Persia. The anecdote is particularly revealing of the relationship between the brothers. For the Persians, in fact, "the chief proof of manliness" is "prowess in fighting" (I.136◊). The king himself justified his power with his qualifications as a warrior; he was a "good bowman" (*DNb* §8h◊). Thus, in the form of a metaphor, Herodotus set forth Bardiya's aspirations to the kingship.

Of course, these observations do not clear away all of the uncertainties; far from it! If Bardiya's ambition was so obvious, we can understand perfectly well that Cambyses would have had him executed, whether before his departure for Egypt (Darius's and Ctesias's version) or after Bardiya's return to Persia (Herodotus's and Justin's version). And it is hard to believe that Cambyses would have sent him back to Persia, permitting him freedom of movement, before thinking better of it. Again we must recall that one author (Justin) places the death of Bardiya after the death of Cambyses and that this version, frankly, is neither more nor less likely than the others.

Having returned to Persia (under our hypothesis)—or not having accompanied his brother to Egypt (another possible hypothesis)—Bardiya revolted during the course of March 522, as Darius notes precisely. But was this a real usurpation, in the strict sense of the word? According to Darius, Cambyses was still alive at the beginning of July. The problem is that we cannot compare Darius to any other indisputable source. Herodotus states that Cambyses received the messenger sent by the usurper with "a proclamation "to the troops . . . that they should take their orders in future not from Cambyses but from Smerdis" (III.61◊) while he was in Syria. We also know that certain Babylonian tablets are still dated by Cambyses until mid-April 522. But these documents (of quite varied nature) do not indicate the date of the death of Cambyses decisively. On the other hand, let us emphasize once more that Justin places the usurpation of Oropastes *after* the death of Cambyses and that, according to Ctesias, "the usurper reigned *after* the death of Cambyses." Darius himself carefully distinguishes two stages: in March 522, Bardiya revolted in Persia; but it was not until July 522 that he "seized royal power." To be sure, the Babylonian tablets provide evidence that he was recognized in Babylon in April. But the expression used by Darius seems to indicate that it was not until the beginning of July that he officially presented himself as the successor to the deceased king, perhaps after an official ceremony had taken place at Pasargadae.

If Cambyses died in the meantime, we may assume that Bardiya had waited for this moment before claiming his legitimate right to the throne, using official protocols. As the son of Cyrus, "the throne was his by right," as Justin explains (I.9: . . . *cui regnum debebatur*). The situation with regard to the succession was at the same time both complex and simple. We know in fact from Herodotus (III.66◊) that Cambyses "had no children, either sons or daughters" (cf. Ctesias §12). As far as we know, this was the first time such a situation had arisen. The fact remains that after the death of Cambyses, Bardiya was the sole male descendant of the royal family. Rebel and usurper for several months, Bardiya had himself named king upon the death of Cambyses. To mark his legitimacy still more clearly, he took the wives of his "predecessor." We can now understand why Darius was motivated to date Bardiya's official assumption of power before the death of Cambyses: it was to transform into a usurper a king who could legitimate his authority by his filiation.

In any event, there is nothing to indicate that this proclamation suffered many objections. Darius himself states on the contrary that the discontent with Cambyses was old and had already begun to appear upon his departure for Egypt. He also stresses that upon the revolt of Gaumata, "all the people conspired against Cambyses"; that the *"magus"* "rallied to himself Persia, Media, and the other countries"; and that no one was able to organize any opposition. He adds, it is true, that "Gaumata" reigned by terror and that he did not hesitate to put many people to death (DB §13). But, here as elsewhere, Darius's claims are subject to caution. He wishes above all to gain credence for the *false* idea that he was the first and only one to dare to oppose the person whom he calls a usurper. The accession of Bardiya to the throne instead implies that he had prepared his coup and that he had sufficient support in Persia to assure him the dynastic loyalty of its inhabitants. It is moreover quite noteworthy that the uprising took place in Persia itself, at Paišiyauvādā, perhaps near Pasargadae, the same place where sometime later the Persian Vahyazdāta would rise up against Darius.

Bardiya and the Persian Aristocracy

The ancient authors' presentation of the relations between Cambyses and the aristocracy leads us to believe that Bardiya succeeded in rallying to himself the great families against whom Cambyses had taken severe measures during his stay in Egypt, at a date when he could not have been unaware of the ambitions of his brother. Did Bardiya give assurances to certain heads of clans, promising them that he would rule in a manner less "despotic" than Cambyses? This is a frequently advanced hypothesis.

In his version, Darius (DB §14) condemns the measures Gaumata had taken in Persia. He takes credit for restoring to its original state the kingdom that had been confiscated by Gaumata: for restoring the 'sanctuaries' (*āyadanā*) destroyed by Gaumata; for restoring to the 'people' (Old Persian *kāra*; Elamite *taššup*; Babylonian *ūqu*) the fields, the herds, the 'workers' (Old Persian *māniya*, Elamite *kurtaš*, Babylonian *agru*), and the 'clan domains' (Old Persian *viθ*) that the *magus* Gaumata had confiscated. And he concludes thus:

> By the favor of Ahuramazda this I did: I strove until I reestablished our royal house on its foundation as (it was) before. So I strove, by the favor of Ahuramazda, so that Gaumata the Magian did not remove our royal House (*viθ*).

This text presents enormous interpretive problems. Let us note first of all that the claims of Darius, here as elsewhere, are a priori affected by a strong coefficient of critical doubt. It is especially clear that, in the very logic of his self-justifying discourse, he needs to present Gaumata as absolutely evil, and he thus congratulates himself for restoring things to the way they were before the usurpation of the *"magus."* He therefore insists on Gaumata's illegitimacy (usurper of the power of the Achaemenids), on his impiety (destroyer of sanctuaries), and on his injustice (confiscator of property from its legitimate owners). This is, traditionally, how every new conqueror as well as every usurper presents himself ideologically to the conquered countries in order to advance his own legitimacy (compare this with Cyrus's contrast of himself with Nabonidus in Babylon). We should also note that Darius's denunciations of Gaumata position Darius within the traditional representations of Iranian society, while they accuse Gaumata of attacking the interests of the army, the priests, and the peasants.

All the same, Darius's accusations are fairly specific, and they cannot be dismissed with a wave of the hand. But their historical interpretation is tricky, insofar as enormous philological problems persist, which generations of specialists have struggled with and still do. The question is simple: what social group(s) did Gaumata/Bardiya have in mind? The word *kāra*, the term used for those Darius names as the victim of Bardiya's measures, has a fairly vague meaning, fitting the sense 'people' (in the broad sense) as well as 'army'. The vocabulary used by the composers of the Babylonian and Elamite versions does not remove the difficulty, for the terms *ūqu* and *taššup* are as vague as *kāra*, just as easily designating 'people' (or 'peoples') or 'troops'. We are immediately tempted to think of the aristocratic clans that without a doubt owned great estates devoted to agriculture and stockbreeding, worked by dependent peasants (*kurtaš*); the term *viθ* (and the corresponding Elamite *ulhi* = 'House') then would refer to the aristocratic Houses. According to this hypothesis, the "sanctuaries" destroyed by Gaumata would be the clan sanctuaries, dedicated to the heroicized ancestors of these powerful aristocratic groups; the term *kāra* would designate the aristocrats more narrowly, those who were devoted in a privileged way to the profession of war.

But this interpretation does raise reservations and feeds insurmountable contradictions, not least by transforming Bardiya into a reformer/social revolutionary who desired to rely on simple peasants to humble the economic privileges of the aristocracy. This is a wholly improbable hypothesis, for Bardiya could not forego the support of the aristocratic class, who at this time governed the Empire under the authority of the king and whose cooperation was indispensable to anyone who wished to claim supreme power. Furthermore, the hypothesis rests on an unstated and totally unacceptable assumption—namely, that in the Persia of 522 social antagonisms were based not only on objective realities but also on a very advanced class awareness, which an outsider like Gaumata would have been able to use. It also depends (without saying so) on the perfectly false parallel of the origin of certain tyrannical regimes in archaic Greece. That Herodotus (III.80–82) later sought to filter the events of 522 through a Greek mental grid is one thing; for the modern historian to follow Herodotus on this path is another. We have as much reason to be skeptical as Herodotus's own audience was (cf. III.80; VI.43).

There is a fairly simple way of resolving this contradiction. The interpretive hypothesis that we will briefly review is implicitly based on the chronology provided by Darius (but even so without insisting on it), namely: (1) usurpation by the *magus*; (2) confiscation of lands; (3) plot against Bardiya. Interchanging stages (2) and (3) is all that is needed to come up with a more reasonable explanation. If we suppose that in fact the plot against Bardiya was hatched in Syria, shortly after the death of Cambyses, it is easy to understand that Bardiya took steps to counter it. Would not the confiscations Darius speaks of first have been aimed at those who sought to remove him? The purpose of the confiscation was thus to take away from Bardiya's opponents their social and economic bases in Persia as well as in other conquered countries where they may have received land. In this framework, we may stress the importance of the Babylonian version (§13). Likewise referring to Bardiya's confiscations, it cites the herds, the workers (*agru*), and the Houses (É/*bītu*). But the parallel with the Persian and Elamite versions stops here, for the logogram É is followed by an expression peculiar to the Babylonian version, namely, *qašātu*. Thus for the first time we find an expression well known from the later Murašû tablets, *bīt qašti*, 'bow estate' (not 'fief', as it is "translated" all too frequently). Besides confirming the existence of military tenancies in the early Achaemenid period (p. 75), the passage offers a most interesting clue. We know in fact that at a later period the royal *dōreai* in Babylonia frequently included bow, chariot, and other estates. What

Bardiya was doing, then, was preventing the rebellious nobles from using military forces connected to the Babylonian *ḫaṭrus* against him. The objective was thus not to confiscate family property; the royal power was revoking the rights of rebellious nobles to land that had been granted to them by the king on a conditional basis (*dōreai*). It was understood that in the case of insubordination these royal grants (*nidintu šarri*) could be reclaimed by the king, who could then redistribute them to loyal nobles. If this interpretation is correct, it would only confirm that the measure taken by Bardiya was based on a positive policy objective: it was meant not only to injure his opponents (confiscations) but also to cement his alliance with the portion of the Persian nobility that had supported him from the beginning (redistributions).

This interpretation presents the undeniable advantage of resolving the apparent contradictions in the documentary record without doing it violence. Bardiya was not so foolish as to turn the Persian aristocracy against him at the very moment when his power was endangered by a conspiracy; he isolated those who opposed him. It was doubtless representatives of these hostile families from whom Herodotus gathered his testimony, according to which, "he was regretted after his death by all the Asiatics under his rule, though not by the Persians themselves" (III.67✧). It was in the interest of the aristocratic Houses who had revolted against Bardiya to promote the idea that Bardiya had aroused unanimous opposition, which was obviously not the case.

Bardiya and Tribute from the Empire

Herodotus makes this remark while citing another decision made by Smerdis/Bardiya after his accession: "To every nation within his dominion he proclaimed, directly he came to the throne, a three years' remission of taxes and military service."✧ Presented by Justin (I.9.12–13) as a demagogic measure, this decision, Herodotus says, gained him the good will of the populace. Elsewhere (VI.59✧), Herodotus mentions the "Persian custom whereby a king, on his accession, remits arrears of tribute from all his subject states." But the two measures cannot be reconciled with each other, for Bardiya did not decree the forgiveness of back tribute as a "gift of joyous accession" but proclaimed an exemption from tribute and military obligations for the three years to come.

The interpretation does not seem open to doubt. Bardiya took a course opposite to that of his predecessors, in particular Cambyses, whose reign had brought an increase in tribute appropriations from the conquered peoples. If Bardiya had taken an equally drastic measure, we would expect discontent among the subject peoples to have surfaced. Darius himself states that, after the departure of Cambyses for Egypt and the execution of his brother Bardiya, the "Lie" (*drauga* = 'rebellion') spread not only among the Persians but also among the Medes and other peoples (*DB* §§10–11). It is true that otherwise he dates the great revolts as beginning in late September 522—that is, after the execution of the person he calls Gaumata. But these revolts themselves can be considered the brutal end of a period of widespread troubles, revealing imperial dysfunction. The enormous levies required by Cambyses for the construction of a navy and for the expedition to Egypt weighed too heavily on the subject peoples, above and beyond the arbitrary requirements of the satraps. To reestablish order and to combat centrifugal forces, Bardiya found himself forced to take a protective measure. With this step, we can suppose, he and his counselors dreamed of reforming the system of imposing tribute—a reform that came about with Darius. It is not out of the question that Bardiya's analyses of the situation were shared by a certain number of nobles who were uneasy with the troubles that were brewing in the Empire and who, for this reason, chose to support his coup d'etat against Cambyses. But it is likely that, at the same time, he aroused the hostility of other Persians, who were unhappy to see the profits of the Empire slip through their fingers even temporarily and doubtless more inclined to repression than to tactical accommodations. This could be the source of Herodotus's suggestion about the poor reputation that Smerdis/Bardiya left among the Persians (III.67). Undoubtedly, the mention of Mardos in Aeschylus (*Persians* 773–775) flows out of this current: "Mardos was fifth to take power, a disgrace to his fatherland and to this ancient throne." This note by Aeschylus is especially interesting because it seems to recognize the legitimacy of Mardos while at the same time condemning his way of governing.

Whatever the particularly difficult imperial and dynastic situation Bardiya found himself in, he never intended to sell off the conquests of Cyrus and Cambyses. The suspension of tribute and military contingents was only temporary. It was intended to calm the uneasiness and discord of the subject peoples in order to set up a new system of assessment. In itself, the tribute policy of Bardiya attests to contradictions in the imperial structure at the time of the death of Cambyses. It also attests to the clear political thinking of the person whom Darius presents as a usurper.

Chapter 3
Trouble, Secession, and Rebuilding (522–518)

1. Darius Comes to Power (522)

The Conspiracy of the Seven: Darius and Herodotus

The ancient sources contain major contradictions regarding the identity of Gaumata/Smerdis, and using them for reconstructing the conditions surrounding the removal of Smerdis and the coming to power of Darius is correspondingly complicated. According to Herodotus (III.68–70), it was Otanes who initiated a conspiracy, being "the first person to suspect that he [Gaumata/Smerdis] was not the son of Cyrus but an impostor" (§68✧). When a conversation with his daughter Phaidime reinforced Otanes' conviction, he "took into his confidence Aspathines and Gobryas . . . and told them of his discovery." The three men then came to an agreement, and each of them chose a fully trustworthy companion: "Otanes chose Intaphernes, Gobryas Megabyzus, and Aspathines Hydarnes." When Darius arrived on the scene "from Persia . . . it was decided to add him to the number" (III.70✧).

In this story, the role of Darius appears singularly minor: until his arrival, Otanes is the central character in the drama. At this point (III.71), the tone of Herodotus's story changes: from now on, he shows Darius and Otanes on opposite sides in the discussions about strategy and tactics held among the Seven. Otanes was particularly opposed to the rapid action urged by Darius. Darius's arguments convinced Gobryas, then the other conspirators (§73). Darius's resolution prevailed once more as the Seven conferred a second time on the way to the palace (§76). Once they had entered Smerdis's quarters, it was Darius and Gobryas who fell on the usurper. In complete darkness, Darius thrust Smerdis through with his sword, as Smerdis was being held by Gobryas (§79). Finally, a few days later, the Seven held a meeting at which Otanes, Darius, and Megabyzus quarreled about the political outcome of the crisis they had stirred up. By arguing in favor of a monarchy, Darius again won the approval of the other four conspirators (§§80–83). In the last phase, Otanes withdrew from the competition (§§83–84) and the royal title was contested by the six remaining conspirators. Darius took it through a ruse effected by his groom (§§85–87): "In this way Darius became king of Persia" (§88✧).

In the text of his proclamation at Behistun, Darius does not embarrass himself with such details. From the beginning, he proclaims loudly and clearly that his royal authority derived from the heritage of his ancestors and the protection of Ahura-Mazda. This is the basic article of self-justification to which he returns incessantly. He also recalls the origins of the usurpation of Cambyses' rule by Gaumata the *magus*, and he stresses that no one, neither Persian nor Mede nor anyone else, dared to rise up against the false Bardiya. In contrast, he, Darius, with the aid of Ahura-Mazda, "with a few men slew that Gaumata the Magian, and those who were his foremost followers. A fortress by name

Sikayauvatiš, a district by name Nisāya, in Media—there I slew him. I took the kingdom from him. By the favor of Ahuramazda I became king; Ahuramazda bestowed the kingdom upon me" (29 September 522; *DB* §§1–13◊). The measures taken by the new king to reestablish the order that was destroyed by Gaumata follow (§14).

Darius thus attributed to himself a role that was not merely dominant but hegemonic: the "few men" who gave him a hand appear only in the background; their subordinate status could only further enhance the royal image of Darius, who presented himself as the only person who could eliminate the usurper. So it continues throughout the long narrative—absent from Herodotus's version—dedicated to the cumulative recital of victories won by Darius. Of course, here and there the king gives the names of the generals who fought under his command, but in every case credit for the victory comes back to him, as a result of the protection that Ahura-Mazda unceasingly provided to his royal person.

Herodotus and Darius would thus be in flagrant contradiction if Darius did not suddenly recognize the other six in a closing paragraph: "These are the men who were there at the time when I slew Gaumata the Magian who called himself Bardiya; at that time these men cooperated as my followers (*anušiyā*)." A list of six names and a solemn declaration follow: "Saith Darius the King: Thou who shalt be king hereafter, protect well the family posterity of these men" (*DB* §§68–69◊ [Kent writes Smerdis for Bardiya]).

Note first that the lists of names given by Herodotus and Darius generally agree:

DB §68	*Herodotus III.70*
Vidafarnah, son of Vāyaspāra	Intaphernes
Utāna, son of Thukra	Otanes, son of Pharnaspes (III.68)
Gaubaruva, son of Marduniya	Gobryas, father of Mardonius (VI.43)
Vidarna, son of Bagābigna	Hydarnes
Bagabuxša, son of Dātuvahya	Megabyzus
Ardumaniš, son of Vahauka	Aspathines

There is a only one disagreement: Ardumaniš and Aspathines are clearly two different people. The former is unknown elsewhere; perhaps he perished in the assault on Smerdis. In contrast, Herodotus's Aspathines is easily recognizable as one of Darius's companions shown bearing royal arms on the king's tomb; an inscription calls him Aspacānā (*DNd*).

In any case, the participants in the plot are all clearly descendants of important aristocratic Persian families (the Persian identity of each of them is indicated by Darius), even though we lack precise indication of the ancestry of some of them; their aristocratic origin is known especially from the status that they and their sons held after Darius's victory. Herodotus (III.68◊) presents Otanes as "one of the wealthiest members of the Persian nobility." One of his daughters, Phaidime, had been taken to wife first by Cambyses, then by Bardiya (III.68); hence the role attributed to him by Herodotus in the denunciation of the fraud (III.68–69). According to Herodotus (II.1; III.2), Cassandane, the wife of Cyrus, was also Otanes' sister. Gobryas and Aspathines are also identified by Herodotus as "two eminent (*prōtoi*) Persians" (III.70◊). Moreover, both are depicted on the tomb at Naqš-i Rustam: the inscription (*DNc*◊) gives Gobryas the title "spear-bearer (*arštibara*) of Darius the king." The inscription does not give his patronym to identify him but calls him Patišuvariš, a designation in which we recognize the Patischorians, a subgroup of the Persian people whom Strabo (XV.3.1) lists in a loose way with the Achaemenids and the *magi* among the Persian tribes (*phula*). Whatever the socio-genetic reality of the Patischorians, there is no doubt that their members were indeed among the *prōtoi* of the Persians.

The Problem of Power

The logic of the plot, as it appears in Herodotus and Darius, cannot be denied. The essential problem to be settled was that of power pure and simple. From the beginning, the problem with the desire to eliminate Bardiya was that there was no heir, since Cambyses, as everyone knew, had died without male issue. According to Herodotus, it was not until after the murder of the "*magus*" and his companions that the Seven addressed the issue: "The conspirators met to discuss the situation in detail. At the meeting certain speeches were made—some of our own countrymen refuse to believe they were actually made at all; nevertheless—they were" (III.80❖). Three theses are then presented, defended respectively by Otanes, Megabyzus, and Darius: (a) establishment of a regime where the 'people' (*plēthos*) and the 'great number' (*pollon*) exercise power; (b) setting up an oligarchic system, whose keystone would be "a group of men chosen from the best" (Megabyzus of course mentions that the Seven would be included); (c) lastly, retaining the monarchic regime. The conclusion of the debate was: "These were the three views set out in the three speeches; the four men who had not spoken voted for the last" (III.83❖).

Like Herodotus's Greek listeners (cf. VI.43), modern historians have given little credence to putting these speeches in the mouths of the three nobles. Their tone and vocabulary are typically Greek. Are we really expected to believe that the supposed excesses of Bardiya/Gaumata against the nobility had caused a resurgence, from a very distant past, of the aspirations of the chieftains of clans and tribes to govern collectively, in other words, to perpetuate the structure of the conspiracy as it is described by Herodotus? This interpretation seems rather farfetched, since it implies that a number of Persian aristocrats would put at risk the fruits of the conquests from which they had so greatly benefited. It is totally shattered if the reconstruction of events presented (as a hypothesis) in the previous chapter is accepted.

In truth, what was at stake was not really the *monarchic* principle; what was at stake, and what the debate must have dealt with, was a *dynastic* problem. In the absence of a direct heir, who should be chosen? This was the only real question. We know the explanation given by Herodotus: Otanes took himself out of the competition, and the other six nobles decided to let fate make the decision: "They proposed to mount their horses on the outskirts of the city, and he whose horse neighed first after the sun was up should have the throne" (III.84❖). Then Herodotus gives the details of the ruse concocted by Oebares, Darius's groom, that led his master to be recognized as king (III.85–88). Obviously, no one could believe that Darius's accession to power was due exclusively to a ruse. The motif of hippomancy was added afterward because it meshes neatly with the notion Darius wished to propagate—namely, his special relationship with the deity. But it is clear from his other qualities and assets that the son of Hystaspes was obliged to seize supreme power with the consent and support of the other conspirators—unanimous support because, basically, Otanes had also given his consent. His companions thereafter had no choice but to recognize the supremacy of Darius, which could only be based on intrinsically superior rights and/or a coalesence of forces in his favor.

The "Rights" of Darius

Darius states that he became king because of and under the protection of Ahura-Mazda and because of the antiquity of his familial rights. He presents himself from the start as "son of Hystaspes, grandson of Arsames, an Achaemenian" (*DB* §1◊). Then he includes his father and grandfather in a sequence going much further back, since it reaches Achaemenes, who is presented as the eponymous founder from whom Teispes and Ariaramnes, father of Arsames and thus great-grandfather of Darius, were directly descended (§2). He simultaneously stresses the antiquity and the distinction of his family: "For this reason, we are called Achaemenians. From long ago we have been noble. From long ago our family (*taumā*) had been kings" (§3◊). And finally he adds: "Saith Darius the King: VIII of our family (there are) who were kings afore; I am the ninth; IX in succession we have been kings" (§4◊). Despite several difficulties in translation, the image Darius wishes to project is perfectly clear. From his viewpoint, there cannot be any disagreement: his right to kingship is rooted in the long duration of the "royal seed," and the purpose of his action was the restoration of his House (*viθ*) to its ancient foundations (§14).

On many counts, Darius's claims are insupportable. He does not mention Cyrus, even though he includes Teispes in his genealogy and presents him as his great-great-grandfather; Cyrus calls Teispes his great-grandfather. The only way to harmonize the two genealogies is to suppose that Teispes divided his kingdom into two branches: the first (beginning with Teispes and Cyrus I) represented by Cambyses and Bardiya; the second by Darius through his father, Hystaspes. But, despite Herodotus (VII.11), the theory of two Persian kingdoms will not stand. Certainly, if this theory were accepted, we cannot see who the eight kings to precede Darius might have been; he is careful not to name them! We know in fact that his father and grandfather, Hystaspes and Arsames, were alive in 522 (cf. *XPf* §3) and that they certainly never bore the title of king. If Darius had a Teispes in his family, the only possibility is that it was a man with the same name as the great-grandfather of Cyrus the Great. There is not one text to demonstrate that Hystaspes' son came from a related line of descent, as is often supposed. Indeed, Plato (*Laws* III.695c) and Aelian (*VH* XII.43) stress that Darius was not the son of a king. This is exactly what Justin suggests (I.10.13–14). Herodotus does not give the slightest hint that Darius had any greater right to the throne than his fellow conspirators. Quite the contrary, he later recalls, using the word *idiōtēs*, that before 522, although he had a prestigious court title (*doryphoros*), Darius was "not yet of any particular importance . . . a person of no power or consequence" (III.139–140◊). By this, he simply means that Darius was not the son of a king; he was an *idiōtēs* ['private person'] (VII.3).

But making Darius into a "usurper," as has been customary, does not make much sense either, for the plain and simple reason that none of the other six conspirators—not even Otanes—could argue for the same dynastic credentials that the son of Hystaspes asserted without discussion. Nor is there much sense in objecting that Hystaspes had more "rights" than his son. It seems clear that, given the occasion of a dynastic vacancy, Darius wished to claim a new foundation for the Persian kingdom and Achaemenid dominion. Therefore, he chose an eponymous ancestor, Achaemenes, which justified his rights a posteriori. It was probably on this occasion that a new "founder legend" was introduced, the legend in which Achaemenes was said to have been fed and raised by an eagle (Aelian, *Anim.* XII.21), an animal whose connections with royal Persian power are well attested. As for the word *Achaemenid* itself, it is clear that Darius uses it in a very narrow sense. For him it does not refer to a clan—which is how we understand Herodotus's *phratries*. It is a name that applies exclusively to the members of Darius's patrilineal family. It is also in this sense that the new king used the word in the fraudulent Pasargadae inscriptions supposedly created by Cyrus (*CMa–b–c* = *DMa–b–c*). By describing Cyrus quite simply as "king" and Achaemenid, Darius was trying to mask his familial manipulations by making Cyrus the fictive ancestor of the new royal family. Here the term clearly referred to the royal family, for we cannot see what Darius would have gained by stressing that Cyrus belonged to the clan/phratry of the Achaemenids.

It is thus totally useless to stress that a man like Otanes would have had as much right as Darius because his father, Pharnaspes, is called "Achaemenid" by Herodotus. Aside from the fact that Herodotus's information is absolutely demolished by the Behistun inscription (§68: Thukra), for Herodotus and Darius the term *Achaemenid* designated different social realities. For Herodotus, it referred to the Achaemenid clan, which was part of the Pasargadae tribe. This is, moreover, the sense in which he described Darius's father as Achaemenid (I.209). In contrast, Darius used the term exclusively to refer to his ancestry in the direct line. As Aelian implies (*Anim.* XII.21), it is by reference to this familial-genetic reality that one must evaluate the nobility (*eugeneia*) of the various Persian families from this time onward. That is, "nobility" was no longer merely a matter of genealogy: the category was thereafter inserted into the political—or, if you like, dynastic—vocabulary.

In other words, Darius did not come into power because of his dynastic ancestry. Quite the converse is true: as a result of the power that he arrogated to himself, he established the dynastic rights of his ancestors. It is not because he was Achaemenid (in the clan sense) that Darius achieved power; it was his accession to royalty that allowed him to redefine the reality of what it meant to be "Achaemenid." At the same time, this redefinition did not wipe out the earlier understanding; it seems clear that the Achaemenid clan continued to function as in the past. But it is also clear that membership in this clan was not enough to claim any sort of right of succession. This decision remained solely in the hands of the "head of the family"—in other words, the reigning king. It was thus the very bases of dynastic reality that Darius modified from top to bottom, as well as the special themes of dynastic ideology, which he did more to manipulate than to restore. It is therefore entirely pointless to judge Darius's candidacy for the throne in terms of a right of succession that he in fact redefined *after* his accession.

The Primacy of Darius

At this point in the discussion, it seems useful and sensible to leave the realm of ideology and propaganda behind. But to decline argument on the terms imposed on posterity by Darius is to find ourselves back at the question posed at the beginning: why, of the seven conspiring nobles, was it the son of Hystaspes who was eventually chosen? It hardly seems legitimate to attribute much credibility to the premonitory dream of Cyrus recorded by Herodotus (I, I.209), which implies that as early as 530 Cyrus feared a revolt by Darius, the son of Hystaspes. If, moreover, we abandon speculation on the "nobility" of his origins, there are other explanations that are worth exploring. It must be assumed that Darius operated from a position of strength, imposed or negotiated. Indeed, contrary to appearances, Herodotus does not at bottom distance himself from the implications of Darius's own statements on this point. Herodotus's phrasing (III.70) and the story of the formation of the conspiracy indicate that from the outset Darius held a special position among the conspirators. Before his arrival, in fact, an organizational chart of the conspiracy could have been diagrammed as a pyramid, drawn up according to the order of appearance on the scene of the first six conspirators, as seen by Herodotus:

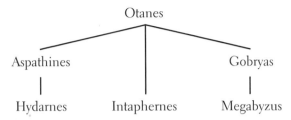

The schema leaves out Darius, who came later. He was then integrated into a conspiracy formed by the heads of six great families without having been recruited personally either directly by Otanes or at a lower level by Aspathines or Gobryas. To put it another way, he was not personally dependent on the other conspirators, particularly not on Otanes. In other words, from the moment of his appearance he occupied a position of strength equal to that of Otanes.

The other observation—a more important one—is that representatives of Darius's family were part of Cyrus's and Cambyses' circle of intimates. According to Herodotus (III.70), Darius's father, Hystaspes, was "governor of Persia" in 522. But this is certainly an error: the Behistun text shows that he held a high military command in Parthia at the time (DB §35). It was perhaps in this capacity that he was part of Cyrus's entourage at the beginning of his final campaign in Central Asia (Herodotus I.209). The career of Darius himself is interesting, to the extent that we can reconstruct it even very imperfectly from remarks in the Classical authors. According to an author who is late but in general well informed about Persian matters, Darius "carried the quiver (*pharētrophoros*) for Cyrus" (Aelian, *VH* XII.43✧). We also know that he accompanied Cambyses on his Egyptian expedition, since Herodotus places him there in a well-known story. Herodotus states that at this date Darius "not yet of any particular importance,"✧ an evaluation that only makes sense in contrast to his position as king, his position when Herodotus first introduces him in the course of his narrative. The author from Halicarnassus states, in fact, that in Egypt Darius had the title "lance-bearer (*doryphoros*) of Cambyses" (III.139). "Lance-bearer" and "quiver-bearer" must be considered not so much duties as court titles by which a king wished to demonstrate the distinction he bestowed on one of his faithful. It was precisely this custom that Darius observed when he placed Aspathines and Gobryas near him on his tomb at Naqš-i Rustam (*DNc–d*). In other words, Darius had acquired first-rank political stature when he seized supreme power in 522. Born around 550, he was able to make a name for himself during the reign of Cambyses.

But the problem remains. That Darius was not a "self-made man" is one thing (and this, after all, is open to question); that he was to become king is another. In a developing situation like that of spring 522, it was within the council of Seven that the decision was made. But to go beyond this simple observation, it would be useful to be familiar

with the inner workings of the group of Seven. Though they came together for the purpose of overthrowing Smerdis, it is also true that there already was a personal and familial solidarity among them, a solidarity that the available evidence allows us to glimpse
faintly in the case of one of the conspirators, Gobryas. The privileged relationship between Gobryas and Darius is illuminated by the place the new king reserved for him on
the façade of his rock-cut tomb at Naqš-i Rustam, where he appears as royal lance-bearer
(*arštibara* = *doryphoros* [DNc]). Indeed, we know from Herodotus that before ascending
the throne Darius had married Gobryas's daughter, who bore him three sons. The oldest
son was named Artobarzanes (VII.2), and another was named Ariabignes (VII.97). Gobryas at an unknown date married a sister of Darius, who bore him Mardonius (VII.5).
These wife-exchanges cemented a solid family alliance. We may also point out that, in
a tradition recorded by Herodotus, Gobryas was Darius's closest and strongest supporter.
He took the floor to second Darius's initial proposals (III.73) and he participated directly
in putting the *magus* to death (III.78). Furthermore, Gobryas was among the four co-
conspirators who approved Darius's "constitutional" proposals (III.83). Keeping in mind
the Greek garb in which Herodotus's report appears, we understand that Gobryas and
three other conspirators (Intaphernes, Hydarnes, Ardumaniš) supported Darius's royal
claims from the beginning, and the other two (Otanes and Megabyzus) did not interfere.
In fact, Otanes then chose to remove himself from the royal competition.

The Elimination of Bardiya

To make headway, we must become familiar with the practical considerations that
led to the execution of Smerdis. All of the ancient authors insist on the fact that the
Seven acted alone, personally facing with weapons in hand first the guards, then Smerdis and his companions. It seems improbable, however, that access to the king was defended only by a few guards at the gate and a few eunuchs. Herodotus, who incorrectly
places the scene in the palace at Susa, composed his tale from heroic motifs, which he
later repeated in his passage on Intaphernes' revolt (III.118). Certain parallels with other
revolts suggest instead that there was in fact a pitched battle. This implies that the Seven
had troops at their disposal. The later example of Intaphernes leads us to think that each
of the Seven had gathered the people of his House (*oikos* = *viθ*), sons and relatives,
around him (cf. III.119). My hypothesis, then, is that for reasons that probably relate to
the state of his prior preparations, Darius would have had the most numerous and best
seasoned "contingent."

At this point in the discussion, it is useful to set aside the tales of the Classical authors
and return to Darius's version. To be sure, it is convenient and justifiable to distinguish
the portion of the Behistun inscription devoted to the revolt of Gaumata from the long
discussion dedicated to the "nineteen battles" with the nine liar-kings that Darius claims
to have won "in a single year." Gaumata is separate from the rest of the kings, who are
represented with ropes around their necks before the Great King: he lies at the feet of
the Great King, who sets his left foot and his bow on Gaumata's body. Nothing else
about him appears except that he is in the list and the victory won over him is apparently
reckoned among the nineteen battles. Darius writes: "I with a few men slew that Gaumata the Magian, and those who were his foremost followers. A fortress by name
Sikayauvatiš, a district by name Nisāya, in Media—there I slew him"✧ (29 September
522). Darius's tale is thus rather different from Herodotus's, which places the scene in

the palace of Susa, or Ctesias's, which claims that the rebel was in bed with one of his Babylonian concubines at the time! If we follow Darius and believe that Gaumata won over a part of the population to himself, then we must doubt that his elimination could have been accomplished simply by a murder in the bedroom of a badly defended palace. It seems more likely that the physical elimination of the rebel was the result of a lost battle, after which Gaumata took refuge in a Median fortress. That is, we can imagine a scenario identical to that of other revolts: a battle, the flight of the vanquished to a fortress, and the execution of the rebel and a few dozen of his associates. If this scenario is valid, the council of the Seven, to whose debates Herodotus limits himself, was nothing other than the general staff who knew they could count on an army capable of doing battle with the forces that were undoubtedly available to "King Bardiya." If this is the case, it must be recognized that, after the death of Cambyses, Darius already held a well-established position that allowed him to take command of certain contingents that he would later call "the Persian and Median army that was with me" (*DB* §25). This hypothesis implies that Darius had planned his violent coup well in advance, at least from the time of the death of Cambyses several months earlier. Perhaps he was among the Achaemenids at Cambyses' deathbed who heard the suffering king exhort them to do battle with the usurper (III.65). It was probably there, or on the road back, that the plot against Bardiya was hatched, the plot that Bardiya attempted to counter by confiscating the property of nobles supporting it (pp. 103ff.). Unfortunately, we have no precise information about the period between the death of Cambyses and the elimination of Gaumata/Bardiya, apart from a few allusions in one of the inscriptions of Udjahorresnet (Posener, no. 1E), who reports that he accompanied Darius in Elam. The new king sent him back from Elam to Egypt. Udjahorresnet would have us understand that, after Cambyses' death, Darius was in charge; but it seems difficult to ascribe too much value to this statement.

A Remark on Method

The comparison of Herodotus and Darius does not bring fully to light an affair that was probably simpler than either of them would have us believe. Once the propagandistic distortions of the new king have been carefully bracketed, his version is far more useful than Herodotus's. The tale of the historian from Halicarnassus is marked by a whole series of literary motifs that he probably wove into a pattern that in turn was built on a series of versions circulating in his time in Asia Minor, or even Greece. The very framework of Herodotus's tale is scarcely credible: a conspiracy of seven aristocrats (the figure 7 is already suspicious), elimination of the *magus* by the Seven, "constitutional" debates, and the selection of Darius by resorting to hippomancy—in all seriousness, not one of the narrative elements presented by Herodotus can hold the attention of a historian for long. New views can only come from a better comprehension of Darius's statements reconsidered in the context of dynastic history.

2. Revolts and Reconquests (522–518)

The Liar-Kings

"This is what I did after I became king": this is how Darius presents his work of "dynastic restoration" (*DB* §10 and 15✧). Herodotus notes, "In this way Darius became king of Persia" (III.88✧). Then, after recalling the marriages Darius contracted and the erection of an equestrian statue, Herodotus turns directly to an account of tribute reform (III.98), which is incorporated into an extensive discussion of the extent of the territories over which the Persian king held sway (III.98–117). Next, he turns to the elimination of Intaphernes (III.118–19) and the revolt of Oroetes (III.120–29). In contrast, he is totally silent about other events of the greatest importance, the revolts of the subject peoples, to which Darius devotes the greater part of his statement at Behistun (§§16–57; V §§71–76). Actually, Herodotus was not unaware that the appearance of Darius ushered in a "time of troubles" (III.126–27, 150). But, for reasons that escape us, he did not see the need to grant the subject much space. Aside from the story of a Babylonian revolt, he makes a single brief allusion to the revolt of the Medes (cf. I.130), who, his informers told him, had already inspired the revolt of the "*magus*" (cf. III.65, 73, 126). The other Classical authors are all equally silent. It is thus to the Behistun inscription that the historian must turn. We have not one version, but four. Along with Elamite (the first to be inscribed), Babylonian, and Persian versions, there is also a badly damaged Aramaic copy, found in Egypt. On the whole, the versions agree, but they also offer a number of differences. The historian is fortunate to have the comparison, for this or that version includes pieces of information that are not found elsewhere. Thus, only the Babylonian and Aramaic versions give the number of people killed and taken prisoner among the rebel armies.

According to Darius's presentation, the earliest revolts broke out in Elam and Babylonia after the elimination of Gaumata. In Elam, Āçina, son of Upadarma, seized power; in Babylonia, the tablets attest that the revolt of Nidintu-Bēl did take place by the beginning of October 522, when he was recognized as king of Babylon under the name Nebuchadnezzar, presenting himself as the son of Nabonidus. While the first revolt was put down without much difficulty (§16), the second was not. At the head of the army, Darius crossed the Tigris, then the Euphrates, inflicting two successive defeats on the rebel Nidintu-Bēl before capturing him and putting him to death (18 December 522; §§18–20). At this point, Darius enumerates the countries that revolted while he resided at Babylon: Persia, Elam, Media, Assyria, Egypt, Parthia, Margiana, Sattagydia, and the Saka of Central Asia (§22). The tale of the victories won by Darius and his lieutenants follows.

The historical use of the Behistun inscription poses a number of problems. If we go by the list of rebellious countries cited by Darius, the revolts embraced the entire Empire from the Mediterranean to the Indus, from the Syr Darya to Babylonia and Elam. But we are not equally informed about all of the fronts. Darius speaks primarily of the troubles in three major regions: Persia and Media, the Iranian Plateau and Central Asia, and Elam and Babylonia. In contrast, he is uncharacteristically laconic about the western regions. We learn from Herodotus that there were troubles in Asia Minor, but these involved the insubordination of a Persian satrap (Oroetes), not a Lydian revolt properly speaking, even though the satrap's administration had previously disaffected part of the population (Diodorus X.16.4). The king is also silent about a rebellion in Egypt, although he alludes to it in his enumeration. It is possible that a local dynast, Petubastis, revolted in 521, and disappeared a few months later, doubtless shown the error of his ways and executed by the satrap Aryandes. It has sometimes been thought that troubles also arose in Judah in concert with the Babylonian revolts. But the prophetic texts adduced for support must be read with care. We might think it unlikely that the Jews, just fifteen or so years after their difficult and harsh return, would have had the men and energy needed to contemplate seriously the restoration of the ancient monarchy for the benefit of Zerubbabel.

It is the chronological aspects that remain most problematic. Each victory is precisely dated to the month and day within the year. But it is not always easy to identify the year. Several times, Darius boasts of having won nineteen victories in a single year. The meaning of this expression continues to be debated. There is hardly any doubt that the repetition of this ideological theme, well known from elsewhere, is first of all meant to magnify a triumphant king. Darius is certainly not overly modest, inasmuch as he proclaims: "Those who were the former kings, as long as they lived, by them was not done thus as by the favor of Ahuramazda was done by me in one and the same year" (§59✧). But at the same time, Darius denies exaggerating or falsifying reality:

> I turn myself quickly to Ahuramazda, that this (is) true, not false, (which) I did in one and the same year. . . . By the favor of Ahuramazda and of me much else was done; that has not been inscribed in this inscription; for this reason it has not been inscribed, lest whoso shall hereafter read this inscription, to him what has been done by me seem excessive, (and) it not convince him, (but) he think it false. (§§57–58✧)

Because the military operations played out on several fronts at the same time, the compilers of the inscription did not follow a chronological plan. They envisaged the confrontations on a regional basis: Elam and Babylonia (§§16–23), Media, Armenia, and Sagartia (§§24–34), Parthia-Hyrcania (§§35–37), Margiana (§§38–39), Persia (§44), Arachosia and Sattagydia (§§45–51), summary (§§52–53). The order in which the liar-kings are represented on the Behistun relief, however, appears to be chronological (Gaumata [Persia], Āçina [Elam], Nidintu-Bēl [Babylonia], Fravartiš [Media], Martiya [Elam], Ciçantakhma [Sagartia], Vahyazdāta [Persia], Arkha [Babylonia], Frāda [Margiana]). But even so, there remain several debates, particularly regarding the date of the elimination of Frāda (December 522 or December 521?).

The Victories of Darius and His Lieutenants (522–521)

The multiplicity of fronts is stressed by Darius himself, doubtless to further exalt the valor of his final triumph: "While I was at Babylon [mid-December–mid-January 521], these are the provinces which became rebellious from me" (§21✧). A list of nine countries (*dahyāva*) follows. In this framework, maneuvers on a grand scale were carried out on fronts sometimes at great distances from each other. Victories were won by Darius's armies a few days apart, or even on the same day: on 15 July 521, the Median general Takhmaspada wiped out a rebel in Sagartia (near Media), and another general, Artavardiya, reconquered Vahyazdāta in Persia. In December 522–January 521, Darius and his lieutenants needed to extinguish numerous brushfires: in the second half of December 522 alone, there were two victories by Darius in Babylonia, the putting down of a rebel in Elam, and another victory in Assyria, not to mention the victory over Frāda of Margiana, if it is actually to be dated to December 522. Nevertheless, Darius cites only the pitched battles. In point of fact, we should probably imagine a campaign characterized by a series of skirmishes.

Even though he presents all the victories very personally ("By the power of Ahura-Mazda, my army wiped out the rebel army"), it is quite clear that the king did not personally lead the operations every time. He was present to put down the Babylonian revolt in December 522, and it was clearly from Babylon that he gave the order to execute the Elamite rebel Āçina. It was at Babylon that he received dispatches from the various fronts and determined his responses. He sent orders to Vivāna, his satrap in Arachosia, to attack the troops sent there by Vahyazdāta, who had taken power in Persia in the name of Bardiya. At the end of December 522, his lieutenant, Vaumisa, won a battle in Assyria over the Armenian rebels, and the next January 12, the Persian Vidarna—dispatched from Babylon—was victorious in Media.

In mid-January 521, Darius left Babylon and decided to establish his general headquarters in Media, where his lieutenants were encountering major difficulties. The Median rebel Fravartiš had clearly achieved some success there and was extending his operations toward Parthia-Hyrcania. Shortly afterward, Vivāna won a second victory in Arachosia (21 Feb.), and Hystaspes, father of Darius, conquered Fravartiš's partisans in Parthia-Hyrcania (8 March). Darius faced the Median chief in person and won the victory (8 May). Following this victory, Darius set himself up at Ecbatana, where the rebellious Median king soon was brought before him after being captured at Rhagae in Media (mid-May). For several months, Darius had to coordinate operations on several fronts. The Armenian rebellion was still going on in June 521, despite several victories won successively by Vaumisa and Dādarši, satrap of Bactria. Several days later (in July), the Sagartian rebel was eliminated, and then the last few outbreaks of revolt in Parthia-Hyrcania were quashed. During this time, Vahyazdāta pursued his offensive in Persia and was halted in mid-July. The king (who had meanwhile returned to Persia) could not relax his efforts; in August 521, the Babylonians rebelled again, under the leadership of Arkha, who took the title King of Babylon. Darius sent an army to Babylon under the leadership of Hydarnes (1 Sept.), who was victorious on 27 November. Finally, if the revolt of Frāda of Margiana is to be dated in 521 (and not in 522), it was at the end of December that Dādarši brought it to an end. It was then that Darius ordered the relief and inscription to be carved on the cliff at Behistun (in their original version), where he could proudly proclaim: "This is what I did by the favor of Ahuramazda in one and the same year after that I became king. . . . These IX kings I took prisoner within these battles" (*DB* §§52–53✧).

The Victories of Darius: A Military Evaluation

Despite the triumphalist character of Darius's proclamations, the gravity of the crisis must not be underestimated. The trial that Darius and his followers survived serves to reveal anew the strengths and weaknesses of the Empire built by Cyrus and his son. What kind of assessment can be made?

Answering this question is no simple task, for the very character of the account inscribed at Behistun defeats any attempt at useful analysis by its one-sided report of the accumulated victories at the expense of any notice of the defeats or an occasional reverse. It is thus difficult to confirm that at the end of 521 all of the fires of revolt had indeed been snuffed out. We may note, for example, that there is no explicit mention of a definitive defeat of Armenia/Urartu. Dādarši defeated the Armenians three times, but obviously none of these victories was decisive, because he waited in Armenia for the arrival of the royal Median army (§28). Another army, led by Vaumisa, beat the Armenians twice more and then in turn waited for Darius to come from Media (§§29–30; *DB Bab.* §24). Since it is not cited separately in the list of rebel countries (§21), Armenia's revolt probably was implicitly considered to be organically linked to the revolt of Fravartiš in Media. Nor is Armenia mentioned in the general recapitulation (§52), and there is no Armenian "liar"-king in the relief. In short, it seems risky to take literally the results of the "pacification," as it is triumphantly described by Darius. An attitude of reserve is all the more justified because in the following year (519) Elam revolted anew, and Darius himself had to lead an expedition against the Saka of Central Asia (V §§71–74).

A simple fact must be underscored at the outset: Darius and his generals in a few months put out several fires of rebellion. On the level of direct results, we may say that the royal and satrapal armies demonstrated their superiority, though even this statement is problematic. Several times, Darius states that he drew various units of his forces from "the Persian and Median army." This doubtless refers to the army of Cambyses, minus the contingents sent to Egypt by the tribute-paying countries. Moreover, Darius could count on his troops to remain loyal. This was even true in Media, where only a minor part of the Persian and Median army refused to engage the rebel. Furthermore, he was able to enlist new soldiers in the course of his victories.

The other figures we possess are the numbers of rebel casualties that are given in the Babylonian and Aramaic versions.

Country	Battle	Killed		Captured	
		DB Bab.	DB Aram.	DB Bab.	DB Aram.
Persia	Rakkha	4,404	35,404 (?)	2...?	??
	Parga	6,246	4,464?		
Media	Maruš	3,827?	5,827?	4,329	4,329?
	Kunduruš	34,425?	[34,42]5	??	1,801[.]
Parthia	Višpauzathiš	6,346		4,346?	
	Patigrabana	6,570		4,192	
Margiana		552.?	5]5,24[3	2.?	6,972
Armenia	Tigra	546	504[6]	520	[520]
	Uyama	427	427	525?	[0]02
	Izala	2,034	2,034		
	Autiyara	2,045	[2,04]6	1,588??	1,578

Some of the figures are impressive. But the problem, as we can see, is that the readings of the figures are far from certain and their interpretation is difficult and even risky. Only one statistic for an army is given in the Babylonian version: the army commanded by the satrap of Arachosia, Vivāna, after winning the second battle against Vahyazdāta's lieutenant is reported to number 4,579 men. We learn elsewhere that the king entrusted an army corps to Hydarnes for putting down the Median rebellion and that this army corps "smote that rebellious army exceedingly" (§25◇). Of course, according to the Babylonian version, the Median losses after this battle (the battle of Maruš) amounted to 3,827 killed and 4,329 captured, which demonstrates that the total of the rebel army was much larger. The best evidence is that Hydarnes thereafter preferred to wait in prudent readiness until the arrival of Darius, whom he would later join near Behistun. Thus either the decisive "victory" was nothing more than an uncertain engagement (or even a defeat), or else the figures in the Babylonian version must be treated with caution. At any rate, the two interpretations are not mutually exclusive. It is proper to consider Darius's propagandistic intent: he loves to repeat that he overcame numerous powerful revolts with an army that he describes several times as "small." It seems clear that the main part of the force remained under Darius's direct command and that he used it to regain Babylonia (October 522–early January 521). As a consequence, he was sending out army units of only a few thousand men under the command of his lieutenants. It is likely that the victory over Phraortes of Media (May 521) was of decisive strategic importance, considering the effect of this battle (the battle of Kunduruš) on the Median rebel army (see the table). It is likely that the securing of the northern front in May–June allowed Darius to redeploy troops against Vahyazdāta in Persia.

If in the end Darius defeated all of the armies that had allied against Persian power, it is apparently because there was no real unified plan for opposing the royal armies. Isolated, some of the rebels were quickly defeated. The first insurgent in Elam, Āçina, surrendered after the dispatch of a message from the king, and the second received no local help. Impressed by the mere approach of the king (Darius says), the Elamites seized their "king" and put him to death themselves. In contrast, other revolutionaries offered long and stubborn resistance. The Armenian insurgents were able to survive five battles in six months; Fravartiš of Media resisted for five months; and Vahyazdāta of Persia was not captured until seven months had passed and two battles were fought in Persia itself.

This is not to say that there was no interregional cooperation; quite the contrary. It is precisely cooperation that helps explain the danger presented particularly by the Median and Persian revolts. One of the dangers was that these revolts prevented Darius, in the beginning at least, from raising fresh troops in these two countries that constituted the base for Achaemenid conscription. Moreover, Fravartiš took command of the Median army stationed in the country (§§24–25), and Vahyazdāta assembled "the Persian army which (was) in the palace" (§40◊). Then, after an initial defeat at Rakha, Vahyazdāta raised a new army at Paišiyauvādā, near Pasargadae (§42). What is more, neither of these rebellions was geographically limited to Media or Persia proper. Vahyazdāta tried to nibble at the eastern part of the Iranian Plateau by sending an army against Arachosia. This offensive and the troubles in Sattagydia (a region located between Arachosia and Gandhara) threatened Achaemenid power on the southern Iranian Plateau as far as Carmania (late 522–early 521). The case of the revolt of Fravartiš in Media is even clearer. In Sagartia, the rebel chief claimed, like Fravartiš, to belong to the family of Cyaxares, and Darius calls the rebel chieftains of Parthia-Hyrcania "the partisans of Fravartiš." It also seems (as we have seen) that the length of the struggle in Armenia was related to the Median rebellion. Fravartiš held the strategic route from Media to Central Asia for awhile. After his defeat, moreover, he decided to march east, which is why Darius detached an army corps that succeeded in catching up with him and capturing him at Rhagae, near the Caspian Gates. Darius understood the danger well: it was the reason he quickly moved to establish himself in Media (January 521)—so that he could coordinate the counteroffensives and prevent Fravartiš from cutting off his communications with Central Asia. It is perhaps because of the importance of the revolt of Fravartiš that Herodotus highlights the Median uprising when he discusses the subjection of Ecbatana by Cyrus: "At a later period [the Medes] regretted their submission and revolted from Darius, but were defeated and again reduced" (I.130◊; cf. Diodorus XI.6.3).

The Political Aspect of the Revolts

Defining the origins and causes of the revolts is especially problematic. The most noteworthy observation is that the various ringleaders all had dynastic aspirations. Each took the title "king": Āçina proclaimed himself "king in Elam," Ciçantakhma "king in Sagartia," Frāda "king in Margiana," etc. In most cases, the rebels took a regnal name that permitted them to connect with the local dynasty that had been erased by Cyrus: in Babylon, Nidintu-Bēl called himself "Nebuchadnezzar, son of Nabonidus"; Fravartiš claimed that he was "of the family of Cyaxares [Uvaxštra]," like the Sagartian rebel. The desire to stir regional sentiments is evident. Even foreigners such as the Persian Martiya in Elam or the Armenian Arkha in Babylon sought to turn the assertion of dynastic continuity to their profit. This choice reflected a clear political intent to resume the course of local history and close what was by implication only a parenthesis of Achaemenid dominion. At Babylon, in fact, for several months private documents were dated to the accession year and first regnal year of a King Nebuchadnezzar (III or IV), and in Persia to the reign of Vahyazdāta/Bardiya (but this may refer to the first Bardiya).

Unfortunately, it is difficult to estimate the popular impact of these manipulations. The impact apparently was not very significant in Elam, where neither of the two "kings" was in a position to raise an army. On the other hand, the recurrence of revolts in the same region (Elam or Babylonia, in particular) suggests that the integration of conquered territories into the Achaemenid Empire was still very imperfect. Until Darius, Susa also remained exclusively Elamite in character. But, generally, we lack information on the breadth and depth of the rebellions. Some historians think that on the basis of the number of people killed and captured—about 100,000 in all—they can draw conclusions regarding the popular and national character of several uprisings. Even setting aside the uncertainty of the readings, the totals for casualties in Media (nearly 50,000) and in Margiana (55,000 killed and 6,972 captured, according to some readings) are especially noteworthy. But does the extent of the losses indicate that the uprising led the entire population to take up arms in a national and popular revolt or, more simply, does it reflect ferocious repression striking out blindly at civilian populations who remained aloof from the movement? There is little doubt that the Persians resorted to the use of terror: Darius boasts of massacring every survivor of the Babylonian armies that he attacked on the banks of the Tigris and the Euphrates (*DB Bab.* §17). In the end, the fact that the leaders raised troops from among the population says nothing about the "national" character of the movement.

According to Darius, the revolts broke out after his victory over Gaumata (29 Sept. 522; §15). But, for reasons already given, the statement of the new king must be considered in perspective, because discontent was previously evident among the conquered populations. The best proof of this is the measure taken by Smerdis to end tribute and military levies for three years (see above, p. 105). The dynastic difficulties at the heart of the Empire represented the ideal occasion for contesting Achaemenid authority. Without rejecting the reasonable idea that some countries clung to the memory of past grandeur, we are inclined to conclude that the deep source of discontent was the system of tribute—as Smerdis had understood. The revolts were led by the local ruling classes, who had been careful to reserve the profits derived from exploiting land and people for themselves instead of the newly dominant class of Persians. Their discontent also related to the excessive burden of the levies, as is demonstrated by the complaints of the Egyptians against their satrap, Aryandes (Polyaenus VII.1.7). It is also useful to note that even in the countries where we can assume strong ethnocultural identity, nothing allows us to assume a unanimous anti-Persian sentiment. During the reigns of Cyrus and Cambyses, many local nobles willingly collaborated with Persian power. Let us recall, for example, that Darius was supported by a Persian-Median army and that one of his lieutenants was the Mede Takhmaspada, who led the army to victory against the Sagartian rebel who claimed to be descended "from the stock of Cyaxares." Darius also names the Armenian Dādarši, who supported him in Armenia. In any event, what was the significance of the revolts at Susa and Babylonia led by a Persian (Martiya) and an Armenian (Arkha), respectively?

Darius and Vahyazdāta

One uprising took on special significance, namely, the revolt of Persia. A man named Vahyazdāta raised the standard of revolt, claiming to be Bardiya, son of Cyrus. As Darius notes (§40), this was the second revolt fomented in the name of the family of Cyrus. Vahyazdāta rallied to himself the army that arrived from Anšan and "became king in Persia." Once again, the unstable dynastic situation was at the root of the revolt. Vahyazdāta was defeated by Artavardiya, who had been sent by Darius. Vahyazdāta nonetheless succeeded in raising a second army and sending troops to Arachosia. It was not until mid-July 521 that he was completely defeated; at that time he was taken prisoner and executed in Darius's presence in the immediate vicinity of the future Persepolis.

The origins and methods of this revolt are problematic. Did the new Bardiya receive aid from certain noble families who were disturbed by the advent of Darius, and/or was he principally supported by the peasant class, distressed by the loss of the other Bardiya? To ask the question is to reopen the matter of the first Bardiya's policy. If the theory that makes Bardiya I the spokesman of particular segments of Persian society is unfounded (above, p. 103), there is no reason to accept the social interpretation of the new revolt without reservation. For reasons already alluded to, the successive raising of two armies in Persia provides no solid indication of the sentiments of the Persian population. Darius himself takes care not to attach any particular importance to the revolt of Vahyazdāta, who receives the same attention as the other "liar-kings." Vahyazdāta has no special place on the relief, unlike Gaumata. Darius thus implicitly denies that his dynastic situation was actually endangered by the rebel Vahyazdāta, who is not distinguished in any way from the other liar-kings.

We may rightly suppose that Darius's account is itself suspect. What appears obvious, nevertheless, is that he was able to gather representatives of the Persian nobility and the Achaemenid administration around him. Vivāna, satrap in Arachosia, and Dādarši, satrap in Bactria, acted on Darius's orders with promptness and determination to repel the assaults led by Vahyazdāta's forces (in Arachosia) and Frāda's troops (in Margiana). Perhaps it was the same for Aryandes in Egypt. Darius's father, Hystaspes, was also at hand, and he led the operations in Parthia-Hyrcania. Four of the six co-conspirators of 522 are listed among Darius's generals: Intaphernes, who put down the rebellion of Arkha in Babylonia (Nov. 521); Hydarnes, who fought against Fravartiš in Media (Jan. 521); Gobryas, who was sent to quash a new Elamite rebellion (the next year) (§71); and Otanes himself, shortly after, led an army to the conquest of Samos (Herodotus III.141–49).

The Rebellion of Oroetes

A single satrap refused to aid Darius—Oroetes, who since Cyrus's time had held the post of satrap of Sardis. This high-ranking person had already become famous when, at the end of Cambyses' reign, he eliminated Polycrates of Samos by treachery (III.122–26). Herodotus provides our only information on the repercussions caused by the rise of Darius in the western lands of the Empire:

> After the death of Cambyses, and throughout the period when Persia was controlled by the Magi, [Oroetes] had lived in Sardis and offered no help to his countrymen in resisting the Median usurpation. Hehad, moreover, during these unsettled times, procured the death of Mitrobates, the governor of Dascylium . . . and also of Mitrobates' son Cranaspes, a man hardly less distinguished than his father (*andres en Perseisi dokimoi*). Nor were these two murders by any means his only acts of violence. (III.126◊)

Then Herodotus specifies that Oroetes even had one of Darius's couriers executed on the road back because "what he ordered him did not suit him." The occurrence takes on special interest because it is the first recorded example of insubordination by a satrap.

The date of these events is given with some precision by Herodotus. "The turmoil still lasted," he writes, and "Darius had just come to power." We are thus at the height of the period of revolts. We may assume that Darius, then at Ecbatana (early 521), had ordered Oroetes to march with the available troops, cross the Halys, and bring aid to the royal troops who were encountering many difficulties in the face of the Median and Armenian revolts. Relying on his satrapal guard (1000 Persians), Oroetes chose to ignore the orders and defy the entirely new authority of Darius. Most unwilling to redeploy contingents on a new front, Darius turned to the Persians of his entourage. Herodotus reports that 30 Persians then rushed forward, "each one eager to do his bidding." Bagaeus was chosen by lot. When he arrived at Sardis, he employed a subterfuge to test the loyalty of the guards. Seeing that they displayed a great deal of reverence for some royal letters that he had the secretary open one after the other, Bagaeus unsealed the last of them: "King Darius orders the Persians of Sardis to kill Oroetes." This they did on the spot, and the property of the satrap was confiscated.

Even cleansed of its fictionalized and bombastic tone, Herodotus's tale is very revealing of relations between the new king and the Persians, not just the Persians who surrounded him but also the Persians of the imperial diaspora. Herodotus accents their loyalty, scandalized as they were by the murder of high aristocrats such as Mitrobates and his son. Reading Herodotus's account does not leave us with the impression that Oroetes would have found many Persians at Sardis ready to follow him in his rebellion. For them, loyalty to the monarchy consisted of the desire to preserve all of the privileges that accrued to them from imperial dominion. Indeed, by refusing to aid Darius and the Persians in maintaining order among the subject peoples, Oroetes put at issue not just the authority of Darius but also the edifice erected by Cyrus and Cambyses, which necessitated the existence of a strong, active, and legitimate central authority.

3. The Aftermath of Victory: The Official Story

Crime and Punishment, Publicity and Propaganda

The measures taken against the liar-kings make the dangers faced by Darius as clear as the absolute will of the new king to wipe them out permanently. At his order, Nidintu-

Bēl of Babylon was impaled, along with 49 of his followers (*DB Bab.* §19). After Hystaspes' victory at Patigrabana, he executed the rebel chief and 80 nobles who accompanied him (*DB Bab.* §29). So also in Margiana, where Frāda was put to the sword along with all his followers (*DB Bab.* §31), and in Babylon where Hydarnes impaled Arkha and the nobles who were with him (*DB Bab.* §39). Vahyazdāta and several dozen of his closest allies were impaled in Darius's presence (*DB Bab.* §35). Two revolts received special treatment, both at the time when Darius happened to be in Media. The Sagartian rebel, Ciçantakhma, was sent to him: "I cut off both his nose and ears, and put out one eye, he was kept bound at my palace entrance, all the people saw him. Afterwards I impaled him at Arbela" (*DB* §33◊). Darius is still more expansive about the fate reserved for Fravartiš the Mede: "I cut off his nose, ears, and tongue and plucked out an eye; he was chained under guard at the gate of my palace and everyone could see him there. [*DB Bab.* §25: Then I impaled him at Ecbatana.] As for his trusted lieutenants, I hung them at Ecbatana in the citadel" [*DB* §32; *DB Bab.* §25: "I hung their heads on the walls of the citadel"; *DB El.* agrees with *DB Bab.*]. The intensity of the punishment should not be surprising; it was customary in the Assyrian period and in the Achaemenid as well. Cutting off the nose and ears was the normal form of torture for rebels and usurpers, the Greek authors would note. What should be stressed instead is the publicity that Darius accorded his executions. The entire population was invited to witness the liarking being tortured at the palace gates. We may recall that, according to Diodorus (XVII.71.6◊), bronze poles, nine meters high, were erected near the gates of Persepolis: "they were intended to catch the eye of the beholder."

This desire to stir the imaginations of the Empire's populations was soon demonstrated again by the new king. He ordered copies of the text inscribed at Behistun to be sent to every country in the Empire (*DB* §70). We now know that the stated will of the king did not remain empty words. At Babylon, fragments of the inscription, parts of what was originally an imposing stela, have been found. Fragments of an Aramaic version of the Behistun text on papyrus have been also been found, this time at Elephantine in Egypt. This is not the original copy sent by Darius to Egypt but probably a student copy, written during the reign of Darius II (422–405), proof that the text continued to be transmitted, even in the form of schoolwork. But access to the royal account was not limited to the literate. At Babylon, a fragment of a copy of the Behistun relief has been discovered, and another tablet has been found at Susa that shows traces of what may be part of another copy.

We may presume that the reliefs and stelas were placed in prominent locations in each satrapy. No doubt the reproductions were protected in the same way as the originals. Addressing those who viewed the monument, Darius adjures them not to destroy the inscriptions or the sculptures; he invokes prosperity for those who protect it and misfortune for those who destroy it (§§65–67). It is clear that by publishing the inscription in all parts of the Empire Darius wished it known to everyone everywhere that he was the uncontested Great King. Again addressing the visitor, he assures him of the absolute truth of his exploits and declares: "Now let that which has been done by me convince thee; thus to the people impart, do not conceal it: if this record thou shalt not conceal, (but) tell it to the people, may Ahuramazda be a friend unto thee, and may family be unto thee in abundance, and may thou live long" (§60◊).

time at Behistun, the 'lie' (*drauga*) is directly connected with the revolt against established, legitimate power. Thus, "when Cambyses had gone off to Egypt, after that the people became evil. After that, the Lie waxed great in the country, both in Persia and in Media and in the other provinces" (§10◇). And, further on, in column IV, Darius repeats: "These are the provinces which became rebellious. The Lie made them rebellious, so that these (men) deceived the people" (§54◇), and he warns: "Thou who shalt be king hereafter, . . . the man who shall be a Lie-follower, him do thou punish well" (§55◇; cf. §64). Darius presents himself as a man who does not lie and who has never lied, and he guarantees it by invoking Ahura-Mazda (§§56–58). The lie (*drauga*) is implicitly opposed to the truth (*arta*), and both terms belong equally to the political and the religious domain—if indeed Darius and his people could ever have distinguished and separated the political from the religious.

There is a figure, placed above the scene, who plays a primordial role. This bearded individual emerges from a winged disk, is clothed in the Persian style, and wears a tall cylindrical headdress, itself topped with a six-pointed star. He holds a ring in his left hand, apparently offering it to Darius. It is currently understood to be a representation of Ahura-Mazda, the god who guarantees the kingdom to Darius by his power and protection and to whom he owes all his victories—this is what Darius incessantly affirms. He is the only individual with whom Darius establishes a dialogue. It is in fact toward the god that Darius raises his hand, as if to receive the ring Ahura-Mazda holds in his left hand. This is a motif well known earlier in Near Eastern royal art: what we see at Behistun is an investiture scene. Darius rightly could exclaim: "It is thanks to Ahura-Mazda that I am king. . . . It is Ahura-Mazda who has granted me the kingdom [or: conferred power on me]." The illustration thus strongly expresses the fact that, without being a god himself, the king is invested with royal power by the god and is Ahura-Mazda's proxy on earth, as the result of a genuine pact they had concluded. Ahura-Mazda is literally the king's god. This is a reality that Darius himself expresses perfectly in his inscription. Ahura-Mazda's name occurs 63 times, but the "other gods that exist" are mentioned only once, in a subordinate form: "This which I did, in one and the same year by the favor of Ahuramazda I did; Ahuramazda bore me aid, and the other gods who are" (§62◇). It is to Ahura-Mazda that royal prayers are always raised in Darius's inscriptions. Though we fully reject the temptation to speak of evolution toward monotheism, we must recognize that in the *official* religion established by Darius, Ahura-Mazda had a supreme position. He is designated as the sovereign deity of the pantheon, and the other deities are invoked only nominally. This privileged alliance conferred absolute power on the king, and no one could question that power, except at the risk of divine displeasure. This is in fact the reason that the lie (*drauga*) and the truth (*arta*) represent political and religious concepts simultaneously. The king rules over the lands and peoples (*dahyāva*) thanks to the protection of Ahura-Mazda, and he must make truth reign and hunt down the lie among them in the name of the same precepts that govern relations between men and gods.

But what is most novel about this monument is quite simply the fact that the Persian language (*arya*) was being written for the first time. Despite the continuing debate over the precise meaning of §70 and the actual act of transcribing a text already inscribed in Elamite, the inclination today is to recognize that Persian writing constituted a major innovation by Darius (who did not hesitate to use it at Pasargadae in order to tap into the prestige of Cyrus to his own advantage). Until this event, the king's deeds were transmitted in Persian exclusively through recitation and song and through the intermediary of masters of memory. To be sure, oral transmission remained a constant throughout the long history of the Persian people, as shown by the notable role of the *magi* in general. But this observation lends still more import to the first indubitable attestation of royal writing, inscribed in the presence of the king (and written on clay and parchment), a model that was followed by all of Darius's successors. By this very action the Great King could claim that he himself was first of all a master of truth. He intended to control the tradition he wished to be transmitted to future generations: the royal word, inscribed for all posterity on the rock, was placed under the aegis of Ahura-Mazda as protection against all those who might want to destroy it (*DB* §§65–67). This is how the king transmitted not only the memory of his unique exploits but also his genealogy. In this way he took appropriate measures to have his word disseminated throughout the lands of his realm (*DB* §70), after having it authenticated—the text had previously been read to him. At the same time, the memory of his royalty was fixed. No one, not even his successors (*DB* §64), would have the right to question it: on the cliff at Behistun, the history of historians is forestalled for all time.

New Campaigns, New Additions: Imperialism and Religion

The composition as a whole would soon be modified to include events that unfolded while the royal artists were still working on the sacred mountain. A new column (col. V) had to be added, in Old Persian only (for lack of room). The text begins: "Saith Darius the King: This is what I did in both the second and the third year after that I became king. A province by name Elam—this became rebellious."✧ For the third time since October 522, the Elamites rebelled, led this time by Atamaita. Gobryas, the king's faithful *bandaka*, was placed at the head of an army. He was victorious, captured Susa, and brought Atamaita before Darius, who put him to death (520). It was perhaps under these circumstances or shortly thereafter that Darius resolved to redesign Susa and erect a vast Achaemenid palace complex there.

The following year, Darius himself took command of the royal army and marched against the Central Asian Saka. The Saka king, Skunkha, was taken prisoner and replaced by another king, apparently hand-picked by Darius. It is likely that the Saka (Darius lists them among the rebellious peoples: *DB* §21) could not be subjugated by the satrap of Bactria, Vivāna, who had been assigned that job, a task that fell to him quite naturally. Or maybe Vivāna was killed during a battle with the Saka? We do not know. The fact is that after his victory Darius returned to Ecbatana and Behistun. Skunkha was added to the relief, behind the liar-kings. He is identifiable by his tall pointed hat, the marker of certain Saka peoples (Tigraxauda). The addition of Skunkha necessitated the destruction of the original Elamite text, which was rewritten to the left of the Persian version. This is also when the text of column V was added.

The most noteworthy novelty of this Old Persian addition is without doubt the religious justification that Darius provides for the two campaigns against Elam and the Saka. The sentence can be understood as follows: "Those Elamites (Saka) were faithless and by them Ahuramazda was not worshipped. I worshiped Ahuramazda [in their lands?]; by the favor of Ahuramazda, as was my desire, thus I did unto them."✧ Or, perhaps Darius is simply recognizing that it was because of his faith in Ahura-Mazda that he was able to conquer populations that did not worship his god. In either case, the politico-religious implications are enormous. In contrast to the royal assertions about the rebels in columns I–IV, in column V the rebels are no longer denounced solely as bearers of the *drauga* ['liars']; they are called *arika*, usually translated 'faithless'. They are described in a clearly pejorative fashion as worshipers of non-Persian deities. This expression is also found in a Xerxes inscription, where the king condemns the cult of false gods (*daivā*) (chap. 13/6).

This statement does not in any way imply that Darius completely altered the ideological strategy of his predecessors in the conquered countries. But what is clear is that in just a few years, at the instigation of Darius, Persian royal authority was endowed with a uniformly steady and coherent politico-religious ideology. More than ever, in times of peace and times of war, the king was the earthly proxy of his god Ahura-Mazda. Furthermore, column V ends with this sentence: "Saith Darius the King: Whoso shall worship Ahuramazda, divine blessing will be upon him, both (while) living and (when) dead."✧ In view of the overall context, this statement promised heaven to whoever served the king loyally.

4. Darius and the Six

Primus inter pares?

We must now return at greater length to the relations between Darius and his companions after his accession to the throne. Reading Herodotus without perspective, one actually receives the impression that Darius was bound by the agreements that had been mutually reached by the Six when he came to power (Otanes having taken himself out of the competition), concessions that basically would have made the new king *primus inter pares*. According to Justin (who had read his Herodotus carefully), as a result of the murder of the *magus*, "the Great ones (*principes*) were equal in merit and nobility" (*virtute et nobilitate . . . pares*; I.10.1–2). This is the version also found in Plato (*Laws* 695c✧) in an otherwise very suspicious passage: "When [Darius] came and seized the empire with the aid of the other six, he split it up into seven divisions, of which some faint outlines still survive today." Are we to conclude that Darius had agreed on limitations to his royal power from the beginning and that he presented himself simply as the chief victor leading an aristocratic restoration that was originally intended to limit the absolute monarchy that had been carried to extremes by Cambyses and Bardiya?

We know that the title "the Seven" continued to be invoked as a sign of distinction among the Persian aristocracy, to the point of making them an integral part of the "pedigree" of certain aristocrats, as given by Herodotus. Thus we have references to Otanes (III.140), Gobryas (IV.132), or even Zopyrus, "son of the Megabyzus (I) who was one of the seven conspirators who killed the Magus" (III.153✧), etc. Diodorus as late as the fourth century specifies that the satrap Rhosaces "was a descendant of one of the seven Persians who deposed the Magi" (XVI.47.2✧), and Quintus Curtius introduces Orsines, chieftain of the tribe of Pasargadae, who was "a descendant of the 'seven Persians' and tracing his genealogy also to Cyrus" (IV.12.8✧). The permanence of the term thus seems assured. But does this mean that the Seven constituted an entity that had the ability to control the activities of the king?

Herodotus often calls the Seven *prōtoi* (III.68–70, 77). The small group of *prōtoi* was often convened by the king in times of peace or war. But it would be a mistake to conclude that the membership of the council was imposed on the king. What we call, purely by convention, the "king's council" had no institutional existence of its own founded on regulations that the king could not overrule; its meetings and deliberations depended solely on the pleasure of the sovereign. Most decisions were made by the king alone, who received advice from these "confidants" who owed him everything. We cannot say that the nobles met in council simply because they were part of the *prōtoi*. It is clear that the king himself selected council members from among the aristocrats: the title "counselor" was included in the court titulature (cf. V.11–24, and especially Aelian, *VH* XII.64). This interpretation is also based on Ezra and Esther, where Ahasuerus is shown convening "the seven administrators of Persia and Media who had privileged access to the royal presence and occupied the leading positions in the kingdom" (Esther 1:13–14◇). It has often been deduced that there was a college of seven judges, a sort of sovereign tribunal, at the court. But this passage is highly suspicious, given the many other references to the number *seven* in the same work: Ahasuerus reigned over 127 provinces (1:2), and also had "seven eunuchs in attendance on his person" (1:10◇), Esther received "seven special maids" in waiting (2:9◇), etc. There is hardly any doubt that the composer was in fact aware of the existence of seven families. In itself, however, this observation constitutes a reinterpretation that the modern historian cannot use as counter-evidence.

The same remark holds true for a Xenophon passage often cited in this context (*Anab.* I.6.4◇): to judge Orontas, Cyrus the Younger convened in his tent "seven of the noblest Persians among his attendants," to whom he adds Clearchus. All we need to do is collect the evidence concerning the royal judges to see that, properly speaking, there was no college of seven royal judges who were systematically chosen from the "Seven families" and who functioned independently of the king. Herodotus defines their function as follows: "These royal judges are specially chosen men, who hold office either for life or until they are found guilty of some misconduct; their duties are to determine suits and to interpret the ancient laws of the land, and all points of dispute are referred to them" (III.31◇). It was they who condemned to death the Egyptians who had just killed a royal herald; it was they to whom Cambyses appealed to determine that he had the right to marry his sister. It was probably also the royal judges who are introduced by the composer of Esther. To judge the behavior of Queen Vashti, Ahasuerus asked his Friends to "pronounce law and judgment." They brought a report to the king proposing that an edict announcing the repudiation of the queen be proclaimed throughout the kingdom. These Friends are called "seven princes [JB: administrators] of Persia and Media" (Esther 1:10ff.).

The connection sometimes made between the royal judges and the privileged status of the seven families who aided Darius is worthless. When Artaxerxes II brought Tiribazus to judgment, "he assigned three of the most highly esteemed Persians as judges" (Diodorus XV.10.1◇). It is clear in fact that the appointment and dismissal of royal judges was solely on the authority of the king, who could reward whomever he wanted with the title of royal judge, including a man of low birth, such as the simple peasant Rhakokes (Aelian, *VH* I.34). On several occasions, judges were condemned to death for handing down iniquitous judgments, particularly for having sold out for money (Herodotus V.25; VII.194; Diodorus XV.10.1◇): "At this time other judges who were believed to have been corrupt were flayed alive and their skins stretched tight on judicial benches. The judges rendered their decisions seated on these, having before their eyes an example of the punishment meted out to corrupt decisions." Even the decision made by the seven judges of Ahasuerus was more of an opinion: "If it is the king's pleasure, let him issue a royal edict." Even though the judges referred to "the law of the Persians and Medes" (Esther 1:19◊), it is clear that the decision was based solely on royal authority.

Their freedom of judgment was also limited because they were objects of surveillance by the king. Although Diodorus states that Artaxerxes II himself was not present at the trial of his son Darius, this was not the rule. Plutarch adds that the king "commanded his scribes to write down the opinion of every one of the judges, and show it to him" (Art. 29.8). Similarly, after the acquittal of Tiribazus the same Artaxerxes "summoned the judges one by one and asked each of them what principles of justice he had followed in clearing the accused" (Diodorus XV.11.1◊). The reasons that the judges gave for their decisions show very clearly that they arrived at their conclusions on the basis of the loyalty and devotion that Tiribazus had previously manifested in furthering royal interests.

Quite often, however, people were condemned by the king without previously being arraigned before a tribunal. This was certainly true for royal judges, who were condemned by the king directly. He could also grant clemency to whomever he wished. On one occasion, we even see the king pronouncing a death sentence on an accused person who had previously been acquitted by the judges (Ctesias, *Persica* §61). Good sense shines through in the reply that the royal judges gave to Cambyses when he inquired about marrying his sister: "They managed to find an answer which would neither violate the truth nor endanger their own necks: namely, that though they could discover no law which allowed brother to marry sister, there was undoubtedly a law which permitted the king of Persia to do what he pleased" (Herodotus III.31◊). Herodotus understood perfectly well that the judges did this so as not to "endanger their own necks." In other words, the king remained the sole source of justice (Plutarch, *Art.* 23.5).

Darius's Point of View: Nobles and King at Behistun

From Darius's point of view, the question of an authoritative council of advisers did not even arise. In the addition in §68, he was very discreet about the role of the six aristocrats: "Saith Darius the King: These are the men who were there at the time when I slew Gaumata the Magian who called himself Bardiya; at that time these men cooperated as my followers (*anušiyā*)" (§68◊). Then, after giving the list, he adds, for the benefit of his successors: "Thou who shalt be king hereafter, protect well the lineage (*taumā*) of these men." In the Babylonian version, the wording is: "Fully protect these men and take care of their descendants" (§54). But this royal statement loses much of its specificity when it is compared with other passages in column IV. Addressing those who behold the inscription, he proclaims: "Now let that which has been done by me convince thee; . . . tell it to the people, may Ahuramazda be a friend unto thee, and may family be unto thee in abundance" (§60◊), or indeed, "If thou . . . shalt protect [this inscription] as long as unto thee there is strength, may Ahuramazda be a friend unto thee, and may family be unto thee in abundance, and may thou live long, and what thou shalt do, that may Ahuramazda make successful for thee" (§66◊). These declarations are not unlike Cambyses' dying words in the presence of "the leading Persians," who had gathered to hear his last will: "If you do as I bid you [depose the *magus* and reduce the Medes to obedience], I pray that the earth may be fruitful for you, your wives bear you children, your flocks multiply and freedom be yours for ever" (Herodotus III.65◊). Indeed, the words of Darius sound like a commitment for him and his successors to maintain the prestigious status of the families of the co-conspirators. But, in contradistinction to other promises of reward or punishment, they do not invoke Ahura-Mazda.

It is also true that Darius is not the only one shown with the liar-kings on the cliff of Behistun. Behind him are two persons (smaller than the king but bigger than the rebels): one is shown carrying a bow in his right hand and the other is holding a lance with both hands, its butt on the ground. They are obviously two Persian nobles, bearing the royal arms. Their names are not given. Could they be, as on Darius's tomb, Aspathines and Gobryas? All theories founder on an obvious fact: if their names have not been included, even though the liar-kings are identified by name, it is because Darius, by design, did not wish to raise these two people above anonymity. They stand metonymically for the nobles who aided him. Although we recognize that the titles "lance-bearer" and "bow-bearer" could distinguish one noble from another, nothing more can be said than that these titles were granted by the king in recognition of services rendered. We are thus closer to court nobility than to clan nobility.

The Six and Court Protocol: The Intaphernes Affair

Of course, we presume that the statements of Darius are nothing but royal propaganda. Let us return to the text of Herodotus, who details in the following terms the privileges that the six conspirators mutually agreed upon before choosing a king from among themselves:

> Permission, namely, for any of the seven to enter the palace unannounced (*aneu eisaggelos*), except when the king was in bed with a woman. They further agreed that the king should not marry outside the families of the seven confederates. (III.84✧)

Even if, despite the unlikelihood of the tale, we accept the reality of the agreement, we would do well to elucidate the implications.

Let us stress first of all that, if indeed it was put into effect, the mitigation of court protocol for the benefit of the Seven did not last very long. This is what is suggested by the Intaphernes affair, which erupted some time later. There can be no doubt that Intaphernes was an important member of the conspiracy; in fact, Darius lists him first among those he calls his followers (*DB* §68). It was this individual who constantly showed loyalty to the new king. We know, for example, that it was he who led a victorious army against a Babylonian rebel in November 521 (*DB* §50).

Herodotus states, however, that Intaphernes was put to death by the king (III.118–19✧). Desiring an audience with Darius, Intaphernes "wished to enter the palace." At this point, Herodotus recalls that the Seven could "visit the king unannounced, provided that he was not, at that moment, in bed with a woman." Meanwhile, "he was, however, stopped by the king's chamberlain and the sentry on duty at the palace gate, who told him that Darius had, in fact, a woman with him at the time." In an angry fit, Intaphernes "cut off and ears and noses." The outcome of the story, which Herodotus reports on the model of the intrusion of the Seven into Smerdis's royal palace, suggests that Darius was not yet totally sure of his power: "Thinking his six former confederates might all be in this business together, he sent for each of them in turn, and sounded them to see if they approved of what Intaphernes had done." Convinced that Intaphernes had acted alone, he took drastic measures: Intaphernes was put to death, along with all of the men of his House (*oikeioi*)—his sons and his relatives (*syggeneis*)—except one of his brothers-in-law, who was saved from execution by his sister.

The tale is marked by a series of repetitive motifs, and thus supports a double reading. We may recognize that Darius's authority was to a degree still tentative for some time because of the privilege granted to the other conspirators. Under the terms in force, the guardians could only refuse Intaphernes access if the king was with one of his wives. But we must also consider the possibility that Intaphernes was flaunting his insubordination by violating rules of protocol that Darius had meanwhile restored to apply even to his old companions. Even given the hypothesis that Darius's authority was still tentative, we are led to the conclusion that the initial privileges were quickly revoked. In fact, no other text suggests that certain Persian aristocrats might be exempt from the rigors of court protocol, which were probably established at the time of Cyrus and Cambyses (pp. 91ff.) and later reinforced by Darius and particularly Xerxes.

The Marriages of Darius

It is also clear that Darius paid no attention to the obligation to take a wife from among the families of the other conspirators:

> The first women Darius married were Cyrus' two daughters Atossa and Artystone; the former had previously been the wife of her brother Cambyses and also of the Magus; the latter was a virgin. Subsequently he married Parmys, a daughter of Cyrus' son Smerdis [Bardiya], and, in addition to these, the daughter of Otanes [Phaidime], the man who had exposed the Magus. (III.88)

The intent and the message were clear: Darius linked himself directly to the stock of Cyrus by marrying Cyrus's two daughters (Atossa and Artystone) and granddaughter (Parmys). As for his marriage to the daughter of Otanes, it seems risky to see it as much of a concession to Otanes; this union is based on the custom whereby a new king took the wives of his predecessor(s) (Atossa, Phaidime)—just as Smerdis/Bardiya had also married Atossa, the sister-wife of Cambyses. What the matrimonial policy of Darius actually reveals is concern for dynastic continuity—however false—rather than a desire for restoration of the aristocracy. Thus, indeed, "Darius entered into family relationships with the old kings. . . . Power appeared less to pass to a stranger than to remain in the family of Cyrus" (Justin I.10.13–14).

It is clear that Darius systematically applied a policy that on the one hand allowed him to link himself fictitiously to the family line of Cyrus and on the other restricted the number of individuals who had rights as members of the Achaemenid family in the narrow sense (i.e., direct descent). Finally, he also married one of his nieces, Phratagune, daughter of one of his brothers, Artanes (VII.224). The single known exception is his marriage to a daughter of Gobryas, but this was before his accession. He had three sons by her before gaining the throne. But the discussions recorded by Herodotus about the royal succession show that there was never any real question of transmitting power to his eldest son, born of this exogamous marriage (VII.2). As we shall soon see, the policy of the Great King consisted of parceling out his daughters, a matrimonial policy that holds exactly the opposite of the meaning attributed to it by Herodotus. And the successors of Darius singlemindedly followed the same policy. It was not until the reign of Darius II that the royal family became open to exogamous marriages (see below, pp. 589–590).

The Saga of Otanes

The use of the term "the Seven" is exclusive to the Greek authors, who wanted to identify the people in their narratives and in some cases needed to distinguish among people with the same name (cf. Diodorus XI.57.1). In some cases, they must have gotten wind of family traditions that tended to exaggerate the prestige of their ancestors. The story of Otanes and his family, revised and corrected between the fifth century and Roman times, may be an illustration of this sort of beguiling distortion.

We know, at least according to Herodotus, that Otanes had played an important role in the conspiracy of 522 and that as a result he had acquired privileges for himself and his descendants. Herodotus says, in fact, that Otanes renounced a position of power on the condition that neither he nor his descendants would be under the orders of whoever would become king, in perpetuity. Referring to this situation, Herodotus then writes:

> To this day, the family of Otanes continues to be the only free (*eleutherē*) family in Persia and submits to the king only so far as the members of it may choose; they are bound, however, to observe the law (*nomos*) like anyone else. The other six then discussed the fairest way of deciding who should have the throne. They agreed that, if it fell to any of themselves, Otanes and his descendants should receive, every year, a suit of Median clothes and such other gifts as are held to be of most value by the Persians, as a mark of honour for the part he had played in the plot against the Magi, of which he was the prime mover and principal organizer. (III.83–84◊)

Later on, a legend of the Cappadocian court recounted the origins of the family and the dynasy in this way:

> The kings of Cappadocia say that they trace their ancestry back to Cyrus the Persian, and also assert that they are descendants of one of the seven Persians who did away with the Magus. Now as to their connection with Cyrus, they count as follows. Cambyses the father of Cyrus had a sister of legitimate birth, Atossa. To her and Pharnaces, king of Cappadocia, was born a son, Gallus; his son was Smerdis, his Artamnes, and his Anaphas, a man of outstanding bravery and daring, who was one of the seven Persians. Such then is the pedigree they trace for their kinship with Cyrus and with Anaphas, to whom, they say, because of his valour the satrapy of Cappadocia was granted, with the understanding that no tribute would be paid to the Persians. After his death a son of the same name ruled. When he died, leaving two sons, Datames and Arimnaeus, Datames succeeded to the throne, a man who both in war and in the other spheres of royal duty won praise, and who, engaging the Persians in battle, fought brilliantly and died in battle. The kingdom passed to his son Ariamnes, whose sons were Ariarathes and Holophernes; Ariamnes ruled for fifty years and died without achieving anything worthy of note. The throne passed to Ariarathes (I), the elder of his sons, who is said to have loved his brother with a surpassing love, and promoted him to the most prominent positions: thus he was sent to aid the Persians in their war against the Egyptians, and returned home laden with honours, which Ochus, the Persian king, bestowed for bravery; he died in his native land, leaving two sons, Ariarathes and Aryses. Now his brother, the king of Cappadocia, having no legitimate offspring of his own, adopted Ariarathes, the elder son of his brother. At about this time Alexander of Macedon defeated and overthrew the Persians, and then died; Perdiccas, who at this point held the supreme command, dispatched Eumenes to be military governor of Cappadocia. Ariarathes (I) was defeated, and fell in battle, and Cappadocia itself and the neighbouring regions fell to the Macedonians. . . . (Diodorus XXXI.19.1–4◊)

Diodorus follows the history of the dynasty down to Roman times and concludes: "And that is enough on the genealogy of the kings of Cappadocia, who trace their origins back to Cyrus." We can thus see that this version was well attested at the time of Diodorus. We recognize in it several historical individuals—from Cambyses, father of Cyrus, to the

Diadochi (and after), including Datames, the criminal satrap, who is incorporated into the genealogy. This genealogy enjoyed wide success, as is evidenced by the Holophernes in the book of Judith.

Whatever the historical reality may have been, the family version has consciously manipulated it. Cyrus is named as the ancestor of the family, and Otanes (Anaphas) becomes the offspring of a Cappadocian king and the aunt of Cyrus (Atossa, who has clearly been confused, deliberately or not, with the daughter of Cyrus and the sister of Cambyses II). While a historian of family oral traditions can profit from this text, obviously someone who is interested in the origin and destiny of the Seven/Six cannot! The court legend was already known at the time of Polybius, who wrote about Mithradates of Pontus: "He boasted of descent from one of the Persian Seven who had killed the *magus*, and he maintained that his line had ever since retained the government that his ancestor had originally received from Darius in Pontus on the Euxine Sea" (V.43). Elsewhere (fragment 166), the same Polybius provides other details from the legend. In a digression devoted to Cappadocia, he records that an unnamed Persian accomplished a magnificent deed during a hunt with Artaxerxes (II). The royal mount was attacked by a lion; luckily, this Persian killed the lion with his *akinakēs* "and saved the king from a great danger." In return, the king gave him a gift (*dōrea*) of all the territory as far as he could see as he stood atop a high mountain. This tale repeats well-known motifs, particularly royal hunts for lions. It resembles the story Diodorus told about Tiribazus's deed at the court of Artaxerxes II (XV.2.3) and the unhappy outcome of the identical action Megabyzus took to save Artaxerxes I (Ctesias §40). The legendary allocation of the land is also found in various forms in Greek (e.g., Polyaenus VI.24; Plutarch, *Mor.* 820d) as well as Iranian tradition. But the tradition is even more ancient. Diodorus, doubtless relying on Hieronymus of Cardia (a contemporary of the Diadochi), states that Mithradates (who took power in Cappadocia despite the opposition of Antigonus) was "a descendant of one of the seven Persians who slew the Magian" (XIX.40.2◊). Appian heard it said that Mithradates "was linked to the Persian royal family" (*Mith.* 9).

We know that Otanes, "who had been one of the Seven," led the conquest of Samos at the beginning of the reign of Darius (III.141–147). But Herodotus says nothing about his receiving territory in Cappadocia. He merely states that the House of Otanes remained "free" and that Otanes would "receive, every year, a suit of Median clothes and such other gifts as are held to be of most value by the Persians, as a mark of honour" (III.83–84◊). The settling of the family of Otanes in Cappadocia is simply deduced from the legend recorded (in different terms) by Diodorus and Polybius. This hypothesis (it is nothing else) is also based on a comparison with other examples of territorial concessions ("without having to pay tribute"): to Bardiya from Cyrus (Ctesias §8), to Zopyrus I from Darius (Herodotus III.160), and to Belesys from Arbaces (Diodorus II.28.4). However, for various reasons, the latter two cases are historically quite doubtful. We know, finally, that around 515–514, the satrap of Cappadocia was called Ariaramnes; it is he whom Darius entrusted with leading the initial expedition against the Scythians (Ctesias §16). Should he be identified as one of the sons of Otanes, called Arimnaeus by Diodorus? But Diodorus "specifies" that upon the death of Otanes it was the other son, Datames, who succeeded him!

From all of this it appears that there is nothing to prove that Otanes received the satrapy of Cappadocia from Darius and still less to support the idea that Darius then approved the creation of an independent kingdom! On the other hand, it is possible that he had been favored with a *dōrea*, as explained in the version known from Polybius; but the repetition of the motif of the hunt makes us suspicious. Perhaps the legend of sovereignty over Cappadocia was grafted onto this original kernel. After all, this would not be the only example of a Hellenistic genealogy that was fictitiously attached to the events of 522 (cf. Strabo XI.14.15). Whatever the case may be, it does seem that manipulation of the tradition had already begun in Herodotus's time, since he represents Otanes as the "son of Pharnaspes" (III.68◊) and father of Cassandane, the mother of Cambyses (III.2). Indeed, the Behistun inscription proves that Herodotus's information is contrived, since Otanes' patronymic is Thukra (*DB* §68). It is likely that this original distortion in Herodotus is responsible for Diodorus's assertion of close family ties between the families of Otanes and Cyrus.

It is true that, according to Ctesias (§20), Xerxes married Amestris, who is represented as the "daughter of Onophas." But is Onophas our Otanes? This seems totally hypothetical. In one case, Herodotus (VII.62) distinguishes the names Otanes and Onophas. Even if we agree that only one Otanes is at issue here, we must stress that this name is very common. Herodotus mentions an Otanes, father of Amestris, who in 480 led the Persian contingent (VII.61), but he lists several others as well. One is Sisamnes' son (V.25), another (or the same one) is married to one of Darius's daughters (V.116), a third is Anaphes' father (VII.62), another is Smerdomenes' father (VII.82), and last, another is Patiramphes' father (VII.40). It would be most strange if Darius had consented to a marriage between his son Xerxes and the daughter of the Otanes of 522. The only certain union between the two families is the marriage of Darius and Phaidime, the daughter of Otanes and previously the wife of Cambyses and Bardiya. This was a marriage that did not carry the political ramifications of the supposed marriage between Xerxes and Otanes' daughter. Marrying Xerxes to Otanes' daughter would have introduced rights for any grandson Otanes might have (which Darius refused to the grandson of Gobryas). Furthermore, if Amestris really was the daughter of one of the Seven, Herodotus (VII.61) would doubtless have mentioned it, because he frequently mentions such family connections (III.153; IV.132), even for Otanes (III.141).

The Family of Gobryas

Let us now turn to Gobryas. We have seen that he played a fundamental role in the conspiracy and that, according to Herodotus, he was the strongest supporter of Darius. We also know that his alliance with Darius was long-standing, since exchanges of wives took place between the two families before 522. Darius's first wife was one of Gobryas's daughters. From this union three sons were born, including Artobarzanes (VII.2). For his part, Gobryas had married one of Darius's sisters. From this marriage Mardonius (VII.5) and Arabignes (VII.97) were born. Gobryas also played a role during the uprisings of subject peoples, since in 520 he was sent to put down a new Elamite revolt (*DB* V §71). He again appears in 513 in the immediate entourage of the king in Scythia, counseling the king to order a retreat (IV.132, 134).

He then disappears from the Classical sources. He reappears in the Persepolis documents. In February–March 498, bearing an authorization from the king, he made use of the royal road between Susa and Persepolis, and he received travel rations at two stations near Susa. His caravan joined (or crossed) another. The document mentions "the wife of Mardonius, a daughter of the king" (PFa 5). By chance this agrees with Herodotus, who says that when Mardonius, the son of Gobryas and one of Darius's sisters, arrived in Asia Minor in 493 to take command, he had married Artozostra, one of Darius's daughters (VI.43). He was thus both the cousin and the brother-in-law of Xerxes. After his expedition in Thrace, Mardonius seems to have fallen out of royal favor. He did not participate at all in the expedition of 490. Later, however, he received an eminent position close to Xerxes. Herodotus judges him severely, and he was lost in the battle of Plataea. We know nothing of Mardonius's family after this event.

The intimacy and permanence of family ties are demonstrated by the constant favor that Gobryas retained in the eyes of Darius and that his son Mardonius subsequently received from Xerxes. The exceptional quantity of travel rations Gobryas received illustrates his eminent position in the court hierarchy, as does perhaps the elaborate nature of the seal impressed on the Persepolis tablet. But his participation in the conspiracy of the Seven does not seem to have given him any freedoms beyond those already experienced by his family, and this status was due to marital alliances made prior to 522 and especially to his unswerving loyalty to the cause of the monarchy. Darius's choice of Xerxes (his son by Atossa) at the expense of Artobarzanes (his son by Gobryas's daughter) to succeed him shows very clearly that the exchange of wives functioned in no one's favor but Darius's.

The Saga of Megabyzus

Megabyzus I is the best known of the other conspirators, because his family traditions were repeated by Herodotus and Ctesias. His son Zopyrus I, according to Herodotus, accomplished a tour de force and captured Babylon in the name of Darius (III.153–60). We might prefer Ctesias's version: he attributes the victory to his son Megabyzus II (Ctesias §22), who had married Amytis, Xerxes' daughter (§22). Three sons of Megabyzus II and Amytis are known: Zopyrus II, Artyphius, and Artoxares (§§37, 39). An analysis of the career of Megabyzus under Xerxes and Artaxerxes indicates that, despite his illustrious birth and his occasional success, he fell out of royal favor for several years. His sons faired no better: after the death of his father, the eldest son, Zopyrus II, left the king and went to Athens; Artyphius was put to death after an ill-fated revolt against Darius II (Ctesias §§50–51). The behavior of both indicates that the reconciliation of Megabyzus and Artaxerxes I depicted by Ctesias (§41) did not eliminate the mutual ill will between Megabyzus's family and the Great Kings.

Hydarnes

We have no explicit mention of Hydarnes after 520. However, some Persepolis tablets attest that he was the satrap of Media under Darius. It is possible that a Hydarnes, son of Hydarnes, who commanded the Immortals in 480 was the son of the conspirator of 522; this may also be the case for a Sisamnes, son of Hydarnes (VII.66). But the relationship between the satrap Tissaphernes and the family must remain hypothetical. A Hydarnes family reappears after the accession of Darius II, but is it the same one? This is far from certain. In any case, the story of the family also gave rise to a court legend in the Hellenistic era. In fact, Strabo records that the Armenian dynasty went back to Orontes, who was himself a descendant of Hydarnes, "one of the Seven" (XI.14.15). However, we know that the ties between Orontes and the Achaemenid royal family in reality went back only to his marriage to a daughter of Artaxerxes II, meaning that his distant descendants could count Darius among their ancestors at Nemrud Dagh. This example proves once again that the traditions of the families of the Seven were systematically used later on for dynastic legitimation.

A Summary of the Discussion

It thus does not appear that the families of the Seven were granted exceptional status in perpetuity by the Great Kings. Even if we accept the hypothesis that Bardiya/Gaumata sought to weaken some of the noble families, we still must avoid concluding that the aristocracy was restored when he fell from power. That some clan chieftains cherished the hope, for a moment, of counterbalancing the powers of the king is a hypothesis that, while insufficiently supported, lies within the realm of possibility. We would still need to explain how Otanes could withdraw with such apparent good will. Only one of the Seven, Intaphernes, tried to free himself from the king's power. But his attempt was doomed to failure because Darius had meanwhile won prodigious victories and was able to attract the loyalty of the Persian aristocracy. Darius exhibited exceptional capacities for authority and command, which his companions do not seem to have seriously contested.

While some descendants of the Seven received honors and special privileges, they were not fundamentally different from the honors that were granted to the other great noble families. This is probably the underlying reality expressed by Plutarch: "To the seven Persians who killed the *magi* the privilege was granted that they and their descendants should wear their headdress tilted forward over the forehead; for this, so it appears, was their secret sign when they undertook their act" (*Mor.* 820d◇; cf. also Polyaenus VII.11.2). This distinction, which Plutarch found a hint of in his evidence, was simply a royal gift that, far from obligating the king, increased the dependence of the nobles on him. This is probably why Gobryas and Aspathines appear bearing the royal weapons on the king's tomb at Naqš-i Rustam: they had been integrated into the court hierarchy (*DNc–d*).

Finally, the phrase *seven families* after 520 is in large part illusory (we should speak of six families after the elimination of Intaphernes and his circle!). The label relates more to family traditions than to dynastic traditions, which, quite to the contrary, tended to push those who participated in the conspiracy that brought Darius to power into the shadows. But even if the Achaemenids (in the clan sense used by Herodotus I.125) were part of the conspiracy, the family of Darius itself (the Achaemenids in the restricted sense imposed by the new king) was still placed above and beyond this small aristocratic circle—which was another way of excluding the aristocrats who had lent their aid to Darius from dynastic competition.

5. Summary and Perspectives

A New Foundation for the Empire

The ways and means of Darius's accession to power—to the extent that we can reconstruct them—are a testimony to the new king's energy and decisiveness. Darius was undeniably an exceptional personality, but he also proved to have organizational ability. During the same time that he was reorganizing the entire tribute system, other projects were carried out in various regions: construction of new capitals, the conquest of Samos, expeditions from the Indus to the Nile; in 518 he also commissioned the satrap Aryandes to gather Egyptian sages to collect the "Egyptian laws"; other measures affecting Jerusalem were effected at the same time.

What is striking is the care with which the king planned for the long term. Darius wanted above all to create a new lineage. To this end, he manipulated dynastic circumstances with a great deal of skill. The redefinition he imposed on the word *Achaemenid* allowed him to exclude those who belonged to the clan of the same name from the line of succession. Henceforth, power could only be transmitted from father to son in one restricted family, which was placed under the blessing and protection of a founder-hero, Achaemenes, invented out of whole cloth. Darius and his counselors were able to carry out political and ideological rethinking that was no less remarkable. From early on, the king was preoccupied with providing an ideological base for his authority and his lineage. Beginning in the late 520s, Achaemenid monarchic ideology was articulated around rules and justifications where politics and religion were fused into a whole of rare consistency. The authority of the king and the rights of his family were henceforth under the protection of Ahura-Mazda, who was invoked as the great god of the king and the Empire. The concept of *arta* ('truth')—in relation to its antithetical corollary, *drauga* ('the Lie')—was the true linchpin of this ideological structure. This is the program we see at work in the new residences in Susa and Persepolis as well as on the royal tomb at Naqš-i Rustam.

Without in the least deprecating the work accomplished by his predecessors (chap. 2), we may thus assert that the advent of Darius marks the foundation of a new dynastic and imperial order. In this regard, the first years of his reign definitely represent a decisive period in Achaemenid history. But at the same time, Darius took care to entrench his reign in the *longue durée*. The projects he undertook at Pasargadae are another testimony to his ambition to place the upheaval he created within the continuity of Persian history. Contrary to what has long been thought, Darius actually never sought to inflict a *damnatio memoriae* on the founder of the Empire. On the contrary, he intended to promote skillful propaganda at Pasargadae that would allow him to establish a fictitious link with Cyrus, just as he did with his matrimonial policy.

Diachrony and Synchrony

I should mention in passing that Darius's activity is attested in numerous domains and in numerous regions of the Empire. But it is impossible to offer an absolutely continuous story from the 520s until 486. I am thus led first to analyze each successive conquest by the new king individually, because it was these that permitted the Achaemenid Empire to achieve its greatest extent (chap. 4). The other aspects of his immense accomplishment will be treated in the course of thematic and regional chapters (chaps. 5–12); these studies will help us better to appreciate as a whole what the Empire was at the death of the Great King and will also lead us to understand better the particular accomplishment of Xerxes (chap. 13).

Chapter 4

Darius the Conqueror (520–486)

1. The Pursuit of Territorial Expansion (520–513)

Darius, Democedes, and the West

Darius did not relax his efforts at extending the imperial realm. There is no question that, after the conquest of Cyrus and even more after the taking of Egypt, the Persians wanted to extend their dominion from the continent to the Aegean Islands. In this sense, Oroetes' attack on Polycrates on the island of Samos, for example, did not conflict with the objectives, overt or covert, of the central government. We have little enough information about the countries of Asia Minor between the execution of Oroetes of Sardis ca. 522–520 and Darius's first direct offensive in Europe in 513. We are indebted to Herodotus for several clarifications of Darius's Aegean policy at the very beginning of his reign. Unfortunately, Herodotus's notes are no more than a subplot, so to speak, in a fairly long but not very scientific digression about the adventures of Democedes, a physician from Crotone in Italy, who had been taken prisoner by the Persians when Oroetes put Polycrates, tyrant of Samos, to death. Brought to the royal court after the execution of the miscreant satrap, Democedes became one of Darius's favorites: "He lived in a large house in Susa, took his meals at the king's table" (III.132◇). He was also friendly with one of the king's wives, Atossa, daughter of Cyrus, on whom Herodotus tries to confer an unusual political position. At Atossa's urging, Darius let his desire to conquer Greece become known. But, before launching an expedition, he decided to send out a reconaissance mission guided by Democedes: Darius "begged him to give the reconnoitering party such guidance and information as they needed, and afterwards to return to Persia" (III.135◇). The Persians left from Sidon and "made a written report of the results of a careful survey of most of the notable features of the coast [of Greece], and finally arrived at Tarentum" (III.137◇). Then Herodotus tells how the Persians, deprived of their guide Democedes, were reduced to slavery in Iapygia (in Italy, then controlled by Greece) before being returned to Darius by Gillus, a Tarentine outlaw, and concludes "These Persians . . . were the first who ever came from Asia to Greece" (III.138◇).

It is hard to separate history from fairy tale in Herodotus's story. In the rationale of his approach, the Democedes affair takes on a particular purpose: to show that the Persian Empire and the Greek world were becoming acquainted well before the onset of the Persian Wars and that, quite early on, Darius cherished notions of conquest in the west.

Darius, Syloson, and Samos

After narrating the adventures of Democedes, Herodotus begins a new digression with these words: "These events were followed by the capture of Samos" (III.139◇). The probable chronological context makes one think that Darius's decision was made shortly after his accession (520–519?). As is often the case with Herodotus, however, what we consider the important causes of a historical event are presented in a personal, anecdotal form.

One of Polycrates' brothers, Syloson, took part in the conquest of Egypt. During this expedition, Darius came to owe Syloson a favor because he had presented a garment to Darius as a gift. After the accession of Darius, Syloson presented himself at the gates of the royal palace, asserting his status as "benefactor" of the king—a term that included all who for any officially recognized reason had the right to request a favor (cf. chap. 8/1). He asked permission to recover Samos, which since the death of Polycrates had been in the hands of Maeandrius, son of Maeandrius, "the man whom Polycrates on leaving the island had appointed to tend to his affairs" (III.139–42◇). "Darius consented to Syloson's request, and dispatched a force under the command of Otanes, one of the seven, with orders to do everything that Syloson had asked; and Otanes, accordingly, went down to the coast to make his preparations" (III.141◇). Otanes reappears here for the first time since his forfeiture of the "royal competition." It is hard to know why he was chosen over the satrap of Sardis (about whom, actually, we know nothing after the execution of Oroetes). As always, the leader of the expedition had received very strict and precise instructions from Darius: "Not to kill or capture any Samian, but to hand the island over to Syloson intact" (III.147◇), instructions that Otanes violated (according to Herodotus) because of a provocation instigated by Maeandrius. The upshot was that Syloson was installed as tyrant of Samos.

The affair was important. Indeed, in theory the conquest was carried out for the benefit of Syloson. But Syloson was in fact an Achaemenid client; he had been installed by a Persian army by order of the Great King. The royal bequest made him obligated to Darius ever after. We can thus consider Samos the first Persian conquest in the Aegean islands. Indeed, it held a very important position both strategically and commercially because of the changes brought about by Polycrates. Behind the anecdotal character of Herodotus's tale we can see the working out of a strategy long entertained by Darius. There is no doubt that Herodotus was anachronistic in attributing to Darius a plan to lead an expedition against the Scythians at that early date. There is also no doubt that Darius, in the footsteps of his predecessors, had early on understood the importance of an Aegean policy, if only because of the proximity of the islands and the close relations they maintained with the mainland towns that were subject to Achaemenid authority at that time.

Darius, the Indus, and the Nile

Herodotus also mentions that Darius launched an expedition that started at the Indus (IV.44) and thirty months later reached Egypt. Though Herodotus's text is clearly based on information received from his compatriot Skylax, it is not entirely clear. According to Herodotus, Darius apparently had two objectives: on the one hand, he wanted to determine whether the extremities of his Empire could be linked to each other and to the center (Elam); on the other, he wanted to organize a reconnaissance mission that would open the way for the projected conquest of the Indus Valley, the *Hinduš* of the royal inscriptions. Herodotus's text certifies that this conquest was led by Darius himself or by one of his armies—we cannot say with certainty which. The date of the conquest is itself uncertain, perhaps just after the campaign against the Sacians of Skunkha, that is, around 518? At any rate, the most recent investigations have shown that no logical, chronological link exists between this expedition and the order to dig a canal between the Nile and the Red Sea.

Aryandes and Barca

Herodotus's long account of the history and peoples of Cyrenaica and Libya (IV, 145–205) includes some information on relations between Aryandes and the Greek leaders of Cyrene and Cyrenaica. One of the town's rulers, Arcesilaus (successor to Battus), was killed in a civil war. His mother, Pheretima, sought refuge in Egypt—which was at that time governed by the Persian satrap Aryandes—taking advantage of the fact that her son had "put Cyrene under Cambyses' control and fixed a rate of tribute" in 525, thus displaying his "friendship with Persia," according to Herodotus (IV.165◊). After obtaining Darius's permission, Aryandes sent a strong army and naval force against Cyrene, led by two Persian nobles named Amasis (a Maraphi) and Badres (a Pasargade). After a long resistance, the Barcaeans agreed to sign a treaty with Amasis. Amasis did not keep his word: the captured Barcaeans "were sent from Egypt to the Persian King Darius, who gave them a village in Bactria to live in. They named the village Barca, and it was still inhabited within my own memory" (IV.204◊). The motivations for the Persian expedition against Cyrene and Libya are not very clearly set out by Herodotus. He records what some of his informants told him: the refuge granted to Pheretima was just a pretext. "Its real object, I fancy, was the subjugation of Libya. The races of men in Libya are many and various, and only a few of them were subject to the Persian king; the greater number never gave Darius a moment's thought" (IV.167◊). However, the Persians never got farther than Euhesperides, near Barca.

The text of the agreement between the Barcaeans and Amasis provides a partial reason. "They promised to pay the Great King a suitable tribute" in return for a commitment (not observed by Amasis, however) to leave the city alone. This commitment indicates that they had ceased to pay the tribute Herodotus attributes to them in his report on tributes paid to Darius: "Egypt, together with the Libyans on the border and the towns of Cyrene, and Barca (both included in the province of Egypt) paid 700 talents" (III.91◊). In other words, Aryandes profited from Pheretima's solicitation by trying to increase his dominion over Cyrenaica, which at that time was still only partial. Because Amasis reminded Badres that "the objective of the expedition had been the single Greek city of Barca" (IV.203◊), we may conclude that this town was picked out for a reason. The leaders of Cyrene from the time of Arcesilaus had also regularly delivered their fixed share of the total amount of the tribute from the Egyptian nome to Aryandes. Moreover, at this point the commanders of the army received Aryandes' order to return. The intervention on behalf of Pheretima was thus aimed at reinstating the subject status of Cyrene. It seems, however, that the Persians did not succeed in getting the Libyans all back in line, since Herodotus writes: "Most of them . . . cared nothing for the king of Persia, any more than they do to-day" (IV.197◊).

2. The Persians in Europe

Darius's Scythian Expedition (513)

In dealing with the evidence for the years 518–517, historians find themselves in a difficult situation. It is virtually impossible to compose a continuous narrative. In fact, Herodotus's tale in book III, after the excursus on Democedes and Syloson, closes with a story bearing on a revolt of Babylonia (III.150–59). This story is repeated by Justin (I.10.15–22) and is difficult to interpret historically and chronologically. Herodotus, Justin, and Ctesias do not return to the course of events until the eve of Darius's expedition against the Scythians. Herodotus opens book IV this way: "After the capture of Babylon Darius invaded Scythia" (IV.1✧; cf. Justin I.10.23). These gaps explain why the chronology after the last events mentioned by Darius at Behistun have always been the subject of much discussion (e.g., the date of Darius's expedition to Egypt). The same situation exists, on the whole, for Darius's expedition against the Scythians. The gaps in evidence make it difficult to date, but there is now good reason to date it ca. 513, a date approximately contemporary with the Persian expedition in Libya. Although the chronology does not pose insurmountable problems, the reasons, objectives, and results of the expedition continue to divide historians.

According to Herodotus, Darius made immense preparations, "sending messengers to every part of his dominions with orders to raise troops here, ships there, and labourers somewhere else to work on the bridge over the Bosphorus" IV.83✧). The number of boats gathered was around 600, according to Herodotus (IV.87), but there as elsewhere the figures must be taken for what they are, because Herodotus was always interested in stressing the immensity of the royal forces (IV.87: 700,000 men, not including the naval forces!). Among the Greek cities, Herodotus enumerates in particular the cities of the Hellespont and the Propontis (Sea of Marmara): Abydos, Lampsacus, Parion, Proconnesus, Cyzicus, Byzantium, and also some of Ionia (Chios, Samos, Phocaea, Miletus) and of Aeolis (Cyme). Herodotus also mentions an Athenian named Miltiades, "who was master of the Chersonese on the Hellespont and in command" (IV.137✧). Leaving Susa, the king arrived with his army in the neighborhood of Chalcedon, then crossed into Europe, after enjoining the Ionians "—who, with other Greeks from Aeolis and the Hellespont, were in charge of the fleet—to sail into the Black Sea as far as the Danube, where they were to bridge the river and await his arrival" (IV.89). Darius marched across Thrace, where some peoples surrendered without a fight and others (the Getae) after fierce resistance (IV.93). Leaving the Ionian tyrants to guard the Danube crossing, the king penetrated Scythian territory. There he encountered a true coalition of peoples who refused to engage in pitched battle. Darius found himself in desperate straits and, with the advice of Gobryas, decided to retreat. Pursued by the Scythians, he nonetheless managed to reach the Danube and cross the river. The Ionian tyrants, despite the cogent arguments of the Scythians, had refused to leave the Persian camp (IV.136–39). The end of the story is quite abrupt: "Darius marched through Thrace to Sestos in the Chersonese, where he took ship for Asia, leaving a distinguished Persian named Megabazus to command in Europe" (IV.143✧).

Darius's expedition poses many questions and has given rise to many divergent interpretations, primarily because our basic source, Herodotus, treats it only very superficially. His main interest is in fact describing the different Scythian peoples. After briefly introducing the Persian expedition, Herodotus launches into one of those digressions so dear to him (IV.1–40). One digression leads to another; he then dedicates several chapters to Libya, the guiding thread of the progression being an inquiry into the limits and configuration of the known world (Asia, Libya, Europe; IV.36–47). It is only in §83 that he returns to Darius, after giving a mass of information on Scythian customs. In the story as a whole, the parts dealing with Darius's expedition appear more as a pretext than as the true subject of the general account.

Despite these conditions, we continue to inquire into the purposes and objectives of Darius, as well as the magnitude of the Persian defeat. Was the Great King preparing to subject the Scythians of southern Russia and integrate them into his Empire, perhaps to return via the Caucasus? or was the march beyond the Danube considered a mere corollary to an objective centered on the conquest of Thrace? Herodotus would give us to understand that Darius had dreamed very early on of conquering Scythia and that Atossa, egged on by Democedes, urged him to turn his attention instead toward Greece (III.134; cf. p. 139 above). But the entire Democedes story is highly suspect. Even if the conquest of Samos around 519 effectively shows that Darius had an Aegean plan, it does not prove that at that date he thought of launching an expedition to Scythia or of preparing a vast offensive against European Greece. Herodotus's other explanation, that Darius's purpose was to avenge the Scythian invasion of Asia (IV.1 and VII.20), hardly deserves the attention of historians. I also have major reservations about Justin's account, that Darius opened hostilities to punish the Scythian king, Ianthyrus, for refusing him the hand of his daughter (II, II.5.9). This is in fact a literary motif, found for example in one of the versions of Cambyses' expedition against Egypt. Ctesias adds information not found in Herodotus: he records that

> Darius enjoined Ariaramnes, satrap of Cappadocia, to penetrate the country of the Scythians and to take men and women captive there. The satrap crossed with 30 fifty-oared galleys (quinqueremes) and took prisoners. He even captured the brother of the king of the Scythians, Marsagetes, whom he had found imprisoned on the order of his own brother for some misdeed. Irritated, Scytharbes, the king of the Scythians, sent a letter of grievances to Darius, who responded to him in the same style. (§§16–17)

It thus seems that the offensive was preceded by a period of tension and a limited expedition led by the satrap of Cappadocia, perhaps for the purpose of gathering information on the country. But in all this foofaraw we do not find any really satisfactory explanation. It is for this reason very tricky to estimate the magnitude of the defeat suffered by Darius. We can hardly trust Herodotus, who received his information from Scythians and Greeks. The difficulties of analysis are further increased by the uncertainties that continue to weigh on the identification of the Scythian peoples introduced by Herodotus.

What seems surprising is that Darius left the Greek fleet at the mouth of the Danube. This strategy implies that his territorial objectives could not have been far away. If they had been, he would have adopted the traditional tactic of having the army and navy proceed together, so that the navy was able to provision the army. But did the fleet left on the Danube represent all of the ships pressed into service by the Great King? Herodotus's narrowly Hellenocentric orientation prevents us from being certain about the matter. Whatever the case may be, the retreat of the Persian armies from Scythia certainly damaged the prestige of the Great King, at least in the short term, as seen in the revolts that then broke out among the Greek cities, in particular the cities on the Hellespont (IV.144; V.1). Among the cities that seceded from the Persians at this point were some that had sent a naval contingent to Darius (IV.138). It is likely that they then returned home, paving the way for an insurrection (cf. V.27). The revolt of these cities could also be explained as a deception, particularly if we agree that at the start the interests of certain tyrants and of the king converged: the tyrants joined Darius's force in the hope that the expedition to the Black Sea would allow them to reenter a region where they had founded colonies but where the Athenian commercial offensive had diminished their influence.

The Persians in Thrace

Whether or not this is a legitimate speculation, it is clear that the bottom line of the Persian expedition was far from negative. In fact, whether Thrace was Darius's primary objective or not (it is impossible to determine), it was conquered by the Achaemenid armies. Darius had already subjugated several Thracian peoples on his path to the Danube. And before reembarking for Asia Minor, he left Megabazus in Europe "with this mission: "to conquer Thrace" (V.2◇). He first " began the reduction of such communities in the [Hellespont] neighbourhood as opposed the Persian power" (IV.144◇), and he seized Perinthus (V.1): "Then Megabazus marched through Thrace, bringing every city and every people in that part of the country under the control of the Persian king" (V.2◇). The Paeonians were the most severely affected by Megabazus's offensive: he seized their principal inland settlements, and he deported some of them to Asia Minor (V.15–16). The task was completed by Otanes, to whom Darius gave "the command of the troops of the coast," just before leaving Sardis (around 510? V.25◇). Otanes seized Byzantium and Chalcedon (the keys to the Bosporus), then Antandrus in Troas, and last, the islands of Lemnos and Imbros (V.27). In contrast, the Ionian towns did not join in the revolt. The reason was doubtless that Darius's expedition marked the end of a degree of autonomy for the cities of Propontis, autonomy that had already been lost by the Ionian cities at the time of the conquest of Samos around 519. Obviously, most of the tyrants shared the opinion of Histiaeus of Miletus, who, when the Scythians asked them to dissociate themselves from Darius, "pointed out that each one of them owed his position as head of a state to Darius, and, in the event of Darius' fall, he himself would be unable to maintain his power at Miletus, and all the rest of them would find themselves in a similar difficulty" (IV.137◇).

A Summary

While we are unable to evaluate the objectives of Darius's expedition, we can evaluate the results achieved. On the northern front, no Achaemenid army would ever again be risked beyond the Danube. Perhaps Darius's objective was simply to safeguard the borders of the empire and to prevent Scythian raids in the regions between the Danube and the Aegean (cf. VI, VI.40). In any case, according to Dino, the Great Kings took the Danube to be the frontier of their dominion (Plutarch, *Alex.* 36.4), which means that, at least in the imperial imagination (cf. chap. 5), all of the Thracian regions south of the river were considered to answer to the authority of the Great King, while at the same time the lands beyond the Danube were banished from the *oikoumenē* and from history.

The seizing of Thrace was an event of major importance for Persian power. The region is rich in strategic materials. Darius had granted Histiaeus a region in Thrace, near Myrcinus, in the canton of the Edonians in repayment for his loyalty. Histiaeus intended to found a town there (V.11). Shortly afterward, Megabazus communicated to Darius his fears regarding the increasing power of Histiaeus. "The site, with its silver mines, and abundance of timber for building ships, and making oars, is a very valuable one. The neighbourhood is thickly populated both with Greeks and other people." Darius was convinced and recalled Histiaeus to Sardis, bringing him back to Susa with him and awarding him the titles "counselor" and "table-companion" (V.23–24◇). The mines of Mt. Pangaeum in Thrace were in fact well known (cf. VII.112), even as well known as the mine at Scapte Hyle worked by Thasos (VI.46). The coinage struck by various Thracian and Paeonian peoples attests to the abundance of precious metals. In brief, these cities and peoples were well able to pay tribute in silver to the Persian administration.

To the west, Persian dominion thenceforth affected Macedonia (cf. VI.44). In fact, Megabazus had sent an embassy to the Macedonian king, Amyntas I, with "a demand for earth and water." Despite favorable legends about the Macedonian royal house collected later by Herodotus (V.17–21), this fact remains: the Macedonian kings had to recognize the sovereignty of the Great King. It was inevitable, given the all-too-close Persian garrisons, the most important and strongest of which were at Eion (at the mouth of the valley of the Strymon) and Doriscus on the Hebrus (VII.59: *basileion*/garrison), where Darius had appointed commanders (VII.105). Thereafter, all of the countries paid tribute to the Great King (VII.108).

Meanwhile, it must be recognized that evidence concerning Persian settlement at this time is highly inadequate. It is commonly thought that the new countries were integrated into a new satrapal district. But was this really the case? Speaking of the march of Xerxes from Doriscus to central Greece in 480, Herodotus states that "the whole country as far as Thessaly had been forced into subjection and made tributary to Persia by the conquests, first, of Megabazus and, later, of Mardonius" (VII.108◇). It is not impossible that this district was not set up until *after* the expedition led by Mardonius, for it seems clear that his enterprises were aimed at stricter oversight by Achaemenid authority in the region. Furthermore, after Megabazus's campaign, Thasos continued to work the mines of his dominion (VI.46), whereas Herodotus notes that in 480 the mines of Mt. Pangaeum were always worked by the Pierians, the Odomanti, and the Satrae (VII.112). In fact, Herodotus himself specifies that a number of Paeonian peoples (from Mt. Pangaeum), Doberi, Agriani, and Odomanti (from Lake Prasias) "were not subjugated by Megabazus" (V.16◇).

Nor is there any sure proof that Macedonia was incorporated into a Persian district. Amyntas I enjoyed a normal reign until 498, when Alexander I succeeded him. According to Herodotus (V.21), Alexander I gave his sister Gygaea in marriage to a Persian named Bubares, who had come to look into a massacre of Persians who had been sent to Amyntas I's court by Megabazus (V.18–20). Bubares was doubtless Megabazus's own son (VII.22), and he apparently stayed in Macedonia for several years (Justin VII.4.1). Amyntas II was born out of his marriage to Gygaea (Herodotus VIII.136). According to Justin, this marriage allowed Amyntas I and Alexander I to maintain good relations with Darius and, later, Xerxes (VII.3.9; 4.1). It seems risky, given the state of the evidence, to conclude that Bubares played the role of a sort of Persian high commissioner in a Macedonian kingdom, which was itself part of a Thracian-Macedonian satrapy.

To sum up, Darius's undertaking in Thrace was obviously neither a secondary nor a temporary objective: the establishment of garrisons, the imposition of tribute (in silver and men), the protectorate imposed on the Macedonian kingdom, as well as the retaking of the region briefly conceded to Histiaeus indicate unambiguously that, in the king's mind, it was an essential phase of his new conquests, just as were the expeditions to the Indus or to Cyrenaica. We do well to stress an important aspect of the strategy followed first by Megabazus and then by Otanes: to strictly control the route joining Asia Minor to their new European conquests. In fact, the Persians took control of the straits, both the Bosporus (Byzantium and Chalcedon) and the Hellespont and the islands that command its entry (Imbros and Lemnos). The city of Lampsacus (on the Hellespont) was held by a tyrant, Hippoclus, "all-powerful before Darius" (Thucydides VI.59.3). At the entry to the Hellespont, Sigeion had long been a dynastic possession of the Athenian tyrants. In 513, Miltiades the Younger, the representative of this Athenian family, had had no option but to take part in Darius's Scythian campaign. A few years later, after Cleomenes I of Sparta drove Hippias out of Athens, Hippias sought refuge with Artaphernes: He "moved heaven and earth . . . to procure the subjection of Athens to himself and Darius" (Herodotus V.96◊).

Before leaving Sardis, Darius had named Artaphernes satrap there, "his brother by the same father" (V.25◊). He received extended powers, to go by what Aristagoras says, as transcribed by Herodotus: "in command of the whole coastal district of Asia" (*pantoi hoi epithalassioi*; V.30◊). Otanes was placed in "command of the coast" (*hoi parathalassioi andres*; V.25◊) and obviously took on some of the authority of Artaphernes, who coordinated all of the Persian forces up to the Halys River (V.102). It is difficult to be certain that Artaphernes supervised the control of the European conquests. In the context of the Ionian revolt, Herodotus (VI.33) refers to the governor of Dascylium, Oebares, son of Megabazus (VI.33). Whatever the uncertainty of the (variable) administrative content of the word *hyparkhos*, there is every reason to think that this Oebares was satrap of Dascylium. Without any doubt, he also had responsibilities in this area, if only by reason of the strategic position of his satrapy, magnificently situated to serve as a bridge between Asia and Europe. Finally, Sestos in the Chersonese of Thrace was a fortified city of decisive importance. The bridge built before 513 by Mandrocles of Samos (IV.87–90) led to a terminus near Sestos, and it was by this bridge that Darius embarked on his return from Thrace some time later. In 480, Sestos and the region were held by Artayctes, who took his orders either from Dascylium or Sardis, or else directly from the king.

3. The Ionian Revolt (500–493)

The Thread of Events and the Problems Posed

"Then trouble ceased for a while, until it broke out again in Ionia. This time it came from Naxos and Miletus" (V.28◊). This is how Herodotus begins a long passage on the revolt of Ionia, with nothing more to say about the period between the conquests of Otanes (V.27: around 510) and the prelude to the revolt (499). Here is Herodotus's version of the chronological sequence of events.

Around 500–499, the tyrant of Miletus, Aristagoras, nephew of Histiaeus (who since 511–510 had remained at the court of Darius; V.24), came to Artaphernes with a proposition that would be to their mutual advantage. Certain Naxian aristocrats, driven from their island by the people, had come to seek aid from Aristagoras on the basis of their friendly relations with Histiaeus. Since he did not have the forces necessary for this undertaking, Aristagoras turned to Artaphernes, showing him the advantages of such an expedition: "You will add to the King's dominions not only Naxos itself but the other islands of the Cyclades, such as Paros and Andros, which are dependent on it. Then with the Cyclades as your base you will have no difficulty in attacking Euboea" (V.31◊). With Darius's consent, Artaphernes gathered a major force whose command he entrusted to Megabates, "a cousin both of Darius and himself."◊ Dissension arose very quickly between Megabates and Aristagoras: the best they could do was leave the exiled Naxians in a fort and return "to the mainland. The expedition had been a failure" (V.30–35◊).

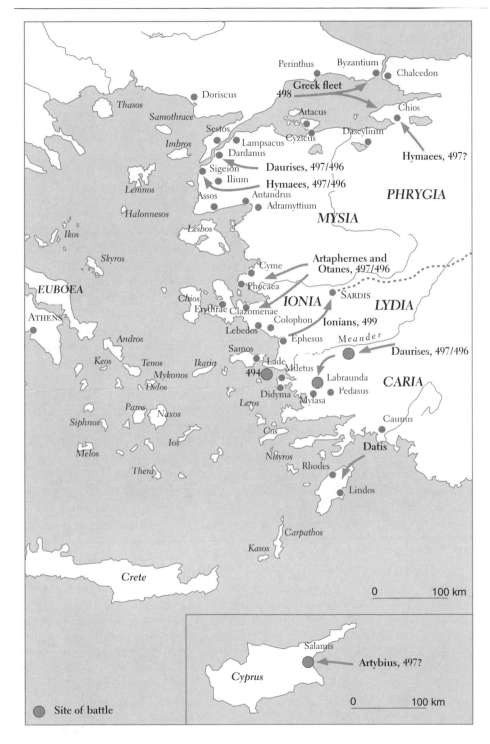

Map 1. The Ionian Revolt.

Motivated by the fear of dismissal and by a message from Histiaeus, Aristagoras decided on open revolt against Darius, despite opposition expressed by the historian Hecataeus of Miletus. After winning over the tyrants who had participated in the expedition to Naxos, "Aristagoras, in open rebellion, set himself to damage Darius in every way he could think of" (V.37◇). One of his first acts was "pretending to abdicate his own position in favour of a democratic government [isonomy], and then went on to do the same thing in the other Ionian cities" (V.38◇). Conscious of his military inferiority, he left for Greece. At Sparta, he was politely turned away by King Cleomenes I, despite tempting promises of booty from barbarians "who have little taste for war" (V.49◇). "From Sparta, Aristagoras went on to Athens" (V.55◇). "Persuaded to accede to Aristagoras' appeal, the Athenians passed a decree for the dispatch of twenty warships to Ionia" (V.97◇), which were soon followed by five from Eretria (V.98).

Hostilities began with a raid launched by the Ionians against Sardis itself (499?). Unable to capture the acropolis, which was defended by Artaphernes in person, the Ionians burned the city below it, then retreated. Pursued by Persian forces, they suffered a major defeat near Ephesus. At that point the Athenians recalled their ships (V.99–103). Soon, however, the revolt spread from Byzantium in the north to Caria in the south (498–497), then to the Cypriot city-states except for Amathus. Persian forces disembarked on the island: the Ionians won a sea battle, but the Persians won on land and after some months took the last resistant cities (V.104–16). On the continent, the Persian generals pursued the land offensive until the Carian declaration of war forced them to send men there. After an initial victory, the Persian army fell into an ambush where its leaders perished (V.116–22). Nonetheless, the remaining Persian generals pursued a systematic reconquest of the Hellespontine and Ionian towns (497). Aware of the impossibility of defeating the Persian forces, Aristagoras relinquished power to Pythagoras, then set sail for Myrcinus, a prior gift from Darius to Histiaeus. He was then lost in a little-known battle against Thrace (V.122–26). These were the conditions, Herodotus says, upon Histiaeus's return to Sardis (496?). He was soon to die by order of Artaphernes. The Ionian fleet was concentrated at Lade but was weakened by overt or covert defections to the Persians. The Persians won a victory at Lade, whereupon Miletus, besieged by land and sea, had to surrender (VI.1–22; 494). The victory was followed by merciless vengeance (VI.22–41; 493). Herodotus ends his tale with a description of the measures taken by Artaphernes to restore law and order (VI.42–43).

This is the bare-bones outline of what Herodotus relates. It is obvious that the importance Herodotus places on these events is out of proportion to Darius's greater concerns in an Empire that thereafter extended from Macedonia to the Indus. Furthermore, between 500 and 493, the Great King was engaged in a number of other enterprises on which the Ionian situation had not the slightest effect. This observation doubtless captures some aspect of historical reality. But it also rouses certain methodological reservations, since it is based implicitly on the silence of both the Greek and Persian sources. Of course this silence means nothing, since royal inscriptions are not narrative texts. By way of comparison, we would have no idea of the extent of the policy carried out by Darius in the Nile Valley if we did not have Egyptian documents. There is one hint of the Ionian revolt found in a Persepolis tablet (Q 1809): a travel voucher indicates in fact that Datis (see p. 158) returned from Sardis in February–March 494, bearing a royal authorization. It is tempting to suppose that he came on Darius's order to make a tour of inspection of Asia Minor on the eve of the final offensive (which was quite certainly ordered by the king himself and his advisers). There can be no further doubt that the Persian forces based in Cilicia were under direct orders from the central administration to launch a vast offensive against Cyprus in 497 (V.108). Herodotus's tale of the final moments of Histiaeus also shows that Darius intended Artaphernes to operate on royal instructions (VI.30), in the same way that he had obtained the king's permission before launching the expedition against Naxos (V.31–32). While it is possible that Darius in the beginning (as Herodotus records in a suspicious passage; V.105) did not harbor great fears, confident as he was of the military superiority of his troops, it is more certain that the operations could not fail to stimulate his irritation and his desire to be done with them. It is in this context that Herodotus reports that Histiaeus persuaded the Great King to allow him to return to Miletus to convince his compatriots to abandon the fight. In fact, Darius's western strategy required him to mount a vigorous effort to retake the coast of Asia Minor. To lose it at this date would have amounted to an infinitely more serious failure than what he had experienced on the Ukrainian steppes. Furthermore, the Ionian revolt poses a series of historical problems whose importance exceeds the limited geographical context of the Asia Minor coast. An analysis of these events can in fact enlighten the political and military situation of the whole Empire at the beginning of the fifth century, as well as the nature of the bonds that united the central, satrapal, and local powers.

To answer all these questions, historians ceaselessly analyze Herodotus, because, except for a few brief allusions elsewhere (e.g., Diodorus IX.25), and despite Plutarch's attacks on him (*Mal. Her.* 24 [*Mor.* 861]), he represents our only source of information. For Herodotus, the description of the revolt is intimately linked to a wider historiographic objective: to explain the origins of the wars between the Persians and the Greeks. And in his mind it is clear that the Ionians, for whom he did not harbor the least sympathy, played a despicable role: their revolt brought on devastation (V.28). The burning of Sardis offered the Persians a pretext for launching a war of reprisals against Eretria and Athens (V.102), and the sending of Athenian and Eretrian reinforcements "was the beginning of trouble not only for Greece, but for the rest of the world as well" (V.97✧). Aristagoras is presented as a crazy man, guided at first by the fear of losing power at Miletus and ready to involve the Greeks in a hopeless revolt (V.35): when he urged the exiled Paeonians in Asia to recapture their countries, it was not to achieve any advantage for the Ionians, it was simply "to annoy Darius" (V.98✧). Herodotus also states (not unmaliciously) that Aristagoras himself did not take part in the raid on Sardis (V.99). And finally, unable to follow through to the end the operations he had initiated, this "poor-spirited creature" left Asia Minor for Thrace (V.124–26✧).

An Economic Crisis?

The problem, obviously, is that Herodotus clearly does not ask the questions to which historians seek answers. Many uncertainties remain, including those of a chronological nature. This is most vexing for those attempting to reconstruct a chain of cause and effect. But the origins and development of a revolt over such a long time are particularly problematic. Many have wondered whether the Persian conquest set in motion an economic crisis in the cities of Asia Minor. Completely opposite responses continue to be offered. But the documentation is so sparse. . . . Herodotus's evaluation is often cited: It "Miletus during the same period had reached the peak of her prosperity and was the glory of Ionia" (V.28◊). But this statement must be placed in context. Herodotus records that some time earlier the city had in fact been torn by civil disorder, which was settled by Parian arbitrators. The discussion clearly shows that in Herodotus's eyes (V.29) the supposed wealth arose solely from planting crops again on land that had previously been laid waste—nothing more. If Aristagoras applied to Artaphernes to lead the expedition against Naxos, it was because Miletus was incapable of bearing the expense by itself (V.30–35). Clearly, Miletus was not "wealthy" enough for it to pursue an independent policy.

Once Histiaeus had returned to Miletus (as always, according to Herodotus), he explained to his compatriots why he had urged Aristagoras to pursue revolt, as follows: "Darius had been planning a transfer of population, intending to settle Phoenicians in Ionia, and Ionians in Phoenicia" (VI.3◊). This passage is sometimes cited to claim that the Persians, after conquering the Mediterranean front, had systematically favored the Phoenicians over the Greek dependencies and that this policy had caused the commercial ruin of the Ionian cities. But this interpetation is not based on any independent sources. For one thing, Herodotus does not conceal the fact that he believes that this explanation is incorrect. For another, we could just as easily suppose that the satrapal courts of Asia Minor created a market that profited the craftsmen of the Ionian cities (see, for comparison, Herodotus VIII.105). And it seems likely that a not insignificant portion of the Greek pottery imported to the Near East was at this time coming from the cities of Asia Minor. Greco-Phoenician competition, which is often made much of, must not be overestimated, no matter how important their political conflicts were in attracting the favor of the Great King (cf. VIII.90). The king never chose one or the other as a privileged commercial partner! A remarkable, recently published (*TADAE* C.3.7) Aramaic document from the time of Xerxes (475) attests that Ionian and Phoenician merchants could be found side by side in an Egyptian port and that, at several sites, Phoenician and Greek pottery types are mixed. Besides, the Ionians also encountered competition in the Greek world, particularly from the Athenians, who during the sixth century had progressively won some of the Aegean trade from the Ionians, in the northern regions. But it is not possible to analyze the consequences of this competition for the economic position of Miletus and other Ionian towns with any precision.

Civic Tensions and Achaemenid Power

What is most surprising is that the troubles arose around 500, whereas conditions might have been more favorable earlier on, during the great upheavals of 522–520 (when Darius came to power), for instance, or during the Scythian expedition (503), for another. While it is true that, during the accession of Darius, Oroetes' power hardly presented conditions that were amenable to the awakening of movement away from the Persians in the Greek cities of Asia Minor, Herodotus explicitly states that, during Darius's Scythian expedition, the Ionian tyrants, who were powerfully pressured by the Scythians to abandon Darius, seem to have had all of the requisites in hand to choose the path of secession. It was this path, according to Herodotus, that was proposed by Miltiades the Athenian, "master of the Chersonese on the Hellespont and in command . . . they should take the Scythians' advice, and so liberate Ionia" (IV.137–38◊). Histiaeus of Miletus (still according to Herodotus) tried to use arguments for democracy to convince his colleagues to secede:

Each one of them owed his position as head of a state to Darius, and in the event of Darius' fall, he himself would be unable to maintain his power at Miletus, and all the rest of them would find themselves in a similar difficulty. Each state would be sure to turn against absolute government, and agitate for democracy. (IV.137◊)

Herodotus's version is not free of imprecision (the role of Miltiades, for example) or anachronism. It is clear that here he puts in Histiaeus's mouth an argument that was actually used by Aristagoras at the beginning of the revolt. This indicates at least that, from Herodotus's point of view, the Greek cities at this time faced an internal political problem, which was closely linked to the relationship they maintained with Persian power. This debate throws singular light on the nature of the contradictions within which the Greek tyrants found themselves, caught between two irreconcilable ambitions: liberation from Persian protection and retention of their own power.

The measures taken by Aristagoras at the beginning of the open rebellion are presented by Herodotus as follows. After having seized the commanders who had participated in the expedition to Naxos, he made the following decision (V.37–38◊):

To induce the Milesians to support him (*hekontes*), he began by pretending to abdicate his own position in favour of a democratic government [isonomy], and then went on to do the same thing in the other Ionian states, where he got rid of the political bosses. Some of them he drove out; those he had arrested on the ships which had joined his expedition to Naxos he handed over to the cities to which they respectively belonged, hoping thereby to get the goodwill of their former subjects. At Mytilene, Coes was taken out and stoned to death the moment the people got their hands on him; at Cyme, however, Aristagoras was allowed to go free, and most of the other cities showed a similar leniency.

Right away we find Herodotus passing judgment without compassion on Aristagoras, in whose democratic fervor he does not believe for a moment ("by pretending"). But, aside from this, his presentations of the situations of 513 and 499 are based on his conviction that an absolute connection existed between the tyrants and Achaemenid authority. From the time that the Achaemenids took power, the expulsion of the tyrants was a prerequisite for rebellion. And, on this point, it is difficult not to agree with Herodotus. To be sure, not all of the tyrants were imposed by Achaemenid intervention. When Histiaeus left for Susa, it was his son-in-law and cousin Aristagoras who took over (V.30). This illustrates the fact that transmission of the job of tyrant proceeded along family lines in the first place. At the same time, as Histiaeus says, it appears clear that the dominion they exercised over their respective cities was directly connected to the support given to them by the Achaemenid power. At any rate, most of the tyrants driven away by Aristagoras's actions immediately turned to the Persian camp (VI.9–10), where they provided the Persians with inside information (cf. VI.13). In the eyes of the Ionians, the dominion to which they were subject was exercised jointly by the Persians and their tyrant (VI.21). The situation was the same in Cyprus: as soon as his brother Onesilus took power and rebelled against the Persians, Gorgus, the king of Salamis, "transferred his allegiance to Persia" (V.104◊). When Herodotus writes that after the Persian victory "the people of [Salamis] restored [it] to their former ruler Gorgus" (V.115◊), he is saying that the power of Gorgus was legitimate (with respect to the monarchic traditions of Salamis), but at the same time he shows that this legitimacy could not be restored without the assistance of Persian military might.

Of course, we cannot see any underlying ideological preference on the part of the Persians, who had simply decided during one period in the history of the Greek cities that alliance with the tyrants was the best way to establish their own dominion. From this point of view, the policy pursued by the Persians in Asia Minor was not fundamentally different from the policy that they followed in the other conquered countries—to support the local elites, as long as they agreed to play the game. But, at the first offense, the king could fire them and name other, more submissive leaders. Furthermore, Darius's policy regarding the sanctuaries of Asia Minor does not seem to have differed essentially from his policy in Babylonia, Egypt, or Judah (chap. 12).

The Naxos affair shows that the power of the great families, from which the tyrants of Asia Minor came, was threatened by popular pressure; then the representatives of this "great" party were removed by the people (*dēmos*; V.30). Whatever the exact sociological realities reflected by Herodotus's words, it is clear that Naxos had just undergone a democratic (or isonomic, the difference is not important here) revolution. These democratic or isonomic tendencies in Asia Minor did not appear suddenly, since, for example, around 575–550, an inscription attests to the existence of magistrates and a "popular" assembly at Chios (ML 8). It is also possible that the nearby example of Athens ("Clisthenian revolution") had again induced the will of the "people" to undo the "tyrannical" protection of the great families. Under these conditions, Aristagoras understood that, to have some chance of success, they had to enlarge the social bases of the rebellion, and in order to do this, they had to give in to the "isonomic pressure" (which, obviously, Miletus also felt, as Herodotus suggests; V.28–29). This policy also allowed Aristagoras to take control of operations: by asking each town to name *strategoi* ('generals'), he could be reasonably sure that these *strategoi* would henceforth operate under his direction.

This decision attests to Aristagoras's political cleverness. The tyrants of 513 made the best choice they could between external dependence and internal democracy. At this time (513), "the liberation of Ionia"—a slogan allegedly defended by Miltiades, though we do not know what motivated him to say this—was certainly not an effective mobilizing slogan any more than it was in 500. In other words, it is not possible to explain the genesis of the Ionian revolt in terms of a (nonexistent) "national consciousness" or in terms of a "hereditary enemy" (i.e., "the Persians have always been our enemy"), two concepts that were forged later in Greece by polemecists such as Isocrates. The Ionian attitude toward Persian dominion was not determined solely by perceiving the Persians to be culturally different. Instead, and more importantly, it was determined by the social status of each group within the context of the Greek city and by the efforts these groups put forth to advance their interests. Aristagoras was able to carry this thought to its logical conclusion: to make war on the Persians presupposed that the social groups who up until the present had been excluded from power were now included. It is appropriate to add a closing remark that allows us to establish another link between internal tensions and revolt against Persia. The remark is fostered by the measures taken by Artaphernes at the end of the revolt. Herodotus states very clearly that "these measures were conducive to peace" (VI.42✧). Given that they related essentially to the idea of tribute (and not just to its amount: chap. 12/5), we are led to think that the exacting of tribute within each city had posed or, more precisely, revealed or even exacerbated internal social tensions. This was a process perhaps not greatly removed from the process in Judah fifty years later (Neh 5:1–3; see below, chap. 14/5): the inequable exacting of tribute from the rich and poor perhaps played the role of accelerating political and social tensions. In the case of the Ionians, at any rate, supporting the revolt promoted a hope for an end to this external pressure and the consequent internal sociopolitical pressure.

The Strategy of Aristagoras: The Beginnings of the Revolt

Supposing that the preceding interpretations partly or fully reflect the truth, we still need to understand why and how, at that particular moment, Aristagoras raised the banner of revolt. To this end, we must first return to the story of the expedition to Naxos. Early on, there was no question of not cooperating with Artaphernes (the satrap of Sardis). Because all of the ships were under the command of Persian captains, Aristagoras's first move was to seek the aid of Artaphernes. The Naxians who were exiled from their island promised financial contributions, and these are the terms under which Aristagoras approached Artaphernes. Upon notification of the mobilization, other towns were required to send oarsmen to the royal fleet. Of course, from the beginning, the alliance betrayed contradictory agendas. Aristagoras hoped to gain in prestige from it; Artaphernes, on the other hand, knew well that the expedition was a Persian expedition, ordered by the king, with a real Achaemenid objective—to take control of an island that Aristagoras represented to him as the key to the Cyclades (V.31). Very quickly, mistrust arose between Aristagoras and the Persian head of the armada, Megabates. It increased some time later, when the Persians found themselves short of money (V.34). In fact, it is likely that, as was customary, Artaphernes had received strict orders from the central authority that released a specific amount of funds calculated on the basis of the number of ships and soldiers conscripted and the expected duration of the expedition.

It was at this moment, according to Herodotus, that Aristagoras decided to revolt. For this, Herodotus provides only explanations of a personal nature. He adds that Aristagoras had received instructions regarding a revolt from Histiaeus, still in his gilded cage in Susa. But the story he gives is highly suspect (V.35◊). In no way was Aristagoras unaware of the superiority of the Persians. The Greeks' only hope—as Hecataeus puts it, but surely Aristagoras was also aware of this—was to take the offensive on the sea: Hecataeus "advised them to work for control of the sea." The only solution was to seize the Persian fleet which, after its unhappy return from Naxos, had just berthed at Myus. Iatragoras was sent to Myus to seize the captains of the ships (i.e., the tyrants who had contributed to the Naxos campaign), and most certainly also to seize the ships by making a daring attack on the naval base. But in seizing the royal fleet, the Greeks also had to settle the budgetary problem. The maintenance of a large armada (perhaps 200 ships) was very expensive (we can estimate the cost as at least 60 talents a month, not counting maintenance and repairs). The Persians had solved the problem by conscription and tribute. The expense is the reason Aristagoras proposed that they seize the treasuries of Didyma: "If that were done, he had good hope that they might succeed in gaining command of the sea" (V.36◊). His proposal was rejected. "They did decide, none the less, to throw off the Persian yoke," says Herodotus.

Though Aristagoras's strategy seems to make sense so far (or at least, if the modern historian can give it meaning!), it is hard to understand why, upon his return from Europe (where he had won the cautious support of Athens and Eretria), he decided to begin an expedition against Sardis after mooring the fleet near Ephesus. The Greeks arrived without mishap near Sardis, thanks to Ephesian guides, who led them by roundabout paths. However, they proved unable to capture the fortress, whose virtually impregnable position is stressed by all of the ancient sources—at any rate, it was inaccessible to a small, hard-pressed troop lacking siege engines. Aristagoras must have been aware that in a very short time Artaphernes would be able to raise mounted troops, "all the Persians stationed west of the Halys" (V.102◊). That is, the army reserve would be sure to advance from the lands awarded to Persian nobles of the imperial diaspora, and, indeed, they did respond: the Greeks had to flee in disorder toward Ephesus before the survivors of the combat were even able to disband (V.102). Shortly, Athenians and Eretrians abandoned the Ionians, who had to face the Persians alone (V.103).

If, taking the opposite tack from Herodotus, we postulate that Aristagoras was *not* crazy, then we must recognize that he had good reasons for acting as he did. For one thing, we should note that he put on the line only a very small part of his forces: the fleet and the soldiers it carried were intact and ready for other battles. Could not the reason for the attack on Sardis be related to an urgent need to give a signal to the populations of Asia Minor? They could not help but be impressed by an offensive so unprecedented that no parallel can be found in the entire history of Persian dominion in Asia Minor, other than Agesilaus's attempt a century later and another led by Alexander more than 160 years later (under very different conditions). In other words, we are suggesting that Aristagoras would have had no illusions about the military effectiveness of the undertaking but that most of all he hoped to gain political advantage from it. The fact remains that the Greek fleet quickly made a veritable propaganda tour of the Asia Minor coast, from the Hellespont to Caria. A large portion of the peoples and cities joined the rebels (V.103), as did all of the Cypriot kings, except the king of Salamis, who fled to the Persians, and the king of Amathus, who was soon besieged by the other Cypriot forces (V.104). The Persians soon won a land victory on Cyprus (aided by the defection of some Cypriot contingents), but the royal Persian fleet, comprising Phoenician contingents, was defeated by the Greeks (V.108–114), and the Ionian fleet then retook Ionia (V.115).

It is also possible that by the incursion of a Greek army at Sardis Aristagoras hoped to damage the prestige and authority of Artaphernes. Herodotus speaks of dissensions in the court at Sardis in a chronological context of the mysterious return of Histiaeus, just after the attack on Sardis by Aristagoras (V.105–7). Herodotus's chronology is suspect, however, and what he says about the Sardis political situation may be pertinent to an understanding of Aristagoras's motives for an attack: Histiaeus sent letters to the Persians who were found in Sardis, as if to men with whom he had previously had conversations on the subject of rebellion. But the intrigues were discovered by Artaphernes, and this time he put a great number of Persians to death (VI.4). Regardless of the uncertainties surrounding these events, they do explain the dissensions that surrounded Artaphernes. It is likely that, although he was the king's brother, he had received less than favorable correspondence from Darius and he no longer had the total confidence of all of the Persians, who must already have been frustrated by the Ionian raid, which implied failure on the part of the intelligence services. It is in any case the first attestation of this kind of atmosphere in the satrapy's leadership circle after the Otanes affair. The execution of numerous Persians is evidence of deep differences over the strategy to follow.

The Persian Victory

We may assume that Aristagoras's plans, whatever they were, so far had gone fairly well. But the problems posed above remained. For one thing, except for a quick defeat in Caria, the Persians retained absolute supremacy on land. Several detachments of troops moved toward the coastal towns, rapidly seizing ("one each day"!) very important ports—Abydos, Lampsacus, Clazomenae, Cyme, and others (Herodotus V.116–17, 123). This deprived the Greeks of the harbors and open ports essential to the fleet, which had to find water and supplies as well as shipyards for repairs (cf. Arrian, *Anab.* I.18–19). Never were the Greeks able to set foot on the Asian continent again. Histiaeus tried to disembark later on, when he left Lesbos, in order to get wheat in the rich territory of Atarnaeus. However, he was defeated by "Harpagus, who was in the neighbourhood at the head of a large army" (VI.28✧). The superiority of the Persian cavalry was total. Only Agesilaus, a century later, was able to challenge it, however ephemerally, by raising a cavalry in the Greek cities and so providing a way "of not hav[ing] to carry on a skulking warfare" (Xenophon, *Hell.* III.4.15✧).

As noted above, the pursuit of naval operations presupposes one has settled his budgetary problems. For this reason, Herodotus says, Aristagoras summoned a council: he "realized that he had no chance against Darius." Herodotus uses this occasion to resume his attacks on Aristagoras, whom he accuses of laying the ground for his own flight (V.124✧). Actually, the tyrant proposed to take Myrcinus in Thrace, where Histiaeus had received a territorial grant from Darius in 513. Against the advice of Hecataeus he took to the sea and died after a battle against the Thracians, whose town he had besieged (V.126). No doubt by this means Aristagoras intended to get his hands on fresh resources of wood and money that would allow him to fund the war by sea (cf. V.23). This moreover is the same reasoning followed by Histiaeus when, preparing for his return to Miletus, he resolved to attack Thasos, which was also renowned for its rich mines (VI.28). Previously, he had attempted to get himself back on the water by requisitioning the merchant ships that plied the Bosporus (VI.5). It is still more remarkable that in 494 the Greeks were still able to put into service 353 triremes, according to Herodotus. However, by then the Persians had had the time and means to rebuild a fleet of 600 ships with the help of contingents sent by the Phoenicians, Cypriots, Cilicians, and Egyptians (VI.6–9). Even though Herodotus's numbers must be taken with a grain of salt, they at least communicate the inequity in forces. The Greeks had obviously thrown the last of their resources into the one battle, because they knew all too well that the outcome would decide the war (VI.6–9).

The Ionians did not have adequate financial resources or excel in unity, despite efforts put forth by Aristagoras at the beginning of the revolt to get a unified command under way (V.38). Several times the Ionians clearly tried to revive the earlier Ionian League artificially, as their meetings at the Panionion (the festival of the Ionian cities) show. This was obviously done with no great success or conviction, the more so because on the one hand not all the Ionian cities were engaged in the combat and on the other because Aeolian and Carian cities had taken part. The battles on Cyprus had already shown that it was every man for himself. Stesenor of Curium, for instance, did not hesitate to switch to the side of the enemy in the middle of a battle (V.113). When at the end of the operations the Persians decided to concentrate their forces against Miletus, the Greeks met one more time at the Panionion. It was there decided to abandon the mainland (the Milesians were left to defend their walls alone) and to gather the fleet at the island of Lade, opposite Miletus. The unified façade quickly crumbled under threats from the Persian generals and under the influence of the tyrants who accompanied them. The fighting spirit that the commander Dionysius tried to instill in his troops rapidly faded, with the soldiers refusing to undergo the difficult discipline he tried to impose on them (VI.12). Under these conditions and faced with increasing disunity, the Samian part of the coalition lent a friendly ear to Aeaces, the old tyrant of their island who had been deposed by Aristagoras, and were persuaded that they could never defeat the Persians. The plaints put in the soldiers' mouths by Herodotus evidence deep discouragement (VI.12). We must observe in this regard that the people were probably exhausted, considering the abandonment of the fields (frequent levies of men as soldiers and oarsmen), ravages of war (the Persians held the flatlands: VI.28), and doubtless also the financial pressure (enormous budgetary needs), which probably conceded nothing to the burden of Persian tribute! All in all, Herodotus remarks, the Samians preferred to return to the joint dominion by the tyrant Aeaces and the Persians. He mentions that the Milesians, on the other hand, were, some time later, against returning to Histiaeus: "the people there had had a taste of liberty and were too well pleased to have got rid of Aristagoras to be willing to welcome another ruler of the same stamp" (VI.5◊). The fact remains that, during the battle engaged by the two fleets near Miletus, a large portion of the Samian vessels left Ladian waters, followed by others: "Most of the allies defected." At least this is Herodotus's version (VI.9–15), who, it is true, harbored no sympathy for the Ionians.

It was soon Miletus's turn to surrender. Besieged by land and sea, the inhabitants had no chance in the face of enemies who had long been masters of the art of siege (VI.18), as they had already demonstrated at Barca (IV.200) and Cyprus (V.115–16): "Five years after the revolt of Aristagoras, [the Persians] made themselves masters of the whole city" ([493] VI.17◊). The last pockets of resistance were mopped up in a relatively short time. Some Carian cities that were still armed folded under the weight of the Persian armies (VI.25). And, at the beginning of 493, the royal fleet took to the sea again and subjugated the last of the holdouts one by one: "In this way," remarks Herodotus, "the Ionians were reduced for the third time to slavery—first by the Lydians, and then, twice, by the Persians" (VI.32◊). Soon, Artaphernes took appropriate measures to restore the stability of Persian dominion in the cities, while maintaining the appearance of their autonomy (chap. 12/5).

4. From Thrace to Memphis (492–486)

The Mission of Mardonius in Thrace

Herodotus records that, in the spring of 492, the king recalled the generals in command in Asia Minor and sent there his son-in-law Mardonius, son of Gobryas. From Cilicia, Mardonius sailed all the way to Ionia, while the army reached the Hellespont overland. When they were reassembled, the Persian forces crossed the Hellespont and were soon operating in Thrace. After a few months, Mardonius returned to Asia Minor, as the result of a campaign Herodotus considers disastrous: his fleet was lost in a storm near Mount Athos and his land army suffered heavy losses to the Brygian peoples. Later, Herodotus even states that Darius relieved Mardonius of his command, for his expedition had had little success (VI.94). But we must note that in Herodotus's opinion the mission entrusted to Mardonius by Darius had been to take Athens and Eretria—obviously because of the aid these two cities had provided to the Ionians in 499. Against this background, the results achieved by Mardonius could hardly be taken as anything other than laughable. This is Herodotus's very personal interpretation: he was eager to incorporate Mardonius's campaign into his broad view of the Persian Wars. He himself adds right away that this was just a pretext: "The Persians intended to subjugate as many Greek towns as they could" (VI.43–45◊). To understand the strategy of Darius, it is important to place it in the broader context of the years 513–492. The conquests in Thrace that had already been achieved, at the instigation of Megabazus and Otanes, were considerable, as we have seen. But they remained relatively fragile because, beyond the regions that were securely held by powerful garrisons, many territories remained de facto outside Persian dominion. Even though we do not have absolute proof, there is hardly any doubt that Thrace and perhaps Macedonia had taken advantage of Persia's difficulties in 499–493 to loosen their bonds. In this perspective, the mission entrusted to Mardonius was at first nothing but the reconquest of the Hellespont and the Propontis in 493–492. Once control of the straits was reasserted, he could retake and more solidly affirm the imperial presence in Europe.

Despite occasional reverses (and a wound received by Mardonius himself), the results must not be underestimated. For one thing, the Persian army "added the Macedonians to the list of Darius' subjects" (VI.44✧). Macedonia was thus no longer simply a protectorate set up by Megabazus, but a conquered country. Actually, Alexander I retained the throne but now was a subject-king, liable for tribute and other assessments. The conquests achieved beyond the Strymon River explain the situation of 480, as Herodotus describes it: "The whole country as far as Thessaly had been forced into subjection and made tributary to Persia by the conquests, first, of Megabazus and, later, of Mardonius" (VII.108✧). However, while wishing to present the fight with the Brygi as a defeat of Mardonius, Herodotus does not conceal the fact that the reality was quite different: "In spite of their initial success, the Brygi were not to escape a crushing blow" (VI.45✧). The implication is that other Thracian peoples were then subjugated. Finally, Herodotus mentions that Thasos surrendered without a fight (VI.44). He confirms this in the story of Xerxes' expedition, where he mentions that, among the peoples of the interior, only the Satrae were then free: all the others sent a contingent to Xerxes (VII.110–11). The "Persian governors [who] held appointments in Thrace and on the Hellespont" (VII.106✧: before 480) probably date to this period. After preparations for the expedition of 480, the Persians were able to set up stores of grain and flour in several places: Leuce Acte in Thrace, Tyrodiza (in the country of Perinthus), Doriscus, Eion, and Macedonia (VII.25). And there is nothing to suggest that during these years the Persians experienced any rebellions in the region.

The following year, Darius was able to complete the conquest begun by Mardonius. Without having to dispatch an army, he sent a message to the Thasians, who had been accused by their neighbors (the Abderans?) of rebellion, "to the effect that its defences should be dismantled and its fleet brought across to Abdera" (VI.46✧). On this occasion, Herodotus states that the Thasians had laid the keels of numerous vessels, thanks to the resources they drew from their property on the mainland and mines: 200 talents per year in all. "The islanders obeyed Darius' order, pulled down their fortifications and sent their whole fleet over to Abdera" (VI.47✧). The Abderans were faithful subjects of the Great King (VIII.120), and Abdera was probably a Persian naval base. This episode confirms that Persian dominion was firmly established at this date: it obviously never occurred to the Thasians to turn a deaf ear. In this way, the Persians obtained access (either directly or via taxes) to the Thasian mines.

From Cilicia to Marathon

The order given to Thasos also meshed with the preparations that the Great King began the following year (491). While royal heralds were sent to ask for "earth and water" from the Greek cities, Darius began the mobilization of his naval forces, instructing his coastal subjects to build long ships and transport vessels (VI.47, 95). The land troops and the fleet were concentrated in Cilicia, under the command of Datis and Artaphernes, son of Artaphernes satrap of Sardis, and thus Darius's nephew (VI.94–95). Departing from Samos, the Persians navigated through the islands up to and including Eretria (VI.95–102). Then came the debarkation on the plain of Marathon, the defeat, and the return to Darius (VI.102–119). This, in skeleton form, is the story Herodotus tells of what is customarily called (from the Greek point of view) the First Persian War.

Herodotus records the orders given to Datis and Artaphernes as follows: "To reduce Athens and Eretria to slavery and to bring the slaves before the king" (VI.94◊). Logically, he concludes his tale with the coming of Datis and Artaphernes before Darius, leading the Eretrians "in defeat" (VI.119◊). The king's desire for vengeance against Athens and Eretria is a recurrent motif in Herodotus (and many other ancient authors following him). Herodotus dates it to Darius's learning of the Greek raid on Sardis (V.105). According to his version, vengeance became a veritable obsession for Darius (VI.94; cf. Athenaeus XIV.652b–c and Plutarch, *Mor.* 173c). Combined with the later exaltation of the battle of Marathon by the Greeks of the fifth and fourth centuries, this interpretation has done not a little to implant the idea that the primary objective of Darius in 491 was to destroy the Greek sanctuaries (particularly the acropolis of Athens), which were designated objects of reprisal for the destruction of the temples of Sardis in 499 (V.102) and, only as a side effect, to conquer Greece.

The Conquest of the Islands

For clarification, it will suffice to reprise events in order. As usual, Herodotus brings his bias to the historical reconstruction. He feels constrained to explain why the Persians chose to head from Samos to Naxos instead of sailing for the Hellespont and Thrace (as Xerxes was to do later on), since this route was clearly difficult to reconcile with a Persian desire to conquer Greece. Naxos "was now their first objective in the war," he writes, stating that it was essential for them to conquer an island against which they had failed in 500 (VI.96◊; cf. V.34). It is necessary at this point to recall the speech that Aristagoras had then addressed to Artaphernes (according to Herodotus): starting from Naxos, the Persians would be able to conquer other islands, the Cyclades (Paros, Andros, and others), and to press as far as Euboea without difficulty (V.31). This is exactly the program that Darius assigned to Datis and Artaphernes in 490. Despite Plutarch's denials (*Her. Mal.* 36 [*Mor.* 869]), Naxos was taken without difficulty, its temples and the city burned, and the inhabitants taken prisoner (VI.96). Then the fleet followed a course from island to island, past Delos, Carystus, and the rest of Euboea (VI.97–101). Cities that resisted, such as Carystus, were harshly punished. Despite the aid of Athenian colonists, Eretria was also forced to surrender: "The Persians there pillaged the temples and set them on fire, avenging the burning of the sanctuaries of Sardis, in conformity with the orders of Darius" (VI.101). Thus, contrary to what Herodotus would have us think, the journey via Naxos was not a detour, but rather the first objective in the conquest of the islands. Darius's objective obviously was to wipe out any competition on the seas. We do not know the precise status of the islands that were thus conquered. There is no doubt, however, that they were required to pay tribute and to send military contingents (cf. VI.99).

In sum, on the eve of the landing in Attica—and the defeat at Marathon did nothing to change this—Darius intended to follow a strategic design through to its logical end, a design that began with the conquest of Samos shortly after his accession. The Scythian-Thracian expedition of 513 (and the following years), expansion of maritime dominance after the Ionian revolt, and then Mardonius's 492 expedition represented further stages in a vast project intended to insure Persian dominance over the Aegean Sea—not just the shores, but the islands as well.

This conquest also marked an essential step in Thucydides' mind. Cyrus, he writes, had subjugated the towns of the continent, but Darius was in a position to seize the islands, thanks to the might of his fleet (I.16.1). Like Polycrates (tyrant of Samos), whom he succeeded, in a sense, as "king of the seas" (I.13.6; 14.2), Darius marked his power by posing as protector of Delos. He had in fact given strict orders to Datis to take care not to land at Delos itself but at Rhenaea. The Delians, who had fled to Tenos at the news of his arrival, were assured that they would be able to return home alive, safe and sound: "Datis followed the message by piling three hundred talents-weight of frankincense upon the altar, and burning it as an offering" (Herodotus VI.97✧). Datis's expedition was also a sort of propaganda tour, intended to show the islands that they had nothing to fear from the new master. Herodotus himself records that, on his return, Datis "sailed in his own ship to Delos" to restore a golden statue of Apollo that a Phoenician sailor had stolen from a Theban sanctuary (VI.118✧). Here we can see the two complementary sides of Persian ideological strategy: patronage granted to the sanctuaries but pitiless repression in case of refusal to submit. Only recalcitrant cities saw their sanctuaries destroyed.

Persian Conquest and Greek Medism

The Persians were able to glean an additional piece of information, or rather a confirmation, from their island campaign. This was that, in the face of Persian aggression, the Greeks did not have a unified patriotic hatred of "barbarians." This was an observation that their experience with the Greeks of Asia Minor had long ago recognized as a certainty. Just as disunified as their companions who had settled on the coast of Asia Minor, the insular Greeks provided the proof. Herodotus records that after six days of siege, Euphorbus and Philagrus, two persons of note (i.e., of wealth) from Eretria, "betrayed (*prodidousi*) the town to the enemy" (VI.100✧). These two people were rewarded by the king, who gave them a grant of land, doubtless in Asia Minor (Plutarch, *Mor.* 510b; Pausanias VII.10.2). This was another example of the exchange of gifts for services rendered between the king and the Greeks that had begun in Cyrus's time (Athenaeus I.30a) and that was to multiply many times later on.

Obviously Datis was also counting on the "Medism" of certain Athenians for the successful outcome of his plans. In fact, Herodotus's discussion leads us to believe that the landing in Attica had a political objective, to install a man in Athens who was devoted to Persian interests. Before Datis, the role of Hippias, son of the tyrant Pisistratus, was quite noteworthy in this regard. He was the one who chose the plain of Marathon (VI.102) and directed the landing and encampment operations (VI.107). The reason obviously was that he was well placed to play a role as military adviser. It was also because over several years he had become one of the most influential political advisers among the Persians. Herodotus depicts him urging the satrap Artaphernes against Athens (V.96). His participation in the expedition was no doubt because he had persuaded Darius that he could reinstall a pro-Persian tyranny in Athens. He certainly knew he could count on allies in the city. Herodotus, strongly denying that the guilty party was of the Alcmaeonid family, records that after the battle of Marathon a signal was sent from Athens to the Persians, indicating that the way to the city was open (IV.115). The signal would have to have been sent by Athenians favorable to the return of Hippias (IV.121). There are no compelling reasons to reject this statement. From multiple sources, we know that there were "friends of tyrants" in Athens. One of them had been elected archon in 496 (Aristotle, *Ath. Pol.* 22.4). Furthermore, the speech Herodotus puts in the mouth of Miltiades (who commanded the Athenian forces) expresses the moral and political uncertainty of the Athenians. Urging the Athenians to join battle without delay, Miltiades insisted that if they waited to do so, they risked "a wind of discord blowing the Athenians toward the Medes"; he also urged them not to wait "until there was something rotten among the Athenians" (VI.109). Herodotus also describes the feeling of terror that the mere mention of the Medes inspired, because their numerous victories were known (VI.112).

Marathon

Datis recalled Darius's orders and, with the advice of Hippias and with great confidence, had his troops disembark on the plain of Marathon. "The part of Attic territory nearest Eretria—and also the best ground for cavalry to manoeuvre in—was at Marathon." As soon as the Athenians heard the news, they and the Plataeans left for Marathon (VI.102–3✧). The Spartans, on the other hand, despite urgent applications made to them, pleaded a ritual feast that forbade them to leave their territory. They would not arrive at Marathon until several days after the battle (VI.105–6).

Herodotus devotes just a few very short pages to the battle proper, which is why Plutarch reproaches him for "detract[ing] from the victory" (*Her. Mal.* 26✧ [= *Mor.* 862b]). In fact, the account is so condensed that major uncertainties remain about the forces involved. The figures offered by Herodotus are entirely suspect, since they concern the number of ships in the royal fleet: 600 (VI.95); and the number killed: 192 Athenians and 6,400 soldiers of Datis (VI.117). One of the most essential details concerns the absence of the Persian cavalry. Its presence in Datis's expeditionary force is beyond doubt (VI.48–95; cf. Pausanias I.32.7). An entry in the *Suda* (s.v. *Khōris hippeis*) indicates that the cavalry had been positioned separately. Shall we conclude from this that they had been instructed to take control of the road to Athens? It is difficult to say. It is no less difficult to understand how Datis could have passed over the factor that made every Achaemenid army superior, especially since Herodotus even states that the plain of Marathon had been chosen because there the cavalry could be deployed with ease.

It is true that the Achaemenid infantry was far from negligible. As was the custom, Datis placed his best soldiers, the Persians and Sacians, at the center of his formation (VI.113). Herodotus remarks that on the other side the Athenians "were the first Greeks, so far as I know, to charge at a run" (VI.112✧). This was in fact the only way to limit the devastating power of the Persian archers, even if some soldiers had to perish in the course of the assault. The Persians prevailed at the center but were penetrated at the wings. They were forced to reboard their ships. Datis attempted to sail quickly for the anchorage at Phalerum, but the Athenians had had the time to ready the city for defense. Datis did not persevere and set sail for Asia Minor. This surprising decision confirms the fact that at this time Darius did not intend to establish long-term dominion over Greece. Datis was simply charged with making a raid, destroying sanctuaries and houses, taking prisoners, and setting sail for the coasts of Asia Minor. In sum, from the Persian point of view, Marathon was nothing but a minor engagement that had no effect whatever on the

Aegean strategy defined by Darius. This was surely the version found in Achaemenid propaganda (cf. Dio Chrys. XI.148).

It is easy to understand why and how the Athenians transformed Marathon into a memorable victory. In later times, it acquired truly mythic force in the collective consciousness of the city. In 490, the victory of the citizen-hoplites signified the reinforcement of a democracy acquired recently and with difficulty; it also enhanced the town's political and military prestige in the eyes of Sparta and the Peloponnesian League. But it was viewed quite differently by the Persians. As has already been said, Darius had attained his fundamental objectives. At any rate, the repercussions of the victory do not seem to have spread beyond the local region. Certainly the Greeks of Asia Minor, who had barely survived a terrible repression, saw no sign of the weakening of Persian dominion in the battle of Marathon. On the contrary, they understood perfectly well that Darius's power had never been greater. The only hint of insubordination is mentioned in the article already cited in the *Suda*: the Athenians were supposedly kept abreast of Datis's tactical dispositions by Ionians in the Persian army. If this information is true, it obviously refers only to a small group acting in the utmost secrecy. Nothing is ever said about anti-Persian activities among the Ionian or Aeolian contingents that Datis brought with him (VI.98).

From Marathon to Memphis

According to Herodotus, Darius immediately drew up a new expedition, which he himself would head, against Greece. To this end, mobilization orders were sent everywhere, "and the whole continent was in uproar for a space of three years" (VII.1◇). It was then (486) that news of an Egyptian insurrection arrived at the court. Darius was preparing to put this insurrection down when he was seized by an illness, in November (VII.4; Ctesias §19). Unfortunately, we have no information on either the causes or the extent of this revolt (Ctesias has nothing to say about it). Herodotus's brief reference is at least a reminder that the Achaemenid history of this period cannot be reduced to the Greek problem. But it also confirms, to the despair of the historian, that in the eyes of Herodotus all that really counted was the Greek perspective on the Persian Wars.

Whatever the case, when Darius died, the Achaemenid Empire had achieved its greatest extent: from the Iaxartes to the Persian Gulf and the First Cataract, from the Danube to the Indus. At the same time that he was pursuing his conquests, the Great King was multiplying reforms and measures pertaining to the organization of Persian authority, both in the center and in the conquered countries.

PART TWO

The Great King

Chapter 5
Images of the World

1. The Builder-King

The Remodeling of Susa

Darius was anxious to exalt his new power and transmit its glorious testimony to posterity; this was expressed in intense building activity, and quite early on he and his advisers conceived the founding of new royal residences at Susa and Persepolis. The urban plan of Susa had undergone no change since Cyrus's conquest and retained the configuration that it had in the Elamite period. The archaeological evidence does not reveal a single irruption of Achaemenid culture until Darius's reign. Then we encounter a sudden change, with the indexes of Elamite culture disappearing suddenly. We can in fact observe a complete redoing of the city around great tells dubbed the "Acropolis," "Royal City," and "Apadana," which overhang the east bank of the Shaur by about 20 meters (fig. 9).

The reasons Darius chose Susa are given as follows by Strabo:

> The Persians and Cyrus, after mastering the Medes, saw that their native land was situated rather on the extremities of their empire (*ep'eskhatois*), and that Susa was farther in and nearer to Babylonia and the other tribes, and therefore established the royal seat of their empire at Susa. At the same time, also, they were pleased with the high standing of the city and with the fact that its territory bordered on Persis, and, better still, with the fact that it had never of itself achieved anything of importance, but always had been subject to others and accounted merely a part of a larger political organization, except, perhaps, in ancient times, in the times of the heroes. (XV.3.2◊)

This text attests above all to the paucity of information available to Strabo about both the chronology of the refounding of the city and the ancient history of Susa and Elam "since the time of the heroes." Only a Greek writer could consider the location of Persia peripheral in the new Empire. In fact, Strabo himself emphasizes (XV.3.3) that the Great Kings were not uninterested in Persian palaces (Pasargadae and Persepolis). Taken in historical context, this decision is better understood as the result of continuous relations between Elam and the high country of Anšan: the construction of the palace at Susa made the victory of the Persians and the unification of the two entities into a single entity evident to everyone. At the date when we think it was undertaken, the labors at Susa also bear witness to the refashioned unity of the Empire around Darius, restorer of the order that had been disrupted by the rebel lands.

The epigraphic record of Darius's activities as a builder is rich. The king appears as both the extender and the restorer of the preceding dynasties, which he does not name. He boasts of rebuilding constructions that had fallen into ruin, particularly fortifications:

> Darius the king says: by the grace of Ahura-Mazda, I completed numerous constructions that previously had been left unfinished. I saw the fortifications at Susa that had been previously constructed fall prey to age; I rebuilt them. These are (in fact) quite other fortifications that I myself have built. (*DSe* 001)

He insists above all on the profoundly novel character of his initiatives:

> At the location where this fortress was built, no other fortress had ever been built. By the grace of Ahura-Mazda, this fortress I built. And, since it was the plan of Ahura-Mazda and all the gods for this fortress to be built, I built it. And I completed it, good and solid, as if it were my own plan. (*DSe*)

In other inscriptions, he presents himself as the builder of a house (*bitu*) and a palace (*ekallu*). Darius's successors were quick to associate themselves with his work. Xerxes states that the gate—now called the Darius Gate—was conceived and erected in his father's time, as was another residence (*XSd*). Artaxerxes II rebuilt the Audience Hall (*apadana*) that was built by his great-great-grandfather Darius and destroyed by fire during the reign of his grandfather Artaxerxes I (A^2Sa).

It is quite difficult to date the beginning of the work precisely. In one of the inscriptions, Darius writes:

> Much of this evil that had been committed, I turned into good. The countries that fought each other, whose peoples killed each other, I fixed, by the grace of Ahura-Mazda, so that their peoples did not kill each other, and I restored each one to its place. And, faced with my decrees, they respected them, in such a way that the strong did not strike nor despoil the poor. (*DSe* 001)

It would be risky to conclude from this that the work began directly after the end of the third Elamite revolt, for Darius's phraseology is stereotypical: every good king boasts of reestablishing order and justice at the beginning of his reign.

At any rate, among the people who were pressed into service were the Ionians and the Carians, who transported Lebanese lumber from Babylon to Susa. If, as is generally thought, these Ionians and Carians represent the Asia Minor populations that were deported to Lower Babylonia and Elam after the Ionian revolt (493–492), the dating must be lowered considerably. But there already were Carians and Ionians in Babylonia before Darius! Herodotus mentions (III.140) that Darius was present at his palace in Susa at the beginning of his reign, which obviously proves nothing. For the sake of prudence, the chronological question must remain open. In any event, the work certainly lasted a very long time. We know, for example, that an interval of several years separated the laying of the foundations of Darius's palace and the foundations of the Apadana, because a comparison of the texts shows that Darius's father, Hystaspes, died in between the two events.

Even if all of the work and all of the building at Susa was not completed during the reign of Darius alone, it is nonetheless clear that the king and his counselors conceived the entire plan as a whole. The new town is organized on three terraces linked to one another. We can identify the palace (on the tell called the Apadana), the residential quarters (Royal City?), and the fortress (Acropolis). Strabo, citing an author from the time of Alexander, states that the city of Susa was 'without fortifications' (*ateikhistos* XV.3.2). The statement may seem a bit fanciful since Darius, as we have seen, boasts of restoring the city walls, building new ones, and "protecting Susa against its enemies." In reality, Darius's city walls do not, properly speaking, constitute a fortification. They are intermingled with the walls that support the various terraces. Nonetheless, the citadel itself occupied a position of strength when defense was required, as the resistance of 317 attests, when Xenophilus, who was in charge of both the citadel (*akra*) and the treasury guard (*thēsaurophylax* = **ganzabara*; Diodorus XIX.17.3; 18.1) defended against the troops of Antigonus.

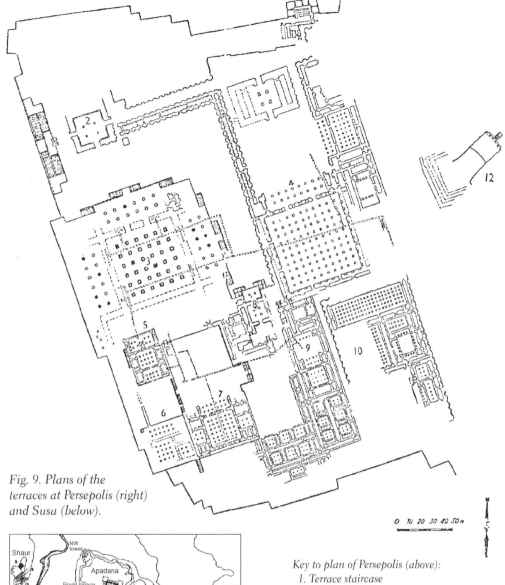

Fig. 9. Plans of the terraces at Persepolis (right) and Susa (below).

0 10 20 30 40 50 м

Susa

0   100 200 300 m

Key to plan of Persepolis (above):
1. Terrace staircase
2. Xerxes Gate
3. Apadana of Darius and Xerxes
4. Hall of One Hundred Columns
5. Tachara ('Palace') of Darius
6. Palace of Artaxerxes III
7. Hadiš ('Abode, Palace') of Xerxes
8. Tripylon
9. Harem (partly restored)
10. Treasury
11. Part of the wall (where the Elamite tablets were excavated)
12. Tomb of Artaxerxes II (or III?)

Immense labors were needed to establish an artificially level surface on which edifices could be built, 70 hectares in extent. Darius himself mentions this in referring to the construction of the palace on the Apadana tell:

> The earth was dug down to bedrock; when the earth was dug [and] the gravel was sufficient, there the gravel was piled up for 40 cubits and for 20 cubits. On the gravel I built the palace. (DSf)

Excavations carried out in the town confirm the existence of these construction methods. The Royal City was supported on a 10–12-meter-high glacis of unbaked brick, 20 m thick at the base. The platform of the palaces, with an area of about 12 hectares (or the equivalent of the terrace of Persepolis), is itself protected by a retaining wall about 15 m high. It was located to the west, overlooking the Shaur, and must have accumulated a veritable breakwater of river gravel that reached 18 m at the southwest corner, since more than a million cubic meters were needed to build this one platform. Some buildings, raised on a terrace of several additional meters of earth that was brought in, had to be provided with mighty foundations. This is especially true for the Darius Gate (fig. 38, p. 260). With a foundation plan of impressive dimensions (40 × 30 m), the gate reached a height of 12–13 m and was supported by stone columns more than 1 m in diameter. There must have been strong unbaked brick foundations, placed on bedrock and protected against erosion by gravel bulwarks. The gigantic character of the undertaking is also shown by the unbaked brick causeway that crossed the 15-meter-deep ravine between the Royal City and the Apadana terrace.

The Beginnings of Persepolis

It was also Darius who undertook the initial work leading to the construction of Persepolis. Before his time, as we have seen (p. 86), all of the building had been done on the plain. Darius decided to put up a new capital there by raising a monumental terrace that would cover 125,000 sq. m upon completion. This gigantic platform abutted the nearby mountain, Kuh-e Rahmat (Mount of Mercy). Four texts have been found on the retaining wall: two in Old Persian, one in Elamite, and one in Akkadian. The Elamite text of this inscription (DPf) refers directly to the planning for which Darius was responsible:

> I, Darius, the Great King, king of kings, king of countries, king on this earth, son of Hystaspes, the Achaemenid. And Darius the king says: "On this site where this fortress was built, previously no fortress had been built there. By the grace of Ahura-Mazda, this fortress, I constructed it according to the plan of Ahura-Mazda, all the gods [being] with him, [namely] that this fortress be built. And I built it, completed it, and made it beautiful and impervious, just as had been ordained of me." And Darius the king says: "I, may Ahura-Mazda protect me, all the gods [being] with him, and also this fortress, and also what was planned for this site. What the hostile man may think, may it not be recognized!"

It is not hard to verify that this statement is almost identical to one of Darius's inscriptions at Susa (DSf). In both cases, Darius boasts of building a fortress that did not previously exist and of having brought the work to completion. In both cases, the word *fortress* refers not to strictly military works but to high walls that bounded and supported the platforms on which he was going to begin to build monuments. Meanwhile, the existence of actual fortifications has been demonstrated archaeologically at Persepolis at least; they must be what Diodorus is referring to, at least approximately (XVII.61.1).

The chronology is no less problematic at Persepolis than at Susa. Several monuments can be securely dated to the reign of Darius. These include the treasury, where a portion of a clay archive has been recovered: the first Elamite tablet is dated 492, but the sole Akkadian tablet of the group is dated to year 20 of Darius (30 December 502; PT 85). Perhaps the (first stage of the) treasury was the first building completed on the site. One of the other constructions was the palace of Darius, so called because several Darius and Xerxes inscriptions attest that the work was begun by Darius and completed by his son. This was also true of the audience court, the Apadana. In fact, foundation deposits, buried in the southeast and northeast corners, have been found there. These deposits contain a series of coins (croesids and various Greek pieces) and silver and gold plaques with the following texts:

> Darius the Great King, King of Kings, King of countries, son of Hystaspes, an Achaemenian. Saith Darius the King: This is the kingdom which I hold, from the Sacians who are beyond Sogdiana, thence unto Ethiopia;, from Sind, thence unto Sardis—which Ahuramazda the greatest of the gods bestowed upon me. Me may Ahuramazda protect, and my house. (DPh✧)

If we accept a nearby building, the Tripylon, as belonging to the same overall plan, we must also credit it to Darius; but the absence of any inscription means that caution must be observed. It appears as though several buildings were conceived during the reign of Darius but constructed or completed only by his successor; this is undoubtedly true of the friezes of the Apadana.

It is much more complex to determine the date of the various monuments. The only attestation of absolute chronology is furnished by the archives called the Fortification tablets, which are precisely dated to 509–494 and provide evidence that by 509 at the latest Persepolis was functioning, though it was still under construction (and it remained under construction until the end of the Achaemenid period). The foundation tablets of the Apadana, on the other hand, still stimulate varying interpretations due to the dates assigned to the coins found with them and the significance of Darius's statement found on them. If we agree that Darius wished to describe his kingdom metaphorically by enumerating the four geographic extremities that it had reached at that point, then we must agree that his statement refers to a date before the Scythian expedition (513), since that is when Sardis constituted the western frontier. Arguing from another standpoint, the way is open for a lower date, around 500, since the Apadana (audience court) of Persepolis is not identical in conception to the one at Susa. In particular, it is raised on a stepped platform, which is absent at Susa. Furthermore, because of uncertainties bearing on the rhythm of the work at Susa, it is not out of the question that the beginning of the first work carried out at Persepolis was almost contemporary with that at Susa. In any case, the chronological discrepancy between the two projects cannot have been very great. This assumes on the one hand that Darius decided to mobilize considerable labor and materials and on the other that construction on both sites was included in an overall plan for reworking the royal residences. This would have made it clear to all eyes that the advent of the king represented, pure and simple, a refounding of the kingdom and the Empire.

Work Carried Out in the Other Capitals

The promotion of Susa and Persepolis did not entail the disappearance of the earlier capitals of Pasargadae, Babylon, and Ecbatana. But we are ill informed about Darius's building activities in those locations. Whatever the chronological uncertainties that continue to burden some of the monuments at Pasargadae, Darius's participation is highly likely. The Persepolis tablets, moreover, mention the existence of a treasury at Pasargadae and the activity of groups of workers (*kurtaš*). We also know that the king had a new palace built at Babylon. As for Ecbatana, Darius lived there for several months in 521. An inscription has been found there whose text and medium (silver and gold plaques) are identical to the foundation plaques discovered under the Persepolis Apadana (*DH* = *DPh*). Two inscriptions of Artaxerxes II are also interesting (*A²Ha* and *A²Hb*): the second records the erection of an *apadana* on the site. Should we conclude from this that Darius had already built this kind of hypostyle hall in the Mede capital, which Artaxerxes II restored? Note as well that, according to Diodorus (II.13.6–8◇), Ctesias attributed some plans at Ecbatana to the mythic queen Semiramis:

> She built in it an expensive palace and in every other way gave rather exceptional attention to the region. For since the city had no water supply and there was no spring in the vicinity, she made the whole of it well watered by bringing to it with much hardship and expense an abundance of the purest water. For at a distance from Ecbatana of about twelve stades is a mountain, which is called Orontes and is unusual for its ruggedness and enormous height. . . . She made a cutting through the base of this mountain. The tunnel was fifteen feet wide and forty feet high; and through it she brought in the river which flowed from the lake, and filled and the city with water.

It is clear that numerous works attributed to Semiramis in fact belong to the Achaemenids, such as the plans for the plain and the mountain at Behistun described in the same chapter (II.13.1–2). Since we know that Ecbatana/Hamadan had always been supplied with water via a network of *qanat*s and that Polybius (X.28) refers to Achaemenid activity in this area, it is tempting to imagine that one of the Achaemenid kings, perhaps Darius, was the initiator. But this is purely hypothetical.

The Royal Tomb of Naqš-i Rustam

The efforts put into all of this are all the more remarkable because Darius was simultaneously working on a site near Persepolis, Naqš-i Rustam. It was doubtless at the beginning of his reign that Darius decided to dig a tomb in the rock some 6 km from Persepolis. He chose for this purpose a 64-m-high cliff. The floor of the tomb is 15 m above the ground, and its façade rises more than 22 m more. He removed a vast amount of rock in the process of excavating the tomb, hollowing out a vestibule from which three vaulted chambers opened, each containing three cists, all excavated from the rock. The façade proper is cross-shaped and is organized in three superposed registers (see fig. 16, p. 211). The lowest register is not sculpted. The middle register has four engaged columns, with a door opening between the two middle columns. It is a copy of the royal palace. Above, borne by representatives of thirty subjugated peoples, the king is shown on a three-step pedestal facing a fire altar, with the entire scene surmounted by divine representations. Other persons—guards (the Immortals?) and aristocrats—are shown; some, unarmed, may metaphorically represent the court's official mourning; others are armed, two of whom are identified by an inscription as Gobryas and Aspathines (*DNc–d*).

Darius's tomb is very clearly identified by two royal inscriptions (*DNa* and *DNb*). His successors followed his example and had other rock-cut tombs prepared nearby, each with its own special arrangements but without altering the original plan a great deal. In the absence of inscriptions, we assume that these belong to Xerxes, Artaxerxes I, and Darius II. On the other hand, beginning with Artaxerxes II, the kings preferred to have their tombs just outside Persepolis, as Diodorus says: "At the eastern side of the terrace at a distance of four plethra [120 m] is the so-called royal hill in which were the graves of the kings. This was a smooth rock hollowed out into many chambers in which were the sepulchres of the dead kings" (XVII.71.7✧). Diodorus also stresses the technological difficulties of the undertaking: "These have no other access but receive the sarcophagi of the dead which are lifted by certain mechanical hoists." This text resembles what Ctesias wrote of Darius's tomb:

> Darius had a funerary monument built on the twin-peaked mountain; it was built there. The desire to visit it having seized him, the Chaldeans and his relatives prevented it; but those close to him wished to climb up there; when the priests who were hauling them to the top saw them, fear caused them to let go of the cables; the king's associates fell and were killed. Darius was deeply affected and had the haulers decapitated, all forty of them. (*Persica* §15)

It is possible, finally, that the site, like Behistun, was then enhanced by the construction of a paradise—if we accept the identification of Naqš-i Rustam with the site *Nupistaš* ['place of writing'] known from some Persepolis tablets.

Royal Art and Imperial Towns

To the historian, the attraction of Darius's building projects (executed and completed by his successors, especially Xerxes) is not limited to architectural structures and urban planning. As the inscriptions and foundation deposits so clearly indicate, the Great King intended first and foremost to publicize the image of his sovereign, unlimited authority. For this purpose, texts and artistic representations repeatedly articulate the organization of the palace and its residences. The artists and craftsmen who worked on the construction had no artistic freedom: they were required to follow rigorously the precise specifications provided by the Great King's counselors, and obvious borrowing from the Assyro-Babylonian, Elamite, and Egyptian repertoires was fused into a new art, a royal art par excellence. Royal art reflects a program that leaves no room for improvisation. This observation also holds for the themes imposed on the seals and stamps of Persepolis and obviously for those used to exalt the royal figure on the coins. In them, the Great King is seen in the two most obvious manifestations of his power: as king and as master of the peoples of the Empire. At Susa, as at Persepolis or Naqš-i Rustam, written proclamations and artistic representations were meant to project a timeless image of the power of the Great King and of Persian power, through an exaltation of the virtues of the king and of Persian dominion over the peoples of the Empire. From this point of view, we must emphasize the uniqueness of the Behistun monument, which constitutes the sole time-bound representation of Darius's power as restorer of dynastic and imperial order, in a precisely demarcated period, against enemies who are also specifically named. Even at Behistun (relief and inscriptions), however, the—as it were—transcendental aspect of the Great King's power is significant. With emphasis on the subjugation of the conquered peoples, many reliefs (peoples bearing the throne, peoples bearing gifts, lists of countries, etc.) very clearly indicate that the new capitals were conceived as localities that gave expression both to Persian power and to the *Pax persica*. Through his virtues, acquired through the privileged protection of Ahura-Mazda, the Great King ensured the idealized unity of one world but at the same time celebrated its ethnocultural and geographic diversity. It is thus merely for convenience that in this book we shall distinguish the representations of imperial power from the representations of royal majesty (chap. 6), though it is clear that the two components overlap and support each other.

2. *The King and His Peoples: Inscriptions and Iconography*

The "Foundation Charters" of Susa

Numerous foundation documents have been discovered at Susa, some fragmentary and some complete. Some were meant to be buried as "foundation charters," and others were meant to be seen by visitors. By way of example, here are Darius's statements as they appear on one of the most recently discovered examples:

> The palace at Susa, it is I who made it; its materials were brought from afar. . . . That which [was made] of molded bricks, people who [were] Babylonians made it themselves. And the beams which [were] cedar, them, from a mountain call[ed] Lebanon, from down there they were brought. The people who [were] Assyrians [Syrians], themselves transported them as far as Babylon, and from Babylon the Carians and Ionians transported them to Susa. And the *yaka* wood of Gandhara was brought, and also of Carmania. And gold from Sardis and Bactria was brought, that which was worked here. And the precious stones which [were] lapis lazuli and also carnelian, which were worked here, from Sogdiana were brought. And the precious stones which [were] turquoise, them, from Chorasmia, were brought [them] which were worked here. And the silver and ebony, them, from Egypt were brought. And the decorative elements with which the terrace was ornamented, them, from Ionia were brought. And the ivory which was worked here, it, from Ethiopia and India and Arachosia were brought. And the stone columns which were worked here, from a town village called Apitaruš, from down there in Elam, were brought. The craftsmen who worked the stone, they, [were] Ionians and Sardians. And the goldchasers who worked this gold, they [were] Sardians and Egyptians. And the men who made the baked bricks, they [were] Babylonians. And the men who decorated the terrace, they [were] Medes and Egyptians. Darius, king, says: "By the grace of Ahura-Mazda, at Susa, much excellent [work] was ordained, much excellent [work] was done. Me, may Ahura-Mazda protect me, me and my country as well." (*DSz*)

The text thus lists sixteen peoples and countries that furnished raw materials (or labor) and eight whose talents as craftsmen were used in the work. Some are found in both groups (Babylonians, Sardians, Egyptians, Ionians); some are only in the first (Syrians, Carians, and Ionians), some only in the second (Medes). Some count twice among the specialists: Sardians worked stone and wood; Egyptians, wood and the palace reliefs; Medes, gold and palace reliefs. Lastly, some were common laborers: Babylonians for foundation work; Syrians, Ionians, and Carians for transporting lumber from Lebanon to Babylon, then to Susa. But the information in the various texts does not always agree. Another Akkadian version (*DSaa*), even though it was buried at the same time as the Elamite version just cited (*DSz*), in its first section simply enumerates the materials used, without specifying their place of origin. A second section gives a list of the peoples "who brought materials for decorating the palace." No less than 23 countries, including Persia, are named.

The Country Lists

In addition to the Susa documents, we also have inscriptions and sculptures that Darius and his successors had carved on their tomb façades, their palace walls, and even on Egyptian stelas and a statue of Darius at Susa. These documents allow us to reconstruct to some extent the idealized image of the world as the masters of the Empire wished it recorded. First of all are what are usually called *empire lists*; they are included in a series of royal inscriptions, most of them dated to Darius's reign: the Behistun inscription

(DB); one of the four inscriptions placed on the south façade of the Persepolis terrace (DPe); one of the two inscriptions on the king's tomb at Naqš-i Rustam (DNa); a Susa inscription (DSe); one of the versions of the Susa foundation charter (DSaa); and finally, a Xerxes inscription (XPh). These lists enumerate the countries that were known to be subjects of the Great King, and they vary in number and order. Here are the countries listed in these six inscriptions:

DB	DPe	DSe	DNa	DSaa	XPh
Persia	Elam	Media	Media	Persia	Media
Elam	Media	Elam	Elam	Elam	Elam
Babylonia	Babylonia	Babylonia	Parthia	Media	Arachosia
Assyria	Arabia	Aria	Aria	Babylonia	Armenia
Arabia	Assyria	Bactria	Bactria	Assyria	Drangiana
Egypt	Egypt	Sogdiana	Sogdiana	Arabia	Parthia
Sealand	Armenia	Chorasmia	Chorasmia	Egypt	Aria
Sardis	Cappadocia	Drangiana	Drangiana	Sealand	Bactria
Ionia	Sardis	Arachosia	Arachosia	Sardis	Sogdiana
Media	Ionia	Sattagydia	Sattagydia	Ionia	Chorasmia
Armenia	Ionians[a]	Makran	Gandhara	Armenia	Babylonia
Cappadocia	Sagartia	Gandhara	Induš	Cappadocia	Assyria
Parthia	Parthia	Induš	Saka H.[c]	Parthia	Sattagydia
Drangiana	Drangiana	Saka H.	Saka T.[d]	Drangiana	Sardis
Aria	Aria	Saka T.	Babylonia	Aria	Egypt
Chorasmia	Bactria	Babylonia	Assyria	Chorasmia	Ionians
Bactria	Sogdiana	Assyria	Arabia	Bactra	Sealand
Sogdiana	Chorasmia	Arabia	Egypt	Sogdiana	Across the sea
Gandhara	Sattagydia	Egypt	Armenia	Gandhara	Makans
Saka	Arachosia	Armenia	Cappadocia	Saka	Arabia
Sattagydia	Induš	Cappadocia	Sardis	Sattagydia	Gandhara
Arachosia	Gandhara	Sardis	Ionia	Arachosia	Induš
Makran	Saka	Ionia	Saka E.[e]	Quadia	Cappadocia
	Makran	Saka E.	Thrace		Dahae
		Thracians	Ionians P.[f]		Saka H.
		Ionians E.[b]	Libya		Saka T.
		Carians	Ethiopia		Skudra
			Makran		Akaufakans
			Carians		Libyans
					Carians
					Ethiopians
23	24	27	29	23	31

a. What the text says exactly is: "The Ionians of the plain and the sea and the lands beyond the sea."
b. European Ionians.
c. *Saka haumavarga*, i.e., the haoma-drinking Saka.
d. *Saka tigraxaudā*, i.e., the pointed-hat Saka—an expression corresponding to Herodotus's *Orthokorybantes*.
e. European Scythians.
f. Ionians who wear/bear the "Petasus" (a broad-brimmed, low-crowned hat).

The People Bearing Thrones

The subject peoples are represented in high-relief sculptures at many Achaemenid sites. They are found primarily as throne-bearers, numbering 30 in all on the royal tombs (Naqš-i Rustam and Persepolis) and at Persepolis itself. They are placed in three rows on each jamb of the east gate of the Tripylon, as well as on the south gate of the Hall of One Hundred Columns (28 figures). On two of the royal tombs (Darius I and Artaxerxes II

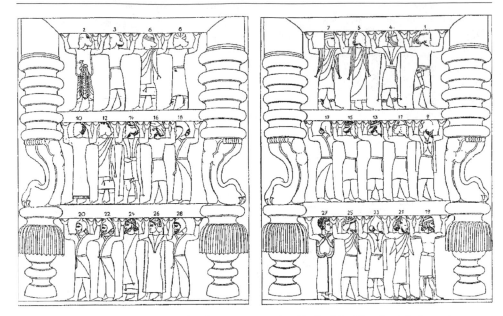

Fig. 10. Peoples bearing the throne (Persepolis: Hall of the Hundred Columns).

[?]), each person is named ("Behold the Elamite," etc.), which considerably facilitates the identification of figures on the other sculptures. On the royal tombs, each person is one meter tall; elsewhere, 40 cm. Each one represents one of the subject peoples. Their arms are raised above their heads, palms up, and together they support the throne on which the king is seated.

A similar presentation of subject peoples is found in several Egyptian documents, the stelas of the Suez Canal (dug by Darius), and the statue of Darius placed at the entrance to a great gate at Susa (the Darius Gate) but carved in Egypt. They number 24 on the rectangular base of the statue (fig. 19, p. 216) and also on the stelas and are placed in two registers in both cases. They are shown in the Egyptian style, each above a crenellated oval containing each one's name in hieroglyphs. They are kneeling, hands above the head, palms up, supporting not the royal throne but the land of the Empire.

The People Bearing Gifts

Finally, we come to the most famous sculptures—the so-called tribute friezes (fig. 12). Two are found on the staircases of the Apadana (Audience Hall): on the west panel of the north staircase and on the south panel of the west staircase. They probably were created (or at any rate completed) under the reign of Xerxes. The peoples—amounting to 23—are represented as delegations. The beginning of the staircase of Artaxerxes I's palace was also decorated with delegations of peoples, in the same form, but numbering 30. The delegations are composed of varying numbers of members. The delegates are preceded by an usher in Persian garb who holds the hand of the leader of the delegation and guides him toward the king, who is enthroned at the center of the composition, in the royal audience rite. The problem of identifying the delegations remains difficult; in the absence of inscriptions, there are various solutions that are generally based on the dress and the objects and animal gifts of the people, as well as on comparison with other depictions. But these comparisons are not always conclusive, so that numerous uncertainties remain. The chart below is one possible reconstruction of the 23 delegations shown on the face of the west panel.

	People	*Qty*	*Gifts*	*Animals*
1	Medes	6	Garments, vessels	Horses
2	Elamites	6	Bows, 1 dagger	Lioness, lion cubs
3	Armenians	5	Garments	
4	Aryans	5	Garments, vessels	1 camel
5	Babylonians	6	Garments, vessels	1 buffalo
6	Lydians	6	Vessel, bracelets, 2-horse chariot	
7	Arachosians	5	Vessel, skin	1 camel
8	Assyrians	7	Vessel, waterskins	2 rams
9	Cappadocians	5	Robes	1 horse
10	Egyptians	6	Garments	1 bull
11	Saka	6	Garments, bracelets	1 horse
12	Ionians	8	Garments, bales, vessel	
13	Bactrians	5	Vessel, skin	1 camel
14	Gandharans	6	Shield, pike	1 buffalo
15	Parthians	5	Vessel	1 camel
16	Sagartians	6	Garments	1 horse
17	Saka	6	Bracelets, axes, daggers	1 horse
18	Indians	6	Axes, spices(?)	1 zebra(?)
19	Scythians	4	Pikes, shields	1 horse
20	Arabs	4	Robes	1 dromedary
21	Drangians	4	Pikes, shield	1 bull
22	Lydians	3	2-horse chariot	1 ibex
23	Nubians	3	Elephant tusks	1 giraffe(?)

3. An Idealized Image of Space and Imperial Power

Space and Administration

The interpretation of these lists and sculptures continues to pose many problems that have arisen and continue to arise in the various analyses. From one list to the next, the number, position, and even sometimes the name vary noticeably. The shortest list, which is also the oldest, from Behistun, includes 23 names: the others have 24 (*DPe*), 27 (*DSe*), and 29 (*DNa*). The longest list dates to the reign of Xerxes (*XPh*). Comparison also shows that the order is not consistent. The same is true for iconographic depictions: 24 peoples on the Egyptian materials, 28 or 30 throne-bearers, 23 and 30 gift/tribute-bearers.

It is not easy to explain the presence or absence of this or that people from one list to another. We might suppose, self-evidently, that the oldest list is the shortest because the imperial conquests had not yet been completed. Thus, it is not surprising that the Hinduš is not found there, since it was conquered several years after the completion of the monument at Behistun. Nonetheless it seems dangerous to employ this sort of explanation automatically, especially since many lists are not precisely dated, and when they are, it is frequently by circular reasoning. Variations in the imperial realm, for example, cannot explain why Persia is missing in four of the five lists or why the country of Ākaufaciyā appears only in the Xerxes list (*XPh*). Similarly, in one of the Akkadian versions of the Susa Charter (*DSaa*) neither India nor Nubia is listed, while other versions attest—or rather allege—that ivory was brought from these countries. In addition, Thrace (Skudra), Libya, the Carians (Karkā), and the European Scythians are also missing. These lists thus do not appear to have been intended as a realistic picture of the state of the imperial possessions at the moment of the foundation of the palace at Susa. It seems as though the variations are particularly striking for regions in the west (Aegean coasts) and north (Central Asia). For example, the nomadic (or seminomadic) peoples of the north are simply called Saka in *DB* and *DPe*; in *DSe* and *DNa*, they are divided into two groups: Saka Haumavarga ('haoma-drinker'?) and Saka Tigraxaudā ('pointed-hat-wearers'), whose name corresponds most closely to Herodotus's *Orthokorybantes* (III.192). Three groups are found in *XPh*, where the Dahae appear, who we know independently are part of the family of Scythians of Central Asia, that is, the Saka. The reduced number of names of peoples from western regions in the same Xerxes inscription does not appear explicable by anything other than territorial advances and retreats.

Fig. 11. Lower register of throne-bearing peoples on the royal tombs.

The same goes for the reliefs, where the problem of identification becomes extremely complicated. The criterion of discrimination by clothing is not always decisive. The composition of certain reliefs seems to depend more on spatial constraints and aesthetic principles than on territorial or administrative realities. The same is true for the number of delegates on the friezes of tribute/gift-bearers. Careful examination shows that the number cannot be taken as a criterion, for example, of the relative importance ascribed to each of the peoples depicted. The number of delegates, in fact, is smaller when the animal brought by the subjects is bigger. The largest delegations (no. 1 with 9 people; no. 12 with 8 people) do not bring an animal as a gift, but the delegations (4, 7, 13, 21) accompanied by a "Bactrian" camel have only 4 members, and the number is reduced to 3 for the Arabs, who bring a dromedary, and for the Nubians, who are accompanied by an unidentified animal (giraffe? okapi?). The case of the Medes makes this analysis clear: on the east staircase of the Apadana, 9 Medes are shown, in contrast with the 6 appearing on the north staircase, quite simply because in the latter case they are accompanied by a stallion, which is absent from the east relief. On the Egyptian stelas, neither the Yaunas nor the Gandharans, who are found in all the lists, are depicted (there was no room to show all the peoples). This is also true for the throne-bearers (fig. 11). Two of them (nos. 29 and 30: Karkā and Maciyā) had to be sculpted outside the field marked out by the legs of the royal throne: one to the right (no. 30) and the other to the left (no. 29).

It must thus be recognized that neither the lists nor the representations
constitute administrative catalogs yielding a realistic image of the imperial
realm. It was not administrative districts
that the Great Kings wanted to represent. The word used in the inscriptions
is *dahyu* 'people'. The kings did not intend to give a list that was either complete or exact. The inscribed lists are
nothing but a selection of subject countries. Darius and his successors are neither archivists nor historians. What
they intend to leave to posterity is not
administrative data. The inscriptions
accompanying the reliefs show instead
that what they wished to transmit to
their contemporaries was a politico-
ideological message.

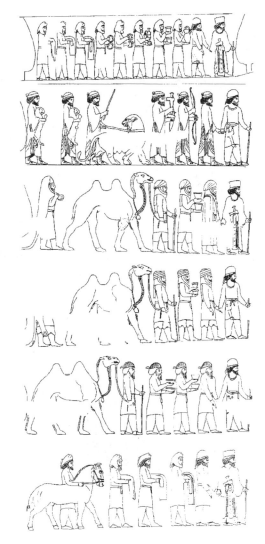

Fig. 12. Some gift-bearing peoples:
Medes, Elamites, Parthians,
Aryans, Bactrians, Sagartians.

Subjugation and Collaboration

Given the perspective that the reliefs
and inscriptions are concerned with
political and ideological issues, the different versions of the Susa inscriptions (*DSz* [Elam.]; *DSf* [OPers., Bab.,
Elam.]) provide considerable clarification. More than a statistical inventory of
the economic resources of the Empire,
they are amenable to what might be
called "images of the world," by means
of which the Great Kings, especially
Darius, intended to impose the idea of
the unbounded nature of their authority
over territories and populations. Here,
for example, is how Darius summarizes
the work in one of the Akkadian inscriptions from Susa (*DSaa*):

> These are the materials that were used for this palace. . . . These are the countries that
> provided the materials for the decoration of this palace. . . . Darius the king says: "By the
> grace of Ahura-Mazda, the materials of this palace were brought from afar and I made the
> arrangements."

In this sort of text, it is the detail "from afar" that is the key to the logic of the discourse. The royal inscriptions from Susa had the principal function of exalting the mobilization into the king's service of the production and manpower of an Empire that
recognized and defined itself through work explicitly called communal and integrative.

These documents eloquently attest to the royal desire to depict every country and every people of the Empire united in harmonious cooperation organized by and surrounding the king. In the enumeration, the far corners of the Empire are recognized: Sardis, Sogdiana, the Indus, and Nubia. Every region is represented: the center (Elam, Babylonia), the far west (Sardis, Ionians), the north (Bactria, Sogdiana, Chorasmia), the east (Carmania, Gandhara, Indus), the west-southwest (Syria, Egypt, Nubia); and each of them contributed its building-stone to the edifice, whose construction was decreed by Darius and realized with the aid of Ahura-Mazda. The same sort of statement is found at Persepolis: "These are the countries that built this, which are gathered here" (*DPg*). Despite the profoundly ideological character of these statements, a realistic component can also be recognized in them. It is in fact beyond doubt that laborers from many countries were gathered at Susa, as they had been at Persepolis. It took thousands of men several years to complete such gigantic projects.

A related idea may be found in the depictions of peoples as throne-bearers, bearers of the soil of the Empire, or gift-bearers. But in these cases the accent is placed more on political subjugation and imposition of tribute than on collaboration. At Naqš-i Rustam, Darius addresses those who contemplate the relief carved on his tomb thus:

> If now thou shalt think that "How many are the countries which King Darius held?" look at the sculptures (of those) who bear the throne, then shalt thou know, then shall it become known to thee: the spear of a Persian man has gone forth far; then shall it become known to thee: a Persian man has delivered battle far indeed from Persia. (*DNa* §4✧)

The relation between military conquest and imperial dominion is just as explicit in the message carved on the pleats of the statue of Darius at Susa: "Behold the stone statue that Darius ordered made in Egypt so that whoever sees it in the future may know that the Persian holds Egypt" (*DSab*). This is also the sense of the statements that open the country lists: "These are the countries which came unto me; by the favor of Ahuramazda I was king of them." Darius ends with these words: "These are the countries which came unto me; by the favor of Ahuramazda they were my subjects (*bandaka*); They bore tribute (*bāji*) to me; what was said unto them by me either by night or by day, that was done" (*DB* §7✧). The formula used by Xerxes (*XPh*✧) is nearly identical: "By the favor of Ahuramazda these are the countries of which I was king outside of Persia; I ruled over them; they bore tribute to me; what was said to them by me, that they did; my law (*dāta*)—that held them firm."

The Empire and the Known World: Representations and Realities

We have seen that all of the royal statements are organized around the phrase "from afar": the Persians conquered "from afar," and the peoples who worked on Susa came "from afar." This phrase all by itself expresses the immensity of the space conquered and controlled by the Great King and the Persians. It is also present in the royal titulature. Darius I appears as "King in this great earth far and wide" (*DNa*✧). But here it is but one element among several: "king of the multitude, only master of the multitude, I am Darius the Great King, King of Kings, King of countries containing all kinds of men" (*DNa*✧); he is also "King of many countries" (*DPe*✧). Here is how this same Darius defined his territorial authority on the foundation tablets of the Apadana at Persepolis: "This is the kingdom which I hold, from the Scythians [Saka] who are beyond Sogdiana, thence unto Ethiopia [Cush]; from Sind, thence unto Sardis" (*DPh*✧).

This sort of presentation is found in several Classical texts. Strabo considers Cyra on the Iaxartes (Syr Darya) to be the farthest point of Persian dominion in Central Asia (XI.11.4: *horion tēs Persón arkhēs*). For Herodotus, Colchis plays the same role in the direction of the Caucasus (III.97). And, among the frontier countries of the Achaemenid world (the *eskhatiai*) where deportees were sent, the Greek authors regularly list Bactria, India, Armenia, and the Persian Gulf. According to the author of the *De Mundo* (398a 25◊), the Asian Empire was "bounded on the west by the Hellespont and on the east by the Indus." From a more Aegeo-centric point of view, Xenophon describes Cyrus's Empire in this way: "Its borders were to the east the Red Sea [Persian Gulf], to the north the Pontus Euxinus, to the west Cyprus and Egypt, and to the south Ethiopia" (*Cyr.* VIII.8.1 = VIII.6.21). Elsewhere, Xenophon attributes the following statement to Cyrus the Younger: "Well, gentlemen, my father's realm extends toward the south to a region where men cannot dwell by reason of the heat, and to the north to a region where they cannot dwell by reason of the cold" (*Anab.* I.7.6◊). This is an explanation often given by Xenophon; in another work, he repeats it to convince his fellow citizens of the excellence of the "central" position of Athens, because of its equidistance between the land of too-hot and the land of too-cold (*Revenus* I.6–8). Labeling the far reaches of the earth by temperature extremes is not exclusively Greek, considering that (as Darius writes) he is also "king over this vast land, in which there are many countries: Persia, Media, and the other countries with other languages, mountains, and plains, from this side of the Bitter River and from the other side of the Bitter River, from this side of the parched land and from the other side of the parched land" (*DPg*). These titulatures stress the immensity of the imperial space and also the ethnic, cultural, and linguistic diversity of the peoples subject to the "king of the countries." At any rate, does not Xenophon stress that Cyrus "ruled over these nations even though they did not speak the same language as he, nor one nation the same as another" (*Cyr.* I.1.5◊)? Did not Darius himself, at Behistun, order that his declaration be publicized in the languages of his peoples (*DB* §70)?

All of these texts are also interesting for the closed representation they give of the Achaemenid Empire, which was bounded by "frontiers." At first sight, this concept seems to contradict the frequently advanced hypothesis that the Great Kings justified their conquests by the affirmation of universal and infinite dominion. In reality, what Darius calls the land (*būmi*)—what the Greeks call *arkhē* '[territorial] dominion' and what we ourselves call the Empire—is notionally merged with the frontiers of the known world: the Empire represents the totality of lands and peoples. This is precisely the reality expressed by Dino, who writes: "The Persian kings had water fetched from the Nile and the Danube, which they laid up in their treasuries as a sort of testimony of the greatness of their power (*arkhē*) and universal empire" (*to kyrieuein hapantōn*; Plutarch, *Alex.* 36.4◊). This concept does not imply that the Great Kings were unaware of the countries located outside of the jurisdiction of their territorial dominion. The attempted circumnavigation of Africa attributed to the Persian Sataspes by Herodotus suggests that they were fully aware of them (IV.43). But here we are in the realm of appearances, whose logic requires that the unconquered countries be considered not to belong to the inhabited world (*oikoumenē*); they are relegated to nonexistence, beyond the "parched lands" and the "Bitter River."

Recognition of the homology between the "frontiers" of the Empire and the edges of the known world allows us to understand that the country lists are not totally devoid of rationality. While the order of enumeration varies from one list to the next, nonetheless the countries are clearly named according to geographical groupings. Taking the Behistun inscription as an example, we can distingish the following subgroups:

A. Center of the Empire (Persia, Elam)
B. South–Southeast Axis (Babylonia, Assyria, Arabia, Egypt)
C. West–East Axis (Those of the Sea, Sardis, Ionia, Media, Armenia, Cappadocia)
D. Center–East Axis (Parthia, Drangiana, Aria, Chorasmia, Bactria, Sogdiana)
E. Southeast–West Axis (Gandhara, Scythia, Sattagydia, Arachosia, Makran)

A closed world, the world of the royal inscriptions was a circular world. To the north, the Saka and Scythian peoples constituted a semicircle from east to west; similarly, to the south, the Libya–Ethiopia–Makran–Karkā [deported Carians at the source of the Persian Gulf] group (attested in *DNa*) form another semicircle. These political representations of the imperial realm are perhaps also integrated into Iranian religious concepts. In *Yasht* 10 of the *Avesta* (Hymn to Mithra), the world watched over by Mithra is bordered by a river to the west and a river to the east. There is also an allusion to the River Ranha, which borders the world. The Iranian world can be diagrammed as a Greek cross in a circle, which is traced by the Ranha.

Center and Periphery: "Aryan of Aryan Stock"

At the same time, this world was organized around a center. In most of the inscriptions, it includes Persia, Media, and Elam (not always listed in the same order), that is, the countries where the sedentary centers of Achaemenid power were located: Pasargadae, Persepolis, Ecbatana, and Susa. These regions are the origins of the axes that radiate in all directions, like the royal roads that link the center to the periphery, as Xenophon puts it: "The tribes that [Cyrus] brought into subjection to himself were so many that it is a difficult matter even to travel to them all, in whatever direction one begins one's journey from the palace (*basileia*), whether toward the east or west, toward the north or the south" (*Cyr.* I.1.15◇).

Even within this group, the subgroup Persia–Media, so often named by the Great Kings, occupies a special place. Darius refers to "this vast land, in which there are many countries — Persia, Media, and the other countries with other languages" (*DPg*). This statement indicates that the pair Persia–Media is bound not only by a common history but also by the closeness of their ethnocultural and linguistic links. This is exactly what the use of the word "Aryan" (*arya*) means in several royal inscriptions and three specific contexts: Darius and Xerxes are presented as 'Aryan[s] of Aryan stock' (*arya arya chiça*; *DNa*, *DSe*, *XPh*); at Behistun, Darius issues an order "to copy onto tablet and parchment the text that already exists in Aryan" (*DB* §70); finally, the Elamite version of Behistun describes Ahura-Mazda twice as 'the god of the Aryans' (*nap harriyanam*; *DB* Elam. §§62–63). Thus the word *arya* refers to a cultural, religious, and linguistic entity.

The word *arya* has a long history that goes back to the origins of what we call the Indo-Iranian peoples, whose common origins are well evidenced by the often-underscored similarities between the *Avesta* and the *Rig-Veda*. From this common trunk (reconstructed solely on linguistic grounds) the so-called Iranian peoples descended. At any rate, regarding the Medes, Herodotus recalls that they "were once universally known as Arians" (*Ariaoi*; VII.62◇). The hellenistic geographers themselves defined a geographic entity they called *Ariana*, which according to Strabo included the peoples of the Iranian Plateau, "further extended to a part of Persia and of Media" (XV.2.8◊). Strabo also describes its unity according to a linguistic measure: "For these speak approximately the same language, with but slight variations (*homoglōttoi para mikron*)." This statement highlights both the linguistic unity and the diversity of dialects, which are well known from philological investigations.

What is the meaning of this usage by Darius and Xerxes? We know that in the Sassanian period King Shapur bore the title *Shahan Shah Eran*, tranposed into Greek in the form *Basileus Basileōn Arianōn*, that is, 'king of the kings of the Aryans [Iranians]'. In the Achaemenid period, however, there is no trace of an Iranian political unity symbolized by the word *Iran*. Of course, the Iranian countries always occupied a special position in the Empire. It was they, for example, that constituted the vanguard of the great Achaemenid armies. Quintus Curtius described the situation in 330: these countries represent a region "which in arms and men, as well as in extent of territory is second to none among those nations; it occupies a third part of Asia, and the number of its men of military age equalled the armies which Darius [III] had lost" (V.10.3◊). Referring in all probability to the Iranian peoples, he adds: "In these nations, the majesty of their kings is extraordinary; in response to his mere name the barbarians assemble, and veneration for his former fortune attends him even in adversity" (§2◊). These very general statements do not imply that from Bactria to Persia the populations believed themselves to belong to a single political entity. But the structure of some country lists under Darius (DNa; DSe), and more so under Xerxes (XPh), separates the Iranian countries (some of them, at least) and places Media at the top.

The Great Kings use the word *arya* to define the power of a superior population. Implicitly, they are characterized by opposition to non-Iranians. Indeed, the word 'non-Iranian' itself (*anairya*)—attested in the *Avesta* and in Herodotus transcribed as *enarees* (I.105; IV.67)—does not appear in the Achaemenid corpus. Nevertheless, Darius sets the Persians and the Medes in opposition to "the other countries with other languages" (DPg). Thus there seems to be, on Darius's part, a desire to archaize, especially if we recognize that the term *arya* originally referred to ancestral nobility.

Center and Periphery: Persia and the Empire

Darius certainly did not intend either to exalt an Iranian political unit [Iran] or to affirm the existence of a Persian-Mede joint sovereignty. When Persia is mentioned in the country lists, it is always at the top; when it is not, its absence expresses its superiority to all other countries. It is perfectly clear, in fact, that the true center of the Empire is the country of Persia alone. This was perfectly understood by Herodotus when he wrote (I.134◊):

> After their own nation they hold their nearest neighbors most in honour, then the nearest but one—and so on, their respect decreasing as the distance grows, and the most remote being the most despised. Themselves they consider in every way superior to everyone else in the world, and allow other nations a share of good qualities decreasing according to distance, the furthest off being in their view the worst.

We cannot imagine a better definition of peripheral peoples! He obviously considers the exemption from tribute granted to Persia in the same general context (III.97). The sage Calanus was also able to give a particularly vivid representation of the decisive importance of the center prior to Alexander (Plutarch, *Alex.* 65.6–7).

In the inscriptions already cited, the complete titulature is as follows:

> Darius the king, one king of many, one lord of many. I am Darius the Great King, King of Kings, King of countries containing all kinds of men, King in this great earth far and wide, son of Hystaspes, an Achaemenian, a Persian, son of a Persian, an Aryan having Aryan lineage. (*DNa*✧)

The pedigree of Darius is thus defined by family (Hystaspes), royal stock (Achaemenids), ethnic group (Persian), and "ethnic" stock (*arya*). We get the impression that here the word *arya* refers narrowly to the Persians or even the royal family. Under this hypothesis, the use of this archaizing vocabulary (*arya*) by Darius would also contribute to founding the irrevocable dynastic rights of his lineage. At any rate, in *DB* §70 the word *arya* 'Aryan language' does appear to be used in a restricted sense, 'Persian language'.

Whatever the case on this point, the inscriptions of Darius and his successors attest to the privileged place of Persia and the Persians in the royal self-perception. At Naqš-i Rustam, the list of subjugated countries is introduced as follows: "By the favor of Ahuramazda these are the countries which I seized outside of Persia" (*DNa* §3✧). A very similar but even more explicit formula is found in the Persian version of the trilingual panel of the southern retaining wall of the Persepolis terrace: "By the favor of Ahuramazda, these are the countries which I got into my possession along with this Persian folk" (*DPe*✧). This individually Persian character of the conquest is clearly highlighted in numerous royal statements, as we have already seen: "I am a Persian; from Persia I seized Egypt. . . . ships went from Egypt through this canal to Persia . . ." (*DZc*✧); "the Persian man/warrior (*martiya*) conquered Egypt" (*DSab*); "the spear of a Persian man has gone forth far . . . a Persian man has delivered battle far indeed from Persia" (*DNa*✧); and so on.

In several inscriptions, Darius favors the "Persian country," and he invokes the protection of Ahura-Mazda:

> Saith Darius the King: "This country (*dahyu*) Persia which Ahuramazda bestowed upon me, good, possessed of good horses, possessed of good men (*martiya*)—by the favor of Ahuramazda and of me, Darius the King does not feel fear of (any) other." Saith Darius the King: May Ahuramazda bear me aid, with the gods of the royal house; and may Ahuramazda protect this country from a (hostile) army, from famine, from the Lie (*drauga*)! Upon this country may there not come an army, nor famine, nor the Lie; this I pray as a boon from Ahuramazda together with the gods of the royal house. This boon may Ahuramazda together with the gods of the royal house give to me!" (*DPd*✧)

Another inscription on the trilingual panel, still in Old Persian, contains the following statement:

> Saith Darius the King: If thus thou shalt think, "May I not feel fear of (any) other," protect this Persian people; if the Persian people shall be protected, thereafter for the longest while happiness unbroken—this will by Ahura come down upon this royalhouse. (*viθ; DPe*✧)

And, at Naqš-i Rustam, this formula is found:

> Me may Ahura-Mazda protect from harm, and my royal house, and this land. (*DNa* §5✧)

All of these proclamations appear to express the establishment of a special relationship between Darius and his country (*dahyu*), that is, Persia *sensu stricto*, defined first of all by its military force ("good horses, good warriors"). It is his country (*dahyu*) and his house (*viθ*) that he calls on the Persian gods to protect. The privileged place of the Persians around the king is also clearly evident in Herodotus's description of Xerxes' royal procession: only Persians precede, surround, and follow the royal chariot; "a host of troops of all nationalities indiscriminately mixed" walked in front, but "a gap was left in the marching column to keep these troops from contact with the king" (VII, 40); (VII.40◇); likewise at the end of the procession: "A squadron of ten thousand Persian horse, after which there was a gap of two furlongs [ca. 400 m] in the column before the remainder of the army, a mass of troops with no particular distinction, brought up the rear" (VII.41◇).

Meanwhile, the royal descriptions are not always in strict agreement. Thus Persia is listed at Behistun and in a Susa inscription (*DSm*) among the countries that had submitted to Darius. In one of the versions of the foundation charter (*DSaa*), it is also mentioned among the peoples/countries "who brought [me] the materials for decorating this palace." On the other hand, in the other versions, the Persians are not listed among the peoples who furnished materials or work details (*DSz, DSf*). They are also absent from the delegations coming to bring gifts to the Great King, but they are represented among the throne-bearers; this indicates that, even though the Persians are special, they are still subjects of the king. For the rest of the inscriptions, such as *DSaa*, this type of enumeration is intended above all to record the cooperation of all of the peoples in a common effort. The very title "king in [of] Persia" appears alone twice: in the Behistun inscription ("I am Darius the Great King, King of Kings, King in Persia, King of countries" [*DB* §1◇]) and in another, minor inscription from the same site (*DBa*).

How can we resolve what seems at first sight to be a contradiction within the royal discourse? Should we propose a distinction between the Empire (*būmi*) and the kingdom (*xšaça*), the latter referring exclusively to Persia? Or should we instead understand the terminological distinction diachronically, with the emphasis on Persia illustrating the conflicting relationships between the king and the Persian aristocracy at the moment of Intaphernes' revolt? Or rather, more simply, can we see the different expressions as a major contradiction? When Darius proclaims himself "Persian, son of a Persian," it is simply because the Persians and his army continue to play a central role in the Empire. It is also because, as Herodotus puts it (I.132), "the king himself is included among the Persians." But, if Darius does not insist on his title "king in Persia," it is because he intends above all to emphasize the universality of his authority, from which Persia cannot be excluded: Persia also is under the jurisdiction of the territorial dominion of the "king of the countries." In the same way, when Herodotus states that "only the country where the Persians dwell enjoys immunity" (*ateleia*; III.97), he is referring only to tribute, meaning primarily politico-ideological tribute (*dasmos*), since recent research has shown that, despite its unquestionable political privileges, Persia was never exempt from all fiscal dues (chap. 11/10).

4. Images and Realities: The King among His Peoples

Peoples and Gifts: An Imperial Festival at Persepolis?

It appears clear that neither the country lists nor the depictions of peoples are intended to give a realistic picture of the administration or the geography of the Empire. Instead, the lists and depictions are primarily the vehicles of the very idea of royal and imperial power. The question remains whether the images also represent ceremonies that were regularly carried out at Persepolis. A positive answer is often given on the basis of the friezes, on which delegations bring to the king objects and animals that are probably typical of their produce. Based on comparisons with medieval Iranian texts (al-Biruni in particular) and Indian texts, there have been frequent attempts to reconstruct, sometimes in considerable detail, the various stages of an annual imperial festival that was observed at the New Year (March).

There can be no doubt about the existence of festivals and ceremonies at Persepolis. In a broad outline of the work of Ctesias, Photius writes: "Having returned to Persepolis (*eis Persas*), Darius offered sacrifices, then died after thirty days of illness" (§19). Despite the allusive character of the passage, it is tempting to relate it to Xenophon's long description of a great parade organized by Cyrus (*Cyr.* VIII.3–4): "Next we shall describe how Cyrus for the first time drove forth in state from his palace" (3.1◊). Descriptions follow of the king's retinue, the protocol that guided it, the king's and the gods' chariots, sacrifices, games, the banquet, and finally the king's gifts. Then Xenophon describes the progress of the king's caravan toward Persia (VIII.5.1–16): "And when, as he continued his journey, he came to the boundaries of Persia, he left the main body of his army there, while he went on with his friends to the capital; and he took along animals enough for all the Persians to sacrifice and make a feast" (VIII.5.21◊). Obviously, this does not describe a unique festival, since, speaking of the death of "Cyrus," Xenophon states that this was the seventh time the king went thus to Persia: "Cyrus performed the customary sacrifice (*ta nomizomena hiera*) and led the Persians in their national dance (*kata ta patria*) and distributed presents among them all, as had been his custom" (VIII.7.1◊).

Quite a few of the details given by Xenophon are found in other Classical authors. Herodotus (VII.40–41) describes the order of march for the royal procession of Xerxes that left Sardis in 480; Quintus Curtius (III.3.8–25) presents the order of the procession of Darius III leaving Babylon in 333. Along with some differences, common elements are found in Xenophon, Herodotus, and Quintus Curtius, which is all the more interesting, given that they clearly derive from different sources. The procession sets out at sunrise (Xenophon, Quintus Curtius; cf. Herodotus VII.54). Cyrus was in his chariot, his charioteer nearby; likewise Darius III was placed in a chariot "in which he rode outstanding (*eminens*) among the rest" (III.3.15◊); Xerxes was "riding in a chariot (*harma*) drawn by Nisaean horses, his charioteer, Patiramphes, son of Otanes the Persian, standing by his side" (VII.40◊); the word used by Herodotus (*harma*) proves that it was a war chariot, not a four-wheel chariot (*harmamaxe*), two vehicles that the author explicitly distinguishes (VII.41). The procession was accompanied by guards and soldiers:

- Cyrus: 4,000 lance-bearers (*doryphoroi*) before the chariot; 2,000 more on each side of the royal chariot; then (after the 200 royal horses), 10,000 cavalry (arranged 100 square), then two more groups of 10,000 cavalry; finally allied troops and chariots (*Cyr.* VIII.3.15–18);

- Xerxes: 1,000 Persian cavalry, 1,000 Persian pike-bearers, 10 Nisaean horses before the chariots of the god and the king; and afterward, other Persian troops: 1,000 pike-bearers, 1,000 cavalry, 10,000 lancers (with gold and silver sashes) and 10,000 Persian cavalry;

- Darius III: the 10,000 Immortals and the *doryphoroi* precede the royal chariot; 10,000 lancers follow the royal chariot.

The king is also accompanied by his associates: near Cyrus are his relatives (*syggeneis*); before Darius III's chariot and after the Immortals walk his relatives (*cognati*); to the right and left of his chariot are placed 'the most noble of those close to him' (*nobi-

lissimi propinquorum). Finally, each of the processions includes divine chariots: one for Zeus, one for the Sun, and a third one followed by a fire altar ("Cyrus"); the sacred chariot of Zeus (Xerxes); fire altars and "a chariot dedicated to Jupiter" (Darius III). It thus seems clear that all three sources transmit credible information on the arrangement of the royal procession, whether during a regular ceremony held in Persia or a relocation of the royal court under other circumstances. In fact, many elements of the Classical descriptions are found on some Persepolis reliefs: guards, royal horses, royal chariot, bearers of royal appurtenances, processions of nobles, and even lines of servants bringing food and drink and vessels for the royal table.

Despite striking, undeniable convergences of the evidence between the Persepolis reliefs and the accounts of Classical authors, numerous objections have been offered against the hypothesis that a New Year festival was celebrated at Persepolis. First of all, the hypothesis is based on the assumption that Persepolis was "a ritual city," dedicated solely to the political exaltation of the power of the Great King. To be sure, this aspect should not be underrated; quite the opposite. But the discovery of the Treasury and Fortification tablets has proved indubitably that Persepolis was also a permanent economic center and the seat of administrative bureaus. We will also find that no contemporary text makes any mention of a New Year festival; but, however legitimate this observation, it must not be allowed to rule out the possibility that one existed, considering how sparse and fragmentary the Achaemenid documentation is. It is obviously more noteworthy that, according to the Classical authors, it was in autumn (and not in spring) that the court resided in Persia. Moreover, at no time does Xenophon mention the arrival of delegations of subject peoples. Instead, he stresses the king's distribution of gifts. The festival he describes obviously takes place in a purely Persian context, where the religious element appears to predominate. As we know from the author of *De Mundo* (398a), the existence of 'receivers of gifts' (*dōrōn apodektēres*) at the court of the Great King probably did not require a ceremony, since the king could receive gifts on many other occasions. The perennial declaration of Darius (and his successors) that "these are the countries that brought me *bāji*" cannot be used to prove anything more than what it says. We note first that the Persian word *bāji* connotes 'the king's share' more than tribute per se. Second, the frequent tabular comparisons set up between the friezes of tributaries/givers and the discussion of tribute by Herodotus are in fact doomed to failure. Herodotus's list of tribute districts actually represents a different logic from the logic governing the composition of the lists and reliefs, even when in the tribute disposition of Darius the *dahyu/ethnos* retains its central position. This is why the depictions are habitually described as Gift-Bearers rather than Tribute-Bearers (anyway, according to all indications, the gifts were paid in money). However, the terminological adjustment obviously does not resolve the problem.

The principal objection to positing an imperial festival is methodological in nature. Iconological and iconographic analysis has shown that, overall, inscriptions and reliefs are intended prima facie to impose and transmit the image of a universal, intangible power. Achaemenid rhetoric is nourished less by administrative realities than by ideological assumptions, which have their own logic. In other words, Persepolitan art is not a simple, quasi-photographic reflection of reality. Though it does capture reality, it does so in order to transform it and make it sublime; it relates less to a scenic scenario than to an ideological discourse on royalty and imperial might organized around themes particularly evocative of the power of the Great King: the king in majesty (audience reliefs, etc.), armed forces (rows of Persian and Elamite guards), the cooperation of the aristocracy (rows of nobles in Persian or Mede garb), and imperial dominion in turn symbolized by the gifts from various populations and by the richness of the royal table. Under these conditions, it is perhaps risky to reconstruct a dynamic reality (observation of a periodic imperial festival around the king) on the basis of depictions that are static and immutable.

We must recognize that the objection is weighty. At the same time, we must carefully observe that even if the royal artists, working according to an imposed model, were not charged with describing a festival and its appurtenances realistically, this does not ipso facto imply that the hypothesis of an imperial ceremony must be abandoned. In order to take into account all of the documented facts, we would do well to return to the Classical sources. Indeed, none of them indisputably corroborates the hypothesis of an imperial festival periodically celebrated at Persepolis (whether or not it took place at the time of the New Year), but some of them describe the bestowing of gifts on the Great King, during the relocations of the court. Let us then set forth first of all the details of this Achaemenid custom in which the Greek authors show great interest.

The Nomadic King

Here is how Xenophon explains the origins of the court migrations:

> Cyrus himself made his home in the centre of his domain, and in the winter season he spent seven months in Babylon, for there the climate is warm; in the spring he spent three months in Susa, and in the height of summer two months in Ecbatana. By so doing, they say, he enjoyed the warmth and coolness of perpetual spring-time. (*Cyr.* VIII.6.22✧)

The same explanation is found in Strabo (XV.1.16) and Athenaeus (XII.513f✧), who sees in this custom an illustration of the luxury surrounding the life of the Great King:

> The first men in history to become notorious for luxurious (*tryphū*) living were the Persians, whose kings wintered in Susa and summered in Ecbatana. . . . In Persepolis they spent the autumn, and in Babylon the remaining portion of the year. So also the Parthian kings live in springtime at Rhagae [Media], but they winter at Babylon, (and pass) the rest of the year (in Hecatompylus [Parthia]).

Aelian sees in this custom evidence of the wisdom of the Great Kings, whose migrations he compares to the annual migrations of fish and birds (*Anim.* III.13; X.16). Conversely, in his very polemical work *Agesilaus* (9.5✧), Xenophon attempts to illustrate once again his thesis of the "moral decadence" of the Great King: "shunning heat and shunning cold through weakness of character, imitating the life, not of brave men, but of the weakest of the brutes." Whatever the Greek interpretations, there is no doubt of the existence of the institution. Furthermore, in a passage on the cuisine of the Great Kings, Polyaenus states that their menus varied with their places of residence (IV.3.32). Aelian also records many anecdotes deriving from the seasonal relocations of the court.

The climatic explanations offered are certainly not irrelevant to this sort of nomadism. We know in fact that Susiana was stifling during the hot season. Strabo, referring to Polyclitus, states, for example: "When the sun is hottest, at noon, the lizards and the snakes could not cross the streets in the city quickly enough to prevent their being burnt to death in the middle of the streets," or again (quoting Aristobulus) "Barley spread out in the sun bounces like parched barley in ovens" (XV.3.10✧)! A report from the time of the Diadochi also shows how oppressive the heat was in June or July: "They walked into a furnace because of the intensity of the heat; many men died and the army fell into despair" (Diodorus XIX.28.1–2; 39.1). Several Hellenistic texts in particular describe the contrast between the Susiana plain and the Iranian Plateau in Fārs. These documents are even more interesting because they are composed from the point of view of a traveler going from Susa to Persepolis (Diodorus XVII.67.1–13; XIX.21.2–3).

There is no reason to doubt that the Great King and his court were looking for more hospitable locations at the height of summer; parallels could be multiplied throughout the Near East. However, there were also historical reasons. With reference to an identical custom of the Parthian kings during his time, Strabo writes: "The Parthian kings are accustomed to spend the winter there because of the salubrity of the air, but the summer at Ecbatana and in Hyrcania because of the prevalence of their ancient renown" (XVI.1.16◊). Likewise, the Achaemenids would not have been able to establish residences at Susa or Babylon without returning to their roots in Media or Persia—especially Persia, where two towns, Pasargadae and Persepolis, remained the ideological apexes of their power.

Aside from these seasonal migrations, the king and court relocated under quite a few other circumstances. This happened especially when the king called up the royal army and led it himself. These armies, in fact, bore only a very slight resemblance to present-day armies. On these occasions, the king was accompanied by his court, family, courtiers, household staff, and even his palace (transformed into tents). The texts bearing on these wartime migrations allow us to reconstruct the pomp and circumstance surrounding the moves and to understand their politico-ideological aspects more clearly.

An Itinerant State

Many texts show that, when the king periodically changed locations, thousands of people also had to migrate. Every member of the royal house, in fact, took part in the trips and moves. Witness the lineup accompanying Darius III when he left Babylon. The end of the procession went like this:

> Next, at an interval of a single stade, one chariot carried Sisigambis, Darius' mother, and in another was his wife. A throng of women of the queens' household rode on horses. Then followed fifteen of what they call *harmamaxae*; in these were the king's children and their governesses, and a herd of eunuchs, who are not at all despised by those peoples. Next rode the 365 concubines of the king, these also regally dressed and adorned. . . . Next to this division rode the wives of his relatives and friends, and troops of sutlers and batmen. (Quintus Curtius III.3.22–25)◊

In fact, "not only the ladies of the royal house but also those of the King's Relatives and Friends, borne on gilded chariots, had accompanied the army according to an ancestral custom of the Persians" (Diodorus XVII.35.3◊). We know that Xerxes brought along some of his illegitimate children on the march against Greece (Herodotus VIII.103–4). Relations and Friends received places of honor in Darius III's procession (Quintus Curtius III.3.14, 21).

Many other elements demonstrate that the king's relocations signified that the State itself was on the march. The king brought with him the insignia of power, namely his royal robe (*kandys*), bow, and shield. He was also accompanied by images of the gods. Xerxes' procession, in 480, included "the holy chariot of Zeus drawn by eight white horses, with a charioteer on foot behind them holding the reins—for no mortal man may mount into that chariot's seat" (Herodotus VII.40✧). This is the official order of march of the royal procession of Darius III:

> In front on silver altars was carried the fire, which they called sacred and eternal. Next came the Magi, chanting their traditional hymn. These were followed by three hundred and sixty-five young men clad in purple robes, equal in number to the days of a whole year; for the Persians also divided the year into that number of days. After that, white horses drew the chariot consecrated to Jupiter; these were followed by a horse of extraordinary size, which they called the steed of the Sun. (Quintus Curtius III.3.9–11✧)

When the procession halted, the royal tent was erected. According to Xenophon, "At the very beginning Cyrus made this rule, that his tent should be pitched facing the east; and then he determined, first, how far from the royal pavilion the spearmen of his guard should have their tent. . . . He himself first took up his position in the middle of the camp in the belief that this situation was the most secure. Then came his most trusty followers, just as he was accustomed to have them about him at home, and next to them in a circle he had his horsemen and charioteers" (*Cyr.* VIII.5.3; 8✧). In this way, the king's tent was at the very heart—the word covering simultaneously both topographic and hierarchical realities. Xenophon also states that each officer had a banner over his tent (VIII.5.13). The royal tent was easily recognizable: "When the day was already bright, the signal was given from the king's tent with the horn; above the tent, from which it might be seen by all, there gleamed an image of the sun enclosed in crystal" (Quintus Curtius III.3.8✧).

When the court was on the move, the royal tent thus became the center of power, identifiable as it was with the king himself. Consequently, the capture of the royal tent by an opponent symbolically represented a transition from one power to another. Quintus Curtius in fact explains "it was an established custom that they should receive the victor in the conquered king's tent" (III.11.23✧). Thus, upon his victory over Astyages, Cyrus the Great entered the tent of the vanquished king, took the throne, and grasped his scepter; then one of his men, Oibaras, placed the *kidaris* (upright tiara), symbol of royalty, on his head (*FGrH* 90 F66.45). The Macedonian victory at Issus in 333 had the same result: "The royal pages now took over the tent of Dareius and Alexander's prepared Alexander's bath and dinner and, lighting a great blaze of torches, waited for him, that he might return from the pursuit [of Darius' enemy] and, finding ready for him all the riches of Dareius, take it as an omen of his conquest of the empire of all Asia" (Diodorus XVII.36.5✧).

Thus, there is no doubt that the king was also accompanied by the high officials who regularly assisted him with all his governmental duties. In one of his anecdotes on the relocations of the court, Aelian tells the following story:

> Note that when travelling the Persian King took with him, in order not to be bored, a small block of lime wood tablet and a little knife to scrape it. This was the activit of the royal hands. He certainly did not take with him a book (*biblion*) or serious thoughts, in order to be able to read something important and improving or meditate on a noble and worthwhile subject. (*VH* XIV.14✧)

We can overlook the polemical slant of the remarks. Here an opposition is set up between books proper (philosophy, history)—"heavy, serious reading"—and the administrative use of writing. The anecdote gives an illustration of the situation we might expect: the king remained in contact with his satraps and subordinates through the intermediary of his chancellery, to which he continued to dictate letters and messages.

To sum up, custom led to the extension and relativization of the very notion of a capital in the Achaemenid Empire. Power was where the king was, whether he was residing in a palace or his tent, at Persepolis or in a paradise, at the heart of the Empire or at Sardis or even Memphis or Bactra.

Royal Arrivals and Departures

The political aspect of these migrations is strongly evidenced by the ceremony surrounding the arrival of the Great King in his cities. There is no doubt that the procession was organized according to strict rules fixed by protocol, as can be seen in the texts of Xenophon, Herodotus, and Quintus Curtius. One of the most interesting texts is the one in which Quintus Curtius (V.1.17–23✧) describes the arrival of Alexander at Babylon in 331:

> Now, as Alexander kept on his way to Babylon, Mazaeus, who had fled to that city from the battlefield [of Gaugamela], met him as a suppliant with his mature children, and surrendered the city and himself. His coming was welcome to the king; for the siege of so strongly fortified a city would have been a great task. Moreover, it was evident that a man of distinction and ready action, who had also gained widespread reputation in the recent battle, would by his example induce the rest to surrender. Therefore the king received him courteously with his children; but he ordered his men to enter the city in square formation, with himself at their head, as if they were going into battle. A great part of the Babylonians had taken their places on the walls in their eagerness to become acquainted with their new king, still more had gone out to meet him. Among the latter Bagophanes, guardian of the citadel and of the royal funds, in order not to be outdone in alacrity by Mazaeus, had strewn the whole road with flowers and garlands, and had placed here and there on both sides silver altars, which he had piled high, not only with frankincense, but with perfumes of all kinds. As gifts there followed him herds of horses and cattle; lions and leopards too were carried before them in cages. Then came the magi, chanting a hymn after their manner, after them the Chaldeans, and of the Babylonians not only the prophets but also musicians with their own kind of instruments; the latter were accustomed to sing the praises of the kings, the Chaldeans, to explain the movements of the heavenly bodies and the appointed changes of the seasons. Lastly followed the Babylonian cavalry, whose apparel and that of their horses met the demands of luxury rather than of magnificence. Alexander, surrounded by armed men, had ordered the throng of townspeople to march after the hindermost of infantry; he himself entered the city in a chariot, and then entered the palace.

This text, clearly based on firsthand description, catalogs the various elements of a minutely organized ceremony. To be sure, like many other Hellenistic-period texts, it presents the displays accorded the king as spontaneous. The reality is quite different. Herodotus states clearly, for example, that before Xerxes arrived at his towns royal heralds were dispatched from Sardis to announce the imminent arrival of the royal procession and to notify the cities of the order to prepare the royal table (VII.32). The roads themselves were made ready: Aelian even states that on this occasion the inhabitants were required to kill all the scorpions on the road from Ecbatana to Persia (*Anim.* XV.26)! There is no trace of improvisation in any of this. Quite the contrary, every stage of the ceremony was prepared in advance, in collaboration with the local authorities. Before receiving Alexander at Susa several weeks later, the satrap sent his son "to meet the king"; for his part, Alexander sent one of his officials to make contact with the satrap Abulites in order to arrange the royal entry in accord with customary Achaemenid protocol (Arrian III.16.6).

In fact, the authorities were required to come before the king outside the ramparts of the city. It was the same at Sardis in the summer of 334: "When he [Alexander] was still about seventy stades [ca. 12 km] away he was met by Mithrenes, commander of the citadel garrison, and the chief citizens of Sardis; they gave up the city, and Mithrenes the citadel and treasury" (Arrian I.17.3◊). In Babylon, the authorities "surrender[ed] the city, the citadel and the treasure" (III.16.2◊). By coming before the king, they clearly indicated that their town was open and that they recognized their subjugation. The authorities were accompanied by corporate bodies: "The Babylonians came out to meet him in mass, with their priests and rulers."

Then came the entry into the town. In Babylon, Alexander rode a chariot. It is also possible that in some cases kings made their entrances on horseback (cf. Plutarch, *Them.* 29.7). Darius saw in one of his premonitory dreams, "Alexander . . . in the garb in which he himself had been made king, . . . riding on horseback through Babylon" (Quintus Curtius III.3.3◊). Established practice, however, required that the Great King parade in his chariot at official ceremonies. Xerxes' chariot was drawn by Nisaean horses (VII.41◊). And Herodotus states: "When the fancy took him, he would leave his chariot (*harma*) and take his seat in a covered carriage (*harmamaxa*) instead." This small detail indicates that the procession described by Herodotus complied with a ceremonial order: it was in fact, according to Quintus Curtius, "an ancestral tradition." Thus, "he rode outstanding among the rest" (III.3.15◊). Diodorus (XVI.24.6) states that in his chariot the king would adopt and maintain a "hieratic" attitude and bearing and that he did not drive his chariot himself. Xerxes was "riding in a chariot (*harma*) drawn by Nisaean horses, his charioteer, Patiramphes, son of Otanes the Persian, standing by his side" (Herodotus VII.40◊). Xenophon does not conceal the king's desire to awe the crowd of spectators, who were massed on both sides of the road:

> His [Cyrus's] hands he kept outside his sleeves. With him rode a charioteer, who was tall, but neither in reality nor in appearance so tall as he; at all events, Cyrus looked much taller. And when they saw him, they all prostrated themselves before him (*proskynese*), either because some had been instructed to begin this act of homage, or because they were overcome by the splendour of his presence, or because Cyrus appeared so great and goodly to look upon. (*Cyr.* VIII.3.14◊)

The king then traversed the streets of the city, which in Babylon "were strewn with flowers and garlands" and redolent with the scent of incense and many other delightful perfumes—which very closely recalls Cyrus's entry two centuries earlier. Likewise, when Xerxes and his train crossed the bridge over the Hellespont, "they burned all sorts of spices on the bridges and laid boughs of myrtle along the way" (Herodotus VII.54◊). This was clearly a victory celebration: at the news of the victory of Salamis, "the Persians . . . strewed the roads with myrtle-boughs, burned incense, and gave themselves up to every sort of pleasure and merrymaking" (VIII.99◊). The king then performed sacrifices to the gods of the town and the country—Alexander never failed to do this, wherever he went. Thus "at Babylon . . . he met the Chaldaeans, and carried out all their recommendations on the Babylonian temples, and in particular sacrificed to Baal [Marduk], according to their instructions" (Arrian III.16.5◊). This ceremony demonstrates that the king was not only received by the population and its leaders, but also by their tutelary deities. Finally, it was the city's difficult task to provide for the royal table—an overwhelming expense, as Herodotus explains at considerable length (VII.118–20).

Court Nomadism and a Survey of the Imperial Realm

It thus seems clear that the movements of the Achaemenid court took on major political and ideological significance. During his travels, the Great King, as it were, visited
the peoples of his Empire. He who was ordinarily so far away could show off to everyone
the might and wealth of his court and army. The Persian custom might be compared
with the "royal entrance" in medieval France, of which it has been said: "At the end of
the Middle Ages, monarchic sentiment was fostered by the numerous entries that the
king made into all his major cities during his progress throughout the kingdom. . . .
First, it was just a festival, then it took on a quasi-religious solemnity; by the end of the
fifteenth century a royal entry had become a great spectacle, wherein the king's councilors intended to lay out all the themes of monarchic propaganda."

During the process of relocating, the king also passed through villages and encountered peasants. Because of the military orientation of the Classical and Hellenistic
sources, we are naturally less well informed on this aspect. But when the royal procession passed through a district, the local people crowded in all along the route. This is
evidenced by the following remark of Quintus Curtius, describing Darius III's retreat toward Media after the battle of Gaugamela, during which he took a side trip: "From the
villages nearest to the road the shrieks of old men and women could be heard, who in
the barbarian manner were still calling on Darius as their king" (IV.16.5◊). Diodorus's
description of the route of Alexander's funeral chariot from Babylon to the Mediterranean coast might also be mentioned:

> Because of its widespread fame it drew together many spectators; for from every city into
> which it came the whole people went forth to meet it and again escorted it on its way out,
> not becoming sated with the pleasure of beholding it. (XVII.28.1◊)

A passage in Herodotus also seems to indicate that, during his stay at Sardis, Darius
held a "seat in state" on the outskirts of the city (V.12◊). There is no doubt in any case
that local populations took advantage of the king's presence to bring petitions and
claims, as Xenophon explains in the *Cyropaedia* while describing the organization of
the royal procession on the occasion of the parade held at Persepolis: "As he proceeded,
a great throng of people followed outside the lines with petitions to present to Cyrus."
Then he "sent them some of his mace-bearers (*skēptoukhoi*), who followed three on either side of his chariot, for the express purpose of carrying messages for him; and he bade
them say that if any one wanted anything of him, he should make his wish known to
some one of his cavalry officers and they, he said, would inform him" (VIII.3.19–23◊).
The same concerns led to Artaxerxes II's instruction that his wife Stateira should travel
in an open vehicle; anyone might seek her out to present a request: her chariot "always
appeared with its curtains down, allowing her countrywomen to salute and approach
her, which made the queen a great favourite with the people" (Plutarch, *Art.* 5.6◊).

Gifts and Presents

Moreover, Arrian explains, "each section of the inhabitants [brought] gifts" to Alexander (III.16.3◊). This meant, notably, presents of animals, including exotic ones: in
Babylon, caged lions and panthers (Quintus Curtius V.1.21); in Susa, "Abulites met him
with gifts of regal splendour. Among the presents were the camels known as dromedaries
and of extraordinary swiftness, twelve elephants imported by Darius from India"
(V.2.10◊). The gifts were often gold and silver crowns, as shown by an inventory of the

Achaemenid treasury at Susa in 317: "There was collected for him [Antigonus], besides, a great amount of money from the crowns and and other gifts, and also from the spoils. This came to five thousand talents" (Diodorus XIX.48.7◇). The inhabitants of the Phoenician towns also greeted Holophernes with crowns as a sign of voluntary submission: in violation of every precedent, however, the Persians "laid their land waste and cut down their sacred trees" (Judith 3:7–8◇).

Note the especially interesting, long passage by Theopompus of Chios, known from a late quotation (*FGrH* 115 F263a), some of which is repeated by Athenaeus (II.77 = F263b). The author was obviously very fond of Persian royal customs and dedicated numerous passages to the luxury of the royal table and to the movements of the Great King. He is the one, for instance, who provides information about the requirement to feed the king and those with him, which weighed on the peoples and cities visited by the king and court (see p. 403 below). The passage that is quoted here at length may refer to the expedition mounted by Artaxerxes III to reconquer Egypt in 343. Here is how—and how enthusiastically!—Theopompus describes the gifts and gift-givers who hastened to the path of the royal caravan on the road:

> Is there any city or people of Asia that didn't send embassies to the king? Is there any produce or any fine and valuable product of their workshops that they did not bring as gifts (*dōron*) to lay down before the king? Many splendid counterpanes, fine blankets, some purple, some multi-colored, some white; many tents fitted out in gold and fully equipped; not to mention many tunics and costly, splendid couches; and on to chased silver and gold worked to perfection, cups and bowls, some covered with precious gems, others appearing to be worked with elegant simplicity. And above and beyond all that, uncountable myriads of arms, both Greek and Barbarian, and an unbelievable number of teams and fatted animals for sacrifice, along with many *medimnes* ['bushels'] of seasonings, many sacks of money, and a large amount of writing-papyrus, and among all the other things everything needed for sustenance, including the meat of sacrificial animals preserved in salt in such quantity that the folks who approached had the impression of seeing mountains and hills raised before them!

Several anecdotes preserved by Aelian describe the obligations that fell on the Persian peasants when Artaxerxes II's royal procession passed near their fields and villages:

> A custom most carefully maintained by the Persians (*nomos persikos*), when the king drives to Persepolis, is that each and every one of them, according to his means (*kata tēn heautou dynamin*), brings an offering. Since they are engaged in farming and toil on the land, living by what they produce (*autourgoi*), they bring no pretentious or unduly expensive gifts, but rather oxen, sheep, or corn, or in other cases wine. As the king passes and drives on his way these objects are laid out by each man, and are termed gifts (*dōron*); the king treats them as such. Men who are even poorer than these farmers bring him milk and dates and cheese, with ripe fruit and other first fruits of local produce. (I.31◇)

It was shameful to disregard the custom (*nomos*; I.32). It was an honor to bring even the smallest present: Aelian tells the story of a particularly impoverished Persian who could offer Artaxerxes no more than a skin of water from the Cyrus River, and another who modestly brought him a single pomegranate. The former was honored with the title Benefactor (I.33; cf. Plutarch, *Art.* 4.4–5; 5.1). The exchanges of gifts that took place on this occasion rendered the generosity of the Great King all the more striking and strengthened his ties with the people.

Gifts to the Great King and Political Submission

There can be no doubt that the offering of gifts took on major political significance. They provided a visible illustration of the submission of the town and population before royal might. Everyone was obligated, especially the rich. On the way to and from his European campaign, Darius crossed Asia Minor and stayed at Sardis. It is quite certainly on this occasion that the wealthy Pythius of Celaenae offered the king the famous golden plane tree. Later, in 480, "at Celaenae [he] was awaiting Xerxes, and on his arrival entertained him and the whole army with most lavish hospitality" (Herodotus VII.27✧). The satrap himself also was required to greet the king regularly. Among other examples we may consider Orxines, who took for himself the title Satrap of Persia. When Alexander neared Pasargadae on his return from Carmania, Orxines came to greet the king "on the Persian border" (Arrian VI.29.2✧):

> He met the king with gifts of every kind, intending to give presents not only to Alexander but to his friends as well. Troops of trained horses followed him and chariots adorned with silver and gold, costly furniture and splendid gems, golden vases of great weight, purple vestments, and 3,000 talents of coined silver. (Quintus Curtius X.1.24✧)

This is confirmed in the tales of Alexander's campaigns. Many peoples and towns awarded him crowns. Every time he turned up at the frontiers of a kingdom or city in India, he was greeted by ambassadors bearing gifts representing the country's products or most valuable possessions. For example, Omphis offered him "fifty-six elephants, . . . besides many head of sheep of extraordinary size and about 3000 bulls." "He entrusted his person and his realm to a prince" (Quintus Curtius VIII.12.7–11✧). Again, these Indian kings were simply following the orders of Alexander, who "having sent a herald in advance to Taxilas [Omphis] and the Indians on this side of the river Indus with orders to meet him, each at their earliest convenience; Taxilas and the other hyparchs complied, bringing the gifts the Indians prize most" (Arrian IV.22.6✧). Poros also received an envoy from Alexander, "to demand that he should pay tribute and meet Alexander at the frontier of his territories" (Quintus Curtius VIII.13.2✧). Open refusal to bring gifts was taken as proof of insubordination. This would have been the case with the Indian king Musikanos, who "had not yet met him to surrender himself and his country, nor had sent . . . any gifts suitable for a great king, nor had he made any request from Alexander." As soon as he heard of the arrival of the Macedonian army, however, Musikanos hastened before Alexander, "bringing gifts of the greatest value among the Indians, . . . submitting himself and his people" (Arrian VI.15.5–6✧).

As the Cyrus of the *Cyropedia* puts it, the satraps were obligated "to send back here what there is good and desirable in their several provinces" (VIII.6.6✧); as for the subject peoples, "those of every nation thought they did themselves an injury if they did not send to Cyrus the most valuable productions of their country, whether the fruits of the earth, or animals bred there, or manufactures of their own arts" (VIII.6.23✧). By coming in person to take possession of these symbolic gifts, the Great King reminded the cities and peoples that their most marvelous products were reserved for him alone. Every available text indicates that in this way the Great Kings periodically reaffirmed their dominion over the peoples they controlled. They recalled their obligations to them and constrained them to exhibit publicly their subjugation by the offering of gifts. In this way, they also staked out the extent of their immediate power over territories and subjects, a power that could only be perpetuated by the delegation of the Great King, who indeed remained far away but who was always able visibly to impose his presence and authority, whether directly by his relocations or indirectly by the intermediary of his satraps.

The Return to Persepolis via Babylon

The nature, function, and methods of presenting these gifts irresistibly make us think of the Persepolis donor friezes. If we agree to set aside the question of the New Year per se (this chronological question is secondary), it is not out of the question that the friezes metaphorically and vividly depict a festival during which delegations of the peoples of the Empire came to present to the king the best-known products of their countries. In the absence of real Achaemenid written documents, this hypothesis tempts us to refer to the delegations received from the "entire world" by Alexander at Babylon in 324:

> From practically all the inhabited world (*oikoumenē*)came envoys on various missions, some congratulating Alexander on his victories, some bringing him crowns, others concluding treaties of friendship and alliance, many bringing handsome presents (*dōreai megaloprepeis*), and some prepared to defend themselves against accusations. Apart from the tribes and cities as well as the local rulers of Asia, many of their counterparts in Europe and Libya put in an appearance. . . . Alexander drew up a list of the embassies and arranged a schedule of those to whom first he would give his reply and then the others in sequence. First her heard those who came on matters concerning religion; second, those who brought gifts; next, those who had disputes with their neighbours; fourth, those who had problems concerning themselves alone; and fifth, those who wished to present arguments against receiving back their exile. . . . receiving their petitions in the order of importance of the sanctuaries. In all cases he made every effort to deliver replies which would be gratifying, and sent everyone away content so far as he was able. (Diodorus XVII.113✧)

Whatever the specifics, this great meeting in Babylon was *perhaps* nothing other than an imitation of an Achaemenid festival of the same kind, a festival of imperial power, during which the many countries known to submit to the Great King came bearing gifts, seeking audience, and requiring his arbitration. Arrian does not conceal the obvious political significance: "It was then more than ever that both in his own estimation and in that of his entourage Alexander appeared to be master of every land and sea" (*Anab.* VII.15.5✧). And we can understand the deep irritation felt by the Macedonian toward the Arabs and the interpretation provided by Arrian: "[Alexander's] naval preparations were directed at the greater number of the Arabs, on the pretext that they alone of the barbarians in these parts had sent no envoys and had taken no other action reasonable or honorific to him. The truth in my own belief is that Alexander was always insatiate in winning possessions" (VII.19.6✧).

However, it is obvious that resorting to a text from Alexander's time—from Babylon, no less—cannot alleviate doubt about the reality of an official ceremony of gift-giving at Persepolis. By way of supplementary evidence, we may cite, not without reservation, a passage from Pliny that lists a locality called Caphrena in Upper Mesopotamia on a road to Syria. Pliny describes it as an old satrapal residence (*satraparum Regia* [= *basileion*] *appellatum*), which by his time had been demoted to a citadel (*arx*); he presents its past political function as follows: 'Where tributes used to be brought' (*quo tributa conferebantur; NH* VI.30.119–20). It thus seems that in the olden days (in the Persian period?) there must have been an official ceremony of tribute-bringing in the satrapal residence. Since most of the rules regulating satrapal court life were copied from central court regulations, we are tempted to think that this kind of ceremony for bringing representative gifts really did take place at Persepolis. However—let us say it one more time—the allusive and late character of the sources means that any conclusion is weak and uncertain. Let us simply stress that the Classical texts require us to leave the question open.

5. Images and Realities: The Imperial Festivals

The Large Army of Xerxes

Among these colorful depictions of the Empire and its peoples is Herodotus's long passage devoted to the description of Xerxes' army (VII.59–101). Herodotus places the scene in Thrace, on the plain of Doriscus, where Darius had established a royal residence (*basileion*) and a garrison. On that spot, Xerxes took a census of the army. "After the counting, the army was reorganized in divisions according to nationality" (*kata ethnea*; §60✧). Then Herodotus gives his readers an exhaustive list of 47 contingents, from the infantry, the cavalry, and also the navy. For each ethnic contingent, he gives a description of the clothing and weaponry, along with the name of the Persian who commanded it.

Among the many problems posed by this most interesting document, we will stress one in particular: the extraordinary diversity of the highly variegated army. Many of the contingents are distinguished by "exotic" uniforms. Some (Caspians, Pactyans, Utians, Myci, Paricanians) "were dressed in skin with the hair on"; the Ethiopians from Africa "in their leopard and lion skins . . . when going into battle they smeared half their bodies with chalk and the rest with vermilion"; the Ethiopians from Asia "wore headdresses consisting of horses' scalps, stripped off with the ears and mane attached—the ears were made to stand erect and the mane served as a crest";✧ "the Thracian troops wore fox skins as a headdress . . . and high fawnskin boots."✧ There was no less diversity in weaponry: some used wicker [*gerrhai*] shields (Persians), others oxhide shields (Paphlagonians), still others "for shields they used crane skins"✧ (Ethiopians of Asia); some wore wooden helmets (Colchians), others bronze helmets (Assyrians), still others "helmets helmets, crested, and decorated with the ears and horns of an ox, also in bronze"✧ (Paphlagonians); there were also wooden clubs embellished with iron nails (Assyrians, Ethiopians of Asia), axes [*sagaris*] (Sacians), "arrows tipped not with iron but with stone worked to a fine point,"✧ or "spears with spearheads of antelope horn"✧ (Ethiopians of Asia), and so on.

The mounted troops also do not seem very homogeneous, in spite of being reduced to a few ethnic contingents. Alongside the literal cavalry were "saddle horses and chariots drawn by horses and wild asses" (Indians), as well as herds of camels (Arabs). Even within the cavalry, Herodotus singles out the Sagartians' peculiar style of combat:

> A nomad tribe called Sagartians, a people who speak Persian and dress in a manner half Persian, half Pactyan; these furnished a contingent 8000 strong. Their custom is to carry no weapons of bronze or iron except daggers; the special weapon on which they chiefly rely is the lasso made of plaited strips of hide. In action, the moment they are in contact with the enemy, they throw their lassos (which have, of course, a noose at the end) and haul towards them whatever they catch, horse or man. The victim, tied up and helpless, is then dispatched. This is their way of doing battle. The Sagartian contingent was organized to form a single unit with the Persians. (§85✧)

One question comes up right away: how were the Persian commanders able to direct operations with such a diversity of troops, considering both their weaponry and their style? One possibility springs to mind immediately: it was exactly this diversity and chaos that enabled the Greeks to beat the Persians or that brought Darius III to defeat after defeat at the hands of the Macedonian armies. But this interpretation must be rejected, because on the one hand it agrees too well with the Greek interpretations and on the other hand, and more importantly, it misunderstands a basic fact: quite simply, most of the contingents described by Herodotus never went into battle at all.

At Thermopylae, the assault was led by elite troops: Medes, Cissians, then the Immortals (ordered to turn the flank) (Herodotus VII.210–11, 215; Diodorus XI.6–8). Here are the contingents picked by Mardonius when Xerxes retook Sardis after Salamis:

> [Along with the Ten Thousand] Mardonius . . . chose . . . the Persian spearmen and the picked cavalry squadron, a thousand strong; and, lastly, the Medes, Saka, Bactrians, and Indians, both horse and foot. These contingents he took over complete; from the troops of other nationalities (*symmakhoi*) he picked a few men here and there, being guided in his choice either by their appearance or by his knowledge that they had distinguished themselves, until he had a total number, including the cavalry, of 300,000 men. The Persians with their necklaces and armlets [the Ten Thousand] provided the largest contingent; next were the Medes—though the Medes were not actually inferior in number, but only in quality. (VIII.113◇)

Further on, Herodotus gives Mardonius's order of battle at Plataea, and he states very clearly that the front lines comprised Persians, Medes, Bactrians, Indians, and Sacians (IX.31). This was also true at Mycale, where the Persians encountered a frontal assault (IX.102). At Plataea, Herodotus identifies the allies selected by Mardonius: Greeks and Macedonians, Phrygians, Mysians, Thracians, Paeonians, and some Ethiopians and Egyptians (IX.32). Regarding the Egyptians, Herodotus includes the following detail: "They had previously served with the fleet, but Mardonius brought them ashore before leaving Phalerum; there were no Egyptian troops in the land force which Xerxes brought to Athens" (IX.32◇). For two reasons, we may not conclude that the contingents from Doriscus had set out: (1) only elite warriors could be chosen, as Herodotus makes very clear regarding the Egyptians themselves; and (2) Herodotus states several times that the *epibates* (marines) were exclusively Persian, Mede, and Sacian (IX.96.184). For reasons that are easily understood, the fighting army per se thus comprised Persian and Iranian troops. It seems equally clear that the 47 ethnic contingents enumerated by Herodotus at Doriscus had never seen battle. We must conclude from this that if Xerxes ever really did impose a general military conscription on his subjects (which itself seems rather doubtful), it was for reasons that had nothing to do with military logic.

Imperial Reviews

An initial review of troops took place at Abydos, before crossing the Hellespont:

> It now occurred to Xerxes that he would like to hold a review of his army. On a rise of ground nearby, a throne of white marble had already been prepared for his use, and at his orders, by the people of Abydos; so the king took his seat upon it and, looking down over the shore, was able to see the whole of his army and navy at a single view. Suddenly as he watched them he was seized by the whim to witness a rowing-match. The match took place and was won by the Phoenicians of Sidon, to the great delight of Xerxes who was as pleased with the race as with his army. (Herodotus VII.44◇)

Xerxes organized another review at Doriscus, in Thrace, after the census of the army:

> When the counting and marshalling of the troops had been completed, Xerxes thought he would like to hold a general review. Accordingly he drove in his chariot past the contingents of all the various nations, asking questions, the answers to which were taken down by his secretaries, until he had gone from one end of the army to the other, both horse and foot. Next the ships were launched, and Xerxes dismounting from his chariot went aboard a Sidonian vessel, where he took his seat under a canopy of gold and sailed along the line of the anchored fleet, asking questions about each ship and having the answers recorded, just as he had done with the army. The ships' masters had taken their vessels some four hundred feet from the beach, and brought up there in a single line with the bows turned shoreward and the fighting men drawn up on deck fully armed as for war. To hold his review, Xerxes passed along between the line and the shore. (VII.100✧)

These examples speak for themselves: Xerxes was not interested in his military forces but in the ethnic and cultural diversity of the peoples of his empire; rather than a review of the troops, this was a review of the Empire. One of the most important elements of the symbolism of this review, we must emphasize with Herodotus, was that the command of the ethnic contingents, hitherto in the hands of native chieftains, was handed over exclusively to Persians, often of very high birth (VII.81, 96). This arrangement marvelously illustrates and reinforces this reality: the Empire of the Great King was a Persian Empire.

It is possible that, by organizing this sort of gathering, the king was also seeking to strengthen the morale of his troops—this, at least, is Quintus Curtius's interpretation (III.2.1). But that is not the heart of it. By passing in front of the contingents arranged by peoples (*kata ethnea*), Xerxes informed himself about the various people/countries (*dahyāva*) whose mobilization in itself constituted a sign of his power and whose diversity accounted for the immensity of an Empire he did not know very well. At this point, one is reminded of Arrian's commentary on the gathering of delegations at Babylon in 324: "It was then that the Greeks and Macedonians first came to be acquainted with their names and appearances" (VII.15.4✧). One also thinks of what Quintus Curtius wrote of Darius III's army prior to Issus: "The Bactriani, the Sogdiani, the Indi, and other dwellers near the Red Sea [Persian Gulf], whose names were unknown even to Darius himself" (*ignotum etiam ipsi gentium nomina*; III.2.9✧). Remember also the army of this same Darius, which was lined up at Gaugamela after being counted in the same fashion as described by Herodotus at Doriscus: "These were followed by other nations (*nationes*), not very well known even to their allies. Phradates came after these nations, leading fifty four-in-hand chariots (*quadrigae*), with a large army of Caspii. The Indi and the rest of the dwellers on the Red Sea [Persian Gulf], mere names rather than auxiliaries (*nomina verius quam auxilia*), were behind the chariots" (IV.12.9✧). These words of Quintus Curtius confirm the truth of the distinction that must have been maintained between two kinds of royal troops: the fighting army (comprising several select ethnic contingents, essentially Iranian), and the ceremonial army (actually a microcosmic representation of the imperial realm, a gathering of all of the conscripts, including those who came from peoples whom the king and court would encounter only in the most unusual circumstances).

The convocation of the royal army *in its entirety* was thus a response to motivations that were more ideological than strategic—never mind that such gatherings generated enormous logistical problems. Just as court nomadism allowed the power and wealth of the Great King to be displayed everywhere, so also these reviews constituted neither more nor less than stagings of the Empire. Furthermore, the notion of "imperial games" is well illustrated by the organization of boat races on the coasts of Abydos. "The greatest pomp and circumstance," Herodotus remarks again, after describing the army's crossing of the bridges, which "occupied seven days and nights without a break" (VII.56–57◊). Note also Xerxes' reaction after the review at Abydos: "When he saw the whole Hellespont hidden by ships, and all the beaches of Abydos and all the open ground filled with men, he congratulated himself"◊ [cf. OPers. *šiyāti*] — that is, he rejoiced in the power that he himself had just staged. The spectacle was designed less to impress the Greeks than to hand the Great King a mirror in which to contemplate his own power.

It must be stressed at this point that the tale of the march of Darius in 513 recounted by Herodotus describes a similar circumstance. After arriving at Chalcedon, "Darius . . . took ship and sailed to the Cyanean rocks . . . seated in the temple which stands by the straits, he looked out over the Black Sea — a sight indeed worth seeing" (IV.85). Then, after contemplating the Bosporus, he raised two white marble stelas on its shore and engraved them — one in Assyrian characters, the other Greek — with the names of all of the peoples he had brought with him; and he had brought with him all of the peoples over whom he ruled" (IV.87). Were there ever such stelas? We might argue. But it is clear that at least in the mind of Herodotus they were intended less to transmit archival-type information than to exalt the territorial power of the Great King — just like, for example, the stelas that (always according to Herodotus) Darius erected at the sources of the Tearus as if to survey his new conquests (IV.91). And just like Xerxes at Abydos, "Darius himself sitting on his throne, with the army crossing over" (IV.88◊).

All in all, we do well to inquire whether the exceptional character of the Doriscus review is not a function first and foremost of the very uneven distribution of our evidence. Would not what we see at Abydos have been reproduced fairly regularly at the royal residences, comparable to the review organized by Cyrus the Younger at Tyriaeum for Epyaxa, queen of Cilicia? Standing in his war chariot, Cyrus passed by the troops, reviewing "the whole front," before pretending to launch his troops into combat. He "was delighted to see the terror with which the Greeks inspired the barbarians" (*Anab.* I.2.14–18◊).

Datames' Staging

An indirect index can be obtained from a passage in the *Life of Datames* by Cornelius Nepos. The satrap Datames had just won a victory over Thuys, dynast of Paphlagonia:

> Datames did not want word of his success to reach the king [Artaxerxes II] from anyone but himself and acted accordingly. This is why, without his entourage's knowledge, he went to the royal residence (*eo uberat rex*). The next day he dressed Thuys, a large man of frightening physique because of his black skin, long hair, and full beard, in the luxurious garment worn by the royal satraps, adorning him also with a gold necklace and bracelets and all the royal jewels. He himself wore just a short, lined peasant cloak and a tunic of coarse fabric, with a hunting helmet on his head and in his right hand a club and in his left a leash attached to Thuys. He pushed him in front of him as if he were leading a beast captured in the hunt. Everyone stared at the prisoner because of the weirdness of his attire and his alien appearance. A great throng of the curious gathered, including some who recognized Thuys and alerted the king. At first the king refused to believe it and sent Pharnabazus to investi-

gate. As soon as he found out, he immediately ordered the procession to enter; he was delighted with the capture and the manner of presentation, and especially that an important king had fallen so unexpectedly into his power. He repaid Datames with magnificent presents. (3.1–5)

Like Herodotus, this author insists on the totally exotic and outrageous nature of the conquered and the utter strangeness of the costume, which was in fact the Paphlagonian peasants' everyday garb. In fact, the context is clearly quite different from Herodotus's descriptions. In Herodotus we are in the domain of a literature derived directly from a familial tradition intended to stress Datames' ingenuity and his feel for the workings of the court (in the political sense—that is, to achieve distinction for the services he had just rendered to the Great King). In C. Nepos, we no longer have a review of the troops but the arrival of a captive with a rope around his neck, like the liar-kings at Behistun.

Nevertheless, these differences in context do not impinge on the rationale of the descriptions, which bear the same symbolic weight. In actuality, this event was also a court spectacle, in which the subjugated people lined up before the king and court. For, make no mistake, Thuys was accompanied by a number of his inner circle and conquered subjects. We might suppose that such a staging—whether or not it actually took place!—could not have had the operative value placed on it by Cornelius Nepos's informants unless the king and court regularly witnessed parades of subjugated peoples, dressed in their traditional costumes. Their foreignness only rendered even more obvious the superiority of the Persians, who wore their splendid robes decorated with costly jewelry, striking symbols of their privileged status in the Empire. In a way, Datames' parade may be considered a muted echo of the imperial festivals regularly held in the royal residences.

From Artaxerxes III to Ptolemy II

Note, finally, that this interpretation of imperial festivals can be presented as no more than plausible. Spirited exaltations of imperial power are found in other contexts as well. Consider, for example, the Athenian festival in which the revenues from the tributes levied each year on the allies of the Delian League were presented (Isocrates, *Peace*, 82). But the *pompē* ['procession'] of Ptolemy Philadelphus is perhaps the most comparable. It was obviously a court festival where the king strikingly demonstrated his wealth and power. "The procession ended with a military parade involving 57,600 infantrymen and 23,300 cavalrymen, all armed, an impressive demonstration of the Ptolemaic army." The link between territorial power and tribute levies was clearly evident in the composition of the procession:

> Each person symbolized a geographic region. This was true for women dressed as Indian captives and others who embodied the Greek towns of Asia, as well as "Ethiopian tribute-bearers." They represented the zones through which Ptolemaic power extended, whether in fact or purely in the imagination (India, Ethiopia). . . . The propaganda brought forth during the festival also had an undeniable political aspect. In part it affirmed the tie that bound Ptolemy II and Alexander, especially the development of the theme of the extension of Ptolemaic power beyond the frontiers of Egypt. The carts for the "barbarian" tents with Indian and other women "held captive" and the "Ethiopian tribute-bearers" embodied the pretensions of the Ptolemaic king to universal dominion; it is quite clear that neither India nor Ethiopia was in his power, but it is striking to observe that under Ptolemy II, as at the time of the Egyptian New Kingdom, the representatives of the foreign countries could only be considered "tributaries" of the Egyptian king. . . . Thus, the images of the festival

evidenced the extent of subject territory; the theme was developed in part on "historical" grounds—the concrete existence of territories occupied by Ptolemaic troops—and in part due to propagandistic amplification. (F. Dunand)

Even though we recognize the Greek elements as the most notable (this is a Dionysiac procession), it would not be surprising if Ptolemaic (or Seleucid: Daphne procession) sovereigns had adapted an Achaemenid festival for their purposes in the same way that the Hellenistic custom of royal entrances seems to have been copied from analogous Achaemenid-period ceremonies. In many ways, the *pompē* of Ptolemy described by Callixenus makes us think of the *pompē* of Artaxerxes III described by Theopompus (*FGrH* 115 F263a), and the preceding analyses show that it is logical to assume that this type of festival organized for the relocating of the Great King also took place more regularly (though not necessarily during the New Year) in the capitals of the Empire.

6. Royal Table and Royal Paradise: Exaltation of the Center and Appropriation of Space

Whatever interpretation we adopt, the message of the "tribute" reliefs of Persepolis is as clear as the image obtained from the Classical texts. In the imperial concept, the subjugated peoples participated in the ostentatious richness of the Great King and his court. This in fact is the understanding offered by all of the ancient authors, fascinated as they were by the gigantic magnet drawing the manpower and products of the conquered peoples toward the center. Of all the symbols of this power to impose tribute, the Greeks were particularly impressed by the splendor and luxury of the king's table. In the polemical portrait of the Great King drawn in the *Agesilaus*, Xenophon writes: "The Persian king has vintners scouring every land to find some drink that will tickle his palate; an army of cooks contrives dishes for his delight" (§9.3✧). Many Greek authors returned to this theme, often stating that the Great King regularly rewarded those who brought new foodstuffs for his table with prizes and payment (cf. Athenaeus IV.144a; XII.529d, 539d, 545d). The king's table in its sumptuousness and variety was in fact considered emblematic of the political and material might of the Great King.

In the mind of the Greek authors, the table was provisioned by taxing the conquered peoples. This is precisely the function assigned by "Cyrus" to his satraps: "Send back here what there is good and desirable in their several provinces, in order that we also who remain here may have a share of the good things that are to be found everywhere" (*Cyr.* VIII.6.6; cf. 6.23). This is also the sense of the apothegm recorded by Dinon via Athenaeus (XIV.652b–c✧):

> They used to set on the king's table all the delicacies produced by the country over which the king ruled, the choice first-fruits of each. For Xerxes did not think that the princes should use any foreign (*xenikos*) food or drink; this is why a custom forbidding such use arose later. Once, as a matter of fact, one of the eunuchs brought as one of the desserts some figs from Attica and Xerxes asked where they came from. When he learned that they were from Athens, he restrained his suppliers from buying them until the time came when he could seize them whenever he wanted without purchasing them. And it is said that the eunuch had done this on purpose to remind the king of the expedition against Athens.

The meaning of the little tale is clear: the king does not buy; he takes. A country that has not surrendered and thus does not send assessments to the royal table is considered "foreign." These assessments are assimilated to tribute by the Greek authors. In his (unfortu-

nately lost) work *On the Tributes Levied in Asia*, Ctesias enumerated all of the products
furnished to the Great King for his meals (*FGrH* 688 F53). He listed, for example,
"acanthus oil from Carmania, which the Great King used" (Athenaeus, II.67a). Amyntas
states that in some districts of Persia "the mountains produce . . . Persian nuts from
which much oil is prepared for the king" (ibid.). It was probably the same for the vineyards planted by the Persians in Syria, near Damascus, whose yield was restricted to
royal consumption, and also the wheatfields of Assos in Aeolis (Strabo XV.3.22). Note
also that, among all the varieties of dates, Theophrastus (*HP* II.6.7) singles out one
called "royal," which was notoriously rare: "It was seen only in the garden of Bagoas (*en
monōi tōi Bagōou kēpōi*), near Babylon." The information is repeated by Pliny (VI.143):

> Of all the dates, the most famous came from Babylon, exclusively from the garden of Bagôas
> (*Babylono natae uno in horto Bagou*), and were honored with the qualification "royal," be-
> cause they were reserved for the kings of Persia.

Another illustration of the centripetal traffic of the products of the Empire is provided
by the royal paradise. The paradises were vacation spots and hunting preserves, and they
also included gardens planted with trees. They were zoological gardens, where kings and
satraps introduced new species of plants and animals, a feature that was well documented already in the Neo-Assyrian period. Many kings boasted of having brought new
lands into production, of having brought in water, and of having planted different trees,
such that they could relax in magnificent gardens and orchards, full "of every sort of aromatic and scented plant" (Sargon; compare Xenophon, *Oec.* IV.21: "sweet scents clung
round them as they walked"). The evidence for the Achaemenid period is less abundant
but equally telling. The paradises are regularly characterized as including every specie
of tree bearing every fruit of the earth (e.g., Xenophon, *Anab.* I.4.10; II.4.14). They are
"groves artificially planted" (Quintus Curtius VII.2.22◊; Xenophon, *Oecon.* IV.21), that
is, carefully tended gardens. They are also encountered in the Persepolis tablets (PFa 1;
33). Aelian compares the Indian kings' paradises with the Persian paradises of Susa and
Ecbatana; always maintaining that the former are still more beautiful than the latter, he
leads us to think that they are characterized by the same wealth of animals and trees as
was brought under the care of 'the kings' superintendents' (*hoi meledōnes hoi basileioi*;
Anim. XIII.17). Elsewhere, he speaks with wonder of the paradises of Susa, where specially trained oxen hoisted the water for the fields (*Anim.* VII.1). As in Egypt and Assyria,
exotic plants and animals from all the subjugated countries were gathered—such as the
"camels known as dromedaries and of extraordinary swiftness, twelve elephants imported by Darius (III) from India" that the satrap of Susa offered to Alexander (Quintus
Curtius V.2.10◊). Aristotle records that Pharnaces acclimated mules to Hellespontine
Phrygia (doubtless in the paradise near Dascylium; *Hist. An.* VI.26.580b). And it was
very likely in his position as superintendent of a paradise that Gadatas received the con-
gratulations of Darius for having planted trees that came from Syria near Magnesia on
the Meander (ML 12).

It is easy to understand that the Achaemenid model was copied by minor local
princes eager to identify with the Great King, such as Polycrates of Samos (pp. 83f.) and
Cotys of Thrace. Theopompus describes one of the dynast's residences thus:

> Onocarsis, an estate in Thrace which included a very beautifully planted grove (*alsos*) and
> one well adapted for a pleasant sojourn, especially during the summer season. In fact it had
> been one of the favourite resorts of Cotys, who more than any other king that had arisen in

Thrace, directed his career towards the enjoyment of pleasures (*hēdypatheia*) and luxuries (*tryphē*), and as he went about the country, wherever he discovered places shaded with trees and watered with running streams, he turned these into banqueting places (*hestiatōria*); and visiting them each in turn, as chance led him, he would offer sacrifices to the gods and hold court with his lieutenants, remaining prosperous and envied. (Athenaeus XII.531e–f✧)

Cotys thus regulated space, the paradise demonstrating symbolically the control and exaltation of his territorial power. The Achaemenid model cannot be doubted: the Great King himself moved from paradise to paradise, where the 'royal stations' were (*stathmoi basilikoi*; cf. Plutarch, *Art.* 25.1). At each stop, the model of the royal table was reproduced (cf. 24.3): Alcibiades understood this perfectly, because he too tried to profit from the symbolism proclaimed by the rules of Achaemenid court nomadism (cf. Athenaeus XII.534d; Plutarch, *Alc.* 12.1). There is hardly any further doubt that the open competition between Straton of Sidon and Nicocles of Paphos over the luxury of their tables was based on conscious imitation of the king's table (cf. Athenaeus XII.531c–e; Aelian, *VH* VII.2).

The same holds for Harpalus, treasurer of Alexander posted to Babylon, who adapted the Persian paradises to the ideological advantage of the Macedonian conquerors:

Harpalus . . . was desirous to adorn the palace gardens and walks with Grecian plants, succeeding in raising all but ivy, which the earth would not bear, but constantly killed. For being a plant that loves a cold soil, the temper of this hot and fiery earth was improper for it. (Plutarch, *Alex.* 35.15✧)

There is little doubt that Harpalus was engaged in imitation and that it was on the orders of Alexander. This is also suggested by Pliny (VIII.44):

Alexander brought under his control, across the entire extent of Asia and Greece, several thousand men who lived for hunting, birding, or fishing, or who maintained breeding-grounds, flocks and herds, apiaries, fisheries, and aviaries, so that no creature remained unknown to him.

Alexander was careful to turn paradises to his advantage as the symbol par excellence of imperial dominion. Paradises in fact constituted a representation in microcosm of the ecological, floral, and faunal variety of the imperial realm. We can easily compare them with this recent semiotic interpretation of the gardens of Versailles under Louis XIV:

The place where [the prince] resides seems to expand to the size of the universe. Garden and palace thus appear to be a miniature compendium of the entire world. . . . This exemplary place contains the most beautiful and rare of what the outside world produces and transforms them into a sign. Versailles becomes the show-window of the world; exotic plants, Dutch flowers, wild animals, rare birds, and objects brought from the four corners of the universe are all perpetually found there. They are presented, they appear together, as a whole, without undergoing the ordinary constraints of merchandise, of payment, of time and space. Not having succeeded in creating a universal monarchy, the kingdom conquered the world in the form of signs; he reconstructed the earth entire in his garden; he played with a scale model of the universe that he could alter as his whim desired. (J. M. Apostolidès)

Table and paradise thus participate in the exaltation of royal splendor. So do human assessments, as seen in the text of the edict (surely apocryphal) recorded by the redactor of the book of Esther. After the repudiation of Queen Vashti, King Ahasuerus made a proclamation throughout his entire kingdom:

Let beautiful girls be selected for the king. Let the king appoint commissioners throughout the provinces of his realm to bring all these beautiful young virgins to the citadel of Susa, to the harem. . . . (2:2–3✧)

The most beautiful women of the Empire were required to come to enchant the nights of the Great King, just as the most celebrated products of the various countries were required to come to enhance the luxury of the royal table, and the scents of the exotic plants accompanied the Great King on his paradisiacal promenades!

Chapter 6

Representations of Royalty and Monarchic Ideology

1. Sources and Problems

The Variety of Evidence: Complementary and Specific

Many and varied are the sources available to the historian who would analyze the constituents and the dynamic of the monarchic ideology established (or more rigorously codified) by Darius and maintained in its essence by his successors. The Great King himself often described, and a number of his inscriptions detail, what constituted the ideological justifications for his power in his own opinion, not just in respect to his dominion over subject peoples (as we have presented above), but also in regard to his royal authority. The Great Kings were also frequently represented in reliefs at Persepolis and elsewhere, in monumental sculpture at Susa, and in both cases sometimes with accompanying inscriptions. Kings' images are also found in various forms in other media, particularly coins and seals. All of these elements taken together constitute what may be called official court art. Along with these imperial sources, the presentations of the Classical sources, which have the advantage of situating royal activity in its historical (or historicizing) context, must also be taken into account.

At first glance, we might consider the convergences between these different sources of information to be striking. From an overall comparison of the various corpora, we can offer a view of Achaemenid monarchic ideology that is both analytical and dynamic. Nevertheless, it is a good idea to keep in mind several methodological caveats. First of all, it is sometimes risky to establish a direct connection between iconographic

Fig. 13. Darius and his court as seen in a Greek painting of the fourth century.

204

depictions and the Classical texts, taking the texts as historiographic commentaries on the reliefs. And even within royal art, we must distinguish the information (1) as a function of the message that the Great King wished to deliver, (2) as a function of the public for whom it was intended, and (3) as a function of the medium (inscriptions, reliefs, seals, etc.).

These distinctions also permit us to reintroduce diachrony into the thematic study. Many iconographic monuments—palaces, reliefs, coins, some seals—are datable and dated (though the dates may be disputed). This does not generally hold for information given by the Classical authors, who most often speak of a generic "king" when discussing a court custom. Most of the Classical sources come from the fourth century (Ctesias, Dinon) and the Hellenistic era (Alexandrine historians), and they aim at analyzing the potential permanence of the ideological systems. When we grant priority to sources specifically dated to the Achaemenid period, we can more clearly recognize what goes back to Darius in the working out and propagation of the monarchic ideology. It will thus be advisable to return to the modifications or adaptations brought about by Darius's successors (for example, the introduction or transformation of an official religion of Mithra and Anāhita during the time of Artaxerxes II) at the end of this chapter.

Lost Persian Monuments, or Greek Reconstructions for Harried Tourists?

There is an additional obstacle to uncritical use of the Classical sources. In some cases, they give information on royal activities that are not represented in the reliefs. There is of course no doubt that many of the decorative elements of the palace have disappeared, whether enameled bricks (known best from Susa but also found at Persepolis) or metal sheathing applied to the monumental gates, gold or jeweled cladding, or color, which can be discerned only from residual traces. Only recently, for instance, has the first physical evidence of fresco-work been discovered in a palace of Artaxerxes II at Susa and on the walls of an apadana ("great hall") in Armenia. This leads to the question, should we or should we not presume that the Classical authors provide firsthand information about monuments that have been lost since ancient times? Or better, should we reconstruct lost Achaemenid monuments in the same way that we might attempt to devise a computer-graphics visual recreation of the battle of Marathon, based on the description given by Pausanias? In some cases, the Greek descriptions are not a real problem. It is not hard to accept, for example, that the palaces were provided with bronze gates, as Diodorus (XVII.71.6) and the author of the *De Mundo* (398a) state. Assyrian precedents, fragments found at Persepolis, and Treasury tablets offer substantiation. The same can be said of the Golden Vine found in the Susa Treasury by one of Alexander's successors. However, among the lost decorative elements, the specific problem of the tapestries must be highlighted. Many Greek authors stress their magnificence. There can hardly be any doubt that in most cases the composition of the woven designs represented the faunal themes so popular in Achaemenid glyptic and goldwork (cf. Aristophanes, *Frogs* 937; Athenaeus XII.538d). For instance, a remarkable illustration is found in a saddlecloth from the Pazyryk kurgan in Siberia, which is understood to be inspired by Achaemenid art.

On the other hand, some statements by Classical authors stimulate critical doubt. According to Plutarch (*Them.* 29.4❖), when Themistocles was granted an official audience with Artaxerxes I, he succeeded in holding the king's attention in this way:

> Themistocles replied, that a man's discourse was like to a rich Persian carpet (*poikila strō-mata*), the beautiful figures and patterns of which can only be shown by spreading and extending it out; when it is contracted and folded up, they are obscure and lost; and, therefore, he desired time.

It is tempting to think that Themistocles was making an implicit but clear reference to the tapestries that decorated the audience chamber of the royal palace. Were these carpets illustrated with drawings and symbolic representations of events? The account of Chares of Mytilene, repeated by Athenaeus (XIII.575f◊), immediately comes to mind. Chares, chamberlain to Alexander the Great, recorded an Iranian folktale that told of a romance between Prince Zariadres and Princess Odatis. Chares says:

> Now this love affair is held in remembrance among the barbarians who live in Asia and it is extremely popular; in fact they picture (*zōgraphein*) this story in their temples and palaces (*basileia*) and even in private dwellings; and most princes bestow the name Odatis on their own daughters.

But, however interesting this may be as evidence for methods of diffusion and preservation of Iranian folklore, the account does not bear on the potential existence of historical scenes. On the other hand, according to a later author, Philostratus, the walls of the Parthian palaces in Babylon were also decorated with embroidered tapestries. Along with mythological motifs borrowed from the Greek repertoire, historical scenes were also found:

> The tapestries also showed Datis snatching Naxos from the sea, Artaphernes besieging Eretria, and, among the deeds of Xerxes, those wherein he claimed victory. Obviously the occupations of Athens and Thermopylae were included, and scenes still more dear to the Medes, of drained rivers, a bridge across the sea, and the manner in which a canal was cut near Athos. (*Vit. Apoll.* 1.25)

What is this kind of evidence worth? Setting aside its late nature, we may legitimately ask whether the author really did see what he describes or whether his claim is pure creative writing. The repetition of the motif by the author of the *Alexander Romance* (III.28.10) strengthens the observer's doubts. Each of the supposed descriptions repeats passages of Herodotus quite precisely, especially the numerous digressions he devotes to rivers drained (he claims) by Xerxes' armies (VII.21, 53, 58, 108). Many modern-day travelers have come to Persepolis armed with passages from Diodorus of Sicily and other ancient sources and—contrary to all evidence at the site—sworn that they saw exactly what their passion for the Classical authors prepared them to "see"!

The fact that a traveler was an eyewitness does not in itself validate his claims. See the conflicting descriptions of Cyrus's tomb given by the companions of Alexander the Great, used by Strabo (XV.3.7–8◊) and Arrian (*Anab.* VI.29). One (Aristobulus) describes the building as "a small tower . . . concealed within the dense growth the trees"; the other (Onesicritus) "states that the tower had ten stories"; a third, later author (Aristus of Salamis) wrote "that the tower has only two stories and is large"! Ever since antiquity, furthermore, all sorts of nonsense (or fictional recreation) has been proffered on the significance of the Behistun relief (it is virtually inaccessible). According to Diodorus (II.13.2◊), "The lowest part of these she [Semiramis] smoothed off and engraved thereon a likeness a herself with a hundred spearmen at her side" (cf. also Isidore of Charax, *Parthian Stations* §5)! And afterward new interpretations were proposed by Arab geographers and European travelers, each more fantastic than the last.

Of course, there can be no doubt that some artists were inspired by the Persian Wars. We know particularly the extent to which the Athenian artists drew their subjects from them—but this was for the purpose of exalting the memory of the Greek victories! Herodotus, for instance, records the story of the architect Mandrocles of Samos, who was richly paid by Darius for designing the bridge of boats across the Bosporus.

> Mandrocles spent a certain portion of what he received in having a picture painted, showing the whole process of the bridging of the strait, and Darius himself sitting on his throne, with the army crossing over. This picture he presented as a dedicatory offering to the temple of Hera, with the following verses inscribed upon it, to serve as a permanent record of his achievement:
>
> *Goddess, accept this gift from Mandrocles,*
> *Who bridged the Bosporus' fish-haunted seas.*
> *His labour, praised by King Darius, won*
> *Honour for Samos, for himself a crown.* (IV.88–89)

It is clear that the picture was not ordered by Darius and that it was not intended to decorate the royal palace walls. Indeed, in doing this, Mandrocles was exhibiting a certain amount of sycophancy and thus contributed to the perpetuation of the memory of Darius's heroic actions near the Greeks. But primarily he intended to leave a monument to his own worth in his city, which had already paid him well by awarding him a crown.

In a long digression, Diodorus of Sicily, following Ctesias, took great interest in the mythical queen Semiramis. Describing one of the palaces in Babylon built by the queen, he writes:

> On both the towers and the walls there were again animals of every kind, ingeniously executed by the use of colours as well as by the realistic imitation of the several types; and the whole had been made to represent a hunt, complete in every detail, of all sorts of wild animals, and their size was more than four cubits [ca. 2 m]. Among the animals, moreover, Semiramis had also been portrayed, on horseback and in the act of hurling a javelin at a leopard, and nearby was her husband Ninus, in the act of thrusting his spear into a lion at close quarters. . . . [In another palace] were also portrayed both battle-scenes and hunts of every kind, which filled those who gazed thereon with varied emotions of pleasure. (Diodorus II.8.6–7♦)

We know that depictions of the Great King often lie behind these descriptions of Semiramis. But no evidence from Susa, Babylon, or Persepolis provides the slightest confirmation. It is possible that Ctesias or one of his informants was talking about hunting scenes that decorated pre-Achaemenid palaces. However, it must be stressed that in the Assyrian palaces war scenes and hunting scenes were sometimes placed in out-of-the-way chambers. It is thus not out of the question that Ctesias took it upon himself to decorate the Babylonian palaces of Semiramis / the Great King with scenes anyone could see on seals and stamps in particular.

Finally, in the course of telling about the expedition of the Emperor Julian against the Sassanian Persians, Ammianus Marcellinus includes a parallel report:

> We halted in rich country lushly planted with fruit trees, vines, and cypress greenery; in the center was found a secluded den, shaded and pleasant, where in each apartment could be seen barbarian paintings showing the king in the act of killing wild beasts in a large hunting party. In fact, these people do not paint or depict any other scenes but massacres and wars of every kind. (XXIV.6.1)

This is also a late text. Study of Sassanid goldwork effectively shows when the hunting theme became part of the monarchic lifestyle. What is more interesting is the country-side described by Ammianus Marcellinus. We are clearly in a paradise, an enchanting place where the king could stop and where hunts were organized in game preserves stocked with wild animals. What the author describes is not a palace in a capital, but a royal residence situated in a paradise. Were these residences decorated with hunting scenes in honor of the king? Possibly. We have no archaeological evidence to confirm the hypothesis. The only information on this point comes from the small courts of Asia Minor, especially Lycia, where the dynasts liked to see portrayals of themselves hunting. But the fact that the artists were partly inspired by the Persians does not necessarily mean that they copied court representations. Perhaps they only imitated and adapted images on seals and impressions.

These preliminary remarks are not intended totally to dismiss the information found in the Classical authors. There is hardly any doubt, for example, that the Greeks of the fifth and fourth centuries knew the splendors of the royal residences. The numerous ex-changes between the Greek cities and the Achaemenid court, quite apart from the abun-dance and richness of the booty, made the Greeks aware of objects symbolic of Persian luxury (garments, vessels, tents, and other things), which upper-class Greeks clearly adopted to their own use. In this, Greek texts and iconography tend to exaggerate the "Achaemenid" corpus but are also careful to separate the source of inspiration from the methods of acquisition and borrowing. On the other hand, we have hardly any informa-tion about just what images of the royal palaces might have been available specifically in Greece. The only exceptions are references by Aristotle (*De Mirab.* 39a.15–26) and Athenaeus (XII.541a–b), who refer to a luxurious *himation* ['cloak'] that Dionysius the Elder was supposed to have bought from a wealthy Sybarite: on the edges of the garment Susa and Persepolis were represented, doubtless in very stylized form, after the fashion of the "city reliefs" that are well known from sculpture (especially Assyrian and Lycian). If correct, the information seems to confirm what might otherwise be questionable: the Greeks of the Classical period had information on the Persian royal palaces and court art. It is sometimes thought, in fact, that the Athenians of Pericles' time adapted the Per-sian style for the Acropolis to emphasize their own imperial dominion. Nonetheless, we must point out that it is not until Alexander's court historians that we have the first writ-ten description of Persepolis (Diodorus XVII.70).

Center and Periphery

It is important to distinguish between evidence that derives from the center and evi-dence that derives from the periphery. The former casts a direct light, springing from the understanding of the Great Kings and their counselors; the latter is more like reinter-pretations, which the historian must try to decipher. We thus need to isolate the "provin-cial" materials, which, though they were clearly inspired by the court art from the center, nonetheless possess distinctive characteristics (the so-called Greco-Persian stamps and stelas from Asia Minor, for example, or Persepolis-like reliefs from Mey-dançikkale in Cilicia). All of these documents assume tremendous importance for any-one who is trying to understand the diffusion of monarchic themes throughout the Empire. What they mostly inform us about, however, is life in satrapal or dynastic courts and the process of acculturation. They will therefore be considered separately (fig. 13).

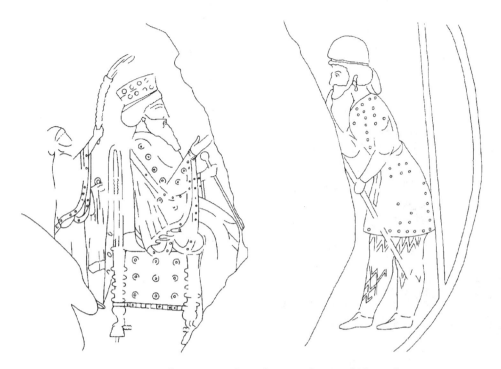

Fig. 14. Audience scene from the sarcophagus of Alexander.

We will only consider depictions that are obviously true copies of depictions found at Persepolis. See, for example, the audience scene on one of the bullas from Dascylium (fig. 15) and the scene found on the shield of a warrior on Alexander's sarcophagus (fig. 14); it has been supposed (not implausibly) that the artist had seen the Persepolis reliefs. On the other hand, it would be a good idea to avoid suggesting that every depiction found in provincial artwork is an exact reproduction of now-lost iconography from the center.

The absence of hunting and war scenes at Susa or Persepolis is particularly striking, especially when we take into account the place the Classical texts and the seal impressions grant to these royal activities and when we recall the strong predilection of the Assyrian kings for this kind of representation. But we must resist the temptation to fill in the Achaemenid lacuna using the Classical texts just presented or the "Greco-Persian" stelas and seals. In the final analysis, all of these texts and interpretations falter in the face of the evidence. Aside from the Behistun relief, the Great Kings never depicted themselves as warriors (or hunters) on the walls of their palaces, and even at Behistun the realistic aspect is secondary. It is exactly this predilection that is of greatest importance for the historian. Neither the reliefs nor the inscriptions were meant to describe the daily life of the king or even to portray explicitly each of the elements of the monarchic ideology. Suffice it to remark that there is not a single royal inscription making even the slightest reference to the Great King's ability as a hunter, except in a few apocryphal inscriptions transmitted by the Greek authors—*transmitted* here meaning "reconstructed" from information

Fig. 15. Audience scene on a seal impression from Dascylium.

they had gathered from other media! This observation constrains our method: although we must use the available sources to understand the functioning of Achaemenid monarchic ideology, we must also distinguish the media, in such a way as to better understand the specificity of the message transmitted by the monumental art of Persepolis, Susa, or Naqš-i Rustam.

2. The Prince in His Own Mirror

Darius at Naqš-i Rustam

Darius himself is responsible for the richest exposition of the ideological justifications for his authority. He presented them first at Behistun, insisting especially on the privileged protection of Ahura-Mazda, his familial rights, and his stature as conqueror. We have already emphasized the considerable interest of the Behistun inscription and relief for the reconstruction of Achaemenid monarchic ideology, and we will have frequent occasion to cite it again in the pages to come, to parallel other royal statements.

But in this regard, a different monument takes pride of place—the sculpted façade of the royal tombs at Naqš-i Rustam (fig. 16). The tombs appear practically identical to each other. In the upper register (the top arm of the cruciform elevation), the Great King is shown standing on a three-step platform. His left hand holds a bow, resting on the ground behind his left foot. His right hand is raised toward Ahura-Mazda, represented here (as elsewhere) as a person rising from a winged disk alongside a lunar crescent. Between the king and the god is a flaming altar. The

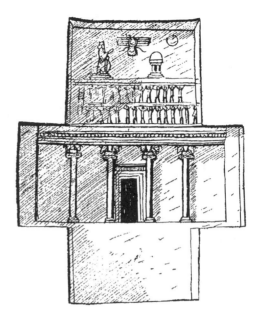

Fig. 16. The tomb of Darius at Naqš-i Rustam.

ground is supported by two rows of thirty figures representing the subjugated peoples as bearers of the throne (or the ground of the Empire). To the left, shown one above the other, are the Great King's arms-bearers Gobryas (Gaubaruva) and Aspathines (Aspacānā), each identified by an inscription (*DNc–d*). Other members of the court appear to the right (perhaps as mourners).

Only Darius's tomb has an inscription, placed behind the king, in several versions. There are three distinct parts. The first (*DNa*) includes an invocation of Ahura-Mazda, "a great god . . . who created this earth, who created yonder sky, who created man, who created happiness for man, who made Darius king [the royal titulature follows]" (§1◊). Then Darius proclaims his dominion over the peoples that he has "seized outside Persia," who "bore tribute to" him, who did what the king ordered them to do: "My law—that held them firm." A country list follows (§2◊). In §3, Darius records his victories achieved with the aid of Ahura-Mazda, and he refers directly to the bearer-peoples, whom the viewer is invited to regard as an attestation of royal power. A final invocation and a prayer to Ahura-Mazda (§5–6◊) follow:

> Saith Darius the King: This which has been done, all that by the will of Ahuramazda I did. Ahuramazda bore me aid, until I did the work. Me may Ahuramazda protect from harm, and my royal house, and this land: this I pray of Ahuramazda, this may Ahuramazda give to me! O man, that which is the command of Ahuramazda, let this not seem repugnant to thee; do not leave the right path; do not rise in rebellion!

Another part (*DNb*◊)—which was later repeated in summary by Xerxes (*XPl*)—is clearly remarkable for its style and inspiration. It comprises a sort of catalog of royal virtues and an exposition of the duties of the king and his subjects. It is thus with good reason that it is considered the Prince's Own Mirror:

§7—A great god is Ahuramazda, who created this excellent work which is seen, who created happiness for man, who bestowed wisdom and efficiency on Darius the King.

§8a—Saith Darius the King: By the favor of Ahura-Mazda I am of such a sort that I am a friend to right, I am not a friend to wrong. It is not my desire that the weak man should have wrong done to him by the mighty; nor is that my desire, that the mighty man should have wrong done to him by the weak.

§8b—What is right, that is my desire. I am not a friend to the man who is a Lie-follower. I am not hot-tempered. What things develop in my anger, I hold firmly under control by my thinking power. I am firmly ruling over my own (impulses).

§8c—The man who cooperates, him according to his cooperative action, him thus do I reward. Who does harm, him according to the damage thus I punish. It is not my desire that a man should do harm; nor indeed is that my desire, if he should do harm, he should not be punished.

§8d—What a man says against a man, that does not convince me, until he satisfies the Ordinance of Good Regulations.

§8e—What a man does or performs (for me) according to his (natural) powers, (therewith) I am satisfied, and my pleasure is abundant, and I am well satisfied. [Xerxes: "And I generously repay men of good will."]

§8f—Of such a sort is my understanding and my command: when what has been done by me thou shalt see or hear of, both in the palace and in the war-camp, this is my activity over and above my thinking power and my understanding.

§8g—This indeed is my activity: inasmuch as my body has the strength, as battle-fighter I am a good battle-fighter. Once let there be seen with understanding in the place (of battle), what I see (to be) rebellious, what I see (to be) not (rebellious); both with understanding and with command then am I first to think with action, when I see a rebel as well as when I see a not-(rebel).

§8h   Trained am I both with hands and with feet. As a horseman I am a good horseman. As a bowman I am a good bowman both afoot and on horseback. As a spearman I am a good spearman both afoot and on horseback.

§8i—And the (physical) skillfulnesses which Ahuramazda has bestowed upon me and I have had the strength to use them—by the favor of Ahuramazda what has been done by me, I have done with these skillfulnesses which Ahuramazda has bestowed upon me.

[§14a—May Ahura-Mazda protect me and my work: *XPl.*]

An isolated paragraph is separated from the body of the preceding inscription by a blank space, which was not repeated by Xerxes. In inspiration, it closely resembles the first part (*DNa*). As in *DNa* §6, the king directly addresses a subject (*marika*) who is not specifically identified, who seems to stand metonymically for all of the populations dominated by the Great King. He dictates his behavior to him:

§9a–b—O menial, vigorously make thou known of what sort I am, and of what sort my skillfulnesses, and of what sort my superiority. Let that not seem false to thee, which has been heard by thy ears. That do thou hear, which is communicated to thee. [O menial], let that not be made (to seem) false to thee, which has been done by me. That do thou behold, which [has been inscribed]. Let not the laws [be disobeyed] by thee. Let not [anyone] be untrained [in obedience]. [O menial], let not the king (feel himself obliged to) inflict punishment (?) [for wrong-doing (?) on the swellers (in the land) (?)].

The Victorious King and the King of Justice

The second text (*DNb*) is more revealing about the specific qualities and virtues of the king. They are defined with reference to two spheres of activity, at once distinct and closely complementary: the palace (*viθ*: or the House) and the battlefield (§8f). Darius is not only a good infantryman and a good horseman, a good archer and a good lancer (§8h), but he is also a good commander-in-chief. If he is able to lead his troops into combat successfully, it is because he possesses particular intellectual qualities: intelligence and a spirit of analysis and decisiveness that free him from the emotion of panic (which any other soldier would be familiar with: §8g) and enable him rapidly to execute the clearest and most effective measures in the heat of battle (§8b.11–13). The king is thus a leader of men.

These statements remind us of many others, such as: "By the favor of Ahuramazda and of me, Darius the King, [this country Persia] does not feel fear of (any) other" (*DPd*◆). In numerous statements, Darius says that it was at the head of the Persian warriors that he conquered and mastered the peoples of his Empire. He refers to himself when he writes, addressing his subjects, "Then shall it become known to thee: the spear of a Persian man has gone forth far; then shall it become known to thee: a Persian man has delivered battle far indeed from Persia" (*DNa* §4). Also: "The Persian Man conquered Egypt" (*DSab*). The ideology of the warrior-king is very well illustrated at Behistun in both text and image. Indeed, "this country Persia which Ahuramazda bestowed upon [him is] good, possessed of good horses, possessed of good men" (*DPd*◆), and all the Persians are known for their valor, as stressed by Herodotus: "Prowess in fighting, the chief proof of manliness" (I.136◆). Thanks to the protection of his god, the Great King was distinguished from all of the Persian warriors: he was not only a first-class horseman, archer, and lancer, but he also possessed the physical and intellectual qualities that made him a commander-in-chief beyond compare.

The same qualities also make Darius a master of justice. As at Behistun, the king contrasts justice with the Lie (§8b). His capacities for comprehension and judgment allow him to dispense justice with complete equanimity, for he is able to transcend anger (§8b). We may compare this royal statement with what Herodotus writes of the way in which the heads of Persian families and the king himself declared judgments: "Custom . . . forbids even the king himself to put a man to death for a single offence. . . . Their way is to balance faults against services, and then, if the faults are greater and more numerous, anger may take its course" (I.137◆). This is exactly the definition Darius himself provides of justice: he repays whoever "does wrong," This punishes "the Lie-follower" and "who does harm" (§8a–c). This obviously relates to a highly monarchical conception of justice: every man is judged in proportion to the aid and assistance he brings to the king's interests—as Herodotus understood perfectly. But Darius's statements go further. He tries to reconcile the interests of the powerful and the poor (§8a). In his eyes, a poor man may behave as worthily as a rich man (§9b). As well as being defender of the peace against enemy attack, Darius is also guarantor and restorer of civil peace (cf. *DSe* 001). If the king can behave in this way, it is because of "regarding himself as divinely appointed for a law to the Persians, and the supreme arbitrator of good and evil" (Plutarch, *Art.* 23.5◆).

Text and Image

Many Achaemenid objects illustrate Darius's statements in pictures. At Behistun and Naqš-i Rustam, Darius holds his bow in his left hand; at Behistun it rests on his left foot, which crushes Gaumata to the ground. The king is also represented as an archer on the royal coinage. In the various designs, he has the bow in his left hand and arrows in his

Fig. 17. Royal Coinage.

right, or sometimes a quiver on his shoulder, or he is kneeling to draw the bow; sometimes he has a lance on the right and the bow on the left, or even, on the run, he has the bow in his extended left hand while drawing an arrow with his right hand from the quiver on his shoulder (fig. 17). It seems clear that this figure is not a specific king, but the king in general.

The contest won by Smerdis in Egypt is indicative of the importance of the bow as an attribute of sovereignty (III.30). Does not Aeschylus call Darius the royal archer? At Naqš-i Rustam the noble Gobryas is Darius's lance-bearer (*arštibara*), while another noble, Aspathines, is the bearer of the bow (*vaçabara*) and the king's battle-axe (*DNc–d*). The bow is expressly listed by the Classical authors as one of the "insignias of royal power," perhaps received by the Great King during the enthronement ceremony.

The theme "victorious king" and the representation in the Behistun style of the people who are conquered is found on several seals (fig. 18). On one of them (attributed to Artaxerxes III), the king, with a lance upright in his right hand and quiver on his shoulder, holds a rope in his left hand that binds the neck of three conquered people (*SA³b*).

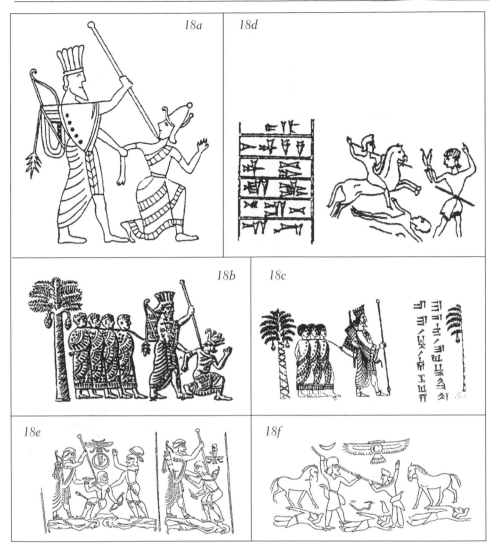

Fig. 18. The King, the Persians, and war.

The text says, "I am Artaxerxes the Great King" (fig. 18c). Another seal, also from Egypt, shows a Persian king, his left hand grasping an Egyptian with an Egyptian hairdo (*pschent*), whom he thrusts through with his lance while holding four prisoners with a rope around their necks (fig. 18a–b); the motif of captives held by a rope is repeated on a seal on the Treasury tablets (PTS no. 28). Perhaps the Artaxerxes seal was meant to commemorate Artaxerxes I's victory over the rebel Inarus. The important thing is to note the persistence of the theme of lionizing the Great King as a hero. The theme of conqueror-king is found on several seals: on one of them, a royal Persian kills a Saka, whom he holds by his pointed hat; a nearly identical scene is found on a cylinder seal from the Oxus treasury (Dalton no. 114, pl. XVI); on another, a king thrusts his lance through a Greek

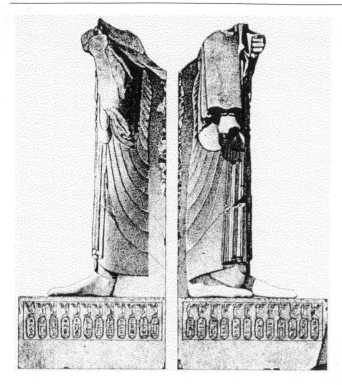

Fig. 19. The statue of Darius discovered at Susa.

warrior, who kneels before him immobilized by the king's left hand (fig. 18e). An image of the warrior king was already represented on the seal of Kuraš of Anšan (fig. 18d); it is also found on the seal of Aršāma, satrap of Egypt (fig. 18f). All of these representations are clearly intended to spread the image of a king endowed with all of the virtues of a fine warrior, just as this fact is expressed in words by Darius at Naqš-i Rustam and Behistun.

3. The King in Majesty

The Statue of Darius

One of the most meaningful objects is the statue of Darius discovered at Susa in 1972 (fig. 19). It was placed on the gate on which construction began under Darius but which was only finished under Xerxes (fig. 38, p. 260). This gate, which dominates the plain at some 15 m high, gave visitors access to the Royal City on their way to the Apadana and the other palaces (fig. 9, p. 167; fig. 19). Probably, two identical statues were originally placed right and left, facing the interior. This is the first known example of Achaemenid monumental statuary; only the head is missing. Although it was carved in Egypt and is characterized both by its origin and its initial installation at Heliopolis, the statue represents the king in a way that is very similar to representations at Persepolis. The king holds a short staff in his right hand and a (lotus) flower in his left. Only the robe looks different, since it has neither decoration nor color.

In fact, in every royal depiction, from Darius I to Artaxerxes I, the king wears the same robe with identical decoration (concentric circles, a row of striding lions). The costume of "Cyrus" is described by Xenophon (*Cyr.* VIII.3.13◊): "A purple tunic shot with white (none but the king may wear such a one), trousers (*anaxyrides*) of scarlet dye about his legs, and a mantle (*kandys*) all of purple." Quintus Curtius features the same choice of colors in describing Darius III's robe:

> The attire of the king was noteworthy beyond all else in luxury; a purple-edged tunic woven about a white centre, a cloak of cloth of gold, ornamented with golden hawks, which seemed to attack each other with their beaks; from a golden belt, with which he was girt woman-fashion, he had hung a scimitar (*akinakēs*), the scabbard of which was a single gem. The Persians called the king's head-dress (*regium capitis insigne*) *kidaris*; this was bound with a blue fillet variegated with white. (III.3.17◊)

Some ornaments do not appear on the Persepolis reliefs. It is not impossible that fashion changed over time (cf. III.3.5). However, the colors noted at Persepolis are also found in this description. The choice of colors was certainly deliberate: in the Indo-Iranian traditions, white, red, and blue corresponded to the three categories of the social fabric, the priests (white), soldiers (red), and farmers (blue).

There is no reason to suppose that the Susa statue was unique in royal Achaemenid art. We know from Herodotus (III.88◊) that, upon his accession, Darius's "first act was to erect a stone monument with a carving of a man on horseback, and the following inscription: Darius, son of Hystaspes, by the *virtue* of his *horse* and *of his groom Oebares, won* the *throne of Persia*. The horse's name was included." Whatever the legitimate doubts concerning the exact content of the inscription, the existence of this sort of relief cannot be ruled out. The craze for equestrian statues among the Persians is attested in a well-known Aramaic document, in which the satrap Aršāma orders the sculptor Hinzanāy, then in Egypt, to "execute a sculpture of a horse with its rider, corresponding to that which he previously executed for me, and other sculptures" (*DAE* 70 [AD 9◊]). We also learn from Diodorus of Sicily (XVII.17.6◊) that Ariobarzanes, "a former satrap of Phrygia," placed his statue in the temple of Athena Ilias. There is thus no difficulty in postulating that other royal statues were found at other sites, including Persepolis (Quintus Curtius V.6.5). Furthermore, Plutarch records that after the sacking of the city one could still see "a large statue of Xerxes" (*Alex.* 37.5◊).

Iconography from Persepolis

The king is also shown in numerous reliefs at Persepolis in conventional poses that are often reflected on the two sides of an entrance, as in a mirror.

He is seated on his throne (supported, as at Naqš-i Rustam, by the throne-bearers). He is sometimes accompanied by another royal figure, who is usually considered to be the crown prince, standing behind him. The king's feet rest on a footstool, and he has his long scepter in his right hand, with its end on the ground in front of the footstool (east gate of the Tripylon: Schmidt, pls. 77–78; fig. 21 here). On other reliefs, the king is shown without the prince; the only figure behind him is a servant holding a parasol over the king with his right hand and a towel in his left (Throne Room: Schmidt, pls. 104–5).

Always seated on his throne in the same pose and holding a lotus flower in his left hand, the Great King is found under a canopy decorated with a lion frieze (surrounding an image of Ahura-Mazda) and friezes of rosettes (fig. 20). Outside of the canopy, guards fill out the scene, two on each side. The royal throne and footstool are placed on a dais. Behind the king, the crown prince stands on the dais, also holding a lotus flower in his left hand, extending his right hand toward his father's throne. Directly in front of the king are two footed censers and a high court official bending toward the sovereign with his right hand to his mouth and a short staff in his left. Behind the crown prince we see two people: a servant holds a towel in his right hand, with his left hand on his right arm; the other probably represents the royal arms-bearer (battle-axe in his right hand, bow and *gōrytos* ['quiver'] on his left shoulder). This was the subject of the reliefs in the Treasury that were originally placed in the middle of the façade of the north portico of the Apadana (Schmidt, pls. 119–21). The crown prince is not found on later reliefs (four audience scenes on the east and west gates of the Hall of a Hundred Columns [or Throne Room] started by Xerxes and built by Artaxerxes I; pls. 96–97); immediately behind the throne is the parasol-holder (fig. 22).

There are also several cases where the king is shown walking, followed by two servants (fig. 23), one holding the parasol over the royal head, the other a towel folded over his forearm (Tripylon: Schmidt, pls. 75–76; Darius's palace: pls. 138–41; Xerxes' palace: pls. 178–84; "Harem": pls. 193–94); a scene showing the king accompanied by his parasol-bearer is also found on a stamp published by Speleers (1917, no. 708; also showing a lion and a trident stuck in the ground).

Finally, on many reliefs a royal figure is depicted confronting real or imaginary animals (lions, bulls; monster with a horned lion's head or bird's head). Most often, the different kinds of combat are depicted side by side as if they constitute the elements of a single iconographic discourse (fig. 24). In general, the combatant grasps the animal's mane (or horns) with his left hand while plunging the sword in his right hand into the belly of the beast (Schmidt, pls. 114–17, 144–46, 195–97). Less commonly, the royal figure smothers a lion with his left arm: his left hand holds a lotus blossom, his right hand a dagger with which he is about to kill the lion (pl. 147, Darius's palace).

It appears that these depictions, taken as a whole, are intended to give an image of the king as at once calm, sovereign, and triumphant. Other motifs in these scenes accord with this view (rows of guards and throne-bearers). Add to these the rows of nobles (fig. 25) and the very idea of an Empire united around the Great King is exalted. Furthermore, the various depictions must not be confused in a too-simple analysis. We may

Fig. 20. Relief depicting royal audience from the Treasury at Persepolis.

Fig. 21. Tripylon (Council Hall),
south jamb of the eastern doorway.

Fig. 22. Throne Hall, east jamb of the
eastern doorway of the southern wall.

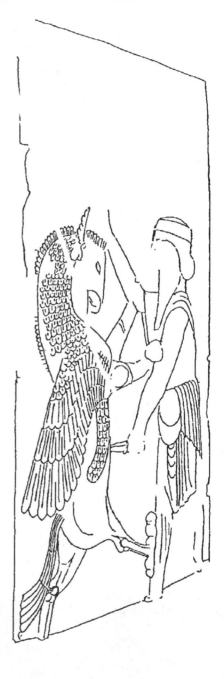

*Fig. 23. Tripylon (Council Hall),
west jamb of the southern doorway.*

*Fig. 24. Throne Hall, south jamb of the
northern doorway in the western wall:
Combat of Royal Hero with a griffin.*

isolate the last category, which is traditionally called "Royal Hero" (fig. 24). In fact, even if the other three representations (figs. 21–23) do not constitute "photographs" (so to speak) of court life, they are no less testimonies to the protocol governing the Great King's court—an aspect absent from the figure of "Royal Hero."

The King on His Throne

The commentary on the first three registers emerges from the images themselves and from details of court life gleaned from the Classical authors. They are intended primarily to express the idea that the king is a man above other men. Each of these reliefs is topped by the disk of Ahura-Mazda. The king himself is shown in a fixed pose, somewhat hieratic. The servants accompanying him are there to relieve him of all of the physical discomforts resulting from the excessive heat (parasol, towel). Only the heir in the audience reliefs is placed on the dais that supports the royal throne. The joint presence of the king and his son further accentuates the immutable character of kingship.

The king is also characterized by material attributes that are his alone. When he is seated on his throne, his feet rest on a footstool. This recalls what Dinon wrote (*apud* Athenaeus XII.514a✧):

> Whenever the king descended from his chariot, Dinon says, he never leaped down, although the distance to the ground was short, nor did he lean on anyone's arms; rather, a golden stool (*diphros*) was always set in place for him, and he descended by stepping on this; and the king's stool-bearer (*diphrophoros*) attended him for this purpose.

The bearer of the royal footstool is represented on the façades of the east and north wings of the Apadana. The footstool itself was well known to the Classical authors, because it was included in the booty seized by the Athenians after the battle of Plataea. According to the Alexandrian tales, this footstool was also used to assist the king in stepping up: when Alexander mounted the royal throne, his feet "dangled in the empty air," to use Quintus Curtius's picturesque and evocative phrase (V.2.13–15). In this way, the king avoided subverting the majesty that needed to be his in whatever pose he assumed. We also know that within the palace the distribution of rooms was such that the king

Fig. 25. Rows of Persian and Median nobles.

was the only one who could use certain corridors or tread on the Sardian carpets reserved for him (Athenaeus XII.514c).

The Royal Audience

The king is also shown seated on his throne in the audience reliefs. Many Classical authors took interest in the audience ritual, leaving the uncertain impression that the official in Mede's clothing who comes bowing before the Great King is none other than the chiliarch, a Greek word translating Iranian *hazarapatiš* (Commander of a Thousand). He was the head of the Great King's personal guard (metonymically represented by the soldiers placed to the right and left of the relief). He was the one who received the petitions of all of those who sought an audience with the king: "Without him, none could gain audience" (Nepos *Conon* 3.2–3; cf. Plutarch, *Them*. 27.2–7). He was the one "who took messages in to the king and presented petitioners" (Aelian, *VH* I.21✧) or passing on their messages to the king if they were not admitted to his presence.

The Classical authors insist that it was necessary to perform a *proskynesis* ['obeisance'] before the sovereign in order to obtain an audience. This, for example, is what was clearly prescribed for Themistocles by the chiliarch Artabanus:

> Amongst our many excellent laws, we account this the most excellent, to honour the king, and to worship him (*proskynein*), as the image of the great preserver (*eikón theou*) of the universe; if, then, you shall consent to our laws, and fall down before the king and worship him, you may both see him and speak to him; but if your mind be otherwise, you must make use of others to intercede for you, for it is not the national custom here for the king to give audience to any one that doth not fall down before him. (*Them*. 27.4–5✧)

The chiliarch Tithraustes addresses Conon in the same words: any man brought before the king must "render to the king a rite of adoration (*venerari*)." Nepos adds, parenthetically, "what in that country is called *proskynesis*" (*Conon* 3.3). It was the same for Ismenias, who was also received by the chiliarch Tithraustes (Aelian, *VH* I.21). These three stories probably go back to a common model by which the Greeks expressed what had become for them a motif illustrating Persian despotism, often also recalled in connection with the satraps and Alexander.

A comparison of the Classical texts and the reliefs nonetheless presents an interpretive problem. Exactly what act must be performed by the person granted audience? In other words, what does the word *proskynesis* mean? In the audience reliefs, the important person in front of the king bends forward and blows a kiss. But in many of the Greek authors, it very clearly refers to an act—also familiar in the pre-Achaemenid Near East and with the Parthians—consisting of falling prone or to one's knees before the royal throne. This is also what Herodotus describes when reporting social differences among the Persians:

> When Persians meet in the streets one can always tell by the mode of greeting whether or not they are of the same rank; for they do not speak but kiss—their equals upon the mouth, those somewhat superior on the cheeks. A man of greatly inferior rank prostrates himself in profound reverence (*prospiptōn proskynei ton heteron*). (I.134✧)

Although the term *proskynesis* implies a kiss, it cannot be reduced to only a kiss. Hence Ismenias's ruse:

> Entering and coming into full view of the king, he surreptitiously took off the ring he happened to be wearing and let it fall at his feet. Looking down quickly he bent to pick it up, as

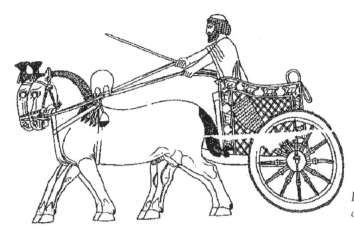

Fig. 26. The royal chariot at Persepolis.

if he were performing the act of homage (*proskynesis*). This gave the Persian king the impression of obeisance (*proskynesis*), but he had not done anything that causes Greeks a feeling of shame. (Aelian, *VH* I.31✧)

This text allows two interpretations. On the model of other Greek tales, it can be taken to imply that *proskynesis* required falling to the ground. On the other hand, it may be taken to imply that bending forward sufficed (since Ismenias did not fall to his knees to recover the ring). A passage in Herodotus preserves this ambiguity (VII.136✧). Introduced before Xerxes, the Spartans Sperchias and Bulis refused to perform the required act despite being so ordered by the guards: They "declared that they would never do such a thing, even though the guards should push their heads down on to the floor. It was not, they said, the custom in Sparta to worship a mere man like themselves, and it was not for that purpose that they had come to Persia." In Greek eyes, *proskynesis* was reserved for the gods.

Whatever the details, there is no doubt about the general meaning of the ceremony: performing *proskynesis* recognized the majesty of the sovereign (cf. Xenophon, *Anab.* I.8.21; [Aristotle] *De Mundo* 398a). The act could be performed outside of the physical presence of the king. We see the satrap Datames make *proskynesis* before a letter he had just received from Artaxerxes II (Polyaenus VII.21.5). But, contrary to what the Greeks deduced from it, the rite did not imply that the king was considered a god.

Royal Horses and Chariots

One of the processions depicted at Persepolis (south wing of the Apadana) is headed by an usher, followed by guards, a bearer of the royal footstool, and squires who bear whips and finely worked saddlecloths. Other squires (on the north wing) lead stallions. They are followed by two highly decorated chariots, each drawn by two horses guided by charioteers holding the reins (fig. 26). These are doubtless some of the famous Nisaean horses found in Xerxes' procession and described by Herodotus in this way:

> Then came ten of the sacred horses, known as Nisaean, in magnificent harness, . . . followed by the holy chariot of Zeus drawn by eight white horses. . . . Then came the king himself, riding in a chariot drawn by Nisaean horses, his charioteer, Patiramphes, son of Otanes the Persian, standing by his side. (VII.40✧)

Fig. 27a–b. The Royal Hero.

This chariot is the two-wheeled war and parade chariot (*harma*), clearly distinguished by every ancient author from the four-wheeled travel carriage (*harmamaxa*). This is the kind of chariot in which Xenophon presents Cyrus to the crowd during the parade at Persepolis. "Cyrus's private stud of horses, with gold bits, about two hundred in all, led along with gold-mounted bridles and covered over with gold-embroidered housings," were also part of the parade (*Cyr.* VIII.3.14–16◇). Wherever the king relocated, he was in fact accompanied by horses from the royal stable, who were quartered near the royal tent (Herodotus IX.70), 400 of them according to Quintus Curtius (III.3.21).

Xenophon stresses the strong impression made by Cyrus, standing in his chariot: "And when they saw him, they all prostrated themselves before him (made *proskynesis*), either because some had been instructed to begin this act of homage, or because they were overcome by the splendour of his presence, or because Cyrus appeared so great and so goodly to look upon" (VIII.3.14◇). Many other texts attest to the majesty assumed by the king on his chariot. That is how he is shown in the celebrated *Mosaic of Naples* (fig. 28 on p. 229). On the verge of the Macedonian victory it commemorates, "the king himself, in extreme peril, caught up the reins, being forced to throw away the dignity of his position and to violate the ancient custom of the Persian kings" (Diodorus XVII.34.6◇). From his chariot, in fact, the king "rode outstanding among the rest" (Quintus Curtius III.3.15◇); Darius III "had entered battle standing high in his chariot" (IV.1.1◇); and to his immediate relations, he stated: "I myself, not only because it is my country's custom, but also that I may be seen of all, ride in a chariot" (IV.14.26◇). All of these texts very clearly express the fact that strict rules governed the movements of the king, all of which were designed to further enhance his stature.

The royal horses and chariot thus do not appear in the Persepolis reliefs simply for decoration. The royal chariot obviously carried ideological weight: the chariot was part of the 'royal insignia' (*insignia imperii*). For this reason, opprobrium was cast on Darius

III in Macedonian propaganda: he had abandoned his chariot to facilitate what the ancient authors called his shameful flight (Quintus Curtius III.11.12). At Gaugamela, the royal coachman was killed by a lance but, "standing as he was high in his chariot, [Darius] blushed to abandon the battle-line of his subjects" (IV.15.30◊). In the end, he took flight. For the second time, Alexander was able to capture Darius's shield, bow, arrows, and chariot (Arrian III.15.5).

The Royal Hero

One of the most frequent themes on seals as well as on the Persepolis reliefs is the Royal Hero fighting real or monstrous animals; the Hero, in the middle, generally holds an animal in each hand (fig. 27b). The placement of these figures on the doorjambs seems to indicate that the king was an apotropaic figure, protecting his palace and his realm (*viθ*) in this way. In contrast to the figures in the seal representations, the main figure at Persepolis does not bear the familiar symbols of the king (robe, crown). Perhaps this is a personification of the victorious Persian Man to whom Darius alludes several times in his inscriptions. But identification with the king is simple and obvious: in a way, it is a variation on the theme of the victorious king.

4. The Good Warrior

A Tall and Handsome King

The Classical sources themselves also abound with notes on the exceptional physical prowess of the Great Kings. For Strabo (XV.3.21◊), Darius I was "the most handsome of men, except for the length of his arms, for they reached even to his knees"! Herodotus paints a no less flattering portrait of Xerxes: "Amongst all these immense numbers there was not a man who, for stature and noble bearing, was more worthy than Xerxes to wield so vast a power" (VII.187◊). As for Artaxerxes, "surnamed the Long-handed, his right hand being longer than his left" (Plutarch, *Art.* 1.1◊), "he owed his chief renown to his imposing appearance and his physical beauty, with which he coupled extraordinary military courage, since of all the Persians he was the one who was personally most worthy" (Nepos, *Reges* 21.4). Darius III was "the tallest and handsomest man of his time" (Plutarch, *Alex.* 21.6◊). Hence the familiar anecdote recorded by Diodorus (XVII.37.5) and Quintus Curtius (III.12.16–17◊): Darius's mother and wife were taken prisoner after the battle of Issus and brought to Alexander's tent, where Haephestion was also present. "Of the same age as the king, he nevertheless excelled him in bodily stature. Hence the queens, thinking that he was the king, did obeisance to him in their native fashion."

The theme is especially prominent during periods of dynastic competition among the various candidates for royal power. As we noted above, this was the background for the anecdote contrasting Cambyses and Smerdis in Egypt, the latter being the only one who could bend the bow sent by the Ethiopian king. The theme would be revived with special vigor in the time of Artaxerxes II and Darius III. All of the texts testify that physical appeal and bravery in combat constituted potent justifications for royal power. This is probably the tradition (widespread in any event) referred to in Strabo's remark: "This, too, is a Medic custom—to choose the bravest man as king; not, however, among all Medes, but only among the mountaineers" (XI.13.11◊). These are obviously *a posteriori* justifications: a man did not become king because he was handsome or a battle-hardened lancer; it was because of his position as king that a man was automatically designated handsome and courageous. If we are to believe Plutarch, the king's physical characteristics were even elevated to the rank of models to be emulated: "The Persians, because Cyrus was hook-nosed, even to this day love hook-nosed men and consider them the most handsome" (*Mor.* 821e◊).

Court artists and officials received strict orders to disseminate the image of a king who was imposing in height and beauty. According to Plato (*Alc.* 121d◊), the eunuchs entrusted with the bodily care of the royal children "attend to all the needs of the infant child, and are especially concerned to make him as handsome as possible, shaping and straightening his infant limbs; and for this they are held in great esteem"! Pliny probably obtained the following information from the same source: "To give to the body the charming appearance," the Persian *magi* and kings coated themselves with an ointment, apparently somewhat unsavory, made from the flowers of a Cilician plant (*helianthes* 'sunflower') steeped in lion fat, saffron, and palm wine (XXIV.165◊). On all of the reliefs, the king is routinely made taller than the other persons. This is particularly obvious at Behistun, but it is also clear in the audience reliefs where, additionally, the king and the crown prince standing behind him are placed on a dais.

Xenophon does not conceal the existence of ruses intended for the physical exaltation of the king. When, during the parade at Persepolis, Cyrus "appeared so great and so goodly to look upon," it was not just because of the special splendor of his garments: "With him rode a charioteer, who was tall, but neither in reality nor in appearance so tall as he; at all events, Cyrus looked much taller" (*Cyr.* VIII.3.13–14◊). Again according to Xenophon, Cyrus also gave this sort of instruction to his closest companions:

> We think, furthermore, that we have observed in Cyrus that he held the opinion that a ruler ought to excel his subjects not only in point of being actually better than they, but that he ought also to cast a sort of spell upon them. At any rate, he chose to wear the Median dress himself and persuaded his associates also to adopt it; for he thought that if any one had any personal defect that dress would help to conceal it, and that it made the wearer look very tall and very handsome. For they have shoes of such a form that without being detected the wearer can easily put something into the soles so as to make him look taller than he is. He encouraged also the fashion of pencilling the eyes, that they might seem more lustrous than they are, and of using cosmetics to make the complexion look better than their nature made it. He trained his associates also not to spit or to wipe the nose in public, and not to turn round and look at anything, as being men who wondered at nothing. All this he thought contributed, in some measure, to their appearing to their subjects men who could not lightly be despised. (VIII.1.40–42◊)

Furthermore, nobles wearing hairpieces appear several times at Persepolis, and this attests to the regular use of fake beards and moustaches. Strabo also mentions hair as a taxable item (XV.3.21). A financial stratagem recorded by Pseudo-Aristotle (II.14d◊) illustrates this practice: Condalus, a governor under Mausolus, "noticing that the Lycians were fond of wearing their hair long, said that a dispatch had come from the king of Persia ordering him to send hair to make false fringes and that he was therefore commanded by Mausolus to cut off their hair." Ctesias knew the story of a eunuch who supposedly conspired against Darius II: "He had a woman fashion a beard and moustache to make him look like a man" (§53). And here is how Xenophon describes the official appearance of Astyages: "Pencillings beneath his eyes, with rouge rubbed on his face, and with a wig of false hair" (*Cyr.* I.3.2◊; cf. VIII.1.41). He also mentions the existence of "beauty-doctors who pencil their eyes and rouge their cheeks for them and otherwise beautify them" in the suites of Persian nobles (VIII.8.20◊). At Persepolis itself, two reliefs show a servant with a (cosmetic) flask in his right hand and a folded towel in the left (Schmidt pls. 148A–149).

The Commander-in-Chief: Representations and Realities

The most important royal personas for Darius were warrior and commander-in-chief. On this point, the testimony of Classical authors is contradictory, however. For instance, as Xenophon puts it, victory is one of the justifications of kingship (*Anab.* I.7.9; I.8.12). But more often the Greeks highlight the reluctance of the kings to place themselves at the head of their armies, such as Artaxerxes III in Diodorus: He, "himself unwarlike, remained inactive. . . . Though regarded with contempt by the Egyptians, he was compelled to be patient because of his own inertia and peace-loving nature" until the moment when "he became enraged and decided to make war upon the insurgents" (XVI.40.4–5◊). Xerxes had a well-publicized reputation for cowardice among his adversaries. So did Darius III, who was guilty of abandoning his chariot and royal insignia (*kandys* and bow) at Issus and Gaugamela.

The judgment of the Classical authors is obviously shaped by a Greek polemical current that resulted in a presentation of the barbarians in general and the Great Kings in particular as weak and worthless men. However, this perspective also is supported by propaganda that issued from opponents at the court during periods of dynastic struggle. This is the framework that explains the strongly divergent images of Artaxerxes II, who is sometimes called a coward (in Cyrus the Younger's propaganda) and sometimes an extraordinary leader of men (in the royal propaganda). The same images and distortions are found in the two versions of the accession of Darius III (chap. 17/1). The very existence of these conflicting versions, moreover, confirms the importance of the warrior function in Achaemenid monarchic ideology.

But the Greek polemical current does not explain everything. While the interpretation found in the Classical authors does in fact reveal Greek assumptions, the avoidance of battle by the Great Kings is confirmed by many examples. Let us note at the outset that only one of all the Achaemenid kings, Cyrus, was lost in a military campaign. It has still not been established whether he was killed in battle. The others died of ill health (Cambyses, Darius, Artaxerxes I, Darius II, Artaxerxes II) or at an assassin's hand (Bardiya, Xerxes I, Xerxes II, Sogdianus, Artaxerxes III, Artaxerxes IV, Darius III). We may also note that during the Greek campaign Xerxes never took part in combat. At Thermopylae, he watched the fighting from his throne (Herodotus VII.212) and at Salamis he followed the battle from the sidelines (VIII.90; Aeschylus, *Persians* 465–67); at the battle of Cunaxa, Artaxerxes soon retired to a nearby hill (Plutarch, *Art.* 11.3, following Ctesias). Even when the king took part in the fighting, he was placed in a spot traditionally assigned to him, in the middle of his forces. Xenophon (who reports that it was the same when encamped: *Cyr.* VIII.3.8–11) does not conceal the fact that this choice was intended to protect the king's life: "For they think that this is the safest position, namely, with their forces on either side of them, and also that if they want to pass along an order, the army will get it in half the time" (*Anab.* I.8.22◊). Similarly Darius III at Issus: "Darius himself held the centre of his whole host, the customary (*nomos*) position for Persian kings" (Arrian II.8.11◊); according to Nicolaus of Damascus, Cyrus made the same choice at a battle with Astyages: "He stayed in the center with the distinguished Persians" (*FGrH* 90 F66.34). It is also clear that great pains were taken to ensure that the king would be able to leave the battlefield safe and sound if things did not go well. Fear of falling into Alexander's hands at Issus found Darius "mounted upon a horse which followed for that very purpose" (Quintus Curtius III.11.11◊; cf. Aelian, *Anim.* VI.48).

The political character of the custom cannot be doubted. Several times, the ancient authors describe discussions about this at the Achaemenid court. According to Herodotus, Artabanus, who had already tried to dissuade Darius from campaigning against the Scythians (IV.83), used the same argument with Xerxes when he was preparing to head the army against the Greeks: he did not think it a good idea to imperil "all the king's affairs" (VII.10). Diodorus, in his tale of the battle of Thermopylae, mentions that the Greeks captured the royal tent and then remarks: "If the king had remained at the royal pavilion, he also could easily have been slain by the Greeks and the whole war would have reached a speedy conclusion" (XI.10.3◊). According to Ctesias (§32), Artaxerxes was similarly dissuaded by his associates from heading the army preparing to march against Egypt. According to Diodorus and Quintus Curtius (III.2.10–19), the same debate unfurled around Darius III after the news of the death of Memnon [Artaxerxes II]:

> Some said that the king must join in battle personally, and they argued that the Persians would fight better in that event. Charidemus, however, the Athenian, . . . recommended that Dareius should on no account stake his throne rashly on a gamble, but should keep in his own hands the reserve strength and the control of Asia while sending to the war a general who had given proof of his ability. (Diodorus XVII.30.2◊)

The ancient authors recount similar discussions in the camps of Cyrus the Younger and Artaxerxes before the battle of Cunaxa (Plutarch, *Art.* 7.3, 8.2).

The exaltation of the fighting abilities of the Great King is thus purely ideological in nature and does not imply that the sovereign exaggerated his acts of valor on the battlefield. During the rare wars in which he did participate, he manifested his abilities less as an elite warrior than as "a good battle fighter . . . first to think with action," to quote Darius himself at Naqš-i Rustam (*DNb* §8g◊). At this point, we may note that Plutarch (*Mor.* 172f◊) records that, in delivering his own testimonial, Darius stated "that in battles and in the face of formidable dangers he became more cool and collected." The performance of Artaxerxes II in the course of a campaign against the Cadusians was exalted in court propaganda in exactly this way:

> With his quiver by his side and his shield on his arm, he led them on foot, quitting his horse, through craggy and steep ways, insomuch that the sight of his cheerfulness and unwearied strength gave wings to the soldiers, and so lightened the journey that they made daily marches of above two hundred furlongs. (Plutarch, *Art.* 24.10–11◊)

Moreover, through his privileged relationship with the deities, whose frequent sacrifices he continued to observe during his expeditions (chap. 6/6 below), he solicited their protection for his army. Finally, heading the army also enabled the king to visit his subjects during the course of one of those peregrinations that brought the court from one end of the Empire to the other (chap. 5/4). For a king who had newly assumed power, it was also a way to assert his authority.

Darius III in Battle: An Agonistic Perspective on Royalty

There is one item that places the Great King on the scene during a battle. This is the famous *Mosaic of Naples*, in which Darius III is standing in his chariot, surrounded by his protective guard, and directly confronts Alexander, who charges on his horse, lance

Fig. 28. Darius III in battle.

in hand (fig. 28). There is in fact a tradition that it took the personal confrontation of the two kings to decide the outcome of the battle. In the reply Alexander issued to his adversary at Marathon, the Macedonian threw down a serious challenge: "If you claim the kingship, stand your ground and fight for it (*agōnisai peri autēs*) and do not flee, as I shall pursue you wherever you are" (Arrian II.14.9◊). The choice of agonistic vocabulary is obviously not innocent. The historian Polybius found this tradition worthless (XII.22.1–7). He quotes Callisthenes, who accompanied Alexander: "Alexander arranged his forces in such a way as to invite personal combat with Darius, who originally had the same intent toward Alexander." According to Chares of Mytilene, the single combat did take place at Issus: "In this battle he was wounded in the thigh, Chares says, by Darius, with whom he fought hand to hand" (Plutarch, *Alex.* 20.8◊). This is the tradition illustrated by the creator of the original scene.

The tradition of the combat of chieftains is well attested among the Greeks and Macedonians, as well as the Persians and Iranians. For example, we know the suggestion of the commander of Persian-Iranian troops in Aria, Satibarzanes, for deciding the outcome of a battle in which none of the adversaries seemed able to prevail: "He challenged to battle anyone who wished to fight in single combat" (Quintus Curtius VII.4.33◊). Erigyius the Macedonian took up the challenge, and the combat (*monomakhia*) took place in an open area between the two armies; Satibarzanes was struck and killed, after which his troops surrendered to the Macedonians (cf. Diodorus XVII.83.5; Arrian III.28.2–3). The theme is also found in Darius III's royal propaganda. One of the versions claims that he owed his throne to his exceptional military valor, which he had proved by his victory in single combat against a Cadusian chieftain (Diodorus XVII.6.1–2; Justin X.3.2–5; perhaps to be compared with Strabo XI.13.11).

Lastly, we may stress the obvious similarities between Callisthenes' and Chares' version of the battle of Issus and what is recorded by several ancient authors about the battle of Cunaxa, where in 401 the legitimate Great King (Artaxerxes II) confronted his brother Cyrus, who claimed superior rights. Although Clearchus had advised against personal combat and had entreated him not to expose himself in this way, Cyrus felt that he must not show himself "unworthy of empire" (Plutarch, *Art.* 8.2◊). Just like Alexander and Darius at Issus, Cyrus and Artaxerxes, "who disputed the kingship (*hyper tēs basileias agōnizomenoi*), were placed at the center of the array. Thus in full view, they fell on each other, eager to decide the outcome of the battle for themselves. Fortune seemed to have reduced the war between the brothers to a single combat (*monomakhia*), comparable to that of Eteocles and Polynice sung by the tragic poets" (Diodorus XIV.23.5).

The texts under consideration primarily express a Greek and/or Macedonian perspective. Note that Diodorus refers explicitly to a Greek custom when he refers to the single combat (*monomakhia*) of Eteocles and Polyneices. We also know that the tradition of single combat was known in Macedonia at the dawn of the Hellenistic era (cf. Athenaeus IV.155a). The documentation thus gives expression to the Greek vision of Persian royal power, but it also transmits a Persian vision known from the court tales that set the Great King to grappling with one of his competitors. As Polybius understood perfectly, court tales deal with the realm of ideological representation and do not report the concrete realities of the battles of Issus and Cunaxa, divergent accounts of which continued to flourish. Actually, the court traditions confirm the central importance of warrior ability in the process of legitimation of royal authority. Whenever two aspirants came into confrontation, the quarrel could not be settled until an individual duel affirmed the aspirations of the winner.

The Hunter-King

The hunt was another occasion when the Great King could demonstrate his bravery. Out of all of Cyrus the Younger's qualifications for kingship, the ones that to Xenophon justified his aspirations the most were his abilities in combat ("military accomplishments, alike the use of the bow and of the javelin") and his love of the hunt: "He was the fondest of hunting and, more than that, the fondest of incurring danger in his pursuit of wild animals" (*Anab.* I.9.5–6◊; cf. *Cyr.* I.3.15; I.4.7–15). Achaemenid inscriptions and iconography are mute on this point, as has already been explained (see 6/1 above). However, texts from the high Hellenistic period can be used. One recurrent theme is that the king himself killed innumerable wild beasts. Quintus Curtius attributes to Alexander alone (*ille*) a kill of 4,000 wild animals (VIII.1.19). This is a theme well known from Assyrian inscriptions as well: Aššurnaṣirpal II boasts of killing no less than 450 great lions and 390 wild bulls with his own hands, and cutting off the heads of 200 ostriches and 20 great lions (*ANET*: 558–60)! Alexander's successors did not fail to take up this theme in turn. Lysimachus was reputed to have killed a lion "of remarkable size" (VIII.1.15◊) with his own hands. An even better story circulated:

> Perdiccas the Macedonian who accompanied Alexander on his mission was apparently so courageous that he once went alone into a cave where a lioness had her lair. He did not catch the lioness, but he emerged carrying the cubs. Perdiccas won admiration for this feat. Not only Greeks, but barbarians as well, are convinced that the lioness is an animal of great bravery and very difficult to contend with. They say that the Assyrian Semiramis had her

spirits raised, not if she killed a lion or leopard or another animal of that kind, but if she captured a lioness. (Aelian, *VH* XII.39✧)

The story clearly originated in circles close to Perdiccas. But it is also very clearly set in a Near Eastern ideological context, as is shown by the reference to barbarians and Semiramis. A legend of Lysimachus portrays him overpowering "a most ferocious lion, by seizing his tongue and smothering him in that way" (Justin XV.3.7–8). Indeed, this motif is also common in the Assyrian period: in one of his inscriptions, Aššurnaṣirpal II boasts of seizing a lion once "by the ears" and another time "by the tail," and this is how the royal artists showed him.

According to protocol, certain prerogatives were reserved for the king. On many occasions Xenophon's Cyrus participates in hunts, particularly at Astyages' court. On one occasion, Cyrus reminds him that it is his right to cast the first spear (*Cyr.* I.4.14). The existence of this protocol at the Persian court is confirmed by Plutarch (*Mor.* 173d). The story of Megabyzus offers a perfect illustration of this court custom:

> Artaxerxes (I) went hunting and a lion attacked him. As soon as the beast leapt, Megabyzus struck him with a javelin and brought him down. The king was angry because Megabyzus had struck the beast before he could touch it himself; he ordered Megabyzus's head cut off. (Ctesias §40)

In doing this, Megabyzus had not just violated the rules of protocol. It is important to state that the scene unfolded during a lion hunt; numerous documents indicate that lion hunts were a special privilege of the king. In other words, Megabyzus had cast doubt on Artaxerxes' abilities as a hunter and thus also his qualification to be king.

This particularly pregnant theme appears again in an account of one of Alexander's hunts:

> When a lion of extraordinary size rushed to attack the king himself, it happened that Lysimachus, who was afterwards a king, being beside Alexander, began to oppose his hunting spear to the animal; but the king pushed him aside and ordered him to retire, adding that a lion could be killed by himself alone as well as by Lysimachus. And in fact Lysimachus, once when they were hunting in Syria, had indeed alone killed a lion of remarkable size, but had had his left shoulder torn to the bone and thus had come into great peril of his life. The king, taunting him with this very experience, acted more vigorously than he spoke; for he not only met the wild beast, but killed him with a single wound. (Quintus Curtius VIII.1.14–16✧)

During royal hunts, then, courtiers had to be circumspect. While someone who came to the aid of the king could be richly rewarded (Diodorus XV.10.3: Tiribazus; cf. Xenophon, *Anab.* I.9.6; Polybius, Frag. 38), the example of Megabyzus indicates that it was not a good idea to appear to be a rival.

No hunting scenes are found in any of the palace reliefs, but they do appear in innumerable seals and seal impressions (fig. 29). The king is sometimes shown hunting from his chariot, as on Darius's cylinder seal (*SDa*) or as described in episodes narrated by Diodorus (XV.10.3) and by Polybius (Frag. 133). But, let us not fool ourselves; an image such as Darius in a chariot confronting an enormous lion (fig. 29a) belongs primarily to the repertory of monarchic ideology. These are not realistic, narrative scenes. Usually, the king hunts on horseback (cf. Aelian, *VH* VI.14), like all the young Persians: "They hunt by throwing spears from horseback, and with bows and slings" (Strabo XV.3.18✧). Herodotus mentions that during a hunting party Darius, jumping his horse quickly,

Fig. 29a–b. Hunt scenes on seals; above (29a), seal of Darius, showing the king hunting a lion; below (29b), inscribed seal, depicting a "Mede" hunting a wild boar.

suffered a severe sprain (III.129). Nevertheless, it was in the hunt as in war that the king proved his exceptional courage and valor. For this reason, the other participants were either completely unknown or else left in the shadows by the court artists.

It must be stressed that in some seals the theme of hunter-king is confused with the theme of Royal Hero. Even when the king confronts lions, the scene is far from realistic. For example, on one seal, the king is perched on a camel and brandishes his lance at a lion rearing up at him on his hind legs (Frankfort 1939, XXXVII, m). The lion is in the same posture on another seal where the king, on foot and armed with a bow, faces the beast (XXXVII h). Nor does the famous seal of Darius constitute a "photograph" of a royal hunt: standing on his chariot, the king launches an arrow toward an immense lion, rearing on its hind feet, while another lion (somewhat miniaturized) lies under the hooves of the horses, already felled by the royal arrow (SDa, fig. 29a). What is more, on some impressions the hunter-king confronts a monster identical to those found at Persepolis. For example, the king, in his chariot, armed with his bow, faces a hybrid winged and horned being (apparently a griffin), also rearing on its hind legs (Frankfort XXXVII, n).

5. *The King, the Earth, and the Water*

The Good Gardener

The elite warrior Great King could also engage in agricultural work and influence the prosperity of the fields. Xenophon develops this theme with particular insistence in the *Oeconomicus*. In order to make his addressee (Critobulos) better understand the combined importance of war and agriculture, Socrates (fictitious mouthpiece of Xenophon) gives the example of the king of the Persians:

> Need we be ashamed of imitating the king of the Persians? For they say that he pays close attention to husbandry and the art of war, holding that these are two of the noblest and most necessary pursuits. (IV.4◊)

Then Xenophon returns indefatigably to this point: "As for the country, he personally examines so much of it as he sees in the course of his progress through it." The mission entrusted to the governors was to ensure "that their country is densely populated and that the land is in cultivation and well stocked with the trees of the district and crops" (IV.8◊). In the shape of a specific illustration of a general policy, Xenophon is careful to include a reference to the paradises:

> "Yet further," continues Socrates, "in all the districts he resides in and visits he takes care that there are (*kēpoi*) 'paradises,' as they call them, full of all the good and beautiful things that the soil will produce, and in this he himself spends most of his time, except when the season precludes it."

"By Zeus," says Critobulos,

> "Then it is of course necessary, Socrates, to take care that these paradises in which the king spends his time shall contain a fine stock of trees and all other beautiful things that the soil produces." (IV.13–14◊)

Elsewhere, Xenophon also states that his Cyrus ordered each of his satraps to establish paradises (*Cyr.* VIII.6.12). In fact, the Classical texts, Babylonian tablets, and also a few tablets from Persepolis show that there was at least one paradise in each satrapy. Among other examples, we may cite Plutarch's description of the paradise of the satrap Tissaphernes at Sardis, "the most beautiful of his parks, containing salubrious streams and meadows, where he had built pavilions, and paces of retirement royally and exquisitely adorned" (Plutarch, *Alc.* 24.7◊). The paradise at Dascylium was known to the Greeks for its fertility and charm (Xenophon, *Hell.* IV.1.15–17). These qualities are depicted on several impressions and seals found at the site. Quintus Curtius wrote this about a paradise near Ecbatana: "The residences in that region have extensive, charming, and secluded parks with groves artificially planted; these were the special delight of both kings and satraps" (VII.2.22◊). However, the paradises were not just hunting preserves; the preserves were only one constituent.

When Socrates was trying to convince Critobulos that Cyrus the Younger "would have proved an excellent ruler" (*Oec.* IV.18◊), he cited several sources in support of this assessment, including a description of Lysander's visit to Cyrus the Younger's paradise at Sardis:

> "Lysander admired the beauty of the trees in it, the accuracy of the spacing, the straightness of the rows, the regularity of the angles and the multitude of the sweet scents that clung round them as they walked; and for wonder of these things he cried, 'Cyrus, I really do admire all these lovely things, but I am far more impressed with your agent's skill in measuring and arranging everything so exactly.' Cyrus was delighted to hear this and said: 'Well, Lysander, the whole of the measurement and arrangement is my own work, and I did some of the planting myself.' 'What, Cyrus?' exclaimed Lysander, looking at him, and marking the beauty and perfume of his robes, and the splendour of the necklaces (*ta strepta*) and bangles (*pselia*) and other jewels that he was wearing; 'did you really plant part of this with your own hands?' 'Does that surprise you, Lysander?' asked Cyrus in reply. "I swear by the

Sun-god that I never yet sat down to dinner when in sound health, without first working hard at some task of war or agriculture, or exerting myself somehow.'" (IV.20–25◇)

There is no doubt that Xenophon's narratives came from a version that sang the praises of Cyrus the Younger's royal qualities and that the link between the Great King and agriculture was thus one of the constituent elements of Achaemenid royal ideology. By systematically underscoring the brutal contrast between the verdure of the paradise and the barrenness of its surroundings, the Classical authors—without being fully aware of it—participated in the exaltation of a sovereign powerful enough to create prosperity and vegetation in the face of unfavorable natural conditions.

But in the passage above, Xenophon—the only Classical author to preserve this *topos*—brings in another characteristic feature: the king himself planted trees. This is not a Hellenizing invention of the author. We may cite a parallel passage from the book of Esther, which records the organization of a feast by Ahasuerus (Xerxes) in his palace at Susa; the author places the festival "in the enclosure adjoining the king's palace" (1:5◇). The Vulgate says: "in the vestibule of the garden and the woods, which had been planted by the royal hands with a magnificence worthy of them" (*horti et nemoris quod regio cultu et manu consitum erat*). More importantly, two iconographic testimonies confirm and illustrate the theme of gardener-king. A cylinder seal from the Achaemenid era shows a Persian using his long staff to guide a pair of oxen with humps drawing a plow. An almost identical scene is found on a coin from Tarsus in Cilicia: the work scene is shown on the obverse, surmounted by a winged disk, with the reverse showing a cow suckling a calf. There is scarcely any doubt that in both cases it is the king himself being shown as a gardener.

Xerxes and the Plane (or Sycamore) Tree

Other texts attest to a special relationship between the Great King and flora. In the course of his story of Xerxes' march between Phrygia and Sardis, Herodotus states concisely, "it was hereabouts that he came across a plane tree of such beauty that he was moved to decorate it (*dōrēsamenos*) with golden ornaments (*kosmos chryseos*) and to leave behind one of his Immortals to guard it" (VII.31◇). The story was clearly very popular among the Greeks; another version has it that during Xerxes' passage through Phrygia (on his return from Europe) a plane (sycamore) tree metamorphosed miraculously into an olive tree (Pliny, *NH* XVII.42). In his *Variae Historiae*, Aelian returns twice to the anecdote:

> The famous king Xerxes was ridiculous (*geloios*), if it is true that he despised sea and land, the handiwork of Zeus, manufacturing for himself novel roads and abnormal sea route, and yet was the devotee (*dedoulōto*) of a plane tree, which he admired. In Lydia, they say, he saw a large specimen of a plane tree, and stopped for that day without any need. He made the wilderness around the tree his camp (*stathmos*), and attached to it expensive ornaments, paying homage to the branches with necklaces (*strepta*) and bracelets (*pselia*). He left a caretaker (*meledōn*) for it, like a guard (*phylakē*) to provide security (*phrouros*), as if it were a woman he loved. What benefit accrued to the tree as a result? The ornaments it had acquired, which were quite inappropriate to it, hung on it without serving any purpose and made no contribution to its appearance, since the beauty of a tree consists of fine branches, abundant leaves, a sturdy trunk, deep roots, movement in the wind, shadow spreading all around, change in accordance with the passing of seasons, with irrigation channels to support it and rain water to sustain it. Xerxes' robes (*chlamydes*), barbarian gold, and the other offerings (*dōra*) did not ennoble the plane or any other tree. (II.14◇)

Aelian judges royal behavior just as severely and condescendingly elsewhere. He includes it among other examples of love "ridiculous (*geloioi*) and bizarre (*paradoxoi*)," for the same reasons as the passion avowed by a young Athenian for a statue of *Tychē* or attachments between humans and animals (IX.39✧). This assessment (no trace of it is found in Herodotus) comes from the nega-

Fig. 30. Seal of Xerxes.

tive vision of Xerxes transmitted by all of the Greek authors who—following the model of their inspiration, Aelian—denounced the immoderation (*hybris*) of a man who did not shrink from affronting the laws of man and god by throwing a bridge across the sea. The same assumption of balance and moderation led Aelian to exalt the laws of nature that did not permit unnatural loves between humans and nonhumans, or personal, emotional relationships between a man and a tree: the growth of vegetation is permitted (or forbidden) by the natural elements (waters, winds, seasons) and by the labor of the peasants (irrigation canals); the personal intervention even of a king as powerful as Xerxes is as nothing in the face of the immutable constraints of nature.

In view of this, it is clear that Aelian understood nothing of the court history that he read, perhaps in Herodotus himself, and that he embellished with a moralizing commentary suitable for reaching his Greek readers. If his account is read back into Persian and Iranian mindsets, it provides another attestation of the special relationship between the king and the vegetable kingdom. The gifts to the plane tree are of exactly the same kind as the gifts that the king presented to his Faithful and his Benefactors (bracelets, necklaces, robes)—that is, to the men who deserved to be recognized for their loyalty and devotion to the Royal House and to the person of the king (chapter 8/1). The Lydian plane tree was thenceforth as richly decorated as the Immortal whom Xerxes appointed as its guard and whose jewelry Quintus Curtius described as follows: "They are especially the ones whom a barbarian luxury of opulence rendered the most imposing: for them gold necklaces, for them robes embroidered with gold and sleeved tunics, also adorned with gems" (III.3.13). But these are also the jewelry worn by the king himself, as Xenophon recalls, stressing that the ornaments did not impede Cyrus the Younger from planting trees.

There can hardly be any doubt that this episode echoes the existence of a tree cult. Several seals convey similar scenes. One of them (inscribed with the name of Xerxes) shows a person dressed and coiffed like a Persian king about to place a crown in front of a stylized tree of life (S*Xe*; fig. 30). One of the Persepolis seals is particularly interesting. Two guards (similar to the guards shown at Susa and Persepolis) stand at attention, lances upright in front of them, on either side of a palm tree, the winged disk surmounting the scene (*PTS* no. 24). We are immediately reminded of the Immortals assigned to guard Xerxes' plane tree!

The Plane (Sycamore) Tree and the Golden Vine of the Great King

The stories told by Herodotus and Aelian were embellished by the decorative elements (now lost) that enhanced the opulence of the Great King's palace. Herodotus records that during Darius's passage through Asia Minor in 513, the fantastically wealthy Lydian Pythius visited the royal entourage and offered the Great King "the golden plane-

Fig. 31. The Assyrian king with the "Tree of Life."

tree and the golden vine" (VII.27✧). The existence of these arboriform decorations was also well known to the Greeks. The Arcadian Antiochus made this derisive reference when he returned from an embassy to the Great King in 367: "He thought that the King's wealth of money was also mere pretence, for he said that even the golden plane tree, that was forever harped upon, was not large enough to afford shade for a grass-hopper" (Xenophon, *Hell.* VII.1.38✧). When Antigonus the One-Eyed inventoried the Treasury in the Susa citadel in 316, "he found in it the golden climbing vine and a great number of other objects of art, weighing all told fifteen thousand talents" (Diodorus XIX.48.6✧).

The reports of Hellenistic authors transcribed by Athenaeus are more precise. Among the testimonies to the luxury of the Great King is Chares of Mytilene, who specifically mentions that "in the bed-chamber a golden vine, jewel-studded, extended over the bed," and Amyntas states "that this vine had clusters composed of the costliest jewels" (XII.514f✧). Phylarcus wrote:

> The famous plane-trees of gold, even the golden vine under which the Persian kings often sat and held court, with its clusters of green crystals and rubies from India and other gems of every description, exceedingly costly though they were, apeared to be of less worth . . . than the expense lavished daily on all occasions at Alexander's court. (XII.539d✧)

Achaemenid palaces were probably the model for the decoration of the palace of the Mauryan king at Pataliputra: "His palace has gilded columns: over all of these runs a vine carved in gold, and silver figures of birds, in the sight of which they take the greatest pleasure, adorn the structure" (Quintus Curtius VIII.8.26✧). We are immediately re-minded of the famous Assyrian banquet under the arbor (fig. 32). There is no doubt that in the Near East (and in many other parts of the ancient world) the vine was recognized and hailed as a symbol of fecundity, and its increase was considered a gauge of power. A good illustration is found in the dream that Herodotus says the Median king Astyages had shortly after his daughter Mandane's marriage to the Persian Cambyses:

Fig. 32. Aššurbanipal and the vine-arbor.

It was that a vine grew from his daughter's private parts and spread over Asia. . . . He told the interpreters about this dream, and then sent for his daughter, who was now pregnant. When she arrived, he kept her under strict watch, intending to make away with the child; for the fact was that the Magi had interpreted the dream to mean that his daughter's son would usurp his throne. (I.108✧)

Such were the favorable auspices under which Cyrus was born. The vine that grew from Mandane's private parts was obviously nothing other than the guarantee of an uncommon destiny for the child and reports of conquests extending across all Asia. This is precisely what the Median king understood: "This dream announced the greatness [of the child about to be born] and presaged to Astyages the end of his crown." Hence the attempts to banish the baby and the happy outcome of the founder legend.

Artaxerxes II in the Paradise

In the Achaemenid ideological context, we have two other testimonies that are particularly evocative of relations between the Great King and arboreal flora. In the *Life of Artaxerxes*, Plutarch tells of the difficulties encountered by the king and his army after their return from an expedition against the Cadusians. The army suffered from so many shortages that the chefs were unable to prepare the royal dinner (24.3). Then Plutarch includes the following anecdote:

> After they had arrived at one of his own mansions (*stathmos basilikos*), which had beautiful ornamented parks in the midst of a region naked and without trees, the weather being very cold, he gave full commission to his soldiers to provide themselves with wood by cutting down any, without exception, even the pine and cypress. And when they hesitated and were for sparing them, being large and goodly trees, he, taking up an axe himself, felled the greatest and most beautiful of them. After which his men used their hatchets, and piling up many fires, passed away the night at their ease. (§25.1✧)

It is clear that this passage is part of a discussion of the royal virtues of Artaxerxes II, whose physical stamina and bravery Plutarch wished to stress, as well as his abilities as a leader (§24.9–11). The connection between the king and the foliage was so well known to the soldiers that they did not dare to raise their axes against the trees, despite the king's authorization. This confirms the role of the king as the trees' protector. A paradise had to remain "undisturbed," that is, free from the ravages of war (Quintus Curtius

VIII.1.13✧; cf. Polybius XXXI.29). The felling of trees in the paradise was considered an affront to the sovereignty and majesty of the Great King. It is quite striking that, according to Diodorus of Sicily (XVI.41.5✧), the first hostile act of the revolt by the Phoenicians against Artaxerxes III was "the cutting down and destroying of the royal park in which the Persian Kings were wont to take their recreation." Similarly, under the guise of reprisals, Cyrus the Younger ravaged the paradise of the satrap Belesys, who had sided with Artaxerxes II (Xenophon, *Anab.* I.4.2), and the Spartan king Agesilaus "ravaged the orchards and the paradise of Tissaphernes" near Sardis (Diodorus XIV.80.2).

Let us also stress that, as in Aelian's version and in many other texts, Plutarch accents the contrast between the aridity of the surrounding countryside and the flamboyant fecundity of the paradise. Of the various tree species, Plutarch also seems to accord special value to pines and cypresses, because these species could only grow in these regions through acclimatization accompanied by intensive care, obviously on the initiative of the royal administration. Strabo, explaining the difficulties that Alexander encountered in 325–324 in procuring wood in Babylonia, states that Babylonia suffered "a scarcity of timber," so much so that Alexander had to sacrifice "the cypress trees in the groves and the parks" (XVI.1.11✧). At Persepolis itself, many reliefs are punctuated by rows of pines (or cypresses).

Clearchus's Tomb

The story of Clearchus, Cyrus the Younger's closest Greek associate, whose abilities as commander-in-chief Xenophon vaunts at length (*Anab.* II.3.11–13; 6.1–15), may also be mentioned in this connection. Shortly after the battle of Cunaxa, Clearchus and other Greek generals fell into the hands of the satrap Tissaphernes (II.5.31–32). Despite the claims of Xenophon (II.5.38), Clearchus was not put to death immediately but was imprisoned, according to Ctesias. Ctesias then established a relationship with the general. Ctesias was undoubtedly following instructions from Cyrus the Younger's mother, Parysatis, who thus once more exhibited her desire to honor the memory of her favorite son. Contrary to Parysatis's wishes, however, Artaxerxes gave in to the repeated importunings of his wife, Stateira, and Clearchus was executed (Plutarch, *Art.* 18.4; Ctesias, *Persica* §60). At this point, Ctesias describes the divine signs that accompanied the burial of Clearchus:

> An extraordinary sight (*teras*) appeared around his body. In fact, spontaneously (*automatōs*), a very high mound rose over his corpse with the breath of a great wind. (§60)

Citing Ctesias, Plutarch records the event with even more detail than Photius, adding an important detail:

> As for the remains of Clearchus, that a violent gust of wind, bearing before it a vast heap of earth, raised a mound to cover his body, upon which, after a short time, some dates having fallen there, a beautiful grove (*alsos*) of trees grew up and overshadowed the place. (§18.7✧)

Plutarch obviously considers Ctesias's information worthless and makes the accusation that "this part of his history is a sort of funeral exhibition in honour of Clearchus." He also points out that if the trees did grow that way, it was not *automatōs* (spontaneously) but because "dates had fallen there." Plutarch's doubts are certainly well founded. But Ctesias did not give these details simply because of his loyalty to Sparta (Clearchus was a Spartan), for which Plutarch denounces him elsewhere (§13.7). It is clear that Ctesias passed on a version that originated in the circle of Parysatis, who once again was trying to enhance the memory of Cyrus by dramatizing a faithful lieutenant's extraordinary destiny. Ctesias even contrasts Clearchus's fate with the fate of other Greek generals, "who were torn apart by dogs and birds" (§7). This detail clearly refers to funerary customs known in eastern Iran and in the *Avesta* (which is more recent), which forbade underground burial and anticipated that animals and birds would strip the flesh from corpses (chapter 2/9). We thus find ourselves in a Persian and Iranian religious context. The punchline of Ctesias's story, as repeated by Plutarch, confirms this: when Artaxerxes saw the luxuriant grove that later graced Clearchus's tomb, he "declared his sorrow, concluding that in Clearchus he put to death a man beloved of the gods" (*theois philos*; §18.8◊). In other words, the propaganda released by Parysatis's supporters repeated, on behalf of Clearchus, the royal ideological theme that we are considering: because of the king's privileged relationship with the deities who guarantee prosperity, he was honored by vegetation that thrived without human intervention (*automatos*). The gods themselves created a paradise in the form of a sacred grove (*alsos*) whose foliage overshadowed a tumulus located in an arid region. Through Clearchus, therefore, as Ctesias wrote, "a sign [was] sent by the gods (*teras*)" that came to provide a striking posthumous confirmation of the royal attributes that Cyrus the Younger liked to claim.

The Rainmaker and Master of the Storm

Royal power was manifested even more directly in the cycles of nature. The clearest reference to this is Polyaenus's discussion of Darius's 519 expedition against the Saka of Central Asia (VII.11.12). Due to the treachery of the Sakian Sirakes, the guide, the Great King's army found itself in an absolutely barren region with neither water nor food supplies, where neither bird nor any other beast could be seen. Salvation came from Darius himself:

> He climbed a very high hill, and after fixing his scepter in the ground, he placed his tiara and the royal diadem on top of his royal robe (*kandys*). This was at sunrise. He prayed to Apollo to save the Persians and to send them water from heaven. The god listened, and abundant rain fell.

The story told by Polyaenus is obviously Persian in origin. Details in it are attested elsewhere: the sacred location (a mountain), the time (sunrise), the interlocutor (the king), the prayers and worship regularly rendered by the Persians to the forces of nature ("They also worship the sun, moon, and earth, fire, water, winds"; Herodotus I.131◊). Furthermore, to mask his evil intent and subterfuge, Sirakes did not hesitate to "call the eternal Fire and the sacred Water to witness" in Darius's presence.

Only the god is unnamed. Polyaenus mentions Apollo, who frequently stands for Mithra in Greek sources. Nonetheless, in this context Polyaenus's Apollo seems to designate a deity specifically connected with rain. Perhaps it was Tištryā, the deity to whom *Yasht* 8 of the *Avesta* was dedicated and who was closely linked to Mithra in Iranian tradition. He was the liberator of the waters and was the deity to whom prayers for rain were addressed, particularly in the hot season. However, Polyaenus's text perfectly expresses the king's role as intercessor between gods and men. Darius strips off all of the attributes of royalty: the royal robe, scepter, tiara, and diadem. It is the scepter stuck in the ground that causes the rain. By granting his prayer, the god confirms and exalts the exceptional position of the king. The story, which the author places in an Iranian-speaking country, is built on a series of motifs that highlight the king's privileged relation with the deities and the power that he drew from his intimacy with the gods who govern the elements of nature.

Ctesias presents further evidence of the cosmic power of the Great King, preserved in Photius's summary. Among all of the marvels he reports about India, Ctesias mentions a "fountain that is filled every year with liquid gold":

> He also talks about the iron found at the bottom of the fountain. Ctesias claimed to have had two swords made from this metal: one was a gift from the king, the other a gift from the king's [Artaxerxes II] mother Parysatis. Regarding this iron he says that if it is thrust into the ground, it deflects thick clouds, hail, and storms. He claims that the king did this twice in his sight. (*Indica* §4)

The two texts have at least one element in common. In order to bring down rain or divert storms, the Great Kings had to drive a royal symbol (scepter, sword) into the ground as an apotropaic ritual.

At one point, the texts of Polyaenus and Ctesias remind us of what Herodotus writes about certain religious customs of the Scythians. He recalls that, based on the model of the Persians, the Scythians do not erect cult statues, altars, or temples to their gods, except for Ares (IV.59), to whom the various Scythian tribes dedicate a sanctuary, a sort of platform with its height limited to the height of a tall heap of firewood. And Herodotus adds: "On the top of it is planted an ancient iron sword (*akinakēs*), which serves for the image of Ares. Annual sacrifices of horses and other cattle are made to this sword" (IV.62✧). Ares, in this case, is both the god of war and the god of storm.

The relationship between the Great King and the storm is also attested in the founder legends. In Nicolaus of Damascus's version, the first encounters between Astyages' Medes and Cyrus's Persians took place in Persia, near Pasargadae, and turned to the disadvantage of the latter, who were soon besieged on a mountain. Cyrus then made his way to the his parents' goatherds' house and made a sacrifice in the courtyard:

> On a base of cypress and laurel trunks he sacrificed barley flour, and he started the fire by friction, in the manner of a poor man with no equipment. Soon, from the right, came lightning and thunder: Cyrus did obeisance [*proskynesis*]. Then, landing on the house, birds (of prey) of good augury appeared, whereupon Cyrus departed for Pasargadae. Then they organized a great meal and stationed themselves on the mountain. The next day, made confident by these birds, they descended toward the enemies at the same time the enemies were ascending toward the summit, and they fought long, vigorously, and courageously. (*FGrH* 90 F66 [41])

To renew the courage of his troops, then, it appears that Cyrus prayed to the storm-god, who legitimated Cyrus's ability as commander-in-chief by manifesting himself to all.

Finally, let us mention the legend of the origin of Mithradates. Plutarch records that a storm broke over his cradle when he was a newborn. The baby's swaddling clothes were burned by a thunderbolt, but the child was safe and sound, though he was left with an indelible mark on his forehead from the lightning (Plutarch, *Quaest. Conv.* I.6.2 [*Mor.* 624a]). This divine sign in itself qualified him to be king.

6. Between Men and Gods

Royal Prayers

Each of the preceding discussions has illuminated one of the most powerful ideological foundations of the Achaemenid monarchy, namely the union and collaboration of the Great King and the gods. Darius states that he obtained his royal power from Ahura-Mazda; he owed his victories and his authority over conquered (or rebellious) peoples to his protection. Contrary to the opinion of some Greek authors, the king himself was never considered a god; but neither was he an ordinary man. By virtue of the specific attributes he received from the gods, he was a man above men. Royal protocol served in perpetuity as a reminder of this (cf. chap. 7). He was situated at the intersection between the world below and the divine world, which communicated through his intercession. Ahura-Mazda was in fact "the greatest of the gods, who created heaven and earth and men, who bestowed all prosperity/happiness/serenity (*šiyāti*) on the men who lived there, who created Darius to be king and bestowed on Darius royalty over this vast land" (*DPg*). After that, the king was the obligatory intercessor between the world of humanity and the world of gods. In this function, Darius addressed Ahura-Mazda to beg him to protect the king, his House, his father Hystaspes, and the crown prince and to provide peace and prosperity to the Persian people, as in this Persepolis inscription (*DPd*◇):

> May Ahuramazda bear me aid, with the gods of the royal house; and may Ahuramazda protect this country from a (hostile) army, from famine, from the Lie! Upon this country may there not come an army (*hainā*), nor famine (*dušiyara*), nor the Lie (*drauga*); this I pray as a boon from Ahuramazda together with the gods of the royal house. This boon may Ahuramazda together with the gods of the royal house give to me!

Here Darius implores Ahura-Mazda "with the gods of the royal house" to protect Persia from both external aggression ("army") and revolt ("Lie"), both of them leading to the wasting away of the fields ("famine"). Here in a nutshell are the royal virtues: the good fighter (who gives chase to an enemy army), a king of justice (who fights the Lie), a protector of the land and its peasants (who is the source of prosperity for the fields).

At this point we must emphasize that, according to Herodotus, one of the rules that governed the Persian sacrifices was: "The actual worshipper is not permitted to pray for any personal or private blessing, but only for the king and for the general good of the community, of which he is himself a part" (I.132◇). This sentence primarily expresses the sense that one belonged to an ethno-cultural community symbolized by its gods. The king no doubt was part of the community; in this expression we also find Darius's insistence on his close and privileged union with his people-country (*dahyu*). But Herodotus's report of this detail attests to another reality—that personal religion itself was invested with the power of the royal majesty, since each Persian had to invoke the gods' blessing and protection on the king whenever he offered sacrifices.

Official Religion

Every royal proclamation attests to the existence of official religious practices in which the king played a central role (cf. *Cyr.* VIII.1.23–26). Xenophon dedicates a long passage to the gods and the sacrifices with which Cyrus honored them (*Cyr.* VIII.3.11–24), and he states that the king's last stay in Persia was his seventh (VIII.7.1◇), implying that "the customary sacrifice" was regular. There is in fact no doubt that the Great Kings returned periodically to Persia and that their presence was marked by religious festivals, the ceremony and scheduling of which were probably regulated by custom in an official religious calendar. This is probably what Ctesias is saying when he describes the end of Darius's life as follows: "Darius, having returned to Persia, made sacrifices" (*Persica* §19). This refers to sacrifices and festivals in honor of the gods that Xerxes celebrated when he was preparing to enter Europe; he invoked the "gods who have our country in their keeping" (Herodotus VII.53◊; cf. Cyr. II.1.1). These gods obviously included "Ahura-Mazda and the other gods" and also quite a few others, such as the Earth, in whose honor Cyrus made sacrifices (Cyr. VIII.3.24).

The diversity of sects observed in Persia is also well documented in two categories of Persepolis tablets (E and K1) that were briefly mentioned above (p. 88). Babylonian and Elamite gods were worshiped alongside Iranian deities, and their attendants were remunerated by the royal administration. In addition to Ahura-Mazda (see below), we have evidence for the worship of Zurvan (Weather), Visai Bagā (a collective divine entity honored in a nonspecific way), Mizduši (goddess related to fertility and power), Naryasanga (related to Fire worship), Brtakāmya (a god unknown elsewhere), Hvarīra (Spirit of the Rising Sun), Ārtca (not included in Persian traditions). Most of the time, the rations delivered to the attendants by the administration were intended for sacrifices in honor of several deities. From this we may conclude that each locality had several sanctuaries. Since the tablets were intended primarily to manage the deliveries of products from the warehouses, they give very few details about the ceremonies themselves. The deity's name is frequently absent. For example, an attendant might receive grain or sheep "for the gods" (e.g., PF 353, 356–65, etc.). A record of the attendants, administrator, and location sufficed for the accountants. The terms describing the sacrifices remain difficult to interpret.

Moreover, the documentation from Persepolis attests to the frequency of sacrifices in honor of the forces of nature, especially mountains and rivers, but also hamlets. For instance:

> 5.7 *marriš* of wine, at the disposal (*kurmin*) of Ušaya, Turkama (?) the priest received, and used them for the gods: 7 QA for [the god] Ahura-Mazda, 2 *marriš* for [the god] Humban, 1 *marriš* for the river Huputiš, 1 *marriš* for the river Rannakara, 1 *marriš* for the river Šaušanuš. (PF 339)

Here we again find agreement with the Classical sources. Herodotus particularly stresses the respect that Persians showed for running water: "They have a profound reverence for rivers: they will never pollute a river with urine or spittle, or even wash their hands in one, or allow anyone else to do so" (I.138◊). We have already mentioned that the Sakian Sirakes refers to Sacred Water. Strabo himself notes that the Persians performed a ceremony that specially honored Water and Fire (XV.3.14).

In addition to performing regular sacrifices, the king was the intermediary with the gods during military expeditions. Xenophon constantly refers to this in the *Cyropaedia*. As the head of the Persian army, "Now as soon as [Cyrus] was chosen, his first act was to consult the gods; and not till he had sacrificed and the omens were propitious did he proceed to choose his two hundred men" (I.5.6◊), telling them: "This, moreover, will, I think, strengthen your confidence: I have not neglected the gods as we embark upon this expedition. For you . . . know that not only in great things but also in small I always try to begin with the approval of the gods" (I.5.14◊). They arrived at the border, and "when an eagle appeared upon their right and flew on ahead of them, they prayed to the gods and heroes who watch over the land of Persia to conduct them on with grace and favour, and then proceeded to cross the frontier" (II.1.1◊). Cyrus never failed to ask the gods for favorable signs (III.3.21–22, 57; VI.3.1; VI.4.12; VII.1.1) or to thank them after a victory (IV.1.2).

The description of Xerxes' expedition in 480 swarms with references to religious and magical practices. Among many possible examples, we may select the rite carried out in Phrygia. To punish Pythius for refusing to send his son to war, Xerxes made the following decision:

> Xerxes at once gave orders that the men to whom such duties fell should find Pythius' eldest son and cut him in half and put the two halves one on each side of the road, for the army to march out between them. The order was performed.
>
> And now between the halves of the young man's body the advance of the army began. (Herodotus VII.39◇)

This "barbaric" custom was found among many peoples and took on magical-religious force. In Herodotus's version, a solar eclipse had stricken the king with terror a little earlier (VII.37). Despite the soothing explanations of the *magi*, the king opted to proceed with a purification of the army, following the practices described by Herodotus. "This measure boded well for the expedition," as le Comte de Gobineau put it. In this way, the evil was left behind, blocked and repulsed by virtue of sacrifice. When a human victim was chosen (in preference to an animal), it was because the matter was serious. It was actually the fate of the army, and thus of the expedition and the king, that hung in the balance.

As Xenophon's Cyrus put it (I.5.14), the king and the army were accompanied by Persian gods, a fact that is also reflected in the descriptions by Herodotus (of Xerxes) and Quintus Curtius (of Darius III). In the official procession, the chariots of the great gods held a preeminent place. Thus, before Gaugamela, Darius called "upon the Sun and Mithras, and the sacred and eternal fire, to inspire [the soldiers] with a courage worthy of their ancient glory and the records of their forefathers" (Quintus Curtius IV.13.12◇), and he addressed his own gods by invoking "the gods of our fatherland, by the eternal fire which is carried before me on altars, by the radiance of the sun whose rising is within the confines of my realm" (IV.14.24◇). "Nothing sways the common herd more effectively than superstition," Quintus Curtius comments aphoristically (IV.10.7◇). In truth, when we know the close connection between royal legitimacy, victory, and divine protection, we understand that the sacral *aura* of the king could well have heightened the courage of the soldiers at his side.

One of the best pieces of concrete evidence of the official religion appears in a passage from the *Mithradatic Wars* (12.66), written by the Roman historian Appian. This is how he describes a ceremony presided over by Mithradates, king of Pontus, after his victory over the Roman Murena:

> He offered sacrifices to Zeus Stratios on a tall stack of wood placed on a high mountain, according to the following traditional custom. To begin, the kings bring wood, and after installing on the nearby plain a mound of less importance, they place on the higher of the two hearths milk, honey, wine, oil, and all sorts of aromatics to burn; as for what is found in the plain, they place on top bread and something for the helpers' meal. This is also the type of sacrifice practiced by the Persian kings at Pasargadae. Then they light the wood. When it burns, it is so great that it can be seen from far off—1000 stadia away—and, as the air burns, they say it is impossible to approach for several days.

The evidence is late. But Pontus was a considerably Iranized country, as Strabo frequently says—and he was from Pontus. Mithradates presents himself as a Hellenized sovereign, without repudiating his Iranian origins. There can be no doubt that behind

33a

33b (right)

33c

33d

33e

33f

Fig. 33. Magi and sacrifices.

Zeus Stratios ['Warrior'] there lurked an Iranian god, albeit partly Hellenized. The author's comparison with the sacrificial practices of Persian kings at Pasargadae is also interesting, even though it involved Persian princes (fig. 36, p. 250) and not Achaemenid kings. The heritage of the Great Kings remained quite vital in Hellenistic Persia.

The King, the Sacrifices, and the Magi

Wherever he went, the king was accompanied by *magi*. Those around Xerxes, for example, interpreted a solar eclipse (Herodotus VII.37), poured libations at Pergamum "to the spirits of the great men of old" (VII.43◇), sacrificed white horses in the Strymon (VII.113), and sacrificed to Thetis to calm the tempest (VII.191). *Magi* around Cyrus "never failed to sing hymns to the gods at daybreak" (*Cyr.* VIII.1.23◇). In Darius III's procession, they went "next [after the Fire altars] chanting their traditional hymn" (Quintus Curtius III.3.9◇; cf. V.1.22). Because of their position, the *magi* were justified in reserving part of the booty for the gods (*Cyr.* VII.3.1; VII.35.1). *Magi* in the *Cyropedia* (VIII.3.11; VIII.1.23) chose the gods to whom the king had to sacrifice, "for the Persians think that they ought much more scrupulously to be guided by those whose profession (*technitai*) is with things divine than they are by those in other professions" (VIII.3.11◇; cf. Strabo XV.1.68, who compares them to the Sages of Mauryan India).

One of the *magi*'s numerous functions in Persian society and in relation to the king was to play an authoritative role in all of the sacrifices. Herodotus says this quite clearly:

> When the [worshipper] has cut up the animal and cooked it, he makes a little heap of the softest green-stuff he can find, preferably clover, and lays all the meat upon it. This done, a Magus (a member of this caste is always (*nomos*) present at sacrifices) utters an incantation over it. . . . Then after a short interval the worshipper removes the flesh and does what he pleases with it. (I.132◇)

Strabo also makes many allusions to the role of the *magi*:

> To fire they offer sacrifice by adding dry wood without the bark and by placing fat on top of it; and then they pour oil upon it and light it below, not blowing with their breath but fanning it; and those who blow the fire with their breath or put anything dead or filthy upon it are put to death. (XV.3.14◇)

Then Strabo gives information concerning the sacrifices that were observed in his time in Cappadocia:

> And to water they offer sacrifice by going to a lake or river or spring, where, having dug a trench leading thereto, they slaughter a victim, being on their guard lest any of the water near by should be made bloody, believing that the blood would pollute the water; and then, placing pieces of meat on myrtle or laurel branches, the Magi touch them with slender wands and make incantations, pouring oil mixed with both milk and honey, though not into fire or water, but upon the ground; and they carry on their incantations for a long time, holding in their hands a bundle of slender myrtle wands. (XV.3.14◇)

An image of Persian origin illustrates Strabo's words to some extent. It is found on a stela discovered near Dascylium in Hellespontine Phrygia, but it appears to be nearly identical to other illustrated items (fig. 33). Two persons (fig. 33b) stand before what appears to be a tall altar on legs. They wear Persian dress; their mouths are covered with a veil, and in their hands they hold a bundle of rods; the heads of a bull and a ram are placed on a bundle of branches in front of them. The veil and the bundle of twigs correspond to objects held by the officiant in the *Avesta*: the *barsom* and the *pādam*, respectively. The officiant bearing the *barsom* is found in several iconographic representations (Dalton XIV.48–49). Nonetheless, not all of the information in Strabo is confirmed. He states, for example, that in "the places where the Fire burns" (*pyratheia*) and "where the Magi keep the fire ever burning . . . the people do not sacrifice victims with a sword either, but with a kind of tree-trunk, beating them to death as with a cudgel" (XV.3.15◊); On the other hand, on a Persepolis seal, an officiant is shown grasping a mouflon [wild sheep with curled horns] in his right hand and holding a short sword in his left (Schmidt II, pl. 15). This "contradiction" serves to remind us on the one hand that Strabo's information is late and on the other that cultic forms were not necessarily identical throughout the Empire (see fig. 33e).

Thus, the *magi* were not strictly priests but ritual experts whose mediation allowed the sacrificer to consume the meat offered to the deity. They are cited several times in this function in the Persepolis tablets. They were responsible to make libations and received the necessary materials from the administration for this purpose:

> 12 *marriš* of wine, at the disposal (*kurmin*) of ?, Irdakurradduš the *magus* (*makuš*), who carried out the *lan* sacrifice, received them for the libation in the *lan* ceremony. From the first to the 12th month, 12 months in all, 19th year. For 1 month, he received 1 *marriš*. (PF 758)

The *magi* were able to do this because of their special knowledge. If, for example, they made sacrifices to Thetis (Herodotus VII.191), it was because they had particular authority in this regard. In one of his polemics against the *magi*, Pliny the Elder describes a precious stone, a form of amethyst: "They keep off hail and locusts if they are used in conjunction with an incantation which they prescribe" (XXXVII.40.124◊). Other precious stones, agates, were reputed by the *magi* to "avert storms and waterspouts and stop the flow of rivers" (XXXVII.54.142◊).

Sacrifices and Banquets

The Classical authors especially describe animal sacrifices: Cyrus offers horses to the Sun, as well as "some exceptionally handsome bulls for Zeus and for the other gods as the magi directed" (*Cyr.* VIII.3.11◊, 24). The importance of meat sacrifices is emphasized by Strabo in many passages dedicated to Persian and/or Iranian sacrifices. Quite another picture emerges, however, from the Persepolis tablets: the administration basically delivered grain, beer, or wine. Sometimes, it is true, the priest traded these products for sheep, but this action seems to have been reserved for a particular kind of sacrifice, the *kušukum*, offered especially in honor of Elamite gods. The liquid products were probably used for the libations, which all of the Classical authors (including Strabo) indicate most often comprised oil, milk, honey, and wine. Note also that, in the images on seals, animal sacrifices are relatively rare.

In Strabo, at the end of the ceremony the meat is divided among the participants; none of it is set aside for the deity, who, the Persians say, desires only the soul (*psychē*) of the sacrificial victim and nothing else (XV.3.13). An illustration of this postsacrificial custom of sharing is also found in several Persepolis tablets that end with the formula "and the *kurtaš* ate [the grain]" (PF 336–37). This probably refers to the organization of a festival. Each great sacrificial festival was in fact followed by a banquet, as Xenophon explains: "To all the winners [of chariot races Cyrus] gave cups and cattle, so that they might sacrifice and have a banquet. . . . When it was all over, they went back to the city to their lodgings" (VIII.3.33–34◊). But one detail given by Xenophon should be stressed: "The victims are omitted when the king does not offer sacrifice" (*Cyr.* VIII.3.34◊). In other words, the sacrifice was not intended solely to honor the gods; the festival and accompanying banquet exalted the might and generosity of the king.

An excellent confirmation of this custom is found in a testimony from the beginning of the Hellenistic era:

> When [the soldiers] had arrived in Persepolis, the capital (*to basileion*), Peucestes, who was general of this land, performed a magnificent sacrifice to the gods and to Alexander and Philip; and after gathering from almost the whole of Persia a multitude of sacrificial animals and of whatever else was needed for festivities and religious gatherings (*panēgyris*), he gave a feast to the army. (Diodorus XIX.22.1◊)

Then Diodorus describes the arrangements made by Peucestes to position the participants at the festival on the occasion of the sacrifice. They were placed in four concentric circles, in accord with their hierarchic and social status:

> In the inner circle with a perimeter of two stades each of the generals and hipparchs and also each of the Persians who was most highly honoured occupied his own couch. In the middle of these there were altars for the gods and for Alexander and Philip. (22.2–3◊)

There is hardly any doubt that Peucestes undertook the organization of Achaemenid religious festivals for his own profit. We know that in encampment and in battle, the Great King was always placed at the center (e.g., *Cyr.* VIII.5.8). The arrangement of the royal processions shows clearly that everyone in them received a place strictly in accord with his titles, his duties, and the status that the Great King afforded to him. Xenophon himself has a long digression on how important Cyrus considered protocol to be during the organization of the banquet that followed a sacrifice (*Cyr.* VIII.4.3). Peucestes had obviously adapted the ceremony to the new conditions arising with the Macedonian conquest. He had the altars dedicated to Alexander and Philip placed in the center, but because he was a recognized partisan of a collaboration loyal to the Persian aristocracy, he accorded them a central place alongside the most eminent Macedonian leaders. What is noteworthy is that the organization of the sacrifice and the banquet were prepared in a context of competition between Peucestes and his rival, Eumenes. It is very clear that the distribution of meat to the soldiers had the objective of maintaining their loyalty (Diodorus XIX.21.3). Some time later, Eumenes himself "performed a sacrifice to the gods and entertained the army sumptuously" (24.5◊). In fact, Eumenes "reason[ed] that Peucestes was playing up to the crowd in furtherance of his desire for the chief command" (23.1◊). And Diodorus specifies further that it was in his capacity as satrap of Persia that Peucestes presided over the ceremonies. It is thus tempting to think that, by doing this, Peucestes had attempted to adorn himself with the prestige that surrounded the Great King during the organization of festivals and sacrificial banquets.

The King and the Cult of Ahura-Mazda

The links between the king and Ahura-Mazda are abundantly attested in the royal inscriptions, as has already been stressed several times. In the prayers of Darius I, Ahura-Mazda, "the greatest of the gods," is most often invoked alone (*DPh, DPe, DSz, DSaa*), less commonly in the company of the "other gods" (*DPd, DPf*). This is confirmed later in the speeches of consolation that a eunuch addressed to Darius III, who was distraught over the fate of the princesses and royal sons after the battle of Issus. Their only suffering, the eunuch explained to the king, was that they missed only "the light of your countenance, which I doubt not but the lord (*kyrios*) Oromasdes [Ahura-Mazda] will yet restore

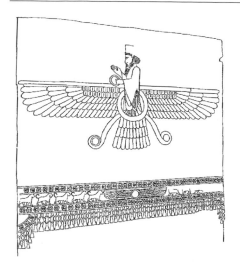

Fig. 34. Ahura-Mazda.

to its former glory" (Plutarch, *Alex.* 30.5◊). Let us also mention an episode from the reign of Artaxerxes II as it is recorded by Plutarch. After the supreme punishment was imposed on a felonious son, "going forth into the court [of the palace], he worshipped the sun, and said, 'Depart in peace, ye Persians, and declare to your fellow-subjects how the mighty Oromasdes hath dealt out vengeance to the contrivers of unjust and unlawful things'" (*Art.* 29.12◊). Ahura-Mazda was indeed the source of royal power and influence (*farnah*).

Outside of these examples, even the name of Ahura-Mazda is rarely mentioned. Sometimes he is recognizable under the name of Zeus. This is certainly the case in Herodotus's digression on the Persian cults: "Zeus, in their system, is the whole circle of the heavens, and they sacrifice to him from the tops of mountains" (I.131◊). We can in fact recognize this as a muted echo of the god "who created heaven, who created earth." It was also certainly Ahura-Mazda to whom were dedicated "the holy chariot of Zeus" brought to Greece by Xerxes (VII.40;◊ VIII.115), the "chariot sacred to Zeus" in Cyrus's procession (*Cyr.* VIII.3.12◊), and again "the chariot consecrated to Jupiter" in the procession of Darius III (Quintus Curtius III.3.11◊). But it would be simplistic to "translate" Zeus automatically as Ahura-Mazda. The Persepolis tablets mention Ahura-Mazda only rarely. In the available documents, an attendant receives items for sacrifice to Ahura-Mazda and other gods. We have only one attestation of a sacrifice honoring Ahura-Mazda alone (*PF* 771). This silence is hard to explain solely on the basis of the uneven survival of the documentation. The following solution has been proposed: one of the sacrifices, the *lan*, was practiced regularly by the *magi* in the context of a official state cult in honor of the great god. This hypothesis offers the advantage of restoring the importance we would expect Ahura-Mazda to have in Darius's Persia. But we must recognize that we lack what might be called tangible evidence.

The iconography and identification of the winged disk remain controversial. Without discounting the opposing arguments, we will here accept the hypothesis that it is indeed a representation of Ahura-Mazda. This winged disk, from which a bearded figure identical to the king frequently emerges (fig. 34), is found on many Persepolis reliefs. But the winged disk appears on nearly every Achaemenid seal, and not only on seals depicting a royal figure. Several seals on Treasury tablets show a scene with two Persians worshiping Ahura-Mazda.

The King and the Worship of Fire

We know that Fire was one of the elements of nature that the Persians worshiped (Herodotus I.131). Strabo also states that Fire and Water were the elements most honored (XV.3.14). He continues: "And to whatever god they offer sacrifice, to him they first offer

Fig. 35. Fire altars and cult.

prayer with fire" (XV.3.16◇). According to Dinon (*FGrH* 690 F28), "of all of the gods, the Persians raise statues (*agalmata*) only to Fire and Water." The Sakian Sirakes was aware of this, for he invoked "the eternal Fire and the sacred Water" to win the confidence of Darius (Polyaenus VII.11.12). It was probably because of the sacred character of Fire that the burning of corpses was forbidden (Strabo XV.3.18; cf. Ctesias §57: *para ton nomon*). In the Persepolis tablets, we find two titles whose roots are related to fire: *āthravapati-* and *ātrvaša*. The holders of the first title filled administrative functions that do not seem to have had anything to do with the religion. The second ('Guardians of the Fire') was different and is mentioned more often. The context is sometimes ritual, but Fire worship as such is not explicitly attested. Note, however, that one of the deities mentioned in the tablets, Naryasanga, maintained a privileged relationship with Fire. The most that is safe to assume is that in each place where these attendants are mentioned there was a Fire sanctuary. Indeed, we have no archaeological evidence from the Achaemenid period, but the importance of Fire sanctuaries in the Hellenistic period (fig. 36) undoubtedly exhibits continuity with the Achaemenid period.

At Naqš-i Rustam, as we have seen (fig. 16, p. 211,) Darius stands before a Fire altar with leaping flames, the scene surmounted by a winged disk and a crescent moon. It is hard to grasp the dynamics of the scene—if it is even intended to portray anything

Fig. 36. Hellenistic Persian coin showing a fire temple.

specific. We may nevertheless suppose that it refers, in a stylized, sacred manner, to a sacrifice offered personally by the Great King before a fire altar. A similar scene is found on numerous stamps on Treasury tablets (fig. 35). One of the most remarkable representations is a seal (fig. 35b) inscribed with the name Zarathustriš. Beneath the emblem of Ahura-Mazda, on each side of a fire altar stand attendants in Persian garb. The attendant on the left holds a bundle of ritual rods (*barsom*) in his hand, and the attendant on the right holds a libation spoon in both hands. This is the only known representation of the sacrifice later known as the *ataš-zohr*.

In any case, the picture at Naqš-i Rustam and the Classical texts together imply privileged relations between the king and Fire. Perhaps it is Fire that Xenophon's Cyrus invokes, using the name Hephaestus, in order to strengthen the courage of the soldiers during the assault led by his hero against Babylon (*Cyr.* VII.5.22). The order of items in the royal processions, spelled out for us by Xenophon, expresses clearly the place that Fire held in the reality of royal power. In Cyrus's cortege, after the chariot of Zeus and the chariot of the Sun, and before the chariot of the king, "followed men carrying fire on a great altar" (*Cyr.* VIII.3.12✧). However, Xenophon says nothing of specific sacrifices in honor of Fire (3.24). Fire assumed an even more eminent position in Darius III's cortege:

> Now the order of march was as follows. In front on silver altars was carried the fire which they called sacred and eternal (*Ignis, quem ipsi sacrum et aeternum vocabant*). Next came the Magi, chanting their traditional hymn. (*patrium carmen*; Quintus Curtius III.3.9–10✧)

Finally, the practice of extinguishing the sacred Fires when the king died (Diodorus XVII.114.4–5) attests to the facts that (1) there were official Fire sanctuaries in all of the satrapies (guarded by the *magi*: Dinon, *FGrH* 690 F28) and (2) that there was an official religion linked very closely to the person and majesty of the king.

The King, Mithra, and the Sun

The Sun was another of the natural elements mentioned by the ancient authors that was worshiped by the Persians (cf. Plutarch, *Art.* 29.12). In the festival organized by Cyrus in Persia was a chariot of the Sun "with white harnesses, crowned like the chariot of Zeus"; the cortege also included horses as "a sacrifice for the Sun," soon to be sacrificed in the fire (*Cyr.* VIII.3.12,✧ 24). Let us also remark in passing that Herodotus (I.216✧) said of the Scythians—an Iranian people—"the only god they worship is the sun, to which they sacrifice horses." Without doubt the Sun was included among "the gods who have our country in their keeping" to whom Xerxes urged the Persians to pray before crossing the Hellespont (VII.53◇). The place of the Sun and its relationship with horses are also clearly brought out in Quintus Curtius's description of Darius III's order of march:

> When the day was already bright, the signal was given from the king's tent with the horn; above the tent, from which it might be seen by all, there gleamed an image of the sun enclosed in crystal. . . . [The Fire altars and the chariot of Jupiter/Ahura-Mazda] were followed by a horse of extraordinary size, which they called the steed of the Sun. Golden wands and white robes adorned the drivers of the horses. (III.3.8, 11)

The relationship between Mithra and horses is also well attested, especially by Strabo. According to him, every year the satrap of Armenia was required to send to the court 20,000 colts to be sacrificed during the festival celebrated in honor of Mithra (*Mithrakāna*; XI.14.9; cf. Xenophon, *Anab.* IV.5.24 and IV.5.35: Helios). The offering of a hecatomb of horses to the Sun by Cyrus occurred at the Mithrakāna. But the sacrifice of horses was not reserved exclusively for the cult of Mithra. Recall, for example, that when the *magi* arrived at the River Strymon in Thrace they "tried to propitiate [it] by a sacrifice of white horses" (Herodotus VII.113◇). Another passage in Herodotus (I.189) also brings together sacred white horses and a river. It is thus risky to establish the identity of a god by the kind of animals offered to him in sacrifice.

It is frequently thought that the Persians assimilated the Sun to Mithra, as claimed by Strabo (XV.3.13), Hesychius, and the *Suda*. Nonetheless, modern debate about this continues at a lively pace, for the documentation is both very heterogeneous and full of contradictions. No sacrifice to the Sun (or to Mithra) is recorded in the Persepolis tablets. Note also that no royal inscription refers explicitly to Mithra (or to Anāhita) prior to Artaxerxes II. Darius sometimes lifts his prayers and thanks to "Ahura-Mazda and the other gods" (*DPa, DPf*). It is generally supposed that this expression includes (among others) Mithra and Anāhita. Two of the *Yashts* of the *Avesta* are dedicated to Anāhita and Mithra, but their use is problematic; it is in fact not easy to distinguish the various chronological strata. This observation holds still more firmly for the Greek and Latin texts, for a number of late ones refer to the solar (and military) cult of Mithra (*Sol Invictus*), which was strikingly popular in the Roman period. In Xenophon, Cyrus the Younger also evokes Mithra in his paradise (*Oec.* IV.24). Artaxerxes acclaimed the exceptional size of a pomegranate offered to him by a simple Persian peasant (Plutarch, *Art.* 4.5; Aelian, *VH* I.33). This was because Mithra, the god of oaths and contracts, a warrior god, was also the god who protected fields and harvests. It was "he who gives favor at his whim, who gives fields at his whim, who does nothing bad to the one who plows, who increases the waters, who hears the appeal, who spreads the waters, who makes the plants grow, who gives increase." He follows the paths "that make fertile fields." In this same *Yasht* 10 of the *Avesta*, he is saluted as "Mithra of the vast pastures." The attributes of just warrior and protector of the earth and peasants were complementarily fused with each other in the person of Mithra, just as they were in the person of the Great King.

We know from Xenophon (*Cyr.* VIII.3.9), Herodotus (VII.54), and Quintus Curtius (III.3.8: *patrio more*) that the royal procession set out at sunrise. But there is nothing to make us think that in doing this the Persians were specifically honoring Mithra. Perhaps they honored the god Hvarīra, who is attested in the Persepolis tablets, if he indeed personified the spirit of the sunrise, as some believe. It is equally improbable that the prayer addressed to the Sun by Xerxes before crossing the Hellespont was in reality directed specifically to Mithra.

One of the most troubling pieces of evidence is late: when before the battle of Arbela Darius III invoked "the Sun and Mithras, and the sacred and eternal fire" (Quintus Curtius IV.13.12✧)—a statement that implies a formal distinction between the two deities, whatever their original genetic relationship may have been. It makes sense at this point to compare this text with another piece of evidence that also dates to the reign of Darius III. A speech put in the king's mouth by Plutarch (*Alex*. 30.7) reveals that, to the Persians, Mithra was both the god who guaranteed contracts (as confirmed by the Iranian and Greek documentation) and the god of light. This indicates that Mithra, among all his functions (warrior, protector of the fields, etc.), maintained a special relationship with the Sun, the source of light. To be sure, Mithra was not the only deity endowed with radiant force. Ahura-Mazda was also (and first of all) the source of light (cf. Plutarch, *Alex*. 30.5). But the two items are not necessarily mutually exclusive, for many (if not all) deities have plurifunctional properties and share common or related characteristics. All in all, the complex case of the identity of Mithra is not closed; the best we can do is to recognize, on the one hand, that, in the Achaemenid period, Mithra was closely related to the Sun and, on the other hand, that there was never either formal or exclusive assimilation (at least not in the official forms of the religion; it is not easy to penetrate into popular beliefs).

We have seen that during the festivals of Mithra (*Mithrakāna*) thousands of horses were offered to the god. This is the only festival for which we are informed about the special role played by the king—that is, about one of the aspects of his participation. In a digression about drunkenness, Athenaeus quotes Ctesias and Duris in these words:

> Ctesias says that in India the king is not permitted to get drunk. But among the Persians the king is allowed to get drunk on one day, that on which they sacrifice to Mithra. On this point Duris, in the seventh book of his *Histories*, writes as follows: "In only one of the festivals celebrated by the Persians, that to Mithra, the king gets drunk and dances 'the Persian'; no one else throughout Asia does this, but everyone abstains on this day from the dance." (X.434e✧)

To tell the truth, the evidence remains difficult to interpret, especially when we compare a fact provided by Demetrius of Skepsis relating to the time of Antiochus the Great. According to him, "it was the habit not merely of the king's friends but also of the king himself to dance under arms at dinner (*deipnon*)" (Athenaeus IV.155b✧). But, from the time of the Great King to the Seleucid king, similar features may have concealed differing functions (in the Persian court, only the king danced the *persica*). We know in any case that, at the Achaemenid court, dances were part of the ritual: when "Cyrus" "performed the customary sacrifice and led the Persians in their national (*kata ta patria*) dance" (Xenophon, *Cyr*. VIII.7.1✧). We also know that the *persica* was widely known. Xenophon presents it as an expression of joy among the Persians (*Cyr*. VIII.4.12). Duris specifies that the Persians regularly gave themselves over to it, in the same way that they took up horsemanship, because it strengthened the muscles. One can well believe this, if one recalls Xenophon's description:

> Lastly, [a Mysian] danced the Persian dance, clashing his shields together and crouching down and then rising up again; and all this he did, keeping time to the music of the flute. (*Anab*. VI.1.10✧)

Let us note in passing that Duris's comparison of the *persica* with riding exercises is perhaps not fortuitous. Aelian, who certainly got his information from Ctesias, records that the Persians banged bronze weapons in front of their horses to accustom them to the clangor of battle (*Anim.* XVI.25). Could this be a fleeting allusion to the shields struck by the soldiers while dancing the *persica*? In any case, it appears that the *persica* was a military dance, quite appropriate for honoring a warrior-god such as Mithra.

It is also noteworthy that on the day of the festival of Mithra, only the king could dance the *persica*. Likewise, only the king could become drunk. Drunkenness was perhaps a common condition among the Persians, including their kings, since according to Plutarch (*Art.* 6.4), Cyrus the Younger—to demonstrate his royal qualities—boasted of holding his liquor better than his brother Artaxerxes. And, according to Ctesias (*Persica* §45), Xerxes II perished at the hand of conspirators "when after a festival he fell asleep drunk in his palace"! It has sometimes been supposed that royal drunkenness on the day of *Mithrakāna* was due to drinking *haoma*, which is considered an intoxicating beverage but whose ingredients remain hotly disputed; but this is sheer speculation. Would not royal drunkenness instead relate to a fertility rite, symbolized by the vine?

The Worship of Anāhita

Anahita, like Mithra, does not appear in the royal inscriptions until Artaxerxes II, but we know that he granted special privileges to her worship in all of the imperial capitals, from Bactra to Sardis. Without devaluing the meaning of Artaxerxes II's decrees, we can surmise, however, that devotion to the goddess did not result simply from a sudden change; worship of her must have evolved over a long period of time.

Other than late attestations of Anāhita in Asia Minor in the form of Anaitis or Persian Artemis, evidence for her worship is basically limited to scenes on seals and rings. One of the seals, belonging to Gorgippa (Anapa), shows (fig. 37a) a king dressed in a long robe and wearing a crenellated crown; he extends both hands toward a woman, who also wears a crenellated crown. She appears in a radiant nimbus, standing on a lion; in her right hand she holds a flower, in the left a baton. Another seal (Louvre, Coll. de Clercq) shows (fig. 37b) a woman seated on a chair with a low back, feet on a footstool; she wears a crown and holds a lotus flower in her left hand; with her right hand she is about to take a dove being presented by a young child standing in front of her; behind the child we recognize a footed censer. Another female figure (also wearing a crenellated crown) fills

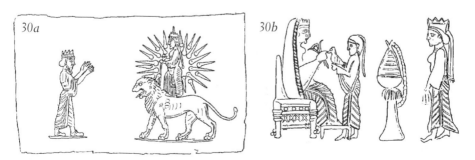

Fig. 37. Anāhita. (a) The king before Anāhita? (b) Representation of Anāhita?

out the scene at the right. These two seals are often compared with a scene on a ring from the Oxus treasury: a woman is seated on a couch with a low back; she wears a crenellated crown; she holds a flower in her right hand and a crown in her left.

Although the interpretation is contested, these are probably three representations of Anāhita. The connections with the dove are well attested. The connection with lions is brought out in an anecdote in Aelian, who records that in a sanctuary of Anaitis in Elymais tame lions roam freely (*Anim.* XII.23). Furthermore, we have a document whose date is more certain: a seal impression on Treasury tablets portrays a woman, a goddess, also surrounded by a radiant nimbus (PTS 91). This document to some extent furnishes the missing link. With this evidence, the figure of the king facing Anāhita riding on her lion can be added to the file on relations between the Great King and the deities. Eventually, we will need to consider certain modifications that Artaxerxes II made to the worship of the goddess (chapter 15/8).

Another equally interesting fact is that the imagery of the first seal very closely resembles Urartian and Mesopotamian depictions. It seems clear, in this context, that Anāhita owes much to Mesopotamian Ištar. Because of this, it is reasonable to suppose that syncretism was at work at least as early as the arrival of the Persians in these regions. This is probably what Herodotus meant when he wrote that the Persians "learned from the Assyrians and Arabians the cult of Uranian Aphrodite" (I.131◇). We are thus led to believe that even though the goddess is not mentioned in the inscriptions of the early kings, she was quite certainly worshiped at an early period. We should also recall that, according to Tacitus (III.62), there was a sanctuary in honor of Anaitis [Persian Diana] in Lydia as early as the reign of Cyrus.

Chapter 7

People and Life at Court

1. Sources and Problems

In the foregoing chapters, I have already offered a partial account of the way that the central court functioned as the locus of power par excellence: it was where the king lived with his family and household, where the nobility had to reside, where administrative and strategic decisions were made, where the satraps were summoned or where they came to consult with the king, where foreign ambassadors were received, where festivals and sacrifices presided over by the king were held, and so on. Paradoxically, documentation of court life is rare and unevenly distributed. The Persepolis tablets occasionally provide indirect but important information, despite their narrowly administrative character (see chap. 11), but it must be said that most information comes directly or indirectly from the Greek authors of the fourth century and from Alexander's historians. The former depend most often on Ctesias and other court writers, such as Dinon; both are abundantly used by two authors we quote frequently, Plutarch in the *Life of Artaxerxes* and Aelian in his *Historical Miscellany*. Many other authors focused on the Achaemenid court (e.g., Heraclides of Cyme, Phylarcus, Theopompus). Their works are lost, but fortunately they are quoted by Athenaeus, to whom we will frequently refer. On the other hand, for the fifth century we know practically nothing specific, because unlike Ctesias, Herodotus is hardly interested in court life, aside from his discussions of Darius's marriages, the (supposed) role of Atossa regarding her royal husband, and the romance of Masistes with which his *Inquiries* ends.

In a very general way, the fourth-century authors and Alexander's historians were guided by the desire to evoke a sense of wonder in their readers by dwelling on what they considered most characteristic of the Great King's court—its opulence, which they took as both a manifestation of its power and proof of its weakness. Also important to us are the numerous details they provide on the organization of the royal banquets and ponderous digressions on the dissolute life and nefarious influence of the Persian princesses. They are much more sparing of details on administrative organization, with the exception of lists. Thus Xenophon enumerates "tax-collectors, paymasters, boards of public works, keepers of his estates, stewards of his commissary department, . . . superintendents of his horses and hounds" (*Cyr.* VIII.1.9✧). The author of *De Mundo* writes: in addition to the guards, servants, and porters, there were "stewards of his revenues and leaders in war and hunting, and receivers of gifts, and others . . ." (398a 20–30✧). But it must be acknowledged that we know nothing more about most of these people than their titles.

The selection of information was obviously carried out as a function of a string of cultural presuppositions and ideological stereotypes. It is clear that it was the king's bed and the king's table that most attracted the Greeks. All we need to look at for confirmation of this is the abbreviated inventory of Darius III's camp (Athenaeus XIII.608a). Using these sources thus poses a methodological problem that has already been pointed out several times in this book. In this particular case, we must not "throw the baby out with the bathwater." That is, in reading the Classical authors, we must distinguish the Greek interpretive coating from the Achaemenid nugget of information. Rejecting the interpretation the Greek writers gave to an Achaemenid court custom does not imply that the custom or practice they were dealing with was pure and simple invention on their part.

Tents and Palaces

Let us also stress the fact that many authors allude to Persian court customs in the context of wars fought by the Persian, Greek, and Macedonian armies. Thus, they were particularly interested in booty, a fact that resulted in fairly exact descriptions (albeit with selective quotation to some extent) of the Persian camps captured after battles. In Alexander's day, the Great King fought far from his palace. He and his court, as we have seen, migrated periodically between the various royal residences. The king relocated with not only his close family, household, and courtiers, but also the various departments of the administration. The mountains of luggage were transported on camelback and muleback, as well as by a special kind of porter whose Persian name, given by Quintus Curtius, is *gangabas* 'treasury porters' (III.13.7◊). The word 'treasury' (Persian **ganza*: III.13.5◊) also refers to all of the paraphernalia that followed the king. In fact, "the greater part of his money and everything else a great king takes with him even on campaign for his extravagant way of living" (Arrian II.11.10◊); "when the Persian king goes to war, he is always well provided not only with victuals from home (*oikos*) and his own cattle" (Herodotus I.188◊).

When the group stopped, specialized workers had to level the ground and erect the royal tent. Xenophon marveled at how quickly "each one has assigned to him likewise the part that he is to do" in packing and unpacking all of the baggage (*Cyr.* VIII.5.2, 4–5◊). The royal tent was erected in the middle of the camp (VIII.5.3, 8–10) and marked with distinctive symbols (cf. Quintus Curtius III.8.7). Each officer also had a tent of his own, recognizable by an ensign flying from a mast (*Cyr.* VIII.5.13). The royal tent was truly monumental, reproducing to the last detail the private apartments of the palace. According to Herodotus (IX.70◊), Xerxes' tent (left in Greece for the use of Mardonius) even contained "the manger used by his horses—a remarkable piece of work, all in bronze" (cf. Quintus Curtius III.3.21). As in any palace, there was a gate, where entry was strictly controlled. There was also a banquet hall; its luxury amazed all the Greeks who had taken possession of Mardonius's tent after the battle of Plataea. This was a cloth and leather monument of impressive dimensions. According to Chares of Mytilene, Alexander's banquet tent was raised on columns 15 m high. The interior of this portable palace measured nearly 700 m in circumference (Athenaeus XII.538b–d, 539d). This was the tent where Alexander held court and granted audiences, after the model of the Great Kings on the road. He sat on a gold seat surrounded by his personal guard (539f), which included 500 Persian *mēlophoroi* 'bodyguards' [lit.: 'apple-bearers'] (Aelian, *VH* IX.3◊). We can understand how the Athenians were later able to conceptualize their own Odeon on the model of Xerxes' tent.

Descriptions by Greek authors go on to provide original information about this tent. Plutarch, for instance, records our only information about the splendor of Darius III's bathing rooms:

Darius's tent, which was full of splendid furniture and quantities of gold and silver, they reserved for Alexander himself. . . . When he beheld the bathing vessels, the water-pots, the pans, and the ointment boxes, all of gold curiously wrought, and smelt the fragrant odours with which the whole place was exquisitely perfumed, and from thence passed into a pavilion of great size and height, where the couches and tables and preparations for an entertainment were perfectly magnificent, he turned to those about him and said, "This, it seems, is royalty." (*Alex.* 20.12–13✥)

The reflection placed on Alexander's lips reminds us of the reaction of Pausanias and the Greeks to the indolent luxury of Mardonius's tent, which they seized after the battle of Plataea (Herodotus IX.82), and many other authors dwell on the splendor of the Persian generals' tents. The descriptions of Alexander's tent are equally rich in information, since he obviously took up a custom of the Great Kings. In general, all the ancient authors' expatiations on the luxury of Alexander's court (reprehensible in their eyes) underline the continuities with Achaemenid practice.

The Classical texts are even more important in that we know so little of the environment within the royal residences. At Susa, a residential quarter containing the royal apartments has been found. Movement between rooms was accomplished with special corridors. But it is generally thought that royal Susa included only a very few permanent residences. The same thinking has been offered about Persepolis. It is sometimes inferred that, during the migrations of the court, the royal entourage stayed in tent cities set out on the plain below the terrace. Indeed, we know that the court included a great number of people because, according to Dinon and Ctesias, 15,000 people, including the soldiers, were fed every day (Athenaeus IV.146c). Nevertheless, these interpretations give rise to several methodological reservations.

First of all, these interpretations rely on gaps in the archaeological record. It is clear that any conclusions regarding the permanent occupation of Persepolis must be considered premature as long as the plain has not been systematically excavated. We know that from Cambyses' time on, palaces and residences were built there. We also know that in Artaxerxes II's time a new palace was built at Susa, down on the Shaur River. There are other ways in which archaeology is not entirely silent. A bathing room has been found at Persepolis. It seems clear that the Great King retired to bathe there regularly (cf. Aelian, *VH* XII.1), as did the Persian nobles (cf. Polyaenus VIII.16.1; Diodorus XIV.80.8), as well as Alexander at Babylon (cf. Plutarch, *Alex.* 76.1–5; Arrian VII.25). Some reliefs (waiters on the royal table) and objects (dishes) imply the existence of reception halls within the palace. The well-known existence of a military quarter indicates that other buildings had been built for the various guard corps. The *kurtaš*, who worked in the many workshops, were perhaps housed nearby as well.

What is more, the Classical texts are sometimes explicit on this subject. The large number of references to the king's bedroom is major evidence: from a passage in Plutarch (*Art.*, 29.3), we can even infer that the walls were not very thick! Again, Diodorus says in his description of Persepolis that "scattered about the royal terrace were residences (*katalyseis*) of the kings and . . . generals, all luxuriously furnished," and he mentions that "private houses (*idiōtikoi oikoi*) had been furnished with every sort of wealth" (XVII.71.8✥, 70.2✥). Bagoas's house (*oikos*), which Alexander gave to Parmenion, should be included among these private residences (Plutarch, *Alex.* 39.10).

A comparison of the descriptions of the Achaemenid palaces with the descriptions of Alexander's tent is also interesting. According to Chares, Alexander took his meals with

his guests in a sumptuous tent at Susa, while the soldiers, foreign ambassadors, and tour-
ists ate in the palace courtyard (*aulē*) (Athenaeus XII.538c). Heraclides writes of royal
Achaemenid meals in which the Great King and his guests dined in two halls (*oikēmata*)
in the royal palace while the soldiers of the guard and other troops shared their rations
in the palace courtyard (*aulē*) (Athenaeus IV.145a–f). We do not know why Alexander
chose to organize his festivities in a tent even though the Persian palaces were still standing. Perhaps the explanation can be found in the permanently mobile nature of Alexander's court? There is general agreement that the Persian royal tent was as exact a replica
as possible of the palaces at Susa and Persepolis. Protocol and the layout of the rooms
corresponded as closely as possible to those of the permanent residences. Furthermore,
there were certainly royal apartments, luxuriously furnished, in each of the major cities
of the provinces in which the king could stay from time to time.

2. Household Staff

The Chiliarch and the Audience Service

The high court officer best known to the Greeks was undoubtedly the officer they
called the chiliarch, whose title may have been rendered in Iranian as *hazarapatiš* 'Commander of a Thousand'. The Persian word is borrowed directly into Greek in the transliterated form *azarapateis* (Hesychius: plural) and also in the less precise form *azabaritēs*
(Ctesias §46). The reason this officer appears so often in the works of the ancient authors
was that (as they have it) every visitor needed his intercession in order to be granted an
audience (see chap. 6/3 above). According to Diodorus of Sicily (XVIII.48.4✧), "The position and rank of chiliarch had first been brought to fame and honour by the Persian
kings." Nepos writes of Tithraustes, chiliarch at Artaxerxes II's court, "that he held the
second rank in the State" (*Conon* 3.2). Thus, we may say that most ancient writers regarded the chiliarch as the highest person in the Achaemenid court, the controller and
supervisor of every department; in short, he acted as prime minister or grand vizier (to
use the traditional expression).

This interpretation is highly improbable. For one thing, the documents usually adduced in its support are of quite unequal value. Furthermore, and most importantly, it
contradicts what is known of the power structure. The king doubtless had a bureaucracy
of scribes and other permanent staff around him. But he never delegated his sovereign
power to anyone. Even Parnaka, head of the economic administration of Persia, was subject to him (see chap. 11/10 below). Every bureau chief was personally responsible to
him, such as the one who ran the Treasury of the Royal House (perhaps distinct from the
imperial Treasuries: see p. 946), whom Nepos calls 'guardian of the royal fortune' (*gazae
custos regiae*; *Dat.* 14.3), or the head of the royal correspondence (*astandēs*; Plutarch,
Alex. 18.8). When the king had to make a decision, either he acted alone or he appealed
to a few men chosen according to their recognized abilities. A council with a permanent
membership never existed (chap. 3/4 above). Every court job was temporary and could
be transferred from one day to the next to another trustworthy man. The author of *De
Mundo* (398a✧) says the same thing: this or that person is put in charge of this or that job
or mission "with all the other necessary functions" (*kata tēs chreias*).

Consequently, it is highly unlikely that the king was ever flanked by a prime minister
who could potentially have assumed a disproportionate role. Like every other court dignitary, the chiliarch was attached to the person of the king and followed him whenever

he relocated and when he went to war. It was doubtless one of the most sought-after titles; hence the expressions used by the Classical authors to characterize it.

But it is customary to distinguish the prestige of the title from the real work of the job; while the work seems to have devolved onto a single person, the title may have been conferred on several. The grammarian Hesychius defined the task of the chiliarchs (*azarapateis*) as follows: "They are the introducers (*eisaggeleis*) among the Persians." The Classical texts on the reception of Greek ambassadors have frequently led to the supposition that it is the chiliarch who is shown in the audience reliefs at Persepolis, standing before the king, bending forward, blowing a kiss with his right hand toward the sovereign seated on his throne (fig. 20, p. 218). On this point, the literary evidence is uncertain. At Astyages' court, seen by Xenophon, the cupbearer Sacas played the role of introducer: He "had the office of introducing to Astyages those who had business with him and of keeping out those whom he thought it not expedient to admit" (*Cyr.* I.3.8,✧ etc.). Xenophon also lists the head of the *skēptoukhoi* 'grand officers' [lit.: 'scepter-bearers'] among the high court dignitaries; they surrounded the king when he left the palace and were entrusted with, among other things, carrying messages to the people who wished to present a petition (VIII.3.19). "Gadatas was chief of the mace-bearers, and the whole household was managed as he directed." He oversaw everything at meals (VIII.4.2✧). *Skēptoukhoi* were also present in the entourage of Cyrus the Younger, but there it is an honorary title rather than a job (Xenophon, *Anab.* I.7.11). It is thus wise to remain cautious about the identity of the person saluting the king in the audience reliefs of the Persepolis Treasury.

However we may define it, the service of the royal audience certainly included many people. Here is how the author of the *De Mundo* pictures and describes the king in his palace:

> The king himself, so the story goes, established himself at Susa or Ecbatana, invisible to all, dwelling in a wondrous palace within a fence gleaming with gold and amber and ivory. And it had many gateways (*pylōnes*) one after another, and porches (*prothyra*) many furlongs apart from one another, secured by bronze doors (*thyrai*) and mighty walls. Outside these the chief and most distinguished men (*hoi prōtoi kai dōkimōtatoi*) had their appointed place, some being the king's (*hoi amph'auton ton basilea*) bodyguard (*doryphoroi*) and attendants (*therapontes*); others the guardians of each of the enclosing walls, the so-called janitors (*pylōroi*) and "listeners" (*ōtakoustai*), that the king himself, who was called their master (*despotēs*) and deity (*theos*), might thus see and hear all things. (398a✧)

This text conveys several conceptions that were firmly anchored in the Greek mind, such as the characterization of the king as god. In the text we also gain an impression of a king, shut inside his palace, but who knows all, thanks to numerous Eyes and Ears. The composer of the book of Esther highlights "those who had privileged access to the royal presence" (1:14✧). Xenophon also insists on it (*Ages.* 9.1–2). One of the measures that the Spartan Pausanias took to identify himself with the Persians was that he "made himself difficult of access, and displayed so violent a temper to every one without exception that no one could come near him" (Thucydides I.130.2✧). Furthermore, Ctesias records the legendary story of Sardanapalus who lived as a recluse in his palace, seen only by his eunuchs and his wives (Athenaeus XII.528f).

The author of the *De Mundo* deserves praise for situating the royal audience in its architectural context, even if not all of the elements of the decor are realistic. The visitor

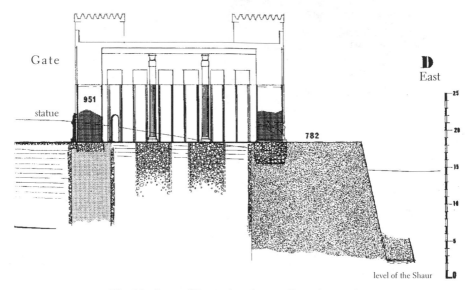

Fig. 38. Gate of Darius's palace at Susa (section).

first arrived at a gate. This term must not be allowed to confuse the reader. The *Gate* was actually an imposing building, distinct in Elamite and Persian vocabulary from the gate of a building. The word became a synonym for the palace and the court, as shown by the expression "Those of the Gate," which became a sort of court title (cf. Esther 2:21, 3:2–3 [JB: Chancellery]), even in Babylonian tablets (e.g., Amherst 258). The best-known example currently is the Darius Gate at Susa, on whose columns Xerxes had a trilingual inscription carved: "Xerxes the king says: 'By the grace of Ahura-Mazda, this *Gate*, Darius the king made it, he who was my father'" (XSd). At the base it measured 40 m by 28 m, and it rose to a height of some 15 m. It comprised three halls. The square central hall measured 21.20 m on a side; it was flanked on the north and south by two oblong halls open to the central hall (fig. 38). At Persepolis, the Gates were decorated with apotropaic reliefs (Royal Hero combating composite animals). At Susa, the passage to the central court was flanked by statues of King Darius. Within the great hall, stone benches were arranged against the walls, where, we suppose, the petitioners waited. In the Gate itself were cut openings, doors giving access to the interior of the palaces. But before gaining access, the visitor had to pass numerous obstacles and go through quite a few checkpoints.

All petitioners and suppliants came to the Gate (Herodotus III.117, 119; cf. Xenophon, *Hell.* I.6.7–7.10; *Cyr.* VI.1.1, etc.). When Syloson wanted to play his titles for all they were worth, "he hurried to Susa [and] sat down at the entrance (*prothyra*) of the royal palace." There he was interrogated by the guardian of the Gate (*pylōros*; Herodotus III.140❖). When the conspirators of 522 arrived at the Gates, they found themselves confronted by the guardians of the gates; they then penetrated into the courtyard (*aulē*), where "they were met by some of the eunuchs—the king's messengers," who reprimanded the guardians for allowing the Seven to enter (III.77❖). This corresponds to the protocol reported in Esther 4:11:❖

All the king's servants and the people of his provinces know that for a man or a woman who approaches the king in the inner court without being summoned there is one penalty: death.

According to a late (Parthian period) text, each visitor had to give his name, homeland, profession, and reason for visiting, and all of this information was written in a register along with a description of the person and his clothing. Each visitor was also asked to prostrate himself (*proskynesis*) before a portrait of the king (Philostratus, *Vit. Apoll.* 1.37). The Greek authors state that in order to be able to obtain an audience one had to commit oneself in advance to making a *proskynesis* before the king; if one would not, one could only communicate by messages (Nepos, *Conon* 3.3) via the message-bearers.

The Royal Guard: Immortals and Bodyguards

It seems clear that the precautions taken before an audience with the king was granted were intended not only to create the image of an omnipotent king but to guarantee his security as well. Xenophon is particularly insistent on this point. "As he deemed this guard insufficient in view of the multitude of those who bore him ill-will," Cyrus created a protective guard of 10,000 lancers (*doryphoroi*) by recruiting lower-class Persians, who "kept guard about the palace day and night, whenever he was in residence; but whenever he went away anywhere, they went along drawn up in order on either side of him" (*Cyr.* VII.5.66–68◊). They were also entrusted with guarding the royal tent while the king was on the move or on an expedition (VIII.5.4). These 10,000 lancers were included in Xerxes' procession in 480:

> chosen for quality out of all that remained—a body of Persian infantry ten thousand strong. Of these a thousand had golden pomegranates instead of spikes on the butt-ends of their spears, and were arrayed surrounding the other nine thousand, whose spears had silver pomegranates . . . the Ten Thousand—a body of picked Persian troops under the leadership of Hydarnes, the son of Hydarnes. This corps was known as the Immortals, because it was invariably kept up to strength; if a man was killed or fell sick, the vacancy he left was at once filled, so that its strength was never more nor less than 10,000. Of all the troops in the army the native Persians were not only the best but also the most magnificently equipped; their dress and armour I have mentioned already, but should add that every man glittered with the gold which he carried about his person in unlimited quantity. They were accompanied, moreover, by covered carriages (*harmamaxai*) containing their women (*pallakai*) and servants, all elaborately fitted out. Special food, separate from that of the rest of the army, was brought along for them on camels and mules. (Herodotus VII.41, 83◊)

This is how Heraclides of Cyme describes those he calls *mēlophoroi* ('bodyguards'; lit.: 'apple-bearers') in his *Persica*:

> These formed his bodyguard (*doryphoroi*), and all of them were Persians by birth, having on the butt of their spears golden apples, and numbering a thousand, selected because of their rank (*aristindēn*) from the 10,000 Persians who are called the Immortals. (Athenaeus XII.514c◊)

When Alexander received people close to him to dine in his tent, "inside it stood in line first of all five hundred Persians, called the apple bearers (*mēlophoroi*), wearing cloaks of purple and quince yellow; then came a thousand archers dressed in flame colour and scarlet" (Aelian, *VH* IX.3◊). Quintus Curtius has a similar description of the Immortals: "No others were more adorned with the splendour of barbaric wealth; theirs were golden necklets, and garments adorned with cloth of gold and long-sleeved tunics adorned even with gems" (III.3.13✧). They are probably the ones shown several times on the Persepolis friezes and the enameled bricks from Susa and on many seals.

The *mēlophoroi* were permanently attached to the king's person. At Gaugamela they fought beside Darius III (Arrian III.13.1) and, along with the Kinsmen, surrounded him during the retreat (III.16.1). In his procession, they marched just behind the royal chariot, after the Kinsmen and the Immortals. Quintus Curtius adds that they were "accustomed to take care of the royal robes" (*vestis regalis*; III.3.15✧), robes that by themelves required a subdivision of the support staff (cf. V.6.5). They remained near the king to guard him during audiences. A portion of the palace interior was reserved for them (Athenaeus XII.514b). To repeat Hesychius's explanation, "among the Persians, they are entrusted with watching over and serving (*therapeia*) the king." The chiliarch probably commanded the thousand bodyguards who constituted an elite within the 10,000 Immortals. This is in fact his only undisputed function (at least etymologically), the function from which his job of introducer probably derived. Because of the close relationship of the *mēlophoroi* with the person of the king, the job of chiliarch could only be given to a person of the utmost trustworthiness; thus, doubtless, the prestigious status accorded him by several ancient authors.

Protocol and Security

When the king left the palace, the royal chariot was surrounded by corps of troops, and the household guard watched over him: "As [Cyrus] proceeded, a great throng of people followed outside the lines" (*Cyr.* VIII.3.19✧). "No one may enter [through the rows of soldiers] except those who hold positions of honour (*hoi timōmenoi*). And policemen with whips in their hands (*mastigophoroi*) were stationed there, who struck any one who tried to crowd in" (VIII.3.9✧). Xenophon also adds this detail: "All the cavalrymen had alighted and stood there beside their horses and they all had their hands thrust through the sleeves of their doublets (*kandys*), just as they do even to this day when the king sees them" (3.10✧). In this way, the author makes a connection between posture and security requirements. The custom is also invoked in an interpolation in Xenophon's *Hellenica* (II.1.8✧); according to the author of this gloss, Cyrus the Younger supposedly put to death some close relatives of Darius II "because upon meeting him they did not thrust their hands through the *korē*, an honour they show the King alone. (The *korē* is a longer sleeve than the *cheiris* and a man who had his hand in one would be powerless to do anything.)" Xenophon, in his obsession with royal security, seems to have devised this interpretation for a custom that may have had a quite different significance. For it is precisely when the hand is concealed that it may hold a weapon invisible to the guards! It is tempting to see this required pose as a manifestation of submission to the king according to rules known later from Iran and elsewhere.

Royal Meals and Protocol

Xenophon also attributes the strict protocol governing "Cyrus" 's dinner guests to security concerns (VIII.4.3). In actuality, it indicated each one's ranking in the king's esteem (VIII.4.4–5). Nevertheless, as Xenophon also remarks elsewhere (VIII.5.59), there is hardly any doubt that the meals themselves placed the king in a weak position relative to any conspirators. In his portrayal of "Persian decadence," he even adds that the young people who were trained to gather medicinal herbs (p. 330) tried to collect poisonous plants, and he concludes: "There is no place where more people die or lose their lives from poisons than there" (VIII.8.14✧). Undoubtedly, this opinion is highly exaggerated. We know of only one attempt to poison a king (Diodorus XVII.5.6). Nevertheless, it does seem that at court there was an officer (*edeatros*) specifically assigned to taste all of the foods offered to the king in order to ensure his security (*eis asphaleion*).

Certain picturesque episodes explain the suspicion that could hover around the palace tables. Ctesias (§69) and Plutarch (*Art.*, 19) portray the meals shared by Artaxerxes II's wife Stateira and mother Parysatis. Here is how Plutarch (based on Dinon and Ctesias) tells how Parysatis got rid of Stateira:

> The two women had begun again to visit each other and to eat together; but though they had thus far relaxed their former habits of jealousy and variance, still, out of fear and as a matter of caution, they always ate of the same dishes and of the same parts of them. Now there is a small Persian bird, in the insides of which no excrement is found, only a mass of fat. . . . It is called *rhyntakēs* [Indian bird about the size of a pigeon]. Ctesias affirms, that Parysatis, cutting a bird of this kind into two pieces with a knife one side of which had been smeared with the drug, the other side being clear of it, ate the untouched and wholesome part herself, and gave Statira that which was thus infected. (19.3–5✧)

One of Parysatis's servants was put to death even though she was acquitted by the judges (Ctesias). With regard to the problem of poisoning, Plutarch states that there was a punishment reserved for poisoners at the court: "There is a broad stone, on which they place the head of the culprit, and then with another stone beat and press it, until the face and the head itself are all pounded to pieces" (19.9✧). The existence of this torture implies that the threat of poison was taken seriously. Ctesias states elsewhere (apud Aelian, *Anim.* IV.41) that a special Indian poison that resulted in a particularly gentle death was kept in the royal apartments, available only to the king and his mother.

The Great King's Water and Wine

One reason the king generally dined alone was to demonstrate his superior position there as elsewhere — above other mortals — but undoubtedly another reason was to ensure his security. On the model of the Immortals' supplies (Herodotus VII.83), the Great King's provisions and foodstuffs were kept and transported separately. Here is what Herodotus has to say on the subject:

> When the Persian King goes to war, he is always well provided not only with victuals from home and his own cattle, but also with water from the Choaspes, a river which flows past Susa. No Persian king ever drinks the water of any other stream, and a supply of it ready boiled for use is brought along in silver jars carried in a long train of four-wheeled mule wagons wherever the king goes. (I.188✧)

Ctesias and many ancient authors confirm the existence of this court practice, whose application obviously was not limited to court travel: it held all year round in the royal palaces. This has often been interpreted from a religious and ritual angle — in his capacity as high priest, the king was subject to food taboos. But this theory does not stand. No ancient author alludes to it, and it is clear that, if necessary, the king could drink some other water, as several anecdotes recorded by Aelian and Plutarch show.

In addition to the constant concern for isolating the king, we also see a concern for protecting his health. In fact, several authors stress that the Choaspes water was "especially clear and tasty." Many remarked that the boiling sterilized the water. In the course of a disquisition on the virtues of different waters, Athenaeus writes: "good water is that which heats or cools in a reasonable time, and when poured into a bronze or silver vessel does not tarnish it" (II.46b◊); Pliny also stresses that prior heating of water allows it to remain fresh (XXXI.40). It thus may be agreed that the recognized healthy properties of boiled water from the Choaspes—"as [the] report says, a fine water" (Quintus Curtius V.2.9◊)—led it to be chosen above any other.

Medical concerns do not explain everything, however. The Great King's water was also poured into receptacles reserved for his own use in order to protect his life. It was the same for his wine. Heraclides states that during a *symposion* 'drinking banquet' following dinner the king drank a special wine (IV.145c), undoubtedly the Chalybonian wine from Syria, the only wine he used to drink (Athenaeus II.28d). We also know from Dinon that the king drank from a special cup shaped like an egg (XI.503f). Bagoas attempted to assassinate Darius III by pouring poison into it, but the king, forewarned, offered his cup to the conspirator as if to award him special honor, and "compelled him to take his own medicine" (Diodorus XVII.5.6◊).

This is why those who poured wine at the court were so important, especially the director of the department, the Royal Cupbearer. He alone had the delicate task of pouring wine into the royal cup, following the immutable rules of royal protocol: "The cupbearers of those kings perform their office with fine airs; they pour in the wine with neatness and then present the goblet conveying it with three fingers, and offer it in such a way as to place it most conveniently in the grasp of the one who is to drink" (Xenophon, *Cyr.* I.3.8◊). He also served as the taster. For example, Xenophon remarks about Sacas, the taster at Astyages' court: "Now, it is a well-known fact that the king's cupbearers, when they proffer the cup, draw off some of it with the ladle (*kyathe*), pour it into their left hand, and swallow it down—so that, if they should put poison in, they may not profit by it" (I.3.9◊). The cupbearer thus had every opportunity to poison the royal drink, which explains the accusations brought against Alexander's cupbearer Iollas (Arrian VII.27.2). This is why men believed to be faithful were chosen, such as Nehemiah at Artaxerxes I's court (Neh 1:11) or the son of the very highly regarded Prexaspes at Cambyses' court (Herodotus III.34). According to one of the founder legends recorded by Nicolaus of Damascus (*FGrH* 90 F66.6–7), Cyrus followed in his adoptive father's footsteps as royal cupbearer in the Median court.

The Court Physicians

Physicians definitely held an important place in the king's trusted household staff. They could only be trustworthy persons, for they too were so well positioned that they would have been able to poison the king (Diodorus XVII.5.3). We know that several Greek physicians practiced at Artaxerxes II's court. One of them is known only by his name, Polycritus (Plutarch, *Art.*, 21.3). Certainly the most noteworthy example is Ctesias himself. This native of Cnidos, which was famous for its medical schools, came from the circle of Asclepiads, who were connected with the sanctuary of the war-god. The exact date and circumstances of his arrival at Artaxerxes' court remain uncertain. Was he drafted by the king because of his medical knowledge, or was he brought to court as a prisoner of war? The fact remains that his presence is attested at least from the time of the battle of Cunaxa, after which he received numerous honors from the king. There is no doubt that he cared for the king, who had been unhorsed during combat (cf. Plutarch, *Art.*, 11.3, 14.1). In any case, he claims "that he himself healed the wound" when his brother Cyrus the Younger assaulted him (Xenophon, *Anab.* I.8.26◊), but the tales of the battle are too propaganda-laden for us to place total confidence in Ctesias's account. He remained at the court until 398–397, when he returned to his homeland and wrote his *Persica*.

To tell the truth, we have little information about Ctesias's medical career. He himself obviously preferred to talk about his role as a favorite, a confidant, even as a diplomatic intermediary (§§63–64). A late passage attests that he cared for Artaxerxes (*Suda*, s.v. Ctesias), and Photius, in his summary of the *Persica*, notes in passing that he was "Parysatis's doctor" (§60). He was obviously very close to Artaxerxes II's mother; he claims to have obtained some of his information from her (§48: succession of Darius II) and to have received gifts of exceptional symbolic value from the king and Parysatis (*Indica* §4). It was certainly because of his intimacy with Parysatis (and not just because of his love for Laconia, which was denounced by Plutarch) that he intervened directly to ease Clearchus's prison conditions (Plutarch, *Art.*, 18.1–4).

Ctesias notes the presence of another Greek physician at Artaxerxes I's court, Apollinides, a native of Cos (an island off the coast of Asia Minor, also famous for its physicians). This reference is interpolated into the saga of the family of Megabyzus. Apollonides was reputed to have healed wounds that Megabyzus received in the fighting that took place within the palace at the time of Xerxes' succession (§30). Later he would fall in love with Megabyzus's widow Amytis, the king's sister, who was famous for her beauty and her extramarital dalliances (Ctesias §28; Dinon apud Athenaeus XIII.609a). Ctesias gives us a glimpse of the Persian court "through the keyhole," as he often does. "Apollonides told Amytis that she would regain her health via congress with men, seeing that she was having trouble with her womb . . ." (Ctesias §41). Later, after Princess Amytis died, her mother had Artaxerxes punish the doctor as an example: "She had him clapped in irons for two months of torture, then buried alive upon the death of Amytis."

But the first appearance of a Greek physician at the court dates to the reign of Darius. Herodotus tells at great length a veritable novella dedicated to the picaresque adventures of the physician Democedes (III.125–38). This native of Crotone in southern Italy practiced his profession freely from town to town in Greece (Aegina, Athens) and was paid from the public funds of the cities that called on his services. Then he settled at the court of Polycrates of Samos. As an outcome of Oroetes' activities against the Samian tyrant, the satrap of Sardis kept Polycrates' retinue close to him, including the foreigners (III.122–25), and he took on the services of Democedes, who was now a slave (III.129). On another occasion, during a hunt, Darius twisted his foot severely. His Egyptian physicians proved unable to heal him, and he appealed to Democedes, whose fame had reached him. Despite his reservations about remaining at the court, the Greek was hardly in a position to refuse his august patient and restored the use of his foot. He thus achieved an enviable status, since he "lived in a large house (*oikos*) in Susa, took his meals at the king's table (*homotrapezos*) . . . great was Democedes' influence with the king (*para basilei*)" (III.132◊). He cured Atossa of an abscess in the breast (III.133). Some time later, he managed to escape his gilded cage (cf. III.130) during the course of a mission Darius sent to Sicily (see p. 139).

According to Herodotus, Darius had already become utterly infuriated by the incompetence of the Egyptian physicians who surrounded him and "who had a reputation for the highest eminence in their profession" (III.129◊). He also states that Democedes had intervened on their behalf with Darius, who wanted to have them impaled.

From the three known examples cited above, we must not draw the premature conclusion that thereafter only Greeks cared for the king and his family. The call for Egyptian physicians had ancient precedent. For Herodotus, in fact, the initial contacts between Cyrus and Pharaoh Amasis anticipated the sending of Egyptian doctors to the Persian court. The Great King "ask[ed] for the services of the best oculist in Egypt" (Herodotus III.1◇). Egyptian medicine and physicians were in fact very well known throughout the ancient Near East; all of the specialties were represented there (cf. II.84). Darius's interest in Egyptian physicians did not weaken. Around 519, he sent Udjahorresnet back to Egypt, who, after pledging allegiance to Cambyses, had accompanied the king on the return road and eventually ended up with Darius in Elam. His mission was to restore the School of Saïs, a well-known Egyptian center for medical studies; in some of his inscriptions, dated to Cambyses and Darius, he bears the title of

Fig. 39. A Scythian cares for his companion (on a vase from Koul-Oba in the Crimea).

Chief Physician. Despite the silence of the sources and the highly partisan orientation of the Greek sources, there is every reason to suppose that Egyptian doctors continued to frequent the court of the Great Kings (pp. 859–861). In the only evidence regarding treatment of a wound in combat, we see the soldiers caring for one of their own: they "dressed his wounds with myrrh, and bound them up with linen bandages" (Herodotus VII.181◇). The treatment chosen (myrrh and linen) points toward Egypt, but it also reminds us of a scene depicted on a Scythian gold plaque (fig. 39).

It is important to recognize that the evidence on hand tells us almost nothing about the most common illnesses. Let us simply note in passing the information that Herodotus gives on leprosy:

> Sufferers from the scab or from leprosy are isolated and forbidden the city. They say these diseases are punishments for offending the sun, and they expel any stranger who catches them: many Persians drive away even white doves, as if they, too, were guilty of the same offence. (I.138◇)

This report is confirmed by a passage in Ctesias. In telling about Megabyzus's exile to the shore of the Persian Gulf, the doctor states: "Megabyzus, after spending five years in exile, escaped by assuming the appearance of *pisagas*; this is the Persian word for 'lepers', and no one can approach them" (§41). These texts imply that there were rules in Persia concerning certain contagious diseases that were considered a divine punishment.

The Magi, Their Herbs, and Their Stones

One of the many decisions Xenophon attributes to his Cyrus is putting the royal Treasury in charge of enlisting physicians, "the very best." They acted as medical counselors, obtaining everything needed in the way of instruments and remedies (*pharmaka*), solid or liquid. Xenophon also says that Cyrus was disturbed by the fact that his soldiers scarcely took any care of their health. To deal with that, he endeavored to stockpile "such things as would be serviceable in case of sickness" (*Cyr.* VIII.2.24–25◇). There is no doubt that these products were basically medicinal plants, which youths were trained to gather during their education (*Cyr.* VIII.8.14; Strabo XV.3.18). In fact, it seems that the Persians made good use of medicinal plants in every circumstance of their daily life. We know from Herodotus (I.138) and Strabo (XV.3.16) that they were not allowed to urinate or spit into running water. An ancient lexicographer states that to solve this problem they took cress, the prescription for stopping any flow (*Suda*, s.v. *kardama*)!

There is little doubt that the specialists to whom Cyrus appealed were none other than the magi. In fact, their knowledge of the stones and plants used in medicine is attested in many ancient texts that explicitly claim to derive from their writings and their knowledge. Note the treatise *On Nature*, attributed to Zoroaster himself (!), or the teachings disseminated by the *magus* Ostanes, who, according to Pliny (*NH* XXX.8), accompanied Xerxes in Greece and who, Diogenes Laertius says, was left with other *magi* at Abdera as tutors for the philosopher Democritus. Pliny says that he himself took much of his information from this Pseudo-Democritus, and thus devotes numerous (highly polemical) digressions to the *magi*'s knowledge of the curative properties of plants. The *magi* also knew about stones. One stone "is prescribed by Zoroaster" for epilepsy (Pliny XXXVII.157✧); other stones fought violence and hot temper or witchcraft (XXXVII.144–45✧).

Regardless of the many distortions this information has suffered over the course of time, there is hardly any doubt that much of it really does goes back to medical practice during the Persian era. Pliny states several times that the use of various herbs was related to the "magical" abilities of the magi. For example, they used the *aglaophotis* "when they wish to call up gods" (XXIV.160✧); placed in a drink, the *theangelis* "to gain power to divine" (XXIV.164✧); certain stones allowed them to battle storms and tempests (XXXVII.142, 155); another stone is "indispensible for the Magi at the installation of a king" (XXXVII.147✧). They also knew herbs' curative powers and used them for the king's health:

> The *theombrotion* grows, says Democritus, thirty schoeni [8 km] from the Choaspes, being like a peacock in its colourings and of a very fine scent. He goes on to state that the kings of Persia take it in drink for all bodily disorders and for instability of intellect and of the sense of justice, and that it is also called semnion from the majesty of its power (*a potentiae maiestate*). (XXIV.162)

This seems to have been a (purgative?) infusion. We also see that the magi's competence in herbalism went beyond health, strictly speaking. The herb Pliny talks about seems to have been reserved for the exclusive use of the king. Furthermore, he draws other benefits from it, even regarding his special capacities as sovereign. Pliny also records that the kings and *magi* made themselves look good with a curious ointment made of a Cilician plant, saffron, and lion fat (XXIV.165). Because of their abilities, the *magi* were fawned over. Pliny records, for example, that a certain herb allowed access to the inner circle of royal favor (*primatum apud reges*; XXIV.165) and that the use of a particular agate offered every chance of success "of petitioners to the king" (XXXVII.169✧)!

Added to other evidence attesting to the *magi*'s functions—in ritual (p. 245), in education (p. 330), especially of the royal children (p. 521), and their continual presence before the king (whose dreams they interpreted), including accompanying him during the enthronement ceremony (p. 523)—the texts bearing on the "pharmacological" activities of the *magi* demonstrate again the central position that the *magi* occupied in the court of the Great King. When Themistocles arrived at Artaxerxes' court, "by the king's command he also was made acquainted with the Magian learning (*hoi magikoi logoi*)" (Plutarch, *Them.* 29.6✧). We have the impression that at the Achaemenid court the *magi* took responsibility for the knowledge, practices, and prestige that at the Neo-Assyrian court had been the province of the Sages and the Literati ("Assyrian scholars"), who were divided into scribes, haruspices, exorcists, doctors, and singers.

3. The Eunuchs

On the Perfidy of Eunuchs

Out of all of the residents of the "oriental" palaces, there was one group of people who stimulated the imagination of European travelers and observers above all others: the eunuchs. They were usually reduced to one job, which could be identified with two words: "harem" guard. Traditionally, "oriental despotism" and the sovereigns' decadence have been attributed to the joint efforts of perverse women and perfidious eunuchs. Ancient Persia has not escaped this stereotype.

Ctesias certainly played a major role in entrenching this view. Every king in Ctesias's writings is flanked by one or more eunuchs, characterized as "the most powerful one(s) near King N": Petesacas, then Bagapates near Cyrus (§5, 9), Izabates, Aspadates, and Bagapates near Cyrus (§9). We find Artasyras in Darius's entourage (§19), Natakas and Aspamithres near Xerxes (§20, 27, 29), Artoxares near Artaxerxes I (§§39–40), and Pharnacyas near Secundianus (§45). Artoxares reappears near Artaxerxes II (§53), in whose entourage another eunuch also named Bagapates is known (§59). Generally speaking, Ctesias's presentation is wholly unsympathetic. The eunuchs participate in many conspiracies. Bagapates conspires against Cambyses (§13) before joining the Seven (§14), Aspamithres participates in Xerxes' assassination (§29), Pharnacyas in Xerxes II's (§45), Artoxares participates in a conspiracy against Secundianos (§47), which helps him become very influential with the new king Darius II (§49), before going on to conspire (aided by a woman!) against his master (§53). The faithfulness of Bagapates, "who died after keeping watch for seven years over Darius's tomb" (§19), appears quite exceptional. Finally, let us not forget Izabates, who denounced the conspiracy of the *magus* and was executed by the usurpers (§13).

Many of Ctesias's stories are pure fiction, especially the Egyptian expedition of the eunuch Bagapates, which allowed Ctesias to portray a battle between two eunuchs, in that Egypt itself was defended by Kombaphis, the head eunuch of Pharaoh Amyrtaeus (sic). Ctesias did not shy away from the most convoluted intrigues; for instance, he did not think twice about making Kombaphis the cousin of Izabates, another important eunuch at Cambyses' court (§9)! We have now entered the realm of imaginative fiction and fairy tale, not history, though paradoxically these flights of fancy are still of interest to the historian. Another very good story concerns the eunuch Artoxares, who had a false beard and moustache made so that he could lead a plot against Darius II. The symbolic weight of this tale is all the more noteworthy because, still following Ctesias (§53), it was a woman who helped him. The alliance of a eunuch and a woman in a court conspiracy could not fail to titillate readers, who were always eager for anecdotes based on "orientalizing" stereotypes.

Ctesias was not the only one to transmit such a negative stereotype. Quintus Curtius speaks "of a herd of eunuchs, who are not at all despised by these peoples" (III.3.23✧);

as for the 360 royal concubines, they were "attended by herds of eunuchs, also accustomed to prostitute themselves (*ipsi muliebria pati adsueti*)" (VI.6.8◊). Quintus Curtius's expression reminds us that, like some other ancient authors, he was particularly scandalized by stories circulating about homosexual relations between certain kings and their favored eunuch. Alexander's historians had much to say about Bagoas, "a eunuch of remarkable beauty and in the very flower of boyhood, who had been loved by Darius [III] and was afterwards to be loved by Alexander" (Quintus Curtius VI.5.23◊). To better express his disgust at these practices, Quintus Curtius puts this speech in the mouth of the Persian noble Orxines, who had just refused to pay his respects to Bagoas: "It was not the custom of Persians to mate with males who had made females of themselves by prostitution" (*qui stupro effeminarentur*; X.1.26◊). Pretty words that certainly do not correspond to reality—despite the polemic on this subject by the ancients, homosexual practices are attested among the Persians.

We also know of a eunuch named Tiridates, portrayed in a magnificent story told by Aelian in the course of a long digression on the fate of Aspasia, Cyrus the Younger's favorite companion, who switched to the camp of Artaxerxes II after the battle of Cunaxa:

> Some time later the eunuch Tiridates died. He had been the most handsome and attractive man in Asia. He ended his days still a youth, emerging from childhood, and the king was said to be greatly in love with him. As a result he lamented bitterly and was in great distress; there was public mourning throughout Asia as a gesture to the king from all his subjects. No one dared to approach or console him. . . . When three days had passed, Aspasia put on mourning and, as when the king departed to the baths stood weeping, her gaze fixed on the ground. . . . The Persian was greatly encouraged by her sympathy and asked her to go to the bedroom and wait for him, which she did. When he came back he put the eunuch's cloak over Aspasia's black dress. Somehow the young man's clothing suited her, and her beauty struck her lover even more powerfully. Once overcome by this sight, he asked her to visit him in this attire until the severity of his grief waned. (*VH* XII.1◊)

How elegant and muted the telling! Delicious food for thought for psychoanalysts-in-training!

Plenty of wicked eunuchs are also found in Plutarch's writings, who takes some of his information from Ctesias himself, as well as from Dinon. The eunuch Sparimazes eggs Mithradates on in his bragging, the better to denounce him and destroy him (*Art.* 15–16). The eunuch Masabates, who cut off Cyrus's head, was won by Parysatis in a dice game with her son Artaxerxes; she calls Masabates an "old rascally eunuch" (17.8◊; cf. Ctesias §59: Bagapates). It is also a eunuch who guides conspirators to Artaxerxes II's bedchamber, though it is true that he first informs the king of the conspiracy (29.1–3). As in Ctesias (§29: Aspamithres), Diodorus's account includes a eunuch (Mithradates) among the conspirators who do away with Xerxes (XI.69.1). Felonious eunuchs are found in the book of Esther (2:21).

But the most famous example is Bagoas (not the same Bagoas mentioned above), whom Theophrastus calls "Bagoas the Elder (*ho palaios*)" (*HP* II.8.7) and whose portrait by Diodorus is disastrous to his memory (XVI.47–50; XVII.5): "A eunuch in physical fact but a militant rogue in disposition" (§5.3◊). During Artaxerxes III's Egyptian campaign, he manifested injustice and rapacity toward the priests and temples and broke promises given to the pharaoh's Greek mercenaries. He acquired the king's full confidence and in 343 he became chiliarch. After the victory, his influence over the king increased further—he received the government of the Upper Satrapies (see p. 1002), and the king "no longer decided anything without his advice." Bagoas thus became the veritable "master of the kingdom/kingship (*basileia*); he was king in all but name." He soon assassinated Artaxerxes III and his brothers and installed the young Arses on the throne; his blows soon fell on the new king and his children, and he chose Codoman/Artašāta to be king (Darius III), whereupon he was poisoned by drinking from the very cup he had just handed to the one he had elevated to the throne (p. 264)!

Indeed, Bagoas does not appear very sympathetic (to say the least!), and his behavior and career, as seen by Diodorus, were not a little responsible for entrenching the notion of Persian decadence in light of palace intrigue (cf. chap. 17/1). But it must also be observed that Bagoas truly became a character in the "oriental romance." An echo is found in an anecdote told by Aelian (VH VI.8✧):

> Artaxerxes, known also as Ochos, was the victim of a plot planned by the Egyptian eunuch Bagoas. They say he was killed, cut to pieces and fed to the cats. Someone else was buried in his place and laid to rest in the royal mausoleum. But Bagoas was not content with killing Ochos; he even made knife handles out of his thigh bones, displaying in this way his murderous instincts. He hated him because, like Cambyses before him, he had killed Apis during a visit to Egypt.

Many details of the story confirm the Egyptian provenance of the Bagoas romance, be it the Egyptian ethnic origin of the Persian or the role of cats. But the romance also includes a Greek layer: the comparison with Cambyses (impious murderer of the Apis, as in Herodotus) and perhaps also the transformation of Bagoas into a protector of Egyptian temples, even though he himself had ransacked them during Artaxerxes III's campaign (Diodorus XVI.51.2). The fact is that the nasty, bloody eunuch became a literary type in ancient romances. For instance, in the Judith romance, the name Bagoas is given to "the eunuch in charge of [Holophernes'] personal affairs" (Jdt. 12:11✧). Furthermore, according to Pliny (XIII.41✧), it was "the Persian word for a eunuch."

Xenophon and the Paradigm of the Faithful Minister

Xenophon develops quite a different picture. His Cyrus was always anxious for his security and chose to entrust it to eunuchs. He explains this with the aid of arguments that seem to be designed to refute point by point the disastrous image these people had in Greece. First of all, the eunuchs had no family ties:

> Those, therefore, who had children or congenial wives or sweethearts, such [Cyrus] believed were by nature constrained to love them best. But as he observed that eunuchs were not susceptible to any such affections, he thought that they would esteem most highly those who were in the best position to make them rich and to stand by them, if ever they were wronged, and to place them in offices of honour (*timai*); and no one, he thought, could surpass him in bestowing favours of that kind. (*Cyr.* VII.5.60✧)

Thus, eunuchs were free of any entanglements relating to family solidarity. This situation made them entirely dependent on a powerful master, toward whom they would be fully disposed to manifest unlimited devotion and loyalty. In fact—continues Cyrus/Xenophon—"inasmuch as eunuchs are objects of contempt to the rest of mankind . . . , they need a master who will be their patron" around whom they know they could achieve a place of honor (§61✧). Their fidelity was demonstrated above all upon the death of their master (§64). To some extent, in this highly hierarchical society, they represent *outsiders*.

Then Xenophon takes issue with the popular opinion that "eunuchs are weaklings." His basis for disagreeing with this notion is the example of animals: a gelded horse, for example, is "none the less fit for service in war." Similarly, eunuchs proved their courage, in both war and the hunt. Armed with a sword or a lance, a eunuch was as good as a man. "Recognizing these facts, [Cyrus] selected eunuchs for every post of personal service to him, from the door-keepers up" (*thyrōroi*; §62–65◊).

In the *Cyropedia*, the Gadatas romance is a lively illustration of the valor, fidelity, and courage of a castrato. Gadatas was a prince subject to the king of Assyria. For an apparently frivolous reason (though the real reason was thinly disguised political opposition), the king had Gadatas castrated (V.2.28). Gadatas then decided to defect to Cyrus and cooperate with him, turning over to him the strongholds he was in charge of in his own principality. He accompanied the army to Sardis and then Babylon. With Gobryas, he captured the town as head of a detachment (VII.5.24–32). He then operated from an exalted position; he participated in the great victory parade, leading a regiment of 10,000 horsemen (VIII.3.17). Shortly thereafter, Cyrus conferred the title "head of the scepter-bearers" (*skēptoukhoi*) on him:

> The whole household was managed as he directed. Whenever guests (*syndeipnoi*) dined with Cyrus, Gadatas, did not even take his seat, but attended upon them. But when they were by themselves, he would dine with Cyrus, for Cyrus enjoyed his company. And in return (*anti touto*) for his services he received many valuable presents (*megala dōra*) from Cyrus himself and, through Cyrus's influence, from others also. (VIII.4.2◊)

It seems pretty clear that Xenophon's stories fit perfectly into the conception of kingship that he was developing throughout the *Cyropedia*: more than anyone else, a eunuch illustrated the theme of royal generosity in response (*anti touto*) to the unlimited devotion of a man who was not concerned about his children's prospects and who therefore exhibited the faithfulness of a pet because he was linked neither to a family clan nor to a court faction.

Xenophon undoubtedly derived his theme of the honest minister from oral tradition and edifying moral tales coming from the Near East. For example, the composers of one of these, the *Ahiqar romance*, situate the story in an Assyrian context, because Ahiqar is presented as the minister first of Sennacherib and then of Esarhaddon. The story is known in several versions, the most important being the Aramaic version (unfortunately incomplete), which is preserved on an Egyptian Aramaic papyrus from the Achaemenid period (*DAE* 106–8 [*AP* pp. 204–48]). The childless Ahiqar adopted his nephew Nādin and had the king recognize him as his successor. His nephew betrayed him and denounced him falsely. Ahiqar was arrested, but the servant who was ordered to kill him actually spared him, though leading the king to believe that he had carried out his mission (this theme of preservation/deception is frequent; it is also found in one version of the Cyrus legend). Then his innocence became known, and he was fully rehabilitated. In the moral precepts he gave his nephew, he stressed obedience and fidelity to the sovereign.

The theme of the falsely accused loyal servant reappears in another romance, known mostly from a Hellenistic-period version included in Lucian's *Dea Syria* (§§17–27). The Seleucid queen Stratonice, wife of Seleucus I, was preparing to undertake a voyage. The king designated his confidant Kombabos to watch over her. Kombabos was afraid that he would later be accused of entertaining illicit relations with the queen and amputated his sexual organs and sealed them in a casket. Thus the (foreseeable!) passion the queen soon avowed toward Kombabos was not consummated. Nevertheless, Kombabos did not go unaccused upon Seleucus's return. Condemned to death by the king, he was able to prove his innocence by opening the casket. Overcome with admiration, the king bestowed the highest honors on him.

We find an allusion to the name Kombabos in Ctesias, who records that the pharaoh's favorite eunuch was called Kombaphis (§19). The word also appears in a hieroglyphic inscription recounting the career of an Egyptian, Ptah-hotep, who allied himself with Darius. The story is repeated in Firdawsi's *Book of Kings* (Shahnameh) in the medieval period. Grafted onto Mesopotamian antecedents, the Kombabos legend is none other than a court tale that had its origin during the Achaemenid period. It exalts both the characteristics of the implacable, just, and grateful sovereign and the unlimited fidelity of a eunuch-confidant. We are very strongly tempted to hear a distant, muffled echo in Xenophon.

The image of the faithful eunuch is also found in other authors. It was already explicit in Herodotus: "In eastern countries eunuchs are valued as being specially trustworthy (*pistis pasē*) in every way" (VIII.105◇). In Ctesias, Izabates denounces the conspiracy of the *magi* (§13), and Bagapates watches over Darius's tomb for seven years (§19). Herodotus presents Hermotimus, "who came to be valued by Xerxes more highly than any other of his eunuchs" (VIII.105◇). The king entrusted him with oversight of his children, who were returned to Asia Minor under the guard of Artemisia of Caria (VIII.107). During the battle of Cunaxa, Cyrus the Younger's eunuchs wailed, and "the most trusty (*pistōtatos*) of them, Pariscas, wept sitting by his corpse" (Plutarch, *Art.*, 12.1). One of Artaxerxes II's eunuchs, Masabates/Bagapates, severed Cyrus's head (17.1), another denounced a conspiracy to Artaxerxes II (29.1), and a third (Satibarzanes) brought water to Artaxerxes when he was consumed with thirst during the battle of Cunaxa (12.4), and so forth. Alexander's authors are also fond of the theme of the faithful eunuch. Darius III's mother's eunuch, Tyriotes, who was captured with many others during the battle of Issus, managed to escape and reach Darius's camp, where he stoically withstood torture (Quintus Curtius IV.10.25–34). One of Darius III's eunuchs dissolved in tears when Alexander mounted the throne of the Great King (Diodorus XVII.66.4–5; Quintus Curtius V.2.14). Even after Darius III's private guard had abandoned him, he remained surrounded by his eunuchs, faithful to the very end (Quintus Curtius V.12.9–13).

The historian clearly does not need to choose between Ctesias and Xenophon. Both views are stereotyped and popularized. Their existence and circulation evidence the ambivalence of both the eunuchs' status and the Greek authors' attitude toward individuals who alternately fascinated and repelled them. What must especially be assimilated from the preceding pages is that, on this topic, the historian must work with texts that are more like court romances than historical narratives.

Eunuchism and Emasculation

Given the nature of the sources, we can only reconstruct the Persian institution inferentially, and the reconstruction can only be partial. In the first place, we need to establish a distinction between the eunuchs who were part of the king's immediate entourage (portrayed by Ctesias in particular) and the many other anonymous eunuchs (the "herds of eunuchs" of Quintus Curtius III.3.23; VI.6.8; cf. Herodotus VII.186–87) who made up the domestic staffs of the king and the royal princesses (e.g., Ctesias §§61–62; Plutarch, *Art.* 15.2; Quintus Curtius IV.10.18). Clearly, eunuchs were individuals whose status was close to slavery, even though their intimacy with the king or the royal princesses conferred a special degree of prestige on them. This fact must be kept in mind when reading what Plutarch has to say about the stakes in the dice game between Artaxerxes II and his mother Parysatis:

> She pressed him to begin a new game for a eunuch; to which he consented. But first they agreed that each of them might except five of their most trusty (*pistōtatoi*) eunuchs, and that out of the rest of them the loser should yield up any the winner should make choice of. (17.6◊)

Like many other court servants, eunuchs came from subject countries (cf. Athenaeus XII.514d). We know that several regions had to furnish human tribute or gifts — boys and girls (500 boys every 4 years from the Ethiopians; 100 boys and 100 girls every 2 years from the Colchians; Herodotus III.97). Each year, Babylonia had to send 500 young castrated men to the court (*ektomiai*; III.92). They could also be included as booty, to go by what Herodotus writes of a punishment pronounced against some rebellious Ionians: "Once the towns were in their hands, the best-looking boys were chosen for castration and made into eunuchs" (VI.32◊).

Because of the market for eunuchs at the satrapal and royal courts, trafficking between the Aegean coast and the inland countries was particularly heavy. Evidence is provided by the case of Hermotimus, who became the eunuch closest to Xerxes. He was a native of Pedasus in Caria who was taken prisoner during a war, then purchased by a man named Panionius of Chios, "a man who made his living by the abominable trade of castrating any good-looking boys he could get hold of, and taking them to Sardis or Ephesus, where he sold them at a high price" (Herodotus VIII.105◊). Caria was always famous for its eunuchs. According to Xanthus, the institution of court eunuchism was ancient in Asia Minor, since it was well attested in the Lydian court (Athenaeus XII.515c). However, the Near East certainly included other centers that served as sources of eunuchs as well.

The eunuchs watched over both the king's chamber and the chambers of the royal princesses (cf. *Alex.* 30.2). This, by the way, is the etymology of the Greek word *eunoukhos* 'guardian of the bed'. The common interpretation, 'guardian of women', is a folk etymology probably based primarily on Esther and on parallels with the Ottoman court. The book of Esther in fact portrays two "king's eunuchs," Hegai and Shaashgaz, both of whom bear the title 'custodian of the women' (*phylax tōn gynaikōn*; 2:3, 8, 14–15◊). We may presume, without actual proof, that these are castrated men. Except for a very fleeting allusion to eunuch-slaves in the service of the 360 concubines in Quintus Curtius (VI.6.8), the only "attestation" is found in Herodotus, in the Democedes romance: Darius sent a physician to the women, and he was escorted by eunuchs (III.130). It is surprising that Xenophon does not mention this task in his discussion of the relation between castration and fidelity. Of course, the wives and concubines of his Cyrus are completely absent from his story. It is also true that the eunuchs were not limited to guarding and maintaining the royal bedchamber; many also served the king during his meals (e.g., Aelian, *VH* II.17; Dinon apud Athenaeus XIV.652c).

Finally, if Plato is to be believed (*Alc.* 121d◊), there were also eunuchs who took care of the royal children:

> Then the boy is brought up—not by some nanny of no account, but by the most highly respected eunuchs in the royal household. They attend to all the needs of the infant child, and are especially concerned to make him as handsome as possible, shaping and straightening his infant limbs; and for this they are held in great esteem.

However, the succeeding discussion makes it appear that the eunuchs were involved with the children only in their earliest years, after which their education was taken over by wise men, that is, *magi* (see p. 330). Here as elsewhere, the eunuchs (here palace slaves) were limited strictly to physical needs. None of them, not even Hermotimus (contrary to what is sometimes said), was charged with the education of the Great King's son.

Title and Duties

It is highly unlikely that all of the people later called eunuchs were actually emasculated slaves. While Hermotimus's unmanning is certain (Herodotus VIII.104–5), serious doubts may be entertained regarding other slaves, especially the so-called eunuchs close to the king. Ctesias tells the story of the eunuch Artoxares, the most powerful of the three eunuchs of the royal entourage (§49), who in his conspiracy against the king "had a woman make a false beard and moustache to give him the appearance of a man" (§53). But not even this story (whatever its veracity may be, no doubt close to zero) proves that he had been emasculated: we know in fact that the king and all the court nobility wore hairpieces. Artoxares may thus have simply procured the collaboration of one of the women who took care of the "court" beards and moustaches to acquire the appearance not of a man but of the king. In the same way, there is nothing to prove beyond the shadow of a doubt that the smooth-faced figures in the Persepolis reliefs (or the Assyrian reliefs) should be identified as eunuchs.

The case of Mithradates, who participated in the plot against Xerxes alongside the chiliarch Artabanus, is even more interesting. Ctesias portrays him (under the name Aspamithres) as highly influential with the king (§29). Diodorus specifies that he was the chamberlain (*katakoimistēs*) in whom the king had the greatest confidence, and he made him the friend and kinsman (*syggenēs*) of Artabanus (XI.69.1). Artabanus was himself the son of Artasyras, a very powerful man close to Darius (Ctesias §19–20). This Artasyras is clearly the same one whom Ctesias calls a Hyrcanian and who was the most influential figure under Cambyses (§9). It is thus virtually certain that he was a noble of Hyrcanian origin, comparable to the Aribazus known during the time of Darius (Aelian, *VH* VI.14). This reference indicates at the very least that certain eunuchs were not without family connections in the palace, contrary to the hopes that Cyrus/Xenophon placed in the castrated eunuchs. It seems rather unlikely that the kinsman and friend of a palace aristocrat would be a castrated slave. Equally striking is the fact that, except in the case of Hermotimus (a case that was inserted by Herodotus into its specific geographical-cultural context), nearly all of the eunuchs mentioned by name have Iranian names. For this there are two possible explanations: either they really were eunuchs who were given Iranian names when they arrived at court, or else they were Iranian nobles integrated into the court hierarchy by being given the label "eunuch." In at least some cases they seem to have been people of non-Persian origin: in addition to Mithradates, we may cite Artoxares, who Ctesias says was Paphlagonian (§39).

It seems doubtful that eunuchs in the functional sense (castrated men of humble status) could have obtained positions as high as the eunuchs mentioned by Ctesias and still more surprising that one of them (Artaxerxes III's Bagoas) could have received the coveted title of chiliarch. Even the title 'chamberlain' (*katakoimistēs*) lent its holder a position of favor near the king. One chamberlain, Satibarzanes (was he Artaxerxes II's eunuch—Plutarch, *Art.* 12.4—or a different one?), advised Artaxerxes II or at least was in his inner circle (cf. Plutarch, *Mor.* 173e and Ctesias §63). It is tempting to think that such an important man would not actually have attended to the king's chamber. The daily work was restricted to the palace eunuchs (cf. Plutarch, *Alex.* 30.2), whom Xenophon describes as "bath-room attendants . . . chamberlains who assist them in retiring at night and in rising in the morning, and beauty-doctors" (*Cyr.* VIII.8.20◊). According to this theory, men like Mithradates and Satibarzanes held a title completely unrelated to the duty it literally represented, as is often true in court hierarchy. On the other hand, the case of Hermotimus seems to contradict this interpretation. However, Herodotus actually says nothing about Hermotimus's functions in relation to Xerxes. He clearly had low status (he had been castrated and sold in Ionia). Despite the phrase used ("valued by Xerxes more highly than any other"), it is not at all certain that he held the same rank as the eunuchs portrayed by Ctesias, since the formula is frequently used for palace eunuchs who were clearly not high court dignitaries (e.g., Plutarch, *Art.* 17.6).

Most often, the ancient authors do not recognize any particular function for the eunuchs of the royal entourage; they simply highlight the hierarchy that distinguished them in regard to royal favor. There are two noteworthy exceptions, however: Mithradates was Xerxes' chamberlain (Diodorus XI.69.2), and Bagoas was chiliarch in Artaxerxes III's court (XVII.5.3). Generally speaking, the position or duties they held easily explain why they were involved in so many conspiracies. They were among the few persons at court with entrée to the royal apartments. This was obviously true for the chiliarch, who was in charge of royal audience (§2 above), but more generally for the eunuchs who guided the conspirators toward the royal bedchamber. Bagapates had all of the keys to the palace, Ctesias writes (§14). Herodotus also reports, describing the conspiracy of the Seven, that when the Seven arrived at the palace courtyard they ran into "the eunuchs—the king's messengers," who attempted to bar the way to the *magus*'s bedchamber (III.77). Ctesias indicates that, in order to obtain an audience, one needed to be assured of the support of a eunuch. This is why eunuchs often appear in the court romances (Ctesias = Athenaeus XII.528f).

Only rarely do we see eunuchs outside of this role. Ctesias mentions two eunuchs who led military expeditions—Bagapates in Egypt (§9) and Nautacas against Apollo of Didyma (§27)—but the former is invention pure and simple. The only indisputable example is the participation of Bagoas in the Egyptian expedition alongside Artaxerxes III (Diodorus XVI.47–50). He was there because of his status as chiliarch, however, not as a eunuch per se. More than once, Ctesias portrays a eunuch as being entrusted with guiding the funeral chariot of the deceased king to the royal tombs: Bagapates for Cyrus (§9) and Izabates for Cambyses (§13). In each case he was the deceased king's favorite eunuch. On one occasion it was a Persian nobleman (not called a eunuch) who had this charge (§§44–46). The case of Batis is also interesting: Darius III entrusted him with the defense of the garrison of Gaza (phrourarch in Josephus, *Ant.* XI.320). An ancient tradition, recorded by Arrian (II.25.4) and the author of the *Itin. Alex.* (§45), refers to him as a eunuch. But on coins he is called "king of Gaza." It is likely in this case that the word *eunuch* is a corruption of a title.

Placing the sources in juxtaposition brings out the fact that the ancient authors some-times used the term *eunuch* for persons who clearly were not. Thus Artapates, "the one among Cyrus' [the Younger's] chamberlains (*skēptoukhoi*) who was his most faithful fol-lower" (Xenophon, *Anab.* I.8.28), was certainly not a eunuch, contrary to Aelian's state-ment (*VH* VI.25), for which, curiously, he credits Xenophon. Perhaps he read in the *Cyropedia* that Gadatas, the head of the *skēptoukhoi* of Cyrus the Elder, was a eunuch (VIII.4.2) — unless Artapates also held the title of eunuch.

It is rather tempting to think that there were two kinds of eunuch at the Persian court: (1) the castrated men, reduced to palace slavery and used in specific contexts (at a higher or lesser rank in the domestic hierarchy); and (2) the eunuchs in the sense of the court hierarchy, that is, nobles (Persian or Iranian) in the king's immediate circle who differentiated themselves according to their own hierarchy (as Ctesias explains several times). At any rate, if we reread Xenophon closely, it seems that Cyrus's castrated men only fulfilled subordinate duties, which acquired importance only because of the king's vulnerability (table, bath, bed; *Cyr.* VII.5.59). They were all servants, "from the door-keepers up (*thyrōroi*)" (§65✧), that is, probably the guardians of the gates of the private apartments. This was apparently the function devolving on the eunuchs who are called porters (*janitores*; Vulgate) or chief bodyguards (*arkhisōmatophylakai*; Septuagint) in the book of Esther (2:21). The prevailing impression is that Xenophon and Ctesias were not talking about the same eunuchs. Xenophon deals with the royalty's use of eunuchs who were sent to the court each year by subject peoples, just as the young Babylonians who were emasculated for this purpose (Herodotus III.92). Ctesias portrays aristocrats bearing a court title that the Greeks, rightly or wrongly, understood to be "eunuch."

All of this leads us to suspect that in many cases those whom the Greek texts call eu-nuchs were nothing other than the holders of high court positions in the king's entou-rage. It is in fact fairly likely that, as in the Assyrian court, the word had become a court title that did not refer to any particular physical characteristics. The real problem, obvi-ously, is that we do not know the Persian vocabulary. The Greek vocabulary itself re-mains uncertain: which Persian word does *eunuch* indicate? It turns out that sometimes copyists confused *oinokhoos* 'cupbearer' with *eunoukhos* 'eunuch', as in the case of Ne-hemiah. In Hebrew, the usual term is *sārîs*, which is borrowed from the Akkadian *ša rēš šarri*, that is, 'he who is stationed at the head of the king'. This is the word that is regularly rendered *eunuch* in the Septuagint of Esther. For more than a century, the debate has raged among Assyriologists as to whether this class of persons automatically consisted of castrated men. The arguments are nearly identical to arguments that can be made re-garding the eunuchs of the Achaemenid court. To interpret *ša rēš šarri* consistently as 'eunuch' leads to a sort of absurdity, as P. Garelli has humorusly expressed it: "Is it nec-essary to castrate half the Assyrian administration and nearly everyone at court?"

We must stress at this point that there are several (often unappreciated) interesting Egyptian documents from the Achaemenid period. The word *saris* is found in several hieroglyphic inscriptions from Wadi Hammamât from the time of Darius and Xerxes. An important Persian administrator there, Atiyawahy, bore the title "*saris* of Persia" (Posener nos. 24–30). He was definitely not a eunuch; *saris* here refers to a high official similar to the powerful minister Potiphar in Genesis 37:36, 39:1 (the title *saris* is trans-lated *dynastēs* 'powerful' in the Greek of the Septuagint). It is possible that the Egyptian title "powerful of Persia" given to Ariyawrata, brother of Atiyawahy, was a "translation" of the word *saris* (Posener no. 34). This is certainly the most convincing testimony, because the Wadi Hammamât inscriptions were not composed without the consent of the persons they honored. If the Persians adopted the foreign word *saris*, would it not have been because it was used at court, no doubt in its Akkadian form? This would be the same word as the word consistently translated into Greek as 'eunuch', perhaps simply because in the everyday speech of Babylonians during the time of Ctesias and other authors of *Persicas* the word would have retained the connotation of a powerful official, long after it had lost its proper institutional or biological definition. A sort of empirical verification of this hypothesis can be deduced from a well-known Babylonian text, the *Dynastic Prophecy*, which alludes to the murder of Arses: "A *ša rēš* [will kill] this king" (*BHLT* 35). This obviously refers to Bagoas, who is regularly called a eunuch in the Classical sources; we know that Bagoas was a high palace official, since he held the title of chiliarch.

To conclude briefly: there is no doubt about the existence of castrated men at the Achaemenid court. The Classical texts are absolutely clear on this point. In most cases, they worked as a part of the palace's immense domestic staff, without our being able to determine precisely whether they were assigned specific tasks. The only exception is that they guarded a particular category of women (called royal *pallakai* by the Greeks), regardless of whether one accepts or rejects the traditional term *harem* (see the next section). It is moreover highly doubtful that all of the counselors and intimates of the Great Kings whom Ctesias and others call eunuchs were castrated men. The most reasonable hypothesis is to accept that *eunuch* is how the Greeks transmitted a term that the court of the Great King considered a court title. The evidence of the Wadi Hammamât inscriptions suggests that, based on the model of the Neo-Assyrian court, this title was *ša rēš šarri* (*saris*).

4. The Women's Side

Wives and Concubines

We know from many examples that the kings, like other Persians, practiced polygamy and that they also had many concubines. In the Persian context, a distinction between the categories of legitimate wife and concubine is often made by the ancient authors, such as Herodotus:

> Every man has a number of wives (*gynaikes*), and a much greater number of mistresses (*pallakai*). (I.135)

or Plutarch:

> When the Persian kings take their dinner, the lawful wives (*hai gnēsai gynaikes*) of the Persian kings sit beside them at dinner, and eat with them. But when the kings wish to be merry and get drunk, they send their wives away, and send for their music-girls and concubines (*mousourgoi kai pallakides*). In so far they are right in what they do, because they do not concede any share in their licentiousness and debauchery to their wedded wives (*gametai*). (*Mor.* 140b✧)

We can also quote Dinon (apud Athenaeus):

> Among the Persians the queen tolerates the large number of concubines (*pallakides*) because the king rules his wife (*gametē*) as absolute owner, and for another reason, according to Dinon in his *History of Persia*, because the queen is treated with reverence by the concubines; at any rate they do obeisance (*proskynesis*) before her. (Athenaeus XIII.556b✧)

In Ctesias's version of the initial relations between the Persian court and the Saite pharaohs, he records that Amasis refused to send one of his daughters to Cambyses, "suspecting that she would not have the station of a wife (*gynaix*) but that of a concubine" (*pallakis*; Athenaeus XIII.560d◇). The story narrated by Xenophon (*Ages.* 3.3) concerning relations between Pharnabazus and Spithridates confirms this point: Spithridates became quite annoyed with Pharnabazus, who was hoping to marry (*gēmai*) one of the king's daughters and was planning to take Spithridates' daughter without marrying her (*aneu gamou*)—that is, we are given to understand that he wanted to take her as a concubine. This manifested considerable disrespect for the girl's father.

The category of "wife" was distinguished from the category of "concubine" by means of an official ceremony and was manifested in the status of the children. The wives bore legitimate children (*gnesioi*), the concubines illegitimate (*nothoi*). In principle, only the former entered into the limited circle of potential heirs (Herodotus III.2). A notable exception occurred in the succession of Artaxerxes I: his wife Damaspia provided only one living legitimate son (*gnēsios*), Xerxes II, the others having died (Ctesias §44). When Xerxes II was assassinated soon after attaining the throne, competition emerged among the *nothoi*, the sons of several Babylonian women (Ctesias §§44–48). In this case, the institution of concubine perfectly met the objectives of polygamy and possessing multiple concubines (*pallakai*), as Strabo puts it: "For the sake of having many children" (XV.3.17◇). The existence of concubines is also "attested" by Ctesias during the reign of Bardiya, since in his tale the *magus* was killed by the Seven while "he was sleeping with a Babylonian concubine" (§14: *pallakē*).

Pallakai and Domestics

But who were these concubines? Or rather, who were these women whom the Greeks murkily call *pallakai*? In the Greek context, the internal differences are well marked, as a famous passage of Demosthenes indicates (*C. Neera* 122): "The courtesans (*hetairai*) we have for pleasure; the concubines (*pallakai*) for everyday cares; the wives (*gynaikes*) to have a legitimate descendant (*gnesiōs*) and a faithful guardian of the hearth." For the female population of the Persian palaces, however, the Greek authors use the word *pallakis/pallakides* nearly uniformly; they use the word *hetaira* very rarely. Let us note meanwhile that in Athenaeus a distinction is made between Cyrus the Younger's two Aspasias: the first, originally called Milto, is called a *hetaira*; the second (the heroine of the romance) is a *pallakis* (XIII.576d). The notorious Thais, supposedly responsible for the burning of the palace at Persepolis in 330, is also called *hetaira* (ibid.).

As Aelian notes regarding the heroine of the romance, the four Greek girls who were introduced to Cyrus the Younger's court received a hetaira's (*hetairika*) education; that is, women of the profession taught initiates to make themselves up, to act a bit coy with men who got together to drink, and undoubtedly to sing and play instruments (harp, flute) as well. It was exactly the reserve of the young, beautiful Aspasia that so seduced Cyrus and prompted him to add her to his concubines (*VH*, XII.1). She came from a poor family, raised by an indigent (*penetēs*) father, Hermotimus. Since the four girls were brought to Cyrus by someone Aelian calls one of his "satraps," who was also her buyer (*agorastēs*), we may presume that they had been sold in a market; the other three girls behaved as though they had been (*kapēlikōs*). Plutarch also speaks of "these women whom the Persians buy for money and make their concubines" (*pallakai*; *Them.* 26.4; cf. Herodotus I.135). Straton of Sidon brought many *pallakai* from Ionia and all over

Greece, and they enlivened his banquets (Athenaeus XII.531b). In Asia Minor (and elsewhere), then, there certainly existed veritable "finishing schools," just as there were centers for the production of eunuchs. There were women who specialized in professional singing and music, and as such they had good reputations in the royal and satrapal courts (see pp. 293f.).

The example of Aspasia shows that one could advance from purchased slave to concubine. This theme recurs in several court romances. The powerful desire of the king for Esther can be paralleled with the story of Aspasia and Cyrus:

> She was very soon preferred to his other mistresses because of her natural manner, reserved disposition, and unstudied beauty. . . . From that time on Cyrus had a greater liking for her than any of the other women he had dealings with. Later he fell very much in love with her, and she returned his affection. The love of the pair reached such a point that they were near to being equals and did not fall short of the harmony and morality of a Greek marriage. His love for Aspasia was celebrated in Ionia and the whole of Greece. (Aelian, *VH* XII.1✧)

Cyrus is so perfectly Hellenized by the storyteller that he was, "contrary to Persian custom (*ou persikōs*), exceedingly pleased with her nobility"!✧ But after all, as everyone knows, life is not very far from fiction, nor kings from men. Does not Herodotus record that, out of all of Darius's legitimate wives, he maintained a special affection for Artystone, in whose honor he had a statue erected (VII.69)?

Most *pallakai* were brought to the palace or the Persian nobles' households as prisoners of war. After the capture of several Ionian towns, "the handsomest girls were dragged from their homes and sent to Darius' court" (Herodotus VI.32✧) by the Persian generals; after the fall of Miletus, "the women and children were made slaves" (VI.19✧). A woman from Cos became the concubine of the Persian Pharandates "by force" (IX.76✧), and a Macedonian woman was taken from Samothrace to Autophradates the same way (Plutarch, *Mor.* 339e). After the Egyptian campaign, a soldier in Cambyses' army sold a female prisoner in Babylonia. After Sidon was taken, in 345–344, Artaxerxes sent a large number of women to Babylon, and the Babylonian Chronicle provides this detail: "They entered the king's palace" (ABC no. 9, 11.6–8). But not all were destined for concubinage in the true sense. They disappeared instead into the huge domestic staff of the palace; the Babylonian texts call these people *arad šarri* 'royal slaves' and *arad ekalli* 'palace slaves'. The women and girl captives without special training worked in various parts of the palace.

They might also join the staffs of the wives and princesses, who were provided with a large number of servants, as shown by the example of Darius III's mother (Diodorus XVII.38.1: *therapeia*). This is presumably the sense of the words that Herodotus places on the lips of Atossa, who wanted Darius to go to war with the Greeks: "I should like to have Spartan girls, and girls from Argos and Attica and Corinth, to wait upon me" (Herodotus III.134✧). The royal concubines themselves had many maids at hand; this is how Esther received "seven special maids from the king's household" (Esther 2:9✧).

There was another method of procuring women. It is explained by the author of the book of Esther. Let us recall that in this court romance Ahasuerus decided to repudiate Queen Vashti, who was guilty of not having attended the royal convocation. In order to find her replacement, he published the following royal order everywhere:

> Let beautiful girls be selected for the king. Let the king appoint commissioners throughout the provinces of his realm to bring all these beautiful young virgins to the citadel of Susa. (2:2–3)

Despite the romanticized character of the work, this method of gathering women does not seem outside the realm of possibility. The motif recurs in a story told by Herodotus to show how Darius dreamed of repopulating Babylon after finally taking it at the end of a very long siege:

> I mentioned at the beginning of my account how the Babylonians strangled their women to save food, and it was in consequence of this that Darius, in order to prevent the race from dying out, compelled the neighboring peoples each to send a certain stated number of women to Babylon. In all, as many as fifty thousand were collected there. (III.159✧)

This again is a "good story" rather than history. Nevertheless, it is woven within a perfectly acceptable political-institutional framework. All Darius did was set up a tribute assessment calculated in proportion to the available resources (in women) in each of the countries taxed. Tribute in human females is attested by Herodotus with regard to Colchis, which had to send 100 young boys and 100 girls to the court each year (III.97). In a way, the royal bed, like the royal table, reflected the immensity of the Empire and the diversity of the populations that it comprised.

On this point, I cannot resist quoting R. H. van Gulik on the concubines of the emperor of China during the T'ang period:

> It would seem that the Palace women consisted of girls offered as tribute, both by the Provinces and foreign and vassal countries; of daughters of prominent families keen on obtaining the Imperial favour; and of women recruited by Palace agents. The Palace agents used to scour the entire Empire for beautiful and accomplished women, and apparently took them wherever they found them, not despising even commercial or government brothels. When a number of such women had been collected, the eunuchs and duennas sorted them out. The best were chosen for the Imperial harem, those skilled in the arts for the *chiao-fang* ['training center'], and the remainder assigned menial tasks in the Palace. (p. 184✧)

But, we must insist, the comparison is shaky, to the extent that the Achaemenid evidence is so sparse. In addition to the book of Esther, we at least can quote Phylarcus, who spoke in this way of a woman named Timosa: She "surpassed all other women in beauty. This girl had been sent as a present by the king of Egypt to Statira, the king's [Artaxerxes II's] wife" (Athenaeus XIII.609✧). She then became Oxyarthes' *pallakis*. Most likely he was infatuated with her and asked his sister-in-law to grant him her lady-in-waiting.

The Great King's 360 Concubines

A real problem arises with the usual interpretation of certain Classical and Hellenistic texts on the number of royal concubines. Plutarch, (*Art.* 27.1), Diodorus (XVII.77.5), Quintus Curtius (III.3.24; VI.6.8), and Dicaearchus (Athenaeus XIII.557b) mention the existence of 360 concubines for Artaxerxes II and Darius III.

The figure 360 is found several times in Herodotus's account about the paying of tribute: the third and twelfth nomes pay 360 talents of silver (III.90,✧ 92); the twentieth (India) annually sends 360 talents of gold powder (III.94). The figure even appears twice regarding the Cilician nome: out of the total of 500 talents of silver demanded, 140 went to maintain the cavalry permanently stationed in their country, the other 360 being sent to the royal court. Additionally, the country had to supply 360 white horses; Herodotus adds the following detail: "one for each day in the year," an expression also found in Diodorus regarding the royal concubines. The comparison of the texts leaves no doubt about the existence of an ideal model, but was it Greek or Persian? Or, more precisely, was there any particular preference for the number 360 in Achaemenid thought? If not, we would have to toss out not only the number of concubines of the Great King but also Herodotus's figures concerning Achaemenid tribute. We would also have to reject Herodotus's story of the punishment that Cyrus inflicted on the Gyndes River, in which a white horse, which had been dedicated to the Sun, drowned: he divided it into 360 tiny streams and thus crossed it easily (I.189–90). We would also have to question the presence of 365 young men in Darius's procession, "equal in number to the days of a whole year" (Quintus Curtius III.3.10✧), as well as the variety (360) of uses the Persians had for the palm tree (Strabo XVI.1.14).

Obviously, this is a symbolic number that is also found in Greek tradition. But it also seems clear that in Persian tradition reference was being made to a solar calendar of 360 days plus 5 epagomenal days that coexisted with the official administrative calendar of the Babylonian lunar type. Some of the texts that include the number 360 (or 365) are situated directly or indirectly in a context of sun worship, especially the horses sacrificed annually during the *Mithrakāna*. It thus becomes apparent that the quantity of 360 concubines attributed to the Great King goes straight back to information from the Achaemenid court (cf. *nomos persikos* in Diodorus). By settling on the number 360 concubines, they once again gave the Great King the image of a man above men because of a perfect proportionality between his own rhythm and cultic time. Thus, more than anything, it was a number pertaining to the sacred character of Achaemenid kingship.

The privileged status of these 360 women is well illustrated by the ancient authors. Custom has it, Diodorus says, that during the relocations of the court the king was accompanied by the women of the Royal House and also by those of the Kinsmen and Friends (XVII.35.3). In Darius III's procession, Quintus Curtius mentions only the king's mother and wife, accompanied by a crowd of mounted women; following were the king's children and their governesses, as well as a crowd of eunuchs. "Next rode the 365 concubines of the king, regally dressed and adorned" (III.3.24✧). We also know from Heraclides that the concubines accompanied the Great King on hunts (Athenaeus XII.514c). This reproduces the custom described by Quintus Curtius (VIII.1.28) for the court of the Mauryan king (Strabo states that the concubines participated in hunts; XV.1.55). The 360 royal concubines constituted an integral part of the king's suite, though definitely at a rank inferior to the blood-related princesses. There can hardly be any doubt, therefore, that out of all whom the ancient authors called "concubines," the 360 royal concubines constituted a group with greater status than the immense horde of palace *pallakai*. We may presume, though without absolute proof, that at the king's death, 360 new concubines were recruited. What became of the earlier group? We know that to humiliate his son Darius, Artaxerxes II banished Aspasia: "he consecrated her priestess of Diana of Ecbatana, whom they name Anaitis, that she might spend the remainder of her days in strict chastity" (Plutarch, *Art.* 27.4✧). But it would be too hazardous to take this episode as a specific illustration of a general practice.

Furthermore, we do not know the criteria by which the concubines were selected. They are always characterized by uncommon beauty. This is already mentioned by the composer of the book of Esther, who adds that they were virgins. Diodorus says explicitly that they were beautiful: They were "outstanding in beauty as selected from all the women of Asia" (XVII.77.6✧). "Selected for their beauty," comments Plutarch in turn

(*Art.* 27.2◇). But this is hardly a distinguishing feature. Timosa and Aspasia are described in the same terms, and so is Amytis, Xerxes' sister and Megabyzus's wife: "Anoutis was the most beautiful of all the women in Asia" (Athenaeus XIII.609a◇). And we recall Alexander's wondering appreciation of the Iranian women: "jestingly . . . terrible eyesores" (Plutarch, *Alex.* 21.10)!

It is difficult to answer the question of selection criteria because the royal concubines are usually mentioned collectively. We know the names of only three of Artaxerxes I's concubines, the ones who bore him children. Smerdis had a concubine who was referred to as a Babylonian (Ctesias §14); similarly, Ctesias refers to Artaxerxes I's concubines as Babylonian, despite the fact that one of them had a good Iranian name, Alogune, which means 'rose-colored'. If they really were among the 360 royal concubines (which is not certain), we may presume, with Diodorus and the composer of Esther, that they were recruited from the subject peoples and princes of the Empire. It seems unlikely, however, that any of them came from the great Persian aristocratic families, considering the indignant reaction of Spithridates, who broke with Pharnabazus on the grounds that he "intended to take his, Spithridates', daughter as a concubine" (Xenophon, *Ages.* 3.3).

The Great King's Sex Life: Images and Realities

One picture of the king's private life comes to us from Diodorus, who describes the following scene: "Each night [the concubines] paraded about the couch of the king so that he might select the one with whom he would lie that night" (XVII.77.7◇). The text implies that each night a new concubine joined the Great King in bed.

Compare the picture presented in the book of Esther. Once Esther arrived at Ahasuerus's court, the eunuch Hegai provided her with perfumes and food and also procured seven select girls for her "from the king's household" (2:9◇)—"concubines" in the sense of domestic staff. For twelve months Esther followed the "regulations for the women"; for six months she was anointed with myrrh and for six months with "spices and lotions commonly used for feminine beauty treatment." When she was summoned by the king, she left in the evening and returned in the morning, but she then stayed in "another harem entrusted to the care of Shaashgaz, the king's eunuch, custodian of the concubines." (2:12–14◇). In theory she would not reappear before the king unless he specifically requested her. Fortunately for the story, this did not fail to happen, for Esther was preferred above all others!

Be that as it may, the preparations required of the girls were probably not fictional. They are found in the book of Judith, when the heroine prepares to join Holophernes:

> Taking off her widow's dress, she washed all over, anointed herself with costly perfumes, dressed her hair, wrapped a turban round it and put on the dress she used to wear on joyful occasions. . . . She put sandals on her feet, put on her necklaces, bracelets, rings, earrings and all her jewellery. (10:3–4◇)

It is not surprising that this sort of preparation was required of women who were about to share the king's bed. The youths who served at the king's table also had to take a bath and wear white clothes, according to Heraclides (Athenaeus IV.145b).

Thus, we see that Diodorus and Esther harmonize fairly well, although the romance does not mention the picturesque promenade featured by the chronicler. But does the modern historian necessarily find this similarity convincing? In an attempt to answer this question, let us turn to Heraclides, who wrote in his *Persica*:

Three hundred women (*gynaikes*) watch (*phyllatousin*) over him. . . . These sleep throughout the day in order to stay awake at night, but at night they sing and play on harps continually while the lamps burn; and the king takes his pleasure of them as concubines (*pallakides?*). [These were admitted to his presence] through the court of the Apple-bearers (*mēlophoroi*). (Athenaeus XII.514b❖)

At first glance, the similarity between Diodorus and Heraclides seems quite pronounced. But we do well to emphasize at the outset that the text is partly restored and that the word *pallakides* is uncertain; other manuscripts have *pollakis* 'often'. The only indisputable word is *gynaikes*. The usual proposals for restoration (sometimes including 360 instead of 300) are based on assimilation to Diodorus, which obviously gives rise to serious doubts regarding the probative value of comparison between the two authors. Diodorus does not mention details given by Heraclides (alert women who sing and play). These differences are all the more noteworthy in that Heraclides was quite familiar with the customs of the Achaemenid court.

The most likely interpretation is that Heraclides is here alluding not to the king's 360 concubines but to the playing and singing *pallakai*, some of whom ornamented the royal dinner with their voices and their harmonies, as we know from Heraclides himself (Athenaeus IV.145c) and other authors. Parmenion seized 329 of these *pallakai basilikai mousourgoi* in Darius III's Treasury in Damascus (XIII.608a). If this interpretation is legitimate, then we are led to believe that Diodorus (or his source) either embellished the story for his readers and/or (intentionally or not) confused facts such as those given by Heraclides. His descriptions integrate perfectly well with one of the favorite images of the Greek authors. As proof of the Great Kings' extreme luxury, Polyarchus did not hesitate to emphasize, for example, their penchant for sexual relations (Athenaeus XII.545f). Another writer, Aelian, compared them to a certain fish in the sea "that has many wives." The Median and Persian barbarians, he wrote, "exhibit their luxury (*tryphē*) in the the pleasures of the bed" (*Anim.* I.14).

It is not easy to distinguish fact from Greek interpretation here. From the number of royal concubines ("the same as the days in the year"), Diodorus draws the conclusion that they took turns in coming to distract the Great King. However, the available texts do not require us to take Diodorus's interpretation literally. We are especially tempted to think that this is how he "rationalized" a number that had supreme symbolic value for the Achaemenids. Perhaps Diodorus's view also derives, at least in part, from Herodotus's detail about relations between the Great King and his women: "In Persia a man's wives (*gynaikes*) share his bed in rotation" (III.69❖). All things considered, if as stated in Esther the girls who were recruited had to be virgins, we may even wonder whether many of them remained virgins even while a part of the harem—and then, perhaps, living in the chastity of a sanctuary of Anāhita (Plutarch, *Art.* 27.3–4).

Cloistered Women? The Myth of the Harem

In conjunction with the Classical texts, the text of Esther has played no small part in giving rise to the idea of a harem at the Great King's court, a harem that is described, or rather imagined, as being similar to the picture of Ottoman harems, peopled with eunuchs and concubines. This sort of presupposition guided the original investigators of Persepolis, who believed that they had discovered a harem—that is, a separate building where the women supposedly lived in individual chambers.

Undoubtedly, the royal princesses and wives generally had their own apartments. In his tale of the murder of Smerdis, Herodotus speaks of the men's apartment (*andreōn*)

(III.77–78), which obviously was separate from the apartments reserved for the women (III.68). The existence of separate apartments is implicit in his story about Democedes' arrival at the court: the Greek physician was taken by a eunuch to the king's wives (III.130: *para tas heautou gynaikas*). Note also Herodotus's detail on Persian infants: "Before the age of five a boy lives with the women (*para tēsi gynaixi*) and never sees his father" (I.136◇).

Speaking of the 360 royal concubines, Plutarch adds the following detail:

> The barbarian people keep a very jealous and watchful eye over their carnal pleasures, so that it is death for a man not only to come near and touch any concubine of his prince, but likewise on a journey to ride forward and pass by the carriages in which they are conveyed. (*Art.* 27.1)

This reminds us of Themistocles' ruse, a tale also told by Plutarch. Once again stressing the jealousy of the barbarians (also noted by Aelian), Plutarch tells how, in order to escape the checkpoints, Themistocles climbed into a covered chariot. Those with him took advantage of the custom of concealing the women and would always say "that it was a woman of Greek origin whom they were taking from Ionia to one of the nobles of the king's Gate." Plutarch specifically comments:

> The barbarous nations, and amongst them the Persians especially, are extremely jealous, severe, and suspicious about their women, not only their wives (*hai gamētai*), but also their bought slaves and concubines (*pallakai*), whom they keep so strictly that no one sees them abroad; they spend their lives shut up within doors (*oikoi*), and when they take a journey, are carried in closed tents, curtained on all sides, and set upon a wagon (*harmamaxai*). (*Them.* 26.5◇)

Plutarch, who was always concerned with the virtue of women, returns to it in his *Life of Artaxerxes*, stating that Artaxerxes was the first to allow his wife, Stateira, to travel in an open carriage (*Art.* 5.6; cf. *Mor.* 173f). He also states that the king's legitimate wives left the hall at the time of the *symposion* ['drinking party'], after attending a banquet; at this time, the concubines and musicians entered (*Mor.* 140b).

There is no good reason to reject the information in the Classical authors totally, however much they may have embellished the details (cf. Herodotus V.18). At the same time, we need to add important qualifications: we must not toss all the women in the palace into a single, undifferentiated category. We do not know much about the life of the royal concubines. The composer of the book of Esther places them in a house called the *gynaikōnos*. There were two houses of this kind, one (run by the eunuch Hegai) where the girls were prepared; the other, "the second women's house" (run by Shaashgaz, "custodian of the royal concubines"), where the women resided after their night with the Great King (2:2–17). Plutarch uses this Greek word when he refers to the satrap of Sardis's concubines (*Them.* 31.2). Aelian also alludes to this kind of building in his analogy between the Great King and a fish of the sea: both the Great King and the wrasse have wives who live in many chambers (*Anim.* I.14). This is also the picture drawn by ancient authors in many passages deploring the effeminacy of Oriental princes, such as Ninyas, "who was never seen except by the eunuchs and his own wives," or Sardanapalus, who lived with his concubines dressed as a woman and spinning wool in their company (Athenaeus XII.528e–f◇).

The word *gynaikōnitis* is usually rendered 'harem'. On this point, the Near Eastern parallels are contradictory. We should note that in pharaonic Egypt words traditionally translated 'harem' actually signify something quite different. One of them in particular refers to groups of musician-singers, including both men and women. It seems on the other hand that in the Mari materials the word *sekretum* means 'confined' (fem.), which could designate the women confined in a particular space (*tubqum* 'interior space'). Thus we see that certain elements found in Esther are legitimate. The royal concubines lived in special apartments that, if we take Heraclides literally, were perhaps separated from the royal apartments by the court of *mēlophoroi* (Athenaeus XII.514b).

It is not certain, however, that the royal princesses lived cloistered in their apartments. The Persepolis tablets attest to their frequent travels. The tablets document travel rations, and the record is that the princesses were treated no differently than the men (husbands, fathers) with whom they relocated from time to time. They certainly had greater autonomy than other women, even if it was only due to their activities as managers of their own houses, which included land and a domestic staff. We may once again mention Amytis—Xerxes' sister and Megabyzus's wife—"the most beautiful of all the women in Asia, and the most licentious," according to Dinon (Athenaeus XIII.609a✧). Ctesias stresses her extramarital adventures, which is why her husband complained to Xerxes (§28). "After Megabyzus's death, she devoted herself to seeking out the company of men, just like her mother Amestris," and she had an affair with the physician Apollonides (§42). Setting aside the Greek authors' criticisms, these examples at least prove that the princesses did not live like nuns shut in a cell!

Generally speaking, the aristocratic women were specially educated. Quintus Curtius mentions that "governesses" (*quae educabant*) of the royal children (III.3.23✧), perhaps of girls in particular (III.13.12), were present in Darius III's procession. Moreover, Ctesias gives the example of Roxanne, sister of Artaxerxes II's son-in-law Teritouchmes: "she was very beautiful and highly skilled with the bow and javelin" (§54). This is a unique and very interesting statement implying that girls received a physical education something like boys', during which they studied traditional martial arts. Note also that in Darius III's procession the princesses are accompanied by "horsewomen" (Quintus Curtius III.3.22) and that, according to Quintus Curtius (V.2.19✧), "there is nothing that the women of Persia feel to be a greater disgrace than to work in wool." When we add to this the fact that the woman warrior played a part in Iranian folk traditions, it is tempting to conclude that aristocratic girls were not prepared for a reclusive life at all, even though they had special apartments in the royal palace or their husband's house. Although the term *harem* must be retained for convenience, the usual meaning cannot be applied to any women other than the royal concubines.

In one way at least, these conclusions are illustrated in visual representations. For reasons we have already mentioned, the absence of images of women in court art is not surprising. They are found in other media. Several Persepolis seals are known to have belonged to Princess Irdabama. The images on them do not distinguish them from men's seals. One of them shows a hunting scene (PFS 51), worked out on a model not unlike the seal of Kuraš of Anšan (PFS 93). Another, used by officials linked to Irdabama, has an audience scene with women only, but the scene is obviously copied from the official Achaemenid court ceremony: it recalls the obligation to perform *proskynesis* at court, perhaps an obligation even imposed on persons of higher status, such as princesses and concubines (cf. Athenaeus XIII.556b). On a seal belonging to Artystone we also find the well-known motif of the Royal Hero. The use of seals and the iconographic themes on them once more attest to the position held by the royal princesses at the Achaemenid court. We should also mention the interesting scenes depicted on a carpet from Pazyryk (obviously of Achaemenid inspiration): two women are praying in front of a footed censer.

5. *At the Great King's Table*

Dining with the Great King

Of all the festive events at court, the luxury and pomp of the banquets particularly captured the imagination of the ancient authors. Their tales vie with one another to celebrate the abundance of the fare. On their birthday, says Herodotus (I.133◊), rich Persians "will have an ox or a horse or a camel or a donkey baked whole in the oven." What can we then say about the royal table, which, as Dinon and Ctesias suggest (Athenaeus IV.146c), fed 15,000 people a day?

We are fortunate enough to have a text that is very informative in this area, in Polyaenus's collection of *Stratagems* (IV.3.32):

> Since Alexander was in the Persian royal residence, the Great King's lunch and dinner were served to him according to what was inscribed on a bronze pillar, which also bore the other rules (*nomoi*) instituted by Cyrus. Here is what they contained:

1.	Wheat flour, pure	400 ardabs
2.	Wheat flour, 2d grade	300 ardabs
3.	Wheat flour, 3d grade	300 ardabs
	Total wheat flour at dinner:	1,000 ardabs
4.	Barley flour, very pure	200 ardabs
5.	Barley flour, 2d grade	400 ardabs
6.	[Barley flour, 3d grade	400 ardabs]
	Total barley flour:	1,000 ardabs
7.	Barley groats	200 ardabs
8.	Very fine flour for beverages	200 ardabs
9.	Minced cress	xxx ardabs
10.	Ptisane [processed barley?]	10 ardabs
11.	Mustard seed	1/3 ardab
12.	Sheep and goats (male)	400
13.	Cattle	100
14.	Horses	30
15.	Fattened geese	400
16.	Pigeons	300
17.	Various small birds	600
18.	Lambs	300
19.	Goslings	100
20.	Gazelles	30
21.	Fresh milk of the day	10 *marriš*
22.	Sweetened whey	10 *marriš*
23.	Garlic	1 talent
24.	Bitter onions	1/2 talent
25.	Herbacious [mercury?]	1 ardab
26.	Juice of silphium	1 talent
27.	Sweet must of sweetened apples	1/4 ardab
28.	Cumin wax	1/4 ardab
29.	Black raisins	3 talents

30.	Dill flower	3 minas
31.	Corn cockle seed	1/3 ardab
32.	Arum seed	2 kapetis
33.	Sesame	10 ardabs
34.	Sweet grape jelly	5 *marriš*
35.	Candied turnips and radishes prepared with salt	5 *marriš*
36.	Candied capers with salt, from which delicious stuffings called *abyrtakai* are made	5 *marriš*
37.	Salt	10 ardabs
38.	Ethiopian cumin	6 kapetis
39.	Dried anise	30 minas
40.	Parsley seed	4 kapetis
41.	Sesame oil	10 *marriš*
42.	Oil extracted from milk	5 *marriš*
43.	Terebinth oil	5 *marriš*
44.	Acanthus oil	5 *marriš*
45.	Oil of sweet almonds	3 *marriš*
46.	Dried sweet almonds	3 *marriš*
47.	Wine	500 *marriš*

(When the king was in Babylon or Susa, half the wine he drank was palm wine, half grape wine.)

48.	Firewood	200 cartloads
49.	Kindling	100 cartloads
50.	Solidified honey	100 square blocks, 10 minas each

When the king was in Media, this is what he distributed:

51.	safflower seed	3 ardabs
52.	Saffron	2 minas

All of the above for beverages and lunch.

Besides this, he distributes:

53.	Fine wheat flour	500 ardabs
54.	Fine barley wheat flour	1,000 ardabs
55.	2d-grade flour	1,000 ardabs
56.	Fine fine wheat flour	500 ardabs
57.	Barley groats	500 *marriš*
58.	Barley for the animals	2,000 ardabs
59.	Chopped straw	10,000 wagons
60.	Hay	5,000 wagons
61.	Sesame oil	200 *marriš*
62.	Vinegar	100 *marriš*
63.	Finely minced cress	30 ardabs

All of the above is given to the soldiers; it is what the king provides each day for his lunch and dinner and for those who receive his allotments.

To evaluate the credibility of this text, two parts should be distinguished at the outset: the numerical information and the commentary in the introduction and conclusion. Polyaenus draws this moral from the story: as his soldiers stared in envious wonder, Alexander burst into laughter, ordered the bronze pillar knocked down, and remarked to his Friends that such an excessive regular diet would weaken the body and the spirit, as proved by the defeats the Persians had just suffered. This discussion, taken in light of the introduction, communicates all of the clichés about the relationship between the *tryphē* (luxury) of the Great Kings and their supposed decadence. It can be compared, nearly word for word, with Herodotus's passage on the reaction of the Greeks to the opulence of Mardonius's tent, which they captured after the battle of Plataea. The words and attitude ascribed to Alexander by Polyaenus correspond very closely to the words and attitude attributed to Pausanias of Sparta by Herodotus:

> When Pausanias saw [the tent], with its embroidered hangings and gorgeous decorations in silver and gold, he summoned Mardonius' bakers and cooks and told them to prepare a meal of the same sort as they were accustomed to prepare for their former master. The order was obeyed; and when Pausanias saw gold and silver couches all beautifully draped, and gold and silver tables, and everything prepared for the fest with great magnificence, he could hardly believe his eyes for the good things set before him, and, just for a joke, ordered his own servants to get ready an ordinary Spartan dinner. The difference between the two meals was indeed remarkable, and when both were ready, Pausanias laughed and sent for the Greek commanding officers. When they arrived, he invited them to look at the two tables, saying, "Gentlemen, I asked you here in order to show you the folly of the Persians, who, living in this style, came to Greece to rob us of our poverty." (IX.82✧)

Both of these citations present a motif that is common to many Greek authors (e.g., Athenaeus IV.150b–c; Aelian, *VH* V.1). The stereotype of a king who is decadent because he is too well fed, repeated for example by Strabo (XV.3.22), reappears in many authors of the fourth century (e.g., Clearchus apud Athenaeus XII.539b).

It is highly unlikely that these rules (attributed to the fictive authority of "Cyrus," as in Xenophon) were inscribed on a bronze pillar. It is far more likely that the information comes from an author who was quite familiar with the court customs of the Achaemenid court, perhaps Ctesias, who we know had written a book in which he described everything that was served at the king's dinner (Athenaeus II.67a), or even Heraclides himself. Even so, all of the information *feels* right. First of all, with each reference to Persian measures (*marriš*, ardabs, *kapeties*, etc.), Polyaenus is careful to give an estimate of their size in terms of Greek measures, and the measures he mentions are known from the Persepolis tablets—at least the ardab and the *marriš*. Furthermore, due to the vast quantities of food needed to provision the royal table, the administrators in charge were required to keep a complete list of supplies and quantities. Since we know how meticulous the administrative control at Persepolis was (chap. 11/1), it is not hard to believe that the administrators of the dining room had to produce a certified official document for the heads of the warehouses in charge of acquisition and disbursement, who had to produce a report for the administration every year, which was then duly verified. At the head of this department were probably those whom Xenophon calls "stewards of his commissary department" (*Cyr.* VIII.1.9✧); Heraclides also mentions an officer whose title in Greek transcription is nearly equivalent (*potibazis*), who was specifically assigned to distributing foodstuffs (Athenaeus IV.145f).

Other details from Polyaenus confirm that he had (indirect) access to a certain amount of original information. He distinguishes the table service according to the location of the court: Persepolis, Susa and Babylon, Ecbatana. This direct reference to the custom of court nomadism constitutes a new measure of the excellence of his sources. We know for sure that wherever the king moved, his table had to be served every day with the same splendor and bounty. We know of only one example to the contrary, the exception that proves the rule. During the army's return from an expedition against the

Cadusians, it suffered food shortages, and on this occasion Plutarch measures the gravity of the destitution by means of a significant formula: "The king's own table failed" (*Art.* 24.3✧). Herodotus further states that, "when the Persian king goes to war, he is always well provided not only with victuals from home and his own cattle, but also with water from the Choaspes" (I.188;✧ cf. VII.83). But the variations introduced in the process of resupply are fairly modest, relating particularly to products that are hard to transport, such as wine, and doubtless also beer and fish, whose use is well attested in Babylonia (cf. Diodorus XVII.108.4).

It appears that, wherever he was, the king's table was always prepared the same way. This seems to be confirmed by an excerpt, supplied by Athenaeus, from an inventory sent to Alexander by Cleomenes, who was in charge of the financial administration of Egypt. It seems actually to be an inventory of the Great King's wealth in Egypt (cf. IX.393c). The *Letter of Cleomenes* (like that of Parmenion, p. 293 below) is quoted briefly in a long digression on birds and their names. The quotation is limited to a short list: "ten thousand smoked coots, five thousand thrushes, ten thousand smoked quails." We are tempted to think that this was originally an inventory of farms operated to raise domestic fowl (well attested in Polyaenus and the Persepolis tablets) near Memphis (or elsewhere) to supply the king's table when he was in Egypt or, on a more permanent basis, the satrap's table. In fact, waterfowl clearly constituted one of the courses commonly consumed at the king's table (cf. especially Herodotus VII.119 and below).

Finally, we can see the overall coherence between Polyaenus's information and the information in Heraclides of Cyme. For one thing, both of them clearly specify that the quantity of food could only be explained as soldiers' rations (cf. also Herodotus VII.119). Polyaenus adds that they also received wood for cooking (nos. 48–49 in the list above) and that they also fed the beasts of burden, presumably including the horses as well (nos. 58–59). Here is Heraclides' list, certainly incomplete:

> One thousand animals are slaughtered daily for the king; these comprise horses, camels, oxen, asses, deer, and most of the smaller animals; many birds also are consumed, including Arabian ostriches—and the creature is large—geese, and cocks. (Athenaeus IV.145e✧)

Heraclides only lists meats here, for the simple reason that the prevalance of meat-eating among the Persians would be especially surprising to the Greeks, who were not accustomed to such a diet (cf. Strabo XV.3.19). The exceptions to the meat menu were sufficiently noteworthy for the ancient authors to mention them explicitly (e.g., Aelian, *VH* I.26.28). Heraclides adds that the soldiers received meat and bread (145f).

Aside from a few differences in detail (there are no ostriches in Polyaenus), it is not hard to say that in both documents the basic diet consists of grains and meats (of a very large variety), and other authors also mention these in passing (cf. Strabo XV.3.18; Herodotus I.133; Aelian, *VH* I.33). Another confirmation is found in the famous text of Herodotus describing the gigantic preparations made by the Greek cities for the arrival of Artaxerxes III in 480: "People in every town . . . employed themselves for months on end in making barley and wheat flour, in buying up and fattening the best cattle they could find, and feeding poultry in coops and waterfowl in ponds" (VII.119✧). In another text, in the only passage in which we see what the king actually ate, "Ochus [Artaxerxes III] stretched out his hands; with the right hand he took one of the knives laid out on the table and with the other he picked up the the largest piece of bread, put some meat on it, cut it up, and ate greedily" (Aelian, *VH* II.17✧). A passage in Plutarch attests to the frequent consumption of small birds (no. 17 in Polyaenus's list; Plutarch, *Art*. 19; cf. Ctesias §61, who transcribes the Persian name of one of them; Athenaeus IX.393c and above).

Category J of the Persepolis tablets (products "delivered to the king") confirms, overall if not in detail, Polyaenus's information. When the king or a member of his family relocated (not necessarily as part of the annual migration of the court), they received products from the administration: cattle (PF 691–94, 710), sheep and goats (696), poultry (697–98, 2033–37), flour (699–704), seed (705–10), oil (727), and other products of uncertain identification. The administration also provided wine (PF 728–32, 735–37; PFa 30, 31). While the number of cattle is not very high (3, 1, 8, 7, 8), the number of sheep and goats is naturally higher (1,124 in PF 696), and so is the quantity of poultry. The amount of flour (in liters) varies from 5,460 (PF 699) to 126,100 (PF 701). The amount of wine furnished varies from 750 liters (PF 728) to 6,900 (PFa 311).

It is true that it is hard to compare these figures with Polyaenus's. Some of the Category J tablets are not clearly distinguishable from Category Q (travel rations), and it is not certain that all of them relate to the annual court migration. At least one of them refers to deliveries to the king at Persepolis—the one with the largest amount of flour (PF 701). Furthermore, they present the same problem as Polyaenus: they do not mention the number of people who had to be fed per delivery. This number can be supplied only by reference to the usual ratio determined from other texts. It has been estimated, for example, that 17,830 liters of flour fed 11,886 people (PF 702).

Polyaenus also lists products not found in the tablets (or not yet identified), especially milk (nos. 10, 22, 42), which could not be stored but was certainly used regularly (cf. in particular Plutarch, *Art*. 22.9: cow's milk). Note that when the king was enthroned, he had to "drink a cup of sour milk (*oxygala*)" (3.2; cf. Polyaenus no. 22). Royalty also ate cheese (Aelian, *VH* I.33) and dairy products (Athenaeus XIII.608a).

Unfortunately, we do not have any of the recipes used by the king's cooks. But the Aelian passage we quoted (*VH* II.17) must not lead us to conclude that the royal table's menu (strictly speaking) was identical to the menu of the soldiers receiving rations. Only the basic ingredients are similar. In fact, Xenophon stresses that the food served to the king was distinguished by high quality: "The food that is sent from the king's board really is much superior" (*Cyr.* VIII.2.4✧), and by way of explanation he emphasizes the specialization of the cooks (VIII.2.6), among whom Athenaeus singles out "the cooks who specialized in preparing dairy dishes" (XIII.608a [Loeb: "pudding-makers"]). Many Greek authors—with a polemical viewpoint identical to Xenophon's (*Ages.* 9.3)—stress that the Great King's cooks were always hunting for new recipes, even bringing them from afar (Athenaeus IV.144b–c; XII.529d; 539b; 545d, f). As Polyaenus's remark regarding capers (no. 36) implies, the birds normally were stuffed. The Persians also served meat in salted form (Athenaeus IX.393c; cf. Plutarch, *Art*. 18.4). Diodorus (XVII.67.4) alludes to "various culinary preparations" that were transported from Persia to Babylonia, undoubtedly to serve the royal table, or again to the manifestation of senseless luxury (*tryphē, hybris*) that led Harpalus to have fish brought from the Persian Gulf (Diodorus XVII.108.4). Obviously, Persian cuisine, like the cuisine of present-day Iran, possessed a delicate subtlety (cf. Athenaeus XII.545e).

Let us emphasize the variety of oils as well (no. 41–46). Ctesias says that an acanthus oil was made in Carmania for the king, and Amyntas noted that in Persia "the mountains produce turpentine [pistachio], squills, and Persian nuts, from which much oil is made for the king" (Athenaeus II.67a◇). On the other hand, Ctesias mentions neither pepper nor vinegar, even though the latter is listed by Polyaenus (no. 62). The last striking thing about Polyaenus's text is the considerable profusion and diversity of condiments and aromatic herbs (nos. 25–26, 28, 30–33, 38–41, 51–52, 63). This is not surprising when we realize their importance to the Persians for medicinal use (p. 266), which does not differ fundamentally from their culinary use. One of these herbs is noteworthy: the terebinth, from which oil is obtained (no. 43; nearly 50 liters). This refers to pistachio nuts, which were very popular among the Persians. Strabo mentions it specifically among the plants that the young people had to learn to recognize (XV.3.18). We also know that it was included in the diet of a crown prince who was preparing to be proclaimed king (Plutarch, *Art.* 3.2). Nicolaus of Damascus records the Medes' pejorative judgment on the Persians, characterizing them as "terebinth-eaters" (*FGrH* 90 F66.34).

The variety of dishes is stressed by Herodotus, who contrasts it with Greek practices:

> The main dishes at their meals are few, but they have many sorts of dessert (*epiphorēmata*), the various courses being served separately. It is this custom that has made them say that the Greeks leave the table hungry, because we never have anything worth mentioning after the first course: they think that if we did, we should go on eating. (1.133◇)

Actually, the ancient authors give several examples of Greeks who were invited by Persians (the Persians call them "barbarian" buffoons!) and stuffed themselves to such an extent that one of them alone ate what had been prepared for the satrap Ariobarzanes and his nine guests (Athenaeus X.413a–c; cf. X.415f). Even Ctesias (if it's the same Ctesias) was famous for gluttony (Aelian, *VH* I.27). Consider also Pharaoh Tachos, who took pains to imitate the Great King—and died of indigestion (Aelian, *VH* V.1)! But, contrary to Greek popular opinion (cf. Aelian, *Anim.* II.11), Heraclides states that the portions taken by the Great King's guests were relatively modest (Athenaeus IV.145e; cf. Strabo XV.3.22). This obviously does not mean that there were no Persians who could be mocked for their dietary habits: one of a dozen men famous for gluttony listed by Aelian (I.27) was a Persian, Cantibaris, who never closed his mouth and whose servants were instructed to shovel the food "into him as into a lifeless vessel" (Athenaeus XV.416b◇)!

Aside from these charming anecdotes, Herodotus's text includes an interesting element on the organization of the meal: the side-dishes were served (as they should be) throughout the meal, punctuating the presentations of the main courses. These side-dishes certainly were included in the hundred dishes served daily by the Paphlagonian prince Thuys, who boasted of setting a table as luxurious as the Great King's (Athenaeus IV.144f). The Persians' sweet tooth is also stressed by Xenophon (who obviously takes it as another argument proving their decadence): "Whatever sorts of bread and pastry for the table had been discovered before, none of those have fallen into disuse, but they keep on always inventing something new besides; and it is the same way with meats; for in both branches of cookery they actually have artists to invent new dishes" (*Cyr.* VIII.8.16◇). Polyarchus praised the "many kinds of cakes" invented by the Persians (Athenaeus XII.545e◇). The honey listed by Polyaenus (no. 50) was probably used for the preparation of these cakes.

The Persians also enjoyed many fruits: dates (Aelian, *VH* I.33), pomegranates (I.33), and figs (Dinon apud Athenaeus XIV.652b–c; Plutarch, *Mor.* 173c), as well as apples (no. 27), raisins (no. 29), and almonds (no. 46). Additionally, a Persepolis tablet reports

Fig. 40. Servants waiting on tables: Persepolis (small staircase south of the Tripylon).

the variety of fruit trees planted in the royal paradises (PFa 33: quince trees, pear trees, etc.; cf. also PFa 1). The Greeks surely knew this, since they transplanted many shrubs from the Near East during the Persian period, such as arbutuses, mulberry bushes, pomegranate trees, and doubtless many others. This is evident in a letter sent to Gadatas rewarding him for planting trees native to Ebir Nāri in Asia Minor (ML 12).

"The Persians "are very fond of wine," Herodotus remarks (I.133◊), and in this he is followed by all of the ancient authors. Cambyses was particularly notorious in this department (Herodotus III.34), and Cyrus the Younger boasted of holding his wine better than his brother Artaxerxes (Plutarch, *Art.*, 6.1). The quantities given by Polyaenus are not particularly high, however (no. 47: about 50,000 liters), if we keep in mind distribution to the soldiers. It is true that the king himself drank a special wine reserved for him (Poseidonius and Heraclides apud Athenaeus IV.145c and I.28d; Strabo XV.3.22). Herodotus mentions this in connection with the *symposia* [drinking feasts], as do Aelian (*VH* XII.1) and Strabo: "They carry on their most important deliberations when drinking wine" (XV.3.20◊). According to Heraclides, it was the same during the *symposia* organized around the king after dinner with his select drinking companions (*sympotoi*; Athenaeus IV.145c). They would go home drunk, he writes, on the model of the drinking companions of Holophernes (Judith 12:20; 13:1). We may presume that the palm wine served during the court's stay at Susa and Babylon would have had the same effect!

Service at the King's Table

The ancient authors also stress the proliferation of domestic staff who specialized in waiting on tables, who are also represented on stairways at Susa and Persepolis (fig. 40).

Xenophon tries not to omit any of the palace servants: "bakers, cooks, cup-bearers, . . . butlers, waiters" (*Cyr.* VIII.8.20◊). The writers concentrate a great deal of their attention on personnel when they describe the Persian kings' and generals' tents. Actually, when the king and court were on the road, the entire kitchen staff went with them: pantry chiefs, cupbearers (Xenophon, *Anab.* IV.4.21), head bakers and provisioners (Plutarch, *Alex.* 23.5), bakers and cooks (Herodotus IX.82), "female cooks" (VII.186–87◊), in short "troops of sutlers and batmen" (Quintus Curtius III.3.25◊).

From this point of view the most interesting (because it is the most precise) text, once more, is a passage from Athenaeus. We know that, before the battle of Issus, Darius took care to leave all of his baggage at Damascus—that is, the women and children and all of the impedimenta that would slow down the army on its march and that one would want to protect from possible pillaging (cf. esp. Quintus Curtius III.13): everything the Greeks called the *aposkeuē* (Athenaeus XIII.607f). After the battle, Parmenion was instructed to take Damascus, which he soon did. He then ordered specialist officials to take inventory, as was normal in such circumstances (Xenophon, *Cyr.* VII.4.12–13; 57; Athenaeus IX.393c; XI.784a–b; cf. Plutarch, *Crassus* 17.9). Thanks to Athenaeus's recounting of the story, we have the unusual opportunity of consulting a quotation from this original accounting document. The quotation is partial: due to the structure of his work, Athenaeus provides only the data relating to kitchen and banquet personnel, as well as a sample of the dishes seized at Damascus (XI.781f–782). Here is the enumeration found in the *Letter of Parmenion* (XIII.608a):

Royal concubine musicians (*mousourgoi*)	329
Chaplet-weavers (*stephanoklopoi*)	46
Cooks (*opsopoioi*)	277
Young kitchen helpers (*khytrepsoi*)	29
Cooks who specialize in dairy dishes (*galaktourgoi*)	13
Beverage-preparers (*potematopoioi*)	17
Wine filterers (*oinoēthētoi*)	70
Perfume makers (*myropoioi*)	14
Total	795

We see that job specialization was well established, even within the category of cooks, young kitchen assistants, and other preparers. The waiters should be added to all of these domestics, of whom Heraclides states: "All who attend upon the Persian kings when they dine first bathe themselves and then serve in white clothes, and spend nearly half the day on preparations for the dinner" (IV.145b✧).

Musicians, Dancers, and Artists

It is not surprising that royal dinners were not confined to taking nourishment. They made an important social and political statement and had much symbolic value. The king's table, truly a symbol of the king's power (see chap. 5/6 above), was the preeminent place for gift-giving and royal largesse. In other words, in Persia as elsewhere, the banquet was a festival in every sense of the word, which at the Great King's court was organized according to the most meticulous rules of protocol. It was a festival organized around the royal person.

This explains the presence of women musicians and other artists who were placed in charge of the festival in Parmenion's inventory. They were an integral part of a banquet (cf. Athenaeus II.48f), just as much as the perfumes and the crowns (Nepos, *Ages.* 8.2). Did not Artaxerxes II honor the Spartan Antalcidas in a very special way by sending him "his own chaplet after dipping it in perfume" (Athenaeus II.48e✧)? In his well-known description of royal meals, Heraclides states that "throughout the dinner his concubines sing and play the lyre; one of them is the soloist, the others sing in chorus" (Athenaeus IV.145c✧). Similarly, Annaros, whom Ctesias portrays as the governor of Babylonia (in a romance that is highly suspect on historical grounds), imitated Artaxerxes by employing

150 women who played the harp and sang throughout the dinner (XII.530d). Likewise, Straton of Sidon occupied his time "drinking and listening to harp-singers and rhapsodists." For this purpose "he used to summon . . . many singing-girls from Ionia, besides girls from every part of Greece, some of whom were singers, some dancers" (XII.531a–b). The musicians (*mousourgoi*) captured by Parmenion were flutists and harpists (XIII.607f). The practice was well enough known to justify entering the word *mosargoi* in the dictionary of the *Suda*, which defines them as musicians specializing in the flute, which they play while others sing; they stop singing when the king drinks, returning to their songs and harmonies when the guests' drinks are poured.

Many other artists entertained the fellow diners, as shown by the accounts of the wedding feast given at Susa by Alexander. According to Polycleitus, male and female flutists always accompanied Alexander, drinking in his company (Athenaeus XII.539a). During the five-day banquet at Susa, Alexander and his guests applauded the famed Indian jugglers, as well as many Greek artists: lyric singers, harpists, flutists, singers, and dancers (XII.538e–f). At Artaxerxes II's court, Ctesias says, Zeno the Cretan was the king's favorite dancer (I.22d). We can understand Polyarchus's envious admiration, emphasizing the variety of spectacles and concerts that punctuated the Great Kings' court life (Athenaeus XII.545f)!

In fact, the most famous artists of the known world were summoned (cf. Herodotus III.137), and they appeared before the king and courtiers, but not necessarily during the banquets. We are put in mind of the athlete Polydamas in Greece:

> But this man . . . is the tallest of our own era. . . . Darius [II] . . . learning when he was king of the exploits of Polydamus, sent messengers with the promise of gifts and persuaded him to come before his presence at Susa. There he challenged three of the Persians called Immortals to fight him—one against three—and killed them. (Pausanias VI.5.7✧)

When he returned to Greece the athlete's great deed was engraved on a stone and depicted on a stela, both of which were placed at Olympia; the stela showed the hero in full action before the king seated on his throne.

Cups and Couches

The royal Persian banquet was surrounded with untold luxury. The Greek authors were particularly struck by the richness of the dishes and cups. In another extract from the *Letter of Parmenion*, Athenaeus quotes the inventory of cups: "Gold cups, weight seventy-three Babylonian talents, fifty-two minae; cups inlaid with precious stones, weight fifty-six Babylonian talents, thirty-four minae (XI.781f–782a✧ [Loeb p. 39]). Elsewhere, as we have seen, he mentions an inventory, sent by Cleomenes to Alexander, perhaps a description for Alexander of the very luxurious royal Persian furnishings found at Memphis that were now in Alexander's possession (cf. Quintus Curtius IV.7.4). As always, Athenaeus's quotation of Cleomenes is abbreviated; Athenaeus selected only the details useful to him at the moment, which in this case was a very long discussion of the various names of drinking vessels. The quotation goes:

> 3 silver *batiakai*, gilded; silver *kondya* 176; of these thirty-three are gilded. One silver *tisigitēs*. Silver spoons, gilded, thirty-two. One silver flask-castor. One ornamented silver wine-container of native manufacture (*barbarikon*). Other small cups of every variety, twenty-nine; drinking-horns, gilded *batiakai* made in Lycia, censers (*thymiatēria*), and bowls. (XI.784a–b✧[Loeb p. 53])

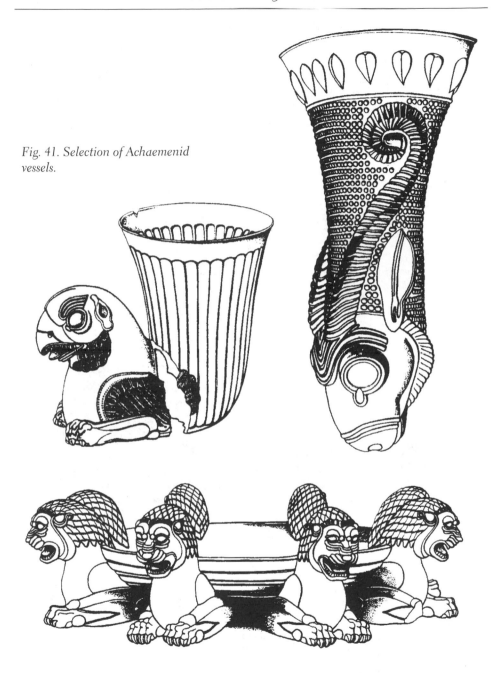

Fig. 41. Selection of Achaemenid vessels.

Athenaeus included explanations of the vessels' names that were unfamiliar to the ears of his Greek readers. The *batiakē* is a Persian vial, he writes (XI.784a). He goes on to describe the vessel called *labrōnia*, so named (in his opinion!) "from the violence (*labrotēs*) which arises in drinking. In design it is flat and large; it also has large handles" (XI.484c◇ [Loeb p. 151]). One author speaks of a *labrōnios* weighing 200 *chrysoi*;

another vessel of this type was said to weigh 120 *chrysoi* (XI.484d–e). The reference to censers (*thymiatēria*) is interesting. They are often shown on Achaemenid reliefs and seals, especially the Persepolis audience reliefs. Elsewhere, Athenaeus mentions them among banquet paraphernalia, along with perfumes, many kinds of garments and carpets, cups, and other utensils (XII.545e). Among the Persian-type cups, the *sannakra* (XI.497e), the *kondy* (XI.478a), and even the *prokhoïs*, are also listed by Athenaeus (XI.496c), who cites Xenophon (*Cyr.* VIII.8.10✧), who wrote in his chapter on "Persian decadence":

> They also had the custom of not bringing [chamber] pots (*prokhoïdes*) into their banquets, evidently because they thought that if one did not drink to excess, both mind and body would be less uncertain. So even now the custom of not bringing in the pots still obtains, but they drink so much that, instead of carrying anything in, they are themselves carried out when they are no longer able to stand straight enough to walk out.

The originator of Athenian New Comedy, Menander, is again quoted by Athenaeus (XI.484c–d✧); in two of his plays, Menander takes inventory of the riches the Macedonians found in the wealthy Persian treasury in Cindya in Cilicia:

> We're living high, and I don't mean moderately; we have gold from Cyinda; purple robes from Persia lie in piles; we have in our house, gentlemen, embossed (*toreumata*) vessels, drinking-cups, and other silver ware, and masks in high relief, goat-stag (*tragelaphoi*) drinking horns, and *labronioi* . . . beakers set with gems and *labrōnia* (were brought in), and Persians stood there holding fly-flaps.

These texts describe the Persian dinnerware abundantly found here and there, including in the Persepolis and Susa deposits. They refer explicitly to the engravings and animal decorations regularly exhibited on the cups that wealthy Persians drank from, except for (1) those who had been demoted, whom the king forced to use a ceramic cup (Athenaeus XI.464a), and (2) the king, who drank from a special egg-shaped cup (*ōion*), according to Dinon (XI.503f). The Greeks were even more familiar with Persian dinnerware because they managed to capture it several times. In a passage that would do an Oscar-winning Hollywood screenwriter proud, Quintus Curtius describes the pillaging of Darius III's Treasury at Issus:

> The Persians call men who carry burdens on their shoulders *gangabae*; these, since they could not endure the severity of the weather—for a storm had suddenly brought a fall of snow and the ground was stiff being then bound in frost—put on the robes adorned with gold and purple, which they were carrying with the money, and no one dared to forbid them, since the ill-fortune of Darius gave licence over him even to the lowest of men. . . . Scattered over all the fields lay the king's riches, the money designed for the pay of a great force of soldiers, the adornments of so many men of high rank, of so many illustrious women, golden vases, golden bridles, tents adorned with regal splendour, chariots too, abandoned by their owners and filled with vast riches. . . . hands of the ravishers were not sufficient to carry the spoil. (III.13.7–11✧)

This passage by Quintus Curtius can easily be compared with Diodorus's (XVII.75) and another of his own (Quintus Curtius V.6.3–8) descriptions of the looting of Persepolis by Alexander's soldiers. In the wreckage of the Persian navy in 480, a Greek "picked up a large number of gold and silver drinking-cups which were washed ashore, and included among his finds Persian treasure-chests and innumerable other pieces of valuable property" (Herodotus VII.190✧). The booty was so attractive that "the most accomplished diver of his day . . . after the wreck of the Persian ships at Pelium had saved agrteat deal of valuable property for his masters—besides getting a good deal for himself" (VIII.8✧)! It was the same in Mardonius's tent, which was filled "with its embroidered hangings and gorgeous decorations in silver and gold" (IX.82✧): in the Persian camp they found "tents full of gold and silver furniture; couches overlaid with the same precious metals; bowls, goblets, and cups, all of gold; and waggons loaded with sacks full of gold and silver basins" (IX.80✧). Likewise, Tiribazus's tent was looted, "with silver-footed couches in it, and drinking cups, and people who said they were his bakers and his cup-bearers" (Xenophon, *Anab.* IV.4.21✧). At Persepolis, according to Quintus Curtius (V.6.5✧), the soldiers "broke with mattocks vases of priceless art."

The Persians took their meals reclining on wonderfully ornate couches, such as the one given by Artaxerxes II to the Cretan Entimus, with all the accessories needed to indicate that he was a favorite: "A silver-footed bed with its coverings, a tent with gaily-coloured canopy, a silver throne, a gilded sun-shade, twenty gold saucers set with jewels, one hundred large saucers of silver, and silver mixing-bowls, one hundred concubines and one hundred slaves . . ." (Athenaeus II.48f✧). There were rugs and cushions on these couches, arranged by a specialist, which is why the king added to the valuable linens "a slave to spread them, alleging that the Greeks did not know how to make a bed" (II.48d✧). In fact, said Heraclides, "the Persians were the first . . . to institute the so- called 'bed-makers' (*strōtai*), in order to secure beauty and softness in the coverings" (II.✧48d). In this matter, too, protocol reserved a distinction for the king: during *symposia*, "his fellow-drinkers (*sympotoi*) sit on the floor, while he reclines on a couch supported by feet of gold" (Athenaeus IV.145c✧), ground that no doubt was provided with comfortable rugs (cf. Xenophon, *Cyr.* VIII.8.16; *Hell.* IV.1.30)! At the wedding in Susa, the guests' couches were silver, but Alexander's couch had gold legs (Athenaeus XII.538c).

6. *The Royal Hunts*

As in every court in the ancient Near East (and elsewhere), kings loved long hunting parties. Clearly they represented one of the privileged loci for aristocratic and court sociability, as symbolized by the thorough training that young Persians received (Strabo XV.3.18). Depictions of the hunt are innnumerable on Achaemenid stamps and stelas.

In one of the many hunting scenes that Xenophon liked so much, he shows the young Cyrus "exhaust[ing] the supply of animals in the park (*paradeisos*) by hunting and shooting and killing them, so that Astyages was no longer able to collect animals for him" (I.4.5✧). Hunts actually took place either in open spaces or in enclosed paradises, as at Dascylium (*Hell.* IV.1.15). At Celaenae in Greater Phrygia, "Cyrus had a palace and a large park full of wild animals, which he used to hunt on horseback whenever he wished to give himself and his horses exercise" (*Anab.* I.2.7✧). The paradises were centers for horticultural experimentation and living symbols of the fertility of the king (chap. 6/5); they also constituted hunting reserves, such as the one in Sogdiana described by Quintus Curtius:

> There are no greater indications of the wealth of the barbarians in those regions than their herds of noble wild beasts, confined in great woods and parks. For this purpose they choose extensive forests made attractive by perennial springs; they surround the woods with walls (*muris nemora cinguntur*), and have towers as stands for the hunters. (VIII.1.11–12✧)

This was also true of the paradise near Ecbatana; guards were stationed at the entrance (VII.2.28). These paradises were quite large. We know this because Cyrus the Younger held a review of his troops in the paradise of Celaenae involving 13,000 men in all (Xenophon, *Anab.* I.2.9) and because Alexander could dine in the Sogdiana paradise with his entire army (Quintus Curtius VIII.1.19). There must have been a considerable number of captive beasts, since, according to Quintus Curtius (VIII.1.19), Alexander and his party killed no less than 4,000. The Macedonians probably borrowed this practice from the Persians:

> The members of the royal house of Macedon had always been devoted to hunting, and the Macedonians had reserved the most suitable areas for breeding game. These districts during the war had been as carefully preserved as formerly, but had never been hunted for four years owing to the exigencies of the times, so there was an abundance of big game of every kind. . . . Aemilius . . . placed the royal huntsmen (*hoi kynegoi basilikoi*) at Scipio's disposal, and gave him complete control over the preserves. (Polybius XXXI.29.1–5◊)

Aristocratic ethics did not exclude the use of traps (cf. Polyaenus VII.14.1). We also know that during their horsemanship training young Persians learned to make human hunting "nets" (Strabo XV.3.18). There is a vivid example of this kind of hunt in Herodotus. Here is how he claims the Persians lowered the resistance of the Greeks at the end of the Ionian revolt:

> Each island, as soon as it was occupied, was gone through with the drag-net—a process in which men join hands and make a chain right across the island from north to south, and then move from one end to the other, hunting everybody out. (VI.31◊)

It seems obvious that the Persians employed a technique in war that was borrowed from the hunt, with its hunters and beaters. Furthermore, the Assyrian reliefs often show hunting with this type of net.

Every royal hunt thus required meticulous preparation, probably carried out under the direction of specialized officials, those whom the author of the *De Mundo* (398a◊) calls "leaders in war and hunting." They had to choose the animals—fed and prepared in select groups (Plutarch, *Alex.* 73.6)—then free them from the cages where they were kept, as we see being done on Assyrian reliefs. They also had to gather the hunting dogs (fig. 42). There were thus many participants at various levels with various jobs, as seen in an episode in the *Cyropedia*: "[Astyages] took [Cyrus] out to hunt; he had got the boys together, and a large number of men both on foot and on horseback, and when he had driven the wild animals out into country where riding was practicable, he instituted a great hunt" (*Cyr.* I.4.14◊). The author emphasizes the security requirements: "[Astyages] let [Cyrus] go out with his uncle and he sent along some older men on horseback to look after him, to keep him away from dangerous places and guard him against wild beasts in case any should appear" (I.4.7◊). It is true that at the time Cyrus was very young and the hunt was taking place in an open space.

Finally, there is the matter of the hunt's royal escort. Even in this situation, there was selectivity among the court nobles: it was a signal honor to be chosen as a hunting companion; Themistocles says: "The king invited him to partake of his own pastimes and recreations both at home and abroad, carrying him with him a-hunting" (Plutarch, *Them.* 29.6◊). The king was surrounded by his most faithful companions (or so he thought: Aelian VI.14). He was surely also accompanied by his bodyguards, since on the hunt the king was more vulnerable than elsewhere. Two court histories report attempts on a king's

Fig. 42. Dogs used in the hunt and in battle by the Assyrians.

life during a hunt (Herodotus III.30; Aelian VI.14). To render the solemnity of the moment still more striking, the king was undoubtedly accompanied by a large escort. Heraclides even claims that he did not go out without his concubines (Athenaeus XII.514c)!

7. *Royal Pomp*

As we keep stressing, the preceding pages are based essentially on the Greek sources, which in some cases can be compared with Persian or "Greco-Persian" iconographic evidence. Two currents can be distinguished in the Greeks' interpretation of the luxury of the royal court. One is represented by Xenophon. In the *Cyropedia*, he analyzes each element of protocol in terms of obsessive concern for the Great King's security, whether it was the institution of the eunuchs, the protocol of the royal table, the audience, or whatever. No doubt this sort of preoccupation was always present. But by constantly referring to security, Xenophon in a way offers his readers a very limited vision, only occasionally mentioning the royal desire to communicate the image of a man above men (e.g., VIII.1.40–42; 3.4, 14).

For most of the Greek authors, the untold splendor of the palace and the rigidity of court protocol constituted first and foremost a striking manifestation of Persian *tryphē* ('luxury'), setting a precedent and example for everyone else: "The first men in history to become notorious for luxurious living were the Persians." Athenaeus sees proof in the nomadism of the Achaemenid court (XII.513e–f◊). In order to animate his account with real-life examples, he has a long discussion in which he quotes a large number of authors who looked into the question (514a–515a◊). These pages represent a sort of dense summary of Greek information on the Persian court, which it is advisable to review here.

Dinon mentions the *labyzos*, a highly aromatic substance more costly than myrrh with which the Great King's hair was done, as one of the visible marks of this *tryphē*. He also mentions the footstool the king regularly used when he descended from his chariot (p. 221). Heraclides states that the king was never supposed to be seen walking on foot in his palace; he only did so to cross the court of the *mēlophoroi*, and even then he walked on carpets that were reserved for him: "When he reached the last court he would mount his chariot, or sometimes his horse." Heraclides also mentions particularly luxurious objects: the footstool, the royal throne made of gold whose four small columns were encrusted with jewels and over which was thrown a rich cloth embroidered with purple. Agathocles mentions the vase containing "water called 'golden'" reserved for the king and his eldest son (see p. 521). Chares of Mytilene describes the famous Golden Vine (p. 235), as does Amyntas, who also mentions a superb gold crater, the work of Theodorus of Samos. Clearchus refers to the eunuchs (whom the Medes/Persians gathered from neighboring peoples), and Heraclides the concubines who accompanied the king on his hunts and charmed his nights. Finally, as absolute proof of unlimited, enervating *tryphē*, Chares speaks of locked Treasuries in rooms that opened onto the royal chamber ("royal pillow" and "royal footstool"; see p. 469). Elsewhere, Athenaeus quotes Aristoxenus's *Life of Archytas*, which refers to Polyarchus, who was famous for his appetite for joys of the flesh. To work out his discourse on the theme of pleasure and *tryphē*, Polyarchus cites the example of the Great King, describing "the comforts enjoyed by the king of Persia . . . , his indulgence in sexual pleasures, the perfumed odour of his body, his elegance and manners of conversation, the spectacles and the entertainments by artists," and he states that, from his point of view, "the king of Persia was the happiest man of the times" (XII.545f◊).

We clearly see that the ancient authors filtered their information through the sieve of their own obsessions—hence the abundance and number of descriptions of the royal table and references to the *pallakai*. Not one of them makes the slightest allusion to the Persepolis reliefs, not even Diodorus, the only one who gives a description of the terrace and palaces (XVII.71.3–8). This choice allowed them to capture the interest of their potential readers, all the while working out their preferred discourse, in which peremptory judgments on the ineluctable dissipating effect of wealth mingled with spellbound admiration for the luxury and might of the Great King. Nevertheless, and in spite of their prejudice and their observational nearsightedness, their accounts also testify to the reality of royal splendor that was enacted daily according to the script of the court regulations. For, in the eyes of the Great Kings themselves, the luxury of the palace, the profusion of Treasuries, the splendor of the festivals, and the richness of the tapestries and clothing were a mark of their ostentatious power. This is just how Heraclides of Pontus understands it in his work *On Pleasure* (*Peri Hēdonēs*), where he provocatively takes on the dominant theory:

> Tyrants and kings, being in control the good things of life, and having had experience of them all, put pleasure in the first place, since pleasure makes men's natures more lordly. All persons, at any rate, who pay court to pleasure and choose a life of luxury are lordly and magnificent, like the Persians and the Medes. For more than any other men in the world they court pleasure and luxury, yet they are the bravest and most lordly of the barbarians. Indeed to have pleasure and luxury is a mark of the freeborn; it eases their minds and exalts them; but to live laborious lives is the mark of slaves and of men of low birth. (Athenaeus XII.512a–b◊)

The same interpretation is found in Plutarch, in a discussion derived directly from the propaganda of Artaxerxes II's court:

The king . . . upon this journey made it appear plainly that cowardice and effeminacy are the effects, not of delicate and sumptuous living, as many suppose, but of a base and vicious nature, actuated by false and bad opinions. For notwithstanding his golden ornaments, his robe of state, and the rest of that costly attire, worth no less than twelve thousand talents, with which the royal person was constantly clad, his labours and toils were not a whit inferior to those of the meanest persons in his army. (*Art.* 24.9–10◆)

In other words, *tryphē* is not reducible to decadent luxury; it is, rather, a striking sign of royal power.

By insisting on the rules of court protocol, the ancient authors do not fundamentally misrepresent reality. All of their details reveal a symbolic Achaemenid vision: whatever he did (walk, sleep, eat, hunt, make love, etc.), the Great King distinguished himself and wanted to distinguish himself from the common mortal. The Greek misunderstanding regarding the divinity of the Great King is understandable. He was a being apart, to whom unlimited respect and submission were due. Court protocol existed to burn this permanently into memory, especially the rules for royal audiences and a table etiquette that reserved a ceremonial couch, special cup, water and wine reserved for his own use, and waiters previously purified by a bath and wearing a white robe. All in all, the Classical authors in their own way have provided a magnificent, lively commentary on court life and royal splendor, or at least they have made it possible for us to do so. For this reason, we would like to suggest to the Great King that—just as he did for Antalcidas—he send Athenaeus and Aelian "his own chaplet after dipping it in perfume"!

Chapter 8

The King's Men

We have seen through text and image that the exaltation of the king's person is a constant theme in the mainstream of the Classical sources. Aristotle, although he does not mention it explicitly, clearly includes the Achaemenid monarchy in the category he calls *pambasileia* 'absolute monarchy', which was found, he writes, "among certain barbarian peoples." Like so many of his contemporaries, he believed that, because the barbarians' character inclines them more to servility than the Hellenes, and the Asiatics more than the Europeans, they endure despotic rule with nary a complaint (Aristotle, *Pol.* VII.6). Within the structure of this *pambasileia*, the king wielded universal authority in obedience to nothing but "his own will" (Aristotle, *Pol.* VII.7). This interpretation streams from the pen or the lips of many Greeks. Among many examples, we may simply note the remark that Xenophon attributes to Jason of Pherae in the context of a stereotypical speech intended to prove that the conquest of the Achaemenid Empire was simple: "I know that everybody there, save one person, has trained himself to servitude (*douleia*) rather than to prowess (*alkē*)" (Xenophon, *Hell.* VI.1.12◇).

In a way, the picture obtained from the Greeks is not much different from the picture that Darius and his successors sought to establish in text and image. But both pictures tend to reduce the problem to the person of the king alone, whether denouncing the despotic regime or exalting the virtues of the man who was able to govern so many peoples and countries thanks to his uncommon virtue. It is obvious that the historian cannot be satisfied with these ideologized approaches. It is important to pose more concretely the problem of the relationships between the king and those who served him and held the highest positions in the Empire.

1. The Giving King

The Royal Statements

On several occasions, Darius and Xerxes give voice to another quality of the good king: he shows favor to those who have aided him or who can be expected to aid him in the course of time. With reference to 'justice' (*arstam*), which guides all his actions, Darius at Behistun exclaims, "The man who cooperated with my house (*viθ*), him I rewarded well; whoso did injury, him I punished well" (*DB* §63◇). He also adjures his successors not to be a friend "of the man who shall be a Lie-follower or who shall be a doer of wrong—. . . punish them well" (§64◇). Likewise, at Naqš-i Rustam: "What a man does or performs according to his powers, (therewith) I am satisfied, and my pleasure is abundant, and I am well satisfied" (*DNb* §8e◇), as well as in Xerxes' parallel inscription: "And I generously repay men of good will" (*XPl* 26–31). The benefits awarded to the men of good will frequently are the protection of Ahura-Mazda and "family in abundance" (*DB* §§60◇–61, §§66◇–67). This recalls the words that Herodotus ascribes to Cambyses on his deathbed, when he adjured those close to him to defeat Smerdis the

302

usurper: "If you do as I bid you, I pray that the earth may be fruitful for you, your wives bear you children, your flocks multiply" (Herodotus III.65✧).

The King's Benefactors

A well-known story of benefaction in the Persian court appears in the biblical book of Esther:

> That night, the king could not sleep; he called for the Record Book, the Chronicles, to be brought and read to him. They contained an account of how Mordecai had denounced . . . two of the king's eunuchs serving as Guardians of the Threshold, who had plotted to assassinate king Ahasuerus. "And what honour and dignity," the king asked, "was conferred on Mordecai for this?" "Nothing has been done for him" . . . [Haman said to the king:] "If the king wishes to honour someone, have royal robes brought, which the king has worn, and a horse which the king has ridden, with a royal diadem on his head. The robes and horse should be handed to one of the noblest of the king's officers, and he should array the man whom the king wishes to honour and lead him on horseback through the city square, proclaiming before him: 'This is the way to treat a man whom the king wishes to honour.'" (Esther 6:1–9✧)

Another story is told by Herodotus. He records that, during the battle of Salamis, Xerxes followed the progress of the fighting from the shore: "Xerxes watched the course of the battle from the base of Mt. Aegaleos, across the strait from Salamis; whenever he saw one of his officers behaving with distinction, he would find out his name, and his secretaries (*hoi grammateis*) wrote it down (*anegraphon*), together with his city and parentage" (Herodotus VIII.90✧; cf. Plutarch, *Them.* 13.1). These are the conditions under which, for instance, Theomestor "was invested by the Persians with the lordship of Samos, and Phylacus was enrolled in the catalogue of the King's Benefactors (*euergetēs basileōs anegraphē*) and presented with a large estate," and Herodotus adds this detail: "The Persian word for King's Benefactors is *orosangae*" (Herodotus VIII.85✧). Whatever the linguistic and etymological reality may be, the reference to a Persian word implies the existence of a recognized court category.

It is clear, then, that there was a register at court in which the names of those who had received the title of Benefactor were written. In a letter he sent to Gadatas, Darius congratulates him on his horticultural achievements, and he states: "For that, you will receive great recognition (*megalē charis*) in the king's house" (ML 12). Likewise in a letter (perhaps) sent by Xerxes to Pausanias of Sparta: "An obligation (*euergesia*) is laid up for you in our house, recorded forever (*es aiei anagraptos*)" (Thucydides I.129.3✧). These are the conditions under which Syloson the Samian went to find Darius shortly after his accession: "He hurried to Susa, sat down at the entrance of the royal palace, and claimed to be included in the list of the King's Benefactors" (Herodotus III.140✧). Darius made the following statement to Coes (commander of a contingent from Mytilene), who had just given him good advice: "When I am safely home again, my Lesbian friend, . . . be sure to come and see me, so that I may make some practical return for your excellent counsel" (Herodotus IV.97✧). On his return from Sardis, Darius did indeed keep his promise (V.11). This is exactly the meaning of the story of the relationship between Ahasuerus and Mordecai as told by the redactor of Esther: when he learned from the Book of Benefactors of the services rendered by Mordecai, the king was astonished that the Jew of Susa had received no honor, and he soon took steps to repair the oversight (Esther 6).

These examples demonstrate the importance of performing a "good deed" under the very eyes of the king—"each striving to appear as deserving as he could in the eyes of Cyrus," remarks Xenophon (*Cyr.* VIII.1.39◇). On this account, the expedition of 480 represents a particularly significant example. For the Greek authors, the combats were veritable spectacles that unfolded before the king's eyes. From the beginning, the scenery and actors were set. At Abydos, they laid out a marble loggia from which Xerxes watched his army march past (Herodotus VII.44); then, at Doriscus, the king reviewed his troops (chap. 5/5 above). From then on, Xerxes was a perpetual spectator: "From the European shore Xerxes watched his troops coming over under the whips" (VII.56◇). At Thermopylae, he was seated on his throne, reacting with passion to the unpredictable turns of events in the combat (VIII.212). Diodorus also did not miss any opportunity to contrast the motives of the Greek soldiers with the Great King's: the former were prodigies of valor because they were infused with the desire to preserve their liberty; the barbarians, however, tried to distinguish themselves because "[they] had the king as a witness of their valour" (Diodorus XI.7.1◇). At Salamis, Xerxes chose "a spot . . . from which he could watch the course of the battle" (XI.18.3◇). He was accompanied by his secretaries, who recorded the names of valiant warriors (Herodotus VIII.86). The soldiers knew that the king's eyes were trained on them, which brought about extraordinary competition: "[They] entered into competition with each other to be the first to win a reward from Xerxes for the capture of an Athenian ship" (VIII.10◇). In fact, "every man of them did his best for fear of Xerxes, feeling that the king's eye was on him" (VIII.86◇). We get the impression that the silent dialogue between the king and his soldiers had a bearing on tactical considerations. Thus, during the escape after the battle: "those astern fell foul of them in their attempt to press forward and do some service for their king" (VIII.89◇). The successful outcome of a maneuver executed by the ship of Artemisia of Caria is particularly spicy: in order to disengage during the battle, she rammed a vessel of the royal fleet, but from the shore it appeared as though she had sunk an Athenian vessel—which "raised her . . . higher than ever in Xerxes' esteem" (VIII.88◇).

Even when the king was not present, people were sure that he would be kept informed: "It is for this reason that there were so many men who undertook to run such risks for Cyrus the Younger, thinking every time that he would know about it" (Xenophon, *Anab.* I.9.15). If the king did not learn it directly, one had to hope that the royal inspectors would bring the king a highly favorable report (Xenophon, *Oec.* IV.6–10). A courtier was always ready to portray his exploits in the most spectacular way, as the later example of Datames shows so well (Nepos, *Dat.* 3; chap. 5/5 above).

The Royal Gifts

The Greeks knew very well that entering the service of the Great King brought great opportunities for receiving gifts and presents in return (cf. Herodotus VII.134–37; VIII.5; IX.18, etc.). Xenophon endlessly revisits this feature of royal Achaemenid ideology and practice. This is how he puts it in the *Oeconomicus*: if the officers in charge of the garrisons and their troops do their work well, the king "promotes [them] in the scale of honour (*tais timais auxei*) and enriches with large grants of money (*dōra megala*)"; the others, however, "he punishes severely, and appoints others to take their office" (IV.7◇). The same was true for the officials in charge of keeping a territory in full production (IV.8). These are the sorts of assumptions on which Xenophon's idealized portrait of Cyrus the Younger is based:

But it was the brave in war, as all agree, whom he honored especially (*diapherontōs timas*)
. . . and whomsoever in his army he found willing to meet dangers, these men he would not
only appoint as rulers of the territory he was subduing, but would honour thereafter with
other gifts (*dōra*) also. . . . As for uprightness, if a man showed that he desired to distinguish
himself in that quality, Cyrus considered it all important to enable such an one to live in
greater opulence than those who were greedy of unjust gain. . . . Again, so surely as a man
performed with credit any service that he assigned him, Cyrus never let his zeal go unrewarded. . . . And surely he of all men distributed gifts most generously among his friends,
with an eye to the tastes of each one and to whatever particular need he noted in each case.
(*Anab.* I.9.14–22✧)

It is clear that the following portrait of Cyrus the Younger is traced from the portrait that
Xenophon drew of Cyrus the Elder:

Though he far exceeded all other men in the amount of the revenues he received, yet he
excelled still more in the quantity of presents he made. It was Cyrus, therefore, who began
the practice of lavish giving (*polydōria*), and among the kings it continues even to this day.
For who has richer friends (*philoi*) to show than the Persian king? Who is there that is
known to adorn his friends with more beautiful robes than does the king? Whose gifts are so
readily recognized as some of those which the king gives, such as bracelets, necklaces, and
horses with gold-studded bridles? For, as everybody knows, no one over there is allowed to
have such things except those to whom the king has given them. (*Cyr.* VIII.2.7–8✧)

These royal gifts were well known to the Greeks, who frequently benefited from
them. The Classical authors referred to them with such expressions as "which are most
prized amongst the Persians" (Herodotus III.160; cf. VII.8✧), "a thoroughly Persian gift"
(Herodotus IX.109✧), or "the highest honours, such as were customary [in Persia]" (Diodorus XV.11.2✧). They are sometimes more specific, as was Herodotus regarding
Otanes and his descendants: "Every year, a suit of Median clothes and such other gifts
as are held to be of most value by the Persians, as a mark of honour" (*tēn pasan dōreēn
. . . en Perséisi timiōtatēn*; III.84✧). In turn, Xenophon puts it thus: "Cyrus gave [Syenne-
sis] gifts which are regarded at court as tokens of honour—a horse with a gold-mounted
bridle, a gold necklace and bracelets, a gold dagger (*akinakēs*)" (*Anab.* I.2.27✧). As for
Ctesias (§22), he states that "the most outstanding gift the king can give among the Persians is a gold millstone" (*mylē khrysē*). We might wonder about the exact significance
of Ctesias's note, but the expression he uses fits perfectly into a series of cases that imply
the existence at the Persian court of a category of gifts, called royal, distinguished from
one another in a subtle hierarchy, and conferred on those whom the king wished to
honor for "good actions" (cf. Aelian, *VH* VIII.8).

Robes and jewelry are archetypal royal gifts frequently attested in the record. Xenophon's Cyrus often resorts to them. Before a major parade, he distributes Median robes
to "those of the Persians and of the allies who held office. . . . And when he had distributed among the noblest the most beautiful garments, he brought out other Median
robes, for he had had a great many made, with no stint of purple or sable or red or scarlet
or crimson cloaks," in such a way that in turn those close to him distributed them to their
friends (*Cyr.* VIII.3.1–3✧). It seems clear that the different colors referred to a hierarchy
defined by the king (cf. VIII.1.40): some jobs at the central court carried the right (and
no doubt the obligation) to wear special robes (Plutarch, *Alex.* 18.8 [*astandēs*]). It is no
less clear that wearing them permitted the recipients to vaunt themselves above other
Persians. Thus Mithradates, overwhelmed with gifts after the battle of Cunaxa, never

Fig. 43. Achaemenid jewelry.

appeared in public without the robe and jewelry that Artaxerxes gave him. Hence this
reflection by a eunuch—at once ironic, envious, and provocative: "A magnificent dress,
indeed, O Mithradates, is this which the king has given you; the chains and bracelets are
glorious, and your scimitar (*akinakēs*) of invaluable worth; how happy has he made you,
the object of every eye!" (Plutarch, *Art.* 15.2✧). Likewise Artapates, the most faithful of
Cyrus the Younger's scepter-bearers, "had a dagger (*akinakēs*) of gold, and he also wore
a necklace and bracelets and all the other ornaments that the noblest (*aristoi*) Persians
wear; for he had been honoured by Cyrus (*etimeto hypo Kyrou*) because of his affection
and fidelity" Xenophon, *Anab.* I.8.29✧). In Persian eyes, in fact, these robes and jewels
were not baubles; they were the resplendent marks of the king's favor granted to them in
return for services rendered. Wearing these ornaments meant accession to the rank of
Persians most esteemed by the king. Thus, the gift of a Median robe to the city of Acanthus by Xerxes in 480 (Herodotus VII.116) bore a rather different significance; the royal

gift was indeed symbolically charged, but its political implications were far from the practical realities of the Achaemenid court.

With all of the Persian nobles wearing sumptuous robes (e.g., *Anab.* I.5.8) and prize jewelry (e.g., Plutarch, *Cimon* 9.5), we should not be surprised that the ceremony of awarding gifts was held in public. Thus Megabyzus, to whom the king awarded a gift of honor (*geras*), is remembered with these words: "Darius had once paid this man a high compliment . . . it was in Persia that Darius paid him this compliment" (Herodotus IV.143◊). Further evidence is available from the story of Mordecai, who received a royal robe and a horse that "the king has ridden." In order to give its full social value to the royal gift, the king issued the following order: "Lead [Mordecai] through the city square, proclaiming before him: 'This is the way to treat a man whom the king wishes to honour'" (Esth 6:8–9◊). Another example of public acclaim is found in the story about Daiphernes' friend's appearance before "Cyrus":

> Cyrus gave him one of the horses that were being led in the procession and gave orders to one of the mace-bearers to have it led away for him wherever he should direct. And to those who saw it it seemed to be a mark of great honour, and as a consequence of that event many more people paid court to that man. (*Cyr.* VIII.3.23◊)

Perhaps it was the king who gave the gold breastplate to Masistius, the rider of a Nisaean horse bridled in gold, described by Herodotus (IX.20–21). The jewelry presented by the king probably bore a distinctive mark, because Xenophon mentions that "no one over there is allowed to have such things except those to whom the king has given them" (*Cyr.* VIII.2.7–8◊). The robes of honor must also have had various special markings, since according to Aelian (*VH* I.22) the "Median" robes given by the Great King were labeled "given as a present" ("dorophoric"). Aelian (*VH* I.22◊) records that court customs regulated the value of the gifts offered to the ambassadors sent to the Great King:

> The presents given by the king of Persia to envoys who came to see him, whether they came from Greece or elsewhere, were the following. Each received a Babylonian talent of silver coins and two silver cups weighing a talent each (the Babylonian talent is equivalent to 72 Attic minae). He gave them bracelets, a sword, and a necklace; these objects were worth 1,000 darics. In addition there was a Persian robe. The name of this robe was *dorophorikē*.

This text leaves the impression that the gifts of jewelry, precious vessels, and gold were calibrated not just according to their symbolic value but also in proportion to the weight of the precious metal from which they were made. There is also every indication that this custom did not hold only for diplomatic gifts. We need only recall the example of the simple Persian peasant who received from Artaxerxes II "a Persian robe, a golden cup, and a thousand darics" (*VH* I.32◊).

Gifts and Honors: The Court Hierarchy

Important as they were, robes and jewelry were but one element of the Great Kings' *polydōria*: Cyrus "used to reward with gifts (*dōra*) and positions of authority (*arkhai*) and seats of honour (*timai*) and all sorts of preferment (*hedrai*) others whom he saw devoting themselves most eagerly to the attainment of excellence (*ta kala*)" (*Cyr.* VIII.1.39◊). Nomination to a high position was in itself a mark of royal favor, as in the case of Xenagoras. He had just saved the life of Masistes, and this action won him "the favor (*kharis*) not only of Masistes himself, but also of Xerxes, whose brother he had saved; and he was rewarded for it by a gift from Xerxes of the governorship of the whole province of Cilicia" (Herodotus IX.107◊).

Obviously, court titles must be included in the category of privileges and honors. Court titles are unfortunately known only from allusions in the Classical sources. We know of "the Friends" (*philoi*); that this was an actual title is implied by the punishment inflicted on Orontes by Artaxerxes II—"exclusion from the company of his Friends" (Plutarch, *Art.* 11.2; cf. Xenophon, *Anab.* IV.4.4; Plutarch, *Art.* 24.9). There was even an internal hierarchy within the category of "Friends," based on the degree of royal favor (Diodorus XVI.52.1). To Histiaeus of Miletus, Darius promised, "Come with me to Susa. All I have will there be yours. You will eat at my table (*syssitos*) and be my counsellor (*symboulos*)" (Herodotus V.24◊). The Greek physician Democedes was himself Darius's Tablemate (*homotrapezos*) (III.131). High Persian aristocrats, such as Megabyzus, also held this title (Ctesias §41: *homotrapezos*).

"Friend" was certainly one of the most coveted court titles. We know in fact that, during certain festivals, many people gathered around the king for the banquet (Athenaeus IV.145c). An example is the banquet given by Ahasuerus in the third year of his reign: "He gave a banquet at his court for all his administrators and ministers" (Esth 1:3◊). This was probably also the case at the "Royal Supper" in honor of the king's birthday (Herodotus IX.110◊). This sort of public banquet is depicted several times by Xenophon in the *Cyropaedia* (cf. VIII.4.1–5). Heraclides' report (Athenaeus IV.145–46) shows that the king generally dined alone in a hall. Some invited guests (the *syndeipnoi*) dined outside, others—still more highly honored (146a; *hoi entimōtatoi tōn syndeipnōn*)—were served in a hall near the royal dining hall. The two halls were separated by a curtain that allowed the king to watch the other side but concealed him from their view. The first group nonetheless accrued considerable prestige, for they dined "in full sight of anyone who wishes to look on" (145b◊). Finally, at the end of the meal, just a dozen or so of the invited guests (the *sympotoi*) were summoned by name by a eunuch and came to a special room to drink in the company of the king—an exceptional honor, because it was during these *symposia* that important matters were discussed (Herodotus I.133; Strabo XV.3.20; Athenaeus IV.144b, V.102c).

It is not certain that the title *homotrapezos* 'Tablemate' was exactly the same as *syndeipnos* 'invited guest'. "Tablemate" was actually a title in the court hierarchy that conferred on its holder a preeminent place before the king. During the battle of Cunaxa, "a very few were left about" Cyrus the Younger, "chiefly his so-called table companions" (*oi homotrapezoi kaloumenoi*; *Anab.* I.8.25◊). The difference between 'Tablemate' and 'invited guest' is clarified by the case of Entimus, which Athenaeus distinguishes from the case of Timagoras. Entimus was invited to the 'luncheon of the Kinsmen' (*to syggenikon ariston*); Timagoras received something from the royal table every day (Athenaeus II.48e): "Not to mention the feast made for [Timagoras] at court, which was so princely and splendid" (Plutarch, *Art.* 22.6◊). Moreover, the two privileges were not mutually exclusive, for Entimus was not merely a *syndeipnos*; he also received necessities every day (Athenaeus II.49a).

This simple example proves that at court there definitely existed a hierarchy of honors. The available texts do not allow us to reconstruct it with certainty, although the title Friend seems to have assumed special importance. We must also beware of confusing titles and duties. Titles that we might expect to be granted to only one person were sometimes held by a great number of people. We must also remain aware of change over time, bearing in mind that most of the sources come from the reigns of Artaxerxes II and Darius III. However, we know from Plutarch that under Artaxerxes I "there happening great alterations . . . at court, and removals of the king's favourites" (*peri tēn aulēn kai tous philous; Them.* 29.5✧) at the start of his reign; other innovations were probably introduced by Artaxerxes II (chaps. 14/1; 15/3).

Also to be counted among exceptional honors was marriage to the king's daughter. We know specifically that Darius married his daughters or sisters to high aristocrats, such as Gobryas (Herodotus VII.2). In 499, the Persian forces in Asia Minor were commanded by three sons-in-law of Darius: Daurises, Hymaees, and Otanes (V.116); another son-in-law of Darius, Artochmes, was one of Xerxes' commanders in 480 (VII.73). Shortly before the battle of Salamis, the Greeks took several high Persian aristocrats (*epiphanoi*) prisoner; they included two (or three) sons of Sandauce, a daughter of Darius, and a daughter of Artayctes (Plutarch, *Them.* 13.2; *Arist.* 9.1–2).

A story told by Plutarch well illustrates the importance of matrimonial problems at court:

> Artaxerxes [II], having many daughters, promised to give Apama to Pharnabazus to wife, Rhodogune to Orontes, and Amestris to Teribazus; whom alone of the three he disappointed, by marrying Amestris himself. However, to make him amends, he betrothed his youngest daughter Atossa to him. But after he had, being enamoured of her too, as has been said, married her, Teribazus entertained an irreconcilable enmity against him. (*Art.* 27.7–9✧)

It is quite obvious that the status of king's son-in-law exalted the social position of a happy few. When Pausanias of Sparta concluded a treaty with Xerxes, he asked to marry one of Xerxes' daughters (Thuc. I.128). Without even receiving a reply on this matter, he considered himself nonetheless part of the inner circle of the dominant socioethnic class. These marriages are thus noteworthy because they clearly express the king's determination to take on and/or officially sanction the loyalty of the families so designated. But they granted no dynastic right to any sons to be born, as is shown by the arguments over the succession of Darius, reported (in his way) by Herodotus (VII.2–4). As it happens, the wife exchange was unequal, since the sons-in-law owed this familial promotion to the king himself: it was a kingly favor, at the king's sole discretion. The disbursal of his daughters constituted one of the elements of his power. Even assuming that he only gave his daughters to members of the highest nobility, anyone who sought to become his son-in-law would have been well advised to prove his devotion and his unfailing loyalty. The relationship was not an acquired right but a royal gift.

There can scarcely be any doubt that these sons-in-law fell into the category of Royal Kinsmen. This term (*syggeneis*) was itself integrated into the court hierarchy. At the time of Darius III, the Royal Kinsmen constituted a corps of elite horsemen, numbering 10,000, whose courage during the battle of Granicus is underlined by Diodorus (XVII.20.2). At Gaugamela, they fought beside the king (*synagōnisthai*), and Diodorus (XVII.59.2✧) explains the criteria for selection as follows: "These were men chosen for courage (*aretē*) and for loyalty (*eunoia*)." They were distinguished by their dress uniform: their lances bore golden apples, they are *mēlophoroi* (Arrian III.11.5). Among their well-known privileges was wearing the diadem; they also had the right to kiss the king on the lips—a sign of significant social achievement, since we know that for the Persians only men of equal rank (*isotimoi*) greeted each other in this way (Herodotus I.134; Strabo XV.3.20). In Darius III's procession, Quintus Curtius (III.3.14, 21) differentiates the *cognati* (numbering 15,000) from the the *propinquii* (numbering some 200); the latter (*nobilissimi propinquorum*) constituted the picked escort of the royal chariot, and obviously they were included among the various troop units (placed just after the Immortals). It is tempting to suppose that the *propinquii* represented the members and in-laws of the royal family, while the *cognati* corresponded to Diodorus's and Arrian's *syggeneis* (court title: *quos cognatos regis appellant*).

But when was this category of *syggeneis* created? The Royal Kinsmen are not attested with any certainty during the time of the first kings. The vocabulary of the Greek authors is necessarily ambiguous, mirroring the use of the term itself at court. In 479, Cimon besieged Eion, where there were "some great men (*andres endoxoi*) among the Persians, of the king's kindred" (*syggeneis basileōs*; Plutarch, *Cimon* 7.1✧); similarly at Byzantium, where there could be found "some connexions (*prosēkontes*) and kinsmen (*syggeneis*) of the king," whom Pausanias sent to Xerxes (Thucydides I.128.5✧). The first term clearly refers to family ties (cf. Xenophon, *Anab.* I.6.1). In a passage taken from Phaenias, Athenaeus reports that Entimus was invited "'to breakfast *en famille*" (*to syggenikon ariston*) during the time of Artaxerxes II (II.48f✧). But once again doubt remains, because Plutarch records that, along with his mother and his wife, the king invited his two brothers, his literal kinsmen, to the table (*Art.* 5.5). Was this an innovation by Artaxerxes II, or was it an arrangement used occasionally by all of the Great Kings (cf. Athenaeus IV.145d)? We may also note that several Aramaic and Akkadian texts (especially from the time of Darius II) refer to the Sons of the House (*br byt'/mār bīti*). This is the term used, for instance, to refer to Aršāma, satrap of Egypt (cf. *DAE* 62ff. [*AD* 1–13]). There we also find the phrase 'princes' (*bny byt'*). The two expressions correspond and render a title applied to exalted members of the royal entourage. But was this a real kinship or a court kinship? It is difficult to decide with certainty. In some Persepolis tablets, moreover, the term 'son of the [royal] house' (*misapuša*) indisputably refers to close relatives of Darius (PF 1793; cf. PFa 24, 29). Nonetheless, granting the title "Royal Kinsmen" even to in-laws implies an extension of the vocabulary of true kinship into the context of a court hierarchy.

The First Circle

The highest aristocrats were endowed with court titles. Just as Darius had been Cyrus's quiver-bearer (Aelian, *VH* XII.43) and Cambyses' lance-bearer (Herodotus III.139), so Gobryas and Aspathines are shown bearing royal arms on the façade of Darius's tomb (*DNc–d*). Prexaspes was Cambyses' message-bearer, and his son "was the king's cupbearer—also a position of no small honour" (Herodotus III.34✧). Patiramphes, son of one of several persons who had the name Otanes, was Xerxes' royal chariot-driver (VII.40). Tiribazus had the privilege of assisting the king onto his horse (Xenophon, *Anab.* IV.4.4). Megabyzus was Xerxes' son-in-law and Artaxerxes I's Tablemate (Ctesias §22, 41). In short, the ambition of the king's men was to be incorporated into the immediate proximity of the king—at court, in the army, or even on the hunt (cf. Plutarch, *Them.* 29.6).

The expressions used by the Greeks are very revealing. Cyrus distributed his royal gifts to those whom Xenophon calls *hoi peri auton* (Cyr. VIII.2.8; cf. VIII.1.36 etc.). In Cyrus the Younger's entourage, Xenophon uses the same term (*hoi peri auton*; cf. I.1.5: *hoi par'eautōi barbaroi*) for the most powerful (*kratistoi*) and best-dressed Persians, who were covered with all sorts of jewels (*Anab.* I.8.1). But there also was an inner circle around the king: "the noblest Persians among his attendants (*Persai hoi aristoi hoi peri auton*)," whom he convened to judge Orontas (I.6.4◊). Pategyas must have been part of this circle: "a trusty Persian of Cyrus's staff" (*anēr Persēs tōn peri amphi Kyron khrestos*; I.8.1◊). Any promotion brought the noble into the circle of cronies, such as Tiribazus after his great deeds during a campaign against the Cadusians, who "set out homewards in the company of the king" (*meta basileōs*; Plutarch, *Art.* 24.9◊), whereas earlier, he stagnated "in humble estate and neglected" (24.4◊). He had already previously bene-fited from royal favor, since he was constantly at the side of the king (*kai hopotē pareiē*; Xenophon, *Anab.* IV.4.4). Likewise Mardonius, "who was part of the entourage of Xerxes" (*par'autōi*; Herodotus VII.5). And, at the beginning of each reign, Ctesias is careful to include the names of the most influential people around the king (*megistos/ dynatos/megas/iskhys par'autōi*) (§9, 20, 29, 45, 53).

In other words, the king's favor was expressed by the degree of proximity one had at-tained with respect to his person: hence the importance of titles that refer to relations of kinship (*syggeneis*) or familiar trust (Friend), to sharing of meals (Tablemate), to a posi-tion that implies being in the king's presence (cupbearer, charioteer, royal arms-bearer, scepter-bearer, etc.). This concentric manifestation of royal favor was realized in three di-mensions by Alexander at Opis (Arrian VII.11.8) and imitated a few years later by Peu-cestes at Persepolis, who placed the participants in four concentric circles around the altars; the innermost circle encompassed "the generals and hipparchs and also each of the Persians who was most highly honoured" (*tōn Persōn hoi malista timōmenoi*; Diodo-rus XIX.22.2–3◊). This royal hierarchy was maintained during all of the activities of the court, including banquets. In the *Cyropaedia*, Xenophon stresses this especially. When his Cyrus gave a victory banquet, "he invited in those of his friends who showed that they were most desirous of magnifying his rule and of honouring him most loyally" (VIII.4.1):

> So when the invited guests came to dinner, he did not assign them their seats at random, but he seated on Cyrus's left the one for whom he had the highest regard (*hos malista etima*), for the left side was more readily exposed to treacherous designs than the right; and the one who was second in esteem he seated on his right, the third again on the left, the fourth on the right, and so on, if there were more. For he thought it a good plan to show publicly how much regard he had for each one (*hōs ekaston etima*), because where people feel that the one who merits most will neither have his praise proclaimed nor receive a prize, there is no emulation among them; but where the most deserving is seen to receive the most prefer-ment, there all are seen to contend most eagerly for the first place (*agōnisai*). Accordingly, Cyrus thus made public recognition of those who stood first in his esteem. . . . And Cyrus felt it a discredit to himself, if the one who sat in the seat of highest honour was not also seen to receive the greatest number of good things at his hands. (VIII.4.3–5◊)

Surely here as elsewhere Xenophon is extolling (through Cyrus) government by the elite, something that he desired for Athens. Meanwhile, the information that he gives on the organization of the royal table is confirmed by much other evidence and there-fore acceptable overall.

An identical hierarchy was in effect in the field. According to Xenophon, Cyrus im-posed very strict regulations in this area. "At the very beginning Cyrus made this rule, that his tent should be pitched facing the east; and then he determined, first, how far from the royal pavilion the spearmen of his guard should have their tent" (VIII.5.3◊). Contrary to what Xenophon's version implies, Cyrus's reasons were not strictly or solely military: "His position in the middle of the camp in the belief that this situation was the most secure. Then came his most trusty followers (*pistōtatoi*), just as he was accustomed to have them about him at home, and next to them in a circle he had his horsemen and charioteers" (5.8✧). It was the same in battle. Principle required the king to be at the center of the troop disposition. The same was true in the (informal) council that the king convened (when he considered it useful). In one of these meetings, for example, after Xerxes, Mardonius took the floor (Herodotus VII.9), who "had more influence with Xerxes than anyone else in the country" (VII.5✧). When he conferred with the heads of the naval contingents before the battle of Salamis, the protocol was no less minutely regulated: "When he had seated himself with all proper ceremony, the rulers of states and commanders of squadrons were summoned to appear before him, and took their seats according to the degree of privilege which the king had assigned them. . . . They sat there in order of rank" (VIII.67–68✧).

Gifts and Redistribution of Wealth

The relationship between the king and his men was also based on the wealth of material advantages they received from him. Some gifts—striking testimony to royal favor—could reflect an often considerable intrinsic economic value. This fact did not escape the Greek authors, who were struck by the luxurious lifestyle of the king and his satraps. That is what Herodotus sought to make his readers understand by recounting the marvelous tale of the physician Democedes, who came to treat Darius for a sprain and was also sent to tend some women:

> They each scooped a cupful of gold coins from a chest and gave them to Democedes. There was such a lot of the money that a servant called Sciton, by picking up the coins which spilt over from the cups, managed to collect quite a fortune. (III.130✧)

Darius provides us with another incident. When he was urging Histiaeus (tyrant of Miletus) to accompany him to Susa, he not only promised him that he would be his Tablemate and his counselor but also encouraged him in this way: "All I have will there be yours" (V.24✧). Phaenias of Ephesus records another case, that of Entimus the Cretan, who switched his allegiance to the Great King and received exceptional honors:

> In his honour Artaxerxes bestowed upon him a tent of extraordinary beauty and size, and a silver-footed bedstead; he also sent rich coverings. . . . The king sent Entimus a silver-footed bed with its coverings, a tent with gaily-coloured canopy, a silver throne, a gilded sunshade, twenty gold saucers set with jewels, one hundred large saucers of silver and silver mixing-bowls, one hundred concubines and one hundred slaves, and six thousand pieces of gold, beside all that was given to him for his daily necessities. (Athenaeus II.48d-f–49a✧)

We also know that ambassadors received regular gifts from the Great King (Aelian, *VH* I.22). The Greeks were all the more aware of this because quite a few ambassadors to the Great King were accused, on their return, of *parapresbeia*, that is, of allowing themselves to be bribed. In 425, Aristophanes alluded to this very clearly in the *Acharnians* (50ff.). Timagoras, ambassador to the Congress of Susa in 369, is mentioned by Athenaeus as having received numerous gifts from Artaxerxes II (II.48e): "And indeed the Athenians condemned Timagoras to death for taking bribes" (Plutarch, *Art.* 22.6; *Pel.* 30.9–13). Conon the Athenian, around 395, was himself honored with magnificent gifts (*dōreai megalai*): "Artaxerxes approved Conon, honoured him with rich gifts, and appointed a paymaster who should supply funds in abundance as Conon might assign them" (Diodorus XIV.81.6✧). This may have been the occasion on which Demos, son of Pirylampes, received a *symbolon* from the Great King in the form of a gold phial, which he used as security for a 16-mina loan (Lysias XIX.25).

There are also two Persepolis tablets, dated 492 and 486, that attest to the distribution of silver to worthy persons. One of them (PT 4) records that on the king's direct order the sum of 5,300 shekels of silver was distributed to thirteen Persians. Some received 60 shekels, others 50, others 30, and others 20. It is hard to identify these people because their names are common. And these were no small gifts: at that time, a sheep was worth 3 shekels; a 300-shekel gift thus corresponds to 100 sheep. To verify this, all we need to do is note the total daily "ration" of sheep (2 head) received by Parnaka, Darius's chief administrator in Persia. The reason for this royal order is doubtless to be found in the next tablet (PT 5), which records the distribution of 9,040 shekels to 113 "cowboys"(?), at the rate of 80 shekels per man. These men were paid in this fashion for seizing a certain Antaka in the region of Tauka. Although various uncertainties about the underlying narrative remain, we can recognize Benefactors among the persons so honored.

The profits of conquest also enriched the king's men. Several of them received concessions of land, which yielded substantial income. Several times Xenophon says that Cyrus divided the booty and spoils of war among his inner circle and his soldiers. The division was undoubtedly unequal, with the king retaining for himself the entire treasuries of conquered kings. But there is also no doubt that the royal favorites got their hands on riches—such as Bagoas, an intimate of Artaxerxes III, who grabbed a quantity of gold and silver taken from the Egyptian temples and then sold back to the priests at an exorbitant price the "ancient sacred annals" that he had just stolen from them (Diodorus XVI.51.2)!

The position held by a satrap was also quite remunerative. Sometimes, the king granted the right of not transferring tribute to the central court. This was the case for Bardiya in Central Asia (Ctesias §8: *ateleis*) and for Zopyrus after his (supposed) exploit in Babylon: Darius granted him the governorship of Babylon, free from tax (*ateleia*), for as long as he lived" (Herodotus III.160✧; cf. Diodorus II.28.4). A satrap also profited from the revenues of his paradise (cf. Xenophon, *Hell.* IV.1.15–17, 33), and he levied a special duty for the purpose of supplying his table (chap. 10/4). He also undoubtedly enjoyed other more irregular (in every sense of the term) revenues. Even though satraps were supervised, we may assume that more than one was tempted to levy a higher tribute than he was obliged to remit each year to the central court. The offering of *baksheesh* (bribes) is regularly mentioned; for example, the parties to a suit tried in this way to sway a governor's decision (cf. DAE 102, 104 [AP 30–31, 33]; Ezra 5:3–4). We may also cite the example of Condalus, high-level administrator of Mausolus, satrap of Caria in the fourth century:

> Whenever during his passage through the country anyone brought him a sheep or a pig or a calf, [he] used to make a record of the donor and the date and order him to take it back home and keep it until he returned. When he thought that sufficient time had elapsed, he used to ask for the animal which was being kept for him, and reckoned up and demanded the produce-tax on it as well. (Ps.-Arist., *Oecon.* II.14a✧)

Condalus's game confirms that satraps and their lieutenants received gifts apart from their periodic inspections. But this was a matter of extorted gifts, which counts as theft pure and simple.

The court titles themselves implied material benefits. First of all, becoming a part of the inner circle made an individual an intermediary to the king, thus someone to be lobbied by means of presents. This explains Xenophon's remark about Gadatas, 'chief of the mace-bearers' (*skēptoukhoi*) at Cyrus's court: "In return for his services he received many valuable presents from Cyrus himself and, through Cyrus's influence, from others also" (*Cyr.* VIII.4.2◇). Some associates of the Great King did not hesitate to profit from their activities. For instance, Satibarzanes, royal chamberlain in the time of Artaxerxes II, was punished for receiving silver from the Cypriot king Evagoras (Plutarch, *Mor.* 173e; Ctesias §63). We also know that royal judges were put to death for rendering decisions for pay (Herodotus V.25; cf. Diodorus XV.10.1).

The royal table (in the administrative sense), symbolic of the territorial and material power of the Great King, was a preeminent location for redistribution, in the form of precedence (when one was invited to take a meal with the king) and in the form of distribution of provisions. Xenophon comes back to this several times. In his eyes, the custom related to royal *polydōria*:

> [Cyrus] recognized from the start that there is no kindness which men can show one another, with the same amount of expenditure, more acceptable than sharing meat and drink with them. In this belief, he first of all arranged that there should be placed upon his own table a quantity of food, like that of which he himself regularly partook, sufficient for a very large number of people; and all of that which was served to him, except what he and his companions at table (*syndeipnoi*) consumed, he distributed among those of his friends (*philoi*) to whom he wished to send remembrances or good wishes. . . . He used also to honour with presents from his table any one of his servants whom he took occasion to commend. . . . He often saw him send even to some of his friends who were not there something that he happened to like very much himself. (Cyr. VIII.2.2–4; 4.6◇)

This was also one of the qualities that Xenophon recognized in Cyrus the Younger, who when he "got some particularly good wine, he would often send the half-emptied jar to a friend. . . . So he would often send halves of geese" (*Anab.* I.9.25–26◇; cf. Aelian, *VH* XII.1). Xenophon again says that the same instructions were given to the satraps: "Let your table, like mine, feed first your own household and then, too, be bountifully arrayed so as to give a share to your friends and to confer some distinction day by day upon any one who does some noble act" (*Cyr.* VIII.6.11◇). Nehemiah 5:17◇ tells us that the governor's table in Judah supplied 150 men every day, Jews and officials, "not to mention those who came to us from the surrounding nations."

These distributions were thus of considerable magnitude. Everyone knows the famous description given by the redactor of Esther (1:3–8◇):

> In the third year of his reign, [Ahasuerus] gave a banquet at his court for all his administrators and ministers, chiefs of the army of Persia and Media, nobles and governors of the provinces. Thus he displayed the riches and splendour of his empire and the pomp and glory of his majesty; the festivities went on for a long time, a hundred and eighty days.
>
> When this period was over, for seven days the king gave a banquet for all the people living in the citadel of Susa, to high and low alike, in the enclosure adjoining the king's palace. There were white and violet hangings fastened with cords of fine linen and purple thread to silver rings on marble columns, couches of gold and silver on a pavement of porphyry, marble, mother-of-pearl and precious stones. For drinking there were golden cups of various designs and the royal wine in plenty according to the king's bounty. By royal command,

however, drinking was not obligatory, the king having instructed the officials of his household to treat each guest according to his own wishes.

It would be tempting to form the obvious conclusion that this is an "oriental legend." However, according to Dinon and Ctesias, whom we have every reason to consider credible, the number of persons served at the Great King's table every day reached 15,000 (Athenaeus IV.146c). These figures are not surprising: Sargon of Akkad boasted of feeding 5,400 men every day (*ANET* ³ 268); Aššurnaṣirpal II records that he gave a huge banquet in which several tens of thousands of people took part: 69,574 for ten days, including 5,000 high dignitaries from conquered countries, 16,000 people of uncertain status, and 1,500 crown officers, along with 47,074 male and female laborers who had just worked on the construction of the new capital (*ANET* ³ 560).

Obviously, not all of the people fed found a place at the royal table. According to Heraclides, "the greater part of these meats and other foods are taken out into the courtyard for the body-guard and light-armed troopers maintained by the king; there they divide all the half-eaten remnants of meat and bread and share them in equal portions" (Athenaeus IV.145e✧; Polyaenus IV.3.32). But aside from these distributions to the soldiers—which Heraclides considered part of their pay (*misthos*)—dishes were sent to persons the king wished to honor, such as Timagoras: "Not to mention the feast made for him at court, which was so princely and splendid" (Plutarch, *Art.* 22.6✧); or Entimus: "some of the food served to the king was merely sent to him from the table" (Athenaeus II 48e✧; cf. 49a). The economic value of these distributions is illustrated well in a story told by Herodotus (the execution of Psammenitus's children; III.14).

To the actual food provided must be added all of the equipment needed for banquets, such as silver-footed couches, tent, blanket, parasol, cups, and staff provided to Entimus (II.48f–49a), or the couch and blanket sent to Timagoras (Plutarch, *Art.* 22.10; *Pel.* 30.10). The custom is also found in the Hellenistic era. Poseidonius records that at the conclusion of the great banquets given every day by the Seleucid king Antiochus VII, "Every one of the feasters would carry home uncarved meat of land-animals, fowls, and creatures of the sea prepared whole, and capable of filling a cart; and after all that, quantities of honey-cakes and wreaths of myrrh and frankincense with matted fillets of gold as long as a man" (Athenaeus XII.540c✧)!

Among the gifts offered by Artaxerxes to the Athenian ambassador Timagoras, Plutarch mentions the following: "Since [Timagoras] needed cow's milk for his health, [Artaxerxes] sent 80 cows after him to milk . . . and cowherds" (*Art.* 22.10; *Pel.* 30.10). This passage makes perfect sense in light of the Persepolis tablets and in turn helps to explain them. A number of Fortification tablets refer to the issuing of food rations, not just to workers (*kurtaš*) but also to administrators and several high figures in the king's entourage: daily rations or travelers' rations were received from the administration by order of the king or the head of economic administration, Parnaka. The study of these tablets shows that here too there was a hierarchy of gifts of an economic nature. This practice was inherited from the Near Eastern monarchies: "The master did not eat alone, and his meal was not solely for nourishment. The Mesopotamian man was required to share his meal, to offer sustenance. . . . Was not the king 'the one who feeds the people, table of the race'? . . . The king maintained the palace personnel and the troops" (J. Bottéro).

2. Unequal Exchange

Gifts and Services

The principle was simple: gifts were given by the king in return for services rendered. This was a reality expressed in all of the texts. "In Persia, any special service to the king is very highly valued," Herodotus remarks (III.154◇). The variety of services is very wide: saving the life of the king (Tiribazus: Diodorus XV.10.3) or of a relative (Herodotus IX.107); generally showing bravery in war and subtlety in council (Diodorus XV.10.3; Nepos *Paus.* 1.2); defending to the death a citadel entrusted by the king (Herodotus VII.105–7); accomplishing a brilliant feat in the presence of the king (III.160; IV.143; VIII.85, 87–88, 90; Plutarch, *Art.* 24.9); and so on. In short, to repeat Xenophon's formulation, if "any one in the olden times risked his life for the king, or if any one reduced a state or a nation to submission to him, or effected anything else of good or glory for him, such an one received honour and preferment (*hoi timōmenoi*)." This same Xenophon pretended to be heartbroken when in his time even morally repugnant acts could be rewarded: "If any one seems to bring some advantage to the king by evil-doing, . . . such are the ones who now have the highest honours heaped upon them" (*hoi tais megistais timais gerairomenoi*; Cyr. VIII.8.4◇).

By giving awards and honor, the king intended to sustain the unfailing devotion of the men who served him. If for Xenophon so many men were faithful to Cyrus (the Younger), it was "because they thought that if they were deserving, they would gain a worthier reward with Cyrus than with the King" (*Anab.* I.9.29◇). This was indeed the function that the same author recognized for Cyrus the Elder's *polydōria* (*Cyr.* VIII.2.9). In his eyes, the distribution of reward-gifts was neither more nor less than a profitable investment. In this way—Xenophon has Cyrus say to Croesus—I "satisfy the wants of my friends; and by enriching men and doing them kindnesses I win . . . their friendship (*philia*) and loyalty (*eunoia*), and from that I reap as my reward (*karpousai*) security and good fame" (*Cyr.* VIII.2.22◇). The promise of reward was actually a powerful motivation, as, for example, during the five-year preparation and mustering of the grand army of Xerxes:

> All the Persian nobles who had attended the conference hurried home to their respective provinces; and as every one of them hoped to win the reward which Xerxes had offered, no pains were spared in the subsequent preparations. . . . Which of the Persian provincial governors received the king's prize for the best-equipped contingent, I am not able to say; nor do I even know if the matter was ever decided. (Herodotus VII.19, 26◇)

The Persians often weighed their merits against royal expectations: for example, Mitrobates and Oroetes (Herodotus III.120) or Masistes and Artayntes (IX.107). Emulation (*agōnisai*) was the foundation of the system, as Xenophon often insists.

Evaluation of Services

Rendering justice, for the king, came down to balancing good deeds against evil acts. For example, this is the basis for the grant of clemency to the royal judge Sandoces: "Darius came to the conclusion that his services to the royal house outweighed his offences, and realizing in consequence that he had acted with more promptitude than wisdom," he let him go (Herodotus VII.194◇). In fact, custom "forbids even the king himself to put a man to death for a single offence. . . . Their way is to balance faults (*ta adikēmata*) against services (*ta hypourgēmata*), and then, if the faults are greater and more numerous, anger may take its course" (I.137✧). This is precisely the quality of which Darius boasts at Naqš-i Rustam (*DNb* §8b). In other words, the prime criterion for judgment was dynastic loyalty.

This is the system that Diodorus Siculus portrays during the trial of Tiribazus, whom Orontes accused of plotting secession (*apostasis*) from the Empire of Artaxerxes II. The king convened the royal judges, who decided that the accused was innocent (XV.8.3–5). At the end of the trial, the judges were interviewed one by one by the king:

> The first said that he observed the charges to be debatable, while the benefactions (*euergesiai*) were not contested. The second said that, though it were granted that the charges were true, nevertheless the benefactions exceeded the offences (*harmatia*). The third stated that he did not take into account the benefactions, because Tiribazus had received from the King in return for them favours and honours (*kharites kai timai*) many times as great, but that when the charges were examined apart by themselves, the accused did not appear to be guilty of them. The King praised the judges for having rendererd a just decision and bestowed upon Tiribazus the highest honours (*hai nomizomenai megistai timai*). (Diodorus XV.11.1–2✧)

The Tiribazus example shows very clearly that the king remained fully in control of the entire process. It was necessary first of all that the feat that had been performed was recognized as such by the king. This is why, for example, the courtiers took care to inform themselves in advance of the desire of the king—neither Coes (Herodotus IV.97) nor Zopyrus (III.154) failed to do this. Before attempting a brilliant feat against Babylon, Zopyrus "went to find Darius and asked him if it was his heart's desire that Babylon be taken." Coes, before offering his suggestion, "determined ahead of time whether Darius would be interested in hearing a suggestion." This is no doubt the explanation for a Persian practice (*nomos*) presented by Aelian (*VH* XII.62✧) as follows:

> Another Persian custom. If someone is about to advise the king on secret or difficult matters, he stands on a gold brick. If his proposal is thought to be necessary, he takes the brick as the reward for his advice and leaves. But he is nevertheless whipped for having contradicted the king.

As Aelian puts it very clearly (*VH* I.31✧), it was in fact up to the king to accept or not accept the offerings that the common peasants of Persia brought him: "These objects . . . are termed gifts (*kai onomazetai dōra*); the king treats them as such (*kai dokei toutōi*)." This is why the gift of some drops of water earned for the peasant Sinetes "a Persian robe, a golden cup, and a thousand darics" from Artaxerxes II (I.32✧), and a simple soldier was honored by Xerxes with the title Benefactor (XII.40).

Gifts with Strings Attached

One could clearly argue that people obtained favors who had previously rendered services (cf. Herodotus IV.115). This is shown by the example of Syloson, as recorded by Herodotus (III.139–140). During Cambyses' Egyptian expedition, Syloson the Greek offered a purple mantle to Darius. After the accession of Darius, Syloson hoped to profit from his gift and reminded Darius that he was one of his Benefactors. However, no one could demand a royal gift in return for services, on one's own terms. This is the moral of the story of Pythius. During Darius's passage through Asia Minor in 513, this extremely wealthy person had already offered magnificent gifts to the king (Herodotus VII.27). With the arrival of Xerxes in 480, he treated the entire army with generosity and he offered the king considerable sums for the success of the war. This gained him the following royal proclamation: "Therefore, as a reward (*anti autōn*) for your generosity, I make you my personal friend (*xeinos*) and, in addition, I will give you from my own coffers the 7000 gold Darics which are needed to make your fortune up to the round sum of 4,000,000. Continue, then, to possess what you have acquired; and have the wisdom to remain always the man you have proved yourself to-day. You will never regret it, now or hereafter" (VII.29◊). Pythius made the mistake of taking these words as a formal agreement that the king would grant him whatever he requested. A little later, he sought out Xerxes. "Emboldened by the presents he had received," he expressed a desire for another royal gift. Xerxes promised to grant it. Pythius then asked the king to exempt one of his sons from military service. Infuriated by such an outrageous request, Xerxes ordered one of Pythius's sons to be sacrificed under particularly horrific conditions (VII.38–39◊). In other words, services rendered did not tie the hands of the king, who had the prerogative of choosing the nature and timing of the reward.

Another example is the fate reserved by Artaxerxes II for two warriors at the battle of Cunaxa. Arguing that he had unhorsed Cyrus, a Carian "su[ed] for his reward" (Plutarch, *Art.* 14.6◊). The king granted him a gift. The Carian made the mistake of publicly showing his annoyance at not having been rewarded more generously; quite irritated, the king sentenced him to death (14.7–10). The same soon happened to Mithradates, "who first wounded" Cyrus; he received royal gifts (robe and gold jewelry) with this proclamation: "The king has honoured you with these his favours, because you found and brought him the horse-trappings of Cyrus" (14.5◊). Mithradates was annoyed and soon boasted during a banquet that he had killed Cyrus with his bare hands (§15); he was thereupon condemned to the horrible torture of the troughs, for by his bragging he had cast doubt on the official version, which attributed the mortal blow to the king himself (§16).

We are thus not in a context where gifts and counter-gifts were being exchanged between equals, in which "there is a functional relationship between the gift and the response, the gift being only one element in a system of reciprocal benefits that are simultaneously free and constraining, the freedom of the gift obliging the recipient to a counter-gift, giving rise to a continual back-and-forth of gifts given and gifts in compensation" (É. Benveniste). The Achaemenid principle is that only the king gives, and only royal gifts place obligations on the recipient. This is the explanation for the aphorism that Plutarch attributes to Artaxerxes I: he "used to say that it is more kingly to give to one who has than to take away (*to prostheinai tou aphelein basilikōteron esti*)" (Mor. 173d◊). Thucydides contrasts the Thracian (Odrysian) and Achaemenid practices: "There was here established a custom opposite to that prevailing in the Persian kingdom, namely, of taking (*lambanein*) rather than giving (*didonai*) . . . it being impossible to get anything done without a present. It was thus a very powerful kingdom" (II.97.3–4◊). Thucydides' proposed contrast is a bit artificial, for the Persian kings also received gifts (cf. esp. Plutarch, *Art.* 4.4–5). But according to the rationale of the system, Thucydides' remark was legitimate. In this system, the Great Kings' *polydōria* was one of the constituent elements of their power, in the sense that the gifts or services received did not further commit the king, although the receipt of honors and royal gifts did oblige the recipient. This was no doubt the source of Democedes' hesitation: at first, he refused to assist the king (III.131). Even though Herodotus states, "I do not myself believe that Darius' motive . . . was anything but genuine and straightforward," he also notes that Democedes did not "accept with open arms everything Darius offered," for he well knew that doing so would obligate him to return to the Great King's court (III.135◊), which was certainly not his intention (III.132, 136). For Democedes, receiving goods and titles ("Tablemate") signified perpetual commitment to the Great King. The same principle operated in the relations established between Alexander and the Athenian Phocion: Phocion responded to Alexander's offer of towns with a refusal. "Alexander was displeased, and wrote back to him to say that he could not esteem those his friends who would not be obliged by him" (Plutarch, *Phocion* 18.6◊; cf. *Alex.* 39.4 and Aelian, *VH* I.25). In another case, it is clear that when Darius invited Histiaeus to Susa to be his counselor and Tablemate, he left him no choice in the matter (Herodotus V.24).

There seem to be only two exceptions to the rule. Herodotus says that once a year there was what he calls the "Royal Supper," whose Persian name he gives (*tykta*; IX.110◊), and he states: "It is the one occasion in the year when the king washes his head and gives presents to the Persians." The latter detail poses a problem. It can be compared with several passages in which Xenophon mentions that, each time Cyrus came to Persia, he gave the gifts customary among the Persians (*Cyr.* VIII.5.21; 7.1). Specifically, we know that, during every stay at Persepolis, the Great King had to give a gold piece to the women of Persia (Plutarch, *Alex.* 69.1–2; *Mor.* 246a–b) in memory of the role that they had played during the first confrontation with the Medes (*FGrH* 90 F66.16–45). But Herodotus's remark can be satisfactorily explained by a detail that comes later: "The law (*nomos*) of the Supper demanded that no one, on that day, might be refused his request" (IX.111◊).

Custom also required that on the day of his official recognition "the heir apparent to the crown should beg a boon (*dōron*), and that he that had declared him so should give whatever he asked, provided it were within the sphere of his power" (*anper ē dunaton*) (Plutarch, *Art.* 26.5◊). The rest of the story shows the importance of the qualification "if it were within the sphere of his power." The eldest son of Artaxerxes, Darius, requested Aspasia, the old companion of Cyrus the Younger: "He gave him her indeed, being constrained by law (*nomos*), but when he had done so, a little after he took her from him. For he consecrated her priestess to Diana of Ecbatana . . . that she might spend the remainder of her days in strict chastity" (27.3–4◊; cf. 28.2)!

A Precarious Favor

The position of the recipients was certainly not stable, because royal gifts and favors were by definition insecure. Speaking of places of honor at banquets reserved by Cyrus for his favorites, Xenophon states this reality, without beating around the bush: "He did not, however, assign the appointed place permanently, but he made it a rule that by noble deeds any one might advance to a more honoured seat, and that if any one should conduct himself ill he should go back to one less honoured" (*Cyr.* VIII.4.5◊). The same author returns to this idea in the *Oeconomicus*: though the king confers honors on worthy persons, "those officers whom he finds to be neglecting the garrisons or making profit out of them he punishes severely, and appoints others to their office" (IV.7◊).

Whatever the nature and size of the gifts and honors received, they could only be retained if the king continued to hold the recipient in high regard—whether court title, decoration, administrative post, or gift of land. Let us take the case of Histiaeus of Miletus. For services rendered during Darius's expedition beyond the Danube, he received the region of Myrcinus in Thrace from the king, "because he wished to found a city there" (Herodotus V.11,◆ 23: *dōreēn*). But soon Megabazus warned Darius that it was dangerous to grant Histiaeus this region "with its silver mines, and abundance of timber for building ships and making oars . . ." (V.23◆). Won over by Megabazus's arguments, Darius recalled Histiaeus to Susa, giving him hope of becoming one of his intimates. Histiaeus obeyed the royal command "and was much flattered at being a King's Counsellor" (V.24◆).

The specific example of Histiaeus is only an illustration of a general practice: lands conceded as a gift carried an insecure title, not a title to private property in the full meaning of the phrase. They could be confiscated whenever the concessionaire disobeyed royal orders (Xenophon, *Cyr.* VIII.1.20). Babylonian tablets from the time of Darius II attest to the revocation of a previous concession granted to a man who turned out to be disloyal. The same certainly was true for court titles (see Ctesias §41) and gifts of honor. In Athenaeus's long disquisition on drinking vessels, Ctesias mentions, for example, that anyone branded with disgrace (*atimia*) by the Great King had to use clay cups (Athenaeus XI.464a) instead of the opulent vessels of gold and silver reserved for the king and his Tablemates (Herodotus VII.119). Even when gifts and honors were granted for the lifetime of the beneficiary (Herodotus III.160) or were transmissible to his heirs (cf. VII.106), it was implicit that their retention depended on future services rendered.

Examples of chaotic careers are legion. Let us first consider the case of Megabyzus II, known especially from the fictionalized tale by Ctesias. He was the scion of a prominent family, since through his father, Zopyrus I, he was grandson of Megabyzus I, one of the Seven conspirators of 522 (Herodotus III.153, 160; *DB* §68). Megabyzus was one of the most influential men around Xerxes; he had wed Xerxes' daughter Amytis, who was known for her fickleness (Ctesias §21, 28; cf. Athenaeus XIII.609a). On the expedition of 480, he commanded one of the three divisions of the army (Herodotus VII.82, 121). When the expedition returned in 479, he put down the revolt in Babylonia—in return for which "Xerxes gave him many presents, notably a heap of gold amounting to six talents; this was the most honorable present among all the royal gifts" (§22). He played a very important role during the accession of Artaxerxes (§30), then won a victory over the Athenians and Egyptians in Egypt (§§33–35). Despite the promises of Megabyzus, the king permitted Amestris to put the Greek mercenaries to death. Displeased, "Megabyzus broke with the king" (§§36–37). He achieved several victories over the armies sent against him (§§37–39), before receiving a royal pardon (§39). Then came the famous episode during a hunt:

> The king went hunting and a lion attacked him. As soon as the beast leapt, Megabyzus struck him with a javelin and brought him down. The king was angry because Megabyzus had struck the beast before he could touch it himself; he ordered Megabyzus's head cut off, but, on the pleas of Amestris, Amytis, and others, Megabyzus escaped death by being exiled on the coast of the Red Sea (Persian Gulf), at Kyrta. Exile was also pronounced against the eunuch Artoxares, who was sent to Armenia for frequently speaking freely to the king on behalf of Megabyzus. (§40)

Megabyzus returned after five years: "Thanks to Amestris and Amytis, the king allowed himself to relent and made him his Tablemate (*homotrapezos*) as before; he died at 76, and the king was greatly moved" (§41).

The fourth-century career of Datames provides a contrasting example. After his victory over the Paphlagonian Thuys, he was rewarded with "magnificent presents," and he was made equal in command with Pharnabazus and Tithraustes (Nepos, *Dat.* 3.5). The rapidity of Datames' recent victory in Cataonia "gained high favour with [Artaxerxes] (*magnam benevolentiam regis*), [but] he incurred equally jealousy from the courtiers, . . . who united in a conspiracy to ruin him" (§5.2◊). He was warned of the plot by Pandantes, who was "keeper of the royal fortune" and who warned him that "it was the habit of kings to attribute disasters to men but success to their own good fortune; that consequently they were easily led to bring about the ruin of those who were reported to have suffered defeat" (§5.3–4◊). Then came the revolt, the traps, the betrayals, and the end.

The course of the career of Tiribazus is equally enlightening. He first appears at the battle of Cunaxa. It was he who advised Artaxerxes to do battle with Cyrus the Younger (Plutarch, *Art.* 7.3), and he was the one who during the battle provided another horse to the king after he had been thrown from his own (10.1). Shortly thereafter, Xenophon refers to him as governor of western Armenia (*Anab.* IV.4.4◊), but perhaps he had gained that position earlier. Or more likely, the unusual position he held resulted from his conduct during the battle of Cunaxa: he "had proved himself a friend (*philos*) to the King and, so often as he was present, was the only man permitted to help the king mount his horse." Around 392, he was commander-in-chief (*karanos*) of the Persian armies in Asia Minor (and perhaps satrap). In this role he received Greek ambassadors; he refused to come to agreement, arguing that he could not do so "without the King's approval." Then he had Conon arrested and went to find the king (Xenophon, *Hell.* IV.8.12–16◊). Though replaced in his administrative post by Struthas, he still retained major responsibilities in Asia Minor (V.1.6). In 387, when the Greeks met at Susa, it was he who read out the royal proclamation (V.1.30).

He appears again at Cyprus, where he commanded all the Persian forces against Evagoras. He was soon accused by Orontes, who was "jealous of his fame." The king put a certain degree of trust in Orontes' letter of accusation and had Tiribazus arrested (Diodorus XV.8; cf. Polyaenus VII.14.1). According to Diodorus, Tiribazus was kept in prison until the return of Artaxerxes II from his expedition against the Cadusians (XV.8.5; cf. 10.1). Plutarch, on the other hand, gives that impression that Tiribazus accompanied the king. But, doubtless because of the charges against him, he stagnated "at that time in humble estate and neglected" (*Art.* 24.4◊). His diplomatic skill made him "deliverer of the king and his army," which won him a new, lightning promotion: "Teribazus, in great honour and distinction, set out homewards in the company of the king (*meta tou basileōs*)" (24.9◊). It was apparently at this time that the trial was held. The royal judges dismissed the charges against him because of prior services rendered to the king (Diodorus XV.11.1). Artaxerxes "bestowed upon Tiribazus the highest honours, such as were customary [in Persia]" (11.2◊).

Among his past services, Tiribazus emphasized the one that "had won him the admiration and distinction of First Friend of the king (*megisthos genesthai philos*). During a hunt, two lions leaped toward the king in his chariot; they had torn apart two horses of the team of four and were about to pounce on the king when Tiribazus appeared, killed the lions, and so saved the king from great harm" (10.3). Plutarch, on the other hand, though recognizing Tiribazus's courage, several times condemns him for his foolishness. He apparently is referring to a different hunt when he describes Tiribazus as "a man often in great favor (*prōtē*) with his prince for his valour and as often out of it for his buffoonery" (24.4◇). He also reports that, during another hunt, the king's robe was torn; at Tiribazus's request, the king donned a new robe and gave him the old one but forbade him to wear it: Tiribazus,

> little regarding the injunction, being not a bad, but a lightheaded, thoughtless man, immediately the king took it off, put it on, and bedecked himself further with royal golden necklaces and women's ornaments, to the great scandal of everybody, the thing being quite unlawful. (5.4◇)

The Great King chose to approach this guilty extravagance with irony.

This fellow's end, like that of Datames, took place in the context of the affairs of court. He was infuriated by the refusal of the king to give him one of his daughters:

> Tiribazus entertained an irreconcilable enmity against Artaxerxes. As indeed he was seldom at any other time steady in his temper, but uneven and inconsiderate; so that whether he were in the number of the choicest favorites of his prince (*homoia tois prōtois*), or whether he were offensive and odious to him, he demeaned himself in neither condition with moderation (*metabolē*), but if he was advanced (*timōmenos*) he was intolerably insolent, and in his degradation not submissive and peaceable in his deportment, but fierce and haughty. (27.9–10◇)

He pressured Darius, the crown prince, to revolt against his father. He was killed during the attack on the royal bedchamber (29.6–7).

Of course, these biographies must be read for what they are: family sagas constructed on a series of royal-hero motifs (in particular dealing with the hunt) designed to praise the greatness of the hero. For instance, Megabyzus's return home, where he was barely recognized by his wife Amytis (Ctesias §41), is reminiscent of a familiar theme, manifested especially in Ulysses' return to Ithaca. We must thus not put good money on all of the information transmitted by Ctesias and Nepos: many episodes that at face value seem factual need to be rewritten. These stories nonetheless point to characteristics of the relationships between the king and the aristocrats. It seems clear that Plutarch's judgments on Tiribazus come directly from the court writers, doubtless Ctesias or Dinon. As such, they express perfectly the qualities and attitudes that characterized faithful servants devoted to the interests of the king. We find nearly the same words in Herodotus's evaluations of Mardonius: he was ambitious (VII.6), boastful (VII.9), a flatterer (VII.9; VIII.97, 100), violent and headstrong (IX.37, 61), quickly exalted by his success (IX.49, 58), clearly lacking in judgment. Numerous other examples of favor/disfavor could be cited. Nothing and no one escaped the king's judgment, not even the people most honored, including a son-in-law of the king (Ctesias §41) or a rebellious heir, such as Artaxerxes II's son (Plutarch, *Art.* 29). In short, for the king's men, the Tarpeian Rock was near the Capitol. From many examples, let us cite the example of Orontes, who was guilty of falsely accusing Tiribazus: "Artaxerxes excluded him from the company of his Friends and showered him with indignity" (*atimia*; Diodorus XV.11.2).

The fictionalized biographies just presented were also intended to illustrate the perennial theme of the king's ingratitude. It appears in this aphorism assigned by Plutarch to the same fellow:

> Orontes, the son-in-law of King Artaxerxes, became involved in disgrace because of an accusation, and, when the decision was given against him, he said that, as mathematicians' fin-

gers are able to represent tens of thousands at one time, and at another time only units, so it was the same with the friends of kings: at one time they are omnipotent and at another time almost impotent. (*Mor.* 174b✧)

An entirely different image was the hallmark of royal propaganda, as can be seen from the tales bearing on Tiribazus. If he suffered the fate he did, it was because he did not show moderation and restraint. We can add to the record an anecdote recorded by Aelian (*VH* VI.14✧):

> I learn of this very kind act of Darius the son of Hystaspes. Aribazus the Hyrcanian plotted against him in alliance with other Persians of note (*ouk aphanoi*). The plot was timed for a hunt. Darius learned of it in advance, but was not deterred; he ordered the men to make ready their equipment and horses and instructed them to hold their weapons at the ready. Looking at them severely he said: "Why don't you do what you set out to do?" Seeing his unflinching gaze they abandoned their plan; fear gripped them to such an extent that they dropped their spears, jumped off their horses and knelt before Darius, surrendering unconditionally. He despatched them in various directions, sending some to the Indian frontier, others to the Scythian. They remained loyal (*pistoi*) to him, remembering his kindness (*euergesia*).

We have no other details about this apparently isolated event. While the text indicates the existence of a plot, we do not know the protagonists or their objectives or motivations. It seems clear that the plot itself was revealed to the king who, because he was surrounded by his guards (which Aelian neglects to mention), was able to exhibit courage tinged even with a certain nonchalance!

At any rate, the text contains little of interest in the way of narrative history. Its primary purpose is an unambiguous ideological message. In fact, it clearly belongs to a very specific genre—royal propaganda or, if you prefer, court literature. It is built on a series of *motifs* linked with monarchic ideology: its intention is to picture Darius as a king who was courageous and just but implacable. The motif of the royal hunt is also interesting, because it is so repetitive. Even one of the versions of the execution of Smerdis/Bardiya claims that Prexaspes (entrusted with the mission by Cambyses) carried out the deed after "he took his victim out hunting" (Herodotus III.30✧). We may also note that the end of the story strangely resembles the denouement of Polyaenus's tale concerning the accession of Darius, who was aided by his stableman's ruse: "The satraps immediately set foot on the ground, performed the *proskynesis*, and made him king of the Persians" (VII.10 [= Herodotus III.85]). As it is transmitted to Aelian, the purpose of the anecdote was to hail the greatness and mercy of the king, not to highlight his weakness and isolation. Moreover, the conclusion is quite moral in itself (in the monarchic sense of the word): thanks to his *euergesia*, the king welcomed the nobles into the circle of his *pistoi*. And, despite being severely punished, the conspirators sing the praises of a sovereign whose greatness they immediately recognize by performing before him the rite of *proskynesis*!

The totality of the evidence thus tends to characterize the individual destiny of the king's men as being closely tied to the sovereign's favor. It is valuable in reminding us that those who held posts and positions were not civil servants in our sense. The only promotions within the system were granted as a result of merit recognized by the king, which was itself defined in relation to the criterion of devotion (*eunoia*).

3. The King and His Faithful: The Rationale of the System

The Faithful and bandaka

We can now return to the central question: the relationship between the aristocratic clans and the dynasty. The political effect of the royal *polydōria* was to constrain the behavior of the aristocrats so that they would act only in the king's interest. The designation of a person as a noble cannot be reduced to his family connections, however prestigious they may have been. It was also defined by the qualities that made a subordinate effective and faithful: "Mardonius, a Mede by birth, satrap and son-in-law of the king, [was also] among the first of all the Persians in deeds of arms and wise counsel" (Nepos, *Paus.* 1.2◊; cf. Diodorus XI.1.3). In Diodorus we find nearly the same words describing Tiribazus: "In wars also, men say, he excelled in valour, and in council his judgement was so good that when the King followed his advice he never made a mistake" (XV.10.3◊).

All of the characteristics attributed to the king's men are wrapped up in a single word: 'faithfulness' (*pistis*). This is the virtue for which Cambyses honored Prexaspes, since he was "the most trusted (*pistotatos*) of his Persian friends" (Herodotus III.30◊). Likewise Artapates, who was "the one among Cyrus' chamberlains who was his most faithful (*pistotatos*) follower" (Xenophon, *Anab.* I.8.28◊). Cyrus the Younger, to be sure, "knew how to judge those who were faithful (*pistoi*), devoted (*eunoi*), and constant (*bebaioi*)" I.9.30◊). It was also according to their faithfulness (*pistotatoi*) that Xenophon's Cyrus arranged his men around him in camp (*Cyropaedia* VIII.5.8). In his letter to Artaxerxes II, Orontas reminded him of the constancy of his "friendship and fidelity (*philia kai pistis*)" (Xenophon, *Anab.* I.6.3◊). One of the virtues required for becoming a Kinsman of the king was also faithfulness (Diodorus XVII.59.1). We find the word in Aelian: the nobles swore to remain faithful (*pistoi*) to Darius (*VH* VI.14). *Pistoi* is also the term used by Xenophon for the men the king ordered to inspect the provinces (*Oec.* IV.6) and by Aeschylus to describe the generals and governors (*Persians* 2). It is clearly for this reason that a man like Boges received from Xerxes "the highest praise" and that his descendants continued to receive honors from the king regularly: "When he was besieged by the Athenians under Cimon, son of Miltiades, and the chance was offered him of leaving the town [of Eion] on terms and returning to Asia, he refused to do so, because he was afraid the king might think that he had shirked his duty to save his skin; so rather than surrender, he held out to the last extremity" before ending his own life (Herodotus VII.107◊). The same was true of Mascames, governor of Doriscus, who alone succeeded in holding out against the Greeks: "Xerxes used to send him a special present every year in recognition of his superiority to all the governors. . . . This is the reason for the annual present from the Persian king" (VII.106◊). The two governors actually proved their faithfulness in every test, comparable to the faithfulness demonstrated later in Alexander's presence by the defenders of Celaenae (Quintus Curtius III.1.7: *pro fide morituros*), by Batis at Gaza (IV.6.7: *fides*), and by Madates in Uxiana (V.3.4: *pro fide*).

It is generally believed that the Classical vocabulary (*pistis/fides*) renders a Persian concept. We know that at Behistun Darius uses the word *bandaka* to describe both subject and loyal peoples and those who supplied aid against rebels. The Persian word itself is hard to translate. In fact, the Akkadian version uses a word (*qallu*) that comes from the vocabulary of slavery or dependence. If, as is generally thought, the Greek translator of Darius's letter to Gadatas encountered the word *bandaka* in the original, he was unable to find any equivalent but *doulos* 'slave'. The Behistun inscription and the translations/ adaptations indicate at least that a *bandaka* was a person simultaneously subject and loyal to the king. The word *pistos* is probably not far removed.

The most concrete example is the relationship between Cyrus the Younger and Oron-tas, commander of the citadel at Sardis. We know that Orontas was a highly exalted in-dividual because of the way he is presented by Xenophon: "A Persian, who was related to the King by birth" (*Anab.* I.6.1◇). Guilty of betrayal to Artaxerxes II, he was tried and condemned by the tribunal called by Cyrus. During the trial, Cyrus recalled:

> This man was given me at first by my father [Darius II], to be my subject (*edōken hypēkoon einai*); then, at the bidding . . . of my brother [Artaxerxes II], this man levied war upon me, holding the citadel of Sardis. (I.6.6◇)

Cyrus's expression illustrates quite clearly the nature of the relationship that was sup-posed to exist between a *bandaka* and his superior. This is also evident in another pas-sage from Xenophon (*Hell.* IV.1.36: *hypēkooi*). When Darius was "giving" Orantas to Cyrus, he loosed Orontas from the ties binding him to Darius and transferred his alle-giance to the person of his son Cyrus. In other words, Orontas was thenceforth obli-gated to be dutifully loyal to Cyrus without reservation. This became the basis of the later accusation leveled against Orontas. Perhaps the same sort of hierarchical relation-ship is suggested by Pharnabazus's desire to take a daughter of Spithridates without the formality of marriage (*aneu gamou*; Xenophon, *Ages.* 3.3), relying on the latter's obliga-tion of loyalty.

Xenophon's text includes other interesting details. The initial reconciliation between Cyrus and Orontas is presented as follows: "Did you not again give me pledges (*pista*) and receive pledges from me?" (I.6.7◇). This makes it appear as though the recognition of a *bandaka* was made official in an official ceremony, during which Orontas gave his right hand to Cyrus, who gave him his (I.6.6). This custom, accompanied by oaths, is well known. It had the status of a guarantee, including, when it involved the king, a guar-antee in regard to an individual or a foreign state (II.4.7; II.5.3; cf. Ctesias §§8, 30). "That is, among the Persians, the sign of an inviolable pledge (*pistis bebaiotatē para tois Per-sais*)," Diodorus remarks (XVI.43.4). A passage in Nepos implies that, in a case in which one party was physically absent, he could send an object to represent his hand. Artaxerxes II "would give him a pledge (*fides*) to that effect in the Persian fashion with his right hand. When [Mithradates] had received that pledge from the king's messenger (*mis-sam*)" (*Dat.* 10.1–2◇). This exchange signifies on the part of the *bandaka* a commitment of loyalty and, on the part of the superior, proof of no less total trust and doubtless also a promise to protect and honor his *bandaka*. At the conclusion of the trial and the conver-sation, "at the bidding of Cyrus, every man of them arose, . . . and took Orontas by the girdle, as a sign that he was condemned to death" (I.6.10◇). In the same way, when Darius III was angered by Charidemus, he "seized [him] by the girdle according to the custom of the Persians, turned him over to the attendants, and ordered him put to death" (Diodorus XVII.30.4◇). For many Iranian peoples, the girdle symbolized the tie between the superior and his *bandaka*: to grasp the girdle signified that the bond was broken.

This concept had very important implications for the political order. It tended to downplay family solidarity in favor of dynastic loyalty and to isolate the nobles in the one-to-one relationship that connected them to the king. Xenophon despairs about this in his picture of "Persian decadence." There he (fictitiously) sets up a before-and-after scenario: "in the olden times," anyone who "effected anything else of good (*kalos*) or glory (*agathos*) for him, such an one received honour and preferment (*timōmenoi*)"; "now . . . if any one seems to bring some advantage to the king by evil-doing, . . . such are the ones who now have the highest honours (*hai megistai timai*) heaped upon them" (*Cyr.* VIII.8.4◇). By way of example, he denounces Mithradates, who without hesitation betrayed his father Ariobarzanes. Furthermore, there are other examples of Persians who, placed in a dilemma of having to choose between allegiance to family and allegiance to the crown, opted to serve the king (e.g., Nepos, *Dat.* 7.1; Diodorus XV.91.3). It was the same for plotters bound to each other by an oath: the attractiveness of royal favor itself eroded the solidity of their plots from within (cf. Herodotus III.71; Ctesias §30; Diodorus XV.91.1). Thus, Xenophon states that at the trial of Orontas even his relatives (*syggeneis*) grasped his girdle (I.6.10).

Clan Nobility and Court Nobility

In a passage devoted to the need for a strict governmental hierarchy, Xenophon presents the famous Chrysantas, who gives a speech before the *homotimēs* ['chief nobles'] and notables gathered by Cyrus (*Cyr.* VII.5.71). Extolling the virtue of obedience, he gave them the following speech: "Let us, therefore, present ouselves before our ruler's headquarters (*archeion*) yonder, as Cyrus bids; . . . Let us offer ourselves for whatever service Cyrus may need us for" (VIII.1.5◇). Chrysantas's proposals were greeted with approval:

> They passed a resolution that the nobles (*entimoi*) should always be in attendance at court and be in readiness for whatever service Cyrus wished until he dismissed them. And as they then resolved, so even unto this day those who are the subjects of the great king in Asia continue to do—they are constantly in attendance at the court of their princes. . . . Accordingly, the nobles came to Cyrus's court with their horses and their spears, for so it had been decreed by the best of those (*hoi aristoi*) who with him had made the conquest of the kingdom. (VIII.1.6, 8◇)

Actually, elsewhere Xenophon recalls one of the obligations that the king laid on the satraps in these words: "To require as many as received lands and palaces to attend at the satrap's court and exercising proper self-restraint to put themselves at his disposal in whatever he demanded" (VIII.6.10◇).

Xenophon makes it quite clear that this was not a choice but a strict obligation. "If any of those who were able to live by the labour of others failed to attend at court, he made inquiry after them" (VIII.1.16◇, 20). Those who did not defer to this command were severely punished by having their goods confiscated and awarded to devoted, obedient nobles (VIII.1.17–21). This is the context in which the obligation laid on Persian nobles to attend the royal table, at least during meals, must be understood (Athenaeus IV.145f–146a). Xenophon makes the significance of these arrangements clear. They existed so that the king could hold up monarchic virtues and greatness in the sight of all. The most devoted nobles of the court received public honors, such as accompanying the king on the hunt: "And thus he inspired in all an earnest ambition, each striving to appear as deserving as he could in the eyes of Cyrus" (VIII.1.39◇).

The process Xenophon describes is nothing more or less than the development of a hereditary nobility into a court nobility. These court nobles were those whom the Greek authors call "People of the Gate" (e.g., Plutarch, *Them.* 26.6), who are incorporated into the court hierarchy, discussed above. It is they whom Themistocles, for example, encountered at the court of Artaxerxes: the chiliarchs Artabanus and Roxanes (27.2–7), the king's cousin Mithropastes (29.7), the Friends of the king (29.5), the powerful personalities (*dynatoi*; 29.5), in short all the People of the Gate (29.1). It is they, depicted in rows on the walls of Persepolis (fig. 25, p. 221), who are so called by the author of the *De Mundo* 398a❖: "The chief and most distinguished men (*hoi prōtoi kai dokimōtatoi*) had their appointed place, some being the king's (*hoi men amph'auton ton basileon*) bodyguard and attendants (*doryphoroi te kai therapontes*), others the guardians of each of the enclosing walls." Each of them received an office and a particular assignment, and, according to this author, they could all be considered 'slaves of the Great King' (*douloi tou megalou basileou*)—in other words, court nobles, *bandaka*.

This kind of organization further increased the nobles' dependence on the king. Watched so closely (*Cyr.* VIII.1.22), the aristocrats had to conform to the dynastic ethic. In the event of revolt, these People of the Gate could also play an important role, as was the case after the battle of Cunaxa:

> During this time Ariaeus' brothers and other relatives (*anagkaioi*) came to him and certain Persians came to his followers, and they kept encouraging them and bringing pledges to some of them from the King that the King would bear them no ill-will because of their campaign with Cyrus against him or because of anything else in the past. (Xenophon, *Anab.* II.4.1❖)

During Megabyzus's revolt in the time of Artaxerxes I, he had with him two of his sons, Zopyrus and Artyphius (Ctesias §37). However, his wife and his youngest son, Artoxares, remained at court (§39). Although Ctesias does not clarify this point, it is apparent that, before signing a treaty with the king (cf. §39), Megabyzus insisted on the return of his wife and son: it was his wife and son (and other people sent by the king) "who convinced him, not without difficulty, to appear before the king." In a way, the relatives of the satraps, who were called "the People of the Gate," served as hostages to ensure the satraps' faithfulness. In this connection, we may quote the case of Memnon, who had retired to Halicarnassus:

> Memnon sent his wife and children to Dareius, because he calculated that leaving them in the king's care was a good way to ensure their safety, while at the same time the king, now that he had good hostages, would be more willing to entrust Memnon with the supreme command. And so it turned out. (Diodorus XVII.23.5)

As a further example, note that, before he left Sardis, Cyrus the Younger remembered to hold hostage at Tralles the wives and children of the commanders of the Greek mercenaries (Xenophon, *Anab.* I.4.8).

Education and Ideological Integration

On numerous occasions, Xenophon stresses the importance of education to the Persians. As he notes several times, participation in education was in principle open to all Persians. But he also states that "all the Persians may send their children to the common schools of justice. Still, only those do send them who are in a position to maintain their children without work; and those who are not so situated do not" (*Cyr.* I.2.15❖). In reality, however, the only ones with access were children of the *homotimēs*, a word used frequently by Xenophon to describe those of upper rank, in contrast to the simple peasants who had to work for a living. In other words, only the aristocratic families could send their children to be educated. The same author says so quite clearly elsewhere: "All the sons of the noblest (*aristoi*) Persians are educated at the King's court" (*Anab.* I.9.3✧), and "it is still the custom for the boys to be educated at court" (*Cyr.* VIII.8.13✧). It was the same in the provinces: the satrap's men had "to have the boys that would be born to them educated at the local court, just as was done at the royal court" (*Cyr.* VIII.6.10✧). It is clear that those who shirked the obligation of being educated found themselves deprived of any chance to ascend to positions and honors, as was true for those who were unable to follow the required courses (I.2.15). This was thus an official system of education, whose successful administration was entrusted to educators (I.2.5) chosen from "their wisest men" (Strabo XV.3.18✧).

The opening chapters of Xenophon's *Cyropaedia* (I.3–5.5) explain the different stages of the education of the young Cyrus at Astyages' court (the book's title means 'Cyrus's education'), from childhood to the time when he was first admitted to the ranks of men and then first took command of an army. This education corresponds very closely to what was prescribed "by the laws of the Persians" (I.2.2). Xenophon indicates that the young Persians passed through several classifications according to age: children (*paides*) until 16 or 17; youths (*ephēboi*) for 10 more years; grown men (*andres*); and then, after 25 years of service, old men.

It is rather difficult to separate what is truly Persian in the *Cyropaedia* from Xenophon's implicit but significant transposition from Spartan institutions, which he has described in another work. The relationship between the two educational systems was also stressed by Arrian (V.4.5), who was a fervent reader and admirer of Xenophon. Fortunately, we can compare Xenophon with Herodotus and Strabo, even though various contradictions remain among the ancient authors about the division into age classes and about the courses taught at the different levels. According to Herodotus, the training of young Persians lasted from the ages of 5 to 20 (I.136); 20 was the minimum age for military service (I.209). According to Strabo, education occupied the youngsters from 5 to 24, with Persians serving in the army from 20 to 50 (XV.3.18–19). According to Herodotus (I.136✧), the Persians taught their children "three things only: to ride, to use the bow, and to speak the truth." Strabo adds: "to throw the javelin" (XV.3.18✧; cf. *Cyr.* I.2.8 and 12). Here is Strabo's view of the training regimen for which they were summoned by brass instruments each morning before dawn:

> They divide the boys into companies of fifty, appoint one of the sons of the king or of a satrap as leader of each company, and order them to follow their leader in a race, having marked off a distance of thirty or forty stadia [5.5–7.4 km]. They require them also to give an account of each lesson, at the same time training them in loud speaking and in breathing, and in the use of their lungs, and also training them to endure heat and cold and rains, and to cross torrential streams in such a way as to keep both armour and clothing dry, and also to tend flocks and live outdoors all night and eat wild fruits, such as pistachio nuts (*terminthos*), acorns, and wild pears. These are called Cardaces, since they live on thievery (*klopeia*), for "carda" means the manly and warlike spirit. Their daily food after their gymnastic exercises consists of bread, barley-cake, cardamum, grains of salt, and roasted or boiled meat; but their drink is water. They hunt by throwing spears from horseback, and with bows and slings; and late in the afternoon they are trained in the planting of trees and in the cutting and gathering of roots and in making weapons and in the art of making linen cloths and hunters' nets. The boys do not touch the meat of wild animals, though it is the custom to bring them home. Prizes are offered by the king for victory in running and in the four other contests of the pentathla. (XV.3.18✧)

This passage of Strabo is much more detailed than any other author's. It also poses a problem of interpretation. Without realizing it, Strabo [and/or an interpolator] in fact distinguishes two diets (wild fruit/daily menu). The former applied to boys called *karda-kes*. They were the ones (exclusively, it seems) who stayed out all night, surviving on foraging and theft. In ordinary times, in fact, the children came home every day (*Cyr.* I.2.8), and the young people slept in a dormitory (I.2.9), except for the married ones (I.2.4). Far from living on the spoils of their thievery, the boys learned justice and honesty (I.2.6), and the youths were used "for seeking out malefactors, and chasing brigands" (*lēstai*; I.2.12).

Whatever the exact meaning of their designation, the *kardakes* were thus clearly a phase, a temporary stage, in the education by age-groups. The similarities with the Lacedemonian *kryptie* are obvious. There we see a court rite of passage during which the youths had to prove their abilities in conditions exactly opposite to those of a soldier: living by night, solitary, surviving on foraging and plunder. After this test, they were admitted to the older age-group. Thus, this must have been a test imposed on those who had undergone ten years of training as youths (cf. *Cyr.* I.2.12). Other rites of passage, far more venerable, are known in Iran, particularly among the Carmanians (Strabo XV.2.14). This process must therefore represent an ancient Persian tribal custom, which was incorporated into the royal education received by the aristocratic youth.

Though it is not included in Herodotus, a certain amount of the information given by Strabo is also found in Xenophon. This includes the importance of the hunt in education, a recurrent theme in the *Cyropaedia* and many other of Xenophon's works. Every time the king goes hunting, some of the youths accompany him, for "in their eyes this occupation is the most authentic training for war. . . . It is difficult to find in war a situation that has not occurred on the hunt. . . . [During hunts] they eat nothing but cress, bread, and water," unless they catch game, which they may then eat (I.2.10; cf. I.2.8). Xenophon also states that they learn "the properties of the products of the earth, so as to avail themselves of the useful ones and keep away from those that were harmful" (VIII.8.14◊).

Training was thus principally physical and military, suitable for turning out good horsemen, good archers, and good lancers. Strabo is the only one to add that the youths were equally devoted to watching over the herds and planting trees. It is impossible to avoid comparing this with one of the royal virtues, the "good gardener" (chap. 6/5). By including agricultural training, young Persians were shaped to the royal model. The equivalence between the aristocratic ethic and the royal ethic could be achieved all the more easily because the royal is derived from the aristocratic. But despite the fact that they share the same values, the king and the aristocrats were not on an equal footing. Though the king was also a fine horseman, a fine archer, and a fine lancer, he was distinguished by superior virtues granted to him by Ahura-Mazda (chap. 6/2, 6/4). It is also significant that the honorary distinctions were awarded to the best youths by the king himself. While the rite of passage just described marked entry into the class of adult warriors (*andres*), the public ceremony of awarding prizes allowed the youths to join those whom the king considered the Faithful (*bandaka*) on an equal footing. Educated at the Gate, "they see and hear the names of those whom the king honors, as well as those who incur his disfavor" (Xenophon, *Anab.* I.9.4).

Now what was the significance of the third instruction the young Persians received: 'To speak the truth' (*alēthizesthai/alētheuein*)? Herodotus himself probably did not know. Xenophon tells us that the children "spent their time learning justice" (*dikaiosunē*), gratitude, and temperance (*Cyr.* I.2.6–8); "they were present at trials conducted according to the law" (VIII.8.13). It is tempting to suppose that the Greek words for truth/justice corresponded to the Persian word *arta*. Based on this assumption, what we hear Herodotus and Xenophon saying is that the youths were educated in the duty of dynastic loyalty. Strabo provides an essential detail: the educators "also interweave their teachings with the mythical element (*mythōdes*), thus reducing that element to a useful purpose, and rehearse both with song and without song the deeds (*erga*) both of the gods and of the noblest men" (*aristoi*; XV.3.18◊). Xenophon adds an extra item, speaking "of tales and songs still heard today. . . . In them, Cyrus is [presented as] having received from nature a very beautiful figure, a very generous soul, a passion for study and for glory to the point of enduring any fatigue, to face all dangers to earn glory" (*Cyr.* I.2.1).

It thus appears that the educators were entrusted with transmitting to the young Persians the oral traditions of their people. These dealt with the heroes as much as with the gods. As Xenophon says, a good part of the traditions dealt with the founder-heroes of Persian grandeur, such as Cyrus (cf. Herodotus III.160). A passage from Athenaeus is most relevant. Within a long digression on the place of music, dance, and hymns in education (XIV.630–31e), Athenaeus recalls that "in days of old," music played a central role (631e–32), especially among the Spartans. More generally, "in days of old . . . it was the acts of heroes and the glory of the gods that the poets set to music" (*di'ōidēs*; 633c). Then, quoting Dinon's *Persica*, he states that this custom has been maintained among the barbarians: "It was the singers (*ōidoi*) who, for example, exalted the courage of Cyrus the Elder and the war he conducted against Astyages." Dinon in fact records that when Cyrus had taken the Persian road that would lead to the founding of the Empire (he was then the head *rhabdophore* ['rod-bearer'] at the Median court), Astyages held a great feast to which Angares, the most renowned singer of the time, was invited. Angares told a story of a powerful beast, lord of all the surrounding regions. In answer to Astyages' question, he replied that this beast was none other than Cyrus (633d–e). Through this passage from Dinon, we gain a specific detail about the oral transmission of founder legends. There is hardly any doubt that, beginning with Darius, the legend of Achaemenes raised by an eagle was added to it; royal propaganda presented this legend as explaining the origin of the nobility (*eugeneia*; Aelian, *Anim.* XIII.21).

There is no longer any doubt that the "wise men" entrusted with this mission were the *magi*, veritable depositories of the collective memory. They specialized in hymns and theogonies (Herodotus I.132; Strabo XV.3.14 [*epōidai*]; Xenophon, *Cyr.* VIII.1.23; Quintus Curtius III.3.9; V.1.22; Pausanias V.27.5–6). We also know that they were entrusted with the education of the royal children (p. 521). Their detailed knowledge of plants and remedies (pp. 266f.) suited them also to teach the value of herbs to Persian youths.

In sum, Persian youths learned throughout their training to become faithful servants of their king, as soldiers as well as subjects. The imperial hierarchy was implicitly present in this training, since the groups of fifty were led by a son of the king or a son of a satrap (XV.3.18). Here, the word *satrap* is taken in its generic sense of representative of the royal elite (cf., e.g., Polyaenus VII.10). Even though Xenophon states that the king's sons also participated in this education (*Anab.* I.9.1–2; *Cyr.* I.3.1), it is clear that, in this as in other ways, they enjoyed a special status.

4. The King and His Faithful: The Dynamic of the Contradictions

Birth and Royal Favor

The preceding discussions lead to a very simple question, which has been glossed over so far—or we have simply assumed the answer: what, exactly, is a noble? We have only the Classical sources to help define the structure and organization of this nobility. Nobles were defined by birth and wealth: "Otanes, the son of Pharnaspes, one of the wealthiest (*chremasi*) members (*genei*) of the Persian nobility (*ho prōtos tōn Perseōn*)" Herodotus III.68); Orxines, in 325, is introduced by Quintus Curtius as follows: "Prominent among all the barbarians for high birth (*nobilitas*) and wealth (*divites*). He traced his descent from Cyrus, formerly king of the Persians" (X.1.22–23✧). Orxines is distinguished by his position as head of the tribe of the Pasargadae. An aristocrat's status was thus defined by his ethnicity (*anēr Persēs*), his father's name, or his tribe and/or clan's name, as shown by the words used by Herodotus to identify the heads of the expedition against Cyrene around 513: "Amasis, a man of the Maraphii tribe, and Badres, of the Pasargadae" (Herodotus IV.167✧). Similarly, at Naqš-i Rustam, the inscription identifying Gobryas refers to the tribe of his origin (Patišuvariš) (*DNc*). And there are many references to people called Achaemenid (in the tribal sense) around Cambyses (Herodotus III.65), Darius, and Xerxes (V.32; VII.62; VII.117, etc.).

The nobility was also defined by contrast with the poor. In two of his inscriptions, Darius refers to certain antagonistic social groups: in his Naqš-i Rustam inscription (*DNb*), the king is presented as mediator between the 'powerful' (*tunavant*) and the 'weak' (*skauθi*), which can also be understood as rich and poor. He and the members of the "royal stock" are placed among those he calls *amata*, a word meaning 'proven', 'excellent', which is usually translated as 'noble'. Another word, *azata*—not found in the royal inscriptions—also refers to nobility of origin, contrasted more generally with persons of inferior status.

The Greek authors make it very clear that "Persian" ethnicity refers to distinct social realities. For Herodotus (I.133) and Strabo (XV.3.19), the social distinction between the directors (*hēgemōnes*) and the people (*hoi polloi*) exists chiefly on the economic level. At birthday banquets, "the rich are served an ox, a horse, a camel, a donkey, all oven-roasted whole; the poor, sheep and goats." One group has rich, colorful garments; the other, mediocre clothing. Joint participation in military expeditions does not efface these distinctions. In Xerxes' army, Herodotus sets up an opposition within what he calls "the king's men": some twenty thousand horsemen "taken from all the Persians" versus the thousand pikesmen who follow Ahura-Mazda's chariot, "all men of the best (*aristoi*) and noblest (*gennaiotatoi*) Persian blood" (Herodotus VII.41✧). We may also mention Heraclides' description of the 1,000 Persian *melophoroi*: "They are chosen by their high birth (*aristidēn*) from the group of 10,000 Persians who bear the name Immortal" (Athenaeus XII.514c).

Within the aristocracy, subtle distinctions are made by the Greek authors using a vocabulary whose apparent diversity makes sociological interpretation difficult. The Persian nobles could be 'esteemed' (*dokimoi*), 'noteworthy' (*logimoi*), 'honored' (*en ainē*), 'worthy' (*axioi*), 'renowned' (*onomastoi*), 'prestigious' (*epiphaneis*), and so on. In reality, these words are often used interchangeably. More interesting are the gradations expressed by the Classical authors with comparatives or superlatives. It is not enough, for instance, to be "esteemed"; one must be among "the most esteemed." Herodotus often describes this superior stratum of aristocracy as *prōtoi*, that is, 'first' or 'princes'. This is the small group the king convenes in peacetime or wartime (Herodotus I.206; III.127; III.65; VII.8; VII.53). The same gradations exist when the king is not present in the theater of operations. In Otanes' army at Samos, Herodotus singles out "the Persians of the highest rank (*tōn Perséōn hoi pleistou axioi*) [who] then had chairs of state placed for them" (III.144◇). After Xerxes left for Sardis, Mardonius was put in command of the army. A rich Theban held a banquet and "invited Mardonius and fifty other distinguished (*hoi logimōtatoi*) Persians" (Herodotus IX.15◇) who, "after Mardonius, were the most honored (*hoi met'ekeinou en ainē eontes*)" (IX.16).

At first sight, this multifarious vocabulary seems to reflect an obvious fact—a genetic reality: one was a noble because one was the son of a noble. But at the same time, the court hierarchy, based on royal favor, necessarily rivaled the clan hierarchies, which derived solely from the privilege of birth. To be distinguished as a noble was not simply a matter of family lineage. Herodotus's vocabulary expresses this double designation. Masistius, lost in the battle of Plataea, is described by Herodotus thus: "a man more highly thought of (*logimōtatos*) both by the king and by his subjects (*kai basilei*) than anyone else in the Persian army except Mardonius himself" (IX.24◇). Herodotus uses comparable expressions several times: the Achaemenid Artachaees was "much respected by Xerxes (*dokimos . . . para Xerxēi*)" (VII.117◇). Prexaspes is not just "in very high honor among the Persians (*en ainē megistē . . . en Persēi*)" and "a distinguished man" (*dokimos*) but also, "the most trusted of [Cambyses'] Persian friends" (III.30◇). We may also quote Artabazus, son of Pharnaces, "who was already an famous man in the Persian army (*en Persēisi logimos*) and was further to increase his reputation as a result of the battle of Plataea" (VIII.126). Even before Plataea, he was already "a Persian of the very highest reputation with Xerxes (*anēr dokimos para Xerxēi*)" (IX.41).

In some way, the two expressions used by Herodotus (more highly thought of than anyone else in the Persian army/of the very highest reputation with the king) refer to the two hierarchies, which continued to coexist: the clan hierarchy (birth) and the royal hierarchy (favor/gift). In other words, royal favor relativized the prestige connected with birth. As Aelian puts it (*Anim.* XII.21), the Persian aristocracy of birth (*tōn Persōn eugeneia*) was defined by reference to dynastic norms. It is also quite characteristic that the grammarian Hesychius explains the Persian word *azatai* 'free, noble' as follows: "Those who are closest to the king." Being held in the king's great esteem was one of the criteria for nobility; moreover, used in the superlative (*eggytatoi*), the word implied the idea of (fictional) relatedness.

Royal Favor and Social Mobility

That there were ways of joining the royal hierarchy apart from being born into it leads us to suppose that it was theoretically possible for a particularly deserving, poor Persian to become integrated into the royal hierarchy. Within Cyrus's army and entourage, Xenophon several times distinguishes the *homotimēs* from the people (*dēmotoi*): the former could live without working, because "they live on the labor of others" (*Cyr.* VIII.1.16); the latter, however, "have to earn their living" (II.1.1). These are the common peasants, whom Xenophon (VII.5.67) and Aelian (*VH* I.32) call the *autourgoi*, that is (by Greek standards), small landowners. For the *homotimēs*: war; for the peasants: farmwork (IV.3.12–13).

Xenophon refers to societal promotions. The people whom Cyrus called on first for his private guard were the *autourgoi* (VII.5.67). And, in a discussion of promotion rewarding individual merit, Xenophon introduces the Persian Pheraulas (II.3.7◊). He was one of the people (*dēmotoi*) "but a man who for some reason or other had from the beginning won Cyrus's confidence and affection; besides, he was well-favoured in body and a gentleman at heart." But because of his origin he did not have access to the traditional education of the Persian nobles. His father was a poor peasant who had to borrow his seed grain (VIII.3.36–38). Although Pheraulas had no choice but to work the land with his father, he was fascinated with the profession of soldiery from childhood (II.3.9–12). Addressing the *homotimēs*, he offered himself as an example and stated that "we are all now starting on an equal footing in a contest of merit" (II.3.8◊). He added: "Cyrus . . . I, for one, shall not only enter this contest, but I shall also expect you to reward me according to my deserts," challenging the other *dēmotoi* of the army to follow his example and "enter with alacrity into the competition with these gentlemen in this sort of warfare" (II.3.15◊). The conclusion was that each would "receive rewards according to his deserts, and that Cyrus should be the judge" (II.3.16◊).

It is difficult simply to take Xenophon's presentation at face value. He has composed a highly political discourse on the merits of a society based on the worth of the individual. At the same time, he seems to promote one of the themes specific to the monarchic ideology. The Achaemenid king, as we have seen at Behistun and Naqš-i Rustam, positioned himself as the conciliator of the interests of the powerful (*tunavant*) and the weak (*skauθi*). Simple soldiers or common peasants could be promoted suddenly to the rank of royal Benefactor and receive royal gifts (Aelian, *VH* I.32; XII.40). But there are no specific examples that might confirm the "society tale" of Pheraulas. Nonetheless, we may cite the example of the poor Mardian peasant Rhakokes, who as a reward for his justice was elevated by the king to the position of royal judge (*VH* I.34). At the same time, it is true that Aelian's anecdote itself emerged from court circles.

Let us also remark that in some of the Persepolis tablets, some Persians are identified not by their tribe name but by their place of residence: Iršena of Anšan (PF 1368), Umizza "son of Halpa, who lives in Hiran" (PF 2070), Uštana of Shiraz (PF 1811), Šadukka of Zappi (PF 1790), Ukama of Paišiyauvādā (PF 330, 2027), and many more. The coexistence of tribal denotations (PF 1797; cf. Herodotus IV.167) and local denotations could well be an indication of a change-in-progress of prosopographic practice. It might also indicate a social differentiation between the old aristocratic families that were attached to their tribes and Persians of lower birth called into service by the king. In fact, the two interpretations harmonize perfectly: the "new social class" represented by the latter would consist of men who rejected the confines of the tribe; the old-stock aristocrats, however, continued to value belonging to a famous tribe until the end of the Achaemenid era. More will be clear when the ethnonyms that appear here and there are better understood. In one tablet, for example, the administration distributes rations to Maraphii and Kušiyans (PF 447). We do not know who the Kušiyans were. On the other hand, according to Herodotus (I.125) the Maraphii were a Persian tribe. It is thus not impossible that they were Persian peasants, whom we do not know whether to distinguish from or compare with the "*kurtaš* living off rations at Marappiyaš" (PF 909–11). Prudence on this score is thus advised. The Persepolis tablets still hold many secrets. The interpretation is all the more insecure because we do not know the exact social origins of many of the Persians of the royal entourage named by the Classical authors.

Furthermore, if such promotions could take place, they did not seriously affect Persian social structures. Two tablets (PF 871, 1137) record the provision of rations to 29 and 15 "Persian boys (*puhu*) [who] copy texts . . . at Pittaman." The word *puhu* always refers to a category of *kurtaš* who received less rations than men. Otherwise, nothing distinguishes these tablets from hundreds of others of the same type. We must thus recognize that some Persians were reduced to the status of *kurtaš* under circumstances we do not understand (impoverishment? royal punishment?). And it is likely that these tablets are only a sample. It is reasonable to imagine that quite a few Persian *kurtaš* are listed anonymously in the tablets. It also seems fairly logical to think that simple Persians worked the lands of aristocrats. They were doubtless also required, as corvée labor, to work the lands in the paradises near their village or to maintain the roads for the passage of the Great King and his court (cf. Aelian, *Anim.* XV.26). We also know that starting with the time of Cambyses, slaves bought at Matezziš had Persian names (see p. 88). The imperial triumph of the dominant ethnic group clearly did not wipe out class differences. The dominant socioethnic class held the preeminent position not just in the Empire but in Persian society itself.

All in all, even when we postulate the possibility of social promotions, there is no doubt that the greater part of the king's men came from the great aristocratic families. The privileges of birth never disappeared. The importance of birth as a criterion is well illuminated by later texts: when the Greeks, after Cunaxa, came to Ariaeus to ask him to take Cyrus's place, he replied as follows: "Many Persians nobler (*beltiones*) than him will not support his becoming king" (Xenophon, *Anab.* II.2.1). When the Spartan king Agesilaus mediated in arranging a marriage between the daughter of the Persian Spithridates and the Paphlagonian dynast Otys, what decided Otys was not the young lady's vaunted beauty but the nobility of her father's ancestry: Spithridates was "from a family inferior to none in Persia" (*Perseōn oudenos endeesteros*); he was "particularly well born (*eugenestatos*)" (*Hell.* VI.1.6–7). And, in Darius III's army, the Persians of distinction (*hoi entimoi Persai*) were distinguished by Arrian from 'the masses' (*to plēthos*; Arrian III.11.8). Alexander later used the same principle to differentiate some Persians who fell into his power after the death of Darius: "Having inquired into the rank (*nobilitas*) of each one, he separated from the common herd (*vulgus*) those who were of high birth (*genus*)" (Quintus Curtius VI.2.9✧).

Persian Aristocratic Houses

Herodotus (I.134) and Strabo (XV.3.20) further indicate that the social hierarchies in Persia cannot be reduced to the opposition rich/poor. Among the elements of social symbolism, in fact, they give special attention to the manner in which Persians greeted each other, according to their place in the social hierarchy. If they were notables (*gnōrimoi*) or 'equal in honor' (*isotimoi*), they kissed on the lips; if one of them was of lower status (*hypodeesteros*, *tapeinoteros*), they kissed on the cheeks; and lastly if one of them was of much lower birth (*pollōi agennesteros*, *eti tapeinoteros*), he was restricted to performing the *proskynesis* before his better. Taken at face value, these practices seem to follow three categories, which we might render, both conveniently and vaguely, with the following expressions: the nobility [*grande noblesse*] (*isōtimoi*; cf. *homotimoi* in Xenophon), the gentry [*petite noblesse*], and the commoners [*gens du commun*].

The first group comprises the heads of the great aristocratic houses. This is the word (*oikos*) used by Herodotus for Intaphernes. He is reputed to have conspired "with all the men of his house" (*hoi oikeioi pantes*), including his sons (III.119). The internal cohesiveness of the great families is well evidenced in the wonderful aristocratic romance of Odatis and Zariadres told by Chares of Mytilene and passed on by Athenaeus (XIII.575). The girl's father opposed the marriage because "lacking male issue, he wished to give his daughter to a young man of his own house" (*eis tōn peri auton oikeiōn*; 575c). It is clear that the aristocrats' power, in Persia as well as in the provinces, was based on possessing land. Perhaps estates of this sort are what underlie the events alluded to in two Treasury tablets (PT 4–5). The late example of Orxines also provides similar confirmation: he came to receive Alexander with great pomp when he arrived from Carmania. As the head of the tribe of the Pasargadae, Orxines represented himself as a descendant of Cyrus. Quintus Curtius includes this detail: "Prominent among all the barbarians for high birth and wealth. . . . He had wealth, both what he had inherited from his forefathers and what he himself had amassed during long possession of sovereignty" (X.1.22–23✧). The example of Orxines also shows that the tribal hierarchies were preserved. We may presume, though there is no definitive proof, that what we have called the nobility pertained to the three tribes (Pasargadae, Maraphii, Maspii) that, according to Herodotus, dominated all of the others. Of these tribes, the Pasargadae, whose members were particularly noble (*aristoi*), retained the preeminence (Herodotus I.125). Should we imagine a distinction between high nobility, which owned ancestral estates in Persia, and another nobility, which basically held its possessions by royal favor?

For the economic organization of the great aristocratic houses, the most revealing text is a passage by Heraclides quoted by Athenaeus. The abundance and variety of the dishes prepared for the king's table every day (IV.145a) were found at the tables of the wealthiest Persians: "A rich Persian (*eudaimones*) on his birthday will have an ox, or a horse, or a camel, or a donkey baked whole in the oven" (Herodotus I.133). While explaining the careful economic management of the food supply for the royal table, Heraclides remarks that it was the same for "the elite Persians" (*hoi en dynasteia*; Athenaeus IV.145e–f). He then explains (145f–146a):

> The entire meal is brought to the table at one time. But when the Tablemates (*syndeipnoi*) have finished their meal, whatever remains on the table, basically meat and bread, is given by the officer in charge of the table to each of the people of the house (*oikeioi*). They take it and in that way receive their daily supplies. This is the reason the most honored Tablemates of the king (*hoi entimōtatoi tōn syndeipnōn*) come to court only for lunch (*ariston*), rather than twice: so that they are able to receive their own *syndeipnoi* ('Tablemates').

All of these statements are unambiguous. The aristocratic houses were directed and organized in a way absolutely identical to the rules that governed protocol in the royal house. Every house had its steward (Berossus apud Athenaeus XIV.639c), as did the royal house (Herodotus III.61). No doubt, these *syndeipnoi* of the great aristocrats were chosen from the men of the house (*oikeioi*) and perhaps also from nobles of a lower rank, who would have been part of their network of alliances and power. The analogy between the aristocratic houses and the royal house is even purer in that the banquets Herodotus describes (I.133✧) are given on the birthday of the head of the house, "of all days in the year a Persian most distinguished his birthday and celebrated it with a dinner of special magnificence." It echoes the importance of the banquet given every year on the king's birthday (IX.110). It is thus not impossible that on that day as well, the heads of houses, like the king, gave gifts to their guests to symbolize and reinforce their power and influence. In sum, Persian society functioned according to a hierarchy that was at once highly diversified and extremely constrained: every great aristocrat also had his own *bandaka* who paid him homage in the form of *proskynesis* (cf. Xenophon, *Anab.* I.6.10).

The similarities do not stop here. Like the kings, the heads of houses practiced polygamy: "Every man has a number of wives, and a much greater number of concubines" (*pallakai*; Herodotus I.135). Strabo adds that polygamy had the objective of providing a large number of children (XV.3.17: *polyteknia*). Herodotus agrees (I.136): "After prowess in fighting, the chief proof of manliness is to be the father of a large family of boys." It is also practically certain that the aristocratic families, following the pattern of the royal family, could enter into endogamous unions. The practice is implicit in a story told by Ctesias: "Teritouchmes [Darius II's son-in-law] had a sister born to the same father and the same mother as he, Roxanne. . . . He became enamored of her and had relations with her" (§54; cf. Athenaeus V.220c).

Herodotus describes the authority that the head of the family had over his children as well:

> They declare that no man has ever yet killed his father or mother; in the cases where this has apparently happened, they are quite certain that inquiry would reveal that the son was either a changeling or born out of wedlock, for they insist that it is most improbable that the actual parent should be killed by his child. (I.137)

The authority of the head of the family is even compared explicitly to the king's: "the custom . . . forbids even the king himself to put a man to death for a single offence, and [it forbids] any Persian under similar circumstances to punish a servant (*mēdeis tōn heautou oiketeōn*) by an irreparable injury" (I.137). In other words, the head of the house seems to have held the power of life and death over the people who depended on him—sons, relatives, and servants—at least for punishments relating to family custom. This may be how we should understand the relationship between Xerxes and Sataspes: presented as an Achaemenid by Herodotus, Sataspes was a close relative of the king, since his mother was Xerxes' sister. Before he was pardoned because of his mother's pleas, he was condemned to death by the king because "he had raped a daughter of Megabyzus' son, Zopyrus" (IV.43◇). Now, we know that Megabyzus himself had married one of Xerxes' daughters (Ctesias §22ff.). It was thus perhaps in his role as head of the royal House that Xerxes intervened in this case.

Family Solidarity and Royal Policy

We thus see that neither the tribal structures nor the privileges of birth ever disappeared. On the contrary, the solidarity of the great Persian houses gave their heads undeniable means of action, as much in the social and economic spheres as in the political. To a certain extent, they even appear to have contradicted the principle of unmitigated royal authority, in particular when they were involved in the process of transmission of imperial orders. By virtue of their riches (and their daughters), the nobles could also gather a clientele by turning the exchange of gifts/favors to their own advantage, which could not help but advance their personal ambitions. This was the "gravest" accusation brought against Tiribazus by Orontes: "To seek by his good deeds to turn to his own cause the commanders of troops and to use honors, gifts, and promises to win them" (Diodorus XV.8.4). Such observations quite naturally specify and confirm the conclusions presented previously on the close dependence that bound the aristocracy to the dynasty by means of royal gifts and honors.

Herodotus and Strabo give some indications of Persian traditional practices regarding wedding ceremonies—for example, on the diet observed by the bridegroom (Strabo XV.3.17). More important, both quite clearly distinguish legitimate marriages from unofficial unions, in the same way that the Greek texts distinguish legitimate children from illegitimate (*nothoi*). It was for this reason that Spithridates was angry with Pharnabazus, who claimed to want his daughter without marriage (Xenophon, *Ages.* 3.3: *aneu gamou*). It is likely that marriages were arranged by heads of families and that the contract was solemnified by oaths and sacrifices (cf. Herodotus IX.108). In some cases, the direct intervention of the king is attested (Herodotus VI.41), not to mention the example of the king's daughters. But the question of what authority sanctioned the legitimacy of the marriage remains. To read Herodotus (III.31), it appears that royal judges could be consulted; however, their involvement, in this area as in others, was limited to "interpreting the ancestral laws." This is the context in which Cambyses approached them to learn whether he had the right to marry his sister.

Let us turn to Arrian, who describes the marriages organized by Alexander at Susa in this way:

> They were celebrated in the Persian way (*nomōi tōi persikōi*); they arranged several rows of armchairs for the future spouses, and after they drank each other's health, each bride sat beside her intended; the men took them by the hand and kissed them, following the king's example. For all the weddings were celebrated at the same time. (VII.4.7)

Of course, this is a late text. But, at the same time, Arrian twice insists on the Persian character of the ceremony (cf. VII.6.2). Furthermore, the political nature of the marriages in Susa makes this interpretation very likely. Shall we infer from this that, in the Achaemenid period as well, all of the weddings were celebrated at the same time, in the presence of the king? On the first point, Strabo gives a positive answer: "Marriages are consummated at the beginning of the vernal equinox" (XV.3.17◆). It is thus not impossible that marriages were recognized by royal authority, or perhaps doubly solemnized—first within the tribe and then by the king in a public ceremony at court.

Herodotus also writes about large Persian families. He notes that, "after prowess in fighting, the chief proof of manliness (*andragathiē*) is to be the father of a large family of boys" (I.136). He immediately adds this detail: "Those who have the most sons receive an annual present (*dōra*) from the king." Strabo uses the word *athla* (XV.3.17), which suggests the idea of a competition between the great families in the same way that the king distributed rewards as prizes for competitions won during Persian youths' education (*athlon*: XV.3.17). As in the case of other gifts and favors, we must consider this occasion and the distribution of prizes to be a form of official recognition. In some fashion, then, a traditional family value was integrated into a demographic policy encouraged by the king. We can easily understand the reasons. To protect their military and political power in the Empire, the Persians had to maintain a large population on which the king could draw to provide his elite cavalry and to serve as a breeding ground for officers and administrators. At the same time, the youth of the aristocracy, called up to the king's service, were molded by the royal education.

On the other hand, the authority of the head of the family was not as absolute as Herodotus would have us think. First of all, several accounts make it clear that, even if youths lived with their father, they had to obey any call to return to the royal army. Twice Herodotus portrays fathers who tried to get a son exempted from military service. Each time, the king's reaction was extremely violent: he reminded them that he himself brought his sons with him (cf. Herodotus VIII.104, 107; Quintus Curtius III.8.12), and he put the young men to death (IV.84; VII.38–39; Seneca, *De ira* XIV.2.4). The principle of familial solidarity had its corollary in judicial order. During a revolt, rebels generally took all the members of their household with them. On the other hand, as already noted (see p. 325), the attractiveness of royal favor frequently led some to breach this solidarity. Nevertheless, this behavior—taking one's entire family along when rebelling—is easily explained by the principle of familial solidarity, for, when all was said and done, the entire family was considered guilty and therefore all would be executed, as the example of Intaphernes already mentioned shows so well (Herodotus III.119; cf. IX.113, and Plutarch, *Art.* 29.8). Under these conditions, we understand how Glus, son-in-law of Tiribazus, might have been afraid of being implicated in the charges levied against his father-in-law (Diodorus XV.9.3).

Finally, let us quote the inexhaustible Aelian:

> A man called Rhacoces, of the Mardian tribe, had seven children. The youngest of them was called Cartomes, who did a great deal of harm to his elder brothers. At first his father tried to correct and restrain him by admonition. But when this failed, the local magistrates (*hoi dikastai tōn perikhourōn*) arrived at the house of the young man's father, and the latter arrested the lad, tying his hands behind his back and taking him into the presence of the magistrates. He made a full and detailed denunciation of all his acts of misbehaviour and asked the magistrates to execute the young man. They were horrified, and decided not to pass sentence on their own authority; instead they brought both before Artaxerxes, the king of Persia. When the Mardian repeated his statement, . . . Artaxerxes commended Rhacoces and made him one of the royal magistrates (*basilikoi dikastai*). (I.34✧)

This court anecdote illustrates quite well the relationship between family justice and royal justice that existed on this occasion. First, Rhacoces attempted to take care of the problem as head of the family; second, he appealed to the local judges, before being received by the king himself. Of course, this anecdote is late: no other document gives any idea of when these circuit judgeships were created (cf. chap. 11/10 [P. 483]: a judge of Parnaka). In addition, this anecdote does not portray an aristocrat; nonetheless, it very clearly poses the problem considered here.

5. King and Satraps

Family Strategies and Royal Control

Among all the Faithful of the king, the satraps ("Protectors of the power/kingdom") played an essential role in the Empire, and the powers and prestige with which they were endued could have provoked them to keep their distance from the king. The solidarity of the great Persian families explains how, once a noble was named satrap, he could take his whole family along with him; it also explains how his sons could cooperate with his government or perhaps participate with him in a revolt against the king (e.g., Ctesias §§37–38, 40). Every head of family had the goal of promoting his children to the highest positions in the Empire (cf. esp. Diodorus XVI.52.3–4). Furthermore, the practice of passing on responsibilities to the next generation is frequently attested. Twice, Ctesias writes: "N became satrap in place of his father" (§§53, 57).

The best-known case concerns the satrapy of Hellespontine Phrygia. In 479, Xerxes appointed Artabazus (Thucydides I.129.1). He was a man of illustrious birth, the son of Pharnaces, who most likely was the same as Parnaka, economic minister of Persia under Darius. Pharnaces/Parnaka was in turn son of Arsames, who all agree was a brother of Hystaspes, father of Darius. Artabazus thus was closely related to the royal family, since he was the son of Darius's cousin. He took part in the expedition of 480 (Herodotus VII.66). He was Xerxes' escort upon the king's return to Sardis; by that time, he was "already a famous man (*dokimos*) in the Persian army" (Herodotus VIII.126). After a setback in Chalcis, he returned to place himself under Mardonius's command (VIII.126–30) but opposed his strategy (IX.66). After the defeat at Plataea, he succeeded, at some cost, in leading some companies of troops to Asia Minor (Herodotus IX.66; 89–90). This is when Xerxes granted him the satrapy of the Hellespont, in the context of his reorganization of his possessions in Asia Minor (see chap. 13/8 below). He played an important part in the 470s (Thucydides I.129.1) and was still on the job in 449 (Diodorus XII.3–4). At an unknown date, he was succeeded by his son Pharnaces, who according to the practice of papponymy bore his grandfather's name. In 412, Pharnaces' son Pharnabazus controlled the satrapy, perhaps for a time jointly with his brothers, since the treaty with Sparta was signed in the name of Pharnaces' sons (Thucydides VIII.58.1). In 387–386, Pharnabazus was recalled to court, and he married Artaxerxes II's daughter Apame. We can follow the family's narrative down to the time of Darius III (and even beyond).

Familial legacy is also known as the basis for other positions. So it was that Otanes succeeded his father Sisamnes (condemned to death by Cambyses) as royal judge (Herodotus V.25). The measures taken by Mardontes and Artayntes, commanders of the fleet in Asia Minor in 479, were also characteristic: "the command was taken over (*autou proselomenou*) . . . together with one other—Ithamitres, Artayntes' nephew, who had been chosen for the position by his uncle" (VIII.130◊). Even if a well-known, esteemed noble's responsibilities were not automatically passed on to his sons, numerous examples show that they were automatically incorporated into the ruling class. One of Xerxes' admirals in 480 was Prexaspes (II), son of Aspathines (I) (Herodotus VII.97). This Aspathines I was probably none other than the person listed (erroneously) among the Seven by Herodotus (III.70, 78), and one of the royal arms-bearers at Naqš-i Rustam (*DNd*). Despite the risk of misidentification (homonymy being no guarantee of identity), it is also tempting to identify him with the person of the same name mentioned in several Persepolis tablets from the time of Darius and Xerxes (PT 12–12a, 14); his seal names him: "Aspathines, son of Prexaspes." He was therefore the grandson of Prexaspes I, who held a choice position in Cambyses' entourage.

Given these practices, the danger of creating little satrapal principalities was great. Oroetes seems to have tried this in Asia Minor, profiting from the void at the center of power (see above, chap. 3/2). Sons naturally tended to behave like successors to a patrimonial estate, as illustrated by the remark placed in Pharnabazus's mouth by Xenophon, addressing these words to Agesilaus: "Everything my father left me, beautiful palaces and paradises full of trees and game, which so delighted me, all this I have seen razed and burned to the ground" (*Hell.* IV.1.33). A further detail (IV.1.40) seems to imply the existence of battles between the heirs apparent to the position of satrap. However, it

appears that the appointment or dismissal of satraps and generals was basically the prerogative of the king alone (cf. Herodotus VI.43). The insertion of a relative (son,
nephew) into the chain of command by a father or an uncle with a position implies that
there also was confirmation (or disallowal) by the king (Arrian II.1.3 and II.2.1). It is
likely that the satraps' power was periodically confirmed (cf. Diodorus XI.71.2). Although satraps were closely watched, the principle of family inheritance of power had
the advantage of preparing the sons to exercise the duties of satrap. It must be added that
the length of the term of the Pharnacids of Hellespontine Phrygia is a highly exceptional
case and that they themselves did not escape royal discipline in the end, in the fourth
century (Diodorus XVI.52.3). The Achaemenid satrap was not merely a civil servant, in
the dismissive sense this term has in our contemporary society. He depended personally
on the king, and he had to behave as a faithful *bandaka*; moreover, he was closely
watched by the central authority.

The Satrap and the Armed Forces

One of the lessons Darius no doubt learned from the insubordination of Oroetes at
Sardis was that, left to his own devices, a satrap had many resources for liberating himself from the central command. One of the advantages Oroetes counted on was the
armed forces available to him—a guard of a thousand Persians and the forces he could
draw from Phrygia, Lydia, and Ionia (Herodotus III.127). But was this power built into
the system, or was it just a consequence of the temporary weakening of the central authority? In other words, did the satrap have full authority over the troops of the satrapy?

In the case of a special military expedition, the answer is clear. The example of
Otanes against Samos as well as Ariaramnes against Scythia and Aryandes against Barca
show unambiguously that the satraps and *strategoi* had to strictly obey orders sent from
the central authority. In some cases, a satrap or high official was commissioned to command troops from a larger territory. These were the leaders whom the Greek authors
called *karanos*—an institution known mostly from a reference by Xenophon. When
Cyrus the Younger was sent to Asia Minor by his father Darius II, he carried with him
the following royal order: "I send Cyrus as *karanos* of those who muster at Castolus," and
Xenophon adds the explanation "*Karanos* means 'vested with full powers' (*kyrios*)" (*Hell.*
I.4.3). We will come back later to the position of Cyrus the Younger. Suffice it to say here
that other titularies of the same military rank are known beginning with the time of Darius I. We know, for example, several leaders in times of conquest who were granted the
title "*strategos* of the men who dwell in the coastal countries" of Asia Minor, particularly
Megabazus and Otanes.

But what about the permanent troops of the territories—the soldier-colonists of
Babylonia, Egypt, and Asia Minor—were these troops available for the use of Persian
magnates who were settled in the provinces, or even the garrisons? This question, unfortunately, can only be answered from late passages in Xenophon, all of them bearing
the mark of generalization and schematization. In the same passage of the *Cyropaedia*
that is dedicated to satraps' duties, Xenophon clearly distinguishes between military and
satrapal duties. According to him, "Cyrus did not want to see the commanders of garrisons in the citadels (*phrourarchs*) and the *chiliarchs* of the guardposts scattered
throughout the territory receive orders from anyone but himself" (VIII.6.1). When
naming satraps, Cyrus clearly specified that the commanders of garrisons were to retain

the missions that had been entrusted to them. These are the instructions given to satraps: "To govern the people, receive the tribute, pay the militia, and attend to any other business that needs attention" (VIII.6.3✧). And further on, as always, Xenophon stresses that the measures taken by "Cyrus" were still respected in his time; for example, "the fashion in which the positions depending on the king (*hai hypo basilei phylakai*) are maintained is identical" (§§9 and 14). The king's goal is defined in this way by Xenophon: "He took this precaution in case any of the satraps, his head turned by his wealth or the number of his subjects, tried to rebel; he would immediately meet opposition on the spot" (§1).

In the *Oeconomicus*, Xenophon devotes a long passage to the complementarity of the "war work" and "peace work" of the Great King. Xenophon wishes to show that, mindful as he was of agriculture and horticulture, the Great King was also passionately concerned with the labors of warriors:

> For all the peoples from whom he collected [tribute], he prescribed to each governor (*archōn*) the number of horsemen, slingmen, and "shieldbearers" (*gerrhophoroi*) he had to maintain (*didonai trophēn*); there had to be enough to keep the subjects obedient and to defend the country against any enemy aggression. Moreover he maintained guards (*phylakai*) in the acropolises. It was the governor entrusted with this duty who had to provision the soldiers of these garrisons (*phroura*); as for the king, each year he reviewed the mercenaries (*misthophoroi*) and all who were required to bear arms; all were gathered, except the garrison soldiers, to the "place of assembly" (*syllogos*) as it is called; then he himself inspected those that were close by his residence. As for those who were distant, he sent some of the Faithful to review them. (IV.5–6)

We see here the distinction between the *phrourarch* ('garrison commander') who had to "defend the country as necessary" and "the governor of civil authority who supervised agricultural work." To Xenophon's way of thinking, the two domains were separate and complementary, for "those who work the earth badly no longer feed the garrisons and cannot pay their tribute." It would all be clear enough if Xenophon had not added the following conclusion: "Wherever there is a satrap, it is he who has the highest authority over both domains, civil and military" (§10–11)—as if, at this point, he was distinguishing archons from satraps. If we imagine that *archon* generically designates what we call a satrap, we see that one of the duties that fell to him was to supervise the maintenance of territorial troops. He was entrusted with furnishing supplies (*trophē*) to the garrison troops, no doubt in the form of rations assessed on the satrapal storehouses.

These passages in Xenophon have stimulated a large number of interpretations, and they raise a good number of difficulties. First of all we must emphasize the general context of the *Oeconomicus*. Discoursing on the ideal lifestyle of a Greek *kalos kagathos* ('beautiful and good'), Xenophon refers to the example of the Great King. In his description, we recognize an idealized image of Cyrus the Elder as well as Cyrus the Younger. His aim is thus not to expound on Achaemenid institutions per se; it is rather to discourse on ideal royalty. The conclusion is contained in the premises: only the king combines the prerogatives and virtues of both gardener and man of war. Terminological exactitude is hardly a dominant concern of Xenophon; here, as in other texts, the word *satrap* seems to be used very loosely. In one case, it seems to denote the head of a satrapy (§11) and in another, an official in the same class as the chiliarchs and phrourarchs (§7).

One of the most difficult problems rests in the hierarchical relationship between the satrap and the garrison commanders. The problem is all the more puzzling in that we lack any evidence for the relationship that we might compare with Xenophon. We know that, after the conquest of Sardis, Tabalus was named commander of the citadel by Cyrus. But what was his relationship with the satrap, who was also appointed by Cyrus? By way of confirmation of the general rule offered by Xenophon (that satraps had authority over military commanders), the later example of Orontas, portrayed by the same author in the *Anabasis* (I.6), is often cited. Accused of treason, Orontas was indicted by Cyrus the Younger before a sham of a royal tribunal. It appears that when Darius II made Orontas general-in-chief, Cyrus held a higher rank than Orontas. As soon as word of Orontas's revolt was received, the new king, Artaxerxes, relieved Orontas of his responsibilities to Cyrus. But the conditions are too specific to be able to draw general conclusions from this late example of Orontas. However, we can conclude that his relations with Cyrus had been modified between the time of Darius II and the time of Artaxerxes II.

But above all, Xenophon's passages, like many other Greek texts, are too allusive to explain the complexity of concrete situations. The only case that is well documented is the case of the garrison of Syene-Elephantine. Originally, the garrison soldiers were organized into companies (*dgalîn*; each numbering perhaps 1000 men); each *dgal* was subdivided into centuries (companies of 100) and decuries (companies of 10), each including soldiers of different ethnic backgrounds. The garrison was led by the *rab haylâ*, which corresponds to the Greek *phrourarch*. The earliest attested incumbent is the Persian Ravaka in 495 (*DAE* 2 [*AP* 1]). The garrison commander was under the orders of the 'governor' (*frataraka*), a subordinate of the satrap. Despite some superficial analogies, the Elephantine documents provide no confirmation for the theoretical views of Xenophon.

Let us now consider a Babylonian tablet dated between about 509 and 500 that is particularly interesting:

> A letter of Guzānu (chief priest of Sippar): To my brother Širku:
>
> May the gods Bēl and Nabū ordain for you health and life.
>
> Every day you have been telling me lies in Babylon. You used to say: "Liblutu, the chariot driver, and your shield-bearer (lit.: third-man-on-the-chariot) are assigned to you in the rolls." But when the commander of the fortress (*rab birti*) came here, he withheld from my contingent not only Liblutu but all the chariot drivers, asserting: "They belong to me!" and he also took away the shield-bearers who were with me. You, who were supposed to assert my claim before him, have in reality handed over to him what belongs to me!
>
> And now Liblutu the chariot driver is in charge of the (transport) of boats for the town Da[. . .]nu. You must not put under his command (my) chariot drivers, shield-bearers, or citizen-soldiers. He must not claim from the commander of the fortress my soldiers illegally. And you, say to Atkal-ana-mār-Esaggil as follows: "Give him (Liblutu other) soldiers in place of (Guzānu's) soldiers!" The curse of King Darius be upon you: release the *gardu*-soldiers as I have already ordered you.
>
> Please consider: at your disposal are the gate guards and all the chariot drivers, also the contingent of Dakūru-tribesmen who are stationed in Babylon; do not claim soldiers which belong to my "chariot fief!" (*bīt narkabti*; VS 6.128; trans. A. L. Oppenheim [Letters no. 143; CT 22: no. 74])

The tablet refers to a struggle over jurisdiction. Guzānu may have been the administrator (*šangu*) of the Ebabbar, the Šamaš temple in Sippar, unless he was governor (*šakin ṭēmi*) of Babylon. He overwhelms Širku, who was supposed to defend his interests, with reproaches. The citadel commander in Babylon had in fact recruited soldiers who were under the authority of Guzānu—soldiers who, apparently, were supposed to be transferred to a different royal official. These soldiers were mustered from a "chariot estate" and, apparently, a "horse estate."

If we needed to rescue some of Xenophon's statements, we might imagine that the commanders of the largest garrisons were appointed by the king, as were the satraps. The reason might be that it was in the citadels in provincial capitals that the treasure was deposited, entrusted to a special officer, the *gazophylax* (guardian of treasure), who apparently reported his activities directly to the central authority. But this observation does not imply that the garrison commanders were independent of the satraps, unless the king issued explicit orders to them (cf. Orontas at Sardis). It is hard to see how else the satrap could have successfully carried out one of his principal tasks, maintenance of order, if the phrourarchs were excluded from the chain of command. In case of mass mobilization of the royal army, it was to the satraps that the phrourarch turned to carry out the levies in their territories, by order of the king. The methods of mobilization ordered by Xerxes indicate this unambiguously (Herodotus VII.19, 26). In times of "peace," the satraps clearly were required not only to feed the garrisons but to ensure logistic and tactical coordination. It was they who were ultimately responsible for the good condition of the troops presented at the annual review. Xenophon also states, "[Cyrus] gave orders to all the satraps he sent out . . . to organize companies of cavalry and charioteers from the Persians who went with them and from their allies" (*Cyr.* VIII.6.10◈), and also, "After showing how each satrap had to carry out his instructions, after giving each an armed force, he sent them out and warned all of them to make ready for the expedition planned for the following year and for a review of the men, arms, horses, and chariots" (§15). Nothing in the *Oeconomicus* passage formally contradicts this interpretation.

The discussions in the *Cyropaedia*, however, can be explained in large part by the author's motives: he wanted to show that Cyrus had taken every measure to avoid the disintegration of central authority (described at length in the last chapter of book VIII), Xenophon included a passage on the relationship between satraps and garrison commanders that is completely consistent with his own approach but for which no sure confirmation can be found anywhere else.

Royal Inspectors

In the same context of the *Cyropaedia*, there is a reference to the periodic inspection of the satraps (*Cyr.* VIII.6.16◈):

> We have noticed also that this regulation is still in force, whether it was instituted by Cyrus, as they affirm, or not: year by year a man makes the circuit (*ephodeuei*) of the provinces with an army, to help any satrap that may need help, to humble any one that may be growing rebellious, and to adjust matters if any one is careless about seeing the taxes paid or protecting the inhabitants, or to see that the land is kept under cultivation, or if any one is neglectful of anything else that he has been ordered to attend to; but if he cannot set it right, it is his business to report it to the king, and he, when he hears of it, takes measures in regard to the offender. And those of whom the report often goes out that "the king's son is coming," or "the king's brother" or "the king's eye," these belong to the circuit commissioners (*hoi ephodoi*); though sometimes they do not put in an appearance at all, for each of them turns back, wherever he may be, when the king commands.

A large number of Greek authors of the fifth and fourth centuries refer to an institution called the king's Eye: Aeschylus, Aristophanes, and Plutarch refer explicitly to a person bearing this title during the reigns of Xerxes, Artaxerxes I, and Artaxerxes II. Herodotus, in his version of the "founder legend," says that among the high officials with which the young Cyrus surrounded himself was a king's Eye. Since later texts state that there were actually numerous Eyes and Ears of the king, it has frequently been deduced that the provinces were watched over by a corps of royal spies, reporting any rebelliousness or dereliction to the king.

That the central authority took measures to control the satraps is certainly beyond question. It was entirely necessary for them to be assured that royal commands were being carried out. Xenophon also touches on the topic in the *Oeconomicus* in the context of troop reviews: "As for the soldiers who are distant [from his residence], the king sends some of the Faithful (*pistoi*) to review them" (IV.6). In the *Cyropaedia*, Xenophon disagrees with the opinion prevailing in Greece:

> Indeed, we are led to think that the offices called "the king's eyes" and "the king's ears" came into being through this system of gifts and honours. Cyrus' munificence toward all who told him what it was well for him to know set countless people listening with all their ears and watching with all their eyes for news that might be of service to him. Thus there sprang up a host of "king's eyes" and "king's ears," as they were called, known and reputed to be such. But it is a mistake to suppose that the king has one chosen "eye." It is little that one man can see or one man hear, and to hand over the office to one single person would be to bid all the others to go to sleep. Moreover, his subjects would feel they must be on their guard before the man they knew was "the king's eye." The contrary is the case; the king will listen to any man who asserts that he has heard or seen anything that needs attention. Hence the saying that the king has a thousand eyes and a thousand ears; and hence the fear of uttering anything against his interest since "he is sure to hear," or doing anything that might injure him "since he may be there to see." So far, therefore, from venturing to breathe a syllable against Cyrus, every man felt that he was under the eye and within the hearing of a king who was always present. For this universal feeling towards him I can give no other reason than his resolve to be a benefactor on a most mighty scale. (VIII.2.10–12◇)

Despite the efforts of Iranists to find vocabulary of Persian origin, not one item in the Achaemenid corpus confirms the existence of such an institution. A word in the Aramaic documents from Egypt, *gaušaka*, has often been thought to parallel the Greek expressions, but the comparison does not seem definitive. The *gaušaka* was actually a satrapal inspector who, upon the summons of a community, came to make an inquiry on the spot accompanied by "judges and policemen(?) who—[like themselves]—are placed over the province of the Southern District" (*DAE* 101 [*AP* 27]).

Royal Letters and Satrapal Subordination

We have also seen how Darius's envoy Bagaeus knew how to impress the Persians at Sardis with royal letters, which were taken metonymically as the royal word itself (III.128). The royal couriers were inviolable in their person—hence the seriousness of the accusation against the same Oroetes (III.127). For the Persians, the reading of a royal message took on a character as impressive as an order given directly by a king in the flesh: did it not start out with "Saith Darius the King"? Polyaenus (VII.21.5) records that the satrap Datames, upon receiving a letter from King Artaxerxes II, performed the rite of *proskynesis* before it and offered the sacrifice customary for good news. Satraps and/or generals received royal instructions that they had to follow to the letter. There are many examples. When Aristagoras brought Artaphernes the proposal to conquer Samos, the satrap gave his approval in principle but made the following response to the Milesian: "The only other thing we need is to get the king's approval." It was not until he received the royal letter that he undertook military preparation (Herodotus V.31–32◊). In a general way, the heads of provinces did not have the right to take the smallest military or diplomatic initiative (e.g., Xenophon, *Hell.* IV.8.16–17). In order to justify their actions, they exchanged many letters with the central authority (e.g., Xenophon, *Anab.* I.5.2–3) or visited the court (e.g., *Hell.* I.3.9; IV.8.16; Diodorus XIV.39, 81; XV.4.2). The generals refer explicitly to royal letters that were composed extremely carefully (cf. Herodotus VI.97, 101). The Persian satraps frequently plead for an exception from royal control in order to make a diplomatic or military decision (cf. Xenophon, *Hell.* I.5.5; III.2.20; 4.5–6, 11, etc.). It was otherwise very unusual for a king's instructions not to be followed word for word. For example, Otanes proceeded to massacre the Samians, contrary to Darius's order, which said "not to kill or capture any Samian, but to hand the island over to Syloson intact" (Herodotus III.147). But there were good reasons for his acting against orders: contrary to assurances that they had given, Maeandrius and his men had massacred "the Persians of the highest rank," who, after making the agreement, "were sitting on their chairs of state" (III.144–45).

If a satrap intended to disobey, he knew well that he risked being denounced before the king—as is shown by the prelude to the revolt of Cyrus the Younger against his brother (chap. 15/2). Many examples in fact show that the satraps or the *strategoi* were frequently denounced, wrongly or rightly, by other satraps or by high provincial officials. In all likelihood, in such cases the suspect satrap was ipso facto called to court—as were, for example, Bardiya/Tanyoxarces by Cambyses and Ochus by Sogdianus (according to Ctesias, §10, 47). The satrap then had to answer the accusations brought against him before the king himself. Moreover, to lead a war presupposes the requisite financial and military means. We can be sure that neither the treasurers nor the managers of storehouses would furnish a speck of merchandise without receiving instructions from the central authority, worked out to the penny. It was not simply up to the satrap himself to order the minting of coins. We will also see that the fixing of a tribute rate by Darius in principle relieved the satraps of any possibility of adjusting the amount of tribute assessments (see also chap. 10/2). While the Babylonian tablets and the Aramaic documents from Egypt show that in each satrapy justice was rendered by the satrap and his subordinates, many examples also show that the Great King could intervene in decisions at any moment if the local populations exercised their right of appeal; this provided a means of tempering and controlling the possible arbitrariness of the satraps (see chap. 12/4).

Satrapal Courts and the Royal Court

Xenophon explains that one of the satrap's fixed obligations was to organize his court on the model of the central court (*Cyr.* VIII.6.10–13). Unfortunately, we have only a handful of documents that portray these satrapal courts, except in the areas that held special fascination for the Greek authors. The luxury and furnishings of the satrapal courts never failed to spark the imagination of the Greeks. The example of Pausanias of Sparta shows that some Greeks were dazzled by the Persian lifestyle in Asia Minor, as had been even more true of Polycrates of Samos at an earlier period (chap. 2/6).

In particular, the Greek authors give consistent accounts of the satrapal paradises, along with their resorts. These allowed a life of luxury characteristic "of satraps and kings" (Quintus Curtius VII.2.22). The description of Cyrus the Younger's paradise at Sardis given by Xenophon (*Oec.* IV.20–25) is familiar, as is Plutarch's description of Tissaphernes' paradises in the same town: "One of them was the handsomest, because its lawns and its refreshing waters, its retreats and its manicured lawns displayed an unimaginable royal luxury" (*Alc.* 24.7). This description is not dissimilar to the description of the paradise laid out near Cyrus's tomb at Pasargadae (see chap. 2/7 above). Every satrapy had at least one, including Persia (chap. 11/5). In Asia Minor alone, in addition to the paradise at Sardis, Xenophon describes others at Celaenae and Dascylium. At Celaenae, Xenophon's companions were able to see "a great park, filled with wild animals . . . and watered by the Meander" (*Anab.* I.2.7). Xenophon's description of the paradise in Dascylium (*Hell.* IV.1.15–16) is particularly evocative:

> That is where Pharnabazus maintained his residence, with handsome, large villages all round, abundantly provided with all the resources, and with game both in enclosed paradises and in the open spaces—magnificent game! Through the whole length flowed a river stocked with every kind of fish. Wildfowl were there in abundance as well, for those who might hunt for birds.

Xenophon's description is illustrated in the scenes on certain bullas from Dascylium (some dating from the reign of Xerxes). Numerous kinds of birds are depicted there, including a falcon holding a lobster in its beak.

One of the satrapal customs that the Greeks often elaborated on (having endured it themselves) was the routine of the satrapal audience. For instance, in order to obtain money from Cyrus the Younger, the Spartan Callicratidas, despite all his proud prejudices, had to resort "to go and beg at the doors of the king's commanders, as Lysander had done." Upon his arrival at the gate of Cyrus's palace, the guard let him know that Cyrus "was busy drinking." He soon endured a new rebuff, and "he took it hardly and set off for Ephesus" (Plutarch, *Lysander* 6◊). In Xenophon's report, Cyrus made Callicratidas wait two days: "Callicratidas was unhappy with this delay, furious with having to wait so long at the Gate." Callicratidas complained later: "When I went to find Cyrus, he put off doing what I asked day after day, and I could not find satisfaction without endlessly going to the Gate" (Xenophon, *Hell.* I.6.6–10). These long delays became proverbial. To highlight the haughty nature of Aspasia (Pericles' companion), a comic author wrote, "You could get an interview with Pharnabazus quicker than with her!" (Athenaeus XIII.570c).

Of course the problem of imperturbable officials was not limited to the satrapal courts of Asia Minor. We can see it in Egypt in the mishaps of the person portrayed in the *Petition of Peteisis*: "For seven months I tried to get justice from the governor or his officials, with no success, because Pkoip, the administrator of Teuzoi, who had gone to Memphis, plotted against me and told everyone, 'Keep him from reaching the governor!'"

The satraps' table-fare was perceived as an additional tax on subject populations (chap. 10/4) and was no less striking to the imagination than other customs. One of the many ways in which Pausanias manifested his "Medization" was by his table, "served in the Persian style" (Thucydides I.130.1). Imitating Xerxes' tent that was captured after the battle of Plataea (Herodotus IX.82), the satraps' tents also served as dining rooms, whose opulence always astonished the Greeks. Tiribazus of Armenia's tent had "silver-footed couches in it, and drinking cups, and people who said that they were his bakers and his cup-bearers" (Xenophon, *Anab.* IV.4.21). As for Agesilaus, he pretended to look down on the luxury flaunted by Pharnabazus, who "had arrived in expensive splendor. . . . His servants spread at his feet those carpets on which the Persians love to loll lazily" (Xenophon, *Hell.* IV.1.30). The best description of a Persian general's tent appears in the book of Judith, namely, the tent of Holophernes, into which the heroine is conducted: "Holophernes was resting on his bed under a canopy of purple and gold studded with emeralds and precious stones." When he left the tent, it was "with silver torches carried before him" (Judith 10:21–22◇). Judith was then taken to the place where his silver dinner service was laid, and quantities of food and wine were ready (Judith 12:1). The looting after the murder of the Persian gives an idea of the richness of his surroundings: "The people looted the camp for thirty days. They gave Judith the tent of Holophernes, all his silver plates, his divans, his drinking bowls and all his furniture" (Judith 15:11◇). All of these texts give an idea of the richness of the satrapal palaces. Satraps arranged banquets according to the royal model, such as Cyrus the Younger's banquet described by Aelian in his story about the adventures of Aspasia (*VH* XII.1).

It is clear, then, that in all of the activities of the satrapal court, the arrangements were identical to those of the central court, whether it was audience rituals (when Cyrus the Younger received people in his palace at Sardis, he was seated on a chair of gold and silver: Xenophon, *Hell.* I.5.3) or organizing banquets or hunts. On this point, the material Xenophon gives in the *Cyropaedia* sounds right: in their provinces, the satraps had to act and behave in the image of the king: "they had to imitate everything they saw Cyrus do" (VIII.6.10). Among all of the measures recorded by Xenophon, there are two that seem particularly significant: "To obligate all those who were to receive land and an official residence to frequent the [satrap's] Gate. . . . To educate at the Gate . . . the children who would be born." To put it another way, the Persian youths of the provinces received at the satraps' Gates the education that the Persians of Persia normally received. The Persian provincial nobility was invited to transform itself into a court nobility. Isocrates also confirms this fact (in his own way); the better to condemn the failings of the barbarians, he writes: "Therefore, those of them who go down to the seashore and whom they call satraps do not appear unworthy of the education of their country and keep the same customs" (*Paneg.* 152). All of these arrangements were intended to conserve the political and cultural homogeneity of the Persians of the imperial diaspora. So this epigram from the Palatine Anthology (IX.423) makes perfect sense: "Sardis, the king's Persia in Asia."

6. The King and His Faithful: The Persians, the Greeks, and the Others

Sources and Problems

Before drawing general conclusions (chap. 8/7 below) from the preceding analyses, we need to broach a question that so far has deliberately been set aside: Were Persians the sole beneficiaries of the imperial system of favors? The question is particularly legitimate because the inquiry has been conducted almost exclusively on the basis of Greek sources, which list many more Greeks than Persians among the Benefactors and among the persons the king honored with court titles, gifts, and favors. Has reality been constructed in a way that fits the corpus of evidence?

To read Herodotus, the Greeks held a decisive place close to the kings. According to him, for example, Demaratus played a major role in the choice of Xerxes as heir, in preference to Artobarzanes (VII.3), and Histiaeus had Darius's ear (V.106–7). Themistocles arrived at court just at the time of the accession of Artaxerxes I, and the new king put total confidence in him. Entirely in character, Herodotus gives the definition of the royal *euergetes* ('Benefactors') with regard to Greeks, who he states were called *orosangae* in Persian (VIII.85). Then he gives the names of Theomestor and Phylacus of Samos, who were rewarded for their valor at Salamis: "Theomestor in reward for this service was invested by the Persians with the tyranny of Samos, and Phylacus was enrolled in the catalogue of the King's Benefactors and presented with a large estate (*khōrē*)." Further on, we again gain the impression that, of all the participants in Salamis whose names the royal secretaries recorded, only the Greeks were honored by Xerxes (VIII.90: Samothracian ship)! Similarly, in his passage on the preparation for Xerxes' expedition, Herodotus appears to assign a disproportionate role to the Athenian diviner Onomacritus (VII.6).

The evidentiary context thus requires a more careful analysis of the place of Greeks in Darius's entourage. In fact, there are several who obtained advantages and preferences: Democedes, the physician from Crotone, was rewarded with gold for healing Darius's sprain, but also with an estate (*oikos*) and a court title, "Tablemate" (Herodotus III.130–32). For giving Darius a purple cloak at the time of Cambyses' expedition to Egypt, Syloson was made tyrant of Samos (III.130–49). Coes was made tyrant of Mytilene in 512 (V.11) because he counseled the king judiciously (IV.97). Another Ionian, Histiaeus of Miletus, was rewarded at the same time with a land grant in the country of the Edonians in Thrace (V.11); then Darius brought him to Susa, promising that he would be his Tablemate and counselor (V.24). Herodotus also records the arrival of Demaratus to see Darius, after he had been exiled from Sparta. Quite a few other Greek exiles are known, especially from the time following the Persian Wars. Many of them—Themistocles is one of the best-known cases—received cities in Asia Minor from the Great Kings, following a procedure already attested in Cyrus's time. Among them were Gongylus, Demaratus, and their offspring, who received lands and towns in Troas from Xerxes. In some cases, even entire Greek communities were collectively honored by the king: "At Acanthus, Xerxes issued a proclamation of friendship to the people and made them a present of a suit of Median clothes, with many expressions of approval for their enthusiastic support of the war and for the work they had done on the canal" (VII.117). In another city, Abdera: "Xerxes is known to have . . . made a pact of friendship with the people there, and to have given them a golden scimitar (*akinakēs*) and a gold-embroidered headband" (VIII.120).

There is no disputing that there were many Greeks at the Great King's court. But the composition of Herodotus's audience (he addressed Greeks principally) and, more generally, the Hellenocentric orientation of the available sources tend to influence our interpretation. It is clear that, although the Great King used Greek representatives, it was only for the relations they maintained with the Greek cities. When Pausanias acquired the (relative) confidence of Xerxes, it was because Xerxes hoped to turn it to his advantage in the continuing war against the Greeks in Asia Minor: "In agreement with the noble Artabazus, whom I sent to you, see to my affairs with full confidence and conduct them most gloriously and however is best for both." So says Xerxes in a letter attributed to him by Thucydides (I.130.3). In other words, Pausanias was subordinate to the initiatives of the Persian Artabazus (who had just received the satrapy of Dascylium), and he had to act in the royal interest. The same was true of Themistocles, who said to the king: "Today, likewise, I have the opportunity to do much good for you, and here I am, pursued by the Greeks, because of my friendship with you" (Thucydides I.137.4). Plutarch in turn comments as follows: "They even say that in successive reigns, in which the affairs of Persia were more closely intertwined with the affairs of Greece, whenever the kings needed a Greek, every one of them wrote letters promising that he would be more prominent at court than Themistocles" (*Them.* 29.9). Furthermore, when Themistocles went back down to the sea, it was "to take up the affairs of Greece" (30.1). "The king hoped, through [Themistocles], to see the Greek world enslaved" (Thucydides I.138.2).

But as Plutarch notes in passing (31.3), the Great King's gaze was not fixed constantly on the shores of the Aegean. And Aelian (*VH* I.22) is careful to state — since it would not be self-evident to his readers! — that the gifts given to ambassadors by the king were not reserved for Greeks alone. There were of course representatives of other peoples at court, such as Udjahorresnet, who followed Cambyses when he departed from Egypt and who resided for some time at Darius's court. When he returned to Egypt, it was because it was profitable to do so. In other words, in every conquered country, the Great King found collaborators (in the neutral sense) ready to serve his interests, as long as they received royal rewards that would bring them wealth and prestige — of which Udjahorresnet boasted: "I was honored by all my masters; [as long as] I lived(?) they gave me finery of gold and made me every useful thing" (Posener, no. 1D).

Foreigners and the Court Hierarchy

The question is, even when Greeks (or other foreigners) had court titles (including Benefactor) or prestige gifts (robes, jewelry), were they on an equal footing with Persian nobles? An explicit passage in Plutarch entertains some doubt. He says that Themistocles was especially honored by the Great King "because he participated in the royal hunts and the palace entertainments . . . , and he even became a friend of the king's mother." The Persian nobles at the court, however, reacted rather badly, and Plutarch explains their irritation: "It is true that the honors he received were nothing like what had been done for any other foreigner" (*hoi alloi xenoi*; *Them.* 29.6). A similar interpretation is found in Thucydides (I.138.2): "Themistocles then took on an important position with the king, as no Greek had ever done before." In fact, as Plutarch explains later on, satiated by the great *dōrea* he enjoyed at Magnesia, the Greek "was honored as an equal to Persians of the first rank" (*timōmenos homoia Persōn aristois*; *Them.* 31.3). We may also recall the case of Entimus the Cretan, who participated in Artaxerxes II's "dinner of the Kinsmen." Phaenias (quoted by Athenaeus II.48f✧) stresses the exceptional nature of such an honor's being granted to a Greek: "The Persians took umbrage at this, because they felt that the honour was being vulgarized (*dēmeuomenē*)."

To illustrate the special position of Themistocles, Plutarch records how the king refused to grant Demaratus the privilege (considered obviously disproportionate) "of making his entry to Sardis, on horseback, with the tiara set in the royal manner upon his head." This request aroused irony in the king's cousin Mithropastes and the anger of Xerxes. Themistocles had to intervene to reconcile the king with the Spartan exile (29.8). Obviously, as a Greek, Demaratus did not know his place, probably supposing that royal favor made him an equal of Persians of the highest distinction. This was also true of the Spartan Pausanias, if Thucydides is to be believed. When Pausanius received Xerxes' letter, his ambition grew in unwonted proportion:

> He grew unable to live in the customary fashion: he left Byzantium dressed as a Mede; he toured Thrace with an escort of Medes and Egyptians; his table was served in the Persian mode; unable to contain his emotions, he revealed through his trivial behavior what he was planning later on a grand scale. Eventually he proved difficult to approach. (Thucydides I.130.1–2)

Pausanias clearly hoped that, through his behavior as a Persian satrap, he would be identified with the dominant socioethnic class. Upon reading Xerxes' (ambiguous) reply, he was perhaps convinced that the king had implicitly agreed to one of his ambitions: to wed a daughter of the Great King (§128.7). There was no clear basis for this—Xerxes was completely silent on this point. Obviously—just like Demaratus—Pausanias had not understood that, despite his assurances of loyalty to the king, his Greek origin prohibited him from ever achieving the position of a Persian aristocrat in the king's entourage.

Persian Ethnicity

To be thorough, we must also mention Metiochus, son of Miltiades, the old Athenian tyrant of the Chersonese. During the reconquest subsequent to the Ionian revolt, Metiochus was captured by the Phoenicians and brought to Darius:

> The king, however, far from doing any harm to Metiochus, treated him with the greatest liberality; he presented him with a house (*oikos*) and property (*ktēsis*), and a Persian wife, by whom he had children who lived as Persians (*es Persas kekosmeatai*). (Herodotus VI.41)

Here we have an extremely rare case of a non-Persian marrying a Persian woman. We also know of the marriage of Gygaea, daughter of Amyntas of Macedonia, to the Persian Bubares. Of this union was born "a son who stayed in Asia, named Amyntas after his maternal grandfather, who enjoyed by the king's gift the revenues of the important Phrygian town of Alabanda" (VIII.136). But the difference between the two examples is obvious. In all probability, Amyntas (who kept a Macedonian name) was not recognized as a Persian, in contrast to the sons of Metiochus. It is also clear that Metiochus's sons' acceptance as native Persians—their "naturalization," as it were—resulted from royal favor, which there is every reason to consider exceptional.

The Ethnic Composition of the High Imperial Personnel

The ethnic composition of the highest ranking personnel clearly illustrates the privileged place that the Persians held in the Empire that they had conquered and the proceeds of which they fully intended to keep for themselves. The fact that local elites were recognized does not contradict this principle, since positions held by local elites were limited, at least under the first kings, to posts without political influence (see chap. 2/6 above). To begin with a region that is better documented than others—Egypt—we see that, beginning in the time of Darius, the leaders of the Egyptian satrapy were Persians. This was true of the satraps themselves (Aryandes, then Pharandates) and also, at Syene–Elephantine, of Parnu and Ravaka, as well as of the leaders of the expedition to Cyrenaica, Amasis and Badres. Even Ariyawrata, *saris* of Coptos, and his brother Atiyawahy were Persians.

The Greek texts, the Elamite tablets from Persepolis, the Babylonian tablets, the Egyptian documents, and several references in the Behistun inscription provide sufficient documentation on the satraps to compile a table that is statistically significant:

Babylonia	Gubāru (535–525), Uštānu (521–516), Ḫuta-x-x (486), to whom Bagapā (503) may perhaps be added
Egypt	Aryandes (522?–ca. 510?); Pharandates (519–492), Achaemenes (484–ca. 462)
Sardis	Oroetes (ca. 525–520); Artaphernes (513–492)
Dascylium	Mitrobates (ca. 525–522); Oebares (493); Artabazus (479)
Cappadocia	Ariaramnes (514)
Susa	Bakabana (ca. 500–495)
Media	Hydarnes (ca. 520[?]–ca. 499) [PF: Miturna]
Bactria	Dādarši (522), Artapan (ca. 500–465?)
Aria	Harbamišša (Arbamisa)
Arachosia	Vivāna (522); Bakabaduš
Carmania	Karkiš

The distribution of military command is also quite impressive. First of all, of course, we have the catalog of Xerxes' army. As Herodotus explains, the commanders of major divisions, in both the infantry (VII.82) and the navy (VII.97), were all king's men, often highborn Persians. Second, a look at the major expeditions leaves no doubt about the ethnicity of the commanders:

Samos (520–519)	Otanes (Herodotus III.142)
Barca (513)	Amasis and Badres (IV 167)
Scythia (514?)	Ariaramnes (Ctesias §15)
Scythia (513)	Gobryas, among those close to Darius (Herodotus IV.132, 134)
Thrace (512)	Megabazus (IV.143; V.1–24)
Head of the shore troops:	Otanes (V.25)
Naxos (500)	Megabates (V.32–35)
Ionia (500-493)	Artaphernes, Artybius, Daurises, Hymaees, Otanes (V.108ff.)
Thrace (492)	Mardonius (VI.43–45)
Europe (490)	Datis (the Mede) and Artaphernes (VI.94)
Europe (480–479)	Mardonius (VIII.100–101)
Asia Minor (479)	Tigranes (IX.96)
Eurymedon (466)	Tithraustes and Pharandates (Diodorus XI.60–61); Ariomardos, son of Gobryas, according to Callisthenes (Plutarch, *Cimon* 12.5)
Egypt (456?)	Pharandates and Artabazus (Diodorus XI.75, 77)

The statistical picture in the Persepolis sources is the same. Except for the administrative workers (*kurtaš*), of course, and specialized jobs (such as Babylonian scribes), the core of the personnel who governed lands, men, and workplaces was of Persian origin.

Despite this fairly substantial documentation, at least two problems remain. For one thing, the description "Persian" may sometimes be ambiguous. In some cases, the label may simply have designated one of the king's men. The uncertainty disappears when the family and/or ethnic background of the person are expressly given—which is fairly frequent in the Greek authors, consistent in the Behistun inscription, and quite noteworthy in a remarkable Persepolis tablet (PT 4). On one occasion, Herodotus includes a very valuable detail: the commanders of the expedition against Barca are described as

"Amasis, a man of the Maraphian tribe, to command the former, and Badres of the *genos* Pasargadae" (Herodotus IV.167◇). For another thing, as we know, the Iranian onomasticon is largely unmarked for ethnicity. Absent any relevant details, therefore, we must remain circumspect about the ethnic background of people, especially since it is not impossible that non-Iranians took Iranian names when they were incorporated (in one way or another) into the dominant socioethnic class.

In any case, the presence of Iranians other than Persians around the king is not open to doubt. Specifically, we know of Datis, to whom nearly all the ancient sources assign a Median origin; two of his sons, Harmamithras and Tithaeus, commanded all the mounted troops of Xerxes in 480 (Herodotus VII.88). We also know that in 522, alongside the Persian generals (Hydarnes, Vaumisa, Hystaspes, Vivāna, Vidafarnah, Dādarši of Bactria, Artavardiya, Gobryas), Darius appointed an Armenian, Dādarši (sent to Armenia) and a Mede, Takhmaspada (sent to Sagartia). This callup of Median generals was nothing new; Cyrus also had several around him. Other sources refer explicitly to non-Persian Iranians: at the heart of the conspiracy against Darius described by Aelian (*VH* VI.14) was the Hyrcanian Aribazus, who was supported by "several of the most distinguished Persians"; among "the most influential persons" around Cambyses, Ctesias lists Artasyras, a Hyrcanian (§9); Artasyras's son Artabanus "acquired around Xerxes the influence his father had had around Darius" (§20).

In sum, the statistical data permit only one conclusion: to direct the satrapies and lead the armies or even to command the garrisons (besides Parnu and Ravaka at Syene-Elephantine, cf. Boges at Eion and Mascames at Drabescus: Herodotus VII.106–7; 113), Darius and, later, Xerxes drew massively on representatives of the Persian aristocracy. The composition of the Empire's highest officials strikingly shows that it was ruled by an ensemble of great aristocratic families united around the dynasty and the cultural traditions of the Persian people. From the inception of the Empire, it was this dominant socioethnic class that held power from the Indus to the Mediterranean and intended to keep it. The elites of the subject nations or the Greek political exiles might receive important positions but not positions of political influence such as satraps or *strategoi*. They collaborated closely with the Persians, but they were not co-wielders of power. The honors and favors they might receive from the king did not place them ipso facto on an equal footing with the representatives of the great families. Finally, among the subject peoples, the Medes doubtless retained a special place, albeit secondary and of diminishing importance.

7. Achaemenid Royalty and Persian Aristocracy

Power and Kinship

To some extent, the Great Kings were able to turn the conflicts that might arise between dynastic power and the power of the great aristocratic Persian families to their advantage. The Persian nobles could closely identify with the dynastic ethic because they shared the guiding principles. By instituting a system of gifts "with strings attached," court hierarchy, and education based on monarchic values, the Great Kings succeeded in insinuating themselves into the aristocratic circles. Family solidarity, though it did not disappear, was diminished by the establishment of a personal relationship (*bandaka*) between each aristocrat and the king. Because of this, the kings had no need for head-on assaults on the solidarity of the aristocratic families, which was the usual matrix for social and demographic reproduction.

Consequently, the aristocratic houses were drawn into the monarchic sphere, though they conserved their social role. Heraclides' account of the organization of the king's table and the tables of the heads of aristocratic houses is full of information. Even when the Persian aristocrats invited their own Tablemates to dinner, they were still obligated to lunch at the royal table, where they were recognized as the most honored of the royal Tablemates (Athenaeus IV.145f–146a). This division of social space/time admirably exemplifies the double allegiance of the Persian aristocrats—toward their family clan and toward their king. But all of the measures taken by the kings (court hierarchy, obligation to attend at court, training of the noble youth according to dynastic norms) strongly prompted the aristocrats to give unfailing priority to the king. A new stage was reached in the integration of the nobility when, at some unknown date, kinship vocabulary infiltrated the court hierarchy.

At the same time, the similarities in the organization of the royal family and the aristocratic families show that the Achaemenid dynasty itself continued to function according to the rules and values common to the entire aristocracy. The kings behaved no differently than a certain Mentor, who took an active part in raising the ten sons of his brother-in-law Artabazus: "Mentor was so enchanted with the large number of children born to the marriage that he promoted the lads, giving them the most distinguished commands in the armed forces" (Diodorus XVI.52.4◊). The highest official in the royal administration of Persia at the time of Darius was Parnaka, whose seal calls him "son of Arsames." He was thus in all probability Darius's cousin through his father Arsames, brother of Hystaspes. This Parnaka/Pharnaces fathered the "satrapal dynasty" of Hellespontine Phrygia, through Artabazus, who was named to the post by Xerxes in 479–478. Darius's father himself held a very important position in Parthia-Hyrcania in 522. One of his uncles, Artabanus, influenced him a great deal; two of Artabanus's sons (Tritantaechmes and Artyphius) commanded units in Xerxes' army (Herodotus VII.26, 66). One of Darius's brothers, "his brother by the same father," Artaphernes I, was satrap of Sardis around 500 (Herodotus V.25◊, 30, 73, 100), and he kept this position until 492 at least (PF 1404–5). To lead the squadron against Samos, he chose his son Artaphernes II, Darius's nephew, who in 490 led the army against Greece with Datis and who in 480 was one of the contingent commanders of Xerxes' army (VII.74). Around 500, another cousin of Darius, Megabates, commanded the fleet (V.33); he may have been the father of Megabazus, who in 480 was one of Xerxes' admirals (VII.97); another(?) Megabates bears the title of admiral in a tablet from the reign of Darius (PT 8).

The number of Darius's sons in Xerxes' army is also very impressive—no less than twelve by five different mothers. Some commanded land or sea contingents; several were killed in action. In the battle of the Eurymedon, the generals were Tithraustes, illegitimate son of Xerxes, and Pharandates, a nephew of the king (Diodorus XI.60.5; 61.3). In Artaxerxes I's entourage, we encounter one of his cousins, Mithropastes (Plutarch, *Them.* 29.7). For the reconquest of Egypt, Artaxerxes I also sent an army commanded by Achaemenes, his own brother by Darius (Ctesias §32; Diodorus XI.74.1). Quite a few satraps were also chosen from the immediate family: Bardiya (Cambyses' brother by Cyrus), Artaphernes (Darius's brother by Hystaspes), Artarios (Artaxerxes I's son), Cyrus the Younger (Darius II's son and Artaxerxes II's brother), and so on. The difference is that, in the case of the royal family, kinship relations were intermingled with the rationale of dynastic succession; the great aristocratic houses were excluded from this, but they were invited to ally themselves devotedly and faithfully in the defense of dynastic continuity.

The Dynastic Pact

The speech that Xenophon writes for Cambyses (father of his Cyrus) illustrates forcefully what might be called a dynastic pact (*Cyr.* VIII.5.22–26). Addressing the Persian aristocracy, he first states that this Empire, conquered by force of arms, is a Persian Empire. He summons the nobles to assist the king in maintaining Persian dominion over the subject peoples. Cambyses especially stresses the common interests that the king and the Persian nobility have in the face of the danger presented by rebellions by the conquered peoples. If Persian dominion is not retained, the nobles risk losing all of the advantages that conquest brought them: "And you, Persians, if any enemy people attempts to bring an end to the dominance (*arkhē*) of Cyrus, or if any conquered people attempts to defect, you shall intervene, both for yourselves and for Cyrus, in accordance with the orders he will issue to you" (§25).

This is also what Chrysantas says to his peers, echoing Cambyses in these words: "It must be understood perfectly that Cyrus will never be able to employ us for his own advantage without it also being for our own, since our interests are the same and our enemies are the same" (VIII.1.5). By the gifts and positions they received, the aristocrats drew economic profit from conquest, profits that they risked losing if they were to dissociate from the king, since they knew perfectly well the precariousness of their position. When Agesilaus tried to persuade Pharnabazus, satrap of Hellespontine Phrygia, to ally with the Greeks against the king, he tried to lure him with the possibility "of no longer reinforcing the king's power but his [own] by reducing his companions to slavery (*homodouloi*) to make them his dependents (*hypēkooi*)." Pharnabazus responded straightforwardly:

> Well! If the king were to send someone else to be general and place me under his orders, I would agree to be your friend and ally. But if he entrusts the command to me—which is, I think, a noble ambition (*philotimia*)—you had better understand that I will make war on you to the best of my abilities. (*Hell.* IV.4.37)

Put another way, the gifts/services exchange was included in the "dynastic pact," by which the king undertook—absent blatant treachery or obvious error by a satrap or a *strategos*—to protect and favor his Faithful (*bandaka*).

Synchrony and Diachrony

The efficacy of the system over the *longue durée* can only be judged in hindsight. While in general the relationship between the monarchy and the aristocracy continued to rest on the foundations described above, there certainly were developments, over the course of time, which we will analyze in their proper place. The transformations may have involved the actual composition of the dominant socioethnic class, because of the ongoing, very close intimacy between the Persians of the imperial *diaspora* and the local elites. Transformations also have occurred during periods of dynastic troubles. Although the "dynastic pact" implied that the balance of power was very strongly tilted in favor of the Great King, it is clear that some periods of turmoil resulting from problems of succession or from external wars created special conditions, to which we shall return at the proper time (see especially chaps. 15/2, 17/2, 18/2).

Part Three

Territories, Populations, and the Dependent Economy

Chapter 9

Territories, Communication, and Trade

1. The Network of Roads

The ancient authors were literally fascinated by the vast extent of the Achaemenid imperial territory. Many of them include full discussions or at least remarks on the communications system within the Empire. They all recognize a relationship between regularity of communication and the ability of the central authority to make its presence felt in the conquered countries. Some, especially in the fourth century, insist—not unpolemically—on the impossibility of the king's mastering the imperial territory, especially since he had to gather his forces from throughout his domain (cf. Xenophon, *Anab.* I.5.9, II.4.3; Diodorus XIV.22.2; Isocrates, *Paneg.* 165; Quintus Curtius III.2.9, etc.). Others, however, were particularly struck by the contrast they saw between the vast extent of the Empire and the rapidity of communication.

The Royal Roads

In his tale of the preparations for the Ionian revolt, Herodotus describes the diplomatic tour of Aristagoras of Miletus to various Greek cities in Europe that he hoped to enlist as allies. In order to persuade King Cleomenes of Sparta, Aristagoras carried "to the interview a map of the world engraved on bronze" (V.49◊). Apparently, Herodotus used a document like this to give details "on the road leading from the sea to the king," that is, the road linking Sardis to Susa, which, he writes, "traverses populated, secure regions." For each region, Herodotus gives the distance in parasangs (a Persian measure equivalent to about 5.4 km), the number of hostels and stopping places found in the stations (*stathmoi*), and the rivers crossed and guardposts placed at regular intervals all along the way (V.52–54◊). This is the route traditionally called the Royal Road.

Regarding the extent and regional divisions of the Achaemenid road network, however, Herodotus's description is fragmentary. In this passage at least, his eastern geographical horizon extends no farther than Susa and Babylonia; he apparently knows nothing of the roads to Persia or *a fortiori* of the roads across the Iranian Plateau and Central Asia. It is particularly unfortunate that Ctesias's work on the subject has not survived: "In it he described the relays (*stathmoi*), days elapsed, and parasangs between Ephesus and Bactra and India," says Photius (*Persica* §64). The Persepolis tablets have the advantage of representing the view from the center—even though not all the information from the tablets has been published yet. While the Susa–Persepolis connections are the most frequently attested, the following also appear: Bactra (2 mentions), Carmania (9 or 10), India (7), Arachosia and Kandahār (11), Aria (4), Sagartia (2), Media (1), Babylonia (1 or 2), Egypt (1), and Sardis (3). The entire imperial territory is covered. The Royal Road from Sardis to Susa is thus just one royal road among many others (cf. also Diodorus XIX.19.2: [*hodos*] *basilikē* between Susiana and Media via Babylonia; Ps.-Arist., *Oecon.* II.2.14b [Caria]; *RC* 20 [Hellespontine Phrygia], etc.). This is why the Hellenistic-period sources are so important: they cover (however unevenly) all the territories formerly dominated by the Great Kings. The chroniclers of military operations enable us to reconstruct the duration of this or that movement of the army on the march: from Babylon to Susa: 22 days (Diodorus XIX.55.2); from Susa to Persia: about 30 days (XIX.17.6); from Susa to Ecbatana via the royal road across Babylonia: 40 days (XIX.19.2); from Susa to Ecbatana by the direct path across the Cossean mountains of Luristan: 9 days (XIX.19.8); from Ecbatana to Persepolis: 20 days (XIX.46.6); etc.

Added to the variety of information given by Herodotus and Xenophon, the data taken from the military authors (both Classical and Hellenistic) enable us to reconstruct generally, if not in detail, the network of major Achaemenid roads—keeping in mind that the accounts of military campaigns only consider roads from the point of view of the provisions the army might be able to find there. We may note first that the capitals of the Empire (Pasargadae, Persepolis, Susa, Babylon, Ecbatana) were linked by major highways, in a rough quadrilateral. The best-known itinerary is Persepolis–Susa, since it can be reconstructed not only by analyzing Alexander's route but also from the Persepolis tablets: there were about twenty stops between Persepolis and Bezitme (near Susa). According to the Hellenistic authors, crossing the Fahliyun region took nine stages, from Parmadan to Dasher. From Susa to Ecbatana, the royal road avoided the central Zagros (Luristan), since the direct route crossing Cossean country was "difficult and narrow, skirting precipices" (Diodorus XIX.19.2◇). The main road took a longer route across the Babylonian plain before veering east to reach the Iranian Plateau near Behistun. From Ecbatana, another road reached Persia by Gabae (Isfahan) and ended up at the Persian Gulf at Bushire.

Furthermore, the variety of countries named in the tablets shows that the capitals were connected to all the provinces in the Empire. Northward, the venerable Khorasan road joined Ecbatana to Bactra, via Rhagae [Teheran], the Caspian Gates, Hyrcania, and Parthia. Southward, leaving Fārs, one could travel to Arachosia (Kandahār) and Gandhara (Kabul area), and from there to Bactra as well as to the Indus Valley. The North Road and the South Road were joined by a transverse road used by Cyrus and then Alexander via Aria (Artacoana/Herat), Drangiana (the Helmand basin and land of Ariaspi), and Kandahār. From Kandahār, another itinerary (used by Craterus in 325) gave access directly to the Indus Valley through the Bolan Pass.

Toward the Mediterranean there were two main itineraries that coincided from Susa to Arbela (east bank of the Tigris). From Arbela, Herodotus's Royal Road reached Sardis via the upper Tigris and upper Euphrates, Armenia, and Cappadocia, the Halys, Greater Phrygia (Celaenae), and the Meander Valley. Here is Herodotus's version:

Region crossed	Parasangs	Stops (stathmoi)
Lydia–Phrygia	94.5	20
Cappadocia	104	28
Cilicia	15.5	3
Armenia	56.5	15
Matiene	⟨137⟩	⟨3⟩4
Cissia	42.5	11

The figures presented here include corrections to the manuscript tradition. The route of Herodotus's Royal Road is still controversial, which is rather surprising, especially within Cappadocia and Cilicia. In all, he writes, the route stretched some 13,500 stadia, if we agree (with him) that 1 parasang equals 30 stadia—thus about 2,500 km. And he ends with: "At 150 stadia per day, the journey would take 90 days." Adding the Ephesus–Sardis leg (140 stadia), he estimates it would take three months and three days to travel from the sea to Susa.

In another itinerary, known mainly from an Aramaic document (*DAE* 67 [AD 6]), to which we shall return at length (chap. 9/2 below, 364ff.), travelers left Arbela for Damascus and Egypt. Some of the stops on the itinerary are the well-known cities of Arbela and Damascus, but also Laḫiru, which is known from several Babylonian texts of the same period (Darius II). We may add that by this route, leaving Thapsacus on the Euphrates, one can travel to Cilicia via Aleppo; this was a route frequently taken by people who landed on the Cilician coast or set sail from there for Asia Minor or Greece. Xenophon's story in the *Anabasis* also shows that a road led from Cilicia to Sardis via the Cilician Gates, Cappadocia, Greater Phrygia, and the Meander Valley, according to the following itinerary, where Xenophon gives the distances in parasangs and the stops (*stathmoi*):

From	Crossing	To	Parasangs	Stops
Sardis	Lydia	Meander	22	3
	Phrygia	Colossae	8	1
Colossae	Phrygia	Celaenae	3	3
Celaenae	Phrygia	Peltae	10	2
Peltae	Phrygia	Ceramon-agora	12	2
Ceramon-agora		Caÿstru-pedion	30	5
Caÿstru-pedion	Phrygia	Thymbrium	10	2
Thymbrium	Phrygia	Tyraeum	10	2
Tyraeum	Lycaonia	Iconium	20	3
Iconium	Cappadocia	Dana	25	4
Dana	Cilicia	Cilician Gates	25	4
Cilician Gates	Cilicia	Psarus River	10	1
Psarus River	Cilicia	Pyramus River	5	1
Pyramus River	Cilicia	Issus	15	2
Issus	Cilicia	Syrian Gates	5	1
Syrian Gates	Syria	Myriandrus	5	1
Myriandrus	Syria	Chalos River	20	4
Chalos River	Syria	Dardas River	30	3
Dardas River	Syria	Thapsacus	15	3
Thapsacus	Syria	Araxes River	50	9
Araxes River	"Arabia"	Corsote	35	5
Corsote	"desert"	Pylae	90	13
Pylae	Babylonia		12	3
?	Babylonia	Cunaxa	3	1
			499	77

It is clear that this itinerary was regularly used long before the expedition of Cyrus the Younger; thus the strategic importance of Cilicia.

Secondary Itineraries

Of course, these itineraries are concerned only with the network of royal roads; many other itineraries, often much shorter and often following mountain or desert routes, are left out. We learn about the latter most often from accounts of military expeditions. This is how, for instance, we know of a road between Miletus and Sardis that enabled the Ionians (with Ephesian guides) to launch a surprise attack on the Achaemenid capital of Asia Minor; the same road was used a century later by the satrap Tissaphernes when he was trying to intercept Agesilaus's army, which was returning from Sardis to Ephesus by the major road that crossed the Karabel Pass. Another example is the itinerary followed by Alexander between Fahliyun and the Persian Gates, while the bulk of the army and its supplies were sent to Persepolis by "the plains route" or the "wheelworthy route." Similarly, in Hyrcania Alexander took the shortest road, over the crest, while he sent the convoy by the military road (*via militaris*). A last example is chosen from many others: when Cyrus the Younger, then at Iconium, sent Epyaxa to Tarsus by the quickest mountain route, some of the escort disappeared. Two explanations were in circulation, each more disturbing than the other: some said the escort was cut to pieces by the Cilicians; others thought that the soldiers had become lost and were unable to find their way. It was in fact impossible to travel by such routes without local guides.

The narrowly military orientation of the Classical sources, however, requires us to be cautious. A route that they considered unusable may not necessarily have been so for everyone in normal times. Here, for example, is what Arrian says (*Indica* 43.3) about a road between Egypt and Babylonia by way of northern Arabia:

> The soldiers of Cambyses' army who were able to reach Susa, the relief troops sent by Ptolemy son of Lagos to Babylonia across Arabia to aid Seleucus Nicator, crossed an isthmus and hurried to traverse that whole parched, desert country in eight days, on camelback. Their pack animals carried the necessary water and they traveled by night; by day they could not endure the open air because of the heat. The region beyond the isthmus just mentioned, between the Arabian Gulf [Red Sea] and the Erythrean Sea [Persian Gulf] is thus far from habitable, since the northern part is desert and sand.

The road just described in fact crossed a terribly inhospitable region. But it must be recalled that when they describe a country as "desert," the Greek authors in context are referring to the march of a major army, which needs supplies of fresh water relatively close together. Xenophon explains this when he recounts Cyrus's march up the east bank of the Euphrates: "Some stages were quite long, because Cyrus always wanted to get to where there was water and fodder" (I.5.7). This is also why Cyrus sought the assistance of the king of the Arabs on his march to Egypt in 525: "[The Arabian king would] fill camel-skins with water, load them on to all his live camels, and so convey them to the desert, where he awaited the arrival of [Cambyses'] troops" (Herodotus III.9✧) — exactly as Esarhaddon had done in 671 on his own Egyptian campaign (*ANET* [3], 292). The people whom the Greeks called Scenite (tent-dwelling) Arabs had dromedaries and a knowledge of the country that enabled them to overcome obstacles that would have appeared truly insurmountable for the commander of an army.

Let us give one more example (from many others). When Alexander found himself in Drangiana (Seistan), he wanted to get a message to Ecbatana in Media. To do this in ten days instead of a month by the main road, the terrible Salt Desert of the Iranian Plateau had to be crossed. Alexander entrusted the mission to Polydamas: "He put off the dress which he was wearing and put on an Arab costume. Two Arabs . . . were given him as companions. They arrived at the designated place on the eleventh day, traversing on camels places which were even made desert by dryness" (Quintus Curtius VII.2.18◊). Here the word "Arab" is used generically: it simply designates the nomadic populations that were accustomed to crossing the desert, "mounted on racing camels [dromedaries]" (Diodorus XVII.80.3).

Road Building and Maintenance

Royal roads, in contrast to the others, were most often broad—what the ancient authors called 'wheelworthy' (*hamaxitos*)—that is, accessible to chariots. This description is used, for example, of the roads from Phrygia to Cilicia, Susa to Persepolis, Susa to Arbela, and across Hyrcania. Horsemen and pedestrians were not the only users of these major roads. Many travelers, civil and military, used chariots, which Aeschylus called "rolling tents" (*Persians* 1000). These traveling chariots, called 'chariot carriages' (*harmamaxa*) by the Greeks, must be distinguished from the light chariots (*harma*) used for war or hunting (Herodotus VII.41; cf. VIII.83; Xenophon, *Anab.* I.2.16).

We must stress that the word *hamaxitos* 'wheelworthy' does not mean that these roads were paved. They no doubt were dirt roads of various widths but well maintained and marked. A Hellenistic text (*RC* 18), for instance, refers to an "old road that the nearby peasants turned to cultivation" in Hellespontine Phrygia. The reference in fact is to a 'royal road' (*hodos basilikē; RC* 20); the detail may be surprising, but Herodotus also mentions that, after 480–479, "The road which King Xerxes took remains untouched to my day; the Thracians hold it in profound reverence and never plough it up or sow crops on it" (Herodotus VII.115◊). Because the roads were dirt, trips became difficult during the rainy season or in more or less swampy locations. This is illustrated perfectly in a passage from Xenophon's *Anabasis* (I.5.7–8◊):

> Once in particular, when they came upon a narrow, muddy place which was hard for the wagons to get through, Cyrus halted with his train of nobles and dignitaries and ordered Glus and Pigres to take some of the barbarian troops and help to pull the wagons out, but it seemed to him that they took their time with the work; accordingly, as if in anger, he directed the Persian nobles who accompanied him to take a hand in hurrying on the wagons. . . . Leaping at once into the mud, they lifted the wagons high and dry and brought them out more quickly than one would have thought possible.

It is quite clear that the management of a system of roads so vast required a sizable, specialized administration. By way of comparison, note that in T'ang China the road network was directed by 21,500 officials assigned to the various roads and 100 high officials at work in the capital. The evidence being what it is, we have only limited information on the comparable department in the Achaemenid Empire. Some of the Persepolis tablets seem to refer to a corps specializing in the maintenance of existing roads and building new ones. About 43 km of the Persia–Media road has been surveyed between Naqš-i Rustam and Mazdaheh (between Shiraz and Isfahan). Traces of Achaemenid roads have also been found south of Pasargadae, in the picturesque gorge of the Tang-i Bulaki on the Pulvar: a 1.7 m–wide road cut sometimes 10 m deep into the rock. It is clear that the construction and maintenance of such roads required a considerable work force. It is likely that in Persia itself the *kurtaš* were called up, but, there and elsewhere, so was the peasantry in the form of corvée (cf. Aelian, *Anim.* XV.26; Diodorus XVIII.32.2). It

fell to the satraps and their subordinates to maintain the roads that crossed their territory, as is implied by a passage in Pseudo-Aristotle (II.2.14b✧) on the administration of
Condalus, one of the satrapal subordinates of Mausolus in Caria:

> And any trees which projected over or fell into the royal roads (*hodoi basilikai*) he used to
> sell . . . the produce taxes.

During military campaigns, it was the army's job. Here is how Xenophon's Cyrus informs the pioneers, or 'road builders' (*hodopoioi*), of their special tasks (*Cyr.* VI.2.36✧):

> You superintendents of the engineering corps have here from me a list of the spearmen, the
> archers, and the slingers, whose names have been stricken from the roster. You must require
> those of them who were spearmen to carry on the march a woodcutter's axe, those who were
> bowmen a mattock, and those who were slingers a shovel. With these tools they are to march
> in squads ahead of the wagons, so that, in case there is any need of road-building, you may
> get to work without delay, and so that, if I require their services, I may know where to find
> them when the time comes.

Herodotus describes road-makers at work in 480. In Pieria, Xerxes gave a third of the
army the job of deforesting the country to build a reliable road (VII.131). Road-makers
show up again in 322–321, when Alexander's funeral chariot left Babylon for the Mediterranean coast: accompanied by many specialists (*technitai*), they were clearly ordered
to prepare and improve the road the chariot was to take (cf. Diodorus XVIII.28.2). A few
years earlier, in 333, the Thracians had opened a road (*hodopoiein*) between Phaselis
and Perga (Arrian I.26.1).

Bridges and Bridge-Builders

The greatest rivers were spanned by permanent bridges, including both the Euphrates and the Tigris (cf. Herodotus I.186). In his description of the Sardis–Susa road, Herodotus takes care to enumerate the rivers the road crossed: the Halys, the Euphrates, the
Tigris, the Little and the Great Zab, the Diyala, and the Choaspes. At least one bridge
was built across the first of them, guarded by a fort (*phylaktērion*) and gates (*pylai*). Obviously, Herodotus is talking about a permanent bridge (V.52). Herodotus calls the other
rivers (Upper Euphrates, Upper Tigris, Little and Great Zab, and Choaspes) 'boat-carry'
(*nēusiperētos*) rivers, which must mean that they were crossed by means of pontoon
bridges (V.52). Xenophon's *Anabasis* clearly shows that this is how all of the rivers were
crossed by Cyrus's troops on the march to Babylonia. Xenophon often gives only the
widths of the rivers, but it seems clear that in most (if not all) cases they were provided
with pontoon bridges, like the bridge of "seven boats tied together" on the Meander
(I.2.5). The Euphrates, about 1000 m wide at the level of Thapsacus, must have been
forded, since the satrap Abrocomas had burned the boats during his retreat to Babylon
(I.4.11–18), as the Persians did later on in the face of Alexander's advance (Arrian
III.7.1–2). On the Tigris, Xenophon also mentions a bridge of 37 boats braced together
(II.4.17, 24), and another bridge at the level of Opis (II.4.25).

In Babylonia, Xenophon distinguishes bridges proper (*gephyra*) from bridges made of
boats tied together (II.4.13). But he includes no details of the construction of the bridges
proper. They may have consisted of a few palm trunks thrown across a canal (II.3.10) or
even some planks resting on piles of rocks (Quintus Curtius V.5.4: near Persepolis).
There must also have been bridges on permanent pilings, like those discovered near Persepolis and Pasargadae. But building a complex bridge of this sort poses difficult technical problems, as Arrian explains in connection with Alexander's crossing of the Oxus
(Amu Darya):

It is the greatest river in Asia, at least of those Alexander and his men had encountered, except for those in India. . . . Alexander tried to cross it, but the river appeared to him absolutely impossible to traverse. It was in fact six stadia [ca. 1 km] wide, but its depth bore no relation to its width, which was proportionately much greater; the bottom was sandy, the current swift, so that the pilings that the men were driving into the bottom were easily carried away by the current, seeing as they were fixed in nothing but sand. (*Anab.* III.19.2–3)

It was much easier to use pontoon bridges on the Mesopotamian rivers, since the water level varied considerably from season to season. Here is how Arrian describes the Roman technique:

On signal, the boats are unfastened and left to the current of the river, not straight and prow-forward, but like boats towed by the stern. The current seizes them, naturally, but they are restrained by a rowboat until they halt at the desired spot. There, pyramidal wicker baskets filled with rough stones are dropped into the water from the prow of each boat, to hold them against the current. When the first boat has been set in this manner, the next, separated from the first by a distance related to the weight it will have to bear, is anchored in turn facing the current; immediately, beams attached to each other by boards nailed across them are placed on these two joined boats; and so the work proceeds, following the line of as many boats as are needed to cross the river. On each side of the bridge proper panels attached to the deck are placed, facing outward, which serve as guardrails for the horses and vehicles, and also to connect the elements of the bridge together more securely. The whole thing is finished in a short time but with a great deal of noise; nonetheless, discipline is not wanting throughout the operation. The cheers for this or that boat do not interfere either with the commands or with the efficiency. (V.7.3–5)

Arrian goes on to say that he cannot report "how Alexander managed to throw a bridge across the Indus, since even those who were on the campaign with him will not talk about it. But, in my opinion, his technique for building the bridge must have been very like the Roman technique, and if he did it some other way, good for him!" We know in any case that Alexander's army included a corps of bridge-builders who, for instance, had to set two pontoon bridges across the Euphrates at Thapsacus to replace the ones the Persians had destroyed (Arrian III.7.1–2). The technique of the Macedonian specialists was likely the same as the Persians', since in this area the Balkan countries seem not to have had any special traditions. The existence of such specialists may be confirmed by a Babylonian document that reports that a group of "bridge-builders" held *ḫaṭru* lands near Nippur.

In 513, to cross into Europe, Darius had a boat-bridge set up on the Thracian Bosporus. The architect was a Samian named Mandrocles (Herodotus IV.87–88). In 480, Xerxes ordered two bridges to be built across the Hellespont at Abydos, at a width of seven stadia. Specialists from several countries worked on it: Phoenicians, who spun cables of white linen; and Egyptians, who brought cables made of papyrus (*byblos*). After the first, unsuccessful attempt (the bridges were carried away by a storm), the engineers succeeded. Here is Herodotus's description (VII.36✧):

The method employed was as follows: penteconters and triremes were lashed together to support the bridges—360 vessels for the one on the Black Sea side, and 314 for the other. They were moored slantwise to the Black Sea and at right angles to the Hellespont—in order to lessen the strain on the cables. Specially heavy anchors were laid out both upstream and downstream—those to the eastward to hold the vessels against winds blowing down the straits from the direction of the Black Sea, those on the other side, to the westward and towards the Aegean, to take the strain when it blew from the west and south. Gaps were left in three places to allow any boats that might wish to do so to pass in or out of the Black Sea.

Once the vessels were in position, the cables were hauled taut by wooden winches ashore. This time the two sorts of cable were not used separately for each bridge, but both bridges had two flax cables and four papyrus ones. The flax and papyrus cables were of the same thickness and quality, but the flax was the heavier—half a fathom of it weighed 114 lb. The next operation was to cut planks equal in length to the width of the floats, lay them edge to edge over the taut cables, and then bind them together on their upper surface. That done, brushwood was put on top and spread evenly, with a laye of soil, trodden hard, over all. Finally a paling was constructed along each side, high enough to prevent horses and mules from seeing over and taking fright at the water.

2. Control of the Imperial Territory

Satrapal Authorizations

The royal roads themselves were "safe to travel by, as [speaking of the Sardis-to-Susa road] it never leaves inhabited country," to repeat a phrase Herodotus used (V.52◊)— which is to say, there was risk of neither famine nor ambush. For the military historians, these were also the routes by which the armies could easily be resupplied. But their use required a prior official authorization, called *halmi* (sealed document) in the Persepolis tablets, Category Q. This is precisely what is contained in the letter provided by Aršāma to his steward Neḥtiḥōr in a well-known Aramaic document (*DAE* 67◊ for the names [text: *AD* 6◊]):

> From Aršāma to Marduk the officer (*peqid*) who is at X [place name], Nabūladanī the officer who is at La'ir, Zātuvyaha the officer who is at 'Arzūḥin, 'Upastabara the officer who is at Arbela, Ḥalṣu and Māt-āl-Ubaš, Bagafarna the officer who is at Sa'lam, Frādafarna and Gawzīna the officers who are at Damascus. And now:—behold! one named Neḥtiḥōr, [my] officer (*peqid*), is going to Egypt. Do you give him (as) provisions (*ptp*) from my estate (*beth*) in your provinces every day two measures [1.7 l] of white meal, three measures of inferior meal, two measures [1.7 l] of wine or beer, and one sheep, and hay according to (the number of) his horses; and give provisions for two Cilicians (and) one craftsman, all three my servants who are going with him to Egypt, for each and every man daily one measure of meal; give them these provisions, each officer of you in turn, in accordance with (the stages of) his journey from province to province (*medinah*) until he reaches Egypt; and, if he is more than one day in (any) one place, do not thereafter assign them more provisions for those days. Bagasarū is cognizant of this order: Rašta is the clerk.

The interest of this letter is that it enables us to reconstruct the administrative process very precisely. Every official leader of a caravan had to have a sealed document that functioned as both a safe-conduct and a permit to travel, *halmi* in Elamite, **viyatika* in Persian (*miyatukkaš = halmi*). The *halmi* included the number of travelers, the amount of their rations, and the path to be followed. The royal roads were in fact marked out in stages, with postal relays and storehouses. This is what Herodotus is saying in his famous description: "At intervals all along the road are recognized stations (*stathmoi basileioi*), with excellent inns" (*katalysies*; V.52◊). This is the background for a financial maneuver reported by the irrepressible author of the *Oeconomica* (II.2.38), who describes Antimenes of Rhodes in Babylonia during Alexander's time: "He ordered the satraps to fill, according to the custom of the country, the storehouses (*thēsauroi*) located along the Royal Roads." The outcome of the story diverges somewhat from the strict rules of the Achaemenid administration: "Whenever an army or some other contingent passed through the country and the king happened not to be there, he would send a sales team to peddle the merchandise that had been deposited in the storehouses!" The storehouse managers were not in fact empowered to disburse goods without satrapal authorization. Upon arrival at each stop, the leader of the caravan was required to produce this document, which allowed him to receive travel rations precisely in the amount indicated in the document he carried. Aršāma's letter also includes this clause: "and, if he is more than one day in (any) one place, do not thereafter assign them more provisions for those days" (*DAE* 67 [AD 6◊]). This provision indicates that, even if the travelers encountered an unforeseen difficulty or if they dawdled en route, they would have no right to supplementary rations. It also confirms that the stops and provisioning locations were generally spaced a day's journey apart.

The tablets of Category Q exactly reproduce the vouchers prepared by the heads of the storehouses at the stops, to record the receipts and disbursements. As an example (chosen from hundreds), here is the text of one of these tablets:

> 4.65 BAR of flour, Dauma received. Each of the 23 men received 1.5 *qa*, and 1 *qa* for each "boy" (*puhu*). Dauma bore a document sealed by Irdarpirna. They were traveling from Sardis. They were headed to Persepolis. Month 9 of year 27. At Hidalu. (PF 1404)

Irdarpirna can be identified as Artaphernes, Darius's brother, who we know from Herodotus was satrap of Sardis. In 495, then, he granted a *halmi* to Dauma, who was going to Persepolis, accompanied by several men and *puhu* (servants). The receipt was written at Hidalu, an important place on the border between Elam and Persia.

Later archival materials include some Aramaic ostraca from Arad, in Palestine, dated (paleographically) to the fourth century. They seem to attest to the existence of a way station where official travelers (doubtless military personnel) could receive rations for their animals.

The Classical sources confirm this practice precisely. Demosthenes, for instance, records that Charidemus reached Sestos only because he bore a safe-conduct (*adeia*) issued by Artabazus (*C. Aristocrates*: XXIII.159). Themistocles explains, in several of the letters attributed to him that, when he was exiled from Athens, he managed to reach the Achaemenid court. He requested authorization from the satrap Artabazus, who granted it to him: "He gave me two horses and the same number of attendants and sent me with 13 other Persians, who were in charge of the road and the provisions. They traveled by camelback" (*Letter* 30). In another version, Themistocles reached the king secretly, after disembarking at Aeolian Cyme (Plutarch, *Them.* 26.1). His prospects were even more unenviable because the king had put a price on his head. Luckily he fell in with a wealthy resident of Aeolian Aegae, Nicogenes, who "had relationships with the Persian nobles of the high country." By conniving this way, Themistocles was able to depart, concealed in an enclosed chariot usually used for women who were traveling. The case of Alcibiades also attests to the difficulty of evading satrapal surveillance. "He determined to go up to Artaxerxes. . . . As for how to travel in total security, he figured that [the satrap] Pharnabazus was most able to make it possible, and he sought him out in [Hellespontine] Phrygia." But, for his own reasons the satrap wanted at all cost to keep the Athenian from seeing the king, so he refused to cooperate with him. Alcibiades then tried to find the "satrap of Paphlagonia" by secretly taking the road from Dascylium, capital of Hellespontine Phrygia. Pharnabazus immediately sent a small contingent in pursuit, and it caught up with him in a Phrygian village, where he was executed. We thus see that access to the roads was jealously guarded. When Themistocles returned to the

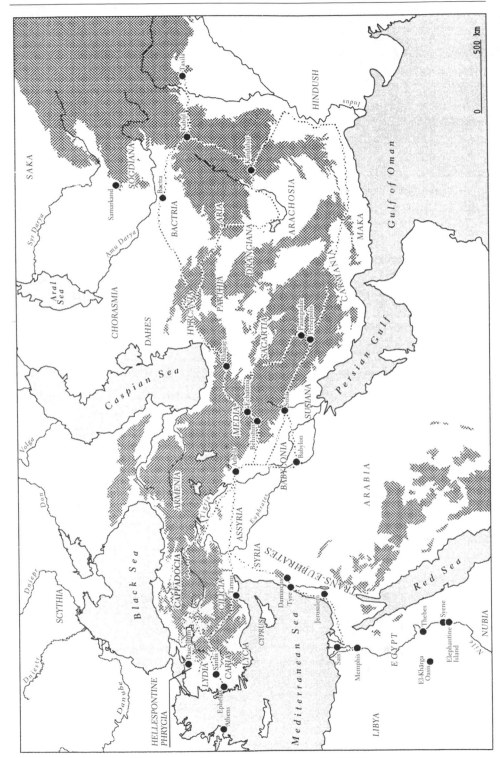

Map 2. The Empire and its principal routes.

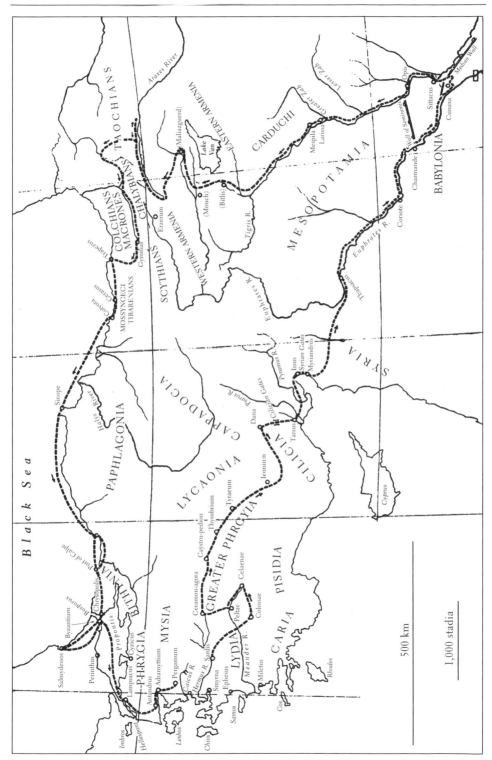

Map 3. *The itinerary of Cyrus and the Ten Thousand.*

coast somewhat later, he found that he was the object of hostility of an important Persian of Greater Phrygia, Epixyes. This man had posted some Pisidians with orders to slaughter the Greek when he appeared at Leontocephalae, a very important stop on the Royal Road. Themistocles was warned and took a back road (Plutarch, *Them.* 30.1). Surveillance was thus perpetual. For instance, the Greeks sent three spies to Asia Minor around 480, but it was not long before they were discovered, at the moment when they made contact with Xerxes' army in Sardis.

A satrap's consent was also required for official travelers, such as foreign ambassadors. When deputies from Athens and other Greek cities were sent to the king in 408, they had to await the goodwill of the satrap Pharnabazus. The first time, he "attempted to take the ambassadors to the king." The caravan wintered at Gordion in Phrygia, a stop on the Royal Road from Sardis to Susa. At the beginning of the following spring, they took to the road again "to seek out the king." As it happens, things did not work out, because the ambassadors ran into Cyrus the Younger, who had been sent by his brother Artaxerxes to take over operations in western Asia Minor:

> Upon receiving this information, the Athenian envoys, especially when they had seen Cyrus, wanted more than ever to seek out the king—or else return home. [On orders of Cyrus,] Pharnabazus was able to detain them for a time, telling them sometimes that he would take them to the king, sometimes that they would return home. . . . After three years he asked Cyrus for permission to return them, saying he had taken an oath, and that he would take them back to the sea, since he would not take them to the king. They were sent off to Ariobarzanes, who was asked to provide an escort; he had them brought to Cius in Mysia, from where they left to join the rest of the army. (Xenophon, *Hell.* I.4.6–7)

This enables us to understand the tenor of a proclamation voted by Athens in the 360s to honor Straton, the king of Sidon, who in fact "had done all he could to see that the ambassadors sent by the people to the king would have as good traveling conditions as possible" (Tod II, no. 139).

Military Escorts

Herodotus writes of the king's highway that it "crossed only inhabited, secure regions," indicating that the routes were closely watched. On the royal roads, traffic was closely monitored by the king's men. Overall, it fell to the king to maintain order and keep travelers safe from highwaymen. This is one of the characteristics of the "good king" as they are cataloged by Xenophon in his idealized portrait of Cyrus the Younger (*Anab.* I.9.11–12◊):

> None could say that he permitted malefactors and wicked men to laugh at him; on the contrary, he was merciless to the last degree in punishing them, and one might often see along the travelled roads people who had lost feet or hands or eyes; thus in Cyrus' province it became possible for either Greek or barbarian, provided he were guilty of no wrongdoing, to travel fearlessly wherever he wished, carrying with him whatever it was to his interest to have.

Nonetheless, despite the severity of punishment incurred by the miscreants, security could never be guaranteed at all times and in all places to the same degree. This is why caravans were usually escorted by armed men. When Nehemiah was sent to Jerusalem by Artaxerxes I, for example, he had "army officers and cavalry" with him (Neh 2:9◊). Previously, Ezra had made the same journey, accompanied by many Jews entrusted with gold and riches for the temple of Yahweh. The way Ezra describes the journey shows that fear of attack was always present. He states in fact: "I should have been ashamed to ask the king for an armed guard and cavalry to protect us from an enemy on the road . . . the favour of our God was with us and protected us on the road from enemies and thieves" (Ezra 8:22, 31).

The Highway Patrol

Surveillance affected not only people but also the messages they were carrying. Three of Herodotus's anecdotes attest to the clever stunts used by people trying to evade the vigilance of the administration. The first portrays Harpagus the Mede when he wished to contact Cyrus secretly in Persia:

> [Because] the roads were guarded, there was only one way he could think of to get a message through to him: this was by slitting open a hare, without pulling the fur off, and inserting into its belly a slip of paper on which he had written what he wanted to say. He then sewed up the hare, gave it to a trusted servant, together with a net to make him look like a huntsman, and sent him off to Persia with orders to present the hare to Cyrus, and tell him by word of mouth to cut it open with his own hands, and to let no one be present while he did so. The orders were obeyed. Cyrus received the hare, cut it open, found the letter inside and read it. (I.123–124◊)

Even more colorful is the subterfuge dreamed up by Histiaeus, who, while he was at Susa, wanted to contact his nephew Aristagoras, tyrant of Miletus, to incite him to revolt against the Persians:

> [Histiaeus] was in difficulty about how to get a message safely through to him [Aristagoras], as the roads from Susa were watched; so he shaved the head of his most trustworthy slave, pricked the message on his scalp, and waited for the hair to grow again. Then, as soon as it had grown, he sent the man to Miletus with instructions to do nothing when he arrived except to tell Aristagoras to shave his hair off and look at his head. The message found there was, as I have said, an order to revolt. (V.35◊)

Last comes the story of Demaratus the Spartan, who was in exile in Susa and wanted to warn his fellow citizens in Sparta of Xerxes' upcoming offensive:

> As the danger of discovery was great, there was only one way in which he could contrive to get the message through: this was by scraping the wax off a pair of wooden folding tablets, writing on the wood underneath what Xerxes intended to do, and then covering the message over with wax again. In this way the tablets, being apparently blank, would cause no trouble with the guards along the road (*hodophylakoi*). (VII.239◊)

Whether these stories are literally true is beside the point (it seems pretty clear that they are just stories). The important thing is whether they are woven on an Achaemenid warp. In each case they give voice to the difficulty an individual would have had in sending a message that did not bear an official seal; in all probability, it would have been seized by the guards along the road.

Royal Mail and Royal Couriers

When the ancient authors wrote of the vastness of the imperial territory, they were particularly struck by the institution of the royal mail. Xenophon (as usual) attributes the origin of the institution to Cyrus the Elder (*Cyr.* VIII.6.17–18):

> We hear of another arrangement, devised to meet the huge size of the empire and enable the king to learn with great celerity the state of affairs at any distance. Cyrus first ascertained how far a horse could travel in one day without being over-ridden, and then he had a series

of posting-stations built, one day's ride apart, with relays of horses (*hippōnas*), and grooms to take care of them, and a proper man in charge of each station to receive the dispatches and hand them on, take over the jaded horses and men, and furnish fresh ones. Sometimes, we are told, this post does not even halt at night: the night messenger relieves the day messenger and rides on. Some say that, when this is done, the post travels more quickly than the crane can fly, and, whether that is true or not, there is no doubt it is the quickest way in which a human being can travel on land. To learn of events so rapidly and be able to deal with them at once is of course a great advantage.

Herodotus in turn (VIII.98✧) gives the following information on a Persian institution, the name of which he transcribes in Greek as the *aggareion*:

> At the same time Xerxes dispatched a courier to Persia with the news of his defeat [at Salamis]. No mortal thing travels faster than these Persian couriers. The whole idea is a Persian invention, and works like this: riders are stationed along the road, equal in number to the number of days the journey takes—a man and a horse for each day. Nothing stops these couriers from covering their allotted stage in the quickest possible time—neither snow, rain, heat, nor darkness. The first, at the end of his stage, passes the dispatch to the second, the second to the third, and so on along the line, as in the Greek torch-race which is held in honour of Hephaestus. The Persian word for this form of post is *aggareion*.

A Persian word, *astandēs*, known from several Greek texts, is the title borne by the future Darius III at court before his accession (Plutarch, *Alex.* 18.7; *Mor.* 326e). This is the definition in the *Suda*: "The *astandai* are the bearers of letters (*grammatophoroi*) who pass the messages successively one to the next (*ek diadochēs*)"; Hesychius calls them *hēmerodromoi* (couriers), *aggeloi* (messengers), and *krabbatoi* (which is much more obscure).

In the Greek stories, we find several examples of the use of such couriers. At the beginning of Aeschylus's *Persians*, the choryphaeus (leader of the chorus) longs for the arrival of a messenger (*aggelos*) or a mounted courier (*hippeus*), up to the very moment that Xerxes' messenger comes to bring the terrible news that "the barbarian army has perished entire" (vv. 13–14; 249–56). A few years earlier, when Darius, who was then at Sardis, wished to communicate his orders to Megabazus, who had been left in Thrace at the head of an army, "a messenger rode off with all speed to the Hellespont, crossed the water, and delivered the letter to Megabazus" (Herodotus V.14✧). The book of Esther shows how royal orders were communicated to every province in Ahasuerus's kingdom: "The couriers, mounted on the king's horses, set out in great haste and urgency at the king's command" (8:14✧).

The existence of these express messengers is confirmed by Persepolis tablets that use the word *pirradaziš*, which covers both the couriers and the horses they rode. This word clearly refers to the royal mail system that operated between the king and his subordinates in the provinces. One of the tablets (from Category Q) is particularly interesting. It reads:

> Datiya received 7 *marriš* of wine as rations. He bore a document (*halmi*) sealed by the king. He came from Sardis on the express service (*pirradaziš*) and was going to the king at Persepolis. Month 11, year 27. At Hidali. (Q 1809)

This was January or February 497. We think that Datiya is none other than Datis, the general who led the European expedition in 490. No doubt Darius had ordered him to make an inspection tour of Asia Minor at the outbreak of the Ionian revolt and to return quickly to Persepolis and report, using the express service.

Orders could reach their destination even more quickly if aural or visual signals were used. The existence of the former is attested in a text from the beginning of the Hellenistic period that shows the operation of a chain of signals between Susiana and Fārs; the text gives us every reason to believe that the use of signals goes back to the Achaemenid period. Then on the embankment of the Pasitigris, Eumenes, one of Alexander's successors, needed to summon reinforcements from Persia; by road, a troop of infantry would take about 24 days to complete the march. To shorten the delay, Eumenes resorted to a procedure described thus by Diodorus (XIX.17.6–7):

> Although some of the Persians were distant a thirty days' journey, they all received the order on that very day, thanks to the skilful arrangement of the posts of the guard (*phylakai*), a matter that it is not well to pass over in silence. Persia is cut by many narrow valleys and has many lookout posts (*skōpai*) that are high and close together, on which those of the inhabitants who had the loudest voices had been stationed. Since these posts were separated from each other by the distance at which a man's voice can be heard, those who received the order passed it on in the same way to the next, and then these in turn to others until the message had been delivered at the border of the satrapy.

In the most urgent cases, the acoustic message was the only one that could surmount a natural obstacle, such as a river. When Darius reached the north bank of the Danube on his retreat, he had to alert the Ionian leaders, who with their boats were on the opposite shore; for this purpose, Darius called on an Egyptian "with a tremendous voice," who was able to transmit the order to rebuild the pontoon bridge (Herodotus IV.141✧). A Persian, Artachaees, was reputed to have "the loudest voice in the world" (VII.117✧), and Persian youths were trained "in loud speaking and in breathing, and in the use of their lungs" (Strabo XV.3.18✧).

Visual relays, using fires kindled gradually, are also reported. This technique—called *pyrseia* by the Greeks—was well known in Judah in the sixth century and in the kingdom of Mari from the beginning of the second millennium on. It developed considerably in fourth-century Greece, as Polybius indicates (X.43–47): "Things that are about to happen can be brought to the attention of those to whom it is important to be kept up to date, whether it be three or four days away or even more." It was commonly used in the Persian Empire as well. It was, for example, "by a chain of beacons through the islands" that Mardonius, left in Greece after Salamis, intended to transmit to Xerxes, then in Sardis, news of the striking victory he (imprudently) expected to win over the Greeks (Herodotus IX.3✧). Aeschylus also alludes to this technique quite clearly in *Agamemnon*: the king let Clytemnestra know of the fall of Troy by fires lit from mountaintop to mountaintop. The entire system of visual relays was restored by one of Alexander's successors, the *Diadoche* Antigonus the One-Eyed, as Diodorus says (XIX.57.5✧): "He himself established at intervals throughout all that part of Asia of which he was master a system of fire-signals and dispatch-carriers, by means of which he expected to have quick service in all his business." The existence of such a system in Ptolemaic Egypt probably also resulted from the Persian heritage.

Lines of Communication and Strategy

From the point of view of Achaemenid power, the great axes of communication and traffic above all fulfilled a political and strategic function. The king's highways were "military roads," to repeat a phrase used by Quintus Curtius (V.8.5). In case of general mobilization, they enabled the various contingents to reach the assembly points that had been established for them (e.g., Herodotus VII.26). It fell to the satraps to construct depots, such as those described briefly by Xenophon in the *Anabasis*, on the Royal Road along the east bank of the Tigris: "Flour, wine, barley accumulated in great quantity for the horses. All this was put in reserve by the satrap of the country" (III.4.31). It was also for strategic reasons that the administration took measures to guarantee a supply of water. The necessity for these provisions is exemplified by a story from southern Palestine, where during the march to Egypt in 525 Cambyses had to resort to the services of the king of the Arabs, who replenished the Persian army's water supply (using a method that irresistibly calls to mind an episode from Esarhaddon's expedition of 671: *ANET*³ 292). Later on, according to Herodotus, the Persians improved the road, providing reservoirs. It is likely for the same reason—at least in part—that the Achaemenid authority supported the digging of *qanats* at the foot of the Elburz Mountains, which ensured permanent stores of water on the main road leading from Media to Central Asia (Polybius X.28).

In case of an attack on royal territory, the lines of communication also proved a decisive factor, both for the Achaemenid general staff and for the leaders of the enemy armies. In fact, control of the main roads provided the logistics necessary for sustaining the progress of armies. For an enemy bent on penetrating the Empire, it was essential to seize these major axes in order to control supply points and access routes. The choice of secondary routes could create surprise, but it could be no more than temporary and circumstantial, since the problem of provisions would soon crop up. Evidence comes to us from Cyrus the Younger's army: as far as Corsote, it could find supplies easily enough. After that, however, the army had to cross a desert on the east bank of the Euphrates, which made it nearly impossible for the soldiers to feed themselves except by buying from the dealers who accompanied the army (Xenophon, *Anab.* I.5.7).

Whenever a vast army crossed a region, it exhausted the region's capacity for supplying it. One example of this is found in the arguments among the Greek leaders after the death of Cyrus the Younger in Babylonia:

> They debated the plan for retreat and the road by which to reach the seacoast together. They
> agreed they could not take the same route by which they had come, because the land they
> had crossed was largely desert, and troops unceasingly harassed by their enemies would have
> lacked provisions. (Diodorus XIV.24.8)

Similarly, to those who counseled Darius III not to confront Alexander in Cilicia and to retreat to Babylonia, he replied:

> There was hardly any way to carry on the war. Such a multitude, at least at the onset of win
> ter, could not find sufficient supplies in a deserted region that had been ravaged alternately
> by his soldiers and by the enemy. (Quintus Curtius III.8.8).

The conditions that determined the strategy adopted by Eumenes in Babylonia in 317 were very much the same:

> He [Eumenes] was forced, however, to cross the [Tigris] because the country behind him
> had been plundered, whereas that on the other side was untouched and able to furnish
> abundant food for his army. (Diodorus XIX.12.4◈)

The same sort of reasons (in part at least) directed Darius III's choice after his defeat at Gaugamela: he reached Media, leaving Alexander to take the royal road to Babylon: "The reason he had chosen to flee to Media was that he thought that Alexander would take the road to Susa and Babylon after the battle, since its entire length crossed inhabited areas, and since the road itself was not hard for the beasts of burden. . . . On the other hand, the Media road did not represent an easy march for a large army" (Arrian III.16.2).

It could thus be said that, for the enemies of the Great King to have any chance of success, they would have to take the Achaemenid theater of strategic operations or, in other words, to turn to their own advantage the logistics the Persian authority had established to ensure its survival. This is the main point of a well-known anecdote told by Plutarch: Alexander once received ambassadors from the Great King during his father's absence, and one of the questions he asked them concerned "the length of the roads and techniques for traveling in the high country" (Plutarch, *Alex.* 5.2; cf. *Mor.* 342b–c). Again, when a defensive strategy was employed by the Persian authorities—or sometimes against them—roads and rivers could be transformed into obstacles in the face of invaders.

From reading Xenophon's *Anabasis*, we discover in fact that both in the Greek imagination and in their actual experiences, rivers represented the obstacles that led them to fear never being able to return to the sea. One of their leaders, Clearchus, addressed the satrap Tissaphernes in terms that make it perfectly clear that he found himself completely unable to master Achaemenid strategy, whether routes, replenishments, or rivers:

> With you, every way is easy, every river is crossable, and there is no dearth of provisions; without you, every way is plunged into darkness, since we know nothing of our route, every river is difficult to cross, every mob is terrifying (II.5.9)

Tissaphernes uses the opportunity to stress ominously in reply:

> The rivers are so numerous that on their banks we are free to pick those of you we choose to fight, and there are some that you could not possibly cross unless we ourselves brought you over. (II.5.18).

This was especially true in Babylonia, where access to the great capitals was contingent on crossing rivers and canals. In wartime, the controlling power could choose to use rivers and canals as means of defense. This was a strategy that was applied from earliest times down to the present—before, during, and after Achaemenid dominion. One example stands out above many others: during the battles of the *Diadochoi* in Babylonia, Seleucus and his side, in order to block their adversaries, "sailed off to a certain ancient canal and cleared its intake, which had been filled up in the course of time. Since the Macedonian camp was surrounded by water and the neighbouring land on all sides was now inundated, there was danger that the entire encamped army would be destroyed by the flood" (Diodorus XIX.13.2◇). It is thus easy to understand the fear expressed by Clearchus, head of the Greek mercenaries, after the death of Cyrus the Younger:

> They kept coming upon trenches and canals, full of water. . . . Clearchus . . . suspected that the trenches were not always full of water in this way, for it was not a proper time to be irrigating the plain; his suspicion was, then, that the King had let the water into the plain just in order that the Greeks might have before their eyes at the very start many things to make them fearful of the journey. (Xenophon, *Anab.* II.3.10–13◇)

The Persians took these considerations into account when Greek mercenaries found refuge in a region encircled by the Tigris and by canals; they feared that

> the Greeks might destroy the bridge and establish themselves permanently on the island, with the Tigris for a defence on one side and the canal on the other; in that case, they

thought, the Greeks might get provisions from the territory between the river and the canal, since it was extensive and fertile and there were men in it to cultivate it; and furthermore, the spot might also become a place of refuge for anyone who might desire to do harm to the King (II.4.22 [Loeb]).

To be sure, a river did not constitute an absolutely impassable obstacle for a determined army. Sometimes it could be forded. This, for instance, is how the Macedonians crossed the Tigris in 331, albeit not without some fears:

> Negotiating the ford, they were in fact in water up to the chest and the rapidity of the current unbalanced many soldiers while they were crossing, making them lose their footing. Many others were carried off by the current which, pounding against their shields, threw them into the gravest dangers. But Alexander thought of an expedient to fight against the violence of the current; he ordered all the soldiers to hold each other firmly by the hand and form a sort of weir by squeezing against each other. The Macedonians did not escape this bold crossing unscathed. (Diodorus XVII.56.3–5)

They could also gamble on luck: collecting all available boats or even crossing on inflated or stuffed animal skins—a procedure widely used in the ancient Near East. Cyrus's Greek mercenaries crossed a Babylonian river on a raft of animal skins to acquire supplies (Xenophon, *Anab.* I.5.10). This is also how Darius I's soldiers crossed the Tigris on their expedition against Nidintu-Bēl in 522 (*DB* §18). And it was also the method Alexander used to cross the Oxus River, when Bessus had burned all the boats after reaching the east bank:

> And the lack of wood was a special source of worry, and it was obvious that they would lose a lot of time if they had to go on distant searches for all the materials needed for building a bridge across the river. Under these conditions, Alexander had the skins collected with which the soldiers covered their tents and ordered them filled with very dry straw and sewn together with tight stitches so that the water could not enter. Thus stuffed and stitched, they enabled the army to cross in five days. (Arrian III.29.4)

A similar technique was suggested by a Rhodian to the survivors of the Ten Thousand, who were anxious to cross the Upper Tigris:

> I will need, he said, 2,000 skins; indeed, I see on every side sheep, goats, oxen, donkeys: slaughter these animals, inflate the skins; we will be able to cross easily. I will also need the straps you use for the harnesses. With these straps I will connect the skins in pairs, I will attach each one to the bottom by hanging rocks from them that will be dropped into the water as anchors. Then, when I have lined them up across, I will attach them to both banks, and over them I will throw bundles of wood on which I will put earth. You will not sink, as you will soon see: every skin can bear two men. And the sticks and soil will keep you from slipping. (III.5.9–11)

The Gates of the Empire and the Network of Garrisons

Guardposts (*phylaktēria*) scattered in strategic locations were another feature of the Persian system of control. In his description of the Sardis–Susa road, Herodotus mentions one guardpost on the Halys, two in Cappadocia, and one in Armenia (V.52). In addition to these posts, there were others that the ancient authors called Gates (similar to the Thermopylae in Greece). Coming from the west (Asia Minor), the first of these, the Cilician Gates, controlled the northern entry to the Cilician plain. They are described by Diodorus, Xenophon, and the historians of Alexander's campaigns: "It is a very narrow, sheer passage, 20 stadia long [ca. 3.6 km]; on both sides, mountains of giddy height, whose walls extend to the edge of the roadway. . . . The road that leads there, wide enough for chariots (*hamaxitos*), was very steep and inaccessible to an army, however slight the resistance it encountered" (Xenophon, *Anab.* I.2.21). These "narrow gorges" were what the natives called Gates, "since the natural site imitates the fortifications built by our hands" (Quintus Curtius III.4.2). It was thus in principle possible for a single garrison to control access. In 401, Cilician soldiers were guarding the pass; Cyrus sent a small unit by a back road to take it from the rear; upon finding out, the Cilician troops deserted their post, which allowed Cyrus to descend to the plain (*Anab.* I.2.21–22). In 333, Alexander attacked the Gates with light troops, who took the unguarded heights (Arrian II.4.3–4); that the heights were left unguarded was severely criticized by Quintus Curtius, for "the satrap should have been able, without risk to his own side, to contain or wipe out an enemy that normally would have dominated him. . . . Alexander recognized that mere rocks would have squashed him, if there had been people to drop them onto his army below. Four men could barely pass abreast" (III.4.4, 11–12).

Once an attacker had arrived in Cilicia, other Gates awaited him beyond Issus, which Xenophon calls the Cilician Gates and the Syrian Gates (pass of the Portelle):

> They consisted of two walls; the one on the hither, or Cilician, side was held by Syennesis and a garrison of Cilicians, while the one on the farther, the Syrian, side was reported to be guarded by a garrison of the King's troops. And in the space between these walls flows a river named the Carsus, a plethrum [30 m] in width. The entire distance from one wall to the other was three stadia [ca. 550 m]; and it was not possible to effect a passage by force, for the pass was narrow, the walls reached down to the sea, and above the pass were precipitous rocks, while, besides, there were towers upon both the walls. It was because of this pass that Cyrus had sent for the fleet, in order that he might disembark hoplites between and beyond the walls and thus overpower the enemy if they should be keeping guard at the Syrian Gates. (*Anab.* I.4.4–5◇)

The entrance to Persia was also defended by several garrisons. A first gate was located near Fahliyun. This was a true stronghold, held in 331 by Madates, a relative of the Great King, "who had decided to risk all for the sake of his honor" (Quintus Curtius V.3.4). With the help of local guides, a small Macedonian detachment used a mountain road and occupied a position overlooking the citadel. Once this position fell, the main road to Persepolis lay open. Alexander sent the bulk of the army, which took the wheelworthy (*hamaxitos*) road across the plain (*iter campestre*) toward Persepolis. Alexander himself, with light troops, used the mountain road in order to be able to take the Persian Gates, where the satrap Ariobarzanes had amassed several thousand men and had built a cross-wall to prevent Alexander's passage. Also worth mentioning are the Caspian Gates (the passes of Sialek and Sardar), located about ten days' march east of Rhagae in Media, which Alexander crossed in 330 in pursuit of Darius.

The strategic value of such transit points is clear. Herodotus notes, for example, that in front of the entrance to the bridge over the Halys—guarded by a fort (*phylaktērion*)— were gates "which have to be passed before one crosses the river" (V.52◇). The relatively small number of permanent pontoon bridges forced caravans to follow the routes laid down by the royal administration. This permitted the administration to easily control the traffic. We must also stress the importance of the location of Thapsacus, where pontoon bridges provided a crossing of the Euphrates River on the main route connecting Babylonia and the Mediterranean coast. Xenophon called Thapsacus a "populous, large, and rich city" (I.4.11). Its exact location remains in dispute, but it must have been near ancient Carchemish, a crossroads city well known from earlier periods. There is no doubt in any case that it was zealously guarded by the Persians. As it happens, an Achaemenid-period cemetery has been found at Deve Hüyük, 27 km southwest of Carchemish, dated to the first half of the fifth century. The objects discovered (arms, horse bits, etc.) show that a fairly sizable garrison existed there, in all probability to guard the crossings and fords of the Euphrates.

At the same time, we need to be subtle in our interpretation of this picture, recalling that our only information on the gates and bridges comes from military reports written by victorious aggressors. These natural fortifications were not impregnable. In every case, they could be circumvented via footpaths pointed out by local peasants and herdsmen—exactly the way that Thermopylae fell into the hands of the Persians in 480. The gates were lightly manned, except for the special case of the Persian Gates in 331, and these were located on a secondary route used by people going from Susa to Persepolis. In the mind of the Persian leaders, the job of the gates was not to halt an enemy offensive, something that was scarcely conceivable anyway. When these gates were properly garrisoned (which was not a permanent condition), they were part of a very dense network of fortified positions that allowed the Persians to hold the level ground and the roads that connected them. These garrisons were in permanent contact through the system of acoustic messages described by Diodorus in connection with the Persian fortifications (*phylakai*) and through visual messages, such as those seen in operation in Mysia at the end of the fifth century, in the Caicus Valley (Xenophon, *Anab.* VII.8.15).

The King's Service

All of these texts, to which many others could be added, have the value of giving— "in a nutshell," we might say—information on the measures taken in peacetime. At first glance, study of the mail and the royal roads confirms the viewpoint of the Greek observers. The main roads constituted one of the methods of territorial control and maintenance of order. Their primary function was political and military: they were used by couriers, armies, tribute-bearers, and also by troops of government workers (the *kurtaš* of the Persepolis tablets; see chap. 11 below) when they were moved from one spot to another. The garrisons placed along them were integrated into a very dense network of fortified locations that organized and structured the territories.

Even when it is stripped of its ideological gloss, the documentation generally testifies to what might be called the political organization of the territory, operated in such a way that the vastness of the Empire did not threaten its survival. Indeed, the moment the Persian presence began to weaken, the roads became less secure. This fact is well illustrated by a passage in the *Life of Datames* (4.1–2): C. Nepos records that in the 370s the satrap Datames was sent to battle the dynast Aspis, who in open rebellion against the Great King controlled Cataonia, a region "full of small strongholds . . . on the frontiers of Cilicia and Cappadocia: if any tribute was being brought to the Great King, they stole it!"

In this respect, then, Herodotus and Xenophon were not at all wrong to stress the political purpose of the Achaemenid mail service. To Greek eyes, the presence and activity of the Achaemenid couriers represented and symbolized the territorial dominion exercised by the Great King. As Plutarch puts it (*Cimon* 19.4), the absence of messengers (*grammatophoroi*) and royal tribute-collectors (*phorologoi*) in a region indicated that it had escaped the dominion of the central authority. In this regard, the Greek texts also express the Persian ideology of dominion. The round-the-clock traffic of messengers immediately brings to mind Darius's boastful proclamation: "These [subject] peoples did what I ordered them, night and day" (*DB* §7)! It is also the picture drawn by the author of the *De Mundo*: "So perfect was the organization and especially the system of visual signals, whose fires succeeded each other from the ends of the Empire to Susa and Ecbatana, that the Great King knew the very same day whatever was happening in Asia" (398a). But this picture gives only imperfect expression to an infinitely more complex reality: it communicates both the Greek fascination with a State that had succeeded in uniting vast territories and a highly idealized vision of the imperial realm, particularly as it emerges from the royal inscriptions (cf. chap. 5).

3. Lines of Communication and Trade

Commercial Arteries?

It is usually supposed that the main royal roads were regularly used by caravans transporting merchandise. The problem is that none of the Persepolis tablets and no Classical texts ever refer to merchants. The only references to long-distance transport are found in political contexts, either tribute or materials gathered at Susa for the construction of Darius's palace. It would perhaps be risky to draw firm conclusions from silence. It is extremely unusual when the tablets themselves give any indication of the purposes of the trips they authorize. We know perfectly well, without (obviously) being able to find any trace in the Persepolis tablets, that the Babylonian firms did business in Elam, Persia, and Media. Moreover, the Classical sources themselves rarely report anything other than the travels of ambassadors or the progress of armies, and they give hardly any information at all on the entire eastern half of the Empire, namely the Iranian Plateau and Central Asia. Indeed, there is every reason to assume that long-distance trade, which is well attested from earlier periods, continued in Achaemenid times. Unfortunately, textual attestations do not exist, apart from a fleeting reference in Ctesias (*Indica* §2) to a Bactrian merchant in India.

By way of indirect evidence, we may turn to Xenophon's *Anabasis*. Cyrus the Younger's route to Babylon was parceled out in stages set up in towns that Xenophon describes very obliquely using modifiers like "populous town" (*polis oikoumenē*; Peltae, Ceramon-agora, Caÿstru-pedion, Thymbrium, Tyraeum), "populous, rich, and great town" (*oikoumenē, eudaimōn, megalē*; Colossae, Celaenae, Dana, Issus, Thapsacus), "great and rich" (Tarsus, Charmande, Caenae), "large" (Opis), or "large and very populous" (Sittacus). On the other hand, Corsote is "a large abandoned town" and Mespila (once the capital of Assyria) is "a large deserted town." The use of such vocabulary— however stereotyped—necessarily takes on a descriptive function in Xenophon's mind. It may be that, for a Greek, the word *oikoumenē* described a town that preserved a certain degree of autonomy—that is, it existed as a city (in the Greek sense). Some of them, in addition, were capitals: Celaenae, capital of the satrapy of Greater Phrygia, site of an immense paradise (where Cyrus organized a review of his troops) as well as a fortified palace built by Xerxes; similarly, Tarsus, where "the palace of the *syennésis* (Cilician dynast) was found." But the adjectives that are organically included in a number of cases—"rich" in particular—clearly refer to an economic fact as well. These towns were rich, first of all, because soldiers could stay there several days and find supplies; a market (*agora*) might also be held there, which would allow the soldiers to escape the clutches of the traveling merchants that followed the army. Some of them are explicitly called commercial towns—primarily the coastal towns, such as those in Cilicia. Tarsus was abandoned by its natives but not by "those involved in retail trade (*kapēlia*) or by those who lived on the seacoast, at Soli and Issus" (Xenophon, *Anab.* I.2.24; Issus is where Cyrus joined up with the ships that had cast off from Ephesus). Likewise, Myriandus— "a town inhabited by Phoenicians"—is called "an *emporion*, where a large number of merchant ships were anchored" (I.4.6). Indeed, these references remain vague. However, considering Thapsacus's position in trade between the Mediterranean coast and Babylonia, it seems appropriate to conclude that, if this town was "populous, great, and rich," it may well have been because it was frequented by merchant caravans. We may also note that the activities of Babylonian merchants are attested in Syria in cuneiform documents from Darius's time. And there can be little doubt that North Arabia was crossed by camel caravans, not just between Arabia Felix and the Palestinian coastal ports (Gaza) that Herodotus calls *emporia* (III.5), but also between the Nile Delta and the Euphrates.

Land Routes and Water Routes

The Classical authors, so loquacious in their admiration of the Achaemenid road and postal system, are rather tight-lipped about communication along rivers and seas. The reason is doubtless to be sought in the strictly military orientation of the available sources, which took rivers and canals far more often as obstacles than as communication arteries. In reality, however, rivers, seas, and canals constituted axes of penetration that were often quicker and more efficient than land routes, especially for transporting heavy items.

First of all, coastal regions are very often rocky and/or marshy, so much so that coastal roads are either nonexistent or else so difficult to access all or part of the year that coastal navigation is an obvious solution. Many historic episodes in Asia Minor testify to this. In 396–395, the Spartan Agesilaus, then in Paphlagonia, negotiated a marriage between the dynast Otys and the daughter of the Persian nobleman Spithridates. She was then living in Cyzicus, a port on the Sea of Marmora. It was impossible to bring the princess by land before spring, because of the cold and snow. Otys, who was in a hurry, pointed out that if they wished they could bring her rapidly by sea: "Immediately Agesilaus fitted out a trireme and ordered the Lacedaemonians to fetch the girl" (Xenophon, *Hell.* IV.1.4–15). The same sort of arguments were put forward by Hecatonymus, a Sinopean, when he tried to persuade Xenophon's soldiers to go by sea to Cotyora in Sinope and then to Heraclea by the Black Sea. He assured his listeners that, if they did not follow his advice, they would encounter obstacles natural (rivers) and human (Paphlagonians) that would sooner or later block their progress, since the land route was "absolutely impossible." "On the other hand," he promised, "if you go by sea, from this country you can hug the coast as far as Sinope, and from Sinope to Heraclea. From Heraclea you can go just as easily by land as by sea, since in this city plenty of boats are available" (*Anab.* V.6.10). Similarly, to bypass the the Cilician and Syrian Gates, whose fortifications reached to the water's edge, Cyrus the Younger relied primarily on his marines: "He wanted to land some hoplites between the two Gates and beyond the second, to surprise and overcome them, if the enemy was guarding the Gates of Syria" (I.4.5). In the same way, Alexander sent his spies by sea to report on Darius III's troop positions on the Plain of Issus in Cilicia (Arrian II.7.1). For rapid connections between Cilicia and the western coast of Asia Minor, it was much more efficient to go by sea. For instance, when Mardonius was entrusted with an expedition to Europe, after he had arrived in Cilicia, "he took ship and continued along the coast in company with the fleet, leaving other officers to conduct the troops to the Hellespont" (Herodotus VI.43◊). Coming from the other direction, Issus is where Cyrus the Younger, having taken the land route, joined up with his fleet, which had set sail from Ephesus.

To get heavy goods out of the back country, there was scarcely any other alternative than using the coastal rivers and hugging the shore until reaching the mouth of another river. Many Greek cities in Asia Minor struck coins showing a river god, often holding a bow, a stern, or a rudder. In northern Asia Minor, the Hypius, Rhyndacus, Lycus, Sangarius, Iris, and Halys rivers were navigable; these were the routes for shipping out the timber cut along their upper reaches. The same was true for the Eurymedon River in southern Asia Minor. Of course, land transport of heavy goods was not unknown in the Near East, as in, for example, king Aššurbanipal's account of his Egyptian campaign and the booty that resulted. He says that he transported two enormous obelisks from Thebes in Egypt to Assyria (*ANET*[3] 295). But only powerful states had the ability to mobilize a labor force both large enough and specialized enough to accomplish such a move. In an example from a later time, Antigonus the One-Eyed made gigantic preparations for an expedition against Egypt in 312. Established at Tyre, he sought the aid of the Phoenician kings: "He himself collected wood cutters, sawyers, and shipwrights from all sides, and carried wood to the sea from Lebanon. There were eight thousand men employed in cutting and sawing the timber and one thousand pair of draught animals in transporting it" (Diodorus XIX.58.2◊). After arriving at the coast, the wood had to be transported by sea to its destination. When Solomon requested lumber from King Hiram of Tyre, he replied that the wood would be conveyed in the form of rafts from Tyre as far as Joppa; it is likely that the same was done with the wood offered by Cyrus for the reconstruction of the temple in Jerusalem. On the Syro-Palestinian coast, several small coastal rivers were also accessible to cargo ships.

The Euphrates Boats

Rivers and canals held a special place in the social and economic life of Babylonia. Except in its upper reaches, which were cut off by rapids, the Euphrates was navigable, as was one of its tributaries, the Khabur. Many cuneiform texts attest to the importance of trade in heavy products (grain, bitumen, wood, stone, etc.) throughout the second and first millennia. Herodotus also took a lively interest in Euphrates navigation. In particular, he gives a fairly precise description of the boats in use in his day:

> I will next describe the thing which surprised me most of all in this country, after Babylon itself: I mean the boats which ply down the Euphrates to the city. These boats are circular in shape and made of hide; they build them in Armenia to the northward of Assyria, where they cut ribs of osiers to make the frames and then stretch watertight skins taut on the under side for the body of the craft; they are not fined-off or tapered in any way at bow or stern, but quite round like a shield. The men fill them with straw . . . and let the current take them downstream. They are controlled by two men; each has a paddle which he works standing up, one in front drawing his paddle towards him, the other behind giving it a backward thrust. The boats vary a great deal in size; some are very big, the biggest of all having a capacity of some hundred and thirty tons [5000 talents]. Every boat carries a live donkey—the larger ones several—and when they reach Babylon and the cargoes have been offered for

sale, the boats are broken up, the frames and straw sold and the hides loaded on the donkeys' backs for the return journey overland to Armenia. It is quite impossible to paddle the boats upstream because of the strength of the current, and that is why they are constructed of hide instead of wood. Back in Armenia with their donkeys, the men build another lot of boats to the same design. (I.194◇).

Herodotus seems to have confused two kinds of small craft well known in both ancient and modern Mesopotamia: the *kelek*, a raft constructed on a series of inflated skins, described several times by Xenophon in the *Anabasis*; and the *quffa* (Akkadian *quppu*), which is a type of round boat covered with leather. Only the kelek can navigate the rapids of the Euphrates. Not all of the boats were built to this pattern. This is shown, for example, by a Neo-Babylonian-period tablet from the archives of the Eanna at Uruk: it states that 5 minas of silver are allotted for the wood for 22 boats that were to transport 30,000 measures of asphalt. The text states that the work squad includes, in addition to unspecialized laborers, a blacksmith, two builders, and four boat carpenters; the latter are a special type of carpenter, distinguished for instance from "door carpenters."

In the Babylonian towns, all economic activity depended closely on numerous waterways, which were often a network of great complexity. They guaranteed the irrigation of the fields and the supply of drinking water as much as the transport of heavy objects. This is documented, for example, in the archives of the Eanna of Uruk. When the temple administrators bought bitumen and asphalt, these materials were transported by boat. The waterways were also used to convey both grain and date harvests to the city quays. The collection centers throughout the year were located on the shores of the navigable routes: "along the high waters," to use the Babylonian expression that referred to canals that were navigable year round. It was the same in Babylon, where materials for the large temple downtown were offloaded at the "Quay of Bēl." Most of the sixty canals near Nippur were navigable. At Uruk, there were flotillas that belonged either to the Eanna or, more often, to professional boatmen who worked for the temple, taking in a fairly high fee for boat and crew rental. Sometimes, peasants and soldiers were required for hauling boats. This could require quite a few craft; on one occasion, for example, we read of the crop-watcher of the Eanna, who needed to transport the barley harvest and contacted a flotilla of 300 small boats, which were immediately placed at his disposal. At Nippur, service lands were granted in concession to the "commander of the boatmen."

Transport on the Tigris

In its upper course, the Tigris River was accessible to large transport ships as far as north of the Nineveh area. The Assyrian kings often used the river to float building timber and enormous sculptures for their palaces. Sennacherib built a fleet at Nineveh; it sailed down the Tigris to Opis, where the boats were transferred to the Euphrates by a canal. In the Achaemenid period, the use of the Tigris is confirmed by Darius III's plans in 332–331. He had decided to concentrate his immense forces in the upper valley of the Tigris at Arbela, a major town on the road connecting Babylon to the West: "He would receive his supplies either by land or by the Tigris" (Quintus Curtius IV.9.8), he thought. The east bank of the Tigris was in fact edged by the king's highway described by Herodotus and taken by the Ten Thousand on their return northward. During this march the soldiers passed near the town of Opis, where there was a bridge; there can be no doubt that Opis was a river port of prime importance. In 539, Cyrus crossed the Tigris and achieved a decisive victory over the Babylonian armies. Xenophon calls it a "considerable city" (II.4.25) and describes the traffic he saw all around: "There are canals that branch off the Tigris. There are four of them. They are a plethra [approximately 30 m] wide and very deep. Boats filled with wheat travel them" (I.7.15). Tablets from the reign of Cyrus also indicate that the town contained a bustling market, where representatives of the House of Egibi went to buy and sell slaves.

From Babylonia to Elam

Navigation was not restricted to the great north–south routes represented by the Euphrates and the Tigris. The two rivers and their tributaries were linked by many canals, which especially facilitated trade between two extremely important Achaemenid centers, Babylonia and Elam (Susiana). Beyond the transverse canals, the Persian Gulf represented a means for privileged communication. This was already evident in the strategic measures adopted as far back as the Assyrian king Sennacherib: desiring to attack Elam from Babylon, he ordered his fleet to descend the Euphrates, skirt the coast of the Persian Gulf, and then land at the mouth of the Karun, on whose banks a decisive land battle was fought. It is likely that the return up the Euphrates was aided by the powerful tides, which at that time reached as far as Uruk.

The comings and goings of the Macedonian fleets in 324 are also informative. After their meeting in Carmania, Nearchus, commander of the fleet, and Alexander agreed to rendezvous at Susa. Guided by a Persian pilot, Nearchus sailed up the Pasitigris (Karun) as far as Ahwaz, then took the Eulaios up to Susa. The next year, Alexander in turn, leaving Susa, went down the Eulaios and reached the mouth of the Tigris; while another part of the fleet went back up the Eulaios as far as the junction with the canal linking the Eulaios with the Tigris and finally entered the Tigris. And Nearchus, who by then had reached the mouth of the Euphrates, met up with Alexander by once more taking the Eulaios. The hazards of navigation—emphasized as early as Sennacherib—made the use of professional pilots obligatory. This is what Nearchus had to say, speaking about the northern section of the Persian coast of the Gulf: "Along the Persian coast, the route was nothing but shoals, reefs, and lagoons" (*Ind.* 38.8). The Susiana coast was similar: "The sea has little depth overall, the reefs extend far from the shores, and it is difficult to enter the ports" (40.10).

Several Babylonian tablets attest to the regularity and vigor of trade. In 505, six men received payment in kind (wool) to take a boat loaded with barley to Elam. In 499, two Babylonians received a fee for taking a boat carrying garments to Elam. The House of Egibi, the commercial company, had agents on the spot. A text from the time of Nabonidus attests that, upon their return, the Babylonian boats brought "fruits of the Elamite orchards" to Babylonia. This document reminds us of what Diodorus Siculus wrote later (XVII.77.4). Speaking of "all kinds of fruit" yielded by the Uxian country (a region of Fahliyun), he wrote: "Because they dry the harvest after it is ripe, the merchants who sail the [Pasi]tigris [Karun] are able to bring down a variety of dishes to Babylonia that are a delight to their customers."

From the Mediterranean to Babylonia

In a letter attributed to him (*Letter* 30), Themistocles describes a trip that took him on an official mission from the coasts of Asia Minor to Babylon and/or Susa:

> During the march, I crossed a hilly country and a deep valley. I saw and passed through deep valleys, whose slopes were inhabited and cultivated. The uninhabited portions sheltered wild beasts and herds of other animals. I navigated many rivers and visited many peoples.

Along with other information, the text explicitly refers to the use of both land and river routes, especially for travelers from Asia Minor to Babylon. Babylonian rivers and canals were closely connected to the Mediterranean coast, because of the combination of three types of transport: river, land, and sea. The source of the Euphrates is no more than about 180 km from the Gulf of Alexandretta [in modern Turkey], with which trade was always active. This is probably what Herodotus was thinking of when he described the cargo of the Babylonian boats as "mostly [Phoenician] wine in palm-wood casks"; he also refers to "anyone today who travels from the Mediterranean to Babylon and comes down the Euphrates" (I.185,◇ 194◇). Merchandise offloaded in Phoenician ports arrived at Thapsacus by land, then went down the Euphrates to Babylon. Regular use of these routes must have been considered normal, considering that the Athenian admiral Conon, who was in Cyprus at one point and wanted to meet the king [Artaxerxes II] as soon as possible, sailed for Cilicia, traveled to Thapsacus overland, and "descended the Euphrates to Babylon" (Diodorus XIV.81.4).

In 324, Alexander had a fleet of 45 ships built in Phoenicia. "These ships were taken in pieces to the Euphrates at the city of Thapsacus, where they were reassembled and went down the river to Babylon . . . where the king had a harbor dug able to receive 1000 warships, as well as arsenals for this harbor" (Arrian VII.20.2–4). From the Achaemenid period proper, we can quote a passage from the Foundation Charter of Darius's palace at Susa: "The wood used here was brought from a mountain called Lebanon. The people from across the river (*Ebir-nāri*) brought it to Babylon; from Babylon, the Carians and Ionians brought it to Susa" (*DSf* §3g). The Lebanese lumber had thus been transported along the route just described: by land, then by river, interspersed with the segment by sea through the Persian Gulf. The Ionians to which this inscription refers may have been the Milesians who were punished as follows after the Ionian revolt (492): "The men [Milesians] in the city who were captured alive were sent as prisoners to Susa; Darius did them no harm, and settled them in Ampe on the Persian Gulf, near the mouth of the Tigris" (Herodotus VI.20◇). This city of Ampe might be identified with Aginis, an important trading post that Arrian locates near the mouth of the Tigris.

Writing in the Roman period, the geographer Strabo cited a third-hand report of an Athenian ambassador, Diotimus, who led an embassy to Susa in 437–436. His story was recorded by his contemporary Damastes, then became known to Strabo by way of Eratosthenes. Strabo intended to demonstrate the unreliability of the information transmitted by Damastes. He polemicized against him in these words:

> Eratosthenes gives us an example of Damastes' stupidity, because he says that the Arabian Gulf is a lake and that Diotimus, son of Strombichos, leading a delegation of Athenians, traveled by water from the Kydnos in Cilicia as far as the River Choaspes that flows past Susa, and that he arrived in Susa in 40 days and that these things had been told him by Damastes himself. (I.3.1)

How, then, can we believe that a water voyage from Cilicia to Susa was possible? Eratosthenes himself and Strabo obviously considered Damastes' assertions to be nonsense pure and simple, and Strabo passed them on simply to show that his colleague was not to be believed. The text has sometimes been understood in the following way: having traveled by sea from Athens to Cilicia, the Athenian ships would then have continued to the Nile Delta, taken the canal from the Nile to the Red Sea, and then retraced the path of the fleet sent by Darius from Egypt to the Persian Gulf (cf. chap. 12/1 below). However, it is far simpler to think that the Athenians followed the traditional route, landing in Cilicia, reaching the Euphrates overland, and sailing from Thapsacus, then reaching lower Babylonia; from there it was possible to reach Susa by an uninterrupted water passage, as we have already seen.

The Phoenician ports played a major role in this whole arrangement, even though their role is not well attested in the High Achaemenid period. Sidon is where Athenian ambassadors docked in the 360s before traveling on to the king, thanks to the assistance the Sidonian king Straton had given them (Tod, no. 139). Sidon is where Democedes left for Greece on Darius's orders (Herodotus III.136). Diodorus (XVI.41.4) says that, toward the middle of the fourth century, Sidon prospered greatly from commerce (*dia tēs emporias*). No less important was a site such as Myriandrus, in the Gulf of Alexandretta. Here is how Xenophon describes it at the end of the fifth century (*Anab.* I.4.5): "A city inhabited by the Phoenicians on the seacoast, it was a trading post (*emporion*) where a large number of merchant ships were anchored." Myriandrus's site was in fact exceptional: "It is located where two economically important roads met: the road that links the Gulf of Issus to the Euphrates via the Gates of the Amanus and the road that links Syria to coastal Cilicia via the Cilician Gates; it was a commercial nerve-center" (G. Kestemont). In a military context, Diodorus also attests to the importance of the traffic between Cilicia and Cyprus in the 380s (XV.3.1).

Archaeology brings regional or interregional commerce to light, much more so than long- or middle-distance trade. The most interesting documents come from shortly before Cyrus's conquest of Babylon. In them we see that Babylonian storekeepers, sometimes on commission from the Eanna of Uruk, imported a number of products from Ebir Nāri, including iron and copper from Yamana (Cyprus?), iron from Lebanon, alum and "Egyptian blue" from Egypt, as well as foodstuffs (honey, wine, spices) and textiles. It seems clear that the Phoenician merchants served as middlemen between the Mediterranean West and the Babylonian merchants in this era. There is no reason to think it was any different in the Achaemenid period.

The Inland Waterways of Egypt:
The Nile between the Mediterranean and the Red Sea?

Herodotus, who was so fascinated by Euphrates boats, also discusses Egyptian boats, whose materials and method of construction he describes. He calls them *baris* and states that "some of them [are] of many tons' carrying capacity" (II.96◊); Herodotus's description has often been compared with an Aramaic papyrus dealing with the repair of a boat belonging to the Persian administration (*DAE* 61 [*AP* 26]). Herodotus makes certain to include pilots among the seven Egyptian hereditary classes (II.164). The Egyptian expression "to be boatless," for that matter, refers to a condition of absolute poverty. As we know, the Nile has always been the essential artery of Egyptian navigation. Diodorus follows Herodotus (II.108) in attributing the most important labors in this area to the pharaoh he calls Sesoosis [Sesostris]:

> Over the entire land from Memphis to the sea he dug frequent canals leading from the river, his purpose being that the people might carry out the harvesting of their crops quickly and

easily, and that, through the constant intercourse of the peasants with one another, every district might enjoy both an easy livelihood and a great abundance of all things which minister to man's enjoyment. The greatest result of this work, however, was that he made the country secure and difficult of access against attacks by enemies; for practically all the best part of Egypt, which before this time had been easy of passage for horses and carts, has from that time on been very difficult for an enemy to invade by reason of the great number of canals leading from the river. (I.57✧)

We will see how the independent pharaohs of the fourth century used this system to bar the Achaemenid armies access to the Delta road (chap. 15/9 below). The role of the Egyptian inland waterways is well attested in the Aramaic papyri, especially in supplying the Elephantine garrison (*DAE* 54–55 [*AP* 2, 24]) but also in mail delivery (*DAE* 14, 17 [*Padua* 1, *AP* 42] and commercial trade (*DAE* 26, 109 [*LH* 2, Berlin 23000]) between Upper and Lower Egypt.

Herodotus (II.99) stresses that the Persians carefully maintained dikes and canals in Egypt, especially to avoid the risk of flooding Memphis. Linked directly to the Nile by a canal, the port of Memphis was extremely busy. It housed not just the administration's military arsenal but also a commercial port, where communities of Carian, Ionian, and Phoenician merchants were located. We also know that on Darius's initiative a canal was (re)opened between the Nile and the Red Sea. The Great King's objective is a bit murky, since it now appears that, contrary to the boastful statement on one of the canal stelas (Posener no. 9), no direct, regular communications link between the Red Sea and the Persian Gulf existed during the Achaemenid period. One of the stelas discovered in the area of this canal came from Tell el-Maskhuta (Posener no. 8). Indeed, recent surveys in the area have produced very interesting results: pottery from various Greek cities of Asia Minor and the islands (Chios, Thasos, Lesbos, Samos) dating from all phases of the fifth century has been noted, as well as from Phoenician cities. Although the purpose is difficult to reconstruct with any certainty, we are led to infer that the canal facilitated the development of trade between the great commercial cities of the Aegean, the Nile Valley, and the Red Sea. Phoenician and Greek (Chios) pottery has also been found at a site (Dorginarti) between the First and Second Cataracts. Finally, a papyrus from the time of Darius I attests to the existence of trade between Elephantine and Lower Nubia (*P. Loeb* 1).

Customs Collection and Trade

As is so often the case, it is the reference to royal taxes that provides information regarding the products and trade on which the taxes are levied. Customs duties are attested at Opis and Babylon in the form of river tolls and bridge tolls. We learn from Pseudo-Aristotle (II.34a) that there were customs duties in Babylonia: having fallen (according to the author) into disuse in Alexander's time, "an ancient regulation (*nomos*) in force in Babylonia required the payment of 10% (*dekatē*) on any product entering the country (*tōn eisagomenōn*)." The book of Ezra (4:20) implies the existence of regular customs duties throughout the Empire. There is little doubt that customs posts were established in the main stopover towns, such as Thapsacus on the Euphrates, as well as many others. Perhaps they were also established in the towns on the frontiers of satrapies, such as Cydrara, which marks the border between Lydia and Caria (Herodotus VII.30), or Iconium, which Xenophon (I.2.19) calls "the last city in Phrygia" (when coming from Celaenae).

Customs Collection on the Nile

We can garner extremely interesting information about customs collection from a very recently published Aramaic document, which the editors date to the reign of Xerxes, around 475 (*TADAE* C.3.7). It consists of extracts from the ledger of an Achaemenid Egyptian customs post that survives as a palimpsest beneath a famous text, the Aḥiqar story (*TADAE* C.1.1). The extracts record the inspection, registration, and taxation of ships that entered and left Egypt. Some ships are explicitly called Ionian (*ywny*); others are not marked by any ethnic label, but, given that they were transporting merchandise probably originating in Phoenicia (wood and especially Sidonian wine), we are led to think that they were Phoenician boats (another undated Aramaic document [*TADAE* C3.12 (DAE 12, AP 72)] attests to the use of Sidonian wine in Egypt). It seems that both the wood and the wine came from ports (in Asia Minor in the first case, in Phoenicia in the second) whose names are given, but there remain many difficulties in identifying them with certainty (Phaselis for the Ionian ships?). Arrival and departure dates of the boats are also given, as are their technical specifications and even the names of their captains. A number of Greek names from Asia Minor are found among the Ionians, and even one apparently Iranian name (Spitaka). All this information was recorded by the royal customs administrators during inspection when the ships arrived and departed. Regardless of their origin or type, every boat was taxed upon entry according to the value of the cargo. The Ionian ships paid a tax called *mndt'*, that is, *mandattu* (an Akkadian word referring to various fiscal levies, including taxes in Achaemenid Egypt); these were duties assessed in gold or silver, to which part (*mnt*) of the cargo of (olive?) oil was added. The Phoenician boats paid 10% (*m'sr'*) of each product carried, a fact that enables us to determine the exact composition of the cargo: it included amphorae (*kd*; Greek *kados*) of wine, different kinds of wood (unfinished wood, boards, etc.), metals (bronze, iron, tin), wool, and (much more rarely) clay (Samos earth?). In addition, each boat paid another fixed tax referred to by the rather mysterious label "silver of the men." On the return trip, every boat paid the "silver of the men," and the Ionian boats paid a tax proportionate to the value of the natron they were exporting from Egypt. All of these assessments were recorded in the accounts of 'the king's house' (*byt mlk'*), that is, the royal administration.

The name of the place where assessments took place is not given. One naturally thinks of Memphis. What is striking is the continuity of the Egyptian system during the Persian period with the customs system known from the Saite period—thanks to several hieroglyphic stelas—and from the period of Egyptian independence in the fourth century known from the Naucratis stela. We know that during the time of Nectanebo I (380), the pharaoh exacted taxes (in gold, silver, or kind) on goods imported from the Mediterranean to Naucratis as well as on the produce of Naucratis itself: one-tenth of the assessment was then transferred to the Treasury of Neith at Saïs. It would not be surprising if, in his "fervor" in regard to Neith, Cambyses had reinstated such regulations. Whatever the case, the extant documents very clearly fit into a chronological and organizational continuum between the Saite period and the fourth century. Since we know that the assessment was made at the entrance to the Canopic Mouth of the Nile Delta in the fourth century, in the city of 'Enwe (Greek Thonis), we may imagine that this was also the case during the period of Achaemenid dominion.

From the Nile to the Euphrates

The aforementioned Aramaic document, exciting in itself, becomes even more informative when we compare two Neo-Babylonian tablets that record the quantities of merchandise imported and sold on the Babylonian market a few years before Cyrus's
conquest. Here is a simplified inventory (based on the groundbreaking study by A. L.
Oppenheim):

YOS 6.168 (550 B.C.)		TCL 12.84 (551 B.C.)	
Copper from Yamana	600 minas	Copper from Yamana	295 minas
Dye	81 minas, 20 shekels		
Tin	37 minas	Tin	37 minas
Blue-purple wool	16 minas, 15 shekels		
Copper from Yamana	205 minas		
Lapis lazuli/"Egyptian blue"	55 minas	Lapis lazuli	55 minas
Fibers	153 minas	Fibers	153 minas
Alum from Egypt	233 minas	Alum from Egypt in sacks	233 minas
Dye	32 minas, 20 shekels		
Iron from Yamana	130 minas	Iron from Yamana	130 minas
Iron from Lebanon	257 minas	Iron from Lebanon	257 minas
Assorted honeys			
White wine	20 'jars': *kandanu*		
Dye	120 minas		
Spice	40 minas		
Spice	1 *kurru*		
Juniper resin	1 *kurru*		

Both tablets refer to the importation into Babylonia of products from the west, as certain place-names make very clear (Yamana, Lebanon, Egypt). Following a route known
well to Herodotus (I.185, 194) when he wrote of the importing of Phoenician wine into
Babylonia, many products imported from various Mediterranean countries were in fact
transshipped in Phoenician ports and from there transported to Babylonia (pp. 382f.
above). We may also note that, both in the Babylonian tablets and in our Aramaic document, the commerce was often in identical products (sometimes more easily identifiable in Akkadian): copper and iron (from Yamana), iron from Lebanon, tin, wine (and
honey from various places in the tablets), and wool (dyed purple and blue). From
Egypt came Egyptian blue (imitation lapis lazuli) and alum. In this regard, *TCL* 12.84
states: "233 minas of Egyptian alum with (its) containers (*aban gabî ša Miṣir adi gu-
rābu*)"—that is, skin or canvas bags. Alum was a product related to natron, and both
were used in Babylonia. From the Neo-Babylonian and Saite periods to the Persian period, then, we find the same products circulating and being traded between Asia
Minor, Egypt, Cyprus, Syro-Phoenicia, and Babylonia—using complex and multi-
faceted procedures and routes. The contextual difference is that the Babylonian documents illustrate the last step in these transactions, the sale in Babylonia carried out by

the merchants (*emporoi*), and they can only suggest the role of the *naukleroi* (Phoenicians, as it happens, in some cases at least) revealed by the Egyptian customs document. The Egyptian customs document, on the other hand, has nothing to say about the mechanisms involved in bringing to market the merchandise imported by this means into the Nile Valley. The merchandise probably was offered for sale by the owners of the boats, not just at Naucratis but also at Memphis, and no doubt at other sites between Thōnis and Memphis.

Conclusion

In the final analysis, it is tempting to conclude that the absence of direct references to commerce and tradesmen on the land routes results primarily from the distorting effect of documentation that is oriented almost exclusively toward the military and political spheres. Our information on customs and tolls seems to confirm the breadth and density of trade. Furthermore, royal assessments could take other forms. We know, for example, that Arab peoples had to pay the enormous quantity of 1,000 talents [ca. 30 tons] of incense to the Great King as a "gift" (Herodotus III.97✧) every year. In reality, this was nothing but a bleeding off of the commercial profits generated by the trade between Palestine and South Arabia.

Chapter 10
Royal Assessments and Tribute

1. *Sources and Problems*

Tribute and Power

It is useful at this point to devote a separate discussion to Darius's fiscal policy, within the context of the overwhelming task that he undertook, which involved reestablishing order and redefining his predecessors' policies. Given the construction work undertaken in his new capitals of Persepolis and Susa, the military expeditions, the gifts he gave, as well as the basic requirements of the court, Darius had to be able to count on significant, regular income. Actually, as we have seen, Cyrus, Cambyses, and Bardiya had also been careful not to neglect fiscal administration. Assessments on subject peoples did not begin with Darius. It is nonetheless true that every ancient text attributes to Darius a determining role in the establishment of tribute. The problem is to try to evaluate with precision the scope of his actions and their consequences for history.

One of the sources bearing on tribute is the royal proclamations; their intent was to glorify the imperial unification accomplished by Darius without taking into consideration any regional particularities. The Greek sources also exhibit this point of view, for the simple reason that they basically assume that the Achaemenid Empire was a unity, from Sardis to Bactra. Generally speaking, the Classical texts are simultaneously indispensable and enormously frustrating. They offer two contradictory pictures of the impact of Achaemenid tribute: some stress the moderation of Darius's taxes; most, however, love to denounce them as an unbearable burden. They likewise offer two images of the king, who is presented now as a just king, fairly compassionate toward his subjects, and now as a shopkeeper (*kapēlos*), "because of his imposition of regular taxes, and other similar measures" (Herodotus III.89◊).

But the royal texts are constructed from an essentially political and ideological viewpoint: they exalt the mythical memory of an ideal king; however, the majority of the Greek authors are led by a desire (often colored by polemic) to denounce the inherent defects of a system that made the Greeks of Asia "slaves" to the Great King, indirectly, via tribute, which was a metaphor for imperial dominion itself (e.g., Herodotus VII.1 [*douleuō*] and VII.7 [*douloterē*]). This approach is nonetheless analytically interesting. The problem is that neither the imperial nor the Classical version is susceptible to mathematically precise proof. This is why Herodotus's long discussion (III.89–97) of the tax reforms undertaken by Darius is so interesting and helpful. This text offers a wealth of information, even on the level of accounting practice, despite the fact that Herodotus himself is no expert in fiscal matters. He is also focused on the political aspect of royal policy — in other words, on the immediate relationship between tribute levying and imperial dominion. For this reason, he never takes a bird's-eye view. This is why his passage on tribute and taxes still poses many difficult interpretive problems, especially regarding other royal assessments and regulation of revenues.

Diachrony and Synchrony

To analyze the dynamic of the system as a whole, it is essential to broaden the documentary base and introduce later texts into the discussion. In doing so, there is obviously a risk of wiping out the diachronic perspective. Therefore, use of texts later than Darius and Xerxes will have to be justified by whether they fit into a logical and coherent whole. In fact, there is every reason to believe that the tribute system did not undergo any revolutionary modifications—except, obviously, the variations in extent and number of satrapies or the allocation of this or that people to this or that district. At any moment, the king might come up with new assignments (e.g., Arrian I.24.5). We should also recognize that temporary adjustments could be made in the base rate or amount of tribute. A specific example of this is the measure taken by Artaphernes in 492 after the revolt of Ionia (see chap. 12/5). But these localized and limited variations do not appear ever to have challenged the operation of the system in toto. This remark is not meant to eliminate the diachronic dimension in favor of an exclusively thematic approach. We will try to indicate, wherever the evidence warrants it, the changes and potential breakdowns.

As it happens, the most numerous and useful sources date to the end of the Achaemenid period, or more precisely, to the transition between the Achaemenid period and the High Hellenistic age. This wide array of evidence derives from the breadth of the reports written by Alexander's historians, who describe the typically Achaemenid institutions that were taken over (in whole or in part) by the Macedonian conqueror. This wealth of documentation also derives from the increasing number of Greek inscriptions from Hellenistic western Asia Minor. In fact, it is not hard to show that in many cases the institutions from the period of the Diadochi (the successors of Alexander) or the Seleucid kings were copied from Achaemenid practices. Achaemenid institutions can then be reconstructed by looking at their reflection in the evidence, always with an awareness of the need for methodological caution: there is a risk of getting lost in a hall of mirrors!

The last quarter of the fourth century is also the period from which the minor work *Oeconomica* dates. It was written by a representative of the Aristotelian school (and for this reason it is usually attributed to the anonymous "Pseudo-Aristotle"). In fact, the *Oeconomica* has the only overall analysis of the operation of the Achaemenid assessment system. The author seeks a model for *economy* in the sense he understands: the ways and means used by an *oekonome*, that is, the manager of a house, to "acquire . . . and to guard . . . [and] order his possessions aright and make a proper use of them. . . . For the preservation of wealth it is best to follow both the Persian and the Laconian methods. . . . The Persian system was that everything should be organized and that the master should superintend everything personally" (I.6.1–3✧). After these general reminders in book I, book II contains a condensed but incisive analysis of the four types of *economy* (II.1.1–8✧): "That of the king is the most important and the simplest, that of the city is the most varied and the easiest, that of the individual the least important and the most varied"; the "satrapal economy" is added, organically linked to the royal economy: the *satrapal economy* concerns receipts (tributes, taxes, etc.), and the *royal economy* has to do with the successful management of goods (what the Greeks call *oikonomia*); the king enjoyed revenues procured for him by his satraps. The common principle of the four kinds of economy is simple: "The expenditure must not exceed the income" (II.1.6✧)! There follows a long series of examples of ruses and subterfuges by which individuals, cities, and satraps amassed the money they were lacking (II.2).

A Greek like the author of the *Oeconomica* took an interest in the Persian Empire because he could thus study the example of an organization where, unlike in Greek cities, the king was never faced with fiscal problems. And it is quite clear that the author saw the reason as being the regularity and size of the assessments imposed by the satraps in the name of the king. This was also the point of view worked out earlier by Xenophon, who, in a work called the *Oeconomicus* on the ideal management of a large estate, highlighted the Great King's interest in his peasants and in "working the land." Xenophon also stressed the way in which tribute afforded the king a means of regularly paying those he owed.

The Documents from the Central Administration

In addition to the Classical sources, we are very fortunate to have documents from the Persian central administration, in particular, the thousands of tablets from Persepolis. In light of this documentation, Pseudo-Aristotle's text may be reevaluated, since the tablets clarify the operation of the royal economy at Persepolis. Babylonia is the best documented region in the remainder of the Empire, even though most of the information on the organization of land and related fiscal matters is later than Darius I. The Babylonian material dates basically to the reigns of Artaxerxes I and Darius II; nonetheless, here too, careful analysis permits us to assume that, basically, the economic structures go back to Darius I and even in some cases to Cyrus and Cambyses. The same methodology applies to the Aramaic materials from Egypt, a fact that assumes decisive importance. The composition and chronological assignment of regional subsets of documents call to mind our basic rule of thumb: despite the global character of the Achaemenid tribute organization implied by Pseudo-Aristotle and Herodotus, it makes sense always to contextualize our analyses by distinct regions. This is why the breadth and specificity of the Persepolis documentation demand separate discussion. At the same time, the questions raised by this documentation lead us to situate them in the framework of the Empire as a whole (chap. 11), before returning to regional studies (chap. 12). Only this sort of "dialogue" between center and periphery will come close to raising, if not resolving, in all their depth, the complicated problems related to the overall functioning of an economic system based on regional tribute.

2. Satrapies and Tributes

Herodotus and the Tributes of Darius

Darius and his advisers tackled the task of tribute reorganization with great speed. Herodotus attests to this haste by writing: " he then proceeded to set up twenty provincial governorships (*nomoi*), called satrapies . . . and assessed [each] for taxes" (III.89✧). The reformed tributes were probably levied for the first time in 518–517, that is, at the end of the moratorium decreed by Bardiya in 522. Following his exposition, Herodotus gives a list of the districts, indicating exactly which peoples belonged to them, as well as the amount of tribute allocated from each (III.90–94). The tabulation is shown on p. 391.

Nomes, Satrapies, and Peoples

This passage from Herodotus has stimulated and continues to stimulate multifarious analyses from historians. Some have maintained that this list contains no credible infor-

Nome	Peoples	Tribute in Talents	Additional Considerations
I	Ionians, Magnesians in Asia, Aeolians, Lycians, Milyans, Pamphylians	400	
II	Mysians, Lydians, Lasonians, Cabalians, Hytennians	500	
III	[Hellespontine] Phrygians, Thracians of Asia, Paphlagonians, Mariandynians, Syrians	360	
IV	Cilicians	500	360 white horses
V	from Posideium to Egypt (Arabs exempted)	350	
VI	Egypt, adjacent Libyans, Cyrene, Barca	700	income from the fish of Lake Moeris + 120,000 *medimnes* of wheat for the Persian garrison at Memphis
VII	Sattagydians, Gandharans, Dadicae, Aparytae	170	
VIII	Susa and the country of the Cissians	300	
IX	Babylonia and the rest of Assyria	1000	500 young eunuchs
X	Ecbatana, the rest of Media, Paricanians, Orthokorybantes	450	
XI	Caspians, Pausicae, Pantimathi, Daritae	200	
XII	Bactrians and . . .(?)	360	
XIII	Pactyans, Armenians, and neighboring peoples as far as the Pontus Euxinus	400	
XIV	Sagartians, Sangians, Thamanaeans, Utians, Myci, and inhabitants of the Erythrean Sea	600	
XV	Saka and Caspians	250	
XVI	Parthians, Chorasmians, Sogdians, Arians	300	
XVII	Paricanians, Ethiopians of Asia	400	
XVIII	Matieni, Saspires, Alarodians	200	
XIX	Moschians, Tibarenians, Macrones, Mossynoeci, Mares	300	
XX	Indians	360	

mation, because its composition is modeled on a Greek literary and poetic tradition going back to Homer's *Catalogue of Ships*. This negative judgment clearly goes too far. For one thing, the comparison frequently made between Herodotus's list and the depictions of peoples at Persepolis and elsewhere is not relevant. These two different kinds of documents clearly pertain to different concepts: one source (documents from the central administration) gives an idealized and ideological representation of the imperial realm (see chap. 5); the other (Herodotus) indisputably refers to an administrative organization. Of course, because he was from Asia Minor, Herodotus clearly Hellenized the facts: it is most striking in particular to note that he begins his list with the Ionian districts, whereas in every Achaemenid document the country lists begin with Persia, which is considered to be the heart of royal power. Similarly, the vitriolic criticisms brought against the figures he provides must be abandoned. It is hardly surprising that

Herodotus encountered various difficulties in converting to talents the amounts that had been furnished to him in darics. But, despite several conversion and arithmetic errors, it is apparent that the numerical information he gives must be considered reliable. The precision suggests quite strongly that he had access—through unknown (and doubtless indirect) channels—to official documents, such as, for example, quotations (written or oral) from the archives of Sardis and elsewhere.

Anyway, even though Herodotus assigns the list of administrative districts to the reign of Darius, it is not certain that some of the information does not date to a later period, that is, the period during which Herodotus was gathering the data to be included in his *Inquiry*. India, for example, was manifestly not included in the system until after Darius's conquest; at the very least, payment of the tribute decided previously could not be imposed until after the conquest. Herodotus (III.96◇) himself states that "as time went on, other tribute came in from the islands and from the peoples in Europe as far as Thessaly"—that is, in the period subsequent to 512–510. But it is very difficult to be sure of the details.

The rationale behind some of the groupings is not always transparent. Furthermore, it can be quite difficult to locate precisely on a map some of the peoples listed by Herodotus, using names that he has distorted. According to him, the *arkhai* (governments) were called *satrapies* by the Persians and were headed by governors (*arkhontes*). The problem is that we do not have any list of satrapies earlier than the death of Alexander that could be used to systematically verify the statements of the historian from Halicarnassus. We are not entirely devoid of information on Darius's satraps, however. Along with the Greek texts, Babylonian documents and Persepolis tablets allow us to prepare a partial list and correlate it with Herodotus's list.

Satrap	Date	Residence	Herodotus's Nome
Mitrobates	525?	Dascylium	III
Oroetes	+521	Sardis and Magnesia	I and II?
Gubāru	522–	Babylonia and Trans-Euphrates	
Uštānu	535–525		V and IX
Ḫuta[. . .]	521–516	Egypt and Cyrenaica	
Aryandes	486	Susa	VI
Bakabana	525–510?	Bactra	VIII
Dādarši	500–499		
Irdabanuš	522	Arachosia	
Vivāna	500	Kandahār	XVII?
Bakabaduš	522	Aria	?
Harbamišša	494	Ecbatana	XVI (in part)
Miturna (Hydarnes)	?		X
	503–499		

In some cases (Dascylium, Sardis, Egypt, Susa, Bactra, and Ecbatana), the agreement between the nomes of Herodotus and the satrapal jurisdictions is adequate, as a first approximation at least. But this is not generally true. For instance, there seems to have been a satrap in Aria in Darius's time, and the existence of a satrapy of Parthia or Parthia-Hyrcania is attested at a later period; furthermore, in a very general way, Sogdiana was connected to Bactria. Despite all these things, the Arians are included with the Parthians, Chorasmians, and Sogdians in Herodotus's immense XVIth nome. Conversely, Herodotus demarcates a Vth division (III.92) whose boundaries correspond fairly closely to what is usually called Trans-Euphrates (Ebir Nāri). In fact, we know that at the date assigned to Darius's reform, Trans-Euphrates continued to be included within the vast administration of Babylonia and Trans-Euphrates. Within this vast satrapy, Trans-Euphrates apparently constituted a tributary subunit, as indicated by a decision of Darius regarding Jerusalem around 518 (Ezra 6:8), involving "tribute from the province of Ebir Nāri" (*middat 'Ābar nahārê*). Nonetheless, we do not possess documentation that could systematically prove Herodotus wrong. One of the main problems is that in later times there was a distinction between satrapal districts and tribute districts. It is likely that in most cases there was no such difference: the responsibility to collect the tribute imposed on the *ethnē* that were supposed to be under a satrap's authority fell to the satrap. Nevertheless, a late passage in Arrian (I.24.5) seems to indicate that, even after the adjustment of a boundary between two satrapies, an *ethnos* belonging to one satrapy was permitted to continue to pay its tribute in a neighboring satrapy (chap. 16/4).

The method that Darius used to determine the boundaries of the districts and their tribute, as reported by Herodotus, is most interesting: "for administrative purposes neighbouring nations were joined in a single unit (*kata ethnea*), outlying peoples were considered to belong to this nation or that, according to convenience" (III.89◇). From the perspective of tribute, the peoples of a nome were "grouped together (*es tōuto tetagemenoi*)" (III.92◇), they "contribute together (*es tōuto sumpherontes*)" (III.92◇), "a particular sum of tribute was set for all the peoples [of a nome]" (III.90). With just one exception—the Vth division (III.91◇)—the borders of the districts are never given with reference to geographical features. A tribute district was first and foremost a combination of neighboring peoples. The term *ethnos* corresponds fairly closely to a word used by the Great Kings in their inscriptions, *dahyu*. Both refer to a community and to the territory in which that community lived and reproduced.

Setting the Amount of Tribute

There are two texts—late but interesting—that inform us of the practical considerations involved in setting tribute amounts at the beginning of the reign of Darius, one from Plutarch and one from Polyaenus. Tradition records the actions taken by Darius on a very auspicious day:

> After fixing the amount of taxes which his subjects were to pay, he sent for the leading men (*hoi prōtoi*) of the provinces (*eparchies*), and asked them if the taxes were not perhaps heavy; and when the men said that the taxes were moderate, he ordered that each should pay only half as much. (Plutarch, *Mor.* 172f◇)

A similar presentation, obviously dependent on the same source, is found in Polyaenus (VII.11.3):

> Darius was the first to levy tribute on his peoples (*ethnē*). In order to make it bearable, he did not set the amounts himself, but had them arrived at by his satraps, who set them at an exorbitant amount. On the pretext of kindness to his subjects, Darius reduced the imposts by half. The peoples regarded the diminution as a considerable benefit awarded by the king and paid the remainder gladly.

There is no overarching reason to doubt this tradition, even though it has probably not escaped the heavy hand of royal propaganda; it is easy to recognize the perennial monarchic aphorism in it: "There are no bad kings, only bad satraps"! By opposing the behavior of his satraps, the king convinced the leaders of the *ethnē* to accept the amount of tribute. In doing so, he very likely broke with previous practice, which doubtless gave too much leeway to the satraps, who were eager to extract from their subjects as much income as possible, so as to enrich themselves personally at their subjects' expense. The king took care to consult both the satraps and the local leaders to *set* the official amount of tribute—hence the repeated use of the verb *tassein* in all its forms by Herodotus, as well as by Plutarch and Polyaenus. We can also better understand the difference that Herodotus points out between the time of Cyrus and Cambyses and the time of Darius: Darius was the first to publish an official tribute list (cf. Herodotus III.89: *epitaxis*; Polyaenus VII.11.3: *prōtos phorous etaxe*). The new king had thus learned a lesson from the revolts he had just quelled, and in this way he also continued the tribute reforms of Bardiya, whom he had just eliminated (see chap. 3/1). It made sense to adopt procedures that ensured the regular payment of tribute without inciting the subjects to challenge Achaemenid domination.

It is difficult to go beyond these general considerations. Nonetheless, several texts explain that the tribute was set 'in proportion to the [subjects'] ability to pay' (*kata to megethos/kata dynamin*). The level of tribute was established in relation to the agricultural resources of the various countries. This is most clearly expressed by Pseudo-Aristotle, analyzing the different aspects of the *satrapal economy*: "Of all these revenues, the most important and interesting is that which derives from the earth; it is called *ekphorion* or *dekatē*" ('tenth'; II.2.4). On the basis of a Hellenistic-period text (the so-called Mnesimachus inscription), it has been suggested that the tribute was set at the rate of $1/12$ per mina of gold [about 500 g], based on a section of land of about 1.5 km^2.

The original Persian document presupposes a remarkable accounting of the diversity of the Empire, which had to have been based on an in-depth preliminary investigation that surely took several years to carry out. Unfortunately, we do not know the details of this operation, which is comparable, but on a wholly different scale, to the analysis conducted by Aristides, the Athenian, in the towns that had just formed the Delian League (in 478). He was instructed "to examine the situation and the revenues of the various territories in order to impose on each what they had to pay in proportion to their resources" (Plutarch *Arist.* 24.1). Aristides' estimate was very likely based on the analysis conducted by the Achaemenid administration at Sardis in 493–492 after the Ionian revolt (cf. Herodotus VI.42). Whatever the case, Darius's tribute principle was simple: every community in the Empire had to turn over part of its produce (*dasmos*) to the king of kings, including the less-known peoples, such as "the inhabitants of the islands in the Persian Gulf [Erythrean Sea], where the king sends those displaced from their homes in war" (III.93✧).

3. Gifts and Tribute

Herodotus's Viewpoint

The exceptions to the rule that all communities had to pay tribute are even more noteworthy. Among those exempt from tribute (*ateleia*), Herodotus lists the country of the Arabs, which is geographically included in the Vth nome (III.91). The explanation is found a bit further on, where he speaks of the category of peoples "upon whom no regular tax (*phoros*) was imposed, [but who] made a contribution in the form of gifts (*dōra*)" (III.97✧): every two years the Ethiopians on the border of Egypt and their neighbors provided 2 quarts of unrefined gold, 200 ebony logs, 5 Ethiopian boys, and 20 elephant tusks; every four years the Colchians and their neighbors as far as the Caucasus sent 100 boys and 100 girls; every year the Arabs sent a 1,000 talents of incense. We know nothing of the reasons for the special treatment of these peoples, except in the case of the Arabs, who had a treaty with Cambyses. These peoples were also included within the Achaemenid imperial realm, as Herodotus emphasizes, distinguishing them formally from other peoples located outside the boundaries, who were "outside the range of Persian influence" (III.97◊; IV.167◊). Like the tributary peoples, they were gathered into administrative districts "with their neighbors." Nor did they enjoy a general exemption; their contributions were added to those of the tributary peoples, though accounted separately (cf. the phrase *parex tou phorou* = 'separately from tribute'). Like the tributaries, they were required to send contingents to the royal army. In fact, in Herodotus's catalogue of Xerxes' army, we note the presence of Ethiopians and Arabs (VII.69◊; 86◊).

The difference between these peoples and the tributary peoples is, first, that "they taxed themselves"—that is, the amount of their contributions was established (in principle) "voluntarily." There is no doubt, however, that the amounts had been determined in accordance with the "desires" of the king (cf. Herodotus III.13◊). Furthermore, in the case of the Ethiopians and Colchians, the payment was biennial or quadrennial. And, in further contrast to the tributary peoples', their contributions were measured not in talents of silver but in raw materials. In this sense, in fact, "they were not taxed to pay tribute": the Achaemenid administration did not establish a level of payment (*taxis*); it was satisfied with requiring delivery (*apophora*). Finally, we may suppose—but this is pure conjecture—that, unlike the tributary peoples, they sent their gifts directly to the central authority without passing through the satrapal intermediary. Whatever the case, in Herodotus's opinion, these examples were nothing but a peripheral, residual exception within the new financial organization set up by Darius. He stresses the contrast with what had happened in the time of Cyrus and Cambyses (III.89). One example seems clear, at least at first reading—the example of the Cyrenians, Barcaeans, and Libyans. When Cambyses arrived in 525, they all "gave themselves up without a battle, agreeing to pay tribute and sending presents" (III.13◊; cf. IV.165◊). In contrast, in his account of Darius's organization, Cyrenians, Barcans, and Libyans bordering Egypt were included as tributaries in the Egyptian nome (III.91). But Herodotus's wording also makes it appear that, already under Cambyses, they paid tribute *and* gifts. This raises questions about the differentiation between gifts and tribute that he seems to make elsewhere.

The Gifts of the Tribute-Paying Peoples

Paradoxically, then, in Herodotus donors tend to show up in clusters at the fringes of the Empire at first, but over time the principle of gift-giving to the king persists and even spreads. This calls to mind what Xenophon (*Cyr.* VIII.6.6◊) writes of the tasks assigned by "Cyrus" to his satraps: "Send back here what there is good and desirable in their several provinces." This request achieved great results: "People of every nation thought they did themselves an injury if they did not send to Cyrus the most valuable productions of their country, whether the fruits of the earth, or animals bred there, or manufactures of their own arts; and every city did the same. And every private individual . . ." (6.23◊). We know from Ctesias that the kings of India—obviously in addition to their tribute—were in the habit of producing items at court that were highly valued by the Great King.

Ctesias names a mythical animal, the *martikhōra*, sent as a gift (*dōron*) to the king of the Persians (*FGrH* 688 F45d; in *Anim.* IV.21, Aelian shows his disdain for the phantasmagorical description by Ctesias). Ctesias also mentions a special kind of iron (*Indica* §4) and a perfume with a powerful, exhilarating scent, "a perfume of which no verbal description can give any idea and which is incomparable. . . . The king of the Indians would send it to the king of the Persians" (*Indica* §28). The Great King also received garments dyed vermilion with an animal dye, whose brilliance surpassed even the famous dye of the Sardians (Aelian, *Anim.* IV.41). Finally, they produced a drug extracted from a bird's excrement that provided a sweet, tranquil, and rapid death; Ctesias states that "the Indian king included it among the valuable gifts he sent to the king of the Persians. . . . The Great King stored it separately (*apothēsaurisei*) and only he himself and his mother had access to it" (*Anim.* IV.46)! Dino in turn reports "that they sent from Egypt to the Great King ammonia salts and Nile water" (Athenaeus II.67b; *FGrH* 690 F25b = Plutarch, *Alex.* 36.4). Nile water was said to be "fertilizing and very sweet." Perhaps Arrian was referring to this custom when, in his description of the oasis of Siwa, he mentions that the locals extracted natural salt. The priests carried it with them from Egypt, he writes, "to be conveyed as a present to the king (*dōron tōi basilei apopherousin*) or to someone else" (III.4.3–4◊).

Nevertheless, these are nothing but fragmentary examples cited by Ctesias's and Dino's informants. They obviously refer to a general practice on which the informants' details agree. The gifts presented to Darius by Pythius the Lydian are in the same category (Herodotus VII.27–28). All of these gifts were part of the Great King's attempt to gather samples of the produce of each of his countries for his paradises, palaces, table, and bed. There were even special court officers whose job was to receive the gifts sent to the Great King (*apodektēres dōrōn*; [Arist.] *De Mundo* 398a)! The principal function of the building in Persepolis that was called the Treasury may even have been to store all of the valuable gifts received by Darius and his immediate successors. In the Hellenistic inventories of royal treasures, we also find artwork (Diodorus XIX.48.7), jewelry and goldwork (Arrian III.19.5), Hermionian purple (Arrian III.16.6–7; Plutarch, *Alex.* 36.2), vessels, and valuable garments (Diodorus XVII.70–71). One of the "gifts" at Susa was the famous Golden Vine offered by Pythius to Darius (Diodorus XIX.48.7; Herodotus VII.27◊). It is doubtless this gift-giving practice that is evoked—metaphorically—by the famous Persepolis reliefs, in which delegations of peoples from the Empire bring presents representative of the commodities of their countries (animals, fabrics, jewelry, precious vessels, arms, chariots, etc.; cf. also Ps.-Arist., *Oec.* II.34a: *dōra polla anagomena*). The debate surrounding these depictions (tributary peoples/donor peoples) is not uninteresting (chap. 5); quite the opposite. But we should ask whether it is legitimate to make a very broad distinction between the two categories, considering the fact that all of the tributary peoples also had to send regular gifts to the central court.

It seems clear that quite often the Great King himself "suggested" the sending of specific products whose renown had reached the court. Given the powers of the king's "suggestions," these gifts might be assimilated to assessments that could not be escaped. This is why it is so hard to distinguish between the gifts and the assessments. This is true also of the gifts that the towns and the peoples had to bring to the king during the movements of the court and the army. It may also hold true for the crowns that the peoples were required to bring to the king at the borders of the country during the travels of the royal court (and doubtless of the satrapal court as well). We know from a late witness that the crowns were also stored in royal treasuries with "the other gifts (*dōreai*) and spoils of war" (Diodorus XIX.48.8). We should ask whether these "crowns" at some point in time also became an annual obligation, following a development that is known from the Seleucid period. We may also consider a (late) anecdote recorded by Pseudo-Aristotle (II.2.14d) to illustrate the rapacity of Condalus, a lieutenant of Mausolus, the satrap of Caria: "He stated to the Lycians that he had received a letter from the Great King requesting hair for making wigs, and therefore Mausoleus had ordered them shaved bald." It would be most imprudent here to distinguish between voluntary gifts and obligatory imposts! Note in this context that hair is catalogued by Strabo (XV.3.21) among the imposts in kind due from some peoples of the Empire, along with drugs, dyes, wool, and even animals—in short, "such things as each country produced." Similarly, the qualitative difference between the gold sent by the Ethiopians as a gift and the gold furnished by the Indians as tribute seems to reflect the politico-ideological domain rather than the purely financial domain. Furthermore, it seems quite clear that refusal to present gifts was punished just as rigorously as failure to pay tribute. We also know that every year Arab peoples had to pay 1000 talents of incense, as a gift (Herodotus III.97). This was in fact nothing other than a tariff imposed by the Great King on the commercial profits generated by trade between Palestine and South Arabia. For the Arabs themselves, the difference between "gift" and "tribute" must have been imperceptible! This is doubtless also the source of the terminological confusion shown by some ancient authors: in Ctesias's eyes, for example, the produce sent by the peoples to the king's table fell into the category of tribute (*phoroi*: FGrH 688 F53), whereas it might better be included in the category of taxes (§4 below).

The foregoing discussion makes it clear that gifts were assimilated into what we call tribute. If it were the other way around, the terminological difference would probably disappear. The later example of the Nabateans shows that, at the end of the fourth century, some ethnic groups still regularly operated under the gift system. They are clearly contrasted by Diodorus (XIX.94.10◊) with the "tribute-paying peoples" (*hoi phorologoumenoi*). They "preserve their liberty" (94.2◊), and they consider any agreement with the central authority as equivalent to a contract for the exchange of gifts/friendship (97.4). Let us reread Herodotus once more, who, after describing the "limits of the known world," writes:

> In any case it does seem to be true that the countries which lie on the circumference (*hai eskhatiai*) of the inhabited world produce the things which we believe to be most rare and beautiful. (III.116◊)

Indeed, all of the donor peoples he names (Arabs, Colchians, Ethiopians) are situated in the *eskhatiai* of the Empire, which were controlled less directly by the central authority and could provide exotic products (or products considered to be exotic by the central authority).

From Persepolis to Babylon

At the end of his passage on tribute, Herodotus writes of Persia, distinguishing it from both tributary peoples and donor peoples: "The one country I have not mentioned as paying taxes (*dasmos*) is Persia herself—for she does not pay any" (*ateleia*; III.97◊). Before the discovery of the Persepolis tablets, it was easy to relate this dispensation to the eminent place that the king himself granted to the Persian country in his decrees. The existence of royal assessments on farm and animal products (including the *baziš*), now revealed by the tablets, calls into question the information provided by Herodotus (cf. chap. 11).

The contradiction between Herodotus's statement and the evidence of the tablets is undeniable, but it is secondary. Herodotus's viewpoint on this subject is first and foremost political: as an *ethnos*, the Persians are not catalogued among the tributaries—not that they are devoid of any obligation to the king (which, for that matter, Herodotus may not have known about!) but that they are not collectively obligated to pay a fixed and itemized annual amount specifically defined as tribute. Of course, the translation of the word *baziš* as 'tribute' is just a useful expedient. The workaday documents confirm that the differences among gifts, taxes, and tributes are only semantic. The labels fluctuate and the differences are uncertain. In the Babylonia of Darius II, communally allotted lands (*ḫaṭru*) were leased to the Murašû family, provided that they collect the royal taxes, which were notated (for example) in the form "[One] barrel of beer, 2 *pan* and 3 *satu* [of wheat] and barley, [2] minas of silver, all the tax (*ilku*) for the king's soldier [. . .] and all the gifts/fees (*nadanātu*) for the house of the king (*bīt šarri*)." In this sort of document, gifts and taxes are still distinguished in the vocabulary, but they are also incorporated into a general financial obligation, each of whose elements preserves an obligatory value.

The Gifts of the Persian Peasants

To gain a clearer understanding, let us turn anew to that inexhaustable court gossip, Aelian. Several times he depicts the Persian peasantry (*autourgoi*) in their relationships with the king. One story, in which the peasant Sinetes brings some drops of water, which he had fetched by hand from the Cyrus River [the modern Kura River], to Artaxerxes II (I.32; cf. Plutarch, *Art.* 5.1 and *Mor.* 172b), is particularly interesting. Aelian takes this opportunity to cite a Persian custom (*nomos persikos*):

> It is a *nomos* among the Persians, and of all the *nomoi* the one that is observed most faithfully, that the inhabitants of places the king passes on his journeys offer him presents (*dōra*), each according to his abilities. (*kata tēn heautou dynamin*; *VH* I.31)

Two features of the text indicate that the payment of these gifts was obligatory. First is the use of the word *nomos*, which, here as elsewhere, refers to a mandatory rule (obligation) of the Achaemenid court; second is the expression "according to his abilities," which, compared with other texts, refers to a rule of a financial kind: the assessment is proportional to individual resources. We can add that the payments must have been annual, since the king and court came to Persepolis at least once a year.

In fact, the example of Persia itself seems unique: the links between the Persians and the king cannot be equated with the relations between the Arabs or the Colchians and the central authority. When the king came to Persepolis, he himself rewarded the Persians with many gifts. In other words, the Persian peasants' gifts were incorporated into the practice of gift and counter-gift (cf. Plutarch, *Mor.* 172b, 173d, *Art.* 4.5). Herodotus also clearly distinguishes Persia from both tributary and donor peoples (III.97). Despite this real distinction, the logic was basically the same: the king determined whether the assessments of this or that people were called gifts or tribute. In this way, the king distinguished his dominion over these peoples from his relationship with the tributary peoples. But the distinction loses much of its value in practice because, for one thing, these gifts were kept on an account and were obligatory; for another thing, the tributary peoples also had to give regular gifts.

One sentence of Aelian's provides the key: "All this is called by the name of gift (*kai onomazetai dōra*) and that is how the king considered them (*kai dokei toutōi*)." What made the difference between a "gift" and a financial assessment was thus not the nature of the gift or the level of taxation or the periodicity of the collection; it was an evaluation by the king, itself based on a rule (*nomos*) that everyone knew and no one could exempt himself from. It was the king's prerogative to call an obligatory payment a gift and then to grant the donor recognition as a Benefactor. In other words—returning to the Achaemenid context—the difference between obligatory payments (whether tribute or other financial levies) and gifts was not an artifact of accounting practices; it emerged primarily from the ideological representations of power.

The impression that prevails is that, far from contradicting the fact of tribute, the practice of gift-giving reinforced it. Each people was required to pay gifts whose obligatory character is well established by all of the evidence. Consequently, the difference between gifts and tribute functioned less as a matter of perception than as a matter of implicit symbolism. Tribute, gifts, and other payments participated in the overall functioning of a *tribute system*, the term being taken this time in its generic sense.

4. Tributes, Gifts, and Assessments

Taxes

In order to clarify the entire fiscal picture, a discussion of taxes really must be incorporated into a fuller and more detailed analysis of Achaemenid finances. As the discussion of customs and tolls (chap. 9/3) has already shown, the king in fact received a great deal of other income that can be classed under two rubrics: regular taxes and special contributions. We are ill informed on the former, since our information basically comes from late texts. It will help one more time to quote the indispensable Pseudo-Aristotle and the four other categories he describes out of the six possible sources of satrapal revenue:

> Thirdly comes that derived from merchandise (*empōria*); fourthly, the revenue from the cultivation of the soil (*gē*) and from market-dues (*agoraia telē*); fifthly, that which comes from cattle, which is called tax on animal produce (*epikarpie*) or tithe; and sixthly, that which is derived from men, which is called the poll-tax (*epikephalaion*) or tax on artisans (*kheironaxion*). (*Oecon.* II.1.4◊)

Several working documents confirm some of the author's information. The existence of royal taxes (*basilika telē*) and tariffs on commercial traffic (*dekatē tēs emporias*) is attested in Caria in the time of the satrapy of Pixodarus. The variety of taxes seems considerable, levied on many products. At the begining of the fourth century in Caria, a tax (*apomoira*) on certain agricultural products was payable to the royal administration. The same tax (on wheat) is mentioned in a text from the city of Telmessus when it was under Ptolemaic rule. Another decree (Seleucid period), found at Aegae of Aeolis, provides an even more impressive enumeration: a *dekatē*, a tax of $1/8$ on fruit, $1/50$ on sheep and goats, $1/8$ on honey, and even "as for the results of the hunt, one leg of each boar and each deer." This sounds a bit too much like an illustration from Pseudo-Aristotle's text regarding taxes levied by the satrap on the fruits of the earth. But aside from some easily explainable diachronic and interregional correlations (royalties levied on the markets or on the transport of merchandise also attested in Achaemenid Babylonia and Assyria), we must ask ourselves whether the author is specifically describing the system in effect in his time in western Asia Minor. Despite obvious continuities with the Achaemenid period, it is impossible to state that all of these taxes already existed during the time of Darius.

This uncertainty is relieved, at least regarding Babylon, by a (short) series of tablets and the commentaries they have received recently. Several texts dated to the reign of an Artaxerxes (undoubtedly II or III) imply that sales of slaves were registered with an office concerned with royal taxes (*bīt miksu ša šarri*); clearly, a special tax was collected on this occasion. This represents a procedure known from Seleucid Babylonia. The establishment of the tax actually goes back to Darius I. Achaemenid–Hellenistic continuities lead us to think that other taxes known from the Seleucid era might go back to the time of the Great Kings; but documentary proof is lacking.

Mines

One of the six kinds of revenue that Pseudo-Aristotle assigns to the *satrapal economy* is "the particular products of the soil in a specific region" (II.1.4). The explanation that follows indicates that he refers only to subterranean products: "This category comprises the particular products of the soil: here gold, there silver, elsewhere copper or whatever is found in the country." This is a basic aspect of royal policy on which we unfortunately have no specific facts. We know of mines worked by the Greek cities themselves, such as the mines known at Lampsacus, the silver mines of Bactria and Cilicia, the lapis lazuli mines of Bactrian Badakhshan, the various mines of Carmania, the iron mines of Ionia and the Lebanon, and the copper mines of Cyprus, which are attested in Neo-Babylonian texts. The Foundation Charters of Susa also hint at mineral resources in this or that region: gold from Sardis and Bactria, lapis lazuli and carnelian from Sogdiana, and turquoise from Chorasmia. Despite the highly ideological nature of such statements (see chap. 5), they probably do refer to well-known resources found in the various regions.

On the operation of these mines, however, we have no precise information. It is certain that the sources of naphtha in Susiana were part of the royal estate (Herodotus VI.119: *en stathmōi heautou*). The Egyptian stone quarries in the Wadi Hammamât were worked under the direction of Persian adminstrators and officials during the time of Darius. It is likely that some mines were under the direct or indirect control of the administration—as, for example, was undoubtedly the case for the iron mines of Niriz, Persia, the site of royal workshops for metallurgical products (arms) in Xerxes' time.

Just about the only mines on which we can gather any information are those in Lydia. They had already been worked by the Mermnadae kings of Lydia, who extracted gold and silver to make electrum. The invention of the process of alloying gold and silver made Croesus famous for his riches throughout the Greek world. It especially made it possible for him to issue gold and silver coinage of high reputation. What happened when Cyrus conquered Lydia? According to Diodorus of Sicily, the Persian was not content with seizing Croesus's royal treasury but also confiscated the Lydians' property for his own profit (IX.33.4: *ktēseis*). This did not necessarily involve every Lydian, but perhaps it involved the mine owners. Nor can we immediately conclude that the Achaemenid administration took control of all of the Lydian mines. It is much more likely that he confiscated the existing gold and silver reserves from the owners—not the mines themselves. In 480, during his march to the sea, Xerxes, his entourage, and his army were treated with extraordinary pomp by Pythius the Lydian (Herodotus VII.27–29). Pythius was well known to persons close to the Great King, and it was from them that Xerxes learned that Pythius had offered Darius magnificent gifts and that he was "the richest man besides the king." At the time of the Greek expedition, Pythius immediately put at the king's disposal his entire fortune, namely, 2,000 talents of silver and no less than 3,993,000 darics. Pythius may have been a descendant of the Lydian royal family; we learn elsewhere that he owned several important mines in the Lydian countryside. Even after the Persian conquest, his family thus retained control of considerable mineral resources. We must conclude that operations after the conquest were just as they had been under the Lydian dynasty: the mines of Lydia were worked by private individuals, who now were required to turn over part of their production to the treasury at Sardis so that the satrap could pass its proceeds on to the royal treasuries (and the royal mints). We assume (in the absence of tangible proof) that the owners/concessionaires were also required to provide a very precise annual accounting of their production; these accounting documents, duly verified by the satrapal administration, were the basis for determining the amount of the levy, at a rate that we do not know.

Corvée

Subjects and peasants had more than taxes to worry about. They were frequently placed in corvée [forced or statutory labor] to work at tasks undertaken by the royal administration. The case of Babylonia is the best known. We have already seen that the sanctuaries could at any time be required to furnish manual labor upon demand of the satrap, especially for the construction and maintenance of canals (chap. 2/4). This is the system referred to as *urāšu* service, which is known from the Neo-Babylonian period. It involved all owners of real estate, whether sanctuaries or private individuals, particularly those whose fields lay along a canal. It was the responsibility of the royal administrator in charge of canals (the *mašennu* in the Achaemenid period) to announce the levies. It is possible that the organization was systematized during the time of Darius I. At that time, *urāšu* service was one of many financial obligations collectively called *ilku*. The officers in charge of *ilku* were the same officers who had the job of requisitioning manual labor to ensure "the corvée of [boat] towing at the quai" or "transport of dues in kind."

Corvée is not unknown elsewhere, although the evidence is less specific. One of the greatest tasks accomplished with corvée labor was the canal across the isthmus at the base of Mt. Athos, by order of Xerxes. Pressed into service were not only contingents of Asian peoples nominally on military duty and grouped *kata ethnē* but also "the natives of [the region of] Athos," probably recruited from the five cities listed by Herodotus (VII.22◊). It is also likely that the digging of the Suez Canal was accomplished by conscripted peasants (II.159; cf. Diodorus I.33). Within the *dōrea* of Mnesimachus, the establishment of which goes back to the Achaemenid period, the villagers were obligated not just to pay *phoros* in cash but also to perform *phoros leitourgikos*—that is, levies of work days. This is confirmed by a letter from Darius to his manager Gadatas. Going against the tradition of privileges recognized by the royal administration for "sacred gardeners," Gadatas subjected the "sacred gardeners" of the temple of Apollo "to pay the tribute (*phoros*) and to work profane land," that is, the territory directly administered by

Gadatas (ML 12). In other words, the peasants as a general rule were subject to tribute and to corvée from which the gardeners of Apollo were exempt because of a royal privilege. One of the tasks imposed on people was the maintenance of royal roads, for which the satrapal administration was responsible, according to Pseudo-Aristotle (II.2.14b). In fact, we read in Aelian (*Anim.* XV.26) that, when the king relocated from Susa to Media, he had to cross a region infested with scorpions: "Three days before his passage, he ordered everyone to hunt down these animals, and he rewarded with gifts those who killed the most." The anecdote is colorful and localized, but it undoubtedly implies a more general system of corvée and labor requisition of all kinds.

The Obligations of Hospitality

Under the heading of contributions that were "above and beyond" regular tribute were the contributions occasioned by the relocations of the court and the army. Among the weighty obligations at that time, the most ponderous of all was the royal dinner. When the king called a halt near a city, in reality he was imposing on that spot the burden of feeding him and his entourage, an extremely heavy burden. One example of this is Herodotus's account of Xerxes' march in 480. Plans for the welcome had been transmitted ahead of time to the cities and peoples: "In Sardis, Xerxes' first act was to send representatives to every place in Greece except Athens and Sparta with a demand for earth and water and a further order to prepare entertainment for him against his coming" (VII.32✧). Herodotus reports the burden of hospitality perfectly (VII.118–120✧):

> Things were even worse for the Greeks who had to entertain the Persian army and provide a dinner for the king. They were utterly ruined, and were obliged to leave house and home. For instance, when the Thasians, on behalf of their towns on the mainland, billeted and fed the army, Antipater, the son of Orgeus, a citizen of the highest repute, to whom the arrangements had been entrusted, proved that the meal cost 400 talents of silver. And similar accounts were returned by the officers in the other towns. A great deal of fuss had been made about the meal, and orders for its preparation had been issued a long time in advance; accordingly, the moment that word came from the officers who carried the king's commands, people in every town distributed their stores of grain and employed themselves for months on end in making barley and wheat flour, in buying up and fattening the best cattle they could find, and feeding poultry in coops and waterfowl in ponds, to be ready for the army when it came. In addition to this they ordered the manufacture of drinking cups and mixing-bowls of gold and silver, and of everything else that is needed to adorn the table. All this, of course, was for the king himself and those who dined with him; for the troops in general the preparations were confined to food. On the arrival of the army, there was always a tent ready for Xerxes to take his rest in, while the men bivouacked in the open; but it was when dinner-time came that the real trouble for the unfortunate hosts began. The guests ate their fill and, after spending the night in the place, pulled up the tent the next morning, seized the cups and table-gear and everything else it contained, and marched off without leaving a single thing behind.

The financial burden was even higher than this, since a formal welcome included the gifts that had to be offered to the king when he reached the outskirts of the city. But peoples and cities had no choice. "Nevertheless the various places along the route did manage to carry out their orders, though not without severe suffering" is Herodotus's pithy comment (VII.120✧)! Any community might be so saddled, including the temples, as seen from several Babylonian tablets from the reign of Cambyses (chap. 2/4). One tablet, dated to the reign of Artaxerxes II, also relates that when the king arrived at

Susa, inhabitants of the neighboring province of Babylonia were also required to contribute. Here too is what Theopompus wrote in his *Philippica*, quoted by Athenaeus
(IV.145a◇):

> Whenever the Great King visits any of his subjects, twenty and sometimes thirty talents are
> expended on his dinner; others even spend much more. For the dinner, like the tribute, has
> from ancient times (*ek palaiou*) been imposed upon all cities in proportion to their popula-
> tion (*kata to megethos*).

Reading Theopompus (who was writing in the fourth century) causes one to wonder
whether these exceptional contributions—at some time or other—were transformed
into a regular duty, such as, for example, the "satrap's table" tax that was levied in coin.
We must remember that a distinction between regular taxes and special contributions is
partly artificial, especially in the case of peoples and cities located on the routes taken
by the king every year from capital to capital.

Royal Taxes and Satrapal Taxes

In addition to all that has been discussed above, the subjects were required to pay
various taxes to the satrap himself. The satrap, image of the king in each province, also
relocated during the year from one residence to another, quite aside from the breaks he
took in his paradise. A text of Polyaenus shows that the satrap traveled with a large retinue and that the populace was required to greet him at the borders. Mausolus, who
wanted to capture Heraclea near Latmus, took the Pygela road: "When he passed by Latmus, the city dwellers came out to watch the order and splendor of the parade. . . . Mausolus's troops found the city empty and the gates open" (VII.23.2). Undoubtedly, on
these occasions the inhabitants and local administrators had to bring gifts to the satrap,
as they did upon the arrival of the king (cf. Xenophon, *Hell.* III.1.12; Plutarch, *Alc.* 12;
Athenaeus XII.534c–d).

Another satrapal tax was called the Satrap's Table. For example, Plutarch reports
(without endorsing) an explanation given by some of Cyrus the Younger's predecessors
for his revolt: "If he broke with the king, it is because he did not receive a sufficient
amount for his meals each day" (*Art.* 4.1). On another occasion, Pharnabazus, satrap of
Hellespontine Phrygia, was so impoverished by the ravages inflicted on his region that
he complained that he had "not so much as a meal in [his] own land" (Xenophon, *Hell.*
IV.1.33◇). These texts may be rather vague, but the meal metaphor conceals a financial
reality that is clearly brought to light in a passage in Nehemiah:

> From the day the king appointed me governor in the land of Judah, from the twentieth to
> the thirty-second year of King Artaxerxes [I], for twelve years, neither I nor my kinsmen ever
> ate governor's bread. Now the former governors, my predecessors, had been a burden on the
> people, from whom they took forty silver shekels each day as their subsistence allowance,
> while their servants oppressed the people too. But I, fearing God, never did this. . . . Jews
> and officials to the number of a hundred and fifty ate at my table, not to mention those who
> came to us from the surrounding nations. Every day, one ox, six fine sheep, and poultry,
> were prepared at my expense; every ten days skins of wine were brought in bulk. But even
> so, I never claimed the governor's subsistence allowance, since the people already had bur-
> den enough [of the construction work] to bear. (5:14–18◇)

'Over and Above the Tribute' (*parex tou phorou*)

Herodotus states that the levies on the peoples who gave gifts were accounted separately from the tribute (*parex tou phorou*; III.97). But he also reports that the peoples

who were subject to tribute were burdened with levies that were "over and above the tribute." In fact, he notes that beyond the tribute of 500 talents of silver, the Cilicians annually had to furnish "360 white horses (one for each day in the year)" (III.90◇). Egypt, in addition to 700 talents (of tribute), furnished the king "with flour delivered separately (*khōris*); the 120,000 bushels of corn [grain] allowed to the troops and their auxiliaries who were stationed in the White Wall at Memphis." The king also had "money from the fish in Lake Moeris"—an amount deducted over and above (*parex*) other amounts payable (III.91◇). Babylonia every year had to present "1000 talents of silver and 500 eunuch boys" (III.92◇). The existence of levies in kind, which were added to the silver tribute, is confirmed by Strabo with reference to Media and Cappadocia: "The reports on the tributes paid [by Media] agree with the size and the [productive] power of the country; for Cappadocia paid the Persians yearly, in addition to the silver tax (*pros tōi argyrikōi telei*), fifteen hundred horses, two thousand mules, and fifty thousand sheep, whereas Media paid almost twice as much as this" (XI.13.8◇).

Parallel information is found in a text from Alexander's time. Alexander ordered inhabitants of the Pamphylian town of Aspendus "to provide fifty Talents for the army as pay, with the horses they bred as tribute (*dasmos*) to the King of Persia [Darius III]" (Arrian, *Anab.* I.26.3◇). This is very much the same system alluded to by Herodotus regarding Cilicia (III.90). Levies of the same kind are known in other satrapies. Strabo writes, in fact, that Armenia had pastures so rich that Nisaean horses were raised there, which had been "used by the Persian kings. . . . The satrap of Armenia used to send to the Persian king twenty thousand foals every year at the time of the festival of the Mithracina" (XI.14.9◇). This fact must be compared with a note by Xenophon recording a conversation with an Armenian village leader (*kōmarch*): "They asked him again for whom the horses were being reared. He answered, as tribute (*dasmos*) for the King" (*Anab.* IV.5.34; cf. IV.5.24). These were horses that Xenophon learned were "consecrated to the Sun (Helios)." Each village had to furnish a certain number of colts (17 in the village allocated to Xenophon and his men). Each year they were collected by the village leaders (*kōmarchoi*) and sent by the satrap of Armenia to the royal court. Notice the vocabulary used in these texts: these levies are not counted as *phoros* but as *dasmos*. Even though the two words are frequently used (and translated!) identically (cf. Herodotus III.97; *dasmophoros*), their etymologies differ: the *dasmos* constituted the "king's part," as in Old Persian *baji*. Arrian clearly distinguishes between the *pharos* and the *dasmos* in regard to Aspendus. Besides the *phoroi* proper (in silver)—from which they were temporarily exempted, in favor of a contribution to the war effort (I.26.3; 27.4)—the Aspendians had to furnish a certain number of horses every year as a *dasmos* for Darius [III].

We do not know why Herodotus chose not to refer to the *dasmos* anywhere other than Cilicia, Egypt, and Babylonia. However, it is logical to infer that this reference to the *dasmos* is an interpolation, because the *dasmos* payments are clearly recorded outside of the tribute proper, which is the topic of his discussion. The information given here and there the Classical texts always seems formally to imply that the levying of a *dasmos* was a general rule. Apart from his development of the tribute theme, Herodotus is eager to highlight the riches of Babylonia and refers both more explicitly and more generally to the Babylonian section of the Achaemenid tax system:

> Apart from the normal tribute, the whole Persian empire is divided into regions for the purpose of furnishing supplies for the king and his army, and for four months out of the twelve the supplies come from Babylonian territory, the whole of the rest of Asia being responsible

for the remaining eight. . . . The governorship (or satrapy, as the Persians call it) of Assyria is by far the most coveted of all their provincial posts.

Then Herodotus details the advantages that the satrap derived from living in Babylonia: stud farms (800 stallions and 16,000 brood mares) and "so many Indian dogs that four large villages in the plain were exempted from other charges (*tōn allōn . . . atelees*) on the condition of supplying them with food" (I.192◊).

Military Levies and the Tax System

The system of levying the public for resources in kind was also the principle underlying the organization of the *ḫaṭrus* [communally held land allotments], which are relatively well known in Babylonia. A military *ḫaṭru* (not all of them were military, to be sure) was required in principle to furnish "the king's soldier" (*ṣāb šarri*), and the holders of a share had to comply with any order for mobilization. Several documents from the reign of Darius show that, when a tenant farmer received royal orders, he had to set out, fully armed and provided with supplies and money; in other words, it was the soldier himself who paid for his weapons and his upkeep. The cost was great: in 513, a horseman was called up for three years; he had to bring with him a mule (purchased for 50 siculi), whose feed cost him 36 siculi, as well as 12 lightly armed men, who provided their own equipment (clothing, blankets, travel bags, shoes, oil, salt, etc.; *Dar.* 253). There are many examples of more or less regular call-ups from the time of Darius and his successors—not to speak of the requisitions by local authorities. In other words, insofar as we can observe its operation in Babylonia, the reserve territorial army was not maintained at the expense of the royal treasury; on the contrary, tenants to whom service lands had been allotted were not exempt from levies, which they were required to pay every year to the administration.

In normal times, the recruiting and maintenance of the armed forces needed by the king did not necessarily strain his budget. In fact, the organization of the navy was based on a simple principle: the royal administration built the ships (with the help of requisition of manual labor), while the tributary coastal peoples (Greeks, Carians, Lycians, Cilicians, Cypriots, and Phoenicians) provided the oarsmen. This represents a considerable commitment of resources. The principle on which the territorial troops were based is also quite simple: one category or another of the populace had to furnish a certain number of outfitted soldiers in exchange for the use of a parcel of land. This was the case for Persian "expatriates" on large estates in Asia Minor, who, when requisitioned by a satrap, had to provide him with a troop of trained horsemen at their own expense. We know that Persian landholders in Egypt also had to pay tribute (*mandattu*: DAE 71–72 [AD 10–11]). It was the same for companies in Memphis. This is a concrete illustration of the familiar saying, "Conquest begets conquest." Obviously, the royal treasury also paid out significant amounts to ensure the provision of foodstuffs (*trophē*) for salaried garrisons. Xenophon (*Oec.* IV.6) refers to them by the ambiguous term *misthophoroi*, by which he meant not mercenaries but "salaried soldiers," such as the garrisons of Syene-Elephantine, who drew rations in kind (*ptp*) and pay in cash (*prs*) from the royal treasury. Actually, according to the principle of payments *parex tou phorou* defined by Herodotus (I.192), even the *trophē* for the troops was levied via assessments in kind.

Tribute and Tribute Assessments

It is thus confirmed that what we (following Herodotus) call tribute represents only a part of the royal assessments or, to borrow R. Descat's image, "the visible part of the iceberg of the Achaemenid financial edifice." This simple observation adds much to the discussion of the functional relationship between gifts and tribute. Each constituted a partial and complementary element of a vastly more complex system. The result of this view is that the distinction between gifts and tribute, which is given excessive weight by Herodotus, is diminished.

5. Payments of Tribute: Metal and Coin

The Phantom of the Natural Economy: Coast and Interior

Let us return to tribute proper. The vocabulary and rationale of Herodotus's text on tributes (III.96) and Strabo's (which, in regard to Armenia and Media, carefully distinguishes between products-in-kind and payments in silver; *argyrikon telos*; XI.13.8) imply that the tribute amount was sent in metal weighed in the treasuries. We then may assume that satraps also required tribute to be paid in silver. On the other hand, one could hypothesize the exact opposite, that a "natural economy" prevailed in the Near East. According to this hypothesis, Herodotus's text gives nothing more than an estimated value in silver of the tribute that was actually paid in kind. But such a broad contrast between a so-called "natural" economy and a monetary economy comes from a Greek outlook that grossly oversimplifies the mechanism of the exchange of goods. One reason for this may be that the tribute obligation posed no technical problem to peoples and cities that were sustained by the circulation of money, especially the Greek cities of Asia Minor: they were able to pay their debts in coin, valued by the satrapal administration according to its weight. In other places, however, tribute was not generally monetized. For example, in the land of Judea toward the middle of the fifth century, the peasants paid their tribute in (weighed) silver, as we know because some complained of having "to borrow money on our fields and vineyards to pay the king's tax (*middat hammelek*)," or having had "to sell our sons and our daughters into slavery" (Nehemiah 5:4–6◊). In Persia itself, payment in weighed silver is attested as early as 502 (PT 85). Even in countries where taxes such as those in the category *parex tou phorou* were basically assessed in kind (e.g., Herodotus III.91), their payment in silver to royal administrators did not pose insurmountable problems. In Babylonia, where the use of weighed silver was normal, there were businesses whose function was to convert levies on agricultural products into silver. In Egypt, where throughout the fifth-century Athenian and Greek coins circulated, monetary exchange was somewhat less (but not unknown), and the common use of weighed silver there is well attested in several Aramaic documents.

There remains a difficult text in Strabo, included in a chapter about the treasuries (*thēsauroi*) and storehouses (*paratheseis*) that, he says, each Persian king had built to stockpile tribute (*phoroi*). Taking his cue from Polyclitus, Strabo distinguishes between coastal peoples (*paralia*) and inland peoples (*mesogeia*). The king collects silver from the coastal peoples, he writes (*prattesthai . . . argyrion*); from the inland peoples, he obtains products in kind according to the country (*ha pherei ekaste khōra*) (dyes, drugs, hair, wool, and other things—even livestock; XV.3.21). The binary opposition silver :: coast / products-in-kind :: interior obviously corresponds to his distinction between treasuries (silver) and warehouses/storehouses (products in kind)—even if the terminological opposition is more formal than functional (cf. Ps.-Arist., *Oecon.* II.38). But what could be the reason for some peoples to make their payments in kind, when it is quite clear that tribute was always transferred to the central court as metal? And above all, what could be the explanation for such a clear-cut distinction between the coast and the interior?

An identical distinction seems to be found in one of Diodorus's passage. Speaking of the "great revolt of the satraps" in the 360s, he stresses that the participants were "nearly all the coastal countries" (*hoi parathalassioi*), as well as "the satraps and *strategoi* who governed the coastal districts" (*hoi parathalattioi topoi*); he adds that, "with the revolt so extensive, half the revenues of the King were cut off and what remained were insufficient for the expenses of the war" (XV.90.3✧). But, not only is the witness of Diodorus historically debatable (chap. 15/7), it hardly clarifies Strabo's text. Even though it is true that, on the level of administrative and military organization, the coastal regions were assigned to a single high commander (within the sphere of military operations) on several occasions, there is no reason to suppose that the Achaemenid financial administration set aside a coastal subregion that was defined specifically by its potential for yielding metals or moneys.

Could Strabo have been referring to populations so distant from the trade routes that they were unable to sell their produce? But even this is no reason to suppose that commercial trade (using weighed silver) was restricted only to ports. Indeed, we know that, despite the use of metals, barter did not disappear: Xenophon, for example, describes populations on the east bank of the Euphrates who "brought to Babylon millstones that they sold, exchanging them for food to feed themselves" (*Anab.* I.5.5). Furthermore, Arrian states that the mountain Uxians had "no money (*khrēmata*) or arable land" (III.17.6✧). But we cannot generalize from these examples (even apart from the fact that Arrian's information on the Uxians is quite unlikely). In fact, a completely different interpretation is suggested by the adventures of the survivors of the Ten Thousand, who several times were able to buy supplies in markets opened by the Persian satrap Tissaphernes. Trade and commerce based on weighed silver existed everywhere, even in countries that might be considered "backward" (e.g., *Anab.* III.5.16). Furthermore, numerous examples show that the interior countries were also well endowed with precious metals (e.g., *Oecon.* II.24a and Polyaenus VII.21.1: a Cappadocian temple pillaged by Datames).

The opposition silver / products-in-kind may reflect a distinction tribute / gifts. Every group of people in the Empire paid both (see above), however, and some donor peoples (in Herodotus's sense) even delivered their "gifts" in metal form (III.97✧). Furthermore, according to Strabo himself (XI.13.8), some inland peoples, such as the Armenians, Medes, and Cappadocians, indeed paid their tribute in silver, but the obligation to raise colts for the royal stud farms was added to this tribute (XI.13.8). Conversely, a strategy described by Pseudo-Aristotle shows that a coastal land such as Lycia had to furnish hair intended for the court of the Great King (II.2.14d), whereas, on the contrary, hair is listed by Strabo among the products in kind specifically levied on the inland countries!

In the final analysis, we cannot really determine the facts of tribute that underlie Strabo's formulation. We are led to think that the interpretations he adopted from Polyclitus primarily express a Greek view of imperial geography. In fact, it was traditional for Greeks to impose a cultural boundary between the coast (*katō*) and the interior (*anō*). We see this clearly in the speech Thucydides puts in the mouths of the Corinthians at the threshold of the Peloponnesian War: the Corinthians urge the interior peoples (*mesogeia*) not to abandon the cause of the coastal peoples (*katō*; I.120.2). Applied to the

Achaemenid realm, this economic-spatial perception leads quite naturally to considering the coast as Greek and the highlands as Persian (e.g., Plutarch, *Cimon* 9.6; *Them.* 26.1 and 30.1). This is why the Greek authors generally admire a man like Agesilaus who—some say (chap. 15/5)—intended to penetrate deep into the highlands (*anōtatō*: Xenophon, *Hell.* IV.1.41) and carry the war "far from the Hellenic sea" (Plutarch, *Ages.* 15.1). This is a recurring viewpoint, expressed many times in the *Anabasis*, as in texts from the beginning of the Hellenistic period. As it happens, the notion of a boundary between the low country and the highlands rested primarily on cultural presuppositions: a cultured, commercial coastal (i.e., Greek) country was contrasted with a highland/interior where a sort of natural (i.e., barbarian) economy reigned—as, for example, in Greece among the Aetolians (Thucydides I.5.3; III.93.3–4). Though this sort of representation is most revealing of the Greeks' idea of civilization, the modern historian has no well-grounded reason to repeat it when reconstructing the tribute organization of the Achaemenid imperial realm.

Royal Treasuries and Tribute

After being collected by the satrapal authorities, some of the tribute remained on location, in satrapal treasuries. Herodotus, for instance, mentions this fact in reference to Cilicia (III.90): of the 500 talents levied in Cilicia, 140 "were spent on the cavalry who were garrisoned there." The rest, that is the larger part, was kept (with the proceeds of gifts, crowns, and booty) in the royal treasuries. Once it was gathered, the tribute was stockpiled:

> The method adopted by the Persian kings of storing their treasure is to melt the metal and pour it into earthenware jars; the jar is then chipped off, leaving the solid metal. When money is wanted, the necessary amount is coined for the occasion. (Herodotus III.96❖)

Contrary to what has long been thought, this passage makes no reference to the transformation of metal into coins. Strabo, speaking of a later period, explains that, even after royal coinage was put into circulation, a minimal part of the annual tribute receipts was minted: "Most of the gold and silver is used in articles of equipment . . . they consider those metals as better adapted for presents and for depositing in storehouses" (XV.3.21❖). This is the exact meaning of Herodotus's statement. The passage describes a mode of operation well known from Babylonian temples: all of the silver received, whether from offerings or from debt management, was sent every month to the temple goldsmiths to be melted into ingots. This became the reserve that was available as a source of metal from which, for example, crowns might be made, or diadems to adorn the statues of gods.

The Problem of Royal Coinage

If tribute was not destined for massive monetization, then what was the reason for minting royal coins, whether silver coins (siculi, i.e., shekels) or gold coins (darics)? The royal coins were sometimes called "archers" by the Greeks, because the king was portrayed as an archer on them (fig. 17, p. 214). Despite continuing discussion regarding the etymology of the word *daric*, the opinion favored today takes into consideration the fact that the first royal coinage was issued by Darius. The date of the initial issue is not known with certainty. We do, however, have a precise benchmark, since a Fortification tablet from year 22 of Darius (500) bears the imprint of a royal coin showing a kneeling archer-king. This coin is of a type (called Type II) whose design may itself be earlier than

500. The discussion of the date of the appearance of Darius's coinage is linked, in part at least, to the purpose attributed to this innovation. The daric and the siculus were struck exclusively at Sardis, at least early on; by transforming Sardis gold into coins, Darius attempted to get some value out of his mining revenues. Perhaps this was why he had the uncomplimentary reputation of 'tradesman' (*kapēlos*), according to Herodotus (III.89). Given these facts, we may assume that Darius made the decision to mint coins on his return from Europe, around 512. There is then, strictly speaking, no relationship between this decision and tribute reform; tribute, we have seen, was paid in weighed silver; the daric was at first a standard of weight (8.30 g). The silver siculus (5.40 g) was different, circulating principally in Asia Minor and probably used to finance military operations in Darius's and Xerxes' time. Issuing the siculus, then, had the effect of driving out the croesids, the coinage that continued to be struck after Cyrus's conquest of Sardis. The siculus, however, was not imposed as the sole coinage; the Greek coastal cities, for instance, continued to strike their own coins, and Greek silver circulated in the Empire more widely than the siculi themselves.

But why create a gold coin whose function was neither to facilitate trade nor to pay soldiers or suppliers? The answer, it is necessary to insist, is the political function of the royal coinage. Not only would the royal image circulate widely by this means but also the innovation would in a way crown the achievements of Darius as a new founder of the Empire. This was the basic idea communicated by Herodotus when he wrote: "Darius wished to perpetuate his memory (*mnēmosynon*) by something no other king had previously done" (IV.166✧). A similar expression is found in Polyclitus, quoted as follows by Strabo (XV.3.21✧): "[Polyclitus] says that in Susa each one of the kings built for himself on the acropolis a separate habitation, treasurehouses (*thēsauroi*), and storage places (*parathesis*) for what tributes they exacted, as memorials of his [good] administration (*hypomnēmata tēs oikonomias*)." In other words, Darius's initiative was not fundamentally economic (in the sense we mean today). It was intended less to pay his expenses than to illustrate his power and expand his prestige; it was at once financial (increasing the value of Sardis gold), political-tributary (imposing an imperial standard), and ideological (establishing himself as a founder). Herodotus and Strabo clearly stress the function of the royal treasuries. The Great King used the treasuries in the context of his policy of redistribution—valuable objects that he could use as rewards; darics could also play this role.

Darius and Aryandes

Herodotus uses the word *mnēmosynon* for Darius's coinage in a story that as a whole continues to pose a number of interpretive problems. He treats it as a revolt by the satrap of Egypt:

> Aryandes, by the way, had been made governor of Egypt by Cambyses; he was the same man who subsequently lost his life as the result of an attempt to rival Darius. Aware by what he had seen and heard that Darius wished to perpetuate his memory (*mnēmosynon*) by something no other king had previously done, Aryandes started to follow his example—but he soon got what he deserved for his impudence. The facts were these: Darius had issued a gold coinage, of which the metal was of the greatest possible purity, and Aryandes as governor of Egypt had followed suit by a similar issue of silver—and indeed to this day the purest silver is the Aryandic. Darius, when he came to know of this, disguised the real cause of his anger by bringing a charge of rebellion against Aryandes, and had him executed. (IV.166✧)

Herodotus's text raises more questions than it securely and verifiably answers. The very existence of Aryandic coins is highly doubtful. For one thing, no specimen has ever been found; for another, Herodotus's text is imprecise on this point.

It is possible that Aryandes changed the standard used in Egypt for paying tribute in weighed silver. This could explain why Polyaenus says (VII.11.7), "unable to bear the severity (*ōmotēs*) of Aryandes, the Egyptians revolted." He proceeds to tell how Darius resumed personal control of the country—a story entirely dedicated to exalting the homage paid to the Apis by the king/pharaoh. The date of these events is not certain, but if we separate—as seems reasonable—these events from the revolt mentioned by Darius at Behistun, we may suggest that they date back to the last decade of the sixth century. Perhaps the Egyptians, exhausted by the burden of assessments imposed by Aryandes, brought their complaint to the Great King, who then came to restore order. According to this hypothesis, Aryandes would have contravened the very strict measures taken by the Great King when, around 518, he implemented a revaluation of tribute in weighed silver, an action that was considered fair by several ancient authors. Let us stress meanwhile that, according to Herodotus himself, it was not this kind of deed that provoked Darius's response. In his view, the king wished to punish the excesses of a satrap who had tried to become his rival in the very area Darius considered the defining characteristic of his reign and his power.

6. The Administration of Tribute: Continuities and Adaptations

Peoples and Territories

Having drawn up a general outline of the organization of tribute established by Darius, let us now proceed to its regional applications. The reforms introduced by the Great King and his counselors can give rise to more than one interpretation. On the one hand, Herodotus wishes to describe the universality of the royal decrees. On the other hand, even if each people corresponded to one territory, the political conception at base was not really territorial but ethnic. This was definitely the state of affairs described by the author of the *De Mundo*: "All the Empire of Asia, bounded on the west by the Hellespont and on the east by the Indus, was apportioned according to races (*kata ethnē*) among generals (*stratēgoi*) and satraps and Kings (*basileis*)" (398a◇). Actually, the term *ethnos/dahyu* must be understood in a broad sense, designating all sociopolitical organizations in their diversity.

We may remark that the ethnic principle was the rule in the military organization of the Empire. When Darius was preparing the proposed expedition against Greece, "without loss of time, he dispatched couriers to the various states under his dominion with orders to raise an army" (Herodotus VII.1◇). Xerxes ordered the same thing some time later: "in the process of assembling his armies, [he] had every corner of the continent ransacked" (VII.19–20◇). The mobilization was thus organized by people, with each ethnic contingent led by a local leader (VII.96), and in every Achaemenid army the contingents were arranged *kata ethnea* (cf. Xenophon, *Anab.* I.8.9; Diodorus XVII.58.1; and Quintus Curtius III.9.5). Similarly, in the organization of work on the site of the Athos canal: "The ground was divided into sections for the men of the various nations (*kata ethnea*)" (VII.23◇). But, once they had arrived at the assembly points, the ethnic contingents were relieved of their native leaders and assigned to Persians (Herodotus VII.96◇):

The men who served with the fleet and those who served with the army had their own native officers (*epikhōrioi*); but, as my story does not require it, I do not propose to mention their names. Some of them were far from distinguished, and every nation had as many officers as it had towns. In any case, these native officers were not really commanders (*stratēgoi*); like the rest of the troops, they merely served under compulsion. The names of the Persian generals who had the real command (*ekhontes kratos*) and were at the head of the contingents sent by the various nations, I have already recorded.

Command of the major divisions also fell to the king's men (mainly Persians; VII.82–83; 88, 97–98). The royal army thus cannot be reduced to an agglomeration with no real unity. However, the regular military organization was also territorialized. Xenophon in fact states that every year the territorial troops were assembled for a review that occurred "at the place of muster (*syllogos*), as it is called" (Xenophon, *Oec.* IV.6✧). He names Castolus or the plain of the Castolus in Lydia (*Anab.* I.1.2; *Hell.* I.4.3), the plain of Caÿster in Hellespontine Phrygia (*Cyr.* II.1.5), and Thymbara in Syria, where "the rendezvous of the king's barbarians from the interior" (*Cyr.* VI.2.11) was located. These assemblies are also well known from Babylonian tablets from the reign of Darius II. It thus appears that the Empire was divided into a certain number of military regions, whose composition was not strictly based on ethnic criteria. Perhaps it was the same for maritime activities, Cilicia and Cyme being the centers of naval districts.

The tribute system set up during the time of Darius also implies that local political structures were maintained—that is, recognition of the authority of the heads and leaders of the various peoples, whether they were called kings (Cyprus, Phoenicia), dynasts (Paphlagonia), ethnarchs, comarchs, or governors of a town (whether Greek or Babylonian). Within each district, the satrap was responsible to the king for the raising and delivery of the general tribute that had been determined. But we may also presume that each "dynast" or "king" or "city" was individually responsible for raising the portion of the total tribute assessed to his *ethnos* in particular. It was his responsibility to parcel out the burden among the various subassemblies that made up the community that he represented before the satrapal authorities. This arrangement allowed the satrap to avoid becoming directly involved in the complications inherent in the internal distribution of the tribute payment among the various communities of his district. He would only intervene directly if the local authorities managed to evade their obligations.

However, this administrative approach can only be envisaged for peoples who had their own recognized political authority. In other cases, the central authority would have had to fix the tribute amounts for each of the constituent entities. We know, for example, that the Carians were included with others in the IInd nome (III.90), but the Carian subassembly was itself parceled out among various dynasts. Herodotus names four in 480. His personal interest in Artemisia, the queen of Halicarnassus, affords us an interesting detail: she was required to provide 5 of the 70 ships requisitioned from the Carians (VII.99). The division of tribute within the Carian subassembly must have proceeded along similar lines (as well as elsewhere; cf. Arrian II.20.2). In this particular case, we know that the division was almost certainly not made without troubles between dynasts, because the central authority had to intervene.

A late text also suggests that tribute-levying had itself been territorialized. This text is the well-known inscription of Mnesimachus, which details the elements of a *dōrea*, located near Sardis, that goes back to the Achaemenid period (*Sardis* VII.1.1). The inscription states that tribute had to be paid to the chiliarchy. The term chiliarchy obviously refers to a territorial military organization, which in this case also served as a tribute district. The late date of the text prohibits us from transposing information from it to the earlier period. Let us merely remark that the territory of ancient kingdoms was often divided into new Persian administrative districts—what the Aramaic texts call a *medinah*, both in Egypt and in the countries belonging to the district of Ebir Nāri. This is probably the sort of situation referred to by several biblical texts that speak of the 120 or 127 *medinah*s of Ahasuerus's Empire. Whether or not one grants credibility to the figures 120 and 127, these texts attest to an effort to territorialize the Empire.

Cadastres in Western Asia Minor

Once it had been territorialized, the Empire could no longer be reduced to the addition and juxtaposition of fully independent ethnic modules. Determining tribute necessitated the establishment of a cadastre (land registry), or at least the setting up territorial boundary markers (*periorismos* in the vocabulary of Seleucid archivists). We know for certain that this was done in western Asia Minor, at least after measures taken by Artaphernes in 493–492 (see chap. 12/5 below), and no doubt such a system already existed at the time of Darius. This is implied, for example, by the confiscation of lands in Miletus in 493 (Herodotus VI.20). It is likely that the royal administration was relying on prior surveys, as suggested by a passage in Herodotus regarding lands and fields in Miletus (VI.29). But, under the Persians, these written documents were recorded by the satrapal administration. The existence of archives at Dascylium is shown by bullas found there inscribed with the name of Xerxes. Cadastres must be assumed for Sardis, where they were known in the Hellenistic period as *basilikai graphai*. At Sardis they were handled by the *bibliophylax*, who was in charge of recording all land transfers, especially transfers resulting from concessions of royal territory (*RC* 19).

The Case of Babylonia

While it is true that the Achaemenid administration was at times relying on previously recorded documents, in particular in countries such as Babylonia and Egypt that had long traditions of accountancy, we should nonetheless inquire whether the introduction of Darius's tribute system led to modifications, even in Babylonia and Egypt. From the moment when the conquest brought with it redistribution of some of the land, we must recognize that the administration had to update records of the real estate on which it imposed many different kinds of taxes. There are some seventy tablets, most of them from Babylon during the time of Darius and referring basically to transfers of real estate, that include along with the text a (sketchy) map of the fields that were the subject of sale or of transfer. This kind of document is not entirely new, but these tablets are unusual in including information generally absent elsewhere—namely, the amount of seed grain needed or the number of palm trees planted in a particular field. Such documents, drawn up privately, could only have been written to provide a guarantee to the purchaser. Since these private documents existed, we must conclude that in Babylon (and doubtless elsewhere in Babylonia) an official cadastre existed as well.

Does the establishment of this cadastre go back no earlier than Darius's tribute reform? This is an attractive hypothesis, simply because of the chronological distribution of the tablets: they come from Darius's time. But the rapid and unpredictable change in the Babylonian corpus should cause us to be cautious in this assertion. In any case, there can be no doubt about the introduction of a financial administration in Babylonia. From the time of Cyrus, we know of a treasurer named Mithradāta. His probable successor was also a Persian, Bagasarū, mentioned in Babylonian tablets from between 518 and 500, where he sometimes has the Akkadian title *rab kāṣir* and sometimes the Iranian title *ganzabara*. Both terms refer to the job of treasurer. Thus he was responsible for managing the treasury of Babylon, and as manager, he had a considerable staff under his direction and control of land that went with the position.

The tablets showing the existence of a royal registry office (*karammaru ša šarri*) also show that the obligation to pay a new, special tax on the sale of slaves first appeared during the reign of Darius. The Iranian etymology of the vocabulary (**kārahmara*) clearly shows that this fiscal innovation originated with the Persian administration. This is also suggested by the technical financial expression *zebēlu ša upiyāta* ('delivery of taxes in kind'); the last word, known from Persepolis (*ukpiyataš*), is clearly of Persian origin (**upa-yata*). At the same time, "like other innovations of Achaemenid rule, the practice of registering sales co-opted existing Babylonian offices and accommodated existing forms of Babylonian legal behavior and recording" (M. Stolper, ZA 79: 91).

The Case of Egypt

Egyptian bureaucratic traditions are ancient and well known. Traditionally, tax in kind was levied on peasants by heads of districts (*nomarchs*), then, step by step, transmitted to the "chiefs of the granaries," and finally, to the palace treasurer. We would like to think that Darius would not have needed to alter a respected financial administration — as Alexander did much later, at least at first: Alexander divided the entire territory of Egypt between two nomarchs (who had nothing to do with the heads of basic districts) but later "instructed [Cleomenes of Naucratis] to permit the nomarchs to govern their own districts in accordance with the ancient practices (*kathaper ek palaiou*), but to exact the tribute (*phoroi*) from them himself, while they were ordered to pay it over to him" (Arrian, *Anab.* III.5.4◊). More important, several demotic documents, some of them dating to the reign of Darius, mention the title *senti*. This title is generally considered to have been applied to a someone who was "director of the fields" or "he who directs the king's scribes who count everything." In some way, these "high bureaucrats inventory the resources, control the level of properties and the apportionment of divine revenues and sacerdotal prebends, organize the raising and allocation of taxes for the king's house" (J. Yoyotte). This *senti*'s area of responsibility was all of Egypt. In Greek, the title was eventually "translated" *dioikētes*, the same title given to the minister of finance in the Ptolemaic period. It seems that, in any event, the Persian administration took over a Saite institution for its own purposes, though we cannot say with certainty whether they adopted it as it was or adapted it to their own needs.

Finally, the existence of a land register, including royal concessions, is atttested in Achaemenid Egypt. For example, several judicial interventions by the Persian authorities imply the existence of an official register of land concessions (cf. *DAE* 2, 18 [*AP* 1, 16]). One document in particular bears emphasis (*DAE* 69 [*AD* 8]). Pamūn, an Egyptian, had asked that he be granted land as a gift (**baga*), land that his father (meanwhile deceased) previously had held. The satrap Aršāma responded that he would grant the request, if "the domain of Pamūn's father, that farm of 30 *ardab*, was abandoned and was not attached to my [= Arshama's] estate or given by me [Arshama] to any other of my servants." The precautions (reflected in the conditional clauses) taken by Aršāma prove that he had ordered his manager to verify Pamūn's rights to the farm—which further implies the existence of a register where the different categories of land were recorded. Aršāma's phrase reminds us of a letter sent by the Seleucid king Antiochus I to his *strategos* Meleagrus, who was ordered to carry out a gift of lands to Aristodicides of Assus: "Thus you will make an inquiry as to whether Petra has not been given to someone else." It turned out that "Petra and the adjacent territory . . . had already been given to Athenaeus" (*RC* 11–12). The inquiry was almost certainly conducted in the royal archives of Sardis (*basilikai graphai*; *RC* 19, lines 14–16), comparable to the archives known in Achaemenid Babylonia (see above). An institution of this sort certainly existed in Egypt as well: we can recognize it in the term for archives (*st-sšw*), which is found in the text of donations at Edfu and in the "archives of the royal scribe of enumerations" mentioned on the *Stela of the Satrap*: "In later times, the 'place of writings' designates in particular the archives where documents relating to real estate transactions were kept" (D. Meeks). The *bibliophylakion*, known in Greco-Roman Egypt, was obviously the successor of the royal scribe of enumerations.

Weights and Measures

It must also be noted that it was in the time of Darius I that the *ardab*, a measure of capacity of Persian origin (Herodotus I.192) but also known from Greek texts and from Elamite tablets from Persepolis, was first used in Egypt. The Elephantine military's rations in kind were calculated in ardabs (*DAE* 54 [*AP* 2]). The yield (or area) of a field was also measured in ardabs (*DAE* 69 [*AD* 8]). Furthermore, in the Saqqara documents (Segal, no. 42a), there is a reference to the *marriš* (Aram. *mry*), a liquid capacity measure well known from Persepolis and often appearing as the Greek loanword *marris*. We may surmise that the introduction of Persian technical terminology in Egypt corresponds to broader changes. It seems in fact that the word *ardab* was applied to an ancient Egyptian measure, the *khar*. To be sure, the assessments imply a noticeable diminution of the relative value of the latter. Consequently, one wonders whether the introduction of the ardab was linked to the establishment of Egyptian tribute in the time of Darius. Paid by the peasants in accordance with a new royal measure, pharaonic tribute would thus have been increased by simply manipulating the weight standard. Whatever the case, it is important to stress that the introduction of the ardab was not limited to Egypt: it was also found in Babylonia during the time of Cambyses as well, and the Mnesimachus inscription (*Sardis* VII.1.1) shows that in the Sardis region, at the end of the Achaemenid period, gardens and *paradeisoi* were evaluated in proportion to the number of ardabs of seed needed to sow crops (compare with *DAE* 69 [*AD* 8]).

Aramaic documents also refer to standards of weight. For instance, a loan of 4 shekels refers to the "royal standard" (*DAE* 4 [*AP* 10]); one sum of 4 *karš* and another sum of 1 *karš* 2 shekels are assessed by the "royal standard" (*DAE* 33, 38 [*AP* 6, 15]); warehouse-keepers had to provide materials (arsenic, sulfur) "at the Persian weight-standard" (*DAE* 61 [*AP* 26]). To be sure, the introduction of Persian weights did not make the other standards disappear. One loan is listed "at the standard of Ptah" (*DAE* 3 [*AP* 11]). The borrower committed himself to pay "out of his salary [in silver] which they give him from the [royal] treasury." But the text also specifies the correspondence between the Ptah weights and the Persian measures. If the tribute was paid to the satrap in weighed silver, it certainly would have required incontestable standards of weight. Several weights of different shapes inscribed with the name of Darius have been found at Susa; others, also stamped with the name of Darius, are known from Persepolis. Their weights range from 1 *karš* (10 shekels) to 70 *karš* (10 minas; cf. Wa–d). Others weights have also been found in various regions of the Empire, such as lion-weights from Abydos (one talent) and Trapezus. There is no doubt that these weights were used for weighing tribute.

The Egyptian and Babylonian examples confirm what the previous analyses strongly suggested, namely, that we cannot reduce the impact of Darius's reorganizations to a simple logical correlation of preexisting elements. However large the contribution of his predecessors, it seems quite clear that the new king was able to integrate all of his acquisitions and inheritance into a coherent, efficient system. Despite Darius's retention of the ethnic module, Herodotus was quite justified in characterizing his tribute organization as one of the most striking manifestations of his territorial might.

7. Tribute Economy and Appropriation: Royal Land and Tribute Land

Royal Territory and Empire

In the eyes of the Greek authors, the tribute system was actually based on a gigantic appropriation of land and people derived from the results of peasants' labor. This is one of Xenophon's favorite themes; he many times states the unlimited rights of the conqueror over peoples and things. It is clear that, from the point of view of Achaemenid imperial ideology, conquered lands without exception came under royal authority. This is what the word *būmi* means. Both Mardonius and Artayctes reminded Xerxes of this, in exactly the same words. Mardonius counseled the king to launch an expedition against the Greeks in retaliation so that "people [would] think twice in future before they invade your country" (*epi gēn tēn sēn strateuesthai*; Herodotus VII.5◊). Artayctes justified the Persian looting of Protesilaus's tomb and *temenos* as follows: he was a Greek "who made war on your [Xerxes'] country" (*epi gēn tēn sēn strateusamenos*; IX.116◊). The same may be said for the objectives of the Delian League, as defined by Thucydides: "Their professed object being to retaliate for their sufferings by ravaging the king's country" (*hē basileōs khōra*; I.96.1◊). By definition, "royal lands" (in the broad sense) had to be kept free from "enemy armies," as Darius himself states quite clearly (*DPd*). Lands that were occupied fell into the category of "enemy territory." Many examples demonstrate that, from the Greek point of view, the king's authority was exercised without discrimination over all of the countries where he exacted tribute, which itself was the very symbol of subjection. It is thus easy to understand how the conqueror justified laying claim to what was his. In the same way, Alexander said to Darius III: "The country is mine (*kai tēn khōran ekhō*), the gods have given it to me" (Arrian II.14.7). From that moment on, Alexander was master (*kyrios*) of all that had been Darius's (II.14.9); he was "the master of all Asia" (*tēs Asias hapasēs kyrios*; II.14.8), as Darius I had been (cf. Aeschylus, *Persians* 763: *pasēs Asidos . . . tagein*). In this sense, "as goes the royal house (*oikos basileōs*), so goes the Empire" (e.g., Thucydides I.129.3: *en tōi hemeterōi oikōi*).

The Great King's Sluices and the qanats of the Hyrcanians

The Greek texts are too propagandistic, however, for us to accept them without some other sort of analysis. Let us return to Herodotus, who wrote:

> There is a plain in Asia surrounded by a ring of hills, which are broken by clefts in five separate places. This tract of land used to belong to the Chorasmians and lies on the boundaries of five different tribes: the Chorasmians themselves, the Hyrcanians, the Parthians, the Sarangians, and the Thamanaeans; but ever since the Persian rise to power (*ekhousi to kratos*) it has been the property of the Persian king (*esti tou basileōs*). Somewhere in the ring of hills a considerable river arises—the Aces—which used to supply water to the five tribes I have mentioned, being split into five channels and flowing out to each of them through a different gorge; now, however, that the Persians are masters of the country (*hypo tōi Persēi*), all these peoples find themselves in a serious difficulty, for the king blocked up the gorges and constructed sluice-gates to contain the flow of water, so that what used to be a plain has now become a large lake, the river flowing in as before but no longer having any means of egress. The result of this for the people who depended upon the use of the water, but are now deprived of it, has been disastrous. In winter, to be sure, they get rain like anyone else, but they need the river water when they are sowing their millet and sesame in the summer. When therefore, they find themselves waterless, they go in a body with their wives to Persia, and stand howling in front of the gates of the king's palace (*kata tas thyras tou basileōs*), until the king gives orders to open the sluices and allow the water to flow to whichever tribe it may be that needs it most. Then, when the land has drunk all the water it wants, the sluices are shut, and the king orders others to be opened in turn, according to the needs of the remaining tribes. (III.117✧)

There is little doubt that Herodotus's tale is not to be taken literally. The oral histories he heard were obviously grafted onto Indo-Iranian (including Achaemenid) legends of sovereignty, in which water held a central place (cf. chap. 6/5). In the same manner, an Indian New Year's festival was organized around a divine hero's combat with a dragon that, barricaded in a fortress, kept the surrounding country parched and arid. The victory of the hero freed the waters from the walls behind which the dragon had kept them plugged up.

But we should also stress the fact that Herodotus's passage is included in his section on tributes. After giving the list of tributary countries (III.89–98), he examines the territorial limits of the authority of the Great King—toward India (III.98–105), which he places at "the remotest parts of the world" (III.106✧), then toward the south, that is Arabia (III.107–13) and toward Ethiopia, "the furthest inhabited country toward the southwest" (III.114✧) and finally, toward the lands of the west (III.115–16✧). Then comes the passage on the Great King's sluices. It is thus clear that in Herodotus's mind, this example especially illustrates the power of Darius and the results of the Persian conquest for the subject peoples' way of life and internal organization. After the conquest, the land "belongs to the king."

The Persian conquest did not merely result in the establishment of tribute. The Great King thereafter controlled the water, which was the determining factor for production in regions dependent on irrigation. Put another way, he thereafter governed the allocation of water within the various communities that, we may presume, had previously organized their own water access agreements. But in this case, royal control was particularly burdensome, since the population had to pay special taxes to be able to use irrigation water, taxes that were in addition to the tribute (*parex tou phorou*). Their dependence is noted by Herodotus, who depicts them as supplicants coming to the Gates of the palace, like the folk thronging an antechamber before obtaining an audience with the Great King or one of the satraps. Even in the form of monarchic fable that it has assumed, Herodotus's presentation expresses a real state of affairs: the deepening of Persian dominion went hand in hand with the development of a tribute economy, the driving force behind royal appropriation.

The connection between Persian dominion and control of water rights is confirmed by Polybius in a well-known passage concerning the *qanat*s tunneled by the Hyrcanian peasants: "At the time when the Persians were the rulers of Asia (. . . *Persai tēs Asias epekratoun*) they gave to those who conveyed a supply of water to places previously unirrigated the right of cultivating (*karpeusai*) the land for five generations" (X.28.3✧). Among other things, this text points out the close relationship between territorial dominion (the right of conquest) and peasants' rights to land and water. In this case, the rights of rural communities do not derive from the category of "property" but only from concessions granted by the king for the use of the produce (*karpeusai*) for a long but limited time. The texts indicate quite clearly that the Persian conquest resulted not in a general confiscation of land but rather, by means of tribute and taxes, in the king's control over the means of production and his acquisition of part of the harvest.

Royal Land and Concession Lands

Concessionary plots were taken from the royal land and given (*dōrea*; *baga*; *dāšna*; *nidintu šarri*) as benefits to favorites or relatives of the king or to colonists (military or not). This is the implication of a Hellenistic text that details the terms of a concession of lands to a man named Aristodicides, of Assus. He obtained a *dōrea* that previously had been conceded to someone else (Meleagrus; *RC* 11, lines 3–5). This *dōrea* had been royal land (*khōra basilikē*; *RC* 12, lines 19–20). The formula used shows that, in principle, royal concessions were revocable. A particularly clear illustration of a revocable royal concession appears in another case, the case of the *dōrea* of Mnesimachus, near Sardis. The case obviously dates back to the Achaemenid period. Mnesimachus had borrowed a large sum from the sanctuary of Artemis. In writing up the guarantee for the debt (secured by the harvests of the *dōrea*), the administrators of the Artemis temple took into account the possibility that the king (Antigonus) would repossess the land. This was necessary because, fundamentally, the land still belonged to the category of royal land (*Sardis* VII.1.1).

The practice of granting concessions of royal land is confirmed by many Aramaic documents from Egypt. For example, we know of the existence of military plots at Elephantine, which are reminiscent of the Babylonian system of *ḫaṭru*s. In addition to rations in kind (*ptp*) and in silver (*prs*), which were received from the royal storehouse, the soldier-colonists of Elephantine had plots of land. The earliest document—dated 495 (*DAE* 2 [*AP* 1])—shows that these plots (*mnt*) were allocated by the administration, sometimes in parts, and that it was the administration's responsibility to adjudicate any litigation that might arise in this connection. Under Artaxerxes (I or II), one colonist represented himself as follows: "Malkiyah, an Aramean holding property (*mᵉhaḥsen*) in Elephantine-the-Fortress" (*DAE* 9 [*AP* 7]). Another document—dated to Artaxerxes I— records a dispute between a colonist and two women. The colonist is complaining to the Persian authorities that the women have not paid him the money owed on a field that, he states, "our company (*dgal*) held from the 24th year to the 31st year of Artaxerxes" (*DAE* 18 [*AP* 16]). The word 'held' (*mᵉhaḥsen*) formally indicates that these plots of land were not the private property of the concessionaire. We suspect that an identical system was in effect at Memphis, because a Saqqara papyrus refers to the "fields of the garrison" (*ḥaylâ*) (Segal, no. 31), on which the garrison's soldiers paid tribute (*mndt*; Segal, no. 18). The same situation obtained for the boatmen who "held" a boat belonging to the administration (*DAE* 61 [*AP* 26]). In another document (*DAE* 69 [*AD* 8]), the Egyptian Petosiris, son of Pamūn, a stableman of the satrap Aršāma, brings a complaint to Aršāma. Petosiris reminds the satrap that his father, before he disappeared in "the troubles," had held an estate. Now the son is making the following petition: "Now give the domain of . . . my father to me; . . . (command that) they assign it to me, (that) I may hold (it)." One of the things that this text shows is that a satrap could concede lands as a gift (cf. *DAE* 62 [*AD* 2]: *dšn'* = **dašna*) but that lands of this sort remained in the category of "holdings"; it was the heir presumptive's responsibility to request confirmation of the previous donation.

The oldest Aramaic document (*DAE* 1 [Bauer-Meissner papyrus]) is also very interesting. It is dated to year 7 of Darius I (515) and was written in a place in El-Hibeh (Teuzoi). It deals with a contract between the holder of a field, named Padi, and a peasant, called Aha. Padi was very likely a member of an Aramaic (or at least Aramaic-speaking) community established at the oasis in either the Saite or the Persian period; Aha was a native Egyptian. Padi provided the land, Aha the seed, tools, and labor; the two parties had agreed to share losses and profits. Now Padi describes his field as being his "portion from the king (*h*[*l*]*qy lmlk*)." Furthermore, the contract is accompanied by a conditional clause: the contract is only valid if the king approves it (or does not oppose it). This clearly indicates that a holder of a concessionary plot had only limited use of the land. In the act of concession, the king did not rescind his own rights. The status of Padi's land was thus quite similar to the status of the colonists' plots at Elephantine.

Darius and Gadatas, Alexander and Priene

Despite all of the examples above, it is still important to remind ourselves that the concept and extent of Persian royal land are difficult to grasp. On the one hand, no Greek literary text actually uses the expression *basilikē gē* 'royal land' or *khōra basilikē* 'royal holdings' to characterize Achaemenid royal land in the sense used here. On the other hand, it is important to stress the relevance of a letter that Darius sent to Gadatas, who in all probability was manager of a paradise near Magnesia on the Meander:

> The sacred gardeners (*phytourgoi hieroi*) have been subjected by you to tribute (*phoros*) and required to work profane land (*khōra bebēlos*). (ML 12)

In this letter reproaching his manager, the king very clearly refers to two categories of land: land that belongs to the sanctuary (what the Hellenistic texts call *hiera khōra*) and "profane land." The latter is also described quite clearly in another passage in this letter. Darius congratulates Gadatas for the care taken in cultivating land 'which is mine' (*tēn emēn gēn*). The same expression is found in a letter sent from Alexander to the city of Priene in 334. In it the king distinguishes several categories of land and population: the city lands (which were exempt from military levy: *syntaxis*) and other (adjacent) land, whose inhabitants (*katoikountes*) were subject to tribute (*phoroi*). Regarding this second category, Alexander states emphatically: "I know that this land is mine" (*khōran* [*g*]*inōskō emēn einai*; Tod 185). In addition to the fact that there are terminological similarities between these letters and the statements of Mardonius and Artayctes (Herodotus VII.5; IX.116; see above), the two letters are especially instructive in that they come from the royal chancelleries.

From a comparison of these documents we can perhaps draw two conclusions: first, the territory of the paradise, about which we were not entirely certain, counted as what the Hellenistic texts call royal land (*khōra basilikē*). Second, royal appropriation did not imply that all the land of the Empire was considered the *property* of the Great King (in the Roman sense of the word *property*). The conquest did not result in a sudden, general confiscation of land. People continued to possess (according to their local standards) their traditional lands. The boundaries of villages, cities, *ethnē*, sanctuaries, or kingdoms were recognized by the administration, and it made these boundaries the basis for taxation. In discussing appropriation, we should be thinking not of rights of ownership but of the Great King's direct or indirect *control* over production and the producers.

Following a revolt, the Great King might confiscate lands and redistribute them however he liked. This happened in the region of Atarnaeus, which around 545 had been conceded to Chios (Herodotus I.160). It also happened in 493 to the territory of Miletus (= *khōra politikē*): "The Persians themselves occupied the land in the immediate neighbourhood of the town, and the rest of the cultivated region which belonged to it, and made over the mountainous interior to the Carians of Pedasus" (Herodotus VI.20◇). Thus we see that the king might award extra land to a deserving city or people, taking it from earlier confiscations. These awards of land are attested frequently in the Hellenistic period. The Great King's gift of a territory to Ešmunazar, king of Sidon (see chap. 12/3), suggests that the same practice existed in the Achaemenid period. The local maintenance of private, community, or civic property did not really contradict the king's right to use the Empire's lands. We might say that all rural property was in a way stamped with a character of revocability. In most cases, the king had no intention of confiscating the lands in question, and so this royal prerogative usually remained theoretical. However, everyone also knew that the prerogative would be exercised without hesitation in the case of an unfaithful or revolutionary individual or population.

Tribute-Producing Lands and Crown Lands

To proceed, we must return to Pseudo-Aristotle, the author of the *Oeconomica*. In this invaluable treatise, he formally distinguishes a particular type of assessment from assessments imposed under the label *tribute*. He writes in fact, regarding the receipt and disbursement of products managed directly by the royal administration, that they "were received by the satraps as *tagē*" (II.1.3). This is a difficult word, which a later lexicographer (Hesychius) understood as "the royal *dōrea* and the entirety of things required for life." Here, the word *dōrea* must be understood in the context of the royal economy, that is, land held by concession, except that this time it was the king himself who was the beneficiary. These lands in *dōrea* are often characterized by the Classical authors as sustaining gifts. The best-known example (but not the only one) is Themistocles, who received revenues from several towns. Each one had to provide him bread, wine, fish, wardrobe, and part of the expenses of his house. This is precisely how Hesychius defined the *tagē*: its revenues went to satisfying the needs of the king. Given the fact that *dōreai* are attested in many satrapies, we must recognize that throughout Imperial territory portions of land were reserved for the needs of the king. This is precisely the system defined by Herodotus in connection with the financial category *parex tou phorou*: "Apart from normal tribute, the whole Persian Empire is divided into regions for the purpose of furnishing supplies (*trophē*) for the king and his army" (I.192◇). It is thus legitimate to conclude that the word *tagē* refers to a specific category of land, which we will call "crown lands," on which the king levied assessments directly. Pseudo-Aristotle makes it clear that these assessments were products in kind. As the author says, it was up to the king to do with these products as he pleased, once they had been stocked in the royal granaries or storehouses (*paratheseis*: II.2.34a).

Another passage from Herodotus, ephemeral though it may be, helps us clarify how *tagē* lands functioned in practical terms. What it says is that from Egypt, along with its tribute, the king benefited from the proceeds (in silver) of the fish from Lake Moeris (III.91). Other concessions of this type were known in Egypt, such as the city of An-thylla, which was "made over ever since the Persian conquest of Egypt to the wife of the reigning monarch to keep her in shoes" (Herodotus II.98✧). In this custom we find an adumbration of the well-known Achaemenid custom of allowing princesses to own lands and villages in the Empire; the revenues from these lands made it possible for them to maintain a household. According to Athenaeus (I.33f), the revenues of the Egyptian city of Anthylla were sent to princesses in the Persian period. Diodorus Siculus (I.52.5✧) said of Pharaoh Moeris, "The income accruing from the fish taken from the lake he gave to his wife for her unguents and general embellishment, the value of the catch amounting to a talent of silver daily." This was not the way it was in the time of Da-rius, when, according to Herodotus (II.149; III.91), the revenues were paid directly to the royal treasury (*to basilikon*).

Unfortunately, apart from this passage, direct references to the category we here call "crown lands" are rare. Let us return to Strabo's materials on animal tribute from Cap-padocia, Armenia, and Media (XI.13.8). They must be compared with what we know about horsebreeding in this region. Strabo had just said (XI.13.7✧), "This . . . is an ex-ceptionally good 'horse-pasturing' country; and a certain meadow there is called 'Horse-pasturing,' and those who travel from Persis and Babylon to Caspian Gates pass through it; and in the time of the Persians it is said that fifty thousand mares were pastured in it and that these herds belonged to the kings (*agelai basilikai*)." Arrian (VII.13.1) in turn gives the figure of 150,000 Nisaean mares (160,000 in Diodorus XVII.110.6). In fact "Nisaean" horses were raised there—named for the Plain of Nisaea between Behistun and Ecbatana; it was famous for its alfalfa, which was called "Median grass" (cf. He-rodotus VII.40✧). This, Polybius says, is the reason for "the royal stud farms being en-trusted to the Medes owing to the excellence of the pastures" (X.27.1✧). Just like the Babylonian stud farms (Herodotus I.191), those in Media were doubtless considered part of the *tagē*, whose produce was furnished "in lieu of tribute in silver." It must have been the same for the stud farms of Aeolis that, being royal property (*ta basilika*), were managed by specialized administrators (Plutarch *Eum.* 8.5).

Perhaps forests, which are included implicitly by Pseudo-Aristotle in the category "products of the earth," were also part of the *tagē*. A decree from the Hellenistic period (213) confirms the existence of royal forests in Asia Minor. To rebuild the city of Sardis, Antiochus III issued the following order: "Let wood immediately be cut for the rebuild-ing of the town and let it be taken from the forests of Taranza." This probably refers to the famous forests of Mount Tmolus, which were quite close to Sardis. The text is clear: if a person was on business for the king, it was not sufficient to allege that he was who he said he was in order to have merchandise delivered; it was necessary to produce a written order from the king (or the satrap) before the managers would release materiel. This was also true of the royal stud farms (Plutarch, *Eum.* 8.5). The existence of royal forests is also attested in Mysia, and the luxuriance of the forests of Trachaean Cilicia is emphasized by Strabo. He notes that the pine wood from this region was regularly used for shipbuilding. The Cilician coast was precisely where the Persians had set up their great shipyards.

Other regions of the Empire, such as Babylonia, were less well off. Strabo refers several times to a lack of timber for construction, except for the trunks of date palms (XVI.1.5 and 11). In 324, Alexander also had to import wood and carpenters from the Lebanon. Nonetheless, Strabo (XVI.1.11) goes on to say that the king was able to set up navy yards in Babylon by making use of cypress that was cut in the woods and paradises. We know that the paradises were famous for the beauty of their trees and forests (cf. Plutarch, *Art.* 25.1–2; Diodorus XVI.41.5), but these woodlands had a greater purpose in life than just to provide shade for satraps and kings! They were also profitable estates. For instance, when Nehemiah was sent to Jerusalem by Artaxerxes I, he bore an official letter addressed to "Asaph, keeper of the king's park" (Neh. 2:8◊), whom we identify as the manager of the royal forests of the Lebanon. This means that, as early as 538, the royal administration ordered "Sidonians and Tyrians to bring by sea as far as Joppa cedarwood from the Lebanon" for rebuilding the temple in Jerusalem. These were the same royal forests from which Antigonus the One-Eyed had thousands of trees cut in 316 to build the fleet with which he intended to conquer Egypt. The forests of the Lebanon remained royal estates through the Hellenistic period, as shown by the order given in 200 by Antiochus III regarding the ornamentation of the temple in Jerusalem.

An Appraisal and Some Uncertainties

Let us review. It is not always easy to identify the boundaries between tribute land and the *tagē*. The texts cited above do not allow us to conclude with full certainty that stud farms and forests were part of the *tagē*, even though that is the interpretation adopted in my hypothesis. The Babylonian tablets refer to a category of lands called *uzbarra*, a word of Iranian origin that is currently understood as "royal land," as opposed to other categories of land. Sometimes the 'king's portion' (*zitti šarri*) was assessed on *uzbarra*. Portions of royal land could also be conceded to court personnel, by way of royal gifts (*nidintu šarri*). But many questions remain about the extent of royal land in Babylonia.

In actuality, *royal land* remains highly ambiguous. Evidence appears in two parallel Hellenistic cases: in one, King Antiochus ordered the concession of land to a favorite (Aristodicides of Assus) and specified that the land be taken from the royal land (*khōra basilikē; RC* 11–12). In the other case, Antigonus reminded the Greek coastal cities that they were strongly urged to purchase wheat that came from tribute land (*khōra phorologoumenē; RC* 3). Were Antiochus and Antigonus referring to two categories of land distinguished by differing terminology or to a single category with only minor distinctions specified by the context? I would suggest that in the politico-ideological sense of the term, "royal land" merged with tribute land—that is, with the Empire in its entirety (this is the understanding held or implied by Herodotus in his tribute discussions). But in a financial-economic sense, royal land was reduced to the royal *dōrea*, or the *tagē*, which I render here with the phrase *crown lands*. Seen in this framework, the Persepolis documents allow us to refine this term's contours.

Chapter 11
Persia: Empire and Tribute Economy

1. *The Persepolis Archives*

Fortification Tablets and Treasury Tablets

In 1933–34 and 1936–38, two lots of tablets were discovered at Persepolis by American excavators, the first in the northeast corner of the terrace, the second in the southeast part. Because of the findspots, they have come to be called the Fortification tablets (PFT) and the Treasury tablets (PTT). The latter were published in 1948 by George G. Cameron, who continued editing them in later years (PF 1957, PF 1963). There are 129 of them, and they date between year 30 of Darius (492) and year 7 of Artaxerxes (458). An Akkadian tablet written in December 502 (PT 85) was also found. The Fortification tablets, dating to years 13 through 18 of Darius (509–494), are much more numerous. In 1968, Richard T. Hallock published 2,087 of them, and another 33 ten years later (PFa). Others have also been published separately since then. In a 1977 article, Hallock announced that he had studied nearly 4,500 of them, but we are still awaiting the publication of the texts he had transcribed before his death. There are, moreover, approximately 500 tablets in Aramaic and 80 Aramaic glosses/dockets on Elamite tablets. Five hundred eighty seals are found on the tablets (86 with inscriptions). Some are published (PTS); others are under study (PFS). Mortars and pestles have also been found at Persepolis, with 163 Aramaic inscriptions, which were published in 1970 by Raymond A. Bowman. They are dated (theoretically) to the reigns of Xerxes and Artaxerxes, between 479/8 and 436/5. Unfortunately, several hundred Aramaic texts and inscriptions remain unpublished. There are also a handful of texts in other languages: 2 Akkadian tablets (PT 85, Fort. 11786), a short Greek text (Fort. 1771), and a text in Phrygian (probably). Thus there are several thousand tablets and inscriptions available to historians of the Achaemenid Empire.

With just one exception—and it is difficult to interpret (PT 4–5)—the Persepolis tablets are not narrative documents. There are no treaties, no recountings of military expeditions, not even any indirect allusions to dynastic history. Basically, the Fortification tablets deal with the collection, warehousing, and distribution of foodstuffs. The recipients are the king and the royal family, high officials in the administration, priests (or religious attendants), cattle, and especially groups of workers (*kurtaš*) in the chancelleries, rural establishments, workshops, and construction sites of Persepolis. An especially complete category (Category Q) records the distribution of food rations to persons and groups traveling from place to place within the Empire. The subjects reappear in three other series: letters, journals, and warehouse accounts. The Treasury tablets, on the other hand, primarily record the distribution of rations to the craftsmen who worked on the construction sites of Persepolis under Darius, Xerxes, and Artaxerxes I. Some of the rations were disbursed (or valued) in silver, instead of only food products, beginning in 493/2.

The entire documentation is extraordinarily concentrated in time and space. Aside from the travelers' provisions (Category Q), they cover a geographic area limited to central Fārs and Susiana, from Susa in the northwest to Niriz in the southeast. The Treasury tablets are almost exclusively concerned with operations in Persepolis itself. Otherwise, the chronological distribution is very irregular, with 46.5% of the Fortification tablets dated to Darius years 22 and 23 (500–499)—72% for Category Q (travelers' provisions). Most of the Treasury tablets are assignable to the reign of Xerxes (486–466), and, within that span, more than 60% date to 466, with 90% of his reign unattested. It is difficult to draw historical conclusions from these percentages. The excavators' spade has obviously uncovered only a tiny portion of the central archives of Persepolis. A significant number of administrative records must have been written on perishable materials. The Fortification tablets frequently mention Babylonian scribes writing on parchment—a method known not only from Classical authors (Herodotus VII.58, Diodorus II.32.5: *diphtherai*) but also from the correspondence of the satrap Arsames, which was written on skin (*DAE* 62–74 [AD]; cf. *FGrH* 115 F263a). Parchment is even explicitly mentioned at Persepolis: a letter on a clay tablet from Princess Irdabama refers to a parchment document (PFa 27). References in Herodotus (VII.239; cf. VIII.90) and Aelian (*VH* XIV.12) state, furthermore, that wax-covered wooden boards, well known in Babylonia from the Neo-Babylonian period (and attested earlier among the Hittites and Assyrians), were still in use. Given these facts, we need to realize that we only have the archives of a few offices. Going by documents surviving from other, earlier Near Eastern kingdoms, we know that we are missing other archives that would have dealt with the care and management of other goods, such as valuable objects, arms, and even clothing. Ancient tales dealing with the sack of Persepolis by the Macedonians clearly confirm our intuitions in this regard (e.g., Quintus Curtius V.6.3–5: textiles, furniture, royal garments, ceramics, etc.).

This documentation will potentially assume enormous importance in the process of conceptualizing Achaemenid history, particularly regarding its economic and tribute organization. In particular, it allows the development of an analysis based on the central authority rather than merely on Classical sources, which, however important they may be, remain spotty and often biased. But, paradoxically, historians have used the Persepolis tablets in no more than piecemeal fashion. The basic reasons for this *relative* neglect are related to language. The first decipherers in fact ran into considerable difficulties that are still far from fully overcome, in spite of the considerable progress already achieved. Aside from a few very rare exceptions, the tablets are written in Elamite, the language of the Anšan and Susa bureaucracies. From the linguistic and syntactic point of view, Neo-Elamite still offers specialists formidable problems, to the point where certain accounting practices implied by the tablets are still so uncertain that sometimes one cannot tell the action from the agent! Moreover, a large proportion of the personal and geographic names and the specialized vocabulary is of Persian origin. And we do not possess a Persian literature from this period that would allow us to compile a complete Persian–Elamite dictionary. The only synoptic texts are the royal inscriptions, which employ a fairly small number of words. Comprehension of the underlying Persian words thus presupposes, on the one hand, an accurate transcription into Persian of the words the scribes wrote in Elamite, and on the other, an etymological analysis that can hardly be undertaken without the assistance of the later corpora (various Iranian languages, including Middle Persian and Modern Persian). But etymology alone does not answer every question, because of the well-known fact that the sense of a word can change considerably over the course of time. A word's etymological meaning must therefore be compared with the context in which it occurs, and then the problems of syntax interfere again. In spite of the loanwords found among the Aramaic documents from Egypt and in the Babylonian tablets, and the terms collected by Greek lexicographers (Hesychius, the *Suda*, etc.), the meaning of a significant number of words used by Elamite scribes serving the Great King still remains unknown or hotly disputed. Meanwhile, it would not be wise to be overcome with skepticism; on the contrary, the breadth of the documentation and the results already achieved drive the historian to interrogate the tablets with both patience and enthusiasm.

Accounts and Archives

The tablets give evidence first of all of the nitpicky, "paper-shuffling" nature of the administrative system established to supervise production and storage. After being gathered in the districts, harvests and livestock were collected in warehouses. Two officials were in charge of each warehouse, one managing the stores (the *tumara* for grain), the other (the *ullira*) authorizing disbursements of merchandise. Each year, the accountants prepared an inventory that they sent to the central office in Persepolis. There also were heads of the warehouses found at each layover on the major routes, where the official travelers could find travel provisions. A duplicate of the records was likewise filed in Persepolis, where the accountants annually registered receipts and disbursements and maintained the books. In principle, then, at any given time, the central authorities were aware of the status of the stores at every location in the territory, and the officials could thus authorize appropriations at this or that warehouse.

Each "county seat" obviously included several warehouses, each one dedicated to the collection and storage of a single product: grains (of various kinds), sesame, wine, beer, wheat, or livestock (sheep, cattle, camels, horses, fowl). The statement of accounts at Hadaran in year 19 lists a total of 2615 BAR [ca. 14 tons] of grain distributed during that year, under 11 categories: distribution to workers (*kurtaš*), to horses, to fowl, to flocks and herds, and delivery to the royal warehouse (PF 1943). At Dur, in year 25, nearly 11,000 BAR [61 tons] of grain left the warehouse (PF 1948[70–71]). Nearly 5,500 liters of wine were appropriated in 503 from the warehouse at Šaramanda (PF 1954). The livestock inventories report each species by sex and age. Under each heading, the accounts give the names of the people in charge of the warehouse along with the name of the administrator who gave the order for disbursement, as well as the amount distributed and the type and number of recipients (priests, *kurtaš*, animals, etc.) and the quantities transported to the warehouses of Persepolis or other sites. Each delivery order coming down the administrative pipeline was sent in a "sealed document" (*halmi*). For example, the record of the grain warehouse at Rakkan, in year 21 (501), mentions 20 *halmi* "signed" by Iršena, one of the chief assessors (PF 1946). Whenever a problem arose, each person's responsibilities were clearly demarcated. Each tablet bore two seal impressions: the seal of the official who provided the merchandise and the seal of the person who received it for distribution. The seals of the highest officials were individualized by an inscription: "Seal of so-and-so, son of so-and-so." In 500, the top official of the administration, Parnaka, let it be known that he had changed his seal: "The seal which hitherto had been mine, this seal has been replaced. From now on, the seal borne by this tablet is mine" (PF 2067–68).

Several documents show that, as elaborate as the system was, it gave rise to disputes. An accountant complains that an official has not provided a sealed document (PF 1957, 1988). There are accusations(?) of "appropriating for themselves" this or that merchandise (PF 1986[37–38], 2074). In May 498, accountants specify that certain female workers have not received their rations for two months (PF 1960). Sometimes the central administration is asked for help in getting this or that administrator his job back (PF 1859–60; 2071). Though quite obscure in detail, there is a letter stating that "the accountants have not furnished a sealed document"; and "the man who was the courier(?) of the tablet has fled." The order is given that he be captured and sent to Media(?), where an inquiry will be conducted. The following order is issued to the administrators: "When you send a tablet to Parnaka, write on it the name of the person responsible for its delivery." It appears, in fact, that previously such precautions had not been taken (PFa 28). The warehouse officials were often called to account. A tablet mentioning the failings of several officials and the adjustments that eventuated ends with this formula: "In conformity with customary law" (PF 1980), where the term translated 'law' (Old Persian *dāta*) here seems to refer to administrative regulations.

2. Administrative Hierarchy and Organization of Production

Parnaka

In charge of the entire administration was a man named Parnaka; documents show that he was in charge between 506 and 497. His seal bears the Aramaic legend "Parnaka, son of Aršāma." It is generally agreed that the Aršāma in question is none other than the grandfather of Darius. Parnaka would thus be the brother of Hystaspes, the paternal uncle of Darius, and the father of Artabazus, whom Xerxes placed in charge of Hellespontine Phrygia. In any case, the size of the daily "rations" he received during his seasonal migrations reveals the eminence of the person and his responsibility: 2 sheep, nearly 90 liters of wine, and nearly 180 liters of flour. Several tablets attest to the large number of letters he sent to his subordinates, most of the time ordering them to release some amount of produce (wine, grain) to specific persons or groups. On two occasions (deliveries to Princess Irtašduna), these letters state that the order came from Darius himself (PF 1793; Fort. 6764). To carry out his duties, he presided over a sizable bureaucracy. Each letter also names its scribe. Several of these letters refer to "Babylonian scribes writing on parchment" who worked directly for him (PF 1807–8, 1810, 1947). A man called Appišmanda may have succeeded him in 497. Several letters, too, were written by the scribes of Ziššawiš, Parnaka's right-hand man (PF 1811–28, 2069). His seal is applied in the name of Darius. His daily rations of course are lower than Parnaka's: less than 3 liters of wine, less than 60 liters of flour, and a single sheep.

The Department Heads

Just below Parnaka and Ziššawiš were several high officials, each of whom was in charge of one area of production and to whom Parnaka or Ziššawiš sent regular letters requiring them to do what was necessary for the delivery of specific products. Armed with this letter, the officials in turn sent sealed orders down the chain of command. As far as we can tell, production was organized into five departments: livestock, grain, wine (and beer), fruit, and fowl.

By way of example, let us take a closer look at the livestock department. It was managed by the head of livestock (*kasabattiš*). At least from 506 to 501, the job belonged to a man named Harrena. In 503, on the orders of Parnaka, who in turn had been instructed by King Darius, Harrena delivered 100 sheep to Princess Irtašduna, one of Darius's wives, whom Herodotus calls Artystone (Fort. 6764). Each district had a bureaucracy like the one in the central offices. At Uranduš in 503, there was a *kasabattiš* called Makama who reported to Harrena (PF 2025) and was in charge of a number of shepherds and stockbreeders. Since the pasturage proper was insufficient—especially during the harsh Persian winter—it was necessary to plan to provide for additional feed (especially grain) in the warehouse stockpiles. Several documents deal with the collection of grain reserves (PF 432, 465, 495–96, 522, 526–27, 535, 538, 542, 545). Several categories of tablets (S1–S3) record rations provided to animals, including special rations anticipating royal migrations (S3). These texts deal with every category (horses, cattle, sheep, camels, and all sorts of poultry). They always follow the same pattern: on orders from above (often a sealed document [*halmi*]), the warehouse manager delivered grain (for example) to a person entrusted with feeding animals. Regarding horses, in year 17 (505), the second-level administrator of rations was Hiumizza, who, in light of a sealed order received from the top administrator, sent orders to the wine-cellar-master Yamakšedda, who was in turn to deliver wine rations to Maudadda, who was in charge of horses at Parmizzan (PF 1833–34; cf. 1687–91). At this same level, those in charge of local horses were the *mudunra* 'stablemasters': they are the ones who received the rations from the warehouse to give to the animals. Other titles sometimes appear—namely, *mudunrabattiš, pasanabattiš, harmanabattiš*—which are often used synonymously but might just as well refer to an internal hierarchy (cf. *battiš* = *pati 'chief'). Reading the individual tablets leads us to believe that each *mudunra* dealt with only a small number of animals. Sometimes this was a single horse, often four or five, rarely ten or more (PF 1635ff.) In every location, there were several horse-tenders. At Rakkan in year 21 (501), rations were entrusted to seven people, whose most common title was *mudunra*. It appears that each *mudunra* was in charge of several groups of horses; one of them, Battišdana, even had to take care of horses, cattle, and sheep (PF 1946).

The rations themselves varied from 1 QA (less than a liter) to 40 QA of grain per day. The horses also received unusual rations: wine (PF 1757–64, 1772–78), beer (PF 1779), grain (PF 1766–68), and flour (PF 1770–71). Provision of wine or beer for horses (even once for camels: PF 1845) is nothing to be surprised about, considering that Aristotle (*Hist. An.* VIII.9) mentions 5 *marriš* of wine as an allocation of elephant feed. This practice is well known in modern times as well. Horses are distinguished by age—"young" and "old"—as well as by function. Two terms are worth mentioning: *pirradaziš* and "[the one] who makes the journey." Both refer to horses normally used in the postal service. The former are the "express horses," famous for their speed and endurance. They were used by the "swift couriers," who were also called *pirradaziš* (chap. 9/2).

The kurtaš Heads (kurdabattiš)

In the Fortification tablets, four officials bear the title *kurdabattiš*: Iršena, Karkiš, Šuddayauda, and Mišparma. The word *kurdabattiš* has received two interpretations: some (the larger camp) think that such people oversaw the laborers who worked in the fields, shops, and construction sites, who in hundreds of tablets are generically called *kurtaš* (OPers. *garda). Others believe that *kurta-* represents not *garda but *grda 'house' and thus that the *kurdabattiš* were chief stewards who headed all five departments and their staff. However, the etymological discussion is of minor importance, since the duties this person assumed clearly lie at the intersection of stock-regulation and administrative staff–regulation, involving one of their most frequently attested roles: distributor of rations. In 494, dates were warehoused in the paradise of Mišdukba, under the supervision of Mišparma, who had the titles *kurdabattiš* and *šaramana*, lower-level administrator/distributor (PF 158). In other words, he would have been responsible for handing out date rations upon receiving an order through channels. In other cases—if this does not involve someone else with the same name—Mišparma was responsible for the stocks of various products that Iršena, also a *kurdabattiš*, quite often distributed for the benefit of groups of *kurtaš* (PF 929–32, 1103, 2041). Having the same title did not imply equality of rank: as in the case of the *kasabattiš* (livestock managers), some people could only carry out their functions within a limited perimeter, under the authority of the head *kurdabattiš*. This was doubtless the hierarchical relationship that existed between Mišparma and Iršena.

Iršena was obviously a very busy, high-ranking person. His ancestry is not known in detail, since he reused a Neo-Elamite seal carved with the name of Humban-aḫpi, son of Šati-Humban. Nontheless, he was a Persian (Ršayana) who, one tablet records, came from Anšan (PF 1368). He is named in more than 70 tablets; the dates of the tablets reveal that he was giving orders at least from 505 to 498. His seal impressions show that he operated with privilege in the Fahliyun region, but he can also be found at work in the Persepolis sector. In essence, his brief was chief financial officer. In this capacity, he sent sealed documents (*halmi*) to various subordinates, whose duty it was to allocate the rations according to his orders. Thus, in 503 he sent more than 10 orders to the warehouse at Hadaran, where the managers were responsible to him. He also planned the transportation of grain from place to place and the delivery of various shipments to the king. In 500, some *kurtaš* in transit received travel rations at an estate (*irmatam*) where Iršena was responsible for the allocation. In other words, it was he who sent the order to the manager of the warehouse (Medummanuš) and to the official (Šiyatiparna) who would receive the grain from him for distribution to the *kurtaš* (PF 1368).

Iršena himself was under the authority of Parnaka and his lieutenant, Ziššawiš, from whom he received letters instructing him to take the steps necessary for the distribution of rations to various people (a *magus*, a warehouse manager, Parnaka's Babylonian scribes, etc.). In 498, he also received a letter from Maraza, who ordered him to distribute grain rations to *kurtaš* (PF 1844). After carrying out major responsibilities in the wine department between 504 and part of 498, and therefore figuring among Parnaka's staff (PF 1789, 1792, 1806–8, 1840), Maraza then was reassigned to the grain department (1841–42, 1844–45). In his capacity as a high official at this time, he ordered Iršena to distribute grain rations to *kurtaš* who depended on him. This simple example shows that the *kurdabattiš* Iršena was not a head steward, in a position in the hierarchy superior to a head of a department. Quite the contrary, on the instructions of the higher authority, he ordered the lower-ranking officials to distribute rations to groups of *kurtaš* placed immediately in his responsibility. The same clearly holds for Karkiš and Šuddayauda, who succeeded him in the Persepolis region, the former from 507 to 503, the latter from 502 to 496. The activities of both of them were in principle limited to a particular region, but they also needed to intervene elsewhere, perhaps because of a scarcity of qualified personnel. In any case, study of the tablets shows the complexity and rigidity of the Persepolis administration's chain of command. It also provides interesting hints about the careers of officials, such as Maraza, who sometimes can be followed for several years.

Treasurerships and Treasurers

The problems posed by another high official, the treasurer, are far more difficult. The only direct information we have comes from the Treasury tablets, which allow us to compile a list of treasurers after 490, when Baradkama took the job, a job that he kept until 466. The Aramaic notes on the Persepolis mortars and pestles allow us to fill out the list of treasurers through 436–435, assuming that the dates proposed by the editor of the inscriptions are fully confirmed, which is not in fact the case. In the Treasury tablets, the treasurer has the Persian title *ganzabara, derived from the word *ganza 'treasure'; in the mortar and pestle inscriptions, "subtreasurers" (*upa-ganzabara) also appear. This may have been Šakka's role alongside Baradkama. Several times treasurers are given the Elamite title *kapnuškira*, which corresponds to *ganzabara (PT 1963$^{3.6}$). They could also be referred to with the phrases "treasurer of Persia" and 'in the fortress' (*hal-marriš*), which unambiguously designates Persepolis. Regularly, at the demand of some official, they released funds for the payment of *kurtaš*. Beginning in 493, in fact, the *kurtaš* were paid partly in weighed silver. The silver came from the treasury, in one instance called the royal treasury (*sunkina*; PT 27). The treasurers' area of activity was confined to Persia itself; in most cases, the *kurtaš* were "craftsmen at Persepolis," where they worked on the construction sites. But the treasury could also provide money/silver for groups who worked at other locations in Fārs, such as the workers who made coats of mail at Niriz (PT 52). Despite these data, their place in the hierarchy is not easy to specify precisely. We do not know exactly what the treasury was or what funds were used to replenish it: funds belonging to Persia proper ("treasury of Parša") or funds deriving from levies of tribute and taxes flowing in from throughout the Empire (as may be suggested by PF 1342, 1357, 1495, and PFa 14; cf. Nepos, *Dat.* 4.2 and *DAE* 71–72 [AD 10–11]). Did the treasurer report to a higher-ranking officer? During Baradkama's tenure, nothing more was said of Parnaka or of any successor to his high responsibilities. On several occasions, Baradkama received orders directly from Darius (PT 4–7). Should we infer that a royal letter was sent in every case?

The Fortification tablets seem to reveal a different state of affairs. The word *ganza-bara is found there only twice. Someone named Mannuya received money/silver at Susa and got orders to take it to Matezziš (PF 1342). Does this refer to the proceeds of taxes levied in Elam? But if so, why take it to Matezziš and not to the Persian treasury in the fortress very close to Persepolis? Another tablet transcribes a statement of accounts set up at Rakkan, which is called a treasury (PF 1947). Among the officials who worked there and received rations there were a treasurer (*ganzabara); an official in charge of authorizing disbursements of goods from the warehouse (*ullira*), who is called *ullira kapnuš-kira*, '*ullira* of the treasury'; and a scribe (*tipira kapnuškima*). The treasury in question, however, was not the treasury of Parša but one of the many local treasuries, which the tablets list throughout the territory of Fārs and Elam. One text refers indirectly to the Persepolis treasury. It records the provision of rations to shepherds who brought "royal sheep" to Susa and who were described as "attached to the treasury [of Persepolis]" (*kan-zaika*; PF 1442). This probably referred to *kurtaš* who were dependent on the authorities of the fortress and who were needed for particular jobs (cf. PT 45, 65–67).

The words *kapnuški* 'treasury' and *kapnuškira* 'treasurer' are attested in 53 Fortification tablets. These treasuries were eleven local treasuries in Persia and apparently have nothing in common with the Persepolis treasury known from the Treasury tablets. These treasuries included warehouses and a sizable staff (as at Rakkan). Attached to them were larger or smaller groups of *kurtaš*—for example, 47 at Shiraz in 504 (then 231 in 500), 677 at Matezziš in 497, 544 at Uranduš in 500, and so on. The local treasuries were thus primarily centers of collection, warehousing, and processing of agricultural and animal products. The treasurer of one of these centers thus did not have much in common with the treasurer of Parša (such as Baradkama), even though both of them were known by the same title, **ganzabara*. Baradkama appears several times in 495–494 as distributor of rations to the *kurtaš* of the treasury (*kapnuški*) of Uranduš and Shiraz (PF 864–67); once, grain was in the control of Iršena; in 495, he was responsible for seven *kurtaš* of the treasury at Kurpun. Obviously, between 494 and 490, he profited from a major promotion that had brought him to the Persepolis treasury. There can be no doubt, then, that the treasuries also involved groups of *kurtaš* who worked in shops, as is suggested by the inscriptions on mortars and pestles found in the treasury.

Apparently, Baradkama had no predecessor in his duties as treasurer of Parša, insofar as we can reconstruct the situation from the Treasury tablets. This is not to say that after Parnaka there was no royal treasury in the sense of a depository for metal and valuable objects. As a matter of fact, the ancient authors often refer to such places as *thēsauroi* and *paratheseis* (cf. Strabo XV.3.21). It is always risky to interpret silence in the sources. The sudden appearance of payments in silver to the *kurtaš* in 493 certainly does not imply that Parnaka did not have sums of money at his disposal. The Akkadian Treasury tablet proves, in fact, that from at least 502 on, dues were collected in weighed silver (PT 85). It seems more reasonable to assume that some of Parnaka's archives have disappeared; moreover, the Fortification tablets are extremely discreet regarding the operations carried out at Persepolis itself.

3. The World of Work: The kurtaš

Kurtaš Craftsmen

An overwhelming majority of the tablets refer to the rations provided to the *kurtaš*. In the Persepolis documentation, the Elamite word *kurtaš* refers generally to the laborers who worked in the fields and shops controlled by the administration or else on construction sites at Persepolis. In most cases, their specialty is not indicated. They are most often listed as *kurtaš* receiving rations in a certain locality or a certain treasury (*kurtaš kapnuškip*). On the other hand, many technical names of occupations are not included, so we have entire lists that are inexplicable (cf. PF 865).

The Treasury tablets basically contain the names of specialized workers in the building trades and ornamental crafts. They are often designated by the expression "*kurtaš*-craftsmen who receive rations from Persepolis." The Elamite word *marrip* 'craftsman' in all probability corresponds to Persian **krnuvaka*. The designation they receive is sometimes very general, such as the 1149 men who are called 'craftsmen of all trades' or 'workers at any task' (PT 79). Their specialty is sometimes indicated more specifically: they work stone, they carve reliefs in wood, they contribute to the completion of a hypostyle hall, they are goldsmiths or smelters. The mass of Treasury tablets attests to the perpetual work on ornamentation and finishing at Persepolis throughout the reign of Xerxes in particular. In the Fortification tablets, the craftsmen (*marrip*) working at Persepolis are also named, but relatively infrequently. Between 507 and 500, certain tablets record the transport to Persepolis of grain, flour, and wine intended for craftsmen's rations; the distributor is Abbateya (1580–84, 1587, 1594, 1614, 1801, 1831; cf. 1049 and 1953). Ethnic background is given once (Lycians: PF 1049); specialties are cited rarely: sculptors in stone (PF 1587, 1633), goldsmiths (PF 872, 1805), woodworkers (PF 1799?). An Aramaic gloss (PF 1587) refers to quarrymen. One is reminded of the Greek graffiti found in a quarry near Persepolis—one graffito carved with the name Pytharcus, another Nikias. Furthermore, the mortars and pestles of Persepolis show that, under Xerxes and Artaxerxes I, *kurtaš* were employed in the fortress's shops to make objects apparently intended for royal tableware.

But not all of the craftsmen were concentrated at Persepolis. The Persepolis treasurer also provided a "salary" to *kurtaš* who made coats of mail at Niriz (PT 52) or who worked at Fasa (PT 53) or Shiraz (PT 42–42a, 60). Like the treasury in Persepolis, the treasuries scattered all around the territory in fact included groups of 'treasury workers' (*kurtaš kapnuškip*) of varying size. A wide variety of trades is found among them: masons at Uranduš (*PTT* 27–33, 67–68), Sardian blacksmiths at Kurra (PF 873), and goldsmiths at Hidalu (PF 874). Among the most specialized groups were the *kurtaš* to whom the administration delivered skins, which they treated to make parchment, which in turn was used by the many chancelleries and accounting offices. Furthermore, 23 texts from various sites refer to groups of *pašap* consisting entirely of women. These were (probably) weavers who worked wool and made a wide variety of clothing.

On the orders of Abbateya in 497, a group of 31 *kurtaš* from the Niriz treasury came to Persepolis, where they worked as masons (PF 1852). These *kurtaš* were not necessarily master masons previously; it is possible that they had been summoned as common laborers and enrolled as workers in squads intended for masonry works. It appears in any case that groups of workers were periodically moved from one spot to another as needed. Such movements are frequently attested in tablets from Category Q (travel rations): from Susa to Persepolis, from Susa to Makkan, from Persepolis to Susa, from Rakkan to Tammukhan, and so on. Relocation of workers is also mentioned in the Treasury tablets. At the end of Darius's reign, construction workers, who were used in the building of a palace at Nupistaš (Naqš-i Rustam? PT 9), were brought from Egypt; in 462–461, a renowned specialist in stone ornamentation was ordered from Susa to Persepolis (PT 78). The groups moved in this way could be sizable: 547 Egyptians from Susa to Persepolis (PF 1557); 108 Cappadocians from Persepolis to Elam (PF 1577); 1500 men from Persepolis to Susa (PF 1542); 150 Thracians, 980 Cappadocians, and 303 Lycians from one place to another within Fārs (PFa 18 and 30); etc.

The change in the number of *kurtaš* on the same site is further evidence of the practice of worker relocation. The orders for distribution of rations in effect allow us to compile an annual census. We can see that some of the treasuries had only small groups attached permanently, such as Hiran (except in 488: 88 *kurtaš*), Kurpun, and even Pasargadae. On the other hand, at Matezziš, rations were distributed to 259 workers in 506, 694 in 499, 702 in 498, and 677 in 497; at Uranduš, the figures are as follows: 15 in 503, 544 in 502, and an average of more than 200 until 497. The variations are sometimes striking: at Parmizzan, where there regularly were very small groups (5 in 505 and 6 in 501), the number reaches 527 in one year (508?). To be sure, the figures must not be taken as a precise reflection of the circumstances, because the archives we have are incomplete and, in particular, they fall silent regarding the number of craftsmen working at Persepolis. Nonetheless, they give an overall idea of the hierarchy of the treasuries and of the movements of laborers from site to site.

Centurions and Foremen

The orders concerning rations and movements of *kurtaš* emanated from 'heads of *kurtaš*' (*kurdabattiš*), who also might carry out the duties of distributors (*šaramana*). Orders could be sent directly from Parnaka's office, sometimes even from the royal chancellery itself. But the groups of *kurtaš*, in particular the best supplied, had their own internal organization, subject of course to the authority of administration officials. Several times in the Fortification tablets products are directed to 'heads of a hundred' (*sadabattiš/*satapati*) and 'heads of ten' (*dasabattiš/*daθapati*), explicitly named according to the formula "the decurion/centurion of such-and-such" (PF 138–43). A 'head of four' (*zatturubattiš*) is even found once (PT 1963: 10). One Treasury tablet records a list of persons (*taššup*/people) divided into hundreds (PT 84). We are tempted to think that it was the job of these centurions and decurions to distribute the rations among their men. Nonetheless, the information drawn from the Treasury tablets does not fully confirm this interpretation. In some exemplars, the centurion is indeed the distributor (*šaramana*; PT 42–42a, 53, 60). But this is not the rule. In 483–482, a group of Syrian, Egyptian, and Ionian *kurtaš* working at Persepolis comprised 201 units in all. The rations were divided unequally among subgroups comprising 46 men each, obviously because of their differing qualifications. The group also includes 63 men called centurions and subcenturions. If we suppose (which is only logical) that each tablet deals with a specific category of workers who received rations, it is obvious that each of the centurions (however many there were) did not command 100 men. They are called more precisely "centurions who [belong to the category] of centurions." This is probably a distinction that entitled one to a larger ration than the 138 other workers (PT 15). This was probably also true for the Egyptian centurion Haradduma, a carpenter/joiner, who in one tablet is the only person specified as receiving a ration (PT 1). He must have been an especially respected craftsman, considering the amount of his ration (the equivalent of 6½ siculi per month), which was much higher than that of other centurions (1 + ¾ + ⅛ siculi per month for each of the 63 centurions and subcenturions of PT 15). It was also much higher than the ration of a particular decorator who, even though he was specially summoned from Susa to Persepolis in 462–461, received only ⅓ siculus per month (PT 78). The modesty of his ration seems all the more inexplicable in that he is called *pirramanakurraš*, which represents the Persian *framanakara*, which is translated 'foreman'. In 466–465, a man named Eškuš was the foreman of 612 carpenters working at Persepolis, but the amount of his ration is not stated (PT 75). In 466, two carpenters' foremen received an allocation of 1⅔ siculi per month (PT 44).

Food Rations and the Organization of Production

According to the Fortification tablets, rations in kind were distributed unequally according to gender and age. In general, men, 'boys' (*puhu*), women, and girls were distinguished, although some uncertainty remains about the exact meaning of *puhu* (defined by age? or by status [servant]?). In an overall analysis, it appears that 83% of the men received 30 QA of grain per month, or about 16.5 kg (figuring 56 kg per hectoliter), the others receiving between 11 and 25 kg; 87% of the women received between 11 and 16.5 kg, nearly all the others drawing 22 kg. But these mean figures do not take into account the diversity of situations. By way of example (among hundreds more), let us consider the amount of grain rations handed out in March 498 to 702 *kurtaš* in Matezziš, who received 1,638.5 BAR, that is, more than 100 quintals (PF 960 [1 quintal = 100 kg]). The allocation was as follows:

1 man	27.50 kg	4 women	27.50 kg
48 men	22.00	120 women	22.00
31 men	18.75	146 women	16.50
23 men	16.50	100 women	11.00
15 "boys" (*puhu*)	13.25	3 girls	13.75
28 "boys"	11.00	13 girls	11.00
38 "boys"	11.00	43 girls	8.25
20 "boys"	5.50	22 girls	5.50
22 "boys"	2.75	17 girls	2.75
		8 *libap*	11.00

We can see differences within each category as well, without in any particular case having any information to help understand the criteria (aside from age, which is clearly not the only consideration). Furthermore, a new category appears here, the *libap*. The *libap* are often mentioned in groups of travelers who are supplied from the warehouses on the royal roads. Two subgroups can be very generally distinguished, the *šaluip* and the *libap*—two categories that correspond to different social statuses but are not defined further—the "gentlemen" and the servants/slaves. The gentlemen usually receive 0.82 kg per day, the *puhu* 0.55 kg, and the servants/*libap* 0.55 kg as well.

While grain was obviously the staple food, some groups also received wine or beer, but this is relatively rare: less than ⅕ of the cases. In March and April 500, for example, 24 *marriš* of wine (ca. 228 liters) were distributed to 8 *kurtaš* of Niriz, as follows: 19.4 liters for each of 2 men, 9.7 liters for each of 2 other men, and 23 liters for one woman (PF 878). We can conclude from these two examples that the women were not systematically less well provided for than the men. The ration of three *marriš* of wine (29 liters) is regularly allocated to women who bore the title *iršara*, which renders the Persian *maθista* 'head'. This title could obviously be applied to men, who therefore received very high rations. But there were often women heads of women *pašap*. These women heads received a very high grain ration of 27.5 kg. On one occasion (PF 1790), 5 of these women received ½ sheep; on another, 544 ordinary female workers of Uranduš earned ⅟₃₀ sheep per month (PF 1794), even though the distribution of meat to *kurtaš* is extremely rare (PF 823–25, 1793). The *kurtaš-pašap* were among the groups that received supplementary rations: one liter of flour per month in one case (PF 1090) and 3 liters of beer for six months in another (PF 1108). Even within the group of weavers—a small number of whom were male—the rations were divided into three subgroups according to job, whether the garments being made were of a more or less fine fabric or texture (superfine, very fine, or other). It was probably the same on the construction sites at Persepolis: it seems quite likely that the work there was divided aaccording to squads and teams, each one assigned to a specific repetitive task.

The Aramaic inscriptions from Persepolis also attest to the administration's efforts to keep close watch on the *kurtaš* and to increase their productivity. These inscriptions, on dishes, pestles, and mortars of green stone ("green chert"), are composed on the following model (according to one of the proposed interpretations):

> IN THE TREASURY OF THE FORTRESS
> ON THE ORDERS OF X, SEGAN
> N MADE THIS MORTAR/PESTLE/DISH
> WHICH HE TURNED
> ON THE AUTHORITY OF Y^1 (TREASURER) AND/OR Y^2 (SUBTREASURER)
> SERIES (OF WORK) OF YEAR A

The procedure can be reconstructed as follows. Workshops for stone vessel-making (doubtless intended to adorn the royal table) were located in rooms in the treasury. Craftsmen whose status is not specifically indicated but who clearly fell under the generic category of treasury workers (*kurtaš kapnuškip*), found so frequently in the tablets, worked there. Some of them, the turner-polishers, were specialists. The *kurtaš* teams—perhaps grouped into decuries (tens) or centuries (hundreds)—were directed and overseen by *segan* 'provosts/guards' who themselves were under the orders of the treasurer (**ganzabara*) and the subtreasurer (**upa-ganzabara*) then in office. The notices written on each object allowed the administrator to verify (and doubtless pay for) the labor of the workers who were involved in the production. They also allowed him to establish a correlation between the weight of stone provided to each workshop and the number of objects produced, thus providing a means of measuring the output. The mention of the date and the serial number confirms the meticulous, detail-oriented character of the administration of the treasury, so clearly attested throughout the Persian documentation. And, were it not marked by an obvious flair for the dramatic, we would not hesitate to use a passage from Diodorus of Sicily to illustrate the administration's concern for "efficiency" (XVII.69.4◊). According to Alexander's historian, as a matter of fact, the Greek *kurtaš* of Persepolis were treated in this way: "They were persons who had acquired skills or crafts and had made good progress in their instruction; then their other extremities had been amputated and they were left only those which were vital to their profession"!

Origins and Status of the kurtaš

We have still not explained the status of the *kurtaš*, and to do so is no easy task. The etymology of the term (*garda*) is not much help. Only context might allow us to attempt some semblance of a description. The first observation is that the *kurtaš* represented a sampling of nearly all of the peoples of the Empire, including Persians in *apparently* limited number. Among the *kurtaš* were Bactrians, Sogdians, Babylonians, Assyrians, Elamites, Arabs, Syrians, Egyptians, Lycians, Carians, Ionians, Sardians, Cappadocians, and Thracians. The occurrences of these different peoples vary in number: while Carians are named only 3 times (PF 1123; PT 37, 1963: 2) and Arabs only 4 (PF 1477, 1507, 1534; PFa 17), others appear in many tablets, especially Lycians (more than 10 times) and Thracians (at least 20 times). But it seems difficult to draw inferences from statistics based on such fragmentary archives.

Why did they come, or why were they brought, to Persia? There is no single answer, and several compatible explanations can be offered. The policy of deportation of conquered populations is attested several times, as it was in the Assyrian and Neo-Babylonian periods (for example, the Judahites under Nebuchadnezzar). After the defeat and destruction of Sidon in 345–344 by Artaxerxes III, men and women of the city were led captive to Babylon, where "they entered the royal palace" (*ABC* no. 9, p. 114). The Classical texts frequently refer to this practice, which the Persian generals sometimes use as the ultimate threat (Herodotus VI.3, 9, 94). The Milesians were subjected to deportation (VI.32, 98), as were the Paeonians of Thrace (VI.98), Barcaeans (IV.204), Eretrians (VI.101, 119), Boeotians, and Carians, not to mention the Branchidae of Miletus who, fleeing Miletus during Xerxes' predations, were settled in Bactria. No document expressly names Persia as a destination to which deportees were sent. They mention instead what the Greeks liked to call "the extremities of the Empire": Bactria, Babylonia, Elam, as well as the islands in the Persian Gulf that were frequently a place of deportation, as much for miscreant Persians as for conquered populations. But there is no doubt that prisoners of war could be settled in Fārs. Alexander, upon his arrival in Persia in 331, made contact with Greeks deported to Persia, as well as with a Lycian shepherd, who told him he had been reduced to this condition after a defeat. We are immediately reminded of the *kurtaš* shepherds known from the tablets. The same is true for the Greeks in Persepolis who "had been carried away from their homes by previous kings of Persia" (Diodorus XVII.69.3✧) and who, mutilated by their masters, complained to Alexander of having been forced to toil in slave workshops (*ergastules;* Quintus Curtius V.5.13).

Quite another picture emerges from the "foundation charters" of Darius's palace at Susa (chap. 5/2). There the king is glorified for bringing raw materials and specialized craftsmen—Ionians, Sardians, Egyptians, Carians, Bactrians, Elamites, Babylonians—from everywhere. Despite the deeply ideological character of these royal proclamations, we can easily agree that Darius utilized ethnic contingents whose specialites were well known. This selective use of specialists is well known from the Neo-Assyrian kings. There is also no doubt that to accomplish his construction projects at Pasargadae, Cyrus himself called on craftsmen from Lydia and Ionia. According to Diodorus Siculus (I.46.4✧), it was the same with Cambyses, who, not content to pillage the temples of Egypt, "[took] artisans (*technitai*) along from Egypt, [and] constructed their famous palaces in Persepolis and Susa and throughout Media." It is unfortunately difficult to confirm whether the ethnic groups mentioned in the tablets were specialized in a particular activity. Though it is true that Babylonians were employed as scribes who wrote on parchment by Parnaka, this was not their only activity. Other Babylonians were "seed merchants" (PF 1811, 1821–22) and still others gravediggers (? PF 1856). Among the Carians, some were stoneworkers (PT 37) and others masons (PT 37, PT 1963: 2). The Egyptians and Syrians worked in various building trades: masonry, carpentry, sculpting, etc. If we add the fact that groups of *kurtaš* were sometimes ethnically mixed, we see that any conclusion regarding ethnic specialities becomes useless and illusory.

The individually named craftsmen constitute a special case, such as, for example, the Egyptian foreman specializing in woodworking who was employed at Persepolis in 490–489 (PT 1) or the decorator foreman who was called posthaste from Susa to Persepolis (PT 78). It is tempting to suppose that some master craftsmen/artists might have come to Persepolis not because they were forced to but because they were requested by Persian officials seeking especially skilled technicians. This was perhaps the situation (later) in the case of the sculptor Telephanes of Phocis, mentioned by Pliny (*NH* XXXIV.19.68), and many other famous Greek artists in various fields (athletes, poets, dancers), even if some of them (the physicians Democedes and Ctesias) were captives. This hypothesis implies that at the end of their engagement (contract?), they could return home or seek another situation. Meanwhile, this process—if it can be proved—could only have worked for a very limited number of highly skilled craftsmen. There was no real labor market (see below, chap. 11/9, the case of Hinzanāy). There must be other explanations for why thousands of *kurtaš* with no particular qualifications other than what was assigned to them were, for example, temporarily moved to the construction sites of Persepolis, where most of them carried out repetitive tasks that involved no particular creativity.

Demographics and Population Growth

Women about to give birth were among the recipients of special rations (PF 1200–37, 1248). Although the term *kurtaš* is not always qualified, there is no doubt that it often refers to women workers, whose specialty is sometimes indicated: for example, weavers (? PF 1200, 1203, 1236; cf. 1224). From time to time they are listed by name. They generally receive wine, beer, and flour. The ration is doubled in the event of the birth of a boy: for example, 10 liters of wine or beer for a boy, 5 liters for a girl; 11 kg of grain for a boy, 5.5 kg for a girl. Some mothers are rewarded with higher allocations (*kamakaš*: 15 liters of wine in one case), for reasons we do not know. Several tablets show that each mother received both wine/beer and grain products. Even though the sample is limited in number and timespan (most of the tablets come from 500–497), it is interesting to observe that the total number of births is 449, 247 of them boys (55%). There do not seem to be any examples of twins. Nevertheless, this documentation testifies to a policy of voluntary supplements on the part of the administration—well attested also (in a quite different political context) for Persian families themselves (cf. Herodotus I.136; Strabo XV.3.17). It is clear that these postnatal rations were over and above normal rations—as it were, a reward. At the same time, the bonuses must have allowed the women to recuperate from childbirth under good conditions and doubtless to nurse their babies—if we suppose that the ancients thought that lactation was optimized by drinking beer!

These documents also show that some of the *kurtaš* of Fārs were quite simply a result of natural population growth, since doubtless the status of mothers was passed on to their children. Unfortunately, we know nothing about the fathers. The actual origin of the mothers is rarely specified: Thracians in one case (PF 1215), Ionians in another (PF 1224). But were the fathers Thracians or Ionians? We may return to the Lycian shepherd who guided Alexander toward the Persian Gates, "whose father was a Lycian, and his mother a Persian," Plutarch states (*Alex.* 37.1◊). There were *kurtaš* who at that time worked in the 'slave-prisons' (*ergastula*) of Persepolis, whose representatives referred to women "whom chance and necessity have joined to [them]" and who had given them children "whom slavery has compelled [them] to acknowledge" (Quintus Curtius V.5.15, 20◊). But can we also apply these details to the Persia of Darius I, and would these accounts then describe a current practice? The Babylonian Chronicle on the taking of Sidon by Artaxerxes III and the Greek texts show that the groups of deportees included men and women.

But what became of the young children? Were they permanently integrated into a group of *kurtaš* that included (hypothetically) their fathers and mothers? Fortunately, we have—as we have seen—a very large number of ration tablets that record amounts differentiated by age and sex, according to categories generally understood as men, women, boys, and girls. On the basis of these documents we can derive some statistics. Taking into account all of the Fortification tablets, M. A. Dandamaev has drawn up the following table:

Total	Men	Women	Boys	Girls
21,576	8,183	8,564	2,687	2,142
100%	37.5%	39.8%	12.7%	10%

Observing that the numerical rations of men to women and boys to girls are approximately equal, the only conclusion that seems possible is that the *kurtaš* lived in families. But the reasoning is not airtight. First of all, the fertility rate seems abnormally low, even if we allow for high infant mortality (cf. Ctesias §49). It also needs to be stressed that any conclusion based on overall percentages has no probative value, since it assumes that the *kurtaš* constituted a fixed, autonomous, and homogeneous community—which was obviously not true. In fact, if we are to inquire into family structure, we must actually analyze the composition of strictly isolated groups of *kurtaš*.

We observe first of all that many *kurtaš* did not have equal numbers of men and women. This is particularly true in the case of the treasury weavers. In 14 tablets from 5 sites, dating between 501 and 496, the percentage of women in the groups is between 63% and 73.5%. The increase in the number of women and children is still more impressive if we take the example of the treasury of Shiraz. We see that a recruitment took place in 505 and then again between 502 and 499. In the first recruitment, the number of men remained unchanged, while the number of women and children grew from 6 to 18. Between 502 and 499, the number of children increased from 16 to 99. Women and children thereafter represent some 90% of the total. This new recruitment led to a reorganization of labor in the group. One tablet shows that the group was divided into 11 subgroups: 6 consisted of men only and 5 of women only, sometimes mixed with a few men. It seems clear that these changes are not due to demographics but to decisions made by the administration, which was interested in increasing productivity by establishing a sexual division of labor. In this reorganization of labor, we presume that women and children were separated from fathers. However, there is also nothing to show that the women were the mothers of the boys and girls who worked beside them.

It also appears that the percentage of children is sometimes abnormally low. One text lists a group of Carian goldsmiths: it includes 27 men, 27 women, 13 girls, and 3 boys (PT 37). Even if we assume (without any proof) that these Carians comprised 27 couples, it is no less true that the proportion of boys is inexplicable, because the texts recording the rations given to the mothers indicate that the number of boys born is slightly higher than the number of girls born. We can multiply the examples of imbalance: there was not one girl in a group consisting of 70 men, 95 women, and 20 boys (PF 951); 103 men, 364 women, 122 boys, and 84 girls composed a group from Matezziš (PF 959; cf. 960); 250 men, 220 women, 18 boys, and 32 girls appear in a group of Thracian *kurtaš* (PF 1010); a group of craftsmen on the construction sites of Persepolis in 466 consisted entirely of 501 men (PT 74).

Let us now consider an aberrant (in the statistical sense) case. It concerns the Persian boys (*puhu*), labeled *kurtaš*, who "copied texts" at Pittaman and who in March and November 499 received grain and wine rations at the order of Šuddayauda (PF 871 and

1137). Apparently, these boys or young men were removed from their families and assembled at a location where they learned the rudiments of the scribal trade. We also see that between March and November their number shrank from 29 to 16 and that within the group there was a hierarchy of rations. It is also true that, in the same year in the same place, two tablets record a group reporting to the same officials that consisted only of men and women (PF 903–4). But we must resist the temptation to see these men and women as the fathers and mothers of the Persian *puhu*: the group in fact comprises just one man and four women. And, what happened to the daughters?

Even though the (sole) reference to the wife (*irtiri*) of a *kurtaš* (PF 999[24]) might possibly lead us to believe that marriages were recognized by the administration, the notion of *kurtaš* living in families must be given up entirely. This simple observation offers much toward comprehending their status. It is in fact clear that the administration was not satisfied with just moving the groups of *kurtaš* from one place to another within the territory. In order to increase productivity, it broke family units or forbade their creation (if any were actually recognized by the authorities). The tablets also show that the bond between mother and child was not permanent. While we might suppose that a mother kept her child near her for the first few years—be it only in apprenticeship to a trade—the texts also prove that the children or youths were taken to other groups that could themselves be broken up according to the needs of personnel management, however these needs were defined by the admininstration.

Finally, the overall deficit in youths (both male and female) makes us think that some of them may have been sent to court to be turned into palace slaves—on the model of the Colchians and Babylonians, who every year had to send 100 boys and 100 girls (Colchians) and 500 eunuch boys (Babylonians) to the king (Herodotus III.92, III.97). There can be no doubt that the various departments of the Achaemenid court included a large number of slaves. Furthermore, the category of royal slaves (*arad-šarrūtu*) is well known from the Babylonian texts, which, for example, mention a slave of Cambyses (before his accession); we also know the category of palace slaves (*arad ekalli*). The Akkadian Fortification tablet (Fort. 11786) includes a clause under whose terms the seller attests that the slave he is selling is not a royal slave (or a free citizen or an oblate), a standard clause in this sort of transaction, but it merits special attention because the tablet was composed in Persia.

Family Breakup and Ethnic Uniformity

A final(?) difficulty remains. The presence of several ethnic groups at the same site is well attested: for example, Lycians and Thracians at Rakkan (PF 1946), where we also find Cappadocians (PFa 30). Among the groups of *kurtaš*, a very small number comprise members of different ethnic groups: Lycians and Thracians (PF 1006, 1172, 1823), Lycians and Bactrians (PF 1947), Egyptians and Assyrians (YBC 16813), to which may be added a group of craftsmen at the construction sites at Persepolis, where side by side one finds Ionians, Syrians, and Egyptians (PT 15). In these groups, the rations are divided according to the traditional categories (men, women, boys, and girls), not by ethnic background. Very generally, then, groups of *kurtaš* for which ethnicity is indicated remained homogeneous. It is tempting to conclude that, while the administration separated parents and children, it did not make a parallel attempt to dilute their collective identity. But is ethnicity an absolute criterion for cultural homogeneity? Doubt on this score is not unreasonable.

Based on analyses of communities of foreigners settled in Babylonia, it is generally agreed that these communities maintained considerable internal cohesion, because the Achaemenid authorities recognized their traditional structures and their cultural peculiarities, particularly their religious practices. How was it in Fārs? Examination of tablets concerning rations given to attendants of various religions shows that the Persians permitted the growth of faith in gods other than their own gods—even though the proportion of Persian deities is overwhelming. The attendants of Elamite gods (Humban, Napiriša, Šimut, Napazapa) and Babylonian gods (Adad, KI) also received rations. Sometimes the rations were given "for the gods," without specifically identifying them. In most cases, products were intended for several gods, and it is not unusual to find rations distributed jointly to attendants of Iranian and non-Iranian gods (PF 338–39, 1956). This may indicate that at some locations there were sanctuaries for both.

Sanctuaries honoring Elamite gods are found in many geographical regions; this is easily explained by the antiquity of the Elamite population in Anšan and the activity of Elamite scribes in the chancelleries. They are found especially in the northwest, of course, which amounted to a veritable Elamite enclave, as is confirmed by the use of Elamite month names for dating documents. The distribution of Babylonian gods is very similar, except that they are less frequently attested. It is generally recognized that the record once more illustrates what we may call the religious policy of the Achaemenids, who were careful not to undermine the religious beliefs of their subjects.

On the other hand, we know nothing of the religious practices of the *kurtaš*. One tablet shows that the *kurtaš* could participate in religious festivals (PF 337). It says: "80 BAR of grain, at the disposal of Bakamira. Bakabana, the priest, received this grain and used it for the religious ceremony: 40 BAR for Ahura-Mazda, 40 for the god Mišduši. Then the *kurtaš* ate it. Year 22." But what is the significance of the presence of *kurtaš* at a festival in honor of Persian gods? Were these Persian *kurtaš*? Or were nearby *kurtaš* simply called together to participate in a festival and the distribution of rations that went along with it? We have no references to Greek, Cappadocian, or Syrian gods. Considering the fact that more than 120 (of the published) Fortification tablets are concerned with priests, gods, and services, it is hard to imagine that the absence of gods other than Iranian, Elamite, and Babylonian deities is due to chance. Nor is there any reason to believe that the Persians forbade the *kurtaš* to honor their traditional gods. However, the available evidence strongly suggests that the administration did not provide grain or wine for their sacrifices.

It thus appears justifiable to consider the example of Elamite and Babylonian religious practice a special case. We must also ask: were the Elamite and Babylonian sanctuaries intended for *kurtaš*? The answer is not clear. The existence of homogenous groups of Babylonians in Persia is well documented. As early as Cambyses' reign, there is evidence of businessmen coming to borrow money and trade in slaves at Matezziš (chap. 2/7). The Akkadian Fortification tablet clearly confirms this point. Though written in Persia, it uses the traditional Babylonian model, and the very titulary of Darius is Babylonian: "Darius, king of Babylon, king of the lands" (Fort. 11786). It shows that the Babylonians of Persepolis preserved a certain ethno-cultural homogeneity. It must again be stressed that the Babylonians portrayed in the Akkadian tablets were not administrative workers; they were free men. Some probably came to Persia to look after their businesses; others came and went from Babylonia to Persia to make deals, just as they would go to Ecbatana or Susa.

This was certainly not the case for the great majority of groups of *kurtaš*. Unlike some "Medizing" Greek communities, the Lycians, Cappadocians, and other Syrians did not move voluntarily to Persia, where they clearly had no autonomy within a system that denied them individual and collective liberty. The administration's vocabulary is quite revealing in regard to the Persians' opinion of them: groups of *kurtaš* constituted an undifferentiated labor force that the administration intended to exploit unhindered. All in all, this was a situation much closer to slavery than the "helot" type of rural dependency, a system in which the local peasants (the *laoi* of the Hellenistic inscriptions) continued to live in their villages with their families and continued to own property.

4. Agriculture: Produce and Levies

Baziš and Other Levies

One category of tablets refers to the receipt of sheep and goats, paid as a tax called *baziš* (PF 267–73). The texts include the number of animals, specified according to kind, age, and sex. The name of the administrator responsible for receiving the animals is also given. In several other tablets we can distinguish two people with the same name, Makama, who can be distinguished by their patronymics: one was the son of Nappunda (PF 268); the other, the son of Wuntiš, held office at Pirritukkaš (PF 269–70). The name appears in an account book (PF 2008) that lists the number of animals received by Makama, who reported to Harrena, in years 15 and 16 (507 and 506). He also appears in an account of year 19 (503), where he has the title 'head of the herds' (*kasabattiš*) at Uranduš (PF 2025). There he received 526 animals turned over to him by Raubasa "and his companions." A man named Umizza, a shepherd, received 48. The previous year (504), Umizza, there called royal shepherd at Hiran, was named in a letter sent by "Raubasa and his companions," by order of Parnaka, to persons who are not clearly identified (PF 2070).

In this letter, Raubasa and his companions have the title "payers(?) of the land(?)." For all its (major!) obscurity, there is no doubt that these men were subject to levies. The text also indicates that they were in charge of *bazikara* (*baziš* collectors), whom they sent into various districts. In other documents, the circumstances remain obscure and difficult to interpret. The word *bazikara* appears in two later tablets (466). In one case, a *bazikara* distributes rations to *kurtaš* (PT 54). In another document, some *kurtaš* are called *bazikara* and receive a salary for their services (PT 41). The *bazikara* (Elamite *matira*) received grain, sometimes explicitly designated for "the royal cattle." For instance, it was a *bazikara*, Kaupiya, who in the same year at Hadaran twice set aside the grain intended for "the royal cattle" (PF 1943, PFa 32). Kaupiya was obviously an important member of the livestock-rearing administration, since on several occasions he delivered sheep to high-ranking persons and to the king (PF 663, 678, 696). The size of the rations awarded to him (PF 843, 1323) shows that he was a high-ranking official. Do these references mean that the *bazikara* were in charge of overseeing the royal flocks and herds (above the shepherds) or that *baziš* was also levied on other animal products as well as agricultural products (which would help us interpret Raubasa's title)? It is hard to know.

It should also be observed that in a warehouse account from Kurkarraka, the title of an official, *rušdabaziš*, appears; this title can be understood as 'levier of tax on land' (PF 1968). The levy of grain deducted for him corresponds to $1/10$ of the total. The existence of a tithe is also verified by several tablets referring to wine (PF 1953–54, 1997–2001).

Every year a portion of the warehoused amount was set aside as a "tithe." On one occasion, the word 'tither' (*daθaiya*) is associated with grain, and the administrator concerned was "named by the king" (PF 1942). In another example, a series of tablets (PF 546–653) mentions the collection of produce (grain, wine, fruit, and sesame) levied in the villages and collected in a warehouse before being transferred to another warehouse probably located in the heart of the district. Part of these levies ($\frac{1}{10}$ for barley, $\frac{1}{30}$ for sesame) was then set aside for seed or for animal feed. Finally, one series of tablets (PF 48–49, 388–96, 428) records the transportation and delivery of various products (wine, various kinds of grain, and sesame). The word for their destination is *ukpiyataš* (*upa-yata*), which refers to payments in kind; in Babylonia there also was a tax called 'transportation of payments in kind' (*zebēlu ša upiyāta*), probably intended for the king's table. On one occasion, the text is a little more specific: "300 BAR of grain-*tarmu*, at the disposal of Babena, received by Manna-Kitin in his capacity of(?) royal *ukpiyataš*. Year 28. He made beer from this grain" (PF 428).

The Levy of Animal *baziš*

Taken in conjunction with other accounts of sheep and goats (PF 2007–12), the documents listing the animal *baziš* invite us to attempt a reconstruction of the various ways that animals were levied, despite major uncertainties that cannot be resolved. The clearest (or least obscure!) text is the previously mentioned letter from Raubasa and his companions (PF 2070) that lists the *baziš* collected in the district of Hiran. It seems that Umizza, the shepherd "who lives in Hiran," was required to collect 48 head of sheep and goats that were entrusted to him by Raubasa. Whatever the case, it is remarkable that the following year he received the same number of animals that Raubasa and his companions had previously entrusted to him (PF 2025). Only the proportion of males and females changed. This seems to imply that each district was assessed the same number of animals each year. Four individuals—including a woman—paid 5, 5, 8, and 9 sheep and goats, respectively: they were attached to (dependents of?) the 'estate' (*irmatam*) of Miturna (Gk. Hydarnes). Two other persons paid 15 and 6 animals: one was a treasury worker (*kapnuški*; from Hiran?); the other was called a "*kurtaš* of the king." It thus seems that sheep and goats were paid as *baziš* 'tribute' each year. Part of the total received was consigned to shepherds (e.g., Umizza) and part to the 'head of herds' (*kasabattiš*) of the district (e.g., Makema). Some animals could be sent to Harrena, the head *kasabattiš* (PF 271). They could be moved long distances, since two tablets mention the transportation of *baziš* to Susa (PF 57, 1495). According to the second tablet, 32 men received travel rations for this purpose: by order of Bakabaduš, they transferred Undana's *baziš* to Susa. These two officials are attested elsewhere as administrators in charge of sheep and goats (PF 62–66). Both were in charge of sheep and goats sent to treasuries.

In fact, another series of tablets (PF 58–77) records the delivery of skins (primarily sheep and goat, but also camel) to treasuries, where they were processed. In the accounts, these are the animals that are listed separately before being slaughtered on site. The hides were then sent to the treasuries under the supervision of officials. Wool probably also came from this source, to be worked by *kurtaš* specialists. The animals that remained alive were raised on the spot by *kurtaš* (cf. PF 848, 1142). The existence of *kurtaš* shepherds is actually attested in several Treasury tablets, which mention two groups: one with more than 370 individuals (men, women, boys, and girls) and the other with 131 (PT 50, 61; cf. PT 1963: 13). Shepherds (*batera*) are also mentioned here and there in the Fortification tablets. We also know of Lycian shepherds who were working near Persepolis when Alexander arrived. We may note that the management of other fauna, such as cattle (PF 2085–86) or fowl (PF 1721), followed the same pattern. The accounts of the Barniš station in particular show that cattle were also divided into various groups: those to be slaughtered, those to be kept alive on the spot, and those to be entrusted to shepherds (*batera*; PF 2013; cf. 1947, 2085, 2087).

The Akkadian Treasury tablet gives us a handle on the extent of the gaps in evidence and on the extent of our ignorance (PT 85). In this text, in fact, we can see that, after the end of 502, a tax (*mandattu*) was paid in weighed silver by three people: (1) a woman named Indukka, mother of Tutu, 'head merchant' (*tamkāru*); (2) Pattemidu the Mede, "son of the shepherd"; and (3) N, "shepherd." In some tablets, the word *baziš* is replaced by the Akkadian word *mandattu*, which in general designates a mandatory tribute assessment. We know that this is also the word used by Aršāma—along with the word for treasury (*ganza)—for the amount of "taxes/fees" levied on his Egyptian estates and the estates of two other Persian nobles (*DAE* 71–72 [AD 10–11]). In the Behistun inscription, *mandattu* is the translation for *baziš*. Of course, *mandattu* and *baziš* are semantically too flexible for us to conclude that Pattemidu and the anonymous shepherd settled the animal *baziš* tax in weighed silver. In any case, PT 85 at least proves that, at Persepolis in 502, two different professional categories—including one or two shepherds—paid their taxes in siculi of weighed silver—a fact that cannot be gleaned from any of the Elamite Fortification tablets.

The Direct Producers

Because of its allusive character, the documentation does not answer an outstanding, haunting question: who paid these different taxes? That is, who grew the produce?

The first thing that needs to be said is that—aside from the shepherds (above)—there are very few explicit references to *kurtaš* dedicated to working the land, although there must have been many in the fields and farms. Since, for example, *kurtaš* received seed from the administration several times (PF 123, 463, 484, 508), we can conclude that they were farmers. There can no longer be any doubt that the labor of cultivation in the paradises required a considerable workforce (PFa 33). But the word 'farmer' itself is absent or not yet recognized in the record. The references to 'nurserymen' (*maršaparra*) or 'irrigation specialists' remain hypothetical or even seriously disputed, since the second of these words is sometimes understood as 'spinner/weaver'. Some Aramaic glosses provide complementary details. In one tablet (PF 855), rations were distributed to *kurtaš* called *pirrasanaš*: the Aramaic inscription says "rations for millers." The reason for this surprising lack of references to farmers is not easy to determine. Perhaps the agricultural workers lived off part of the harvest and so did not receive rations, or at least the rations were not recorded by the administration. On the other hand, the situation was different for the *kurtaš* who worked at processing agricultural products: winemakers, brewers, millers, oil-pressers, bakers(?), and those who were used in the warehouses or to transport the products from place to place, as well as those who worked in the bureaucracy (accountants, scribes, etc.).

In any case, the *kurtaš* were certainly not the only people working the land. Persian peasants are in fact portrayed several times by the Classical authors, unfortunately in references that are quite indirect. Among the reforms attributed to "Cyrus," Xenophon describes the establishment of a corps of 10,000 lancers in the royal guard; according to

Xenophon (*Cyr.* VII.5.67), Cyrus chose Persians who lived in abject poverty; Xenophon calls them *autourgoi*, that is, farmers working their own small parcels. This is also the word used by Aelian (*VH* I.31). These peasants are sometimes mentioned by name (Sinetes, Omises, Rhakokes); they worked hard (I.31) in their gardens (*paradeisoi*) and farms (*epauleis*; I.32). They raised animals (cattle, sheep) and cultivated wheat and the vine, fruit (I.31–32) and vegetables (lettuce: I.34). This is obviously the social class Xenophon's Pheraulas comes from. His father was a poor peasant, forced to borrow seed in the difficult gap between two harvests (*Cyr.* VIII.3.36–38).

The importance of these texts, however, is in providing a concrete picture of a little-known segment of the population, namely, free smallholders, since the entirety of the documentation from Persepolis leads us to suppose that the land was worked entirely by the *kurtaš*. But what possible relationship to the information found in the tablets can be discovered? We might, for example, contrast the case of Pheraulas's father with the *kurtaš* who received seed from the administration (PF 123, 463, 484, 508). However, what is the informational value of the rags-to-riches tale of Pheraulas? We know, again from Aelian, that the Persian smallholders were required to give gifts to the Great King when he crossed Persia (*VH* I.31–32). Is it possible that the recently proposed meaning 'gift' for *nutanuyaš/nadānu* allows us to understand Aelian?

It has also been proposed that the growers entered into a farming contract with the administration each year. They kept and fed the animals entrusted to them and in return kept part of the increase. But it must be noted that no such system is set forth in the documentation available to us. All we have is two accounts (PF 2010–11) that give lists of persons (12 and 22). Some of these people's names are found in other documents, where they are clearly labeled administrators. One of these was Mannuka, who in 493 was responsible for the flour paid for tanning work. To be sure, the potential for men with the same name counsels caution. But do these data really have to do with free smallholders? According to this theory, the boundary between the produce of farmers or landowners and the produce raised on lands controlled directly by the administration is not clear. Did the agricultural *kurtaš* simply have to pay part of their produce, keeping a fixed percentage for themselves?

In sum, the uncertainties remain so great because we do not know the answer to a basic question: can all of the assessments that can be identified in the tablets be considered fiscal levies (whether they are called tribute or not, which remains a subsidiary discussion)? Indeed, this question raises another, which is also very important, of the status of lands and persons in the Persian countryside. The observations presented above represent only partial answers, which now must be considered more systematically.

5. Lands and Estates

Partetaš

Despite the stress placed on agricultural and animal produce, the tablets hardly ever refer explicitly to the soil—apart from a few (uncertain) references to pastureland. Nonetheless, three words deserve special attention: *partetaš*, *irmatam*, and *ulhi*. There can no longer be any doubt that the *partetaš* corresponds precisely to what the Greek authors meant by "paradise," which in turn is clearly a loanword from Persian (**paradaida*). The criticisms that had been leveled against this interpretation were based on the belief that the Persian paradises were solely hunting preserves. However, the Classical sources prove indubitably that paradise use was much more varied. Paradises also included plantations and farmlands, especially produce gardens and orchards. For Xenophon, the paradise was a specific kind of garden (*kēpos*; *Oec.* IV.13). The notion of gardens/fields is what Aelian means by the word (*VH* I.32), referring to small holdings in Persia proper, and it is the meaning of "market gardens" that the Greeks retroject to the Hellenistic period. At any rate, this is the sense of the word in a Greek inscription from Sardis, of Achaemenid origin (*Sardis* VII.1.1), that records the various components of a "gift estate" (*dōrea*).

Favorable locations were chosen for the *partetaš*: , in particular, places with running water—rivers and springs. Several parts of Persia offer these features. Following Nearchus, Strabo (XV.3.1) and Arrian (*Ind.* 40.2–5) divided Persia into three major climatic and ecological regions. The Persian Gulf coast was described as "sandy and sterile owing to the heat." The northern mountainous zone was "wintry and snowy." In contrast, Arrian emphasized the fertility of the central zone, what Strabo called Coele-Persis, which he placed in the neighborhood of Pasargadae (XV.3.6):

> The country is grassy with water meadows, many vines and all other fruits except the olive; it is rich with all sorts of gardens (*paradeisoi*), has pure rivers flowing through and lakes, and is good for all sorts of birds that haunt rivers and lakes, and for horses; it provides pasture for the other domestic animals, is well wooded, and has plenty of game. (Arrian, *Ind.* 40.3–4◊)

Quintus Curtius described the Persepolis area as "a spacious plain . . . , a fertile land, and abounding in many villages and cities," watered by the Araxes, edged with "plane trees also and poplars," "and the soil was very rich and abounded in fodder" (V.4.6–7, 20◊).

This was also true of the region of Fahliyun, within Persia and Susiana. The eyewitnesses (of Alexander's time and later) have left enthusiastic descriptions: "Rich, watered by numerous streams, and productive of many fruits of all kinds" (Diodorus XVII.67.3◊). After describing the road between Susiana and Persia as "steep-sided, sunscorched, offering no respite," Diodorus of Sicily notes the sudden change that welcomes the traveler entering the Fahliyun basin.

> [The second part of the road] was over high land, blessed with a very healthful climate and full of the fruits appropriate to the season. For there were glens heavily overgrown and shady, cultivated trees of various kinds in paradises, also natural converging glades full of trees of every sort and streams of water, so that travellers lingered with delight in places pleasantly inviting repose. Also there was an abundance of cattle of every kind. . . . In density of population, too, this country far surpassed the other satrapies. (XIX.21.2–3◊)

There can be no doubt that such a paradise was the location for an Achaemenid-period pavilion that has been discovered in the Fahliyun region. It was also in paradises that the king and court very often halted during their relocations (e.g., Plutarch, *Art.* 25.1). Of course, the fertility of these paradises also relied on hydraulic installations such as have been uncovered by archaeologists in the paradise near Pasargadae. We even know that Cyrus's tomb was so equipped: "A grove had been planted round [the paradise] with all sorts of trees and irrigated, and deep grass had grown in the meadow" (Arrian, *Anab.* VI.29.4◊). Achaemenid-period canals and reservoirs have also been discovered in the Persepolis plain.

One Fortification tablet (PFa 33) is particularly illuminating. It is an inventory (referring to seed?) of 6,166 fruit trees (quince, pear, apple, date, mulberry, etc.) that were to be planted in three paradises close to Persepolis. Two other texts (PF 1946, PT 38) apparently refer to *kurtaš* whose job was "guarding trees" (cf. also PT 49 and 1963: 9). Another tablet (PF 1815) mentions rations to be given to four *kurtaš* whose job had to do with trees in a paradise near Persepolis. The paradises were also potential sources of lumber (cf. esp. Plutarch, *Art.* 25.1–2), which was especially impressive in lands such as Babylonia that had no forests (Strabo XVI.1.5, 11).

Aside from these occurrences (which are the easiest to interpret), the word *partetaš* reappears in a series of 15 tablets (PF 144–58). Some of the paradises named in these tablets seem to be located in the Persepolis area, one of them at Nupistaš (Naqš-i Rustam?). But the tablets deal only with administrative matters, not with estate management. They are actually records of storage of several products: various fruits, dates, figs, and grain-*tarmu* were placed in the care of an administrator for later distribution (as rations) on orders to be received by the distributor (sometimes explicitly named). We may note that on ten occasions the products are called royal (*sunkina*). But this point is difficult to interpret, because the adjective "royal" is not used systematically; it appears to modify less the storage depot than the origin of the products collected—which for that matter represents another problem (chap. 11/10 below). From this elliptical record, it seems likely that the administration of the paradises—which must have had a specific manager, in Persia as in other regions—was included in the general management of produce that circulated between different administrative levels and different districts; in this respect, then, paradise administration functioned as just another branch of government, at least under certain conditions.

Irmatam

The second category of "estate," the *irmatam*, poses more difficult problems. We are not certain of the Old Persian equivalent. In the Elamite version of the Behistun inscription, the word appears in connection with Vivāna, who was said to "perform the function of satrap in Arachosia" (*DB* §47). In the great revolts of 522, Vivāna won a battle with the rebels near the fortress of Aršādā in Arachosia, and this fortress is called Vivāna's *irmatam*. This usage is difficult to interpret, for two reasons. First, there is no equivalent for this phrase in the Old Persian version, which has nothing but 'fortress' (*didā*), as in the Akkadian version (*birtu*). It is also hard to determine, from all the evidence, just what the Elamite writer had in mind. Given that in the tablets from Susa from the time before Achaemenid dominion the word *irmatam* referred to a kind of "estate" (in a vague sense) and that the word appears to be borrowed from Old Persian in the first place, there is no reason to think that its meaning would be any different in the Behistun inscription. But if so, why would the Persian version have the word *didā*? And what was the relationship between a fortress and an *irmatam* in a satrapy in 522? It is possible that, as in the Persepolis tablets, the word 'fortress' (Elam. *halmarriš*) refers to both a military headquarters and an established administrative center, something like a county seat that collected the produce of the surrounding region. If the satrap Vivāna held an "estate" there, we can understand why the rebels would have made it the prime objective of their offensive. The text also makes it clear that these estates existed before the reign of Darius, a fact that could not be known for certain from the Susa tablets.

The word appears in 30 Fortification tablets (9 of them unpublished). Each time, it is associated with a person's name: the *irmatam* of Ištimanka, of Irtuppiya, of Dayaka, of

Mišparma, etc. In most cases, the texts record the deposit of merchandise in an *irmatam* (PF 2079), or the *irmatam* is at the disposal (*kurmin*) of a specific administrator. These products are 'set aside' (*nutika*; e.g., PF 1857) before being distributed in ration form by a distributor, who is also named (PF 331, 1256, 1892). These rations can be distributed to *kurtaš* (1368, 1802) or to animals (331: camels), sometimes on sealed orders of the king (PF 1256). On one occasion, one of these estates is called simply "the one where Iršena, the head of the *kurtaš* (*kurdabattiš*), is the organizer/distributor (*šaramana*)" (PF 1368). The same tablet also shows that the estate in question served as a stopping-place for troops of *kurtaš* who were being moved from one place to another; they received travel rations for one day.

From this perspective, the *irmatam* are included within the general administration, just like the *partetaš*. Both served as collection, storage, and distribution centers for local produce. In addition, *irmatam* and paradises are sometimes associated. In six tablets (PF 150–55) dated to year 22 (500), the destination of grain deposited in some paradises is given as follows: "To be used in the *irmatam* of Šutezza." Two of these tablets can be connected with three others that are included in the series concerning levies on agricultural products of the nearby villages or farms (PF 152/640–41, 153/637). In these tablets Šutezza appears to be in charge of produce that was collected around Mutrizaš (PF 640) or Šaurakkaš (PF 641) and stored in the paradises of Mutrizaš and Kutkuš. At Kutkuš, Šutezza again was in charge of the grain set aside for seed (PF 520–21).

Nevertheless, there is no doubt that the *irmatam* were also agricultural estates. Most were located in the central region, near paradises, which implies that they had been carved out of fertile, irrigated land. We are led to suppose that they were granted by the king to administrators. They were thus perquisites, including the one Vivāna had been granted in Arachosia because he was satrap. Given all these factors, the gift can hardly be considered entirely free. The concessionaires were not free of obligation to the administration; they were mere cogs in the machinery. In some inventories, the *irmatam* are located in a district (*batin*) and near villages (*humanuš*). The structure of the text on one tablet (PF 1857) seems to imply that they were also accounted as financial units by the administration. This tablet also indicates that the concessionaires of "estates" were required to turn over part of their produce (grain in this instance) to the administration's warehouse. Another tablet (PF 2070) concerning the levying of *baziš* confirms that these estates did not enjoy any sort of financial immunity: four "taxpayers" are actually referred to as "being at the *irmatam* of Miturna(?)," who himself carried out official tasks; this may be why he had this estate.

Ulhi

The third word is *ulhi*. In the royal inscriptions, *ulhi* corresponds to Old Persian *viθ* and Akkadian *bītu*, two synonyms that can be translated 'house', which is less a building than the ensemble of people who live and work on an "estate," which includes lands and various kinds of farms and which is headed by the master of the house. This is exactly the sense of the word in §16 of the Behistun inscription: where the Old Persian has *viθ*, the Elamite has *ulhi*. In his prayers to Ahura-Mazda (cf. *DNa* §6, *DPe*), Darius beseeches the god to protect him and the people of Persia (*dahyu*) and his house (*viθ*). And certain decorative elements in the palace (window frames, door hinges) bear the inscription "Made in the house (*viθ*) of the king" (*DPc, DPi, A¹I*). The word corresponds exactly to Greek *oikos*, which is what the Greek texts frequently call the Persian royal house (e.g., ML 12). It also appears in this meaning in several Persepolis tablets. In 506, Parnaka, under orders from King Darius, sent the following order to Harrena, head of the flock department: "Give Irtašduna, the princess, 100 sheep [to be taken] from my house" (*ulhi*; Fort. 6764). In another tablet (PF 1987[30–32]), sheep are transferred to the royal house (*ulhi sunkina*) and entrusted to the care of a shepherd.

Other people operated in an estate referred to as an *ulhi*. This was the case for Irtašduna, one of Darius's wives, known to Herodotus as Artystone, who had two of this kind of estate, at Mirandu and Kuknaka (PF 1835–37), and also for Arsames, a son of Darius (unpublished tablet), and also for a woman called Irdabama, who held an *ulhi* at Šullake (PFa 27). It is likely that Irtašduna also held interests near the village of Matannan, where she sent a letter requesting a supply of grain (PF 1857). Twice grain was apparently set aside at her request (PF 166 and 168). In the second example, the organizer (*šaramana*) is named Šalamana; this was probably the same person who transmitted Artystone's orders for the delivery of produce "taken from her *ulhi*" on three separate occasions (PF 1836–38). Two other individuals had this kind of estate: Rammanuya (PF 1855) and perhaps Naktanna(?; PF 2075). Unfortunately, we know nothing of their circumstances. In every case, these estates appear in letters in which the master or mistress of the *ulhi* orders the delivery of a certain amount of produce to a particular person, specifying that they were to take the grain or wine "from my *ulhi*." One letter from Irdabama is addressed to accountants (PFa 27), and one from Artystone expects rations for her accountant Kamšabana (PF 1837). Physically, the agricultural estates connected to an *ulhi* cannot have been different from an *irmatam* or a paradise. The terminological distinction may not be random, however, since members of the royal family never receive an *irmatam* but always an *ulhi*. But this observation—which may be overturned by the publication of additional tablets—does not help explain the actual difference in status. In the village of Matannan, it even appears as though some of the produce was paid to the administration on Artystone's orders (PF 1857).

The house of the princesses included much more than farms. They obviously had a personal retinue and a sizable staff. Evidence for this is the large quantities of foodstuffs placed at their disposal for travel (PF 730–39, 2019, 2035). The same was true for other royal princesses (PFa 5), who doubtless also headed houses. Arsames is named in these contexts, along with Artystone (PF 733–34, 2035). He also had horses (PFa 24, 29[10]). Furthermore, several tablets list the payment of rations to *kurtaš*, who are called *kurtaš* of Artystone or Irdabama (PF 1236, 1454; 849, 1002, 1028–29, 1041–43, 1098, 1109, 1198, 1221, 1232). These documents are problematic, because they do not make clear the relationship between the princesses and these workers, who do not seem to be distinguished from other identical groups. They work in a specific place (Shiraz, for example); they perform the same labor (for example, the women-*pašap* of Artystone: PF 1236). It is possible that these *kurtaš* were generally attached to the administration but that their services may have been required by the beneficiaries of the temporary assignment. On the other hand, members of the royal family surely also had subordinates who were permanently assigned to work in their house, such as the person "attached to the house (*viθ*) of Hystaspes," father of Darius (PF 1596), who may be compared with the people attached to the royal *viθ*, among whom were included personnel holding important positions in the palace economy (PF 1946[73–77]).

6. The Persepolis Tablets and the Imperial Administration: Sources and Problems

After reconstructing the organization of labor and production in Fārs, especially in the time of Darius, a basic problem remains. Should the picture derived from the tablets be confined to Persia proper, or can it be extended to all (or to some parts) of the Empire, albeit taking into account local circumstances? Or, in other words, does the Persepolis documentation specifically reflect, however mechanically, organizational peculiarities of Persia proper only? Let us stress from the start that the question has a decisive importance: from the answer two contradictory pictures of the Achaemenid Empire follow. One picture reveals a very lax organization of countries that continued to carry on according to their traditional ways, without any impact of Persian dominion detectable. The other—the so-called "hard" view—turns the Achaemenid Empire into an imperial construct in the fullest sense—that is, a State within which the conquerors established and unified rules of administrative organization and economic exploitation that, without a head-on assault on local traditions, nevertheless infiltrated them from within and modified them profoundly, at least in several key ways that permitted the dominant socioethnic class to enjoy hegemony in alliance with the local aristocracies.

Let us begin by dismissing a fallacious argument based on the narrowness of the chronological and spatial extent of the tablets (chap. 11/1 above). The dating of the tablets (between 509 and 458) does not in the slightest imply that the administrative organization known in Darius's time suddenly vanished in the seventh year of Artaxerxes I, nor, of course, that it was not in place before 509. For reasons already given, it is clear that we have only a tiny sample of a mass of documentation that must have been enormous. As for the geographic range of the tablets, here too we must beware of the vagaries of preservation. First of all, it cannot be denied that there were archival deposits in every satrapal territory. Herodotus inserts this detail, as an aside, regarding the secretary of Oroetes: "an officer who forms part of every governor's establishment (*grammatistai basileioi*" (III.128◊). Xenophon also alludes to this institution when he mentions the presence of Megaphernes, a "royal scribe," in Cyrus the Younger's service (*phoinikistēs basileios; Anab.* I.2.20). In Babylonian, biblical, and Egyptian documents, we also find exalted persons in the satrapal administration bearing the titles (sometimes multiple) *bēl ṭēmi* and *sipīru*, that is, 'chancellor' and 'scribe'. It is thus very clear that all the satrapal chancelleries were organized on the same model and that they were responsible for dispatching letters and orders and receiving and preserving letters from the royal chancellery.

It is true that no satrapal archive in the strict sense has been found intact and complete. This gap is due first to the chances of discovery but also and especially to the perishability of the commonly used materials (papyrus, parchment, wooden tablets coated with wax). An episode from the *Life of Eumenes* (2.6–7) very concretely attests to the fragility of these archives: after the destruction of Alexander's tent by fire, "the king wrote to all the satraps and *strategoi* to send copies of the destroyed documents, which were all collected, following his orders, by Eumenes." And at Dascylium, satrapy of Hellespontine Phrygia, a group of bullas bearing cuneiform and Aramaic inscriptions and sealings has been found. Some of them are written in the name of Xerxes. The impressions left by papyrus and thread attest to the existence of letters and documents written on parchment or papyrus deposited in the satrapal archives; only the clay envelopes (the bullas) have survived to this day.

The spatial extent of the tablets is considerably widened by Category Q (travel rations), which covers all the imperial territories. The very operation of the system implies that the archives associated with warehouses that supplied the road network were numerous throughout every satrapy. But it is likely that many items were recorded on papyrus or parchment. It was the same for the travel voucher given by Aršāma to his steward Neḥtiḥōr when he sent him to Egypt (*DAE* 67 [AD 6])—and the relationship of this text with the tablets of Category Q has long been recognized. Other documents, such as the Aramaic ostraca of Arad, confirm—if there were any need—that the organization of travel on the royal roads relied on a unified imperial system. Elsewhere, though exceptional, several discoveries are noteworthy, in particular an Elamite tablet from Susa, another from Kandahār, others in Armenia(?). Paradoxically, the random character of these finds testifies to the fact that they are representative (cf. chap. 16/18).

It is thus possible that the specificity of the Persepolis documentation does not imply that the bureaucratic organization of production was limited to Persia or to the Persepolis–Susa axis. Obviously, this remains to be proved, on the basis of better-assembled regional corpora. It would in fact be bad methodology to extend mechanically any analysis drawn from the tablets to the entire Empire. The reason is not simply that Persia and the Persians constituted a country-people (*dahyu*) with an out-of-the-ordinary political and ideological status. It is also because, on some points, the interpretations of the tablets are burdened with a degree of uncertainty. Under these conditions, to be grounded, any extension of the results of analyzing the tablets must come from comparison with other documents that are themselves unequivocal.

7. The Management of Property and the Royal Warehouses in Egypt

Egypt's very arid climate means that only its documentary record is comparable to that of Persepolis. In addition to a quantity of letters on papyrus or skin from the archives of the satrap Aršāma, we have several official letters attesting to the minutiae of the satrapal administration, especially concerning the receipt and disbursement of products that require the existence of warehouses. We will illustrate this topic through five documents. Some of them are late (reign of Darius II), but all of them allow us to imagine that the organization they depict goes back at least to the reign of Darius I.

The Resupplying of the Garrison of Syene–Elephantine

The first document is a demotic papyrus from the last year of Darius I (486; *P. Loeb* 1). It states that the Egyptian Khnumemash, son of Horwenmefer, had been instructed along with the Persian Artaban to seek out commodities, especially wheat, in the mountainous region (*jebel*). The grain was to be stored, probably at Syene, in the house of the man who had given the order, another Egyptian, Osoreris. The letter of claim/complaint is addressed to Parnu, "chargé of the southern district," who was Osoreris's immediate superior. We can imagine that Khnumemash was an Egyptian boatman and that he worked for the administrators responsible for feeding the soldiers of Syene–Elephantine, under the direction of Parnu.

The resupplying of the garrison is also the topic of an Aramaic document (*DAE* 54 [AP 2]) dated to year 2 of Xerxes (484). Two people with Jewish names, Hōsea and Aḥi'ab, received commodities (barley and lentils) directly from an Egyptian named Espemet, "servant(?)" of the commander Hananī—commodities that he was ordered to transport by boat to Elephantine. The barley and lentils were intended as rations for the soldier-colonists: 22 soldiers belonging to two different military units (centuries). Hōsea and Aḥiʾab were instructed in Espemet's presence to deliver the commodities "before the officials of the house of the king and before the scribes of the warehouse"; it was the responsibility of the latter to organize the division among the 22 garrisoneers envisioned by the document. The document is authenticated by numerous named witnesses and also specifies the amount of individual rations and the total of commodities received: 32.38 hl, of which 6.16 hl was lentils. The warehouse scribes were to repay the cost to Espemet. In the corresponding case, Hōsea and Aḥiʾab undertook to pay Espemet 100 karš of refined silver. As a deposit, they put up as collateral the salary they received from the house of the king as well as their houses and property, which, if there were a default, Espemet would have the right to seize. We thus see that in Egypt the various ranks of the hierarchy were personally responsible for the goods in their charge: in case of loss or theft, they had to repay the value out of their own pocket.

Another document (*DAE* 55 [*AP* 24❖]) permits a better understanding of the procedure, although it comes from a later period (May 419). It concerns the accounts of the garrison of Syene–Elephantine. The scribes and accountants summarized the total of rations distributed to the soldiers of Syene and Elephantine in one year. The barley in question came from various locations, from the province of Thebes and the southern district (of which Elephantine was the capital). It had been brought to Syene through the efforts of several people with Egyptian names, probably boatmen whose status was analogous to that of Espemet or Peteisis, another boatman known from an Egyptian scal. Part of the cargo was deposited in the granary; the rest was distributed to soldiers of the garrison as food rations (*ptp*). As far as we can reconstruct, the traffic in goods was thus handled at Syene in a manner clearly similar to the process reflected in the Persepolis tablets. The document under consideration is very like general accounts prepared at Persepolis. A fourth document, moreover, indicates that the local administrators—the scribes—were required to send " each item month by month" to Memphis (*DAE* 60 [*AP* 17❖]). The local administrators were reimbursed by the central office in Memphis on the basis of this document. Inspectors (*azdakara*) were responsible for overseeing the regular ration distribution procedure on the spot.

The Repair of an Administration Boat

The fifth document (*DAE* 61 [*AP* 26❖]) is an especially rich illustration of the bureaucratic nature of the satrapal administration. Dated 411, it concerns the repair of a boat. The boat was operated by two Egyptians, Psamsineith and another boatman whose name is not preserved, both of whom have the title "boatmen of the fortifications"—the latter word referring to Syene and Elephantine. The boatmen are not the boat-owners: they have "charge of it" in the same way that the soldier-colonists have "charge" of land. The boat thus belonged to the administration. The Egyptian boatmen use it for official business, such as transporting foodstuffs to Syene, a service for which they receive payment.

We also note that at this time Psamsineith and his partner's boat was in need of repair: its deckwork needed to be entirely replaced. The work could only take place in an administration dockyard, at Elephantine, and to this end the managers had to commit to expenses that in the last analysis could only be authorized by the satrap Aršāma. This was the reason the letter was sent by Aršāma to the Egyptian Wahpreʾmahi, who seems to have been responsible for the management of materials at the Elephantine navy yard. But the final decision was preceded by a voluminous exchange of letters and orders between Syene and Memphis. First of all, Psamsineith and his partner had sought out their immediate superior, the Persian Mithradāta, who had the (Persian) title *nav-pati*, or head sailor; he had authority over the numerous boatmen in his district. They had informed Mithradāta of the state of disrepair of their craft. After an initial inspection of the boat, which had run aground "in front of the fortress," a report had been sent to Aršāma by Mithradāta's boss. But, before authorizing the repair, the satrap required an inspection to be made and a very detailed estimate drawn up. These operations had to be carried out jointly by the treasury accountants (*ganza*), the "foremen" (*framanakara*; Šamašillek and his colleagues), and the head carpenter in charge of the district, an Egyptian called Šamaw, son of Konūfi.

After the inspection of the boat—carried out in the presence of Mithradāta and the two boatmen—a very precise estimate was communicated to the office in Memphis. Thereupon, the satrapal office sent an order to Wahpre'mahi authorizing him to furnish the materials to the head carpenter Šamaw: the number and quality of wooden boards needed for the repair of different parts of the boat are listed, as well as other supplies (sails, bronze plates, etc.)—even the number of nails: 425 bronze nails for the gunwale, 200 for attaching metal elements. Additionally, they were required to provide arsenic and sulfur, whose weight would be calculated "according to the standard weight of Persia." It was also specified that, in exchange for the new wood, "they shall bring to the treasury the used wood and broken (boards)." This detail bespeaks the rarity of wood in Egypt. The text also indicates that among the boards provided to the carpenter were "used pine boards." But it also shows that the administration would not allow the waste of any items that were its property; for example, they did not want the boatmen (or the shipyard workers) to resell the used boards for their own profit! There is no doubt that, upon completion of the repairs, the administration in Memphis required from Wahpre'mahi an equally detailed written proof of the use of the materials. This implies yet another inspection of the boat by the head carpenter and the treasury accountants; it was up to them to determine whether the administration warehouses should receive back any unused nails! And this entire bureaucratic apparatus was deployed for a total expense of not more than one talent ten minas!

Royal Dockyards and Workshops

Other dockyards are known in Egypt, particularly the dockyard in Memphis, which is attested in an Aramaic document that unfortunately is poorly preserved. It is called "house of boats." The text itself is a sort of journal in which the movements of the personnel are minutely recorded. The personnel are multi-ethnic and, as at the Elephantine colony, the dockyard workers are grouped in "thousands" (*dgalîn*), which were perhaps in turn divided into centuries (as at Persepolis). One of these thousands reported to an Iranian, Bagapāta. As it stands, the document supplies no direct information on the status of the workers garrisoned in the Memphis dockyard. There is nothing that permits us to equate them with the *kurtaš* of Persepolis, though this theory is attractive. Nor do we know anything of their actual relationship with the military *dgalîn* attested at Memphis in more recently published papyri.

The existence of royal workshops in Egypt is strongly implied by the discovery, at Susa in particular, of many aragonite vases with hieroglyphic inscriptions with the names of Darius, Xerxes, and Artaxerxes I, in a simple form "Xerxes Great King" or a more elaborate form, such as "King of Upper and Lower Egypt, Lord of the Two Lands,

Darius, may he live forever." The vases of Xerxes and Artaxerxes have a quadrilingual text (Persian, Elamite, Babylonian, and Egyptian). Several of these vases are dated by regnal year. Two of them indicate the contents in Egyptian measures. It is virtually certain that these vases were made in Egyptian workshops and sent to the central court. Perhaps the manufacturing process was organized in Egypt after the pattern of the Persepolis workshops that specialized in stone vessels (chap. 11/3 above). Royal stone tableware has also been found at Persepolis. The inscribed objects bear the name of Xerxes exclusively, in four languages. Their shape and the engraving of the inscriptions are very similar to earlier Egyptian vases. But it is difficult to say whether they were made in Egypt, rather than in Persepolis by Egyptian craftsmen.

Manufacture of weapons is known in Memphis already during pharaonic times. Vases inscribed with the names of Psammetichus and Amasis have been found at Persepolis, part of the booty seized by Cambyses. They are very like the vases dated to the time of Darius and his successors. Shipyards are also very well attested in pharaonic Egypt. The boatyards were controlled by the "master of the shipping," whose duties and powers were assumed by the satrap of Egypt. Nonetheless, the obvious continuity must not cause us to lose sight of the innovations introduced by the Persians. The abundance of Persian-origin administrative terminology in the Aramaic texts provides specific evidence of this; the meaning of these terms can often be recovered by comparison with the Persepolis tablet lexicon. The treasury (**ganza*) named in the papyri seems to operate in a fashion identical to that of the treasuries found in Persia. It can be referred to with the terms "warehouse," "king's warehouse," or "king's house." In each case, it includes both a treasury proper and warehouses, since the military received salaries in silver (*prs*) as well as rations in kind (*ptp*). The treasury is where the reserves are deposited, "before the authorities of Government House and before the clerks of the treasury" (*DAE* 54 [*AP* 2✧]). This provides us with an illustration of a procedure well known in Persepolis, where the produce is "at the disposal" (*kurmin*) of an official, who then provides it to the official in charge of distribution (*šaramana*).

Titles well attested at Persepolis are also found. At Elephantine, the disbursement from the warehouse of the materials needed for repairing the boat is authorized by officials who bear the Persian title **hamarakara*, a title also found in the texts from Persepolis and in Akkadian documents. These officials are simultaneously archivists and accountants who according to the Treasury tablets are in charge of groups of *kurtaš*. Among the officials responsible for drawing up the estimate (also a Persian word) were Šamašillek and his colleagues, who bear the title *framanakara* 'foremen'—a term that also appears in the Persepolis materials. Analysis of the documents shows that these borrowings are not only linguistic; they relate to an identical organization for managing produce and its distribution among the warehouses and treasuries.

8. *Management of Surpluses*

Back to Pseudo-Aristotle

At this point, a parallel with another source is inescapable: the *Oeconomica* of Pseudo-Aristotle. When the Treasury tablets were published by G. G. Cameron in 1948, one of the first reviewers (F. Altheim)—soon followed by Cameron himself—pointed out the similarities between Pseudo-Aristotle's analysis and the practices of the administration in Persepolis. The proposed comparisons deal with the payment of rations in silver to the *kurtaš*, interpreted in light of an expression in the *Oeconomica*. We will soon come back to this passage. Let us simply note that it is included within a broader discussion of the royal economy, which embraced four sectors: "coinage, exports, imports, and expenditure" (II.1.3✧). At this point, the author refers very tersely to the management of surpluses in kind generated by the assessments imposed by the administration. The Persepolis tablets, especially the Fortification tablets, provide both a striking confirmation and a precise commentary on Pseudo-Aristotle's analysis, because these four categories relate to the basic, central operations that may be reconstructed from them: assessments/warehousing/archiving/distribution.

For the administration responsible, the first duty was to oversee the preservation and recording of products collected. To stay within the same geographical and chronological framework, we may cite a Greek parallel dating to the very beginning of the Hellenistic period (320), a text that echoes Pseudo-Aristotle as much as the Persepolis tablets. The Diadoche Eumenes of Cardia—who at the time was under attack by Antipater, who considered himself the supreme representative of the imperial order—was reinforcing his cavalry from the royal stud farms of the Ida, in Troas:

> He took as many [horses] as he had occasion for, and sent an account of his doing so to the overseers, at which Antipater is said to have laughed, calling it truly laudable in Eumenes thus to hold himself prepared for giving in to them (or would it be taking from them?) strict account of all matters of administration (*ta basilika*). (Plutarch, *Eum.* 8.5✧)

Antipater's reaction might be understandable; he was surprised to learn that Eumenes, even during such a chaotic period, showed himself to be so legalistic and hopeful of his political survival. That is, Eumenes, careful to display his loyalty, took care to apply the accounting rules that the Macedonians had carried over from the Achaemenid administration. At the same time, the episode strongly suggests that the political disturbances had done nothing to modify bureaucratic routines; the bureaucrats knew well that at any moment they might be asked for accounts of their management—that is, a ledger of receipts and outflow.

Surplus in Kind and Exchanges

The author of the *Oeconomica* not only discussed the stocking of produce of the *tagē* in the royal warehouses (*paratheseis*), such as those located at stages along the royal roads (II.2.34a: *thēsauroi*) or the strategic reserves deposited by the satraps in their territories (e.g., Xenophon, *Anab.* III.4.31), but also considered their marketing. The phrase "consider at what moment and in what way it will be advantageous to sell them" refers to one of the missions of the royal economy, which operated equally on the *exagōgima* and the *eisagōgima* (II.1.2). These two words designate not what we call exports and imports, but rather the shipment of produce out from and receipt into the royal warehouses. Perhaps the author was thinking of the needs of the State apparatus (army units on the move, official travel on the royal roads, royal table, transfers of produce from one satrapy to another, etc.), maintenance of which required permanent inventories. But his analysis goes further: the verb used, *diatithestai*, comes from the vocabulary of the market. What the author is referring to, then, is a method that made it possible for the king to make money by selling off surplus from his granaries at the right moment (II.1.3).

There is no hint of a theoretical approach. It is clear that, aside from massive requisitions like those of the Great Kings for their expeditions, or aside from particularly bad years, the inventories of wheat (or other products) were subject to precise management: what was to be done with the surplus? This is exactly the question answered by the author: the administration profited from circumstances favorable to releasing inventories to the market. The author clearly found this problem very interesting, as is shown by one of the financial strategies he attributed to Antimenes of Rhodes, in Alexander's time: "Antimenes ordered the satraps to keep the storehouses along the royal roads filled according to the custom of the country; but whenever an army or any other body of men unaccompanied by the king passed along, he used to send one of his own men and sell the contents of the storehouses" (II.38✧). Though Antimenes' behavior appears rather reprehensible from the perspective of administrative regulations, it at least recalls the principle set forth by Pseudo-Aristotle—namely, the marketing of wheat from the royal granaries.

A concrete illustration of the procedure is found in another document from western Asia Minor in the last quarter of the fourth century. In a reply to the ambassadors from the town of Lebedos, Antigonus the One-Eyed answered that he was not favorably disposed toward the maintenance of wheat reserves by the towns themselves: this system would prove too costly to them, he wrote. And he recalled his policy in the following words:

> Until now, we have not been willing to grant to any town the right of importing wheat or establishing wheat reserves. . . . Again in the present case, our initial thought was not to authorize this operation, inasmuch as the tribute land (*khōra phorologoumenē*) is nearby, and thus it is easy, we believe, to seek out there whatever may be desired. (RC 3[80–85])

In other words, the king profited from the existence of a nearby market (Greek cities) by selling surplus wheat derived from tribute (to use the word in a general sense). At this date, he even had sufficient political means to impose what appears to have been a sort of monopoly; since the towns did not have the right to buy overseas, they were required to buy from the administrators of the royal granaries. We have one other attestation from the beginning of the Hellenistic period, in a decree in honor of Thersippos: one of the good deeds for which he was recognized by the city was the provision of wheat to the city during a famine (*sitodeia*): "He obtained from the satrap the right to import wheat (*eisagōga[n sito]*)" (*OGIS* 4). This wheat clearly came from the satrapal administration's reserves, and the previous example strongly suggests that Thersippos negotiated the purchase with the satrap. Other inscriptions published more recently confirm the frequency of such sales in the Seleucid period.

It is clear that these practices were inherited from the Achaemenid period. This assertion of continuity is not simply hypothetical. First of all, the existence of satrapal inventories is explicit in the instructions issued by Darius regarding Jerusalem (Ezra 6:9; cf. Josephus, *Ant.* XI.16). We have decisive evidence for the practice itself (that has been entirely overlooked). It comes from an Athenian decree of disputed date (probably toward the middle of the fourth century) that honors the satrap Orontes, who at the time held a post in Asia Minor (presumably in Mysia). Orontes was awarded Athenian citizenship because he had responded favorably to a request from the town. The Athenian armies at the time were fighting in the regions near the Straits; because they were in extreme financial difficulty, the *strategoi* found themselves unable to pay the *misthos* (part of which was to be paid in kind) to their soldiers. Athens then turned, quite naturally we might add, to the Persian satrap, because every Greek knew that he had vast reserves of wheat (like any other satrap). Athenian ambassadors then came to present this request to Orontes. The decree clearly shows that Orontes did not donate the wheat but sold it—because the decree states which funds the necessary payment was to be taken from, and it gives instructions to the treasurers regarding the repayment of the funds to the satrap (*IG* II² 207a). It thus seems clear that Antigonus and the Seleucid kings were merely following the example of the satraps of Asia Minor: they would regularly offer for sale the surplus of the royal granaries on the Aegean market—with, no doubt, the prior assent of the central authority and on condition that the price be high.

The Fish of Lake Moeris

Several passages in Herodotus provide further indication of the conversion into silver of levies in kind. He notes—as we have already seen—that the profit on fish from Lake Moeris paid a talent a day to the royal treasury (*to basilikon*; III.91). To put it another way, every day the "royal fish" were sold on the nearby market, in Memphis or elsewhere. This is of course a special case, since it was difficult to preserve fish, except as salted fish, which the Egyptians were very fond of (II.77). But in the long term, it was a general problem for the administration: how can we turn a profit on the yield of income in kind?

The Athos Canal Workers

We might ask whether war was an excellent opportunity for selling one's inventory. Perhaps part of the answer may be found in Herodotus's description of the immense preparations made by Darius and Xerxes. On hearing the news from Marathon, Darius ordered the mustering of troops as well as the gathering of "warships, transports, horses, and foodstuffs" (VII.1◇). Several years later, Xerxes reprised his father's work:

> Provision dumps were being formed for the troops, lest either men or animals should go hungry on the march to Greece. For these dumps the most convenient sites were chosen after a careful survey, the provisions being brought from many different parts of Asia in merchantmen or transport vessels. (VII.25◇)

It is unfortunate that Herodotus does not provide further details. But we may suppose that the wheat came primarily from the royal granaries, and that the king had authorized stewards at the granaries to make 'disbursements' (*exagōgima*).

We learn that the food supplies for the Immortals, "separate from that of the rest of the army, [were] brought along for them on camels and mules" (VII.83◇). It is particularly unfortunate that we know nothing of the distribution of supplies to the soldiers. Did they receive rations free, or did they have to pay for them? This question may be surprising, but it is legitimate. From numerous examples, we know that ancient armies—including the Achaemenid armies—did not have, properly speaking, a quartermaster corps. Most often, the soldiers lived off the land, either by pillage or by purchase from the locals. This is how Cyrus the Younger's mercenaries survived; the only preparation he undertook was to plan for flour and wine wagons in case the Greeks were unable to find supplies on the spot (*Anab.* I.10.18). Cyrus's actual army was accompanied by merchants who presided over the "Lydian market": at a time of scarcity, the Greek mercenaries came to resupply themselves, but they were discouraged from buying by the prices asked (*Anab.* I.5.6). We also know of Phoenician merchants in Alexander's army (Arrian VI.22.4).

One of the most interesting examples involves satrapal troops in Cyprus in 386–385:

Since Evagoras had such advantages, he entered the war with confidence. First, since he had not a few boats of the sort used for piracy, he lay in wait for the supplies coming to the enemy, sank some of their ships at sea, drove off others, and captured yet others. Consequently, the merchants (*emporoi*) did not dare to convey food to Cyprus; and since large armaments had been gathered on the island, the army of the Persians soon suffered from lack of food and the want led to revolt, the mercenaries of the Persians attacking their officers, slaying some of them, and filling the camp with tumult and revolt. It was with difficulty that the generals of the Persians and the leader of the naval armament, known as Glōs, put an end to the mutiny. Sailing off with their entire fleet, they transported a large quantity of grain from Cilicia and provided a great abundance of food. (Diodorus XV.3.1–3✧)

Indeed, at this time, as in the time of Darius, the Cilician coast constituted a supply base for the Persian armies; it was from Cilicia that the Persian generals drew on royal wheat reserves to bring supplies to Cyprus. When the sea was free, it fell to the *emporoi* to ensure the supplies. We may imagine that in this era merchants went to buy wheat in the royal granaries and then resold it to the soldiers at, no doubt, a considerable profit. In other words, according to this theory, part of soldiers' pay returned to the royal treasury via the royal granaries, minus the traders' cut. Of course, Darius's and Xerxes' soldiers were not mercenaries. But this does not mean that they had less money (in the form of weighed silver). We have already seen that raising royal soldiers in Babylonia did not cost the royal treasury anything, since they furnished their own equipment and the equipment for their staff, and they were required to bring foodstuffs for several days (chap. 10/4). It would not be surprising if troop movements created their own market, permitting the administration to peddle its surplus to its own soldiers.

This is in fact how the system operated that was set up to ensure supplies for the labor force working on the Athos canal, a labor force consisting of contingents of subject peoples and squads requisitioned in the Greek towns of the region:

> In a meadow near by the workmen had their meeting-place (*agora*) and market (*prētērion*), and grain ready ground was brought over in great quantity from Asia. (VII.23✧)

It thus seems certain that the workers purchased their rations. Perhaps they received a salary (in whatever form: silver or tokens), which they hastened to spend in the military warehouses!

Return to Persepolis

It is not impossible that Herodotus's text describes a procedure similar to the process seen in action in the Treasury tablets. Beginning in 493, payments were made to the *kurtaš* in silver, at least for part of their salary. The *kurtaš* apparently received silver and foodstuffs (beer, grain, wine). Some obscurity remains concerning the practical operation. What is certain, however, is that the mode of payment implies the establishment of fixed prices for commodities at the rate of 3 siculi for 1 sheep and 1 siculus for 1 *marriš* (9.7 liters) of wine. This method of payment is often compared to one of the principles of the royal economy, which is reported in these words by Pseudo-Aristotle: "In regard to expenditure, what expenses ought to be curtailed and when, and whether one should pay what is expended in coin (*nomisma*) or in commodities which have an equivalent value" (*anti nomismatos ōnia*; 2.1.3✧)—with the slight but essential difference that the Persians certainly did not use coined silver but weighed silver. Taking this principle together with another rule ("The expenditure must not exceed the income": 1.6.7✧), it is clear that the primary goal of the royal economy was to increase the central authority's revenues.

Given these factors, we may suppose that the silver allocated to the administration workers would buy foodstuffs that would eke out the rations in kind that they received normally. But from whom would they buy? It is not impossible that a private market existed in Persia, since several Babylonian texts refer to merchants in Persia. Also, it is likely that, for example, the court was not fed exclusively by levies in kind, since Dinon (apud Athenaeus 14.652c) alludes to royal buyers (*hoi agorastai*) who came to the market to buy (*ōneisthai*) figs. However, if it existed at Persepolis, this market was not "free" in the usual sense, since the prices were fixed by the administation. Other documents attest to transactions carried out by administrators. Thus, in 503, the head of the warehouse of Udarakka set aside grain and in return received "one top-quality mule and one top-quality cow" (PF 1978). The trade was probably with another warehouse (even perhaps within the Udarakka fortress), not with private merchants. Every case involves exchange of merchandise—never silver. Otherwise, the minuteness of some silver allocations (1/18 siculus) makes it unlikely that the admininstration actually weighed and calculated such small payments. It seems more likely that these payments were strictly "paper" transactions; that is, the *kurtaš* had credit that they could spend in the administration warehouses. If so, it was a win–win situation for the administration, since it could fix the prices and require the *kurtaš* to shop there. Living conditions for the *kurtaš* became more and more difficult as prices rose, as can actually be seen at Persepolis between December 467 and August 466. The texts display extraordinary variation in the price of grain. The price rose to five times normal and then grew still more; it did not return to normal until August 466. We know nothing of the circumstances. All we can say is that the quality of life of the *kurtaš* eroded drastically because of the administration monopoly. Overall, this example seems to confirm that there was no free market that could (possibly) have lowered prices by massive imports from nearby regions (such as Babylonia).

Compared with the Herodotus text we started with, the Persepolis documents throw a stark, empirical light on the methods involved in managing the surplus goods stocked in the royal granaries. Were these methods applied systematically in every satrapy? Meanwhile, an Aramaic document from Egypt poses a real problem (*DAE* 54 [*AP* 2✦]). Recall that two Egyptian boatmen received barley and lentils from Espemet, servant(?) of the commander Hananī, to transport to the Elephantine warehouse. In fact, the document explicitly provides that the clerks of the Elephantine warehouse were to "reimburse the price" to Espemet, in the amount of 100 *karš*. It shows that a warehouse (Syene) could "sell" merchandise to another warehouse (Elephantine) following a procedure known from documents from Persepolis. Were these goods purchased at Syene on the Egyptian market? It is possible that this is the case, because the provision of produce to the garrisons from tribute paid in kind (Herodotus III.91) would probably not suffice to ensure regular resupply.

9. Lands and Peasants

Kurtaš, garda, gardu

Comparison of texts from other sources can also deepen our analysis of another series of Persepolis tablets. The word *kurtaš*, in the form *garda/gardu*, appears in Aramaic documents from Egypt and in Babylonian tablets. Both sources are often used to clarify the meaning of the word *kurtaš* in the Persepolis tablets.The word *garda* is used in three

Aramaic letters dated 420–410. One was sent by Aršāma to Neḥtiḥōr, manager of the satrap's estates in Egypt (*DAE* 68 [*AD* 7]). Aršāma complains about Neḥtiḥōr's behavior, which he compares unfavorably with that of his previous steward, Psammešek, who despite difficulties had "carefully protected our *garda* and property"; he had even sought elsewhere for *garda* to replace those who had died or fled. Likewise for other stewards in Lower Egypt. Hence Aršāma's order: "Seek diligently elsewhere for *garda*—all kinds of artisans; bring them into my courtyard, mark them with my sign, and appropriate them for my estate (*bēt*), just as the former superintendents used to do" [Whitehead]. The second letter was sent by another Persian noble, Varfiš, who also held lands in Egypt. It is also addressed to Neḥtiḥōr, who, defying Aršāma's order, had not given a group of Cilicians to Masapāta, Varfiš's steward. Masapāta had complained thus: "He has assaulted my lady's *garda* and taken goods from them." Hence Varfiš's anger, which is vented in the following words to Neḥtiḥōr: "Now then, *you* have no business with my *garda*! Give back what you forcibly took from the *garda* . . ." (*DAE* 73 [*AD* 12; Whitehead]).

The third letter was sent by the satrap of Egypt, Aršāma, to his steward Neḥtiḥōr and his accountants in Egypt (*DAE* 70 [*AD* 9]):

> From Aršāma to Neḥtiḥōr, Kenzasirma and his colleagues [accountants]. Now then, I have a servant, a sculptor (*patikara-kara*) named Hinzanāy, whom Bagasarū brought to Susa. Give him and his staff (*bēt*) the same rations as my other *garda*-personnel [polishers?] so that he will make reliefs of a mounted soldier . . . , and make a relief of a horse with its chariot, just as he formerly made for me, among other reliefs. Let them be dispatched and brought to me immediately! Artōhī knows about this order. Scribe: Rašta. [Whitehead / transliteration of names, Grelot]

Aršāma's letter is constructed on the same pattern that the princesses Irtašduna and Irdabama used when drafting letters to the accountants of their house (cf. PFa 27). The sculptor Hinzanāy, 'servant' (*ʿlym*) of Aršāma, and the women of his house (*bēt*) were to receive rations in kind (*ptp*) from Aršāma's steward, "the same as my other *garda*." The sculptor in question—certainly a Mesopotamian—was famous enough to have been summoned to Susa by Aršāma before being dispatched to Egypt. We also see that he was an itinerant artist who took his family with him when he moved. He had laborers under him, specialists in stonework, like the "foremen" of Persepolis (cf. PT 75). His status is not clearly indicated. It is undoubtedly dangerous to make him into a prototype of a free wage-earner. Aršāma calls him a slave-servant (*ʿlym*); the vocabulary is vague (cf. *DAE* 69 [*AD* 8]), to be sure, but we might compare Hinzanāy's case with several others known from the tablets, where certain individuals are said to be "attached to the house" (PF 1946). Rather than being a free itinerant craftsman, Hinzanāy seems to have become a dependent craftsman, whom Aršāma moves around at will in his own interest.

One of Aršāma's phrases, "*garda*—all kinds of artisans," is a virtual Aramaic calque of a Persian phrase known from a Treasury tablet (PT 79) in its Elamite calque (*kurtaš marrip mišbazana*). But the lexical comparison provides no indication of the *garda*'s status; the word *garda* is used here in its generic sense of 'personnel'. The Cilicians, named in the second letter and in other documents, are included among these 'personnel'. In two documents they are described with sufficiently vague words (*ʿbd*, *ʿlym*) that they can be considered slaves as much as servants (*DAE* 66, 67 [*AD* 5, 6]). We do not know how the stewards recruited new "slaves": by purchase in Egypt, or at some other market after being captured in war? It is likely that a large majority worked in the fields, but the estates of nobles also employed a staff with very diverse skills. A certain number—such as those who were assigned to Masapāta's wife—must have been domestic servants. All in all, the prevailing impression is that here the word *garda* is more a label than a technical term whose judicial status can immediately be defined. We may note in passing that *garda* owned personal property, since Neḥtiḥōr is accused of having taken some of it for himself (*DAE* 73 [*AD* 12]). We can conclude, however, that they were not free men but dependents and/or slaves who worked the lands and the estate for rations provided by the stewards.

Another fact needs to be brought up: the mention of a brand or mark that these people were required to wear. It is paradoxically via a passage in Quintus Curtius that we can indirectly establish a functional link between the Aramaic documents and the Persepolis tablets. Describing Alexander's arrival in 331, Quintus Curtius (like Diodorus) devotes a passage (meant to be moving) to the Greeks who had been deported to Persepolis and who, he writes, worked in the slave shops (*ergastules*). He adds an interesting detail: they were "branded with the characters of barbarian letters" (V.5.6◊). This practice is well known in Babylonia; just as slaves (*širku*) and the Eanna temple's flocks were marked with the goddess's star, private slaves were frequently branded with the name of their master. The only Akkadian text from the Fortification archives confirms this custom (Fort. 11786). A Babylonian document from Cambyses' time even states that the hand of a slave of Itti-Marduk-balāṭu "bears an inscription in Akkadian and [another] in Aramaic" (*Camb.* 143). Two other Aramaic documents from Egypt offer striking parallels. A case involving division of property among heirs mentions a male slave (*ʿbd*) whose hand bears a *yod* and an Aramaic word reproducing the name of the deceased owner (*DAE* 41 [*AP* 28]). Another letter confirms that slaves were branded on the arm with the names of their successive owners (*DAE* 22 [Bodleian ostracon 1]). The information given by Quintus Curtius thus certainly appears to be legitimate. But should we conclude from this that every *kurtaš* was branded? It is difficult to say. A passage in Herodotus nonetheless seems to imply that this was in fact the case for prisoners of war (VII.233: Greek prisoners marked with 'royal marks' [*stigmata basileia*]). What cannot be doubted, on the other hand, is that slaves proper (sold, bought, tattooed) are known from one of the two Akkadian tablets from Persepolis and, previously, from tablets from the time of Cambyses and Bardiya written at Matezziš (chap. 2/7). But in every case this concerns private slaves, who obviously had to be clearly distinguished from the *kurtaš* belonging to the administration.

The word *kurtaš* is also found in several Babylonian tablets, in the form *gardu*. But, as always, it is used allusively and erratically, sneaking furtively into contexts whose very logic most often escapes us and which always assume that we know exactly the thing we are hoping to find out. One document, dating to Darius I (between 507 and 500), states that *gardu* can be enrolled into the army reserve. The other attestations are later and appear in documents from the archive of the house of Murašū under Artaxerxes I and Darius II. What we find in these texts first is that *gardu* could farm plots of land that they had rented from the Murašū. We also find technical terms that are borrowed from the Persian vocabulary well known from Persepolis. We have terms such as royal *gardu*, for example, as well as a head *gardu* (*gardupatu = kurdabattiš*); another official has the title *pitipabaga* of the *gardu*, or 'distributor of rations in kind' (*ptp*)—a title recognizable from Dinon in the transcription *potibazis* (Athenaeus XI.503f = *FGrH* 690 F4). In two documents, these officials levy taxes on lands of the royal prince worked by the Murašū, who have rented the land to *gardu*. The *gardu* are themselves hierarchically subordinate to three higher persons. One has the title *šaknu* of the *gardu*; on the model of the *segan* who oversee the *kurtaš* of the workshops in Persepolis, he was, as it were, their "foreman." Another is called satrap (a very flexible term in the Babylonian documents). Both are royal officials. We are thus tempted to conclude that the nobles and the *gardu* who worked on the estates of the king and the nobility in Babylonia were organized on a socioadministrative model very like that of Persepolis: they received their rations from the royal administration.

At the same time, the Babylonian documents show that, in lieu of rations, other *gardu* received land to farm from within the *ḫaṭru* system. So it was, for example, for a *gardu* called Šalammanu. Elsewhere, the same person was called "*Gardu* of the fourth year of Darius [II]." This is a rather mysterious expression; one attempted explanation has compared this phrase with the use of the word *rabbap*, which at Persepolis modifies some *kurtaš*. Thanks to the Behistun inscription, the basic meaning of the word is fairly clear: 'connected/attached/dependent'. It has been translated 'conscripted', a word that would qualify groups of *kurtaš* temporarily requisitioned for state corvées in Fārs. Of course, the corvée system is known in Babylonia. It is also known that, in the time of Darius I, Babylonians could receive orders to perform military service in Elam for a specified duration. But too much uncertainly remains to be able to be certain about the interpretation of the word *rabbap* in the (dim!) light of the Babylonian tablets, especially since in this example the mutual support the Persian and Babylonian documents seem to provide rests instead on circular reasoning.

Kurtaš and laoi: Tissaphernes and the Peasants of Parysatis's Villages

However allusive, a passage in Xenophon also deserves to be included in the discussion. After the Greek mercenaries retreated from Babylon, they arrived near "villages of Parysatis" (probably not far from Opis). Xenophon wrote:

> Tissaphernes, by way of insulting Cyrus, gave over these villages—except that it was forbidden to enslave the inhabitants (*plēn andrapodōn*)—to the Greeks to plunder. In them there was grain in abundance and cattle and other property. (*Anab*. II.4.27)

Politically, Xenophon's explanation fits well enough into the post-Cunaxa context, Tissaphernes being an enemy of Cyrus and hated by Parysatis. The prohibition he then imposes takes on a certain interest, at least giving us something to reflect on.

Among all the documents bearing on the *laoi* 'common people', we may cite the so-called Mnesimachus inscription (*Sardis* VII.1.1), which refers to a *dōrea* near Sardis. In the inventory are listed many villages (*kōmai*) and *laoi*, with each village paying a *phoros* to the military district (chiliarchy) to which it belonged. All the available documents testify that, even in the case of a donation, the peasants remained attached to their village, which, in Xenophon's Armenia, was governed by a *kōmarch*, who was required to transmit the *dasmos* 'tribute' to the royal administration (*Anab*. IV.5.9–10, 24). Elsewhere, very often, the literary and epigraphic texts from Asia Minor confirm this arrangement, and it is implicit in Darius's letter to Gadatas (ML 12): bound to their village, the peasants (*laoi, laoi basilikoi* 'palace slaves', *hierodouloi* 'temple slaves') are protected by the administration—in no case may they be captured or sold on the slave market (cf. chap. 12/4). We are then led to inquire whether this is the context that lies behind Tissaphernes' behavior in Babylonia. Tissaphernes' behavior can be contrasted with Mithradates': to make his rebellion (*apostasis*) against the Great King obvious, Mithradates pillaged the villages (*kōmai*; Polyaenus VII.29.1; cf. Nepos, *Dat.* 10.2). Another example leaps to mind: we know that deeds recording slave sales in Babylonia regularly included a restrictive clause: the sale (duly registered in the royal archives) was only valid if the slaves in question were not royal slaves, free citizens, or temple oblates. If the comparison with the Babylonian example is valid, we must recognize that the villagers assigned to gift land also benefited from this kind of safety clause and thus that their sociolegal status was comparable to the status enjoyed by the *laoi* and *hierodouloi* known in Anatolia in the Hellenistic period and later.

To finish up on this point, we must also stress, nonetheless, that the conclusion just offered cannot be generalized. It cannot be applied to anyone other than the peasants who because of the concession of land continued to live in their traditional villages and cultivated their ancestral territories. Xenophon also refers to them in the *Cyropaedia*, composing the following speech for "Cyrus," who has just laid his hands on regions subject to the "Assyrians":

> There are two things that it were well for us to look out for: that we make ourselves masters of those who own this property, and that they stay where they are. For an inhabited country (*oikoumenē khōra*) is a very valuable possession, but a land destitute of people becomes likewise destitute of produce. Those, therefore, who tried to keep you off, you slew, I know, and you did right. . . . But those who surrendered you have brought as prisoners of war (*aikhma-lōtoi*). Now, if we should let them go, we should, I think, do what would be in itself an advantage. For, in the first place, we should not have to keep watch against them nor should we have to keep watch over them, nor yet to furnish them with food; . . . and in the second place, if we let them go, we shall have more prisoners of war than if we do not. For, if we are masters of the country, all they that dwell therein will be our prisoners of war; and the rest, when they see these alive and set at liberty, will stay in their places and choose to submit rather than to fight. (IV.4.5–8◇)

In other words, the tribute economy made it necessary to maintain the system of liberty-dependence that characterized the *laoi* so well. Hence the words spoken by "Cyrus" to the "Assyrian" prisoners:

> You shall dwell in the same houses and work the same farms; you shall lie with the same wives and have control of your children just as now. But you shall not have to fight either us or any one else. (IV.4.10–11◇)

The comparisons with other corpora lead us to think that Xenophon merely transmitted a Greek vision of village dependence: the measure taken by Tissaphernes seems to be a concrete illustration of the policy attributed to "Cyrus." Booty was limited to harvest and stock, and the villagers are explicitly excluded; in the opposite case, the satrap would have negated the economic benefits granted by the king to Parysatis, since a gift of land without peasants was useless. This fact provides a measure of the distance from the status of the *laoi* to the status of the *kurtaš*.

Irmatam, ulhi, and Gift Lands (dōreai)

Similarly, we are tempted to compare the tablets with other documentary corpora to try to dispel some of the uncertainty surrounding the exact status of the estates (*irmatam*, *ulhi*) allotted to princes, princesses, and high-ranking persons who belonged to Darius's inner circle.

As we have just seen from a passage in Xenophon, the Classical authors often testify to the existence of lands and/or revenues granted to Persian princesses. This holds, for example, for the revenue from the fish of Lake Moeris in Egypt, which Herodotus mentioned in his passage on tribute (III.91). Xenophon uses comparable expressions to describe the villages near Aleppo that belonged to Parysatis, wife of Darius II: "They had been given her for girdle-money" (*Anab.* I.4.9◊; cf. II.4.27). Likewise in Plato:

> I once spoke with a reliable man who travelled over to the Persian court, and he told me that he crossed a very large and rich tract of land, nearly a day's journey across, which the locals called "the Queen's girdle." There's another one called "the Queen's veil," as well as many others, all fine and rich properties, each one named for a part of the Queen's wardrobe, because each one is set aside to pay for the Queen's finery. (*Alc.* 123b–c◊)

Many other ancient authors refer to this practice, which Cicero considered (pejoratively) to be specific to Oriental kings (*Verr.* III.33).

Whatever limitations there are on our use of Classical sources, in every case they explain that the princesses had lands and villages in various regions of the Empire from which they drew revenue that was allocated to their own house. Confirmation is found in numerous Babylonian tablets from the reigns of Artaxerxes I and Darius II that refer to houses (*bītu*), that is, estates assigned to members of the royal family (as well as to Persian nobles). We know in Artaxerxes I's time about an "estate of the lady of the palace" (perhaps one of the king's wives), as well as an "estate of the king's son" (*mār šarri*; reign of Darius II). Let us notice in particular several references to estates of Parysatis, among which we may quote the following:

> 60 KUR of barley, farm rent imposed, rent in kind of the lands [of Parysatis], (located) along the Addu-ab-usur canal, right [and left] banks, [from its sluicegate to] its mouth, where [its] water [flows out], from year 3 of Dar[ius the king, (lands) that (are) in the hands of] Mattani-Iāma [slave of Ea-bullitsu the steward (*paqdu*)] of Parysatis, (and) who (are) [at the disposal of Rīmūt-Ninurta son of] Murašû; the barley in question, [60 KUR, farm rent imposed on] these [lands] for year 3, [Mat]an[ni-Iāma from the hands] of Enlil-itannu and Mu[tīr-gim-milli treasurers] of Rīmūt-Ninurta received, it has been paid; Mattani-Iāma will have drawn up a receipt (for) 60 KUR, farm rent imposed on these lands for year 3 (and) coming from Ri-[. . .] and Ea-bullitsu the steward of Parysatis to Enlil-itannu and [Mutīr-gimilli he will give (it)]. [Names of the witnesses and the scribe.] Nippur, 12-ix-3 of Darius. (PBS II/1.50; trans. after G. Cardascia)

Various estates allocated to Aršāma, prince of the (royal) house, are also mentioned between 425 and 404. If the tablets relating to Parysatis echo Xenophon and Plato, those citing Aršāma quite naturally remind us of several Aramaic letters from him when he was satrap of Egypt, where he also had estates (*bēt; DAE* 62–73 [AD 1–12]). In addition, he was not the only one: some documents refer to two other Persian nobles, Varfiš and Varohi, who also had lands in Egypt (*DAE* 71–73 [AD 10–12]). Of course, these documents are much later than the Persepolis tablets; nevertheless, the comparison with Babylonian tablets from the reign of Darius I leads us to think that the internal organization of the Babylonian estates did not change noticeably between Darius I and Darius II.

The translation of *bēt* (Akk. *bītu*) as 'estate' should not give rise to any confusion. Lands allocated to estates of this sort did not necessarily comprise a homogeneous territorial entity, set apart and individually identified as such in the countryside. These were not "rural estates" or manors surrounded by high walls. These "houses" included various cadastral elements, including *ḫaṭru* lands (bow lands, for example) and portions of 'royal land' (*uzbarra*). This is also the picture portrayed in a Greek inscription from Sardis (*Sardis* VII.1.1) that lists the different elements of a *dōrea* of Achaemenid origin: the concessionaire was one Mnesimachus from the end of the fourth century and his allotment included villages, *klēroi* (military lots?), gardens for rent (*paradeisoi*), etc. This suggests that the king did not grant his family members and favorites rural farms in units as we would understand them: the administration allocated revenues to them from a certain number of cadastral units, which could be increased or diminished. The origin and status of the lands allocated in this fashion make it clear at the same time that the concessionaires—whether nobles or princesses—were not relieved of financial obligation to the king: even if *ḫaṭru* lands were granted to a prince of the royal house, they retained their original obligations, namely, various taxes and royal service (furnishing soldiers when called up by the king and/or the satrap). Likewise, the *dōrea* of Mnesimachus remained subject to the payment of tribute (*phoroi*) that burdened the villages and *klēroi* of his *dōrea*. This is the sense in which the accounts of the Greek authors preserve some of the institutional reality: what the king gave was not so much the land and the peasants but part of the revenue; in the eyes of a Xenophon or a Plato, the villages allocated to Parysatis represent nothing more than what is nowadays called a civil list. It was the same for the revenue from the fish in Lake Moeris. Even though they were grants, from the outset these concessions were clearly understood as revocable; they were not private property in the full sense.

That the grants were revocable does not imply that the beneficiaries did not actively concern themselves with managing them. In general, they entrusted management to stewards (*paqdu*), such as Neḫtiḫōr, Psammešek, Hatūbašti, or Masapāta in Egypt, or Lābāši, steward of the Babylonian estates of a royal prince, and Ua-buliṭsu, steward of Parysatis. Their mission was to watch over the lands, property, and workers—and thus produce and revenues. In exchange for their services, they received grants of land (cf. *DAE* 69 [*AD* 8]). It thus was the responsibility of the beneficiaries to exploit their estates in such a way as to extract the maximum profit after deducting the taxes payable to the royal administration. This was in fact the goal that Aršāma and the other Persian nobles set for their stewards (*DAE* 68, 71 [*AD* 7, 10]).

Even when gathered in compact and incomplete form, these facts are incomparably more detailed than what can be extracted from the Persepolis tablets. Setting aside the word *ulhi* (which corresponds to the Akkadian *bītu*) and setting aside the status of the concessionaires (princesses), it is in fact difficult to build sturdy bridges between the various pieces of the documentary record. The relationships are only partial and uncertain. As an example, let us examine the data from a single tablet. It records the provision of travel rations to 71 'boys' (*puhu*) of Abbamuš and Irtašduna, servants "who transport a treasury (*kapnuški* = **ganza*) from Kerman to Susa" (PFa 14). Whoever the first of these two women may be (she is certainly high-ranking), the information is problematic. Another tablet (PF 1357) records the transportation of a treasury (*kapnuški*) from Babylon to Persepolis, but it is silent regarding the administrative background. There is a similar event in PF 1342 (a treasurer [**ganzabara*] transports silver from Susa to Matezziš). It is tempting to compare the first of these documents (PFa 14) with a letter from the satrap of Egypt, Aršāma, ordering the 'treasury' (**ganza*), consisting in part of the proceeds of taxes (*mandattu*) assessed on the Egyptian estates of the Persian nobles, to be brought to Babylon (*DAE* 71 [*AD* 10]). Perhaps Irtašduna and the other princess possessed estates in Carmania, and the "treasury" designated either the revenues they extracted or else the proceeds of taxes they owed to the royal administration, or perhaps both at once.

The letter Aršāma entrusts to his steward Neḥtiḥōr (*DAE* 67 [*AD* 6]) wonderfully illustrates the ambiguities of the word 'house' (*bītu*). By sending him back to Egypt, the satrap entrusts him with nothing less than a travel voucher. Addressing the stewards in charge of the stations that lined the road from Babylonia to Egypt (from *medinah* to *medinah*), he required them to deliver to Neḥtiḥōr and his companions rations (*ptp*) taken "from his house (*bēt*)." But to what does this refer? The fact that the steward of his estates in Egypt (Neḥtiḥōr) and the stewards of the various cities involved had the same title (*peqid/paqdu*) does not imply that the duties of the two were the same. Nor does the fact that the personnel of Aršāma's estates also received rations (*ptp*) prove that the "houses" of Arbela or Damascus were assimilated to the satrap's Egyptian estates. For how else can we explain the fact that travel rations were taken from "private" funds, whereas the Persepolis tablets show that travel rations were provided by the administrators of state warehouses?

The tablets allow us to offer an answer, albeit a hypothetical one. These "estates" must have been comparable to *irmatam*, that is, estates whose status was at the convergence of private and public interests. We have seen that they functioned as centers for the collection and distribution of the products of owners who were exempt from *irmatam* assessments. We may suppose that the house of Aršāma had "credit" at Laḫirū, Arbela, or Damascus, which he was able to use to support activities in which his satrapal interests proper mingled with his personal interests. We can easily use the parallel example of the status of satrapal paradises. Here is how Pharnabazus reacted after the damage caused by Agesilaus's soldiers in his paradise at Dascylium:

> And the beautiful dwellings and paradises, full of trees and wild animals, which my father left me, in which I took delight, — all these paradises I see cut down. (*Hell.* IV.1.33◇)

Pharnabazus's wording seems to imply that, from his perspective, the paradise had been transmitted to him by inheritance. In reality, what he had "inherited" was the position of satrap. The paradise was not his personal property; it remained attached to the position he held directly by royal favor, not from his father. But, as it happens, the practice of passing on the post within the family tends to obscure a basic fact: the paradise was an estate accompanying the job that, like the estates of Aršāma in Egypt, was located at the convergence of the interests of the king and the concessionaire.

10. The King's House

The King's Sheep, Camels, and Horses

But what are the circumstances underlying Darius's order to take 100 sheep from his house (*ulhi*) and provide them to Artystone (Fort. 6764)? The easiest answer is the most obvious, which is to suppose that the royal house was at the confluence of power in both the political and economic senses. This observation seems even more obvious when we consider that the order was given to Parnaka, who was in charge of managing production and the labor force in Fārs. In a letter sent by Darius to Gadatas, the steward of a paradise in Asia Minor, the Greek translation reads: "You will have great recognition in the king's house" (*en basileōs oikōi*; ML 12). The word is *oikos*, which is very close to Persian *viθ* and often was used by the Greeks to label what they thought of as the patrimonial management system of the Empire. The same conclusion seems to emerge from the Babylonian financial formula "taxes paid, the king's soldier, the king's flour, the *bārra* and all sorts of rent for the king's house (*bīt šarri*)."

However, the vocabulary of the tablets prompts us to be cautious. We may briefly note that some texts refer to 'royal shepherds' (*batera sunkina*; PF 2025, Fort. 1091), "sheep of the king" (PF 775, 1442), "cattle of the king" (1946, 1965, 1991; PFa 32), "horses and mules of the king and princes" (1793), "royal horses" (1668–69, 1675, 1784–87; 1942), and a "horse of Ariaramnes" (PFa 24, 29). Some stable heads (*mudunra*) are "attached to the royal estate" (PF 1946[73–77]) or else named as specifically dealing with the king's horses (1765) or "horses and mules of the king and princes" (PF 1793). The lower courtyard at Persepolis (or part of it) is said to "belong to the royal warehouse" (PF 1797). Some lots of products deposited in the warehouses are also called "royal" (PF 150–56, 158–60), etc. One of the most interesting documents is a "transportation authorization" that records the passage of a considerable flock (more than 100,000 head) that was brought from Persepolis to Susa by about 700 shepherds (PF 1442), accompanied no doubt by scores of dogs (cf. PF 1264–66, 1904). This document certainly refers to *kurtaš*, since they are described as "belonging to the treasury" and the sheep are "royal sheep." The same analysis may also hold for other tablets that mention the movement of flocks over long distances (PFa 31).

The question posed by the documentation is thus very simple—simple to formulate, at least. Why is the word 'royal' (*sunkina*) used in only a minority of cases? What does this word mean? Is it definitive, or simply a passing reference to a well-known fact? Were there other flocks and other shepherds that were not "royal" even though they belonged to the royal administration and received rations from it? Or should we think that the omission of the adjective *sunkina* has no particular significance and is due simply to the haste of the scribes, who had no need to specify what everyone knew? The latter notion is the opinion, for example, of the editor of the Fortification tablets, who in the tablets referring to delivery of products to warehouses inserts the word "royal" in some cases (PF 2–4, 30–32, 53, 378–83, 385–87) but not in others (PF 435, 459–60, 488, etc.). Meanwhile, there is nothing to prove that one of the words for warehouse (*huthut*) must always be considered to refer to a "royal warehouse." Because the word *sunkina* describes some warehouses (PF 42, 133, 431, 533, 543, 650, 729, 1796–97, 1943[15–16]) but not others, is it not more likely that not all of them are royal? And if some administrators were "named (*damana*) by the king" (1942[23–24]), was it not because they had a privileged relationship with the royal house?

It is true that the reasons for the presence or absence of the adjective "royal" are difficult to bring to light. Why, for example, is the *baziš* called "royal" only once (PF 2025)? And why is another tax, the *ukpiyataš*, called "royal" only 6 of 13 times (PF 48–49, 388, 395, 396, 428)? We, like the editor of these texts, are obviously tempted to assume that the adjective is implicit everywhere. Comparison of parallel tablets sometimes permits us to observe that certain words were omitted by the scribe from one or the other. Umizza is called "royal shepherd" at Hiran in one tablet (PF 2070) and simply "shepherd" in a text from the following year (PF 2025), even though the context is exactly the same. We may also cite the captivating example of the 33 camels that were brought from Persepolis to Susa "toward the king" (PF 1787), then sent back to Persepolis a month later (PF 1786, PFa 26 and 29). In the first text they are called "royal" but not in the other three, which, like an echo, record the flour rations they received on the return trip. And even the texts of these three tablets are not precisely identical: the destination is sometimes Persepolis, sometimes Matezziš (which is, to be sure, a suburb of Persepolis); the name of the official in charge is not always given, nor that of Bakabada, who gave the travel authorization. Nor are the purposes of the three tablets identical. In the general account (PFa 29), the scribe omitted certain details but added others, though we do not know just which documents lay before him. Whatever the case, it is not clear why some camels called "royal" on the inbound journey could have lost this characteristic a month later on the way back!

But the situation appears less simple as soon as we consider the longer series of texts. Of the hundreds of tablets recording rations paid to the *kurtaš*, only 4 refer explicitly to royal *kurtaš* (PF 1092, 1127, 1211, 2070[23-25]), and of more than 100 texts concerning rations given to horses, only 5 list rations to horses of the king or princes (PF 1669–70, 1775, 1784; PFa 24 = PFa 29). Some ration accounts make it look as though some of the rations were reserved for the "royal cattle" (sesame: PF 1991, 2082). But in the larger account books, feed for the royal cattle is only part of the total (PFa 32); this is especially clear in PF 1792, where Šuddayauda, the head of the *kurtaš*, addresses Parnaka through his superior, Harrena, and states that he has set aside 60 BAR of grain for cattle expressly identified as "royal." Similarly, in another general account (PFa 29), the rations allocated to "a horse of Ariaramnes" represents only a specific subgroup of a general account (cf. PFa 24) in which other horses received their travel rations. It states simply that the ration of 5 BAR of grain to which he is entitled includes his travel ration of 2 BAR. It is clear that this ration was much higher than that of other horses named previously (0.7 BAR). In other words, among all the horses fed by the administration, the royal (or princely) horses constituted a special, recognized category. This observation holds for sheep, poultry, and cattle that are called royal as well. We should especially note the description of some head stablemen (*mudunra*): they are "attached to the [royal] house" (PF 1946[73-77]), as others are "attached to the house of Hystaspes" (1956[5, 7]; *viθ = ulhi*).

Two Economic Domains?

But if royal and princely houses really existed, distinct from the general administration, what was their relationship? In this regard, one tablet is particularly interesting. It says:

> One ox, under the responsibility (*kurmin*) of Rumada, at the warehouse(?), [was] paid (*zakke*) to the king, [to] Anzamanakka. Year 19. Iškumipanna [was] the shepherd (*batera*). (PF 692)

The editor includes it among the texts referring to deliveries to the king, specifically, in fact, to the royal table (PF 691–740). Despite clear onomastic connections with the next tablet (PF 693) and translation difficulties, it *may* have to do with a completely different operation. The word *zakke* is fairly rare in the tablets and its usage is ill defined. In some cases, *zakke* has to do with distributions to *kurtaš* (1178–81, 1986–87: "He paid [amount] to [specified] *kurtaš*"), but we cannot clearly distinguish a difference from the ordinary distributions (though there certainly must have been one!). In four cases, *zakke* involves "purchase" by an administrator of an animal in exchange for grain (PF 1976–78, 1980), thus apparently referring to transactions between two warehouses. This is perhaps what is going on: the document seems to mean simply that on one occasion an ox was requisitioned from administration livestock and transferred to the royal estate (perhaps in a trade). If so, this could be how an ox became "royal," with the named shepherd being either the royal shepherd who received the ox in the name of the king or (more likely) the warehouse shepherd. It must have been a fairly common operation that allowed the men in charge of the royal herds to (re)build their livestock with carefully selected animals. One tablet (PF 198732) seems to report that administrators exchanged grain for sheep that were then transferred to the royal house (*ulhi sunkina*) and placed in the care of a shepherd, no doubt one in charge of royal flocks. Another states that Darius's shepherd received 55 animals from the *irmatam* of Irtuppiya, in Parmadan (Fort. 1091).

Let us return to the particularly interesting example of Umizza, a 'royal shepherd' (*batera sunkina*) whose situation is very clearly spelled out in one tablet (PF 2070): "Umizza, son of Halpa, who lives in Hiran, in [the district] called Halkukaptarriš." He appears in two tablets dated to different years (504 and 503) but reflecting the same context, since the same administrators' names are found in both (PF 2025 and 2070) and both deal with the collection of *baziš* (labeled "royal" once: 2025). In each case, Umizza receives sheep and goats, while others were delivered to the local "head of flocks." If, as seems logical, a royal shepherd deals with royal sheep, we can conclude that some (small: less than 1/10) part of the sheep and goats resulting from the *baziš* (and not immediately slaughtered) was requisitioned yearly to rebuild the royal flocks, the rest going quite naturally to the heads of the administration's flocks.

Other transfers between royal property and the administration's property are attested. In some cases, "royal" products were placed in reserve in the paradise warehouses (PF 150–56, 159–60). On one occasion, royal grain was reserved for seed to be divided among four officials, including a head stableman (*mudunra*; PF 440). Much more numerous are the documents that describe providing the king or his family members with various products from the warehouses. The products in question could be delivered to a royal warehouse: wine (PF 42, 729), grain (PF 1796, 384(?)), fruit (PF 133), as well as animals (PF 1797: horses). Sometimes, grain or sesame is "set aside" "in the royal warehouses(?)" (PF 533, 543) or simply "for the king" (PF 1846). The fruit deposited in this way sometimes comes explicitly from levies assessed on the surrounding villages (PF 650). We have also seen that "royal" animals were frequently fed from the administration's reserves. This was the case for an enormous flock of royal sheep that was taken to Susa by *kurtaš* "attached to the treasury" (PF 1442). Another series of tablets (PF 691–740, 2033–35) records the provision of foodstuffs in the course of relocations of the king or members of the royal family: Irtašduna, Arsames, Irdabama (PF 730–40, 2035), or even Darius's sisters (PFa 5, 31).

Parnaka, Persia, and Darius

We have seen that the royal inscriptions reserve a separate position for Persia among the peoples (*dahyāva*) ruled by Darius. Herodotus, for one, confers a special tribute status on it in a passage (III.97) in which limitations and gaps have already been highlighted. A priori, the special place of Persia within the Empire does not imply ipso facto that it was devoid of any state administration. But we cannot be sure, since the documents do not deal directly with the problem of territorial administration of the country raised by some Persepolis tablets.

Nevertheless, the special status of Persia raises the question of the place of Parnaka. Did he exercise a sort of economic high command, with the right to intervene in the strictly political realm? We have no clear reference to a satrapy in Persia at the time of the first kings. Three times, the tablets refer to "satraps" (PF 679–81). They record the payment of rations to three people; the first two are called "satrap carrying out his duties at Makkash"; the third is referred to as "satrap carrying out his duties at Pura(?)." The rations of wine and grain that they received are unusually high. But this information cannot be used to define their status; in fact, these rations were travel rations probably used to feed members of their entourage (even though they are not mentioned; cf. PFa 4, PFT 23). If they really were satraps in the administrative sense (and the label not just a generic title), they seem nevertheless to have carried out their duties far from Persia.

The Classical texts are silent. The information given by Herodotus on the duties of the "governor" (*hyparkhos*) of Persia, the duties that Hystaspes is supposed to have performed before 522, is clearly erroneous (III.70; cf. *DB* §35). Not until the time of Alexander is any information available, and not until then do we learn that there was a satrap of Persia, Ariobarzanes; again, it is important to stress that only Arrian uses this title (III.18.2), which is not without its own problems of interpretation. At this date, there was also a garrison guarding Persepolis, and Persia was peppered with citadels that Alexander had to overthrow by force. We also learn that someone called Tiridates was 'guardian of the royal fortune' (*custos pecuniae regis*) and that another Persian, Gobares, was 'prefect' (*praefectus*) of Pasargadae. Diodorus says of Tiridates that he "governed the town" of Persepolis, probably in the absence of Ariobarzanes, whom he forbade to reenter the town because he himself was negotiating with Alexander. All the same, he turned over to the king the treasury that he guarded (cf. chap. 16/12). Tiridates' Persian title would have been **ganzabara*.

At first sight, the information given by the Hellenistic authors does not contradict the (scarce) information gleaned from the tablets. First of all, the citadels are mentioned many times. The citadels (*halmarriš*) were not solely centers for collection and redistribution of products derived from taxes on the countryside but also—doubtless originally—full-fledged military sites that also served as relay stations for the transmission of acoustic signals (Diodorus XIX.17.6: *phylakai*). Two tablets (PF 1591, 1812) list the payment of rations (beer, grain) to the 'guards of the fortress' (*halmarriš nuškip*), including the one at Persepolis; in one case, the group consisted of three squads (10, 20, and 70 men), each headed by a named commander. These soldiers are to be distinguished from the *kurtaš* attached to the workshops of a treasury (*kapnuškira*) or the *kurtaš* who oversaw the workshops (PF 874), as well as from the guardians of the paradises or rural estates, who are also *kurtaš* (*puhu*).

Limited as it is, this information proves (if that were necessary) that the garrisons revealed in 331 had not suddenly been positioned to stave off the Macedonian advance. But by itself this information does not permit us to conclude anything regarding the political status of Persia in the time of Darius I. What is problematic, obviously, is that no satrap is ever cited in his official capacity in the tablets among the high-ranking persons who receive rations. It is true that the absence of any title connected with the name Parnaka is a basis for nothing more than an argument from silence; and this argument is less definitive, obviously, than the approach proposed by some interpreters, who refer to some as satraps who never had the title because of the role they played in the distribution of *halmi* to travelers who used the royal roads. Nevertheless, the argument from silence is not without value, because, as we have seen, the word *satrap* is present in the Persepolis archives.

The tablets also inform us of the existence of several bodies of administrators entrusted with judicial tasks. Three tablets refer, for example, to *šamidakurra*, a word that is sometimes understood as "peace officers/conciliators" (PF 1311, 1374, 1461). Other persons seem to perform the functions of police. One tablet (PF 1272) reports the delivery of wine rations to a certain Bakabada, called "judge (*databara*) of Parnaka." Since he received rations for 20 days, it is likely that his job took him from one place to another within Persia. The expression "judge of Parnaka" should occasion no surprise. The same construction is found in Babylonian tablets—as in "*dātabaru* of Artareme," a person who clearly carried out official duties (Artarius/Artareme was satrap of Babylonia), or the "judge of Gubāru," satrap (or high administrator) of Babylonia at the time of Darius II.

From Aelian (*VH* I.34) we know of the existence of itinerant judges in Persia at the time of Artaxerxes II. However, the tasks of Bakabada appear different in kind. There is no proof that Bakabada actually was an official acting on the spot in the name of a satrap. This theory, in fact, would not help us understand why the tablets never give Parnaka the title of satrap; he is never so identified. Parnaka's duties were very wide-ranging, but at the same time they were limited to the administration of property and government workers. This is undoubtedly the context in which the "judge of Parnaka" operated. It seems likely, in fact, that in administrative usage the word *dāta* 'law' referred to rules governing the behavior of bureaucrats, including their calculations of their fiscal accounts (PF 1980). It is thus likely that Bakabada, in the name of Parnaka, was given the task of ruling on disputes internal to the administration and ensuring that accountants and warehouse heads adhered to the rules and obligations of their positions. In this sense, the relationship between Bakabada and Aelian's itinerant judges must not lead us to identify the former's job with the missions assigned to the latter: Bakabada was part of the general administration; the others belonged to the royal administration. The modesty of his daily ration (less than a liter of beer) does not lead us to attribute an eminent position in the administrative hierarchy to him. From all this, we can firmly conclude that Parnaka had neither the title nor the responsibilities of a satrap, insofar as we define these based on our analysis of the satraps located in the various provinces of Darius (cf. chap. 12).

Two further observations may be added to this one. First, it is doubtful that the great aristocratic Persian families would have been subject to the same administration that was responsible for the life and work of the *kurtaš*. Their way of life was more "tribal," in the sense that Herodotus lends to the Persian *genē* (I.125), than territorial. At this point we should recall that Quintus Curtius writes of Orxines in 325: "From there they [Alexander and company] came to Pasargada; that is a Persian race (*gens*), whose satrap was Orsines" (X.1.22✧). Of course, Quintus Curtius's terminology is not certain. The continuation of the story shows that Orxines was the head of the tribe of Pasargadae. But at the same time, in every language, the administrative content of the word *satrap* itself is uncertain. All things considered, it would not be inconceivable for the title to be borne by the chiefs of the great aristocratic families that doubtless controlled the peasants who worked on the land attached to the tribe. Whatever the reality of this (secondary) terminological usage, it is reasonable to think that alongside the territorial division belonging to the administration headed by Parnaka, the old division familiar to the Persian clans and tribes continued to operate, whether their chiefs did or did not bear the title "satrap." Furthermore, within the civil society of the Persians, the name of the tribe continued to be linked to the name of the ancestor, as seen in the example of "Masdayašna of the Maraphi" (PF 1797) and the (contemporaries) of Amasis of the Maraphii and Badres of the Pasargadae (Herodotus IV.167). According to this theory, the later creation of the position "satrap of Persia" significantly reinforced royal power in Persia itself at the expense of the hereditary chiefs of the tribes; but too many uncertainties remain on this point to be able to sustain such a theory.

We should also keep in mind that the geographical and political area covered by the Persepolis tablets does not include all of Persia. The Persian *ethnos* included subgroups located on the margins of the royal domain itself. While some of these groups, such as the Sagartians or the Yautiyans, are listed by Herodotus among the tributary peoples, others are not—in particular, the Mardians and Uxians. The former lived in the mountains not far from the heart of royal power, the latter in the mountains abutting Susiana and Persia, close to a region firmly administered by the royal administration, the basin of Fahliyun. Both populations were short-ranging nomads connected with basic valley agriculture. For example, "the mountain Uxians" are described thus by Arrian: "They had no money or arable land, but were mostly herdsmen (*nomeis*)" (III.17.6◇). The amount of annual tribute imposed on them by Alexander reveals the extent of their livestock: 100 horses, 500 pack animals, and 30,000 sheep (Arrian III.17.6). They were neither tribute-payers nor donors; on the contrary, it was the Great Kings who paid them gifts or tribute when they crossed their territory, according to the Hellenistic authors (chap. 16/11). In sum, one conclusion seems inevitable: not all of Persia was managed directly by the administration headed by Parnaka.

Royal House, Persia, and Empire: A Hypothesis

When Darius ordered that 100 sheep be delivered to Irtašduna from his house (*ulhi*), we are tempted to suppose that he was not referring generically to property managed by the administration but rather that he was instructing Parnaka to charge these animals to a specific account. The orders given by Irtašduna, Irdabama, and Arsames to charge merchandise taken from their house (*ulhi*) and designated for specific persons seem to be a similar case. It is perhaps possible to locate traces of a royal house distinct from the general fiscal administration in the Classical texts. We know that when the Great King relocated, he was accompanied by his entire court, including a treasury transported by hundreds of animals. Of course, it is not certain that this treasury could be confused with the treasuries kept in the capitals of the Empire—the very treasuries Alexander seized in 331–330. This at any rate is what is suggested by a passage by Chares of Mytilene, quoted by Athenaeus in a long discussion of the *tryphē* of the Persian kings:

> Near the royal bed, beyond the head of it, was a chamber large enough to contain five couches, wherein were stored 5000 talents of gold coin filling the whole, and it was called the royal cushion. At the foot was a second, three-couch chamber, containing 3000 talents in silver money, and called the royal footstool. (XII.514e–f◇)

This text reveals the formulas commonly employed by the Greek authors to designate the revenues assigned by the king to the official list of Persian princesses (the veil, the queen's slipper, etc.). The comparison is interesting; in fact, it suggests that the king had a treasury available for his own needs that we should not confused with the treasuries managed by the treasurers appearing in the Persepolis tablets.

This interpretation is based on the distinction we suggested between *tagē* and tribute-producing land (chap. 10/7). Although all of the territories—what we call the Empire—belonged to the conquering king (by way of tribute assessments), parts were reserved for him (the *tagē*) as *dōrea* for the specific needs of his own house. It is our suggestion that Persia itself was organized on the same model—namely, within the country, we can distinguish the territories of the *ethnē*, the estates of the nobles (established by inheritance and/or by royal gift), the lands managed by the administration, and the royal land (taken in the restricted sense implied by the word *tagē* in Pseudo-Aristotle). The *tagē* is the phenomenon referred to by the tablets naming the royal *ulhi*, otherwise known as the royal house (*oikia basileōs*). This Persian royal *tagē* was indeed a *dōrea* in Pseudo-Aristotle's sense—that is, it was not distinguished in the landscape of the administration's land. Lands and villages were assigned to the royal house, and they undoubtedly were also managed by their own stewards. Revenues from these properties fed the personal treasury of the sovereign and permitted his patrimony to flourish. Darius told Parnaka to charge the 100 sheep he gave to Irtašduna to this account. Our hypothesis—which we offer here solely for the purpose of discussion—implies that the king was not only the master of the Empire but that he also had a separate life as a private person or, rather, as the head of a house (*ulhi*); its funds are not to be confused with what is normally called the royal economy.

The ambiguity of the vocabulary perhaps reflects the ambiguity of the situation, which simultaneously distinguishes and confuses. The sense of the word *ulhi* cannot be reduced to a rural estate, in contrast to a working estate (*irmatam*), of which the satrapal paradise is a well-known example. Originally, the royal house must have consisted of family property—just like any aristocratic house (*oikos*: Herodotus III.119; chap. 8/4). In principle, the king's house was sustained by the produce coming from the part that, etymologically, means 'the king's part', paid to the king in the form of a "gift" according to a process that is probably distantly echoed in the *nomos persikos* so carefully defined by Aelian (*VH* I.31; chap. 10/3); this is in fact the original meaning of *baji-baziš*. This "division" must be very ancient, since the word *baziš* appears in the name of the fifth Persian month (July–August), **drnabaziš* 'month of *baziš* on the harvest'. During the course of reinforcement of royal power, only the word *baziš* remained, though it came to signify only one of the financial levies.

This hypothesis does not imply the existence of two rigidly distinct economies. It was Parnaka whom Darius ordered to take sheep from his *ulhi* and transfer them to Irtašduna's account. In fact, the king's house had resources other than the income from particular estates. Every year, part of the produce or profit was set aside and placed in a special account belonging to the king's house. Despite the activity of a staff "attached to the king's house," many functions were carried out by administrators working directly for Parnaka. The royal shepherd Umizza himself appears to have had (unclear) hierarchical relationships with Miššumanya, who, on the authority of Harrena (PF 2025, 2070), had responsibilities in the administration of herds (PF 267, 2012). What makes the interpretation so difficult is that the houses—royal and princely—are included at the same time and in different forms within the purview of the royal economy, because it was precisely from the king that princes and princesses enjoyed the revenues of their houses, in the same way that Parnaka's authority derived from royal delegation. Somehow, by virtue of his position, Parnaka found himself at the intersection of the two spheres that the king dominated without making a clear distinction between them. At this point, it is tempting to think that this was the reality hinted at by Darius when he simultaneously distinguishes and combines in a condensed formula the two elements that are his country (*dahyu* = Persia) and his house (*viθ* = *oikos*; cf. DPe, DNa).

From a historical point of view, we may ask, finally, whether the ambiguity of the vocabulary also accounts for the (difficult and conflicting) gestation and development of state bureaucracy, originating from a world that was, in the end, considered to be the personal property of the sovereign. Within the dynamic of tribute, the ideological representations and the politico-economic realities were fused because, by means of tribute, gifts, and assessments, the Great King revealed and exercised his unshared authority not so much over the lands themselves as over the wealth they produced through the labor of his subjects.

11. Transition

As viewed by a Greek author writing toward the end of the fourth century in Asia Minor, the structure of the royal economy was very much the same as the operation two centuries earlier in Fārs or Achaemenid Egypt. Analyzed in light of the Persepolis documents, the regional corpora show an undeniable internal coherence. This conclusion has the advantage of restoring an imperial universality to what is usually considered a simple reporting of local income. In particular, we have seen the considerable contribution of the Aramaic documents from Egypt to the discussion. Indeed, there is no decisive historical reason to consider Egypt a special case within the Empire. On the contrary, the evidence from Egypt fully reveals the limitations of the argument that would mechanically link the quantity of documentation with the degree to which a country was integrated into the imperial structures. Actually (and noting that the quantity of evidence is purely accidental), Egypt was the only country that succeeded in detaching itself politically from the center for two generations? Despite gaps in the documentation, and whatever the extent of local peculiarities, we may reasonably suppose that the management of royal property was organized identically in every satrapy in the Empire. The obvious concurrence of the analysis by Pseudo-Aristotle, the information in the Egyptian and Babylonian documents, and the Persepolis model leads us to think that this organization had been in place since the time of Darius.

These observations do not necessarily imply that the installation of an imperial administrative machine always obliterated local traditions, particularly in the socioeconomic and cultural realms. It is clear, for example, that the existence of a category called *gardu* did not obliterate other categories of worker in Babylonia. In the Achaemenid period, as before, we encounter in Babylonia as many free laborers and owners as slaves proper and groups of dependents (often linked to the economy of the sanctuaries), whose status, to repeat the famous formula of the lexicographer Pollux, puts them "between free and slave." In other words, the approach adopted here does not eliminate regional approaches; it makes them still more necessary. The inquiry has already been initiated in the course of the previous chapter (chap. 10/7). It will now be pursued more systematically.

Chapter 12
The King of the Lands

1. *Darius and Egypt*

Satraps and Satrapy

Our sources on Darius's policy in Egypt are abundant and varied. The texts (Egyptian, Aramaic, Greek) and the archaeological data (statue of Darius, paintings and sculptures, stelas, *naoi*) eloquently testify to Darius's varied activity on the shores of the Nile and in the Eastern and Western Deserts: sanctuary-building, codifying "Egyptian law," digging a canal between the Nile and the Red Sea, and so forth. Whatever uncertainties remain about the conditions leading to Egypt's revolt in 522, it is clear that Aryandes was confirmed as satrap by Darius at that time and that he ruled at least until 510, the date when he was deposed and put to death under conditions that Herodotus's narrative (IV.166) does not fully clarify. In fact, Demotic texts show that in 492 Pharandates assumed the role of satrap (*Berlin P.* 15339-15340) until later, in 484, when Xerxes installed his own brother, Achaemenes, in Egypt (Herodotus VII.7).

After the conquest by Cambyses, the Persian satrap held court in Memphis, the site of the offices and various administrative branches. The citadel, or White Wall (*Jnb ḥd*), was held by a garrison of Persians and auxiliaries, and in order to support them, the Egyptians had to pay 120,000 bushels of wheat in addition to tribute (Herodotus III.91). The basic territorial organization (villages, nomes) underwent no apparent modification. But, under the supreme authority of Memphis, Egypt itself was divided into a number of districts that the fifth-century Aramaic texts call 'provinces' (*medinah*). The Aramaic documents show that the southern district (Tšetreš) had Elephantine as its capital and was distinct from the province of Thebes (*DAE* 55 [*AP* 24]). A garrison was stationed at Syene-the-Fortress and, opposite it, on the island of Elephantine. At the top of the hierarchy, but dependent on the satrap, we know of the *frataraka* 'governor' who lived on Elephantine, while the garrison commander (*rab ḥaylâ*) lived in Syene. The first garrison head we know of appears in an Aramaic papyrus dated 495, a contract among three women of Jewish origin; the first two women refer to "half the share which was granted to us by the king's judges and Ravaka the commander" (*DAE* 2 [*AP* 1]). "Commander" was undoubtedly also the position held by Parnu (a Persian or Iranian), who is named in Demotic papyri dated 487 and 486; he was designated as the "representative of the southern district, to whom the fortress(?) of Syene is entrusted" (*Berlin P.* 13582; *P. Loeb* 1).

In all probability, Ravaka's decision involves a part of the share (*mnt*) allocated by the administration to the soldier-colonists of Elephantine, which also involved rations in the form of foodstuffs (*ptp*) and weighed silver (*prs*). The intervention of the Achaemenid authorities in civil and/or private judicial affairs is frequently attested. For instance, in a petition (ca. 410) the members of the Jewish community in Elephantine demand that "an inquiry be conducted by the judges, the police, and the informers (*gaušaka*) in charge of the Southern District province" (*DAE* 101 [*AP* 27]).

The troops and garrison at Syene-Elephantine, just above the First Cataract, had to maintain order as part of their brief and at the same time had to guard the southern frontier with Nubia. The Nubian frontier, however, was not particularly close, as we infer from one of the documents mentioning Parnu that refers to a convoy of wheat coming from south of the First Cataract (*P. Loeb* 1).

Udjahorresnet's Return to Saïs

Overall, the Egyptian documentation testifies to a fair degree of continuity from Cambyses to Darius. Our earliest evidence—partial, to be sure—comes from the biography of the famous Udjahorresnet, whom we saw in action after the conquest of the country in 525. It appears that he accompanied Cambyses when he left Egypt in 522 but then found himself in the entourage of Darius, who soon sent him back to the Nile Valley (fig. 44). He writes:

> His royal Majesty of Upper and Lower Egypt, Darius, may he live forever, ordered me to return to Egypt—while his Majesty was in Elam, when he was Great King of all the foreign countries and great sovereign of Egypt—to put back in order the institution of the scribal bureau . . . after its

Fig. 44. Statue of Udjahorresnet.

destruction. The barbarians carried me from country to country and eventually brought me to Egypt, as had been ordered by the Lord of the Double Land. (Posener no. 1E)

Thus, like Neḥtiḥōr, steward of Aršāma, who returned to Egypt "through province after province" (*DAE* 67 [AD 6]), Udjahorresnet, armed with a royal authorization, used official services to return to the Nile Valley "through country after country." There, he writes, he restored an institution for teaching medicine (House of Life), providing the students with all they needed to pursue their studies, "as it had been before." And the Egyptian specifies: "His Majesty did this because he knew the usefulness of this art for reviving every sick person." We have indeed seen that Egyptian physicians were highly regarded at the Achaemenid court (chap. 7/2); it is they who were brought to Darius when he suffered a major sprain while dismounting from his horse during a hunt, since they "had a reputation for the highest eminence in their profession" (Herodotus III.129◊). Udjahorresnet stresses that the work of restoration undertaken at Darius's initiative encompassed the entire sanctuary of Neith at Saïs: "His Majesty did this . . . to preserve the names of all the gods, their temples, the income from their *wakf* properties, and the observance of their festivals, for all time." In Udjahorresnet's eyes, Darius thus continued the work of Cambyses, who had manifested a pronounced piety toward the goddess Neith.

Darius and the Egyptian Laws

It was just about the same date, 519, that Darius sent a letter to his satrap in Egypt, which we know (in fragmentary form) from a text on the back of the *Demotic Chronicle*. Darius ordered his satrap to assemble Egyptian sages, chosen from among priests, warriors, and scribes. They were instructed to gather in writing all of the old laws of Egypt down to year 44 of Pharaoh Amasis, that is, 526—the eve of the Achaemenid conquest. The commission worked for sixteen years (519–503) and produced two copies of its work, one in Demotic, the other in Aramaic.

The text does not detail the exact content of the book that they produced. It simply distinguishes "public (or constitutional) law," "temple law," and "private law." It is helpful to compare this text with other papyri of the Ptolemaic era that may have been composed on the model of Darius's code. One of them, in Demotic, is known as the "legal code of Hermopolis West." More than a law code in the strict sense, it is a collection of legal precedents dealing basically with leases and property disputes. The judge could easily find the path to follow in each case that might turn up. It is practically certain that these collections were edited by religious personnel, who had available to them documents preserved in the Houses of Life—such as the one that Udjahorresnet restored at Saïs.

Pharandates and the Sanctuary of Khnūm at Elephantine

Settling disputes apparently was a common role for Darius and his governor in Egypt and so it is that they came to intervene in a matter of the sanctuary of the god Khnūm at Elephantine later on, in 492–491. Two Demotic letters found at Elephantine attest to relations between the administrative council of the sanctuary and a man called Pharandates, "to whom Egypt is entrusted" (*Berlin P.* 15339-15340). This cannot refer to anyone other than the satrap, the successor of Aryandes. The matter in question was the naming of a *lesonis* at Elephantine; the *lesonis* was not strictly a priest but an administrator of temple property—comparable, as it were, to the *neocore* [administrator] of a Greek temple. In the first letter, Pharandates reminds the college of priests of Khnūm of the conditions (social and moral) required of candidates for the post and for being considered "in agreement with what Darius the pharaoh commanded." Eight months later, the priests of Khnūm wrote to Pharandates. Without referring directly to the satrap's previous letter, they let him know the name of the one they had chosen.

The intervention of Darius and his representative in Egypt was thus not onerous. To judge by the chronology of the letters and their content, the people of Khnūm did not, strictly speaking, submit their candidate for the approval of the government; all they did was to communicate the name of their choice to the satrap. Pharandates was satisfied with the prior reminder that the choice had to conform to conditions known to both sides. There is no doubt that in doing this, Pharandates was simply reprising a role that traditionally was the responsibility of the pharaoh, a fact that is reflected in the name "Darius the pharaoh."

Furthermore, the well-known text called the *Petition of Peteisis* seems to record limits on the exercise of royal power in these domains. In the ninth year of Darius (512), Peteisis III was imprisoned by Ahmose, who had come to make an inquiry at El-Hibeh (Teuzoi) alongside the *lesonis* Zeubestefonk, son of Jenharoü. Peteisis was a temple scribe at the time. His report was forwarded to the governor (the satrap of Memphis?). A little later, Pkoip came to El-Hibeh, where he denounced Peteisis before the priests. Moreover, "He relieved the *lesonis* of his duties, threw him in prison, and bolted the door of our prison. Subsequently he replaced the *lesonis* with Jenharoü, son of Petehapi." After many difficulties, Peteisis gained an audience with the governor, to whom he brought charges regarding the activities of the priests of Teuzoi. On his return, Peteisis found his house burned down. The governor then convened the priests at Memphis. Only the *lesonis* responded to the summons. He was punished with fifty strokes of the rod, but finally he was allowed to return to Teuzoi in the company of Peteisis who, despite the promises of the *lesonis*, was unable to assert his rights (*P. Rylands* IX).

Darius in the Temple of Hibis (El Khārga)

Darius's activity as builder is easily spotted at a number of locations in Egypt. At El-Kab, the imperial sanctuary of Upper Egypt, where the new Horus, the pharaoh, received the white crown, the temple was rebuilt by Darius. On a counterweight found at Karnak, the king bears the epithet "beloved of Haroëris," who was the lord of Upper Egypt. A fragment of ritual furnishing also bears an inscription in the name of Darius. More recently, in the same sanctuary, a half-drum of a column inscribed with the name of Darius has been found: "He who performed the rites, the king of Upper and Lower Egypt, Darius."

The presence of Darius is particularly significant in the oasis of El Khārga, about 200 km west of the Nile Valley on the same latitude as Luxor. An Egyptian-style temple has been found there, the only intact Egyptian-style temple known from the New Kingdom to the Ptolemaic period. The initial work there was done by the last pharaohs of the Saite dynasty, but most of the construction dates to Darius. Decorated with representations of hundreds of Egyptian deities, the sanctuary was dedicated primarily to Amon-Rê. Darius is shown as pharaoh many times, wearing the crowns and traditional appurtenances, presenting various offerings to the gods and goddesses of the Egyptian pantheon (incense, wine, water, land). Two hymns to Amon are inscribed there, as well as a hymn to the Sun that the king recited in the course of the ceremonies. Darius is saluted in it as follows: "The Master of the diadems, son of Amon, chosen of Râ . . . , the gold Horus 'Lord of the Lands, beloved of all the gods and goddesses of Egypt,' king of Upper and Lower Egypt, 'ray of Râ,' Râ's own son who loves Darius, may he live forever, beloved of Amon-Râ, lord of Hibis, great god rich in vigor, may he live forever." On the exterior wall, several inscriptions celebrate Darius's work as a builder. Amon-Rê manifested his satisfaction as follows:

> Amon-Rê, his disk appeared in life-power in the morning, illuminating the Two Lands with the splendor of his eyes. . . . The gods are cheerful. He has seen the precious, splendid, and comfortable chambers of his temple. There is no other prince who is great like the king of Upper and Lower Egypt. Son of Rê, Darius, sovereign of all the princes of [all] the foreign countries. He [made] this as his monument to his father Amenebis, great god, powerful of arms, by making for him . . . of good white stone from Meska, place of eternity, whose walls were founded by Sechar, built with labor perfect for eternity, whose decoration was executed by Resi-inbef, who created the beauty of its gates, and in which the Sun shines for ever and ever.

Many reliefs portray privileged links between the gods and the pharaoh, who in this case was Darius. For example, four panels mounted on the east wall of hypostyle hall B show Darius and several specific gods: Mut takes the king's hand and gives life to his nostrils; we also see the god Imy-wet extending his scepter toward Darius's nostrils; below,

Darius is embraced by Isis, who addresses him as her well-beloved son. Furthermore, the goddess Neith of Saïs nurses the young Darius while Hathor of Hibis holds him by the arms. Two inscriptions explain the scene: "Words spoken by the great Neith, the divine mother, lady of Saïs who presides at Hibis," and (behind her): "Take, O youth, her nipples with your mouth; she is the powerful one who heads Saïs." The same scene is repeated in room L of the sanctuary: "Words spoken by the great Neith, lady of Saïs: "I suckle your body with [my] milk, in such a way that you gather the Double Land with all the *Rekhyt* [subject peoples] to your breast, O my son!" Elsewhere (hypostyle hall N), it is Mut who nurses Darius. This well-known pharaonic rite confers divine status on the new king.

Darius at Heliopolis

A recently published object, a statue of Darius (fig. 19), was eventually placed at the entrance to the Gate of Susa known as the "Darius Gate." However, a statement by Darius himself makes it clear that the statue came from Egypt, where it had been carved. Engraved on the segments of the belt, the folds of the tunic, and the edge of the base are four hieroglyphic inscriptions. One of them refers to:

> The portrait made in the exact image of the perfect god, master of the Two Lands, which His Majesty had made so that a monument to him might be permanently established and so that his appearance might be remembered before his father, Atum, Heliopolitan lord of the Two Lands, Râ-Harakhte, for all eternity. May he accord to him in return all life and all power, all health, all joy, as Râ [enjoys].

The longest inscription underlines still more clearly the links between Darius and Atum, even as it intermingles Pharaonic and Persian titulary:

> The king of Upper and Lower Egypt, master of the Two lands, Daraywesh, may he live forever! The great king, the king of kings, the supreme lord of the earth [in its totality, the son of the] father-of-a-god Wishtapa [Hystaspes], the Achaemenid, he who appeared as king of Upper and Lower Egypt on the seat where Horus reigns over the living, like Râ at the head of the gods, eternally!

The god confers a universal power on Darius:

> I give you all the countries of plain and mountain united under your sandals. I give you Upper Egypt and Lower Egypt, who address adorations to your handsome face, as to Râ's, eternally.

Darius's Pharaonic Reputation

In every case, the Classical sources paint Darius as a pharaoh highly respectful of the customs of his Egyptian subjects, in contrast to the behavior of Cambyses. Thus the statue of Darius from Susa makes us think of what Herodotus (II.110) and Diodorus Siculus (I.58.4✧) wrote of relations between Darius and the priests of the sanctuary of Hephaestus [Ptah] in Memphis. This sanctuary, according to the Greek authors, is where reliefs extolling the exploits of the pharaoh Sesostris, who was famous for his Asiatic conquests, had been placed. Darius wished to place his own statue above the statue of Sesostris. The priests would hear of no such thing: "The chief priest (*arkhihiereus*) opposed it in a speech which he made in an assembly of the priests, to the effect that Darius had not yet surpassed the deeds of Sesoösis." Darius seems to have taken this quite well and abandoned his plan for the moment. If this popular tradition has any significance at all, it indicates that, in Egypt, Darius attempted to assimilate for his own benefit the prestige of earlier pharaohs, particularly Sesostris, who was presented by Herodotus and Diodorus as the greatest of conquerors and administrators. Before launching into the conquest of the inhabited world, Sesostris, after "dividing the entire land into thirty-six parts which the Egyptians call nomes, set over each a nomarch, who should superintend the collection of the royal revenues and administer all the affairs of his division." He surrounded himself with men of his generation who were totally devoted to him: "And upon all these commanders he bestowed allotments of the best land in Egypt, in order that, enjoying sufficient income and lacking nothing, they might sedulously practice the art of war." His conquests encompassed an immense space, from the Ganges to the Danube. He conquered Thrace and also the rest of Asia and most of the Cyclades, and in Thrace he erected inscribed columns bearing representations of the conquered peoples. "He dealt gently with all conquered peoples and, after concluding his campaign in nine years, commanded the nations to bring presents each year to Egypt according to their ability (*kata dynamin*)" (Diodorus I.54–55◇). Diodorus again insists on the peacetime accomplishments of this pharaoh; by using the workforce assembled after military campaigns, "in the whole region from Memphis to the sea, he dug many canals all opening into the Nile, in order to facilitate the transport of the fruits and the commercial relations of all the inhabitants; but, more importantly, he safeguarded the country from enemy invasions" (I.56–57). It is quite tempting to see in the portrayal of the exploits of Sesostris implicit references to the achievements of Darius in many domains, in the same way that Diodorus (following Ctesias) dealt with the mythic queen Semiramis in the light of Achaemenid reality.

Similarly, Diodorus situates Darius's codification of Egyptian law within the pharaonic *longue durée*, succeeding the work of prior pharaohs such as Mneves, Sasyches, Sesostris, and Bocchoris (I.94–95):

> A sixth man to concern himself with the laws of the Egyptians, it is said, was Darius the father of Xerxes; for he was incensed at the lawlessness which his predecessor, Cambyses, had shown in his treatment of the sanctuaries of Egypt, and aspired to live a life of virtue and of piety towards the gods. Indeed he associated with the priests of Egypt themselves, and took part with them in the study of theology and of the events recorded in their sacred books (*hierai graphai*); and when he learned from these books about the greatness of soul of the ancient kings and about their goodwill towards their subjects he imitated their manner of life. For this reason he was the object of such great honour that he alone of all the kings was addressed as a god by the Egyptians in his lifetime, while at his death he was accorded equal honours with the ancient kings of Egypt who had ruled in strictest accord with the laws.

In parallel, Herodotus (II.158–59◇) and Diodorus (I.33◇) stress that, by establishing a waterway between Bubastis and the Red Sea, Darius repeated the accomplishment of Necho II, the pharoah who, according to Herodotus, "began the construction of the canal, . . . a work afterwards completed by Darius the Persian." Herodotus mentions that Necho was forced to interrupt the work because of opposition from the Egyptians; an oracle had proclaimed "that his labour was all for the advantage of the 'barbarian,'" by which it was sometimes understood that it was the foreign merchants who would reap the benefits of the direct link. Diodorus repeats the tradition, but he adds that "Darius left it unfinished," for he had been convinced by his advisers "that if he dug through the neck of land, he would be responsible for the submergence of Egypt" because of the difference in level between the Red Sea and Egyptian territory! This approach allowed Diodorus to credit Ptolemy alone with finishing the earlier projects.

The Pharaoh and the Great King

On the canal stelas, Darius is designated "born of Neith, mistress of Saïs. . . . He whom Râ placed on the throne to finish what he had started." His "mother," Neith, bestowed the bow on him "to repel his enemies every day, as she had done for her son Râ" (Posener no. 8). The pictorial compositions at Hibis (El-Khārga) speak to the ideological objectives of Darius and his counselors in Egypt. Another bit of evidence is interesting. A small wooden *naos* (shrine) was found at Hermopolis bearing inscriptions in the name of "perfect god, lord of the Two Lands, Darius," "the king of Upper and Lower Egypt, Darius," and "Long live the perfect god, lord of the Two Lands, Darius, living eternally." All of these texts and other evidence together lead us to think that Darius wished to signal a continuity with the traditions of pharaonic power.

On the other hand, the ideological discourse is sometimes ambiguous. The two Niles are depicted under the Egyptian winged disk on the Tell el-Maskhuta stela. The gods address Darius in these words: "I give you all the lands, all the subjected countries, all the foreign countries, all the Bows. . . . I give it to you to appear as king of Upper and Lower Egypt. . . ." Darius is "born of Neith, mistress of Saïs; image of Râ; he whom Râ placed on his throne to finish what he had started." The hieroglyphic text, however, repeats the Persian titulature of Darius: "Great King, king of kings," and he is also hailed as "king of kings, son of Hystaspes, the Achaemenid" (Posener no. 8); similarly, on the Susa statue, even Hystaspes is Egyptianized with the attribute "father-of-a-god." The Persian quality of Darius's rule is also expressed by the trilingual (Persian, Elamite, Akkadian) inscription arranged on the left portion of the royal robe of that statue: "This is the stone statue that King Darius ordered to be made in Egypt in order that anyone who sees it in the future will know that the Persian Man ruled Egypt" (*DSab*). This arrogant proclamation of dominion by force of arms leaves no doubt regarding the Persian nature of the new master. It recalls the words that this same Darius had inscribed at Naqš-i Rustam, metonymically addressing an unnamed subject: "Observe the statues that carry the throne. . . . Then you will know that the spear of the Persian warrior has reached far, just as you will know that far from Persia, the Persian warrior has made war" (*DNa*). It is no less striking that, on a statue carved in Egypt by Egyptian craftsmen, the Great King wears Persian ceremonial dress. In fact, in all probability the statue was originally placed in the sanctuary of Atum in Heliopolis. The goal could only have been to impress the Egyptians with an unambiguous representation of Persian power.

The digging of the canal at Suez is generally set in the context of the mission Darius entrusted to one of his squadrons. We are informed about this by Herodotus (IV.44✧), who doubtless received his information from his Carian compatriot, Scylax of Carianda, who took part in the expedition:

> The greater part of Asia was discovered by Darius. He wanted to find out where the Indus joins the sea—the Indus is the only river other than the Nile where crocodiles are found—and for this purpose sent off on an expedition down the river a number of men whose word he could trust. Led by a Caryandian named Scylax, the expedition sailed from Caspatyrus in the district of Pactyica, following the course of the river eastward until it reached the sea; then, turning westward, the ships followed the coast, and after a voyage of some thirty months reached the place from which the king of Egypt had sent out the Phoenicians, whom I have already mentioned, to circumnavigate Libya. After this voyage was completed, Darius subdued the Indians and made regular use of the southern ocean. In this way all

Asia, with the exception of the easterly part, has been proved to be surrounded by sea, and so to have a general geographical resemblance to Libya.

This passage in Herodotus is inserted, obviously, in a more general discussion of the limits of the known world and the configuration of each of the major geographical entities (IV.36–46), and this discussion itself is included within a vast panorama of Darius's European conquests. As best we can tell, the mission entrusted to his squadron consisted of reconnoitering the Indus preparatory to the conquest of the country (around 518?). Herodotus sets up a direct connection with a decree issued by Pharaoh Necho after the cessation of work on the canal: Necho ordered some Phoenicians to circumnavigate Africa via the Austral Sea (Indian Ocean), returning via the Pillars of Hercules (Gibraltar), a voyage that they were to complete in three years (IV.43). According to Scylax's tale, the fleet sent by Darius would have circled the Arabian Peninsula before reentering the Red Sea. But, whatever the reality of this circumnavigation may have been, it is too much to imagine that at the same time the king would have ordered the digging of the canal in order to establish a regular shipping line between Egypt and the Persian Gulf. If it ever took place, the sending of boats filled with tribute certainly was an unusual event. Darius's order, affixed to the stela of Shaluf (Posener, no. 9), is more closely related to the sort of thing we see in the royal inscriptions: it represents a symbolic takeover of the space delimited ideally by the wakes of ships. Furthermore, the inscriptions are accompanied by Egyptian-style depictions of the peoples theoretically subject to the power of the Great King. However, the construction of the canal need not be reduced to a political vision; exploratory campaigns demonstrate that there was significant expansion of trade in the region of Tell el-Maskhuta throughout the fifth century.

From Cambyses to Darius

The Classical authors love to sharply contrast the Egyptian policies of Cambyses (impious) and Darius (respectful of Egyptian religion). The opposition is noted explicitly by Diodorus when he discusses Darius as legislator. Following Cambyses' model, Darius concerned himself with the interment of an Apis in year 4 of his reign (Posener no. 5) as "King of Upper and Lower Egypt, lord of the Double Country, endowed with life [like] Râ [eternally? . . .] . . . Indeed, His Majesty loved [the living Apis] more than any king." Although the chronological context raises some problems, we may recall what Polyaenus wrote in this regard (VII.11.7).

> The Egyptians could not tolerate the oppression of the satrap Aryandes, and, for this reason, they rebelled. Darius crossed Arabia Deserta. He arrived at the very moment when the Egyptians were in mourning, for, on that very day, the Apis had ceased to "appear." Darius issued the following order: 100 talents of gold would be given to whoever could restore Apis. Pleasantly surprised by the piety of the king, the Egyptians submitted voluntarily to Darius.

It is interesting to compare this text with the hieroglyphic inscription just mentioned, whose text is as follows (fig. 45):

> Year 4, third month of the season Shemu, day 13, under the Majesty of the king of Upper and Lower Egypt Darius, endowed with life like Râ eternally (?) . . . , this god was led in peace toward the beautiful West and laid to rest in the necropolis, in his place which is the place his Majesty had prepared for him—nothing like this had ever been done before—after all the ceremonies had been performed for him in the embalming chamber. Indeed, His Majesty glorified him as Horus had done for his father Osiris. They made him a great sarcophagus

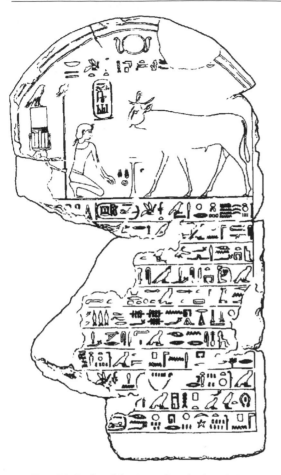

Fig. 45. Stela of the Apis that died in 518.

of solid, costly material, as had been done previously; they dressed him in garments, they sent his amulets and all his ornaments of gold and every superb precious substance, they were more beautiful than had been made before. Indeed, His Majesty loved the living Apis more than any king. . . . May Darius be able to be for the Apis a recipient of life and prosperity forever (?). (Posener no. 5)

A more recently discovered inscription shows additionally that, in year 33 of Darius, there was a solemn procession for the interment of the mother of an Apis.

This comparison of Polyaenus and the Apis stela raises chronological questions that are still disputed. Furthermore, given that the Polyaenus passage reports the opposition shown by some Egyptians to the policy of Darius's satrap, we must inquire into the exact reasons for this unpopularity. What is principally found in the passage is the traditional picture, setting the good king in opposition to the evil satrap. We tend to doubt that Darius could have suppressed what is presented as an uprising (*apostasis*) with such ease.

Diodorus, on the other hand, as we have seen, notes that the priests of the sanctuary of Ptah in Memphis refused to allow Darius to erect his statue alongside Sesostris's. While Diodorus did affirm that Darius abandoned his plan without bitterness, it would be naive to conclude from this that Darius's relations with the priests were unclouded, inasmuch as Diodorus wished to stress Darius's "benevolence" toward Egyptian religion. Furthermore, if the anecdote is based on a specific event, it tends instead to prove that the priests were far from reconciled to allowing a foreign king, even a pharaohized one, to impose any decision on them. The contrast between Cambyses and Darius is only relative, in view of the reevaluation of Cambyses' policies already presented (chaps. 1/8–9; 2). They both wanted to be considered in Egypt simultaneously as Great Kings and as legitimate sovereigns.

We can no longer state with certainty that Darius suppressed Cambyses' measures regarding Egyptian temple revenues, even though the contrast between the two kings is implicit in the viewpoint found in the text on the back of the Demotic Chronicle. Of course, in the temple of Hibis at El-Khārga, Darius is shown several times offering fields and lands to various Egyptian gods. But these are atemporal representations of the pharaoh, which do not necessarily imply actual donations, though they do not exclude them. In regard to the temples, Darius found himself with the same problem as Cambyses: he wanted to attract the temples' support without conceding too much power to them, which would be counter to the interests of the royal authority. Moreover, a Demotic document from 486 seems to indicate that titularies of benefices in the sanctuary of Khnūm at Elephantine were obliged to make payments into the account of the commander, Parnu (in this case for myrrh; *Berlin P.* 13582).

Persians and Egyptians

Contacts between conquered peoples and the central authority were not established via an administration in the abstract. The imperial administration was represented locally, not by satraps alone, but by an entire bureaucratic staff. At least as early as the time of Cyrus and Cambyses, Persians were sent by the king into every one of his provinces. All high-ranking administrators of the Egyptian satrapy were Persian, be they satraps, governors, or garrison commanders of Syene-Elephantine, governors of Coptos, or even military officers sent against Barca in Libya in 513. But at the same time, the Persians had Egyptians in their service, for reasons already suggested. For instance, one of the high officials of the tribute administration, the *senti*, was Egyptian; we also know of an Osorwēr, one of Parnu's subordinates, at Syene. And the Peteisis Romance only gives names of Egyptians at the governor's court in Memphis (*P. Rylands* IX).

As in Cambyses' day, Egyptians accepted work in the service of the pharaohized conqueror without apparent difficulty. In addition to Udjahorresnet himself, we can mention Khnemibre, who in a series of more than a dozen inscriptions gives valuable information on his origins and duties (Posener nos. 11–23). These inscriptions were carved in the rock in Wadi Hammamāt, a place that, traditionally, the pharaohs used as a source for stone for statues and buildings. This is also the source from which the block was quarried that was eventually carved into the statue of Darius discovered at Susa. In Egypt, Khnemibre held the title "head of labor of Southern and Northern Egypt," at least as early as the last year of Pharaoh Amasis. In a fictional genealogy, he claims family links with predecessors in the New Kingdom and the Ethiopian period. Some of his inscriptions date to years 26 (496), 27 (495), 28 (494), and 30 (492) of Darius. Some are dedications to the gods Min, Horus, and Isis of Coptos. He gives himself grandiose titles such as "commander of the soldiers, commander of the work of the troops." It is possible that this title refers to the military organization of expeditions for quarrying stone. It is equally likely that the title does not correspond to the exact powers bestowed on him. We also have a series of texts inscribed in the name of a Persian, Atiyawahy, "son of Artames and the lady Qanju," whose activity in Wadi Hammamāt spans 51 years, from Cambyses 6 (524) to Xerxes 13 (473). He hails Darius as follows: "The good god, lord of the Double Country, Darius, endowed with life like Râ, beloved of Min the Great, who dwells at Coptos" (Posener no. 24). It is likely that his job was to supply stone to the construction yard at El-Khārga. He bears the title "*saris* of Persia": doubtless he was governor of Coptos and the entire region of the Wadi Hammamāt.

Another Egyptian, Ahmose, gives himself prestigious titles: "Honored before the Apis-Osiris, the sole companion, the head of soldiers Ahmose . . . ," and he states that he played a very prominent role during the interment of an Apis:

He stood before the Apis, in charge of the archers and directing the troop and the elite soldiers to be sure this god achieved his place in the necropolis. I am a servant active for your
ka. I spent every night on watch without sleeping, seeking how to do all the things needful
for you. I placed respect for you in the hearts of the people and the foreigners of all the foreign countries who were in Egypt by what I did in your embalming chamber. I sent messengers to the South and others to the North to summon all the governors of towns and
provinces bearing their gifts to your embalming chamber. . . . (Posener no. 6)

Once more, the traditional terminology must not lead us into error. The primary function
of this type of inscription is to preserve the memory of an important person among the
Egyptians—to whom the inscriptions are addressed. The words used by Ahmose do not
imply that he personally organized all the ceremonies that accompanied the interment
of an Apis. The titles themselves say more about his prestigious status in Egyptian society
than about his actual place in the political-administrative hierarchy of the country.

On the model of Darius himself, Persians in Egypt could adopt Egyptian customs. It
is particularly striking to note that Amasis, whom Herodotus refers to as a member of the
illustrious Persian tribe of Maraphii, had an Egyptian name (IV.167). Since Polyaenus
calls him Arsames (VII.28.1), we are led to believe that he adopted the Egyptian custom
of double naming. We also know of Ariyawrata (brother of Atiyawahy), who in a later inscription (461) presents himself as follows: "The Persian Ariyawrata, nicknamed Jeho,
son of Artames, born of the lady Qanju" (Posener no. 31). Such naming practices doubtless facilitated Persian contact with the Egyptians, but we cannot conclude with certainty that the conquerors were Egyptianized on the basis of the names.

We will make the same cautionary remark regarding certain Persians' invocations of
Egyptian gods. This is the case with Persian administrators who officiated in the Wadi
Hammamāt: Atiyawahy, mentioned above, who is attested under Cambyses, Darius, and
Xerxes; and his brother Ariyawrata, under Xerxes and Artaxerxes I. The two brothers in-
voked, or at least referred to, Egyptian gods in this formula:

> Min the great, who is on [his] altar
> Year 10 of the Lord of the Double Country Xerxes
> Made by the *saris* of Persia, Atiyawahy and Ariyawrata

or:

> Made by the *saris* of Persia, Atiyawahy, may he dwell before Min who is on [his] altar.
> (Posener nos. 27–28).

It seems risky to take this as an index of Egyptianization in the strict sense. It was only an
imitation of the Great Kings, all of whom adopted an Egyptian titulary. Since the brothers were governors of Coptos, it was logical for them to invoke the god of the city, Min.
Votive bulls found in Egypt indicate that some Persians, imitating Cambyses and Darius,
also showed respect for Apis.

Conversely, Egyptians tried to assimilate to the dominant socioethnic class. In addition to Udjahorresnet, we may cite the case of Ptah-hotep. His statue bears an inscription
with the title of treasurer, but it is difficult on this basis to know the exact position he
held in the satrapal administration. On his Egyptian robe, he wears typically Persian
jewelry (a torque), doubtless a royal gift. Elsewhere, a seal carved with the name of Peteisis, an Egyptian boatman, also testifies to the interweaving of Egyptian and Persian
traditions. In particular, we can make out the image of Ahura-Mazda, in the form of a
body breaking away from horizontal wings.

Generally speaking, the representatives of the Egyptian elite had few problems becoming supporters of Cambyses and Darius, because the practice of conferring royal gifts was well known among the pharaohs. One of the most interesting documents in this regard is an inscribed statue found in the vicinity of Priene. It appears that the dedicator, a man named Pedon, performed a service for Psammetichus. As a reward, the pharaoh bestowed on him as "prize for his value (*aristeia*), a gold bracelet and a town, by reason of his courage (*aretēs heneka*)." He had his image portrayed in Egyptian style, and the statue itself was certainly made in Egypt. It was in fact typical for a pharaoh to decorate faithful subjects with necklaces or bracelets. The gift of a town is also known from other texts. We are instantly struck by the fact that the manner of distinction and the objects themselves correspond closely to what is known of Achaemenid royal gifts (lands, towns,

Fig. 46. Egyptian votive stela.

bracelets, necklaces; see chap. 8/1). The decoration of Ptah-hotep's robe also reflects the encounter between Pharaonic and Achaemenid practices. It is no less noteworthy that a sculptor portrayed the jewelry worn by Udjahorresnet in the Egyptian style. In other words, neither Udjahorresnet nor Ptah-hotep would have felt a sense of "betrayal" if they received gifts and honors from the Great King, for from their point of view, it was just another pharaoh who was honoring them in this way. This is precisely the meaning of one of Udjahorresnet's statements: "I was a [man] honored before my masters; [as long as] I lived(?) they gave me gold jewelry and made every useful thing for me" (Posener no. 1F). It is clear here as elsewhere that Udjahorresnet did not distinguish the Saites from the Great Kings; in other words, the latter are situated in the *longue durée* of pharaonic history.

The allegiance of the Egyptians to Darius sometimes took more personal forms. One of the most interesting items is a votive stela showing an Egyptian praying before the Horus falcon (fig. 46). The dedicator addresses him as Darius, who was assimilated to the Egyptian god. This was a private monument, which seems to show that, in the popular Egyptian consciousness, Darius was thoroughly and genuinely divinized.

A Brief Evaluation

All in all, the nature of Darius's power in Egypt elicits a mixed evaluation. The desire for pharaonic continuity cannot be denied, but perhaps we should no longer insist on this factor to the exclusion of others, especially because Udjahorresnet so suspiciously insists on it. He must have seen only advantage in thus exalting his loyalty to Cambyses and Darius, both of whom he intentionally situates within Egyptian continuity. The statements of Darius himself are more ambiguous: even while presenting himself as legitimate sovereign, he never fails to stress that he is the conqueror who does not owe his power simply to the good will of Udjahorresnet and his ilk. The passage from Saite power to Persian dominion was not achieved without upheavals and changes. Together with Cambyses' decree, the disappearance of foundation stelas seems to illustrate Persian repossession of the Egyptian sanctuaries. The suppression of the "Divine Consort" should perhaps be placed in the same context. It was a religious and dynastic institution that obviously no longer suited the new conditions after the conquest and the "appearance" of a pharaoh whose interests encompassed a horizon infinitely vaster than the Nile Valley and its surroundings.

2. Babylonia under Darius

Sources

Despite the large number of tablets dated to the reign of Darius I, the history of Babylonia is rather poorly known after Intaphernes (Vidafarnah) regained control of the region in 520 (*DB* §50). This is because in many cases the mention of Darius's regnal year—"king of Babylon, king of the countries"—is nothing more than an element in the dating formula of documents coming from the private sector. Thus, only rarely and indirectly are we able to detect the presence and actual operation of the Achaemenid administration. In comparison with the previous period, we suffer from the loss (or nonpublication) of the temple archives, especially for the Eanna of Uruk. Darius's accession to power coincided with Gimillu's appointment to the *ferme générale*. This dishonest oblate carried out his dubious operations under the usurper Nebuchadnezzar IV, before being dismissed in 520. After this date, the materials are painfully lacking, aside from sporadic documents from 511–510 that mention the name (Murānu) of the king's principal at the Eanna. Given the state of the evidence, no conclusions of a historical nature can be drawn concerning the relationship between the Persian authority and the towns and sanctuaries of Babylonia, although the number of published tablets increases each year.

Satraps and Governors

The administrative system set up by Cyrus in 535 survived the troubles of 522–520. The "governor of Babylonia and Ebir Nāri [Trans-Euphrates]" continued to rule an enormous district extending from the Tigris to the borders of Egypt. It was ruled by an individual whom the Babylonian texts call 'governor' (*piḫatu*) and whom the Greek texts call "satrap": "The government of this region—the satrapy, as the Persians call it—is of all the governments the most considerable," writes Herodotus, for example (I.197; cf. III.161), underlining the considerable profits that the satrap could draw from the region. There are tablets attesting that, between 521 and 516, Uštanu held the post. He disappeared at an undetermined date; a text shows that in October 486, a few weeks before the death of Darius, the government was secured by Ḫuta[. . .], son of Pagakanna. The territory of Babylonia proper was itself subdivided, testimony to persistent continuities. We know for example of the existence of the "country of the Sea" (Māt Tāmtim) in the marsh region of the Lower Tigris. The great towns were still administered by local governors, the *šakin ṭēmi*, Babylonians who must have come from the class of *mār banê*, the citizen-landowners with full rights in the Babylonian cities. In the time of Darius I, they are known at Ur, Borsippa, and Babylon.

At the same time, these local governors appear to have been more and more fully integrated into the satrapal administration. First of all, after 521, the *šandabakku* disappeared, though until this date the position had represented the highest territorial office in Babylonia. It appears that after Darius came to power, he replaced many of the Babylonian holders of high office. Babylon remained one of the capitals of the Empire where the king and court were periodically in residence. A tablet from 496 refers to the new palace. This royal presence was also symbolized by the erection of a replica of the monument and inscription of Behistun in the capital of Babylonia. The growing integration of the country into the imperial administration is also marked by the increasing number of Persian names, particularly in the areas of finance and justice. It is interesting to note that one of the governors of Babylon, Iddin-Nergal, had the Persian title **vardana-pāti* 'chief of the town'. A series of tablets also mentions a certain Bagasarū, who held the post of treasurer in Babylon between 518 and 501. His title is given in its Babylonian form, *rab kāṣir*, then in its Iranian form, **ganzabara*, in tablets from 511 to 501. Bagasarū was one of the Persians who held land in Babylonia, doubtless company land. His house was run by a majordomo (*rab bīti*) called Piššiya, who had a large staff under him. Several tablets show that Bagasarū did not work his lands directly: he had them managed by representatives of the Egibi business concern, who returned part of the harvests (or their value) to him as farm rent. That is, beginning with Darius I, a system was in place for managing lands and revenues. Documentation from the house of Murašū during the reigns of Artaxerxes I and Darius II allows us to analyze this system more precisely. It was a system that implied close cooperation between the aristocracy and the Persian power and the representatives of Babylonian business firms. On this topic, one of the representatives of the Egibi family, Marduk-naṣir-apli, who bore the nickname Širku, also acted as the administration's intermediary: for example, he levied taxes on land held in Babylonia. He also collected certain royal taxes, as is concretely shown in a tablet (*TCL* 13.196):

> [Concerning] the collection of tolls on the bridge and the quai [for boats] going downstream and upstream, prerogative of Guzānu, the governor of Babylon, which is at the disposal of Širku, for the half of the part that returns to him of the revenue on the bridge of Guzānu, the governor of Babylon, which he shares with Murānu, son of Nabû-mukīn-apli, Nabû-bulissu, son of Guzānu, as well as Harišānu and Iqūpu [and] Nergal-ibni, the guardians of the bridge. Širku, son of Iddinaia, descendant of Egibi, and Murānu, son of Mabû-mukīn-apli, descendant of . . . ? . . . in farm rent for 15 shekels of white silver of ⅛ alloy, of current quality, have given [this collection] to Bēl-asūa, son of Nergal-uballit, descendant of Mudammiq-Adad and to Ubaru, son of Bēl-ahhē-erība, descendant of . . . ? . . . Bēl-asūa and Ubaru will tax the boats that dock at the bridge. Bēl-asūa and Ubaru will not transfer the silver from the monthly revenue from the bridge belonging to Širku and Murānu, owners of part of this [revenue], without Širku's agreement. Bēl-asūa and Ubaru will show Širku and the [other] guardians of the bridge every written instruction concerning this bridge. (after F. Joannès)

The document sheds light on the river tolls in Babylonia, the concession of revenues to elevated persons, and the way certain taxes were collected.

Estates and *ḫaṭru*

We have several tablets showing that during the time of Darius the same system of military lots that had been set up in the time of Cyrus and Cambyses existed; the system was newly extended beginning at the end of the 520s. Each "estate" was burdened with

Fig. 47. Some Babylonian seal impressions, from Cyrus to Xerxes.

a series of fees that, taken together, were called *ilku*. In principle, each military lot allowed the administration to draft soldiers who are described in the same way as their "estates"; for example, horsemen were drafted from a horse estate. Several documents from Darius's reign show that the Babylonian soldiers could be subject to exceptional mobilizations, such as to serve in Elam. In every case, they had to equip themselves according to the standards set by the administration, bearing their own associated costs, which could be quite high. The soldiers could be requisitioned "at the head of ships," which meant that they had to escort them, or maybe even haul them, in the guise of *urašû* service. This was a requisition for manual labor, which in Darius's time was an element of *ilku*.

In the later documents (Artaxerxes I and Darius II), the enumeration of charges assessed on military allotments was regularly recorded in the following way: "Full taxes, the king's soldier, the king's flour, the king's *bārra*, and all kinds of contributions/gifts (*nadānu*) for the king's house." There is every reason to believe it was the same under Darius I. The terms used indicate that the assessment involved taxes in kind. But several documents reveal that, beginning with the reign of Darius I, some property owners paid in silver equivalents. This is how the role of the Egibi was established. They also managed working land, such as the military allotments. Thus, Širku (that is, Marduk-naṣir-apli) collected the tax on lots around Babylon between 497 and 495. It was also the Egibi who worked the estates of "the house of the royal son" (*bītu ša mār šarri*). This activity was quite lucrative, judging by the shares drawn by Bagasarū and the Egibis from the orchards between 518 and 500: one-third for the former, and he was the landowner; two-thirds for the latter, and they were the managers!

Persians and Babylonians

For Babylonia, the onomastic information that has been gathered to date allows us to state that the number of Persians and Iranians increased between 521 and 483 but that it remained relatively modest, nonetheless, in view of the considerable number not only of Babylonians but also of representatives of various countries. As for the processes of Iranian–Babylonian acculturation, they are especially evident in later documentation (tablets and seals of the house of Murašû). Nonetheless, they are also detectable in the earlier period, even though the scenes on seals remain predominantly Babylonian (fig. 47). From the beginning of the fifth century on, we observe the practice of intermarriage and the consequent adoption of Iranian names by Babylonians and vice versa.

To be sure, Persian–Babylonian contacts are old. The importance of Babylonia in the Empire and the frequent presence of the court in Babylon could only have encouraged contacts and mutual influence.

3. *Trans-Euphrates*

The District of Trans-Euphrates

Within the immense district whose central seat was at Babylon, Trans-Euphrates was ruled by a governor who was both a private individual and a subordinate governmental official. At the beginning of Darius's reign, the book of Ezra mentions "Tattenai, satrap of Transeuphrates [Ebir Nāri], Shethar-bozenai [Satibarzanes] and their [Persian] colleagues" (5:3◊). In tablets dated 502, he also has the title 'governor' (*pihatu*) of Ebir Nāri. It is likely that his residence was in Damascus, on which our information is both paltry and late. We know that Damascus was an important stage on the road between Babylonia and Egypt. The form sent by Aršāma with Neḥtiḥōr mentions the presence of two stewards there (*DAE* 67 [*AD* 6]); this might explain (if not confirm) Josephus's statement (*Ant.* XI.2.2) that Cambyses died in Damascus during his return from Egypt. We also know that at the time of Darius III, the town was governed by a "prefect" (Quintus Curtius III.3.2). Finally, Strabo describes it as "the most famous of the cities in that part of the world in the time of the Persian empire" (XVI.2.20◊). It is evident from a passage in Berossus (*FGrH* 680 F11) that the town was important in the imperial regime at the time of Artaxerxes II.

Despite the similarity between the (generic) titles for governor, *pihatu* and *pehā*, Tattenai did not rule a completely distinct satrapy, but there is no document to clarify the nature of his relationship with the governor of Babylon and Ebir Nāri. Darius's reply to Tattenai nonetheless refers to the "royal revenue—that is, from the tribute of Transeuphrates [Ebir Nāri]" (Ezra 6:8◊), which shows that the management of tribute was organized by subregions. Ebir Nāri, we know, corresponds fairly precisely to Herodotus's Fifth Nome—from Posideium (Ras-el Bassit) to the borders of Egypt (III.91). Even within these large regions, peoples and territories were in turn divided into *medinahs*— a term conveniently rendered 'provinces'. The redactor of the book of Esther (1:1) refers to the 127 provinces of the Empire of Ahasuerus. The term is also found in the letter from Aršāma to the stewards ordered to deliver rations to Neḥtiḥōr and his servants, who were returning to Egypt: "Give them these rations, from steward to steward, following the route that goes from province to province (*medinah*), until Neḥtiḥōr arrives in Egypt" (*DAE* 67 [*AD* 6]); it is a pity that the document says nothing of the stages dotting the journey from Damascus to the Nile Valley.

The Province of Judah

There is no doubt that, beginning with the time of Cyrus or Cambyses, the land of Judah by itself constituted a *medinah*. But until Nehemiah's arrival in the time of Artaxerxes I (chap. 14/5), we have no specific information on its organization. Nehemiah himself refers to it as follows: "The former governors, my predecessors, had been a burden on the people, from whom they took forty silver shekels each day as their subsistence allowance"; in contrast, he says that he himself "never ate governor's bread" (Neh 5:15–18). There is no doubt that the Jewish community was subject to paying tribute to the kings, as well as various taxes, such as "the satrap's table." But who were the former governors? The theory that makes Judah a dependency of Samaria at this date seems to have little foundation. A series of seal impressions and bullas has been found in Judah on which explicit references to the province of Judah (Yehūd) and a governor (*peḥā*) can be read. On the basis of this evidence, a list of the governors of the province between Zerubbabel and Nehemiah has been reconstructed: Elnathan (perhaps Zerubbabel's successor), Yeho-ezer (early fifth century), Ahzai (early fifth century)—all of them Jews (as were Zerubbabel and Nehemiah). Numerous seals attest to Persian presence, but they are probably later (second half of the fifth century and the fourth century).

The province of Judah and its governor came under the authority of the governor of Ebir Nāri. At the beginning of Darius's reign, Governor Tattenai, accompanied by his chancellery and court, made a tour of inspection of Jerusalem. They found the Jews busy rebuilding the temple of Yahweh. Questioned by Tattenai, the Elders justified the labor by referring to an old decree from Cyrus. Unconvinced, the governor sent a letter to Darius asking him to search "in the king's [royal archives] in Babylon" (Ezra 5:17◊). It was actually in the citadel of Ecbatana that evidence of the document was found. As a result, the Great King ordered Tattenai to let the Jews complete the construction work. Here is the order from Darius, as it is transmitted by the redactors of Ezra (6:6–12◊):

> Wherefore, Tattenai, satrap of Trans-Euphrates, Shethar-bozenai and you, their colleagues, the officials of Trans-Euphrates, withdraw from there; leave the high commissioner of Judah and the elders of the Jews to work on this Temple of God; they are to rebuild this Temple of God on its ancient site. This, I decree, is how you must assist the elders of the Jews in the reconstruction of the Temple of God: the expenses of these people are to be paid, promptly and without fail, from the royal revenue—that is, from the tribute of Trans-Euphrates. What they need for [sacrifices] to the God of heaven: young bulls, rams and lambs, as also wheat, salt, wine and oil, is to be supplied to them daily, without fail, as required by the priests of Jerusalem, so that they may offer acceptable sacrifices to the God of heaven and pray for the lives of the king and his sons. I also decree this: If anyone disobeys this edict, a beam is to be torn from his house, he is to be pilloried upright on it and his house is to be made into a dung heap for this crime. May the God who causes his name to live there overthrow any king or people who dares to defy this and destroy the Temple of God in Jerusalem! I, Darius, have issued this decree. Let it be obeyed to the letter!

Darius thus repeated the measures ordered by Cyrus, providing new donations, since the expenses were charged to the tributes collected by the government of Trans-Euphrates. In return, the priests of Jerusalem were to invoke the protection of their god on Darius and his sons. The work was completed in March 515, and the Jews were able to celebrate Passover right away. The Jerusalem community thus continued to enjoy internal autonomy, as had been the case since Cyrus, while at the same time it had to exhibit its submission to Achaemenid authority (in particular in the area of tribute).

Cyprus

We are considerably less well informed about other subregions, such as Cyprus and Phoenicia, which were also subordinate to the government of Trans-Euphrates. Both had to pay tribute (Herodotus III.91) and furnish naval contingents. Both were divided into numerous city-states. Herodotus (VII.98) selectively names the rulers he considers the most important: two Cypriot kings (Gorgus and Timonax) and three Phoenician kings (Tetramnestus of Sidon, Matten of Tyre, and Merbalus of Aradus).

It is clear that Cyprus, because of its close relations with Cilicia (see below), always represented a strategic location that was essential to Persian Mediterranean policy; thus, we can extend to the entire period the reflections that Diodorus assigned to Artaxerxes II in the 380s: "The king understood the advantageous position of Cyprus, being able to furnish a considerable fleet and serve as an outpost in the Asian war" (XVI.42.4). The island also had old ties to Phoenicia. There was a town there called "Carthage of Tyre" (Amathonte or Kition), and the evidence of Phoenician influence in it is considerable, alongside Greek influences and ancient Eteo-Cypriot roots. Moreover, many dynasties were of Phoenician origin and continued to use the Phoenician language in their inscriptions.

We learn a little more about Cyprus at the time of the Ionian revolt. Onesilus, brother of Gorgus, king of Salamis, seized power and persuaded the Cypriot cities, except Amathus, to join the revolt (Herodotus V.104). At this point, Herodotus gives the genealogy of the king of Salamis—a kingdom that appears to have been the most important on the island. The king of Salamis, Gorgus, and his brother Onesilus were sons of Chersis, grandsons of Siromus, great-grandsons of Euelthon (V.104). Power thus passed from father to son. But on at least one occasion we see that the Great King intervened in these internal affairs. According to Herodotus, the Persian victors had the Salamisians return power to Gorgus (V.115). Since Gorgus had fled to the Persians (VII.104), he must have recovered his throne due to the direct support of Darius. At the end of the revolt, Herodotus writes simply, "after a year of freedom Cyprus was once more brought into subjection" (V.116◊). But Herodotus's vocabulary tells us nothing of the status of the Phoenician cities. We know that Persian garrisons were stationed on the island, but it is likely that they were already present before. We are prompted (without proof) to repeat the judgment formulated by Diodorus on the position of the Cypriot kings in the fourth century: "In this island were nine populous cities, and under them were ranged the small towns which were suburbs of the nine cities. Each of these cities had a king who governed the city and was subject to the King of the Persians" (XVI.42.4◊). At the same time, the expedition led by Artaxerxes II demonstrates that the Great King could not allow a Cypriot king to formally declare his independence and stop paying tribute (cf. Diodorus XV.9.2).

Phoenicia

Like the Cypriot city-states and Syria–Palestine, the Phoenician city-states are included in the Fifth Nome of Herodotus (III.91). Their prime appearances in the sources are to furnish large, renowned naval contingents, from Cambyses' conquest of Egypt to Xerxes' expedition (525–479). According to Herodotus (VII.89), the Phoenicians, grouped with "the Syrians of Palestine," provided Xerxes with the biggest contingent (300 ships). "Next to the [Persian] commanders the following were the best known of those who sailed with the fleet:" the kings of Sidon, Tyre, and Arad (VII.98◊), and he states that "the fastest ships were the Phoenician—and of these the Sidonian were the best" (VII.96◊): the only comparable ships were those of Artemisia of Halicarnassus, which "were the most famous in the fleet, after the contingent from Sidon" (VII.99◊). It was the Phoenicians of Sidon who won the rowing match organized near Abydos (VII.44). It was a Sidonian ship from which Xerxes reviewed the navy at Doriscus (VII.100) and which he boarded when the fleet departed (VII.128). The reputation of the Phoenician ships was well founded. A sealing on a Persepolis tablet (PT 8) from the reign of Darius shows a vessel shaped very like the Sidonian vessels known from later Sidonian coins (fig. 50f, p. 606).

Fig. 48. Inscribed sarcophagus of Ešmunazar.

The most interesting document comes from Sidon: the sarcophagus of King Ešmunazar II, which is of Egyptian origin (fig. 48). The king presents himself as follows:

> I, Eshmunʿazar, king of Sidon, the son of king Tabnit, king of Sidon, the grandson of king Eshmunʿazar, king of Sidon, and my mother, Amoʿashtart, priestess of Astarte, our mistress the queen, the daughter of king Eshmunʿazar, king of Sidon. (Rosenthal, *ANET* 662)

Then, referring to his numerous benefactions in honor of the city, he states:

> The Lord of Kings gave us Dor and Joppa, the mighty lands of Dagon, which are in the Plain of Sharon, in accordance with the important deeds which I did. And we added them to the borders of the country, so that they would belong to Sidon forever.

The inscription thus attests to the allocation of lands to Sidon by the Great King. But the date and, therefore, the circumstances of the gift remain in dispute. The Phoenician ships had indeed played an important role from Cambyses down to Xerxes and beyond. Moreover, according to Herodotus (VII.98), in 480 the Sidonian contingent was led by Tetramnestus, son of Anysus. Even if some linguistic deformation of the personal names has taken place, there is no way to make this into a reference to Ešmunazar, son of Tabnit, who, moreover, died at the age of 14. Since we have no independent gauge for fixing the chronology of the kings of Sidon at the end of the sixth and beginning of the fifth century, the question remains open.

Moreover, Herodotus says the king of Sidon enjoyed a special position under Xerxes. Before the battle of Salamis, he was the first one Xerxes went to for advice among "the rulers of states and comanders of squadrons . . . [they] took their seats according to the degree of privilege which the king had assigned them—the lord of Sidon first, the lord of Tyre second, and so on in their order" (VIII.67–68✧). But, contrary to what has sometimes been supposed, the king of Sidon was not the admiral of the Persian fleet, which remained under the control of high-ranking Persians. Herodotus names four of them (including two sons of Darius), and he states that the Phoenician contingents (and others) reported to Prexaspes and Megabazus. If the local chiefs (including Artemisia) were consulted, it was because of their expertise in plying the sea; the privileged place of the king of Sidon was due simply to the well-known maneuverability of the ships he had provided to the Great King. But responsibility for strategy rested solely with the Great King and his associates.

4. From Jerusalem to Magnesia on the Meander

Darius, Gadatas, and the Apollo of Aulai

Between Otanes' conquest of Samos (ca. 520–519) and Darius's stops at Sardis on the way to and from his European expedtion, we have not one factual word about Persian policy in Asia Minor. This is why there is so much interest in a document traditionally called the Letter of Darius to Gadatas, which we present and discuss at this point, whatever the doubts surrounding its actual date. It reads:

> The king of kings, Darius, son of Hystaspes, to his servant (*doulos*) Gadatas speaks as follows: I understand that you do not obey every point of my instructions. Without doubt you exercise care in cultivating the land that belongs to me, since you transplant into the regions of Lower Asia trees that grow on the other side of the Euphrates: on this point, I praise your intent, and, for that, there will be great recognition in the king's house. But, on the other hand, since you choose to disregard my desires as regards the gods, I shall cause you to experience, if you do not change, my wrath excited by an injury. The sacred gardeners (*phytourgoi hieroi*) of Apollo have been subjected by you to tribute (*phoros*) and required to work profane land (*khōra bebēlos*); that is to disregard the sentiments of my ancestors toward the god who said to the Persians — — — [lacuna] — — —. (ML 12)

The authenticity of the document is no longer really challenged. It might appear surprising to find a Greek version of a royal letter, especially since the inscription is engraved according to standards that date it to the Roman imperial period. It is actually the re-engraving of a document whose original does go back to the reign of Darius, since the characteristics of the epistolary composition are close to the style of the Achaemenid chancellery. At the time of the Roman conquest, the cities and temples had to produce proof of preexisting privileges and immunities that they wished to renew. Of course, the editor-translators Hellenized some words for which they had no equivalent. It is quite likely, for example, that the modifier *doulos*, by which Darius addresses Gadatas, represents Old Persian *bandaka*, which in turn designates the king's Faithful. There is similarly no doubt that the name Gadatas is the imperfect transcription of a Persian name (Bagadāta?). One uncertainty remains: the date within the reign of Darius. We have no benchmark that would allow us to place it either before or after the Ionian revolt (500–492) or before or after Darius's traversal of Asia Minor in 513–512. It is tempting simply to suppose that the royal statement was recorded in a series of measures decided during his stay in Sardis on his return from Europe. Herodotus shows the king sitting on the throne (*proasteion*) of Sardis while receiving delegations (V.12). It is possible that the directors of the sanctuary of Apollo came to him at this time to ask him to take a position on the matter that was troubling them.

The letter itself is in two parts, both distinct and linked. First the king makes known his satisfaction with Gadatas for the horticultural work he has conducted so well. Gadatas's job is not indicated. It has sometimes been supposed that he held the position of satrap of Sardis after the death (undocumented) of Artaphernes around 493–492. It is true that in Magnesia on the Meander there was a residence used by the satrap of Sardis, under Oroetes (Herodotus III.122, 125) around 525 and again by Tissaphernes more than a century later (Thucydides VIII.50.3). According to the *Oeconomicus* of Xenophon, it is also true that the governors' job was to keep the land under cultivation and increase the yield of the soil—otherwise "the garrisons are not maintained and the tribute cannot be paid" (IV.11◇). Nonetheless, the letter concerns a specific territory, where Gadatas is praised for acclimatizing "exotic" plants from *peran tēs Euphratou* ('across the Euphrates', or Trans-Euphrates)—a Greek phrase rendering (in its way) the Akkadian word Ebir-Nāri. It is difficult not to see this as a reference to the famous Persian paradises that included, among other components, a botanical garden dedicated to experiments with rare species. Given these circumstances, Gadatas was most likely the steward of the royal/satrapal paradise close to Magnesia on the Meander—comparable to "Asaph, keeper of the king's park" (*pardes lammelek*) in Syria, in the time of Artaxerxes I (Neh 2:8◇). The grounds of this paradise are what Darius refers to in the second part as "profane land," corresponding to another phrase at the beginning of the text, "the land that belongs to me" (chap. 10/7). The curious expression "profane land" is justified by the fact that obviously it adjoins the territory belonging to a Greek sanctuary, the sanctuary of Apollo. This is the Apollo of Aulai, near Magnesia on the Meander. Darius scolds Gadatas for commandeering "sacred gardeners," whose privileges can now be reconstructed: the sanctuary enjoyed fiscal immunity, because the "sacred gardeners" did not pay tribute and were not subject to satrapal requisitions under the corvée system.

Darius, Tattenai, and Gadatas

Darius's letters to Tattenai and Gadatas testify first of all to the limits placed on satrapal whim. When the king granted privileges to a community, royal letters were sent to the local representatives of the administration. When, some time later, Nehemiah was sent to Jerusalem by Artaxerxes I, he bore letters for the governors of Trans-Euphrates; he also had a letter addressed to Asaph, steward of the royal paradise (who had to furnish wood for construction; Neh 2:7–8). The royal and/or satrapal officers had to conduct an inquiry before making any decision whatsoever. Tattenai did not neglect to do so; he came to question the Elders of Jerusalem, asking them who had authorized the work of rebuilding the temple. Apparently neither the Jews nor the provincial government offices had a written copy of Cyrus's order, and thus Tattenai sent a letter to Darius to ask him to have a search made in the central archives. In the case of Darius's letter to Gadatas, the recognized privileges of the sanctuary of Apollo of Aulai were very old, since Darius attributed them to his "ancestors." It is possible that during the conquest of Asia Minor Cyrus had established good relations with the priests, and they in return had received fiscal immunity. Darius's letter was thus probably sent to Gadatas after the sanctuary administrators had appealed to the Great King to reverse the decision of the steward of the paradise. The royal letter thus was the confirmation of recognized privileges, which Gadatas could no longer ignore under pain of extremely severe sanctions, however laudable his efforts in the horticultural realm may otherwise have been.

The royal missives also show the continuity of the policy of the Great Kings from Cyrus to Darius, which we have every reason to believe held for relations with the Babylonian temples as well. The Gadatas letter provides a rare, explicit example of fiscal immunity bestowed on a sanctuary. The only comparable example is the immunity later granted to the personnel of the temple in Jerusalem: "It is forbidden to impose tribute, customs or tolls" on them (Ezra 7:24◇: *phoros* in the Septuagint). Darius's letter to Gadatas thereby testifies both to an overall ideological strategy and to the specificity of its local applications. If Cyrus granted the sanctuary at Aulai such a privilege, perhaps it was because it had originally been granted by the Lydian kings. The probably limited extent of the lands associated with the sanctuary meant that the loss to the royal treasury was small; as for political risk, it was negligible in comparison to the ideological benefits the crown could draw from this privileged alliance with a respected sanctuary located near an Achaemenid administrative residence.

The sacred gardeners (*hieroi phytourgoi*) of the Apollo of Aulai could easily be compared with the thousands of sacred slaves (*hierodouloi*) who worked the lands of the great sanctuaries of Anatolia. Strabo, speaking of the hierodules of Comana in Pontus (XII.3.34), states that the master of the sanctuary had full rights over them, except for the right to sell them (*kyrios plēn tou pipraskein*). It was certainly with reference to such implicit precedents or parallels that Antiochus of Commagene, when he founded the dynastic sanctuary at Nemrud Dagh, specified:

> It shall not be permitted to anyone—king, dynast, priest, magistrate—to reduce these hierodules to slavery (*katadouleisthai*) . . . whether their children or their descendants, who belong to this class forevermore, nor may they alienate them (*apallotriōsai*) in any way, nor maltreat them (*kakōsai*) to any extent, nor extort corvée from them (*leitourgia*), but the priests and the magistrates shall take charge of them and the kings, the magistrates, and every private individual shall protect them. (*OGIS* 383, lines 171–85)

The villages where the hierodules lived, which the king granted to the sanctuary as *dōrea* (cf. *IGLS* VII, no. 4028), were similarly protected. Looting and war certainly figured among the possible causes for enslavement or mistreatment that the king and his administration had in mind (which could endanger the regularity of revenue from the affected villages at the shrines and the sanctuary). We should also recall at this juncture what Strabo wrote about the hierodules of the sanctuary of Zeleia (dedicated to Anaitis): as a result of all sorts of misdeeds, their number had diminished (XII.3.37).

Did every Anatolian sanctuary—some of which were Persianized (e.g., Anaitis)—also enjoy privileges such as those conferred on the Apollo of Aulai? The existing evidence does not provide an answer to this question. We must simply emphasize that the consecration of a few sanctuaries is evident during the Persian period (cf. Plutarch, *Art.* 27.4; Strabo XI.14.16). Another document (also late) may provide a parallel: a Greek inscription from Cappadocia reveals the existence of a sanctuary dedicated to an Iranian goddess, Anaitis Barzochara, to whom hierodules were consecrated. It states that they were to be exempt "from molestations on the part of anyone, with their descendants forever." Such customs and regulations forcefully recall the facts of Darius's letter to Gadatas, as well as clarify them. But, unfortunately, nothing can be said about the fiscal status of these Anatolian sanctuaries at the time of Achaemenid rule. The looting that was organized by Datames in some of them and that may well be an illustration of his rebellion against the Great King (Ps.-Arist. [*Oecon.*] II.24a; Polyaenus VII.21.1)—which remains to be proved—does not imply that the sanctuaries were normally exempt from any obligation to the imperial power.

5. Western Asia Minor: Cities, Dynasts, and Empire after the Ionian Revolt

The Measures of Artaphernes and Mardonius (493–492)

The nature of the reconquest carried out at the end of the Ionian revolt (chap. 4/3) also shows that the attention paid to local sanctuaries found its limit in the subjects' loyalty. The reconquest was pursued bluntly by the Persians, in a pitiless fashion that could not have surprised the Greeks. Herodotus reports that the Persians had let it be known that those who resisted to the end would suffer exemplary punishment: reduction to slavery, deportation, land confiscation, and demolition of private houses and sanctuaries (VI.9). This was the fate of Miletus:

> Most of the men were killed . . . ; the women and children were made slaves, and the temple at Didyma, both shrine and oracle, was plundered and burnt. . . . The Persians themselves occupied the land in the immediate neighbourhood of the town, and the rest of the cultivated region which belonged to it, and made over the mountainous parts of the interior to the Carians of Pedasus. . . . In this way Miletus was emptied of its inhabitants. (VI.19–20, 22◇)

The islands of Chios, Lesbos, and Tenedos, then mainland towns, and then the towns of the Hellespont were systematically burned and laid waste (VI.32ff.). In contrast, the Samians, who had deserted at the urging of Aeaces, were favored: "Samos itself was not burnt by the Persians, neither their town nor the temples" (VI.25◇).

At the conclusion of these expeditions of reconquest, in the same year (493), Herodotus states, "Something was done greatly to [Ionia's] advantage":

> Artaphernes, governor of Sardis, sent for representatives from all the Ionian states and forced them to bind themselves by oath to settle their differences by arbitration, instead of being continually at one another's throats. In addition to this, he had their territories surveyed, and measured in parasangs (the Persian equivalent of 30 furlongs) and settled the tax which each state was to pay at a figure which has remained unaltered to within living memory. The amount was, moreover, much the same as it had previously been. These measures were conducive to peace. (VI.42–43◇)

Then, after mentioning the appointment and arrival of Mardonius as military commander the following spring (492), Herodotus refers to another measure he took: Mardonius "ejected the irresponsible despots from all the Ionian states and set up democratic institutions in their place" (VI.43◇). Diodorus, giving the impression that these measures were taken by Artaphernes after a conversation (certainly invented) with Hecataeus, alludes to the reconquest in the following words: "Artaphernes . . . restored (*apedōke*) to the cities their laws and laid upon them (*epetaxen*) fixed tributes according to their ability to pay (*kata dynamin*)" (X.25.4◇).

Border Wars and Arbitration

Let us make an initial examination of the decisions explicitly attributed to Artaphernes by Herodotus. It is clear that though he calls these decisions 'conducive to peace' (*eirēnaia*), Herodotus was no apologist for the Persian Artaphernes. He was content to note what for him was evidence that the satrap initiated a noteworthy amelioration of relations between cities. The Halicarnassus native knew very well that border wars were one of the most acute problems of the Greek cities. He went on to give a concrete example of "rape and pillage" by reporting what befell some soldiers from Chios who survived the battle of Lade: trying to return home, "they entered the territory of Ephesus" at the moment when the women were celebrating the Thesmophoria: "Seeing that a company of armed men had crossed their borders, [the Ephesians] at once supposed them to be brigands who were after their women. They therefore hurried to the rescue with every available man, and all the Chians were killed" (VI.16◇).

The dearth of arable land provoked the constant envy of neighboring cities. A Hellenistic inscription (283–282) records this fact especially clearly: King Lysimachus had to intervene to arbitrate a violent quarrel that arose between Samos and Priene over possession of a district (Batinetis; *RC* 7). Summoned by the king, the delegations of the two cities pleaded their cause, and the Samian envoys presented a history of their rights going back to the seventh century, in the process producing "stories, testimonies, and other judicial documents" that convinced the king of the legitimacy of the ancestral rights of their city!

It is even more interesting that we have a concrete illustration of the measures imposed by the satrap in a Milesian inscription dating to the beginning of the fourth century, thus a century after Artaphernes. It records a decision made by the king (Artaxerxes II) and Struses, "satrap of Ionia," aimed at definitively settling the many territorial disputes between Miletus and Myus concerning an area in the plain of the Meander. The two cities appealed to the king, who ordered Struses to adjudicate. Initially, the problem was passed by Struses to the Ionian judges (whose names are included in the inscription). Miletus and Myus each sent a delegation instructed to plead its cause with the aid of witnesses and evidence. The judges traveled around the area to mark off the territories, then forwarded their decision (or rather, their proposal) to Struses: "after hearing the Ionian judges, Struses decided (*telos epoiēse*) that this area belonged to Miletus" (Tod no. 113). This document confirms the quality of information that Herodotus received. It testifies admirably to the relationship that the satrap established with the cities. The administration officially recognized their autonomy, inasmuch as Struses did not act on his authority alone but delegated responsibility to a local authority traced back to the old Ionian League (which had never officially disbanded). At the same time, the proceeding makes clear that the power resided at Sardis.

The arbitration forced on the Ionian states by Artaphernes was in full harmony with Achaemenid methods, which aimed less at directly governing the cities than at controlling them. Maintenance of order and stability were the foundations of Artaphernes' policy; he strove to ensure imperial order, which could not be maintained in the middle of on-going frontier disputes. But the autonomy of the cities was in turn kept in check by higher orders, since recourse to arbitration no longer relied on their good will but instead on a policy advocated by the satrap, who kept a close watch over its application. As soon as a judgment was handed down, no city could evade it without risking being considered a rebel. It was up to the satrap to enforce the judgment, if necessary by force of arms.

The Question of Tribute

The interpretation of tribute reorganization poses more complex problems. First, reorganization did not lead to an increase in the amount of tribute. Herodotus's remark, that the amount of tribute remained unaltered, seems perfectly credible, since it is impossible to see how Artaphernes could have dreamed of increasing the fiscal pressure on cities that had just been bled dry by their long rebellion. As Herodotus's formulation implies, the arrangements introduced by the satrap did not concern the increase of tribute but its distribution. Diodorus, logically, indicates that tribute was apportioned according to the ability of each city—that is, in relation to the area and productivity of the territories (*kata dynamin*). As we know, at the core of tribute pressure was agricultural revenue (Ps.-Arist. [*Oecon.*] II.1.4). This was the reason why the Achaemenid administration surveyed each city's territories; the surveys, logically, used parasangs as the unit of measurement. Overall, the amount of tribute imposed by Darius in 518 *kata ethnē* ('on each nation') was not modified. On the other hand, the portion paid by this or that city might have increased or decreased in proportion to the estimate established by the royal surveyors.

Herodotus was thus not wrong to link two measures that seem so different (forced arbitration and reapportionment of tribute). The stability of intercity relations presupposed that civic territories were clearly defined and that their boundaries were recorded in official documents preserved in the satrapal archives in Sardis (*basilikai graphai*). Every modification was recorded there, including, for example, the confiscations and bestowals determined after the fall of Miletus (Herodotus VI.20). Ever afterward, it was the only document that would provide validation: to commence a border war was tantamount to contesting it. This sort of precaution also guaranteed the regularity of tribute payment—an advantage not only to the royal administration but also to the cities, which on the one hand were taxed more equitably and on the other could file appeals based on a satrapal document. Simultaneously, these measures also did away with some of the systemic dysfunctionality that had doubtless played a role in triggering the revolt.

Democracies and Tyrannies

But it is the third measure (deposing tyrants) that creates the greatest difficulties and raises the deepest questions. Moreover, this was so already in the time of Herodotus, who exercised prudence when he introduced his statement in the following way: "[Otanes] did something which will come as a great surprise to those Greeks who cannot believe that [he] declared to the seven conspirators that Persia should have a democratic government" (VI.43✧). To tell the truth, in the eyes of the historian, the comparison set up by Herodotus is rather unsettling, so great is the skepticism, ever since antiquity (III.80), about the democratic fervor attributed to Otanes! Let us also note a discrepancy between Herodotus and Diodorus: if, as we think, Diodorus's phrase ("restored to the cities their laws") is the equivalent of the measure Herodotus describes (deposition of tyrants and establishment of democracies), then Diodorus credits Artaphernes as the initiator; for Herodotus, it was Mardonius.

A preliminary remark: It is pointless to suggest, on the model of Herodotus's audience, that this measure is not believable on account of the political attitude attributed to the Persians. Because the Persians did not entertain any ideological preference regarding their subjects' form of government, they could at any given moment perfectly well support (or: not oppose) the birth of a democratic regime. The only question is obviously the following: Did they really do so? On this point, the evidence is contradictory, at least on first analysis. To begin with, it is clear that the tyrants driven out by Aristagoras who sought refuge among the Persians recovered their previous status. This fact is certain for Aeaces of Samos, who was reestablished on the island "as a reward for the great and valuable services which he had rendered" to the Persians (VI.25✧). And many other tyrants are known to have had power later in other cities (e.g., Chios, Lampsacus), and several were established later by Xerxes (cf. VIII.85). If the information given by Herodotus is not simply hot air—and the rest of his discussion does lead us to believe that he collected his information carefully—then we must admit that the measure he describes, even if it was limited to Ionia (but what exactly does this name mean?), does not merit the general character he attributes to it. What also seems clear is that the introduction of democratic regimes was not the result of an authoritarian decision by the Persian administration. Rather, it can easily be imagined that the Persians learned a lesson from the revolt. The start of the revolt had overtly demonstrated that tyrannical regimes in many cities had been crippled—a circumstance that Aristagoras had used admirably (chap. 4/3). To reintroduce tyrants by force in cities that wanted nothing to do with them at any price (cf. VI.5: Miletus) would necessarily have led, in the short or long term, to the reappearance of grave internal difficulties, and this would only have damaged the *Pax Persica* that had only just been restored by Artaphernes. Being the pragmatists that they were, the Persians had sometimes restored particularly loyal tyrants such as Aeaces, who had been able to persuade his citizens to abandon the side of the revolt during the battle of Lade; and sometimes they recognized democratic governments that had taken root in other cities after 499.

Perhaps what Herodotus wanted to say was quite simply that, at the end of the revolt, the Persians had not systematically reimposed the tyrants—nothing more; but this was quite enough in the eyes of a fifth-century Greek! It was apparently the same situation that Diodorus refers to when he speaks of "the restoration of the laws of the cities"—that is, autonomy—in the sense that the Persians did not intervene in the establishment of regimes in the cities that had just been conquered. This sort of attitude came from a "peace-making" policy (in the sense Herodotus intended) fully in harmony with the general activity of Artaphernes, to whom Diodorus attributes the measure, perhaps not wrongly. If, as Herodotus states, the decision was made by Mardonius, this simply indicates that he had been instructed to proclaim a royal policy officially, perhaps responding to a request for clarification made earlier by Artaphernes, who certainly did not make any of his decisions without prior consultation with the central authority. After all, at the end of the Ionian revolt, Darius knew just how much he could trust in the loyalty of tyrants, and he was not unaware that a democratic city was perfectly amenable to paying tribute! But, conversely—need we say it?—there was nothing to stop him from installing tyrants in the future, even in Ionia, if he felt that such a policy would be in his interest.

Autonomy and Military Control

The Greek cities, though autonomous, were no less closely controlled. Although direct evidence is scarce, there is no doubt that Persian garrisons were stationed at several points on the shore. Thus we learn from Herodotus that Sandoces was the governor (*hyparkhos*) of Cyme in Aeolis in 480. In 499 (or a little after), Cyme had joined the revolt; it was rapidly (497?) retaken by the army commanded by Artaphernes and Otanes (V.123). Cyme was one of the naval bases for the royal fleet: before 480, Xerxes ordered the ships to gather at Cyme and Phocaea (Diodorus XI.2.3), and Cyme was where the fleet wintered in 480–479 on returning from Salamis (XI.27.1; Herodotus VIII.130). The presence of a governor in the city limited its autonomy considerably. The Persians could not permit the slightest indiscretion at their fleet's bases and/or in the shipyards, which were scattered all along the Mediterranean coast.

Imperial Power and Dynastic Powers

But Asia Minor cannot be reduced to its narrow western shore, nor to its civil structures. In the interior of Asia Minor, the Persian conquest and occupation did not signify the annexation and incorporation of all the dynastic territories into the network of the new imperial organization. Our information is unfortunately scanty on the relations between the territories and satrapal power. Obviously, the catalog of Xerxes' army can be cited, as it is given by Herodotus. In Xerxes' infantry were a large number of peoples (already given in the list of peoples included in the tributary nomes). Some of them continued to be ruled by dynasts/kings, a fact that is known from later documents: the Paphlagonians, for instance, mobilized with the Matieni (VII.72); the Mysians and Pisidians are also included (VII.74, 76), as well as the Moschians, the Macrones, and the Mossynoeci (VII.78–79), who the fourth-century Greek texts like to stress enjoyed total independence from the central authority but of whom we know nothing (or next to nothing) during the time of Darius and Xerxes—except in Diodorus (XI.61.4), where the Pisidians are portrayed ca. 466 in the image that they were to retain, as enemies of the king.

Among the naval contingents, Herodotus names the Cypriots (50 ships), Cilicians (100 ships), Pamphylians (30 ships), and Lycians (50 ships) (VII.90–92). Although he declines to give the names of the heads of ethnic contingents in the army (VII.96), Herodotus names the heads of the naval contingents. In addition to the Phoenicians and Cypriots, he lists "Syennesis son of Oromedon, from Cilicia; Cyberniscus son of Sicas, from Lycia; . . . and Histiaeus son of Tymnes, Pigres son of Hysseldomus, and Damasithymas son of Candaules from Caria" (VII.98✧). The rest of the discussion shows that, within these countries, the power in turn was parceled out among small principalities. Herodotus once again fails to name the rulers one by one. Nonetheless, he makes an exception for Artemisia: "She was the daughter of Lygdamis, a Halicarnassian; on her mother's side she was Cretan. She sailed in command of the men of Halicarnassus, Cos, Nisyros, and Calydna, and furnished five ships of war" (VII.99✧). At the time of the Ionian revolt, we learn of the existence of "Pixodarus, son of Mausolus, a man of Cindya, who had married a daughter of the Cilician king Syennesis" (V.118✧). He was probably an ancestor of Mausolus of Mylasa, who is well known from the beginning of the fourth century. According to Herodotus's version, it appears that the Carians were not able to unite except under the pressure of external aggression. They had a general gathering "at a place called White Pillars (*Leukai Stēlai*) on the [river] Marsyas" (V.118✧); after the battle against the Persians, the survivors "shut themselves up at Labraunda, in the great grove of sacred plane trees known as the precinct of Zeus Stratius," where they deliberated about the strategy to take (V.119✧). We also know that Lycia was divided among many dynasties, among which the dynasty of Xanthus was constantly trying to achieve hegemony, at least in western Lycia.

We are very poorly informed about Cilicia. The region seems to have preserved some sort of autonomous government. This is at least suggested by the existence of a local dynast referred to as *syennesis* by the Greek authors. He was doubtless the heir of the "king of the Cilicians," who Herodotus says mediated between the kings of Lydia and Media around 585 (I.74). The same author calls him "Syennesis, king of the Cilicians" in 499 (V.118). Among the most important people in Xerxes' fleet, again according to Herodotus, was "the Cilician Syennesis, son of Oromedon" (VII.98)—who, according to Aeschylus (*Pers.* 327), died in the battle of Salamis. We must wait until the end of the fifth century for further evidence. In 401, Cyrus the Younger entered into relations with "Syennesis, king of the Cilicians" (Xenophon, *Anab.* I.2.12, 23; Ctesias §58)—whose wife Epyaxa came to find him at Tyriaeum, at the head of his army (I.2.14–20). Syennesis had a residence (*basileion*) at Tarsus (I.2.23). An agreement was reached with Cyrus: he gave Syennesis gifts of honor, "promising him, further, that his land should not be plundered any more and that they might take back the slaves that had been seized in case they should chance on them anywhere" (I.2.27✧).

One should not be quick to conclude from this that the *syennesis* and Cilicia stood outside the Achaemenid imperial realm or that their integration was merely theoretical or fictitious. First of all, Cilicia is included in Darius's tribute organization, making up the entire Fourth Nome by itself; each year, it paid Darius "500 talents of silver, together with 360 white horses" (III.90◇). Furthermore, the *syennesis* had to furnish soldiers and sailors: with 100 ships, the Cilician contingent equaled the contingent of the Ionians and the contingent of the Hellespontines (Herodotus VII.91, 94–95). Finally, Cilicia was a region of strategic importance for the Persians. From the time of Darius on, it was the region through which all had to pass on the great road linking Babylonia with Asia Minor, as shown by the procedure followed by Mardonius in 492:

> [He went] down to the coast in command of a very large force, both military and naval. . . . Reaching Cilicia at the head of his great army, he took ship and continued along the coast in company with the fleet, leaving other officers to conduct the troops to the Hellespont. (VI.42◇)

Throughout Achaemenid history, Cilicia retained its role as crossroads and nerve center between the Mesopotamian lands and Anatolia. This emerges clearly again during the preparation for the expedition of 490:

> The new commanders [Datis and Artaphernes] left the court and with a powerful and well-equipped force made for the Aleian plain in Cilicia. Here they halted and were joined by the naval contingent—all the ships and men which the various subject communities had been ordered to supply—including the horse-transports which Darius had requisitioned from his tributary states the year before. The horses were embarked in the transports, the troops in the ships of war, and they sailed to Ionia. The fleet . . . consisted of six hundred vessels. (VI.95◇)

It was the same in the 460s. Artabazus and Megabyzus were ordered to prepare for war against the Egyptian rebels, and they left the homeland with strong contingents of foot-soldiers and horsemen and established camps in Cilicia and Phoenicia. They organized a fleet, requisitioning boats from the Cilicians, Cypriots, and Phoenicians; they camped in Cilicia for a year, where they could proceed to train the troops before setting out for Egypt via Syria and Phoenicia (Diodorus XI.74.6–75, 77.1).

In his passage on tribute, Herodotus also states that, of the 500 talents due annually from the Cilician nome, "140 were used to maintain the cavalry force which guarded Cilicia" (III.90◇). The occupying troops and the garrisons (including the one posted at the Cilician Gates) were able to resupply amply in this way, as suggested by Xenophon:

> [Cyrus] descended to a large and beautiful plain, well-watered and full of trees of all sorts and vines; it produces an abundance of sesame, millet, panic, wheat, and barley, and it is surrounded on every side, from sea to sea, by a lofty and formidable range of mountains. (*Anab.* I.2.22◇)

This is the Aleian Plain, watered by the Pyramus (cf. Arrian II.5.8–9 and Strabo XIV.5.17).

Control of the island of Cyprus also presupposes that the Persians had a firm hold on the Cilician coast. For example, it was from Cilicia that the Persian troops crossed to rebellious Cyprus in 499 (III.109). We may also cite the later example of the war waged against the large island by Tiribazus and Orontes in the 380s: they "took over the armaments in Phocaea and Cyme, repaired to Cilicia, and passed over to Cyprus, where they prosecuted the war with vigour" (Diodorus XV.2.2◇). Cilicia is where the Persian generals sought to restock food for their troops fighting on the island; in normal times, the merchants made the round trip between Cyprus and the Cilician coast (XV.3.1–2). From Cyprus it was always by way of the Cilician coast that one regained the great road leading to Babylon (XV.4.2; cf. XIX.79.4–6). Maritime Cilicia was not only a location for the concentration of troops; the Persians also located arsenals (*neōria*) and shipyards there. They were able to acquire quality wood in abundance from the famous Cilician cedar forests. Cilicia was rich in other strategic materials: the Assyro-Babylonian sources in particular show that the Mesopotamian sovereigns found horses in quantity there, as well as well-known iron and silver mines.

For the period considered here, we have no direct information on the possible presence of Persians in Cilicia Trachaea ("mountainous"). The irrefutable epigraphic and archaeological evidence of Achaemenid presence comes from the fourth century at the site of Meydançikkale, which is located on a spur 900 m high in the Cilician Taurus. It would thus be very unwise to transfer the conclusions drawn from this fourth-century evidence back a century or more to the first decades of the fifth century (that is, if the Artaxerxes mentioned in the Aramaic inscription is not really Artaxerxes I, a possibility that paleographic analysis does not exclude). Let us simply note that the site is very old: the name Kiršu, used for the site in the Aramaic inscription, is already known from a campaign of Neriglissar (557–556), at which time it was the residence of the local king, Appuašu. It is thus not impossible that the Persians had erected a fortress (*byrt'*) there at a very early date.

The Persians in Asia Minor

While the existence of an imperial diaspora in Asia Minor is undeniable, it is more difficult to specify the individuals, aside from the satraps themselves and a few isolated cases. When the Greek authors refer to them, it is most often in a very general way, such as "the Persians of Sardis" (Herodotus III.128; VI.4; cf. Xenophon, *Hell.* III.4.25). Sometimes the allusions are a bit more specific. When Cimon took Persians prisoner at Sestos, "a little while after, the friends and kinsmen of the prisoners coming from Lydia and Phrygia, redeemed everyone his relations at a high ransom" (Plutarch, *Cimon* 9.6✧). Plutarch also called them "powerful ones of the high country" (*hoi anō dynatoi*). These were the same people with whom Themistocles' host at Aegae, Nicogenes, maintained regular relations (*Them.* 26.1), and Themistocles also took to the road leading to the Great King in the company of a "Coast-Persian" (*meta tōn katō Persōn tinos*; Thucydides I.137.3).

The best-known example (because it is the most concrete) of Persians settled in the provinces is Asidates, who, right at the beginning of the fourth century, had an "estate" in Mysia, on the plain of the Caicus (Xenophon, *Anab.* VII.8.7–22✧). This was a very rich agricultural estate, peopled with slaves and dependents. The Greeks, unable to take a tower (*tyrsis*) "high and large, and furnished with battlements and a considerable force of warlike defenders," attacked the fortified enclosure (*pyrgos*), which was surrounded by walls "a thickness of eight earthen bricks." The fortification was further integrated into the defense system of the satrapy, since its defenders were able to use signal lights (fires) to call for the assistance of troops posted in nearby royal garrisons. Many Persian estates in Asia Minor must have been organized similarly, to go by the description of farms (*epauleis*) and "castles" (*tetrapyrgia*) near Celaenae that, "together with the men and beasts with which they were filled," could only be taken with siege engines (Plutarch, *Eum.* 8.9✧).

The system is described simply and realistically by Xenophon. A satrap himself was surrounded by a large number of Persians as, for instance, at Sardis (Herodotus VI.3–4). Furthermore, there were Persians who had received lands in the conquered countries (these Persians included nobles attached to the central court) so that a house and its revenues would be available when they had to stay there during a mission (*Cyr.* VIII.6.4–5). It also included even more Persians who came to settle:

> In times past it was their national custom that those who held lands should furnish cavalry-men from their possessions and that these, in case of war, should also take the field. (VIII.8.20✧)

We can see the system in action at the very beginning of the Ionian revolt, when the Ionians attempted a raid on Sardis: "All the Persians stationed west of the Halys, on hearing news of what had occurred, mustered for the defence of the Lydians" (Herodotus V.102✧); here, "Lydians" means "Persians of Sardis." They were under the authority of the satrap (*Cyr.* VIII.6.10), and apparently they were summoned (with other troops) for annual reviews in "the places of assembly." In this way the Persians of the diaspora were included in the organization of the territorial occupation troops, and they contributed to the defense of the imperial territories—all the more efficiently given that in Asia Minor the Greeks, with some fleeting exceptions (Xenophon, *Hell.* III.4.15), were usually unable to counter the Persian cavalry furnished by the nobles of the provinces on the other side of the Halys.

The example of Nicogenes is one of the rare, explicitly individual evidences of the Persian presence in the high country. This example also proves that coast and high country, although constituting two very different categories in the eyes of the Greeks, were not truly separate from each other. It is even more remarkable that we do not have a single case of a marriage between Persians and Greeks (for example). The only available evidence concerns the presence of Greek concubines in the satrapal court. Aside from the case of Harpagus in Lycia, we can note that personal names may suggest mixed marriages in Caria in the fifth century: Megadates [Persian], son of Aphyasis [Greek]; or Letodorus [Greek], son of another Megadates [Persian].

The basic information relating to the Persian diaspora in western Asia Minor dates from a later period; in fact, as we know, the documentation that gives us some idea of the density of Persian and Iranian settlement in certain favored regions is very late (mostly Roman period). But it is quite difficult to date precisely the settlement of large families in this or that region of Asia Minor, except for the Pharnacids of Hellespontine Phrygia; the major Persian projects at Celaenae in Greater Phrygia may date to the time of Xerxes (see chap. 13/9). Place-names incorporating the name "Darius" also offer some leads in this area. Among other information, the late texts include evidence about the establishment of Persian cults. But undoubtedly this process was set in motion at the time of the initial conquests—especially if we recognize, with Tacitus (III.60), that the sanctuary of Persian Artemis at Hierocaesarea (Hypaipa) goes back to Cyrus. But we have no information on Persian cults during this period in a center like Sardis, for example. The best-known evidence is a stela from the region of Dascylium depicting a Persian sacrifice that corresponds quite well to Herodotus's and Strabo's descriptions. It is unfortunately difficult to date with precision—perhaps the second half of the fifth century. In any case, it is a motif found in several areas of the Achaemenid world (cf. fig. 33a–e, p. 244), particularly on a gold plate from the Oxus treasury and a relief found near Kayseri (chap. 16/6 and fig. 60, p. 712).

One particularly interesting piece of evidence is a stela found in 1981 near Dascylium (Sultaniye Köy). Dated around 500, it constitutes the earliest example of a long series of reliefs called "Greco-Persian." In two stacked registers, it shows a funerary banquet scene and a hunting scene. Below these is an Aramaic inscription composed and inscribed by Ariyābama in honor of Addā. The former is clearly a high-ranking Persian and the latter is one of his colleagues. It seems that Ariyābama laid the remains of Addā in or near the funerary mound that the latter had built for himself when he was alive. This inscription is comparable to another inscription — perhaps fairly contemporary, perhaps much later — in Aramaic, also found near Dascylium: a funerary inscription that evokes the memory of the deceased, Elnap, son of Ašya, and invokes the gods Bēl and Nabū (Gibson II, no. 37).

The main interest of the first stela is the introduction of what may be called the first generation of high-ranking Persian officers residing in the districts of Asia Minor, although we are not able to establish direct relationships with the Persians named (in very limited number) by the Classical sources for the Dascylium region. The two stelas also show that non-Iranians were included among the satrapy's personnel: Addā is a Semitic name; Elnap may be of Jewish origin (but the reading of the name is uncertain): perhaps this man was part of the Jewish diaspora known to have been in Lydia in the fourth century. If this was the case, the second inscription provides evidence of an apparent religious syncretism. Like some of his compatriots at Elephantine, Elnap (if he really was Jewish) did not hesitate to invoke Babylonian gods. There is no longer any doubt that the satraps of Sardis had many Lydians among their collaborators, such as Myrsus, son of Gyges, who was active between the time of Cambyses (and certainly Cyrus) and the beginning of the Ionian revolt, when he died in an ambush (Herodotus III.122; V.121).

Satrapal Art and Local Artists

The stelas just discussed fall into a category traditionally known as "Greco-Persian" because of the central role attributed to Greek artists. This interpretation needs to be modified, however, just like the interpretation that assigns a crucial place to Greek artists in the royal studios. On the one hand, it is true that the appeal to Greek artists, in Dascylium and elsewhere, is very appropriate. In this frontier region, the contacts between the Persians of the satrapal court and the Greeks of the coast were surely intense, as shown for instance in the case of Nicogenes, discussed above. The Greek market was where the Persians of Sardis went to buy *pallakai* and eunuchs (cf. Herodotus VIII.105; Aelian, *VH* XII.1). No doubt, much other merchandise and many people circulated between the coastal Greeks and "the powerful of the high country" (Plutarch, *Them.* 26.1). It is likely that, from this period on, the Persians themselves began to come for long or short vacations to Greek cities such as Ephesus that had been under Iranian influence after the conquest of Cyrus. The settlement of many Greeks in this area on the initiative of the Great King, particularly in Xerxes' time (chap. 13/9), must have favored the growth of all sorts of interactions in the cultural arena.

Moreover, the subjects depicted on the stelas and seals are typically Persian. The Persians particulary delighted in being shown participating in activities related to banquets and the hunt. Scenes of Persian sacrifices are also found. The Persians were the patrons; the Greeks the craftsmen. The same observation can be made for other regions of the Empire. When Aršāma ordered his sculptor Hinzanāy to make equestrian statues (*DAE*

70 [AD 9]), clearly he must have put considerable constraint on the artist's creativity. This was also true, for example, for the artists and craftsmen working in the provincial workshops attached to the satrapal courts and for those who made vases inscribed with the names of the Great Kings in the workshops of Memphis and elsewhere and sent them to the central court: the pattern is the same as the pattern required in the workshops of Persepolis or Susa. Likewise, the small wood and ivory objects found in Egypt evidence typically Persian themes and borrowed typically Persian forms, as does the goldsmithery. The existence of these satrapal workshops would explain the relative uniformity of Achaemenid-period objects found in many regions. The jewelry and small objects dug up at Manisa and Sardis confirm the existence of workshops in the Lydian capital.

Conceived and organized in imitation of the central court (see chap. 8/5), the satrapal courts were relay stations for Achaemenid court art. The inscribed bullas of Dascylium (some dating to Xerxes) are good evidence. Several display scenes evoking the famous aquatic paradise surrounding the satrapal palace. Others carry images of royalty. A large number, for example, show the image of the Royal Hero (fig. 56b, p. 700) so frequently attested on the seals from Persepolis (and elsewhere). Another has an audience scene (cf. fig. 15, p. 210) comparable not only to scenes from Persepolis but also to a painting that was mounted on the inside of the shield of a Persian soldier depicted on Alexander's sarcophagus (cf. fig. 14). It has been proposed, not implausibly, that the artist worked from sketches that came directly from contact with the art of Persepolis. This suggestion is even more plausible because a nearly identical scene appears on several Persepolis seals (cf. chap. 6/1–3).

Royal Persian Art and Lycian Dynastic Art

At the same time, there is evidence from several monuments at Xanthus in Lycia of the diffusion of Persian themes, particularly on the monument referred to as Building G. In addition to showing a group of youths with fly-whisks, one frieze shows a procession of archers and horsemen (fig. 49a); the pose of the squires (arm above the horses they are leading) is amazingly close to what is seen at Persepolis (fig. 49b–c), so much so that it has been hypothesized that "in risking such an un-Greek gesture, the Lycian sculptor relied on a study of an Oriental original" (P. Bernard).

The influences of Achaemenid court art are also easy to discern on one of the best-known monuments at Xanthus, which, since its discovery, has been known as the Monument of the Harpies. It is a funerary column, mounted on a massive substructure, that may originally have stood more than ten meters tall. It is usually dated between 480 and 470. Each of the four sides displays sculptures in the round. Those on the east side are especially interesting: we see a bearded prince seated on a sculpted throne, who is holding a long scepter in his left hand, with its end on the ground; the right hand lifts a lotus flower toward his face; his feet rest on a low footstool. Two people, clearly servants, are seated behind the throne. In front of the prince kneels(?) a young boy offering a rooster; behind him we can see another young man, standing, leaning on a staff, with a dog nearby. On the north side is a prince with beard and mustache, seated on a throne; he is younger-looking, holds a scepter, and also has his feet on a footstool; facing him, a hoplite holds a fully feathered Corinthian helmet; the relief is surrounded by sirens who are leading children away. The west side shows several women: one is seated on a throne,

Fig. 49. Relief from Building G at Xanthus (top) and two Persepolis reliefs (bottom).

while three come to meet her, and another woman, also seated on a throne, is facing a door, probably the door of the tomb.

We must emphasize, finally, the interesting frescoes found on the wall of a tomb at Karaburun, Lycia, not far from another tomb at Elmali (discussed above, chap. 2/6). The tomb at Elmali dates to about 525; the date of the Karaburun tomb, however, is clearly close to the dates proposed for Building G and the Monument of the Harpies at Xanthus (ca. 480–470). From Elmali to Karaburun the evolution appears quite clear: while the Near Eastern (Assyrian) elements are not lacking at Elmali, the workmanship and iconographic repertoire are basically Greek; at Karaburun, on the other hand, the Persian influences are incontestably more evident. The various paintings show scenes from the life of a local dynast: he is reclining on a banqueting couch, in combat on a horse against a Greek warrior, or traveling seated on a chariot drawn by two horses. In the banqueting scene, he wears a long, colored robe and a diadem; two servants wear Persian clothing, while another waves a fan, and a woman (behind him) bears an alabastron and a purple sash. The Iranian influence appears not only in the costumes and poses but also in the floral and faunal decoration: the dynast wears a lion-headed bracelet and holds a cup decorated with floral motifs in his hand; one of the servants brings a goblet decorated with griffins, while the third one's fan has a ram's head on the tip. The

Monument of the Harpies is similar. There is little doubt that the artist who carved the east side, in particular, was inspired by a Persepolis model, since the similarities between it and the audience reliefs of the Persepolis Treasury that date either to Darius or to Xerxes are obvious.

From Xanthus to Karaburun, then, we have very clear indications of Iranian cultural influence. The local dynasts wanted to have themselves shown in the image of the Great Kings. It is true that the case of Xanthus is a bit special, since it is generally believed that the local dynasty descended from Cyrus's lieutenant Harpagus, who conquered Caria, Caunus, and Xanthus and doubtless the towns near the Xanthus Valley. Iranian influence is notable beginning with the reign of Kprlli (485–440), whose coins bear a motif taken from the Iranian repertoire, a striding lion-griffin.

6. Population Resettlement and Deportation

Deportation of Greeks and Other Peoples

Provincial Persians and local peoples were not the only ones to confront each other. Much more than under the Neo-Assyrian and Neo-Babylonian kings, peoples or groups of peoples moved or were moved from one place to another within the Empire. The Greek authors, naturally, were struck by the many times that inhabitants of Greek cities were deported as the result of a royal command. We know of the pronouncement with which the Persians threatened the Ionians who revolted (493): "their boys will be made eunuchs, their girls carried off to Bactria" (Herodotus VI.9✧); and similarly, the threat of "Nebuchadnezzar," transmitted to the Jews by Holophernes: "I will lead them captive to the ends of the earth" (Judith 2:9✧).

The earliest case on record is the case of the Barcaeans, who after the Persian victory (513) were taken first to Egypt and then to Darius, "who gave them a village in Bactria to live in. They named the village Barca, and it was still inhabited within my own memory" (Herodotus IV.202, 204✧). After the conquest of Miletus (493), "the men in the city who were captured alive were sent as prisoners to Susa; Darius did them no harm, and settled them in Ampe on the Persian Gulf, near the mouth of the Tigris" (VI.20✧). Many Greek authors have also preserved the example of the Eretrians taken prisoner during the expedition of Datis and Artaphernes in 490:

> Before their capture, Darius had nursed bitter resentment against the Eretrians, because they had injured him without provocation; now, however, when he saw them brought before him in defeat and knew that they were in his power, his anger vanished. He did them no further harm, but settled them on some land of his, called Ardericca, in Cissia, about twenty-six miles from Susa." (VI.120✧)

Ancient authors mention the presence of Boeotian deportees and also deportees from "Carian villages" near Susa (Diodorus XVII.110.4–5). During what Herodotus calls the Second Ionian Revolt (479), the Branchidae of Miletus took Xerxes' side; in the face of Greek victories, they chose to flee in the wagons of the royal army. Xerxes settled them in Bactria and, according to tradition, they were later severely punished by Alexander (Strabo XI.11.4; Quintus Curtius VII.5.28–35). There is obviously no reason to suppose that the Greeks were the only ones so treated; the ethnic roll-call of the Persepolis tablets is proof (chap. 11/3). Herodotus also lists among the deportees the Paeonians, whom Darius had settled in Asia Minor (V.12–14); according to Diodorus Siculus,

Cambyses also deported Egyptian craftsmen (I.46.4), and according to Pliny (VI.29.116), Darius is supposed to have transferred *magi* to Media (but this may be an echo of a suspect tradition concerning the revolt of the Median *magi* and the measures taken against them [the *Magophonia*] by Darius; Herodotus III.79). According to late, highly untrustworthy sources, Jews were also supposed to have been deported during the time of Artaxerxes II (see chap. 15/7).

The Status of Displaced Communities

It is not easy to determine the status of deported populations. We will set aside the texts from Alexander's time, which indicate the presence of Greeks and Lycians in the Persepolis workshops and agricultural establishments (animal husbandry), since it is impossible to date their arrival. Diodorus simply explains that their presence went back to "previous kings of Persia" (XVII.69.2✧; see also chap. 16/12). However, the presence of Greeks in Persia during the time of Darius I is evidenced not only by certain texts and graffiti written in Greek but also by several tablets (cf. PF 2072). One tablet refers to maternity rations provided to Ionian women (PF 1224). Others refer to a person using the ethnicon Yauna as a personal name; this was certainly a Greek, who apparently held jobs in the administration, because he handled grain (PF 1942, 1965) and in 499–498 he was a member of the staff of Parnaka and Zissawis.

The older texts illuminate the fact that in every case the Greek deportees were provided with a permanent settlement and the use of land. Their situation was doubtless not fundamentally different from that of any other ethnic community settled in Babylonia under the *ḫatru* system. The members of these organizations were not exclusively soldiers, and a wide variety of ethnic groups are known: Iranians, Indians, Saka, and people originally from Anatolia as well. A document from Cambyses' reign suggests that Egyptians settled near Nippur had an autonomous organization ruled by elders and recognized by the Achaemenid administration. The same was true for the Jewish diaspora, some of whom remained active even after the others returned from exile. Many Jews, thoroughly integrated into the commercial and cultural context, actually preferred to stay where they were rather than attempt the risky return to Judah. We may make the same observation for the Babylonians settled in Persia beginning with the reign of Cambyses. It seems quite likely that the deported Greek communities enjoyed a status identical to that of other deported groups, or nearly so—which would explain Herodotus's insistence that Darius "did them no (further) harm" (VI.20, 119✧). In the time of Darius III, the Euboeans of Susiana furnished a contingent for the royal army (Quintus Curtius V.1.2). This must have been a general practice, because the deportees (*anaspastoi*) settled on the islands in the Persian Gulf were integrated into Darius's tribute organization (Herodotus III.93) and sent a contingent to Xerxes' army (VII.80).

The Garrisons of Egypt

The placement of royal garrisons throughout the imperial territories also shows that, like groups alloted land under the *ḫatru* system, garrisons comprised a variety of ethnic groups. The best-known case is Syene-Elephantine. The presence of Jews on Elephantine goes back to a period before the Persian conquest, since in a petition that the Jews sent to the governor of Judea in 407, they recalled that, "when Cambyses entered Egypt, he found this sanctuary already built" (*DAE* 102 [*AP* 30–31]). Although by the nature of things the Aramaic documents come from privileged Jews, they also show that soldiers of many ethnicities were present: Persians of course, and also other Iranians, Medes (*DAE* 46 [*BMAP* 5]), Caspians (nos. 36, 44–46 [*AP* 13, *BMAP* 3–5]) Khwarezmians (nos. 33–34 [*AP* 6, 8]), not to mention Egyptians (no. 101 [*AP* 27]), Arameans (nos. 6–9 [*AP* 29, 35, 43, 7] etc.), and even Babylonians (no. 33 [*AP* 6]). The company (*dgal*) commanders frequently have Iranian names (nos. 11, 33–36, 38, 41 [*AP* 45, 6, 8, 9, 13, 15, 28]), but others have Babylonian names, such as Nabûkuddurî (nos. 7, 9, 53 [*AP* 35, 7, *BMAP* 12]) or Iddinabû (nos. 39, 48 [*AP* 20, *BMAP* 7]). We observe the same ethnic diversity at Memphis, both in the garrison and in the royal workshops. Without doubt, even though the Egyptian case is the best known, it is not unique. In addition to the Babylonian example, we know that there were Egyptians, Assyrians, Hyrcanians, and Bactrians among the garrisons in Asia Minor. The excavations at the cemetery of Deve Hüyük (30-odd km from Carchemish) have shown that most of the soldiers there came from northern Iran.

All of the texts also show evidence of the mixing of populations. The military organization itself (the *dgal*) was not a mask for ethnic unity: each company included soldiers of various origins. Naming practices provide a reference point: for example, the Babylonian Nabûkuddurî had a son called Bagadāta (*DAE* 32 [*AP* 5]); Nabûre'i and Mannuki had fathers with Iranian names (no. 37 [*AP* 14]). The Jews' adoption of Egyptian, Aramean, or Canaanite ritual practices or gods is further evidence of ethnic mixing.

7. Unity and Diversity

Imperial Administration and Multilingualism

Coming on the heels of Cyrus's and Cambyses' efforts, the reorganization and reconstruction carried out by Darius radically accelerated the movement toward administrative unification of the conquered territories. Analysis of income from tribute proves that, beginning with Darius, one may speak of an imperial enterprise in the full sense of the word. However, the unification of administrative practices on an imperial scale does not imply a loss of local traditions, which supposedly melted and alloyed into an Achaemenid *koinē*. The conquest and dominion played out on two levels, which are only apparently contradictory: unification and maintenance of diversity.

The documentation from the reigns of Darius and Xerxes reveals the general spread of Aramaic in the satrapal bureaucracies: in Persepolis itself, Babylonia, Egypt, Sardis, Dascylium, and all the way onto the Iranian Plateau. Nonetheless, the administrative spread of Aramaic did not displace the local languages. Naturally, we are reminded of the command given by Ahasuerus in the book of Esther, "to each province in its own script and to each people in its own language" (3:12◇; cf. Daniel 3:4, 7; 6:26) and of the order given by Darius at Behistun: "Afterwards this inscription I sent off everywhere among the provinces. The people unitedly worked upon it" (§70, OPers◇ and Elamite). The versions found in Babylonian at Babylon and in Aramaic at Elephantine prove that the royal order was efficiently carried out.

It is quite clear that local languages and scripts continued to be used heavily, in private texts as well as in official documents sent out by the central authority—for example, the hieroglyphic texts of Darius and Xerxes. There are many witnesses to this continuity, in Asia Minor, Babylonia, Phoenicia, and even Persepolis: for instance, the Egyptian code of jurisprudence was published in Aramaic and Demotic; among the documents of daily life, there was the slave in Cambyses' Babylonia on whose wrist was an inscription in Akkadian and Aramaic (*Camb.* 143).

Analysis of the correspondence in 492 between Pharandates, satrap of Egypt, and those in charge of the sanctuary of Khnūm at Elephantine illuminates this matter very clearly. It shows concretely that Aramaic could not systematically be used as the exclusive linguistic vector between the administration and the subject peoples. The satrap's letter was written in Aramaic by the Memphis offices, under the direction of a high chancellery official (a non-Egyptian, perhaps a Persian), and then was actually translated phrase by phrase by an Egyptian secretary (Peftu'uneith) familiar with Demotic; he ran into some difficulty in this task, resulting in the translation problems encountered by modern scholars. However, the Elephantine priests' reply was rendered directly in Demotic. In other words, to make themselves understood, the satrapal administration needed recourse to local scribes.

Under these conditions, the translations of official documents were not always done with the legal precision, especially if the target language did not have an equivalent for some Persian word. Thus, the Greek translator of Darius's letter to Gadatas could not find any other word to render *bandaka* than *doulos*, and, semantically, the Greek word is only very distantly related to the Persian word assumed to underlie it (cf. also Xenophon, *Anab.* I.6.6). The translations may have been even more complicated because there often was an Aramaic intermediary between the Persian original and the version in the local language. The bilingual and trilingual inscriptions demonstrate the difficulties of rendering: the best example from this time period is the Behistun inscription in its differing versions and, for a later time, the Xanthus Trilingual.

We know of very few examples of language-learning. Themistocles is the best-known example. He learned Persian when he entered the entourage of Artaxerxes I (*Them.* 28.5; Thucydides I.138.1)—so well, in fact, that, according to Nepos (*Them.* 10.1✧), "It was much easier . . . to speak in the presence of the king than to those who were not born in Persia"! Herodotus mentions Histiaeus of Miletus, who spoke Persian, at least well enough to identify himself to a Persian soldier (VI.29). Of course, he had spent more than ten years at the court of Darius. Nonetheless, the known examples are both anecdotal and isolated. All indications are that the Persian language was not widely spoken. Xenophon, to be sure, relates that in Armenia he addressed a village chieftain through an interpreter speaking Persian (*persisti*: *Anab.* IV.5.10) or Persian-speaking (*persizōn*: IV.5.34). But the evidence should not be overestimated. Xenophon does not in fact state that the *kōmarch* actually spoke Persian. We may just as well suppose that an Armenian could, without much difficulty, comprehend a simple conversation in a language closely related to his own.

Strabo states that the populations of the Iranian Plateau (Aria) spoke the same language (*homoglōssoi*), mentioning also that there were minor dialect variations (*para mikron*; XV.2.8). It is likely that Persian was used by some peoples of the Plateau; this is certain for the Sagartian nomads, who spoke Persian (*phōnē*), according to Herodotus; of course he also says that they were descended from a Persian people (*ethnos persikos*; VII.85), in all their tribal diversity (I.125); they preserved methods of combat, for instance, that did not differ greatly from the royal cavalry. The language and traditions of the other Persian tribes, such as the Mardians of Persis (cf. Aelian I.34) probably also had not changed greatly over the years. Strabo notes that the inhabitants of Drangiana were also acculturated to the Persians (XV.2.10). The word he uses (*persizontes*) could lead us to think that he is referring to adoption of the Persian language, but the context does not require this interpretation. Herodotus (I.125) mentions the Persian tribes of "laborers" called the Germanii; Strabo calls them Carmanians (XV.2.14◊) and says that they adopted agricultural practices similar to those of the Persians. But Strabo's story also shows the extent to which the Carmanians retained their own customs. In particular, a rite of passage that he describes is very different from the Persians' rite (chap. 8/3): before marrying, a young man had to prove his virility by "cut[ting] off the head of an enemy and [bringing] it to the king; and the king stores the skull in the royal palace"!

Aside from the specific case of the Sagartians, there is nothing to indicate widespread use of the Persian language among the Iranian peoples. This is why, for example, Alexander needed to use an interpreter accustomed to the form of speech (*phōnē*) used by the inhabitants of Maracanda in Sogdiana (Arrian IV.3.7). Furthermore, all of the later documents report the vigor of the Bactrian and Sogdian languages, as well as the maintenance of funerary customs in eastern Iran entirely different from the customs of Persia (such as desiccation of corpses).

The maintenance of multilingualism resulted in the use of interpreters. There were many interpreters in the royal army (e.g., Xenophon, *Anab.* I.2.17; 8.12) as well as at the central court, and not just during the reception of foreign ambassadors. For example, during Themistocles' first audience, he addressed the Great King through an interpreter (*Them.* 28.1). The presence of interpreters at the meetings between Cyrus and Croesus (I.86) and Darius and the Greeks (III.38) is also reported by Herodotus. Obviously, Darius I did not bother to learn Greek, although his distant successor Darius II did (at least according to Quintus Curtius V.11.5). There were some Persians who learned to handle the local languages, such as the Greek-speaking Persian at the banquet at Thebes in 479 in honor of Mardonius (Herodotus IX.16), or Pategyas, in Cyrus the Younger's entourage, who knew enough Greek to give an order to the mercenaries (Xenophon, *Anab.* I.8.1). However, at the end of the fifth century, the satrap Tissaphernes still used an interpreter to communicate with the Greeks (Xenophon, *Anab.* II.3.17).

A Babylonian tablet (Amherst 258) dated (theoretically) to the beginning of the fifth century seems to suggest that knowledge of local languages was not a widespread accomplishment among the Persians. It lists rations issued to a series of people, mostly Persians, clearly high-ranking (among them Uštānu, probably none other than the satrap of Babylonia and Ebir Nāri); these Persians may have been passing through Elam and Babylonia or may have completed a mission there. In any case, the tablet mentions a scribe-interpreter (Libluṭu), a translator (Mardukā) attached to Uštānu's retinue, as well as Artapāti's interpreter (Bēl-ittannu). Apparently, these Persians were unable to communicate directly with those they were governing and had to call on Babylonian interpreters to do so. It is also true that the document can be interpreted differently: perhaps the Persians, though they could utter a few words in Babylonian, had not mastered the language sufficiently to give specific orders; or perhaps they insisted on speaking Persian to maintain their prestige; or perhaps the word used (*sipīru*) for the Persians' associates refers primarily to their secretarial function, which is not necessarily linked to the job of translator-interpreter.

Perhaps it would be a good idea not to assign too much importance to this text. Even though oral communication between the Persians and their subjects was in fact hobbled by a whole series of obstacles, linguistic and/or political, it must be stressed that the use of Aramaic and the work of secretaries and interpreters allowed them to pass easily over the obstacles in administrative affairs, and even in daily life. When Persians made a commercial deal with Egyptians, the text was written in Aramaic (*DAE* 109); so too for a contract between an Aramean from El-Hibeh (Teuzoi) and an Egyptian peasant (*DAE* 1). In other words, the perpetual linguistic diversity did not imperil the political unity of the Empire: written or proclaimed in Greek, Babylonian, Lycian, or Demotic, a royal or satrapal order retained its full *Persian* effective value—just as, despite the use of craftsmen from every land and borrowing from various Near Eastern iconographies, Persepolis art is *Royal Achaemenid* art, in the full sense of the term.

Royal Law and Local Law

Because Darius decreed the "codification" of the Egyptian "laws," it is sometimes said that he must have intended to issue a common set of judicial precepts, known as the "royal law," throughout the Empire. This interpretation gives rise to many reservations. The jurisprudence collected by the Egyptian sages does not actually equal a law code, in the usual sense this idea has in the context of Roman law. Moreover, this Egyptian jurisprudence was meaningless outside the Egyptian context; it was useful exclusively to the lawyers and judges of the Nile Valley. The satrapal authorities had to conform to it when they chose to intervene in an Egyptian proceeding (see chap. 14/8).

We also know of the existence of judges in Babylonia (*dātabaru, dayyānu*, etc.). But the use of Persian loanwords (*dātabaru/*dātabara*) does not in itself prove that the royal law functioned in Babylonia. The existence of these officials, whose duties are ill-defined anyway, does not imply that Babylonia was subject to an imperial law code. Whatever their titles, the judges rendered their decisions in accord with local law, as long as the case did not leave the regional system. Moreover, the phrase "according to the king's law (*datu ša šarri*)," which recurs in several Babylonian tablets, may primarily designate fiscal obligation—that is, obligations closer to rules and regulations than to actual laws. The same terminology lies hidden in the Aramaic papyri from Saqqara (*dtbry', dayyēnē*); in all likelihood, these judges were to preside over civil trials, as in the southern provinces (*dyny'* in the Aramaic documents from Elephantine). Of course, on rare occasions they appear at Elephantine as 'royal judges' (*dyny mlk'*; cf. *DAE* 2 [*AP* 1]). But the temptation to equate them with the category of royal judges, as it is known from the Classical sources, must be resisted: royal judges were named by the king and acted only in a Persian context (Herodotus III.31; *hoi patrioi thesmoi*). In Egypt, judges, provincial judges, and royal judges presided over cases and their appeals under the authority of the governor, satrap, and, ultimately, of the king.

The Persian word *dāta*, translated 'law', is itself responsible for some of the ambiguities. For example, in a Persepolis tablet, it designates "regulations" that the heads of warehouses had to follow (*PF* 1980: Elamite *datam*). This is also the framework in which we must understand the tasks entrusted to the judge (**dātabara*) of Parnaka (*PF* 1272). In the book of Esther, the word *dāta* appears nineteen times to refer to a court regulation (e.g., 1:8: wine reserved for the king *kata prokeimenon nomon*) or to refer to established custom (1:15: judgment of Esther *kata ton nomon*) or to the king's edict (1:19: *prostagma*). Here the translation of *dāta* by *nomos* is perfectly appropriate. In the Greek authors, in fact, the word *nomos* simply refers to Persian practices (e.g., Ctesias §57:

funerary practice; Herodotus I.131–40, etc.) and/or Achaemenid court practices—as in Aelian, who was fond of these court regulations: I.21 (*nomos epikhōrios: proskynesis*), I.31–32 (*persikos nomos*: obligatory gifts from the Persian peasantry to the king), XII.62 (*nomos persikos*: obligations of the king's councilors). To get to the bottom of these comparisons, including a playful one, let us come back to the Elamite phrase *datam appukana*, which is usually understood as 'according to the usual/traditional regulations' rather than as 'according to the former law' (PF 1980). One can see how a Greek author trying to render it in his own language would have used a formula such as *kata ton (persikon) patrion nomon*!

In a passage with little historical credibility, the redactor of the book of Esther contrasts the laws of the Jews with the laws of the king (3:18: *nomoi tou basileōs*). But here, the accent is on the political rather than the judicial aspect: there was no question of imposing the Persian laws everywhere; instead, the royal edict explicitly recognizes the laws of the various peoples (*nomoi . . . para panta ta ethnē*), in the same way that the royal edicts were published in all of the languages of the Empire, "declaring that every man should be master in his own house" (1:22). One final example, the one most often quoted, is Ezra 7:25–26◊, in which we find the royal order in the following form:

> And you, Ezra, by virtue of the wisdom of your God, which is in your possession, you are to appoint scribes and judges (*kritai*) to administer justice for the whole people of Trans-Euphrates, that is, for all who know the Law of your God. You must teach those who do not know it. If anyone does not obey the Law of your God—which is the law of the king—let judgement be strictly executed on him.

There is no trace here of a desire to extend a "code of imperial laws," since the king recognizes and protects the laws of the Jews (the Torah), according to which the judges appointed by Ezra will render their decisions, including regarding Jews living outside the territory of Judah ("all the [Jewish] people in the Trans-Euphrates province"). The explanation is quite different: as soon as they are recognized by the Great King, local customs are included in the general category of "royal law." In other words, they acquire ipso facto (and first of all with respect to the satrapal administration, to which the king speaks) an authority that does not proceed exclusively from the local people's own traditions. In a way, from the perspective of the rulers of local communities (*ethnos*, city, sanctuary), the label "royal law," far from being considered a limitation on their autonomy, constituted a sort of royal guarantee against satrapal arbitrariness. In this sense, Darius's tribute reforms can be included in the category of "royal law": while they symbolized and marked submission, they also strictly limited the unfortunate impulses of satrapal authorities.

In sum, we must firmly conclude that there was in the Empire no law code imposed on every population without distinction. In this sense, the concept of royal law belongs in the sphere of politics, not of law. This is how Darius's statement at Behistun must be understood: "By the power of Ahura-Mazda, these peoples respected my law (*dāta*), they did as I ordered" (§8). Here, *dāta* is nothing more than the requirement of loyalty (*arta*) and the obligation to pay the "king's portion" (= *baji* [*baziš*] 'tribute'). The word obviously reflects politico-religious ideology, not judicial organization; it designates and exalts the unshared domination of the Great King over his countries and his peoples.

PART FOUR

From Xerxes to Darius III:
An Empire in Turmoil

Chapter 13
Xerxes the Great King (486–465)

1. Sources and Problems

The Year 479 and Xerxes' Reputation

Traditionally, modern historiography has presented a terrible image of Xerxes' personality and reign. This image was already fully fashioned in Rawlinson's *Five Great Monarchies*, a work published in 1867: with Xerxes began the disorders of the harem, assassinations, and conspiracies; around him were unleashed the passions of the court princesses and the growing influence of the eunuchs, with the result that "the character of Xerxes sank below that of any of his predecessors." The king was weak, easily influenced, immature in his appetites, egotistical, cruel, superstitious, licentious. All this explains the decline of the Empire, which had become exhausted by the bloodletting of the Second Persian War. This decadence was visible not only in the territorial and military realms but also in the area of administration and "national spirit." "With Xerxes began the corruption of the court," evident in the growth of luxury and the effeminacy of the customs. Rawlinson is willing to concede that the king was able to demonstrate his aptitude as a builder, but at the same time he emphasizes that most of the buildings dated to his reign were probably planned by his father, Darius. We can see that, despite the clearest warnings, this image of Xerxes has continued to be set forth even in recent articles and books. My concern with this presentation of Xerxes can be put in the form of one direct, simple question: What is the significance of the year 479 in Persian history? In answering this question, we must first inquire into the origin of the above point of view, since any reexamination presupposes a historiographic consideration of the way that the viewpoint came into being.

Persian History and Hellenocentrism

It is easy to see that the traditional view is based primarily on an uncritical reading of the Classical sources. Aside from Herodotus's passage on the choice of a crown prince (VII.2–3) and a very brief allusion to Xerxes' reconquest of Egypt (VII.7), all of books VII, VIII, and IX of his *Histories* are dedicated to examining the king's preparation for and the Persian defeats at Salamis (480), Plataea, and Mycale (479). Herodotus's narrative stops suddenly with Xerxes' preparations for leaving Sardis after the defeat at Mycale. What is more, the last chapters of Herodotus have played no small part in establishing the picture of a decadent king. Herodotus relates, in fact, that during the king's stay at Sardis when he returned from the European expedition, he fell in love with his sister-in-law, the wife of his brother Masistes; unable to seduce her, he "arranged a marriage between a daughter of Masistes and this woman and his own son Darius, under the impression that by this means he would be more likely to get her" (IX.108◊). Herodotus then introduces Amestris, Xerxes' wife, and her fateful influence on the spirit of her husband, as well as her untold cruelty (IX.109–12). This adventure touches on the revolt of Masistes, which led to the massacre that took not only Xerxes' life but also the lives of his children and his forces (IX.113). Injected into the story of the Greek victories in Asia Minor, these tales fostered the image of a king subject to the nefarious influences of the women of the palace and more interested in slaking his guilty passions than in defending the territorial inheritance of Darius. In reality, placing such an emphasis on the story of Xerxes and his sister-in-law results from a highly questionable methodology. On the one hand, the story is a romance, characterized by a whole series of repetitive motifs on which it is extremely imprudent to base any historical extrapolation. On the other hand, Herodotus's tale contains many other informative elements that are much more convincing about the policy and strategy followed by Xerxes after his return from Salamis—at least if the historian chooses to free himself from the overwhelming weight of stereotypes.

Of course, we have already pointed out Herodotus's inadequacies several times. But his disappearance (as historiographer) after 479 also suggests that we need to reevaluate his place in the reconstruction of Achaemenid history. We lose the narrative thread that has guided historians ever since the conquests of Cyrus and Cambyses. And no other Greek author represents a viable alternative. As narrative, Thucydides' famous chapters on the formation of Athenian power (I.89–95) and the careers of Pausanias (I.128–30) and Themistocles (I.135–38) to some extent take up where Herodotus leaves off. But Thucydides never claimed to be writing a history of Persia. He touches on Persia only peripherally, when it allows him to answer the question he proposes with regard to the trigger of the Peloponnesian War: How did Athens acquire the power it wielded in 432, during the period known as the Fifty Years (*Pentakonta*) (I.89.1; 118)? Of course, his analysis does offer passages that also touch on the history of Persia, such as the story of the Athenian expedition to Egypt (I.104, 109). But to privilege these passages is likely to accord too much weight to the Mediterranean region of the Empire. The same considerations hold for the works of other authors, such as Diodorus Siculus or even Plutarch (*Themistocles, Aristides, Cimon*). The reigns of Xerxes and his successors cannot be reduced to the ups and downs of Persian battles with Athens in the Aegean Sea (cf. Plutarch, *Them.* 31.3).

Ctesias's narrative contribution is weak and dubious, and Photius's summary, aside from the mention of a Babylonian revolt (§§21–22), illustrates the same glaring inadequacies as Ctesias. Not only does Ctesias's tale of Xerxes' expedition swarm with errors (§§23–27), but the period 479–466 is covered in a couple of sentences on the extramarital affairs of his daughter Amytis (wife of Megabyzus) and the plot in which the king lost his life (§§28–29). It seems clear that beginning with §22, Ctesias is less interested in dynastic history than in the saga of the family of Megabyzus, to which he devotes long passages, up through the death of the last son of Megabyzus, Zopyrus II, during the reign of Artaxerxes I (§43). No other Classical author fills in the gaps. We find the same imbalance in Justin (III.1.1) and Aelian (*VH*, XIII.3): "Xerxes, king of Persia, formerly the terror of the world, began to be despised even by his subjects" (Justin); "against the Greeks he came off badly, and on his return he suffered a most shameful death, murdered one night in bed by his son" (Aelian✧).

The Idea of Decadence

In every case, the year 479 is presented implicitly or explicitly as a crucial date, after which began the long death-throes of the Empire created by Cyrus, Cambyses, and

Darius. Plato, who widened the interpretation to Achaemenid history in its entirety, also believed this. In his passage on the link between Persian decadence and the way that the royal children were educated, he highlights the case of Xerxes and concludes: "Ever since then, hardly any king of the Persians has been genuinely 'great,' except in style and title" (*Laws* 695e◊). Plato also compares Xerxes and Cambyses; the parallel is found in Arrian as well (IV.11.6). In Greek eyes, both were typical examples of mad despots. Plato also contrasts Xerxes with Darius, who, not being the son of a king, was not subjected to the deplorable influence of the palace women and so was able to maintain a robust policy and "added to the territory Cyrus had bequeathed at least as much again" (*Laws* 695d◊).

The same contrast is also found in Aeschylus, who is responsible for an equally powerful contribution to the dismal reputation of Xerxes. Darius was a "king without peer" (650), a "benevolent father" (665–70), "the beloved head of Susiana" (555–56), "the all-powerful, benevolent, invincible, equal to the gods" (853–55). By contrast, Xerxes was weak, childish in his tactical choices (353–64); he was a coward, inasmuch as immediately after the defeat at Salamis, "he hurled himself into headlong flight" (469–70). To organize the contrast more clearly, the poet brings on the ghost of Darius, who denounces his son, who has lost his senses (829–31), and repeats the typically Greek accusation of immoderation (*hybris*) against Xerxes, who had had the gall to throw a bridge across the sea (715–25, 740ff.). Xerxes himself despairs of his defeats and failings (908–15, 934ff.). He is responsible for unspeakable disaster, for the loss of a multitude of men, many of high birth (441–44, 765ff.). All of Asia is stripped of its substance (550), "an entire people lost in combat" (728–31); "only a handful of survivors" can be counted (510). In Aeschylus's version, the consequences of the defeats are catastrophic for the Empire of the Great King. Salamis is "the tomb of Persian power" (596). At last comes the familiar apostrophe of the chorus:

> And for a long time, on the land of Asia, the law of the Persians will no longer be obeyed; tribute will no longer be paid under imperial duress; one will no longer fall to one's knees to receive commands; the force of the Great King is no more. Tongues will no longer be gagged. A people is released and speaks freely, as soon as the yoke of force is removed. (585–95)

It is passing strange that even in modern works this passage of Aeschylus is cited to justify a conclusion that the Achaemenid Empire was in irreversible decline and that Xerxes was extremely weak, reduced to busying himself with his construction projects at Persepolis and to wallowing in delight in the dissolute charms of the harem!

Furthermore, the Hellenocentric view has infiltrated Iranian studies. Consider the interpretation traditionally suggested for Xerxes' *daivā* inscription (see below, 519). The weak, cruel, and licentious Xerxes moreover became the very symbol of religious intolerance: "A new note sounds, a note peculiar to Xerxes: the note of a profound but intolerant religiosity." Reliance on Hellenistic-period sources leads to the insistence that Xerxes seriously modified the policy of his predecessors, whether in Babylonia or Egypt. "Once he had suppressed the Egyptian rebellion, he stripped himself of his Egyptian royal name and treated this land of venerable culture as an ordinary satrapy; by demolishing the Mardūk temple, he broke the hearts of the Babylonian priests, who had opened their gates to Cyrus." To be sure, the Empire "remained standing," but "its internal erosion is the only way, in the eyes of a disconcerted world, to understand how all this magnificence crumbled to ruins under the gigantic fist of Alexander" (M. Mayr-hofer). And so we have come back to Plato, after a winding detour through the sources from the center, themselves revisited by Alexander's *Vulgate*!

History and Documentation

It has been possible to propose such reconstructions only because the very idea of decadence pervades all of Western literature on "Asiatic despotism." Nonetheless, the reconstructions are not based solely on blind confidence in the Greek sources. Method-ologically, they also depend on mechanically appropriating unevenly distributed evi-dence directly into narrative exposition. For, beginning with Xerxes, the sources from the center are significantly less abundant and diverse than under Darius. The number of Babylonian and Egyptian documents is drastically reduced. The archaeological evi-dence, most of the Treasury tablets, and a number of the royal inscriptions basically refer to the building activities of the Great King. Not all of the royal inscriptions are concen-trated at Susa and Persepolis; one text refers to the existence of royal workshops at Ecba-tana (*XH*); another, located close to one of Darius's inscriptions (*DE*), is carved on the Mt. Elvend near Ecbatana (*XE*); and lastly, a third has been discovered near Lake Van in Armenia (*XV*). But it is a delicate task to draw consistent historical inferences from such inscriptions. The fact remains: the sources for Xerxes' reign are inadequate and fragmentary; consequently, it is impossible to reconstruct a continuous narrative history. But to deduce from this that beginning in 479 Xerxes lost interest in political problems and devoted himself solely to the embellishment of Persepolis is the result of a peculiar sort of historical method based, one might say, on the fact that the narrative evidence falls silent. To put it another way, the obvious distortions of the polemical Greek sources' memory of Xerxes lead the historian to question this still-lively thesis and to take another look at the historical significance of Xerxes' reign.

2. From Darius to Xerxes

Herodotus's Presentation and Xerxes' Statement

"Upon returning to Persia, Darius offered sacrifices and died. . . . The throne passed to his son Xerxes." With these simple words, Ctesias, or at least Photius, treats the suc-cession of Darius (§§19–20) — leaving the historian grasping at straws. Though the king was a man above men, he himself was no less subject to political constraints. The con-flict between Cambyses and Bardiya and then the accession of Darius had eloquently il-lustrated the difficulty of transferring royal power, even when the successor of the king (Cyrus) had been chosen during his lifetime. The basic question is this: Did the Achae-menid court have rules for the transmission of power? At Behistun, as we have seen, Darius insists (not without fabrication) on the importance that he accorded to succes-sion. In his mind, there was no doubt that his power had to be passed to one of his sons in such a way as to guarantee dynastic continuity.

At the beginning of book VII (2–4), Herodotus dedicates a long passage to Darius's preparation for his succession, which he places at the moment of the Egyptian rebel-lion, four years after the battle of Marathon (486) (VII.1):

> A violent quarrel (*stasis*) broke out between Darius' sons on the question of priority and suc-cession (*peri tes hegemoniēs*). . . . Darius before his accession had three sons by his former wife, Gobryas' daughter, and four more after his accession by Atossa the daughter of Cyrus. The eldest of the first three was Artobazanes, and of the last four Xerxes. It was between these two, therefore, being sons of different mothers, that the dispute arose. (VII.2✧)

Whom to choose? Artobarzanes argued "that he was the eldest of all Darius' sons (*presbutatos . . . pantos tou genou*)" (VII.2◊). Xerxes stressed the prestige of his ancestry, which, through his mother, went back to the founder of the Empire, Cyrus. Still following Herodotus, we learn that Darius was uncertain, and his hesitancy was fanned by arguments whispered to Xerxes by the Spartan Demaratus (driven out of his homeland, he had just appeared before the king). Referring to the Spartan model, Demaratus argued that Xerxes' rights were unsurpassed because he was born when his father, Darius, was king, which was not the case for Artobarzanes, who was born when his father was just an ordinary person (*idiōtēs*: VII.3). The end of the story is:

> Xerxes adopted the suggestion and Darius, recognizing the justice of the argument, proclaimed him heir to the throne. Personally, I believe that even without this advice from Demaratus, Xerxes would have become king, because of the immense influence of Atossa (*eikhe to pan kratos*). Xerxes, then, was publicly proclaimed as next in succession to the crown, and Darius was free to turn his attention to the war. . . . (VII.5◊)

Xerxes in turn referred to his father's choice in a famous inscription (*XPf*). After recalling the accession of his father, while Hystaspes and Arsames were still alive, he wrote:

> Saith Xerxes the king: Other sons of Darius there were, (but)—thus unto Ahuramazda was the desire—Darius my father made me the greatest (*maθišta*) after himself. When my father Darius went away from the throne [died], by the will of Ahuramazda I became king on my father's throne. (*XPf* §4◊)

There is at least one point on which Herodotus and Xerxes agree: that Darius chose between several of his sons. Contrary to Herodotus, who presents the succession as a duel between Xerxes and Artobarzanes, Xerxes refers to his other brothers in such a way as to deny implicitly that any of them had a special right to argue against him. Xerxes was certainly thinking (without naming them) of his three full brothers, the only ones who shared the same ancestry; according to Herodotus, they were Achaemenes (VII.7, 97), Masistes (VII.82; IX.107), and Hystaspes (VII.64). But even on this point divergent traditions were in circulation because, as we shall see, some authors introduce an Ariaramnes. At the same time, the very fact that Xerxes inscribed such a statement (which has no parallel) and the fact of his insistence on his "victory" over his brothers also seem to confirm that he had overcome some form of opposition.

Chronology and nomos

The importance of Herodotus's text must not be underestimated. But his presentation also poses several problems of interpretation, as much on the modalities as on the reasons for the choice of royal heir. Herodotus places the succession decision at the moment of "Darius' resolve to go to war, not only against Greece but against Egypt too." It was under pressure from his sons that Darius decided to settle the succession, "for [they said] according to Persian law (*kata ton Perseōn nomon*) the king may not march with his army until he has named his successor" (VII.2◊). No other example confirms the existence of this custom. To be sure, before crossing the Araxes, Cyrus had sent his son Cambyses home to Persia, under the guard of Croesus: "He intended to bestow royalty on Cambyses," Herodotus remarks, clearly letting it be understood that in case of misfortune, Cambyses would succeed Cyrus (I.208). But Cyrus had made his choice many years earlier, as is shown by his granting Cambyses the title "king of Babylon" for a short time in 538–537. And above all, this was not Cyrus's first campaign. The same, obviously, holds for Darius. If the date given by Herodotus is correct, we must conclude that

Darius had waited quite a long time: in 486, he was about 65 years old (cf. Herodotus I.209); Xerxes must have been around 30 or 35 (his parents' marriage was in 522). It seems hard to believe that, if Darius was about to found a new royal stock and a new dynastic legitimacy, he had not long since taken measures to ensure continuity with the son he had chosen. We may thus suppose that official recognition predated 490–486, without being able to prove this or to suggest a more precise date. In other words, what Herodotus calls a *nomos* was not in any way obligatory; furthermore, this is an observation that can be made on the basis of an analysis of the word *nomos* in the context of each succession (see chap. 17/1).

Darius, Xerxes, and Atossa

Furthermore, it is clearly erroneous to state that the prince's mother, Atossa in this case, had a right to interfere. Although in actuality the mother of the crown prince (and then of the reigning king) had prestigious status at court (cf. Aelian, *Anim.* IV.46), there was strictly speaking no Achaemenid queen (despite, e.g., Athenaeus XIII.556b). The mother of the crown prince had no special rights. She could perhaps wield her personal influence, but nothing more. In addition, Xerxes in his declaration of legitimacy breathes not a word about Atossa, which he could not have failed to do had she exercised the sort of power sometimes accorded her on the basis of Herodotus. On the contrary, he insists on the patrilinear transmission of power (XPf §3). Dynastic legitimacy was not established by way of the mother. The prestigious status that Atossa had at court was because one of her sons held the status of heir. Darius chose Xerxes for entirely different reasons, which have already been discussed (chap. 3/4). To choose Artobarzanes would have been to confer on the family of Gobryas a distinction absolutely in opposition to Darius's objectives as revealed by his policy of endogamy: to retain power only for his own direct descendants.

The Crown Prince

The designated son did not become designated heir until a special ceremony, alluded to by Plutarch: "It was the rule and usage of Persia, that the heir apparent to the crown should beg a boon, and that he that declared him so should give whatever he asked, provided it were within the sphere of his power" (*Art.* 26.5✧). If we recall the rules covering the King's birthday banquet (Herodotus IX.110), we can see that it is likely that this proclamation was made during this banquet or during the feast marking the crown prince's birthday. Thereafter, the prince, like his father, had the right "to wear the upright hat (*kidaris*), as they called it," adds Plutarch.✧ His prestigious status is demonstrated by his presence behind his father in the audience reliefs in the Persepolis treasury. It is also possible that from then on he bore a special title (**visa-puthra*) that distinguished him from all of the other princes of the [royal] house (*br byt'*). But this Old Persian title is a reconstruction, unattested in any Old Persian text. Xerxes simply states that Darius awarded him the title or designation *maθišta* 'the greatest [after him]', a word rendered in the Classical sources 'second after the king'.

A Principle of Primogeniture?

But which of his sons did the king choose during his lifetime to succeed him? In other words, does the example of Xerxes illustrate a general rule? According to Plutarch—who makes a point of recalling the precedent of Demaratus at this point—identical arguments were made at the court of Darius II to decide between Cyrus the Younger and the future Artaxerxes II (*Art.* 2.4). The similarity between the successions of Darius I and Darius II becomes even more striking when we note that, like Atossa, Parysatis (mother of the princes) vigorously intervened in the discussion, with quite different results. Plutarch says that to decide the succession of Artaxerxes II, appeal was made to primogeniture, "as he himself [Artaxerxes] had received the [kingdom]" (26.1◊). The difference between Atossa and Demaratus is that the arguments proffered by Parysatis in support of the child born to the purple had no effect whatsoever.

Several other texts imply that the oldest child held a position of special prestige. A text by Agathocles of Cyzicus, quoted by Athenaeus (XII.515a◊), provides the following information: "In Persia there is also water called 'golden.' This water consists of seventy bubbling pools, and none may drink of it save the king and his eldest son (*presbyatos*); if anyone else drinks it, the penalty is death." The custom is difficult to understand precisely, but the comment is unambiguous regarding the privileged place of the oldest son. Let us also quote Plato: "When the eldest son (*ho presbytatos pais*) and heir to the throne (*houper hē arkhē*) is born, all the king's subjects have a feast day" (*Alc.* 121c◊). For Plato, the king's birthday banquet (Herodotus IX.110) was nothing but a repetition of the original feast: "Then, in the years that follow, the whole of Asia celebrates that day, the king's birthday, with further sacrifice and feasting."◊

Plato also states that from birth the newborn was entrusted to hand-picked eunuchs: "They attend to all the needs of the infant child, and are especially concerned to make him as handsome as possible, shaping and straightening his infant limbs" (121d◊). Behind the picturesque description is a political idea: the first son, called to succeed his father, must be made into the image of a king, who by definition is tall and handsome (chap. 6/4). Plato goes on to say that later the child was entrusted to educational specialists. Like other young men, he received a military education (horsemanship, hunt, courage, Truth) (*Alc.* 121e–122a). Additionally, Strabo says that the heads of groups are chosen from "among the sons of the king or satrap" (XV.3.18◊). At the same time, Plato mentions the existence of "royal pedagogues" to whom the crown prince was entrusted at the age of 14. Even though Plato does not use the word, apparently some of these royal pedagogues were *magi*, since one of them (the wisest [*sophōtatos*]) "instructs him in . . . the Magian lore" (122a;◊ cf. Plutarch, *Art.* 3.3). It is a *magus* who "instructs him . . . in what a king should know (*didaskei de kai ta basilika*)" (*Alc.* 122a◊) and, according to Cicero (*Div.* 1.41.91), "no one could be king of Persia who had not previously received instruction in the wisdom of the magi." In short, from earliest childhood on, the oldest son was prepared to take up his royal duties and to assume his rank in the political, military, and religious hierarchy. The preference given the oldest is confirmed statistically as well. The custom is easy enough to understand. First and foremost, succession to the throne was no different from familial succession: to take one's father's throne was also to receive and make fruitful the heritage of the royal House, which quite naturally was entrusted to the oldest. In a way, Darius's choice did not formally contradict this point: once Artobarzanes was out of the picture, for political reasons that have been cited, the king's choice fell on the oldest of his sons born to Atossa.

At the same time, analysis of the concrete situations leads us to offer several corrections. Plato's expression ("heir to the throne") is certainly exaggerated. The oldest son was not the only one entrusted to "royal pedagogues" (Plato himself uses the plural).

Plutarch introduces the *magus* from whom Cyrus the Younger received lessons (*Art.* 3.3); Cyrus was "educated with his brother and the other boys" (Xenophon, *Anab.* I.9.2✧). Given the risk of infant mortality (cf. Ctesias §49), any heir, whether or not he was the oldest, would normally have received a royal education. Moreover, in every case, the king's choice remained entirely free. The exclusion of Artobarzanes, the arguments exchanged, and the frequently attested intervention of the court cabal in favor of one or another competitor seem to confirm that there was no fixed rule and that the preference for the oldest son (Artaxerxes I and Artaxerxes II) related more to incidental conditions than to mandatory rules. And last but certainly not least, the official recognition of a crown prince in no way signified a sharing of power: the king was One. Despite the crown prince's undeniably prestigious status, he himself was not exempt from royal disfavor. This is clearly seen in the story of the relations between Artaxerxes II and his son Darius, who was convicted of treason and was put to death (Plutarch, *Art.* 26–29).

Funeral Ceremonies

The death of the king was observed by the extinguishing of the sacred Fires, as shown in the steps taken by Alexander after the death of his beloved friend Haephestion:

> He proclaimed to all the peoples of Asia that they should sedulously quench what the Persians call the sacred fire, until such time as the funeral should be ended. This was the custom of the Persians when their kings died, and people thought that the order was an ill omen, and that heaven was foretelling the king's own death. (Diodorus XVII.114.4–5✧)

This decree was a way of symbolizing that life was temporarily suspended until a new king was proclaimed. It was the start of a period of mourning, like the period decreed by Alexander in the same circumstances: he "commanded mourning throughout the whole barbarian country" (Arrian VII.14.9✧); or the period proclaimed at the death of Alexander (Quintus Curtius X.5.18); or the one ordered by Artaxerxes II when the eunuch Tiridates died (Aelian, *VH* XII.1). It was customary for Persians to shave their heads as a sign of affliction (cf. Herodotus IX.24; Arrian VII.14.4; Plutarch, *Alex.* 72.1).

Herodotus compares Spartan and barbarian customs: "One custom is observed on the occasion of a king's death, which is the same in Sparta as in Asia." In Sparta, the whole population gathers "wailing as if they could never stop" (VI.58;✧ cf. III.65 and IX.24 for the Persians). The contributions of subject peoples (including financial contributions) when a Great King died appears to be well established (Diodorus XVII.114.4). Herodotus continues: "If a king is killed in war, they make a statue (*eidōlon*) of him, and carry it to burial on a richly-draped bier."✧ The construction of an *eidōlon* of the deceased Persian king may also be alluded to by Aelian (*VH* XII.64). The dead king's remains were prepared by specialists. So it was with Alexander's body, which was embalmed by Egyptians and Chaldeans, "after their manner" (Quintus Curtius X.10.13✧). Since the royal tombs contained no bodies when they were discovered, we cannot say with certainty that the Great Kings were treated similarly. Herodotus (I.140) and Strabo (XV.3.20) say that the Persians coated the body with wax before burial, which probably provides another similarity with Lacedaemonian customs (cf. Plutarch, *Ages.* 40.1; Nepos, *Ages.* 8.7; Diodorus XV.93.6).

We know that the body of a deceased king was carried to the place of interment on a sumptuously ornamented chariot that must have resembled the funeral chariot of Alexander that is so carefully described by Diodorus (XVIII.26–28.1), before which the entire populace crowded. It was the crown prince's responsibility to conduct the funeral rites. By presiding over them, he officially demonstrated his position as heir to the throne; he showed at the same time that the dead king continued to exist through his own life. It is also likely that each king in turn repeated Cambyses' custom of establishing permanent sacrifices around the tomb of the deceased king (cf. Ctesias §19).

Royal Investiture

At the end of all of these ceremonies came the royal investiture. For this topic our only source is Plutarch, who described the investiture of Artaxerxes II as follows:

> It was not long after the decease of Darius [II] that the king, his successor, went to Pasar-gadæ, to have the ceremony of his inauguration consummated by the Persian priests. There is a temple dedicated to a warlike goddess, whom one might liken to Minerva, into which when the royal person to be initiated has passed, he must strip himself of his own robe, and put on that which Cyrus the first wore before he was king; then, having devoured a frail of figs, he must eat turpentine, and drink a cup of sour milk. To which if they superadd any other rites, it is unknown to any but those that are present at them. (*Art.* 3.1–2✧)

Plutarch's last sentence confirms that the Greeks had sometimes heard of Persian cultic ceremonies, which they called "secret," on which they had nothing but inadequate oral information (cf. Herodotus I.140). It is clear that the enthronement ceremony in particular took place in the presence of only a small number of people. In addition to the prince himself, there were those whom Plutarch calls priests (*hiereis*), doubtless meaning the *magi*. According to Cicero, "no one could be king of Persia who had not previously received instruction in the wisdom of the magi" (*Div.* 1.41.90). Pliny mentions a certain stone "as being indispensible for the Magi at the installation of a king" (XXXVII.147✧). Plutarch (*Art.* 3.3) even seems to imply that these were the same *magi* who cared for the education of the crown prince.

Plutarch's interesting text nonetheless raises some questions. The ritual practices, basically, seem to have been well anchored in very ancient traditions, as shown by the reference to the robe of Cyrus the Great. The "initiate's" menu testifies to this as well, with its basis in milk and herbs (in which the *magi* also specialized; see chap. 7/2). But was the initiation ceremony he described immutable, or did it undergo alterations during the time of Artaxerxes II or earlier? It is the location of the ceremony that is questionable. The warrior goddess is easily recognized as Anāhita. Since this goddess's cult seems to have assumed new importance at the time of Artaxerxes II (chap. 15/8), we may well ask whether the ceremony took place in a different location prior to Artaxerxes II. It is also likely that the ceremony included an invocation of Ahura-Mazda. Several times, Darius used the formula "Ahura-Mazda granted me the kingdom." Perhaps this referred to a portion of the ceremony in which the insignia of power were handed to the new king—namely, his robe (*kandys*) and shield.

In essence, the ceremonies took on two clearly visible characteristics. On the one hand, they showed that Achaemenid royalty was sacred: through the agency of the *magi*, the new king was invested with divinity. On the other, they exalted dynastic continuity by insisting that it was based on relationship with Cyrus the Elder. The transmission of the robe best illustrated and symbolized the transmission of power itself. By means of a garment "magically" considered to be the power itself, the prince changed from heir designate to Great King. It is possible that at the end of the ceremony he appeared in a tour of Pasargadae to be acclaimed by the assembled crowds. To mark his accession, he remitted the people's tribute-debts (Herodotus VI.59). Doubtless he also confirmed (or revoked) the power of the satraps and governors of the Empire (Diodorus XI.71.2; Josephus, *Ant.* XI.185). Thus the great officials of the kingdom served at the pleasure of the reigning king and personally pledged their fealty to him.

The Successor of Darius

"After his death the crown passed to his son Xerxes." Herodotus puts it so simply (VII.4◇). But it must be noted that Justin (II.10.1–11) and Plutarch (*Mor.* 173b and 488d–f) offer a version that differs at several points from that of Herodotus. They describe the debate as following the death of Darius, introducing (in the same words) an Ariaramnes in place of Artobarzanes; this Ariaramnes appears to have held a position in Bactria (173b; cf. 488d: "come down from Media" to meet Xerxes). The ancient authors insist that this was not a real revolt. Ariaramnes simply intended to put forward his claim as oldest son. Plutarch even sees this as an illustration of brotherly love. Xerxes sent gifts to Ariaramnes and had his envoys transmit the following message: as soon as Xerxes was recognized as king, he would recognize Ariaramnes as "second after the king." The dispute was settled by a paternal uncle (Artabanus in Plutarch, Artaphernes in Justin), who decided in favor of Xerxes. The judgment was accepted with good grace by Ariaramnes. Clearly, this version represents a corruption of Herodotus's version. Possibly Plutarch's and Justin's sources had blended in the romanticized story about Xerxes and his brother Masistes in 479, as reported by Herodotus (IX.108–13). Masistes appears to have been satrap of Bactria; he was humiliated by his brother, rebelled against him, and then was massacred along with "his sons and his army" by troops sent by the king. It is also possible that in the Greek tradition the name Masistes represents the Persian word *maθišta*, so that Masistes and Ariaramnes were one and the same person, since according to Plutarch Xerxes conferred on Ariaramnes the title 'second after the king'—that is, *maθišta*. While Plutarch's and Justin's version is scarcely credible overall, perhaps it is built upon a fact: that the naming of a crown prince did not necessarily eliminate competing brotherly ambitions. Plutarch times the quarrel between the death of Darius and the official recognition of the new king. This was a sensitive period, marked by official mourning throughout the Empire. Only afterward, it seems, could the coronation ceremonies at Pasargadae begin.

Several statements demonstrate the care with which the new king connected himself with the work and person of his father. Along with all the new buildings he says that he erected "after he [I] became king" (*XPf* §4; *XSc*), the new king mentions finishing and completing the work of Darius (*XPf, XPg, XV*). This was certainly true of the Susa Gate (*XSd*). References to work exclusively his own are fairly rare (*XPb; XPd*). Often, on his own buildings, he also invokes the protection of Ahura-Mazda on buildings that were built by his father (*XPa, XPc, XSa, XSd*) or that were built jointly: "What had been built by my father, that I protected, and other building I added. What moreover I built, and what my father built, all that by the favor of Ahuramazda we built" (*XPf◇*). This statement is even more interesting because it is placed just after the reminder of his selection as crown prince and his accession. These statements are not unique: let us particularly recall an inscription in which Artaxerxes II links himself with his great-great-grandfather, Darius (*A²Sa*). It was a way of placing oneself in the dynastic line; Xerxes also never missed an opportunity to recall that he was the son of Darius, an Achaemenid.

Crushing Rebellions

Xerxes began by devoting himself to pursuing his father's imperial enterprise. Upon his accession, in fact, some territories were threatened not so much by the defeat at Marathon as by the Egyptian revolt that had arisen in Darius's time. In Herodotus's version, the Egyptian campaign was just a minor episode that delayed the Greek expedition a few months, an expedition that had been decided on shortly before, under the pressure of Mardonius and Medizing Greeks (VII.5–6). It appears nonetheless to have become sufficiently dangerous that Xerxes took personal command of the army (of course, this also allowed him to inaugurate his reign with a military expedition). Moreover, though it subsequently took another four years to prepare the army that was to march against Greece (VII.20), this was only because the troops and materiel assembled by Darius over the previous three years (VII.1) had been expended in the Egyptian expedition. After his victory, the king made his brother Achaemenes satrap in Egypt (484) (VII.7).

Some years later, perhaps in 481, another rebellion broke out in Babylonia, led by Bēl-šimānni, who took the title "king of Babylon, king of the lands." The uprising was very short, lasting only some fifteen days. Nevertheless, it too reflects a troubled atmosphere, though we cannot state precisely either its origin or its causes. Despite this mood, however, the theory of a coincident revolt by Judah around 484 is inadequately grounded. It certainly goes too far to speak of a generalized state of insurrection, which would seriously have damaged preparations for the European expedition. We must simply say once again that the troubles in Egypt and Babylonia indicate that Darius's imperial policy had discovered its natural limits.

Returning to the Greek Affair

Xerxes was then able to return to his father's plan (VII.1) to march against Greece. Herodotus refers to reservations about such a plan on the part of the new king, but they were due solely to the need to put down the Egyptian rebellion first (VII.5, 7). He also refers to many disputes on the subject within the royal entourage. According to Herodotus, Xerxes made his decision under pressure from Mardonius and Greek exiles (VII.6–7). Herodotus also states that, after Xerxes returned from Egypt, he convened the highest Persian officials (*aristoi*). After announcing his decision to move against the Greeks (VII.8), he gave the floor to the most prestigious Persians. Mardonius supported the king, in particular stressing the weakness and disunity of the Greeks (VII.9–10). Artabanus, on the other hand, stressed the dangers of such an expedition, as he had done with Darius when he was preparing to move against the Scythians (VII.10); he was harshly dismissed by the king, who took him for a coward. However, after a dream, Xerxes reversed his original decision and decided not to march on the Greeks (VII.12–13). After dreaming the dream a second time, Xerxes had Artabanus put on his royal apparel, sit on his throne, and sleep in his bed. Artabanus had the same dream; thereafter, he urged Xerxes to conduct the expedition and, as a result, the king gave the order (VII.14–18). Herodotus then records that, after making his decision, Xerxes had a third vision; the *magi* who were consulted determined "that it portended the conquest of the world. . . . Xerxes, in the process of assembling his armies, had every corner of the continent ransacked" (VII.19✧).

This entire discussion by Herodotus raises strong suspicions, since both the speeches given and the arguments exchanged totally derive from a judgment *post eventum*. Herodotus insists that he got his information from the Persians (VII.12). It is entirely possible that Mardonius had a bad reputation among the Persians themselves. We know, for example, the opposition that his strategy awoke in Artabazus in 480–479 (IX.41–42, 58, 66) and that Artabazus was honored by Xerxes after the war (Thucydides I.129.1). Perhaps the order that Xerxes gave to Artabanus is an example of the well-known Babylonian custom of substitute kings. But generally, Herodotus's tale is structured around literary motifs and human stereotypes that were easy for his listeners and readers to interpret. It was standard practice to contrast two counselors, one ambitious and stupid, the other wise and deliberate. This had the result, if not the intention, of portraying Xerxes as indecisive, even cowardly, which fits well with the traditional Greek presentation.

In truth, for Xerxes the situation was very clear. First of all, he had to take responsibility for the projects that his father had already gotten under way (cf. VII.1). He was confronted with rebellions and also had to prove his royal ability to lead a victorious military expedition. It must also be kept in mind that conducting an expedition on such a scale allowed the king to visit a large number of subject lands and to reconfirm the chains of command (see chap. 5/4). Furthermore, up to the borders of Greece, his itinerary scarcely differed from the periodic relocations of the court. When Xerxes left Sardis, the order of the royal procession was established according to traditional protocol, Xerxes himself "riding in a chariot drawn by Nisaean horses" (VII.40✧), and this order held until after "crossing the bridge of boats" (VII.55). He was accompanied by his sons (VII.39; VIII.103–4) and many members of his immediate family. Peoples and tribes came to the royal caravan to pay homage to the sovereign and to offer him their gifts and presents (cf. VII.27). Cities and peoples received orders to prepare the King's Table in the appropriate manner (VII.32, 118–120). The king even played his role as protector of greenery (VII.31). In a way, this first portion of Xerxes' march assumed the primarily political nature that emerged from specifically Achaemenid concerns: it was on the same order as the reviews of the Empire conducted at Abydos (VII.44–45) and Doriscus (VII.59ff.). Throughout the journey, Xerxes showed off the power of the king and the Empire. While marching against Greece, he surveyed his territory and peoples, as he had already done on the journey between Babylon and Memphis: "He rejoiced in his prosperity" (VII.45; VII.100; cf. VII.57). To lead his army was to exalt his power as well as to seek to increase it with new conquests that would only impress the subject peoples even more. From this perspective, we can accept the rationale (if not the exact words) of the speech that Herodotus puts in the mouth of Mardonius, speaking to Xerxes: "When you have tamed the arrogance of Egypt, then lead an army against Athens. Do that, and your name will be held in honour all over the world, and people will think twice in future before they invade your country" (VII.5✧).

Of course, the military objective was clearly defined: it was not merely a matter of exacting vengeance on Athens but of actually conquering the Greeks (cf. VII.138). For this reason, Xerxes' expedition assumes a quite different character from the expedition that Datis had led ten years earlier. The magnitude of the preparations and the king's personal participation leave no doubt about it. By participating, Xerxes took on Darius's objectives; according to Herodotus, Darius had decided shortly after Datis's return to conquer Greece and had begun active preparations for the campaign, before the Egyptian revolt and his own demise temporarily interrupted the Persian plans (VII.1).

"The Unconquerable Swell of the Seas"

As soon as Xerxes returned from Egypt, he instituted a military draft throughout the Empire (VII.8, 19). Several times Aeschylus stresses the immensity of the army headed by Xerxes: "monstrous human herd" (line 74), "broad human tide," comparable to "the unconquerable swell of the seas" (line 90). Herodotus gives statistics on the royal army as it approached Thermopylae: 277,610 soldiers on the warships (1,207 warships listed at Doriscus: VII.89); 240,000 men in the crews of the transport ships; 1,700,000 infantrymen, 80,000 horsemen, 20,000 Arab camel-riders and Libyan charioteers; add the troops drafted by Xerxes in Europe (300,000), and the total is 2,617,610 men. Herodotus also says that an equal number of "servants and camp followers, the crews of the provision boats and of other craft" have to be counted, and he thus reaches a total of more than five million men, not to mention, he adds, "as for eunuchs, female cooks, and soldiers' women, no one could attempt an estimate of their number . . ." (VII.184–87✧). Finally, feeding this immense horde (not counting the women, eunuchs, beasts of burden, or dogs) took more than five million liters of flour per day. We are thus not terribly surprised at Herodotus's assessment that "the rivers sometimes failed to provide enough water" (VII.187✧)—a particularly powerful image, extremely popular throughout Antiquity (cf. Philostratus, *Vit. Apoll.* 1.25).

For a long time, Herodotus's statistics were judged unacceptable, if only for purely logistical reasons. It is clear that some of the figures reflect ancient models, such as the number of ships (1,207 in Aeschylus and Herodotus), which may go back to the Homeric Catalogue of Ships. Furthermore, to stress the utterly novel character of Xerxes' army, Herodotus explicitly refers to the Trojan War (VII.20). Other ancient authors' statistics seem no more credible: from 700,000 (Isocrates) to 3,000,000 (Simonides). All share a Greek perspective when they calculate the armies of Darius III; their motive is to exaggerate the glory of the Greek warriors who defeated them.

Everyone agrees with this assessment. But the problem is that most attempts to interpret Herodotus rely on dangerous assumptions and comparisons, and as a result, the modern estimates differ considerably from one another. The state of affairs thus requires us to argue for plausible solutions. If we agree on the one hand that, for reasons already given (chap. 5/5), the review at Doriscus should be set aside, and on the other, that in the only battle fought on Greek soil (Plataea), the Persian forces did not greatly outnumber the Greek forces, then we arrive at a figure of about 60,000 men for the army of Mardonius. We agree that this is no more than one guess among many; but the advantage of this estimate is that it is based on the account of a battle and that it renders the forces involved considerably more even. We may make the same comment regarding the warships. The figure 1,207 is traditional, even mythical, and Herodotus doubtless took it from Aeschylus. It seems clear that the triremes in the royal fleet could not have greatly outnumbered the Greek warships at Salamis. Taking into account the Persian losses at Artemisium, a figure around 600 is probably much closer to reality than the 1,207 of Aeschylus and Herodotus.

As Herodotus rightly says, it makes sense to add the noncombatants to the fighting forces. There were certainly many of them, since every relocation of the king and court required an immense staff. But if we do not try to give an overall estimate, as Herodotus himself refused to do (VII.187), then out of this whole crowd we could simply consider the army's servants. A Babylonian document from 513 (*Dar.* 253) allows us to offer a plausible estimate: a horseman obeying the summons was accompanied by twelve lightly-armed men to equip and protect him (on the model of the *helots* in the Spartan army).

Logistical Preparations

According to Herodotus, the preparations lasted no less than four years (VII.20). It was not just a matter of assembling the men; it was also necessary to mobilize immense production capacity to guarantee the logistics of the expedition. A number of supply depots were set up in well-chosen locations—Leuce Acte in Thrace, Tyrodiza (near Perinthus), the strongholds of Doriscus and Eion, and Macedonia. Numerous transport ships were assembled for the purpose, with the supplies coming "from throughout Asia" (VII.25; 37). Thousands of workers were needed to dig a canal across the Mount Athos (Acte) Peninsula (because the king's advisers remembered the wreck of Mardonius's fleet in 492) and to build bridges across the Strymon (VII.22–24). Constructing two bridges across the Bosporus certainly required long months of labor, and the first attempt was ruined by a storm (VII.33–37). Meanwhile, the Great King and his generals had assembled the contingents, initially at Critalla in Cappadocia and then at Sardis (VII.26). After wintering at the Lydian capital (481–480), the king and the army set out for the Hellespont and Greece at the beginning of the spring of 480 (VII.37).

3. From Sardis to Sardis (480)

The Persian Advance and Greek Strategy

From Doriscus, Xerxes set out for Thrace, gradually conscripting new contingents from the subject peoples. He crossed the Strymon on the bridge that had been built previously (VII.105, 118–16). The troops had been divided into three contingents, each assigned to a high official (VII.121). When they reached Acanthus, he sent the navy to await him at Therma at the mouth of the gulf (VII.121). After the armies were recombined in this town, the force turned toward Pieria, where he learned that most of the peoples and cities of central Greece had agreed to "give [tokens of submission of] earth and water" (VII.132◇). Of course, as Herodotus explains (VII.172), they scarcely had any choice. Shortly before, the Greeks gathered at the Isthmus of Corinth had sent a contingent near Tempe to bar the way. But as soon as they learned from King Alexander of Macedonia that the royal army was able take a different route, the troops departed: "The result of it was that the Thessalians, finding themselves without support, no longer hesitated but whole-heartedly worked in the Persian interest, so that in the course of the war they proved of the greatest use to Xerxes" (VII.174◇). Herodotus was certainly simplifying. It is clear that from the start some of the Thessalian leaders (the Aleuadae) favored alliance with the Persians (VII.6). As in 490, the Persians understood how to exploit internal differences among the Greek states, many of which were prepared to "Medize." In a passage that is very favorable to Athens, Herodotus even goes so far as to say, whether his listeners would believe him or not, that the majority of Greeks "were all too ready to accept Persian dominion," since the inequality of the military forces appeared to be an insurmountable problem (VII.138◇). As for the Phocaeans, if they were the only central Greek people who did not join the Persian cause, it was, Herodotus says, because of their age-old enmity toward the Thessalians (VIII.30). Let us also recall that Demaratus of Sparta remained in Xerxes' entourage, and there were also representatives of the family of the Pisistratids with him. One of the objectives of the expedition, therefore, must have been to install client governments in many of the Greek states (cf. VIII.54–55).

After lengthy discussions, the Greeks decided to face Xerxes at a line of defense on land at Thermopylae and at sea at the Artemisium Promontory, two sites very close together (VII.175). When a detachment of royal ships sailed as far as Therma, the Greeks left Artemisium and dropped anchor at Chalcis, "intending to guard the Euripus, and leaving look-outs on the high ground of Euboea" (VII.183✧). As Xerxes continued his march toward Thermopylae (VII.198–201), part of the fleet (moored near Cape Sepias) was destroyed by an unexpected storm (VII.190–92)—a real disaster according to Herodotus, since a large number of warships and grain transports were lost, "and men beyond reckoning." On land, despite the resistance of the Greeks (to whose heroism Herodotus devotes a passage of disproportionate length: VII.201–39), the Persians took the pass at Thermopylae. Meanwhile, the Greek navy (commanded by the Spartan Eurybiades) had dropped anchor near Artemisium. Herodotus says that the Athenian Themistocles managed to persuade the Greeks to hold their position despite the defeat at Thermopylae. Persian losses were heavy, not only at the hands of the Greeks, but also because another storm had struck a portion of the royal ships that were attempting to skirt Euboea to fall on the Greeks from behind. Nonetheless, from the perspective of the Persian general staff, the objective had been achieved: the road to Greece was open (August 480). The royal army immediately entered central Greece, receiving the support of the "Medizers" (VIII.34–39).

From Thermopylae to Salamis

The most significant result of the Persian victories was probably on the political plane. On the authority of Themistocles, the Greek ships had moored in the harbor of Salamis. According to Herodotus, the Athenians were disheartened by the attitude of the Peloponnesians, who rather than advancing into central Greece had fortified the Isthmus of Corinth to create a barrier against the Persian advance. The Athenians' "object was to give themselves an opportunity of getting their women and children out of Attica, and also of discussing their next move" (VIII.40✧). To make a long story short, the Athenian/Spartan quarrel, which had already surfaced in the context of choosing a commander, broke out again. The question regarding strategy was taken to the council of the commanders of the Greek naval contingents that had meanwhile all returned to Salamis. Despite Spartan reluctance to do battle far from their bases, Themistocles managed to convince Eurybiades that the only solution was to confront the royal fleet in the Bay of Salamis. Additional plans were formed: on land, the Lacedaemonians would continue to mass their forces on the isthmus (VIII.70–74); the Athenian population was forced to leave the town and countryside and go into exile (VIII.40–64). The battle that ensued in the Bay of Salamis ended with a resounding defeat of Xerxes' fleet (VIII.76–96; September 480).

From Salamis to Sardis

Not content to celebrate the victory—understandably—every Greek author, to a man, stresses the indecision and cowardice shown by Xerxes, who was concerned more than anything else with "impassioned flight" (Aeschylus) in order to escape the consequences of the defeat. It is clear that the news of the defeat at Salamis dumbfounded the Persians, who were undoubtedly very conscious of their superiority, including the Persians remaining in the royal residences who, according to Herodotus, were already preparing to receive Xerxes in triumph (VIII.99). These are the circumstances on which

Herodotus built the exchange that he recounts between Mardonius and the king after the battle (VIII.100–101). Mardonius, anxious to clear himself of the accusation of having recommended an expedition that turned out badly, suggested to Xerxes (of whose preparations for flight he was not unaware: VIII.97) that he leave him an army with which he would "deliver Greece to him in chains" (VIII.100❖). Again according to Herodotus, Xerxes had his young illegitimate sons leave for Asia Minor under the protection of Artemisia of Caria (VIII.103–4). And, several days after the battle, he departed Attica with the army (VIII.113). When he arrived in Thessaly, he left Mardonius an army of elite troops and traveled to the Hellespont in 45 days (VIII.115), after which he pressed on to Sardis (VIII.117). Herodotus portrays Xerxes' retreat apocalyptically:

> He reached the crossing in forty-five days, but with hardly a fraction of his army intact. During the march the troops lived off the country as best they could, eating grass where they found no grain, and stripping the bark and leaves off trees of all sorts, cultivated or wild, to stay their hunger. They left nothing anywhere, so hard were they put to it for supplies. Plague and dysentery attacked them; many died, and others who fell sick were left behind. . . . The Persians having passed through Thrace reached the passage over the Hellespont and lost no time in getting across to Abydos. They crossed, however, in ships, as they found the bridges no longer in position, bad weather having broken them up. Food was more plentiful at Abydos than what they had been making do with on the march, with the result that the men over-ate themselves, and this, combined with the change of water, caused many deaths in what remained of the army. The remnant proceeded with Xerxes to Sardis. (VIII.115, 117❖)

Herodotus probably got this version—repeated by many ancient authors (e.g., Justin II.13.11–12)—from Aeschylus (lines 480–515). First of all, it is a literary theme, doubtless bearing only the most tenuous connection to reality. Even if the retreat faced difficult climatic conditions, it is hard to believe that the quartermasters' stocks were completely exhausted. Herodotus records other versions that were circulating in his day, suggesting that Xerxes had returned to the Asian coast by sea. Each version highlights the Great King's cruelty (VII.118–19). But Herodotus rejects these stories, contending that Xerxes had indeed passed through Abdera and thanked the inhabitants with a pact of friendship and with a gift of a gold *akinakēs* ('sword') and a gold-embroidered headband (VII.120). Nonetheless, Classical tradition preserves the versions contested by Herodotus, as in Justin's tale, which is both dramatic and moralizing (II.13.9–10):

> Xerxes found the bridges broken and crossed hastily in a fishing boat. This was quite a sight, and it really brought the men's circumstances home to them, after an amazing turn of events, to see him huddled in a little craft—a man that formerly the entire ocean could barely contain and that had overworked the land with his countless ground troops—and now he was without a single slave to serve him.

The potential criticisms of the ancient stories should not lead us to believe, however, that the Persian situation was the same in September 480 as it had been a few months earlier. The defeat had certainly weakened some imperial positions. When he returned to Asia Minor (where he had accompanied Xerxes), Artabazus besieged Potidaea (albeit unsuccessfully): "The people of Potidaea . . . had openly thrown off the Persian yoke as soon as Xerxes passed them on his march to the eastward and they knew of the flight of the Persian fleet from Salamis" (VIII.126❖). Herodotus's story of the king's retreat makes it very clear that several Thracian peoples had severed their ties of allegiance (VII.115–16). It probably goes too far to suggest that the cities of Asia Minor were ready to rebel at this date: this idea comes from a somewhat suspect view worked out by Herodotus and fourth-century authors, especially Ephorus, who was extensively used by Diodorus. Some time before the defeat at Salamis, according to Herodotus (VIII.19, 22–23), Themistocles had attempted to detach the Ionian contingents from the royal navy—with no success (VIII.85). We also know that after Salamis, the Greek victors sent ships to the Cyclades, besieging Andros there and extorting money from the other islands (Herodotus VIII.111–12); but Herodotus explains that they were not in a position to undertake an assault on the islands that Datis had conquered in 490.

All in all, despite the resounding defeat, the military outcome was not catastrophic. The Persian army was practically intact; it was able to hold the countryside, even to move against the fortifications raised by the Lacedaemonians at the entrance to the isthmus (as the Spartans were perfectly well aware). As for the navy, it was certainly not completely destroyed: the Greeks still feared it. One of the reasons offered by the Greek authors for Xerxes' retreat to Sardis was that he feared the Greeks would cut the bridges at the Hellespont, which would trap him in Europe (VIII.97). According to a widespread (but surely imaginary) tradition of the Greek authors, it was Themistocles himself who secretly had a message sent to Xerxes to that effect, in order to force him and the Persians to return to Asia. Many Greek leaders believed, after the battle, that the Persian general staff was preparing a new offensive.

But Xerxes and his advisers chose a different strategy: they decided to divide their forces. Mardonius was given the job of pursuing the offensive in Greece, with the army. Xerxes returned to Sardis, along with the navy. He must have remained there throughout the summer of 479. Thus, there was never the possibility that the Great King would hurl himself into "headlong flight." At Sardis he was in constant communication with Mardonius, and he continued to oversee the entire operation. The plan had a further advantage: the presence of Mardonius in Greece prevented the Greeks from embarking on a cruise through the islands, and thus everyone knew that the decisive battle would take place on Greek soil.

4. Xerxes between Two Fronts (480–479)

Xerxes in Sardis and Mardonius in Europe

In the spring of 479, it appears, Mardonius was definitely ready to take the offensive. He was certainly convinced of his military superiority. He did not come to this conclusion simply because he was a vain and conceited character, as so conveniently highlighted by Herodotus (cf. IX.3); instead, he must have been aware that the Spartans were putting all their effort into completing the wall across the isthmus that they felt was the utmost priority (IX.7): "The wall was not complete—they were still working at it, in great fear of the Persians" (IX.8❖). And meanwhile, Mardonius had received a letter from Xerxes ordering him to contact the Athenians, with the following words:

> The king's orders to him are, first, to restore to Athens her territory, and, secondly, to allow her to choose in addition whatever other territory she wishes, and to enjoy her liberty. Let Athens but come to terms with the king, and he has his instructions to rebuild the temples which have been destroyed by fire." (VIII.140❖)

The goal of the Persians, as Mardonius understood it, was to divide the Greeks more deeply—specifically, to prevent real military cooperation between the Athenians and the Spartans: "If only he could form an alliance with them [the Athenians], he would have no difficulty in getting the mastery of the sea . . . while he was already confident of his superiority on land" (VIII.136◇). The Persians probably also felt that pro-Persian elements were at work in Athens, as before. They had already won the allegiance of the Tegeates, who were committed to preventing a Spartan army from entering the isthmus (IX.12). In order to be sure he was holding all the cards, Mardonius entrusted the mission to Alexander of Macedonia, who on the one hand was related by kin to the Persians and on the other had more than an official relationship with the Athenians (VIII.136).

The Spartans were uneasy. They had also sent a deputation to Athens, and they spoke to the Athenian council after Alexander. The Athenians rebuffed the overtures from Mardonius, but they presented the Spartans with an ultimatum: if, as the Spartans had threatened, they refused to send an army to assist the Athenians, they would have to take their chances with the Persians (VIII.141–44). When Mardonius received the Athenians' response, he marched against Attica, which once again was evacuated, and he made Xerxes aware of his victory by means of signal fires from island to island (IX.3). Another diplomatic initiative had no more success than the first, despite isolated attempts by a few Athenians to provide a favorable response (IX.4–5). Once more the Athenians had to send an embassy to Sparta to complain of its inaction and to let the Spartans know that their behavior would force the Athenians to reopen negotiations with Mardonius. At last, a Lacedaemonian army left the Peleponnesus commanded by the regent Pausanias (IX.6–11).

Persian strategy never ceases to amaze. Why did the Persians not attempt to profit from what would appear to be their position of strength, beginning in spring 479 (cf. VIII.113)? The contrast between a wait-and-see attitude and an offensive strategy is emphasized by Herodotus somewhat later. He introduces Artabazus and Mardonius: Artabazus suggests waiting quietly, distributing gold and riches among the Greek leaders: "Soon enough, they will surrender their freedom" (IX.41). Mardonius, on the other hand, being of "violent and headstrong character," counsels attack without further delay. But tactical and strategic debates regarding matters that did not become clear until several months later cannot be transferred, in retrospect, to the spring of 479. Nevertheless, it is clear that the description of Mardonius is highly suspect, given its systematic presentation of Mardonius in opposition to Artabazus (chap. 13/6 below).

The decision was actually made in Sardis. The king made his choice not only on the basis of European conditions but also on the basis of conditions in Asia Minor and the eastern Aegean. And the danger there was equally pressing, or at least could be considered so. Upon his return to Sardis, Xerxes had ordered his navy to winter in the waters of Cyme, with some ships spending the bad season at Samos. In spring 479, the whole navy was sent to Samos "to keep watch . . . upon the cities of the Ionians who were suspected of hostile sentiments" (Diodorus XI.27.1◇; cf. Herodotus IX.130). Xerxes and his advisers could have had no illusions about the restlessness of the Asia Minor Greeks. The appointment of tyrants, such as Theomestor at Samos (VIII.85), was not sufficient to ward off the danger. Xerxes must have been aware of the attempt to overthrow Strattis, the pro-Persian tyrant of Chios. The conspirators managed to escape and sought out the Spartans, in the name of the Ionians, "to ask them to deliver Asia." They then met with the leaders of the Greek navy at Aegina, commanded by the Spartan Leutichydes, to entreat them "to come land in Asia" (VIII.132). Herodotus then states that the Chios delegation, not without difficulty, persuaded the Greeks to sail as far as Delos. He says that the Greeks did not dare to venture beyond Delos, nor the Persians beyond Samos, so that "their mutual fears stood sentry over the whole intervening area" (VIII.132◇). More likely, the Greeks could not leave Europe without forcing Mardonius's hand, and Xerxes at Sardis found the situation sufficiently worrying that he kept his navy safe from the Ionians. Taking all this into account, the king decided to order Mardonius to make his overtures to Athens. But this was not a proposal to negotiate as equals: what was demanded of the Athenians was that they accept Persian dominion, a necessary condition for the recognition of their "autonomy.

Plataea

After destroying whatever Athenian structures remained standing, Mardonius withdrew toward Thebes, "where he could fight in good cavalry country" (IX.13◇). He decided to set up an entrenched camp near the city (IX.15). The first engagements demonstrated the known superiority of the Persian cavalry (IX.19–23). Against the advice of Artabazus, Mardonius decided to commit to battle near Plataea, again relying on the cavalry; the battle was decisive (IX.49). Artabazus, observing the inevitable (or so it was later said to be) defeat, left the battlefield at the head of his divisions, "with the intention of reaching the Hellespont as quickly as possible" (IX.66). After the death of Mardonius, the Persian divisions took refuge in the entrenchment, which was soon seized by the Athenians and Lacedaemonians (IX.70). The Greeks captured Mardonius's camp and Xerxes' tent and were amazed by the tent's riches (August 479). Meanwhile, Artabazus reached Abydos by forced march (IX.89–90). He must have arrived shortly after the Persians were defeated "again.

The Asia Minor Front: Mycale

"It so happened that the Persians suffered a further defeat at Mycale in Ionia on the same day as their defeat at Plataea" (IX.90◇). While the synchronicity generally fits a well-known literary theme (cf. IX.100), this time it must correspond to reality, if not to the exact day. The victory at Plataea freed the Greek navy from the constraints that had previously kept it from leaving European waters. Meanwhile, the Greek commanders, who were at Delos, received messengers from Samos who—unknown to the tyrant Theomestor—communicated the following arguments:

> that the mere sight of a Greek naval force would be enough to make the Ionians revolt, and that the Persians would offer no resistance to it—or if they did, they would provide the Greeks with as rich a prize as they were ever likely to get. (IX.90◇)

An alliance (*symmakhia*) was then formed between the Samians and the Greeks (IX.92), and the fleet cast off and dropped anchor off Samos (IX.96).

The speech Herodotus provides for the Samian envoys is curiously similar to the arguments offered twenty years earlier by Aristagoras of Miletus to Cleomenes of Sparta: "These foreigners have little taste for war . . . how easy they are to beat! Moreover, the inhabitants of that continent are richer than all the rest of the world put together" (V.49◇). True, Herodotus's rationale leads him to describe what he calls the Second Ionian Revolt, which he places at the same time as the battle of Mycale (IX.104). It is hard to estimate the actual state of readiness of the Persian forces. Tigranes' army, which Xerxes had ordered to guard Ionia (IX.96), had been reinforced with conscripts from Sardis and its environs (Diodorus XI.34). These must have been military colonists and divisions that the Persians of the plain had to provide when required. The Persian commanders decided not to do battle at sea but to disembark their soldiers; united with Tigranes' troops, they hoped to win a land battle that they thought would be decisive. As soon as the Greek leaders arrived, they put pressure on the Ionians to join them. Their entreaties succeeded with some, as shown by the measures then taken by the Persians. The Samian contingent was disarmed (Herodotus IX.99, 103):

> Next, the Persian command ordered the Milesians to guard the tracks which lead up to the heights of Mycale—ostensibly because the Milesians were familiar with that part of the country, but actually to get them well out of the way. Then, having taken these precautions against the Ionian troops who they thought might cause trouble if they got the chance, they proceeded to make their own dispositions. (IX.99✧)

But most of the Ionians waited cautiously. They knew that Xerxes had never left Sardis (Diodorus XI.35), and they were not unmindful that if the outcome was in favor of the Persians, the reprisals would be merciless. Nothing came of it. The Persians were beaten (mid-August 479), and the surviving divisions fell back to Sardis, close to Xerxes (IX.107; Diodorus XI.36).

The "Second Ionian Revolt"

"Thus this day saw the second Ionian revolt from Persian domination" (IX.104✧)—this is how Herodotus reflects, after describing the behavior of the Ionian divisions during the battle. Instigated by the Samians, "the other Ionians . . . defected as well and attacked the Persians" (IX.103). The Milesians took advantage of the position assigned to them by the Persians before the battle to lead the suvivors toward the Greek camp: "and finally joined in the slaughter and proved their bitterest enemies" (IX.104✧). After the battle, a reunion took place at Samos. The Lacedaemonians, hoping to return to the Peleponnesus as soon as possible (IX.114), advised the Ionians to choose exile, since they would be unable to resist the inevitable Persian counterattack. The Athenians objected to this strategy, and their arguments won out:

> Thus they brought into the confederacy (*symmakhia*) the Samians, Chians, Lesbians, and other island peoples who had fought for Greece against the foreigner; oaths were sworn, and all these communities bound themselves to be loyal to the common cause. This done, the fleet sailed for the Hellespont with the purpose of destroying the bridges, which, it was supposed, were still in position across the strait. (IX.106✧)

Thus was born what was to become the Delian League, but which at that date was no more than an extension of the Hellenic League established in 481 at Corinth after the news of Xerxes' arrival. Few cities in Asia Minor joined at that time, and then only the cities that were on islands, secure in their locations and with their navies. Other islands participated as well; they must have been added to the Greek alliance during the voyage between Delos and Samos somewhat earlier (cf. IX.101).

Xerxes from Sardis to Babylon

We can see that the events have been reconstructed almost exclusively from the Greek point of view. We have no precise or unbiased information on the actions and reactions of Xerxes. After discussing the guilty passions of the Great King and his sister-in-law, Herodotus leaves it at this: "He left Sardis for Susa" (IX.108✧). Diodorus in turn writes: "And when Xerxes learned of both the defeat in Plataea and the rout of his own troops in Mycalê, he left a portion of his armament in Sardis to carry on the war against the Greeks, while he himself, in bewilderment, set out with the rest of his army on the way to Ecbatana" (XI.36◊). Had Xerxes thus chosen, "one more time," to flee the theater of operations and seek repose in his harem and among his architects? Or, when did he leave Sardis, and why?

It is clear that the presentations by the ancient authors are shaped primarily by polemical impulses. In reality, Xerxes did not return to the heart of his Empire as soon as he came back from Attica. Between his return from Salamis and his march toward Babylon, in fact, he undertook the fortification of the acropolis of Celaenae and built a residence there (Xenophon, *Anab.* I.2.9)—proof that he had not left Sardis in a fit of panic. Actually, as we shall see, after Mycale the Great King remained at Sardis. We learn from Ctesias (§27) that shortly afterward he sent a detachment of troops to waste the sanctuary of Didyma, a very famous sanctuary connected with Miletus. It is clear that by doing so Xerxes was mounting a counterattack against the rebellious Ionians, specifically the Milesians, after their treachery in the battle of Mycale (Pausanias VIII.46.3). We also know that the Branchidae, the sanctuary administrators, sought refuge with him: they had openly supported the Persians, and they feared reprisals from their fellow citizens. Ctesias says that Xerxes intended to reach Babylon. The reason for Xerxes' choice of this option must be sought in the situation prevailing at that time in that region. There are Babylonian tablets that indicate that a new revolt was under way, led by a man named Šamaš-eriba, who assumed the titles "king of Babylon, King of the Lands." It is highly likely that these events should be dated to 479, specifically August–September 479. At the very moment that he was trying to put down the Ionian revolt, the Great King received a message at Sardis informing him of the Babylonian insurrection.

So once again he was caught between two fronts. After the conference at Samos, the Greek navy had sailed toward the Straits, seizing Sestos, before returning to Greece in advance of the beginning of the chilly season (September 479: Herodotus IX.114–21). Given the choice of Ionia or Babylon, the king opted for the latter, surely because of the central importance it held in the imperial structure. The offensive was led by Megabyzus, who took the city (October 479). But even so, Xerxes did not abandon the Asia Minor front but left well-trained troops there.

5. The Persian Defeat: Its Causes and Consequences

Some Questions

We have seen how from the perspective of the Greeks, and of a large number of modern-day historians, 479 was a crucial year in the course of Achemenid history (chap. 13/1 above). We have also stressed the distortions introduced in the old analyses. However, our ideological decoding of the Greek sources must not take the place of proof, since—once we eliminate the spectre of "decadence"—even the most biased texts can communicate some measure of reality. It thus fitting that we return to a series of questions as easy to formulate as they are hard to answer. How can the Persian defeat be explained? What were the magnitude and consequences of the defeat? How is Xerxes' position around 479 to be evaluated? We will stress beforehand that the state of the evidence permits at the most a few remarks and interpretive hypotheses, all (or nearly all) marked by a more-or-less high degree of uncertainty.

Arms and Tactics

At the risk of stating the obvious, the Persian defeats immediately reveal their military and tactical inferiority, at least at that point in time. It is unfortunately not easy to state the reasons for this, because the fragmentary and contradictory state of the ancient sources makes it especially difficult to reconstruct Persian tactics in detail, including those employed at the most important land battle, Plataea.

First of all, it seems clear that the Persians placed unlimited confidence in their cavalry. With their swift steeds—swifter than the best of the Greek mounts (the Thessalian horses), says Herodotus (VII.196)—the horsemen were in a position to harry the enemy army, as at Plataea. A detachment encircled the Phocian division:

> The Persian cavalry surrounded the unfortunate men, and began to close in with weapons ready poised, to make an end of them. A few spears were actually let fly; but the Phocians stood firm, drawing close together and packing their ranks tight. (IX.18✧)

A contingent of Megarians, who were fighting with the Phocians, were unable to cope and soon had to ask to be relieved of the post to which they had been assigned (IX.20). The cavalry was armed with spears and bows (IX.49; cf. Xenophon, *Anab.* I.8.3). They attacked by squadron (IX.22) and hurled spears and shot arrows, avoiding hand-to-hand combat (IX.49, 52). They did not charge, properly speaking, which would have been impossible without stirrups anyway, but continuously harassed (IX.57). The form of combat described by Herodotus reminds us somewhat of the tactics of the Sakan cavalry, against which Alexander's generals suffered extreme difficulties in Central Asia. The Saka, true mounted archers, showered the Greco-Macedonian infantrymen with arrows, panicking them by encircling them, howling and spewing shafts, then rapidly breaking off the combat only to return over and over (e.g., Arrian IV.5.4–9). The Sakan cavalry also distinguished themselves at Plataea (IX.71).

Not only was the Persian cavalry extremely mobile, it was just as securely armored. Here, for example, is how Xenophon describes Cyrus the Younger's Persian cavalry:

> In the centre Cyrus and his horsemen. . . . These troopers were armed with breastplates and thigh-pieces and all of them except Cyrus, with helmets—Cyrus, however, went into the battle with his head unprotected—and all their horses had frontlets and breast-pieces. . . . (*Anab.* I.8.6✧)

Herodotus describes the rich breastplate worn by the Persian Masistius, who was brought down by the Greeks at Plataea. They tried to kill him, but "the reason why they could not kill him at once was the armour he wore—a corslet of golden scales under his scarlet tunic. No blow upon the corslet had any effect . . ." (IX.22✧). A Babylonian document dated to Darius II adds some interesting details later: each horseman summoned to the king's review had to be provided with an iron breastplate, a gorget(?), an armored headdress, a nape-cover, a copper shield, and 120 arrows (UC 9/3).

But the use of such a force involved, or could involve, a number of disadvantages. First of all, it placed a spatial constraint on the leadership: the force could only maneuver on wide, nearly level plains. Herodotus says that Miltiades advised Datis to land at Marathon in 490 because he thought (rightly or wrongly) that "the part of Attic territory nearest Eretria—and also the best ground for cavalry to manoeuver in—was at Marathon" (VI.102✧). Mardonius left Attica because "it was bad country for cavalry" (IX.13✧). The Megarians suffered a thousand dead during the engagements prior to the battle at Plataea because "it so happened that the point in the Greek line which was most open and vulnerable to a cavalry charge was held by the Megarians" (IX.21). But it seems quite likely that the Greeks knew exactly how to choose a location that would render many of Mardonius's divisions impotent (Diodorus XI.30.6). Much later, Arrian wrote that the Persian defeat at Issus could be explained by the poor choice of ground, which was not appropriate for deploying the cavalry and Darius III's many divisions (II.6.3; II.6.6). It was quite different at Gaugamela, "an empty plain, suitable for cavalry. . . . If there was any eminence in the plains, [Darius] gave orders that it should be levelled and the whole rising made flat" (Quintus Curtius IV.9.10◇; Arrian III.8.7).

Furthermore, this heavily armored cavalry was hard to set in motion, as explained by Xenophon, a technician well informed on military and equestrian matters and eyewitness to Cyrus the Younger's exploits:

> In no instance did the barbarians encamp at a distance of less than sixty stadia [ca. 11 km] from the Greek camp, out of fear that the Greeks might attack them during the night. For a Persian army at night is a sorry thing. Their horses are tethered, and usually hobbled also to prevent their running away if they get loose from the tether, and hence in case of any alarm a Persian has to put saddle-cloth and bridle on his horse, and then has also to put on his own breastplate and mount his horse—and all these things are difficult at night and in the midst of confusion. (*Anab.* III.4.34–35◇)

The jambeaus, pieces of scaled armor for both rider and mount protecting both the horse's chest and the man's legs, were especially dangerous. The moment a horse was wounded or panicked, the rider was thrown and often was wounded by the jambeau. On the ground, a Persian cavalryman was as good as dead (Herodotus IX.22). We may add that, in order to achieve some degree of effectiveness, the cavalry had to move with rigid discipline. The death of the leader of a division left the horsemen on their own, as we can see from the description of Masistius's death: "They missed him—for there was no one to give the commands." Instead of charging by squadron (*kata telea*), the entire force rode in again in a mass attack (IX.22◇). Consequently, the Persians were unable to retrieve Masistius's body (IX.23).

What is most striking is that the Persian leaders were unable or unwilling to conceive of tactics that would closely unite the cavalry and infantry, other than in spur-of-the-moment engagements that were not really coordinated (IX.23). It appears that the cavalry was never able to disrupt the compact mass of Greek infantry (IX.60–61). At Plataea, Mardonius on horseback led his infantry on the double, but he was soon followed by other detachments that swept forward in the utmost disorder, "without any attempt to maintain formation . . . a yelling rabble, never doubting that they would make short work of the fugitives" (IX.59◇). The Persians' favorite tactic was to set up a sort of wall consisting of their shields rammed into the ground; with this protection, they let fly arrows and spears at the intimidated attacker (IX.61, 100). But as Pausanias reminds us (IX.46), the Greeks had had the experience of Marathon, "where they were, as far as we know, the first to advance toward the enemy at a run . . ." (VI.112). As soon as the Greek hoplites carried off this maneuver, the rampart of shields was quickly breached. Forced to unstring their bows, the Persian infantrymen no longer measured up, as at Plataea (IX.62) and Mycale (IX.102). On this point, Herodotus's analysis is unambiguous:

> In courage and strength [the Persian infantry] were as good as their adversaries, but they were deficient in armour, untrained, and greatly inferior in skill. Sometimes singly, sometimes in groups of ten men—perhaps fewer, perhaps more—they fell upon the Spartan line and were cut down. . . . The chief cause of their discomfiture was their inadequate equipment: not properly armed themselves, they were matched against heavily armed infantry. (IX.62–63◇)

Similarly, in his tale of the battle of Mycale, Herodotus stresses the Persians' courage, but he clearly shows at the same time that the moment the rampart of shields was downed, they had nothing but their courage with which to oppose the well-oiled machine of the phalanx (IX.102). Indeed, in both battles, and contrary no doubt to Persian expectations, the infantry won the day (cf. IX.28–31). At the end of the battle of Plataea, for example, Mardonius's cavalry was nearly intact (IX.69). Once they were repelled, the troops of Mardonius (who was now dead) were reduced to seeking refuge behind the palisade their leader had built for this purpose before the battle (IX.15). However, they were soon dislodged by the Athenians, "who knew [how] to attack the fortifications" (IX.70).

The Persians and the Others

Herodotus stresses the courage of the Persians several times. At Mycale, after their rampart of shields collapsed, "the enemy made no further serious resistance; all of them turned and fled, except only the native Persian troops" (IX.102◇). At Plataea, Mardonius was surrounded by an elite Persian corps, who mounted an unflinching resistance (IX.62). Herodotus opines as follows, stating that the Persians' allies (i.e., the other ethnic contingents) had not fought spiritedly, and he adds regarding Plataea:

> It is perfectly obvious that everything depended on the Persians: the rest of Mardonius' army took to their heels simply because they saw the Persians in retreat, and before they had even come to grips with the enemy. (IX.68◇)

This analysis probably goes too far. Herodotus certainly sometimes uses the word "Persian" in an extended sense. For instance, according to him, all the navy crew were Persians, Medes, and Sakians (VII.96, 184). He also states regarding the battle of Plataea: "Of the enemy's infantry, the Persian contingent fought best; of the cavalry, the Sacae" (IX.71◇). It is undeniable that every commander depended primarily on the Persian contingent. Opposite the Lacedaemonian contingent, certainly the most warlike by reputation (IX.58), Mardonius placed the Persian infantry (carefully distinguished from the Medes) and within this group, "the best of them" (IX.31◇). It was at their head that he led them in the offensive (IX.59).

Should we infer that this difference in attitude also reflects political motives? We might *a priori* imagine that the Persians fought with great resilience because they were defending the interests of their own people and their king (cf. Diodorus XI.35.4), interests that did not necessarily converge with those of the peoples drafted to fill out the army. We know the Greek authors' predilection for one particular image: contingents forced to march under the whip, opposing Greeks who were fighting for their liberty. But it is hard to be certain about any of these matters, however basic. The behavior of some of the Ionian contingents during the battle of Mycale, particularly after the Greek victory, seems to be too specific an example to be able to generalize from it about the behavior of other peoples. Even at Salamis, Herodotus had to recognize, there was a small minority of Greeks who longed to change sides (VIII.11) among those who fought in Xerxes' navy, but he focuses instead on those who fought valiantly under the eyes of Xerxes, from whom they expected and received rewards and benefits (VIII.85, 90). It is also true that the presence of perfectly loyal contingents of marines (Persians, Medes, Sakians) certainly contributed to maintaining discipline on the ships. However, Herodotus puts forward explanations on the tactical level, similar to what he stressed at Plataea: in Salamis Harbor, the barbarians fought in disorder, breaking ranks, in contrast to their Greek allies (VIII.86, 89).

The decisions of the general staff must be explained on purely military grounds. When Herodotus states that the Persians were "deficient in armour, untrained, and greatly inferior in skill" (IX.62✧), he cannot be referring to the Persians proper, whose education on the contrary prepared them to be distinguished horsemen (see chap. 8/3), accustomed to the sort of activities demanded of them in battle (cf. Aelian, *Anim.* III.2; XVI.25). We may make the same assumption about the infantry. It is also likely that, like the Persian generals in Cilicia at the end of the 460s (Diodorus XI.75.3) and Darius III before Gaugamela (Diodorus XVII.53.4, 55.1), Xerxes took care to drill his troops. It is also likely that many of the Sakians in Xerxes' army had not been drafted directly from Central Asia but came from the military colonies settled in Babylonia and elsewhere; their armament was thus matched to the Persians'. When Herodotus labels the marines Persians, Medes, and Sakians (VII.96, 184), this implies that they were armed the same and drilled together, which is less certain for some other marines of different origin (Egyptian) who are named in one of Herodotus's summaries (VIII.32).

This, then, was the disposition of the Achemenid armies. At Marathon, the Persians and Sakians were placed at the center of Datis's formation; they were excellent fighters, but "the Athenians on one wing and the Plataeans on the other were both victorious," and thus were able to encircle the Persians and Sakians (VI.113✧). Unfortunately, we do not know which divisions were assigned to the wings. At Plataea, Mardonius had placed the Iranian contingents at the center: Sakians/Indians/Bactrians, then the Medes and Persians; the allies were placed on the flanks (Europeans on the left flank; the others on the right flank, including the Egyptian marines). As soon as the royal cavalry found it impossible to break the disciplined ranks of the phalanx and the infantry adopted the traditional tactic of the rampart of shields, the outcome of the battle was assured, especially when the disastrous effect of the loss of the leaders responsible for organizing the divisions' offense is taken into account (IX.22–23]).

Artabazus and Mardonius

Herodotus introduces a heated debate between Artabazus and Mardonius in 479. Artabazus, portrayed as one "of the small number of Persians whom Xerxes held in particular esteem," advised against battle; Mardonius invoked "the good old Persian way"—"to engage in battle" (IX.41✧)—in a (reconstructed) conversation reminiscent of the speeches attributed by Diodorus to the Persian satraps in 334 (XVII.18.2). Herodotus says Artabazus was "a man of some foresight."✧ Later on, he attributes Artabazus's defection in the heat of battle to jealousy (IX.66). The contrast between the two men in Herodotus seems too stereotyped to reflect reality, and the details are unavailable to us. Herodotus also says of Artabazus that he "was already a famous man in the Persian army and was further to increase his reputation after the battle of Plataea" (VIII.125✧). In fact, we know that he was soon awarded the satrapy of Dascylium (Thucydides I.129.1). He certainly did come to Sardis to criticize Mardonius to Xerxes. This, paradoxically, is why the defeat at Plataea earned him a promotion within the king's entourage.

But even though Artabazus' career seems to indicate that Mardonius was no longer fondly remembered by the Persians (cf. VIII.99), this does not mean that the strategy advocated by Artabazus was the best one to adopt in 479, unless we follow the *post eventum* reasoning conveniently followed by Herodotus. Could the Persians have waited even longer, possibly spending another winter in Europe, just as the Greek navy was beginning to get under way in the Aegean? Commander-in-chief Mardonius probably had received orders from Xerxes in the meantime. Given these circumstances, it seems difficult to follow Herodotus (and other ancient authors) when he assigns sole responsibility for the defeat at Plataea to Mardonius. It is likely that any Persian general in the same situation would have made the same tactical decision, quite simply because this decision corresponded to requirements relating to the armaments and the combat style of the royal army. The Persians were accustomed to gaining victories because of their cavalry, which had nearly always provided them superiority in their fights against the Greeks in Asia Minor. The Persian commander in 479 made two errors: first, he did not make the best use of his cavalry (which even seems not to have participated at Marathon and Mycale); second, he seems not to have understood that this adversary was quite different. Obviously, the Persians, despite their experience at Marathon, did not realize the effects of the hoplite revolution in Greece—or at least they had not drawn the necessary conclusions. But how could they?

The Consequences of the Defeats: Persian Losses

The magnitude of Persian losses, which if true would have caused lasting weakness in the military sphere of the Empire, is frequently stressed among the consequences of the defeats. But we have no credible evidence whatsoever that allows us to estimate with any probability the number killed. It seems to us that the impression of massive losses basically comes from Aeschylus, who states several times that the entire youth of Persia was lost (chap. 13/1 above). We have very little information beyond the deaths of nobles and leaders, who are listed by Aeschylus after the defeat at Salamis. But this list is not confirmed by Herodotus (*Persians* 303–30; Herodotus VIII.89✧), who simply writes, "Amongst the killed in this struggle was Ariabignes, the son of Darius and Xerxes' brother, and many other well-known men from Persia, Media, and the confederate nations." Masistius and Mardonius died at Plataea (IX.22–23, 64); two of the four commanders at Mycale, Mardontes and Tigranes, were killed (IX.102–3); Herodotus notes the death of two half-brothers of Xerxes, Abrocomas and Hyperanthes, at Thermopylae (VII.224). There is no doubt that many other names could be added to these selective lists (cf. Plutarch, *Them.* 14.3–4, *Arist.* 9.1–2, etc.). But these losses were not in any way decisive: the Persian people continued to thrive, and the nation was perfectly able to replenish the population in the normal way.

The Consequences of the Defeats: Territorial Setbacks

When we consider territory, the outcome is different. If we compare the situation after Mycale to the territory governed by the Persians at the time of the death of Darius, the most important losses are in the Aegean, where the naval defeats left the field free for the Greeks. Probably even before Mycale, most of the islands conquered in 490 had left the Persian side. We must also note, however, that when Xerxes left Sardis, and even at the end of 479, the losses in Asia Minor proper were minimal. What Herodotus calls the Second Ionian Revolt is negligible alongside the First; this time, the mainland cities remained under Persian control. On the other hand, and contrary to the interpretation that might be derived from the silence of the Greek sources, Xerxes did continue to take an interest in the western front. Before leaving Sardis, he took military and strategic measures, according to Diodorus—who unfortunately does not provide the details (XI.36.7).

Obviously, the breadth of the defeats and setbacks must not be underestimated, nor should we underestimate the errors made by Xerxes and his advisers. However, we would like to stress at this point that, in 479, the book was not yet closed. No one knew, at that time, that the Athenians would launch a vast offensive between 470 and 460 — or at least it is doubtful that the Persians had any awareness of it then. They were certainly aware that the Spartans had resolved not to remain in Asia Minor, since despite their Greek experiences in 490 and 480–479, the Persians were well enough situated to know that the Spartans were reluctant to leave their Peloponnesian domain. Even in the Peloponnesus, Xerxes had the active friendship of the people of Argos (VII.151; IX.12). In other words, there is no reason to say that by leaving Sardis Xerxes had reached a turning point regarding the western front or that he had decided to dedicate himself exclusively to matters in the heartland. And at any rate, in the strategic thinking of the Great King, where would the periphery have begun?

The Consequences of the Defeats: The Great King's Prestige

The fact remains that during the summer of 479, the Great King had just suffered three defeats in a row and that he had to leave the Asia Minor front to put down a new revolt in Babylonia. We do not know the exact causes of the revolt. But we may suppose that the Persian defeats were a trigger, an event from which the Babylonians tried to profit. In the same way, the "Second Ionian Revolt" was a logical consequence of the Greek victories. These revolts, following the revolt in Egypt in 486, remind us of the fragility of the Achaemenid imperial structure, while at the same time the reconquests illustrate the resilience of the Persian machinery, in particular the military superiority of the Persians compared with their Near Eastern neighbors.

But did the defeats also weaken the Great King in the eyes of the aristocracy and the Faithful? It is quite difficult to answer a question so delicate at this point, though the analyses below will flesh out a response. Two contrary approaches can be taken successively, neither of which, it must be recognized from the outset, can provide a fully satisfactory answer. We know the Greek response. The breadth of Xerxes' defeat was symbolized for the Greeks by certain items of booty, symbols of royal power, that fell into their hands. Most important were the royal tent and Xerxes' footstool. In Herodotus's dramatic tale of Xerxes' retreat after Salamis, he also mentions that on the inbound journey Xerxes had left the sacred chariot of Zeus/Ahura-Mazda at Siris in Thrace (VIII.115), the very chariot that had held a place of honor in the official procession of the king when he left Sardis (VII.40). Herodotus adds that Xerxes was not able to retrieve it, "because the Paeonians had given it to the Thracians and, when Xerxes demanded it, pretended that the mares had been stolen at pasture by the up-country Thracians, who live near the source of the Strymon."❖ The entire passage about the retreat is highly suspect: it tries to show not only the Great King's distress but also the disloyalty of the subject peoples (cf. VIII.116). Nonetheless, there is no reason to doubt the truth of the episode of the chariot. Indeed, as we have seen (chap. 6/3), the chariot was a striking manifestation of the sacred character of Achaemenid royalty and its privileged relationship with Ahura-Mazda. To an extent, Xerxes' situation was comparable to Darius III's (seen through Macedonian propaganda) who, after Issus and Gaugamela, abandoned the insignia of his power on the spot. But, however evocative the episode was in Greek eyes, is it likely that it discredited the Great King in Persian eyes?

Undoubtedly, royal propaganda denied the defeats. The list of countries in the *daivā* inscription (XPh §3), though it undoubtedly dates to a later period, includes (as if nothing had happened) the Ionians living near the sea, the Ionians living beyond the sea, and the inhabitants of Skudra. It was certainly the same in 480–479. The tenor of the letter sent to Mardonius (VIII.140) in fact implies that in Xerxes' eyes the devastation on the Acropolis and the spoils he had carried off from there were significant symbolic and political markers of the success of his expedition (cf. VIII.55). It may have been when he returned to Sardis that he deposited a bronze statuette the Persians had captured at Athens in the sanctuary of the Mother of the Gods (Plutarch, *Them.* 31.1). This righted the wrong committed against the sanctuary of Sardis twenty years earlier by the rebellious Ionians (cf. V.102). The official Persian version of the events is probably close to what Dio Chrysostom reports much later (XI.149):

> During his expedition in Greece, Xerxes achieved victory over the Lacedaemonians at Thermopylae and killed King Leonidas there. Then he took and laid waste to Athens, of which he sold into slavery all the inhabitants who had not succeeded in escaping; and after these successes, he imposed tribute (*phoroi*) on the Greeks and returned to Asia.

This appears to be a biased report but, as is easy enough to understand, it is entirely possible that the king had ordered that the story be spread among the High Country peoples (*ta anō ethnē*) in such a way that they would not incite unrest. Xerxes also states in the *daivā* inscription that, like the other peoples reputed to have submitted, the Ionians brought him their *bāji* 'tribute/gift'.

Like Aeschylus, Herodotus describes the despair of the Persians at Susa when they learned of the defeat at Plataea. He contrasts it to their rejoicing at the news of the capture of Athens: "They strewed the roads with myrtle-boughs, burned incense, and gave themselves up to every sort of pleasure and merrymaking" (VIII.98◊). The festival described here corresponds in all its details with the order of the royal procession when the Great King solemnly entered his residences or when he was greeted by his peoples and cities. Everything leads us to believe that, upon his return, bearing spoils and booty taken from Greece, Xerxes again appeared in triumph. He deposited the booty in the various capitals of his realm, as conspicuous signs of his "victory" (cf. Arrian III.16.7–8; VII.19.2; Pausanias I.8.5, 16.3; VIII.46.3).

Of course, royal proclamations do not constitute a fully satisfactory answer, either, since they present an image of the Empire as the Great Kings wanted it to be, not necessarily as it was. Nonetheless, they have the undeniable advantage of introducing us to the Persian presentation of events in contrast to the meaning these events had for the Greeks. Note, too, that this was not the first time the Great King had suffered a military reversal. Cyrus had died on an expedition in Central Asia, and Darius had returned from the Ukrainian steppes without conquering the Scythians. Moreover, there is no evidence of the slightest hint of disloyalty on the part of leaders or soldiers. The generals were always quite anxious to serve the King's House and just as anxious to avoid royal ire after a defeat (IX.107). The only known "revolt," that of Masistes (IX.113), appears in a context that is too suspect to be used as a criterion. It is obviously out of the question to suppose, as do Justin (III.1.1) and Aelian (*VH* XIII.3), that the assassination of Xerxes thirteen years later was the outcome of a loss of prestige due to the defeats of 480 and 479. In short, in 479, the undeniable military defeats and initial territorial losses were, in the Persians' eyes, neither overwhelming nor conclusive. We have every right to think that, on the contrary, they were ready to go to war anew.

6. Xerxes and His Peoples

A Problem of Method

Also generally attributed to the first years of Xerxes is a sudden and radical transformation of royal policy toward conquered lands. The dominant theory may be presented as follows. The decrees attributed to Xerxes in Egypt and Babylonia after their rebellions had several intentions: to abandon the traditional titles of pharaoh and king of Babylon that his predecessors had borne; to destroy their temples and sanctuaries; and to transform countries that until then had retained their own pre-Achaemenid structures into thorough-going satrapies. For Babylonia, these conclusions are extracted from Classical texts and from Babylonian tablets; for Egypt, from a passage in Herodotus, from hieroglyphic inscriptions . . . and from the (supposed) silence of the sources.

This interpretation is also based on a famous inscription of Xerxes, recovered in several exemplars in several languages (Persian, Akkadian, Elamite) at Persepolis and Pasargadae (*XPh*). In this inscription, the Great King states on the one hand that he had brought order back to a country in which turmoil had spread after his accession; on the other hand, he writes that he had destroyed the sanctuaries of the *daivā*, a word understood in general as 'demons' or 'false gods'. It is most often inferred that this country was none other than Babylonia—even though some authors have considered Bactria, Media, Egypt, and even Athens. The various sources are deemed to complement each other and to give Xerxes the image of an intolerant king who made a violent break with Achaemenid ideological strategy by obstinately warring against the sanctuaries of the subject peoples, instead of respecting them as his predecessors had.

So we see that the texts and arguments have been mechanically jumbled together to produce a coherent picture that—moreover—corresponds with the view that the Greek authors wished to impose (cf. chap. 13/1)—not, incidentally, a point in its favor. This methodological point is the focus of our criticism. The coherence of the body of evidence must not in fact be the basis for postulation or preconception. If such coherence exists, it must emerge from distinct, and thus regional, analyses of the various assemblages. We shall thus begin with a careful examination of the Babylonian and Egyptian examples and add to them the Greek example. Only after this first stage can we arrive at an interpretation of the statements by Xerxes.

Xerxes and Babylonia: The Babylonian Materials

Let us first open the Babylonian file, stating at the outset that it is a good idea to separate the information transmitted by the Greek sources from the data in the tablets. Three conclusions have long been drawn from the tablets: the Great King abandoned the Babylonian royal titles, he stopped presiding over the New Year festival, and he separated Babylonia from Trans-Euphrates and made them both distinct entities. Finally, the scarcity of Babylonian tablets from the time of Xerxes and later and the apparently sudden break in certain private archives are attributed to all sorts of upheavals caused by the king in Babylonia.

Yet not one of these arguments holds water. The retention of the traditional titles is now certain for the time of Xerxes, and the title King of Babylon is even attested in the 24th year of Artaxerxes I (441). It is also true that the titulature of Xerxes exhibits adaptation, but there is no reason to relate it directly to the Babylonian revolts (chap. 13/7 below). As for the New Year's rite, the supposed abstention of Xerxes signifies nothing, since the participation of his precedessors is not recorded either. There remains the third argument, based on the disappearance of the district of Babylonia and Trans-Euphrates in the time of Xerxes as a consequence of the revolt. However, this is an interpretation, not a commentary on specific tablets. One recently published tablet witnesses to the existence of the title and the position "Governor of Babylon and Ebir Nāri" in October 486, two months before the death of Darius, 25 years after the mention that had long been thought to be the latest (BM 74554). Indeed, the extant documentation does not rule out an administrative change in Xerxes' time, nor does it support it any longer. When we recognize the transitory character of our knowledge of Babylon due to the changing and unforeseeable state of the cuneiform documentation, any conclusion of this sort is suspect, since it clearly proceeds from a preconception about the behavior of Xerxes: the supposed link between the Babylonian revolt and the creation of a separate satrapy (which might, with just as much "verisimilitude," be interpreted in exactly the opposite way). Finally, the state of the documentation also reminds us not to link political inferences mechanically to the number of tablets, reign by reign. The case of Kish alone is convincing: at this site the number of tablets *currently* dated to Xerxes' reign (21) is nearly twice the number coming from Cyrus and Cambyses combined (11) and somewhat lower than the number of tablets from Darius (30). Moreover, recent publications continue to increase the Babylonian corpus from the time of Xerxes.

Xerxes and Babylonia: The Greek Materials

As has been mentioned, the revolt that forced Xerxes to leave Sardis during the summer of 479 was led by Šamaš-erība, who between August and October bore the traditional titulary ("King of Babylon, King of the Lands"). Only Ctesias gives the story of the events themselves, and it is briefly summarized by Photius. Megabyzus son of Zopyrus was at Sardis with Xerxes, and he was entrusted with putting down the rebels; this feat earned him considerable royal rewards (Ctesias §22). Xerxes' depredations in the Babylonian sanctuaries are presented as follows by Herodotus. In his depiction of Babylon, he describes the sanctuary of Zeus, whom we must understand to be Mardūk; he states that there was a large gold statue (*agalma*) there of the seated god; there were also a table, a throne, and a footstool of gold, and outside the temple two altars (one gold) on which sacrifices were offered by the Chaldeans. He ends:

> In the time of Cyrus there was also in this sacred building a solid golden statue of a man (*andrias*) some fifteen feet high—I have this on the authority of the Chaldaeans, though I never saw it myself. Darius the son of Hystaspes had designs upon it, but he never carried it off because his courage failed him; Xerxes, however, did take it and killed the priest who tried to prevent the sacrilege. (I.183✧)

Contrary to what is frequently stated, Herodotus's text does not allow the conclusion that Xerxes deported the statue (*agalma*) of Mardūk to Susa; in his time, this statue was still in the temple. Did Xerxes steal the other statue (human, not divine: *andrias*), which was located outside the sanctuary proper? This is possible, but we cannot conclude this on the evidence of Herodotus alone. In fact, it is clear that he got his information from representatives of the sanctuaries more than a generation after the alleged events. Let us add two remarks: the contrast between Darius and Xerxes is repeated by Herodotus himself in the case of Egypt (VII.7), and Darius's fear in the presence of a statue seems to reflect a popular theme, since it is found again in Herodotus (II.110) and Diodorus of Sicily (I.58.4), both referring to relations between Darius and the priests of the sanctuaries of

Ptah at Memphis. In other words, Herodotus's text is built on a series of motifs that hardly convince the commentator to accept it at face value.

Xerxes' sacrileges are especially developed by the Hellenistic authors, who got their material from Alexander's historians. They all contrast the Macedonian's behavior with the Great King's: Strabo (XVI.1.5) and Diodorus (XVII.112.3) mention the destruction of the tomb of Belus but do not date it precisely. Arrian is more explicit: after describing the king's entry into Babylon, where he is greeted by, among others, the priests (III.16.3; Quintus Curtius V.1.22), he writes:

> On entering Babylon Alexander directed the Babylonians to rebuild the temples Xerxes de-
> stroyed, and especially the temple of Baal, whom the Babylonians honor more than any
> other god. . . . At Babylon too he met the Chaldaeans, and carried out all their recommen-
> dations on the Babylonian temples, and in particular sacrificed to Baal, according to their
> instructions. (III.16.4–5◊)

He reverts to the subject during Alexander's second stay in the city (324–323). He recalls that Xerxes "had destroyed Babylonian sanctuaries," including that of Belus, dating these destructions to Xerxes' return from Europe—that is, 479 (VII.17.1–3).

There is no need to argue about the propagandistic character of the Hellenistic texts; the contrast emphasized between Alexander and Xerxes could only enhance the piety of a king who later on would also allow the Greeks to retrieve "all the statues or images or other votive offerings Xerxes removed from Greece" (VII.19.2◊). For Arrian, as for many other Greek authors, Xerxes is pictured as a destroyer of sanctuaries and a king overcome by excesses, just as Cambyses was, for that matter (cf. Arrian IV.11.6; VII.14.6). In fact, by entering Babylon, Alexander was doing nothing more than repeating the attitudes and decisions of any conqueror, condemning the memory of his predecessors and dem-onstrating his piety toward the gods of the "liberated" population. This is precisely what Cyrus had done in 539 on the same spot (cf. chaps. 1/5, 18/3). It was no less usual for a king to claim to have restored structures that had fallen into ruin (e.g., *DSe* 001). It was said that Alexander "had it in mind to rebuild it [the temple of Belus], some say on the original foundations . . . others say that he wished to make it even larger than the old one" (Arrian VII.17.2◊). In other words, although it can easily be suggested that Alex-ander took action on behalf of the Babylonian temples, nothing shows that their "de-struction" was due to Xerxes.

And even if we admit that the Classical texts are not simply bearers of false propa-ganda spread later by the representatives of the temples, it goes too far to state that Xerxes entirely destroyed the sanctuaries, since their subsequent vitality is well attested right through the Hellenistic period. Taking reprisals against the sanctuaries of a rebellious country was a general custom that cannot be considered specific to either Xerxes or the Achaemenids. Xerxes demonstrated his power in this way only at Athens and Didyma. Such decisions—whose ins and outs have already been explained—do not at all preju-dice the king's religious sentiments; still less do they imply that Xerxes had decided to persecute Babylonian religion.

Xerxes and Egypt

The theory that an "identical" policy was carried out in Egypt is primarily founded on the gaps in a *narrative* documentary record that, to be quite strict, is based on nothing more than an imprecise sentence in Herodotus. He simply writes that, after reconquer-ing the Nile Valley, and "having reduced the country to a condition of worse servitude [*pollon douloterēn*] than it had ever been in in the previous reign, [Xerxes] turned it over to his brother Achaemenes," the son of Darius (VII.7◇). From Herodotus's point of view, the expression is indisputably condemnatory. We may also note that he had already introduced the contrast between Darius's behavior and his son's at Babylon (I.183). But he is silent on the measures actually taken by the son. Should we infer from this, as is usually done, that beginning with Xerxes the Egyptian policy was radically altered, with the king harshly punishing the Egyptian sanctuaries, abandoning the pharaonic titulary, and removing Egyptians from positions within the administration? In short, was Xerxes transforming Egypt into a satrapy after it (according to this hypothesis) had remained an autonomous region under Cambyses and Darius?

A preliminary remark: if the theory discussed here has awakened any echoes, it is in part because argument *e silentio* (or supposed silence) has been used *ad nauseam*, and it is especially because an interpretation formed on the basis of a study (a faulty study; see above) of the Babylonian materials has been plastered onto Egypt. We will not insist on this last observation, even though it leaps out at the wary observer. As for the silence of the sources, this is an argument born of desperation, whose vanity (we may even say, the danger) has just been illustrated in the Babylonian example. It is true that, apparently, no temple construction is attested in Egypt after the work done by Darius. But what are we to conclude from this? Should we not cautiously wait for the evidence to take on some degree of comparability? We may mention, for example, that a bronze carrying handle has been found with an inscription in the name of Xerxes (in Persian: 'Xerxes the king, *vazraka*'); according to the author who published the piece, "this carrying pole . . . would thus have served to bring a *naos* or some other portion of the sacred equipment offered by Xerxes to an Egyptian temple." Of course, the object is tiny and the interpretation susceptible to revision. But if we consider the example of Karnak, Darius's building activity is attested there only by a few modest bits of evidence, the latest of which was only discovered recently. If we add to this the fact that in year 1(?) of Xerxes a Demotic document (also recently published) provides evidence of the existence of an official ceremony of burial of the mother of an Apis, we see how certain historical inferences have been drawn from nothing more than a simple statistical illusion.

In any event, the evidence is not absent! But the potency of the supposed Babylonian parallel and the picture of Xerxes previously drawn have led to the neglect of the actual evidence, or to biased interpretation. In actuality, no abandonment of the pharaonic titles is attested. Quite to the contrary, two groups of documents argue against such a theory. First are the hieroglyphic inscriptions from Wadi Hammamāt, which come from a Persian (and sometimes his brother), Atiyawahy, who held the post of governor of Coptos under Darius, Xerxes, and Artaxerxes. Between Darius and Xerxes, no major modifications of the titles are noticeable (cf. Posener nos. 24–25: 486 and 484). In 476 and 473 (nos. 27–28), Xerxes is called "Lord of the Double Country." In 474, Atiyawahy refers to Cambyses, Darius, and Xerxes as bearers of the title "Lord of the Double Country" (no. 28). The following year, the inscriptions name Darius and Xerxes together, with the same title: "Lord of the Double Country, son of Râ, master of the crowns, may he live forever" (no. 30). There is no essential difference in the picture given by the inscriptions on stone vases found at Susa and Persepolis (and elsewhere). There we find: "King of Upper and Lower Egypt, Lord of the Double Country, Xerxes, may he live forever" (nos. 43–48). Some, to be sure, say only "Xerxes, Great King" (nos. 49–76). But, given that they are undated, a chronological-thematic division into two distinct groups to illustrate a change in royal policy must remain hypothetical, presently unverified. As in the case of Babylonia, gaps in the documentation must be considered in the case of Egypt; a recently published inscribed vase proves the existence of the title "Pharaoh the Great" under Artaxerxes I (A*¹Orsk*).

Some changes are undeniable. Under Darius, for example, the vase inscriptions are in hieroglyphics only, but they are quadrilingual in the times of Xerxes and Artaxerxes. It is also true that Xerxes' title is less rich than what Udjahorresnet, for instance, acknowledges for Cambyses and then Darius. But this does not necessarily reflect a policy change; the cause is due to the source (Atiyawahy), the purpose of the object, and the identity of the recipient of the message (a stone vase is a very different sort of medium than an Egyptian's autobiographical inscription). In sum, the fact remains that the content and dating of the inscriptions currently known indubitably prove that the reconquest of Egypt was not followed by the sudden abandonment of the pharaonic titles.

It must be stressed, finally, that we have no truly trustworthy document that could serve as the basis for assessing Xerxes' behavior in respect to the Egyptian temples. The only text available for this purpose is the famous *Stela of the Satrap*. Dated to year 4 of Alexander IV, this hieroglyphic inscription exalts the virtues of the good pharaoh, whom the priests of the goddess Wajet of Buto identified with Ptolemy, then satrap of Egypt. The inscription reports that, at the end of an Asian campaign, a pharaoh brought back statues of gods and ritual objects, "as well as all the ritual paraphernalia and the books of all the temples of Northern and Southern Egypt, and returned them to their original place." He is especially praised for confirming and extending a land concession made to the sanctuary. The text reports that the (unnamed) pharaoh "expelled the profaner Xerxes from his palace with his eldest son."

Few documents have excited Egyptologists as much. The interpretations vary widely, and great uncertainty lingers, partly due to purely epigraphic and philological problems. Let us provisionally set aside all of the counterarguments and agree for the sake of argument that the inscription really is about Xerxes. At this point, it is enough to recall what was said earlier, on the basis of the Greek sources dealing with Xerxes' policy toward Babylon: if in either case, above and beyond the obvious apologetical prejudice in favor of Alexander and Ptolemy, respectively (borne by means of the same literary motifs and ideological clichés), they transmit any scrap of truth, this cannot come as a surprise. All that can be deduced from the text is that after the reconquest of Egypt the Great King retaliated against the Egyptian temples (assuming that the case reported here can be extended). Nothing further can be added.

Xerxes and the Greek Gods

By way of confirmation of Xerxes' religious policy during these years, it is useful to review his ritual practices during the Greek war. At the beginning, the king was accompanied not only by Persian *magi* but also by Greek diviners and specialists. Herodotus mentions that one of his advisers was the oracle-collector Onomacritus, who had been thrown out of Athens with the Pisistratids. To egg Xerxes on to war, Herodotus says, Onomacritus spoke oracles favorable to the future expedition (VII.6). The same was true for Mardonius, during the battle of Plataea: while the diviner Teisamenos officiated on the Greek side, Mardonius had with him the Aelian diviner Hegesistratus, whom he had hired at great cost. He could also count on the services of another diviner, Hippomachus of Leucas, who was with his Greek allies. It was due to the urging of Hegesistratus "that he interrogated the future by offering sacrifices in the Greek fashion" (IX.37–38). We also know, again from Herodotus, about Mardonius's care in consulting the Greek oracles (VIII.133–35). The practice was widespread, at least from the time of Croesus, including Cyrus and Darius.

Xerxes too made many sacrifices to the local gods. At Ilion, "he sacrificed a thousand oxen to the Trojan Athena," while the *magi* made libations in honor of the heroes (VII.43). This clearly refers to the "Asiatic" heroes, Priam and his companions. In contrast, the *temenos* at Elaeus dedicated to Protesilaus, Greek hero of the Trojan War, was laid waste by Artayctes, governor of Sestos. Herodotus, referring twice to this person he despises for his damnable impiety and harshness, represents his deeds as driven by his personal zeal and claims that Xerxes was unaware of his trickery (VII.33; IX.115–16); but it seems more likely that the devastation of a *temenos* dedicated to a Greek hero reflects honoring the memory of Priam.

Throughout the expedition, the *magi* and Greek specialists performed sacrifices, each in his own domain. But it is not always easy to determine whether Xerxes was addressing Iranian or Greek gods; for example, when he arrived at the Hellespont:

> All that day the preparations for the crossing continued; and on the following day, while they waited for the sun which they wished to see as it rose, they burned all sorts of spices on the bridges and laid boughs of myrtle along the way. Then sunrise came, and Xerxes poured wine into the sea out of a golden goblet and, with his face turned toward the sun, prayed that no chance might prevent him from conquering Europe or turn him back before he reached its utmost limits. (VII.54◊)

Herodotus then states that Xerxes ritually threw several objects into the sea (the goblet, a bowl, and a Persian sword). These ritual acts presented Herodotus with several interpretive problems:

> His prayer ended, he flung the cup into the Hellespont and with it a golden bowl and a Persian *acinaces*, or short sword. I cannot say for certain if he intended these things which he threw into the water to be an offering to the Sun-god; perhaps they were—or it may be that they were a gift to the Hellespont itself, to show he was sorry for having caused it to be lashed with whips. This ceremony over, the crossing began. (VII.54◊)

The reference to the Sun obviously refers to Persian worship (see chap. 6/6). But the episode cannot be reduced to this alone. This is probably what caused Herodotus's dilemma. We can easily compare Xerxes' deed with the sacrifices carried out by Alexander at the Indian Ocean near the mouth of the Indus:

> Then he sacrificed bulls to Posidon, and cast them into the sea, and after the sacrifice poured a libation and cast into the sea the cup made of gold and golden bowls as thank-offerings, praying that Posidon would safely convoy the naval force he intended to dispatch with Nearchus towards the Persian Gulf. (Arrian, *Anab.* VI.19.5◊)

Aside from a few differences (bull/Dionysus), the texts correspond: the king makes a libation, then throws the ritual cup, accompanied by golden bowl(s), into the sea. Xerxes adds a Persian sword. Rather than thinking (as is sometimes done) that Xerxes was honoring Iranian water gods in this way, we are tempted to think that this refers to Greek sea gods. We also know from Herodotus (VII.191◊) that, in order to deflect a storm, the *magi* were not satisfied by "putting spells on the wind, [but] by further offerings to Thetis and the sea-nymphs"—gods who for the Greeks were among the descendants of the Tide of the Sea (*Pontos*). The Wind himself was honored both by the Persians (I.131) and by the Greeks (cf. VII.13). It thus appears more likely that the Persian offerings were intended to procure the favor of Greek gods for Xerxes and his army; these gods had already exhibited their wrath by destroying the first bridges, which, according to Herodotus, had led to royal reprisals against the sea itself and against the engineers (VII.33–36). It was obviously to counteract this disturbing memory and to open for himself the gates of Darius III's Empire that Alexander "sacrific[ed] a bull to Posidon and the Nereids in the midst of the Hellespont strait, and pour[ed] into the sea a drink offering from a golden bowl" (Arrian I.11.6◊).

This was a common practice. Whenever a conqueror wanted to seize an enemy country, he needed to invoke the protection of the local gods to guarantee his future success. Alexander did not fail to do this, for example, before the battle of Issus (Quintus Curtius III.8.22). Datis, eager to placate the Apollo of Delos, did the same (Herodotus VI.97). Conversely, all who resisted or rebelled also had to be punished in the presence of their gods. This is why Didyma was destroyed after Mycale; it is also, of course, why the sanctuaries of the Acropolis were destroyed and the votive statues deported (VIII.52–54), deeds that cannot be reduced to the motif of revenge. Herodotus actually failed to grasp the political significance of one order that Xerxes gave:

> He summoned to his presence the Athenian exiles who were serving with the Persian forces, and ordered them to go up into the Acropolis and offer sacrifice there according to Athenian usage; possibly some dream or other had suggested this course to him, or perhaps his conscience was uneasy for the burning of the temple. (VIII.54◊)

Actually, Xerxes' behavior was not illogical. After conquering Athens (taking civic sanctuaries), he installed his clients there; only by acknowledging the local gods could the Persians' client rulers have legitimate power. Herodotus repeated this pious tale: "When the Athenians, who were ordered by the king to offer the sacrifice, went up to that sacred place, they saw that a new shoot eighteen inches long had sprung from the stump [of the sacred olive tree]. They told the king of this" (VIII.55◊).

From Cyrus to Xerxes

In the final analysis, when marching against or alongside his peoples, Xerxes behaved no differently from his predecessors: he appealed to local religious specialists, sacrificed to local gods, destroyed sanctuaries in cities and countries that disturbed the imperial order. In no place— Babylonia, Egypt, or Greece—do the orders of the king that have survived (or those attributed to the king) reveal any sort of fundamental or insurmountable hostility toward the gods honored by the local peoples. Having come this far in the analysis, there is no longer any need to contrast Xerxes' methods of government with Darius's. Furthermore—let's get it out of the way now—the theory of a "satrapization" of Babylonia and Egypt comes from a mistaken understanding of the policy pursued successively by Cyrus, Cambyses, and Darius. By 486, neither Babylonia nor Egypt constituted a kingdom linked weakly by nothing more than a personal relationship with the Great King. However great its consequences, the changes made, especially no doubt in the time of Darius, had already adapted and transformed the political-administrative structures of these two countries, both of them having been turned into satrapies directly after conquest, one in the time of Cyrus (Babylonia), the other in the time of Cambyses (Egypt).

7. Xerxes, Ahura-Mazda, and Persia

The daivā Inscription: Study of the Content

Having clarified the debate, we may now approach a basic document, the famous *daivā* inscription (*XPh*). In the first part (§§1–2), Xerxes repeats practically word for word the introductory paragraphs of Darius's first inscription at Naqš-i Rustam (formulas of the creations by Ahura-Mazda, genealogy, titles). Then follows a list of 31 countries that were subject to him and brought him tribute (*bāji*) (the only country list among this king's inscriptions). Then come the paragraphs that have stimulated countless debates:

> (§4a) Saith Xerxes the King: When that I became king, there is among these countries which are inscribed above (one which) was in commotion (*ayauda*). Afterwards Ahuramazda bore me aid; by the favor of Ahuramazda I smote that country and put it down in its place. (§4b) And among these countries there was (a place) where previously false gods (*daivā*) were worshiped. Afterwards, by the favor of Ahuramazda, I destroyed that sanctuary of the demons, and I made proclamation, "The demons (*daivā*) shall not be worshiped!" Where previously the demons were worshiped, there I worshiped Ahuramazda and Arta reverent(ly). (§4c) And there was other (business) that had been done ill; that I made good. That which I did, all I did by the favor of Ahuramazda. Ahuramazda bore me aid, until I completed the work. (§4d) Thou who (shalt be) hereafter, if thou shalt think, "Happy (*šiyāta*) may I be when living, and when dead may I be blessed (*artāva*)," have respect for that law (*dāta*) which Ahuramazda has established; worship Ahuramazda and Arta reverent(ly). The man who has respect for that law which Ahuramazda has established, and worships Ahuramazda and Arta reverent(ly), he both becomes happy while living, and becomes blessed when dead. (§5) Saith Xerxes the King: This that I have done, all this was by the will of Ahuramazda. Ahuramazda brought me aid, until I finished the work. May Ahuramazda protect me from harm, and my royal house, and this land: this I pray of Ahuramazda; this may Ahuramazda give to me!◈

During the course of this statement, with many elements copied from *DNa*, Xerxes thus introduces a passage distinctly his own, in which he claims: (1) to have reestablished order in a troubled country; (2) to have destroyed the sanctuaries of the *daivā*; (3) to have reestablished the worship of Ahura-Mazda; and (4) to have reestablished order in another "business." And he adjures those who "will come hereafter" to follow his example in doing what will ensure happiness on earth and after death.

The text has posed numerous historical problems and continues to do so; the problems are made still more difficult by epigraphic and philological problems that remain controversial, in particular the meaning of the phrase *artācā brazmaniya*. Comparison with the fragmentary Babylonian and Elamite versions does not resolve this problem, since the number of lexical borrowings from Persian is much higher in them than in the inscriptions of Darius. Despite the fact that the discourse forms a whole, we must, at least initially, answer three questions: What historical circumstances does the royal statement fit into? What is the king referring to with the word *daivā*? What instruction and advice is the king giving to those he addresses? It would be better not to focus on the discussion of the first question at the outset, because its answer depends in large measure on the answers to the other two questions.

The King, Ahura-Mazda, Life, and Death

The first interesting point about Xerxes' proclamation is that it contains the only occurrence of the word *artāvā* in the Achaemenid inscriptions. The importance of the concept of *arta* for the Persians is well evidenced by three observations: (1) Herodotus says, formerly "the Persians ... were known to themselves and their neighbours as Artaei" (VII.61✧); (2) Hesychius defines the word as "the heroes among the Persians"; (3) moreover, one of the courses of instruction given to young Persians was Truth.

What is noteworthy in the use of *artāvā*, which can also be understood as 'virtuous death', is that it expresses a belief in an afterlife whose course is determined by judgment of the person's behavior during his life on earth. "The message is as follows: whoever performs acceptable sacrifices to Ahura-Mazda can during his lifetime be assured of his fate after death, and upon dying, will find his *artavanité* officially recognized" (J. Kellens). Already at Behistun, Darius clearly expresses the link between a person's behavior on earth (relations with the king) and happiness/prosperity (*šiyāti*). In fact, he promises the person numerous descendants and long life, adding, "May Ahuramazda be a friend unto thee" (*DB* §60;✧ cf. §66). A contrary invocation is aimed at whoever would destroy the sculptures or would not care for them (§67). The idea of fecundity/prosperity is found again in Herodotus's version of Cambyses' last words (III.65). Darius's statement is expanded at Naqš-i Rustam, where the king promises to repay "him who cooperates" and punish "him who does harm" (*DNb* 5–13, 17–23✧). This promise is repeated, as we know, by Xerxes (*XPl*), who adds a clause giving it extra weight: "I generously repay men of good will" (*XPl* 26–31). These statements by Darius, repeated by Xerxes, are linked to the role of judge that the king assumed (*DNb* 5–15; *XPl* 5–17). If the king could act in this way, it was because he "regard[ed] himself as divinely appointed for a law (*nomos*) to the Persians, and the supreme arbitrator of good and evil (*aiskhra kai kala*)" (Plutarch, *Art.* 23.5✧). This is recognized as the giver/redistributor quality of the Great King, who rewarded the service of his own and severely punished rebel-Liars (see chap. 8/1).

In the last column, Darius goes further: "Whoever worships Ahuramazda, divine blessing will be upon him, both (while) living and (when) dead" (V §§73, 76). Xerxes takes another step by using the word *artāvā*. To earn the attribute of *artāvā*, a man must be both loyal to his king and faithful to Ahura-Mazda's law. In other words, passage from the world of the living to the world of the dead is mediated by the person of the king.

Ahura-Mazda and the daivā

The connections between the last column of Behistun and Xerxes' inscription do not stop with these considerations. It is in the same column (partly restored from *XPh*!) that Darius denounces the Saka and the Elamites as faithless (*arika*) because they do not worship Ahura-Mazda (V §71–76). Still more directly, a related idea is expressed by Xerxes when he claims to have destroyed the sanctuaries of the *daivā* to restore a cult in honor of Ahura-Mazda. The word *daivā* in particular is the starting-point for endless argument on the Zoroastrianism of the Achaemenids. In fact, we know that in the *Gāthā* the *daēuua* are described disparagingly, because their believers perform a bad ritual. This observation is doubtless the basis of the complementary references to the *daivā* and *artācā brazmaniya*, if we agree (which seems to be a given) that the phrase originally refers to correct methods of sacrifice: the *daivā* sectaries, in the *Gāthās*, are accused specifically of 'error, breach' (*aēnah*) because of the form of their sacrificial practice. It is thus confirmed that Xerxes principally had in mind the method of sacrifice to Ahura-Mazda. It does seem likely that this detail reflects a more rigid codification of an official cult in honor of the great Persian god, whose guarantor and maintainer Xerxes presents himself to be, even more firmly than had Darius.

The Land of the daivā: The King's Time and History's Time

Without claiming to have exhausted the debate, let us now return to the first of the three questions: Into what historical circumstances does the inscription fit? None of the proposals regarding the identification of the country in commotion is genuinely justifiable, first of all for the reasons that emerge from the above analysis of the relations between Xerxes and Babylon (the most frequent hypothesis); and the same rationale applies to relations between Xerxes and Egypt, as well as Media, Greece, or any other country. But the real question is this: Did Xerxes really intend to identify a specific country? If so, why did he not name it explicitly? In fact it remains deliberately vague; the syntax does not even make it certain that the place where the sanctuaries of the *daivā* were located was the very country that he says was in commotion (*XPh* §4b). Nor is it absolutely certain that the phrase "when I became king" refers specifically to the first year of his reign; it is a very vague chronological phrase that could just as well refer to any point during his reign, without any other detail (cf. *XSc* 2–5). Furthermore, internal examination of the inscription does not require a high date.

Xerxes' phrase is thus deliberately imprecise, both chronologically and geographically. This is not the only example. In one of the Susa inscriptions, Darius writes:

> Saith Darius the King: Much which was ill-done, that I made good. Provinces were in commotion; one man was smiting the other. The following I brought about by the favor of Ahuramazda, that the one does not smite the other at all, each one is in his place. My law— of that they feel fear, so that the stronger does not smite nor destroy the weak. Saith Darius the King: By the favor of Ahuramazda, much handiwork which previously had been put out of its place, that I put in its place. A town by name . . . [PB: Susa], (its) wall fallen from age, before this unrepaired—I built another wall (to serve) from that time into the future. (*DSe* 001.22–35 [◇ Kent *DSe* §§4–5 lines 30–49])

The generality of the inscription does not permit us to deduce that Darius was specifically referring to the revolts of 522–521, which he describes much more precisely at Behistun. Furthermore, just like Xerxes, at Susa (in the Persian version: *DSe* §4.33) he uses the word *yaud* ('agitation' in a verb form), which is not exactly interchangeable with *hamiçiya* 'revolt', which in contrast is the word regularly used at Behistun to designate the rebellious countries warring against the king. At Susa, we have instead an exaltation of the transcendental virtues of the sovereign that by definition do not need to be illustrated with a historical situation. The sovereign is first and foremost the one who makes order proceed from disorder. The countries "in order" are those that follow the king's law and Ahura-Mazda's law. The word *dāta*, here as elsewhere, illustrates not a judicial-administrative state of affairs but a political-ideological depiction that challenges History.

Darius's statements at Susa obviously relate much less closely to those at Behistun than to the statements he had engraved at Naqš-i Rustam and that Xerxes adopted: "It is not my desire that the weak man (*skauθi-*) should have wrong done to him by the mighty (*tunavant*); nor is my desire that the mighty man should have wrong done to him by the weak" (*DNb* 5–13; *XPl* 5–14). Clearly, in Darius's Susa inscription just quoted, he is not referring to rebellions against his authority but to the virtues of a king who guarantees the social and cosmic order, quite apart from any reference that might be precisely located in History's time. This sort of statement is also found in the *daivā* inscription, in a sentence that also does not provide much of a narrative: "And there was other (business) that had been done ill (*kartam*); this I made good" (*XPh* §4c). Even though the word *kar-*

tam is fairly vague in meaning, it very much looks as though here it can be understood as 'what I built', alluding to the virtues of the builder-king so abundantly attested at Persepolis and Susa—and this observation contributes to extension of the chronological range addressed in the inscription to the entire reign of Xerxes.

In the final analysis (without failing to recognize its originality), the *daivā* inscription fits perfectly into the corpus of royal inscriptions. Except for *DB* (and only in part, the part that was not necessarily most important to Darius), the royal inscriptions do not constitute narrative texts in the modern historian's sense. They are first and foremost ideological assertions that, situated in the King's time, do not fit into History's time. In other words, to use the inscriptions judiciously, the historian must understand that they never claim to preserve narrative or purely descriptive information. In the *daivā* inscription, Xerxes makes no allusion to a rebellious country or to royal activities specifically located in space and time. His inscription is instead intended to illustrate the permanence of his power and the transcendence of his royal virtues. The repetition of formulas borrowed from Darius contributes to anchoring this impression of permanence and at the same time further legitimates Xerxes' power. The most noteworthy difference is that the list of countries begins not with "These are the countries I conquered" but with "the countries of which I became king." Xerxes dwells on the inheritance from Darius by leaving the impression (by omission) that he had kept it intact. However, to boast more about the size of his Empire, he adds countries that had never been listed before him (the Dahae and Ākaufaciyā), though we are not able (or necessarily required) to relate this reference to some fact located precisely in History's time.

Xerxes and Persia

These observations do not drain the *daivā* inscription of its historical interest. In fact, it expresses both the significance of Darius's legacy and the originality of his successor. Even if Xerxes was broadly inspired by Darius, he did not slavishly copy his father's statements. He added what must be considered ideological innovations, which completed the work on which his father had already made great progress. All in all, the *daivā* inscription gives the impression of accentuating the religious justifications for the power of a Great King, the true representative on earth of Ahura-Mazda, in whose worship he asserts his authority to intervene directly. But it is also clear that Xerxes' religious authority holds only in Persia—"this land"—with respect to Persians' worship of Persian gods. This restriction certainly held for the Persians of the imperial diaspora as well. Did Xerxes set about erecting sanctuaries for Ahura-Mazda in the Persian provincial communities and/or regulating ritual practice, in a way similar to what Artaxerxes II did later on, on behalf of Anāhita (chap. 15/8)? This is not impossible, but it must be recognized that we do not have any clear information in this area.

For a long time, a transformation in the titles in Babylonia has been observed, and more recent discoveries have confirmed this point. Added during year 1 to the traditional title used at the start of every reign, "King of Babylon, King of the Lands," is a more complex formula, such as "King of Persia, Media, and the Lands" or "King of Persia, Babylon, and the Lands." These changes certainly reflect some political intent, but what? For reasons already set out previously, a connection with a supposed overturn of the Great King's Babylonian policy seems unlikely. In fact, these modifications and adaptations took place before the revolts themselves. Let us emphasize that Xerxes was the only successor of Darius to revive the sobriquet "Aryan of Aryan stock." Moreover, the sole occurrence of the formula is in *XPh*. It was his intention to state still more strongly the ideological and political hegemony of the central authority of the Iranian countries—especially Persia proper. In a way, this titulature reveals both continuity with his predecessors and a toughening of the Achaemenid monarchic ideology.

Of course, Xerxes' self-justification is, to an extent, as suspect as the systematic denigration of him found in the Greek sources. By itself it cannot provide us with a realistic picture of the relations between the central authority and the provinces, since the king was completely silent, for example, on the Babylonian revolts. The historian's position is all the more difficult because the nature of the evidence prevents plunging into the details of regional daily life. Nonetheless, the official Achaemenid sources by their very existence serve to remind historians not to be satisfied with the panorama viewed from the heights of the Acropolis in Athens. They demand rereading the Greek, Egyptian, and Babylonian sources, which are all too often molded willy-nilly to the chapter so regrettably initiated by Plato on the theme of Xerxes and the decadence of the Achaemenid Empire.

The Builder King

At the same time, Xerxes ardently pursued construction at Persepolis, frequently putting his work in continuity with that of his father, as did all the kings after him. His activity as a builder is shown not only by the royal statements, from which we generally infer that Xerxes was responsible for completing Darius's palace, but also by new structures such as the "Harem," a new palace that was completed by Artaxerxes I (cf. *XPj*). Many sculptures were also finished during his reign. The excavations at Susa in the early 1970s have also shown that Xerxes' efforts were not restricted to Persepolis. Thus far, two short inscriptions attest to Xerxes' construction of a palace on the acropolis at Susa. We now know that he also completed the Darius Gate (*XSd*).

Xerxes' activities are also demonstrated by the Treasury tablets. They show that activity continued uninterrupted. The earliest tablets date to 484–482 (PT 12–13, 15, 17, 18; PT 1957: 1), and there is a chronological concentration of tablets during the last years, 467–466, when groups of workers were frequently shifted around the Persepolis construction yards. As in the preceding period (PF), these workers come from various countries (Caria, Syria, Ionia, Egypt, Babylonia). Sometimes the workers simply have generic titles, such as "*kurtaš* craftsmen" or "*kurtaš* of the Treasury." But they are also listed according to their technical specialties. It is quite striking to notice that these were basically not construction workers per se (although construction workers are found as well) but craftsmen working on decoration and finishing (sculptors in wood and stone, makers of iron and wood gates, specialists in inlaying precious stones, etc.).

8. Athenian Offensives and Royal Territories (478–466)

The Creation of the Delian League and the Royal Territories

All continuous narrative falls silent after 479 (chap. 13/1 above), so no narrative presentation of the years leading to the death of Xerxes can be offered. The nature of the evidence forces us to focus on events in Asia Minor. At the risk of boring the reader, we must once again emphasize that the situation in Asia Minor is known to us only from Greek sources that, generally speaking, are interested in spotlighting the victorious war of liberation conducted by the united Greeks and Ionians against the Persians. Thucydides, for instance—the only one to provide a chronological framework (albeit often challenged)—had only one aim: to recount the great stages of Athenian imperialism.

The bare outline of the main events is well known, even though several noteworthy chronological obscurities remain. In the spring of 478, the Greek navy cast off once more, under the command of Pausanias. It consisted of Peleponnesian, Athenian, and "other allies'" ships (Thucydides I.94.1✧)—that is, those of island cities that in the summer–fall of 479 "had now revolted from the king" (I.89.2✧). According to Diodorus, Pausanias's mission was "to liberate the Greek cities which were still held by barbarian garrisons" (XI.44.1✧). And so it was in several cities on Cyprus. Then the squadrons took Byzantium, which could not resist long. Then comes the story of Pausanias of Sparta who, because he was suspected of collaborating with Xerxes, was recalled to Sparta. He was replaced by Dorkis. According to all of the ancient authors, Pausanias's behavior had bothered the allies, so they turned to Athens for leadership, and the Spartan authorities decided to concentrate their efforts in the Peleponnesus once again. This is how what is called the Delian League was founded. It was financed by a tax levied on each member city in proportion to its resources; the most important cities furnished ships instead of money (Thucydides I.96.1).

The first question raised by the evidence is the extent of Persian territorial losses. Debates proceed apace about the composition of the League at its founding and afterward, but it seems clear enough that what Herodotus called (not without emphasis) the Second Ionian Revolt had no lasting effect on Persian positions on the mainland. The Greeks knew the power of the Persian army, and the harsh punishment imposed on Didyma implies that Miletus itself remained under Achaemenid dominion. At first, the Delian League essentially consisted of island members. It does not appear that the Athenians attempted to extend their operations on the mainland any further after 478. In addition to Byzantium, the Greeks succeeded in taking Eion, one of the Persian garrisons remaining in Thrace, after a long siege (476?). On the other hand, despite all their efforts, they failed at Doriscus, as stressed by Herodotus, who notes that Mascames the governor successfully resisted; "this is the reason for the annual present from the Persian king" (VII.106✧). According to Thucydides (I.94.2✧), the Greeks also "subdued most of the island" of Cyprus. But this statement can scarcely be believed. Diodorus mentions only the expulsion of barbarian garrisons from several cities (XI.44.2). The Greek navy was not strong enough and the expedition was too short to make total subjection of the island possible. What is more, the isolated successes of 478 were without sequel. It seems in fact that the Persians managed to take back control of the Cypriot kingdoms during the 470s. Last, it is entirely in character with the times that, until the campaign of the Eurymedon in 466, Thucydides does not mention a single Athenian offensive expedition in Asia Minor; after the taking of Eion, the only campaigns he notes are against Carystus on Euboea and then against Naxos; but the latter already belonged to the League and had tried to throw off the Athenian yoke (467–466; I.98), so this was not a matter of territorial expansion.

What Thucydides says about the reasons for the creation of the League must also be stressed: "Their professed object (*proskhēma*) being to retaliate for their suffering by ravaging the king's country" (I.96.1✧). There is no compelling reason to doubt Thucydides here. Even though the League is presented later on as the instrument for the liberation of the Greek cities of Asia, this perspective was not relevant in the 470s. Athens did not have the resources to support such a policy. The tribute levied in 478 could not sustain a permanent naval force capable of successfully facing the fleets that the Great King could mobilize in an instant. The main objective of Cimon's expeditions in the 470s seems to have been to collect booty to pay his forces (Plutarch, *Cimon* 9.6). The taking of Naxos (466–465) is what Thucydides gives as the beginning of a gradual change. He highlights the policy of some allies who preferred "to pay their share of the expense in money instead of in ships, and so to avoid having to leave their homes. Thus while Athens was increasing her navy with the funds which they contributed, a revolt always found them without resources or experience for war" (I.98.3✧). It was thus only gradually that the Athenian tribute system—adapted from the Achaemenid system—produced results favorable entirely for Athens.

Of course, Thucydides' tale is partial (and does not pretend otherwise). He selected facts that appeared to illustrate the stages marking Athenian imperialism. But there are no other sources that would permit us to reach dependable conclusions. In particular, it is very dangerous to reconstruct the expansion of the League back to its beginnings by calculating backward from the first "Athenian tribute lists" (ATL), the first of which dates to 453. That mainland towns entered the Athenian League is beyond doubt, but which towns and when? In a famous passage in the *Life of Cimon* (§12), Plutarch, like many other ancient authors, extravagantly praises Cimon's conquests:

> Nor did any man ever do more than Cimon did to humble the pride of the Persian king. He was not content with getting rid of him out of Greece; but following close at his heels, before the barbarians could take breath and recover themselves, he was already at work, and what with his devastations, and his forcible reduction of some places, and the revolts and voluntary accessions of others, in the end, from Ionia to Pamphylia, all Asia was clear of Persian soldiers. (12.1✧)

The significance of this passage for Achaemenid history depends on the date assigned to it. Plutarch had no problem placing this campaign just before the battle of the Eurymedon in 466, which he describes at length. It is the same in Diodorus: after reinforcing his fleet at Athens, Cimon set sail for Caria:

> He at once succeeded in persuading the cities on the coast which had been settled from Greece to revolt from the Persians, but as for the cities whose inhabitants spoke two languages and still had Persian garrisons, he had recourse to force and laid siege to them; then, after he had brought over to his side the cities of Caria, he likeweise won over by persuasion those of Lycia. (XI.60.4✧)

Doubts have been expressed that Cimon could have accomplished all these conquests in a single campaign in 466. To tell the truth, there is no way to say with certainty. In any case, even if we acknowledge that Plutarch and Diodorus are referring to actions carried out several years earlier, we may legitimately question the breadth assigned to them, expressed in stereotypical formulas. It is clear that the *Life of Cimon* is nothing but a long eulogy, which emphatically praises the great deeds of a man "after [whose] death there was not one commander among the Greeks that did anything considerable against the barbarians" (19.3✧). Moreover, even Plutarch's version reports as much raiding and plunder as conquests proper. He also reports resistance against the Athenian offensive. The case of Phaselis (located exactly in the context of the Eurymedon campaign) clearly shows that the cities were far from agreeing to surrender voluntarily: "though inhabited by Greeks, yet would not quit the interests of Persia, but denied his galleys entrance into their port. Upon this he wasted the country, and drew up his army to their very walls" (§12.4◊). While it is not possible to achieve certainty on the extent of Persian losses, both Plutarch and Diodorus imply that, at this time (which may be 466!), many mainland cities remained in the Persian orbit and, furthermore, Achaemenid garrisons were scattered throughout.

The Eurymedon and Its Consequences (466–465)

The Great King was not unaware that at the same time the Athenians were experiencing increasing difficulties with their most powerful allies. In the passage devoted to this development, Thucydides names the revolt of Naxos, "the first instance of the engagement being broken by the subjugation of an allied city. . . . Next we come to the actions by land and by sea at the river Eurymedon" in Cilicia (I.98.3; 100.1◊). The island was once again conquered by Cimon in 467. During this time, the Achaemenid general staff had gathered vast assemblies of troops in the Cilician, Cypriot, Phoenician, and Pamphylian bases (Didorus XI.60.5; Plutarch, *Cimon* 12.2). High-born generals had been selected by the king: Ephorus names Tithraustes, who headed the royal navy, and Pharandates, who headed the ground troops (*Cimon* 12.5), the former presented as an illegitimate son of Xerxes (Diodorus XI.60.5). Callisthenes names Ariomandes, son of Gobryas, as supreme commander (*kyriotatos*) of the Persian forces (*Cimon* 12.5). The breadth of the preparations and the quality of the commanders show that the king was not content with a defensive strategy but that he intended to lead a counteroffensive in order to profit from the Athenian troubles. The various confrontations proved favorable to Cimon, on both land and sea.

> This success of Cimon so daunted the King of Persia that he presently made that celebrated peace, by which he engaged that his armies should come no nearer the Grecian sea than the length of a horse's course, and that none of his galleys or vessels of war should appear between the Cyanean and Chelidonian isles. (Plutarch, *Cimon* 13.4◊; cf. 19.4)

Even though Plutarch emphasizes the scope of the victory at the Eurymedon, he also notes that Callisthenes said nothing of such a treaty but that the king meanwhile "kept off so far from Greece that when Pericles with fifty and Ephialtes with thirty galleys cruised beyond the Chelidonian isles, they did not discover one Persian vessel" (12.4◊). Plutarch says he chose the version with a treaty because its text was included in the collection gathered by Craterus. Plutarch is responsible for starting the familiar debate on the Peace of Callias, which is most often dated to 449–448 and attributed to the mediation of Callias (Herodotus). But was such a peace ever concluded? And was Callias's embassy simply a renewal of an accord sealed in 467–466, shortly before the death of Xerxes?

I have no intention here of reopening the entire, extremely complex debate; a torrent of writing has already washed up utterly contradictory opinions. The principal arguments pro and con are well known. Pro: (1) We find the Greek sources to be relatively coherent on this subject—so much so that it seems difficult to believe it was simply invented by fourth-century historiography, however rich it is in errors of every kind; (2) the king and Athens would both have found it advantageous to conclude a treaty after the Eurymedon. Con: (1) Theopompus states that the treaty is a forgery; (2) Thucydides does not mention it; (3) we cannot see why Athens and the Great King would have

behaved thus; (4) it was not customary for the Achaemenid court to conclude such treaties. Each argument, as is well known, can be completely turned on its head, since at the
present time no "proof" is generally and unreservedly convincing. Let us at least agree
that there was merely an agreement in fact (and not *de jure*), as a result of the initiatives
of the Greek generals and the satraps, even though this is a somewhat desperate solution
that cannot in itself illuminate everything.

The basic question lies in the realm of strategy and policy: What form could such an
accord have taken, and was it in the Great King's interest at this time? Plutarch's answer
cannot satisfy us (the king was utterly daunted by the defeat). It fits too well into the imagery of Xerxes and the propagandistic frenzy after the victory at the Eurymedon to be
convincing. Testing other possible solutions raises quite a few difficulties, however, especially chronological problems. As anyone can see, after the battle Cimon did not seek
to take advantage of the victory, but on the contrary merely skirted the coast of Thrace.
There he conquered the Persians who were resisting, aided by Thracians, then sailed for
rebellious Thasos (Plutarch, *Cimon* 14.1–2). But dating the Thasos revolt remains problematic because of the vagueness of Thucydides' phrasing: "Some time afterwards occurred the defection of the Thasians" (I.100.2✧). If we agree that the Thasian revolt does
date to the period immediately after the Eurymedon, we must then also agree that the
Great King, despite his defeat, had no reason to subject himself to such a humiliating
treaty, since Athens again found itself in a situation as difficult as in 467, after the revolt
of Naxos. Furthermore, other fronts were again demanding Athens' attention back in
Greece, and the city was soon to suffer an unprecedented disaster in Thrace (Drabescus;
Thucydides I.100.2; IV.102).

But Diodorus (who dates the aforementioned peace to 449–448) recounts the Persian reaction after the battle of the Eurymedon entirely differently from Plutarch: "But
the Persians, having met with so great reverses, built other triremes in greater number,
since they feared the growing might of the Athenians" (XI.62.2✧). Diodorus (doubtless
relying on Ephorus) reverts to this in his presentation of the beginning of the reign of
Artaxerxes (465): "Artaxerxes . . . concerned himself with both the revenues and the
preparation of armaments" (XI.71.2✧). The second passage, to be sure, could be related
to the Egyptian rebellion. However, since the Egyptian rebellion did not break out before Xerxes' death (71.3), and since, therefore, the king could not have decided to put
down his arms or to fall shamefully back from the coast of Asia Minor after the Eurymedon and allow an Athenian navy to grow there without opposition while it was occupied
with more urgent tasks, it seems difficult to date the treaty (if there ever was one) after
the Eurymedon.

The Case of Lycia: Text and Image

It is difficult to find any other access point, because the sources are so impoverished.
Between the battle at the Eurymedon and the death of Xerxes, the Classical sources are
silent on Greco-Persian relations and thus on the gains and losses of royal territory in
Asia Minor during this period. A preliminary assessment cannot be compiled until 453,
when the Athenian Tribute List (ATL) series begins. As has already been noted, however, any backward argumentation on the basis of such a source is burdened with a high
level of uncertainty. For instance, we know that the Lycians provided ships to Xerxes in
480 but paid tribute to the Delian League from 452/451 to 446/445, along with the Tel-

messians. But at what date did the Lycians switch from the Persian to the Athenian side, and what were the implications of such a change? It is generally thought that the new ties to Athens were due to the activity of Cimon before and after the Eurymedon, activity that can be confirmed archaeologically in the destruction layers at Xanthus. But the so-called destruction layers are themselves dated by reference to the supposed activities of Cimon, so the mutual support of textual and archaeological "facts" turns out to be illusory.

Iconographic studies are also full of traps, insisting now on Athenian influence, now on Achaemenid. But what cultural relationship can be established between iconographic borrowing and Achaemenid political influence? Perhaps there was none to speak of, especially if we agree that these works were produced at a time when Lycia was free of the Persian yoke. We must stress, on the one hand, that there is not a single exact copy of an Achaemenid model; however, there was selective borrowing of elements from the Persepolis iconographic repertoire. Attic influence is also very clear, as much in the execution of some reliefs as in the choice of some images. We have another illustration in the evidence of increasing flow of imports of Attic pottery at the site of Xanthus. In a way, the Lycian example shows that the Hellenization of Lycia proceeded side by side with its Iranization, both being grafted onto a Lycian stock that remained extremely vital. The Lycian dynasts and aristocrats borrowed the elements of an Achaemenid iconographic repertoire that allowed the dynasts to exalt their political status within Lycian society and the aristocrats to depict a lifestyle punctuated by banqueting and the hunt. It is quite striking to observe that the buildings at Xanthus, generally dated later than 480–470, show very prominent Achaemenid influence. But this appropriation does not necessarily imply political subjugation, any more than the adoption of Greek motifs presupposes some sort of allegiance to Athenian interests in the region.

9. Xerxes' Western Strategy

Xerxes and the Asia Minor Satrapies

In order to make progress, it will be prudent to adopt complementary access points, beginning with one simple observation, suggested by the preceding discussions: we must assume that, faced with Athenian offensives, the imperial authorities (both central and satrapal) devised a strategy. Attempting to reconstruct the strategy might appear to be quite a challenge, since the Greek sources cared not a whit about it. At most, we learn from Diodorus that before leaving Asia Minor, Xerxes "left a portion of his armament in Sardis to carry on the war against the Greeks" (XI.36.7✧). Only by gathering fragments of information can we see that the Great King then, or a little later, took a series of actions—apparently disparate but only because of the character of our evidence. These actions are in fact very widely cited by the Greek authors outside the context of the confrontation of the 470s. For example, in Xenophon's description of the march of Cyrus the Younger, he mentions in passing, regarding Celaenae: "It was here also, report has it (*legetai*), that Xerxes, when he was on his retreat from Greece after losing the famous battle, built the palace (*basileia*) just mentioned and likewise the citadel of Celaenae" (*Anab.* I.2.9✧). When we recognize the strategic importance of this city, it is hard not to see in this comment an echo of Persian military reinforcement.

Herodotus mentions a royal decree during his recounting of the Masistes romance. He reports that a Halicarnassian, Xenagoras, son of Praxilaus, had saved the life of

Masistes and that "this action won Xenagoras the favour not only of Masistes himself but also of Xerxes . . . ; and he was rewarded for it by a gift from Xerxes of the governorship of the whole province of Cilicia" (IX.107◊). Obviously this information must be set within what little we know of the Persian occupation of Cilicia at this time (chap. 12/5). It seems impossible that a Carian would have been named satrap. We know on the contrary that it was family ties between the Syennesis family and the Carian dynasts that were old and close, since around 500 "Pixodarus, son of Mausolus, a man of Cindya, had married a daughter of the Cilician king Syennis" (V.118◊). Perhaps it was after the death of the Syennesis at Salamis that Xenagoras laid claim to his dynastic rights. Under this hypothesis, it was the Great King himself who made the decision. This would not be the only example of this sort of direct intervention, since the Saka campaign of Darius resulted in the replacement of one rebel king (Skunkha) with another, in accordance with the Great King's wishes (*DB* V §74). The same thing was done at Cyprus during the Ionian Revolt (Herodotus V.115). Under this hypothesis, the naming of Xenagoras was tantamount to asserting royal presence in Cilicia. We may presume that this decision by Xerxes fitted into an overall plan that had the more specific intention of better protecting and controlling Cyprus, which was threatened by the Athenian offensive of 478. It is also likely that this decision fostered ties with Caria. Although we know nothing of Artemisia after Salamis, it is clear that she remained the king's faithful ally, since he made her the guardian of his illegitimate sons (Herodotus VIII.101–3). There is in fact nothing to indicate that Halicarnassus and the Dorian cities that were its dependencies (VII.97) belonged to the Delian League from the start; quite the contrary, the discovery of a potter's vessel inscribed with the name of Xerxes "Great King" in the city (Posener no. 51; XVs) leads us to think that ties with Persia were not loosened (but we must recognize that the evidence is slight).

Xerxes' concern to maintain the Achaemenid position in Asia Minor is also well illustrated by the decisions he was soon to make in Hellespontine Phrygia. Thucydides, in his very important excursus on the adventures of Pausanias, in fact mentions that then (478–477) "Xerxes . . . sent off Artabazus, son of Pharnaces, to the sea with orders to supersede Megabates, the previous governor in the satrapy of Daskylion" (I.129.1◊). Artabazus was a high-ranking person since his father, Pharnaces, is probably none other than the Parnaka of the Fortification tablets—that is, Darius's uncle. Artabazus took part in the campaign of 480: he accompanied Xerxes as far as the Straits, then left the battlefield of Plataea after a disagreement with Mardonius about strategy. His appointment to Dascylium began a long stretch of satrapal government retained in the same family. Thucydides says simply that Artabazus was ordered to communicate with Pausanias. But the royal order was certainly part of a larger strategic undertaking, especially at a time when the Persians had lost Sestos and Byzantium. The fact remains that the "royal presence" at Dascylium is well illustrated by the inscribed bullas discovered in 1952–55 (but still unpublished), which constitute residual traces of the satrapal archives. Several of them have royal motifs (the "Royal Hero," fig. 56b, p. 700) and inscriptions in Old Persian: "Xerxes the king."

Xerxes and Pausanias

It is time to take up the story of Pausanias, since it provides a very fine illustration of another of Xerxes' trump cards, the allegiance of some Greeks. According to Thucydides, Pausanias was given the command of the Greek navy in 478, but after Byzantium was taken by the Persians, he was recalled to Sparta. He had aroused the opposition of the allies because he exercised authority "tyranically." Moreover, he was accused of "Medism," "to all appearances one of the best-founded charges against him. The Lacedaemonians did not, however, restore him to his command" (I.94.3–6◇). This "Medism" is explained further on: after the capture of Byzantium, Pausanias had returned the high-ranking Persian prisoners to Xerxes; among them were relatives and allies of the king's family. With the Greek Gongylus as intermediary, he had also sent a letter to Xerxes requesting the hand of Xerxes' daughter and offering in return "to make Sparta and the rest of Hellas subject to you" (I.128◇). Xerxes delightedly sent Artabazus to Dascylium with the reply, assuring Pausanias of recognition and asking him to collaborate with Artabazus, promising him great sums of money and extensive support. Puffed up with pride, the Spartan adopted the lifestyle of the Persian nobles: "He went out of Byzantium in a Median dress, was attended on his march through Thrace by a bodyguard of Medes and Egyptians, kept a Persian table. . . . He also made himself difficult of access." This aroused the ire of the allies and resulted in his recall to Sparta (I.128, 129.1◇). Despite the accusations, he was acquitted and, acting as a private citizen, took to the sea again toward the Hellespont (I.128.3); driven out of Byzantium, he set himself up at Colonae in the Troad, where, they say, he "was intriguing with the barbarians." He was then recalled again to Sparta and convicted, particularly because he was accused further of "intriguing with the Helots" (I.131–34◇).

Some of Thucydides' discussions have long given rise to suspicion, not least because Herodotus says that Pausanias intended to marry a daughter of Megabates, a cousin of Darius, who doubtless can be recognized as Artabazus's predecessor (though Herodotus adds, "if what they say is true"; V.32)! It is clear that nearly fifty years later the image of Pausanias had become symbolic in Greece, particularly his adoption of Persian customs. But Thucydides' tale rings substantially true, so there is no reason to deny the exchange of letters between Pausanias and Xerxes. We can see perfectly the advantages that the Persians could have drawn from his agency, since they were already accustomed to using skilled Greeks in their service—which was what the Greeks called "Medism." According to Justin (IX.1.3), "Byzantium, originally founded by Pausanias, king of Sparta, remained in his power seven years." If this information is correct, we must understand that he was installed in this city by the Persians, just as they had installed tyrants elsewhere, and that he remained there between ca. 478/477 and 472/471. The takeover of Byzantium doubtless allowed the Persians to mount a counterattack in Thrace, an attack that also depended on their base in Doriscus.

Gifts of Lands and Towns: Colonization and Territorial Control

Xerxes could count on the support of additional Greeks. Thucydides mentions Gongylus as well, the person who acted as intermediary between Pausanias and the Great King (I.128.6). From a casual remark by Xenophon about the campaign led by the Spartan Thibron in Aeolis at the very beginning of the fourth century, we learn a bit more about this person:

> Gorgion and Gongylus gave their allegiance to Thibron, they being brothers, one of them the ruler of Gambrium and Palaegambrium, the other of Myrina and Grynium; and these cities were a gift from the Persian king (*dōron para basileōs*) to the earlier Gongylus, because he espoused the Persian cause,—the only man among the Eretrians who did so,—and was therefore banished. (*Hell.* III.1.6◇)

We know that in 490, in Eretria, Datis had found rich inhabitants who would have turned over the city to him, "having an eye to the main chance— . . . for Persian pay" (Herodotus VI.100–101◊). But Gongylus's "treason" dates instead to 480. This was the year he returned with Xerxes and so was able to serve as intermediary to Pausanias. Other Greeks were rewarded at this time, such as Theomestor, who was installed by the Persians as tyrant of Samos, and the other Samian, Phylacus, who "was enrolled in the catalogue of the King's Benefactors and presented with a large estate (*chōra*)" (VIII.85◊). In the same *Hellenica* passage, Xenophon also cites the case of other towns that fell into the hands of Thibron: "Pergamus by voluntary surrender, and likewise Teuthrania and Halisarna, two cities which were under the rule of Eurysthenes and Procles, the descendants of Demaratus the Lacedaemonian; and this territory had been given to Demaratus by the Persian king as a reward (*dōron*) for accompanying him on his expedition against Greece" (III.1.6◊). We know that Demaratus had arrived at the court earlier, during the reign of Darius, "who welcomed him with a magnificent gift of land and cities" (Herodotus VI.70◊). But the gift referred to by Xenophon was clearly a new reward granted to him by Xerxes, because we know that Demaratus was at the king's side during his expedition in 480.

These gifts forcefully illustrate the king's policy of attracting Greeks to his service. As it happens, the gift of towns was not entirely new. We know that Cyrus had already favored one Pytharcus of Cyzicus in this fashion, in a historical context that we cannot precisely identify but that probably fits into the conquest of Asia Minor (Athenaeus I.30). In exchange, the concessionaires became faithful clients of the Great King, to whom they were also linked by military obligations: they were an integral part of the system by which the royal territories were occupied. These clients can be compared with Zenis and his wife Mania of Dardanus, who under Pharnabazus's authority administered (*satrapeuein*) part of Aeolis at the beginning of the fourth century, in exchange for which they were obligated to pay tribute from their territory and to furnish military contingents (Xenophon, *Hell.* III.1.10–15). Indeed, it is noteworthy that the towns granted both to the Gongylids and to the Demaratids were all in the Troad, in the part that, as we have just seen, was a dependency of the satrap of Hellespontine Phrygia. It is no less noteworthy that Colonae, the town where Pausanias established himself after leaving Byzantium, is also located in the Troad: it was one of the three towns taken by Mania in the name of Pharnabazus II (*Hell.* III.1.13). It is hard to believe that this was coincidental. The Troad and its neighbors (Aeolis) constituted a region of the utmost importance: one of the main Persian naval bases was at Cyme of Aeolis, commanded by a specific hyparch (Herodotus VII.194); this is where the Persian fleet was moored when it returned from Salamis. The region was also rich in timber, as Pharnabazus says (*Hell.* I.1.22). Herodotus's story of Xerxes' march from Sardis to the Hellespont is also rich in information. The caravan set out toward the valley of the Caicus and Mysia, passing successively by Atarnaeus, Thebe, Adramyttium, and Antandrus before arriving at the plain of Ilion on the banks of the Scamander (VII.42). It was in "the Pergamum of Priam" that the king sacrificed to Athena Ilias and that the *magi* poured libations in honor of the heroes ("Asiatic" heroes of the Trojan War).

After Cyrus, on the other hand, islands received land on the mainland. For example, around 545, Chios received the region of Atarnaeus in Mysia from Mazares (Herodotus I.161), a territory where the Chians retained interests throughout the fifth century and where exiles sought refuge. Other incidents show that during the period of Athenian do-minion the Persians could intervene in this way—directly or indirectly—in the island cities close to the coast. There is little doubt that the territories mentioned above were placed under the command of Artabazus, the new satrap of Dascylium. Perhaps it was at his initiative that someone named Arthmios, from Zeleia, was sent with money to the Peleponnesus to support some allies.

We must thus conclude that royal concessions were part of a strategic design to pro-tect Achaemenid interests in a vitally important region. This colonization movement did not contradict the expansion of the imperial diaspora; on the contrary, it reinforced it. Persian colonies were founded in particularly large numbers in the valley of the Cai-cus and its tributaries.

Themistocles at the Court of the Great King

Xerxes won a new Greek ally in the person of his opponent of the 480s, Themistocles. The victor of Salamis, banished from Athens, first sought refuge at Argos; then, pursued by the Athenians, he reached Macedonia. There he took ship at Pydna, made the cross-ing off Thasos (then under siege by the Athenians), and landed at Cyme in Aeolis (Plu-tarch, *Them.* 26.1). We may note in passing the reaction of the Greek inhabitants of Cyme, who tried to capture Themistocles, a man with a price placed on his head by Xerxes. Themistocles then fled to Aegae, a small town of Aeolis, where he made contact with his host, Nicogenes, "who had relations among the powerful (*dynatoi*) of the High Country," which probably means that they were Persians of the court of Dascylium. This episode confirms the importance of Artabazus and his satrapy in the strategy developed by Xerxes after 479 in Asia Minor, and it was Artabazus who authorized Themistocles to meet the king in an official caravan (*Letter Them.* 30).

According to Thucydides, Themistocles wrote a letter to King Artaxerxes, "who had just come to the throne" (I.137.3◇). Other authors (cf. Plutarch, *Them.* 27.1◇) "write that he came to Xerxes." Perhaps Themistocles landed in Asia Minor shortly before the death of the king (August 465), before being received somewhat later by his successor. Whatever the case, the Athenian was welcomed with great acclaim by the king, who saw him as a heaven-sent adviser on Greek affairs (*Them.* 29.3, 9): "He awoke in the king the hope of seeing, thanks to him, the Greek world enslaved" (Thucydides I.138.2). Whether from Xerxes or Artaxerxes (the latter is more likely), gifts were bestowed on Themistocles: he received the revenues of several towns in Asia Minor, including Magnesia, Myus, and Lampsacus. This royal gift in itself implies that the Persians still held and always had held a good number of coastal towns, including the most important ones.

10. From Xerxes to Artaxerxes

The Assassination of Xerxes: The Literary Motifs

Xerxes died during these events, the victim of a bloody plot. Though the king's assas-sination is mentioned by many authors, it is sometimes solely as the post mortem con-demnation of a king who was burdened by the weight of the defeat at Salamis. For example, Aelian (*VH* XIII.3) simply writes that the king ended life miserably, cut down in his bed by his own son. Our primary sources for these events are versions from Justin (III.1), Diodorus (XI.69), and Ctesias (§§29–30), who partly agree. The affair is all the more interesting because it concerns the first assassination of a king, except for the case of Bardiya. We should pause at this point, not so much to reconstruct these events in minute detail (an impossible task), as to understand how the stories that came from the Achaemenid court might have been transmitted to the Greeks (and thus on to us).

In essence, the ancient authors agree on the broad picture:

—The initiator of the plot was called Artabanus, introduced as a Hyrcanian by Diodorus and Ctesias, and given the title of chief bodyguard by Diodorus (*praefectus* in Justin); according to Justin and Diodorus, he aspired to the kingship; Ctesias and Diodorus say he enjoyed royal favor.

—He included his (seven, in Justin) sons in the plot, as well as the eunuch Aspamithres (Ctesias); Diodorus calls him Mithradates, making him Xerxes' chamberman (*katakoimistēs*); Justin calls him Baccabasus and introduces him into the plot only after the murder of Darius.

—Xerxes is assassinated by the conspirators (Ctesias) in his bedroom (Diodorus, Justin, Aelian) with the help of Mithradates (Diodorus).

—Artabanus convinces the youngest son, Artaxerxes, that it was his oldest brother, Darius, who killed his father. Diodorus adds that the third son, Hystaspes, was then off in his satrapy in Bactra. Despite Darius's protestations of innocence (Ctesias), he is put to death by his brother, accompanied by guards (Diodorus), when he (Darius) comes looking for Artaxerxes (Ctesias) or when he is about to fall asleep (Justin).

—Artaxerxes becomes king (Ctesias). Artabanus continues his intrigue, attempting to seize the throne; he takes Megabyzus into the plot, and Megabyzus reveals all to the king (Ctesias); in Justin, it is Baccabasus who reveals the plot. Subsequently, there are several versions of the death of Artap(b)anus: (1) he is executed with Aspamithres (Ctesias); (2) Artaxerxes summons the army and kills Artabanus himself after Artabanus is stripped of his armor (Justin); then Artaxerxes arrests his sons; (3) wounded by the conspirator, Artaxerxes kills him with his bare hands (Diodorus).

—According to Diodorus and Justin, Artaxerxes then reigns without further ado. According to Ctesias, a quarrel arises between the accomplices—Artabanus's sons on the one hand, the other Persians on the other; Megabyzus is gravely wounded but survives, thanks to the Greek physician Apollonides; Bactria revolts, led by a different Artabanus; Artaxerxes wins and subdues Bactria (Ctesias §31).

Before going on, we should note that Aristotle also analyzes the elimination of Xerxes in a long passage on the reasons that might drive someone to assassinate a tyrant or a king:

> Thus, Artapanes conspired against Xerxes and slew him, fearing that he would be accused of hanging Darius against his orders—he having been under the impression that Xerxes would forget what he had said in the middle of a meal, and that the offence would be forgiven. (*Pol.* V.10.1311b◈)

Obviously, except for the name Artabanus and a reference to Darius, Aristotle's version has nothing in common with the just-mentioned authors. It does show, however, that numerous versions of an event were circulating and had made a deep impression on the Greek imagination.

It is obvious at any rate that the tales of Justin, Diodorus, and Ctesias are built on common heroic-literary motifs: a high-ranking plotter secures an accomplice in the palace, then kills the king in bed (a motif used by Justin twice), is betrayed by his principal ally (Justin, Ctesias), and is eliminated. Dynastic order has the last word. This structure is repeated many times. If the conspirators planning to assassinate Artaxerxes II manage to penetrate the bedroom, it is partly because the crown prince himself admitted them and partly because they were assisted by a eunuch close to the king (Plutarch, *Art.* 29). So also with the assassination of Xerxes II, killed as he lay drunk in his palace. Once again the plot is organized by intimates of the king (Ctesias §45). As Ctesias had told it— as fancifully as Herodotus—the Seven penetrated all the way to Smerdis/Bardiya's bedroom (where he lay with a Babylonian concubine) with the collaboration of one of the most highly placed eunuchs, Bagapates, "who held all the palace keys" (§13).

The repetition of the motif of murder in the bedroom is suspect. There is another common element in the murders of Smerdis (Ctesias, Herodotus) and Xerxes: the figure *seven*, Justin's number of the sons of Artabanus (three in Ctesias). The killing of the conspirator in Diodorus (single combat) is also scarcely credible; Justin also refers to it, but he states that Artaxerxes took the precaution of summoning the entire army. It must be stated, lastly, that in Ctesias the story is enfolded in a long exposition of the Megabyzus family saga. It was the infidelities of his wife Amytis, daughter of Xerxes (§28), that drove him to the plot, in which he played the role of denouncer before his heroic behavior in the face of the armed conspirators. Justin obviously got the framework of his tale from Ctesias. The surprising name Baccabasus is obviously just a transcription of Bagabuxša, in a form that is closer to the Persian (likewise Bagabazus in Dinon in Athenaeus XIII.609a) than Megabyzus, the name transmitted by Ctesias himself (or, Photius).

The repetition of literary motifs does not immediately disqualify all the information the narrators convey. Undoubtedly, the king was particularly vulnerable when he was in his private apartments. Xenophon refers several times to Cyrus's unease about his security: "He realized that men are nowhere an easier prey to violence than when at meals or at wine, in the bath, or in bed and asleep" (*Cyr.* VII.5.59◊; cf. VIII.4.3). At the same time, the narrative structure of the ancient texts calls for special vigilance on the part of the commentator.

The Assassination of Xerxes: The Dynastic Problems

There is no a priori reason to doubt Diodorus's information. Xerxes had three sons (assumed to be born of Amestris, since no other official wife is attested), besides his illegitimate offspring (cf. Herodotus VIII.103; Diodorus XI.60.5). According to Justin, Darius was still an adolescent (*adulescens*) and Artaxerxes but a child (*puer*). The third son, Hystaspes, must have been older than Artaxerxes, since he was then satrap in Bactra, although several examples seem to indicate that the second son normally would have received a satrapal post as compensation. This would more easily explain why, after the accession of Artaxerxes, Hystaspes (called Artabanus by Ctesias) would have rebelled, thinking he had more right to the throne than his younger brother.

Justin makes it clear that Darius was the designated heir (*quo maturius regno potiretur*). But, in fact, we have no direct confirmation of Darius's primacy—except perhaps implicitly in Aristotle's version (*Pol.* 1311b). The "rule" reported by Herodotus (VII.2: the king must designate his heir before entering a campaign) has no more foundation in this context than in the succession of Darius (cf. chap. 13/2 above). Not one ancient author mentions the naming of a crown prince before Xerxes left for Greece in 480. Herodotus states that Xerxes "bestowed his scepter" on his paternal uncle, with this mission: "Keep safe for me my house and dominions (*tyrannis*)" (VII.52✧). It is excessive to speak of regency in this case. As has already been said, royal power was not divisible or delegable. Whether in Europe or in Sardis, the king continued in unshared rule. It is likely instead that Artabanus was entrusted with both applying the orders he received from Xerxes (VIII.54) and keeping his house safe (which, on this occasion, is not strictly synonymous with the Empire). To go by Herodotus (VIII.103–4: *nothoi*), the legitimate children did not accompany Xerxes to Greece, perhaps because they were too young; they probably remained in the royal residences with their mother, Amestris, all of them entrusted to Artabanes. We may then imagine that the naming of Darius as crown prince happened after 479.

Furthermore, Justin and still more clearly Diodorus state that the conspirator Artabanus planned on taking the royal title (*in spem regni adductus*/*kai tēn basileian eis heauton metastēsai*). Africanus (in Pseudo-Manetho, Frag. 70 = Syncellus) goes even further, stating that Artabanus was the sixth king (of the XXVIIth Dynasty of Egypt) and reigned for seven months. If this were true, it would be the sole example in all of Achaemenid history of the accession of a king who was not a scion (one way or another) of the Achaemenid stock, and we would be led to inquire once more into the conflicted relationship between the aristocracy and the dynasty. It is difficult to be certain about a solution to this problem. In the Babylonian tablets, Artaxerxes succeeds his father, with no break in continuity. Xerxes died at the beginning of August 465; his son Arses (who took the throne name Artaxerxes) succeeded him, without a single tablet's recording any Artabanus. The same is true for the Egyptian documents. The absence of a usurper from the tablets does not imply that there was no trouble after Xerxes' death (at Artaxerxes I's death, neither Xerxes II nor Sogdianus appeared on a single tablet, either); it does seem to imply, however, that the possible usurper was never officially recognized. On the other hand, Justin, Diodorus, and Ctesias do not report such an event. Ctesias states to the contrary that, after the assassinations of Xerxes and Darius, "Artaxerxes became king (*kai basileuei Artoxerxēs*)," simply saying that he owed the throne to the "ardent zeal (*spoudē*)" of Artabanus (§30). To sum up, we are strongly tempted to believe that Africanus's information is not credible. It is difficult to know where he got this datum, which curiously recalls what Herodotus said of the *magus* who ruled for seven months (III.67; Eusebius in Pseudo-Manetho Frag. 71a–b)—except, obviously, that the reign of Barzia was recognized in Babylonia.

The actual circumstances under which Xerxes was put to death are quite difficult to determine. Ctesias makes Artabanus out to be the son of the Hyrcanian Artasyras, who was very influential during the reign of Cambyses (§9) and was associated with the conspiracy of the Seven (in 522) (§14), held an enviable position at the time of Darius, and died shortly after his master (§19). These recollections scarcely speak in Ctesias's favor, since he uses the same name to refer to Hystaspes, one of Xerxes' sons. The only possible comparison is the chiliarch Artabanus, who received Themistocles upon his arrival at the Court (Plutarch, *Them.* 27.2). In any case, the Artabanus of the conspiracy seems appropriate to have taken on this charge, since he was the chief bodyguard. If we exclude (for the sake of argument) the idea that he was acting on his own initiative, his behavior must be situated in conflicts between the king's sons regarding the succession. We will simply note that Artaxerxes comes out looking good in all the stories: he is cleared of any accusation (he was Artabanus's pawn); following a familiar motif, he justified his power by winning in single combat (Justin); and in the sequel, his military prowess is spotlighted (Nepos, *Reges* 1.4). Can we infer that this presentation comes from the propaganda that was developed after his accession and that would have shifted all the responsibility onto Artabanus, whom the new king hastened to put to death (cf. also Diodorus XI.71.1)? This would not be the only such example. But to go further risks leading to the construction of a romance just as unworthy of belief as the one preserved by the ancient authors.

The episode confirms that the succession will always remain one of the most difficult problems in Achaemenid history—as is shown, for example, by the impressive number of royal assassinations. The recurrence of attempts on the reigning king demonstrates the fragility of power, despite all the respect surrounding the royal person (chaps. 6–8); at the same time, it testifies to the troubles that surrounded the dynastic succession. Even the methods of recognizing a crown prince introduce an element of uncertainty, which can be illustrated by this simple question: what would have happened if Xerxes had died during the European expedition? In fact, the answer is easy to give, and it confirms perfectly, as if there were any need, that Achaemenid royalty was not a constitutional monarchy. Dynastic wars, already frequent during anticipated successions, would have raged, despite the role Artabanus (Xerxes' uncle) might have been able to play. Perhaps it was to ward off just such a danger that the king would never expose himself in the front lines of battle; but no amount of precaution can avoid all risk!

11. An Assessment

Whatever the case may be, we cannot judge Xerxes' reign in terms of dynastic difficulties, nor, a fortiori, can we postulate with the Classical authors that his assassination was destiny's just punishment of a man guilty of immoderation. We must renounce, once and for all, the Greek vision of Xerxes' reign. At bottom, his policy does not appear fundamentally different from his father's, even if the defeats suffered on the western front betoken an incontestable shrinkage of Darius's imperial realm. Again we must stress that, seen from the center, these setbacks were only temporary and that Xerxes never gave up the idea of reconquest. Because the general concept of the palace at Persepolis (A^IPa) built by Xerxes and completed by his son Artaxerxes I goes back to Xerxes, we realize that, as if to claim an extent never achieved by the Empire, even under Darius, the Great King installed a frieze of tributaries/gift-bearers, where the number of delegations (30) and delegates (300, versus 138 on the Apadana) was greater than ever before.

Although faced with constraints and contradictions, Xerxes was able to promote a robust policy of colonization with the goal of establishing Persian dominion more solidly, a policy that included appealing to Greek supporters, especially in Asia Minor. Difficult though it is to date the archaeological and iconographic evidence precisely ("Greco-Persian" stelas and impressions), it nevertheless seems that Xerxes' reign marked a quantitative and spatial increase of the Persian imperial diaspora in the provinces; this at least is the impression gained from the data coming from Asia Minor, and more specifically from the region of Dascylium, which at this date appears to have been more important than it had been previously.

The Great King's authority was further strengthened by ideological propaganda that tied religion (Ahura-Mazda) and throne closer and closer together by proclaiming the

Great King to be the regulator of Persian rituals. Although the accent on the "Persian" character of the Empire did not, properly speaking, constitute a novelty, it nonetheless appears to have been affirmed with a new force. This insistence, we have seen, does not imply that Xerxes sought to "persecute" local religions or to "convert" his peoples to Mazdaism. The message was perhaps primarily addressed to the Persians, those in Persia and those in the imperial diaspora, in such a way as to bind together still more closely the dominant socioethnic class around its king.

Chapter 14

From the Accession of Artaxerxes I to the Death of Darius II (465–405/404)

1. One King after Another (465)

Sources and Problems

With the accession of Artaxerxes I, the historian faces a continual dwindling of *narrative* evidence. Ctesias is much more interested in the history of Megabyzus's family than the history of the dynasty: the framework of §§30–43 is constructed around Megabyzus and his sons, from this fellow's contradictory participation in the plot against Xerxes to the death of his youngest son, Zopyrus II, after the death of Artaxerxes. So once again our best information is about Aegean affairs, thanks especially to Diodorus of Sicily and Thucydides, who follow the vicissitudes of the Athenian-Persian conflict from Asia Minor to Egypt. Because of the biblical books of Ezra and Nehemiah, we can also analyze the internal situation in Judah—with the reservation that many exegetical difficulties appear insurmountable today. Two regions are documented best. The first is Babylonia, thanks to the archives of a business, the Murašū; the records cover the reigns of Artaxerxes I and Darius II. The second is Egypt, thanks to the Aramaic evidence, which comes mainly but not exclusively from Elephantine; this evidence has survived on leather, and within this we can easily isolate the correspondence of the satrap Aršāma (*DAE* 62–74 [*AD*]). We may also add that for the first time since the beginning of the reign of Darius I, we have a fleeting reference to events in eastern Iran. At the same time, the number of documents from Persepolis diminishes: though the most recent excavations have led to a reevaluation of Artaxerxes I's role as builder, the historical interpretation of the excavation results remains problematic.

Quite apart from its fragmentary and random nature, the available evidence presents a major difficulty: dating it with precision. Many Babylonian and Aramaic documents are dated to the reign of an Artaxerxes. But since both Artaxerxes I and Artaxerxes II had very long reigns, it is often impossible to arrive at an absolute chronology; this observation holds for some Babylonian documents dated to a Darius as well. Sometimes there is scarcely anything other than personal names that might provide clarification, since most often neither the orthography nor the paleography provides adequate criteria. We encounter similar difficulties with Greek and Aramaic inscriptions in Asia Minor dated to an Artaxerxes, even when they are historical sources of critical importance. This is true, for instance, of the Greek inscription from Sardis that records the dedication of a statue by a high satrapal official, as well as an Aramaic inscription from Cilicia that attests to the existence of an Achaemenid power center in the mountains. We may add that the Greek authors themselves from time to time appear to have introduced confusion among the two or three Artaxerxes, and it is this very possibility that has served as partial justification for the endless debate on the chronology of the missions of Ezra and Nehemiah to Jerusalem.

The Position of the New Great King

One of the new king's first acts was to give up his private name and take the throne name Artaxerxes, a custom that is first attested with his reign. The choice of a name meaning 'whose power [is established through] Arta' appears to indicate a desire to exalt the political-religious value of "truth" and dynastic loyalty, as his father and grandfather did—which was probably welcome after the difficulties in the succession. Similarly, the new king's inscriptions obviously do not breathe a word of the bloody struggles that cleared his path to the throne. Artaxerxes repeats the creation formulas of Ahura-Mazda known from Naqš-i Rustam and other previous installations and presents himself simply as follows: "I am Artaxerxes the Great King, king of kings, son of Xerxes the king, grandson of Darius, an Achaemenid"; at the same time he is careful to position his work as a builder in continuity with his father's (A¹Pa; cf. A¹I). The court propaganda also endowed the new king with all of the traditional royal virtues. We get an idea of the propaganda's impact in the description given by Nepos: "Macrochir is principally known for his imposing and handsome figure, which he enhanced by incredible valour in war; for no one of the Persians excelled him in deeds of arms" (*Reges* 1✧). Plutarch also was glad to stress that "the first Artaxerxes, among all the kings of Persia [was] the most remarkable for a gentle and noble spirit" (*Art.* 1.1✧; cf. 4.4). Diodorus also refers to the attribute of gentleness, stressing the great acclaim achieved by the new king among the Persians (XI.71.2). Like many other authors, Plutarch recalls that he was nicknamed "the Long-Handed" (*Machrokheir*), giving the explanation "his right hand being longer than his left."✧ Another writer, Pollux, comments as follows: "with a power that extends far," an expression that seems more in keeping with royal Persian thought, since the phrase is often found in the inscriptions of Darius and Xerxes (see chap. 5/3). The fact remains that Artaxerxes had to fight hard to reinforce his new authority. Plutarch mentions that, shortly after his accession, the king was unable to turn his full attention to the Aegean front, "being taken up with the affairs of" the High Country (*anō; Them.* 31.3✧). This High Country is what the Greek authors, especially in the Hellenistic period, called the Upper Satrapies. Fortunately, Ctesias provides several supplementary details: "Bactra with its satrap, another Artabanus, seceded from Artaxerxes; a great, indecisive battle ensued. But with the resumption of combat, the wind came up in the face of the Bactrians and victorious Artaxerxes accepted the surrender of all Bactria" (§31). This Artabanus was probably none other than Artaxerxes' brother Hystaspes, who was then satrap in Bactra, according to Diodorus (XI.69.2). This event, then, was not properly speaking the rebellion of a subject country but a dynastic struggle. The victory could only have reinforced the authority of Artaxerxes, who thus proved his mettle as a fine warrior and restorer of imperial and dynastic order.

Diodorus mentions other aspects of reorganization carried out by Artaxerxes at his accession: He "first of all punished those who had had a part in the murder of his father and then organized the affairs of the kingdom to suit his own personal advantage. Thus with respect to the satraps then in office, those who were hostile to him he dismissed and from his friends he chose such as were competent and gave the satrapies to them" (XI.71.1✧). Josephus states that the king appointed the commanders of 27 satrapies, from

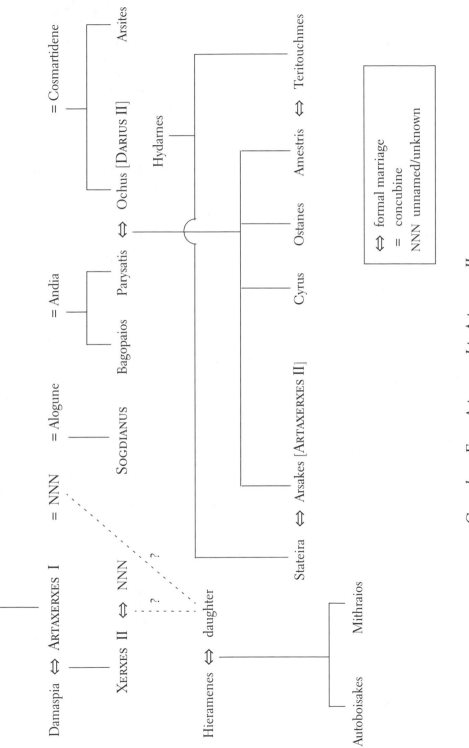

Genealogy: From Artaxerxes I to Artaxerxes II

India to Ethiopia (*Ant.* XI.185). But was this act circumstantial or structural? The general impression we have is that whenever a new ruler came to the throne, he confirmed or disaffirmed the powers of the officials currently in office, and they thereafter served at his pleasure. No other document suggests that Artabanus the chiliarch's "revolt" or, subsequently, that the revolt of Hystaspes created a general occasion of insurrection or that these events resulted in a sudden shift in the holders of satrapal posts.

In the *Life of Themistocles* (29.5✧), Plutarch states that Artaxerxes made "great alterations at court and removals of the king's favourites." The sole objective of Plutarch's comment is to explain how Themistocles was able to obtain extraordinary favor at court, which gave rise to jealousy on the part of the nobility among the royal entourage (*Them.* 29.5–6). Whatever the case, we are tempted to compare this information with what Plutarch says elsewhere about Artaxerxes:

> He was the first to issue an order that any of his companions in the hunt who could and would might throw their spears without waiting for him to throw first. He was the first to ordain this form of punishment for those of the ruling class (*hoi hēgemonikoi*) who offended: Instead of having their bodies scourged and the hair plucked from their heads, they took off their outer garments and these were scourged, and put off their head-dress and this was plucked, . . . as the tearful owners beg for mercy. (*Moralia* 173 d;✧ 565a✧)

The same information is found in nearly identical terms in Ammianus Marcellinus, in a passage dedicated to Artaxerxes "the Long-Handed"'s gentleness, which he contrasts with the cruelty of punishment imposed by the other Persian kings (XXX.8.4). It is also possible that some Babylonian tablets illustrate the "new" royal punishments.

The tradition is thus relatively consistent. It must, however, be noted that some measures attributed to Artaxerxes I must be credited to Artaxerxes II. Note in particular that it was precisely because he was the first to shoot an arrow at a wild animal that Megabyzus was condemned to death the first time by Artaxerxes I (Ctesias §40). Of course, the story of Megabyzus encompasses an entire series of clichés and monarchical motifs (the theme of the lion hunt in particular), all of which must be located outside History's time; but it is hard to see why the storyteller would attribute this punishment to a king who was also known for having relaxed the protocols of the royal hunt. It is not impossible that this modification simply dates to Artaxerxes II; Plutarch in particular stresses that he lightened certain court regulations (*Art.* 4.4–5; 5) and that he based this on an identical policy of Artaxerxes I (§4.1).

Though there does not seem to be any doubt that Artaxerxes I redefined the court hierarchy, it is more difficult to infer a political interpretation from this. At first sight, it is tempting to see the change in form of punishment as a sign that court protocols were being relaxed, as well as a hint of the weaving of new relationships between Artaxerxes and the Persian aristocracy, which could also be interpreted as a symptom of the weakening of the new king's position. But we do well to stress that the penalties pronounced against the aristocrats are quite serious, because they concern the very symbols of social distinction and royal favor: robes, hairstyles, and wigs (hair!). If we add that these punishments without any doubt were applied in public, it becomes clear that the aristocrats could not have considered such measures to be a real concession on the part of the king, who, in any event, remained the source of justice and law (cf. Plutarch, *Art.* 23.5).

Artaxerxes I at Persepolis

At the same time, tablets provide evidence of the pursuit of work at Persepolis, between summer 464 (PT 76–77) and 460–459 (PT 79), the date when the Elamite tablets stop. According to the accepted chronology, the last Aramaic inscriptions on stone vessels date to 432–431. An inscription on a fragment of a silver vessel confirms activity at the royal workshops of Persepolis (A^{1}I). The available tablets show the extent of construction, since, for example, in 460–459, 1149 craftsmen received rations on the site (PT 79). The recent excavations have also confirmed the king's statements claiming that he completed the works begun by his father Xerxes (A^{1}Pa); we now know that he finished Palace H. Furthermore, a foundation inscription in Babylonian also states that he was the builder of the Hall of a Hundred Columns.

The reliefs installed on his buildings basically reprise the form and message of those of his predecessors, with, however, several noteworthy modifications. The theme of the procession of tributaries/donors is found on the staircase of Palace H, but the number of delegations (30) is greater than it ever was in the structures erected by Darius or Xerxes. The Royal Hero victoriously confronting a composite animal (Schmidt, pls. 114–17), as well as the king on his throne supported by 28 representatives of conquered peoples (pls. 96–99), are both found on the doors of the Hall of a Hundred Columns. We also find four copies of an audience scene, but its composition is different from the scene that originally adorned the central panel of the Apadana of Darius: in particular, the king is no longer accompanied by the crown prince (usually behind him; only a parasol-bearer is depicted behind the throne; pls. 103–7; fig. 22, p. 219 above).

It is quite difficult to assign a political interpretation to these changes. It is also not absolutely proved that Artaxerxes was actually responsible for the relocation of the central relief from the north and west staircases of the Apadana to the Treasury, even if the theory is appealing for the political implications it suggests: namely, the new king would have relished the disappearance of the image of his brother Darius from alongside the throne of his father, Xerxes. But is it actually Xerxes, Darius I, or some royal person consigned to anonymity who is shown seated on his throne in the Treasury audience scene? There we are, faced with a narrow skein of iconographic interpretations, each of which has some elements of plausibility but none of which achieves total acceptance; and all of this gives rise to several doubts about the overall coherence of the argument. Given the breadth of uncertainties that remain, it seems quite injudicious to imagine that, beginning with Artaxerxes I, Persepolis lost the political role it had played before, only to be transformed into a sort of "provincial Versailles" and become "a sanctuary rather than a capital." The role assigned to Susa in this theory is paradoxical, since the new king does not appear to have carried out greater building activities there than at Persepolis. From one of Darius II's inscriptions we learn simply that he began the construction of a palace at Susa (D^{2}Sb); one of Artaxerxes II's inscriptions shows that Artaxerxes I did not bother to rebuild the Apadana of Darius, which was destroyed by fire during his reign (A^{2}Sa).

2. The Egyptian Revolt (ca. 464–454)

The Revolt of Inarus and the Athenian Intervention

After achieving victory in Bactria, it was in the west that Artaxerxes would see the greatest threat to his imperial authority, particularly in Egypt (cf. Plutarch, *Them.* 31.4).

The facts are known to us essentially through Diodorus and Thucydides; Ctesias's report is marked by a series of repetitive motifs and onomastic and chronological improbabilities (§§32–35). According to Diodorus, the news of the assassination of Xerxes and the subsequent turmoil incited the Egyptians to try to win back their freedom. Their first rebellious act was to expel the Persian tribute-collectors and to bestow royal authority on a Libyan, Inarus (463–462). He gathered an army conscripted from the Egyptians and Libyans, reinforced by mercenaries from everywhere. He was aware of the disproportion of forces and sent an ambassador to Athens empowered to negotiate an alliance (*symmakhia*) and to promise the Athenians considerable future benefits and even a share in the control of Egypt (*koinē basileia*). The Athenians responded enthusiastically to Inarus's request and soon sent a fleet to the Nile (XI.71.3–6). Thucydides supplies the following details:

> Meanwhile Inarus, son of Psammetichus, a Libyan king of the Libyans on the Egyptian border, having his headquarters at Marea, the town above Pharos, caused a revolt of almost the whole of Egypt from King Artaxerxes, and placing himself at its head, invited the Athenians to his assistance. Abandoning a Cyprian expedition upon which they happened to be engaged with two hundred ships of their own and their allies, they arrived in Egypt and sailed from the sea into the Nile, and making themselves masters of the river and two-thirds of Memphis, addressed themselves to the attack of the remaining third, which is called White Wall. Within it were Persians and Medes who had taken refuge there, and Egyptians who had not joined the rebellion. (I.104◇)

Diodorus reports that the Persians took refuge in the Memphis fortress after being defeated. To put down the revolt, Xerxes then sent an army under the command of Achaemenes, "son of Darius and his own uncle" (XI.74.1)—that is, the very person who had been made satrap of Egypt by Xerxes after the revolt of 486–484 (Herodotus VII.7). Reinforced by the Athenian contingents, Inarus's army achieved victory at Papremis in the Delta, and Achaemenes lost his life there (Herodotus III.12, VII.7; Diodorus XI.74.1–4; cf. Ctesias §32).

Thucydides' account has the advantage of placing the revolt within the wider framework of Athenian politics. Though in Greece itself the break with Sparta was final and the circle of belligerents continually increased, Athens continued to maintain its maritime operations. This is shown by a list of Athenian soldiers who died in the years 460–459 in areas as far-flung as Greece, Cyprus, Phoenicia, as well as Egypt (ML 33). Taking into account the new international situation, Artaxerxes, who was busy preparing a new army, reasonably sent Megabyzus to Sparta with money "to bribe the Peleponnesians to invade Attica and so draw off the Athenians from Egypt" (Thucydides I.109.2◇; cf. Diodorus XI.74.5). These efforts did not have the expected results. The Persian army and navy prepared and trained in Cilicia, Cyprus, and Phoenicia and set off in a convoy commanded by Megabyzus and Artabazus. Throughout this time, the garrison at Memphis continued to stand firm, while the Athenians and their allies continued exercises—and Thucydides is very unforthcoming about their nature and extent (I.109.1). The Persian navy reached Memphis by sea and river and broke the blockade. Soon discord dominated relations between the Egyptians and the Athenians: the former surrendered, and the latter were convinced to make a truce with Megabyzus, who allowed some of them to return to Greece by crossing the Libyan Desert. The Athenian disaster soon climaxed when another squadron was surprised at the entrance to the Mendesian Mouth of the Nile and almost completely destroyed: "Such was the end of the great expedition of the Athenians and their allies to Egypt" (Thucydides I.110.4◇). It had lasted six years (460–454; I.110.1).

Characteristics and Consequences of the Revolt:
Persian Egypt and Egyptian Egypt

Thucydides states that the Athenian's initial success enabled them to become "masters of Egypt" (I.109.2◇). There is nothing to this claim. Inarus himself was only able to seize control of part of Egypt (I.109.1). There is no trace of rebellion anywhere but the Delta. In 461, for example, the Persian Ariyawrata had an inscription placed in Wadi Hammamāt, dated as follows: "Year 5 of the king of Upper and Lower Egypt, lord of the Double Country, Artaxerxes, may he live forever, beloved of the gods" (Posener no. 31). Identical inscriptions are known from the following years (nos. 32–34). Nor is any trace of trouble detectable in the Aramaic papyri from Elephantine dated to the reign of Artaxerxes.

In actuality, the revolt was limited to the Delta. Inarus was careful to present himself as the son of Psammetichus, who himself represented a program of restoration of Egyptian independence as it existed before the conquest by Cambyses. He ordered the expulsion of Persian tribute-collectors, who were visible signs and symbols of subjection. But first he established himself in Libyan bases before setting foot in the western Delta; his insurrection thus was the latest in a long history of Libyan dynasties in Egypt. Moreover, he obviously was aware that in the present circumstances the Athenians had as their highest objective "to humble the Persians as far as they could" (Diodorus XI.71.5◇). But he never succeeded in attracting the loyalty of all the Egyptians. We have seen that, despite the length of the siege and the Athenian successes, Egyptian auxiliaries remained faithful to the Persians in the White Wall at Memphis (I.104.2). Inarus went so far as to promise the Athenians a sort of power-sharing in Egypt (Diodorus XI.71.4). Because of these considerations, it seems impossible to consider this revolt a manifestation of what is customarily called "Egyptian nationalism." It is likely that the promises made to the Athenians did nothing other than to alienate a certain number of Egyptians. In the end, Inarus was betrayed to the Persians and crucified (I.110.3).

The events also reveal gaps in Persian territorial dominance. Thucydides writes that, after the Persian victory, "Egypt returned to its subjection to the king," but he adds this crucial reservation: "except Amyrtaeus, the king in the marshes, whom they were unable to capture from the extent of the marsh; the marshmen being also the most warlike of the Egyptians" (I.110.2◇). In fact, we know from Herodotus that the best Egyptian soldiers came from the Delta nomes (II.164–65). These "marsh kings" became part of the Egyptian *longue durée*: according to both Herodotus (II.152) and Diodorus (I.66), Psammetichus I himself had been exiled to the marshes, and he regained power with the aid of Ionian and Carian mercenaries. This was the same strategy taken by Inarus. Among the considerable advantages that it dangled before the Athenians (Diodorus XI.71.4) perhaps was the availability of plots of land in Egypt, comparable to what Psammetichus had distributed to the Ionian and Carian mercenaries after his victory (Herodotus II.154). It is clear that after the death of Inarus another marsh king, Amyrtaeus, retained power locally, and the Persians did not attempt to vanquish him because of the operational difficulties. This Amyrtaeus may be the other Egyptian who, Ctesias (§32) says, rebelled at the same time as Inarus. The fact remains that Inarus's line did not die out, since in 445–444 another dynast, also named Psammetichus, sent shipments of wheat to Athens, indicating that at this date he controlled rich farmland in the Delta. The same situation existed in 412 (Thucydides VIII.35.2).

The events of Artaxerxes' reign thus show that the Persians worked out a highly uneven scheme for territorial occupation in Egypt. Their first concern was to keep open the riverways linking Memphis to the sea. This, anyway, was Herodotus's observation when he visited Egypt some time after the revolt (cf. III.12): "To this day the elbow which the Nile forms here, where it is forced into its new channel, is most carefully watched by the Persians, who strengthen the dam every year; for should the river burst it, Memphis might be completely overwhelmed" (II.99✧). Thus, by exercising control over the Egyptian river fleet, they prevented any rebel from turning it against them (cf. Diodorus XVI.47.6). Because they collaborated with Egyptian engineers, they were in a position to use dikes and canals against rebels (Thucydides I.110.4; Diodorus XI.77.1). Finally, garrisons allowed them to keep the road to Palestine open, as well as the mouths of the Nile, through which warships and transport vessels traveled freely.

The Persians were aware of their inability to impose direct dominion over the western Delta (or, perhaps they merely wanted to pursue their traditional policy) and therefore gave up the idea of military occupation. This is probably what underlies Herodotus's remark regarding Egyptian dynasts:

> For the Persians are in the habit of treating the sons of kings with honour, and even of restoring to their sons the thrones of those who have rebelled against them. There are many instances from which one may infer that this sort of generosity is usual in Persia: one obvious one is the case of Thannyras, the son of Inarus the Libyan, who was allowed to succeed his father. Pausiris, the son of Amyrtaeus, is another example: to him, too, his father's kingdom was restored—and all this in spite of the fact that nobody ever caused the Persians more trouble and loss than Inarus and Amyrtaeus. (III.15✧)

In other words, after the execution of Inarus, the Persians did not attempt to dislodge his son. The requirement, obviously, was that he agreed not to rise up against the Persians and that he would not attempt to extend the territory allocated to him. He was to some extent a client king, as were Amyrtaeus and his son. In addition to other obligations, they were required to send the famous Egyptian marsh soldiers, whom Herodotus calls the Hermotybians and Calasirians (II.164–65), to the Great King. These soldiers had participated in the campaign of 480; they were even included among the *epibates* ('marines') in Mardonius's elite army (IX.32). It is practically certain that this system had been in place since the time of Cambyses' conquest. Let us emphasize in fact that Inarus is referred to as a Libyan dynast who was "king of the Libyans on the Egyptian border" (Thucydides I.104.1✧). Indeed, the adventures of the Persian army when it had retreated from Cyrenaica in 513 show that, even at that time, "most of them [the Libyans], at the time of which I write, cared nothing for the king of Persia, any more than they do to-day" (Herodotus IV.197✧).

The system managed to work to the Persians' advantage for several decades. For one thing, they kept in place several concurrent dynasts, following a method they had applied in other parts of their Empire (cf. Plutarch, *Art.* 24.5–9). For another, the Delta dynasts by themselves were unable to seize waterways or Memphis; until the arrival of the Athenians, the unrest fomented by Inarus does not seem to have been widespread. On the other hand, the Persian strategy had enormous risks that were evident as soon as the marsh kings found support from a state such as Athens that could dispatch a fleet capable of sailing the Nile as far as the seat of Persian power (cf. Thucydides I.104.2). As it happens, a few years later, an Athenian squadron once again headed for the Delta in response to an appeal from Amyrtaeus, "the king in the marshes" (I.112.3✧). In other words, maintenance of dominion over Egypt very much depended on the abilities of the royal navy. To deal with these circumstances, the central power was able to mobilize men and materiel from its Levantine subjects (Cilicians, Cypriots, Phoenicians). It also benefited from the multiple fronts faced by the Athenians, who were more interested in weakening Artaxerxes (Diodorus XI.71.5) than in conquering Egypt. It was exactly the same motivations, in reverse, that led the Persian embassy headed by Artabazus to act as it did in the Peleponnesus; Artaxerxes and his successors thereafter always attempted to take advantage of the new situation created by the rupture between Sparta and Athens.

The fact remains that the Egyptian strategy was an important success for the Great King. According to Ctesias, before leaving Egypt, Megabyzus left Sarsamas there as satrap (§35). We are tempted to think that he is the same Aršāma who is mentioned in several Aramaic documents as the satrap of Egypt under Darius II. Apart from a new and fruitless attempt by Amyrtaeus (Thucydides I.112.3), Egypt remained calm throughout the reign of Artaxerxes I.

3. Trans-Euphrates Matters

Artaxerxes and Megabyzus

These events in Egypt form the chronological context of the obscure affair of Megabyzus, which is narrated at great length by Ctesias in a story with the following outline. Amestris (here confused by Ctesias with Amytis) was unhappy with the agreement between Megabyzus and Inarus and the Greeks in his service (§34). Her only goal was to get the king to punish the murderers of her son Achaemenes, and she achieved this aim five years later: Inarus and fifty Greeks were crucified (§36). Megabyzus was utterly distraught at this and received permission from the king to leave the court and settle in Syria, which is referred to as 'his territory' (*he heautou khōra*). With the aid of Inarus's Greek mercenaries, whom he had hired, he seceded, supported by his sons Zopyrus and Artyphius. Their forces routed two successive armies sent by Artaxerxes, the first commanded by Usiris, the second by Menostanes, a nephew of the king (§37–38). Negotiations took place: "The king granted him a pardon" (§39). Following this, Ctesias reports the episode of the lion hunt, the exile of Megabyzus to the Persian Gulf, his wild escape, his reunion with his wife Amytis, his return to favor, and then his death (§§40–42).

The story thus told is not without interest. It clarifies the relationships between the king and an aristocrat of distinguished lineage who was a descendant of one of the conspirators of 522, who had achieved a preeminent position close to Xerxes (he married one of Xerxes' daughters and successfully suppressed the Babylonian revolt), and who had played an important though unclear role after the accession of Artaxerxes. We also note that, before opening negotiations with the king, Megabyzus was careful to make sure that his wife and young son were present with him; otherwise, they might have been considered hostages held at court to guarantee loyalty. Furthermore, Ctesias's tale introduces people (Artarius, Menostanes) whose historical existence is confirmed by Babylonian tablets. We know, for example, that the emissaries sent to Megabyzus, Petisas and his son Spitamenes, at that time had the concession on lands in the Nippur area (the names are Pātēšu and Ispitāma in the tablets). But taken as a whole, despite the veracity of some details, Ctesias's tale is far from believeable. As has been mentioned several times already, it is clearly a family saga. Ctesias even follows the adventures of Megabyzus's sons Artyphius and Zopyrus II. Zopyrus left royal territory and sought refuge in Athens; he later died in an obscure attempt on Caunus (§43). The entire narrative is built on a series of literary motifs (cruel Persian princesses seeking vengeance for their child, royal favor/disfavor, wound in the thigh, lion hunt, theme of return).

Even if we conclude that there really was a revolt by Megabyzus, it is still not easy to analyze it with total equanimity. We do not even know Megabyzus's position during these events. We get the general idea from Ctesias that he was satrap of Syria (Trans-Euphrates), which we think had previously been separated from Babylonia—and this in fact seems likely (Artarios is called "satrap of Babylonia," §38). But when Ctesias calls Syria "his territory," he might just as well be thinking that estates had been granted to Megabyzus in the region. It is true that the two interpretations (satrap; estate-holder) are not mutually exclusive, given how difficult it is to distinguish personal estates from government lands (see chap. 11/9). If we agree that he really was a satrap, we should stress that he is the first example since the still mysterious case of Aryandes in Egypt (Herodotus IV.166) of someone undertaking a rebellion. One of the most noteworthy aspects of the revolt is that Megabyzus recruited Greek mercenaries. This is the first attestation of a practice that was to be repeated some years later under Pissuthnes.

Troubles in Judah?

According to the Chronicler, at just about the same time, troubles continued to rock Judah (Ezra 4:7–24◇). The Jews, who he says (4:4–6) already had been denounced in Xerxes' time, were again criticized in the time of Artaxerxes. A letter was sent by Rehūm the governor and Shimshai the scribe, with the support of representatives of other peoples neighboring Judah. They let the king know that the Jews were continuing to rebuild the town and raise walls, and they foresaw that these activities risked a serious attenuation of Artaxerxes' power in the region, because Jerusalem was a "rebellious and wicked" town and, therefore, soon, if they were not careful, its inhabitants would refuse to "pay tribute, customs or tolls." The governor asked Artaxerxes to look into the royal archives, which would prove that Jerusalem had always been seeking independence under the leadership of their own kings. This was done. Convinced, the king ordered the suspension of construction work and ordered Rehūm and his colleagues to carry out the decree.

But what should we make of this passage? The problem is that its chronological placement is anomalous, since immediately afterward comes the discussion of the acts of Darius I. It is possible that the Chronicler wanted to make a point here, to which he keeps returning during the missions of Ezra and Nehemiah—namely, that Judah was surrounded by neighbors ready to condemn them to the satrapal authorities, who were inclined to lend them a receptive ear. The story of Tattenai's inspection tour is built on the same motif—he too asked Darius to research something in the royal archives (5:3–17). If we concede (though not without reservations) the historicity of the episode, it is possible that the construction carried out at Jerusalem greatly exceeded the prior royal authorization, which referred only to building a temple. On the other hand, the connection often suggested between this episode and the Egyptian insurrection and the possible revolt of Megabyzus must remain hypothetical, since no external evidence has yet been found to confirm it.

4. The Asia Minor – Eastern Aegean Front

Athenian-Persian Hostilities (the 450s)

After the Egyptian campaign, Athens' position was certainly weakened, both as a result of the losses suffered in the campaign (cf. Thucydides I.110.1) and as a result of the dangers encumbering its position in Greece itself. It is likely, too, that Artaxerxes profited from his success in Egypt. This is what Plutarch leads us to believe: he "despatch[ed] messengers to Themistocles at Magnesia, to put him in mind of his promise, and to summon him to act against the Greeks" (*Them.* 31.4; ◇ cf. 31.3). To read Plutarch, it appears as though Themistocles did not accede to the royal instructions (31.5; *Cimon* 18.6; but cf. Thucydides I.138.4). The conclusion of a five-year truce with Sparta (454 or 451?) allowed Athens to return to the offensive, at the goading of Cimon, who had returned from exile (451?):

> Released from Hellenic war, the Athenians made an expedition to Cyprus with two hundred vessels of their own and their allies, under the command of Cimon. Sixty of these were detached to Egypt at the instance of Amyrtaeus, the king in the marshes; the rest laid siege to Kitium. (Thucydides I.112.2–3◇)

These events are also known from a passage in Plutarch (*Cimon* 18.5–9) and a report in Diodorus; Diodorus, unfortunately, seems to have partly confused this episode with the Eurymedon campaign (XII.3–4.1–3).

The Persian forces were commanded by Artabazus and Megabyzus. Artabazus was awarded the overall command and led the fleet anchored at Cyprus, while the latter led the army encamped in Cilicia (Diodorus XII.3.2). If Diodorus's information is correct, it implies that the two Persian commanders were ordered to maintain the troops in war-readiness at the end of the Egyptian campaign (cf. XI.74.6). The siege of Kition was fruitless. After the death of Cimon, the Athenians won two victories on land and sea: "Being victorious on both elements, they departed home, and with them the returned squadron from Egypt" (Thucydides I.112.4◇). For Thucydides, the Asia Minor front disappeared precisely at the time of the settlement of the Thirty Years' Peace with Sparta (446–445). After the death of Cimon, there was a change in strategy, under the aegis of Pericles: the Greeks turned away from mounting major expeditions against the Persians, such as those that Cimon had led, because this only reinforced the dependency of the subjects of the Empire.

Return to the "Peace of Callias"

In the course of his tale about the Cyprus expedition, Diodorus refers to Athenian-Persian negotiations (XII.4.4–5). When he heard the news of the Cyprus defeats, Artaxerxes gathered his Friends and decided that it would be to his advantage to open peace talks with the Greeks. He then sent the generals and satraps written instructions that allowed them to discuss the terms of a treaty. For their part, the Athenians dispatched ambassadors with full authority, the leader of whom was Callias, son of Hipponicus. Here, according to Diodorus, are the principal articles of the agreement that was reached:

All the Greeks cities of Asia are to live under laws of their own making; the satraps of the Persians are not to come nearer to the sea than a three days' journey and no Persian warship is to sail inside of Phaselis or the Cyanean Rocks; and if these terms are observed by the king and his generals, the Athenians are not to send troops into the territory over which the king is ruler. After the treaty had been solemnly concluded, the Athenians withdrew their armaments from Cyprus. (XII.4.5–6✧)

Let us underscore it one more time: Thucydides does not breathe a word about this. Furthermore, Herodotus refers to the presence—at the same time, at Susa—of an Argive embassy (which had come to ask the king to confirm the traditional alliance), Callias son of Hipponicus, and other Athenian deputies, who had come "on some mission, which had nothing to do with the business we are now considering" (VII.151✧). But he does not date the episode precisely ("many years after" [Xerxes' expedition in Europe]). The Argive diplomatic mission possibly should be dated to 466–465. The ancient literature on this treaty dates primarily to the fourth century. But we may provisionally agree that there may well have been negotiations between Athens and Artaxerxes around 449. We will then observe that, setting aside the distortions introduced by later Athenian propaganda, this was apparently a limited accord: the Athenians evacuated Cyprus and Egypt in exchange for formal agreement by the satraps not to intervene directly in the Greek cities that at that time were parties to the Athenian Alliance. There is certainly no question that this was an Athenian triumph, especially at a moment when Pericles obviously thought the chapter of the Persian Wars was at an end. From the Persian perspective, then, we can imagine that continuing control of the eastern Aegean heavily outweighed any provisional concessions that were granted; the central power certainly thought, on the one hand, that these concessions were limited and temporary and, on the other, that none of them commited the Persians to abandoning the king's eminent rights to "the territory over which he was ruler." The Great King never relinquished his tribute prerogatives, even when the Athenian occupation temporarily prevented the satraps from collecting the annual levies in the Alliance cities (Thucydides VIII.4.5; 6.1). All the same, the Great King himself did not participate directly in the agreement; the Athenians had to enforce it on the satraps. We may also suspect that at court it was also thought that the situation in Greece opened up numerous prospects for weakening the Athenian position.

The Persians had even fewer reasons to accept a diplomatic "Waterloo" because they were far from unaware of the difficulties Athens was experiencing with its allies, difficulties they themselves had nurtured. We know, in fact, from a decree (ML 40) dated (hypothetically) to 453–452 that the members of the council of the city of Erythrae had to agree "not to receive [into the city] any of the exiles who sought refuge from the Medes." Some time later (451–450?), another decree guaranteed Athens' assistance to Sigeion against any enemy coming "from the mainland," a phrase that generally refers to the Persians, or Greeks aided by the Persians (*ATL* III:255). Conflicts between the allied cities were thus used by the satraps of Sardis or Dascylium, who then tried to install factions favorable to secession from the Athenian Alliance; these factions would naturally seek support from the mainland Persian satraps.

Obviously, the signing of the supposed "Peace of Callias" did not interrupt the activities of the satraps. In 441, a border conflict broke out between Miletus and Samos. The Athenians did not intervene (in the spirit of actions taken by Artaphernes in 493—see chap. 12/5 — the two cities would have had to appeal to the satrap, if they recognized his authority at the time). The defeated Milesians appealed to Athens, which installed a democratic regime in Samos. As usual, the Samian exiles sought refuge with Pissuthnes, the satrap of Sardis. An alliance (*symmakhia*) was formed; under the terms of the agreement, Pissuthnes furnished 700 auxiliaries, and they allowed the exiles to regain their footing in Samos, "after which they revolted [against Athens], gave up the Athenian garrison left with them and its commanders to Pissuthnes"; soon Byzantium joined the revolt (Thucydides I.115.2–5◊). It is clear that the Samians counted on massive Persian support. When Pericles set sail for Samos, he rerouted part of the squadron to Caria "upon the news that the Phoenician fleet was approaching," and a Samian, Stesagoras, was sent to meet it (I.116). It is possible that this news came from a Persian attempt at disinformation; at the least it indicates that the Athenians had no illusions about one of the clauses of the "Peace" that in principle prohibited an Achaemenid navy from patrolling the coasts of Asia Minor. Further, there is nothing to indicate that Pissuthnes was required to return the Athenian garrison that had been taken off to Sardis.

In any case, the Samian and Erythraean examples prove that the Great King had instructed the Persian satraps to profit as much as possible from Athenian setbacks. It is quite clear that in each allied city there was a group of "Medizers" ready to work for the advantage of the Persians against the Athenians. In 430, exiled Ionians sought out the Lacedaemonian admiral Alcides and let him know that he could easily provoke the defection of Ionia from the Athenian side: "They would probably induce Pissuthnes to join them in the war" (Thucydides III.31.1◊). This is the context of Thucydides' report that "Itamenes and the barbarians, who had been called in by certain individuals in a party quarrel" (34.1◊) moved into Colophon's upper town; at Notium, exiles "called in Arcadian and barbarian mercenaries from Pissuthnes, and . . . formed a new community with the Median party of the Colophonians who joined them from the upper town. . . . Paches [an Athenian] then gave up Notium to the Colophonians not of the Median party (*hoi mēdisantes*)" (34.2–4◊).

The outbreak of the Peloponnesian War would soon enough offer the Great King new possibilities for intervention. Thucydides (II.7.1) presents the hopes of the Lacedaemonians and their allies as follows: "They resolved to send embassies to the king and to . . . others of the barbarian powers." Some time later, they actually sent embassies to Artaxerxes "to persuade the king to supply funds and join in the war" (II.67.1◊). They planned to go to Pharnaces of Dascylium, "who was to send them up the country to the king." A Thracian named Sadocus turned the Lacedaemonian ambassadors over to the Athenians, who were very anxious to block such contacts (67.2). In 424–423, the Athenians seized a Persian ambassador, Artaphernes, "on his way from the king to Lacedaemon" (IV.50.2◊). The tenor of the captured letter indicated that the king remained puzzled because of the conflicting information he was receiving from the ambassadors who had sought him out: "If however they were prepared to speak plainly they might send him some envoys with this Persian [i.e., Artaphernes]" (50.2◊). It thus seems that, at least after the time of the Egyptian campaign at the beginning of the 450s, diplomatic contacts between Spartans and Achaemenids had never ceased (I.109.2–3), even if the Spartans had thus far refused to take decisive action, because they were concerned above all not to have to fight far from their Peloponnesian bases (cf. III.31.2). The Athenians themselves were very careful to ensure the safe travel of Artaphernes to Ephesus with all the honor due one of his rank; included in his escort were representatives who clearly had been instructed to make contact with Artaxerxes (IV.50.3). Strabo (I.3.1) mentions Diotimus's embassy to Susa; Aristophanes mocks the presence of Athenian ambassadors in Persia and Persian ambassadors in Athens in 425 and 424. Nevertheless, we cannot conclude that the Great King had already become the arbiter of Greek affairs, as he clearly would be in the fourth century; but the process had been set in motion.

In short, if there ever was a "Peace of Callias" in 449–448, it particularly functioned to the advantage of the Persians, who on the one hand could thereafter enjoy their Egyptian and Cypriot possessions in peace and on the other would no longer make the mistake of interfering in the internal affairs of the Athenian alliance. We may thus ask whether, from the Persian point of view, the agreement reached around 449–448 actually had a totally different meaning from the significance put forward by the Greek authors of the fourth century. We may recall that, according to Diodorus himself, Artaxerxes intended to initiate talks not with Athens alone but with all of the Greeks (XII.4.4). The context does not exclude the possibility that several Greek cities had already sent deputations to the Great King. Is it possible that this situation provided a precedent for the congress that was gathered by Artaxerxes II at Susa in 387 and before which he had his decree read (Xenophon, *Hell.* V.1.31)? Of course, the circumstances were different, not least with respect to power relationships. But from the Great King's perspective, the difference was insignificant. The clause granting autonomy to Asian cities—which Diodorus and others present as a striking Greek victory—could just as well be considered as targeting Athens, since, applied systematically by the Persians, its purpose was to achieve dominion over Athens; we are tempted to think that it was by brandishing it as a slogan that the Persian satraps of Asia Minor supported the intrigues of those among the allies who wished to escape the unbearable yoke of Athens (cf. Thucydides II.63.2: *tyrannis*). In other words, it is not impossible that the 449–448 agreement was interpreted in totally opposite senses in Athens and Susa: in Athens, it was lauded as an unprecedented victory; at Susa, it was seen as a royal correction. Anyway, it appears from the way that Plutarch reports it that the Athenians were fully aware of the limits imposed on them by the agreement (and/or the balance of power!), because Plutarch writes regarding Pericles: "he did not comply with the giddy impulses of the citizens . . . when . . . they were eager to interfere again in Egypt, and to disturb the King of Persia's maritime dominions" (*Per.* 20.3✧). In the final analysis, we are led to believe that if there really were diplomatic negotiations in 449, the result was not so much a Peace of Callias as a Peace of the King.

Artaxerxes in 449 was no more ready than his father in 466 to accept conditions that were unilaterally determined by Athens. Despite gaps in the evidence, we see nothing that might justify the notion that there had been an Achaemenid diplomatic/military disaster. From Artaxerxes' perspective, it appears that on the one hand his rights over Asia Minor were never abandoned, and on the other, he commanded the satraps of Sardis and Dascylium to attempt to regain the lost territory. We do not know why the Great King did not initiate a mass mobilization to lead a more energetic reconquest. Perhaps more than anything he had not forgotten recent defeats in pitched battle; no doubt he also believed that such efforts would be pointless and that he could in any case hope that divisions among the Greeks and the Athenians' military, political, and financial difficulties would lead to the same result in the long run. In fact, throughout Achaemenid history, the mobilization of a royal army proved to be the rarest of exceptions.

Return to Xanthus

It is difficult, even impossible, to plot exactly on a map the Persian gains and losses in Asia Minor at the end of Artaxerxes' reign. The Attic tribute lists show that from year to year the positions could change very rapidly, in either direction. Between 428 and 425, Athens clearly put great effort into firmly controlling the islands. We learn at the same time that the Athenians lost some very important positions, such as Caria and Lycia, the latter disappearing from the lists at the end of the 440s. The failures to reinstall Athenian dominion there were as frequent as the attempts. In 428, leading "collection ships" (*argyrologoi*), the strategos Lysicles suffered a reverse in Caria, in the plain of the Meander (Thucydides III.19.2). In 430–429, the Athenian strategos Melesander was given command of a squad of six ships with the mission of going to Caria and Lycia

> to collect tribute in those parts, and also to prevent the Peloponnesian privateers from taking up their station in those waters and molesting the passage of the merchantmen from Phaselis and Phoenicia and the adjoining continent. However, Melesander, going up the country into Lycia with a force of Athenians from the ships and the allies, was defeated and killed in battle, with the loss of a number of his troops. (Thucydides II.69.1–2◊)

The first point of interest in Thucydides' text is that hostilities did not interrupt commerce with territories belonging to the king—an observation generally confirmed elsewhere. It also reveals the importance that the Athenians attached to Lycia in their strategic planning. Last, it shows that despite their efforts, the Athenians were never able to bring the region back to the heart of the alliance.

But the passage is interesting for another reason, and a very unusual one at that: we find an allusion to the episode in a famous text, the Xanthus Pillar inscription (*TL* 44). Even though the Lycian text is only partially deciphered, the name Melesander (Milasantra) can be read; he was defeated by an army commanded by a person named Trbbenimi, a Lycian name also known later (a descendant?) from coins and a tomb inscription (*TL* 128, 135). Another passage refers to a victory won (probably much later) by the Kheriga dynasty. Obviously, nothing proves that the dynasts of Xanthus and surrounding towns had acted at the instigation of the Persian satraps; that they consistently portrayed themselves as descendants of Harpagus is not sufficient proof. The proud exaltation of their victories over the Athenians certainly primarily expresses that they wished to appear as fully independent leaders; this of course also played into the hands of the Persian. Certainly, the Persian authorities must immediately have attempted to profit from the situation, only stopping short of claiming, as did Isocrates (*Paneg.* 161◊), that "Lycia no Persian has ever subdued"! Perhaps the Persian leaders intervened just as they had in Ionia, providing support for agitators who wished to break with Athens.

5. *Ezra and Nehemiah in Jerusalem*

Ezra's Mission

Meanwhile, life in the provinces went on, with no apparent connection to the events in Asia Minor. What we have to go by, primarily, are the biblical books of Ezra and Nehemiah. They report that, with the express permission of Artaxerxes, these two Jews carried out missions to Jerusalem: Ezra in the seventh year of Artaxerxes (458), Nehemiah in the twentieth (445). Ezra was "a scribe versed in the Law of Moses" (Ezra 7:6◊), "the priest-scribe, the scribe who was especially learned in the text of Yahweh's commandments and his laws relating to Israel" (7:11◊). Accompanied by a new caravan of returnees (7:7, 8:1–12), Ezra went to Jerusalem bearing a royal letter (7:12–26). The king allocated materials in order to allow the temple and sacrifices to regain their former splendor: offerings from the king himself and the court, gifts sent by the Jews living in Babylonia, and vessels for the temple. Furthermore, the order was given to the Trans-Euphrates treasurers to provide Ezra with whatever he asked—up to 100 talents of silver, 400 liters of wine, 400 liters of oil, 400,000 liters of wheat, and "salt as requested." Part of the sacrifices were intended to ensure divine protection for the king, his sons, and their Empire. In all respects, the steps taken by Artaxerxes conformed to those enacted previously by Cyrus and Darius. It is possible, even likely, that Ezra was also authorized to continue work on building the temple (cf. 6:14, 9:9). But Artaxerxes went further: the satrapal authorities were prohibited "to levy tribute, customs or tolls" on the temple personnel. As has already been pointed out (chap. 12/4), only one parallel is known: the exemption from tribute and corvée that Darius's ancestors awarded to the "sacred gardeners" who worked the land of Apollo of Aulai (ML 12).

From the point of view of both the Jews and the royal power, the principal mission entrusted to Ezra was in the legal realm. He was in fact ordered to appoint judges and magistrates "to administer justice for the whole people of Transeuphrates"; exemplary punishment was promised to any who did not carry out "the Law of your God—which is the law of the king" (7:25◇). We must still ask about the content of this law, though doubtless it refers to the Torah. In order to "purify" the people of Judah, Ezra promulgated the law prohibiting mixed marriages and, during an official ceremony of renewal of the Covenant, the men repudiated their foreign wives and sent away the children they had borne (Ezra 10). But what is especially noteworthy is that thereafter the laws of the country were placed under the protection of the king and thus were included in the all-encompassing category of royal law (see chap. 12/7). As Artaxerxes' review puts it (7:25), all who opposed the law (by rejecting the decisions made by the judges appointed by Ezra) would find themselves subject to royal punishment. As in many other examples, this case forcefully illustrates the connection between internal autonomy of a subject community and royal dominion. The king became the protector and guarantor of local customs, as long as they did not contradict Persian interests; even more, by returning harmony to Jerusalem, Ezra served the cause of imperial order.

Nehemiah's Mission

Thirteen years later, at his own request, Nehemiah also was sent to Jerusalem by the Great King. He had been alerted by his brother Hanani to the deplorable state of the community and the town. Artaxerxes gave letters to Nehemiah as he had to Ezra. Some were addressed "to the governors of Transeuphrates" and instructed them to facilitate the trip for the Jew and his companions. Others were addressed to Asaph, "keeper of the king's park," who was ordered to furnish timber "for the gates of the citadel of the Temple, for the city walls," as well as for the house in which Nehemiah planned to live (Neh. 2:1–10). The work soon began: "The wall was finished within fifty-two days, on the twenty-fifth of Elul" (October 445; 6:15◇). Nehemiah put his brother Hanani in charge of Jerusalem and Hananiah in command of the garrison (7:2). Then he proceeded to take a census of the population (7:6–68). Steps were taken, in the presence of Ezra(?), to restore the splendor of the rituals and daily life of the temple and its personnel. After twelve years, Nehemiah returned to the king (433).

He soon had to return to Jerusalem (ca. 430–425), having discovered that the rules he had instituted were not being enforced. In particular, the Jews no longer paid the tithe owed to the temple personnel. Nehemiah once more had to take action requiring respect for the Sabbath and forbidding mixed marriages (13:6–31). Such is the outline of Chronicles, which is apparently based on the memoirs of Nehemiah himself.

Above and beyond the many debates about a text filled with traps and pitfalls, one point seems certain. Like Ezra, Nehemiah had received orders from the Great King; unlike Ezra, he held an official position: 'governor' (*peḥā*). He emphasizes the contrast between himself and the governors who preceded him in the position (5:14–17). His jurisdiction was "the country of Judah" (5:14), that is, the province (*medinah*) that on fourth-century coins is called Yehūd. Apparently the province, including Jerusalem itself, was divided into districts (*pelek*), which probably were tribal in origin but perhaps also corresponded to fiscal subdivisions. Like the governors of other provinces in the region, Nehemiah acted under the authority of the governor of Trans-Euphrates, who was undoubtedly based at Damascus. This governor, it seems, held an estate within the jurisdiction of the province that was something like a satrapal paradise, and the inhabitants of the province were required to perform corvée on his estate (3:7). Nehemiah, it seems, was accompanied by a "king's commissioner for all such matters as concerned the people" (11:24◊)—as it happens, a Jew—but the breadth of his jurisdiction vis-à-vis the governor is not clearly established. Following the model of a "real" satrap, the governor of Judah received a special tax ("the governor's bread") that permitted him to supply his table every day and to entertain his guests (5:14–18). One of his main tasks was to levy the royal tribute (cf. 5:3). He also had a military function, since he put Jerusalem in a state of military readiness and entrusted the citadel to one of his close associates.

Nehemiah had instructions from the Great King specifically to reestablish political and social order. The description given by Nehemiah himself reveals extremely sharp social conflict. The common people complained of having to indenture their children to be able to eat; some had to mortgage their fields and vineyards to pay the royal tribute. In order to restore peace, Nehemiah took astonishing measures: he no longer collected the "governor's bread" tax. But this act had primarily symbolic (and self-justification) value, even though it takes into account the combined effect of the royal levies and satrapal taxes. The basic problem lay at the level of relations between rich and poor: by lending money at interest, the former starved the latter. Like a Judahite Solon, Nehemiah was not a social revolutionary: though he proclaimed the abolition of debt and required the rich to return the mortgaged fields, vineyards, and olive groves to the small land-holders (5:10), there was no thought of actually dividing up the land. The impoverishment of the small land-holders was thus not simply an automatic result of the imposition of tribute: tribute only played a role of revealing and accelerating what already existed in the context of class relations specific to Jewish society. The various taxes also converged in that everyone had to pay for maintenance of the temple and its personnel: a one-third shekel head tax (10:33), as well as "first-fruits and tithes, . . . those portions . . . awarded . . . to . . . the cantors and gatekeepers too . . ." (12:44–47◊). The burden was so heavy that during Nehemiah's absence the Jews had stopped bringing "the tithe of corn wine, and oil to the storehouses" (13:12◊).

It thus appears that from Cyrus to Artaxerxes there was considerable consistency in royal policy, though we are not able to say that the Great King took special interest in this small region. The importance of Judah is only an "optical illusion" created by the uneven distribution of evidence. In particular, there is nothing to prove that Susa or Persepolis considered Judah a bulwark of Persian dominion against fickle and unruly Egypt. More likely, from the Persian point of view, Nehemiah's mission was to establish a new basis for assessing tribute and guaranteeing regular payment: mutatis mutandis, and keeping in mind their purposes, his reforms can be compared with those carried out by Artaphernes in 493 in the cities of Ionia that had been ravaged by war and social tension (cf. chap. 12/5).

From Jerusalem to Elephantine

The principles on which Jewish autonomy and the limits of its effectiveness were established are clarified by Aramaic documents from Egypt during the reign of Darius II. In 410, during a murky affair (to which we return below in chap. 14/8) that found them in opposition to the governor of Syene, the Jews of the Elephantine garrison sent a petition addressed jointly to "Johanan the high priest and his colleagues the priests who are in Jerusalem, and to Ostana the brother of ʿAnani and the nobles of the Jews"—that is, to everyone who constituted the internal government of the community of Jerusalem, alongside the "governor of Judah" proper (*DAE* 102 [*AP* 30–31◇]). The people of Elephantine received no reply to their plea. The reason was probably because in their rituals they had violated the "Law of Moses," as had recently been proclaimed so forcefully by Ezra and/or Nehemiah. Their petition in fact concerned the reconstruction of the temple of Yahweh that they had built on the island in the Nile, contrary to the principle of the uniqueness of the center of worship. One document, certainly from 419, shows that the Jews of Elephantine paid a head tax intended to sustain the expense of the temple service, conduct that was even more reprehensible because this money would serve to honor not only Yahweh but also Aramean gods (Betʾel and Anat; *DAE* 89 [*AP* 22]). In contrast, when Ezra was sent to Jerusalem, the Jewish settlers in Babylonia had given him offerings for the temple in Jerusalem (Ezra 7:16).

The Jews (or, rather, Judeo-Arameans) of Elephantine probably had appealed to the authorities in Jerusalem at an earlier time because the Great King had conferred on the rulers of Jerusalem the authority to intervene in purely religious affairs of the Jewish diaspora in the Empire. Anyway, the royal edict sent to Ezra said: "Appoint scribes and judges to administer justice for the whole people of Transeuphrates, that is, for all who know the Law of your God. You must teach those who do not know it" (Ezra 7:25◇). We find an illustration of this state of affairs in an Aramaic papyrus from Egypt. In 418, one Hanani (Nehemiah's brother?) came to Elephantine bearing a very important document that regulated the celebration of Passover by the Jews (*DAE* 96 [*AD* 8]). It does seem that in this case the initiative came from the authorities in Jerusalem, who wanted to unify ritual throughout the diaspora. Hanani's letter states that the order came from the king and was sent to Aršāma, the satrap of Egypt. But the central government was not in a position to intervene in a purely internal religious matter of the Jewish communites of the Empire. All it did was to grant official sanction ("royal law") to a local ruling ("laws of the countries").

The Enemies of Nehemiah and Judah

To read the Chronicler, the arrival of Nehemiah did not disarm the hostility of Judah's neighbors; quite the reverse. As in the previous episode (cf. above, chap. 14/4),

Judah's neighbors intended to communicate to the Great King their condemnation of the royal ambitions they attributed to Nehemiah, in light of the fortifications he had just provided for Jerusalem (6:6–7). The danger was even greater because many neighbors of Judah had family members in the province because of the many intermarriages that all of Ezra's efforts (if he really did precede Nehemiah) had obviously failed to suppress. Even the high priest's son took a wife from outside Judah. On his second mission, Nehemiah had to renew the prohibition.

A coalition against Judah and Nehemiah developed: the Chronicler names "Sanballat the Horonite, Tobiah of Ammon, and Gašmū the Arab" (Neh 2:19, 6:1–7). The first was the leader of "troops from Samaria" (3:34 [Heb.; 4:2 Eng.]). We know that in 410 someone else called Sanballat was "governor of Samaria" (*DAE* 102), and he must have been a descendant. Papyri and inscribed bullas from Wadi ed-Daliyeh, north of Jericho, provide an additional reference point: dated between 375 and 335, they mention yet another Sanballat, who in all likelihood belonged to the same family. In the Elephantine document from 410, we see that Sanballat I had his sons Dalayah and Šelemyah beside him. There was thus a veritable dynasty that governed Samaria, at least between the reigns of Artaxerxes I and Darius III. The bullas and papyri of Wadi ed-Daliyeh and coins show that these men bore the title "governor (*peḥā*) of Samaria"; Samaria was the name of the province (*medinah*) as well as the town (*qryt*'), which is sometimes called "Samaria the fortress" (*byrt*'), according to a formula frequently found in Achaemenid-period documents, at Sardis, Xanthus, and Meydançikkale as well as at Syene-Elephantine. Here, as elsewhere, the Persians recognized a local dynasty, but there is no question that its members received the title of governor directly from the central power. Like their colleagues at Jerusalem, the dynast-governors of Samaria depended on the higher authority of the governor of Trans-Euphrates.

The other two members of what the book of Nehemiah portrays as an anti-Judahite coalition are harder to identify. The name of Gašmū the Arab is usually related to the same name found in dedications inscribed on silver vessels found at Tell el-Maskhuta in Egypt. One is inscribed with the name "Qaynū, son of Gašmū, king of Qedar" (*DAE* 68 [AD 7]). But the extent of the Arab Qedarite kingdom and its relationship to the Achaemenid authorities remains problematic. As for Tobiah, he was probably part of a dynasty also known from later Aramaic inscriptions found in Transjordan (Iraq el-Emir); perhaps he was recognized by the Persians as governor of the region.

Sanballat's hostility does not seem to have been religious in origin. At this time, the word *Samaritan* had not yet acquired the sectarian significance it took on in the Hellenistic period when the sanctuary on Mount Gerizim, Jerusalem's rival, was founded; it refers exclusively to the inhabitants of the province (*medinah*) of Samaria. Furthermore, when the authorities in Jerusalem remained deaf to their plea in 410, the Jews of Elephantine did not hesitate to send a letter to the sons of Sanballat (*DAE* 102). Thus, it seems that the governor of Samaria and his neighbors (Gašmū, Tobiah) were uneasy about the strengthening of the governor of Judah's power, which is why they attempted to stir up the fears of the Persian government. Without being able to prove it, we may suggest that these local jurisdictional squabbles can be compared to the tensions seen in Asia Minor between the satraps of Sardis and Dascylium, who were continually disputing control over frontier territory (the Troad). If this is true, perhaps Nehemiah had received guarantees on this point from the central government.

6. One King after Another (425–424)

Ctesias and the Babylonian Tablets

According to Ctesias (§44), Artaxerxes and his wife Damaspia (unknown elsewhere) perished on the same day. They had only one legitimate son, who took the throne under the name Xerxes (II). But several of Artaxerxes' illegitimate sons who had strong ambitions challenged Xerxes II. The main challenger was Sogdianus, son of Alogune. He fomented a conspiracy against his half-brother with the help of Pharnacyas, Menostanes, and several others; 45 days after his accession, Xerxes was assassinated, "while he lay drunk in his palace," and Sogdianus took the royal title (§45), naming Menostanes chiliarch (*azabaritēs/hazarapatiš*; §46). One of his half-brothers, Ochus, also born to a Babylonian woman (Cosmartidene), had received the satrapy of Hyrcania from his father and married one of his half-sisters, Parysatis, daughter of a third Babylonian concubine, Andia. Ochus refused to attend the meetings called by Sogdianus and won several important people to his side, including Arbarius, the commander of Sogdianus's cavalry. He soon seized power and took the throne name Darius II (§§47–48). This is a sketch of the tale told by Ctesias.

The Babylonian tablets, moreover, allow us to conclude that the events between the death of Artaxerxes and the accession of Darius II unfolded between the end of December 424 and February 423 and also that the reigns of Xerxes II and Sogdianus were not officially recognized by the Babylonian scribes. Many details elude us. It is likely that Xerxes took the throne because of his parentage and perhaps also because his father had recognized him as crown prince. It seems that, presented with the accession of the new king, Sogdianus and Ochus announced their pretensions simultaneously. Ctesias's report shows that the aristocrats had to choose sides, and in the ensuing battle, Ochus managed to win over very important men, such as Arbarius, the commander of Sogdianus's cavalry; Arsames (Aršāma), the satrap of Egypt; and even Artoxares, who at the time of Artaxerxes I had been exiled to Armenia because he had spoken to the king on behalf of Megabyzus (§40).

It just so happens, by extraordinary coincidence, that many of the people just named are also known from Babylonian tablets belonging to the archives of the Murašū, a business establishment that during the reigns of Artaxerxes I and Darius II dealt specifically with the management of land around Nippur, including land granted by the king to members of his family and high crown officials. Alongside the "house of the woman of the palace" in the time of Artaxerxes I and the "house of Parysatis" (after the accession of Darius II), we also can identify Aršāma, who in addition to his estates in Egypt kept land and livestock in Babylonia under Artaxerxes I and Darius II. We can also identify Menostanes, son of Artarios; he was a brother of Artaxerxes I and satrap of Babylonia at the time of Megabyzus's rebellion. His son Menostanes had at that time been defeated by Megabyzus's troops (§38), then defected to Sogdianus, who made him his chiliarch (§§45–46). Menostanes, a nephew of Artaxerxes I who is known as Manuštānu in the Babylonian tablets, is called *mār bīt šarri* 'royal prince'; he died soon, shortly after the defeat of Sogdianus, and his estates then passed to one Artaḫšar, who is none other than Artoxares; according to Ctesias, he had declared himself a compatriot of Ochus (§47). (Arbareme in the tablets) was similarly rewarded for switching to Ochus's side lock, stock, and barrel (Ctesias §47).

Although Ctesias is not explicit on this point, it appears that Artarios and Menostanes did not succeed in winning over Babylonia to Sogdianus, who very likely lived at Susa after his accession. It seems clear at the same time that the Babylonian troops supported Ochus (cf. §§46–47). The Babylonian tablets lead us to believe that Ochus did muster the soldiers who in return for the use of land (within a *ḫatru*) were required to respond to any call-up. To go by Ctesias's story, there does not seem to have been a pitched battle. Just as Tanyoxarces had eventually done (§10), Sogdianus agreed to give himself up when ordered by the new king, and he was executed "after reigning 6 months 15 days" (§48). Darius then had to face two other rebels: his full-brother Arsites (like him, the son of Artaxerxes and Cosmartidene) and Artyphius, the son of Megabyzus, who some 30 years earlier had already participated in the revolt against Artaxerxes I alongside his father (§37). They were soon put to death, as well as Pharnacyas, one of Sogdianus's lieutenants. Menostanes chose suicide (§§50–51).

Families and Powers

The succession after Artaxerxes I both confirms the persistence of dynastic problems and constitutes a special case. It is surprising that Artaxerxes and Damaspia had only one legitimate son. Others may have died young, as did thirteen of the children of Darius II and Parysatis (§49). Whatever the case, after the disposal of Xerxes II, power was contested among the illegitimate sons of the dead king—Sogdianus and Ochus, and later Arsites. According to Herodotus (III.2), a 'rule' (*nomos*) disqualified illegitimate sons from the succession. But like many other Persian royal *nomos* he mentions (cf. VII.2), this regulation did not have the critical force that Herodotus imputes to it. There is no doubt, for one thing, that the *nothoi* (illegitimate children) enjoyed high status in the court (cf. Herodotus VIII.103; Diodorus XI.61.5), and for another, the important thing in every case was to ensure family continuity. It is also remarkable that no great family ever attempted to seize control: the Great Ones were content to side with one or another of the contestants, a sign that Ochus and Sogdianus were truly considered sons of Artaxerxes and as such endowed with a certain familial, and thus dynastic, legitimacy.

While most of the nobility was satisfied with the rewards granted by the new king (court titles, land grants), one family was singled out to receive considerably greater benefits. At an unknown date, in fact, Darius married his son Arsaces to Stateira, daughter of Hydarnes, and at the same time the king's daughter Amestris married Teritushmes, son of Hydarnes. In Ctesias a long passage follows on the adventures of the two couples, culminating in the death of Teritushmes (in battle) and the torture of his entire family (sister, mother, brothers, and two more sisters; §§54–55). Ctesias charges all these murders to Parysatis, archetype of the "cruel princess," who had been infuriated by Teritouchmes' behavior. According to Ctesias, Teritushmes had fallen in love with his sister Roxanne and executed Amestris, the daughter of Darius and Parysatis (§54). Ctesias also says that Darius wanted to kill Stateira, the daughter of Hydarnes and wife of his son Arsaces, but Parysatis allowed herself to be moved by the appeals of her son: "Darius yielded to him as well, but warned Parysatis that she would regret it" (§56). We know that during the reign of Artaxerxes II, Parysatis finally did away with Stateira (§61; Plutarch, *Art.* 19), before approving a union between Artaxerxes II and her daughter Atossa (*Art.* 23.3–7). Nonetheless, the entire family was not exterminated, since in 400 a brother of Stateira was in the entourage of Tissaphernes (Xenophon, *Anab.* II.3.17).

The cross-marriages with the family of Hydarnes constituted a noteworthy novelty in Achaemenid family policy. At least from the time of Cambyses, marriages had been based on strict endogamy. The exchanges of wives with Hydarnes in themselves granted him exceptional personal power. Unfortunately, we know nothing about him. It cannot be said for sure that he was indeed a descendant of Vidarna, one of the conspirators of 522. Whatever the case, he must have provided a great deal of assistance to Ochus during the war of succession. At the same time, the bloody actions soon taken by Darius and Parysatis show that they were far from granting permanent arrangements. Their own marriage was destined to give meaning back to the policy of endogamy and prevent a great family from one day claiming royal power. In other words, the matrimonial concessions made to Hydarnes were purely based on the moment; as soon as he was sure of his power, Darius was quite willing to lop off potential rival branches. At the same time, the events demonstrate the Achaemenids' capacity for rebuilding the dynastic stock. In fact, Artaxerxes I married Ochus to his half-sister Parysatis, and from this union a new Achaemenid branch was intended to sprout. Before coming to power, Ochus and Parysatis had produced two children: a daughter, Amestris; and Arsaces, the future Artaxerxes II (§49).

Legitimacy and Propaganda

It is clear that Ochus's victory resulted from a combination of forces he had managed to gather on his side; but it also appears that each competitor was able to conduct a skillful propaganda campaign on the theme of his own legitimacy. Perhaps Pausanias's curious incidental citation (II.5) comes from this tradition, according to which "Darius, illegitimate son (*nothos*) of Artaxerxes, with the support of all of the Persian people (*ho Persōn dēmos*), dethroned Sogdianus, legitimate son (*gnēsios*) of Artaxerxes." Did Sogdianus attempt to deck himself out with a (highly debatable) genetic legitimacy? Possibly, but we know nothing of him before the death of Artaxerxes. Does his name ("the Sogdian") mean that he was born during his father's campaign in eastern Iran at the beginning of his reign? Did Artaxerxes make contingency arrangements, before he died, in case Xerxes died suddenly? According to this theory, did he recognize Sogdianus's rights as eldest son? And was naming Ochus to the satrapy of Hyrcania a sort of compensation to the younger son? All these questions (and others, too) remain unanswered.

The "Persian people" referred to by Pausanias are doubtless the army, which Ctesias states was hostile to Sogdianus (§45). Ctesias makes this observation during a passage that clearly comes directly out of propaganda spawned in Ochus's circle. Ctesias says that Sogdianus gave a certain Bagorazus the task of driving the funeral chariot on which the remains of Artaxerxes I and Xerxes II were placed: "In fact, the mules that drew the funeral chariot, as if they had been waiting for the remains of the son [Xerxes] as well, refused to move; but when Xerxes' body arrived, they moved on in high spirits" (§45). Then, Ctesias says, Sogdianus got rid of Bagorazus, "on the pretext that he had abandoned his father's body" (§46). Even though Photius's summary is somewhat less than clear, it seems that some controversy arose over what to do with the royal remains; in fact, organization of the funeral solemnities reverted to the heir. What Bagorazus had cast doubt on was neither more nor less than the legitimacy of Sogdianus. A passage in Polyaenus (VII.7.17) confirms that from Ochus's point of view, it had become his responsibility, after ten months, to "proclaim the royal mourning according to Persian custom." Polyaenus also says that during this time Ochus sealed documents with his father's seal. In fact, as we know, Ochus was recognized as king in February 424. What Ctesias and

Polyaenus transmit, in their own way, is probably a scrap of the official version that circulated after Ochus's accession. In the same vein, a Greek tradition passed on the image of Darius II as a king with little interest in ostentatious luxury, someone who said on his deathbed that he had "practised justice before all men and gods" (Athenaeus XII.548e◊).

Darius the Great King

The reuse of the throne name "Darius" conferred additional legitimacy on the new king. In his few inscriptions, Darius II, imitating his predecessors, uses almost word for word the titles of Darius I at Naqš-i Rustam and presents himself as son of and successor to Artaxerxes I (D^2Sb). At Susa he claims to have built an *apadana* (D^2Sa) and to have completed another palace (*hadiš*) begun by his father (D^2Sb), and he had his tomb excavated near his father's, on the cliff at Naqš-i Rustam. On the other hand, he did not rebuild the palace erected by Darius I, which had been destroyed by fire during the reign of Artaxerxes I (cf. A^2Sa). In the absence of written evidence, we know nothing of any possible building activity at Persepolis.

7. Affairs on the Western Front

The Situation in Asia Minor (424–413)

In the absence of evidence from the center, we are reduced to narratives that refer almost exclusively to Asia Minor and Egypt. We have seen that just before the death of Artaxerxes the Athenians had sent Artaphernes to Ephesus, obviously wishing to open talks with the Great King (Thucydides IV.50.3). Andocides, an Athenian orator of the fourth century, refers very generally to a treaty consummated between Athens and the Great King after Artaxerxes' accession: "We concluded a truce (*spondai*) with the Great King and we established friendship (*philia*) with him forever; the agreement was negotiated by Epilycus, son of Teisandrus, my mother's brother" (*Pace* 29). Whether this report refers to a renewal of the so-called Peace of Callias or a new treaty is not easy to determine in the absence of any external confirmation (aside from an Athenian decree commending Heraclides—but the date itself is debated). All the same, we may agree that at the presumed date, around 424–423, the Great King and Athens both had reasons to avoid overt conflict.

This may be the context of the revolt of Pissuthnes, which Ctesias alone mentions in his story of the difficulties encountered by the king shortly after his accession. With the aid of Athenian mercenaries commanded by Lycon, the satrap of Sardis revolted. Darius sent an army against him commanded by three generals, including Tissaphernes. Pissuthnes was betrayed by Lycon and executed, and the satrapy of Sardis was bestowed on Tissaphernes (§52). Perhaps Pissuthnes had tried to profit from Darius's setback (Ctesias had just described the revolt led by Arsites and Artyphius before mentioning an obscure intrigue planned by Artoxares; see §§50–51, 53).

Nonetheless, although cordial relations had been declared between the Athenians and Darius, the Athenians violated the agreement a few years later, as Andocides states: "After that, we hear of Amorges, slave of the king and exile. . . . Result: the angry king became the ally of the Lacedaemonians and provided them with 5,000 talents to underwrite the war until they were able to destroy our power" (*Pace* 29). We know in fact from Thucydides (VIII.54.3) that the Athenians had sent aid to Amorges (who is also named on the Xanthus Pillar inscription), and we learn from him as well that this Amorges was the illegitimate son of Pissuthnes and that Tissaphernes had been ordered by the king to bring the rebel to him, dead or alive (VIII.5.5). It appears that the Athenian decision to aid Amorges was made before the expedition to Sicily—that is, in 414.

The Aftermath of the Athenian Debacle in Sicily

The defeats suffered by the Athenians in Sicily (September 413) soon provided the Great King with an opportunity to take revenge. In a magnificent account, Thucydides describes the shock that the disaster caused in Athens: the Athenians were fearful that "their adversaries at home, redoubling all their preparations, would vigorously attack them by sea and land at once, aided by their own revolted confederates" (VIII.1.2◊). Hopes were high, in fact, in Sparta and Greece (VIII.2). There soon were envoys in Lacedaemon from Chios and Erythrae, as well as ambassadors from Tissaphernes and Pharnabazus,

> who [Tissaphernes] invited the Peleponnesians to come over, and promised to maintain their army. The king had lately called upon him for the tribute from his government, for which he was in arrears, being unable to raise it from the Hellenic towns by reason of the Athenians; and he therefore calculated that by weakening the Athenians he should get the tribute better paid, and should also draw the Lacedaemonians into alliance with the king; and by this means, as the king had commanded him, take alive or dead Amorges. . . . (VIII.4.5◊)

Thucydides describes similar hopes on the part of Pharnabazus, who hoped to "procure a fleet for the Hellespont" (VIII.6.1◊). With this goal in mind, his envoys brought a sum of 25 talents (VIII.8.1). At Sparta, a great battle for influence broke out between the two delegations. The Lacedaemonians "decidedly favored the Chians and Tissaphernes," led in that direction by the influence of Alcibiades and even more by the hope of gaining access to powerful fleets at Chios and Erythrae (VIII.6.3–5◊). In the spring of 412, after many difficulties, Lacedaemonian ships arrived below the walls of Chios, commanded by Chalcideus and Alcibiades and soon aided at Teos by Stages, one of Tissaphernes' lieutenants. Thus began the Ionian War.

If we accept Thucydides' explanation, Pharnabazus and Tissaphernes had both "lately" received the order to levy tribute on the Greek cities. In theory, the king had never given up his rights, but the new situation offered him the possibility of putting them into practice. This mission involved launching overt operations against Athens so as to reaffirm Achaemenid dominion over the Asia Minor coast; in other words, all prior treaties, if any had ever really existed, were declared null and void by Athens' own actions.

The Spartan–Achaemenid Treaties (412–411)

Soon (summer of 412), Tissaphernes reached an initial formal agreement of alliance (*symmakhia*) with Chalcideus between Lacedaemon and the king. The two allies agreed to wage war or be at peace jointly, and the rights of the king were reaffirmed in the following way: "Whatever country or cities the king has, or the king's ancestors had, shall be the king's; and whatever came in to the Athenians from these cities, either money or any other thing, the king and the Lacedaemonians and their allies shall jointly hinder the Athenians from receiving either money or any other thing" (VIII.18◊). In return, the Persians were to treat any who left the Lacedaemonian alliance as enemies. But it is clear that in general the treaty favored the Persians and Tissaphernes and that they were able to reestablish their dominion without major cost, other than the financial expenditures.

Even though the terms of the treaty were not restricted to Tissaphernes' domain, he as satrap of Sardis intended to be first to take advantage of it. Despite the Athenians and with the aid of the Peleponnesian armies, Tissaphernes soon captured Amorges on Iasus, allowing his allies to take plunder and impress the rebel's mercenaries, before establishing a garrison on Iasus (VIII.28.2–5; 29.1). Because Tissaphernes was reluctant to pay off their troops, the Peleponnesians requested a new treaty, which was drawn up in the winter of 412–411 (VIII.37). In reality, the differences between the two versions are scarcely noticeable, aside from the fact that this time the treaty is made in the name of the king and his sons. At the beginning of 411, one of the Spartan commissioners, Lichas, considered the second treaty outrageous and null and void (43.3–4). Alcibiades also advised Tissaphernes not to become too closely involved with the Lacedaemonians: He "generally betrayed a coolness in the war that was too plain to be mistaken" (46.5◇). But the Spartans scarcely had a choice of allies; Lichas also objected to the Milesians "that [they] ought to show a reasonable submission to Tissaphernes and to pay him court, until the war should be happily settled" (84.5◇)! At the same time, Alcibiades, always eager to return to Athens in triumph, urged Tissaphernes to settle with Athens. It did not happen. On the contrary, Tissaphernes concluded a third treaty in the summer of 411. The satrap of Hellespontine Phrygia was directly involved, and Tissaphernes promised the arrival of a Phoenician squadron; from that moment onward, the Peloponnesians had to support their own ships, because Tissaphernes had agreed to lend them funding only until the end of the war (VIII.58).

The Athenian Reconquest (411–407)

In truth, not the slightest trace of a Phoenician navy was seen in Asia Minor during these years; Thucydides thought that Tissaphernes had never intended to provide a fleet (VIII.87). Given the situation, the Lacedaemonians decided in the end to respond favorably to Pharnabazus's repeated demands, since he had promised to "provide for their support" (VIII.81.2). But the Athenians piled victory upon victory. At the same time, contention between the satraps was predominant. Tissaphernes made a special trip to the Hellespont: he apprehended Alcibiades and placed him under arrest at Sardis, "saying that the King ordered him to make war upon the Athenians" (Xenophon, *Hell.* I.1.9◇). But until the arrival of Cyrus in 407, the generals were in disarray, so much so that the Athenians were able to embark on a victorious counterattack under the command of Thrasybulus and Alcibiades. Flush with success, Alcibiades finally had his triumphal return to the city. Pharnabazus was unable to counter the situation and in 408 came to an agreement with the Athenian leadership: he would give them 20 talents, authorize them to levy tribute on the town of Chalcedon, and commit himself to take their ambassadors to the king (*Hell.* I.3.9). During this time, the Athenians captured Byzantium. The following spring (407), when they expected to depart to see the king, the Athenian ambassadors saw none other than Cyrus the Younger arrive at Gordion, accompanied by Lacedaemonian ambassadors led by Boeotius, who stated that they "had obtained from the King everything they wanted" (*Hell.* I.4.2◇).

Darius II and His Satraps

It must be recognized that, until Cyrus's arrival at Gordion, tentative and disorganized initiatives by Tissaphernes and Pharnabazus had not led to any great success, apart from the treaties with Sparta—and Tissaphernes did not seem very eager to apply them.

Darius had indeed secured recognition of his dominion over Asia Minor from the Lacedaemonians, but the Athenian reconquests in 407 appeared to render this accomplishment partly moot.

One of the reasons for this was the dogged competitiveness that motivated Tissaphernes and Pharnabazus. Though this trait first appeared in 413 at Sparta, it never flagged during these years. Thucydides highlights Tissaphernes' anxiety when the Spartans decided to send forces into the Hellespont, "being also vexed to think that Pharnabazus should receive them, and in less time and at less cost perhaps succeed better against Athens than he had done" (VIII.109.1◊). In fact, Tissaphernes' ambition did not exceed his rival's: "Pharnabazus was inviting [the Peleponnesians] to come, and making every effort to get the fleet and, like Tissaphernes, to cause the revolt of the cities in his government still subject to Athens, founding great hopes in his success" (VIII.99◊). For both of them, the important thing was to succeed in a way that would ensure the king's favor (VIII.6.1). This is why Pharnabazus's envoys refused "to take part in the Chios expedition" (VIII.8) in 413. At the same time, Tissaphernes' primary objective was to capture Amorges. And, of course, the Peloponnesian allies did not pass up the opportunity to take advantage of this rivalry from time to time (cf. *Hell.* I.1.31–32).

These inter-satrapal competitions are frequently attested, especially between Sardis and Dascylium, which had long-standing border disputes. For the Great King it was certainly a convenient way to keep a satrap from getting inordinately important (cf. Xenophon, *Anab.* I.1.8); but a corollary of this convenience was a degree of inefficiency. It seems particularly strange that Alcibiades managed to escape from his prison in Sardis with his Athenian companion Mantitheos shortly after his arrest by Tissaphernes: they "provided themselves with horses and made their escape from Sardis by night to Clazomenae" (*Hell.* I.1.10◊). Taking into account the strength of the garrison at Sardis and the difficulty of travel on the region's roads, we are tempted to think that Alcibiades had the benefit of help from inside accomplices. It is quite likely that the Persians of Sardis were hostile to Tissaphernes' strategy, like the Persians of the early 490s who seem to have conspired with Histiaeus of Miletus against Artaphernes' enterprises (Herodotus VI.4). It is also likely that Tissaphernes' hesitancy reflects more general dissension about the course of action to take with regard to Athens and Sparta.

Another reason for the inter-satrapal rivalry is the fact that neither Tissaphernes nor Pharnabazus had sufficient military forces to allow them to really win the day. This is why each of them attempted to invite the Peleponnesians into their own territory in 413. Furthermore, even on land, the Persian cavalry was not always the uncontested king of battle; in 409, for instance, the plentiful cavalry of Pharnabazus was defeated by Alcibiades' army of horsemen and hoplites (I.2.16). In the same year, the Athenian Thrasyllus was able to make a foray into Lydia, "when the grain was ripening"; Stages, Tissaphernes' subordinate, was able to take only a single prisoner, despite the strength of his cavalry (I.2.4–5◊).

But it was on the sea that Persian incompetence was most glaring and most crucial. Apart from the case of the mysterious Phoenician fleet promised by Tissaphernes—which no one ever managed to see!—the satraps had no navy at all. At most, they could hire crews (though not without frequent mutual recriminations) and let their Peloponnesian allies build ships using timber cut from the royal forests (*Hell.* I.1.24–25). Thus, because of their naval inferiority, they participated only marginally in a war that unfolded between the Athenian and Peloponnesian navies. In 411, when there was an amphibious battle between Athenians and Lacedaemonians, we have a picture of Pharnabazus reduced to "riding his horse into the sea as far as possible, [where he] bore a share in the fighting and cheered on his followers, cavalry and infantry" (I.1.6◇). The Athenians took control of the Straits and were even able to impose customs duties (in the form of a tithe) on the grain-ships that passed by Chalcedon (I.1.22). The agreement between Pharnabazus and Alcibiades the following year expresses perfectly the satrap's inability to repel an attack on his territory (I.3.8–13).

Of course, the satraps had significant resources that enabled them to hire mercenaries (though fairly limited in number) and especially to pay the Peleponnesian soldiers fighting at their side. But it is not certain that their financial capacity was unlimited. It seems in fact that, from Tissaphernes' and Pharnabazus's viewpoint, the important thing was to carry on operations with the least possible expense (cf. Thucydides VIII.87.5; 109.1). The Peleponnesians and Tissaphernes himself also appear often to have relied on levies collected from the Greek cities of Asia Minor, which in turn exhibited some reluctance to cooperate (cf. VIII.36.1; 45.5). On at least one occasion, Tissaphernes refused to increase the mercenaries' pay while waiting, he claimed, for an answer from the king (VIII.29.1), letting it be understood that he would raise wages if any money arrived from Darius (45.5–6). On several occasions, the Peleponnesian allies complained that they did not receive enough regular income to live on (cf. VIII.78). Later on, Alcibiades addressed the representatives of the allies as follows:

> He also pointed out that Tissaphernes was at present carrying out the war at his own charges (*ta idia khrēmata*), and had good cause for economy, but that as soon as he received remittances (*trophē*) from the king he would give them their pay in full, and do what was reasonable for the cities. (VIII.45.6◇)

These "own charges" were doubtless the funds available to the satrap in his personal account. Considerable sums are involved, since some years later Tithraustes was able to pay some troops by withdrawing 220 talents of silver from "the personal resources of Tissaphernes" (*ek tēs ousias tēs Tissaphernous; Hell. Oxyr.* 19.3). This must have been a fortune that existed somewhere on the borderline between state structure and personal property (as did the paradises, for example). Whatever the case, the king thought that the satraps ought to use these "own charges" to pay their soldiers. Perhaps the king also thought that the order he had given to Tissaphernes and Pharnabazus to collect tribute from the cities (VIII.5.5; 6.1) implied that he did not have to finance the war. The author of the *Hellenica Oxyrhynchia* (19.2) complains, moreover, about the Great King's great avarice, referring explicitly to the time of Darius II (and his successor):

> The soldiers were paid by the *strategoi* in a deplorable fashion. Anyway, this was their habit, as in the War of Decelia when they [the Persians] were allied with the Peloponnesians; they provided money on a scale both mean and shabby, and their allies' triremes would often have been sent back had not Cyrus acted swiftly. Responsibility for this state of affairs lies with the Great King: every time he decided to make war, he sent a small sum of money at the beginning to those who were to carry it out, but he did not take into account subsequent events, so much so that if they were not able to use money of their own (*ek tōn idiōn*), the generals had to disband their armies.

In other words, the king made an initial investment that the satraps were required to manage as best they could. If they were not able to get the business taken care of in the time allotted, they had to pay from their own funds (see also *Hell.* I.5.3). In time of war, just as in time of peace, the Great King was quite *economical*—he kept a careful eye on his own fortune. We thus have the impression that we are seeing in this a specific illustration of a more general policy by which imperial revenue was managed. It might be compared, *mutatis mutandis*, with an instruction included in the travel voucher that Aršāma gave to his steward Neḥtiḥōr: "And if he is in a place more than one day, on the later days do not give them extra provisions" (*DAE* 67 [*AD* 6]). An Aramaic document from Egypt (*DAE* 54 [*AP* 2]) demonstrates the same principle. Thus, the personal financial responsibility of administrative functionaries seems to have extended all the way up to satraps, even when they made war! This was one of many ways of limiting satrapal ambition.

Darius II, Asia Minor, and the Other Fronts

It is difficult to understand the expectations and objectives of the strategy set in motion by the Great King. Too much remains unknown. A Babylonian tablet dated November 407 illustrates the extent of our ignorance: it refers to a "state of siege" at Uruk, and we have no idea what this refers to. Other tablets, dated to 422, refer to a gathering of soldiers at Uruk. The discrepancy in date prevents relating it to the 407 tablet; furthermore, it alludes to regular reviews, the existence of which does not imply that the region was then in turmoil (see below). Moreover, incidental passages in Xenophon's *Hellenica* refer to a Median revolt that was put down at the end of 407 (I.2.19) and to a war that Darius II waged against the Cadusians in 405 (II.1.13). It is true that, generally speaking, we know practically nothing of military activities outside of the Asia Minor region. It is only because Plutarch wrote a life of Artaxerxes II that we learn, for example, that he too led an expedition against the Cadusians in the 380s (*Art.* 24). Then again, some recently published Babylonian astronomical tablets (*ADRTB* nos. −369, −367) also lead us to distrust the deafening noise created by the Classical sources on matters of the western front (cf. also chap. 15/1).

In Asia Minor itself, the satraps faced other dangers for which our only information is circumstantial. Xenophon mentions that, several years later, a subordinate of Pharnabazus named Mania, the wife and successor of Zenis of Dardanus, governed the region in Aeolis that was subject to Dascylium; in addition to other services she rendered to the satrap, "she also accompanied Pharnabazus in the field, even when he invaded the land of the Mysians or the Pisidians because of their continually ravaging the King's territory" (*Hell.* III.1.13✧). The failure of the Mysians and Pisidians to be submissive, frequently highlighted by the fourth-century Greek authors, explains the frequency of the expeditions against them. When Cyrus the Younger wanted to conceal from his troops the fact that he was actually leading them against Artaxerxes II, he led them to believe that he was leading them against the Pisidians (Xenophon, *Anab.* I.2.1). And, according to Diodorus, during the battle of the Eurymedon, the Persian troops believed for a while that they had been attacked by the Pisidians (XI.61.4). But the stereotypical nature of a number of Classical references to the irredentism of the "mountain peoples" alerts the critical caution of the historian (cf. chap. 16/11, 16/18).

Finally, according to Diodorus (XIII.46.6✧), the reason that the Phoenician navy never appeared in Asia Minor was because they had learned that "the king of the Arabians and the king of the Egyptians had designs upon Phoenicia." Did the danger oblige

Tissaphernes—or rather, Darius—to reroute the squadron toward the Nile Valley? In truth, there is no formal proof of this interpretation. A passage in Thucydides (VIII.35.2) simply makes us think that merchant ships carrying wheat arrived in Asia Minor from Egypt in 412; but it is difficult to conclude from this that an Egyptian dynasty had already taken the Athenians' side against the Persians. We are also completely in the dark as to the identity of this mysterious "king of the Arabians." The travel voucher Aršāma provided to his steward implies that at this time (around 411–410) the road between Babylonia and Egypt was safe (*DAE* 67 [*AD* 6]). On the other hand, it is likely that in the Delta the Persians continued to pursue the policy that we have already discussed (see chap. 14/2 above), namely, to leave the local dynasts in place. But we have absolutely no information about the details. Aramaic papyri from Elephantine mention troubles in 410 and the quartering of troops (*hndyz*) in the citadel as a result of the intrigues of someone named Anudarū (*DAE* 66 [*AD* 5]). Aršāma's estates suffered damage (*DAE* 68 [*AD* 7]); Pamūn, an Egyptian steward in the service of the satrap, was killed (*DAE* 69 [*AD* 8]). For their part, the Jews mention that "detachments of the Egyptians rebelled" in 410 (*DAE* 101 [*AP* 27◊]). But the actual troubles related here appear to be of limited extent, without a clear connection to the war that supposedly provoked sending a royal fleet to the Delta.

In the final analysis—without totally rejecting such an interpretation—we are led to think that the reasons for the apparent passivity of Darius II on the Asia Minor front are to be found neither in Egypt, nor among the Cadusians, Medes, or Pisidians. Two explanations can be offered, one political-diplomatic, the other military. We can imagine that, together with with Tissaphernes' timidity, the fluctuating strategy of the Spartans sowed turmoil and uncertainty among the king's advisers. The Lacedaemonian strategy must have appeared foreign, opaque, and contradictory to Darius II, just as it had to his father, Artaxerxes (cf. Thucydides IV.50.2). As far as we can tell, the Great King seems not to have fully comprehended the situation; like Tissaphernes, he seems to have expected that the Greeks would wear each other out.

Darius II and His Armies

The second explanation puts the accent on the Great King's military weakness. This, we know, is a recurrent stereotype in the Greek view of Persia, especially in the fourth century, beginning with Xenophon in the last chapter of the *Cyropedia*. A similar perspective is found in many other Greek authors, such as Plato (*Laws* 697d). But taking into account the deeply polemical character of these appraisals, historians must instead base their work on external evidence, which allows them to test the validity of such interpretations.

We generally turn to the Babylonian sources. It is frequently stressed, in fact, that within the framework of the development of the system of military land allotments (the *ḥaṭru* system) the plot-holders, instead of providing the military service connected to the property they controlled, apparently preferred to pay the entire cost (*ilku*) in the form of money ("paid service"). This phenomenon can be detected from the time of Darius I on, but it tended to become more widespread in the time of Artaxerxes I and Darius II. This observation also can be connected to increasing reliance on Greek mercenaries. The totality of the reconstruction tends to validate Xenophon's critical remarks about the Persians' abandonment of the ancestral rules requiring landholders to "furnish cavalrymen from their possessions and that these, in case of war, should also take the field, while those who performed outpost duty in defence of the country received pay for their services," so much so that "enemies may range up and down their land with less hindrance than friends" (*Cyr.* VIII.8.20–21◇).

Even if we do not insist that Xenophon's comments are essentially a caricature, we still need to stress that the Babylonian evidence is more ambivalent than it appears. Insofar as it can be reconstructed from the tablets, the situation at the time of Darius II's accession shows that the *ḫatru* system was already fully operational. For one thing, we know that Ochus (the future Darius II) was ruler of Babylonia and that he could gather a huge army. The tablets also indicate that, in order to respond to mobilization orders, the tenant farmers had to borrow vast sums from the house of Murašū—and there are many examples of this process. We know in fact that most of the time the plot-holders did not work the land themselves but turned the management over to the Murašū or other business concerns of the same type. So while the documentation implies that the financial position of the grant-holders was not spectacular, it also indicates that they were nevertheless committed to the military obligations they had taken on.

Several documents from year 2 of Darius (422) show that at that time, by royal order, the tenants in the Nippur region were required to furnish the 'king's soldier' (*Ṣāb šarri*) to take part in a review that would be held at Uruk (UC 9/3; 10/61–62; PBS II/1:54, 162). Another tablet belonging to the same lot is even more explicit:

> Gadal-lāma, son of Raḫūm-ili, declared of his own free will to Rīmūt-Ninurta, descendant of Murašū, as follows: "Because Raḫūm-ili adopted your brother Elli-šum-iddin, you now possess the share of Barik-ili in the plow and fallow land held in tenure as 'horse land' (*bit sīsi*) by Raḫūm-ili. Give me a horse with harness and reins, a *suḫattu* coat with neckpiece and hood, an iron armor with hood, a quiver, 120 arrows, some with heads, some without, a sword(?) with its scabbard, 2 iron spears, and I will perform the service attached to your share in the tenure land." Rīmūt-Ninurta agreed and gave him a horse and the military equipment mentioned above, as well as 1 mina of silver for his travel provisions, in order to obey the royal order to go to Uruk in connection with this "horse land." Gadal-lāma bears responsibility for presenting the equipment given to him. He will show it for registration to Sabin, the man in charge of the secretaries of the army, and he will give the deed of registration to Rīmūt-Ninurta. [Names of witnesses and scribe] Nippur, 18 Tebet, year 2 of Darius. ([422] UC 9/68; trans. F. Joannès/P. Beaulieu)

Through adoption, a member of the house of Murašū thus acquired part of a horse estate. Rīmūt-Ninurta had no desire to fulfill the military service associated with the land granted by the king (in the *ḫatru* system) and entered into an agreement with the son of the holder of the other part: Gadal-lāma attended the assembly with a horse and the entire required weaponry (compare Xenophon, *Hell.* III.4.15!).

This document is transparent: it explains very clearly that at this time, at Nippur, estates were subject to active military service, though the identity of the person who performed it did not matter to the administration. The core of the administration's concern was that each estate recorded in the archives furnish the soldier(s) whose service justified the very rationale for the system. And, compared with other documents dated to the same months of the same year, it is not possible to argue that this text could be taken as illustrating a special or unusual case. Even if we cannot prove it, it seems highly unlikely that the order to assemble at Uruk was issued in preparation for a military expedition; it is more plausible that there actually were annual assemblies, which Xenophon several times says took place regularly in each military region at "the place of assembly" (*syllogos*).

Finally, later tablets from the reign of Artaxerxes II imply the general continuity of the system. The archives of the barber Kuṣur-Ea, son of Sin-aḫḫe-bulliṭ, include (among others) seven texts referring to a practically identical procedure between the years 399 and 363. One of his relatives, Nidintu-Sin, made a contract with the barber, asking Kuṣur-Ea to furnish him with all of the equipment that citizens of Ur were required to furnish for military service; in exchange, he would appear at the royal assembly held in the 8th year of Artaxerxes II (397; UET 4.109). Kuṣur-Ea was in fact subject to service because he held one quarter of a 'bow estate' (*bīt qašti*; UET 4.106 [363 B.C.]). Here, the word 'assembly' renders the Old Persian word **handaisa*, which is also found in the Elephantine archives (*DAE* 36, 66, 101 [*AP* 13, *AD* 5, *AP* 27]; Aram. *hndyz*). Whether the service was carried out directly by the plot-holder or by a substitute (who was armed by the former), the Babylonian document thus incontestably shows that the plots were perpetually tied to the original royal obligation.

Reliance on Greek mercenaries at this date remained fairly limited. Tissaphernes and Pharnabazus counted on the Lacedaemonian contingents primarily to fulfill the mission entrusted to them by Darius: to gather the tribute from cities still under Athenian control. They also were able to utilize levies of horsemen from Persians living in the imperial diaspora, following a well-known, long-lived system. Furthermore, there is no doubt that the colonization strategy actively pursued from the time of Darius and Xerxes had a major impact in the military realm; striking confirmation is found through the study of the composition of Cyrus the Younger's army (see chap. 15/2). Evidence no longer requires us to believe that there was a significant deterioration in the system of military plots in Egypt, either in Elephantine or in Memphis. The campaigns of Darius and his armies against Media and the Cadusians provide strong confirmation that the central authority could place as much military force on active duty as strategy required. In short, it does not appear that the undeniable Persian military shortcomings in Asia Minor have to be explained by recourse to the convenient but simplistic theory of the decadence of the Great King's army. Similarly, the observation that the Great King did not send funds to his satraps in Asia Minor is woefully insufficient evidence to support the conclusion that the royal coffers were empty!

All of this evidence seems much more to be a result of a policy decision made at the center, which for reasons that remain to be clarified did not wish to commit powerful armies on the Aegean front. We could offer an entire series of interpretations of a technical sort (burden and cost of levies, for example), but no single element was determinative. Given the rarity of general mobilizations throughout Achaemenid history, we perhaps should not be overly surprised that Darius II did not consider an Empire-wide conscription useful now. It seems especially clear that the Great King and his advisers thought that the Lacedaemonian alliance would have to provide sufficient support for the Asia Minor satraps to get the upper hand, and that the subsequent reconquests would have to finance military operations, since they would provide the basis for the reintroduction of tribute assessments in the Greek cities. The only exception to this presumed rule was the assembling of that famous Phoenician navy we have already mentioned in Cilicia, and it obviously functioned under direct orders from the central authority (Thucydides VIII.88.5).

Cyrus in Asia Minor

When the Great King decided to send Cyrus to Asia Minor in 407, it was perhaps to calm dissension that was brewing between his sons; he was certainly aware of the need to pursue a more energetic policy. It is possible that the Spartan Boeotius and his colleagues had apprised him of the situation, persuading him to act. Nevertheless, the powers entrusted to Cyrus and the amount of money offered to him to conduct the war leave no doubt regarding the royal intent: Cyrus in fact "brought with him a letter, addressed to all the dwellers upon the sea (Asia Minor; *katō*) and bearing the King's seal, which contained among other things these words: 'I send down Cyrus as *karanos*'—the word '*karanos*' means 'lord' (*kyrie*)—'of those whose mustering-place is Castolus'" (*Hell.* I.4.3;✧ cf. *Anab.* I.1.2). In other words, Pharnabazus and Tissaphernes were thereafter his subordinates. His mission was clear: "In order to be ruler of all the peoples on the coast and to support the Lacedaemonians in the war" (*Hell.* I.4.3✧). The time for royal hesitation and inter-satrapal rivalry was over. Cyrus immediately ordered Pharnabazus to detain the Athenian ambassadors in such a way as not to alert Athens to the Great King's new intentions; it was not until three years later that they were allowed to leave Asia Minor, at a time when the fate of the Athenian armies had already nearly been sealed.

The appointment of Cyrus coincided with the arrival of a particularly energetic and decisive Lacedaemonian admiral, Lysander. The two men soon came to trust each other, and with Persian support Lysander was able to reinforce his army and navy. When he was absent, during the summer of 406, the Athenians achieved a victory in the Arginusae islands. However, they were not able to benefit from the victory: the *strategoi* were doomed! Lysander's return (summer of 405) marked the beginning of a new stage in Spartan–Achaemenid relations. Some time later, Cyrus the Younger was recalled to his father's sickbed. Before leaving, he gave Lysander large sums of money and, according to Xenophon, "assigned all his authority to him" (*Hell.* II.1.14–15). In September of the same year, Lysander won a decisive sea battle over the Athenians at Aigos-Potamos. Some months later (April–May, 404), Athens fell to Lysander. Meanwhile, Darius died (between September 405 and April 404).

8. The Great King in His Countries

The Murašū, Babylonia, and the Royal Administration

At this point, we would do well to pause for a moment and attempt to draw up a new imperial balance-sheet, which should not be reduced to territorial and military considerations alone but should be drawn from regional realities. One of the best-documented countries is Babylonia. In fact, we have several hundred tablets from the archives of a Babylonian business concern, the Murašū, whose activities are particularly well attested between year 25 of Artaxerxes I (440–439) and year 7 of Darius II (417–416). Some other tablets, dating between 413 and 404, provide evidence for the activity of an old subordinate of the house of Murašū, but it is difficult to establish in what capacity he functioned. The cessation of the archives probably reflects the dissolution of the business, although we should not necessarily infer that there was a major modification of the pattern, since the Murašū, whose activities were centered around Nippur, were no doubt only one of the firms that did business in Babylonia at this time.

The Murašū were not a bank in the modern sense. Their basic activity was managing land, and this is why their archives are a prime source as much for reconstructing land management as for fiscal organization. The tenant-farmers, rather than devoting themselves directly to working their lands, entrusted the land's management to the Murašū, and in return the latter turned over the rent to the tenants. The Murašū themselves generally sublet the land to farmers, and this explains the large number of farming contracts found in the archives. Some of the parcels exploited in this system are identified as "royal lands," as well as 'royal gifts' (*nidintu šarri*)—which benefited highly placed persons (primarily members of the court and Iranians). Well-known people are found among them, including Parysatis and Prince Aršāma (satrap of Egypt), as well as many other important persons, some of them known from Ctesias. Also among the tenants were members of the *ḫaṭru* (military and nonmilitary), who also utilized the services of the Murašū, whether as land managers or moneylenders. The debts incurred were calculated not on the plot itself—which, though it could be transferred by inheritance, remained inalienable—but on future harvests. The Murašū thus played a very important role: both they and the tenants had a mutual interest in increasing the yield of the land. Furthermore, they sold the produce of the farms, which was perishable, on the open market, allowing the tenants to pay their interest in silver, without having to bother themselves with carrying out a difficult transaction.

Bēlšunu

One of the notables of the period is a Babylonian, Bēlšunu, who is known from a series of tablets gathered into an "archive" that was deposited under one of the citadels of Babylon (the Kasr); the archive dates from 438 to 400. He was a son of Bēl-uṣuršu and was called "governor (*piḫatu*) of Babylon" between 421 and 414. The title is not the same as what we call satrap; in Babylon, the satrap was the Persian Gubāru/Gobryas, who is attested until 417. Bēlšunu was thus one of the satrap's subordinates (a Greek author, probably referring to him, calls him *hyparchos*). Then, between 407 and 401, his title was "governor of Ebir Nāri," which the Greek authors transcribe as "satrap of Syria." In all probability, then, we can identify him with the Belesys whom Xenophon calls "satrap of Syria" during Cyrus the Younger's offensive against his brother Artaxerxes II in 401 (*Anab.* I.4.10; cf. Diodorus XIV.20.5). Perhaps this Babylonian's new title was the reward that Darius II gave him for his aid.

The tablets provide very important information on the role and possible activities of Bēlšunu. One of them, dated around 416–415, is particularly interesting (TBER, AO 2569):

> [*broken lines* . . .] we displayed(?) the stolen property (?) [. . .] [. . . Ea-iddin, Marduk-z]ēr-līšir, and Bēl-lūmur, the accountant[s of the temple of Uraš and(?) . . . , son] of Ṣihā(?), discovered the stolen property that had been carried off by(?) Bēl-ittannu, [son of Bulluṭu, and] his son [Bēl]-uṣuršu and Uraš-nāṣir, son of Nidintu, in Dilbat [in their houses(?)], {seized(?)} it, and put it under seal in the treasury of (the god) Uraš, and [. . .]. They held Bēl-ittannu, son of Bulluṭu, and his son Bēl-uṣuršu in detention(?) in Dilbat, and they put their houses under seal. [Uraš-nāṣir and (?). . .(?)] their [. . .] escaped and {came} to Babylon, to Bēlšunu, the [governor of Babylon]. Then Marduk-zēr-lišir and Bēl-lūmur [. . .] displayed to the assembly of Esagil [the stolen goods that] they had seized in their [. . .] and had [. . .] and [put under seal(?)] in the treasury of Uraš. Subsequently, the [assembly(?)] addressed {Bēlšunu}, governor of Babylon, as follows: "Uraš-nāṣir, who [. . .] the stolen goods [. . .] and then escaped from Dilbat and came to you [. . .]." Uraš-nāṣir and [. . .] to the assembly of Esagil [. . . Uraš]-nāṣir, (and) along with him(?) the goods that(?) he carried off [. . .] year 8 of Dar[ius. . .] they interrogated [. . .] sw[ore(?) an oath] by the iron dag[ger(?)]

. . .] [Ea-iddin, Marduk-zēr-lišir, and] Bēl-lūmur, accountants and [overseers] [of the temple of Uraš] . . . to Dilbat, to Uraš-nāṣir, [son of Nidintu(?),] [Bēl-ittan]nu, son of Bulluṭu and his son, Bēl-uṣuršu [. . .] . . . investigate and in lieu of [. . .] that was given to the estate of Uraš [. . .] in year 2 of King Darius. Ea-iddin, Marduk-z[ēr-lišir (. . .)] [and Bēl]-lūmur, the accountants and overseers of the temple of Uraš [and?] the accountants and overseers, and the collegium of the temple [. . .], [. . .] with the concurrence of the assembly of Esagil . . .[. . .]. . . of Uraš-[nāṣir . . .] Bēl-uṣuršu, son [of . . .] [. . . remainder broken . . .]. (trans. M. Stolper)

In summary: a theft took place in the sanctuary of the god Uraš at Dilbat. The thieves were captured, and the recovered stolen goods were put under seal in the god's treasury. One of the thieves went to find Bēlšunu, the "governor of Babylon." At the same time, the sanctuary treasurers sent the case to the assembly of the Esagila in Babylon, which in turn applied to Bēlšunu to turn over the miscreant. The guilty parties were sentenced to repay the treasury of Uraš out of their own funds. The text throws some light on a city, Dilbat, that is relatively little known at this period, and on the continuity of administrative practices from the time of Cyrus and Cambyses on, particularly the role of the "civic" assembly of the Esagila and its relationship with the governor. It also illustrates the length of the process, since apparently four years elapsed between the event and the punishment of the criminals.

In parallel with his public activities, Bēlšunu actively pursued business in the private sector, which was reminiscent of what the Murašû had done previously. Not only was he actively involved with his land, which he possessed as a 'royal gift' (*nidintu šarri*), but he also worked other land of the same type, which generally belonged to people with Iranian names. Bēlšunu's integration into Babylonian society is also well illustrated by another tablet (that does not mention his title): a subordinate/servant of Bēlšunu is directed by his master to ensure regular offerings in honor of the gods Zababa and Ninurta throughout the twelve months of year 5 of Artaxerxes II (*TCL* 13.204).

Darius II in Egypt

Turning to Egypt, we note that the epigraphic evidence is not comparable in extent to that known from the reigns of Cambyses, Darius, and Xerxes. The latest inscriptions from the Wadi Hammamât and the latest inscribed vessels date to the reign of Artaxerxes I (Posener nos. 33, 78–82; A*l*Orsk). But, paradoxically, numerous Aramaic documents date to the tenure of Aršāma in the time of Darius II, and they allow us to reconstruct as faithfully as possible the various levels of Persian officials in Egypt, the system of soldier-colonists, and the management of royal property (see chap. 11/7). A few isolated bits of evidence also attest to the "presence" of Darius II in the country. First, there is the cartouche of Darius II that appears in the temple of El-Khārga, as if he wished to take credit for the policy of his distinguished predecessor. It also seems that the sanctuary of Horus at Edfu benefited from major land grants. A seal found at Memphis appears to be carved with the name of Darius (II), showing a Royal Hero triumphing over two sphinxes (*SD²a*). We may stress, finally, that the Aramaic version of the Behistun inscription and part of the Naqš-i Rustam inscription were written on the back of a papyrus that can be dated with certainty to Darius II (before 418). We cannot be sure that this was an expression of the royal desire to disseminate anew the deeds of his ancestor to make a political connection; perhaps instead the papyrus was only a schoolboy exercise. If this is the case, the document shows even more eloquently the practical ways and means through which diffusion of Achaemenid monarchic ideology took place among the children of the Judeo-Aramean colonists of Elephantine. It would be very risky to conclude, as sometimes happens, that the gaps in the evidence mechanically represent the central authority's lack of interest in a province whose intrinsic importance had not diminished. Putting it together, the existing evidence instead suggests that there were no noteworthy changes in royal policy during the fifth century, after the reconquest by Artaxerxes I.

The Persian Authorities Confront Jews and Egyptians in Elephantine

We learn a bit more about one particular point from an Aramaic dossier from Elephantine. In year 14 of King Darius (410), the Jews of Elephantine, during the satrap Aršāma's absence in Babylonia, sent a complaint to Memphis regarding both the Egyptians and the governor of Syene, Widranga (*DAE* 101 [*AP* 27◇]). They state that the administrators of the sanctuary of Khnūm had made an agreement with Widranga, to whom "they gave money and valuables." As a result, the Egyptians "will not allow [the Jews] to bring meal-offering and incense and sacrifice to offer there to Ya'u the God of heaven . . . but they made there a fire(?) and the rest of the fittings they took for themselves, all of it"; in short, "they destroyed the altar house." The Jews thus asked to have the sanctuary rebuilt in its prior location. To underline the illegality of the Egyptians and Widranga conniving together, the Jews also state that their enemies had raided royal property, since they destroyed "part of the king's stores which is in the fortress of Yeb, . . . and they built a wall in the midst of the fortress of Yeb." Finally, they stopped up a well that had supplied the garrison whenever the troops were assembled there (*hndyz*).

Widranga's accountability was fully established: according to the Jews, it was he who ordered the destruction of Yahō's sanctuary at the request of the priests of Khnūm. In order to accomplish this, he sent a letter to his son Nafaina, who had succeeded him as head of the garrison (*rab ḥaylâ*) at Syene-the-Fortress. Nafaina led a troop of Egyptians "with the other forces" and proceeded to destroy the temple totally and seized the sacred vessels (*DAE* 102 [*AP* 30]). As a result, the Jews requested the opening of an "inquiry . . . by the judges, police, and informers who are set over the guard of the southern District" (*DAE* 101 [*AP* 27]).

At the same time, the Jews sent a complaint to the Jerusalem authorities, namely, "to Johanan the high priest and his colleagues the priests who are in Jerusalem, and to Ostanes the brother of 'Anani, and the nobles of the Jews." The letter went unanswered (*DAE* 102 [*AP* 30] lines 17–18◇). Three years later, in 407, they turned to both Bagohi, "governor of Judah," and "Dalaiah and Šelemiah the sons of Sanballat governor of Samaria." They remind the governors that the Jewish community had been in mourning for three years and specify that they had made "neither offering, nor incense, nor holocaust" in the sanctuary. They implore Bagohi to intervene with "his friends in Egypt" to give them permission to rebuild their temple. The dual approach to Bagohi and Samaritan authorities associated with Aršāma (who had meanwhile returned to Egypt; *DAE* 103 [*AP* 32]) finally got results. The satrap made a decision that provided for terms under which the temple could be rebuilt "as it was built before." On the other hand, though the incense and the offering could be carried out normally, this was not the case for the "holocausts of rams, oxen, and goats." The Jews agreed to give some money and 1,000 ardabs of barley to the house of Aršāma (*DAE* 104 [*AP* 33]).

The matter presents formidable interpretive problems. We must first pay attention to the makeup of the available material. We have the details only from the Jews themselves—that is, from the arguments they presented to the authorities. The materials are necessarily incomplete and undoubtedly biased. The Jews continually contrast their loyal behavior with the Egyptians' felonious behavior: "We are free from blame, and anything harmful of this kind has not been found in us" (*DAE* 101 [*AP* 27] lines 14–15✧). That is, the Jews state that they are not rebels, in contrast to various groups of the Egyptians (lines 1–2). But the modern historian cannot take an advocate's arguments as a court clerk's record. The Jews also accuse the Egyptians of buying off Widranga. Though it is true that the Classical texts refer to the king's condemnations of judges who embezzle, we must also remember that the payment of *baksheesh* was ubiquitous in Egypt and Babylonia. In this case, the Jews themselves made major gifts to the house of Aršāma to thank him for his services. Finally, the very nature of the documentation (letters and memoranda) does not clarify episodes for which we would like to have more information. In their 407 petition to Jerusalem and Samaria, the Jews say of Widranga: "The dogs tore off the anklet from his legs, and all the riches he had gained were destroyed, and all the men who had sought to do evil to that temple, all of them, were killed and we saw (our desire) upon them" (*DAE* 102 [*AP* 30] lines 15–16✧). Despite some uncertain points of reading and translation, it thus seems that Widranga and the temple's vandalizers received serious punishment. But we do not know who punished them or why, especially since Widranga seems to reappear, complete with the title "commander of the garrison," in one or possibly two documents dated 398.

What emerges clearly is that during these years a conflict broke out between the leaders of the Jewish community of Elephantine and the leaders of the temple of Khnūm. But why? Another document, unfortunately fragmentary, refers to a visit to Memphis. It alludes to troubles at Thebes: the Jews "fear robbery," and investigators are accused of taking bribes from the Egyptians (*DAE* 97 [*AP* 27]). In another text, a Jew complains that Widranga, now commander of the garrison at Syene, imprisoned him at Abydos "because of a precious(?) stone which they found stolen in the hand(s) of the dealers" (*DAE* 98 [*AP* 38✧). But these isolated and fragmentary data are difficult to interpret and to connect to the events at Syene-Elephantine. Let us linger especially on this imprisoned Jew's complaint to his colleagues at Elephantine: "It is known by you that Khnūm is against us from the time that Hanani was in Egypt till now." Was this a religious conflict? Did the destruction of the temple and the Jews' houses (*DAE* 100 [*AP* 34]) mean that Widranga and the Egyptians shared anti-Jewish sentiments? Hypotheses such as these seem difficult to sustain. Although Widranga was able to demonstrate a certain amount of devotion to Egyptian gods, for reasons shared with high Persian officers of the satrapy from Darius on, there is nothing to indicate that he was so Egyptianized that he sided with the priests of Khnūm for purely religious reasons.

We would do well now to return to basics. As governor, Widranga had to adjudicate a dispute that had arisen between the representatives of the Jewish community and the administrators of the temple of Khnūm. There must have been a trial, after which Nafaina, acting in his official capacity, was required to carry out the sentence pronounced by his father, who also was acting in his official capacity. What was the purpose of the litigation? Several earlier documents show that judges often had to make decisions regarding property disputes, and a number of these disputes involved land adjacent to the sanctuaries of Yahō and Khnūm (*DAE* 32–36 [*AP* 5, 6, 8, 9, 13]). The Jewish sanctuary in fact abutted Khnūm's estate. It appears that the litigation between the two sanctuaries pertained purely to property, since the new buildings put up by the priests of Khnūm were encroaching on some royal properties (granary and a well) as well as on Yahō's estate. When it proved impossible for the two sides to arrive at a compromise, they submitted the matter to the governor for arbitration.

As any other judge, Widranga would have referred to the corpus of local jurisprudence that Darius had ordered collected more than a century earlier. If we concede the relationship between this book of jurisprudence and Egyptian customary law of the Hellenistic period, we may stress that a very important part of the latter is devoted to conflicts relating to land ownership. One section is expressly dedicated to cases involving buildings erected on land that is later on claimed by someone else. Without being able to prove it completely, we can imagine that the Egyptians claimed to be the actual (because they were the first) owners of the parcel on which the temple of Yahō had been built.

This theory is partially confirmed by the Jews themselves. In one of their petitions, they in fact provide one component of a rebuttal. Looking back on the destruction of their sanctuaries, they state:

> Already in the days of the kings of Egypt our fathers had built that temple in the fortress of Yeb, and when Cambyses came into Egypt he found that temple built, and the temples of the gods of Egypt all of them they overthrew, but no one did any harm to that temple. (*DAE* 102 [AP 30] lines 12–13✧)

Because it is included in a petition that was intended to plead their cause to recognized authorities (Judahite and Samaritan), the statement should be seen as an argument shaped by its administrative context. In this case, the Jews were trying to prove that the building of their temple had been authorized first of all by the Saite pharaohs and later confirmed by Cambyses. We recognize this as a well-known form of legal defense: to validate their rights, the managers of a temple (or a city) refer to prior privileges, of which the present authorities require them to furnish proof (cf. Tacitus, *Annals* III.61–63). We may recall the behavior of Tattenai at Jerusalem or even Darius's letter to Gadatas; in the first case, the Jews referred to Cyrus's edict; in the second, the authorities of the temple of Apollo recalled that their privileges went back to Darius's ancestors (cf. chap. 12/4). It is the same here: the Jewish leaders came before Widranga's tribunal because they faced adversaries who demanded the demolition of the temple of Yahō; they reminded the governor that the existence of the temple had been officially confirmed by Cambyses. If the Jews lost the trial, it was very likely because, unlike the people of Jerusalem who appealed to Tattenai, they were unable to produce a written document. If Widranga decided in favor of the Egyptians, it was perhaps quite simply because the documents they were able to produce were immeasurably superior to the Jews' purely oral statements. The decision and the rationale for it were as follows: the Jews were required to dismantle the temple, because the parcel was declared the property of Khnūm.

The episode is very instructive regarding the relationship between the administration and the various ethnocultural communities of the Empire and regarding the procedures that protected the rights of each of them. We do not know what grounds Aršāma had for nullifying Widranga's decision, because we do not have the text of the satrap's decision—only an indirect and fragmentary citation (*DAE* 104 [AP 33]). But we must stress that in this case the Persian authorities of Syene and then Memphis had to choose between two rationales: one giving priority to a royal decision (Cambyses' decree), the other resting on recognizing the "law of the countries" (Egyptian jurisprudence).

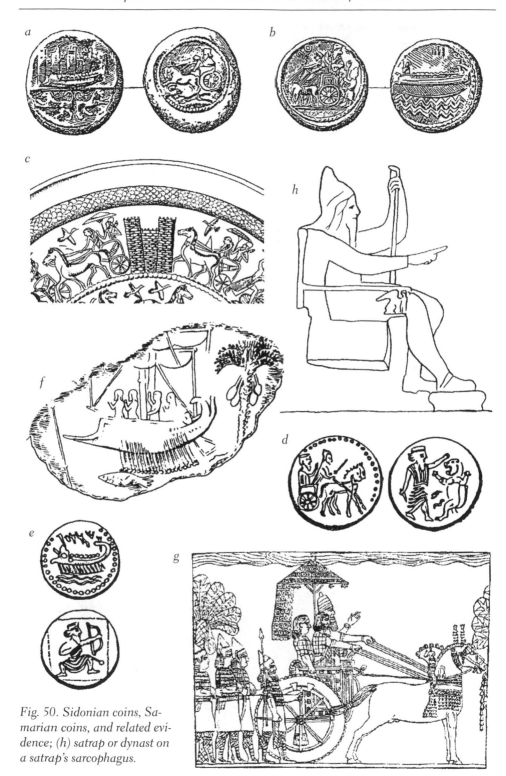

Fig. 50. Sidonian coins, Samarian coins, and related evidence; (h) satrap or dynast on a satrap's sarcophagus.

Widranga opted for the latter, for reasons that probably had less to do with personal preference for the Egyptians and their gods than with the need to maintain order, which in an Egyptian context could only be achieved by conforming to Egyptian law.

A Business Letter

We have an especially vivid illustration of everyday relations between Persians/Iranians and other peoples living in Egypt in an undated Aramaic papyrus that retranscribes a letter sent by Spendadāta, son of Fravartipāta, to Hôri and Petemehû:

> To my brothers Hôri and Petemehû, your brother Spentadāta. May all the gods grant at all times the prosperity of my brothers! And now, I have a boat, common to me and to its owner, which is in your hands. Be advised that Armaidāta will tell you that I have given him charge of the boat, and let him do whatever he wants. Also, give him my share of the rent of [this] boat [which is ours]. There is [a total] of 8 shekels, I gave [it] to [. . .] to give it [in exchange] for grain to bring to me. And there is 1 karsh 8 shekels of silver that I gave you to buy wheat for Yatma. Total of money: 1 karsh, 8 shekels. If you bought grain with this amount and brought it into your houses, good! If not, give the money to Armaidāta. He will bring it to us. And if [this] grain remains available to you, tell Armaidāta and give it to him in such a way that he can sell it. (*DAE* 109)

The transaction seems fairly simple: two Iranians or Persians got together to buy and transport wheat, which they intended to sell; it seems that a third person, Yatma (an Aramaic name) also contributed money to the deal. The two sailors are Egyptians, as in every other known case. Many details escape us. Nonetheless, the text has the advantage of providing concrete information on the commercial activities of two Persians/Iranians, who no doubt held important posts at Elephantine, and on their relations with two Egyptians. The document allows us to see that the Persians of Egypt, following the pattern of the Persians of Babylonia, had no problem thoroughly integrating themselves in the commercial environment and profiting from it. Perhaps the wheat was partly intended to feed the garrison reserves?

The Great King in Sidon and Elephantine

Sometimes only the iconography makes it possible to identify the Persian presence in one region or another, especially in regions where other sources are silent during the time of Artaxerxes I and Darius II. This is the case for Sidon. On the city's earliest coins, which date to the third quarter of the fifth century, the Great King is depicted in various poses (fig. 50a–b). Some show a Sidonian ship on the obverse, sometimes moored at the foot of fortifications; the reverse shows the following scene: "The king of Persia standing in his chariot drawn by four horses galloping to the left; he is capped with the five-pointed *kidaris* and dressed in a *candys*; he raises and extends the right hand; the charioteer is in the chariot beside the king holding the reins in both hands. Beneath the horses, the carcass of an ibex" (Babelon II.2, no. 889; cf. nos. 890, 892–93, 895). On other coins, two lions, on the obverse, spring backward, and a ship is moored at the base of the fortress; on the reverse: "The king of Persia standing battling a lion; he is capped with the crenellated *kidaris* and dressed in the *kandys*; in his right hand he brandishes the short sword [*akinakēs*]; in his left hand he holds a lion by the mane, his arm straining; the lion is rearing in front of him on his two hind legs. Empty square" (nos. 891, 894, 896). On still others, he is shown standing, drawing a bow, opposite a head-and-neck view ibex (no. 897), or, half-kneeling, holding a spear in his right hand and a bow in his left (no. 898).

These scenes correspond quite closely to nearly identical depictions in court art (Royal Hero confronting a lion) or on seals (king in his chariot) and coins (king as archer and lancer; cf. chap. 6). The iconographic influence also shows up in reverse—if we may put it that way: a seal on some Treasury tablets (*PTS* no. 32) shows a ship very much like those found on Sidonian coins (fig. 50f). This specific example indicates that the iconography of Sidonian coins spread into other regions. To remain within the period we are considering here, we may note in particular that the Sidonian types were copied at Elephantine with, on the obverse, a Sidonian ship (and the name Syene in Aramaic: *swyn*), and on the reverse, the Royal Hero fighting the lion, with a cock poised between them. We also know of Elephantine imitations of Milesian coins with a Persian archer on the reverse. The Sidonian types are also found in Samaria (fig. 50d–e).

There is no doubt that the kings of Sidon deliberately copied motifs from the Achaemenid iconongraphic repertoire when they had coins struck. There is no room for uncertainty about the political significance. Sidonian coinage is in fact entirely unique; in the other Phoenician cities, the coins from this time show nothing but local symbols. The iconographic distinctiveness expresses the special place held by Sidon within the (very poorly known) organization of Phoenicia at this time. It certainly reflects an older heritage, since the inscription on Ešmunazar's sarcophagus shows that there were close connections between the Great King and the city (see chap. 12/3). The presence of the king of Sidon beside Conon before, during, and after the battle of Cnidos at the beginning of the fourth century further demonstrates that since the time of Cambyses the Sidonian navy had maintained a prime position in the Great King's strategic thinking (Diodorus XIV.79.8; *Hell. Oxyr.* 9.2). We may stress that seals with royal Achaemenid images have also been found in the territory of Dor, which had previously been given to Ešmunazzar.

Meanwhile, it must be emphasized that the interpretation related above always raises doubts because of debates about the identfication of the person standing in the chariot: some authors suggest that it is Baal of the city rather than the Great King. Even though this is the minority opinion (and probably unsupportable), we must stress that the arguments brought up on this topic are very similar to the arguments put forward on the political significance of the scenes on a Sidonian sarcophagus known as the sarcophagus of the satrap, which dates to approximately the same period (late fifth, early fourth century). Is the person on the throne (fig. 50h) the satrap (or even the Great King himself) or the king of Sidon, portrayed in the image of the Great King? Or to put the problem another way: in the absence of any written evidence, does iconographic evidence permit us to establish the nature of political relationships that existed between the local dynasts and the Achaemenid authorities?

The Lycian Case

The same question underlies every discussion of the political significance of the Lycian texts from the end of the fifth century. Although they are only partially deciphered, the Lycian inscriptions of the Xanthus Pillar (which was created at the beginning of the fourth century) reveal familiar names like Amorges, Tissaphernes, Hieramenes, Iasus, Caunus, Darius II, and Artaxerxes II. Despite much obscurity regarding the details, there is hardly any doubt that the inscriptions refer to events that took place in Lycia and southwestern Asia Minor during the Ionian War; they also provide evidence of the involvement of the dynast of Xanthus, who at the time was Gergis/Kheriga, son of Harpagus. The dynast probably aided Tissaphernes, specifically by supplying triremes for the battle in 412 in which the satrap opposed the Persian traitor Amorges, who had taken refuge in Iasus (Thucydides VIII.28.2–4). Furthermore, evidence of Tissaphernes' activity in the region is provided(?) by a coin that bears his name in Lycian (partly restored) and that also bears the name Xanthus (Arnna), though it is difficult to decide whether it dates to the period before or after Cyrus's arrival in Asia Minor, since this event restricted Tissaphernes' authority to Caria, under the supreme command of Darius's younger son. Unfortunately, this numismatic evidence does not permit us to describe the relationship between Tissaphernes and the Lycian dynasts—particularly the dynast of Xanthus— with complete certainty. The analysis of the relationship between the satrap and Xanthus depends fundamentally on the interpretation placed on the "portraits" on certain coins struck at Xanthus by the dynasts. The thesis of relatively strict Persian control is derived from another thesis that sees the coin-portraits as representing the satrap himself; but however appealing this interpretation may be, it has not been unanimously accepted.

The ambiguity of the Lycian evidence is constant. The available evidence reveals clear, growing Greek cultural influence at the Xanthus dynastic court. This holds for the dynastic coinage, and it holds also for a Greek epigram that exalts the military excellence of Gergis, son of Harpagus. It holds even more for the poem of Arbinas, which was written at the beginning of the next century by the Greek diviner Symmachus of Pellana. Symmachus may have arrived at Caunus with the Peloponnesian navy around 412, before entering the service of Gergis and, later, his son Arbinas. The subject of the poems is purely domestic, we might say, since they transmit for posterity the victories won by the dynasts of Xanthus over their relatives and neighbors and celebrate the rebuilding of a Xanthian princedom that extended through the valley of the Xanthus. There is no trace in all of this of specifically imperial interests. The composition suggests that the domestic life of Lycia went on under Persian dominion as if nothing had happened.

But it is a good idea to provide a more nuanced perspective. When Arbinas celebrated his own and his father's virtues, he had no reason to refer to the Persian political presence; this is in sharp contrast to the Lycian Chronicle (Pillar Inscription). But the two propositions should not be set sharply in opposition to one another: the Persians apparently did not interfere in purely domestic dynastic matters, as long as the victorious dynast did not challenge his submission to the Great King. Even in the cultural realm, increasing Greek influence need not be interpreted as marking the increasing autonomy of the Xanthian dynasts. On the contrary, their continued dependence on Persia is illustrated, for example, by one of the poems celebrating the victories of Arbinas: "Arbinas is distinguished over all in all human knowledge, archery, warriorhood, and expert horsemanship." One is immediately reminded of the royal virtues as presented by Darius: the good warrior and the good horseman. Of course, Symmachus, the author of the elegy, certainly did not slavishly copy the Naqš-i Rustam inscription (or some copy that might have circulated in one form or another). Let us say rather that the vocabulary used *also* reveals, in Greek garb, the stamp of the aristocratic Persian ethic that had been present in Lycia since the beginning of the fifth century (chap. 12/5 end). In order to establish their legitimacy, the Xanthian dynasts borrowed their literary themes and iconographic repertoire from both Iran and Greece, in equal measure. In short, this sort of evidence does not allow the historian either to assert or to exclude the influence of the Achaemenid authorities in Lycia in the last decades of the fifth century. The only texts that provide information about this are naturally those that belong to the narrative genre (Thucydides, Pillar inscription). They suggest that when external danger loomed, the Lycian dynasts were included in Persian planning, and, simultaneously, that the Lycians might have been able to profit from this, achieving their own goals.

The Cilician Case

In other regions, we have only very difficult fragmentary, heterogeneous, and poorly dated evidence. This remark is particularly true of Cilicia, a region that we have every reason to believe continued to play the military role it had always had throughout Achaemenid history. We have no specific example at this date, but an episode in the Cypriot War, a few decades later, removes any doubt about this point (Diodorus XV.3.1–3). After Xenagoras's appointment by Xerxes in 479 (Herodotus IX.107), the documentation is singularly lacking. Not until the campaign of Cyrus the Younger do we have access to any information. Cyrus was joined at Caÿstru-pedion by Epyaxa, "the wife of Syennesis, the king of the Cilicians" (Xenophon, *Anab.* I.2.12◊). The Cilician dynast himself refused to defend the Cilician Gates (I.2.21) and fell back to Tarsus, where his palace was located (I.2.23). According to Xenophon, he made an agreement with Cyrus in which he gave great sums of money to him in return for the promise that his territory (*khōra*) would not be ravaged by Cyrus's troops (I.2.27). Ctesias's and Diodorus's passing references are not particularly explicit on the nature of the *syennesis*'s power and his relations with the Persians, other than that in principle he owed respect to the Great King.

We have long known of series of Cilician coins that traditionally have been viewed as dynastic coinage, even though they bear no name other than that of their place of issue, usually Tarsus (fig. 51). A person believed to be the dynast is depicted on his horse, often holding two spears and wearing a *bashlyk*. The reverse is most often decorated with the image of a Greek hoplite in combat (Babelon nos. 504–20). One series dated (hypothetically) to the last decades of the fifth century always has the mounted dynast on the obverse, but on the reverse we see royal images, described thus: "The king of Persia as archer on one knee facing right and drawing the bow; he is bearded, bare-headed, dressed in the pleated candys gathered at the waist; his quiver full of arrows is on his back; in the field at left the handled cross" (Babelon no. 521; cf. nos. 522–25; fig. 51 here). On several other coins, two royal figures are depicted: "Two kings of Persia, standing facing each other; both are bearded and dressed in the candys; each rests on his spear with both hands; they have the bow and quiver on their back . . ." (no. 526; cf. no. 527). On three other examples, the royal images occupy front and back; on the obverse, the Royal Hero battles the lion, seizing him by the mane with his right hand and plunging his short sword into the lion's flank with his left hand (no. 528; cf. nos. 529–30); on the reverse, the standing king leans on his spear. The Cilician mint is marked by the presence of the cross with handle, which the king holds in his left hand on the later coins, and by the inscription "Tarsus" in Aramaic (in Aramaic and Greek on some examples: nos. 528–30).

Because of ongoing chronological uncertainties, it is difficult to come to firm conclusions on the basis of this numismatic evidence. Nonetheless, two noteworthy observations may be made: on the one hand, royal images were diffused throughout various

Fig. 51. Dynastic(?) coinage from Cilicia.

parts of the Empire, from Sidon to Cilicia, and this diffusion was achieved in a privileged way by means of coins and seals; on the other, the frequent connection, on obverse and reverse, of the images of the dynast and the king (or Royal Hero) was an association that had obvious political significance but that informs us only imperfectly about the relationship between the two.

The Persians and the Kings of Cyprus

Located a stone's throw or two from the Cilician coast—from which the Persians kept an eye on it—Cyprus remained in the Achaemenid sphere of influence. We learn from Isocrates (*Evag.* 18–20) that a man of Tyrian origin (who was probably a Phoenician from Cyprus) deposed the king of Salamis and seized power shortly after 450. In his eagerness to promote the militant Hellenism of his hero Evagoras, Isocrates gives the impression that Salamis and the other cities previously had never been subject to the Persians. He writes, in fact, that the new master hastened to "deliver the town to the barbarians and to subject the island to the slavery of the Great King." Actually, the Cypriot cities appear never to have left Persian dominion after the the Ionian Revolt was quashed (cf. Diodorus XII.3.2; 4.2). Around 415, another "Tyrian" named Abdemon came to power in the city, probably by renewing his allegiance to Darius II, since Diodorus considered him "a Friend of the King of the Persians" (XIV.98.1✧). He tried to kill Evagoras, whom Isocrates presents as the legitimate descendant of the Teucrid dynasty. Evagoras sought refuge at Soloi in Cilicia. There he recruited a small force, left for Cyprus, and managed to drive out Abdemon (Diodorus XIV.98.1; Isocrates, *Evag.* 26–32). Contrary to what Isocrates says, the new king of Salamis did not immediately try to rebel; we even find Evagoras acting as mediator between Tissaphernes and Athens in 410, which implies that he had good relations with the satrap. During this period, his status is exactly what we can draw from Diodorus's subsequent discussion: he was the sole ruler of Salamis and had to pay tribute to the Great King, who granted him the royal office at Salamis (XV.8.2–3). This was clearly true for other petty kings of Cyprus as well, such as the case of that Agyris whom Diodorus some years later presents as an ally (*symmakhos*) of the Persians (XV.98.2). Obviously, viewed from the heartland, the convulsions that Cyprus was suffering were considered purely local affairs that did not affect the facts of Persian power over Cyprus. As in the previous period, the Persians unthinkingly continued to rely on the populations of Phoenician origin, pitting them against the Greek communities on the island.

Chapter 15
Artaxerxes II (405/404–359/358)
and Artaxerxes III (359/358–338)

1. The Reign of Artaxerxes II: Sources and Problems

The Greek Authors' View

The accession of Artaxerxes at Darius II's death inaugurated the longest reign in Achaemenid history. Once again, it is up to the historian at the outset to stress the gaps and serious distortions in the evidence, which first and foremost bears the stamp of the dominant position held by the Classical sources, which quite naturally pay disproportionate attention to affairs on the western front. Fortunately, Cyrus the Younger's recruitment of Greek mercenaries provides us with many descriptions of his rebellion until his death in the battle of Cunaxa (404–401). We might speculate, however, that the young prince had been on the offensive since Bactra—the silence regarding matters on the Iranian Plateau (aside from fleeting allusions to raising troops) being especially significant. In this earlier case, of course, Cyrus would not have been able to recruit Greek mercenaries, with the result that all we have on these events are a few scattered sentences, similar to Plutarch's comments on Ariaramnes' "rebellion" against Xerxes (see chap. 13/2).

The Classical authors are much less loquacious on the next forty years—that is, on virtually the entire reign of Artaxerxes. We have a few narrative sources, but none of them really answers either the questions or the needs of the historian of the Achaemenid Empire. In the *Hellenica*, Xenophon continues his history of relationships among the Greek cities until 362–361. Because of Xenophon as well as the anonymous author of the *Hellenica of Oxyrhynchus*, we are informed about the Greco-Persian conflicts in western Asia Minor and the Great King's increasing role in Greek affairs. On the other hand, Xenophon is no more truly interested in the internal life of the Empire than his predecessors. Diodorus's very limited discussions of these same Greco-Persian matters probably come from Ephorus, all of them stamped with the theme of the political and military weakness of the Great Kings. Ctesias's work, again in the same vein, covers events down to 382. Dinon, another author of a *Persica*, is "a historian in whose account of Persian affairs we have the most confidence," according to C. Nepos, who wrote a *Life of Datames* (*Conon* 5.4◊); but Dinon is scarcely known and then only from fragments, which give the impression that he was particularly interested in court protocols. We know that Ctesias also inspired Aelian, many of whose stories take place in the Persia of Artaxerxes II.

Plutarch turned to Ctesias, Dinon, Xenophon, and a few others when he wrote his *Life of Artaxerxes*, the only biography of a Great King that has reached us. Twelve of its thirty chapters are devoted to relations between the king and Cyrus the Younger (§§2–13) and five to the succession of Artaxerxes II (§§26–30). Diplomatic and military matters do not receive much attention: he only writes about relations with the Spartans

(§§20–22) and an expedition against the Cadusians (§§24–25) and makes a very fleeting allusion to an Egyptian campaign (§§24.1). The composition is basically structured around court personalities and affairs and one person in particular, Parysatis. She gave Cyrus her unconditional support—hence the chapters devoted to the savage revenge carried out against those who opposed her favorite son, especially those who boasted of killing him on the battlefield (§§14–17). At the same time, she used her influence to ease the imprisonment of Clearchus (§18). Stateira soon became the target of Parysatis's vengeful wrath, and she died, poisoned by her mother-in-law (§19). Plutarch was also greatly interested in personal affairs, including Artaxerxes' marriage to his daughter Atossa (§23) and conflict with his oldest son, Darius, regarding Aspasia, Cyrus's former companion (§§26–27.1–5).

The Achaemenid court as seen by Plutarch (and Ctesias) was dominated by the personalities of two exceptional women, Stateira and Parysatis, whose hatred for each other continually smoldered. Parysatis "detested her [Stateira] more than any other person, and because she wished to have no one so powerful as herself" (§17.4◊). After the elimination of her daughter-in-law, her political influence, which had been far from negligible, grew considerably: "She obtained great power with him [Artaxerxes], and was gratified in all her requests," and she was quick to use her influence to grant prerogatives to those who loved the king and his daughter Atossa (§23.1–5◊). The king's anger after the murder of Stateira did not last; after he exiled Parysatis to Babylon (§19.10), he "was reconciled to her, and sent for her, being assured that she had wisdom and courage fit for royal power" (§23.2◊). Another woman, the king's daughter-wife Atossa, seems to have been motivated by a feverish lust for power: Plutarch reports that she supported Ochus more than her other brothers, and she had an affair with him (§26.2–3). Her ambition grew still higher after the execution of the oldest son, Darius, who had spun a plot against his father because he had stolen Aspasia away from him (§§26–27). Ochus was thereafter "high in his hopes, being confident in the influence of Atossa" (§30.1◊). Throughout the biography of Artaxerxes, the Persian court appears to be consumed by the hateful and cruel ambitions of the women, by the conspiracies of eunuchs and courtesans, by assassinations and executions that piled horror on horror, by general recriminations, and by wearisome amorous intrigues. It is thus easy to understand the narrative's disastrous end, coming after the tale of the suicide of one of Artaxerxes' sons and the murder of Arsames by his brother, Ochus: "When [Artaxerxes] heard of the fate of Arsames, he could not sustain it at all, but sinking at once under the weight of his grief and distress, expired" (§30.9◊).

The reign of Artaxerxes was also the heyday of an Athenian orator, Isocrates, another of those largely responsible for the idea of "Persian decadence." Isocrates was a champion of Pan-Hellenism and the war against Persia, and he never ceased urging the Greeks to mount an assault on the Empire he described as decaying. This is especially clear in the *Panegyricus*, which was written at the end of the 380s: if it is to be believed, the Persians no longer controlled a single western land, from the Straits to Egypt. Like many others—especially Xenophon in book VIII of the *Cyropedia*—the Athenian orator found reason for hope in the expedition of the Ten Thousand (a phrase only later applied to Cyrus's Greek mercenaries); the expedition is offered as absolute proof of the Persians' inability to defend even the heart of their Empire. What is customarily called "the great Satraps' Revolt" in the 360s has long seemed to confirm that Artaxerxes II exercised nothing more than ficticious authority over provinces mangled by Greek assaults and the autonomous tendencies of the governors.

We must emphasize once more: ideological decryption of the Classical texts does not by itself license a simplistic reconstruction that would be the exact mirror image of the Greek perspective. It is again appropriate, if we are to make full use of the texts, to ask them questions that go beyond the problem of Greco-Persian relations. In other words, if the Persian situation did seem to worsen, additional sources are needed to prove it. The situation is even more paradoxical because gaps in documentation from the center at the same time require the historian to use the Classical record itself to correct the very vision to which it gave rise. But, when all is said and done, the contradiction is only an illusion, due principally to the Greek authors themselves. A few chapters apart, Plutarch stresses both the Great King's military weakness (20.1–2) and then his eminent prowess as a warrior (24.9–10). The second of these passages derives directly from the royal propaganda. It is thus the historian's duty to try to come to an understanding on the basis of highly ideologized texts that fluctuate between denigration and apologia. To put it another way, the best we can do is to bring to light a few scattered shreds of historical reality.

The View from Susa, Babylon, and Persepolis

The task is particularly delicate because, compared with the Classical sources, the sources from the center remain inadequate. They are not, however, totally absent. Once again, most of our information is on the king's activities as builder, due to inscriptions found at several sites. At the same time, though the royal inscriptions maintain their nonnarrative character, they also exhibit noteworthy innovations that deserve special examination; for example, for the first time a Great King explicitly invokes the protection of Anāhita and Mithra. Finally, it must be remembered that the Classical sources sometimes transmit (more or less precisely and adequately) documents and decrees that came from the royal bureaucracy. An example is the very important reference in Berossus to a royal order concerning the worship of Anāhita in the various regions of the Empire, from Bactra to Sardis. Finally, Plutarch and his sources got wind of regulations and court histories that have made it possible for us to trace the organization of the central court (see chap. 7). It is also Plutarch who provides our only information about the royal investiture ceremony at Pasargadae. The period of Artaxerxes II and his immediate successors is also clarified by the sometimes copious regional bodies of evidence, especially in Asia Minor and Judea–Samaria, but in Babylonia as well. There are even some tablets that offer the only echo, distant and faint though it is, of Cyrus's campaign against his brother, for Xenophon's Belesys can be none other than the Bēlšunu who is now well known from a group of Babylonian tablets.

At the same time, allusions in other Babylonian documents reveal our ignorance. A tablet dated to year 38 of Artaxerxes refers to a battle won by "the king's troops" (*ADRTB* no. –366); another (no. –369), from the seventh month of the 36th year of the same king, mentions that Artaxerxes assembled his troops and left to fight in the territory of Razaunda, probably in Media. Together with some Classical texts that also mention, erratically and incidentally, expeditions of Darius II and his successor in Media (Xenophon, *Hell.* I.2.19) and among the Cadusians (II.1.13; Plutarch, *Art.* 24), these tablets contribute (albeit modestly) to restoring a breadth and depth to the imperial presence that the Greek tradition generally tends to efface from the memory of the reader. Paradoxically, the astronomical tablet that is (albeit modestly) one of the most informative, at least in narrative terms, deals with affairs taking place on the western front, on the island of Cyprus (ADRTB no. 440)!

2. The War of the Two Brothers (404–401)

From Darius II to Artaxerxes II

In addition to illegitimate children born to his concubines (cf. Xenophon, *Anab.* II.4.25), Darius II had several sons from his marriage to Parysatis. The marriage was quite prolific, since according to Ctesias (§49), Darius and Parysatis had thirteen children, most of whom died prematurely. A daughter (Amestris) and at least four sons survived: the oldest, Arses, who was born before 424; then Cyrus, Ostanes, and Oxathres (Plutarch, *Art.* 1.2; Ctesias §49). "Now when Darius lay sick and suspected that the end of his life was near, he wished to have both his sons with him. The elder, as it chanced, was with him already; but Cyrus he summoned from the province over which he had made him satrap" (Xenophon, *Anab.* I.1.1–2◊). Cyrus came, accompanied by Tissaphernes and a troop of Greek mercenaries (I.1.2).

Plutarch says that Cyrus was summoned by his mother, who favored him over his older brother (*Art.* 2.3–4). He also says that she tried to persuade her ill husband to choose Cyrus, using the same arguments that Herodotus attributes to Demaratus when Darius's succession was in question (VII.3). The explicit repetition of the motif is highly suspicious. It is unlikely that Darius II waited until the end of his life to decree the succession. Even though we are not able to determine the exact date, we must assume that the appointment of Arses as crown prince took place several years earlier. The exact reasons for Darius's choice are not available to us, but it is likely that Arses' status as oldest weighed heavily in his favor. In any case, after his father's death, the oldest son seated himself on the throne and took the name Artaxerxes. At this time, he was inaugurated at Pasargadae, in a ceremony described for us only by Plutarch (*Art.* 3.1–2; chap. 13/2).

One tradition states that Arses heard his father's last words on his deathbed (Athenaeus XII.548e). Of course, this scenario very much reminds us of the scene Xenophon depicts (imagines!) at the end of the *Cyropaedia* (VIII.7.5–28◊): sensing his declining vigor, Cyrus summoned Cambyses, Tanaoxares [Bardiya], and the highest officials. Xenophon wrote a long speech for the king, and at the end of this utterance he breathed his last. In the speech, he divides his powers between his two sons: the older, Cambyses, received the kingship, and the younger, an immense satrapal territory. Cyrus, who was fully aware of the potential dangers surrounding his succession, adjures his sons to live in harmony, especially impressing on the second-born the requirement "to let no one more readily than yourself yield obedience to your brother or more zealously support him." The tradition recorded by Athenaeus thus very likely represents a component of court propaganda that originally was intended to legitimate Artaxerxes II rather than Cyrus the Younger.

Another tradition states that the real motive for summoning Cyrus was quite different from the motive that Plutarch reports. Cyrus was accused of executing two members of the royal family (Autoboisaces and Mitraeus) at Sardis (Xenophon, *Hell.* II.1.8). According to this theory, he was summoned to answer for his actions. These data are both unverifiable and probable. There is in fact hardly any doubt that, while remaining completely loyal to his father, Cyrus garnered all the profit he possibly could from the very high position that Darius had awarded him at Sardis. A series of coins apparently issued during this period is quite remarkable: they are Athenian "owls" (tetradrachms) overstruck with a portrait of a king, who surely must be Darius II. More interestingly, some individual examples bear a second portrait. This much smaller portrait has two characteristics: it does not wear the royal *kidaris*, and it is beardless. It is thus highly likely that it represents Cyrus. This definitely is not coinage of revolution—that is, these imitations of Athenian owls were without doubt struck at Sardis by the *karanos* to pay the wages of Peloponnesian military units. Nonetheless, they also demonstrate the very high opinion that Cyrus had of himself and of his own authority.

According to Plutarch, it was shortly before Artaxerxes' investiture ceremony that Cyrus first overtly displayed his ambition. Tissaphernes relied on the testimony of the *magus* who had overseen the education of Cyrus and thus brought charges against him: "as though he had been about to lie in wait for the king in the temple, and to assault and assassinate him as he was putting off his garment [in order to don the robe of Cyrus the Elder]. Some affirm that he was apprehended upon this impeachment, others that he had entered the temple and was pointed out there, as he lay lurking by the priest." He was rescued from execution only by the immediate pleas of Parysatis: "Artaxerxes . . . sent him away again to the sea" (*Art.* 3.3–6◊). The *magus*'s accusations appear particularly legitimate because he "was likely to be as much disappointed as any man that his pupil did not succeed to the throne" (*Art.* 3.3◊). Even though this story gives the impression that Cyrus had other support at court besides his mother's (which can hardly be doubted), it remains hard to believe. It is hard to imagine a pretender to the throne defiling the sanctuary of Anāhita. The story was doubtless invented later as a part of the royal propaganda that was designed to smear the memory of the rebellious brother. However, the existence of conflict at this time cannot be denied. Though Xenophon does not repeat the story presented by Plutarch, he reports that, after Artaxerxes' accesssion, Cyrus was (falsely) denounced by Tissaphernes and that he owed his survival to the intervention of his mother (*Anab.* I.1.3).

Cyrus's Preparations and Artaxerxes' Response: From Memphis to Sardis

After his brother was inaugurated, Cyrus returned to Sardis, which, "however, could no longer content him; . . . his resentment . . . made him more eagerly desirous of the kingdom than before" (*Art.* 3.6;◊ cf. Xenophon, *Anab.* I.1.4). Tissaphernes, whom he (formerly) "considered a friend" (*Anab.* I.1.2), was always at his side. Recent events had just proved to him that Tissaphernes in fact wanted only to get rid of him. At first, then, Cyrus considered it wise to act in great secrecy, "so that he might take the King as completely unprepared as possible" (*Anab.* I.1.6◊). He continued to correspond regularly with his brother (*Anab.* I.1.8; Plutarch, *Art.* 4.3), and he entertained his envoys lavishly, hoping to entice them to his side (I.1.5). Additionally, he remitted the tribute to the court regularly (I.1.8).

In order to amass troops, he entered into secret agreements with mercenary commanders who were his guests; he asked each one to keep his contingent ready and to respond immediately to any summons that might be sent (I.1.6–11). At the same time, he parleyed with the Spartan authorities, reminding them of the services he had rendered them earlier during their fight against the Athenian districts in Asia Minor. Lacedaemon responded positively to his contact: it officially authorized Clearchus to place himself at the service of Persia (*Art.* 6.5) and ordered the head of the navy "to hold himself under

Cyrus' orders, in case he had any request to make" (*Hell.* III.1.1◊). It appears that the Lacedaemonian authorities were careful not to declare themselves too openly, preferring to await the outcome of the pending confrontation between the two brothers (Diodorus XIV.21.1; cf. 11.2). Finally, both Diodorus (XIV.35.2) and Xenophon indicate that a large number of Greek cities defected to Cyrus, abandoning Tissaphernes, to whom they "had originally belonged . . . , by gift of the King" (*Anab.* I.1.6◊). Cyrus immediately besieged Miletus when it refused to accept his authority (I.1.7).

Cyrus came up with all sorts of excuses to justify his military preparations. First of all, he said that he was preparing to make war on Tissaphernes, who had exiled the opposition in order to hold onto Miletus (*Anab.* I.1.7). This was the explanation that he gave two of the Greek mercenary commanders, "saying that he intended to make war upon Tissaphernes with the aid of the Milesian exiles" (I.1.11◊). Next, when he gathered his troops at Sardis in the spring of 401, "the pretext he offered was that he wished to drive the Pisidians out of his land entirely" (I.2.1◊). This ruse was intended for the Greek mercenaries, who had no interest in marching against the Great King personally. It was also meant to allay the suspicion of the king's men, since expeditions against the Pisidians were becoming quite a routine affair. Tissaphernes was not taken in, since he "had taken note of these proceedings and come to the conclusion that Cyrus' preparations were too extensive to be against the Pisidians; he accordingly made his way to the King as quickly as he could, with about five hundred horsemen. And when the King heard from Tissaphernes about Cyrus' array, he set about making counterpreparations" (I.2.4–5◊). This at any rate is Xenophon's summary version of Persian affairs in Asia Minor between 404 and 401.

In Xenophon's reading, Artaxerxes possessed a strange blindness: "The King failed to perceive the plot against himself, but believed that Cyrus was spending money on his troops because he was at war with Tissaphernes. Consequently he was not at all displeased at their being at war" (I.1.8◊). It is hard to believe, despite Plutarch (*Art.* 4.3), that the influence of Parysatis was sufficient to deceive Artaxerxes regarding Cyrus's true intentions. The comings and goings between Sardis and the central court imply that numerous reports reached the Great King. It is true that Xenophon's remark could be explained by a royal policy that was intended to counterbalance one satrap's power with another's. But it is difficult to understand why Artaxerxes chose to support his brother, whose ambition had long been known to him — even though Cyrus was careful to send to the court "the tribute which came in from the cities he chanced to have that belonged to Tissaphernes" (I.1.8◊). Nothing suggests that Artaxerxes ever replied favorably to Cyrus, who "urged . . . that these Ionian cities should be given to him instead of remaining under the rule of Tissaphernes."◊ Instead, one gets the impression that these interpretations are integrated a little too successfully into the tendentious portrait of the king found especially in the opening chapters of Plutarch, who delights in contrasting the irresolute and dithering (*mellēsis*) character of Artaxerxes (§4.4) with his brother's energetic ambition (§6.1).

The case of Orontas brings very different thoughts to mind. Here is how Cyrus himself later portrays this person, whom he is judging on grounds of treason in summer 401: "This man was given me at first by my father, to be my subject; then, at the bidding, as he himself said, of my brother, this man levied war upon me, holding the citadel of Sardis" (I.6.6◊). Orontas, the phrourarch of Sardis, had at some point received royal orders to engage in armed combat against the followers of Cyrus, who even accused him of deserting to the Mysians and ravaging territory subject to Cyrus's control (I.6.7). The example strongly suggests that the war between Artaxerxes and Cyrus began—albeit in embryonic form—long before the departure from Sardis in March 401 and that Tissaphernes and Orontas had been ordered by the king to thwart the ambitions of his younger brother.

Ephorus provides a version of the dating and source of the accusations against Cyrus that is completely different from Xenophon's; it is transmitted by Diodorus (XIV.11.1–4), Nepos (*Alc.* 9.3–4), and Plutarch (*Alc.* 37.8–39). According to Ephorus, Alcibiades was exiled from Athens and driven completely away; he took refuge at the court of Pharnabazus at Dascylium, who (in accordance with a longstanding Achaemenid policy) gave him the town of Grynium so that he could provide for his needs. At this point, Alcibiades sought an alliance with the Great King in order to reopen the war against Sparta. When he learned of Cyrus's preparations, he saw a way of garnering the favor of Artaxerxes, and he pestered Pharnabazus for an official safe-conduct (*halmi* in the PF, *adeia* in Demosthenes XXIII.159), and Pharnabazus authorized it. However, according to Diodorus, Pharnabazus "usurped the function of reporter and sent trusted men to disclose the matter to the King." He also assassinated Alcibiades while he was en route, with the assistance of a mysterious "satrap of Paphlagonia" (Diodorus XIV.11.3◊). According to this version, Artaxerxes was already informed of his brother's military preparations by 404–403.

So we are faced with two contradictory accounts. It is likely that, as on a previous occasion (Themistocles' arrival in Asia Minor: chap. 13/9), one comes from the court of Sardis, the other from the court of Dascylium. How can we choose one? We might eliminate the second account by suggesting that in this passage, as in at least one other case (XIV.35.1), Diodorus (Ephorus) simply confused Pharnabazus and Tissaphernes. But an analysis of Alcibiades' route confirms that he did indeed leave from Dascylium. We might nonetheless conclude that the Dascylium version was invented later in order to reinforce Pharnabazus's status vis-à-vis Tissaphernes, who received wide authority in Asia Minor after the battle of Cunaxa. This is a perfectly reasonable hypothesis—apart from the fact that the competition between the two satraps is attested beginning at least as early as 412. We may add that the actions taken by Darius II in 407 could only have aroused Pharnabazus's hostility against Cyrus, who, as general commander of the maritime regions, had taken control of "Aeolis, and the neighbouring territories" (cf. Diodorus XIV.19.6◊); these regions had always been disputed by Dascylium and Sardis. It is logical to prefer Pharnabazus's version, to the extent that it offers a picture of the central authority that is consistent with the policy it was then following at Sardis against Cyrus. The only counterargument comes from Diodorus himself—probably still following Ephorus: after describing Cyrus's march to Babylonia, he presents Artaxerxes' situation as follows: he "had learned some time before (*palai*) from Pharnabazus that Cyrus was secretly collecting an army to lead against him, and when he now (*tote*) learned that he was on the march [toward the High Country (*anabasis*)], he summoned his armaments from every place to Ecbatana in Media" (XIV.22.1◊). By stating once more that Pharnabazus had warned the king much earlier, Diodorus also implies that he had done nothing in the interim—although the expression used could also be understood to mean that the order quoted by Diodorus consisted simply of ordering already-mobilized troops to move to their mustering stations.

At the same time, it is clear that the tales of the Greek authors are devoted exclusively to Cyrus's campaign. This leads to another theory: the Classical sources pass over important events in other regions of the Empire in silence, which would explain Artaxerxes' apparent lack of activity better than does a secret undertaking by Cyrus. This interpretation is easy to test, if not to establish with complete certainty. In fact, at this time, another front required the full, vigilant attention of Artaxerxes—Egypt. We know for a fact that, after Cyrus's arrival in Cilicia (summer of 401), the *strategos* Abrocomas turned toward the Euphrates and then toward Babylonia, having "turned about in his journey from Phoenicia" (*Anab.* I.4.5◊). The meaning is clear: as in many later episodes, the concentration of an army in Phoenicia signified an offensive against the Nile Valley. The Elephantine documents confirm that there was an Egyptian revolt. The last document dated to Artaxerxes II at Elephantine is from the end of 401 (*DAE* 53 [*BMAP* 12]). Another, from September 400, refers to year 5 of King Amyrtaeus (*DAE* 7 [*AP* 35]), who therefore must have been proclaimed pharaoh during 404. He must have been a descendant of the rebels that we know were in the Delta during the fifth century—specifically, a grandson of Amyrtaeus I (cf. Herodotus III.15). The Elephantine documents show that between 404 and 400 (or even 398) Upper Egypt remained under Persian control but that, conversely, Amyrtaeus dominated all or part of the Delta. It was obviously in order to subdue him, probably shortly after his accession, that Artaxerxes assembled an army in Phoenicia under the command of Abrocomas (cf. Isocrates, *Phil.* 101). This was not the first time that the Egyptian dynasts of the Delta tried to profit from a disputed succession (cf. Diodorus XI.71.3). But as it happens, circumstances were particularly favorable to them. It is, moreover, not impossible that Cyrus had consciously taken advantage of the situation then prevailing in the Nile Valley; he was certainly not unaware of events in Egypt. We know in fact that one of his closest lieutenants was Tamos, probably an Egyptian-born Carian from Memphis. Indeed, we learn that, after Cyrus's death, Tamos feared Tissaphernes' vengeance and fled to Egypt with his family and his wealth. He expected to take refuge with Psammetichus, "king of the Egyptians, who was a descendant of the famous Psammetichus." There is no reason to challenge this testimony from Diodorus (XIV.35.4◊) on the grounds that he confused Amyrtaeus and Psammetichus; as in previous periods, the Delta was divided among several rival dynasts. Indeed, it is quite interesting to observe that, according to Diodorus, Tamos expected the protection of Psammetichus, "because of a good turn he had done the king in the past." Diodorus offers no relevant details, but we might ask whether Tamos had previously been instructed by Cyrus to initiate a relationship with the Egyptian dynast on the chance that he might thus strike a fatal blow to Achaemenid interests in Egypt. In any case, Cyrus could not have been unaware that, whatever Abrocomas would decide (whether to submit to him or to remain faithful to the Great King), the offensive he was leading against his brother would interrupt the reconquest of Egypt already in progress.

It is thus easy to understand why the Great King did not immediately in 404–401 use the information provided by Pharnabazus. He first ordered a mobilization to reconquer Egypt. We thus also understand why Xenophon and Ephorus agree on one point: Artaxerxes was not able to proceed with his preparations until later, because he was otherwise occupied (*Anab.* I.2.4–5; Diodorus XIV.22.1). In order to do battle with his brother between 404 and 401, then, Artaxerxes was only able to count on the loyalty of his people in Asia Minor, such as Tissaphernes, Orontas, and certainly Pharnabazus as well, in the hope that open warfare at Sardis and in Ionia would deter Cyrus from marching against him. This explains the king's satisfaction at seeing Cyrus and Tissaphernes at each other's throats (I.1.8), an observation that Xenophon expanded into an incomplete and probably erroneous interpretation. When Tissaphernes left Asia Minor in the spring of 401, it was not really that he intended to inform the king of Cyrus's already well-known preparations; more simply, once Cyrus's revolt had officially begun, he decided immediately to place himself under the authority of the Great King, who awarded him a very high command in the army he had assembled (*Anab.* I.7.12, 8.9).

Cyrus the Younger's Army

The contingents summoned by Cyrus assembled at Sardis. Each mercenary commander brought his men; they came from Asian cities but mainly from the Peloponnesus—8,100 troops all together (*Anab.* I.2.3–4). At Colossae, Menon of Thessaly joined up, leading 1,500 more soldiers (I.2.6); at Celaenae in Greater Phrygia, the army was filled out with the men of the exiled Lacedaemonian Clearchus (2,000), Sosis the Syracusan (300), and Agias the Arcadian (1,000). The Greek army reviewed by Cyrus in the capital of Greater Phrygia thus amounted to 12,900 men, and at Issus the 700 hoplites of the Spartan Cheirisophus joined them, arriving by sea (I.4.2). It is this assemblage that a later tradition marked by apologetic tendencies refers to collectively as the Ten Thousand. They are the main topic of Xenophon's narrative, along with the contentious relations among its leaders (especially Clearchus and Menon) and their persistent reluctance to follow Cyrus beyond Tarsus and the Euphrates. At first sight, the attraction of using Greek infantrymen (hoplites and peltasts) is easily explained: they had especially good reputations as a result of their long combat experience (cf. Diodorus XIV.23.4), and Cyrus himself adopted some of the Greek equipment (breastplates and swords) to equip the elite of his cavalry (XIV.22.6; cf. *Anab.* I.8.7). In comparison with everything known before, this is the first time a Persian leader made such massive use of mercenaries.

Xenophon's (and other Greeks') view needs several major corrections. As he himself notes, Cyrus's army included Greeks and barbarians (I.2.16). There were two armies side by side, Greek and barbarian (Ctesias §58), just as there were two navies, with the barbarian navy under the command of Tamos (Diodorus XIV.19.5). There were two distinct commands, though Cyrus himself remained commander-in-chief (XIV.19.9). At Cunaxa, the two armies took up separate positions (Xenophon, *Anab.* I.8.14); only 1,000 of the barbarian army, men from the Paphlagonian contingent, were arrayed alongside Clearchus, commander of the Greeks (I.8.5; Diodorus XIV.22.5). On the left flank were the Paphlagonians—whose cavalry was particularly famous (*Anab.* V.6.8)—as well as the troops drafted from Phrygia and Lydia, as well as 1,000 horsemen under the command of Ariaeus. Cyrus placed himself at the center of the formation, surrounded by the bravest of the Persians and the other barbarians (*Anab.* I.8.5; Diodorus XIV.22.5–6). Also in the center were contingents led by faithful subjects such as Procles, "the ruler of Teuthrania" and a descendant of the Demaratus to whom Xerxes had granted territory in Aeolis (*Anab.* II.1.3◊). In sum, Cyrus had assembled all the territorial forces of Asia Minor: contingents of subject peoples (Paphlagonians), horsemen levied from the Persians of the imperial diaspora, and soldiers provided by families who had settled in Asia Minor after the time of Xerxes (see chap. 13/9). Cyrus was thus not content with gathering Greek mercenaries; he also ordered a general mobilization throughout Asia Minor (Didorus XIV.19.7), and this enabled him to recruit a cavalry, without which he would never have been able to commence such an enterprise (cf. *Anab.* II.4.6).

Propaganda and Legitimation

For his project to succeed, the young prince, while assembling a cohesive fighting force, had to generate personal loyalty strong enough to break the links that bound the Persians to the Great King. Without being fully aware of the fact, all the ancient authors report that the armed conflict was accompanied by a vigorous propaganda war:

> Yet busy, factious men, that delighted in change (*hoi neōteriskoi kai polypragmones*), professed it to be their opinion that the times needed Cyrus, a man of great spirit, an excellent warrior, and a lover of his friends, and that the largeness of their empire required a bold and enterprising prince. (Plutarch, *Art.* 6.1◊)

Though Plutarch's words confirm that he unfailingly favors stability and order, the themes he conveys are the very ones that Cyrus's camp undertook to propagate. The passage is even more significant because it is embedded within a comparison of Cyrus and his brother, who appears to be known for his "natural dilatoriness . . . which was taken by many for clemency" (4.4◊). To illustrate his thesis, Plutarch cites the king's *polydōria* and gifts offered him by the simple peasants, albeit without understanding their significance, at least in this passage (cf. *Mor.* 172b and Aelian, *VH* I.31–33). He also notes that Artaxerxes allowed his younger brothers to partake of his table, and his wife to travel in an open carriage (§4.4–5; 5; cf. *Mor.* 173f). Cyrus is contrasted to the king, who was criticized as weak in character:

> among many other high praises of himself, . . . said he had the stronger soul; was more a philosopher and a better Magian; and could drink and bear more wine than his brother, who, as he averred, was such a coward and so little like a man, that he could neither sit his horse in hunting nor his throne in time of danger. (§6.5◊; cf. *Mor.* 173e–f)

This quotation does not call for much comment, because it is obvious that by proclamations of this sort Cyrus intended to legitimate his claim to supreme authority by disqualifying his brother with respect to traditional Achaemenid royal ideological attributes.

The thesis is consciously and systematically laid out by Xenophon in his eulogy for Cyrus: Cyrus from his youth was regarded as "the best of them," courageous in both the hunt and war; he was loyal in his commitments, merciless toward delinquents of any stripe, bringing order and security throughout his territory. Xenophon and others particularly stress that he was diligent in rewarding excellence, that "he never let . . . zeal go unrewarded," that he displayed unparalleled *polydōria*, sending his Friends food from his table (*Anab.* I.9.1–28◊). Moreover, Cyrus was also a "good gardener" (Xenophon, *Oec.* IV.20–25)—a virtue later exalted by the propaganda that came from Parysatis's entourage (chap. 6/5). In short, "no man, Greek or barbarian, has ever been loved by a greater number of people" (*Anab.* I.9.28◊), and, "if Cyrus had only lived, . . . he would have proved an excellent ruler" (*Oec.* IV.18). Though the clear similarities with the *Cyropaedia* indicate that Xenophon is here painting a portrait of the ideal king, what we know about the monarchic ideology also shows that the materials used to paint this portrait were the virtues that all genuine Achaemenid documents ascribe to the Great King (cf. chap. 6).

The gods themselves legitimated the pretender's royal ambitions, and this can be gleaned from a story told by Xenophon. In July 401, Cyrus's army arrived at Thapsacus on the Euphrates, "the width of which was four stadia [ca. 700 m]" (*Anab.* I.4.11◊). In the course of his retreat, Abrocomas had burned the bridges (4.18◊): "Cyrus proceeded to cross the river, and the rest of the army followed him, to the last man. And in the crossing no one was wetted above the breast by the water." There is nothing remarkable about this, since at that time the river was at a low flow, and the soldiers waded across. What is more interesting is the ensuing interpretation of this "stunt":

> The people of Thapsacus said that this river had never been passable on foot except at this time. . . . It seemed, accordingly, that here was a divine (*theios*) intervention, and that the river had plainly retired before Cyrus because he was destined to be king. (I.4.18◊)

We have a parallel episode in Plutarch's *Life of Lucullus*. During his Armenian campaign, the Roman Lucullus too found himself at odds with unenthusiastic soldiers (§24.1). The army reached the Euphrates at flood, "finding the waters high and rough from the winter." During the night, inexplicably, the level of the waters fell, and at dawn the river had returned to its bed:

> The inhabitants, discovering the little islands in the river, and the water stagnating among them, a thing which had rarely happened before, made obeisance to Lucullus, before whom the very river was humble and submissive, and yielded an easy and swift passage. (§24.2◊)

The tradition is particularly interesting in that the Lucullus episode is set in Iranian territory (Acilisene) at the very location of a famous sanctuary of Anāhita, who would soon issue an additional favorable omen to the Roman—a heifer branded with the mark of the goddess, a torch, offered herself up. Lucullus sacrificed her; "besides which, he offered also a bull to Euphrates, for his safe passage" (§24.4–5◊). We can end with another parallel, taken from Tacitus (*Ann.* VI.37): Vitellius and Tiridates reached the banks of the Euphrates with their troops; the Roman Vitellius offered a *suovetaurile* to the gods, according to Roman custom, while Tiridates "sacrificed a horse in honor of the river":

> The inhabitants proclaimed that without any rain the Euphrates had just risen all by itself beyond measure, and that the cleansing foam formed circles that looked like nothing so much as diadems, portent of a favorable omen.

All of these stories reflect *topoi* that are well grounded in royal Near Eastern literature. How often, for example, do the Assyrian kings claim to have crossed torrents or precipices without hindrance! Furthermore, privileged relationships between the king, the waters, and the rivers are found in these stories, and these relationships also appear in a story regarding Cyrus the Elder that Herodotus transmits (I.188).

Personal and Dynastic Loyalty

It is clear, at least to hear Xenophon tell it, that Cyrus's vaunted *polydōria* toward "the barbarians of his own province" was designed to ensure that they "should be capable soldiers and should feel kindly (*eunoia*) toward him" (I.1.5◊). There is no doubt that Cyrus surrounded himself with men in whose loyalty he was completely confident (cf. Diodorus XIV.19.9). His purpose was to generate loyalty toward himself that would rival the loyalty any Persian might show to their king (*Anab.* I.6.6–8). But does Cyrus's propaganda imply that he was successful, or does it show that he needed to persuade those who were reluctant to embrace his cause? This question is somewhat artificial, since the two possible answers are not mutually exclusive. Nevertheless, the question has decisive importance, which can be stated a bit more precisely: Were all of the Persians of Asia Minor unreservedly committed to the cause of the one who already considered himself the equal of a king?

There is no doubt regarding the ones who joined him. His closest confidants were those whom Xenophon calls his 'Faithful' (*pistoi*; cf. I.5.15)—his *bandaka*, those bound to him by personal ties, symbolized by a handclasp before the gods (I.6.6–7). The small group that remained faithful to the end were his Tablemates (*homotrapezoi*) (I.8.25), a title that by itself indicates that Cyrus had re-created a court hierarchy based on the royal court. Among his "Faithful," Xenophon singles out Artapates, "the most faithful of Cyrus' chamberlains" (6.11,✧ 8.28); the rebel Orontas was executed in Artapates' tent (6.11). One tradition claims that Artapates killed himself on his master's corpse: "he had a dagger (*akinakēs*) of gold, and he also wore a necklace and bracelets and all the other ornaments that the noblest Persians (*hoi aristoi Persōn*) wear; for he had been honored (*timē*) by Cyrus because of his affection (*eunoia*) and fidelity (*pistotēs*)" (8.29✧). The gold *akinakēs* was clearly a "royal" gift (cf. I.3.27), which distinguished him from other Persian aristocrats, who all wore glittering robes decorated with sumptuous jewels (I.5.8).

The Persians of Asia Minor who sided with Cyrus generally are referred to by Diodorus as "satraps" (XIV.35.2). Alongside unnamed Persians who held subordinate commands (XIV.19.9: in the army), Diodorus refers to relatives (*syggeneis*) of Cyrus who were governors of Lydia and Phrygia (XIV.19.6). On rare occasions, a few Persians are explicitly named by the ancient authors: Artaozus and Mithradates, for example, "who had been most faithful friends of Cyrus" (II.5.35✧); also Satiphernes, "a noble man and a faithful friend to Cyrus" (Plutarch, *Art.* 11.2✧); Ariaeus, "Cyrus's satrap," who was one of his Friends (11.1✧) and commanded the cavalry on the left flank in the battle of Cunaxa (Diodorus XIV.24.1; cf. *Anab.* I.8.5: *Kyrou hyparkhos*). He was "most highly honoured by Cyrus" (III.2.5✧), and he was certainly of noble origin (cf. II.1.1–4). Xenophon also mentions Pategyas, "a trusty Persian of Cyrus' staff" (I.8.1✧).

But the problem remains unresolved: Do these examples indicate a general eagerness to march against Artaxerxes? For Xenophon, the question answers itself. The best proof of Cyrus's kingly merit, he says, is the following observation: "Although Cyrus was a slave, no one deserted him to join the King . . . ; on the other hand, many went over from the King to Cyrus after the two had become enemies" (*Anab.* I.9.29;✧ cf. *Oec.* IV.18). Ctesias provides confirmation: "Many turncoats changed from Artaxerxes to Cyrus, but not one changed from Cyrus to Artaxerxes" (§58). Here we find one of the justifications that Alexander later offered to contest the legitimacy of Darius III's authority (Arrian II.14.7): the true leader must know how to inspire the loyalty and devotion of his followers.

What was the truth? In fact, though "tens of thousands" of turncoats are mentioned (*Oec.* IV.18), none but the 400 Greek mercenaries of Abrocomas can be pinpointed, and they no doubt were attracted by hope for high wages (*Anab.* I.4.3). Though hardly representative politically, this shift in allegiance compensated to some extent for the defection of two mercenary leaders, Xennias and Pasion, who, as soon as Cyrus's real destination became known, chose to board ship and return to Greece (I.4.7). Cyrus was so unsure of his Greeks that he had taken the precaution of holding the wives and children of the *strategoi* hostage, at Tralles (I.4.8). It is perhaps for the same sort of reason that the Lydian market, where the soldiers could provision themselves, was located "in the barbarian army" (I.3.14, 5.6). To stimulate the Greeks to follow where he wanted to lead them, Cyrus constantly resorted to ruse and deception. The Pisidian goal (see p. 617) proved to have been a decoy as soon as the army arrived at Tarsus. The soldiers refused to return to the road for 20 days, "for they suspected by this time that they were going against the King" (I.3.1◊). A real riot erupted against Clearchus, because many of the mercenaries wanted to return on their own (I.3.1–14). At this point, Cyrus claimed that he was marching only against Abrocomas on the Euphrates and that, once they got there, they would see what the appropriate course of action would be (I.3.20); according to Diodorus, he announced that he was leading them "against a certain satrap of Syria" (XIV.20.5◊). Not until they arrived at Thapsacus did he openly unveil his plans; there he calmed the reawakening uneasiness with promises of increased pay (I.4.11–13). Apparently Cyrus's promises failed to persuade all of the Greeks (4.13). In other cases, their loyalty remained conditional, as is seen by the assurances Cyrus proceeded to give: "he promised that he would give every man five minas in silver when they reached Babylon and their pay in full until he brought the Greeks back to Ionia again" (*Anab.* I.4.13◊).

Now let us return to the perspective of the Persian aristocracy. The reality is that Ctesias gives but a single example of defectors to Cyrus: Arbarius apparently defected shortly before the decisive battle. But we do not know whether this is the same person as the Arbarius who twenty years later betrayed Secundianus to join Ochus/Darius II (§47). And even this example is scarcely convincing, since Ctesias states that this Arbarius "was denounced" (§58), an indication that he was an isolated case, even if some of his compatriots then joined Cyrus's side (*Anab.* I.7.2). Xenophon, as an exception to the rule he had just illustrated, gives the example of Orontas, who was convicted of treason against Cyrus. The author places the episode in Babylonia (I.6). Orontas was a member of the highest nobility and enjoyed immense prestige: "a Persian, who was related to the King by birth and was reckoned among the best of the Persians in matters of war" (§6.1◊). Under the pretext of hindering the activities of marauders from the royal army, he had asked Cyrus to entrust a corps of horsemen to him. At the same time, he sent a letter to Artaxerxes, announcing his change of allegiance. But he was betrayed by the messenger and arrested, convicted, and executed.

Cyrus convened a tribunal to try him, comprising the seven most distinguished Persians among his attendants; he included Clearchus, the most faithful of the Greek *strategoi* (§6.4–5). The verdict was signaled in the traditional way: "Every man of them arose . . . and took him by the girdle, as a sign that he was condemned to death" (§6.10;◊ cf. Diodorus XVII.30.4). Xenophon interjects that even the relatives (*syggeneis*) of the accused had to perform the fatal gesture. Some additional details indicate that Orontas had a large network of associates. Xenophon notes, for instance, that even after his sentencing, "when the men who in former days were wont to do him homage saw him, they made their obeisance even then, although they knew that he was being led forth to death" (§6.10◊). The end of the episode is equally revealing: "Now after he had been conducted into the tent of Artapates, the most faithful of Cyrus' chamberlains, from that moment no man ever saw Orontas living or dead, nor could anyone say from actual knowledge how he was put to death,—it was all conjectures, of one sort and another; and no grave of his was ever seen" (§6.11◊). The confidentiality imposed by Cyrus was probably intended to forestall any official mourning in honor of the condemned man. It is also quite noteworthy that Cyrus did not call on Persian troops, but on Greek detachments that were not susceptible to being torn between conflicting loyalties, to guard the tent where the trial was being conducted (§6.4). The inclusion of the Greek Clearchus among the judges was certainly also due to the same considerations. Convening the seven most distinguished Persians was probably intended to assure the support of fully faithful Persians; by including kinsmen of the accused, Cyrus was also attempting to compel them to restate publicly their personal loyalty to him.

Furthermore, it can be deduced from Xenophon's tale itself that Orontas was not the only one to exhibit misgivings regarding Cyrus. Without stressing it, Xenophon in fact notes that a few weeks earlier, in Lycaonia, "Cyrus put to death a Persian named Megaphernes, who was a wearer of the royal purple" (*phoinikistēs basileios*; I.2.20✧). We know nothing further about this person; his job may have allowed him to set up a relationship with Artaxerxes' camp. Xenophon adds that someone else was put to death at the same time. He describes him with a less than clear phrase: "another dignitary among his subordinates" (*heis tōn hyparkhōn dynastēs*; 2.20✧). Could this have been one of the officers in charge of a district (cf. *Hell.* III.1.12)? Cyrus did in fact need their support in order to have access to the treasuries and well-stocked storehouses along the route. So far, he had not encountered any major obstacles. The authorities at Celaenae (cf. Plutarch, *Them.* 30.1), for example, clearly did not oppose his requests (*Anab.* I.2.7–9). This interpretation is supported by an action that Cyrus took in Lycaonia: "This country he gave over to the Greeks to plunder, on the ground that it was hostile territory" (*polemia khōra*; 2.19✧). This phrase very plainly refers to a land that could be ravaged because it had not submitted. This was also the case in Cilicia prior to the submission of the *syennesis*; as soon as he had submitted, Cyrus promised "that his land should not be plundered any more and that they might take back the slaves that had been seized in case they should chance upon them anywhere" (I.2.27✧).

Earlier on, in fact, the *syennesis* had refused to ally himself with Cyrus. He was soon forced to do so by the simultaneous arrival of Cyrus's army and navy (I.2.21–26). According to Xenophon, the *syennesis* agreed to give Cyrus large sums of money for his army, and Cyrus in return presented such gifts of honor as the Great Kings usually bestowed (2.27). Clearly, the *syennesis*'s alliance was purely tactical. Ctesias stresses it: "He fought (*synemakhei*) both at the side of Cyrus and for the side of Artaxerxes" (§58). Photius's summary, fortunately, is filled in by the information given by Diodorus (XIV.20.3✧):

> On learning the truth about the war [Syennesis] agreed to join him as an ally against Artaxerxes; and he sent one of his two sons along with Cyrus, giving him also a strong contingent of Cilicians for his army. For Syennesis, being by nature unscrupulous and having adjusted himself to the uncertainty of Fortune, had dispatched his other son secretly to the King to reveal to him the armaments that had been gathered against him and to assure him that he took the part of (*symmakhia*) Cyrus out of necessity, but that he was still faithful (*eunoia*) to the King and, when the opportunity arose, would desert Cyrus and join the army of the King.

The *syennesis* was certainly not the only one to adopt an attitude guided by an eye on the future. Diodorus notes, for instance, that "the Lacedaemonians had not yet openly entered upon the war, but were concealing their purpose, awaiting the turn of the war" (XIV.21.2✧).

The ancient authors were merely sharing in the anxiety of the Greeks, who, it must be noted, were especially intimidated by the Empire's vastness: "The word had got about that it was a four months' march for an army to Bactria" (Diodorus XIV.20.4✧)! We know nothing of the reactions of the "barbarian army." According to Diodorus, the Persian high command had been informed of the true objective ever since Cyrus's departure from Sardis (XIV.19.9). Diodorus's phrasing implies that the ordinary troops (*to plēthos*) had been left out of this confidence, just like the Greeks. Of course, it was legitimate to answer the call of the *karanos* to march against the Pisidians (or "some rebellious Cilician tyrants": Diodorus XIV.19.3), but it was dangerous to take arms against the Great King. It is true that no proof can be offered, but it is possible that stirrings of discontent or reluctance saw the light of day among the "barbarian" contingents as well.

Xenophon states that "no man, Greek or barbarian, has ever been loved by a greater number of people" (I.9.28◇). It is possible that he is here referring, in an apologetic fashion, to the support Cyrus received from the Greek cities of Asia Minor (I.1.7; Diodorus XIV.35.2). In any case, Cyrus's entourage included non-Persians as well (cf. I.9.28). The processes by which mercenaries were enlisted show that Cyrus entered into personal hospitality pacts with several Greeks: Aristippus the Thessalian, Proxenus the Boeotian, Sophaenetus the Stymphalian, and Socrates the Achaean (I.1.10–11). Before the revolt started, Xenias the Arcadian "commanded for him the mercenary force in the cities" of Ionia (I.2.1◇). Cyrus attempted to gather around him the Greek exiles, such as the Milesians (I.2.2), and Clearchus as well, who had been exiled from Lacedaemon and who gathered a troop of mercenaries for his own purposes (I.1.9). Cyrus considered him "the man who was honored above the rest of the Greeks" (I.6.6◇) and certainly the most faithful of the mercenary leaders—which is why he later enjoyed the special protection of Parysatis. We also know of a certain Gaulites, "a Samian exile who was there and was in the confidence of Cyrus" (I.7.5◇); during the Ionian War, he had worked closely with Tissaphernes; Thucydides represents him as "a Carian, who spoke the two languages" (VIII.85.2◇). We can also mention the Carian-Memphite Tamos, "trusted friend" of Cyrus, who appointed him governor "of Ionia, Aeolis, and the neighboring territories" before he departed (Diodorus XIV.19.6◇) and also "commander of the barbarian fleet" (XIV.19.5◇; *Anab.* I.2.21). His son, Glos, participated in the expedition against Artaxerxes (*Anab.* II.1.3).

Does the presence of a significant number of non-Persians around Cyrus indicate a growing intimacy of relationships between the Persians of Asia Minor and their neighbors, and/or does it reflect a specific policy of Cyrus, who was anxious to fend off the hostility of some Persians of the western region? It is difficult to answer these questions with complete certainty. A man such as Tamos, for example, began his career well before Cyrus's arrival at Sardis. One can hardly fail to be fascinated, though, by the division of powers Cyrus decided on before beginning his campaign. Though Persians were put in charge of Lydia and Phrygia, Tamos, as we have just seen, received the command "of Ionia, Aeolis, and the neighboring territories" (XIV.19.6◇). In particular, it is remarkable that he governed Aeolis and its neighbors, but there is no doubt that this arrangement goes back to 407. On the other hand, the version of Ephorus (analyzed above) implies that Pharnabazus was inducted into the "Faithful" of the Great King after Cyrus's return to Asia Minor. Furthermore, if, as Diodorus maintains (XIV.19.6), Cyrus gave Lydia and Phrygia to some of his kinsmen (*syggeneis*), this disposition implies that Pharnabazus must also have lost his satrapy or that he was demoted to a subordinate position—and for this and other reasons he sided with the king.

When he arrived in Cilicia, Cyrus suffered another huge reverse. Abrocomas (having been entrusted with the expedition to Egypt), rather than joining Cyrus—who certainly must have made contact with him—retreated instead toward the Euphrates with his army, burning the bridges at Thapsacus to slow the rebel's advance (*Anab.* I.4.18). Abrocomas was not the only one to side with the king. So did Belesys (Bēlšunu), the governer of Syria (Ebir Nāri), as is unambiguously implicit in Cyrus's order to lay waste the satrapal residence and paradise that were idyllically sited at the springs of the Dardas (I.4.10). We may also note that according to Diodorus (XIV.20.5), in order to mislead them one more time (*Anab.* I.2.1), Cyrus revealed his goal in the following words at Tarsus: "He was leading the army, not against Artaxerxes, but against a certain satrap of Syria" (Diodorus XIV.20.5✧). He certainly made the same claim with regard to the satrap of Babylonia, who perhaps is the Gobryas who was one of the commanders of the royal army during the battle of Cunaxa (I.7.12). Tiribazus also sided with the Great King (Plutarch, *Art.* 7.3, 10.1); Xenophon represents him as "governor of Western Armenia" (*Anab.* IV.4.4). Artasyras, "the king's eye," was also with the king (Plutarch, *Art.* 12.1–3✧). In fact, this Artasyras was the father of Orontes (*OGIS* 264, 390–92), who seems to have been a governor in eastern Armenia (cf. Xenophon, *Anab.* III.5.17; cf. IV.3.4); this Orontes had brought a contingent to the king (II.4.9).

Even though the evidence is partial in both senses of the word, one conclusion it tempts us to draw is that Cyrus did not succeed in gaining the support of officers stationed beyond his official jurisdiction. A second conclusion is that an unknown number of his peers and subordinates refused to cut their ties of allegiance to the one they considered the sole Great King, Artaxerxes II. Finally, some of his other allies committed themselves only with much caution or many second thoughts. The record does not confirm the hopes that Plutarch claims Cyrus nourished in 404: that he would be able to win to his side not only "those of his own province near the sea, but . . . many of those in the upper countries" (*Art.* 6.2✧).

Artaxerxes and Cyrus Face Off

The arrival of Cyrus and his army in Babylonia created a political and strategic situation unprecedented in Achaemenid history. The Great King was threatened at the very heart of his Empire by a single enemy at the head of a major force intent on seizing supreme power. The danger was thus even more pressing than that faced by Darius in 522–521, when disorganized rebels never tried (or never succeeded) to unify for a march on the center of the Empire (see chap. 3/2). Cyrus's expedition thus represents a sort of prefiguring of Alexander's conquest. Just like Darius III in 331, Artaxerxes lost control of Asia Minor and regions beyond the Euphrates, including Egypt. His response to this challenge evokes the measures taken by the Great King seventy years later.

Artaxerxes had less time for preparation than Darius III, who was able to gather and train an army while Alexander pursued his conquest of Syria–Phoenicia and Egypt, before returning to the road to the Euphrates (late 333 – autumn 331). Just like the Persians in 331, the Great King ordered Abrocomas to destroy the bridges over the Euphrates to slow down Cyrus's march (I.4.18). And, just like Mazaeus when faced with the Macedonian, Artaxerxes decided to apply a scorched-earth policy in advance of Cyrus (I.6.2). At the same time, he proceeded to prepare the defenses of Babylonia. According to Xenophon, during the third day's march in the country, they came upon "a deep trench, five fathoms in width and three fathoms in depth. . . . This trench extended up through the plain . . . reaching to the wall of Media. . . . The trench had been constructed by the Great King as a means of defence when he learned that Cyrus was marching against him" (I.7.14–16;✧ cf. Plutarch, *Art.* 7.2). Further on, Xenophon explains that "the so-called wall of Media . . . was built of baked bricks, laid in asphalt, and was twenty feet wide and a hundred feet high; its length was said to be twenty parasangs, and it is not far distant from Babylon" (II.4.12✧). Cyrus's propaganda spread the news that, having built the wall, Artaxerxes turned tail and refused combat (I.8.19). While certain obscurities concerning the course of this wall do exist, it actually appears that the Great King reused prior construction to good effect and that he adopted a well-known strategy—using the waterways to cut off access to Babylon (see chap. 9/2)—however, apparently with no great success.

Xenophon stresses the speed of Cyrus's march. The prince stopped only to secure provisions (I.5.9) in the villages along the route (I.4.19; 5.4, 10): "Cyrus sometimes made these stages through the desert very long, whenever he wanted to reach water or fresh fodder" (I.5.7✧). Choosing a route for its swiftness forced the army to cross inhospitable territory, called "Arabia" by Xenophon (I.5.1–3), and brought them to the edge of famine, which particularly upset the Greeks: "It was not possible to buy any [grain] except in the Lydian market attached to the barbarian army of Cyrus, at the price of four *sigli* for a *capithē* of wheat flour or barley meal" (I.5.6✧). There is no doubt that the price went up sharply in such contexts (cf. Plutarch, *Art.* 24.3). The soldiers were unable to indulge in such luxury and "therefore managed to subsist by eating meat" (*Anab.* I.5.7✧), probably from hunting (I.5.2–3). Cyrus's haste is explained above all, according to Xenophon, by his need to prevent the Great King from assembling his forces: "His thought was that the faster he went, the more unprepared the King would be to fight with him, while, on the other hand, the slower he went, the greater would be the army that was gathering for the King." Like so many ancient authors, Xenophon thought that "while the King's empire was strong in its extent of territory and number of inhabitants, it was weak by reason of the greatness of the distances and the scattered condition of its forces, in case one should be swift in making his attack upon it" (I.5.9✧). Cyrus's haste contrasts dramatically with the relative leisure of his march until he reached the Euphrates: he stayed 7 days at Colossae (2.6), 30 days at Celaenae (2.9), 3 days at Peltae (2.10), 5 days at Caÿstru-pedion (2.11), 20 days at Tarsus, 3 days at Issus (4.2), and 5 days at Thapsacus (4.11)—73 days in all. It is unlikely that the length of the stopovers can simply be explained, with Xenophon (I.3.21), by the alleged ill will of the Greek mercenaries, who were often left waiting for their pay. Beginning with the crossing of the Euphrates, the army proceeded at a forced-march pace, even though Cyrus must have already been growing uneasy at the preparations of Artaxerxes, which unsubstantiated rumors at Tarsus indicated were considerable (Diodorus XIV.20.4). When Cyrus chose to follow a swift route that did not have many resupply points, it was because a decisive strategic factor had arisen in the meantime. According to Xenophon (I.4.5✧), Cyrus expected Abrocomas to bar his passage through the Syrian Gates: "Abrocomas, however, did not do so, but as soon as he heard that Cyrus was in Cilicia, he turned about in his journey from Phoenicia and marched off to join the King, with an army, so the report ran, of three hundred thousand men." Continuing with Xenophon's account, Abrocomas arrived five days after the battle of Cunaxa (I.7.12). His delay was not due to dawdling: quite simply, he had chosen to take the Royal Road, which, though much longer, allowed him to resupply his troops (cf. Arrian III.7.3). After he left the Euphrates behind, Cyrus had taken a speedy route that was intended to prevent Abrocomas's army from joining up with the royal army.

According to Diodorus (XIV.22.1◊), Artaxerxes "summoned his armaments from every place to Ecbatana in Media" as soon as he got wind of Cyrus's departure. This detail does not imply that the king was then at his summer residence (it was early spring). More likely, he was at Babylon. The mention of Ecbatana as the assembly point is easy to explain: just as Darius III was to do later on, Artaxerxes II ordered the mobilization of troops from the Iranian Plateau as far as the Indus. Diodorus states that the troops from those distant places did not arrive in time "because of the remoteness of those regions" (XIV.22.2◊). This is confirmed by Xenophon: as the Greek mercenaries who had survived the battle passed Opis on the Tigris, they "met the bastard brother (*nothos adelphos*) of Cyrus and Artaxerxes, who was leading a large army from Susa and Ecbatana to the support, as he said, of the King" (*Anab.* II.4.25◊). The rapidity of Cyrus's march had also prevented Artaxerxes from carrying out his initial plans, which had apparently included Abrocomas's forces, since Abrocomas is named by Xenophon as one of the four commanders (along with Tissaphernes, Gobryas, and Arbaces; I.7.12).

The royal army drawn up at Cunaxa thus did not include the forces from western Asia Minor (preempted by Cyrus), Abrocomas's army (still on the road), or the eastern Iranian contingents (who would also arrive too late). It had been mustered exclusively from the closest regions: Babylonia, Susiana, Media, Persia; the Cadusians also sent a cavalry contingent commanded by Artagerses (Plutarch, *Art.* 9). For reasons already discussed in connection with Xerxes' army, it is impossible to provide reliable estimates of the size of the king's forces (cf. Plutarch, *Art.* 13.3–4). We may simply surmise, with Xenophon (I.8.13), that they were superior in number to Cyrus's. Contrary to one of the favorite claims of the Greek authors (and contrary to the mercenaries' expectations: they were "full of confidence and scorn"), Xenophon (I.8.14) and Plutarch (*Art.* 7.5◊) both stress the discipline and training of Artaxerxes' soldiers: "The very manner in which [Artaxerxes] led on his men, silently and slowly, made the Grecians stand amazed at his good discipline; who had expected irregular shouting and leaping, much confusion and separation between one body of men and another, in so vast a multitude of troops"! Plutarch's sources instead attribute the defeat to Cyrus's overweening pride and Clearchus's lack of discipline (*Art.* 8.2–6).

Just as Darius III and his advisers were to do later on, Artaxerxes placed great confidence in his scythe-equipped chariots: "and the scythes they carried reached out sideways from the axles and were also set under the chariot bodies, pointing towards the ground, so as to cut to pieces whatever they met; the intention, then, was that they should drive into the ranks of the Greeks and cut the troops to pieces" (I.8.10◊). The success rate was not as high as expected: just as Alexander's soldiers were to do, "whenever the Greeks saw them coming, they would open a gap for their passage" (I.8.20◊). The Greeks were ranged on the right flank with a detachment of 1000 Paphlagonian horsemen and gave chase to the enemy; as a result, they escaped the deluge of shafts fired by the king's archers and spearmen (I.8.19; cf. I.8.9 and II.1.6; Diodorus XIV.23.1–2). The hand-to-hand fighting favored Clearchus's Greeks, who too confidently threw themselves into pursuit of their opponents. Xenophon tells us (I.8.24) that this is when Cyrus, fearing that the Greek contingent would be surrounded, attacked in the middle; he was killed in circumstances that the conflicting traditions do not permit us to reconstruct (I.8.24–29). On the left flank, Ariaeus, after initial successful engagements, was stunned into retreat by the news of the death of Cyrus and was afraid that he would be encircled by the king's contingents (Diodorus XIV.24.1). The death of Cyrus sealed the fate of the battle and the expedition.

3. Artaxerxes the Victor

The Process of Relegitimation

After the death of Cyrus on the battlefield at Cunaxa, Artaxerxes immediately took actions designed to extirpate the memory of him who, after his initial victories, "was already being saluted with homage as King by his attendants" (I.8.21✧). "And when he had come near the dead body, and, according to a certain law of the Persians, the right hand and head had been lopped off from the trunk, he gave orders that the latter should be brought to him, and, grasping the hair of it, which was long and bushy, he showed it to those who were still uncertain and disposed to fly. They were amazed at it, and did him homage; so that there were presently seventy thousand of them got about him, and entered the camp again with him" (Plutarch, *Art.* 13.2✧). Artaxerxes showed clearly that he was the one who had won the loyalty of thousands and the one whose legitimacy was proved by the victory.

A court tradition transmitted by Dinon even claims that Cyrus was killed by the hand of the king himself (Plutarch, *Art.* 10.3). "For it was his desire that every one, whether Greek or barbarian, should believe that in the mutual assaults and conflicts between him and his brother, he, giving and receiving a blow, was himself indeed wounded, but the other lost his life" (§16.2✧). This is why, as Plutarch reports it, Artaxerxes was very irritated to hear that a simple Caunian soldier and a young Persian, Mithradates, each made the claim or let it be understood that it was he who had done the deed. Artaxerxes "was greatly enraged at it, as having the lie given him, and being in danger to forfeit the most glorious and most pleasant circumstance of his victory" (§16.1✧). Throughout his reign, no opportunity to portray the king as a proven general and an accomplished leader of men was missed (§24.9–11).

At the same time, the royal inscriptions show that Artaxerxes followed the model of not only his father Darius II (A^2Sb, A^2Sd) but, like his predecessors, also the model of Darius I. He insisted on dynastic continuity, particularly in this sort of inscription from Susa (A^2Sa✧): "Saith Artaxerxes the Great King, King of Kings, King of Countries, King in this earth, son of Darius the King, of Darius (who was) son of Artaxerxes the King, of Artaxerxes (who was) son of Xerxes the King, of Xerxes (who was) son of Darius the King, of Darius (who was) son of Hystaspes, an Achaemenian: This palace Darius my great-great-grandfather built; later under Artaxerxes my grandfather it was burned; . . . this palace I (re)built . . ." (cf. also A^2Hc).

Reward and Punishment

After the first treaty with the Greeks, "the King led his army off to Babylon. In that city he accorded fitting honours to everyone who had performed deeds of courage in the battle" (Diodorus XIV.26.4✧). First among the persons honored was Tissaphernes, because he had joined the king as early as spring 401 and played a decisive role at Cunaxa: at least in one version, he was head of one of the four divisions (I.7.12) and was said to have taken over the army when Artaxerxes was wounded: "He slew great numbers of the enemy, so that his presence was conspicuous from afar. . . . [The King] judged Tissaphernes to have been the bravest of all. Consequently he honoured him with rich gifts, gave him his own daughter in marriage, and henceforth continued to hold him as his most trusted friend" (XIV.23.6;✧ 26.4✧). He certainly was one of the king's favorites, since he was permitted shortly afterward to let the Greeks pillage "the villages of Parysatis" at Tikrit, not far from Opis (cf. II.4.27). Another noble, Orontes, the satrap of Armenia, married Rhodogune, a daughter of the king (*Anab.* III.4.13; Plutarch §27.7; *OGIS* 391–92). Perhaps it was at the same time that the king promised two other daughters to Pharnabazus and Tiribazus (27.7). The latter was one of the Friends of the king and had played a major role at Cunaxa (Plutarch, *Art.* 7.3), where he saved the king's life (according to one of the versions; §10.1). It was not until fifteen years later that Pharnabazus gained the noteworthy dignity of becoming the king's son-in-law (Xenophon, *Hell.* V.1.28).

Tissaphernes received an even greater promotion: "Now . . . Tissaphernes, who was thought to have proved himself very valuable to the King in the war against his brother, was sent down as satrap both of the provinces which he himself had previously ruled and of those which Cyrus had ruled" (Xenophon, *Hell.* III.1.3✧). He then set about regaining control of the cities and dignitaries who had taken the rebel's side as rapidly as possible. Tissaphernes abandoned the Greek survivors at the Gates of Armenia and returned to Sardis by the Royal Road (Diodorus XIV.27.4). All the leaders except Tamos, who chose to flee to Egypt (35.4), came to pay homage to the new *karanos*; Tamos's son Glus, who had received a royal pardon, was even put in charge of the armed forces (35.3). Ariaeus, another old companion of Cyrus, received a command: in any case, some years later he was the satrap of Phrygia (cf. Diodorus XIV.80.8; Polyaenus VII.11.6); later still (around 394), he held a post at Sardis (*Hell. Oxyr.* 14.3). His status as a former enemy of the king even worked to his advantage to some extent, since rebels would seek refuge with him at Sardis, obviously hoping that he would mediate for them with the king to obtain a royal pardon (Xenophon, *Hell.* IV.1.27).

We note with interest that the Great King did not hesitate to pardon a number of rebels. Do these decisions speak to the uncertainty of his power after the victory at Cunaxa? It is difficult to answer this question. It is true that all of the ancient texts insist on the "gentility" of Artaxerxes II and on his practice of royal gifts. But the distribution of the evidence may be deceptive. It is possible that the king, at an unknown date, promulgated a relaxation of certain court regulations, particularly regarding royal hunts; but even on this point chronological uncertainties remain. We may simply note that after Cunaxa the Great King hardly had any choice regarding ways of winning over to himself nobles who had followed Cyrus (by choice or by force). Under other circumstances, however, Artaxerxes did not shrink from using drastic measures even against those close to him (cf. Plutarch, *Art.* 25.3). Even Tissaphernes did not escape royal punishment some years later after losing the battle outside Sardis against Agesilaus (§5 below), though Artaxerxes "continued to hold him as his most trusted friend" (Diodorus XIV.26.4✧).

The Great King and His Armies

Arguing that the return of the survivors of Cyrus's mercenaries to the sea demonstrated quality of character, Plutarch offers this thought to his readers:

> Making it plain to all men that the Persian king and his empire were mighty indeed in gold and luxury and women, but otherwise were a mere show and vain display, upon this all Greece took courage and despised the barbarians. (*Art.* 20.1–2✧)

This comment conveys an idea that was equally dear to Xenophon, whether in the last chapter of the *Cyropaedia* or in the *Agesilaus*, a small work dedicated to singing the praises of a Greek hero whose human qualities contrasted in every way with the Great King, who was viewed as mired in luxury and sloth. Magnifying the deeds of the Ten Thousand is a common topos of fourth-century authors, who brought them forward as proof that "any one who is engaged in war with [the Persians] can, if he desire, range up and down their country without having to strike a blow" (*Cyr.* VIII.8.7✧)—and that because the Persians had been rendered effeminate by a dissolute life, they "can conduct their wars only with the assistance of Greeks" (8.26✧). This point of view is particularly stressed by Isocrates (*Paneg.* 138–49), who ends his discussion of the softness of the Persians thus: "They made themselves objects of derision under the very walls of their King's palace" (§149✧).

Even if we invoke the ritual reminder that the state of the evidence leaves everything in doubt, the status of the Greek mercenaries during the battle of Cunaxa and in the following weeks poses real problems. In Xenophon's version, they prolonged the battle until evening, winning several engagements with detachments of the royal army (I.10.4–19). They were sure of having won and even raised a monument (Diodorus XIV.24.4) before returning to their camp, where they discovered that the enemy's light infantry had pillaged the food reserves (*Anab.* I.10.18–19). It was not until daybreak that Procles and Glus informed them of the death of Cyrus (II.1.2–3). The battle lines were so strained that there had evidently been two different battles: on the left flank, Ariaeus had retreated; from there, he had sent Procles and Glus to request that Clearchus and the Greeks join him, proposing that they organize a joint return to Ionia (II.1.3). Clearchus refused, even offering to put Ariaeus on the Persian throne, and he sent messengers to inform him (II.1.4–5). Ariaeus replied that this was out of the question (II.2.1). An agreement was finally reached, with both swearing to an alliance, and Ariaeus agreed to guide the Greeks to the coast (II.2.8–9). At the same time, emissaries from Tissaphernes and the king parleyed with the Greeks, demanding that they lay down their arms. Clearchus arrogantly refused, emphasizing that his forces were intact (II.1.7–13); it was even said that not a "single man among the Greeks [got] any hurt whatever in this battle" (I.8.20✧). Nonetheless, the mercenaries were not in full agreement; a few groups agreed to surrender (II.1.14; 2.17). Xenophon's account continues: he says that the king himself was afraid of the army of Clearchus and Ariaeus (II.2.18; 3.1). This is why Tissaphernes and a brother-in-law of Artaxerxes showed up on his behalf with orders to come to an agreement: if the Greeks agreed not to fight, the Persians would supply them (II.3.17–29). The Greeks were fully aware that without guides they would never manage to overcome the obstacles or resupply themselves in the country. So it was that they set out for the west bank of the Tigris Valley under the watchful eye of Tissaphernes (II.4.8–28).

Why, then, had the Great King failed to order his generals to begin the battle? Should this be seen as proof of his weakness? This is clearly Clearchus's perspective, which was accepted by Xenophon. Mercenaries quoted by Xenophon thought that the king was waiting until all of his troops were reunited (II.4.3). Not until some time later was the recombination of the various royal contingents completed: "the troops of Orontas . . . , the barbarians whom Cyrus had brought with him on his upward march, and those with whom the King's brother had come to the aid of the King [II.4.25–26], besides these contingents Tissaphernes had all the troops that the King had given him; the result was, that his army appeared exceedingly large" (III.4.13✧). Nevertheless, Tissaphernes did not organize his army into battle order; he was content to mount occasional attacks on the Greeks, shadowing them as far as the Upper Tigris.

Meanwhile, basic strategic changes had taken place. According to Diodorus, Tissaphernes submitted the following plan to Artaxerxes: He "promised him that he would destroy them one and all, if the King would supply him with armaments and come to terms with Aridaeus, for he believed that Aridaeus would betray the Greeks to him in the course of the march. The King readily accepted this suggestion and allowed him to select from his entire army as many of the best troops as he chose" (XIV.26.5✧). The first order of business was the recovery of Ariaeus and the large body of troops under him that Cyrus had levied in Asia Minor. "Ariaeus' brothers and other relatives came to him and certain Persians came to his followers, and they kept encouraging them and bringing pledges to some of them from the King that the King would bear them no ill-will because of their campaign with Cyrus against him or because of anything else in the past" (*Anab.* II.4.1✧). The negotiations between the two camps soon succeeded. Ariaeus and his companions, Artaozus and Mithradates, "who had been most faithful friends of Cyrus,"✧ laid a trap for the Greeks: several *strategoi* and *lokhagos* summoned to Tissaphernes' tent were seized and put to death (II.5.31–6.1). By winning Ariaeus's troops over to him, eliminating the main Greek *strategoi*, and gathering a large army, Tissaphernes was in a position of power from that time forward. He left the Greeks at the frontier of the land of the Carduchi to return to his territory at Sardis (Diodorus XIV.27.4). At this point, it was impossible for the Greeks to return directly to Ionia; they could only march north. There is no doubt that the Persians were certain that the survivors would not overcome the natural barriers (rivers, mountains), the attacks of the mountain peoples, or the attacks of the troops of the Armenian satrapy.

Events suggest contrasting conclusions regarding Artaxerxes II's military situation after Cunaxa. The very make-up of the armies of Cyrus and Artaxerxes indicates that the system of conscription continued to operate perfectly from Asia Minor to India, even though the delay of the eastern Iranian contingents demonstrates that it was not possible to organize a general muster in a few months. Given the relatively limited geographic distribution of the conscripts who did fight at Issus, there is hardly any doubt that the Great King, for his part, was able to count on the soldiers provided by the Babylonian *ḥaṭrus*, among others. The reliance on thousands of Greek mercenaries in Cyrus's army constituted a decided novelty, quite apart from the important role Cyrus assigned them in the battle, in combination with his cavalry. It is no less true, however, that the confrontation at Cunaxa was not a duel between Cyrus's Greek mercenaries and Artaxerxes' regulars; it was the clash of two royal armies.

As in the battles in Greece and Asia Minor in 490 and 480–79, the Greek foot soldiers *seemed* to exhibit clear superiority over the infantrymen they faced. This observation, however, needs to be tempered: for one thing, let us recall that Plutarch (*Art.* 7.5) and Xenophon (I.8.14) stress the maneuverability of the royal army; for another, Tissaphernes' actions after the battle can be accounted for by his fear of the army commanded by Ariaeus, or, to put it another way, he feared joint maneuvers involving the inter-satrapal army and the Greek army. The Persian leaders thus adroitly chose to separate them and then forced the Greeks onto an itinerary that they could assume would prove fatal. After Megabyzus's victory over Amyrtaeus, he had acted no differently. He reached an agreement with the Egyptian rebel's Greek mercenaries: "No ill shall be done them by the king's men, and the Greeks shall return home whenever they wish" (Ctesias §34); they took the road to Cyrene and, according to Thucydides (I.110.1◇), "most of them perished" (there is a different version in Diodorus XI.77.5).

But there is a difference in scale: in 401, the Greeks were in Babylonia. The Persians were anxious to see them out of the heart of the Empire. At the same time, we may observe that the Persians never pretended to accept the offers of services that the heads of the mercenaries had made to them several times, emphasizing that they would be very useful in a fight against the unsubdued peoples (*Anab*. II.1.14, 5.13–14). At this time, it appears that the Persian leaders did not even consider including the Greek mercenaries in the royal army. Did the Great King fear that mercenaries could be used by an ambitious man, as Cyrus had done? This is the burden of Tissaphernes' convoluted speech to Clearchus: "The King alone may wear upright the tiara that is upon the head, but another, too, with your help, might easily so wear the one that is upon the heart" (II.5.23◇). The mercenaries themselves seem to have been persuaded that they could make and unmake kings, as shown by the offers they made along these lines to Ariaeus (II.1.4); they were convinced, Clearchus says, that "to those who are victorious in battle belongs also the right to rule" (II.1.4◇). But the proposals they sent to Ariaeus were rather naive, and the Persian let them know, in ironic understatement, that "there were many Persians of higher rank than himself and they would not tolerate his being king" (II.2.1◇). It is clear that not a single Persian had the slightest notion of abandoning Artaxerxes; on the contrary, all hoped to obtain from him favor or pardon from him.

4. Conditions in Asia Minor and Artaxerxes II's Strategy (400–396)

From Sardis to Memphis

As we have seen, after Cunaxa and the "expulsion" of the Greek mercenaries, Tissaphernes returned to his governorship in Sardis (Diodorus XIV.27.4). It was his job, in fact, to restore order to Asia Minor. Diodorus stresses that the Greek cities that had supported Cyrus were scared to death (XIV.35.6). And with good reason: one of Tissaphernes' first acts was that he "demanded that all the Ionian cities should be subject to him." They refused and appealed to Sparta for help (Xenophon, *Hell*. III.1.3◇). Without delay, Tissaphernes devastated the territory of Cyme and laid siege to the town; at the beginning of winter (400–399), the Persian accepted heavy ransoms for the prisoners and lifted the siege (Diodorus XIV.35.7). The following spring (399), the first Spartan expeditionary force landed on the Asia Minor coast. Greco-Persian hostilities thus broke out once again on the coast of Asia Minor.

For reasons we have already discussed, the Great King had to deal with the Egyptian front at the same time. When the Greek mercenaries offered their services to Tissaphernes, they had not neglected to bring up the matter of the Egyptians, with whom the Persians were "especially angry" (*Anab*. II.5.13;◇ cf. II.1.14). If the king wished to march against Egypt—said Clearchus—"I do not see what force you could better employ to aid you in chastising them than the force which I now have" (*Anab*. II.5.13◇). A contract attests that Pharaoh Amyrtaeus was recognized at Elephantine in 400 (*DAE* 7 [*AP* 35]). In 398, Nepherites founded the XXIXth dynasty (*DAE* 105 [*BMAP* 13]) and reigned until 393. It is surprising that no source mentions an attempted Persian reconquest. Not until the reign of Hakoris (392–380), around 385(?), is there evidence for the assembling of an army to march against Egypt (cf. Isocrates, *Paneg.* 140). Meanwhile, Egypt had entered into the coalition put together by Sparta against Artaxerxes as an equal partner. As in the 460s (see chap. 14/2), from that point forward Egypt was included in a much wider front, with the important difference that this time the Persians no longer had a base in the country. The Elephantine garrison, for example, had gone over with both weapons and supplies to the side of the independent pharaohs (*DAE* 7, 105). Artaxerxes' task was even more difficult because Tamos, Cyrus's lieutenant, fled Asia Minor in 400 and took refuge with the pharaoh, along with his fortune and the fleet he commanded (Diodorus XIV.35.4–5)—"fifty triremes which had been fitted out at great expense . . . [but Psammetichus took] for his own both Tamōs' possessions and his fleet" (XIV.19.5◊).

Artaxerxes, His Satraps, and the Asia Minor Front

At the very moment when Amyrtaeus was extending his power into Upper Egypt, Thibron, the Lacedaemonian commander-in-chief, landed in Asia Minor (spring, 399). He was leading a smaller force but recruited troops in the Greek cities, and then soon joined up with the Greek refugees of the *Anabasis* (*Hell.* III.1.4–6). He could then "draw up his troops against Tissaphernes even on the plains" and took many towns and strongholds in Mysia, Aeolis, and the Troad (III.1.8◊). Complaints from Greek cities that he fleeced soon resulted in his replacement by Dercyllidas, who resurrected a traditional tactic: he played Tissaphernes off against Pharnabazus. He then headed for "the Aeolis, in the territory of Pharnabazus, without doing any harm whatever to his allies" (III.1.10◊). Pharnabazus was very unhappy at being stripped of this region and "secretly envied Tissaphernes his position as general" (III.2.13◊); he agreed to a truce with Dercyllidas, "thinking that Aeolis had been made a strong base of attack upon his own dwelling-place (*oikēsis*), Phrygia" (III.2.1,◊ 9). In short, they were back to a situation very like what prevailed in 412–407, with the two satraps in perpetual competition. Obviously, Tissaphernes had not succeeded in gaining the upper hand, as had Cyrus the Younger at Sardis.

The dissension surfaced once again some time later, during preparation for a pitched battle near Magnesia. The two satraps had combined their forces: "The entire Persian force which chanced to be at hand, all the Greek troops which each of the two satraps had, and horsemen in great numbers, those of Tissaphernes upon the right wing and those of Pharnabazus upon the left" (III.2.15◊). According to Xenophon, Tissaphernes (in contrast to Pharnabazus) was not particularly eager for combat and offered to negotiate with Dercyllidas (III.2.18). One of the reasons undoubtedly was that war threatened to ravage Caria, where Tissaphernes' estates were (*oikos*; III.2.12). The talks between the Persians and Dercyllidas led to a truce: the Persians demanded that the Lacedaemonian troops and the governors (*harmostes*) who had been stationed in the Greek towns since Lysander's victories depart; Dercyllidas demanded autonomy for the Greek cities. Both sides decided on consultations—with the Great King and the Spartan leadership, respectively (III.2.20). In effect, the Persians were asking that the treaties with the king and his representatives agreed to by Sparta during the Ionian War fifteen years earlier be put into effect.

Pharnabazus was instructed to sound out the king regarding his intentions (Diodorus XIV.39.6). The satrap of Dascylium, Diodorus tells us, favored a vigorous sea offensive. Just after the first truce with Dercyllidas, he had sought out the king and persuaded him to fund him (in the amount of 500 talents of silver) and to appeal to the Athenian Conon

(XIV.39.1). Ever since the Athenian defeats of 405, he had taken refuge with Evagoras of Salamis, on Cyprus, at the very time when Evagoras had been doing everything he could to increase the city's prosperity and had inaugurated vast arms programs. There is no indication that the Cypriot king was trying to escape from the Persian yoke. His original objective was to extend his power throughout the island at the expense of the other petty kinglets. It is nonetheless possible that he took advantage of the war between the brothers to take certain liberties with his obligations as a subject. In 398, contacts were established between Evagoras and Artaxerxes, perhaps with Ctesias as go-between. Evagoras agreed to resume payment of tribute (*Persica* §63), since under the present circumstances he shared the Persians' hostility to Sparta, whose power was a check on his ambitions. These were the conditions under which Pharnabazus arrived in Cyprus, bearing a letter from the king ordering all the kings of the island to prepare about one hundred triremes. Conon accepted an appointment as admiral of the fleet. He then set sail for Cilicia, where he began his preparations for the war that was about to commence against the Peloponnesian navy (Diodorus XIV.39.2–4).

This was an important event. As far as we can determine, this was the first royal navy that seems to have been assembled since the famous Phoenician navy of 412 (not considering Cyrus the Younger's fleet in 401). This royal navy (*basilikos stolos*) did not comprise Cypriot ships alone; somewhat later, Conon was joined by a Cilician contingent, as well as a Phoenician squadron commanded by the king of the Sidonians (Diodorus XIV.79.8; *Hell. Oxyr.* 4.2). Sparta soon got wind of these massive naval preparations through a Syracusan merchant who was in Phoenicia on business at the time:

> Seeing Phoenician war-ships—some of them sailing in from other places, others lying there fully manned, and yet others still making ready for sea—and hearing, besides, that there were to be three hundred of them, . . . [he] reported to the Lacedaemonians that the King and Tissaphernes were preparing this expedition; but whither it was bound he said he did not know. (*Hell.* III.4.1✥)

The methods used to assemble the royal fleet indicate that Persian authority, however shaken by Cyrus's revolt, was fully operational among its Levantine subjects. We see that, as in earlier times, the king of Sidon played a very important role for the Persians. On the other hand, the theory that the *syennesis* in Cilicia was in political decline at this date must be viewed with some hesitancy, since no independent evidence supports it.

At the same time, the king continued to raise the troops needed to fight in Asia Minor (Nepos, *Ages.* 2.1; Xenophon, *Ages.* 6.1). He also decreed that the command be unified in such a way as to avoid repeating previous errors: Tissaphernes was named commander-in-chief (*stratēgos tōn pantōn*). Despite the hatred that Pharnabazus, now back in Asia Minor, nursed toward Tissaphernes, he did not shrink from "assuring him that he was ready to make war together with him, to be his ally, and to aid him in driving the Greeks out of the territory of the King" (*Hell.* III.2.13✥). But the competition between Pharnabazus and Tissaphernes was more complicated than this, since (according to several ancient authors, e.g., Nepos, *Conon* 2.2), Pharnabazus received command of maritime operations, thus doubling up on the Athenian Conon. It seems clear that the command assigned to Tissaphernes was reduced to the ground troops.

To carry out his objective, the king also released considerable resources. Some time later, to be sure, we learn that a riot broke out in Conon's army when the soldiers complained about not receiving their pay (*Hell. Oxyr.* 15; cf. Isocrates, *Paneg.* 142). Justin was probably not wrong to see this as the result of machinations by the "king's lieutenants, who were in the habit of defrauding the soldiers of their pay" (VI.2.11). To deal with the problem, Conon appealed directly to Artaxerxes, promising to destroy Lacedaemonian sea power if Artaxerxes would grant him sufficient money and equipment: "Artaxerxes approved Conon, honoured him with rich gifts, and appointed a paymaster who should supply funds in abundance as Conon might assign them" (Diodorus XIV.81.6;✧ cf. Nepos *Conon* 4.2 and *Hell. Oxyr.* 19). So it appears that, quite atypically, Conon received permission to draw on royal supplies without checking each time with the central court (cf. Nepos, *Conon* 4.1). Access to such resources could hardly avoid arousing great hope among the enemies of Sparta, who were numerous in both Greece and the Aegean. This is why Sparta had to wage war against Elis during the expedition led by Dercyllidas (400–398; *Hell.* III.2.21–31), and then later had to deal with an attempted *helot* revolt (397; III.3.4–11). And despite being at peace with its former enemy, Athens sent an embassy to the Great King and provided secret reinforcements (sailors) to Conon, who was then at Caunus (*Hell. Oxyr.* 7.1).

We are unable to discern, then, the strange passivity in Artaxerxes that the ancient sources attribute to Darius II (see chap. 14/7). Obviously, Artaxerxes made the firm and irrevocable decision to fight energetically to regain control of the Aegean coast. There is no doubt that the king's objective embraced the entire Aegean as well. Confronted by this threat, Sparta sent King Agesilaus to Asia Minor in 396. At the same time, it dispatched ambassadors to Pharaoh Nepherites, who provided the equipment for 100 triremes and 500,000 measures of wheat—which soon fell into the hands of Conon, who had just taken Rhodes (Diodorus XIV.79.4–7; cf. Justin VI.2.1–2). The pharaoh realized that his survival depended on a Spartan victory. Conversely, Artaxerxes knew that retaking Egypt presupposed the reestablishment of hegemony over the Aegean Sea, which his predecessors had gradually lost during the course of the previous century. From this point of view, the Great King's actions after Cunaxa represent a sort of strategic turnabout: the hour of reconquest was at hand.

5. Agesilaus in Asia Minor (396–394)

The Defeat of Tissaphernes

Sparta was confronted with imminent danger and decided to prosecute the war on a grander scale (cf. Diodorus XIV.79.1). King Agesilaus was sent at the head of a 12,000-man expeditionary force, and he soon reached Ephesus (*Hell.* III.4.1–5; spring, 396). His mission was clear: to ensure the autonomy of the cities of Asia Minor (III.4.5). At first, Tissaphernes agreed to a truce, with the excuse that he had to get the king's permission. In reality, he was completely aware of Artaxerxes' intention: he was stalling for time until the king's troops could reach him (III.4.6; cf. Nepos, *Ages.* 2.4). He also needed to gain enough time for the Phoenician shipyards to complete the craft promised to Conon, as well as to free the fleet that the Lacedaemonian admiral Pharax had blockaded at Caunus; this he accomplished (Diodorus XIV.79.4–8; *Hell. Oxyr.* 9.2–3). When the truce expired, then, Tissaphernes was able to demand that Agesilaus pull back from the Asia Minor territories; the Spartan responded immediately that this was out of the question (*Hell.* III.4.11]).

Agesilaus assembled the Carian, Aeolian, Ionian, and Hellespontine contingents at Ephesus (III.4.11). Tissaphernes thought that the Spartan intended to ravage his estates in Caria, so he sent his infantry to Caria and concentrated his cavalry on the plain of the Meander, expecting to cut off the Greek troops there. Contrary to expectations, Agesilaus took the Phrygian route. A battle took place near Dascylium: Pharnabazus's lieutenants, Rhathines and Bagaeus, won a cavalry engagement but had to retreat when the hoplites charged. Agesilaus then returned to Ephesus (III.4.11–15). The purpose of this offensive was not to conquer towns and territory; all of the ancient authors instead stress the amount of booty seized by the Spartan (Xenophon, *Hell.* III.4.12; Nepos, *Ages.* 3.2; Plutarch, *Ages.* 9.4). Diodorus (XIV.79.2) also states that the army was accompanied by a large number of merchants (*agoraios . . . okhlos*), who clearly had been instructed to find ways to market the booty (cf. Plutarch, *Ages.* 9.8; Xenophon, *Hell.* IV.1.26). It is clear that first and foremost Agesilaus had decided that money was to be the ultimate means of achieving his real objectives. With this reinforcement, he then decided to send out an army capable of successfully opposing the Persian forces:

> Perceiving that, unless he obtained an adequate cavalry force, he would not be able to campaign in the plains, he resolved that this must be provided, so that he might not have to carry on a skulking warfare. Accordingly he assigned the richest men of all the cities in that region to the duty of raising horses; and by proclaiming that whoever supplied a horse and arms and a competent man would not have to serve himself, he caused these arrangements to be carried out with all the expedition that was to be expected when men were eagerly looking for substitutes to die in their stead. (*Hell.* III.4.15✧)

At the same time, the Ephesus workshops were operating at full capacity: "The market was full of all sorts of horses and weapons, offered for sale, and the copper-workers, carpenters, smiths, leather-cutters, and painters were all engaged in making martial weapons, so that one might have thought that the city was really a workshop of war" (III.4.17✧). The soldiers themselves were given daily drills.

Agesilaus announced that he was prepared to march on Sardis (spring, 395). Curiously enough, Tissaphernes did not believe a word of it and one more time sent his troops to defend Caria. A battle on the banks of the Pactolus ended with an advantage to the Greeks. From this point on, Xenophon's story is very sketchy. According to him, after the battle, Tissaphernes was indicted by the Persians of Sardis and was soon condemned to death by Artaxerxes. Tithraustes was sent to Sardis, and Tissaphernes was beheaded (*Hell.* III.4.21–25; Diodorus XIV.80.1–8; *Hell. Oxyr.* 11.2–12.4) and his possessions (*ousia*) confiscated to provide funds with which to pay the soldiers (*Hell. Oxyr.* 19.3). The new commander once again informed Agesilaus of the king's demands: "That the cities in Asia, retaining their independence, should render him the ancient tribute" (III.4.25✧). A six-month truce was then agreed to. Agesilaus received supplies from Tithraustes that made it possible for him to march to Hellespontine Phrygia. At this moment, the order from Sparta to take complete command of the navy reached him; he then issued orders to the coastal cities to provide ships and entrusted their command to his brother-in-law Peisander (III.4.25–28).

The "Anabasis" of Agesilaus

Diodorus provides further details about Agesilaus's plans after the battle of the Pactolus: he "was about to attack the satrapies farther inland (*anō*), but led his army back to the sea when he could not obtain favourable omens from the sacrifices" (XIV.80.5✧). The much more detailed report in the *Hellenica Oxyrhynchia* shows us that these sacrifices took place when, fresh from the plain of Sardis (accompanied for part of the journey

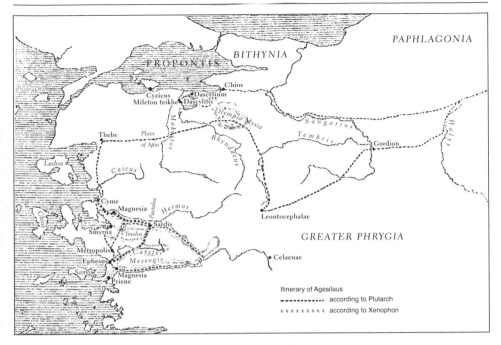

Map 4. The expedition of Agesilaus.

by Tissaphernes), Agesilaus went up the valley of the Cogamus before arriving on the banks of the Meander (12.1). Sacrifices were then offered to discover whether it was auspicious to move against Celaenae, the fortified capital of Greater Phrygia (12.4). When the gods provided a negative indication, Agesilaus went back down the Meander Valley to Ephesus (cf. also Diodorus XIV.80.5). In reality, the omens simply confirmed a prior decision: to march against Celaenae would be terribly risky. Agesilaus had had a twofold goal: to make an impression on the inland populations and to collect sizable booty.

He seems to have had some success in meeting these goals. Artaxerxes suffered some anxiety at the initial results of the land engagements (Diodorus XIV.80.6) because he had received information concerning the Greek predations on the plain of Sardis and beyond, including Tissaphernes' paradise (80.2). No doubt the Persians of Sardis were even more displeased with Tissaphernes because this was the first time since the Ionian raid in 499 that such unheard-of events had taken place. Moreover, according to the anonymous author (§21.1), Tithraustes agreed to the truce on the condition that Agesilaus would not pillage the Lydian countryside. It appears that more than anything else the Persians wished to keep Sardis and Lydia safe from war. As in earlier episodes, the leaders of Sardis were happy to see the theater of operations shift to the coast of Hellespontine Phrygia!

Nonetheless, Agesilaus did not give up his plan to advance on the interior. While Peisander was readying the navy, "Agesilaus continued the march to Phrygia" (*Hell.* III.4.29✧). He hoped to be able to count on the Mysians, who were said to be unsubmissive to the Great King. For this reason he ravaged their territory, but this action did not have the anticipated result: only a portion of the Mysians placed themselves under his command; another portion did severe damage to his troops (*Hell. Oxyr.* 21.1–3). Agesilaus did not let up on ravaging Pharnabazus's lands. He was soon joined by the Persian Spithridates, who had broken with the satrap of Dascylium some time earlier (Xenophon, *Hell.* III.4.10; *Ages.* 3.3; *Hell. Oxyr.* 21.3–4):

> And when Spithridates said that if he would come to Paphlagonia with him, he would bring the king of the Paphlagonians to a conference and make him an ally (*symmakhos*), Agesilaus eagerly undertook the journey, since this was a thing he had long desired—to win some nation (*ethnos*) away from the Persian King. (*Hell.* IV.1.2◇)

Accompanied by his new allies, Agesilaus took the interior road to Greater Phrygia and rejoined the royal way at Leontocephalae. Though he was able to extort some booty, he failed to take the town (*Hell. Oxyr.* 22.5), one of the most secure in Phrygia (Appian, *Mith.* 10: *khōrion okhyrotaton*). He then advanced against Gordion, "a fortress (*khōrion*) built on a hill and well supplied," but there too he had to fall back in the face of resistance put up by Rhathines (21.6), a subordinate of Pharnabazus (cf. Xenophon, *Anab.* VI.5.7 and *Hell.* III.4.13).

The Spartan next returned to Cius in Mysia and then Hellespontine Phrygia (*Hell. Oxyr.* 22.1–3). At this point Xenophon (and many other authors follow in his wake) devotes a long digression to relations between Pharnabazus and Agesilaus. At first, Pharnabazus's cavalry and scythe-equipped chariots won total victory, but then the Greeks managed to plunder the satrap's camp (IV.1.15–26). The author of the *Oxyrhynchus Hellenica* indicates that, meanwhile, Agesilaus had tried to take Dascylium, "a very strong place (*khōrion okhyron*), fortified by the king, where they said Pharnabazus kept the silver and gold he had" (22.3). Agesilaus brought the boats of the Peloponnesian navy from the Hellespont and ordered the commander to load all of the booty and take it to Cyzicus; then he sent his soldiers to their winter quarters, ordering them to regather the following spring (394; 22.4). The Spartan was unable to capture the citadel and so proceeded with controlled pillaging of the surroundings, particularly the prosperous, game-rich satrapal paradise (*Hell.* IV.1.15–16). We are then told that Pharnabazus complained to Agesilaus in these words: "I have not so much as a meal in my own land unless, like the beasts, I pick up a bit of what you may leave" (IV.1.33◇)! These words were spoken, Xenophon would have us believe, during a conversation between the leaders that was arranged by a Greek who had invited them both. After the meeting, Agesilaus left the country and encamped in the plain of Thebe near the Gulf of Adramyttium (spring, 394), and this is where he was when he received the order from the Spartan authorities to return immediately to Greece.

According to *Hell. Oxyr.* (22.4), his goal then was to march on Cappadocia: despite the obvious geographical mistake about the layout of Asia Minor, the datum indicates clearly that Agesilaus had decided to resume the march to the interior. Xenophon says no different: "He was preparing to march as far as he could into the interior (*anōtatō*), thinking that he would detach from the King all the nations (*ethnē*) which he could put in his rear" (Xenophon, *Hell.* IV.1.41◇). A similar appraisal is found in Plutarch: He "now resolved to carry away the war from the seaside, and to march further up into the country, and to attack the King of Persia himself in his own home in Susa and Ecbatana; not willing to let the monarch sit idle in his chair, playing umpire in the conflicts of the Greeks, and bribing their popular leaders" (*Ages.* 15.1;◇ cf. *Pel.* 30.3). The words used by Nepos are no less grandiose: "He was already planning to march against the Persians and attack the King himself" (*Ages.* 4.1–2✧). Finally, Isocrates, going on about the remarkable military weakness of the Persians, as was his wont, stated "that Agesilaus, with the help of the army of Cyrus, conquered almost all the territory this side of the Halys river" (*Paneg.* 145✧). Note that he took the opportunity of this comment to connect Agesilaus with Cyrus the Younger. We know in fact that the escapades of these two leaders—Cyrus (that is, the Greek mercenaries!) and Agesilaus—were constantly cited in Greece as especially eloquent precedents: both "brought the King to extremities" (Xenophon, *Hell.* VI.1.12✧)! Similarly, in the *Agesilaus*, the Spartan hero is systematically contrasted with a decadent Great King. If we follow Xenophon in this panegyric, Agesilaus was a Greek (Spartan) hero whose adventures explicitly matched those of the Homeric heroes: Agesilaus embarks on nothing less than a new Trojan War; emulating Agamemnon, he set sail from Aulis (cf. Plutarch, *Ages.* 6.6–8; Xenophon, *Hell.* III.4.3; Diodorus XIV.79.1).

In all of these Greek accounts we can recognize the traditional stereotypes of the Persians and the Great King (cf. *Hell.* III.4.19). But, above and beyond the Greek polemic and the private fantasies of the Lacedaemonian king, there is no doubt that from the moment of his arrival in Asia Minor he intended to pursue a very different war from the war that had been fought by his predecessors in the fifth century. With the exception of a brief appearance by Lacedaemonian troops in the Meander Valley and an Athenian raid on the fields of Lydia (*Hell.* I.2.4–5), the fifth-century Greek generals had always confined their operations to the coast and to pillaging in the areas of royal territory closest to the sea. It is possible that the very recent example of the Ten Thousand was actually interpreted in Greece and Asia Minor as proof of the relative permeability of the Empire's land defenses (cf. Xenophon, *Hell.* III.4.2). But it is important to distinguish the Achaemenid reality from the impression gathered from the Greek portrayals (which, moreover, are badly informed about facts of geography, as has just been seen and as is well confirmed by passages in the *Anabasis*). And this is why the historian of the Achaemenid Empire is interested in Agesilaus's operations: they provide an opportunity to take stock of Persian control of territory in western Asia Minor.

Persian Defenses Confronting Agesilaus's Offense: Satraps and ethnē

Xenophon's account is partial (in both senses of the word); according to him, the campaigns of his hero unfolded without major opposition (e.g., *Hell.* IV.1.17). Quite another picture emerges from the *Oxyrhynchus Hellenica*, which fortunately is closer to an arid campaign journal than an expansive and often misleading literary reconstruction. If Agesilaus really did have a momentary notion of retracing Cyrus's progress (whose trail he would follow between Sardis and the frontier of Greater Phrygia), he must have been a cockeyed optimist. The Persian leaders clearly adopted a traditional tactic to confront him: avoiding giving battle (cf. Xenophon, *Hell.* IV.1.17), allowing him to wander the countryside until necessity forced him to return to the coast. Agesilaus's main goal seems never to have been anything more than amassing booty in order to feed and pay his soldiers (*Hell. Oxyr.* 22.4). His greatest fear was lack of supplies (22.4). To be a threat to Persian dominion, he would have had to attack major towns. As it happened, every time he set up his battle line in front of a fortification held by the king's men, he was unable to conquer it, whether at Leontocephalae, Gordion, or Miletu teikhe (21.5–6; 22.3)—not to mention Sardis, Celaenae, or Dascylium. This series of failures illustrates the disconnect between the ambitions attributed to him and military reality. Agesilaus obviously had no siege engines, and, furthermore, no citadel commander was of a mind to desert the king.

Agesilaus clearly was counting on winning the allegiance of the peoples of the interior, whose independence from the central authority is smugly stressed by all the fourth-century authors. But we may inquire whether in this regard, too, the Spartan was the victim of his informers and/or his own fantasies. We have seen that the Mysians did not flock to him en masse, and that several communities even opposed him openly (*Hell. Oxyr.* 21.1–3; 22.3). The reaction of the Mysian people could perhaps be explained by their desire to preserve their lands and villages from the ravages of war; it could just as well be explained by fear of Persian reprisals — the satrap of Dascylium regularly led expeditions against Mysians who rebelled overtly (Xenophon, *Hell.* III.1.13). Moreover, many Mysians were serving in Pharnabazus's army (IV.1.24). Agesilaus scored greater success with the dynast-king of Paphlagonia, who provided a thousand horsemen and a thousand peltasts (soldiers armed with light shields). This dynast seems already to have broken with the central authority, since Xenophon states that "he had been summoned by the Persian King and had refused to go up to him" (IV.1.3◊); an invitation of this sort, of course, could bode no good! To refuse the king's invitation was tantamount to crossing the line one more time into rebellion, since in normal times Paphlagonia was also required to furnish a troop contingent whenever a satrapal requisition was issued (cf. Diodorus XIV.22.5). At any rate, Agesilaus wanted to cement the Paphlagonian alliance still more solidly, so he negotiated a marriage between the dynast and Spithridates' daughter (Xenophon, *Hell.* IV.1.2–15). It must again be remarked that, according to *Hell. Oxyr.* (22.1), Agesilaus concluded a truce (*spondai*) with the Paphlagonians, which implies that not all of the groups considered the dynast their leader. Like Mysia, Paphlagonia must have been split among several rival chieftains. This reality — that some regions had multiple local chieftains — certainly applied to various locales in Asia Minor and is well illustrated by Artaxerxes' war several years later against the Cadusians; in this case, there were two local kings, and each was anxious to obtain for himself "the friendship and alliance of the king" (Plutarch, *Art.* 24.6◊; cf. chap. 16/18).

Furthermore, the Persians may have kept an eye on Mysia and Paphlagonia more directly than the ancient texts suggest. In the context of preparations for Cyrus the Younger's expedition, Diodorus mentions a "satrap of Paphlagonia" who furnished Alcibiades with a safe-conduct that Pharnabazus had refused to him (XIV.11.3). Diodorus also, discussing the beginning of the Satraps' Revolt (which he places at the end of the 360s), refers to Orontes, the leader of the rebels, as the "satrap of Mysia" (XV.90.3◊3). These comments clearly could be simple mistakes by Diodorus, who is quite free with the word "satrap." But the term might also designate officials subordinate to a satrap (of Dascylium and/or Sardis). Let us recall the parallel case of Zenis of Dardanus, the "satrap" who was appointed by Pharnabazus in the part of the Aeolis that fell under his jurisdiction and who was responsible for overseeing the country, levying tribute (transferred to Pharnabazus), leading contingents of the satrapal army, and scheduling ostentatious receptions for the satrap of Dascylium during his inspection tours (Xenophon, *Hell.* III.1.10–15). In short, Zenis acted like a satrap (*satrapeuein*: III.1.10) accountable to Pharnabazus; Zenis (who was succeeded by his widow Mania) was one of the governors dependent on the authority of Pharnabazus (III.1.12: *pantōn tōn hyparkhōn*). If we follow this theory, we might ask whether Ariobarzanes fulfilled the same function in Paphlagonia in 407; Ariobarzanes, a relative(?) of Pharnabazus, was ordered in 407 to bring the Athenian ambassadors, whom the satrap of Dascylium had detained for three years, to Cius in Mysia (*Hell.* I.4.7).

Ambiguity also results from the confusion between geographic regions and ethnic groups. We have already pointed out that neither Mysia nor Paphlagonia was unified. Several episodes reveal that certain parties in Mysia were firmly under the thumb of the Persians. Many military establishments had been set up there beginning in the time of Darius and Xerxes (chap. 13/9). The survivors of the Ten Thousand had had rough times there as soon as they reached Pergamum, which Xenophon places in Mysia, in the plain of the Caicus (*Anab.* VII.8.8), the same place where the work of Orontes ("satrap of Mysia") is attested (*OGIS* 264, lines 6–9). The Persian Asidates had a very large rural estate, peopled with slaves and dependents, on this plain. The estate was fortified (*tyrsis, pyrgion, teikhos; Anab.* VII.8.12–14). Moreover, the defenders were able to communicate with other positions in the surroundings, using signals beacons:

> There came to their assistance Itamenes with his own force, and from Comania Assyrian hoplites and Hyrcanian horsemen—these also being mercenaries in the service of the King—to the number of eighty, as well as about eight hundred peltasts, and more from Parthenium, and more from Apollonia and from the nearby places (*khoria*), including horsemen. . . . And Procles also came to the rescue, from Halisarna and Teuthrania, the descendant of Damaratus. (VII.8.15, 17✧)

The men of Gongylus of Eretria soon joined in; he had been established in the region during the time of Xerxes (VII.8.17; cf. *Hell.* III.1.6). This example is a perfect illustration of the density of Achaemenid territorial occupation in this Mysian region: it was populated with military colonists and garrisons, and bristled with small forts. Confirmation is found in a passage in Polyaenus (VI.10) in the context of Thibron's expedition in Aeolis; it too appears to have been covered with a dense network of small forts commanded by a "phrourarch of the strongholds (*khōria*) of the Aeolid."

Of course, these observations do not answer the subsidiary question of whether there were governments of Mysia or Paphlagonia. But though we note that the satraps could at any moment count on contingents of horsemen led by the Persians of the diaspora, we can easily agree that the imperial territories were not as empty of defenses as the Greek authors would have us believe or as Agesilaus himself perhaps imagined. Despite the victory near Sardis, he was unable to appropriate for himself any Achaemenid strategic space (roads, storehouses, citadels; see chap. 11/2). If he really did cherish the dream of marching once more on the interior in 394, his chances of success were practically nil.

The Persians and Agesilaus Face Off

Agesilaus was unable to seize the strong towns in the interior, but the theoretical possibility of creating enough unrest that some Persians would desert the king remained. But even the hopes of this possibility that he might have harbored were dashed. When he returned from his expedition, as we have seen, he conversed at length with Pharnabazus. According to Xenophon, he emphasized to the satrap, "It is within your power by joining with us to live in the enjoyment of your possessions without doing homage to anyone or having any master" (*despotēs; Hell.* IV.1.35✧). And he adds:

> We urge upon you . . . to increase, not the King's empire, but your own, subduing those who are now your fellow-slaves (*homodouloi*) so that they shall be your subjects (*hypēkooi*). (IV.1.36✧)

In context, this speech was intended to convince Pharnabazus to make himself into an independent prince by transforming the other Persians in his satrapy into *bandaka*. Pharnabazus replied simply that, if the king named another general, he would agree to be Agesilaus's friend and ally; if not, his connection to the Great King could not be severed (IV.1.37). The satrap's dilatory response in fact left Agesilaus with no hope, even more so because Pharnabazus had much earlier been promised one of Artaxerxes' daughters (Plutarch, *Art.* 27.7)—a promise that was kept some years later (Xenophon, *Hell.* V.1.28).

The only attested defector was Spithridates. He was a high-born Persian who broke with Pharnabazus when the latter proposed to take his daughter as concubine (Xenophon, *Ages.* 3.3); when Lysander approached, he fled to Cyzicus, where he left his whole family, his treasure, and his following of 200 horsemen and, along with his son Megabates, joined Agesilaus (Xenophon, *Hell.* III.4.10; IV.1.6–7; *Hell. Oxyr.* 21.4). His duties under Pharnabazus are not precisely known: *Hell. Oxyr.* notes simply "that he lived with Pharnabazus and served him" (21.4). He thus belonged to the circle of landed aristrocrats used by the satrap of Dascylium for occasional missions. We know that in 410 he shared command with Rhathines of the contingents who, with the Bithynians, were mustered by Pharnabazus to prevent the survivors of the Ten Thousand from entering Phrygia (*Anab.* VI.4.24, 5.7). But the missions accomplished by one or another satrapal official say nothing at all about their permanent job; during Agesilaus's expedition, this same Rhathines was in command of Gordion (*Hell. Oxyr.* 21.6). Most notable is the fact that Spithridates agreed to marry his daughter to the Paphlagonian dynast (*Hell.* IV.1.4–15). We are tempted to conclude from this that he had had a long and close relationship with Paphlagonia.

The alliance between Agesilaus and Spithridates did not last. After the successful attack on Pharnabazus's baggage and caravan (394), Spithridates and his Paphlagonian allies took booty. They were soon relieved of it by Agesilaus's lieutenant, on the excuse that it had to be placed in the hands of the "officers in charge of sale of booty." According to Xenophon, this practice is what drove Agesilaus's allies to abandon him (IV.1.26–27). In reality, this complaint was probably just a pretext. Contrary to Xenophon, Spithridates and the Paphlagonians had certainly drawn their own conclusions from recent events, which held out little hope of victory to the Lacedaemonian. Their concern from that moment onward was to obtain the king's pardon. So they left immediately for Sardis to meet with Ariaeus, the former companion of Cyrus the Younger; when Ariaeus had left Lydia, Tithraustes had given him a command alongside another Persian, Pasiphernes (*Hell. Oxyr.* 19.3), and he had recently displayed his loyalty by actively participating in the execution of Tissaphernes (Diodorus XIV.80.8). They had decided to put "their trust in Ariaeus because he also had revolted from the King and made war on him." Xenophon lets it be known that this desertion sounded the death knell for Agesilaus's hopes: "Nothing happened during the campaign which was more distressing to Agesilaus than the desertion of Spithridates, Megabates, and the Paphlagonians" (*Hell.* IV.1.28❖).

Agesilaus: A Summary

Agesilaus was recalled in haste to Sparta, which was threatened by a coalition of Greek cities (including Athens) that wanted to escape its dominion; he left Asia Minor with a less than impressive resumé. Aside from a contingent commanded by Dercyllidas that he sent to the Hellespont shortly after his departure (*Hell.* IV.3.3) and the garrisons still found here and there, he had had to abandon to their fate the cities he had come to liberate from the Persian yoke. The only positive point in the record is the existence of the navy that the Spartan chief had ordered built the year before and had entrusted to his brother-in-law Peisander (III.4.28–29). It is true that he had also demonstrated that the Persians controlled the roads to Sardis only imperfectly. Thibron had already shown the way by campaigning against Magnesia and Tralles (Diodorus XIV.36.2–3). Agesilaus went further, since he had understood that he needed a cavalry to confront the Persians. Some time later, the Spartan Diphridas even succeeded in capturing Struthas's son-in-law "as they were journeying to Sardis" (*Hell.* IV.8.21✧). Meanwhile, all in all, even if the Spartan had exhibited boldness by developing an "anabasis" strategy [driving for the interior], he does not seem ever to have believed that he could drive the Persians from the satrapies of Sardis and Dascylium. In any case, this goal was unrealizable both because the imperial defenses were solid and because the very idea of an expedition of this kind had certainly never entered the mind of the Spartan leaders. In short, despite the Trojan setting, neither geographically nor politically was Agesilaus a prototype of Alexander.

6. Achaemenid Successes and Failures: From Asia Minor to Egypt (ca. 396 – ca. 370)

The Defeat of Sparta

During the same period, after being named admiral of the royal navy (§4 above), Conon completed his preparations and began his offensive. His first success (396), after obtaining funds from Tithraustes and the Great King, was to incite a Rhodian party to rise up against the Spartans and welcome his fleet (Diodorus XIV.79.5–6). This was a major victory because of the commercial and strategic importance of the island. In concert with Pharnabazus, Conon piloted the navy to the Cnidian Chersonese to confront the Lacedaemonian navy that was moored at Cnidos. The ensuing battle proved a striking victory for his squadrons (Diodorus XIV.83.4–7; Xenophon, *Hell.* IV.3.11–12). The conquerors gained immediate profit from driving the Lacedaemonian garrisons from both the islands (Cos, Nisyros, Teos, Mytilene, Chios) and the coast (Ephesus, Erythrae; Diodorus XIV.84.3):

> Pharnabazus and Conon . . . made a tour of the islands and the cities on the sea coast, drove out the Laconian governors, and encouraged the cities by saying that they would not establish fortified citadels within their walls and would leave them independent. And the people of the cities received this announcement with joy and approval, and enthusiastically sent gifts of friendship to Pharnabazus. (*Hell.* IV.8.1–2✧)

Only Dercyllidas was in a position to resist the offensive of Pharnabazus when he returned to his territory (IV.8.5). The following spring (393), Conon and Pharnabazus's navy returned to sea. Pharnabazus's goal was to wreak vengeance on Sparta: his navy took Cythera, liberating the Cyclades in the process (Diodorus 84.5), then "sailing to the Isthmus of Corinth and there exhorting the allies to carry on the war zealously and show themselves men faithful to the King, he left them all the money that he had" (IV.8.8✧). The Persian may even have been hailed at Athens with an honorary decree (cf. Tod no. 199). This was the first time since 480 that an Achaemenid navy had come to support the "Medizers"! The Persian triumph seemed resplendent.

The Persians Caught between Athenians and Lacedaemonians

In truth, however, the Persian victory was fragile and uncertain. The Persians, willy-nilly, were once again squeezed between Sparta's desire to maintain its dominion and Athens's wish to reestablish its own. The victory at Cnidos and those that followed were also the work of Conon, who since 405 had dreamed of nothing but restoring the glory of his homeland. On his insistence, Pharnabazus agreed to leave a part of his fleet and money with him, and Conon was soon to use it to rebuild the walls of Athens and Piraeus that had been destroyed by the Spartans in 404 (*Hell.* IV.8.9–10). The Lacedaemonians used this new opportunity to break their alliances and to try to arrange a new treaty with Artaxerxes against Athens. Playing on dissension among the Persian leaders, something they were very good at, they sent Antalcidas to Tiribazus at Sardis; meanwhile, the king had made Tiribazus head of the royal troops in Asia Minor (Diodorus XIV.85.4).

Antalcidas arrived, and right behind him arrived ambassadors from Athens and from the cities that fought alongside it against Sparta as well. Each delegation addressed Tiribazus in turn, making him their arbitrator. Antalcidas offered peace, "just such a peace as the King had wished for. For the Lacedaemonians, he said, urged no claim against the King to the Greek cities in Asia and they were content that all the islands and the Greek cities in general should be independent" (*Hell.* IV.8.14◇). As the speeches of the other delegates show, the Spartan offer encompassed the problems of the cities of Europe. The Athenians opposed it strongly, quite rightly thinking that such a peace would prevent them from achieving their ambitious goals.

The Persian leaders were not all in agreement about strategy at this time. Tiribazus brought Conon to Sardis and threw him in prison (Diodorus XIV.85.4). He provided money to the Lacedaemonians secretly because he could not make a decision to do this without consulting with the king (*Hell.* IV.8.16◇). Obviously, Tiribazus would not have been able to persuade Artaxerxes, who sent Struthas to Sardis, who "devoted himself assiduously to the Athenians"; his hostility toward the Spartans surely grew when, shortly afterward, the Lacedaemonian Diphridas seized his son-in-law Tigranes and held him for ransom (IV.8.21)! The following years brought an escalation of hostilities between Athenians and Lacedaemonians in Asia Minor, and the Persians scarcely appear to have been in a position to arbitrate. The Lacedaemonians reinstalled governors (*harmostai*; IV.8.29).

But the truth is doubtless more complicated than Xenophon indicates, for his account is devoted entirely to Athens-Sparta hostilities. In fact, we learn from an inscription that we have already discussed (see chap. 12/5) that during these years Struthas (Struses) arbitrated a territorial disagreement between Miletus and Myus, which he submitted to judges from twelve Ionian towns (Tod no. 113), a sign that at that date Sardis could impose its own arbitration on the cities of the Ionian coast, along the lines of the decrees made a century earlier by Artaphernes. It is very likely that an important administrative change took place during these years (between 395 and 391) as well: Caria, hitherto a dependency of Sardis, was made into an autonomous satrapy and entrusted to Hecatomnus, heir to a dynastic power centered on Mylasa, capital of the *koinon* ('federation') of the Carians. It is possible that Artaxerxes did this to render war on Sparta more efficient.

From Cyprus to Egypt

Seen from Susa or Babylon, matters cannot be reduced to the contradictory ambitions of Athens and Sparta on the coast of Asia Minor. The Great King was primarily preoccupied with the events then unfolding in Egypt and Cyprus. In fact, it is in the context of 391–390 that Diodorus discusses the fears of the Great King, who was alerted by some Cypriot kings (Amathus, Soloi, and Kition). They were desperately fighting off the assaults of Evagoras's forces and sought Persian aid:

> They accused Evagoras of having slain King Agyris, an ally of the Persians, and promised to join the King in acquiring the island for him. The King, not only because he did not wish Evagoras to grow any stronger, but also because he appreciated the strategic position of Cyprus and its great naval strength whereby it would be able to protect Asia in front, decided to accept the alliance (*symmakhein*). He dismissed the ambassadors and for himself sent letters to the cities situated on the sea and to their commanding satraps to construct triremes and with all speed to make ready everything the fleet might need. (XIV.98.3✧)

Ever since he had come to power (see chap. 14/8), Evagoras of Salamis had methodically pursued his goal—to extend his power over the other cities on the island. Moreover, since 398 he had collaborated with Artaxerxes II in the war against Lacedaemonian forces. But the effective disappearance of the Spartan threat to the Aegean coasts after the battle of Cnidos changed the situation drastically. Diodorus's text is very clear: the break did not come from Evagoras (who no longer had any interest there); it was a cold decision of Artaxerxes. Isocrates agrees (*Evag.* 67–68). At the moment he regained control of Asia Minor, the Great King at all costs wanted to avoid seeing an economic and military power arise on his flank that threatened to reduce to nothing the maritime strategy he had pursued consistently since Cunaxa; thus, control of the island presupposed that power there would be fragmented among a number of simultaneous kinglets who, as we have just seen, would inform on each other to the central authority.

A recently published Phoenician inscription provides several clarifications regarding the initial battles on Cyprus. The inscription, dated to year 1 of Milkyatōn (son of Baalrōm), the king of Kition, commemorates the erection of a monument after a victory won by the king "and all the people of Kition" over "our enemies and their Paphian auxiliaries." There can hardly be any doubt that the term "enemies" designates Evagoras and his allies—among whom only the Paphians are named. We thus have a direct echo of the open warfare between Kition and its allies (Amathontes, Soloi) on the one side and Salamis and its allies on the other. It is quite noteworthy that it was after this victory that Milkyatōn took the title of king (392?), founding a royal dynasty that can be followed down to 312. Unlike an older inscription from Idalion, which dates to somewhere between 470 and 440, the "Medes" are not named. But we cannot doubt that the new ruler of Kition received aid and support from Artaxerxes, as Diodorus reports (XIV.98.3). It is nonethless likely that this success came in a period before the direct intervention of Persian forces; it was not until several years later that the Persians won a naval battle near Kition (cf. XV.3.4–5). At any rate, this sort of dynastic monument clearly highlights the close cooperation between the new king and "all the people of Kition." Moreover, seen in the context of Persian–Cypriot relations, the battles against Evagoras of Salamis also (primarily?) belong to the history of Cyprus in the *longue durée*—a history that cannot be reduced to the vagaries of dominion by the Great King.

One essential element certainly played a part in Persian policy: if Cyprus were not retaken, any expedition against the Nile Valley was doomed to failure. And, in fact, the reconquest of Egypt was the topmost priority for Artaxerxes. Just as negotiations between the Greeks and Tithraustes were beginning, power was changing hands in Egypt. In 394–393 (or 392–391), Nepherites perished in dynastic turmoil. Two dynasts proclaimed themselves pharaoh simultaneously: Muthis, son of Nepherites, and Psammuthis. The debate was soon settled by a third person, Hakoris (perhaps a relative of Nepherites), who took power at the beginning of 392 (or 392–391). His titles and the breadth of his building program show his desire to connect himself with the glorious tradition of the Saite period and to pursue the war against the Persians doggedly; he knew that they had never abandoned the idea of reconquest. The reign of this sovereign (whom he calls Pakōrios) is the topic of the lost twelfth book of Theopompus's *History*, in which "the story of the deeds and acts of the Greeks and Barbarians down to his time is found" (*FGrH* 115 F103).

The Initial Operations (391–387/386)

It is quite noteworthy that in 391–390 the Great King wanted to act rapidly (Diodorus XIV.98.3: *kata spoudēn*). He probably hoped to prevent Evagoras from receiving external aid. Theopompus notes the alliance between Hakoris and Evagoras. It is possible that Evagoras had sent ambassadors to Hakoris, as he had to Athens (Lysias XIX.21–23), but it seems quite unlikely that the pharaoh was in any position to send him reinforcements at that time. On the other hand, the unleashing of the Cypriot operation could only help Hakoris, since it gave him time to consolidate his power and prepare his country for the inevitable Persian offense.

It is possible, as Isocrates suggests (*Paneg.* 161), that Tyre took the side of Evagoras, because a few years later Tyrian ships fought alongside his (Diodorus XV.2.4); but Tyre's defection from Persia may have come several years after the onset of hostilities. At one point, Evagoras also received aid from Athens: in 390–389, Athens sent ten ships that were hailed for inspection by a Lacedaemonian admiral (Xenophon, *Hell.* IV.8.24; Lysias XIX.21ff., 43). Some time later (388–387), Athens sent new reinforcements to Evagoras—10 triremes and 800 peltasts commanded by Chabrias (V.1.10)—but we know nothing of the outcome (probably nothing happened). At almost the same time (388), the Athenian Thrasybulus advanced with a squadron along the southern coast of Asia Minor as far as Aspendus on the mouth of the Eurymedon, where he tried to levy taxes on the inhabitants. They, however, became fed up with the soldiers' predations and slew the Athenian general in his tent (IV.8.30; Diodorus XIV.99.4). These occasional military operations clearly belong more to the history of the Athens-Sparta conflict than to the affairs of Cyprus. In any case, the strange behavior of the Spartans and Athenians, with respect to the ships sent by Athens to Cyprus in 390–389, was stressed by Xenophon: "Both parties were acting in this affair in a manner absolutely opposed to their own interests; for the Athenians, although they had the King for a friend, were sending aid to Euagoras who was making war upon the King, and Teleutias, although the Lacedaemonians were at war with the King, was destroying people who were sailing to make war upon him" (*Hell.* IV.8.24◊)! In short, in 391–390, Evagoras could not count on any external allies.

The Persian troops had two commanders: the Persian Autophradates (land army) and Hecatomnus, the "Carian dynast" (as admiral; Diodorus XIV.98.4; Theopompus *FGrH* 115, F103). We know practically nothing about this first campaign. According to Isocrates, the results were not commensurate with the enormous financial sacrifices to which the Great King consented, since during the war Evagoras "took Tyre by storm, caused Cilicia to revolt from the Great King" (*Evag.* 60–62◊). Of what value, then, are the words of the Athenian polemicist? Perhaps they simply convey that one of the results was that Tyre was captured by the king of Salamis. Let us simply recall that all the ancient authors, especially Diodorus, imply that between about 390 and 387–386 the Great

King and his generals primarily used the time to complete their preparations. A navy was assembled in Asia Minor, at Phocaea and Cyme, and troops were gathered in Cilicia, where the entire army was concentrated before crossing to Cyprus (XV.2.1–2). The sequence and rationale of Diodorus's presentation imply that during this time Evagoras also gathered reinforcements with the aid he found among his neighbors (2.3–4).

The King's Peace (386)

Meanwhile, Antalcidas, who had accompanied Tiribazus all the way to the King, obtained from him "an agreement that the King should be an ally of the Lacedaemonians if the Athenians and their allies refused to accept the peace which he himself directed them to accept" (V.1.25◇). Most of the Greek cities were worn out by the continual wars and yearned for peace: "So that when Tiribazus ordered those to be present who desired to give ear to the peace which the King had sent down, all speedily presented themselves. And when they had come together, Tiribazus showed them the king's seal" and read the following document:

> "King Artaxerxes thinks it just that the cities in Asia should belong to him (*heautou einai*), as well as Clazomenae and Cyprus among the islands, and that the other Greek cities, both small and great, should be left independent, except Lemnos, Imbros, and Scyros, and these should belong, as of old, to the Athenians. But whichever of the two parties does not accept this peace, upon them I will make war, in company with those who desire this arrangement, both by land and by sea, with ships and with money." (V.1.30–31◇)

With the exception of the Thebans, all the participants "[swore] that they would abide by the treaty which the King had proposed; thereupon the armies were disbanded and the naval armaments were likewise disbanded" (V.1.35◇).

From a Greek point of view, the peace (also known as the Peace of Antalcidas) certainly meant a victory for Sparta, which lost no time in proclaiming the leagues created around Athens and Thebes obsolete, because they were contrary to the clause guaranteeing the autonomy of the cities. From the Persian point of view, the victory was no less complete. The peace brought an end to the era that began with the creation of the Delian League in 478–477: the cities in Asia returned wholly to the Achaemenid fold, and the cities in Europe agreed that they would no longer attempt to get them to leave. The king's territories, so often pillaged and threatened since 478–477, remained safe and protected thereafter. In a way, Artaxerxes II succeeded in bringing to completion the program Alcibiades had suggested to Tissaphernes nearly forty years earlier: to play the Greeks off against each other (Thucydides VIII.46.1–4). The Great King owed this victory not just to the internal weakening of the Greek cities or the distribution of "royal-archer" coins (silver siculi and gold darics); he owed it first and foremost to the resoluteness and constancy of his policy and deeds.

A Universal Conflagration?

It is easy enough to understand how the open hostilities at the end of the 390s could resume stronger than ever after 387. According to Justin (VI.6.2), Artaxerxes was so eager to impose peace around 387 because, "preoccupied with the war against Egypt, he feared that if he sent aid to the Lacedaemonians against his satraps, his armies would be tied up in Greece." Even if Justin is especially interested in illustrating the king's cynicism, the thought he ascribes to him should not be surprising: it reminds us of a comparable decision made by Artaxerxes I in the 460s (Thucydides I.109.2; Diodorus XI.74.5). Diodorus in turn says that the peace that the king imposed on the Greeks left him able to operate with a free rein, and he "made ready his armaments for the war against Cyprus. For Evagoras had got possession of almost the whole of Cyprus and gathered strong armaments, because Artaxerxes was distracted by the war against the Greeks" (XIV.110.5✧). In addition, Theopompus says the fighting on Cyprus continued even more vigorously after the peace of 386 (*FGrH* 115 F103). The text read to the Greek delegations also explicitly stated that Cyprus was part of the king's territory (*Hell*. V.1.31).

The ancient authors are unanimous in emphasizing that Artaxerxes then found himself facing multiple rebellions, which they characterize as not merely simultaneous but coordinated. Diodorus says Evagoras had a very wide network of alliances: the king of Egypt, Hakoris, sent significant forces, and Hecatomnus of Caria secretly provided him with large amounts of money for hiring mercenaries. Evagoras also possessed Tyre and "several other towns," which furnished ships. As Diodorus tells it, the entire Levant was seceding, since Evagoras also received aid from "such others . . . as were at odds with the Persians, either secretly or openly," and "not a few soldiers were sent him by the king of the Arabs and by certain others of whom the King of the Persians was suspicious" (XV.2.3–4✧). A similar narrative is found in Theopompus: he reports "how Hakoris the Egyptian made alliance with the Pisidians" (*FGrH* 115 F103). In the *Panegyric* (380), Isocrates lays out a catastrophic review of Persia's status in the Levant:

> Are not Egypt and Cyprus in revolt against him? Have not Phoenicia and Syria been devastated because of the war? Has not Tyre, on which he set great store, been seized by his foes? Of the cities in Cilicia, the greater number are held by those who side with us and the rest are not difficult to acquire. Lycia no Persian has ever subdued. Hecatomnus, the viceroy of Caria, has in reality been disaffected for a long time now, and will openly declare himself whenever we wish. From Cnidos to Sinope the coast of Asia is settled by Hellenes, and these we need not to persuade to go to war—all we have to do is not to restrain them. (§§161–62✧)

Isocrates' chronologically rather imprecise presentation certainly need not be taken absolutely literally; his purpose was to persuade the Greeks to launch an offensive in Asia Minor. To that end, he was attempting to prove the Persians' extreme military weakness, which was illustrated particularly by their defeats in Egypt, as well as by the exploits of Cyrus's mercenaries and Agesilaus's troops (§§138–59).

The existence of unrest in this period is well illustrated by the biography of Datames presented to us by Cornelius Nepos. Datames, son of Camisares, "governed that part of Cilicia which adjoins Cappadocia and is inhabited by the Leucosyri, or 'White Syrians'" (§1.1✧); he was a member of the royal palace guard and displayed his valor as a soldier for the first time "in the war which the king waged against the Cadusii," during which his father died (§1.2✧). This Cadusian war is also mentioned by Diodorus, in the context of the Cyprus war, so it took place about 385–384 (Diodorus XV.8.5; 10.1). Plutarch (*Art*. 24) seems to refer to a second Cadusian war, which he places at the time of the second Egyptian expedition, in 374 (*Art*. 24.1; cf. Trogus Pompeius, *Prol*. X). Nepos goes on to say that his hero once again demonstrated his bravery "when Autophradates, at the king's command, was making war on the peoples that had revolted" (§2.1✧). Nepos says nothing about the identity of these peoples. On the other hand, we know that Datames led another expedition after 387, this time against Thuys, dynast of Paphlagonia, who "did not own obedience to the king" (§2.2✧).

While the existence of unrest is established, there is nothing to suggest that it constituted a vast common front formed at the instigation of Hakoris and/or Evagoras. We must in fact stress that the Greek authors were fond of this sort of catalogue, as is illustrated particularly well by the systematic review that Diodorus lays out (XV.90.2–4) of the rebellions fomented against Artaxerxes about twenty years later (see chap. 15/7 below). The evidence implies that Artaxerxes' campaigns in the Zagros were a local affair injected into the *longue durée* of Cadusian affairs (see chap. 16/18). And, while the alliance between Hakoris and the Greeks and Evagoras is undeniable, it nonetheless appears strange that the pharaoh would be so interested in acting in concert with the Pisidians, as Theopompus states; this allusion indicates no more than that at this point the Pisidians (or some of them at least) were opposed to royal forces—which is a given throughout Achaemenid history. Similarly, the example of Thuys is not isolated; the Paphlagonian dynasts were frequently opposed to Persian authority, as shown by the very recent example of Agesilaus and Spithridates. Other information given by the ancient authors must be taken with a grain of salt. For instance, there is nothing to indicate that Cilicia was ever totally endangered, aside from the unfortunate raid by Thrasybulus in the region of Aspendus in Pamphylia (*Hell.* IV.8.30; Diodorus XIV.99.4). It is clear that at this date, as before, Cilicia was utilized by the Persians virtually as a military base (Diodorus XV.3.3), and this is also indicated by the coins struck by Tiribazus in several Cilician cities (Tarsus, Issus, Soloi, Mallus). Furthermore, the peace of 386 prohibited the Greeks from interfering. It must also be recalled that Cilicia itself included distinct subregions (see chap. 16/6). We may recall, for example, that Datames was ordered by Artaxerxes to defeat Aspis, "the ruler of Cataonia; . . . [who] far from acknowledging allegiance to Artaxerxes, even overran the regions neighbouring to Persia and carried off what was being brought to the king" (Nepos, *Dat.* 4.1–2◊). This again refers to a minor, local problem, which one is tempted to compare with the false goal that Cyrus announced to his expedition in 401 to deceive his mercenaries: they were "leading the army to Cilicia against the despots who were in rebellion against the King" (Diodorus XIV.19.3◊). Moreover, it is quite noteworthy that Datames landed in Cilicia on the way from Syria, before marching against Aspis (*Dat.* 4.4). Finally, the matter of the Carian satrap Hecatomnus also remains uncertain. During the first offensive in 393–392, he was entrusted with military operations (Diodorus XIV.98.4), in cooperation with Autophradates, according to Theopompus (*FGrH* 112, F103). Diodorus places him among Evagoras's secret allies in 387, the one to whom Evagoras sent great sums of money to hire mercenaries (XV.2.3); and Isocrates, in the *Panegyric* (§162◊), believes he had "been disaffected for a long time now." But formal proof of his rebellion is singularly lacking.

However difficult the task, it is still necessary to distinguish these purely local troubles from genuine networks of alliances (Hakoris/Evagoras, Evagoras/Tyre). Among those involved in alliances we should include the person Diodorus calls the "king of the Arabs" (XV.2.4), who is also mentioned in a similar context earlier, in 411–410 (XIII.46.6); he may have been the head of the tribe whose territories adjoined the road between Gaza and Egypt. But nothing allows us to state with certainty that the disturbance embraced all of Syria–Palestine or all of Phoenicia. Mounting an expedition to Egypt around 385–384 (below) presupposes, on the contrary, that the Persians were able to requisition ships in Phoenicia and that they controlled traditional logistical bases (Sidon, Acre, Gaza). It is nonetheless true that Artaxerxes II's situation at that date was difficult and filled with potential dangers, since he needed simultaneously both to carry out local expeditions and to gather considerable forces to overcome Evagoras and Hakoris.

The Offensive against Evagoras (387/386–383/381)

After lengthy preparations, land and sea forces were entrusted to Orontes and Tiriba-zus, who were ordered to subdue Evagoras. The breadth of preparations carried out in both camps (Diodorus XV.2) indicates that the confrontation was expected to be deci-sive. On Cyprus, the Persian navy scored a victory at Kition, and then the army laid siege to Salamis (Diodorus XV.3.4–6; 4.1). At this point, Evagoras sought out Hakoris in Egypt "and urged him to continue the war energetically and to consider the war against the Persians a common undertaking" (XV.4.3◊). He brought back nothing from this contact except pretty words and a piddling amount of money (XV.8.1). Fresh from his victory over the Persian forces (or perhaps still in the middle of the fight), the pharaoh obviously considered the Cypriot front a secondary matter.

After lengthy negotiations, peace was imposed by the Great King under the following conditions: "Evagoras . . . should be king of Salamis, pay the fixed tribute annually, and obey as a king the orders of the King" (XV.9.2◊; around 383–381). Diodorus presents as one of Evagoras's achievements that he was recognized as king of Salamis (XV.8.2–3; 9.2). Actually, on the political and strategic level, down the line Evagoras had to retreat, since the terms of his surrender forbade him to undertake any future offensive against the other Cypriot kings, all of whom from then on would be the Great King's preferred allies on the island. Like them, Evagoras thereafter had to bend to the Achaemenid au-thorities in all things and provide tribute and naval contingents. In sum, matters in Cy-prus were back to the place they had been some twenty years earlier, before Evagoras had begun to extend his dominion over other kingdoms on the island. Combined with the outcome of the peace of 386, the Cyprus victory was crucial to Achaemenid author-ity because of the central strategic importance of the island of Cyprus to the Persian po-sition in the eastern Aegean. Undoubtedly, it also allowed them to retake the Phoenician cities that had joined Evagoras, particularly Tyre.

The Egyptian Defeats

At the same time, however, the Great King suffered a defeat in his principal objec-tive, the reconquest of Egypt. In his *Panegyric*, Isocrates (our only source, unfortunately) in fact alludes to an operation against Egypt in the 380s:

> Take, first, the case of Egypt: since its revolt from the King, what progress has he made against its inhabitants? Did he not dispatch to this war the most renowned of the Persians, Abrocomas and Tithraustes and Pharnabazus, and did not they, after remaining there three years and suffering more disasters than they inflicted, finally withdraw in such disgrace that the rebels are no longer content with their freedom, but are already trying to extend their do-minion over the neighbouring peoples as well? (*Paneg.* 140◊)

The date of this fruitless expedition is uncertain; it appears, however, that it was carried out at the same time that the Persian troops were in action against Cyprus. The fact re-mains that it was a considerable setback. An independent Egypt would be a perpetual threat to Persian dominion over the lands of Ebir Nāri. It would also be a natural ally to anyone who wanted to take on the Persians, including subordinates of the Great King. So it was when Glus, Tiribazus's son-in-law, chose to rebel against the king at the end of the 380s, because he was afraid of being swept up in the accusations against his father-in-law. As commander of the Cyprus fleet (Diodorus XV.3.2), he had played a decisive role in the battle of Kition against Evagoras (XV.3.6). Endowed with an abundance of money and soldiers, he entered into alliance with Hakoris and the Spartans (XV.9.3–5) but fell to an assassin's hand (XV.18.1). To be sure, his case is special, because he was the son of the Carian-Memphite Tamos, Cyrus's old admiral, who had sought refuge with Psammetichus in 400. But it is also worth observing that, according to Diodorus (XV.18.1), Glus's plans were taken up by a certain Tachos, whose name indicates that he had an Egyptian background; he had founded a city in land located on the borders of Cyme and Clazomenae (18.2–4). It thus appears that Glus and, later, Tachos attempted to set up with the aid of the pharaohs a sort of "dynasty" in Asia Minor, situated not coincidentally very close to Cymae, Persia's very important naval base in Asia Minor.

The danger was even more serious in that Hakoris apparently continued his preparations, gathering a large number of Greek mercenaries and even recruiting the Athenian Chabrias, who was engaged privately, because at this time Athens was far from anxious to engage in hostilities with Artaxerxes. According to Diodorus, the pharaoh gathered his troops "for the campaign (*pros tēn strateian*) . . . and with great dispatch made preparations to fight the Persians" (XV.29.1–2✧). Does the phrase indicate that Hakoris had decided to go on the offensive? We cannot say with certainty. What is certain, however, is that Artaxerxes did not abandon his plan to reconquer the Nile Valley, especially in view of the fact that, from this point on, Egypt could no longer count on external allies.

Pharnabazus, who was ordered to advance against Egypt, set up his logistical base at Acre in Palestine and gathered a massive navy, since it was said that no expedition against Egypt could succeed without the support of a navy, both for resupplying the troops and for negating the defenses of the Delta. The ships must have been built in Phoenicia (cf. Polyaenus III.9.63) as well as Cyprus and Cilicia, where Pharnabazus's coinage also attests to the enlistment of troops. During his preparations, Pharnabazus sent an embassy to Athens, demanding that Chabrias be recalled from Egypt and Iphicrates be sent to Acre; his demands were met (XV.29.4). These are the reasons why (still following Diodorus; XV.38.1✧) Artaxerxes intervened directly in 375 to stop the hostilities that were ripping the Greek cities apart, "intending to make war on the Egyptians and being busily engaged in organizing a considerable mercenary army."

In 373 the full force of Persian intervention was set in motion. In Egypt, after a confused period of infighting after the death of Hakoris (380), Nectanebo was recognized as pharaoh, thus founding what is conventionally called the XXXth Dynasty, and he soon adopted Hakoris's strategy toward the Persian threat. The Egyptians, expecting Pharnabazus's attack, had fortified the Delta: "Nectanebôs . . . was emboldened, chiefly by the strength of the country, for Egypt is extremely difficult of approach, and secondly by the fact that all points of invasion from land or sea had been carefully blocked" (XV.42.1✧). The Egyptian leaders had erected fortifications on each of the mouths of the Nile; near the Pelusiac mouth, the principal point of entry, walls interrupted the navigable channels, and land routes were flooded in order to prevent their use: "Accordingly it was not easy either for the ships to sail in, or for the cavalry to draw near, or for the infantry to approach." Pharnabazus therefore decided to attack by the Mendesian mouth, where his troops leveled the fortification (42.3–5✧). Shortly afterward, the Egyptians regained their footing on the site; the annual flood had forced Pharnabazus to evacuate Egypt (43.1–4).

According to Diodorus (XV.41.2), one of the reasons for the defeat lay in the length of the Persian preparations (several years). "For Pharnabazus marched slowly and had given plenty of time for the enemy to prepare"; and he explains the attitude of the Persian leader as follows: "Indeed it is the usual custom for the Persian commanders, not being independent in the general conduct of war, to refer all matters to the King and await his replies concerning every detail" (41.5◊). This is a remark made by many Greek authors, and it certainly reflects part of the truth: for one thing, the assembly of so large an army, the construction of a navy, and the training of soldiers is a long-term affair; for another, the Persian generals traditionally had to apply to the court for every expense that exceeded the budget that had been allocated (see, e.g., Diodorus XV.4.2). But this explanation is also polemical in nature: it fits comfortably into the predominant Greek presentation of Persian military incompetence. It is doubtful that Pharnabazus was idle throughout this period. If the Egyptian revolt spread toward Palestine, it is likely that the Persian general took advantage of his presence in the region to restore Achaemenid order in such a way as to secure his rear. Anyway, the construction of fortifications in Egypt goes back to an earlier period; we know, for example, that Chabrias (who left Egypt at the latest in 379) had directed the construction of earthworks near Pelusia and Lake Mareotis (Strabo XVI.2.33; XVII.1.22). In fact, the Egyptian pharaohs had been preparing for many years already, which doubtless also explains Pharnabazus's aforementioned failure. Because of the inferiority of their forces, the Egyptians needed first and foremost to prevent the Persian army and navy from entering the Delta. This is exactly the same strategy they adopted toward Artaxerxes III in 343, also profiting at that time from the long duration of Persian preparations (cf. Diodorus XVI.46.7).

Diodorus also presents what he describes as the incompetence of the Persian high command. According to him, Iphicrates, head of the Greek mercenaries in the army, had proposed a different strategy. After they took the fort at the Mendesian mouth, he suggested going up the Nile to take Memphis, which at that point was undefended, taking advantage of the situation to seize the town with his troops. Pharnabazus's refusal was, for Diodorus, the reason that the expedition failed (XV.43). But it is risky to accord too much credibility to a story so fully devoted to singing the praises of the Greek *strategos*. We get the primary impression that Diodorus, under the influence of his sources, wants to express the idea so often found in the fourth-century authors that the Persians were incapable of winning a battle without the advice and counsel of Greek leaders. He even repeats the same explanation to account for the defeat of Nectanebo II by Artaxerxes III in 343 (XVI.48.1–2); the theme of the rivalry between Persian and Greek leaders is also found in this story (XVI.49.1–4; cf. 50.4–6 and XVII.18.2–4).

Contrary to what Diodorus would have us believe, Iphicrates was certainly not Pharnabazus's equal. Iphicrates was entrusted with training recruits (Nepos, *Iph.* 2.4) and, under the authority of Pharnabazus and other Persian leaders (Diodorus XV.43.2; Nepos, *Dat.* 3.5: Tithraustes and Datames himself), he oversaw preparation of the Greek troops and their maneuvers, seconded by other mercenary leaders (*Dat.* 5.6: Mandrocles of Magnesia). In sum, the structure of Pharnabazus's army was similar to the organization of Cyrus the Younger's army in 401, except that Iphicrates probably did not enjoy the prestigious status under Pharnabazus that Cyrus had accorded Clearchus. Diodorus's text seems to indicate simply that Iphicrates was asked for his opinion during a war council held after the capture of the Mendesian fortification; his opinion apparently differed from the views held by Pharnabazus and his Persian lieutenants. Diodorus's version continues, explaining the attitude of Pharnabazus and the other Persian leaders as jealousy: they were afraid Iphicrates would seize Egypt for himself (§43.2). This presentation scarcely convinces. Pharnabazus might have had excellent strategic reasons for turning down this plan, first among them the need to justify himself later to the king—which accounts for the thought ascribed to him: he responded to Iphicrates "that it was because he was master of his words but the King was master of his actions" (§41.2◇). In other words, he preferred not to risk losing everything in a raid that would cut him off from his rear bases, since the essential thing, in his eyes, was to return to the king totally crowned with victory. Setting aside the personal antagonism portrayed so dramatically by Diodorus, the simplest explanation is to suppose that the Persian command had underestimated the capacity for prolonged resistance by the Egyptian defenses in the Delta, as well as the logistical difficulties connected with the deployment of such extensive forces in a land where first the enemy and second the force of nature (flood) would render unusable the preferred access approach via the Nile.

It seems strange that Pharnabazus's army would leave Egypt so quickly, in contrast to what the Persians had done around 460, when several years of fighting had been needed to put down the rebellion (see chap. 14/2). It seems clear that this was not a decision born out of a moment of panic. Despite what Diodorus would have us believe (XV.43.4), no one need fear that Pharnabazus was ignorant of the timing of the Nile flood! We can imagine that the central authority feared that its army would get bogged down in an interminable war of inches in Egypt. Nor, in fact, was it a withdrawal pure and simple. On the contrary, the Persian army retreated to their Palestinian bases, where they prepared a new offensive. But it is not until the last year of Artaxerxes II that we hear fleeting references to a new attempt, in an entirely different strategic context. Meanwhile, Persians and Egyptians were encamped face to face, on the brink of war, and we cannot exclude the possibility of confrontations suppressed by the Classical sources. Whatever the case, the fact remains that the Achaemenid armies proved unable to regain their footing in the Nile Valley. This was a painful failure for Artaxerxes, who had cherished the project ever since his victory over his brother, Cyrus.

Artaxerxes and the Greeks

A basic, tangible result was achieved nonetheless—the victory on Cyprus. The military activity of the Persian armies in Syria–Palestine and the disarray of the Greek cities in Europe left the pharaohs to face Persian power alone. Neither Sparta nor Athens (despite the presence of Chabrias alongside Hakoris) sought to carry out military operations in the royal territories after 386. After the unfortunate Egyptian campaign, Pharnabazus even sent a message to the Athenians, setting forth Iphicrates' accountability and urging them to judge him. The Athenians refused the satrap's request but sent a courteous and respectful reply nonetheless (Diodorus XV.43.6). Since they were thoroughly occupied with settling the problem of hegemony, Sparta, Athens, and Thebes held scrupulously to the terms of the King's Peace, even after Athens (in 378–377) formalized the new naval alliance that it had begun to create in the 380s. The peace of 386 was reaffirmed twice on the initiative of Artaxerxes: first in 375 and then in 371. In the first year, a congress was held at Sparta at the insistence of the Great King's envoys; one of the Athenian ambassadors took the opportunity to refer to the autonomy clause of the peace of 386 solely to denounce the behavior of the Lacedaemonians (Xenophon, *Hell.* VI.4.9). The general peace of 371 encompassed all of the Greek cities except Thebes (Diodorus XV.50.4), which a few weeks later was to inflict a memorable defeat on Sparta at Leuctra (371). Artaxerxes II had become the the the Greeks' arbitrator.

7. *Artaxerxes II, His Satraps, and His Peoples (ca. 366–359/358)*

Diodorus and the "Great Revolt" of the Satraps: The Empire in Flames?

This general peace in Greece is the context in which Diodorus presents what is conventionally called the "great revolt of the satraps" (XV.93.1). He dates the beginnings of the uprisings to 361. As he puts it, the Empire was on the brink of implosion and disaster:

> During their term of office the inhabitants of the Asiatic coast revolted from Persia, and some of the satraps and generals rising in insurrection made war on Artaxerxes. At the same time Tachôs the Egyptian king decided to fight the Persians and prepared ships and gathered infantry forces. Having procured many mercenaries from the Greek cities, he persuaded the Lacedaemonians likewise to fight with him, for the Spartans were estranged from Artaxerxes because the Messenians had been included by the King on the same terms as the other Greeks in the general peace. When the general uprising against the Persians reached such large proportions, the King also began making preparations for the war. For at one and the same time he must needs fight the Egyptian king, the Greek cities of Asia, the Lacedaemonians and the allies of these,—satraps and generals who ruled the coastal districts and had agreed upon making common cause with them (*koinopragia*). Of these the most distinguished were Ariobarzanes, satrap of Phrygia, who at the death of Mithridates had taken possession of his kingdom (*basileia*), and Mausolus, overlord of Caria, who was master of many strongholds and important cities of which the hearth and mother city was Halicarnassus, which possessed a famous acropolis and the royal palace of Caria; and, in addition to the two already mentioned, Orontes, satrap of Mysia, and Autophradates, satrap of Lydia. Apart from the Ionians were Lycians, Pisidians, Pamphylians, and Cilicians, likewise Syrians, Phoenicians, and practically all the coastal peoples (*ethnē*). With the revolt so extensive, half the revenues of the King were cut off and what remained were insufficient for the expenses of the war. (XV.90✧)

It is immediately plain to see that, with respect to evidence, we are in a situation similar to the one we are placed in by Isocrates with regard to the 380s (*Paneg.* 161–62; cf. p. 650 above). The historian is thus faced with the same problem as in the earlier context. Diodorus's presentation arouses the greatest reservations *a priori*. The last sentence of the catalogue of woes in particular eloquently illustrates the distortions brought about by a Hellenocentric viewpoint, and it reminds us of a remark of Polyclitus that is mentioned incidentally by Strabo (XV.3.21). But no one can believe that the revolt (whatever magnitude is ascribed to it) exhausted the Great King's monetary reserves and prevented him from making war on the rebels.

Apart from this grandiose fresco painted by Diodorus, we have neither continuous nor complete documentation of any kind, except for a summary of the work of Trogus Pompeius. The summary covers an expedition of Artaxerxes II against the Cadusians and then explains how the Great King "pursued his dignitaries (*purpurati*) who had defected (*defectores*) in Asia: first of all Datames, satrap of [Paphlagonia], a land whose origin is presented; then the satrap of the Hellespont, Ariobarzanes; and next in Syria the governor of Armenia, Orontes; how he conquered them all and died, leaving the throne to his son Ochus" (*Prol.* X). This information is not found in Justin, who unfortunately was engrossed in Greek (VI.6–9), Macedonian (VII), and Greco-Macedonian (VIII–IX) affairs, and did not consider it necessary to explain; he did not take up the course of Artaxerxes II's reign except to cover the royal succession (X.3.1–2), before arriving very quickly at the accession of Darius III (X.3.3–7). Justin's method does not diminish the value of the summary of Trogus Pompeius, but it is unfortunately too fleeting to constitute a basis for historical reconstruction.

Trogus Pompeius places Datames first among the rebels, but Diodorus omits his role entirely, at least in the catalogue of rebels. Diodorus does name Datames, but apparently assigns him a personal role only in repelling the counterattack mounted by Artabazus (XV.91). We learn more about this person from C. Nepos's biography of him, which dates his revolt (wrongly) to the return of the expedition against Aspis of Cataonia (§5.1–6). The life and works of Datames are also cited by Polyaenus (VII.21.1–7; VII.29.1–2; cf. VII.28) and Pseudo-Aristotle (*Oecon.* II.24a–b = Polyaenus VII.21.1) to illustrate the theme of military deception and fiscal stratagem as practiced by the satraps and generals. Again in Polyaenus we find several short stories introducing Orontes (VII.14.2–4), Ariobarzanes (VII.26), and Autophradates (VII.27.1–3). Each is an anecdotal tale with a major defect: none is situated in the chronology precisely. The biography by Nepos belongs to the genre of *saga*: it is entirely devoted to singing the praises of a hero who is haunted by the king's ingratitude and his associates' betrayals.

References to the satraps and countries in revolt also decorate several discourses delivered by Athenian orators and politicians, which at least have the advantage of being situated more precisely in the chronology. In 354, Demosthenes beseeches his fellow citizens to shoulder a financial burden and makes it clear that the Athenians had nothing to fear from the Great King:

> Nor is there, as it appears to me, any ground for what some persons fear, that, having money, he will collect a large body of mercenaries. I do indeed believe, that against Egypt and Orontes, and any other barbarians, many of the Greeks would be willing to serve in his pay. . . . Against Greece, however, I do not believe that any Grecian would march. For whither could he betake himself afterwards? Go to Phrygia and be a slave? (*Sym.* 31–32✧)

In an oration delivered in 352, this same orator strongly opposed a decree issued by Aristocrates, who had proposed protective measures that would be to the advantage of Charidemus, the head of the mercenaries. On this occasion, Demosthenes recalled several recent deeds of Charidemus, who, he writes, had hired his services to Mentor and Memnon, brother-in-law of Artabazus, who himself had just been captured by Autophradates. Later, the mercenary leader received a safe-conduct pass from the satrap, permitting him to cross into Chersonesus in Thrace (*C. Arist.* 154–59). The following year (351–350), Demosthenes made a resounding plea for Athens' intervention on behalf of Rhodian democrats who had been banished from their city on Mausolus's initiative. By doing so, the orator claimed, he opposed those who, nevertheless, "counseled the republic to turn to the Egyptians for aid against the king of Persia" (*Lib. Rhod.* §5); he recalls that "Once, O Athenians, you sent Timotheus out to assist Ariobarzanes" (cf. also Isocrates, *Ech.* 111):

> Timotheus, seeing that Ariobarzanes had openly revolted from the king, and that Samos was garrisoned by Cyprothemis, under the appointment of Tigranes, the king's deputy (*hyparkhos*), renounced the intention of assisting Ariobarzanes, but invested the island with his forces and delivered it. And to this day there has been no war against you on that account. (*Lib. Rhod.* §§9–10✧)

What can we make of these brief allusions? First of all, we note that they extend the time of troubles considerably. In turn, this chronology (correlated in Demosthenes and Isocrates with the ongoing Egyptian secession) again accentuates the impression, implicit in Diodorus, that the central authority in the western provinces was deeply and permanently disorganized. The impression is also reinforced by the use of the word *basileia* 'kingdom' to describe Ariobarzanes' power in Phrygia (Diodorus XV.90.3) and by a comparison between two of Isocrates' discourses—one from 380 (*Paneg.* 161), the other from 347 (*Phil.* 100–101; cf. p. 683). As in Diodorus in 361, the entire Mediterranean region seems to have been united in rebellion for nearly the entire fourth century. But the orators' insistence seems suspicious, since the goal of their argument was precisely to demonstrate to their hearers (*ekklēsia*) and correspondents (Philip II) that the Great King was merely a paper tiger. To accomplish this, they did not even hesitate to contradict themselves within a few paragraphs (Demosthenes, *Sym.* 3–9 and 29–32) or within a few years: in 347, Isocrates praised Artaxerxes II's reign to the skies, at least in comparison with the reign of his successor (*Phil.* 99–100); in 380, he had ridiculed it (*Paneg.* 138–66). Even if we separate these discourses from the ideological current that bears them along, they provide very few precise details—very few details, at any rate, that can easily be integrated into a framework that could be constructed independently. The fact is that the references (in Demosthenes in particular) are merely incidental and accidental, offering nothing more than a few names and a few hints as to how the Greek politicians envisaged the possible consequences of the occasional interventions of some of their *strategoi* and/or mercenary chiefs in the internal affairs of the Achaemenid Empire.

There are also two Greek inscriptions that very indirectly allude to satraps. One (found at Argos and now lost) comprises the statement of several Greek states that had just agreed to a common peace (*koinē eirēnē*). The parties affirm that a state of war did not exist between them and the Great King and that, if he meant them no ill, they would remain at peace with him; on the other hand, if the king or anyone coming from his territories (*ek tēs ekeinou khōras*) were to march against the Hellenes, they would organize a common defense. The broken beginning of the text includes (perhaps) a reference to an envoy who came from the satraps' side ([*para t*]*ōn satrapōn*; Tod no. 145). Additionally, an Athenian inscription, unfortunately perennially burdened by arguments about establishing the text itself and its chronology, refers to the granting of honors (including citizenship) to Orontes because he had sold wheat to Athenian *strategoi* following an exchange of ambassadors and negotiations (IG II^2 207). This decree provides fodder for the debate on the satrapal duties of Orontes in Mysia, but the connection with the story of his revolt is tenuous: there is nothing to indicate either that by issuing the decree Athens was exhibiting any sort of military alliance with Persia, or that the sale of wheat to the city clearly illustrates secessionist tendencies on the part of the satrap. The first decree cited here (whose authenticity has sometimes been doubted) first of all shows that the Greek cities were very anxious to prove their eagerness for the common peace renewed under the aegis of the Great King; the beginning of the text especially seems to confirm that there was a *koinopragia* ('joint enterprise') between satraps at this date, as Diodorus mentions in his catalogue (XV.90.3). But because the stone was broken at the top, the date of the decree, the restoration of the text (*para* or *peri?*), and the subsequent interpretations are themselves largely based on Diodorus's text—which removes considerable weight from the pile of evidence thus constructed!

The outcome of the foregoing investigation, we can see, is not very encouraging: the Classical sources are sparse and allusive and are not interested in the internal history of the Achaemenid Empire. There is one apparently more informative text (Diodorus), but its structure and typology make the historian highly suspicious. There are two allusive Greek inscriptions, but their readings are very uncertain and so is their date. Finally, there are no Achaemenid sources at all, apart from a large number of coins minted by *strategoi* and satraps, and whether these individuals were revolutionary most often remains to be demonstrated. Moreover, the chronology of the activities can never be reconstructed with complete certainty. Indeed, what good are proposals regarding chains of causality if the actual order of events cannot be established? It is thus quite understandable that major disagreements among historians remain regarding the development, breadth, and purposes of the revolt (or better: the revolts).

Schematically, we can consider this in terms of two opposing views—one maximalist, one minimalist. The former tends to present the rebellions as a vast unified movement that had an ultimate goal of raising a frontal assault on the power of Artaxerxes and perhaps even marching on Babylonia to destroy him. In addition to Diodorus, the proponents of this theory appeal to Trogus Pompeius (*Prol.* X) and Polyaenus (VII.21.3). Trogus Pompeius states that Artaxerxes II defeated Orontes in Syria; Polyaenus says that Datames marched beyond the Euphrates during his war against the Great King. If we postulate that all of these offensives (and the Egyptian rebellion) are organically connected, we get the impression that Artaxerxes' authority was threatened in its very own strongholds. A few years ago, however, dissenting views were expressed, and these tend to reduce (sometimes drastically) the various revolts and rebellions to localized affairs that never really threatened the Great King. Both views run into difficult chronological problems, not to mention the fragility of arguments based on evidence that is not only heterogeneous and anecdotal but also puts far too much stock in the Greek portrayals (the quasi-structural weakness of Achaemenid evidence) and in the self-interest of the Greek states (which were peripherally involved in the quarrels in Asia Minor). All this is as good as to say that the following discussion traffics more in the wealth of our ignorance than in the poverty of our certainty.

The Initial Revolts: Datames

The career of Datames marvelously illustrates the breadth and complexity of the historical and chronological arguments. Let us recall first of all that Diodorus does not list him among the satraps and *strategoi* who reached agreement on a treaty of cooperation (XV.90.3). He discusses Datames in a separate chapter, implying quite clearly that his rebellion occurred while the traitorous satraps were busy polishing their weapons (91.2)—that is, during the 360s. Diodorus's purpose is not to offer a connected narrative of events, but simply to give other examples of treason that embellished the revolts (91.1–2). Thus he reports that a royal *strategos*, Artabazus, penetrated into Cappadocia, where Datames was satrap; despite being betrayed by his father-in-law, Mithrobarzanes, Datames was victorious (91.2–6). On the rest of Datames' career, Diodorus is laconic to a fault: "As for Datames, though even before this he was admired for his generalship, at that time he won far greater acclaim for both his courage and his sagacity in the art of war; but King Artaxerxes, when he learned about Datames' exploit as a general, because he was impatient to be rid of him, instigated his assassination" (91.7✧).

Mithrobarzanes' betrayal and Datames' end are also found in the biography by Nepos, who offers a more detailed story of the background of the satrap and the first part of his dazzling career (§1–3.4). After his victory over Thuys of Paphlagonia (in the 380s), Datames was sent to Acre in company with Pharnabazus and Tithraustes, who were then readying the Egyptian expeditionary force; then, after the recall of Pharnabazus (certainly after the defeat in 374), Datames was placed at the head of the army (§3.5). At this point, the king ordered him to bring an end to the disorders caused by Aspis of Cataonia. After he was successful, he returned to Acre (§4–5.1). This, Nepos says, is when the rupture with the Great King took place: Datames was warned by his friend Pandantes, the "keeper of the royal treasury," of a plot by courtiers, so he 'determined to leave the king's service' (*descicere a rege*) without letting anything betray his intentions. He left with his entire household for Cappadocia, and "then he secretly (*clam*) came to an understanding (*amicitia*) with Ariobarzanes" (5.6❖). Then comes the tale of his father-in-law Mithrobarzanes' betrayal—not during a war against Artabazus but in a battle against some Pisidians (§6). His oldest son Sysinas soon abandoned him and switched to Artaxerxes' side, and Datames found himself under attack by Autophradates, who had received orders from the king to deal with Datames but, finding himself unable to win, made a truce with Datames (§§7–8). A story of new betrayals follows (§9), the last of them planned by Mithradates, son of Ariobarzanes, who at the king's command enticed Datames into a trap and killed him (§§10–11).

As we have already stressed several times, the biography by Nepos must not be taken at face value. Nepos (just like Diodorus) was eager to extol the worth and the virtues of his hero and built his tale on a series of repetitive motifs: Datames' strategic brilliance, the kings' ingratitude, and a series of betrayals (his father-in-law; his oldest son). Veracity and historic coherence count for little. From author to author, the chronology and the characters vary, and this is why serious doubts have been raised about the conditions and chronology of the revolt. According to Nepos, the revolt took place (but secretly) at the end of the 370s—that is, at a date much earlier than that fixed by Diodorus for the general conflagration and the royal armies' campaigns against Datames. Nepos's only explanation for Datames' defection is quite surprising: when he was at the zenith of royal favor, the announcement of a courtiers' conspiracy was all it took for him to decide to make the break, because he was afraid that a setback in Egypt would alienate Artaxerxes' favor.

That Datames was considered a rebel by the court can scarcely be doubted. But when, and under what conditions? According to Nepos, a secret treaty was first concluded with Ariobarzanes, satrap of Hellespontine Phrygia. However, nothing indicates that Ariobarzanes had declared his independence from the Great King as early as the 370s. It seems instead that it was the subsequent accusations of his son Sysinas that persuaded the Great King (§7.1), who then ordered Autophradates, the satrap of Sardis, to move against the rebel (§§7.1–8.5). If we date the campaign to approximately 367, it is rather difficult to elucidate the nature of the relationships that had previously maintained Datames' loyalty to the central authority. The paucity and contradictory nature of the information make perfectly contradictory interpretations possible. We could suppose, for example, that his campaign against the Pisidians (*Dat.* 6)—or, more precisely, against unidentified groups of Pisidians (cf. §6.1)—related to periodic Achaemenid army sallies against a traditionally unstable people; but it *might* also clearly reflect a rebel's desire to enlist Pisidians in his service (cf. §4.4). Furthermore, several anecdotes and coins imply that there were campaigns in northern Asia Minor (Sinope, Amisus) at a date that is very hard to pin down. Polyaenus records an interesting anecdote: while he was besieging Sinope, Datames received a letter from Artaxerxes ordering him to call off the operation. He immediately "made obeisance before the letter and offered the sacrifice usually offered for good news" (VII.21.5). One is tempted to see this as proof of the satrap's loyalty, as a perspective exactly opposite the one that Nepos presents—as long as Artaxerxes' letter does not point to Datames' rebellion-in-progress and the satrap's obeisance before the royal letter is not simply mockery! We also know that Datames was not afraid to seize even the wealth of Cappadocian sanctuaries in order to finance his campaign (Polyaenus VII.21.1; Ps.-Arist., *Oecon.* II.24a). Once again, this is an episode that can support two readings. It might illustrate a banal fact—namely, a lack of cash that forced the satraps and generals to stopgap measures in order to pay their troops. But it might also be seen as proof of rebellion.

This is a good point at which to bring up an important question: what exactly is a rebel? One of the best definitions—the most forthright, in any case—is found in Nepos's text and also appears in nearly identical words in an anecdote in Polyaenus (VII.29.1). Nepos says that finally, greatly frustrated, the Great King gave Mithradates carte blanche to get rid of Datames. Mithradates tried to act like a rebel, because he knew that Datames was extremely wary. So Mithradates adopted attitudes and made decisions that would advertise his open break with the king:

> Mithradates prepared his forces and made friends (*amicitia*) with Datames without meeting him. He then began to raid the king's provinces (*regis provincias vexat*), and storm his fortresses (*castella expugnat*), gaining a great amount of booty (*magnas praedas capit*), of which he divided a part among his soldiers and sent a part to Datames; he likewise handed over several fortresses (*castella*) to the Carian. By continuing this conduct for a long time he convinced Datames that he was engaged in implacable war against the king (*se infinitum adversus regem sucepisse bellum*). (§10.2–3✧)

Polyaenus similarly uses the words *phrouria basileōs/kōmai/phoroi/leia*: the attacks on the royal garrisons, the villages, and the tribute proved that he was an enemy of the king (*polemios einai basilei*). Many texts, Xenophon's in particular, in fact show that a satrap's fundamental duty was to use the garrisons (*castella/phrouria*) to maintain order, and this in turn allowed the peasants (cf. *kōmai*) to work and to maintain production without being subjected to raids (cf. *praedae/leia*), so that they would be able to pay tribute (*phoroi*). The robbing of tribute is also why Aspis of Cataonia had been pursued by the royal armies: he "even overran the regions neighbouring to Persia and carried off what was being brought to the king" (*Dat.* 4.2✧). This behavior was the opposite of the conduct of a good satrap, who would protect his country from the ravages of war (cf. Quintus Curtius III.4.5: *terra quam a populationibus vindicare debebat*). This was one of the justifications given (it appears) by Arsites in 334 to oppose the scorched-earth strategy proposed by Memnon: "He would not suffer one house to be burned belonging to his subjects" (Arrian I.12.10✧).

Clearly, this definition of "rebel" is no less partial. More generally, one was considered guilty or unworthy if one did not defer to royal orders or if one carried out a mission badly. The line between loyalty and rebellion was thus both fine and porous: it was the judgment of the king that counted, as is so clearly shown by Tiribazus's appearance when he was criticized by Orontes, who was "envious of Tiribazus' high position" (Diodorus XV.8.3;◊ cf. 10–11). This example also demonstrates the role of formal accusations, which could come from local populations who were unhappy with an administrator's demands, or from royal inspectors and delegates, or from a jealous colleague. This was how the king stayed informed regarding the progress of the provinces. In short, while Datames' rebellion must undoubtedly be dated a few years before 361, its exact chronology and concrete circumstances remain indecipherably hazy.

The Troubles in Western Asia Minor (366–361)

Conflict also broke out in western Asia Minor before 361. According to Nepos (*Dat.* 5.6), Datames' first ally was Ariobarzanes; Diodorus's catalogue for 361 (p. 656 above) designates Ariobarzanes as satrap of Phrygia (XV.90.3). In truth, by then Ariobarzanes had lost the siege of Dascylium. According to Demosthenes (*Lib. Rhod.* §§9–10), he had overtly declared himself in rebellion when the Athenian Timotheus was sent to lend him a hand in 366; he also received aid from the Spartan Agesilaus. This may be the context in which Ariobarzanes, his son, and two of his Greek subordinates received Athenian citizenship. The king had sent a fleet and an army to confront the rebel; the fleet was commanded by Mausolus, the satrap-dynast of Caria, and the army was led by Autophradates, the satrap of Sardis, after his return from the fruitless expedition against Datames. Some time later, the king ordered the rebel captured, and he was crucified (364?). He seems to have been betrayed by his own son, Mithradates. We also learn that the satrapy of Dascylium passed to Artabazus, son of Pharnabazus and Apame—that is, Artaxerxes' grandson (363–362?). One of the new satrap's first campaigns (during his voyage to Dascylium?) was to fight Datames, without success. Meanwhile, we lose track of Ariobarzanes until he is named by Diodorus in the catalogue of rebellious satraps in 361.

Perhaps it was also in these years that Orontes began to assert his power in Mysia, in the region of Pergamum. But the sources for this are also poor. We know for sure that Orontes was satrap of Armenia in 401 and that around 384 he took part in the Cyprus campaign, and this is when he accused his colleague Tiribazus of carrying out private operations. The judgment favored Tiribazus: "The King . . . bestowed upon Tiribazus the highest honours, such as were customary. Orontes, however, he condemned as one who had fabricated a false accusation, expelled him from his list of friends, and subjected him to the utmost marks of degradation" (Diodorus XV.11.2◊). Orontes then vanishes from sight (from our sources!) until the moment when, in 361, Diodorus calls him "satrap of Mysia" (XV.90.3). Whatever authority had been conferred on him (satrap in his own right, lieutenant governor), Orontes must have been transferred from Armenia to western Asia Minor at a date unknown to us, perhaps as a repercussion of the disfavor that had befallen him after the Cyprus affair. His private activity in Mysia near Pergamum is attested in a Greek inscription (*OGIS* 264): the date is not given, but the person is unambiguously described as a rebel against the Great King (*apostas*). His coinage at Adramyttium and Cisthenes shows that he was enlisting mercenaries, who made it possible for him to take Cyme, despite the cavalry dispatched by Autophradates to oppose him (Polyaenus VII.14.3). Another anecdote reports him leading harassing operations near Sardis (VII.14.2). It appears that these skirmishes and offensives must be dated before 362–361; furthermore, they indicate that, despite the opposition of Autophradates and other "generals of the king" (VII.14.2), Orontes was trying to enlarge the bases of his territorial authority.

As meager and uncertain as it is, the information we can glean already gives us reason to increase our doubts about Diodorus's version. The satrapal turmoil did not burst out suddenly in 361; instead, it reflects unrest that was both endemic and localized. Furthermore, the participation of some of the rebel leaders whom Diodorus catalogues could have been temporary. We know hardly anything about Autophradates except for a badly dated passage (362–361?) in which Demosthenes (*C. Arist.* 154) mentions that, when Charidemus arrived in Asia Minor, Artabazus was taken prisoner by Autophradates and shortly afterward released—which constitutes a very feeble hint. Finally, still according to Diodorus, Orontes' revolt ended as quickly as it had begun. After collecting money to hire mercenaries (XV.91.1) and sending Rheomithres to Egypt to request money from Pharaoh Tachos (92.1), Orontes suddenly changed his plans:

> He . . . proceeded to betray his trust. For suspecting that he would obtain from the King not only great rewards (*dōreai megalai*) but would also succeed to the satrapy of all the coastal region if he should deliver the rebels into the hands of the Persians, he first arrested those who brought the money and dispatched them to Artaxerxes; then afterward he delivered many of the cities and the soldiers who had been hired to the commanding officers who had been sent by the King. (91.1✧)

His example was soon followed by Rheomithres, who, when he returned from Egypt, made landfall at Leucae with his navy:

> To this city he summoned many leaders of the insurgents. These he arrested and sent in irons to Artaxerxes, and, though he himself had been an insurgent, by the favours that he conferred through his betrayal, he made his peace with the King. (92.1✧)

This behavior appears strange, to say the least. It is likely that here, as elsewhere, Diodorus has shortened the chronology to the point of caricature. Nonetheless, Orontes' surrender seems to be completely confirmed by the Pergamum Chronicle, which also mentions the death of the ex-rebel (*OGIS* 264). But how is this mindset to be accounted for? Could contemporary events on other fronts put us on the right track? Of course, we immediately think of Egypt, since Orontes and his group had made contact with Tachos.

The Egyptian Front

In 359, Tachos, ruler of Egypt since 361, decided to go on the offensive against the Persians (cf. Diodorus XV.90.2; Xenophon, *Ages.* 2.28). He began immense preparations (and/or completed those of his predecessors), which, according to Diodorus (XV.92.2✧), included assembling "two hundred triremes expensively adorned, ten thousand chosen mercenaries from Greece, and besides these eighty thousand Egyptian infantry." He had sent emissaries to Athens and Sparta in order to recruit these mercenaries. Athens had little interest in breaking with the Great King and made no agreement with the pharaoh; nonetheless, it authorized Chabrias to enter into Tachos's service privately (XV.92.3; Plutarch, *Ages.* 37.5). Sparta, on the other hand, made an alliance with the pharaoh; Agesilaus hired mercenaries with the Egyptian funds and met with Tachos, accompanied by 30 advisers and 1000 Spartan hoplites (*Ages.* 36.5; Diodorus 92.2). Chabrias was placed in charge of the navy, and Agesilaus received command of the mercenaries. Tachos retained for himself general oversight of military operations (92.3), a choice that appears to have generated some friction between the two Greek *strategoi*.

Against the advice of Agesilaus (at least according to the version that puts the Spartan in a very favorable light), the pharaoh decided to launch the offensive "far afield and was encamped near Phoenicia," while his lieutenant Nectanebo (his nephew) was ordered "to besiege the cities in Syria" (92.3–4◊). At this point, a conspiracy began to unfold back home. Tachos had left Egypt in the charge of his brother Cha-hap-imu, the father of Nectanebo. Cha-hap-imu won over to himself the soldiers that Tachos had put under his command in order "to besiege the cities in Syria" and asked Chabrias and Agesilaus to support him; Agesilaus did so, since Sparta had given him free rein. Nectanebo soon had himself named pharaoh. As a result, Tachos sought refuge with Artaxerxes II, who "not only cleared him of the charges against him but even appointed him general in the war against Egypt" (92.5◊). Diodorus places the death of Artaxerxes II (between November 359 and August 358) and the accession of his son, Ochus, under the throne name Artaxerxes III, in this time period (XV.92.3–5; 93; cf. Plutarch, *Ages.* 37.3–11); at the same time, fighting in Egypt continued, because another leader whose origin was in Mendes rose up to oppose Nectanebo. After these events, Diodorus (XV.93.2–6: note the confusion of the names Tachos and Nectanebo) and Plutarch (*Ages.* 38–40) shine the spotlight on the leading role played by their Spartan hero, Agesilaus, in Nectanebo II's victory over his rival.

Orontes and the Egyptian Front

Let us return to the problem of a possible collaboration between the Asia Minor rebels and Tachos. We may simply remark that the pharaoh agreed to supply money and ships to Rheomithres, "who had [previously] been sent by the insurgents to King Tachôs in Egypt" for that purpose (XV.92.1◊) and that Rheomithres left his wife and children hostage at the pharaoh's court (Xenophon, *Cyr.* VIII.8.4). Just like his predecessors, Tachos, because he was at war with Persia, sought alliance with the Greek cities of Europe and supported those that were in revolt against the Great King with his own money (cf., e.g., Diodorus XV.9.4–5). But did he really put plans for joint action against Artaxerxes into operation? The only reference comes from a very confused passage (a resumé, actually) in the *Summaries* of the work of Trogus Pompeius (book X), indicating that "Orontes, satrap of Armenia" was among the enemies Artaxerxes II subdued, "on whom he had inflicted a defeat in Syria, after a victory over Ariobarzanes (*deinde in Syria*)." The conclusion sometimes drawn from this is that Orontes actually did march south in order to join up with the pharaoh's army. The importance of the problem posed is clearly evident, since a whole series of historical inferences of the utmost importance cascades from the response one chooses: if any such plan in fact existed, the implication is that Orontes, together with other rebels, was considering nothing less than advancing against Babylon.

However, restraint seems the best policy in considering whether or not Tachos's revolt extended to Syria. We cannot state with certainty that the Egyptian offensive incited all of the Phoenician cities to revolt. We know that Athens issued a decree in honor of King Straton of Sidon during these years, thanking him for facilitating the passage of ambassadors who were traveling to the Great King (Tod no. 139). We also know that Tachos, before joining the Great King's court, had taken refuge in Sidon (cf. Xenophon, *Ages.* 2.30). None of these data permits us to state that Straton was included among the declared enemies of the Great King at this time; in contrast, a later text (Hieron. *Adv. Iovinian.* I.45) seems to state that the king of Sidon broke his treaty of alliance (*fœdus*) with the Great King—thereby implying that in the era under consideration amicable relations obtained with Egypt. However, there still is Diodorus's allusion to Nectanebo's "besieg[ing] the cities of Syria" (XV.92.4✧), by order of Tachos. It is possible that Tachos, then on the coast (*hē Phoinikē*), ordered Nectanebo to turn toward the interior (*tas poleis en tēi Syriai*), the "cities" perhaps designating Achaemenid fortresses such as Arad or Beer-sheba; but archaeological excavations have not revealed any destructions at this date. The real problem is that it is very difficult to understand what Diodorus means by the term "Syria." Elsewhere, he speaks of "Phoenician Syria" (in which he includes Acre), which he distinguishes from "Syria" (within which he lists Joppa, Samaria, and Gaza; XIX.93.6). If we take this distinction seriously, Nectanebo's mission would have been to subdue fortresses located on the coast in "Phoenician Syria"; but this is just a guess. All in all, however, it is clear that the little information available is flimsy and incomplete, but there is nothing to prove that the campaign by Tachos and Nectanebo put Syro-Phoenicia to fire and the sword, Diodorus notwithstanding (XV.90.3: Syrians and Phoenicians).

More than anything, the Greek tales, partial in both senses, leave us completely in the dark about a possible response from the Great King (aside from the subsequent agreement between Artaxerxes and Tachos). Diodorus does not return to the Egyptian theater until much later (during 351–350) and then only with a very vague and very suspect flashback on the perpetual inaction of Artaxerxes Ochus [III] (XVI.40.2–5). A late source (but one which there is no reason to doubt), however, briefly mentions that Ochus "made a campaign against Egypt while his father was still alive" (Syncellus, p. 486.20)—and this no doubt is the source of the error of Trogus Pompeius (*Prol.* X) or his epitomizer, who attributes the victory to Artaxerxes II. This campaign can be dated to 360 or 359, and it was obviously mounted to counter the offensive by Tachos. These are clearly the facts that Lyceas is referring to in his *Egyptian History* as well, when he writes: "The Egyptians undertook a campaign against Ochus, king of Persia, but were defeated. Their king was taken prisoner, but Ochus treated him kindly and even summoned him to dinner" (Athenaeus IV.150b–c✧). This Egyptian king is obviously Tachos, as comparison with an anecdote told by Aelian shows (*VII* V.1). This is probably also the context of Artaxerxes II's demand that Athens recall Chabrias (Nepos, *Chab.* 3.1; cf. Plutarch, *Ages.* 37.4–6). Artaxerxes II thus repeated a traditional policy when confronting internal disorder in Egypt: he supported one of the competing pretenders (Tachos) against the other (Nectanebo). We may note in fact that, according to the ancient authors, the failure of Tachos's expedition was due to internal problems in Egypt. The breadth of these problems truly must not be underestimated. The overbearing fiscal requirements imposed by Tachos in order to build up his war chest had alienated the Egyptian administrative classes and no doubt awakened the hostility of the ordinary peasants. But we could just as well ask whether the rebellion of Cha-hap-imu and his son Nectanebo was not in fact triggered by the military losses inflicted by the Persian forces of Prince Ochus.

In short, the historian is faced with an unfortunately common dilemma: having to interpret the information offered by Trogus Pompeius or to reject it pure and simple. Two answers remain theoretically possible:

(1) The mention by Trogus Pompeius is a mistake; the summarizer in haste conflated two events that Trogus Pompeius treated as successive—the demise of Orontes (in Asia Minor) and the campaign of Ochus in Syria. To justify this position, we might say that Orontes' march appears inexplicable on the strategic level, because it would require the assumption that all the Persian leaders of Asia Minor would have come to his aid—but

there is no evidence for this. It is much simpler to imagine that the news of Tachos's difficulties convinced Orontes that the revolt had no chance of success, and that his best opportunity was to try to win the king's pardon. It is likely in any case that Orontes got his information from Rheomithres, since the "betrayals" of the two leaders were obviously coordinated.

(2) Orontes and his troops did advance toward Syria, where they arrived after the defeat and surrender of Tachos to Ochus. Orontes would then have agreed to side with Ochus. This solution has two points in its favor: first, it does not dismiss an "awkward" text; and second, it provides an explanation for Diodorus's incomprehensible passage about the treason of Orontes and Rheomithres (XV.91.1; 92.1). It is clear that Diodorus has excessively condensed the chronology. We might reconstruct the events as follows: (a) the sending of an embassy to Egypt and return of Rheomithres; (b) the defeat of Tachos becomes known; (c) Orontes and Rheomithres gather some conspirators and decide to march to the king, not to fight him but to exhibit their new-found fidelity (which would explain how they were able to pass through the breadth of Asia Minor unchallenged); (d) when they arrive in Syria, they come upon Ochus, with Tachos in his train, and pay homage to Ochus. Because Artaxerxes died between November 359 and November 358, it is possible under this theory that the encounter took place at the moment of a difficult dynastic transition and that Orontes offered his aid to Ochus (or at least that the news of the death of Artaxerxes II was precisely what led Orontes suddenly to shift his allegiance to Ochus—hence his betrayal and march to Syria to meet the prince).

While this hypothesis (which we will follow here) offers the advantage of taking Trogus Pompeius into account (by interpreting him) and "reconciling" him with Diodorus, we can see that it does not at all imply that Orontes ever considered marching on Babylonia to depose Artaxerxes II; still less does it imply that this initiative was coordinated with the plans sometimes imputed to Datames. Orontes' behavior fits well enough into the dynastic difficulties known to have surrounded the accession of Artaxerxes III Ochus (chap. 15/8 below); Orontes was among those who sided with Ochus (cf. also chap. 17/1–2).

Back to Datames

In an unknown chronological context, Polyaenus (VII.21.3) describes an offensive led by Datames across the Euphrates to pursue the war against the Great King (*epolemei megalōi basilei*). He was pursued by "a great army" and recrossed the river with difficulty before the king arrived on the east bank, quickly taking his enemies. Does this mean that Datames, at a given moment, decided to end his defensive strategy in his Cappadocian provinces and launch a vast offensive against Babylonia, which some historians think was coordinated with the grandiose plans imputed to Orontes? All the ancient authors, to be sure, stress the king's desire to be done with an adversary whom they present as superior because of his merit and strategic brilliance. But their apologetic mission dissuades us from placing blind confidence in tales that are completed devoted to hailing the virtues of the rebel and denouncing the ingratitude of the prince. There is no choice but to agree that, by itself, Polyaenus's anecdote does not license us to answer the question in the positive. Let us say that at the very least many other interpretations are possible, any of which could reduce the operations to a minor slap on the wrist with no lasting consequence.

What about the numismatic sources? In addition to the coins minted by Datames at Sinope and Amisus, a Cilician coinage usually attributed to him has been discovered—

struck with the Luvian name Tarkumawa. Some of this "karanic" coinage has no distinctive features when compared with coins of the same type struck by other Persian generals during the military preparations carried out in Cilicia between 390 and 380. Some coins, however, bear more original scenes. They show a person dressed in Iranian style, seated on a throne, his feet resting on a sort of cushion, examining an arrow and holding a bow in his hand; at the top is the disk of Ahura-Mazda (fig. 52). Another coin shows a temple and two people: one is naked and bearded and gestures toward the other, who is dressed in Greek fashion and makes a deferential gesture toward the former; the coin has an Aramaic legend that reads "Ana" or "Anu."

Fig. 52. Coin with Aramaic inscription of the name of Tarkumuwa.

One scholar has recently proposed the following explanation: both coins illustrate Datames' status as rebel. While the first dates to the early part of the revolt, when Datames had not yet defined his plans (hence the retention of the Persian symbols), the other hints at propaganda invoking the Babylonian god Anu, and it could be explained by the Polyaenus passage in which Datames crosses the Euphrates. The implication would be that Datames thus claimed that he would "liberate" Babylonia in the name of the god Anu.

However, this interpretation gives rise to some reservations. For one thing, the idea that the arguments derived from the Datames coin and the Polyaenus text are mutually supporting is artificial, because neither piece of evidence is unequivocal (to say the least). For another, the fact that a person in Persian clothing was represented with his own name can in no way be considered indisputable evidence of a desire for secession; the exact opposite argument could be offered with the same potential for veracity. As for the other coin: if the reading of the Aramaic epigraph is correct, the legend "Anu" is very worrisome. In fact, we know that there was a notable enhancement of the position of the god Anu in the fourth-century pantheon at Uruk, and this is particularly noticeable in personal names. But the reasons for this change remain obscure, so a logical connection with the Datames coin would be a matter for deliberation. In any case, it would be hard to explain why the satrap would have chosen a Babylonian divine symbol over that of Ahura-Mazda in a fight against Artaxerxes, given that, according to this theory, his purpose would have been to win over the Persian aristocracy. Could we say that the hypothetical modesty of his origin and his hypothetical "Luvian" underpinning (Tarkumawa) prohibited him from hoping for the assistance of the Persian nobility? But then, in the name of what common interests and on what ideological bases could he have hoped to mobilize the Babylonian population around him? It is thus better not to accord too much importance to the Polyaenus passage that "justifies" an interpretation of the numismatic evidence, which in turn is based on premises that we have just contested.

Mausolus and the Revolts

We must now say a few words about Mausolus of Caria, "who was master of many strongholds and important cities," and whom Diodorus includes among the conspirators (XV.90.3◊). This gentleman inherited the title of satrap from his father, Hecatomnus, in

377. Mausolus's place in the Achaemenid Empire was relatively original, since he was both dynast and satrap, so that the position of satrap was transmitted within the family. However, the example is not unique; for example, the governors of Samaria also inherited their positions. Quite a few decrees issued by Carian cities (including Mylasa, the Hecatomnids' original center of power) or by the Carian *koinon* are silent about the very existence of the Achaemenid State, while others bear a heading of the form "In year *n* of King Artaxerxes, Mausolus being satrap." These formulas express the dual nature of the prerogatives of Mausolus. This is without doubt why Mausolus, in a statement placed in his mouth, declares that he is sending gifts to the Great King in order to preserve "the ancestral power" (*patrōa arkhē*; Polyaenus VII.23.1). Could this incident refer to gifts to the Great King on the occasion of Artaxerxes III's accession, after which the king confirmed (or dismissed) the satraps and officials in their positions (cf. Diodorus XI.71.1 and Josephus, *Ant.* XI.185)?

Mausolus was also probably striving to enhance his own power and prestige, while maintaining Achaemenid order. This is demonstrated particularly well by the transfer of his capital to Halicarnassus, where he created a genuine court that followed the model of satrapal courts and adorned it with sumptuous monuments on which Greek, Anatolian, and Achaemenid traditions mingle. It is also evidenced by external initiatives that brought him up against nearby islands and cities, at dates that are poorly known. But the information we possess on the external activities of the satraps of Sardis and Dascylium does not allow us to say that Mausolus's behavior was essentially idiosyncratic, much less that the satrap of Halicarnassus exhibited separatist tendencies by carrying on these activities, because his ambitions could (at least in certain cases) mesh perfectly with Achaemenid interests. After all, was not the traditional mission of the satraps to enlarge the royal territories (cf. Herodotus III.120; V.31)? Despite the way that the fourth-century Greek authors frequently present their information, Mausolus was certainly not an independent dynast. We have only sparse information on his activities as satrap, but it at least shows that he was trusted by the central authority to maintain order in Caria; he furnished ships and military units and collected and transmitted tribute and other taxes (cf. *Ps.-Arist., Oec.* II.14d) and even maintained royal roads (II.14b). He also levied taxes within the satrapal jurisdiction, comparable to satrapal imposts, such as the required gifts that the inhabitants of countries crossed by the caravan of the satrap or of one of his subordinates had to provide (II.14a; cf. Polyaenus VII.23.2). Many of the anecdotes found in the *Economics* illustrate Mausolus's legendary fiscal rigor (*Oec.* II.14; cf. Polyaenus VII.23.1). This is the context of several anecdotes that attest (though poorly) to his relations with the central administration. For example, he received an order from the king to send a tax (gift) in kind (II.14d); he tapped the richest of his friends and ordered that all of these collections be sent to the Great King (Polyaenus VII.23.1). More precise details are found in an epigraphic text dated to his successor, Pixodarus. The inhabitants of Platasa (in Caria) granted a tax exemption to one Dion and his descendants; the decree states that this exemption pertained only to civic taxes—Dion and his descendants still had to pay the royal taxes (*basilika telē; BE* 1973, no. 408); this datum is confirmed by other decrees. Like any satrapy, Caria was thus obligated to pay tribute, gifts, and a string of other taxes, piled on top of the city taxes, and it was obviously Mausolus and his successors who were required to pass on the sum to the royal administration.

We can single out from the epigraphic record a most interesting decree from Mylasa, dated to year 39 of Artaxerxes (367–366). It says:

> Whereas, Arlissis, son of Thyssolos, having been sent to the king by the Carians, was convicted of breach of trust (*parapresbeuse*) during his embassy; and whereas he conspired (*epebouleuse*) against Mausolus, who is himself a benefactor of the city of the Mylasians just like his father Hecatomnus and his ancestors; and whereas the king adjudged Arlissis guilty (*adikein*) and condemned him to death; whereas the city looks after his possessions, according to the traditional laws (*kata tous nomous tous patrious*); having allocated them to Mausolus, they called down curses on their subject: that nothing be suggested and said aloud running to the contrary; if anyone violates this, he shall be put to death, he and his. (Tod 138.1)

We do not know the substance of the charges brought against Mausolus; there is nothing to prove that the satrap could have been accused of rebellion at this date, even if Arlissis felt that he could bring accusations of this sort in so sensitive a sphere. It must have been an internal affair, perhaps related to Mausolus's fiscal concerns. There are other texts (Tod no. 138.2–3) that refer to such conspiracies, in which the guilty are regulary condemned and their property confiscated. What is more interesting about the Arlissis affair is the illustration of relationships among several spheres of power: the satrap-dynast, the *koinon* of the Carians (who sent the embassy to Artaxerxes), the city of Mylasa (which made the decision), and the Great King. It is especially noteworthy that it was Artaxerxes who condemned Arlissis, probably reversing an earlier judgment in which the accusations brought by the informer had been judged legitimate. The role of the Mylasa assembly, which no doubt was closely controlled by Mausolus, was simply to record the king's sentence and to issue a further penalty (confiscation of goods), which was purely local in nature. This latter penalty did not fall under the purview of the central authority, which had no particular acquaintance with specifically Carian institutional behavior. The new trial entered into at Mylasa includes an accusation of *parapresbeia*, an accusation that was quite common in the Greek cities: they frequently condemned ambassadors sent to the court of the Great King, who agreed to accept gifts, following Achaemenid custom (Aelian, *VH* I.22)—which upon their return were considered bribes. For all these reasons, the text fits perfectly into the ample record of relations involving judicial jurisdictions between the central authority and the subject communities.

However, there is no choice but to recognize that no evidence explicitly confirms Diodorus's statements about Mausolus's active participation in the revolts. Altogether, we have just a few sentences in the *Agesilaus* of Xenophon (2.26–27). There we learn (1) that, during the campaign against Ariobarzanes in 366, Autophradates was assisted by Mausolus's navy—a matter of cooperation between land and sea forces—as previously was the case in 391 during operations against Cyprus (Hecatomnus and Autophradates); and (2) that the sieges of Assos and Sestos were carried out jointly by their troops. It is thus clear that in this situation Mausolus was acting alongside loyalist forces in the context of a mission that was maintaining imperial order. The sequel to the passage is more obscure, in regard to both the text itself and its interpretation. Mausolus abandoned the siege of Assos and Sestos, at the urging of Agesilaus (an ally of Ariobarzanes) and after taking money from both parties; then he gave funds to the Spartans; last, Tachos and Mausolus organized the return of Agesilaus with great pomp. Without going into this point in detail, we may simply note that any triangular relationship among Mausolus, Tachos, and Agesilaus that might be posited raises virtually insoluble chronological problems.

Let us try to collect the points that are more or less reliable: (1) no indisputable evidence can be detected of a supposed secessionist mindset in Mausolus's acts and initiatives; (2) on the contrary, we observe that the only action in which we see him take part was directed against the rebel Ariobarzanes, in close cooperation with the royal forces (into which the Carian contingents are integrated); (3) the Arlissis affair shows that, even in Caria itself, there were many enemies who were ready to criticize Mausolus to the Great King; it also eloquently shows that adroit, unscrupulous accusers could hurl accusations at satraps for debatable motives, and the king had to make a decision based on his inner convictions.

From Caria to Lycia

Diodorus also counts the Lycians among the coastal peoples in rebellion, a fact that to some extent recalls a categorical declaration made by Isocrates in 380, in one of his many digressions on the weakness of the Achaemenid Empire: "Lycia no Persian has ever subdued" (*ekratēsen*; *Paneg.* 161✧). However, the fact that Diodorus and Isocrates concur grants no authority to their common interpretation. To be able to make a judgment, we need to go back several decades, in order to situate this brief period in the *longue durée* of Lycian history and in the context of its relations with Persian might after the end of Darius II's reign (see chap. 14/8).

At that time, Lycia was fragmented among a large number of dynasts. But as in previous periods, one can glimpse attempts at hegemony on the part of some of them. The beginnings of a dynast called Pericles (we do not know his Lycian name) date to around 380; he sought to enlarge his territory after setting out from his base at Limyra in eastern Lycia. He was well enough known that Theopompus thought it worthwhile to devote a passage to him in the twelfth book of his *History*, of which we have the following summary: "The Lycians, under the leadership of their king (*basileus*) Pericles, made war on Telmessos and did not cease fighting until they had surrounded its inhabitants within their walls and forced them to negotiate" (*homologia*; *FGrH* 115 F103). Pericles quickly succeeded in building himself a well-organized little principality, as is confirmed by the rock-cut necropolises and the ruins of his residence at Limyra, which magnificently dominated the sea (fig. 54). Moreover, the royal titles accorded him by Theopompus are confirmed by a Greek inscription recently found at the site: it states that "Pericles, who reigns over Lycia (*Lykias b[asileuōn]*), raised an altar in honor of Zeus Hypatos, son of Chronos and Rhea."

It seems quite likely that the urbanization program and the boastful declarations of Pericles were meant to respond to the accomplishments of the Xanthus dynasts who had always held a privileged place in Lycian politics after the Persian conquest. The particularly rich Xanthus documentation reflects both internal troubles and the radiance of the Xanthian principality between 400 and 360. The Pillar Inscription is traditionally dated to ca. 400, and its authorship is attributed to Kheriga. Although the Lycian text has still not been fully deciphered, parallel Greek texts provide a wealth of information. One of the pillar's inscriptions celebrates the valor in combat and exploits in war of Gergis/ Kheriga, son of Harpagus, of the lineage of Karikas: "He conquered many acropolises and gave his relatives (*syggeneis*) a share in his royal domain." This last formula and the inscriptions of his successor, Arbinas, actually show that instability was the norm, encouraged by the practice of distributing the domain of a decedent among the members of the family. Arbinas/Erbbina, who presents himself as the son of Kheriga, claims that he had to conquer Xanthus itself in his youth, as well as Pinara and Telmessus. Another

53a

Fig. 53. Monument of the Nereids
at Xanthus: (a) audience scene;
(b–d) banquet scenes.

53b

monument "recalls [how] he established his power over [Lycia] ... spreading fear among the Lycian masses and imposing himself as master over them (*etyrannei*)"; the rest of the inscription celebrates his intellectual, moral, and physical virtues.

Kheriga was almost certainly responsible for the erection of the monument to the Nereids [daughters of the sea god]. Without once more describing in detail the icono graphic composition of this re markable structure, we will stress its obvious thematic unity, which il lustrates dynastic ideology very well. While the Greek imprint is obvious in the iconography, as in the inscriptions on the same edi fice, we may also note the signifi

53c

cance of themes dependent on Persepolis specifically and on Achaemenid court art generally, including audience scenes, hunting scenes, banquets, gift-bearing, and war and siege (fig. 53a–d). These last-mentioned images seem to depict visually the dynast's

53d

written assertions. In order to exalt his power, the Xanthian dynast simultaneously summoned the Greek gods, memories of the Persian Wars (repetition of an epigram in honor of the victory at the Eurymedon), and the pageantry of the scenes shown in Persian reliefs and seals. The monument can be dated to approximately 390–380—that is, a period shortly before Pericles began to consolidate his power at Limyra and started to publicize his own glory, using themes and methods parallel to those used by Arbinas at Xanthus. Furthermore, the two men were certain to clash: according to Theopompus, Pericles conquered Telmessus, the very town Arbinas had taken at the beginning of his reign. Both wanted to be proclaimed king of the Lycians. In a way, their rivalry can be compared to the hectic competition that, at almost the same time and not far from Lycia, made rivals of Straton of Sidon and Nicocles of Paphos, each desperate to outdo the other in the splendor and brilliance of life at their court. Contrary to Theopompus's claim (apud Athenaeus XII.531a–e; Aelian, *VH* VII.2), this *tryphē* was not simply luxury and pleasure; it was first and foremost the image of power that these kinglets could outwardly show by exhibiting a symbolism of power that was strongly inspired by the ideological and iconographic codes that regulated the court of the Great King. However, from another perspective, as we have already said, the many thoughtful borrowings from Achaemenid court art do not *necessarily* imply that the dynasts were thus acknowledging their submission to satrapal authority. It is in fact tricky to establish a sound political connection on the basis of an iconographic program; the dynasts of Xanthus and Limyra primarily were anxious to exalt their dominant position in Lycia. We will simply note that the dynast of Xanthus was far from attempting to flatter the Persians by implicitly referring to the victory at the Eurymedon (to his own benefit). It is true that the poem was written by a Greek, Symmachus of Pellana, but he certainly must have submitted the text to his patron in advance! Anyway, as with the coins, one of the problems is the identification of the people who appear, for example, in the audience scenes (fig. 53a): the satrap or the dynast?

Fortunately, another Xanthian monument, the sarcophagus of Payava (so-called by the name of its Lycian occupant), relieves part of the difficulty. The Persian borrowings are significant once again, and they are particularly obvious in an audience scene: several people dressed in Greek style appear before a dignitary, who wears Persian clothing and appurtenances (kandys, *akinakēs*, tiara, beard); and two other people stand behind him. On the lid's ridge, a Lycian inscription names "Autophradates, Persian satrap," and describes the delivery of an object(?) to a person whose name is missing but who could not be anyone other than Payava; either he or the other person appears to have "captured a Lycian general" (?) (*TL* 40). The presence of Autophradates at Xanthus is not surprising on an institutional level, because Lycia was a dependency of the satrap of Sardis at that time, and another funerary inscription (of Phellos) is dated by the phrase "under the command(?) of Autophradates" (*TL* 61). It is nonetheless highly noteworthy to see Autophradates represented on a Lycian monument, which implies that Payava was his dependent (he probably was the dynast of Xanthus at the time). We get the impression that the sarcophagus scene depicts one of the ceremonies surrounding the arrival of a satrap in his province. But what is the date of the scene: before, during, or after the revolts? Study of the sarcophagus itself does not allow us to date it more precisely than from about 370 to about 350. Does the evidence lead us to make a distinction (ensured many times over by other evidence through the years) between western

Fig. 54. Parade on Pericles' monument at Limyra.

Lycia (loyal to or reconquered by the Persians) and a central and eastern Lycia (ruled by a dynast in open revolt, who would be Pericles)?

A number of commentators have answered this question in the affirmative, even suggesting that there was cooperation between Pericles and Datames. But the fragmentary and poorly-dated record authorizes no such inference. We may note first (but without provable connections with the events we are trying to analyze here) that texts from the time of Alexander suggest that the Persians campaigned in Lycia at about this time and took prisoners, some of whom were deported to Persepolis (Diodorus XVII.68.5; Plutarch, *Alex.* 37.1; Polyaenus IV.3.26; chap. 16/12). We will next recall that Theopompus mentions an attack on Telmessus by Pericles, which assumes that there was a war against the Xanthus dynast, seeing that Arbinas considered Telmessus within his domain. In addition, Pericles' territorial expansion is confirmed by inscriptions found at several sites in central and eastern Lycia. An inscription from Limyra refers to Pericles' victory over one Artumpara, whose coins have been found at several Lycian sites; but we cannot establish with certainty his (possible) relationship with Autophradates. The handful of solid evidence instead gives an impression only of alluding to squabbles between Lycian dynasts, with no dependable connection with the Satraps' Revolt, even if we might make the suggestion that the Revolt could have provided some advantage to the dynasts. The chronological doubts, in any case, do not allow us to deduce that Autophradates directly intervened (even though they do not exclude this possibility, either). A recently published inscription has even brought into question the role usually attributed to Pericles. It shows that, after his death, his family and descendants continued to occupy a position of great prestige in Limyra, an obvious sign that his power had not been destroyed. All by itself, this text wipes out any theories that might have been constructed regarding the fate reserved by the Great King for a dynast guilty of rebellion.

A *Summary of the Discussion*

While we cannot forget the persistent uncertainties that have been pointed out all along the way, we can at least state with certainty that Diodorus's thesis is not confirmed by the rest of the evidence. We are not dealing with a general, coordinated conflagration on the western front in 361 but rather with a series of limited local revolts over the course of a decade. Despite the motives attributed to Orontes and Datames, there is no evidence that the satraps ever planned to unite their forces with the Egyptians' in an attempt to dethrone Artaxerxes II. In any case, if any plans for united action ever existed over the long term and distance, they were never put into practice. If Orontes ever really was acknowledged as *strategos* of a coalition, we never see him at the head of a united army confronting the king's army. It is nonetheless quite striking to observe that the only military operations mentioned are in Aeolis and the Troad, on the one hand, and in the regions bordering Datames, on the other. In northwestern Asia Minor, the unrest may belong in the context of the long history of conflict between Sardis and Dascylium. We often see the Persian leaders of Asia Minor at each other's throats—hardly ever cooperating, except during the loyalist campaign of Autophradates and Mausolus. Datames himself also engaged in individual operations, apart from an agreement with Ariobarzanes—but we can only guess at its duration and practical effectiveness. The only royal army seen operating in the west is the force that Prince Ochus led to victory over Tachos in the last months of his father's reign. Given the information that reached Artaxerxes from Asia Minor, he, as best we can judge, believed that the forces of his loyal satraps were sufficient to calm any unrest.

The end of the earlier revolt of Pissuthnes, as reported by Ctesias (§52), is quite significant. He was betrayed by the head of the mercenaries who fought by his side, an Athenian named Lycon: "He also received towns and lands as the reward for his betrayal." In fact, this example is not unique. We again must emphasize the frequency of the theme of betrayal in the ancient sources. The case of Datames is particularly noteworthy because he suffered successive betrayals by his father-in-law, his oldest son, many of his companions, and finally by Mithradates, who pretended to join the rebellion, the better to betray him. But his case was not isolated, because Ariobarzanes himself was betrayed by his son, and Orontes and Rheomithres themselves surrendered and turned over many conspirators to the royal officials. Mistrust of other Persian leaders certainly appears to have been common to all of the protagonists. It would be a mistake to consider the theme nothing but a moralizing *topos*, whatever the intentions of the Classical authors may have been. The motives imputed to Orontes and Rheomithres are very clear: the former desired "great rewards" from the king (in particular, an extensive jurisdiction); the latter wanted "to ma[k]e his peace with the King" (Diodorus XV.91.1;✧ 92.1✧). In other words, the Persians continued to frame their activities within the ideological structure of the system of royal loyalty/favor that so many texts evidence throughout Achaemenid history (see chaps. 8, 17/2).

Is it necessary to state that these remarks are not intended to deny the existence of rebellions? The problem is to interpret rebellions in relation to the Great King's territorial dominion. From this point of view, the situation is twofold. On one side, we stress once more that the Persians, despite the King's determination and great preparations, proved incapable of retaking the Nile Valley; moreover, at one point, the pharaoh even took the offensive. This inability is difficult to understand: though the theory of Persian military decadence is hardly tenable (see chap. 17/3), we can emphasize the insufficiency of Persian territorial control. Already in the previous century the Persians did not seem to have genuine control of the Delta in its entirety (see chap. 14/2); in addition, Hakoris's power, which was based both in Egypt and in a network of alliances, forced the satrapal armies to fight on various fronts at the same time. On the other side, it seems difficult to assert that the satrapal revolts attested in Asia Minor illustrate a deep and irreversible degradation of the control that the central authority exercised over the governors. This was not the first time, after all, that discontented satraps took up arms: let us recall, for example, the (hypothetical) revolt of Megabyzus (see chap. 14/3), or the revolts of Arsites (Ctesias §50), Pissuthnes (Ctesias §52), and then his son Amorges. None of these occasional revolts constituted any great threat to Artaxerxes I or Darius II, despite the external assistance they sometimes received (for example, the Athenians' support of Amorges). Contrary to an interpretation that would see Orontes as the image of a new Cyrus the Younger, he did not, properly speaking, endanger either Artaxerxes or the Achaemenid dynasty; there was in fact no alternative to Achaemenid dynastic continuity. Nor do we see one or another Persian rebel ever endangering the imperial structures by attempting, for example, to found a private principality, let alone an independent kingdom—contrary to the impression that the vocabulary (*basileia*) used by Diodorus might create (speaking of Hellespontine Phrygia; XV.90.3); he was obviously anticipating the situation in the Hellenistic period (cf. XVI.90.2; XX.111.4; XXXI.19.1–5). In short, as well as they can be reconstructed, the events of the 360s provide evidence of the symptoms of imperial instability (the satrapal revolts and the offensive of Tachos of Egypt), their limited and contradictory nature (the internal collapse of the revolts; dynastic squabbling in Egypt), and the intact capacity of the center to overcome these changes through offensives that were military (victories of Ochus in Syria) or political (defections to Ochus and Artaxerxes II).

8. At the Heart of Power

In the Royal Residences

As we have stressed several times, the focus of attention on affairs on the western front in the preceding pages (as in the previous chapter) is not the author's choice: it derives from the nature of the evidence. Furthermore, dealing with revolts, insurrections, and reconquests constitutes one of several touchstones that exposed the functional capabilities of imperial structures. We would like, nonetheless, to be able to carry out an equally detailed inquiry into the heart of the Empire.

Once again, it is royal building projects on which we are best informed. We know that Artaxerxes II had an apadana built at Ecbatana (A^2Ha–b–c). He was probably also the builder of a new Achaemenid palace in Babylon. But it was at Susa that his activity is most certain. We know that he rebuilt Darius I's apadana, which had perished in flames during the reign of Artaxerxes I (A^2Sa). Even more important, excavations and inscriptions prove that he built a new palace, below the terrace, on the banks of the Shaur (A^2Sd). Neither the building nor the decoration of any palace can be attributed to him at Persepolis. On the other hand, he was the first to build his tomb above the terrace, and he was followed in this by his successor. These are the tombs to which Diodorus Siculus refers (XVII.71.7). Unfortunately, we do not know all of the reasons that led Artaxerxes II to abandon the site near Naqš-i Rustam. The king's decision at least illustrates the fact that, alongside Pasargadae, Persepolis endured as a dynamic capital of the Empire. At any rate, we may note, by way of anticipation, that Artaxerxes III continued to carry out the work of his predecessors there (A³Pa, Pb): he added a western stairway to Darius's palace, selectively reusing the reliefs of gift-bearers.

Artaxerxes II, Mithra, and Anāhita: Sources and Problems

Like his predecessors, Artaxerxes II consistently invoked Ahura-Mazda—for example, by repeating the formulas of Darius I (A²Hc, 15–20). But more noteworthy is the fact that he invokes the great god of the dynasty jointly with Anāhita and Mithra in several of his statements (A²Sa, Sb, Sd, A²Ha). For the first time, the "other gods" invoked anonymously by Darius I and his successors are explicitly named. The historical significance of this innovation has been continuously investigated. Traditionally—and not unreasonably—one of Artaxerxes II's edicts is cited; Berossus mentions this edict and its gist has been transmitted by a late author (Clement of Alexandria; *FGrH* 680 F11). After recalling that the Persians and Medes did not pay homage to statues of wood or stone, Berossus says:

> Later, however, after many years they began to worship statues (*agalmata sebein*) in human form. . . . Artaxerxes, the son of Darius, the son of Ochus, introduced this practice. He was the first to set up (*anastēsas*) an image of Aphrodite Anaitis in Babylon and to require such worship (*sebein*) from the Susians, Ecbatanians, Persians [Persepolis] and Bactrians [Balkh] and from Damascus and Sardis. (§5.2✧)

This text—which certainly derives from an official source—without doubt pertains to a role that traditionally belonged to the Great King: regulator of Persian worship. This said, serious problems of interpretation remain. The royal inscriptions themselves are not unambiguous: the formulas can differ from one inscription to the next. Ahura-Mazda continues to occupy first place, especially in the inscription that refers to building the new palace at Susa (A²Sd✧): "By the favor of Ahuramazda this is the palace which I built. . . . May Ahuramazda, Anaitis, and Mithras protect me from all evil . . ."; it is said rather differently in the inscription describing the reconstruction of the apadana of Darius I at Susa: "By the favor of Ahuramazda, Anaitis, and Mithras, this palace I (re)built" (A²Sa✧; cf. A²Ha).

However, why does the sole inscription of his successor at Persepolis read simply: "Me may Ahuramazda and the god Mithras (*Mithra baga*) protect, and this country, and what was built by me" (A³Pa✧)? Why is Anāhita no longer mentioned? And why does Berossus say not a word about Mithra? The "omission" of Mithra seems even more odd because it is solely in regard to the public worship of Mithra that we have any corroborative information. We know from Strabo (XI.14.9) that, during the Achaemenid era, the satrap of Armenia had to send 20,000 colts each year to the Great King at the time of the *Mithriaka*, that is, the official celebrations in honor of Mithra. Some passages in Xenophon show that this practice was in effect at least beginning with the time of Artaxerxes II, because each village in Armenia yearly had to send colts as royal *dasmos* (*Anab.* IV.5.24) and that (some of?) these colts were dedicated to the Sun (IV.5.35). We also learn of these official festivals in honor of Mithra from Duris, who stresses the central role played by the king (Athenaeus X.434e). Most Classical references to Mithra date approximately to the reign of Artaxerxes II (e.g., Xenophon, *Oec.* IV.24; Plutarch, *Art.* 4.5; Aelian, *VH* I.33). But does this necessarily imply that there was a close chronological connection to the change in royal formulary that appears at the time of Artaxerxes II? Nothing could be less certain.

Behind these questions lurks a basic problem, already posed by Plutarch's well-known text on the enthronement of Artaxerxes II at Pasargadae in a temple dedicated to Anāhita, here called "warlike goddess" (*Art.* 3.2◇): precisely how new was the novelty introduced by Artaxerxes II? What, for example, is the meaning of Berossus's distinction between towns (Babylon, Susa, Ecbatana) that received the order to erect (*anastēsas*) statues versus other towns (Persepolis, Bactra, Damascus, and Sardis), in which apparently the accent is placed solely on worship (*sebein*), as if statues already existed (or as if one could worship without a statue)? And, if such statues did exist here and there, how are we to appraise the novelty of the edict? Or again: if Berossus does not mention Mithra, is it because we have only a partial quotation of the royal edict, or because the worship of Mithra was not concerned with holy statues—even though statues seem to have represented the most noteworthy novelty to Berossus himself?

This observation in turn poses another problem. *A priori*, Berossus's text does not harmonize perfectly with what Herodotus, for example, says (I.131◇): "The erection of statues (*agalmata*), temples, and altars is not an accepted practice among them [the Persians]. . . . [T]hey sacrifice . . . from the tops of mountains" (cf. likewise Strabo XV.3.13). But are these peremptory statements legitimate? We can overlook Strabo's assertion (XV.3.15) that statues (*xoana*) of Anāhita and Omanus were transported with great pomp during festivals in the Persian sanctuaries in Cappadocia; his comment refers to a later period. More important is a passage by Dinon (also cited by Clement of Alexandria), written in the fourth century, with information at variance with Herodotus: according to Dinon, though Persians, Medes, and *magi* did indeed sacrifice on the heights, they worshiped two gods in the form of statues (*agalmata*)—namely, Fire and Water (*FGrH* 690 F28). Dinon's chronology does not allow us to determine that he is describing a change initiated by Artaxerxes II. Nevertheless, he does not mention Mithra or Anāhita, except to suggest that Fire designated the former and Water the latter, which seems very unlikely: Water and Fire are two clearly individualized gods whose central place in Persian sacrificial practice is stressed by Strabo (XV.3.14, 16). So we are back to the basic question regarding the innovation introduced in the time of Artaxerxes II.

Droaphernes and the Sardis Statue

It is easy to see the problem's stumbling block: we are utterly unable to find confirmation or illustration anywhere else of the change suggested by the royal inscriptions and made explicit in the Berossus quotation. To confirm the change, in fact, we would need to have some precisely dated evidence that would allow us to demonstrate that official sanctuaries of Anāhita, complete with cultic statues, were erected in the towns listed by Berossus beginning in the time of Artaxerxes II. However, this is not the case; though the spread of sanctuaries of Persian Anaitis/Anāhita in western Asia Minor certainly goes back a long time (cf. Tacitus, *Ann.* III.62), we have no direct evidence of the existence of a sanctuary of Anāhita at Sardis itself before 322 (Pausanias VII.6.6: Persian Artemis). A recently published text from Sardis has been claimed as a parallel (*SEG* XXIX.1205); it is a Greek inscription, in which three parts can be identified—a dedication and two prohibitions:

(1–5) In the 39th year of Artaxerxes, Droaphernes, son of Baraces, *hyparkhos* of Lydia, [dedicated] the statue (*andrias*) to Zeus of Baradates.

(5–11) He(?) orders the *nēocores therapeutes* [temple administrators] [of Zeus] who have the right to enter the adyton and who crown the god not to participate in the mysteries of Sabazios of those who bring the victims to be immolated and of Angdistis and of Mā.

(11–13) They(?) order the *nēocore* Dorates to abstain from these mysteries.

The Greek text was (re)carved during the Roman Empire period for reasons that remain unclear. This peculiarity probably explains several puzzles that remain. Basically, the text records a decision made by Droaphernes, who is unknown elsewhere but bears a typically Iranian name; he must have been an important person in the satrapal administration of Sardis (though the word *hyparkhos* alone does not allow us to determine his exact position). As the formula "Zeus of Baradates" implies, the decision involves a family cult comparable to the "Men of Pharnaces" known to have been in Pontus from Strabo (XII.3.31). Baradates, according to this hypothesis, must be considered the ancestor of Droaphernes, son of Baraces.

It is especially noteworthy to observe that Droaphernes dedicated a statue. But must it necessarily be seen as a concrete expression of a general policy that had the goal of multiplying cult statues throughout the Empire? To imagine that the statue was even the statue of a god—a conclusion hardly permitted by the word used (*andrias*: statue of a human)—is not supportable in any respect. In the first place, the date of the inscription is problematic: apart from the suggested comparison with Berossus, not a single feature allows the text to be assigned to Artaxerxes II (ca. 366–365) rather than Artaxerxes I (ca. 427), since the copy we have comes from several centuries after Droaphernes' decree. As for the Zeus who is honored, there is nothing to allow an *interpretatio graeca* claiming that Ahura-Mazda appeared in the original version. It is much more likely that Zeus here refers to a local god, who could quite simply be the Lydian Zeus, who is well attested at Sardis from the beginning of the sixth century on. Given all of these factors, there is no reason to submit the inscription to a close comparison with the decision Berossus ascribes to Artaxerxes II.

Anāhita and Ištar

Moreover, it is quite paradoxical that not one text refers to any official celebration in honor of Anāhita—and this festival was supposedly established precisely in the time of Artaxerxes II. Or to be more precise, we have one piece of evidence, which is not without its own interpretive problems. Plutarch states that Artaxerxes II took the following action against Aspasia, the former companion of Cyrus the Younger: "He consecrated her priestess to Diana of Ecbatana, whom they name Anaitis, that she might spend the remainder of her days in strict chastity" (*Art.* 27.4◊). First, the passage formally implies that the sanctuary of Anāhita of Ecbatana, known from other later texts, already existed at least in the time of Artaxerxes, and it even gives the impression that it had been founded earlier. It is tempting to compare Plutarch's evidence with a much earlier text from the time of the Assyrian, Esarhaddon: it names a woman who bears the title 'royal oblate' (*šēlūtu ša šarri*) in the sanctuary of Ištar of Arbela. To be sure, we do not know whether a sanctuary of Ištar still existed in Achaemenid Arbela, but the significance of the town makes the supposition likely.

A priori, the comparison appears to go hand in hand with the representations of Anāhita on several iconographic objects (seals, sealings, rings) already presented (fig. 37a–b,

p. 253); these objects exhibit syncretisms between Anāhita and Ištar, the great Mesopotamian goddess, that had doubtless been operative for a very long time. Must we, however, infer that the goddess whose statues and worship Artaxerxes II intended to spread throughout the Empire was none other than a Babylonicized Anāhita? This theory is hard to believe, in the same way that the related theory postulating a "Babylonicization" of the Achaemenid dynasty during the fourth century, usually connected with the half-Babylonian origin of Darius II and Parysatis, is hard to believe. We may also note that Ištar is not the only goddess to whom a woman was consecrated; on the contrary, it was a very widespread custom. Strabo mentions that it was practiced in the temples of Anāhita in Cappadocia (XI.14.16), and he reports similar practices at Zeleia, in the sanctuary of Anaitis founded by the Persians (cf. XI.8.4); furthermore, hierodules are also found in other sanctuaries dedicated to Persian gods (XII.3.37): a Greek inscription from Cappadocia attests the consecration of hierodules to "the great goddess Anaitis Barzochara."

What would be the significance of this decree for peoples from eastern Iran to western Asia Minor who were not affected in the slightest by the syncretism between Anāhita and Ištar? In Lydia, for example, the assimilations and syncretisms in progress involved the goddesses Anāhita and Artemis. Could it have been precisely because of her mutable character that Anāhita was the goddess of choice for a king who wanted to diffuse among his peoples the worship of a goddess that each of them could recognize as their own?

Back to Berossus

While the political nature of the royal decree scarcely seems to offer any room for doubt, the fundamental problem in fact remains: to whom was Artaxerxes' decree addressed? It seems rather improbable that Artaxerxes II departed from the policy of his predecessors and tried to impose the worship of Iranian gods on the regions named by Berossus. Moreover, though Anāhita was certainly the object of syncretisms with local gods, as we have seen, it was not the intention of the Great King to confuse the official worship of the goddess with local gods. While such syncretisms already existed, the Great King's purpose clearly was to transplant the worship and images of a *fully Iranian* goddess. Berossus's list provides a key: we immediately recognize it as a list of the main centers of Achaemenid dominion: Babylon, Susa, Ecbatana, Persepolis, Bactra, Damascus, and Sardis. Given these facts, the most likely explanation—at least, the one we accept here—is that Artaxerxes was addressing his decree to the Persians who had settled in the various provinces of the Empire. By exalting the goddess who dispensed royal legitimacy, Artaxerxes was seeking to bind the imperial Persian diaspora still more closely to himself. His pronouncement served to reinforce the function that Xenophon quite rightly attributes to the satrapal courts: they were to be the guardians of Persian mores and the locus of ideological perpetuation of the dominant socioethnic class—that is, "Persia in Asia Minor for the king," to repeat the poet Bianor's colorful phrase characterizing Sardis (*Anth. Pal.* IX.423).

One more question remains: when and why? Does the existence of an edict allow us to suggest that Artaxerxes was responding to an internal crisis in the Empire by promulgating the edict? What historical circumstances would lie behind it, according to this hypothesis? The edict might have been an outcome of the ideological contest with his brother Cyrus the Younger or might have been connected with the satrapal unrest. However, recalling the precedent of Xerxes and the *daivā* (see chap. 13/6–7), we must point out that another interpretation is possible: Artaxerxes II was reaffirming the sacral nature of royal power that was indissolubly linked to the protection of the gods, outside of all concrete historical time. Let us end with this acknowledgment: the interpretation that we have just presented leaves many questions hanging, and we ourselves are incapable of providing well-founded answers.

The Imperial Realm

Berossus's text is interesting in another way, which we will consider briefly—the world of administration. His list of sites also comprises a sort of inventory of the imperial realm, organized around traditional residences (Persepolis, Susa, Babylon, Ecbatana) and capitals of vast regions: Bactra (Iranian Plateau), Damascus (Trans-Euphrates), and Sardis (Asia Minor and Anatolia). The omission of Memphis confirms *a contrario* the accuracy of Berossus's information.

Though the importance of Damascus or Sardis could already have been known through other sources, we will stress specifically that this is the first explicit mention of Bactra since Artaxerxes I's campaign there at the beginning of his reign (Ctesias §31). Berossus's reference confirms what we could learn (or guess), beginning, on the one hand, with the role attributed to Dādarši in 522–521 and, on the other, with the situation that seems to have prevailed in the time of Darius III—namely, that the responsibilities of the satrap of Bactra extended far beyond the horizon of Bactria proper. This mention in turn can be connected with other information (also very unspecific) dating to the reigns of Artaxerxes II and his successor. Let us recall in particular that, when he had to face the advance of Cyrus the Younger, Artaxerxes mustered troops at Ecbatana (Diodorus XIV.22.1–2), though these troops arrived too late. They were led by an illegitimate brother of the king (Xenophon, *Anab.* II.4.25), which at least proves that the Iranian Plateau and Central Asia continued to furnish soldiers whenever a general mobilization was decreed; further confirmation will be found in the disposition of troops by Darius III in 333–331.

Of course, the texts are far from eloquent, and the interpretation of some of them is uncertain, but they opportunely remind us that, seen from the center, the Empire extended as far as Central Asia. India itself is not completely absent from the evidence that dates to the reign of Artaxerxes II. The work Ctesias devoted to this region is filled with fantastic stories that must have captivated his listeners. Nonetheless, we will stress that, whether directly or through Aelian, we learn that the kings of the Indus were required to send gifts to the Great King regularly; this may be how Darius III obtained Indian elephants (cf. Quintus Curtius V.2.10). Let us add, finally, that in Ctesias's lost work dedicated to the royal roads and stages, he followed an itinerary from Ephesus to Bactra and India (*FGrH* 688 F33: *apou Ephesou mekhri Baktrōn kai Indikēs*). By itself, this information remains vague; nonetheless, the implication is that at this date the connections between Susa and the Indus Valley had not been broken, and the Indian kings continued to show their subjection to the Great King.

From Artaxerxes II to Artaxerxes III

According to Plutarch, the old king's last years were strewn with pitfalls and conspiracies. Plutarch first of all relates that Artaxerxes had three legitimate sons from his marriage to Stateira: Darius (the oldest), Ariaspes (called Ariarathes by Justin X.1.1), and Ochus (the youngest; *Art.* 26.1–2; cf. 30.2). His concubines bore him a great number of illegitimate children as well (115 sons according to Justin X.1.1, 5), among them Arsames (Plutarch §30.1, 8). "Being willing to put down in good time his son Ochus's hopes, lest . . . wars and contentions might again inflict his kingdom," the king named Darius crown prince (Plutarch §26.4–5◊). Soon, an intense resentment impelled Darius, egged on by Tiribazus, to weave a plot against his father (§27–28). The prince expected that many courtiers would be ready to follow him (§29.1), including, according to Justin (X.1.5), fifty of his illegitimate brothers. The conspiracy was uncovered through information provided by a eunuch; Darius was brought to trial before the royal judges and put to death (Plutarch §29), "along with the wives and children of all the conspirators" (Justin X.2.6). Following this, in Plutarch, is an account of the contemptible schemes of Ochus, who was bolstered by his lover Atossa; she was both his sister and his stepmother (§23.3–7; 30.1; cf. Val. Max. IX.2.7). Through his stratagems and accusations, Ochus managed to drive his legitimate brother Ariaspes mad, and he chose to take his own life (§30.1–5; different version in Aelian, *VH* IX.42). Soon he had his illegitimate brother, Arsames, who was the king's favorite, killed (§30.7–8). These were the circumstances at the time of Artaxerxes' death of old age, after a long reign (between November 359 and April 358, according to Babylonian tablets).

Behind the frantic romanticism of Plutarch's tale, we can observe several realities. First of all, following the model of his predecessors, Artaxerxes II was careful to designate a crown prince during his lifetime—his oldest son, as it happens. Second, the selection of a crown prince did not result in sharing power (despite Justin X.1.2). Finally, and as a corollary to our second point, the status of crown prince was itself unstable. Plutarch, in contrast, breathes not a word about the designation of a new heir after the deaths of Darius and then Ariaspes. He is content to note that the king showed a preference for one of his illegitimate sons, Arsames. In reality, everything leads us to believe that, when Artaxerxes II died, everything was ready for the transition. If, as we may reasonably suppose, Ochus had been placed by his father at the head of the army sent to fight Tachos (Syncellus, p. 486, 20: "while his father was still alive"), this designation all by itself removes our doubts. Without dwelling on it, Diodorus (XV.93.1) simply notes that, when Artaxerxes II died, Ochus succeeded his father. This is not to say that the succession was welcomed by everyone. One late author, for example, mentions that on his accession the new Artaxerxes "buried Atossa alive, who was both his sister and his stepmother. He locked his uncle and more than 100 sons and grandsons in an empty courtyard and had them killed in a hail of arrows" (Val. Max. IV.2.7; cf. Justin X.3.1). This presentation fits perfectly with the despicable image of Artaxerxes III in the ancient literature (e.g., Plutarch §30.9). However, even if we suppose that the tradition transmitted by Valerius Maximus is accurate, all that can be concluded from it is that Ochus had made enemies at court before his accession. Furthermore, Plutarch himself also notes that, as at the time of the succession of Darius II (§6.1–2), the court was disrupted by the activities of opposing factions favoring Darius or Ochus (§26.1).

9. *The Wars of Artaxerxes III (351–338)*

Artaxerxes III and Artabazus

It appears that the new Great King found himself beset with troubles in Asia Minor shortly after his accession—or perhaps the troubles had always been there in latent form. In the course of Diodorus's discussion of Athens' war against its rebellious allies between ca. 357 and 355 (XVI.7.3–4; 21–22.1–2), he states that the Athenian *strategos* Chares, who hoped to alleviate the financial burden of the military operations, had entered into an agreement with the satrap of Hellespontine Phrygia, Artabazus, who was then in revolt (*apostas*) against the king. With Chares' help, the satrap won a victory over the royal army (§22.1). Soon thereafter, facing threats from Artaxerxes, Athens ceased its intervention. Traces of these events can also be found in anecdotal fragments that provide a few additional details: the royal forces were led by Tithraustes, whose status is not clarified; he had a *khōra* ('position') in Phrygia, and he had just overpowered Chares (*FGrH* 105 F4). After the Athenian's departure, Artabazus received aid from the Thebans, who sent him a force commanded by Pammenes, and with Pammenes' help he achieved victory over "the satraps who had been dispatched by the king" (Diodorus §34.1–2).

Though it seems certain that Artabazus received no assistance from the other satraps in Asia Minor, the reasons for and origins of his rebellion remain thickly cloaked in mystery. According to the Scholia on Demosthenes (4.14), the king ordered the satraps to disband their mercenaries. However, aside from some problems posed by this information (see chap. 17/3), it explains nothing about Artabazus's behavior. Instead, we must imagine, as in the previous period, that Artabazus was accused by one of his colleagues, for reasons that totally escape us but that apparently persuaded the king (cf. Diodorus XVI.52.3: *egklēmata*). Under unspecified conditions, Artabazus, with his entire family, chose exile at the court of Philip II of Macedon (ibid.).

Failure in Egypt, Revolt in Phoenicia and Cyprus (351–345)

While these minor flareups were being extinguished in Asia Minor, the new king was primarily engrossed with the situation in Trans-Euphrates and Egypt. Even though at the time of his accession he might have guessed that he had a free hand in dealing with Egypt, he in fact knew nothing about the destructive effects of Nectanebo II's rebellion or about the difficulties that the pretender faced when his attempt to assert his authority was challenged. We do not know much about the intentions of Artaxerxes III. In a highly suspect passage that was intended to illustrate the cowardice of the Great King, who was reluctant to assume leadership of operations himself, Diodorus simply notes that Persian generals were once again defeated when they tried to regain a foothold in Egypt during the period from 361 to 351 (XVI.40.3–5). But we have not a shred of corroborative evidence of their attacks on Egypt prior to the moment when Artaxerxes himself summoned his army and suffered a defeat in 351 (Isocrates, *Phil.* 101; Demosthenes, *Lib. Rhod.* §§11–12); he avenged the insult a few years later.

In 347, Isocrates addressed a stirring tribute to Philip II of Macedon. He promised that the king would win victory after victory, for the Persian Empire was moribund following the failure that the Great King had just experienced in Egypt (351):

> Furthermore, Cyprus and Phoenicia and Cilicia, and that region from which the barbarians used to recruit their fleet, belonged at that time to the King [Artaxerxes II], but now they have either revolted from him or are so involved in war and its attendant ills that none of these peoples is of any use to him; while to you, if you desire to make war upon him, they will be serviceable. And mark also that Idrieus [of Caria], who is the most prosperous of the present rulers of the mainland, must in the nature of things be more hostile to the interests of the King than are those who are making open war against him; . . . but if you should cross over to the mainland . . . you will also induce many of the other satraps [besides Idrieus] to throw off the King's power if you promise them "freedom" and scatter broadcast over Asia

that word which, when sown among the Hellenes, has broken up both our [Athens'] empire and that of the Lacedaemonians. (*Phil.* 102–4✧)

In this speech we find one of those catalogues of countries that were unsubmissive to the Great King of which the Athenian orator was so fond; on this occasion, however, he did not hesitate to provide a contrast by elevating the reign of Artaxerxes II, which he had ridiculed in a discourse in 380 (*Paneg.* 161; see p. 650 above; cf. p. 658). Nonetheless, behind the outrageousness of the thinking, Isocrates is alluding to undeniable facts that Diodorus, in particular, treats in book XVI.

According to Diodorus, in fact, the stimulus for the Egyptian conflict came from the Sidonians, who persuaded the other Phoenicians to take up arms against the Persians and to make a treaty (*symmakhia*) with the pharaoh, Nectanebo, before engaging in an immense war effort. The war officially commenced when the Sidonians devastated the Persian paradise located near their town and destroyed the stocks of fodder stored by the satraps with the Egyptian war in mind; they also executed several leading Persians (XVI.41). At the same time, a revolt connected to the earlier rebellion on the island broke out on Cyprus, with the nine kings declaring independence (42.3–4). While Artaxerxes was gathering an army at Babylon (§42.1), he ordered Idrieus of Caria to lead an army and a navy to Cyprus (§42.6–9), just as Mazaeus, "governor of Cilicia," and Belesys, "satrap of Syria," were conducting the first operations against Phoenicia. Tennes, "king of Sidon," had meanwhile acquired considerable reinforcements through levies on the Sidonian population and the arrival of a contingent of mercenaries sent by the pharaoh and commanded by Mentor; Mazaeus and Belesys were forced back (42.1–2). They later combined their forces with the royal army that arrived from Babylonia. According to Diodorus, the Great King did not really have to fight, since the king of Sidon, Tennes, who soon joined up with Mentor, preferred to betray his fellow citizens. He delivered one hundred Phoenicians to Artaxerxes and then opened the gates of the city; he was soon put to death. The Sidonians chose to kill themselves, their women and children, and to put their houses to the torch; appalled by the king's savagery, the other Phoenicians surrendered (§§43–45.6). Shortly after(?), the Cypriot cities were recaptured or surrendered; Pnytagoras of Salamis alone held out, but he too soon submitted (§46.1–3).

Interesting and detailed though it is, Diodorus's tale poses many problems. First of all, the chronology is often fluid, as it is throughout book XVI. The only external chronological evidence is a fragment of the Babylonian Chronicle (ABC no. 9, p. 114), dated to year 14 of Artaxerxes III, that refers to the sending of Sidonian prisoners to the royal palace in Babylon in October 345. We deduce from this that Sidon was taken some weeks or months earlier, perhaps even in 346, at the same time acknowledging that Isocrates refers to a revolt still in progress in 347 (*Phil.* 102). The revolt certainly lasted quite a while, since Mazaeus and Belesys were ordered to suppress it at first; but it is hardly possible to fix a precise chronology or to state with certainty that the Phoenician revolt broke out immediately after the defeat by the Egyptians in 351, because Diodorus's phrasing leads us to believe otherwise—that several years elapsed between the two events. It is clear in fact that, after the failure on the Nile, the Persians immediately began to prepare an immense force, for the Great King had determined to put an end once and for all to secessions by the pharaoh (Diodorus XVI.40.5–6). Artaxerxes' real purpose in leaving Babylonia was to advance against Egypt (cf. §§43.2; 44.1–5). Sidon was clearly one of the bases for Persian logistical preparations; it was there that the navy and troops were assembled and the cavalry's fodder stored (§41.5). Diodorus's story clearly indicates that Persia's preparations were already well under way when the revolt broke out. In short, it does not seem that the revolt lasted as long as from 351 to 346, as is sometimes stated.

The preparations of the army partly explain some of the causes of the beginning of hostilities. Diodorus indicates that Tennes of Sidon was counting on the militias levied in the city and on Greek mercenaries, some of whom had been sent by Nectanebo under Mentor's command (§§41.4; 42.2; 44.6). He also says that, because of its unparalleled wealth, Sidon was in a position to gather triremes, mercenaries, all sorts of arms, and quantities of provisions (§§ 41.4; 44.5)—indicating that Tennes had been able to take advantage of the slowness of the Great King's preparations. Without denying Sidon's own strengths, we must nonetheless stress that its leaders had been able to profit from the fact that the Persians had chosen their city as the place for their preparations for the Egyptian expedition. It is clear that the Sidonians seized some strategic imperial supplies (§41.5). Given this background, we are tempted to think that its 100 triremes and pentaremes (§44.6) constituted the contingent it had been required to prepare for the war in Egypt. The inhabitants burned their ships after Tennes' betrayal, and the goal of this action must have been more to weaken the royal navy than to prevent some of them from fleeing (§45.4). In other words, like Aristagoras in 499 (see p. 153 above), the Sidonian leaders had deprived the Persians of the means that were intended to sustain the offensive that the Great King was preparing to launch against Egypt.

We are less well informed regarding the origins of and reasons for the revolt, inasmuch as we know little of the history of Sidon and Phoenicia in the preceding decades; we know only of the participation of the Sidonian navy in Conon's war and the equivocal behavior of Straton during Tachos's offensive, some ten years earlier. Diodorus highlights the hatred that the Persian leaders who lived in the city had aroused. The arrogant orders and requisitions, he says, had created or strengthened a strong mood of discontent regarding the imperial war taxes (§41.2, 5), which were severely depleting the profits that the city drew from its commercial activities (*dia tas emporias*; §41.4). Nor was this the first time Sidon had been forced to contribute; they had suffered fiscally ever since Cambyses' first Egyptian expedition in 525. Does the huge extent of Persian preparations, stressed by Diodorus (§40.6), suffice to explain the decision of the Sidonian leaders to burn their bridges when they devastated the royal paradise and to execute high Persian officials? They must have known even at that moment that the war the Great King would wage against them would be merciless (cf. §41.6).

This and several other questions remain unanswered. In fact, it is hard to explain why Tennes chose to betray the city when he received the news of the arrival of Artaxerxes' army. According to Diodorus (§43.1◊), as soon as he was informed of the size of the royal army, the king of Sidon "thought that the insurgents were incapable of fighting against it." We cannot explain this sudden change of direction by assuming that Tennes had previously been unaware of the king's preparations; this is an obviously unsupportable hypothesis. Does his attitude reveal that there was internal conflict in the city? Furthermore, we never see the other Phoenician cities joining the rebellion, even though Diodorus, without explicitly saying so, *seems* to suggest that the Sidonians were united with Aradus and Tyre (§41.1; cf. §45.1). In fact, only Sidon seems to have opposed the Persians; it was the only one of the three cities to be severely punished. In short, the blindness of the Sidonian leaders is hard to explain. Perhaps the hoped-for support of

Nectanebo must be considered. Had he promised them that he would intervene directly? It is possible, given that the pharaohs were generally not parsimonious with such promises; the Sidonians must also have recalled Tachos's recent offensive. For Diodorus, at any rate, it certainly was the Egyptian example that impelled the Phoenicians and, later, the Cypriots to revolt (§§40.5; 42.5). Last, it is very likely that, during the period when the Great King was preparing his army at Babylon, the Persian forces in Phoenicia itself were not very numerous; this would explain how the Sidonian forces and their mercenaries managed to repel the initial counterattack led by Mazaeus and Belesys.

From Sidon to Jerusalem and Jericho

It would also be quite interesting to discover whether the Sidonian and Cypriot rebellions extended to neighboring countries—a theory that might help to explain the Sidonians' apparent optimism. However, it must also be recognized that we have only meager and contradictory evidence about this point. Several late authors refer to the deportation of Jews to Hyrcania, carrying out orders issued by the Great King. Another author (Solinus) speaks of the destruction of Jericho in the time of Artaxerxes III (during his return from Egypt). But aside from the fact that these texts are suspect or contradictory (on the chronological level), there is no external evidence to confirm the existence of a revolt that would have excited Judah and Samaria.

The Reconquest of Egypt (343–342)

As a part of the Great King's strategy, calming Phoenicia and Cyprus was definitely an important matter. Nonetheless, he remained obsessed with the Egyptian problem, and he had begun enormous preparations to deal with it some years earlier (XVI.40.6). Accompanied by a war flotilla and considerable transport (§40.6: stereotypical numbers), the Great King set out on the road to Egypt at the end of 343. Some months later (summer 342), he entered Memphis, whereupon Nectanebo fled to Upper Egypt and then Nubia (§51.1–2). From the point of view of Achaemenid history, one of the most important questions is why Artaxerxes succeeded at what had eluded so many Achaemenid armies since the beginning of the fourth century. In answering this question, we have nothing to rely on but Diodorus Siculus's detailed report (XVI.46.4–9, 47–51), which can easily be compared on many points with his own accounts of the expeditions led by Pharnabazus (XV.41–43), by Perdiccas against Ptolemy (XVIII.33–36), and even by Antigonus against the same Ptolemy in 306 (XX.73–76). It is also a good idea to mention—before returning to it at greater length (chap. 18/3)—that the entire passage in Diodorus is vitiated by the decisive importance he attributes to the Greek mercenaries throughout the course of the campaign.

Diodorus states that the Achaemenid army suffered from the same handicaps that he had already stressed in the descriptions of previous expeditions. Before even arriving in the Nile Valley, the enemy troops had to overcome many obstacles. First, they had to cross the terrifying "region without water" that stretched south of Gaza. We know that Cambyses had recourse to the services of the "king of the Arabs" when he crossed this region (Herodotus III.5–9), just as Esarhaddon had, in his time (ANET[3] 292), and Antigonus in 306 (Diodorus XX.73.3); we do not know what happened in 343. Next came the region of quicksand, the Barathra (Diodorus I.30.4–7; XX.73.3; cf. Polybius V.80.1), in which Artaxerxes III lost a number of soldiers (XVI.46.5) because, Diodorus says, the

Persians had no idea of the topography of the area. He states elswhere that, when Tennes of Sidon entered into negotiations with Artaxerxes III, he emphasized that he could guide the royal army (XVI.43.3). We are further amazed that the Persians did not seek out local guides (cf. XVI.48.3). In this case, we have the impression that Diodorus was reusing a motif illustrated earlier by the role that Herodotus assigned to Phanes, the head of the mercenaries who accompanied Cambyses in 525 (III.4).

The only advantage Diodorus grants to Artaxerxes—and this is a deeply rooted *topos*—is the crushing numerical superiority of his army: Nectanebo had 20,000 Greek mercenaries, 20,000 Libyans, and 60,000 Egyptian *makhimoi* ('soldiers') (XVI.47.5–7), facing an "uncountable" royal army, as implied by the conventionalized numbers cited (300,000 infantrymen, 30,000 cavalry, 300 triremes, and 500 other transport vessels: XVI.40.6). He recalls the most memorable episodes, at least in his eyes: early on, it seems, an army corps, aided by Egyptian guides, managed to cross the river and establish a bridgehead on the opposite bank (XVI.48.3–5); this was what Nectanebo had feared, and he hastened to Memphis in order to ready its defenses (§48.6). This fallback in turn aroused uncertainty in the Egyptian camp and led some Greek mercenaries to negotiate terms of surrender. This resulted in the fall of Pelusium, which was soon followed by the taking of Bubastis and other fortified cities (§49.7–8; 51.1). Thereafter, the way to the Nile was free, and the royal fleet was able to sail up the river as far as Memphis (cf. Thucydides I.104.2).

Moreover, Diodorus stresses that the royal army set off very late because of the length of the preparations, which allowed the ruler of Egypt to continue building up the country's defenses (XVI.46.7; 49.7; cf. XV.41.2, 5). Behind this cliché there certainly lies a truth, for the offensive against Egypt did not take place until the winter of 343–342. For one thing, after the conquest of Sidon the king probably waited for the surrender of the Cypriot cities (46.1–3); for another, further preparations doubtless were completed in the midst of some confusion because of the Sidonian revolt (cf. 45.4: destruction of the ships). Diodorus also states that, before his departure from Babylon (or when he arrived in Phoenicia), Artaxerxes sent messengers to Greece to recruit mercenaries; Athens and Sparta declined nonconfrontationally, but Thebes and Argos sent contingents (44.1–3). This was also the period when the contingents from the subject cities of Asia Minor were joining the royal army (44.4; cf. 46.4). After the fall of Sidon, the Great King also welcomed Mentor and his 4,000 men (42.2; 47.4).

These delays encouraged Nectanebo to use traditional tactics: like all of the pharaohs, he sought to take advantage of the topography. Thus, to render the river uncrossable and to prevent landings on the beaches of the Delta, fortifications were placed on all the mouths of the Nile, especially the Pelusian branch, which had the most beaches (XVI.46.6–7, XV.47.2–4; XX.76.3). A large quantity of boats that were well suited for river combat had been gathered from along the Nile (XVI.47.6); these boats also transported troops from one point to another to prevent enemy troops from landing on the beaches (XX.75.1; 76.3–4). The banks of the river itself were fortified in such a way as to prevent passage (XVI.47.7; cf. XV.47.3; XVIII.33.6, 34.1–4). It looks as though, in order to cover all bets, the Great King chose a favorable season, just as Antigonus had in 306, when he left Palestine at the rising of the Pleiades—that is, at the beginning of November (XX.73.3), a time when the army would not be endangered by the Nile flood (cf. XV.48.4). But in itself this auspicious choice was not a token of success: Antigonus still faced failure and even suggested retreating and returning "with more complete preparation and at the time at which the Nile was supposed to be lowest" (XX.76.5✧). Pharnabazus's failure had also shown that sustained resistance by Egyptian defenses could force an attacker to defer the assault too long, resulting in the collapse of the attack (XV.48.1–4).

Does Diodorus's very unfavorable portrayal of Nectanebo reflect, to a greater or lesser extent, the feelings of the Egyptians? It is impossible to answer such questions: that Artaxerxes used Egyptian guides does not tell us anything specific about their attitude toward the pharaoh; and, even Nicostratus, after all, took hostages as a part of his strategy (XVI.48.3). We may simply note, with Diodorus (§§48.6; 49.2–3), that Nectanebo's withdrawal to Memphis demoralized his soldiers. Finally, Nectanebo very quickly lost hope and gave up on defending Memphis to the death, preferring to flee to Nubia in the belief that many cities were ready to betray him (§51.1). We may wonder whether the internal weakening of pharaonic authority (the subject of military edicts throughout the fourth century) was not in fact one of the most important reasons for the Egyptian failure; but this is simply a guess, and the existing evidence does not permit us to arrive at a more certain conclusion. Diodorus states that Nectanebo was scarcely inclined to take the risks necessary to maintain hegemony (*hyper tēs hēgemonias*; 51.1). This attitude seems entirely opposite to the thoughts that Diodorus imputes to Artaxerxes, who resolved to head the army himself in order to personally lead the fight to preserve his kingdom/kingship (*agōnas hyper tēs basileias*; §40.6). Even though Diodorus's presentation and aggressive vocabulary express royal propaganda, there is little doubt that Artaxerxes III had made it his personal goal not only to reestablish order in Phoenicia but also to reconquer Egypt. He had reached power in troubled circumstances, and now he was determined to prove his military prowess, which in turn would provide justification of his power. A passage in Theopompus illustrates the importance attached to the march on Egypt. It was an occasion when the Great King summoned representatives of the subject peoples as he passed by, and they came to bring him gifts and ritual presents (*FGrH* 115 F263a–b). This meant that Diodorus was able to write, correctly, that when he returned from Egypt, laden with booty, the Great King acquired great renown for his victories (§51.3). In other words, he had reinforced his authority and prestige among his family and his peoples. On this occasion, a royal seal exalting the king's personal victory over the Egyptians was engraved (*SA*³*a*; fig. 18b, p. 215).

Artaxerxes III in Egypt

And so Egypt returned to the Achaemenid fold, nearly sixty years after Amyrtaeus's secession. A Persian administration under the direction of Pharandates was reinstalled in the country (XVI.51.3); however, we cannot say with certainty that Pharandates was a descendant of the satrap with the same name from the time of Darius I (chap. 12/1). Traditionally, Artaxerxes III had an appalling reputation in both the Egyptian and the Classical traditions; in this respect, he is like Cambyses, with whom he is frequently compared in the ancient texts. The origin of this negative reputation is surely to be found in the actions he took, reported by Diodorus as follows:

> After . . . demolishing the walls of the most important cities, by plundering the shrines [he] gathered a vast quantity of silver and gold, and he carried off the inscribed records from the ancient temples (*tas ek tōn archaiōn hierōn anagraphas*), which later on Bagoas returned to the Egyptian priests on the payment of huge sums by way of ransom. (XVI.51.2✧)

Artaxerxes was even accused, just as Cambyses was, of killing the sacred bull Apis; according to Aelian (*VH* VI.8), Bagoas assassinated Artaxerxes in order to punish the king for his disgraceful Egyptian deeds! Coins show that the new conqueror bore the title of pharaoh.

Mentor in Asia Minor

When he had returned, Artaxerxes sent Mentor to Asia Minor. After Mentor had interceded with the King, asking that Artabazus and his family be allowed to return (XVI.52.3–4), his prime objective was to march against Hermias, "the tyrant of Atarnaeus, who had revolted from the King and was master of many fortresses and cities" (§52.5◊). Then, without going into detail, Diodorus writes that Mentor brought other leaders (*hēgemōnes*) who had broken with the Persians back to their senses and that, by force or by stratagem, he soon subdued them all (§52.8◊). This statement obviously refers to localized disturbances of no great importance. Mentor fulfilled the customary mission of maintaining order in the face of local "dynasts," who were recognized by the Achaemenid authority but also had to exhibit steadfast loyalty on every occasion. Although Diodorus's text does not allow us to arrive at a sure conclusion, it does in fact seem that, after the submission of Hermias, Mentor's activities were located on the periphery of the old domain of this "tyrant"—that is, in Aeolis and the Troad, regions traditionally governed from Dascylium.

Artaxerxes III and Philip II

The initial diplomatic and military interactions between Artaxerxes III and Philip II apparently date to the years after the reconquest of Egypt. But did the court have a Macedonian policy, and if so, at what date did it take shape and achieve consistency? Let us stress from the start that the answer to this question risks being only a reflection, as in a distorted mirror, of an image that comes out of a prophetic or eschatological history— that is, a history that presumes that Alexander's conquest was a matter of necessity. At the same time, let us stress that we have no direct evidence that would allow us to reconstruct in detail the picture of Philip's progress in Greece and Thrace as it was seen by the Achaemenid authorities.

The first indication of direct relations between the Persian Empire and the Macedonian kingdom is that Artabazus and his family took up exile status with Philip II (Diodorus XVI.52.3). There is no reason to infer from this that Philip II intended to show animosity toward Artaxerxes at that date, especially since Artaxerxes had recently come to power under highly irregular circumstances. That Philip II accepted a Persian exile does not necessarily imply a rupture with the Great King. A Persian refugee from Dascylium could scarcely find refuge anywhere other than in Europe. We can name at least two Persians of distinction who had sought refuge in Athens during the fifth century in order to escape royal punishment (Plutarch, *Cimon* 10.9: Rhoisaces; Ctesias §43: Zopyrus). Artabazus's choice of Macedon as a place to settle was due in part to its proximity to a region nearly on the border of his satrapy; despite the defeats of 479, relations among Dascylium, Thrace, and Macedon were undoubtedly not simply cut off. Furthermore, a Persian noble could find a structure and way of life among the local aristocracy in Macedon rather like that to which he was accustomed. Furthermore, we are aware of at least one other Persian, Amminapes, who found asylum at the court of Philip II, for reasons unknown to us (Quintus Curtius VI.4.25).

The context of Artabazus's return to the Great King has sometimes been taken as an indication of Philip's activities in the Empire. In a harangue delivered in 341, Demosthenes offered his listeners an argument for the policy of alliance with the Great King that he favored:

> Secondly, the agent and confidant of all Philip's preparations against the king has been snatched off (*anaspastos*), and the king will hear all the proceedings, not from Athenian accusers, whom he might consider to be speaking for their own interests, but from the acting minister himself. (*Phil. IV* 32◇)

This "agent," we know, was Hermias, who is presented by Diodorus in the context of the mission entrusted to Mentor by Artaxerxes III after his victory in Egypt. There has been a tendency to take Demosthenes literally and infer that Philip, through his intermediary Hermias, planned to disrupt the Achaemenid position in western Asia Minor. This theory deserves little credit. It is in fact remarkable that in his version Diodorus does not breathe a word of possible Macedonian collusion with Hermias, the tyrant of Atarnaeus, and reduces Mentor's mission simply to restoring the imperial order that was disturbed in some locales (XVI.52.5–8); and this comes from the very same Diodorus who elsewhere did not hesitate to state that, when the king of Macedon had triumphed at Delphi in 346–345, he dreamed that he would be recognized as *stratēgos autokratōr* of the Greeks and then would march against the Persians (XVI.60.5). Although Philip's "Persian policy" is as opaque to us as Artaxerxes' "Macedonian policy," nothing in Philip's behavior at this date confirms that he was immediately ready to take action on the goal that Isocrates vigorously advocated in 347 — to mount an expediton to Asia Minor.

In the same harangue, Demosthenes stressed for his audience another circumstance unfavorable to Philip: "Those whom the king trusts and regards as his benefactors are at enmity and war with Philip" (*Phil. IV* 31◇). This clearly alludes to the hostilities then going on at Perinthus, as is even more clearly set forth in an (apocryphal) response to an (apocryphal) letter from Philip: "The satraps of Asia have just thrown in mercenary troops for the relief of Perinthus . . ." (*Reply* 5◇). Diodorus confirms the existence of these hostilities:

> Philip's growth in power had been reported in Asia, and the Persian king, viewing this power with alarm, wrote to his satraps on the coast to give all possible assistance to the Perinthians. They consequently took counsel and sent off to Perinthus a force of mercenaries, ample funds, and sufficient stocks of food, missiles, and other materials required for operations. (XVI.75.1–2◇)

Pausanias (I.29.10) adds a significant detail: it was Arsites, satrap of Hellespontine Phrygia, who coordinated operations; this seems logical, given the strategic location of the territories of Dascylium. Moreover, in 334 we find this same Arsites directing the operations against Alexander, again in consultation with his colleagues (Arrian I.12.8–10).

The aid provided to Perinthus was among the charges leveled by Alexander against Darius in a letter he sent after the battle of Issus. According to the text preserved by Arrian (II.14.5), Ochus was also accused of sending an army into Thrace. The Macedonian king even went so far as to put the responsibility for the murder of his father on the Persian court. Darius recalled that previously there had been a treaty of friendship and alliance (*philia kai symmakhia*) between Artaxerxes III and Philip II (II.14.2). The absence of any corroborative evidence for any such treaty has opened the way to speculation, and the overarching characteristic of these speculations is that they contradict each other; it would be useless to add one more item to this house of cards—it is a miracle that it has not already collapsed! We must remain content to note only that embassies were certainly exchanged between the two courts, though we are not able to identify their missions, which perhaps were limited to good- or bad-neighborliness (cf. Plutarch, *Alex.* 5.1–3; Quintus Curtius III.7.1). Certainly, the two capitals, Pella and Susa, were not unfamiliar with each other. The record contains just one certainty—the Persian-Macedonian hostilities at Perinthus, which was besieged about 341 by Philip. But even here we must be careful: Demosthenes attempted to make an argument from the situation at Perinthus that would persuade his fellow citizens that the Great King was ready to enter into an alliance with them and send them money for the war; but by no means does this make the orator an objective observer of the "Macedonian policy" of Artaxerxes! For, when all is said and done, at least according to Aeschines (III.238), Artaxerxes was quick to let the Athenians know that he would not be sending them any money!

Let us summarize. There is no doubt that Artaxerxes III, like his predecessors, followed a policy toward the Greek cities that involved sending fairly frequent royal embassies. It is also beyond doubt that Macedon's opponents, such as Demosthenes, thought that the support of the Great King represented the only credible alternative with which to oppose Philip II's progress. Last, it is certain that the arrival of Macedonian armies at the Straits aroused the anxiety of the satrap of Dascylium, who certainly shared his concern with the Great King. The king took limited defensive steps, restricting himself to sending relief to Perinthus. Did he perhaps also send a body of mercenaries into Thrace, as in Alexander's accusation? We cannot say, but is this not simply one more stylistic redundancy? In short, the court was kept informed about Philip's operations. It seems difficult to go beyond these observations, since, after all, it is not obvious that Philip's intentions were any clearer to the Great King and his advisers than they are to us today. Persia's expert consultants on Balkan policy must have often been bewildered by the incomprehensible contradictions of the European powers (cf. Thucydides IV.50.2). We must await Philip's victory at Chaeronea (338) and then the founding of the Corinthian League (337) before things become entirely clear. Meanwhile, Artaxerxes III had died by an assassin's hand, and one of his sons, Arses (Artaxerxes IV), had succeeded him (August–September 338).

PART FIVE

The Fourth Century and the Empire of Darius III in the Achaemenid *longue durée*: A Prospective Assessment

Chapter 16

Lands, Peoples, and Satrapies:
Taking Stock of the Achaemenid World

Introduction: In the Steps of Alexander and on the Trail of Darius

Another "Achaemenid" Source: The Alexandrian Historians

Before beginning the final chapter, which is my account of the confrontation between Darius III and Alexander, I would like to pause to synthesize and integrate the
facts, interpretations, and theories that have been presented in the preceding chapters.
The inquiry can also move forward because of the contributions of a "new" corpus—the
ancient historians of Alexander. Thus far, we have deliberately limited use of them, except in the chapters in part 2 that are devoted to relatively stable aspects of the Persian
tradition. We consider "stable" those things that constitute the very principles of royal
Achaemenid ideology, whether it be royal virtue, representations of the imperial realm,
or even the people and life of the court—all those aspects that the texts from the time of
Darius III imply go back to "ancestral custom" (e.g., Diodorus XVII.34.6; 35.3; Quintus
Curtius III.3.8; III.8.12; IV.13.26, etc.). Two examples may quickly clarify this point.
(1) Quintus Curtius's famous description (III.3.8–25) of the royal procession before the
battle of Issus is amazingly like the somewhat parallel descriptions provided by Xenophon (of "Cyrus") and Herodotus (of Xerxes; see chap. 5/4 above). (2) Similarly, the description, again by Quintus Curtius (V.1.17–23), of Alexander's entry into Babylon could
be integrated, at a stage before careful analysis, into a discussion of "royal entries," which
we have every reason to believe did not change significantly in either principle or organization. There is even one place where Quintus Curtius himself compares Darius III
with Xerxes—in regard to the methods that the Great Kings used for counting and enumerating the contingents of the royal army (III.2.2). This example must not, however,
lead us to imagine that royal customs were completely static. For one thing, Quintus
Curtius's comparison does not necessarily commit the modern historian to the same
conclusion; for another, it does not imply a general paralysis of royal protocol, which, as
we have seen, underwent several modifications over time, any more than the apparently
repetitive character of the royal inscriptions should lead us to conclude that nothing
changed between Cyrus and Darius III; we have observed, for example, that innovations
were introduced in the times of Artaxerxes I and Artaxerxes II (chaps. 14/1, 15/8).

On the other hand, the sources going back to the time of Alexander, situated within
the *longue durée* of the fourth century, are of decisive importance in our attempt to determine the state of the Empire at the time of the accession of Darius III. Of course, just
like the Greek authors of the fourth century, the courtier-historians often transmitted a
biased view of the conquest and the conquered. We will come back to this point several
times. We will see that in some cases the information offered by the Hellenistic writers
must be taken with as much caution as is required for the writers of the fourth century.

For example, caution is called for when they introduce us to the little-known peoples of the Zagros, whom they identify using the undifferentiated and reductive label of "savage brigands," or more generally when they try to contrast, one final time, Achaemenid stasis with the innovations spurred by Alexander (work on the Babylonian canals and rivers). The primary reason for this is that the ideology promoted by Alexander's Companions is homologous with that which runs through the writings of the fourth-century authors. But the responsibility also belongs to the historian who reads and makes use of them. In fact, many of the details reported by the ancients can only be understood when they are located in the *longue durée* of Persian history. Here is how the Alexander histories constitute an "Achaemenid" source: they illuminate Achaemenid history, which in turn helps the historian to understand the sense and significance of the information they provide. To take but a single example, it is obvious that Arrian's and Quintus Curtius's descriptions of Alexander's entries into Sardis and, later, Babylon take on their full historical meaning only when they are placed in the context of the "royal entries" well known from the Achaemenid period (primarily), and earlier periods as well. This Achaemenid perspective has the effect of ruining the traditional interpretation of this information about the relationships that Alexander developed with the elites of the conquered countries.

Beyond these distortions (which the Achaemenid context allows us to examine and thus to correct), Alexander's historians (used, each in their own fashion, by Plutarch, Arrian, Quintus Curtius, Diodorus, Justin, and several others) considerably modify the way we look at the Empire—for very simple reasons. First, following Alexander step by step, they carry us along the trail of Darius and lead us to discover the Upper Country, about which the Classical authors are all but silent, except for Cyrus's march from Sardis to Babylon and the return of the Greek mercenaries from the Tigris Valley and the Black Sea by way of the Armenian mountains, Bithynia, and Paphlagonia. This time, (nearly) every satrapy is traversed. As a result, the Achaemenid world takes on a breadth and depth that we have been unable to examine since the time of Darius I, because of an abundance and variety of evidence unequaled throughout the fifth and fourth centuries. It suffices to recall, for instance, that the Companions of Alexander were the first to provide written descriptions of Persepolis and Pasargadae. Furthermore, the Iranian Plateau and Central Asia are no longer *terra incognita*. Of course, the modern historian would prefer to have more detailed sources; it is nonetheless true that the information drawn from the fourth-century writers makes it possible for us to attempt a tour of the Great King's entire domain from the geographical, ecological, and ethnographic points of view concurrently (even if, on this last point, Asia Minor once again takes pride of place). For the first time since Herodotus (VII–IX), because of these sources we can, for example, compile a *Who's Who* of the imperial elite.

There is obviously a flip side to this coin. By definition, the military historians follow the conqueror and exalt his memory. At best, Darius's territorial dominion appears only as a chimera, in a context that often suggests it never represented more than a feeble bulwark against the victorious progress of the Macedonian armies. The descriptions are thus very uneven from one region to the next, in direct relationship to the obstacles encountered by Alexander. We glean only meager information on Cappadocia and Armenia, for example, which in large measure remained satrapies *in partibus* [*barbarorum*], whereas the resistance encountered in the course of several weeks between Susa and Persepolis yields valuable notes on Uxiana, the Uxians, and the Persian Gates. This is especially true for the Iranian Plateau, Central Asia, and the Indus Valley. When Alexander traversed Aria, Arachosia, Bactria, and Sogdiana, Darius III was dead, and the royal proclamation of Bessus had not aroused the Achaemenid loyalist sentiments that he had expected. And so the impression prevails that Persian dominion in these regions was light, and this in turn reinforces certain conclusions that have sometimes been drawn from the silence of the Classical sources. But was the sense of emergency felt in Bactria and Sogdiana when Alexander invaded a reflection of the situation that prevailed earlier? This example illustrates one of the major difficulties in using the Alexandrian sources: bringing Achaemenid conditions to light is a sometimes delicate problem, insofar as in each case we cannot assume complete continuity with the past.

In sum, the Hellenistic sources (Babylonian, Egyptian, Greek, etc.), in comparison with the Greek sources of the fourth century, are exceptionally rich in Achaemenid data. To be sure, we have not one royal inscription, nor can we identify a single structure that can be attributed with certainty to Darius (not even the incomplete tomb at Persepolis: fig. 64, p. 735). But many texts and depictions—from Asia Minor, Egypt, and Samaria, in addition to Babylonia—enlarge and enrich the corpus, anchoring it to a regional foundation. Without being paradoxical, we might even say that the reign of Darius III is particularly well documented. The devaluation (nearly a *damnatio memoriae*) to which the last representative of the Achaemenid dynasty was subjected is thus not simply a mechanical reflection of the poverty of our evidence; it is primarily due to the unbridled Alexandrocentrism that modern historiography has long fed on. This fixation arises not from imitation of the Macedonian conqueror's courtiers but from an excessive focus on just one of the protagonists—who thus appeared to travel through an empire that had no prior existence.

Methods and Aims

The problem is well known: Darius III is often presented as a weak king who controlled (badly) a decaying Empire, unable to rely on the faithfulness of his satraps or on an army worthy of the name or on the support of the subject populations, who endured an unbearable financial burden, which was then simply hoarded (hence the economic stagnation)—the totality of the interpretation tending to create the all-too-well-known "colossus with feet of clay." We know that the image comes directly from the polemical Greek authors of the fourth century and that it was taken up and even magnified by the historiography of colonial Europe. We have already had several occasions to bring up the specific problem posed by the use of these documents, as well as their success in modern historiography. Though we must conclude that the Greek interpretation generally falsifies the landscape, the problem of tracing internal changes that the Achaemenid imperial structure must have undergone from the time of Darius I on remains. This assessment is the burden of two chapters here (16–17), which parallel the chapters above that assess the Empire during the times of Darius and Xerxes (chaps. 5, 13). In between, partial assessments have been furnished, especially in the area of territorial dominion of the Great Kings. It is now appropriate to broaden them and extend them in different directions: the lands and populations (chap. 16) and the instruments of authority (chap. 17). This is a prospective assessment, for these varying approaches will be taken up again and discussed, in context, in the last chapter (18), which will attempt to understand more precisely why the Great King was conquered by Alexander. This intermediate assessment is absolutely indispensable if we wish to avoid the well-known vicious circle: the Empire was conquered because it was in a state of profound structural crisis ("Achaemenid decadence"), and this state of crisis is "confirmed" by the defeat.

1. Sources and Problems

It is for the reign of Darius III and the subsequent Macedonian dominion that we have the most information on the administrative organization of the Empire. The first complete list of satrapies, as they existed at the time of Alexander's death, dates to the age of the Diadochi. In a famous passage that is part of a geographical discussion, Diodorus differentiates the satrapies "sloping to the north" from the satrapies sloping "to the south" (XVIII.5◊). Even more useful are the lists of satrapies as they were divided among the Companions of Alexander in 323 and 320 (e.g., XVIII.3.1–2). All of these documents are very interesting (we will use them), but they are not enough. In fact, they do not necessarily reflect the exact state of affairs in 334; Alexander had already made some changes, and so did Perdiccas, who, for example, in 323 conferred on Eumenes all of the Anatolian territories that had not submitted to Alexander (XVIII.3.1◊).

Other texts and contexts provide further essential information that permits us to get back to the situation prevailing at the accession of Darius III. First, of course, there are the tales that follow Alexander step by step, always naming the satraps in office and the region or regions over which they held sway. Next, we have the mobilizations ordered by Darius III. At the battle of the Granicus, we find contingents led by the satraps of Asia Minor; at Issus, the contingents were drafted from the central and western portions of the Empire; at Gaugamela, we find troops that were enrolled from as far away as India (Arrian III.8.3–6◊):

Name	Position	Contingents
Bessus	satrap of Bactria	Bactrians, Sogdians, Sakians
Barsaentes	satrap of the Arachotians	Arachotians and Indian hillmen
Satibarzanes	satrap of the Areians	Areians
Phratapharnes		Parthians, Hyrcanians, Tapyrians
Atropates		Medes, Cadusians, Albanians, Sacesinians
Orondobates, Ariobarzanes, Orxines		peoples bordering the Persian Gulf
Oxathres	son of Abulites the satrap	Susianians and Uxians
Bupares		Babylonians, deported Carians, and Sittacenians
Orontes and Mithraustes		Armenians
Ariaces	satrap?	Cappadocians
Mazaeus		Syrians

These lists pose several interpretive problems. There are obvious discrepancies from one list to another, and it is not always easy to come to a decision; for instance, when Arrian describes the Persian order of battle at Gaugamela (III.11.3◊), he reports that

"Aristobulus tells us that a document giving the order as Darius drew it up was afterwards captured." Furthermore (again in the context of the military units brought to Darius prior to the battle of Gaugamela), it is not certain that the person named as the leader of the contingent must automatically be considered the satrap of the regions from which the troops were drawn: in some cases, Arrian actually calls them satrap (Bessus, Barsaentes, and Satibarzanes); in the other (more numerous) cases, he uses a phrase that refers primarily to their position as head of the contingents (*agein, arkhein*; III.8.3–6); in at least one case, it is not the satrap (Abulites of Susa) but his son Oxathres who is ordered to lead the satrapal contingent. Parallel passages sometimes permit resolution of the ambiguity (e.g., III.23.7).

In any case, an inventory of the Empire cannot be restricted to a simple enumeration of districts. It is necessary to gather concurrent data on the human and material resources available to the Great King. For this purpose, Strabo provides essential information on both the extent and the human geography of the lands of the Near East. His report of course represents a late state of affairs, but Strabo quite often positions his data diachronically and usually also provides some material specifically dated to the period of Achaemenid dominion. Many other sources (literary, archaeological, epigraphic, and iconographic) dating from various times (from the fourth century to the Greco-Roman period) allow us to fill in the picture, particularly of the peoples who lived in the Empire and of the contacts they wove among themselves—thus permitting us to place all of this information in the *longue durée*. Following the steps of Alexander, we proceed from west to east—that is, from the least poorly understood to the most poorly investigated; because of the uneven spread of the data, the accounts are of highly variable importance. In any case, our intention here is not to draw up an exhaustive regional and microregional assessment (which would require a book in itself) but to isolate and integrate the data that will permit us to apprehend the reality of Achaemenid territorial dominion between Artaxerxes II and Darius III.

2. *The Satrapy of Dascylium*

As in previous periods, the residence of the satrap of Hellespontine Phrygia was in Dascylium, on the edge of Lake Manyas (Dascylitis), which was accessible to warships by way of the Rhyndacus (*Hell. Oxyr.* 22.3–4). It was defended by a stronghold (22.3: *khōrion okhyron*), furnished with a garrison (Arrian I.17.2), and famous for the immense paradise, teeming with fish and game, in which Pharnabazus took great delight (Xenophon, *Hell.* IV.1.15–16). In 334, its satrap was Arsites, who may have been in place beginning with the exile of Artabazus (who had taken refuge at the court of Macedon after his abortive revolt against Artaxerxes III around the middle of the 350s: chap. 15/9). If we carefully follow the argument of Diodorus's text on Mentor's operations in Asia Minor after the reconquest of Egypt (XVI.52), it appears that his mission was limited to setting the affairs of the satrapy of Dascylium back in order. This is the context of his fights with Hermias of Atarnaeus and other petty local chieftains in the Troad and Aeolis (chap. 15/9), as well as the recall from exile of Artabazus, Memnon, and all of their abundant progeny. Artabazus did not regain his post at Dascylium, but he became an influential adviser to the Great King and enjoyed an exalted position alongside him in the court hierarchy (cf. Arrian III.23.7). Meanwhile, the family remained solidly settled in the region. For one thing, Arsites himself may have been a relative. For another, we know that

Memnon had land and estates in the Troad in 334 (cf. Polyaenus IV.3.15 and Arrian I.17.8: *khōra tou Memnōnos*); it is possible that he received them from his brother Mentor (as a reward from Artaxerxes), who disappears from the scene after his victories. In this connection, it is not uninteresting to note that when one of the Companions of Alexander arrived at the sanctuary of Athena Ilias, before the battle of Granicus, he "noticed in front of the temple a statue of Ariobarzanes, a former satrap of Phrygia, lying fallen on the ground" (Diodorus XVII.17.6◇). Just like Xerxes (Herodotus VII.43), Ariobarzanes sacrificed to the goddess; but he had gone further by placing a statue there, thus placing a Greek sanctuary under the goddess's protection and in the process causing prestige to redound to himself. His statue also served to mark a territory, the Troad, to which his ancestors in Dascylium had always laid claim in opposition to the ambitions of the satraps of Sardis.

In addition to being charge of the Troad, the satrap of Dascylium had responsibility for part of Mysia (which may have been placed under the authority of a lieutenant governor or even, for a time, a satrap of its own [Orontes]: chap. 15/5). The Paphlagonians also were a dependency of Dascylium; they were famous for their cavalry (Xenophon, *Anab.* V.6.8) and had provided a contingent to Cyrus the Younger (I.8.5; Diodorus XIV.22.5); in 334, they placed themselves under the orders of the satrap Arsites (Diodorus XVII.19.4). According to Quintus Curtius and Arrian, the Paphlagonians rushed an embassy to Alexander while he was staying at Ancyra, a town near Gangra, which is believed to be the capital of the lieutenant governor of Paphlagonia. They offered their people's submission and requested that Alexander not invade the country; the king ordered them to place themselves under the authority of Calas, whom he had named satrap of Hellespontine Phrygia in place of Arsites some months earlier (Arrian II.4.1–2; cf. I.17.1 and Quintus Curtius III.1.24). Quintus Curtius adds that the Paphlagonians sent hostages to Alexander and "obtained freedom from the obligation of paying tribute, which they had not rendered even to the Persians" (1.23◇), while the king "order[ed] the inhabitants of the territory Arsites ruled to pay the same taxes as they used to pay to Darius," apparently including "natives who came down from the hills" (Arrian I.17.1◇). This interpretation is difficult to confirm, because we have no information on the region after the events relating to the passage of Agesilaus and Datames' campaign against Thuys. Nonetheless, it is doubtful that the Paphlagonians, who sent a contingent to Calas, no longer paid tribute in 334. It seems more likely that Quintus Curtius's source was referring to the well-known fact that Paphlagonia, which had not been invaded by Alexander, was included among the unsubmissive countries in 323 (cf. Diodorus XVIII.3.1). In the eyes of the fourth-century Greek authors, the region had always been considered independent of the Persians—a generalization that is obviously inappropriate. During the Persian counterattack after Issus, Paphlagonia was one of the recruiting bases used by Darius's generals (Quintus Curtius IV.1.34; 5.13). The discovery of a Greco-Persian relief in the region (fig. 55) even seems to imply the presence of an imperial diaspora. The Paphlagonian marriage of Camisares, the father of Datames (Nepos, *Dat.* 1–3), and the matrimonial designs of Spithridates (Xenophon, *Hell.* IV.1.4–5) in themselves suggest that connections were common and fairly close between the representatives of the imperial diaspora and the Paphlagonian aristocracy.

On the coast, the main town was Sinope, which had several dependent tributary cities: Trapezus, Cerasus, and Cotyora (Xenophon, *Anab.* IV.8.22; V.3.2; V.5.3). Sinope had a rich and famous port and thus was broadly open to the sea; the town was also closely linked to the back country and exported its timber resources (Strabo XII.3.12). Cappadocian ocher was exported by way of Sinope as well (XII.2.10). Isocrates' phrase (*Phil.* 120: "Asia from Cilicia to Sinope") illustrates the extent of its commercial relations—as far as southern Asia Minor—and this is also attested by discoveries of coins. It was also at Sinope that the rebellious Datames had coins struck in his name; around 332, some Persian

Fig. 55. Persian relief from Paphlagonia.

generals also issued coins there, with Aramaic legends. Between 334 and 330, the Sinopeans continued to consider themselves subjects of Darius (Arrian III.24.4;✧ Quintus Curtius VI.5.6); they were not considered to be "part of the Greek league" (*to koinon tōn Hellēnōn*) by Alexander. Let us note finally that Iranian personal names frequently appear on the seals marking ownership of amphorae from the city.

Bithynia, another country on the Black Sea coast, was in principle a dependency of Dascylium; it was west of Paphlagonia and its best-known town was Heraclea, in the territory of the Mariandynians (cf. Strabo XII.3.4, 9; Xenophon, *Anab.* VI.2.1). We know little about relations between the Bithynian leaders and the satrap of Dascylium. In 400, Pharnabazus sent a cavalry troop to aid the Bithynians against the Greek mercenaries (*Anab.* VI.4.24). In other circumstances, however, we find the same Pharnabazus at war with the Bithynians (*Hell.* III.2.2). Their relations with the satrap of Dascylium must have been as irregular and contradictory as the relations between Dascylium and the various Paphlagonian chieftains (chap. 15/5). In 334, the region seems to have been ruled by the local prince Bas; and Calas, the Macedonian satrap of Dascylium, led an unsuccessful expedition against Bas, in the course of which Calas met his end. Bas was succeeded by his son Zipoithes. Heraclea always exhibited great loyalty to the Achaemenid authority. In the course of the fifth century, the Heracleans at first refused to pay tribute to Athens, "because of their friendship toward the Persian kings" (*ob amicitiam regum persicorum*; Justin XVI.3.9), and then yielded to Athenian threats. Around 364, Clearchus took power with the help of a force led by Mithradates, son of Ariobarzanes, the satrap of Hellespontine Phrygia, and he renewed a traditional policy of alliance with the Achaemenid authorities, as is illustrated in particular by the sending of several embassies to Artaxerxes II and III. His "Persianization" is demonstrated by the discovery of a portrait carved in Persian style that probably represents the tyrant himself. Clearchus's successors did not modify the substance of his policy, not even after the victory at the Granicus. According to the local historian Memnon, Dionysius of Heraclea actually profited from the battle at the Granicus (*FGrH* 434 F4); the requests presented to Alexander by the Heraclean exiles obviously fell on deaf ears.

The satrapal court at Dascylium had certainly been wide open to Greek influences for several generations. This is eloquently evidenced by many "Greco-Persian" stelas,

Fig. 56a–c. "Greco-Persian" objects from Dascylium.

bullas, and seals (fig. 56a–c). At this point, we cannot help recalling that around 360 the satrap Artabazus married a sister of the two Rhodians, Mentor and Memnon. The marriage was fruitful, producing eleven sons and ten daughters, including Pharnabazus, who fought alongside his uncle Memnon on the Asia Minor front in 334–333 before succeeding him as commander of naval operations. One of the daughters was Barsine, who successively married her uncles Mentor and Memnon before becoming a Companion of Alexander, to whom she may have given the famous Heracles. According to Plutarch (*Alex.* 21.9✧), "she had been instructed in the Grecian learning" (*paideia hellēnikē*). The societal promotion of the two Rhodians is all the more remarkable in that through his mother, Apame, Artabazus was grandson of Artaxerxes I.

3. From Sardis to Ephesus

The satrapy of Lydia, bordering on Hellespontine Phrygia, had its capital at Sardis. The administrative organization of the satrapy continues to pose problems that are difficult to resolve, particularly regarding the name attributed to Spithridates' territory: "satrap of Lydia and Ionia" (Arrian I.12.8✧). From the beginning of the fourth century, whenever an inscription refers to a "satrap of Ionia" (Tod no. 113), the exact relationships that link the two components are far from clear: in 334, the Macedonian Asandrus received "Lydia and the rest of Spithridates' district" (*arkhē*; Arrian I.17.7;✧ chap. 18/2). The satrap in place in 334, Spithridates (Spithrobates in Diodorus XVII.19.4), had succeeded his father Rhosaces (I) at an unknown date; the latter was "a descendant of one of the seven," who had taken part in the Egyptian campaign in 343 (XVI.47.2:◇ "satrap of Ionia and Lydia"). Another son, Rhosaces (II), aided Spithridates in his territory (XVII.20.6). The garrison was commanded by Mithrenes, who handed over the citadel and treasury to Alexander a few weeks after the battle of the Granicus; this was a veritable godsend for the Macedonian, for everyone knew of the virtual impregnability of the position (Arrian I.17.3–8). The Persians had also erected a lookout on Mount Tmolus (Strabo XIII.4.5), and several military colonies of diverse origins had been stationed there, as is attested by (among other things) the existence of a Hyrcanian plain (named for the people who settled there).

The available evidence provides a particularly large amount of information on the depth and breadth of intercultural contact in Lydia and Ionia. That is what, in its way, Plutarch's description of Ephesus around 407–405 points toward; the description occurs within a discussion that is very critical for Lysander the Spartan, who was accused of imitating the behavior of the satraps:

> Being at Ephesus, and finding the city well affected towards him, and favourable to the Lacedaemonian party, but in ill condition, and in danger to become barbarised by adopting the manners of the Persians, who were much mingled among them, the country of Lydia bordering upon them, and the king's generals being quartered (*diatribein*) there for a long time. (*Lys.* 3.3◇)

The passage is uncommonly interesting in that it deals with daily life. It is easy to imagine that the essentially permanent presence of the Persians led to close intercultural encounters of the sort that Plutarch deplored, because in his eyes they threatened the Hellenism of the city (compare *Agis* 3.9). In a rather derogatory discussion, Democritus also condemned the "effeminate" character of his fellow citizens, which was manifest particularly in the richness and delicacy of their clothing, highlighted with colors and bordered with pictures of animals; among these clothes, Democritus specifically names typically Persian garments, such as the long robes called *kalasireis*, as well as the *sarapeis* and the *aktiai*, which he considers "the most costly among Persian wraps" (Athenaeus XII.525c–e◇).

Illustrations of Persian-Ephesian contacts are found in several passages touching on Tissaphernes. In 411–410, before reaching the Hellespont, the satrap "went first to Ephesus and offered sacrifice to Artemis" (Thucydides VIII.109.1◇). About two years later, he decided to go once more to Ephesus, which was then threatened by the Athenian Thrasyllus: "When Tissaphernes learned of this plan, he gathered together a large army and sent out horsemen to carry word to everybody to rally at Ephesus for the protection of Artemis" (Xenophon, *Hell.* I.2.6◇6). Meanwhile, he returned to the Troad. This was probably the occasion when he struck bronze coins in his name at Astyra, a small city on the Gulf of Adramyttium: he is shown on the obverse (one time mounted); the reverse of two of the coins bears a sacred image of Artemis.

Ephesus was connected to Sardis by the royal road (Ctesias §64; cf. Herodotus V.54) and enjoyed long and continuous relations with the satrapal capital. We may recall first of all that the administrator (*neocore*) of the sanctuary there bore a name-title of Iranian origin, the Megabyzus — that is, Bagabuxša 'who serves the god'. He is the one to whom Xenophon paid the tithe that he had withheld from the booty and dedicated to Apollo and Artemis of Ephesus in 400–399 (*Anab.* V.3.5–7). It also appears that the Great Kings themselves held the sanctuary in great honor: according to Strabo (XIV.1.5), Xerxes spared it when he destroyed the sanctuary at Didyma. Furthermore, we know from Tacitus (III.61) that in Tiberius's time the Ephesians mentioned an immunity granted to the sanctuary of Artemis by the Persians. The respect that Tissaphernes showed toward the great Ephesian goddess is comparable to the respect demonstrated in Egypt by high Persian leaders of the satrapy (chap. 12/1).

In an opposite sense, if we may put it that way, a Lydian-Aramaic funerary inscription from Sardis dated to the tenth year of an Artaxerxes (III? 348?) invokes the protection of Artemis Coloe and Ephesian Artemis on the funerary vault and the adjoining *temenos*. The existence at Sardis of a sanctuary of Artemis of Ephesus is confirmed by Lydian inscriptions and by a now-famous inscription from Ephesus called the "Inscription of Sacrileges" (*I. Ephesos* 2). It reports that a number of Ephesian sacred envoys had been sent to Sardis to perform ceremonies according to ancestral custom (*kata ton nomon ton patrion*) in a sanctuary of Artemis at Sardis, described as "that which was founded by the Ephesians," obviously to distinguish it from the sanctuary of Sardian Artemis. It appears that on this occasion the Ephesian sacred envoys were attacked by some Sardians, who subsequently were sentenced by the Sardian tribunals in the presence of witnesses to the crime who had come from Ephesus. A list of about fifty condemned men follows. Another Ephesian inscription adds confirmation and some detail. It records a decree granting citizenship to an inhabitant of the town who had provided assistance to the sacred envoys sent to the sanctuary of Ephesian Artemis at Sardis. The texts, unfortunately, are not dated; we are inclined to place them at the beginning of the last quarter of the fourth century, either just before or just after the Macedonian conquest. A more precise date would of course be important, but we must note that in any case the sanctuary had long existed. Furthermore, relations between Sardis and Ephesus were nothing new; they were clearly frequent and encouraged throughout the Achaemenid dominion.

The record gives rise to several historical reflections—first of all, on the status of Sardis at the end of the Achaemenid period and the very beginning of the Hellenistic period. Insofar as we can reconstruct, the procedure followed by the Ephesians mentioned in the inscriptions cited above necessarily implies that there were tribunals—deliberative institutions—at Sardis, and this in turn demonstrates that Sardis constituted a political community (albeit not a Greek city). Another decree, also dated to this period, verifies this. This inscription is from Miletus and records an agreement between that city and Sardis: Sardis guaranteed access and security to the Milesians. A commission was named in each city to guarantee the enforcement of the agreement, and the text includes the formula "Here are those of the Sardians who have been named in accordance with the decree (*kata to psephisma*)" (*Syll.*³ 273). The way in which Alexander arrived in 334 confirms that Sardis had local authorities, not to be confused with the Persian authorities, since the town was handed over to Alexander by the chief citizens (*dynōtatoi tōn Sardianōn*), while the Persian *phrourarch* Mithrenes handed over the citadel and treasury to the conquerer (Arrian I.17.3◊). Whatever uncertainties about details may remain in the texts, we must conclude that Sardis under Achaemenid dominion enjoyed some degree of autonomy, comparable in some respects to the autonomy that the texts imply was enjoyed by Babylon. Just like Babylon, Sardis also had a district where peasants and workmen labored, and they lived in villages (Hieracome, Village of the Hibis, Tamasis), as shown by the "inscription of sacrileges"; these villages obviously were dependent on the city, since the guilty parties were tried at Sardis. Other villages on the plain of Sardis are listed in the Mnesimachus inscription (*Sardis* VII.1.1); they regularly have Lydian names (Tobalmura, Kombdilipia, Periasasostra), some of them partially Hellenized (Ilucome, Tanducome); the peasants also had Lydian names. All of this evidence gives the impression that there was extensive Lydian continuity; in this connection, we may also cite the participation of the Lydian Adrastos in the struggles of the Diadochi in 322 (Pausanias VII.6.6).

Actually, the population of Sardis and environs was ethnically mixed. Among the names in the Mnesimachus inscription is a Babylonian name (Beletras/Bēl-ēṭir). The list at the end of the "inscription of sacrileges" includes Greek, Lydian, "Asianic," and five Iranian names. One of the guilty persons is a Carian; the presence of Carians at Sardis is attested by many other documents. They were basically common people and craftsmen: bath boys, sellers of soles (of shoes), a sandal merchant, a butcher, as well as a goldsmith and an oil merchant; people with religious titles are found there as well: the son of a priest (*hiereus*) and even a sacred herald (*hierokēryx*). Not everyone with an Iranian name was necessarily an aristocrat: one, Mithradates, was the slave of a man with a Lydian name, Tyios; another, Ratopates, was the son of a man named Papes, a name that marks him as Lydian. From this we must conclude that personal names are not enough to identify anyone's ethnicity. Marriage and the borrowing of foreign names probably contributed to this mélange. Consider a fourth-century Greek-Lydian bilingual inscription where someone named Nannas, son of Dionysopolis, makes a dedication to Artemis/Artimus.

This does not seem to be the case for Sisines, whose father also had an Iranian name, Eumanes/Vohumāna, and who the "inscription of sacrileges" says lived in Hieracome. This is the name of the village known later as Hierocaesarea. Much evidence from the Roman period attests to the existence of a sanctuary dedicated to Persian Artemis, otherwise known as Anāhita, at Hieracome. According to Tacitus (III.62), the original privilege of immunity was granted by Cyrus the Great, which probably was the time when the sanctuary was founded as an accompaniment to the settling of an originally Iranian populace. The privileges were confirmed by the Hellenistic kings, as suggested by a letter of Attalus III that refers both to his ancestors and also to earlier kings (*RC* 68). The same is true of Hypaipa, a site very close to Sardis and Tmolus. Pausanias reports that even in the Roman period the *magi* (who are also found in the inscriptions of this period, including an *archimagus*) continued to preside over sacrifices, invoking the god "in a foreign language" (V.27.5). Many other inscriptions report the spread of sanctuaries of Anāhita/Anaitis in the Lydian and Meonian countryside. Behind apparent stability, the available evidence shows elaborate processes of syncretism between Anāhita and local gods, including Artemis. Though the coins at Hierocaesarea show an almost completely Hellenized Anaitis, at Hypaipa the goddess is represented with authentically Iranian characteristics.

We know that Sardis also had a sanctuary devoted to the worship of Sardian Artemis, who was distinct from Ephesian Artemis, as we have seen. The fifth/fourth-century sanctuary has not yet been discovered. We find evidence for it in several fourth-century Lydian inscriptions and a well-known passage in Xenophon: Cyrus the Younger recalls that, after Orontas's second reconciliation with him, he "[went] to the altar of Artemis and [said he was] sorry" (*Anabasis* I.6.7✧). The sanctuary was very wealthy, as a well-known inscription from the beginning of the Hellenistic period shows: it says that a

certain Mnesimachus had inherited as a royal gift a vast *dōrea* near Sardis, and it is clear
that the antecedents of this property must be sought in the Achaemenid period (*Sardis*
VII.1.1). Mnesimachus borrowed large amounts of money from Artemis of Sardis; she
clearly held sacred land (*hiera khōra*) to which the Persians had perhaps granted a privilege of immunity, like that of Anaitis of Hieracome (Hieracaesarea); the sanctuary's
holdings were administered by *naopes* ('temple overseers'). Although it remains mysterious, a Lydian inscription from the Achaemenid period also seems to refer to a loan
by sanctuary administrators to someone with an Iranian name, Mitradastas, son(?) of
Mitratas.

Does this mean that the Persians identified Artemis of Sardis with Anāhita? This is
not at all certain. There is no doubt that there was a sanctuary dedicated specifically to
Artemis Persica, even though the earliest literary attestation dates to 322 (Pausanias
VII.6.6). Perhaps it was distinct from Artemis Coloe, who is named in the "inscription
of sacrileges," the Lydian-Aramaic funerary inscription mentioned above, and a Greek
inscription dated to Caesar. The sanctuary is located 200 stadia north of Sardis by
Strabo, who mentions the very well-known festivals celebrated in honor of the goddess
(XIII.4.5). It was situated on the shores of a lake rich in fish. A dedication to Artemis Persica has been found there, along with proof of the existence of an Iranian community,
the Maibozenoi (who perhaps originally were from Cappadocia), at an early period. It is
thus not impossible that Artemis Coloe was more or less assimilated to Iranian Anāhita,
who was also a water goddess.

Whatever the case may be, we can see that the totality of the evidence attests first of
all to a dense settlement of Persians and Iranians not only in the great satrapal residences
but also in the west Asia Minor countryside. The evidence also demonstrates the intimacy of daily relations between the Persians and the local peoples. Although much of
the evidence is late in date (from the Roman period), there is hardly any doubt that contact between peoples of different cultures was regular and permanent from the Achaemenid period onward. This was already implied by Droaphernes, who dedicated a statue
to a Zeus who could well be a local god, perhaps Lydian Zeus. The Lydian-Aramaic inscription from Sardis dated to either Artaxerxes II or Artaxerxes III is also worth considering. The dedicator, Manes, son of Kumli, grandson of Siluka, is quite certainly a
Lydian; while the heading of the inscription includes a formula close to the Aramaic
version of the Xanthus trilingual, we also see that the month name (Marshewan) is cited
in Lydian: Baki (assimilated by the Greeks to Dionysius). We also note the borrowing
of several Persian words for both the stela and the sacred enclosure. Another Manes

is found on a seal showing a typically
Achaemenid scene of a Royal Hero with
lions (fig. 57). Another Lydian seal is
carved with the Iranian name Mitratas.
The Lydian seals amply testify to the association of Lydian and Persian elements,
as well as the participation of Greek artists — or artists working in the Greek style.

The intimacy of these relations must
have had political repercussions. Thus, in

Fig. 57. Seal bearing the name Manes.   Asia Minor, many Greeks were among the advisers or diplomatic intermediaries at the courts of Sardis and Dascylium (cf. Thucydides VIII.6.1; 85.2; Xenophon, *Hell.* IV.1.29). We also know of a number of (private) agreements of hospitality between Persian aristocrats and prominent Greek citizens that were formalized by the exchange of gifts and oaths (cf. *Hell.* I.1.9; IV.1.39–40). It was because they had ancient bonds of hospitality that Antalcidas received military reinforcements from Ariobarzanes of Lesser Phrygia (V.1.28); furthermore, all of the mercenary captains from Cyrus were hosts (*xenoi*; *Anab.* I.1.10–11). But were the Persians themselves merely residents (Plutarch, *Lysander* 3.3: *diatribein*) at Ephesus and elsewhere, or had they by this time established institutional relationships with the city? We do not have sufficient evidence from Asia Minor to clarify the question, aside from the Ephesus decree granting citizenship to a Sardian for the role he had played in the affair of the sacrileges. On the other hand, several Athenian texts and decrees deserve to be mentioned. We know that Orontes received Athenian citizenship for himself and his descendants because he sold wheat to the city at a difficult moment (*IG* II², 207a). The same was true for the satrap of Dascylium, Ariobarzanes, his three sons, and two of his Greek advisers, Philiscus and Agavus. An Athenian inscription dated 327 attests that Pharnabazus and Artabazus, though they did not necessarily bear the title, were considered benefactors (*euergetountes*) because of their actions on behalf of Athens in wartime (Tod, no. 199). We may also remark that, according to Ctesias (§43), Zopyrus, son of Megabyzus, sought refuge at Athens "because his mother had dispensed her benefactions toward the Athenians" (*eis autous euergesia*). In any case, it was not the first time that a Persian aristocrat broke with the Great King and found asylum at Athens (cf. Plutarch, *Cimon* 10.9). Thus, we cannot exclude the possibility that similar decisions were made in Asia Minor from time to time to the advantage of high dignitaries from Sardis and Dascylium, even though we have no indisputable evidence.

4. From Celaenae to Halicarnassus

In the winter of 333, Alexander arrived outside Celaenae, the capital of Greater Phrygia. The satrap Atizyes was no longer there; he had taken part in the battle at the Granicus, then joined Darius, probably at the head of what remained of his contingent; he then fought at Issus and died during the battle. Arrian (I.29.2) and Quintus Curtius (III.1.6–7) tell of the strength of Celaenae's location. We know that the construction of a residence (*basileion*) and the restoration of the acropolis go back to the time of Xerxes (Xenophon, *Anab.* I.2.9). Celaenae had a major Iranian settlement and was also well known for its enormous paradise, watered by the sources of the Marsyas (I.2.7–9), as well as for the great fortified estates (*tetrapyrgia*) immediately around the town (Plutarch *Eum.* 8.5). These estates, comparable to Asidates' estate in Mysia, evince the richness of the agriculture and husbandry of a country "abounding in villages rather than in cities" (Quintus Curtius III.1.11◇). To the west, the town of Cydrara permanently marked the border between Phrygia and Lydia (Herodotus VII.30). When Cyrus the Younger crossed it, Lycaonia belonged to Celaenae, because Iconium was called "the last city of Phrygia" (*Anab.* I.2.19◇).

To the north and northeast, the royal road ran toward Gordion, where it reached the Halys, which marked the Phrygian-Cappadocian border (cf. Herodotus V.52). The old capital of the kingdom of Phrygia, located on the Sangarius, certainly took on major importance in the Achaemenid period. It was a "stronghold (*khōrion*), built on a hill and well fortified," that was defended by the energetic commander Rhatanes, who was able to successfully resist the timid attempts of Agesilaus to take it (*Hell. Oxyr.* 21.6). Because of its strategic location, Gordion had certainly been well supplied with an abundance of granaries and storehouses—which is enough to explain why Alexander chose to winter there in 334–333. This was the occasion when the king ascended the acropolis, "where the palace of Gordion and his son Midas was situated" (Arrian II.3.1◊), before taking the road to Ancyra (modern Ankara; II.4.1; cf. Quintus Curtius III.1.14–15). Archaeological, numismatic, and iconographic evidence points to the Persian presence at Gordion and the area surrounding it that was crossed by the royal road.

We do not know the exact date of the creation of the satrapy of Greater Phrygia; perhaps it was during the fourth century. On this point, a valuable note in Arrian (I.24.5◊) must be quoted. In his description of Alexander's march through southern Asia Minor, Arrian says this about the Milyan district: "It belongs to Greater Phrygia, but was then reckoned part of (*syntelei*) Lycia by the Persian king's orders." Milyas had close cultural links to Lycia (cf. Herodotus I.173) and seems to have had dual status, since even though it was an administrative dependency of Celaenae, it nonetheless remained fiscally connected to Lycia: the word *syntelei* indicates that it paid its tribute together with the Lycians. In other words, Darius I's tribute organization, as presented by Herodotus (III.90), had been partially retained, since Lycians and Milyans were at that time part of the First Nome (along with the Ionians, Magnesians of Asia, Aeolians, Carians, and Pamphylians); but successive reorganizations created satrapal territories that no longer necessarily corresponded in detail to the original tributary territories. An *ethnos* could be transferred to a newly created satrapy even though its original tribute accounting might be preserved. Even though the Great King goes unnamed by Arrian, it is tempting to think that the reorganization goes back a few decades at most. The decision might have been made in connection with the creation of the satrapy of Greater Phrygia, which also must have resulted in a change of status for Lycia.

In fact, a now-famous document, the Xanthus trilingual, shows that Lycia was the object of a major administrative reorganization under Artaxerxes III. At the time of the decree that it records (337), Lycia was included in a satrapy along with Caria, because the official (Aramaic) version bears the following ascription: "In the month of Sivan in year 1 of King Artaxerxes, in the citadel of Orna [Xanthus], Pixoda[ro], son of Katomno, the satrap who [governs] in Karkā [Caria] and Termila [Lycia], said. . . ." Here we recognize Pixodarus, well known from many Greek and Lycian texts as the satrap of Caria beginning in 341–340. Thus, at some time, certainly within the reign of Artaxerxes III, Lycia was joined to the satrapy of Caria, and the satrap of Caria was thereafter also satrap of Lycia. The reasons for the reform are obviously not presented in any part of the inscription. We must simply stress that the rulers of Halicarnassus had harbored ambitions toward Lycia from ancient times and that the region of Caunus in particular was claimed by both the satraps of Caria and the dynasts of Xanthus. As a result, the Great King had to resolve these territorial disputes between neighboring peoples (e.g., Arrian I.27.4 and Diodorus XVI.113.3) in a way that would stabilize the situation to the advantage of the central authority. We can imagine that these were the conditions under which the administrative status of Milyas was redefined, perhaps to settle an overt problem between Halicarnassus and Celaenae. A new and important decision was made in the time of Darius III. When Alexander arrived at the borders of Caria, he was greeted in the traditional way by Ada (Diodorus XVII.24.2), the daughter of Hecatomnus and wife of Idrieus; "Pixodarus, however, turned her out of the government. . . . On his death Orontobates, his brother-in-law, was sent down by the king and assumed the government" of Caria (Arrian I.23.7–8◊). Without naming him, Strabo also refers to Orontobates in the course of a passage on Hecatomnid dynastic history: he states that, "having espoused the side of the Persians" (*persisas*), Pixodarus had asked the Great King to send a satrap to share power cooperatively (*koinōnia*). "And when he [Pixodarus] departed from life, the satrap [that is, Orontobates] took possession of Halicarnassus. And when Alexander came over, the satrap sustained a siege" (XIV.2.17◊). The historical circumstances of the episode continue to pose several interpretive problems in the context of relations among Pixodarus, Philip II, and Darius III. But the texts appear relatively clear on one point at least: by "Persianizing" himself, Pixodarus displayed his submission to the Great King. The Great King (as he had certainly done during the accession of Pixodarus) intervened directly in the succession, with the result that a satrap of Persian origin was named at Halicarnassus: Pixodarus and later Orontobates were the delegates of the central authority in Caria (Arrian I.23.8).

5. Pixodarus at Xanthus

Let us return to the Xanthus trilingual (fig. 58). The document's importance warrants presenting it in detail, since it provides very important information on the satrapal administration, the satrap's relations with the political community of the Xanthians, and the ongoing process of acculturation in Lycia. We know that the stela (which can be seen today in the museum in Fethiye) includes three versions: the official Aramaic version (inscribed on the front) and two translations, Greek and Lycian, on the sides. We also know that the topic of the decree is a matter internal (in principle) to Xanthus: the founding of service for and a sanctuary dedicated to Basileus Caunius and to Arcesimas. To this end, the Xanthians and their neighbors chose to appoint a priest, assign land to the new sanctuary, and specify the sacrifices to be rendered to the god.

The texts pose many interpretive problems, which we will not go into in detail here. We will pay particular attention to the light the documents may throw on relations between a satrap and a Lycian town. The reasons for and nature of the satrap's intervention continue to be problematic. We will especially stress that the civic version of the text (the Lycian and Greek versions) is rather different from the satrapal chancellery's version. The civic version presents the event in the context of decisions relating to the political community (*polis* in the Greek version), though it acknowledges the authority of Pixodarus at the end of the text: "May Pixodarus have the high hand in these decisions." In contrast, the Aramaic version presents the Xanthian decision as a simple proposition, and it states: "This law (*datah*), he (Pixodaro) has inscribe[d], who is master [of the decision]." The authority of the satrap in Lycia is highlighted by details given in the Greek and Lycian versions. We learn in fact that Pixodarus named two commissioners/archons in Lycia: Hieron and Natrbbyemi (Apollodotos); he also named a chargé d'affaires/governor (*epimelētēs*) at Xanthus, Erttimeli (Artemelis) by name, obviously a Lycian. The heading of the Aramaic version is unambiguous: "In the month of Sivan in year 1 of King Artaxerxes, in the citadel of Orna, Pixoda[ro], son of Katomno, the satrap who (governs) in Caria and Lycia, sa[id]. . . ," where the formula "said" obviously introduces a satrapal decree. The text illustrates very well the relations between a civic community

Greek Inscription

(1–2) When Pixodarus, son of Hecatomnos, became satrap of Lycia, he established (3) (as) archons of Lycia Hieron and (4) Apollodotos and (as) governor of Xanthus (5–6) Artemelis. The Xanthians and their dependents decreed to found (7) an altar for the King of Caunos and for Ar(8)kesimas.

And they chose (as) priest Simis, (9) son of Kondorasis, and him who (10) will be the closest to Simias always.

(11) And they gave him, on all his property, (12) exemption from taxes.

And the town gave the land (13) that Kesindelis and Pigres wo(14)rked and all that adjoins the field (15) and the buildings, for that which belongs to the King (16) of Caunos and to Arkesimas.

And are given (17) each year three half(18)minas on the part of the town.

And all those who (19) will be freed will pay (20) to the God two drachmas.

All things that (21) have been inscribed on the stela (22) have been consecrated to belong in totality to the King (23) of Caunos and to Arkesimas. And on all the profits (24) that accrue from it, one sacrifices (25) each new moon a sheep (26) and annually an ox.

And (27) the Xanthians and their dependents have made oaths (28–30) to do exactly all that is inscribed on the stela for those gods and for their priest, and to remove nothing (31) from it nor to permit another to do so. (32) And if anyone changes [the rule], (33) may he be guilty with respect to those gods (34) and to Leto and to (his) descendants and to Nym(35)phs!

Lycian Inscription

(1–2) When Pigesere, son of Katamia, became satrap of Lycia and when he had (3) for the Lycians established (as) commissioners (4) Iyeru and Natrapiyẽmi and (5) for Arna (as) governor Ertimeli, (6–7) the citizens and the dependents of Arna decreed(?) to found this(?) sanctuary for the King (8) of Caunos and for Arkazuma the (9) King.

And they made priest for (10) these gods Simias, son of Kondorahi, (11) and him who would be close to Simias.

And (12) they gave him free what is his.

And (13) the town and the dependents added to it (14–15) fields of the town. Lo, Khesentedi . . . . . . and Pigres irrigated them. (16) And all that is added—and that which is built—(17) (will be) property of the King of (18) Caunos and of Arkazuma.

And Arna (19) gives him annually 18(?) *adas* for salary.

(20) And he requires (that) the slaves(?)—(21) all those who will thereafter be freed—(22) give him (two?) *sigloi*.

And one has consecrated (23) everything written on this stela (24) to the King of Caunos and to Arkazuma.

(25) And he who receives this benefit, (26) one will sacrifice month by month (27) ritually with a sheep and yearly (28) with an ox to the King of Caunos and Arka(28)zuma. And it is Simias who sacrifices, and he (30) will be close to Simias.

(30–32) And the town of Arna and the dependents of Arna have made him their oath for this law; thus, one (33) establishes this law; (that) all that (34) is inscribed on this stela, no one (35) will abrogate it, neither this with respect to these gods (36) nor that with respect to that priest. May, if (37) someone abrogates it, one require the penalty from those gods (38) and from the Mother of the enclosure of here, (39) the *Pentrenni*, and from her children and (40) from the Eliyana.

Aramaic Inscription

(1) In the month of Sivan in year 1 (2) of King Artaxerxes, (3) in the citadel of Orna, Pixoda[ro], (4) son of Katomno, the satrap (5) who (governs) in Caria and Lycia, sa[id]:

(6) "The citizens of Orna planned (7) to make a sanctuary(?) for the King (8) the God of Caunos and his Companion.

(9) "And they made priest Simias, (10) son of Koddorasi.

"And there is an est[ate] (11) that the citizens of Orna gave (12) to the King the God.

"And year by year, (13) on the part of the town (are) given in silver (14) a mina and a half.

"The said priest (15) sacrifices at the beginning of the month a sheep (16) to the King the god, and he immolates(?) (17) year by year one ox.

"And the said estate (18) is emancipated, (the estate which is) his."

(19) This law, he (Pixodarus) has inscribed, who is master (of the decision). Moreover, (20) if ever anyone steals (something) (21) from the King the God or from the (22) priest (then) in office, (may he), by the King (23) the God and his Companion, (be) stolen! (24) And, by the god, Lato, Artemis, (25) Hšatrapati and other (gods), (may) someone (26) (be) stolen! And may these gods (27) require of him (expiation)!

Fig. 58. Xanthus Trilingual Inscription (FdX VI, 1974).

and the Achaemenid authority. The participation of Pixodarus in this matter does not appear to be any different from other known satrapal or royal initiatives or involvement in internal matters of local religious practices throughout the Achaemenid period. The Xanthians' proposal was probably brought to the attention of the satrap because the permanence of the regulation was placed under the protection both of the gods and of the satrap, who also was considered the guarantor.

Despite uncertainties on the administrative level, the political organization reflected in the Xanthus trilingual attests to a major transformation of the situation in Lycia, even if the existence of two archons may be attributed to the traditional division between western and eastern Lycia. The disappearance of dynastic coinage illustrates the fact that Lycia had been thoroughly "satrapized." Other evidence clarifies the satrap's administrative practices. A Greek-Lycian bilingual from Xanthus (probably originally a trilingual; *TL* 45) also refers to a regulation (Lycian *mara*) engraved on a stela and invokes curses on those who would contravene the regulatory provisions. It appears that at some date (probably close to that of the trilingual), Pixodarus granted a considerable favor to the towns of the valley (Xanthus, Tlos, Pinara, Kandaynda)—to be refunded, "in whatever manner they choose," a commercial tax (*dekatē emporias*) that in normal times would obviously have belonged to the category of royal and/or satrapal taxes. A decree of the Carian community of Plarasa, also dated to the rule of Pixodarus (*Pixadaro[u] xaitrapeuontos*), grants a fiscal exemption to a person named Dion, from Cos, except for "royal taxes (*basilika telē*)." Other texts make it clear that the cities, which were in charge of civic taxes (in the best of circumstances), were not in charge of royal taxes that had to be paid one way or another. Arrangements of this sort certainly held for all of the cities and communities subject to the "tribute of Darius"; only special situations allowed for variation—for example, a decree from Alexander allowed the Ephesians to dedicate to Artemis the tribute they traditionally paid to the Great King (Arrian I.17.10).

6. From Tarsus to Mazaca

Other administrative reorganization can be detected, beginning with Tarsus. We know that around 350 Mazaeus was put in charge of Cilicia, while Belesys was governing Trans-Euphrates (Diodorus XVI.42.1). To the extent that we can date them with certainty, the coins of Mazaeus indicate that, after the fall of Sidon, he saw his power spread, since the Aramaic legend on his coins struck in Cilicia bear the formula "Mazdai [governor] of Trans-Euphrates and Cilicia," the title he still bore when Alexander arrived. The combination of the two provinces is certainly logical, because Cilicia had always looked more toward Syria than toward Asia Minor. The satrap governed from Tarsus, where he had a residence (cf. Xenophon, *Anab.* I.2.23). He undoubtedly had a subordinate at Damascus (cf. Quintus Curtius V.13.11), a fortified town that had a governor in 333 (III.13.2) and that after 323 continued to retain the importance it had held in the Achaemenid period on the road between Babylonia and Egypt (*DAE* 67 [AD 6]; cf. Arrian, *FGrH* 156 F9.28).

The breadth and depth of Persian territorial control in Cilicia are generally underestimated. To evaluate it, we must begin by emphasizing that the use of the term "Cilicia" artificially confers political unity on a region within which, beyond any doubt, many different statuses overlapped (cf. Diodorus XIV.19.3: *tyrannoi*). The Classical and Hellenistic authors loved to emphasize a contrast between the Cilician coast and the Cilician

Fig. 59. Cilician civic coins.

highland in their descriptions of the Empire. This is what Strabo does (XIV.5.1) when he distinguishes Cilicia Pedias from Cilicia Tracheia, the former running from Soloi to Tarsus and Issus. This interpretation is also found in Arrian, who speaks of an expedition led by Alexander in 333 that set out from Soloi: at the head of light detachments, Alexander led a campaign against "the Cilicians holding the heights. In no more than seven days he drove some of them out, induced others to enter into agreements (*homologia*), and returned to Soli" (II.5.6◆).

Persian dominance on the coast is abundantly attested from the end of the sixth century onward. On the coast, in particular, the Persians had military bases and royal arsenals. It seems quite clear that the creation of a full-fledged satrapy at Tarsus signified a weakening—nay, the disappearance pure and simple—of the power of the old *syennesis*; though the date cannot be fixed precisely, it must have been no later than the time of the installation of Mazaeus. Mazaeus's authority over the coastal cities is illustrated by the coins he struck at Tarsus, Soloi, Mallus, and Issus. These cities also had to pay taxes and tribute, following the pattern of Aspendus of Pamphylia, who each year furnished a certain number of horses as royal *dasmos* ('tribute'), according to a statute well attested in Cilicia itself (Herodotus III.90) and also in Armenia (Xenophon, *Anab.* IV.5.34; cf. 5.24 and Strabo XI.14.9). The existence of a royal tribute imposed on Mallus is confirmed by Arrian (II.5.9); it seems quite likely that the fine imposed on Soloi by Alexander (II.5.5) was in addition to the normal tribute. It also appears that kings and satraps recruited mercenaries from this area, particularly at Aspendus in Cilicia, a town that was famed for the valor of its archers (cf. Nepos, *Dat.* 8.2; Xenophon, *Anab.* I.2.12). The towns of the Cilician coast were also integrated into the imperial military organization, with each of them required to send a specific contingent to the royal navy (cf. Arrian II.20.2: Soloi and Mallus). The coinage of the Cilician cities simultaneously demonstrates the significance of local tradition (cf. Quintus Curtius III.8.22), the introduction of Persian themes, and the adoption of Greek models (fig. 59).

Turning to Cilicia Trachaea, Alexander's campaign there can be read in two different ways. The fact that he campaigned in this region does not imply that there had been an expansion of imperial dominion into a region previously left to itself by the Persians. It is nonetheless likely that the satrap of Cilicia periodically led expeditions against peoples who were taking advantage of the strength of their mountain positions to remove themselves from the control of the central authority. This in fact was one of the missions entrusted by Alexander to Balacrus, his satrap of Cilicia, who led an unsuccessful campaign against Isaura and Laranda (Diodorus XVIII.22.1). Persian presence is in any case attested in the high country, at the site of Meydançikkale, where the only provincial example of Persepolis-type reliefs has been discovered. Two Aramaic inscriptions have been found there as well; one of them, badly damaged, is dated to the reign of an

Artaxerxes and includes the word *datah*; it is likely that the site was occupied at a very early date, because it is attested from the time of the Neo-Babylonian period under the name Kiršu (found in the Aramaic text). This is also the case for the royal treasury at Cyinda, on the Cilician coast.

Among the political subunits we must also consider the great sanctuaries, which are known especially (later) from Strabo—particularly the sanctuary of Artemis Perasia at Castabala, which was later called Hierapolis and was located in the valley of the Pyramus. An Aramaic inscription dating to the Achaemenid period has been found there, and it describes the limits of the sanctuary's territory. This is where, at the height of the Roman period, the local authority of the dynasty of the Tarchondimontos was recognized. The dynastic name recalls their distant Luvian origins, similar to the name (Tarkumawa) that, according to the most widely accepted theory, appears in Aramaic on Cilician coins attributed to Datames. Strabo locates Hierapolis-Castabala in Cataonia (XII.2.2–7✧), an area whose geographic and administrative outlines are poorly specified in the Achaemenid period. "A broad hollow plain, and produces everything," Cataonia is watered by the Pyramus, a navigable river that reaches the sea in Cilicia, and also by the Carmalus. The region is surrounded by mountains and had few cities, but "they have strongholds (*phrouria*) on the mountains." This is confirmed by Nepos: the country was thickly wooded and covered by a dense network of *castella* (*Dat.* 4.2). Among its strongholds, Strabo names Nora, "where Eumenes held out against a siege for a long time" (XII.2.6✧). Nora was known for the strength of its position at the very beginning of the Hellenistic period and certainly must have been occupied since the Achaemenid period, just like many other neighboring citadels that, similar to the garrisons of Mysia (Xenophon, *Anab.* VII.8.15), could easily lend assistance (cf. Diodorus XIX.16.3).

At a much later time, the region of Castabala constituted an administrative subdivision, the Castabalitis, and we know of the existence of a "*strategos* and high priest of Cataonia"—an organizational structure that may be compared with the organization described several times by Strabo in the "temple states" of Greco-Roman Anatolia (XII.2.3). For the Achaemenid period proper, the most evocative text is a passage in Nepos, who describes the territory of Aspis, against whom Artaxerxes II sent Datames: "ordering him to attack Aspis, the ruler of Cataonia (*Cataoniam tenebat*); that country lies beyond Cilicia, next to Cappadocia" (*jacet supra Ciliciam, confinis Cappadociae*; *Dat.* 4.1✧). The outcome of the tale shows that the country was crossed by major roads, since Aspis took advantage of its location to seize tribute that was being sent to the Great King (§4.2). We should stress the importance of one of these roads, the road that led from Cataonia to the Cilician Gates via Tyana (Strabo XII.2.7–9; cf. Xenophon, *Anab.* I.2.20–21 [Dana]). Datames was probably chosen as Artaxerxes' agent because his father, Camisares, had himself held an official position: Camisares had in fact "governed (*habeat provinciam*) that part of Cilicia which adjoins Cappadocia (*partem Ciliciae iuxta Cappadociam*) and is inhabited by the Leucosyri, or 'White Syrians'" (§1.1✧). This region obviously is Cataonia, which was located in a frontier area between Cappadocia and Cilicia and apparently was at that time a dependent of the satrapy of Cilicia—although, according to Quintus Curtius (IV.12.11–12), the Cataonians were among the contingents placed under the authority of Darius III at Gaugamela. This is where the main town, Mazaca (later called Eusebeia-near-the-Argaeus after the volcano that towers 3900 meters over it) was located (Strabo XII.2.7). Some 35 km northeast of the future

Fig. 60. Persian relief found near Kayseri.

Caesarea (Kayseri), Mazaca in the Achaemenid period may have been the seat of the lieutenant governor of Cataonia—namely, Camisares and, later, Aspis.

Not far from Mazaca, an altar base has been found; on its four faces typically Persian scenes are carved: sacrificing *magi*, very similar to the scene on one of the stelas from Dascylium (fig. 60). It is possible that the Persians established Fire worship on the volcanic Argaeus, thus assimilating a worship of heights to their advantage—a theory that calls to mind the sanctuary of Anaitis Barzochara, the Iranian divine name designating a high mountain known in nearby Cappadocia. Nearby, in the town of Hanisa—which was built on the site of ancient Kanesh—a late inscription provides evidence for the density of Iranian population very like that of neighboring Cappadocia. The "governor and high priest" of Cataonia, also known from a late inscription, had an Iranian name, Arsames, and a local patronymic, Iazemis. It is also within the confines of Cappadocia and Cataonia (Farasa) that late Greek inscriptions attest to a "Luvian/Castabalian" personal name, Tarkondaios; and it was here that a Greek-Aramaic inscription in honor of "Sagarios, son of Maiphernes, commander/garrison chief (*stratēgos / rab ḥaylâ*) of Ariaramneia, who became *magus* of Mithra" was recopied (first century A.D.?). This material shows the retention of Iranian names (Maiphernes, which is also found at Hanisa and Celaenae) and their mixture with local names (Sagarios, also known at Sardis), as well as the continuity of Aramaic language and Iranian religion—each component obviously going back to the Achaemenid period.

All of this evidence shows that Achaemenid territorial occupation was much more dense than is generally postulated on the basis of a convenient but partly illusory dichotomy between plain and mountain (or coast and interior). In the interior of Cilicia, there were political subunits, ruled by lieutenant governors, such as Camisares and Aspis of Cataonia, who can be compared with a person named in an Aramaic inscription of the Achaemenid period found at Hemite, which was close to Hierapolis-Castabala: "[X so]n of Sarmapiya the satrap." The title *satrap* may indicate that the person (who has a Luvian name) held some sort of official position in the region; and even if the title was only a status identifier, it is remarkable that the person improved his social status by using a Persian word. Other evidence—though the date is always difficult to pin down—shows that there was a Persian diaspora in various subregions of Cilicia (and/or borrowing of the Persian lifestyle): "Greco-Persian" reliefs; an Aramaic inscription (at Saraidin: Gibson II no. 35), where someone boasts of his hunting prowess (in a paradise? cf. Nepos, *Dat.* 5.4); and a late Greek inscription that mentions an Iranian religious title (*satabara*) not previously attested. We may emphasize, finally, an interesting, isolated, and undated Cilician coin depicting a gardener-king.

7. *From Tarsus to Samaria via Sidon and Jerusalem*

Artaxerxes III's reconquest of Egypt led to other administrative reorganizations in Trans-Euphrates. Thereafter, Mazaeus's authority also extended south, from his original base in Cilicia as far as the Egyptian border. After Cyprus was retaken, the island's kings, including Pnytagoras of Salamis, were permitted to retain their positions (Diodorus XVI.46.1–3), but they certainly were required to renew their oaths of allegiance (cf. XV.9.2). This then brings up the question of the Sidonian problem. Contrary to what Diodorus would have us understand (XVI.45.4–6—there taking up well-known narrative motifs; cf. Herodotus I.176; Diodorus XVIII.22.4–8), Sidon was not obliterated from the map nor was its population entirely eliminated. The deportation of Sidonian women "to the royal palace at Babylon," which is referred to in a Babylonian chronicle (*ABC*, Chronicle 9, p. 114) simply confirms the reality of the kind of retaliatory measure that was customary in such circumstances. After all, there is hardly any doubt that the city was required to provide a naval contingent for the armada accompanying Artaxerxes to the Delta. The scarcity of direct evidence prevents us from reaching a decisive conclusion regarding the status granted to or imposed on Sidon. The question is, after the reconquest by Artaxerxes III, was the town administered directly by the Persians, or did it retain the relative independence it enjoyed before the revolt? It is frequently thought that the Great King rescinded the grant one of his predecessors had conferred on King Ešmunazar (chap. 12/3), but the documentation remains very elliptical. On the other hand, there is no doubt that a few years later (342–341) Sidon was once more led by a king whose name was Straton (II), because his coins have been found. We also know that Mazaeus struck coins at Sidon and that his coins continue without interruption between 343 and 333. But there is nothing to prove that we must interpret this as evidence of a drastic limitation on Sidonian privileges. The reports of Alexander's authors make it clear that Straton, the king of Sidon installed by the Great King, was perfectly loyal to the Persian cause (cf. Quintus Curtius IV.1.16 and Diodorus XVII.47.1). In Achaemenid strategic planning, the Phoenician coast, in combination with Cyprus and Cilicia, always constituted an important naval recruiting base, as is demonstrated by the composition of the Persian navy in 334–332 (cf. Arrian I.19.7; II.16.7; II.20.1). Shipyards (*neōria*) are attested at Tripolis (II.13.3–4), and the timber of Lebanon was close by (cf. Quintus Curtius IV.2.18). The importance of this area for naval operations carried over to Alexander, whose Indus fleet was made up of Phoenician, Cypriot, Carian, and Egyptian equipment (Arrian VI.1.6). When Alexander was planning for the expedition against the Arabs, he once more called on the Phoenician shipyards (e.g., VII.19.3), and these shipyards, supplied by the forests of Lebanon, remained active during the age of the Diadochi (cf. Diodorus XIX.58.2–5).

Achaemenid authority was also well established in Samaria, though we have no official information after the Jews' appeal to Sanballat and his sons Dalayah and Šelemyah in November 407 (*DAE* 102–3 [*AP* 30/31–32]). Aramaic papyri, seals, sealings, and coins add important details. Papyri and some seals were found in 1962 in one of the caves in the Wadi ed-Daliyeh, near Jericho. Coins have been discovered in two hoards, one from Nablus (now disperesed) and one at Samaria. Several of these coins mention Mazaeus: none from the Samaria hoard (apparently predating 345), but four in the Nablus hoard (CS nos. 14, 16, 21, and 48), dated between 345 and 333–332. Sidonian coins (or imitations) struck in the name of Mazaeus were also found in the Nablus hoard. Among the items from Wadi ed-Daliyeh is a coin from Tarsus depicting Baal of the city and stamped with the name of Mazaeus. The papyri from Wadi ed-Daliyeh record private business and are dated to the reigns of several Great Kings and also name the governor (*peḥā*) of Samaria. One of the most interesting and best preserved has the following heading: "The twentieth day of the month of Adar, second year, accession year of Darius the king, in Samaria the citadel (*byrt*), which is in Samaria the province (*medinah*)"; and then, along with clauses of warranty and authentication, a formula appears: "Before Yeshu'a, son of Sanballat, governor (*peḥā*) of Samaria, and Hananyah, the prefect (*šangu*)" (SP 1). To start with, the document has the unique advantage of being dated to the very moment of the transition between Arses/Artaxerxes IV (year 2) and Darius III (year 0)—that is, March 19, 335. It is the latest of the documents; most of them date to Artaxerxes III, some to Artaxerxes II, and the oldest goes back to 375. Furthermore, we observe that Samaria (the term refers equally to the town [*qryt'*], the citadel [*byrt'*], and the province [*medinah*]) was still administered by a governor assisted by a prefect. Finally, it is clear that the line of Sanballat I had remained in place at least since Darius II: Yeshua is in all probability Sanballat I's grandson through his son Sanballat II (CS 41–45), or through Delayah (CS 49?); Hananyah the prefect was Sanballat II's brother, whom he succeded as *peḥā* of Samaria (cf. SP 7, 9 and CS 29–30). According to Josephus (*Ant.* XI.302), yet another Sanballat was made satrap of Samaria by Darius III; if he ever existed, he would have to be considered Sanballat III, the son of Hananyah. Thus we see here a succession of several generations that is somewhat reminiscent of the Hecatomnids of Caria; in that case, members of the same family passed on the title of governor, though there is no doubt that at each succession the new title was bestowed directly by the royal authority, who always retained the sovereign right to confer power on whomever he wished. If the same family maintained this preeminence, it was obviously because it had proved its unbroken loyalty to the Great Kings from Darius II (at least) to Darius III. Information on Judah as well comes from coins: coins were struck in the name of "Yehizqiyyah the governor (*peḥā*)," and others in the name of "Johanan the high priest." The relative dates of the coins and the relational hierarchy between the governor and the high priest (who both used the same types of coins) unfortunately continue to be problematic. However, it is worth recalling that this joint administration was quite venerable, because in 410 and 407 the Jews of Elephantine sent two successive petitions, one to the leading citizens of Judah and (a different) "Johanan the high priest," and a second to Bagohi the governor (*DAE* 102 [*AP* 30/31]).

What must be stressed is the broad diffusion of Persian motifs on the coins and seals (fig. 61a–g), sometimes by way of imitation of Sidonian coins (the Sidonian ship is found several times: CS 16–17, 44–45, 49, 54). One of the most common scenes is the Royal Hero, who is so well known from Persepolis and elsewhere: he confronts lions (CS 16, 44–45, 48–51, 59–60), sometimes winged lions (cf. WD 4, 17), or a bull (CS 19, 31–33).

Fig. 61. *(a–e) Coins from Samaria and (f–g) sealings from the Wadi ed-Daliyeh.*

We also find, as on royal coinage, the archer- and/or lancer-king (CS 17, 22, 21, 56–57, related images on front and back of CS 52), as well as the king on his throne (CS 18, 21), before a footed censer (CS 33), in his chariot (CS 35, 48), or standing with his scepter (CS 37). The Persian motifs (lion-hunting and others) are sometimes united on a single coin (CS 18, 21, 31–33, 36–38, 48, 52, 57). In one case (CS 50), a royal scene (king killing a lion) is combined with a head of Athena (fig. 61b). This serves to recall the diffusion of Athenian models in the coinage and the Greek influence evident in particular in the "Greco-Persian" seals from Wadi ed-Daliyeh (fig. 61f–g). The Jerusalem coins of Yehizqiyyah and Johanan themselves include motifs that are scarcely Jewish: an owl and a female mask. Some motifs are harder to define "ethnically," such as a man killing a horse rearing in front of him (CS 58); we might be tempted to see this as a reference to horse sacrifice in Mithra-worship—if the man were wearing Persian garb, which is not the case (fig. 61e).

8. *From Gaza to Petra*

After the fall of Tyre, Palestine fell into Alexander's hands, except for Gaza, which put up a lengthy resistance (September to November 332) that is described by all the ancient historians, including Polybius, who praises the locals' fidelity to the imperial power, going all the way back to Cambyses' conquest (XVI.22a). The reports show that Gaza was heavily fortified and that its governor, Batis, had a sizeable garrison, including both Persians and Arab auxiliaries (cf. Arrian II.25.4–26.1; Quintus Curtius IV.6.7). After taking the city, Alexander—they say—sent 500 talents of incense and 100 talents of myrrh to his tutor, Leonidas (Plutarch, *Alex.* 24.6). The presence of Arab mercenaries, the existence of inventories of incense and myrrh, and the finds of coins lead us to recall that Herodotus had compared Gaza's prosperity to the wealth of Sardis (III.5); the city was at that time the main center of all the emporia that, again according to Herodotus (III.5✧), "belong to the king of Arabia." This king of the Arabs was certainly none other than the one who in Cambyses' time controlled the desert road leading from Gaza to Egypt (III.7). Other evidence shows that the merchandise of the Minaeans (of South Arabia) found an outlet in Gaza; we have long known about a Minaean inscription (*RÉS* 3022) that refers to a merchant caravan that had returned from trading in Egypt, Assyria, and Trans-Euphrates (*'br Nhr'*); the inscription reports that the Minaean merchants "rescued their goods from the heart of Egypt during the conflict that broke out between the Medes (*Mdy*) and Egypt (*Mṣr*)." If the text is to be dated to the Achaemenid period—which seems probable—it most likely refers to one of the campaigns against Egypt, which unfortunately cannot be dated more precisely than to the time between Cambyses and Artaxerxes III.

We also know, again from Herodotus, that Cambyses had entered into an agreement with the king of the Arabs (III.7, 9). We then might suppose that it was because of this agreement that Herodotus included the Arabs among the donor peoples: "The Arabians brought a thousand talents of frankincense every year" (III.97✧); even though they were officially included in Trans-Euphrates, their territory was exempt from tribute (III.91). It is likely that the "king of the Arabs" retained his privileged status throughout the Achaemenid period. But between Herodotus and Alexander we have hardly any direct information; twice Diodorus simply mentions that the "king of the Arabs" was aligned with the pharaoh and his allies against the Persians; around 410, he allied himself with Amyrtaeus (XIII.46.6); and around 382, he sent reinforcements to Evagoras of Cyprus (XV.2.4). It would be going too far to conclude from this that the Persians had deliberately chosen to abandon the region. Gaza's resistance permits us to think that, at least after the reconquest of Egypt (343), the town had again become a fortified place of great importance that was directly controlled by the Great King. Furthermore, Quintus Curtius states that Batis was exceptionally loyal to Darius III (IV.6.7✧). Two collections of Aramaic ostraca from Beer-sheba and Tell Arad, two sites in Idumea, date to the fourth century, perhaps even to the reign of Artaxerxes III, and reflect Achaemenid settlement in the region. The second collection includes partial summaries of the distribution of food rations to men and animals (horses, donkeys); workers were organized into *dgalîn* (companies), something well attested at Elephantine; similar to the Persepolis tablets (PF, Category Q), these ostraca clearly show that the territory was organized logistically around major centers that commanded smaller centers that had storehouses and garrisons (Tell Arad). The case of Beer-sheba is no doubt different, since the presence of a garrison is not, properly speaking, attested; the foodstuffs mentioned in the ostraca could be deliveries from farmsteads in the surrounding areas to a collection center. The recent (and still unpublished) discovery of hundreds more ostraca of the same type, also from the fourth century, may confirm that Achaemenid settlements (military or not) in the province (*medinah*) of Idumea were quite dense—the area that Diodorus, at the very beginning of the Hellenistic period, calls "the district (*eparchias*) of Idumea" (XIX.95.2✧). It is also immediately striking that the personal names betray very thorough mingling of the peoples clustered at these sites (Arabs, Edomites, Hebrews, Phoenicians, and some Persians).

The political geography of North Arabia at this time poses a number of other problems that continue to be hotly debated, and we cannot enter into the details of the debate here. One of the most interesting texts is the long passage that Diodorus of Sicily (XIX.94 97) devotes to the Nabateans in the context of his description of the campaign that Demetrius, a lieutenant of Antigonus the One-eyed, launched against them from Idumea (§95.2). They were nomadic herders (camels, sheep): "while there are many Arabian tribes who use the desert as pasture, the Nabataeans far surpass the others in wealth . . . ; for not a few of them are accustomed to bring down to the sea frankincense and myrrh and the most valuable kinds of spices, which they procure from those who convey them from what is called Arabia the Fortunate" (§94.4–5✧). So they profited from their role as intermediaries between southern Arabia and the Mediterranean ports, principally Gaza. Demetrius had launched an attack against a natural stronghold (*petra/Petra*), where the trading posts were set up (§95.1). After sending Antigonus a letter (in Aramaic; §96.1), the Nabateans offered Demetrius the following deal: Demetrius was to withdraw his army, and the Nabateans would give him gifts (*dōreai*; §97.4). This was done, and hostilities ceased (§97.6). We can imagine that the situation prevailing at this time was no different from the situation prevailing at the end of the Achaemenid period: the Nabateans were not tributaries (*phorologoumenoi*; §94.10), but they presented gifts to the Persian administration, just as the "king of the Arabs" did in the time of Herodotus. It may be this king of the Nabateans that Heraclides of Cumae was referring to when he recalled that he was "independent and subject to nobody" (Athenaeus XII.517b–c✧). However, if this theory is valid, by referring to him as ruling "the country where frankincense is produced" (*libanophoros khōra*), Athenaeus would be guilty of confusing the production and the distribution of this commodity.

9. *Egypt from Artaxerxes III to Darius III*

We are little and poorly informed about the history of the Egyptian satrapy after Artaxerxes III's reconquest. Not a single Classical text refers to the region in this period: all we know is that the satrap of Egypt in 333 was named Sabaces, but we do not know when or how he replaced the satrap who had been appointed ten years earlier by Artaxerxes III. At this point, we cannot avoid turning to a well-known document—namely, the

Satrap Stela, which dates to the seventh year of Alexander IV (312–311)—though its reading and interpretation continue to exercise modern scholars. This hieroglyphic stela describes the good deeds of the satrap Ptolemy, particularly his benefactions that honored the temple of Ejo, near Buto, in the Delta. Not only did he "bring back from Asia the images of the gods and the books that belonged to the temples of Egypt," but he also renewed a land grant that had been made (renewed?) previously by someone named Khabbabash. This person in fact had come to inspect the Delta, "to become familiar with all the branches of the Nile that flow into the sea, in order that the *kbnt*-boats of the Asians might be cordoned off from Egypt." Given this information, the editors of the inscription recall that "the age-old enemy, Xerxes," had nullified a previous grant.

Some of the details indicate that the inspection of the Delta took place at the exact moment when it was threatened by the invasion of a navy from Syria–Palestine; the terminology and date of the stela show that Khabbabash feared an expedition headed by an Achaemenid fleet—hence his concern to inspect and improve the defenses of the Delta, which was the entryway to the Nile and Memphis, following the example of his predecessors when they had faced similar situations in the past (see chap. 15/9). But what is the date of this enigmatic Khabbabash? The few documents that name him do not allow us to answer the question; all we can say is that he was a pharaoh in the full sense, though we are not able to say that he controlled all of Egypt. It seems highly unlikely that he can be placed in the time of Xerxes. The context of the text leads us instead to suggest that the time of Khabbabash was not long before the time of Ptolemy. As a result, there have been several attempts to place him around 342–338, or between 338 and 336, and to suggest that "Xerxes" in the inscription actually refers either to Artaxerxes III or to his successor, Arses/Artaxerxes IV. Whatever the (disputed) identity of Xerxes, we have to conclude that, at some date that we cannot establish (Artaxerxes III, Artaxerxes IV, or Darius III), the Achaemenid armies must have once again mounted an expedition of reconquest. Nevertheless, we can say nothing about the magnitude of the revolt, because after his fleeting appearance, Khabbabash completely disappears from the historical record. Furthermore, we cannot be certain that Pharandates, the satrap appointed by Artaxerxes III, died as a result of this uprising.

We have very little information on the organization of Egypt when Alexander arrived, apart from the account of administrative measures taken in 332–331, which included the appointment of two nomarchs, Doloaspis and Petisis (the latter declined the offer), and a phrourarch at Memphis. Cleomenes of Naucratis "was instructed to permit the nomarchs to govern their own districts in accordance with the ancient practices (*ek palaiou*), but to exact the tribute (*phoroi*) from them himself, while they were ordered to pay it over to him" (Arrian III.5.4◊). One of the nomarchs, Doloaspis, actually appears to have had an Iranian name. Was he a Persian, or a Persianized Egyptian? Though two people are named "nomarch," confusion arises over the sense of the title when it appears in the second half of the text, where it designates the heads of the 42 basic administrative regions of Egypt; it seems clear that these jurisdictions had not been altered by the Persians, nor were they modified by Alexander. It was these district rulers who turned over the proceeds of the tribute to Cleomenes (cf. Ps.-Arist., *Oecon*. II.33a [1352a]). We may note finally that, when Alexander arrived, Elephantine was still "open for business," because the king deported some of his political adversaries there (Arrian III.2.7).

10. From Arbela to Susa

After being defeated at Gaugamela, Darius returned to Media, leaving open the road that led from Arbela to Babylon and Susa (Arrian III.16.1–2); the conqueror's progress was aided by the fact that the road was well provided with resupply stations. We know that Mazaeus and the Babylonian authorities surrendered the town to Alexander (Arrian III.16.3; Quintus Curtius V.1.17–23). The same fate soon befell Susa, a twenty-days' march from Babylon; it was surrendered to Alexander by Darius's satrap, the Persian Abulites, who retained his post (III.16.6, 9; Quintus Curtius V.2.8, 17), just as Mazaeus had been made satrap at Babylon (Arrian III.16.4; Quintus Curtius V.1.44). It was at Babylon that Darius had twice assembled his forces—before entering Cilicia in 333 and Upper Mesopotamia in 331. In 331, Oxathres, the son of Abulites, led the Susianan and Uxian troops, while Bupares (then satrap of Babylonia?) was in charge of the Babylonian contingents (Arrian III.8.5). We know that Babylon and Susa were two of the most important centers of Achaemenid presence at this date; the projects carried out there by Artaxerxes II demonstrate this fact (chap. 15/8). An "Achaemenid residence" recently uncovered north of Sippar belongs to the end of the Achaemenid period.

We have very little detail about the satrapal administration of Babylonia and Susiana. As in the time of Darius I (chap. 12/2), there was a treasury managed by a treasurer at Babylon (Quintus Curtius V.1.20: Bagophanes, *arcis et regiae pecuniae custos* = **ganzabara*); the same was certainly the case at Susa (cf. Diodorus XIX.18.1: Xenophilus *thēsuurophylax* [**ganzabara*]; cf. §48.6). It is likely that the satrapy of Babylonia was divided into several subdistricts, as in earlier times; we know very little about these districts, aside from the explicit mention of detachments from Sittacene and "transplanted Carians" among the troops in the unit commanded by Bupares (Arrian III.8.5◊). These transplanted Carians were settled in "villages called Carae" that Diodorus (XVII.110.3◊) locates on the great road leading from Susa to Ecbatana along the east bank of the Tigris, close to Sittacene, which was probably a subdistrict (in Steven of Byzantium, Sittacus is called *persikē polis* 'a Persian city'). While following his itinerary, Alexander came into contact with the transplanted Eretrians (not Boeotians, as Diodorus has it) who had been settled by Darius in the community of Ardericca in Kurdistan, which was near naphtha wells (cf. Herodotus VI.119–20). These are probably the people that Quintus Curtius calls Gordyans and that also sent a contingent to Darius at Gaugamela (IV.12.11; cf. Strabo XVI.1.25). We may also note that, after the division of 323, Mesopotamia and Babylonia were two separate satrapies (Diodorus XVIII.3.3); and after the division of 320, Mesopotamia was united with Arbelitis (XVIII.39.6). It is likely that this arrangement went back to the Achaemenid period and that the region around Arbela at that time constituted a specific administrative subdivision; Strabo includes it in what he (in confusion) calls Assyria (XVI.1.3). The travel voucher given by Aršāma to his steward when he sent him back to Egypt from Babylon makes it clear that the Arbela region was among the 'provinces' (*medinah*) crossed by the royal road (*DAE* 67 [AD 6]). The strategic importance of the region—where the ruins of ancient Assyrian towns remained (Xenophon, *Anab.* III.4.6–9)—is illustrated by its easy communication with Babylonia (Quintus Curtius IV.9.8) and by the presence of Achaemenid colonies that were integrated into the imperial military organizations. It is likely, finally, that the marshy southern portion of the lower Tigris and Euphrates valleys also constituted a province, named Māt Tāmtim ("Sealand"), within the Babylonian satrapy.

The sources from Alexander's time provide considerable information regarding navigation and water management. Some of them deserve careful examination if only because they are sometimes used as evidence for the claim that Persian territorial control of Babylonia was weak. We may begin with a well-known passage from Arrian. Alexander sailed up the Tigris with his navy as far as Opis:

> In the voyage upstream he removed the weirs in the river and made the stream level throughout; these weirs (*katarrhaktai*) had been made by the Persians to prevent anyone sailing up to their country from the sea and mastering it with a naval force. The Persians had constructed them because they had no naval power (*nautikoi*), and the weirs, built up at such regular intervals, made the voyage up the Tigris impracticable. Alexander, however, said that contrivances of this kind were the work of men lacking military supremacy; he therefore regarded this precaution as of no advantage to himself, and showed by his action in destroying with ease works on which the Persians had spent their energy that it was of no value. (VII.7.7◇)

The same information, similarly told, is found in Strabo (XVI.1.9; cf. XV.3.4). If it is correct, we would have to conclude that the Persians did not control southern Babylonia, which would have been continually at risk from any foreign enemy that was able to assemble a navy powerful enough to sail up the Babylonian rivers and challenge the Achaemenid forces at the heart of the Empire. But Arrian's and Strabo's presentation is highly suspect. Two facets must be distinguished: the facts provided (the construction of artificial weirs) and the historical commentary. It is clear that Arrian's passage contains all of the traditional literary stereotypes about the weakness of the Persians: like the fourth-century Egyptian pharaohs (see chap. 15/9), they primarily trusted defensive emplacements to repulse invasions, since the Great Kings were incapable of demonstrating any sort of military supremacy. Furthermore, the claim that the fourth-century Persians were not sailors is an evaluation that does not make much sense; we suspect that Arrian has taken over nearly word for word the phraseology used by Herodotus when he describes the Persians at the beginning of the reign of Cambyses (I.143). Finally, it is hard to imagine which enemies from the Persian Gulf region were strong enough to threaten the rich lands of Babylonia and endanger the royal residences at Susa and Babylon at this time. In reality, there is every indication that the observers relied on by Arrian and Strabo took as permanent defensive works what were nothing more than light structures set out by the satrapal administration each year to regulate the river at the time of high water. In fact, it seems likely that in this era the structures only temporarily hindered river traffic between the Gulf and Susa (cf. Strabo XV.3.4)— but did not prevent it (XV.3.5; Quintus Curtius IV.9.8; Diodorus XVII.67.3).

Arrian and Strabo describe other hydraulic projects carried out at Alexander's initiative at this time. Strabo (quoting Aristobulus) states that the king went down the Euphrates, sometimes closing, sometimes opening the canal diversion dams (XVI.1.11). Arrian gives details of a canal well known from the Babylonian evidence, the Pallacopas, and he says that the king set projects in motion to create a new outlet (VII.21). Once more, Greek ingenuity is implicitly but clearly contrasted with Achaemenid practice:

> The satrap of Babylonia used to dam the outlets of the Euphrates into the Pallacopas with considerable effort, even though they were easily opened, since the earth there is muddy and mostly soft clay, such as lets through the river water and makes it none too easy to turn the river back; for over 2 months more than ten thousand Assyrians (*Assyriōn andres*) used to be engaged on this task. (VII.21.5◇)

According to Strabo (XVI.1.10❖), Alexander's actions were characteristic of "good rulers" (*hēgemōnes agathoi*), who harnessed the water to irrigate the arable land. Arrian says the same thing: "When this was reported to Alexander, it incited him to improve the land of Assyria" (VII.21.6❖). Both take up one of the most powerful tenets of Mesopotamian royal ideology. They make Alexander the heir to this tradition, and they distance the Persians from it—with regard to both the Tigris and the Euphrates. Once again, the presentation is highly suspect. For one thing, Arrian's text very clearly indicates that in the early Achaemenid period, as throughout history, the satrapal authorities undertook major construction and maintenance projects related to water management, and this necessitated the use of local labor, which was requisitioned by way of corvée (cf. also Pliny VI.30.120). There was indeed a changeover between the Achaemenids and Alexander, but it was not what Arrian and Strabo claim. Alexander undertook such projects, not really to improve irrigation, but quite simply because at this time his principal concern was to prepare for the Arabian expedition. Thus, he had a new port built at Babylon to serve as a place where the boats could be gathered, including those that had been transported in pieces from Phoenicia to Thapsacus on the Euphrates. This, at any rate, is quite clearly the goal Strabo assigns to Alexander (XVI.1.11), and Arrian as well: he went down the Pallacopas canal in the direction of Arabia as far as the lakes and founded a city there (VII.21.7). The change between the Achaemenids and Alexander is that the latter used the Babylonian rivers and canals for military purposes, and the traditional (irrigation-oriented) waterworks either were inadequate for his navy to sail from Babylon to the Gulf (via the Pallacopas canal) or else impeded the movements of his warships (*katarrhaktai* on the Tigris). In the short term, the conqueror only had to provide the barest of necessities for irrigation. All we can conclude from this is that the Great Kings did not sail their navy up the Tigris to Opis or up the Pallacopas to Babylon. But why should they have? In the long run, their dominion and the enormous tribute assessments laid on Babylonia (cf. Herodotus I.192) made it imperative that the satrap pay attention first of all to irrigation projects. Placed in their military and ideological context, these remarks by Arrian and Strabo precisely prove that it was this way throughout the time of Darius III and also—note well!—during the first years of Macedonian dominion (cf., among others, *ADRTB* nos. –332B, –328, –324A)!

Apart from these discussions, the sources from Alexander's time dealing with Babylonia are far from explicit—quite apart from the problem of relations between the Macedonian conqueror and the Babylonian authorities during his two sojourns, in 331 and 325–323 (chap. 18/3). This is why we need to glean as much information as we can from sources related to the Babylonian temples, as well as the incidental mention of an (unnamed) sanctuary in Susa (Arrian VI.27.5). A corrupt passage in Pseudo-Aristotle (*Oecon.* II.34a [1352b]) mentions a tithe on goods imported into Babylonia, which appears to have fallen into obsolescence; but the text is too allusive and fragmentary to provide an overall picture of the situation. Thus, it is necessary to give primary attention to the cuneiform tablets. The insufficiency of the evidence and the chronological uncertainty relating to the various Artaxerxes make it difficult to take stock of the situation in Babylonia and Susiana in the time of Darius III; nonetheless, recent publications of astronomical texts provide some important additional information. Taken as a whole, the Babylonian record of the fourth century provides a picture of unwavering continuity. This is especially apparent in the religious, economic, and administrative organization

*Fig. 62. Some Murašū seals
(here and on facing page).*

of the great sanctuaries, which appear to have continued to operate as in the past. It can also be observed in the continued high prestige of the Sages, who observed the planets, and the haruspices and diviners—those whom the Classical authors call Chaldeans and who, they say, had academies at Uruk, Borsippa, Babylon, and Sippar (e.g., Strabo XVI.1.6; Pliny, *NH* VI.123). But this picture—however accurate it may be—risks missing elements of development and change. It has been observed, for example, that in Seleucid Uruk the god Anu seems to have taken on a new importance, and this probably goes back to the Achaemenid period; but the historical interpretation of this observation poses problems that have not yet been resolved.

Classical sources and Babylonian tablets indicate both the existence of many foreign communities in the region and also the depth of intercultural relations. The initial picture comes from Alexander's historians' descriptions of Greek populations settled in Babylonia/Mesopotamia from the time of Darius I. While Herodotus could write about the Eretrians of Ardericca around 450 that they "still speak their original language" (VI.119◊), this was no longer the case in the time of Darius III; by then they had put down roots and "were now degenerate" (Quintus Curtius IV.12.11◊): "They are bilingual and speak like the natives in the one language, while in the other they preserve most of the Greek vocabulary, and they maintain some Greek practices" (Diodorus XVII.110.5◊). This refers to the easily understandable development of a population that had long been cut off from its roots (cf. also Quintus Curtius V.5.13, 19; VII.5.29; Strabo XI.11.4). Persians themselves had settled in Babylonia in large numbers. In addition to the evidence from the tablets, there is Berossus's passage on the erection of sacred statues of Anāhita at Babylon in the time of Artaxerxes II; despite remaining uncertainties (chap. 15/8), it seems clear that all of this evidence attests to the importance of the Persian diaspora in Babylonia. What does this evidence say about the relations between the Persian diaspora and the Babylonians?

Contacts between the Babylonians and Persians are attested to by seals and sealings; the most important corpus is the group collected from the Murašū tablets (second half of the fifth century). They include themes that are specifically Persian (Royal Hero, Persian soldiers), as well as Babylonian themes (fig. 62). We may note in passing that two seals on Persepolis tablets show boats (Phoenician ships) in a Babylonian setting, indicated by palm trees (fig. 50f, p. 606). This typically Babylonian plant seems to have been injected into Persian tradition; according to Strabo (XVI.1.14), a Persian song (a counting rhyme?) listed the 360 uses of the palm tree. Furthermore, it is quite remarkable that many seals also testify to the activity of Greek artists in Babylon, just as is the case at Dascylium, Sardis, Sidon, and Samaria. Paradoxically enough, we get the impression that, at least on this level, Greek artists (or better: artists working in the Greek style) created a sort of meeting-point between Persians and Babylonians. On this point, the Susa sealings are explicitly different from the Babylonian, since "the impressions found at Susa show hardly any Greek influence. . . . There is only one that might be considered 'Greco-Persian'" (P. Amiet).

The study of personal names also results in several interesting observations—even when the ancient authors take a rather casual approach toward the names or encounter various difficulties in transcribing into Greek the Babylonian names they only knew by hearing them pronounced. For example, Plutarch (*Art.* 19.2) says one of Artaxerxes II's eunuchs was called Belitaras according to Ctesias (Bēl-ēṭir? cf. *Sardis* VII.1.1) but Melantas according to Dinon (Greek adaptation of

a nickname?). As a result, sometimes we find personal names in curiously mixed forms, such as Belephantes, who according to Diodorus (XVII.112.3) was the head of the school of Chaldeans that tried to dissuade Alexander from entering Babylon. This said, it is quite noteworthy that Abulites, the satrap of Susa in 331, although he is called a Persian by Arrian (III.16.9), has a Babylonian name, while his son's name, Oxathres, is indisputably Persian (III.8.5). The situation regarding one of the sons of Mazaeus, who was a Persian, is identical, in reverse: this son, the second-in-command in Syria, was named Brochubelus (Quintus Curtius V.13.11); two more of his sons had Babylonian names, Antibelus (Arrian III.21.1) and Artibelos (VII.6.4), while another had the inarguably Persian name Hydarnes (VII.6.4). However, Bagistanes, who was called "a Babylonian and a noble" (Arrian III.21.1✧), had a typically Persian name (cf. also Quintus Curtius V.13.3). It is not certain that these apparent contradictions should automatically be attributed to errors or guesses by the Greek and Roman authors. The Babylonian evidence in fact shows that people who belonged to the foreign communities who settled in the country frequently gave Babylonian or Semitic names to their children. Between 482 and 331, we find four people with Babylonian names and Iranian patronymics, eleven people with Semitic names and Iranian patronymics, and eight people with Iranian names and Babylonian patronymics. The Murašû archives also demonstrate that personal names are not an absolute guide to ethnic origin. In the archives, 71% (463) of the seals are held by men with Babylonian names, of whom 80% also have a Babylonian patronymic; 14% are men of West Semitic origin; 3% are of Egyptian origin; 7% (48) of the seals belonged to a person with an Iranian name, but only 1/3 of these have both an Iranian name and Iranian patronymic. This obviously reflects both mixed marriages and the desire to identify with the dominant ethnic group. At the same time, the distribution of images on the seals shows a specific preference on the part of each ethno-cultural group: the Iranians preferred hunting scenes and narrative representations of the sort introduced into Babylonia at the time of the Achaemenid conquest.

If we accept Arrian's judgment about the "Persian" ethnicity of Abulites, the satrap of Susa (III.16.9), and if we take into consideration the name of his son (Oxathres: III.8.5), he might actually have been a Persian who, like Ariyawrata/Jeho in Egypt (Posener no. 34), adopted a double name, Persian and Babylonian. If this theory could be verified, it would add to our understanding of the breadth of Persian-Babylonian intercultural encounters. But, since the theory cannot be proved, the most likely interpretation is different: it seems more likely that a certain number of "Persian" dignitaries in Babylonia and Susiana at the end of the Achaemenid period were of Persian stock but, given the frequency of polygamy in this context, married both Persian and Babylonian wives, whose children had sometimes Persian, sometimes Babylonian names. Contrariwise, the dignitaries with Babylonian names probably were genuine Babylonians (perhaps the offspring of mixed marriages), who, as a result of marriage to a Persian woman, or for political reasons, may have given a Persian name to some of their sons. The example of Bēlšunu, son of Bēl-uṣuršu (chap. 14/8), reminds us that Babylonians were able to reach high positions in the imperial hierarchy; the case is even more striking if we recognize that the Belesys who was satrap of Syria around the middle of the fourth century (Diodorus XVI.42.1) was actually the son (or some other descendant) of Bēlšunu. In each case, we can imagine that there were intimate contacts between the Persian aristocracy of the imperial diaspora in Babylonia and the elite leaders of the satrapy; this perhaps explains, *in part* at least, Mazaeus's attitude in 331 (chap. 18/3, 18/5).

It is clear that examples such as these attest to active exchanges between the Persian diaspora of Babylonia and the Babylonian elite, which must have involved marriage as well, going back at least to the fifth century. May we go so far as to speak of the "Babylonization" of the Persians of Babylonia, pure and simple? Even if indicators that point in this direction can in fact be found, it must be stressed, on the one hand, that cultural borrowings took place in both directions (cf. Strabo XVI.1.20) and, on the other, that unlike the deported Greeks, the Persians of Babylonia clearly continued to maintain close relations with their nearby homeland—where they could always return to their roots. However, the "Babylonization" of the dynasty, which is sometimes suggested on the basis of Darius II's Babylonian heritage through his mother, raises thornier problems, particularly on the political level. We may stress first of all that the theory is implicitly connected to another theory—that the Great Kings were losing interest in Persepolis and Persia already in the fifth century and instead were orienting themselves more and more to Babylonia. But there is nothing to confirm a perspective so schematic (cf. chaps. 14/1 above and 16/12 below). Moreover, a passage in Plutarch (*Art.* 19.10) even seems to portray Babylon as a backwater used for banishment, far from the court of Artaxerxes II! In the case of Darius III, the only text that might possibly support recent Babylonian borrowings is an extract from Quintus Curtius's long description of the royal procession prior to the battle of Issus: he states that "both sides of the chariot were adorned with images of the gods . . . ; the yoke was ornamented with sparkling gems, and on it rose two golden images a cubit high of the king's ancestors, one of Ninus, the other of Belus" (III.3.16✧). The (incoherent) reference to Ninus is surprising enough, but this item is completely out of place in a description that is marked indelibly and thoroughly by a typically Achaemenid symbolism. ‖According to the editor of the Loeb Classical edition, the dual reading Ninus and Belus, *alterum Nini, alterum Beli*, is a suggested emendation of the unintelligible *alterinalterutrum* by the 16th-century scholar Joseph Scaliger.—TRANS.‖ In the prayers that Darius III regularly offered during his campaigns, there is nothing that might suggest the introduction of a Babylonian god (Bēl) into the royal pantheon; exactly the opposite is true (e.g., Quintus Curtius IV.13.12–14; 14.24; Plutarch, *Alex.* 30.12).

Quintus Curtius (V.1.22✧) offers another example of this kind of meeting between Persian and Babylonian components. In the procession that greeted Alexander at Babylon, Quintus Curtius (unlike, for example, Justin XII.13.3–5, who confuses them) very clearly distinguishes the Chaldeans from the *magi* ("accustomed to sing the praises of the kings"; not found in Arrian III.16.3). But the parallel with Quintus Curtius's first example (the procession prior to Issus) is lame, since in the second case it is Persian features that are introduced, at Babylon, into a Babylonian context—which obviously has a political significance utterly different from that which can be inferred from the earlier example. In this case, the participation of *magi* and Chaldeans is in the context of the organization of a procession in which Achaemenid and Babylonian authorities appear side by side (hence the absence of *magi* in Arrian, who refers only to the Babylonian procession). The entire account simply serves to remind us that, at the end of the Achaemenid period, those whom the ancient authors refer to as Chaldeans always occupied a prominent place in the sanctuaries and towns of Babylonia. The Chaldeans were "scholars . . . who have gained a great reputation in astrology and are accustomed to predict future events by a method based on age-long observations [of] the configuration of the stars" (Diodorus XVII.112.2✧). In contrast, only the *magi* appear in Darius III's royal procession: they are near the chariot consecrated to the Fire and "chanting their traditional hymn (*patrium carmen*)" (Quintus Curtius III.3.10✧). The reference to Ninus and Belus thus has every chance of being a late interpretation; we may wonder whether here as elsewhere (the description of Babylon) Quintus Curtius might have been depending, via Clitarchus, on Berossus's Babylonocentric perspective in which Belus is the founder of Babylon and urban civilization in general.

It is also possible, even though there is no textual evidence, that until the end of the Achaemenid dynasty its representatives bore the title "king of the countries": in a tablet dated to 331, Darius III is called "king of the world" (*ADRTB* no. 330). At the same time, as shown by the royal inscriptions, the ideological attributes of Achaemenid kingship could not be limited to their Babylonian component. This poses a real problem. What was the "status" of the Great King when he officiated at Babylon in accord with Babylonian tradition? Let us specifically consider the rite of the substitute king, which certainly was practiced in the time of Xerxes, according to Herodotus (VII.15–18), and which is also very clearly alluded to, much later, by well-known texts that are clearly from the context of Alexander's last year at Babylon. We may remark on this point that, when a "substitute" took the throne, the eunuchs of Alexander's entourage did not evict him, because, according to Arrian (VII.24.3✧), they were respecting "some Persian custom" (*kata de tina nomon persikon*). This is a surprising phrase (we expect mention of a "Babylonian custom" instead), but its ambiguity is significant, exactly like the apparent discontinuity between the (Babylonian) names and (Persian) ethnicity sometimes attributed to one and the same person. Furthermore, we observe the same imprecision in some authors who speak of the (mysterious) feast of the Sacaea, which Strabo, through a dubious etymological operation, attributes to Cyrus, who supposedly instituted a celebration in the sanctuaries of Anāhita to commemmorate a victory over the Saka (XI.8.4–5). Ctesias also mentioned the Sacaea (Athenaeus XIV.639c); but the more credible information provided by Berossus is unambiguous: it was a Babylonian feast celebrated every year at the end of August/beginning of September (Athenaeus XIV.639c). Whatever the (very uncertain) connection of this feast with the New Year, it seems clear that, for many Greek authors, any custom encountered in the Achaemenid Empire was automatically described as "Persian." Perhaps there was also a "feast of fools" in Persian tradition like that described by Berossus and by Dio Chrysostom (IV.66–68). Whatever the case, there is no choice but to observe that we do not have a single piece of evidence for the participation of the Great King in the Babylonian New Year festival.

11. *The Great King, Alexander, and the Peoples of the Zagros Mountains*

At the end of 331, Alexander left Susa and led his army toward Persia, using the road that is well known expecially from the Persepolis tablets but also from many Hellenistic texts. Diodorus, for example, states that it took 24 days to march from Susa to Persepolis (XIX.21.2), but that a system of voice relays permitted messages to travel rapidly between the two (XIX.17.7). This is the region where Alexander first encountered military opposition: Madates, a relative of Darius III, commanded a stronghold that was eventually taken. Then Alexander himself stormed the mountain and clashed with the "Uxians of the mountain." This is a good point to pause and analyze the policy that Alexander adopted toward this population and to comment on the historical interpretations often

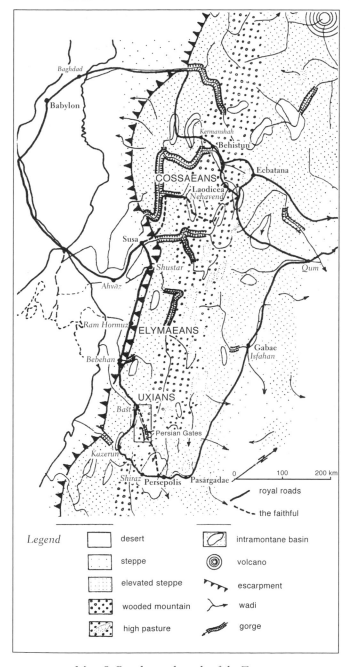

Map 5. Peoples and roads of the Zagros.

drawn from it concerning the weakness of the Great Kings' authority at the very gates of Persepolis.

Of all the accounts, Arrian's (III.17) is the most detailed—although the parallel versions by Diodorus (XVII.67) and Quintus Curtius (V.3.1–16) permit clarification of some points left in shadow by Arrian. Arrian starts by clearly distinguishing two groups of Uxians. The first group lived on the plain: the gorges of Uxiana controlled the first pass that would permit the traveler to enter Persia from Susiana (Strabo XV.3.4; cf. Arrian, *Indica* 40.1). Quintus Curtius says of the territory of the Uxians that "this adjoins Susa, and extends into the first part of Persia" (V.3.3◇). Persia begins on the far side (Diodorus XVII.68.1)—that is, the region dominated by the fortress commanded by Madates: they "had obeyed the Persian satrap, and now surrendered to Alexander" (§17.1◇). Quintus Curtius states that Alexander "left the city intact, and allowed it to cultivate its fields without tribute" (*sine tributo*); then the king "incorporated the subdued race of the Uxii in the satrapy of the Susiani" (V.3.15–16◇). It is likely that, prior to Alexander's action, Uxiana constituted a special subdistrict entrusted to Madates (cf. Quintus Curtius V.3.4: *praefectus regionis*; Arrian III.17.1: satrap). Alexander's connection of the area with Susiana can be accounted for even more easily because of the fact that in the Persepolis tablets the region appears to be strongly marked by Elamite influence. This also explains the name "Susian Gates" that Diodorus (XVII.68.1) uses for what are usually called the "Persian Gates." The old connections between Uxiana and Susa are also demonstrated by the common command that the satrap of Susa exercised over both the Susianian and Uxian contingents (Arrian III.8.5).

The second group of Uxians lived in the mountains; Alexander had to lead an expedition against them, and it ended in their submission. Here is Arrian's version (III.17.1–2, 6◇):

> But the Uxian hillmen, as they are called, were not subject to Persia, and now sent a message to Alexander that they would only permit him to take the route towards Persia with his army if they received what they used to receive from the Persian king on his passage (*hosa kai para tōn Persōn basileōs epi tei parodōi*). Alexander sent them away, with orders to go to the pass, their control of which made them think that the way through to Persia was in their hands, in order to receive from him too what was prescribed. . . . [defeat and massacre of the Uxians] . . . These were the gifts of honour (*ta gera*) they received from Alexander; and it was only with difficulty that they obtained from him their request to retain their own territory, paying annual tribute to Alexander. . . . The tribute assessed was a hundred horses every year with five hundred transport animals and thirty thousand from their flocks and herds. For the Uxians had no money or arable land, but were mostly herdsmen (*nomeis*).

Strabo confirms that, when the Great King went from Susa to Persepolis, the Uxians extracted payments from him (XV.3.4: *misthoi*). But, for Nearchus (cf. *Indica* 40.1), who is quoted by Strabo (XI.13.6◇), the Uxians were just one in a series of peoples who had made equally strange arrangements with the Great King. Nearchus lists four predatory tribes: "The Mardi were situated next to the Persians; the Uxii and Elymaei next to the Mardi and the Susians; and the Cossaei next to the Medians";

> and that whereas all four extracted tribute (*phorous prattesthai*) from the kings, the Cossaei also received gifts (*dōra*) at the times when the king, after spending the summer in Ecbatana, went down into Babylonia; but that Alexander put an end to their great audacity when he attacked them in the winter time.

We know nothing in detail of the Elymaeans (a name known especially from a much later period) and very little of the Mardians, aside from Quintus Curtius's mention of Alexander's campaign against them in winter 331–330, which he carried out from Pasargadae (V.6.17–19). They were obviously the people whom Herodotus describes as one of the "tribes of nomads" among the Persian tribes (I.125). A founder's legend claimed that Cyrus the Great's parents were miserable Mardians whose lives were devoted to raising a few goats and to living as brigands (*FGrH* 90 F66.3). The Mardians clearly had the same reputation in 330, since Quintus Curtius describes them as "a warlike people, differing greatly from the rest of the Persians in their manner of life" (V.6.17✧). Actually, the Mardians also practiced agriculture and even horticulture on small family farms (Aelian, *VH* I.34), and they regularly provided fighting units to the army (Herodotus I.84), including Darius III's army (Arrian III.11.5). At Gaugamela, they were placed at the center of the battle formation, alongside the Cosseans (Diodorus XVII.59.3). The Cosseans are better known, since they are twice referred to in context by Diodorus. At Ecbatana after the death of Haephestion, Alexander led a campaign against the Cosseans, who were a warlike and courageous people who had remained independent throughout the Persian monarchy. Alexander seized the routes of access into their country and subdued them, requiring them to submit to his authority (XVII.111.4–6✧). Then, in 317, when Antigonus intended to travel from Susiana to Media, he chose not to use the royal road (which was blazing hot) but to take a more direct mountain road; this cooler route crossed the land of the Cosseans—an enemy (that is, unsubjected) country (*polemia* [*khōra*]):

> It is not easy for an army to follow this route without having gained the consent (*aneu tou peisai*) of the tribesmen who inhabited the mountain ranges. These men, who have been independent from ancient times (*autonomoi gar ontes ek tōn palaiōn khronōn*), live in caves, eating acorns and mushrooms, and also the smoked flesh of wild beasts. Since Antigonus regarded it as beneath his dignity to use persuasion on these people or to make them presents (*dōrodokein*) when he had so great an army following him, . . . [difficulties encountered by the army] . . . Antigonus regretted that he had not heeded Pithon when he advised him to purchase the right of passage with money (*khrēmatōn priasthai tēn parodon*). (XIX.19.3–4, 8✧)

The historian is thus faced with a homogeneous tradition. The mountains of Persia and Media were inhabited by peoples defined by a specific way of life that was based on animal husbandry and highway-robbery, to the exclusion of agriculture. This may explain the curious diet of the Cosseans, who seem to have lived solely on the results of hunting and gathering. Furthermore, these peoples never acknowledged the dominion of the Great Kings; when the royal caravan crossed their territories, the Great Kings had to pay a "travel fee" that was designated by various terms (*misthoi, phoroi*). Moreover, the Cosseans were accustomed to accepting gifts (*dōra*). But they were not alone in this regard, because the Uxians expected to receive gifts of honor (*ta gera*) from Alexander. The Great Kings had to pay fees to these peoples because they controlled impregnable defiles. The example of the Uxians is even more noteworthy because it implies that the Great Kings did not even control the road between Susa and Persepolis. We could not ask for a better illustration of the weakness of the Great Kings, which is certainly the message of the Hellenistic war correspondents.

The problem is all the more important because the four peoples named by Nearchus could easily be included in a much longer list. We know the offer that Clearchus—apparently!—made to Tissaphernes after the battle of Cunaxa, in these words:

> I know that the Mysians are troublesome to you, and I believe that with the force I have I could make them your submissive servants; I know that the Pisidians also trouble you, and I hear that there are likewise many other tribes (*ethnē polla*) of the same sort; I could put a stop, I think, to their being a continual annoyance to your prosperity. (Xenophon, *Anab.* II.5.13◊)

Xenophon returns to the topic elsewhere:

> The Mysians and Pisidians, occupying very rugged country in the Great King's territory and lightly armed, contrive to overrun and damage the King's territory and to preserve their own freedom. (*Memorabilia* III.5.26◊)

As for the Lycaonians, "they had seized the strongholds in the plains and were reaping for themselves the lands of these Persians" (*Anab.* III.2.23◊). The mountain peoples are always characterized as independent from royal authority; this is true for the Mysians (*Hell. Oxyr.* 16.22), and also for the Carduchi, Taochians, and Chaldeans (of Armenia; Xenophon, *Anab.* V.5.17). The Carduchi "were not subjects of the King" (III.5.17◊); "they were enemies of the King and a free people" (Diodorus XIV.27.4◊). The Mardian territory on the Caspian Sea had never been invaded (Arrian III.24.2); and the same was true of the Iberians, "never subject to the Medes or Persians, and they happened likewise to escape the dominion of the Macedonians" (Plutarch, *Pompey* 34.7◊). The permanent nonsubmission of the Pisidians is made clear, for example, by the (false) goal announced by Cyrus the Younger to his mercenaries (*Anab.* I.2.1); this incident recalls the fear of the Pisidians that Diodorus (XI.61.4) attributes to the Persian leaders at the Eurymedon sixty years earlier. Alexander's campaign does seem to confirm that the Pisidians continued their incursions, using their strongholds as bases from which to launch attacks (Arrian I.24.6; 27–28). The Persians' inability to subdue these peoples is also illustrated by failures in battle: according to Xenophon (*Anab.* III.5.16), an immense army (thirty myriads!) was annihilated during a campaign against the Carduchi; the many Cadusian wars were apparently just as inglorious (see immediately below and chap. 16/18).

These examples at first appear to illustrate the limits of military occupation of the imperial realm; control of some areas could not be guaranteed by the establishment of numerous royal garrisons alone, at least not without multiplying them exponentially. But at the same time, the presentation by the ancient authors—all of whom were impressed by the notion of Persian military impotence—must be qualified, at the very least. For one thing, as has already been stressed in connection with Mysia and Paphlagonia (chap. 15/5), not all of the territories of these peoples lay beyond the reach of satrapal oversight, and the existence of a district of Mysia is nearly certain, even apart from references to the mysterious "satrap of Paphlagonia." Furthermore, all of these peoples were included, says Herodotus, within tributary districts (III.90, 92), including the Moschians, Tibarenians, Macrones, Mossynoeci, and Mares (III.94◊). Of course, we have no direct information on payments of tribute coming from these districts; let us simply note that in his work *On the Tributes of Asia* (which is actually about the taxes levied for the king's table), Ctesias refers to the wine of the Tapyrians (*FGrH* 688 F54). Finally, as "autonomous" as these peoples may have been, they regularly provided military units to the Great King, usually as mercenaries (chap. 17/3). Cadusian contingents participated at Cunaxa, led by Artagerses, who used the opportunity to demonstrate his loyalty to Artaxerxes II (Plutarch, *Art.* 9–10). They were also present at Gaugamela, alongside Albanians and Sacesinians, all led by Phratapharnes of Media (e.g., Arrian III.8.4; 11.3–4).

At the same time, the ancient authors were obviously guilty of simplification. First of all, the ethnographic descriptions of these peoples are located within a dominant stream of ancient historiography that tends to reduce the social dynamic to the "law of need": on poor soil, a group of people is necessarily poor; to survive, the group therefore draws on the wretched results of hunting and gathering and, toughened by the very causes of its poverty (soil and climate), it is "naturally" aggressive and profits or survives from raiding. But this is an extraordinarily reductionist perspective. In reality, the Zagros peoples whom we have just been discussing had fields and villages as well; subsistence agriculture was practiced in combination with extensive animal husbandry (cf. the tribute imposed on the Uxians by Alexander). The lifestyle attributed to them by the ancient authors can be explained by the circumstances: when they were attacked by a mighty army, the mountain dwellers fled their villages, surviving in an exceptional and atypical way, and waited out the end of the offensive.

The problem of "royal tribute" remains. The texts indicate that encounters between the Uxians, the Cosseans, and the Great King took place regularly, since the presentation of gifts/tribute was related to the periodic relocations of the court from residence to residence. But it is especially noteworthy that neither the Uxians nor the Cosseans actually controlled the royal roads from Susa to Persepolis or Susa to Ecbatana. Their territories were remote. It must therefore be recognized that every year the Great King (or his personal representative) intentionally detoured to meet the representatives of the Uxians and Cosseans. Obviously, the Uxians were taken in by Alexander's promises, and they waited for the Macedonians at the defile where they expected to receive the promised amount (as in the time of Darius). Alexander violated the custom. From this time on he imposed tribute on the mountain Uxians and required the Cosseans to acknowledge their submission. But his action did not have lasting results, because both the Cosseans and the Uxians were fully "autonomous" by 317 (Diodorus XIX.17.2). Despite Pithon's wise advice, Antigonus demonstrated the same blindness as Alexander: he too was unable to understand any language other than that of military might and considered the tradition an unbearable stain on his military pride—wrongly considering the gift to be extortion for the right of passage. In fact, the customary, regular relations between these peoples and the Great King were not based on war; they were based on "controlled hostility," which itself was based on gift and counter-gift (*dōra, dōrodokein, geras*), which guaranteed that it would go on indefinitely. Arrian's tale enables the process to be reconstructed: every year, the king or his representative would meet with the Uxian leaders at the entrance to the defile; there was a ceremony in which each party made a commitment to the other. The bestowal of royal "gifts," here as elsewhere, implied no recognition of royal "weakness"; on the contrary, it created a link between the receiver and the giver. Through this ceremony, the Uxians (in a way) committed their loyalty to the king. The arrangement was advantageous to the King because he received the submission of the Uxians and Cosseans without investment of military resources; furthermore, both groups probably sent soldiers to the king whenever conscription was ordered.

The Uxians were thus definitely not isolated from the Achaemenid world. The size of their animal production (horses, sheep, cattle), which presupposes that they were able to market the surplus, implies that they were connected. Arrian provides two relevant pieces of information that require interpretation: the Uxians had no money (*khrēmata*), and the tribute imposed by Alexander was 100 horses, 500 pack animals (humped cattle?), and 30,000 sheep. The size of the tribute leads us to conclude that, on the one hand, it was related to the ability of the Uxians to pay, and on the other, the amount was not worked out by Alexander in a few hours but goes back to the Achaemenid period. At that time, the tax in head of cattle was not regarded as tribute but as if it were a contractual matter—the money paid by the Great King (aside from the gifts) corresponded to a "purchase price" (cf. Diodorus XIX.19.8: *priasthai*). This may be the sort of exchange Xenophon had in mind when he wrote of the Carduchi: "Whenever they made a treaty with the satrap in the plain, some of the people of the plain did have dealings with the Carduchi and some of the Carduchi with them" (*Anab.* III.5.16◊).

It would nonetheless be risky to state that relations between the king and the "mountain people" were governed by similar customs in every case, because only the relationship between the Great King and the Cosseans and Uxians is actually documented. Recourse to force is well attested elsewhere, without, unfortunately, our being able to analyze the reasons (broken contract?) or methods. Only the case of the Cadusians permits us a basis for reflection and theorizing. The recurrence of Cadusian wars is particularly noteworthy because the theme appears in one of the Cyrus legends (Nicolaus of Damascus, *FGrH* 90 F66.11–16). We have no details about Darius II's mission (Xenophon, *Hell.* II.1.13). Artaxerxes II's expedition is mentioned by several authors, but their accounts are difficult to harmonize. Diodorus's allusions (XV.8.5; 10.1) seem to imply that the expedition lasted some time, and Trogus Pompeius specifically says that Artaxerxes II lost (*Prol.* X). It was probably during this war that Camisares perished and his son Datames was rewarded by the king for his great deeds (Nepos, *Dat.* 1.2). Plutarch, on the other hand, does not mention any fighting: the royal expedition was concluded with a treaty, based on "friendship and alliance," that was agreed to by Tiribazus and two Cadusian kings (Plutarch, *Art.* 24.6◊). As a result, Artaxerxes left the country, obviously satisfied with the outcome (§24.9). The treaty clearly implies that the king's goal was not to challenge the existence of local chieftains. For instance, after the death of Artagerses at Cunaxa, Artaxerxes "sent goodly and magnificent gifts to his son" (14.1◊), and this clearly was another way of legitimizing the succession of the Cadusian king (see chap. 16/18 below).

We also know that Artaxerxes III led a campaign against the Cadusians. The account is included by Justin (X.3.2–5) and Diodorus (XVII.6.1–2) in the official version of the accession of Darius III. Without mentioning battles, both seem to reduce the confrontation to single combat (*monomakhia*) undertaken by Darius III (Codoman) in response to a challenge from a Cadusian giant. Single combats of this kind are well attested, particularly in stories by Diodorus (XVII.88.4–6) and Quintus Curtius (VII.4.33–38) about Satibarzanes' conflict with the Macedonians in Aria. Facing the prospect of continued uncertainty over the outcome of the battle, Satibarzanes proposed settling the struggle by single combat; Erigyius accepted and won, and Satibarzanes' soldiers surrendered without further fight. These monomachies recall what M. Mauss wrote: "The people present at the contract are moral people: clan, tribe, and families who confront and oppose each other either as a group facing each other on the land itself, or in the person of their leaders, or in both ways at once." We could ask whether Codoman's single combat with the Cadusians reflects the practice of "organized hostility," whether it consists of the confrontation of two armies pure and simple, or (more likely) whether the duel follows a battle (according to this theory, a battle adhering to custom). Following the confrontation, the Cadusians renewed their allegiance to the Great King in a treaty that was formally egalitarian. But we must be cautious: the theory must take into account the fact that Diodorus's and Justin's tales are basically constructed on monarchical motifs (cf. chap. 17/1). They are found in part in Diodorus's Median *logos* (II.33): a Persian named Parsondas, who was close to the Median King Artaeus, sought refuge with the Cadusians, "to one of whom, the most influential man in those parts, he had given his sister in marriage." Heading a force of 200,000 men(!), Parsondas vanquished king Artaius, whose army numbered 800,000 men(!): "And for this exploit he was so admired by the people of the land that he was chosen king" (§33.4◊). Diodorus concludes as follows: "The Cadusii were always inveterate enemies of the Medes, and had never been subjected to the Median kings up to the time when Cyrus transferred the Empire of the Medes to the Persians" (§33.6◊). Obviously, Diodorus was dependent on the version found in Nicolas of Damascus—and both no doubt go back to Ctesias. It is hard to understand why so many stories about the relationship between the Persians and the Cadusians were in circulation in the time of Artaxerxes II.

12. Persepolis, Pasargadae, and Persia

After the stronghold defended by Madates was taken, Alexander sent Parmenion and the supply caravan by the wagon road through the plain (*hamaxitos; iter campestre*) that led to Persepolis (Arrian III.18.1; Quintus Curtius V.3.1). He himself took the high road. After defeating the Uxians in the mountains and throwing the forces massed at the Persian Gates into disorder, he joined up with Parmenion at Persepolis. Alexander's long stay in Persia (end of 331 to spring 330) gave rise to a plethora of ancient accounts that provide a great deal of information of great interest. We return to the itinerary followed by Alexander from Susa and note first of all that Diodorus's descriptions emphasize the contrast between the sweltering plain and the refreshing climate of the plateau, a difference immediately evident to any visitor. His descriptions particularly feature the splendor and verdure of the Fahliyun region, which abounded in rivers, springs, paradises, and all sorts of plantations (XVII.67.3; XIX.21.2–3). These were the natural features that also impressed Nearchus (*Indica* 40.4; Strabo XV.3.1). The affluence of the countryside and the fertility of the fields—stressed as well by Quintus Curtius for the surroundings of Persepolis (V.4.20; 5.4)—are complemented by the vigor of the people. Based on eyewitness testimony (from Hieronymus of Cardia) and speaking of the area between Fahliyun and Persepolis, Diodorus in fact remarks: "Those who inhabited this country were the most warlike of the Persians, every man being a bowman and a slinger, and in density of population, too, this country far surpassed the other satrapies" (XIX.21.3◊). This note accounts for the vigor of demographic growth and the maintenance of the country's military resources. We can well imagine that the Great Kings' "birth rate incentive policy" (cf. Herodotus I.136 and Strabo XV.3.17) was highly effective. Plutarch also states that Alexander maintained the custom, first established by the Great Kings, of awarding a

Fig. 63. Tomb of Artaxerxes II (reconstruction).

gold piece to pregnant women on the occasion of each visit to Persia (*Alex.* 69.1–2; *Mor.* 246a–b).

Whatever debates persist regarding their breadth and significance, Alexander's policies and activities show that both Pasargadae and Persepolis remained major ideological centers of Persian power and the might of the Great King—a position they had never truly lost (despite Plutarch's quaint but simplistic remark: *Alex.* 69.2). This was again recognized by Alexander when he ordered that Darius III be buried in the royal tombs of Persepolis (fig. 63), as were his predecessors (Arrian III.22.1). That they were still major centers is also eloquently evidenced by the work that continued at Persepolis throughout the fourth century (including during Darius III's time, if, as is possible, the incomplete tomb is to be attributed to him; fig. 64) and by the maintenance of regular sacrifices around

Cyrus's tomb at Pasargadae (VI.29.7). The replication of iconographic patterns (including those on seals), from the earliest in the time of Darius I to the latest in the time of Artaxerxes III, displays the stability of Achaemenid monarchic ideology at the heart of the Empire. At the same time, the reliefs on Artaxerxes III's tomb show that the borrowings were also selective: while some "peripheral" peoples (Nubians, Libyans) are found on all of the tombs, Artaxerxes III's tomb reliefs do not include Armenians, Lydians, Egyptians, or Indians—for reasons that obviously have nothing to do with facts concerning territorial dominion. The lists and depictions do not claim to represent a statistical abstract of the Empire, any more at the end of the Empire than in earlier eras (chap. 5/3); basically, the peoples shown are a representative group, just like those who took part in the banquet of Opis: "Next to [the] Persians, . . . any persons from the other peoples who took precedence for rank (*kat'axiōsin*) or any other high quality" (Arrian VII.11.8◊).

Moreover, the ongoing construction and rebuilding pose a specific problem. During the reigns of Darius I, Xerxes, and Artaxerxes I, the basic resource for this construction activity was the forced labor provided by *kurtaš* and the organization of workshop and farm production—even if the latter did much more than feed the workers in the construction yards. The "sudden disappearance" of the tablets that record these processes

Fig. 64. Unfinished tomb at Persepolis.

obviously cannot be ascribed to elimination of the royal economy in Persia (an absurd conjecture in itself). However, it appears that other texts from Alexander's time provide information that might enrich the debate. When Alexander was stymied at the Persian Gates, he appealed to prisoners that his troops had just captured. One of them was introduced as bilingual, a speaker of Greek and Persian and probably Lycian as well. His father had in fact originally come from Lycia, where he had previously been taken prisoner by the Persians; since his youth he had known the mountains like the back of his hand, because he was a shepherd (Quintus Curtius V.4.3–4, 10–12; Diodorus XVII.68.4–6; Plutarch, *Alex.* 37.1; Polyaenus IV.3.27). Some time later, as Alexander neared Persepolis, he was approached by Greeks who "had been carried away from their homes by previous kings of Persia," about 800 of them according to Diodorus (XVII.69.3◊) and Justin (XI.14.11), 4,000 according to Quintus Curtius (V.5.5). They had been mutilated (to enhance their ability to carry out their manual labor, according to Diodorus; XVII.69.4), and they were also "branded with the characters of barbarian letters" (Quintus Curtius V.5.6◊). They worked in "ergastula" (V.5.13)—that is, (slave) workhouses. Some came from Cyme, others from Athens (V.5.9, 17). Their settlement in Persia went back some time, since they had taken wives there and raised children (V.5.13, 20) and refused repatriation. The shepherd seems to have been in the same situation, because Plutarch says that his "father was a Lycian, and his mother a Persian" (*Alex.* 37.1◊).

Once they have been stripped of their emotive language, these Classical texts do not deserve to be rejected in principle. It is far more likely that, one way or another, these Greeks and Lycians in these stories should be compared with the *kurtaš* known from the tablets. According to this theory, the Hellenocentric orientation of the ancient sources leads us to think that these Greek and Lycian expatriates were nothing more than a sample of the population who, once freed from captivity, chose not to abandon the settlements in Persia that had resulted from mass deportations; they were used by the royal administration in the fields and pastures and in the workshops and construction yards. We do not claim that nothing had changed since the time of Darius I, but we are confident in the (reasonable) idea that the administration put in place by the first kings did not miraculously disappear. This is confirmed by the passage in which Arrian very precisely gives the quantity of rations allocated to the *magi* who were responsible for the sacrifices around the tomb of Cyrus, as well as the number of horses they had to sacrifice (VI.29.7)—information that clearly had been received directly from the royal administrators (cf. Diodorus XVII.69.8), as in the time of the Fortification tablets.

At the same time, the information we have on the administration of the region and on the high officials who were in place there in the time of Darius III provokes us to inquire into possible changes in the status of Persia over the course of Achaemenid history. At Gaugamela, three generals—Orontobates, Ariobarzanes, and Orxines—commanded the contingents raised from "the tribes bordering on the Red Sea [Persian Gulf]" (Arrian III.8.5;◇ cf. Quintus Curtius IV.12.7). The Persians are not listed as such in this line of battle, even though they participated en masse, separate from the Persian Gulf natives (Arrian III.11.3–7). Once more we find Ariobarzanes entrusted with the defense of the Persian Gates; on this occasion, Arrian entitles him "satrap of Persia" (III.18.2). Among the other notables, we can point out Tiridates, head of the Treasury (**ganza*) at Persepolis, who sent a letter to Alexander offering him the town (Quintus Curtius V.5.2; 6.11; Diodorus makes him "governor of the city," XVII.69.1◇); and also Gobares, whom Quintus Curtius calls 'governor' (*praefectus*) of Pasargadae (V.6.10). If Arrian's information is correct, we must conclude that at some unknown date, under some unknown circumstances, Persia was turned into a satrapy—which was not the case at the time of Darius I.

But many uncertainties remain on this point, because only Arrian (alone among Alexander's historians; cf. Quintus Curtius V.3.17 and Diodorus XVII.68.1) grants Ariobarzanes this title, which is not attested with certainty, however, until after the conquest, when the king named the Persian Phrasaortes, son of Rheomithres, "satrap of Persia" (Arrian III.18.11◇). According to Polyaenus, who makes him the leader of the Persian troops at the Persian Gates, this Phrasaortes was "a close relative of Darius" (IV.3.27). We may also note that there was an eminent person alongside Ariobarzanes—Orxines, who was "in charge of the whole . . . , a descendant of the 'seven Persians' and tracing his genealogy also to Cyrus, that most renowned king," according to Quintus Curtius (IV.12.8◇). For this reason, during Alexander's Indian expedition, after the death of Phrasaortes, Orxines proclaimed himself satrap of Persia "because he felt that he was the right person, in the absence of any other governor, to keep the Persians in order for Alexander" (Arrian VI.29.2◇). This is the point in Quintus Curtius's narrative where he grants him the title "satrap" (X.1.22◇)—which simply means that we must understand that Orxines was the chief of the Pasargadae tribe (*Persica gens, cuius satrapes Orsines erat*). This example at least demonstrates that ancient social and tribal stratification survived in Persia. It is clear that the heads of the great families continued to hold first rank (e.g., Plutarch, *Alex.* 37.1; Diodorus XIX.22.2). Moreover, according to Quintus Curtius, Orxines was the one who led the Persian contingents; but if this is true, what exactly did Ariobarzanes do? Does the word "satrap" relate to nothing more than the command he received at the Persian Gates?

The problem is all the more difficult because, aside from the appointment of a satrap of Persia, the presentation of administrative actions taken by Alexander at Persepolis is very brief—whether Quintus Curtius's or Arrian's. Quintus Curtius simply notes that Tiridates kept his job of treasurer (*gazophylax*) even when the fortress was handed over to the Macedonian Nicarchides (V.6.11). On the other hand, not one author says anything about any tribute from the satrapy, although this information is regularly provided elsewhere. At this point, all we can do is to mention three pieces of information that are hard to relate to each other: the plains Uxians were exempt from tribute (Quintus Curtius V.3.15); but the mountain Uxians had to pay tribute (Arrian III.17.6); and once they were freed, the Greek *kurtaš* of Persepolis were exempt from royal tribute (*ateleis . . . basilikou phorou*), according to Diodorus (XVII.69.8). But what can we conclude from this about the situation prior to Alexander? The only obvious fact we have (see above) is that the mountain Uxians had not paid tribute to the Great King but now had to pay Alexander; furthermore, the context leads us to believe that the exemption granted to the plains Uxians was confirmation of a preexisting status (it was very unusual that Alexander agreed not to impose tribute). The case of the Greeks of Persepolis remains: does Diodorus's note imply the existence of tribute before Alexander, or does it imply that after the conquest Alexander imposed tribute on a country that, Herodotus (III.97) says, was exempt at the time of Darius I? This is a rather difficult question. Let us recall that the Greeks received seed and livestock from Alexander "in order that the land assigned to them (*ager attributus*) might be cultivated and sown" (Quintus Curtius V.5.24◊). This provides the context for the exemption from royal tribute (Diodorus XVII.69.8), which clearly relates only to a very specific case: Alexander as conquerer took lands (from the royal estate or from the estates of noble Persians) and allotted them to a community. This constituted the foundation of a colony, a process that was frequently associated in the Hellenistic period with the distribution of seed and the granting of temporary fiscal exemption. So it seems difficult to draw general conclusions about the tributary status of Persia either before or after Alexander from these data. If, as has been suggested, the Greeks were only a small part of a large population of *kurtaš*, Alexander certainly did not intend to free them all because, if the royal economy was still vital in 331–330, there would have been no reason to take action that was likely to weaken it. The few texts dating from Alexander's second residence in Persia generally illustrate the continuity of Achaemenid practices (Arrian VI.29.7; Plutarch, *Alex.* 69.1–2 and *Mor.* 246a–b; Strabo XV.3.7–8).

13. From Persepolis to Ecbatana

In the spring of 330, Alexander hurried along the major plateau road leading to Media, which he reached in twelve days (Arrian III.19.3)—a journey that an army traveling at a normal pace could accomplish in twenty days (Diodorus XIX.46.6). He crossed and subjected the land of the Paraetacae, which was made into a separate satrapy (Arrian III.19.2). He also crossed the Gabiene, which Strabo places in the northern reaches of Persia, where we know of a royal residence (*basileion*) at Gabae/Tabae (Strabo XV.3.3; cf. Quintus Curtius V.13.2: *oppidum in Paraetacene ultima*; Polybius XXXI.9.3). It was a rich region, where the armies could resupply (Diodorus XIX.26.2). Then he arrived at Ecbatana. At Gaugamela, the Median contingent (along with peoples coming from Ecbatana: Cadusians, Albanians, Sacesinians) was led by the Mede Atropates (Arrian III.8.4), the future founder of Atropatian Media (Strabo XI.13.1). Was he at this time the satrap of Media? We cannot say with certainty. We simply know that Alexander named the Persian Oxydates to the position some time later (Arrian III.20.3), before replacing him with Atropates himself (IV.18.3). At any rate, this is the first attestation we have of a satrap of Media since the reign of Darius I (at that time, it was Miturna/Hydarnes:

PFa 18). The last mention of the operation of the city is the reference to the royal archives located in Ecbatana the Fortress in Ezra 6:1–2 in the time of Darius I (DB II §32: *Hagmatāna didā*). This is because Media, located far from the Greco-Persian theaters of operations, scarcely attracted the attention of the Greek writers of the Classical period, though they did know about the fabled splendor of Ecbatana, and they also knew that it was one of the intermittent residences of the Great King and his court. The gap is only partly filled by the Alexandrian historians, since the Macedonian paid only brief visits to Ecbatana.

Polybius, on the other hand, left enthusiastic descriptions of Media and Ecbatana in several of his discussions of Seleucid history. He stresses the unusual strategic situation of the region and its resources: it "might rank as a kingdom" (V.44–45◊). It was, he says, "the most notable principality in Asia, both in the extent of its territory and the number and excellence of the men and also of the horses it produces. It supplies nearly the whole of Asia" (X.27◊). The lushness of the Median pastures stressed by Polybius was well known to the Companions of Alexander. The famous Nisaean stud farms were located six days' march from Ecbatana (Nisāya district; *DB I* §13); in the times of the Great Kings, they supported more than 150,000 animals grazing freely (Diodorus XVII.110.6; Arrian VII.13.1; Strabo XI.13.7). Despite the raw climate, Media included quite rich districts, the plains and fields of which were farmed by peasants who lived in hundreds of villages (Diodorus XIX.32.1–2; 37.2; 39.1; 44.4; cf. Strabo XI.9.1). As Strabo tells it (XI.13.8), Atropatian Media alone (in his time it was distinct from Greater Media) delivered to the Great King, in addition to money tribute, an impressive amount of livestock, every year: 4,000 mules, 3,000 horses, and 100,000 sheep. Strabo again stresses the size of the military resources of the region, which could easily raise 10,000 horsemen and 50,000 infantrymen (XI.13.2). Strabo's note seems to imply that the territory that was to become Atropatian Media already constituted a (tribute) administrative subdistrict in the Achaemenid period. We may also note Diodorus's use (XIX.44.4) of the term *eparchy*: Rhagae is called one of the eparchies of Media (*dahyu* in DB II §32). Because of the date of the events Diodorus is describing (beginning of the age of the Diadochi), it is tempting to think that the term goes back to some Achaemenid administrative arrangement—perhaps a unit identifiable with *medinah*, which in the Aramaic documents from Egypt refers to the internal subdivisions of a satrapy (see Diodorus XIX.95.2, referring to Idumea).

Polybius is responsible for the best description of Ecbatana. Quintus Curtius (V.8.1) simply presents it as the capital of Media (*caput Mediae*), and Diodorus (XVII.110.7) presents it as a very large town (circumference of 160 stadia = ca. 30 km) and the seat of a royal residence (*basileion*) and a very well stocked treasury (Alexander had brought some of the treasuries of Susa and Persepolis to Ecbatana). Polybius (X.27◊) says that the town, though unfortified, included a citadel (*akra*) defended by strong walls. From the walls of this citadel (OPers. *didā*; Akk. *birtu*), Darius hung the mutilated bodies of the rebel Fravartiš and his accomplices in 521 (*DB II* §32; *Bab.* §25). Polybius also describes the untold wealth of the palace: its ceilings, beams, and columns, made of cedar or cypress, "were with plated with either silver or gold." Even after being pillaged by the Macedonian soldiers, the columns of the Anais temple's peristyles "were still gilded and a number of silver tiles were piled up in it." Anais must have been none other than Anāhita; Artaxerxes II had ordered a cult statue of her erected in Ecbatana (*FGrH* 680 F11) and had consigned Aspasia to her sanctuary as "priestess to Diana of Ecbatana, whom they name Anaitis, that she might spend the remainder of her days in strict chastity" (Plutarch, *Art.* 27.4◊). The sanctuary is also mentioned later by Isidore of Charax (*Parthian Stations* §6), and perhaps it is this goddess who is called Median Artemis in a Hellenistic inscription (chap. 16/3 above). There is no doubt that there were many temples and sanctuaries in Ecbatana and the rest of Media (cf. Arrian, *Anab.* VI.27.4). On the other hand, we wonder about the Iranian identity of an "Asclepius" who supposedly had a temple in the capital of Media (Arrian VII.14.5). As Polybius implies, many of the buildings undoubtedly were built by the Great Kings; furthermore, their building activity at Ecbatana is attested in several inscriptions, three of which come from Artaxerxes II (A²Ha–b–c). However, the lack of organized excavations prevents us from providing any detail. Finally, following the pattern of all their colleagues, the satraps and the representatives of the imperial elite had located enchanting paradises close to the town, "charming . . . with groves artificially planted" (Quintus Curtius VII.2.22–23◊). Additional paradises served royal stations (*stathmoi basilikoi*) along the major roads (Plutarch, *Art.* 25.1). Without question, the most famous of these was the one at Behistun; its fame caused Alexander to turn aside from the road from Babylonia to Ecbatana (Diodorus XVII.90.5). Behistun was located in the Kampanda district (DB II §25), a place-name easily recognizable behind Isidore of Charax's Gambadene (*Parthian Stations* §5) and perhaps Diodorus's Gadamala (XIX.37.1).

In Polybius's eyes (V.44), Ecbatana owed its reputation and riches to its position as a crossroad. To the east lay what Quintus Curtius (V.8.5) calls a *via militaris*, the Khorasan road that led to Bactra and Central Asia via the rich region of Rhagae, the Caspian Gates, and Hecatompylus (cf. Arrian III.19.1–2, 20.2, etc.). From Ecbatana, Armenia and Cappadocia could easily be reached (Plutarch, *Eum.* 16.1–2), as well as Persepolis, via the Gabiene. One could also get to Upper Mesopotamia by a mountain road that had only poor opportunities for resupply (Arrian III.16.1); it crossed the land that an astronomical tablet dated 331 refers to with the archaizing term "land of Guti" (*ADRTB* no. −330). One could also take the road, described by Herodotus (V.52), that originated at Sardis and the Halys, crossed part of Cappadocia, had fifteen stations (*stathmoi*) in Armenia, and after Arbela went down the east bank of the Tigris (cf. *DAE* 67 [AD 6]) crossing many of its tributaries on pontoon bridges (V.52). Quite naturally, it was at Ecbatana that Darius stopped after his defeat at Gaugamela, because he hoped that he could assemble additional forces coming from the satrapies of the Iranian Plateau there (chap. 18/4). Ecbatana also was the place where, in 401, Artaxerxes II gathered troops from the eastern regions and then ordered them to advance against Babylon (Diodorus XIV.22.1; Xenophon, *Anab.* II.4.25). Throughout Achaemenid history, the strategic role of Ecbatana (and of Rhagae) recurs, particularly clearly in the wars of Darius in 522–521, because the king stayed there for several months to organize counterattacks from Ecbatana against Rhagae and Parthia (DB II §§31–32, §35; III §36). Alexander also considered the town to be crucial; we know this because he left Parmenion and several *strategoi* at Ecbatana and had part of the royal treasuries of Susa and Persepolis brought there. There is every reason to believe that the Median capital did not simply serve as the summer residence of the Great Kings but always functioned as a place for the Empire's east and west to meet. Merchandise from Central Asia, such as lapis lazuli from distant Badakhshan (Bactria), was conveyed through Ecbatana. Tablets from the time of Cyrus and

Cambyses reveal the activities of Babylonian businessmen in the Median capital. Similar documents date to the time of Darius II (including an inscription supposedly from Hamadan: *D²Ha*); it is likely that the Babylonian business establishments followed the annual relocations of the court.

Like many peoples of the Empire, the Medes provided military contingents that were permanently settled in garrison-colonies in Asia Minor (Diodorus XVII.19.4) or Egypt (*DAE* no. 46 [*BMAP* 5]). Several Medes also appear in fifth-century Babylonian tablets. Conversely, the presence of a Persian diaspora in Ecbatana can perhaps be deduced from the Berossus text discussed above (chap. 15/8). On the other hand, we know practically nothing of the place that the Median aristocracy held in the Empire or of their relations with the Persians. Of course, we can imagine that, one way or another, the wealthy, great families of the Median aristocracy were obliged to cooperate (*principes*: Quintus Curtius X.1.3). But for what reason and with what duties? The problem is even more difficult to deal with because, from the time of the earliest kings, it is impossible to find men who are described as Medes among the high-ranking imperial personnel. Exactly three are identified in the Alexandrian historians: Atropates (Arrian IV.18.3), Baryaxes (VI.29.3), and one named either Cobares (Quintus Curtius VII.4.8) or Bagodaros (Diodorus XVII.83.7; alongside Bessus); in contrast, references to *anēr Persēs* are fairly common. On first analysis, this seems to be in striking contrast to the position of the Medes in the time of Cyrus and Cambyses, and even in the reigns of Darius and Xerxes — both of whom liked to include the Medes and Media in the "first circle" (chap. 5). Furthermore, we cannot say whether the title "king of the Persians and Medes," which is known from the time of Xerxes, was maintained throughout Achaemenid history — or not, even though, according to Arrian (VI.29.3✧), this was the title that the Mede Baryaxes awarded to himself during Alexander's absence in India. Finally, the place of Medes in Darius III's army seems much less prominent than it was in the time of Darius I and Xerxes. But what can be concluded from such poorly documented observations? Should we infer a relative depreciation of Media and the Medes in the imperial whole? It is hard to say, since Media continued to retain its prime position in the country lists — though we should remember that they were copied by rote (*A²P*). Moreover, the absence of Medes in the fourth-century imperial *Who's Who* is perhaps nothing more than a misleading reflection of the gaps in the evidence and our uncertainties about personal names.

The record is weakly fed by a handful of isolated and elliptical texts located in the period between Darius II and Alexander. We may start with the information offered by an interpolation in Xenophon's *Hellenica* (I.2.19), which says that, at the end of 409–408, the rebellious Medes were brought back under control by Darius II. But we know nothing about the causes or the extent of any such revolt, so that it is nearly impossible to situate the episode in the *longue durée*; nothing leads us to suppose (or deny) that, from 521–520 on, Media was periodically wracked by separatist tendencies. We might nonetheless recall that an astronomical tablet from the reign of Artaxerxes II (*ADRTB* no. 369) mentions an expedition in the land of Razaunda, which is in Media, and that Baryaxes wore the "upright tiara" and proclaimed himself "king of the Persians and Medes" (Arrian VI.29.3✧). But what significance does this claim have in view of the long history of relations between Persians and Medes, especially at a moment when one or more Persians attempted to swing the course of Persian history back to Persia (VI.27.3;

Quintus Curtius IX.10.19; X.1.9)? We may recall, finally, that Bessus was sent to Ecbatana for execution after he was sentenced by Alexander (Quintus Curtius VII.10.10), "to be put to death there in the assembly (*syllogos*) of Medes and Persians" (Arrian IV.7.3✧). It is obviously tempting to deduce the existence of a sort of Persian-Mede joint sovereignty in the earlier Achaemenid period from this statement—supposing that Alexander's practice was modeled on Achaemenid practice. But as it happens, it is more likely that what we have here is a typical example of "false continuity," because we do not have evidence that there ever was a regularly convened assembly of the Median and Persian nobility in the Achaemenid period. It is also highly unlikely that Alexander intended to symbolize the obliteration of Persia and Persepolis by choosing Ecbatana and by doing this to restore Media's previous luster. In fact, on the one hand, he only unwittingly agreed to torch some palaces (cf. Arrian VI.30.1; Quintus Curtius V.7.11; Plutarch, *Alex.* 38.8); on the other, he had sent the remains of Darius III to Persepolis to be buried "in the royal tomb, " like his ancestors (Arrian III.22.1✧). Assuming that Arrian's version of the death of Bessus is accurate, the choice of Ecbatana (which was then acting as rear base) can be explained primarily by the ease of communication between Ecbatana and Bactria, where the Macedonian was at the time. In the final analysis, we are tempted instead to offer a totally different interpretation: at the moment when Alexander wished to present himself as Darius's avenger, he symbolically handed over the regicide to those he would call on to cooperate in the new empire, in this way cobbling together an "institution" as new as it was transitory.

14. From Ecbatana to the Halys

Adjacent to Media on the west was Armenia, which in turn was bordered by Cappadocia; the Euphrates marked the boundary between the two countries, and the Halys marked the traditional line between Cappadocia and the Phrygias. According to Strabo (XII.1.1✧), "Cappadocia, also, is a country of many parts (*merē*) and has undergone numerous changes"; it was the Persians who divided it into two satrapies, Greater Cappadocia (or Tauric Cappadocia) and Pontic Cappadocia (XII.1.4). But Strabo's statement has to be taken with a grain of salt, because it is possible that he chose this expression to locate in the distant past the birth of the two Cappadocian kingdoms known to him. It is difficult to reach a conclusion, because we know virtually nothing of the country after Ctesias's comment (§16) that Ariaramnes, satrap of Cappadocia, was ordered by Darius I to campaign on the northern shores of the Black Sea shortly before 513 (cf. chap. 4/2). Even Datames' adventures are not very forthcoming about the Cappadocian regions. In 332–331, the Cappadocian contingents were led by a single leader named Ariaces (Arrian III.8.5). In contrast, the Armenian forces were led by Orontes and Mithraustes (ibid.). It is possible that this arrangement reflects an internal division within Armenia: around 400, Xenophon says, Orontes (an ancestor of Darius III's satrap) held the reins in Armenia (*Anab.* III.5.17), where he had an official residence (*basileion*) and a paradise (IV.4.2), while Tiribazus (still following Xenophon) was hyparch in western Armenia (IV.4.4). Codoman (Darius III) also received command of the two Armenias after his adventure in the Cadusian war fought by Artaxerxes III (Justin X.3.4). But Xenophon's phraseology leaves open the possibilty that there was a single satrapy within which there were several subdistricts (hyparchies).

It must be said that we know little about these Cappadocian and Armenian districts in the time of the Great Kings. The sparse information that we do have can support contradictory readings. The presence of the imperial and satrapal administration is inferred from scraps of evidence, and, until some recent discoveries, we must admit that the evidence was fairly unhelpful. The two countries are regularly included in the lists of subject lands, where they are listed as Katpatuka and Armina, though the latter is called Urartu in the Babylonian versions. Actually, the original Urartu, near Lake Van, yields the only official evidence of royal presence—the inscription carved by Xerxes on a rock face (XV); in the inscription, the king recalls that he had completed the work of his father Darius. Perhaps this inscription expresses the specific importance of the (capital?) district within the satrapy. The strategic value of Cappadocia and Armenia is also attested by the route (the details are disputed) of the royal road described by Herodotus (V.52) and by Xerxes' order to assemble the military contingents at Critalla in Cappadocia (VII.26). Like other countries, Cappadocia and Armenia were included in the imperial tribute scheme, though population groups were combined for this purpose in a way that does not correspond (Herodotus, III.93–94) to satrapy boundaries that we can reconstruct (badly) for later periods. According to Strabo (XI.13.8◊), "Cappadocia paid the Persians yearly, in addition to the silver tax, fifteen hundred horses, two thousand mules, and fifty thousand sheep." The existence of a royal *dasmos* in Armenia (in horses) is attested in Xenophon (*Anab.* IV.5.24, 35). The Persian presence in Armenia and Cappadocia is deduced primarily from late texts and late evidence, which in itself illustrates the extent and vigor of the imperial diaspora. This is most especially indicated by the density of Iranian personal names in Cappadocia, by the use of Aramaic in official correspondence (cf. Diodorus XIX.23.3: satrap of Armenia) and private memos, and above all by the spread of Persian gods and religion, especially the worship of Anāhita, both in Zeleia (Strabo XI.8.4; XII.3.37) and in the Armenian district of Acilisene (Strabo XI.14.16; Plutarch, *Lucullus* 24.2–5). We may add that, in a story repeated by Ctesias (§§40–41), the central authority considered Armenia to be a place of exile and deportation, in addition to being a place to colonize.

In contrast, other evidence, at least at first sight, would lead us to stress the weakness of Achaemenid territorial dominion in these regions. First, we have Xenophon's tale of the adventures of the Greek mercenaries in Armenia. Though Xenophon does not entirely forget to mention that satrapal officers (Orontes, Tiribazus) were present, accompanied by significant forces, he does focus his tale on the opposition mounted by a whole series of peoples that he usually identifies via ethnographic characteristics that flaunt their exotic barbarity. This is the case for the Carduchi and Colchians and for the Macrones and Mossynoeci as well. But, here as elsewhere (chap. 16/11 above), the author's presentation must be qualified: these peoples also furnished contingents to the satrapal and royal armies—for example, in the Gaugamela campaign (Arrian III.8.4: peoples subsidiary to Media). Furthermore, a large number of Achaemenid luxury goods have been found in Colchis; their presence in the tombs probably is a result of gift exchanges between the Colchian aristocracy and the Great King's court. After all, these exchanges are made explicit in Herodotus's discussion of the donor peoples (III.97). The second argument in favor of the ongoing independence of these regions is derived from the presumed autonomy of all or part(s) of Cappadocia and Armenia when Alexander arrived, as well as their relations with the central authority during the Macedonian campaign and throughout the age of the Diadochi. But care is required in this case, too, and the material needs to be placed in context. For both Cappadocia and Armenia, we primarily have foundation legends that were situated in the Hellenistic period and were intended to justify the establishment of independent dynasties, each of them fictively connected to one of the Seven. Thus, it is clear that this literary genre must be handled with a great deal of caution (chap. 3/4). Moreover, we observe that the old satrap Orontes continued in his position in Armenia in 323 (Diodorus XIX.23.3; Polyaenus IV.8.3), and Cappadocia was (along with Paphlagonia and adjacent territories) among the still-unconquered regions that were granted to Eumenes at Cardia. But there is no reason to conclude from this that the situation was the same in the time of Darius III, who, as we have seen, drew many contingents from these regions. Armenia and Cappadocia remained beyond the control of Macedon quite simply because "Alexander did not invade, having been prevented from doing so by the urgency of his affairs when he was finishing the war with Darius. . . . Ariarathes, the ruler of Cappadocia . . . , had been overlooked by Alexander, owing to the struggle with Darius and its distractions, and he had enjoyed a very long respite as king of Cappadocia" (Diodorus XVIII.3.1; 16.1◊). The Macedonian thought it was enough to name Persian satraps: Sabictas/Abistamenes in Cappadocia (Arrian II.4.2; Quintus Curtius III.4.1) and Mithrenes in Armenia (Arrian III.16.5; Diodorus XVII.64.6; Quintus Curtius V.1.44). It seems clear that these satraps' power was largely fictitious or else limited to a subdistrict. Cappadocia, at any rate, was one of the recruiting bases used by the Persian generals who had escaped after the battle of Issus and attempted to launch a counterattack on the Macedonian rear (cf. Quintus Curtius IV.1.34). This was also the time when some of them struck coins at Sinope.

We heartily welcome the truly remarkable surge of new evidence, both inscriptional and archaeological, that has emerged, especially from ancient Armenia. The latest archaeological and ceramic investigations appear to confirm the presence of highly developed Achaemenid settlements, especially at sites near Lake Van. At Altintepe, the only example of an apadana in a satrapal capital has been found, and at Arin-Berd very rare wall paintings have been discovered in an Achaemenid building. An even more remarkable discovery is the find of fragments of three Elamite tablets at Armavir-blur; according to the most recent (but already disputed!) interpretation, they are very similar to the Persepolis tablets and deal with levying taxes (tithes?) in kind (head of cattle; grain) and depositing them in the quartermaster's storehouses. These documents testify to the existence of imperial archives at the excavated site and also to the presence of a developed provincial administration (perhaps a *frataraka*). If we add that the site of Armavir-blur (Urartian Argištihinili) was continuously occupied from the Urartian period to the Hellenistic period, that the Hellenistic seal impressions from Artašāt attest to both the Achaemenid legacy and so-called "Greco-Persian" influence, and that even more recently Achaemenid column bases have been discovered at another site, we must at some point realize that the perception of Achaemenid Armenia that we have hitherto held is in the process of total reorganization.

15. From Ecbatana to Cyropolis

The eastern Iranian contingents used the *via militaris* to join Darius at Babylon in preparation for the battle that was about to take place at Gaugamela. As we have already emphasized, apart from a few scattered notes dating to the reigns of Artaxerxes I (Ctesias

Map 6. Lands and peoples of the Iranian Plateau and Central Asia under Achaemenid rule.

§31; Plutarch, *Them.* 31.3) and Artaxerxes II (chap. 15/8 on the imperial realm), the Hellenistic reports break a lengthy silence regarding the lands of the Iranian Plateau. We must again emphasize that, before Alexander's arrival at Bactra (modern Balkh), data on the plateau satrapies are limited to mere summaries because Alexander's march was so rapid. Other than the name of the ruling satrap, we receive meager information on the boundaries of the satrapies and the names of the official residences (*basileia*), which were often fortified (Zadracarta in Hyrcania; Artacoana in Aria). The excavations at Old Kandahār, where an Elamite tablet of Persepolis type has been found, and Dahan-i Ghulaman (Seistan) nonetheless attest to Achaemenid presence on the Plateau. The descriptions of the countries are unfortunately very incomplete: not a single author, for example, makes the slightest reference to the network of Bactrian canals discovered by the archaeologists. The reason is quite simple: first, Alexander's march to Bactra was fairly rapid, and furthermore, the military historians were interested only in features of the countryside to the extent that they figured in Alexander's campaigns or, possibly, if they exhibited "exotic" characteristics that might stimulate the imagination of their readers. Because they were following Alexander step by step, the ancient authors aim their spotlights on certain peoples that they differentiate on the basis of their country's ecology and/or the resistance that they put up to the Macedonians. This, for example, explains the long discussions of the Mardians of the Caspian and, conversely, of the Ariaspi/Benefactors of the Helmand Delta; the latter were rewarded by Alexander to commemorate their "good deeds" in honor of Cyrus and because of the aid that they had provided to Alexander himself. Not even the reports on Bactria and Sogdiana are particularly detailed. The Oxus (Amu Darya) seems to have been the boundary between the two regions (Arrian III.28.9; IV.15.7; 16.1), and the Iaxartes (Syr Darya) was 'the boundary of the Persian Empire' (*horion tēs Persōn archēs*); the border was also marked in the countryside by the town of Cyropolis, "the last city founded by Cyrus" (Strabo XI.11.4◇). The strongly fortified Cyropolis was actually just the largest (Arrian IV.2.2) of a series of seven fortified towns located on the Iaxartes, and Alexander and his generals had to subdue these towns arduously, one by one (Arrian IV.1–3). A large number of unnamed fortified towns or fortresses are also reported by the ancient authors and by archaeologists in both Sogdiana and Bactria.

First of all, the texts from the times of Alexander and the Diadochi allow us to draw up a list of what the Hellenistic authors (especially Diodorus) call (though not without confusion) the Upper Satrapies. In 323, Diodorus names Paropamisadae, Arachosia and Gedrosia, Aria and Drangiana, Bactria and Sogdiana, Parthia and Hyrcania, Carmania (XVIII.3.3: most of them in pairs). The enumeration of 320 scarcely differs (XVIII.39.6): Carmania, Parthia, Aria and Drangiana, Bactria and Sogdiana, Paropamisadae; and the list is similar around 317–316 (XIX.14.6): Carmania, Arachosia, Paropamisadae, Aria and Drangiana, Bactria. These data correspond by and large to the situation at the time of Darius III, so far as we can reconstruct it on the basis of the ancient reports: Parthia-Hyrcania (including the Tapyrians), Aria, Drangiana, Arachosia, Bactria, Sogdiana, Carmania, Gedrosia. At the battle of Gaugamela, Arrian (III.8.3–4◇) lists the Bactrians and Saka (led by the satrap of Bactria, Bessus), the Arachotians and "Indian hillmen" (led by Barsaentes, satrap of Arachosia), the Aryans (led by Satibarzanes, satrap of Aria), the Parthians, Hyrcanians, and Tapyrians (commanded by Phratapharnes; we find out later [III.23.4; 28.2] that he was satrap).

Such a catalog in itself can inform us only very imperfectly about the Persian administrative organization of these regions. The main interpretive problem comes from the context of the Macedonian campaigns in Bactria-Sogdiana. Let us briefly review them. Bessus, a relative of the Great King and satrap of Bactria, was the driving force behind the conspiracy that led to the murder of Darius in July 330, along with Nabarzanes, chiliarch of the royal cavalry, and Barsaentes, satrap of Arachosia and Drangiana (III.21.1). Bessus backtracked to Bactria to lead the resistance to the Macedonian offensive, where he had himself proclaimed "King of Asia" (III.25.3◇)—that is, Great King—under the name Artaxerxes (Diodorus XVII.74.1–2; 78.7; Quintus Curtius VI.6.13). He enlisted Satibarzanes, whom Alexander had retained as satrap of Aria (III.25.1), in his cause:

Satibarzanes soon perished in the Macedonian counterattack, and the same fate befell Barsaentes, who was executed after the Indian hill peoples turned him over to Alexander. Meanwhile, at first at least, disturbances continued in Alexander's rear: the new satrap of Aria, Arsamenes, showed no loyalty to the Macedonians (III.29.4); he probably stayed in communication with Bessus. Moreover, Bessus, who had assumed supreme authority (albeit falsely), had named a satrap in Parthia (IV.7.1).

Should we conclude from this that the authority of the satrap in Bactra extended throughout the Upper Satrapies and thus that his command extended eastward from Ecbatana? We know for certain that this was true in the Seleucid period, but was it also the case earlier, under the later Achaemenids? It is hard to offer a defensible response to this question, since the texts are open to conflicting interpretations. The only evidence along these lines is a passage in Diodorus (XVI.50.8), where the information (that Bagoas was entrusted with the Upper Satrapies under Artaxerxes III) seems dubious—which is not to say that it should be thrown out. We must note that aside from this text we see nothing that would establish a bridge between the Achaemenid period and the Hellenistic era with any certainty. Until more evidence appears, we can stress only that the Seleucid innovation itself goes back to the age of the Diadochi, because the earliest attestation comes from 316, when Pithon took on the duties of both satrap of Media and "*strategos* of the Upper Satrapies" (Diodorus XIX.14.1). The satraps of these regions combined their contingents and held common council (XIX.14–15). But the political context (their joint opposition to Eumenes) is very specific, and the fact that they joined forces does not necessarily imply that by doing so the satraps were following an Achaemenid precedent. For one thing, in 331 the eastern Iranian contingents were led by several satraps (Bessus, Barsaentes, Satibarzanes; Arrian III.8.3); for another, the motivations of the satraps allied with Bessus do not seem to have derived from the fact that the satrap in Bactra was regularly granted authority over the entire area but basically from personal motives—not least the desire to preserve their own position (cf. Arrian III.21.5). In any case, the death of Darius III created an entirely new situation, and Bessus's proclamation of kingship obviously did not make the situation any better. Finally, after Darius's death, Bessus's personal authority held priority with his Bactrian horsemen (III.21.4; cf. Diodorus XVII.74.1) and over the alliance with some of the Saka chiefs (III.8.3).

The only thing that seems clear is that the military responsibilities of the satrap in Bactra went beyond the usual boundaries of Bactria, since at Gaugamela he led all of the Bactrians, the Sogdians, a Sakian contingent, and a unit provided by the Indians who were adjacent to Bactra (III.8.3). The differing accounts allow us to think that in the time of Darius III, the authority of the satrap in Bactra extended to Sogdiana, where no separate satrap is ever named, either before or after Alexander. The satrap in Bactra appears to have undertaken active relations with some of the Saka in this official role: thus, he was their supreme commander when the Bactrian contingent and a Sakian troop led by their chief Mauaces joined Darius III in 332–331, on the basis of a *symmakhia* entered into with Darius (Arrian III.8.3). Throughout Alexander's war in Sogdiana-Bactria, Bessus and later Spitamenes would find aid among some of the Sakian peoples. Cooperation between the Sakians and the Persians, which is known from even before Alexander's offensive beyond the Iaxartes (Syr Darya), obviously belonged to the long-standing relationship between the Achaemenid authorities and the Saka, who were usually divided into many groups but who put up a united front in the face of attacks by their enemies. If, as Strabo writes (XI.11.4), and according to Darius I (*DPh*), the Syr Darya represented the boundary of direct Persian dominion, no general state of permanent hostility between the Persians and Saka can be inferred. In fact, the information provided by Alexander's old historians must be placed in context. Arrian, recalling what he took to be Alexander's intentions when he planned to found a town on the Syr Darya, wrote: "The site was suitable for the city to rise to greatness, and it would be well placed for any eventual invasion of Scythia and as a defence bastion (*prophylakēs*) of the country against the raids of the barbarians dwelling on the other side of the river." (IV.1.4◊). That hostilities frequently broke out between the Persian forces and some Sakian peoples does not seem open to doubt. Darius I's campaign is irrefutable testimony to this fact, and the action taken in that case (replacement of one Sakian king with another: *DB* V §74) illustrates a general practice. But to deduce that there were permanent hostilities is to attribute to the word "boundary" a modern sense and to postulate that there was a break pure and simple between the sedentary world and the nomadic world—which was certainly not the case. Some Sakian peoples (who had in part become sedentary) lived in close contact with the populations of Sogdiana (e.g., Arrian III.28.8). Furthermore, the mobilization of the Saka against Alexander was a response to a brand-new situation created by both the "Achaemenid void" and the Macedonian offensive—two phenomena that happened to coincide. The fortified towns founded by Cyrus on the Iaxartes did not merely function to defend against Saka "aggression," contrary to what Arrian and many others would have us think. These citadels also served as refuges for the "barbarians near the river" (IV.1.4;◊ 2.6; 3.1). It seems quite likely that there were also many Sakian/Scythian refugees. Note, too, that in Cyropolis alone 15,000 fighters were massed (IV.3.4: *makhimoi*); in this case, again, the theory of Sakian participation in the defense of the town seems reasonable—perhaps something like the Arab mercenaries (*misthōtoi*) who contributed to the defense of Gaza alongside Batis the governor and Persian soldiers (Arrian II.25.4). This is the context of the *symmakhia* between Darius and Mauaces.

The Syr Darya, "boundary of Persian power" (because the satrapy ended on the western bank), was certainly not an impregnable boundary; the towns founded by Cyrus were also trading posts between the world of the steppes and Bactria-Sogdiana—which accounts (very specifically, even) for the carpets with Achaemenid motifs discovered in a Uralic tomb in Pazyryk; these carpets could have come from weavers in Sogdiana-Bactria. From this perspective, Alexander's policy represents a break from, rather than a continuation of, the policy that can be attributed to the Great Kings. Whatever his long-term goals may have been, Alexander was driven by an immediate concern—not to leave a single pocket of resistance behind him (Arrian IV.3.5). The Great Kings, on the other hand, had learned during the long course of their administration that they were well advised to maintain order on the "boundary" and that it was best to establish cooperative relations with the Saka chiefs, some of whom had been granted an autonomous status that went hand in hand with imperial military obligations (to furnish military contingents during satrapal and royal mobilizations). The tales of Herodotus show that the Saka were among the elite of the royal army, alongside other Iranian contingents, such as the Bactrians themselves, the Persians, the Medes, and even the Indians (e.g., VIII.113). At Gaugamela, Sakian horsemen fought alongside the Bactrian horsemen (Arrian III.13.3). We also know that after the establishment of Achaemenid dominion, many Saka had been settled in Babylonia as a part of the *ḥaṭru* system.

But what authority did the satrap have over the territories placed directly under his authority because of the position conferred on him by the Great King? On this point, we have relatively coherent, though indirect, indications. Generalized attempts at resisting Alexander's advances developed, led successively by Bessus and Spitamenes; but other resistance was organized locally by senior individuals whom Arrian often identifies as hyparchs. According to Arrian, the number of hyparchs was quite large; this is implied in his report, for example, that "many other hyparchs had taken refuge" on the Rock of Chorienes (IV.21.1✧). The phrase also seems to imply that there was an internal hierarchy within this category. But we know that the word hyparch is highly polysemous. Referring to the same people, Quintus Curtius uses the word "satrap" several times: in the Sogdian district of Nautaca, "the satrap was Sisimithres" (VIII.2.19✧); Oxyarthes the Bactrian was "an illustrious satrap" (VIII.4.21✧); elsewhere, Quintus Curtius himself uses the word "satrap" to describe Orxines, though in this case it is clear from the context that he is using the term for the chief of the Pasargadae tribe (X.1.22). Thus, the vocabulary by itself will not help advance the discussion of the relationship between hyparchs and satraps any more, for example, than the use of the words "satrap" (in a verb form) and "satrapy" in Xenophon (*Hell.* III.1.10, 12) by itself allows us to determine the nature of the connections created, in Aeolis, between Pharnabazus, Zenis, and Mania.

In each case, the terms refer to authority exercised over a territory. This is very clearly confirmed by all of the texts dealing with hyparchs: each hyparch had a more or less extensive territory organized around a princely residence that was located on a fortified acropolis. The hyparch's authority was expressed in two ways: first, the huge amounts of food reserves that he built up show that he imposed duties on farm produce (cf. especially Quintus Curtius VII.11.1 and Arrian IV.21.1); second, he enrolled the people who worked his lands into militias. His territorial authority is also attested by the steps taken, after their surrender, against those whom Arrian calls hyparchs and Quintus Curtius satraps: the territory of Ariamazes and its inhabitants were handed over to the new towns (Quintus Curtius VII.11.29). The examples of Sisimithres and Oxyartes confirm this point: in both cases, their power is called *imperium* [= *arkhē*] and the context makes it clear that their power was territorial (Quintus Curtius VIII.2.32; VIII.4.21), and the same was true for the hyparchs listed by Arrian (cf. Arrian IV.21.9). It is obvious that the local chiefs had all the lands at their disposal (cf. Quintus Curtius VIII.1.1).

A crucial question remains: were these hyparchs fully independent of the satrap? We may begin our answer with a famous passage in Arrian (IV.1.5✧): after Spitamenes handed Bessus over to the Macedonians, he stirred up the Sogdians and attempted to incite a Bactrian revolt in Alexander's rear. He met with some success, since "it was a pretext they gave for the revolt that Alexander had instructed the hyparchs of that country (*hoi hyparkhoi tēs khōras ekeinēs*) to come to a joint conference (*syllogos*) at Zariaspa, the greatest city, and that this conference (*syllogos*) was not for their benefit." The word *syllogos* poses an obvious problem: does it refer to an institution borrowed by Alexander from the Achaemenid period, or does it simply refer to an ad hoc meeting? We may remark that Arrian uses similar words to describe an incident in India: through a herald, Alexander ordered Taxilas and the other Indians to come to a meeting, "each at their earliest convenience; Taxilas and the other hyparchs (*kai hoi alloi hyparkhoi*) complied, bringing the gifts the Indians prize most" (IV.22.6✧). However, the word *syllogos* does not appear here; furthermore, the context is not exactly the same: in the incident in

India, Alexander let it be known that, according to custom, the Indian leaders had to come submit to him, bringing ritual gifts; in the situation in Bactria, the hyparchs had already surrendered to Alexander, and Bactria was already essentially calm (e.g., Arrian III.28.1). While we could imagine that Alexander might have wanted to require new proofs of loyalty from the Bactrian hyparchs, we also have the strong impression that the gathering in the *syllogos* reveals additional motives.

We know that the word *syllogos* is used several times for the meeting that was period-ically organized in several gathering places (*syllogos*) in the Empire. It was at the *syllogos* that territorial troops were reviewed. This is quite clearly explained by Xenophon: "The king annually reviews the mercenaries and all the other troops ordered to be under arms, assembling all but the men in the citadels at the place of muster (*syllogos*), as it is called" (*Oec.* IV.6✧). It is clear that the word takes on a technical and institutional sense in this reference. Other passages in Xenophon confirm that these reviews were held regularly (*Cyr.* VIII.6.15), and he mentions some of the locations: Castolus (*Hell.* I.4.3) or Cas-tolou Pedion in Lydia (I.9.7) and Thymbara in Syria/Ebir Nāri (*Cyr.* VI.2.11). There is hardly any doubt that such assembly points existed in every satrapy or military region (which could include several satrapies). This is almost certainly the context of the Baby-lonian texts regarding military levies (at Ur and Uruk). The word used, *andēsu*, which appears in its Aramaic form (*hndz'*) in the documents from Egypt, was borrowed from Old Persian *handaisa 'convocation' (in a place fixed by the administration).

Does this information provide the background for the *syllogos* of Zariaspa? To answer the question, we must turn to the texts dealing with relations between Bessus and the Bactrian horsemen—who, we know, played an important role alongside Bessus in the plot against Darius; according to Arrian (III.21.4), it was the Bactrians who recognized Bessus's unrivaled authority, and as a result he had seven or eight thousand Bactrian horsemen on his side (III.28.8; Quintus Curtius VII.4.20). When he made the decision to cross the Oxus (Amu Darya), Bessus was abandoned by most of his horsemen. The parallel passages in Quintus Curtius and Arrian are entirely typical. The former writes: the Bactrians "slipped away each to his own village" (*in suos quisque vicos dilapsi*; VII.4.20✧); and the latter: the Bactrian horsemen "dispersed in different directions to their homes" (*allos allēi epi ta sphōn*; III.28.10✧). It is clear that the phrases used are con-nected with the conscription procedure: Bessus's (satrapal) contingent was composed of subgroups, each of which was levied in a particular territory (compare Arrian III.19.2 and VII.15.2). This implies that some of a satrapy's territory was divided into "modules" that formed the basis of the administrative organization. The simplest explanation is that conscription was organized locally in each of these "modules" by those whom Arrian calls hyparchs. This is confirmed by Quintus Curtius's parallel passage on the Zariaspa meeting. He also took notice of the rumors spread around Bactria by Spitamenes and his allies, writing in fact that they "had spread abroad the report that all the Bactrian cavalry (*bactrianos equites . . . omnes*) were being sent for by the king, in order that they might be slain" (VII.6.15✧). It thus seems clear that the Bactrian *syllogos* was one example of an Achaemenid institution known elsewhere: each hyparch brought the contingent he had mustered in his territory (cf. also Arrian III.28.10). When Quintus Curtius used the phrase "all the Bactrian cavalry," he might have had in mind a fact about the wealth of the territory that he cites elsewhere: "The cavalry of the Bactriani had amounted to 30,000" (VII.4.30✧). Whatever value is accorded (or not) to the number given, we have the impression that the information presupposes the existence of an archive on which, in Bactria as elsewhere, the administration was able to base its orders for meeting at the "place of muster." Furthermore, from this viewpoint, Sogdiana constituted a special sub-district, even though it was included in the same district: in Arrian (III.28.10✧), 'the horsemen from Sogdiana' (*hoi ek tēs Sogdianēs hippeis*) are distinguished from the Bactrian horsemen. Whatever the circumstances, the conclusion seems inevitable: on the one hand, by convening a *syllogos* of the Bactrian hyparchs at Zariaspa, Alexander intended to reinforce his army just as he was preparing to launch a trans-Oxus campaign; on the other hand, because he had just named a satrap in Bactria (III.29.1), all he had to do in order to achieve this goal was to take advantage of an Achaemenid institution that Bessus himself must certainly have used when he received the order from Darius III to assemble all of the contingents of his district (cf. Arrian III.8.3).

If this interpretation holds up, it suggests a number of reflections, and they in turn stimulate further investigations. First of all, Bactria did not escape the central authority's organizational energy, which can be observed in other satrapies. The conscription system resembles, in form at least, the method described by Xenophon in a passage that has already been quoted many times (*Cyr.* VIII.8.20✧): "In times past it was their national custom that those who held lands should furnish cavalrymen from their possessions and that these, in case of war, should also take the field." Thus, when the satrap issued an order to assemble, the Persians of the imperial diaspora who had received lands from the king each had to supply his contingent of horsemen (e.g., Xenophon, *Hell.* III.4.10). Generally, anyone who held a *dōrea* was subject to this obligation (e.g., Diodorus XVII.19.4); this was true of Persians and even of Greek beneficiaries in Asia Minor (this explains the presence of Gongylids in Cyrus the Younger's army: Xenophon, *Anab.* II.1.3). The Bactrian *syllogos* thus was just one instance of a general practice. It was apparently unique in one respect: as far as we are able to determine, the role of the hyparchs was anchored in Bactria's long history. They came from a local aristocracy that undoubtedly possessed broader territorial authority than that enjoyed by the recipients of donations. But, at the same time, as would be true for any subordinate, the hyparchs themselves were certainly bound by duty to be absolutely loyal. For this reason, some of Alexander's directives may reflect practices that were not specific to the Macedonian conquest.

In particular, let us recall how Ariamazes and his people were punished. He and those close to him were put to death; then "a multitude of those who had surrendered, together with the booty in money, was given to the settlers in the new cities. Artabazus was left to govern the rock and the region adjacent to it" (Quintus Curtius VII.11.29✧). The only unique item in this account involves the beneficiaries of the allotments: the settlers in the newly founded cities. The remainder of the story accords well with many examples taken from Achaemenid history, which show that at any time, particularly in case of a rebellion, a beneficiary of lands might find himself dispossessed by the Great King. No allocation of land was guaranteed to be permanent, whether it was a gift or a territorial right that might reach back before the conquest. Even the fiscal assessment imposed by the hyparchs in their territory was not really anything new; obligations imposed on holders of *dōrea* were also the same as they had been in the past. If this were not true, who would have paid the Bactrian tribute? To be able to attach certainty to our conclusion, we would have to know why the local elites were motivated to ally with the conquering kings, Cyrus and Darius. But there does not seem to be any reason why, a priori, the process had to be utterly unique in Bactria. Instead, we are led to think that after the conquest the Great Kings had acted no differently than Alexander did in his time; after Chorienes' submission, he "entrusted (*edōke*) this very stronghold (*to khōrion*) to him and made him hyparch of the people he had previously administered" (Arrian IV.21.9;✧ cf. Quintus Curtius VIII.4.21 [Oxyarthes]). In Alexander's thinking and practice, this action derived not from any desire to perpetuate an independent local power but instead was simply a confirmation of a position Chorienes had already held in the Achaemenid period. In another case, the Macedonian confiscated a hyparch's land and allocated it to the inhabitants of the new towns (Quintus Curtius VII.11.29) as an expression of the rights of the conqueror over land and peasantry. For Alexander, in fact, the conquests were considered "land conquered at spearpoint" (Arrian VII.6.1). The Great Kings certainly had not acted any differently. Or are we supposed to think that Bactria was the only one of all the conquered territories that was not part of the *tagē* system (cf. chaps. 10/7, 11/10)?

The available evidence refers, albeit allusively, to other ways in which the central authority intervened in the life of the satrapy. First of all, it is clear that there was a Persian diaspora in the country. This is implied by Berossus's mention of the erection of statues of Anāhita in Bactra (chap. 15/8). All of the satraps were Persian, sometimes relatives of the Great King's family. However, it is difficult to go any further on this point because of the relative similarity of Iranian personal names. Aside from the case of the hyparchs who opposed Alexander, it is difficult to distinguish men who are identified as Bactrians. Scarcely any can be named other than the Orontes who, according to the Pergamum Chronicle (*OGIS* 265), was of Bactrian background (*to genos baktrios*); and even this example raises more questions than it answers. Let us simply say that it is certain that Bactrians had settled in other satrapies, either on their own or as garrison-colonists. In addition, Bactria itself did not escape the colonization system set up elsewhere in the Empire. After 479, Milesians (the Branchidae) had been resettled by Xerxes in Sogdiana. They at that time lived in a fortified town, held territory, and were incorporated into the local population (Quintus Curtius VII.5.28–35; Strabo XI.11.4). Herodotus (IV.202, 204), in his passage on the Persian expedition in Cyrenaica in 513, recalls that the Barcaeans, who had been brought to Susa as prisoners of war, received from Darius a village (*kōmē*) in Bactria as a gift (*edōke*), and they still lived there in the time of Herodotus. Like other 'border regions' (*eskhatiai*; cf. Aelian, *VH* VI.14; Diodorus XVII, Contents), Bactria was perceived by the Greeks as a place to which people were banished (cf. Herodotus VI.9)—which is to say, from the Achaemenid point of view, a land for colonization.

To be sure, this handful of evidence looks pathetic; but it is quite clear that the ancient sources offer nothing more than a highly partial sample of the state of affairs, because of their orientation. The information in them only makes sense when it is placed in a general imperial perspective. Although it cannot be proved, it is likely that, following the pattern of the deportees who were settled in Babylonia (cf. Quintus Curtius V.1.2; Arrian III.11.5) and the Persian Gulf (Herodotus III.93; VII.80), the deportee-colonists of Achaemenid Sogdiana and Bactria were included in the military and tribute organization of the satrapy. There is no longer any doubt that the fortified town of the Branchidae was part of a network of fort-towns and citadels that the ancient accounts unanimously agree was extremely dense. Work at the site of ancient Samarkand (Afrasiab) in particular confirms the strength of the citadel's position during the Achaemenid period. It is likely that, as in Mysia (Xenophon, *Anab.* VII.8.15), Cataonia-Cappadocia (Diodorus XIX.16.3), and Margiana (Quintus Curtius VII.10.15), these fortresses maintained easy communication with each other.

We must now address a major interpretive problem posed by the archaeological discovery of a very dense network of canals in eastern Bactria—a problem that has already been briefly mentioned (chap. 2/5). From the archaeological point of view, the Achaemenid imperial administration had nothing to do with either the conception or the development of the irrigation canals. This conclusion is based on a series of observations and inferences that we may review briefly. First, the works that can be dated to the first half of the first millennium belong to the *longue durée* of Bactrian history, because the first irrigation canals go back to the Bronze Age. Second, the pottery is specifically Bactrian and does not show the slightest imperial influence. At this point we bring other evidence to bear and refer to Diodorus; in a story on the deeds of Semiramis, he states that the queen's expedition against Bactria met with resistance from Bactrians led by a certain Oxyarthes, who is called king (II.6.2). Without saying in so many words that royal institutions were perpetuated after the conquest, archaeologists nonetheless think that both before and after the Achaemenid conquest there was what they call a "Bactrian entity"; the only evidence of a Bactrian central state, however, appears as military and tribute assessments. In the opinion of the archaeologists, it was the representatives of this "entity" who were in charge of the canalization and irrigation projects that were carried out throughout the Achaemenid period—what they call the "Achaemenid" period, the quotation marks indicating that the term serves only to define a chronological point of reference rather than making any claim about a political fact. In this interpretation, the real break took place after the Greek conquest (apparently even later than Alexander's conquest); archaeological data of every kind (including pottery) show that at the point of discontinuity a genuine colonization policy was established, and there is no evidence that it went back to the previous period. Finally, in response to objections, the archaeologists sometimes state that Bactria's status was not really different from that of other regions of the Empire, because the real and active presence of the central authority in the provinces is very poorly documented and, in any case, does not imply an actual takeover of land and people other than in the form of military and tribute assessments, establishment of garrisons, and installation of a small number of administrators—the basics of real power continued to be exercised by the local "entities."

We see immediately that these theories support and orient the general discussion of Achaemenid imperial development that has been carried on, especially in the last few years. However, we can respond that to draw parallels with other satrapies in the Empire, without undertaking regional analysis beforehand, seems singularly unwise. There is a passage in Polybius that implies that the Great Kings took an interest in transporting water and irrigation in Hyrcania (X.28); and furthermore, the Babyonian tablets inarguably show that management of the canals belonged to a branch of the royal administration. All by themselves, these reminders rule out the generalizations that in reality are derived from a very "Bactrocentric" vision—as will be confirmed by a careful cataloguing of archaeological discoveries in the various lands of the Empire over the last twenty years or so (chap. 16/18 below). We may add, without needing to put too much emphasis on the point, that it is utterly indefensible, methodologically speaking, to resort to Diodorus for support. But these criticisms do not exhaust the subject; far from it! The real problem is that it is extremely difficult to build bridges between the literary evidence and the archaeological evidence, each of which supports a picture that contradicts the other—or, more precisely, pictures that the historian and the archaeologist have not done well at reconciling. If a "Bactrian entity" really was active around 330, there is no trace of it in the texts. Nevertheless, a recent presentation of archaeological discoveries in the region refers to it as "a still poorly known and badly defined entity that existed well before the Persians" (B. Lyonnet). However, as we have seen, the ancient evidence portrays Bactria as a country basically divided among "hyparchs" who derived their authority from the satrap. As soon as the Wittfogel model is invoked (as archaeologists are regularly wont to do), we cannot see how the minor and major hyparchs of Bactria could have taken responsibility for operations of this sort, which necessitated interregional cooperation and the drafting of thousands of workers.

Furthermore, the contrast between the Achaemenid and Hellenistic periods, which is archaeologically clearly marked and absolutely undeniable, must not be pushed too far. We should first of all recall that the physical presence of the Achaemenid administration in the provinces (aside from the *strategoi* and the garrison commanders) is often known only from incidental and accidental discoveries such as, for example, the discovery of an Elamite tablet in the fortifications of Old Kandahār. If we take the example of Persia itself, the discovery of the Persepolis archives completely altered the prior view of the strength of bureaucratic tradition at the heart of the Empire. As has already been explained at length (chap. 11/6–7), the extension of administrative practices to the provinces is proved in some cases and extremely likely in others (even if attested only in tablets that mention official travel between the imperial capitals and the eastern Iranian satrapies, including Bactra). Could Bactria have escaped the trend toward integration of the satrapies into the Empire? Only the discovery (which is statistically rather unlikely) of the satrapal archives of Bactra would allow us to answer the question with certainty; the theory proposed here is that the administration would have included (as in Babylonia) a special department of water and canals. It is true that in Babylonia we know of this department only from indirect references that show up in private files (the Murašū archives)! In the absence of such evidence from Bactra, we must be content with an observation: the Achaemenid tablet and the Greek-Aramaic bilingual from Kandahār demonstrate that there were archives in the capital of Arachosia and that the language of the Achaemenid chancelleries spread throughout the Iranian Plateau: "Two centuries after the Great Kings, we find [at Kandahār] the same sort of documentation [that we find in Achaemenid Egypt], the same language similarly suffused with Iranian words. . . . The use of Aramaic shows that we are actually in an Iranian province where the traditions of the Achaemenid chancelleries were maintained" (É. Benveniste). At Ai-Khanūm itself, an Aramaic ostracon appears to be residual evidence of this. Furthermore, the inscriptions (in Greek and Aramaic) of the treasury give expression to an elaborate financial administration that must have owed much to Achaemenid precedents. Thus, we would simply like to emphasize one more time that the silence of Achaemenid evidence from this area must be interpreted with great caution and care. These observations obviously do not allow us to suggest that there was a satrapal department of water and canals in Achaemenid Bactria; they merely allow us to not exclude the possibility.

Let us then return to the argument from pottery, which appears to rule out imperial involvement. If we imagine that this argument is decisive *in itself*, there is no reason to continue the discussion. Conversely, the undeniable break (in the long run) that accompanied the Macedonian conquest must be explained. The multiplicity of archaeological traces of the Greek presence reflects a colonization policy that contrasts with the Achaemenid practice (we can make the same observation for Egypt). But this very notable difference does not necessarily imply that from the Achaemenid era to the Hellenistic period they passed from a lax and superficial dominion to micromanagement of land and water. In the Achaemenid period, in fact, imperial power was molded into the local traditions (particularly on the technical level); it thus cannot be immediately "read" in the layout of the canals or the shape of the pottery—so much so that the Achaemenids appear strangely absent. If we grant these premises, we must also grant that the uses of Bactrian pottery and satrapal intervention are not mutually exclusive. This interpretation offers the advantage, at least in the historian's eyes, of spotlighting the single authority presented by the texts (the satrap) and relegating to the wings a "Bactrian entity" of which not the slightest trace has been found—even though the time when the Great King disappeared provided circumstances that were particularly favorable to political affirmation of and resurrection of evidence for the "entity." It is safe to say that the discussion is not over. . . .

16. *From the Punjab to the Indus Delta*

As difficult as the state of the evidence is in Bactria-Sogdiana, it becomes even more desperate in the Indus Valley. After the royal catalogs (lists and depictions of peoples of the Empire) and the many references in the Persepolis tablets and Herodotus, the lands of the Indus are hardly ever mentioned in the extant documentation. Let us recall, however, that some texts from the time of Artaxerxes II imply that the Indian kings at that time continued to demonstrate their submission by sending gifts and tribute (chap. 15/8) and that these countries also sent contingents to Darius III (cf. Arrian III.8.4, 6; Quintus Curtius IV.9.2). When Alexander arrived in the Punjab, the ancient texts make hardly any allusion to the presence of authorities installed by the former central authority. We are tempted to infer from this that the Achaemenids had lost control of these lands. But is this certain? We do well to be cautious. On the one hand, as we have already emphasized, there no longer was an Achaemenid State; on the other, it is difficult to claim that authorities about whom we know nothing after Darius I had simply disappeared. Without going into detail (which often escapes us anyway), it is clear that the regions and peoples of the Indus Valley and between the Indus and Hydaspes Rivers enjoyed a wide variety of internal organization and external relationships. This is evident in the diversity of vocabulary: alongside kings and kinglets (*reguli*: Quintus Curtius X.1.1), we find *ethnē*, cities, etc., though we are not always able to distinguish clearly the articulation of their powers. Arrian often mentions hyparchs, who could head a more or less extensive *khōra* (IV.22.8; 24.1; 25.5; 25.7; 30.5). The problem, here as elsewhere, consists in understanding what part of Alexander's decrees represent continuities with Achaemenid administration; that sorting this out is not easy is an understatement. All we can do is to offer a few incidental remarks.

Even before crossing the Khyber Pass, Alexander sent a herald to to Omphis of the Taxila tribe, ordering him to come to him. Omphis "and the other hyparchs" did not fail

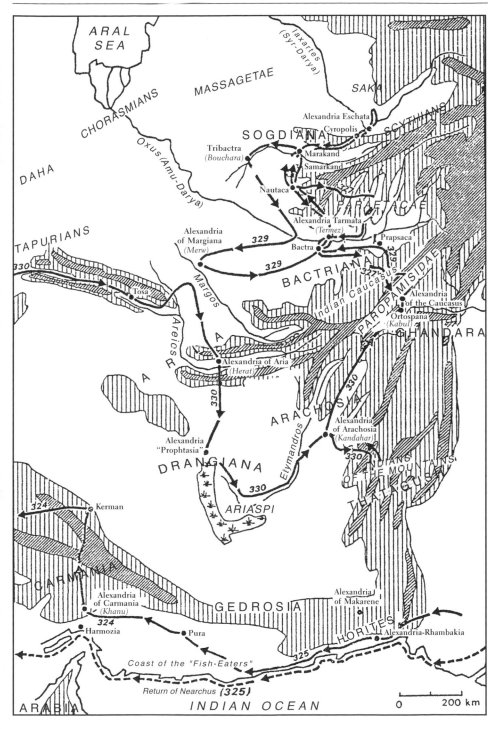

Map 7. Alexander in India and eastern Iran.

to do this, bringing what were considered very valuable gifts to Alexander (Arrian IV.22.6;✧ V.3.5–6). This ceremony was repeated all along Alexander's march: the presentation of *dōra* at a country's border was the very mark of submission to a king (e.g., V.8.3; 20.5; 29.4; 15.6). This clearly reflects an Achaemenid heritage: traditionally, when the king relocated among his peoples (chap. 5/4), the local authorities and the satrap were required to greet the royal caravan at the border with gifts (cf. VI.29.2). These gifts also bring to mind Ctesias's materials on the valuable gifts regularly sent to the Great King by the Indian kings in the time of Artaxerxes II. Elephants are mentioned frequently as one of the gifts offered to Alexander. No doubt this is how Darius obtained the twelve elephants (*a Dareo ex India acciti*) that were included among the gifts offered to Alexander by the satrap of Susa (Quintus Curtius V.2.10); the context leads us to believe that they were ceremonial beasts, perhaps retirees from a paradise at Susa. Moreover, Achaemenid submission was not limited only to offerings of this sort. The ambassador that Alexander sent to Abisares was instructed to summon the Indian king to "pay tribute (*stipendium pendere*) and meet Alexander at the frontier of his territories" (Quintus Curtius VIII.13.2✧). Later, Alexander set the amount of tribute that Abisares was required to pay him (Arrian V.29.5). It probably was the same in the Achaemenid period: the gifts regularly sent to the court were added to the tribute itself, in accord with general practice (chap. 10/3).

The reality of Achaemenid power in the countries on the west bank of the Indus can hardly be doubted. In a passage on the countries of the Iranian Plateau (Ariana), Strabo gives a list of peoples that he says runs from north to south, west of the Indus: the Paropamisadae, the Arachosians, the Gedrosians, "with the other tribes that occupy the seaboard"; and he adds the following detail: "The Indus lies, latitudinally, alongside all these places; and of these places, in part, some that lie along the Indus are held by Indians, although they formerly belonged to the Persians" (XV.2.9✧). The Babylonian versions of the royal lists lead us to conclude that the Paropamisadae occupied the country known as Gandhara in the Persian text. These Paropamisadae inhabited the entire Kabul Valley as far as the Cophen River. In 327, Alexander appointed the Persian Proexes as satrap there, and he was soon succeeded by Tyriaspes (Arrian III.28.4; VI.15.3).

Then we reach the border of the country of those whom Arrian rather vaguely calls "the Indians on this side of the river Indus" (IV.22.6✧), among whom he counts "Taxilas and the other hyparchs" (22.6✧), including the hyparchs of the city of Peucetis (22.8) and of the Aspasians (24.1). At the end of his "mountain campaign," the king made Nicanor "satrap of the region this side of the river Indus" (28.6✧). At the town of Taxila, finally, he named Philip, son of Machatas, "satrap of the Indians of this region" (V.8.3✧)—that is, "the country west of the Indus towards Bactria" (VI.2.3✧). It seems clear that the kings and local dynasts—to whom Alexander "restored" their kingdoms—submitted to him (VI.27.2; Taxila and Eudamus). It is quite likely that in whole or in part this was also the situation during the Achaemenid period. The composition of the military contingents brought to Gaugamela by Bessus of Bactria and Barsaentes of Arachosia is quite typical; Bessus was at the head of "those Indians who bordered on the Bactrians," and Barsaentes led "the Indian hillmen, as they were called" (III.8.3–4✧)— both of whom belonged to what in the Parthian period would be called White India.

The relationship between these countries is reflected in other details. We know that Taxilas was in contact with Alexander while the latter was in Sogdiana, promising the

Macedonian "to join him in a campaign against his enemies among the Indians" (Diodorus XVII.86.4;✧ cf. Quintus Curtius VIII.12.5–6). Sisicottus, who apparently came from the region of the Assacenians, was one of the Indians who had provided soldiers to Bessus; in Bactria, he joined Alexander (IV.30.4; V.20.7). Relations between the satrap of Kandahār and the "Indian hillmen" are also well attested. We know in fact that when Alexander arrived in Drangiana, Barzaentes fled to India (Quintus Curtius VI.6.36). Later, during his stay in Taxila, Alexander handed over "Barzaentes, the instigator of the revolt of the Arachosii . . . , as well as thirty elephants which had been captured at the same time with him. . . . Samaxus also, the king of a small part of India" (VIII.13.3–4✧). This king seems to have been pardoned by Alexander, if he is in fact the same person as the Sambus whom the king made "satrap of the Indian hillmen" (Arrian VI.16.3✧). He would have controlled the major passages between the southern Indus Valley and Arachosia, including the Bolan Pass, which must have been the one used by Craterus (VI.15.5). Arrian includes these two groups of people among those he calls the "self-governing Indians" (V.22.1–2;✧ 24.8). This phrase seems to refer to fully constituted states that had cities and leaders (*hēgemōnes*), nomarchs, and a ruling elite (V.22.1). We know that Alexander appointed a satrap over the Mallians and Oxydracae (Arrian VI.14.3). However, the Oxydracian delegates considered themselves self-governing, since they had not been governed by a satrap and had not paid tribute (VI.14.2). But, this does not mean that the Achaemenid state was completely absent (especially because self-government is defined in this context more with respect to the Indian kings than with respect to the Great King). Let us recall in particular that the Persians regularly hired mercenaries (in the Achaemenid sense; see chap. 17/3) from the (Ox)ydracae (Strabo XV.1.6) and that both peoples paid tribute to the Arachosians (Quintus Curtius X.7.14), which seems to imply that the Mallians and Oxydracae were subject to the authority of the satrap of Kandahār, a dependent relationship that may have been mediated by Samaxus/Sambus. According to this theory, Sambus would have been the Persians' agent in the lower Indus Valley, hiring mercenaries and collecting tribute and military payments such as the various elephants brought to Gaugamela by "the Indians on this side of the Indus" (Arrian III.8.6;✧ *FGrH* 151 F12–13), as well as the celebrated dogs of war (e.g., Diodorus XVII.92)—which the Great Kings raised on a large scale in Babylonia (Herodotus I.192).

Overall, then, though the literary sources lead us to believe that Achaemenid tutelage was not gone from the Indus Valley under Darius III, it is far more difficult to determine the breadth and depth of its influence in the absense of epigraphic and archaeological evidence. Let us simply mention, at the end of this section, a recently published late Indian coin. It has a legend in the Kharoṣthi script and the image of a person who has several Persian/Iranian characteristics: "Perhaps the satrap of the region, depicted in Achaemenid style with some Greek influence. . . . A hundred fifty years after the downfall of the Achaemenid Empire, among the Indians living between the Indus and the Jhelam, the official image of the person exercising supreme authority in the province was still that of a Persian-style satrap" (P. Bernard). There is almost no doubt that there was an imperial Persian diaspora in Taxila; an echo of this diaspora may possibly be found in the "Greco-Persian"-style sealings that are found in this country, similar to those found elsewhere.

17. From Pattala to Susa and Babylon: The Persians and the Persian Gulf

The tales of Nearchus provide some information, albeit fleeting and uncertain, regarding the Persian coast of the Persian Gulf. After the (Persian?) governor of Patala fled, Alexander took possession of the town and citadel (Arrian VI.17.5; 18). From Patala he set out for Baluchistan, shortly before the departure of the squadron led by Nearchus. The purpose of Nearchus's Memoirs was "to record . . . the way in which Alexander's navy reached Persia from India" (Arrian, *Indica* 17.7◊). With this goal in mind, he gives information on the fleet that the king had built, which was manned by sailors of Phoenician, Cypriot, and Egyptian origin (*Indica* 18.1; cf. Arrian, *Anab.* VI.1.6). Nearchus several times very clearly states the mission entrusted to him: "To reconnoitre the coasts that lay on the line of the voyage and the roadsteads and islets, to explore thoroughly every bay which they found, to learn about all the cities on the sea-coast, and to discover which land was fruitful and which desert" (*Indica* 32.11;◊ *Anab.* VII.20.10). To do so, the army and navy proceeded in convoy. Alexander had to provide food and water supplies for the sailors on a coast that had none (cf. *Anab.* VI.18.1; 20.4–5; 21.3; 22.3; 23.1; 23.3–8). On the first part of the voyage, Alexander and Nearchus came upon barbarian—i.e., "savage"—peoples. Although the local tradition in Gedrosia was that the region had already been traversed by Cyrus and Semiramis (*Anab.* VI.24.2–3; Strabo XV.2.5), there does not seem to have been any trace of the central state before they reached Pura, the official residence (*basileia*) of Gedrosia (VI.24.1). When Alexander reached Gedrosia, he appointed satraps for Gedrosia and Carmania (VI.27.1–2). Nearchus in his account describes the parallel progression of civilization (marked by the appearance of regions under cultivation) and the conditions for navigation. In Gedrosia—where for the first time he notes "cultivated trees, and inhabitants not quite like animals" (*Indica* 27.2◊)—Nearchus was able to employ a pilot, Hydraces, who promised to guide the navy as far as Carmania (§27.1). It was only when they arrived in Carmania that Nearchus's sailors, like Alexander's soldiers, could be certain they had returned to a civilized nation, not far from Cape Maceta (§32.4–7). At Harmozia (Hormuz), which had "an abundance of products of all kinds" (§33.2), Nearchus contacted 'the hyparch of this district' (*hyparkhos tēs khōrēs tautēs*; §§33.8;◊ 36.1); this is the first reference to an official who must have reported to the satrap of Carmania. Shortly afterward, we become aware of another governor (*hyparkhos*), Mazenes, who undoubtedly was a Persian who was in charge of the island of Oaracta; here the locals showed Nearchus the tomb of Erythras, whom local tradition took as the eponym of the Sea (§37.2–3). Mazenes served as pilot for the navy at this point (§37.2). Leaving Carmania, Nearchus noted that "the people live like the Persians, as they are their neighbours, and have the same military equipment" (§38.1◊). Arrian stresses that the Persian shore proper, even in the middle of winter, was especially "sunny and well supplied with all necessaries" (*Anab.* VI.28.7◊). Then, after a difficult sail along a coast littered with hazards, the navy "anchored at Taoce on the river Granis. Inland from here there was a Persian royal residence (*Perseōn basileion*), about 200 stades from the mouth of the river" (*Indica* §39.3◊). Nearchus and Alexander joined up not far from Susa, at a place called Pontoon Bridge (*Indica* 42.7–10).

But what can we conclude about Persian dominion in the Gulf, starting with the Iranian coast, from this meager information? It appears that, during the first part of the voyage, until the first contact between Nearchus and Alexander in Carmania, the coast was inhospitable: there were neither anchorages nor ports, at least as far as Cape Maceta (Ras Musandam). Notes on trade are also quite scarce. Those who lived near Cape Maceta assured Nearchus that "it was from there that cinnamon and other such commodities were imported into Assyria" (§32.7✧), but the Persian port of Apostana is the first place where Nearchus notes the presence of many transport/trading ships (§38.5: *ploia*). Furthermore, Nearchus's mission seems to imply that Alexander did not yet have any information about this region. These observations tempt us to conclude that the Persians controlled only part of the Iranian shore of the Gulf—that is, the Carmanian and Persian coasts. But silence must be interpreted cautiously. It is not very likely that Alexander would have thrown himself into this operation without any prior knowledge. We may note, for example, that a Persian—Bagoas, son of Pharnuches—was among the commanders of triremes (*Indica* 18.8) and that only from Gedrosia onward did the navy employ a pilot—whose name (Hydraces) sounds quite Iranian (§27.1). Furthermore, Nearchus was clearly picking and choosing in his descriptions of lands and peoples in accordance with the interests of his readers (he compares areas with Greek regions) and in terms of cultural stereotypes about the varying degrees of barbarism. Furthermore, Nearchus's own *Journal* was surely more detailed than the simple summary provided by Arrian and other authors. Pliny, for example, says that the river Anamis (*Indica* 33.2) was navigable and roiled with gold (VI.107). Strabo, also quoting Nearchus, states that the traditions about the founder Erythras on the island of Ogyris (Oaracta, where the hyparch Mazenes was in charge; *Indica* 37.2–3) were provided to Alexander's admiral by "Mithropastes, the son of Aristes, which latter was satrap of Phrygia; and that the former was banished by Dareius [III], took up residence in the island." (XVI.3.5✧). Together with the presence of the hyparch Mazenes, this reference serves to remind us that part of the Persian Gulf was still in Persian hands: the deportation of Mithropastes was just one in a long series of such actions that go back to the deportation of the Milesians to the head of the Gulf at Ampe (Herodotus VI.19–20)—which is surely to be identified with the village of Aginis at the mouth of the Tigris (*Indica* 42.4). We also know about the exile of Megabyzus to Kyrta, which Ctesias locates in the Persian Gulf (*Persica* §40). These deportations must have been numerous, because Herodotus names "the inhabitants of the islands in the Persian gulf where the king sends prisoners and others displaced from their homes in war (*anapastoi*)" (III.93✧) among the tribute subdistricts of the Fourteenth Nome. The same phrase reappears in the catalog of Xerxes' army (VII.80). Herodotus's phrase implies actual imperial colonization activity, which never stopped throughout the duration of the Achaemenid Empire.

　　These observations in themselves certainly do not allow us to claim that Persian dominion over the eastern shore of the Gulf was uniformly effective. Instead, we should rank in order the degrees and methods of territorial dominion. It seems clear that influence over Carmania was especially strong. Arrian notes that "the people live like the Persians, as they are their neighbours, and have the same military equipment" (*Indica* 38.1✧). This note recalls what Strabo (XV.2.14✧) writes about the same people: he quotes Nearchus as saying that "the language and most of the customs of the Carmanians are like those of the Medes and Persians" and, though he notes the existence of very different social mores, adds (following Onesicritus?) that their farming practices (*geōrgia*) are identical with the Persians'—including viticulture (Carmanian wine was particularly renowned). This "Persianization" of the Carmanians is explained all the more readily because Herodotus (I.125✧), referring to them as the Germanii, includes them with the Persian tribes "attached to the soil." Finally, Strabo stresses the richness of the Carmanian mines (silver, copper, vermilion, salt, arsenic), which no doubt had been worked since ages past—certainly throughout the Achaemenid period (cf. Pliny IV.36, 98). The Persian coast proper was definitely under firm control. The coast had easy communication with the interior; for example, Alexander took the road to Pasargadae, which was close to the border between Persia and Carmania (*Anab.* VI.29.1; cf. Quintus Curtius X.1.22–24 and Strabo XV.3.6). Strabo (following Nearchus, *Indica* 39.9) also comments on one of the noteworthy geographical features of the Persian coast—the size of the Oroatis River, "the largest of the rivers in that part of the world" (XV.3.1✧). It is entirely typical that Cyrus established a residence at Taoce, right next to Bushire, where the Seleucids later planted a colony (Antioch of Persis). It is not impossible that the canal that archaeologists have found there goes back to the Achaemenid period. In short, the Carmanian and Persian coasts were certainly linked intimately to the nearby Persian countryside. These coastal areas were certainly the regions from which the soldiers came who were mustered from the inhabitants of the Persian Gulf and who were brought to Gaugamela by high Persian officials (*Anab.* III.8.5; 11.5). Persian dominion in Gedrosia was certainly less evident, but it is still important to remember once more that the pilot (Hydraces) hired by Nearchus had an Iranian name.

Cyrus's founding of Taoce proves that Achaemenid interest in the Persian Gulf and its coasts was long-standing, and the Persepolis tablets frequently refer to missions to and from these regions in the time of Darius I. Though we can observe continuity throughout Achaemenid history (which itself probably owed much to its predecessors) on this point, it is more difficult to draw up an account of the places that drew Achaemenid interest on the basis of such meager information. The only literary testimony, which dates to the period close to Darius III, is not terribly eloquent: in his quest for *tryphē* (here: opulence to the point of absurdity), Alexander's treasurer Harpalus "fetched all the long way from the Red Sea [i.e., Persian Gulf] a great quantity of fish" (Diodorus XVII.108.4✧). It is likely that maritime trade with India was quite extensive under the Achaemenids, but it must be noted that direct evidence is very weak, aside from a few nuggets gleaned from the Susa Foundation Charter. The land routes (like the route taken by Craterus) must also have represented a significant connection. It is also true that transport may have been provided by Indian sailors as far as Cape Maceta (cf. *Indica* 32.7–8). At the head of the Persian Gulf, near the mouth of the Euphrates, Nearchus mentions "a village of Babylonia, called Diridotis; here the merchants (*emporoi*) gather together frankincense from the land of Gerrha and all the other sweet-smelling spices Arabia produces" (41.6–7;✧ Strabo XV.3.5). Despite these notices, it is not impossible that some of these spices in fact were imported from India.

What about the Arabian shore? Do descriptions of the expeditions that Alexander sent out from Babylon provide any clarification of the question?

> Alexander was planning to colonize the coast along the Persian Gulf and the islands there. . . . The prosperity of the country was also an incitement, since he heard that cassia grew in their marshes, that the trees produced myrrh and frankincense, that cinnamon was cut from the bushes, and that spikenard grew self-sown in their meadows. . . . He was informed . . . that there were many islands off-shore and harbours everywhere in the country, enough to

give anchorages for his fleet, and to permit cities to be built on them, which were likely to prosper. . . . He thought that it would become just as prosperous a country as Phoenicia. (Arrian VII.19.5; 20.2✧)

This information was provided by the leaders of missions he had previously sent: Archias, who had gotten no farther than Tylus (Bahrein); Androsthenes (who "sailed around part of the Arabian Peninsula"); and especially Hieron of Soloi, whose "sailing orders were to coast round the whole Arabian Peninsula . . . to reconnoitre the coast lying on the Ocean, the inhabitants of the coast, its anchorages, water supplies." He did not pass the promontory toward which Nearchus had refused to set sail (VII.19.7–10;✧ *Indica* 43.8)—that is, Ras Musandam. Similarly, ships had on occasion cast off from the head of the Red Sea (Gulf of Aqaba), but they were forced to turn back, and we cannot say how far they sailed (Arrian, *Indica* 43.7). The voyages along the Arabian coast of the Persian Gulf a priori look like explorations of unknown territory. But this perspective will certainly need to be modified. As Arrian (VII.19.6) and Strabo (XVI.1.12) noted, Alexander's objective was basically military—to subject the Arabs who had not voluntarily submitted. Thus, the navigators' mission was to catalog the ports and water supply points for the navy that was to make the run from Babylon. There certainly never was an actual plan to circle Arabia and reach Egypt.

Unfortunately, the archaeological evidence is not very eloquent. Achaemenid strata have indeed been found at Failaka (Kuwait), in Bahrein, and in Oman, but the results do not really allow us to identify a significant Achaemenid influence. It is also true that, here as elsewhere, excavating for Achaemenid archaeological evidence proper is a rather pointless exercise—Achaemenid dominion over a region does not necessarily imply that Persian artifacts were borrowed. We know that when the Macedonians approached Failaka they found a sanctuary there ("a shrine of Artemis"; Arrian VII.20.3–4✧). The discovery of Babylonian and Achaemenid pottery proves that the sanctuary had existed there for quite some time, at least since the Neo-Babylonian period. An Aramaic inscription from the site of Tell Khazneh seems to offer a fifth–fourth-century benchmark. So it is tempting to conclude that, like the Neo-Babylonian kings (Nabonidus had a governor at Dilmun and Nebuchadnezzar II a residence and temple at Failaka), the Great Kings ruled Dilmun, or, more precisely, that they maintained frequent, active relations with this region. Babylonian–Achaemenid continuity is also evident at the head of the Persian Gulf. The town of Ampe, to which Darius deported the Milesians (Herodotus VI.20), was probably none other than the village of Aginis, which Arrian (*Indica* 42.4) and Strabo (XV.3.5) locate 500 stadia from Susa. Ampe itself must have been located not far from Durine; its name and description (*urbs regia*) indicate that it went back to the Assyrian period (Dur-Yakin). It is likely that this site not only served as the Great King's naval base but also functioned as a trading post with the Arabs of the east coast of the peninsula. At the end of the Achaemenid period, the Gerrhaeans came by sea and then by river to trade directly in Babylonia (Aristobulus, quoted by Strabo XVI.3.3). Unfortunately, we do not know much about these Arabs during the Achaemenid period, since Strabo's other comments refer to a much later epoch. When Antiochus III came into contact with the Gerrheans, we know that a treaty was entered into by the two parties: the king recognized their "autonomy" and the Gerrheans gave him a "gift" of 500 talents of silver, 1,000 talents of incense, and 200 talents of myrrh (Polybius XII.9). If these relations go back to the Achaemenid period—of which we cannot be sure—they could easily be compared with the connections between the Great Kings and the "king of the Arabs" in Palestine (chap. 16/8 above).

18. An Appraisal and Some Questions

At the conclusion of this Achaemenid "grand tour," several highly contrasting images emerge that can and do feed a variety of historical interpretations, which we have been presenting concisely ever since the opening pages of this book. The images of Persepolis are not the only ones that have established an impression of permanence. Once they have been cleansed of their polemical distortions, quite a few of the Classical and Hellenistic texts also lead us to trace many continuities from Darius I to Darius III: monarchic ideology, military and tribute administration, and satrapal organization. The roll call of Darius III's military contingents at Issus and later at Gaugamela very clearly implies that in 334 the Great King still held sway from the Indus to the Aegean. But what was the depth of territorial dominion? Was it, as is often claimed, limited to the appointment of satrapal administrators and the maintenance of a network of outposts and garrisons that enabled the Achaemenids to control the roads and a few territories? This question in turn provokes consideration of the methods inherent in our analytical tools. It may seem paradoxical to raise the problem after the regional inventory and not before. This choice was born of simple necessity: the debate cannot really be presented as a whole without evidence that has already been analyzed in its temporal and spatial contexts. Thus, the following reflections have no other purpose than to take stock of the uncertainties and various possibilities.

The discussion of Bactria (chap. 16/15) has shown that the picture of a lax imperial organization has given pride of place to the archaeological evidence. This line of argument appears frequently: the small amount of archaeological evidence regarding the Persians is thought to illustrate just how thin the territorial coverage achieved by the central power was. More than twenty years ago, this interpretation was elucidated by P. R. S. Moorey as follows:

> Material traces of the two hundred years of Persian rule in the Near East are still generally elusive. In many regions of their far flung empire this period is among the least known archaeologically. This might be explained most easily by the subsequent profound and everywhere evident impact of Hellenic art and culture in areas previously ruled by the Persians; but the available evidence only partially sustains such an interpretation. Persian influence was geographically restricted and socially superficial in all but a very few areas over which they at one time or another had authority. In government and administration they adopted and modified rather than radically changed what they had gained by conquest or annexation. Existing administrative hierarchies were crowned and reinforced with imperial civil servants and military officers, not transformed to a standard pattern. In religious matters the Persian administration was usually tolerant and accommodating, sympathetic to traditional custom and practice, nowhere seeking to force their own cults by edict. . . . The Persian contribution was generally confined to the reconstruction of existing administrative buildings or to the creation of parks and palaces in the Iranian manner, particularly in satrapal capitals. . . . In some regions, notably Egypt, Persian cultural influence was very slight, confined to decorative features which need sharp investigation to detect them. . . . (1980: 128)

This kind of argument seems to reflect the facts that we find on the ground exactly. One need merely to walk the site of Sardis to ask, "But where were the Persians?" Nonetheless, the truth is more complex than it appears, because it is precisely at and around Sardis that the Persian/Achaemenid presence is particularly well attested by literary texts and late inscriptions. Thus, there is a contradiction between the archaeological picture and the text, and it is up to the historian to take into account and resolve this issue, without simply having recourse to a simplistic either-or perspective. It is also necessary to pay attention to vocabulary. Because, generally speaking, the Persians anchored themselves in local tradition, it is sometimes difficult to distinguish evidence of centrifugal tendencies in an iconographic representation from what might demonstrate the presence of the central state apparatus (cf. the case of the Lycian and Phoenician monuments). Furthermore, for decades, excavations at major sites (such as Babylon) have never really had the goal of uncovering Achaemenid remains—or the remains discovered have often been underestimated because of dubious assumptions. Imagine, for instance, that it took until 1993 for the initial results of scientific examination of the pottery collected in 1955 at two Armenian sites (Altintepe; Cemin Tepe) to be published. The reexamination of the evidence now proves that Achaemenid ware (long called "Urartian") existed at the site—and recent investigation has uncovered Achaemenid buildings, sometimes constructed on top of older Urartian structures. Fragments of Elamite tablets have also been found at one of the sites (chap. 16/14 above). This is not an isolated example. Consider, for example, that the discovery—first pointed out in 1967—of stone balls from the siege of the town of Paphos by the Persians in 497 has been practically "forgotten"—even though these artifacts lead us to wonder whether the catapult might have been invented by the Persians (and not by Dionysius of Syracuse at the beginning of the fourth century). It required the recent discovery of the same sort of ball at Phocaea—a relic from the Persian siege of 546—for this remarkable material to become fully integrated into the technical debate. Other "forgotten" publications of Achaemenid objects found at sites in ancient Assyria, etc., might be mentioned. All of the new discoveries point in the same direction—that is, toward the theory that Achaemenid imperial occupation was much more dense than has been imagined in the past on the basis of spotty, varied, and disparate evidence.

Because of restoration of the Hellenistic and especially Roman remains of older sites (especially in Asia Minor: cf. Sardis), the Achaemenid stratum has often disappeared, leading to great hope (already partly realized) in the results from "virgin" sites, such as Dascylium. Another example is highly instructive: the condition and context of the Persepolis reliefs from Meydançikkale in Cilicia (the only materials of this type recovered within imperial territory). Even though the initial reports are not terribly detailed, it appears that the blocks were reused in the Hellenistic period, probably in Building A (which was built on the foundations of previous construction). It is thus only by the merest chance that the reliefs have been preserved to this day, perhaps because some peasants tried unsuccessfully to move them from the acropolis; the block engraved with an Aramaic inscription (from which we learn the ancient name of the site: Kiršu) has probably been recarved. This is a perfect illustration of the random nature of the most remarkable discoveries of recent years. Consider another example, an Elamite-Persepolitan-type tablet from the Achaemenid fortifications at Old Kandahār, which *all by itself* manages to destroy the argument *a silentio* that is sometimes carried *ad absurdum*. Furthermore, Elamite tablets of the Persepolis type have also been found quite recently at the Armenian site of Armavir-blur!

Statistical evaluation—which in principle is not entirely reliable—of imperial presence thus runs up against the proof of new discoveries and publications. The examples we have just briefly run through (excavations at Dascylium; Armenian sites; reliefs and inscriptions from Meydançikkale; Elamite tablets from Kandahār and Armavir-blur) in fact illustrate a basic reality of the life of scholarship: over the last twenty years, the number of objects, monuments, and written materials—in short, the quantity of evidence—has continued to grow in the lands that belonged to the Achaemenid Empire. Even if we consider only the new evidence (including new publications about previously known evidence), the list (pp. 1029–1031) is quite impressive. The publications concern all sorts of evidence: inscriptions, tablets, papyri, excavations, surveys, iconography, and coins. They concern every region of the Empire, although Fārs, Elam, Babylonia, Egypt, and western Asia Minor are especially favored, while Central Asia remains the poor cousin (though we await the final publication of the French explorations in eastern Bactria, and the new excavations in Samarkand are promising). Syria is emerging from semioblivion; the evidence for Palestine, especially Judea and Samaria, has increased considerably.

However, the discoveries just mentioned must not be evaluated only in quantitative terms. What is most striking is that many of the new materials have exceptional historical significance: the Elamite tablets from Kandahār and Armavir-blur, the Darius statue from Susa, the Xanthus trilingual, and the Aramaic memorandum on Egyptian customs duties—to single out just five examples, to which may be added the publications of new Babylonian tablets that sometimes shatter accepted perspectives. Even if they do not provide all of the answers (the most interesting items, naturally, raise new questions), some of them do change our view of Achaemenid territorial coverage. For example, who would have thought that the remote site of Meydançikkale in the Cilician mountains would yield reliefs of the same type that we find in Persepolis? Since this only second-rate site had them, can we not assume that similar reliefs also existed at the great regional centers (Sardis, Dascylium, Damascus, Bactra, etc.)? Even more decisive are the discoveries of Persepolis-style administrative tablets in Arachosia and Armenia (for reasons already presented; see chaps. 11/6 and 16/15). Furthermore, considering the state of affairs since the beginning of the 1970s (over about 25 years), it is easy to see that the tempo of discovery and publication increased significantly during the 1980s, and the harvest of the 1990s also looks excellent. Bearing this in mind and knowing that the research programs and the vision of archaeologists and museum conservators are in part determined (and sometimes overdetermined) by general research trends, we may reasonably hope that there will be a meaningful cumulative effect from the progress of Achaemenid studies in both the short and middle term. In all of this, one observation that amplifies the reservations already expressed above stands out: precisely because of rapid change in the body of evidence, the (pseudo-)statistical hypothesis of a scanty Persian presence and an inconsequential imperial occupation, based on bodies of evidence that are obsolete or reduced to a regional perspective, demands to be questioned more and more pointedly and fundamentally by historians of the Achaemenid Empire.

This resolutely optimistic appraisal should not conceal the methodological and interpretive difficulties, however. What are the "signs" of imperial presence in the provinces and countries? What paths should a qualitative evaluation take? One possible path is to investigate the density of Persian and Iranian personal names and attestations of sanctuaries dedicated to Persian gods. Both of these types of data obviously illustrate the settlement of colonists (of different types), whose presence in turn implies control of territories and populations. For historical reasons, it would be preferable if this investigation were carried out in Greek-speaking lands—that is, basically, Asia Minor; but the Babylonian tablets also shed interesting light on this question. (To carry this a little further, it would be useful to inaugurate exhaustive research into the distribution of Iranian personal names and vocabulary, including, of course, their presence in Hellenistic-period tablets.) Another element must be taken into account: in addition to the spread of Achaemenid iconographic motifs (which could be attributed to Persians settling in the provinces), we also need to consider the borrowing of these motifs by local elites. Of course, it is not easy to link cultural borrowing to political control. The case of Lycia, which has been mentioned several times, shows both the fascination and the limitation of this argument—particularly because in some cases (e.g., the tomb of Petosiris), the local taste for Achaemenid-type items lasted beyond the political fall of the Empire of Darius III. In other cases, there is no doubt about the political nature of the evidence. For example, when the kings of Sidon adopted royal motifs for their coinage, we cannot escape the conclusion that it was their way of demonstrating their particular integration into the Empire. And can we really deny that the spread of such images (into Samaria, for example) during the fourth century is an Achaemenid "marker"? Of course, all by itself this marker is insufficient, but when we can refer to the spread of artistic motifs, the construction of administrative residences, the exploitation of land, etc.—all in the same region—it is only reasonable to situate these features in their imperial context. Indeed, this statement may easily be applied to several regions of the Empire of Darius III.

Analysis of texts, as we have said again and again, poses just as many methodological problems. By way of example, let us return to the claim that some areas were poorly controlled, such as the territories of the Zagros peoples. There is no doubt that, beyond the apparently universal use of the satrapal unit and the natural integration of regions into the Empire that resulted, Darius III's administration—like Darius I's—continued to recognize the existence of peoples (*ethnē*). This was true during the military review at Doriscus in 480 (Herodotus VII.60) and later at Cunaxa (Xenophon, *Anab.* I.8.9); the various contingents at Gaugamela were arranged *kata ethnē* (Diodorus XVII.58.1); and Darius was concerned about communication among groups speaking such diverse languages (53.4). This heterogeneity also explains the formula "kings, cities, dynasts, and peoples," which is represented frequently in the diplomatic correspondence of the Seleucid kings but also was a reality of the Achaemenid period (cf. Nepos, *Ages.* 7.3). The Achaemenid conquest did not result in the downfall of all these kings and dynasts, whoever they were—Cadusians, Saka, Indians, or even the rulers of the western Delta.

But even this reflection cannot be reduced to these remarks. Darius III's army was no more a "countless and undisciplined horde" than the armies of Xerxes (chap. 5/5) or Artaxerxes II (Plutarch, *Art.* 7.5; Xenophon, *Anab.* I.8.11)—no matter what Alexander's earlier historians say. Once the army was assembled and counted, the ethnic contingents partly gave up their individuality and were reorganized into regiments (cf. Quintus Curtius IV.12.7). It is enough to compare two passages in Arrian to explain this: the enumeration of Darius's army (III.8.3–6) and his order of battle (III.11.3–7). It is also clear that some contingents organized *kata ethnē* were considered less than useful (cf. II.8.8). The Great King counted first of all on the elite contingents—the Persians, Saka, and

Bactrians—and within the Persians, certain particularly reliable regiments, such as the Kinsmen of the king and the *mēlophoroi* (III.16.1; cf. Diodorus XVII.20.2). In addition to the Persians, some ethnic contingents enjoyed privileged positions. The drafting of other contingents, who were of little military use (e.g., Quintus Curtius IV.12.9), reflected political considerations—the Great Kings wanted to give a picture of the immensity of the Empire (see chap. 5/5)—rather than strategic necessity. Alexander provided a vivid illustration of this hierarchy of peoples at the banquet at Opis: first, the Macedonians, "next to them Persians, and then any persons from the other peoples who took precedence for rank or any other high quality" (Arrian VII.11.8✧). It seems clear, on the one hand, that Alexander was following an Achaemenid protocol (like Peucestes, later on; Diodorus XIX.22.2–3) and that, on the other, the order was determined on the basis of the rank and loyalty of each the Empire's peoples (compare Tacitus, *Ann.* XIII.54.2). Thus, the composition and operation of the royal army illustrate the two components of the Empire: unity and diversity—the latter not necessarily in contradiction to the former.

The example of the Zagros peoples and some others (chap. 16/11 above) must therefore be considered with some caution. Because relations between the Great King and the Uxians and Cosseans were unusual, they clearly demonstrate that the configurations of imperial dominion were very supple and flexible. Far from constituting an obstacle to the Great King's dominion, though, the diversity served to enhance the unity of the Empire—which in fact proves the folly of the attacks by Alexander and Antigonus. Because of the Achaemenids' keen understanding of the differing situations, it was out of the question to attempt to impose centralization of the sort found in modern states, which are based on the "national" ideal—a notion that was utterly foreign to a multiethnic, multicultural Empire. Furthermore, even though the "ethnic unit" retained nearly all of its significance (cf. Arrian I.24.5), changes during the fourth century did not lead in the direction of disintegration of the central power; on the contrary, some countries, such as Caria, Cilicia, and Lycia, were "satrapized." In fact, at the dawn of the Macedonian expedition, Caria was governed by a Persian satrap (Orontobates) for the first time. Berossus's famous passage on the introduction of ritual statues of Anāhita into the great capitals of Artaxerxes II's Empire (chap. 15/8) suggests that there were large administrative regions. Additionally, the existence of military-tribute districts (chiliarchies) in the Sardis Plain shows the progress of territorialization at the end of the Achaemenid period (*Sardis* VII.1.1). This is also suggested by Diodorus's (XIX.44.4; 95.2) use of the word *eparchy* (within Media and of Idumea), which may reflect the administrative entity known in Aramaic as the province (*medinah*).

What about the kings/dynasts whom the Achaemenids left in place? We ought to inquire into the dependency relations that linked them to the central authority. To focus on their revolts is not enough to settle the interpretive problem. The wars that the Great Kings waged against them simply demonstrate that the alliance could be rocky at times; they do not prove that these petty kingdoms remained either fully independent or hostile throughout the Achaemenid period. These peoples were more like the client-kingdoms of the Assyrian period or the "friendly" kingdoms that propped up Roman imperialism in one of the phases of its history. At any rate, 'friendship and alliance' (*philia kai symmakhia*) was the very basis on which Artaxerxes reestablished his authority after the Cadusian campaign (Plutarch, *Art.* 24.5–9✧). A relationship based on *philia kai symmakhia* is also attested for Ephesus (Arrian I.19.1: *philoi kai symmakhoi*) and Sidon (Diodorus

XVII.47.1: *philia*), both in the time of Darius III. Darius IIII also entered into relations of *symmakhia* with the Cadusians and Saka, and on the strength of these he demanded that military contingents be furnished (Arrian III.19.3). We could ask whether a treaty of *philia kai symmakhia* is the Greek form that corresponds more or less to the loyalty oaths (*ādū/ē*) by which the Neo-Assyrian and Neo-Babylonian kings imposed dominion and hegemony—flexibly and in considerable variety but nonetheless with significant weight. This theory in fact fits some of our data—the annual meeting (as we have reconstructed it in chap. 16/11 above) between the Great King (or his representative) and the leaders of the Uxian and Cossean communities. In any case, there is no doubt that, within the framework of an imperial policy that Herodotus transmitted without fully understanding it (III.15), the Great Kings would intervene in the dynastic successions of these kinglets; they did not hesitate to legitimate successors (cf. Plutarch, *Art.* 14.1) or even, in cases of rebellion, to install a new dynast who was completely devoted to Achaemenid interests (e.g., *DB* V §74; Herodotus V.104). These are all techniques that we have already seen being systematically applied in the Neo-Assyrian period (e.g., *ANET*[3]: 291–92). As a result, the kinglet-friend was one of the cogs in the imperial machinery—sometimes integrated even more closely by means of matrimonial alliances with representatives of the dominant socioethnic class (cf. Nepos, *Dat.* 1.1.3; Xenophon, *Hell.* IV.1.1–15).

In order to understand the bivalent nature of these local powers better—and by way of comparison—we may point out that in a ninth-century bilingual inscription (Tell Fekheriye) inscribed on the statue of a Syrian dynast, he presents himself (in Aramaic) as a 'king' (*mlk*) but is called 'governor' (*šaknu*) in the Assyrian text. *Mutatis mutandis*, this example is reminiscent of the principle we have just analyzed and, more specifically, of a familiar text—the Xanthus trilingual. There are two points of comparison. The first has to do with the relationship between the satrap and Xanthus and the picture that the Xanthians had of themselves: while they overtly presented themselves as a civic community (*polis*), the satrap's version of the inscription makes the town into a mere fortress (*byrt*) in which the satrap Pixodarus had installed a governor (*epimelētēs*); this governor represented Pixodarus alongside the two archons/commissioners, who had also been appointed by the satrap and had responsibilities in the Lycian district. The second point of comparison is concerned with the dual status of the satrap: the satraps of Caria had been appointed from the same dynastic family from the beginning of the fourth century until Darius III installed a Persian, Orontobates, who had previously married one of Pixodarus's daughters (Arrian I.23.8; Strabo XIV.2.17). We can then understand why later authors asked questions about and argued over the political status of a man like Mausolus: "According to M. Tullius [Cicero], Mausolus was king of the Carian country (*rex terrae Cariae*), or else, as authors of Greek histories say, the prefect of the province [of Caria], what the Greeks call a satrap (*provinciae praefectus satrapēn Graeci vocant*)" (Gellius Aulus, N.A. 10.18.2). If we compare this text with the Tell Fekheriye inscription, *rex* corresponds precisely to *mlk*, and *praefectus/satrapes* to *šaknu*, with respect both to vocabulary and to history. In reality, Mausolus was both (cf. Strabo XIV.2.17), just as the representatives of the Sanballat family were Samaritan dynasts and Achaemenid governors—except that, within the imperial framework, both were *first and foremost* the authorized representatives of the central authority (hence the titles they bear in the official documents: "satrap"; "governor"). In other regions, the maintenance of kinglets and "autonomous" dynasts need not necessarily lead to the conclusion that the central power's territorial control was limited; nor is it true that Artaxerxes II's treaty with the Cadusian kings illustrates "Achaemenid decline"—the contraction of the imperial territories like crepe during the fourth century (contrary to an interpretation that resurfaces from time to time in historiography, against the increasing weight of the evidence). Pericles of Limyra's assumption of the title "king of the Lycians" can no longer be interpreted as a sign of his rebellion against the central power. As we have already noted (chap. 15/7), his proclamation was aimed at his Lycian competitor in Xanthus—not at Artaxerxes II. We can also interpret in this way the traditions about the kings of Lydia (Arrian I.17.6), Caria (Diodorus XV.90.3; XVII.24.2), and Phrygia (Arrian II.3) that were transmitted down to Darius III.

In sum, the central authority may have been perfectly happy to permit these kinglets and dynasts to continue to function and may even have taken advantage of them in establishing its territorial control. This is perfectly illustrated by the case of the dynast-tyrant of Pontic Heraclea who succeeded his brother in 338–337: "Dionysius increased his territorial dominion (*arkhē*) because of the defeat inflicted on the Persians by Alexander in the battle of the Granicus, a defeat that allowed anyone who wished to expand by profiting from the diminution of the Persian might that until then had impeded them" (Memnon, *FGrH* 434 F4). This text, presenting an interpretation offered by a local historian, supports a perspective totally antithetical to the stereotype of "Achaemenid decadence," because Memnon of Heraclea explicitly attributes the process by which the territories gained their autonomy to the shock of the Macedonian conquest, which seriously destabilized Achaemenid dominion—a dominion that the author had considered as a durable guarantee of territorial continuity and imperial solidity.

Chapter 17

The Great King, His Armies, and His Treasures

1. *The Accession of Darius III*

From Artaxerxes III to Darius III: Diodorus and Bagoas

One of the reasons often advanced for the weakening of the central authority is the multiplication of dynastic crises and assassinations, and the accession of Darius III would be a striking example. Is this claim reasonable? In order to come to a decision, we need to go back several years. The Classical authors are rather subdued about most of Artaxerxes III's reign, but they are less so about the brutal circumstances of his death. The character Bagoas, in fact, reemerges into the light of day—this character who, as we have seen, already has had a preliminary introduction from Diodorus in book XVI:

> He rose to such power because of his partnership with Mentor that he was master (*kyrios*) of the kingdom (*basileia*), and Artaxerxes did nothing without his advice (*gnōmē*). And after Artaxerxes' death he designated (*apedeiknyto*) in every case the successor (*diadokhoi*) to the throne and enjoyed all the functions of kingship save the title. (XVI.50.8✧)

Diodorus keeps his promise (§50.8) by returning to Bagoas in book XVII in an account dedicated to the recent history of the Achaemenid dynasty. He stresses that Artaxerxes III's implacable character had rendered him loathsome to the Persians and then re-introduces the chiliarch Bagoas as "a eunuch in physical fact but a militant rogue in disposition" (§5.3✧); he poisoned the king with a physician's assistance and had the assassinated king's sons murdered, except for Arses, who very likely took the name Artaxerxes [IV] (§5.4; cf. XV.93.1). According to Diodorus, the cruel Bagoas assumed that the sovereign's youth would make him easily manipulated, but he most certainly was not! But at the very moment when the king was planning to eliminate Bagoas, he resorted once more to murder:

> [He] killed Arses and his children also while he was still in the third year of his reign. . . . [He] selected a certain Dareius, a member of the court circle, and secured the throne for him. . . . Pursuing his habitual savagery he attempted to remove Dareius by poison. The plan leaked out, however, and the king, calling upon Bagoas, as it were, to drink to him a toast and handing him his own cup compelled him to take his own medicine. (XVII.5.4–6✧)

This account is found, often in less precise wording but still in complete harmony, in practically every ancient report. The murder of Arses after two years of rule is also mentioned (without citing his name) in a well-known Babylonian text, the *Dynastic Prophecy*, which states that the murder was committed by a *ša rēši* (obviously Bagoas), after which a prince seized power and ruled for five years (Darius III) (*BHLT* 35, III.4–8). Because the reality of these conspiracies and royal assassinations cannot be doubted, what conclusions on the political plane is the historian able to draw?

Darius III's Illegitimacy: The Macedonian Version

An initial interpretation is found in one of the accusations against Darius III that is included in the letter that Alexander sent to the Great King after the initial Persian diplomatic overtures following the battle of Issus. At this point in the discussion, it is not particularly important to highlight the extremely dubious nature of the document. It is clear that we have a magnificent piece of Macedonian propaganda, in which Alexander and his "communications directors" attempted to legitimate the Macedonian king's imperial pretentions. As a matter of fact, it is precisely the fabricated nature of the letter that lends the present text so much interest. In Arrian's version, we find the following charge against Darius:

> You assassinated Arses with the help of Bagoas (*meta Bagōou*), and seized the throne unjustly (*ou dikaiōs*), and in actual contravention of Persian law (*para tōn Persōn nomon*), doing wrong to Persians (*adikountos Persas*). (II.14.5✧)

As portrayed in Macedonian propaganda, Darius III was delegitimated on the basis of three criteria: (1) he had seized power "in contravention of Persian law," (2) against the will of the Persians, (3) and the Persians' opposition was proved by their later behavior, when they defected to Alexander and fought by his side "of their own free will"; thus, the defeats Darius suffered disqualified him, proving that he had lost the help of the gods (§14.7–8). The Macedonian discourse thus took on a rare Achaemenid coherence: Darius III had no right to the throne because he was unable to claim the traditional justifications for royal authority as they are expressed at Behistun and Naqš-i Rustam: (1) he could not prove blood ties to his predecessors; (2) he had not exhibited the virtues of a good soldier; and (3) his Faithful and the gods had abandoned him. In short, Darius III was delegitimated in the same way that Gaumata had been by Darius I.

The same accusation is found in a speech that Quintus Curtius places in Alexander's mouth in 330: "Not even Darius received the rule of the Persians by right of succession (*hereditarium . . . imperium*), but he was admitted to the throne of Cyrus by the favour of Bagoas, a eunuch . . . vacant [is thus] the kingdom (*vacuum regnum*)" (VI.3.12✧). Even though this speech is placed after the death of Darius, the rationale of the text makes it clear that the last words also apply to the previous period (cf. Justin XI.5.7: *matura imperia*). Moreover, this is also the meaning of the symbolic actions performed by Alexander when he landed (Diodorus XVII.17.2; Arrian I.11.7; Justin X.11.5). Strabo also refers directly to the "illegal" character of Darius III's accession: after recalling that the Persians "are governed by hereditary kings (*hypo tōn apo genous*)" (XVI.3.17✧), he goes on to say that "the successors of Dareius [I] came to an end with Arses. Arses was slain by Bagoüs the eunuch, who set up as king (*katestēse*) another Dareius, who was not of the royal family (*ouk onta tou genous tōn basileōn*)" (XV.3.24✧). The same account is in Diodorus: after Arses' murder, the royal house was vacant/extinct (*erēmou . . . tou basileōs oikou*); there was no one who could inherit power by virtue of family ties (*kata genos*); and this created the context for Bagoas's resolve to bring one of his friends, Darius, to power (XVII.5.5). Finally, in some of the other authors, the accusation emphasizes the modesty of Darius's background: he "was a slave (*doulos*)" (Aelian, *VH* XII.43✧); he was "a slave and courier (*astandēs*) of the king" (Plutarch, *Mor.* 326e✧, 337e, 340b), or simply *astandēs* (Plutarch, *Alex.* 18.7); he was thus nothing more than the creation of Bagoas, who "took up the kingship of Persia": Arses and Darius were merely "puppet kings" (337e✧).

The Accession of Darius: The Persian Version

We also have the unusual opportunity of consulting an opposing perspective that clearly derives from the Persian camp. Justin (X.3.4) and Diodorus (XVII.6.1–3✧)—the latter is quick to present the two versions side by side—both state in similar words that, entirely on the contrary, Darius came to power because he had previously displayed striking personal courage: during one of Artaxerxes III's wars against the Cadusians, Darius (called Codoman by Justin) was the only one of the Persians around the king who dared to answer the challenge thrown down by a Cadusian of Herculean strength. He won this single combat (*monomakhia*) "and restored to his people, with the victory, their glory that had nearly perished" (Justin). Because of his personal deed, he was "honoured in consequence by the king with rich gifts (*megalai dōreai*), while among the Persians he was conceded the first place in prowess (*andreia*)" (Diodorus). According to Justin, Codoman was then awarded "the command of the two Armenias" (X.3.4). Again in nearly identical words, Justin and Diodorus say that when Ochus died and Darius was placed on the throne, it was because his striking courage was remembered. Justin goes on to say that "the people honored him with the name Darius" because of his courage.

It is easy to see that the Persian propaganda responds precisely to the Macedonian propaganda—or at least that the latter was not a counterattack against propaganda spread by Darius after his accession (see below). But this does not alter the facts of the situation. What we find here is in fact one of the most common Achaemenid justifications for kingship: personal bravery in combat. At the same time, we can note how frequent the repetition of the theme of *monomakhia* is—well attested among the Iranians and particularly among the Persians in the context of dynastic contests. It is thus understandable why neither Justin nor Diodorus, at this point at least, makes the slightest allusion to Bagoas's machinations or the broken line of succession: when Ochus died, power devolved quite naturally onto Darius Codoman.

Darius III and the Achaemenid Royal Family

We obviously cannot simply choose one version in preference to the other. Neither is acceptable *in toto* because both are patently propagandistic. Codoman's *monomakhia* reflects a monarchic motif, while at the same time serial murder by and large reflects historical reality. Let us begin by examining the texts that present the humble origins of the new king. The Aelian passage (*VH* XII.43) must be placed in context. It is in fact a list of leaders and kings who came to power by rising from anonymity. Thus, we can see that it conforms to one of the most common motifs of monarchic literature, particularly in the Hellenistic period, when authors loved to contrast kings born to kings (*ek basileōs basileus*) with kings whose fathers were commoners (*ex idiōtou basileus*; cf. *Letter of Aristeas* 288). At any rate, even Plato stresses that Darius I, in contrast to Cambyses and Xerxes, was able to exhibit virtues precisely because he was not the son of a king (*Laws* III.694c–695d). Similarly, Herodotus, speaking of Darius I before his accession, calls him *idiōtēs* (VII.3). This is not to say that Darius at that time was vegetating in anonymity, because he was in Egypt as a spear-bearer (*doryphoros*) for Cambyses (III.139). We also find Darius I in Aelian's list of those who rose from anonymity to power (XII.43), and Aelian says that, under Cyrus, Darius was a royal quiver-bearer (*pharētrophoros*; XII.43). This is evidence for the striking titles so clearly displayed at Naqš-i Rustam (*DNc, DNd*). The same was true for the future Darius III: he was not called *astandēs* 'courier' because he had been a letter-carrier! Instead, this was his court title, and the prestige of the office was symbolized and enhanced by the special robe he wore (cf. in particular Plutarch, *Alex.* 18.7; *Moralia* 340b; and Quintus Curtius III.3.5). The use of the adjective *doulos* does not throw this evidence into doubt; on the contrary, this adjective is precisely how the Greek authors frequently translate/transmit the Persian phenomenon of *bandaka* (e.g., [Arist.] *De Mundo* 398a, which counts the royal couriers [*hēmerodromoi*] among the king's *douloi*). In short, Darius III, who was born around 380 (cf. Arrian III.22.6), had been part of the royal inner circle probably since the end of the reign of Artaxerxes II and certainly during the time of Artaxerxes III. Thus we may usher out the unknown person manipulated into power by his "friend" Bagoas.

The dynastic-familial illegitimacy put forward by the Macedonian propagandists, on the other hand, is clearly nothing but fiction. Diodorus himself states that Darius "was the son of Arsanes, and grandson of that Ostanes who was a brother of Artaxerxes [II] who had been king" (XVII.5.5✧); he was thus Artaxerxes III's cousin. Darius was born to a brother/sister marriage (Arsanes/Sisygambis), and he himself married his sister Stateira. The alleged "Persian law" cited in Alexander's letter also reflects a biased interpretation of Achaemenid succession practice. If in fact the male descent of Artaxerxes III was reduced to its simplest form (namely, Bisthanes, the older half-brother of Artaxerxes IV) when Arses and his children had died, then the royal house was not limited to the sons of the dead king. In fact, when Arses/Artaxerxes IV died, the situation was quite similar to the conditions after the demise of Artaxerxes I (see our analysis in chap. 14/6). Artaxerxes I left only one legitimate son (Xerxes), who was soon assassinated; in order to confine power to the royal family, the throne passed to an illegitimate son of the deceased king (and half-brother of Xerxes II)—namely, Ochus, who soon seized power from his half-brother Sogdianus and took the throne name Darius II. With regard to the "Persian law"—that is, more precisely, Achaemenid succession practice—Darius III was thus perfectly legitimate.

Violence and nomos

Another Macedonian accusation referred to the fact that Darius III seized the throne by violence, against the will of the Persians. In truth, the vocabulary used by Arrian reflects some hesitancy from the beginning. The contrast between violence and *nomos* in fact recurs regularly in the Hellenistic texts that wish to delegitimate any rival to Macedonian tradition (cf. Diodorus XVIII.33.3). Of course, the accusation is not specifically Greek. Let us recall, for example, that in the *Cyrus Cylinder* Nabonidus is denounced for mistreating the Babylonians, and Gaumata is also delegitimated at Behistun because of his violence against the Persians. But under Arrian's pen the accusation takes on a more Macedonian tone, because during the famous debate on the *proskynesis*, Callisthenes recalls that the Macedonian king had to rule "not by force but in accordance with custom (*oude biai, alla nomōi*)" (Arrian IV.11.6✧).

Even more noteworthy is the fact that the reference to a Persian *nomos* in this area does not have much significance. In fact, very few royal successions occurred without problems. The existence and machinations of court cabals that supported one candidate over another are frequently attested (cf. Herodotus VII.2–4; Plutarch, *Art.* 6.1–2; 26.1–2, 27–28, etc.). Furthermore, the murders of Artatxerxes III and Arses were part of a long series. All we need to do is to draw up the list: one king dead on a military expedition (Cyrus), five kings dead of natural causes (Cambyses, Darius I, Artaxerxes I, Darius II,

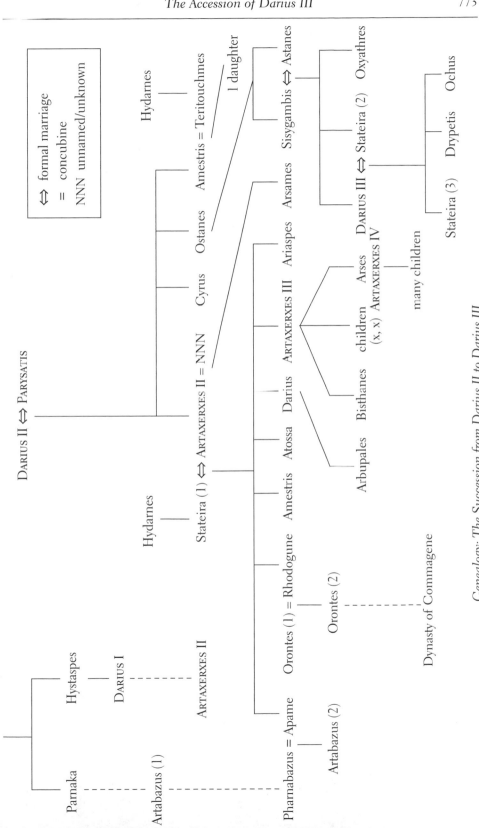

Genealogy: The Succession from Darius II to Darius III

Artaxerxes II), and seven kings assassinated (Bardiya, Xerxes I, Xerxes II, [Sogdianus], Artaxerxes III, Artaxerxes IV, Darius III), to whom may be added Darius, oldest son of Artaxerxes II, who was surely guilty of plotting against his father and was executed. The excessive "cruelty" attributed to Artaxerxes III by the ancient authors does not appear to have been unique to him, if we also recall the serial murders of the representatives of the Hydarnes family, which were initiated jointly by Darius II and Parysatis (chap. 14/6).

Whether we condemn it or not (this is not the problem), the physical elimination of opponents and presumed rivals was also part and parcel of Achaemenid court practice; Ctesias in particular liked to emphasize the wanton cruelty of the punishment and executions, which were as terrible as the actions taken by Darius I against some of the "liar-kings." Moreover, the legitimacy of a king who came to power through blood and iron was not *ipso facto* marked as invalid—as was demonstrated quite clearly by Darius I, Artaxerxes I, Darius II, and Artaxerxes III. All that a king had to do was to demonstrate his authority, which was a matter less of *nomos* than of results achieved in the political and military realms. This authority could later be challenged if the king did not succeed in creating a coterie of Persian aristocrats that supported him. This is the background to the other disqualification hurled against Darius III by Alexander: "As I have conquered in battle first your generals and satraps, and now yourself and your own force, . . . I hold myself responsible for all of your troops who did not die in the field but took refuge with me; they are with me of their own free will (*hekontes*), and voluntarily serve in my army (*xustrateuontai met'emou*)" (Arrian II.14.7✧). This reiterates one of the common motifs of the false propaganda put out by Cyrus the Younger's camp against Artaxerxes II (chap. 15/2). Comparison of the two incidents tends to reinforce our suspicion about the arguments brought by Alexander in favor of his own royal legitimacy. Let us simply note that Alexander himself was not in the best position to wield this weapon because his own accession was accompanied by bloody purges of the Macedonian nobility; these purges can hardly be considered less excessive than the Persian behavior on this score, and Darius III himself sought to take advantage of the troubled context that resulted from the killings by encouraging conspiracies in his adversary's camp.

Darius and Bagoas

One article of the indictment against Darius remains to be examined: that he became king only because he had been hoisted onto the throne by Bagoas, the "militant rogue" eunuch, in Diodorus's words (XVII.5.3)—words that are both picturesque and damning. As we have already seen, the word *eunuch* by itself disqualified the person so called from being human in the eyes of most of the Greek authors. The *Dynastic Prophecy* shows that Bagoas actually bore the title *ša rēši*, the very word automatically "translated" *eunuch* by the Greek authors (chap. 7/3)! Bagoas certainly was an important person at court, since Diodorus calls him "the most faithful of his [the king's] friends (*ho pistotatos tōn philōn*)" (XVI.47.3–4). Thus, he was a privileged counselor to Artaxerxes III (§50.8). If Ctesias had had to mention Bagoas, he would certainly have used the generic phrase he was so fond of: "the most influential eunuch alongside [Artaxerxes III/IV]." In contrast, the words Diodorus uses to describe Bagoas's promotion after the Egyptian campaign are extremely suspect. In the context, Diodorus sets up a totally artificial parallel between Mentor and Bagoas, who are dividing the Empire through an agreement of *koinopragia/koinōnia* that they had supposedly reached in Egypt: the West was to be Mentor's, the East was to go to Bagoas (XVI.50.6–8). The parallel comes from a biased source (certainly Ephorus) who tended to exaggerate the Rhodian Mentor's position and devalue royal authority. In reality, Mentor was certainly never commander-in-chief of Asia Minor, and the general command of the Upper Satrapies attributed to Bagoas is also very doubtful.

The only official title borne by Bagoas was chiliarch (Diodorus XVII.5.3). In this position, he held lands in Babylonia (cf. Pliny XIII.43; Theophrastus, *HP* II.6.7; Plutarch, *Alex.* 39.10). His responsibilities certainly provided opportunity to organize and carry out a plot against the king. But there is nothing to prove that he was the sole instigator on each occasion. Furthermore, Diodorus's own presentation, which suggests that he was actually "master of the kingdom" and a kingmaker (XVI.50.8◊), must not be overvalued. And when Plutarch compares Bagoas with the (supposed) role played by Atossa in the accession of Xerxes (a comparison that creates consternation for the modern historian!), he goes even further, stating that Bagoas "took up the kingship of Persia and bestowed it upon Oarses and Darius" (*Moralia* 337e◊). This presentation is already found in the ancient authors who reported the succession of Xerxes: the chiliarch Artabanus was at the heart of the conspiracy that led to the accession of Artaxerxes I, but some of the Greeks claimed that he himself aspired to the royal title and even that he seized it for himself (chap. 13/10). We have the impression that we are faced with an interpretation that was very popular in Greece and that was articulated with a series of repeated motifs. A frequently used motif is poison: Bagoas poisoned Artaxerxes III with the complicity of a physician, and Darius III poisoned Bagoas by handing him the cup from which the "rogue eunuch" had intended Darius to drink (Diodorus XVII.5.3, 6◊). Given the frequency of the theme of poison in the Achaemenid court, it is surprising that Diodorus, referring to the elimination of Bagoas, presents the circumstances as "making a moral point" (*mnēmēs axios*)! Even Parysatis was reputed to have poisoned her sister-in-law Stateira by offering half a roast fowl to her (Plutarch, *Art.* 19.2–6; Ctesias §61).

The murder of Artaxerxes III certainly implies that at the outset there was opposition to the king, which Diodorus presents, in his own way, by stressing the hatred generated among the Persians by the king's cruelty (XVII.5.3). We can imagine that there were rival factions at the court and that, for reasons unknown to us, one of these factions favored the youngest son, Arses. In this we recognize a well-known pattern, one that is also illustrated at the end of Darius II's reign and again in the last years of Artaxerxes II. Another possible interpretation is thus opened up. We could also imagine that Arses, who was eager to seize power, propped himself up on Bagoas—just as Artaxerxes I had received the aid of the chiliarch Artabanus. We cannot be certain which of these possibilities matches the facts, since we know nothing at all of Arses before his accession. Was there opposition toward some other son, who may have received the title of crown prince? Whatever the case, the physical elimination of the new king's brothers certainly cannot be blamed on Bagoas alone: Artaxerxes IV himself certainly saw to the disappearance of all rivals. In any case, it has not been conclusively proved that he was the pawn of the chiliarch, since Diodorus himself states that the young king was far from willing to permit Bagoas free rein, and he even planned to bring an end to the latter's career (XVII.5.4). These were the circumstances under which Artaxerxes IV himself fell victim to an attack (late 336 – early 335).

Diodorus once again assigns responsibility to Bagoas alone, citing only "his habitual savagery (*synēthēs miaiphonia*)" (XVII.5.6◊). Of course, the phrase seems quite appropriate as one of the qualities attributed to this person, the "militant rogue eunuch" (§5.3; cf. Plutarch, *Art.* 17.8). Furthermore, the word used (*miaiphōnia*) carries another negative judgment, since it connotes the notion of degradation. But the explanation is a bit brief and no more convincing than Plutarch's claim that attributes the accession of Ochus/Artaxerxes III to his "hot, violent, no less treacherous than bloody" character (*Art.* 26.2;✧ 30.2–3✧)! In reality, Ochus's acquisition of supremacy was the result of a well-handled strategy that he had used to attract committed partisans (§26.2). At this point, we can mention the interesting phraseology used for the ancestry of the very close relatives of Artaxerxes III who figure in Darius III's retinue: thus, the surviving son, Bisthanes, in Arrian (III.19.4✧) is called "son of Ochus, the predecessor of Darius [III] as King of Persia" (*tou pro Dareiou basileusantos Persōn*); the same idea is also found in Quintus Curtius (III.13.12✧) regarding the three daughters and the widow of Ochus, "who had reigned before Darius" (*qui ante Dareum regnaverat*). Arses is not mentioned in any of these cases; he had apparently become the victim of a sort of *damnatio memoriae* in the court of Darius, who certainly seems to have wanted to connect himself directly to Artaxerxes III. This may explain why, in the Persian version transmitted by Justin (X.3.3–5), Codoman succeeds Artaxerxes III, without resolving the issue of continuity. Along the same lines, there is other disturbing evidence. First of all, given the breadth of the purge widely attributed to Artaxerxes III upon his accession (Justin X.3.1), it is noteworthy that the branch Darius belonged to was not touched. It is tempting to conclude from this that Darius's branch sided with Ochus and that its members (including the future Darius III) were among those who, in Artaxerxes II's palace, had been fervent supporters of Prince Ochus (cf. Plutarch, *Art.* 26.2; cf. 30.1–2). This then calls to mind one of the royal legends about Darius: it was during one of Artaxerxes III's campaigns that Darius/Codoman displayed his valor against a Cadusian—for which he was honored with *megalai dōreai* by the reigning king (Diodorus XVII.5.1). We are thus led to think that the prestigious court title (*astandēs*) and the distinction he enjoyed before his accession had been awarded to him by Artaxerxes III because of the assistance he provided to the king when Artaxerxes II died (359–358).

If, as Justin (X.3.4) says, Darius III actually was satrap of the two Armenias at the death of Artaxerxes II, he also held a territorial base and controlled armed forces. If this theory is valid, we may compare it to the situation of Ochus/Darius II, who was satrap of Hyrcania when his father Artaxerxes I died, according to Ctesias (§44). Therefore, it is even more doubtful that Bagoas himself placed Darius on the throne—though there is no doubt that he did lend his aid to the conspirators. Alexander himself, in his letter, "recognized" that it was Darius who had killed Arses, and the role attributed to Bagoas is that of accomplice rather than ringleader (*tou meta Bagōou*; Arrian II.14.5). Darius III was no more the puppet of the chiliarch than Artaxerxes I, at his accession, was the tool of Artabanus. Rather than, with Diodorus (XVII.5.5), making Darius III a "friend" of Bagoas, it is more correct to understand that the chiliarch was counted in the court category of Friends of Darius III, in the same way that he had been close to Artaxerxes III (XVI.47.3). Darius was a close relative of Artaxerxes III and IV, and therefore about 44 years old. As we have seen, he was a member of the "inner circle," especially in the time of Artaxerxes III, and he was much more certainly the real head of the conspiracy; when the conspiracy succeeded, he did away with a henchman (Bagoas) who was probably judged overly burdensome.

The New Great King

The tradition transmitted by Diodorus (XVII.5.6) only enhances the prestige of Darius, because it was the king himself who put the chiliarch to death. Without doubt, this lovely story was invented from whole cloth by the royal propagandists. Thus, we understand why Diodorus thought it would "make a moral point"; but Diodorus (who nevertheless was depending on Persian tradition) seized on the phrase, thinking only that he wanted to enhance the memory of Darius, not of Bagoas! Furthermore, in keeping with the rule after a dynastic struggle, a classic royal legend then was promulgated at court and gained broad distribution, describing the monomachy won by Codoman over a formidable Cadusian adversary. The propagandists attributed to Darius, as to all his predecessors (chap. 6/4), a "regal" physical appearance: he was "the tallest and handsomest man of his time" (Plutarch, *Alex.* 21.6✧).

Finally, it is certain that Darius III underwent the royal investiture in the regular fashion, during which he put off the robe of the *astandēs* (cf. Quintus Curtius III.3.5: *in eodem habitu Dareus fuisset, cum appellatus esset rex*), then put on "that which Cyrus the first wore before he was king" (cf. Plutarch, *Art.* 3.2✧), since only this sequence can explain the rationale of the dream attributed to Darius (cf. also Plutarch, *Alex.* 18.7–8). This is exactly what Plutarch says: he states that Bagoas "stripped from [Oarses] the garb of a courier (*astandēs*) and put upon him the royal raiment (*stolē basilikē*) and the tiara that ever stands erect" (*Moralia* 340c✧). This certainly must have been when he abandoned his former name (Artašāta) to take the throne name Darius. Although he attributes the name Codoman to him (we do not know why), Justin also provides the information: "the people honored him with the name Darius, so that he would lack nothing of regal majesty" (X.3.5). It is quite noteworthy that he did not take the name Artaxerxes, because, according to Diodorus (XV.93.1✧), "Artaxerxes [II] had ruled well . . . , [and] the Persians changed the names of those who ruled after him and prescribed that they should bear that name." We wonder whether the new king, following Darius II, wanted to indicate by his throne name that, like Darius I, he was founding a lineage that, though it belonged to the progeny of his distant ancestor (the "royal stock"), had its own legitimacy. If so, the new king's ambitions were not small.

The Accession of Darius III in Achaemenid Dynastic History

It is thus a good idea to treat cautiously and skeptically the pseudolegal context in which Alexander's letter and the other writings record the circumstances of Darius's accession. Of course, Arrian is not the only one who refers to a Persian *nomos*. Herodotus, for example, mentions a *nomos* that required the king to name a successor before going on a military campaign (VII.2). Herodotus, referring to a Persian *nomos*, also claims that a bastard has no right to the throne (III.2). It clearly is to *nomos* that Demaratus (VII.3), Parysatis (Plutarch, *Art.* 2.4–5), and the partisans of Darius (son of Artaxerxes II; §26.1) appeal for support when they refer to the absolute right of the oldest son or to the right (no less absolute) of the child "born to the purple" (once in a while, the contrast between the son of a king and the son of an *idiōtēs* turns up; see above, p. 771). The circumstances of the accessions of Xerxes and Darius II illustrate the point at which these (reconstructed) debates become surreal and mask conflicting ambitions that end up being settled by the decision of the ruling king or by the fortunes of war. The only bulwark against the threat of a family coup d'état was the proclamation of a crown prince (cf. Plutarch, *Art.* 26.4), but the dynastic history eloquently proves that this barrier was often breached (or threatened) by the sharp ambition of a younger son who was seething over being deprived of supreme power (examples: Bardiya, Cyrus the Younger, Ochus). The basic reason for this situation is easy to uncover: the Persian kingdom was not a constitutional monarchy with continuity determined by written rules of succession that were strictly applied by a sort of Supreme Court. This obviously would put us in the realm of total fiction: the justifications that Darius I gave for his authority, as we have seen (chap. 3/1), did not derive from a "right of succession" established for all time; they simply fleshed out his victory, which was confirmed *a posteriori* by proclamations that impress no one but their author. The same was true for Darius III: because he was king, he belonged to the royal House without having to prove anything. If there really were *nomoi*, then in an absolute monarchy (Aristotle's *pambasileia*), they would have no force of law with respect to the authority of the ruling king or the power relationships set up in regard to one of his rivals. Here as elsewhere (chap. 12/8), to render *nomos* as 'law' reflects the work of traducer rather than translator! As far as Darius III is concerned, the routine "legal" interpretations of the ancient authors were in every case completely overturned.

The only absolute rule binding the Achaemenids was that royal power was transmitted through the womb of the family. But, as we have seen, this was not a constitutional right; on the contrary, this conviction was built deeply into the family structure of Persian society and was expressed in the practice of endogamy (of which Darius III was a product and an exemplary performer). From this perspective, Achaemenid dynastic history after Darius I displayed a remarkable consistency: when there was no (or no longer a) legitimate son, the dead king's illegitimate sons disputed the succession among themselves, and one of them revived the royal stock by endogamy (Darius II); when the oldest son had died, one of the younger sons attained power (Artaxerxes I, Artaxerxes III, Arses); and when the king died without male descendant, either a competitor triumphed by force of arms and it became necessary to invent a prestigious ancestry after the fact (Darius I), or else power passed to a collateral branch and it was considered *a posteriori* as deriving without contest from the royal House (Darius III). All in all, the descendants of Darius I managed to bring to realization the dynastic program their ancestor had defined: the battles for supreme power were played out exclusively among members of the royal House. Never did an outsider manage to impose himself. As it turned out, the actual bases of the "dynastic pact" (chap. 8/7) remained solidly anchored.

At the same time, one might think that these practices weakened the central power, at least at the actual moment when contests were under way. There is hardly any doubt, for example, that secessionist tendencies (which were already manifest) took on new vigor after the execution of Bardiya; in addition, Diodorus states that the Egyptians took advantage of the unsettled succession after Xerxes to initiate a revolt (XI.71.3). But, in fact, the real threat came less from subject peoples than from the attitude of the Persian aristocracy, which was in the habit of supporting one candidate or another. This leads us to believe that each candidate had to make promises to the families that gave him their support. Did this practice necessarily weaken the new king? This is not at all certain, at least in the short term, if we recall the situation when Darius II and Parysatis wiped out nearly every representative of the Hydarnes family (chap. 14/6).

An Assessment

Whatever uncertainties remain about the details, the dynastic history between Artaxerxes III and Darius III provokes several reflections. First of all—and one more time—

about the Classical and Hellenistic sources: contrary to their claims, Darius III was an indisputable member of the "royal stock." He was an elite warrior, supported by broad segments of the court, the aristocracy, and of course the army; thus, he was indeed a legitimate Great King. But in these sources, the bases of disqualification from Persian royal power is found in at least two traditions that both appear (without mingling) in Diodorus. The first clearly goes back to the Greek polemicists of the fourth century, and especially Ephorus, who was Diodorus's inspiration in book XVI; in all of their activities, the fourth-century Persian kings are weak and little inclined to war or work. We would not insist on this point, which is rarely in evidence, were it not that the same theme is found in Ctesias, who is followed by Plutarch and many others. The problem is that this tradition has been taken up and magnified by Alexander's ancient historiography, which had the goal of exalting the Macedonian conqueror and was quite willing to use (or pretend to use) the Persian discourse of royal legitimation against Darius III.

At the same time, the discussions devoted to the accession of Darius III are included within a more general narrative that is designed to denigrate the memory of the last Great King. One illustration (of many) is found in Arrian, who transmits Alexander's fabricated arguments from 333; in Darius III's "funeral oration," he stresses that he was "dishonourable" in the battle of Gaugamela (because he fled), that "his life was one series of disasters," and finally that his fate was explained by his very character (or rather by his lack thereof): "No man showed less spirit or sense in warfare." Arrian then simply concedes that "in other matters he committed no offence." But the implicit contrast to other kings (Artaxerxes III in particular) does not really play in Darius's favor, since if he did not offend, it was "for lack of opportunity, since the moment of his accession was also the moment of the attack on him by the Macedonians and Greeks. So even if he had the will, he was no longer free to play the tyrant to his subjects, as his position was more dangerous than theirs" (III.22.2✧)! Let us stress in passing that the lack of "offence" (= firmness) was not really a royal attribute, as the propagandists of Cyrus the Younger and Ochus/Artaxerxes III emphasized in their time—they loved to denounce the "gentleness" (= weakness) of Artaxerxes II and his son Darius (Plutarch, *Art.* 2.1; 4.4; 6.1, 4; 26.1–3; 30.1–2).

The modern historian's task, obviously, is not compensatory exaltation of the memory of the last Great King. It is to attempt to understand why Darius lost the war. This is where, in the historiographic *longue durée*, the presentations by Alexander's authors have played a disastrously distorting role. It is tempting in fact to link the two traditions—the supposed weakness and the illegitimacy of Darius, the former "explained" by the latter—because Darius supposedly acceded to the throne contrary to Persian custom and only because he was propelled there by the eunuch Bagoas, who is thought to have been the real wielder of power. Textual and contextual analysis actually tends to prove that we have far too often promoted as conclusions what are nothing more than assumptions inherited directly from Macedonian propaganda. Obviously, we can assume that the same suspicions bear on the propaganda from the Persian side, which exalted Darius's courage in the face of Alexander (Justin X.3.6) and stressed his meticulous preparations for the impending military confrontation (Diodorus XVII.7.1–3). Meanwhile, the simultaneous disqualification of both traditions breeds its own contradictions, since the positioning of Darius III's accession in Achaemenid dynastic history makes quite a few of the details disappear—the very details that since antiquity have regularly been attributed to the event. As for the reality of the authority that might be boasted about, "both in the palace and in the war-camp" (*DNb* 27–31◇), Darius did not long delay proving it by eliminating Bagoas; his authority was also demonstrated by the fact that the recent conspiracy of Bagoas was quickly made the topic of a denunciation (Diodorus XVII.5.6).

2. The Great King and the Persian Aristocracy

The circumstances when Darius took power presuppose that he had support among the Persian aristocracy. Quite luckily, we have considerable information preserved by Alexander's writers that illustrates this point. We will not discuss all the details of this large mass of data: on the one hand, not all of the notes are equally useful; on the other, our concern here is to analyze the composition and function of the dominant socioethnic class in general and to observe possible changes.

In the innermost circle of royal favor, the primary group was the Kinsmen. As we have already seen (chap. 8/1), the word itself refers to two distinct things that are well illustrated in Darius's procession before the battle of Issus: one of the groups preceding the royal chariot was "those whom they call the king's kindred (*cognati regis*), 15,000 men. . . . About two hundred of the noblest relatives (*nobilissimi propinquorum*) of the king attended him on the right and on the left [of the chariot]" (Quintus Curtius III.3.14, 21◇). The respective quantities and the different positions indicate clearly that the first group comprised the Kinsmen, as a class in the court hierarchy, and the second group was the actual relatives. At Gaugamela, the Kinsmen (*syggenesis*) were placed at the center, close to Darius (Arrian III.5), 10,000 of them who were "chosen for courage (*andragathia*) and for loyalty (*pistis*)" (Diodorus XVII.59.3◇). There were 40 of them at the Granicus (XVII.20.2), but these represented only the Persian nobility from Asia Minor. Also among the most coveted titles was Friend, a category that itself was crisscrossed with internal hierarchies. For example, Mazaeus was not simply a Friend of Darius (Diodorus XVII.55.1), but he also was "the most influential man at the court of Dareius" (Plutarch, *Alex.* 39.9◇). This hierarchy obviously developed as a function of royal favor (cf. Diodorus XVI.52.1: *Artaxerxēs proēgen* [*Mentōra*] *malista tōn philōn*); special positions resulted from an honor (*timē*) and at the same time illustrate the way royal favor worked (cf. Arrian I.12.10). It is easy to distinguish the inner circle of "very highly placed Persian officers of Darius (*hoi amphi Dareion Persōn hoi epiphanestatoi*)" (Arrian III.23.4◇). Artabazus was certainly one of these Persians. According to Quintus Curtius (III.13.13◇), he was "chief of the courtiers" (*princeps purpuratorum*); the word *princeps* renders the Greek *prōtos*, as Arrian III.23.7 shows: "he [Alexander] kept Artabazus and his sons by him in an honourable position (*timē*), as they were among the most eminent (*prōtoi*) Persians and especially because of their loyalty (*pistis*) to Darius." These handpicked examples prove that the relationship between the king and the aristocrats was always based on the exchange of gift/service (favor/loyalty) and that the nobles continued to define themselves in terms of their own origin and by the degree of intimacy connecting them to the king. Orxines, who commanded the Persian troops at Gaugamela, boasted that he descended from the Seven Persians (Quintus Curtius IV.12.8) and that he belonged to the lineage of Cyrus through his position as head of the tribe of Pasargadae (X.1.22–23). Under Artaxerxes III, Rhosaces was eager to let it be known that he "was a descendant of one of the seven Persians who deposed the Magi" (Diodorus

XVI.47.2✧). The example of Artabazus, among others (e.g., Arrian III.23.7), also proves that Alexander, within the framework of his policy of cooperation with the Iranians, took over the rationale of the Achaemenid system for his own advantage. By awarding the collective title "Kinsmen" to the Persians in his retinue (Arrian VII.11.1), and then to the Macedonians (§11.6–7), Alexander was merely stretching to the breaking-point a change that had already gained ground during the course of Achaemenid history—a change that tended to make the place of the nobility in the ranks of the court hierarchy more and more intimate in relation to the king.

Because a single word (*syggenesis*) is used in Greek for both categories, it is not always easy to distinguish kinsmen from Kinsmen, except when family ties are explicitly mentioned; when two texts supplement one another (e.g., Diodorus XVII.67.4 and Quintus Curtius V.3.12); when the author uses a complementary term (e.g., Diodorus XVII.73.9: "the brother and other relatives [*syggeneis*] of Darius"); or finally, when the author uses a specific term: according to Arrian (III.21.5), Bessus had family ties (*oikeiotēs*) to Darius—though even this word can mean 'ties of familiarity'. The title is sometimes associated with "friend," as in the "kinsmen" and "friends." In some cases, it is difficult to tell which kinsmen/Kinsmen are involved (e.g., Diodorus XVII.31.1). Sometimes, the use of an apparently more precise term (*propinquus*) leads us to believe that the author is referring to a relative (Quintus Curtius III.3.25, compared with III.3.21), but this criterion is not always definitive (cf. IV.11.1). The number of relatives (200) in Darius's procession should not surprise us: the numerous illegitimate sons of the king must have been included since, according to Justin, Artaxerxes II had no fewer than 115 of them (X.1.1). The phrase used by Quintus Curtius (III.3.21: *nobilissimi propinquorum*) seems to imply the existence of an internal hierarchy, probably based on closeness of blood ties. This helps explain several other phrases used by the same author: "Darius sent ten envoys, the leading men (*cognatorum principes*) of his court" (IV.11.1✧) to contact Alexander. Quintus Curtius (V.3.12✧) writes about Madates: he "had taken to wife her [Sisygambis's] sister's daughter, and thus was a near relative of Darius" (*Dareum propinqua cognatione contingens*); Madates was apparently married to a granddaughter of Ostanes (the brother of Artaxerxes II and father of Sisygambis); finally, Polyaenus calls Phrasaortes "a close relative of Darius" (IV.3.27).

Darius also had many representatives of his immediate family around him. First, we note the presence of members of Artaxerxes III's family. Bisthanes, the sole surviving son, seems to have held a special position near the king (Arrian III.19.4–5). Three daughters and the wife of Ochus were also among Darius's followers (Quintus Curtius III.13.12–13); they must also have been among the "wives of his relatives and friends (*propinquorum amicorumque conjuges*)" (III.3.25✧) who appeared at the end of the royal procession. We may also name a granddaughter of Ochus [Artaxerxes IV] "who had lately been king of the Persians"; she was born to one of the (unnamed) sons of this king. Moreover, her husband, Hystaspes, was "a kinsman (*propinquus*) of Darius [III]" and in this capacity had received a high military command (Quintus Curtius VI.2.7). We may also note Arbupales, a son of Darius who was himself a felonious son of Artaxerxes II (Arrian I.16.3). Apparently, Arbupales had escaped the purge that followed Darius's execution. The already-cited examples of Bessus (satrap in Bactra), Madates (governor of Uxiana; Quintus Curtius V.3.4), Bisthanes, and Hystaspes show that the Great King systematically distributed important posts to his relatives (cf. Diodorus §31.1:

philoi kai syggeneis). Furthermore, Arbupales was one of the Persian leaders at the Granicus. We also know that a son-in-law of the king, Mithradates, was unhorsed and grievously wounded by Alexander (Arrian I.16.3). Among his closest family, Darius's son Ochus was too young to have held any job at all. In contrast, Oxathres, brother of the Great King, was known to have performed heroically at Issus (Diodorus XVII.34.2–3; Quintus Curtius III.11.8). He remained close to Darius until the final catastrophe (Quintus Curtius VI.2.9–11).

This is the way it also was in the great Persian aristocratic families. The association of sons and brothers with the responsibilities of fathers or brothers was everyday practice (cf. Arrian VII.6.4–5). At the Granicus, for example, Memnon arrived with his sons at the head of his horsemen (I.15.2), and Rhosaces came to the aid of his brother Spithrobates [Spithridates], satrap of Lydia and Ionia (Diodorus XVII.20.3–6). Memnon himself was in all probability the son of Rhosaces, who held the same post during the time of Artaxerxes III (XVI.47.2). Orontes, who (together with Mithraustes) led the Armenian contingent at Gaugamela (Arrian III.8.5), appears to have been a descendant of the satrap with the same name who, as son-in-law of Artaxerxes II, ruled Armenia around 400 (Xenophon, *Anab.* III.4.13; 5.17; IV.3.4). At Babylon, Mazaeus came to greet Alexander "with his mature children" (Quintus Curtius V.1.17–18◊). One of them, Brochubelus, had previously assisted him in his district of Cilicia–Trans-Euphrates (V.13.11). But the best example, because it is the best known, certainly is Artabazus and his family; he was a distant descendant of Pharnaces (the uncle of Darius) and grandson of Artaxerxes II by one of the king's daughters. We know that after his revolt Artabazus lost his satrapy of Hellespontine Phrygia, which his ancestors had ruled since the time of Xerxes. He had had to leave his country for Macedon with his entire family; this included not just his wife and many children but also two captains of Rhodian mercenaries, Memnon and Mentor, whose sister he had married (Diodorus XVI.52.4). After his exalted deeds in Egypt (343), Mentor had obtained a pardon for Artabazus from Artaxerxes III, and as a result Artabazus was able to return, along with his numerous progeny (eleven sons and ten daughters). Artabazus did not regain his satrapy (which then belonged to Arsites) but did regain royal favor, which reached its zenith in the time of Darius III (Quintus Curtius III.13.13; Arrian III.23.6). When they had returned, Mentor actively concerned himself with promoting his nephews, "giving them the most distinguished commands in the armed forces" (Diodorus XVI.52.4◊). The entire family appears again in the time of Darius III. Artabazus was too old to take part in battle, but the situation was quite different for his brother-in-law and his children. Even if it is hugely exaggerated by Diodorus (chap. 17/3 below), Memnon's role after the battle of the Granicus was quite noteworthy, until he died in the assault on the walls of Mytilene in the summer of 333. Before dying, he entrusted his authority to his nephew Pharnabazus, while awaiting Darius's decision (Arrian II.1.3; 2.1)—literal nepotism, which irresistibly leads us to an episode narrated by Herodotus (VIII.130). As ordered by Darius, who had confirmed him in his position, Pharnabazus turned over contingents of mercenaries to his cousin Thymondas (son of Memnon) and then led vigorous operations in the Aegean until he was captured at Chios in the summer of 332. Cophen, another son of Pharnabazus, had been the king's quartermaster at Damascus in 333 (Arrian II.15.1); he reappears in 330 close to Darius along with two of his brothers, Ariobarzanes and Arsames (Arrian III.23.7). Another son, Ilioneus, was taken prisoner after the battle of Issus, along with the wife and sons of Pharnabazus, three daughters of Mentor, and the wife and sons of Memnon; Quintus Curtius comments: "Hardly any house of a member of the court (*domus purpurati*) escaped that great disaster" (III.13.13–14◇). According to Diodorus, Memnon had intentionally sent his wife and son to Darius: "He calculated that leaving them in the king's care was a good way to ensure their safety, while at the same time the king, now that he had good hostages, would be more willing to entrust Memnon with the supreme command" (XVII.23.4◇). The last part of Diodorus's comment is probably not true; the phrase instead alludes to a general rule that the wife and minor children of those in high positions at the center of the Empire usually remained at court, including occasions when the father was on a mission in the provinces or with the army or when the court itself was on the road, in time of peace or time of war.

The composition of the high imperial personnel of Darius III suggests several contrasting reflections. For one thing, continuity with the state of affairs in the time of Darius I and Xerxes is obvious—so much so that it can be reconstructed primarily on the basis of notes on personal names offered by Herodotus (cf. chap. 7). The continuity is illustrated especially well by the example of the descendants of Pharnaces/Parnaka at Dascylium and by the insistence some placed on connecting themselves to the time of Darius I (as a "descendant of the Seven": Rhosaces, Orxines). Continuity was created and sustained by the persistent custom of passing assignments through the same families and/or by the association of one or more sons with the satrapal responsibility of the father (or a nephew his uncle's). At the same time, the dominant Persian socioethnic class was open to some non-Persians (in the ethnic sense), as is illustrated by the promotion of Bēlšunu in Babylonia (chap. 14/8), the matrimonial alliances between the satrapal family of Dascylium and the Rhodians Mentor and Memnon (chap. 16/2), and personal names (cf. Abulites of Susa and the names of some of Mazaeus's sons; chap. 16/10). This certainly reflects a major trend to which we shall return when we consider its political significance, particularly beginning with the example of Mazaeus. Conversely, in 334 the satrapy of Caria, which had long been held by the Carian Hecatomnid family, was ruled for the first time by a satrap of Persian origin, Orontobates (cf. Strabo XIV.2.17).

3. *The Royal Armies*

The Greek Thesis

We know that from the Greek point of view—which is repeated ad nauseam in modern works, including some of the most recent—one of the most visible manifestations of Persian decadence was the inability of the Great Kings to put an army worthy of the name into the field against Greek troops, who were superior in both arms and courage. Under these conditions, the Great Kings would have had no alternative when they wished to make war than to rely first and foremost on corps of Greek mercenaries, who were the only ones capable of slowing the advance of the Greek armies sent against the imperial territories. This smug thesis was developed particularly by Xenophon and Plato, along with many fourth-century authors—hence the unbridled use of the "glorious" precedents for the Ten Thousand and the *anabasis* of Agesilaus.

We have already touched on the problem in previous chapters while analyzing the composition of the armies of Darius II, Artaxerxes II, and Cyrus the Younger (in 401). We noted there that the thesis is not tenable and that nothing in particular demonstrates a connection between resorting to mercenaries and disintegration of recruiting bases for soldiers for the royal army in Babylonia or elsewhere. It is nonetheless important to re-open the discussion generally, because the thesis has been widely advanced, by ancient authors and again by modern authors in the context of Darius III's army. We may recall in particular that, according to Arrian (I.14.4), the Persian satraps at the Granicus had a force of 20,000 foreign mercenaries (*xenoi misthophoroi*), a number equal to the force of Persian horsemen. Quintus Curtius (III.8.1◇) writes that, on the eve of the battle of Is-sus, the Greek soldiers led by Thymondas (cf. Arrian II.2.1) were Darius's "principal and almost sole hope" and that the Great King had 30,000 mercenaries at that time (III.2.9). Does this mean that during the fourth century the military capacity of the Empire had shrunk critically?

In order to answer this question, we should first of all analyze the genesis of this thesis and identify its real creator. While Plato, Xenophon, and Isocrates certainly did much to support its credibility, the person really responsible for it is Diodorus, who is correctly thought to have used as his basis the work of Ephorus, an author whose anti-Persian bias is well known (cf. XVI.76.5–6). Diodorus, in fact, frequently presents the Greek merce-naries in action, particularly during the Egyptian expeditions, by using a form of narra-tive that tends, apparently at least, to provide objective, concrete details. These passages in Diodorus are quite widely paraphrased by modern historians. In order to lay bare the system of Diodorus, let us begin with his long account of Artaxerxes III's expedition against Egypt (XVI.46.4–9, 47–50; cf. 40.3–6, 41–45). We will study it alongside the sto-ries of other Persian expeditions against Egypt transmitted by the same author: the expe-ditions of the 460s (XI.77.1–4) and the 370s (XV.41–44). Fragments about the operations with and against Artabazus in the 350s will be added, since they also appear to derive from Ephorus. It is easy to show that in every case Ephorus's thesis is illustrated by the same arguments and the same stereotypes:

(1) The pharaoh and the Great King reinforced their armies with the help of Greeks: there were 10,000 in Artaxerxes III's army (XVI.44.4) — 4000 of them mercenaries sent by Greek cities in Europe at his request (1000 Thebans under the command of Lacrates, 3000 Argives commanded by Nicostratus), to whom must be added the 4000 men of Mentor, the former mercenary commander of Nectanebo II (§42.2; §45.1); and the latter in turn had gathered another 20,000 Greek mercenaries (§47.6). In 373, Necta-nebo I had "collected a large mercenary force": 20,000 according to Diodorus (XV.29.1◇), 12,000 according to Nepos (*Iph.* 2.4); and Tachos repeated this in 360 (XVI.92.2–3). The Sidonians also managed to recruit a multitude (*plēthos*) of mercenar-ies (XVI.41.4◇), and the same was true of the army sent by the Great King against Cy-prus (§42.7–9). Furthermore, the army of Inarus in the 460s used mercenaries: the Egyptian rebel counted on military aid (*symmakhia*; XI.71.4) sent by Athens (cf. Thucy-dides I.104, 109), and his mercenaries are specifically portrayed by Ctesias within the framework of the Megabyzus saga (§§32–37).

(2) The Greeks always appear in the forward elements of the army. According to Dio-dorus, in 343 only the Greek army (*hellēnikē dynamis*) was engaged in the front lines and "the rest of the army" was held in reserve under the command of Artaxerxes III. The Greek army itself was divided into three regiments, each commanded by a Greek and a Persian: Lacrates and Rhosaces, Nicostratus and Aristazanes, Mentor and Bagoas. Given the prominent role attributed to the Greek leaders, we get the impression that the Per-

sian leaders were subordinate to them (XVI.47.1–4). This is also what Diodorus wants us to believe when he states that Artaxerxes was being very careful when he acquired mercenaries and their commanders because he remembered his previous defeat with great acrimony (§44.1–2). This is a curious conclusion, suggesting that on his previous expedition the Great King had had no mercenary troops, given that Diodorus himself continually exalts their role in all of the Egyptian campaigns (cf. XV.41ff.). Of course, Diodorus also notes the presence of "barbarian forces" in the Great King's army (XVI.47.2, 4; §50.3; XI.74–75), but in every case he highlights the special value and courage of the Greek leaders and in every case he also introduces the contrast between the Greeks and their employers (whether Egyptian or Persian). Furthermore, the parallelism between the two armies that Diodorus wishes to present becomes even more striking when we consider the order of battle he presents: Nectanebo II and Artaxerxes both kept themselves in reserve, behind the front lines (XVI.47.5–6), as if the Greek mercenaries constituted the heart of their respective forces.

A similar scheme is also found in the tales concerning the participation of Chares in the rebellion of Artabazus. When Diodorus states that Chares fought alongside (*symma-khōn*) the satrap (XVI.22.1; 34.1), it is clear that he attributes the glory of the victories to Chares. He treats the Theban Pammenes similarly some time later: "By defeating the satraps in two great battles, [he] won great glory for himself and the Boeotians" (§34.2✧). The one (Ephorus?) who inspired a scholia to Demosthenes 4.19 even passes over the presence of Artabazus alongside Chares in silence: it is Chares alone who led 10,000 mercenaries to a stunning victory over Tithraustes, who commanded a considerable force of 20,000 Persians, most of whom were horsemen (cf. also *FGrH* 105 F5). We may emphasize in passing that this kind of presentation is not applied only to Persians; Diodorus adopts it for the pharaohs' armies as well as for the Phoenician army that rebelled against the Persians. Using a stereotyped expression, he reports on the throngs of mercenaries raised by the authorities in Sidon (XVI.41.4). But, in reality, only Mentor's 4000 mercenaries are specifically named (§42.2), and they primarily belong to the category of citizen-soldiers (*stratiōtai politikoi*)—who in fact do seem to have taken the main role in all of the fighting (§44.5–6; cf. §45.4–5).

(3) As Diodorus reports them, the confrontations of the 343–342 campaign thus seem to be reduced to fights between Greek mercenaries from the two sides. Though he mentions the presence of Libyans and Egyptians in Nectanebo II's army (XVI.47.6), he scarcely brings them onto the scene in what follows; it is the Greeks who defend Pelusium courageously (§49.2), even as we learn incidentally that the garrisons comprised Greeks and Egyptians (§49.7). When Diodorus mentions this, it is primarily to illustrate the stark contrast between Greeks and Egyptians (§49.8; §50.2). The Persian side is handled similarly. The Thebans faced the Spartan Philophron, who commanded the garrison at Pelusium, and they threw themselves boldly into the battle, "being eager to show themselves the best of the Greeks that were taking part in the expedition" (46.8–9✧). The Argive Nicostratus was first to cross the Nile and thus determined the success of the operations, and it was another Greek, Cleinius of Cos, who opposed him in the Egyptian camp (§48.3–5). Similarly, Lacrates the Theban actively pursued the siege of Pelusium (§49.1–3), and Mentor the Rhodian took Bubastis and other nearby cities (§49.7–8). Likewise, again, in 371, Iphicrates dashed at the head of his men against a fortification on the Mendes Mouth of the Nile (XV.42.5).

(4) This presentation is articulated on the basis of a single assumption: the superiority of the Greeks, both soldiers and officers—who were so superior that victories were due entirely to them and defeats were attributable solely to their employers. Thus, Hakoris sent for Chabrias only because he "ha[d] no capable general" (XV.29.2◊). Similarly, it was certainly because Pharnabazus insisted that the Athenians sent him Iphicrates (XV.29.2), and Diodorus devotes an entire chapter to Iphicrates' valor (XV.44). Likewise, Artaxerxes III himself asked the Argives to give the command to Nicostratus, who was famous for his bravery and valor (XVI.44.2–3). Chabrias and Agesilaus, alongside Tachos, are treated in the same way (XV.92.2–3), etc. Furthermore, Nectanebo II was conquered in 343 because of his military incompetence combined with overconfidence resulting from previous victories; in fact, Diodorus thinks, his earlier victory (in 351) was due to the fact that he had turned over command of the troops to commanders of Greek mercenaries, the Athenian Diophantus and the Spartan Lamius (XVI.48.1–2). The same explanation appears in this context that Diodorus had given for the failure of Tachos in 361–359; Tachos had ignored the "wise counsel" of Agesilaus (XV.92.3). Similarly, Pharnabazus had ignored the judicious suggestions of Iphicrates (XV.43). The Greek leaders were in fact swift and brave (XV.43.1–2, 5–6; 44.2), in contrast to the Persian generals, who were "cowardly and inexperienced" (XVI.40.4) and who were further characterized by their hesitancy and timidity (XV.43.1–2)—they were unable to march quickly on the enemy because they lost much time readying their armies and ceaselessly seeking the advice of the Great King (XV.41.2–5; XVI.46.7; cf. XVII.18.2). This resulted in frequent clashes between Persian and Greek leaders, the former supposedly envious of the latter (XV.43.2, 6), and this is the background for presenting the disputes between them in 343 (XVI.50.1–4) and again in 334 (Arrian I.12.10; cf. Diodorus XVII.18.3). The uncommon bravery of the Greek soldiers is illustrated primarily as a contrast to the cowardice of the Egyptian soldiers, who after the initial clashes could think of nothing other than trying to make peace with the Persians (XI.77.3; XVI.49.7–8).

(5) The superiority of the Greeks was recognized by the Persians themselves. This was already the significance of the description presented by Xenophon of the military review organized in Cilicia by Cyrus the Younger. It was the Greeks of his army—and they alone—who incited panic among the barbarians (*Anab.* I.2.17–18). The case was the same during the Egyptian campaigns: because he admired Greek valor, Megabyzus agreed to a treaty with them, for he feared direct confrontation (Diodorus XI.77.4). The Greeks saved their lives "by their courage" (*idia aretē*; §77.5◊). Some anecdotes from Polyaenus—who himself may have been dependent on Ephorus—also promulgate this stereotype. For instance, facing the Persians, Gastron, a Spartan leader in Egypt, armed the Greeks in Egyptian style and the Egyptians in Greek style and put the latter in the front line: "The Persians actually taking them for what they appeared to be, threw themselves into disorder and fled" (II.16). In a similar situation, Orontes was facing Autophradates: he hoped to impress his enemy and make him believe that a reinforcement of Greek mercenaries was on their way, so "he armed the most vigorous of the barbarians in Greek style" and mingled them with the Greeks: "Seeing the Greek arms, Autophradates convinced himself that these were the reinforcements he had heard tell of: not daring to risk combat, he struck camp and fled" (VII.14.4). The first anecdote is all the more striking in that it is not based on any sort of military rationale, even a false one (in contrast to Orontes' actions): instead, we get the impression that the author was using the parable for purely ideological ends.

(6) The valor of the Greeks is even more noteworthy because, generally speaking, they were minority participants: in 343, there were 10,000 Greeks within the immense royal army (XVI.40.6: stereotyped figures; cf. XI.74.1); on the Egyptian side, again in 343, we find 20,000 Greeks alongside 20,000 Libyans and 60,000 Egyptian *makhimoi* (XVI.47.6).

The Use of Mercenaries and "Decadence": Achaemenid Truth and Athenian Filter

The coherence, and thus the apparent credibility, of the thesis we have just schematically laid out is even more noteworthy because it was already worked out in the fourth century by all of the Greek authors. But this only *seems* paradoxical—it is this very unanimity that casts grave doubt on every one of its constituent elements and thus on the totality of the thesis. In fact, it seems clear that it is built on a radical antithesis between Greek and barbarian that is quite frequently asserted by the masters of Panhellenism (Isocrates, Ephorus) and the advocates of the theory of "Persian decadence" (Isocrates, Ephorus, Plato, Xenophon in the last chapter of the *Cyropaedia*). The "analysis" of the decadence itself proceeds through convenient, effective stereotypes: wealth and opulence (*tryphē*) inexorably made the Persians effeminate and caused them to abandon their traditional warrior virtues. It is thus abundantly clear that this theory is embedded in the *longue durée* of Greco-Persian relations;. We recall that it is already fully present in the speech that Herodotus gives Aristagoras of Miletus to deliver to Cleomenes of Sparta: the barbarians are not only immensely rich but they also "have little taste for war (*Oute* [. . .] *alkimoi*) . . . how easy they are to beat! you . . . are the strongest power in the Greek world" (V.49✧). It is clear, finally, that this certainty was conceived in the heart of the battles at Thermopylae, Salamis, Plataea, and Mycale, because we know that the memory of all of these clashes was both piously preserved and cannily transformed by the fourth-century Athenian authors. At any rate, it is enough to recall the explanation offered by Diodorus/Ephorus for the behavior of the Greeks in Egypt: at the time of their participation in the battles alongside Inarus, the Greeks hoped to be worthy of their predecessors' example at Thermopylae (XI.77.3–4). The precedent of the Persian Wars was also cited by Chares: after "his" victory over Tithraustes, he did not flinch from presenting it to the Athenians as "the sister to the battle of Marathon" (scholia on Demosthenes 4.14; cf. Plutarch, *Aratus* 16.3)!

The intellectual frailty and the implications of the ideological assumptions of this presentation no longer need to be pointed out. All the same, other authors have worked out totally different theories about the political components of the *tryphē* (symbol of power) and/or underlined the valor and courage of the Persian combatants, whether confronting the Greeks in 490–479 [480–479?] or Alexander's Macedonians. Nevertheless, to understand the logic and effectiveness of these stereotypes better—in order to reder them harmless—they must be placed into an even more precise context. When they are put into the context of the 350s, these narratives on the use of mercenaries also reflect a debate internal to the city. Though there are several possible corpora to consider, it is enough to consider the harangues that Demosthenes delivered during the course of wars and conflicts with Philip II. In these harangues, the Macedonian king's power (just like the Great King's; cf. *Symm.* 3–9; 29–32) is sometimes highlighted and sometimes devalued, not as a function of observable change, but simply as a function of the orator's own forensic requirements. If the orator felt the assembly's resolve weakening, he would try to strengthen it by emphasizing the "decadence" of the kingdom of Macedon, which he describes with the same stereotypes that were described as flaws in the Achaemenid system. For instance, Philip behaves like a barbarian, surrounding himself with buffoons—"The rest about him are brigands and parasites, and men of that character, who will get drunk and perform dances which I scruple to name before you" *Olynt.* II.19✧)! This moral weakness is accompanied "quite naturally" by the decadence of the Macedonian army. Demosthenes appealed to testimony that was both anonymous and false (and against all probability) and was quite willing to slander the king's soldiers, Macedonian infantry (*pezhetairoi*) and mercenaries (*xenoi*) alike: "His mercenaries and guards, indeed, have the reputation of admirable and well-trained soldiers, but, as I heard from one who had been in the country, a man incapable of falsehood, they are no better than others" (§17✧).

It is not difficult to notice that, within his own civic rationale, the use of mercenaries was passionately opposed by Demosthenes. Mercenaries were eager for cash and booty, and their leaders often took initiatives contrary to the city's interests (e.g., *Olynt.* II.28; Isocrates, *Peace* 44). In the *First Philippic*, delivered in 351, he urged his fellow citizens to re-create citizen armies, and he denounced the leaders of the mercenaries who did not hesitate to sell themselves to the highest bidder: "they go off to Artabazus or anywhere" (§24✧), which the scholiast renders (4.24) with a very tendentious statement: "Not wishing themselves to fight because of the danger, the Athenians engaged paid outsiders (*xenoi misthōmenoi*)." The same evaluation is found in Diodorus (X.34.8–13), where it is included in a general discussion contrasting the Greek cities with the tyrants and kings. The author, who here also is presenting Ephorus's opinion, urges the Greeks not to resort to the deplorable habit of drafting mercenary troops (*xenikai dynameis*) in place of civic armies (*politikai dynameis*). Diodorus tirelessly embroiders the stereotype of the Greek (Athenian) vision of the Persian Wars, and he in fact stresses the superiority of valor/courage (*aretē* = Greeks) over number (*plēthos* = barbarians). In nearly identical words, Demosthenes and Diodorus describe the appeal to mercenaries as one of the symptoms of the decadence of civic spirit. Like Xenophon when he discusses the Persians in the last chapter of the *Cyropaedia* or the Spartans in the last chapter of the *Constitution of the Lacedaemonians* (the Spartans of "the olden days" and the Persians "of today" are themselves contrasted comprehensively in the *Agesilaus* IX), Demosthenes enjoys contrasting the virtue of the ancients with the moral decadence he sees in the Athens of his day. In ancient times, "the king of this country [Macedon] was submissive to them, as a barbarian should be to Greeks" (*Olynt.* III.24✧); in ancient times, instead of appealing to mercenaries, the people "dared to campaign for themselves" (III.30). The discourse is all-encompassing and takes on universal value: it applies to any state suspected of being unable to mobilize its own people against an enemy. This explains why the pharaohs counted less on their troops than on their country's natural defenses (Diodorus XV.42.1–3; XVI.46.7–8, 47.6–7, 48.7). This is also a well-known motif in Greek literature—condemnation of cities that put all their hope in their fortifications instead of counting first on the courage of their citizens. The same charge is brought against the Persians by Alexander (cf. Arrian VII.7.7).

Of course—and we have already repeated it several times here—the ideological decryption of the Greek sources cannot take the place of proof: Achaemenid reality is not the mirror image of Greek portrayals. But it is necessary to state that the many references to the Great King's Greek mercenaries do not in themselves have probative value; their primary purpose is to charge the Persians with decadence of civic spirit, which is paralleled by the assumed weakness of the satraps' and Great Kings' armies—and both of these are presented in a convenient opposition between a "then" (virtue) and a "now" (decadence) that is constructed from whole cloth, whether it concerns Athens, Sparta, or Persia. In the logic of this discourse, the Persian (or Egyptian) reference thus primarily plays a supporting role; it does not require proof derived from verified or verifiable facts. But then, though no one would ever consider viewing the effectiveness and organization of Philip's army solely through the distorting prism of Demosthenes' harangues, how could any historian be so credulous as to portray the Persian Empire on the basis of the words of the Athenian orators and polemicists? We can only imagine that the ancient orators would be thoroughly amazed to learn that probative value is sometimes still today granted to an "analysis" of the Empire of Artaxerxes III or Darius III as a city unable to defend itself on its own and that put its security into the hands of foreign mercenaries without batting an eyelash!

Command Structure

We remain equally skeptical about Diodorus's presentation of the command structure when the leaders of Greek mercenaries took part in combat. We have seen that Diodorus claims that the command of the three regiments created by Artaxerxes III in 343 was entrusted to three Greek-Persian pairs; he even wants us to believe that the Greeks were in charge of the maneuvers. The vocabulary he uses does not give rise to the ambiguities because, in principle, the Greek was the *stratēgos* and the Persian was the *hēgemōn* (XVI.47.1), which implies that authority belonged to the latter. However, Aristazanes is said to "share the command (*synarkhōn*)" with Nicostratus (47.3), and Bagoas "fought alongside (*synestrateuto*) Mentor" (§47.4). Regardless of what their titles were, the actions of commanders in some other cases erase the doubts that Diodorus's vocabulary and presentation generate: after Lacrates made an agreement with the mercenaries of Pelusium, "Artaxerxes dispatched Bagoas with barbarian soldiers to take over (*paralambanein*) Pelusium" (§49.4;✧ cf. 6: *paradidōmi*). The term used is clear: a Persian was officially responsible for taking possession of the town in the name of the king. At Bubastis, the Greeks of the garrison sent emissaries to Bagoas; again, he was the first to enter the town, at the head of the barbarian soldiers (§50.1, 4).

Furthermore, Diodorus portrays conflict that arose due to the coadministration of Persians and Greeks, such as the disputes between Lacrates and Bagoas (49.1–6) or Mentor and Bagoas (50.1–6). This evidence is also found in the campaign of 373: "Pharnabazus became suspicious of his [Iphicrates'] boldness and his courage for fear lest he take possession of Egypt for himself. . . . Some generals [on Pharnabazus's staff] indeed bore a grudge against him and were attempting to fasten unfair charges upon him" (Diodorus XV.43.2✧). The participation of the mercenary leaders in the staff's deliberations is also attested for Cyrus the Younger, but in every case the final decision rested with the chief of staff, who was always a Persian. So this much is clear: under the King's supreme authority, it was the Persians who retained command. Who can doubt it when Diodorus emphasizes the royal favor enjoyed by the three Persian generals in 343, all of them "preferred above the others for valour and loyalty" (XVI.47.1✧)? Rhosaces boasted of descent from one of the Seven (§47.2); Aristazanes "was an usher (*eisaggeleus*) of the King and the most faithful of his friends (*pistotatos tōn philōn*)" after

Bagoas" (§47.3◇); and as for the last of the three, it was he "whom the King trusted most" (§47.4◇).

The Greeks appear as often as they do in part because of the highly partisan orientation of the work of Ephorus. We have also seen that an anonymous author attributes the direction of military operations against Tithraustes to Chares and Pammenes. Because of an incidental reference, we learn that, after a raid led by Pammenes, Artabazus awarded command of the troops to two of his brothers, Oxythras and Dibictus (Polyaenus VII.33.2). The Greeks might also be at the fore because the Persian leaders preferred to sacrifice the mercenaries before engaging their own "barbarian" troops. Finally, Greek commanders appear often because, as in Cyrus the Younger's army, the Greek leaders retained command of the unit they had themselves recruited (cf. XVI.48.3: Nicostratus *tōn Argeiōn stratēgos*). Nevertheless, this limited command was incorporated into a chain headed by Persians, and the general direction of operations and strategic decisions remained with the Great King himself (§49.6–7).

Memnon, the Persian Satraps, and Darius III

It is quite striking to observe that, once more, Diodorus—this time in book XVII—repeats the same sort of explanation to account for the unusual position of the Rhodian Memnon at the beginning of Darius III's reign. At the time of the first Macedonian offensive in 336–335, only Memnon seems to have been able to counterattack: he was the one who put Parmenion to flight near Pitane in Aeolis (§7.8). Even though Darius chose 'his best commanders' (*aristoi hēgemones*; unnamed), he selected Memnon as the one to whom he gave 5000 mercenaries "and ordered him to march to Cyzicus and try to get possession of it" (§7.2–3◇). What was the reason for this choice? Memnon was "outstanding in courage (*andreia*) and in strategic understanding." His special position is also evident during the war council at Zeleia, which is described by both Diodorus and Arrian. It is clear that Diodorus strongly preferred the scorched-earth policy that was promoted, against the rest of the Persians, by Memnon, whom Diodorus presents once more as "famed for his military competence"—portraying the Persian generals once again as incompetent, because they delayed making decisions and launching a campaign (§18.2–3◇). Memnon again was the one who appeared to direct the Persians' retreat to Miletus (§22.1) and then Halicarnassus, in the course of which it was he who repelled the initial assaults (§24.5), made a sortie, and inflicted heavy losses on the Macedonians (§25.5). He called a council of the officers (*hēgemones*) who surrounded him (*hoi peri ton Memnona*; §25.3), who elsewhere (§27.5◇) are called 'generals and satraps' (*stratēgoi kai satrapai*). These officers, clearly, were first and foremost the commanders of mercenaries, among them the Athenians Ephialtes and Thrasybulus (§25.6; §26.2–3). Darius recognized Memnon's exceptional valor and sent a letter "to those who dwelt next to the sea, directing them one and all to take orders from Memnon. [He] assumed the supreme command" (*tōn olōn hēgemonia*; §23.6◇). To support him, Darius provided huge sums of money (§29.1). It is thus easy to understand the end result: "With his death Darius's fortunes also collapsed" (§29.4◇)—and with his death Alexander's confidence rose (§31.4). This is the point at which Diodorus depicts a war council assembled by Darius. The Athenian Charidemus proposed sending an army to the coast to be commanded by "a general who had given proof of his ability" (himself! §30.3), but Darius flew into a towering rage and decided to take the head of his troops himself: "he searched for a competent general to take over Memnon's command but could find no one, and finally felt constrained to go down himself to take part in the contest for the kingdom (*eis ton hyper tēs basileias kindynon*)" (§30.7✧). This is exactly the same explanation that Diodorus himself had given (XVI.40.5–6✧) for the choice Artaxerxes III had made prior to the Egyptian revolts: Artaxerxes was hobbled by the cowardice and incompetence of his generals and so had to get beyond his own weakness and laziness; thus, he "adopted the plan of carrying out in person the struggles to preserve his kingdom" (*tous hyper tēs basileias agōnas*).

The presentation in its entirety provides a portrait of Darius as an irresolute man who put all of his confidence in the Rhodian and his mercenaries. However, a single comment serves to destroy the presentation by Diodorus's source: Darius was able to set out for Cilicia in the summer of 333, obviously, because he had already begun preparing his army at Babylon many months before, unable to anticipate that Memnon's death would require him to do so. It is also clear that Diodorus focuses his story on Memnon and never names the Persian generals who abandoned the battlefield at the Granicus. This is not unlike what happens at Halicarnassus, where Diodorus very conveniently (for the consistency of his discourse) "forgets" to mention the active presence of Orontobates, the satrap of Caria (cf. Arrian I.23.1). It is also quite obvious that the arguments exchanged in the war council at Zeleia strangely recall the disputes between Greek and Persian leaders in Egypt, also reconstructed by Diodorus: in 334 at Zeleia, the accountability of the Persian leaders was criticized, just as Tachos and Pharnabazus had been condemned for refusing to adopt the strategic planning ("wise counsels") offered by Chabrias (XV.92.3) and Iphicrates (XV.43), respectively. It is also clear that Memnon's unusual position is conceptually parallel to the status that Diodorus conferred on his brother Mentor after the Egyptian campaign (XVI.50.7; 52.1–2)—which is hardly convincing. Furthermore, the Great King's absolute confidence in Memnon singularly recalls what Diodorus (again) wrote about the assistance that Artaxerxes III expected from the arrival of the Argive Nicostratus at the beginning of the Egyptian campaign (XVI.44.2–3). Of course, Diodorus was not the only author to ascribe such importance to Memnon's activities; but the support of Arrian and Quintus Curtius does not by itself confer validity on a theory that they are the only ones to develop with such consistency. We will return later to an analysis of the role played by Memnon at the beginning of Alexander's offensive. Here let us simply observe that the many repetitions of motifs found in both books XVI and XVII of Diodorus lead us to consider with some caution the preeminence that the author attributes to the Rhodian and the Greek mercenaries—not to mention his judgment regarding the incompetence of the Persian generals and the cowardliness of the Great King.

The Great King and the Satraps' Mercenaries

Furthermore, the stories concerning the mercenaries of Artabazus and Orontes have given rise to a more truly political analysis that carries a much more formidable weight because it is attributed to the Great King himself. In his presentation of the beginnings of Artabazus's revolt against Artaxerxes III in the mid-350s (cf. chap. 15/9 above), the anonymous scholiast (Schol. Dem. 4.19) provides the following information:

> The king of the Persians sent an order to the coastal satraps to disband their mercenary armies (*ta mistophorika strateumata*), on the grounds of the enormous expenses they were incurring; as a consequence, the satraps dismissed the soldiers (*stratiōtai*). Numbering about 10,000, these soldiers presented themselves to Chares, the Athenian general, who was

then leader of a mercenary army (*xenikē dynamis*), and they placed themselves under his command. Then in revolt (*apostas*), the Persian Artabazus was fighting against the king; he summoned Chares to take his army into the king's territory.

At first sight, the king's order seems to illustrate the thesis that the central authority was weakening in the face of satraps who could build up armies of their own using mercenaries. This interpretation in turn has sometimes been cited in support of the broader idea that there was a shift toward the creation of personal satrapal armies, such as can be seen in the Hellenistic period. This interpretation is also bolstered by noting one of Alexander's orders, as presented by Diodorus (XVII.106.3✧): "He wrote to all his generals and satraps in Asia, ordering them, as soon as they had read his letter, to disband all their mercenaries instantly." We may add that, at an earlier time, several satraps revolted with the assistance of mercenaries (e.g., Ctesias §37, §52).

However, this theory is weak. The comparison with Alexander's order, though obviously tempting, is purely formal. Diodorus's account is in fact quite clearly placed in the very unsettled context of Alexander's return from India; at that time, we know, the king had to take draconian measures against both usurpers (in Persia and Media) and satraps who had taken advantage of his absence to plunder and pillage the people. It is in this context that Diodorus reveals the fears of some of the generals: "Some who had mercenary troops revolted against the king's authority" (XVII.106.2✧). By giving the order that Diodorus reports, then, Alexander was trying to deny satraps and generals who had *already* entered into revolt the use of their mercenaries. There is nothing of this in the scholiast's text. Instead, for one thing, Artabazus recruited mercenaries *after* his revolt; and for another, the satraps (we do wonder who exactly they might have been) do not offer any objection to obeying the king's order. The impression prevails in the scholiast's account, that no one had challenged the king's authority and no one, at that time, was really threatened.

These observations lead us to view the information with considerable skepticism. We are tempted to think that the author has attributed to Artaxerxes III an attitude often attributed to the Persians by the Greeks, who loved to criticize the Great King's avarice (cf. Plutarch, *Alex.* 69.2) and his unwillingness to pay the Greek soldiers in his service (*Hell. Oxyr.* 19.2). Even if we grant the information credence, it must be observed that the scholiast contradicts Diodorus (XVI.22.1–2)—and this has certainly created difficulties for the commentators. Moreover, the scholiast has quite freely interpreted a passage in the *First Philippic*, where Demosthenes denounces the leaders of the mercenaries, who were quite willing to abandon the mission entrusted to them in order to set sail "to Artabazus or anywhere" (§24✧). While still following the course of Demosthenes' argument, the scholiast adds details found only in his account: departing from a discourse on civic concerns (see above), the inspirer of the gloss (Ephorus?) establishes a connection with a "fact" that appears to condemn the same evils among the Persians; and/or, perhaps, the gloss simply illustrates the policy that Demosthenes is proposing vis-à-vis the mercenaries—namely, to dismiss them. In sum, the text of the scholium does not make a contribution that solidifies the basis of the historical interpretation drawn from it.

Mercenaries and "Mercenaries": The Greeks and the Others

Of course, the presence of mercenary troops within the fourth-century royal and satrapal armies is beyond doubt. However, it is still necessary to inquire into the central role attributed to them by the Greek authors, as well as into the internal changes in the Empire that might have fed the theory of the decadence of the Achaemenid military. Discussion of this point requires us to answer two preliminary questions: What was a mercenary in the Achaemenid armies? and were all the mercenaries Greek? These questions are not usually asked, even though it is obvious that the problem has (nearly) always been considered in the context of its Greek component—the significance of the use of mercenaries with respect to the internal sociopolitical development of the Greek cities. Indeed, neither the vocabulary used nor historical probability provides serious support for this interpretation—which nonetheless is confidently and assuredly proclaimed as certain. In order to make the proof more convincing, here we shall select examples taken exclusively from the Mediterranean theater of the Empire's operations, because we would like to believe that no one would dream of arguing that the garrisons of Babylon, Susa, Persepolis, Ecbatana, or Bactra comprised primarily Greeks!

Though we cannot claim to have performed a complete census, let us present some noteworthy examples taken from Alexander's ancient historians. Arrian, referring to the mercenaries (20,000 according to him) that were one of the components of the satrapal army in 334, uses the generic term *xenoi pezoi misthophoroi* 'foreign infantry mercenaries' (I.14.4✧; I.16.2); the Macedonians found themselves faced with *misthophoroi* at Ephesus (I.17.9), *xenoi hoi misthophoroi* at Miletus (I.19.1), *xenoi* at Halicarnassus (I.20.2; 23.5), *xenoi misthophoroi* at Hyparna (I.24.4), and so on. But were all these *xenoi* and/or *misthophoroi* actually Greeks? The presence of Greek mercenaries is certainly mentioned quite often, but they clearly constituted only a part of the *misthophoroi* (I.19.6; I.29.5; III.6.2). Several phrases used to describe these troops are unambiguous: at Sylleion, Arrian clearly distinguishes the *xenoi misthophoroi* from the [*xenoi*] *epikhouroi* 'natives' (I.26.5✧), the latter clearly referring to soldiers that were recruited on the spot; at Celaenae, we find 1000 Carians and 100 *misthophoroi hellēnes* (I.29.1), and at Gaza *Arabes hoi misthōtoi* (II.25.4; cf. II.27.1 and Quintus Curtius IV.6.15: *Arabs quidam, Darei miles*), mixed with Persians (Quintus Curtius IV.6.30). It is thus undeniable that, even in the western regions, the mercenaries in Persian service were not exclusively of Greek origin. Furthermore, this fact could also be gained from reading Xenophon's general description of the occupation troops in the satrapies: "The king annually reviews the mercenaries (*misthophoroi*) and all the other troops ordered to be under arms" (*Oecon.* IV.6✧): the mercenaries are explicitly distinguished from the soldiers of the garrisons; but there is absolutely no reason to catalogue them all as Greeks (even if there must have been Greeks among them, at least in western Asia Minor). Here is another significant example: Diodorus, in the tale of the expedition against the Cypriot kings in the 350s, writes that the wealth of the island attracted hordes of "soldiers (*stratiōtai*) . . . in the hope of gain" (XVI.42.8–9✧). The context and vocabulary ensure that these were soldiers fighting for pay and a share of the booty, and it is just as clear that the passage does not refer to Greeks exclusively, because Diodorus states that they came from the mainland—namely, Syria and Cilicia. There obviously were plenty of people in those regions quite ready to sign up.

Where did these non-Greek mercenaries come from, and how were they enrolled? The answer seems obvious: mercenaries were hired in every region of the Empire and, more precisely, by the satraps and generals in the territories that came under their authority, such as the Arab *misthōtoi* who were hired by Batis at Gaza; the Chalybian and

Taochian *misthōtoi* in the army of Tiribazus of Armenia (Xenophon, *Anab.* IV.4.18); the Armenian, Mardian, and Chaldean *misthophoroi* found among the troops of Orontes and Artuchas (IV.3.4); and probably the Mysians in Pharnabazus's army (Xenophon, *Hell.* IV.1.24). Elsewhere, Xenophon writes that the Chaldeans of Armenia "serve for hire *(misthou strateuontai)* when any one wants them" *(Cyr.* III.2.7✧). The hiring of mercenaries was thus certainly a very general practice, and Strabo mentions that the Persians hired mercenaries *(misthophoroi)* among the Hydraces of India (XV.1.6); there are many examples of the use of mercenaries in India at this time (e.g., Arrian IV.26.1 and 27.3; Diodorus XVII.84; Plutarch, *Alex.* 59.3–4). This is perhaps what Ctesias is describing as well *(Indica* §22). Mercenaries are the troops that Xenophon refers to with the entirely characteristic description *hoi basileōs misthophoroi (Anab.* VII.8.15✧). This passage shows quite clearly that the author was specifying the territorial troops and garrisons of Mysia, who came to the aid of Asidates from all of the strongholds in the region; they included, for example, "Assyrian hoplites and Hyrcanian horsemen." We also know about the existence of Median, Hyrcanian, and Bactrian military colonies in Asia Minor in 334 (Diodorus XVII.19.4), Hyrcanian settlements in Lydia are attested by Strabo (XIII.4.13), and Bactrian settlements in the same region are mentioned indirectly by Athenaeus (XIV.636a–b). These examples first of all—as if it were really necessary—confirm that not all of the paid garrison soldiers of the Empire were Greeks. Furthermore, it seems clear that all of the soldiers permanently settled in this fashion are vaguely identified by the Greek authors as *misthophoroi*, which is translated by the quite ambiguous term 'mercenaries'. To some extent, the Greek word is not totally misleading, since these Achaemenid "mercenaries" received pay (in the form of rations: *trophē*). We can easily imagine that, if the Greeks had had the occasion to mention the garrison at Elephantine, they would have designated them as mercenaries, because they received rations in kind and money. But at the same time, the Greek word is misleading and introduces confusion, because the *basileōs misthophoroi* are not mercenaries in the precise sense that this word had in ancient Greece.

Let us return for a moment to Artaxerxes III in 345–343. Diodorus mentions that, alongside the mercenaries raised in Greece (and the ones led by Mentor), the king raised 6000 *stratiōtai* from the coastal lands of Asia Minor, adding that the army thus included 10,000 Greeks as *symmakhoi* 'allies' (XVI.44.4). These details elicit two remarks. First, the phrase used *(hoi tēn parathalattion tēs Asias oikountes* 'inhabitants of the seacoast of Asia Minor') does not necessarily imply (despite Diodorus: *Hellēnes)* that all 6000 soldiers were Greek; among them might have been Carians or Lycians (for example). Second, and more generally, Diodorus's merging of the mercenaries and the *symmakhoi* is highly doubtful. Even though the word *symmakhoi* can take on the broad and neutral enough sense of 'military reinforcements', it could also refer to something more specific. We know, for example, that during Darius III's (incomplete) reinforcement of Ecbatana, he received Cadusian and Scythian *symmakhoi* (Arrian III.19.3). Later, Bessus hoped to attract Saka to himself as *symmakhoi* (III.25.3), just as Spitamenes had counted on the *symmakhia* he formed with the Saka, to whom he had promised a share in the booty (IV.5.4–5). In addition, Bessus had brought some Saka to Gaugamela, and Arrian states that they had not been registered as 'subjects' *(hypēkooi)* but had sent a contingent 'on the basis of an alliance with Darius' *(kata symmakhian tēn Dareiou;* III.8.3✧). These last examples lead us to believe that the 6000 soldiers enlisted by Artaxerxes III were not mercenaries in the Greek sense but "mercenaries" in the Achaemenid sense—that is, they were soldiers who signed up not on their own initiative but because of an imperial obligation placed on them collectively (as on the Arabs, Mysians, Taochians, Chaldeans, Mardians, Chalybians, and other Indians). The 6000 "mercenary" *symmakhoi* of the army in Egypt were probably nothing other than troops enrolled in the cities and among the subject coastal peoples by the Asia Minor satraps; they were then sent to the Great King, who was in Phoenicia at the time. Furthermore, it is entirely characteristic of Diodorus that he distinguishes them and collectively refers to them with the phrase *hoi tou basileōs Hellēnes* 'the King's Greeks' (XVI.47.4), which clearly echoes Xenophon's *hoi basileōs misthophoroi*. The distinction that he introduces does not refer primarily to the ethnic origin of the soldiers but to the institutional method of their recruitment.

In Achaemenid reality, the "royal mercenaries" must be distinguished, for example, from the soldiers of the Babylonian *ḥaṭrus*, who were required to bear the costs of enrollment themselves; in turn, these are distinct from the Persians of the imperial diaspora, who had to provide troops whenever they were requisitioned. The "royal mercenaries" in fact received their rations (*trophē*) from the central administration (Xenophon, *Oec.* IV.5–7). We thus should distinguish the levies that were organized in the framework of general or partial mobilizations (assessments comparable to tribute levies: cf. Herodotus III.67 and Justin I.9.12–13) from the enrollment of paid soldiers from subject peoples, even if both were constituents of the royal army (or a satrapal army). If this description of the system is accurate, the existence of troops of "royal mercenaries," far from constituting a symptom of the withering of the Great King's miltary resources, must instead be considered proof of the Empire's ability to renew them. This also reminds us of the diversity of methods used by the central authority to control and exploit the peoples of the Empire: Carduchi, Taochians, and other Chaldeans, all of whom Xenophon (*Anab.* V.5.17) refers to as nonsubjects (*hypēkooi*) of the king, provided soldiers in the category of "royal mercenaries."

"Greek Army" and "Barbarian Army"

In order to define the participation of the mercenaries more precisely, it is important to define the composition of the royal armies in the fourth century. Unfortunately, the ancient terminology is often muddled. The name "Persians" itself is ambiguous: the 20,000 Persians—especially horsemen—commanded by Tithraustes when he fought Artabazus (Schol. Dem. 4.19) were certainly not all of Persian origin, even though there is no doubt that he had recourse to mobilizing contingents that were led by representatives of the Persian aristocracy who had settled permanently in Greater Phrygia. Here, as in many other cases, "Persians" means 'loyal soldiers levied within the framework of imperial structures' (including ethnic Persians, obviously). In the case of Diodorus, he is most often satisfied to speak of the barbarian army, without further specification; nonetheless, apart from the obvious precedent of the "barbarian" army of Cyrus the Younger (chap. 15/2), the methods of enlistment used by Artaxerxes III in Babylon imply that forces levied in Mesopotamia and the east of the Empire were combined (XVI.42.1). As usual, the king was joined en route by satrapal contingents that came from Asia Minor (probably in Cilicia), including "a large force of cavalry and no small body of infantry composed of barbarians" led by Rhosaces, "satrap of Ionia and Lydia" (§47.2✧). It is also possible that Mazaeus and Belesys, who had previously been defeated by the Sidonians (§42.1–2), led the contingents from Cilicia and Syria (if Belesys had not died in the meantime). In Phoenicia, they joined the mercenaries, as well as the *symmakhoi* of Asia Minor (§44.1– 4). The royal army comprised the totality of these contingents, within which the portion singled out by Diodorus under the term "Greek army" (as in the army of Cyrus the Younger) constituted a numerical minority.

Other examples may be added that testify eloquently to the undiminished abilities of the military resources belonging to the satraps and Great Kings up to and including the reign of Darius III. One of the most interesting comes from the reign of Artaxerxes II, a period when it is generally agreed that the satraps very largely depended on the enlistment of (Greek) mercenaries. There is a very precise inventory in Nepos (*Dat.* 8.1–2✧) of contingents that Autophradates put on the line against the rebel Datames:

> Of [Persian] barbarians he had twenty thousand horse and a hundred thousand foot, of the troops that the Persians call Cardaces, besides three thousand slingers of the same nationality; and in addition, eight thousand Cappadocians, ten thousand Armenians, five thousand Paphlagonians, ten thousand Phrygians, five thousand Lydians, about three thousand Aspendians and Pisidians, two thousand Cilicians, the same number of Captiani, and three thousand Greek mercenaries, along with an enormous number of light-armed troops.

This document, which there is no reason to doubt, is very clear. Nepos carefully distinguishes the Persians proper (barbarians, Persians, Cardaces) from the other contingents; he no less precisely distinguishes the Greek mercenaries from the troops levied from the Asia Minor satrapies as imperial assessments (Cappadocia, Armenia, Lydia, Cilicia; we do not know which *ethnos* is concealed behind the name "Captiani" [Cataonians?]). It is possible that the Pisidians and Aspendians were enrolled as "mercenaries" (in the Achaemenid sense; see above). Note, finally, that, whatever doubts may legitimately be nurtured about the absolute numbers, the share of Greek mercenaries is proportionally very small.

The composition of the satrapal contingents at the battle of the Granicus is stripped of all ambiguity. If at first we set aside the problem of foreign mercenaries—to which we shall shortly return—the methods of assembling satrapal troops provide information that is generally consistent from source to source. The Asia Minor satraps (those who are named are Arsites of Hellespontine Phrygia, Spithridates of Lydia and Ionia, Atizyes of Greater Phrygia, and Mithrobuzanes of Cappadocia) mustered their troops from everywhere: among them were Hyrcanian horsemen, Medes, and Bactrians (which may all have come from permanent colonies and garrisons)—that is, the "royal mercenaries" (above); the masters of *dōreai* (such as Memnon, and probably Arsames as well) brought their "own horsemen"; subject peoples provided a contingent to the satrap who ruled them (a contingent of Paphlagonian horsemen alongside Arsites). In the methods used to raise it and in its very composition, the army commanded by Arsites in 334 matches feature for feature the "barbarian" army assembled by Cyrus the Younger in Asia Minor.

Let us now consider the armies led in person by Darius at Issus and Gaugamela. The evidence poses two preliminary methodological problems. First, the numbers are immoderately exaggerated by the ancient authors (though by differing amounts). We may recall here what was said about the armies of Xerxes in 480 and suggest that it is impossible to establish a numerical value that is certain. Furthermore, we can note in passing that Quintus Curtius explicitly compares the review organized by Darius III with the census of Xerxes' army at Doriscus (III.2.2), leading to the comment: "An all but innumerable mass of cavalry and foot, which gave the appearance of being greater than it actually was" (2.3✧)! Second, the analysis of the initial disposition of the troop formations and the unfolding of the battles in principle should have provided some basic information. Unfortunately, in this case as in so many others, the ancient tales are fragmentary and contradictory—so much so that reconstructing the maneuvers continues to divide the war-game specialists. This is especially the case for the battle of the Granicus, on which the reports of Arrian and Diodorus disagree from beginning to end.

In any event, the ancient texts are in sufficient agreement that we may state, without fear of error, that Darius created his armies with the help of ethnic contingents levied in every satrapy of the Empire that he controlled at the time (cf. the phrase *kata ethnē*: Arrian II.8.8; Diodorus XVII.58.1 [Gaugamela]). In order to prepare for the battle that was about to take place at Issus, the Great King brought troops from everywhere to Babylon. Though the extended time that the process took prevented the arrival of the contingents from the Iranian Plateau, the troops included in his army were (according to Quintus Curtius) Persians, Medes, Barcaeans, Armenians, and Hyrcani (Quintus Curtius III.2.4–9; order of battle: III.9.1–6; and Arrian II.8.5–8). Similarly, between 332 and 331, Darius once again convened his troops at Babylon, before bringing them close to Arbela. This time, the contingents from the Iranian Plateau had arrived in time (cf. Quintus Curtius IV.9.1–3), and they seem to have formed, according to Arrian (who refers to an official document preserved by Aristobulus), the heart of the new royal army (III.11.3–7); each satrap brought his own contingent(s) (III.8.3–7). Without analyzing each situation in detail, the conclusion is obvious. from 334 to 331, Darius employed all of the military resources of the Empire—all of which leads us to think that the troops at that time were both highly diversified (colonies, garrisons, soldiers of the imperial diaspora, contingents of the subject people, "royal mercenaries") and quite large.

The problem of the Darius III's Greek mercenaries remains—a problem that we have deliberately set aside until now. The ancient texts present three well-known problems: the number, the ethnic origin, and the technical specialization of these troops. We should first of all present the information on these problems provided by Alexander's authors, distinguishing them chronologically.

(1) Alone among the ancient authors, Arrian twice mentions the presence of 20,000 "foreign mercenary infantry" in the satraps' army at the Granicus, in addition to 20,000 "Persian" infantrymen (I.14.4;✧ II.7.6). These mercenaries were commanded by the Persian Omares (I.16.3). Diodorus speaks of 100,000 Persian foot soldiers (XVII.19.5✧). Plutarch alludes to foot-soldier combat when he states that the Persian infantry was not slow to flee: only the Greek mercenaries stood their ground, only to be massacred by Alexander (*Alex.* 16.12–14); according to Arrian, none survived, except for 2000 who were taken prisoner (I.16.2).

(2) After he decided to oppose Alexander directly, Darius ordered Pharnabazus, the nephew of and successor to Memnon (who had died in the summer of 333), to send foreign mercenaries (*peregrini milites/xenoi misthophoroi*) to him. Pharnabazus followed these instructions and brought them from Mytilene to Lycia, where he turned them over to Thymondas, son of Mentor, his close relative (Quintus Curtius III.3.1; Arrian II.2.1–2). The mercenaries seem to have been brought by sea to Tripolis in Phoenicia, and there they joined the royal army (Arrian III.13.3). Quintus Curtius stresses that Darius put all of his hope in these mercenaries (III.3.1; III.8.1). Just like Arrian (II.8.6), Quintus Curtius says that there were 30,000 mercenaries who, in his opinion, constituted "the undeniable elite of the army." They were placed under the command of Thymondas on

the right flank, while 20,000 barbarian infantrymen were placed on the left flank (III.9.2–3). Arrian states that the 30,000 Greek mercenaries were placed at the head of the "hoplite troops," facing the Macedonian phalanx, while 60,000 "Cardacian hoplites" were placed on the other side (II.8.6). Behind the Greek mercenaries and the "Persian phalanx," the other contingents were ranged *kata ethnē* (Arrian II.8.8).

(3) After the defeat, several thousand Greek mercenaries accompanied Darius in his train: the number was 4000, according to Arrian (II.13.1). Another 8000 left the battle-field on the orders of their leaders (Amyntas the Macedonian, Thymondas, Aristomedes of Pherae, and Bianor of Acarnania) and reached Tripolis in Phoenicia (Arrian II.13.2–3). At Gaugamela, close to Darius (at the center), there was a contingent of Greek mercenaries alongside his Persian troops, opposite the Macedonian phalanx (Arrian III.11.7). Quintus Curtius, who places Darius in the left flank (IV.14.8), is not explicit, but like Arrian (III.16.2) he mentions that foreign mercenaries accompanied Darius when he fled (V.8.3: 4000; 2000 in Arrian). According to Arrian, they were led by Paron of Phocaea and Glaucus the Etolian (III.16.2). Quintus Curtius also mentions this Paron (Patron) and gives him a speech in which he recalls that only a very small number of mercenaries remained out of the 50,000 that had begun the battle (V.11.5); he presents them as the last bulwark of royal legitimacy against conspirators (V.8.3; 10.7; 11.12). There is clearly much smugness in this claim about faithfulness—which is also found in Aelian (*Anim.* VI.25) when he speaks of the unconditional faithfulness of the Great King's dog, which he directly compares with the faithfulness of Cyrus the Younger's Tablemates at Cunaxa!

The numbers provided are both scarcely credible and difficult to check (cf. Polybius XII.17–22). It is clear that Quintus Curtius overstates the number of mercenaries in the Great King's service—he has Patron refer to 50,000. Even if we assume that Quintus Curtius was totaling the 20,000 mercenaries from the battle of the Granicus (Arrian) and the 30,000 from Issus (which is not at all certain), each of these figures by itself is problematic. Throughout his story, the mercenaries occupy a special position alongside Darius, because he loves to contrast their courage and faithfulness with the cowardice of the barbarians (cf. III.9.11; 11.17–18). The barbarians are opulently clothed ("like women"), but they are far from courageous (see III.3.14; compare V.1.23). Arrian's number (20,000 mercenaries at the Granicus) has long been rightly doubted, though he points out that he is referring to foreign mercenaries—not just Greek mercenaries (even though he later tends to "Hellenize" them). That the Asia Minor satraps had Greek mercenaries at their disposal is indisputable, but that they arrayed 20,000 of them at the Granicus is utterly impossible. Finally, let us stress that this infantry force does not seem to have held a significant place in the strategic thinking of the satraps, because they are never reported as having participated (except quite incidentally in Plutarch). It is thus risky to state that the Greek mercenaries were never as numerous in the Achaemenid armies as between 333 and 331. Though Alexander's ancient historians strongly insisted on the number and valor of Darius III's mercenaries, on the one hand, they did so because, by calling them Greeks, they could sing the limitless praise of Alexander's "pan-Hellenic" merits (Arrian I.16.6); on the other hand, they did so because they loved to stress the unshakable devotion that some Greek leaders showed to Darius. Finally, for reasons already given, the "royal mercenaries" may have been included in the count of the *xenoi misthophoroi*, just like the colonists levied in Asia Minor (Diodorus XVII.19.4).

Since the problem of the numbers seems insoluble, we would do better to examine the function of the mercenaries at Issus and Gaugamela. First of all, it is clear that the Persian high command had no illusions about the military abilities of some of the contingents that were organized *kata ethnē*, despite the training sessions that all of the royal troops regularly received (Diodorus XI.75.3; XVII.55.1). At Issus, these groups were placed far from the front line indeed (Arrian II.8.8). Obviously, the Persians relied most of all on the contingents of Persian and Iranian horsemen, as is clearly seen in the three set battles. At Issus, there is no reason to doubt the order that Darius gave to Pharnabazus and Thymondas to assemble (some of) the mercenaries in Cilicia for the impending battle. The ancient authors state several times that Darius believed that they were the only force capable of stopping the Macedonian phalanx. Here again we see the classic theme of Greek tactical superiority in infantry combat, which in turn implies that the Persians had only poorly-prepared infantrymen. Does this mean that after the defeats of 480–479, the Persians never attempted to put an infantry worthy of the name into the field? On this point, we have serious reservations.

The order of battle at Issus and Gaugamela in fact suggests a considerably different interpretation. At Issus, the Greek mercenaries were not alone against the Macedonian phalanx; not far from them, in fact, "60,000 of the so-called Cardaces, who were also hoplites," were placed (Arrian II.8.6✧). Together they constituted the "Darius phalanx" (II.8.10). Even though Arrian reduces the infantry combats to a duel between Greeks and Macedonians (II.10.5–7), there is no reason to follow him across this terrain that is so well known to the entire Greek tradition (cf. II.10.7: *tois genesi tōi te Hellēnikōi kai tōi Makedonikōi philotimia*, comparable with Diodorus XVI.46.9: *agōn/philotimia* between the Spartans and Thebans before Pelusium in 343). At Gaugamela, Darius also had a phalanx (Arrian III.14.1) that faced the Macedonian phalanx and comprised Greek mercenaries and "Persian troops" (III.11.7✧). Unfortunately we do not know exactly who the Cardaces were, but we could legitimately think that they made up the Persian phalanx. In support of this idea, we may note that they already appear in the army that Autophradates set against Datames some 40 years earlier; there were 100,000 of them, as Nepos would have it (*Dat.* 8.2: . . . *quos illi* [the Persians] *Cardacas appellant*). The term also appears in Strabo's passage (XV.3.18) on the education of young Persians, which is perhaps an interpolation. According to Strabo, the term *Kardakēs* refers to military and physical attributes; in his context, it seems to refer, originally at least, to young men who had completed the rite of passage from adolescence to adulthood. But later (or simultaneously), it more likely refers to elite infantry troops who underwent training comparable to that of the Greek and Macedonian infantry.

Intermittent and accidental though they may be, several other pieces of information indicate that the Persians attempted to adapt their armaments and their tactics to Macedonian techniques. Diodorus, for example, states that Darius introduced some innovations in 332–331: "He had fashioned swords (*xiphē*) and lances (*xysta*) much longer than his earlier types because it was thought that Alexander had had a great advantage in this respect in the battle in Cilicia" (XVII.53.1✧). This tactic might seem to be too little, too late. Quintus Curtius explains that Darius actually had been doing this sort of thing since the beginning of his reign: he "had ordered that the form of the Persian scabbard of the scimitar (*acinacis/akinakēs*) should be changed to that shape which the Greeks used" (III.3.6✧). The adaptations go back even earlier: Cyrus the Younger's elite horsemen, who were the best equipped, carried Greek breastplates and swords (Diodorus XIV.22.6✧).

This evidence stimulates some reflections. While there is no reason to reject the evidence, it is important to stress the limits of its applicability. Diodorus and Quintus Curtius, who are dependent on their Greek and Macedonian informants, report only what they consider interesting from the Greek point of view—namely, that in order better to withstand Alexander, Darius had tried to mimic certain Greek tactics. Though the remark *may* (though far from certainly) imply a positive evaluation of the Great King within the rationale of one of Diodorus's sources (XVII.7.1), this says nothing more than that the information was meant to support the notion that the only hope for survival for Darius's Empire was "Hellenization." However, should we not recognize that the Persian general staff wanted to improve the tactical capabilities of their troops by adopting many other practices apart from those they could copy from the Greeks? To ask the question is to answer it. Arrian, for example, mentions the presence of elephants in front of the Persian battle line (III.11.6; see §15.6 and *FGrH* 151 F5). We can legitimately question the practicality of elephants in battle, but the novelty of the deployment (on the western front at least! [Ctesias §6]) and its Indian origin are beyond doubt. Similarly, all of the ancient authors report that Darius relied heavily on his scythed war chariots to disrupt the Macedonian battle line. This was a specifically Persian tactic (Xenophon, *Cyr.* VI.1.29–30) that the Greek troops, to their horror, had already experienced in Asia Minor when fighting Pharnabazus (*Hell.* IV.1.17–19) and at Cunaxa against Artaxerxes II (Plutarch, *Art.* 7.6). The occasional borrowing of Greek weaponry must not lead us to the conclusion that the Achaemenid army was suffering from technical stagnation, and the (limited) recourse to Greek mercenaries should not lead us to imagine a withering away of imperial military forces, and even less that Persia's native abilities were drying up. According to eyewitness testimony (Hieronymus of Cardia) about the region of Fahliyun, "Those who inhabited this country were the most warlike of the Persians, every man being a bowman and a slinger, and in density of population, too, this country far surpassed the other satrapies" (Diodorus XIX.21.3✧)—and this does not include the contingents that the Diadochi were able to draw from the country (e.g., XIX.17.4: 10,000 archers). There is thus no longer any reason to follow Xenophon in his reconstructed speech on the decadence of the education offered to young Persians at the heart of the Empire.

In sum, in 334 as before, the Great King could rely on considerable military strength. To confront the Greek and Macedonian phalanx, he could deploy his own phalanx, and there is nothing to lead us to believe that from the beginning of the fourth century on the Achaemenid infantry had lost the maneuverability that had so impressed some of the Greek observers of the battle of Cunaxa (cf. Plutarch, *Art.* 7.4–6). We shall return to this later (chap. 18/5); but let us say for now that the defeats inflicted by Alexander must not be considered either proof, or even a significant indication, of military disarray in the Empire of Darius III.

4. Subject Populations and Tribute Economy

Hoarding and Stagnation: Obvious but False

One of the most frequently suggested causes for the weakening of the Empire and the victory of Alexander certainly is the structural crisis inflicted by the tribute economy. This crisis, which was bitterly resented by the subject population, would in turn explain their disaffection with the Great King and their defection to the Macedonian conqueror. This theory was first formulated by Olmstead, who gave his chapter on royal assessments a title that left no room for ambiguity: "Overtaxation and Its Results." Olmstead begins with Herodotus's tribute list, which he contextualizes not at the heart of Darius's reign but at the pivot between Xerxes and Artaxerxes, as if to demonstrate more dramatically the notion of a general crisis that would be illustrated by the assassination of the Great King and bloody struggles for the succession. Olmstead's idea may be summarized as follows. The imperial fiscal administration created a unidirectional flow of wealth, from the periphery to the center, symbolized by the size of the treasuries captured by Alexander. This "surtax" created a shortage of money in the provinces—hence, he says, simultaneous inflation and price increases that are especially observable in Babylonia. This led to many revolts by the subject peoples and is even reflected in the need that the Babylonians found themselves faced with—to auction off their daughters (Herodotus I.196).

It is worth noting that this theory, despite the criticisms it has received from time to time, continues to permeate many recent works about both the Achaemenids and Alexander. It therefore might be worthwhile to investigate its origins. Droysen's publications deserve special consideration. One of the most remarkable innovations attributed to Alexander by Droysen, the "inventor of the Hellenistic period," was the "extent of economic success," which he explains first and foremost as a result of the fact that Alexander put the Persian treasuries into circulation. We cannot help quoting Droysen's splendid sentence on this topic:

> When Alexander liberated these riches that had previously been sequestered, when [the new power] let them escape its bosom, as the heart pumps blood, it is easy to understand that labor and commerce spread them around, in faster and faster circulation, among the long-ligatured members of the Empire; we see how, by this means, the economic life of the peoples, from whom Persian dominion had sucked the life force like a vampire, had to recover and prosper.

It is quite noteworthy that Droysen is content to support his suggestion by referring only to Plutarch's *De Fortuna Alexandri* (I.8 [*Moralia* 330d✧]). In his delirious panegyric to the Conqueror, he emphasizes that Alexander did not come to Asia simply to turn it into booty; his true desire was "to render all upon earth subject to one law of reason and one form of government and to reveal all men as one people"!

However, although we can comprehend how, given both the rationale of his historical-philosophical vision and the state of the evidence in his time, Droysen was able to maintain the theory of the "vampirization" of the Empire, how can we explain why such a simplistic, not to mention poorly argued, position could have known (and could still know) such success? We can imagine that two historiographic streams, however generally contradictory, played a decisive role. First there is what might be called European colonial historiography, which in its search for models and precedents often turned to the "great colonizers" of Antiquity, such as Alexander. Mimicking Plutarch's presentation, historians have presented Alexander as a generous, chivalrous conqueror who brought progress to a stagnant Asia. The reestablishment of peace, opening of roads, founding of towns, and monetization of the Persian treasuries were the vectors and methods of unprecedented economic and commercial expansion. We will not dwell long on the failings of this reconstruction, which is based primarily on the assumption that a conquering and commercial Europe was culturally superior. What is more surprising—at least at first sight—is that Marxist historiography has contributed in no small measure to spreading the model as well. We know that Engels and Marx conceived the theoretical model of the "Asiatic mode of production." "Asiatic" societies are fundamentally characterized by "stagnation"; in fact, to repeat the words of J. Chesneaux, Marx "was literally haunted—the word is not too strong—by the problem of 'Oriental stagnation.'" While Marxist scholars (aided by Wittfogel's analyses, which they also adduced) in the 1970s and 1980s vigorously rejected this notion, it is no less true that it has not disappeared at all—it is attested by the (highly politicized) use of the word "stagnation" in the language of *perestroika*. Even though Marxist thought has scarcely touched on the study of the Achaemenid Empire and Alexander's conquests, historians have nonetheless long made reference (most often implicitly) to a model that postulates both over-exploitation of tribute and economic stagnation, as seen in Olmstead.

It is true that the ancient sources also may be used to illustrate the centripetal circulation of resources. This is in fact the basic idea underpinning the ancient discussions of the king's table and the royal paradises: the untold wealth of the Great King is explained as coming from conquest and taxes (chap. 5/6). For example, Strabo, following Polyclitus, explains that each king had to build at Susa not only a residence (*oikēsis*) but also treasuries (*thēsauroi*) and storehouses (*paratheseis*), where they deposited the tribute money in hope of managing it wisely (*oikonomia*; XV.3.21). Diodorus states that the treasuries seized by Alexander at both Susa and Persepolis were the result of ceaseless accumulation from the time of Cyrus onward (XVII.66.1; 71.1). And Plutarch reports that at Susa "Alexander found . . . five thousand talents' worth of Hermionian purple, that had been laid up there an hundred and ninety years, and yet kept its colour as fresh and lively as at first" (*Alex.* 36.2✧). In the thinking of Pseudo-Aristotle, the good operation of the royal economy is the purpose and justification of the tribute system he analyzes. The royal economy, he writes, "is universal in scope." According to Pseudo-Aristotle, the Great King understood perfectly how to apply the maxim he records in these words: "The expenditure must not exceed the income" (II.1.6✧). We can also cite the passage where Herodotus explains how the Great King kept the gold and silver tribute in his stock (III.96; cf. Strabo XV.3.21). According to Strabo, the king used a very small part of tribute income for his well-known policy of redistribution through gifts and to enhance the opulence of his table and palaces. Both explain the political and ideological function of the Great King's treasuries. However, this is obviously only a partial explanation: the expenses to which Pseudo-Aristotle alluded were not limited to luxury goods. Even though the Greek authors took court expenditures into account, it is easy to understand why they considered the method of managing the royal wealth to be particularly "frugal," because the Great King had immense stores of precious metals at any point in time; as Strabo put it when describing a later period, he never struck more coins than he needed for anticipated expenses, bit by bit (XV.3.21). This was precisely the situation in the time of Darius III. In short, the king had no need for recourse to the financial strategies used by the cities, satraps, or generals—which are described and deplored by the author of the *Oeconomica*.

Each of these texts contributes to establishing a picture of a Great King who was stingy, if not greedy—someone who could part with his riches only with the greatest difficulty. In Greek eyes, in fact, the Great King was a model *economist*, in the sense of a careful administrator of a great estate (*oikos*), and they assimilate the Empire to this model in a manner that is both simplistic and suggestive. In fact, the Great King took care of his expenses "with economy (*oikonomikōs*) and even with parsimony (*akribōs*)," as Heraclides of Cyme put it (Athenaeus IV.145d✧), and the Greek soldiers engaged in his service—so it seems—complained about it (*Hell. Oxyr.* 19.2). In the same vein, Plutarch does not even hesitate to state that the Great Kings (insofar as he knew!) rarely visited Persia, and Artaxerxes never went there at all, because they hated having to hand out gold pieces to pregnant women as royal custom demanded (*Alex.* 69.2). But the theory of hoarding/vampirization goes too far when both economic stagnation and violent, generalized discontent against Persian authority among the subject peoples are derived from it—all of which is marshalled to provide a historical interpretation of the Macedonian victory.

Even when it is stripped of its rhetorical excesses, this interpretation raises many doubts. First of all, it tends to minimize the very rationale for the operation of a system based on redistribution. At any rate, this is partially explained by Strabo himself: in the context of noting, like Herodotus, that the Great King spent gold or silver only at the moment it was needed, Strabo explains that only a very small portion was turned into coinage (as confirmed by the treasury inventories of 331–330) and that most of the precious metal was transformed into pieces of equipment (*kataskeuai*; furniture); furthermore, "they consider those metals as better adapted for presents (*dōreai*) and for depositing in storehouses" (*pros keimēliōn apothēsin*; XV.3.21✧). Indeed, as we have seen (chap. 8), "royal gifts" were the very essence of the king's relationship with the Faithful. In addition, it is certainly a mistake to state that the royal treasure was derived exclusively from the yield of tribute and gifts; some of it was the booty of war. After a conquest, the Great Kings seized the treasuries of the defeated kings and brought them to their capitals, which is exactly what Alexander did. Finally, though it is no doubt true that part of the tribute actually was taken all the way to Persia (Susa, Babylon), it is also clear that, despite the inadequacy of the ancient sources, the amount in the treasuries seized by Alexander in the great capitals was far less than the amount of tribute that we might theoretically reconstruct had been collected since Cyrus or Darius. It is obvious that a major portion of the tribute remained in the treasuries of the satrapal capitals, and Alexander took possession of these as well.

Moreover, the contrast often invoked between Achaemenid hoarding and the sudden circulation (monetization) of the royal wealth by Alexander should be evaluated carefully. The conclusions drawn, which are based on analysis of partial sources, come from two assumptions that are both open to challenge. The first assumption is that economic prosperity requires the use of coined money; but the case of Babylonia (which is not unique: e.g., PT 85) shows that weighed silver played a similar and equally effective role. The second assumption (which is almost dead) is that the Achaemenid Empire did not know the use of coined money; but this is false on two counts. First, in the Mediterranean lands, cash money was common and became more and more widespread beginning in the second half of the fifth century, as shown, for example, by the Cilician, Cypriot, Phoenician, Judean, and Samaritan issues. Moreover, small denominations appeared in more and more dense distribution, which in themselves were obviously one of the vectors for local monetary trade (even if trading was not limited to the monetary level). In addition, Athenian coinage (originals and imitations) circulated widely from Egypt to Central Asia. Assuming that this is really the basic point (which is far from certain), the least one can say is that the Achaemenid lands did not lack for means of

payment and trade. It is quite surprising that Olmstead, based on the Babylonian material, connects the lack of silver and coin to inflation, on the one hand, and to rising
prices, on the other. Even if we assume that the word *inflation* is justifiable, we do not
see how inflation could be connected with the lack of liquid assets. Instead, stagna-
tion/deflation is a more likely result. It seems clear enough that the analytical tools commonly used (not without error and approximation!) in our capitalist societies are not
directly applicable to Babylonia at the end of the fifth century. We have elsewhere discussed the difficulties faced by the historian in interpreting the "price increase" that took
place at Persepolis around 466 (see chap. 11/8).

Let's face it: though it is easy enough to expose the failures of one's predecessors, it is
vastly more difficult to offer an alternative positive reconstruction. The basic reason is
the crying inadequacy of the sources and the absence of truly functional theoretical
models; at least, the profusion of models reveals nothing more than our inability to describe and explain the general operation of an Empire where unity and diversity inter-
acted dialectically. It is extraordinarily difficult to draw a picture of the flow of exchange
that is both supportable and satisfying. However, we cannot be satisfied with a simplistic
picture (such as the one painted by Alexander's colonial historiography), which combines the opening of roads, the spread of peace, and the circulation of merchandise. We
reject this simplistic explanation quite simply because the sources do not allow it—not
the literary sources, not the numismatic evidence, and not the results of archaeology. It
is enough here to observe that, for example, the texts (Greek or Elamite) bearing on the
roads never associate the use of the great imperial highways with the traffic of merchants
and merchandise. Only very rarely are we (fleetingly) informed about commercial prosperity of the sort achieved by Sidon around the middle of the fourth century (cf. Diodorus XVI.41.4: *dia tēs emporias*). Certainly, no historical inference is to be drawn from
this silence; it can be explained first of all by the narrowly political (Persepolis tablets)
and military (Greek and Hellenistic sources) orientation of the available evidence. Another factor is that a major portion of transportation was by water (seas and rivers), for
which direct evidence is rare, except in Babylonia. The recent discovery of a customs
memorandum from Egypt dating to the time of Xerxes reminds us of the dangers of any
argument from silence (*TADAE* C.3.7; chap. 9/3: *Customs Collection and Trade*,
above). Babylonia remains the best-documented region, and this presumably is why
Olmstead made it the basis of his interpretations. But even in the case of Babylon, it is
necessary to emphasize the gaps in the documentation, which primarily relate to the uneven chronological distribution of the tablets. Because of this, any attempt to follow the
fluctuations of the Babylonian economy from Cyrus to Darius III will be at risk.

Center and Periphery

At the same time, it seems clear that the theory of Achaemenid hoarding/vampiriza-
tion is based on another certainty—that the Great Kings, who were jealous for their
power and authority more than anything else, had no interest in pursuing a policy that
would develop the conquered countries, which were considered sources of revenue first
and foremost. It is true that each of the elements of the interpretation that has just been
presented in summary can be supported by evidence, whether it concerns the ostentatious luxury of the Great Kings or the severity of the assessments. After all, to Pseudo-
Aristotle, the royal economy appeared to operate as a gigantic financial sump fed by the

satrapal economy. On the other side of the issue, we tend to distrust principles derived from monarchic ideology, which bestows on the king the image of a benefactor and defender of the workers in the fields. Even after the evidence has been gathered, the problem remains unsolved. The Empire was in fact not merely a "symbolic capital" but also a collection of means of production (primarily land and water) and productive powers (in particular human productive powers). In the vision—which was necessarily their vision—of an Empire destined to perdure, the Great Kings certainly did concern themselves with guaranteeing the regularity of their income; they were determined to preserve and increase their capital and to bequeath it to their successors magnified and enriched. The term *capital* must not send shivers down our spines; whether conquered, bought, or given, a city (or a territory) "could not be anything more than a productive organism susceptible to appreciation" (J.-M. Bertrand) and thus subject also to the calculation of profitability, which in the case of the Great King (his predecessors, his successors) was measured by the scale of its yield in tribute. This is in fact the significance of some Hellenistic inscriptions: for example, by guaranteeing that the inhabitants of a city retained possession of land that was contested by "barbarians," a royal governor reminded the citizens (Arsinoe in Cilicia) that they had to "fully cultivate the land and make plantations (*phyteu[santes]*), in order to live in prosperity and in order to pay the king greater revenues (*prosodoi*) than before" (SEG XXXIX.1426). Here, the gift of land, which often has been reduced to its political component, is explicitly considered by the king to be a long-term investment—and this will soon be confirmed by Polybius (X.28.2–4; below).

It is true that Xenophon presents a picture of the Great King as a wise economist: he was eager to see the tribute pour in regularly; he rewarded the governors charged with receipt of tribute, as well as the military leaders, who were responsible for seeing to the security of the fields. In the Great King's eyes, good governors, whom he rewards, are those "who are able to show him that their country is densely populated and that the land is in cultivation and well stocked with the trees of the district and with the crops" (*Oec.* IV.8✧). Xenophon highlights the fact that the Great King's interest in maintaining and developing the population and increasing the value of regions cannot merely be assigned to the ideological category of the "good gardener" (see chap. 6/5). The paradises were not merely striking evidence of the king's authority over the growing cycle, nor simply hunting preserves; they also were agricultural estates, places for horticultural experimentation carefully undertaken and cultivated by the villagers assigned to them (cf. Xenophon, *Anab.* IV.4.7; *Hell.* IV.1.15; PFa 33; ML 12). The granting of *dōreai* itself tended to improve production. The evidence frequently portrays holders of land grants as absentee landlords and simple farmers. But even if the Murašū tablets can support this interpretation, it nonetheless remains partial. First of all, even when they delegated responsibilities, the Murašū were concerned both with generating personal profit from renting land and gathering the royal duties. On the other hand, the "owner farm" grant holders had great interest in good yield from their lands, as attested by the Aršāma correspondence (*DAE* 68 [AD 7]).

In his discussions of the conquests of "Cyrus," Xenophon often mentions the conqueror's policy that had the goal of generating profit from the land and peasants. Thus, "Cyrus" stated with respect to the "Assyrian" peasants: "No change whatever shall come to you except that you shall not have the same ruler over you as before; but you shall dwell in the same houses and work the same farms; you shall live with the same wives and have control of your children just as now. But you shall not have to fight either us or any one else" (Cyr. IV.4.10–11;✧ cf. III.3.22). Of course, Xenophon's model can be criticized, but is it anything other than a praise of "good kingship"? The ideological theme of "defense of the peasants" conceals a basic practicality in that the lands and peasants regularly filled the royal coffers with tribute. The maintenance of existing social structures (village communities) represents both a purpose and a means of gaining political and tribute dominion. In this respect, the ideology of peace is not a simple distortion of the truth: the king and his satraps were "protectors of the peasants," and this contributed to the maintenance of the level of production capability and guaranteed harvest and tribute, as Xenophon rightly insists. He has "Cyrus" speak the following words: "An inhabited country is a very valuable possession, but a land destitute of people becomes likewise destitute of produce" (*Cyr.* IV.4.5✧). This confirms the "birth-rate incentive policy" (cf. p. 733) attested in Persia both among the Persians themselves and among the *kurtaš*—a policy designed to increase human reproduction that, pursued throughout the Achaemenid period (Plutarch, *Alex.* 69.1–2; *Mor.* 246a–b), had some success, as attested by Diodorus Siculus at the beginning of the Hellenistic period (XIX.21.3).

It is quite clear that this evidence is disparate, vague, and susceptible to varying interpretations. Can we really speak of profitable investments that must have been financed directly by the royal administration, which then skimmed off part of the profits or derived tribute while hoping to generate additional future profits? Aside from the Persepolis tablets (chap. 11), the available evidence is terribly inadequate. The inadequacy is not simply quantitative but qualitative as well, in that no document explicitly speaks of a policy of economic development (and certainly none would be expected). The same evidence can support varying interpretations as a function of the assumptions and models used. The case of the canal from the Nile to the Red Sea is entirely typical in this regard. Once it has been proved that the goal of creation of the canal was not to establish a direct, permanent link between the Nile Valley and Susa, must we conclude that Darius's decison was based purely on political-ideological motives? Recent explorations in the Tell el-Maskhuta region has produced evidence of a rather sizable influx of pottery from various Greek cities (Chios, Thasos, Lesbos) and especially from Phoenicia. Was development of trade in the region Darius's goal, or does it merely represent a side effect of an action that emerged primarily from the political sphere? It is obviously impossible to offer a sure answer. However, if we place Darius's policy in the *longue durée* between Necho (cf. Diodorus II.158–59) and the Ptolemies (e.g., Diodorus I.33), it is not likely that we would think that the Great King had no commercial (fiscal) interest in the matter at all.

The evidence regarding water-resource policy seems clearer. At all times, in the great irrigated valleys, the king and his administration took charge of the great water works. This was true in Babylonia—a case that we have already had occasion to discuss (chap. 16/10)—as is shown by Arrian (VII.7.7; VII.21) and Strabo (XVI.1.11). The Babylonian texts reveal that there was a special Water Department. For Egypt, we have nothing but a single passage in Herodotus (II.90), which is interesting at least because it shows that the royal administration maintained and reinforced the levees that protected Memphis and environs each year (an activity that we might be inclined to doubt); in all likelihood, we once again have only a partial view of much more extensive work. There is another text that adds to this topic, a passage in Polybius that by pure chance preserves direct information on the Great Kings' initiatives regarding the water supply. Within an account of Antiochus III's campaign against the Parthian king Arsaces, Polybius offers the following information on methods of bringing water to a part of Hyrcania that is referred to as desert:

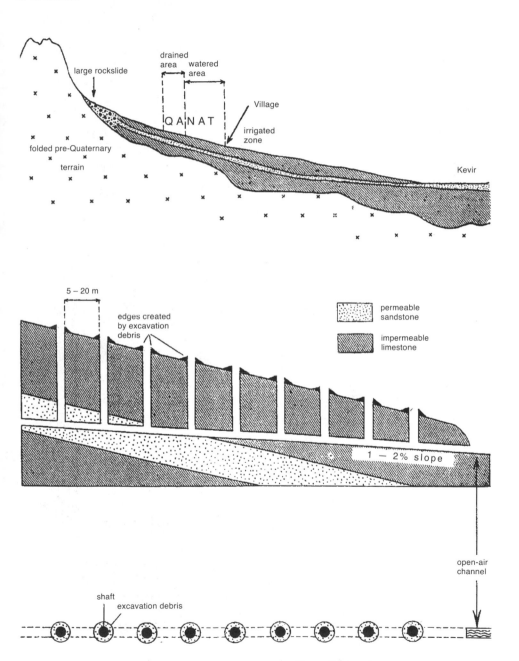

Fig. 65. Plan of a qanat *(showing profile and vertical views).*

> In the region I speak of there is no water visible on the surface, but even in the desert there are a number of underground (*hyponomoi*) channels communicating with wells (*phreatiai*) unknown to those not acquainted with the country. About these a true story is told by the inhabitants. They say that at the time when the Persians were the rulers of Asia they gave to those who conveyed a supply of water to places previously unirrigated the right of cultivating (*karpeusai*) the land for five generations, and consequently as the Taurus [Elburz] has many large streams descending from it, people incurred great expense and trouble in making underground channels reaching a long distance, so that at the present day those who make use of the water do not know whence the channels derive their supply. (X.28.2–4◊)

Polybius describes quite precisely installations called *qanats* that have been used for centuries in Iran: they are subterranean corridors that sometimes run tens of kilometers to water sources lying under the slopes of well-watered mountains. The technology certainly goes back before the Persian conquest, but Polybius includes a very important clarification of a well-thought-out policy of the royal administration. This work did not require the mobilization of a vast labor force (unlike the great Babylonian, Egyptian, and Bactrian canals); instead, it was carried out by the local populations. In exchange for investment in the form of labor, Hyrcanian communities received not ownership but use (*karpeusai*) of the land. The royal administration drew benefit from it in several ways. It is obvious, for one thing, that arrangements like this made it possible to place water reserves along the high road from Media to Central Asia. Furthermore, it enabled lands to be planted that had previously been unproductive and thus supported a policy of agrarian colonization. Finally, nothing suggests that the Hyrcanians received a tax exemption. The word *karpeusai* indicates only that they had the right to cultivate a plot of which they were not the real owner; it does not imply they were free of all royal assessments. In reality, the administration certainly expected to receive revenue from these parcels in the form of tribute and/or water taxes (cf. chap. 10/7). The fact that the description is an isolated example should neither surprise us nor create a statistical illusion; we have access to this information in the first place only because the *qanats* played a role in military strategy. Thus, we may draw the inference, without much risk, that the royal administration followed an identical policy in other parts of the Iranian Plateau and perhaps in other parts of the Empire (Arabia, Egypt). Of course, the form of royal involvement is different from what one would find in Babylonia; in Iran we find encouragement rather than direct intervention, but the contrast is essentially more formal than structural.

There is today every indication that the scope of the imperial administration cannot be reduced to extracting tribute. On the contrary, it is easy to see that many regions of the Empire, far from falling into somnolence, were actually in a stage of expansion and population growth, whether Syria, Babylonia, Susiana, or Bactria; whether Hyrcania or the *medinah* of Samaria or Arachosia (despite Plutarch [*Mor.* 328c], the Arachosians did not have to wait for Alexander to bring them agriculture!). Archaeological explorations have instead revealed a picture of sustained development from the time of the inception of the Empire on, even though in Babylonia it is not always easy to distinguish an Achaemenid phase from a Neo-Babylonian phase. Xenophon's account largely confirms that around 400 Babylonia was fully irrigated and cultivated (e.g., *Anab.* II.3.10–13; 4.13) by a dense population divided among prosperous towns and villages (II.4.13, 22, 25); it had paradises (§4.14) as well as lands held by Parysatis (II.4.27). Of course, the case of Bactria, to which we will not return here, shows that the development of production capability cannot always be put into a direct causal relationship with imperial control—even though the contrary is more obvious in Babylonia. But the fact remains: even when the two spheres, political and economic, are kept apart on methodological grounds, we must observe that the long Achaemenid dominion did not lead to general impoverishment that could be explained by "vampirization."

In the end, Xenophon's perspective is not so far from reality; his view of the economy coincides with that very likely held by the Great Kings: it is the careful management of an estate (*oikos*). The Great Kings understood that, to ensure the regularity—nay, the increase—of their revenues, they needed to take measures that would promote the development of production capabilities. However, we will not conclude that they followed an "economic policy." For one thing, economic development cannot be reduced to central interference in matters; not all of the productive capability is controlled by the royal administration; far from it. Furthermore, the decisions made by the Great Kings do not belong exclusively to the economic sphere, which always was subordinated to political-military concerns. It would thus be better to speak of "tribute policy," which implies that the income from development was primarily destined to exalt royal splendor in all of its aspects and manifestations. We could without difficulty add all kinds of activities related to construction (in the center and the provinces) to the sphere of indirect encouragement. For instance, the splendor of satrapal residences presupposes considerable development of artistic technique (well displayed by the activity of Greek artists, or artists working in Greek style, in many regions of the Empire); these royal and satrapal courts certainly created a market, especially for luxury goods intended for the Great King and the imperial and court elite (cf. Herodotus VIII.105; Athenaeus XII.531b; XIV.652b–c; Aelian, *VH* XII.1; Diodorus XVII.67.3 and 108.4). This example serves to illustrate one of the operating rules of the tribute economy, which Parmenion recalled for Alexander at Persepolis (Arrian III.18.11✧): the circulation of the Empire's products cannot be reduced to its centripetal component, since the (undeniable) sucking of riches from the periphery to the center requires that the periphery not be ruined by the demands and assessments of the center. If the center were sucking the periphery dry—as Parmenion puts it—the king would not be acting as a good manager of his property (*ktēmata*), and "the Asians would not so readily adhere to him." If, in fact, the periphery fed (the "royal table") and exalted the center, the center for its part contributed, by means of the State apparatus, to maintaining—even developing, and in any case favoring—the activities of the periphery.

"Overexploitation of Tribute" and Revolt

Let us return to one of the components of the argument brought by Olmstead and his followers: the growing burden of tributes and taxes would have generally stirred up discontent in the Empire and thus facilitated (in the long run) Alexander's conquest. The real problem is that it is very difficult to assess the actual burden imposed by the various tributes and taxes paid to the Great King in relation to the production capacities of the countries; without this information, it is also difficult to infer that the tribute and taxes were an exhausting burden on the peoples. Sometimes (following Plutarch, *Mor.* 172f and Polyaenus VII.11.3) it is claimed that Darius's tribute was fairly moderate, sometimes that it was (or became) unbearable—both without the claims' being based on actual numerical analysis. The reason is obviously that the state of the evidence does not really permit such calculations. Even if we can make some assumptions about the level of tribute, we still somehow need to add in the multiple taxes, which themselves are generally not quantified by the ancient texts, with only one exception (Neh 5:15). There is hardly any doubt that the special payments would heavily burden the resources of the people and cities; we are thinking particularly about the expenses occasioned by the visits of the court and about Herodotus's comment on the condition of the Greek cities visited by the royal caravan in 480: "The Greeks who had to entertain the Persian army and provide a dinner for the king . . . were utterly ruined, and were obliged to leave house and home" (VII.118✧); Herodotus emphasizes the resignation of the downtrodden: "The various places along the route did manage to carry out their orders, though not without severe suffering" (VII.120✧)!

In addition, the weight of tribute, taxes, and satrapal requisitions was added to the assessments already in effect in any given area (whether the land belonged to a sanctuary, an *ethnos*, or a city). We might think, for example, that in the Greek cities the system of double taxation—civic and royal—led to tensions between the civic government and the royal administration; we are thinking here of the tensions that are better known for the Hellenistic period, when cities begged the king or his representative to grant them control (*kyrioi*) of taxes that Pseudo-Aristotle considers among the satrapal levies. We know, for example, that when a city granted an 'exemption' (*ateleia*) to an individual, it stated that the royal taxes (*basilika telē*) were excluded from the scope of the decree. Part of production and wealth were ever after diverted to the royal treasury, with nothing but negative consequences for the immediate producers, especially the peasants, because the source of all wealth is in the land, as Pseudo-Aristotle insists several times. One of the aspects of the creation of the *dōreai* had the same effect, since the holders of the land grants only had to pay a fixed tribute and thus had every reason to increase the yield resulting from peasant labor. Let it suffice for now to make a brief reference to just one example—the tragic situation of the Jewish smallholders, who around the middle of the fifth century complained in these words: "We have had to borrow money on our fields and our vineyards to pay the king's tax (*middā/phoroi tou basileōs*)" (Neh. 5:4✧). The tribute charged was all the heavier because it was a surcharge on top of the satrapal taxes (governor's bread: 5:14–15) and the various assessments paid to the Temple and its personnel (13:10–13).

The connection between regional crisis and imperial dominion is never simple to expose. We may observe, for example, that around 418 the price of foodstuffs suffered an exorbitant increase in several Babylonian towns. But who can say that this (brief and localized) "subsistence crisis" was due to royal taxation and not (e.g.) bad harvests? Astronomical tablets regularly refer to the unlucky consequences of torrential rains in some years, using a formula like: "There was a famine in the land. The people [sold their children]" (*ADRTB* no. –373; cf. nos. –366 and –369). We wonder to what extent these practices explain what Herodotus says in a passage (I.196) often used by Olmstead to connect Persian conquest with impoverishment of simple Babylonians. We obviously lack direct evidence of the perception that Babylonian peasants might have had of Persian control of tribute. We might nevertheless quote a tablet (*YOS* 7.128) from the time of Cambyses (528) that records a dispute brought before the *mār banî* of Uruk; in it, a priest of Ištar is accused by a shepherd from Uruk of stealing 60 sheep from the flock of Ištar and threatening that he would choke the shepherd with the cord of his necklace while whispering into his ear, "This is how Gubāru and Parnaka break the backs of people." Whoever Parnaka may be (the future administrator at Persepolis under Darius?), he was the confederate of Gubāru, who can only be the satrap of Babylonia and Ebir Nāri. Should we see in the priest's threatening words evidence of the implacable nature of imperial coercion as it was experienced by the subject-administrators? Perhaps; but if the threat does refer to an actual event and is not merely a metaphor, we also wonder what perception the Babylonian social elite might have had about their relations with the satrapal administration and, more broadly, with the imperial organizational structures. We should also emphasize that historiography has long been affected by the theory of continued price increases in Achaemenid Babylonia; however, a recent study has cast doubt on this "certainty," because it finds that prices of some staple products fell between Artaxerxes I and Darius III. Other investigations on the same topic are in progress, and they no doubt will nuance and complement the analyses that have been based on a newly published but narrow corpus (the astronomical tablets). In short, it seems unlikely that there will ever be a return to the traditional theory.

Another interesting example just referred to comes from Judah in the time of Nehemiah. The peasants complain of "hav[ing] had to borrow money on [their] fields and [their] vineyards to pay the king's tax" (Neh 5:4◊). But the context makes it very clear that the overburdening of the peasantry is not due solely to the royal tribute: internal class warfare and temple assessments contributed just as much to the impoverishment of the Jewish peasantry (see chap. 14/5). Similarly, in the Greek cities (and elsewhere), in addition to the royal tribute, the city authorities levied civic taxes. More than anything, it was the totality of the various tax systems that explains various situations, whether in Judah or the Greek cities; and in Babylonia, it was the totality of state taxes and the profits siphoned off by the Murašū (and other land managers). But not all of the inhabitants of a community suffered equally, because the tribute drain did not accrue only to the Great King and his Faithful (even if they were the main beneficiaries, on both the political and the economic levels). An analysis of one example of the circulation of the income from assessments (in kind) of the *tagē* (sale of royal wheat: *IG II*^{2}, 207) implies that the Greek cities received back some benefit from the purchase of royal wheat (according to Antigonus, it was cheaper than the wheat available on the Aegean market: *RC* 3). While the political and financial advantage for the Great King and his satraps is obvious, the operation also profited the cities themselves and the richest citizens, who were adept at negotiating the situation to their advantage. In the same way, in Babylonia, the Murašū earned some of their profit from converting taxes paid in kind into silver, and their operations also contributed to the enrichment of the Persians who had received land there. An Aramaic document from Egypt records an association between Persians and non-Persians in a commercial enterprise (*DAE* 109)—a fact also well attested in the Babylonian evidence. In other words, the tribute system was not by itself the cause of tensions between the dominators and the dominated. Peasants, who certainly were part of the dominated (as seen in Babylonia), did not gain any advantage from the circulation of goods; rather, they suffered from it. This probably explains Herodotus's interpretation of the impoverishment of the Babylonian people (I.196: *pas tis tou dēmou*), even if the connection that he makes between conquest and impoverishment must be discounted, to say the least. In contrast, the local elites, who were closely linked to the imperial elite (or part of it), themselves profited from the circulation of the products paid into the royal tax system. This is probably one of the reasons for the long life enjoyed by local dynasties and, more generally, client regimes; Persian authority was to some extent concealed behind the screen of the local gentry, who were entrusted with levying tribute and taxes locally, with the result that any possible discontent on the part of the peasants was aimed at these gentry (as seen in Nehemiah's Judah). In a way, the king's strategy for dealing with the sanctuaries and social elites of his provinces was nothing other than the political-ideological component of a much larger imperial project, and the success of this project presupposes both political centralization and social and cutural polycentrism.

It is important to observe that there is no evidence that would permit us to attribute the known revolts to the cause of tribute alone. The burden of tribute may be why the great revolts of 522 broke out (cf. Justin I.7.2), and this happens to be Bardiya's analysis—he exempted his peoples from tribute and military expenses for three years (Justin I.9.2; Herodotus III.67). It has also been suggested that the Ionian revolt was connected, at least in part, to tribute; if we have properly understood the meaning of the measures taken by Artaphernes, we can see that the royal administration was able to discern the consequences and thus reform the allocation of tribute, while maintaining the total amount (chap. 12/5). This is, after all, an explanation that would confirm that, like Bardiya, the administration of Darius was able to adapt to the needs of the hour. But the only explicit reference along these lines comes from Diodorus, who describes the revolt that was born in Egypt at the time of Inarus in these words: "Mustering an army, they revolted from the Persians, and after expelling the Persians whose duty it was to collect the tribute from Egypt (*kai tous phorologountas tēn Aigypton tōn Persōn ekbalountes*) . . ." (XI.71.3✧). There is no significant reason to reject this statement, even though it is embedded in a stream that is both dominant and suspect, a stream that says that the Persians "governed avariciously and arrogantly" (Quintus Curtius IV.7.1;✧ cf. Diodorus XVII.49.1 and Polyaenus VII.1.7). But are we really certain that all of the tribute-collectors in Diodorus's text were "Persians"? The available evidence implies that it would have been Egyptians who were in charge on the local level (cf. Arrian III.5.4; Ps.-Arist., *Oec.* II.33a). In Diodorus's version, the tribute-collectors were the primary symbols of Persian authority, whatever their ethnic origin. In another case (Sidon), the insurgents first attacked the satrapal paradises (Diodorus XVI.41.5✧). Even if the action had the additional purpose of destroying Persian fodder reserves, the symbolic import was considerably greater than a slap in the face. This is very clearly explained by Diodorus: "The first hostile act was the cutting down and destroying of the royal park in which the Persian Kings were wont to take their recreation"; this was neither more nor less than a declaration of war (cf. Plutarch, *Art.* 25.1–2). The same motivations probably prompted the leaders of the Egyptian revolt to put the "Persian" (that is, imperial) tribute collectors to death.

5. Transition

Whatever point of view one chooses, one irrefutable conclusion emerges: Darius III's Empire was not moribund, as it was smugly described by the Greco-Hellenistic authors. Whether the topic is the authority and aura of the Great King, his financial and military abilities, the productive activity of the various countries, or the cooperation of local elites, there is nothing to suggest that, from Darius I to Darius III, the internal capabilities of the Empire were crumbling. This observation confirms at the least that the theory of "Achaemenid decadence" must definitively be relegated to a display case in the museum of historiographic wonders. But clearly this is no more than a partial conclusion that leaves the way open to another interpretation: the defeat at the hands of the Macedonians does not reveal a cyclic crisis of the Empire but a structural weakness. This is the hypothesis that we propose to test in the next chapter, which is dedicated to the imperial response to Macedonian aggression. The task is not a simple one because, like the Persian Wars, the war of Darius III is known to us only from authors entirely committed to the European cause. It is thus only in a vacuum that we can reconstruct the Achaemenid view of Alexander's conquest, after a close decryption of the ancient sources. To try to resolve the problem that has been raised, we will discuss three points in order, resituated diachronically: Darius's strategy, the Persian aristocracy's attitude, and the position taken by the local elites when they were confronted by the Macedonian's overtures.

Part Six

The Fall of an Empire (336–330)

Chapter 18

Darius and the Empire Confront Macedonian Aggression

1. Territories, Armies, and Strategies

The First Macedonian Offensive (336–335)

We know that after the victory at Chaeronea Philip set about creating a league of which he was *hēgemōn*. The officially announced purpose of the league was to carry out an offensive: the goal was to campaign against the Persians in revenge for the devastation of 480 and thus to liberate the Greek cities of Asia (Diodorus XVI.89). To this end, the king of Macedon sent an advance army corps to Asia Minor in 336 commanded by Parmenion, Attalus, and Amyntas, who were to prepare for the landing of the royal army (XVI.91.2; Justin IX.5.8). We are quite poorly informed about the operation, since the ancient authors (Diodorus and Polyaenus) cast their spotlight exclusively on Memnon of Rhodes. The first actions, certainly, were not favorable to the Persians; this is quite certainly when pro-Persian governments were ejected from Lesbos, Chios, Ephesus, and perhaps also Iasus. In the temple of Artemis at Ephesus and in several towns on Lesbos, statues of Philip were erected at this time, and Parmenion settled factions there that are referred to as "democratic" (cf. Arrian I.17.11). Perhaps the statue that Ariobarzanes had erected in the sanctuary of Athena Ilias was pulled down during the fighting in Troas (Diodorus XVII.17.6). The assassination of Philip II and the accession of Alexander did not interrupt the operations, but these events certainly created conditions more favorable for Darius III to mount a counterattack. At the beginning of his reign, Alexander sent a new detachment to Asia Minor led by Hecataeus; he joined Attalus and Parmenion, though his actual mission was to see to the death of Attalus, who had fallen under the suspicion of the new king (Diodorus XVII.2.3–6). Attalus's machinations were stirring up trouble in the Macedonian army up to the moment he was assassinated, either by his own men (§5.1–2) or on Parmenion's initiative (Quintus Curtius VII.1.3; VIII.7.5). Nevertheless, throughout 335, Parmenion's advances were reduced to almost nothing. Although Memnon did not manage to take Cyzicus (Diodorus XVII.7.8; Polyaenus V.44.5), pro-Persian tyrants were reestablished in the cities of Lesbos and at Ephesus (cf. Arrian I.17.12: Syrphax and his brothers). In Troas, Callas also suffered several defeats (Diodorus XVII.7.10). At the beginning of 334, apparently only Abydos was in Macedonian hands (cf. Arrian I.11.6).

Despite being poorly documented, these events stimulate several reflections. On the military level, the situation is mixed. Initially, the Macedonian expeditionary corps won major victories. Apparently, Parmenion had even been able to advance as far as Magnesia ad Sipylum (Polyaenus V.44.4), and this confirms the relative permeability of the Persian defenses (at least at an early stage)—something that was already apparent in the Greek offensives of the fifth and fourth centuries. At the same time, we need to stress that our sources remain partial, in both senses of the word. Darius "thought to turn the coming war back upon Macedonia," according to Diodorus (XVII.7.1◇), "and began to pay serious attention to his forces. He fitted out a large number of ships of war and assembled numerous strong armies, choosing at the same time his best commanders." This is the context in which he turned to Memnon, who was "outstanding in courage and in strategic grasp. The king gave him five thousand mercenaries and ordered him to march to Cyzicus and to try to get possession of it" (§7.2–3◇). However, Diodorus's presentation must at least be nuanced and supplemented. First of all, Memnon was certainly not the only campaign leader. The financial strategems attributed to the Rhodian (Ps.-Arist., *Oec.* II.29 [1351b]) are evidence of the fact that he was acting as the head of a troop of mercenaries in the service of the Persians. Memnon paid and fed his men by imposing taxes on the cities; this perhaps explains the reaction of the inhabitants of Cyzicus (Polyaenus V.44.5), who had no desire to give in to extortion. Furthermore, it was not only Greek mercenaries that were hired, and Memnon was not made commander-in-chief of the royal troops. Specifically, it is impossible to think that Arsites, the satrap of Hellespontine Phrygia, did not participate in fighting that mostly took place in his territory, and we can make the same observation about Spithridates of Sardis. It is even extremely likely that, as in 341–340 (Pausanias I.29.10), so also in 334 (Arrian I.12.8–10) Arsites was the one who received the Great King's direct orders. Moreover, Diodorus seems to imply that the Persians did not really get under way until after Alexander's accession (§7.2), which occurred at almost the same time as Darius's accession (summer, 335). However, the notion that the Persians responded slowly is also dubious; whatever the extent of the troubles at the center and in some provinces (Egypt?)—certainly less than is usually suggested—the central authority had probably been alerted by Arsites and taken appropriate action. The Xanthus trilingual and the appointment of Orontobates to the satrapy of Caria-Lycia (Arrian I.23.8) testify that the reign of Arses/Artaxerxes IV and the beginning of the reign of Darius were marked by more than palace intrigues. It simply turns out that Diodorus and Polyaenus, fixated on the personality of Memnon, had nothing to say about the operations of 336—and from this we cannot necessarily infer passivity on the part of the Great King. On the contrary, there is every reason to believe, with Diodorus (XVII.7.1–3), that even if other fronts (Egypt?) might have required their attention, Artaxerxes IV and Darius III very quickly became aware of the problems on the Asia Minor front.

Darius, His Satraps, and Alexander's Landing (May–June 334)

Alexander was secure in his European rear and thus he and his army took the Thracian route in the early spring of 334 and crossed the Hellespont (Arrian I.11.6–8; 12.1–7). Parmenion was given the largest part of the army, which crossed unopposed from Sestus to Abydos with the aid of 160 triremes and a substantial number of cargo boats (*ploia*). Meanwhile, Alexander, assisted by a small troop, landed in Troas, where he carried out his "Homeric pilgrimage" (cf. Diodorus XVII.17.1–3; Plutarch, *Alex.* 15.7–9). Next, he came to Arisbe and Percote, before taking a position on the banks of the Granicus (Arrian I.13.1). Persian "satraps and generals" had gathered their forces near Zeleia, where they considered what action to take in response to Alexander's landing (I.12.8–10).

One of the most controversial problems is: Why did the Persians not attempt to prevent the Macedonian landing? Diodorus is the only one to ask the question explicitly, and he has a ready answer: "The Persian satraps and generals had not acted in time to prevent the crossing of the Macedonians, but they mustered their forces (*athroisthentes*) and took counsel [Council of Zeleia]. . . . So they decided to fight it out, and summoning forces from every quarter (*tas pantakhothen dynameis metapempsamenoi*) . . . , they advanced in the direction of Hellespontine Phrygia" (XVII.18.2, 4◊). This delay seems quite surprising, because both the initial Macedonian offensive of 336–335 and the preparations and public proclamations of Alexander left no doubt about his intentions. We recognize this as one of the favorite motifs of Diodorus as well as of Xenophon and other Greek authors: the deliberate pace of the Persian armies was a crippling handicap (e.g., XV.41.2). However, though this remark really can be applied to the assembling of immense royal armies (as at Issus and Gaugamela, for example), it is much less convincing for the army of the Granicus, which comprised territorial troops (military colonies, horsemen provided by the Persians of the diaspora and land-grant holders) and contingents of subject peoples (such as the Paphlagonians), all of whom could be brought together in a short time. Moreover, these troops (some of them, at least) had been mobilized before 334, since they must have taken part in the fighting in 336 and 335. Depending on the date assigned to the battle (April or May), we can imagine that the Persians might have assembled their troops in their winter quarters, which might have been rather far apart (compare XIX.44.4; 68.2). However, paradoxically, apart from the fact that this hypothesis would naturally lead to confirmation of the idea that the Persians had taken many months to assemble their army, a comparison with Arrian leads to a much more reasonable solution. In fact, as Diodorus writes, a war council was held at Zeleia; all the satraps of Asia Minor took part, and the list is given by Arrian (Diodorus names only Memnon). Arrian very clearly states that the Persian troops had already pitched their camp near the city at that time (I.12.8: *katestratopedeukotes*). In short, despite Diodorus's claim, the Persian generals certainly did not wait until their strategy was planned before issuing the order to mobilize. The reason for the situation was quite different. We quite simply doubt that a land army alone would have been adequate to prevent a landing, even if we recall that a Persian commander did challenge Greek ships with his horsemen on one occasion, near Abydos, as a last resort (Xenophon, *Hell.* I.1.6) and also that land troops could occasionally prevent a fleet from gaining access to water supplies (e.g., Arrian I.19.8). They would still have had to know which beachheads the Macedonian army intended to use for landings—something that would have been very difficult to determine, because Alexander, for reasons that might not have been due solely to his desire to pay homage to the Greek heroes of the Trojan War, chose to split his forces (Arrian I.11.6; 12.6). In short, the Persian generals did not bring their troops to the sea "to prevent the crossing of the Macedonians" (*diabasis*: Diodorus §18.2◊) quite simply because the very idea never crossed their minds.

If the Persians had decided to prevent the crossing by the Macedonian army, they obviously would have had to appeal to their sea power. To be sure, not one ancient text refers to the existence of even one Persian boat in the area. This is even more surprising because at that time, in comparison with the 160 triremes (and cargo boats) Alexander controlled (Arrian I.11.6), the Persians had undeniable naval supremacy. They dominated the sea (*thalassokratein*), writes Arrian (I.18.6) of the situation a few weeks later when Alexander was at the gates of Miletus. Arrian numbers the royal navy at 400 ships (§18.5) that were manned by well-trained crews, who had come from Cyprus and

Phoenicia in particular (§18.7; II.13.7). There also were contingents from Greek cities (I.19.11: Iassus). Arrian states that this fleet "[arrived] too late" at Miletus (§18.5), which indicates that the Achaemenid squadrons were already on the Asia Minor front; but this tells us nothing of their comings and goings in the previous weeks, because we do not know from what region they had set sail for Miletus. As a result, we continue to be surprised about the absence of the fleet from the Hellespont; most often, it is attributed to Khabbabash's revolt in Egypt. While this theory is not unattractive, it should be recalled at the same time that the only available evidence—the *Satrap Stela*—does not permit a certain date to be assigned to events in the Delta. Obviously, to date this revolt on the basis that it delayed the arrival of the fleet on the coast of Asia Minor is to adopt circular reasoning that is historically attractive but methodologically has little to recommend it. As a result, we must conclude that we have no answer to the question or, more precisely, that none of the possible answers transcends the limit of probability, absent additional evidence.

Whatever the case, it is clear that the Persian generals did "hold a council of war," to use Arrian's phrase (I.12.8◊). He describes the meeting as follows: against the advice of Memnon, who recommended a scorched-earth policy, Arsites, with the support of the other Persian commanders, chose to give battle. Memnon's suggestion was based on two considerations: first, "the Macedonians . . . were far superior in infantry"; second, "Alexander would not stay in the country for want of provisions." In rebuttal, "it is said (*legetai*) that Arsites stated in the Persian council that he would not suffer one house to be burned belonging to his subjects." He was supported by the other Persians, moreover, who "suspect[ed] Memnon of deliberately holding up warlike operations for the sake of the honour (*timē*) he held from the king." The war council is also reported by Diodorus, who presents Memnon's speech identically (XVII.18.2–4◊). Diodorus strongly supports the Rhodian's strategic choice: "This was the best counsel, as after-events made clear." Then Diodorus offers his explanation of the (in his eyes unreasonable) attitude of the satraps and generals: they rejected the Rhodian's suggestions as "beneath the dignity (*megalopsykhia*) of the Persians" (§18.3◊).

The ancient tales and simple reasoning invite a number of questions, as much about the role of Memnon as about the reasons for the strategic choice of the Persians and about Darius's participation. First, let us note that, while the versions of Arrian and Diodorus essentially agree, Diodorus has once more outrageously favored Memnon, who is once again presented as "famed for his military competence" (§18.2;◊ cf. §7.2 and §20.7). He makes Memnon the key person of the war council, without naming a single one of the Persian satraps and generals! The role that Diodorus attributes to Memnon and his evaluation of Memnon's proposals are very much like other meetings he describes, particularly the discussions between Iphicrates and Pharnabazus in Egypt. In that case, too, the Greek's advice (which is considered especially judicious by Diodorus) is rejected by Pharnabazus and the Persian leaders near him, for motives that strangely resemble those Diodorus attributes to Arsites and his colleagues: "Pharnabazus became suspicious of his [Iphicrates'] boldness and his courage for fear lest he take possession of Egypt for himself (*kat'idian*). . . . Some generals indeed bore a grudge against him and were attempting to fasten unfair charges upon him" (XV.43.2◊). In an observably similar manner, Diodorus exalts the figure of Memnon and confers on him an authority and influence he certainly did not have in the spring of 334. On the same occasion, Diodorus credits him with plans ("transfer entirely the theater of the war to Europe") that were certainly not appropriate at that date. In reality, Arrian makes it clear that the council comprised Persians (*syllogos tōn Persōn*; 12.10) and that within it, logically, pride of place was held by Arsites, the satrap of Hellespontine Phrygia; it was he who bore primary responsibility for conducting operations, as he had in 341 (Pausanias I.29.10). In 334, Memnon was nothing more than the leader of a contingent of horsemen levied on the land he held in Troas (Diodorus XVII.19.4). If his opinion was asked for, it was only one opinion among many. It would be of great interest to know where the ancient authors got their information. If, as is likely, Arrian is depending on the same source as Diodorus, he has at least used it more circumspectly (*legetai* 'it is said') and with less partisanship, although he too reports that the Persian leaders feared the ambition of the Rhodian, who enjoyed royal favor.

The arguments exchanged by Memnon and the Persians continue to raise various critical doubts. A *posteriori*, we are tempted to agree with Diodorus that Memnon's strategy would have been effective. Alexander certainly needed to resupply his forces from the land, and all of the ancient authors stress that he was short of funds at the time. According to Quintus Curtius (X.2.24) and Arrian (VII.9.6), he had even inherited a debt of 600 talents from his father. The spoils of war and income from mines in Macedon had alleviated the situation, and at his landing, he had enough funds to allow him to sustain his army for 30 days. In other words, it was absolutely necessary that he gain a rapid victory that would allow him to get his hands on satrapal treasuries. Against these arguments, which seem both rational and reasonable, the Persian leaders, according to Diodorus and Arrian, advanced two arguments, which *a priori* appear to be rather inconsistent. Arsites' proclamation can be compared with other texts to show explicitly that a satrap's primary mission was to protect the land from the ravages of war (e.g., Quintus Curtius III.4.5); this is how he earned and retained the confidence of the Great King and was the basis on which he could expect promotions in royal favor (Xenophon, *Oec.* IV.8–11). These assumptions prevented him, in principle, from adopting Memnon's tactic. But we doubt that Arsites would have reached such a decisive conclusion simply by referring to these considerations. The debate is similar to the one between Artabazus and Mardonius in 479, reported by Herodotus (IX.41◊). Artabazus countered Mardonius's argument by proposing that they not give battle but instead persuade the Greeks to drop out of the coalition. Herodotus strongly takes Artabazus's side, describing him as "a man of some foresight," whereas Mardonius "expressed himself in much more uncompromising terms": he was certain that "the Persian army was much stronger than the Greek . . . it would be best . . . to engage in battle in the customary Persian way (*nomos tōn Perseōn*)." From Herodotus to Diodorus and from Mardonius to Arsites, the similarities are obvious. The *megalopsykhia* ('arrogance') of the satraps in 334 clearly corresponds to the *nomos tōn Perseōn* invoked by Mardonius; the satraps considered it unworthy of their rank and valor to refuse combat.

In spite (and/or because) of the striking convergence of the reports on Zeleia with Herodotus's story, it would be very unwise to adopt Diodorus's interpretation without nuancing it. The concept of Persian *megalopsykhia* that he invokes is developed in real life in the athletic-contest perspective that he imposes on the battle of the Granicus; its outcome was determined, as he presents it, by the result of a *monomakhia* that pitted Alexander against Spithrobates [Spithridates], "a Persian of superior courage. . . . To the

Persian, it seemed as if this opportunity for a single combat was god-given. He hoped that by his individual gallantry Asia might be relieved of its terrible menace" (XVII.20.2–3◊). The duel took place in the sight of the transfixed soldiers (§20.5) and is presented according to a model that Diodorus (XVII.83.5–6) and Quintus Curtius (VII.4.32–38) use elsewhere—the same model that several ancient authors apply as a way of interpreting the battle of Issus (Polybius XII.22.2; *FGrH* 125 F6). However, aside from the fact that Diodorus's tale is easily challenged, if the word (*megalopsykhia*) he employs is applied without discernment, we are likely to be led onto shifting and uncertain ground—the "psychology of peoples." Though the courage of the Persians is hailed by all of Alexander's authors, there is nothing embedded in an aristocrat's genes that requires him to give battle at any cost! Perhaps contrary to what Diodorus intended, or in any case contrary to what some have made him say on one occasion or another, the Persians were not regularly stripped of common sense—whatever we may think of the tactical disposition they adopted in the battle. Their aristocratic ethic (*megalopsykhia*)—for which parallels may easily be found among the Macedonians—did not necessarily lead them to make "uncompromising" decisions (Herodotus IX.41◊) completely divorced from military rationality. Furthermore, Herodotus cannot hide the fact that Mardonius's decision was also based on a reasonable objective (to keep the Greeks from assembling their forces). Like all the *nomoi*, the *nomoi persikoi* [*tōn Perseōn*]—which was invoked, it seems, by Mardonius—were subordinate to the principle of reality. We can list many cases where the Persian leaders either applied the scorched-earth strategy (e.g., Quintus Curtius III.4.3; including Darius himself: e.g., Quintus Curtius IV.9.14; Diodorus XVII.55.2) or displayed tactical caution (e.g., Diodorus XV.43.1–2), or refused combat that they considered lost in advance (e.g., Xenophon, *Hell.* IV.1.17). Arsites and his colleagues certainly were aware of the relevant fact that, above and beyond (rather airy) discussions of traditional ethics, the Great King was interested in only one thing: victory. Thus, the situation certainly could appear favorable to them in 334 (the judgments *post eventum* pronounced by Diodorus and Herodotus in favor of Memnon's and Artabazus's choices were of interest only to their authors). The Persians had in fact achieved noteworthy successes over the Macedonian forces in the previous year; in addition, Arsites could legitimately estimate that his numerical superiority and the valor of his horsemen would confirm his optimistic view of the future.

But let us go further and ask a simple question: Was Arsites completely free to adopt the strategy of his choice? The ancient authors do not say a word about Darius III. If we consider that Diodorus states that the Great King had previously ordered a general mobilization (§7.2) and that elsewhere he never stops emphasizing (if only to deplore) the fact that the Persian generals depended on the king's orders for everything (e.g., XV.41.2), can we really imagine that Darius III was not interested in the situation as it stood in the spring of 334 and that he permitted Arsites to make the strategic decisions on his own? Only one author, Justin, alludes to this, and he does so very indirectly and, in the context, recalls the tenor of the arguments exchanged at Zeleia: "Meanwhile, King Darius, trusting in his forces, disdained to have recourse to a ruse and stated that to conceal his plans was to devalue the victory. . . . The first encounter therefore (*igitur*) took place in the plain of Adraste" (Justin XI.6.8.10). While Justin's formulations can be subjected to criticism, they at least suggest that Arsites had received orders from the Great King that he should plan for battle in Phrygia. This conforms with Achaemenid practice: though the *tactics* in fact came from Arsites (who consulted his colleagues on this point), the *strategy* was imposed by Darius (cf. the exact parallel in Diodorus XVI.75.1–2)—just as in Greece Mardonius made his decisions on the basis of orders sent to him by Xerxes (chap. 13/4–5). This leads us very much to doubt that the Council of Zeleia was really called to choose between two strategies: it is far more probable that the main purpose was to decide on what tactics to adopt (choice of location, the disposition of the contingents, the role and position of each of the commanders). The satraps engaged in combat quite simply because they had been ordered to do so and because they feared that disobedience would look like treason to the royal cause and result in severe punishment by the Great King (*FGrH* 151 F1.1; *Itin. Alex.* §19). Even if we agree that a debate took place in the terms recorded by Diodorus and/or Arrian, their interpretation of it (given in different words) is certainly incorrect. We may simply imagine that in the course of the debate there was an incidental "ethical" discussion. But the purpose of this discussion was not to define strategy or to question a royal decree that the Persians would easily accept because the battle would give them the opportunity to demonstrate the *megalopsykhia* that, according to Diodorus, was so important to them. It would also provide Arsites with an opportunity to display his valor before Darius III, although the opportunity came with a well-known risk (Arrian I.16.3 [suicide of a satrap, due to his failure]).

Darius in Babylon and the Asia Minor Front (334–333)

From the Achaemenid point of view, the defeat at the Granicus was not really a decisive event. On the other hand, taking into account the difficulties Alexander faced when he landed (on the financial level, for instance), the victory freed him from many of his fears. He had not been driven back into the sea, and he now had additional assets that he could use to pursue his goal. The victory was followed by a series of impressive successes: he took possession of Dascylium, which had been abandoned by its garrison, and he made Calas satrap of Lesser Phrygia and ordered the inhabitants to pay "the same taxes as they used to pay to Darius" (Arrian I.17.1–2◊). He soon made his official entry into Sardis, which Mithrenes had surrendered to him without a fight (§17.3–8), and he seized its treasuries (Diodorus XVII.21.7). At least for the short term, the Macedonian had no more financial woes. It was soon the turn of Ephesus, Magnesia, Tralles, and many other coastal cities (Arrian I.17.9–13; 18.1–2), and then of Miletus, which the Persian fleet could not really rescue, because it arrived after the Macedonian fleet, which was commanded by Nicanor. After some resistance, the garrison surrendered (§18.3–9; 19; cf. Diodorus §22.2–4).

From the Persian perspective, the military losses were appreciable though, as always, they are difficult for us to quantify (1000 horsemen according to Arrian I.16.2). Brave leaders fell: Arrian mentions Niphates, Petenes, Spithridates, Mithrobuzanes, Mithradates, Arbupales, Pharnaces, and Omares (I.16.3); Rhosaces (Spithridates' brother) was also gravely wounded during the battle (I.15.7). Arsites fled the battlefield and chose suicide (I.16.3). Of the participants at the war council of Zeleia (I.12.8–9), only Rheomithres and Arsames survived, in addition to Memnon (and perhaps his sons: I.15.2). Rheomithres returned to Darius's camp. Atizyes, the satrap of Greater Phrygia, also left the battlefield safe and sound after, it appears, stopping in his capital, Celaenae (I.25.3), which he had abandoned when Alexander arrived (I.29.1). Arsames, after trying to get

Cilicia into a state of defensive readiness, also joined Darius, who was then on the march toward Cilicia. Rheomithres, Arsames, and Atizyes later died in the battle of Issus (II.11.8). A major portion of the army nonetheless managed to retreat to the south; the units commanded by the escapees, including Memnon, fell back to Halicarnassus, a powerfully fortified city that was watched over by the satrap Orontobates. The arrival of the troops from the Granicus allowed the town to post an impressive garrison of Persians and mercenaries (I.20.2), and it was also reinforced by soldiers transported by the navy (§20.7). Alexander and his troops suffered several sizable reverses; for instance, at Myndus, despite promises made by deserters at the outset, the city refused to surrender (§20.5–7). The Macedonian efforts were ultimately successful, but only in part. When he left Halicarnassus at the end of 334, Alexander left behind a troop of 3000 infantry and 200 horsemen commanded by Ptolemy, who was ordered to take the two citadels that remained in Persian hands (§22.1–6; cf. Diodorus XVII.24–27).

The Empire at this time found itself in an utterly unheard-of strategic situation, the only possible precedent being Cyrus the Younger's offensive. It was not the first time satraps had known defeat in Asia Minor or that an enemy had camped just outside the walls of Sardis; but it was the first time that the citadel at Sardis had fallen and that the adversary had continued his march with no noticeable obstacles as far as the walls of Halicarnassus, proclaiming long and loud the entire time that his ambitions went well beyond the "liberation of the Greek cities." We would love to know how Darius and his advisers reacted to this avalanche of catastrophic news. We are quite poorly informed about this (to say the least), because the ancient authors follow Alexander step by step without paying the least attention to the Great King. We learn that, when Alexander took his winter campaign to Pamphylia-Lycia, the Great King attempted to stir up a conspiracy against his enemy: he sent a messenger to Alexander Lyncestes, who he had learned was prepared to betray Alexander. The royal envoy fell into the hands of Parmenion, the Lyncestian was arrested, and from the Persian point of view, that was the end of the matter (Arrian I.25). But the story itself should be taken with a grain of salt, because Persian participation in the plot may simply represent a later accusation. There is no doubt that the Great King sent messengers to certain leaders to urge them to resist to the end—this, at least, is what can be gleaned from the statements of the defenders of Celaenae (Quintus Curtius III.1.8). Nevertheless, it must be noted that we are certain about one specific major strategic decision: in the summer of 334, the Great King appointed Memnon (then at Halicarnassus) "to the command of lower Asia [coastal regions] and the whole fleet" (Arrian I.20.3;◊ II.1.1; Diodorus XVII.23.5–6).

The title "commander of the fleet" reminds us that at this time the Persians held hegemony of the sea. At Miletus, in fact, Alexander ordered his navy to disband, except for the Athenian squadron and some cargo boats. According to Arrian (I.20.1◊), Alexander had long been certain of his inferiority on the water (cf. §18.6–8) and, furthermore, "he was then short of money"; lastly, "he reflected that as he now controlled Asia with his land troops, he no longer needed a navy, and that by capturing the cities on the coast he would break up the Persian fleet, since they would have nowhere to make up their crews from, and no place in Asia where they could put in" (§20.1◊). Alexander's decision to take this course of action was already questioned in Antiquity (cf. Diodorus XVII.23.1–3). The plan to destroy Persian naval power by conquering the coastline in fact presented considerable risk. The success that Alexander's troops had enjoyed when they prevented a Persian landing near Miletus was quite unusual, because it simply required them to defend an area that was both well-defined and quite circumscribed—the isle of Lade and the port of Miletus (Arrian §§18.5; 19.2–3); the result was that the Persians were forced to seek water far away, at Samos (§19.7–10). But to extend this strategy to the entire Mediterranean front was a major gamble. It was impossible to control the entire area, at the cost of tying down thousands of garrison troops, because this would have considerably weakened the army as it moved forward (cf. Quintus Curtius IV.1.35). The conquest of Lycia, which was carried out, according to Arrian (I.24.3◊), "to render the enemy's navy useless," did not impede Pharnabazus at all when he proceeded to meet up with Thymondas's ships in August 333 (II.2.1–2). Furthermore, when Alexander left Caria at the end of 334, he had not deprived the Persians of all of their mainland bases: Orontobates and Memnon still held two acropolises at Halicarnassus (I.23.1–6); the Persians also held the island of Cos, from which Memnon set sail some time later (Diodorus XVII.27.5), as well as Samos (Arrian I.19.8). Southern Caria constituted a first-class base for the Persians—especially after the Macedonian forces certainly suffered several defeats; the evidence for the defeats is that by September of the following year (333), Orontobates was in control of "the citadel of Halicarnassus, . . . Myndus, Caunus, Thera and Callipolis" (II.5.7;◊ cf. Quintus Curtius III.7.4). Thereafter, Alexander's strategy, at least in the short term, left the way entirely open to the Persian navy, which meant that, in the middle term, Persian naval superiority threatened to wipe out Alexander's control of the Asia Minor coast. Alexander quickly became cognizant of this danger because, even before the death of Memnon (July–August 333), he ordered a new war fleet to assemble: "He gave Amphoterus command of the fleet at the shore of the Hellespont and Hegelochus of the land-forces, in order that these officers might free Lesbos, Chios and Cos from the enemies' garrisons. . . . And the allies were ordered, as was provided by their treaty, to furnish ships to guard the Hellespont" (Quintus Curtius III.1.19–20◊). Meanwhile, Memnon had gone on the offensive and taken Chios, and the towns on Lesbos also surrendered, except for Mytilene.

It seems quite obvious that Darius and his advisers were kept up to date about the situation and that the appointment of Memnon to head the fleet and to defend the coast was intended to use him to the best possible advantage. Was Darius hoping that success would force Alexander to turn back? Or, was he beginning to build an army from this moment on? We know that around the end of the summer of 333 Darius departed from Babylon at the head of the royal army, accompanied by the entire court, "according to the traditional custom of the Persians" (Diodorus XVII.25.3). According to Diodorus, the decision to summon the royal army was made late, after a council that was held when the news of Memnon's death was received in the summer of 333 (§§30; 31.1; Quintus Curtius places it when Darius was in Syria: III.8.2–11). However, as they are recorded by Diodorus, the terms of the discussion provoke suspicion because the presentation carries with it accusations against Darius that are identical to those brought previously against Artaxerxes III (XVI.40.5–6). Should we also be suspicious of the chronology? It is difficult to decide. When we realize how long these general mobilizations took (as often stressed by Diodorus himself: cf. XV.41.2), it seems difficult to believe that the army of 333 could have been gathered, armed, and trained in only a few months. In another respect, the draft of troops was not universal, because, to use Quintus Curtius's phrase (III.2.9; cf. IV.9.1–2), the speed (*festinatio*) with which the assembly took place prevented the contingents from the Iranian Plateau and Central Asia from being summoned. So two interpretations become available: (1) from this moment on, Darius began to levy his troops to prepare for any eventuality, or (2) he thought (or hoped) that leaders and troops in Asia Minor would be enough to deal with the problem. According to the second theory, Darius was behaving no differently from his predecessors: never, after Xerxes in 480–479, had the regions of Asia Minor seen a royal army. But if this be the case, we must also conclude that the Great King had not taken the measure of either the situation or his adversary's determination.

To be able to make a judgment regarding Darius's state of mind, we would have to know the content of Memnon's mission. In the course of a report that Diodorus provides regarding a council that Darius held when he learned of the Rhodian's death, he states that, until the Great King received the news, he "had counted on Memnon's transferring the impact of the war from Asia into Europe" (§30.1✧). The same information appears in Arrian (II.1.1). Diodorus adds that Memnon's initial successes encouraged many island cities to send delegations and even stirred up unrest as far as Euboea and Greece, whose leaders received bribes from the Rhodian (§29.3). Finally, according to Quintus Curtius (III.1.19–20) and Arrian (III.2.3), Alexander, while at Gordion in the spring of 333, ordered a navy to be rebuilt precisely because of the dangers posed by the situation; he agreed to considerable expenditures for this purpose and sent money to those in Greece who were looking after the cities. There can be no doubt, in fact, that on the eve of the battle of Issus some Greeks believed that the balance of forces tipped in favor of the Great King (cf. Aeschines III.164); in addition, Athens, Thebes, and Sparta had sent ambassadors to the Great King (Arrian II.15.2–4; Quintus Curtius III.13.5). However, that Memnon's campaign aroused such hope (in Greece) or fear (in Macedon) might simply have resulted from untrammeled rumor of the kind that Arrian passes on (II.2.4); whether the Rhodian actually carried out this strategy is a different question. In the spring of 333, Memnon reconquered Chios and then concentrated his forces on Lesbos: only Mytilene resisted, and it was during the siege of this town that Memnon died of an illness (July–August 333). This, in any case, is the skeletal narrative provided by Arrian (II.1.1–2) and Diodorus (§29.2: with an error). Clearly, Memnon at this time had no intention of taking advantage of his crushing superiority by carrying the war into Europe; instead, he dedicated many weeks to completing the blockade of Mytilene. Memnon's activities lead us to believe that his goal in the short term was to retake the coastal cities and the islands, foiling Alexander's appraisals of the situation (Arrian I.20.1)—thus explaining the Macedonian's reaction when he learned that his adversary was threatening not Europe but his prior conquests in Achaemenid territory. All in all, we can imagine that Memnon's military activities corresponded to the mission Darius gave him—a mission that is implicit in the geographical range of the expertise that brought Memnon the Great King's recognition in the first place, namely, the coast of Asia Minor.

It is likely that the European designs attributed to Memnon came from a Greek tradition that was originally concerned only with his and his family's memory (cf. Tod II no. 199) and that this tradition is best represented by Diodorus (chap. 17/3 above). Diodorus even says (and this seems quite unlikely) that the Rhodian had proposed carrying the fight to Europe already in the war council at Zeleia (§18.2). Diodorus (§29.4) and Arrian (II.1.3), in almost identical terms, present the death of the Rhodian as a major relief to Alexander (Diodorus §31.3–4) and a full-scale disaster for Darius, so that he now had to take the leadership of the army himself (Diodorus §30; cf. also Quintus Curtius III.2.1). From this it is sometimes inferred that Darius at this time decided to abandon his maritime strategy in favor of a mainland strategy. However, none of these interpretations appears to be valid. First of all, Memnon's succession had already been dealt with: before he died, he had turned his responsibilities over to Autophradates and Pharnabazus son of Artabazus, his nephew, anticipating that Darius would confirm these arrangements (Arrian II.1.3)—and Darius did so soon afterward, confirming Pharnabazus in his position (II.2.1). In addition, the death of Memnon did not interrupt the maritime offensive at all, even though the dispatch of mercenaries to Darius probably weakened Pharnabazus's and Autophradates' capabilities. The operations that took place in the interim prior to the battle of Issus on the contrary demonstrate that Memnon's successors abandoned his strategic, somewhat dilatory caution and threw themselves more vigorously into the assault on Macedonian positions. Autophradates and Pharnabazus vigorously pursued the siege of Mytilene, which soon fell; the city became "allies of Darius on the basis of the peace of Antalcidas," a garrison was established, a friendly district was entrusted to one of the oligarchs who had been exiled by Alexander the previous year, and taxes were levied on the inhabitants (II.1.4–5◊). The terms of the treaty imposed on Chios (and shortly afterward on Tenedos: Arrian II.2.2) show that Darius was not in the least willing to accept the initial Macedonian conquests. On the contrary, the Great King tended to interpret the dictum imposed on the Greeks in 386 by his grandfather Artaxerxes II very broadly. The conquest of Tenedos was probably part of a much wider goal—to cut off the wheat supply coming from the Hellespont, a danger that Alexander had already prepared for even before the death of Memnon (cf. Quintus Curtius III.1.19–20). Nevertheless, it was only later that the Macedonian fleet became fully operational (cf. Arrian II.2.3), and this is clear from the fact that, even though Datames suffered a reverse of no great magnitude at Siphnos (II.2.4–5), it had no lasting consequences, and the Achaemenid fleet retained its superiority. The most painful setback for the Persians took place in Caria. When he was in Cilicia (September 333), Alexander to his great relief learned about the victory that Ptolemy and Asandrus (the satrap of Caria) had won over Orontobates, who went on to lose his positions at Myndus, Callipolis, Caunus, Thera, Triopium, and Cos (II.5.7; Quintus Curtius III.7.4). This was certainly a setback of the first magnitude; nevertheless, either Halicarnassus remained in Persian hands or they recaptured it shortly afterward (cf. Arrian II.13.6).

To answer the question raised earlier, we can be sure that Darius, at least from this time onward—but surely already since the preceding year—was perfectly well aware of the danger presented by the Macedonian offensive. To counter it, he and his counselors had devised a strategy that was both maritime (reconquering the coasts of Asia Minor) and mainland (preparing an army that would take the offensive). Despite Diodorus's statement (XVII.30.7), Darius decided to take the leadership of the army and lead it "toward the coast" not because he thought that the death of Memnon represented a decisive blockage of his goals at sea; on the contrary, while Pharnabazus, Autophradates, and their lieutenants led the offensive by sea, he personally prepared to confront the Macedonian army. However, as everyone knows, a strategic plan, however well conceived it may appear (especially as reconstructed by the modern-day historian!), is only worth the means that are actually available to carry it out and any advantage that the plan may grant the creator of the plan vis-à-vis the enemy. From this perspective, the situation was ambiguous. First, it is clear that Alexander, who had just welcomed major reinforcements at Gordion, was not dissuaded from pursuing his march to the south, and he resumed doing so around June–July 333. At the same time, it must be stressed that the Macedonian still found himself in a precarious situation, caught, as it were, between a rock and a hard place: the Persian navy was still operating off the coast and the royal army was approaching from Cilicia. The fact that he summoned several garrisons that had been left in the rear (Quintus Curtius IV.1.35) shows that in some respects he had his back to the wall. In the short term, the success of his plan to conquer the coasts assumed that he would be able to take some Phoenician towns. Darius also understood this; the best proof of his eagerness (*festinatio*) to reach Cilicia is that he chose not to wait on the contingents from the Iranian Plateau and Central Asia (Quintus Curtius III.2.9). In order to compensate for their absence, the Great King in the summer of 333 ordered Pharnabazus to bring some of the mercenaries who were fighting on the Mediterranean front, despite the fact that this risked depleting a critical position, his Aegean rear (cf. Arrian II.1.2; Quintus Curtius III.3.1). The presence of Sabaces, the satrap of Egypt, at Issus implies that he had brought a contingent with him, and this probably weakened Persian positions in the Nile Valley (Arrian III.1.2; cf. Quintus Curtius IV.1.28). As long as we do not conclude from the results of the battle of Issus that the fate of the Achaemenid Empire was already definitively sealed, we must recognize that the battle about to unfold in Cilicia would take on critical importance for Alexander.

From Issus to Gaugamela (November 333 – October 331)

Alexander's victory at Issus made it possible for him to march on Phoenicia, and many Phoenician towns opened their gates to him: Aradus, Marathus, Sigon, Mariamme, then Byblus and Sidon (Arrian II.13.7–8; 15.6–7; Quintus Curtius IV.1.15–16). The Tyrians, however, offered him a pro forma rejection (Arrian II.16.7–8). In response, Alexander basically concentrated on capturing Tyre, a success that validated his strategic plan, which was to take the coasts before conquering the interior (Arrian II.17). The Macedonians did not even have to wait for the powerful Phoenician city to fall; the kings of Aradus and Byblus were ready to capitulate and "left Autophradates and his ships and joined Alexander with their own fleet, along with the Sidonian triremes; thus some eighty Phoenician sail came over to him. In the same days nine triremes came from Rhodes, . . . three from Soli and Mallus and ten from Lycia." It was soon the turn of the kings of Cyprus, who commanded 120 ships; they also joined Alexander because "they were alarmed at the whole of Phoenicia being already in Alexander's power" (Arrian II.20.1–3;✧ early 332). The concomitant arrival of a Macedonian ship marked the return of Alexander's navy in force to Aegean waters, commanded by Amphoterus and Hegelochus (Quintus Curtius IV.5.14). The successive defections of these forces confirmed the success of the strategy that was initiated by the disbanding of the navy at Miletus in the summer of 334.

But meanwhile, the Persians had not been taking it easy. They launched a vigorous counterattack in Asia Minor. We have only meager information about this land offensive in Quintus Curtius and Diodorus (but not Arrian). We know that quite a few of Darius's regiments had left the battlefield safe and sound, still under his command—4000 men, according to Arrian (II.13.1). Several mercenary units commanded by Amyntas (a

Macedonian exile), Thymondas, Aristomedes, and Bianor had managed to reach Tripolis in Phoenicia, where they gained reinforcements. One of them, Amyntas, on his own authority then led a fruitless attack on Egypt (Arrian II.13.2–3; Diodorus XVII.48.2–5; Quintus Curtius IV.1.27–33; cf. §7.1). Diodorus and Quintus Curtius include the adventures of these mercenary leaders in a more general discussion of Persian counteroffensives after the battle of Issus:

> His [Amyntas's] experience was paralleled by those of the other officers and troop leaders who escaped at the head of their military units from the battle at Issus and attempted to maintain the Persian cause. Some got to important cities and held them for Dareius, others raised tribes (*ethnē*) and furnishing themselves with troops from them performed appropriate duties in the time under review. (Diodorus XVII.48.5–6◇)

Quintus Curtius returns to these events on several occasions:

> The generals of Darius who had survived the battle of Issus, and all the force that had followed them in their flight, with the addition of vigorous young soldiers of the Cappadocians and Paphlagonians (*assumpta etiam Cappadocum et Paphlagonum juventute*), were trying to recover Lydia. The governor of Lydia (*Lydiae praeerat*) was Antigonus, one of Alexander's generals; he, although he had sent very many soldiers from his garrisons to the king, nevertheless scorned the barbarians and led his forces out to battle. There also the fortune of the contending parties was the same; in three battles fought in one region and another, the Persians were routed. (Quintus Curtius IV.1.34–35◇)

Quintus Curtius (IV.1.36) says that these last events happened at the same time (*eodem tempore*) that

> a fleet of the Macedonians, which had been summoned from Greece, defeated Aristomenes, who had been sent by Darius to recover the coast of the Hellespont, and captured or sank his ships. Then (*deinde*) Pharnabazus, commander of the Persian fleet, having exacted money from the Milesians and put a garrison into the city of Chios, sailed with a hundred ships to Andros and from there to Siphnos. These islands also he occupied with garrisons, besides fining them. (IV.1.36–37◇)

Quintus Curtius comes back to this later, in the context of the celebration of the Isthmian Games (IV.5.11)—that is, June–July 332, after the fall of Tyre (during the siege of Gaza?). But the chronological connection is expressed quite loosely, as follows:

> But not only was Alexander himself proceeding to reduce the cities which still rejected the yoke of his rule, but his generals also, distinguished leaders, had invaded many places: Calas Paphlagonia, Antigonus Lycaonia; Balacrus, having vanquished Hydarnes, Darius' satrap, had recovered Miletus; Amphoterus and Hegelochus with a fleet of 160 ships had brought the islands between Achaia and Asia under the sway of Alexander. (IV.5.13–14)

From this gap-filled but consistent and perfectly credible information we must conclude that, after the battle of Issus, Persian generals took positions in Cappadocia and Paphlagonia and carried on conscription efforts there. With the armies thus raised they launched an initial offensive that Antigonus thwarted. His victories, however, did not settle the problem: the second Quintus Curtius quotation shows that the Persians continued to occupy Cilicia, Paphlagonia, Lycaonia, as well as the Aegean coast (Miletus). It was not before mid-332, *at the earliest*, that the Persian danger was definitively overcome as a result of the Macedonian offensive that was carried out as much on land as by sea.

In fact, Pharnabazus and Autophradates were able to pursue objectives in the Aegean. Until the defection of the Cypriot, Phoenician, Lycian, and Cilician contingents, at the beginning of 332 (Arrian II.20.1), they had a nearly intact strike force. When Alexander appeared below their walls, at any rate, the Tyrians thought that "the Persians were still supreme at sea" (Arrian II.18.2✧). This was also, according to Arrian, Alexander's view (II.17.2–3). They could also count on support from their mainland bases in Caria—Halicarnassus and Cos (Arrian II.13.4) and probably Miletus as well (Quintus Curtius IV.5.13). In the autumn of 333 (before Issus), they had left Cos for Siphnus, where Agis of Sparta, who was planning to rebel against Antipater, had come to join them. They were in Siphnus when they received the stunning news of the defeat at Issus, and Agis was sent to Crete "to stabilize the situation." Pharnabazus reinforced the guard at Chios (some of whose inhabitants were considering a revolt), occupied Andros (Quintus Curtius IV.1.37–40), and then rejoined Autophradates at Halicarnassus (Arrian II.13.4–6; Quintus Curtius IV.5.15–16). This is *perhaps* when Autophradates carried out an operation in the region of Ephesus (Polyaenus VII.27.2) and launched a raid on Samothrace (Plutarch, *Mor.* 339e; cf. *Alex.* 48.4). Despite the presence of the Macedonian navy, then, the Persian leaders after Issus continued to actively pursue their objectives, even though it is difficult to follow their trail in detail because the evidence is fragmentary.

Thus, between the end of autumn 333 and the end of spring 332, combat continued unrelentingly on the mainland as well as along the coast and in the islands. In order to try to understand these conflicts on the various fronts, it is attractive to think that they all pursued the same strategy. According to this theory, the strategy could only have been defined by Darius himself, but two observations appear to argue against this interpretation. First, Amyntas's attack on Egypt reflects his own purely personal motives (cf. Arrian II.13.3), which Quintus Curtius thinks were based on his own interpretation of "finders-keepers" (IV.1.27: *velut certo jure possessum*). Second, the content of the diplomatic offers attributed to Darius after the battle of Issus seems to imply that he was deeply depressed. But neither of these obervations actually would prevent alternative explanations. If Amyntas's designs on Egypt really were personal, it is very strange that when he reached Pelusium he presented himself as having been ordered to go there by Darius himself (Diodorus §48.3). Furthermore—precisely as Arrian implies (II.13.1–3)—the other leaders who accompanied Amyntas as far as Tripolis and Cyprus did not follow him to the Nile; in all probability, then, they were subsumed under Pharnabazus's command at Siphnos. Finally, we will return to Darius's diplomatic overtures later, because rather than being able to infer from them that the Great King was weak, we can only interpret them in the context of a *preliminary* elucidation of the royal strategy after Issus.

Of course, there are several accounts of Darius's involvement on the Aegean front after Issus. After his retreat from Issus, the Great King returned to Babylon, where he immediately began to assemble a new army, appealing particularly to contingents from the Iranian Plateau and Central Asia (Diodorus XVII.39.1–4; Quintus Curtius IV.6.1–2; 9.13). It seems utterly impossible that he was cut off from information about the progress of operations on the Aegean front, because he was fully aware that the fall of Tyre would obliterate all of his hopes of seeing Alexander turned back. We must therefore stress the reasoning that Diodorus attributes to the Tyrian leaders: "They wanted to gratify Dareius and keep unimpaired their loyalty to him, and thought also that they would receive great gifts from the king in return for such a favour. They would draw Alexander into a protracted and difficult siege and give Dareius time for his military preparations" (XVII.40.3◇). It is also not impossible that the problems Alexander had to deal with in Syria (the Beqaʿa Valley) during the siege of Tyre can also be attributed to Achaemenid fomentation. Alexander may have taken the risk of "dividing his forces" because he thought the danger was real (cf. Quintus Curtius IV.2.24; 3.1, 7). In addition, the fall of Damascus and the naming of a satrap of Syria shortly after the battle of Issus (Arrian II.13.7) certainly did not signify the total submission of the country, as the revolt of Samaria made clear a short while later (332–331; Quintus Curtius IV.8.9–11). We also know that when Amyntas arrived in Egypt his attack was repelled by Mazaces, who must have been named satrap of Egypt shortly after Issus to replace Sabaces, who was killed during the battle for Cilicia (cf. Arrian III.1.2). Finally, we will stress Quintus Curtius's explanation of operations in the Hellespont at the beginning of 332: the Macedonian navy won a victory over Aristomenes, "who had been sent by Darius to recover the coast of the Hellespont (*qui ad Hellesponti oram reciperandam a Dareo erat missus*)" (IV.1.36◇).

The totality of the evidence thus leads us to conclude quite definitively that after his defeat Darius did not abandon the strategy he had formed in 334, which consisted of pushing hard to assemble a royal army and continuing offensives in Asia Minor in Alexander's rear. He could correctly believe that Alexander's territorial control in Asia Minor was very superficial, especially in the regions (Paphlagonia and Cappadocia) where his own generals had raised their armies. Quintus Curtius names only one of these generals, Hydarnes. But we have long known of coins from Sinope that were struck with names that can be identified as Mithropastes, Orontobates, and Hydarnes (in Aramaic). Mithropastes may be the son of Arsites, the former satrap of Dascylium, of whom we know only that he was exiled by Darius to the head of the Persian Gulf at an unknown date and under unknown circumstances (Strabo XVI.5.5). This Orontobates may have been the satrap of Caria who disappears from the sources after the fighting in Caria. Hydarnes, finally, may be one of the sons of Mazaeus, the former satrap of Cilicia-Syria. Whatever the case, we doubt that these generals took the offensive on their own initiative; it is far more likely that they were sent by Darius, who gave them letters authorizing the levying of troops and the use of any treasury funds that remained intact (without doubt in Cappadocia). According to a well-documented practice (cf. Ps.-Arist., *Oecon.* II.24a), the generals would strike coins to pay their troops in a coastal town, Sinope, which at that time still maintained its Persian alliance (Arrian III.24.4; Quintus Curtius VI.5.6). The goal entrusted to them clearly was to reestablish Achaemenid authority in Asia Minor, to cut Alexander's lines of communication, and to advance toward the coast (cf. Hydarnes to Miletus). This is probably why in Quintus Curtius's first discussion (IV.1.35) only Antigonus is named; it was his responsibility as satrap of Greater Phrygia and ruler of the strategic town of Celaenae to defend the royal road. The task attributed to Antigonus by Quintus Curtius (*Lydiae praeerat*), despite the terminological imprecision it implies, may indicate that he was ordered by Alexander to coordinate the Macedonian defenses.

It is also possible that royal orders reached the coast at the same time, as evidenced by Quintus Curtius's statement concerning the mission assigned to Aristomenes in the Hellespont (IV.1.36); furthermore, it was also on Darius's orders that Thymondas had come to Pharnabazus at Siphnos and there turned over the mercenaries under his command. This interpretation would provide an even better explanation of why, during his private adventure in Egypt, Amyntas could claim to have been assigned an official mission by the Great King: "He proclaimed that he had been sent by King Dareius as military commander because the satrap of Egypt had been killed fighting at Issus in Cilicia" (Diodorus XVII.48.3◊). Amyntas thus would have been attempting to evict the satrap who had recently been named by Darius (that is, Mazaces; cf. Quintus Curtius IV.1.28), even though he had probably simply been ordered by the king to take mercenaries to Egypt to reinforce the garrisons there. Diodorus also says (§48.2◊) that Agis had "received from the Persian king ships and money," but Arrian does not mention a royal order and attributes the initiative to Pharnabazus alone (II.13.4–5). One of Pharnabazus's problems at this time was financial (cf. Quintus Curtius IV.1.37: levies of taxes at Miletus, Andros, and Siphnus by Pharnabazus). It is probable that, unlike the generals who struck coins at Sinope, the Persian coastal commanders did not have access to treasury funds, which in that region were controlled and used by Alexander. But it must not necessarily be concluded that communication between the Great King and Pharnabazus was cut off at that time, especially if we acknowledge, as seems obvious, that the Persian land and sea offensives were coordinated.

The initial victories of Antigonus and then, several months later (in the first months of 332?), of Balacrus (satrap of Cilicia) and Calas (satrap of Hellespontine Phrygia) marked the fall of Persia in Anatolia. Nevertheless, Cappadocia and Armenia responded to the royal order to mobilize; in the months after Issus, both regularly sent their contingents to the Great King, under the leadership of Ariaces (Cappadocia) and of Orontes and Mithraustes (Armenia) (Arrian III.8.5). At the same time, the Macedonian navy continued its offensive. Nonetheless, it was not before the end of 332 that the navy's admiral, Hegelochus, was able to report to Alexander, who was then in Egypt: he and Amphoterus had managed to take, successively, Tenedos, Chios (where Pharnabazus and Aristonicus, tyrant of Methymna, had been taken prisoner), Mytilene, and Cos (Arrian III.2.3–7; Quintus Curtius IV.5.14–22). Pharnabazus disappears (until 322) from the sources after his escape from Chios, and it thus appears that nothing remained of the Persian naval forces except perhaps some small residual groups of "pirate" ships. Only Agis continued the struggle in Europe, though without any direct connection with the Persian front.

Meanwhile, Alexander captured Gaza, and then Egypt was surrendered by the satrap Mazaces, who did not have sufficent forces to resist (cf. Arrian III.1.1–2). In 331, Alexander was able to take the road to Tyre and Babylonia and to confront Darius, and along the way he bloodily quashed the rebellion in Samaria (Quintus Curtius IV.8.9–11).

Darius and Alexander: War and Peace (333–331) — Another Reading

All of the ancient authors say that during the same period diplomatic negotiations between the two camps opened and that they were initiated by Darius. The number and date of the diplomatic missions and letters sent by the Great King vary from one to the next. Here is a summary of the information that the ancient authors report.

(1) According to Arrian (II.14.1–3◊) and Quintus Curtius (IV.1.7–14), the Great King sent a message to Alexander immediately after the battle of Issus, and the Macedonian would have received it when he was at Marathus (around November–December 333).

The Great King requested that the members of his family (mother, wife, children) imprisoned at Damascus (Arrian) be restored, for ransom (Quintus Curtius), and suggested a treaty of "friendship and an alliance."

(2) A second mission arrived during the siege of Tyre (Arrian II.25.1◊). Quintus Curtius (IV.5.1) dates it after the fall of the town, though without certainty (*isdem ferme diebus*). Once again the king offered ransom (10,000 talents) and a treaty of friendship and alliance, and for the first time he agreed to give up some territory, though the amount varies among the sources: "all the country west of the Euphrates to the Greek sea" (Arrian, *Itin. Alex.* §43); "the entire region lying between the Hellespont and the Halys River" (Quintus Curtius IV.5.1;◊ cf. Diodorus §39.1). Quintus Curtius and Arrian state that the Great King proposed sealing the treaty by a marriage between his daughter Stateira and Alexander, and Quintus Curtius adds the detail that the territory conceded (Lydia, the Ionians, Aeolis, the coast of the Hellespont," IV.5.7◊) was to be the dowry (IV.5.1, 7). Some of these proposed terms also appear in an anonymous author (*FGrH* 151 F3).

(3) With the notable (but logical) exception of Arrian, all of the authors speak of a third diplomatic overture, which took place when Alexander had already crossed the Euphrates. In addition to ransom for his mother and daughters (his son also remained hostage in Alexander's hands, according to Quintus Curtius IV.11.6) and a treaty of friendship and alliance, the Great King offered "all the country between the Hellespont and the Euphrates" and the hand of one of his daughters (Quintus Curtius IV.11.5;◊ Justin XI.12.10; Diodorus §54.2). Quintus Curtius reiterates that this territory would be the princess's dowry (IV.11.5). Diodorus adds: "Alexander would become Dareius's son-in-law and occupy the place of a son, while sharing in the rule of the whole empire" (*koinōnon genesthai tēs holēs basileias*; §54.2);

(4) Plutarch, on the other hand, makes only one allusion to these negotiations, which he places at Tyre during Alexander's second stay (around June 331). He mentions the ransom (1,000 talents), "all the countries on this side the river Euphrates," a marriage, and amity and alliance (*Alex.* 29.7◊).

These data have long attracted the attention of historians, but they have not received an exhaustive treatment recently. While we can easily understand that Darius might have sent letters and ambassadors to Alexander, is the content, as recorded by the ancient authors, credible? Though the request that Alexander free captives does not present many problems, can we agree on the other hand that the Great King almost certainly would never have offered to give up part of his kingdom to Alexander, let alone that he would have offered to share his kingship with the victor of Issus (Diodorus)? Again, to put it more clearly: do the texts we have reflect, whether in whole or in part, the true nature of the relationship between the two kings at this time, or is it nothing but a piece of Macedonian propaganda?

The first task, obviously, is to establish a relationship between the concessions offered by the king and the military and political situation, both as the modern historian might analyze it now and also as Darius would have envisaged it then (the latter is not an easy task). The offers attributed to Darius by the ancient authors in fact necessarily imply that he felt that he was in an inferior position; thus, giving up territory appeared to him to be the only option. The ancient authors present the king's concessions as graduated: (1) the request to return prisoners, (2) the abandonment of territory as far as the Halys, and

(3) then the Euphrates. The progression actually seems logical: as Alexander ironically remarks, the Great King each time abandons only territories that he had already lost. There is an identical gradation in the varying amounts of ransom offered. But does the internal logic followed by the ancient presentations actually match what Darius decided? This is the crux of the problem.

Like the Tyrians (Arrian II.16.7◇), we today rightly believe that after the battle of Issus "the issue of the war . . . was still obscure." As Diodorus explains (§39.1), Darius's determination was steadfast. He still had immense resources in both men and money; specifically, he could count on the arrival of the contingents from the Iranian Plateau and Central Asia (cf. Quintus Curtius IV.6.1–2; Diodorus §39.3). In 331, the contingents available to him came from every imperial territory under his control, from Cappadocia to the Indus (cf. Arrian III.8.3–6). Alexander's ongoing siege of Tyre immobilized him and allowed Darius to oversee the assembling of troops undisturbed. At the same time, as we have seen, Darius did not abandon his Aegean strategy. In addition, despite Alexander's statements in his letter from Marathus (II.14.7), there is nothing to indicate that the Great King had suffered significant defections among the high-ranking Persian aristocrats (chap. 18/2 below). Between the end of 333 and spring–summer of 332 (the presumed date of the second embassy), the situation had partly reversed—to Alexander's advantage—primarily because of the defection of Phoenician and Cypriot units from Pharnabazus's navy and the renewed activity of the Macedonian navy. Meanwhile, the siege of Tyre dragged on; Quintus Curtius mentions twice that Alexander was even on the brink of despair and turning back (IV.3.11; IV.4.1). Despite some victories won by Antigonus, the Persian offensives in Alexander's rear were not yet totally neutralized (cf. the chronological alignments in Quintus Curtius IV.5.11–14). Beyond Tyre, Alexander knew that he would also have to conquer Gaza, which was commanded by Batis; he had made considerable preparations that would probably let him put up a lengthy resistance (cf. Arrian II.25.4), and Quintus Curtius (IV.6.7◇) hails him as "a man of exceptional loyalty to his king (*eximiae in regem sui fidei*)"; the use of this phrase implies that he had received instructions from Darius (cf. V.3.4).

At Babylon, meanwhile, Darius actively pursued his military preparations; he even introduced technical innovations in the arming of his troops (Diodorus §53.1–3; Quintus Curtius IV.9.3–4). He and his advisers carefully chose the field of battle, at a spot (near Arbela) on the great road (*DAE* 67 [AD 6]) that they knew Alexander would take due to logistical considerations (Arrian III.7.3; Quintus Curtius IV.10.13). The royal army trained there every day (Diodorus §§53.4; 55.1). Supply logistics were meticulously organized (Quintus Curtius IV.9.8). In order to avoid the errors made at Issus (cf. Quintus Curtius IV.13.6), the ground was leveled (IV.9.10; Diodorus §53.4) to permit the cavalry and chariots to maneuver easily (Arrian III.8.7). According to Polyaenus (IV.3.17) and Quintus Curtius (IV.3.36), iron caltrops (a device with four metal points) had been driven into the soil as a hazard to the maneuvers of the Macedonian cavalry. The Great King took other measures to impede Alexander's march. For instance, Mazaeus had been ordered to guard the Euphrates, and he did such a good job that the Macedonian pontoon-builders were not able to finish their work before Alexander arrived (cf. Arrian III.7.1–2). When he retreated, Mazaeus tried to apply a scorched-earth policy (Quintus Curtius IV.9.13; 10.10–13; Diodorus §55.1–2). Quintus Curtius repeats an unverifiable tradition and even adds that Darius tried to organize an assassination

plot against Alexander (IV.10.16–17). In conclusion, we see nothing in the deeds and behavior of Darius that might illustrate that he had a sense of panic or despair. Though the
repeated successes of Alexander were undeniably nothing but failures for Darius, after
Issus, he was still completely determined to confront the Macedonian army once more,
and he did everything possible to prepare. It was Darius who determined the strategy at
this time; Alexander had to adapt to the plans worked out by the Persian staff—not the
other way round. Diodorus acknowledges this with the following appreciation: "He was
not crushed in spirit in spite of the tremendous setback he had received" (§39.1◇). In
short, the Great King was not in the sort of desperate situation that might be expected
from the breadth of territorial concessions attributed to him.

The ancient authors clearly realized that they had a problem, because if the offers of
territory (even "reduced," contra Arrian, to the Halys border) are dated to the time of the
siege of Tyre, they were made at a time when Darius had already issued the general mobilization order (hence the coordinated decision made by the Tyrians, following Diodorus §40.3; cf. *FGrH* 151 F1.7: *dia to speudein epi ton Dareion*). The ancient authors,
even though they generate their own contradictions, all sidestep the problem by stating
that it was the breakdown of negotiations that forced the Great King to prepare an army,
"despairing of peace, which he had believed that he could obtain through letters and envoys" (Quintus Curtius IV.6.1;◇ cf. Arrian II.25.3; Diodorus §55.1). The problem is that
Arrian dates this attitude of Darius to spring–summer 332 (approximately), while Diodo
rus dates it to summer–fall 331, at a time when the royal army had already been assembled (Diodorus) or was well along in the process (Arrian). The offer of the Euphrates is
literally incomprehensible: at this time, it was evident that Darius had in fact decided to
fight, because, as even Quintus Curtius avers, he left Babylon for Arbela (IV.9.6) before
sending the third embassy to Alexander (IV.11.1; cf. Diodorus 54.1–2). The ancient authors offer two intepretations to explain the inexplicable.

(1) Darius preferred to arrange a peace rather than confront Alexander. This is the
picture that drives Alexander's responses, which are constructed on a consistent model.
Thus, he refuses all of the territorial concessions, which would do no more than authen-
ticate the conquests that had already been achieved. He aspired to control the entire
kingdom and to wield undivided power. He goads Darius to another battle that will decide the contest. It is clear that this image is built on a very popular motif: Alexander
never stops pursuing an enemy who slinks away in flight; and this motif was consistently
driven home by the sources close to the Macedonian camp and spread wide in many depictions. Quintus Curtius even claims that for a moment (end of 332 – beginning of
331?) the Great King considered leaving Babylon and seeking refuge in the Iranian Plateau countries; he gave up this plan only because he understood that, because he faced
so firm a foe, all flight was futile (IV.9.1–2). But whatever interpretation is put on the
"flights" of Darius III at Issus and Gaugamela (chap. 6/4), the information on the Great
King's military preparations offered by Quintus Curtius and Diodorus themselves
(above) impugns the interpretations that they suggest.

(2) The later overtures (for instance, the Euphrates as border) are explained by Darius's passionate admiration for Alexander; after all, he had just learned from one of his
eunuchs about the care with which Alexander had surrounded his wife Stateira, who
had just died (cf. Quintus Curtius IV.10.18–33). This is presumed to explain the senseless speech given to the Great King: "O Gods of my fathers, . . . may no one, I pray, be

king of Asia, rather than that enemy so just" (§10.34◊), and the following: "Accordingly (*itaque*) . . . overcome by his enemy's continence, Darius sent ten envoys" (§11.1;◊ cf. Justin XI.12.6–9: *itaque*). None of these laborious and/or rhetorical comments could convince anyone. Furthermore, it is clear that the speeches attributed to the Great King's ambassadors at this time are improbable reconstructions that bear no evidentiary value (cf. in particular Quintus Curtius IV.11.2–9). Whatever the (political or personal) importance Darius attached to the members of his family who were held in Alexander's camp, it is hard to believe that at the moment his army was actively training on the battlefield of Gaugamela he could imagine exchanging them for half of his territory. The offer is even more unbelievable because, under this "exchange theory," the Great King's prime concern would have to have been the fate of his son; indeed, according to Quintus Curtius (IV.11.6), Darius asked Alexander to return his mother and daughters but would be willing to let him keep the young boy hostage. This is all incredible—unless we assume that the Great King "had the virtues of a private citizen more than the attributes of the leader of an empire" (G. Radet)! It is easy to find two of the favorite components of Macedonian propaganda in the words and thoughts attributed to Darius by Quintus Curtius and Justin: the greatness of spirit and moderation of Alexander on the one hand, and on the other, the voluntary dismantling of the Empire by Darius, who with his dying breath charged his "chivalrous" conquerer to punish Bessus, the satrap who committed regicide (Diodorus §73.4; cf. Plutarch, *Alex.* 43.4; Justin XII.11.5).

In short, the ancient comments on the (imagined) personality of the Great King do nothing to clarify the political decisions attributed to him. Alexander's historians could provide no credible explanation for the strategy that they thought the Great King followed. The reason is simple: Quintus Curtius and Diodorus in particular faced an insurmountable paradox: they were unable to reconcile two very different pictures of the Great King—a decisive commander-in-chief on the one hand and a completely panicked head of state on the other. Only Arrian escapes the internal contradictions. His negative evaluation and judgment of Darius never varies and brooks not a single exception: the speeches he gives Alexander always contain canonical images of weak and effeminate Persians, in contrast to tough Macedonians and glorious Greeks (II.7.3–7)—a practice that is reminiscent of the precedent of the Ten Thousand (II.7.8–9; cf. I.12.3) and that certainly is dependent on his source, one of his favorite authors, Xenophon. Darius is presented as a pawn in the hands of his advisers (II.6.4); he has a defeatist mentality (§10.1); he is unwilling to part with any of the royal paraphernalia of opulence (*tryphē*), "even on campaign" (§11.10◊). All of these judgments about Darius are repeated in his funeral oration—"No man showed less spirit or sense in warfare" (III.22.2◊); and he was guilty of infamous cowardice at Gaugamela: "he himself was among the first to flee dishonourably at Arbela, and lost the greatest army of the whole barbarian race" (§22.4◊). Arrian had already developed all of these themes in the (highly suspect) text of the letter he had Alexander send to Darius from Marathus (II.14). The letter amounts to an organized attack on the legitimacy of Darius, composed according to the canons of dynastic propaganda. The Great King is contrasted with the powerful, victorious Alexander (who, however, is compassionate toward the members of Darius's family) and is disqualified on every count: he is not a legitimate king; he is abandoned by those close to him, who "voluntarily" turned to Alexander (Arrian II.14.7◊); he not only was vanquished on the battlefield but in his ignominious flight he abandoned the symbols of his authority (bow and arrows, mantle, chariot), with the result that thereafter their symbolic power redounded to Alexander's glory (II.11.6; 12.4–5; III.15.6). In this context, the abandonment of territory would crown the entire picture, because Darius himself agreed to divide the Empire and even to grant Alexander an equal share of authority (Diodorus).

All of this confirms that there were two contradictory views of the personality of Darius III in Antiquity. It seems obvious that the tradition of abandoning territory emerged from a stream of Macedonian propaganda that obligingly emphasized the Great King's weakness and cowardice. Arrian followed this stream unswervingly. Diodorus and Quintus Curtius also adopted it, but they melded it with information from another, more "Persocentric" source. Because they inherited two traditions, their narratives are marked by many contradictions and awkward explanations. Moreover, we have already seen that Diodorus provides both versions of Darius's accession a few lines apart without realizing that they are mutually exclusive (§§5.3–6; 6–7.1–2). The only point on which the two agree is the notorious abandonment of territories, but it is probably accidental that Arrian is the only one who dates the offer of the Euphrates as a boundary to the siege of Tyre (II.25.1). Modern commentators almost unanimously reject Arrian's version and in so doing validate the other version, which describes the ceding of Trans-Halys Anatolia. But does this version really have better foundations? Is it more credible? This is indeed the problem.

The choice of the Halys and the Euphrates as the borders offered by Darius is no gauge of Achaemenid authenticity. The Greeks had known since the time of Herodotus (I.74◊) that the Halys was considered the border between the kingdoms of Media and Lydia, and the diplomatic agreement between the two had been sealed with a marriage between the son of Cyaxares and the daughter of Alyattes because "treaties seldom remain intact without powerful sanctions [family bonds]." Moreover, the territory thus "ceded" corresponds almost exactly to a theme, dear to Isocrates, by which conquest could be measured (*Phil.* 120: "Asia from Cilicia to Sinope"). The notion of the Euphrates as a border seems at first sight to have been transferred from the administrative term Ebir Nāri—that is, 'beyond the river', which is rendered in Greek as 'beyond the Euphrates' (*peran Euphratou*) in Darius's letter to Gadatas (ML 12). But the formulas used by Alexander's historians—"between the Euphrates and the Greek sea" (Arrian), "this side of the Euphrates" (Diodorus, Plutarch), "between the Hellespont and the Euphrates" (Quintus Curtius), and "as far as the Euphrates" (Justin)—clearly represent an Aegeocentric view of the Achaemenid world, simultaneously betraying a Greek or Macedonian hand (just like the phrase "this side of the Halys"). Furthermore, in Greek representations of Achaemenid space, the Euphrates was traditionally perceived as a cultural boundary beyond which deepest Asia, both mysterious and unsettling, commenced (cf. in particular Chariton of Aphrodisias, *Chaereas and Callirhoe* 5.1.3). There can be no doubt that these at least in part are the political-geographic assumptions that lie behind the construction of the (conventional) dialogue between Alexander and the elderly Parmenion, who here as elsewhere appears in his (entirely conventional) role of "peasant from the Danube" (Arrian II.25.2; Diodorus 54.4–5; Quintus Curtius IV.11.11–13). These observations lead us to take the probative value frequently accorded to the gradated nature of Darius's territorial concessions with considerable reservation. In reality, the theme of "gradated response" in the ancient authors typically relates to the category of contrived evidence; it essentially serves as *a posteriori* legitimation of the successive phases of Alexander's conquests. To this end, the writers have deliberately taken over geographical-administrative terminology that would establish an apparent continuity with existing Near Eastern formulas, but they have reinterpreted them from a European perspective on imperial space.

If we attempt to see things from the Persian point of view, the preceding discussions invite us once more to reread the texts that, rather than portraying the thoughts of Darius, reveal the afterthoughts of Alexander. We must especially stress that never in Achaemenid history had there been a precedent for relinquishing territory in this fashion. To this observation one obviously might retort that no Great King had ever found himself in a similar situation in the past. The only parallel that might be suggested is when Artaxerxes II faced Cyrus the Younger. Of course, the two examples are not fully congruent, because this one concerns two royal sons—though on the military and strategic level, Artaxerxes II's position in the summer of 401 was at least as serious as Darius's (although, unlike Darius III, Artaxerxes did not have the contingents from the Iranian Plateau and Central Asia). Nevertheless, there never was a question, even for a moment, that the Great King would abandon an ounce of his sovereignty, even in favor of a younger brother. Diodorus's gloss (XVII.54.2) on the sharing of power (*koinōnon genesthai tēs basileias*) is highly suspicious; strangely enough, it recalls a promise of the same type that (also according to Diodorus; XI.71.4) Inarus supposedly made to the Athenians in the 460s (*koinēn autois parexesthai tēn basileian*). Power-sharing and joint regency are in fact notions absolutely foreign to the Achaemenid concept of monarchy. The parallel sometimes suggested on the basis of the position that Diodorus (once again) attributes to Mentor after the Egyptian campaign (XVI.50.8) is built on sand: there never was a vice-regency at any time in the entire history of the Achaemenid dynasty.

Does Quintus Curtius's insistence on the idea of "dowry," in connection with the supposed offer of Darius's daughter to Alexander, allow us to alleviate the difficulty? To put it another way, to what extent would ceding land as a dowry possibly limit Alexander's future rights? To answer the question with any finality, we would have to understand "matrimonial law" among the Persians with some precision, which is not really possible. But to formulate the dowry theory is also to acknowledge that the conditions for devolution of power would have been understood by Darius and his entourage. In other words, adopting Quintus Curtius's theory raises new difficulties: who would reign after Darius's death—his own son or Alexander? And when Alexander died, would not power depart from the Achaemenids forever: would not a son born to a Macedonian father and an Iranian mother be considered a Macedonian, as is demonstrated by the Susa marriages? We do not really think that Darius could have been naive about this point. We are even more wary because the dissipation of a kingdom through dowry is one of the favorite motifs in monarchic literature that has a goal of justifying a conquest *post eventum* by claiming family rights. Let us simply recall the stories circulating in Persia and Egypt of a Persian-Egyptian marriage (cf. Herodotus III.1–2) or the fiction that made the Persians the heirs of the Median kingdom through an engagement agreed to by "Cyaxares" in the presence of his future son-in-law "Cyrus": "With her I offer you all Media as a dowry, for I have no legitimate male issue" (Xenophon, *Cyr.* VIII.5.19✧). This is a rather banal motif that probably goes back to Ctesias, because it is found word-for-word in Nicolas of Damascus (*FGrH* 90 F66.8): Astyages gives his daughter in marriage to Spitamenes with "Media for a dowry." For all of these reasons, the dowry theory raises great reservations.

Nevertheless, it is not impossible that the Great King offered one of his daughters in marriage to Alexander. But on what basis and with what intent? First of all, we may note that in second-millennium Near Eastern interdynastic matrimonial practice, every dowry had a functional (and thus inseparable) association with the bride-price paid simultaneously by the future son-in-law. At the same time, it must be stressed that, in the Achaemenid context itself, to hold the position of king's son-in-law never conferred any special authority: instead, the position was a royal gift that obligated the recipient vis-à-vis his royal father-in-law (and not vice versa; see chap. 8/1). Is this how Darius would have understood it? From Darius's point of view, this union would in fact have served as a bargaining chip ensuring a retreat by the Macedonian forces. The response that Alexander seems to have made to this proposal (cf. Arrian II.25.3) implies that a marriage of this kind offered by Darius alone could in no way be considered equivalent to a sharing of power and/or territories. Alexander was both smarter and more ambitious than Pausanias (cf. Thucydides I.128.7)! Furthermore, the tradition of the dowry is repeated by an anonymous author, though in a form slightly different from Quintus Curtius's: Darius wanted to obtain the freedom of some captives and sent (apparently immediately after the battle of Issus) an embassy to Alexander seeking peace: "He gave him (*didous*) all the territories this side of the Halys, and whichever one of his daughters Alexander would choose to marry, and 20,000 talents by way of dowry (*emproikia*)" (*FGrH* 151 F1.5). In this account, the dowry is formally distinct from the ransom and it consists solely of a gift of money.

If, then, there is no doubt about the reality of diplomatic overtures, we nevertheless do not see how this would justify, from the Persian perspective, Darius's offers of territory—at least in the terms recorded by Alexander's historians (cession pure and simple, or as a dowry). Instead, we are led to conclude that the territorial concessions attributed to Darius between 333 and 331 were falsely promoted by Macedonian propagandists. Obviously, it is always difficult to reject a unanimous tradition on the basis that we consider the tradition improbable—an idea that itself comes from the historian's personal interpretation or his own conviction. But the agreement of Alexander's ancient historians is not sufficient ground to support their theory. In fact, the agreement essentially results from an illusion, if we agree that they used the same source for this detail. Furthermore, the agreement is no more than partial, because only Quintus Curtius and an anonymous author (*FGrH* 151 F1.5) provide the dowry clause, and they do so in different terms. Finally and most importantly, textual and contextual analysis nearly inevitably lead to this theory, because it is the only approach that actually takes into account the activities and decisions actually attested for Darius (in contrast to his assumed and reconstructed thoughts), the change in power relations, Achaemenid political traditions and concepts, and the internal contradictions found in the Hellenistic and Roman authors. The interpretation is made even less desperate by the fact that one tradition has echoed it even in Antiquity. According to Diodorus (XVII.39.2◊), in fact, when Alexander gathered the council of his Friends, he "concealed the real letter. Forging another more in accord with his interests he introduced it to his advisers." The chronological uncertainty of the passage does not lessen the force of the objection that it generates: the fabrication of forged letters (not to mention speeches!) was a practice well known in the time of Alexander and in the Hellenistic period. The improbability of the strategy and of the thoughts attributed to Darius reinforces the conviction that we are dealing with a Macedonian fraud—a conclusion that is no more difficult to accept than the impossibility of proposing truly credible alternative explanations.

The Consequences of Gaugamela (331–330)

Despite his immense, intense military preparations, Darius was once again vanquished on the battlefield at Gaugamela. This defeat had considerably more serious consequences than the defeat at Issus. When the Great King returned to Arbela, he and his advisers held a conference. According to the ancient authors, they faced a dramatic choice: either to return to Babylon, where Mazaeus and his contingents were soon coming to seek refuge (cf. Quintus Curtius IV.16.7), and there take advantage of the strength of the position to prepare Babylon defensively and thus block Alexander's advance; or else to attempt to assemble a new army and thus prepare for a final confrontation. Because of the recent rout, both options presented major disadvantages: leaving open the Babylon road would in the end allow Alexander to seize the great capitals, their treasures, and the rich plains of Babylonia and Susiana; but to fall back to Babylon would be equivalent to recognizing that the fall of the city—however long the siege might take— would signify the end of Achaemenid dominion and the conclusive defeat of Darius III, who would then fall into the hands of the conqueror. Darius chose, against the advice of some of his intimates, it appears (cf. Quintus Curtius V.1.7), to fall back to Ecbatana, taking the road from Arbela across the mountains of Armenia (V.1.9; Arrian III.16.1; ADRTB no. –330). According to Arrian (III.16.2), this option was based on two considerations. First, Darius knew that Alexander would soon attack Babylon; the good road from Arbela to Babylon offered Alexander the supplies that his troops needed, which were not available on the route chosen by Darius; given these factors, the Great King was quite aware that his adversary was intent on capturing rich, prestigious towns such as Babylon. Second, Darius counted on rebuilding an army at Ecbatana, aided by a new mobilization that had been launched in the East Iranian satrapies (Diodorus §§64.1–2; 73.1), especially Bactria, which according to Quintus Curtius (V.10.3◊) "occupies a third of Asia, and the number of its men of military age equalled the armies which Darius had lost."

We know that, when Alexander arrived in Babylonia, Mazaeus did not really attempt to organize the town's resistance, even though it was well fortified, and he capitulated to Alexander; the satrap of Susiana soon followed his example. Quintus Curtius, describing the surrender of Susa to Alexander by the satrap Abulites, muses that he did this "whether by order of Darius, . . . or of his own volition" (V.2.8◊). This is basically the problem faced by the modern historian as well. Diodorus, also commenting on Abulites, reveals varying traditions about his voluntary surrender to Alexander:

> Some have written that he did this in compliance with orders given by Dareius to his trusted officials. The king of Persia hoped by this policy, it is suggested, that Alexander would be kept busy with dazzling distractions and the acquisition of brilliant cities and huge treasures, while he, Darius, won time by his flight to prepare for a renewed warfare. (§65.5◊)

A little earlier, Quintus Curtius had offered his own interpretation, in the context of his discussion of the debate between Darius and his circle at Arbela after the retreat from Gaugamela. He says that, when he left the road to Babylon open, the Great King's thinking was as follows:

He himself had learned from experience that costly equipment and concubines and trains of eunuchs were nothing else than burdens and hindrances. Alexander, dragging these same clogs after him, would be inferior in the resources by which he had formerly conquered. (V.1.6✧)

This is obviously a personal gloss by Quintus Curtius (or his source) that regurgitates all of the clichés about *tryphē*, built on a litany of evocative terms: "costly," "concubines," "eunuchs." Quintus Curtius and the other ancient historians would soon use the same images to criticize the "orientalization" of Alexander. Moreover, coming as it does from a Latin historian's pen, the passage is very reminiscent of the description of Hannibal and "the delights of Capua" (cf. V.1.36–38). It is also difficult to make sense of the thoughts attributed to Darius by Diodorus, because the best way to gain time would obviously have been to order Mazaeus and Abulites to continue to resist as long as possible. Arrian also refers to the strategy of the Great King, who was then at Ecbatana:

> Darius had determined, if Alexander were to remain at Susa and Babylon, to wait himself where he was in Media, in case there were any new developments [*neōterizein*: disaffection?] on Alexander's side, but if Alexander were to march straight against him, he proposed to go up country to the Parthyacans and Hyrcania, as far as Bactra, ravaging all the country and making further progress impossible for Alexander. . . . He stayed himself in Ecbatana with the force he had collected. . . . [Alexander] was informed on the road that Darius had decided to meet him in battle and fight it out again. . . . (III.19.1–3✧)

Arrian's passage raises several difficulties, because it is placed at a late time (May–June, 330) and confuses several stages of Darius's strategy (which is perhaps the source of the chronological inversion of Susa and Babylon). The thoughts that Arrian gives to Darius do not mean that he believed that Babylon and Susa would not resist; the word used (*neōterizein*) even makes it possible to believe that the Great King hoped that Alexander might still find himself in the grip of difficulties. These thoughts are only understandable if in the meanwhile the Great King's hopes had not been realized and he had learned of the fall of the capitals (by swift courier, the news could have reached him at Ecbatana in a day or two, via Persepolis and Gabae). This is probably the situation that lies behind the statements of Quintus Curtius and Diodorus: Darius hoped that for whatever reason (logistics, perhaps) Alexander would stay awhile in Babylon. It is only *post eventum* that Arrian (III.16.2) is able to state that, according to the Great King himself, since early October 331, Babylon and Susa comprised the 'prize of the war' (*tou polemou ton athlon*)—a phrase from the world of sports that gives Darius the false image of a competitor who recognizes, sportsmanlike, the victory of his opponent. On the contrary, as Arrian recognizes without attempting to evade the implications, it is clear that, throughout the winter of 331–330, the Great King did not abandon his initial plan, which was to raise an army and give battle: "Darius was preparing himself for battle rather than for flight" (Quintus Curtius V.8.2;✧ cf. Diodorus 73.1). Only later did he make the decision to withdraw toward the Upper Satrapies.

We can now answer Quintus Curtius's question about Abulites' behavior: "whether by order of Darius, . . . or of his own volition" (V.2.8✧). Whether it concerns Babylon or Susa, the first possibility—that Abulites acted on orders from Darius—seems even less likely, because the Great King was quite aware that a new mobilization would take quite a few months. We must thus assume instead that, quite logically, Darius had sent orders to Mazaeus and Abulites instructing them to put up the strongest possible resistance to

Alexander. In fact, Darius must have written to all of the satraps while at Ecbatana. According to Diodorus (§64.2◇), "he posted couriers to the satraps and generals in Bactria and the upper satrapies, calling upon them to preserve their loyalty to him." The same applies to Madates, who was in command of a fortification on the road from Susa to Persepolis: he was "a man by no means a time-server; for he had decided to endure the utmost to the best of his loyalty" (*ultima pro fide*; V.3.4◇). This phrase reveals that he was personally involved with Darius (cf. IV.6.7), as Mazaeus and Abulites certainly had been; and this explains the uncertainty expressed by Quintus Curtius (V.2.8) and Diodorus (65.5), who, moreover, may be providing the excuse offered at the time by the rebellious satraps. The behavior of these two men poses other problems, to which we shall soon return, but we must not conclude that their actions reflect the position of the Great King; on the contrary, their deeds took him by surprise. By organizing the defense of the territories in his rear, Darius clearly hoped to gain the time needed to prepare a new army. Babylonia, Susa, and Persia were endowed with many strongholds, and the size of contingents placed at the Persian Gates show that the region was not devoid of officers and men. Mazaeus himself headed a force of Babylonian horsemen who figured in the procession that went to welcome Alexander (Quintus Curtius V.1.23). Perhaps these cavalrymen were among the troops that had followed Mazaeus all the way to Babylon (IV.16.7). For that matter, Alexander himself was much less optimistic than many modern-day historians. Before Mazaeus defected, he was quite fearful that the siege of Babylon would immobilize him for a long time (cf. Quintus Curtius V.1.17). Despite the successive surrenders of Babylon, Susa, Persepolis, and Pasargadae, Alexander was still uneasy in the spring of 330, which helps to explain the forced march that brought him to Media in twelve days. At the end of this march, he learned that Darius had decided to retreat toward the interior (Arrian III.19.4–5). We shall return later to Darius's last weeks (chap. 18/4 below), but as a provisional conclusion, we must insist on a fundamental observation: there is no doubt that the victory at Gaugamela represented an essential step for Alexander—and was actually experienced as such (cf. Plutarch, *Alex.* 34.1)—and that the defeat was, *in the long run*, a catastrophe for Darius. Nevertheless, as of the evening of October 1, 331, the story had not yet been written. The battle seems decisive only because we know the rest of the story and only if we assume that Darius was totally discouraged after the defeat—a picture that all of the ancient authors throw into doubt. If any event can be called decisive, it was the surrender of Babylon, nearly a month after the battle; but, it was never anticipated that Mazaeus would surrender the town without a fight.

2. Darius and His Faithful

Mithrenes and the Persians of Asia Minor (334–333)

In his letter from Marathus, Alexander, according to Arrian (II.14.7◇), made his superiority evident in these terms: "I hold myself responsible for all of your troops who did not die in the field but took refuge with me; they are with me of their own free will (*ouk akountes*), and voluntarily (*hekountes*) serve in my army." We can see that this is one of the well-known articles of royal justification. The voluntary (*hekousiōs*: e.g., Diodorus §65.5 [referring to Abulites]) defection of personnel close to a rival reinforces the right of the one who wishes to claim supreme authority. This has already been shown in the case of all of the ancient authors who calmly record the propaganda issued by Cyrus the Younger against his brother Artaxerxes (chap. 15/2). As in the case of Cyrus, Alexander's statements must be viewed with caution. The behavior of the Persian satraps prior to the battle at the Granicus had already shown how much the Persian aristocrats were united around their king and how determined they were to carry out the orders given to them.

There are few examples of voluntary (*hekousiōs*: Diodorus XVII.21.7) defection; we can cite only the case of Mithrenes, phrourarch of Sardis, who after his defection was always considered a traitor (*proditor*) to the Great King (Quintus Curtius III.12.7). When Alexander arrived, Mithrenes, accompanied by nobles (*dynōtatoi*) from Sardis, sought the king outside the walls and "gave up . . . the citadel and treasury" (Arrian I.17.3◊). Mithrenes' reasons escape us. His attitude was entirely different from the mood of Hegesistratus, "to whom Darius had entrusted command of the Milesian garrison, [and who] had previously sent a letter to Alexander surrendering the city, but he had taken heart again, because the Persian force was no distance away; his intention was now to save the city for Persia" (Arrian I.18.4◊). But Mithrenes was aware that the town's position was virtually impregnable and that, in any case, Alexander would have to lose many weeks in order to force its surrender (because he obviously could not continue his march and leave such an important position behind him). Moreover, Mithrenes certainly did not realize that the fall of the citadel would allow Alexander to recover from his financial straits (cf. Diodorus §21.7). The death at the Granicus of Spithridates, the satrap of Lydia and Ionia, does not explain everything. In other words, given the nature of the balance of power at the time, Mithrenes' decision was extremely risky, especially if there had been a successful Persian counterattack. We would better be able to resolve the problem if we knew the personal and political pedigree of the phrourarch of Sardis — which, unfortunately, we do not. Mithrenes obviously thought that Alexander's offers were sufficiently attractive, and we know that in exchange for his surrender he received a prestigious position: "Mithrenes remained with him, with the honours (*timē*) of his rank" (I.17.4;◊ cf. III.23.7).

The Mithrenes episode and the vocabulary used indicate that after his landing Alexander was convinced that the conquest of the Empire and lasting dominion presupposed that he would be able to attract the support of the dominant Persian socioethnic class that, aside from occasional revolts, had remained closely tied to the Great King throughout Achaemenid history. The Hegesistratus episode implies that he had made contact with many important officials shortly after the victory at the Granicus (compare Arrian III.16.6). To bolster his attempts to win converts, he had devised a quite simple ideological stratagem that was copied from the technique that the Great Kings themselves had applied to the elites of conquered countries. Thus, Mithrenes was welcomed into the royal entourage, and he retained the perquisites of prestige that he had enjoyed in Darius's service. Alexander did not go so far as to integrate Mithrenes into the new ruling class; he did not receive a satrapy until 331. Up until 331, the high satrapal posts were exclusively reserved for Greeks and Macedonians. Even at that date, the Macedonians were certainly not ready to accept the Iranians as equals; from this, we can infer that, in these first years, an Achaemenid-style court hierarchy was created parallel to the Macedonian court hierarchy. An anecdote about Memnon recorded by Polyaenus (IV.3.15) also seems worth mentioning. After his landing, Alexander "ordered his troops to spare Memnon's lands . . . in such a way as to make him suspect." Alexander's policy was quite different after the victory at the Granicus: at that time, he sent troops "to Memnon's territory (*epi tēn khōran tēn Memnonos ekpempei*)" (Arrian I.17.8◇)—which implies that the Rhodian had been dispossessed. This was a signal intended for those who were considering resistance: if they did not yield, they would also lose the economic advantages that they had enjoyed as a result of the favor shown to them by Darius (cf. Arrian I.12.10). These were probably the factors that Mithrenes took into account.

Alexander's policy may be easy to understand, but we need to evaluate its impact and success. Apparently, aside from Mithrenes, there were not many defectors; we know only that someone named Sabictas/Abistamenes was put in charge of part of Cappadocia in the summer of 333 (Arrian II.4.2; cf. Quintus Curtius III.4.1), but we know nothing about him. Overall, the high officials' faithfulness to Darius is verified throughout 334–332. The generals and satraps who survived the battle at the Granicus remained loyal to Darius: some came to defend Halicarnassus, others returned to their satrapy or country (Atizyes to Greater Phrygia, Arsames to Cilicia) before returning to Darius's camp, and still others met their end in violent counterattacks against Macedonian positions before and after Issus. We also need to be able to trace the activities of the Persians of the imperial diaspora who were settled in large numbers in Asia Minor. They no doubt were confronted with the same problem that Mithrenes had to face. Unfortunately, we have no way of knowing what their attitude might have been at that time. Not until 332 do we have any interesting evidence: a Greek inscription from Amyzon, which reveals the granting of citizenship to someone named Bagadates and his naming as *neocore* of a civic sanctuary dedicated to Artemis. The context suggests that Bagadates was a Persian settler in Caria who, during the turmoil surrounding the collapse of Achaemenid dominion, managed to retain a prestigious position by being integrated into the civic ranks. But the late date of the inscription (after the death of Alexander) keeps us from making generalizations about the attitude of the Persians of Asia Minor after the Macedonian army had passed through in 334 and after the confrontations of 334–332.

The Surrender of Mazaces (332)

The first recorded surrender by a satrap is the case of Mazaces, who capitulated in Egypt in 332. Quintus Curtius indicates that Mazaces came to welcome the king outside the ramparts of Memphis, as Mithrenes had done at Sardis: he "delivered to Alexander 800 talents of gold and all the royal furniture" (IV.7.3–4◇). Arrian explains Mazaces' decision as follows:

> Mazaces . . . on learning how the battle of Issus had gone, of the shameful flight of Darius, and that Phoenicia, Syria, and the greater part of Arabia were in Alexander's hands, and being without any Persian force, received Alexander in a friendly way into the cities and the country. (III.1.2◇)

We should establish a hierarchy for the reasons offered by Arrian and make distinctions among them. It is likely that Mazaces had been negatively influenced by the defeat at Issus, but the explanation nonetheless seems forced. In fact, it was only because Sabaces, the satrap of Egypt, had fallen at Issus, that Mazaces had been named satrap in his place, in the context of measures taken by Darius III after his Cilician defeat. Arrian's bizarre explanation is also suspect because of the generalization it implies about the attitude of the Persians after Issus. It is built on one of the common themes of Macedonian propaganda that has already been highlighted in the letter from Marathus, as well as in the descriptions of the battle of Issus (and then Gaugamela): Darius III was completely discredited by abandoning the symbols of royal authority when he fled. There is hardly any doubt that Alexander at this time had mounted a psychological campaign that was intended to force a split between the Persian aristocracy and the Great King, but there is no evidence that he achieved any degree of success in this area. There is in fact nothing to show that the Great King's prestige was deeply affected. The defeat, we have already seen, did not result in terrified flight among the high officials, who were certainly reassured by the energy that Darius displayed. The only "traitor" we can name is the governor of Damascus, who after the battle of Issus betrayed the confidence of the Great King (Quintus Curtius III.13.2–4); however, he was slain by one of his accomplices, "reverencing the majesty of the king" (§13.17◊), who brought his head to Darius. We also know that Batis, who was in charge of Gaza, maintained his commitments to the Great King to the end (Quintus Curtius IV.6.7), despite the shock of the fall of Tyre. On the other hand, we do know the name of a Persian (Oxydates) who had been imprisoned by Darius at Susa—"this made Alexander trust him" (in 331; Arrian III.20.3◊); but no general conclusion can be drawn from this incident, because we know nothing about the time or circumstances of the affair.

Along with his appointment, Mazaces would certainly have received orders from Darius to resist if the occasion arose, and Egypt had been a troubled theater ever since he had been assigned there. After the battle of Issus, Amyntas, a Macedonian deserter who was in the service of Darius, reached the Nile Valley accomanied by his mercenary troopunit. He claimed to have been named *strategos* by Darius; there was a battle, in which Amyntas perished (Diodorus XVII.48.2–5; Quintus Curtius IV.1.27–33). The affair probably reinforced the satrap's position, and he probably enrolled Amyntas's mercenaries in his service. The need to pay mercenaries is perhaps confirmed by the coins bearing his name that he issued in Egypt. At the same time, Alexander's crushing military and naval superiority must have worried Mazaces, who was now completely cut off from the Persian camp. We know about one of his subordinates, Amminapes, a Parthian, who according to Arrian "was one of those with Mazacus, who had surrendered Egypt to Alexander" (III.22.1◊). Quintus Curtius (who calls him Manapis) places the appointment of Amminapes at a later date and adds that he had been exiled during the reign of Ochus and had stayed at Philip's court during that time (VI.4.25). It would be risky to infer that Amminapes abandoned Memphis and took the side of Alexander because of his Macedonian past. Artabazus and his family, who also were exiled in the time of Artaxerxes III, exhibited unfailing loyalty to Darius III, despite the fact that their wives and daughters had been taken prisoner at Damascus (Quintus Curtius III.13.13–14).

It is far more likely that the motivations of the Persian leaders in Egypt are to be explained by the same considerations as those that motivated Mithrenes: they wanted to preserve their privileges, especially ownership of the estates from which they profited in the arable land (cf. Diodorus §48.4). However, unlike Mithrenes, they could claim that the balance of power had tilted decisively in Alexander's favor.

The Defections of Mazaeus and Abulites (331)

When Alexander arrived in Babylonia and Susiana in October and November 331, he accepted the surrender of the two capitals from Mazaeus and Abulites, respectively. The surrender followed the well-known royal-entry ceremony: Mazaeus came with his children to greet the victor, accompanied by an official procession; then Alexander made his triumphant entry into the town (Quintus Curtius V.1.17–23; 1.44; 2.8–10;

Arrian III.16.3–4). The same sequence took place at Susa, preceded by Abulites' coming to pay him homage "with gifts of regal splendour" (Quintus Curtius V.2.9✦). In both cases, the organization of the processions shows that prior negotiations with the satraps had taken place. The negotiation phase is attested in the case of Abulites at Susa; he surrendered voluntarily (*hekousiōs*; Diodorus §65.5; Quintus Curtius V.2.8) and promised to give up the town without a fight:

> He himself [Alexander] set out [from Babylon] for Susa. On the way he was met by the son of the satrap of Susa and a letter-carrier from Philoxenus, whom Alexander had sent to Susa directly after the battle. In Philoxenus' letter it was stated that the people of Susa had handed over the city and that all the treasure was in safe-keeping for Alexander. (Arrian III.16.6✦)

This is when Quintus Curtius (V.2.8) and Diodorus (§65.5) express their uncertainty about the reasons for Abulites' behavior (pp. 840–842 above). Nothing, however, is mentioned about prior correspondence between Mazaeus and Alexander. Interestingly, there is a Babylonian tablet that, despite its uncertain reading, shows that Alexander had entered into communication with Babylon (*ADRTB* no. –330). This leads us to believe that Mazaeus had in fact made contact with Alexander, following a practice that is attested a few times. At the same time, certain details supplied by the ancient authors are problematic. First, Mazaeus included Babylonian horsemen in his procession (Quintus Curtius V.1.23). Second, Arrian (III.16.3✦) and Quintus Curtius (V.1.19) state that, when Alexander arrived near Babylon, he placed his army "in battle order (*hōs es machēn/velut in aciem*)," and Quintus Curtius adds that Alexander entered the town "surrounded by armed men" (V.1.23✦). While the organization of Mazaeus's procession poses no special problems (the presence of sumptuously caparisoned Babylonian horsemen was obviously part of the parade), this is not true for Alexander's formation. Does the notable presence of troops ready for battle imply that Mazaeus initially refused to surrender and/or that Alexander was afraid that Babylon would resist? This seems to be the interpretation held by the author of the *Itin. Alex.* §65. But how, then, can we harmonize this possibility with the earlier exchange of messages between Alexander and Babylon? In order to reach a conclusion, we will need to establish certain parallels that themselves will open the way to varying interpretations.

The events at Babylon and Susa evoke what happened when Alexander arrived at Taxila (chap. 16/16). Omphis, the king of Taxila, had previously (as was customary) made contact with the Macedonian, to let him know that he would offer no resistance (Quintus Curtius VIII.12.5). When Alexander arrived, "he went out to meet him with his army. . . . And Alexander at first thought that not an ally but an enemy was coming, and he also had already ordered his soldiers to take arms and the cavalry to withdraw to the wings, and was prepared for battle" (§12.7–8). The rest of the story shows that Alexander had misinterpreted the arrangements made by Omphis. It was obviously the general practice that, when a king or satrap was in the process of surrendering a town or a kingdom, he surrounded himself with his army, not to project ill will but, on the contrary, because political submission presupposes that the command of an army is symbolically handed over to the victor. The surrendering army is then incorporated into the triumphal procession, though in a subordinate place—at the end (Quintus Curtius V.1.23)—according to a symbolic hierarchical arrangement that *mutatis mutandis* can be observed in Xerxes' order of march as reported in Herodotus (VII.40–42✦). In Xerxes' procession, the royal chariot was preceded, followed, and surrounded exclusively by Persian troops; at a distance of two stadia it was followed by "the remainder of the army, a mass of troops of no particular distinction." Generally speaking, when the Great King entered a town (in a chariot, like Alexander: cf. Quintus Curtius V.1.23), he too was surely surrounded by men at arms, if only for his security. This is proved by the details of the practice during a royal parade in Persia that are supplied by Xenophon (*Cyr.* VIII.3.9–10): "Rows of soldiers stood on this side of the street and on that" (cf. also Herodotus VII.40–41). Because the royal entrances we have discussed come from the Achaemenid period and nearly always took place in times of war, we may conclude that in these cases also the king was surrounded by his army (as Xerxes was when he left Sardis in great style). The king's goal, quite simply, was to display his own glory, just as the showcasing of his luxury was an aspect of making his authority evident to all (cf. Herodotus I.188; Aelian, *VH* XII.40).

Unfortunately, neither the parallel with the royal parades in Persia nor the surrender at Taxila allows us to draw confident conclusions about the situations at Babylon and Susa. Though the example of the royal parades allows us to understand why guards would be present around the king, it does not resolve the biggest problem: why did Alexander originally put his army into combat formation? As it happens, Arrian and Quintus Curtius add a noteworthy detail—"in battle order"—but the problem remains, because even in this form the military formation adopted raises some questions. When Alexander arrived at Taxila, he waited until the last moment to put his army in order, when he realized his mistake. Furthermore, we note that Quintus Curtius (V.2.8–10) does not record Alexander taking any action of this kind at Susa. It is true that Quintus Curtius's report (interesting because of the dromedaries in the satrap's procession!) may be incomplete. The case of Sardis, on the other hand, is presented in detail by Arrian: Alexander placed his camp on the outskirts of the town; at the camp, Mithrenes and the Sardian nobility surrendered the citadel and the city; while they were in his camp, Alexander sent Amyntas to take possession (*paralambein*) of the citadel in his name; finally, the king entered the town (I.17.3–5). The episode provokes two reflections: first, there is no mention of lining up the army, at any stage; second, Alexander exhibits a degree of caution.

Of course this is easily explained, because the surrender of Babylon was part of a long series of similar events. Experience had in fact taught Alexander that the promise (even in writing) of a peaceful surrender was not a guarantee that capitulation was certain. Four examples can be offered.

(1) Hegesistratus, the defender of Miletus, had sent a letter proposing peace to Alexander but changed his mind when he felt that the balance of power favored him (Arrian I.18.4).

(2) Alexander received a promise from some defenders of Myndus that they would abandon the town to him on the condition that he arrive by night, but when he arrived, the garrison showed no sign that they were willing to surrender (Arrian I.20.5–6).

(3) When the scoundrel governor of Damascus sent a letter to Parmenion, the latter's fears were not allayed—especially after the messenger absconded. Parmenion "feared a plot"; the governor himself "was already in a state of fear lest he had not been trusted"; as a precaution, he had the town evacuated, which signaled that he himself intended to flee (Quintus Curtius III.13.2–5✧). The governor's fears had a legitimate basis, because shortly afterward he was killed and his head was brought to Darius (III.13.17).

(4) At Persepolis, Tiridates sent a letter to Alexander (Diodorus §69.1), but he was afraid that other Persians would be prepared to resist, so he sent another message to Alexander, urging him to hurry (Diodorus §69.1–2; Quintus Curtius V.5.2).

Each of these four examples proves that betrayal by the head of a town was most often done in secret and that his promises bound only himself (or a small group of collaborators in the betrayal); this explains the advice of the Myndus traitors that Alexander should arrive at night. Alexander thus had to be cautious. The situation was very likely the same at Babylon, and this explains the deployment of the army in a way that was intended to forestall any risk if Mazaeus had changed his mind or been deserted by his compatriots. This explanation may converge with another: we can imagine a staged engagement—an imitation battle—suggested by Mazaeus and agreed to by Alexander; this would allow Mazaeus to pretend that he had resisted to the end (even if it would fool no one). We might argue against this interpretation by observing that Mazaeus's procession was organized according to an age-old, unchangeable ritual. Nevertheless, the contradiction can easily be resolved if we recognize that the ceremony *also* had the purpose of preventing those conquered from losing face.

This interpretation in turn gives rise to two important observations, which nonetheless cannot be presented as more than theories. First, the authority and prestige of Darius were still potent enough that the defector was motivated to conceal his betrayal under cover of defeat; he did not wish to be considered a traitor (*traditor*) by the Persian camp, like Mithrenes (cf. Quintus Curtius III.12.6–7) and like Mazaeus himself, according to Quintus Curtius (V.8.9–12) who in a speech that he gives to Darius combines the cases of the two "traitors." Second, and more importantly, we wonder whether Mazaeus had experienced difficulty in convincing the other Persian officials in Babylon to accept his position; this may lie behind Darius's hope for 'any new developments' (*neōterizein*; Arrian III.19.1◊). It is obviously difficult to decide whether this is true, since the ancient authors shine the spotlight on Mazaeus and the only reference to another official does not support this theory. This official, Bagophanes, is mentioned only by Quintus Curtius; he was the *ganzabara* ('treasurer') who turned over the citadel to Alexander (V.1.44), and he also was the one who had set about decorating the streets of the town, apparently all on his own (V.1.20). Mazaeus thus obtained the cooperation of at least one colleague, and the behavior of this colleague makes it clear that, though he was still operating in concert with Mazaeus, he intended to show Alexander that he was acting on his own, perhaps because of a separate agreement he had reached with the king on his own (solely to ensure his personal future). This reconstruction also suggests that we should reflect on the attitude of the Babylonian elites. We will return to the question later (chap. 18/3 below), but for now we may offer one remark: even though it is fragmentary, the Babylonian tablet referred to earlier (*ADRTB* no. −330 reverse) in fact seems to concern only relations between Alexander and the inhabitants of Babylon (including the officials of the Esagila)—not the Persians. If we agree, as seems obvious, that Alexander made promises to the Babylonians, the Persian leaders of Babylon would have found themselves in a difficult situation. Given this context, we can understand how Mazaeus and Bagophanes, perhaps against the advice of some other Persians, may well have calculated that the possibilities of resistance were now illusory, as soon as they opposed those whom Arrian calls the city's "priests (*hiereis*) and rulers (*arkhontes*)" (III.16.3◊).

In order to understand the situation better, a few words must be said about the protagonist, Mazaeus; we know nothing about the prior career of Abulites. However, we know that Mazaeus had been satrap of Cilicia and Syria since the time of Artaxerxes III (chap. 16/6–7) and had become an intimate of Darius and was considered one of his Friends (*philoi*; Diodorus §55.1). Plutarch even calls him "the most considerable man in Darius's court (*ho megistos para Dareiōi*)" (*Alex.* 39.9◇). He thus belonged, beyond the shadow of a doubt, to the royal inner circle. Perhaps he was among those "suitable" men, Friends and Kinsmen, with whom the king surrounded himself before the battle of Issus (Diodorus §31.1◇). The relationship continued after the battle, and after the loss of Cilicia and Syria the king entrusted Mazaeus with crucial missions. It was Mazaeus who was instructed to lay waste the countryside in advance of the Macedonian troops who had crossed the Euphrates. He held a top-level position at Gaugamela, even winning an engagement on his flank, before falling back to Babylon at the head of his retreating troops. At Gaugamela, he commanded units drawn from Mesopotamia and Syria (Arrian III.8.5). It does not appear that he had been named satrap of Babylonia prior to Gaugamela, however, because the Babylonian contingents there were under the command of Bupares (III.8.4). However, if Bupares fell at Gaugamela, Darius may have conferred the position of satrap on Mazaeus (by letter) *after* the battle; his high rank in the court hierarchy and the prestige inherent in his recent military accomplishments (cf. Quintus Curtius V.1.18) would easily have justified his selection—but this is mere guesswork. We may add a remark that itself bears some importance: like Abulites of Susa, two (Artibelus, Brochubelus) or three (Antibelus; or is this name simply a result of confusion with the first?) of Mazaeus's sons had Babylonian names; from this we might deduce that their father at least had cultivated close contacts with Babylonian society and perhaps that their mother was Babylonian. Thus, in Babylon and Babylonian society, Mazaeus was a man of both power and influence. If we note that "the siege of so strongly fortified a city would have been a great task" (Quintus Curtius V.1.17◇) and that Mazaeus commanded troops, then his defection truly was a decisive strategic event for Alexander. Quintus Curtius was certainly not wrong in thinking that Alexander hoped that the defection of Mazaeus "would by his example induce the rest to surrender" (V.1.18◇). We can easily understand why the Macedonian was ready to pay the price.

Apart from the (uncertain) case of Sabictas/Abistamenes, it was at Babylon and Susa that Alexander for the first time appointed as satraps men who had served Darius: Abulites retained his satrapy at Susa, the turncoat (*transfuga*) Mazaeus was named satrap of Babylonia, and the traitor (*proditor*) Mithrenes was appointed over the district of Armenia (Quintus Curtius V.1.44; 2.17; Arrian III.16.4; 16.9). In contrast, the old treasurer Bagophanes ended up losing his post (it was given to a Greek/Macedonian: Arrian III.16.4), though he received preferential treatment as compensation: Alexander "ordered [him] to follow him" (*se sequi jussit*; Quintus Curtius V.1.44◇)—in other words, he was admitted to Alexander's entourage, just as Mithrenes had been after his defection at Sardis. The same was true for a son of Abulites Susa, Oxathres, who had been his father's right arm (Arrian III.8.5) and who probably had been sent to meet Alexander on the road from Babylon (III.16.6). The following year, Oxathres was made satrap of the Paraetacae (III.19.2). At this time, still remaining with Darius were Bagistanes, "a Babylonian and a noble," and Antibelus, one of Mazaeus's sons, who undoubtedly had accompanied the Great King on his retreat after Gaugamela (cf. Arrian III.21.1;◇ Quintus Curtius V.13.3). Mazaeus's other sons had been with their father since he defected to Alexander (Quintus Curtius V.1.17). Several years later, two of them, Artibelus and Hydarnes, were accepted, along with some other Persians, into a mixed cavalry regiment

(Arrian VII.6.4)—which implies that they had also been incorporated into the king's entourage. Another son (or one of these?) was also rewarded by Alexander (cf. Plutarch, *Alex.* 39.9). In conclusion, let us emphasize that Mazaeus's career under Alexander was marked by two noteworthy characteristics. Though Alexander, at Babylon as elsewhere, named Greco-Macedonians to key positions (command of troops, levying taxes; Arrian III.16.4), the numismatic evidence shows that the new satrap was granted a unique privilege: he was authorized to issue coins of Cilician type bearing his name at Babylon. Second, he was one of the few former Achaemenid officials to retain his satrapy until his death (in 328) without apparently incurring any blame from Alexander for maladministration, unlike Abulites, for instance, who was executed (along with his son Oxathres) because of his failure to follow royal orders (Arrian VII.4.1; cf. Plutarch, *Alex.* 68.7). The overwhelming evidence is that, in contrast to many Iranian satraps, the satrap of Babylon displayed unfailing loyalty to his new master.

The Persians of Persia between Darius and Alexander

Flush with success, Alexander took to the road for Persia at the end of 331. He twice ran into opposition. At the entrance to Uxiana (Fahliyun region), he had to assault a citadel commanded by the Persian Madates, who had sworn to the Great King that he would resist to the end (Quintus Curtius V.3.4). When Madates capitulated, he and the survivors were granted their lives, and the Uxian region was declared exempt from tribute and was attached to Susiana (V.3.15–16; cf. Diodorus §67.4–5 and Arrian III.17.1). Then, after sending Parmenion, the equipment, and the majority of the army to Persepolis by the high road (III.18.1; Quintus Curtius V.3.16) and subjecting the mountain Uxians to tribute (Arrian III.17.1–6), Alexander arrived in front of the Persian Gates, where Ariobarzanes (the satrap of Persia, according to Arrian III.18.2) was stationed with a large force (no less than 40,000 infantry and 7,000 cavalry according to Arrian; 25,000/ 300 according to Diodorus §68.1). After fierce fighting and a classic trick (wrong directions from a shepherd), the Macedonian army opened up the road to Persepolis, where the king linked up with Parmenion (chap. 16/12).

In its matter-of-fact approach, the tale presents the Persians as having mounted the sort of resistance in Persia that neither Mazaeus nor Abulites thought wise at Babylon or Susa. This observation is based on reality, but it needs to be nuanced. According to Arrian (III.18.9), Ariobarzanes fled to the mountains with a band of horsemen; Quintus Curtius says he was "in haste to take possession of the city of Persepolis, the capital of the region. But shut out by the garrison of the city . . . ," he was soon killed in a battle with the Macedonians (V.4.33–34◇). Meanwhile, Alexander received a letter from Tiridates, "who was in charge of Darius's finances" (Quintus Curtius V.5.2◇) and/or "governor of the city" (Diodorus §69.1◇): he promised to surrender the town; he made arrangements for the transfer to happen quickly so that "those who planned to defend the city for Dareius" (Diodorus) would not be able to seize power and/or to prevent the townsfolk from pillaging its treasures (Quintus Curtius). Obviously, then, dissension occurred among the high Persian officials, some (Ariobarzanes) wishing to defend the town, others (Tiridates) thinking that surrender was open to negotiation. Some time later, another official followed Tiridates' example: Gobares, the governor of Pasargadae, turned over the town and the treasury to Alexander (V.6.10). The "traitors" were repaid: "For Tiridates, . . . the same rank was continued which he had held under Darius" (Quintus Curtius V.6.11).

The new satrap, Phrasaortes, son of Rheomithres (Arrian III.18.11), was obviously also one of those who aligned themselves with the new master (according to Polyaenus IV.3.27, who no doubt has confused him with Ariobarzanes, ; he had fought at the Persian Gates and "he was a close relative of Darius"). Finally, the wealth still enjoyed by Orxines, head of the Pasargadae tribe, in 325 clearly implies that he too had kept his possessions and position through the turmoil (Quintus Curtius X.1.22–25). Thus, we cannot speak of a general uprising of the Persians of Persia against the Macedonian invasion.

However, aside from the fact that we know nothing about any opposition Parmenion may have met on the road to Persepolis, the various episodes should be situated in the chronology and more clearly placed in the context of Alexander's political and ideological strategy. Even after the capture of Persepolis, the matter had not played out. Many points of resistance remained in Persia, and Alexander set out to subdue them during a hard springtime campaign (330). This campaign is fully described by both Quintus Curtius and Diodorus (despite the latter's chronological error). Quintus Curtius writes: the Macedonians "devastat[ed] the fields (*agri*) of Persia and reduc[ed] many villages into his power" (*vici*; V.6.17✧); and Diodorus: "Alexander visited the cities (*poleis*) of Persis, capturing some by storm and others by his own fair dealing" (XVII.73.1✧). When he used the word *poleis*, Diodorus must have been referring to the network of citadels and strongholds that were successors to those we know from the Persepolis tablets. Diodorus's matter-of-fact account shows that some phrourarchs agreed to submit (probably after negotiations) and others put up stubborn resistance. Quintus Curtius reveals that the campaign also targeted the Mardians, "a warlike people (*gens* = *ethnos*) differing greatly from the rest of the Persians in their manner of life" (V.6.17✧). Let us recall that the Mardians were included by Nearchus as one of the "four predatory tribes [who] exacted tribute from the kings" (Strabo XI.13.6✧). The Mardians were regularly conscripted into the royal armies (Quintus Curtius III.13.2), especially as archers (cf. Arrian III.11.5), and certainly resisted Alexander strongly, as did the mountain Uxians and later (324) the Cosseans (chap. 16/11).

When Alexander returned to Persepolis (around April–May 330), he could believe that all military resistance was over. Indeed, we know that in May 330 he performed an action that bore great symbolic import: he set fire to the palaces of Persepolis. We will not rehearse in detail the historiography of the matter. Everyone agrees that it was a political decision that was carefully considered by Alexander. As far as we can tell, this act of destruction had no precedent during Alexander's entire Asian campaign, from the landing in 334 on. Everywhere, especially at Babylon, Alexander wanted to present himself as a preserver and restorer. In his mind, this act was certainly not a symbol of "Panhellenism" (even if his propaganda could lead to this interpretation), nor generally a signal pointed at the conquered populations. The royal order was clearly situated in a specifically Persian context. Indeed, Alexander could not have been unaware that, despite the importance attached to Babylon and Susa, Persia and its capitals had always represented the ideological center of Persian authority and dynastic grandeur (chap. 16/12). The matter is all the more intriguing because Alexander spared nothing to win the approval of the population. Even though most of the texts deal with Alexander's second visit, when he had returned from India, there is no doubt that, after taking Pasargadae, the Macedonian did everything he could to cultivate the memory of Cyrus and instructed the *magi* to maintain the regular sacrifices in front of the founder's tomb (cf.

Arrian VI.29.7; Strabo XV.3.17). His devotion to Cyrus was so well known that it gave rise to the epithet *philokyros* ('friend of Cyrus'; Strabo XI.11.4). It is clear that earlier, at the time when Darius was attempting to assemble a new army and Alexander had little information on events at Ecbatana (cf. Arrian III.19.4–5), he wanted to spark widespread defection of Persians. This did not happen. Quintus Curtius (V.7.2✧) and Diodorus (§71.2✧) very clearly set up a cause-and-effect relation between Alexander's decision to burn the royal palaces and the enmity of the Persians. Quintus Curtius writes that "those whom he had conquered were but lately subdued and were hostile to the new rule." It is true that this is a stereotypical expression (cf. IV.1.5), but Diodorus's statement is unambiguous: "He felt bitter enmity (*sphodra allotriōs*) to the inhabitants (*egkhōrioi*) [of Persia]. He did not trust them." It is difficult to read this evaluation as anything other than the reflection of deep apprehension on the part of the Persians toward the Macedonian conqueror. They had surrendered militarily—some of them voluntarily—but remained attached to their history, which was a mixture of the legends of kings and the great deeds of the dynasty—and Darius III was certainly in their eyes the lone representative of this heritage. Given the impossibility of achieving acceptance by the Persians, Alexander decided to burn the palaces. He thus demonstrated to the recalcitrant Persians that the age of imperial grandeur was over, unless they turned to him *en masse*. The regrets that the Macedonian expressed later imply that, from his point of view, the destruction decree of 330 was vengeance for a political failure.

3. The Local Elites, Darius, and Alexander: Popularity and Unpopularity of Achaemenid Dominion

Sources and Problems

Although it was very specific, Alexander's policy toward the Persians was part of a wider project—to win over the leaders of the cities, peoples, and communities that had been subject to Darius's dominion. Generally, the ancient authors insist that he was successful in this area, most often attributing his achievements to the anti-Persian sentiments of the Near Eastern peoples. "The Sidonians who loathed Persia and Darius," for example, "called him in themselves" (Arrian II.15.6✧). Diodorus especially likes to develop this theme with respect to Egypt and the Egyptians. He stresses the misdeeds of Cambyses (I.46.49) and Artaxerxes III (XVI.51.2) against the temples and the religion of the Egyptians. He broadens his perspective, beginning with the example of Cambyses, and also writes: "The Persians . . . ruled for one hundred and thirty-five years, including the periods of revolt on the part of the Egyptians which they raised because they were unable to endure the harshness of their dominion and their lack of respect for the native gods" (I.44.3✧). Using identical words and concepts, Diodorus (XVII.49.2✧) and Quintus Curtius (IV.7.1–3✧) describe the feelings of the Egyptians when they heard the news of Alexander's arrival:

> For since the Persians had committed impieties against the temples and had governed harshly (*biaiōs*), the Egyptians welcomed the Macedonians.   //   The Egyptians, hostile of old to the power of the Persians—for they believed that they had been governed avariciously and arrogantly (*avere et superbe imperitatum*)—had taken courage at the prospect of Alexander's coming, since they had welcomed even Amyntas, although a deserter coming with authority depending on favour. Therefore a vast multitude of them had assembled at Pelu-

sium, where they thought that Alexander would enter the country. . . . The Persians did not await his coming, being greatly alarmed also by the revolt of the Egyptians.

The reference to Alexander's entry into Egypt obviously calls to mind his entry into Babylon, where, according to Diodorus (§64.4◊), "the people received him gladly, and furnishing them billets feasted the Macedonians lavishly." We know that Mazaeus and his children had come to greet him outside the ramparts (Quintus Curtius V.1.17–18). But Mazaeus was not alone:

> The Babylonians came to meet him in mass, with their priests (*hiereis*) and rulers (*arkhontes*), each section of the inhabitants bringing gifts and offering surrender of the city, the citadel and the treasure. (Arrian III.16.3◊)

For some reason unknown to us, Arrian does not refer to Mazaeus's surrender, which is so well described by Quintus Curtius, who is careful to mention the presence of the Chaldeans and the Babylonian horsemen (V.1.22–23) in the procession (alongside Persian *magi*). In his arrangement, the delegation must have been functionally equivalent to the reception Alexander received outside Sardis, where Mithrenes was accompanied by "the chief citizens of Sardis (*Sardianōn hoi dynōtatoi*)" (Arrian I.17.3◊). Then came the triumphal entry into the town:

> Bagophanes . . . , in order not to be outdone in alacrity by Mazaeus, had strewn the whole road with flowers and garlands, and had placed here and there on both sides silver altars, which he had piled high, not only with frankincense, but with perfumes of all kinds. As gifts there followed him. . . . (Quintus Curtius V.1.20–21◊)

Just as Alexander—in contrast to the impious Persians—respected and maintained the "native customs" in Egypt (Quintus Curtius IV.7.5◊), in Babylon he is presented as the restorer of the rights of the sanctuaries, which had been violated by the Persians:

> On entering Babylon Alexander directed the Babylonians to rebuild the temples Xerxes destroyed, and especially the temple of Baal, whom the Babylonians honour more than any other god. . . . At Babylon too he met the Chaldaeans, and carried out all their recommendations on the Babylonian temples, and in particular sacrificed to Baal, according to their instructions. (Arrian III.16.4–5◊)

The picture of Alexander as a restorer of traditions, one who is greeted as a liberator, recurs at every stage. At Sardis, "the Sardians and the other Lydians were granted the use of the old Lydian customs (*hoi nomoi te hoi palai Lydoi*), and allowed to be free" (Arrian I.17.4◊); after this, Alexander climbed the citadel and founded a temple there dedicated to Olympian Zeus (§17.5–6). At Ephesus, he dedicated the tribute that the city had been paying to Darius to the sanctuary of Artemis (§17.10) and then issued a general proclamation to the Greek coastal cities: "He ordered the oligarchies everywhere to be overthrown and democracies to be established; he restored its own laws to each city (*tous nomous tous sphōn hekastois apodounai*) and remitted the tribute they used to pay to the barbarians" (§18.2◊). "Straightway all the cities sent missions and presented the king with golden crowns and promised to co-operate with him in everything" (Diodorus §24.3◊). In Phoenicia, "their inhabitants accepted him willingly" (§40.2◊).

At the same time, the ancient authors also mention resistance and revolt. For Alexander, there were only two categories of communities: those who agreed to surrender voluntarily, after reaching an agreement (*homologia*; e.g., Arrian I.24.4), and those who offered resistance. But several times, those who resisted were showing the effect of

Persian coercion. For example, when Tenedos was retaken by Pharnabazus, Arrian analyzes the event as follows:

> The inclination of Tenedos was rather towards Alexander and the Greeks; but at the moment there seemed no hope of safety but in joining the Persians. . . . It was in this way, rather by terrorism (*phobos*) than by their consent, that Pharnabazus brought Tenedos over. (Arrian II.2.3◊)

Thus, because Alexander assumed that collaborators with Persian authority actually were hostile toward their masters, he readily granted them pardon. This was also true for the Cypriot and Phoenician kings who in the spring of 332 abandoned Pharnabazus and rejoined Alexander with their ships:

> To all of them Alexander let bygones be bygones, supposing that it was rather from necessity (*hyp'anagkēs*) than their own choice (*kata gnōmēn*) that they had contributed to the Persian fleet. (II.20.3◊)

There would be no point in multiplying quotations from the ancient authors ad infinitum: from the Troad to the Indus, the picture of the conqueror is reproduced with perfect consistency. It is also clear that this consistency is the result of Macedonian propaganda that had the goal of legitimating Alexander's authority. Just like some Persians (Diodorus §§21.7; 76.1), local leaders came to surrender voluntarily (*hekousiōs*) to the one they considered the new master. This attitude of cooperation and "spontaneous" adherence tended to consolidate the conqueror's authority (cf. Arrian II.14.7: *hekontes*). Furthermore, these evaluations are certainly grounded in reality. Alexander always made many symbolic gestures toward cities and peoples that capitulated, "winning over the cities that lay on his route by kind treatment" (*philanthrōpiai*; Diodorus §24.1◊). The slogan "war of liberation" was obviously just one special aspect, in Asia Minor, of a strategy that Alexander followed systematically throughout the Achaemenid domains, and this was a strategy, as we have already noted, that was cast in the same mold as the plan that the Great Kings had always followed. Everywhere, Alexander took care to invoke the appropriate deities; he always made votive offerings intended to gain victory and recognition, such as before the battle of Issus (Quintus Curtius III.8.22: *patrio more*). That he carried out sacrifices "according to the Chaldeans' recommendations" (Arrian III.16.5) at Babylon should thus not be at all surprising.

This leads to an apparent contradiction: the presumed "enthusiasm" of the local leaders seems to imply that they had a visceral hostility to the Persians. Furthermore, the thesis is explicit in the cases of the Egyptians and the Babylonians: both are said to have been fundamentally opposed to the Persians, who had trampled their privileges under foot and violated or destroyed their sanctuaries. Of course, there is not a trace of this policy throughout Achaemenid history, except when it is a case of punishing a population that had just revolted. For example, we do not see what Arrian (I.17.4◊) means when he says that "the Sardians and the other Lydians were granted the use of the old Lydian customs," as if they had been abolished in the time of Persian dominion, which was obviously not the case. More generally, the tales of the ancient authors must be analyzed in the framework of Achaemenid (and, more widely, Near Eastern) institutions. As we have already stressed several times, the ceremony of the royal entry does not, *a priori*, imply any enthusiasm (other than that generated on command!) for the conquerors or visceral hostility to the former master. These processions accomplished nothing other than official symbolic sanction of the existence of a new authority. Furthermore, it must be stressed that not all of the peoples and cities accepted the arrival of the Macedonians with gladness of heart. Examples of resistance and revolt are rife, as, for example, at Miletus (Arrian I.18.3–9), or during the winter campaign in Lycia-Pamphylia-Pisidia. Similarly, at Aspendus: initially, the ambassadors agreed to surrender the city on condition that it would not be occupied by a garrison. Alexander consented, but the Aspendians were required to provide 50 talents and as many horses as the city had provided as a *dasmos* to the Great King (I.26.3). When the Aspendians exhibited ill will about fulfilling these terms, Alexander toughened them: the Aspendians would thereafter have to obey Alexander's satrap and pay an annual tribute to the Macedonians (I.27.4). We also know that Tyre put up a lengthy resistance (we will return to it) and that, in circumstances for which we lack precise details, the inhabitants of Samaria burned alive the governor of Syria that Alexander had appointed (Quintus Curtius IV.8.9). When Alexander had returned from Egypt, he sent a punitive expedition (§8.10), directed by either himself or Perdiccas, which led to massacres and, no doubt, to the foundation of a town or a military colony. Many Samaritan families had to take refuge in caves in the Wadi ed-Daliyeh—and as a result, we now possess documents of the greatest interest!

However, these acts of resistance can themselves be read in several ways. While the Tyrians' resistance was coordinated with Darius (cf. Diodorus §40.3), it is not certain that the Aspendians and Samaritans wanted to remain faithful to the Great King at all costs. The attitude of both groups was primarily dictated by their analysis of the balance of power, and this is what Arrian says with respect to the case of Hegesistratus of Miletus (I.18.4) and the Tenedians (II.2.3). The Aspendians were aware that Halicarnassus still held and that Alexander had no siege engines (cf. I.27.3). And, after Darius's arrival in Syria-Cilicia, "the people of the country . . . abandoned Alexander and came over to Dareios" (Diodorus §32.4;✧ cf. Quintus Curtius IV.1.5). For the inhabitants of Phaselis, whose ambassadors came to offer Alexander golden crowns, it seems primarily to have been a matter of obtaining protection from the king against attacks by the neighboring Pisidians (Arrian I.24.6)—protection that traditionally was provided by the satraps. Because it is impossible for us to elucidate every case, we have chosen here to analyze in more detail a few of the less poorly documented cases.

Ephesus, Miletus, and Aspendus

Alexander's arrival at Ephesus was marked by scenes of massacre so violent that the king himself had to intervene to bring them to an end (Arrian I.17.11–12). The massacres were initiated by partisans of the tyrants whom the Persians had reinstalled in the hope that they would displace the Macedonian forces after they had reconquered the region in 336–335: "Seldom did Alexander win a higher reputation than he did on that occasion by his treatment of Ephesus," concludes Arrian (17.13✧). Let us simply note that the Ephesians' rage was not really directed against the Persians themselves but against the "oligarchs," whom Alexander drove out and replaced with the Ephesian exiles who were in his camp. This is a typical example of the confusion that arises for us regarding the difference between conflicts internal to a city and conquest by an external force. It is thus hard to draw a general conclusion about the genuine reaction of the Ephesians, who had long been associated with the Persians of the high country (chap. 16/3). At the same time, we should note that the Ephesians turned down Alexander's offer to assume responsibility for the cost of rebuilding the temple of Artemis—so long as they met his demand that his name be inscribed on the stone (Strabo XIV.1.22). The

Ephesians obviously had no desire to pass from one dominion to another, even though they were only able to express their reaction symbolically.

Generally, the enthusiasm of the Asia Minor Greeks for the "war of liberation" must be considered from the perspective of hindsight. We must first recall that, beginning with the events of 336–335, this Macedonian slogan would have had only limited effect in the cities of Asia Minor. For instance, though the inhabitants of Cyzicus apparently were hostile to Memnon (Polyaenus V.44.5), not all of the towns spontaneously opened their gates to Parmenion, especially after the Persian counterattack was launched. Pitane withstood the siege victoriously. In the case of Grynium, which also resisted, "Parmenion . . . sold its inhabitants as slaves" (Diodorus XVII.7.9✧)—which left no doubt about the Macedonian king's ambition to dominate totally and destroyed any possible advantage he had expected from the slogan ("liberation of the Greek cities") that had been officially promulgated. Lampsacus—which still favored the Persian cause when Alexander arrived (Pausanias VI.18.2–4)—was also among the cities that had no interest in passing from Persian dominion to Macedonian dominion, after the Persian reconquest (Ps.-Arist., *Oec.* II.2.29a [1351b]). The events that transpired in the towns on Lesbos and at Ephesus are especially revealing of the bitter internecine struggles that occurred; the Persians and the Macedonians each successively attempted to play the situation to their own advantage. By depending on the support of tyrant families, the Persians managed to reestablish their authority in the cities that had been taken by Parmenion and the Macedonians. Garrisons were stationed in them. It is possible that from this time onward the leaders of the reconquered cities had to agree to "become allies with Darius on the basis of the peace of Antalcidas with (the Persian) king" (Arrian II.1.4;✧ 2.2 [in 333]). Of course, the granting of power to "tyrants" may seem like a fragile recovery. But these great families also relied on the support of local partisans, as is evident at Ephesus (Arrian I.17.11). Furthermore, the Persian reconquests in 334–332 demonstrate that the recovery by Alexander was also quite uncertain. Whatever the case, the events of 336–334 show that Persian dominion in western Asia Minor was not generally rejected—or (probably more precisely) it was not rejected as long as the Persians retained the means of forcing their dominion to be respected.

We also think it unlikely that the Macedonians were greeted with open arms because of Persian "overtaxation" (see chap. 17/5). This theory seems to be based on blind faith, supported by dubious arguments, that the local rulers of Asia Minor hoped—or had even received promises from Alexander—that the amount of tribute would be lowered. However, to make this argument would be to attribute considerable naiveté to the local rulers, and Alexander's first actions in Asia Minor do not justify this presumption: in every conquered satrapy, a tribute administration was established and tribute collectors were appointed (e.g., Arrian I.17.7; cf. III.5.4; 16.4). Generally speaking, these officials were assigned to collect "the same taxes as they used to pay to Darius" (I.17.1;✧ I.27.4). When exemptions were granted, it was always in connection with tribute paid to Darius (I.17.10; 18.2; II.5.9). Sometimes, the tribute paid to Darius was increased (I.27.4). An inscription from Priene records a decree issued by Alexander at this time (Tod no. 185): his sovereign rights over the territory are reconfirmed ("I know that this land is mine") with an ardor that matches the intensity Darius I demonstrated in the letter that he had sent to Gadatas (ML 12). The Macedonian king also reinstated the Achaemenid practice of the gift of towns, with himself as beneficiary (cf. Aelian, *VH* I.25; Plutarch, *Pho-*

cion 18.7). When favors were granted from time to time (see also the example of Babylon below), they were only given in the guise of a "Panhellenic" or "dynastic" beneficence (e.g., Arrian II.5.9) or when a community found itself in a balance of power that the Greek cities of Asia could never tip to their own advantage.

Only Miletus attempted to "sit on the fence." The Milesians were reassured by the proximity of the Persians in their ships (so-called "friends and allies") and sent Glaucippus, "one of the notables" (*dokimoi*) of the city, to Alexander. The Milesian offer to the king, relayed by Glaucippus, was "to open their walls and harbours to Alexander and the Persians in common" (I.19.1◊), but the proposal was rejected by Alexander. In a way, the offer by Glaucippus of Miletus expressed what must have been the deepest desires of the Asia Minor Greeks: though they were unable to claim the illusion of liberty, the Milesians imagined that there might be a sort of Persian-Macedonian co-administration. Did they hope that this status, which was acceptable in reality neither to the Persians nor to Alexander, would accord them some room to maneuver? Nevertheless, after the failure of the Persian navy, Miletus fell into the Macedonian's hands. Its leaders were not able to negotiate properly, even when the military situation again permitted it. The Aspendians committed a similar error (I.26.3; 27.4).

From Sidon to Tyre

After the battle of Issus, the first Phoenician towns (Aradus and its dependencies; Byblus) surrendered without a fight (Arrian II.13.7–8; Diodorus §40.2; Quintus Curtius IV.1.15). The Sidonians also put up no resistance; they appealed to Alexander because they "loathed Persia and Darius" (Arrian II.15.6◊). This is the first mention of strong opposition to Persian dominion from a subject community. The Sidonians' attitude can obviously be explained as due to the implacable treatment that Artaxerxes III had reserved for them after he retook their city (Diodorus XVI.45.5–6)—a severity that, we emphasize in passing, could certainly not have come as a surprise to the Sidonians, who had themselves declared that the war would be merciless (§41.5–6; cf. §45.2). But the matter is a little more complicated than it seems. The Sidonians were in fact divided regarding what position to take. King Straton—Quintus Curtius explains (IV.1.16◊)— "had surrendered rather at the desire of the people than of his own accord (*sua sponte* = *hekousiōs*) . . . [he was] supported by the power of Darius," and he was in a relationship of "friendship for Dareius" (Diodorus XVII.47.1◊). In other words, the situation at Sidon seems quite comparable to what prevailed at Ephesus, with Straton playing the role held by the tyrant Syrphax at Ephesus, with respect to Persian authority. The decision made by Alexander in this case is also comparable: he placed a man (Abdalonymus) on the throne who would be totally loyal to him (cf. Quintus Curtius IV.1.18–26; Diodorus XVII.47); he "gave orders that not only the regal equipment of Straton should be assigned to him, but also many articles from the Persian booty" (Quintus Curtius IV.1.26◊). The Sidonians were drafted by Alexander (IV.4.15).

Then Alexander turned toward Tyre. At first, the "community" (*to koinon*) sent ambassadors to Alexander with this message: "Tyre had decided to accept Alexander's orders" (Arrian II.15.6◊). The difficulties mounted as soon as Alexander let it be known that he intended to sacrifice in the sanctuary of Heracles/Melqārt: "The Tyrians decided to obey all Alexander's other commands, but not to admit any Persians or Macedonians within their city" (§16.7◊). This initial attitude of the Tyrians seems quite similar to the

Milesians', at least at first sight. Furthermore, their request could count on some precedents: the Paphlagonians, for example, convinced Alexander "not to enter their country in force" (§II.4.1◇) and, initially, the Aspendians were assured that Alexander would not station a garrison (I.26.3). But, when the threat of the Persian navy was becoming increasingly acute, and when the Tyrians ships commanded by King Azelmicus were fighting under the orders of Pharnabazus (II.15.7), Alexander understood that he needed to take possession of the city (cf. Quintus Curtius IV.2.5). To tell the truth, the Tyrians could not be unaware of his intentions, but they believed that they were in a position of strength: "This decision would be the easiest to excuse in the existing circumstances, and safest for the future and for the issue of the war, which was still obscure" (Arrian II.16.7◇). We know, in fact, that according to Diodorus (§40.3◇), "They wanted to gratify Dareius and keep unimpaired their loyalty (*eunoia*) to him, and thought also that they would receive great gifts (*kharis*) from the king."

Egypt and the Egyptians

We have seen the enthusiasm with which Diodorus (XVII.49.2) and Quintus Curtius (IV.7.1–3) describe the warm reception that the Egyptians, according to them, reserved for Alexander. In many respects, the Egyptians' situation appears unique. Not only had they revolted against Persian dominion several times during the fifth century, but they had rewon their independence between the end of the fifth century and 343, when Artaxerxes III succeeded in retaking the Nile Valley. Moreover, if Khabbabash is to be dated to this period (which is practically certain), a pharaoh was once more proclaimed and reigned for an undetermined period of time, some time between 343 and 336–335. The renewed Persian rule had been contested anew quite recently, during Amyntas's adventure after the battle of Issus. This, at least, is what Quintus Curtius and Diodorus say. According to Quintus Curtius, the Egyptians "had welcomed even Amyntas" (IV.7.1◇). He stresses that "the Egyptians [were] always at odds with their governors" (IV.1.28◇); nevertheless, next, while accusing them of being unstable, he tells how they battled Amyntas's troops, who were then ravaging the countryside. Amyntas forced them to retreat into Memphis, and this is when the satrap Mazaces victoriously led his troops into battle (IV.1.30–33). Diodorus, on the other hand, attributed the victory to the Egyptians alone (§48.4), without mentioning Mazaces. Nevertheless, it seems clear that it was indeed Mazaces who led the operations. In the White Wall, the satrap had Egyptian auxiliaries, who fought alongside the Persian troops, as their ancestors had more than a century before—those whom Thucydides (I.104.2◇) refers to as "Egyptians who had not joined the rebellion."

The contradictions between Diodorus and Quintus Curtius may appear uninteresting, but they are revelatory of the partiality of the ancient sources as soon as they touch on Persian–Egyptian relations. When the Egyptians revolt against the Persians, it is always a unanimous uprising. Thucydides makes it clear that this simplistic presentation cannot be accepted. The notion that the Egyptians intensely hated the Persians goes back at least to Herodotus, if we recall his interpretation of Cambyses' policy in Egypt (see chap. 1/9). Artaxerxes III himself was accused of impiety in regard to the Egyptian temples (see chap. 16/9). Ptolemy certainly took advantage of this idea, which conformed so well to his interests: in the *Satrap Stela*, he insists that he had restored the privileges of the sanctuary of the goddess Wajet of Buto that had been suppressed by

"Xerxes." Furthermore, in the same document these words are found: "He brought back the images of deities that had been found in Asia, and restored them to their original place. . . . And this great satrap excelled in benefactions toward the gods of Upper and Lower Egypt." His successors constantly repeat the theme of the return of deported statues. There is no doubt that Alexander, when he came on the scene, followed a policy designed to conciliate the sanctuaries. When he arrived in Memphis, "he sacrificed to the gods, especially Apis" (Arrian III.1.4◊), and several stelas dating to his reign refer to burial ceremonies for the mother of an Apis. He ordered and completed work in several Egyptian sanctuaries. The most spectacular accomplishment was the chapel of Luxor, where Alexander is represented with the attributes of the pharaoh. From Cambyses to Alexander, we can identify a general continuity in the conquerors' Egyptian policy.

However, how can we know the Egyptians' deepest sentiments? The plethora of revolts is a clue that obviously should not be disregarded. But in itself, this is not sufficient to answer the question. Fortunately, we have several autobiographical Egyptian inscriptions. Along the sides of the *dromos* of the Serapeum in Memphis, there are several private tombs that were discovered in the nineteenth century. One tomb belonged to Onnophris, son of Painou, whose memory lives on in posterity because of the inscriptions found there. This physician, who lived during the XXXth Dynasty, specialized in the prevention and cure of snakebite. One of his titles specifically is "prophet of the statues of the king's father, general Cha-hap-imu," who is known from other sources to be Nectanebo II's father. It seems that sometime around 360–359 Onnophris accompanied Tachos during the Egyptian offensive in Syria. The Egyptian war fleet (*kbnt*) is mentioned, and Onnophris embarked in order—he says—"to reach the place where the Sovereign of the Two Lands was. I found him in the land of Su[. . .]." In all probability, Onnophris's fate then matched the fate of Tachos, who was defeated by Prince Ochus and then dethroned by the revolt of Nectanebo; thus, he followed his conqueror to the court, where the Great King "appointed him general in the war against Egypt" (Diodorus XVI.92.5◊). We can imagine, without being able to prove it, that he was then able to demonstrate his medical abilities at the Persian court, just as Udjahorresnet had done 165 years earlier. Later, he returned to Egypt under these circumstances:

> I remained silent. Then he said to me: "Do not be sad because of this. (Here is) my order: Hurry back to the land of your birth!" . . . Thereupon, I reached Egypt. I found a messenger from the Great One who governs Egypt; he embraced me, showered me with kisses, passed the day with me, and the day flew by, questioning me about everything.

Even though the subject ("he") is lost, it is likely that the order to return to Egypt was given by the Great King, perhaps Artaxerxes III, who may have assigned him a diplomatic mission to the pharaoh. Unfortunately, the fragmentary state of the text prevents us from being certain about what this could be. As in the two following examples, Onnophris may have intended to say that the idea of returning to the Nile Valley had been suggested to him by an Egyptian deity; to claim that this was the case was certainly more acceptable, specifically because it allowed the speakers "to completely disengage from responsibility for their stay with an enemy sovereign" (J.-J. Clère).

A small statue of the eldest son of Nectanebo II, the pharaoh conquered by Artaxerxes III, has also been found. Speaking of the goddess Isis, he states: "When I was among the foreign peoples, she caused me to win the esteem of their prince. She brought me back to Egypt." The chronological uncertainty remains great. Perhaps this person also lived at the Great King's court. This possibility is inferred from another autobiographical inscription that was carved for another doctor, Samtutefnakht (a wāb-priest of Sekhmet, like Onnophris). Samtutefnakht addresses the god Herishef-Re, who intervened on his behalf "an infinitude of times" (trans. after O. Perdu):

> You freed my walk to the royal palace,
> the heart of the Perfect God being content with what I said;
> You distinguished me before the multitude while you turned away from Egypt;
> You inspire my affection in the heart of the Prince of Asia, while his courtiers complimented
>   me, when he gave me the position of chief of the wāb-priests of Sekhmet, in replacement
>   of my brother by my mother, the chief of the wāb-priests of Sekhmet for South and North,
>   Nakhthenbeb.
> You protected me in the offensive of the Greeks until you repelled Asia;
> they killed a mob around me without a single one raising his hand against me.
> Subsequently I saw you in a dream, Your Majesty saying to me:
> "Go then to Heracleopolis, I am with you."
> I traversed the foreign countries being alone,
> and crossed the sea without fear, knowing that thus I would not violate your order;
> and I reached Heracleopolis without a hair on my head being harmed.

The historical context is far less certain in this case. We recognize an allusion to a Persian reconquest ("while you turned away from Egypt"), probably the one carried out by Artaxerxes III (but it could also refer to the Persian expedition that put down Khabbabash). The direct reference to a struggle and a battle between the "Greeks" and the Prince of Asia is dubious: Samtutefnakht was captured in the turmoil of Alexander's invasion. Moreover, he was in the Persian camp when the Prince of Asia's troops were defeated. There is no question that this refers to the battle of Issus, in which Sabaces, the satrap of Egypt, took part and during which he died (cf. Arrian II.11.8). We do not know when Samtutefnakht returned to Egypt, though perhaps it was in the train of Alexander, or earlier with Amyntas, who certainly needed Egyptians with him as guides in the Nile Valley. Whatever the case, Samtutefnakht previously had been a favorite of the Great King (who may have been Artaxerxes III or IV or Darius III, depending on whether his career is related to Artaxerxes III's reconquest or to the expedition led by either Artaxerxes IV or Darius III against Khabbabash). He received an appointment as chief physician. In this, too, even if he was not associated with the same sanctuary, the parallel with Udjahorresnet is striking: Udjahorresnet, we will recall, had been made chief physician at Saïs by Cambyses. In the pattern of Nectanebo's oldest son (if the parallel is legitimate), Samtutefnakht takes care to cleanse himself of the accusation of collaboration with the Asiatics. He no longer grants a pharaonic title to the Prince of Asia. He continually proclaims, however, that wherever he was, he enjoyed the protection of the god. This is explained easily enough by his later return to Egypt and by the dating of the inscription to the beginning of the Ptolemaic period. But the fact remains: we have a clear example of an Egyptian who turned to the Great King after the reconquest—or who at least did not refuse to serve him and take personal advantage of his relationship with him.

The many inscriptions found in the tomb of Petosiris at Hermopolis provide access to the preserved memory of a veritable dynasty of high priests of Thoth, because Petosiris (who exercised his chief priesthood and the position of *lesonis* [administrator] at the beginning of the Macedonian period) had succeeded his brother Djethotefankh and his father, Sishu, who himself inherited the office from his father, Djethotefankh the Elder. Some inscriptions in honor of Petosiris, moreover, are the work of his grandson, Padikam. What is very interesting is that the careers of Sishu and his two sons unfolded between the times of Tachos and of Alexander and Philip Arrhideus. In the inscriptions, which are devoted to singing their praises, Sishu and Petosiris are depicted as men filled with wisdom and virtue, lovers of order and justice. This is not exactly the case for Djethotefankh, who in all probability succeeded his father at the end of Nectanebo II's reign and thus watched the reconquest of Artaxerxes III play out. His brother Petosiris had to defend his memory by giving him this speech: "I did not steal the ritual offerings, I never did any wrong against this country, for Maat is with me and will not be separated from me for all eternity." When Petosiris succeeded him, however, he encountered a compromised situation:

> When a head of foreign countries [Artaxerxes III] exercised his protectorate over Egypt, there was no longer anything that was in its former place; since battles broke out in the interior of Egypt, the South being in agitation and the North in a state of revolt, men walked in bewilderment, there was no longer a temple that was available to its attendants, and the priests were distant (from the sanctuaries), in ignorance of what was going on.

Petosiris was able to reestablish the prosperity of the sanctuary not only because of his remarkable merits but also because of the sudden change in political conditions·

> [I spent seven years] as *lesonis* of Thoth . . . doing everything excellently in his temple, expanding the importance of his priests, to fill his granaries with barley and wheat and his valuable reserves with all perfect things, beyond what existed before foreigners became governor of Egypt. (after trans. by G. Lefebvre, revised by B. Menu)

Though his older brother had had to deal with the disorders connected with the defeat of Nectanebo II by the armies of Artaxerxes III, Petosiris must have lived in the period of transition between Achaemenid dominion and the Ptolemaic period. He probably received the responsibility from his brother after Alexander's arrival. From the father (Sishu) to the younger son (Petosiris), the inscriptions are intended to provide an image of Egyptian history that is characterized by rectitude. There was a period of calm in the time of Nectanebo II, followed by a period of disorder in the time of Artaxerxes III and his successors, and then a return to order with the arrival of Alexander. Other Egyptians of this period celebrated the return to order. However, specifically because they were composed in a Hellenistic context, these declarations have only limited value as evidence: "It is difficult not to suspect the existence of a propaganda favoring these behaviors within the upper clergy and giving them all the means (notably economic) of succeeding, propaganda emanating from the high Macedonian administration and maintained by Ptolemaeus son of Lagus" (B. Menu). A general consideration of the fourth-century autobiographical inscriptions also leads to the conclusion that, as in the time of Cambyses and his successors in the fifth century, Egyptians did not hesitate to collaborate with the Persians. For the same reasons, they turned just as easily to Alexander, then Ptolemy. In other words, when Alexander took Egypt, it was not because there was a general Egyptian uprising that supported him; more simply, it was because the Persian officials in charge of the satrapy had no military means of opposing him. Thus, the behavior of the Egyptian aristocrats was entirely predetermined.

The Babylonians, Alexander, and Darius

The attitude of the Babylonians is much better documented. We would not return to Alexander's situation after Gaugamela were it not to reaffirm that the balance of power allowed the Babylonian leaders (present in the procession that came to greet the conqueror) to hope that they would receive significant compensation in exchange for their defection. An astronomical tablet (*ADRTB* no. −330) provides proof that, after Gaugamela, negotiations were opened between Alexander and the Babylonians. On October 8, a week after the battle, a text seems to refer to the arrival at Babylon of an envoy who delivered a message regarding the Esagila and its property. On October 18, Alexander is at Sippar, and he seems to promise (to the Babylonians?) that he will not allow his soldiers to break into their houses. Next, there is an allusion to the presence (participation?) of Greeks (*Iamana*) at a sacrifice. Finally, there is the entry into Babylon of Alexander, who bears the title "King of the Universe." Alexander came to sacrifice to Marduk and conversed with the Chaldeans on everything concerning the great god of the city (cf. Arrian III.16.5).

This is the context in which the Classical texts mention the destruction effected by Xerxes in the Babylonian temples as a contrast to Alexander's "benevolent" behavior. We need not tarry long on Xerxes' policy, except to recall that the presentation by Alexander's historians is erroneous and partial (see chap. 13/5). Instead, the attitude of the conqueror is situated in general continuity with the traditional policy of the Great Kings. Following the example of Cyrus, Alexander made contact with the leaders of the great sanctuaries—"their priests and rulers (*hiereis kai arkhontes*")" (III.16.3◇). In order to weaken the elites' will to resist, just after the victory, Alexander had begun negotiations with Mazaeus (and Bagophanes) and the Babylonian leaders. He promised the officials that he would respect the city and be sure to care for the sanctuaries, as Cyrus had done. This strategy is also shown by the rituals of the triumphal entry (Alexander in his chariot; Quintus Curtius V.1.23), which astonishingly resemble the protocols of Cyrus's official entry into Babylon in 539. At the same time, there is no doubt that Alexander began work on the Babylonian sanctuaries. Whatever its nature and extent may have been, this work could not have been begun until after the "Chaldeans" had been consulted, because this work in itself symbolized that Alexander was supported and accepted by the gods of Babylon. This is perhaps what Arrian is describing when he writes: He "carried out all their recommendations on the Babylonian temples, and in particular sacrificed to Baal, according to their instructions" (III.16.5◇).

Good relations between Alexander and the Babylonian leaders did not wane. Two episodes illustrate their relationship, both during the king's last years. Many ancient authors relate that the Chaldeans wanted to dissuade Alexander from entering Babylon, arguing against it on the basis of bad omens taken from examining the stars and constellations. According to an ancient tradition, Alexander did not give in to their pleas, because he suspected that they wished to keep for themselves the funds he wanted to dedicate to the reconstruction of the temples (Arrian VII.17.1–4). This anecdote has sometimes been thought to reveal that bad relations prevailed between Alexander and the sanctuaries at this time. In truth, when the warning from the Chaldeans is situated in the *longue durée* of Babylonian tradition, it appears that the Chaldeans were simply behaving consistently in the role that they had played throughout Antiquity: the Chaldeans, who were entrusted with observing the skies and drawing omens from them, simply wished "to report to the king the danger which threatened . . . that he must under no circumstances make his entry into the city; . . . but he must abandon his intended route and pass the city by" (Diodorus XVII.112.2–3✧).

Some time later, another incident made an unfortunate impression on the Greek observers, who then misinterpreted a Babylonian custom that they did not know existed. The ancient authors tell the same story in sometimes varying words. One day, a Babylonian of uncertain status, who was condemned by common law, managed to approach the king's throne and seat himself upon it: He "put on the royal dress and bound his head with the diadem, then seated himself upon the chair and remained quiet" (Diodorus §116.2–3✧). Arrian records the eunuchs' reaction as follows:

> Owing to some Persian custom (*nomos persikos*) they did not drag him off the throne but rent their garments and beat themselves on their breasts and faces as if some terrible disaster had happened. (VII.24.3✧)

Once again, Arrian confirms that Alexander understood nothing about the matter. He suspected a plot and had the man questioned, but "he would only say that the idea had come to him to do so"; and Arrian adds, in the same vein, "This actually made the seers readier to interpret what had happened as portending no good for Alexander" (VII.24.3✧). According to Diodorus, conversely, Alexander then remembered the initial warning that the Chaldeans had given him, and he showered the advisers who had urged him to disregard it with reproaches, while he himself "was impressed anew with the skill of the Chaldaeans and their insight" (§116.4✧). For Diodorus, in both cases, it was a sign from the gods—a "portent about his kingship" (§116.5✧). Diodorus was well informed. Despite some (easily understandable) differences, the episode fits into a well-fed stream of Mesopotamian tradition—that of the substitute king. When omens regarding the life of the king were disturbing, a man of low birth was chosen, and he received all of the outward appurtenances of power: the raiment, the scepter, a queen, and a court—though the real power was exercised by the king who, in principle, was sequestered elsewhere. When the risk was believed to have passed, the substitute was put to death. We can thus reasonably imagine that this episode in 323 did not result from the spontaneous initiative of a poor wretch—as is implied in any case by Arrian's reference to a *nomos persikos* (actually, in this case, a venerable Babylonian tradition). The Chaldeans were more and more disturbed by the multiplication of omens and resorted to the substitute king ritual (with Alexander's consent) and thus cleansed the king of the threats accumulating around him. All of these episodes attest to Alexander's acceptance by the local elites at Babylon—the only condition being that he rule according to local tradition, as "King of the Lands," as the Great Kings always had.

While the reality of the "Babylonization" of Alexander seems generally to be well established, at the same time, other texts dissuade us from concluding that the reaction of the Babylonian elites harmonizes completely with the image of "liberator" that the ancient texts conventionally ascribe to Alexander. First, we may note that in a tablet dated to 329 Alexander is called "king of the Haneans," which highlights his foreign origin (*ADRTB* no. –328). However, another text is even more interesting—the famous *Dynastic Prophecy*. Though the text is difficult, because the tablet is broken and fragmentary, this prophecy (obviously *post eventum*) devotes several lines to the reign of Darius III. The composers record the invasion of the Macedonians (here also referred to as Haneans) and a defeat by Darius; they continue:

Afterwards, he (the king) will refit [his] army and ra[ise] his weapons; Enlil, Shamash, and [*Marduk*] will go at the side of his army [and] the overthrow of the army of the Hanaean he will [bring about]. He will carry off his extensive booty and [*bring (it)*] into his palace. The people who *had* [*experienced*] misfortune [*will enjoy*] well-being. The mood of the land [will be a happy one]. Tax exemption (*zakutu*). (*BHLT*, p. 35 [col. III.12–23])

There would be no point in comparing this text with the Alexander historians in an attempt to determine which historical events are referred to. Recording of events per se is in fact not the purpose of this kind of literature, which simply sets out "good" and "bad" reigns alternately. However, it is quite notable that here Darius (the king), aided by the Babylonian gods, in the end is victorious over Alexander (the Hanean), and this triumph is received with joy in Babylon, whose inhabitants then regain their prosperity. The person of Darius III has thus been reintroduced in the context of a traditional narrative on good Babylonian kingship. The text shows that the attitudes of the elite were at least ameliorated with respect to new masters.

One perfectly reasonable theory is that the text itself was composed at the beginning of the Hellenistic period in the context of the inauguration of Seleucus's rule in Babylonia. Thus, we cannot conclude that it reflects the perspective of the Babylonians in 331; it is more likely that it expresses the change in relationship between Macedonians and Babylonians in the time of the wars that ravaged the country at the beginning of the age of the Diadochi. The text certainly does confirm that the Achaemenid period was not seen as particularly oppressive (at least in comparison with Macedonian dominion). It also stresses that the Babylonian leaders' submission to Alexander was linked to royal behavior that was in accord with the country's traditions — just as in Udjahorresnet's Egypt, Cambyses and Darius had to follow the precepts of "right kingship" ("as did every previous benevolent king"). This obligation is reflected in the Macedonian propaganda, which described Alexander's hydraulic constructions in Babylonia as worthy of "good rulers (*hēgemōnes agathoi*)" (Strabo XVI.1.10✧; cf. Arrian VII.21.6). In other words — and in conclusion — the defection of the leaders to Alexander did not occur because they were pressured by the enthusiasm of a population that craved liberation; the surrender was conditional, because it was based on negotiations that the Babylonians certainly came to with great caution. After all, the (subsequent) message of the *Dynastic Prophecy* was not particularly favorable to Alexander or, in general, to the Macedonian conquest, which the editors present as a (vain!) attempt to interrupt the happy course of the reign of the "good king," Darius.

4. The Death of a Great King (330)

Darius at Ecbatana

Taking into account all of these elements — both military and political — makes it possible to evaluate Darius's situation at Ecbatana. When Alexander suddenly left Persepolis in May 330, he had only a very small amount of information about the Great King's actual situation; he thought that Darius, since October of the previous year, had been completing his preparations for a battle that would have to determine the final outcome of the war. When Alexander arrived in Gabiene (Gabae/Isfahan), at the Median Gates, he received urgent news that was delivered by Bisthanes (son of Artaxerxes III), "who reported that Darius had fled four days before, with his treasure from Media of seven thousand Talents and with about three thousand cavalry and about six thousand infantry" (Arrian III.19.5◊). Quintus Curtius states that the news-bearer was a Babylonian, Bagistanes, who told Alexander that Darius "was in danger either of death or of fetters" (V.13.3◊). It is likely that Quintus Curtius confused the two messengers. It was only later (when Alexander reached the Caspian Gates) that Bagistanes and Antibelus, one of the sons of Mazaeus, informed him that Darius had been thrown in irons by the chiliarch Nabarzanes, Bessus the satrap of Bactria, and Barsaentes the satrap of Arachosia (Arrian III.21.1).

In October 331, Darius planned to gather a new army. He had with him some soldiers who had followed him on his retreat, and among them were several thousand Greek mercenaries—whose faithfulness the ancient authors like to exalt unreservedly—as well as the Bactrian cavalry, some Persians from the royal Kinsmen, and his guard of *mēlophoroi*—that is, those who had surrounded him during the battle (Arrian III.16.1; cf. 11.5). The Great King expected to draft soldiers in the regions near Ecbatana, particularly from the Cadusians and Saka, who in fact did send him contingents (Arrian III.19.3). Nevertheless, he was primarily counting on troops levied in eastern Iran (cf. Diodorus XVII.73.1). Quintus Curtius calculates his army at 30,000 infantry (including 4000 Greeks), 4000 slingers and archers, and more than 3300 horsemen, "mostly Bactrian" (V.8.3–4◊); Diodorus speaks of 30,000 men, "Persians and Greek mercenaries" (§73.1◊); Arrian counts 3000 horsemen and 6000 infantry (III.19.5). It is always difficult to compare the numbers. Meanwhile, when Darius learned that Alexander had arrived by forced march, Darius decided to set out for the Upper Satrapies. The change in the balance of power led some contingents—Saka and Cadusians—to abandon the royal army (III.19.4). Then, when Alexander resumed his pursuit of Darius from Ecbatana, "many of those who shared his flight deserted him during its course, and went off to their homes, and a good number had surrendered to Alexander" (III.19.4; 20.2◊).

The military collapse primarily reveals the continued weakening of the Great King's political position. Quintus Curtius, in an account that is very favorable to Darius, writes that Darius's prestige continued to be solid: "In those nations the majesty of their kings is extraordinary; in response to his mere name the barbarians assemble, and veneration for his former fortune attends him even in adversity" (V.10.2◊); or this: "the reply of all the Persians was about the same, that it was impious for the king to be deserted" (V.9.16◊). These are fine phrases, but they account for only a part of the situation and, as a result, distort it. Quintus Curtius himself also explains that Darius's decision to abandon Babylonia after Gaugamela had not been greeted enthusiastically by all who were close to him (V.1.7–9). Nonetheless, Darius's royal authority remained strong enough among the satraps, generals, and subject peoples that he was still able to issue a new order to mobilize and could urge the satrapal leaders to remain faithful to him (Diodorus §64.2). But internal opposition did not miraculously vanish. Though we are unable to date the conspiracy precisely, we may reasonably suggest that the successive capitulation of Babylon, Susa, and Persepolis, without a fight, dealt a direct blow to the King's authority, because these surrenders signified the failure of the strategy adopted after Gaugamela. The failure was military, but also and especially political, as first Mazaeus, then Abulites, Tiridates, and several others went over to Alexander. It is also likely that the torching of the palaces at Persepolis contributed even more to unsettling what had once been certain. Finally, the Persians of Ecbatana had certainly discovered by now that Alexander had warmly welcomed officials who had transferred into his service, and he had entrusted high posts to them. Despite their attachment to the glorious memory of the Achaemenids, they must have thought that Alexander looked more and more like a credible alternative. This thought was reinforced even further after the conspiracy against the Great King.

The Conspiracy against the Great King

The sources are unanimous in naming Bessus as the one at the heart of the treachery that, already long in preparation, broke out during the retreat to the Upper Satrapies. At this time, Darius was already the hostage of the satrap of Bactria, who had absolute personal control over his contingent of horsemen (Quintus Curtius V.10.5, 12; 12.6). Against them, Darius basically could count on the loyalty of Artabazus, "the oldest of his friends" (V.9.1◊), who attempted to organize his defense (cf. V.9.13), aided by the Persian contingent (§9.16) and Greek mercenaries (who feared Alexander's vengeance). Henceforth, there were two camps and two armies face to face. As Alexander's progress became known, the treachery was soon in the open: the conspirators put Darius under arrest. It appears that initially the primary objective of the conspirators was to deliver Darius to Alexander, in the hope of obtaining large rewards (Quintus Curtius V.5.2; 12.1; cf. Arrian III.21.5 and 30.4). But they had so few illusions about the Macedonian's response that they were preparing "to kill Darius, and make for Bactra with the forces of their nations" (V.10.6◊); they were counting on the reserves of men in Bactria . . . and "they expected to regain the power of the empire, should they succeed in getting possession of the province" (V.10.4◊). Arrian is probably closer to the truth when he presents the plan of Bessus and his companions as follows: their intent was to "preserve their power in common" (III.21.5◊), by which it must be understood, on the one hand, that any idea of counterattack was ruled out, and on the other, that operations would be directed jointly by Bessus, Barsaentes, and Nabarzanes (cf. III.30.4).

Nevertheless, Bessus's position was already preeminent. According to Arrian, he "had been recognized as commander by the Bactrian cavalry and the other barbarians who had fled with Darius, except by Artabazus and his sons and the Greek mercenaries. . . . Bessus was in command for the moment because of his relationship to Darius and because the act was done in his satrapy" (§21.4–5). These are the circumstances under which some of the Persians in Darius's entourage decided to change their allegiance to Alexander (§21.1). The agreement among the conspirators scarcely lasted. Nabarzanes and Barsaentes assassinated the Great King. They then fled with several hundred horsemen (§21.10). Barsaentes returned to his satrapy, thinking that he would be able to organize resistance to benefit himself; Nabarzanes soon came, accompanied by "other very highly placed Persian officers of Darius," to surrender to Alexander (§23.4◊). The third conspirator, Bessus, for his part, reached Bactra with his troop of Bactrians and turncoat Persians; he had himself proclaimed Great King under the name Artaxerxes (§25.3; Diodorus §74.2; Quintus Curtius VI.6.13). Despite this royal claim by the satrap of Bactra, the assassination of Darius marked once and for all the end of the dynasty and the Empire.

5. *The Fall of an Empire*

Once the historian has recognized that the "decadence" explanation must be permanently discarded, he finds himself at a loss when he is required to throw the light of day onto the causes and origins of an event as spectacular as *the fall of an Empire*. The massive symbolic weight of this phrase certainly describes a responsibility that belongs to the historian—but this fact does not make the task any less intimidating.

The Cornelwood Lance

It is necessary to observe that the Empire fell primarily because the royal and satrapal armies were conquered on the battlefields of the Granicus, Issus, and Gaugamela. The Great King found himself unable to parry militarily—or, more precisely, none of the imagined parries fulfilled all of the hopes he placed in them. Indeed, in 334, Darius had held naval superiority, and his armies and financial resources gave him a considerable strike force. At this same time, neither the energy nor the stability of the Great King, nor his strategic and military abilities, nor the connection of the officials to the dynasty could reasonably be challenged. In order to explain these defeats, we might invoke an entire series of more or less valid military causes. Arrian gives the following explanation for the victory at the Granicus: "Alexander's men were getting the best of it, not only through their strength and experience but because they were fighting with cornelwood [dogwood] lances against short javelins" (I.15.5◇). This is why, according to Diodorus, during the preparation of his army at Babylon in 332–331, Darius "had fashioned swords and lances much longer than his earlier types because it was thought that Alexander had had a great advantage in this respect in the battle in Cilicia" (§53.1◇). However, even metaphorically, the historian is reluctant to reduce the Persian defeat to the superiority of the Macedonian cornelwood lance. This purely technical explanation is notoriously frustrating, even when we take into account the superior maneuverability of the Macedonian army and the clear vision, not to say genius, of its leader.

We may add—and this is surely more important—that the Empire was not prepared for the military and strategic challenge posed by Alexander. Agesilaus's incursions had already proved that the imperial space was relatively permeable. In any case, the military cautiousness and the political impediments imposed on him after Sparta had prevented him from stirring up the *ethnēs* as a whole and shattering the dynastic loyalty of the Asia Minor Persians. Thus, because of these restrictions, as we have seen, Agesilaus's attempt was doomed to failure (see chap. 15/5). However, as soon as an adversary had decided to wage total war against the Achaemenid armies and garrisons and had gained a firm foothold in Asia Minor, it was extremely difficult to dislodge him; now he was the one who was able to take advantage of the organization of Achaemenid strategic space around strongholds, treasuries, and storehouses—places where the Great King's enemy could find ample supplies of money and materiel that had originally been created for the defense of the imperial territories (see chap. 9/2). Only a Persian victory in the open field of battle could have ended the Macedonian offensive. So we have come around to the starting-point: once all of these details have been gathered into a coherent argument (or, at least a credible one), they allow us to understand *how* the Great King and his satraps lost the battles. But the fundamental question remains: *Why* did Darius lose the war?

Persian Royal Power and Multicultural Empire

We must stress the absolutely novel character of the Macedonian offensive. For the first time in its history, the Empire found itself confronting an adversary who was resolved to pursue total war to the end—that is, a war of conquest. Furthermore, the adversary also understood that a victory in pitched battle was not enough to dethrone so powerful a Great King, and he knew that war also proceeds by means other than arms. After each victory, Alexander, who had a connoisseur's appreciation of the Empire, would try all means possible to achieve political success, taking advantage of the structural weaknesses of the Achaemenid imperial structure. This is demonstrated by the attitude of the local elites—as long as it is not misinterpreted. Contrary to the repeated affirmations of Macedonian propaganda, the leaders of the subject peoples were not longing for a liberator. Not one of the countries of the Empire—not even Babylonia or Egypt—was imbued with an acute national awareness that drove them irresistibly toward independence. In fact, in each of these countries (and others), the population remained committed to its own norms and continued to cultivate the memory of its own glorious past. It is true that we should at this point note several distinctions. The case of Egypt, which over two generations returned to the course of pharaonic history, cannot be equated with the case of Babylonia, where the royal residences symbolized that Persian authority was taking root, or with the case of Susiana, which was linked closely by a long common history to the Persian high country (which itself was partly Elamized). In any case, the leaders of these great centers were not so naive as to believe that the Macedonian conquest signified a return to a Babylonia or an Egypt as it was before the conquest by Cyrus the Great. The choice was simply between one overlord and another. Finally, in the course of more than two centuries of subjection/cooperation, these peoples had woven often close relationships with the Persians and had themselves profited from the imperial system. In brief, the fall of the Empire was not due to general discontent on the part of the subject populations and their elites.

The weakness of the Empire at the point of the Macedonian invasion was perfectly wedded to the force that had held it together throughout the period from Cyrus to Darius III. The Persians had never attempted to attack the recognized traditions of their subjects: the multiethnic Empire remained multicultural, as is shown, for example, by its extraordinary linguistic diversity (e.g., Diodorus §53.4). Even if the political unity and the mixing of peoples in the Empire yielded remarkable intercultural achievements, it still is the case that, fundamentally, a Greek felt that he was a Greek and spoke Greek, an Egyptian felt that he was Egyptian and spoke Egyptian, and so on—for the Babylonians and every other people, including the Persians, who never attempted to spread their language or impose their religion. On the contrary, throughout their history, the Great King and the Persians demonstrated their desire for them to maintain their own ethnocultural traditions. The unity of the Empire was thus accomplished by means of the uncontested, but personal, supremacy of the Great King. Thus, Alexander relentlessly attempted to capture Darius himself after each battle, and the Great King certainly made every effort to escape his enemy (as was his duty)—both goals perfectly illustrate the fragility of the system (which was quite evident, at any rate, from the Macedonian side).

Thus, while there actually was an ideology of the King that continued to function perfectly at the center, an ideology of the Empire did not really exist, even though royal images were spread by means of seals and coins and by popular storytellers who narrated the court histories from land to land, echoes of which are found in Aelian's *Historical Miscellany*, as well as in Esther, Judith, and the *Tale of Aḥiqar*. In other words, there was no Achaemenid identity that might have induced the peoples, in all of their diversity, to rise up and defend some common norms. In other kinds of state—nation-states, for instance—a defeat in pitched battle did not signify the end of the community; the community might even organize a war of resistance in the adversary's rear. However, this strategy presupposes conditions that were foreign to the Achaemenid State. On the contrary, the political-ideological structures that organized and governed the territories and populations by definition abandoned the destiny of the Empire to the fate of arms, and this would quickly convince the country's elites to turn to the conqueror and transfer their allegiance to him. As soon as the royal military was conquered, local leaders found themselves with a simple choice (which their ancestors had known since the conquests of Cyrus): to negotiate with the victor a way to maintain their dominant position within their own society. Negotiation was feasible for the victor because he acknowledged the ideological attributes of the community's identity—namely, the potency of the sanctuaries and the perpetuation of traditional worship. These were concessions that Alexander was not only entirely prepared to grant but that he himself solicited.

The Dynastic Pact and Its Limits

Moreover, Alexander developed the same strategy toward the Persians. In its very structure, the Empire was organized around the supremacy of the Great King—who in Persia was king. Around him revolved all of the activities of the representatives of the aristocracy, who were provided with commands and economic advantages of all sorts. They were what we have called the dominant socioethnic class, united around the dynasty and values of the Persian community. Generally, the system continued to function satisfactorily throughout the Achaemenid Empire; analysis of the high-ranking personnel of Darius III shows that managing the Empire remained mostly a family matter. Despite occasional crises, the dynastic problem did not deeply or permanently alter the loyalty of the Persian aristocracy to the Great King. The known satrapal revolts were localized and never had a goal of imposing a king who was not of royal stock. The attitude of the Persian population (reconstructed on the basis of the policy followed by Alexander in the country) attests that Persia was always the heart of royal and imperial power. Finally, in every manifestation of his power, Darius III clearly had prestige and authority as great as that of his predecessors.

However, the shock of the conquest also demonstrates the fragility of this structure, whose erectors had obviously never given thought to a challenge of such magnitude and scope. Indeed, during the first years of Alexander's campaign, there was no generalized desertion; on the contrary, the example of Mithrenes of Sardis remains an exceptional, basically inexplicable case. However, it also serves to reveal an attitude that many aristocrats were to adopt after defeat, especially after Gaugamela. Though the Persians constituted a highly homogeneous ethnocultural community, they were not formed into a nation. Their loyalty to the Great King was based on personal relationships, which could be transferred to another person who was endowed with the prestige of victory. As the military defeats accumulated, men like Mazaeus and Abulites, following Mithrenes, were anxious to conserve their prestigious positions and their economic privileges. Indeed, in his approach to them, Alexander had long understood (even before his landing) that the *political* defeat of the Achaemenid Empire would emerge from the reproduction of gift-for-service relations that had always cemented the close alliance between the Great King and the Persian aristocracy—according to practices quite similar to those known in the Macedon of Philip and Alexander (cf. Arrian I.5.4 and Plutarch, *Eum.*

8.12). Alexander was able to create the conditions for a balance between his own ambition and the nobility's desire not to perish in the turmoil. Even though a circle of aristocrats remained faithful to the Great King until the end, their attitude does not contradict this general tendency. Alexander's success is not measured simply in the number of defections; more importantly, he was able to attract to himself men who, like Mazaeus and Abulites, held key posts at decisive moments and could thus tip the balance of power one way or the other.

Furthermore, the way in which the loyalty of a man like Artabazus was expressed—"the oldest of his Friends"—can support two readings. He certainly seems to have resolved not to abandon his king, and there is no question that he upheld this resolve. But the reasons that Alexander gave for granting him an eminent position in his administration are also very interesting: "He kept Artabazus and his sons by him in an honourable position, as they were among the most eminent Persians (*en tois prōtois Persōn*) and especially because of their loyalty to Darius" (*kai tēs es Dareion pisteōs heneka*; Arrian III.23.7✧). Of course, Arrian is speaking from Alexander's point of view. But who could seriously imagine that, in the period between the death of Darius and the change in allegiance of Artabazus and his children, the Persian aristocrat did not enter into discussions with Alexander's camp? In one way or another, Artabazus was able to negotiate with Alexander for the loyalty that he had once demonstrated toward Darius. Because of his battlefield victories, Alexander had managed to persuade the Persians little by little to transfer their allegiance to him in exchange for concessions that are easy to imagine: land, power, and prestige (cf. Plutarch, *Alex.* 34.1). Moreover, the Persians had the same perspective as the elites of the conquered countries: in the process of transferring their allegiance, they did not wish to alter the nature of the relationships that traditionally had connected them to the sovereign. Thus, the "orientalization" of the Macedonian king and his court was the necessary compensation for his Iranian policy.

Mazaeus Once Again

Above and beyond the uncertainties that remain, the examples of Mazaeus and Abulites stimulate further reflection. The available evidence in fact strongly suggests that a man like Mazaeus, though inarguably of Persian origin, was also intimately immersed in Babylonian society; the names of some of his sons are irrefutable proof. There is no doubt that the same holds true for Abulites at Susa. Both are probably representatives of a human and political type: Persians who had woven close contacts with the elites of the countries they were sent to govern (though in the second case, perhaps, we have a "Persianized" Babylonian—hence the name of Abulites' son, Oxathres). With respect to the *ideal type* of an ethnically and culturally homogeneous socioethnic class, these examples might seem to be examples of the failure of Persian authority. But, as always, historical reality is contradictory. The maintenance of imperial dominion was also accomplished by personal connections and by non-Persians' access to command positions (of which the Babylonian Bēlšunu is the prime example). These men—who, based on all of the evidence, were always considered Persians and considered themselves Persians in the political sense of the word—were at the same time a sign of the success of the imperial enterprise. In their position as *cultural mediators*, they symbolized and accelerated the creation of a new governing elite, and this elite's origin and composition paradoxically favored the permanence of Persian dominion. In this respect, too, the overwhelming challenge of the Macedonian conquest drove the contradictions to surface. If we assume that we have correctly understood the situation in Babylon in 331 following the defeat at Gaugamela, we may also imagine that the combined defections of Mazaeus and the Babylonian elites were coordinated, involving negotiations and discussions between the satrap and his friends and relatives in Babylonian society. At the very least, we can imagine this hypothesis.

Bessus in Bactria

Finally, let us return to the paramount case of Bessus. Unfortunately, his background is unknown to us, apart from the fact that he was related by blood to Darius and that Darius had made him satrap of Bactria, one of the richest and most powerful regions of the Empire (cf. Arrian III.21.5). His proclamation of himself as king obviously did not have much effect on his authority. On the other hand, it is interesting to note how he acquired his hegemony in the conspiracy: he had been acclaimed leader by his Bactrian contingents (§21.4) who, throughout the last weeks of Darius, had constituted a shadow army. Bessus intended to turn Bactria into a redoubt, with himself as the master. According to Diodorus (§74.1◊), "being known to everyone because of his administration, [he] now called upon the population to defend their freedom." We must not see this as setting in motion a "war of nationalism" that would ultimately give way to a permanent "Bactrian independence." In his books on the history of the Diadochi, Diodorus frequently uses the same sort of phrase: when Seleucus wanted to set foot in Babylonia, "most of the inhabitants came to meet him, and declaring themselves on his side, promised to aid him as he saw fit" (XIX.91.1◊). Peucestes, who was named satrap of Persia by Alexander, is described in the same way: despite the opposition of the other Macedonian leaders, he had learned Persian and adopted all of the Persian customs, with the result that he "had gained great favour with the inhabitants" (XIX.14.5◊)—so much so that Antigonus was irritated to see "that Peucestes was enjoying great favour among the Persians." When Antigonus had decided to deprive him of his satrapy, "Thespius, one of their leading men (*henos de tōn epiphanestatōn*), even said frankly that the Persians would not obey anyone else" (XIX.48.5◊). We can easily list other examples from the age of the Diadochi that illustrate the ambition of some Macedonian leaders who wanted to create personal power on the basis of support from a country and a people with which they had woven relationships of confidence and intercultural cooperation. Diodorus's phrase suggests that this was Bessus's ambition in Bactria. In this respect, after the Great King had died, Bessus served as something akin to a prefiguring of the Diadochi after Alexander's death. This shift was perhaps present in embryo in people such as Mazaeus who were closely linked to the governing elites of their satrapies. Nevertheless, in 334, the problem did not really arise; it is enough to consider the example of Artabazus and his family to realize that no matter how close connections with the local populations might be, they did not diminish in the least the Persian and imperial loyalty of the king's men. The dominant socioethnic class, insofar as we know its composition under Darius III, remained united around its king and Persian power. Only the challenge posed by the totality of the Macedonian conquest led these people, one by one, to join the camp of the victor.

Conclusion

From Nabonidus to Seleucus

Within the framework of ancient Near Eastern history, the Achaemenid phase takes on special significance. For the first time, countries that were hitherto divided among hostile rival kingdoms were gathered into a single, unified state, from the Indus to the Aegean Sea. Over the *longue durée*, this is the fundamental contribution of the conquests of Cyrus and Cambyses. The successive capturing of Ecbatana, Sardis, Bactra, Babylon, and Memphis marked the incorporation of kingdoms into the wider framework of an empire. Whatever may have sometimes been claimed, this creation was not simply a façade. The prior kingdoms, as such, disappeared. For various reasons, the Great Kings simply acknowledged that at Babylon and Memphis they were putting on the older garb of Nabonidus and Psammetichus. Nevertheless, at the same time (or after a very short delay at Babylon), Babylonia and Egypt were transformed into satrapies governed by a satrap who held his position and made his decrees on the basis of direct orders from the Great King. The same was true at Sardis and Bactra (whatever state organization might have existed previously); so it was at Ecbatana, with the difference that, at least under the first kings, Media and the Medes continued to have a special place in the Empire. No ancient heritage—whether of Babylonia, Egypt, Media, or Elam—had been denied; each had, on the contrary, been integrated into the dynamic force of a new state construct, as is shown specifically by our analysis of Achaemenid court art; it was not a simple juxtaposition of preexisting Near Eastern elements but a genuinely new elaboration in which the stylistic and iconographic diversity, far from delivering a blow to the unity of the whole, managed to reinforce it into an integrated exaltation of the unlimited power of the Great King. In the same way, we can easily discover many elements within the royal ideology to which we can find parallels in the Assyro-Babylonian and Elamite kingdoms (warrior king, gardener-king, king of justice). However, they were incorporated into a new ideology for which, at its heart, the specifically Iranian and Persian elements constituted a driving force. Recall in particular the central role accorded to the great god Ahura-Mazda and, later, Anāhita and Mithra. We can make the same observations regarding Darius's tribute organization: it was grafted both onto realities already observable in earlier times and onto the initial tinkerings carried out by Darius's predecessors; however, by the organizational power that it presupposes and that was its impulse, his system went well beyond simple borrowing of accounting practices. The inverse thesis, which reduces the Achaemenid structure to borrowings from preceding kingdoms, is based, it seems to me, on a historical and methodological error. So I have already written about Alexander, some years ago. I hope the reader will excuse me for quoting myself: "The danger of isolating components or structures that were supposed to have been borrowed by Alexander is in fact great. . . . We cannot historically isolate one structure from an overall system of ideological representations, and a system is more than the sum of its parts" (*RTP* 359). What is true for Alexander with respect to

Achaemenid ideology also is true for Cyrus, Cambyses, and their successors with regard to the organizational structures of the kingdoms they would literally engulf in the same way that white blood cells engulf bacteria. The Empire was in fact a new single-celled organism that grew by absorbing scattered, hostile cells that then cooperated within a new cellular dynamic.

In order to ensure the continuance of their power and rule, the Great Kings were first and foremost supported by the Persian aristocracy. Within the aristocracy, each family entity had privileged access to positions of power that were endowed with a genuine capacity for initiative — under the direction of the Great King. I have frequently (including in this book) referred to this group as the dominant socioethnic class, which was connected to the king through unequal relationships that were based on gift-and-service exchanges. Throughout Achaemenid history (including during the time of Darius III), the system continued to operate, because it was based on interests common to the dynasty and the aristocracy (the "dynastic pact"). At the same time, the Great Kings did not deny local elites access to the sphere of power. On the contrary, they received positions in the imperial hierarchy, sometimes at a high level. In parallel with the Great Kings' treatment of local personnel, the central authority also recognized local forms of organization, whether dynastic powers or sanctuaries or religion. The only limit on recognition of local traditions was the adherence of the imperial elites to the means and goals of the Persian authority, for which they served as local representatives and indispensable contact points. Nevertheless, the Great King did not hesitate to take drastic measures against communities tempted by revolt (*drauga*), which since the time of Darius I had been identified with calling into question a Great King, who was the representative and earthly defender of the values of Truth-Justice (*arta*) that were exalted by Ahura-Mazda.

To repeat a banal cliché, the Empire was characterized by both unity and diversity. This can be seen especially in its cultural manifestations, which are so well exemplified by the large number of languages and religions. This is why it is so difficult to analyze the Achaemenid imperial evolution as a whole: we end up alternately stressing the Empire's integrative power and its centrifugal tendencies. For reasons already discussed, these two aspects are not necessarily mutually exclusive. Across the long course of Achaemenid history, the creation of a Persian imperial diaspora in the provinces accelerated the processes of acculturation, even when the processes were not limited to the Persians and the elites of the subject populations. Marriages and many kinds of personal contact (cf. Artabazus of Greater Phrygia) led to closer and closer relationships, which can be illustrated, for example, by the rise to command positions of non-Persians (Bēl-šunu), of men who emerged from two cultures (Abulites), or of those who still participated in two cultures (Mazaeus, Orontobates). This development does not seem to have threatened the unity of the Empire. On the contrary, it tended to create a dominant imperial class that was not limited to its Persian component; at the same time, whatever their ethnic origins had been, the leaders always considered themselves Persian in the political sense — Persians, that is, who were linked to the Great King by the same unequal gift-and-service relationship and by common political and material interests. Even young people born to a mixed marriage could gain full Persian status (cf. Datames) through a privilege granted by the king (cf. Herodotus VI.41), following a procedure similar to that by which a Seleucid king granted the honor of a Greek name to a man of Babylonian origin (YOS 1.52). I am tempted to think that this development explains the state of equilibrium that was the Empire's when Alexander conquered it. By using the phrase "state of equilibrium," I obviously do not intend to project an image of peaceful, unbroken cooperation (cf. the revolts) but I intend instead to express what was a political desire of the center (in the long term) to overcome the conflicts that could not be avoided within an imperial dynamic that was founded on both the Persians' supremacy and their cooperation with the local ruling classes. The Macedonian victory, then, provides no basis for any inference about a "crisis" of the Achaemenid Empire in 334 and even less basis for any claim about its "decadence" throughout the fourth century. Put more simply, the genesis and nature of the Macedonian conquest prevented it from metamorphizing into a Nation-State that would have been able to consolidate itself through ideological norms that were common to all the peoples of the Empire in all their diversity.

Situated within the Achaemenid *longue durée*, Alexander's conquest takes on two conflicting characteristics. On the one hand, the short period initiated by the arrival of the Macedonian was the prolongation of that *longue durée*, from the geopolitical point of view; this observation further devastates the theory of "Achaemenid decadence." The Macedonian in fact took over, for his own benefit, the principles and organization of an empire whose structures were totally alien to the Balkan world. One piece of evidence —the *Oeconomica* of Pseudo-Aristotle—which we are inclined to think was compiled in the last quarter of the fourth century in Asia Minor—demonstrates that, for the Greeks, the royal and satrapal economies represented a form of tribute organization that no Greek State had ever managed to get off the ground; the only exception was the Athenian *arkhē* of the fifth century that itself borrowed much from the Achaemenid model. This is the context in which we must, to a great extent, seek the origins of the Macedonian conquest. As has often been noted, Philip II had already borrowed from the Achaemenid world, but in his time, these were nothing more than scattered borrowings that were not reintegrated into an overall dynamic. This dynamic was forced upon them by the conquest of the Achaemenid territory and the destruction-absorption of the imperial organization of the Great Kings. Whatever may have been the intentions of the King of Macedon when he launched the initial offensive against the royal territories in 337– 336, his son pursued to completion a goal of unprecedented breadth that was based on the complete usurpation of the territorial and ideological forms of organization of Darius III's Empire, as well as the cooperation of the former ruling class.

However, by posing as the heir of Darius, Alexander at the same time caused insurmountable conflicts to erupt. First, some of the Macedonian nobility were hostile to the idea of accepting Iranians as totally equal partners. Despite all his efforts—symbolized by the grandiose Iranian-Macedonian marriages at Susa—Alexander never really succeeded in creating a new ruling class that was as homogeneous and stable as the socioethnic class that ruled the Empire of Darius III and his predecessors. The defection of local elites was not due in any respect to a deep disaffection with Persian power but was simply a function of the Great King's military defeat; it had also been conditioned by the deep and lasting acceptance of local norms by the new masters. Alexander's long absence in India had already shown that satraps (Macedonian or Iranian), thinking that the king's quest had failed, were quick to violate the agreements Alexander had made with the local elites. When Alexander died, none of the problems were resolved.

Furthermore, we should consider the dramatic inability of the Macedonian authority to organize any dynastic succession—thus demonstrating an extraordinary structural weakness, in contrast to the remarkable Achaemenid capacity for renewal even in times of the most intense dynastic crises. We know what happened to the Empire's unity, which was more and more torn apart by the rival Diadochi under cover of defending the sovereign prerogatives of the two putative successors to Alexander. It took just a few years for the geopolitical situation to revert to one that, even taking into account intervening historical changes, was reminiscent of that which prevailed in the Near East before Cyrus: the Empire was shattered into several rival kingdoms. The Macedonian enterprise, which in the short term was a continuation of Achaemenid imperial history, would soon dig the grave of the political unity the Great Kings had been able to establish and safeguard through the preceding two and a half centuries. From the point of view of Near Eastern imperial geopolitics, Alexander was indeed "the last of the Achaemenids."

At the same time, the invention of the great Hellenistic kingdoms was carried out in partial continuity with Achaemenid practice. We know that Peucestes, who was appointed satrap of Persia by Alexander, ingeniously attempted, despite the objections of other Macedonians, to adopt the social practices of the Persians over whom he was satrap in order to create a commonality of culture and destiny with the aristocracy of the country. Even though Persia did not recover its former independence at this time, it represents a sketch of the developments observed in other Near Eastern Hellenistic countries. Alongside other evidence (such as that of Diodorus), the *Dynastic Prophecy* suggests that Seleucus, with the assistance of his Iranian wife Apame, was able to win over the cooperation of the ruling elite in Babylonia; the latter were growing more and more frustrated by the destruction throughout the country that was a result of the continual wars of Eumenes and Antigonus. It was as a "King of the Lands"—not as a foreign conqueror—that Seleucus was recognized in Babylonia; he took up for his own benefit the political and ideological strategy that the Great Kings had faithfully followed.

However remarkable it may have been, the Seleucid enterprise was on a far smaller scale than that of the Achaemenid Empire—and it found itself in a context where all at once traditional hostilities with Egypt reappeared and centrifugal tendencies increased, set loose by the deaths of Darius III and then Alexander. This is what we see, for example, in Cappadocia and Armenia: here, where the Achaemenids defaulted sooner than elsewhere, their satraps were quick to establish dynasties with close connections (that they loved to stress) to the Achaemenid family. In a Greek-Armenian inscription from Agaça Kale, men who may have been direct descendants of the Ariaces who led the Cappadocian contingents at Gaugamela were quite ready to adorn themselves with the nostalgic title "legitimate satraps."

Research Notes

Prologue
The Persians before the Empire

- *General bibliography.* Briant 1984a has been repeated here only to a rather small degree and in a largely reworked and modified form to take into account more recent specialized articles, particularly Miroschedji 1985 and 1990a.

1. Why Cyrus?

- *Discontinuous Documentation and the Longue Durée.* "Scandal of history" of the disappearance of the Assyrian Empire: see the discussion by Garelli (Garelli and Nikiprowetzky 1974: 125–28 and 239–42), and the summary of the topic in a more closely argued form in Zawadski 1988a: 14–22; and the interpretive suggestions of Na²aman 1991. The problem of the beginnings of Persian history is very well stated by Harmatta 1971 (even if stressing Median influence exclusively is debatable; see below); see also the reflections of Delaunay 1985: 71–81, on the reasons why Aramaic scribes were used during the time of Cyrus.
- *Persian History and Greek Representations.* See Briant 1989a; on Median-Persian relations, see also §§6–7, pp. 21–27.

2. The Founder Legends

Version of Ctesias in Nicolaus of Damascus: *FGrH* 90 F66; version of Dinon in Athenaeus XIV.633d–e; Cyrus legend and Sargon legend: Drews 1984 and B. L. Lewis 1980; on the theme of the abandoned child, cf. also Widengren 1966 and Binder 1964: 17–28; on royal legends in Iranian literature, in particular in Firdawsi, see Christensen 1936 (who finds similar traits in the legends reported by Herodotus and Ctesias), Davidson 1985, Duleba 1987, Krasnowolska 1987; remembrance of Cyrus among the Persians: Xenophon, *Cyr.* I.2.1; Herodotus III.160; Strabo XV.3.18; and Athenaeus XV.633d–e: cf. chap. 8/3 on the education of young Persian aristocrats.

3. The Kings of Anšan

Inscriptions of Ariaramnes and Arsames: cf. summary of the topic in Lecoq 1974a: 48–52, who concludes that "the inauthenticity [of these texts] has not been proved" (cf. also Herrenschmidt 1979a); the discussion is directly connected to the interpretation given to Darius's dynastic claims, which are extremely suspect (on the genealogy recorded by Darius, see the keen reflections of Miroschedji 1985: 280–83): we return to these problems at greater length in chapters 2/10 and 3/1; seal of Kuraš of Anšan: Hallock 1977: 127, Miroschedji 1985: 285–87, Bollweg 1988; and most recently Garrison 1992: 3–7 (and n. 22).

4. Anšan and Susa

Arrival of the Iranians in the Zagros: cf. summary of the topic and bibliography in Briant 1984a: 79–83; add Sumner 1994, who prefers a higher dating (middle of the second millennium); on relations between the lowlands and the highlands, see Vallat 1980; Carter and Stolper 1984: 32ff.; Miroschedji 1990a; Tall-i Malyan tablets: Stolper 1984b; site of Malyan: Sumner 1988; coexistence of several Elamite "kings" at the beginning of the seventh century: cf. Stolper 1986;

"royal cities": Miroschedji 1986 and 1990a: 65–69; battles of Elamite kings against the Assyrians: Carter and Stolper 1984: 44–53, as well as Gerardi 1987 and a brief presentation in Frame 1992: 255–56; assuming the title "king of Anšan": Miroschedji 1985: 296–99; chronology and succession of the first kings: without denying that they are just hypotheses, I follow on this point the interpretations of Miroschedji 1985: 280–285 (who refuses to recognize Cyrus in the Aššurbanipal inscription published by Weidner 1930), but there remain uncertainties and discussion on absolute chronology: cf. Bollweg 1988: 56 (genealogical tree; explicitly denying the reconstruction of Miroschedji); the discrepancies explain why Cyrus the Great is sometimes numbered II, sometimes III (just as his father is sometimes designated Cambyses I, sometimes Cambyses II), depending on the weight given to Herodotus VII.11.

5. Persian Society before the Conquests: Herodotus and Archaeology

• *Herodotus and Persian Society.*   Text of Herodotus: Briant 1984a: 105–10, 1990a: 77–84; tribal organization: see also the reports of Xenophon (twelve tribes!) (*Cyr.* I.2.5) and Strabo XV.3.1: cf. Von Gall 1972; Iranian terms: Dandamaev 1989a: 13; note that the term **zantu* does not occur in the Old Persian texts; according to Dandamaev and Livshits 1988: 459, it appears several times in the Elamite tablets from Persepolis as a constituent element in personal names, but see *contra* Schmitt 1990b; Greek (and Mesopotamian) view of the opposition nomads/farmers: Briant 1976 and 1982b: 9–56; *kāra* in OPers. can designate the army as well as the people (whence the problems posed by *DB* §14: see below, chap. 2/10); the title *karanos* appears in Xenophon to describe a military head with exceptional powers: Haebler 1982, Petit 1983, Sekunda 1988: 74; military prestige of the king: Briant 1984a: 114–17.

• *The Findings of Archaeology.*   Absence of sedentary populations: Sumner 1972: 264–65, 1986: 4–7 (without enthusiasm: "unsatisfactory . . . assumption . . . hypothetical explanation"); conclusions repeated and strengthened by Miroschedji 1985: 288–94 ("radical sedentary depopulation"); see also Miroschedji 1990a; agricultural activities in Persian month names: cf. the analysis of Hinz 1973: 64–70; maintenance of pastoral populations in Achaemenid Fārs: Sumner 1986: 30–31; cf. Briant 1976. On the very incomplete character of explorations in Fārs: cf. the remarks of Miroschedji 1990a: 54–55; Elamite influences: Briant 1984a: 92–95, Miroschedji 1982 and 1985: 296–305, Calmeyer 1988b (dress), Bollweg 1988 and Garrison 1992 (seals); archaeological results in Khūzistān: Carter 1994; tomb of Arjan: Vallat 1984, Alizadeh 1985 (criticism by Vallat, *AbIran* 10 [1987], no. 217); cf. also Miroschedji 1990a: 55 and the article by Majizadeh 1992 (publication of a bowl with scenes of hunting, tribute-bearers, and banquets: the author stresses Phoenician and Assyrian influences); according to Duchêne (1986), Arjan is to be identified with Huhnur, halfway between the future site of Persepolis and Susa, by proposing a relationship with the place-name Hunair known from the Fortification tablets (cf. Koch 1990: 198–200). The Susa tablets were published in 1907; their dating was and is uncertain: Hinz (1987) defends a high date (before 680); 600–540 is suggested by F. Vallat (1984: 11, n. 26); see also Miroschedji 1982 and 1990a: 79, and Stève 1986, from whom I take the term "Neo-Elamite IIIB (ca. 605–539)" (pp. 20–21); quotation: Ghirshman 1976b: 160; Iranian metallurgical tradition: Moorey 1984; on the term *irmatam*, cf. below, chap. 11/5, 11/9; Persians and Iranians in Babylon: Zadok 1977: 66–67; Babylonian populations in Khūzistān: Stolper 1986; importance of intercultural contacts before Cyrus: cf. Briant 1984a.

6. Anšan, Ecbatana, Babylon, and Susa

• *The Consequences of the Fall of the Assyrian Empire.*   On the events that led to the demise of Assyria, see (besides Goossens 1952 and Garelli 1974: 125–28, 239–42) the recent analyses by Zawadski 1988a and Naʾaman 1992. It will immediately be seen that the interpretations continue to differ on very important points: but it would not be appropriate to review the debate here, in the course of a discussion devoted specifically to the kings of Anšan. It will have to suffice to put in a nutshell some facts and analyses that, even indirectly, might contribute to the understanding of the Near Eastern world upon the arrival of Cyrus II; downfall of the Assyrian capitals: see Goossens 1952: 90–93; Kuyper 1981; Scurlock 1990b; Dalley 1990, 1993; Kuhrt 1995 (now bringing into the discussion the tablets from Tall Sēḫ Ḥamad [valley of the Khabur]), which prove that the political end of imperial power did not mean the instant annihilation of the language or more generally of Assyrian culture: cf. the articles collected in *SAAB* 7/2 [1993]); on the role of the Medes after 610, see Baltzer 1973 (and Joannès 1995b, with the subsequent remarks of Gasche 1995 on the name and dating of the "Median Wall"); Astyages/Alyattes treaty of 585: the Labynetus of Herodotus cannot be Nabonidus (556–539) (to whom he gives the same name): cf. discussion in Beaulieu 1989a: 80–82; the Medes and Central Asia: Briant 1984b: 35–42; reconstruction of an Elamite kingdom centered on Susa: Miroschedji 1982, Vallat 1984, Stève 1986; the notion of the submission of Susa to Ecbatana is defended by Zawadski 1988a: 138–43 (cf. also Lukonin 1989: 61, according to whom Astyages imposed his domination over Elam in 585); but the evidence is contradictory: some take the opposite view, that there are a number of links between Susa and Babylon (Lukonin 1989: 58–59; Wiseman 1956: 36; and Carter-Stolper 1984: 54); in any event, it is quite possible that Elam was itself not unified, with various princes, who were not necessarily strictly under the control of Susa, controlling local territory; Babylonian conquests in the west: Wiseman 1956; name of the last Elamite king (Ummaniš): Miroschedji's hypothesis 1982: 62–63.

• *Anšan on the World Stage.* Classical texts on the fall of the Assyrian Empire: in the final analysis, all that can be agreed to are a few contemporary notes (cf. Scurlock 1990b); we may add that the version of Amyntas is already found in part in Xenophon (*Anab.* III.4.8–13), who identifies the ruins he viewed in Assyria with the cities captured by Cyrus from the Medes; on the "Arabs" of Mesopotamia, cf. Briant 1982b: 120–22 and Donner 1986.

• *Median Dominion.* The hypothesis that the *Dream of Nabonidus* (cited below, chap. 1/1, p. 881) identifies Cyrus as *ardu* ('slave') of Astyages (so Dandamaev 1984b: 82–86) derives from a faulty reading: cf. Baltzer 1973; tribute under Median domination: cf. Justin I.7.2 (very general); on Herodotus's Median dynastic chronology, see most recently Scurlock 1990a.

• *Dynastic Marriages?* Identification of Aryenis, daughter of Alyattes: Herodotus I.74 and especially a *scholion* to Plato (Pedley 1972: no. 96); note also that one of the daughters of Darius was called Mandane, at least in a court novel recorded by Diodorus XI.57.1. Another marriage tradition is found in Diodorus (II.10.1) and Berossus (apud Josephus, *Ag. Ap.* I.19): a "Syrian" king landscaped the Hanging Gardens of Babylon to please his wife "who was originally from Persia" (Diodorus) or Media (Berossus): cf. also Quintus Curtius V.1.35. The diminution of foundation legends attests above all to the vigor of the oral traditions.

7. From the Medes to the Persians

• *Borrowing and Inheritance.* The theory of Medo-Persian linguistic inheritance is found already in Meillet and Benveniste 1931 (cf. particularly p. 7: "For historical, geographic, and dialectal reasons, it can be nothing other than Median"); cf. also R. Schmitt, *RlA* 7/7–8 (1990): 617–18 s.v. "Medische [Sprache]"; this is the basis on which Harmatta 1971 reconstructed Median state organization, which supposedly was copied by the Achaemenids; on this point, see the critique of Sancisi-Weerdenburg 1988a: 208–10. The theory was strongly challenged by Skjærvø 1983 (summarized here), as well as by Lecoq 1987, who elsewhere (1974b) sets forth the idea of a Perso-Median *koinè*; on the name Mede applied to the Persians, cf. Graf 1984, and Tuplin 1994.

• *The Structure of the Median Kingdom: Mēdikos logos of Herodotus.* Cf. Helm 1981 (oral traditions and Persian propaganda); Brown 1988: 78–84, Sancisi-Weerdenburg 1993a, also Scurlock 1990a (on the Median chronology of Herodotus, judged perfectly acceptable); note that Ctesias also devoted part of his *Persica* to Median history: cf. Diodorus II.32–34; cf. also IX.20.4, where he mixes information from Ctesias with some attributed explicitly to Herodotus, but which he cites in a faulty way; on the problems posed by the "Scythian interregnum," see now the detailed analysis of Lanfranchi 1990 and the interpretations of Vogelsang 1992: 181–90, 310–12; Medes and Assyrians: cf. chronological table drawn up by Brown, *RlA* 7/7–8 (1990): 620; role of Cyaxares: Brown 1988: 81–86; also Sancisi-Weerdenburg 1988a: 202–3, 211. Note that Ctesias calls Cyaxares "founder of Median hegemony"; but given that Diodorus (II.32.3) cites Herodotus, this is obviously a confusion with Deioces; the same author claims (II.34.6) that Astyages is the name the Greeks gave to a certain Aspandas; finally, note in passing that Diodorus (II.34.1) cites a certain Astibaras among the Median sovereigns: this involves the evidence of a personal name copied from an Achaemenid title (*arštibara* = Gk. *doryphoros* 'lance-bearer') familiar from an inscription of Naqš-i Rustam (*DNc*) and from Babylonian tablets (Stolper 1985a: 55 n. 12). Scarcity of Median archaeological remains: see several articles of Muscarella (1987, 1994) and the refinement of Genito (1986), with the criticism of Vogelsang (1992: 177; but the use of country lists leaves me methodologically unconvinced) and especially Medvedskaya 1992, who concludes on the basis of observations of ceramics and geography that Bābā Jān can no longer be considered a Median site. On "Median art," see the convenient presentations of P. Calmeyer in *RlA* 7/7–8 (1990): 618–19 and *EncIr* II (1988) 565–69 and D. Stronach, 1977: 688–98, 1981 and *EncIr* II (1988) 288–90. The theory of very limited spread of Median power is supported especially by Sancisi-Weerdenburg (1988a, 1993a); Brown (1986, 1988) considers the impact of Assyrian levies on the passage from a tribal society to a state society, beginning with the eighth century. The theory of the rewriting of history by the Babylonians in an anti-Median direction is very strongly supported by Zawadski 1988a: 132–48, dated by the author to exactly 576 (p. 148); the interpretation seems attractive but does suffer from a significant weakness: it postulates that the composers of the *Nabopolassar Chronicle* systematically designated the Medes with the name Umman-Manda (cf. pp. 127–29); however, this interpretation appears very doubtful (cf. Baltzer 1973); under these circumstances, the reassessment of the role of the Medes in the anti-Assyrian coalition does not carry much conviction.

   • *Appraisal of the Discussion.*   The importance of the Elamite legacy to the Persians has been stressed by numerous authors (P. Amiet, F. Vallat, M.-J. Stève, M. Garrison); cf. also Stolper 1984b: 4, regarding the tablets from Tall-i Malyan ("They supply a distant historical antecedent for Elamite administrative recording in Fārs under the Achaemenids"), and Miroschedji 1982 and 1985. Miroschedji concludes that the Persian administration in Fārs "was probably set up by Cyrus II in the middle of the sixth century, when the Empire was established" (1985: 301; see below, chap. 2/9, p. 895, on the organization of the sacrifices around the tomb of Cyrus); perhaps we should even consider that it was set up before the first conquests (cf. Briant 1984a: 118)? Note in this regard that two high officials in Persia at the time of Darius continued to use seals engraved with an Elamite name, Humban-aḫpi (cf. Hinz 1972b: 281), and that the seal of Kuraš of Anšan himself is applied to six tablets (cf. on this seal most recently Garrison 1992: 3–10); on the other hand, the Median borrowings (arms, clothing) are usually reconstructed on the basis of later documents, in particular the Greek authors and the representations of Persepolis (cf., for example, Trümpelmann 1988; also Calmeyer, *RlA* 7/7–8 [1990] 615–17). On all these problems, see now also the interesting treatment by Tuplin 1994: 251–56.

8. Conclusion

   It must be stressed that many of the hypotheses of the (supposed) relations between Nabonidus and Cyrus (cf. summary of the topic in Baltzer 1973: 87–88) are implicitly based on the assumption of the recognition of Anšan as a military power by the other kingdoms (specifically Neo-Babylonian and Median).

Chapter 1

The Land-Collectors: Cyrus the Great and Cambyses

1. Medo-Persian Hostilities, the Defeat of Astyages, and the Fall of Ecbatana (553–550)

• *General Bibliography on Cyrus.* Dhorme 1912; Olmstead 1948: 34–85; Mallowan 1972; Stronach 1978: 285–95; Cook 1983: 25–43; Cuyler Young 1988: 28–46; Dandamaev 1989a: 10–69.

• *Sources and Problems.* The *Dream of Nabonidus* is part of a long inscription of that king (Inscription 1 in Beaulieu 1989a: 22; translation, p. 108, and commentary, pp. 108–10); other Babylonian sources referring to the victory of Cyrus over Astyages: *Nabonidus Chronicle* (text edited and translated by Grayson, *ABC*: 104–11; cf. p. 106; cf. also the English translation in *ANET*: 305 and the important remarks of Tadmor 1965 on the literary models on which the text is built). The *Dream* (with other Babylonian texts) poses an interpretive problem regarding the generic term Umman-Manda; the problem has been discussed extensively and remains debatable: cf. Baltzer 1973; Zawadski 1988; Lanfranchi 1990; it looks as though a general identification as the Medes is no longer acceptable; but here, whatever the intentions of the author, it is clear that he intended to identify the Medes (and their king Astyages) by the generic pejorative Umman-Manda; the role of Harpagus is also stressed in a Greek tradition from Asia Minor that uses a chronological formula of the form "when Harpagus urged Cyrus son of Cambyses to revolt [against Astyages]" (Mazzarino 1947: 197 and 225); the tradition is suspect, because it could well come directly from Harpagus himself, whose links with Asia Minor are well attested; the problem consists entirely of determining when Harpagus seceded: at the beginning of (or even before) the revolt, or at the end of the Medo-Persian war? In the first case, one must suppose the war to have been very short (Herodotus); in the second, one must suppose that the defection of Harpagus can be explained by the defeats suffered by the Median armies after a series of victories: this is in fact the version of Diodorus IX.23; the date of the beginning of overt Medo-Persian hostilities is disputed, depending on the interpretation of the vague and contradictory chronological indications found in the *Dream of Nabonidus* (cf. Drews 1969; also Cook 1983: 27, 144; and especially Tadmor 1965). Nabonidus's departure from Teima: Beaulieu 1989a: 149ff. Presumed relations between Nabonidus and Cyrus: Beaulieu 1989a: 109, 144: to explain the wait-and-see policy regarding Nabonidus at the beginning of his reign, the author notes: "It is likely that Nabonidus was waiting for Cyrus' revolt to start, a welcome event which would give him total freedom of action in Syria, Palestine, and Arabia." But we do not actually know whether in 556 anyone thought a Medo-Persian war was inevitable.

• *Offensives and Counteroffensives.* Cf. Stronach 1978: 282; the *Cyropaedia* of Xenophon does not mention a revolt; quite the contrary: once elevated to the court of his grandfather Astyages, Cyrus cooperated fully with his uncle Cyaxares, successor of Astyages(!), to the point that he commanded the united army in his campaigns against Sardis and then Babylon; despite several clashes due to the touchiness of Cyaxares, the agreement continued to hold until Cyrus married the daughter of Cyaxares (who was without male heir) and received all of Media as dowry (VIII.5.19); Xenophon was following or himself inventing a scenario that is obviously quite removed from reality—although from time to time he can supply an interesting piece of information (to the extent that it can be confirmed by an independent source; cf. below on the story of Gobryas).

• *The New Master of Ecbatana.* Tent and treasures of Astyages: Nicolaus of Damascus, *FGrH* 90 F66.45; cf. *Nabonidus Chronicle* II.3–4; on the symbolism of entering the tent of the vanquished: Briant 1988c: 269; fate of Astyages and of Media: Herodotus I.130: "Cyrus kept him near him until his death and did him no other harm"; Justin I.6.16: "Cyrus was content to deprive him of royalty and treated him like a grandfather rather than a defeated enemy, and since Astyages did not wish to return to Media, he gave him the government of the great nation of the Hyrcanians ("Barcaeans" in Ctesias §4; cf. Briant 1984b: 56–58); Ctesias, *Persica* §2: "Cyrus honored him like his father"; submission of the Central Asian peoples: Nicolaus of Damascus, *FGrH* 90 F66.46, and Ctesias, *Persica* §2; cf. Briant 1984b: 35–41; retention of Ecbatana as capital: cf. Strabo XI.13.5 ("it continued to preserve much of its ancient dignity; and Ecbatana was winter residence for the Persian kings"✧: cf. Briant 1988c); on the business conducted at Ecbatana by the Egibi during the reign of Cyrus, see p. 72. [See now Tuplin 1994: 253–56.]

2. The New International Situation and Cyrus's Projects

• *The Median Territorial and Diplomatic Heritage.*   On the Lydian kingdom, see the old work of Radet 1893, still useful though outdated; cf. also Mazzarino 1947 and Talamo 1979; one should also recall that Lydia's participation in Near Eastern international life was long-standing and is well attested, especially in the Assyrian inscriptions; see the convenient summary in Frei 1979.

• *Chronological Problems and Cyrus's Strategy.*   Very clearly set forth by Cargill 1977 and Kuhrt 1988b: 34; Cargill concludes (p. 110): "There exists . . . no clear evidence for the exact date of the conquest of Lydia"; most recently, and of the same opinion, Stork 1989; Nabonidus at Teima and Belshazzar at Babylon: Beaulieu 1989a.

3. The Defeat of Croesus and the Establishment of a Mediterranean Front

• *The Successful Counterattack by Cyrus (547–546).*   On the Lydian alliances: with Nabonidus: cf. Beaulieu 1989a: 79–82 (discussion of the identification of King Labynetus mentioned by Herodotus I.74, 77, 188); with Sparta: discussions in La Bua 1977: 40–43; with Amasis: La Bua 1977: 43. Campaign of Cyrus: Radet 1893: 242–59; Balcer 1984: 95–117; attitude of the Greek cities: La Bua 1977: 44–61; Pytharcus of Cyzicus: Athenaeus I.54 (cf. Briant 1985b: 50; Austin 1990: 296–97); defeat of Cyrus (before his final victory): Polyaenus, VII.8.1; Eurybates: Diodorus IX.32.

• *Takeover of the Lydian Kingdom.*   On the siege of Sardis, cf. the recent publication of a helmet by Greenwalt-Heywood 1992, and Greenwalt 1992; fate of Croesus: Herodotus I.153, 155; Xenophon, *Cyr.* VII.2.9–14, 29, but the ancient tradition is highly contradictory (Wiesehöfer 1987a: 116–17), because it was marked by quasi-mythical reconstructions in Athenian imagery (Francis 1980: 67–70; Miller 1988); gift of a town to Croesus: Ctesias, *Persika* §4 and Justin I.7.7 (cf. Briant 1985b: 56–58). Treasures of Sardis: Xenophon, *Cyr.* VII.2.14, 3.1, 4.12–13, 5.57 (their arrival in Babylon, because Xenophon dates the conquest of Asia Minor after the taking of Babylon; perhaps it should be Ecbatana: cf. Herodotus I.153, or "the country of the Persians": I.157); Diodorus (IX.33.4) speaks of the confiscation of properties (*ktēseis*) of the inhabitants of Sardis for the royal treasury (cf. also Herodotus I.153: . . . *kai ton khryson tōn allōn Lydōn*); perhaps this refers to the confiscation of the product of the mines of Lydia; Tabalus: Herodotus I.153 (cf. Petit 1990: 34–35).

• *The Revolt of Pactyes.*   Herodotus I.154–61 and the anti-Herodotian polemic of Plutarch *De Mal. Her.* 20 (*Moralia* 859a–b); duties of Pactyes: Legrand (ad loc.) understands that Pactyes had been detailed by Cyrus to transport (*komizein*) the riches (*khrēmata*) of Croesus and the Lydians to Babylon; but the term used by Herodotus (*komizein*) can also refer to the action 'look after' as well as 'transport'; since Pactyes remained at Sardis after Cyrus left, Picard (1980: 34–36) concludes that Pactyes was "the intendant for Persian revenues in Asia Minor"; he would have been concerned with "the tax due on the royal lands and the other domains"; the suggestion goes back to P. Naster, cited and discussed by Lombardo 1974: 718 and n. 131; demobilization of the Lydians: cf. the remarks (in large part metaphorical) of the ancient authors stating that, at the suggestion of Croesus himself (Herodotus I.155), Cyrus decided to transform the Lydians, who previously were considered the most "virile" and "courageous" people in Asia, into "effeminate shopkeepers"

(I.79); identical discussions are found in Polyaenus, Justin, and Plutarch (the last, however, speaking of Cyrus's policy toward Babylon); the tradition is linked to Greek stereotypes bearing on the relation between wealth and military weakness and is thus suspect (cf. Briant 1989a: 42–43). It is often suggested that after the defeat of Pactyes, some Lydians were deported to Babylon (van der Spek 1982: 281); Wiesehöfer 1987a: 117); but there is no certain proof that the Lydian communities found in Babylon in the second half of the fifth century (Eph'al 1978: 80–83) date from the time of Cyrus; to be prudent, the suggestion must remain just that; on the presence of Lydian craftsmen at the construction of Pasargadae, cf. especially Nylander 1970; Cyrus and the Greek temples: Branchidae (Parke 1985: 59–61); Aulai (ML 12, lines 26–27; Boyce 1982: 47–48; Boffo 1983: 63–64); Claros (Picard 1922: 29, 116, 120, 129–30, 422, 606–7; Boffo 1983: 11).

• *Harpagus in Asia Minor.* On the administrative position of Harpagus: Petit 1990: 36–38; submission of the Greek cities: Diodorus (IX.35) says that it was before Harpagus that the Spartan delegation appeared; on these chronological problems, see the discussion of Boffo 1983: 10ff. (who, pp. 48–51, considers unlikely the assembly of Ionians at the Panionion, the center of the Ionian League: Herodotus I.141); conquests of Mazares and Harpagus: Boffo 1983: 26–45 and 56–58; situation of the islanders: note meanwhile that Mytilene and Lesbos sent a naval contingent for the campaign against Egypt in 525 (Herodotus III.13)—which implies some sort of subjection to Persian power (which had to have been established between 546 and 525).

4. Cyrus in Central Asia

On the possibility (enunciated by Ctesias) of an expedition by Cyrus in Central Asia before the conquest of Lydia, see above, p. 34; the situation of the countries of Asia Minor before Cyrus: Briant 1984b; Bactriana and the Saka before Cyrus: Briant 1982b: 182–90ff.; 1984b: 13–43; chronology and problems of Cyrus's conquests in this region: Mallowan 1972: 8–9; Cook 1983: 19–30, Francfort 1985 and 1988: 170–71 (who thinks there was only one expedition led by Cyrus in Central Asia, that it should be dated after the capture of Babylon, and that it resulted in the death of the conqueror); note that according to Polyaenus (VII.6.4) and Justin (I.7.3–5) it was Babylon that Cyrus marched against upon leaving Sardis.

5. The Capture of Babylon (539)

• *Sources and Problems.* Critical presentation by Dougherty 1929: 167–85; more recently Sack 1983; Kuhrt 1983, 1988b: 120–125, and 1990c; as well as Rollinger 1993; translation of the *Cyrus Cylinder*: Eilers 1974; cf. Kuhrt 1988c: 63–66; *Chronicle*: Grayson, *ABC*: 104–12; *Panegyric*: *ANET*: 312–15 (cf. Lackenbacher 1992); *Dynastic Prophecy*: Grayson, *BHLT*: II.24–33; although in this text, as in the other three, Nabonidus is portrayed as an oppressive king, the difference is that Cyrus is also denounced in the same way (Grayson, *BHLT*: II.22–24), which raises some questions about the identity of the composers and the date of composition (Sherwin-White 1987: 10–14; Kuhrt 1990a: 181–82). Beginning with an analysis of Deutero-Isaiah, Sidney Smith (1944) and Morton Smith (1963) went a long way toward spreading the historical interpretation of Cyrus as a liberator; see the criticism of Kuhrt 1990c: 127 and 144–46. On Babylonian affairs, see MacGinnis 1994: 213, who appears to take up in turn the idea of a general hostility of the "priestly powers" of the Babylonian temple against Nabonidus and their siding with Cyrus, but his observations are not convincing; see rather Beaulieu 1993a: publication of tablets showing that, at least four months before Cyrus's attack, Nabonidus had brought to Babylon divine statues coming from several Babylonian sites (including the Eanna of Uruk), accompanied by staff and attendants; hence the mention in the Cylinder of the return of these statues under a decree of the victorious Cyrus.

• *The Military Conquest.* Possible Persian-Babylonian hostilities before 539: Beaulieu 1989a: 197–203 (the presence of Belshazzar in a locality called "fortified military camp [Dūr-karāšu]" suggests that the text actually alludes to hostilities between Cyrus and the Neo-Babylonian army, stationed at the fortifications at the north of the kingdom); but see Gadd 1958: 76–77, citing an inscription of Nabonidus that refers to the treaty made not only with Egypt and the Arabs but also with "the city of the Medes," an expression designating the new power of Cyrus after the capture of Ecbatana; this would thus indicate a treaty between Nabonidus and Cyrus; but the interpretation remains tentative (it is not discussed or refuted by Beaulieu 1989a: 173); cf. on these problems also the analysis of Von Voigtlander 1963: 194–95 and the remarks of Kuhrt 1988b: 120–23; Delaunay (1985: 80) states that around 545 Cyrus took Subaru and Ḫarran and on this occasion he enlisted Aramaic scribes in his service; but the documentary evidence is lacking. [At this writing (1992), vol. 2 of Delaunay's work, which will contain the scholarly apparatus, is not available.] Fortifications ("Median Wall") north of the Neo-Babylonian kingdom: Barnett 1963; Vallat 1989b; the archaeological articles in *NAPR* 1 (1987) and 2 (1989); and most recently Gasche 1995; hostilities at Uruk: Beaulieu 1989a: 219–20. Ugbaru/Gobryas: Kuhrt 1988b: 122–23; Beaulieu 1989a: 226–30, 1989b; Petit 1990: 49–55; Dandamaev 1992a: 72–73; the taking of Susa is not precisely dated: 539 is generally accepted (Zadok 1976: 61–62, followed by Miroschedji 1985: 305 and n. 161), but cf. Briant 1994f: 54 n. 20; note simply that the *Dynastic Prophecy* calls Cyrus "king of Elam" before the conquest of Babylon; but this mention after the fact may be nothing but a "deliberate archaism" (Grayson 1975a: 25 n. 7). Siege of Babylon and resistance of Nabonidus: Kuhrt 1990c: 131–35; the information of the Classical authors about the resistance in Babylon does not seem to square with the chronological information in the *Chronicle*; cf. Glombowski 1990. The book of Daniel also contains a number of direct allusions to Babylonian events: note in particular that it was at the end of a feast and a banquet that King Belshazzar (son of Nabonidus) was assassinated; Belshazzar's feast has often been compared with Xenophon's indication that Cyrus took advantage of a feast and drinking-party to send Gobryas to seize Babylon (*Cyr.* VII.5.15–30); it was in this assault that the "king" (i.e., Belshazzar) would have been killed (ibid. 30; cf. Daniel 5:30 and the remarks of Yamauchi 1990: 59 on the identification [which has been debated for so long] of "Darius the Mede"; cf. also Dandamaev 1992a: 73); on the fate of Nabonidus, cf. discussion by Beaulieu 1989a: 231; cf. also Briant 1985b: 57 n. 3; dating of the tablets relating to the capture of Babylon: Petschow 1987; administrative status of Babylonia after the Persian conquest: see below, chap. 2/3, pp. 67ff..

- *From Nabonidus to Cyrus.* Entry of Cyrus and Alexander into Babylon: Kuhrt 1988b: 68–71, 1990b: 122–26; Briant 1988c: 257–63; propaganda of Cyrus in the *Cylinder*: Kuhrt 1983, 1988a–b, 1990c; Nabonidus and Ḫarran: Beaulieu 1989a: 62–65, 205–9; Kuhrt 1983: 90 and 1990c: 135–46; construction by Nabonidus at sites that Cyrus claims to have restored: Beaulieu 1989b; *Cylinder* and Aššurbanipal texts: Walker 1972; Harmatta 1974; Kuhrt 1983; Cambyses and the New Year: cf. *Chronicle* III.24–28 (but the text is very broken); position of Cambyses: Kuhrt 1988b: 126 ("an interim measure to cope with the problems raised by the conquest of such a large and politically complex area") and Peat 1989.

6. Cyrus, Trans-Euphrates, and Egypt

- *Trans-Euphrates after the Capture of Babylon.* Policy of Nabonidus and his predecessors concerning the countries of Trans-Euphrates: Wiseman 1956, Bing 1969: 144–63, Ephʿal 1982: 170–91, Briant 1982a: 153–61, Beaulieu 1982a: 149–85, Hoglund 1989: 9–40; importance of raw materials: Oppenheim 1967; summary of the history of Judah: Oded 1977a–b–c; Weippert 1988; see also Wiseman 1956: 21–39; Judah between Egypt and Babylon: Malamat 1988; on the situation of the king of Judah at the Babylonian court: Weidner 1939.

- *Cyrus and Jerusalem.* The text of Second Isaiah poses numerous historical and chronological problems: cf. Kuhrt 1990c: 144–45; edict of Cyrus: de Vaux 1937, Bickerman 1946, Yamauchi 1990: 89–92; doubts about its authenticity in Wiesehöfer 1987: 113–14 and Grabbe 1991 and 1993; the problem is linked to complex questions regarding the date and authorship of the books of Nehemiah and Ezra: cf. Ackroyd 1968, 1984, 1988; Oded 1977d (note incidentally that the decrees of Cyrus are also recorded by Josephus, *Ant.* XI.104); on the policy of Cyrus, cf. also van der Spek 1982 and 1983. Sheshbazzar and Zerubbabel: Japhet 1982; Petit 1990: 64–66 (*tiršata*: Skjærvø

1994b: 501); status of Judea: Avigad 1976, MacEvenue 1981, Williamson 1988; chronology of the construction of the temple: the hypotheses of Bickerman 1981 are contested by Kessler 1992; deportations in the Assyrian period: Oded 1979; deportations and returns of statues: Cogan 1974; the return of the Jews to Jerusalem has sometimes been compared with the return of a Syrian community exiled in Babylonia to Neirab (cf. Eph'al 1978: 84–87); but the Neirab texts continue to pose major chronological and historical problems that necessitate some care in their interpretation: most recently Oelsner 1989 and Cagni 1990.

• *Cyrus and the Trans-Euphrates.* On Cyrus and Arabia, despite recent reaffirmations (Beaulieu 1989a: 180 and n. 23), a Persian conquest of the Arabian oases before 539 is highly doubtful: Eph'al 1982: 201–4; Briant 1982b: 162–63; Graf 1990a: 138; satrapy of Babylonia and Trans-Euphrates: Stolper 1989b, especially pp. 296–97 (cf. also Heltzer 1992b); on the 5th *nomos* of Herodotus: critical view in Calmeyer 1990b; Cyprus: see the proof by Watkin 1987; according to Herodotus (II.82), Pharaoh Amasis "was the first king in the world to capture Cyprus and reduce it to paying tribute": Wallinga 1987: 60 thinks this conquest happened in 539; Sidon and the Phoenician cities: discussion of the date of submission to the Persians in Elayi 1989: 137–38, who prefers the high dating (Cyrus).

• *Cyrus and Egypt.* Egyptian doctor and dynastic marriage: apart from Herodotus, see Athenaeus XIII.560d–f, who relates the contradictory opinions of Ctesias (daughter of Amasis requested by Cambyses) and Dinon and Lyceas of Naucratis (Cambyses, son of Nitetis); see also Polyaenus VIII.29 (Nitetis married by Cyrus, who would have been the first to think of vengeance by attacking Amasis); Lloyd 1983: 286 and 340 (considers the possibility of a marriage); Atkinson 1956 (Persian propaganda started in Cambyses' time); at the same time, it seems clear that these legends were created in a Near Eastern context (Zaccagnini 1983 positions the episodes recounted by Herodotus in the *longue durée*); Amasis's fear in the face of Persian might is not surprising; sending an Egyptian doctor to the court of the Great King is not in itself unlikely: for one thing, the reputation of Egyptian physicians had long been celebrated in courts throughout the Near East; for another, the story of this Egyptian oculist ("plucked from his wife and children") is included in a long series of "diplomatic gifts" of this kind between Egypt and Babylonia (cf. Zaccagnini 1983: 250–56); the "gift" in question seems to illustrate the inequality of the relations established between Cyrus and Amasis; it is the same with the sending of an Egyptian princess, a request with which Amasis would not have complied had not "the power of the Persians made him uneasy and he took fright" (III.1); in analogous cases known from the history of Egypt, it was foreign princesses who came to Egypt to marry. Otherwise, the fact that the "winged genius" of Pasargadae wears the Egyptian crown and shows Phoenician influence does not require us to think that Cyrus actually conquered Egypt; this characteristic simply indicates the intensity of cultural exchange, which goes back to a time before the Achaemenids (Nylander, in a comment after Donadoni 1983 [pp. 41–43], suggests that in doing this Cyrus symbolically signified his claim "to worldwide dominion, to the four corners of the earth, the ancient heritage of the Assyro-Babylonian kings"); on Cyrus and Egypt, see now the fine summary by Tuplin 1991a: 256–59.

7. From Cyrus to Cambyses

Last campaign and death of Cyrus: Francfort 1985 (who thinks that this was the first and only expedition of Cyrus in these regions); on the differing oral versions of the death of Cyrus, cf. Sancisi-Weerdenburg 1985; "apanage" of Bardiya: Briant 1984b: 75–76 and 1985b: 55–56; the extent of this government is described differently by Xenophon (*Cyr.* VIII.7.11: "satrap of the Medes, the Armenians, and the Cadusians") and Ctesias (*Persika* §8: "Bactrians and territory of the Choramnians, Parthians, and Carmanians"); both traditions are difficult to interpret (we cannot see how Bardiya could have controlled both Bactriana and Carmania at the same time). From reading Ctesias, it would appear that Bardiya's center of power was located at Bactra. It is possible that after this date the satrap of Bactra had special strategic responsibilities from the Syr Darya to the Hindu Kush (Briant 1984b: 71–74). Portrait of Cambyses: Hoffman and Vorbichler 1989; Brown 1982; Munson 1991; balanced summary by Lloyd 1988. Greek authors and "Persian decadence": Briant 1989a; and Sancisi-Weerdenburg 1987a–b.

8. The Egyptian Campaign (525–522)

• *The Egypt of Amasis.*   Conquest of Cyprus by Amasis: in 539 according to Wallinga 1987: 60; Egypt under the Saites: Lloyd 1983; Naucratis and Greek and Carian mercenaries in Egypt: Austin 1970; cf. also Masson-Yoyotte 1988 and Ampolo-Bresciani 1988; on the American excavations at Naucratis, cf. Coulson-Leonard 1981, with the very important remarks of Yoyotte 1993: 634–44; trade in Greek wine in Saite Egypt: cf. Quaegebeur 1990: 259–71; Saite customs: Posener 1947; role of Polycrates and relations with Amasis: Labarbe 1984, Wallinga 1987: 60–62 and 1991, König 1990, Villatte 1990; on his coinage in relation to historical events, cf. Barron 1960: 35–39; reorganization of the navy under Necho II: Perdu 1986: 33; Chevereau 1985: 319–22; Lloyd 1972; Wallinga 1987: 55–66; Darnell 1992.

• *The Conquest of the Nile Valley and Its Approaches.*   Cambyses, creator of the royal Persian navy: Wallinga 1984, 1987, and 1993: 18–129; Cambyses, the king of the Arabs, and Gaza: Briant 1982b: 163–65; the vital importance of a fleet for seizing Memphis and Egypt is clearly illuminated by Thucydides' story about the Athenian expedition (I.104.2; 109.4; 110.1–4). Memphis: *LÄ* 4 (1980), s.v. "Memphis"; its direct links with the sea: Goyon 1971 and 1974: 136–45. Note also that, in an unusually confused story, Ctesias (*Persica* §9) states that the Egyptian campaign was conducted by Bagapates, who managed to defeat Pharaoh Amyrtaeus [*sic*] "thanks to the eunuch Kombaphis, powerful minister of the king of the Egyptians, who surrendered the bridges and betrayed all of Egypt's interests in order to become its governor"; we might think that behind the legend of Kombaphis lies a reference to the treason of Udjahorresnet, but the connection remains suspect; perhaps it is better to see it as a fictionalized reminiscence of the Phanes episode (Schwartz 1949: 72). Cambyses and Cyrene: Mitchell 1966 (Cambyses' designs on Carthage [Herodotus III.19] have been doubted by several historians, in my opinion with good reason). Saite precedents for Cambyses' campaign to the south: expedition of Psammetichus toward the Fayyum and Libya: Perdu 1986: 23–37; of Amasis toward Nubia in 529–528: Zauzich 1983: 423–25; Cambyses and Nubia: Desanges 1978: 229–33; see also Tuplin 1991a: 261–64 and Morkot 1991, especially p. 327 (very carefully: "The fall of Egypt to Persian rule may have led the Cushite kings to attempt an expansion into Lower Nubia. Beyond this, we can say little at present"); the article by Levrero 1992 adds nothing new; on Cambyses' expedition against Ammon, see also the texts and commentaries of Leclant 1930: 210–18, who says (p. 215) Cambyses had the intention "[of] occupying the strategic position of the oases in the west, Egypt's outer bulwark and gate to the continent of Africa." On the excavations at Dorginarti and the historical implications that can be drawn from them, see above all Heidorn 1991 and 1992 (I am very grateful to the author for sending me a copy of her dissertation), which include a detailed treatment of Saite policy (pp. 123–32) and of Cambyses' campaign (pp. 132–34); while remaining circumspect about the "Achaemenid" purpose of the fortress, the author concludes clearly: "There is little doubt that Level II at Dorginarti remained active into the fifth century" (p. 146); she also thinks that the orders must have come from Elephantine. Since most of the documentation (relatively inexplicit nonetheless; *P. Loeb* 1) comes from the reign of Darius (Cush in the royal lists), it might just as well be supposed that the initial attempts by Cambyses were followed up by Darius.

9. Cambyses and the Egyptian Traditions

• *The "Madness" of Cambyses.*   "Ozymandias" is nothing but the mythical representation of Ramses II (Drews 1973: 123–125); deportation of statues: cf. the remarks of Morschauser 1988: 216–19 and Devauchelle 1995; funerary rites of the Apis: Posener 1936: 30–47, Vercoutter 1962; disorder linked to the Persian invasion: at Saïs: Posener 1936: 167–69; at Elephantine: *DAE* 102

[*AP* 30–31], lines 12–13 (Briant 1988a: 146–47); Lüddeckens 1971. Booty seized in Egypt by Cambyses' soldiers: cf. the text translated by Dandamaev 1984b: 107–8, and see Tuplin 1991a: 260–61; burial by Cambyses of the Apis that died in 524: Posener 1936: 30–36, 171–75; according to Polyaenus (VII.11.7), upon his arrival in Egypt, Darius exhibited a great reverence for Apis: Atkinson (1956: 170–71) thinks that the episode actually refers to Cambyses: see summary by Tuplin 1991a: 265–66, who gives full weight to the chronological difficulties in Polyaenus's text; Cambyses' Egyptian seal: Hodjache-Berlev 1977.

• *Udjahorresnet and Cambyses.* Inscriptions of Udjahorresnet: Posener 1936: 1–29 (edition and annotated translation: 164–71); French translation only in Lalouette 1984: 187–91; historical commentaries: Lloyd 1982 and Briant 1988a: 158–66; Persian propaganda: Atkinson 1956; *damnatio memoriae* of Amasis: Meulenaere 1938 (doubts of Tuplin 1991a : 257–58); "cult" offered to Udjahorresnet one hundred sixty years later in Memphis: Bresciani 1985a; on the recently discovered tomb, cf. Verner 1989 and Bareš 1992.

• *Collaboration and Resistance*: the Persian kings and the insurgent Egyptian "dynasties": Briant 1988a: 149–50; donation stelas: Meeks 1979; on their disappearance as of 525, see ibid. 655: the author remarks that they reappear under Darius I; their "disappearance" in 525 is thus perhaps nothing but an automatic reflection of fragmentary documentation; whatever the case, the corpus in its current state of preservation seems to indicate a desire on the part of the Great Kings to control and limit the economic and financial power of the Egyptian sanctuaries; "decree of Cambyses": Spiegelberg 1914: 32–33; Bresciani 1989: 31–32; Bresciani (1983) thinks that the three temples cited are not the only three to have been exempted; the text simply mentions three temples of the region of Memphis; if this is true, the extent of the royal activity ought to be fundamentally reevaluated; fiscal pressure under Cambyses: Wallinga 1984; nomination of Aryandes: Herodotus IV.166; on the basis of a text published by Strassmaier (*Camb.* 344), Ebeling, *RlA* 1.454C §36 thinks that we have from this period mention of a "governor of Egypt" who, moreover, has a typically Babylonian name; but, as F. Joannès and A. Kuhrt have pointed out (personal communications), this represents a faulty reading (cf. Kuhrt 1992): it really is a governor (of Egypt?), but his name is not given (on this point at least, Stolper [personal communication of 31 May 1993] agrees with Kuhrt and Joannès). The events surrounding the death of Cambyses have given rise to two hypotheses: suicide or natural circumstances; it is clear that Herodotus's text repeats a series of motifs, such as the wound in the thigh (cf. Sancisi-Weerdenburg 1985: 467); but examination of the terminology used by Darius at Behistun and of Herodotus's text has decided in favor of the second: Walser 1983 (and Bresciani 1981b on the allusion to the event in the unclear text on the verso of the *Demotic chronicle*, as well as Malbran-Labat's remark 1994: 109 n. 103 on the formal analysis of the passage corresponding to *DB Bab.* §10).

There is a French translation of the text on the verso of the *Demotic Chronicle* in Devauchelle 1995: 74–75 (also Bresciani 1996)—the "decree of Cambyses." Otherwise, beginning with chronological observations (dates on the Apis stelas, methods of succession of Apises), the author comments (cf. also Devauchelle 1994b: 102–3) that doubts must remain as to the now standard theory (which I have included in the text) absolving Cambyses of all blame: "It is thus not possible to definitively exclude the hypothesis of the murder of a 'young' Apis before he succeeded the Apis who died in Year 5—doubtless before his enthronement, which would explain the fact that memory of him would have been erased—but it remains subject to caution" (p. 70). Starting from the same premises, Depuydt 1995a arrives independently at the same conclusion, in a still clearer form; according to him, there is no contradiction between Herodotus and the archaeological evidence; the murder of a young Apis thus remains perfectly imaginable: "In light of the evidence, I would personally rather believe that Cambyses is to be presumed guilty until proven innocent" (p. 126). If this hypothesis concerning the defections to the Persian conqueror, is accepted, I am somewhat less sorry about suggesting that the fiscal measures taken by Cambyses responded perhaps to the opposition of certain sanctuaries, and not the reverse: if the "murder" of the young Apis is accepted—whatever the narrative schema implicit in such an expression—we can without doubt think of the same chain of causation: Egyptian resistance followed by reprisals from Cambyses. We then recall another politico-religious situation well known throughout Achaemenid history: drastic punishment of peoples and sanctuaries guilty of resistance and rebellion; that is, a situation exactly the opposite of the one generally reconstructed on the basis of the statements of Udjahor-resnet. It is true that not all of the sanctuaries and their authorities necessarily reacted in the same way to the Persian conquest. This also means that this interpretation does not completely invalidate the earlier one, which is *also* based on an irrefutable official document, the stela of the Apis buried in Year 6 of Cambyses (on which, see the reservations of Devauchelle 1995: 70 and n. 15). We ought rather to think of two stages or two sides of royal policy defined and executed either simultaneously (in one sanctuary or another: e.g., Memphis vs. Saïs) or successively (the policy represented by the stela and the inscriptions of Udjahorresnet following a period of repression). Although all of the authors stress that doubts remain (the process of "putting to death" is obviously explained only by Herodotus), it would be a good idea to modify my text, to take into account new discussions on a question that had seemed fully closed (the historiographic analysis of Depuydt is quite interesting); nonetheless we must (at least!) avoid speaking of an "inevitable conclusion"! I remark finally that this interpretation adds fuel to the counterattack recently remounted by W. K. Pritchett against Fehling 1989 and more generally against all those (Kimball Armayor, S. West, etc.) whom Pritchett calls (collectively and rather misleadingly) *The Liar School of Herodotus* (Amsterdam, 1993).

Chapter 2
The Conquest and After: An Interim Summary

1. From Cyrus to Darius: Sources and Problems

• *Cyrus and the Persian Gulf.* An Achaemenid palace similar in structure to the residential palace at Pasargadae has been discovered at Borazjan, about 70 km northeast of the port of Bushire, on the road between central Persia and the Iranian coast of the Persian Gulf; it is no doubt an unfinished residence dating to the reign of Cyrus the Great (cf. Sarfaraz 1971, Stronach 1978: 293–94, Boucharlat and Salles 1981: 66–70). Pasargadae inscriptions: texts in Kent 1953: 116 and, more fully, Lecoq 1974a: 53–63 and Stronach 1978: 97–103, 136–37. I do not wish to enter into a discussion that exceeds my competence in epigraphy and linguistics; innumerable articles have been written about Behistun §70, trying to decide whether Darius was the creator of Old Persian cuneiform writing (see Lecoq 1974a for a history of the debate; most recently Herrenschmidt 1989b and Malbran-Labat 1992b); I tend to agree with Stronach (1990), essentially for reasons related to my understanding of the word *Achaemenid* (cf. p. 111 above). Ghirshman (1965) worked out the theory of a *damnatio memoriae* intentionally inflicted on Cyrus by Darius, but a number of documents make it clear that this theory is unsupportable: cf. Root 1979: 55, 62, 92 n. 147, 297–99 (cf. p. 900 below). Two related comments: (1) In a recent article, C. Herrenschmidt (1989b) suggests that the Old Persian inscription at Behistun was based on an earlier version taken from royal annals, similar to the *basilikai diphtherai*, which (according to Diodorus) would have been used or consulted by Ctesias. But for reasons already given elsewhere (*RTP* 497), I do not believe that any such annals existed (cf. also Sancisi-Weerdenburg 1987a: 38–39); at this period as well as later, the attested archives were administrative (cf. Ezra 6:1), not a written record of the deeds and accomplishments of the Great Kings. (2) Several Greek authors from Alexander's entourage claim to have copied inscriptions from the tomb of Cyrus, some of which were even supposedly written in Greek! But (pace Heinrichs 1987) we can grant no credibility to this kind of testimony, which must remain irrelevant to the discussion of the inscriptions actually found in Cyrus's capital (cf. *RTP* 389–90 and, most recently, Schmitt 1988).

2. Satraps and Satrapies

• *The Satraps of Cyrus and Cambyses.* See the recent review by Petit 1990: 13–97 (I will indicate in passing a few disagreements); also Lehmann-Haupt 1921. Xenophon (*Cyr.* VIII.6.7) gives a list of satraps Cyrus is supposed to have appointed: "Megabyzus in Arabia, Artabatas in Cappadocia, Artacamas in Greater Phrygia, Chrysantas in Lydia and Ionia, Adousios in Caria"; but for many reasons, this information is historically worthless: cf. Leuze 1935: 5–10. According to Petit (1990: 41–42, 182), there was no satrapy of Dascylium at the time of Mitrobates; but the arguments are debatable. Satrapy of Gubāru: Stolper 1989b; links with Media: ibid. 302. Subdivisions of satrapies: cf. Tuplin 1987b: 122; see also Stolper 1989b: 298 on Babylonia and Trans-Euphrates. Cilicia before the Persian conquest: Albright 1950, Houwinck ten Cate 1967: 17–30, and especially Bing 1969; more recently Davesne, Lemaire, and Lozachmeur 1987: 372–77; and Beaulieu 1989a: 22, 117, 127 (campaigns of Nabonidus); Erzen (1940: 98) thinks the military bases known at the end of the sixth century go back to the time of Cyrus, but the documentary proof is lacking. We have no information on the territorial control exercised by the *syennesis* or on the relations set up between the Persians and the Cilician coastal cities (on these, cf. Bing 1971). Note that in Cambyses' navy there was no Cilician detachment, in contrast to what is known from the time of Darius and Xerxes. On the importance (evident later) of the Cilician coast in Achaemenid military organization, cf. pp. 497–500. Lycia: according to Treuber (1887: 98), there was no Persian occupation at this time, but the proof is weak. For a long time, it has generally been thought that the dynasty known at Xanthus from the 480s resulted from the marriage of a Lycian woman and Cyrus's general, Harpagus the Mede (Bryce 1982: 331–32), mostly because of a reference to a Harpagus in the ancestry of a Xanthian dynast at the beginning of the fourth century (cf. Bousquet 1975 and 1992). According to Bryce (1983: 33–34; 1986: 100–101), it is even quite likely that this Xanthian dynasty was established by the Persians, who would thus have been able to control the country without recourse to direct administration. The "Irano-Lycian" origins of the Xanthian dynasty are strongly emphasized by Shahbazi (1975: 32–46), principally on the basis of an analysis of a later monument, dating to 480–470, traditionally called the monument of the Harpies, on which Persian influence is undeniable (cf. already Tristch 1942; pp. 503–505). I will note meanwhile that the hypothesis of descent from the Mede Harpagus has again been cast in doubt by A. G. Keen (1992b: 58), who thinks, first, that the Xanthian dynasty was installed by the Persians and that, then, under Cambyses assistance was provided for a change of dynast, to the benefit of Kheziga (Kossikas?). Caria: Hornblower 1982: 2–21.

• *The Duties of the Satrap.* Words for 'satrap' in various languages of the Empire: Schmitt 1976a; in Demotic: Smith 1988; for the Greek, see Tuplin 1987b: 114 and n. 22 (in Greek, the term is often used to designate a high person of noble origin: e.g., Polyaenus VII.4; Strabo XV.3.18; Aelian, *VH* XII.1, etc.). In Akkadian, the term *piḫatu* (like Greek *satrapēs*) does not necessarily refer to the satrap per se (Stolper 1987: 398–99, 1989b: 291; also Petit 1988b and 1990: 15–20). As for the transcription *aḫšadrapānu*, it can just as well be applied to a subordinate officer (Stolper 1985a: 58; 1987: 396; cf. Dandamaev 1992b); *bandaka*: cf. Herrenschmidt, *EncIr* III (1988), s.v.; and above, pp. 324–326. Military forces of the satraps: according to Tacitus (*Annals* III.63), the sanctuary of Persian Diana [Anāhita] at Hierocaesarea [Lydia] went back to the time of Cyrus. Indeed, in a general way, the establishment of sanctuaries dedicated to Persian divinities or divinities of Persian origin goes hand in hand with the founding of Persian settlements (*RTP* 457–62). On the garrisons, see especially the impressive collection of sources by Tuplin 1987c; garrison of Babylonia: Xenophon, *Cyr.* VII.5.33–34; "commander of the citadel" at Babylon (under Darius): Joannès 1982: 24–25; Egyptian garrisons: at Elephantine: Grelot 1972: 33–43; at Memphis: Herodotus III.91; cf. Segal 1983; other Egyptian garrisons: Tuplin 1987c: 185–86; on the site of Migdol, see the results of exploration and excavation by Oren 1985; Tabalus at Sardis: Herodotus I.153–54; citadel of Sardis: Mierse apud Hanfmann 1983b: 46–47; texts collected by Pedley 1972; garrisons of Asia Minor: Xenophon, *Cyr.* VII.4.1–11; cf. *RTP* 176–78; on the citadel of Kapišākaniš, where Vivāna won a victory over Vayahazdāta, see Bernard 1974 (Kapisa taken as the citadel of the capital of Arachosia, Arachôtoi); garrisons on the Iaxartes: *RTP* 244–45; Francfort 1988: 171; in northern Bactriana: Gardin 1995. On satrap/phrourarch relations, cf. the remarks of Tuplin 1987c: 168–71, 228–31; we return to this point more fully below (pp. 340–343). Satrapal secretaries: in the satrapy of Babylon (under Darius), see Stolper 1989b: 298–303; exchange of correspondence between Gubāru and an officer in Media: Stolper 1989b: 302.

3. Tributes and Gifts

• *Revenues and Fiscal Administration.* On the treasures of vanquished kings: Astyages: p. 33; Croesus: Herodotus I.153–54; cf. Xenophon, *Cyr.* VII.4.12–13 (inventory), VII.5.57 (delivery of the treasure of Sardis); Cambyses in Egypt: pp. 55–57; treasure of Babylon: Ezra 1:7. Various votive objects of Mesopotamian origin have been found in the Persepolis Treasury (Schmidt 1957: 57–65); these may have been derived from booty brought back by the conquerors. Mithradāta: his duties certainly correspond to those of Bagasarū, who was very likely his successor during the time of Darius (Dandamaev 1969c); according to Petit (1990: 41), "Oroites had complete authority over the finances of the territories he was in charge of"; but the text adduced for support (Diodorus X.16.4) says nothing about this. Treasuries, tributes, and gifts: cf. *RTP* 202–6; exemption of Ariaspi: Wiesehöfer 1989: 187.

• *Tribute-Paying Peoples and Gift-Giving Peoples.* The passage of Herodotus on gifts/tributes has long stimulated confusion and ingenuity among commentators; see recent commentaries in Tuplin 1987b: 140; Dandamaev 1989b: 177–78; Sancisi-Weerdenburg 1989b: 129–30; Wiesehöfer 1989: 186; also the relevant analyses of Eph'al 1982: 207–8; the discussion is taken up again on pp. 394–399 above. On exemptions: Wiesehöfer 1989; Near Eastern precedents: Zaccagnini 1989: 195–98; Liverani 1979 (difficulties of rendering the polymorphous reality of Egyptian terminology); also Descat 1989a: 83. Similarities between Achaemenid and Athenian tribute: Balcer 1989b; Wallinga 1989b; and the remarks of Kuhrt 1989a: 218.

• *From Cyrus to Darius. Kapēlos.* Wallinga 1984: 411; and Descat 1989a: 80–81 (but see now Descat 1984); fiscal oppression under Cambyses: Wallinga 1984 and 1987.

• *Tribute and Coinage.* The role of the satraps under Cyrus and Cambyses is deduced from the presentation by Polyaenus (VII.11.3). Problem of the "Croesids": Picard 1980: 66; Price 1989; Descat 1989; Stronach 1989; Carradice 1987; Alram 1993: 23–24; Le Rider 1994b; Descat 1994: 164–66. According to Wallinga (1984: 412–13), Cambyses began to monetize tribute, but I do not see how he arrives at this idea.

4. Continuities and Adaptations: The Case of Babylonia

• *Changes and Integration.* Government of Babylonia at the beginning of the reign of Cyrus, and Cambyses' titulature: San Nicolò 1941: 21–22, 51–64; Petschow 1988; also Kuhrt 1988b; Joannès 1990a: 176–77; Peat 1989; and Graziani 1983, 1989. Petit (1990: 54–55), on the contrary, thinks that Gubāru became satrap upon the conquest of Babylon in 539, but the documentation is incomplete: see Stolper 1989b. On relations between Nabonidus and his son, cf. Beaulieu 1989a: 185–97. Babylonian archives—private archives: cf. Joannès 1989a (p. 121); temple archives: Joannès 1982. References to regulations from the Neo-Babylonian period: Durand and Joannès 1989; Beaulieu 1989b (cf. 1989a: 111–27); Dandamaev 1984b: 500–501; and now more fully, Frame 1991. Retention of Babylonian administrators after the Persian conquest: see especially San Nicolò 1941. Sippar scribe: Dandamaev, *Orientalia* 55/4 (1986) 466. Širikti-Ninurta at Nippur: Joannès 1982: 3; cf. Stolper 1988b: 129.

• *Craftsmen's Charter.* Weisberg 1967 (cf. pp. 48–49, but the political context outlined by the author generates some reservations). Activities of the Egibi: Bogaert 1968; at Ecbatana and in Iran: Stolper 1990c; at Matezziš: Zadok 1976: 67–78; and Stolper 1984a: 306–8 (but on the identification of the king, see now Zawadski 1995a: Bardiya, not Vahyazdāta). Dandamaev (1972b: 259) cites a document of 538 (*Camb.* 143) that according to him shows that Itti-Marduk-balāṭu bought a slave in Elam that he resold at Opis on the Tigris; but this interpretation is based on a reading that has been questioned by Greenfield (1991: 183): the wrist of the slave in question bears an inscription "in Akkadian and Aramaic" (not Elamite, as Dandamaev [1984b: 230–31] claims).

• *Temple Lands and Royal Administration.* Fields and orchards of the Eanna: Cocquerillat 1968: 14–36; Joannès 1982: 115–260; Frame 1991. Administration of the temple and its properties: San Nicolò 1941: 24 (*qīpu*), 26 (*šatammu*), 29–30 ("royal commissioner . . ."); on the hierarchical relations between the royal commissioner and the *šatammu*, see Saggs 1959; Joannès 1982: 131–36; Garelli 1974: 159–61; and, more recently, Frame 1991: 69–79. Role of the *mār banê* and the assembly (*puḫru*): Dandamaev 1981. *Ferme Générale*: Cocquerillat 1968; Joannès 1982: 126ff. (quotation, p. 126); also Van Driel, *JEOL* 30 (1987–88) 61–64. Nabonidus's policy: Kuhrt 1990c: 146–50; Frame 1991. On all these problems, consult MacGinnis 1994 and especially 1995, on the administration of the sanctuary of the Ebabbar of Sippar during this period.

• *The Fiscal Obligations of the Babylonian Temples.* See especially Dandamaev 1966; also idem 1994a; and Tuplin 1987b: 150–51. Problems of the tithe: cf. Dandamaev 1967 and Giovinazzo 1989a. Deliveries to the palace: San Nicolò 1949; Dandamaev 1984a, 1989b: 363 (text in translation) and most recently 1992b: 119–22; but MacGinnis (1994 and 1995: 185–86) shows quite clearly that, even under Darius, the royal administration sent important offerings to the Babylonian temples. Guardpost archers: Joannès 1989a: 179–91; corvées: Joannès 1989a: 157–59 (temple); Dandamaev 1984b: 250–51 and 315–26 (private); canal digging and maintenance: Joannès 1982: 193–201.

• *The Justice of Gubāru.* Letter from Gubāru to Ardīya: Cocquerillat 1968: 73; Gubāru's order regarding canal-digging: ibid. 100; cf. also Giovinazzo 1983 (many texts in translation); and Dandamaev 1992a: 74–80. Gubāru's intervention between the Eanna and Uruk: Saggs 1959: 35 and Dandamaev 1984b: 518–19 (text in translation). The Gimillu affair: San Nicolò 1933a; Olmstead 1948: 72–73; Cocquerillat 1968: 102–3; Dandamaev 1984b: 533–37. Note that a "canal of Gubāru" is known from a tablet of Cambyses' time and another dated to Xerxes: Joannès 1982: 325–26; Van Driel, *JESHO* 32, 205–6; should it be compared with the passage where Pliny (VI.30.120) mentions the "prefect" Gobares, to whom he attributes major hydraulic works in Babylon? Or is this Gobares the Gubāru known in a comparable administrative situation in the time of Darius II? Cf. chap. 16/10, research notes, below.

• *Administration of Land.* In general: Dandamaev 1967. Babylonian paradises: Dandamaev 1984a; Gubāru's estates: text in translation in Dandamaev 1979: 101–2, but perhaps this actually deals with lands allotted to communities settled in Babylon (Van Driel 1989: 205–6); Gubāru's canal is known from later texts (Joannès 1982: 326). Other Iranians' estates near Nippur: Zadok 1977: 93; origins and development of the *ḫaṭru* system under Cyrus and Cambyses: see summaries and discussions in Dandamaev 1967, 1983, and 1989a: 147–51; Kuhrt 1988b: 128–29; Stolper 1989c; Van Driel 1989: 205–8; Zaccagnini 1989: 203–8 (precedents; on this point cf. also Stolper 1985a: 98 n. 113 and 71 n. 6). Lands in Nippur: Stolper 1988b: 140–41. Reverting to an interpretation first presented in 1967, Dandamaev recently reaffirmed (1989b: 150) that the *ḫaṭru* system began to break down during the reigns of Cambyses and Darius; but this is an interpretation that has neither documentary weight nor logical probability in its favor. See the reflections of Stolper 1989c (esp. pp. 150–52) and above, pp. 597–599; *bīt qašti* in the Babylonian version of Behistun: p. 104 above.

5. From Bactra to Sardis

• *Bactrian Polity and Achaemenid Power.* On the Persian impact in Central Asia, cf. summary of the topic and discussions in Briant 1984b and, since then, reaffirmation of the archaeologists' position in Gardin 1986 and Lyonnet 1990, 1994; cf. also Vogelsang 1992; the discussion will be taken up again in chap. 16/15 below.

• *Central Authority and Cultural Polycentrism.* Briant 1987c and 1988a. Imperial Aramaic: e.g., Delaunay 1985; Cambyses' navy: Wallinga 1984 and 1993; Near Eastern legacy and Achaemenid planning at Pasargadae and Persepolis: cf. especially Nylander 1970 and Root 1979; also Nylander 1991 (diffusion of the toothed chisel in Achaemenid construction) and Stronach 1978: 43 (Cyrus's tomb). Pasargadae gardens: Stronach 1989a.

• *Text and Image.* Greek authors and regions of the Iranian Plateau: Briant 1984b: 63–68.

6. Persians and Conquered Populations

• *Military Conquest and Ideological Strategy.* Number of Persians: Xenophon (*Cyr.* I.2.15) states that "the Persians, it is said, number about 120,000"; but I cannot see what this estimate is based on; and does it refer exclusively to adults, or to the whole population? In any case, the estimate is obviously very rough. Interpretation of the archaeological data led W. Sumner (1986: 11–12) to estimate "the sedentary Achaemenid population" in Fārs as 43,600. On the flourishing demographics of the great Persian families, cf. Briant 1987c: 21–22. The religious policy of the Achaemenids has often been scrutinized: Duchesne-Guillemin 1967–68; Gnoli 1974; Dandamaev 1975c; Tozzi 1978a; Briant 1986a, 1987c, and 1988a; Firpo 1987; Heinz 1987; see the discussions of the policy adopted by Cyrus and Cambyses (above) and the analyses sited in their particular historical contexts (below). Resistance to the conquest: pp. 59–61 above. Defection of Lydian aristocrats: Myrsos, son of Gyges: Herodotus III.122 and V.121; cf. (in Xerxes' time) the case of Pythius of Celaenae, son of Atys, perhaps a descendant of Croesus (Herodotus VII.27); companion of Psammetichus: Herodotus III.14 (Briant 1989b: 42).

• *The Political Personnel of Cyrus and Cambyses.* Babylonia: cf. Kümmel 1979 and Zawadski 1990; cf. also Weisberg, *JAOS* 104/4 (1984) 739–43 (review of Kümmel 1979). Persians and Egyptians in Egypt: Briant 1988a: 160–64; cf. de Meulenaere 1987 and 1989. "Petition" of Peteisis: Griffith 1909. Medes in the Empire: Mazares and Harpagus: Herodotus I.156 (*Mēdos*), 162 (*genos . . . Mēdos*); Takhmaspada: *DB* §82 (*Mada*). Datis, also cited in a Persepolis tablet (Lewis 1980), is regularly called "Datis the Mede" (without patronym) by Herodotus (VI.94, 199 etc.); but is this really an ethnonym or simply a surname (Suidas, s.v., has Datis *Persēs*)? Marriage of Cyrus and Amytis, daughter of Astyages and widow of Spitamas: Ctesias, *Persica* §2, who wrongly makes her (ibid. 10) the mother of Cambyses and Bardiya; he also states (§8) that Cambyses had made the two sons of Spitamas and Amytis satraps before his death: Spitaces supposedly "satrap of the Derbices" and Megabernes "satrap of the Barcaeans"; but this version (Median in origin) is extremely doubtful. Place of Media in later royal lists: Vogelsang 1986: 131–35; Media in the tale of Darius and the problems it poses, cf. Dandamaev 1989a: 95–99; satrap of Media: Stolper 1989a: 302. In the course of his work, Ctesias gives the names of royal favorites, often eunuchs (but see pp. 274–277): the eunuch Petesacas "who enjoyed the full confidence of Cyrus" (*Persica* §§5–6) and, after the death of Petesacas, Bagapates (also a eunuch), who, with Artasyras and the eunuchs Izabates and Aspadates, was among the "most influential men around Cambyses" (§9). All of the personal names sound "Iranian"; on a single occasion Ctesias gives an ethnic background: he calls Artasyras a Hyrcanian (cf. also Aelian, *VH* VI.14). Are we to think that, as Xenophon indicates several times in the *Cyropedia*, the Hyrcanians held a special place near the Great King? Why? But here as elsewhere the analysis of personal names is troublesome, for the Iranian onomasticon we have is largely undifferentiated, so that in the absence of an ethnonym it is difficult to identify a Mede, a Bactrian, or a Persian. In some texts, even the mention of an ethnic background does not provide an absolute guarantee (cf. Briant 1984b: 89–91). Perhaps Pharnaces/Parnaka should also be counted among the Achaemenids serving under Cyrus and Cambyses; he was the chief administrative official at Persepolis, according to Elamite tablets from the reign of Darius I and in all probability was the son of Arsames and thus the uncle of Darius (cf. Hallock 1972: 11–14); according to Dandamaev (1972c: 19 n. 81), Pharnaces/Parnaka is found on a Babylonian tablet from 528 (*YOS* 7.128), as a subordinate to the satrap Gubāru (repeated in Dandamaev 1992a: 108–9; confirmed to me by F. Joannès [personal communication]).

• *Contacts and Acculturation.* Personal names at Matezziš: Zadok 1976: 73. Babylonian concubines: Ctesias §14 (Smerdis/Bardiya: but Ctesias's chronological references are always subject to caution). Polycrates: cf. Athenaeus XII.515e, 540; Vilatte (1990) exclusively insists on the Greek aspect of Polycrates' power; see Briant 1991b: 235 n. 45. On the paradise: cf. Briant 230–36 with references. Tombs of Sardis and Taš-Kule: Ratté 1992 and Cahill 1988; tomb of Kizilbel: Mellink 1979.

7. The Seats of Power

• *The Old Royal Residences.* On Herodotus's description of Ecbatana, see the remarks of Gnoli 1974: 118 (the colors indicate Babylonian influence, which implies that Herodotus himself received the tradition from Babylonian informants). Ecbatana as a royal residence: cf. the Babylonian tablets studied by Stolper 1990c (see also Chevalier 1989 on the results of early explorations, and Brodersen 1991 on the very late traditions regarding hypothetical structures of Cyrus at Ecbatana). On Ecbatana in the time of Cyrus, see also the reflections of Tuplin 1994: 253–54. Royal residences and paradises in Babylonia: Dandamaev 1984a. Xenophon's point of view: to be compared with the reasons he gives for the "central" position of Athens in *Revenus* I.3–8. On Greek notions of the "periphery" in the Achaemenid Empire, cf. Briant 1984a: 64–66. Moves of the Achaemenid court: chap. 5/4, pp. 183ff. Beginning of construction at Susa: Miroschedji 1982 and

1985; place of Susa before Darius: according to Herodotus (III.70), Smerdis was assassinated in the palace at Susa, but this information is worthless, for Darius himself states specifically that the drama played out in Media (cf. Briant 1993b).

• *Palace and Gardens of Pasargadae.* In general, see above all Stronach's 1978 monograph; also Treidler 1962 (especially useful for the critical presentation of textual sources on the city). Date of Palace P: opposing points of view expressed (prudently) by Stronach 1978: 95–106 (Darius) and Root 1979: 49–58 (end of Cyrus's reign), respectively; see also discussion by Farkas 1974: 7ff. In a general way, the date of construction of Pasargadae has not been securely placed within Cyrus's reign; archaeological evidence of the presence of Lydian craftsman leads us to adopt a date after 546 (conquest of Sardis): cf. Nylander 1970: 53–70, 101–2, 126–28; Stronach 1978: 21–23. Alexander at Pasargadae: *RTP* 386–92. Gardens of Pasargadae: Stronach 1977: 108–12, and 1989a. Babylonian paradises: Dandamaev 1984a.

• *The Beginnings of Persepolis.* Tilia 1972: 73–91; Sumner 1986; Stolper 1984a: 306–9; Stronach 1978: 302–4 (Takht-i Rustam); Koch 1990: 25–30. Lydian and Greek workers at Pasargadae: Nylander 1970; on the process, cf. Diodorus I.46 (referring to Cambyses' pillaging of the Egyptian temples): "He carried off with him Egyptian artists to build the royal palaces that are so famous at Persepolis, Susa, and in Media." We may add that deportation of specialist craftsmen is already attested in the Neo-Assyrian and Neo-Babylonian periods (Oded 1979: 54–59; Weidner 1939). Ration system: cf. Arrian, *Anab.* VI.29.7 (whose information agrees best with the specifics in the Persepolis tablets: p. 95).

• *Persian Society and Empire.* Persian agro-pastoral populations in the Achaemenid period: Briant 1976, and 1982b: 57–112. Babylonian tablets: Zadok 1976: 67–78 (but on the date—Bardiya, not Vahyazdāta—see Zawadski 1995a); *tamkāru*: Dandamaev 1971 and 1989b: 219; Greek texts on the absence of markets among the Persians: Strabo XV.3.19, Aelian, *VH* X.14; Herodotus I.153. In a discussion of the education of young Persian aristocrats Xenophon states that merchants (*agoraioi*) existed in Persia but that the markets themselves were "relegated to some other spot, so that the hurly-burly would not disturb the concentration of those who were being instructed" (*Cyr.* I.2–3: cf. also Stolper 1988b: 142–43).

8. Royalty and Authority

• *Royal Representations and Titles at Pasargadae.* Sculptures of Palace P: Nylander 1970: 124–38 (time of Cyrus); Stronach 1978: 95–97 (about 510); "Winged genius": Barnett 1969; Nylander 1970: 126; Mallowan 1972: 1–3; Stronach 1978: 47–50; Root 1979: 47–49 and 300–303; seal of Cyrus of Anšan: Miroschedji 1985: 285–87; Stève 1986; Bollweg 1988; Garrison 1992: 3–7. King of Anšan: Miroschedji 1985: 296–300. Bardiya's titulature in the Babylonian version: Schmitt 1980: 110.

• *Royal Protocol.* The thesis that the privileges accorded to the Seven existed from the time of Cambyses is offered by (e.g.) Dandamaev 1989a: 101–2, but see above, pp. 131–132. Although incomplete, a Pasargadae relief (fig. 5, p. 89) indisputably shows an official procession (cf. Stronach 1978: 66ff.; Root 1979: 51–58), which could be taken to indicate a system of court protocol at the time of Cyrus (if it dates to Cyrus and not Darius).

• *From One King to the Next.* See Briant 1991a and below, chaps. 13/2 and 17/1.

9. The King and the Gods

• *Persian Religion and Iranian Traditions.* Interpretation of the archaeological evidence: cf. Boyce 1982: 50–61; measured viewpoint in Boucharlat 1984: 124–26; cf. also Stronach 1984 and 1985a. Zendan-i Sulaiman and "Zoroastrian Kaʿaba": cf. Sancisi-Weerdenburg 1982, as well as the remarks of Bernard 1974b: 279–84. Zoroaster in Classical texts: Bidez-Cumont 1938; and recently Kingsley 1995. Composition and date of the books of the Avesta: Kellens 1988a–b and 1991a–b; let us note here an interesting cylinder seal from the fourth century B.C. with the name Zarathustriš and a typically Persian cultic scene: two *magi* sacrificing to the Fire (Bordreuil 1986a: 104 and 1992: 152; fig. 35b, p. 249 below). Cyrus and Mithra: Duchesne-Guillemin 1974; Herrenschmidt 1990a (with caution). Replacement of Mithra by Ahura-Mazda as "great god" as a result of the Mazdian reform: Kellens 1976b: 127–31. Cyrus in Zoroastrian context: Boyce 1988.

• *The Tomb of Cyrus and Persian Funerary Practices.* "Stripping" of corpses and funerary customs: Widengren 1968: 156–58; Grenet 1984: 31–42; cf. also Bernard 1985a: 32 n. 1 (texts from the start of the Hellenistic period) and Jacobs 1992. Note that a Greek-Aramaic inscription from Limyra in Lycia, carved on the façade of a rock-cut tomb in the name of Artimas and his family, refers to the tomb (Greek *taphos*) with the Iranian word *astōdana* (cf. Lipiński 1975: 162–71). This is the oldest attestation of an "Avestan" word that basically means 'receptacle for bones, ossuary'. In a somewhat speculative discussion of Artimas and his family, Shahbazi (1975: 125–34; followed by Boyce 1982: 210–11) notes on the one hand that the word can also mean 'tomb' and on the other that it refers here to an ossuary. He thinks that the evidence (both literary and archaeological) for burial refers rather "to exceptional circumstances, that is, after a campaign" (p. 126), and he highlights the Herodotus passage I cite in the text. He also takes into account the dimensions of funerary cists, which he says make it impossible for Artimas to have been buried. If so (but after a visit to the site I am not entirely convinced), it would make sense to reverse his hypothesis and to claim that the case of Artimas is the exception, since the attestations of the other custom are numerous and definitive (cf. also Grenet 1984: 108 n. 20). On funerary practices, cf. also the case of Clearchus analyzed above, pp. 238–239. Susa tomb: de Morgan 1905 (on the date, see most recently J.-G. Elayi 1992a). Deve Hüyük cemetery: cf. Moorey 1975 and 1980, who also refers to other Achaemenid-period cemeteries; at Persepolis: Schmidt 1957: 115–23.

• *The Sacrifices around the Tomb of Cyrus.* Strabo (XV.3.17) also refers to sacrifices and *magi*, but he erroneously states that horses were included in the *magi*'s rations. Pliny (VI.29.116) seems to refer to the 'small structure' (*oikēma smikron*) reserved for the *magi* as 'Phrasargis, citadel' (*castellum*), where the tomb proper was located. Persepolis tablets: cf. Hallock 1969 = PF 336–77 and 2029–30 (Category E); 741–74 and 2031 (Category K1). On these texts, cf. Koch 1977 and 1987a. Sheep rations: compare them with what was received by Parnaka, the highest administrator of the Persepolis region at the time of Darius: 2 sheep a day, as well as 90 measures of wine and 180 of flour (Hallock 1972: 11). Horse sacrifices: cf. Widengren 1968 (index, p. 419); Armenian horses: see also Xenophon, *Anab.* IV.5.24 and 35 (horse dedicated to the Sun). *Magi*: cf. Benveniste 1938; Clemen 1928; Bickerman and Tadmor 1978; Gnoli 1989; the Classical texts are collected in Bidez and Cumont 1938. We will return to the *magi* several times in different contexts (cf. the index). Cambyses' tomb: Ctesias (§13) states that the mortal remains of the king were returned to Persia; it has long been thought that Cambyses was buried in the (unfinished) monument near Persepolis called Takht-i Rustam, on account of its great resemblance to Cyrus's tomb: cf. Stronach 1978: 302–4 (with caution).

10. Bardiya's Usurpation (522)

• *Bibliography.* The bibliography on this topic is huge. See especially Sancisi-Weerdenburg 1980: 84–110; Dandamaev 1976 and 1989a: 83–113; Wiesehöfer 1978; Balcer 1987, where complete prior bibliography will be found (on Bardiya in Babylonia, cf. the recent publication by Graziani 1991, with the critical remarks of Jursa 1993). I will avoid systematically listing my agreements and disagreements with this or that author, in order not to bloat the discussion excessively and uselessly. I reject the "Median" explanation of the revolt: even though Darius calls Gaumata/Bardiya simply "*magus*" (DB §11), Herodotus (III.65, 73) follows some of his informants in stating that Gaumata/Bardiya is a Median *magus* and that Cambyses exhorted the Persian nobles "not to tolerate hegemony passing anew to the Medes" (§65). Several authors have nevertheless denied any truly Median character to the revolt (cf. Dandamaev 1976: 133ff. and Wiesehöfer 115ff.). We may note that the theory of a Median revolt makes sense only if Gaumata is exactly what Darius says! It is true, as Schmitt (1980: 111) emphasizes, that in the Babylonian version (§10) Gaumata is explicitly called a Mede; but in the same version Bardiya is presented as "Barziya, the son of Cyrus, king of Persia" (Schmitt 1980: 111). Given the Persian origin of Bardiya, the revolt does not necessarily imply a desire for restoration of Median power: Herodotus seems to have confused this situation with the importance of the Median revolt of 522–521, after the death of Gaumata/Bardiya. He probably also fell victim to an oral version that was circulating in his time. On the problem of "Median *magi*," cf. the (somewhat overly-subtle, it seems to me) interpretations of Bickermann, in Bickermann and Tadmor 1978.

• *The Reputation of Cambyses.* Burying people alive: a religious rite seems to figure in Herodotus VII.114, since it is presented as an offering to a subterranean deity. It is difficult to say what divinity is concerned. Xenophon mentions sacrificial victims (animals) with throats cut in honor of Earth (*Cyr.* VIII.3.24); the Earth cult is also mentioned by Herodotus (I.131) and Strabo (XV.3.13): but this does not seem to allude directly to the subterranean world. Several Greek authors (Aristotle, Plutarch) identify their Hades with Ahriman. In the *Gāthās*, Ahra Mainyu is opposed to Ormazd (Ahura-Mazda) in every regard. He is a liar (*drugvant*) where Ahura-Mazda is master of truth; he symbolizes darkness and evil, while the other blossoms in light and good. It is because of their characteristics that in Plutarch the kings invoke Oromazes (Ahura-Mazda) (*Art.* 29.12, *Alex.* 30.5) or Areimanios (*Them.* 28.6). Opposing Boyce (1982: 157), who thinks that Herodotus (VII.114) alludes to Yama, "king of the dead," Gnoli (1980: 151 n. 164) thinks he refers to Areimanios (following Bidez and Cumont 1938: 1.9 n. 3). On the infernal deities, see also Bivar (1975a: 60–63), who proposes that the motif of the lion and his prey (bull, stag)—present at Persepolis and very widely represented on stamp seals and coins—symbolizes the gods of death in different cultures, but the argument is not fully convincing. On Ahriman in the Classical sources and the Iranian texts, cf. Rapp 1865: 77–89; Duchesne-Guillemin 1953. Whatever may be the case, we are not required to conclude that human sacrifice, which was also known among the Scythians in connection with royal funerals (IV.71–72), was a regular practice among the Persians for exclusively religious motives. Amestris buried the physician Apollonides alive (Ctesias §42); Parysatis gave the same treatment to several members of the family of Teritouchmes, son of Hydarnes (§45). These two cases obviously involve torture, and this is doubtless also true of the episode concerning Cambyses in Egypt in Herodotus (III.35).

• *Smerdis, Tanyoxarces, Mergis, Mardos.* The name Tanyoxarces (Ctesias) refers to the physical and warlike characteristics of its bearer (Wiesehöfer 1978: 47; Dandamaev 1989a: 85 n. 5).

• *Cambyses and Bardiya.* In addition to Herodotus, see Ctesias (*Persica* §12): "Cambyses offers a sacrifice, but the blood does not flow from the slaughtered victims; he is distressed. Now Roxane bears him a headless baby; his distress increases. The *magi* interpret the signs; he will leave no successor to the throne." Wives of Smerdis: he married women who had previously been married to Cambyses—Atossa, daughter of Cyrus; and Phaidime, daughter of Otanes (Herodotus III.88).

• *Bardiya and the Persian Aristocracy.* On the Babylonian version of Behistun, cf. von Voigtlander 1978: 17, who believes that the word *ūqu* when construed as a plural refers specifically to the army. Nonetheless, I note that, even though she refers (1978: 109 n. 101) to Voigtlander's interpretation without apparent disagreement, Malbran-Labat (1994: 110, 163–64) translates 'the people'; likewise for the Elamite *taššup*, translated 'the people' by Grillot-Susini, Herrenschmidt, and Malbran-Labat 1993: 44, even though they take it as 'troops, army' in many other unambiguous passages in DB Babylonian and Elamite. The word *taššup* is translated 'army' once by Hallock (PF 200), more often 'people' (e.g., PF 1600), without clearly stating the reasons for the choice; the context is exactly the same in PF 200 and PF 1600. Nor am I convinced by Dandamaev's 1972c: 24 commentaries on the meaning of *taššup*/troops in PF 113, 1602; I do not see how, given the available materials, he can write: "From all the evidence, this concerns troops." I mention in passing that in an entirely different context, exactly the same discussion has gone on about the meaning of Greek *plēthos* and Latin *populus*, when ancient authors refer to gatherings of what is customarily called the "Macedonian assembly." Does this refer to 'people', to the 'army', or even to 'armed people' (cf. Briant 1973: 291–92, 303–7)? On the word *agru*, cf. Stolper (1985a: 57), who identifies it with *kurtaš*. Dandamaev (1989a: 110) thinks that the formulation of the Babylonian compilers is difficult to understand, but he offers no real alternative explanation (he thinks that Bardiya was supported by the lower class [see particularly 1976: 170–207, his analysis of DB §14] — an interpretation that is absolutely contradicted by the rest of his argument). On the other hand, Stolper (1985a: 154) poses a relationship between Bardiya's confiscation of land from nobles who had revolted and redistributing it to loyal supporters and the decision, reported by Herodotus III.67, to grant a three-year exemption from tribute and military levies; but in my opinion these are two completely distinct spheres of activity (Persian nobles/subject peoples). On the system of *dōreai* and the *ḫaṭru*, cf. in particular Stolper 1985a: 52–69, 90–91, 100–103 and Briant 1985b (but it must be noted, as pointed out by Stolper, that the word itself is not attested in this meaning until the time of Artaxerxes I? Darius II?, in the Murašū archives: cf. below, chap. 14). It is likely that the Babylonian version refers specifically to the Babylonian situation (von Voigtlander 1978: 17), but it cannot be excluded that the same kind of measures were taken for the *dōreai* located in other regions of the Empire. Malbran-Labat's (1994: 110, 134) translation of é *qašātu* as 'domaines [estates]' seems strange to me; in any case, remarkably imprecise.

• *Bardiya and Tribute from the Empire.*   Cf., e.g., Dandamaev 1976: 134–35 and Wiesehöfer 1989: 184.

Chapter 3
Trouble, Secession, and Rebuilding (522–518)

1. Darius Comes to Power (Summer–Autumn 522)

• *General Bibliography.* Dandamaev 1976 and 1989a: 103–13; Gschnitzer 1977; Wiesehöfer 1978; Herrenschmidt 1982; Balcer 1987.

• *The Conspiracy of the Seven: Darius and Herodotus.* On the different versions used by Herodotus, see Gschnitzer 1977. The names of the conspirators are given very inaccurately by Ctesias §14: Onophas [Otanes], Idernes [Hydarnes], Norondobates, Mardonius [likely confusion with his father, Gobryas], Barisses, Artaphernes [Intaphernes?], Darius. Gobryas's role in the murder of Smerdis is also illuminated by Justin (I.9.22–23), who elsewhere (9.14–18) also makes Otanes (Hostanes) the inspiration and instigator of the conspiracy. Aeschylus (*Persians* 776–77) makes "Artaphernes" (Intaphernes?) the conqueror of the *magus*—helped "by several friends who came together for this purpose." Obviously there were many family versions that were embellished and subsequently circulated among the Greeks. For introductions to the conspirators: Dandamaev 1976: 159–61; Wiesehöfer 1978: 168–74. Darius gives not only the name and ethnic group of the six nobles (they are all called Persians) but also their patronymic; these details are not found in Herodotus, except for Otanes. But where Darius and Herodotus disagree about Otanes, it is obviously Darius who must be followed, for he and his counselors knew Otanes' ancestry perfectly well. When Herodotus makes him the son of Pharnaspes elsewhere (III.68), he has obviously become confused—understandably so, since the risk of homonymy in the case of Otanes was considerable (cf. the list compiled by Legrand, *Herodote: Index analytique*, pp. 60–61).

Aspathines and Aspacānā: *DNd*: "Aspacānā, *vaçabara*, bears the battleaxe of Darius the King" (the meaning of *vaçabara* is disputed ['chamberlain' or 'bow-bearer']: see Hinz 1973: 57–59; Schmitt 1980: 125; also Gschnitzer 1977: 20, 25). Aspathines may be the son of Prexaspes, who, Herodotus says (III.74–75), denounced the fraud of the *magus* (see sources in Dandamaev 1976: 158 n. 666). Gobryas (not to be confused with Gubāru I or Gubāru II): the Babylonian version of DB (§54) gives his complete family status: "Gubāru, son of Marduniya, Persian, Padišumariš [Pastichorian]" (Schmitt 1980: 125). On the term *Pastichorian*, see also Briant 1984a: 108 and 1990a: 83–84. The term *prōtoi*: Briant 1990a: 74–75 and Calmeyer 1991b; cf. Justin I.9.18: *optimates Persarum*, and I.10.1: *principes*; Ctesias §14: *episēmoi*. Cf. also Stolper 1993: 10–11 on Bab. *parastāmu.*

• *The Problem of Power.* The bibliography on the "constitutional debate" is considerable (cf. Gschnitzer 1977: 30–40; Wiesehöfer 1978: 203–5). Many authors think that Herodotus (who states that he received his information from Persian sources) has passed on a Persian reality in Greek form (cf. Dandamaev 1989a: 106). This interpretation is itself closely linked to the assumption that Bardiya was a bitter enemy of the nobility. It is also based on the theory of the existence of an Assembly of nobles, to whose decrees even the kings had to submit. For various reasons, this "feudal" theory seems to me unsustainable. On the structure of Herodotus's story of Oebares' ruse, see Köhnken 1990. Dumézil (1984) insists that there are Indian parallels, but the parallel of King Rusa of Urartu seems much more apposite (cf. Wiesehöfer 1978: 205 n. 2). We may note in passing that the sun motif is also found in Justin XVIII.3.8–14 (arrival of Strato of Tyre).

• *The "Rights" of Darius.* The various "genealogical" hypotheses are conveniently presented by Miroschedji (1985: 280–83, with references to the previous literature). On the founder legend repeated by Aelian, cf. Binder 1964: 45–46. The "premonitory" dream that Cyrus reported to Hystaspes, the father of Darius, perhaps belongs to this tradition: "I saw your eldest son with wings on his shoulders, and one overshadowed Asia, the other Europe" (I.209). On the relationship between the eagle and royal power, cf. Harmatta 1979 and Nylander 1983: 22–27. On the Pasargadae inscriptions, cf. most recently the convincing demonstration of Stronach (1990). The mounting doubts explain why Mayrhofer (1975: 12–13) has suggested new sigla (*DMa, DMb, DMc*) for the inscriptions traditionally ascribed to Cyrus (*CMa, CMb, CMc* in Kent).

• *The Primacy of Darius.* Aeschylus uses the name *Artaphernes* for the man who, "helped by several friends who came together for this purpose," put an end to the reign of Mardos (*Persians* 775–77). It is nearly unanimously postulated that *Artaphernes* is a mistake for *Intaphernes*, and this is seen as further proof of the false character of Darius's version. This lie might be considered a further indication of Darius's secondary role in the conspiracy and of the deeply aristocratic nature of the elimination of Smerdis (see particularly Dandamaev 1976: 162, who recalls that Hellanikos calls him Daphernes; along the same lines, Wiesehöfer 1978: 205–6). Ctesias (§14) also includes Artaphernes in an admittedly imprecise list, and he seems to have confused him with Intaphernes. But if we recognize that Darius (like the other conspirators) was accompanied by men of his House, we can also hypothesize that the name in Aeschylus in fact identifies one of Darius's brothers who is well known elsewhere (this is also the position of Balcer 1987: 115 and 159 n. 12, without discussion).

The execution of Smerdis might be compared with what the ancient authors say of the murder of Xerxes and subsequent episodes (cf. particularly Ctesias §30, *makhē*) and especially with the veritable civil war that led to the accession of Darius II (see chap. 16/6). On the position of Darius, we will not go so far as to propose (pace Balcer 1987: 100) that Darius himself killed Cambyses or that he gave the job to a friend; as has now been established with certainty, Cambyses died of natural causes (cf. Walser 1983).

• *The Elimination of Bardiya.* For the victory over Gaumata in the Behistun inscription, cf. Vogelsang 1986: 127–31.

• *A Remark on Method.* On the symbolism of the numbers, cf., for example, Root 1979: 201 n. 55. It would be excessive to pile up examples of the number 7 in conspiracies (e.g., Appian, *Mith.* 2.9). On the actual formation of the conspiracy of 522, a very similar schema will be found in Arrian's tale (IV.13.3–4) of the conspiracy of the pages (cf. also Quintus Curtius VIII.6.9).

2. Revolts and Reconquests (522–518)

• *The Liar-Kings.* Herodotus (III.150–59) records a Babylonian revolt, which he places at the beginning of the reign of Darius while distinguishing it (§150) from the "*magus*" period and presenting the final fall of Babylon as the "second" (§159), that is, after the conquest of Cyrus in 539. Considered in a context furnished by Ctesias and some others, Herodotus's text poses problems that remain debated (cf. Balcer 1987: 125–30, Briant 1992a: 9–13). The Babylonian and Aramaic versions of DB have been published by Von Voigtlander (1978) and Greenfield and Porten (1982), respectively. The Persian version has been reedited by Schmitt (1991b), who is also responsible for fundamental studies comparing the different versions (1980 and 1990c). A French translation of the Elamite version has been prepared by Grillot, Herrenschmidt, and Malbran (cf. JA 1993; also Malbran-Labat 1994 [DB Bab.], and Porten and Yardeni 1993 [DB Aram.]).

On the chronology of the Babylonian revolts, see Parker and Dubberstein 1956: 15–16; Weisberg (1980: xvi–xxiii) sheds doubt on the existence of a second Nebuchadnezzar (on the chronology of Nebuchadnezzar III and IV, cf. Dandamaev 1993a and 1995a; Zawadski 1995b–c). Egypt: reasonable solution in Tuplin 1991a: 264–67 (followed here). Jerusalem: cf. Bickerman 1981 (propounds a revolt at the end of 521); doubts in Dandamaev 1989a: 127–28 (following Ackroyd). Bickerman's chronology is now strongly challenged by Kessler (1992), who thinks there is nothing in Haggai to justify postulating an anti-Persian movement in Judah.

"In a single year": the bibliography is considerable. Cf. the summary of the topic in Wiesehöfer 1978: 213–20; Bickerman and Tadmor 1978: 240–42 (Mesopotamian precedents); Nylander 1994;

Vogelsang (1986: 121–27, against Borger 1982) thinks that the order of liar-kings on the relief is not strictly chronological.

- *The Victories of Darius and His Lieutenants (522–521).*   Story of the events: Burn 1984: 96–103; Dandamaev 1989a: 114–31; Vogelsang 1992: 119–32. Cf. also Koch 1993a: 49–69.

- *The Victories of Darius: A Military Evaluation.*   On the figures, cf. Schmitt 1980: 108. The text of *DB* on the Armenian events presents many chronological and historical problems, which were recognized by Poebel 1937–38: 152–62 (and the publication of the other versions does not provide a solution). On Herodotus and the Median revolt, cf. also III.65 (speech of Cambyses) and 126. But Herodotus (who says nothing about the great revolts of 522–521) is very confused about Median affairs (cf. III.73).

- *The Political Aspect of the Revolts.*   Babylonian tablet dated to 19 Nisān, Year 1 of Barzia, king of the countries: Zadok (1976: 74–76) thinks this is Vahyazdāta, because the transaction took place at Matezziš, very close to the site of Persepolis. (On the tablets dated to Barzia, cf. now Graziani 1991, with the critical remarks of Jursa 1993; still more recently, Zawadski 1995a has cast doubt on Zadok's interpretation: the tablets actually date to the reign of Bardiya I). Popular participation in the revolts, cf., for example, Dandamaev 1989a: 119 (Media), 126 ("the revolt in Margiana was one of the important popular uprisings of antiquity"). Regarding Martiya: he might be an Elamite with a Persian name (Zadok 1976: 74). On Arkha, cf. Dandamaev 1989a: 122–23. Aryandes and the Egyptians: Briant 1988a: 141–42, and below, chap. 10/5: Darius and Aryandes.

- *Darius and Vahyazdāta.*   The social character of the Vahyazdāta revolt (supported by the peasants against the nobles): the theory is worked out at great length by Dandamaev 1976: 170–86. It should be emphasized that this presentation of Vahyazdāta's policy is closely linked (cf. p. 186) to an analysis of §14 of *DB*, to which (pp. 186–206) it is the prelude, and to the presentation of Darius as the head of an aristocratic restoration (206–14); cf. Briant 1993c: 407–8, 421–22.

- *The Rebellion of Oroetes.*   On Oroetes' refusal to do obeisance, I follow the persuasive hypothesis of Poebel 1937–38: 159–61.

3. The Aftermath of Victory: The Official Story

- *Crime and Punishment, Publicity and Propaganda.*   Fragments of the Behistun inscription at Babylon: Voigtlander 1978: 63–66. Date of the Aramaic copy: Greenfield and Porten 1982: 1–4 and Porten 1990: 17. Fragments of the relief at Babylon: Seidl 1976; at Susa(?): Canby 1979; and Muscarella in Harper, Aruz, and Tallon 1991: 218 n. 2, 221 n. 14.

- *Truth and Lies at Behistun: Darius and Ahura-Mazda.*   Since Rawlinson, the monument at Behistun has stimulated a vast number of studies (see the interesting historiographic discussion in Dandamaev 1976: 1–22). The analysis has been renewed by the German archaeologists, who were able to examine the relief at close range in 1963–64 and distinguished five chronological phases in the erection of the monument and the carving of the various versions (cf. Trümpelmann 1967 and Luschey 1968; more recently, Borger 1982). Many analyses and important reflections are also found in Root 1979: 58–61 and 182–226 (with references to the earlier bibliography). Site of Behistun, cf. Bernard 1980. On Semiramis at Behistun, cf. Briant 1984b: 30. Functional relationships between the inscriptions and the relief: Root 1979: 186–94. On *arta/dāta*, cf. Bucci 1972; P. O. Skjærvø (*EncIr.* 3 [1990] 696, s.v. "Old Persian Arta") emphasizes the surprising rarity of the term *arta* in the royal inscriptions (a single occurrence in *XPh* in the form *artāvan*); nevertheless, in the royal narrative taken as a whole, the frequency of references to the antonym *drauga* (Av. *druj* 'lie') confers on *arta* ('order, ordinance') a central place in Persian religious and political thought (cf. especially Kellens [1995], who even creates the [French] neologism *artavanité*, p. 30). Cf. also Pirart 1995 on the ethnonym *Artaioi*.

Individual in the winged disk: for a long time, historians have engaged in debates on his identity (e.g., Shahbazi 1974, 1980b); Lecoq's (1984) demonstration that the figure is Ahura-Mazda has convinced me completely (cf. also Root 1979: 169–76). Rite of investiture at Behistun: Lecoq

1984: 306–7; Vanden Berghe 1987: 1513–14 (who thinks that the ring represents the *Kh^varnah*, the Glory/Radiance that, according to other authors, is represented by the individual rising from the winged disk). Darius and Ahura-Mazda: cf. the interesting reflections of Gnoli 1974: 163–79 (and pp. 170–75 on the wiping out of the idea of *Kh^varnah* beginning in Darius's reign; also Gnoli 1990). In a personal communication (July 27, 1992), A. Kuhrt expresses doubts about the nature of the object held by Ahura-Mazda in the relief; in her opinion, it is not a ring: "In Mesopotamian usage, [it is] a thing called *șerret* = 'halter' or 'leading rope'; its character as a rope of some kind is fairly clear on the stele of Urnammu." On the passage of oral memory into writing, cf. the reflections of Herrenschmidt 1989b: 207 and Cardona 1980: 282–83 (following Gerschevitch), as well as the analyses of Sancisi-Weerdenburg 1980: 103–13.

- *New Campaigns, New Additions: Imperialism and Religion.* Campaign against the Saka: the major lacunae in the text have resulted in an inflated number of studies bearing principally on the identity of the Saka. Are they really the Saka of Central Asia (called Scythians by the Greeks: Herodotus VII.64), or is the text instead a description of the campaign of 513 by Darius against the Scythians of Europe, narrated at great length by Herodotus? We cannot give a long list of references here; pace Cameron (1975), there is no longer any doubt that the text is about an expedition led by Darius in Central Asia in 519: cf. Harmatta 1976, Shahbazi 1982. It is certainly this campaign to which an anecdote of Polyaenus (VII.11.14) refers. Religion and politics in *DB* V: Kellens 1987 (followed here); see already the lucid analyses of Sancisi-Weerdenburg 1980: 16–21, repeated and developed in Sancisi-Weerdenburg (in preparation).

4. Darius and the Six

- *Primus inter pares?* The theory of a restoration of the aristocracy was developed particularly by Dandamaev (1976: 210–12), who alongside Herodotus and Plato cites Aeschylus (*Persians* 956–960) and Esther 1:14. But these last two citations add nothing to the discussion. Dandamaev presses his hypothesis very hard because he sees the basic reason for the structural weakness of the Achaemenid Empire in this restoration (pp. 210–14): cf. Briant 1993c: 421–22. On the so-called Council of Seven, cf. the appropriate doubts of Lewis 1977: 23. I remain hesitant about the interpretations of Petit (1990: 222–26) in what he presents as the birth "of a new aristocracy" (the Six) at the expense of the "tribal nobility"; the statistical analyses Petit uses are, strictly speaking, worthless. The existence of a title understood as "guardian of one of the seven parts" in Achaemenid Egypt (*DAE* 49 [*BMAP* 8]; Bogoljubov 1967) cannot in any case support the views of Plato on a division into seven parts, whatever, e.g., Gnoli (1981: 271 n. 33) thinks of it (cf. Calmeyer 1987b: 133–40); it simply confirms that the figure 7 possessed a particularly productive symbolic meaning in Iranian cosmological thinking (compare, for example, Shahbazi 1983, with the remarks of Calmeyer 1983a: 199–203). I would add that I scarcely believe the "feudalist" theses of Widengren (1969: 102ff.), who would have the king elected by a noble *Landtag*, because the Achaemenid sources adduced for support are hardly probatory and because the consultation of later sources (pp. 108ff.) follows an unreliable method. Quite the opposite, we may suppose that the reunited nobility would acclaim the new king (cf. chap. 13/2: The Royal Investiture). On the "*syllogos* of the Medes and the Persians" known to Arrian, cf. Briant 1994e: 286–91. Regarding royal judges, we may note in passing that, according to Diodorus (XI.57), Mandane, the daughter of Darius, demanded that Xerxes punish Themistocles, who was considered responsible for the death of her children in 480. In this she was joined by "the noblest Persians" and incited the 'mob' (*okhlos*) to gather in front of the palace to demand of the king a trial in right and proper form. Xerxes gave in and agreed to form a tribunal (*dikasterion*) made up *ek tōn aristōn Persōn*, whose verdict he would accept in advance; Themistocles was ultimately acquitted. But this entire story is scarcely credible (likewise the marriage of Themistocles to a Persian woman: Diodorus XI.57.6). Apart from the factual errors, we recognize a well-known motif: the Persian princess who demands the punishment of a rebel guilty of killing her children (cf. Ctesias §35–36; cf. also §59 = Plutarch, *Art.* 14.9–10, 16–17).

- *Darius's Point of View: Nobles and King at Behistun.* The word *anušiyā* itself is not specific, because it also qualifies the members of the immediate entourage of the liar-kings (DB §13, 32, 42, 47). See on this the summary of Gnoli 1981, who thinks that the word is very close in meaning to *bandaka*; see also the very interesting remark of Malbran-Labat (1994: 121 n. 165) on the Babylonian vocabulary. The compiler did not use *qallu*, the "equivalent" of *bandaka* in DBBab. Identification of the bearers of royal arms at Behistun: Luschey (1968: 68–71) suggests Gobryas and Intaphernes, but the reasons given are purely speculative.

- *The Six and Court Protocol: The Intaphernes Affair.* See the analysis of Gschnitzer 1977 (although I do not agree with every step of his argument); see also the remarks of Sancisi-Weerdenburg 1983: 30–31.

- *The Marriages of Darius.* Darius's marriage to Gobryas's daughter was before 522 (Herodotus VII.2); this union produced Artobarzanes, Darius's eldest son (VII.2), who was thus born when his father was a 'an ordinary commoner' (*idiōtēs*; VII.3), that is, before 522. We do not know when Gobryas himself married one of Darius's sisters (VII.5), but neither case supports the thesis that the king was required to choose a wife from the conspirators' families. The only uncertainty concerns Xerxes; we do know that he married a "daughter of Onophas" (Ctesias §20): see below.

- *The Saga of Otanes.* See first of all the argument of Meyer 1879: 31–38 (followed by Reinach 1890a: 1–4); also Marquardt 1895: 489–512; and, on the fragment of Polybius and the demarcation of the land, compare the legend recorded by al-Biruni, where the royal concession is measured with respect to the flight of an arrow shot by the recipient (cf. Panaino 1988: 233). On the fiscal concessions granted to Otanes, cf. Briant 1985b: 55 (compared with other cases of the same type) and 1990b: 88; Wiesehöfer 1989: 187. Other examples of hereditary royal grant: Herodotus VII.106–7. It does not seem possible to conclude that Otanes and his family "were not compelled to obey the king as long as they did not infringe Persian laws" (so Dandamaev 1989a: 104, who paraphrases Herodotus very freely). On the identification of Xerxes' father-in-law, the controversy continues at full tilt; but it seems presumptuous to claim with great confidence that this Onophas/Otanes is even the same as the conspirator of 522 (cf. doubts presented by Burn 1984: 334–35; see already Marquardt 1895: 497). The reconstructions proposed by Herrenschmidt (1987b: 58–62) seem weak to me, since they are based on the assumption that the name *Thukra* is a nickname ("the Red"), which thus would not contradict Herodotus's statement. The proposal is interesting but remains unprovable and not even very likely. In fact, I would point out again that the pedigrees given for the conspirators at Behistun are precise, so it is hard for me to believe that Darius would have simply given Utāna's father his nickname.

- *The Family of Gobryas.* Cf. Lewis 1985: 110–11. Seal of Gobryas: cf. Root 1991: 19–21. Among the Persian chieftains at the Eurymedon, Callisthenes lists an "Ariomardos, son of Gobryas" (Plutarch, *Cimon* 12.5), but it is difficult to place him in the genealogy of Darius's lieutenant; nor do I know what to do with "Mardonius the Elder (*ho palaios*)," enumerated by Ctesias among those close to Xerxes at his accession (§19). It seems as though it could only be the son of Gobryas, but why this epithet *palaios*? Was there another, younger Mardonius? This is not certain, for the expression could just as well distinguish two persons not necessarily linked by family ties (cf. Theophrastus *HP* II.6.7). On Mardonius's lands in Babylonia, cf. Stolper 1992d. Petit (1990: 186–88) finds our Gobryas in Gubāru, "*piḫatu* of Babylonia and Trans-Euphrates" in the time of Cyrus, but the hypothesis (also postulated by Dandamaev 1992a: 79) seems unfounded to me. We know that the satrap Gubāru had a son associated with him as his deputy, named Nabūgu (Dandamaev 1992a: no. 206), but whatever the Iranian form of this name, it is not to be found in the family of Gobryas. That this Nabūgu was in all probability the oldest son of Gubāru seems to me to raise a very strong objection to this hypothesis, for the oldest son of Gobryas was in all probability Mardonius.

- *The Saga of Megabyzus.* Brown's article on Megabyzus (1987) adds nothing new.

• *Hydarnes.*   Satrap of Media according to Lewis 1977: 84 n. 14 (comparing the Miturna of the Persepolis tablets; cf. now unpublished tablets used in this sense by Koch 1993a: 12–13). On Tissaphernes, cf. ibid. 83–84, but there are many uncertainties (the ascendancy of Tissaphernes is induced from the inscribed Column of Xanthus, which calls him son of Hydarnes). On the ancestors of Orontes, cf. Reinach 1890b; Dörner 1967; Osborne 1973: 519–21.

5. Summary and Perspectives

• *A New Foundation for the Empire.*   On Darius's memory of Cyrus: in addition to Herodotus III.160, see the reference to Cyrus in the stela of Tell el-Maskhuta (Posener no. 8, p. 61), which remains regrettably mysterious because of the deplorable condition of the stone. It is also certain that Cyrus was among the ancestors (*progonoi*) that Darius invoked collectively and anonymously as glorious precedents in his letter to Gadatas (ML 12; and see chap. 12/4, pp. 491ff.).

Chapter 4
Darius the Conqueror (520–486)

1. The Pursuit of Territorial Expansion (520–513)

• *Darius, Democedes, and the West.* On the deeds of Democedes and the structure of Herodotus's tale, see the interesting analysis of Griffiths 1987, and the comments of Asheri 1990: 341–48.

• *Darius, Syloson, and Samos.* Asheri 1990: 256ff. and 348–54; Descat (1989: 79 and 1990a) thinks that after the execution of Oroetes at Sardis, Darius was supported by Otanes and Cappadocia; but this interpretation (which is based explicitly on the very suspect text of Diodorus XXXI.19.2) assumes that Otanes was in fact satrap of Cappadocia, which in my opinion is very doubtful for the reasons given above, chap. 3/4: "The Saga of Otanes," pp. 132ff.. [Herodotus's tale of Syloson: Van der Veen 1995.]

• *Darius, the Indus, and the Nile.* On the date of the conquest of India, cf. Shahbazi 1982: 233 n. 218 (519 B.C.) and Tuplin 1991a: 270–71 (around 518); on the expedition of Skylax and the suggested connections with the creation of the canal from the Nile to the Red Sea, see especially the very strong warnings of Salles 1988: 79–86 (p. 84: "The periplus of Skylax must be kept strictly separate from the stelas of Suez"), and Salles 1990: 117–18 (p. 118: "In the present state of our knowledge, it is better to see the periplus of Skylax as only an adventure, sufficiently daring to have struck the imagination, but only a unique adventure"); on Darius's canal, the basic reference is now Tuplin 1991a, which, while adding (p. 271 n. 23) some nuances to Salles's skepticism, nonetheless agrees with him overall (cf. his conclusion, p. 278) and, moreover, stresses quite opportunely (p. 242) that Herodotus's passage does not imply that Darius wished to establish direct communication; see also chap. 12/1.

• *Aryandes and Barca.* The date is disputed: cf. discussion in Mitchell 1966; on Amasis the Maraphi, cf. Briant 1988a: 160; on Herodotus's Cyrenian excursus, cf. Corcella and Medaglia 1993: 332ff.

2. The Persians in Europe

• *Darius's Scythian Expedition (513).* The bibliography is expanding but continues to lack consensus, except that there is no doubt about the date, for it is now acknowledged (*pace* Cameron 1975) that the expedition led by Darius against the Sacian Skunkha (*DB*) had nothing to do with the one against Scythia in Europe (cf. Harmatta 1976; Shahbazi 1982; the contrary attempt pursued by Petit [1984 and 1987; cf. 1990: 108–9] has not convinced anyone). *Pace* Petit (1990: 205 n. 421), the mission entrusted to Ariaramnes of Cappadocia (Ctesias §§16–17) seems perfectly understandable to me, including the geographical aspects. In contrast, the objectives and consequences of the Scythian expedition remain widely disputed; to the bibliography cited by Gardiner and Garden (1987), add the important article of Momigliano (1933) and the balanced perspective found in Nenci (1958: 144–156) and, since then, Fol and Hammond (1988: 235–43); on the geographical and logistical aspects, see the article of Nowak (1988), who depends too much on the assumptions of Engels (1978); Gallota's 1980 article adds nothing. We may mention in passing that an inscription on clay attributed to Darius has been found at Gherla in Romania [*DGh* in Mayrhofer 1978: 16] and published, with many restorations, by Harmatta (1953); how much Darius had to do with the stelas that were inscribed during his expedition (Herodotus IV.87, 91) remains very hypothetical, since the authenticity of the stelas in question is far from proved (*RTP* 390 n. 278, as well as West 1985: 296 and Schmitt 1988: 32–36). [Paintings showing the Scythian expedition: Calmeyer 1992a.]

- *The Persians in Thrace.* Castritius 1972; Fol and Hammond 1988; on the Paeonian tribes on the lower Strymon River, see Samsaris 1983. The existence of a satrapy of Thrace at this date (a theory defended by Hammond 1988a–b) is generally deduced from the reference to western peoples in some lists of countries: the "Saka beyond the sea" (*paradraya*; *DSe, DNa*), "Those beyond the sea" (*DPe*), and Skudra (*DSe, DNa, DSab, XPh*), Yauna "with a hat in the shape of a shield" (*Yaunā takabarā*; *DNa*), Yauna "who live beyond the sea" (*DSe, XPh*). But it must be stressed that a reference to a people does not necessarily imply the existence of a satrapal government (cf. the following chapter); it must also be stressed that the identification of these peoples continues to be problematic: Castritius (1972: 9–15) thinks (not without good arguments) on the contrary that the satrapal government dates simply from the Mardonius expedition. The theory of the integration of Macedonia into the satrapy is defended by Hammond (1979: 59–60), based especially on the case of Bubares, "governor or adviser to the governor of the satrapy"; on these problems, see the summary of Balcer (1988) who, *contra* Hammond, approves and specifies Castritius's interpretations; and Borza (1990: 100–103); read also the related discussion of Hatzopoulos and Loukopolou (1992: 15–25). Status of Oebares at Dascylium: hyparch and not satrap according to Balcer (1988); doubts of Petit (1990: 183–85). On the Achaemenid influence in Thrace (discernible basically in the fourth century), cf. Briant 1991c: 234 n. 42, where a bibliography is found; and a suggestion on the use of the word "parasang" by Arrian I.4.4.

3. The Ionian Revolt (500–493)

The bibliography is impressive, and there is no possibility here of carrying out a systematic (and vain) review; an analysis can be found in Tozzi (1978b) and Murray (1988); see also Burn 1984: 193–217; Will 1972: 86–89; Walser 1984: 27–35; on the position and sources of Herodotus, consult the always pertinent pages of Nenci (1956: 156–91) and Tozzi (1978a: 23–74); Nenci 1994 (commentary on book V of Herodotus) reached me too late to be properly used here.

- *The Thread of Events and the Problems Posed.* Persepolis tablet Q 1809: see Lewis 1980; in contrast, to look for an allusion to the revolt in certain "lists of countries" (so Stève 1974: 25) seems to me a hopeless exercise for, contrary to what Stève assumes, a diachronic analysis of the country lists in royal inscriptions does not permit the historian "to follow the fluctuations of Persian expansion, the establishment of recently acquired provinces, the dismantling of ancient administrative units and their reorganization into a new ensemble." On this question, see chap. 5/2–3. The gaps in Herodotus leave some chronological problems open: cf. Tozzi (1978b: 100–13) and Murray (1988: 473): "Within these limits [499–494] any detailed chronology is to some extant arbitrary." The author rightly stresses that there is a gap of several years in Herodotus's tale. This documentary situation makes it difficult to answer the question "Why did the revolt last so long?"

- *An Economic Crisis?* The theory of the economic weakness of the Ionian towns as an aftershock of the Persian conquest has recently been revived by Tozzi (1978b: 113–28) and Murray (1988: 477–78); the exact opposite theory in Roebuck 1988: 453–53; see also Picard 1980: 81–95 (but his conclusion on p. 90 seems to me too sudden); Ionians at Memphis, cf. Segal 1983 no. 26; on Ionians and Phoenicians doing business side by side in a delta port at the time of Xerxes: see the very clear text *TADAE* C3.1–29 (cf. Porten and Yardeni 1993; Yardeni 1994; and Lipiński 1994); Greek pottery from Asia Minor in the Near East: Perreault 1986; Ionian and Phoenician pottery on the site of Tell el-Maskhuta: Paice 1986–87 (although the Phoenician pottery is much more abundant).

- *Civic Tensions and Achaemenid Power.* The link between social problems and revolt has already been put forth by Hegyi (1966, 1971); social conflicts and tensions at Miletus (last quarter of the fifth century): cf. Robertson 1987: 375–77; *contra* Graf (1985), Austin (1990) expresses the idea that the Persians were in fact systematically supported by the tyrants; I am not sure that the two interpretations are really antithetical, as I hope I have shown in the text; on the slogan "liberty for the Greeks of Asia" and its history, cf. Seager and Tuplin 1980. I note also that according to

Murray (1988: 475–76), the Persians in Asia Minor could not find support from a "priestly caste," contrary to the situation in Babylon, Egypt, and Jerusalem; but, aside from the fact that the expression "priestly caste" is not really appropriate, I believe that the contrast he emphasizes (based on the letter from Darius to Gadatas: ML 12) is hardly substantiated (on this document, see below, chap. 12/4).

• *The Strategy of Aristagoras: The Beginnings of the Revolt.* Concerning the logistical problems related to the fleet, I have accepted the fascinating explanations of Wallinga 1984. Otherwise, it seems that the Athenians and Eretrians did not play a very important role, despite the claims of Lysanias of Mallus, cited by Plutarch (*Mor.* 861a–c; cf. Tozzi 1978b: 60–61). On the relations between Histiaeus, Artaphernes, and Darius, the mystery continues unabated, especially because Herodotus's chronology is very uncertain: Hegyi (1971) sees here a clash between two strategies, Darius's and his satrap's, regarding the relationships to be established with subjugated populations; I am not convinced. On the role of Histiaeus, see also the reflections of Burn 1984: 207–8; Murray 1988: 486–87 [and Kienast 1994].

• *The Persian Victory.* On the very lax character of the organization at the heart of the Ionian League: Roebuck 1955; Neville 1979; Lateiner 1982; the Ionian League was not suppressed by the Persians after the revolt (cf. Tod no. 113), which implies that it did not represent much of a threat in their eyes (Murray 1988: 489). The existence of a revolutionary coinage (Gardner 1911) has now been cast in doubt (cf. Graf 1985: 103 n. 22; but see Tozzi 1978b: 81–92). Reconquest: the excavations at Old Paphos on Cyprus have confirmed that the Persians destroyed sanctuaries there (cf. Tozzi 1978a); they also illustrate the technical abilities demonstrated by the Persians during sieges (cf. Herodotus IV.200); in the excavations of the siege ramp, 422 stone shot weighing between 2 and 12 kg were found—a discovery of something totally new, since it was generally believed that the invention of machines for hurling, such as the catapult, dated to Dionysius the Elder at the beginning of the fourth century (a point of view once again expressed by Y. Garlan, *CAH* VI[2] [1994]: 682–84, where rather surprisingly there is no reference to the discussion started by the Paphos discoveries); the recent find of a stone ball at Phocaea dated to the siege of the town by Cyrus in 546 (Ozyigit 1994) now provides reinforcement for the hypothesis (cf. bibliography and summary in Briant 1994h).

4. From Thrace to Memphis (492–486)

• *The Mission of Mardonius in Thrace.* See especially Castritius 1972; Balcer 1988; Hammond 1988b: 493–96; and now Zahrnt 1992. Regarding the expression used by Herodotus (VI.43) to describe Mardonius in 493 ("newly married to a daughter of the king, Artozostra"), cf. *PFa* 5 with the remarks of Hallock 1978: 110 and Lewis 1984: 596.

• *From Cilicia to Marathon.* On the different stages of Darius's strategy, one may read with profit the lucid remarks of Will 1964: 73–78.

• *The Conquest of the Islands.* The famous *Chronicle of Lindos* (cf. Blinkenburg 1912: 379–85; 1941: 177–200 = *FGrH* 532), which lists donations to the sanctuary by Datis, has long posed many problems; we start off by questioning the reality of the deeds reported: several authors believe it is a useless fake; cf. Baslez 1985: 138–41, remarking in particular that the Delian dedication attributed to Datis is certainly a later falsification; same opinion, Murray 1988: 468–69; but not all doubts have been resolved: see Bresson, *REA* 1985/1–2: 155, explicitly opposing Baslez; Burn (1984: 218) places the episode during the Ionian revolt, Datis having acted on the initiative of Mardonius; citing for support information found on some Persepolis tablets, Heltzer (1989a) suggests the date 497, at the time of the attacks on Cyprus; an alternate hypothesis would be to date these donations to the time when Datis left Cilicia and headed toward Naxos.

• *Persian Conquest and Greek Medism.* Cf. Graf 1979 and 1984; the work of Gillis 1979 is of little interest.

• *Marathon.* On the battle, cf. Hignett 1963: 55–74; Burn 1984: 239–53; Hammond 1988b: 506–17; Lazenby 1993: 48–80; on the absence of the cavalry, cf. the hypotheses of Whatley 1964 and Evans 1987; on the exaltation of Marathon and historical distortions among the Athenians, cf. Loraux 1981: 157–73.

• *From Marathon to Memphis.*   On the Egyptian revolt: Aristotle's phrase (*Rhet.* II.20.3 = 1393B) does not add much to the discussion (cf. Tuplin 1991a: 266). Date of the death of Darius (Nov. 486): it is established with the help of Babylonian tablets (Stolper 1992a); it is noteworthy that the most recently published tablets show that for three weeks after the death of the king (until 21 Dec.), scribes at Sippar continued to date their documents according to the reign of Darius, although at Borsippa the first document dated to the reign of Xerxes is from 1 December 486: cf. Zawadski 1992.

Chapter 5
Images of the World

1. The Builder-King

• *The Remodeling of Susa.* See the special issue of *Dossiers Histoire et archéologie* 138 (1989), with dense summaries by the best specialists as well as an up-to-date bibliography (p. 90). Archaeological evidence for the break between the Elamite and Achaemenid levels: Miroschedji 1987. The Susa epigraphy is published by Stève 1984 and 1987. *DSf, DSz, DSaa* are published with commentary by Vallat 1971, 1972, and 1986; trilingual inscription of the Darius Gate: Vallat 1974b. Copy of the Behistun relief at Susa: Canby 1979, and Muscarella in Harper, Aruz, and Tallon [1991]: 218 n. 2 and 221 n. 4 (a reconstruction based on a minuscule fragment). Date of the beginning of construction of Susa: high date (beginning in 520) according to Stève 1974: 27, followed by Vallat 1986: 281; I find the hypothesis tempting, but the Classical texts adduced in support do not have the value claimed by these authors (cf. Briant 1993b). Death of Hystaspes: Stève 1974: 168–69 and Vallat 1986: 221. Urban planning at Susa: Perrot 1981 and Boucharlat 1990a; work on Susa: Perrot 1974; Perrot, Ladiray 1974 (Darius Gate).

• *The Beginnings of Persepolis.* See in general Schmidt 1953: 39ff. *DPf*: Herrenschmidt 1990; date of *DPh*: Stronach 1985a and Root 1988 and 1989; cf. also Root 1979: 76ff., as well as Koch 1987b (cf. p. 157); see especially the detailed suggestions of Roaf (1983: 127–59), who attributes the beginnings of construction of the Apadana, the Treasury, and the palace of Darius to the reign of Darius (but at the beginning of the fifth century)—all projects completed by Xerxes; among the evidence used in the dating, Roaf (p. 150) includes the Treasury tablets (PF): the earliest attestation of craftsmen (*marrip*: cf *PFT*: 45–46) receiving rations at Pārsa is dated to Year 15 (PF 1580), or 508–507; but the significance of the statistical distribution of the tablets ought to be taken into account; on these problems, see also the important suggestions offered by Garrison 1988: 383–85, 391–93, and 474–75. Persepolis fortifications: Schmidt 1953: 206–11, Shahbazi 1976b: 8–9, and now Mousavi 1992 and Kleiss 1992b.

• *Work Carried Out in the Other Capitals.* Chronological problems relating to building Pasargadae: Nylander 1970; cf. most recently Koch 1987b: 158; Treasury and *kurtaš* at Pasargadae: Koch 1990: 30–31. The construction of a new palace at Babylon is attested by a tablet dated to Year 26 of Darius (*BRM* 1.81), referring to the "new palace" (Joannès 1990a: 186); on the other hand, the *Perserbau*, often attributed to Darius (Haerinck 1973), was the work of Artaxerxes II (Vallat 1989a); *apadana* at Ecbatana: cf. Stronach, *EncIr*, s.v. "Apadana."

• *The Royal Tomb of Naqš-i Rustam.* Methodical description by Schmidt 1970; also Calmeyer 1975; Root 1979: 72–76 and 162–81; and Von Gall 1989; text of Ctesias (§15): Balcer (1972: 117–19) thinks that Ctesias has definitely confused it with the cliff at Behistun; meanwhile, the funerary nature of the monument described hardly leaves any room for hesitation; *Nupistaš* (**Nipišta-*): Gershevitch 1969: 177–79 (with reflections on the chronology extracted from the tablets); Hinz 1970: 425–26 (in the form of a question); but see Hallock 1977: 132 and Koch 1990: 49 (n. 235).

• *Royal Art and Imperial Towns.* On the dynastic and imperial program, see especially the analyses of Root 1979, 1980, and 1990 (largely repeated here).

2. The King and His Peoples: Inscriptions and Iconography

• *The "Foundation Charters" of Susa.* Vallat 1971 (*DSf, DSz*), 1972 (*DSaa, DSz*), 1986 (*DSaa*); also Stève 1974 and 1987, as well as Kent, *OP.* The sigla for Susa inscriptions (e.g., *DSc* 001) are taken from Stève 1974 and 1987.

- *The Country Lists.* From the burgeoning bibliography, see especially Herrenschmidt 1976–77 and 1980c; Calmeyer 1982, 1983a, and 1987b (where numerous comparisons with Classical texts will also be found).
- *The People Bearing Thrones.* Reproductions and analyses in Schmidt 1970 and Walser 1972; Susa statue: cf. *CDAFI* 1974 (exhaustive analysis by Roaf) and Calmeyer 1991a; on the canal stelas, cf. Posener 1936: 48–87 and 181–88 and Tuplin 1991a: 242–46; the written and visual documents are also analyzed at great length by Vogelsang 1992: 94–119 and 132–65 (who probably uses the criterion of dress too systematically). In general, see the very important contribution on this topic by M. Root (1979: 227–84: "The Tribute Procession"). The table presented on 175 is taken from Shahbazi 1976b: 24–25.

3. An Idealized Image of Space and Imperial Power

- *Space and Administration.* Synoptic lists are found in Roaf 1974: 149 and Calmeyer 1982 107; on the meaning of *dahyu* in the royal inscriptions, see especially Cameron 1973, whose conclusions have been universally accepted; cf. most recently Lecoq 1990a.
- *Subjugation and Collaboration.* See especially Nylander 1979 and Root 1979.
- *The Empire and the Known World: Representations and Realities.* *Eskhatiai* of the Empire: Briant 1984b: 64–65; the interpretation of *būmi* as 'Empire' comes from Herrenschmidt 1976: 43–65; this interpretation has been challenged by Frye 1977: 75–78. Periplus of Sataspes: Desanges 1978: 29–33 and recently Colin 1990. Circular schema of representations of the world: first proposed by Goukowsky (1978: 222–24), repeated (with minor modifications) by Herrenschmidt 1980c and Calmeyer 1982. Space and religious concepts· the hypothesis is proposed by Shahbazi 1983, on which see the reservations of Calmeyer 1983a: 199–203. These images of peoples subject to the Great King may be compared to monuments from the Roman period, in particular the *simulacra gentium* of Aphrodisias of Caria (R. R. R. Smith, *JRS* 78 [1988]: 50–77; cf. p. 77: "It seems clear that in the Sebasteion the selection of outlandish peoples was meant to stand as a visual account of the extent of the Augustan empire, and by the sheer number and impressive unfamiliarity of the names, to suggest that it is coterminous with the ends of the earth"); among the numerous studies of the Assyrian depictions, cf. in particular Calmeyer 1983a: 181–90; much thoughtful material is also found in Liverani 1990: 33–102.
- *Center and Periphery: "Aryan of Aryan Stock."* Persians, Medes, and Iranians: the word *Arya*: see various articles by Gnoli (1983, 1988a, and 1990) that deny any existence of a concept of "Iran" in the Achaemenid period; cf. also the articles "Arya" (Bailey) and "Aryans" (Schmitt) in *EncIr* II (1988); more recently, Lamberterie 1989; Schmitt 1991c; and Skalmowski 1993, 1995. On the place and role of the Iranian peoples in the country lists, see in particular Herrenschmidt 1976: 59–61 and Calmeyer 1982: 135–39 (cf. also pp. 164–66; 1983a: 220–21 and 1987b: 141); the former writes, for example: "The non-Persian Iranians are subject to the Persians like the others, pay tribute, furnish soldiers; but they have an advantage on the other peoples by reason of their Iranian origins"; according to the latter, six countries always listed together (Parthia, Aria, Bactriana, Sogdiana, Khwarezm, Drangiana) represent historical Aryanē (p. 138); on the various proposed interpretations, see the analyses of Calmeyer 1983a: 194–214.
- *Center and Periphery: Persia and the Empire.* See many analyses by Herrenschmidt (1976, 1977, 1980a, 1980b, 1980c), in which the author presents the hypothesis of a "Persian kingdom" formally distinct from the concept of Empire (*būmi*); this interpretation has been challenged by Frye 1977 and Schmitt 1978b; cf. also Gschnitzer 1988 (p. 989 n. 12 quoting *DPh* in particular), who suggests a very tempting chronological rearrangement of the inscriptions; but we know the difficulties involved in dating these texts precisely: the proposed method (p. 101 n. 18, based on the countries listed) does not really work (cf. Vallat 1986: 282); see also his reflections (pp. 99–101) on *DPe.* On the administrative situation in Persia during the time of Darius (a problem also mentioned by Gschnitzer, p. 114 and n. 37), see chap. 11. According to Herrenschmidt (1976: 61), the

place of the Medes shows that "the rapidity and importance of his [Darius's] conquests extended the reach of his power so far that there were not enough Persians qualified for political, administrative, and military leadership. They thus had to turn to the Medes"; this interpretation has been criticized by Vogelsang 1986: 131–35, who throws in relief the exceptional position of the Persian country [cf. also Tuplin 1994].

4. Images and Realities: The King among His Peoples

• *Peoples and Gifts: An Imperial Festival at Persepolis?* The bibliography on this topic is huge. Here let us simply recall that the so-called New Year ceremony was reconstructed by Pope 1957 and Ghirshman 1957 (followed since then, much more systematically even to the point of caricature, by Fennelly 1980); on comparisons with Indian rites, see most recently Musche 1989 (coronation festivals). See now the very clear summary by Sancisi-Weerdenburg 1991b, where both a clear presentation of the sources and problems and a fascinating history of the hypothesis based on the reports of European travelers since the seventeenth century will be found (cf. also 1987 [ed.] and 1991a); I note only that she does not systematically use the sources that I analyze here, particularly in the last subsection, "Return to Persepolis"); see also Calmeyer 1979b: 156–57 and 1986: 77–79 (where the passages of Theopompus and Aelian are cited), as well as Root 1979 (278–79: on the hypothesis of the Now Ruz; 236–40: unity of the whole composition, taking into account the central location of the audience relief). M. Root and P. Calmeyer both insist on a timeless, nonspecific analysis of the reliefs (whatever that is). But we must remain open to the hypothesis of an imperial festival, not completely excluded by M. Root (p. 157) and more definitely indicated by H. Sancisi-Weerdenburg: "It is clear that no Nowruz is attested for the Achaemenid period. This, however, is not proof that it did not exist at that time" (1991b: 201). As for the proposed timing of royal visits to Persepolis (summer), I note simply that Darius came to Persepolis, where he died (Ctesias §19) in November 486 (on the date, Stolper 1992a and Zawadski 1992), which provides confirmation—if any were needed—that the Great King frequently stayed at Persepolis throughout the year, in accordance with the official cultic calendar (confirmation of this point is now found in Koch 1993a: 61–91, esp. pp. 88–89); on the parades described by Xenophon, Herodotus, and Quintus Curtius, cf. the synoptic comparison prepared by Calmeyer 1974: 51–54 and 1986: 79–82; on the relationship between Xerxes and the Persepolis depictions, see especially Sancisi-Weerdenburg 1980: 184–216.

• *The Nomadic King.* I have treated this problem at length in Briant 1988c; additional references to ancient texts and modern studies are found there (cf. also Briant 1991c: 233 and n. 34); on Aelian, *VH* XIX.41, cf. Briant 1992b; entries of Cyrus and Alexander into Babylon, cf. Kuhrt 1990b; on the gifts of Persian peasants, cf. Briant 1993c. Many interesting analyses are also found in the work of Koch 1993a: 61–91, which uses the Persepolis tablets, including many unpublished ones; it turns out that the information drawn from the tablets does not completely agree with the claims of the ancient authors on the chronology of the annual visits of the court to this or that capital; while the sojourns at Susa and Persepolis are amply attested, the same cannot be said for the visits to Babylon and Ecbatana: cf. pp. 89–90. [Migrations of Darius to the east of Iran: Giovinazzo 1994b.]

• *The Return to Persepolis via Babylon.* The embassies received by Alexander are also described by Arrian VII.14.6; 15.4–5; 19.1–2 (the author admits some doubts about the reality of some of them) and by Justin XII.13. On Pliny VI.30.119–20, see also Dilleman 1962: 168–70, 245 (cf. *RTP* 453).

5. Images and Realities: The Imperial Festivals

• *The Large Army of Xerxes.* The interpretation presented here has already been published in preliminary form (Briant 1990a: 81 n. 20; cf. Briant 1988b: 175); since then, I have learned that Burn (1984: 470), without working it out, offered a similar observation (the levying of ethnic contingents relates to "considerations of royal prestige"); he nevertheless thinks (cf. also p. 324) that these contingents, though they did not actually fight, accompanied Xerxes to Attica; he argues for this based on the fact that Artabazus exercised command over the army that accompanied Xerxes to the Hellespont (Herodotus VIII.126◊), recalling that at Doriscus Artabazus is called the chief of the Parthians and Chorasmians (VII.66◊). But it is precisely this style of argument that appears questionable to me because it assumes that Artabazus retained the command of the Parthians and Chorasmians, who do not appear in any battle. I am rather inclined to believe that, for one thing, the Doriscus contingents (which need not be more than small squads, purely representative of their peoples) returned to Asia after the parade, and for another, the Persian chieftains were then integrated into the organizational chart of the elite troops as "commanders of thousands and myriads of men" (VII.81◊). Some may also have soon gotten their civil authority back: thus, Herodotus calls Artayctes, who at Doriscus "commanded" the Moschians and the Tibareni (VII.78◊), governor of Sestos in Hellespont at this time (IX.115); in fact, he still had that job in 479–478 (VII.33; IX.115–18), and there is no sure evidence that he actually participated in the march to Athens. I note finally that Armayor (1978: 6–7) also thinks that it was a parade, but he adds that Herodotus's description comes from a Greek model that has no relation to Persian reality—a conclusion that seems excessive to me, even if the memory of the parade really did take on additions and exaggerations; cf. especially Josephus, *Ag. Ap.* I.172–73◊; quoting Choerilus of Samos, Josephus even assumes that the Jews also sent a contingent, whose clothing and general appearance were no less surprising than those of the contingents described by Herodotus; what is most interesting is that the citation of Choerilus (who wrote toward the end of the fifth century) shows that the composition of the army had been reworked by tradition, because he lists the inhabitants of the Solymian hills (assimilated to Jews by Josephus), an ethnonym not found in Herodotus. On the grand army of Xerxes, see also chapter 13. [[On this point at least—nonparticipation in battle of the ethnic contingents listed by Herodotus—I find myself in agreement with Barkworth 1992.]]

• *From Artaxerxes III to Ptolemy II.* On the Isocrates passage, cf. Meiggs 1972: 433–34; on the transportation of tribute, cf. the scene on the Darius Vase and the remarks of Villanueva and Puig 1989: 289–96; and, regarding bags (containing the Athenian tribute), the judiciously proposed comparisons of Bernard and Rapin 1980: 20 n. 3. *Pompē* of Philadelphia: the quotations are taken from F. Dunand, "Fête et propagande à Alexandrie sous les Lagides," in *La Fête, pratique et discours*, Paris (1981): 18, 21, 24–25; on Persian borrowings (tent), cf. Lavagne 1988: 96–99 and Perrin 1990.

6. Royal Table and Royal Paradise: Exaltation of the Center and Appropriation of Space

• *On the Royal Table.* Cf. Briant 1989b and 1993c; on the paradise, cf. *RTP* 453–56, Fauth 1979, and Stronach 1989a; for the Assyrian period: Oppenheim 1965; Albenda 1974; Wiseman 1983a; see also Lackenbacher 1990: 91–96 ("Canaux, vergers et jardins") [[I note in passing that the text of Aelian (*Anim.* VII.1) on the oxen of the paradise at Susa gives strength to the interpretation of Cardascia (1951: 132 n. 1) on the existence of norias in Achaemenid Babylon (on this, see now Stevenson 1992, esp. pp. 48–51, although unaware of the Aelian text)]]; on the ideological function of the royal gardens in pharaonic Egypt (appropriation of the known world), cf. Beaux 1990: 314–17; on Cotys, cf. Briant 1991c: 232–35; on Alcibiades, cf. Briant 1985b: 59; Alexander: Pliny VIII.44 is discussed by Bodson (1991: 132–33); the author thinks that the connection between Alexander and Aristotle (made explicit by Pliny) must be reviewed, which seems reasonable; meanwhile, I do not believe that we can simply use Pliny's passage to show the impact of the Macedonian conquest on the development of the natural sciences in Europe; the principal goal of the conqueror seems to me to be consistent with the (Near Eastern) model of the paradise, which, after all, he probably knew about before 334 (cf. my discussion of this point in Briant 1991c: 230–36). Gardens of Versailles: quote from J.-M. Apostolidès, *Le Roi-machine: Spectacle et politique au temps de Louis XIV*, Paris (1981): 136–37.

Chapter 6
Representations of Royalty and Monarchic Ideology

1. Sources and Problems

• *The Variety of Evidence: Complementary and Specific.* On the relationship between Classical sources and the reliefs, cf. the relevant critical remarks of Calmeyer 1979b. A large number of fragmentary objects (gate decorations, precious stones, jewelry, etc.) have been found at Persepolis that originally must have been ornaments on the reliefs: Schmidt 1957: 70–80; colors at Persepolis: Tilia 1978: 31–68; Krefter 1989: 131–32 (and pl. 1 in color, with Calmeyer's brief comment in *AMI* 9 [1989]); at Susa: Stève 1974: 144–45; in the palace of Artaxerxes II at Susa, fragments of a painted frieze showing a line of donor peoples has been found, similar to those sculpted at Persepolis: Boucharlat-Labrousse 1979: 67–68 (cf. photos in Briant 1992d: 50); wall paintings in an Armenian apadana from the Achaemenid period: cf. Summers 1993: 94; reconstructions of the tablet that decorated the *Stoa Poikilē* in Athens in Pausanias's time: C. Robert, *Die Marathonschlacht in der Poikilè*, Halle, 1895 (cf. Briant 1992d: 148–49). Persian tapestries decorated with "woven figures": Athenaeus V.179b; cf. IV.138c; images of monsters and griffins in Persian style: Athenaeus XI.477d; cf. Daumas 1985: 293; high Persian garments in color (*poikilmata*): Aelian, *Anim.* 5.22; Pazyryk carpets: see good color photos in Gryzanov 1969: 132–35; some motifs on carpets found at Pazyryk have nearly identical correspondences at Persepolis: Tilia 1978: 49–52 (see now Lerner 1991). Plutarch's text on Themistocles (*Them.* 29.4): some translators (cf. *Vies de Plutarque*, II, CUF, Paris [1961]: 135) understand *poikila strōmata* as 'historiated carpets', but the primary sense of *poikilos* remains 'variegated' (e.g., Ps.-Arist., *Oecon.* II.1.2, with the remarks of Descat 1990b: 86–87). Evidence of Philostratus: cf. the appropriate critical remarks of Bigwood 1978b: 41 and n. 37; the *Alexander Romance* is quoted from the edition by G. Bounoure and B. Serret (Paris: Les Belles Lettres, 1992); we may remark on this passage that it also contains a reference (entirely imaginary, in my opinion) to a painting of Xerxes (II.15.8). On the distortions introduced by travel accounts, cf. Sancisi-Weerdenburg 1991a–b, who studied particularly striking examples, and the documents in Sancisi-Weerdenburg (ed.) 1987c. Semiramis: see Bigwood 1978b: 41–43. On Herodotus IV.88–89, cf. Hölscher 1973: 35–37. Among the errors (or approximations) of the ancient authors, let us mention also that Ctesias (§15) placed Darius's tomb "on the mountain with two peaks," i.e., at Behistun (cf. Balcer 1972b: 117–18). Diffusion of Persian images ("perseries") in the Greek world, cf. especially the painstaking study by Miller 1985 (also Miller 1989 on the adoption/adaptation of objects from the Achaemenid court [parasols] in Athenian high society); on the *himation* (garment) of Denys the Elder, cf. Jacobsthal 1938 (whom I follow despite Robertson 1939) and the remarks of Childs 1978: 80; on the Greek use of Achaemenid motifs on the Acropolis (a hotly debated issue), see Lawrence 1951 and most recently Root 1985 (who has edited a book [still unpublished] on this question); on the references to Persepolis in the Classical-period text, cf. the appropriate remarks of Cameron 1973: 56. Darius vase (fig. 13, p. 204): Villanueva and Puig 1989 (with prior bibliography) and, most recently, Ghiron and Bistagne 1992–93.

• *Center and Periphery.* On this theme, see the stimulating reflections of Root 1991, as well as the remarks and analyses of Jacobs 1987: 52–58 (but I do not share the views expressed on pp. 15–23); audience scene on a shield on Alexander's sarcophagus: Gabelmann 1984: 68 and von Graeve 1987; pictures of Sassanian hunts: Harper 1986; Assyrian hunts: Magen 1986: 29ff.; absence of reference to the hunter-king in the inscriptions: see my remarks in *RTP* 389–91 and, since then, Schmitt 1988: 29. The hypothesis of exact identity between the hunting scenes on the

"Greco-Persian" stelas and hunting scenes formerly present (?) in the royal residences is developed in particular by Cremer 1984 (based on Classical texts), but I think it is better to be cautious about proof in this matter; the immutable, fixed, and timeless character of Achaemenid court art has quite specifically been stressed by M. Root and P. Calmeyer in many articles (with the regional exception analyzed in Calmeyer 1992a: 16); on court art and royal propaganda in different media, and on the relationship between the "Court style" of stamps and monumental art, cf. in particular Garrison 1988: 383–93 and Garrison 1992; on the propagandistic program systematically developed on the royal coinage, cf. Stronach 1989b.

2. The Prince in His Own Mirror

• *Darius at Naqš-i Rustam.* Description of the façade of the royal tombs: Schmidt 1970: 79ff.; Root 1979: 72–76 and 162–81; see also Houtkamp 1991: 24–25 and 38–39 (fire altars). The translation of *DNb* is taken from Herrenschmidt 1985: 134; the third part (here §14b) poses major translation problems; the discovery of the Aramaic version in the Behistun papyrus from Elephantine allowed Sims and Williams (1981) to resolve a significant number of difficulties; the translation of the last sentence is adopted from Hinz 1988.

• *The Victorious King and the King of Justice.* Bow, royal insignia: *RTP* 374–75; perhaps awarded to the king at his enthronement: Briant 1991a: 8.

• *Text and Image.* The different poses of the king on the coins are graphically presented by Vanden Berghe 1987: 146–47, and by Stronach 1989b: 260 (here fig. 17, p. 214). Artaxerxes' seal: cf. Porada 1979: 88–89 (fig. 46); combat with a Saka: cf Porada 1979: 86 n. 68; king against Greek warrior: ibid., 89, fig. 47; seal of Kuraš of Anšan (PFS *93): e.g., Bollweg 1988 and Garrison 1992: 3 7; Aršāma's seal: drawing in Moorey 1978: 149 fig. 8, where a drawing of the Oxus cylinder will also be found (fig. 7).

3. The King in Majesty

• *The Statue of Darius.* I return to the articles published in *JA* 260/3–4 (1972) and *CDAFI* 4 (1974); see also chap. 12/1 below for the Egyptian context; *DAE* 70: cf. Fleischer 1983 and Roaf 1979: 72; the authenticity of the inscription on the statue of Darius (Herodotus) is put in doubt (not without good reason) by Schmitt 1988: 30–32; on the symbolism of the colors of Darius III's robe, cf. Dumézil 1985; on the statue of Xerxes mentioned by Plutarch, cf. the remarks of Calmeyer 1979b: 60 and n. 51; we may also note the statue carved in honor of Artystone [Darius's favorite wife] according to Herodotus VII.69. On the statue of Darius and especially on residual traces of Achaemenid statuary (including at Susa), see also Spycket 1981: 394–401; and Harper, Aruz, Tallon (eds.) 1992 = French edition 1994: 219–21 (fragment of a royal head from Susa) [and Traunecker 1995 on a "Perso-Egyptian" head in the Strasbourg Museum].

• *Iconography from Persepolis.* On the audience relief found in the Persepolis Treasury, cf. Tilia 1977: 69–74, and chap. 14/1, with the notes (Artaxerxes I at Persepolis).

• *The King on His Throne.* Diphros of Xerxes, cf. Miller 1985: 110–11 (war booty); Frost (1973: 118–19) tries to show, based on Dinon, that the translation 'throne' is incorrect; but his proof is inconclusive, since it is clear that the word *diphros* designated not only footstools but also seats (cf. in particular Herodotus III.146, where the word seems to be used as a synonym for *thronos*: III.144); it is thus not impossible (contrary to Frost's conclusion) that Xerxes sat on his gold *diphros* (cf. Plutarch, *Them.* 13.1); Alexander and the royal Achaemenid throne: cf. Calmeyer 1973: 137–46; on the Achaemenid throne, cf. Jamzadeh 1991.

• *The Royal Audience.* The texts are given and analyzed by Gabelmann 1984: 7–21; role of the *hazarapatiš*: cf. texts and commentaries in Briant 1994e: 291–98, and chapter 7/2 below; problem of the *proskynesis*: see Bickerman 1963 who, with others (cf. Frye 1972a), considers the *proskynesis* to be precisely the rite shown on the audience reliefs; disagreeing, Gabelmann 1984: 15–16, 88–95 (though the author unfortunately shows no awareness of Bickerman's article); I note in passing that in some Mari tablets there is a hierarchy among ambassadors, with some of them exempt from *proskynesis* and others having to bow three or two times: cf. J. M. Durand, *NABU* 1990/1, no. 24.

- *Royal Horses and Chariots.* Cf. *RTP* 374–75; Calmeyer 1974; also Stamatiou 1989.
- *The Royal Hero.* Root 1979: 118–22 (seals) and 303–8 (the interpretation followed here); Garrison 1988 and 1992; also Porada 1979: 82–85, Boardman 1970a: 30–37, Bivar 1970, and Stronach 1989b: 272.

4. The Good Warrior

- *A Tall and Handsome King.* On the (supposed) length of Darius's arms, see also the nickname *Makrocheir*, which Pollux interprets as 'grasping power from afar' (Schmitt, *EncIr*, s.v. "Artaxerxes I"); it is thus not certain whether Strabo has confused Darius I and Artaxerxes I. Dynastic competitions: cf. chapters 14/1, 14/6, 15/2, 17/1. Garments of the king and Ahura-Mazda at Persepolis: Tilia 1972: 41ff.; colors: Widengren 1968: 179–80 and Dumézil 1985. Hairpieces (cf. Miller 1985: 283–85): all the iconographic evidence shows the care with which the Persepolis sculptors delineated beards and moustaches: Tilia 1972: 39.
- *The Commander-in-Chief: Representations and Realities.* See the accurate reflections of Widengren (1968: 179) regarding Darius III: "The battle lost, he fled, for his duty was not to fight, but simply to survive to rule. It would be wrong to view this as cowardice, which it absolutely was not. In the Mahābhārata, Yudisthira, a model king, does not participate in combat; he is content to supervise and direct it"—to be read with both the critical and the assenting remarks of Nylander 1993: 150–51; on the importance of the theme of the victorious campaign in the first regnal year among the pharaohs, cf. Zaccagnini 1990: 39.
- *Darius III in Battle: An Agonistic Perspective on Royalty.* I repeat here some earlier reflections (*RTP* 373 n. 113); on the *Mosaic of Naples* , cf. especially Nylander 1982, 1983, and 1993.
- *The Hunter-King.* Cf. Briant 1991c (where I tried to collect the documentation without claiming exhaustiveness), and below, chapter 7/6. The seal showing the king's combat with a griffin is discussed by Hill 1923 (also Briant 1991c: 220; photo in Briant 1992d: 102–3).

5. The King, the Earth, and the Water

- *The Good Gardener.* On Xenophon's text, see *RTP*: 176–88, 455–56; on the paradise, cf. ibid., 451–56 and Fauth 1979; see chap. 11/5 and the index, s.v., and Pomeroy 1994: 237–54 (following Briant and Fauth); paradise scenes on the Dascylium stamps: Kaptan-Bayburtluoglu 1990; work scenes: the cylinder seal (in the Louvre) is reproduced on the back cover of *RTP* and in Briant 1992d: 103; a photograph of the Tarsus coin is found in Franke-Hirmer 1966: 124 and no. 194 [[cf. also Casabonne 1995b n. 6]]; the relationship between the two documents was judiciously proposed by Sancisi-Weerdenburg 1990: 266.
- *Xerxes and the Plane (or Sycamore) Tree.* On the texts offered, see a few preliminary remarks in *RTP* 447–48 and 456; see also Eddy 1961: 27–30. Stamps: *PTS* 24–25; king before the tree of life: Menant 1878: 71; cf. *SXe* (with the critical remarks of Schmitt 1981: 26–32); such scenes are also common on Babylonian seals of the Achaemenid period: Legrain 1925: 43; cf. also Delaporte 1909 no. 633. In every case, the tree is a palm tree: cf. the remarks of Schmidt 1957: 8; Porada (1979: 85) offers the hypothesis that the theme could have been borrowed from Egypt by Darius (the seal is supposed to have come from Egypt: Yoyotte 1952); on this theme, cf. also Garrison 1992: 19–20; but the theme of the palm tree seems instead to emerge from the Babylonian inventory, later reintegrated into Persian thought (cf. Strabo XVI.1.14).
- *The Plane (Sycamore) Tree and the Golden Vine of the Great King.* The texts on the Golden Vine are collected by Jacobsthal 1927: 102–11; cf. also R. Vallois, *L'architecture hellénique et hellénistique à Délos*, Paris (1944): 290–98, 427.
- *The Rainmaker and Master of the Storm.* Tištryā and Mithra: cf. the recent articles by Panaino 1986 and 1988 (without referring to Classical texts), and his edition of the *Yasht* dedicated

to this god (Panaino 1990; volume 2 is in press); see already Bidez and Cumont 1938: 115 n. 3, 124–27; my note in Briant 1994f: 61 n. 30 [Mithra?] must now be corrected. After this discussion was written, I became aware of Calmeyer 1989 [1991], who also, with even more documentation, proposes identifying Tištryā as lying behind Polyaenus's Apollo. On the theme of rain and storm, cf. also Widengren 1968: 75–77, 264–67, 349–50; Nicolaus of Damascus's text on Cyrus: cf. the remarks of Binder 1964: 25.

6. Between Men and Gods

It is not my intention in the pages that follow to treat Persian religion *in extenso* or to offer solutions to all of the pending problems. Such an enterprise—which exceeds my competence—requires an entire book. Here, my topic is centered primarily on the religious component of Achaemenid monarchic ideology, even if I am led here and there to delve into the file on this or that deity. I have made great use of the following works: Rapp 1865; Clemen 1929a–b; Duschesne-Guillemin 1952 (cf. also 1972); Widengren 1968; and Boyce 1982—while of course many specific studies will be cited where appropriate. Cf. also chapter 2/9 above, where the innovative articles of J. Kellens are cited (in the research notes). [Ahn's 1992 book reached me too late for me to be able to incorporate his analyses and discussions, but at first sight he seems to me to lay too much weight on the later Avestan texts.] Let us remark at the outset that no building at Persepolis is identifiable as a temple (cf. Boucharlat 1984: 130–32); the interpretation of Darius's *tachara* as 'sanctuary' offered by Fennelly (1980: 143–47) smacks of fiction; I remain equally cautious about the proposal of Roaf (1974: 96), repeated by Moorey (1979: 221), suggesting that the live animals carried by servants on some Persepolis reliefs were intended for sacrifice (on these reliefs, cf. the remarks of Sancisi-Weerdenburg 1993c). Herodotus (I.131) and Strabo (XV.3.13) tell us that the Persians erected neither statues (*agalma*: Strabo) nor altars (*bōmos*: Strabo, Herodotus) nor temples (*naos*: Herodotus) to their gods but sacrificed in the open air on high places (cf. also Polyaenus VII.11.12 analyzed above). If this information is correct, research into Persian sanctuaries becomes even more difficult, since they did not give rise to construction. It is true that Herodotus may be referring to popular religion—the oldest stratum of Persian beliefs (cf. Briant 1984a: 103–4); later documents (fourth century) seem to indicate, however, that these regulations did not last the entire time of the Achaemenid Empire (cf. the order given by Artaxerxes II: chapter 15/8 below); the clearest text (but just as problematic!) is a fragment of Dinon (*FGrH* 690 F28): in repeating the prohibition evoked by Herodotus and Strabo, Dinon adds that the Persians erected statues only in honor of Fire and Water. A final remark: the specific example of Anāhita (discussed on p. 253) reminds us of the general problem of the constituent elements of Achaemenid monarchic ideology, which I cannot treat fully here (it would require a specialized work). Disagreeing with the Indo-European interpretation (frequently offered by Benveniste, Dumézil, and even Widengren), Gnoli (1974) has strongly emphasized the Mesopotamian and Babylonian borrowings; Root (1979) has introduced the significance of the Near Eastern iconographic repertory in royal Achaemenid art, but at the same time she rightly stresses that these are not simply borrowings and copies but elements reinterpreted in the framework of a new and original concept (cf. also the reflections of Kuhrt 1984: 159 and Calmeyer 1994, and chaps. 15/8 and 16/10 in this volume).

• *Royal Prayers.* See especially the articles of C. Herrenschmidt (1977, 1985, and 1990a–b), which I have used extensively; nondivine character of Persian royalty: cf., e.g., Calmeyer 1981; on the "trifunctional" prayer of Darius in *DPd*, cf. Benveniste 1938b: 538–43 and Dumézil 1986: 617–21; on the relationship between private and public cults, cf. already the remarks of Gnoli 1974: 181 and Herrenschmidt 1991: 14–16.

• *Official Religion.* Xenophon's Cyrus and the sacrifices: cf. Sancisi-Weerdenburg 1980: 184–216, 1985; also Eddy 1961: 53–54 (but some of his interpretations are moot); the existence of an official cultic calendar (which I deduce from Ctesias §19) is fully confirmed by Koch's (1993a: 86–89) analysis of the Persepolis tablets. Gods and cults in the Persepolis tablets: see the specialist studies by H. Koch (1977, 1987a, and 1991); cult of natural forces: Rapp 1865: 75–77; cult of the mountains and waters in the Persepolis tablets: Koch 1977: 96–100, 1991: 93–95, with my remarks in Briant 1994f: 48, 61 (also p. 47 n. 8 on hydromancy among the Persians according to Strabo XVI.2.39). On the rite of purification of the army, cf. Masson 1950. Achaemenid legacies in Hellenistic Persia : cf. Wiesehöfer 1991a and 1994.

• *The King, the Sacrifices, and the Magi.*   Mentions of *magi* in the tablets: Koch 1977: 156–58; the Dascylium stela was published by Macridy 1913: 348–52 and has frequently been discussed since then (cf. Nollé 1992: 93–96); another fairly similar scene (altar base found near Kayseri, described in chapter 16/6 here): cf. Bittel 1952.

• *Sacrifices and Banquets.*   On Strabo XV.3.14–15, cf. Benveniste 1964: 53–58; sacrifice scenes on seals and sealings, see the documents collected and interpreted by Moorey 1979; the seals affixed to Treasury tablets with cult and religious scenes are described by Schmidt 1957: 9–10. Postsacrificial banquet: see also the text of Nicolaus of Damascus, *FGrH* 90 F66.41. Sacrifices and banquet presided over by Peucestes at Persepolis: cf. *RTP* 80 n. 4 and, since then, Calmeyer 1982: 185–86 (followed by Wiesehöfer 1991a: 130).

• *The King and the Cult of Ahura-Mazda.*   Boyce, *EncIr.*, s.v.; Ahura-Mazda in the Classical texts: Rapp 1865: 47–53; in the Persepolis tablets: Koch 1977: 81–85; *lan* sacrifice: Koch 1977: 129–41, 1987a: 241–45, and 1991: 89–91; Persepolis seals: Schmidt 1957: 8–9.

• *The King and the Worship of Fire.* On the Fire in the Classical texts, cf. Rapp 1865: 73–74 (with the important remarks of Benveniste 1964: 53–58 on the terms *pyraithoi* and *pyraitheia* in Strabo XV.3.15); titles in the Persepolis tablets: Koch 1977: 159–70 (but, as Benveniste 1964: 57 stresses, *aθravan* is simply "the generic and archaic term for priest, with no connection with fire"); Darius at Naqš-i Rustam: Root 1979: 177–79 and Jamzadeh 1991: 95–97; representations of fire altars, cf. Houtkamp 1991; fire altars on the Treasury tablets: Schmidt 1957: 9–10; Zarathustriš seal: Bordreuil 1986a, no. 136 (fig. 33b, p. 244 here); extinguishing the Fire at the death of a king: Briant 1991a: 2.⟦Contrary to the hypotheses developed by Pitschikjan 1992, the Bactrian temple at Takht-i Sangin (whose construction he places solidly in the Achaemenid period: p. 35) is probably not a Fire temple but a sanctuary dedicated to the cult of the deified Oxus River (Bernard 1994a), so that any comparison with the very doubtful "Fire temples" of Susa or Persepolis is based on circular reasoning (cf. Bernard, p. 96 n. 51). Pitschikjan's article has spawned another, by H. Koch (Koch 1993c [1995]); after a very skeptical survey of the archaeological literature on Achaemenid-period Fire temples, Koch also rejects Pitshikjan's interpretation; she proposes an architectural connection between the building of Takht-i Sangin and the Persepolis Treasury and suggests rather surprisingly that the "temple" could have been the headquarters of "a high officer, or even a satrap of the Achaemenids," which would have been occupied in the third century by a Seleucid satrap (p. 186).⟧

• *The King, Mithra, and the Sun.*   The Classical texts on the Sun are collected by Jacobs 1991; cf. the important study of Rapp 1865: 53–60. Mithra and the horse sacrifice (in this volume, chapter 2/9 on the sacrifices around Cyrus's tomb). We should note a very interesting coin from fourth-century Samaria with a very unusual scene in which an unidentified person confronts a horse (CS 58; fig. 61e, p. 715 here): cf. Meshorer and Qedar 1991: 23 and 55 (a theme apparently absent from the seal impressions at Wadi ed-Daliyeh: cf. the annotated list prepared by Leith 1990: 475–76). Relationship between the Sun and Mithra: cf. the study of Gnoli 1979; *Yasht* to Mithra: Gershevitch 1967 and Benveniste 1960; Hvarīra: Koch 1977: 94–95; drunkenness of the king at the Mithra festival: the hypothesis of *haoma* [an intoxicating beverage?] is offered by Bowman 1970: 8 (cf. already in this sense Eddy 1961: 55, and my remarks in Briant 1994f: 47 n. 7); on the *persique*, L. Séchan (*La danse grecque antique*, Paris [1930]: 100–101) is unfortunately highly condensed, and he does not cite the Dinon text; M. H. Delavaud-Roux is also silent about this in *Les Danses armés en Grèce antique*, Aix-en-Provence (1993).

• *The Cult of Anāhita.* I have drawn much profit from the clear remarks in Moorey 1979, where drawings of the two stamps described in the text are found; however, I will not conceal the fact that this cultic interpretation has always suffered several difficulties, brought out by Brosius 1991: 190–93 (whose conclusion is opposite to Moorey's); for the Oxus ring, cf. Dalton pl. XVI (p. 103) and the commentaries on pp. 26–27 (the iconography of the goddess with the lions is found later at Hierapolis Bambyke: Oden 1977: 51–53); Anāhita and the dove: cf. Shepherd 1980, who cites the Achaemenid seals (pp. 56–58); see also the very suggestive article by Hanaway 1982; we may add the tale of the young Semiramis fed by doves, as it is presented by Diodorus (II.4.4–6); cf. also the story of Derketo in Ctesias (Strabo XVI.4.27), which was probably the inspiration for Diodorus (Oden 1977: 69–73); a dove also plays a role (in relation to Aphrodite [Astarte]) in the story of Aspasia in Aelian, *VH* XII.1. We may note that Isidore of Charax (*Parthian Stations* §1) mentions the existence of a sanctuary of Artemis founded by Darius in Babylon on the site of a royal residence (*basileia*; on the location, cf. Galikowski 1988: 82); Artemis was probably Anāhita disguised (even though in §6, speaking of Ecbatana, the author refers to her with the more usual name Anaitis [cf. Polybius X.27]); but it is difficult to be sure that this story actually relates to Darius I. Policy of Artaxerxes II: chapter 15/8.

Chapter 7
People and Life at Court

1. Sources and Problems

• *The Greek Authors and Persian Court Organization.* On the contribution of the Persepolis tablets, cf. most recently Koch 1993a, esp. pp. 61–91.

• *Tents and Palaces.* See especially Briant 1988c: 263–67; on the word *gangabas*, cf. Mancini 1987: 9–60, esp. 43–55 (= **ganzapa*; cf. Elam. *kanzabara*, Aram. *gnzbr'*); Odeon and Xerxes' tent: cf. most recently the (prudent) clarification of Miller 1985: 116–24; on Alexander's and Ptolemy's tents (*pompē*), cf. Lavagne 1988: 95–99 and Perrin 1990. Private apartments in Susa: the interpretation is worked out by Perrot 1981: 86–89; doubts in Amandry 1987: 161; Boucharlat (1990a: 153–57) stresses the weakness of the permanent settlement; settlement in the Persepolis plain: Tilia 1978: 73–91; Artaxerxes II's palace on the bank of the Shaur: *CDAFI* 10 (1979); bathing rooms at Persepolis: Tilia 1977: 74; military quarter at Persepolis: Schmidt 1953: 206–10 and 1975: 97–101; dishes: Schmidt 1957: 81–95; the word *katalyseis* used by Diodorus (XVII.71.8) may imply that habitations were used only temporarily during the periodic stops of the central court: cf. for comparison Herodotus V.52 and Aelian, *VH* I.33; Alexander's banquet is evoked by Boucharlat 1990b: 225 n. 1, in the wider context of the history of the Susa palace during the Hellenistic period. Royal furnishings in various cities of the Empire: cf. references in Briant 1988c: 267 n. 16.

2. Household Staff

• *The Chiliarch and the Audience Service.* On the hypotheses regarding the chiliarch, I refer to my discussion in Briant 1994e: 291–98 (where the bibliographic references will be found). The words *gate* and *door*: cf. Vallat 1974b: 176; on the Darius Gate, cf. the precise description by Perrot and Ladiray 1974; on the terms *Porte* and *Sublime Porte* in the Ottoman Empire, cf. J. Deny and U. Heyd, *EncIslam* I (1960): 859–60.

• *The Royal Guard: Immortals and Bodyguards.* On the guards portrayed on the bricks at Susa, cf. de Mecquenem 1947: 53–54, who also remarks that their garments differ noticeably from the descriptions in the Classical authors; on the word *Immortals* and its probable meaning in Persian, cf. the clarification by Gnoli 1981 and 1982.

• *Protocol and Security.* On the interpretations in Xenophon's *Hellenica*, cf. Santoro 1979, whose conclusions I accept.

• *Royal Meals and Protocol.* The taster (*progeustēs*) was called *edeatros* according to several grammarians; the texts are excerpted and discussed by J. Kalléris, *Les Anciens Macédoniens: Études linguistique et historique*, I (Athens, 1954): 162–69 (who concludes, rather too dogmatically, that the career was Macedonian and not borrowed from the Persian court: cf. Briant 1994e: 284 n. 2).

• *The Great King's Water and Wine.* See my article on this specific topic: Briant 1994f; we may remark on this passage that the cupbearer was required to pour the drops into his left hand, considered by Cyrus (Xenophon) "as more exposed to attack than the right" (*Cyr.* VIII.4.3).

• *The Court Physicians.* The recent article by Huyse (1990) is very unclear and adds nothing on this question; on the chronological problems posed by Ctesias's biography, see the recent clarification by Eck 1990; the Democedes romance has been interpreted with panache and humor by Griffiths 1987: this clearly was a very popular story (cf. Athenaeus XII.522a–d); Egyptian physicians and their specialties: cf., e.g., P. Ghalioungui, *BIFAO* (Bulletin du Centenaire) (1980): 11–18; Udjahorresnet, cf. Posener 1936: 21–26; on leprosy and related diseases in the ancient Near

East, cf. M. Stol, "Leprosy: New Light from Greek Sources," *JEOL* 30 (1987–88): 22–31; according to Dandamaev 1992c: 19, tablets from the archives of the barber Kuṣur-Ea show that several barbers had to take care of people struck by leprosy [but Stolper 1994c and Joannès 1995a show that this represents incorrect readings]. We know far more of the diagnostics and treatments practiced by the physicians of the Assyrian court: see particularly Parpola 1983: 230–38; one text seems to allude to the fear of being poisoned by a prescription: ibid., 131.

• *The Magi, Their Herbs, and Their Stones.* Cf. Bidez and Cumont 1938 II: 106–30, 167–74, 188–91; see also Delatte 1936 and Bidez 1935; on *kardamum* ('cardamom'), cf. Sancisi-Weerdenburg 1993d and 1995; on the Sages at the Neo-Assyrian court, cf. Parpola 1983: xiv–xxi.

3. The Eunuchs

• *Bibliography.* There is no specialized monograph, but in Guyot (1980: 80–91) there are several pages on the eunuchs at the Achaemenid court, as well as an entry on each eunuch named in the ancient sources (pp. 181ff.); also several pages in Miller 1985: 280–82 and Schnoll 1987: 115–18; by way of comparison, one might also consult the articles "Eunuque" in *DictBib.* II (1899): 2044 and *"Khasi"* in *EncIslam* IV (1978): 1118–24, as well as "Homosexualität" in *RlA* 4: 459ff. (J. Bottéro).

• *On the Perfidy of Eunuchs.* On homosexuality among the Persians and an overly simple text of Herodotus (I.135: Persian borrowing of Greek morals), cf. B. Sergent, *L'Homosexualité initiatique dans l'Europe ancienne,* Paris (1986): 192–98, who collects the Classical texts (add Sext. Emp. *Pyrrh.* I.152); see also Petit 1961: 62–63 and notes; on the eunuch Bagoas, lover of Darius III and then Alexander, cf. Badian 1958; on the Egyptian legend of Bagoas, cf. Schwartz 1948; Bagoas as a generic name: cf. Maas 1921: 458–60.

• *Xenophon and the Paradigm of the Faithful Minister.* On the *Dea Syra,* I have closely followed Benveniste 1939 (on the work of [Lucian], cf. the commentary of Oden 1977, esp. pp. 36–40 on Kombabos); Ptah-hotep's inscription: Posener 1986; I do not think anyone has previously attempted a comparison with Xenophon; on the theme of the faithful minister in the romanticized framework of the Achaemenid court, cf. also the curious Qumran text published by Eisenman and Wise 1992: 99–103 (I owe the reference to Amelie Kuhrt).

• *Eunuchism and Emasculation.* Caria: cf. Maas 1921: 458; on the education of royal children, we may note that Quintus Curtius notes the presence "of the king's children and their governesses" (*et quae educabant eos*) in Darius III's procession (III.3.23); this could just as well refer to the king's daughter's (*mārat šarri*) nursemaid, named in a Babylonian tablet dated to Xerxes' accession year (Graziani 1986, no. 8; let us emphasize that this nurse's name, Arṭim, could be Iranian or Anatolian [cf. Artimas] and that in Babylonian the king's daughter's name is transcribed Ittaḫšaḫ, or Rataḫšaḫ: Dandamaev 1992a: no. 51, 252, and 265).

• *Title and Duties.* Batis: sources collected by Berve II, no. 209, and Guyot 1980, no. 23, who call him a eunuch (cf. also Schnoll 1987: 115–16, who is rather imprudent in definitively excluding all sources that call him "king"); Josephus gives his name in the form Babemesis: Marcus (*Josephus* 6, Loeb. Class. Lib. 6 [1966]: 468 note c) reconstructs an Iranian name, Bagamisa, but coins unambiguously confirm the name Batis (cf. M. Delcor, *VT* 1 [1951]: 118–19). On beardless persons at Persepolis, cf. the apposite remarks of Yamauchi 1980: 138–39 (repeated in Yamauchi 1990: 260–64); we may also note that elsewhere Ctesias records the story of the totally effeminized Sardanapalus, who shaved his beard as close as possible (Athenaeus XII.528f); on this theme, cf. also Chiasson 1984; on the beard/beardless problem in Assyrian reliefs, see the very careful interpretations of Reade 1972 (who still postulates the presence of many eunuchs on the reliefs); on the Assyriological discussions, summaries are found in Oppenheim 1973 (who, while obviously acknowledging the existence of eunuchs, rejects the systematic interpretation of *ša rēši* as eunuchs), Tadmor 1983 (who does not want to take a position on the basic problem [cf. n. 10]), Garelli 1974: 276–77 (quotation from p. 277), who opposes Kinnier Wilson's interpretation (1972: viii–ix, 46ff.);

generally speaking, the theory of a large number of eunuchs at the Assyrian court seems to have fewer supporters these days (cf. the long critical note of J. A. Brinkman and S. Dalley, ZA 78 [1978]: 85 n. 27), but it remains hardy nonetheless: the theory of "eunuchization" of the Assyrian court has been revived by J. M. Durand in *Dossiers d'archéologie* 171 (1992): 6; Parpola (esp. 1983: 20–21), on the other hand, continues to think that the *ša rēši* has to be considered a eunuch and nothing else; this is based in part on Classical sources (including Ctesias), or at least he includes references to them; but the connection he suggests between the two corpora overlooks the interpretive problems examined here. On the Hebrew word *saris*, see Yamauchi 1990: 261–62; in the hieroglyphic inscriptions, cf. Posener 1936: 118–19 (court title, "probably borrowed from Aramaic"); cf. also Ray's (1988: 273 n. 47) remark: there is nothing to suggest the translation of *saris* as 'eunuch'; the author suggests understanding it as equivalent to *peḥā*; and Vergote 1959: 40–42; to my knowledge, Levy (1940) was the first and only person to use the evidence of the Wadi Hammamât inscriptions. Let us note, finally, that the term *ša rēš šarri* is also found in Achaemenid-period Babylonian tablets as an attribute of high persons (including the one sometimes translated 'the king's principal', who was entrusted with overseeing the administration of the sanctuary of the Eanna): there is no reason to think these persons were eunuchs (cf. Brinkman 1968: 309–11; Oppenheim 1973: 329; see several attestations of LÚ *rēš šarri* in Dandamaev 1992a: 220, s.v.).

4. The Women's Side

Thanks to the Maria Brosius's generosity, I have been able to consult her unpublished monograph (1991), which discusses the Persepolis tablets at great length along with the Classical texts; I will cite it only occasionally and not discuss some of its interpretations, because the author is currently working on a publication version.

• *Wives and Concubines.* The title *dukšiš* is given to Irtašduna (Artystone), one of Darius's wives, in the tablet Fort. 6764 (cf. also PF 1795); the word must not be translated 'my daughter' (as Cameron 1942 does); it must include the meaning 'princess', as shown by Benveniste 1966: 43–50; but, probably under the influence of Greek vocabulary, he is also inclined to interpret it as 'queen', which is wrong: for one thing, the title *dukšiš* is known for several high-ranking women (wives, sisters, and probably daughters of the king) in the Fortification tablets (PF 823; Q 812; PFa 31; see Brosius 1991: 29–32); to speak of 'queens' (Königinnen) in regard to Darius's wives, as Koch 1994 regularly does, risks leading us into error: later on we will return to the place of the king's mother at court and the political role of the princesses (chapter 13/2: Darius, Xerxes, and Atossa). On the slaves of the king (*arad šarri*) and the palace (*arad ekalli*), cf. Dandamaev 1984b: 561–64 and 565–67. On depictions of women in Achaemenid art, cf. the preliminary remarks of Spycket 1980 and the annotated collection of documents in Brosius 1991, chapter 5; we may add to the category of female statuettes (cf. Amiet 1972: 173–80 and Cooney 1965) the recent discoveries in the "Achaemenid residence" of Abū Qubūr north of Sippar: Spycket 1991; additionally, the Olympia relief erected by Lysippus in honor of Polydamas (who had just fought the Immortals at Darius II's court: Pausanias II.5) showed, according to the original editors, the king seated on his throne along with four women (cf. *Historische und philologische Aufsätze E. Curtius* [Berlin, 1884]: 240–42; drawing p. 240; cf. most recently Gabelmann 1984: 80–82); but the highly damaged condition of the sculpture allows serious doubt about the interpretation; in the drawing, hardly anything is visible except for the king on his throne and the bottoms of several robes, but are they women's—or do they instead belong to the Immortals referred to directly by the sculptor?

• *The Great King's 360 Concubines.* On the figure 360 in tributes, see the reflections of Asheri 1991: 49–53 (followed here) and Nylander 1993: 157 n. 62; the doubts raised by Schwartz (1986: 273) on Herakleides' text do not strike me as justified; on the other hand, the author does a good job of showing the interpenetration of the various versions in Josephus and the book of Esther.

• *Cloistered Women? The Myth of the Harem.* On the social activities of the princesses, cf. Brosius 1991: 91ff. The word *gynaikōnitis* is found in Diodorus's description of the oasis of

Ammon: "The second enclosure contains the court of the *gynaeceum*, the dwellings of the children, women, and relatives, as well as the bodyguards of the overseers of the *gynaeceum* . . ." (XVII.50.3); on the Egyptian vocabulary, cf. Ward 1983; on Mari, cf. Durand and Margueron 1980; Weidner's use of the term *harem* (1956: 261–62) has no semantic justification; letter (i.e., the private chancellery) of Atossa, cf. Briant 1992b; theme of the woman-warrior: in addition to Ctesias, cf. the curious text of Polyaenus VIII.60 (within a chapter dedicated to fighting women); Polyaenus introduces one Rhodogune, whose story is copied from Semiramis's (VIII.26), and the author concludes: "This is why the impression of the Persian royal seal shows Rhodogune with her hair hanging down and attached with a knot": this has no basis in fact (cf. Baldus 1987)! Women warriors in Iranian literature: Hanaway 1982. Seals and depictions of women: see especially Brosius 1991: 179–93 and Garrison 1988: 477–78 (Artystone) and 1992: 4–10.

5. At the Great King's Table

• *Service at the King's Table.* Polyaenus's text has not received a great deal of study (aside from a curious note signed L. L. in *CJ* 30 (1827): 370–74); D. Lewis (1987) deserves credit for recognizing its importance: the author is especially interested in comparisons with the tablets, without offering a detailed commentary on the passage; he rightly establishes a correspondence with a well-known inscription of Aššurnaṣirpal II (cf. Wiseman 1952 and Grayson 1991 no. 30); on the royal banquets and consumption of ostriches, see also Sancisi-Weerdenburg's note 1993c [on the same point for the Neo-Assyrian period, see Mallowan 1966, I: 119–21 and Joannès 1995: 186–88, and for the Achaemenid period, Bennett and Blakely 1989: 263] — and, by way of comparison, K. Wilson 1972: 32ff. (as well as Mattila 1990) and especially the remarkable study of Milano 1989; on this subject, see most recently Sancisi-Weerdenburg 1995. On Polyaenus's source (cf. Lewis 1987: 81 and n. 3): the reference to an inscription of Cyrus seems to confirm that Polyaenus acquired his information from a companion of Alexander (on epigraphic propaganda in Alexander's time, cf. *RTP* 389–91); on the use of the *marriš* in Polyaenus, cf. Bernard's note 1985b: 93–94; abundance of the table and "decadence" in the Greek authors: Briant 1989a; redistributions: cf. Briant 1989b and Sancisi-Weerdenburg 1989b; on the word *potibazis*, Xenophon's vocabulary (*Cyr.* VIII.1.9), and their relationship to Akkadian vocabulary, cf. esp. Eilers 1940: 64–81; see also Stolper 1985a: 57–58 (Wiseman 1983b: 85 n. 26 notes that the word *potibazis* is also found in the Nisa materials); on administrative aspects, see also Heltzer 1979, who uses a Babylonian tablet dated to the "month of Ayar [of the] first year of Darius, king of Babylon and king of the countries" [= D. Owen, *Mesopotamia* 1975, no. 33]; the text anticipates the delivery of dried apples and raisins to the cooks, with each of the 28 named cooks receiving a given quantity. On dairy products, cf. also *RTP* 349–50; raising waterfowl in Babylonia: Cardascia 1951: 173; on beer in Mesopotamia, cf. Stol 1994; on fish-farming in Babylonia (Neo-Babylonian and Achaemenid periods), cf. Dandamaev 1981b; tablets from Category J and the seals on them (including Kuraš of Anšan's: PFS 93): cf. Garrison 1992: 2–3. Distribution of Near Eastern arbutuses in the West Anatolian and Greek region: cf., e.g., Cousin and Deschamp 1889: 536–37; on the terebinth/pistachio tree, cf. Amigues 1995: 71–72.

• *Musicians, Dancers, and Artists.* For the preceding periods, cf. the entries *nārtu* (female musicians), *nāru* (male musicians), and *nārutu* (music) in the CAD; I am strongly tempted to think that the pseudo–personal name Annaros in Ctesias (Athenaeus XII.530d) was formed on this Akkadian root—which would give even more sense to the popular story Ctesias heard in the Babylonia of his time. [M. Stolper reminds me, following Roth, *CSSH* 29 (1987): 740ff., that many Neo-Babylonian occurrences of SAL.NAR = *nārtu* mean not 'women musicians' but 'girls'; this remark does not formally invalidate the hypothesis I present here on the possible etymology of Annaros.] On Polydamas, cf. Gabelmann 1984: 80–82 and my remarks above.

• *Cups and Couches.* On Achaemenid dinnerware, cf. especially Amandry 1958a–b; Culican 1971; von Bothmer 1981; Moorey 1984, 1985, 1988: 82–89; also Miller 1985: 124–37; Gunter

1989: 22–30; Prfommer 1991; Miller 1993; Rozenberg 1993. On the reclining banquet and the special position of the king, cf. Dentzer 1982: 64–69; cf. also Lavagne 1988: 96–101 and Perrin 1990: 224–26 (the king is placed under an *ouraniskos*).

6. The Royal Hunts

Cf. Briant 1991c and 1993b, where more complete references will be found; cf. also pp. 230ff. above on royal hunt protocol; on hunting with nets, cf. Meuli 1975. It is likely that, as with the Assyrians, the hunters were accompanied by dogs: Xenophon mentions 'those in charge of the horses and the dogs' (*hippōn kay kynōn epimeletai*; *Cyr.* VIII.1.9); it is also possible that two Persepolis tablets (PF 1264–65) refer to hunting dogs (*PF*: 40). We especially have information on the breeding of dogs of war, such as those mentioned by Herodotus in Babylon (I.192: Indian dogs), and by Pliny (VIII.61) in Colophon and Cilicia (later period); but it does appear that these are the same dogs that were taken hunting (cf. Aelian, *VH* XIV.46), as Xenophon indicates in *On Hunting* (9.1; 10.1). On Darius III's pet dog, cf. Aelian, *Anim.* VI.25. On the dogs (statues) at Persepolis, cf. Kawami 1986: 260–63.

7. Royal Pomp

On the Greek concepts of royal *tryphē* (Achaemenid or Hellenistic), cf. Briant 1989a.

Chapter 8
The King's Men

Bibliography

This chapter constitutes a considerably expanded rewriting of analyses presented in preliminary form in Briant 1987a: 21–31 and Briant 1990a.

1. *The Giving King*

• *Bibliography.* See Sancisi-Weerdenburg 1988b and 1989b in particular. [Also van der
Veen 1995 debating Gould 1991 on the story of Syloson.]

• *The King's Benefactors.* Cf. Wiesehöfer 1980, who reminds us (p. 8) that the likely etymology of the Iranian word (corresponding to *orosangae*) goes back to **varusanha-*, i.e., 'highly renowned'; register: cf. also Josephus, *Ant.* XI.248 (plagiarizing Esther).

• *The Royal Gifts.* See for comparison the article "Hiba" in *EncIslam* III² (1971): 353–60
(there are many similarities); on Herodotus IX.109, cf. Sancisi-Weerdenburg 1988b; the gift of
robes of honor is also well known among the Incas: cf. J. V. Murra, "Cloth and Its Functions in the
Inca State," *Amer. Anthrop.* 64 (1962): 710–28; on the importance of dress as social indicator for the
Persians, cf. esp. Plutarch, *Mor.* 173c.3 and 565a; cf. also Sancisi-Weerdenburg 1983: 27–30 (on
Herodotus IX.108–13); a hierarchy of gifts in relation to the value/weight of the object is well attested at the court of Hammurabi of Babylon: see the very interesting note Joannès 1989d (to which
I return below in the research note to chap. 10/5, royal coinage); Masistios: Briant 1990a: 100; on
Ctesias §22, could the "gold millstone" be, if not the same as, at least comparable to the *plinthos
khrysē* on which the royal counsellor stood, before receiving it as payment "if his counsel was
judged good and useful" (cf. Aelian, *VH* XII.62, with the remark of Villanueva-Puig 1989: 293)?

• *Gifts and Honors: The Court Hierarchy.* On the king's table, cf. also chaps. 5/6 and 7/5;
Ptolemaic court hierarchy and its probable Persian antecedents: cf. the (careful) discussion by
Mooren 1977: 17ff.; on *philos*, cf. Wiesehöfer 1980: 11–14; titles and functions: cf. the very wide
diffusion of the title "lance-bearer" (*aštebarriāna*) in the Babylonian tablets: Stolper 1985a: 55 and
n. 12; king's relatives: cf. Benveniste 1966: 22–26, who on the *br byt'* of the Aramaic papyri writes:
"'Sons of the House' no longer applies to a single person, the crown prince, son of the king, but to
a class of royal princes who probably had no immediate kinship with Darius II"; cf. also on this
subject the analyses in Gauger 1977 (whose conclusions I do not follow in every respect) and the
thoughts of Mooren 1977: 40–41.

• *Gifts and Redistribution of Wealth.* Gold phial of Demos, cf. Vickers 1984 and Sancisi-
Weerdenburg 1989b: 134, as well as C. Gronatelli's interesting remarks in *Scienze dell'antichità* 2
(1988): 249–50; this document seems to indicate, as seems logical (cf. Xenophon, *Cyr.* VIII.2.8),
that the royal gifts bore a distinguishing mark which in some cases (vessels) could be an inscription: cf. Nylander 1968: 124–27; Sancisi-Weerdenburg 1989b: 134, 142 and n. 14; Gunter and Jett
1992: 69–73. PT 4–5, cf. Hinz 1973: 75–76 (who offers a highly speculative narrative explanation)
and Cameron PTT 89–91 (but I doubt that the Parnaka listed in PT 4 is the high official found
throughout PF); land grants, cf. Briant 1985b; Sancisi-Weerdenburg 1989b and below, chapters
10/7 and 11/9; Satibarzanes: on the date see Briant 1994e: 309–10. Royal table and redistribution:
Briant 1989b, Sancisi-Weerdenburg 1989b: 133–35; 1993e; and 1995; Aššurnaṣirpal's banquet:
published in Wiseman 1952 (latest edition in Grayson 1991: 292–93); distribution of foodstuffs at
the Neo-Assyrian court, cf. also Fales-Postgate 1992, no. 157. Quotation from J. Bottéro, *RlA*, s.v.
Mahlzeit, 260.

2. Unequal Exchange

• *Gifts with Strings Attached.* In general, see M. Mauss, *Essai sur le don*, Paris 1923–25 (= *Sociologie et anthropologie*, 1968); on the Thucydides passage, cf. Mauss 1921, who compares the Thracian practice described by Xenophon, *Anab.* VII.2.35–38 and VII.3.21–34 (Seuthes festival); the Benveniste quotation comes from "Don et échange dans le vocabulaire indo-européen," *Annales de Sociologie* 1948–49 (p. 7); cf. Briant 1982b: 88–94; on the royal banquet (*tykta*), cf. Sancisi-Weerdenburg 1980: 147–51 and 1989b: 132.

3. The King and His Faithful: The Rationale of the System

• *Faithful and* bandaka. On the Persian word and its connotations, see the articles "banda" (W. Eilers) and "bandaka" (C. Herrenschmidt) in *EncIr* III: 682–85; on the belt, cf. Widengren 1968 who, here as elsewhere, insists without much support on the "feudal" character of Persian society; the importance of Xenophon's passage on Orontas has been rightly stressed by Petit 1909: 148–49 (n. 161); right hand: cf. Sherwin-White 1978; rows of nobles at Persepolis: cf. Roaf 1983: 83–114; Trumpelmann 1983: 231–37, and 1988; Calmeyer 1991b.

• *Education and Ideological Integration.* See *RTP* 449–51; see also Widengren 1969: 82–86 and Knauth and Najamabadi 1975: 76–92, who also compare the rite of passage with the Lacedae-monian *kryptie* (on which, cf. the rich analyses of Vidal-Naquet 1983: 125–207 and 1989 who (p. 402) suggests lines of comparison with Iranian societies, following Davidson 1985: 81–87); on the *kardakes*, see the discussion by Knauth and Najamabadi 1975: 83–84; and the texts quoted by Segre, *Clara Rhodos* 9 (1938): 193–94 (n. 2); and Bosworth 1980a: 208 (we will return later to this military category, which poses many interpretive problems; cf. Index s.v. *kardakes*); on the diet and the identification of *terminthos* = pistachio nut, see Amigues 1995: 71–72 and Sancisi-Weerden-burg 1995. On *alētheia*, cf. also *RTP* 381–83, 449, and Sancisi-Weerdenburg forthcoming (2); and on the name *Artaioi* previously given to the Persians according to Herodotus (VII.61), cf. Pirart 1995. On the name Angares: I do not recall ever having seen any commentary on the Athenaeus passage presented in the text; I am tempted to offer the same hypothesis that I presented on Annaros (above, p. 921). On the role of the *magi* as preservers of memory, cf. also the hypotheses of Gershevitch 1969: 181, s.v. *pirramasda* ("It would be a possible designation of priest who had learned to recite the largest number of hymns required") and, on memory transmission, Cardona 1980: 282; in this context, some importance is sometimes accorded to Persepolis tablets that mention in such-and-such a year, Persian *puhu* "copied texts at Pittaman" (PF 871, 1137)—which would seem to imply that writing was widespread among the Persians. But such documents are not conclusive; in fact, they concern *kurtaš* who were probably trained in the scribal craft, which does not imply extensive literary knowledge or direct access, for example, to royal inscriptions (cf. Cardona's remarks 1980: 280 n. 6). Let us also recall that, according to Pausanias (V.27.5–6), in his time a *magus* sang the invocations in a foreign language in the Persian sanctuaries of Hiero-caesarea and Hypaipa, reading them from a book (Robert 1976: 28–29). The last detail may imply a development toward writing down the songs that the *magi* had traditionally transmitted orally (cf. Briant 1985a: 192 n. 71 following Cumont); on the epithet Mnemon given to Artaxerxes II, cf. Schmitt, *EncIr*, s.v. Artaxerxes II (p. 656). A final remark on the youths: based on an erroneous (in my opinion) interpretation of Arrian IV.13.1 (Briant 1994e: 298–307), a hypothesis was developed by Kienast (1973) according to which the institution of royal pages (*basilikoi paides*) was borrowed from the Achaemenid court by Philip II. Since I wrote my article in *AchHist* VIII, I have learned that Clamer (1952) used the French word *page* for the persons who were in Ahasuerus's service in Esther 6:1. But this translation is unwarranted; in any case, it is not clearly relevant to the thesis of the existence of "royal pages" at the Achaemenid court. For one thing, the Septuagint uses the word *diakōnos* (better translated 'servant' by L. C. L. Brenton, *The Septuagint Version: Greek and English* [1970]: 658–59); as for the Hebrew word *naʿar* (pl. *neʿārim*), it simply refers to a "group of young men, or youths, in the service of a patron" (Bordreuil 1992: 190); it thus expresses a hierarchy based on both age and rank (cf. Bordreuil and Israel 1991–92); we find the same ambivalence in Greek *pais* as well as Elamite *puhu* (on which cf. Hallock 1960: 93–94, and PFT: 38–39, 47, 746; also the remarks of Lewis 1994: 24, 26; and Giovinazzo 1994a–b, who translates it with 'valet'). Although the word *page* in French or English renders the word used in Greek (*paides*) to designate the well-known Macedonian institution of "royal pages," I see no need to modify my former conclusion; on the contrary, I restate that the institution of royal pages is inserted into a political context quite different from the context of the Achaemenid court (cf. on this exact point Briant 1994e: 302–7). Finally I will add that since this note was written, Kienast's interpretation has been repeated by Borchhardt 1993c: analyzing a sculpted block of the *hérōon* of Limyra, he proposes (pp. 352–53) that we find portrayed there the corps of *basilikoi paides*—a Macedonian institution created, he claims, after an Achaemenid precedent; starting with this belief, Borchhardt then inappropriately overlays the texts about Macedonian pages onto the supposed Persian institution, claiming (as if to provide better backing for his Lycian interpretation) that the central institution had been adopted in "every court within the Persian Empire"; I think that, if my proof is recognized, it becomes more interesting to ask why so many people on the Limyra frieze (including those in the scene analyzed by Borchhardt: cf. fig. 54, p. 673) wear the low-brimmed hat (i.e., a Macedonian fashion).

4. The King and His Faithful: The Dynamic of the Contradictions

• *Birth and Royal Favor.* *azata ('nobility'): cf. F. de Blois 1985; the word has been found in an Aramaic document from Egypt (Benveniste 1954: 298–99); *amata* ('noble'): cf. Harmatta, *Entretiens Hardt* XXV (1990): 106–7; on social distinctions, cf. Briant 1990a: 71–77, followed now by Calmeyer 1991b (who also uses the Persepolis reliefs)—as well as Stolper's remark (1993: 10–11) on the Babylonian word *parastāmu*, which he tentatively suggests comparing with *prōtoi* ('princes, aristocracy').

• *Royal Favor and Social Mobility.* Cf. Sancisi-Weerdenburg's reflections 1989a: 139; on Maraphii/Marappiyaš, cf. Benveniste 1958a: 56–57.

• *Persian Aristocratic Houses.* On styles of greeting, see, from the point of view of comparative history, the recent work of Y. Carré, *Le Baiser sur la bouche au Moyen Âge: Rites, symboles, mentalités* (Paris, 1992); on the Athenaeus passage (IV.145f–146a), cf. the important suggestions by Eilers 1940: 73.

5. King and Satraps

• *Bibliography.* Lehmann-Haupt 1921; Petit 1990.

• *Family Strategies and Royal Control.* On the Pharnacids of Hellespontine Phrygia, cf. Lewis 1977: 52 and Hornblower 1982: 145ff.; for other examples, cf. Briant 1987a: 25–28; Aspathines: cf. Cameron PTT 103 and Schmitt 1957, seal no. 14; see Lewis 1985: 115.

• *The Satrap and the Armed Forces.* This is a much-debated problem, on which see the overview by Tuplin 1987b, esp. pp. 228–32 (who rightly judges that the satrap had to count on the aid of the garrison commanders); Petit's position (1990: 109–19) appears to me insufficiently qualified (diminution of satrapal powers under Darius; separation between civil and military powers); it relies heavily on reconstructions of Xenophon (cf. RTP 176–88); *karanos*: cf. Petit 1983 and 1990: 133–44 (once again too schematic, on the presumed date [Darius] of the institution: pp. 143–44); on the chain of command at Elephantine, cf. most recently Wiesehöfer 1991b (and on *rab haylâ*, Lipiński 1975: 176: in a Greek-Aramaic bilingual from Farasa, the word is rendered by Greek *stratēgos*); the Babylonian tablet VS 6.128 is translated and annotated by Joannès 1982: 24–25 and 1990b: 187 n. 60 (with some changes); cf. also Van Driel 1989: 207 (who makes Guzānu the *šākin tēmi* of Babylon); on the dependency of the *gazophylax* ('guardian of the treasury') with regard to the central authority, cf. the Hellenistic texts quoted in RTP 211; satrap and coinage: cf. my remarks in Briant 1989c: 328–30 [[and the brief considerations of Mildenberg 1993: 58–60]].

- *Royal Inspectors.* Cf. Hirsch 1985a: 101–34.
- *Satrapal Courts and the Royal Court.* A few summary pages appear in Petit 1990: 147–52; and an attempt at synthesis in Borchhardt 1990; on the paradise (a theme often broached in the course of this work), cf. index s.v.; Dascylium bullas: Kaptan-Bayburtluoglu 1990. Satrapal audiences: Gabelmann 1984: 35–61 (Lycian documents); on the throne of Cyrus the Younger, we may mention that a throne of Achaemenid type (but certainly made locally) was found in the excavations of Samaria (Stern 1982b: 143–44); further, Nehemiah 3:7 refers to "men of Gibeon and Mizpah (belonging) to the throne (*lᵉkisseʾ*) of the governor of Trans-Euphrates"; whether this concerns land connected directly to the governor (Briant 1985b: 67) or a satrapal residence (Lemaire 1990: 39–40), we must stress that the "throne" symbolizes satrapal power itself (comparable with a Babylonian formula: Joannès 1982: 28 n. 1).

6. The King and His Faithful: The Persians, the Greeks, and the Others

An entry on each of the Greeks listed below will be found in Hofstetter 1978; cf. also Wiesehöfer 1980 and Herman 1987: 106–15 (on the *dōreai* of the Achaemenid and Hellenistic periods; summary table, pp. 109–10). The story of Themistocles at the court of the Great King and the jealousy shown toward him by the Persian aristocrats has a parallel (or a copy) in the story of Daniel at the court of Nebuchadnezzar (Daniel 6); another imaginative "good story" on the theme of Themistocles at the court of the Great King: Diodorus XI.57 (marriage and judgment of Themistocles). The list of satraps compiled in the text was drawn up using information from the Persepolis tablets by recognizing with Hinz (1970: 430) and many others that the person who provides a sealed authorization (*halmi*) to travelers is in fact the satrap of the place of departure (cf. Briant 1991b: 70 n. 13 and 1992c). On this point, see Koch 1993a: 5–48, where analyses will be found dealing with nine provinces of the Iranian Plateau as well as India and Syria; summary table, p. 47; list of the satraps of Babylonia and Trans-Euphrates: Stolper 1989b: 290–91. [[I note that my very tentative conclusion on the place of the Medes among the imperial political personnel (chap. 8/6, last sentence) agrees very closely with the position laid out by Tuplin 1994: 255–56.]]

7. Achaemenid Royalty and Persian Aristocracy

- *Power and Kinship.* On Parnaka, see below, chap. 11; the distinguished place of Hystaspes, father of Darius, in Parthia-Hyrcania in 522 is deduced from DB §35 (cf. Koch 1993a: 33–34), information that seems to contradict Herodotus's mention of Hystaspes *"hyparkhos* of Persia" (III.70); we may rightly suppose that the DB version is more accurate than Herodotus (whose mention probably comes from a version of the Founder Legend; cf. Nicolaus of Damascus, FGrH 90 F66.10: Cyrus makes his father Atradates the satrap of the Persians); on the status of Persia, cf. below, chap. 11/10. On the relatives of Darius and Xerxes in Herodotus's catalog, cf. Burn 1984: 333–36; Megabates: Lewis 1985: 115; satraps from the royal family: Briant 1984b: 75–76.

Chapter 9
Territories, Communication, and Trade

- *Bibliography.* An up-to-date and virtually exhaustive bibliography is found in Briant 1991b and Graf 1993, 1994. The existence of these recent works (cf. also Wiesehöfer 1993: 350–51) leads me to limit the number of bibliographic references given here.

1. The Network of Roads

- *The Royal Roads.* On the PF (Category Q), see especially Koch 1986, 1993a [and now Giovinazzo 1994a–b]; use of military historians to reconstruct the landscape (RTP 141–45) and itineraries: cf. Engels 1978 (to be used with extreme caution); Seibert 1985; and, on Xenophon's sources and method, Tuplin 1991b: 46–48 and Briant ed. 1995b; among the most useful works, although late and concerned solely with the central and eastern part of the Empire, is the *Mansiones Parthicae* of Isidore of Charax (ed. Schof), on which see Dillemann 1962, Khlopin 1977, Chaumont 1984, Walser 1985, and Galikowski 1988. Persepolis–Susa road: cf. Mostafavi 1960, Hallock 1977, Koch 1986, and Sumner 1986: 17, 28; also RTP 161–73 (use of Classical sources); Briant 1976 and 1988c (roads between the royal residences); on the Cossaean road, cf. Briant 1976 and 1982b: 81ff.; the course of Herodotus's Sardis–Susa road continues to sustain long-fought problems: cf. Briant 1973: 49–53; Seibert 1985: 18–19; Graf 1993a; Chaumont 1986–87 (Matiene: region between Lake Urmia and the headwaters of the Little Zab); also Mutafian 1988 I: 113–18; route of Cyrus the Younger: see Cousin 1904; Manfredi 1986; Mutafian 1988 I: 119–21; [and Müller 1994, Graf 1994: 173–80, Debord 1995; Syme 1995: 3–23 was actually not written recently]; place-name Laḫirū (Laʾir) in *DAE* 67: cf. Dandamaev 1993c.

- *Secondary Itineraries.* References in Briant 1976: 197 and 243–44 n. 52; 1991b: 74–75; Arrian, *Ind.* 43.3; cf. Tarn, *CR* 40 (1926): 13–15; Briant 1982b: 117–19, 129, 132; and now the arguments of Winnicki 191: 193–97; Esarhaddon, Cambyses, and the Arabs: Ephʿal 1982: 137–42; Briant 1982b: 163–64.

- *Road Building and Maintenance.* Hamaxitos: Briant 1991b: 74; search for Achaemenid roads: Schmidt 1957: 20–21; Kleiss 1981; Mousavi 1989; to fill out the information, one might be tempted to use what the ancient authors wrote about Semiramis's road-building activities (Diodorus sII.13.5; Polyaenus VIII.26), but this is an uncertain method, despite the concurrence between Achaemenid achievements and the achievements legendarily attributed to Semiramis; on the problems posed by the vocabulary of some Persepolis tablets, cf. Briant 1991b: 73 n. 20. The figures regarding ancient China come from J. Needham, *Science and Civilisation in China* (Cambridge 1954): IV, 36 (the entire chapter, pp. 1–38, should be read).

- *Bridges and Bridge-Builders.* Bridge near Persepolis: Nichol 1970 (cf. Sumner 1986: 13–16); Pasargadae: Stronach 1978: 113–16; "bridge-builders" at Nippur: Stolper 1985a: 76 and 1992c: 76–77 (publication of tablets; the author notes, p. 74, that elsewhere the head of the "bridge workers" has the title "Head of the tolls at Opis[?]"); Mazzarino (1966: 78) stresses that, unlike the Greeks, the Persian engineers had some knowledge in this area; they had probably learned a great deal from their predecessors, as Parpola rightly stresses (1983: 245 and 295; he also notes that a tablet from the time of Darius mentions a bridge at Borsippa); on the bridge at Babylon, cf. Wiseman 1983b: 63–64. [On Arrian V.7.3–5, see now Bosworth 1995: 219–27.]

2. Control of the Imperial Territory

- *Satrapal Authorizations—Military Escorts—The Highway Patrol.* Cf. Briant 1991b: 70–73 and Briant 1992c (The *Letters* of Themistocles are edited, translated, and annotated by Doenges

1981); on Alcibiades' flight and his route, cf. Robert 1980: 257–307; on the journeys of Ezra and Nehemiah, cf. Williamson 1991: 54–61 (a reading of the biblical texts in the light of PF). The Arad ostraca were published by Naveh 1981; cf. also Aharoni 1981 and Temerev 1980 (studies of rations, compared with those known from Elephantine); see also the Beer-sheba ostraca: Naveh 1973 and 1979 (hundreds of Aramaic ostraca of the same type and date [fourth century] as those from Beer-sheba have recently come on the antiquities market originating from unknown sites in Idumea; some are in the course of publication: André Lemaire, pers. comm.); meanwhile, there is some doubt about the interpretation of the post as a station on a road (see on this subject the reflections in Tuplin 1987c: 187 and de Salles 1991a: 221–22); on one of Herodotus's anecdotes on the highway patrol (V.35), cf. Foucault 1967a.

• *Royal Mail and Royal Couriers.* *Aggareion*: Rostowzew 1909; also D. Sperber, "Angaria in Rabbinic Literature," *AC* 38/1 (1969): 162–68, and Herrenschmidt 1993a–b; *astandēs*: Chantraine *DELG*, s.v., and most recently Happ 1992; *pirradaziš*: PFT 42; Q 1809: the tablet is published and commented on by Lewis 1980; visual signals in the Empire: Aschof 1977a; also P. Girard, "Les signaux lumineux dans l'*Agamemnon* d'Eschyle," *REA* 11 (1909): 289–95; in Judea: Lemaire 1977: 113–14; at Mari, G. Dossin, "Signaux lumineux au pays de Mari," *RA* 34 (1938): 175–76; Egyptian post in the Seleucid period: Preisigke 1907: 241–77, and Van't Dack 1962: 338–41 thinks that the spread of the system to Egypt goes back to the Persians, including pyro-telegraphy. It is clear that in all these areas the Persians themselves borrowed much from their Assyrian predecessors. On the royal roads (*harrān šarri*), the relays and postal stages (*mardītu*), and the express couriers (*kallē*) in the Neo-Assyrian kingdom, cf. esp. Weidner 1966, Wilson 1972: 57–58, Malbran-Labat 1982: 12–29, and *harrānu* and *mardītu* in CAD; *harrān šarri* ['royal road'] passing very close to Nippur in the Achaemenid period: Zadok 1978: 286–87; but we may also go back much further in time, as is shown very instructively in M. Sigrist's article "Les courriers de Lagaš" in *Fragmenta Historiae Elamicae* (Paris, 1966): 51–63, where the administrative system described (assignments, couriers, tablets, archives) resembles very closely what can be discerned in the Category Q tablets; by way of comparison, see also the synthesis by A. D. Crown, "Tidings and instructions: How news travelled in the Ancient Near East," *JESHO* 17/3 (1974): 244–71, as well as the article *Barid* in *Enc-Islam* I² (1961): 1077–78 (D. Sourdel); on Diodorus XIX.17.6–7, see the doubts expressed on this tradition by Aschoff 1977b (with the comments of Graf 1994: 168).

• *Lines of Communication and Strategy.* *Via militaris* in Quintus Curtius: cf. Briant 1984b: 66–68; stores of water: Briant 1982b: 164 and Briant 1984b: 67; cf. also more generally Briant 1986c. [[Baslez 1995.]]

• *The Gates of the Empire and the Network of Garrisons.* On the Cilician and Syrian Gates, cf. the discussion in Mutafian 1988 1.125–29; see also Bosworth 1980a: 198–204; Manfredi 1986: 74–77; Hammond 1994; Caspian Gates: Bosworth 1980a: 333–41 [[bibliography in Bernard 1994b: 483 n. 11]]; Gates at the entrance to Persia: cf. discussion and bibliography in RTP 161–73; on the garrisons, see Tuplin 1987c and 1991b: 54–57; site of Thapsacus: cf. Briant 1991b: 77 and 78 n. 37 with Lendle 1988 and Manfredi 1991; Deve Hüyük: Moorey 1975 and 1980 (with the critical remarks of Mazzoni 1991–92: 66–67, who stresses that the history of the site extends throughout the *longue durée* from the time of Iron I). The limits of using the military historians to reconstruct the network of permanent Achaemenid garrisons are well laid out by Tuplin 1987c: 209–10 (on the Cilician Gates and the Persian Gates); cf. also Tuplin 1991b: 56 (who notes that many garrisons could have been located in the flat country and remarks that the lack of supplies and difficulty in crossing rivers were sufficient obstacles in normal times in the face of a strong enemy).

• *The King's Service.* Xenophon (*Cyr.* VIII.6.17) and Herodotus (VIII.98) state that the royal couriers traveled day and night; this information is sometimes compared with a passage in the Behistun inscription: "What was said to them [subjects], day or night, they did" (*DB* §§19–20); but Darius's statement rests on a very different foundation than a simple roadway metaphor: "These lines implicitly say that the Achaemenid king offers his empire the same protection as some deities:

he is alert and issues orders in the night to forestall the threats of the Druj [*drauga*] and to conserve Order [*arta*] during the time when it is invisible" (Kellens 1995: 25). For what it's worth, the highly ideologized concept transmitted by the Greek authors of the dominion exercised by the Great King thanks to the roads and the postal service can be compared with what (it seems) Confucius says of the Empire of the Chou High Kings: "The radiation of virtue is faster than the transmission of [imperial] orders by stages and couriers (*chih yu*)"; J. Needham, *Science and Civilisation in China* (Cambridge, 1971) vol. IV, part 3: 35, from whom I take the quotation, observes that "this remark [of Confucius] would have been made, it is curious to note, at a time exactly contemporary with the functioning of the Persian Royal Road, ca. 495."

3. Lines of Communication and Trade

- *Commercial Arteries?* I touched on this problem briefly in Briant 1991b: 79–82: I largely withdraw my earlier remarks; cf. also Wiesehöfer 1982 (with my remark in Briant 1991b: 81 n. 44); Xenophon's *Anabasis*: the hypothesis about the phrase *polis oikoumenē* ("autonomous" city) was developed by Geysels 1974, but to me it seems to be only a partial explanation; the problem was touched on in several presentations at the international conference *Dans le pas des Dix-Mille: Peuples et pays du Proche-Orient vus par un Grec* (Toulouse, 2–3 February 1995) = Briant 1995b.
- *Land Routes and Water Routes.* See Briant 1991b: 75–79, where many additional bibliographical references will be found.
- *The Euphrates Boats.* De Graeve 1981: 5–93; also Fales 1983 (Neo-Assyrian period) and Frame 1986 (Neo-Babylonian– and Achaemenid-period contracts); in the Eanna's archives: Joannès 1982: 198–202, 252–53 (cf. 328–29); and the very interesting texts published by Beaulieu 1993a (use of waterways and location of boats to transport divine statues and personnel, shortly before the arrival of Cyrus's Persian troops in 539); networks of canals in Babylonia: Cocquerillat 1968, 1981, 1983; Joannès 1982: 117; Zadok 1978 (who stresses [p. 275 n. 53] among other things the importance of Nippur in the trade network between Babylonia and Elam); "commander of the boatmen": Joannès 1982: 10; on the price of boats in Babylonia, cf. Dubberstein 1939: 40, Joannès 1982: 328–29, and Giovinazzo 1983: 563–65; on the *kelek*, cf. also *EncIslam*[2], s.v.
- *Transport on the Tigris.* Cf. Briant 1986b (p. 21 n. 15 on Opis).
- *From Babylonia to Elam.* Briant 1986b; Joannès 1990a: 183; Babylonian tablets: Dandamaev 1972b (but on *Camb.* 143, cf. Greenfield 1991: 183); on the Diodorus passage (XVII.77.4), cf. Bosworth 1987: 545–46.
- *From the Mediterranean to Babylonia.* Briant 1991b: 77–79 (with Joannès's [1995: 182–83] remarks on the difficulties of navigation at certain places and at certain times of the year); on the *Letter of Themistocles*, cf. Briant 1992c; importance of the site of Myriandrus: Kestemont 1983: 66; 1985: 135–37; Babylonian merchants in Syria (Neirab tablets): see overviews in Oelsner 1989 and Cagni 1990; on the Tell Tawilan tablet (Dalley 1984), cf. the critical remarks of Joannès 1987 (Dalley's reply 1990: 79–80); caravan commerce and importance of the site of Gaza: Briant 1982b: 142–45, 150–52 and Eph'al 1982: 195–96; Charter of Susa and presumed role of the Ionians: Mazzarino 1966: 76–77; Aginis: Högemann 1985: 153 (= Dur-Yakin); Neo-Babylonian tablets and commerce between Phoenicia and Babylonia: see the illuminating article of Oppenheim 1967, as well as Joannès 1982: 235–60; on regional trade in the eastern Aegean in the Achaemenid period, cf. Salles 1991a, 1994; cf. also Salles 1991b (on Elayi 1988).
- *The Inland Waterways of Egypt: The Nile between the Mediterranean and the Red Sea?* The pharaoh Sesostris could be none other than Darius (cf. chap. 12/1); boatbuilding: cf. *DAE* 61 [*AP* 26] (commentaries by Grelot 1970b; 1972: 296–95; and Whitehead 1974: 119–54); river commerce: Milik 1967: 551–57; Memphis: Segal 1983: 8–9; 41–42; *DAE* 109: Porten 1988b; connections between Memphis and the Nile, cf. Goyon 1971. Naucratis: cf. Yoyotte 1993; on Darius's canal between the Nile and the Red Sea, see chap. 12/1; on the surveys in the area of Tell el-Maskhuta, cf. Holladay 1982 and 1992, and Paice 1986–87; in a more recent article, the same

author (Paice 1993) suggests that from the Saite period to the Ptolemaic period the canal linked Red Sea trade (incense for example) with the Nile Valley; on Dorginarti, cf. Heidorn 1991 and especially 1992.

• *Customs Collection and Trade.* On the Pseudo-Aristotle passage (assessment of a tenth: *dekatē kata ton nomon*), cf. Andréadès 1929: 5–8; Van Groningen 1933: 194; tolls at Opis: Joannès 1982: 10 and Stolper 1992c: 74 n. 22; at Babylon: Joannès 1990a 186 and n. 56 (translated text); on Asia Minor, we may note the tax mentioned by Pseudo-Aristotle, who notes the existence of sales taxes (*agoraia telē*; i.e., assessments) in the satrapal economy (*Oecon.* II.1.4); we have available mostly indirect but nevertheless revealing documents, for instance those by which a satrap (or perhaps also a town) exempts this or that community from import-export duties: see esp. the Greco-Lycian inscription published by Bousquet 1987: Pixodarus abandons the *dekatē tēs emporias* to the cities of the Xanthus Valley—that is, 10% assessed on commercial trade; let us also mention that in the now-famous Roman regulation of customs in Asia, reference is made to earlier documents going back at least to the Attalids (cf. *BE* 1976 no. 595 and 1991 no. 480); we may also note that the regulation of the tax farm in the territory of Colophon (third century B.C.) also refers to royal regulations (*BE* 1991, no. 476); although it is impossible to prove, it would not be unexpected if such regulations go back to the Achaemenid period (on these continuities, cf. chap. 10/1 with the notes). The new Aramaic document (announced in Porten 1990: 17) is published by Porten and Yardeni 1993 (I heartily thank the authors for providing me with an advance copy): see also Yardeni 1994 and Lipiński 1994; I think the natron came from traditional areas west of the Delta, such as the Wadi el-Natroun (cf. Aufrère, Golvin, Goyon 1994: 167–72): in this case, it must be recognized that the customs post was also located at the outlet of the western Delta (I may also note in passing that companies of garrison soldiers in Memphis paid part of the taxes due to the royal Treasury in the form of "eastern natron": Segal 1983: 5, 40). On Saite customs, cf. Posener 1947; the Saite regulations were in essence repeated by Nectanebo I, at least at Naucratis: Lichtheim 1980: 86–89 [[and Yoyotte's remark 1994: 683]]. On caravan commerce and royal assessments, I follow the compelling interpretation of Eph'al 1982: 206–10 (despite the reservations of Graf 1990a: 138–39). Perhaps it would make sense at this point also to recall some hypotheses on caravan commerce in Egypt in the Persian period: according to Aufrère, Golvin, and Goyon 1994: 83, "The oases seem to benefit, beginning in the Persian period, from the introduction of new technology that simplified transportation, desert travel, and agriculture. The Persians introduced a new kind of ceramic travel container shaped like a cask with the opening on top, well adapted to a pack animal's packsaddle. This kind of container was very popular among the general population, in the oasis and elsewhere. What we are referring to here is the *ciga*. Also, the Persians brought with them the camel, native to Bactria, which was hardier than the donkey and allowed the crossing of much greater distances"; they also suppose (p. 148) that during his expedition against the oasis, Cambyses sought to "check Cyrene on the commercial level" (on this point, cf. also chap. 2/8); I will simply note in passing that the chronology of the diffusion of the so-called Bactrian camel in the Near East is a very complicated problem (cf., e.g., Briant 1982b: 221–22 and 1984b: 20) and that the date suggested for Egypt by these authors is but one suggestion among many (i.e., the introduction of the camel to Egypt could just as well go back to the Assyrian period).

Chapter 10
Royal Assessments and Tribute

1. Sources and Problems

• *Diachrony and Synchrony.* Hellenistic sources and Achaemenid institutions: besides *RTP* passim, see, e.g., Préaux 1954; Descat 1985; Briant 1993b and 1994e; also the treatments of Hellenistic decrees by Wörrle (1977: 60; 1978: 223–24; 1979: 110–11; 1988: 458–65) and the remarks by Savalli 1987 and de Gauthier 1989: 28–29. Study of the Babylonian tablets of the Hellenistic period offers comparable results: see Stolper 1989a, 1993 (esp. 68, 84–85: first attestation of a Babylonian calque, *azdakarri*, on Old Persian *azdakara in a tablet dated to Antigonus the One-Eyed) and 1994a. The *Oeconomica* of Pseudo-Aristotle: van Groningen 1933; Rostovtzeff 1941: 440–46 and 469–72; Altheim and Stiehl 1963: 137–49; Cracco Ruggini 1966–67; Thillet 1969; Corsaro 1980a; Descat 1990b.

2. Satrapies and Tributes

• *Nomes, Satrapies, and Peoples.* I will not list and discuss the entire bibliography that has been dedicated to Herodotus's text. Nor will I discuss here the geographical aspects—not that they are devoid of interest but simply because doing so would not result in sufficient depth of analysis of the system's operation and because discussion of the geographical issues presupposes extremely detailed analysis that would be out of place here (cf. Toynbee 1954; the book by Högemann 1992, received belatedly, has a very deceptive title [matching its content]). Generally speaking, the commentators have attempted to combine Herodotus's list with the lists and depictions of peoples found here and there on the walls, a method that does not stand up to analysis; the views of Kimball Armayor (1978a) are not devoid of interest, but the arguments are not always systematic (cf. my remarks in *AbIran* 3 [1980], no. 197). I would add that according to Pirart (1995: 65–68) the total of 20 satrapies (actually: *nomoi*) in Herodotus can be explained by Iranian mythological notions. Concerning the amounts of tribute and Herodotus's method, cf. Picard 1980: 70–72 and Descat's (1985) demonstration. The (hypothetical) list of satraps provided here is based in part on the "travel texts" of Persepolis, by postulating that the persons who granted safe-conducts (*halmi*) to travelers were in fact the satraps of the region; the suggestion goes back to Hinz 1970: 430 (cf. Briant 1991b: 70 n. 13), and it is amply worked out by Koch (1993a), where much valuable information will be found, taken (in part at least) from unpublished tablets; for the satraps of Babylonia-Trans-Euphrates, cf. Stolper 1989b: 290–91; meaning of *dahyu*: most recently, Lecoq 1990.

• *Setting the Amount of Tribute.* See Descat 1989a: 80–81; *kata to megethos*: Theopompus apud Athenaeus IV.145a (contributions for the king's Table); Diodorus uses a synonymous formulation: *kata dynamin* (IX.25.4: Artaphernes in Ionia in 492—compare Plutarch, *Aristides* 24.1: *kat'axian ekastōi kai dynamin*: tribute of Aristides; see also I.55.10: tribute obligations [gifts] imposed annually by Pharaoh Sesostris on the subject peoples of his empire, see also XVII.114.4: exceptional "contributions" imposed by Alexander on the cities of Babylonia to help pay for the expenses incurred by the funeral rites of Haephestion); cf. also Aelian, *VH* I.32 (*kata tēn hautou dynamin*: obligations laid on the simple Persian peasants [gifts to the king]), and Strabo XI.13.8 (*megethos kai dynamis tēs chōras*: tribute charges compared between Cappadocia and Armenia during the Persian period); applied to a specific region in a financial context, the word *dynamis* refers unambiguously to the region's ability to contribute: cf. Herodotus I.192. Measurement of tribute: suggestion by Descat 1985; cf. also Heltzer 1991 (who discussed the interpretation of the inscription *Syll.*[3] 302 that Descat proposed in Ann Arbor in 1990 but did not retain in Descat 1994).

3. Gifts and Tribute

• *Herodotus's Viewpoint.*   In this section I am bringing the discussion begun above in chap. 2/3 to its logical conclusion.

• *The Gifts of the Tribute-Paying Peoples.*   Nile water: cf. Briant 1993c; on Arrian (III.4.3), cf. Leclant 1930: 246–47; functions of the Persepolis treasury: Cahill 1983 (though I largely agree with the critical remarks of Tuplin 1987b: 139); crowns: cf. Briant 1988c: 261 n. 9 (for the Seleucid period, cf. Bickerman 1938: 112).

• *From Persepolis to Babylon.*   "Gifts" in Babylonian financial documents: cf. Dandamaev 1979: 102–6 (translated texts), Cardascia 1951: 98–99 (translated as 'redevances' [rent, taxes]; see also pp. v–vi, 69–70, 125, etc., on the polysemy of the word *nadānu* 'give, remit'); on *nidintu šarri* 'royal gift' (*dōrea basilikē*), cf. Stolper 1992b: 126; according to Giovinazzo 1989b, the Akkadian word should be transcribed *nadānu* in the Persepolis tablets, rather than *nutanuyaš* ('breeding place'). Exemption for Persia: I abandon the interpretation presented in *RTP* 344, for reasons relating to the interpretation of the Persian nobility's relations with Bardiya and then with Darius as developed above in chap. 2/10 (Bardiya and the Persian aristocracy); see also Wiesehöfer 1989: 183–84.

• *The Gifts of the Persian Peasants.*   On Aelian's texts, cf. Briant 1988c: 256–57 and 1993c: 62–63; Calmeyer (1979b: 57) sees in these texts a reflection of the donor reliefs at Persepolis; Tuplin (1987b: 143) proposes (carefully) comparing them with certain Persepolis tablets that record payments made for royal provisions (Category J; cf. *PFT*, pp. 24–25 and Garrison forthcoming); gifts made by the king to the Persians: cf. Xenophon, *Cyr.* VIII.3.3–8, etc.; cf. also Plutarch, *Alex.* 69.1; *Mor.* 246a–b; and Nicolaus of Damascus, *FGrH* 90 F77.43 (gifts to pregnant Persian women).

4. Tributes, Gifts, and Assessments

• *Taxes.*   Royal taxes in the cities of Asia Minor: Hornblower 1982: 161–62; Corsaro 1985; Bousquet 1987 (*dekatē tēs emporias*); Wörrle 1978: 223–24 (*apomoira*; Achaemenid continuities) and 1979: 91–94 (epigraphic attestation of *kheironaxion*; Achaemenid precedents); the decree of Aigai has been published by Malay 1983; one of the problems posed by the Hellenistic decrees is that they generally refer to civic taxes, which are not necessarily the equivalent of royal taxes (they are often distinguished, when a town is under the authority of a king, by an expression such as "the taxes controlled [*kyrios*] by the town"). Taxes on the sale of slaves in Babylonia: I follow closely the explanation of Stolper 1989a. [[On other potential Achaemenid-Seleucid financial continuities in Babylonia, cf. Rostovtzeff (1941: 470), who seems to suggest that the salt tax might go back to the Achaemenid period; but while this suggestion fits well into current historical perspectives (i.e., Hellenistic adaptations of Achaemenid states of affairs: cf. Stolper 1989a: and 1993; Kuhrt and Sherwin-White 1994), to my knowledge we have no unequivocal documentation of such a tax (we may simply note that Ezra 7:22 implies that stocks of salt were found in the royal storehouses; similarly, in the fortresses: *RTP* 21 n. 11; at most, we might find an indication in the gifts of salt sent to the king by the Egyptians: Arrian III.4.3).]] We may note in passing that no tax on the sale of slaves (at least not in so many words) is listed by Pseudo-Aristotle; a Greek inscription from Caria (*BE* 1979, no. 466) is sometimes considered proof of its existence, at the end of the Achaemenid period or the beginning of the Hellenistic (cf. Hornblower 1982: 161), but the text does not require this interpretation (cf. the very tempting suggestions of Hahn 1985, that the inscription actually concerns a complete financial exemption [*ate*[*lē*] *einai*] except for the *phoroi basilikoi*, conceded to those of the slaves [hierodules according to Hahn] who took care of the tomb of a man named Skoranos, who [with his wife] had dedicated an estate to Apollo and Artemis); Corsaro 1985: 90 (followed by Gauthier 1991: 66) observes that, in the cities of Asia Minor, the only known taxes were not on the sale of slaves but on their labor (we may simply add that the Xanthus regulation provides that "those who are to be freed [*apeleutheroi*] will pay the god two drachmas":

lines 18–20 of the Greek version; siculi in the Lycian version). As for the head-tax (*epikephalaion*) listed by Pseudo-Aristotle, it is known from the Hellenistic period (Bickerman 1938: 111; and now the in-depth consideration by Gauthier 1991 in the context of Greek towns), but we have no attestations from the Achaemenid period; however, we must cite a passage of Theocritus (apud Plutarch, *Mor.* 11a–b): one of the obligations that Alexander imposed on towns and peoples was a head-tax in silver; but the question is, to what extent was this a continuation or an innovation?

• *Mines.*   Mines of Lampsacus: Polyaenus II.1.26; silver mines of Bactria: Ctesias, *Indica* 12; of India: ibid. and 5; Cilicia, Lebanon, Ionia, Cyprus: Oppenheim 1967; Joannès 1982: 255 (Ionian iron cost 8 or 9 times as much as Lebanese iron); Wadi Hammâmât quarries: Posener 1936: 179–80; Goyon 1957: 1–9, 28–29, 128–30; Niriz workshops: PT 52 (with commentary by Cameron, *PTT* 166); Pythius: see Descat 1989b: 25–26; also Sekunda 1991: 119–21.

• *Corvée.*   *Urāšu* system: Joannès 1989a: 151–59 (cf. also Stolper 1977: 254–59); *phoros leitourgikos*: *RTP* 106 (I note in passing, with Gauthier 1991: 56–58, that the tax known in the Greek towns from the exemption formula [*ateleia tou sōmatos*] has nothing to do with service at a sanctuary or temple); on Aelian, *Anim.* XV.26, cf. Briant 1988c: 259 (the late texts relative to the *aggareion* imply the existence of taxes and corvées: Rostovtzeff 1909; cf. Mitchell 1976).

• *The Obligations of Hospitality.*   See in general Briant 1988c. Aside from Herodotus's text, we have a striking description of hospitality customs in Theopompus (*FGrH* 115 F263a), quoted extensively above in chap. 5/4; tax paid by Babylonian oblates during a visit by Artaxerxes II to Susa: Joannès 1988 and 1990a: 183; on the tablets of Category J and their relationship with the royal Table, see Garrison forthcoming.

• *Royal Taxes and Satrapal Taxes.*   On the texts concerning the migrations of Alcibiades, cf. Briant 1985b: 59; on the Nehemiah passage (5:15–17), cf. the evaluation offered by Heltzer 1992a.

• *Military Levies and the Tax System.*   War expenses: cf. Briant 1986c; financial and military obligations of the tenant farmers of *ḥaṭrus*: cf. Cardascia 1958 and 1978; Joannès 1982: 16–26; Stolper (1985a: 98–99) stresses that the *ḥaṭrus* did not constitute military colonies alone: "The main concerns are the production of crops, taxes and rents" (p. 99); levy on the companies of Memphis: Segal 1983: 5, 7; on the operations of the military *ḥaṭrus* during the time of Darius II and later, cf. chap. 14/7 (Darius II and his armies) and chap. 17/3.

5. Payments of Tribute: Metal and Coin

• *The Phantom of the Natural Economy: Coast and Interior.*   The vocabulary deserves a historical investigation; I will simply note in passing the reservations of M. Mauss (1921: 388), who discusses barter as follows: "a system which it is customary to distinguish with the term 'natural economy,' without being certain that there has ever been a society where such an economy operated exclusively or regularly"; regarding Herodotus's tribute list, Will (1960: 269) believes that it is "a monetary evaluation, Greek style, of payments made largely in kind" (an idea recently repeated by the same author, *RPh* 65/2 [1991]: 35): but see the apt remarks of Picard 1980: 76–78 and Descat 1989a: 83; Will's article nevertheless poses a real problem, that of the transformation into silver of certain payments provided in kind outside tribute proper (*parex tou phorou*), including some of the *tagē* (on this point, see chap. 11/8, and Briant 1994d: sale of "tribute" wheat on the Aegean market)—additionally, an Aramaic papyrus from Saqqara (Segal, no. 24 and p. 7, 40) shows that the Memphis garrison paid a tribute (*mndt*) in "industrial" products: natron and alabaster. Role of the Babylonian business firms: this is well known from the time of Artaxerxes I and Darius II through the Murašū archives; but beginning with the reign of Darius I, the lands of the treasurer Bagasarū were entrusted to the management of the Egibi: Dandamaev 1969c. Strabo XV.3.21: in a brief discussion of this passage, Descat (forthcoming) judges that Polyclitus "had a good understanding of financial matters" (n. 5), and he seems to think that the author was referring to the shipment of exotic items to the central court; but this remark does not resolve the difficulty of the text; I do not see on what Wallinga (1984: 412–13) bases his claim that Polyclitus's text refers to "the monetization of tribute"; I agree instead with Tuplin (1987b: 138–39), who thinks that Polyclitus's representation is "certainly false" and perhaps derives from the observation that money was preferred in the coastal regions; purchase of merchandise by Cyrus's Greek mercenaries: *Anab.* I.5.10; agreements with Tissaphernes and the opening of markets (*agora*): II.3.26–27; "It is against payment that you will have our goods": II.4.5, 9; pillages or markets: IV.5.16–18; V.7.13ff.; coast and interior in Hellenistic texts: *RTP* 74–81.

 • *Royal Treasuries and Tribute.* Transportation of tribute to the central authority: cf., e.g., Nepos, *Datames* 4.2; PF 1342 (transport of silver between Susa and Matezziš), PF 1357 ("treasure" of Babylon transported to Persepolis), PFa 14 ("treasure" transported from Kerman to Susa), and the unpublished tablets (Q 1898, 2149, 2580) used by Koch 1993a: 23–25; also *DAE* no. 71–72 [AD 10–11] (transport of taxes from Egypt to Babylon); the exact interpretation of Herodotus's wording (III.96) comes from Schlumberger 1953: 14; Near Eastern precedents: Torrey 1943; Oppenheim 1946; gold and silver in the Babylonian temples: Joannès 1982: 236; 1992b: 174–76; and Beaulieu 1989c.

 • *The Problem of Royal Coinage.* I am aware that my discussion of this subject is brief and perhaps superficial. Doubtless it reveals the difficulties I feel in approaching these questions, which remain largely the province of specialists. I must say that despite numerous recent contributions on the subject (particularly those collected in *REA* 1989 = R. Descat [ed.] 1989), I remain perplexed due to the breadth and complexity of the problems raised by such studies (however fine they may otherwise be). I have attempted to synthesize as much as possible to get to the heart (or at least what appears to me to be the heart!) of the matter. On the monetary policy of Darius, I have made considerable use of the various works of Descat (1985, 1989a–b, 1994, forthcoming), through which the development of the author's ideas can be followed on important points; see also Root 1988 and 1989 (impression on a tablet and evolution of the types emerging from studying the Persepolis seals), Carradice 1987 (attempt at relative chronology), Stronach 1989b (ideological-iconographic analysis), as well as O. Picard's chapter on the topic (1980: 65–79: "The Persians and Coinage"), the article by Alram (1993: 25–29), and last but not least Schlumberger (1953), who in particular points out, by analyzing the treasuries known in his time, the limited distribution of the siculus in contrast to Athenian coins; I note finally that G. Le Rider touched on several of these problems in his 1995 lectures at the Collège de France (text to appear in *ACF*: I thank the author for sending me an offprint). On the political-ideological function of the daric (and the ideas about Darius that it suggested to me), see F. Joannès's (1989d) conclusions regarding stamped "medals" distributed by Hammurabi during a festive reception in his palace: "One should . . . note the parallel with the gold daric of the Achaemenid period, which the specialists consider a true coinage: the weight of the daric was also based on the Babylonian siculus [. . .]; it was provided with a mark and did not appear in general commerce but seems to have been reserved for particular uses." ⟦At this point the author is referring to the use of the daric by Cyrus the Younger to pay his mercenaries; actually, in the context, the word *daric* refers to the weight standard; we might more appropriately compare a custom of the Achaemenid court that established quite precisely the value and weight of gifts made by the Great King to foreign ambassadors (Aelian, *VH* I.22): cf. Joannès p. 80: "The gifts to the Mari military personnel [were distributed] after a precise codification establishing the relationship of the rank of each one with the value of the gift he received."⟧ The author thinks that Hammurabi's pieces of silver were not coins (unlike the darics), even though their nominal value (greater than their actual weight) was set by the royal administration; however, I would ask what, precisely, in the context of royal policy, distinguishes a silver medal from a gold coin? Not to press the paradox, but one might as well say that the darics were not coins (in the usual sense of the word) but "medals" used by Darius in the context of a policy of (re)distribution that exalted his ostentatious splendor and the attribute of donor par excellence (cf. the annual distribution of gold pieces [darics] by the Great Kings to pregnant Persian women: Plutarch, *Alex.* 69.1; *Mor.* 246a–b; also the gift of a gold vessel and 1000 darics from Artaxerxes II to a simple Persian peasant: Aelian, *VH* I.33). Let us stress, to finish up on this point, that the thought-provoking comparison proposed by F. Joannès also calls to mind an old yet still vital debate on potential Near Eastern forerunners of coinage (e.g., Powell 1978; Parise 1987; also Joannès 1994a): while the archer siculus clearly was born out of the culture of Lydia (chap. 2/3), it is not as easy to determine the derivation of the daric. We might also mention the debates that sprang up concerning the origins of Achaemenid coinage after the discovery of small inscribed silver bars at Nūš-i Jān (Bivar 1971; Curtis 1984: 11–14). Compare this discovery with other discoveries of inscribed pieces of metal that have all too rapidly been called *coins* by some (cf. the debates among Figulla 1954, Hulin 1954, 1972, and Henning 1972); I would add that metal bars perhaps comparable to those from Nūš-i Jān were discovered near the site of Cemin Tepe in Armenia (and subsequently lost: Summers 1993: 87); however interesting these sources and the reflections they stimulate may be, they cannot themselves answer the question: why at a specific date did Darius decide to create the royal archer coins? To be sure, the commentators mentioned give due weight to the political function of coinage, unlike other interpreters, who insist on its economic function. But I must emphasize that the case of the darics must be distinguished from the case of the silver siculi, and western Asia Minor from Babylonia or Persia; at the time of Darius and Xerxes, the creation of royal coins did not lead to any monetary economic advances in Persia itself, contrary to what was thought in the first stage of commenting and reflection on the Treasury tablets, since it is obvious that the silver given to the *kurtaš* (if in fact it really was given!) was weighed and not minted (cf., e.g., Cameron 1958: 161, 168–72; Naster 1970a and 1990; error of Martin 1985: 120 n. 120; also chap. 11/8 here: "Return to Persepolis").

• *Darius and Aryandes.* The episode of Darius and Aryandes has stimulated a flood of articles; the problem is extensively treated by Tuplin 1989, who includes discussion of the minting of coins by the satrap; on the other hand, Descat (1989b: 27–28) and Price (*REA* 1989: 82–83) think that Aryandes did not mint coins but that he manipulated the value of silver in Egypt (cf. also Descat 1989a: 85–86); on the Polyaenus text (VII.11.7) and the assumed date of Darius's arrival in Egypt, see the overview by Tuplin 1991a: 265–66.

6. The Administration of Tribute: Continuities and Adaptations

• *Peoples and Territories.* Military regions: cf. Briant 1990b: 50–51; maritime regions: Wallinga 1991; chiliarchies: *RTP* 210–11; *medinah*: texts in Dandamaev 1989b: 103 n. 4, who wrongly speaks of "120 to 127 satrapies"; satrapal subdivisions: cf. Tuplin 1987b: 120–27.

• *Cadastres in Western Asia Minor.* Sardis archives: *RTP* 191–92 (on potential Hellenistic continuations, cf. Wörrle 1988: 465).

• *The Case of Babylonia.* It is now agreed that, contrary to the traditional interpretation (e.g., Joannès 1982: 224), the administrator called *zazakku* was not in charge of the cadastre (Dandamaev 1994a; Joannès 1994b). Royal real estate archives in Babylonia in the time of Darius I: Stolper 1985a: 29–31 and 1989a; Babylonian fields: Nemat-Nejat 1982: 1–24, 277–79; the texts are related by Dandamaev 1985 (94–95) to the reforms of Darius; but we note that from year 2 of Darius (520), tablets of this type are known for transactions concerning houses (Joannès 1990c); Bagasarū the treasurer: Dandamaev 1969c and 1992a, nos. 98a and 197e; tax on the sale of slaves: Stolper 1989a (quotation from p. 91) and 1977: 259–66 (on **kārahmara*).

• *The Case of Egypt.* Egyptian *senti*: Yoyotte 1989 (followed here); military lots at Elephantine: Porten 1968: 35; Grelot 1970a: 122–23. DAE 69: Briant 1985b: 68 and Whitehead 1974: 77–84 (compare with the Babylonian example analyzed by Stolper 1985a: 67: transmission of the *dōrea* [*nadnu*] of Pitibiri in the house [*bīt*] of Sitūnu; military lots at Memphis: Segal 1983: no. 31; on the office of writing in Egypt, cf. Meeks 1972: 58 (which clearly compares to the *basilikai graphai*).

• *Weights and Measures.* Ardab: Malinine 1950: 17–19 (whose suggestion is taken up here, without reopening the whole matter of the Egyptian ardab:, e.g., Vleeming 1981); weight standards: cf. in general Bivar 1985; at Elephantine: Porten 1968: 62–72; Grelot 1970a: 124; see also (in other contexts) Heltzer 1991 and Eph'al and Naveh 1993; weights from Susa and Persepolis: Stève 1987: 83–85; Schmidt 1957: 105ff.; lion weights from Abydos: cf. Mitchell 1973 and Descat 1989b: 18–20; weights from Trebizond: Kunkel and Haas 1986.

7. Tribute Economy and Appropriation: Royal Land and Tribute Land

• *Royal Territory and Empire.* The discussion begun here is the result of thinking that has been developing for many years (cf. *RTP* passim) on the problem of knowing what lies behind the expressions "royal land" and "tribute land" (in particular in the Hellenistic inscriptions). I have already tried to make the point in another work (Briant 1982c: esp. p. 307 n. 81, on the distinction that must be made between "*ownership* of the means of production" [false debate on "Asiatic despotism"] and "*control* of the means of production"). On all of these problems, cf. also the basic overview of Zaccagnini 1981, and the work of van der Spek, most recently 1995: 195–97; see also C. Herrenschmidt's reflections on the term *būmi* in the royal inscriptions: she interprets it in the sense of empire (cf. Herrenschmidt 1976 and 1977); even though these articles suffer from some weaknesses (the Wittfogelian expression "hydraulic Persian royalty" [1977: 52] seems especially unfortunate to me) and even though Herrenschmidt has been debated fiercely (e.g., Frye 1977: 75–78), the perplexities that drive her strike me as illuminating; her conclusions in a way answer Altheim and Stiehl's statements, in the course of their interesting discussion on the relationship between private and public domains among the Achaemenids: "Bezeichnend, daß sich kein Ausdruck für das 'Reich' der Achaimeniden ermitteln läßt" (1963: 178). The discussion continues in chap. 11/10.

• *The Great King's Sluices and the* qanats *of the Hyrcanians.* Cf. *RTP* 418–30 (also chap. 11/10).

• *Royal Land and Concession Lands.* See also chap. 10/6 (on Egypt), where I compare *RC* 11–12 and *DAE* 69 [*AD* 8], and chap. 11/9; generally, see my overview in Briant 1985b [add to the bibliography Wörrle's essential 1978 article, and now the comments of Savalli 1987] with the remark (p. 70) on a Hellenistic detail, namely, that in some cases the donor returned to a town land conceded as a gift (but I must ask whether we might not detect a comparable process in the gift to Ešmunazar of Sidon, who returned "forever" the conceded territory: Gibson III, no. 28); on *DAE* 1, see the republication by Szubin and Porten 1992, where a detailed commentary is found (whose conclusions are accepted completely here).

• *Darius and Gadatas, Alexander and Priene.* On ML 12 compared with Tod 185, cf. already a few words in *RTP* 361; on Tod no. 185, cf. Sherwin-White 1985, esp. p. 83 (Alexander's retaking of Achaemenid royal estates), and Marasco 1987: 68–73; on the word *bebēlos*, cf. Chantraine, *DELG*, s.v. (the word is very clearly the opposite of a sacred territory); attributions of lands to towns in the Hellenistic period: *RTP* 244ff. and Jones and Habicht 1989; on the implications of *attributio* in the Roman period, cf. Bertrand 1990 (pp. 139–45 on Hellenistic practices).

• *Tribute-Producing Lands and Crown Lands.* On the *tagē*, see especially Descat 1989a: 81–83 (whose conclusions I incorporate); the expression "crown lands" was first suggested to me by a hypothesis in Thillet (1969: 578) on a possible Iranian etymology of *tagē* ('diadem'); although I am a bit skeptical of this suggestion (a Greek etymology from *tassō* and *tagos* [*DELG*, s.v., without explicitly referring to *tagē*] seems more likely), I have kept the phrase, since it allows me to avoid the ambiguous form "royal land" [[on the etymology of *tagē*, see most recently B. Helly, *L'État thessalien* (Lyon, 1995): 19–38, without reference to the use of the word by Pseudo-Aristotle]]. Life-supporting gifts: cf. Briant 1985b and below, chap. 11/9; on the Lake Moeris fish, cf. Dumont 1977; royal stud farms: *RTP* 209 (Aeolian stud farm), 354–55; royal forests: for Sardis, the Seleucid inscriptions are edited and annotated by Gauthier 1989: 22–32 (who also quotes the texts regarding Mysia, Cilicia, and the Lebanon); I translate *exagagesthai* with 'cause to leave' rather than 'export' for reasons explained in chap. 11/8.

• *An Appraisal and Some Uncertainties.* Royal lands in Babylonia: on the vocabulary of the Babylonian tablets, cf. Stolper 1985a: 35ff. and 1992b (p. 126 on *nidintu šarri* translated 'crown-grant' [[but one could adopt the literal translation 'royal gift']]); see also the (deceptive) focus of Cagni 1988 and Oelsner's 1988 article.

Chapter 11
Persia: Empire and Tribute Economy

1. The Persepolis Archives

One preliminary detail: my interest in this material is longstanding (cf. my articles of 1977 [1979] and 1978–79 reprinted in *RTP* 202–11 and 331–56), but I have no special philological competence in the area. Because of the numerous differences among specialists and because of my lack of competence in Elamite, I do not claim that the following pages are anything more than an attempt to take a position on a series of problems that appear to me to be essential for understanding the operation of the royal economy in Persia and the Empire. Individual articles are numerous, but I have not come across any satisfactory synthesis; despite its obvious interest, the recent book by Koch (1990) contains less than the title promises: it is much more a matter of *Verwaltung* than *Wirtschaft*; the author also has reprinted several earlier articles (cf. Koch 1988a) in the framework of a synthesis: Koch 1992, esp. pp. 25–72, 264–85; she continues her analyses in Koch 1993a (which appeared after this chapter was written); Cardascia (1978: 6) announced a work by J. A. Delaunay, *La Place des Iraniens dans l'administration royale à Persepolis* (forthcoming), "which studies the two thousand documents published by Hallock from the administrative and economic point of view"; but by the time my manuscript was finished, it had still not appeared (I imagine Delaunay 1976 constitutes a preliminary study). I will simply explain that I decided in each case to start from the texts (in transliteration and translation) while trying to take into account the findings of philological and etymological studies (cf. Hinz and Koch 1987), but I cannot claim to have read everything or even to have grasped all of the subtleties of the specialists' arguments; when I have chosen among several interpretations, it is sometimes on the basis of "historical probability," and the subjective nature of this process is well known. [A magnificent illustration of this phenomenon appeared at the very moment that I was ready to put the final touches on the additions and corrections. Some tablets found in Armenia (Armavir-blur) had been read by the *editores principes* as a fragment of the Gilgamesh Epic (Diakonoff and Jankowska 1990); three years later, H. Koch (1993a) "proved" that they were actually tablets of the Persepolis-Achaemenid type, and I therefore used this interpretation in this book (cf. chap. 16/14)—partly, also, because it reinforced some of my views on imperial organization (cf. chaps. 11/6, 16/18); later, F. Vallat published a note (Vallat 1995) in which, while announcing a detailed study in preparation, he states that neither hypothesis is acceptable; according to him, the text is a private letter dating probably from the first half of the sixth century. Vallat, a renowned authority, concludes as follows: "By the way, this threefold interpretation of a single document shows very clearly that Elamite remains the least well known language of the ancient Near East!" I do not know whether this remark is supposed to reassure or frighten off the outsider!] We can hope, finally, that the Chicago tablets will be made available to scholars within a reasonable time. The longer that these texts remain unpublished, the more each scholar will have to resort to quoting isolated unpublished tablets, and the more his results risk being questioned; cf., for example, the statement in Vallat 1993: vii: "Without this considerable contribution [unpublished Hallock transcriptions] . . . , the RGTC would have been a mere skeleton for the Achaemenid period"—which probably also accounts for his judgment (p. cxliv) on Koch 1990, which did not utilize unpublished tablets (Koch 1990: 2 n. 3).

• *Fortification Tablets and Treasury Tablets.* In addition to the introductions and commentaries on PTT, PFT, PFa, and Hallock's (1972) both general and detailed presentation, an excellent introduction to the archives will be found in Garrison 1988: 168–84, who (p. 162) estimates the number of unpublished tablets at 25,000–30,000; on the PFT, see also the long and important reviews by Hinz (1970) and Dandamaev (1972c and 1973), and on the PTT the reviews of Goossens (1949), Hallock (1950), and Altheim (1951); see also Benveniste 1958a, the many articles by Koch, Giovinazzo, Kawase, Uchitel, Vallat, etc., and the excellent introductions by the late and sorely missed David Lewis (1977: 3–13; 1984: 592–600; 1985; 1990a; and 1994), who at the end of his life was working on a manuscript on the tablets of Category Q); many interesting comments will also be found in Brosius 1991. Isolated publications of tablets: Lewis 1986 (Q 1809), Grillot 1980 (no indication of provenance), Vallat 1994 (2 tablets from the Fribourg University museum), Balcer, *BiOr* 36/3–4 (1979): 280 (Fort. 1771). Aramaic texts and legends: Bowman 1970; cf. Stolper 1984a: 300 and n. 5 (there is an unpublished manuscript by Bowman); wood tablets: Briant 1992b (wood and ivory tablets in the Assyrian period: cf. Mallowan 1966, 1: 149–63; on the wood tablet found in the wreck of an ancient boat at Ulu Burun, cf. the detailed presentation by Symington 1991); references to documents on parchment in Babylonian tablets: cf. Stolper 1985a: 158–60 and 1992b: 120; on the disappearance (or nondiscovery) of part of the Persepolis archives, cf. the reflections of Hallock 1973; on the chronological division, cf. Hallock, PFT: 51 (Category Q); the other percentages are the result of personal evaluations; the seals on the Treasury tablets (*PTS*) were published by Schmidt 1957: 4–49, plates 1–19 (reviewed by Porada 1961); the seals on the Fortification tablets (PFS) have been studied by M. Root and M. Garrison (cf. programmatic presentation by M. Root, *DATA* 1993 n. 14).

• *Accounts and Archives.* The conversion of Persepolis weights and measures into the metric system poses many problems, since we do not really know (for example) what kind of barley is involved (and the translations of ancient words for grain are very often uncertain); as a result of all sorts of variables (dry vs. moist grain, for example), the proposed equivalences can vary considerably (these problems are treated in a thesis being prepared by M. Gabrielli at Toulouse under my direction); here I conventionally use the equivalents proposed by Hinz (1970: 431): 1 BAR = 10 QA = 9.7 liters, and 100 liters of barley weigh about 66 kg (on metrology, cf. also Hinz 1973: 101–4; Hallock PFT 72–74; and Lewis 1987: 86); on the *marriš* (a word occurring in the only tablet in Greek, Fort. 1771, and in a Saqqara papyrus, Segal no. 42a), cf. Bernard 1985b: 93–94; on the *šaumarriš* measure, see most recently Giovinazzo 1993. The use of seals and even the method of archiving continue to pose major problems (cf. Garrison 1988: 181 n. 3), so research on the geographical-administrative partition of Persia leads to notably different results: cf. Hallock 1972: 17–21 and 1977; Sumner 1986 (also utilizing the facts derived from archaeological exploration and ecology); Koch 1990 (synthetic summary, pp. 247–310, with maps): the author stresses (p. 311) that the current state of research deals with "relative topography"—that is, sites are located in accord with their relationships to other sites; see also the useful reflections of Tuplin 1987b: 115–16 and now Vallat 1993. *Halmi*: Hallock 1950: 247–48; Benveniste 1958a: 63–65; Vallat 1994: 269–70; Giovinazzo 1994a (Category Q). PF 1980: translation (customary law) taken from Grillot-

2. *Administrative Hierarchy and Organization of Production*

• *Parnaka.* Hallock 1972: 11–13 and Lewis 1977: 7–11; on the administration for which he was responsible, see also Hinz 1972: 301–11 and Koch 1990: 229–34. Irtašduna: Cameron 1942 (with an error on the title *dukšiš* borne by Irtašduna: 'princess' not 'daughter'; note that at the same time, Irtašduna received 200 *marriš* of wine, on order of the king transmitted by Parnaka to the wine-cellar-master Yamakšedda: PF 1795); Hallock 1969: 52 and 1972: 11 and n. 1; cf. Lewis 1985: 110. The large amount of daily "rations" given to Parnaka poses a problem (so also for other high persons; cf. figures collected by Koch 1983: 45–47); at one time, Hallock thought, in a very plausible and tempting hypothesis, that Parnaka fed his entourage; he later reversed this opinion when he published a tablet (*PFa* 4) showing (along with other, still unpublished tablets) that Parnaka's *puhu* received their own rations (cf. Hallock 1978: 110; cf. also the remarks of Lewis 1987: 80). I wonder, however, whether the payment of these quantities of foodstuffs and sheep really took place daily in physical form; I am now much less sure (cf. Briant 1985b: 64) that the comparison made by Dandamaev (1972c: 20–21) with the food gifts known to the Classical authors (e.g.,

Themistocles) is really appropriate; keeping in mind the example of the "house of Aršāma" in *DAE* 67 [*AD* 6] (§5: *irmatam*; *ulhi*; §9: *irmatam*; *ulhi*, lands in gift; analyzed below), I propose instead, as a hypothesis, that these "rations" were quite simply transferred on a "paper" accounting basis to the "house of Parnaka"—that is, that Parnaka had credit that he or his subordinates could draw on at the warehouses during relocations organized on his initiative (similar to the credits on which Aršāma and his steward Neḥtiḥōr could draw, as well as Irtašduna or Irdabama).

• *The Department Heads.*   On animal husbandry, cf. Hinz 1972: 288–90, *RTP* 331–56; and Kawase 1980 (but cf. Giovinazzo 1989a: 203–6, who proposes a radically different interpretation of the word *nutanuyaš*, generally understood as stockyard; cf. *PFT*, s.v.; and Hinz 1973: 86–87); Giovinazzo sees the word instead as a transcription of the Akkadian word *nadānu* 'gift', that is, a form of tax); a recently published tablet with Harrena and Parnaka (distribution of sheep rations to a goldsmith: 1 sheep per month for 6 months): Vallat 1994: 264–71; on the related words *mundurabattiš*, *harmabattiš*, etc., see Gershevitch 1979: 170, 174, 179; names of horses: *PFT* 47; cf. Lewis 1980; their rations in wine or beer: cf. the remarks of Delaunay 1976: 19 n. 38 (from which I also take the translation of several administrative terms) and Bernard 1985b: 93–94 (on rations given to elephants).

• *The kurdaš Heads (kurdabattiš).*   Hinz understands as 'majordomo' (1972: 280); cf. review of viewpoints in Stolper 1985a: 57; list in Koch 1990: 237–45; Iršena and Šuddayauda: Hallock 1972: 14–15; Hinz 1972: 282–85.

• *Treasurerships and Treasurers.*   Cf. Hinz 1972: 261–64; Koch 1982 and 1990: 235–37; the remarks of Tuplin 1987b: 130–31; and the note of Lewis 1994: 23 n. 38; the list of treasurers and sub-treasurers in the Aramaic texts on mortars and pestles was compiled by Bowman 1970: 56–62, but the dates proposed must remain hypothetical, as noted by Delaunay 1975: 194–95. Bowman dated the first texts to 479/8; but in reading the rather surrealistic comments he wrote on the close connection he postulates between what I will call the "*haoma* chronology" and the chronology of defeats of Xerxes (pp. 60–62), I have the very clear impression that his proposal emerges from his desire to show at any cost that "[the Persians] desperately sought support and victory. They needed the wise guidance and support of Mithra . . . in such a context the *haoma* ceremony became meaningful . . ." (p. 62): in short, the institution of the *haoma* cult was supposedly a response to the defeats of Salamis, Plataea, and Mycale! Of course, Bowman's cult theory has never found much acceptance (see, e.g., Delaunay 1975; Boyce 1982: 149; Dandamaev 1989b: 334–35; curiously enough, Koch 1993a: 26 and 1993c: 181 nonetheless continues to believe that the mortars and pestles were ritual objects [*Kultgegenstände*]); but, other than confirming the fecundity of ideas on the enormous importance generally accorded to the year 479 (cf. chap. 13/1, below), my note here is simply intended as a reminder that the chronology of the texts remains open, since, among other things, palaeography cannot decide it (Delaunay 1975). Transportation of tribute: in addition to the documents cited in the text, cf. the unpublished tablets (Q 1898, 2149, 2580) quoted and used by Koch 1993a: 23–25. Workshops: cf. Hinz 1972: 234ff. and Koch 1982. Kawase (1986) interprets the word *kapnuški* in the narrow sense of specialists in the treatment of hides (cf. critical remarks of Uchitel 1989: 234); on the words *kapnuškip*, *ganzabara*, and *ganzaba*, cf. also Mancini 1987: 46–54 (in a discussion of the word *gangabas*, which Quintus Curtius [III.13.7] says means 'porter'); on the role of the treasury-fortresses, cf. also *RTP* 202–7 and, on the meaning that must be assigned to the word *birtā* (*halmarriš* in the tablets), Lemaire and Lozachmeur 1987.

3. *The World of Work: The kurtaš*

Surprisingly, the subject of the *kurtaš* has hardly ever been treated on its own; until recently (Kawase 1984 and 1986; Uchitel 1989 and 1991), there was virtually nothing but Dandamaev's excellent 1973 review article on *PFT*, which he reprinted without evident change in Dandamaev 1975a and 1989b.

- *Kurtaš Craftsmen.* More or less detailed discussions will be found in any treatment of the tablets. Craftsmen on the construction sites of Persepolis in the PT: cf. Roaf 1979; craftsmen in the treasury-fortresses: Hinz 1972: 266–68; Koch 1982: 244–46 and 1990: 238–39 (tables); Uchitel 1989 (partial tables) and 1992; much is to be found in Kawase 1984 as well (women-*pašap*) and 1986 (*kapnuški*), even though the interpretations presented have been strongly contested by Brosius (1991) in the first case and Giovinnazo (1989a) in the second; Greeks at Persepolis: Lewis 1977: 12–14; also Delaunay 1976: 24 (someone named Philippos in PF 1276?) and Nylander and Flemberg 1989.

- *Food Rations and the Organization of Production.* Rations: cf. Koch 1983 and 1994 (rations given to women); Dandamaev 1989b: 161–65; cf. also Guépin 1963–64, with summary and synoptic tables of rations known from the PT. We may also note in passing that the workers doubtless also received clothing from the administration (*sig-ba* 'wool rations' in the Mesopotamian terminology: Gelb 1965: 235), but these archives have been lost (Hallock 1973: 323); on the rations and their value, see most recently Giovinazzo 1993. Meat rations: let us note in passing that, although the testimony of PF 1793–94 is not equivocal (despite the absence of the word *kurtaš*), the process implied in PF 823–25 (without using the word *kurtaš*) is not absolutely certain (cf. PFT 27); see especially PF 823, where Bakeya receives 2 sheep with Ištin, a woman with the title *dukšiš* 'princess'; in these circumstances, Bakeya is probably a high-ranking person (Lewis 1984: 600 and 1985: 112 thinks he was the princess's husband, perhaps recognizable in Bagaeus, son of Artontes, in Herodotus 3.128); see also the tablet published by Vallat 1994: 264–71 (a goldsmith receives a sheep each month for 6 months). Organization of labor among the women-*pašap*: I accept the interpretation of Kawase 1984, which has been criticized by Brosius 1991: 154ff.; teams on the Persepolis construction sites: cf. Roaf 1983 (some of whose methodological choices are strongly contested by Sancisi-Weerdenburg 1992). Manufacture of stone objects at Persepolis: I faithfully follow the proof of Delaunay 1975, but I must state that this is only one possible interpretation out of several—since the debate remains lively and complex and the materials are difficult, which can open the door to interpretations that vary widely (see, for example, Williamson 1990 on the Aramaic gloss *gll* on PF 1587, challenging [p. 84] Delaunay's interpretation of the word); following Bernard 1972, some authors (Vogelsang 1992: 169; Williamson 1991: 43; Koch 1993a: 26) stress that the treasurers Dātamithra and Bagapāta bear the title "treasurer who is in Arachosia" (see already the doubts expressed by Bowman 1970: 28–30); they conclude that the objects were made in various places in Arachosia, then deposited at Persepolis as gifts presented to the Great King by high officials of the province; mortars and pestles would then no longer have any connection with the Persepolis workshops.

- *Origins and Status of the kurtaš.* On the deportations of peoples and the "extremities of the Empire" (*eskhatia*), cf. Briant 1984b: 64–65; on the status of laborers at the construction sites of Persepolis, see also the thoughts of Guépin 1963–64: 38–40, who thinks that they cannot have been free workers.

- *Demographics and Population Growth.* In his most recent work (1989b: 160), Dandamaev repeats without change an interpretation he had presented earlier (see 1973: 6–8, detailed table; p. 9, table in percentages); as he himself notes (1973: 9 n. 28, using the tablet PT 37: Carian goldsmiths), the hypothesis of *kurtaš* living in families goes back to Guépin 1963–64: 36; it has recently been repeated in Kawase 1984: 19–20; but meanwhile, an important article by Zaccagnini (1983) has come out, though it has not received the circulation it deserves; in this article (pp. 262–64), Zaccagnini seriously challenges Dandamaev's conclusions (which I followed previously); Zaccagnini's article also includes a major discussion of the concept of free labor in the ancient Near East; for the figures and percentages quoted, in part I used the calculations of Kawase 1984 and 1986; royal slaves and palace slaves: Dandamaev 1984b: 565–67.

- *Family Breakup and Ethnic Uniformity.* On the status of communities settled in Babylonia, see especially Eph'al 1978; cf. also Heltzer 1981; on the Babylonians in Persia, cf. Stolper

1984a; Elamite and Babylonian gods in Persia: Koch 1977: 101–19, repeated and developed in Koch 1987a and 1991; see also Dandamaev 1975: 196–97. On PF 337: Vallat 1994: 272 believes that "the grain was not intended for the 'religious ceremony' itself, but rather for the workers concerned with divine service"; on the *laoi*, cf. *RTP* 93–133, and below, chap. 11/9; PF 999: I owe the note on the wife of a *kurtaš* to Brosius 1991: 28.

4. Agriculture: Produce and Levies

• *Baziš and Other Levies.* The meaning of *baziš*, compared with *baji*, has been discussed frequently; it is generally recognized that the word goes back etymologically to a gift rather than a tribute, properly speaking; more precisely, it concerns 'the [king's] part', as in Akkadian *zitti šarri*, for example (see *RTP* 215 n. 75; Herrenschmidt 1989a; Sancisi-Weerdenberg 1989b: 137–38); as for the complex problem that is more basically financial (including the problem of the *bazikara*), there is little hope of agreement (cf. opposing views in Herrenschmidt 1989a and Koch 1989). In a recent article, Giovinazzi (1989b) proposes that the *baziš* and *mandattu* are equivalent, and she thinks that the Elamite *nutayunaš* is a transcription of Akkadian *nadānu*; her research has also brought to light the existence of another tax referred to by the Akkadian word *ḫallat*; one of her other articles (1989a) is an excellent clarification of the methods of collecting produce within districts, thanks to her new interpretation of the phrase *ha duš ha duka* in the tablets; on Raubasa: cf. Herrenschmidt 1989a: 113–14, who thinks (contra Hinz and Koch) that the *bazikara* do not levy taxes but are responsible for the royal flocks; I am not convinced that the two explanations are mutually exclusive (see below, chap. 11/10); *rušdabaziš*: hypothesis of Hinz 1973: 96; contra Herrenschmidt 1989a: 118 n. 4, who understands the word as 'who has part of the harvest' and concludes: "Exit tribute. But there are other problems with this word"; tithe: Koch 1981: 123–24; *ukpiyataš*: Hinz 1973: 88; Stolper 1977: 254–59; Joannès 1989a: 153–54.

• *The Direct Producers.* Tuplin (1987b: 143) proposes interpreting Aelian I.31 in light of the Category J tablets; *nutanuyaš/nadānu*: Giovinazzo 1989b: for this author, the *nadānu/nutanuyaš*, in animal form, is "delivered to the gate/before the portico" of the palace; taken literally, the phrase seems to mean that every year the producers had to deliver formally, as a "gift," part of their flocks to the king or his representatives. Can we establish a link between small Persian peasants and these deliveries "at the gate"? In the absence of irrefutable confirmation, I remain cautiously optimistic. On farm rent: the hypothesis was developed by Koch 1981 (repeated in Koch 1992: 269–72); it is strongly contradicted by Vallat, *AbIr* 4 (1982) no. 166 (cf. also Herrenschmidt 1989a: 116–17); since the discussion is based on philological facts, I am not competent to participate; I will simply observe that there certainly was terminology for farm rent in Old Persian, since it is found in the form of calques in an Aramaic papyrus from Egypt (Benveniste 1954: 304). On the question raised at the end of chap. 11/4 (assessments vs. taxes), cf. the position of Herrenschmidt 1989a n. 6: "In sum, I do not believe at all that the grain that circulates in the Persepolis tablets comes from 'tribute'. It comes from fields cultivated under royal authority and circulates from one branch of the administration to another for various needs"; I have myself expressed some reservations with reference to Giovinazzo's 1989a article (Briant, *AbIr* 13 [1990] no. 94: "Meanwhile, it seems there is nothing to prove that 'these documents illustrate the levying of a special tax' [p. 15]—at least to take the word 'tax' in such a general sense that it loses its descriptive meaning"); at the same time, Herrenschmidt's model appears to me to be too positive, since it implies that all the land in Persia belonged to the category of *royal land*—which is exactly what remains to be proved (see chap. 11/10).

5. Lands and Estates

• *Partetaš.* Despite the doubts expressed here and there (PFT 15, quoting a letter from Benveniste withdrawing his previous interpretation: Benveniste 1954: 309), I see no persuasive arguments against the equation of "paradise" and *partetaš*; on the other hand, the "paradise" of Artaxerxes' inscription at Susa (A²Sd) must be excluded from the discussion (Stève 1987: 98;

Lecoq 1990b); "paradise" in Classical sources: *RTP*, index, s.v.; Fauth 1979; also Briant 1991c: 230–36; *paradeisos* and market gardens in the Mnesimachus inscription: Buckler and Robinson 1912: 78–79 and Briant 1991c: 231 n. 30; on *kēpos*, see also Caroll and Spilleke 1989; Fahliyun region in the Classical sources, cf. *RTP* 161–70 and 206–7; in the tablets: Hallock 1977: 131–32; Koch 1986 and 1990: 135ff.; hydraulic improvements: in the parks: *RTP* 453; at Pasargadae: Stronach 1985d: 108–10; Kleiss 1992a; in Persia: Sumner 1986: 13–17; Kleiss 1988 and 1992a; administration of the *partetaš*: Koch 1981: 119–20.

- *Irmatam.* In the Susa tablets, cf. Hinz 1987: 130–32, who calls Vivāna's *irmatam* the "feudal residence" (*Lehenssitz*); cf. also Hinz 1973: 60–63; in the Persepolis tablets, cf. Sumner 1986: 26–27 (also using 9 unpublished tablets); the rebel attacks on Vivāna's *irmatam* can certainly be related to the devastations of the satrapal parks often mentioned in the Classical texts (*RTP* 456); the associations of tablets PF 152/640–41 and 153/637 were suggested to me by Giovinazzo's 1989a article.
- *Ulhi.* On princesses' houses, cf. Brosius 1991: 131–34, and pp. 137ff. on their *kurtaš* (add text B published by Vallat 1994: 271–74: *kurtaš* of Irdabama); see also Koch 1994: 134–40 (who unfortunately continues to call them "queen," or even "Mitkönigin," throughout: p. 137).

6. The Persepolis Tablets and the Imperial Administration: Sources and Problems

Cf. already *RTP* 207–11; on the importance of the problem, cf. also Lewis 1990a: 5 and Koch 1990: 311; "chancellor and scribe," cf. Stolper 1989b: 298–303; *phoinikistēs*: Lewis 1977: 25 n. 143; Chantraine, *DELG* 1218; and G. P. Edwards and R. B. Edwards, *Kadmos* 6 (1977)· 131–40 (with bibliography); Dascylium bullas: Akurgal 1956; Balkan 1959; Kaptan and Bayburtluoglu 1990; Arad ostraca: Avigad and Naveh 1981. Discoveries of Elamite tablets: Briant 1984b: 59 (to the best of my knowledge, the tablet found at Kandahār has not been the subject of a single publication); cf. also a tablet found at another site in Fārs: Wilkinson 1965: 344 (the seal impressed there has a "Royal Hero" scene), the Elamite tablet (YBC 16813 published by Jones and Stolper 1986: 248–53); the Susa tablet MDP 11.308 republished by Garrison (forthcoming), and the Elamite tablets of Armavir-blur in Armenia (Koch 1993b; chap. 16/14 below [but cf. Vallat 1995!]); on Category Q tablets, cf. also Briant 1991b: 69 n. 8. (M. Stolper and C. E. Jones are currently preparing an article that assembles all of the documents that are identical or comparable to Persepolis documents).

7. The Management of Property and the Royal Warehouses in Egypt

- *The Resupplying of the Garrison of Syene–Elephantine.* P. Loeb 1, cf. Hughes 1984: 75–77; on the resupply boats, cf. also Milik 1967: 554–55; seal of Petosiris the boatman: Duchesne-Guillemin and van de Valle 1959–62.
- *The Repair of an Administration Boat.* Cf. Grelot 1970: 23–31; 1972: 283–95; and especially the detailed commentary by Whitehead 1974: 119–54.
- *Royal Dockyards and Workshops.* Memphis dockyard: Aimé-Giron 1931: 54–63 and Bowman 1941; Egyptian vases from Susa: Posener 1936: 137–51, 189–90; Amiet 1990; Persepolis vases: Schmidt 1957: 81ff.; pre-Achaemenid Egyptian dockyards: Griffith 1909: 71ff.; cf. also *BIFAO* 76 (1976): 1–15; 54 (1954): 7–12; 78 (1976): 17–35; **hamarakara*: cf. Eilers 1940: 43–59; Greenfield 1972; Stolper 1977: 259–65; *dgalîn* at Memphis: Segal 1983: 8.

8. Management of Surpluses

- *Back to Pseudo-Aristotle.* Eumenes and the royal stud farms of the Ida: cf. *RTP* 209.
- *Surplus in Kind and Exchanges.* Letter from Antigonus to Teos: cf. the commentary of Préaux 1954 (followed here; cf. already Briant 1986c: 47–48 n. 23, where the reference to Strabo XV.3.21 is irrelevant, for the reasons laid out above, chap. 10/5), to be compared with a letter from Antiochus III to Heraclea by Latmus (Wörrle 1988: 468–69); Orontes and Athens: the text is given

by Osborne 1982: 52–54; 1983: 65–80 (without touching on the problem discussed here; the text has primarily been used in the context of the "great satrapal revolt" and the reconstruction of Orontes' career); on all these documents, see now Briant 1994d.

- *The Athos Canal Workers.* Cf. already a few words on this subject in Briant 1986c: 47 n. 14.

- *Return to Persepolis.* See the review of the various hypotheses in Dandamaev 1989b: 165–67, to which may be added the discussion by Naster 1990; comparisons with Pseudo-Aristotle: Altheim 1951, followed by Cameron 1965: 168–72; cf. Altheim and Stiehl 1963: 157–67. The hypothesis put forth here (credits to the warehouses expressed in weighed silver) is taken in part from Guépin 1963–64: 37, who, noting the tiny amounts of some silver rations, suggests: "It is just possible that the silver was not 'given'—paid out—at all, but that the earner could pay with a kind of check (or scrip) received from the treasury." To explain better the process proposed here, I would like to compare what is known about the payment of wages in the Hellenistic armies: (1) Soldiers sometimes received *symbola* [a kind of token] from the administration that constituted evidence of their right to receive rations (cf. Launey 1949, 2: 776 n. 4, 770–71, 773). (2) Compared with the Herodotus text on the people of the Athos Peninsula (VII.25), the administrative machinery glimpsed at Persepolis could be considered a pale reflection of the *adaeratio* in the Hellenistic armies (cf. Launey 1949, 2: 1280 s.v.): in this system, part of the wages in kind was calculated in silver, at a rate established by the military administration; in principle, the ratio was advantageous, since the prices were lower than in the market (Launey 2: 735–40, 779); in some cases, however, the soldiers lost out in the exchange (p. 771); following this hypothesis, the disadvantage would clearly be greater for the workers, if we agree (as I believe: see below) that there was no free market, properly speaking, at Persepolis (in any case, the profits earned by the administration on this occasion are stressed by Cameron 1958: 172). Prices in the year 467–466: cf. Hallock 1960: 94–95 and 1972: 25, who thinks that the price explosion must be seen in relation to the military operations in Asia Minor (battle of the Eurymedon)—which seems to me to be a desperate hypothesis: cf. Briant 1993c: 414 and nn. 47–49); transfers between warehouses: cf. Hallock 1960: 92 and 1972: 27, who suggests instead that the head of warehouses made the exchange with a private merchant (on these transfers, cf. also Giovinazzo 1993 and Vallat 1994); the existence of a private market is also suggested by Hinz 1970: 432–33, followed by Dandamaev 1973: 16 n. 7 = 1989b: 166. It is true that the phenomenon of increasing prices at Persepolis raises thorny interpretive problems. But I have the impression that the usual explanations presuppose that the market played a determinative role, which appears highly unlikely to me; see by way of comparison the article by Gentet and Maucourant 1991, who, contesting previous interpretations, describe the operation of the Egyptian economy as follows: "The Egyptian economy is an economy of redistribution. A center, consisting of the administration and the granaries of the public and religious institutions, assesses and redistributes the majority of the wealth produced. . . . The Egyptian economy is not a merchant economy" (pp. 13–14); we could repeat this definition for the Achaemenid palace economy nearly word for word, insofar as it can be seen operating in Persepolis; the authors stress (p. 17) "that a price increase concerning grain" would not be the same as inflation; they also note: "Price increases must no longer be taken as sufficient proof of famine, since in a redistributive economy it would not have an automatic effect on prices" (p. 22); nor does the existence of a scribal evaluation of the change in value of commodities in monetary form imply that there was a change in cash commodities (p. 25); as the authors note at the end (p. 30), "increase in prices always implies a transfer of resources." For all these reasons, an interpretation that calls on market mechanisms to explain what we see at Persepolis seems to me to have been firmly refuted.

9. Lands and Peasants

- *Kurtaš, garda, gardu.* On the care required when facing terminological identity, see the apt reflections of Stolper 1985a: 31 n. 115; on the Aramaic documents, cf. the notes of Whitehead 1974: 72ff.; on Hinzanāy, cf. also Roaf 1979: 72, and Briant 1988a: 167–68; see especially the reflections of Zaccagnini 1983 (without referring to this example) on itinerant artists and crafts-men in the ancient Near East. "Craftsmen of all kinds": Benveniste 1958a: 60–63. Cilicians: on their ethnic origin, cf. Goetze 1962: 54 n. 55 (opposing the opinion of Cazelles 1955: 93, which I followed in Briant 1988a: 143 n. 10). Tattoos: in an earlier article (*RTP* 311 n. 89), I followed the opinion of Harmatta (1963: 207), who says that the term *tattoo* comes from an incorrect reading; but this isolated opinion does not seem acceptable (cf. Whitehead 1974: 75); on the practice of marking Babylonian slaves with the names of their successive masters, cf. Cardascia 1951: 172; tat-tooed Babylonian slave (*Camb.* 143): reading by Greenfield 1991: 183.

- *Garda and gardu.* See mainly Dandamaev 1984b: 568–73 and Stolper 1985a: 55–59; *piti-pabaga* and *potibazis*, see mainly Eilers 1940: 73–81, with the complementary remarks of Stolper 1985a: 57–58. *Rabbap*: Dandamaev 1984b: 173 (free workers); cf. also Sumner 1986: 30 ("local people . . . temporarily assigned to work groups") and more recently Uchitel 1992; but see Ger-shevitch 1969: 184, who thinks, however, that *rabbap* cannot refer to free workers; he thinks that the word *zamip* refers to free workers, but with many questions.

- *Tissaphernes and the Peasants of the Villages of Parysatis.* On the Xenophon passage and its translation, cf. *RTP* 61 n. 3; on the *Cyropaedia* passages, cf. *RTP* 176–81 and 480–81.

- *Irmatam, ulhi, and Gift Lands (doreai).* See Briant 1985b and Stolper 1985a: 52–69; *dōrea* of Mnesimachus: Descat 1985. *DAE* 67: cf. *RTP* 311 n. 89 and Whitehead 1974: 60–66, who inde-pendently reach similar conclusions (Briant 1985b: 66); on the relationship proposed in the text between *DAE* 67 and certain Persepolis tablets regarding princesses' subordinates, see also De-launay 1976: 19: "Only . . . the princesses can thus pay out of the public coffers and require either directly or by intermediary (*šaramana*) that the assets they control be released." In disagreement with Dandamaev's position (e.g., 1972a: 29–31; 1974), I continue to believe that land concessions, just as in the Hellenistic period, could be revoked by the king (cf. *RTP* 58–59 [note], 93; and Briant 1985b). [*Additional note* on Aršāma's "estates": in a recent article, Dandamaev (1993c: 122), who seems not to know my 1979 note reprinted in *RTP* 311 n. 89 and my article 1985b, ends up agreeing with Whitehead's opinion, quoted (p. 122) via Stolper 1985a]; on this point cf. also Porten 1987: 43, 47 (on *dšn'* in *DAE* 62): "It was thus not a grant to be held by the father and his estate, but a gift subject to revocation by the sovereign benefactor. . . . Thus *dāšna* is a royal grant, especially of land, of *usufructum* but not of absolute ownership in fee simple or fee tail. . . . It is revocable at the will of the sovereign benefactor" (on the word *°dāšna* in *DAE* 62 [earliest attesta-tion], see also Benveniste 1954: 300–301; note that this Persian word is probably found in a Perse-polis tablet [PF 337] in the sense of sacrificial offering for Ahura-Mazda: cf. PFT index s.v., p. 681). On Parysatis's property, see Cardascia 1991, who also believes that the royal princess was simply the beneficiary of the income from rather than the owner of the lands from which she received the revenue; on the land concessions made to the stewards of the houses, cf. Stolper 1985a: 65; he compares the case of Babylonian stewards with those known in Egypt—on which see now Porten 1985 (on *DAE* 69); cf. also Szubin and Porten 1988: 42–43.

10. The King's House

- *The King's Sheep, Camels, and Horses.* On the warehouses, cf. Hallock's position, PFT 19; following him, Dandamaev (1972c: 14–16) thinks that the absence of *sunkina* is not particularly significant. "On all evidence," he writes, "there was not the slightest boundary between govern-mental property and royal property, between imperial revenue and royal property" (also, see Dan-damaev 1973: 20 on royal *kurtaš*); this is also the basis of the presentation given by Altheim and Stiehl (1963: 177–79), but in a form both more nuanced and more conceptual; I note that Lewis (1977: 11 n. 40) also expresses certain prudent reservations about Hallock's interpretation of the Category E texts (warehouses); on scribal practices (regarding PFa 29), cf. Hallock 1978: 114 (comparable, in an entirely different context, with remarks by Bernard and Rapin 1980: 19–20); on the phrase "attached to the house," cf. Gershevitch 1969: 175–77, followed by Hallock 1978: 112;

on the other hand, the examples from the PT first put forward by Cameron must now be excluded: cf. Cameron 1965: 176.

• *Two Economic Domains?* On the exchange of produce, cf. also Hallock 1972: 26–27 and PFT 62, as well as Giovinazzo 1993 (on the *sut* process; Hallock thinks these exchanges were carried out in the context of a private market, but this interpretation does not convince me; cf. above); on the word *zak/zakme*, cf. Hallock 1960: 92; Fort. 19191: I know this unpublished tablet only from Hallock's 1972: 22 n. 4 reference. On the tablets naming Umizza, I am close to the interpretation suggested by Herrenschmidt 1989a: 114 (although I am reluctant to follow her on the meaning of *bazikara*, p. 115).

• *Parnaka, Persia, and Darius.* On Parnaka's position and the nonexistence of a satrapy in Persia, I agree basically with Lewis 1977: 8–9 (correctly contesting the previous hypothesis of Hinz); cf. also Tuplin 1987b: 115, and now Koch 1993a: 16–22 (on the satraps of Pura/Puruš and Maka(š) named in some tablets); peace officers and police: Gershevitch 1969: 169, 181–82; Hinz 1973: 72–75; *datābaru* in Babylonia: Stolper 1985a: 91; on the word *dayyānu* in the tablets, cf. Eilers 1940: 6–7 (note).

• *Royal House, Persia, and Empire: A Hypothesis.* As the title of this section indicates, I must stress that the interpretations proposed here are nothing more than hypotheses, since they in turn raise several difficulties of which I am aware and which the above analyses do not entirely dispel; but it seems to me that even if my solutions do not convince the readers, the problem that inspired them remains. Some additional remarks:

1. On the text of Chares of Mytilene (Athenaeus): On the expressions used by the Greeks to describe the royal gifts (belt, slipper, etc.), cf. Briant 1985b: 59–62. Without being aware of my article, Cardascia (1991) recently returned to this question, and he too understands them as "for her maintenance" or "for her personal privy purse," what I have called here "civil list." Nor am I persuaded that the formulations of the Greek authors have to be rejected (despite his note, p. 365 n. 16) or that the accounting procedures they describe smack of "improbability" (cf. Briant 1985b: 61–62); I also note the existence of comparable formulas in Egyptian texts: cf. Meeks 1972: 68–71 on the lands whose revenues are dedicated to the care of animals (institutions known from Diodorus I.83.2: *epimeleia, trophē*), to be compared with the examples enumerated in the Achaemenid Empire and presented in Briant 1985b: 60–61; cf. Meeks 1972: 109ff.: "lamp fields. Doubtless fields whose revenues were applied to the maintenance of lamps in the temple." The identity of the formulas implies that, from the point of view of Chares of Mytilene, the king's pillow and footstool took on the same political-economic significance as the queen's girdle or slipper, that is, assessments reserved for the personal maintenance of the king: we there find the definition given by Hesychius for the *tagē* (*basilikē dōrea kai hē syntaxis tēn pros to zēn anagkaiōn*); if we pursue this interpretation to the end, we are led to believe that the king's cushion and footstool were supported by the revenues (in metal) of the *tagē*, that is, the royal land in the strict sense. (I hesitate, however, to conclude that the title *custos regiae pecuniae* [Quintus Curtius V.5.2, V.1.20; Nepos, *Dat.* 5.3] names the manager of this private treasury; they seem rather, at least in the first two examples, to be *gazophylax*.)

2. Rapin (1992a: 273–74) is the only author I know of who has commented on the Chares passage, in the context of a discussion of the architectural organization of the palace, where he distinguishes "the actual royal treasury" or the "specifically royal treasury" from the warehouses, but without clearly explaining what he means by "actual royal treasury."

3. Of course, the basic problem posed by my hypothesis is that it implies the existence of a *patrimonium* of the prince. I note that this is Bickerman's position (1938: 180), who, for the Seleucid era, argues for the existence of "the royal estate proper . . . called, it seems, *khōra basilikē*. This patrimony consisted of the old property of the Achaemenids, Alexander, and his successors." Against this position, Corsaro (1980a: 1165 n.13) suggests that "the entire

khōra phorologoumenē [tribute land] must be considered *khōra basilikē*." Without repeating the entire discussion presented above (chap. 10/7), I will observe that Corsaro's too-clear-cut position is disputable, especially after Descat's studies of the *tagē*, which clearly imply a difference between the two categories of land and taxes—in silver for the tribute, in kind for the *tagē*.

4. In the suggested development toward the installation of a state system, it is difficult to determine what goes back to Darius: it is possible that the restricted sense of the word *Achaemenid* (chap. 3/1) signified that, from that point on, the property of the royal family was distinguished from the lands of the Achaemenid clan (at least lands of the latter that were not included within the royal house). Herodotus reports that Darius included among his wives Phratagune, daughter of his brother Artanes, who was also a son of Hystaspes, and he states, "By marrying his daughter to Darius, he had given him his entire *oikos* as dowry, since she was his only child" (7.224). It is sometimes thought (cf. Lloyd in the discussion of Briant 1990a; also Brosius 1991: 66 n. 123) that Herodotus imposed the purely Greek phenomenon of the *epiclère* daughter [daughter with an additional name] on Persia; the objection is obviously possible, but in my view, the story can be understood just as well in the Persian context (cf. the thoughts of Atkinson 1956: 173–77) and in what we know of the internal organization of the Persian aristocratic houses (cf. chap. 8/4); the conclusion I draw from this would instead be the following: the Achaemenid practice of endogamy had the additional purpose of keeping the property of the various princely houses within the broader framework of the royal house. On the other hand, and even though my interpretation agrees in general lines with that proposed by Herrenschmidt 1989a, I have some reservations regarding part of her argument: I do not think, in particular, that one can date the shift in meaning of the word *baziš* from king's part to tribute [on **drnabāziš*, Hinz 1973: 66] so specifically (after *DB*: p. 115); if the development did happen (which I also believe), we can think only of the *longue durée*, especially if we recognize (or suppose) that the royal administration in Persia did not begin with the first dated tablet (cf. my reflections on this in chap. 2/9 above, regarding Cyrus's reign).

5. It is possible, finally, that the royal house was also distinct in the religious area; I note in fact that in addition to the deities of the official pantheon (for example, Ahura-Mazda), Darius III invokes the 'gods of [his] ancestors' (*theoi genethlioi*; Plutarch, *Alex.* 30.12; the explanation given in *RTP* 379 n. 166 is obsolete because it used an outdated translation of *DPd*): if Plutarch's formulation corresponds to reality, we are led to suppose that, as in the Hellenistic period (cf. Gauthier 1989: 67–73), the *theoi genethlioi* were specifically the protective gods of the royal family.

11. Transition

On the Egyptian documentary context and its characteristics, cf. Briant 1984b: 58.

Chapter 12
The King of the Lands

1. Darius and Egypt

• *Bibliography.* The basic references will be found in Bresciani 1958, 1984, 1985c; Briant 1988a; Ray 1988; and Tuplin 1991a; see also Kienitz 1953; Kraeling 1953: 32–40; and Bianchi 1982.

• *Satraps and Satrapy.* Persian titles in Egypt: cf. Wiesehöfer 1991b; Demotic documents: Hughes 1984 (on P. Loeb 1, cf. also Heidorn 1992: 130–32); Memphis: cf. *LÄ,* s.v. "Memphis" and "Saqqara"; Petrie 1909–10; Segal 1983; on the internal organization of the garrison at Syene–Elephantine, see especially Kraeling 1953: 41–48; Porten 1968: 28–61; Grelot 1972; and Tuplin 1987c: 225.

• *Udjahorresnet's Return to Saïs.* Posener 1936: 21–29, 175–76; Blenkinsopp 1987; Briant 1993e; on his recently discovered tomb, cf. Verner 1988 and Bareš 1992.

• *Darius and the Egyptian Laws.* Besides Spiegelberg's publication of the text and his commentary 1914: 30–32 and the old article by Reich (1933), see especially Bresciani 1981; Allam 1986, 1993; and Mélèze and Modrzejewski 1986, both of whom suggest (cautiously but explicitly) a relationship between Darius's code and the Demotic customary laws of the Ptolemaic period [likewise Johnson 1994: 157–58 and Devauchelle 1995: 76 (see also Briant 1996b); a translation of the Demotic text is also found in Devauchelle pp. 74–75 (and in Bresciani 1996)]; on the "sacred law" and the role of the priests of the Houses of Life, cf. Quaegebeur 1980–81 (with a comparison, pp. 239–40, with the codification ordered by Darius); on a possible use of these customs at Elephantine in the time of Darius II, cf. the hypothesis proposed below in chap. 14/8 (taken up and elaborated in Briant 1996b).

• *Pharandates and the Sanctuary of Khnūm at Elephantine.* Hughes 1984; on the Petition of Peteisis, cf. Griffith 1909: 43–110; French translation by Capart 1914; cf. also Lloyd 1983: 304–5 [and now Chauveau 1996]; on the site of Teuzoi, cf. Szubin and Porten 1992: 72–73; on the Aramaic papyrus studied by Milik 1960, cf. the corrections in Porten 1985b: 438–39.

• *Darius in the Temple of Hibis (El Khārga).* Winlock 1941; Davies 1953 (with many drawings of the depictions of gods that she surveyed; some are reprinted in Briant 1992d: 62); Cruz-Uribe 1988; Aufrère, Golvin, and Goyon 1994: 88–94; see also El-Sayed 1982, 1: 92ff.; 2: 421–22 (with the translations used here); ritual of divine suckling: J. Leclant in *Mélanges Mariette* (1961): 251–84; French translation of the Darius inscriptions at El Khārga: Drioton, *ASAE* 40 (1940): 339–77. Without going into detail, I note that the chronology and interpretation of the buildings and reliefs are somewhat problematic (cf. Cruz-Uribe 1986); the most recent commentator (Cruz-Uribe 1988: 192–98) thinks that the absence of Neith points to some reworking of Darius's Egyptian policy—which privileged the gods of Upper Egypt (Thebes region) over those of the Delta; I must say that, in relation to everything I have read elsewhere, this author's interpretations are problematic; but we probably should await the publication of vol. 2 before deciding. We may also note that networks of *qanats* for supplying the oasis with water have been discovered; they are generally thought to date to the Persian period and thus to Darius (cf. Goblot 1979: 113–14, who quotes and uses earlier studies made on the spot by archaeologists; on Goblot's work, cf. Planhol's criticism [1992]); on the *qanats* in the oasis, see also Aufrère, Golvin, and Goyon 1994: 85 (Persian period), and also the article by Bousquet and Reddé 1994 (site of Douch). Meanwhile, in a private letter dated July 1, 1992, for which I am grateful, M. Betro (Pisa) alerts me to investigations by A. Fakry at Bahria (*ASAE* 40 [1940]: 855–96 and *Recent Discoveries in the Oases of the Western Desert* [Cairo, 1942]: 71–87), whose results may imply that the system of *qanats* known at El Khārga predates the conquest. ⟦I will also mention the discovery of Demotic ostraca in a recent excavation at Douch; some are dated to Darius I (pers. comm. from N. Grimal, February 1995).⟧ Sporadic mentions of Darius at other sites: Yoyotte 1952; Traunecker 1973–77; Ray 1988: 264.

• *Darius at Heliopolis.* Yoyotte 1972, 1974 (publications of hieroglyphic inscriptions); on the iconography, cf. Roaf 1974 and Calmeyer 1991a (distinguishing the Persian and Egyptian elements).

• *Darius's Pharaonic Reputation.* On Darius and Sesostris: cf. Posener 1934; Malaise 1966; Lloyd 1982a: 37–41; Gaggero 1986; Morschauser 1988; Obsomer 1989: 151–58; and West 1992—with the authors disagreeing to some extent.

• *The Pharaoh and the Great King.* On the *naos* of Hermopolis, see the detailed commentary by Mysliwiec 1991 (but the interpretation of the role attributed to Pharandates in the matter makes me wonder); another Darius *naos*: photo in Briant 1992d: 60 ⟦another interesting object recently republished by Traunecker 1995: a carved head melding Persian and Egyptian traditions⟧. On Darius's position, cf. the valid remarks of Tuplin 1991a: 243–47; Darius and the Suez Canal: cf. Posener 1936: 48–87 (canal stelas), 180–89 (interpretation of the lists), and Posener 1938; see clarification in Salles 1990: 117–18; Tuplin 1991a; also Briant 1991b: 78–79; surveys in the region of Tell el-Maskhuta: cf. Holladay 1982, 1992; Paice 1986–87, 1993 ⟦as well as Redmount 1995 on the route of the canal⟧.

• *From Cambyses to Darius.* On Polyaenus VII.11.7, cf. Tuplin 1991a: 265–66; on the stela mentioning the interment of the mother of an Apis, cf. Smith 1988: 188–89; 1992. The decree on the back of the *Dem. Chron.* concerning Cambyses' taxation and the possible role of Darius is not clear (did or did not Darius overturn Cambyses' decree?): cf. Bresciani 1983, 1989 ⟦and Devauchelle 1995: 76; Bresciani 1996⟧; *P. Berlin* 13582: Hughes 1984: 84–85 (but the text contains several obscurities). ⟦On Cambyses' Egyptian policy, see now Devauchelle 1995 and Depuydt 1995a, analyzed above, chap. 1/9, Research Notes, pp. 887f.⟧.

• *Persians and Egyptians.* Cf. Briant 1988a, esp. pp. 160–66; on the titles given to the Egyptian elite, see also Meulenaere 1989: 569: the titles "Venerable before the king" and "Truly known to the king" "fell out of use after the Persian invasion, just as the 'Known to the king' disappeared from Egyptian autobiography under the invaders. Only an avowed 'collaborator' like the famous Udjahorresnet could boast, with good reason, of having been a 'Truly known to the king'"; on Persian names in Egypt from later papyrological sources, cf. Huyse 1990b, 1991. See also the interesting funerary document (drawing in Ray 1988: 273; photo in Briant 1992d: 90–91) from Memphis showing the deceased dressed in Persian (Median?) style: cf. Martin and Nichols 1978: 66–80; another funerary stela evidencing acculturation (Greco/Carian[?]-Egyptian) was published by Gallo and Masson 1993. ⟦In this regard, the most fascinating new evidence is the funerary stela discovered in 1994 at Saqqara and briefly described on p. 1031 below thanks to information kindly provided by H. S. Smith and A. Kuhrt (published in *JEA* 81 [1995]); the inscription seems to attest to an Iranian-Egyptian marriage, which (along with other considerations) leads me to retract what I wrote in Briant 1988a: 166⟧. On Ahmose/Arsames, cf. Posener 1936: 177 and Briant 1988a: 160; Egyptian *senti*: Yoyotte 1989. Knemibre: besides Posener (1936: 88–116), see Guyon 1957: 17–20 (on the military nature of the expeditions that gathered and transported stone from Wadi Hammamât; cf. ibid., 28–29: inscriptions of Atiyawahy); I note that new Aramaic documents found in the Wadi Hammamât are published by Bongrani Fanfoni and Israel 1994, who also republish the hieroglyphic texts (though some of the historical commentaries seem questionable to me); origin of the stone for the statue of Darius: Trichet and Vallat 1990 (results of petrographic analysis). Votive bulls: Michaelidis 1943: 99 (Mithrobaios), who interprets it as an object dedicated to the Mithra cult, but see the critical remarks of Yoyotte 1952: 167 n. 5. The only evidence for Persian religion in Egypt is the mention of two *magi* (Mitrasareh and Táta) as witnesses in a private contract from 434 (*DAE* 45 [= *BMAP* 4]; cf. Lipiński 1981–84; cf. also Kakosy 1977). But obviously no historical inference can be drawn from this lacuna, which results solely from the nature of the available sources. Ptah-hotep: Cooney 1954a; Ray 1988: 272; on his duties, cf. most recently Bresciani 1989: 30–31 [and Devauchelle 1995: 78]. Seal of Peteisis (uncertain date): Duchesne-Guillemin and van de Valle 1959–62, comparable to the Persian-Egyptian seal published by Barnett and Wiseman 1969: 95 no. 49 (a falcon in front of a footed censer, and in front of it an ibex-horned bull, in a field bordered by *udjat* eyes); statue and inscription of Pedon: Ampolo and Bresciani 1988; and Masson and Yoyotte 1988; concerning the gift of the town, the latter authors think that it was the gift of ruling a town and that this sort of gift cannot be integrated into a Greek context; in any case, we can only stress the striking parallel with the gifts of towns in the Achaemenid period (Briant 1985b; cf. the careful considerations along these lines of Bresciani [p. 241], who nonetheless thinks it had to do with a land concession within the framework of the "colonization" policy followed by Psammetichus: Herodotus II.154); the remark about Udjahorresnet's jewelry comes from Amandry 1958a: 16 n. 55 (the author's entire long note is important; see also the remarks of Muscarella 1980: 26–27, 35–36; and Musche 1992: 278, drawing). Egyptian votive stela: published by Burchardt 1911: 71–72 (plate VIII, 1; cf. drawing in Ray 1988: 265), who thinks it really does relate to a cult of the king; the importance of the object is stressed by Lloyd 1982b: 174–75; compare monuments from the reign of Nectanebo in relation to the cult of kings of the XXXth dynasty: Nectanebo II is frequently awarded the epithet "falcon" there (cf. Meulenaere 1960, who relates the royal cult to the pharaoh's building activity).

• *A Brief Evaluation.* On the institution of the "Divine Consort," cf., e.g., Gitton 1984; on its disappearance after the Persian conquest, see the brief but clear remark in Meulenaere 1938: 187 (the last known seems to be Ankhnesneferibre, who, according to the author [p. 187 n. 2] "still lived under Psammetichus III"); unfortunately, as far as I know, this extremely important remark has never been followed up; I will simply observe that, without quoting Meulenaere, Tuplin (1991: 267) proposed to see in it an illustration of the decline of Thebes in Egyptian policy—a point of view that seems to me somewhat paradoxical, since Thebes continues to be an important center during the Achaemenid period [in addition, see Johnson 1994: 150 n. 5, and the whole article on the problems of continuities/discontinuities]; nonetheless, Tuplin's general opinion is completely relevant: "Darius did not aim to return everything to its pre-525 status quo." On the problems posed by the official enthronement of a foreign pharaoh, see the reflections of Burstein 1991 (concerning Alexander).

2. Babylonia under Darius

• *Sources.* Clear analysis by Kuhrt 1988b: 129–33; also Joannès 1990a: 173–74; Cocquerillat 1984b: 154–55 (Murānu). On the nonpublication of private documents from the time of Darius, see the impressive figures provided by Dandamaev 1992c: 172; he also notes (quite rightly) that it is not certain that Darius destroyed the Eanna, and he suggests that beginning with this king the Eanna kept its records on wooden tablets [same reasoning on the Ebabbar of Sippar in Dandamaev 1995b], but this last point remains to be proved. [See also McGinnis 1994, 1995, which I received late.]

• *Satraps and Governors.* Petit 1990: 186–96 must be completed and filled out by Kuhrt 1988b: 130–32 and Stolper 1989b; *šandabakku*: Stolper 1988b: 128–30; new palace: Joannès 1990a: 186 and n. 159; **vardana-pāti*: ibid., 178 n. 21; *Bagasarū*: Dandamaev 1969c, 1992a no. 98b; *širku*: Joannès 1990a: 186 (and n. 56 for the translation of *TCL* 13.196); and Abraham 1995. Concerning the office of *zazakku* (on which, see Joannès 1994b: royal secretary, not cadastre officer), Dandamaev (1994a: 40) thinks it was abolished by the Persian conquerors; this is possible, but the reasons given are not particularly convincing.

• *Estates and ḫaṭru.* Cardascia 1951, 1958, 1978; Stolper 1985a; Van Driel 1989: 206–8; Joannès 1982: 21–22; service in Elam: Dandamaev 1972b: 260; Joannès 1982: 22–23; *urāšu* service: Joannès 1982: 23–25, 1989a: 151–59; payment of taxes in silver-equivalent from the reign of Darius I: Joannès 1982: 21–22 (see chap. 14/7, Darius II and his armies).

• *Persians and Babylonians.* See Zadok 1977 and Dandamaev 1989b: 303–4, 1992a: 166–67; Joannès 1990a: 179–80 insists on the hegemonic role of the Persians, especially starting with Xerxes, but I am not sure that the available documentation allows us to draw such firm conclusions (cf. chap. 13/6); on the seals and the information that can be gleaned from them, see Zettler 1974, who says that beginning with Darius a large number of seals exchange traditional images for images known elsewhere from Persian seals; but see Graziani 1989 and esp. 1991: 164–65, who concludes that, on the contrary, 31 of 32 sealed tablets dated to Darius continue to bear Babylonian scenes (cf. also his remark on p. 161); on this point, see also the recent article by MacGinnis 1995: 164–81, and on the seals on the later tablets of the Murašû archives (to which I will return later, chap. 15/8), see now the detailed study of Bregstein 1993. I will add one remark: even though in Babylonia we have no evidence as clear as the inscription of Pedon in Egypt (above), we may note that the practice of royal gifts can equally as well be inserted without difficulty into the Assyro-Babylonian *longue durée*: see, e.g., Fales and Postgate 1992 no. 58 and pp. xxii–xxiii.

3. Trans-Euphrates

• *The District of Trans-Euphrates.* The period between the accession of Darius and the arrival of Nehemiah is the most lacking in documentation; see the recent collection of sources in Weippert 1988: 682ff. Tattenai: Olmstead 1944; cf. Rainey 1969; Ephʿal 1988; Stolper 1989b; Petit 1990: 189–90; Heltzer 1992b; see critical doubts about Herodotus's Vth *nome* expressed in Calmeyer 1990b. On Damascus: I am aware that it has been suggested that Sidon may have been the capital of Ebir Nāri, but I must say that the theory, based on a late and not very convincing text of Diodorus (XVI.41.2), has always seemed strange to me: see also Ephʿal 1988: 154–55, who agrees; in a discussion that is not always clear, Elayı (1989: 144–46) seems to agree that the Damascus theory is well grounded but at the same time thinks that the problem "is badly posed because the capital . . . need not have been unique and fixed": this remark could only hold for the paradise-residence that Xenophon places at the sources of the Dardas (*Anab.* I.4.10), not for the permanent headquarters of the satrapy. Concerning the government of Ebir Nāri, a recent article by H. Koch (1993a: 39) poses some problems; after mentioning that an unpublished tablet (Q 1888) refers to Cypriot *kurtaš* in Persia around 495, she compares this tablet with another (PF 1527) that deals with the movement of 1150 *kurtaš*, where the name of the person who delivered the *halmi* (Dā-tāna) is the same as the one in Q 1888; from this she deduces that this person was then satrap of Syria (of which Cyprus was a dependency). But: (1) this conclusion is based on the assumption that people who deliver *halmi* must always be considered satraps—which sometimes raises problems: cf. Briant 1991b: 70 n. 13; (2) in PF 1527, the ethnicity of the *kurtaš* is not stated, so this tablet and the other (Q 1888) could simply involve two people having the same name.

• *The Province of Judah.* Governors of Judea before Nehemiah: the inscribed bullas were published by Avigad 1976, and his interpretation has found widespread agreement (e.g., Laperrousaz 1982; Greenfield 1988; Lemaire 1989b: 95–96, 1994: 16–18; Meyers 1985 suggests that Elnathan is none other than the son-in-law of Zerubbabel); meanwhile Avigad's datings have been contested by Bianchi 1989, who concludes from analyzing the archaeological context that they are the Hellenistic period. Administration of Judea: cf., e.g., McEvenue 1981; Williamson 1988; and Lemaire 1990: 29–45 (the entire documentation is collected and interpreted, and the province of Judah is set among the other provinces [*medinah*] that make up Trans-Euphrates; revised version in Lemaire 1994a); seals with Achaemenid motifs struck (sometimes) with Iranian names have been found in the region, but the dates are not all precise: see Bordreuil 1986a no. 125ff.; Shaked and Naveh 1986; Stern 1971, 1982b: 196ff. Darius and Jerusalem: cf., e.g., Yamauchi 1990: 155–59; Bickermann's (1981) chronology has been seriously questioned by Kessler (1992). I mention in passing—not wanting to launch into a thorough-going critical analysis of Ezra and Nehemiah (cf. chap. 14/5 Research Notes)—that in a recent article Dequeker 1993 maintains that the reconstruction of the temple in Jerusalem should be dated to Darius II, not Darius I.

• *Cyprus.* The Phoenician presence in Cyprus is amply attested; see Masson and Snyczer 1972; Maier and Karageorghis 1984; and the articles by Destrooper and Giorgiadès, Hermary, Greenfield, and Yon in *Studia Phoenicia* 5 (1987), as well as Collombier 1991; the Cypriot kingdoms are clearly presented in their environment by Collombier 1990 (she stresses [p. 31] the uncertainties surrounding the function of the palace at Vouni, interpreted by Gjerstad as the residence of a Persian governor who would have been appointed after Cyprus's participation in the Ionian Revolt); cf. also Wiesehöfer 1990; Petit 1991; Reyes 1994: 85–97; Maier 1994: 297–308. I recall (above) that, according to Koch 1993a: 39, an unpublished Persepolis tablet (Q 1888) provides evidence of the presence of Cypriot workers (*kurtaš*) in Persia around 495; she also says that the adjective *kupirriyaip* does not refer to the place-name Gaufriya but to Cyprus [cf. the Babylonian astronomical tablet *ADRTB* -440, where Cyprus is called KUR *ku-up-ru*].

• *Phoenicia.* Generally speaking, Jidejian's syntheses on Tyre (1969) and Sidon (1971) are useful but very general; likewise Katzenstein's 1979 article; one may also consult the many studies by J. Elayi (cf. bibliography); the earlier, Assyrian sources allow the study of the extension of Phoenician occupation in the Gulf of Alexandretta (Myriandrus): cf. Kestemont 1983: 53–78, 1985: 135–65 (cf. also Bunnens 1983b); sources for the early Achaemenid period are scarce, aside from the role played by the Phoenicians in the Ionian Revolt and their relations with Carthage (cf. Ferjaoui 1992: 56–62), and aside from an Akkadian tablet found at Tyre dated 492 (sale of a female ass; Wilhelm 1973); not until the start of coinage, beginning in the second half of the fifth century, and the Classical texts bearing on the fourth-century revolts and Alexander's conquest do we have documentation (still indirect) dealing with the nature of the relationships between the Phoenician kings and the Great King; however, I note that quite recently Dandamaev (1995c) thinks that he has found mention of a governor of the town of Tyre [LÚ-NAM ša^{uru} gub-ba-al^{ki}] in a Babylonian tablet from the reign of Darius (CT 55, no. 435); the governor has a Babylonian name, and the text proves that the first Achaemenids kept very close watch over the Phoenician cities—all interpretations that require confirmation. Seal and tablet from Persepolis: PT 7; cf. Schmidt 1957 no. 32; cf. p. 11 (drawing in *CAH* IV² [1988]: 157 [fig. 50f, p. 606 here]). Ešmunazar inscription: text in Gibson III no. 28; the French translation is taken from Lemaire 1990: 56 (see also Lemaire 1994a: 31–32; text and photo of the sarcophagus in Briant 1992d: 85); on the date and the circumstances of the allocation to Sidon, see Kelly 1987, who reviews the previous interpretations and concludes that it was due to the activity of the Phoenicians against the Ionian rebels; to Kelly's bibliography add Garbini 1984 and Coacci Polselli 1984 (who places Tetramnestus between Ešmunazzar I [490–481] and Ešmunazzar II [475–461]); finally, in the course of a lucid article, Bondi (1974: 154–55) sees the first indication of Sidon's special place in the Achaemenid administrative system in Phoenicia in the royal concession (which he dates to the Egyptian revolt of Inarus); this special status could be based on the absolute fidelity of the kings of Sidon, which is clearly shown later on by the place of the Great King on the city's coins: cf. chap. 14/8. The king of Sidon close to Xerxes: I repeat here the conclusions of Hauben 1970, 1973 (compare the theories of Wallinga 1984, 1987, 1993 on the construction and organization of the royal fleet).

4. From Jerusalem to Magnesia on the Meander

• *Darius, Gadatas, and the Apollo of Aulai.* The inscription was published by Cousin and Deschamps 1889 (cf. Cousin 1890) and gave rise to many analyses: cf. Boffo 1978; the identification of the sanctuary referred to in the letter comes from L. Robert 1987: 42–43; the authenticity of the document has been reconfirmed by Wiesehöfer 1987b, soundly refuting Hansen 1986 [but some doubts remain in Tuplin 1994: 238]; the letter in Iranian context: Brandestein and Mayrhofer 1964: 91–98; the identification of Gadatas as satrap (claimed, for example, by Tuplin 1987b: 145) is offered once again by Petit 1990: 179–80 and Chaumont 1990: 588–90, but the arguments are far from convincing; Gadatas, steward of a paradise: Dandamaev 1984a: 114 ("probably"); on the date proposed here (Darius at Sardis during the return from Europe): suggested by comparison with the embassies sent by the sanctuaries to the Roman Senate: Tacitus III.60ff. (cf. Briant 1993a: 11–12); note that on this occasion "the Milesians invoked an order of King Darius" (III.63), which obviously gives us every reason to think it predated the Ionian Revolt.

• *Darius, Tattenai, and Gadatas.* On the founding of Nemrud Dagh by Antiochus of Commagene and the status of the hierodules, cf. Dörrie 1964: 83–88 and Debord 1982: 85–87; [[and Sanders (ed.) 1996]] Artemis Barzochara: *BE* 1970, no. 538 and *BE* 1971, no. 669.

5. Western Asia Minor: Cities, Dynasts, and Empire after the Ionian Revolt

• *Border Wars and Arbitration.* See already Briant 1987a: 3–4; *RC* 7: cf. the illuminating comments of Curty 1986 on the value the judges ascribe to the writings of local historians; on Tod 113, see also Picirilli 1973: 155–59.

• *The Question of Tribute.* Let us remark at the beginning that here as elsewhere the word *Ionians* is problematic: it seems difficult to believe that the tribute reorganization was limited to Ionia; it is quite a bit more likely that the measure extended to the other coastal regions of Asia Minor. Herodotus VI.20 is frequently referred to, but primarily in the context of the continuity between Achaemenid and Delian tribute (Evans 1986; Wallinga 1989, with the remark by Kuhrt 1989a: 218), less frequently in the framework of an independent investigation of Achaemenid tribute organization (see, however, Thompson 1981); on this, see the important contribution by Murray 1966 and the remarks by Descat 1989a: 81 and 1989b: 29 (monetization of tribute, in relation to the introduction of the daric; according to Descat, a reduction in tribute when compared with prior payment methods in weighed metal. Herodotus does make a statement about the slight difference between the earlier tribute and the tribute established by Artaphernes; but I am not sure I fully understand what Descat means by "monetization of tribute"); cf. also the suggestions about quantity made by Descat 1985: 99–103 and the remarks by Tuplin (1987b: 148), who thinks that Artaphernes' measure does not imply that the satrapal administration later interfered in the internal affairs of the cities. It was the responsibility of each city to determine the means of raising the tribute according to their own rules (cf. also pp. 145–46); the author might be right about this point, as long as it is always kept in mind that, according to the Greek epigraphic formula so often encountered in Asia Minor (including in the Achaemenid period), a city was not 'master' (*kyrios*) of "royal tribute [taxation]"; it could not grant an exemption on this part of its obligation (cf., e.g., *BE* 1971 no. 622, 1973 no. 408; Corsaro 1985; Savalli 1987); in other words, the city's autonomy in the matter is reduced to setting the rules governing the raising of an *obligatory* tax whose amount is *fixed* by the imperial authority!

• *Democracies and Tyrannies.* Besides Briant 1987a: 4, cf. Graf 1985 and critical remarks by Austin 1990: 306; cf. also Frei 1990: 162–64.

• *Autonomy and Military Control.* On Phocaea and other naval bases, cf. Wallinga 1984: 408, 1987: 68, 1991; on the presence of Persian garrisons in other cities, cf. Diodorus XI.60.4 (in the 460s).

• *Persian Power and Dynastic Powers in Asia Minor.* Cilicia: Erzen's study (1940) remains important; Desideri and Jasink's book (1990) provides nothing new on the status of the *syennésis* (pp. 178–202), a point to which I will return (chaps. 14/8 and 16/6); on the other hand, Desideri takes an interest in situating the Achaemenid period in the *longue durée* (on the Assyro-Babylonian period, see also Bing 1969, 1971, as well as Hawkins and Postgate 1988); for an overview taking into account epigraphic, archaeological, and numismatic data, cf. Lemaire and Lozachmeur 1990; Persian arsenals in Cilicia: Wallinga 1991; Cilician tribute: Asheri 1991; Cilician horses imported to Egypt: cf. Milik 1960 (but the readings are disputed by Porten 1985b); Meydançikkale: see Laroche and Davesne 1981 and Davesne, Lemaire, and Lozachmeur 1987. I am not taking into consideration here the identification of Cilicia on the gift-bearer frieze at Persepolis, since there is no certain textual basis; on the other hand, following many authors, Asheri (1991: 41–42) thinks that behind the *Yaunā drayahā* and the *Yaunā tyaiy drayahā* of the royal inscriptions an indirect allusion to Cilicia may be found, the Cilicians being included there with Cyprus "and the other inhabitants of the sea"; cf. also Wallinga 1991: 278–79, who thinks that the phrase represents an actual administrative and strategic unit including Cyprus–Cilicia–Phoenicia; he rejects the nonetheless convincing interpretation of Schmitt (1972), for whom "those from the sea" designates the peoples of the satrapy of Dascylium (Hellespontine Phrygia). But this discussion accords perhaps too much administrative value to the vocabulary of the royal inscriptions (cf. chap. 5 above); the Achaemenids seem to have adapted the Assyro-Babylonian vocabulary, which frequently uses the phrase "kings of the coast" to refer not only to the Phoenician kings but also to all the princes of southern Anatolia, Syria, and Palestine; as for the Cypriot princes, Esarhaddon (Prism) calls them "those who are beyond the sea."

• *The Persians in Asia Minor.* On the military levies, in addition to the Herodotus passage (V.102) and the example of Asidates (cf. Tuplin 1987c: 213), see Xenophon, *Hell.* I.2.6; III.2.15; also probably Diodorus XI.34.3; I note in passing that a late Greek inscription (*BE* 1983 no. 359) mentions a place called Tetrapyrgia in the plain of Castolus (Castolou Pedion in Meonia), which Xenophon (*Anab.* I.1.2; I.9.7) names as one of the assembly locations (*syllogos*) for territorial troops in western Asia Minor. Pharnakides near Dascylium: Sekunda 1988a: 178; Celaenae: Sekunda 1991: 120–21; for place-names incorporating Cyrus and Darius, see the reasonable interpretations of Sekunda 1985: 20–23. Many sources are assembled in the works of N. Sekunda (1985, 1988a, 1991), but for the most part the documents date to the fourth century and thus will be taken up later; cf. also Briant 1985a (Greco-Roman sources); Baslez (1985) stressed the dangers in the use of Iranian onomastics from Asia Minor (cf. also Sekunda 1991: 87–88), but I must say that I do not follow her all the way to the end of her argument; the method used by L. Robert (cf. RTP 458ff.) continues to appear valid to me (to reconstruct Iranian settlement on the basis of late documentation: Iranian personal names and sanctuaries dedicated to Persian Artemis/Anaitis). Mixed marriages in Caria: Hornblower 1982: 26 and Sekunda 1991: 96. Dascylium stela: first published by Macridy 1913: 348–52, who also published two other stelas—a procession of women on horseback and a banquet; and a hunting scene; Macridy dates them to the end of the fifth century (on the very difficult chronological problems, cf. also Dentzer 1969: 200ff.); gold plaque from the Oxus treasury: Dalton 19–20 and pl. XIV; Sultaniye Köy stela: Altheim et al. 1983 (Nollé 1992: 19–22); Elnap stela: Lipiński 1975: 150–53 and Nollé 1992: 15–16 (but the problem of the date must remain open).

• *Satrapal Art and Local Artists.* On the entire question of "Greco-Persian" art and its relation to court and satrapal art, see Root's stimulating thoughts (1991); she begins with a well-known though generally badly treated problem, that of the Persian presence in the Empire, considered in relation to its archaeological and iconographic vestiges (cf. Briant 1984b: 57–68, 1987a: 6–11; Sancisi-Weerdenburg 1990a; Root 1991; chap. 16/18 below). The crucial importance of the "intermediate zone" in the cultural exchanges between Iranism and Hellenism has been particularly emphasized and brilliantly illustrated by Asheri 1983a, 1983b: 15–82; on Ephesus and its "barbarization" (Iranization) at the end of the fifth century, cf. Plutarch's evocative text *Lysander* 3.3 and my remarks on this text in Briant 1985a: 181–82 and 1987a: 16, as well as chap. 16/3 below; at an earlier date, Herodotus's statement (VIII.105) describes the place of the town in trade between Greeks and Persians; we also know that the highest official (*neocore*) of the Artemision bore a name-title borrowed from Persian: Megabyzus, i.e., Bagabuxša (Benveniste 1966: 108–13); on the Iranization of Ephesus, see Papatheophanes 1985, who, following Picard 1922 and Boyce 1966, poses hypotheses that seem rather adventurous to me. The Greco-Persian stelas have been published in many scattered places, which I cannot exhaustively list here [cf. Nollé 1992]: cf. Metzger 1971; Starr 1977; Sekunda 1988a, 1991; von Gall 1981–83 [1990]; likewise for the seals: cf. Boardman 1970b; on the hunting scenes and their relationship to lost monuments at Persepolis, as suggested by Cremer (1984: 91–99), cf. my reservations expressed in chap. 6/1 above; Aršāma and Hinzanāy (*DAE* 70 [= AD 9]): cf. Briant 1988a: 168; also Fleischer 1983 and Roaf 1979:

72. Workshops in Asia Minor: Melikian-Chirvani 1993; royal workshops in Egypt: chap. 10/6 above; wood and ivory objects: Bernard 1976 and Stucky 1985; goldsmithery (cf. also Pfromann 1990 and McKeon 1973): Amandry 1958a: 16 n. 54, 1958b: 44–46, who notes: "It is true that in the Achaemenid period a certain unity was established, in motifs and style, throughout the entire Empire" (p. 16); objects from Manisa and Sardis: Akurgal 1961: 170–71 (photographs); cf. also the very interesting, still unpublished stela in the museum of Manisa in Greenwalt and Heywood 1992: 16 (photo); still with respect to the workshops, which in my opinion were located throughout the Empire, we may note an interesting passage in Athenaeus (XI.486c), who in the course of an inventory from the time of Alexander refers to typically Persian vases made in Lycia (*lykiourgeis*; but the text is uncertain). [[I now see the same interpretation in Tsetskhladze 1994:99, who thinks that the inventory might come from a letter written by Nearchus when he was satrap of Lycia.]] Dascylium bullas with scenes of paradises: Kaptan and Bayburtluoìglu 1990; scenes of the Royal Hero: Akurgal 1961: 174, fig. 122; and Mellink 1988: 220 (drawings [here fig. 56b, p. 700]); audience scene: Miller 1988: 85–86, who rightly notes, "Pictorial elements of Achaemenid imperial iconography were reproduced on a smaller scale"; an excellent drawing appears in Musche 1989: 147 [here fig. 15, p. 210]; scene on the shield: von Graeve 1987 [here fig. 14, p. 209]; audience scene on Persepolis seal impressions: PTS no. 26.

 • *Royal Persian Art and Lycian Dynastic Art.* See in general Asheri 1983b, esp. pp. 64ff.; and Jacobs 1987. I note that the Xanthian documents pose other problems of a more specifically political sort, and these will be taken up in subsequent chapters. Building G: description in Demargne and Coupel 1963: 49–61 (ca. 460); on the Achaemenid influences, see esp. Bernard 1965 (quotation, p. 285; cf. p. 287; on this particular point, see Rodenwalt 1933: 1031); Monument of the Harpies: Demargne 1958. 37–47; on the Iranian influences, the basic work remains Tritsch 1942, whose interpretation is repeated (and amplified) by Shahbazi 1975: 15–50 (who refers to the monument as Monument of the Harpagide, on the basis of the identification that he suggests); tomb of Karaburun: cf. Mellink 1979, 1988: 222 (475 B.C.); see color photos provided by the author in Briant 1992d: 66–67; also the detailed analysis in Dentzer 1982: 227–30; Persian iconography on the coinage of Kprlli: Mørkholm and Zahle 1972: 90–98; Zahle 1991: 150; and now Keen 1992a, chap. 5.1, who locates Kprlli around 480–440. We may add that Iranian names are common in Lycia (cf. Bernard 1964: 210–11; Briant 1984b: 94–96; Sekunda 1991: 97–105; [[now add REG 107 (1994): 325–26]]); however, there is much disagreement on this point: according to Schmitt 1982, they do not seem to have spread widely beyond the imperial diaspora properly so called; and, contrary to P. Bernard, Bryce (1986: 162–63) thinks that the settlement of many Persian families after Harpagus's conquest cannot be assumed (cf. also Zahle 1991: 152); if with Keen (1992b: 58 and n. 24) we agree that Harpagus the Mede is not the founder of the dynasty, then the discussion self-evidently takes an entirely different direction: "The evidence for Iranian settlement in Lycia is minimal" (Keen 1992a chap. 2.2: "The Repopulation of Xanthos").

6. Population Resettlement and Deportation

 • *Deportation of Greeks and Other Peoples.* There is no general treatment; Ambaglio 1975 remains partial; on the other hand, there is much to be found in Asheri 1983b: 33ff.; on Persian policy (settlements in the *eskhatiai* of the Empire), which was also applied to rebellious Persian nobility, cf. Briant 1984b: 64, 97; deportation of the Branchidae to Bactria, cf. Bernard 1985a: 123–25; on the deported Eretrians, the abundance of Greek documentation has stimulated some specialized studies: cf. Grosso 1958, Penella 1974; the deported Greeks in Lower Babylonia are compared with the Ionians and Carians listed in the Foundation Charter of the palace at Susa by Mazzarino (1966: 76–77); language problem: Briant 1984b: 95; the tale of the deportation of the Paeonians in Herodotus provokes numerous questions: cf. Foucault 1967b.

 • *The Status of Displaced Communities.* Greeks in Persepolis in 330: cf. *RTP* 329 n. 161, 343–44, and chap. 16/12 below; Yaunas in the tablets: Delaunay 1976: 24, Lewis 1977: 12–13 (who reviews the existence of other texts attesting to Greek presence on the construction sites: cf. Roaf 1979: 70); on the graffiti, cf. Nylander and Flemberg 1981–83. Ethnic diversity among the *ḫaṭrus*: Stolper 1985a: 72–79; on the Saka: Dandamaev 1979, 1992a: 159–62 (and the whole book on the subject mentioned here); the ethnic diversity of Achaemenid Babylonia is well attested, especially by the onomastics, but it is not due only to massive deportations (see Zadok's articles, *BASOR* 230 [1978]: 57–63, *Tel-Aviv* 6/3–4 [1979]: 164–81, *Assur* 4/3 [1984]: 3–28); on Arab penetration into Mesopotamia, cf. Eph'al, *JAOS* 94 (1974): 108–15 (eighth century) and Fales 1989; on the status of foreign communities in Babylonia, cf. esp. Eph'al 1978; also Heltzer 1981 (Jews in Babylonia) and Dandamaev 1992a: 176–77 (who sees it as the precedent for the Hellenistic *politeumata*); Babylonians in Persia: Stolper 1984a: 309–10 (cf. also chap. 11/3: "Family Breakup and Ethnic Uniformity," p. 437).

• *The Garrisons of Egypt.* See esp. Kraeling 1953: 49ff.; Porten 1968: 28ff.; Grelot 1971b, 1972; each of these authors discusses at length the phenomenon of intercultural encounters; on Jewish ritual practices at Elephantine, cf. also Vincent 1937 and Milik 1967; on the Caspians, Grelot 1971: 101–17; Memphis garrison: Segal 1983: 7–9; Memphis workshops: Aimé-Giron 1931, 1939; Asia Minor: Assyrians and Hyrcanians: Xenophon, *Anab.* VII.8.15; Bactrians: Briant 1984b: 92–94; Deve Hüyük: Moorey 1975, 1980 (but see the critical remarks of Mazzoni 1991–92: 65–66). Tuplin 1987c: 218–22 focuses on the ethnic origins of the garrisons in various regions of the Empire.

7. Unity and Diversity

• *Imperial Administration and Multilingualism.* There is no point in providing an exhaustive bibliography on the spread of Aramaic throughout the Empire: see Fitzmyer and Kaufman 1991 (on Palestine, cf. the exhaustive list in Lemaire 1989b); I consider this claim by Petit (1990: 152) a complete fantasy: "The use of Aramaic as administrative language is doubtless to be included among the reforms of Darius" (referring, curiously, to Tiratsian 1981: 160); it skips over the developments of the Assyro-Babylonian period; Aramaic on the Iranian Plateau: see esp. Benveniste 1958b: 43–44, Briant 1984b: 59–61, Rapin 1992a 111–12; inscribed wrist of a Babylonian slave: Greenfield 1991: 183, contesting the reading of Dandamaev 1984b: 230–31; correspondence of Pharandates: Hughes 1984: 77–84. Linguistic exchanges: I do not see the basis for Dandamaev's statement (1989b: 296) that "Cyrus the Younger . . . spoke fluent Greek"; Plutarch, *Per.* 24, which he cites, says nothing of the sort, while Xenophon (*Anab.* I.8.12) implies just the opposite (cf. Cousin 1904: 123); Iranian languages: cf. (e.g.) Maricq, *JA* 1958: 395–99 and G. Fussman, *BEFEO* 1974: 3–38; see also Benveniste 1958b (Aramaic version of the Asoka inscription, filled with Achaemenid Iranian words) and Rossi 1981; on the concept of Ariane in Strabo, see chap. 5/3 above; on the Mardians and other Persian ethnic groups, cf. Briant 1976, esp. p. 233 n. 125; on the East Iranian dialects and Alexander's interpreter, see Briant 1984b: 61, 94–96 [but doubts in Bosworth 1995: 25]. It is likely that some *kurtaš* learned Persian, not only those who worked in the administrative offices (e.g., Yauna: Lewis 1977: 10–11) but also people involved in production (cf. Quintus Curtius V.4.4). Example of Tissaphernes: Lewis 1977: 101 n. 72. On the interpreters, Mosley 1971 offers nothing new, despite the attractive title of the article; cf. Asheri 1983b: 20–22, 68. Babylonian tablet Amherst 258: published by Ungnad, *AfO* 19 (1960): 79–81 (partial translation in Dandamaev 1989b: 112). The doubts stated in the text were suggested to me by M. Stolper (pers. comm.); see also some remarks in Tuplin 1987c: 179 and n. 29, and, on the Persians or Iranians who were close to Uštānu, the notes of Dandamaev 1992a nos. 8, 29, 42, 61, 100a, 272, 336a.

• *Royal Law and Local Law.* The thesis of the spread of a royal law or common precepts throughout the Empire was developed by Olmstead 1935, 1948: 119–34 (beginning primarily from the spread of the phrase *dātu ša šarri* in the Babylonian documents and a supposed connection with Hammurabi), whose positions were strongly contested by (e.g.) Dandamaev 1989b: 117; cf. also the careful remarks of Kuhrt 1988b: 132 and Petit 1990: 164; the interpretation developed here concurs with what Frei 1984 presented (the discussion is connected with relations between royal [satrapal] authorities and local sanctuaries; cf. Briant 1986a). On the judges (*dātabaru*) and *dātu ša šarri* in Babylonia, cf. Dandamaev 1989b: 116–18, 122–25; Joannès 1990a: 179; cf. also Stolper 1985a: 91, Tuplin 1987b: 118–20, and more recently Dandamaev 1992a: 42 and no. 341b; CAD (s.v.) translates 'royal edict (concerning a particular matter)', which corresponds much better to the concrete realities; but, to offer a truly justifiable conclusion, one would have to inventory every tablet with the word *dātu*; I will add that my reservations about translating *dātu* as 'law' are also inspired by the remarks of Bottéro 1987 on the "code" of Hammurabi (cf. esp. pp. 218–20 on the phrase *simdat šarrim* 'decisions of the king', which reminds us of the Babylonian-Achaemenid category *dātu ša šarri*). ⟦On the problems connected with the use of the calque *dātu* in the Babylonian tablets, see Stolper 1993: 60–62, 1994a: 338–41.⟧ Judges in the Saqqara papyri: Segal 1983:5; in the Elephantine papyri: cf. Wiesehöfer 1991 and Porten 1968: 47–50 (who makes an erroneous comparison with Persian royal judges, p. 49; cf. the justifiably critical remark of Petit 1990: 164 and n. 253). The word *dāta* in PF 1980: see the commentary by Giovinazzo 1993: 124 n. 28 (which I learned of at the last minute, well after this section was written); while taking over the translation 'according to the former law' from Grillot and Susini 1987: 71, the author also emphasizes the importance of the phrase in line 20: *meni inni huttik šutur*, which, contrary to Hallock and Grillot, she understands as 'then [the count] was not done [according to the] rules' — a phrase she compares with *datam appukaka*; this interpretation, it seems to me, tends to confirm my understanding of *dāta* in PF 1980. The word *datah* also appears in two Aramaic inscriptions from Asia Minor: one is too broken to offer commentary (cf. Davesne, Lemaire, and Lozachmeur 1987: 368–70; Lemaire 1991c: 206); the other occurs in the Aramaic version of the Xanthus Trilingual; it perfectly confirms the relationship that existed between the "law" of the satrap and the local laws; as Bousquet (1986: 105) correctly notes, the satrapal decree on the trilingual "is not exempt from financial preoccupation" (I independently developed the same interpretation in Briant 1986a: 435–37; cf. now also the remarks of Lemaire 1995c); while regretting that there is no exact equivalent in the Greek version, we note especially that in this text the Persian-Aramaic *dāta*/*dath* is rendered in Lycian by *mara*, which in another Lycian text (Bousquet 1986: 101) refers to a fiscal decree by the same Pixôdaros in Lycia (on the word *maraza* 'arbitrator/conciliator' in the Pilier inscription, see Melchert's 1993 suggestions). All of these comparisons confirm that the translation of *dāta* as 'law' is at best ambiguous; in every case, the translation 'regulation' is probably closer to the administrative reality. *Dath* in the biblical texts: the word also appears several times in Daniel 2:9, 13–15; 6:9, 13–16, with the same meaning it has in Esther; once again it refers to "the law of the Medes and Persians," which held for example that "no edict or decree can be altered when once issued by the king" [JB]; on the phrase *patrios nomos* in the context of Hellenistic Judaism, cf. Briant 1990a: 58–60 (following Bickerman's work). Last, I observe that some of Darius's acts are presented by Plato (*Laws* III.695c) as a 'law' (*nomos*): "He also included in his code regulations (*nomos*) about the tribute (*dasmos*) promised to the people by Cyrus" [Hackett]; but, contrary to what is frequently stated, it is not certain that Plato was really referring to the tribute form properly speaking; the context actually makes it clear that his acts are being discussed exclusively in the context of relations with the Persians and Persia (*ouk . . . dasmophoros*: Herodotus III.97), so that the *dasmos* (and not *phoros*!) that the author speaks of could just as well refer to the gifts given to the king by the Persians, which we know from Aelian (*VH* I.31) were strictly codified by a *nomos persikos* (on the word *nomos* and its polysemy, cf. in particular Modrzejewski 1966: 149–56). Two closing remarks concerning the "legislator/nomothete" king (Diodorus I.94–95): (1) According to Robert (1975: 314), in a Greek inscription from Sardis, the word Baradates is an *epiclēse* [additional name] of Zeus, the entirety being understood by him as "Ahura-Mazda Legislator"; but, aside from the fact that Gschnitzer (1986) has shown that it is a personal name, we would expect to find *databarès* (*dātabara*) in the Greek instead; (2) Grillot (1990) recognized the word *te-nu-[um-ta-ut-ti-ra]* in DSf (Elamite) and translated it 'sole legislator among many', although Hinz (1950: 3) and Vallat (1972: 9) translate 'sole lord among many' (on this word, cf. also Gershevitch 1983 analyzed by Grillot, *AbIran* 7 [1984] no. 159).

Chapter 13

Xerxes the Great King (486–465)

1. Sources and Problems

• *The Year 479 and Xerxes' Reputation.* I have learned much (relating to this entire chapter) from Sancisi-Weerdenburg 1980, 1987a, 1989a, 1991a–b, 1994; on the sources for the reign of Xerxes, cf. also Yamauchi 1990: 187–92; on the romance of Masistes, cf. Sancisi-Weerdenburg 1980: 48–83; I note in passing that the relations between Amestris and Xerxes, as seen by Herodotus, have a nearly exact duplicate in the story of the relations between Semiramis and the king of Assyria reported by Aelian (*VH* VII.1) after Dinon; on a specific point (gift of an army), Sancisi-Weerdenburg 1988b; on Ctesias and the Persian Wars, cf. Bigwood 1978a; Ctesias and Xerxes at Babylon: Briant 1992a.

• *Persian History and Hellenocentrism.* According to the *Suda,* Dionysius of Miletus wrote a work called *Ta met' Dareiou,* but the content of this lost work continues to be problematic (cf. Hignett 1963: 12–13; Moggi 1972); Thucydides and the Persians: cf. Andrewes 1961; also Schmitt 1983b.

• *The Idea of Decadence.* Sancisi-Weerdenburg 1987a; Briant 1989a; quotations in the text (on Xerxes' "intolerance"): Mayrhofer 1974 (cf. idem, 1973b: 282); see also Olmstead's surprising claim 1939: 318: "[After Salamis, Xerxes] completely lost his head"; on the relationship between the year 479 and the institution of the "haoma cult" at Persepolis according to Bowman 1970, see my critical discussion above, chap. 11/1 Notes. The theory of Persian decadence is still found in recent work: cf. Briant 1993e, 1994b (on the significance of Droysenian historiography among Iranists, cf. my remarks in *RTP* 318–23). *Daivā* inscription: see chap. 13/7 below.

2. From Darius to Xerxes

• *Chronology and nomos.* On the date of Xerxes' selection as crown prince by Darius: according to Calmeyer (1976b: 83), Xerxes was "king and co-regent" for twelve years beginning in 498; but, aside from the fact that I am skeptical of the author's general thesis of "double kingship" (the king never shares power), the archaeological evidence offered is hardly probative: the Babylonian tablet to which he refers (in Olmstead 1948: 215 n. 4), and which he considers "very seductive" evidence, speaks only of a new palace at Babylon (*BRM* 1, 81; Joannès 1990a: 186 and n. 59), and it has not been directly related to the naming of a "co-regent" at this date; we may note further in passing that it dates to 496 (*Dar.* 26), not 498. Another document that has been brought to bear on the question is inscription *XPk,* which is carved on the clothing of the royal figure on the east stair of the Median gate of the *tacara* of Darius: "Xerxes, son of King Darius, Achaemenid king," but it is especially difficult to draw chronological conclusions from the inscription (cf. the discussion of Roaf 1983: 138; cf. also Root 1979: 73–75); but the hypothesis offered (Darius at first chose Artobarzanes) comes from a misinterpretation of the phrase "leave the throne"; for the same reasons, the suggestion (Porada 1979: 81 n. 51) to identify Artobarzanes on a Persepolis seal (*PTS* 26) becomes void. On possible satrapal duties that Artobarzanes would have assumed, cf. Koch 1993a: 40, who also suggests on the basis of an unpublished tablet (Q 931) that the person would have borne the title **visa-puthra.* This remains a real problem, for which Herodotus offers no solution.

• *Darius, Xerxes, and Atossa.* See especially Sancisi-Weerdenburg 1983: 25–27 (faithfully followed here; her intrepretations have been challenged by Carney [1993, esp. n. 20], but in the course of a comparison that raises several criticisms, to the extent that it is not free of circular reasoning). On the title "queen" falsely attributed by Classical authors, see chap. 7/4: "Wives and Concubines," Research Notes, p. 920.

- *The Crown Prince.* On the king's birthday banquet (*tykta* in Herodotus IX.110), cf. Sancisi-Weerdenburg 1989b: 132–33, who suggests that it might have served as the setting for an annual renewal of royal power (the king's birthday party is also attested in the Seleucid period: Bickerman 1938: 246; Gauthier 1989: 67–68); on the *kidaris*, cf., e.g., Quintus Curtius III.3.19 and Atkinson's commentary 1980: 128–29 (we may note in passing the phrase used by Antiochus of Commagene: *prōtos analabōn tēn kidarin*: Wagner 1983: 199, 201); on the title for the person we know as the crown prince (terminology not found in ancient documents; cf. Briant 1994d: 466 n. 22), cf. the thoughts of Benveniste 1966: 22–26, 51–65; as M. Stolper notes (pers. comm.), the title is reconstructed from the Akkadian form *umasupitrū* and the Elamite *misapušaš*, "translated" into Akkadian as *mār biti* 'Son of the House' and into Aramaic as *br byt'* 'Prince of the House', titles that do not necessarily imply actual kinship (Benveniste 1966: 22–26); on the title **viθ(a) puça* in Demotic, cf. recently Vittmann 1991–92; on "second after the king," cf. also Briant 1993b: 292–93.

- *A Principle of Primogeniture?* On the text by Agathocles of Cyzicus, cf. some remarks in Briant 1994f: 47–51. I now wonder whether the term "oldest son" is as unambiguous as it appears. I was originally led to raise the question while reading Goedicke's remarks (1985: 42 n. 46) on the Egyptian phrase "oldest son," which is found applied to the son of a Great King in the famous *Stela of the Satrap*: "This designation expresses importance rather than physical age" (no comment on this point in Clère 1951); see also Bonhême-Fargeau 1988: 264: "The phrase 'oldest son of the king' does not designate the firstborn of the sovereign but all the royal principles [princes? P.B.] in the Old Kingdom and only some of the king's sons in the New Kingdom, including the future pharaoh, chosen from among the sons from time to time. Because of very high infant mortality, it was the oldest surviving son who sometimes inherited the kingdom; this was the case for the future Ramses II. Furthermore, the title 'oldest son of the king' did not really have a precise meaning, as seen for Amenophis II: the future king is called 'oldest son of the king' and 'royal son' in the same text. Cross-checking information and the attribution of the title should allow us to disentangle the uses of this appellative, taking into account diachrony, and to know whether some sense of primogeniture must be applied to it, in addition to its role of classifying the royal sons." Then, on another occasion, these thoughts recurred upon rereading a well-known document that curiously had never been brought to bear on the problem under consideration here. In fact, in a bilingual inscription from Kandahār (whose Aramaic version is crammed with Persian-Achaemenid words), the Greek *presbyteros* renders the Persian *maθišta* (cf. Benveniste 1958b: 42–43; I do not know why Benveniste does not make any comparison at all with the Xerxes inscription, either here or in 1966: 64–66); the "translation" can be interpreted two ways: either we take it as confirmation of the place of the oldest son in the succession, or else the word that (following the Greek authors) we render 'oldest son' was a title rather than a biological-familial designation; under this hypothesis, the crown prince would automatically be called the oldest son using the term (with two meanings) *maθišta*. I leave it to those more expert than I am to judge the validity of this suggestion; I will simply observe that in the PF (e.g., 1063–64), the word *matištukkašpe*, built on *maθišta*, clearly refers not to the age but to the status ('head'; Elamite *iršara*) of the *kurtaš* so labeled (PFT 34–35).

- *Funeral Ceremonies.* Briant 1991a: 4–6; we have no original documents to prove that the king's corpse was embalmed (Goukowsky's translation [1976, ad loc] of Diodorus XVII.71.7 as 'embalmed body' is unjustified [*ta nekra*]); but the texts from Alexander's time strongly suggest it, as does comparison with the custom carefully described by Firdawsi in the *Shahnameh* (the Firdawsi passage is analyzed by Shahbazi 1975: 154–57).

- *Royal Investiture.* On the "magical" importance of the royal robe, cf. Sancisi-Weerdenburg 1983a: 29; among the Persian nobility: Plutarch, *Mor.* 173c, 545a; Ammianus Marcellinus XXX.8.4; cf. also the incidental remark of Kuhrt and Sherwin-White 1987: 74–75 on a royal Assyrian custom.

- *The Successor of Darius.* Xerxes and Ariaramnes: cf. the analyses by Sancisi-Weerdenburg 1980: 67–74; also Briant 1984b: 75–77, 1991a: 8–9 and n. 6. We may note that in connection with the accession of Xerxes, Plutarch uses the word *anagoreusai*, that is, 'acclaim' and not 'recognize [as king]' (compare Briant 1973: 309–10; henceforth, I challenge views expressed previously [Briant 1984a: 112–13] on the role of a *Landtag* such as had been put forth on several occasions by Widengren; cf. Briant 1994e: 286–91): perhaps the word *anagoreusai* refers to a ceremony of acclamation that then took place at Pasargadae: cf. Sancisi-Weerdenburg 1983b and my additional remark in Briant 1991a: 8–9 n. 6; on the potential dangers between the death of the king and the enthronement of his successor, cf. Briant 1991a: 4–6 (in order to interpret the delay between the death of Darius and the first mentions of Xerxes in Babylonia, Zawadski 1992 suggests that the scribes awaited the official proclamation, namely, news of the enthronement ceremony); inscriptions on the Darius Gate: Vallat 1974.

• *Crushing Rebellions.* The causes and extent of the Egyptian revolt are very badly documented: cf. remarks in Briant 1988a: 140–43 (it is possible that the interment of the mother of an Apis must be dated to Xerxes' first year, but the reading of the figure is uncertain: Smith 1992a: 205–6); the dating suggested here for Bēl-šimāni's rebellion is a hypothesis I worked out in Briant 1992a. The theory of a Judean revolt (put down by Xerxes on his way back from Egypt) goes back to Morgenstern 1956–57, 1960; but this thesis is based on biblical texts that do not demand this interpretation (cf. Oded 1977d: 525–26; Hoglund 1989: 90–109); Morgenstern's theory has recently been followed by Balcer (1989a: 133) in the context of discussion of the generally insurrectional state in the Empire, which might partially explain the defeats of 480–479; but Balcer's arguments are scarcely cogent.

• *Returning to the Greek Affair.* On the debates at Xerxes' court, cf. the remarks by Legrand, vol. VII: 15–23 and Hignett 1963: 90–91; on Xerxes' dream and the Babylonian practice of substitute king, cf. Bottéro 1978: 3–4, Germain 1956, and Parpola 1983: xxix–xxxii (cf. Briant 1991a: 4); according to Wallinga (1987: 73 n. 77), Xerxes' prime objective was to annihilate Greek naval power; on the phrase "earth and water" and the persistent uncertainties, see Orlin 1976, Kuhrt 1988a. With many others, I doubt the existence of a Persian-Carthaginian alliance confronting a Greco-Syracusan alliance: cf. Asheri 1988: 766–74 (on the traditions of the Himera–Salamis parallel, cf. Gauthier 1966).

• *"The Unconquerable Swell of the Seas".* The discussions are too many and too varied to all be mentioned here: one may profit from the (obviously contradictory) foci of Hignett 1963: 345–55, Burn 1984: 325–33, Cuyler Young 1980, Cook 1983: 113–17, Hammond 1988c: 532–35, and Yamauchi 1990: 194–200. Everyone (at least since Beloch, quoted by Hignett 1963: 354–55) agrees on the decisive importance of the number of soldiers commanded by Mardonius at Plataea (cf. Hammond 1988b: 534: "our only yardstick"); I note that Wallinga (1987: 72) accepts the figure of 1,200 triremes in Xerxes' navy; on these problems, see most recently the discussions by Lazenby 1993 and Barkworth 1992 (both received late); on the tablet *Dar.* 253: Joannès 1982: 18.

• *Logistical Preparations.* On the Athos Canal, cf. Isserlin 1991; Isserlin et al. 1994; and the remarks of Nicolet-Pierre 1992.

3. From Sardis to Sardis (480)

• A preliminary remark: in the following pages, we have not attempted to enter into all the military-historical debates (cf. the overall analysis in §5 below) or to analyze the problems that directly concern the Greek viewpoint (for example the famous decree of Trezene); my aim is first of all to center the discussion on the viewpoint of the history of Xerxes and the Achaemenid Empire. On the chronology of operations, cf. table in Hammond 1988b: 591, and thorough discussion in Hignett 1963: 448–57; on Greek Medism in 480–479, cf. Gillis 1979: 59–81 and especially Graf 1979: 141ff.

• *From Salamis to Sardis.* Hignett 1963: 240–47 refutes (successfully) the old thesis that the Phoenicians regained their cities after the battle; Burn 1984: 470–71 (compare Xerxes' decision to the decision of Darius, who upon returning from the Danube left Megabazus in Thrace while he himself resided at Sardis); Hammond 1988b: 581–88 (if Xerxes changed his plans, this was in part because of the cool weather that was about to set in; in Hammond's way of thinking, Xerxes would undoubtedly have already decided to return to Europe—as proved by the fact that all of the royal equipment was left with Mardonius: Herodotus IX.82).

4. Xerxes between Two Fronts (480–479)

- *Xerxes in Sardis and Mardonius in Europe.* Cf. especially Hignett 1963: 240–344.
- *Xerxes from Sardis to Babylon.* Cf. Briant 1992a (where more detailed references will be found; see most recently the clear historiographic focus of Rollinger 1993: 52–56, 218–26, unaware of my article); on the factuality of the settlement of the Branchidae in Bactria, cf. Bernard 1985a: 123–25.

5. The Persian Defeat: Its Causes and Consequences

- *Some Questions.* On the difficulties of reconstructing the battle of Plataea (even though it is the best documented), consult especially the long analysis by Hignett 1963: 289–344; cf. also Barron 1988: 599–611; see especially on this point the caustic observations of Whatley (1939); most recently, the sensible and balanced pages of Lazenby 1993: 248–61.
- *Arms and Tactics.* The analysis that follows derives a number of suggestions from Rahe 1980: 79–87 (where additional bibliographic references will be found; but I hardly believe "that there were few imperial divisions of well-trained and disciplined archers," p. 79) and Evans 1987; on what credibility can be granted to Herodotus, cf. Jackson 1894; Sakian military practice: Briant 1982b: 199–202; Babylonian horseman: cf. Joannès 1982. 16–17 (who compares Herodotus VII.67); on the vulnerability of the Persian cavalry in precipitous retreats, see also Quintus Curtius III.11.15 and Arrian II.11.3. Although he does believe that the cavalry was indeed created by Cyrus (disagreeing with Tarn on this point), Bernard (1964: 207–8) nonetheless thinks that the Persian horsemen at Plataea do not seem to have worn these heavy breastplates but that the cavalry on this occasion seem to have been "light horse" (elsewhere, he stresses that cataphractaries did not appear until late in Central Asia: *BEFEO* 68 [1980]: 60–63); but Herodotus VII.84, which he quotes, does not seem probative to me ("The Persian cavalry were equipped like the infantry . . ."): the example of Masistios ensures at least the use of breastplates by the Persian cavalry at Plataea; the same author (Bernard 1964) has given an excellent description and definition (repeated here nearly word for word) of the jambeaus worn by the Persian horses and riders.
- *The Persians and the Others.* On the role of the epibates, I repeat a suggestion by Wallinga (1989: 175); on the Saka in Babylonia and their armament, cf. Dandamaev 1979, 1992a: 159–62; on the basic role of the Iranian contingents, cf. already Briant 1988b.
- *Artabazus and Mardonius.* The adoption of Greek arms by the Persians is not attested before Cyrus the Younger (Diodorus XIV.22.6); Darius III also introduced them at the beginning of his reign (Quintus Curtius III.3.6): see below, chap. 17/3, end. On the "Persian custom" invoked (according to Herodotus) by Mardonius, see also chap. 18/1, "Darius, His Satraps, and Alexander's Landing (May–June 334)," pp. 818ff.
- *The Consequences of the Defeats: Persian Losses.* The thesis of lasting military weakness is embraced for example by Cook 1983: 125, who estimates the loss as 25,000 men; he wisely comments: "The numbers might be made good in a generation," but he soon adds (without any proof): "But the former military ascendancy could be never regained"; on the persistent vigor of the Persian population, cf. in particular Diodorus XIX.21.3 (see Briant 1987a: 21–22; 1994b: 128).
- *The Consequences of the Defeats: Territorial Setbacks.* We will return below (§7) to the affairs of Asia Minor; Argive alliance: cf. Burn 1984: 349–50; Badian 1987: 2. Wallinga (1987: 72–74) thinks that after Xerxes' vain efforts to fight the Athenian navy in 480–479, the organization of the royal navy established by Cambyses was abandoned; but, to my way of thinking, analysis of the policy followed by Xerxes and then by Artaxerxes I at the beginning of his reign does not appear to

fully confirm "this drastic weakening of Persian sea-power"; or, in any case, it seems hazardous to attribute responsibility for it to Xerxes or to date the alteration precisely to 479; if there were changes in 479, they were primarily because Athens from then on had sufficient funds to combat the royal fleets: Persian weakness is thus above all relative. On the concept of periphery in Persian strategic thinking, cf. my reflections in Briant 1993f: 412.

• *The Consequences of the Defeats: The Great King's Prestige.* Regarding the List of Countries in *XPf*, it must be kept in mind that none of these documents is archival in nature, and they were not meant to give a faithful picture of the peoples who were actually subject at the time of preparation of the inscription: cf. chap. 5 and, on the Xerxes inscription, the reflections in this direction by Sancisi-Weerdenburg forthcoming (1) (where the problem of the date of the inscription is treated in detail); Achaemenid version: cf. Briant 1993c: 411–12; Greek booty from the Persians, most recently Miller 1985: 105ff.; on the chariot episode: Tripodi 1986; Darius III after Issus and Gaugamela: *RTP*: 373–75; booty brought back by Xerxes: Perdrizet 1921 (cf. Briant 1988a: 153 and n. 28); statue of the Mother of gods at Sardis: Perdrizet 1921: 71–74.

6. Xerxes and His Peoples

• *Xerxes and Babylonia: The Babylonian Materials.* The proof is borrowed in toto from A. Kuhrt (cf. Kuhrt and Sherwin-White 1987; Kuhrt 1988b: 134–35) and Stolper 1989b (on the problem of Babylonia–Trans-Euphrates; cf. also Kuhrt 1988b: 135 n. 174); on the Kish materials and the methodological remarks suggested by them, see McEwan 1983; among other possible cases, we may also cite Agade: until the recent publication of a Hellenistic tablet (Beaulieu 1989b), it was believed that Agade disappeared at the end of Darius's reign (cf. Durand and Joannès 1988); on the increase in tablets dated to Xerxes, cf. Graziani 1986; Kuhrt 1988b: 133; Stolper 1991 and 1992d; on a statistical attempt to classify the tablets under Cyrus and Cambyses, cf. Cagni, Giovinazzo, and Graziani 1985 (but the political inferences drawn on p. 582 leave me skeptical); the theory of the sudden loss of a private archive at Borsippa as an aftereffect of Xerxes' measures is offered by Joannès 1989b: 118–26 (followed by Van Driel 1992); cf. idem 1990a: 175–76, in drawing from it very sure conclusions on Xerxes' measures in Babylonia (cf. chap. 13/7: "Xerxes and Persia," pp. 553ff.). Today we can no longer accept an argument like Olmstead's (1948: 237): "So thoroughly was Babylonia ravaged that hardly a half-dozen tablets have survived from the remainder of his [Xerxes'] reign." 〚On these problems see also now McGinnis 1994, and the end of the following section.〛

• *Xerxes and Babylonia: The Greek Materials.* According to Ctesias (who places the event before the Greek expedition (wrongly in my opinion: cf. Arrian VII.17.2; Briant 1992a)), Xerxes was then at Ecbatana, in the Great Kings' summer residence. Diodorus (who was not aware of the Babylonian revolt) for his part writes that, after leaving Sardis, Xerxes reached Ecbatana (XI.36.7). This was probably the occasion on which he deposited certain ritual objects there that had been taken from the Greeks. Thus it is not certain that the Great King himself went to Babylon; but, given the fragmentary nature of the documentation, this is not impossible. It would even be surprising if, once the revolt was quashed, the king did not make a ceremonial entry into the town. Ctesias also gives indications on the relations between the Great King and the Babylonians, at a period he continues to place before the 480 expedition: "He reached Babylon and expressed a desire to see the tomb of Belitanas. Mardonius showed it to him, but Xerxes was unable to fill the sarcophagus with oil as prescribed by the inscription" (§21); there follows the mention of the revolt of Babylon put down by Megabyzus (§22). The tale is found in Aelian (*VH* XIII.3), who sees it as a warning of the unfortunate destiny of the European expedition. It is difficult to draw firm conclusions from the stories Ctesias certainly heard in the Babylon of his time; he may have turned into unfavorable signs what was nothing but the carrying out of a ritual regularly carried out by the king of Babylon in the sanctuary of Marduk (cf. McGinnis 1987b); the mention of the presence of Mardonius, who was considered to be the man truly responsible for the upset at Plataea (so considered by the Persians as well, says Herodotus VIII.99), makes us think the story was reworked after the defeats of 479: at this point I note an observation presented by Perdrizet (1921: 58 n. 4), in the Greek context: "In sum, in the time of Pausanias, more than ten centuries after the Persian Wars, the tradition lays at the feet of Xerxes and Mardonius much destruction that they had nothing to do with"; of course, Ctesias was writing only a century after the events, but across such a timespan the Babylonian stories had certainly been considerably embroidered: we may remark, for example, that the motif of a king violating sepulchres is very widespread (cf. I.187: Darius violating the tomb of Nitocris; on this, see Marquardt 1892: 574–75 and the interesting comparisons in Krappe 1928, and now Dillery 1992). This is why I also remain very skeptical about the illustration of the anti-Babylonian policy of Xerxes that has sometimes been sought in the book of Esther (Littman 1975). On the interpretation developed here, see basically Kuhrt and Sherwin-White 1987b and Kuhrt 1990b; among other sources, Diodorus (II.9.9) repeats the theory of Persian pillaging, but the construction of the sentence may imply that he is referring only to ritual implements; Plutarch (*Mor.* 173c) merely transmits a *topos* on the fate reserved for rebels (transformed into "women": Herodotus I.155–56; Justin I.7.11–13, Polyaenus VII.6.4: Cyrus and the Lydians). [[After this section was written, I was able to become acquainted with Dandamaev 1993d at the last minute; he thinks that Kuhrt and Sherwin-White's 1987 article "is not indisputable" (p. 43) and that, all in all, "the problem of Xerxes' policy in relation to Esagila remains, and only future discoveries of Babylonian texts may help to provide a solution." If in fact no interpretation ("working hypothesis" according to D.) can be considered proved once and for all, and if everyone agrees in hoping for the publication of new tablets (cf. also Briant 1992a: 15), we must also agree on the necessity of understanding and interpreting the documentation as it exists today, without constant recourse to the argument *a silentio* (contrary to what Dandamaev does, p. 43: "It is true that there is no contemporary Babylonian documentary evidence that corroborates Greek sources [on the destruction carried out by Xerxes], but it is also important to note that Babylonian documents do not refute the Greek accounts"); for one thing, the dating of the Babylonian revolts is considerably less certain than the author seems to say, p. 41; for another, one of the arguments developed by Kuhrt and Sherwin-White concerns the interpretation of Herodotus I.183; against their position, Dandamaev (p. 43) lets it be understood that Herodotus's statement could well refer to the removal, by Xerxes, of a statue of Marduk from the Esagila—but on grounds that are very weak methodologically: in fact, instead of referring to the text in the original Greek (cf. *agalma* vs. *andrias*) and discussing the actual textual argument of Kuhrt and Sherwin-White (pp. 71–72), Dandamaev quotes only a sentence from Ravn (which in itself proves nothing). I will add that here as elsewhere (cf. Briant 1993c), the author has scarcely tried to gather the recent articles actually bearing on the subject; no mention is found, for example, of Stolper 1989b (on the satrapy of Babylonia and Ebir Nāri), Kuhrt 1990b (on the texts bearing on Alexander's Babylon policy), or Briant 1992a (examination of the cuneiform and Greek texts bearing on the Babylonian revolts against Xerxes).—I will note, finally, that the hypothesis of the destruction of the Esagila in Xerxes' year 2 again serves as the basis for the suggestion for dating an unpublished tablet (BM 68777) in MacGinnis, *NABU* 1993 no. 93. But at the same time, it is quite remarkable to observe the evolution across a decade or so of the historical interpretations proposed by the Assyriologists: all or nearly all of them used to think that the loss of the archives had to be related to Xerxes' reprisals; it seems that since then this opinion is all but universally abandoned (see most recently Dandamaev 1995b, McGinnis 1995: 188); this visible shift simply strengthens me in my interpretation (presented in Briant 1992a), at the end of which, as Arrian very clearly says (VII.1.1), the Second Babylonian Revolt dates to 479; in fact it very much seems, *at least at the present moment,* that no Babylonian documentation (or: interruption thereof) is going to call into doubt this interpretation.]]

    • *Xerxes and Egypt.* I have already provided some information on this topic in Briant 1988a: 164–65; I find myself in basic agreement with the arguments presented briefly by Kuhrt and Sherwin-White 1987b: 77–78—except for their doubts concerning the Egyptian origin of the statue of Darius (which is now proved: cf. Trichet and Vallat 1990); but it is also true that we know nothing of the circumstances under which it was transported to Susa; there is nothing to prove that it was relocated by Xerxes in 486 (despite Vallat 1974a); the foundations of the Gate in fact go back to the reign of Darius (on this see Perrot and Ladiray 1974: 52–53); it is thus also entirely likely (1) that the order goes back to Darius and (2) that the statue (or statues) at Susa were simply replicas of statues that had been left in place in Heliopolis: under these conditions, the link (sometimes suggested) between the relocation of the statue and the Egyptian revolt is just a false argument; for identical methodological reasons, I remain highly skeptical of the absolute dating (486) suggested by Holladay (1982: 25–26) for the Persian abandonment of the site of Tell el-Maskhuta: it appears to me that the chronological hypothesis is based first of all on a preconceived view of Xerxes' Egyptian policy. The theory of the satrapization of Egypt can be discovered in nearly every article and book dealing with the question: it was formulated by Kienitz 1953: 66–69; among the most recent works, cf., e.g., Cook 1983: 99–100 and Dandamaev 1989a: 178–87 (cf. Briant 1993c: 413). The bronze carrying handle was published by Michaèlidis 1943: 95–96 (the source of the quotation in the text); on Darius at Karnak, cf. Traunecker 1973–77, who, notwithstanding, infers from the poverty of documentation the "proof" that the Achaemenid power displayed "reserve with respect to Thebes, the religious capital and possible seat of nationalist movements" (cf. also Traunecker and Le Saout 1981: 13–15): this, in my opinion, is a groundless suggestion (compare Cruz-Uribe 1988: 192–98, who thinks on the contrary that Darius favored the Theban cults, to the detriment of the Delta cults). Beyond the texts presented here, texts dated to Xerxes are rare in Egypt: on the hieroglyphic documents, cf. Posener 1936: 131–36 and, on this text (full of gaps and still a mystery), the remarks and suggestions of Smith and Kuhrt 1982; Aramaic documents: Gibson 1982 no. 23 (funerary inscription); *DAE* 85 (Saqqara stela dated to year 4 of "Xerxes, king of kings"), *DAE* 3 ([= *AP* 11] certainly 479) and *DAE* 54 [= *AP* 2], dated to year 2 of Xerxes; the publication of a new Aramaic document dated to Xerxes (*TADAE* C.3.7; Aharoni 1994; Lipiński 1994) once again reminds us of the weakness of any statistical conclusion; similarly, the recent publication of a stela from Memphis: the document deals with the interment of the mother of an Apis in year 1(?) of Xerxes (Smith 1992a: 205–6). [[We can obviously stress that no stela of the interment of an Apis is known between 487 and 398 (except, perhaps, one under Darius II in 412); but, as Devauchelle himself remarks (1995: 70), to whom I owe the information, "[this lack] is perhaps due only to the chance preservation of ancient monuments"; see on this the arguments laid out in Devauchelle 1994b: 104–6.]] We may add Herodotus IV.43, on the adventures of Sataspes, a text that seems to imply that, in imitation of Necho, Xerxes took an interest in circumnavigating Africa, but I must admit to my perplexity faced with a discussion built on a series of motifs (cf. Desanges 1978: 29–33 and, most recently, Colin 1990, on the geographical aspects). The inscriptions of Wadi Hammamât are published by Posener 1936; the distinction between two series of vessels (A and B) based on their titulature was suggested by Posener himself (1936: 140–41); but the argument concerning Artaxerxes (ibid., 146) no longer holds since the publication of the vessel of Orsk (by Salieva, apud Ray 1988: 233 = A*ˡOrsk*; cf. Mayrhofer 1978: 28–29). Whatever the case, it is quite extraordinary to see how this rich documentation has been used: Olmstead 1948 (a posthumous work to be sure, based essentially on Herodotus: p. 235 n. 17) from Posener's (obviously cursory) reading retains only the title "Xerxes, the Great King" (p. 237). He also refers (p. 236 and n. 18) to Gunn 1926, and he says that upon the death of an Apis the Egyptian priests "forgot" to place Xerxes' name in the cartouche on a sarcophagus, to work vengeance on a king who had refused to accept the pharaonic titulature; but there is nothing of the sort in Gunn's article (cf. 1926: 90). To return to Dandamaev, he seems to have grasped the difficulty but, concerned primarily to reiterate his theory (which he continues to proffer, nearly unaltered, with respect to Babylonia [1989a: 183–87]), evades it by means of a disarmingly candid expression (ibid., 182): "The stone, however, which was quarried there, was not used for buildings, but rather for sarcophagi"! I add in passing that I do not see what basis the same author (p. 95) has for stating that the rebellious Egyptians were aided by the Athenians; nor do I understand why he says (p. 182) that "the sources lend not support for [the] hypothesis . . . that Xerxes commanded the punitive expedition himself"; but what sources is he referring to? The *only* available source is Herodotus VII.7, which does not exhibit the slightest ambiguity on this point (*stratiēn poieetai*); finally, his conclusion that "after Darius I the Persian kings were basically uninterested in the internal affairs of Egypt" (p. 243) defies plain common sense. (Conversely, it is just as surprising to find Kraeling [1953: 30], referring to Olmstead, stating: "The reign of Xerxes [486–465] saw the zenith of Persian power.") On the *Stela of the Satrap*, cf. the discussion below, chap. 18/1, pp. 820ff., with the Research Notes.

• *Xerxes and the Greek Gods.* A late tradition claims that upon leaving Abdera (doubtless during his return from Salamis: cf. Herodotus VIII.120), Xerxes left the *magus* Ostanes and other *magi* there "as private tutors" (cf. Bidez-Cumont 1938, 1: 167–74); Xerxes and the Hellespont: the adventuresome interpretations of Reinach 1905 were rightly demolished by Perdrizet 1912; the Iranian interpretation (Sun = Mithra; Water = Apām Napāt) suggested by Briquel and Desnier (1983: 22–30) and recently repeated by Desnier (1995: 20–21) has not convinced me, any more than the (terribly systematic) interpretations of Boyce 1982: 166–67; sacrifice of a bull to a river in the Iranian context: cf. Plutarch, *Lucullus* 24.5; prayers of Alexander before Issus: cf. Bing 1991.

• *From Cyrus to Xerxes.* On the modifications of Xerxes' titulature at Babylon, see Joannès 1989a: I have deliberately not introduced this discussion here, for as F. Joannès himself remarks (following A. Kuhrt), "There is no relationship between the revolts . . . and a modification of the titulature."

7. Xerxes, Ahura-Mazda, and Persia

• *The daivā Inscription.* The following pages owe a great deal to the pioneering work of Sancisi-Weerdenburg 1980: 1–47, now repeated and expanded in Sancisi-Weerdenburg forthcoming (1). It is quite noteworthy and damaging that this work has been so little read, or at least so little cited (I already reported and followed it in Briant 1986a; cf. also Papatheophanes 1985: 109–10); she was the first, as far as I know, to come up with the idea that *XPf* is not a narrative text; a related idea is found in Kellens 1987 (who does not quote Sancisi-Weerdenburg), as well as (in a different form) in Bianchi 1977.

• *The King, Ahura-Mazda, Life, and Death.* On the word *artavān*, cf. (among others) Duchesne-Guillemin 1953: 51–54, Menasce 1974, and Herrenschmidt 1991: 17–18; on the eschatology, cf. also Bianchi 1977: 7–12 and Kellens 1988b: 344–47 (in the *Gāthā*), and quite recently Kellens 1995 (from which, p. 36, the quotation in the text is taken); on *šiyāti*, the position of Herrenschmidt 1991 has been definitively rebutted by G. Gnoli, EW 42/2–4 (1992): 528, and subsequently by Kellens 1995: 34–39; on the phrase *artācā brazmaniya*, cf. most recently Herrenschmidt 1993c (followed by Kellens 1995: 36 n. 40) and Skalmowski 1992–93.

• *Ahura-Mazda and the daivā.* On the *daēuua* in the *Gāthā*, I follow faithfully the analyses of Kellens 1988b: 360–63, where (pp. 347–48) clarifying reflections on the correct methods of sacrifice in the *Gāthā* in relation to the discussion of the *daēuua* are also found.

• *The Land of the daivā.* Locating the *daivā*: in Greece was defended by Levy 1939; the Median hypothesis was developed especially by Ghirshman (1976a; 1976b: 169–77); he wishes to distinguish the "rebellious" countries (Egypt and Babylonia, he says) from the country of the *daivā*, which he says is Media; he proposes to find archaeological proof in the excavations of Nush i-Jān: cf. their publication by Stronach 1977, at the end of which Ghirshman, pp. 608–10 repeats his interpretation; but D. Stronach (1981: 126–27; 1984: 479–83) himself expressed (convincingly) very strong reservations about this interpretation. Contra Ghirshman and several others, Sancisi-Weerdenburg (1980 and forthcoming [1]) proposes lowering the date of the inscription and a new interpretation of it (adopted here in its essentials); the comparison of *DB* (V) and *XPh* is due to the same author; it is also found in Kellens 1987: 681; Bianchi 1977 stresses the Iranian cultural context of the royal statements; the translation of *DSe* 001 is taken from Stève 1987: 61–62; let us remark incidentally that, just like the introductory sentences of *XPf*, the first paragraphs of *DSe* (§1–2) reproduce the first lines of *DNa*; these observations make me think that it would be wrong to use *DSe* and *DSe* 003 to date the beginning of work at Susa (cf. chap. 5/1); *yaud* and *hamiçiya*: cf. Kent 1953: 204, 213; cf. also *DAE* 69 ([= AD 8] Grelot 1972: 316 note e; and Whitehead 1974: 73–74); perhaps the two words differ in the same way as Greek *tarakhē* 'trouble' and *apostasis* 'secession, revolt': cf. also Briant 1988a: 142–43 (on the Egyptian word *bks*).

• *Xerxes and Persia.* On Xerxes' royal ideology, cf. Sancisi-Weerdenburg forthcoming (1). The modification of the Babylonian titulature is presented in Joannès 1989b, who draws from it the conclusion that it was adopted here to promote "an imperial ideology of Iranian dominance much more clearly than under his predecessors," rightly remarking (in the wake of Kuhrt and Sherwin-White 1987) that no relationship with the revolts may be seen in it, since they are later; cf. also the important remarks of Stolper 1992d: 214, on scribal practice: "Not only was the change in titulary not an immediate consequence of the Babylonian revolts, not abrupt, and not consistently applied, but it was also not perceived as obligatory or even meaningful." In another article, however, F. Joannès (1990a: 175–76) alters his position considerably: even while remarking in passing that "the sources are much less numerous than under Darius," the author in fact makes a series of statements not one of which appears to me well founded: (1) The cessation of documentation at several sites reveals a sudden change after rebellions; (2) "The system of land ownership changes consistently so as to turn it over nearly exclusively to Persian hands"; (3) "The socioeconomic autonomy of Babylonia ends, and Xerxes, then his successors, succeed in wiping out any trace of the ancient powers"; (4) "The effort pursued by Xerxes and his successors bore fruit, since the beginnings of the Hellenistic period show that, if the region is prosperous, any trace of local ideological autonomy has disappeared." But: (1) We recall (above) that the quantitative diminution of documentation bears no logical relation to the modification of the titulature (cf. Van Driel 1987: 162–63); (2) In Xerxes' time we see no proof of a sudden change in the property system: onomastic investigations show nothing relevant (cf. the chronological classifications drawn up by Zadok 1977); I do not preclude that the reign of Xerxes marks an extension of the Persian diaspora in Babylonia (similar to what is found in Asia Minor: see below), but the Babylonian documentation from Xerxes' reign is still too sparse to confirm this hypothesis; (3) The author frequently refers to the Murašū archives and to Xerxes' successors: that there were changes is certain, but nothing allows us to ascribe all the changes to the reign of Xerxes: these things must instead be envisaged over the long term, that is, since Cyrus, Cambyses, and Darius; (4) The end of socioeconomic and ideological autonomy of Babylonia is a matter for speculation: it is rather the perseverance of Babylonian traditions that strikes the observer of the beginnings of the Hellenistic and Seleucid periods (cf. most recently Beaulieu 1989c; Kuhrt and Sherwin-White 1991, 1993, 1994; also Beaulieu 1989c, 1992; Stolper 1993, 1994a); in sum, I prefer to adhere to the prudent remarks of Kuhrt and Sherwin-White 1987: 77. [Concerning the "disappearance" of private archives toward the beginning of Xerxes' reign, I observe, incidentally, that in a more recent article (1992b: 160–61) F. Joannès makes a very different interpretive suggestion from the one I challenged above. Cf. also McGinnis 1994, 1995: 188 (contra Joannès), but I am very skeptical about the alternative explanation offered by this author: a changeover from cuneiform to Aramaic and from clay tablet to perishable media (the same explanation in Dandamaev 1992c: 172 with reference to the archives of the Eanna [and 1995b for the archives of the Ebabbar of Sippar]); while the use of wooden tablets is actually attested in the Achaemenid period (cf. Briant 1992b), it is in fact very ancient in Mesopotamia (cf. Mallowan 1966, 1: 149–63); for another thing, the use of Aramaic obviously does not date to the Achaemenid conquest (even if it expanded at that time), and finally, everyone knows that cuneiform on clay remained in widespread use all the way into the Hellenistic period (including vouchers and notarized documents), so much so that it seems to me utterly impossible to imagine a sudden change happening at the beginning of Xerxes' reign; if such a changeover did take place, it obviously could only have been gradual and over a long period. And, in any case, another possibility must not be forgotten: quite simply, these "missing" archives are still underground (or even sometimes "mislaid" on museum shelves).]]

• *The Builder King.* The dates of construction of several buildings in Persepolis continue to pose complex problems, which my lack of competence in the area prevents me from rehearsing here: I refer to Roaf's summary 1983: 138–40; on the tablets, cf. Roaf 1979; Xerxes at Susa: cf. Vallat 1974. Add the inscription published by Shahbazi 1985b: 11–12 ("Darius the Great King, King of Kings, son of Hystaspes, an Achaemenid": *DPb.h*), which does appear to show that, contrary to another theory, the *hadiš* was built by Darius, not Xerxes (cf. Henkelman forthcoming).

8. Athenian Offensives and Royal Territories (478–466)

• *The Creation of the Delian League and the Royal Territories.* The following pages should also require long discussions of Athenian policy, which I cannot treat here *in extenso*; it is no longer possible to provide an exhaustive bibliography (given its exponential increase!); I will thus mention recent work in which state-of-the-art reviews can be found [[cf. Briant 1995a]]. On the (highly contested) chronology, see most recently Badian 1988 and Delorme 1992; according to Loomis 1990, the League was created in 477 (not 478). A lot of ink has been spilled on the origins and original composition of the Delian League: see Meiggs 1972: 50–58, 459–64; also Rhodes 1985: 6–11; the "minimalist" view of the extent of the League was presented by Sealey 1966, not without good arguments (but see Meiggs *contra*); on the danger of using the ("so-called") ATLs without caution, cf. the strong reflections by Pritchett 1969, especially p. 20: "Our information about the Athenian Alliance between 476 B.C. and 454 B.C. is so limited that any interpretation of the period is like grasping at straws in the wind"! The same author reasonably thinks that we cannot permanently "correct" Thucydides and remarks: "Now the picture in Thuc. I.99 is clearly one of slow development of the Confederacy or Alliance" (p. 21). Cyprus: an inscription in the Cypriot syllabary refers to a siege of Idalion by "the Medes and the people of Kition"; but, through arguments from pottery and numismatics, the inscription is dated either to the 470s or later to the 440s, so it cannot support an argument for a Persian counterattack in the region at the high date (cf. summary in Meiggs 1972: 476ff.; see also Wiesehöfer 1990: 245; Collombier 1990: 34–35; and Petit 1991: 163–65). The amount 460 talents of silver given by Thucydides for the first levying of tribute poses extremely difficult problems (cf. Meiggs 1972: 58–67; Finley 1978: 109–14); Persian and Achaemenid tribute: cf. Evans 1978 and Wallinga 1989. On Plutarch's chronology in *Cimon*: cf. Meiggs's strongly stated reservations (1972: 73–75), who thinks Cimon's first conquests on the Asia Minor shore date to the 470s; but, in my opinion, doubt remains; for Eurymedon, I adopt the most commonly accepted date (466) (Meiggs 1972: 80–82; Badian 1987: 4–7).

• *The Eurymedon and Its Consequences (466–465).* On the Persians' offensive strategy, cf. Meiggs 1972: 78–83 (opposing the most commonly advanced theory). On a Peace concluded after Eurymedon, cf. Badian 1987 (add to the bibliography Schrader 1976, an opponent to the "Peace of Callias"); since then, see Bosworth 1990, who offers some (good) remarks on the meaning that ought to be found in the statements Plutarch ascribes to Callisthenes; to judge by the English summary (VDI 1991/1: 168), V. M. Strogetsky's recent article does not seem to add anything particularly new. Contrary to the interpretation offered here, Badian (1987: 3) states that both adversaries desired peace, but he offers no arguments to persuade the reader, and he does not quote the Diodorus passages that give exactly the opposite impression for the Great King; what is the basis for the author's bald statement, "We are told in fact that Xerxes was eager for peace"? It seems clear, from reading what follows, that Badian hypothesizes that the Egyptian revolt had already begun, which is far from being proved. [[Contrary to Badian's interpretation, see most recently Bloedow 1992 and the critical remarks of G. Shrimpton, *EMC* 13 (1994): 415–18 = review of Badian 1993, which comprises the revised republication of Badian 1987 and 1988.]] Finally, contrary to Meiggs's opinion (1972: 80), I see no compelling reason to exclude the testimony of Plutarch (*Cimon* 14.1), that after Eurymedon the Persians still held parts of the Chersonesus, with the assistance of Thracians: cf. Fol and Hammond 1988: 249; let us add that if with Pritchett (1969) we date the transfer of the Treasury to the League before Eurymedon, the ancient texts refer to the Persian threat in the Aegean (Plutarch, Per. 12.1; Diodorus XII.38.2); on Greek propaganda after Eurymedon: cf. especially the vase published by Schauenberg 1975 (cf. on this document the remarks of Francis 1980: 70–71 and Daumas 1985: 300–302). All these uncertainties lead us to remark (among other things) that it is fortunate that no specialist in the Peace of Callias (meanwhile see Cahill 1985: 381 n. 40) seems to have happened on the interpretation given (although with some reservations) by Hallock (1960: 95) of the rising prices in Persepolis in 466: he sees it as a direct consequence of the Persian defeats at the Eurymedon, which would have caused a shortage of grain at the heart of the Empire; we may imagine what grist such a theory, instantly transformed into a factoid, could bring to the mill of those who continually insist on the notion of "Persian decadence" and think that the Great King was then forced to sign a humiliating treaty with Athens!

• *The Case of Lycia: Text and Image.* Destructions at Xanthus causally related to Cimon's expedition: cf. Demargue and Coupel 1963: 27, 80–81; doubts of Bryce 1986: 103–4; I note that the problem posed by the Lycian case is methodologically similar to that very clearly attacked by Zettler 1979, regarding Babylonia, the problem "of the relation between political-historical change and changes in material culture" (cf. also on this theme Briant 1984b, and chap. 16/18 below); the idea of a strict correlation between Persian cultural influence and subjection to the Great King was developed by Borchhardt 1979; it is based partly on a questionable interpretation of the east face of the Monument of the Harpies: the author thinks the seated prince is none other than the Great King, but this analysis is scarcely acceptable, as has rightly been shown by Gabelmann 1984: 41–42, who thinks on the one hand that the frieze of the Monument of the Harpies is not properly speaking an audience scene (even if the Persepolis influence is undeniable) and on the other hand that the person cannot be anyone but a dynast of Xanthus (cf. also with this opinion Tritsch 1942; Demargne 1958: 44 suggests identifying him as Cyberniscus, who led the Lycian ships to Xerxes: Herodotus VII.92, 98; *contra* Shahbazi [1975: 47–49], who thinks that the one he calls "the elderly prince" of the east Face is Harpagus, the founder of the dynasty, and recognizes Cyberniscus on the north Face, with the erection of the structure ascribed to the Sppndaza dynasty known only from coins). Borchhardt's theory is repeated (in a highly weakened form) by Metzger 1987: 15 (concerning Lycian dynastic iconography): "Perhaps the similar development [of Elmali and Kizilbel] should be ascribed to a stronger Iranian grip despite the Persian defeat at the Eurymedon, and to a possible sharing of influence between Athens and the Great King"; a related idea is found in Childs 1980: 56–62, who, p. 61, issues some reservations on Borchhardt's position (while calling it interesting, "though probably premature to accept"); on the basis of an examination of monetary standards, the author offers the hypothesis that only western Lycia was "probably" subject to the Delian League (pp. 57–61); but the rarity of Lycian evidence for this period certainly prevents us from mapping Persian and Athenian "zones of influence." In any event, in each of the monuments that we have considered, the Greek influences are also very noticeable (Metzger 1983); quite rightly, Metzger (1987: 14) also highlights the specifically Lycian foundation, regarding the "Harpies" (Sirens): "The artists working in Lycia, painters [Elmali] or sculptors, often grafted onto local themes images borrowed from the western world, the world of Greece"; on this, cf. also Dentzer 1982: 230 (on the tombs of Elmali and Karaburun)—but neither does the diffusion of Greek images imply Athenian political domination (cf. with this opinion Eddy 1973: 242–43); in this context see the wise remarks of Miller (1985: 59–60) on "the difficulties of reading" facts on the basis of pottery; in particular she remarks that the influx of Greek pottery is found on many other sites, such as Sardis and Gordion, that clearly remained within the Achaemenid orbit! To end for a moment with this point, we must stress here that the political inferences proposed to be drawn from stylistic and iconographic analyses cannot in every case be placed too precisely within the chronology, for the simple reason that buildings as important as Building G, the Monument of the Harpies, or the tomb of Karaburun are dated only approximately, within a bracket of 20 to 30 years, on the basis of stylistic relationships, always difficult to establish, and archaeological evidence that is not always certain (I note for example that Bryce [1986: 103–4] thinks that the Monument of the Harpies is earlier than the arrival of Cimon, disagreeing on this point with the reconstruction of Metzger 1958: 81); on the difficulty of dating the Lycian coins of the first half of the fifth century, cf. the revision proposed by Zahle 1991. From all this, we must conclude that the greatest prudence is still required on the question of the "status" of Lycia at the end of Xerxes' reign—Lycia which was for all that certainly not united, despite the presence (to some extent concomitant) of Iranian themes at Xanthus and Milyas (on the relations between Milyas and Lycia, cf. Hall 1986: 142–44): cf. Childs 1980: 57–62 analyzed above. One last remark: the Lycian *kurtaš* (from Termila) are especially numerous at Persepolis and environs, but the available documentation lists them only in the years 501–499 (PF 857–62, 1000–6, 1141–42, 1172, 1565, 1823, 1946–47; cf. Uchitel 1989: 236; 1992: 127–29).

9. Xerxes' Western Strategy

• *Xerxes and the Asia Minor Satrapies.* Celaenae: cf. Briant 1973: 74–89; on the colonization, cf. Sekunda 1991: 110–13, 119–23 (basically I share some of the conclusions, but others seem a bit adventurous to me; I do not believe [p. 112] that the Arsames listed by Polyaenus VIII.28.2 can be identified with the other Arsames who, in the same chapter of Polyaenus, leads the army to Barca around 513; this is probably Polyaenus's confusion with the story of Datames given by Diodorus XV.91.2–6). Xenagoras: I repeat here a suggestion by Erzen (1940: 112); Xerxes' vessel at Halicarnassus: Kent 1953: 115; while noting the existence of this vessel, Hornblower (1982: 25) thinks that Halicarnassus joined the League at the start, referring to Meiggs 1972: 54ff., but this author is fairly cautious on the subject (even if he finally ends up with the hypothesis of sticking with the high date); on the other side, correctly in my view, Wallinga (1991: 279) stresses the strategic implications of Xerxes' measure in Cilicia. Artabazus: cf. Lewis 1977: 51–52; the discussion by Petit 1990: 181–86 serves only to complicate matters unnecessarily; the Dascylium bullas are presented in summary by Balkan 1959; the author (n. 4 and p. 127) suggests (without arguments) that they date to the satrapy of Megabates and illustrate the importance of the satrapy during the invasion of Greece in 480: I have the strong impression that this dating is itself inferred from the "retreat" postulated for Xerxes after 479! On the bullas, cf. also Kaptan and Bayburtluoglu 1990, who leaves open the date of the documents (p. 25).

• *Xerxes and Pausanias.* The problems relating to the career of Pausanias are well presented by Graf 1979: 212–25; the Justin passage has alway given rise to numerous problems, made more difficult still by the absence of any other direct source (cf. Sealey 1966: 248–52). We will not enter here into the interlacing of the arguments, simply remarking that many authors, today, admit the validity of Justin's information as well as the (ill-defined) breadth of the Persian reconquests in the 470s (cf. Meiggs 1972: 466–68); Badian 1988: 300–302; Schumacher 1987); on the interest and credibility of Justin's text, see especially Fornara's proof (1966: 267–71), whose conclusions I have adopted here; Balcer 1986 (with others) thinks that the letters quoted by Thucydides are fakes forged by the *ephors* ['overseers, supervisors'], but the argument is not very convincing (cf. Olmstead 1933; Westlake 1977: 102–3; see also Nylander 1968).

• *Gifts of Lands and Towns: Colonization and Territorial Control.* On the policy of colonization carried out systematically by the Persians with the aid of exiled Greeks, see the excellent work of Asheri 1983b: 51–54, 78–80; status of Gongylus and Demaratus, cf. Briant 1985b: 62–64; on the Gongylus, cf. also the note by Fogazza 1972a, Robert 1973, and Pareti 1961; on Mania, cf. Lewis 1977: 55 n. 32 and 128 n. 3; in the fifth century we may also note that Pharnaces, a son of Pharnabazes, gave lands to the Delians at Adramyttium (Thucydides V.1.1; cf. discussion in Lewis 1977: 80 n. 198 and Asheri 1983b: 79). The case of Arthmios of Zeleia raises several problems, because the Athenian decree condemning him is known only from quotations by fourth-century authors: cf. Meiggs 1972: 508–11 (followed cautiously by Lewis 1989: 230 n. 9) and

Manes 1982, both of whom accept the reality of the episode (whatever its date, which is difficult to fix precisely).

• *Themistocles at the Court of the Great King.* Role of Artabazus: cf. Briant 1992c; we may note that according to Thucydides (I.135.2), Themistocles landed at Ephesus, not in the Aeolid, as in Plutarch; the authors of *ATL* III:111–12 express doubts on the central role attributed to Artabazus in the *Letters* attributed to Themistocles (meanwhile, see Nylander 1968); it is obvious that many versions circulated, more or less romanticized (cf. Diodorus XI.57), but, on this point at least, I see no compelling reason to prefer Thucydides' version. Moreover it is not impossible that the differing versions go back to contradictory information that the Greek authors could have collected later, perhaps in the Dascylium satrapy, perhaps the Sardis, which had always been circulating, and which were incessantly disputed in the neighboring territories (cf. Weiskopf 1982: 350–53; 1989: 41–43, on the southern Troad); under this theory, the "Letter of Themistocles" and Plutarch's version stems from Dascylium, and the Thucydides version comes from the satrapal circles of Sardis. At any rate, it is not possible to infer from the documentation that Artabazus had then replaced the satrap of Sardis, since our sources are silent on Sardis until the end of the 440s, aside from a fleeting allusion to an (unnamed) satrap of Sardis in Plutarch (*Them.* 31.1–2) at the beginning of Artaxerxes' reign. On chronological disputes, I refer (*inter alia*) to Badian 1987: 4–5; but I will add one observation (already suggested by Olmstead 1948: 289–90): if the chiliarch Artabanus who received Themistocles upon his arrival is the same Artabanus who conspired against Xerxes and was put to death by Artaxerxes (chap. 13/10 below), we must conclude that Themistocles was indeed received by Xerxes. On the towns received as a gift by Themistocles, cf. Briant 1985b: 59–62, with the critical supplements of Savalli 1987; these donations have always been used as an argument by those who oppose the theory of an Athenian-Achaemenid peace (e.g., Meister 1982: 32ff.; contra, e.g., Badian 1987: 20; see also the discussion of Frost 1980: 220–23, and already *ATL* III:113); on Themistocles' coinage, cf. Cahn-Gerin 1988 and Cahn-Mannsperger 1991.

10. From Xerxes to Artaxerxes

• *The Assassination of Xerxes: The Literary Motifs.* We may remark that an Athenian vase painting (inscribed with the name Artoba[ ] = Artabanus?) is sometimes considered a depiction of the murder of Xerxes (cf. Hölscher 1973: 48–49): this would confirm that the event attracted special attention in Greece.

• *The Assassination of Xerxes: The Dynastic Problems.* Youngest son and satrapy of Bactra, cf. Briant 1984b: 75–77; Hystaspes, satrap of Bactra: cf. PF 1287, 1555 (Lewis 1977: 19 n. 96); Xerxes and his son Darius: the problem of knowing whether the former had named his son as successor during his lifetime remains very complicated, being very badly documented (if it really is Xerxes who is named in the *Stela of the Satrap*, and if the expression "oldest son" really refers to the oldest son [but see above, chap. 13/2, Research Notes], this would be the only attested association of Xerxes and Darius!). Even if we agree with some people that the audience relief on the central panel of the Apadana of Persepolis represents Xerxes and his son (and not Darius and Xerxes: below), this theory gives no precise chronological information; despite Legrand (ad loc.), I am tempted to think that the task entrusted to Artabanes was close enough to what Herodotus says Cambyses conferred on the *magus* during the Egyptian campaign (III.61: *meledōn tōn oikiōn*; cf. Wiesehöfer 1978: 49–50; on the title *meledōn* [also found in Greek inscriptions], cf. Lévy 1940: 237 and n. 5; in an "Achaemenid context," cf. Aelian, *VH* II.14 and *Anim.* XIII.18). Post-accession propaganda: we may recall at this point that several authors (cf. Tilia 1977: 70–71; Calmeyer 1976: 78–79) think that the shifting in the Treasury of the audience relief from the central panel of the Apadana is due to Artaxerxes; this theory is based on another one supposing that the royal persons represented are not Darius I and Xerxes, but Xerxes and his son Darius: under these circumstances, Artaxerxes would have removed from view a scene that was an unpleasant reminder that his brother Darius, whom he had assassinated, was the legitimate heir. But I hesitate to use the argument, given the risk of circular reasoning—especially since the kings shown might have had an urge toward anonymity [??] (see Henkelman forthcoming). Africanus: without digging deeper into the question, Badian (1987: 3 n. 8) thinks: "This can hardly be wholly invented" (cf. also Calmeyer 1976: 77, without taking a firm position; Dandamaev [1989a: 234] does not rule out that Artaxerxes "was only formally the king"). But comparative study of the information from the chronographers about the XXVIIth dynasty does not in the slightest confirm such confidence in Africanus: cf. Waddell 1966: 70–71; a fragment of a Greek papyrus repeats the datum on Africanus (cf. Bilabel 1924: 35–48), but this lends no weight to such a highly suspect tradition. We have not a single datum showing that Xerxes' power was weakened in his last years. Dandamaev (1989a: 233–34) brings in two items: (1) for one thing, we have known since Hallock 1960: 94–95 that a sharp increase in grain prices is visible at Persepolis at the end of 467 and the start of 466; Hallock proposed to see it as a consequence of the Persian defeats at the Eurymedon, but this is a very unlikely theory: in any case, the connection between a *relative* increase in prices and economic weakening remains to be proved; (2) referring to Hinz (1979: 24), Dandamaev cites numerous dismissals/appointments (about one hundred) of high-ranking administrators in Persia, which he interprets through the royal desire "to pacify the discontent in Persia." The theory goes back in part to Bowman (1970: 27–28, 57), who concludes from an examination of the datings of the *segan* and treasurers in the Aramaic texts (inscribed objects) that there was a general alteration of job titles in 467–466. But, for one thing, the absolute dates proposed by Bowman must remain hypothetical; for another, the examples given hardly allow us to state that the change was sudden and general or that they have to be closely related to the shortage of 467 (despite Hinz 1972: 308)—especially since the very existence of a shortage has to be evaluated with great care; in any case, it is hard to see the connection that might be established between appointments to high positions and discontent in Persia, and still less the relationships among the price increase, discontent, crisis, and the assassination of Xerxes (despite Cahill 1985: 381 n. 40, who, moreover, even suggests a link with the Peace of Callias!): actually, the replacement of administrators can just as easily be interpreted as a proof of royal authority (cf. Diodorus XI.71.1: accession of Artaxerxes I). Accession of Artaxerxes: the Babylonian documents are presented by Parker and Dubberstein 1956: 17; cf. also Stolper, *CAH* VI²: 237; Aramaic documents in Egypt on the transition between the two kings: Porten 1990: 26–27.

11. An Assessment

• On the Frieze of tribute-bearers on the façade of the palace of Xerxes–Artaxerxes I, see especially Tilia 1974: 132–33 and 1977: 74–76; cf. also Shahbazi 1976b: 57–58; Root 1979: 108–10; Roaf 1983: 140.

Chapter 14

From the Accession of Artaxerxes I to the
Death of Darius II (465–405/404)

1. One King after Another (465)

• *Sources and Problems.* On the difficulty of dating the Babylonian documents, cf., for example, the remarks of Joannès 1982: 331–32, 358; cf. also pp. 5–6 (dating of a trove from the reign of Artaxerxes II); see also on this subject the remarks of Kuhrt 1987a: 152, Stolper 1990b: 561–62, and the striking example presented by Sachs and Hunger 1988: 69, with the comments of van der Spek 1993a: 96; on the dating of the Aramaic texts from Egypt, cf., for example, Porten 1987b (on *DAE* 9 [= *AP* 7], dated by Grelot to Artaxerxes I, by Porten to Artaxerxes II) and Lemaire 1991c: 199–201 (*DAE* 75); even if the question has not really been reopened recently, I recall the arguments over the dating of the Aramaic texts from Persepolis: cf. Bowman 1970: 56–62 and my remarks above, p. 940; same difficulties in dating the Demotic papyri: Lüddeckens 1965, Cenival 1972 (palaeographic criterion); on the Greek inscription from Sardis, cf. chap. 15/8: Droaphernes and the Sardis Statue, pp. 677ff.; the Aramaic inscription from Cilicia (Meydançikkale) was published by Lemaire and Lozachmeur (Davesne, Lemaire, and Lozachmeur 1987: 365–70); it is dated to year 16(?) of Artaxerxes; the editors remain prudently uncertain about the identity of this king (I or II? cf. also Lemaire 1991c: 206); on Ezra–Nehemiah, cf. chap. 14/5, pp. 583ff.

• *The Position of the New Great King.* On royal metonomasia [use of throne names] (known from several Classical texts and attested more specifically in Babylonian tablets): cf. Schmitt 1982c (correcting Schmitt 1977), and now van der Spek 1993a: 95–96; dynastic nature of the Bactrian revolt: cf. Briant 1984b: 76–77; identification of Artabanus: cf. remarks of Lewis 1977: 19 n. 96; changing satraps at the beginning of a reign: Briant 1991a: 9 〚hence my doubts on the recent commentary on Diodorus XI.71.1 by Balcer 1992b (1995)〛; court measures attributed by Plutarch to Artaxerxes I: cf. my discussion in Briant 1994e: 307–10 (on rules regarding royal hunts); comparison with Babylonian tablets: cf. Stolper 1985a: 270 and the note regarding text no. 91 dated to Darius II (the similarity in punishments is striking; the comparison implies that royal decisions were not limited to the Persian aristocrats—which poses new problems, which M. Stolper returned to in 1995a).

• *Artaxerxes I at Persepolis.* The works accomplished by Artaxerxes I at Persepolis have been brought to light by the investigations of Tilia: cf. Tilia 1972: 191–208; 1974; 1977; as well as Calmeyer 1990a: 15–16. The hypothesis of a change in the function of Persepolis is developed by Frye 1974, who thinks that, from this time on, Artaxerxes I chose Susa as his capital, but the supporting arguments do not carry conviction: whether they concern the reception of Greek ambassadors at Susa (Herodotus VII.151) or the absence of tablets: is it necessary to repeat that the gap is accidental? We may also stress that in Herodotus the seat of power of the Great King is regularly placed at Susa, which for him is the very symbol of royal power (cf. Briant 1993b); in supposing that the other kings until Artaxerxes II did not use Persepolis frequently (p. 384), Frye fails to take into account the entirety of Classical documentation (cf. Cameron 1973), or lets himself be misled by a worthless moralizing tradition, without quoting it, such as is repeated by Plutarch, *Alex.* 69.2 (same distortion in Dandamaev 1989a: 312; cf. Briant 1993c: 421); as for the suggestion that Artaxerxes I "perhaps found mid-March on the plateau too cold to live there" (p. 385), this reckons on the one hand on the royal presence exclusively at the time of the New Year's festival (cf. chap. 5), and on the other on the special "sensitivity to cold" of the Great King that is pure fiction (if Ctesias §19 transmits truth, we see that in November 486, Darius was in Persepolis; the text also suggests that the king regularly went to Persepolis in accordance with the ritual calendar [[on this point, see now Koch 1993a: 61–91, who contrasts the information given by the Classical authors on the relocations of king and court [Briant 1988c] to the facts provided by the Persepolis tablets; the study particularly confirms [pp. 88–89] the theory that I drew from Ctesias on the requirements of the ritual calendar]); lastly, I remark that, in the framework of Frye's interpretation, it is hard to understand why beginning with Artaxerxes II the Great Kings chose to have their tombs dug above the Persepolis terrace (cf. Calmeyer 1990a: 13–14). Based on all other arguments, the theory of a change in function of Persepolis is also offered by Cahill 1985, who takes into consideration the relocation of the audience reliefs and what he considers "the cessation of bringing gifts into the treasury" (a point on which I remain skeptical); at the same time, the author rightly remarks that the remaining uncertainties require great caution on the part of interpreters (pp. 388–89).

2. The Egyptian Revolt (ca. 464–454)

• *The Revolt of Inarus and the Athenian Intervention.*   On Ctesias, cf. Bigwood 1976, whose conclusion (p. 21) is unexceptionable: "This account of the Egyptian episode may afford us some amusement. But there is no major historical problem which it helps us to resolve"; on the Athenian intervention, Meiggs 1972: 101–4, 473–76; on the revolt itself, cf. Kienitz 1953: 69–72 (the role attributed to the Nile–Persia maritime link, p. 69, comes from an erroneous understanding of the canal's function), Salmon 1965: 90–192 (long and heavy), and most recently Hoglund 1989: 250–87.

• *Characteristics and Consequences of the Revolt: Persian Egypt and Egyptian Egypt.*   Cf. Briant 1988a: 140, 147–51, 171–72 (repeated here for the basics); on the origins and relations of the marsh kings, cf. the articles "Amyrtaios" (de Meulenaere), "Psammetichus IV, V" (Spalinger) in the *LÄ* (on the Delta, cf. also Yoyotte 1961, Bertrand 1988, Favard-Meeks and Meeks 1992); despite Dandamaev (1989a: 242–43), the hypothesis (taken from other authors whom he cites) of a high dating of the archives of Aršāma must be abandoned, as well as the hypothesis of a reference to Inarus in an Aramaic papyrus (DAE 66 [= AD 5]) in connection with some troubles in Upper Egypt: cf. Cazelles 1955: 97–99; the name must no doubt be read Anudarū and not Inarus: Grelot 1972: 309, Whitehead 1974: 57 (on the absence of troubles in Upper Egypt, cf., for example, Porten 1968: 26–27 and Grelot's remark 1972: 81, who replies to Kraeling 1953: 31, without mentioning him, regarding the use of "weights of Ptah"); Artaxerxes' seal: according to Porada (1979: 88–89), the seal of the Hermitage Museum in St. Petersburg, fig. 18a–b, p. 215 here (a Great King, bow and quiver on his back, a lance in his hand, holding in his hand a rope that wraps around the necks of four captives, while the king brandishes his lance against a kneeling man with Egyptian hairstyle [*pschent*]), could represent Artaxerxes I and Inarus, but it is not impossible that it could be Megabyzus (on this seal, cf. also Nagel 1963: 134 and fig. 11, and the remarks of Henkelman forthcoming); we may note that a seal on the Treasury tablets (*PTS* no. 28) bears a similar scene, with the difference that the captives bound with a rope around their necks and the warrior on his knees killed by the king are Greeks: Schmidt 1957: 10, 29; a nearly identical scene on a Babylonian impression (communication from L. Bregstein and M. Stolper) and even on a bulla of (or: from?) Artašāt of Armenia (Root, DATA 1993, p. 13, and the forthcoming articles by Khatchatrian and Manukian).

3. Trans-Euphrates Matters

• *Artaxerxes and Megabyzus.*   On the literary motifs constituting Ctesias's tale, cf. Bigwood 1976: 19–21; the ill-informed article by Brown (1987) provides nothing new; Petit (1990: 194–95) strongly insists that Megabyzus held the position of satrap at the time, but by means of arguments that do not convince (in particular he has not considered Stolper 1989b); Petesas and Spitamas: cf. Stolper 1985a: 94; the importance of the episode in the framework of the history of the Greek merchant class in the Achaemenid Empire is analyzed by Seibt 1977: 35–39; Rahe (1980: 88–90) thinks that Megabyzus (followed by his son Artyphius) was the first (before Pissuthnes and Cyrus the Younger) to understand the importance of organizing joint maneuvers by the Persian cavalry and the Greek infantry, but I am not sure that the existing evidence allows us to attribute this innovation to a particular person (which moreover presupposes the decadence of the royal Achaemenid army: cf. pp. 79ff.; but cf. chap. 14/7: Darius II and His Satraps, pp. 593ff., and chap. 17/3); Lewis (1977: 51) thinks that the revolt weakened the king's position (but see below, chap. 14/5, on Nehemiah's mission); see most recently Hoglund 1989: 196–299 (he denies a revolt by Megabyzus; I have not been able to consult Hoglund 1992).

• *Troubles in Judah?* Cf. Oded 1977d: 527; see also Yamauchi 1990: 251, who, following others (cf. Blenkinsopp 1987: 416), compares the Egyptian affair with the revolt of Megabyzus, thinking in particular that, if a few years later the king allowed Nehemiah to rebuild the fortifications of Jerusalem, it was because meanwhile the revolts had been suppressed: the basic problem remains: should we or should we not accord explicit historical value to what appears to be an interpolation (cf., e.g., Ackroyd 1984a: 9; 1988a: 41–42)? On possible troubles in the time of Xerxes, cf. my skeptical remarks, chap. 13/2: "Crushing Rebellions," p. 525.

4. The Asia Minor – Eastern Aegean Front

• *Athenian-Persian Hostilities (the 450s).* Controversy exists in regard to the condition of the Athenian and allied forces after the Egyptian campaign: Meiggs (1972: 104–8) thinks that the campaign was a disaster that had weakened Athens in the eyes of its allies; starting with this belief and examination of several texts (Erythrae, Miletus, Sigeion), Meiggs factors into this context the support that Athens's opponents found in the Asia Minor satraps (1972: 109–28); an opposing position on the consequences of the Egyptian campaign has been worked out anew by Holladay 1989. Without being able to cover the whole bibliography here (cf. Briant 1995a), I will simply stress that most of the arguments (including mine) are burdened by a whole series of chronological difficulties (whether involving the historians' texts or epigraphic documents). On Cimon's campaign in Cyprus, cf. the clarification by Wiesehöfer 1990: 246–47.

• *Return to the "Peace of Callias."* Cf. the bibliography cited above, in the Research Notes to chap. 13/8 (pp. 967ff.), as well as Dandamaev 1989a: 250–55 [contrary to what the author states (p. 254), Demosthenes, *Amb.* 273 does not imply that the Athenians were unhappy with the terms of the treaty negotiated by Callias], and especially Lewis 1992a: 121–27, who, not without exhibiting a certain impatience with those who hold the opposite opinion (p. 126), thinks that the historicity of the Peace cannot be doubted; he makes three arguments: (1) the Peace of Epilycus that renewed the Peace of Callias is "now virtually certain"; (2) the missing year in the ATL is very likely 448; this gap is to be linked to the conclusion of the Peace; (3) the Periclean building program was financed by the League's funds transferred to Athens: "The only conclusion which can be drawn is that the Athenians were confident before starting work on the Parthenon that the Persian War was over, by mutual consent. Beside this conclusion, the details are relatively unimportant" (p. 126); without neglecting the relevance of Lewis's arguments, I remark that: (1) the first argument *risks* being one segment of a circular argument; (2) in the opinion of Lewis himself, doubts remain regarding the identification of the missing year (p. 125: "Clearer evidence would be welcome"); (3) the use of the allies' tribute for building the monuments on the Acropolis, denounced by Plutarch and long disputed, is an interpretation that has just been challenged, not without excellent reason, by Giovannini 1990. The dating of Herodotus VII.151, which is in close chronological relation to the Peace, is placed in doubt by the theory's opponents: cf., e.g., Meister 1982: 22–24, who dates the Argive embassy to the beginning of the reign of Artaxerxes I. I stress that several authors have rightly warned against the temptation to interpret too rapidly the gaps in the ATL by reference to a Peace of 449 and to believe, with circular reasoning, that the Peace explains the gaps (and vice versa): cf. Robertson 1987: 386 ("The Peace of Callias is a joker in the pack; it makes a better game to play without it"), Piérart 1987: 296 and Giovannini 1990: 146 and n. 43; on the activities of the satraps, cf. Meiggs 1972: 111–18, 188–90, 314–15; on the Miletus affair, see the important corrections to Meiggs's theory on the basis of the publication of a new fragment of the decree: Piérart, *REA* 87/1–2 (1985): 42; also Robertson 1987: 384–90 (in fact, the decree concerns an internal crisis and not a revolt against Athens); on the Colophon and Notium affairs, cf. Piérart 1984: 168–71; these various episodes are also reviewed by Badian (1987: 19–26), who, strongly supporting the notion that a peace concluded after Eurymedon, thinks that the sa-trapal actions do not imply a declared state of hostility between the satraps and Athens—a presen-tation that appears to me to be based on a legal fiction (which I am tempted to attribute to the author and not to Artaxerxes or Pissuthnes; see on this subject also the analysis of Eddy 1973 and the reflections of Lewis 1977: 59–62). It would be good to add that two other very important aspects remain unresolved: (1) Thucydides mentions several times that the cities of Ionia were deprived of fortifications: was this dismantling brought about by a treaty imposed by the king, or was it the result of an Athenian decision? (Meiggs 1972: 149–50 prefers the second interpretation; Wade-Gery [1968: 215–16], by contrast, imagines that Athens accepted this condition in exchange for the Great King's agreement not to send the royal army to fight in western Asia Minor; in agree-ment Lewis 1977: 153 n. 118): it is impossible to decide; (2) did the cities allied with Athens con-tinue if not actually to pay tribute (though some authors admit even this possibility) then at least to owe the Great King tribute? (cf. Meiggs 1972: 148, who answers in the affirmative, and the re-marks of Frost 1980: 220–29 on cities granted to Themistocles). On the strategy of Pericles, cf. the remarks of Giovannini 1990: 145–46. On the diplomatic contacts between Sparta and Artaxerxes: cf. the analysis by Lewis 1977: 63–70; between Athens and the Great King: Hegyi 1983. We may note that in the context of the traditional interpretation of the Peace of Callias, the question why the Great King did not send an army to the coast receives an answer if we agree that the treaty for-bade the royal army to interfere there—a standpoint developed by Wade-Gery 1968: 215ff., but al-ways on the foundation of (contradictory) texts whose credibility can be doubted. For his part, following Wallinga (1987: 47–48), Descat (1990a: 544) thinks that after Salamis and Mycale "the Achaemenids no longer had a permanent navy"; aside from the fact that this interpretation re-mains hypothetical, all it does is push the problem back, or rather raise another: when and why did the central power decide on such a sudden change of strategic direction?

• *Return to Xanthus.* On the Tribute Lists, cf. the tables prepared by Meiggs 1972: 538–61, and the cautious and wise observations of Piérart 1987: 294–95 (and n. 14) on the change in Caria's tribute beginning in 446, then after 440–439; Athenian efforts in the islands between 428 and 425: Piérart 1984; disappearance of Lycia: Meiggs 1972: 246–47; on Caria and Lycia: cf. also Eddy 1973 and Keen 1993a (who stresses the strategic value of the Lycian coast; on this point, cf. also Zimmermann 1992). We may mention regarding Caria/Lycia that a passage in Ctesias is problematic; in his presentation of the Megabyzus saga, he notes that his youngest son, Zopyrus, left the king's camp to seek refuge in Athens: "With those who accompanied him he fled toward Caunus and demanded that they turn over the town to him. The people of Caunus replied that they would hand the town over to him but not to the Athenians with him" (§43): the date of this expedition is not certain, but it was before the death of Artaxerxes (§43), perhaps between 430 and 425: cf. Eddy 1973: 255, who reasonably thinks that Caunus rose up against Athens, perhaps with the aid of Pissuthnes (the counterarguments of Badian 1987: 23–24 do not appear valid to me); see also Meiggs 1972: 436–37 (who proposes linking the episode to Melesander's mission); Descat (1991: 39) sees in the Zopyrus affair the expression of a break between Athens and the Great King; my opinion on this question is not very settled: all I would like to stress here (even without collect-ing all of the examples) is that the available documentation (Greek texts and Pillar inscription: cf. Shevoroškin 1977 and Melchert 1993) attests to the exceptional importance of Caunus in Persian strategic thinking in the southwest corner of Asia Minor (up to and including Darius III [cf. also Descat 1994b]); at the time of the Diadochi, one of the two magnificent citadels defending the city and access to the port (cf. Diodorus XIX.75.5) was called the *Persikon* (Diodorus XX.27.2). Pil-lar Inscription of Xanthus, cf. Demargne 1958: 79–105; on the author (Kheriga) and date (around

400), I adopt the position of Bousquet 1992: 167–74; on the events, cf. Childs 1981: 62–66 and Bousquet 1992: 175; on the status of Lycia during this entire period, see now the detailed work of Keen 1992a (consulted through the author's generosity), chap. 5/2 (he adopts the hypothesis of a Peace of Callias in 462–461): "It seems likely that Lycians returned to Persian allegiance when they left [the allegiance] of Athens"; on Melesander's (then Lysicles') expedition and the information gleaned from the Pillar Inscription, cf. ibid., chap. 6, and Keen 1993b.

5. *Ezra and Nehemiah in Jerusalem*

• As a result of various kinds of argument, it has often been proposed that Ezra actually carried out his mission under Artaxerxes II, in 398: a summary may be found in Oded 1977d: 503–9 (which adopts the low chronology), Yamauchi 1990: 253–56 (which inclines rather toward the dating adopted here, without denying that the other interpretation is not unappealing), Williamson 1987: 69–76, and Hoglund 1989: 73–80 (Ezra before Nehemiah). Among the arguments sometimes adduced in support of the low chronology is the Egyptian situation at the beginning of the fourth century, and it is thought that Ezra's mission fits with the king's desire to protect the approaches to the Nile Valley (cf. Cazelles 1954: 114–19); this is a traditional explanation, often offered also to explain Cyrus's measure of 538 (cf. chap. 1/6); but this is a simple argument of similarity, without any evidence as a basis: at the risk of appearing naïve (or ill informed), I must insist that even and especially after studying a map, I have never really understood what decisive strategic advantage against Egypt the small land of Judah could have had in the eyes of the Achaemenid central authority (or in the eyes of certain modern interpreters?); other historical arguments are equally weak: thus the admission of Dor (near Sidon) to the Delian League (accepted by Meiggs 1972: 420–21), sometimes interpreted as an argument in favor of Ezra's high dating (cf. studies cited by Yamauchi 1990: 254 n. 60), is anything but certain (cf. Lemaire 1990: 56 n. 135; the note is not repeated in Lemaire 1994: 33). The debate, finally and especially, is part of a subtle and complex discussion of the content of the "Memoirs" of Nehemiah and, thus, the work and chronology of the Chronicler; long under way, the discussion seems to have taken on new life these last few years (cf. the articles collected by P. R. Davies 1991), perhaps under the influence of the rebirth of Achaemenid studies (cf. Hoglund 1989, 1991; Williamson 1991; Weinberg 1992a, b; Grabbe 1992b [seen too late]); my lack of competence in the material keeps me from participating (cf. the clear summary by Ackroyd 1988; developments can be followed by means of the *Chronique* by P. Abadie, *Trans.* 1 (1989): 170–76 and 4 (1991): 141–45; see most recently Dequeker 1993, who, dating Ezra to the Artaxerxes II period, thinks that the reconstruction of the temple took place under Darius II and not Darius I [and Lemaire 1995a: 57–61, who, on the basis of the Egyptian situation and the Elephantine documents, chooses the date 398]); I will state nothing but an impression: to go by the recent literature, the nonspecialist would not do well to intervene in the discussions and polemics, whose scientific bases escape him more and more as the readings multiply (cf. Dequeker's baffling 1993 article); we have the impression that at the present time no tradition enjoys the status of "historical fact" (cf. in particular Grabbe 1994): in short, the dates in the text have been adopted purely by convention: my only justification is that I am in good company; but I would be no less so if I held the exact opposite position!

• *Ezra's Mission.* See the discussions in Cazelles 1954 (who sets Ezra in 398); Oded 1977b: 535–36; Purvis 1988: 169–70; Yamauchi 1990: 256–57, who following Blenkinsopp (1987) sets up a parallel with the mission entrusted by Darius I to Udjahorresnet and the similarity of the "Egyptian laws": but, with Grabbe 1994: 294–95, the parallel does not seem particularly legitimate to me; see also other reflections by the same author, who has multiplied the warnings and reservations on currently accepted interpretations of Ezra's mission; I find myself agreeing with one of his observations (p. 297): "The closer one looks, the more enigmatic Ezra's mission becomes," and "We have to conclude that Ezra's mission is a puzzle" (p. 298).

• *Nehemiah's Mission.* It is impossible for Nehemiah to have been a eunuch; it is even highly unlikely that he was a cupbearer to the king (cf. Oded 1977b: 528 and, both more detailed and more certain, Yamauchi 1980b, 1990: 260–64). The literature on his mission is considerable: a summary may be found in Yamauchi 1990: 264–78; on the governors before Nehemiah, cf. chap. 12/3 above; on the extent of the province of Judah, cf. a summary of the issue in Lemaire 1990: 32–45 (cf. pp. 39–40 on *pelek* and the satrapal residence at Mizpah and Gibeon, with the remarks of Briant 1985b: 67); the duties of the commissar (Neh 11:24) remain mysterious (cf. Heltzer 1989: 346 n. 71, and now Heltzer 1994: a summary will be found there [pp. 109–13], and comparisons [interesting, but in my opinion not very convincing] with Udjahorresnet, Histiaeus of Miletus, and Arlissis of Caria); on relations with the central authority, cf. also the reflections of Graf 1985: 92–93 and Weinberg 1977: 32–38 (who thinks that Nehemiah was not *peḥā* of the province of Judah, but rather head of what he calls the "Bürger-Tempel-Gemeinde": cf. now Weinberg 1992a, b): on Weinberg's views, cf. Dion 1991 and the critical remarks of Blenkinsopp 1991; on Nehemiah's social reforms, cf. (inter alia) Yamauchi 1980a, 1990: 272; Kreissig 1973; Kippenberg 1982: 54–77; Heltzer 1989b; on Nehemiah's fortification, cf. Laperrousaz 1979.

• *From Jerusalem to Elephantine.* DAE 89: cf. Grelot 1972: 354–67, Porten 1986: 12–13; on the *Pascal Papyrus* (DAE 96), cf. Grelot 1955, 1972: 378–86, 1981; most recent restoration in Porten 1986: 7; on the interpretation, cf. also Vincent 1937: 249–61, Briant 1986a: 432–34, Frei 1984: 16–17, and, quite recently, the (to say the least) surprising proposals of Dequeker 1993: 89–92 (who connects the document to the reconstruction of the Jerusalem temple, which he places under Darius II and not Darius I, on the basis of textual exegesis in which I refuse to get involved [and Lemaire 1995a: 60]); finally I do not believe that we can say, with Porten and Yardeni 1993: 59, that the document attests to the favor that Darius II in particular is supposed to have manifested toward the Jewish community of Elephantine. On the Jews in Babylonia, cf., e.g., Coogan 1974, Purvis 1988: 154–62 (who poses, pp. 158–60, the problem of the possible existence of a temple).

• *The Enemies of Nehemiah and Judah.* On the province of Samaria and the information coming from Wadi ed-Daliyeh, see the various publications of Cross (1963, 1966, 1971, 1974, 1985); some of the papyri have been studied by Gropp 1986, but we are still waiting for the final publication; the coins were recently published by Meshorer and Qedar 1991 (we will return at a suitable point to this rich material: chap. 16/7); see also Lemaire 1990: 64–67 (on the province of Samaria) and Lemaire-Lozachmeur 1987 (on *byrt'/hirtā*); summary and review on Gašmū and Tobiah in Lemaire 1990: 45–54, 68–72. Tobiah: on his residence at Iraq el-Emir, cf. the publication by Will and Larché et al. 1991: 5–9. Gašmū the Arab: on the vessels and dedications of Tell el-Maskhuta, cf. Dumbrell 1971, Briant 1982b: 172–73 (with some doubts on the generally proposed reconstructions), and, since then, Graf 1990a: 139–40; Knauf 1990: 207; as well as Holladay 1992: 590; Paice 1993 [cf. Lemaire 1995a: 54–55]; Sanballat's hostility is easily explained if we accept the theory (worked out by Alt) that before Nehemiah, Judah was a dependecy of Samaria; but the discovery of bullas inscribed with the names of governors before Nehemiah has done away with this interpretation (unless the datings are challenged, as was recently done by Bianchi 1989): on Alt's position, see also the critical remarks of Hoglund 1989: 123ff.; [on relations between Judah and the Samaritans, cf. also Macchi 1994: 33–44]. Lastly, I note that in several works (cf. 1965, 1985), M. Dunand connected the edifices built by Nehemiah in Jerusalem with a vast royal project to defend the "Mediterranean front of the Empire" such as, for example, some Sidonian buildings (temple of Eshmun), both of them characterized by the presence of a "Persian podium"; but this whole reconstruction is purely hypothetical, without solid foundation (cf. my remarks in *AbIran* 12 [1989] no. 229, and J. Elayi's, *Trans.* 1 [1989]: 190–91, as well as the doubts of Mazzoni 1991–92: 66).

6. One King after Another (425–424)

• *Ctesias and the Babylonian Tablets.* Cf. Lewis 1977: 71–76, Stolper 1985a: 104–24, as well as my remarks in Briant 1994b: 118 n. 20; on the chronology, see the summary by Stolper 1983,

1985a: 116–20, and most recently Depuydt 1995b; on the estates of the princes and princesses, cf. Stolper 1985a: 54ff., 64–66 (Aršāma), 89–93 (Artarios, Menostanes, Artoxares), 96 (Arbarius/ Arbareme); on these people, cf. also the notices of Dandamaev 1992a nos. 16, 26, 33, 43, 185, 250, and on Menostanes (and his brother or associate, Uštapānu), the text published by Donbaz and Stolper 1993.

• *Families and Powers.*   Cf. also Briant 1990a: 95–96 (and n. 49); like Lewis (1977: 83–84), I doubt that Hydarnes, father of Tissaphernes (Xanthus Pillar Inscription), can be the father-in-law of Darius II: it is highly unlikely that Ctesias would not have mentioned the fact in the context.

• *Legitimacy and Propaganda.*   Cf. Briant 1991a: 4–6; Lewis (1977: 77 n. 77) stresses that the epithet "illegitimate" is applied to Darius II by late sources.

• *Darius the Great King.*   Lewis (1977: 78 and n. 182) published an inscription of Darius II that is said to come from Hamadan (= D^2Ha; cf. Mayrhofer 1978: 17, 29–30).

7. Affairs on the Western Front

• *The Situation in Asia Minor (424–413).*   On the various problems, cf. Andrewes 1961: 1–7, Lewis 1977: 80–82, Cartledge 1987: 187ff., Briant 1995: 116–32; on the Peace of Epilycus, cf. most recently Descat 1991, who stresses its novelty, and Lewis 1992a: 122, 1992b: 422 n. 132; on the problems posed by the Athenian aid for Amorges, cf. the discussion of Lewis 1977: 85–86, and the readings of the Pillar inscription by Shevoroškin 1977: 127–28 n. 1 (but several have now been dismissed by Melchert 1993, analyzed in the next paragraph); on the Ionian War, I have made much use of Lewis 1977: 86–135 as well as Westlake 1979 and, on some chronological problems, Robertson 1980 (who places the mission of Arthmios of Zeleia in the context of 408–407; cf. also on this point Walbank 1982, 1983, 1989).

• *The Spartan–Achaemenid Treaties (412–411).*   Lewis 1977: 90–107; Levy 1983; cf. also Canfora 1990 and Cartlege's doubts (1987: 187) on the character of "treaty": the author speaks of an "agreement." While the author's suggestion along these lines remains very modest (p. 34), it is perhaps in this context that we might locate the new readings of several lines of the Pillar Inscription by Melchert 1993: he thinks the text refers to an accord sworn between Tissaphernes, son of Hydarnes, and his Lacedaemonian allies; presided over by the dynast of Xanthus (who speaks in the first person), who acts as arbitrator/conciliator (*maraza*) between the two allies, the agreement would have been written on two stelas, one deposited at Hytenna [a reading that removes from the text the pseudo-Persian personal name Utāna/Otanes] in the sanctuary of Maliya, the other at Caunus in the sanctuary dedicated to Maliya, Artemis, and Basileus Caunius; it is thus possible that there we have, seen from the Lycian side and expressed in Lycian, a reference to the negotiations opened at Caunus between Tissaphernes and the Spartan leaders (Thucydides VIII.58.1), but it could also deal with a different episode. Whatever the case, an article like Melchert's, coming after many others (e.g., Shevoroškin 1977), once again sharpens the historian's hope of one day having a complete text that hopefully would fatten the skinny file of non-Greek narrative sources for the Achaemenid period.

• *Darius II and His Satraps.*   Concerning his escape from Sardis, Alcibiades claimed "perfidiously that Tissaphernes had let him go" (Plutarch, *Alc.* 28.1); on the diplomatic hesitations of Tissaphernes, cf. Lewis 1977: 129–31; on the military inferiority of the satraps, cf. Westlake 1979: 37–40; cf. ibid. on the fiscal levies imposed on the Greek cities, which, he says, were one of the reasons for the limited enthusiasm on the part of those cities for participating in the war against Athens. The phrase *idia khrēmata* is not unreminiscent of others used later by Xenophon: in 405, Cyrus the Younger "assigned to Lysander all the tribute which came in from his cities and belonged to him personally (*tous phorous tous ek tōn poleōn, hoi autōi idiōi ēsan*)" (*Hell.* II.1.14◇); when he arrived in Asia Minor with 500 talents released by Darius II, Cyrus also declared himself ready to "use his *idia*" if the royal funding proved insufficient (*Hell.* I.5.3); and, later, Cyrus begged his brother Artaxerxes II "that these Ionian cities should be given to him instead of remaining under the rule of Tissaphernes" (*Anab.* I.1.8◊): "for, in fact, the Ionian cities had originally belonged to Tissaphernes, by gift of the King (*dedomenai*)" (I.1.6); the phrases used by Xenophon are problematic; but I am not certain that the author is thus referring to a gift of towns, comparable to what was given to Themistocles (a theory defended cautiously by Lewis 1977: 119–22, thinking that the gift was given to the person, not the satrap); I am tempted rather to think that in this way the king allowed the satrap entrusted with the war to finance it with the profit of the tribute, which comes down to authorizing him not to pay the full amount to the royal treasuries—an obligation that, by contrast, fell on Cyrus (*Anab.* I.1.8), doubtless the source of his discontent; on these problems, cf. also Tuplin 1987a: 133–35; on the financing of military campaigns in these years, see especially Lewis 1989: 231–34; on Cyrus's coinage, cf. Weiser 1989 (with the strong objections of Casabonne 1995b).

• *Darius II, Asia Minor, and the Other Fronts.* State of siege at Uruk: Stolper 1990b: 572 (with caution, since the parallels invoked date to the seventh century); the royal concern for the other fronts is particularly stressed by Lewis 1977: 133–34; in an earlier article, the same author (Lewis 1958) presented the idea that the Phoenician navy was rerouted to Egypt in 411: on this point, cf. my critical remarks in Briant 1988a: 143; moreover, the text of Thucydides VIII.35 is less forthcoming than supposed by Kienitz 1953: 73 (which I made the mistake of following too closely in Briant 1988a: 150). Indeed, the absence of documents from the center and certain recently published Babylonian tablets must lead the commentator to caution and not overestimating the Aegean front in the imperial strategy of these years. But, on the one hand, the orders given by Darius II to Pharnabazes and Tissaphernes show that the decision to reassert authority over the Greek coastal cities was indeed made by the king; on the other, an expedition such as the one against the Cadusians certainly did not take on such military importance that it could endanger the Achaemenid engagement on the western front (on the "Cadusian Wars," cf. my interpretive remarks in chap. 16/18). In short, it seems to me reasonable to doubt that these fronts could have led Darius to neglect the affairs of Asia Minor (cf. also the reflections along these lines in Tuplin 1987a: 139–42 and Cartledge 1987: 189–90).

• *Darius II and His Armies.* On the Greek stereotype of Persian military decadence, cf. Briant 1989a and the systematic analysis carried out in chap. 16/3; on compensated service (repayment in silver for the *ilku* charges), cf. Joannès 1982: 20–21, who, while noting that it is already known in the time of Darius I (p. 21), thinks that "it even became the rule from the reign of Artaxerxes I" (p. 20) and that the contrary texts (convocations at Uruk under Darius II: texts pp. 19–20) constituted nothing but "a few exceptions"; cf. also pp. 25–26: "Under Artaxerxes I and Darius II, this is the system that prevailed and, at least under unusual circumstances, the feudatories of the Nippur region were not normally compelled to do anything but pay the *ilku* in silver"; this interpretation had already been presented by Cardascia (1951: 8) and Dandamaev (1967: 41–42) and it is widely accepted among those who study the development of the Greek institution of mercenaries under the Achaemenids: cf. Picard 1980: 222–23 (with several notes of caution nonetheless, p. 223); also Rahe 1980: 90–93, and Petit 1993 (cf. Briant 1994b: 120–22); in contrast, more cautious regarding the Greek texts, Seibt (1977: 121–38) does not know the Babylonian material; on the Gadal-lāma affair, cf. Cardascia 1951: 179–82 (but I vehemently reject the conventional "feudal" interpretation) and 1958, from which I take the translation of UC 9/68 by P. Beaulieu in Joannès, *CANE*, p. 1481 (cf. also Cardascia 1977); regarding the translation 'secretaries of the army' ['army cashiers' *sipīru ša ūqu*], Cardascia 1951: 58 n. 2 mentions but does not accept San Nicolo's interpretation (*non vidi*), which compares the phrase *grammateis tōn dynameōn*; the suggestion seems quite sensible to me: in the Hellenistic period, these *grammateis* (scribe/*sipīru*) were required to take the function of soldiers (*hoi grammateis tōn tagmatōn*): cf. Launey 1949 II: 672, and pp. 778–79 on their role in the distribution of military rations; on the Babylonian phrase, cf. also Stolper 1985a: 31 n. 116 and 93; convocations at the *syllogos*: cf. texts gathered by Widengren 1956: 152–60; texts dated to Artaxerxes II: analyzed by Dandamaev 1992a: 18 (on the barber's archives, cf. Van Driel 1987: 164–67). The circumstances of tenants' indebtedness at the time of the fight between Sogdianus and Ochus are analyzed in detail by Stolper 1985a: 104–24; he develops the idea (pp. 106–14) that the tablets record that the members of the *ḫaṭru* had to pledge their plots (or more precisely the revenues derived from their plots) to the Murašû to be able to outfit themselves during the events relating to the succession. I stress that Joannès (1982: 22), Picard (loc. cit.), and Rahe (1980: 92) all refer to Stolper's work (who in turn cites Parke and Seibt, p. 150 n. 69, in a sort of "bibliographic tautology"); but Stolper's analysis does not necessarily lead to the conclusions they come to: cf. the critical remarks by Van Driel (1987: 174–76; 1989: 223–24); it furthermore seems to me that, more recently, Stolper has modified his initial proposal a bit (cf. Stolper 1989c: 150, discussing Dandamaev 1967); on the (limited) use of Greek mercenaries in Asia Minor before the revolt of Cyrus the Younger, cf. Seibt 1977: 35–51. To these remarks I will add one more (in the form of a suggestion): we might in fact ask to what extent the "pessimistic" interpretation of the generalization of payment in silver is not a distorted view, derived from a "flat" use of the evidence considered. On the royal taxes incumbent on the *ḫaṭru*, in fact, we have nothing but tablets from the archives of the house of Murašû (and other houses from at least the time of Darius). More specifically they relate to the category analyzed by Cardascia (1951: 98–120) under the name "tax receipts": managing lands entrusted to them by the concessionaires, the Murašû took their profit in the form of rent, and it was they who, for this reason, paid the taxes to the *šaknūtu*, who, in turn, paid it to the royal treasury (cf. the clear analysis by Cardascia 1951: 188–98). This procedure calls forth three remarks: (1) we have no trace of the "normal" procedure, in which the concessionaire paid the tax directly to the *šaknu* (Cardascia 1951: 192); (2) to pay the tax in silver, the Murašû had to transform the farm produce, either by sale (cf. Cardascia 1951: 198) or by the transformation of some agricultural products into "industrial" products, dates and beer in particular (Van Driel 1989: 211, 235–36); in this way they played a central role in the system (as Van Driel 1989 rightly insists), since the royal treasury preferred to deal with silver rather than agricultural products (see also Briant 1994d); (3) the payment in silver by the Murašû thus does not necessarily mean that the concessionaires did not owe actual military service; on the contrary, this was an obligation that cost quite dearly and that required purchases from craftsmen (arms, etc.): it was through the Murašû as intermediaries that they got this silver, for, besides the taxes, the Murašû obviously paid a fee to the concessionaires for the lots they were managing. In other words, the generalization of the land management system (and thus of payment in silver) did not conflict with the military capacities of the *ḫaṭru* (which is by and large concealed by the nature of our evidence); quite the contrary, it was a primary condition of their maintenance. — On all of these problems, see also the clear reflections of Kuhrt 1989: 220 and the important comments by Tuplin 1987b: 153–56, in particular pp. 155–56 on "compensated service"; the author, it seems to me, has reservations similar to those I suggest here (citing the tablets relating to the barber Kuṣur-Ea), while agreeing nonetheless that the actual levy of the "king's soldier" became rarer and rarer in favor of the appeal to mercenaries (p. 157). I maintain meanwhile that the available documentation does not allow such statistical inferences: from recently published tablets, we learn for example of a convocation of the army by the king in 370 (*ADRTB* no. –369), or of the existence of fighting in 368 (no. –367); this suffices to exemplify the accidental nature of military events showing up in the Babylonian documentation; anyway, it is not impossible that every year the members of certain military *ḫaṭru* had to send fully armed soldiers, such as the sumptuously equipped "Babylonian horsemen" who regularly came to welcome the king on his frequent visits to Babylon (cf. Quintus Curtius V. 1.23; cf. also my reflections in *RTP* 45 and n. 2, as well as Kuhrt and Sherwin-White 1994: 312): according to Xenophon, in any case, speaking in general of troop reviews, they were annual reviews (*Oec.* IV.6); besides, such regularity would certainly make it possible to maintain the troops' military readiness at an appropriate level. [On paid service, see most recently the text BM 49718 explained by Jursa 1995, who compares it with the texts concerning Kuṣur-Ea.]

• *Cyrus in Asia Minor.* The theory of a new treaty between Sparta and Darius (the so-called treaty of Boiotios) was developed by Lewis 1977: 124ff.; it has found strong and reasoned opposition from Tuplin 1987a (some of whose arguments appear to me to be conclusive); on the amounts Cyrus received from the king, cf. Lewis 1977: 131 n. 138; 1989: 231 (he notes the interest of the passage *Hell. Oxyr.* 19.2 and stresses that for the first time the king brings into play his own resources); on Cyrus and Lysander: cf. Bommelaer 1981; the title *karanos* borne by Cyrus: cf. Petit 1983; Haebler 1982; and most recently Bernard 1994b: 500 and n. 53 (on the coins of the first Parthian kings, we find the word *karanos* in Aramaic, rendered in Greek by *autokratōr*).

8. The Great King in His Countries

• *The Muraŝû, Babylonia, and the Royal Administration.* I summarize here with broad strokes the work of Cardascia 1951, Joannès 1982, Stolper 1985a, and Van Driel 1989 (who have just been quoted above with respect to mercenaries and *ḫatru*; cf. also Stolper 1990c, 1992c; *CAH* VI^2: 245–53). Much information and analysis will also be found in Bregstein 1993, in particular pp. 114–207, where the author with great precision presents the functional identity of the owners of a seal: it thus constitutes the most detailed presentation of the administrations and administrators in Achaemenid Babylonia; I mention in passing that in 418 we observe a price increase in some Babylonian towns; it is possible that it lasted until 416, but the sparse available documentation does not allow us to infer a deep structural crisis (cf. Joannès 1982: 276–79): there is in any case no trace of a Babylonian revolt in these years, contrary to what the mistaken reading of a tablet had led us to believe (cf. Stolper 1988a: 197–98).

• *Bēlŝunu.* On his career, cf. especially Stolper 1987, 1990a, 1995, and the remarks of Graf 1993: 153–54; I thank F. Joannès for providing me with a translation of the document TBER AO 2569 (cf. also English translation by Stolper 1992b: 123–25; the translation 'governor of Babylon' seems to me better than 'satrap of Babylon'): in another article (1989b: 298), Stolper raised doubts about his earlier reconstruction, stressing that Bēlŝunu seems to have remained subordinate to the satrap of Babylon (on the uncertainties of Persian administrative vocabulary and its Akkadian calques, cf. Stolper 1985a: 58; *CAH* VI^2: 252–53; Dandamaev 1992b); on Bēlŝunu's activities as manager, cf. also Stolper 1985b (with doubts now expressed in Stolper 1990a: 205), Van Driel 1989: 223–26; *TCL* 13.204: Stolper 1987: 392 and n. 17.

• *Darius II in Egypt.* On the paradoxical situation concerning evidence in Egypt, cf. Briant 1984b: 58; Aramaic documents of the reign of Darius II: list in Bresciani 1958: 187 (add Segal 1983: 4, probably Darius II); Darius II at El-Khārga: Kienitz 1953: 73–74; Winlock (1941: 7ff.) thinks that it relates to Darius I instead, but, more recently, Van Wijngaarden (1954: 69–70) attributes the document to Darius II (cf. Bresciani 1958: 181, who also cites a sherd inscribed with the name "[–], son of Artaxerxes"; she thinks it could relate to Darius II but does not exclude Arses); according to Grelot (1972: 398, referring to Posener 1936: 78–79), Darius II had a hymn to Amon carved in the sanctuary of El-Khārga; I do not know where this information comes from (not found in Posener): we thus see that some uncertainty remains regarding the possible presence of Darius II at El-Khārga. Furthermore, Cazelles (1955: 87 n. 3) asks whether the *naos* found at Hermopolis Magna could be attributed to Darius II (rather than Darius I), but Mysliwiec 1991 seems to exclude this hypothesis. Darius II's gifts at Edfu, cf. Meeks 1972: 20, 55, 133–35; on *SD^{2}a* and the uncertainties of dating, cf. Schmitt 1981: 33–34; Aramaic version of Behistun (and Naqš-i Rustam: Sims-Williams 1981), cf. Greenfield and Porten 1982: 2–4; Porten and Yardeni 1993; Porten 1990: 17 on the date; I add that in their new publication of the Aramaic text of Behistun (*TADAE* C.2.1), Porten and Yardeni 1993: 59 repeat the theory already presented in Greenfield and Porten 1982 of copies for student use (for *DB* and *DNa* [Sims-Williams 1981]), and they add this political explanation: "Perhaps the text was read periodically on public occasions"; observing that the earliest date in the text on the verso is 417, they suggest that the new copy "may have been written to commemorate the 100th anniversary of the great victories of Darius I which fell shortly after the accession of his later namesake, etc." Even though the idea of a political impetus that had its source at the center came to my mind as well, I did not believe myself able to adopt this suggestion when I wrote the text of this note, and I do not believe myself able to sway from this rule of interpretive caution, quite aside from the fact that the authors' comparison between the revolts put down by Darius I and those faced by Darius II seems excessive to me. Lack of interest in Egypt on the part of the Great Kings in the fifth century is suggested, for example, by Kienitz 1953: 73–74 (based—astonishingly!—on the presumed silting up or filling with sand of the canal from the Nile to the Red Sea); a similar idea is found in Dandamaev 1989a: 243: "After Darius I, the Persian kings were basically uninterested in the internal affairs of Egypt" (referring to the limited number of documents dated to Artaxerxes I); it is clear that this position comes directly from the traditional view of the rupture introduced by Xerxes, a point of view that does not stand up to analysis (cf. chap. 13/6). Regarding the absence of stelas for the interment of an Apis or the mother of an Apis after those dated to Darius and Xerxes, then their reappearance beginning with Hakoris in 391, Smith (1992a: 207) suggests that one must see this as testimony to the restoration of the sanctuary, which "could well have been one of the principal preoccupations of the local government after the end of Achaemenid dominion in 404"; this is obviously a tempting interpretation, because of the historical inferences it suggests; I will simply allow myself three remarks: (1) Smith himself stresses the special character of the stela that refers to Darius and Xerxes (cf. Smith 1988: 188; 1992a: 205), a sort of official document, as opposed to the stelas of the fourth century (up to and including Alexander), which were inscribed by the masons at work during the interment of the mothers of Apises; moreover, the first stela was reused later on, which opens the way to a different interpretation, namely, that the stelas dating from the first Persion dominion were destroyed after 404; the final publication will certainly provide important information on this point; (2) meanwhile, I note that in the time of Artaxerxes I we see no evident change in the position of the Great King in Egypt: in the quadrilingual inscription on a vase (A¹Orsk), the hieroglyphic text calls him "Artaxerxes the great pharaoh" (*vazraka* in the reconstructed Persian version: Mayrhofer 1978: 28); these remarks do not alleviate the difficulty, but they might awaken interpretive caution; (3) [[lastly I will take up what D. Devauchelle has very recently written (1995: 70): "We may remark the absence of attestations concerning the three or four Apises who lived at the end of the first Persian dominion; this is perhaps due only to the chance preservation of ancient monuments"; nonetheless the author thinks it is possible that according to the recollections found on a stela of the Ptolemaic era, the interment is dated either to ca. 412 or to the reign of Darius II (he develops and explains this point in Devauchelle 1994b: 104–6)]].

   • *The Persian Authorities Confront Jews and Egyptians in Elephantine.*   I repeat here the basics of my proof in Briant 1988a: 144–47 (where the bibliography may be found), which I amend and complete in some points; the relationship between the "code" of Darius and the Syene–Elephantine affairs were suggested to me by reading Allam 1986, 1993; Mélèze-Modrzjewski 1986, 1989; I also note in passing that the phrase "in the time of Cambyses" is found in a Saqqara papyrus but not in any explanatory context: cf. Segal 1983: 4. The fate and career of Widranga raise many problems; first of all, the punishment that he is supposed to have received (humiliation?) is inferred from a very difficult passage in the petition sent by the Jews to the governor of Judah (*DAE* 102 [= *AP* 30], line 15): the variety of solutions imagined by the translators is considerable (cf. Kraeling 1953: 105 n. 15; Porten 1968: 288 n. 19; Grelot 1972: 410 notes s and t); besides, Widranga seems to be named in a (badly damaged) letter dated to the accession of Nepherites (Kraeling no. 13 = *DAE* 105), which seems to imply that he had not lost his job and in any case that he had not been executed, since he would have been present and active on Elephantine in 399 or 398 (cf. Kraeling 1953: 111–13; Grelot 1972: 422 with doubts about the identification of this Widranga; [[Lemaire 1995a: 53–54 with some annoying typos in the dates]]). The question was reopened by Lemaire 1991c: 199–201, who proposes dating the Aswan stela (*DAE* 75) to Artaxerxes II (398), not Artaxerxes I (458); he makes basic corrections: rather than seeing in it the erection of a Persian sanctuary, he thinks that Widranga dedicated a sanctuary to "Osiris the powerful" — hence his note (p. 201 n. 7) on *DAE* 98 [= *AP* 38] and Widranga's "Egyptophilia": for reasons already given in Briant 1988a: 167, the Persians' marked devotion to Egyptian practices does not seem to me sufficient proof of Egyptophilia (in the political sense implied by the authors who use the word: e.g., Donadoni 1983: 35, referring specifically to Widranga); all we can think is that, after the end of Persian dominion, Widranga (just like the garrison) allied himself with the new masters: but from this nothing can be inferred about his "Egyptophilia"; after all, when the Persians switched sides to Alexander (cf. chap. 18/3), no one dreamed of accusing them of "Macedonophilia": they simply obeyed whoever it seemed to them at the moment to be in their interest to obey; for all these reasons, I do not think that the new readings proposed by Lemaire in themselves allow us to understand the reasons for Widranga's decision against the Jewish sanctuary at Elephantine. I consider the entire matter in detail in Briant 1996b.

• *A Business Letter.*   Besides Grelot's commentary, see Porten 1888b and Briant 1988a: 169–70; on "joint ventures" in Babylonia (without any Iranians), cf. Dandamaev 1984a: 321, 332, 371.

• *The Great King in Sidon and Elephantine.*   On the coinage, besides Babelon (1910 II.2: 545–58), see more recently Betlyon 1982: 3–9 and J.-A. G. Elayi 1993: 125–61; the beginning of coinage at Tyre and Sidon is dated ca. 450 by Mildenbert 1990: 144 n. 30 (cf. also J.-A. G. Elayi 1992b). *PTS* 32: cf. photo in Briant 1992d: 74 and drawing in Eph'al 1988: 157, who thinks it shows a "Phoenician trireme" (on the presence of fortifications on some of these coins, cf. Childs 1978: 79, Elayi 1986); seals from Dor: Stern 1990, 1994c: 190–92; coins of Syene–Elephantine: Lipiński 1982: 27. Debate on Sidonian coins: beginning with study of the later coins, where another person (with Egyptian hairstyle) walks behind the chariot (Babelon no. 906ff.), Seyrig (1959) offered the hypothesis that the king in the chariot is not the Great King but an image of the god Baal of the city; this interpretation was cast into doubt by Schlumberger 1971, using arguments that seem very strong (cf. also Betlyon 1982: 10); it should be recalled that the motif of the king on his chariot is also found in Phoenician imagery before the Achaemenid period: cf. a Cypriot-Phoenician bowl from Praeneste (drawing in Childs 1978: fig. 29 = fig. 50c, p. 606 here): hunt near the royal city (represented by two towers); standing under a parasol, the king rests his right hand on the driver's shoulder who, leaning forward, holds the reins of the horse (two horses?); there as elsewhere, the imagery beyond doubt owes much to Neo-Assyrian models (on these bowls, cf. Childs 1978: 54–56, who is not directly interested in the motif of the king on his chariot). Sarcophagus of the satrap: the date and interpretation are controversial; against Kleeman 1958 (around 430), Gabelmann 1979 proposes the decade 380–370, after a stylistic comparison with the Lycian monuments: the comparison is also systematically done to extract a historical interpretation from it (see most recently the discussion by Stucky 1993); the "theory of dependency" (principal person = Great King) was worked out over several years by Borchhardt (cf. in particular 1983, and most recently 1993a: 50–52); against this position, see Kleemann (1958: 163–65), Gabelman (1984: 63–68, on the audience scene), and Jacobs (1987: 71–73).

• *The Lycian Case.*   On the Lycian texts of the Xanthus Pillar and the Greek epigraphic corpus, cf. the analyses by Childs 1981: 62–69; Bryce 1986: 105–8; and now Bousquet 1992 (discussed by Keen 1992a, chap. 17); according to Childs (1981: 69), the sarcophagus of Merehi should be attributed to Kheriga, because of an inscription on it; but Demargne (1974b: 96) thinks the iconography leads to a lower date. Coin of Tissaphernes at Xanthus: publication by Hurter 1979: 100–101, 108; on the uncertainties of the historical interpretation, cf. Harrison 1982a: 391–96; the theory of the satrapal portrait has been developed particularly by Cahn in many works (cf. Cahn 1975, repeated in 1985: 594; 1989): on this subject, see in particular many works of Zahle: 1982, most recently 1989: 175–76: contra Cahn, the author thinks it is a portrait of the dynast plain and simple; at the same time he agrees that such coinage explains the military participation of Lycians with the satrap and that, according to him, it was the satrap himself who supplied the silver for the minting; entirely opposed, Savalli (1988: 118 and n. 78) stresses the uncertainty of the restoration

"Tissaphernes" on the Xanthus coin, and she writes: "For this entire period [440–380 approx.], there is no trace of any control on the part of the Achaemenid kings and/or their satraps, other than [this coin]"; the suggestion seems incautious to me because of the generalization it draws, especially from analyzing the Greek poems from Xanthus (interestingly, for all that); cf. the opposite position of Bryce 1986: 109 (the author of the pillar was "an ally, if not a vassal, of the satrap Tissaphernes"), and the appreciation of Keen 1992a: chap. 7 ("In general the ruling dynasty at Xanthus seems to have become more pro-Persian, both politically and culturally, after the accession of Kheriga"). On the poems celebrating the deeds of Gergis and Arbinas, cf. now especially Bousquet 1992 (from whom I take much); on the poem of Arbinas: the theory of a direct borrowing from Persian concepts is developed (following Robert 1975: 328–30) by Herrenschmidt 1985; against this position, Savalli (1988: 106–10) exhibits the deeply Greek character of the poem; I am closer to the subtle position of Bousquet, who while challenging Herrenschmidt's interpretation, describes Arbinas as "a dynast brought up in the Iranian fashion" (1992: 181); on the Xanthus dynasts' own objectives during the Ionian War, cf. the historical reconstructions of Bousquet: "On the occasion of the war in Caria, Gergis had to lay his hands on the land of Caunus," from which, later, Arbinas perpetrated his conquests in the Xanthus Valley (1992: 175–78, 180), but see now Melchert 1993, analyzed above.

• *The Cilician Case.*   On Cyrus the Younger in Cilicia, cf. Erzen 1940: 116–20, where the sources are gathered; according to Kraay (1976: 9–11), several Cilician coins of Tissaphernes were issued to finance the (famous) Phoenician navy in 411–410, but the hypothesis remains very dubious: cf. Harrison 1982a: 46–51; Capecchi 1991: 68–69; Price, *REA* 91/1–2 (1989): 106; on the "dynastic" coinage, cf. the doubts brought out by Harrison 1982a: 440–50 and Moysey 1989: 127 n. 5; on this coinage, see also Capecchi 1991: 68–72 (and 72–85 on the coinage of the Cilician cities) and Weiser 1989: 278–81 (who thinks this might be coinage of Cyrus the Younger during his passage through Cilicia); according to Davesne (1989: 161), the Cilician coinage in its entirety expresses "the adoption of a common standard, derived from the Persian shekel, [which] seems to indicate that the Achaemenid power was at the root of this production"; but this political interpretation seems weak to me. On these numismatic and monetary problems, see now Casabonne 1995a, b.

• *The Persians and the Kings of Cyprus.*   Cf. Wiesehöfer 1990a and Collombier 1990, 1991. A Babylonian astronomical tablet (*ADRTB* no. –440) refers directly to events taking place around Salamis on Cyprus; it has been dated (not without reservations) by the editors to the reign of Artaxerxes I (hence its numbering); but I am persuaded by the arguments of van der Spek (1993a: 96) who tends to date it to the reign of Artaxerxes II; the text will thus relate to the affairs of Cyprus in the 380s (chap. 15/6: "The Offensive against Evagoras (387/386–383/381)," p. 652; also chap. 15/1).

Chapter 15

Artaxerxes II (405/404–359/358) and
Artaxerxes III (359/358–338)

1. The Reign of Artaxerxes II: Sources and Problems

• *The Greek Authors' View.* Cf. Briant 1987b, 1989a, 1994b, and Sancisi-Weerdenburg 1987a; on Plutarch's *Life of Artaxerxes*, cf. Orsi 1979–80, 1988, Manfredi and Orsi 1987, Tagliaferro and Manganelli 1991–92; as for the stereotyped view of Artaxerxes II and the court conspiracies (fanned by the inescapable Parysatis!) discussed by Dandamaev 1989a and Petit 1993, I have explained elsewhere what I think of it (Briant 1993c; Briant 1994b: 118–19); for all these reasons (laid out as needed in the course of this chapter), I do not share the confidence Moysey 1992 asks us to place in Plutarch, or that the same author (1991: 112–14) grants to Ephorus on the grounds that he is an "eyewitness" (see chap. 15/7: A Summary of the Discussion, pp. 674ff.). On Dinon (*FGrH* 690), cf. Stevenson 1987; on the *Oxyrhynchus Hellenica*, cf. Bruce 1967 and McKechnie-Kern 1988; on Xenophon's *Hellenica*, cf. Krentz 1989 and now Tuplin 1993 (who centers his proposal on Greek matters); on the phrase "Ten Thousand," see Masqueray 1928.

• *The View from Susa, Babylon, and Persepolis.* On Belesys/Bēlšunu, see several articles by Stolper (most recently *CAH* VI²: 238–39 and Stolper 1995). *ADRTB* no. –369: on the place-name Razaunda, I owe the suggestion (Media) to Stolper, *CAH* VI²: 239. *ADRTB* no. –440 is dated to Artaxerxes I by the editors (despite the doubts already expressed by Schmidt 1982c: 87); the tablet should instead be dated to Artaxerxes II, as suggested in turn by van der Spek 1993a: 96, who places it in the context of the Persians' battle against Evagoras known from Diodorus XV.2ff.; if we were able to date precisely Diodorus's phrase "this year" (§2.1✧), we could also place the tablet within Artaxerxes II's reign (the editors' suggestion "year 24?" is no more than that). Obviously we can inquire why a Babylonian scribe would look to the Aegean front for a chronological marker, given that generally speaking references to events are strictly Babylon-centric (Sachs and Hunger 1988: 36). It is obviously not easy to discover why at this point the scribe felt it would be useful to mention a fact that (for us) belongs to imperial history (cf. van der Spek 1993a: 93–95). My suggestion (all else being equal) is as follows: examination of the astronomical tablets and other Babylonian chronicles of the Achaemenid and Hellenistic periods suggests (it seems to me) that extra-Babylonian regions are referenced only when the king or a member of the royal family was on the spot: this holds, for example, for *ABC*, Chronicle no. 9 (p. 114), which deals with Artaxerxes III's expedition against Sidon and Phoenicia (Diodorus XVI.40.6ff.), or *ABC*, Chronicle no. 13, reverse: expedition of Seleucus in Asia Minor and Macedonia (Sherwin-White, *JNES* 42/4 [1983]: 266–67; Briant 1994c: 463–67), as well as some astronomical tablets, such as *ADRTB* no. –273 (Sherwin-White and Kuhrt 1993: 46–47), or another one (no. –255) that announces the death of Queen Stratonice in Sardis ("That month it was heard in Babylon: queen Stratonikè died in Sardis"). I thus conclude from this that, if van der Spek's proposed dating is correct (which it has to be if the reading is [Ar]šu), then *ADRTB* no. –440 refers to a time when Artaxerxes II led the troops in person against Cyprus (or at least that he was at the front at the beginning of the war); although we can never be absolutely certain, it is what Diodorus writes (XV.2.1): *Artaxerxēs . . . estrateusen ep' Euagoran ton Kuprou basilea*, where *estrateuse* should be taken in its primary sense of 'make (or participate in) a military expedition', that is, for a king, to lead at the head of his troops (compare Diodorus XVI.40.4–6; cf. Herodotus VII.3–6); doubtless it is this presence that the tablet is referring to with the unfortunately broken formula ". . . of the land Iamuniammu which the king made [. . .]." Thus no conclusion can be drawn from this text about the suggestion that Babylon was concerned with the "particular" importance of the Aegean front; for a Babylonian scribe, it was equally noteworthy in other years to indicate that the king had led his troops against the country Razaunda (*ADRTB* no. –369), or that the "king's troops had given battle [somewhere]" (no. –366), and far more interesting to mention planetary conjunctions, the level of the Euphrates flood, or the price of barley on the Babylon market (cf. Slotsky 1993).

2. The War of the Two Brothers (404–401)

• *From Darius II to Artaxerxes II.* We know nothing of the reasons for Parysatis's preference for Cyrus (on the relationships of Parysatis, Cyrus, and Artaxerxes, the ramblings of Hüsing 1933 must be relegated to dead storage, despite the echoes that still are occasionally encountered today): an ancient tradition (Aelian, *Anim.* VI.39; Plutarch, *Mor.* 328c) holds that she engaged in incestual relations with her younger son; this tradition doubtless goes back to Ctesias (cf. *FGrH* 688 F44). The name (Aršu) of Darius II's first son (called Arsices by Ctesias and Oarses by Dinon: Plutarch, *Art.* 1.4) is confirmed by Babylonian tablets (cf. Schmitt 1982c: 84–85; 88–89, and now van der Spek 1993a: 95–96); lands belonging to the "son of the king (*mār šarri*)" are attested in the Nippur area by tablets dating between years 1 and 7 of Darius II (Stolper 1985a: 54–62), but the designation used does not require us to suppose that Arses had been recognized as crown-prince from that date; although in fact the translation-interpretation 'crown prince' (adopted by Stolper) can be justified for the Seleucid period, when the custom of associating an heir-designate with the throne—and even double kingship—existed [[Sherwin-White and Kuhrt 1993: 23–24; Sherwin-White, *JNES* 32/4 [1982]: 265–66; Briant 1994d: 466 n. 22]], things were quite different in the Achaemenid period, for which nothing indicates that the person called *mār šarri* actually was the one who was recognized by his father in the ceremony described by Plutarch, *Art.* 26.4–5 (it is even excluded in the case under analysis here): the problem is doubtless different for the title *uma-supitrū*, which is also translated 'crown-prince' by Stolper, pp. 59–61, following Eilers: cf. on this point also chap. 13/2, p. 520. Concerning Athenaeus XII.548e, doubts remain, because of the various men called Ochus; it could refer to either Darius II or Artaxerxes III (the same problem with Polyaenus VII.17; see chap. 15/8: From Artaxerxes II to Artaxerxes III, pp. 680ff.); but the characteristics attributed to the dying king, the insistence on the length of his reign, and especially the conditions surrounding the succession of Artaxerxes II make us prefer to believe that the author is actually referring to the transition from Darius II to Artaxerxes II; Justin V.11.1 may derive from the same tradition: "In his last instructions, Darius left the throne to Artaxerxes, and to Cyrus the towns of which he was governor." On the interpolation included in the *Hellenica* (II.1.8), cf. the doubts of Lewis 1977: 104 n. 83; but, if Xerxes is corrected to Artaxerxes, the datum can be accepted (cf. Cousin 1904: 32–33); on this point, we may also stress the curious detail included by Thucydides (VIII.37.1) in the text of the second treaty between the Persians and the Lacedaemonians, in winter 412–411: the contractual parties swearing to it on the Persian side are listed as: "The king [Darius], the sons of the king (*hoi paides tous [tou] basilōs*), and Tissaphernes." Altheim and Stiehl (1963: 150–51) think that the phrase designates Autoboisaces and Mitraeus, who the *Hellenica* interpolator says were "sons of Darius's sister"; they also think that this (unnamed) woman was Artaxerxes I's daughter—hence the murders of Autoboisaces and Mitraeus by Cyrus: these are a lot of assumptions (it might also simply be a diplomatic formula just like the one doubtless found in Ezra 6:10). On anti-Cyrus propaganda, cf. Orsi 1979–80; Cyrus's coinage at Sardis: Weiser 1989.

• *Cyrus's Preparations and Artaxerxes' Response: From Memphis to Sardis.* I know of no investigation intended specifically to place the events in the framework of Achaemenid history proper; recent studies are particularly interested in the itinerary of the Ten Thousand, on which they provide often important and interesting commentary: see Cousin 1904: 213–33; Manfredi 1986; Donner 1986; Lendle 1984 and 1986; Debord 1995; Joannès 1995; etc. In contrast, Cook

(1983: 211–13) and Dandamaev (1989a: 274–85) offer nothing new on the level of historical interpretation, other than sometimes surprising suggestions; in particular, I do not see the basis for Dandamaev's (1989a: 274) "It is possible that he [Cyrus] hoped to diminish the influence of the Persian nobility and to create a centralized government, comparable to those which were established in the Hellenistic period": on this point, cf. Briant 1993c: 421–22; despite its age and a few faults, Cousin's book (1904) sometimes offers more interesting questions than many recent studies. Cyrus and Tissaphernes: according to Lewis (1977: 120–21), control of the cities was taken from Cyrus to be given by Artaxerxes II to Tissaphernes; see the critical remarks of Tuplin 1987a: 142–45; on the hierarchical relationship between the two men, cf. the discussion by Ruzicka 1985a, who offers several important suggestions. Alcibiades and Pharnabazus: on the record and its contradictions, cf. Hatzfeld 1951: 341–49 (who thinks, contrary to the position defended here, that Cyrus's intentions were unforeseeable by anyone in 404; cf. also Ruzicka 1985a: 211 n. 22); on the path followed by Alcibiades, cf. Robert 1980: 257–99; the Pharnabazus theory is adopted by Cousin (1904: 63–68). Egyptian revolt: we may note that, according to Xenophon's sources (*Anab.* I.8.9; II.1.6), Egyptian soldiers fought in the royal army at Cunaxa: but this might refer to Egyptians who had settled in Babylonia; on the date of *DAE* 7 [AP 35] (September 11, 400), see Porten 1990: 19. Psammetichus and Amyrtaeus: cf. valid remarks of Kienitz 1953: 76, and now Lloyd 1994: 337 and 347 n. 48; on the chronology of the Egyptian revolt and the Persian retreat, see Lemaire 1991c: 200–1 and 1995a: 51–56. Tamos and Psammetichus: despite Cloché 1919: 222, there is no reason to infer from the murder of Tamos that Psammetichus was a "Persophile"; the Tamos episode has quite recently been cited by Lloyd 1994: 347, who believes that Diodorus's text is too allusive to support historical interpretation; this justifiable caution leads me to stress once more that the idea (discussed in my text) of an alliance sought by Cyrus is simply hypothetical; on the other hand, the existence of a privileged relationship between the Egyptian dynasts and Carian-Memphites in the service of the Persians is confirmed by Diodorus XV.9.4, who places himself some twenty years after Cyrus's revolt: Glus, son-in-law of Tiribazus, makes a *symmakhia* with Pharaoh Hakoris; of course, Glus was himself the son of Tamos (Xenophon, *Anab.* II.1.3; Briant 1988a: 161).

- *Cyrus the Younger's Army.* There are a great many studies on Cyrus's Greek mercenaries: one may especially consult Roy 1967, Seibt 1977: 51–69, and Marinovic 1988: 24–36; cf. also the analysis by Cousin 1904: 133–212, which has the (rare) distinction of considering Cyrus's "barbarian" army (pp. 108–32): on this point see also Briant 1985b: 62–63; among the available sources, Westlake (1987) with good reason reevaluates Diodorus Siculus's contribution. On the size of Artaxerxes II's and Cyrus the Younger's armies: as usual, the figures offered by the ancient authors are both contradictory and barely usable: Diodorus (XIV.19.7) makes the ratio between mercenaries and barbarian army 1 : 7, Xenophon (I.7.10) 1 : 10, proportions leading to evaluations that are much too high (if only for logistical reasons); just as with Xerxes' army in 480, there is virtually no way of coming to a decision, other than by appealing to the eminently subjective notion of "reasonable figures": cf. most recently G. Wylie 1992: 123, who (following others) suggests the sum total of 30,000 for the rebel army. Is it necessary to add that the ancient estimates concerning Artaxerxes II's army are equally unacceptable? On these problems, see also now the discussions and analyses of Gabrielli 1995 and Descat 1995.

- *Propaganda and Legitimation.* On the crossing of the Euphrates and Xenophon's tale, cf. some remarks along these lines by Desnier (apud Briquel 1981) and by Briquel and Desnier 1983 (which I do not follow for all their interpretations) [[taken up again in Desnier 1995: 21–22, 25–26 (received at the very moment our final revision was being completed)]]; on the date of the event, cf. Cousin 1904: 307–8; on the crossing of the Euphrates by Lucullus, cf. Cumont 1905a. According to Weiser 1989, Cilicia was where Cyrus first struck coins with his image, coiffed with the royal *kidaris*. If the theory is correct, the message was clear: Artaxerxes was not facing any ordinary satrapal revolt. In his mind, Cyrus was already acting as a Great King would. But it must be recognized that the interpretation is highly speculative: anyway, see now Casabonne 1995b. In any case, I have the very clear impression that Cyrus was seriously in need of metal reserves: it is no doubt not out of the question that promises of bonuses were predicated on the victory to come (*Anab.* I.4.13; on these problems, cf. also Descat 1995).

• *Personal and Dynastic Loyalty.*   Cousin (1904: 92ff.) also holds grave doubts about the scale of defections to Cyrus, and he thinks (p. 92) that "the true strength of the king lay in the loyalty of his people," rightly supposing that it was a case of propaganda intended to legitimate the rebel's kingly pretensions; unfortunately, the author does not exhibit the same critical attitude when he characterizes Artaxerxes II as a weak prince, isolated within his harems (pp. 99–100); on Megaphernes' title *phoinikistēs*, cf. Lewis 1977: 25 n. 143; on the phrase "enemy land," cf. *RTP* 58 n. 4; on Tamos and Glus: cf. Briant 1988a: 161; administrative position and family of Orontes of Armenia: Osborne 1973: 517–22; Belesys and Gobryas in 401: at that date, Bēlšunu/Belesys was "governor of Ebir Nāri" (cf. Stolper 1987); the case for Gobryas is less certain; a man with that name was "governor of Babylonia" or "governor of the country of Akkad" in the first years of Darius II, with the last (currently available) mention dating to 417; it might be the same person (Stolper 1987: 396–98). [I wonder whether this Gobryas could be identified with the Gobares (*praefectus*) of whom Pliny (VI.30.120) recalls that he dug a canal to protect Babylonia from the Euphrates flood; according to him this was the Narmalchas (*regium flumen*). It is true that the risks of homonymy are great (as much in personal names as in river names) and that the text might just as well be referring to Gubāru in the time of Cyrus and Cambyses, both because several tablets mention a "Gubāru canal" (Joannès 1982: 326) and because there were confusions in the Classical authors among the various "royal" canals (cf. the presentation of the problem in van der Spek 1992: 236–39). Pliny might also be echoing a memory of the major works carried out by (the later) Gubāru in redigging/improving an older canal (cf. for comparison the text from the time of Xerxes, quoted by Joannès 1982: 326: recruitment of workers "for digging the Gubāru canal," not to mention that the canal is already found in a text from the time of Cambyses). The question must remain open.] I also note that according to Bivar (1961), one Artimas (he publishes a seal of his bearing his name in Aramaic), whom the author presents as holding an official position in Lycia, defected to Cyrus (subsequently, Shahbazi 1975: 119–24 connects him to Megabyzus's family); but the use of the "satrapal list" in *Anab.* VII.8.25 is very risky, and Bivar's theory thus carries a very high coefficient of uncertainty, especially because Artimas is not a specifically Persian name (cf. also the incidental remark of Dandamaev 1992a: 45); the name is very common in Caria (cf., e.g., Lipiński 1975: 166; Blümel 1990); furthermore, Robinson (editorial note following Bivar) stresses that the Lycian origin of the document is far from proved. Bivar's theory has nonetheless been repeated quite recently by Melikian-Chirvani 1993: 114–15; the latter, moreover, makes him the descendant of the Artimas whose name is written in Lydian on a footed censer, whose text (Artymalim) was published with commentary by Gusmani 1983: this all makes for quite a rickety scaffolding of hypotheses! Three final remarks: (1) If as I suggested in the previous paragraph Cyrus had run out of money (until the moment he was partly rescued by the *syennesis*), it has to be admitted that he did not succeed in winning over all the treasurers and other gazophylaxoi along the route, who continued to demand an authorized chit from the royal chancellery before turning over funds, which Cyrus was unable to provide (cf. for comparison the texts quoted in RTP 29 n. 3 and 49 n. 2, as well as my remarks in Briant 1989c: 328–29): a process of resistance no doubt illustrated by Cyrus's retaliative acts (studied in the text) in Lycaonia; (2) if Cyrus recruited so many Greek mercenaries, I am not convinced that it was only because of some intrinsic technical superiority that he recognized in them—it may also have been because a certain number of regular contingents from Asia Minor refused to defect to him; under this hypothesis, the call to the Greek mercenaries would reflect less a tactical choice than a political constraint; (3) some of the problems treated in this section have just been broached by Joannès 1995, who wonders (pp. 183ff.) why Cyrus took a secondary road along the east bank of the Euphrates; Joannès suggests a possible element of surprise (p. 185); he also thinks that this choice proceeded from Cyrus's distrust of some of his close associates.

- *Artaxerxes and Cyrus Face Off.* On the Median Wall, cf. Barnett 1963; see also Lendle 1986: 211–14 and Vallat 1989b, as well as the articles on the subject in NAPR 1 (1987) and 2 (1989), and now Gasche 1995; on the word "Arabia" in Xenophon, cf. Briant 1982b: 121–22 and Donner 1986 (also Joannès 1995); on the delays in Cyrus's progress, cf. the remarks in Cousin 1904: 317–21. It is particularly difficult to reconstruct the battle of Cunaxa, because of the contrasting and contradictory descriptions: cf. Bigwood 1983; G. Wylie 1992; and Erhardt 1994, whose discussion (pp. 1–2) bears a title ("Who won the battle of Cunaxa?") that says a great deal about the persistent uncertainties, and whose conclusion deserves to be quoted: "In short, Tissaphernes won at Cunaxa."

3. Artaxerxes the Victor

- *The Process of Relegitimation.* Royal propaganda in Plutarch's biography, cf. Orsi 1979–80. According to Cameron 1955: 96, these were the circumstances under which Artaxerxes authorized a foundation legend that made Cyrus into Mardes, the son of common peasants, and had fake inscriptions carved in the names of Ariaramnes and Arsames in order to discredit Cyrus's lineage. But, for all sorts of reasons (in particular, the way foundation legends are embellished), Cameron's interpretation is far from convincing. Besides, according to Shahbazi 1972b, the tomb of Gur-i Dukhtar (in the valley of Buzpar, southwestern Fārs), published by Vanden Berghe 1964 [whose high dating, before Cyrus the Great, is no longer accepted today: cf. Nylander 1966], was raised by Parysatis, on the model of Cyrus the Great's tomb (cf. fig. 2, p. 87 here), to lay to rest the meager remains of Cyrus the Younger (head and right hand); but, aside from the fact that the monument could just as well date to the end of the Achaemenid period or even the Hellenistic period (Stronach 1978: 302) and that the Ctesias passage (§59) quoted by the author actually seems to refer to a burial at Susa, one might reasonably doubt whether after such a fierce struggle the king would have authorized the erection of such a monument to the honor of Cyrus, which could have become a dangerous rallying-point within Persia itself (compare the political measures taken by Cyrus against the memory of the "rebel" Orontas: *Anab.* I.6:11◊: "no grave of his was ever seen"); in fact, the king had already made an exceptional concession to Parysatis by securing the head and right hand that had been cut off according to custom (Ctesias §58; Plutarch, *Art.* 13.2), since normally the head and hand of a usurper would simply be discarded/exposed (Strabo XV.3.17: *riptetai*), which is to say, probably left for the animals: cf. the fate of Cyrus's Greek *strategoi* who were decapitated (in Xenophon's version, *Anab.* II.6.29) and then "torn in pieces by dogs and birds" (Plutarch, *Art.* 17.7◊; above, p. 239 and chap. 2/9, pp. 93ff., on Persian funerary customs); this was probably the fate meted out so secretly by Cyrus the Younger on Orontas (entrusting it to the faithful Artapates), whence Xenophon's sentence, "From that moment no man ever saw Orontas living or dead, nor could anyone say from actual knowledge how he was put to death,—it was all conjectures, of one sort and another; and no grave of his was ever seen" (I.6.11◊).
- *Reward and Punishment.* On the career of Ariaeus, cf. Lewis 1977: 119 n. 78 and Hornblower 1994a: 78–79; on the possible modification of royal protocol and the chronological problems posed by the ancient texts, see Briant 1994e: 307–10 and chap. 14/1 above.
- *The Great King and His Armies.* On the Persians and their "military weakness" in Plutarch's *Artaxerxes*, Xenophon's *Agesilaus*, and Isocrates, see some reflections in Briant 1987b and 1989a; on the role of the Greek mercenaries, see the reflections of Seibt 1977: 63–69; and Rahe 1980, who makes the mistake, to my way of thinking, of considering it an established fact that the Babylonian *ḫaṭrus* no longer furnished soldiers: on the *ḫaṭrus* in the time of Artaxerxes II, cf. the material investigated by Joannès 1982: 4ff.; also Dandamaev 1992a: 18, and chap. 14/7: Darius II and His Armies, pp. 597ff.; we will return to all these problems later: chap. 17/3.

4. Conditions in Asia Minor and Artaxerxes II's Strategy (400–396)

- *From Sardis to Memphis.* Return of Tissaphernes to Sardis, cf. Lewis 1977: 138–39; Amyrtaeus at Elephantine, cf. Porten 1990: 19, who dates the papyrus *DAE* 7 [*AP* 35] to September 11,

400; but Lemaire (1991c: 200–201) proposes redating the Aswan stela (*DAE* 75) and considers it possible that Persian control of Syene could have lasted until 398; on the chronology of the first independent pharaohs, cf. also Traunecker 1979 and most recently Lloyd 1994; we may note finally that perhaps these pharaohs did not make a sharp break with the Persian court, if we go by an anecdote preserved by Phylarcus (apud Athenaeus XIII.609b): an (unfortunately unnamed) Egyptian king sent the famous courtesan Timosa to Stateira, the wife of Artaxerxes: the word used (*dōron*) without doubt refers to a "diplomatic gift," the kind well known between the pharaohs and Near Eastern kings. [The record of the Egyptian break was reviewed by A. Lemaire in a talk given in Paris at the colloquium "Égypte et Transeuphratène" (May 10–11, 1993) = Lemaire 1995a: 51–56.]

• *Artaxerxes, His Satraps, and the Asia Minor Front.* On the Sparta policy, cf. Lewis 1977: 139ff. and Westlake 1986; on Tissaphernes and Pharnabazus, cf. Westlake 1981; Evagoras's attitude: cf. Costa 1974: 46–50; *syennesis* of Cilicia: the theory of his political demise goes back to Erzen 1940: 114–20, but the author rightly remarks that no document exists to positively support it (at least until the nomination of Mazaeus/Mazdai around 350: cf. Briant 1994b: 124); it is however not entirely certain that at that time (400) Cilicia was transformed into a satrapy in the full sense, since the coins struck in Cilicia by Tiribazus, Pharnabazus, and Datames are not satrapal coins properly speaking but "karanic" coins (cf. Briant 1989c: 329); on the doubts that do need to be retained on this point, cf. Lemaire and Lozachmeur 1990: 146–47; and now Casabonne 1995b.

5. Agesilaus in Asia Minor (396–394)

• *The Defeat of Tissaphernes.* Agesilaus's offensive and the circumstances of the battle of the Pactolus continue to pose topographic and historical problems, because of contradictions in the ancient sources: see Dugas 1910, Foss 1978, and the analyses of Bruce 1967 (ad loc.), particularly pp. 150–56 on the battle of Sardis; most recently, cf. Cartledge 1987: 215–17; Botha 1988; Wylie 1992; De Voto 1988; Dillery 1995: 109–14.

• *The "Anabasis" of Agesilaus.* See especially Dugas 1910 and Bruce 1967, as well as Wylie 1992 (who rightly holds Agesilaus's strategic ability in low esteem); on the man and his campaigns, cf. the synthesis by Cartledge 1987, esp. pp. 180–218 (who also, pp. 217–18, revises downward the territorial ambitions assigned to Agesilaus by the ancient authors).

• *Persian Defenses Confronting Agesilaus's Offense: Satraps and ethnē.* On relations between the Persians and the interior peoples, cf. Briant 1976 and 1982b: 57–112 (chap. 16/18, pp. 762ff.). Orontes' title ("satrap of Mysia") has caused much ink to be spilled in the service of studies dedicated to reconstructing the "Satraps' Revolt" (chap. 15/7, pp. 656ff.); the validity of the information provided by Diodorus is accepted by Osborne 1973 (fully empowered satrapal government centered at Pergamum: cf. *OGIS* 264, lines 4–9), although Hornblower (1982: 176–78) thinks (unconvincingly, in my opinion) that toward 361, Orontes was still satrap of Armenia; cf. also Osborne 1982: 65–80 (where a profound discussion of the opposing views is found, in particular a vigorous reply to Hornblower, who thereupon reiterated his view in Hornblower 1994b: 220); Osborne's viewpoint is adopted by Moysey 1987; see also Weiskopf 1982: 108–18 and 1989: 70–76, who, while admitting that Orontes received a position in Mysia, denies the existence of an autonomous administration and compares Orontes' position to that of an Asidates, who was provided with land and estates; the author recalls that Diodorus's phraseology is very elastic and suggests that the same holds for Diodorus's mention of a "satrapy of Paphlagonia" (1982: 114); on this point, cf. also Robert (1980: 265ff.; cf. also 203–19), who without attacking head on the problem discussed here thinks it self-evident that the satrap of Paphlagonia resided at Gangra, not far from Ancyra, the very spot—we may note in passing—where the Paphlagonian leaders went to submit to Alexander in 334, with the king ordering them to obey the satrap of Dascylium, as in the past (Arrian II.4.1–2); let us add in passing that Paphlagonia is not devoid of Persian iconographic evidence: cf. Doncel-Voute 1984 (chap. 16/2, fig. 55, p. 699) and von Gall 1966; on Polyaenus VI.10 (Aeolid) and the fortifications of Asidates (Mysia), see RTP 190; Tuplin 1987c: 212–13; and Debord 1994.

• *The Persians and Agesilaus Face Off.*   On Spithridates and his estates, cf. Sekunda 1988a: 178–80; on his relations with Agesilaus and the limited character of the threat he posed at the time, cf. Weiskopf 1989: 23–25; coins struck in the name of a Spithridates are known, but this one's precise identification is problematic; he might be a satrap known from Classical sources in 334 (cf. Harrison 1982a: 416–18, Cahn 1989: 101); on Pharnabazus's reply to Agesilaus (*Hell.* IV.1.35–36), cf. the reflections of Lewis 1977: 150–51, and chap. 8/7: "The Dynastic Pact," p. 354.

6. Achaemenid Successes and Failures: From Asia Minor to Egypt (ca. 396 – ca. 370)

• *The Defeat of Sparta.*   Conon at Rhodes: Berthold 1980: 35–38 and Westlake 1983 [[and now *CAH* VI²: 67–70; 103–6]]; on the military operations in Asia Minor, cf. Lewis 1977: 142–47.

• *The Persians Caught between Athenians and Lacedaemonians.*   The position of Struthas (called "satrap of Ionia" in Tod II, no. 113) raises several problems that support an abundant litera-ture on the holders of the satrapy of Sardis and on the administrative delimitation of this jurisdic-tion during these years (cf. Lewis 1977: 118 n. 75; Weiskopf 1982: 88–93; Hornblower 1982: 37 n. 10; Petit 1988: 309–11; Chaumont 1990: 598; Hornblower 1994a: 77–78), but each of the solu-tions that has been suggested runs up against difficulties that appear difficult to surmount with cer-tainty. On the creation of the satrapy of Caria, cf. Hornblower 1982: 34–38 and Ruzicka 1992b: 16–20; against this (universally accepted) position, Petit (1988) has defended a paradoxical thesis: he says the Hecatomnids were never officially recognized as satraps by Artaxerxes; but, to use a li-totes, the proof lacks conviction (cf. my brief remarks in *Abst. Iran.* 12 [1989] no. 283 and Descat's, *Topoi* 3/1 [1993]: 265–66, as well as Hornblower 1994b: 215–16; on the status of Mausolus, see also chap. 16/18, pp. 767f.).

• *From Cyprus to Egypt.*   On Evagoras's policy, cf. Costa 1974: 48–56, Weiskopf 1982: 154–56, Collombier 1990: 35–37, and Maier 1994: 312–17; dynastic affairs in Egypt: Traunecker 1979: 401ff. (on the chronological problems, cf. also Tuplin 1983: 185–86 and Lloyd 1994); on the Athe-nian intervention in Cyprus (according to Lysias), cf. Tuplin 1983 (who dates the operations to 390–389). Phoenician inscription from Kition: published with commentary by Yon and Snyczer 1991, 1992 (I follow here the gist of their interpretation here).

• *The Initial Operations (391–387/386).*   The entire period ca. 391–381 poses major chrono-logical and historical problems, on which see Tuplin 1983 and the focus by Shrimpton 1991; the dates adopted in the text are with reservations (examination of the numismatic evidence [coins struck by Tiribazus] leads Harrison [1982a: 304–15] to date the second Cyprus expedition to 382–380 [and not 387–386], but his arguments are no longer compelling).

• *The King's Peace (386).*   See most recently the focuses of Urban 1991 and Badian 1991.

• *A Universal Conflagration?*   On the logical connection between the King's Peace and the resumption of Persian preparations for the Cyprus matter, cf. Sinclair 1978, and the interesting re-marks of Ruzicka 1983a (on the Clazomenae problem treated by this author, cf. also Aikyo 1988); concerning ancient texts on the general nature of the revolt, see the suitable thoughts of Weiskopf 1982: 161–92 (who I think, however, underestimates the threat posed at this date by Evagoras: cf. p. 190); Datames: Sekunda 1988b; on Cilicia and the numismatic evidence (coins struck by Tiri-bazus), cf. Lemaire and Lozachmeur 1990: 147, and Davesne 1979: 162 (but the proposed connec-tion with the elimination of the *syennesis* must, I think, be given up, for reasons stated above), and especially the systematic presentation by Harrison 1982a: 304–15, as well as Capecchi 1991: 85–95; on Datames' first campaigns, cf. Sekunda 1988b: 38–40; on the role of Hecatomnus, cf. Weiskopf 1982: 157–60 (who thinks that the 391–390 campaign ended quickly via an agreement with Evagoras, and that there is no trace of a rebellion by Hecatomnus, who, he suggests perhaps a bit excessively [p. 167], did not even participate in the expedition: "Diodorus interpreted his ab-sence as secret support"), and Ruzicka 1992b: 26–29 (also rebuts Diodorus's and Isocrates' presen-tations); on the "king of the Arabs," cf. Briant 1982b: 163–64. The theory of a quasi-collapse of

Persian domination in Palestine beginning with Artaxerxes II is presented (e.g.) by Eph‘al 1982b: 205–6, but on the basis of archaeological evidence that does not appear to me to support this conclusion with certainty (cf. also Stern 1982b: 254–55, whose chronology seems to me to apply instead to a later phase of the reign of Artaxerxes II, though it will remain unverified nonetheless, because archaeology has a strange tendency to require written documentation as corroboration; I am equally at a loss to understand the relation that Betlyon (1986: 636) seeks to establish between the appearance of the first Jewish coins around 400 and the "decadence" of the Empire. We must particularly emphasize the cruel absence of written evidence on the history of these regions in these years; the only possibility of glimpsing the intervention of the central authority is to date Ezra's mission to the 7th year of Artaxerxes II and to see it as an index of unrest stirred up by the Egyptian revolt (e.g., Cazelles 1954 [[Lemaire 1995a]]); here we will not reopen this debate, which is far from ready to die out (cf. chap. 14/5).

 • *The Offensive against Evagoras (387/386–383/381).* On the terms of the treaty imposed on Evagoras, cf. Weiskopf 1982: 178–92. For reasons presented in chap. 15/1 above, the tablet *ADRTB* no. −440 probably refers to the very beginning of the war against Evagoras; the text reads: "[. . .] the land Saminē, a famous city of the land Kupru, which for making [. . .]sundu of the land Iamuniammu which the king made [. . .]."

 • *The Egyptian Defeats.* See especially Kienitz 1953: 80–92 and Lloyd 1994: 346–48; the date of the campaign of Pharnabazus, Tithraustes, and Abrocomas against Egypt (Isocrates) primarily derives from the fact that Pharnabazus was recalled to the court around 387 (Xenophon, *Hell.* V. 1.28), from which it is deduced that Ariobarzanes succeeded him at that time (cf. Weiskopf 1982: 120–27 and 1989: 27–28); but many uncertainties remain (cf. Cloché 1919: 230–32 and 1920: 85–88); according to Moysey (1986: 10, 15), some coins attributed to Pharnabazus might have been struck in Cilicia between 386 and 383, at the time of preparation for the Egyptian expedition, but other possibilities exist: cf. Harrison 1982a: 315–21 and Lemaire and Lozachmeur 1990: 147, who suggest dating them instead to the 370s (that is, to the second expedition); concerning the possible offense-oriented mindset of Hakoris: note the discovery in Phoenicia of altar bases with the cartouche of Hakoris, which are generally taken to indicate an attempt at an Egyptian offensive (cf. Traunecker 1979: 435), but the interpretation remains uncertain (Lloyd 1994: 347 n. 50). On the Greek mercenaries on the Egyptian expedition, see Seibt 1977: 80–83, who notes particularly that it was the first time a Persian army included so large a number of Greeks but without offering a more detailed interpretation; according to Sekunda (1988b: 42), Datames adopted some components of Greek arms, and it was also he who first established a Persian infantry corps (Cardaces: Nepos, *Dat.* 8.2): on all these problems, see chap. 17/3 below. Nectanebo I's coming to power: Traunecker 1979: 435–36, Meulenaere 1963, Lloyd 1994: 357–59; possible kinship (by marriage) between Chabrias and Nectanebo I: Kuhlmann 1981: 276–78 [[but for the convincingly argued contrary view, see now Huss 1994b]]. Pharnabazus's expedition in 373: Cloché 1920: 88–99; Datames' participation in Pharnabazus's expedition is inferred from Nepos (*Dat.* 3.5; 5.1), but the text poses certain problems of interpretation that are presented and treated by Sekunda 1988b: 40–41; no one could believe that Artaxerxes would have endangered the Egyptian expedition to distract Datames in a campaign without glory against a Cataonian dynast (*Dat.* 4; 5.1–5), or that Datames would have suddenly rebelled at the very moment when he received the command of the army of Egypt on the pretext that a court cabal had sworn to lose it (§5.2–5): this would grant a rather naïve confidence to a text belonging to the genre of family saga; for these reasons, Weiskopf's reconstruction of Datames' career (1982: 205–7) strikes me as more satisfactory (even if it includes its share of speculation: we are now in the realm of comparison of likelihoods, nothing more: the author [pp. 207–9] thinks that after the victory over Aspis, Datames was promoted to satrap of Cappadocia).

 • *Artaxerxes and the Greeks.* See now also Seager, *CAH* VI²: 156–58.

7. Artaxerxes II, His Satraps, and His Peoples (ca. 366–359/358)

• *Diodorus and the "Great Revolt" of the Satraps: The Empire in Flames?*   In all that follows, I have been greatly influenced by Weiskopf's analyses (1982, 1989), which contain very innovative, very convincing interpretations rendering largely obsolete previous work (particularly Judeich 1892 and Meloni 1951); an up-to-date bibliography is found there, so I will not systematically provide references; but it must be recognized that Weiskopf's theses have been vigorously criticized by Moysey 1991–92; I must say that this is not my point of view (cf. Briant 1994b: 127 n. 45), while admitting that Weiskopf's work suffers here and there from certain weaknesses (cf. below on Orontes' planning): the problem is that Weiskopf 1982 (doctoral dissertation) has not been published, and the evaluations have been made exclusively on the basis of the minor work of 1989 (had it been the other way around, I doubt whether Moysey 1991: 120 could have criticized Weiskopf for not using the numismatic evidence, which, moreover, does not fully support some of the historical conclusions that Moysey 1989 believes he can draw concerning Datames' plans: below; see also Hornblower's criticisms, *CR* 40 [1990]: 363–65; 1994a: 84). On Diodorus's text specifically, see in particular Weiskopf 1982: 337–41, as well as Moysey 1975: 96–99 and 116–17; cf. also Briant 1989a: 38–39; on *IG* II² 207, see in particular the epigraphic and historical analyses by Osborne 1971, 1981: 52–54, 1982: 61–80, Moysey 1975: 254–65, 1987, Weiskopf 1982: 401–5, and myself in Briant 1994d; on Tod 145, cf. the contradictory views of Moysey 1975: 143–48 and Weiskopf 1982: 398–401 ("a display of diplomatic fantasy"), 1989: 84–85 (an analysis that has stimulated the lively criticism of Moysey 1991: 120; but, because of major uncertainties I recognize in the text, I do not think that this document, in any case, can be considered "a major stumbling block to W.'s thesis," unless one supposes, as Moysey does through a very willful formulation, that "only one context makes sense").

• *The Initial Revolts: Datames.*   In addition to Sekunda 1988b (which I do not follow on the beginnings of the revolt), I have been greatly influenced in this section by Weiskopf 1982: 197–220 and 418–25; on Datames' coinage struck at Sinope, cf. Harrison 1982a: 263–65 (by comparison with stratagems described by Polyaenus and Pseudo-Aristotle).

• *The Troubles in Western Asia Minor (366–361).*   Ariobarzanes: texts and commentary in Osborne 1983: 50–53, who raises the problem of the date; on relations between Ariobarzanes and Athens, cf. also Moysey 1975: 80–84 and Weiskopf 1982: 353–80; on Ariobarzanes' demise, cf. theories of Weiskopf 1982: 381–85, who thinks that his son Mithradates then went over to Datames' camp (on Weiskopf's genealogical theories, I must say that in part I share the reluctance of Moysey 1991: 117). Orontes: Weiskopf 1982: 395–98; 1989: 89–90; on the coinage attributed to Orontes, cf. ibid., pp. 388–94; see also Troxell 1981, but his dating to the 350s is certainly wrong: cf. Moysey 1989: 123–25; the role of leader that Diodorus says (XV.91.1) was accorded to Orontes by the other satraps is not explained; the argument fails if we recognize with Hornblower (1982: 176–78) that Orontes remained satrap of Armenia: but, on Hornblower's arguments, cf. the convincing critical remarks of Osborne 1982: 67ff. (despite Hornblower 1994a: 86); Artabazus and Autophradates: cf. Moysey 1975: 119; see especially the discussion of Weiskopf 1982: 423–29; death of Orontes: cf. Osborne 1973: 542–51; contra Moysey 1975: 109, who thinks that Orontes regained his command in Mysia. On *IG* II² 207 (sale of wheat by Orontes to Athens): cf. Briant 1994d, where I demonstrate that the deed does not in the slightest reveal a secessionist policy on the part of the satrap (see also Moysey 1987: 100 n. 100, but in the context of a chronological proof that does not persuade me: see chap. 15/9: "Artaxerxes III and Philip II," Research Notes, pp. 1005f.).

• *The Egyptian Front.*   On the (disputed) chronology and the problems raised by Tachos's offensive, cf. Cloché 1919: 212–18; 1920: 99–107, as well as Kienitz 1953: 96–100 and 180–81; Weiskopf 1982: 405–12; and Hornblower 1982: 174–75; on Cha-hap-imu and his kinship with Tachos and Nectanebo, cf. Meulnaere 1963; Tachos's offensive is the context in which was written (with an unfortunate degree of uncertainty) the (fragmentary) biographical inscription of the Egyptian Onnophris, "prophet of the statues of the father of the king, the general Tcha-hap-imou," who apparently accompanied Tachos (who is not named) when he "went to Asia"; comparison with Diodorus's version does not resolve all of the difficulties in the text, and it is not even impossible that Onnophris accompanied Tachos to the Great King's court (cf. von Känel 1980 and 1984: 198–201, who compares Onnophris with Udjahorresnet and Samtutefnakht; cf. chap. 18/4).

• *Orontes and the Egyptian Front.* Regarding Orontes in Syria (Trogus Pompeius, *Prol.* X), see the critique of Weiskopf (1982: 405–12; 1989: 81–84), who, however, in my opinion goes too far: I think it is misguided to throw out the only direct evidence in the record; cf. in contrast the unconvincing remark of Osborne 1973: 537; for his part, Moysey (1975: 106) thinks that Orontes tried to join the Egyptian forces in Syria; on the decree honoring Straton of Sidon, cf. in particular Moysey 1975: 244–53 and Weiskopf 1982: 458–59; Austin's (1944) attempt to infer from the decree that Athens had then taken part in the revolt against Artaxerxes is hardly persuasive; on the other hand, cf. Moysey 1987: 99 n. 27 and 1989: 120–21 on Hieron., *Adv. Iovinian.* I.45; on Straton's coinage, which has sometimes, since Babelon 1910, been thought to illustrate a pro-Egyptian policy, cf. Betlyon 1982: 9–10, 29–30: but the interpretation poses certain difficulties (cf. Moysey 1989). According to Diodorus (XV.92.5◇), "Tachôs . . . made bold to go up to the King by way of Arabia"; this mention immediately recalls what Arrian wrote (*Indica* 43.5) concerning Cambyses' soldiers and Ptolemy's troops, who chose to return to Babylon by the fearsome route crossing North Arabia (cf. Briant 1982b: 129, 132): but why choose this itinerary, if Tachos was then at Sidon (on the "normal" route, as also suggested by the decree honoring Straton, cf. Briant 1991b: 77–79)? I must declare myself incapable of responding reasonably to the question, which, moreover, may be moot anyway because of the meaning (unknown to us) that Diodorus assigns to the name "Arabia" (on the use of this word by Classical authors, cf. Briant 1982b: 120–22); not to mention "Syria" (cf. Sartre 1988). Ochus's campaign in Syria: Cloché 1919: 245–46; Weiskopf 1982: 410 and 460 n. 109; Tachos at the Great King's court: Briant 1985b: 57–58. On Tachos's and Chabrias's fiscal measures and their political repercussions in Egypt, cf. Will 1960; on the fragile internal situation of the pharaohs, cf. Meulenaere 1963: 93; Ray 1986: 149 and 256; 1987; as well as Briant 1988a: 155–58 and the reflections of Yoyotte 1992.

• *Back to Datames.* "Grandiose" plans of Datames: Olmstead 1948: 419, followed by Moysey 1975: 107–8 (n. 25) and Harrison 1982a: 411–13; cf. also Osborne 1973: 537 n. 104, who draws the rather surprising conclusion from Polyaenus's text that Datames, just like Orontes, got as far as Syria; position contrary to Weiskopf 1982: 424 (now see also the doubts of Hornblower 1994a: 87); on the coins of Tiribazus and Pharnabazus struck in Cilicia, cf. Harrison 1982a: 304–20 and Moysey 1986. The interpretation of Datames' coins (discussed in the text) is from Moysey 1989: 108–19, esp. 109–12; while emphasizing that it is a "conjecture," the author thinks that the comparison with Polyaenus is "a plausible explanation, given the long enmity toward the king and the precedent for such an invasion established by Cyrus the Younger" (p. 110); the author, without explanation, appears to think that Datames' goal was to drive Artaxerxes II from the throne, which appears to me highly debatable (Moysey 1975: 113–14 offers the same reasoning regarding Orontes, but neither is there anything in Orontes' coinage to suggest it proclaims royal ambition on his part: cf. Weiskopf 1982: 388–94; Hornblower 1982: 178–79; Moysey 1989: 123–25). Anu at Uruk (problem unknown to Moysey 1989): cf. Stolper 1990b: 561 (in the context of a strictly chronological argument); cf. also Kuhrt 1987a: 151 (observation made by Oelsner), and now especially Beaulieu 1992: 54–60; for the basis of his interpretation, the author compares (p. 110) the policy he attributes to the satrap with what he considers the spread of the cult "of the *Mesopotamian* goddess *Anāhita*" by Artaxerxes II (emphasis added): but, for all sorts of reasons, this comparison is totally invalid (chap. 15/8: Anāhita and Ištar, pp. 678ff.). On Datames' background, cf. Briant 1987a: 19 n. 47 and 27 n. 116, and (independently) Sekunda 1988b: 35–36, as well as Lemaire's studies on the Luvian name Tarkumawa found on certain coins *attributed* to Datames: cf. Lemaire 1989: 144–49 and 1991c: 203–5: "Datames was a local dynast carrying out the job of satrap, then commander-in-chief at the heart of the Persian Empire" (but without summarily excluding the other hypothesis: "Tarkumawa was a local Cilician dynast of whom we have not a single echo anywhere else").

• *Mausolus and the Revolts.* In general, see Hornblower 1982, Weiskopf 1982: 221ff., and Ruzicka 1992b: 15–75; discussions will be found there of many controversial aspects of Carian institutions (the existence or not of a Carian *koinon*, for example), which I do not think it useful to treat here in detail (on Mausolus's relations with the Carian cities, see now the remarkable document published by Blümel 1990); accession of Mausolus: Hornblower 1982: 34–40; regarding the phrase *patrōa arkhē*, it can without doubt be compared with a formula used in an inscription (*hoposēs [gēs/khōras] Maussōlos arkhē*), on which see the appropriate reflections of Hornblower 1982: 154; let us simply emphasize that the terminology does not imply that Mausolus occupied an exceptional situation vis-à-vis other satraps; from the Greek point of view, in fact, a satrap's territorial power could be designated perfectly with the word *arkhē* (cf. IG II² 207a line 15: *ek tēs Orontou arkhē*: see Osborne 1982: 73–74); on Mausolus's building projects, see Hornblower 1982: 223ff. (the degree of Hellenization and its forms are the topic of polemic between Gunter 1985 and Hornblower 1990a; cf. also the useful remarks of Sherwin-White, *CR* 34/2 (1984): 257–59, where additional bibliographical references will be found, as well as the analysis by Stamatiou 1989: 379–85 on borrowings from the Achaemenid iconographic repertoire and their injection into Greek forms; cf. also the remarks of Von Gall 1989: 505 and n. 2, and now the articles collected in Isager 1994)—a problem well illustrated elsewhere, in particular at Xanthus but at Sidon as well; on his foreign policy, cf. Hornblower 1982: 107ff. (with the reflections, pp. 152–53, on the possible "normalcy" of Mausolus's initiatives); on this point, cf. also Weiskopf 1982: 270–85, as well as the useful commentary by Moysey (1989: 126–30) on Mausolus's coinage; also, on a specific point (Mausolus's interference in Lycian affairs), Borchhardt 1993a: 78: a stela with the Carian double axe, he says, is evidence of burial on the spot of a Carian phrourarch who had settled at Limyra— a theory that seems rather weak to me; on satrapal duties of Mausolus, cf. Hornblower 1982: 137ff. and 161–65 on the problem of royal/civic taxes, on which point, see also Corsaro 1985 and Frei 1990: 166–68 and the text published by Bousquet 1986 (on Mausolus's position in the Empire, see also chap. 16/18 below, at the end). On the interpretation (Mausolus as a rebel) sometimes given to these anecdotes, cf. Weiskopf 1982: 232–35; on the texts mentioning conspiracies, cf. ibid. 252–56, who quite rightly stresses (pp. 230–31) that the Arlissis affair shows rather that at this date Artaxerxes supported Mausolus and that thus there was no proof there of any rebellious mindset on the part of the dynast (on Arlissis's position in the royal court, cf. the highly speculative remarks of Heltzer 1994: 116–19); on Tod 138.2, cf. also *BE* 1990: 276; on the accusations of lying made against ambassadors to the Great King, cf. Hofstetter 1972: 102–4; on Mausolus's behavior during the revolt, cf. Hornblower 1982: 170–82 (the passage is primarily devoted to a general discussion of the revolt: but cf. Osborne 1982: 67–72); while fully stressing the paucity of the record, Hornblower suggests that Mausolus did indeed enter into revolt (likewise Ruzicka 1992b: 76–89 in a discussion that is not the most satisfactory portion of the book); contrary position (which I adopt here overall) of Weiskopf 1982: 263–70 and 1989: 45–46 and 65–68 (a position contested by Moysey 1991: 119); we may add at this point that Mausolus's participation in the revolt has also been deduced from the Xanthus trilingual (cf. Dupont-Sommer 1979: 166–67); but this inscription must be left out of consideration, for it now appears that its date is later (below and chap. 16/5).

• *From Caria to Lycia.* On what follows, discussions will be found (often contradictory because of the weakness of the documentary record) in every article and work devoted to Lycia in the fifth and fourth centuries: Houwinck ten Cate 1961: 8–13; Childs 1981: 70–80; Bryce 1980 (article devoted specifically to Pericles) and 1986: 109–14; on Pericles, see the sources gathered by Borchhardt 1976b: 99–108, in the context of a description and interpretation of the dynast's *herōon*; the results of surveys at Limyra (compared with other satrapal or official residences) have recently been presented by Borchhardt 1990 and in Borchhardt (ed.) 1990: 75–84 (cf. now Borchhardt 1993a); the recent inscriptions pertaining to Pericles are published by Wörrle 1991 and 1993; on the Lycian dynastic coinage, see most recently Zahle 1989 and Moysey 1989: 130–34. On the place of Pericles (before his supposed revolt): in the very detailed and interesting description he gives of the friezes on the *hērōon* of Pericles, Borchhardt (1976b: 121–23) sees the west frieze of horsemen as an illustration of the parades held regularly in the satrapal courts imitating ceremonies in the central court (fig. 54, p. 673 here); according to the author, alongside Pericles the horseman dressed in Persian style (no. 22) can be identified as Artaxerxes III, "co-regent with his father, Artaxerxes II" (cf. color photograph [restoration] on the cover and p. 169 of Borchhardt [ed.] 1990, and also in Borchhardt 1993a: 49: "It is the young Artaxerxes III, who put down the Satraps' Revolt," and plate 21): there we have an expression of the "thesis of dependency" so often discussed by Borchhardt (cf. his 1983 article) — namely, that by doing so, Pericles recognized Persian sovereignty; on the political level the interpretation might be acceptable, because Pericles' urbanization program did not conflict with Persian supervision — a position recently restated by Wörrle (1991: 215–17), according to which Pericles' building activities at Limyra and especially his royal titulature (cf. also Wörrle 1993) should be seen as existing in the context of a political-ideological competition with Xanthus; on the other hand, as Borchhardt suggests, the identification of the future Artaxerxes is rather dubious (why Ochus, rather than his father, Artaxerxes II?). Pericles' conquests at Limyra: Weiskopf 1982: 289–90 and 332–33 (and pp. 211–13 on the problems posed by Artumpara/Artembares: stresses the uncertainty of the evidence; on this point, cf. also Wörrle 1993: 189–90 and the position of Keen 1992a below). Xanthus: on the Arbinas inscriptions, see their publication by Bousquet 1975 and 1992 (who, in agreement with Laroche and against Childs 1979, convincingly restates the restoration Kheriga/Gergis and not Kherei in the Lycian inscription on the Pillar); see also Savalli 1988; on the conquests of Arbinas, cf. Robert 1978b (with the important reservations of Bousquet 1975: 145, developed in Bousquet 1992: 177–78, 180–81: Arbinas used Caunus as the base for his departure); on the monument of the Nereids, its iconographic program, date, and author (Arbinas), see from now on the exhaustive publication of Demargne-Childs 1989 (which renders obsolete the interpretations of Shahbazi 1975: 104–8); I note in passing that in a recent update (*Topoi* 2 [1992]: 322), P. Demargne writes: "I must say that for the sculpted decoration which Childs and I described, many points appear open to criticism," and again, on Persian influences, "that resembles Persepolis, by bringing Persepolis to life; similarly in the hunting and war scenes"; on the siege scenes, cf. Childs 1978 (who stresses [pp. 91–93] that these are really historicizing scenes); on the audience scenes, cf. Gabelmann 1984: 43–49; concerning the political interpretation of Lycian dynastic monuments and inscriptions, we may also stress that the invocation of Greek gods is not unambiguous (cf. Demargne 1975 and Wörrle 1991: 216–17); the same may be true for some invocations of Lycian gods (Melchert 1993: 34 n. 4). Sarcophagus of Payava: cf. Demargne 1974: 61–87, as well as Bryce 1986: 111, and Shahbazi 1975: 135–48; on the Persian armaments in some of the war scenes, cf. Bernard 1964; on the Lycian inscriptions, cf. Laroche 1974a: 137–39; on the audience scene of Autophradates, cf. Gabelmann 1984: 59–61, who stresses its specificity, since according to him on the audience scene on other Xanthian monuments the dynast, not the satrap, is shown (cf. the presentation of the methodological problem on pp. 61–62, with discussion of Borchhardt's "dependency theory"); on the date (and its uncertainties), cf. Demargne 1974: 86 (Gabelmann 1984: 61 places it too assuredly at the moment of the Satraps' Revolt; Chaumont's chronological hypotheses 1990: 600–602 are baseless); on Autophradates and Xanthus, cf. also Weiskopf 1982: 290–91. On the "revolt" of Pericles, see Hornblower 1982: 181–82 (who stresses the thinness of the evidence), and particularly the painstaking analysis of Weiskopf 1982: 286–91, whose conclusions (local struggle and no participation in a general revolt) strike me as highly convincing. Cf. now the important work of Keen 1992a (chap. 7 is dedicated specifically to Pericles of Limyra), which I was able to consult through the author's kindness, but only after my manuscript had already been finalized; I will simply mention that, concerning the dynast's policy toward the Persians and the satrapal revolts, Keen develops views different from those espoused here; while he too thinks that the building program established by the dynast at Limyra and his own political ambitions did not at first conflict with the acceptance of Achaemenid supervision (illustrated by the Persianizing decoration of the *herōon* of the acropolis), nonetheless he believes that the dynast really did revolt around 370; according to him, this rebellion was caused by a desire on the part of the central authority to increase imperial supervision of the region (upon the death of Arbinas, two Persians, Artembares and Mithrapates, were sent by Autophradates to take command of western and eastern Lycia, respectively: the author makes it a precedent to the organization known from the Xanthus Trilingual under the satrapy of Pixodarus); Pericles would have been conquered around 361 and executed. There is nothing surprising about interpretive differences, because the documentation is hopelessly fragmented and ambiguous. Nevertheless, I stress that Keen was not aware of the new epigraphic discoveries published by Wörrle 1991, particularly, in this context, the inscription concerning the dynast's family: in his commentary, Wörrle (1991: 215 n. 62) resolutely takes the side of Weiskopf: as for the second document (the letter), the editor (whom I follow in the text) shows how it modifies our view of the dynast's power before and especially after his death (1991: 224–33, esp. 232–33).

• *A Summary of the Discussion.*   Basically, I object to the views recently expressed by Dandamaev 1989a and Petit 1993, for reasons laid out elsewhere (Briant 1993c; 1994b: 123–25). I must also share my doubts about a recent article by Moyses (1992; cf. also 1991) setting out his hesitation about Weiskopf 1989 and restating the grand ambitions of Orontes and the coordination of the revolts (pp. 162–64). Moyscy uses several passages in Plutarch's *Life of Artaxerxes* to state that the power of the aging Artaxerxes was considerably weakened by court conspiracies and that this situation certainly encouraged the rebellious satraps; all the while stressing (as in Moysey 1991) that "this new perspective on the health of the Persian Empire at the end of the 360s and the beginning of the 350s does not reinforce the traditional theory of the end of the Achaemenid dynasty as the 'sick man' of the fourth century" (p. 165), he nonetheless thinks that the king's physical and psychological weakness explains the vigor of the satrapal revolts: "The struggle within the court, the king's advanced age, [and his] paranoid nature ignited the volatile mixture of satrapal ambition and the forces of imperial disunity." This, I think, grants too much importance to Plutarch's view of the court conspiracies (cf. p. 161). Moysey 1991 criticizes Weiskopf for his hypercriticism of the fourth-century Greek sources that speak of the Achaemenid Empire (setting up, moreover, on p. 122, a very surprising comparison between Weiskopf 1989 and Balcer 1987, judging the latter more "plausible" [*sic*]); but on the level of historical method, it seems to me far more arguable that he himself accords this merit to a flat reading of such ideologized texts as Plutarch's *Life of Artaxerxes* and Nepos's *Life of Datames*: "In any case, there is no good reason for denying the validity of Plutarch's and Nepos' evidence" (Moysey 1992: 166; 120 and n. 23, and more specifically on Plutarch, see chap. 15/1: The Greek Authors' View, pp. 612ff. and chap. 15/2: Propaganda and Legitimation, pp. 621ff.. Comparison of the texts shows that Plutarch's "psychological portrait" of the aging Artaxerxes II is not truly descriptive but instead is included within an ideologically homogeneous whole, contrary to what the author suggests when like many others he contrasts Artaxerxes II and Artaxerxes III, while he himself objects to the "weakness" of Arses and Darius III (1991: 121; 1992: 167); but, if we read Diodorus XVI.40.5–6 in comparison with Diodorus XVII.30.7, we must "conclude" that Artaxerxes III was just as "weak" as Darius III or Artaxerxes II (cf. chap. 17/3: "Memnon, the Persian Satraps, and Darius III," p. 790). In other words, and even if we may regret the fact, the fourth-century Greek documentation does not truly allow us to prepare royal portraits that are properly individualized from each other. Finally, as I have tried to show, the king was actively supported by high officials, including the son that Plutarch portrays in the most unfavorable light—namely Ochus, to whom Artaxerxes II (in 360 or 359, or just before his death) entrusted an army to fight Tachos (successfully). Despite the obvious importance of the Great King's person, the survival of the system was thus not linked solely to his physical and mental health; the system possessed its own dynamic (illustrated, as it happens, by the role played by the crown prince: or, the prince who proclaims himself crown prince); this dynamic appears to me to have acted more in the direction of imperial unity than disunity. This is in a way confirmed by the end of the story, since, after all, if there really were several revolts (but not a coordinated general insurrection), it must be observed that the central authority prevailed! Rather than using Plutarch uncritically to derive the impression that since perhaps 370 the central power had been paralyzed by its dynastic struggles (1992: 164), the author might have taken a look at the Babylonian texts (see chap. 15/1 above): he would have taken into account that in 370 the king led his army in a campaign against Razaunda in Media (*ADRTB* no. –369; Stolper, *CAH* VI²: 239), and that three years later another tablet refers to a battle won by "the royal army, " *ADRTB* no. –366).

8. At the Heart of Power

• *In the Royal Residences.* On the building works at Babylon, cf. Vallat 1989a and Stolper, *CAH* VI²: 259–60; new palace at Susa: Vallat 1979 (inscriptions), Labrousse and Boucharlat 1972, Boucharlat and Labrousse 1979, Boucharlat and Shahidi 1987; and on the tomb (generally) attributed to Artaxerxes II at Persepolis: cf. Schmidt 1970: 99–102 and Calmeyer 1990a: 13–14 (under this theory, the inscription naming the bearer peoples published by Kent under the siglum A²P must be attributed to Artaxerxes II); on Artaxerxes III's buildings at Persepolis: cf. Tilia 1977: 68, 74, Roaf 1983: 128, and Calmeyer 1990a: 12–13; we may add in passing that according to Frye 1982 the Aramaic inscription on Darius I's tomb at Naqš-i Rustam *may* date to Artaxerxes II or III.

• *Artaxerxes II, Mithra, and Anāhita: Sources and Problems.* On the texts and depictions illustrating these divinities, I refer to the discussion in chap. 6/6 above; I remark in passing that, always following Plutarch (*Art.* 23.7◇), during the illness of Atossa (his daughter-wife), Artaxerxes II prayed to the Goddess Hera, "to this one alone of all the deities he made obeisance, by laying his hands upon the earth; and his satraps and favourites made such offerings to the goddess by his direction, that all along for sixteen furlongs, betwixt the court and her temple, the road was filled up with gold and silver, purple and horses, devoted to her"; Chaumont (1958: 165–66) thinks that Anāhita is hiding behind Hera; I do not see the basis for such a theory (already proposed without discussion by Hüsing 1933: 18), for never in Classical texts is Anāhita so designated, as well as the fact that earlier on (§3.2), Plutarch refers to Anāhita with the name Athena (Clemen 1920b: 87 and Boyce 1982:220 suggest identifying Spenta Armaiti behind Hera, for reasons that escape me altogether); it is true that seeking a pertinent goddess behind her Greek veil poses very delicate problems (on Hera at Hierapolis Bambyke, cf. Oden 1977: 55–58). Dinon' s mention of the *agalmata* of Water and Fire (confirmed for Fire by Maximus of Tyre: Clemen 1920a: 66): Rapp (1865: 45–46) sets himself to proving it does not contradict the statements of Herodotus and Strabo (I imagine a similar theory is followed by Boyce 1982: 221: ". . . fire, the only icon permissible for a true follower of Zoroaster," but without quoting Dinon; doubtless she is referring to the beliefs of the Parsees); I stress simply that in this case it is necessary to explain what the Greeks meant by the word *agalma(ta)* applied to Fire and Water, since the word is not at all ambiguous, and if (as is usual) we accept the the meaning 'cult statue' in Berossus, why should it be rejected in interpreting Dinon? As I stress in the text, the problem comes from the fact that we cannot assign a single monument to the command of Artaxerxes: on this point, cf. also the remarks of Rapin 1992b: 108–16. On the sanctuaries of Anāhita in Asia Minor: we have no reason to think that they go back to Artaxerxes alone; besides, Cooney's analysis (1965) of a female statuette found in Egypt suggests considering it a replica of one of the statues of Anāhita erected throughout the Empire in the time of Artaxerxes II—a theory that seems paradoxical to me, since Egypt was then outside the Empire. It is moreover entirely typical that Memphis is not precisely named in Berossus's list—which merely confirms the administrative value of the evidence ("The Imperial Realm," p. 680). A few supplementary remarks on Mithra, without venturing too deeply into a difficult and delicate subject:

1. On the basis of examining iconographic materials, Bivar often stressed the importance of the motif of the combat of lion and bull, in which he sees a reference to the gods of death in

various cultures and a sort of Mithraic syncretism; he also sees a Mithraic reference on some coins struck by Masaeus in Cilicia (Bivar 1975a; cf. also Bivar 1970); the theory makes me wonder;

2. The most fascinating document is certainly the Xanthus Trilingual: we know that the Aramaic version names the divine triad as follows: "L'TW (Latô), 'RTMWŠ (Artemis), and ḤŠTRPN' (*xšaθrapāti-*)," the last of which obviously names Mithra with the epithet "Lord of Power"; the discovery prompted important remarks from Mayrhofer (1973b: 277, 279; 1979: 184–85), a detailed commentary by Dupont-Sommer (1976), and a theory by Bivar (1988b; on the identification of this "god-satrap," Mithra and Sarapis, an equation that the author believes was widespread in the Achaemenid period); against Dupont-Sommer's position, Downey (1986: 304–5) supposes that it is unlikely "because of the lack of evidence of the presence of Mithra in Asia Minor at the date of the Xanthus stela"; but, precisely, I am convinced that Mithra was quite widespread, for reasons given elsewhere: *RTP* 460–62, based on late evidence to be sure, but nonetheless usable; on epigraphic documents of an earlier period naming Mithra in Asia Minor, see also Lipiński 1975: 176–84 (*magus* of Mithra in Cappadocia in a Greek-Aramaic inscription) and *BE* 1983 no. 437 (*kata magous Mithrēn*, in Cappadocia as well);

3. Michaélidis (1943: 99) suggested the presence of a Mithra cult in Egypt in the Achaemenid period, but see the contrary arguments of Yoyotte 1952: 167 n. 5; Schaeder's theories (apud Aimé-Giron 1939: 36) appear no more solid; it is clear that the presence of *magi* at Elephantine (*DAE* no. 45 [*BMAP* 4]) does not necessarily imply the existence of a sanctuary dedicated to Mithra; on this point, cf. also M. Boyce in Boyce and Grenet 1991: 359–60 (but on the basis of very late documents that in themselves have little to say);

4. In Babylonia, we know little (Bivar 1975b refers mostly to late documents); according to McEwan 1983: 122–23, a Babylonian has a name meaning 'servant of Mithra'— evidence that the author considers "an important document for the existence of a Mithraic cult in Babylonia" at the time of one of the Artaxerxes; but see *contra* Dandamaev 1992a: 171 (Babylonian name and patronymic);

5. The title found in A³Pa (*Mithra baga*) has long presented many problems, both philological and historical (relation to the seventh month of the Persian calendar, *Bagayādi-*): on this point I refer to the recent treatment by Sims-Williams 1991 (with note 18 on A³Pa);

6. The existence of a monumental statue of Mithra in the main temple of Ai-Khanūm remains too hypothetical (Grenet 1991) to erect theories on it of possible antecedents in the Achaemenid period (evidenced, by the way, by a frieze of walking lions, p. 148).

• *Droaphernes and the Sardis Statue.* The inscription was published by L. Robert 1975, who dates it to Artaxerxes II; it is clear that he was led to this dating by his theory of an "Ahura-Mazda (Zeus) Lawgiver (*Baradates*)" rather than a "Zeus of Baradates." Robert's theory was first contested by Frei 1984: 19–21 (whom I quoted without following him in Briant 1986a: 439 n. 9); Gschnitzer (1986) shows that it concerns a family cult, but, regarding Men of Pharnaces, I have reservations about following the theory he develops (pp. 50–51) on the basis of an identification (unlikely, in my view) with the Parnaka of the Persepolis tablets and the ancestor of the satrapal dynasty of Hellespontine Phrygia (I note in passing that A. van Haeperen-Pourbais [1984] works out a theory of the Indo-Iranian origin of the deity Men, not failing to cite the Men of Pharnaces [pp. 236–39], which she interprets in a completely different fashion from Gschnitzer). I add, as I have remarked above (chap. 12/7 on *dāta*, p. 510), that 'lawgiver' would instead be rendered *dātabara*. By setting up a direct relationship with Berossus, L. Robert has quite naturally, we might say, dated the inscription to Artaxerxes II (1975: 314–17; cf. p. 310: "I opt for Artaxerxes II Memnon"); but, inasmuch as a number of historical-religious inferences suggested by the editor no longer hold, on grammatical rather than speculative grounds (besides Frei 1984 and Gschnitzer 1986, see Schmitt quoted by Chaumont 1990: 580–81, and Briant 1996b), the dating of the inscription could just as well be as early as 426 or as late as 365 (cf. remarks to this effect by Chaumont 1990: 583–84, 591, 608; it is surprising that Gschnitzer [1986: 45 and n. 3] did not consider this)—all the more so in that the chronological location of the dedicator (Droaphernes) in the satrapal *Who's Who* poses problems that cannot be resolved at the present time (cf. the discussion by Weiskopf 1982: 98–107 and 1989: 91–93 [low date], without knowing the works of Frei, Gschnitzer, or Chaumont 1990; he finally ends up favoring the low date but without persuasive argument, because his reasoning is essentially based on an extremely unconvincing discussion of the word *hyparkhos*: I do not see what keeps us from thinking that Droaphernes held a subordinate position during Pissuthnes' satrapy: cf. *Ead.* 593). Whatever the case may be on this point, the Zeus–Ahura-Mazda theory of L. Robert (1976: 314) no longer holds if we eliminate the rest of the argument (which has unfortunately eluded Boyce in Boyce and Grenet 1991: 205; Boyce seems not to know the work of Gschnitzer and knows Frei's only from my reference to it in Briant 1985a: 189 n. 13, where I made the mistake of arguing against Frei): it is strange indeed that Gschnitzer (1986: 46) continues to think, quoting L. Robert, that Zeus does designate Ahura-Mazda, since this would appear utterly unlikely in view of his own interpretation; it is hard to imagine a Persian in Sardis founding a family cult in honor of an "Ahura-Mazda of Baradates"; Corsten (1991: 175–78), even though he knows and quotes the work of Frei and Gschnitzer, also adopts the Ahura-Mazda theory (by thinking, in order partly to resolve the contradiction, that it might be an Ahura-Mazda assimilated to a local god: p. 177 n. 66), and he suggests that the inscription reports the institution of a state cult that he places in close parallel with Berossus, because the king would have been simultaneously promoting the worship of both Ahura-Mazda and Anāhita; but, and this is exactly the point, at Sardis there was no state cult; more convincingly, Frei (1984: 21) imagines instead an indigenous deity (*einheimische Gottheit*)—perhaps quite simply Lydian Zeus, as I have suggested elsewhere (Briant 1993a note 19; this example shows once more the difficulties in recognizing an epichoric deity [whatever it may be] behind the polysemous name of Zeus and the risks in postulating syncretisms: cf. CS 38 with the commentary of Meshorer-Qedar 1991: 18). To end on this note: there is no longer any basis for the chronological link postulated ever since L. Robert between Artaxerxes II's edict and Droaphernes' initiative (see also "Back to Berossus," p. 679): I take up the matter and discuss it in Briant 1996b, where I return in particular to *andrias* (human not divine statue, in my opinion).

• *Anāhita and Ištar.* On the iconography, cf. chap. 6/6 above; on Plutarch, *Art.* 27.4: I note to begin with that the story is also told by Justin (X.2.4), but in a very different version: Aspasia "was dedicated to the cult of the Sun, which forbade her any carnal relations with men"; it seems that here we encounter a confusion between Mithra and Anāhita, as in the Herodotus passage (I.131) over which gallons of ink have been spilled (most recently Corsten 1991, who if I am not mistaken does not know Justin's text); royal oblate at Arbeles: cf. Lipiński 1982: 117–21; dedication to Anaitis Barzochara: *BE* 1968 no. 538 and Schmitt 1970 (*BE* 1971 no. 669); cf. also *BE* 1979 no. 432, close to Sardis (hierodules of Artemis and Persian names). M. Boyce (1982: 201–4) thinks that Plutarch's text on the royal initiation implies that Anāhita-worship existed in Persia before Artaxerxes II (which appears beyond doubt); from this she draws the conclusion that the reform actually went back to Darius II, and Parysatis played the principal role, because Darius II's wife is depicted as rendering "burning devotion to Ištar-Anāhita" (p. 218); this theory, which is not based on a *single* document, is totally unlikely (Hüsing 1933, which Boyce [p. 218 n. 50] did not use, already attributed to Parysatis a decisive religious role, with the aid of mostly disastrous arguments): M. Boyce (1982: 203–4) in fact suggests that the cult statues (whose spread she attributes to Darius and Parysatis, then to Artaxerxes II in the context of the war against Cyrus) were copied from the Babylonian model of Ištar; this interpretation was already defended by G. Gnoli (1974: 126ff.): Anāhita was somehow fused with Mesopotamian Ištar—an interpretation that, in my opinion, poses several historical problems; Gnoli (1974: 129) also locates Artaxerxes' decree in the war against Cyrus the Younger; he too sees in it "the realization of a process of assimilation of Mesopotamian traditions begun long ago and going back to the Medes"; the Babylonian theory seems to me difficult to sustain when at the same time the same author insists on Anāhita's role as "dispenser of the royal investiture" (pp. 127, 129: confronting Cyrus the Younger); the assertion is also found in Moysey 1989: 110, who on the basis of this conviction proposes a highly doubtful interpretation of Datames' revolt (see chap. 15/7: "Back to Datames," p. 666). The links between Anāhita and Ištar cannot be denied (the iconography is sufficient evidence), but, in my opinion, the Berossus text cannot really be understood unless it is placed in its properly Persian context; under this hypothesis, it is in fact Persian Anāhita, and not a Babylonized Anāhita, whose statues Artaxerxes II ordered erected and whose worship he promoted. On the "Babylonization of the dynasty" and the ambiguities of this phrase, see my reflections in chap. 16/10 below. [[I will note finally that the identification Artemis/Anāhita in the Xanthus Trilingual, as has just been proposed by Desnier 1995: 33–36, raises considerable reservations, which I will explain elsewhere.]]

- *Back to Berossus.* I repeat here, adding some detail, an interpretation already presented in Briant 1984b: 98–99 and 1986a: 430–31. Gnoli (1974: 129) and Boyce (1982: 203–4) place Artaxerxes' edict (Berossus) in the context of the war against Cyrus the Younger; for his part, Weiskopf (1982: 107, writing before the work of Gschnitzer and Frei, but repeated in Weiskopf 1989: 91–93) sees in the Droaphernes inscription a response of Autophradates, satrap of Sardis, to the revolt of Ariobarzanes; he even bases his preference for the low dating on this argument, the weakness of which he had previously stressed (apud Hanfmann and Mierse 1983: 256 n. 10): this suffices to state the unreliability of the theory, which no longer had a basis from the moment when it became virtually impossible to hold that Zeus designated Ahura-Mazda (above, and Briant 1996b).

- *The Imperial Realm.* On the responsibilities of the satrap of Bactra, cf. Briant 1984b: 71–74, on Darius III's Indian elephants, cf. Briant 1995d. On the Upper Satrapies, I believe I must now abandon an interpretation presented earlier (1990b: 50–51), because a reexamination of the context leads me to qualify my suggestion and envision an alternative theory, which I consider more acceptable, because of the general context of Diodorus's statements (which I had not analyzed sufficiently in Briant 1990b). Here is what is going on: upon returning from his Egyptian expedition, Artaxerxes III generously rewarded the men who had distinguished themselves there. Diodorus spotlights Mentor and Bagoas especially, who achieved exceptional positions in the court hierarchy, greatest "of all the friends (*philoi*) and relatives (*syggeneis*) . . . Bagoas . . . administered all the king's affairs in the upper satrapies (*en anō satrapeiais hapanta dioikōn*)" (XVI.50.7–8◊). It is quite striking to find the expression *Upper Satrapies* appearing in this context, which Diodorus uses so often in the era of the Diadochi and which is found in a number of Hellenistic authors to designate the countries of the Iranian Plateau and Central Asia. Does the intended parallelism with the naming of Mentor imply that at Bactra a general command of the satrapies of the Iranian Plateau was created, or already existed? In other words, did there exist a precedent for the situation so described in the Seleucid period, with a royal representative at Bactra and another at Sardis (on this Seleucid organization [a theory formulated by Bengtson 1946], cf., e.g., Robert 1983: 177–78, but the traditional title "viceroy" strikes me as unfortunate; besides, Bengtson's theory has been challenged by Musti 1965: 157–60 and 1966: 107–11; reply by Robert, *BE* 1966, no. 377bis)? As preparation for responding, it is a good idea to place these mentions by Diodorus into the textual and contextual logic that governs his entire discussion of Egyptian affairs and the weakening of the royal power. He reports how in Egypt Mentor and Bagoas, reconciled after a serious altercation, had entered into an agreement of cooperation (*koinopragia/koinōnia*), which, according to Diodorus, explains their joint power before the king (§50.6–7). The mention of the missions and powers that are then granted them leads the reader quite naturally to think that Artaxerxes dumped the running of the Empire on them, from Bactra to Susa; for example, "Bagoas . . . rose to such power because of his partnership with Mentor that he was master of the kingdom (*tēs basileias kyrios*)" (50.8◊). This discourse itself must be placed in a larger context, since—in the highly directed vision of Diodorus—the cooperation between Bagoas and Mentor is obviously the particular expression, or even the realization, of a general policy that in Egypt had led the king to divide the command among three Greek-Persian teams (cf. chap. 17/3: "Command Structure," p. 789). Diodorus's entire discourse structure (or that of his source) is thus perfectly coherent, but it is precisely this coherence that lets fly serious doubts about his credibility. We may remark in fact that Bagoas seems to have resided principally at the central court, to go by the tale of Diodorus himself and as is implied by his title of Chiliarch (I do not see that this justified Goukowsky's statement, 1978: 33, that Bagoas participated in the siege of Perinthus in 341; his n. 47 on p. 258 does not cite any relevant document). Furthermore, Mentor was certainly not some sort of governor general of Asia Minor posted to Sardis—where Rhosaces, "satrap of Ionia and Lydia," who had also taken part in the Egyptian campaign, certainly did reside (Diodorus XVI.47.2✧); Rhosaces was succeeded at an unknown date by his brother Spithridates/Spithrobates in the same position (Diodorus XVII.20.6; Arrian I.16.3). The titles Diodorus assigns to Mentor vary from one line to the next: "chief command in the coastal districts of Asia (*en tois parathalattiois meresi tēs Asias hēgemōn megistos*)" (XVI.50.6–8), or *satrapēs tēs kata tēn Asian paralias* (as usual, Diodorus uses the word *satrap* in a very vague way), and again *stratēgos autokratōr* (52.5). Diodorus again states a little further on that Mentor "was in charge of the war against the rebels." At first sight, then, it appears that Mentor received assignments normally entrusted to a *karanos*, namely, the coordination of troops based in western Asia Minor, on a temporary mission. But this is certainly an illusion, once again created by the partiality and imprecise terminology of Diodorus's source. It seems clear that in Greece Mentor's place in the imperial hierarchy has been distorted in the same way as Memnon's (cf. chap. 17/3: Memnon, the Persian Satraps, and Darius III, pp. 790ff.): it can scarcely be doubted that it comes from an Athenian source, as is shown in particular by a decree enacted by Athens in an anti-Macedonian context (327–326), which exalts the members of Pharnabazus's family through a descendant, Memnon II (Memnon I's grandson or nephew): in this decree, it is recalled that Mentor "saved those Hellenes who fought in Egypt, when Egypt was taken by the Persians" (Tod no. 199; Schwenk 1985 no. 58). At the same time, it must be stressed that the significance of the phrase *Upper Satrapies* itself is not entirely devoid of ambiguities, to the extent that it depends on the point of view of the observer (cf. Briant 1990b: 49 and n. 15), as emerges very clearly in another Diodorus passage (XIV.98.4; cf. Hornblower 1982: 37 n. 10 and Petit 1988: 311), and as is also implied by the vocabulary used by the ancient authors to exalt the *Anabasis* of Agesilaus. Given this situation, I am led to conclude that: (1) Diodorus's source was thinking rather of the hegemonic role he attributes to Bagoas in conducting affairs at the center of power (XVI.50.8; cf. XVII.5.3–6 and chap. 17/1)—a center of power that, in relation to the assignment attributed to Memnon in Asia Minor, was naturally considered to be in the High Country (*anō*); (2) the distortion that leads Diodorus astray is intended above all to magnify Mentor's role, by placing him parallel to the position attributed (wrongly) to Bagoas in the east of the Empire. (It is also true that the discrediting of the Mentor text does not necessarily discredit the position attributed to Bagoas; nonetheless, both the general context and the pervasive distortions of Bagoas's role at court tend to discredit all the information transmitted by Diodorus.)

• *From Artaxerxes II to Artaxerxes III.* Artaxerxes II's date of death: cf. Parker and Dubberstein 1956: 18–19; Plutarch (§30.9) has Artaxerxes die at the age of 94, after a reign of 62 years, which is manifestly erroneous (cf. Lucian, *Macr.* 15; Moysey 1992: 161 n. 10); it may also be doubted whether Darius was 50 years old when he was seated as crown prince (Plutarch §26.4); Plutarch's presentation implies on the contary that the decision goes back to shortly after the battle of Cunaxa; Darius was without doubt born around 424 (cf. Ctesias §45), so he was about 25 around 400 (hence the attempts to correct the manuscripts in this direction); besides, Justin's version (X.1.2) can scarcely be accepted: he claims that the naming of Darius ran contrary to established practice (*contra morem Persarum*), which was "that the scepter does not pass to other hands until the death of the prince"; on the contrary, "Artaxerxes crowned his son Darius during his lifetime": obviously, Justin (same source as Plutarch) was confused by Artaxerxes' bestowing the *kidaris* on his son (Plutarch); there is certainly nothing in this tradition to confirm the *Doppel-königtum* defended by Calmeyer 1976b (cf. pp. 69–70); on Justin's text, cf. also the critical remarks of Ritter 1965: 22–23. Change of Ochus's name to Artaxerxes (regnal name; Diodorus XV.93.1): cf. Schmitt 1982c: 85 and 89–90 and Stolper, *CAH* VI²: 239 n. 17; like his predecessors, the new king connected himself to his father and ancestors (*A³Pa*). We may note that Polyaenus tells the story of an Ochus who, upon the death of his father Artaxerxes, with the collusion of high court officials, "concealed his father's death for ten months . . . and sent letters in his father's name ordering the recognition of his son Ochus as king. When Ochus was recognized as king everywhere, he then revealed to all the death of his father and ordered royal mourning according to Persian custom." The text could refer either to Artaxerxes I's succession or to Artaxerxes II's; despite the contrary opinion of Lewis (1977: 71 n. 144, not without reservations), I have chosen the former solution for reasons given in Briant 1991a: 5–6 and recalled in chap. 14/6: "Legitimacy and Propaganda," p. 590. The Artaxerxes II/Artaxerxes III theory is also adopted by Moysey 1992: 165 (who, n. 28, seems to suggest, for no good reason, that Justin 10.3 reinforces Polyaenus 7.17), to better support his theory that the Achaemenid court was utterly disorganized because of the weakness of an aged king (he even has to push the dynastic struggles back toward 370); here I will simply remark that the character traits attributed by Polyaenus to Artaxerxes ("feared by his subjects") and Ochus ("feared being scorned") are scarcely in harmony with the portrait painted by Plutarch, to whom Moysey grants so much credit throughout his article (cf. my criticisms in the Research Notes to chap. 15/7: "A Summary of the Discussion," p. 997).

9. The Wars of Artaxerxes III (351–338)

• *Artaxerxes III and Artabazus.* The sources for Artabazus's revolt and Chares' role are conveniently gathered by Moysey 1975: 295–317. Recent research has shown that what has traditionally been called (wrongly) the "Second Satraps' Revolt" never became widespread or particularly disturbing to the central power. The disagreements concern three points of unequal importance: (1) First, the possible participation of Orontes; aside from the fact that his presence is never mentioned, the evidence that remains in dispute (IG II² 207: sale of wheat by Orontes to the Athenian strategoi) does not prove in the least that Orontes rebelled a second time, whether the decrees are dated to the 360s (so Osborne 1983: 72–80 and Weiskopf 1982: 401–5, with nuances) or to 349–348 (so Moysey 1987 and Ruzicka 1992b: 121), since, even under the second hypothesis the satrap's behavior fits perfectly with ordinary administrative behavior (Briant 1994d). It must be recognized that we know nothing of Orontes after the brief mention in the *Pergamum Chronicle* (OGIS 264): cf. the differing reconstructions by Osborne 1973: 546–51 and Moysey 1975: 189–95 and 1987. The *Pergamum Chronicle* mentions (line 9) that "then Orontes, having given over/entrusted the town [Pergamum] to Artaxerxes, died"; this could refer to Artaxerxes II or Artaxerxes III, and the act could relate to the moment when Orontes returned to the king's side (Diodorus XV.91.1); if, as has been presumed above (chap. 15/7: "Orontes and the Egyptian Front," p. 664), Orontes in fact returned to Ochus/Artaxerxes III, he must have received his reward, which could well have been his reintegration in Armenia, where his son was in 331 (Arrian III.8.5) and apparently still was in 316 (Diodorus XIX.23.3); (2) Mausolus's participation in the revolt (which Moysey 1975: 170–74 does not rule out, although not without contradictions) is also not attested anywhere; the aid he offered the rebellious allies against Athens in 357–355 (cf. Hornblower 1982: 211–15) does not at all imply a break with the Great King (as Moysey has to recognize; see Ruzicka 1992b: 95–96); as in the previous period, Mausolus's policy does not conflict with Achaemenid interests proper; (3) the interpretation of the evidence of the Scholiast to Demosthenes 4.19 (order given by Artaxerxes III to his satraps to discharge their mercenaries) poses many problems: on this, see chap. 17/3: "The Great King and the Satraps' Mercenaries," p. 791. On Artabazus's exile in Macedon, I do not understand the doubts about this tradition raised by Hammond and Griffith 1979: 309 n. 4.

• *Failure in Egypt, Revolt in Phoenicia and Cyprus (351–345).* Let us emphasize that we know nothing about the expedition against Egypt in 351, except for its unhappy outcome (this expedition may be what Aristotle is referring to [*De Inund. Nili* §6, ed. D. Bonneau 1964]: planning to attack Egypt, Artaxerxes Ochus "prepared to reroute the Indus as though it were the same river as the Nile, when he learned it had crocodiles like the Nile"; on this passage, see some remarks by Calmeyer 1982: 169–70, and more recently Bosworth 1993: 415–16). On its disastrous consequences for morale at Sidon, according to Diodorus: Kienitz (1953: 101) thinks that "it made an enormous impression on the eastern Mediterranean world," because he postulates that the Phoenician revolt dates to 350 or 349, as an *immediate* response to the Egyptian events, which is exactly what remains to be proved; on the chronological problems, cf. the remarks of Leuze 1935: 193–95 (where there is also a discussion [193ff.] of the functions of Mazaeus and Belesys); on the origins of the Phoenician revolt: Elayi (1987: 63ff.) wonders at length about the burden of tribute but without being able to draw any conclusion, given the poverty of evidence; as I suggest in the text, if the revolt is to be placed in this context, it is instead because of the burden of war contributions; on Tennes' policy: the contradictions in Diodorus's text (Mentor's role) have been well set forth by Weiskopf 1982: 505–9; Tennes' coins confirm his revolt, since after a few years they no longer show the king in his chariot (cf. Babelon 1910 II.2: 575–77; also Betlyon 1982: 16–17, not without some chronological guesses); Aradus and Tyre: Diodorus refers to the existence of an important city (*polis axiologos*) called Tripolis, made up of three distinct cities, named for Tyre, Aradus, and Sidon, where the Phoenicians met from time to time (*synedrion*; §41.1), but without making a direct connection with the revolt (it seems instead to be a digression about Phoenicia in this period); some time later, to justify abandoning the city, Tennes claims to be going to "a common meeting of the Phoenicians" (§45.1◇); in fact, Diodorus notes that Tennes had pressed the Phoenicians to make a bid for their independence (§41.3◇) and that after the destruction of Sidon, the other Phoenicians made their submission to Artaxerxes (§45.6), appalled by the fate meted out to Sidon (§45.2), but it must be emphasized that at no point does he mention the presence of contingents from Tyre or Arad alongside the Sidonians: did the other Phoenician cities remain anxiously cautious? The texts, finally, pose two administrative problems: (1) concerning the possible status of Sidon as Achaemenid satrapal capital (hotly disputed), I will simply mention that the Berossus passage analyzed above (see chap. 15/8: "The Imperial Realm," p. 680) as well as its importance in the time of Darius III (e.g., Quintus Curtius III.13) appear to me to confirm unambiguously that Damascus then remained the capital of the satrap of Trans-Euphrates—which obviously does not exclude the possibility that high Persian officials resided at Sidon, as Diodorus XVI.41.2 has it anyway (on the paradise at Sidon, cf. Clermont-Ganneau 1921; the contrary reasoning by Petit 1991: 173–74 is circular); (2) the structure of Tripolis continues to support differing analyses: cf. Galling 1964: 191–94 and 204–9, against which Elayi 1987: 78–81 takes a position; see also Elayi 1990b, J.-A. G. Elayi 1992b, the remarks of Stern 1982b: 242, and Verkinderen 1987: 293; let us stress in any case that Tripolis, certainly, represented an Achaemenid naval base of the utmost importance (cf. Arrian II.13.2–3: *neōria*).

• *From Sidon to Jerusalem and Jericho.* The ancient texts on the Jewish deportations and the revolt of Jericho are quoted by M. Stern 1974: 194 and 1980: 421–22, and by Barag 1966: 8–9; Barag (as well as Kienitz 1953: 102 and several others) sees it as proof of the revolt of Judea, but it must be remarked that the archaeological evidence offered by Barag is much less conclusive than he thinks: on this, see Stern 1982b: 242 and 255, as well as the short but clear summary by Oded 1977a: 500–1; more recently a (papyrus) document has been found in a cave near Jericho; the editors (Eshel and Misgav 1988: 175–76) suggest (by quoting in turn the texts on the exiles of the Jews) that the presence of a document in a cave cannot be explained except by a very unstable situation in the country, thus repeating the sort of argument followed to explain the presence of documents in the Wadi ed-Daliyeh; but these are precisely dated, and the reality of a Samaritan revolt at that time (332–331) cannot be doubted: the inferences drawn from this purely hypothetical comparison thus appear to me to be subject to caution (on the document, cf. also Heltzer 1992c: 174–75); furthermore, like their predecessors, the authors do not fail to note the internal chronological contradictions of the literary corpus (p. 176 n. 54). What might be supposed is that at a late date, among the Jews, the figure of Artaxerxes III took on odious characteristics that came to be dressed up with Greek and Egyptian traditions (cf. Josephus, *Ag. Ap.* I.194; II.129–33); without wishing here to review all the discussions that have taken place on this subject, we might in fact imagine that the expedition led by Holophernes in the book of Judith represents a sort of historical romance created on the background of the Persian expedition against Phoenicia in 350–340 (we find "the same" Holophernes in the Cappadocian court legend transmitted by Diodorus Siculus XXXI.19.2–3: Holophernes comes to aid Ochus in a battle against the Egyptians); under this theory, "Nebuchadnezzar, king of the Assyrians," represents Artaxerxes III; on this subject, see *inter alia* Clamer 1952: 491–93; most recently Heltzer 1989a: 99–100, who also thinks of Artaxerxes III, while postulating a Jewish revolt at this date, which does not appear necessary to me at all; cf. also Schwartz 1949: 75–77, who, citing Jerome, thinks that Nebuchadnezzar represents Cambyses, while Sulpicius Severus prefers Artaxerxes III: p. 77 n. 3; there remains the story reported by Josephus (*Ant.* XI.297–301): a conflict between Bagoses and the high priest Jōannēs; but, contrary to a theory that connects Bagoses with Bagoas, the chiliarch of Artaxerxes III, we would do better today to consider that he was Bagohi, governor (*peḥā*) of Jerusalem, to whom the Jews of Elephantine sent a petition in 410 and another in 407 (*DAE* 102–3 [*AP* 30/31–32]): cf. Marcus 1937: 457 note g and 499–501, Oded 1977a: 501, and more recently Grabbe 1992a. On the Judea and Samaria of this period, see also chap. 16/7.

• *The Reconquest of Egypt (343–342).* Bickerman (1934b: 77–82) dates the expedition to winter 343–342, which is generally accepted today (cf. Lloyd 1988b); on strategic and tactical matters and for a comparison with the expedition led by Antigonus in 306, cf. Hauben 1975/76.

• *Artaxerxes III in Egypt.* Coin of Pharaoh Artaxerxes (written in Demotic), see Mørkholm 1974, Shore 1974, and Lloyd 1974: 352 (drawings); we may also note that among certain chronographers the reign of Artaxerxes is not recognized in Egypt before 339–338 (Lloyd 1994: 359 and n. 110); on the later reputation of Artaxerxes, see above all Schwartz 1949, esp. pp. 69–70 (traces the tradition back to Manetho).

• *Mentor in Asia Minor.* For reasons given above (see the Research Notes on chap. 15/8: "The Imperial Realm," pp. 1001f.), I can hardly believe that Mentor, with the title of *karanos*, would have received the command of western Asia Minor (viewpoint expressed *inter alia* by Ruzicka 1992b: 120–22). On Philip and Hermias, I will not list all the bibliography, but I am very hesitant about the interpretation that makes this affair a revelation of Philip II's Achaemenid ambitions (e.g., Hornblower 1994a: 94); I prefer to follow the conclusions of the fine analysis carried out by Weiskopf 1982: 516–21.

• *Artaxerxes III and Philip II.* The problems broached in these paragraphs have generated innumerable studies; I will cite them only selectively (on Philip II's policy toward Persia, I find myself close to the "minimalist" analyses of Hammond-Griffith 1979: 458–62, 484–88, 517–22; see chap. 18/1). From the Achaemenid point of view, does the order given to the "satraps on the coast (*hoi epi thalattēs satrapai*)" (Diodorus XVI.75.1◇) imply that a general mobilization of the forces of Asia Minor had been decided on (so Hornblower 1982: 45 n. 69 and 1994a: 95–96)? We must remark that the phrase recurs frequently in Diodorus/Ephorus, and it does not necessarily have a technical sense, just as the usage of the word *satrapēs* is vague and lax in this author (cf. Weiskopf 1982: 307–8 and 473–74). Treaty between Philip II and Artaxerxes III: accepted, for example, by Momigliano (1992: 154–55 and n. 13, p. 192), who without excluding it entirely, is much more cautious about the truth of the collusion between Philip and Hermias (1992: 155 and n. 15); on the treaty (also accepted by Wirth 1972: 143), see the serious doubts of Hammond and Griffith 1979: 485–87; cf. also Bosworth 1980a: 229–30, who, presenting the various chronological theories, suggests that the treaty might have been made by the satrap of Hellespontine Phrygia (which merely defers the problem and, I stress, presupposes that a satrap could conclude a treaty of this sort on his own initiative, which I doubt). The greatest difficulty, it will be understood, comes from the rather hopeless nature of our evidence: it is quite difficult for example to date the "Persian plans" of Philip II (see the interesting reflections of Errington 1981b: 76–83 [Philip's decision came late; cf. also Ruzicka 1985b], with the discussion by Borza 1990: 228–30); historians sometimes tend to plaster equivocal documents onto ideas *a priori* (if they're not doing the opposite!): so Moysey (1987: 97), who thinks that IG II^2 207 is from 348 and infers from this that at that date the satrap (Orontes) sent wheat to Athens because "he wished to stop Philip before he became a threat to his own territory"; the sole objective of this entire (in my opinion disastrous) reconstruction is to justify the chronology that Moysey proposes for the Athenian decree and consequently for the change in Orontes' career. I return below to the initial Macedonian operations in the time of Philip II: chap. 18/1 (pp. 817ff.).

Chapter 16
Lands, Peoples, and Satrapies: Taking Stock of the Achaemenid World

Introduction: In the Steps of Alexander and on the Trail of Darius

• These introductory pages do not requre long, erudite notes. [[On the use of sources from the beginning of the Hellenistic period, see already chap. 10/1: Diachrony and Synchrony, pp. 389ff. with the corresponding Research Notes.]] I would simply like to add two correctives of the historiographical kind:

(1) I have long insisted on the absolute necessity of close familiarity with Achaemenid history in order to be able to deal with Alexander's conquest (and with Alexander's historical sources for supplementing the Achaemenid materials)—since the first edition of my *Alexander the Great* (1974) and my study of the Zagros peoples (Briant 1976): cf. particularly in a 1977 article (= RTP 357–403; cf. Nylander 1993: 146, who ranks me implicitly and good-naturedly [p. 143] among the "renegade" Classical scholars); still more explicitly in a 1979 article = RTP 291–330; cf. p. 306: "as detailed a knowledge of the Achaemenid Empire as possible is an absolute research necessity"; it is in fact clear that progress achieved in our knowledge of Achaemenid history is immediately reflected in the field of Alexandrine history (cf. the prefatory notes to my *Alexander the Great*[3, 4] = Briant 1986d and 1994a)—especially so because I continue to think that, despite being so specific, the period 334–323 is a special phase of the Achaemenid history of the ancient Near East (RTP 328–30). [[On the Achaemenid–Hellenistic transition, see most recently the articles in *AchHist* 8: *Continuity and Change* and, on the decolonization of Achaemenid (and Hellenistic) history, the viewpoint of Oestergaard 1991.]] I note with satisfaction that this opinion, which I have long held, preached, and illustrated [[cf. my interview in *L'Histoire*, May 1995]], is now widely shared, by "Classicists" (not the "renegades"!) as well, who for a long time had not kept up with the Achaemenid problematics and evidence (cf. RTP 505 n. 41): see, for example, F. Will, *Gnomon* 64/1 (1992): 68–70, who, reviewing a work on the Hellenistic period, writes, "Indeed, can we understand Alexander's Empire, and then the Hellenisitc kingdoms, without good knowledge (I know it has its limits) of the Achaemenid Empire?" (p. 68); while lamenting that the progress of the author's reflections is not explicitly located in historiographical continuity, we may measure it by recalling what he previously wrote of "the psychology of Alexander, without which no understanding will ever be possible of this series of events that was to change the face of the world" (*AncSoc* 10 [1979]: 79); I hope that reading and taking into account the output of the Achaemenid scholars of the '80s and '90s will push back the "limits" that, not without a certain subjectivity, É. W. assigns to knowledge of Achaemenid history (see the skepticism in Hornblower 1994a: 48, who, for reasons that escape me, thinks that, "in the present state of our knowledge, it is not possible [to write] a history of the Achaemenid Empire in the fourth century").

(2) In the following pages (and more in chap. 17 than chap. 16), there will be much question of a suspect notion and an obsolete phrase, "Achaemenid decadence" (a problem already touched on in the preceding chapters and Briant 1989a; cf. also Sancisi-Weerdenburg 1987a–b and 1989a, who rightly insists on the ideological heritage transmitted by Rawlinson 1871; in a very different ideological contest, I would gladly add Gobineau 1869: 340–41; 348–49; 352, who, referring to the fourth century, speaks of "bloody palace intrigues, . . . general demoralization, . . . a court less and less concerned with the Empire's affairs, . . . the use of Greek, Carian, Phoenician, Egyptian, Thracian *condottieri* . . . [so much so that the Empire was nothing more than] an enormous mass that could no longer hold up under its own weight": it gives us the impression of a preview of the

1007

"colossus with feet of clay"!). Concerning the phrase, I share the hesitation of H. Sancisi-Weerdenburg (1990: 267), who recommended eliminating the words "growth" and "decline" from the discussion and concentrating on a problem expressed more neutrally—namely: Did or did not the system continue functionally and efficiently (cf. Briant 1994b: 116 n. 18)? This is precisely the problem that guides me in the following chapters. The problem is that this historiographic phase is not yet universally recognized: I would like to say that reading recent books and articles (Dandamaev 1989a and Petit 1993, on which see Briant 1993c and 1994b) has convinced me, even if other more nuanced opinions are available today (e.g., Hornblower 1994a: 45–46), that it is necessary once and for all to wring the neck of this historiographical ghost of "Achaemenid decadence," hoping that I will be able to strike the deathblow (but on this point I maintain a reasonable skepticism, as I do for the closing statement of Badian 1987: 38 concerning the arguments over the Peace of Callias). I am fully aware that the discussion risks trapping me on the terrain chosen or imposed by those who adhere to the notion of decadence (or decline!), but I believe that the exceptional fecundity of this interpretive approach makes it necessary once and for all to systematically and exhaustively carry out the task consisting of demonstrating the extreme methodological weakness of their arguments, to which the first prerequisite is the construction of an exhaustive catalog of the sources (which they have not done themselves), and to conduct a detailed textual and contextual analysis—that is, an analysis that is not reduced to purely impressionistic evaluation (cf. already chap. 12 above on Xerxes, chap. 14/7 [Darius II and His Armies, pp. 597ff.], and chap. 15 *in toto*).

1. Sources and Problems

• On the satrapal organization of Darius III (and Alexander), we already have several good analyses: Julien 1914, Berve 1896: 1, 253–90 (table); the article by Petit 1990: 206–19 is incomplete, and that by Jacobs 1994b reached me too late to be able to take into account; a useful collection of information will also be found in Seibert 1985; I will not systematically refer to it in the notes (nor to the notices of Berve, which obviously I have used, as well as those of Heckel 1992); I will merely point out in passing my criticisms and reservations on this or that interpretation (to the extent they fit into the framework of my presentation); conversely, I do not think it worthwhile systematically to cite Engels 1978, which appears to me marred by disastrous method: has the author ever asked himself what the Achaemenid Empire was? I seriously doubt it: a reading of his section on Persia in 331 will show this; as for the mathematical-statistical postulates he claims to employ, they rest on illusion, which is a pity, since the work's primary objective remains extremely interesting.

2. The Satrapy of Dascylium

• Weiskopf (1982: 483) discusses the idea that Arsites belonged to the satrapal dynasty of Dascylium; his position of satrap of Dascylium is not always textually certain until after 341–340 (Pausanias I.29.10); Greco-Persian relief from Paphlagonia: Doncel-Voûte 1984; see also von Gall 1966 on Persian-type tombs in the region; on Sinope, cf. the appropriate remarks of Descat 1990b: 546–47; coins of Datames and Persian generals at Sinope: cf. Harrison 1982a: 255–65 and Harrison 1982b; on the Bithynian princes Bas and Zipoithes, cf. the notes of Berve nos. 208 and 338; on Heraclea, consult Burstein 1976, where the sources are quoted and commented on (one of the main sources is Memnon of Heraclea: *FGrH* 434); on the portrait of Heraclea, cf. Akurgal 1986; "Greco-Persian" stelas: the literature is considerable (cf., e.g., Borchhardt 1968; Metzger 1971; Starr 1977; von Gall 1981–83; Radt 1983; Cremer 1984; Sekunda 1988a: 188–94): see now Nollé 1992; seal impressions from Dascylium: cf. most recently Kaptan-Bayburtluoglu 1990 (who is preparing an edition of them); on the label "Greco-Persian," cf. the critical remarks and illuminating suggestions of Root 1991 and 1994; on the Rhodians and their Persian relatives, cf. the notes of Berve nos. 152 (Artabazus), 206 (Barsine), 497 (Memnon); on the role of Memnon and Pharnabazus between 334 and 332, cf. chap. 18/1. Without being able to achieve full certainty (given the conditions of the discovery in a private collection), it is possible that the wood beams bearing paintings published by Calmeyer 1992a come from a tomb in the Dascylium region; whatever the facts are, the interest of these paintings cannot be overestimated; the author sees them as one of the very rare examples of *narrative* representation in Achaemenid art (here "Greco-Persian" in the traditional sense): one of the scenes (procession, pp. 9–12) recalls identical scenes on stelas from the Dascylium region: according to Calmeyer, the war scenes (pp. 13–17) reflect Darius's expedition against the Scythians; the material could also be dated around 490 (pp. 16–17); no doubt this item will (justly) stimulate many comments in years to come (including perhaps in the context of studying relations of influence between the satrapy of Dascylium and Macedon).

3. From Sardis to Ephesus

• On Spithridates' district, we also have coins (perhaps) struck in his name: Harrison 1982a: 416–18 (with caution) and Cahn 1989: 101; Achaemenid military colonies: cf. Briant 1984b: 92–94; lookout on Mt. Tmolus: cf. Greenwalt 1995 (archaeological indications). Excavations at Sardis: they have been published regularly in the series *Archaeological Exploration of Sardis* and synthesized in Hanfmann and Mierse 1983; we can follow their progress in the reports in *BASOR*, and most recently Greenwalt, Ratté, and Rautmann 1994 and Greenwalt 1995. On Plutarch's text (*Lysander* 3.3): cf. already Briant 1985a: 181–82; Megabyzus/Bagabuxša: Benveniste 1966: 108–13; the coins of Tissaphernes at Astyra have been published by Cahn 1985; the author places them in 400–395, but the date adopted here is more easily justified (cf. Descat 1991: 36); on Thucydides' and Xenophon's passages on Tissaphernes, cf. Lewis 1977: 108; cf. also Picard 1922, esp. pp. 606–18, but his comment (p. 160; cf. p. 610) on the *Hellenica* (I.2.6) is sheer fantasy: "Tissaphernes [proclaimed], in the *hiera khōra*, a holy war: this assured him the support of the rustics, who hastened without delay to the aid of the endangered goddess" (Xenophon's phrasing instead leads us to believe that the satrap ordered the Persians of the low country to bring their contingents); nor can I see the basis for the author's claim (p. 611) that the Megabyzus "was in fact the equal, in Ionia, of the satraps or principal local delegates of the great king." On the sanctuaries of Anāhita in Lydia, cf. L. Robert's many articles (1948a, b, c; 1975, 1976; *BE* 1963 nos. 219–23) as well as Diakonoff 1979, Briant 1984b: 92–94, 1985a, and *RTP* 460–61; since then Robert 1987 and Boyce and Grenet 1991: 197ff.—while nonetheless stressing that the late date of the evidence poses a methodological problem as soon as the intention is formed to study cultural contacts between Persians and local populations (cf. presentation of the problem in Briant 1985a: 176–81; M. Boyce's contrary position in Boyce and Grenet 1991: 236–39, esp. p. 238); I think the hypothesis of total fixedness of Iranian religious traditions in Lydia is untenable, especially as soon as we recognize (*contra* Boyce, p. 205) that the Droaphernes inscription makes no reference at all to Ahura-Mazda and that the religious prohibitions were added long after the Achaemenid period (cf. Briant 1996b, which withdraws certain earlier interpretations, in particular Briant 1986a: 429–30 and 1987a: 20–21). Ephesian Artemis and Sardian Artemis: the Lydian-Aramaic inscription (Cowley 1921) has been republished by Lipiński 1975: 153–61; we may also note that a Greek funerary inscription of the third century B.C. (of unknown provenance) invokes "Artemis—Median Artemis and Ephesian Artemis and all the gods" (inscription published by Oikonomides 1982); Sherwin-White 1982 suggested seeing Median Artemis (attested nowhere else) as a reference to a Persian deity, "probably Anāhita"; after seeming to have made the same suggestion (*BE* 1982 no. 280 ["Anāhita?"]), L. and J. Robert treated Sherwin-White's suggestion quite cavalierly (*BE* 1984 no. 339), without providing any justification for their ironic skepticism; the theory (adopted, for example, by Corsten 1991: 171 n. 45) seems appealing to me nonetheless: it would be another example of a joint prayer to "Anāhita" and Ephesian Artemis: under these conditions, would the former designate the Persian Artemis of Sardis, attested in 322 by Pausanias VII.6.6? On the inscription of the sacrileges, see basically Masson 1987b and Hanfmann 1987, and the commentaries on a previous publication in *BE* 1963 no. 211, 1965 no. 342, 1966 no. 369; the Ephesus inscription in honor of a Sardian has been republished and commented on by Robert 1967: 32–36; the dating of both comes from palaeographic analysis (cf. Robert 1967: 34, "second half of the fourth century, and doubtless toward the beginning of this period"); on the status of Sardis, cf. my discussion in Briant 1993b (where full bibliographical references will be found; to the arguments offered there, add Herodotus IV.45✧: existence of a "tribe called Asias in Sardis," which is also attested epigraphically: Briant 1995c); on the place and personal names of the Mnesimachus inscription, cf. Buckler and Robinson 1912: 28–58 (on Beletras, cf. Masson 1969); on the personal names in the inscription of sacrileges, see Hanfmann 1987: 5–7 and especially Masson 1987b: 231–39; also Benveniste 1966: 105 on Ratopates, and Grenet 1983: 376 on Oumanes/Vohumāna, found at Ai-Khanūm (without knowing the Ephesus inscription but recalling concerning him, after Robert 1975: 323 n. 60, that an Omanes is known at Magnesia around 244; cf. RTP 196); Carians at Sardis: Pedley 1974, Greenwalt 1978b: 42–45, and Gusmani 1975: 79–111, 1982; Nannas inscription: Masson 1991: 670; Hieracome and Hierocaesarea: Robert 1948b, 1976: 36ff. ⟦Wikander (1946: 85), Chaumont (1956: 169) and Boyce (1982: 201–2) think that Tacitus's Cyrus (III.62) is not Cyrus the Great but Cyrus the Younger, a position that seems scarcely necessary to me (cf. already RTP 459); this view is connected (particularly by M. Boyce) with a very dubious interpretation of the role attributed to Parysatis in this matter (see chap. 15/8: "Anāhita and Ištar," p. 678); the hypothesis is repeated by Corsten (1991: 171 and n. 43) in the course of a (very strict) argument that tries, taking off from a comment by Herodotus (I.131), to establish that the worship of Anāhita was introduced to Lydia in the time of Xerxes or shortly thereafter⟧; Hypaipa: Robert 1976; on the Artemis sanctuary in the Mnesimachus inscription, cf. Buckler and Robinson 1912: 26–28 and Descat 1985; Mitradastas: cf. Gusmani 1964: 23–24 and Barnett 1969; Artemis and Anāhita at Sardis: the assimilation is suggested by Hanfmann 1987: 5, but I find no decisive evidence (cf. Briant 1993a n. 22); Artemis Coloe: Lane 1975, Robert 1987: 297–314, 323–25 and Merkelbach 1991 (the inscription dating to Caesar was published and commented on by Hermann 1989); archaeological and iconographic evidence of Persians in Sardis: cf. Akurgal 1961: 171, Mierse in Hanfmann and Mierse 1983: 100–106, Melikian-Chirvani 1993; Persian words in the Lydian-Aramaic inscription of Manes: cf. Lipiński 1975: 156–58 (the author suggests Artaxerxes III, while Mierse [Hanfmann and Mierse 1983: 105] dates the document to Artaxerxes II); seal of Manes: Masson 1987b (fig. 57, p. 704 here); seal of Mitratas: Barnett 1969a and, more generally, Boardman 1970; add Pœtto 1985 (scene of Royal Hero killing a lion) and Lemaire 1992 (Persian-inspired seal with a Lydian legend). On the process of Persian-Lydian acculturation and the preservation of Lydian traditions, see also the provocative articles by Ratté (1989) and Melikian-Chirvani (1993). To finish with this point, I note that in the inscription of sacrileges Hanfmann (1987: 5) wants to see evidence of "a forceful missionary expansion undertaken by the Ephesian Artemis during the Persian era," but the bases of this interpretation seem evanescent to me; nonetheless, the attack on the Ephesian sacred envoys poses a real problem: given the long history of relations between Ephesus and Sardis, it may relate to special circumstances of which we have no knowledge; by way of *hypothesis*, I wonder whether the episode might not have taken place in the context of the first Macedonian expedition, during which Ephesus was occupied by the Macedonians and then retaken by the Persians (cf. Arrian I.17.11); in any case, the facts themselves trace the political limits on relations between Sardis and Ephesus, which were certainly not idyllic, whether or not Ephesus had gotten caught up in the Greco-Persian wars. Greek advisers to the satraps: cf. the remarks of Lewis 1977: 14; on the naturalization of Orontes, Ariobarzanes, his sons, and their advisers, cf. Osborne 1982: 52–54 and 1983: 50–53.

4. From Celaenae to Halicarnassus

• On Alexander's siege of Celaenae, cf. Briant 1973: 45–46 and Billows 1990: 41–42; *tetrapyrgia*: Briant 1973: 80–89 and *RTP* 56–62 (not without contradictions); on the route of the royal road, see most recently Müller 1994, and Debord 1995 (who thinks it did not pass by Celaenae); on Gordion, see especially Mellink 1988: 228–30, who evaluates the many Persian or Persianizing iconographic discoveries in the city and its environs (see also Sekunda 1991: 129–40); on the excavations of Gordion, cf. also De Vries 1990, who suggests that the destructions of buildings around 400 were due to an earthquake (and not to Agesilaus's attacks); at Gordion have been discovered [and excavations continue], aside from a hoard of siculi (still unpublished) and many seals (whose publication was assigned to E. Porada: cf. Masson 1987: 110), two Aramaic inscriptions, one on a seal (cf. Mellink 1988: 228), the other in ink on a fragment of Greek pottery (perhaps including an Iranian name derived from *dāta*: De Vries 1990: 400); finally, a name appearing in Hellenistic inscriptions (Mistraboutas) could be Iranian (ibid. 404; but cf. Roller 1987: 128 and BE 1990 no. 770: "a good Phrygian name"). On the boundaries of the satrapy, cf. Briant 1973: 47–53; we have no evidence that would allow us to date the creation of the satrapy of Greater Phrygia: Weiskopf (1982: 476) thinks that Xenophon, *Anab.* I.2.7–9 attests to its existence in 401, which seems to me far from certain (no more than for Plutarch, *Them.* 30.1, can one go back to Artaxerxes I); my theory is based mostly on the Arrian text I use (I do not understand how or why Petit [1990: 207–8] denies satrapal authority to Atizyes and seems to suggest that Greater Phrygia belonged to Sardis in 334); I note in passing that the Iranian diaspora of Celaenae (Robert 1963: 349) appears in the *Persica* of Timothaeus, around 400 (cf. Francis 1980: 53 n. 1, 69, 79 and Henrichs 1986: 287; see also Weiskopf 1982: 476–77 on Tithraustes, who he thinks was not satrap, and p. 526 n. 13 on the Arsames of Polyaenus VII.28.2); the Persian presence in Phrygia is also attested in late documents: two dedications (*BE* 1979 no. 512 and 519), one invoking the *theoi Hellēnōn kai Per sōn*, the other, various Greek deities and *tōn idiōn pantōn Dii Persōn*. On the cultural ties between Lycia and Milyas, see the example of Karaburun (chap. 13/8: The Case of Lycia: Text and Image, pp. 558ff.); on the region, cf. Bosworth 1980a: 157–58 and, more specifically, Hall 1986 (but the theory [p. 144 n. 16] that the connection of Milyas to Lycia signifies the Great King's recognition of the conquests of Pericles of Limyra seems to be void of all foundation); Arrian (I.24.5): P. Savinel (*Arrien*, Paris, 1984) translates: "Milyas, which is part of Greater Phrygia (*esti men tēs Megalēs Phrygias*), but which, at this time, was connected to Lycia (*syntelei de es tēn Lykian*)"; the translator appears to me to introduce a chronological distinction (nebulous at that) that is not explicit in the Greek text; this distinction is even clearer with Robson (LCL): "It belongs to Greater Phrygia, but was reckoned then as part of Lycia" [the current edition of LCL, trans. P. A. Brunt (1976), reads similarly]; but I maintain that the Greek text is construed with two present indicatives; the opposition signaled by *men* and *de* thus is not diachronic but synchronic; therefore, we must, it seems to me, grant to *syntelein* a sense it frequently has, 'to contribute [financially]', with the formula *eis Lykian* expressing that Milyas was part of the same tribute district as Lycia (many examples listed in LSJ, s.v. *synteleō* III.2; also Bertrand 1990: 149 n. 29), from which I infer that Milyas, attached to the satrapy of Greater Phrygia, paid its portion of tribute with Lycia, from which it had thus recently been separated (on this point, cf. also the discussion by Berve 1926, I: 256). It is easy to understand that when Halicarnassus and other Carian strongholds continued to resist obstinately, Alexander had to make changes: Nearchus was made "satrap of Lycia and the country bordering on Lycia as far as Mount Taurus" (Arrian III.6.6✧); subseqently (after 331), Lycia was attached to Greater Phrygia (cf. Quintus Curtius X.10.2: Briant 1973: 75–76). On Ada, see most recently the discovery of the tomb of "a Carian princess" (Özet 1994); the identification on the basis of skeletal remains (Prag and Neave 1994) is, as is frequently the case, inconclusive (cf. the addendum p. 109). *Xanthus Trilingual*: on the texts and translations, I am obviously close to the edition by Dupont-Sommer, Metzger, and Laroche in *FdX* VI (1979) [[to which should now be added the new suggestions of Lemaire 1995c]]; the date of the inscription has been fixed in June–July 338, that is, year 1 of Artaxerxes III, by Dupont-Sommer (1974: 138–42); but this date brings on insurmountable historical and chronological difficulties, since, on the one hand, all the other sources show that Pixodarus became satrap in Caria in 341–340 and, on the other, this new date in any case cannot be reconciled with what is known of the history of the Hecatomnids (except by imagining, with Dupont-Sommer, rather unbelievable circumstances); the only way to resolve these contradictions is to imagine, as Badian (1977b) does, that the Artaxerxes in question is

Artaxerxes IV, the throne name taken by Arses, son and successor of Artaxerxes III (it is especially vexing that SP 1 does not give his name; on the Babylonian text carefully cited by Badian, cf. now van der Spek 1993a: 96, who expressly reinforces Badian's position); in his most recent article (1979: 166–69), Dupont-Sommer repeats his suggestion, without fully discussing Badian's theory (cf. 1979: 166 n. 1); for excellent reasons, most historians (but see Asheri 1983: 108–10, and more recently FdX 9/1 [1992]: 37, as well as Borchhardt 1993a: 7) nonetheless think that 337 is by far the most reasonable date (cf. BE 1977 no. 472 and 1980 no. 486; Weiskopf 1982: 293–97, Hornblower 1982: 46–49, and Ruzicka 1992b: 125). Concerning the date of the satrapal reform, I observe that there is nothing in the inscription to prove that Pixodarus had just received Lycia; the reorganization could just as well go back several years (cf. wise remarks along these lines by Badian 1977b: 45; contra Laroche 1979:37: but only the Greek text uses a formula [*egeneto*] taken up in the Lycian version [Laroche 1979: 60], which might support the theory of a reform that was recent and/or in progress; but this formula does not appear in the Aramaic text [Dupont-Sommer 1979: 141–42], the only usable text, since neither the Greek nor the Lycian version states that Pixodarus was satrap in Caria); according to Keen 1992a, chap. 7, the institution of two Achaemenid representatives even goes back to the beginning of the 370s. In any case, an anecdote indicates that since the time of Mausolus the satrap of Caria had had tribute prerogatives in Lycia (cf. [Ps.-Arist.] *Oec.* II.14d [1348a?]; see Weiskopf 1982: 291–93); on cultural and political contacts between Caria and Lycia, cf., for example, the presence of Basileus Caunius on the Inscribed Pillar (early fourth century; Dupont-Sommer 1979: 168; Melchert 1993), the same god whose worship was the subject of the trilingual (below); on the region of Caunus (in eastern Caria, Telmessus being the traditional boundary with Lycia), cf. Bousquet 1992: 176–78 and 180–81 (conquest of the region by Gergis/Kheriga, then the starting point of Erbbina-Arbinas), as well as Melchert 1993: from all these indications, I am tempted to think that Artaxerxes' decision is chronologically involved with the recognition of Pixodarus as satrap in Caria, hence around 341, and I suggest that the incorporation of Lycia into Caria was part of a vast administrative reorganization ordered by Artaxerxes III after his expedition to Phoenicia and Egypt.

5. Pixodarus at Xanthus

• The tasks assigned to the two archons remain in the realm of theory (cf. Asheri 1983b: 111); Hellenistic evidence might provide some materials along these lines (but with the risk of circular reasoning): cf. Wörrle 1977: 59–60; see also Keen 1992a, chap. 7. The reasons for Pixodarus's interference in the religious matter have stimulated many analyses (which differ somewhat among themselves); Asheri 1983b: 110–23, Frei 1984: 21–23, Briant 1986a: 434–37, and now Lemaire 1995c; on relations between the Carian dynasts and Basileus Caunius, cf. Dupont-Sommer 1979: 168–69, but it must be stressed, with Bousquet (1992: 175 n. 48), that the introduction of Basileus Kaunios to Xanthus was much earlier and more likely due to Kheriga than to a fifth-century Carian dynast; on the word *dāta* and its relation to the Lycian *mara*, cf. chap. 12/7: Royal Law and Local Law, pp. 510ff. *TL* 45: cf. the restorations and commentaries by Bousquet 1986; Plarasa's decree and other related ones, cf. BE 1973 no. 406; Hornblower 1982: 161–64; Weiskopf 1982: 293ff.; Corsaro 1985 and 1989. Last, I will state that synoptic comparison between the two parallel texts, the Greek and Lycian (which is certainly the original: Blomqvist 1982), permits several observations on linguistic borrowings and adaptation: one of the most surprising is the following: where the Lycian author wrote *sicle* (line 22), the Greek author "translated" with *drachme* (line 20)—which makes me doubt the restoration "⟨two?⟩ sigloi" proposed by Metzger (on these problems, cf. Frei 1977).

6. From Tarsus to Mazaca

• Since the early work of Erzen 1940, Bing 1969, and Houwinck ten Cate 1961 (pp. 17–35), Cilicia of this period has received little attention or specialized investigation. Conversely, they have boomed in recent years: aside from the special number of *Quaderni Storici* 76/1 (1981) and

the volume *De Anatolia Antiqua* (Istanbul and Paris, 1991), we have the book by Desideri and Jasink 1990, to which we may add the general but useful book by Mutafian 1988 and, on a special
point, the suggestive article by Bing 1991. This reawakening of interest in the region is no doubt
largely due to several spectacular discoveries, not the least being the site, the "Persepolis" reliefs,
and the Aramaic inscriptions of Meydançikkale (cf. Laroche and Davesne 1981; Davesne, Lemaire, and Lozachmeur 1989); this reawakening of interest has itself stimulated new explorations,
which, currently led by M. H. Sayar in eastern Cilicia, have quite recently brought about the discovery of several Aramaic funerary inscriptions not far from Castabala (Sayar 1990), two of which
have just been published by A. Lemaire (1993), who is preparing the edition of other documents
[= 1994b]; the interest of the region also lies in the abundance and diversity of coinage from the
Achaemenid period found there (Harrison 1982a: 304–77; Levante 1994; Casabonne 1995b, etc.).
In the recent bibliography, we will see first of all the overview by Lemaire and Lozachmeur 1990,
where the sources are presented and commented on; on the Aramaic documents from Cilicia, cf.
Dupont-Sommer 1964 (Castabala) and Lemaire 1991c: 205–6 (Hemite and Meydançikkale); on
the coins of Mazaeus and his district in Cilicia, then in Cilicia and Trans-Euphrates, consult also
the discussion of Leuze (1935: 234–35), who shows that after the revolt Belesys died, and Mazaeus
took back Trans-Euphrates with Cilicia, and that of Weiskopf 1982: 498–500; coins struck by Mazaeus in the Cilician cities: cf. Lemaire 1989a: 142–44 and 1991d, Chuvin 1981, Harrison 1982a:
346–77, Mildenberg 1990–91: 10–13. Concerning Mazaeus, we may consider four specific problems in passing: (1) According to Quintus Curtius V.13.11, it looks as though one of his sons, Brochubelus, assisted his father in Syria (*Syriae quondam praetor*); doubtless this was not an official
title (Mazaeus's coins are very clear) but one of many examples of cooperation between father and
son (Briant 1987a: 26–27) in a satrapal administration bestowed on the former (cf. Petit 1990: 209–
10). (2) We have long known about an Athenian stela whose upper register shows a Royal Hero
scene, and the lower register exhibits a scene of lion/bull combat (photo in Briant 1992d: 122): Bivar (1970: 59–61) thinks the lower scene reproduces Mazaeus's seal and the stela represents the
naming of a *proxenos* to the satrap at Athens (cf. also Bivar 1975a: 63–64); but the argument seems
to me highly speculative. (3) Quintus Curtius (III.4.3) describes Arsames as follows in the spring
of 333: *qui Ciliciae praeerat*, but the phrase does not imply that he was then satrap of Cilicia (cf.
on this point Leuze 1935: 242–50 and Weiskopf 1982: 495–98). (4) On the basis of the role that
Mazaeus played in Babylon after the arrival of Alexander, it is sometimes thought that after the fall
of Tarsus he headed Syria–Phoenicia and Babylonia: this suggestion appears to me to have little
basis; in the catalog transmitted by Arrian III.8.3–6◊ in fact, "the Syrians of Hollow Syria and all
from Mesopotamian Syria" were led by Mazaeus, while the Babylonians were commanded by Bupares; even though Arrian's phrasing raises a few problems, it appears that Mazaeus did not command Babylonia. Plain and mountain in Cilicia according to Strabo: cf. Desideri 1986; we will
stress above all that the opposition is very common in Classical and Hellenistic authors, contrasting at the same time the Achaemenids' inability and Alexander's facility in subduing the mountain
peoples (cf. Briant 1976: 194–200 and cf. chap. 16/11 and 16/18); archers of Aspendus: Foss 1975:
30 (Aspendus belongs in principle to Pamphylia, although between 331 and 323 it was a dependency of Lycia, which in turn was attached to Greater Phrygia: Quintus Curtius X.1.2; in any case,
we find Aspendians in the guard of Epyaxa, wife of the *syennesis* in 401: Xenophon, *Anab.* I.2.12).
Coins of Cilician cities: e.g., Chuvin 1981, Capecchi 1991, Casabonne 1995b; among the things
most evocative of the borrowing and adaptation of Persian motifs, we may consider some coins
from Issus struck with the name Tiribazus in Aramaic that bear an anthropomorphic representation of Ahura-Mazda: the divine representation is repeated in many other regions (cf. in particular
the coinage of Samaria: below), but what makes the Issus coins so remarkable (even though this is
not an iconographic *hapax*) is that the Persian god is depicted nude, with typically Greek concep-
tualization and workmanship (Brindley 1993: 4–5); on the theme of Persian loans, see also Casabonne 1995a. Meydançikkale: Davesne, Lemaire, and Lozachmeur 1987 and Lemaire 1991c:
205–6 (photo of a relief reprinted in Briant 1992d: 87) [final publication of the Persepolis reliefs

and Aramaic inscriptions currently in press]; Kyinda: cf. Bing 1969: 129–30 and *RTP* 49 n. 2 and 93; Tarkondimontos: Robert 1964; Nora and other garrisons: *RTP* 20–21; Castabalitides and Cataonia strategy: Robert 1963: 436–37 and 1964: 39, and Boffo 1985: 54–60; cf. Devine 1984 on the passage of Alexander. Jobs of Aspis and Camisares, cf. Sekunda 1988b: 36 and 42–44; on the altar found at Bünyan (not far from Kayseri), cf. Bittel 1952 (the author makes Mazaca the center of the official power of Camisares and Aspis; I include the suggestion in my text but only as a theory); we may note in passing that a treasury found at Kayseri contained several Pamphylian coins (Aspendus, Side), one of Datames, and one of Mazaeus (Davesne 1989: 167): this last may confirm that the region belonged to the satrap of Tarsus; I also note that according to de Planhol 1992: 136–37 the *qanat*s known at Kayseri (and Ancyrus) could go back to the Achaemenids; Anaitis Barzochara: *BE* 1968 no. 538 and 1971 no. 669 (Schmitt 1970; but see Wikander 1972); Hanisa inscription and Iranian personal names: cf. Robert 1964: 457ff. (cf. p. 516, the name Maibouzanes is found at Comana in Cataonia, a personal name that in Lydia, not far from Sardis, is applied collectively [Maibouzanoi] to an Iranian community: Robert 1987: 333–35); Iazamis/Arsames: Robert 1963: 433–45; Farasa inscription: cf. Grégoire 1908 and Lipiński 1975: 173–84 (the inscription was found in the valley of the Carmalas, which according to Strabo (XII.2.6) flowed through Cataonia; on the site of Ariaramneia [doubtless in Cataonia], cf. Grégoire 1908: 441–43). Hemites and Saraïdin inscriptions: cf. Lemaire and Lozachmeur 1990: 153 and Lemaire 1991c: 205 (and pp. 203–5 on Datames/Tarkumawa): note that the personal name Sarmapiya has recently been found in an Aramaic funerary inscription from near Hemites (cf. Lemaire 1993: 12–14 with suggestions on the possible familial relations); Lemaire (1991c: 205), regarding the Hemites inscription, writes: "We are thus probably faced with a new case of a 'dynast-satrap'"; my reservations expressed in the text come from the observation that in several imperial corpora (Akkadian, Greek), the word *satrap* does not necessarily refer to the head of the satrapy, but it can designate a very highly placed person within a satrapy (cf. Stolper 1985a: 58; and *CAH* VI²: 252–53; Dandamaev 1992b) or a Persian aristocrat (e.g., Strabo XV.3.18). Greco-Persian reliefs from Cilicia: Borchhardt 1968 and Hermary 1984; *satabara*: Dagron and Feissel 1987: 36; gardener-king coin: Franke and Hirmer 1966: 124 and no. 194 (Sancisi-Weerdenburg 1990: 266; Casabonne 1995b note 6; and chap. 6/5, pp. 232f.).

7. From Tarsus to Samaria via Sidon and Jerusalem

• Aside from the Phoenician cities (e.g., Elayi 1987b, 1989, 1990c), Judah, Samaria, and Palestine (besides Stern 1982b, 1994c, see the recent collection Laperrousaz-Lemaire [ed.] 1994), evidence bearing on the Achaemenid presence in northern Syria in the fourth century is rather rare and generally unforthcoming, and we have no synthesis on the question (Eph'al's [1988] overview barely deals with Achaemenid dominion in all its diversity): the discussions in Millar 1987 seem to me somewhat "defeatist" on the situation in Syria before (and during) the Hellenistic period (see now the explicit criticisms of Lund 1993: 27–28, 40); Sartre's 1989 article is summary and disappointing; Mazzoni 1991–92: 55 laments the absence of special studies on the region in early volumes of *Achaemenid History*. See now the volumes of *Transeuphratène* and the assessment prepared by Elayi and Sapin 1991. Aside from a few late indications of the presence of an imperial diaspora in the region (cf. Boyce and Grenet 1991: 354–57), the written sources are abjectly poor (once more we may list the travel voucher given to Neḥtiḫôr [*DAE* 67 (= AD 6)] and the text of Berossus, which confirm that Damascus was indeed at this date a major provincial capital [chap. 15/8: "The Imperial Realm," p. 680; see also chap. 12/3: "The District of Trans-Euphrates," p. 487; I recall that according to Josephus, *Ant.* XI.2.2, Cambyses died there; Herodotus (III.64) places this event at Ecbatana-in-Syria, identifiable with the future Epiphania on the Orontes by Mazzoni 1991–92: 62, referring to Pliny V.82]; —the existence of a Syrian satrapal paradise at the sources of the Dardas [Xenophon, *Anab.* I.4.10], lands belonging to the house of Parysatis near Aleppo [I.4.9; Manfredi 1986: 97–98; Mazzoni 1990–91: 67–68; Graf 1993: 152–254], and the place-name Triparadeisos that implies the presence of paradise structures at the sources of the Orontes [on the location, cf. Seibert 1983: 109]—all these observations lead us to think, with Seyrig 1970: 301, that royal Achaemenid land was well represented in northern Syria: and cf. now Sapin 1990). New information is thus basically provided by regional and microregional archaeological excavations and surveys: see especially Lund 1993 (region of the Orontes in the fourth century) and Mazzoni 1990 and 1991–92, who, by examining the distribution of habitats between the Phoenician coast and the Khabur Valley, concludes overall that there was an increase in the number of sites; the detailed study (1990) of Tell Mardikh/Ebla is especially interesting, since a new ("rustic") palace was built in the late Achaemenid period (fourth century) within "a complete restructuring of the acropolis" (1990: 190; cf. also *Les dossiers histoire et archéologie*, no. 83 [1984]: *Ebla retrouvée*, esp. p. 31; ironically, the headless inscribed statue of Prince Ibbit-Lim that provided the identification of Ebla was discovered within the Persian-period structure as a reused block; cf. ibid., pp. 13 and 88). All the recent discoveries point in the same direction: "It was with the blossoming of the Achaemenid phase that the economic surge and transformation of the region came about, rich with promise" (Mazzoni 1990: 193; following a traditional practice [cf. RTP 230–33], several Hellenistic towns [Apamaeus, Epiphania on the Orontes] were founded on already inhabited sites that had been put to good use in the Achaemenid period: Mazzoni 1991–92: 61–62, 67–68; on these Achaemenid-Hellenistic continuities, see also Lund 1993). On an especially important site (a Euphrates ford?), the cemetery of Deve Hüyük, see Moorey 1975 and 1980, with the critical remarks of Mazzoni 1991–92: 66–67.

- *Phoenicia.* The discussions on the status of Sidon after the revolt are dense and contradictory, though the evidence is poor (cf. Elayi 1989: 147–48), in particular the textual evidence (as far as I know, the Persian-period cuneiform tablet found at Tell Mikhmoret [Stern 1993] has never been published): theories are thus primarily built on numismatic evidence (which poses enormous problems (and which I feel particularly incompetent to examine); see also the Achaemenid-style column capital found at Sidon, which is sometimes related to the satrapal paradise (Clermont-Ganneau 1921 and, most recently, the observations of Yon-Caubet 1993: 51). It seems unlikely (contrary to Babelon's theory) that Artaxerxes granted Sidonian kingship to Evagoras of Cyprus, who, after striving in vain to reinstall himself at Salamis in Cyprus, received from the king "another and higher command in Asia" before fleeing to Cyprus (Diodorus XVI.46.2–3; cf. on Babelon's position Betlyon 1982: 19–20); the confiscation of the gift to Ešmunazar is inferred from Quintus Curtius (IV.1.25), who says that Alexander granted to the new king (Abdalonymus) "a territory adjacent to the city," a phrase that is sometimes seen as a restoration of the prior Achaemenid concession (cf. Barag 1966: 8 n. 8 and Lemaire 1990: 58–59 in the same sense; while he discusses the passage, Verkinderen 1987: 306–7 does not take a position on the question); we may note with Stern (1990: 154, 1994c: 151ff.) that the Persians, aware of the importance of Sidon and Dor, rebuilt the Phoenician cities' fortifications (the author also thinks that Dor was returned to Sidon, implying that it had previously been confiscated, but cf. Stern 1982b: 243; 1994b: 79); on the coinage of Straton II: cf. Betlyon 1982: 18–20; coinage of Mazaeus at Sidon (I restrict myself here to the recent bibliography, without rehashing studies of the Six): Betlyon (1982:18), whose argument is vitiated by chronological errors, thinks that after the institution of martial law (*sic*), Mazaeus took control of the city market; but as Harrison 1982a: 353–54 (whose dating of the satrap's Sidonian coins I use) rightly stresses, we see that the last kings of Sidon were striking coins at the same time as Mazaeus, so that we can imagine the latter's coins "were struck for needs other than civic" (p. 354): these considerations lead us to think that, as in many identical situations in other countries, the Great King was satisfied with changing the dynast/king, without questioning the prior status of Sidon (on which we are, after all, ill informed); for his part, Mildenberg (1990: 138) thinks that Mazaeus, by placing his name on Sidonian coins, was acting as "regent of the city," but the author (note 4) remarks at the same time that on the coins struck in their name by the Sidonian kings, Mazaeus does not indicate his satrapal position (cf. also Mildenberg 1990–91: 14: "It is noteworthy that . . . Mazaeus respected the civic prerogative of coin production in every respect even a short time after the revolt led by Sidon had been crushed"; similarly in Mildenberg 1994: 65); on these complex problems of Sidonian coinage, cf. also Elayi 1989: 215–19 and J.-A. G. Elayi 1993: 146–47.

• *Samaria.* On the Wadi-ed Daliyeh documents, see the various articles by Cross in the bibliography; nine papyri concerning slave sales have been published and translated by Gropp 1986 (SP 1–9); the coins were published by Meshorer and Qedar 1991 (= CS), including many coins that did not come from Wadi ed-Daliyeh, which the authors attribute to studios in Samaria; the sealings from Wadi ed-Daliyeh have been published and commented on by Leith 1990 (= WD); I refer the reader to these highly detailed studies, being satisfied here to use them selectively (on the spread of Persian or Persian-inspired motifs and objects in these regions, see also various articles by Stern (1971, 1982a, 1994a, and 1994b: 190–92 on the seals), and also the recent interesting publication by Rozenberg 1993 (Achaemenid ivories). Three additional remarks on evidence: (1) The Aramaic papyrus found near Jericho (Eshel and Misgav 1988) is too broken to sustain historical interpretation—despite the editors, who wish to see in it indications of a Samarian revolt in response to the Phoenician revolt around 350; the fiscal interpretation proposed by Heltzer 1992c (allusion to royal taxes at the end of the Achaemenid period) is hardly more convincing; Lemaire (in Laperrousaz and Lemaire [1994]: 276) anyway thinks the document should be dated to the Hellenistic period; (2) I note that, in *Michmanim* 6 (1992): 41, E. Stern announces a new(?) discovery: "A hoard of Persian period bullae from the vicinity of Samaria"; (3) On Samarian coins with cuneiform legends, cf. Lemaire and Joannès 1994 (we may note that the two coins examined are new examples of CS 58 [fig. 61e here] with the very interesting image I discuss in the text).

• *Judah.* Coins of Yehizqiyyah and Johanan: cf. the analyses and interpretations (often contradictory) of Rappaport 1981, Barag 1985, Betlyon 1986, Mildenberg 1979, 1988, [[Machinist 1994: 366–70]]; the Johanan of the coins is sometimes compared with the person of the same name introduced by Josephus (*Ant.* XI.297–301): in competition with his brother Jeshua (who had obtained the support of the Persian *strategos* Bagoses), Johanan killed his brother, and in retaliation Bagoses defiled the temple; but Josephus's tale is too romanticized to be able to serve as the basis for historical reconstruction (cf. Oded 1977d: 501); it is difficult to incorporate these characters into a genealogy of the high priests (ibid., 506–9; meanwhile, see the proposals of Barag 1985: 167–68 and Betlyon 1986: 639–41, following Cross 1975); Grabbe 1992a thinks that Josephus's Bagoses is actually Bagohi, *peḥā* of Judah; on possible coins of this person, cf. Lemaire in Laperrousaz and Lemaire (1994): 285. One last remark: recent discoveries seem to give support to the theory that there was a province of Ammonitides (Herr 1992; cf. also Heltzer 1989c; Lemaire 1990: 48–71; 1994: 46–47).

8. *From Gaza to Petra*

• On the history of Gaza in the Achaemenid period, see an overview (without great originality) by Katzenstein 1989; on the siege of Gaza, see the sources collected by Bosworth 1980a: 257–60 (cf. also Romane 1988 on aspects of military history); on the Minaean inscription *RÉS* 3022 and the historical and chronological difficulties, cf. most recently Robin 1991–93: 61–62 [[in a presentation at the conference on Egypt and Trans-Euphrates (Paris, April 1993), A. Lemaire drew attention to the fact that the inscription refers to a revolt (not simply a war)—which, as he said, still does not allow us to pin down the events to Artaxerxes I vs. Artaxerxes III = Lemaire 1995a: 55, inclining more toward the revolt of Amyrtaeus at the end of the fifth century]]; on the coins of Gaza, cf. Mildenberg 1990 (distinguishing coins of the Arabs from coins of the city); on the "kings of the Arabs" and Gaza, cf. Briant 1982b: 150–52, 169–70; Eph'al 1982: 195–97, 206–10 (but the theory, recalled pp. 212–13, identifying the king of the Arabs of Palestine with the king of Qedar named in *DAE* 78–79, rests on a very weak argument); Graf 1990a: 142–43; Lemaire 1990: 45–47 and 1994a: 28–29. The Beer-sheba ostraca were published by Naveh 1973 and 1979, as were those from Arad (Naveh 1981), on which see also the observations of Aharoni 1981: 141–51; some Beer-sheba texts are dated to year 7 of a king; on the basis of palaeography, Naveh (1979; cf. Naveh 1981) opts for Artaxerxes III. On the organization of Arad, cf. Graf 1993: 160–61 (comparison with the PF: cf. also RTP 505; this evidence is fully interpreted in light of the Hebrew inscriptions of Lachish and Arad: Lemaire 1977); Beer-sheba: the existence of a garrison is doubted by Tuplin 1987c: 187 (followed by Salles 1991: 222); discovery (not yet published) of new ostraca like the Beer-sheba ostraca (fourth century): I owe the information to the generosity of A. Lemaire [who is currently preparing the edition], whose general historical evaluation (1994a: 29–30) I quote as well: "The Aramaic ostraca of Arad and Beer-sheba, probably dating around the middle of the fourth century, attest quite clearly to Persian military and administrative control over this region which probably was reorganized between 385 and 352, and this reorganization brought about the end of the kingdom of Qedar and its partial replacement by the Nabateans"; cf. also Stern 1982b: 253–55, who thinks that after the destructions of the 380s the Persians reinstalled garrisons in these regions. On the Persians in northern Arabia, see the overviews of Knauf 1990 and Graf 1990a; the former (pp. 214–15) thinks that, beginning around 400, because of the loss of Egypt, the Persians decided to abandon Arabia (cf. also Högemann 1985: 17); while it may hold for the major oases (but the chronological and terminological uncertainty about the sparse evidence is great: Briant 1982b: 172), this idea seems to me to need considerabe nuancing, at least in order to take into account the Arad and Beer-sheba ostraca (not used by Knauf): cf. Graf's treatment, 1990a: 160–61; on the creation of the province of Idumea, cf. Lemaire 1994a: 28–29 (creation after 380); on the eparchy of Idumea in the age of the Diadochi and Diodorus's text (XIX.95.2: *eparchy*; 98.1: *satrapeia*), see the discussion of Bengtson 1964, 3: 35–36 (he thinks that only the first of the terms comes from the original source). On the Nabateans (too controversial a topic to be treated here *in extenso*), cf. most recently Bartlett 1990, Graf 1990b, MacDonald 1991, Roche 1994; among the Achaemenid traces in Nabatea we must recall the presence of a cuneiform tablet at Tell Tawilan dated to the inaugural year of a King Darius (Dalley 1984; Joannès 1987, with the reply of Dalley 1990: 79–80); an important find of jewelry was also found there, worked like the jewelry of the Achaemenid court (Maxwell-Hyslop 1984, with remarks of interpretive caution offered by Graf 1993: 158; cf. also the recent interpretations of Roche 1994: 42–43: evidence of the nomadic Nabateans' wealth).

9. Egypt from Artaxerxes III to Darius III

• On Sabaces, cf. Nicolet-Pierre 1979 (coinage) and Schmitt 1987a (name); Pseudo-Aristotle (*Oecon.* II.32 [1352a◊]) names one "Evaeses, the Syrian" as satrap of Egypt (apparently in the Persian period), but the mansucripts are problematic (cf. van Groningen 1933: 182–83). The literature on the *Stela of the Satrap* is considerable (it is mentioned in recent articles by Spalinger 1978a; Goedicke 1985; and most recently Huss 1994a: see now the new suggestions by Duvauchelle forthcoming, whom I heartily thank for providing his manuscript; on a detail [*kbnt* vessels], cf. Darnell 1992: 73–78 [to the attestations of the word in documents of the Saite-Persian period (p. 78), add the Onnophris inscription in von Känel 1980: 44, who translates it 'warships']; the publication of the stela goes back to Brugsch in 1871 (reedited by Kamal 1905: 168–71). The arguments over the date are old: Wilcken (1897: 85) already highlighted the weakness of some aspects of Brugsch's argument and thought that Khabbabash must have come after Xerxes; Spalinger thinks (following others) that "Xerxes" must be understood as Artaxerxes III and Khabbabash rebelled at the end of this Great King's reign (cf. also Michaèlidis 1943: 97–99 and Bresciani 1958: 167). Spalinger's readings have been briskly contested by Ritner 1980, who thinks there is no reason to suppose that Khabbabash was a contemporary of Ḫšryš: an interpretation that is interesting because it demolishes the historical argument for the identification of Xerxes as Artaxerxes III while at the same time allowing a late date for Khabbabash; Ritner's position has had many repercussions: cf. Ray 1988: 271 n. 42. Goedicke (1985) places Khabbabash in the reign of Arses, specifically in the autumn of 336, so that it was Darius III who carried out the reconquest [similar viewpoint in Huss 1994a]; in his opinion, the word used is a metathesis of "Arses" in hieroglyphics. It is necessary to state that the arguments between the Egyptologists bear on the most important clauses, and that when all is said and done it seems that no one can answer such important questions as: Who is speaking? To whom? I am thinking particularly of differences about the meaning of the phrase (concerning this king and his eldest son) "expelled from his palace": for Spalinger (1978a: 151–52), it is the clerics of Buto who pressed Khabbabash to drive Artaxerxes III and Arses out of Egypt; for Ritner (1980), the clerics of Buto let it be known that the god himself had already driven the king (Xerxes) and his son out of Egypt (this would refer to the palace of Horus, "the seat of the contention between Egypt and Persia"); finally, Goedicke (1985: 41–42) thinks that the text refers to the murders of Arses "in his residence" (Susa or Persepolis) and his eldest son—hence the very precise dates he assigns to Khabbabash's revolt (autumn of 336) and the reconquest by, for him, Darius III (February–March 336), p. 53: but why would the Egyptian writers have referred to an event so distant from their concerns? It seems more logical to think that they are alluding to a "fact" (?) that took place in Egypt. I have no competence to participate in the epigraphic and philological discussion; I will simply indicate that, from the historical point of view, the Artaxerxes III (or Artaxerxes IV/Arses) theory appears more comprehensible than the Xerxes theory (would the fourth-century Egyptian pharaohs have done nothing on behalf of Buto after Xerxes' confiscations?); but, at the same time, the text is built on such a series of repetitive motifs that it is difficult to place all of the episodes in time; this is why we hesitate, for example, to establish a direct relationship between the abduction of the sacred archives by Artaxerxes III (Diodorus XVI.51.2) and their repatriation by Ptolemy (*Stela*), particularly because, according to Diodorus, Bagoas returned them to the priests for ransom. The theme of the return of statues is so frequent in the official literature of the Ptolemaic period that it is difficult to distinguish what relates to the narrative genre in the text from what belongs to the area of Egyptian ideological depictions and Ptolemaic propaganda (neither of them with any particular interest in "historical accuracy"!). Finally, I wonder whether it should not be suggested that, as in some Greek texts, "Xerxes" had become a generic term for the Egyptians (cf. Isocrates, *Phil.* 42 and the note by Brémond, *Isocrate*, CUF, 4 [1962]: 30 n. 1). Most recently, using other arguments (from the chronographers), Lloyd 1988b thinks that Artaxerxes III led another reconquest of Egypt, and Lloyd 1994: 344–45, without ruling out the other possibilities, suggests that Khabbabash might have reigned between the reconquest of Artaxerxes III (343–342) and his recognition in Egypt—namely, 339–338: p. 359 n. 110. To finish up on this point, I will mention that the dating also bears a certain interest for the reconstruction of other aspects of Achaemenid history: (1) on relations between the Great King and his son and thus on the date at which Xerxes, Artaxerxes III, and even Arses/Artaxerxes IV recognized their oldest sons as crown prince (on the phrase "oldest son," cf. also chap. 13/2: "A Principle of Primogeniture?," p. 520); (2) several authors think that the obstacles on the Egyptian front might have affected Darius III's disposition in Asia Minor in 334 (chap. 18/1: Darius, His Satraps, and Alexander's Landing (May–June 334), pp. 818ff.).— Measures taken by Alexander in Egypt and Achaemenid continuities: cf. Harmatta 1963: 208–10 and Burstein 1991 and 1994 (among the recently published documents, we may note a Demotic graffito dating to Alexander that seems to refer to a satrapal order and names one Pediese [Smith 1988: 184–86]; perhaps this is Peteisis, who we know from Arrian [III.5.2] was made "nomarch" by Alexander: cf. on this point Burstein 1994); we may also note that the personal names later testify to a Persian and Iranian diaspora in Egypt (cf. Huyse 1990b and 1991, where an overview of the famous *Persai tēs epigonēs* will be found), corresponding in part at least to the Iranian names found in the fifth century, not just in the Aramaic papyri but also in the Demotic documents (cf. Smith 1992b and Huyse 1992); we also know of Egyptians who defected to the last Persian kings: cf. chap. 18/3: Egypt and the Egyptians, pp. 858ff.

10. From Arbela to Susa

• "Achaemenid residence" near Sippar: we can follow the results of the explorations in *NAPR* 4 (1989) and 7 (1991): cf. also Pons 1993 and Gasche 1995; Artaxerxes II's building projects at

Babylon: Stolper, *CAH* VI²: 259–60; on Babylon in this period, cf. also Schachermeyr 1970: 49–73. The Achaemenid administrative system in Upper Mesopotamia is particularly difficult to uncover because, on the one hand, the data are very thin and, on the other, the vocabulary of the ancient authors is rarely consistent (cf., for example, Tuplin 1991b: 51–54 on *Sittakē* in Xenophon, and Helm 1980: 27–41 and 276–312 on the very elastic use of the word *Assyria* in the Classical authors: see Zadok 1984 for the cuneiform sources in the Neo-Babylonian and Achaemenid periods): cf. the pages (to be used carefully) of Herzfeld 1968: 10ff.; on the deported Eretrians and Carians, cf. ibid., 11–12, as well as Grosso 1958 (where all the Greek materials will be found), and Stolper 1985a: 73, 79, 86 (cuneiform sources: Ḫaṭru). The importance of Arbela is well established, in the Achaemenid period, by the role it played in 522–521 (*DB* §33), its role in communications (*DAE* 67 [= *AD* 6]), Darius III's leaving his baggage there (cf. Quintus Curtius IV.9.9; IV.16.9; V.1.10; Diodorus XVII.64.3; Arrian III.15.5), and Darius I's decision upon returning from the war against the Saka to dedicate the revenue from several villages to the maintenance of the camel that had brought him back safe and sound from the expedition (Strabo XVI.1.3; Plutarch, *Alex.* 31.7); on Assyria in the Achaemenid period, see most recently Kuhrt 1995. On Susa and Susiana, cf. Le Rider 1965: 254–80 and Boucharlat 1990a–b, as well as Joannès 1990b (publication of tablets dated to an Artaxerxes; presence of many Egyptians; mention of a treasurer; use of the word *bandaka* in a personal name); Lower Babylonia: on the "Sealand," cf. Joannès 1990a: 177–78 (note). On the hydraulic projects carried out by Alexander in Babylonia, cf. Briant 1986b, the main conclusions of which I repeat here, without rehashing the detailed argumentation *in extenso* (the bibliography will also be found there; I see no point in repeating it here; add the prudent correction of Boucharlat [1990a: 162] on irrigation agriculture in Susiana); I will add briefly that since then I have discovered – by a chance reading – that the Hellenistic tradition is repeated by Ammianus Marcellinus XXIV.6.1–2: as he describes the work carried out by Trajan in redigging the Narmalcha ("royal river"), the author recalls that "once upon a time the Persians, fearing similar [military] operations [against them] blocked [the Narmalcha] with an enormous mass of rock." Independently, Högemann 1985 proposed a radically different theory; throughout his book, he works out the idea of a structural antagonism and permanent hostilities between the Achaemenid authority and the Arabs of the north of the peninsula: in this framework, the works carried out by Alexander prove that the Achaemenid administration no longer had the will to finish them (pp. 144–49); Alexander's urbanization policy provides additional proof of Arab aggression (149–58), with Arabs regularly plundering and pirating in Achaemenid Lower Babylonia (p. 155); the "Sealand" had been completely abandoned to them by the Great Kings, who were unable to deal with the danger (189–93); Alexander's vigor and his Arab project thus had to lead to a "Babylonian renewal" (p. 207: "Neuerschließung Babyloniens"). It would take too long to respond point by point to all his arguments; I will content myself here with accenting the methodological aspects. It is clear that the author believes he can use the Hellenistic texts "as is," without ever examining the political-ideological context of their creation. However, on the evidence, the initiative for the offensive came from Alexander, because the Arabs were the only ones who had not hastened to send an embassy to him (Aristobulus apud Strabo XVI.1.11)—that is, had not shown prior submission to him by sending delegates bearing gifts (cf. Arrian VI.15.5); under these conditions, all that can be inferred from Alexander's behavior compared with the Achaemenids' is that the Arabs had manifested the "same hostility," and Alexander had no choice but to respond. At any rate, it is entirely characteristic that the author (who has obviously not kept up with the literature on the subject) compares the "Arab danger" with the "danger" posed, according to him (p. 155), by the Cossean and Uxian mountaineers, both of whom constituted a permanent threat to Babylonia: but the case of the Uxians and Cosseans, to whom we shall soon return (chap. 16/11), shows precisely that the Hellenistic tales have led to the same sort of misinterpretation, though reversing the poles of aggression. The author returns several times to earlier periods, when pretenders were supported from their bases in Lower Babylonia in their challenge to the Neo-Assyrian or Neo-Babylonian kings: it still remains to be proved that the same held true in the Persian period, which is often suggested but never proved (see chap. 16/17 on Persian policy in the Persian Gulf). Besides, I observe that the view of contacts between "sedentary" and "nomadic" peoples emerges from a reductionist view (cf. Briant 1982a: 9–56; Eph'al 1982; and most recently Fales 1989): that there were "infiltrations" of Arab populations in the Achaemenid period (as in other periods) can scarcely be doubted (cf. Zadok 1978, 1979), but they do not necessarily prove that there was a state of permanent hostility: some were settled in Babylonia under the *ḫaṭru* system (cf. Stolper 1985a: 78, 85–87; also Eph'al 1982: 188–90); and concerning the Gerrheans, Aristobulus refers especially to their trading voyages to Babylonia (Strabo XVI.3.3), which on the contrary implies cooperative relations (see also remarks of Teixidor 1993: 290). Some parts of southern Babylonia may have been under threat of marauders, as implied by tablets from the time of Nabonidus, Cyrus, and Cambyses bearing on troops assigned to watch over distant pastures in the north (cf. Joannès 1982: 179–83, where the danger represented by the "mountain brigands" nonetheless seems to me highly overrated), but it concerned localized, circumscribed disturbances, quite different from the victorious general threat suggested by Högemann in Lower Babylonia (on this point, cf. also the critical remarks of Salles 1990: 125–26); we no longer see that these Arabs had the ability to launch naval expeditions on the Tigris and Euphrates (Aristobulus [Strabo XVI.3.3] simply speaks of little raft-like boats). Högemann's interpretation looks like part of a predetermined discourse on the image of an Achaemenid authority that was moribund and unable to deal with the threats weighing on it: I stress in particular that the theory of Babylonia's and Babylon's decadence at the end of the Achaemenid period will certainly be pounced upon by all those who over the last few years have demonstrated, using cuneiform evidence, that there was no such thing. Last, I will mention that recent work supports my 1986 conclusions: see first of all the noteworthy remark of Joannès 1995: 194 n. 17: the *katarrhaktai* of the Tigris were the "foremost waterworks known on this river"; next, in van der Spek 1992: 238 n. 15, a list of occurrences of Pallukatu/Pallacopas in the astronomical tablets *ADRTB*, repeated by van der Spek 1994: 17–18: examination of tablets dated 333, 329, 325 on waterworks maintenance, compared with the Classical texts I examine in the text; besides, these very tablets (*ADRTB* nos. –332, –328, –326) are mentioned by Slotsky 1993 (pp. 233–34) in the course of a discussion (pp. 231–51) of variations in the level of the Euphrates in the astronomical tablets—which imply the existence of what we might call a sort of "Euphratometer" at Babylon.

• On the *Babylonian sources* under the last Great Kings, see Kuhrt 1987a, van Driel 1987, and Stolper, *CAH* VI²: 234–35; on the astronomical tablets (published by Sachs and Hunger 1988), cf. the already cited Bernard 1990b, Slotsky 1993, and van der Spek 1993a, 1994; it is obvious that the unequal distribution of the sources through time must not lead us to risky historical conclusions of the "statistical" type (cf. appropriate remarks along these lines by MacEwan 1983 on Kish; Beaulieu 1989b on Agade; and van der Spek 1992 on Sippar); an exhaustive treatment of the subject would require profound knowledge of the Babylonian materials from the Achaemenid and Seleucid periods (which I do not have), to the extent that analyses carried out for the beginning of the Seleucid period often allow us to trace continuities with the end of the Achaemenid period: cf., for example, the articles by Kuhrt, Sherwin-White, and van der Spek gathered in Kuhrt and Sherwin-White 1987, as well as Kuhrt and Sherwin-White 1994 and the analyses by Stolper 1989a, 1993, and 1994a and the more recent work of van der Spek; administration of the temples at the beginning of the Seleucid period (compared with the Achaemenid period): cf., e.g., MacEwan 1981, Beaulieu 1989c, and Kuhrt and Sherwin-White 1991; on the Chaldeans, cf. van der Spek 1992: 236–43; the author, pp. 241–42, also gives a transliteration/translation/commentary for an interesting tablet dated 308–307: traditional organization of the Ebabbar of Sippar, with its lands, its *šatammu*, in the context of a dispute with the treasurer of Babylon; on continuities of Babylonian religious practices and thought patterns: cf. the texts published by Nougayrol 1947 and Labat 1960, as well as the remarks of Joannès 1992c; problem of Anu: cf. Kuhrt 1987a: 151 (but the link speculatively suggested with Artaxerxes II's reform does not appear obvious to me), as well as

Stolper 1990b: 561, Beaulieu 1992: 54–60 and 1993b: 48–49. On the near-absence of "Greco-Persian" scenes in the Susa impressions, cf. Amiet 1972b: 285 (quotation in the text). The Persian diaspora, which was certainly sizable in Babylonia, is nonetheless poorly known: cf. the elements gathered (for the period 482–331) by Zadok 1977: 96–107 (but most of the material dates to the fifth century; cf. p. 106); the author (p. 91) says that the number of people with Iranian names or patronymics tends to increase throughout the Achaemenid period, but a reading of his work does not tend to prove this formally, even if the assumption does seem logical (cf. also Stolper 1987: 393–95 and 1992b: 126: names of several Persians or Iranians who owned lands in Babylonia at the end of the fifth century: Mitratu, Artašāta, Spitamas; also Stolper 1992b, the examples quoted by Dandamaev 1983: 137–40, and now the synthesis in Dandamaev 1992a, on which see Stolper 1994b); for Susa, cf. the publication of the tomb by Morgan 1905 (Persian jewelry), a tomb whose date has just been pushed back to the end of the fifth century by J.-A. G. Elayi 1992a; we may add several mentions of *magi* in the tablets: Dandamaev and Livshits 1988 (with the remarks of Schmitt 1990b) and Dandamaev 1992a: 166–67. Babylonian seals: see remarks by Kuhrt 1987c: 50–51 (where further bibliographic references will be found); some Babylonian data on names and personal names are taken from Zadok 1977; all the others are drawn from the rich analysis of Bregstein 1993, particularly pp. 218–38 (I very heartily thank the author for sending me a copy of his dissertation); on Bēlšunu: Kuhrt (1987a: 153–54) asks whether he might not be a "Babylonized" Persian: but his patronymic would seem to rule out this suggestion; on the theory about Antibelus of Susa, I note in passing that the use of the double name is known in Seleucid Babylonia: cf. Sherwin-White 1983 (cf. pp. 213–14 on Babylonian usage); this practice (known in Egypt: cf. Briant 1988a: 160–61) could explain the case of Datames/Tarkumawa: cf. a theory along these lines in Lemaire 1989a: 149 and 1991c: 204–5. "Babylonization" of the dynasty (see already chap. 15/8 above on Anāhita/Ištar): on the "Babylonian" concubines of Artaxerxes I and the problem posed by Ctesias's vocabulary, cf. Briant 1990b: 54 and n. 30; the word "Babylonization," which tends to find its context in a recurring view of "decadence" (e.g., Athenaeus XII.530d), must be wielded with caution: we may recall for example that at a date when we recognize that the portraits on royal coins were individualized, Babelon (1910: II.2: 50) claims to recognize Darius II by "his big Semitic [*sic!*] nose," stressing (by way of "explanation") that the king was born of a Babylonian woman; cf. conversely (and equally ideologized) his description of the "portrait" of Cyrus the Younger (ibid., 51–52); such postulates stir unpleasant memories (cf. *RTP* 265–76). Of course these bad habits do not *ipso facto* condemn the word "Babylonization," but its content remains nebulous and fickle. On Bēl and Ninus on Darius III's chariot: aside from the brief, unclear remarks of Boyce (1982: 287–88), the only commentary I know is by Harmatta (1978: 317–18), who draws from it a straightforward conclusion on the change in Achaemenid monarchic ideology: "This fact proves that from Artaxerxes II on (who was of half-Babylonian origin, and under whom the golden eagle first appeared), Old Persian royal ideology underwent some changes and was adopted to Babylonian ideas more than before. The Achaemenid family tree was enlarged with Ninus and Belus, and the Babylonian royal standard, representing the eagle Anzu with outspread wings, was adopted as the royal emblem of the Old Persian Great King." This is an interesting suggestion, but it runs up against some serious objections: (1) It is based (more or less implicitly) on the belief that Artaxerxes II's act rested on an assimilation between Anāhita and Ištar, which appears to me far from obvious (cf. chap. 15/8); (2) I am not certain that Quintus Curtius's information should be considered a "fact" (on Berossus's influence on Diodorus and Quintus Curtius, cf. Schnabel 1923: 35–66; and, on Berossus's purposes, the fundamental consideration by Kuhrt 1987c); (3) as for the royal standard, it seems to me that Nylander's (1983) investigation of the *Mosaic of Naples* leads us to see in it the attestation of persistent Iranian (Persian) traditions rather than the introduction of Assyro-Babylonian traditions ⟦at any rate, see now the remarks along these lines of Nylander 1993: 151, who, without citing Harmatta's article, thinks that Quintus Curtius was confused and that Ninus and Bēl actually represented Ahura-Mazda and Mithra, the eagle being known as a specifically Achaemenid emblem; cf. also his note 67, p. 158]. In the same vein, I will make two additional remarks: (1) According to Sims-Williams (1991: 182–83), the festival in honor of Mithra could have been created "in imitation of the Babylonian festival in honor of Šamaš"; (2) the texts of Ctesias (*Persica* §21) and Aelian (*VH* XIII.7) might attest to the perseverance (at any rate likely and logical) of pre-Achaemenid royal rituals in Babylonia (cf. Macginnis 1987b). On Arrian VII.24.3 and the *nomos persikos*, cf. also along these lines Smelik 1978–79: 107; on the Sacaea, cf. Langdon 1924 and Labat 1939: 98–102; cf. also Briant 1991a: 3–4; Labat (1939: 102) doubts that this Babylonian festival could be confused with the New Year; cf. also Bottéro 1978: 17, who is reserved about the possibility of identifying it with the substitute king ritual: on this, see more clearly Parpola 1983: xxxi (on Berossus: the author thinks on the contrary that Dio Chrysostom IV.66–68 does refer to the substitute king ritual); on the Sacaea, see most recently Boyce and Grenet 1991: 290–92 (but the suggested interpretation does not really take into account the Babylonian traditions on the matter); on the New Year festival and the policy (falsely) attributed to Xerxes concerning it, cf. the proof by A. Kuhrt in Kuhrt and Sherwin-White 1987a: 73–76.

11. The Great King, Alexander, and the Peoples of the Zagros Mountains

• On the roads and routes between Susa and Persepolis, see *RTP* 163–68; Mostafavi 1960; Hallock 1977; and Koch 1986. On the point discussed here, I refer to my proof in Briant 1976 (with the critical remarks of Sancisi-Weerdenburg and van der Vliet, *BiOr* 36/1–2 [1979]: 119–21; cf. also *RTP* 206–7 on Madates in Briant 1982b: 57–112. The interpretation is adopted by, e.g., Boucharlat 1990a: 162–63; it is ignored by Badian 1985: 441–42 note, but referred to more explicitly in Badian 1994, even though his chronological reconstruction ought to have led him to examine more closely what he calls (deliberately) without differentiation "the Uxian interlude" (p. 279); it is quite strange that the author (who, moreover, on p. 287 acknowledges Uxian assessments on the Great King) has not understood (cf. notes 40–41) that the entire episode makes sense only if we recognize two Uxian populations and two battles (as I proved in Briant 1976, repeated in *RTP*— an article also unknown to Bosworth 1980a quoted by Badian, but quoted and accepted in Bosworth 1988: 89–90). On Elymeans and Elymais (and its sanctuaries), cf. Holleaux 1968: 255ff. and Boyce and Grenet 1991: 40–48 (with some guesses, p. 40); on the Cadusians, the sources are collected by G. Meyer, *RE* Suppl. 7 (1940): 316–17; cf. also Syme 1988 (not too useful); the theory on monomachy was already presented in brief in Briant 1976: 239 n. 103. [The stories of relations between Alexander and the Uxians have recently been restudied by Atkinson 1994: 68–83, who disagrees with some of my interpretations; the book reached me too late to be discussed here; I shall return to it elsewhere.]

12. Persepolis, Pasargadae, and Persia

• On the roads, cf. *RTP* 163–68, where complete bibliographic references will be found. Alexander at Persepolis and Pasargadae: cf. *RTP* 384–403, Wiesehöfer 1994a: 23–49, and chap. 18/2 below; Persian demography: Briant 1987a: 21–22; fourth-century work at Persepolis: cf. Calmeyer 1990a; tomb of Artaxerxes III: Schmidt 1970: 102–7, and the commentaries of Roaf 1983: 128 and Calmeyer 1990a: 12–13 (on the number of delegates, see also the remarks of Borchhardt 1993b, to be compared with those of Calmeyer 1990a: 12); on the incomplete tomb, cf. Kleiss and Calmeyer 1975 (time of Artaxerxes II) and Calmeyer 1990a: 11–12 (Darius III?, with huge doubts). I will make three additional remarks on this matter: (1) It is sometimes suggested that the reliefs on Artaxerxes III's tomb attest to the "decadence" of Achaemenid artistic traditions; but if, in effect, they are nothing more than copies of the reliefs on Darius I's tomb, the concept of "decadence" seems particularly inappropriate in this area (cf. the remarks of Calmeyer 1990a: 13); the idea seems to go back to Herzfeld's highly "Alexandrocentric" interpretations, on which see the critical remarks of Root 1994: 17; (2) similar reflections have often been offered on the "deplorable" syntax of the last royal inscriptions; I am not competent to participate in this debate; I will simply remark, on the one hand, that according to some authors (Lecoq 1974a: 60–61; Mayrhofer 1974: 109), knowledge of the language of the inscriptions had been deteriorating since Xerxes, and on the other, that in at least one case what has long been held to be a syntactic mistake by the royal authors actually came from a wrong reading on the part of modern epigraphers, who then spoke of "barbarism" (cf. Benveniste 1954: 309): cf. now Stève 1987: 98 and Lecoq 1990b on the false "paradise" in A²Sd; (3) we no longer discern "negative" change in the royal images on the siculi and darics dated between Artaxerxes III and Darius III, even if these late coins are obviously not free of variation (as after all has been the case since Darius I): most recently Alram 1993. On the Greek *kurtaš* of Persepolis: I have long been directing attention to these texts (without much effect, I must admit): cf. in particular *RTP* 329 n. 161; on Arrian VI.29.7 and its comparison with the facts in the tablets, cf. chap. 2/9, pp. 95–96. On the nonexistence of a satrapy at the time of the tablets, cf. chap. 11/10: Parnaka, Persia, and Darius, pp. 466ff.; on Ariobarzanes' title, cf. also the doubts of Tuplin 1987b: 115, and the caution of Lewis 1977: 9; somewhat confused presentation by Petit 1990: 212–13 (I do not see the basis for Berve [II no. 115] to make this Ariobarzanes the son of Artabazus, nor why he thinks that Ariobarzanes might have joined his father close to Darius [cf. Arrian III.23.7]: Quintus Curtius clearly says that this person died soon after in battle: V.4.34); on relations between Persia and the lands of the Persian Gulf, cf. chap. 16/17, pp. 758ff. On the status of the plains Uxians, the basic text is Quintus Curtius V.3.16 (cf. *RTP* 162–63): the exemption from tribute is granted when the conqueror Alexander might have imposed it—which leaves open the hypothesis that it was already the rule in the Achaemenid period. One final remark: the exile of Persepolis architects to India, as suggested by Wheeler 1974, is based on very debatable indications: Nylander 1988.

13. From Persepolis to Ecbatana

• On the Median royal stud farms, cf. *RTP* 354–56 (and on the *Suda*'s surprising note on Nisaean horses [coming from the Persian Gulf], cf. Goukowsky 1974: 136 n. 104); on Nisāya: the word may be used as a personal name: Nesāya, that is, something along the order of "the Nisaean" (*DAE* 46 [= *BMAP* 5] lines 16–17, where Ātarfarna, son of Nesāya, is called a Mede). Strabo XI.13.7 stresses the excellence of the "Medic grass" that nourishes horses the best; it is generally identified as common alfalfa; perhaps it may be identified in the Iranian word (borrowed into Akkadian) *aspastu*, but the translation 'alfalfa' is not absolutely certain: cf. Jursa 1993 and Donbaz and Stolper 1993. Medes in the Babylonian tablets: cf. Zadok 1977: 112–13 and Dandamaev 1992a: 153–56. On the word *eparchy* in the Hellenistic texts, cf. Bickerman 1938: 197–99, 203 and chap. 16/8 above (but in *DB* §32, *dahyu* seems to have the meaning 'people' instead: Lecoq 1990a: 133–34, who emphasizes that Kent's translation 'district' is erroneous). Media in the Persepolis tablets (many of them still unpublished), see Vallat 1993: 161–62 and Koch 1993a: 12–14. The adjective *ateikhistos* applied by Polybius (X.27.6) to the town of Ecbatana as opposed to the man-made citadel (*akra*) "admirably constructed and fortified" merits a few remarks: for one thing, the same word, *ateikhistos*, is used by Polycleitus about Susa (Strabo XV.3.2), which obviously does not mean there were no walls in Susa but instead refers to walls that hold up terraces, walls "that on the inside scarcely projected above the occupation level" (Boucharlat 1990a: 150).—Susa, which like Ecbatana had an acropolis (Strabo XV.3.2; Diodorus XIX.48.7); besides, a passage from Aelian (*VH* VII.8) deserves to be quoted, because he says that, after the death of Haephestion, Alexander "destroyed the acropolis of Ecbatana and knocked down its walls (*teikhē*)"; Plutarch (*Pel.* 34.2; *Alex.* 72.3) refers only to throwing down the battlements; the word used by Aelian (*perikeirō*) could well be an allusion (in the form of a pun) to a debated measure taken (it appears) by Alexander, to cut the mane and tail of the horses and mules "as a sign of mourning"; taking into account the many versions of this episode that were circulating, Arrian (VII.14.4) reports that some said Alexander even shaved (*keirasthai*) his own head completely; it is in this critical passage that he describes the order for "the temple of Asclepius at Ecbatana to be razed to the ground"

(§14.5◇); perhaps we ought not bother to inquire too closely into the identity of this god, since Arrian rejects this tradition, which, he says, better fits Xerxes' destructions, and which perhaps was constructed out of the arrival of a delegation from Epidaurus to whom the king entrusted "a votive offering to take back to Asclepius" (14.6◇, to his sanctuary in Epidaurus); finally it is clear that the story has been intertwined with that of Glaucias, the physician put to death for not saving Haephestion (on these contradictory traditions, cf. Heckel 1992: 87–91). In short, all we have is Polybius's description, which must correspond by and large to Achaemenid Ecbatana—which in any case archaeology has not revealed to us: Hamadan has never been systematically excavated; all we have is a little evidence from temporary, limited expeditions (cf. Chevalier 1989), and all the Achaemenid-type objects (tableware in particular) that supposedly come from Hamadan (by way of clandestine digging and antiquities dealers) cannot be considered authentic (see especially Muscarella 1980: 31–35); quite recently (summer 1994) rumors circulated in the press of archaeological discoveries in the town of Hamadan [and a recent visit to the site, April 1995, confirmed that deliberate excavations were currently underway]. Rock-cut tombs have also been found in Media dating to the Hellenistic period that demonstrate Achaemenid influence in the region (cf. presentation and discussion in Boyce and Grenet 1991: 94–106): perhaps these are the tombs that were plundered by Alexander's generals (Arrian VI.27.4). On Behistun and its names, cf. Bernard 1980. Babylonian tablets from the time of Darius II at Ecbatana: Stolper 1990c: 164–71; see also Joannès 1990b: in one of the Babylonian tablets from Susa published by the author (no. 1; p. 177), dated to an Artaxerxes, one of the parties asks the other "to give him the maidservant Šammandu as wife by bringing her from Ecbatana to Susa" (on the Murašû texts from Susa, see Stolper 1992c); *ADRBT* no. –369: Stolper, *CAH* VI²: 239. Khorassan road: see Briant 1984b: 36–40; Caspian Gates: Bosworth 1980a: 334–35 and Bernard 1994b: 483 and n. 11–12. The "special" size of the Median contingents in Darius III's army, as suggested by Vogelsang (1992: 229–34), appears to me based on circular reasoning, which grants disproportionate value to the testimony (which at any rate is far from clear) of Quintus Curtius III.2.4–9. On the "*syllogos* of Medes and Persians," cf. Briant 1994e: 286–91 (where I recall other possible but, in my opinion, less convincing interpretations than the one chosen here; in any event, it must not be forgotten that the death of Bessus gave rise to a large number of versions in Antiquity).

14. From Ecbatana to the Halys

• I do not understand why Petit 1990: 205 n. 421 disallows Ctesias's evidence on Ariaramnes; as for his attempts (pp. 207–8) to deny the existence of a satrapy of Cappadocia in the time of Darius III, they are doomed to failure: cf. his very strange argument, p. 208 n. 429. The historical geography of Cappadocia and Armenia presents many problems, several of which still appear insurmountable even today: on Cappadocia cf., for example, Planhol 1981; on Achaemenid Armenia, Tiratsian's 1981 article is not useless, but he nonetheless adds little on the specific conditions of the country under Achaemenid dominion (cf. pp. 153–54 on the Van region); we also have the work of Hewsen 1983 (cf. p. 142 on Van), who calls some of his own reconstructions "speculative" (p. 143); cf. also Hewsen 1984, Schottky 1989: 4–43 (Atropatene Media and Greater Armenia at a later time), Boyce-Grenet 1991: 69–84, and the recent article of Zimansky 1995 (continuities with Urartu); on the status of Armenia, see also the remarks of Osborne 1973: 518–22; on the route of the royal road in these regions, see most recently Chaumont 1986–87; Iranian personal names in Cappadocia, cf. especially Robert 1963: 433ff.; see also the interesting Greek–Aramaic inscription of Agaça Kale (cf. Lozachmeur 1975), published by Cumont 1905c: a funerary inscription in honor of the "legitimate (faithful) satraps, Oromanes son of Ariuces, and Ariuces, his dear son"; Lipiński (1975: 197–208) relates this Ariaces to the person by the same name who in 332–331 led the Cappadocian contingents to Darius III (Arrian III.8.5); the Ariaces of the inscription, under this theory, was perhaps the son of the commander of 331 (the Aramaic text gives Ariaces II the title "sat[rap of Ar]menia": Lipiński 1975: 200–203); on the spread of Aramaic, cf. also Dupont-

Sommer 1948. On the cults, see the evidence cited in chap. 16/6 above (in Cataonia and Cappadocian regions near and far), as well as Reinach 1905 (Acilisene); Boyce 1982: 274–75; and Boyce and Grenet 1991: 262–304. Achaemenid-type objects in Colchis: Tsetskhladze 1992b, 1993/94, and 1994; Rehm 1993. Eumenes of Cardia and Perdiccas against Ariarathe of Cappadocia: *RTP* 15ff.; on Alexander's activities beyond the Halys, Arrian II.4.2 is clearly erroneous (cf. Bosworth 1980a: 189); see in particular Appian's doubts (*Mith.* 2.8), thinking that Alexander "left in place the leaders of these peoples, on the condition that they pay tribute, because he was forced to march against Darius"; even if we accept Appian's idea, it is clear that Ariarathe never paid tribute (cf. Diodorus XVIII.16.2); I wonder whether Abistamenes/Sabictas didn't simply receive the command of Cataonia (the border area between Cappadocia and Cilicia: chap. 16/6), a region that Alexander had to cross; on the satraps named by Alexander, see also Anson 1988; Persian generals' coins at Sinope: Harrison 1982b; Reinach (1890: 1–8) saw Ariarathe as a descendant of what he calls "a dynasty of tyrants" installed at Cius in Mysia during fourth-century disturbances; but while the existence of a large Persian family endowed with lands around Cius can scarcely be doubted (cf. Sekunda 1988a: 180–81), the independence of their "principality" in the Achaemenid period is deduced from late texts, which tend to qualify (by anticipation) as "hereditary kingdoms" certain satrapies or subdistricts: cf. in particular Diodorus XV.90.3 ("Great Satraps' Revolt") and XVI.90.2 (death of Ariobarzanes, succeeded by his son Mithradates); it seems clear that here and there Diodorus (XX.111.4) depends on the Cappadocian royal legend, to whose publication he himself strongly contributed (XXXI.19.1–5): see the analysis of Meyer 1879: 31–38, and chap. 3/4 above. — The results of Armenian excavations and of the pottery analyses mentioned (selectively) in the text are presented in detail by Summers 1993 (with bibliography); see ibid. p. 86 on the site of Argišti-hinili, where the Elamite tablets were discovered; they were initially interpreted (Diakonoff and Jankowska 1990) as a tale from the *Gilgamesh Epic*; but one of the editors (Diakonoff, p. 103) had first thought it might be an "administrative or business letter": this is exactly what Koch 1993b shows—I repeat his conclusions briefly here (very heartily thanking the author for sending me his article in proof [but see now Vallat 1995!]). Among the 8000 stamped bullas found at Artašāt, several bear "Greco-Persian"-inspired scenes, including a scene of prisoners lined up [Root, DATA Feb. 1993: 13], a Behistun-type image also found on an inscribed royal seal (SA^{3}b) and a Babylonian seal [pers. comm., M. Stolper and L. Bregstein]; on the Artašāt bullas, see now Khatchatrian forthcoming and Manukian forthcoming, about which I know thanks to M. F. Boussac. The Persepolis-type column bases were recently found at the site of Beniamin; the fifth–fourth century "is the date of the foundation on the hill of a large rectangular palace": Ter and Martirossov 1994. On workshops for Achaemenid-style pottery in Armenia, cf. Melikian-Chirvani 1993: 125–27.

15. From Ecbatana to Cyropolis

• To avoid filling the text with multiple, massive references to the ancient texts, I have chosen on the one hand to quote Arrian primarily (to the extent that he is not contradicted by other evidence), and on the other to refer the reader to existing overviews of the satraps and satrapies (Berve I, Seibert 1985, Vogelsang 1992: 219–44; cf. also the inventory in Dobbins 1984); besides, I have already touched elsewhere on several problems treated here (cf. Briant 1982b: 181–234; 1984b; and 1987a: 6–11): I will not automatically refer to them, except in discussions where my point of view has changed or on which new and/or different points of view have been suggested meanwhile (on the sanctuary of Takht-i Sangin and the treasury of the Oxus, cf. the recent publication of Pitschikjan 1992, which I received too late to discuss its interpretations; I note that the author's theses are discussed by Rapin 1992b, and strongly contested by Bernard 1994a, 1994b: 507–9, as well as Koch 1993c (who suggests seeing here a residence of the Achaemenid satrap); satrapies of the Iranian Plateau in the Persepolis tablets: Koch 1993a: 22–35 [and Giovanazzo 1994b]; finally, I have not tried to mention all of the chronological and/or topographic problems posed by Alexander's campaigns in eastern Iran: on this point (to restrict myself to recent references, where the earlier literature will be found), I refer basically to Bernard 1982 (replying to Bosworth 1981 on the Margiana problem), Seibert 1985, Fischer 1987, Bosworth 1988: 106–19; also Bosworth 1995 (received at the last moment). Excavations at Kandahār and Dahan-i Ghulaman, cf. Genito 1986b and Vogelsang 1992: 255–57, 260–67. On Peithon's position at Ecbatana and the *strategos* of the Upper Satrapies, see Bengtson 1964, I: 176–86 and II: 79–89, as well as Briant 1990b: 48–51; Vogelsang (1992: 240) thinks that Bessus (in the northwest) and Barsaenties (southeast) are the two main representatives of Achaemenid authority on the plateau, and compares the situation in 522 (Dādarši and Vivāna); on the positions of Bessus and Barsaentes, cf. also Briant 1984b: 71–74. On the boundary between eastern Bactria and Sogdiana, cf. the suggestions of Bernard 1975: 67–69; on the administrative unit Bactria-Sogdiana, see the thoughts of Bernard 1990a: 26; like Bactra, Maracanda included an official satrapal residence (*basileia tēs Sogdianōn khōras*; Arrian III.30.6); besides, according to Arrian (IV.15.7✧), when Alexander returned to Sogdiana he wished to punish those among the inhabitants who had refused to obey "the satrap set over them by" him: doubtless referring to Artabazus (IV.16.3), who some time earlier had been made satrap in Bactra (IV.15.5), or possibly to a subsatrap residing at Maracanda. On the significance of Alexander's offensive in the context of relations between Achaemenid Bactria and the Saka: cf. Briant 1982b: 203–30: my interpretation has been accepted, basically, by Holt 1988: 52ff.; P. Bernard (1990a: 22–25), on the other hand, has expressed reservations about it, writing "that the participation of the nomads in the anti-Macedonian revolt was more than once dictated by the lure of plunder (Arrian IV.16.4–7; 17.7)": but, exactly, does Arrian's evidence on the "natural" aggressiveness of the Saka have to be taken at face value? This is what I (like Holt) doubt; nor have Bloedow's counterarguments 1991a–b done any more to convince me. On Pazyryk, see most recently Hiebert 1992, who stresses that the tombs published by Rudenko in 1953 are, after the latest excavation campaigns, among hundreds of kurgans that allow us to define a "Pazyryk culture" based in a semi-nomadic lifestyle that may be located mostly in the fifth century; technical analyses (Böhmer and Thompson 1991) have shown that the famous carpets were not imports but were local handcrafts: "The parallels with the Greek and Achaemenid style and iconography are variants of the local style rooted in long-term interaction with Central Asia" (p. 127); on the same subject, see the special number of *Source (Notes in the History of Art)* 10/4 (1991) dedicated to Pazyryk, especially the article by J. Lerner, who conducts a very detailed iconographic analysis of the Pazyryk carpet and also concludes that it was locally made, by which she means it was not a product that came from Pesepolis workrooms (or another great imperial center); rather, she thinks that, whatever its date, the carpet might come from workrooms "in Bactria or Sogdiana, where the Achaemenid artistic koiné had penetrated and been adapted to local taste" (p. 12); this theory (which goes hand in hand with the investigation of local creation of objects with Achaemenid workmanship: e.g., Francfort 1975; Root 1991, 1994; Melikian-Chirvani 1993) fits well into the picture I am trying to draw of these interchanges between the east-oriental satrapies and the world of the steppes of Trans-Iaxartes (on the identification of Cyropolis and other Achaemenid towns of the Syr Darya, cf. Bernard 1990a: 28–29). Saka in the Babylonian *ḫaṭrus*: cf. Dandamaev 1979, 1992a: 159–62; Zadok 1977: 120–24. On the hyparchs, cf. *RTP* 241–47 and Briant 1984b: 81–88, which I repeat here with (sometimes significant) modification of certain interpretations (on the word *hyparch* in Arrian, cf. the important analysis by Bertrand 1974): the comparison on pp. 85–86 of the *syllogos* of Bactrian hyparchs with the *"syllogos* of Medes and Persians"* (Arrian IV.7.3) must be abandoned, for reasons implied by the analysis in chap. 16/13 above; *syllogos* = place of assembly, cf. Widengren 1956: 157ff. and Petit 1990: 133–36; on **handaisa*, cf. Dandamaev 1992a: 18. The theory of large Achaemenid military regions (four of them, one of them being the Upper Satrapies) goes back to Meyer, repeated by Bengtson 1964, III: 176–77: cf. Briant 1990b: 50–51 (but the support found in Diodorus XVI.50.8 must be kept in perspective for reasons already presented in the Research Notes to chap. 15/8: "The Imperial Realm," pp. 1001f.): on Quintus Curtius VII.11.29, cf. *RTP* 242–43, and on the meaning of *attribuere/attributio* see the important article of Bernard 1990 (esp. p. 157: "Attribution is only one of the means allowing the elements of the Empire to be hierarchized"), who suggests (n. 177) a completely justified comparison with Persian practice (cf. Briant 1985b); for all these reasons, the doubts expressed by Tuplin 1987c: 185 do not appear to me to be fully justified, even though he is correct in stressing the uncertainty of the sources; on the Persians in Bactria and Bactrians elsewhere in the Empire, cf. Briant 1984b: 89–96; exile of the Branchidae, cf. Bernard 1985a: 123–25 and Briant 1992a: 14; strongholds in Sogdiana and Bactria: cf. list in Francfort 1979 and Tuplin 1987c: 240 (where the sources are collected), and now Gardin 1995; Achaemenid fortifications at Samarkand: cf. Bernard 1990a: 29–30, Bernard, Grenet, and Isamiddinov 1990 (366–69) and 1992, and most recently Rapin and Isamiddinov 1994 (where the authors recall structures of the period they term "Achaemenid"); network of fortresses, cf. *RTP* 190–91 (on Quintus Curtius VII.10.15, cf. the correction of Bernard 1982, opposing Bosworth 1981 on Margiana: cf. most recently on the "Achaemenid palace" of Merv, Usmanova 1992). Achaemenid administration and irrigation works: I repeat here the essence of arguments worked out in Briant 1984b (and 1993c); the contrary position of the archaeologists has been restated by Gardin 1986 (who thinks [p. 88] the opposite position is "intellectually lightweight"), Francfort 1989: 438–46, and Lyonnet 1990, 1994, though they do not analyze the basis of my arguments because of what they consider the decisive nature of the pottery calibration (I will further remark that Lyonnet's 1990: 87 recourse to Boucharlat 1990a is misplaced, because it greatly exceeds the author's interpretive intent; he himself [p. 162] bases his suggestions on a parallel with Bactrian archaeology, so that the suggested support loses much of its probative force; I also continue to question the formulation used in Lyonnet 1994: 545 on northern Syria); on the famous "Bactrian entity": the reaffirmation by Vallat 1993: cxxxvii–cxlii, 42, 161–62, of the historical character of Diodorus II.5–7 on pre-Achaemenid Bactria does not seem to me particularly fortunate, whatever other validity his analysis of the Assyrian sources may have (the two arguments have to be conducted separately); the quotation in the text from B. Lyonnet comes from Lyonnet 1994: 542; on this point, see also Vogelsang 1992: 245–303, esp. pp. 270–74 on northern Bactria, who comes to the same overall conclusion as Gardin and Lyonnet, all the while emphasizing (pp. 302–3) "that an apparent cultural autonomy of the subject territories cannot be directly used to suggest political autonomy with respect to the same territories"; this is the position I have defended for years (cf. also pp. 1–9 above, where my position is somewhat simplified); on the methodological problems posed by the contrast of two pictures (textual and archaeological) in the general framework of the Empire, cf. Briant 1984b; 1987a: 6–11; Sancisi-Weerdenburg 1990a and chap. 16/18 below. Imperial Aramaic in Kandahār and Central Asia: cf. Briant 1984b: 60 (with references to the previous literature, including Benveniste 1958b quoted in the text); Rapin 1992a: 105, 111–12; and Bernard 1987: 187 (also notes the attestation of the custom of birds stripping the flesh from cadavers [Strabo XV.1.62] and concludes that these two continuities [religious and linguistic] "testify to the profound impress left on the country by two centuries of Achaemenid hegemony"); on the inscriptions from the Treasury of Ai-Khanūm and the theory of borrowings from the Achaemenid administration, see now Rapin 1992a: 273–79 (architecture) and 108–13 (fiscal operations and use of Aramaic): I will allow myself to point out that I made a suggestion along these lines back in 1979 (*RTP* 317–18). On the (very widespread) theory of "Bactrian autonomy" at the end of the Achaemenid period (supposedly proved by Bessus's policy), cf. the counterarguments I presented in 1984b: 76–80.

16. From the Punjab to the Indus Delta

• India and its neighbors in the Persepolis tablets: see Koch 1993a: 36–38. On the Indo-Iranian borderlands and the Indus Valley at the end of Achaemenid dominion, cf. Vogelsang 1992: 75–95, 236–41, 246–55; cf. also 1990, where he thinks (pp. 107–8) that the silence of the sources does not necessarily imply that India completely escaped Persian domination; he quite rightly remarks that the Persian authority's methods of intervention were flexible and adapted to the traditions of the countries; the complex problem of Alexander's Indian satrapies has been presented by Bosworth

1983 and Dobbins 1984; on Strabo XV.2.1, cf. Bernard 1985a: 85ff.; on Sambus/Samaxus, cf. Eggermont 1975: 16–22 and Briant 1984b: 71–74 (powers of the satrap of Bactra); on the problems relating to the route taken by Craterus, cf. Goukowsky 1981: 105–7; dogs from India: cf. the note of Goukowsky 1976: 248–49; among those who provided elephants was certainly Eudamus (cf. Bernard 1985b); on the Indian elephants at the Achaemenid court and in Darius III's army, cf. Bigwood 1993, Bosworth 1993: 413, and Briant 1995d; Indian coin "with satrap": Bernard 1987: 190; seals and impressions of "Greco-Persian" type: Callieri 1992. On all these problems, see most recently Fleming 1992, whose provocative title perfectly expresses the difficulty of the situation regarding evidence; it includes an overview of several works published in India on the question, a presentation of the pottery data, and the (cautious) reaffirmation that the Achaemenid capital may have been located at Taxila (on which, one might consult the discussion between Wheeler 1974 and Nylander 1988).

17. From Pattala to Susa and Babylon: The Persians and the Persian Gulf

• On the return of Nearchus: cf. the older, careful analysis of Schiwek 1962; see also Bosworth 1988: 139–53 and the remarks of Salles 1988a: 86–87, as well as Potts 1990b: 2–4, and quite recently Besenval 1994: 525–29 (texts related to explorations on the Gedrosian coast); on the complementary nature of Nearchus's and Alexander's expeditions, cf. also Bosworth 1987 (who, p. 560 n. 56, rightly stresses the total misinterpretation of Engels 1978: 118 on the question; see also Kraft 1971: 106–18); on Arrian's text, see also Briant 1987b: 2. The question of the presence and activity of the Achaemenids in the Gulf has been the topic of several overviews by J. F. Salles (cf. Salles 1990, where the sources are presented and commented on; also 1988a, 1992a–b); also consult the summaries by Boucharlat and Salles 1981 and 1987, the recent synthesis by Potts 1990a–b, and Tuplin 1991a: 275–78; on the legend of Erythras, cf. also Agatharcides (Strabo XVI.4.20), who states that the legend was transmitted to the Athenians by a Persian, Boxus, who had left his homeland in the Hellenistic period (on this, see Goukovsky 1974 and Burstein 1989: 42–45); the etiological legend may well have preserved the memory of Persian dominion in the Gulf. On the interest of the Persepolis tablets, see particularly Koch 1993a: 16–21. The ancient geography of the head of the Persian Gulf continues to pose major problems: cf. Briant 1986b and Bosworth 1987; on the islands of deportees: Potts (1990a: 351) thinks they might be Bahrein and Failaka and (p. 355) that a reorganization of the central Persian Gulf took place after the Achaemenid conquest or at the time of Darius's tribute reform at the latest; on the canal near Bushire, cf. Whitcomb 1987; as for the contingents' coming from "the tribes bordering on the Red Sea" (Arrian III.8.5❖: *prosoikoi tēi Erythreai thalassēi*; cf. 11.5: *hoi pros tēi Erythreai thalassēi*), they must, I think, be distinguished from those whom Herodotus (III.93❖; VII.80❖) calls "the inhabitants of the islands in the Persian Gulf [*anaspastoi*]"; but Arrian's text is no less problematic (Bosworth 1980a: 290–91 suspects a lacuna): at Gaugamela, the inhabitants of the Persian Gulf fought separately from the Persians (Arrian III.11.3–7), which implies that their contingents constituted a special subgroup (cf. Quintus Curtius IV.12.8: *partibus copiarum*); I am tempted to think that, under the general command of Orxines (ibid.), Ariobarzanes led the Persian troops and Orontobates the troops from the Gulf coast (Persian and Carmanian), the former even including those whom Quintus Curtius (IV.12.9❖) calls "the Indi and the rest of the dwellers on the Red Sea." On incense from India, cf. Salles 1987: 90. Archaeological discoveries on the Arabian coast of the Gulf: overview by Salles 1990: 119–23; the Achaemenids and Oman: Potts 1990a: 394–400 (the interpretation of the Persepolis tablets offered by Potts 1990a: 391–92 poses formidable problems because of the uncertainty of the place-names—as stressed by the author himself; it seems rather unlikely that a name such as Ti-ul-ma-in-to or Ti-li-man could refer to Dilmun: cf. Koch 1990: 304: Tirman); "Achaemenid" *qanat*s in Oman: most recently Planhol 1992: 137; voyages of Archias, Androsthenes, and Hieron: Högeman 1985: 88–93, and Salles 1988: 86ff. (the author thinks [p. 88] that it is a matter of "true explorations of virgin territory"—a phrase that seems excessive to me, given the fact that the author recognizes that the Seleucids behaved there as "heirs of the Achaemenids": 1987: 89); see also Potts 1990b: 5–10; on Aginis/Ampe/Durine, cf. Högeman 1985: 153–55 (but the conclusions that the author draws about Arab-Achaemenid hostilities do not appear valid to me: cf. chap. 16/10 Research Notes, p. 1018 above); on Gerrha, cf. ibid., 85–97; and Sherwin-White and Kuhrt 1993: 97, 200. One last remark: against the position defended (for example) by Rouché and Sherwin-White 1985, Hornblower (1990b: 95) thinks it not impossible that the Greek garrison at Failaka (*SEG* XII.556) dates to the end of the Achaemenid period—which would require recognition that the Great King had settled Greeks there; without being able to justify it, I must reveal my skepticism about this suggestion (on the text, cf. most recently Sherwin-White and Kuhrt 1993: 173–78).

18. An Appraisal and Some Questions

• *List of evidence recently discovered*: (I have not attempted systematically to gather isolated discoveries/publications of Babylonian tablets, or coins.)

At the Center

Pasargadae: Final publication: Stronach 1978 (cf. also 1985b, 1989a).

Persepolis and Fārs: "Rediscovery" of the central panel of the Persepolis Apadana: Tilia 1974–78; walls of Persepolis: Mousavi 1992; Kleiss 1992b; publication of the Fortification tablet seals in progress: Hallock 1977; Garrison 1988–92, forthcoming; Root 1989–93; Keel 1990: 90; inscribed royal seals (catalog): Schmitt 1981; first supplement to the PFT: Hallock 1978 [[list of tablets transcribed and transliterated by Hallock before his death: apud Vallat 1993: lxxv–ci]]; isolated publications of unpublished Fortification tablets: Grillot 1986; Lewis 1980; Vallat 1994; Akkadian tablet from the Fortification archive: Stolper 1984a; new edition of the various versions of Behistun: Von Voigtlander 1978; Greenfield Porten 1982; Schmitt 1991b; Porten-Yardeni 1993; Grillo-Susini, Herrenschmidt, and Malbran-Labat 1993; Malbran-Labat 1994; Aramaic version of *DNa*: Sims-Williams 1981; archaeological discoveries in Fārs: Kleiss 1981, 1991, 1992a, 1993; Sumner 1972, 1988.

Susa: Statue of Darius, Darius Gate, and inscriptions: *JA* 1972 and *CDAFI* 1974; palace of Artaxerxes II at Susa: Boucharlat et al. 1979f; stratigraphic investigations: Miroschedji 1978–90; residual traces of a copy of the Behistun relief: Canby 1978 and Muscarella in Harper, Anuz, and Tallon (1991): 218 n. 2, 221 n. 14; new inscriptions of Artaxerxes II: Vallat 1979; final edition of the royal inscriptions of Susa: Stève 1987; Elamite tablet with seal from the reign of Darius (MDP 11 308): Garrison forthcoming; small objects: Amiet 1972a, 1990; seals: Amiet 1972b: 284–87; Babylonian tablets: Joannès 1990b.

Ecbatana: Chevalier 1989; Babylonian texts relating to commercial activities at Ecbatana: Dandamaev 1986c; Stolper 1990c; Joannès 1990b no. 1. Excavations in progress on the tell (1995).

Babylon: Inscription of Artaxerxes II: Vallat 1989a; remains of a copy of the Behistun relief: Seidl 1976; cf. Von Voigtlander 1978: 63–66.

In the Provinces

Babylonia: Cadastral documents: Nemet-Nejat 1982; Joannès 1990c; temple archives: e.g., Cocqerillat 1968–85; Frame 1984–91; Joannès 1982, 1992b; Beaulieu 1993; Stolper 1992b; Zawadski 1986; McGinnis 1994, 1995; private archives: Stolper 1985–92; Joannès 1989a, 1992c; van Driel 1987–89; Wunsch 1993; astronomical tablets: Wiseman 1983: 116–21; Brinkman 1987; Sachs and Hunger 1988; publication of texts by reign: Cagni, Giovinazzo, and Graziani 1985; Giovinazzo 1983; Graziani 1983–86, 1991; Weisberg 1980; coins: Reade 1986; seals and impressions: Wooley 1962; Porada 1979a; Graziani 1989; Bregstein 1993; results of explorations: Adams and Nissen 1972; Adams 1981; Gibson 1972; Achaemenid residence near Sippar: *NAPR* 1987–92, Gasche 1995.

Assyria: archaeological evidence of Persian presence: see, e.g., Goldstein 1980 (on the glass objects); collection of data by Kuhrt 1995.

Persian Gulf: archaeological discoveries: Salles 1988–90; Potts 1990a–b.

Asia Minor and Anatolia

Evidence of uncertain provenance: Hoard of 1491 siculi: Alram 1993; wood beams decorated with "Greco-Persian" style paintings: Calmeyer 1992a [from a tomb near Dascylium?].

Cilicia: Reliefs from Meydançikkale and Aramaic inscriptions: Laroche and Davesne 1981; Davesne-Lemaire-Lozachmeur 1987; Sayar 1990; Lemaire 1991c, 1993, 1994b; Lemaire and Lozachmeur 1990; Iranian religious title (not previously attested) in a Greek inscription: Dagron and Feissel 1987: 36; "Greco-Persian" reliefs: Hermary 1984.

Lycia: Xanthus Trilingual: *CRAI* 1974 and *FdX* VI; other evidence from Xanthus: Bousquet 1975–92; Childs and Demargne 1989; archaeological and epigraphic evidence from Limyra: Borchhardt 1976–93; Wörrle 1991–93; tombs of Elmali and Karaburun: Mellink 1979.

Caria: Discovery of a fourth-century female's tomb and its contents, including a diadem similar to the one from tomb 2 of Vergina in Macedon: Özen 1994; Prag and Neave 1994.

Lydia and Sardis: Greek inscriptions from or relating to Sardis: Robert 1975; Hanfmann 1987 and Masson 1987; Lydian inscriptions from Sardis: Gusmani 1964–83; Lydian helmet from Sardis [dated 546]: Greenwalt 1992 and Greenwalt and Haywood 1992; publication of the pyramidal tomb of Sardis: Ratté 1992, and of the tomb of Taš-Kule: Cahill 1988; "Greco-Persian" stelas: Radt 1983; Greenwalt and Heywood 1992: 16.

Hellespontine Phrygia and Dascylium: "Greco-Persian" reliefs in the Dascylium area, several of which were discovered in the 1980s (Altheim-Stiehl, Metzler, and Schwertheim 1983; Cremer 1984; Altheim-Stiehl and Cremer 1985): Nollé 1992 (others have been discovered since then but are not yet published; oral information from T. Bakir); Dascylium excavations: in progress: T. Bakir 1995; tomb(?): Calmeyer 1992a.

Paphlagonia: "Greco-Persian" relief: Doncel and Voute 1984.

Gordion and Phrygia: State of excavations of Gordion: DeVries 1990.

Armenia: Achaemenid sites: Summers 1993; Elamite tablets from Armavir-blur: Koch 1993b [[cf. Diaknonoff and Jankowska 1990; and now Vallat 1995!]]; Hellenistic seals with Persian motifs: Manukian forthcoming; Achaemenid bell-shaped bases found at the site of Dastakert, whose founding goes back to the fifth–fourth centuries: Ter-Martirossov 1994; Achaemenid-type silver vessel: Melikian-Chirvani 1993: 125–26.

Georgia: Many valuable objects of Achaemenid make found in the tombs of the local elite: Tsetskhladze 1993–94 and 1994 (with Rehm 1993).

Syria-Palestine, Judea-Samaria: State of archaeological discoveries: Stern 1982b; *Transeuphratène* 1–9 (1989–95); excavations of cemeteries in Syria: Moorey 1975, 1980; Persian levels at Tell Mardikh/Ebla: Mazzoni 1990, 1991–92; *Dossiers Histoire et archéologie* 83 (1984): 29–31; archaeological publication of the Persian period at Tell el-Hesi: Bennett and Blakely 1989; ostraca of Beer-sheba and Tell Arad: Naveh 1979–81; publication of the coins from Samaria: Meshorer and Qedar 1991; Lemaire and Joannès 1994; hundreds of Aramaic ostraca similar to the Aramaic ostraca from Beer-sheba (fourth century), dispersed from Idumea, in course of analysis and publication (oral communication from André Lemaire); publication of the Wadi ed-Daliyeh papyri: Cross 1985; Gropp 1986; of the Wadi ed-Daliyeh seal impressions: Leith 1990; Jewish coins: Barag 1985–87; Spaer 1977, 1986–87; various coinages in the countries of Ebir Nāri: Mildenberg 1979–94; Babylonian tablet dating to Cambyses year 5 found at Tell Mikhmoret: Stern 1993: 1044–45.

Phoenicia and Cyprus: Excavations at Dor: Stern 1994b–c; monuments: Stucky 1984; von Graeve 1987; Dunand and Saliby 1985; coins: J.-G. Elayi 1993; new Phoenician and Aramaic inscriptions: Deustch and Heltzer 1994; new Phoenician inscription from Kition: Yon and Snyczer 1991 and 1992.

Egypt: New edition of Demotic texts: Hughes 1984; new Demotic texts from Saqqara and Memphis: Smith 1972, 1992a–b, in preparation; Devauchelle 1994a–b, Bresciani 1996; new epigraphic and archaeological evidence from Wadi Hammamât: Bongrani-Fanfoni and Israel 1994, from Nubia: Heidorn 1991–92, from Wadi Tumilat: Paice 1986/87–93; Holladay 1982–92; Redmount 1995; approximately 90 Demotic ostraca dated between year 32(?) of Darius I and year 22 of Artaxerxes I found at the site of Ayn Manâwir 5 km west of the tell of Douch (personal communication from Nicolas Grimal); new editions of Aramaic texts from Elephantine and elsewhere: Porten 1986–90; Porten and Yardeni 1986–93; Szubin and Porten 1988–92; Lemaire 1991c, 1995b; new publications of the Aramaic version of Behistun: Greenfield and Porten 1982 and Porten and Yardeni 1993 (*TADAE* C.2.1); discovery of the Aramaic text of the Naqš-i Rustam inscription on an Elephantine papyrus: Sims-Williams 1981; memorandum of Egyptian customs duties in the reign of Xerxes: Porten and Yardeni 1993 [*TADAE* C.3.7]; Yardeni 1994; Lipiński 1994; Aramaic documents from Saqqara: Segal 1983. Tomb of Udjahorresnet: Bareš 1992; Verner 1989; new publication of the temple of El-Khārga: Cruz-Uribe 1986–88, forthcoming; a *naos* of Darius I: Mysliwiec 1991; evidence from Karnak from the time of Darius I: Traunecker 1973–77 [1980]; autobiographical hieroglyphic inscriptions: von Känel 1980; Lloyd 1982b (reedition); Perdu 1985 (reedition); Sherman 1981; Menu 1994 (new readings); *Satrap Stela*: Duvauchelle forthcoming; Carian-Memphite and Helleno-Memphite funerary stelas: Martin and Nicholls 1978; Gallo and Masson 1993; funerary stela found in October 1994 at Saqqara, whose lower register shows a high Persian dignitary seated on a throne, with a hieroglyphic inscription, "Djedherbes, son of Artjam, born of Tanofrether" (personal communication, H. S. Smith and A. Kuhrt); coins from Elephantine: Lipiński 1982; coins in the name of Artaxerxes III: Mørkholm 1974; Shore 1974; Delta fortresses: Oren 1982–85 (Migdol); Valbelle 1989, Valbelle and Defernez 1995 (forthcoming); small objects: Bernard 1976a; Stucky 1985; Pfrommer 1991, Traunecker 1995 (royal head).

Central Asia (excavations and explorations): Gardin et al. 1976–86; Gardin 1995; Francfort 1989; Lyonnet 1990, 1994; Genito 1986b; Bernard et al. 1990–92; Pitschikjian 1992 [[Bernard 1994a]]; Ricciardi 1980; Usmanova 1992; Vogelsang 1992; Elamite tablet from Kandahār: Helms 1978 [[cf. Briant 1984b: 59]].

Indus countries: Indian bronze coin with an official dressed in Persian style on the reverse: Bernard 1987; "Greco-Persian" impressions: Callieri 1992.

Many small objects, coins, and vessels from museum storerooms or appearing in dealers' showcases or gallery catalogs: e.g., McKeon 1973; Foss 1975; Francfort 1975; Moorey 1978; Gunter 1988; Gunter and Jetts 1992; Moorey 1982–88; Porada 1989, Tanabe 1989; Keel 1990: 90; Lemaire 1991d, 1992; Rozenberg 1993 etc.; Persian artillery ball dating to 546 at Phocaea: Ozigyit 1994; Briant 1994g.

Comments

• On the problems touched on here (I would note that the discussion stands in logical relation to that in chap. 11/6 above, pp. 447ff.), cf. Briant 1984b: 59–61 (Kandahār tablet: conclusions already reinforced by Jones and Stolper 1986, and now by Koch 1993b [Elamite tablets from Armavir-blur: chap. 16/14 above, p. 743], and Vallat 1995 too, as well as Garrison forthcoming [Susa tablet]), and Briant 1987a: 7–11 (critical analysis of the views of Moorey 1980 on what I call the "(pseudo-)statistical vision" of Achaemenid dominion), also Sancisi-Weerdenburg 1990a; add Postgate 1993: 257–61 on the Assyrian Empire ("Archaeological visibility") and Postgate 1994. On Dascylium: I have benefited from two visits to the site (July 1993, July 1995), and I was able to become acquainted with the initial results thanks to the generosity of Tomris Bakir, who has directed the excavations there for several years (she reports on them in Bakir 1995); Armenian sites: Summers 1993. Concerning the surprising rarity of Achaemenid evidence at Sardis, I will permit myself to quote at length the introductory sentences of the paper presented by C. H. Greenwalt, Jr., at the Toulouse symposium in February 1995 (= Greenwalt 1995):

> The only explanation can be the chance of survival and recovery. Conspicuous architectural monuments and stores of wealth (tombs) have been intensively pillaged; more significantly, only a small fraction of the large site has been archaeologically explored, and exploration has concen-

trated on monuments of other cultural eras. In addition, a difficulty in distinguishing Persian from Lydian in the archaeological record, due partly to continuity in building and ceramics traditions, partly to inadequate chronological references, obscures the surviving record.

I will also remark that, concerning Babylon, recent investigations tend to reevaluate the genuinely Achaemenid involvement (even of Susian origin) in the structures built in the town after the Persian conquest (Gasche 1991b and 1995 promising a dedicated study), and that, according to Fleming 1989, it was during the Achaemenid period that there appeared in Babylonia a ceramic known as "eggshell ware." —On museums' hoards, many recent examples deserve to be mentioned (and considered): first, the four cedar beams covered with "Greco-Persian" paintings and published by Calmeyer 1992a; he mentions, without further detail, that these remarkable objects were given in 1989 to a museum in Munich after being in a private collection "for several decades" (p. 7); second, the cache of 1491 siculi published by Alram 1993 was acquired in 1990 by the same museum in Munich after belonging to a private collector (most of the time, treasures are scattered when they are auctioned, or even when they are found); yet another, the two Persepolis Elamite tablets (one bearing a seal inscribed in Aramaic belonging to Parnaka) that belong to the collection of the Biblical Institute of the University of Fribourg, and whose existence was recently revealed (Keel 1990: 90; publication by Vallat 1994). To these examples may be added, despite its being a special case, the pottery collected in Armenia by C. A. Burney during his 1955 explorations: it has remained in storage in the British Institute in Ankara for several decades (Summers 1993: 87). It might perhaps be worthwhile to mention, finally, that according to information received by Summers (1993: 96), twenty silver bars were discovered in 1938 near Cimin Tepe, some of them (apparently) with cuneiform inscriptions [[I wonder whether they might not be comparable to the "ingots of silver" found at Nūš-i Jān, one with a cuneiform inscription: Bivar 1971, esp. pp. 102 and 107]]; but apparently these objects are now lost! In short, there is no doubt that "excavations in the museums" will reveal many surprises (cf. also the painstaking and passionate inquiry into the "Athos Treasure" by Nicolet-Pierre 1992). The stela found in 1994 at Saqqara (for which I owe knowledge, a brief description, and a photograph to H. S. Smith and A. Kuhrt) was to be published in JEA 81, 1995; the information reached me at the last moment, and I was not able to integrate it into the discussions of chap. 12/1. On the ādē, the literature is considerable: cf. Tadmor 1982, Grayson 1987, Parpola 1987, and most recently Parpola and Watanabe 1988 (French translation of the treaties in Briend, Lebrun, and Puech 1992: 67ff.), and the historical comments of Cogan 1993 on the methodology of Assyrian imperialism: although the investigation cannot be carried through in detail here, reading these works has persuaded me that a systematic comparison would add much to the analysis of relations between the Achaemenid central authority and the kings and communities of the Achaemenid Empire called "independent"; Tell Fekheriye statue and dual title of the "king-governor," see already the remarks of Abou-Assaf, Bordreuil, and Millard 1982: 109–12; since then, Liverani 1988: 88–89 (the entire article raises a series of problems that might equally bear on the discussion of Achaemenid imperial formation: cf. Postgate 1993 [reply to Liverani]); on the "friendly" kingdoms of Rome in the Near East, cf., for example, Braund 1984, who notes (p. 116): "The king's relationship with Rome was the very foundation of his position [in his kingdom]": I am also tempted to think that it was the same for the kings recognized (or even appointed) by the Achaemenid authority, and obviously also for dynasts who at a particular moment received the title satrap/governor. —To sum up, no significant progress will be accomplished until after the completion of regional and even microregional analyses taking into account the various "markers" and weighting them appropriately: the attempt in the chapter ending here is nothing but an outline that will also need to be inserted, in the future, into the framework of the comparative history of imperial formations in the Near East of the first millennium.

Chapter 17

The Great King, His Armies, and His Treasures

1. The Accession of Darius III

• *From Artaxerxes III to Darius III: Diodorus and Bagoas.* I have never encountered an in-depth analysis that departs to any extent from a simple paraphrase of the ancient authors. Generally speaking, historians simply see in these events the proof and illustration of the weakening or even disintegration of the central authority (e.g., Badian 1985: 421–23; Bosworth 1988: 18, etc.).

• *Darius III's Illegitimacy: The Macedonian Version.* On Arrian II.14.4–9, see already my analysis in RTP 371–84, which I amplify here on several points.

• *Darius III and the Achaemenid Royal Family.* On the theme of the origin of kings and on Aelian XII.43, cf. some remarks in Briant 1973: 19–24.

• *Violence and nomos.* On this theme too, see Briant 1973: 179–80.

• *Darius and Bagoas.* On the chronology of the reigns: Babylonian texts put the accession of Arses in August–September 338 (Stolper, *CAH* VI²: 240; van der Spek 1993a: 86); thus his year 1 began in April 337 (Badian 1977a: 49–50); the date of Arses' assassination is generally fixed at the end of 336: the *Dynastic Prophecy* states that Babylon fell into Alexander's hands when Darius was in the fifth year of his reign, and another tablet (*ADRTB* no. –330) dates Gaugamela to Ululu 24 of year 5 of Darius, or October 1, 331 (Bernard 1990b: 516); we may also stress that a Samaria papyrus (SP 1) is dated as follows: "The twentieth day of Adar, the second year, accession year of Darius the king"; the text thus refers directly to the moment of transition between Arses/Artaxerxes (not called by name) and Darius: it dates to March 19, 335 (Cross 1985: 10; Gropp 1985: 6). On support for Darius: I do not see the basis on which Berve (no. 763) makes Hystaspes a descendant of the satrap of Bactria at the beginning of Artaxerxes I's reign or how Quintus Curtius VI.2.7 shows that he "belonged to the Achaemenid family"; the marriage of Darius to a representative of the family of Artabazus of Hellespontine Phrygia (Berve no. 116) must remain in the realm of unverified hypothesis; on the *damnatio memoriae* of Arses: Dandamaev (1989a: 313) thinks that he is denounced by the *Dynastic Prophecy*; but the passage he cites (*BHLT* II.22–24) quite certainly does not designate Arses but Cyrus instead (cf. Sherwin-White 1987: 10–11; Kuhrt 1990a: 181–82; Briant 1993c: 18).

• *The New Great King.* On Darius's name before his accession, cf. Schmitt 1982c: 86, 90–91 (a discussion of the name Codoman attributed to him by Justin).

• *The Accession of Darius III in Achaemenid Dynastic History.* Several authors think that the transition from Arses to Darius was marked by Babylonian and Egyptian revolts: cf., for example, Bosworth 1988: 18, 34, who draws very confident conclusions that "the military weakness of the Persian empire was a commonplace"; but this is to register as "facts" what are merely theories based on fragmentary and elliptical evidence; on the Egyptian revolt (Khabbabash) and the considerable uncertainties that remain, including on the chronology, cf. chap. 16/9 Research Notes, p. 1018 above; the Babylonian revolt is inferred from a Babylonian tablet (of uncertain reading; Royal list of Uruk), which simply mentions the name, Nidin-B[ēl], of a king preceding Darius III; see on this text the very cautious remarks of Kuhrt 1987a: 148–49 and Stolper, *CAH* VI²: 240: "He may be one of the rebels from the reign of Darius I, misplaced by manuscript corruption; but he may also be an otherwise unrecorded local usurper who claimed power in Babylon during the unstable period of the assassinations that brought Darius III to the throne." These remarks obviously do not imply that the dynastic troubles that emerged between the assassination of Artaxerxes III and the accession of Darius III (August–September 338 – late 336) had no detrimental repercussions here and there (cf. Kuhrt and Sherwin-White 1994: 316 n. 13); but it is necessary to observe that the available evidence does not authorize the opposite conclusion of generalized rebellion or collapse of imperial structures shortly before 334.

2. The Great King and the Persian Aristocracy

• See the discussions in chap. 8 above and chap. 18/3, pp. 852ff.

3. The Royal Armies

• *The Greek Thesis.*   See already chap. 14/7: Darius II and His Armies, pp. 597ff. (where the Babylonian evidence from the reign of Artaxerxes II has already been introduced *in extenso*), and chap. 15/3: The Great King and His Armies, pp. 631ff. The Greek interpretation is systematically repeated in recent work: Dandamaev 1989a: 312, for example, is a concentration of all the stereotypes on Persian military decadence (on the Egyptian expedition in 343): "it should not be forgotten that the unity of the empire was fought in the main with the assistance of Greek mercenaries, instead of with the Persian army, who for a long time had drawn its military quality and strength from the Greeks, both in tactics and weaponry. It is significant that to crush the rebellion in Egypt, Artaxerxes not only used Greek mercenaries, but also appointed Greek generals as the commanders of his forces. Persian generals were only added to the staff as a precaution." No less caricatured are the snap judgments of Bosworth (1988: 17–18): not content to state that at the end of the 360s "practically the entire empire west of the Euphrates was alienated from the Great King at Susa" (source? Isocrates?), the author paraphrases Diodorus and writes, without batting an eyelash, that the reconquest was due solely to Greek leaders' leading Greek troops; as a result, "Persian success depended on the Great King's ability to pay and keep mercenaries"; this interpretation is already found in Parke 1933: 165–69; it is unfortunately repeated, without much change, by Seibt 1977: 122–45 and 194–204; likewise in Marinovic 1988: 106–23 and, in part, in Picard 1980: 217–24, more nuanced to be sure (cf. pp. 288–90); most recently, Petit 1993: 54–55, with my critical remarks (Briant 1994b: 120–22). It is remarkable that aside from an inconsequential remark by Marinovic (1988: 123 n. 39), these authors do not in the slightest question the credibility accorded to Diodorus (which all of them copy more or less); all of them quote favorably the famous passages in Plato and Xenophon on "Persian military decadence" (Plato's text, *Laws* 697e, is even made the epigraph of Parke's chapter 18 [1933: 177] on Greek mercenaries in the Achaemenid army between 340 and 330). The recent article of Landucci Gattinoni 1994 adds nothing to this discussion; I will simply note that the author stresses, as if it were his own idea, the very important role played by the Greek mercenaries in Darius III's army (p. 33). Happily, the article by Tuplin 1987c is far better informed and sets forth many real problems (see below).

• *Diodorus/Ephorus and the Greek Mercenaries.*   On the inspirer (Ephorus) of the passages devoted to the revolt of Artabazus of Hellespontine Phrygia, see Moysey 1975: 303–5, 307; Ephorus probably also underlies many anecdotes in Polyaenus and Pseudo-Aristotle introducing Greek mercenaries in satraps' armies: cf. Cracco Ruggini 1966–67.

• *The Use of Mercenaries and "Decadence": Achaemenid Truth and Athenian Filter.*   On theories regarding the Persian *tryphē*, cf. Briant 1989a, and chap. 7/7, pp. 299ff. above; Athenian use of the victories in the Persian Wars: in general Loraux 1981 (partial quotation in Briant 1992d: 148–49), particularly in the fourth century (use of Persian references in civic discourse: Briant 1987b and 1989a: 39; cf. also Nouhaud 1982 [e.g., pp. 321–24] on the polemical use of the memory of the Ten Thousand in Isocrates); and again in the Hellenistic period: R. Étienne, M. Piérart, *BCH* 99 (1975): 51–75 (pp. 63–75); on Arrian VII.7.7, cf. Briant 1986b: 13–15.

• *Command Structure.*   On the terms *paralambanein/paralepsis*, cf. Holleaux 1968: 88–90: the term has to be translated 'taking possession' and not 'taking by assault' (cf. also, following Holleaux, *RTP* 18–19); as I indicate in the text, the use of this technical vocabulary, in Diodorus, perfectly explains the jurisdictional relations between Greek and Persian leaders: the operations led by the former are under the strategic and political supervision of the latter; for all these reasons, it is not possible (despite Nepos, *Dat.* 5.6, adopted without discussion by Sekunda 1988b: 44) that upon his departure from Acre, Datames awarded command of the army to Mandrocles of Magnesia.

• *Memnon, the Persian Satraps, and Darius III.* On the position of Memnon in 334, see the appropriate remarks of McCoy 1989 (cf. in particular, p. 425 n. 40); the fact that Arrian also seems to make Memnon the linchpin of Darius III's strategy (II.1.3, to be compared with Diodorus XVII.29.4) does not necessarily rehabilitate Diodorus: on Memnon's role, cf. chap. 18/1, pp. 817ff.

• *The Great King and the Satraps' Mercenaries.* The theory repeated in the text (precursor to the Hellenistic armies) is presented by Seibt 1977: 90–92; at the same time, Seibt needs to recognize (somewhat conflictingly) that the apparently easy application of the royal order illustrates what he calls a restoration of the authority of the central power; for his part, Moysey (1975: 299–300), like other historians (whom he quotes), is quite wrong to believe that the satraps really did let their mercenaries go, which leads him to propose purely speculative reconstructions (it is true that he thinks that, because Ephorus was an eyewitness, an inspirer of the scholiast [1975: 301–3], he was historically "generally accurate": Moysey 1991: 113–14—an assessment directed specifically against Weiskopf 1989 that leaves me speechless: chap. 15/7, Research Notes on "A Summary of the Discussion," p. 997); the most abrasive counterattack was made in fact by Weiskopf 1982: 473–75, who thinks that the order attributed to Artaxerxes actually risked creating disorder in Asia Minor and Greece, just as it did in 326–325 (on Diodorus XVII.106.2: cf. Badian 1961: 27–28, who thinks that Alexander then enrolled the mercenaries into his own service); cf. also Briant 1994b: 121–22.

• *Mercenaries and "Mercenaries": The Greeks and the Others.* I would note that the place of Greek mercenaries in the Near East before the Achaemenid conquest has frequently been overestimated as well, whereas they obviously constituted only a very small part of the mercenaries levied by, for example, the Assyrian kings (on this, cf. the useful discussion by Helm 1980: 135–60); in any case there does not seem to be a specific word that can be translated 'mercenary' (on the foreign contingents in the Assyrian armies, cf. Malbran-Labat 1982: 89–101 and 103–4); on the variety of ethnic origin of the Achaemenid garrisoneers and on the mercenaries in Xenophon's *Cyropaedia* and *Oeconomicus*, see especially the thorough discussion of Tuplin 1987c: 168–75, who, without concealing the difficulties, thinks that in the *Oeconomicus* Xenophon distinguishes the "pure mercenaries from the military communities" (p. 175), the latter designating the military colonies (Iranian, for example) settled in the *khōra* (cf. pp. 173–74 and 232–34); in a discussion of satrapal forces, he does not neglect to raise the case of Orontes' and Tiribazus's armies, stressing that "the Armenians and Mardians are not mercenaries in the sense [of Greeks hired by a satrap or the king]" (p. 195); later he returns to this important point, inquiring into Xenophon's phrase *hoi basileōs misthophoroi* (*Anab.* VII.8.15), which he thinks applies exclusively to the Hyrcanian and Assyrian troops of Comania: at the same time he emphasizes the difficulties of the interpretation (pp. 222–23; on this topic, see also Petit 1990: 128–32 and the incidental remark of Hornblower 1990b: 95: "the tricky word mercenary"); on the existence of East Iranian colonies in Asia Minor, cf. Briant 1984b: 92–94 (where references to earlier studies will be found, in particular those of L. Robert; cf. also Tuplin 1987c: 195 n. 98. On *symmakhoi* in Artaxerxes III's army (Diodorus XVI.44.4): Seibt (1977: 98 n. 1 and 221) equally well distinguishes mercenaries proper but without drawing any particular inferences. On Arrian III.8.3, Bosworth (1980a: 289) concludes that the Saka "were independent of the satrapy of Bactra" and contrasts the situation in the fifth century, when they were subjects of the Great King, referring to the tribute catalog of Herodotus III.93; Arrian's vocabulary actually raises several questions about the status of the Saka (cf. Briant 1982b: 198–203 and 1984b: 71–72); I note meanwhile that the use of the word 'ally' (*symmakhos*) is frequent in Xenophon when he is speaking of contingents brought by subject peoples: this particularly the case in regard to the Hyrcanians (*Cyr.* IV.2.21: *symmakhoi kai koinōnoi*), who he says switched voluntarily to Cyrus (IV.2.4); they are "those who first became our allies," states "Cyrus" (IV.5.53◇); for this reason, still following Xenophon (IV.2.8), they had a special place in the Empire; the word 'ally' is also found in Herodotus, where, it appears, *symmakhos* is simply a label for anyone opposed to Persia (cf. in particular VIII.113 [including the Saka]; also V.32) and thus does not designate a particular political status. It is obviously possible that from the narrowly Hellenocentric point of view of Diodorus's source, the Greeks of Asia Minor were *symmakhoi* (in the sense of voluntary allies) and not subjects: but this changes nothing about the fact that they, like all the subject peoples, had to furnish contingents in the form of imperial levies (royal armies) or "mercenaries" (in the Achaemenid sense); under these conditions, the Saka brought by Mauaces (Arrian III.8.3) might have been levied by Bessus as "mercenaries" (= paid imperial soldiers): but I strongly doubt that the satrap of Bactra offered them the choice of not participating in the campaign of 333–331: in the context in which *symmakhia* appears, we see on the contrary that the sending of troops resulted from an obligation—even if it was expressed in the form of an official treaty with the Great King (e.g., Plutarch, *Art.* 24.6 and chap. 16/18 above, pp. 766ff.); on the word *symmakhia*, see also Launey 1949, I: 36–42, particularly 41–42 on the contingents sent by the towns to the Hellenistic kings, which I see as a situation very close to that evoked by the *symmakhoi* of Artaxerxes III in Diodorus XVI.44.4. One last observation: the discussion here holds equally as well for the *xenoi misthophoroi* so often referred to by Arrian in Alexander's armies; it seems clear that the term can also designate soldiers levied in the subject populations of the Macedonian king (cf. Berve I: 144–49, with the critical remarks of Parke 1933: 186–98 and Griffith 1935: 27–32).

 • *"Greek Army and Barbarian Army."* On Autophradates' army, Burn (1985: 377), by way of explaining what seemed to him inexplicable, suggests that in this exact case the limited number of Greek mercenaries has to be connected to the consequences of the war in Arcadia! The remark is repeated by Sekunda 1988b: 49, who adds that Autophradates really did command the expeditionary force of which he took command at Acre: but the (purely hypothetical) remark does not remove the difficulty (cf. also Sekunda 1992: 27, who thinks that the decision to raise 120,000 "mercenary *kardakes*" as hoplites was made because of the shrinkage of the number of available Greek mercenaries; but, I stress, the word "mercenary" does not appear in Nepos, who simply uses the word *kardake*: *Dat.* 8.1.2); on the satrapal contingents at the Granicus, cf. Bosworth 1980a: 111–13, 125 and "Mercenaries and "Mercenaries": The Greeks and the Others," p. 792; on the battle of the Granicus and the contradictions between Diodorus and Arrian, see the lucid analysis of Badian 1977a; the various phases of the battle of Gaugamela present equally difficult problems: cf. Marsden 1964 and Wirth 1980, but Bernard 1990b: 515–25 adds much that is new. The number of (Greek) mercenaries around Darius III has caused the spillage of much ink: according to an argument already put forward by Grote and Parke, Seibt (1977: 180) thinks that the figure 50,000 is the sum of the 20,000 mercenaries at the Granicus and the 30,000 at Issus, figures that he recognizes as accurate (pp. 180–94), which leads him to note that this is the highest percentage of mercenaries ever observed in an Achaemenid army. But it has long been remarked that the totals offered by Arrian and Quintus Curtius are at the least subject to caution, as noted for example by Badian 1977a: 284–85 for the Granicus; for his part, Devine (1988: 7–10) reduces the number of Greek mercenaries in 334 to 4000–5000, figures given by Diodorus (XVII.7.3) and Polyaenus (V.44.4) for the mercenaries sent by Darius at the beginning of the campaign led by Memnon in 337 against the first Macedonian expeditionary force; as for the figure of 30,000 mercenaries at Issus, it clearly goes back to Callisthenes, whose tale of the battle is vigorously criticized by Polybius (XII.18–22), but Polybius cites Callisthenes' figure without skepticism or criticism (18.2); the figure is rejected by Devine (1985b: 47), who thinks that the number of mercenaries and Persian infantry (*kardakes*) could not have been larger than the number of Macedonian phalangists (12,000); another reduced figure, no more than 10,000, according to Beloch, cited by Parke 1933: 183–84; it is easy to observe that all of the estimates are the result of a narrow skein of hypotheses that fit together without necessarily reinforcing each other. The ancient sources on the *kardakes* are collected by Segre 1938: 191–92, Bosworth 1980a: 208, and Knauth and Najmabadi 1975: 82–83; the lexicographers' notes are not particularly precise: "They are soldiers in Asia" (Photius) or "the barbarians that fight under the command of the Persians" (Hesychius); Polybius's incidental mention (V.82.11) does not add any decisive element (it is not possible to suppose, with Launey [1949, II: 486] and some others, that the word *kardakes* conceals Carducian ethnicity). We must fall back on Nepos and Arrian: the *kardakes* are Persian infantry, armed like hoplites, in contrast to the light infantry (*psiloi*; Arrian II.8.6). The relationship with Strabo's Cardaces (XV.3.18) is problematic, but it must be noted that in Strabo the Persian *agōgē* touches on the selection of the best of the young people in the eyes of the king, who conferred gifts and honors on them. In any case, in the military context they were clearly an elite corps. Three additional remarks concerning them:

(1) Devine (1985b: 48) identifies them with the 20,000 barbarian infantrymen placed by Quintus Curtius on the left flank under the orders of Aristomedes (III.9.3); meanwhile, Aristomedes is named with several others, including Thymondas, as leaders who managed to escape the battlefield with their troops (*stratiōtai*; Arrian II.13.2–3); even though Arrian does not specify the identity of these *stratiōtai*, it seems clear that they were mercenaries (of whom Thymondas was in command) and not *kardakes*.

(2) Sekunda (1988b: 42) suggests attributing to Datames the creation of this corps of *kardakes*, among other innovations (borrowing of Greek arms) that the author also credits him with, but the evidence for this theory is singularly lacking; the same author (1992: 52–53) thinks that the *kardakes* numbered 120,000, but for various reasons the appeal to Xenophon, *Anab.* III.5.16 is totally unjustifiable; nor do I see the basis for his suggestion that the *kardakes* can be assimilated to the *misthophōroi basileōs* of Xenophon; on this topic, see also the remarks and theories of Head 1992: 42–44.

(3) Let me suggest a *hypothesis*: we know that, in Central Asia, Alexander had 30,000 young men drafted, who must have been armed and trained in Macedonian fashion (cf. Quintus Curtius VIII.5.1); they are called *epigonoi* by the authors, who report their arrival at Susa in 324 (cf. Arrian VII.6.1; Diodorus XVII.108.1–2; Plutarch, *Alex.* 71.1); it is possible that the order extended to all the satrapies, including Egypt (Suda, s.v. *basileioi paides*), and that the system had been adapted from the Macedonian institution of Royal Pages (cf. Hammond 1990: 275–80; Thompson 1992: 50 and nn. 15–16); but I am tempted instead to think (without being able to prove it) that if Alexander was able to put this system in place so easily and quickly, it was because it already existed in the Achaemenid period (the transformation introduced being simply the "Macedonization" of these levies): that is, the military instruction of the young recruits was more or less already in the satraps' hands; under this theory, the *kardakes* designate nothing more than the Persian subset of an age class, or else the term would have been extended to all the young men raised and educated in Persian fashion; hence the definition found in Photius and Hesychius: *Kardakes: hoi strateusamenoi barbaroi hypo Persōn.*

• *Persian Technical and Tactical Innovations (Especially in the Infantry).* Cf. Head 1992: 39–42; Darius's elephants: Briant 1995d; chariots: Sekunda 1992: 25–26 and Head 1992: 44–48 (the question deserves to be reopened *in toto*; a war chariot has recently been found near Sardis, at the site of Bin Tepe [cf. Greenwalt 1995] and a scythed chariot in the Granicus Valley: they are both being analyzed). Besides, while publishing a lead sling ball inscribed with the name Tissaphernes, Foss 1975, starting with Xenonphon, *Anab.* III.3.16, thinks that around 400 the Persian slingmen (in contrast to the Rhodian slingmen) used not lead balls but stone balls. He strongly suggests (and this is an understatement) that it was on the example of the archers in the corps of Greek mercenaries that Tissaphernes introduced lead balls in his armies in Asia Minor, when he was sent there after Cunaxa and its consequences (cf. chap. 15/4). I must say that Foss's position (which is not really discussed by Pritchett 1991: 46–47 in his discussion of lead sling balls, pp. 43–53) leaves me perplexed and skeptical. He mentions (p. 26) that the Greeks "providentially" (*sic*) came upon a supply of lead in a nearby village (the mercenaries were then marching along the east bank of the Tigris), but providence had nothing to do with it! Xenophon in fact states that in the village they found "gut [for bowstrings] in abundance and lead for the use of their slingers" (III.4.17◊); it is obvious that as in another case (III.4.31: supplies of food for men and horses, stockpiled by the satrap) these were strategic stocks controlled by the administration (see Briant 1986c: 37–38); in this case, it was clearly an arms depot—specifically an arsenal specializing in hurling-weapons; from this we may conclude that the lead was stockpiled for the manufacture of lead balls, and the theory of Persian borrowing of Greek technology loses much of its credibility (many sling balls have been found at Dascylium—some of them with Greek inscriptions [personal names]; they remain unpublished; I owe my knowledge of them to the kindness of Tomris Bakir). Persian demographics: Briant 1987a: 21–22. Persians in the Hellenistic armies: Launey 1949, II: 563–80 (Medes and Persians).

4. Subject Populations and Tribute Economy

• *Hoarding and Stagnation: Obvious but False.* See Olmstead 1948: 289–99; against Olmstead's position, see the critical remarks of Stolper 1985a: 143–46 (my inspiration); see Center and Periphery, pp. 804ff. On Droysen and his disciples (not that the founder desired disciples!), cf. *RTP* 291–96 and 281–90 (colonial historiography); on Marx and "Asiatic stagnation," cf. *RTP* 419–22 and 477–79; central treasuries and the accumulation of tribute: see the calculations offered by Altheim and Stiehl 1963: 120–37: even if the numerical results seem rather shaky, the authors have the merit of recalling that the ancient authors' presentation (uninterrupted stockpiling of tribute from the time of Cyrus) rests on nothing (on this point, cf. also Tuplin 1987b: 138–39); on the inventory of Darius's treasuries from Classical sources, cf. Bellinger 1963: 68–69, De Callatay 1989: 260–61, and Price 1991: 25–27; on the term *akribōs* in Heraclides of Cyme quoted by Athenaeus IV., 145d, and more generally in the Greek "economics" literature, see the very interesting essay of Farraguna 1994, especially pp. 567–76, and his definition of the *akribeia*, p. 588: "The attention given to economic calculations down to the smallest detail." The theory of the sudden monetization of Darius III's treasuries by Alexander has recently been revived by De Callatay 1989, but on this presentation I share the methodological criticisms of M. Price and A. M. Prestianni-Giallombardo (after Callatay's contribution: pp. 274–75); cf. also the remarks of Bellinger 1963: 68–73; the subtitle of De Callatay's article ("motionless cash or circulating cash?") is obviously inspired by Schlumberger 1953, but he simply contrasted, in the fifth and fourth centuries, royal money ("nearly motionless") and Greek coins ("living money"); on the use of weighed silver in Hellenistic Babylonia, cf., e.g., Sherwin-White and Kuhrt 1993: 63–65, Stolper 1994a (although the tablets also refer to the use of coins), Joannès 1994a; local fractional currency: cf. in particular Mildenberg 1979, 1988 (with Lemaire in Laperrousaz and Lemaire, 1994: 283–84 and 287) and the royal coins (fractions of siculi) described in the catalog *Münzen und Medaillen AG*, November–December 1988, no. 73–74 (I owe the reference to R. Descat). On models: see that of the *Early State*, presented by Claessen 1989, and used by Sancisi-Weerdenburg (e.g., 1988a); the discussion of the concept of feudalism (an old debate) by Petit (1990: 243–53) appears to me to be marked by much confusion (cf. on this point also the remarks of Stolper 1985a: 146–49, who stresses the differences between medieval rents and the Babylonian system of plots managed by the Murašū). The roads/commerce problem: cf. chap. 9/3: Customs Collection and Trade, pp. 384ff., as well as the reflections of Tuplin 1991a: 278–81; on the difficulty of interpreting the archaeological evidence for reconstructing the regional and interregional commercial roads, cf. in particular Salles 1991a, 1991b: 53–58, and 1994; we may certainly consider the Babylonian temples as special points of contact: e.g., Joannès 1982: 235–60 (origin of gold and silver as imports; cf. p. 255 on the role of Babylon as a place of redistribution of merchandise).

• *Center and Periphery.* I have often touched on the problem of the development of productivity: cf. *RTP* 475–89, Briant 1982c (more advanced German version) and 1994g; on Xenophon's view, cf. *RTP* 176–88; on the economic character of the conquered countries (or those acquired by gift), cf. the reflections of Bertrand 1990: 134–35 (quotation); inscription of Arsinoe in Cilicia: Jones and Habicht 1989 (lines 6–9), which can be compared with other evidence (cf. Sherwin-White and Kuhrt 1993: 67–71); paradises, garden estates: *RTP* 452–54; king and satraps as protectors of peasants: *RTP* 365–70; *dōrea* and putting to seed: Stolper (1985a: 148) stresses that in Babylonia the concession-holders("feudatories") did not reap economic advantage from possible increases in yield; but this is not the case with the Murašū, who, on the contrary, had every opportunity to increase the productivity of the lands; on the concession of Mnesimachus, see the remarks of Descat 1985: 108–9 (there too, it is not so much the concession-holder himself as the usufructor [Artemis temple] that carried out the work of improvement); this is also implied by the case of the city of Telmessus, which obtained from Ptolemy the right never to be given in *dōrea* — "neither the city, nor the villages, nor any of the territory of the Telmessians" (Wörrle 1978, lines 20–23), because they feared the installation of a tyrannical regime with the certain increase in charges (cf. Wörrle 1978: 207–12 and Savalli 1987). On the explorations in the area of Tell el-Maskhuta: cf. Paice 1986–87, 1993 and Halladay 1992. —Polybius X., 28.2–4 and the *qanats*: cf. *RTP* 94–100 (analysis of the text), 492, 499–500 (method of transmission of information down to Polybius), also Briant 1984b: 67 (military aspects of the royal decree); the text is also used by Goblot 1979: 70–72, who suggests (rightly, it seems to me) that the Achaemenids extended the system of *qanats* on the Iranian Plateau; but it must also be recalled on the one hand that many *qanats* go back to an earlier period (it is not an Achaemenid invention) and, on the other, that the dating of these works poses major problems (in B. Geyer [ed.], *Techniques et pratiques hydrauliques traditionelles en domaine irrigué* [Paris, 1990]: 328, P. Sanlaville writes: "As for me, I would like to think that we must go quite far back in time, several millennia before the Common Era no doubt, for the origin of these *foggara*, these subterranean channels"); hence the careful proof needed before concluding (as Goblot automatically does) that the spread of *qanats* far and wide was automatically the work of the Great Kings: cf. for Oman the remarks of Salles 1990: 132 and Potts 1990a: 388–92 [[Goblot, p. 71, wonders whether the place-name Canate in Arrian, *Indica* 29.4 might render the word *qanat*; I will simply observe that the technical term *diōryx* used by Arrian can refer to a channel open to the sky: cf. *Indica* 39.1 and Whitcomb 1987: 330–31]]; *qanats* in northern Arabia: e.g., Graf 1990a: 137, and in the oasis of El-Khārga, Bousquet and Reddé 1994 (cf. also chap. 12/1: "Darius in the Temple of Hibis (El Khārga)," p. 475); on these problems, see most recently the minute analysis of Planhol 1992, who (while criticizing Goblot) thinks overall that "the technology of the drainage channels . . . was the basis of Achaemenid power." On the royal administration of water in Achaemenid Babylonia, cf. Stolper 1985a: 36–51 and Bregstein 1993: 116–30. Economic life in Babylonia: Stolper (1985a, chap. 6) concludes that even though the evidence points to an increase in indebtedness of some individuals (for reasons he presents), "The Neo-Babylonian and Achaemenid periods [can be considered] the beginnings of a long phase of general growth [expansion of population, resettlement and cultivation of long-abandoned territory]" (p. 133); in particular taking into account the results of surveys (Adams 1965: 58–61; 1981: 185–92; Adams and Nissen 1972: 55–57; Gibson 1972 [Kish region: cf. also McEwan 1983], and Lendle 1986; on explorations in Susiana, cf. Boucharlat 1990: 157–66), all the specialists now agree on the fact that the Babylonia of the end of the Achaemenid period was not affected at all by an economic crisis, quite the contrary (cf. van Driel 1987 and 1989: 226; but I am not sure I understand what the author means to say when he writes, challenging Stolper's view of the end of the Murašū archives, that the Achaemenid period "seems to have been a time of privatization, tempered, perhaps, we might concede, by tyranny"); Joannès 1995 emphasizes that it is very likely in the Achaemenid period that the system of two harvests, winter and summer, was introduced. Hydraulic works in Hyrcania: cf. Ricciardi 1980 and Vogelsang 1992: 293–98; Arachosia: Vogelsang 1992: 255–67; on the development of Samaria, cf. Zertal 1990 (who, pp. 15–16, thinks the Achaemenid administration was highly visible); to Samaria may be added the case of northern Syria, recently studied by Sapin 1990 (Achaemenid precedents), and Mazzoni 1990, 1991–92, who writes: "It is with the blossoming of the Achaemenid phase that produced a boom and an economic transformation of the region, rich with promise" (1990: 193). —To finish up on this point, in a word, the problems I have just presented are also faced by the Assyriologists who deal with the (economic and political) significance to be attributed to the water policy followed by the Neo-Assyrian kings: on the work of Oates 1968 (particularly chap. 3), cf. the reflections of Reade (1978: 173–75) and Liverani (1971: 155–59); see also, regarding the Roman Empire, Nicolet 1978: 899–902, and regarding the Hellenstic world, the debate between É. Will on one side, A. Kuhrt and S. Sherwin-White on the other, in *Topoi* 4/2 (1994): 432 and 452, as well as the remarks (of rather Finleyesque inspiration) of van der Spek 1994.

• *"Overexploitation of Tribute" and Revolt.*   Level of tribute: cf. Descat 1985; on the burden of tribute, cf. also Tuplin 1989b: 140–45 and Nixon-Price 1992: 177–78 (for these authors, the theory of the heaviness of Persian tribute is implicit but significant in the contrast they make with the moderation of Athenian tribute when it began). Dandamaev (1989b: 193) suggests that in the fourth century "the collection of taxes turned into flat-out pillage and coercion, which caused many uprisings against Persian domination," but the texts offered in support (pp. 193–94) regarding Egypt do not appear terribly eloquent to me: I stress especially that, for Dandamaev, this judgment goes back to his initial analyses of what he considered the "parasitic" role of the Persian nobility which, after the "aristocratic restoration" carried out by Darius in 522, was gratified with immense privileges in the provinces—which had "very negative consequences for the economy of the conquered countries," and hence—the final consequence—"the weakness of the Achaemenid empire" before Alexander (Dandamaev 1976: 212–14); but, for reasons already given (chap. 2/10: "Bardiya and the Persian Aristocracy," p. 103, and chap. 3/1, pp. 107ff., and 3/4, pp. 128ff., above), the "aristocratic restoration" is nothing but a myth, such that the author's entire construct, in my opinion, never gets off the ground (cf. also my remarks in Briant 1993c: 421–22). On the revolts, cf. Briant 1988a: 139–43 (I alter some aspects); see also Stolper (1985a: 155–56): the author rightly stresses that, on the one hand, the activity of the Murašû without doubt resulted in the impoverishment of small proprietors, but that, on the other, this segment of the population had no political influence; the tablet from the reign of Cambyses (*YOS* 7, 128) which I present was pointed out to me by F. Joannès, who also provided a translation: I thank him very heartily. Aside from remarks of Joannès (1982: 278–79) on prices in 418, the price rise in Babylonia has been studied by Dubberstein 1939 and Dandamaev 1988b: the former inquires into the reasons for the increase (p. 43), evoking one by one "the increasing wealth of individuals, the expansion of capitalism, the Persians' monetary policy, their wars . . ."; for his part, Dandamaev stresses on the contrary that it was a long-lasting feature, which has no implication of an economic crisis (p. 58); a position somewhat contradictory to that of the same Dandamaev (1989b: 194), who attempts to establish a relation between Persian dominion and the price increase in Babylonia "and very likely the same way in the other countries": on this last point, it is necessary to remark that the author offers not one real piece of evidence to justify his position. More important: the initial observation (continuous price increase) is now thrown in doubt by the work of Slotsky 1993 (which I became acquainted with only quite late), who has studied the changes in price of the products mentioned in the *ADRTB*. Her conclusions (which I evoke in my text) totally contradict everything that has so far been written about the "continuous price increase" in Babylonia during the Achaemenid period; price decrease is rather what the author finds, for barley (pp. 70–71, 84–85), dates (pp. 94, 101: lowest price under Darius III), mustard (pp. 128–29), cress (p. 152), sesame (pp. 178–79), and wool (pp. 204–5): for all these products, the author observes that the price is lower under Darius III than under Artaxerxes I (p. 219); among the reasons advanced, she suggests taking into account the increase in agricultural production and yield (p. 228). In expectation of an anticipated study by Vargas (p. 3) based on wider and more varied evidence (Vargas forthcoming), we must obviously remain cautious (P. Vargas takes up the problem again in a communication presented at the *Deuxièmes Rencontres de Saint-Bertrand sur l'économie antique*, May 4–5, 1996). Nonethless, this study by

M. L. Slotsky is clearly part of a reevaluation of many hypotheses established on the basis of too-narrow evidence, in particular since the work of Dubberstein 1939, which henceforth must clearly be considered obsolete. On the economic and commercial activity of the Murašû, cf. in particular Cardascia 1951: 189–98, Stolper 1985a: 27–35, 143–56, and van Driel 1989; sale of royal wheat to the Greek cities: Briant 1994d (which van der Spek 1994: 23 cannot have known); local taxes and double taxation in the Hellenistic cities: cf. Corsaro 1985; Wörrle 1988: 461–64; Carian cities (under Achaemenid dominion) and royal taxes: Hornblower 1982: 161–63; Tuplin 1987b: 148–49.

Chapter 18
Darius and the Empire Confront Macedonian Aggression

1. Territories, Armies, and Strategies

• *A Preliminary Detail.* No more than in the preceding chapters do I intend to rehearse here the detailed narrative of Alexander's campaigns, except to the extent that the information and interpretations of the ancient authors and modern historians touch on the discussion of the Achaemenid Empire's situation during this period. Where the weave of the narrative seems certain, I will not multiply references to the ancient or modern authors, which will be found conveniently gathered in, e.g., Bosworth 1988; cf. also Bosworth 1980a, 1995, and Berve 1926, II. As I said in the introduction to this volume, this chapter attempts to offer elements of a response to a question that with others I have long been considering on the reasons for Alexander's defeat of the Persians.

• *The First Macedonian Offensive (336–335).* See especially Badian 1966: 39–46, Ruzicka 1985b, Heisserer 1980 (where the decrees are analyzed that allow us to reconstruct the events on Lesbos, Chios, and Iasus), and most recently Ruzicka 1992a and 1992b: 129–34; on the role and place of Memnon and the date of the Persian counterattack (perhaps already in Arses' time), see also the apt remarks of McCoy 1989: 422–27. On the chronology of the invasion of Egypt against Khabbabash, in synoptic relation to the events of Asia Minor, the interpretations of Anson 1989 remain subject to caution because of the persistent uncertainty governing the date and extent of the Egyptian revolt (cf. chap. 16/9, pp. 717f. above); on the very hypothetical Babylonian revolt (which, according to Bosworth 1988: 34, would explain Darius's inaction until the end of 335), see Stolper, *CAH* VI^2: 240; on Ephesus and its relations with Sardis (at this date?), see the theory presented in chap. 16/3 above on the Inscription of Sacrileges from Sardis (p. 702). I note in passing that the initial operations pose the additional problem of Pixodarus's attitude: we know that Plutarch (*Alex.* 10.1–3) says that Pixodarus intended to marry his oldest daughter to Arrhideus for political goals (*eis tēn Philippou symmakhian*), and that Alexander married the satrap's daughter; this "Pixodarus affair" has generated a considerable number of interpretations, especially in the context of relations between Alexander and his father; I have no desire to venture into this labyrinth (cf. the overview of Hatzopoulos 1982, but contra French and Dixon 1986); in the context of Achaemenid history, the only question is: in carrying out these negotiations, was Pixodarus demonstrating secessionist tendencies? Or better: in 336, was Pixodarus cleverer than the Achaemenid rulers, and was he already preparing for post-conquest Macedon (cf. the discussions of Weiskopf 1982: 308–10; Ruzicka 1992b: 130–32)? Using Strabo's (XIV.2.17) comments as his basis, Hornblower (1982: 49 and 221) thinks that *persikas* means 'adopting a political attitude favorable to Persia', but as the author himself admits (p. 49 n. 89) in quoting Arrian VII.6.3, the meaning of the word is open to discussion: cf. the reservations expressed by Weiskopf 1982: 306 (without knowing Hornblower), who translates it 'turning to Persia': the word may also signify 'adopting Persian customs, Persianizing', as in Arrian VII.6.3 (quoted ["by contrast"] by Hornblower 1982: 49 n. 89), but also and especially by Strabo himself: cf. in particular XV.2.14; in any event, I think Ruzicka (1992b: 131–34) is right to think that we must not grant excessive credence to the phrase used by Strabo and that the sending of Orontobates was solely the idea of Darius III, who was concerned to make preparations to resist the coming Macedonian offensive (cf. also 1992a: 90–91). If Pixodarus's contacts with the Macedonian date to this period, we may simply suggest (with Weiskopf 1982: 308–9) that Philip was trying to prepare, though diplomatic means, a (limited) beachhead in Asia Minor; but then we plunge back into the problem of Philip's reason for sending an army corps to Asia Minor.

• *Darius, His Satraps, and Alexander's Landing (May–June 334).* Delay of the Persian navy: an overview and bibliography will be found in the article by Anson 1989: he thinks the fleet had returned from Egypt but was not able to participate because of the lack of continental bases; against the position of Badian 1966, Anson in fact thinks that the Persian reconquest of 335 was very incomplete: but both this theory and his chronological estimates about the revolt of Egypt do not seem to me imbued with great certainty, which is merely confirmed by the state of the evidence (even if, by way of "probability," the explanation he offers is worthy of interest). Goukowsky 1976: 180 thinks he can explain Diodorus XVII.18.2 by referring to Diodorus XV.41.5 and the "(customary) slowness of the Persians": cf. apt critical remarks of Seibert 1987: 442; Grzybek 1990: 61–66 (who, p. 63, fixes the date of the battle of the Granicus at April 8) insists on the element of surprise that would explain the absense of opposition to Alexander's landing; but, while the chronological proof is interesting, I am not convinced by the author's historical argumentation. Proclamation of Arsites: cf. *RTP* 363–65 (while recognizing [Briant 1976: 238 n. 61] that the satrap's decision was also based on other considerations); on his supremacy in the hierarchy at Zeleia, cf. the remarks of Badian (1977a: 283–84), who rightly rejects the theory of collegiality (the objection of McCoy 1989: 433 n. 65 is not matched with any proof); on Alexander's financial situation at the beginning of the campaign, cf. Rebuffat 1983, followed by Price 1991: 25; *megalopsykhia*: Goukowsky (1976: 30) translates (very freely) with 'chivalric spirit': I suspect this translation/interpretation derives directly from the "feudal" theories of Schachermeyer 1973: 166–74 (*Junker gegen Junker*).

• *Darius in Babylon and the Asia Minor Front (334–333).* On Darius's maritime operations and policy, see Thomassen 1984 and the excellent criticism of Ruzicka 1988 (both correctly reevaluate Darius's strategy, and the former insists, no less correctly, on the exaggeration by the ancient authors [and modern ones: e.g., Badian 1966: 48] of the role of Memnon: pp. 28ff.); cf. also Heisserer 1980: 87–111 (Chios), 169–203 (Iasus). The exact reconstruction of certain conquests and reconquests poses chronological problems, into the details of which I shall not enter, at least where the major paths of change appear well enough established; on the decommissioning of the navy, cf. Bosworth 1980a: 141–43, who thinks it reflects a "colossal error [on Alexander's part] that the Persians exploited, but inadequately"; see also Thomassen 1984: 8–18, who insists on Alexander's long-range perspective.

• *From Issus to Gaugamela (November 333 – October 331).* Persian land counterattack after Issus: cf. Burn 1952 and Briant 1973: 53–74: this interpretation (all of the conclusions of which I do not repeat here) has stimulated some objections (cf. Ruzicka 1983b): as Atkinson (1980: 286) notes, Burn makes several chronological approximations on the maritime operations of Pharnabazus and Autophradates *before* and *after* Issus, but this observation does not ruin the hypothesis (cf. Ruzicka 1988: 144 n. 41); for his part, Anson 1988 thinks the Persian counterattack was not as important as Burn and Briant suggest; in the opposite case, Anson thinks, Antigonus would not have been able to win these victories, because he himself was undermanned; according to him, the Persian generals could count on neither Ariarathe of Cappadocia (who remained, he says, cautiously neutral: but cf. below) nor satrapal forces: but these observations do not invalidate the interpretation, since the Persians established a conscription in Cappadocia and Paphlagonia (which comprised nothing more than a mobilization of satrapal contingents); on Antigonus's position as I have proposed it (1973: 63–66: given a general command in Asia Minor), see the varying evaluations of Anson (1989: 474) and Billows (1990: 44 and n. 80); it is clear that the state of the evidence leads to interpretive caution; it has not yet been fully gathered: it is surprising that none of the authors I just cited knows (at least they do not quote) the articles of Harrison 1982a: 265–84 and 1982b on the (long known) coins of Sinope: Harrison thinks (by way of hypothesis, which I follow here) that on the coins we have the names of certain Persian leaders who led the counterattack after Issus; note also that we know coinage of Ariarathe from Sinope (cf. also Alram 1986: 55ff.): even if Harrison thinks that this coinage is somewhat later than these events (1982a: 289–90), the chronology remains in dispute (as the author recognizes, p. 290), and this evidence requires at least the nuancing of Anson's hypothesis (1988: 473) on the (presumed) "neutrality" of the Cappadocian dynasty during the Persian counterattack (how would the Persians have been able to levy the youth of Cappadocia without [at least] the consent of Ariarathe?); on Orontobates: it seems to me impossible (despite Berve no. 594) to find him at Gaugamela in charge of some of the troops that came from Persia (Arrian III.8.5). On the situation in Syria after Issus, cf. the remarks of Harrison 1982a: 368–69; on Thymondas, cf. the apt proposals of Ruzicka 1988: 146–47 and n. 44; on Agis's Cretan war (which interests me here only marginally), cf. van Effenterre 1968: 244–47 and Badian 1967, 1994; on all of these problems I reject the conclusions of the recent (ill-informed) article of Bloedow 1994.

• *Darius and Alexander: War and Peace (333–331)—Another Reading.* See the bibliography and overview in Bosworth 1980a: 227–33, 256–57 (but without discussion of the possibility of a forgery); cf. also Bosworth 1988: 64–65 and 75–76 (simple paraphrase of the ancient texts); on Diodorus XVII.39.2, cf. Griffith 1968 (without considering the possibility of an overall forgery); to my knowledge, the latest article is that of Bernhardt 1988 (the author suggests a parallel with an episode from Sassanian history; the parallel is not without interest, but it does not provide the solution to the problem; the author himself displays much skepticism on the question: pp. 181, 198); note the near total, quite surprising silence (p. 451) of Seibert 1987 in an article reevaluating the historical stature of Darius III. On Darius's preparations and the coherence of his strategy, see now the important article of Bernard 1990b: 519–24, which rightly reevaluates (against the traditional theory: p. 522) the role and choices of Darius. On the theme of the expiring Darius handing over the Empire to Alexander, cf. *RTP* 401–3; on the Greek representations of the imperial realm and the Euphrates as frontier, cf. *RTP* 78 and Briant 1984b: 64–65. Theory of the dowry and "gradated" concessions was developed especially by Radet 1925 and 1930; no more than other more recent authors (including me: Briant 1987c: 36–39, modified in 1994a: 47–48) does Radet ever inquire into the authenticity of the tradition; the reason for this is obviously that historians generally do not attempt to locate the evidence in the framework of Achaemenid history, except sometimes by referring to Achaemenid dynastic practices ("vice-regency"), which the Persian evidence proves never existed; Radet thinks (1925: 196 n. 7) that the ancient authors other than Quintus Curtius, including Arrian, were irresponsible for not connecting the marriage and the dowry: a contestable evaluation, to say the least; he also quotes (1925: 194 n. 2) the anonymous author ("Anonymous from Jerusalem" = *FGrH* 151 F3) but is not aware of the problem posed by the text (which also stimulated a presentation by Reinach 1892, but the author's remark [pp. 309–10] is unaware of the specificity of Quintus Curtius and Anonymous); the Suda, s.v. *Dareios*, also shows the extent to which successive confusions are piled on top of each other, because, according to the text, Darius asks Alexander to conclude a treaty (*koinōnia*) and, for this purpose, offers him his daughter Roxanne—although we know from Anonymous (*FGrH* 151 F3) that Darius's daughters who fell into Alexander's hands were named Stateira and Drypetis: cf. Berve II nos. 290 and 722. On Darius's matrimonial offers, see also the (partial) remarks of Vogt 1952: 175. The problem of the dowry is evoked by Atkinson 1956: 171–77, who, without referring to the example of Darius III, but by studying the texts on the Median marriages (Xenophon, Nicolas of Damascus, which I quote in the text), concludes that the practice of transference of property by dowry reflects a Persian custom—which does not appear to me to be established at all; I remark in passing (since I cannot deal with the case here) that a somewhat similar discussion has long been continuing on a tradition that attributes the Ptolemaic rights to Syria–Phoenicia to a dowry: cf. presentation of the sources and problems in Cuq 1927, who quite curiously does not invoke the "precedent" of Darius and Alexander; accepted by Cuq, the theory of the dowry is refuted by Bickerman 1938: 29–30. On dowries/gifts in the ancient Near East, cf. Zaccagnini 1973: 24–30, especially using the rich evidence from El-Amarna (the dowry can only be understood as an exchange for bride-prices sent by the future husband). I add that in the gifts to Persian princesses (such as Parysatis), Cardascia 1991 would like to see an ancient form of *Morgengabe*: the idea is interesting; I note meanwhile that the hypothesis was suggested to him especially by medieval and modern judicial texts; so I wonder whether the "Franco-Achaemenid" glosses he uses (cf. nn. 26–30) provide the requisite guarantees of reliability, even when the comparisons he stresses appear captivating, at least on the terminological level.

• *The Consequences of Gaugamela (331–330).* Darius's retreat to Media and Alexander's arrival in Babylon are also evoked in the tablet ADRTB no. –330, presented and interpreted by P. Bernard 1990b: 525–28 (cf. chap. 18/3, pp. 852ff.); on the word *neōterizein* in Arrian (III.19.1), cf. the remarks of Bosworth 1980a: 333, who translates "in the hope that some disaffection might break out around Alexander," asking justifiable questions about the hopes attributed to Darius; but I doubt that the word can be explained by arguments linked to Darius's "third embassy" or by an evocation (by anticipation) of the problem of Philotas; I am rather tempted to think that Darius hoped Alexander would encounter some difficulties in establishing his dominion in Babylonia and Susiana (see chap. 18/3). On the vision contemporary writers have of the "decisive" (or not) character of the battle, I recall the aptly cautious remarks of Borza 1972: 243: "It may be only our own post factum judgments that see the battle of Gaugamela as decisive because it was in fact decisive. Alexander may not have felt so certain. It is conceivable that Darius loomed as a much more serious threat to the king than he appears to us in retrospect." I note finally that, according to Gasche 1991a: 6, the "Achaemenid residence" found to the north of Sippar was built at the end of the Achaemenid period and that it was never occupied by its owner: "This abandonment is without doubt to be related to Alexander's campaign"; the history of this residence, built "by a noble at the very end of Darius III, perhaps shows in its way how the Persians had been surprised by the rapid progress of the Macedonian troops" (Gasche 1995: 208). We know that about fifteen days after Gaugamela, Alexander was at Sippar, carrying out his policy of collaboration with the Babylonian elites (Bernard 1990b: 526). It is possible that no one really expected that the Great King, leading an army prepared so well, could lose the battle, and that, furthermore, the strategic retreat to Media ordered by Darius, connected with the news of the defeat, could have caused a panic in Babylonia, particularly in the countryside, at least in the first days (this in any case is a *possible* reading of Quintus Curtius V.1.7). Can these considerations really explain the phase of abandonment identified by the archaeologists? I do not dare to give an answer, because, as every one knows, it is extremely risky to relate archaeological data (however precisely dated they are, as in the present case) to a historical narration that is only a skeleton (even if the recent publication of the astronomical tablets has just recently added flesh to it!).

2. Darius and His Faithful

• *Mithrenes and the Persians of Asia Minor (334–333).* See Briant 1985a: 167–69 and 1993a (it is surprising to observe that, aside from an incidental remark of Higgins 1980: 130, the case of Mithrenes continues to be ignored by historians studying Alexander's Iranian policy, as if he had not thought of this necessity until after his arrival in Babylon: e.g., Bosworth 1980a: 128 and 1980b, Hamilton 1987); on Memnon: Bosworth (1980a: 131) chronologically relates Polyaenus (IV.3.1) and Arrian (I.17.8), thinking that, at Sardis, Alexander sought to detach Memnon from the Persian officials; but, for one thing, the two passages are explained much better if Polyaenus is connected to the moment of the landing (when Alexander landed in Troad); for another, Arrian's phrase (*epi tèn khōran tou Memnonos*), used in an obvious military context, appears to me quite clearly to designate an offensive action: Alexander had certainly already understood that Memnon would not surrender; Bosworth adds that Polyaenus's anecdote may be apocryphal: but it could more simply be a piece of the tradition concerning Memnon, which is easy enough to integrate into Arrian I.12.10: hostility of the Persians toward Memnon, who was suspected of wanting to drag out the war because of the honors (*timē*) he held from Darius. On Bagadates and the Amyzon inscription, cf. Robert 1983: 113–18 and Briant 1985a (which I nuance here on the question of the exemplary quality of the document in relation to the Mithrenes affair). Recognizing that the *dōrea* of Mnesimachus near Sardis (*Sardis* VII.1.1) is of Achaemenid origin, which can hardly be doubted (cf. Descat 1985), it is possible that his (probably) Persian titles were stripped from him at some point, though we are not able to say with certainty that happened at the time of Alexander's visit to Sardis (even if the hypothesis is seductive); the transfer may have taken place in the era of the Diadochi (cf. Buckler and Robinson 1912: 22–25); in any case, the document, which dates about twenty years after Alexander's passage, strongly suggests what the situation of the Persian aristocrats of the imperial diaspora might have been—summed up as having to choose between keeping their position, on the one hand, and unfailing faithfulness to Darius III and confidence in the Persian armies' capacity for counterattack, on the other.

• *The Surrender of Mazaces (332).* Mazaces and his predecessor, Sabaces, are also known from several coins inscribed with their names in Aramaic (Nicolet-Pierre 1979; Harrison 1982a: 384–87; Schmitt 1987); the problem posed by the coins of Mazaces is all the more difficult to resolve in that some of them, it appears, were struck at Babylon: see most recently Price 1991: 452, who (despite Bellinger 1963: 66, not without hesitation) appears to revert to the theory (adopted, for example, by Berve II, no. 485) that Mazaces received an official position in Babylonia from Alexander. On Alexander's propaganda after Issus, cf. *RTP* 371–84.

• *The Defections of Mazaeus and Abulites (331).* The tablet *ADRTB* no. –330 is presented and used by Bernard 1990b: 525–28; the author also considers the problem treated here: he thinks that the military disposition adopted by Alexander was intended solely "to show off his force by having the army parade before the eyes of the Babylonians," and "not because the king expected resistance" (p. 526); while agreeing that P. Bernard's position is perfectly defensible, I have been convinced by the remarks, brief but illuminating, of Kuhrt 1990b: 125–26, who concludes that the ceremony described by the ancient authors was "merely the final result of complex negotiations"; I add that I do not see why Bosworth (1980a: 314) thinks it "improbable" that the appointment of Mazaeus was the price of his surrender; I think nonetheless that this position fits into the very reductive view of Alexander's Iranian policy that he develops elsewhere (Bosworth 1980b); opulent display in the royal processions: see also Briant 1994f; on Plutarch, *Alex.* 39.9: Alexander offers one of the sons of Mazaeus (not named) a "satrapy larger . . . than that with which he previously had been provided": Berve (1926: I, 84 n. 5) rejects the mention, on the grounds that no son of Mazaeus was ever a satrap: but it could refer to Brochubelus, who, to follow Quintus Curtius (V.13.11), was *praetor Syriae* (under the direction of his father); we may note in passing that Plutarch's note throws a vivid light on the negotiations opened between Alexander and the high Achaemenid dignitaries who agreed to defect to him; and if the Brochubelus of Quintus Curtius is the same as the Artiboles of Arrian (which is not certain), this son of Mazaeus would have preferred to be (and was) admitted to Alexander's entourage (Arrian VII.6.4). On Mazaeus's Babylonian coinage, cf. the discussions of Bellinger 1963: 60–65 (who, while observing it, does not explain the political reasons for this issue), Harrison 1982a: 361–70 (with some doubts), and most recently the summaries of Price 1991: 453–57 and Mildenberg 1990–91: 15–17; Mazaeus coins have also been found in the "Achaemenid residence" recently excavated at Sippar: cf. Amandry 1989 and 1991. I mention finally that in a speech given to Alexander (response to the Great King's ambassadors), Quintus Curtius lets it be known that the daughter of Darius offered to Alexander had already been promised to Mazaeus (IV.11.20); we are tempted to see this as an allusion to a personal quarrel beteween Mazaeus and the Great King, similar to the one Plutarch describes between Tiribazus and Artaxerxes II (*Art.* 27.7–10): but Quintus Curtius's rhetoric is very hazy and the context very dubious (embassy supposedly sent by Darius to offer the Euphrates border); and even if we recognize the existence of a rumor, it would not in itself explain Mazaeus's behavior.

• *The Persians of Persia between Darius and Alexander.* On Madates and the campaigns against the Uxians, cf. *RTP* 171–73 and 206–7 (with n. 62 on Parmenion's route); on the Mardians, cf. Briant 1976; on Alexander's policy, I repeat here basically what I wrote in *RTP* 384–403, where more detailed analyses will be found, and the bibliography; I have modified my position on two points: (1) I was not sufficiently attentive to the voluntary surrenders (such as the surrender of Tiridates); (2) I am less sure that the regrets later expressed by Alexander (Arrian VI.30.1; Quintus Curtius V.7.11; Plutarch, *Alex.* 38.8) mean that he then hoped to assume the title of Great King. The Persepolis matter has given rise to some analyses recently, on which I will provide a few quick comments:

(1) Hammond's 1992a chronological reconstruction appears totally unacceptable to me (we must stick with Borza 1972); the author, furthermore, is not really concerned (here or elsewhere) with providing an exhaustive historiographic inquiry.

(2) I find the same casualness in Badian 1994, where the author reexamines (and eventually confirms) his 1967 conclusions concerning the chronology of Agis's war against Antipater; in this framework, he devotes one discussion (pp. 277–81) to Alexander's chronology between Gaugamela and Ecbatana and another (pp. 281–85) to the burning of Persepolis, concluding that Alexander's order had to be connected with events in Europe (Agis war); in the opposite case, he finds no possible explanation (pp. 289–92), in particular rejecting the hypothesis of Persian resistance (pp. 283–84; without examination of texts); but the author seems not to know my 1977 article, reprinted in *RTP*; in any event, he does not mention or discuss it at all, and apparently does not consider it to be among "the major contributions of other scholars" (p. 292): which is certainly within his right, as long as he explains why!

(3) The most innovative study is by Sancisi-Weerdenburg 1993 who, while recalling the various interpretations, suggests examining the archaeological traces of the fire; they show (a) that the buildings attributed to Xerxes are the ones that suffered most; (b) she thinks that the main objective was to destroy not palaces but the valuable furnishings and other royal paraphernalia they contained: if this was really Alexander's concern, it was thus to prevent the use of these luxury objects in the framework of a policy of *polydōria*, which was a constituent element of the Great King's power. The article is very thought-provoking and raises some questions (in particular the last sentences [p. 185] on the image of Alexander as "conqueror, not . . . a ruler who has the safekeeping of the governmental apparatus foremost in his mind"—clauses that leave me wondering); the author (p. 178 and n. 12) refers to my interpretation, but she thinks that Diodorus XVII.71.3 "does not allow conclusions as to Persian hostility towards Alexander. . . . It merely says something about Alexander's mood": but, after reading and rereading the Diodorus passage, it still seems clear enough to me: if Diodorus is actually describing the situation from Alexander's point of view, it is because the mistrust and bad relations are also the deed of the *egkōrioi*; furthermore, I now willingly add to the discussion Diodorus XIX.14.5✧: speaking of the support given to Peucestes (named satrap of Persia when Alexander returned from India), Diodorus states that Alexander "wish[ed] to please the Persians and believing that through Peucestes he could keep the nation in all respects obedient (*kata panth'exein to ethnos hupēkoon*)"; the text no doubt refers implicitly to the rebellions that arose during Alexander's absence in India (Arrian VI.27.3; Quintus Curtius IX.10.19; X.1.9), but we may also wonder whether this passage is not additional evidence that also confirms that Alexander faced opposition in Persia in 330 that had not yet died down by 325 (thus, no doubt, leading to the "regrets" he then expressed for having carried out the destruction in 330).

(4) An extremely valuable and well-informed summary is found in Wiesehöfer 1994: 23–49 (cf. pp. 38–39, comparison of the interpretations of Briant and Sancisi-Weergenburg).

(5) On the inscription from Philippi published in 1984 by C. Vatin, M. Hatzopoulos thinks (*BE* 1987 no. 714; without touching directly on the problems I treat in this section) that the city's embassy sought out Alexander when he was in Persia (*Persis* restored on the stela), and it was during his stop in Persepolis that the king decided to change his plans; having initially resolved to pursue Darius, "whose capture would have to mark the end of the expedition," Alexander would have resolved at Persepolis "to pursue the war until the complete submission of the Persian Empire." I

will admit to some doubts about this reconstruction of Alexander's plans, but I prefer not to discuss the author's note, in the expectation of the publication of a more detailed argument.

3. The Local Elites, Darius, and Alexander: Popularity and Unpopularity of Achaemenid Dominion

The subtitle of this section is obviously inspired by the many studies devoted to this theme in the context of Athenian dominion in the fifth century (cf. bibliography in Briant 1995a: xlvi).

• *Sources and Problems.* I know of no satisfactory overall study of this problem: that of Schachermeyr 1975 is quite general and quite deceptive: marked by tenacious stereotypes, it insists solely on the character of "Benefactor" that Alexander intended to project; but the real problem (what were the reactions of the populations other than the Greeks of Asia Minor?) is not really treated in depth. I will not dwell here at length on Alexander's policy toward the Greek cities: from an abundant bibliography, I refer to Bickerman 1934, Badian 1966, Heisserer 1981, and Corsaro 1980b; cf. also Briant 1994a: 27–32 and 68–72 (it is self-evident in particular that the [somewhat vain] question of their possible connection to the Corinthian League does not interest me here at all). On Quintus Curtius III.8.22 (sacrifices of Alexander before the battle of Issus), cf. Bing 1991; on Alexander at Sardis, cf. Briant 1993a; on the Samaritan revolt and the documents from Wadi ed-Daliyeh (chap. 16/7), cf. the studies of Cross, e.g., 1971: he also recalls (p. 57) that according to Josephus (*Ant.* XI.321–22), after Issus, Sanballat of Samaria abandoned the cause of Darius III and sought out Alexander at Tyre; he received permission to construct a sanctuary on Mt. Gerizim, before dying, "since the siege lasted 7 months"; but I am not certain that Josephus's "information" is particularly credible (and still less so, obviously, the tradition that he records (*Ant.* XI.325–39) of Alexander's visit to Jerusalem—even if the procession welcoming Alexander was copied from the ceremonial of the royal entries); on Perdiccas in Samaria and the foundation of Gerasa, cf. Seyrig 1966 (unknown to Cross 1971: 57 n. 22) and Macchi 1994: 38–40.

• *Ephesus, Miletus, and Aspendus.* On Macedonian behavior during the preconquest, cf. Badian 1966: 39–42 (and p. 45 on Alexander at Ephesus); Alexander at Priene: see Sherwin-White 1985 (discussion of the composition and date of the materials), Heisserer 1981: 155–68 and, most recently, Marasco 1987, in particular pp. 67–73 on the problem of the land: on this point, cf. also my remarks in RTP 360–62, as well as Corsten 1994 (on the gifts given by Alexander to Phocion).

• *From Sidon to Tyre.* On the internal conflicts at Sidon and the position of Straton, see especially Bondi 1974: 152–57; on the Phoenician cities opposing Alexander, see also Verkinderen 1987; on Abdalonymus, cf. von Graeve 1970: 125–28; on the events at Tyre, cf. especially Lemaire 1991e, who, on the basis of numismatic sources, concludes that after his surrender (Arrian II.24.5) King Azelmicus kept his throne and title.

• *Egypt and the Egyptians.* On Khabbabash: cf. the discussion above, chap. 16/9, p. 718; a Demotic papyrus dated to year 2 of Darius III is known (Bresciani 1958: 185). On the theme of the return of statues and the partial nature of Hellenistic Egyptian sources, cf. Lorton 1978, Briant 1988a: 152–54, Morschauser 1988: 216–19, and, most recently, Winnicki 1989, 1990, and 1991 (and Winnicki forthcoming); on the policy of Alexander and Ptolemy I, cf. Swinnen 1973, van Voss 1993, and the summary of Burstein 1994, who stresses quite firmly the ideological distortions of the evidence coming from Alexander's side (Burstein [1991] also thinks that the theory of the pharaonization of Alexander must be abandoned), as well as, on the Egyptian religious policy of Ptolemy, the major analyses of Yoyotte 1994 that emphasize in particular that the satrap launched this strategy; inhumation of the mother of an Apis under Alexander: Smith 1988 and 1992a; another document refers to one Peucestes, who we might imagine is the Macedonian named commander of the troops left in Egypt by Alexander (along with Balacrus; Arrian III.5.5); this Peucestes seems to have sent an order concerning the prohibition of entry into the *hiereōs oikēma* (Turner 1974; cf. Thompson 1992: 106)—a measure that can be compared with that taken by Cambyses in the sanctuary of Neith, at the insistence of Udjahorresnet (Posener no. 1 B-b); chapel of Alexander at Luxor: Abd el-Raziq 1984. Inscription of Onnophris: my presentation is taken *in toto* from van Känel 1980. Statuette of Nectanebo's son: Clère 1951, who stresses the difficulty in dating but thinks that the parallel with the inscription of Samtutefnakht is striking; the inscription of the latter is published by Tresson 1931, then by Perdu 1985 (unfortunately, as far as I know the second half of the article never appeared); translation and commentary are also found in von Känel 1984: 120–25; Tresson (pp. 388–89) thinks the battle was Arbela, but the Issus suggestion seems more likely to me (cf. Perdu, p. 108, while recognizing there is "no decisive indication one way or the other"); on the meaning of the inscription, see also Lloyd 1982b: 179–80 (but I doubt that Samtutefnakht's oratorical warnings about Persian dominion can be considered "an exact reflection of his inmost feelings at a first state [of Persian dominion]" (p. 179). Petosiris inscriptions: see still the exemplary publication of Lefebvre 1924; see also on the date of the tomb and its decorations Picard 1930 and Muscarella 1980: 28–29 and pls. VIII–IX on Achaemenid influence: "The reliefs inform us about the manufacture of Achaemenian objects in Egypt around 300 B.C."; see also some comments in Lloyd 1982b: 177–78, to which I owe the comparison with the Udjahorresnet inscription (Posener 1936: 21); I had access to Menu 1994 (quotation is from p. 327) at the last moment, and I have used it extensively here; he will continue his analysis in the next issue of *BIFAO*. Another interesting inscription, Djedhor the Savior's: Jelinkova and Reymond 1951: 102 and Sherman 1981 (with the comparison, p. 100, with Udjahorresnet, but I scarcely believe that another part of the inscription [which she quotes] expresses "religious persecution by the Persians in the administration of their empire": this interpretation of a very allusive text is, as it seems, based on a traditional, canonical, but highly outmoded view of Achaemenid policy). Finally, I will mention that another inscription may refer to Artaxerxes III's reconquest (Vercoutter 1956; cf. p. 114), but it adds nothing to the discussion here. Four additional remarks on the documents just considered.

(1) A statue fragment found at Memphis (Mit Rahina) in 1955 bears an inscription in which the dedicator (Minirdis?) recalls that he restored a statue of Udjahorresnet "a hundred seventy-seven years after his time"; through the absolute date assigned to the episode, the exaltation of the figure of Udjahorresnet could possibly be considered the indication of adherence (after the reconquest of 343) to loyalist ideology (i.e., in favor of Artaxerxes III), just as it underlies the declarations of Udjahorresnet in favor of Cambyses and Darius: so Godron 1986; but see the reservations of Bresciani 1985a: 3, where the new document is presented in detail.

(2) On Samtutefnakht, the interpretations of Dandamaev (1989a: 324) are unacceptable because they are based on an indirect, partial, and mistaken reading of the inscription (cf. Briant 1993c: 18).

(3) I remain cautious about the explanations offered by Valbelle 1990: 266, who, suggesting that the second Persian dominion was even more resented than the first by the Egyptians, states that Samtutefnakht "surrendered at Issus . . . and flung wide the gates of Egypt [to Alexander]"; there is nothing in the text to justify this comment; as for claiming that he and the Egyptians did not consider the Greeks "potential invaders" because of the long (Saite period)-established links with the country, and thus that Samtutefnakht probably had no awareness of giving up "Egyptian independence"—these are very speculative theories and (in my opinion) hard to accept.

(4) Two talks on the subject under discussion in this section, one by B. Menu and one by D. Duvauchelle, were presented at a conference in Paris in April 1993, *L'Égypte et la Transeuphratène*; they are slated to appear in *Trans.* 9, 1995 [[see now Devauchelle 1995 and Menu 1995]].

• *The Babylonians, Alexander, and Darius*   See most recently Bernard 1990b: 525–28; I will simply indicate that the judgment on Sippar's decadence at this date (p. 526) must at least be nuanced: on this, see van der Spek 1992; a chronicle fragment may also allude to the war between the Macedonians (Haneans) and Darius, but the widely differing readings of Grayson (*ABC* no. 8; cf. p. 24) and Glassner (1993 no. 29) lead me not to use a text that is so fragmentary; on Alexander at Babylon and his relations with the sanctuaries, I borrow the proof from Kuhrt 1990b (on Cyrus at Babylon, cf. Kuhrt 1983b); see also Kuhrt and Sherwin-White 1994. The Chaldeans and Alexander: see the arguments of Smelik 1978–79; the sources are gathered and interpreted by Smelik, as well as the prior bibliography; on the substitute king, all the sources, including the Classical sources, are collected and discussed by Parpola 1983: xxii–xxxii (cf. also Labat 1939: 103–10 and Bottéro 1978 repeated in Bottéro 1987: 170–90; the ancient authors depict several other episodes (Alexander's diadem) that I do not think it useful to analyze here in detail: I refer to Smelik 1978–79. *Dynastic Prophecy*: an edition and translation was published by Grayson 1975: 24–37 (pp. 34–35); since then, several studies have allowed improved readings; the translation presented here is based on Grayson's translation; see also Sherwin-White 1987: 12–13 and the recent French translation by Tallon 1994: 101–2 (who rightly stresses the difficulties of the material); Marasco 1985 saw a direct reference to Babylonian opposition to Alexander after Gaugamela in the text; but this view is hardly acceptable today: the interpretation I develop here is essentially based on the analyses of Sherwin-White 1987: 10–15 and Sherwin-White and Kuhrt 1993: 8–9; cf. also Kuhrt 1987a: 154–55 and Kuhrt and Sherwin-White 1994. But it must be recognized that this interpretation is not accepted by every scholar: according to Geller 1990: 5–6, followed by Stolper, CAH VI²: 241 n. 24, the *Dynastic Prophecy* refers not to a "prophecy" concerning a "defeat" of Alexander by Darius but to the war between Antigonus and Seleucus in Babylonia in 310–308 and 307: I am not convinced by the argument. On *ADRTB* –328, cf. my reflections in Briant 1994d: 463–64. Two last remarks on Babylonian matters:

(1) With regard to Plutarch's description (*Alex.* 34.1) of the consequences for Alexander of his victory at Gaugamela and his royal proclamation (for which, see Hammond 1986), see also Aelian, *VH* II.25, and the comments by Grzbek (1990: 42–43): "We arrive at the conclusion that Alexander chose the Babylonian New Year—in the Macedonian calendar we are in the month of Daisos—to officially proclaim the deposition of the Great King and his decision to assume the Achaemenid succession" (p. 43).

(2) In a recent article, Bosworth (1992: 75–79) offers a hypothesis that calls for a remark here; by way of explaining the apparent inconsistencies in the dating of the reign of Philip III Arrhideus in Babylon, the author thinks that Alexander gave his half-brother the title "King of Babylon" (in 324), and Bosworth compares this with the situation that (according to him) prevailed in the months that followed the conquest of Babylon by Cyrus in 539, when for several months Cambyses bore the title "King of Babylon" (but see Petschow 1987). No doubt these hypotheses will arouse the interest of the specialists in the Babylonian documentation of the Achaemenid and Hellenistic periods [[cf. Stolper 1993: 80]] and also specialists in the political history of the Diadochi (Bosworth connects this with the high chronology, which I defended in Briant 1973, and which since then has been nearly unanimously rejected); not wishing here to get into an analysis that transcends the framework of this book, I will simply mention that I am entirely opposed to the Babylonian interpretation that Bosworth wants to put on Quintus Curtius X.7.2; I continue to think very firmly that, by expressing himself thus regarding Arrhideus (*sacrorum caerimoniarumque consors*), Quintus Curtius (his source) is thinking very specifically of the tasks and prerogatives of the Macedonian kings (cf. Briant 1973: 326², 330–31). [[Without knowing Bosworth's article, Kuhrt and Sherwin-White 1994: 323 n. 19 stress quite rightly the deep difference between association with the Seleucid throne and for example the (temporary) nomination of Cambyses as "King of Babylon"; cf. also Briant 1994c: 466 and n. 22.]]

5. The Fall of an Empire

• *The Cornelwood Lance.* Technical problems: chap. 17/3: "'Greek Army' and 'Barbarian Army,'" pp. 795ff.

• *Persian Royal Power and Multicultural Empire.* I have already suggested elsewhere the theory developed here: cf. Briant 1988a: 172–73.

• *Bessus in Bactria.* On the nature of the war conducted by Bessus, cf. Briant 1984b: 77–80 (cf. also *RTP* 401–403); on Seleucus in Babylonia, Peucestes in Persia, and, more generally, the policy of the Diadochi, cf. *RTP* 41–54 (and now on Peucestes, Wiesehöfer 1994a: 50–56).

Conclusion

Alexander the "last of the Achaemenids": cf. in particular RTP 318–30; on the position of the Seleucids, profoundly Babylonized in Babylonia, cf. Sherwin-White and Kuhrt 1993, and, on their relations with their Macedonian origins, my remarks in Briant 1994c. The Greek-Aramaic inscription mentioning "legitimate satraps" was first published by Cumont 1905c, then by Lipiń-ski 1975: 197–208 (who proposes the identifications of the people that I use here); the Greek word used (*euthemitoi*) is translated by Cumont (1905c: 96) as 'pious, fair', that is, 'legitimate'. Of course, the interpretation suggested in the text (implicit but intentional continuity with the Achaemenid era) is a mere hypothesis.

List of Abbreviations

AA	*Archäologischer Anzeiger*
AAAS	*Annales Archéologiques (Arabes) Syriennes*
AAH	Acta Antiqua Academiae Scientiarum Hungaricae
AASOR	Annual of the American Schools of Oriental Research
ABC	A. K. Grayson, *Assyrian and Babylonian Chronicles*, 1975 [reprinted, 2000]
AbIran	*Abstracta Iranica*
AC	*L'Antiquité Classique*
AD	G. R. Driver, *Aramaic Documents of the 5th Century* B.C.
AchHist	*Achaemenid History*, vols. 1–8 (Leiden), 1987–1994
Acta Sum.	*Acta Sumerologica*
ADRTB	A. J. Sachs, H. Hunger, *Astronomical Diaries and Related Texts from Babylonia*, I, 1988
AfO	*Archiv für Orientforschung*
AHB	*The Ancient History Bulletin*
AIIN	*Annali dell'Istituto Italiano di Numismatica*
AION	*Annali dell'Istituto Orientale di Napoli*
AJA	*American Journal of Archaeology*
AJAH	*American Journal of Ancient History*
AJBA	*Australian Journal of Biblical Archaeology*
AJPh	*American Journal of Philology*
AJSL	*American Journal of Semitic Languages*
AK	*Antike Kunst*
AM	Athenische Mitteilungen
AMI	*Archäologische Mitteilungen aus Iran* (Berlin)
AnAnt	*Anatolia Antiqua* (Istanbul)
AncSoc	*Ancient Society*
ANET³	J. B. Pritchard, *Ancient Near Eastern Texts Relating to the Old Testament* (Princeton), 1969
ANSMN	*The American Numismatic Society Museum Notes*
AnSt	*Anatolian Studies*
AO	Antiquités orientales (Musée du Louvre)
AÖAW	*Anzeiger der Österreichischen Akademie der Wissenschaften Vienna*, Ph.-Hist. Kl.
AOF	*Altorientalische Forschungen*
AOr	*Archiv Orientální*
AP	A. E. Cowley, *Aramaic Papyri of the Fifth Century* B.C. (Oxford)
ARID	*Analecta Romana Istituti Danici*
ASAE	*Annales du Service des antiquités d'Égypte*
ASNP	*Annali della Scuola Normale di Pisa*
Athen.	*Athenaeum*
ATL	*Athenian Tribute Lists*, vols 1–4 (Princeton)
AUSS	*Andrews University Seminary Studies*
AW	*Ancient World*
BA	*The Biblical Archaeologist*
Babelon	E. Babelon, *Traité des monnaies grecques et romaines*

BABesch	*Bulletin Antieke Beschaving* (Leiden)
BAGB	*Bulletin de l'Association Guillaume-Budé*
BAH	Bibliothèque Archéologique et Historique
BAHIFAI	Bibliothèque archéologique et historique de l'Institut français d'archéologie d'Istanbul
BAI	*Bulletin of the Asia Institute*
BASOR	*Bulletin of the American Schools of Oriental Research*
BBR	*Bulletin of Biblical Research*
BCH	*Bulletin de Correspondance Hellénique*
BE	*Bulletin épigraphique de la Revue des Études Grecques*
BEFAR	Bibliothèque des Écoles françaises d'Athènes et Rome
BEFEO	*Bulletin de l'École française d'Extrême-Orient*
BES	*Bulletin of the Egyptian Seminar*
BgM	Baghdader Mitteilungen
BHLT	A. K. Grayson, *Babylonian Historical and Literary Texts*, 1975
BICS	*Bulletin of the Institute of Classical Studies* (London)
BIDR	*Bolletino dell'Istituto di diritto romano* (Milan)
BIFAO	*Bulletin de l'Institut français d'Archéologie orientale*
BiOr	*Bibliotheca Orientalis*
BM	Tablets in the collections of the British Museum
BMAP	*The Brooklyn Museum Aramaic Papyri: New Documents of the Fifth Century* B.C. *from the Jewish Colony at Elephantine* (New Haven)
BMB	*Bulletin du Musée de Beyrouth*
Bonn. Jahrb.	*Bonner Jahrbücher*
BOR	Babylonian and Oriental Records
BSA	*Annual of the British School at Athens*
BSFE	*Bulletin de la Société française d'égyptologie*
BSL	*Bulletin de la Société de linguistique de Paris*
BSOAS	*Bulletin of the School of Oriental and African Studies*
BZ	*Biblische Zeitschrift*
CAD	Assyrian Dictionary of the University of Chicago
CAH	*Cambridge Ancient History*
Camb.	J. N. Strassmaier, *Inschriften von Kambyses, König von Babylon*, 1890
CANE	J. M. Sasson (ed.), *Civilizations of the Ancient Near East*, vols. 1–4 (New York), 1995 [reprinted, 2000]
CBQ	*Catholic Biblical Quarterly*
CDAFI	Cahiers de la Délégation archéologique française en Iran
CdE	*Chronique d'Égypte*
CHI	*Cambridge History of Iran*
CHJ	*Cambridge History of Judaism*
CHM	Cahiers d'Histoire Mondiale
CII	Corpus Inscriptionum Iudaicarum
CJ	*The Classical Journal*
CPh	*Classical Philology*
CQ	*Classical Quarterly*
CRAI	Comptes rendus de l'Académie des Inscriptions et Belles-Lettres
CS	Y. Meshorer and S. Qedar, *The Coinage of Samaria*, 1991
CSCA	*California Studies in Classical Antiquity*
CT	Cuneiform texts from Babylonian tablets in the British Museum
DAE	P. Grelot, *Documents araméens d'Égypte* (Paris), 1972

Dar.	J. N. Strassmaier, *Inschriften von Dareios, König von Babylon,* 1897
DBS	*Suppléments au Dictionnaire de la Bible*
DdA	*Dialoghi di Archeologia*
DHA	*Dialogues d'Histoire Ancienne*
EA	*Epigraphica Anatolica*
EI	*Encyclopaedia of Islam*
EMC	*Echos du monde classique*
EncIr	Encyclopaedia Iranica
EPRO	Études préliminaires aux religions orientales
EVO	*Egitto e Vicino Oriente*
EW	*East and West*
FdX	Fouilles de Xanthos
FGrH	F. Jacoby, *Die Fragmente der griechischer Historiker* (Berlin–Leiden), 1923–1958
FO	*Folia Orientalia*
Fort. no.	unpublished Fortification Tablets from Persepolis
Frankfort	H. Frankfort, *Cylinder Seals,* 1939
GGA	*Göttingische Gelehrte Anzeigen*
Gibson II, no.	J. C. L. Gibson, *Textbook of Syrian semitic inscriptions* II, 1982
Gibson III, no.	J. C. L. Gibson, *Textbook of Syrian semitic inscriptions* III, 1982
GIF	*Giornale italiano di Filologia*
GNS	*Gazette Numismatique Suisse*
GR	*Greece and Rome*
GRBS	Greece, Roman and Byzantine Studies
HSCIP	Harvard Studies in Classical Philology
HThR	*Harvard Theological Review*
HUCA	*Hebrew Union College Annual*
IA	*Iranica Antiqua*
ICS	Illinois Classical Studies
IEJ	*Israel Exploration Journal*
I. Ephesos	H. Wankel (ed.), *Die Inschriften von Ephesos,* part Ia: *Inschriften griechischer Städte aus Kleinasien,* II/1 (Bonn), 1979
IFAO	Institut français d'Archéologie orientale
IFEA	Institut français d'Études anatoliennes
IG II²	*Inscriptiones Graecae,* II (Attica), 2d ed.
IGLS	Inscriptions grecques et latines de Syrie
IIJ	*Indo-Iranian Journal*
IM	Istanbuler Mitteilungen
IMJ	*Israel Museum Journal*
INJ	*Israel Numismatic Journal*
IOS	*Israel Oriental Studies*
ISMEO	Istituto per il Medio e Estreme Oriente
JA	*Journal Asiatique*
JANES	*Journal of the Ancient Near Eastern Society*
JAOS	*Journal of the American Oriental Society*
JARCE	*Journal of the American Research Center in Egypt*
JB	*Jerusalem Bible*
JBL	*Journal of Biblical Literature*
JEA	*Journal of Egyptian Archaeology*
LEC	*Les Études classiques*
JEOL	*Jaarbericht . . . Ex Oriente Lux*

JESHO	*Journal of the Economic and Social History of the Orient*
JfW	*Jahrbuch für Wirtschaftsgeschichte*
JHS	*Journal of Hellenic Studies*
JJP	*Journal of Juristic Papyrology*
JJS	*Journal of Jewish Studies*
JNES	*Journal of Near Eastern Studies*
JQR	*Jewish Quarterly Review*
JRAS	*Journal of the Royal Asiatic Society*
JRGS	*Journal of the Royal Geographical Society*
JRS	*Journal of Roman Studies*
JS	*Journal des Savants*
JSJ	*Journal for the Study of Judaism*
JSOT	*Journal for the Study of the Old Testament*
JSS	*Journal of Semitic Studies*
LCL	Loeb Classical Library
LCM	*Liverpool Classical Monthly*
JCS	*Journal of Cuneiform Studies*
LÄ	*Lexikon der Ägyptologie*
LdP	*La Lettre de Pallas*
MBAH	Münchener Beiträge zur Handelsgeschichte
MDAFI	*Mélanges de la Délégation archéologique française en Iran*
MDAIK	Mitteilungen der Deutsche Archäologische Institut, Kairo
MDFP	Mémoires de la Délégation française en Perse
MDP	Mémoires de la Délégation en Perse
MEFRA	*Mélanges de l'École française de Rome—Antiquité*
MH	Museum Helveticum
MIFAO	Mémoires de l'Institut Français d'Archéologie Orientale du Caire
MJBK	Münchener Jahrbuch der bildenden Kunst
ML	R. Meiggs and D. Lewis, *A Selection of Greek Historical Inscriptions*, 1980
MMAI	Mémoires de la Mission Archéologique en Iran
Mnem.	*Mnémosyme*
MSS	Münchener Studien zur Sprachwissenschaft
MUSJ	*Mélanges de l'Université Saint-Joseph*
MVAG	Mitteilungen der vorderasiatisch-ägyptischen Gesellschaft
NABU	*Nouvelles assyriologiques brèves et utilitaires*
NAPR	Northern Akkad Project Reports
NAWG	*Nachrichten von der Akademie der Wissenschaften in Göttingen*
NC	*Numismatic Chronicle*
NTZ	*Nachrichtentechnische Zeitschrift*
OA	*Oriens Antiquus*
OGIS	W. Dittenberger, *Orientis Graeci Inscriptiones Selectae*, 1903–1905
OIP	Oriental Institute Publications
OLA	Orientalia Lovaniensia Analecta
OLP	*Orientalia Lovaniensia Periodica*
OLZ	*Orientalische Literaturzeitung*
OpAth	*Opuscula Atheniensia*
OPers.	Old Persian
OpRom	*Opuscula Romana*
PAPS	*Proceedings of the American Philosophical Society*
PBS	Publications of the Babylonian Section (University Museum, University of Pennsylvania)

PCPS	*Proceedings of the Cambridge Philological Society*
PdP	*La Parola del Passato*
PEQ	*Palestine Exploration Quarterly*
PF, no.	*Persepolis Fortification Tablets*, 1969
PFa, no.	R. T. Hallock, *Selected Fortifications Texts*, CDAFI 1978
PFS	Persepolis Fortification Seals
PFT	R. T. Hallock, *Persepolis Fortification Tablets*, 1969
P. Loeb	Loeb Papyrus
Posener, no.	G. Posener, *La Première Domination perse en Égypte* (1936), no. inscriptions
PT, no.	Persepolis Treasury Tablets
PT 1963, no.	Cameron, *JNES* 1965
PTS	Persepolis Treasury Seals
PTT	G. Cameron, *Persepolis Treasury Tablets*, 1948
Q-000	Fortification Tablets from Persepolis; unpublished transcriptions by Hallock
QCSC	*Quaderni Catanesi di Studi Classici e medievali*
QS	*Quaderni di Storia* (Bari)
QuadStor	*Quaderni Storici* (Urbino)
QUCC	*Quaderni Urbinati di Cultura Classica*
RA	*Revue archéologique*
RAL	*Rendiconti dell'Academia dei Lincei*
RAss	*Revue d'assyriologie et d'archéologie orientale*
RB	*Revue Biblique*
RBN	*Revue belge de numismatique*
RBPh	*Revue belge de philologie et d'histoire*
RC	C. B. Welles, *Royal correspondence in the Hellenistic period*, 1934
RDAC	Reports of the Department of Archaeology of Cyprus
RdE	*Revue d'égyptologie*
RE	Real-Enzyklopädie der Altertumswissenschaft
REA	*Revue des études anciennes*
REArm	*Revue des études arméniennes*
REG	*Revue des études grecques*
REJ	*Revue des études juives*
RÉS	*Répertoire des études sémitique*
RFIC	*Rivista di Filologia e di Istruzione Classica*
RGTC	Répertoire géographique des textes cunéiformes
RH	*Revue historique*
RhM	Rheinisches Museum
RHR	*Revue de l'histoire des religions*
RIDA	*Revue internationale des droits de l'Antiquité*
RIL	*Rendiconti dell'Istituto Lombardo*
RlA	*Reallexikon der Assyriologie*
RN	*Revue numismatique*
RPh	*Revue de philologie*
RSA	*Rivista di Storia Antica*
RSF	*Rivista di Studi Fenici*
RSI	*Rivista storica italiana*
RSO	*Rivista degli Studi orientali*
RT	*Recueil de travaux relatifs à la philologie et à l'archéologie égyptiennes et assyriennes*
RTP	P. Briant, *Rois, tributs et paysans* (Paris), 1982
SAA	State Archives of Assyria

SAAB	State Archives of Assyria Bulletin
SAK	Studien zur Ägyptischen Kultur
Sardis VII, 1	W. H. Buckler, D. M. Robinson, *Sardis VII* (1): *Greek and Latin Inscriptions*, 1932
SB Berlin	Sitzungsberichte der Akademie der Wissenschaften (Berlin)
Schmidt	E. Schmidt, *Persepolis* [number of the photographic plate]
SCO	Studi Classici e Orientali
SEG	Supplementum Epigraphicum Graecum
Segal	J. B. Segal, *Aramaic Texts from North Saqqâra* (London), 1983
SELVOA	Studi epigrafici e linguistici sul Vicino Oriente Antico
SII	Studien zur Indologie und Iranistik
SKPAW	Sitzungsberichte des König. Preuss. Akad. d. Wissensch. (Berlin)
SNR	Swiss Numismatic Review
SO	Symbolae Osloenses
SRA	Silk Road and Archaeology
STIR	Studia Iranica
Syll³.	W. Dittenberger et al., *Sylloge Inscriptionum Graecarum*, 3d ed., 1915–1924
TADAE	Porten-Yardeni, *Texts and Aramaic Documents from Ancient Egypt* (Jerusalem; vols. A [1986], B [1992] C [1993])
TAM	Tituli Asiae Minoris
TAVO	Tübinger Atlas des Vorderen Orients
TB	Tyndale Bulletin
TBER	Textes babyloniens d'époque récente
TCL	Textes cunéiformes, musée du Louvre
TL	Tituli Asiae Minoris: Tituli Lyciae lingua lycia conscripti
TMO	Travaux de la Maison de l'Orient (Lyon)
Tod	M. N. Tod, *A Selection of Greek Historical Inscriptions* (Oxford)
TPhS	Transactions of the Philological Society
Trans	Transeuphratène
UCP	University of California Publications in Semitic Philology (Berkeley)
UET	Ur Excavations, Texts
UF	Ugarit-Forschungen
VDI	Vestnik Drejnev Istorii
VO	Vicino Oriente
VS	Vorderasiatische Schriftendenkmäler der Königlichen Museen zu Berlin
VT	Vetus Testamentum
WO	Die Welt des Orients
YBT	Yale Babylonian Texts
YClS	Yale Classical Studies
YNES	Yale Near Eastern Studies
YOS	Yale Oriental Series, Babylonian Texts
ZA	Zeitschrift für Assyriologie
ZÄS	Zeitschrift für ägyptische Sprache und Altertumskunde
ZAW	Zeitschrift für die alttestamentliche Wissenschaft
ZDMG	Zeitschrift der Morgenländischen Gesellschaft
ZDPV	Zeitschrift der Deutsche Palästina-Vereins
ZPE	Zeitschrift für Papyrologie und Epigraphik
ZVS	Zeitschrift für Vergleichende Sprachen
WD	M. J. V. Leith, *Greek and Persian Images in pre-Alexandrine Samaria: The Wadi ed-Daliyeh Seal Impressions*, 1990

Bibliography

Abd el-Razik, M.
1984 *Die Darstellungen und Texte des Sanktuars Alexanders des Grossen im Tempel von Luxor.* Mainz am Rhein.

Abou-Assaf, A.; Bordreuil, P.; and Millard, A. R.
1982 *La Statue de Tell Fekheriye et son inscription bilingue assyro-babylonienne.* Paris.

Abramenko, A.
1992 "Die zwei Seeschlachten vor Tyros: Zu den militarischen Voraussetzungen für die makedonische Eroberung der Inselfestung (332 v. Chr)." *Klio* 74: 166–72.

Achaemenid History 1
1987 *Sources, Structures and Synthesis,* ed. H. Sancisi Weerdenburg. Leiden.

Achaemenid History 2
1987 *The Greek Sources,* ed. H. Sancisi-Weerdenburg and A. Kuhrt. Leiden.

Achaemenid History 3
1988 *Method and Theory,* ed. H. Sancisi-Weerdenburg and A. Kuhrt. Leiden.

Achaemenid History 4
1990 *Centre and Periphery,* ed. H. Sancisi-Weerdenburg and A. Kuhrt. Leiden.

Achaemenid History 5
1990 *The Roots of the European Tradition,* ed. H. Sancisi-Weerdenburg and J. W. Drijvers. Leiden.

Achaemenid History 6
1991 *Asia Minor and Egypt: Old Cultures in a New Empire,* ed. H. Sancisi-Weerdenburg and A. Kuhrt. Leiden.

Achaemenid History 7
1991 *Through Travellers' Eyes: European Travelers on the Iranian Monuments,* ed. H. Sancisi-Weerdenburg and J. W. Drijvers. Leiden.

Achaemenid History 8
1994 *Continuity and Change,* ed. H. Sancisi-Weerdenburg, A. Kuhrt and M. Root. Leiden.

Ackroyd, P. R.
1968 *Exile and Restoration.* London.
1984a "Historical problems of the Early Achaemenid period." *Orient* 20: 1–15.
1984b "The Jewish community in Palestine in the Persian period." *CHJ* I: 130–61.
1988a "Problems in handling of Biblical and related sources in the Achaemenid period." *AchHist* 3: 33–54.
1988b "Chronicles-Ezra-Nehemiah: the concept of Unity." *ZAW* 100: 189–201.

1990a "The written evidence for Palestine." *AchHist* 4: 207–26.
1990b "The Biblical portraits of Achaemenid rulers." *AchHist* 5: 1–16.

Adams, R. McC.
1965 *Land behind Baghdad: A History of Settlement in the Diyala Plain.* Chicago.
1981 *Heartland of Cities: Surveys of Ancient Settlement and Land Use of the Central Floodplain of the Euphrates.* Chicago.

Adams, R. McC., and Nissen, H. J.
1972 *The Uruk Countryside.* Chicago.

Afshar, A., and Lerner, J.
1979 "The horses of the ancient Persian Empire at Persepolis." *Antiquity* 207/3: 44–47.

Aharoni, Y.
1967 *The Land of the Bible: A Historical Geography.* Philadelphia.

Aharoni, Y. (ed.)
1981 *Arad Inscriptions.* Jerusalem.

Ahn, G.
1992 *Religiose Herrscherlegitimation im Achamenidischen Iran: Die Voraussetzungen und die Struktur ihrer Argumentation.* Acta Iranica 31, Textes et Mémoires 17. Leiden-Louvain.

Aikio, K.
1988 "Clazomene, Eritre ed Atene prima della Pace di Antalcida (387 a.C.): Un'analisi di due decreti attici." *Acmè* 41/3: 17–33.

Aimé-Giron, N.
1931 *Textes araméens d'Égypte.* Paris.
1939 "Araméen: Additions et corrections aux textes araméens d'Égypte." *BIFAO* 38: 33ff.

Akurgal, E.
1956 "Les fouilles de Daskyleion." *Anatolia* 1: 20–24.
1961 *Die Kunst Anatoliens von Homer bis Alexander.* Berlin.
1966 "Griechisch-persische Reliefs aus Daskyleion." *IA* 6: 147–56.
1976 "Les fouilles de Daskyleion." *Anatolia* 1: 20–24.
1986 "Bärtige Kopf mit Tiara aus Herakleia Pontica." Pp. 9–13 in *Archäische und klassische griechische Plastik (Akten des Intern. Kolloquiums, Athens 1985).* Mainz.

Albenda, P.
1974 "Grapevines in Ashurbanipal's garden." *BASOR* 215: 5–17.

Albright, W. F.
1950 "Cilicia and Babylonia under the Chaldean Kings." *BASOR* 120: 22–25.

Alexandrescu, P.
"MHΔIZEIN: À propos des importations et de l'influence achéménides en Thrace." *Dacia* 30/1–2: 155–58.

Alizadeh, A.
1985   "A tomb of the Neo-Elamite period at Arjan near Behbehan." *AMI* 18: 49–73.

Allam, S.
1986   "Réflexions sur le 'Code légal' d'Hermopolis dans l'Égypte ancienne." *CdE* 61: 50–75.
1993   "Traces de 'codification' en Égypte ancienne." *RIDA* 40: 11–26.

Alonso-Nuñez, J. M.
1988   "Herodotus' ideas about world Empires." *AncSoc* 19: 125–33.

Alram, M.
1986   *Nomina propria iranica in nummis.* Vienna.
1993   "*Dareikos* und *siglos*: Ein neuer Schatzfund achaimenidischer *sigloi* aus Kleinasien [mit einem metrologischen Beitrag von St. Karwiese]." *Res Orientales* 5 [Circulation des monnaies, des marchandises et des biens]: 23–50.

Altheim, F.
1951   Review of Cameron 1948, *Gnomon*: 187–93.

Altheim, F., and Stiehl, R.
1963   *Die aramäische Sprache unter den Achameniden.* Frankfurt.
1969   *Geschichte Mittelasiens im Altertum.* Berlin.

Altheim, F.; Stiehl, R.; and Cremer, M. L.
1985   "Eine gräco-persische Türstele mit aramäischer Inschrift aus Daskyleion." *EA*: 1–15.

Altheim, F.; Stiehl, R.; Metzler, D.; and Schwertheim, E.
1983   "Eine neue gräko-persische Grabstele aus Sultaniye Köy und ihre Bedeutung für die Geschichte und Topographie von Daskyleion." *EA*: 1–22.

Amandry, M.
1989   "Les monnaies [Abû Qubûr]." *NAPR* 4: 34–37.
1991   "Abû Qubûr et Tell al-Hargâwî: Les trouvailles monétaires." *NAPR* 5: 57–59.

Amandry, P.
1958a   "Orfèvrerie achéménide." *AK*: 9–22.
1958b   "Toreutique achéménide." *AK*: 38–56.
1987   "Le système palatial dans la Perse achéménide." Pp. 315–26 in *Le Système palatial en Orient, en Grèce et à Rome.* Strasbourg.

Ambaglio, D.
1974   "Il motivo delle deportazione in Erodoto." *RIL* 109: 378–83.

Amiet, P.
1966   *Élam.* Anvers-sur-Oise.
1972a   "Les ivoires achéménides de Suse." *Syria* 49: 167–91 and 319–37.
1972b   *Glyptique susienne des origines à l'époque des Perses Achéménides: Cachets, sceaux-cylindres et empreintes antiques découverts à Suse de 1913 à 1967, I: Texte.* Mémoires de la DAI XLIII; Mission de Susiane. Paris.

1973   "La glyptique de la fin de l'Élam." *Arts asiatiques* 28: 3–32.
1990   "Quelques épaves de la vaisselle royale de Suse." Pp. 213–24 in F. Vallat (ed).
1992   "Sceaux dans l'ancien Orient." *DBS* 12: 66–86.

Amigues, S.
1995   "Végétation et cultures du Proche-Orient dans l'*Anabase*." Pp. 61–78 in P. Briant (ed.), *Dans les pas des Dix-Mille: Peuples et pays du Proche-Orient vus par un Grec* (Actes de la Table ronde de Toulouse, 3–4 février 1995). Pallas 43.

Ampolo, C., and Bresciani, E.
1988   "Psammetico re d'Egitto et il mercenario Pedon." *EVO* 11: 237–53.

Andreadès, A.
1929   "Antimène de Rhodes et Cléomène de Naucratis." *BCH* 53: 1–18.

Andrewes, A.
1961   "Thucydides and the Persians." *Historia* 10/1: 1–18.
1992a   "The peace of Nicias and the Sicilian expedition." *CAH* 5²: 433–63.
1992b   "The Spartan resurgence." *CAH* 5²: 464–98.

Anson, E. A.
1988   "Antigonus, the satrap of Phrygia." *Historia* 37/4: 471–77.
1989   "The Persian fleet in 334." *CPh* 84/1: 44–49.

Aschoff, V.
1977a   "Optische Nachrichtenübertragung im klassischen Altertum." *NTZ* 30/1: 23–28.
1977b   "Die Rufposten im Alten Persien: Historische Wirklichkeit oder nachrichtentechnische Legende?" *NTZ* 30/6: 451–55.

Asheri, D.
1983a   "Fra ellenismo e iranismo: il caso di Xanthos fra il ve iv sec. a.C." Pp. 486–500 in *Modes de contacts et processus de transformation dans les sociétés anciennes.* Pisa-Rome.
1983b   *Fra ellenismo ed iranismo: Studi sulla società e cultura di Xanthos nella età achéménide.* Bologna.
1988   "Carthaginians and Greeks." *CAH* 4²: 739–80.
1990   *Erodoto: Le Storie. Libro III: La Persia* (a cura di D. Asheri et S. Medaglia; traduzione di A. Fraschetti), introduzione e commento, Fondazione L. Valla.
1991   "Divagazione erodotee sulla Cilicia persiana." *QuadStor* 76: 35–65.

forthcoming   *Lo stato persiano: Ideologie e istituzioni nell'Impero achemenide.* Turin.

Asmussen, J. P. (in honor of)
1988   *A Green Leaf: Papers in Honor of Prof. J. P. Asmussen.* Acta Iranica 28. Leiden.

Atkinson, J. A.
1980   *A Commentary on Q. Curtius Rufus' Historiae Alexandri Magni, Books 3 and 4.* Amsterdam-Uithoorn.

1994   A Commentary on Q. Curtius Rufus' His-
        toriae Alexandri Magni, Books 5 to 7.2.
        Amsterdam.
Atkinson, K. M. T.
1956   "The legitimacy of Cambyses and Darius
        as Kings of Egypt." JAOS 76: 167–77.
Atlan, S.
1958   "Eine in Sidè geprägte lykische Münze."
        Anatolia 3: 89–95.
Atti del Convegno sul tema
1965   "La Persia e il mondo greco-romano."
        (Roma 11–14 aprile 1965.) RAL 363.
Auberger, J.
1991   Ctésias: Histoires de l'Orient (translation
        and commentary). Paris.
1993   "Ctésias et les femmes." DHA 19/2: 253–
        72.
Aufrère, S.; Golvin, J. C.; and Goyon, J. C.
1991   L'Égypte restituée. I: Sites et temples de
        Haute-Égypte. Paris.
1994   L'Égypte restituée. II: Sites et temples des
        deserts. Paris.
Aurell, M.; Dumoulin, O.; and Thelamon, Fr. (ed.)
1993   La Sociabilité à table: Commensalité et
        convivialité à travers les âges. Publication
        de l'université de Rouen 178. Rouen.
Austin, M.
1970   Greece and Egypt in the Archaic Age. PCPS
        suppl. 2. Cambridge.
1990   "Greek tyrants and the Persians." CQ 40/2:
        289–306.
Austin, R. P.
1944   "Athens and the satrap revolt." JHS 64: 97–
        100.
Autran, C.
1951   "L''Œil du Roi': concept politico-adminis-
        tratif commun à l'Iran, à la Chine et à
        l'Hellade." Humanitas 3: 287–91.
Avigad, N.
1976   Bullae and Seals from a post-exilic Judean
        Archive. Qedem 4. Jerusalem.
Azarpay, G.
1972   "Crowns and some royal insignia in early
        Iran." IA 9: 108–15.
Babelon, E.
1907–10 Traité des monnaies grecques et romaines.
        Part 2: Description historique, I–II. Paris.
Badi, A. M.
1963–91 Les Grecs et les Barbares: L'autre face de
        l'Histoire. Payot (Lausanne) puis Geuth-
        ner. Paris. 12 volumes.
Badian, E.
1958   "The eunuch Bagoas: a study in method."
        CQ 8: 144–57.
1961   "Harpalus." JHS 81: 16–43.
1966   "Alexander the Great and the Greeks of
        Asia." Pp. 37–69 in Ancient Studies and In-
        stitutions presented to V. Ehrenberg. Oxford.
1967   "Agis III." Hermes 95: 170–92.
1975   "Nearchus the Cretan." YClS 24: 147–70.
1976   "Some recent interpretations of Alexan-
        der." Pp. 279–311 in Alexandre le Grande:

images et réalités (entretiens Hardt 22),
Geneva.
1977a   "The battle of the Granicus. A new look.
        II: the battle." Pp. 271–93 in Ancient Mace-
        donia II. Thessalonica.
1977b   "A document of Artaxerxes IV?" Pp. 40–50
        in Greece and the Eastern Mediterranean
        in Ancient History and Prehistory: Studies
        presented to F. Schachermeyr. Berlin–New
        York.
1985   "Alexander in Iran." CHI 2: 420–501 and
        897–903.
1987   "The Peace of Callias." JHS 107: 1–39.
1988   "Towards a chronology of the Pentekontae-
        tia down to the renewal of the Peace of
        Callias." EMC 23: 289–320.
1991   "The King's peace." Pp. 25–48 in Geor-
        gica: Greek Studies in Honor of G. Cawk-
        well = BICS Supp. 58.
1993   From Plataea to Potidea: Studies in the His-
        tory and Historiography of the Penteconta-
        etia. Baltimore-London.
1994   "Agis III: revisions and reflections." Pp.
        258–92 in I. Worthington (ed.), Ventures
        into Greek History. Oxford.
Bakir, T.
1995   "Archäologische Beobachtungen über die
        Residenz in Daskyleion." Pp. 269–95 in
        P. Briant (ed.), Dans les pas des Dix-Mille.
        Peuples et pays du Proche-Orient vus par un
        Grec (Actes de la Table ronde, Toulouse,
        3–4 février 1995). Pallas 43.
Balcer, J. M.
1966   "The medizing of the regent Pausanias."
        Pp. 105–14 in Actes du Ier congrès d'études
        balkaniques. Sofia.
1972a   "The Persian occupation of Thrace 519–
        491." Pp. 241–58 in Actes du IIe congrès in-
        ternational des études du Sud-Est européen
        II.
1972b   "The date of Herodotus IV, 1: Darius'
        Scythian expedition." HSCIP 76: 99–132.
1977   "The Athenian episkopos and the Achae-
        menid 'King's eye.'" AJPh 391: 252–63.
1983   "The Greeks and the Persians: The process
        of acculturation." Historia 32/3: 257–67.
1984   Sparda by the Bitter Sea: Imperial interac-
        tion in Western Anatolia. Chico, Califor-
        nia.
1985   "Fifth Century Ionia: a frontier redefined."
        REA 87/1–2: 31–42.
1987   Herodotus and Bisotun. Wiesbaden.
1988   "Persian occupied Thrace (Skudra)." His-
        toria 37/1: 1–21.
1989a   "The Persian wars against Greece: a reas-
        sessment." Historia 38/2: 127–14.
1989b   "Ionia and Sparda under the Achaemenid
        Empire: The sixth and fifth centuries trib-
        ute, taxation and assessment." Pp. 1–27 in
        Briant and Herrenschmidt (eds.).
1990   "The East Greeks under Persian rule: a re-
        assessment." AchHist 6: 57–65.

1993a   A Prosopographical Study of the Ancient
        Persians Royal and Noble, c. 550–450 B.C.
        Lewiston-Queenston-Lampeter.
1993b   "The Ancient Persian satrapies and satraps
        in Western Anatolia." AMI 26 [1995]: 81–
        90.
Balensi, J.; Dunaux, I.; and Finkielsztein, G.
1990   "Le niveau perse à Tell Abu Hawam:
        résultats récents et signification dans le
        contexte régional côtier." Trans 2: 125–36.
Balkan, K.
1959   "Inscribed bullae from Daskyleion-Ergili."
        Anatolia 4: 123–27.
Baltzer, D.
1973   "Harran nach 610 'medisch'? Kritische
        Überprüfung einer Hypothese." WO 7: 86–
        95.
Barag, D.
1966   "The effect of the Tennes rebellion on Pal-
        estine." BASOR 183: 6–12.
1985   "Some notes on a silver coin of Johanan
        the High Priest." BA: 166–68.
1986–87 "A silver coin of Yohanan the High Priest
        and the coinage of Judaea in the fourth
        Cent. B.C." INJ 9: 4–21.
Bareš, L.
1992   "The shaft tomb of Udjahorresnet: An in-
        terim report." ZÄS 119: 108–16.
Barkworth, P. R.
1992   "The organization of Xerxes' army." IA 27:
        149–67.
Barnett, R. D.
1960   "Assyria and Iran: The earliest representa-
        tion of Persians." Pp. 2997–3007 in A Sur-
        vey of Persian Art XIV.
1969a   "A new inscribed Lydian seal." Athenaeum
        47 (= Studi P. Merigi): 21–24.
1969b   "Anath, Baʿal and Pasargadae." MUSJ
        45/25: 407–22.
Barnett, R. D., and Wiseman, D. J.
1969   Fifty Masterpieces of Ancient Near Eastern
        Art in the Department of Western Asiatic
        Antiquities. London.
Barocas, C.
1974   "Les statues 'réalistes' et l'arrivée des Perses
        dans l'Égypte saïte." Pp. 113–61 in Gurura-
        jamanjarika: Studi in onore di G. Tucci.
        Naples.
Baron, S. W.
1956   Histoire d'Israël: Vie sociale et religieuse
        (French trans.). Paris.
Barron, J.
1990   "All for Salamis." Pp. 133–41 in Owls for
        Athens: Essays on Classical Subjects pre-
        sented to Sir K. Dover. Oxford.
Barron, J. P.
1966   The Silver Coins of Samos. London.
1988   "The liberation of Greece." CAH 4²: 592–
        622.
Bartlett, J. R.
1990   "From Edomites to Nabateans." ARAM
        2/1–2: 25–34.

Baslez, M. F.
1985   "Présence et traditions iraniennes dans les
        cités de l'Égée." REA 87/1–2: 137–56.
1989   "La circulation et le rôle des dariques en
        Grèce d'Europe à la fin du vᵉ et au ivᵉ siè-
        cles: Apport des inscriptions phéniciennes
        et grecques." REA 91/1–2: 237–46.
1995   "Fleuves et voies d'eau dans l'Anabase."
        Pp. 79–88 in P. Briant (ed.), Dans les pas
        des Dix-Mille: Peuples et pays du Proche-
        Orient vus par un Grec (Table ronde, Tou-
        louse, 3–4 février 1995). Pallas 43.
Bausani, A.
1980   "La scrittura pahlavica fruito di bilin-
        guismo aramaico-iranico?" VO 3: 269–76.
Beal, R. H.
1992   "The location of Cilician Ura." AnSt 42:
        65–73.
Beaulieu, P. A.
1989a   The Reign of Nabonidus, King of Babylon
        (556–539 B.C.). YNES 10. New Haven–
        London.
1989b   "Agade in the Late Babylonian period."
        NABU, note no. 66.
1989c   "Textes administratifs inédits d'époque hel-
        lénistique provenant des archives du Bīt
        Reš." RAss 83: 53–80.
1992   "Antiquarian theology in Seleucid Uruk."
        Acta Sum 14: 47–75.
1993a   "An episode in the fall of Babylon to the
        Persians." JNES 52/4: 241–61.
1993b   "The historical background of the Uruk
        prophecy." Pp. 41–52 in The Tablet and the
        Scroll: Near Eastern Studies in Honor of
        Prof. W. W. Hallo (M. E. Cohen, D. C.
        Snell, and D. B. Weisberg, eds.). Bethesda,
        Maryland.
Beaulieu, P. A., and Stolper, M.
1995   "Two more Achaemenid texts from Uruk
        are to be added to those edited in Bagh.
        Mitt. 21 (1990), pp. 559–621." NABU, note
        77.
Beaux, N.
1990   Le Cabinet des curiosités de Thoutmosis III.
        OLA 36. Louvain.
Beck, P.
1972   "A note on the reconstruction of the Achae-
        menid robe." IA 9: 116–22.
Bejor, G.
1974   "La presenza di monete nei depositi di
        fondazione de l'Apadana a Persepoli."
        ASNP 3d series 4/3: 735–40.
Bellinger, A. R.
1963   Essays on the Coinage of Alexander the
        Great. New York.
Bengtson, H.
1964   Die Strategie in der hellenistischen Zeit, I³–
        II³–III³. Munich.
Bengtson, H. (ed.)
1968   The Greeks and the Persians. New York.
1974   Kleine Schriften zur Alten Geschichte. Mu-
        nich.

Bennett, W. J., and Blakely, J. A.
1989 *Tell-el Hesi: The Persian Period (Stratum V)* (ASOR excavations reports; The Joint Archaeological expedition to Tell-el Hesi, III). Winona Lake, Indiana.

Benveniste, É.
1929 *The Persian Religion according to the Chief Greek Texts.* Paris.
1934 "Termes et noms achéménides en araméen." *JA* 225: 177–19.
1938a *Les Mages dans l'ancien Iran.* Paris.
1938b "Traditions indo-iraniennes sur les classes sociales." *JA* 230: 529–49.
1939 "La légende de Kombabos." Pp. 249–58 in *Mélanges syriens offerts à R. Dussaud.* Paris.
1954 "Éléments perses en araméen d'Égypte." *JA* 242/3–4: 297–310.
1958a "Notes sur les tablettes de Persépolis." *JA* 246/1: 49–65.
1958b "Une bilingue gréco-araméenne d'Asoka, IV: les données iraniennes." *JA* 246/1: 36–48.
1960 "Mithra aux vastes pâturages." *JA* 248: 421–29.
1964 "Sur la terminologie iranienne du sacrifice." *JA* 252: 45–58.
1966 *Titres et Noms propres en iranien ancien.* Paris.
1969 *Le Vocabulaire des institutions indo-européennes,* I–II. Paris.

Bernand, A., and Masson, O.
1957 "Les inscriptions grecques d'Abou-Simbel." *REG* 70: 1–46.

Bernard, P.
1964 "Une pièce d'armure perse sur un monument lycien." *Syria* 41: 195–212.
1965 "Remarques sur le décor sculpté d'un édifice de Xanthos." *Syria* 47: 261–88.
1969 "Les bas-reliefs gréco-perses de Daskyleion à la lumière de nouvelles découvertes." *RA:* 17–28.
1972 "Les mortiers et pilons inscrits de Persépolis." *STIR* 1: 165–76.
1974a "Un problème de toponymie antique dans l'Asie centrale: les noms anciens de Qandahar." *STIR* 3/2: 171–85.
1974b "Trois notes d'archéologie iranienne." *JA:* 279–97.
1975 "Note sur la signification historique de la trouvaille [Trésor d'Aï-Khanum]." *RN* 17: 58–69.
1976a "À propos des bouterolles de fourreaux achéménides." *RA:* 227–46.
1976b "Les traditions orientales dans l'architecture bactrienne." *JA:* 245–55.
1980 "Héraclès: le grottes de Karafto et le sanctuaire du mont Samboulos en Iran." *STIR* 9/2: 301–24.
1982 "Alexandre et Aï-Khanum." *JS:* 125–38.

1985a *Fouilles d'Aï-Khanoum, IV: Les Monnaies hors-trésors. Questions d'histoire gréco-bactrienne.* Paris.
1985b "Le monnayage d'Eudamos, satrape grec du Pendjab et 'maître des éléphants.'" Pp. 65–94 in *Orientalia G. Tucci memoriae dicata.* Rome.
1987 "Les Indiens de la liste d'Hérodote." *STIR* 16/2: 177–91.
1990a "Alexandre et l'Asie centrale: Réflexions à propos d'un ouvrage de F. L. Holt." *STIR* 19/1: 21–38.
1990b "Une nouvelle contribution de l'épigraphie cunéiforme à l'histoire hellénistique." *BCH* 114: 513–41.
1994a "Le temple du dieu Oxus à Takht-i Sangin en Bactriane: temple du feu ou pas?" *STIR* 23/1: 81–121.
1994b "L'Asie centrale et l'Empire séleucide." *Topoi* 4/2: 473–511.

Bernard, P., et al.
1978 "Fouilles d'Aï-Khanoum (Afghanistan)." *BEFEO* 63: 5–51.
1992 "Fouilles de la mission franco-ouzbèque à l'ancienne Samarkand (Afrasiab): deuxième et troisième campagnes (1990–1991)." *CRAI:* 275–311.

Bernard, P., and Grenet, F. (eds.)
1991 *Histoire et culte de l'Asie centrale préislamique: Sources écrites et documents figurés.* CNRS. Paris.

Bernard, P.; Grenet, F.; and Isamiddinov, M.
1990 "Fouilles de la mission franco-soviétique à l'ancienne Samarkand (Afrasiab): première campagne (1989)." *CRAI:* 356ff.

Bernard, P., and Rapin, Cl.
1980 "Le Palais, la Trésorerie." *BEFEO* 68: 10–38.

Bernhardt, R.
1988 "Zu den Verhandlungen zwischen Dareios und Alexander nach der Schlacht bei Issos." *Chiron* 18: 181–98.

Berthold, R. M.
1980 "Fourth Century Rhodos." *Historia* 29/1: 32–49.

Bertrand, J. M.
1974 "Notes sur les hyparques dans l'Empire d'Alexandre." Pp. 25–34 in *Mélanges W. Seston.* Paris.
1988 "Les *Boucôloi* du Nil ou le monde à l'envers." *REA* 90/1–2: 139–49.
1990 "Territoire donné, territoire attribué: note sur la pratique de l'attribution dans le monde impérial romain." *Cahiers G. Glotz* 2: 125–64.

Berve, H.
1926 *Das Alexanderreich auf prosopographischer Grundlage,* I–II. Munich.

Besenval, R.
1994 "Le peuplement de l'ancienne Gédrosie, de la protohistoire à la période islamique." *CRAI:* 513–35.

Betlyon, J. W.
1982   *The Coinage and Mints of Phoenicia: The Pre-Alexandrine Period*, Scholars Press.
1986   "The provincial government of Persian period Judea and the Yehûd coins." *JBL* 105/4: 633–42.

Bianchi, F.
1989   "Bolli e monete ellenistici in Giudea." *OA* 18/1–2: 25–40.
1994   "Le rôle de Zorobabel et de la dynastie davidique en Judée du VIe siècle aus IIIe siècle av. J.-C." *Trans* 7: 153–65.

Bianchi, R.
1982   "Perser in Ägypten." *LdÄ* 4: 943–51.

Bianchi, U.
1977   "L'inscription des *daiva* et le zoroastrisme des Achéménides." *RHR* 192/1: 3–30.
1988   "Dieu créateur et vision universaliste: le cas de l'Empire achéménide." Pp. 191–200 in Gignoux, Ph. (ed.), *La Commémoration: Colloque du centenaire de la section des sciences religieuses de l'EPHE.* Paris.

Bickerman, E. J.
1934a   "Alexandre le Grand et les villes d'Asie." *REG* 47: 346–74.
1934b   "Notes sur la chronologie de la XXXe dynastie." Pp. 77–84 in *Mélanges Maspero* I. MIFAO 66. Le Claire.
1938   *Institutions des Séleucides.* Paris.
1945–46 "The edict of Cyrus in Ezra 1." *JBL* 64–65: 249–75.
1981   "En marge de l'Écriture. I: Le comput des années de règne des Achéménides (Neh. I.2; II.1 and Thuc. VIII.58)." *RB:* 19–28.
1984   "The Babylonian captivity." *CHJ* 1: 342–57.

Bickerman, E., and Tadmor, H.
1978   "Darius I, Pseudo-Smerdis and the Magi." *Athenaeum* 56/3–4: 239–61.

Bidez, J.
1935   "Plantes et pierres magiques d'après le Pseudo-Plutarque, *De Fluviis*." Pp. 25–39 in *Mélanges O. Navarre.* Toulouse.

Bidez, F., and Cumont, F.
1938   *Les Mages hellénisés: Zoroastre, Ostanès et Hystaspe d'après la tradition grecque,* I–II. Paris.

Bigwood, J. M.
1964   *Ctesias of Cnidus.* Ph.D. Harvard University.
1976   "Ctesias' account of the revolt of Inarus." *Phoenix* 30: 1–25.
1978a   "Ctesias as historian of the Persian Wars." *Phoenix* 32/1: 19–41.
1978b   "Ctesias' description of Babylon." *Phoenix* 32/1: 32–52.
1980   "Diodorus and Ctesias." *Phoenix* 34/3: 195–207.
1983   "The Ancient accounts of the battle of Cunaxa." *AJPh* 104: 340–47.
1986   "P.OXY 2330 and Ctesias." *Phoenix* 40: 393–406.

1993a   "Aristotle and the elephants again." *AJPh* 114: 537–55.
1993b   "Ctesias' parrot." *CQ* 43/1: 321–27.

Bilabel, F.
1924   *Griechische Papyri.* Heidelberg.

Billows, R. A.
1990   *Antigonus the One-Eyed and the Creation of the Hellenistic State.* University of California Press.

Binder, G.
1964   *Die Aussetzung des Königskindes, Kyros und Romulus.* Beitr. z. Klass. Philol. 10. Meisenheim am Glan.

Bing, J. D.
1969   *A History of Cilicia during the Assyrian Period.* Ph.D. Indiana University.
1971   "Tarsus: a forgotten colony of Lindos." *JNES* 30: 99–103.
1991   "Alexander's sacrifice *dis praesidibus loci* before the battle of Issus." *JHS* 111: 161–65.

Bisi, A. M.
1990   "Quelques remarques sur la coroplastie palestinienne à l'époque perse: tradition locale et emprunts étrangers." *Trans* 3: 77–94.

Bittel, K.
1952   "Ein persischer Feueraltar aus Kappadokien." Pp. 18–29 in *Satura: Früchte aus der antiken Welt (FS O. Weinreich).* Baden-Baden.

Bittner, S.
1985   *Tracht und Bewaffnung des persischen Heeres zur Zeit der Achaimeniden.* Munich.

Bivar, A. D. H.
1961   "A 'satrap' of Cyrus the Younger." *NC:* 119–27.
1970   "A Persian monument at Athens and its connections with the Achaemenid State seals." Pp. 43–61 in *W. B. Henning Memorial Volume.* London.
1971   "A hoard of ingot-currency of the Median period from Nush-i Jān, near Malayir." *Iran* 9: 97–110.
1975a   "Document and symbol in the art of the Achaemenids." *Acta Iranica: Monumentum H. S. Nyberg,* I: 49–67.
1975b   "Mithra and Mesopotamia." *Mithraic Studies* 2: 275–89.
1985   "Achaemenid coins, weights and measures." *CHI* 2: 610–29.
1988a   "The Indus lands." *CAH* 4²: 194–210.
1988b   "An Iranian Sarapis." *BAI* 2: 11–17.

Blenkinsopp, J.
1987   "The mission of Udjahorresnet and those of Ezra and Nehemiah." *JBL* 106/3: 409–21.
1991   "Temple and society in Achaemenid Judah." Pp. 22–53 in P. R. Davies (ed.).

Blinkenberg, C.
1912   *La Chronique du temple lindien.* Explor. arch. de Rhodes, Fondation Carlsberg. Copenhagen.

1941 *Lindos: Fouilles de l'Acropole (1902–1914),* II: *Inscriptions,* I (n°s 1–281). Berlin-Copenhagen.

Bloedow, E. F.
1991a "Alexander the Great and Bactria." *PdP* 256: 44–80.
1991b "Alexander the Great and those Sogdianaean horses: prelude to hellenism in Bactria-Sogdiana." Pp. 17–32 in J. Seibert (ed.), *Hellenistische Studien: Gedenkschrift für H. Bengtson.* Münchener Arbeiten zur Alten Geschichte 51. Munich.
1992 "The peaces of Callias." *SO* 67: 41–68.
1994 "Alexander's speech at the eve of the siege of Tyre." *AC* 43: 65–76.

Blois, F. de
1985 "'Freemen' and 'nobles' in Iranian and Semitic languages." *JRAS*: 5–15.

Blomqvist, J.
1982 "Translation of Greek in the trilingual inscription of Xanthos." *OpAth* 14/2: 11–20.

Blümel, W.
1990 "Zwei neue Inschriften aus Mylasa aus der Zeit des Mausollos." *EA* 16: 29–42.

Boardman, J.
1970a "Pyramidal stamps seals in the Persian Empire." *Iran* 8: 19–45.
1970b *Greek Gems and Finger Rings.* London.

Boardman, J., and Roaf, M.
1980 "A Greek painting at Persepolis." *JHS* 100: 204–6.

Bockisch, G.
1959 "Die Karer und ihre Dynasten." *Klio* 51: 117–74.

Bodson, L.
1991 "Alexander the Great and the scientific exploration of the Oriental part of his Empire: An overview of the background, trends and results." *AncSoc* 22: 127–38.

Boffo, L.
1978 "La lettera di Dario a Gadata: I privilegi del tempio di Apollo a Magnesia sul Meandro." *BIDR* 3d series 20: 267–303.
1983 "La conquista persiana delle citta greche d'Asia Minore." *RAL* 7th series 26/1: 6–70.
1985 *I re ellenistici e i centri religiosi dell'Asia Minore.* Florence.

Bogaert, R.
1968 *Les Origines antiques de la banque de dépôt.* Leyde.

Bogoliubov, M. N.
1974 "Titre honorifique d'un chef militaire achéménide en Haute-Égypte." Pp. 109–14 in *Acta Iranica* 1st series (Hommage universel Cyrus). Tehran-Liège.

Böhmer, H., and Thompson, J.
1991 "The Pazyryk carpet: a technical discussion." *Source* 10/4: 30–36.

Bollweg, J.
1988 "Protoachämenidische Seegelbilder." *AMI* 21: 53–61.

Bolšakov, A. O.
1992 "The earliest known gold pharaonic coin." *RdE* 43: 3–9.

Bommelaer, J. F.
1977 *Lysandre de Sparte.* BEFAR 240. Paris.

Bondi, S. F.
1974 "Istituzioni e politica a Sidone dal 351 al 332 a.C." *RSF* 2: 149–60.

Bongrani Fanfoni, L., and Israel, F.
1994 "Documenti achemenidi nel deserto orientale egiziano (Gebu Abu Queh-Wadi Hammamat)." *Trans* 8: 75–92.

Bonhême, A. M., and Fargeau, A.
1988 *Pharaon: Les secrets du pouvoir.* Paris.

Bonneau, D.
1964 "Liber Aristotelis de inundatione Nili: Texte, traduction, étude." *Études de Papyrologie* 9: 1–33.

Borchhardt, J.
1968 "Epichorische, gräko-persische beeinflusste reliefs in Kilikien." *IM* 13: 161–211.
1976a "Zur Deutung lykischer Audienzszenen." Pp. 7–12 in *Actes du Colloque sur la Lycie antique.* Paris.
1976b *Die Bauskulptur des Heroons von Limyra: Das Grabmal Königs Perikles.* Ist. Forsch 32. Berlin.
1983 "Die Dependenz des Königs von Sidon vom persischen Grosskönig." Pp. 105–20 in *Beiträge zur Altertumskunde Kleinasiens* (*FS K. Bittel*), I. Mainz.
1990 "Zêmuri: Die Residenzstadt des lykische Königs Perikles." *IM* 40: 109–43.
1993a *Die Steine von Zêmuri: Archäologische Forschungen an der Verborgenen Wassern von Limyra.* Vienna.
1993b "Lykische heroa und die *pyra* des Hephestions in Babylon." Pp. 252–59 in J. Borchhardt, G. Dobesch (ed.), *Akten des II. Intern. Lykien-Symposions.* ÖAW, Denkschr. 231 Bd. Vienna.
1993c "Zum Ostfries des *heróons* von Zêmuri/Limyra." *IM* 43: 351–59.

Borchhardt, J. (ed.)
1990 *Götter, Heroen, Herrscher in Lykien.* Vienna.

Borchhardt, J.; Neumann, G.; and Schulz
1989 "Das Heroon von Phellos und TL.54 mit der Weihung einer Statue des udalijr, Sohn des Muraza." *BM* 39: 89–96.

Bordreuil, P.
1986a *Catalogue des sceaux ouest-sémitiques inscrits de la Bibliothèque nationale, du Musée du Louvre et du Musée biblique de Bible et Terre sainte.* Paris.
1986b "Charges et fonctions en Syrie–Palestine d'après quelques sceaux ouest-sémitiques du second et du premier millénaires." *CRAI*: 290–308.
1992 "Sceaux inscrits des pays du Levant." *DBS* 12: 86–212.

Bordreuil, P., and Israel, F.
1991–92 "À propos de la carrière d'Elyaqim: du page au major-dome(?)." *Semitica* 41–42: 81–87.
Borger, P. R.
1975 "Der Kyros-Zylinder mit dem Zusatzfragment BIN Nr 22." *ZA* 64: 192–234.
Borger, R.
1982 "Die Chronologie des Darius-Denkmals am Behistun Felsen." *NAWG, Phil. Hist. Kl.*: 105–31.
Borza, E. N.
1972 "Fire from Heaven: Alexander at Persepolis." *CPh* 67: 233–45.
1990 *In the Shadow of Olympus: The Emergence of Macedon.* Princeton University Press.
Bosworth, A. B.
1974 "The government of Syria under Alexander the Great." *CQ* 24: 46–64.
1980a *A Historical Commentary on Arrian's History of Alexander,* I. Oxford.
1980b "Alexander and the Iranians." *JHS* 100: 1–21.
1981 "A missing year in the history of Alexander." *JHS* 101: 17–37.
1983 "The Indian satrapies under Alexander the Great." *Antichton* 17: 37–46.
1987 "Nearchus in Susiana." Pp. 542–67 in *FS G. Wirth,* I. Amsterdam.
1988 *Conquest and Empire: The Reign of Alexander the Great.* Cambridge University Press.
1990 "Plutarch, Callisthenes and the peace of Callias." *JHS* 110: 1–13.
1992 "Philipp III Arrhidaeus and the chronology of the successors." *Chiron* 22: 55–81.
1993 "Aristotle, India and the Alexander historians." *Topoi* 3/2: 407–24.
1995 *Commentary on Arrian's History of Alexander,* II: *Commentary on Books IV–V.* Oxford.
Botha, L.
1988 "The Asiatic campaign of Agesilaus: the topography of the route between Ephesus and Sardis." *Acta Classica* 31: 71–80.
Bottéro, J.
1978 "Le substitut roal et son sort en Mésopotamie ancienne." *Akkadica* 9: 2–24 [cf. Bottéro 1987: 170–90].
1987 *Mésopotamie: L'écriture, la raison et les dieux.* Paris.
Boucharlat, R.
1984 "Monuments religieux de la Perse achéménide: État des questions." Pp. 119–35 in *Temples et Sanctuaires.* TMO 7. Lyon.
1985 "Suse, marché agricole ou relais de grand commerce? La Susiane à l'époque des grands empires." *PaléoOrient* 11/2: 71–81.
1990a "Suse et la Susiane à l'époque achéménide: Données archéologiques." *AchHist* 4: 149–75.

1990b "La fin des palais achéménides de Suse: une mort naturelle." Pp. 225–34 in Vallat (ed.).
1994 "Continuité à Suse au Ier millénaire av. n.è." *AchHist* 8: 217–28.
Boucharlat, R., and Labrousse, A.
1979 "Le palais d'Artaxerxès II sur la rive droite du Chaour à Suse." *CDAFI* 10: 19–154.
Boucharlat, R., and Salles, J. F.
1981 "The history and the archaeology of the Gulf from the fifth century B.C. to the seventh century A.D.: a review of the evidence." *PSAS* 11: 65–94.
1987 "L'Arabie orientale: d'un bilan à un autre." *Mesopotamia* 22: 277–309.
Boucharlat, R., and Shahidi, H.
1987 "Fragments architecturaux de type achéménide: découvertes fortuites dans la ville de Suse 1976–79." *CDAFI* 15: 313–27.
Bousquet, B., and Reddé, M.
1994 "Les installations hydrauliques et les parcellaires dans la région de Tell Douch (Égypte) à l'époque romaine." Pp. 73–88 in B. Menu (ed.), *Les Problèmes institutionnels de l'eau en Égypte ancienne et dans l'Antiquité méditerranéenne.* Bib. d'Études de l'IFAO 110. Cairo.
Bousquet, J.
1975 "Arbinas, fils de Gergis, dynaste de Xanthos." *CRAI:* 138–50.
1986 "Une nouvelle inscription trilingue à Xanthos?" *RA:* 101–6.
1992 "Les inscriptions gréco-lyciennes." *FdX* 9: 147–99.
Bovon, A.
1963 "La représentation des guerriers perses et la notion de Barbare dans la première moitié du vᵉ siècle." *BCH* 87: 579–602.
Bowman, R. A.
1941 "An Aramaic journal page." *AJSL* 58: 302–13.
1970 *Aramaic Ritual Texts from Persepolis.* OIP 91. Chicago.
Boyce, M.
1975 "On Mithra, Lord of fire." *Acta Iranica* 1 (*Monumentum H. S. Nyberg*): 69–76.
1982 *A History of Zoroastrianism,* II: *Under the Achaemenids.* Leiden-Cologne.
1984 "A tomb for Cassandane." Pp. 67–71 in *Orientalia Duchesne-Guillemin.*
1984 "Persian religion in the Achaemenid age." *CHJ* 1: 279–307.
1988 "The religion of Cyrus the Great." *Ach Hist* 3: 5–32.
Boyce, M., and Grenet, F.
1992 *A History of Zoroastrianism,* III: *Zoroastrianism under Macedonians and Roman Rulers.* Leiden.
Brandestein, W., and Mayrhofer, M.
1964 *Handbuch des Altpersischen.* Wiesbaden.

Braund, D. C.
1984   *Rome and the Friendly King: The Character of Client-Kingship.* London-Canberra-New York.

Breebart, A. B.
1967   "Eratosthenes, Damastes, and the journey of Diotimos to Susa." *Mnem.* 20: 422–31.

Bregstein, L.
1993   *Seal Use in Fifth Century B.C. Nippur, Iraq: a Study of Seal Selection and Sealing Practice in the Murašû Archive.* Ph.D. University of Pennsylvania.

Breitenbach, H. R.
1966   *Xenophon von Athen.* Stuttgart.

Bresciani, E.
1958   "La satrapia d'Egitto." *SCO* 8: 132–88.
1960   "Una statua in 'abito persiano' al Museo del Cairo." *RSO*: 109–18.
1967   "Una statua della XXVI dinastia con il cosidetto 'abito persiano.'" *SCO* 16: 273–80.
1972a   "Annotazioni demotiche ai *Persai tès epigonès*." *PdP* 144: 123–28.
1981a   "Frammenti da un 'prontuario legale' demotico da Tebtuni nell'Istituto papirologico G. Vitelli di Firenze." *EVO* 4: 201–12.
1981b   "La morte di Cambise ovvero l'impietà punita: a proposito della 'Cronica demotica,' verso, col. 7–8." *EVO* 4: 217–22.
1983   "Note di toponomastica: i templi di MN-NFR, WH-HN, PR-H'PJ-MHT." *EVO* 6: 67–73.
1984–85 "Il possibile nome del figlio maggiore di Nectanebo II." *JANES* 16–17: 19–21.
1984   "Egypt: Persian satrapy." *CHJ* 1: 358–71.
1985a   "Ugiahorresnet a Memphi." *EVO* 8: 1–6.
1985b   "I Semiti nell'Egitto di età saitica e persiana." Pp. 93–104 in *Egitto e società antica = Vita e Pensiero.* Milan.
1985c   "The Persian occupation of Egypt." *CHI* 2: 502–28.
1989   "Osservazioni sul sistema tributario dell'Egitto durante la dominazione persiana." Pp. 29–33 in Briant and Herrenschmidt (eds.).
1996   "Cambyse, Darius Iᵉʳ et les temples égyptiens." *Méditerranées* 6.

Briant, P.
1973   *Antigone le Borgne.* Paris.
1976   "'Brigandage,' conquête et dissidence en Asie achéménide et hellénistique." *DHA* 2: 163–259.
1982a   *Rois, tributs et paysans: Études sur les formations tributaires du Moyen-Orient ancien.* Paris.
1982b   *État et pasteurs au Moyen-Orient ancien.* Paris-Cambridge.
1982c   "Produktivekräfte: Staat und tributäre Produktionsweise im Achämenidenreich." Pp. 351–72 in J. Hermann and I. Sellnow (eds.), *Produktive-kräfte und Gesellschaftsformationen in vorkapitalistischer Zeit.* Berlin.

1984a   "La Perse avant l'Empire: Un état de la question." *IA* 19: 71–118.
1984b   *L'Asie centrale et les royaumes moyen-orientaux au premier millénaire av. n.è.* Paris.
1985a   "Les Iraniens d'Asie Mineure après la chute de l'Empire achéménide: À propos de l'inscription d'Amyzon." *DHA* 11: 167–95.
1985b   "Dons de terres et de villes: l'Asie Mineure dans le contexte achéménide." *REA* 87/1–2: 53–71.
1985c   "La Bactriane dans l'Empire achéménide: L'État central achéménide en Bactriane." Pp. 243–51 in *L'Archéologie de la Bactriane ancienne.* Paris.
1986a   "Polythéismes et Empire unitaire: Remarques sur la politique religieuse des Achéménides." Pp. 425–43 in *Les Grandes Figures religieuses.* Paris.
1986b   "Alexandre et les *katarraktes* du Tigre." Pp. 11–22 in *Mélanges M. Labrousse.* Toulouse.
1986c   "Guerre, tribut et forces productives dans l'Empire achéménide." *DHA* 12: 33–48.
1986d   *Alexandre le Grande³.* Paris.
1987a   "Pouvoir central et polycentrisme culturel dans l'Empire achéménide: quelques réflexions et suggestions." *AchHist* 1: 1–31.
1987b   "Institutions perses et histoire comparatiste dans l'historiographie grecque." *AchHist* 2: 1–10.
1988a   "Ethno-classe dominante et populations soumises dans l'Empire achéménide: le cas de l'Égypte." *AchHist* 3: 137–73.
1988b   "Contingents est-iraniens et centre-asiatiques dans les armées achéménides." Pp. 173–75 in *L'Asie centrale et ses rapports avec les civilisations orientales des origines à l'âge du fer.* Paris.
1988c   "Le nomadisme du Grand Roi." *IA* 23: 253–73.
1989a   "Histoire et idéologie: les Grecs et la 'decadence perse.'" Pp. 33–47 in *Mélanges P. Lévêque*, II. Paris.
1989b   "Table du Roi: tribut et redistribution chez les Achéménides." Pp. 35–44 in Briant and Herrenschmidt (eds.).
1989c   "Remarques finales." *REA* 91/1–2: 321–35.
1990a   "Hérodote et la société perse." Pp. 69–104 in *Hérodote et les peuples non grecs.* Entretiens sur l'Antiquité classique 35. Geneva.
1990b   "The Seleucid kingdom, the Achaemenid Empire and the history of the Near East in the first millennium B.C." Pp. 40–90 in *Religion and Religious Practice in the Seleucid Kingdom*, ed. P. Bilde et al. Aarhus University Press.
1991a   "Le roi est mort: vive le roi! Remarques sur les rites et rituels de succession chez les Achéménides." Pp. 1–11 in J. Kellens (ed.).
1991b   "De Sardes à Suse." *AchHist* 6: 67–82.

1991c "Chasses royales macédoniennes et chasses
       royales perses: le thème de la chasse au
       lion sur la *Chasse de Vergina.*" *DHA* 17/1:
       211–55.
1992a "La date des révoltes babyloniennes contre
       Xerxès." *STIR* 21/1: 7–20.
1992b "Les tablettes de bois du Grand Roi et les
       lettres d'Atossa." *DATA*, note 1.
1992c "Thémistocle sur la Route royale." *DATA*,
       note 4.
1992d *Darius, les Perses et l'Empire.* Paris.
1992e "Ctésias." *The Anchor Bible Dictionary* 1:
       1211–12.
1992f "Persian Empire." *The Anchor Bible Dictio-
       nary* 1: 237–44.
1993a "Alexandre à Sardes." Pp. 1–15 in *Alex-
       ander the Great: Myth and Reality.* ARID
       suppl. 21. Rome.
1993b "Hérodote, Udjahorresnet et les palais de
       Darius à Suse." *DATA*, note 7.
1993c "L'histoire politique de l'Empire aché-
       ménide: problèmes et méthodes (À propos
       d'un ouvrage de M. A. Dandamaev)." *REA*
       95/3–4: 399–423.
1994a *Alexandre le Grande*[4]. Paris.
1994b "L'histoire achéménide: sources, mé-
       thodes, raisonnements et modèles." *Topoi*
       4/1: 109–30.
1994c "De Samarkand à Sardes et de la ville de
       Suse au pays des Hanéens." *Topoi* 4/2: 455–
       67.
1994d "Prélèvements tributaires et échanges en
       Asie Mineure achéménide et hellénis-
       tique." Pp. 69–81 in *Premières Journées de
       Saint-Bertrand-de-Comminges sur l'écon-
       omie antique* (ed. J. Andreau, P. Briant, and
       R. Descat). Saint-Bertrand-de-Comminges.
1994e "Institutions perses et institutions macé-
       doniennes: continuités, changements et
       bricolages." *AchHist* 8: 283–310.
1994f "L'eau du Grand Roi." Pp. 45–65 in L. Mi-
       lano (ed.), *Drinking in Ancient Societies:
       History and Culture of Drinks in the An-
       cient Near East.* Padua.
1994g "Travaux hydrauliques et contrôle de l'eau
       dans l'Empire achéménide." Pp. 91–101 in
       B. Menu (ed.), *Les Problèmes institution-
       nels de l'eau en Égypte ancienne et dans
       l'Antiquité méditerranéenne.* IFAO, Biblio-
       thèque d'études 110. Cairo.
1994h "À propos du boulet de Phocée." *REA*
       96/1–2: 111–14.
1995a "La guerre et la paix." Pp. 17–132 in P. Bri-
       ant and P. Lévêque (eds.), *Le Monde grec
       qux temps classiques,* I: *Le ve siècle,* coll.
       "Nouvelle Clio." Paris.
Briant, P. (ed.)
1995b *Dans le pas des Dix-Mille: Peuples et pays
       du Proche-Orient vus par un Grec* (Actes de
       la Table ronde internationale, Toulouse, 3–
       4 février 1995). Pallas 43.

1995c "Legal and social institutions of Ancient
       Persia." in *Civilizations of the Ancient Near
       East* (ed. J. M. Sasson et al.). New York.
1995d "Les éléphants de Darius III." *DATA.*
1995e "Les institutions de Sardes achéménide:
       Une note additionnelle." *LdP* 2, note 2.
1996a "Une curieuse affaire à Éléphantine en 410
       av. è. Widranga, le temple de Yahweh et le
       sanctuaire de Khnûm." *Méditerranées* 6.
1996b "Droaphernès et la statue de Sardes." In
       M. Brosius and A. Kuhrt (eds.), *David
       Lewis Memorial Volume.* Leiden.
Briant, P., and Herrenschmidt, C. (eds.)
1989   *Le Tribut dans l'Empire perse* (Actes de la
       Table ronde de Paris, 12–13 décembre
       1986). Trav. Inst. d'études iraniennes de
       l'université de la Sorbonne Nouvelle 13.
       Paris-Louvain.
Briend, J.
1990   "L'occupation de la Galilée occidentale à
       l'époque perse." *Trans* 2: 109–24.
Briend, J.; Lebrun, R.; and Puech, É.
1992   *Traités et Serments dans le Proche-Orient
       ancien.* Suppl. to Cahier de l'Évangile 81.
       Paris.
Brindley, J. C.
1993   "Early coinages attributable to Issus." *NC*
       153: 1–10.
Brinkman, J. A.
1987   "BM 36761: the astronomical diary from
       331 B.C." *NABU,* note 63.
1968   *A Political History of Post-Kassite Babylo-
       nia.* Rome.
1986   "The Elamite-Babylonian frontier in the
       Neo-Elamite period, 750–625 B.C." Pp.
       199–207 in *Fragmenta Historiae Elamicae.*
       Paris.
1989   "The Akkadian words for 'Ionia' and 'Ion-
       ians.'" Pp. 53–71 in *Daidalikon: Studies in
       Memory of R. V. Schoder, S. J.* Wauconda,
       Illinois.
Briquel, D.
1981   "Sur un passage d.'Hérodote: prise de
       Babylone et prise de Véies." *BAGB:* 293–
       306.
Briquel, D., and Desnier, J. L.
1983   "Le passage de l'Hellespont par Xerxès."
       BAGB: 22–30.
Brixhe, C.
1993   "Le grec en Carie et en Lycie au ive siècle:
       des situations contrastées." Pp. 59–82 in
       C. Brixhe (ed.), *La Koinè grecque antique,*
       I: *Une langue introuvable?* Nancy.
Brodersen, K.
1991   "Ein Weltwunder der Antike in Iran." *AMI*
       27: 53–55.
Brosius, M.
1991   *Royal and Non-royal Women in Achaeme-
       nid Persia.* Ph.D. Oxford.
Brown, S.
1986   "Median and secondary State formation in
       the neo-Assyrian Zagros: an anthropologi-

cal approach to an Assyriological problem."
JCS 38/1: 107–19.

1988 "The *Medikos logos* of Herodotus and the evolution of Median State." *AchHist* 3: 71–86.

1990 "Media in the Achaemenid period: the late Iron Age in Central West Iran." *AchHist* 4: 63–76.

Brown, T. S.
1978 "Suggestions for a vita of Ctesias of Cnidus." *Historia* 27/1: 1–19.

1982 "Herodotus' portrait of Cambyses." *Historia* 31/4: 387–403.

1986 "Menon of Thessaly." *Historia* 34/4: 387–404.

1987 "Megabyzus son of Zopyrus." *AW* 15: 65–74.

Bruce, I. A. F.
1967 *An Historical Commentary on the* Hellenica Oxyrhynchia. Cambridge.

Bruns-Özgan, C.
1967 *Lykische Grabreliefs des 5. und 4. Jahrhunderts v. Ch.* 1st. Mitt. Beih. 33. Berlin.

Bryce, T. R.
1979 "Lycian tombs families and their social implications." *JESHO* 22/3: 296–313.

1980 "The other Pericles." *Historia* 29/3: 377–81.

1981 "Lycian relations with Persians and Greeks in the fifth and fourth centuries re-examined." *AnSt* 31: 55–80.

1982 "A ruling dynasty in Lycia." *Klio* 64/2: 329–37.

1983 "Political unity in Lycia during the 'dynastic' period.'" *JNES* 42/1: 31–42.

1986 *The Lycians in Literary and Epigraphic Sources.* Copenhagen.

Bucci, O.
1972 "Giustizia e legge nel diritto persiano antico." *Apollinaris* 45: 157–72.

1978 "L'attività legislativa del sovrano achemenide e gli archivi reali persiani." *RIDA* 3d series 25: 11–93.

1984 *L'impero pesiano come ordinamento giuridico sovranazionale, I: Classi sociali e forme di dipendenza giuridica e socio-economica.* Rome.

Buckler, H. V., and Robinson, D. M.
1912 "Greek inscriptions of Sardis." *AJA* 26: 15–84.

1932 *Sardis VII: Greek and Latin Inscriptions.* Leiden.

Buijs-Zeist, J. A. J. M.
1983 "Abermals Persepolis." *Gymnasium* 90: 313–29.

Bunnens, G.
1983a "Tyr et la mer." *Studia Phoenicia* 1/2: 7–21.

1983b "Considérations géographiques sur la place occupée par la Phénicie dans l'expansion de l'Empire assyrien." *Studia Phoenicia* 1/2: 169–93.

1985 "Le luxe phénicien d'après les inscriptions royales assyriennes." *Studia Phoenicia* 3: 121–33.

Burchardt, M.
1911 "Datierte Denkmäler der Berl. Sammlung aus der Achämenidenzeit." *ZÄS* 49: 69–80.

Burn, A. R.
1984 *Persia and the Greeks*[2]. Oxford.

1985 "Persia and the Greeks." *CHI* 2: 292–391.

Burstein, S. M.
1976 *Outpost of Hellenism: the Emergence of Heraclea on the Black Sea.* University of California Press.

1978 *The Babyloniaca of Berossus.* Sources for the Ancient Near East 1/5. Malibu, California.

1989 *Agarthacides of Cnidus on the Erythrean Sea.* London.

1991 "Pharaoh Alexander: a scholarly myth." *AncSoc* 22: 139–45.

1994 "Alexander in Egypt: continuity or change?" *AchHist* 8: 381–87.

Bury, J. B.
1897 "The European expedition of Darius." *CR*: 277–82.

Cagni, L.
1988 "Aspetti dell'economia regia nella Mesopotamia achemenide." Pp. 156–66 in *Stato, Economica, Lavoro nel Vicino Oriente antico.* Milan.

1990 "Considérations sur les textes babyloniens de Neirab près d'Alep." *Trans* 2: 169–86.

Cagni, L.; Giovinazzo, G.; and Graziani, S.
1985 "Typology and structure of Mesopotamian documentation during the Achaemenid period." *AION* 45: 547–83.

Cahill, N.
1985 "The treasury at Persepolis: gift-giving at the city of the Persians." *AJA* 89: 373–89.

1988 "Taš Kule: a Persian-period tomb near Phokaia." *AJA* 92/4: 481–501.

Cahn, H. A.
1975 "Dynast oder satrap." *GNS* 25: 84–91.

1985 "Tissaphernes in Astyra." *AA*: 587–94.

1989 "Le monnayage des strapes: iconographie et signification." *REA* 91/1–2: 97–105.

Cahn, H. A., and Gerin, D.
1988 "Themistocles at Magnesia." *NC* 148: 13–20.

Cahn, H. A., and Mannsperger, D.
1991 "Themistocles again." *NC* 151: 199–202.

Callatay, Fr. de
1989 "Les trésors achéménides et les monnayages d'Alexandre: espèces immobilisées ou espèces circulantes?" *REA* 91/1–2: 259–64.

Callieri, P.
1992 "La glittica greco-persiana nelle regioni orientali dell'impero achemenide." Pp. 63–72 in *Studi di egittologia e di antichità puniche* 11 (ed. E. Acquaro and S. Pernigotti). Pisa.

Calmeyer, P.
1973   "Zur Genese Altiranischer Motive." *AMI*
        6: 135–52.
1974   "Zur Genese Altiranischer Motive, II: Der
        leere Wagen." *AMI* 7: 49–77.
1975   "Zur Genese Altiranischer Motive, III:
        Felsgraber." *AMI* 8: 99–113.
1976a   "Zur Genese Altiranischer Motive, IV:
        'Persönliche Kröne' und Diadem." *AMI* 9:
        45–95.
1976b   "Zur Genese Altiranischer Motive, V: Syn-
        archie." *AMI* 9: 63–95.
1977a   "Zur Genese Altiranischer Motive, V: Syn-
        archie. Korrekturen und Nachträge." *AMI*
        10: 191–95.
1979a   "Zur Genese Altiranischer Motive, VI:
        Toxotai." *AMI* 12: 303–13.
1979b   "Textual sources for the interpretation of
        Achaemenian palace decorations." *Iran*:
        55–63.
1981   "Zur bedingten Göttlichkeit des Gross-
        königs." *AMI* 14: 55–60.
1982   "Zur Genese Altiranischer Motive, VIII:
        Die 'Staatliche Landcharte des Perser-
        reiches,' I." *AMI* 15: 105–87.
1983a   "Zur Genese Altiranischer Motive, VIII:
        Die 'Staatliche Landcharte des Perser-
        reiches,' II." *AMI* 16: 109–263.
1983b   "Zur Rechtfertigung einiger Grosskönig-
        licher Inschriften und Darstellungen: die
        Yauna." Pp. 154–67 in *Kunst, Kultur und
        Geschichte der Achämenidenzeit und ihr
        Fortleben*. AMI suppl. 10. Berlin.
1985   "Zur Genese Altiranischer Motive, IX: Die
        Verbreitung des Westiranischen Zaum-
        zeugs im Achaimenidenreich." *AMI* 18:
        125–44.
1986   "Dareios in Bagestana und Xerxes in Per-
        sepolis: zur parataktischen Komposition
        achaimenidischer Herrescherdarstellung-
        en." *Visible Religion* 4: 76–87.
1987a   "Greek historiography and Achaemenid re-
        liefs." *AchHist* 1: 11–26.
1987b   "Zur Genese Altiranischer Motive, VIII:
        Die 'Staatliche Landcharte des Perser-
        reiches'—Nachträge und Korrekturen."
        AMI 20: 129–46.
1988a   "Aufreihung-Duplik-Kopie-Umbildung."
        AchHist 3: 101–20.
1988b   "Zur Genese Altiranischer Motive, X: Die
        elamisch-persische Tracht." *AMI* 21: 27–51.
1989   "Der 'Apollon' des Dareios." *AMI* 22: 125–
        29.
1990a   "Das Persepolis der Spätzeit." *AchHist* 4:
        7–36.
1990b   "Die sogennante Fünfte Satrapie bei Hero-
        dot." *Trans* 3: 109–29.
1990c   "Madjdabad: zur Datierung von Stein-
        bruch-Arbeiten im Persepolis." *AMI* 23:
        185–90.
1991a   "Aegyptischer Stil und Reichsachaimeni-
        dische Inhalte auf dem Sockel des Darios-

        Statue aus Susa/Heliopolis." *AchHist* 6:
        285–303.
1991b   "Zur Darstellung von Standesunter-
        scheiden in Persepolis." *AMI* 24: 35–51.
1992a   "Zwei mit historischen Szenen bemalte
        Balkan der Achaimenidenzeit." *MJBK* 53:
        7–18.
1992b   "Zur Genese Altiranischer Motive, XI:
        'Eingewebte Bildchen' von Städten." *AMI*
        25 [1994]: 95–124.
1993   "Die Gefässe auf den Gabenbringer-
        Reliefs in Persepolis." *AMI* 26 [1995]: 146–
        60.
1994   "Babylonische und assyrische Elemente in
        der achaimenidische Kunst." *AchHist* 8:
        131–47.
Calmeyer, P., and Eilers, W.
1977   "Von Reisehut zur Kaiserkrone." *AMI* 10:
        153–90.
Caltabiano, M. C., and Colace, P. R.
1989   "Darico persiano e nomisma greco: differ-
        enze strutturali, ideologiche e funzionali
        alla luce del lessico greco." *REA* 91/1–2:
        213–26.
Cambridge Ancient History, 4²
1988   *Persia, Greece and the Western Mediter-
        ranean, c. 525–479 B.C.* (ed. J. Boardman,
        N. G. L. Hammond, D. M. Lewis, and
        M. Ostwald). Cambridge.
Cambridge Ancient History, 5²
1992   *The Fifth Century B.C.* (ed. D. M. Lewis,
        J. Boardman, J. K. Davies, and M. Ost-
        wald). Cambridge.
Cambridge Ancient History, 6²
1994   *The Fourth Century B.C.* (ed. D. M. Lewis,
        J. Boardman, S. Hornblower, and M. Ost-
        wald). Cambridge.
Cambridge History of Iran, 2
1985   *The Median and Achaemenian Periods* (ed.
        I. Gershevitch). Cambridge.
Cambridge History of Judaism, 1
1984   Ed. W. D. Davies and L. Finkelstein. Cam-
        bridge.
Cameron, G. G.
1941   "Darius and Xerxes in Babylonia." *AJSL*
        58: 314–25.
1942   "Darius' daughter and the Persepolis in-
        scriptions." *JNES* 1: 214–19.
1943   "Darius, Egypt and the 'lands beyond the
        sea.'" *JNES* 2: 307–13.
1948   *Persepolis Treasury Tablets*. OIP 65. Chi-
        cago.
1955   "Ancient Persia." Pp. 79–97 in *The Idea of
        History in the Ancient Near East* (ed. R. C.
        Dentan).
1958   "Persepolis Treasury Tablets old and new."
        JNES 17/3: 161–76.
1965   "New tablets from the Persepolis treasury."
        JNES 24: 167–92.
1973   "The Persian satrapies and related mat-
        ters." *JNES* 32: 47–56.

1974 "Cyrus the 'Father' and Babylonia." *Acta Iranica* 2: 45–48.

1975 "Darius the Great and his Scythian (Saka) expedition: Bisitun and Herodotus." *Acta Iranica* 1 (= *Monumentum H. Nyberg*): 77–88.

Campanile, E.
1974 "Ant. Pers. XSAYATHIYA XSAYATHIY-ANAM." Pp. 110–18 in *Studi linguistici in onore di T. Bolelli*. Pisa.

Canby, J. V.
1979 "A note on some Susa bricks." *AMI* 12: 315–20.

Canfora, L.
1990 "Trattati in Tucidide." Pp. 193–216 in *I trattati nel mondo antico: Forma, ideologia, funzione* (ed. L. Canfora, M. Liverani, and C. Zaccagnini). Rome.

Cannizzaro, F. A.
1913 *Il capitolo georgico dell'Avesta, Vendidád, III*. Messina.

Capart, J.
1914 *Un roman vécu il y a 25 siècles*. Paris-Brussels.

Capecchi, G.
1991 "Grecità linguistica e grecità figurativa nella più antica monetazione di Cilicia." *QS* 76/1: 67–103.

Cardascia, G.
1951 *Les Archives des Murašū: Une famille d'hommes d'affaires babyloniens à l'époque perse (455–403 B.C.)*. Paris.

1958 "Le fief dans la Babylonie achéménide." Pp. 55–88 in *Recueils de la Société Jean-Bodin, I²: Les Liens de vassalités et les immunités*. Brussels.

1978 "Armée et fiscalité dans la Babylonie achéménide." Pp. 1–10 in *Armées et Fiscalités dans le monde antique*. Paris.

1983 "Lehenswese, B: in der Perserzeit." *RLA*: cols. 547–50.

1991 "La ceinture de Parysatis: une *Morgengabe* chez les Achéménides?" Pp. 363–69 in *Marchands, diplomates et empereurs: Études sur la civilisation mésopotamienne offertes à P. Garelli* (ed. D. Charpin and F. Joannès). Paris.

Cardona, G. R.
1980 "Etnografia della communicazione e documenti antici: il caso dell' antico pesiano." *VO* 3: 277–86.

Cargill, J.
1977 "The Nabonidus chronicle and the fall of Lydia." *AJAH*: 97–116.

1981 *The Second Athenian Confederacy: Empire or Free Alliance?* University of California Press.

Carney, E. D.
1993 "Foreign influence and the changing role of royal Macedonian women." *Ancient Macedonia* (Thessalonica) 5/1: 313–23.

Carradice, I.
1987 "The 'regal coinage' of the Persian Empire." Pp. 73–95 in I. Carradice (ed.), *Coinage and Administration in the Athenian and Persian Empires*. BAR Int. Ser. 343. London.

Carroll-Spillecke, M.
1989 *Kēpos: Der antike griechische Garten. Wohnen in der klassischen Polis* 3. Munich.

Carter, E.
1994 "Bridging the gap between the Elamites and the Persians in Southeastern Khuzistan." *AchHist* 8: 65–95.

Carter, E., and Stolper, M.
1984 *Elam: Surveys of Political History and Archaeology*. NEA 25. University of California Press.

Cartledge, P.
1987 *Agesilas and the Crisis of Sparta*. Baltimore.

Casabonne, O.
1995a "Sur une coiffure de Nergal de Tarse à l'époque achéménide." *LdP* 1, note 9.

1995b "Le *syennésis* cilicien et Cyrus: l'apport des sources numismatiques." Pp. 147–72 in P. Briant (ed.), *Dans les pas des Dix-Mille: Pays et peuples du Proche-Orient vus par un Grec* (Actes de la Table ronde de Toulouse, 3–4 février 1995). Pallas 43.

Castritius, H.
1972 "Die Okkupation Thrakiens durch die Perser und die Sturz des athenischen Tyrannen Hippias." *Chiron* 2: 1–15.

Cattenat, A., and Gardin, J. C.
1977 "Diffusion comparée de quelques genres de poterie caractéristiquesde l'époque achéménide sur le Plateau iranien et en Asie centrale." Pp. 225–48 in *Le Plateau iranien*. Paris.

Cazelles, H.
1954 "La mission d'Esdras." *VT* 4: 113–40.

1955 "Nouveaux documents araméens d'Égypte." *Syria*: 75–100.

Cenival, F. de
1972 "Une vente d'esclaves de l'époque d'Artaxerxès III." *RdE* 24 (= *Mélanges M. Malinine*): 31–39.

Chaumont, M. L.
1958 "Le culte d'Anāhita à Stāxr et les premiers Sassanides." *RHR* 153: 154–75.

1962 "Recherches sur les institutions de l'Iran ancien et de l'Arménie." *JA* 250: 11–22.

1973 "Chiliarque et curopalate à la cour des Sassanides." *IA* 10: 139–61.

1984 "Études d'histoire parthe, V: La route royale des Parthes de Zeugma à Séleucie du Tigre d'après l'itinéraire d'Isidore de Charax." *Syria* 61: 63–106.

1986–87 "L'Arménie et la route royale des Perses." *REArm* 20: 287–307.

1990 "Un nouveau gouverneur de Sardes à l'époque achéménide d'après une inscription récemment découverte." *Syria* 57/3: 579–608.

Chauveau, M.
1996   "Violence et répression dans la *Chronique
        de Pétéïsé*." In B. Menu (ed.), *Égypte pha-
        raonique: pouvoir, société*. Méditerrannées
        6. Paris.
Chevalier, N.
1989   "Hamadan 1913: une mission oubliée." *IA*:
        245–51.
Chevereau, P.
1985   *Prosopographie des cadres militaires égyp-
        tiens dans la basse époque*. Paris.
Chiasson, C. C.
1984   "Pseudartabas and his eunuchs: *Achar-
        nians* 91–122." *CPh* 136–37.
Childs, W. A. P.
1978   *The City-Reliefs of Lycia*. Princeton.
1979   "The authorship of the inscribed pillar of
        Xanthos." *AnSt* 29: 97–102.
1980   "Lycian relations with Persians and Greeks
        in the fifth and fourth centuries re-exam-
        ined." *AnSt* 31: 55–80.
Childs, W. A. P., and Demargne, P.
1989   *Fouilles de Xanthos*, VIII: *Le Monument
        des Néréides*. Le décor sculpté 1–2. Paris.
Choksy, J. K.
1990   "Gesture in Ancient Iran and Central Asia
        I: the raised hand." Pp. 30–61 in *Papers
        Yarshater*.
Christiensen, A.
1936   *La Geste des rois dans les traditions de
        l'Iran antique*. Paris.
Chuvin, P.
1981   "Apollon au trident et les dieux de Tarse."
        JS 269: 305–26.
Claessen, H. J. M.
1989   "Tribute and taxation, or: how to finance
        Early States and Empires." Pp. 45–75 in
        Briant and Herrenschmidt (eds.).
Clamer, A.
1952   *La Sainte Bible*, IV. Paris.
Clemen, C.
1920a   *Fontes Historiae Religionis Persicae*. Bonn.
1920b   *Die griechischen und lateinischen Nach-
        richten über die persische Religion*. Giessen.
Clère, J. J.
1951   "Une statue du fils ainé de Nectanébo."
        RdE 6: 138–55.
1983   "Autobiographie d'un général gouverneur
        de la haute-Égypte à l'époque saïte."
        BIFAO 83: 85–100.
Clermont-Ganneau, C.
1921   "Le *paradeisos* royal achéménide de Si-
        don." *CRAI*: 106–9.
Cloché, P.
1919–20 "La Grèce et l'Égypte de 405 à 342–341
         av. J.-C." *RdE* 1: 210–58; 2: 82–127.
Coacco Polselli, G.
1984   "Nuove luce sulla datazione dei re sido-
        nii?" *RSF* 12: 169–73.
Cocquerillat, D.
1968   *Palmeraies et Cultures de l'Eanna d'Uruk
        (559–520)*. Berlin.

1973   "Recherches sur le verger du temple cam-
        pagnard de l'Akîtu." *WO* 7/1: 96–134.
1981   "Compléments aux *palmeraies et cultures
        de l'Eanna d'Uruk*." *RAss* 75: 151–69.
1983   "Compléments à la topographie d'Uruk au
        temps de la Ferme générale." *RAss* 77:
        163–68.
1984a   "Compléments aux *Palmeraies et Cultures
        de l'Eanna d'Uruk* (II): l'aménagement de
        la campagne d'Uruk et son peuplement
        avant l'époque des Fermes générales (VIIIᵉ–
        VIᵉ s. av. J.-C.)." *RAss* 78: 49–70.
1984b   "Compléments aux *Palmeraies et Cultures
        de l'Eanna d'Uruk* (III)." *RAss* 78: 143–67.
1985   "Compléments aux *Palmeraies et Cultures
        de l'Eanna d'Uruk* (IV)." *RAss* 79: 51–59.
Cogan, M.
1974   *Imperialism and Religion: Assyria, Judah
        and Israel in the eighth and seventh cent.
        B.C.* Missoula, Montana: Scholars Press.
1993   "Judah under Assyrian hegemony: a re-
        examination of *Imperialism and Religion*."
        JBL 112/3: 403–14.
Colin, F.
1990   "Le récit de Sataspès s'inspire-t-il de sources
        égyptiennes?" *ZPE* 82: 287–96.
Collombier, A. M.
1987   "Céramique grecque et échanges en
        Méditerranée orientale: Chypre et la côte
        syro-palestinienne (fin VIIIᵉ–fin IVᵉ s. av.
        J.-C.)." *Studia Phoenicia* 5: 239–48.
1990   "Organisation du territoire et pouvoirs lo-
        caux dans l'île de Chypre à l'époque
        perse." *Trans* 4: 21–43.
1991   "Écritures et sociétés à Chypre à l'âge du
        fer." Pp. 425–47 in *Phoinikeia grammata:
        Lire et écrire en Méditerranée*. Studia Phoe-
        nicia 13. Liège.
1993   "La fin des royaumes chypriotes: ruptures
        et continuités." *Trans* 6: 119–48.
Coogan, M. D.
1974   "Life in the diaspora: Jews at Nippur in the
        fifth century B.C." *BA* 37/1: 6–12.
Cook, J. M.
1983   *The Persian Empire*. London/Melbourne/
        Toronto.
1985   "The rise of the Achaemenids and estab-
        lishment of their Empire." *CHI* 2: 200–
        291.
Cooney, J. D.
1954a   "The portrait of an Egyptian collaborator."
        Bull. Brooklyn Museum 15: 1–6.
1954b   "The lions of Letopolis." *Bull. Brooklyn
        Museum* 15: 17–30.
1965   "Persian influence in Late Egyptian Art."
        JARCE 4: 39–48.
Corcella, A., and Medaglia, S. M. (eds.)
1993   *Erodoto, Le storie, Libro IV: La Scizia e la
        Libia*. Rome-Florence.
Corsaro, M.
1980a   "*Oikonomia* del re e *oikonomia* del satrapo:
        Sull'amministrazione della *chērō basilikē*

d'Asia Minore dagli Achemenidi agli Attalidi." *ASNP* 3d series 10/4: 1163–1219.
1980b "Un decreto di Zelea sul recupero dei terreni publici (*Syll.*³ 279)." *ASNP* 3d series 14/3: 441–93.
1985 "Tassazione regia e tassazione civica dagli Achemenidi ai re ellenistici: alcune osservazioni." *REA* 87/1–2: 73–96.
1989 "Autonomia cittadina e fiscalità regi: le città greche d'Asia nel sistema tributario achemenide." Pp. 62–75 in Briant and Herrenschmidt (eds.).
1991 "Gli Ioni tra Greci e Persiani: il problema dell'identità ionica nel dibattito culturale e politico del V Secolo." *AchHist* 6: 41–55.
Corsten, T.
1991 "Herodot I.131 und die Einführung des Anāhita-Kultes in Lydien." *IA* 26: 163–80.
1994 "Zum Angebot einer Schenkung Alexanders an Phokion." *Historia* 48/1: 112–18.
Costa, E. A., Jr.
1974 "Evagoras I and the Persians, ca. 411 to 391 B.C." *Historia* 23/1: 40–56.
Coulson, W. D. E., and Leonard, A., Jr.
1981 *Cities of the Delta, I: Naukratis.* ARCE Reports. Malibu, California: Undena.
Cousin, G.
1890 "Correction à l'article intitulé 'Lettre de Darius fils d'Hystaspes.'" *BCH* 14: 646–48.
1904 *Kyros le Jeune en Asie Mineure (printemps 408–juillet 401).* Nancy.
Cousin, G., and Deschamps, G.
1889 "Une lettre de Darius, fils d'Hystaspes." *BCH* 13: 529–42.
Cowley, A. E.
1921 "L'inscription bilingue gréco-lydienne de Sardes." *CRAI*: 7–14.
1923 *Aramaic Papyri of the Fifth Century B.C.* Oxford.
Cracco, Ruggini, L.
1996–67 "Eforo nello Pseudo-Aristotele, *Oec.* II?" *Athenaeum* 44/34: 199–237; 45: 2–88.
Cremer, M. L.
1984 "Zwei neue graeco-persische Stelen." *EA*: 87–99.
Cross, F. M.
1963 "The discovery of the Samaria papyri." *BA* 26/4: 110–21.
1966 "Aspects of Samaritan and Jewish history in Late Persian period and Hellenistic times." *HThR* 59/3: 201–11.
1971 "Papyri of the fourth century B.C. from Dâliyeh." Pp. 44–69 in D. N. Freedman and J. G. Greenfield (eds.), *New Directions in Biblical Archaeology.* New York.
1975 "A reconstruction of the Judean restoration." *JBL* 94: 4–18.
1985 "Samaria Papyri I: an Aramaic slave conveyance of 335 B.C. found in the Wâdi ed-Dâliyeh." *Eretz-Israel* 18: 7–17.

Cruz-Uribe, E.
1986 "The Hibis Temple project, 1984–85 field season: Preliminary report." *JARCE* 23: 157–66.
1988 *Hibis Temple Project, I: Translations, Commentary, Discussion and Sign-List.* San Antonio, Texas.
Culican, W.
1965 *The Medes and the Persians.* New York.
1971 "Syro-achaemenian ampullae." *IA* 11: 100–112.
Cumont, F.
1905a "Notes sur le culte d'Anaïtis." *RA*: 24–31.
1905b "La Persée d'Amisos." *RA*: 180–89.
1905c "Une inscription gréco-araméenne d'Asie Mineure." *CRAI*: 93–104.
Cuq, E.
1927 "La condition juridique de la Coelè-Syrie au temps de Ptolémée V Épiphane." *Syria*: 145–52.
Curtis, J.
1984 *Nush-i Jān: The Small Finds.* London.
Curty, O.
1989 "L'historiographie hellénistique et l'inscription no. 37 des *Inschriften von Priene*." Pp. 21–35 in *Historia Testis: Mélanges T. Zawadski.* Fribourg.
Cuyler Young, T., Jr.
1980 "480/479 B.C.: A Persian perspective." *IA* 15: 213–39.
1988a "The early history of the Medes and the Persians and the Achaemenid Empire to the death of Cambyses." *CAH* 4²: 1–52.
1988b "The consolidation of the [Achaemenid] Empire and its limits of growth under Darius and Xerxes." *CAH* 4²: 53–111.
Dagron, G., and Feissel, D.
1987 *Inscriptions de Cilicie.* Paris.
Dalley, S.
1984 "The cuneiform text from Tell Tawilan." *Levant* 21: 19–22.
1990 "Cuneiform and Assyria after 612 B.C." Pp. 74–84 in E. Aerts and H. Klengel (eds.), *The Town as Regional Economic Center in the Ancient Near East.* Studies in Social and Economic History 20. Louvain.
1993 "Nineveh after 612 B.C." *AOF* 20/1: 143–47.
Dalton, O. M.
1926 *The Treasure of the Oxus*². London.
Dandamaev, M. A.
1966 "Temple et État en Babylonie" (Russian). *VDI*: 17–39.
1967 "Die Lehnsbeziehungen in Babylonien unter den ersten Achämeniden." Pp. 37–42 in *FS W. Eilers.* Wiesbaden.
1969a "Achaemenid Babylonia." Pp. 296–318 in I. M. Diakonoff (ed.), *Ancient Mesopotamia: Socio-Economic History.* Moscow.
1969b "Der Tempelzehnte in Babylonien während des 6–4 Jh.v.u.Z." Pp. 82–90 in *Beiträge zur Alten Geschichte und deren Nachleben (FS F. Altheim),* vol. I. Berlin.

1969c "Bagasarū ganzabara." Pp. 235–39 in *Studien zur Sprachenwissenschaft und Kulturkunde: Gedenkschrift für W. Brandestein*. Innsbruck.

1971 "Die Rolle des *tamkārum* in Babylonien im 2. und 1. Jahrtausend v.u.Z." Pp. 69–78 in H. Klengel (ed.), *Beiträge zur sozialen Struktur des Vorderasiens*. Berlin.

1972a "Politische und wirtschaftliche Geschichte." Pp. 15–58 in Walser (ed.).

1972b "Connections between Elam and Babylonia in the Achaemenid period." Pp. 258–64 in *The Memorial Volume of the Vth Intern. Congress of Iranian Art and Archaeology*. Tehran.

1972c "Nouveaux documents de l'économie royale en Iran (509–494 av.n.è.)." *VDI*: 3–26 (Russian).

1973 "Les ouvriers des exploitations royales en Iran (fin VIe-seconde moitié du Ve s. av. n.è.)." *VDI*: 3–24 (Russian).

1974 "The domain-lands of Achaemenes in Babylonia." *AOF* 1: 123–27.

1975a "Forced labour in the palace economy in Achaemenid Iran." *AOF* 2: 71–78.

1975b Review of Mayrhofer 1973, *GGA* 277/3–4: 225–39.

1975c "La politique religieuse des Achéménides." Pp. 193–200 in *Monumentum H. S. Nyberg*, I. Leiden-Tehran.

1976 *Persien unter den ersten Achämeniden*. Wiesbaden.

1977a "The dynasty of the Achaemenids in the early period." *AAH* 25: 39–42.

1977b "State and temple in Babylonia in the first millennium B.C." Pp. 586–89 in E. Lipiński (ed.).

1979 "Data of the Babylonian documents from the 6th to the 5th centuries B.C. on the Sakas." Pp. 95–109 in *Prolegomena to the Sources on the History of Pre-Islamic Central Asia*. Budapest.

1981a "The neo-babylonian citizens." *Klio* 63/1: 45–49.

1981b "Die Fischerei in neubabylonischer Texten des 6. und 5. Jhdt.v.u.Z." *JWG*: 67–82.

1983 "Aliens and the community in Babylonia in the 6th–5th Cent. B.C." Pp. 133–45 in *Les Communautés rurales*. Recueils de la société Jean-Bodin 41/29. Paris.

1984a "Royal *paradeisoi* in Babylonia." Pp. 113–17 in *Orientalia J. Duchesne-Guillemin Emerito Oblata*. Hommages et Opera Minora 9. Leiden.

1984b *Slavery in Babylonia from Nabopolassar to Alexander the Great (626–331 B.C.)*. Northern Illinois University Press.

1984c "Babylonia in the Persian age." *CHJ* 1: 326–34.

1985 "Herodotus' information on Persia and the latest discoveries of cuneiform texts." *Histoire de l'historiographie* 7: 92–100.

1986 Review of Pinches 1982, *Orientalia* 55/4: 464–68.

1986b "Neo-Babylonian archives." Pp. 273–77 in Veenhof (ed.).

1986c "Some Babylonians in Ecbatana." *AMI* 19: 67–82.

1988a "Royal economy in the Achaemenid Empire." Pp. 145–55 in *Stato, Economia, Lavoro nel Vicino Oriente antico*. Milan.

1988b "Wages and prices in Babylonia in the 6th and 5th centuries B.C." *AOF* 15: 53–58.

1989a *A Political History of the Achaemenid Empire*. Leiden.

1989b *The Culture and Social Institutions of Ancient Iran* [= M. A. Dandamaev and V. G. Lukonin 1989]. Cambridge.

1989c "The old Iranian PASA'DU." Pp. 563–65 in Meyer and Haerinck (eds.).

1990 "The old Iranian *azarapanata*." Pp. 60–61 in *Papers Yarshater*.

1992a *Iranians in Achaemenid Babylonia*. Columbia Lectures on Iranian Studies 6. Costa Mesa/New York.

1992b "The title *aḫ šadrapànu* in Nippur." Pp. 29–32 in M. DeJong Ellis (ed.), *Nippur at the Centennial: Papers read at the 35th RAI (Philadelphia, 1988)*. Philadelphia: The University Museum.

1992c "Was Eanna destroyed by Darius I?" *AMI* 25 [1994]: 169–72.

1993a "The latest evidence for Nebuchadnezzar III's reign." *NABU*, note 11.

1993b "Lu zinabarra." *NABU*, note 12.

1993c "Achaemenid estates in Laḫiru." *IA* 27: 117–23.

1993d "Xerxes and the Esagila temple in Babylon." *BAI* 7: 41–47.

1994a "The neo-babylonian *zazakku*." *AOF* 21: 34–40.

1994b "Achaemenid Mesopotamia: traditions and innovations." *AchHist* 8: 229–34.

1995a "The earliest evidence for Nebuchednezzar IV's reign." *NABU*, note 34.

1995b "An unidentified document from Xerxes' reign and the Ebabbara temple." *NABU*, note 35.

1995c "A governor of Byblos in Sippar." Pp. 29–31 in K. Van Lerberghe and A. Schoors (ed.), *Immigration and Emigration within the Ancient Near East: Festschrift E. Lipiński*. OLA 65. Leuven.

Dandamaev, M. A., and Livshits, V.
1988 "Zattumešu, a maguš in Babylonia." Pp. 457–59 in *A Green Leaf (Papers Asmussen)*. Leiden.

Daressy, G.
1900 "Stèle de l'an III d'Amasis." *RT* 1–3: 1–9.

Darnell, J. C.
1992 "The *Kbn. wt* ships of the late period." Pp. 67–89 in J. H. Johnson (ed.).

Daumas, F.
1977 "Le problème de la monnaie dans l'Égypte antique avant Alexandre." *MEFRA* 89: 425–42.

Daumas, M.
1985 "Aristophane et les Perses." *REA* 87/3–4: 289–305.

Davesne, A.
1989 "La circulation monétaire en Cilicie à l'époque achéménide." *REA* 91/1–2: 157–68.

Davesne, A.; Lemaire, A.; and Lozachmeur, H.
1987 "Le site archéologique de Meydançikkale (Turquie): du royaume de Pirindu à la garnison ptolémaïque." *CRAI*: 359–83.

Davidson, O. M.
1985 "The crown-bestower in the Iranian Book of the Kings." Pp. 61–148 in *Papers Mary Boyce*, vol. I. Leiden.

Davies, N. de Garis
1953 *The Temple of Hibis in El Khargeh Oasis*, Part III: *The Decoration*. New York.

Davies, P. R. (ed.)
1991 *Second Temple Studies*, I: *Persian Period*. JSOT suppl. 117. Sheffield.

Davies, P. R.
1991 "Sociology and the second temple." Pp. 13–19 in Davies 1991 (ed.).
1992 "Defending the boundaries of Israel during the second temple period, 2: Chronicles 20 and the 'Salvation army.'" Pp. 43–54 in *Priests, Prophets and Scribes: Essays on the Formation and Heritage of the Second Temple Judaism in Honor of J. Blenkinsopp*. Sheffield.

Davis-Kimball, J.
1989 *Proportions in Achaemenid Art*. Ph.D. Berkeley.

Dayton, J.
1984 "Herodotus, Phoenicia, the Persian Gulf and India in the first millennium B.C." Pp. 363–75 in R. Boucharlat and J. F. Salles (eds.), *Arabie orientale: Mésopotamie et Iran méridional de l'âge du fer au début de la période islamique*. Paris.

Debord, P.
1982 *Aspects sociaux et économiques de la vie religieuse dans l'Anatolie gréco-romaine*. EPRO 98. Leiden.
1994 "Le vocabulaire des ouvrages de défense: Occurrences littéraires et épigraphiques confrontées aux *realia* archéologiques." *REA* 96/1–2: 53–61.
1995 "Les routes royales en Asie Mineure occidentale." Pp. 89–97 in P. Briant (ed.), *Dans les pas des Dix-Mille: Peuples et pays du Proche-Orient vus par un Grec* (Actes de la Table ronde internationale, Toulouse, 3–4 février 1995). Pallas 43.

Debord, P., Varinoglu, E., et al.
forthcoming *Les hautes terres de la Carie du Sud*. Bibl. de l'IFEA. Istanbul.

Delaporte, L.
1909 *Cylindres orientaux: Catalogue du musée Guimet*. Annales du musée Guimet 33. Paris.
1910 *Catalogue des cylindres orientaux et des cachets assyro-babyloniens, perses et syro-cappadociens de la Bibliothèque nationale*. Paris.
1920 *Musée du Louvre. Catalogue des cylindres, cachets et pierres gravées de style oriental*, I: *Fouilles et missions*. Paris.
1923 *Musée du Louvre. Catalogue des cylindres, cachets et pierres gravées de style oriental*, II: *Acquisitions*. Paris.

Delatte, A.
1936 "Herbarius." *Acad. royale de Belgique: Clase des Lettres* 22: 227–348.

Delaunay, J. A.
1974 "L'araméen d'Empire et les débuts de l'écriture en Asie centrale." *Acta Iranica* 1: 219–26.
1975 "À propos des 'Aramaic ritual texts from Persepolis' de R. A. Bowman." *Acta Iranica* 2: 193–217.
1976 "Sur quelques noms de personnes des archives élamites de Persépolis." *STIR* 5/1: 9–31.
1985 *Genèse de l'araméen d'Empire*, I. Paris.

Delorme, J.
1992 *Histoire des Cinquante Ans: Commentaire sur la Pentekontaètie de Thucydide*. Toulouse.

Demargne, P.
1958 *Fouilles de Xanthos*, I: *Les piliers funéraires*. Paris.
1974a "Le décor des sarcophages de Xanthos: réalités, mythes, symboles." *CRAI*: 263–69.
1974b *Fouilles de Xanthos*, V: *Tombes-maisons, tombes rupestres et sarcophages*. Paris.
1975 "Athéna, les dynastes lyciens et les héros grecs." Pp. 97–101 in *Florilegium anatolicum*. Paris.
1976 "L'iconographie dynastique au monument des Néréides de Xanthos." Pp. 81–95 in *Recueil Plassart*. Paris.
1983 "Serviteurs orientaux sur deux monuments funéraires de Xanthos." Pp. 167–70 in *FS K. Bittel*. Mainz.

Demsky, A.
1983 "Pelekh in Nehemiah 3." *IEJ* 33: 242–44.

Dentzer, J. M.
1969 "Reliefs au 'banquet' dans l'Asie Mineure de Vᵉ siècle av. J.-C." *RA*: 195–224.
1982 *Le Motif du banquet couché dans le Proche-Orient ancien et le monde grec du VIIᵉ siècle av. J.-C.* BEFAR 246. Paris-Rome.

Depuydt, L.
1995a "The story of Cambyses' mortal wounding of the Apis bull (*ca.* 523 BCE)." *JNES* 54/2: 119–26.
1995b "The date of death of Artaxerxes I." *WO* 26: 32–42.

Dequeker, L.
1993 "Darius the Persian and the reconstruction of the Jewish temple in Jerusalem (Ezra 4,24)." Pp. 67–92 in J. Quaegebeur (ed.), *Ritual and Sacrifice in the Ancient Near East.* OLA 55. Leuven.

Desanges, J.
1978 *Recherches sur les Méditerranéens aux confins de l'Afrique.* Paris.

Descat, R.
1985 "Mnésimachos, Hérodote et le système tributaire achéménide." *REA* 87/1–2: 97–112.
1988 "Aux origines de l'économie grecque." *QUCC* n.s. 28/1: 103–19.
1989a "Notes sur la politique tributaire de Darius Ier." Pp. 77–93 in Briant and Herrenschmidt (eds.).
1989b "Notes sur l'histoire du monnayage achéménide sous le règne de Darius Ier." *REA* 91/1: 15–29.
1990a "Remarques sur les rapports entre les Perses et la mer Noire à l'époque achéménide." Pp. 539–48 in *Ikinci Tarih Boyunca Karadeniz Kongresi Bildileri* (Samsun, 1988). Samsun.
1990b "De l'économie tributaire à l'économie civique: le rôle de Solon." Pp. 85–100 in *Mélanges P. Lévêque*, vol. V. Paris.
1991 "Colophon et la paix d'Épilykos." Pp. 33–39 in *Erol Atalay Memorial* (ed. H. Malay). Izmir.
1994a "Darius le roi *kapélos.*" *AchHist* 8: 161–66.
1994b "Les forteresses de Théra et de Kallipolis de Carie." *REA* 96/1–2: 205–14.
1995 "Marché et tribute." Pp. 99–108 in P. Briant (ed.), *Dans les pas des Dix-Mille: Peuples et pays du Proche-Orient vus par un Grec* (Actes de la Table ronde internationale, Toulouse, 3–4 février 1995). Pallas 43.
forthcoming "Darius Ier et la monnaie." *AIIN.*

Descat, R. (ed.)
1989 *L'Or perse et l'histoire grecque. REA* 91/1–2.

Desideri, P.
1986 "Le città dela pianura di Cilicia in Strabone (14,5,8–19)." *Studi Tardoantichi* 2: 331–46.

Desideri, P., and Jasink, A. M.
1990 *Cilicia: Dall'età di Kizzuwatna alla conquista macedone.* Turin.

Desnier, J. L.
1995 *De Cyrus à Julien l'Apostat: Le passage du fleuve. Essai sur la légitimité du souverain.* Paris.

Destrooper-Giordiades, A.
1987 "La Phénicie et Chypre à l'époque achéménide." *Studia Phoenicia* 5: 339–55.
1993 "Continuités et ruptures dans le monnayage chypriote à l'époque achéménide." *Trans* 6: 87–102.

Deutsch, R., and Heltzer, M.
1994 *Forty New West-Semitic Inscriptions.* Tel Aviv–Jaffa.

Devauchelle, D.
1994a "Les prophéties en Égypte ancienne." Pp. 6–30 in *Prophéties et Oracles, I: En Égypte et en Grece.* Suppl. *Cahier Évangile* 89. Paris.
1994b "Les stèles du Sérapeum de Memphis conservées au musée du Louvre." Pp. 95–114 in *Acta Demotica: Acts of the Fifth International Conference for Demotists* (Pisa, 4th–8th September 1993). Pisa.
1995 "Le sentiment antiperse chez les anciens Égyptiens." *Trans* 9: 67–80.
forthcoming "La stèle dite du satrape (Caire CG 22182)." *BIFAO.*

Devine, A. M.
1984 "The location of Castabalum and Alexander's route from Mallus to Myriandrus." *Acta Classica* 27: 127–29.
1985a "The strategies of Alexander the Great and Darius III in the Issus campaign." *AW* 12: 25–38.
1985b "Grand tactics at the battle of Issus." *AW* 12: 39–59.
1986 "The battle of Gaugamela: a tactical and source-critical study." *AW* 13: 87–116.
1988 "A pawn-sacrifice at the battle of the Granicus: the origins of a favourite stratagem of Alexander the Great." *AW* 18: 3–20.

De Voto, J. G.
1988 "Agesilaos and Tissaphernes near Sardis in 395 B.C." *Hermes* 116: 41–53.

DeVries, K.
1990 "The Gordion excavations: Seasons of 1969–73 and subsequent research." *AJA* 94: 371–406.

Dhorme, P.
1912 "Cyrus le Grande." *RB* 9: 22–49.
1913 "La religion des Achéménides." *RB* 10: 15–35.
1928 "Les tablettes babyloniennes de Neirab." *RAss* 25/2: 53–82.

Diakonoff, I. M.
1979 "Artemidi Anaeiti anestesen." *BABesch* 54: 139–75.
1985a "Elam." *CHI* 2: 1–24.
1985b "Media." *CHI* 2: 36–148.

Diakonoff, I. M., and Jankowska, N. B.
1990 "An Elamite Gilgameš text from Argišti-ḫenale, Urartu (Armavir-blur), 8th cent. B.C." *ZA* 80/1: 102–23.

Dillemann, L.
1962 *Haute Mésopotamie orientale et Pays adjacents.* Paris.

Dillery, J.
1992 "Darius and the tomb of Nitocris (Hdt. I. 197)." *CPh* 87/1: 30–38.
1995 *Xenophon and the History of his Time.* London–New York.

Dion, P. E.
1991 "The civic and temple community of Persian period Judaea: neglected insights from Eastern Europe." *JNES* 50/4: 281–87.
Dobbins, K. W.
1984 "Alexander's Eastern satrapies." *Persica* 11: 73–108.
Doenges, N. A.
1981 *The Letters of Themistokles.* New York.
Donadoni, S.
1983 "L'Egitto achemenide." Pp. 27–40 in *Modes de contact et Processus de transformation dans les sociétés anciennes.* Pisa-Rome.
Donbaz, V.
1987 "Deux nouvelles inscriptions de Nabonide, roi de Babylone." *AnAnt* 1: 15–21.
1989a "The question of the Murašū texts dated at Susa." *NABU*, note 86.
1989b "One Murašū document from Lagaš." *NABU*, note 87.
Donbaz, V., and Stolper, M.
1993 "Gleanings from the Murašu texts in the collection of the Istanbul Archaeological Museum." *NABU*, note 102.
Doncel-Voute, P.
1984 "Un banquet funéraire perse en Paphlagonie." Pp. 101–18 in Doncel-Lebruin.
Doncel, R., and Lebrun, M. (eds.)
1984 *Archéologie et Religions de l'Anatolie ancienne: Mélanges en l'honneur du Prof. P. Naster.* Louvain.
Donner, F. M.
1986 "Xenophon's Arabia." *Iraq* 48: 1–14.
Dörner, F.
1967 "Zur Rekonstruktion der Ahnengalerie des Königs Antiochos I. von Kommagene." *IM* 17: 195–219.
Dörrie, H.
1964 *Der Königskult des Antiochos von Kommagene im Lichte neuer Inschriften-Funde.* Göttingen.
Dossin, G.
1938 "Signaux lumineux au pays de Mari." *RAss* 35: 174–86.
Dothan, M.
1985 "A Phoenician inscription from Akko." *IEJ* 35/2–3: 86–94.
Dougherty, H. P.
1929 *Nabonidus and Belshazzar: A Study of the Closing Events of the Neo-Babylonian Empire.* YOS 15. Yale University Press.
Downey, S. B.
1986 "A stele from Hierapolis-Bambyce (?)." *BM* 17: 301–8.
Drews, R.
1969 "The fall of Astyages and Herodotus' chronology of the Eastern kingdoms." *Historia* 18/1: 1–11.
1973 *The Greek Accounts of Eastern History.* Cambridge, Massachusetts.

1974 "Sargon, Cyrus and Mesopotamian Folk History." *JNES* 33: 387–93.
Drioton, E.
1952 "Le théâtre égyptien." *Pages d'égyptologie* (= *Revue du Caire* 1943): 217ff.. Cairo.
Driver, G. R.
1957 *Aramaic Papyri of the 5th Century B.C.* Oxford.
Dubberstein, W. H.
1939 "Comparative prices in Later Babylonia (625–400 B.C.)." *AJSL* 56: 20–43.
Duchêne, J.
1986 "La localisation de Ḫuhnur." Pp. 65–73 in *Fragmenta Historicae Elamicae: Mélanges offerts à M. J. Stève.* Paris.
Duchesne-Guillemin, J.
1952 *La Religion de l'Iran ancien.* Paris.
1953 *Ormazd et Ahriman: L'aventure dualiste dans l'Antiquité.* Paris.
1967–68 "Religion et politique de Cyrus à Xerxès." *Persica* 3: 1–9.
1972 "La religion des Achéménides." Pp. 59–82 in Walser (ed.).
1974 "Le dieu de Cyrus." *Acta Iranica: Commémoration Cyrus* III: 11–21.
1979 "La royauté iranienne et le x^varanah." Pp. 375–86 in *Iranica* (ed. G. Gnoli). Naples.
Duchesne-Guillemin, J., and Van de Valle, B.
1959–62 "Un sceau-cylindre irano-égyptien." *JEOL* 16: 72–77.
Dugas, Ch.
1910 "La campagne d'Agésilas en Asie Mineure." *BCH*: 56–95.
Duleba, W.
1987 "The epos and history of the story of Feridoun in Shahnahmeh." *FO* 24: 159–72.
Dumbrell, W. J.
1971 "The Tell el-Maskuhta bowls and the 'kingdom' of Qedar in the Persian period." *BASOR* 203: 33–44.
Dumézil, G.
1984 "L'intronisation de Darius." Pp. 143–49 in *Orientalia Duchesne-Guillemin.*
1985 "Le costume de guerre du dernier Darius." Pp. 261–65 in *Orientalia, I: Tucci memoriae dicata* (ed. G. Gnoli and L. Laniotti). ISMEO I. Rome.
1986 *Mythe et Épopée: L'idéologie des trois fonctions dans les épopées des peuples indo-européens5.* Paris.
Dumont, J.
1977 "La pêche dans le Fayoum hellénistique: traditions et nouveautés d'après le papyrus Tebtynis 701." *CdE* 103: 125–42.
Dunand, M.
1965 "Nouvelles inscriptions phéniciennes du temple d'Echmoun à Bostan ech-Cheikh, près Sidon." *BMB* 17: 105–9.
1968 "La défense du front méditerranéen de l'Empire achéménide." Pp. 43–51 in *The Role of the Phoenicians in the Interaction of*

Mediterranean Civilizations (ed. Ward). Beirut.

1973 "Le temple d'Echmoun à Sidon: Essai de chronologie." *BMB*: 7–25.

Dunand, M., and Saliby, N.
1985 *Le Temple d'Amrith dans la Pérée d'Aradus.* Paris.

Duncan-Jones, R. P.
1979 "Variation in Egyptian grain-measures." *Chiron* 19: 347–75.

Dupont-Sommer, A.
1948 "Deux inscriptions araméennes trouvées près du lac Sevan (Arménie)." *Syria* 25/1–2: 53–66.
1964 "Une inscription araméenne et la déesse Kubaba." Pp. 7–15 in A. Dupont-Sommer and L. Robert, *La Déesse de Hiérapolis Castabala (Cilicie).* BAHIFAI 16. Paris.
1966 "Une inscription araméenne inédite d'époque perse trouvée à Daskyleion (Turquie)." *CRAI*: 44–57.
1974 "La stèle trilingue récemment découverte au Létôon de Xanthos: le texte araméen." *CRAI*: 132–49.
1976 "L'énigme du dieu 'Satrape' et le dieu Mithra." *CRAI*: 648–60.
1978 "Les dieux et les hommes en l'île d'Éléphantine près d'Assouan, au temps de l'Empire des Perses." *CRAI*: 756–72.
1979 "L'inscription araméenne [de Xanthos]." Pp. 129–78 in H. Metzger (ed.).

Durand, J. M., and Joannès, F.
1988 "Contrat babylonien d'Agadè." *NABU*, note 74.

Durand, J. M., and Margueron, J.
1980 "La question du harem royal dans le palais de Mari." *JS*: 253–80.

Eck, B.
1990 "Sur la vie de Ctésias." *REG* 103/2: 409–34.

Eddy, S. K.
1961 *The King Is Dead: Studies in the Near Eastern Resistance to Hellenism.* Lincoln, Nebraska.
1973 "The cold war between Athens and Persia, ca. 448–412 B.C." *ClPh* 68/4: 241–58.

Eggermont, P. W. L.
1993 *Alexander's Campaign in Southern Punjab.* OLA 54. Louvain.

Ehrhardt, C.
1994 "Two notes on Xenophon, *Anabasis.*" *AHB* 8/1: 1–4.

Ehtecham, M.
1946 *L'Iran sous les Achéménides: Contribution à l'étude de l'organisation sociale et politique du premier empire des Perses.* Fribourg.

Eilers, W.
1935 "Das Volk der *karka* in der Achämenideninschriften." *OLZ* 38/4: 202–13.
1940 *Iranische Beamtennamen in der keilschriftliche Überlieferung.* Abhand. für die Kunde des Morgenlandes. Vienna.

1974 "Le texte cunéiforme du cylindre de Cyrus." *Acta Iranica* 2: 25–31.

Eisenmann, R. H., and Wise, M.
1992 *The Dead Sea Scrolls Uncovered.* Shaftesbury-Rokport-Brisbane. [French trans., *Les Manuscrits de la mer Morte révélés.* Paris, 1995]

Elayi, J.
1978 "L'essor de la Phénicie et le passage de la domination assyro-babylonienne à la domination perse." *BgM* 9: 25–38.
1980 "The Phoenician cities in the Persian period." *JANES* 12: 13–28.
1981a "The relations between Tyre and Carthage during the Persian period." *JANES* 13: 15–29.
1981b "La révolte des esclaves de Tyr relatée par Justin." *BM* 12: 139–50.
1982 "Studies in Phoenician geography during the Persian period." *JNES* 41/2: 83–110.
1983 "Les cités phéniciennes et l'Empire assyrien à l'époque d'Assurbanipal." *RAss* 77: 45–58.
1986 "Les éléments d'architecture sur les monnaies phéniciennes préalexandrines." *QTNAC* 15: 61–75.
1987a "Al-Mina sur l'Oronte à l'époque perse." *Studia Phoenicia* 5: 249–66.
1987b *Recherches sur les cités phéniciennes à l'époque perse.* AION suppl. 47/2. Naples.
1988a *Pénétration grecque en Phénicie sous l'Empire perse.* Nancy.
1988b "Les sarcophages phéniciens d'époque perse." *IA* 23: 275–322.
1988c "L'exploitation des cèdres du mont Liban par les rois assyriens et néobabyloniens." *JESHO* 31: 14–41.
1989 *Sidon: cité autonome de l'Empire perse.* Paris.
1990a "The Phoenician cities in the Achaemenid period: remarks on the present state and prospect of research." *AchHist* 4: 227–37.
1990b "Tripoli (Liban) à l'époque perse." *Trans* 2: 59–72.
1990c *Économie des cités phéniciennes sous l'Empire perse.* AION suppl. 50. Naples.

Elayi, J., and Elayi, A. G.
1992a "Nouvelle datation d'une tombe achéménide de Suse." *STIR* 21/2: 265–69.
1992b "La première monnaie de TR/Tripolis (Tripolis, Liban)." *Trans* 5: 142–51.
1993 *Trésors de monnaies phéniciennes et circulation monétaire (ve–ive siècles avant J.-C.).* Paris.

Elayi, J., and Sapin, J.
1991 *Nouveaux Regards sur la Transeuphratène.* Paris.

El-Sayed, R.
1982 *La Déesse Neith de Saïs,* I–II. Cairo.

Emery, W. B.
1971 "Preliminary report on the excavations at North Sâqqara 1969–70." *JEA* 37: 3–13.

Engels, D.
1978 *Alexander the Great and the Logistics of the Macedonian Army.* University of California Press.

Eph'al, I.
1978 "The Western minorities in Babylonia in the 6th–5th centuries B.C.: maintenance and cohesion." *Orientalia* 47/1: 74–90.
1982 *The Ancient Arabs: Nomads on the Borders of the Fertile Crescent (9th–5th cent. B.C.).* Jerusalem-Leiden.
1988 "Syria–Palestine under Achaemenid Rule." *CAH* 4²: 139–64.

Eph'al, I., and Naveh, J.
1993 "The jar of the Gate." *BASOR* 289: 59–65.

Erdmann, E.
1977 *Nordosttor und persische Belagerungsrampe im Alt Paphos, I: Waffen und Kleingefunde.* Ausgrabungen im Alt-Paphos auf Cypern 1, ed. G. Maier, part 1. Berlin.

Errington, R. M.
1981a "Alexander the Philhellene and Persia." Pp. 139–43 in *Ancient Macedonian Studies in Honor of Ch. F. Edson.* Institute for Balkan Studies. Thessalonica.
1981b "Review-discussion: four interpretations of Philipp II." *AJAH* 6/1: 69–88.

Erzen, A.
1940 *Kilikien bis zum Ende der Perserherrschaft.* Leipzig.

Eshel, H., and Misgav, H.
1988 "A Fourth Cent. B.C. document from Ketef Yeriho." *IEJ* 38/3: 158–76.

Evans, J. A. S.
1978 "The settlement of Artaphrenes." *CPh* 71/4: 344–48.
1987 "Cavalry about the time of the Persian Wars: a speculative essay." *CJ* 82/2: 97–106.

Fales, F. M.
1983 "Il taglio e il transporto di legname nelle lettere a Sargon II." Pp. 49–92 in O. Carruba, M. Liverani, and C. Zaccagnini (eds.), *Studi orientalici in ricordo di F. Pintore.* Pavia.
1989 "Pastorizia e politica: nuovi dati sugli Arabi nelle fonti di età neo-assira." Pp. 119–34 in A. Avanzi (ed.), *Problemi di onomastica semitica meridionale.* Pisa.

Fales, F. M., and Postgate, J. N.
1992 *Imperial Administrative Record, Part I: Palace and Temple Administration.* SAA 7. Helsinki.

Faraguna, M.
1994 "Alle origini dell'*oikonomia*: dall'Anonimo di Giamblico ad Aristotele." *RAL* 5: 551–89.

Farkas, A.
1969 "The horse and rider in Achaemenid art." *Persica* 4: 57–76.
1974 *Achaemenid sculpture.* Leiden.
1980 "Is there anything Persian in Persian art?" Pp. 16–20 in Schmandt-Besserat (ed.).

Farrell, J. B.
1961 "A revised itinerary of the route followed by Cyrus the Younger through Syria, 401 B.C." *JHS* 81: 153–55.

Fauth, W.
1978 "Der königliche Gärtner und Jäger im Paradeisos: Beobachtungen zur Rolle des Herrschers in der vorderasiatischen Hortikultur." *Persica* 8: 1–53.

Favard-Meeks, C., and Meeks, D.
1992 "L'héritière du Delta." Pp. 22–33 in *Alexandrie, IIIᵉ siècle av. J.-C.* (ed. Ch. Jacob and Fr. de Polignac), ed. Autrement, Mémoires 19. Paris.

Fehling, D.
1989 *Herodotus and his "Sources": Citation, Invention and Narrative Art.* Leeds.

Fennelly, J. M.
1980 "The Persepolis ritual." *BA* 43/3: 135–62.

Ferjaoui, A.
1992 *Recherches sur les relations entre l'Orient phénicien et Carthage.* Carthage.

Figulla, H. H.
1954 "A 'coin' of Cyrus." *NC* 14: 173.

Finet, A.
1969 "L'Euphrate, route commerciale de la Mésopotamie." *AAAS* 19: 37–48.
1985 "Le port d'Emar sur l'Euphrate, entre le royaume de Mari et le pays de Canaan." Pp. 27–38 in *The Land of Israel: Cross-Roads of Civilizations.* Louvain.

Finley, M. I.
1978 "The fifth Century Athens Empire: a balance-sheet." Pp. 103–26 in P. A. Garnsey and C. Wittaker (eds.), *Imperialism in the Ancient World.* Cambridge.

Firpo, G.
1986 "Impero universale e politica religiosa: Ancora sulle destruzioni dei templi greci ad opera dei Persiani." *ASNP* 3d series 16/2: 331–93.

Fischer, F.
1983 "Thrakien als Vermittler iranischer Metallkunst an die frühen Kelten." Pp. 191–302 in *FS K. Bittel.* Mainz.

Fitzmyer, J. A., and Kaufman, S. A.
1991 *An Aramaic Bibliography,* vol. I. Baltimore-London.

Fleischer, R.
1983 "Ein Bildhauerauftrag unter Dareios II." *AK*: 33–37.

Fleming, D.
1989 "Eggshell ware pottery in Achaemenid Mesopotamia." *Iraq* 51: 165–85.
1993 "Where was Achaemenid India?" *BAI* 7: 67–72.

Fogazza, G.
1972a "Sui Gongilidi di Eretria." *PdP* 27: 129–30.
1972b "Datame di Cappadocia." *PdP* 27: 130–31.

Fol, A., and Hammond, N. G. L.
1988 "Persia in Europe apart from Greece." *CAH* 4²: 234–53.

Fornara, C. W.
1966   "Some aspects of the career of Pausanias of Sparta." *Historia* 15/3: 257–71.

Foss, C.
1975   "A bullet of Tissaphernes." *JHS* 95: 25–30.
1978   "Explorations in Mount Tmolus." *CSCA* 11: 21–60.

Foucault, J. de
1967   "Histiée de Milet et l'esclave tatoué." *REG* 80: 182–86.

Foucher, A., and Foucher-Bazin, E.
1942   *La Vieille Route de l'Inde de Bactres à Taxila.* Paris.

Frag, A. J. W., and Neave, R. A. H.
1994   "Who is the Carian princess?" Pp. 97–107 in J. Isager (ed.), *Hekatomnid Caria and the Ionian Renaissance.* Odense.

Frame, G.
1984   "Neo-Babylonian and Achaemenid texts from the Sippar collection of the British Museum." *JAOS* 104/4: 745–52.
1986   "Some Neo-Babylonian and Persian documents involving boats." *OA* 25: 29–50.
1991   "Nabonidus, Nabū-šarra-uṣur and the Eanna temple." *ZA* 81/1: 37–86.
1992   *Babylonia 689–627 B.C.: A Political History.* Leiden.

Francfort, H. P.
1975   "Un cachet achéménide d'Afghanistan." *JA* 263: 219–22.
1979   *Les Fortifications en Asie centrale de l'âge du bronze à l'époque kouchane.* Paris.
1985   "Note sur la mort de Cyrus et les Dardes." Pp. 395–400 in *Orientalia I: Tucci memoriae dicata.* Rome.
1988   "Central Asia and Eastern Iran." *CAH* 4²: 169–93.
1989   *Fouilles de Shortugaï: Recherches sur l'Asie centrale protohistorique.* Paris.

Francis, E. D.
1980   "Greeks and Persians: the art of hazard and triumph." Pp. 53–86 in Schmandt-Besserat.

Franke, P. R., and Hirmer, M.
1966   *La Monnaie grecque* [French trans.]. Paris.

Frankfort, H.
1939   *Cylinder Seals: A Documentary Essay on the Art and Religion of the Ancient Near East.* London.
1946   "Achaemenian Sculpture." *AJA* 50: 8–14.

Frei, P.
1977   "Die *Trilingue* vom Letoon, die lykische Zahlreichen und das lykische Geldsystem." *SNR* 56: 5–17.
1979   "Die Rolle des Lyderreiches im internationalen System des 6. Jahrhunderts v. Ch." Pp. 375–82 in *VIII. Türk Tarih Kongresi.*
1984   "Zentralgewalt und Lokalautonomie im Achämenidenreich." Pp. 7–43 in P. Frei and K. Koch, *Reichsidee und Reichsorganisation im Perserreich.* Göttingen.

1990   "Zentralgewalt und Lokalautonomie im achämenidischen Kleinasien." *Trans* 3: 157–71.
1992   "Die epichorischen Namen im griechisch-römischen Inschriftenbestand der Region von Eskisehir." Pp. 181–92 in H. Otten et al. (eds.), *Hittite and other Anatolian and Near Eastern Studies in Honor of Sedap Alp.* Ankara.

French, V., and Dixon, P.
1986   "The Pixodaros affair: another view." *AW* 13/3–4: 73–86.

Frost, F. J.
1973   "A note on Xerxes at Salamis." *Historia* 22/1: 118–19.
1980   *Plutarch, Themistocles: a Historical Commentary.* Princeton.

Frye, R. N.
1963   *The Heritage of Persia.* Cambridge, Massachusetts.
1964   "The charisma of kingship in Ancient Iran." *IA* 4: 36–54.
1972a "Gestures of deference to royalty in Ancient Iran." *IA* 9: 102–7.
1972b "The institutions." Pp. 83–93 in Walser (ed.).
1974   "Persepolis again." *JNES* 33: 383–86.
1975   "Mithra in Iranian history." *Mithraic Studies* 2: 62–67.
1977   "Remarks on kingship in Ancient Iran." *AAH* 25: 75–82.
1982   "The 'Aramaic' inscription on the tomb of Darius." *IA* 17: 85–90.
1983   "Achaemenid echoes in Sasanian times." Pp. 247–52 in H. Koch and D. McKenzie (eds.), *Kunst, Kultur und Geschichte der Achämenidenzeit und ihr Fortleben.* AMI suppl. 10. Berlin.
1984   *The History of Ancient Iran.* Munich.
1985   "Zoroastrian incest." Pp. 445–55 in *Studi Tucci,* vol. I. Rome.

Gabelmann, H.
1979   "Zur Chronologie der Königsnekropole von Sidon." *AK* 94: 163–77.
1984   *Antike Audienz-und Tribunalszenen.* Darmstadt.

Gabrielli, M.
1995   "Transports et logistique militaire dans l'*Anabase.*" Pp. 109–22 in P. Briant (ed.), *Dans les pas des Dix-Mille: Peuple et pays du Proche-Orient vus par un Grec* (Actes de la Table ronde de Toulouse, 3–4 février 1995). Pallas 43.

Gaggero, G.
1986   "Considerazione sulla legende di Sesostri nella tradizione greco-romana." Pp. 1–19 in *Sesta Historia Antiqua* 15. Rome.

Galikowski, M.
1988   "La route de l'Euphrate d'Isidore à Julien." Pp. 76–98 in *La Géographie historique du Proche-Orient.* Paris.

Galling, K.
1963 "Echmunazar und der Herr der Könige." *ZDPV*: 140–51.
1964 *Studien zur Geschichte Israels im persischen Zeitalter*. Tübingen.

Gallo, P., and Masson, O.
1993 "Une stèle 'hellénomenphite' de l'ex-collection Nahman." *BIFAO* 93: 265–76.

Gallota, B.
1980 *Dario e l'Occidente prima della guerre persiane*. Milan.

Garbini, G.
1984 "Tetramnestos, re di Sidone." *RSF* 12: 3–7.

Gardin, J. C.
1980 "L'archéologie du paysage bactrien." *CRAI*: 480–501.
1986 "Migrateurs et porteurs de pots en Bactriane de l'âge du bronze à nos jours." Pp. 79–94 in M. T. Barrelet (ed.), *À propos des interprétations archéologiques de la poterie*. Paris.
1995 "Fortified sites of Eastern Bactria (Afghanistan) in pre-hellenistic times." Pp. 83–105 in A. Invernizzi (ed.), *In the land of Gryphon: Papers on Central Asian Archaeology in Antiquity*. Florence.

Gardin, J. C., and Gentelle, P.
1976 "Irrigation et peuplement dans la plaine d'Aï-Khanoum de l'époque achéménide à l'époque musulmane." *BEFEO* 63: 59–99.
1979 "L'exploitation du sol en Bactriane antique." *BEFEO* 66: 1–29.

Gardin, J. C., and Lyonnet, B.
1978–79 "La prospection archéologique de la Bactriane orientale (1974–78): Premiers résultats." *Mesopotamia* 13–14: 99–154.

Gardiner, A. B.
1938 "The mansion of life and the master of the King's largess." *JEA* 24: 83–91.

Gardiner, A. B., and Garden, J.
1987 "Dareios' Scythian expedition and its aftermath." *Klio* 69: 326–50.

Gardner, P.
1911 "The coinage of the Ionian revolt." *JHS* 21: 151–60.

Garelli, P., and Nikiprowetsky, V.
1974 *Le Proche-Orient asiatique: Les empires mésopotamiens. Israël*. Paris.

Garlan, Y.
1974 *Recherches de poliorcétique grecque*. BEFAR 223. Paris.

Garrison, M.
1988 *Seal-Workshops and Artists at Persepolis: a Study of Seal Impressions preserving the Theme of Heroic Encounter on the Persepolis Fortification and Treasury Tablets*. Ph.D. University of Michigan.
1992 "Seals and elite at Persepolis: some observations on Early Achaemenid Art." *Ars Orientalis* 21: 1–19.

forthcoming "A Persepolis fortification seal on the tablet MDP 11.308 (Louvre Sab 13078)." *JNES*.

Gasche, H.
1989 "Une résidence achéménide à 10 km au NNO de Sippar." *NABU*, note 12.
1991a "Fouilles d'Abū Qūbur. Quatrième campagne (1990). I: Chantier F. La 'résidence achéménide,' nouvelles données." *NAPR* 7: 5–9.
1991b "Héritages susiens dans l'architecture achéménide en Babylonie (sommaire)." *Orient-Express*: 20–21.
1995 "Autour des Dix-Mille: vestiges archéologiques dans les environs du 'Mur de Médie.'" Pp. 201–16 in P. Briant (ed.), *Dans les pas des Dix-Mille: Peuples et pays du Proche-Orient vus par un Grec* (Actes de la Table ronde internationale, Toulouse, 3–4 février 1995). Pallas 43.

Gauger, J.-G.
1977 "Zu einem offenen Problem des hellenistischen Hoftitelsystems: Ein persische Ehrentitel *suggenès*?" Pp. 137–58 in *Bonner Festgabe J. Straub*. Beihefte d. Bonner Jahrbücher 39. Bonn.

Gauthier, P.
1966 "Le parallèle Himère-Salamine au ve et au ive siècle av. J.-C." *REA*: 5–32.
1989 *Nouvelles Inscriptions de Sardes*. Geneva.
1991 "Ateleia tou sômatos." *Chiron* 21: 49–68.

Gelb, I. J.
1965 "The ancient Mesopotamian ration system." *JNES* 24: 230–43.

Geller, M.
1990 "Babylonian astronomical diaries and corrections of Diodorus." *BSOAS* 53/1: 1–7.

Genito, B.
1986a "The Medes: A reassessment of the archaeological evidence." *EW* 36/1–3: 11–81.
1986b "Dahan-i Ghulaman: une città achemenide tra centro e periferia dell'Impero." *OA* 25: 287–317.

Gentet, D., and Maucourant, J.
1991 "Une étude critique de la hausse des prix à l'ère ramesside." *DHA* 17/1: 13–31.

George, A. R.
1993 "Babylon revisited: archaeology and philology in harness." *Antiquity* 67: 734–46.

Gerardi, P.
1987 *Aššurbanipal's Elamite Campaigns: a Literary and Political Study*. Ph.D. University of Pennsylvania.
1988 "Epigraphs and Assyrian palaces." *JCS* 40/1: 1–35.

Germain, G.
1956 "Le songe de Xerxès et le rite babylonien du substitut royal: Étude sur Hérodote VII 12–18." *REG* 69: 303–13.

Gershevitch, I.
1964 "Zoroaster's own contribution." *JNES* 23: 12–38.

1967   The Avestan Hymn to Mithra. Cambridge.
1969   "Iranian nouns and names in Elamite
       garb." TPhS: 165–99.
1979   "The false Smerdis." AAH 27: 337–52.
1983   "Extrapolation of Old Pedrsian from Elam-
       ite." Pp. 51–56 in H. Koch and D. M. Mac-
       kenzie (eds.), Kunst, Kultur und Geschichte
       der Achämenidenzeit und ihr Fortleben.
       Berlin.
Gese, W.
1984   "Wisdom literature in the Persian period."
       CHJ 1: 189–218.
Geysels, L.
1974   "Polis oikoumenē dans l'Anabase de Xéno-
       phon." LEC 42: 29–38.
Ghiron-Bistagne, P.
1992–93 "À propos du 'Vase des Perses' au musée
       de Naples: Une nouvelle interprétation?"
       Pp. 145–58 in P. Ghiron-Bistagne, A. Mo-
       reau, and J. C. Turpin (eds.), Les Perses
       d'Eschyle. Cahiers du GITA 7. Montpellier.
Ghirshman, R.
1945   "À propos de l'écriture cunéiforme vieux-
       perse." JNES 24: 244–50.
1951   L'Iran des origines à l'Islam. Paris.
1954   Village perse-achéménide. MDFI 36. Paris.
1957   "Notes iraniennes VII: à propos de Persé-
       polis." Artibus Asiae 20: 265–78.
1958   Review of V. M. Masson, Istoria Midii (Le-
       ningrad, 1956). BiOr 15/5: 257–61.
1962   Perse: Proto-Iraniens, Mèdes, Achéménides.
       Paris.
1976a "Les Daivadâna." AAH 24: 3–14.
1976b Terrasses sacrées de Bard-è Nechendeh et de
       Masjid-i Solaiman. MDFAI 45. Paris.
Gibson, J. C. L.
1982   Textbook of Syrian Semitic Inscriptions, I:
       Phoenician Inscriptions. Oxford.
1987   Textbook of Syrian Semitic Inscriptions, II:
       Aramaic Inscriptions. Oxford.
Gibson, McG.
1972   The City and Area of Kish. Miami.
1992   "Patterns of occupation at Nippur." Pp. 33–
       54 in M. de Jong Ellis (ed.), Nippur at the
       Centennial: Papers Read at the 35th RAI
       (Philadelphia 1988). Philadelphia: The
       University Museum.
Gignoux, P.
1977   "Le dieu Baga en Iran." AAH 25: 119–27.
Gillis, D.
1979   Collaboration with the Persians. Wiesbaden.
Giovannini, A.
1990   "Le Parthénon: le trésor d'Athènes et le
       tribut des alliés." Historia 39: 129–48.
Giovinazzo, G.
1983   "28 testi della Mesopotamia datati al regno
       di Ciro." AION 43/4: 534–89.
1989a "L'expression ha duš ha du ka dans les
       textes de Persépolis." Akkadica 63: 12–26.
1989b "Présence babylonienne dans les textes
       économiques de Persépolis." AION 49/3:
       201–7.

1989c "NP hiše dans les textes achéménides."
       AION 49/3: 209–17.
1989d "The tithe ešrû in Neo-Babylonian and
       Achaemenid period." Pp. 95–106 in Briant
       and Herrenschmidt (eds.).
1993   "Les saumarraš dans les textes de Persépo-
       lis." AION 53/2: 121–27.
1994a "Les documents de voyage dans les textes
       de Persépolis." AION 54/1: 18–31.
1994b "Les voyages de Darius dans les régions ori-
       entales de l'empire." AION 54/1: 32–45.
Girard, P.
1909   "Les signaux lumineux dans l'Agamemnon
       d'Eschyle." REG 11: 289–95.
Gitton, M.
1984   Les Divines Épouses de la 18e dynastie.
       Paris.
Glassner, J. J.
1993   Chroniques mésopotamiennes. Paris.
Glombiowski, K.
1986   "Fragments de Ctésias de Cnide chez Dio-
       dore et chez Élien non cités par Jacoby
       (FGrHIST 688)." Eos 74: 77–83.
1990   "Die Eroberung Babylons durch Kyros im
       orientalischer und griechischer Überliefer-
       ung." Das Altertum 36/1: 49–55.
Gnoli, G.
1967   Ricerche storiche sul Seistan antico. Rome.
1974   "Politique religieuse et conception de la ro-
       yauté chez les Achéménides." Acta Iranica
       1/2: 117–90.
1979   "Sol persice Mithra." Pp. 725–40 in Myste-
       ria Mithrae. EPRO 80. Leiden-Rome.
1980   Zoroaster's time and homeland. Rome.
1981   "Antico-persiano anušiya e gli Immortali di
       Erodoto." Pp. 266–80 in Mon. Morgen-
       stierne I. Acta Iranica 5.
1982   "Le 'Fravasi' e l'immortalità." Pp. 339–47
       in La Mort: les morts dans les sociétés anci-
       ennes. Cambridge.
1983   "Le dieu des Arya." STIR 12/1: 7–22.
1984a "L'évolution du dualisme iranien et le
       problème zurvanite." RHR 201/2: 115–38.
1984b "Note sullo 'Xvaranah-.'" Orientalia Du-
       chesne-Guillemin: 207–18.
1985   De Zoroastre à Mani: Quatre leçons au
       Collège de France. Travaux de l'Institut d'é-
       tudes iraniennes 11. Paris.
1988a "Basileus Basileôn Arianôn." Pp. 509–32 in
       Orientalia: Studi Tucci, III. Rome.
1988b "A note on the Magi and Eudemus of
       Rhodes." Pp. 283–88 in A Green Leaf (Pa-
       pers Asmussen).
1988c "Cyrus et Zoroastre: une hypothèse." Pp.
       201–16 in P. Gignoux (ed.), La Commémor-
       ation: Colloque du centenaire de la Sec-
       tion des sciences religieuses de l'EPHE.
       Paris.
1989   The Idea of Iran: An Essay on its Origin.
       ISME, Seria Orientale Roma 62. Rome.
1990   "On Old Persian Farnah." Pp. 83–92 in Pa-
       pers Yarshater.

Gobineau, J. A. de
1869 *Histoire des Perses d'après les auteurs orientaux, grecs et latins* II. Paris. [Repr., Tehran 1976]

Goblot, H.
1963 "Dans l'ancien Iran: les techniques de l'eau et la grande histoire." *Annales ESC:* 499–520.
1979 *Les Qanats: Une technique d'acquisition de l'eau.* Paris–La Haye.

Godron, G.
1986 "Notes sur l'histoire de la médecine et de l'occupation perse en Égypte." Pp. 285–97 in *Hommages à Fr. Daumas.* Montpellier.

Goedicke, H.
1985 "Comments on the Satrap Stela." *BES* 6: 33–54.

Goetze, A.
1962 "Cilicians." *JCS* 16: 48–58.

Goldman, B.
1965 "Persian fire temples or tombs?" *JNES* 24/4: 305–8.
1974 "Political realia on Persepolitan sculptures." *OLP* 5: 31–45.

Goldstein, S. M.
1980 "Pre-persian and Persian glass: some observations on objects in the Corning Museum of glass." Pp. 47–52 in Schmandt-Besserat (ed.).

Gomme, A. W.; Andrewes, A.; and Dover, K. J.
1981 *Historical Commentary on Thucydides, V: Book VIII.* Oxford.

Gonda, J.
1975 "Mitra in India." *Mithraic Studies* 1: 40–52.

Goossens, G.
1940 "L'histoire d'Assyrie de Ctésias." *AC* 9: 25–45.
1949 "Artistes et artisans étrangers en Perse sous les Achéménides." *La Nouvelle Clio* 1–2: 31–44.
1950 "Le sommaire des *Persica* de Ctésias par Photius." *RBPh:* 513–21.
1952 "L'Assyrie après l'Empire." Pp. 84–100 in *3ᵉ RAI.* Leiden.

Goukowsky, P.
1974 "Les juments du roi Érythras." *REG* 87: 111–37.
1976 *Diodore de Sicile: Livre XVII.* Paris.
1978 *Essai sur le mythe d'Alexandre (336–270 av. J.-C.),* I: *Les Origines politiques.* Nancy.
1981 *Essai sur le mythe d'Alexandre (336–270 av. J.-C.),* II: *Alexandre et Dionysos.* Nancy.

Gould, J.
1991 *Give and Take in Herodotus.* The fifteenth J. L. Myres memorial Lecture. Oxford.

Goyon, S.
1957a "Les ports des pyramides et le grand canal de Memphis." *RdE* 23: 137–53.
1957b *Nouvelles Inscriptions du Wadi Hammamat.* Paris.
1971 "Kerkeasôre et l'ancien observatoire d'Eudoxe." *BIFAO* 74: 135–47.

Grabbe, L. L.
1991 "Reconstructing history from the Book of Ezra." Pp. 98–106 in P. R. Davies (ed.).
1992a "Who was the Bagoas of Josephus (Ant. 11.7.1, 297–301)?" *Trans* 5: 49–61.
1992b *Judaism from Cyrus to Hadrian, Vol. I: The Persian and Greek Periods.* Minneapolis.
1994 "What was Ezra's mission?" Pp. 276–89 in T. Eskenazi and H. R. Richards (eds.), *Second Temple Studies, II: Temple and Community in the Persian Period.* JSOT suppl. 175. Sheffield.

Graeve, M. C. de
1981 *The Ships of the Ancient Near East (c. 2000–500 B.C.).* OLA 7. Louvain.

Graf, D.
1979 *Medism: Greek Collaboration with Achaemenid Persia.* Ph.D. University of Michigan.
1984 "Medism: the origin and significance of the term." *JHS* 104: 15–30.
1985 "Greek tyrants and Achaemenid Politics." Pp. 79–123 in *The Craft of the Ancient Historian: Essays in Honor of C. G. Starr.* Lanham.
1990a "Arabia during Achaemenid times." *AchHist* 4: 131–48.
1990b "The origins of the Nabateans." *ARAM* 2/1–2: 45–75.
1993 "The Persian royal road system in Syria–Palestine." *Trans* 6: 149–68.
1994 "The Persian royal road system." *AchHist* 8: 167–89.

Grayson, A. K.
1975a *Babylonian Historical-Literary Texts.* Toronto Semitic Texts and Studies 3. University of Toronto Press.
1975b *Assyrian and Babylonian Chronicles.* Locust Valley, New York.
1987 "Akkadian treaties of the seventh century B.C." *JCS* 39: 127–60.
1991 *Assyrian Rulers of the Early first Millennium B.C., I: 1114–859 B.C.* ARIM, Assyrian Periods 2. Toronto-Buffalo-London.

Graziani, S.
1978 "Su un'interpretazioni achemenide di Bes." *AION* 38/1: 53–61.
1979 "Ancient Near Eastern seals from the Nayeri collection." *EW* 29: 177ff.
1983 "I testi mesopotamici achemenidi del regno di Ciro contenuti in BE VIII." *AION* 43/1: 1–31.
1986 *I testi mesopotamici datati al regno di Serse (485–465 a.C.).* Rome.
1989 "Le impronte di sigilli delle tavolette mesopotamiche del British Museum pubblicate da J. M. Strassmaier, datate a Ciro, Cambise, Dario e Serse." *AION* 49/3: 161–200.
1991 *Testi editi ed inediti datati al regno di Bardiya (522 a.C.).* Suppl. AION 67. Naples.

Greenfield, J. C.
1972 "*Hamarakara > 'Amarkal." Pp. 180–86 in *Henning Memorial Volume.*

1977 "On some Iranian terms in the Elephantine papyri: Aspects of continuity." *AAH* 25: 113–18.
1985 "Aramaic in the Achaemenian Empire." *CHI* 2: 698–713.
1986 "Aspects of archives in the Achaemenid period." Pp. 289–95 in Veenhof (ed.).
1988 "Découvertes épigraphiques récentes au service de l'histoire, du retour de l'exil à la révolte de Bar-Kokhba." Pp. 41–53 in E. Laperrousaz (ed.), *Archéologie, art et histoire de la Palestine.* Paris.
1991 "Of scribes, scripts and languages." Pp. 173–85 in *Poikila grammata: Lire et écrire en Méditerranée.* Studia Phoenicia 13. Louvain.

Greenfield, J. C., and Porten, B.
1982 *The Bisutun Inscription of Darius the Great: Aramaic Version.* Corpus Inscriptionum Iranicarum 1: Inscriptions of Ancient Iran. London.

Greenwalt, C. H., Jr.
1978a "Lydian elements in the material culture of Sadis." Pp. 37–45 in *The Proceedings of the Xth Congress of Classical Archaeology.*
1978b *Ritual Dinners in Early Historic Sardis.* University of California Publ., Class. Studies 17. University of California Press.
1992 "When a mighty Empire was destroyed: the common man at the fall of Sardis, ca. 546 B.C." *PAPS* 136/2: 247–71.
1995 "Sardis around 400 B.C." Pp. 125–45 in P. Briant (ed.), *Dans les pas des Dix-Mille: Peuples et pays du Proche-Orient vus par un Grec* (Actes de la Table ronde internationale de Toulouse, 3–4 février 1995). Pallas 43.

Greenwalt, C. H., Jr., and Heywood, A. M.
1992 "A helmet of the Sixth Cent. B.C. from Sardis." *BASOR:* 1–31.

Greenwalt, C. H., Jr.; Ratté, C.; and Rautman, M. L.
1994 "The Sardis campaigns of 1988 and 1989." Pp. 1–43 in W. G. Dever (ed.), *Preliminary Excavation Reports: Sardis, Paphos, Caesarea Maritima, Shiqmim, Ain Ghazal.* AASOR 51.

Grégoire, H.
1908 "Note sur une inscription gréco-araméenne trouvée à Farasa (Ariaramneia-Rhodandos)." *CRAI:* 434–47.

Grelot, P.
1955 "Le papyrus Pascal et le problème du Pentateuque." *VT* 5: 250–65.
1964 "L'huile de ricin à Éléphantine." *Semitica* 14: 63–70.
1967 "La reconstruction du temple juif d'Éléphantine." *Orientalia:* 173–77.
1970a "La communauté juive d'Éléphantine." *CdE* 45: 120–31.
1970b "Essai de restauration du papyrus A.P. 26." *Semitica:* 23–32.
1971a "Études sur les textes araméens d'Éléphantine." *RB* 78: 515–41.
1971b "Notes d'onomastique sur les textes araméens d'Égypte." *Semitica* 21: 95–117.
1972 *Documents araméens d'Égypte.* Paris.
1981 "Sur le 'papyrus Pascal' d'Éléphantine." Pp. 163–72 in *Festschrift H. Cazelles.* AOAT 212.

Grenet, F.
1983 "L'onomastique iranienne à Aï-Khanoum." *BCH* 107/1: 373–81.
1984 *Les Pratiques funéraires dans l'Asie centrale sédentaire, de la conquête grecque à l'islamisation.* CNRS. Paris.
1991 "Mithra au temple principal d'Aï Khanoum?" Pp. 147–51 in P. Bernard and F. Grenet (eds.).

Griffith, G. T.
1968 "The letter of Darius at Arrian 2.14." *PCPS* 14: 33–48.

Griffith, J. G.
1953 "*Basileus basileôn:* remarks on the history of a title." *ClPh* 48/3: 145–54.

Griffith, L.
1909 *Catalogue of the Demotic Papyri in the John Rylands Library, III: King-Lists, Commentaries and Indices.* Manchester-London.

Griffiths, A.
1987 "Democedes of Croton: a Greek doctor at Darius' court." *AchHist* 2: 35–71.

Grillot, F.
1986 "Une tablette achéménide inédite." *AMI* 19: 149–50.
1990 "Les textes de fondation du palais de Suse." *JA:* 213–22.

Grillot-Susini, F.
1987 *Éléments de grammaire élamite.* Paris.

Grillot-Susini, F.; Herrenschmidt, C.; and Malbran-Labat, F.
1993 "La version élamite de la trilingue de Béhistoun: une nouvelle lecture." *JA* 281/1–2: 19–59.

Gropp, D. M.
1986 *The Samaria Papyri from Wadi ed-Daliyeh: The Slave-Sales.* Ph.D. Harvard University.

Gropp, G.
1984 "Herrscherethos und Kriegsführung bei Achämeniden und Makedonen." Pp. 32–42 in *Festschrift K. Fischer: Aus dem Osten des Alexanderreiches* (ed. J. Ozols and V. Thewalt). Cologne.

Grosso, F.
1958 "Gli Eretriesi deportati in Persia." *RFIC* 86: 351–75.

Gryaznov, M.
1969 *Sibérie du Sud.* Geneva-Paris-Munich.

Grzybek, E.
1990 *Du calendrier macédonien au calendrier ptolémaïque: Problèmes de chronologie hellénistique.* Basel.

Gschnitzer, F.
1977 *Die Sieben Perser und das Königtums des Dareios.* Heidelberg.
1986 "Eine pesische Kultstiftung in Sardeis und die 'Sippengötter' Vorderasiens." Pp. 45–54 in *Im Bannkreis des Alten Orients (Festchr. K. Obenhuber).* Innsbruck.
1988 "Zur Stellung des persischen Stammlandes im Achaimenidenreich." Pp. 87–122 in *Festschrift Deller.* AOAT 220.

Gubel, E.
1990 "Tell Kazel (Sumur/Simyra) à l'époque perse: Résultats préliminaires des trois premières campagnes de fouilles de l'Université américaine de Beyrouth (1985–87)." *Trans* 2: 37–50.

Guépin, J. P.
1963–64 "On the positions of Greek artists under Achaemenid rule." *Persica* 1: 34–52.

Gunn, B.
1926 "The inscribed sarcophagi in the Serapeum." *ASAE* 26: 82–91.
1943 "Notes on the Naukratis stela." *JEA* 29: 55–59.

Gunter, A.
1985 "Looking at Hekatomnid patronage from Labraunda." *REA* 87/1–2: 113–24.
1988 "The Art of eating and drinking in Ancient Iran." *Asian Art* 1/2: 7–54.

Gunter, A., and Jetts, P.
1992 *Ancient Iranian Metalwork in the Arthur M. Sackler Gallery and the Freer Gallery of Art.* Washington, D.C.: Smithsonian Institution.

Gunter, A. C.
1990 "Models of the Orient in the art history of the orientalizing period." *AchHist* 5: 131–48.

Guralnik, E. (ed.)
1987 *Sardis: Twenty-Seven Years of Discovery.* Chicago.

Gusmani, R.
1964 *Lydisches Wörterbuch.* Heidelberg.
1975 *Neue epichorische Schriftzeugnisse aus Sardis (1958–1971).* Arch. explor. of Sardis, Monograph 3. Cambridge, Massachusetts.
1980 *Lydisches Wörterbuch: Ergänzungsband. I Lieferung.* Heidelberg.
1982 "Zwei Graffiti aus Sardis und Umgebung." *Kadmos* 21/2: 125–29.
1983 "Ein Weihraucher mit lydischer Inschrift im Metropolitan Museum." *Kadmos* 22: 56–61.

Guyot, P.
1980 *Eunuchen als Sklaven und Freigelassenen in der griechisch-römischen Antike.* Stuttgarter Beiträge zur Geschichte und Politik 14. Klett-Cotta.

Gyles, M. F.
1959 *Pharaonic Policies and Administration (663–323).* Chapel Hill, North Carolina.

Haebler, C.
1982 "Karanos: Eine sprachwissenschaftliche Betrachtung zu Xen. Hell. I 4, 3." Pp. 81–90 *Serta Indogermanica = FS Neumann.* Innsbruck.

Haerinck, E.
1973 "Le palais achéménide de Babylone." *IA* 10: 108–32.
1984 "L'Iran méridional, des Achéménides jusqu'à l'avènement de l'Islam: Bilan des recherches." Pp. 299–306 in R. Boucharlat and J. F. Salles (eds.), *Arabie orientale: Mésopotamie et Iran méridional de l'âge du fer au début de la période islamique.* Paris.
1987 "La neuvième satrapie: archéologie confronte histoire?" *AchHist* 1: 139–46.

Hahn, I.
1981 "Periöken und Periökenbesitz in Lykien." *Klio* 63: 51–61.
1985 "Zur Frage der Sklavensteuer im frühen Hellenismus." Pp. 56–64 in H. Kreissig and F. Kühnert (eds.), *Antike Abhängigkeitsformen in den Griechischen Gebieten ohne Polisstruktur und den Römischen Provinzen.* Schrift. z. Gesch. und Kultur der Antike 25. Berlin.

Hall, A. S.
1986 "RECAM, notes and studies no. 9: The Milyadeis and their territory." *AnSt* 36: 137–57.

Hallock, R. T.
1950 "New light from Persepolis." *JNES* 9: 237–52.
1960 "A new look at the Persepolis treasury tablets." *JNES* 19: 90–100.
1969 *Persepolis Fortification Tablets.* OIP 92. Chicago.
1972 *The Evidence of the Persepolis Tablets.* Cambridge.
1973 "The Persepolis fortification archive." *Orientalia* 47: 320–23.
1974 "Persepolis again." *JNES* 33: 383–86.
1977 "The use of seals on the Persepolis fortification tablets." Pp. 127–33 in McG. Gibson and D. Biggs (eds.), *Seals and Sealings in the Ancient Near East.* Malibu, California: Undena.
1978 "Selected fortification texts." *CDAFI* 8: 109–36.

Hamilton, J. R.
1969 *Plutarch, Alexander: A Commentary.* Oxford.
1987 "Alexander's Iranian policy." Pp. 467–86 in *FS G. Wirth,* I.

Hammond, N. G. L.
1967 "The origins and the nature of the Athenian alliance of 478/7." *JHS* 87: 41–61.
1986 "The kingdom of Asia and the Persian throne." *Antichton* 20: 73–85.
1988a "The expedition of Datis and Artaphernes." *CAH* 4²: 491–517.

1988b "The expedition of Xerxes." CAH 4²: 518–91.

1990 "Royal pages, personal pages and boys trained in the Macedonian manner during the period of the Temenid monarchy." Historia 39/3: 261–90.

1991 "The Macedonian defeat near Samarkand." AW 22/2: 41–47.

1992a "The archaeological and literary evidence for the burning of Persepolis palace." CQ 42/2: 358–64.

1992b "Alexander's charge at the battle of Issus in 333 B.C." Historia 41/4: 396–406.

1994 "One or two passes at the Cilicia-Syria border?" AW 25/1: 15–26.

Hammond, N. G. L., and Griffith, G. T.
1979 A History of Macedonia, I–II. Oxford.

Hanaway, W. L.
1990 "Alexander and the question of Iranian identity." Pp. 93–103 in Papers Yarshater.

Hanfmann, G. M. A.
1966 "The new stelae from Daskylion." BASOR 184: 10–13.

1975 From Croesus to Constantine: The Cities of Western Asia Minor and their Arts in Greek and Roman Times. Ann Arbor, Michigan.

1978 "Lydian relations with Ionia and Persia." Pp. 25–35 in The proceedings of the Xth International Congress of Classical Archaeology.

1983a "On the gods of Lydian Sardis." Pp. 219–31 in FS K. Bittel. Mainz.

1983b Sardis from Prehistoric to the Roman Times: Results of the Archaeological Exploration of Sardis 1958–1975. Cambridge, Massachusetts–London.

1985 "Les nouvelles fouilles de Sardes." CRAI: 498–519.

1987 "The sacrilege inscription: the ethnic, linguistic, social and religious at Sardis at the end of the Persian era." BAI 1: 1–8.

Hanfmann, G. M. A., and Mierse, W. E.
1983 Sardis from Prehistoric to Roman Times. Cambridge, Massachusetts–London.

Hanfmann, G. M. A., and Waldbaum, J. C.
1969 "Kybebe and Artemis: Two Anatolian Goddesses at Sardis." Archaeology 22/4: 264–69.

1975 Archaeological Exploration of Sardis: A Survey of Sardis and the Major Monuments outside the City Walls. Harvard.

Hannaway, W. L.
1982 "Anàhita and Alexander." JAOS 102: 285–95.

Hansen, O.
1986 "The purported letter of Darius to Gadatas." RhM 129/1: 95–96.

Hansman, J.
1972 "Elamites, Achaemenians and Anshan." Iran 10: 101–25.

1975 "An Achaemenian stronghold." Acta Iranica 16 (= Monumentum H. S. Nyberg, III): 289–309.

1985 "Anšan in the Median and Achaemenid period." CHI 2: 25–35.

Hanson, R. S.
1968 "Aramaic funerary and boundary inscriptions from Asia Minor." BASOR 12: 3–11.

Happ, H.
1992 "Zu asgandès, askandès, astandès = "Bote." Glotta 11: 198–201.

Harmatta, J.
1953 "A recently discovered Old Persian inscription." AAH 2/1–2: 1–14.

1959 "Irano-Aramaica: Zur Geschichte des frühhellenistischen Judentums in Ägypten." AAH 7: 337–400.

1963 "Der Problem der Kontinuität im frühhellenistischen Ägypten." AAH: 199–213.

1964 "Das Problem der Sklaverei im altpersischen Reich." Pp. 3–11 in Neue Beiträge zur Geschichte der Alten Welt, I.

1971 "The rise of the Old Persian Empire: Cyrus the Great." AAH 19: 4–15.

1974 "Les modèles littéraires de l'édit babylonien de Cyrus." Acta Iranica 1: 29–44.

1976 "Darius' expedition against the Saka Tigraxauda." AAH 25: 15–24.

1979 "Royal power and immortality: The myth of two eagles in Iranian royal ideology." AAH 27: 305–19.

Harper, P. O.
1978 The Royal Hunter: Art of the Sassanian Empire. The Asian Society.

Harper, P.; Aruz, J.; and Tallon, F. (eds.)
1992 The Royal City of Susa: Ancient Near Eastern Treasures in the Louvre. New York.

Harrison, C. M.
1982a Coins of the Persian Satraps. Ph.D. University of Pennsylvania.

1982b "Persian names on coins of Northern Anatolia." JNES 41/3: 181–94.

Hartner, W.
1985 "Old Iranian calendars." CHI 2: 714–92.

Hatzfeld, J.
1946 "Agésilas et Artaxerxès II." BCH 70: 238–46.

1951 Alcibiade. Paris.

Hatzopoulos, M.
1982 "A reconsideration of the Pixodaros affair." Pp. 59–66 in Macedonia and Greece in Late Classical and Early Hellenistic Time. Studies in History of Art 10. Washington.

Hatzopoulos, M., and Loukopolou, L. D.
1992 Recherches sur les marches orientales des Téménides (Anthémonte-Kalindoia). Athens-Paris.

Hauben, H.
1970 "The king of the Sidonians and the Persian imperial fleet." AncSoc 1: 1–8.

1973 "The chief commanders of the Persian fleet in 480 B.C." AncSoc 4: 23–37.

1975–76 "Antigonos' invasion plan for his attack on Egypt in 306 B.C." Pp. 267–71 in Miscellanea in honorem J. Vergote. OLP 6–7.

1976 "The expansion of Macedonian sea-power under Alexander the Great." *AncSoc* 7: 79–105.

Hawkins, J. D., and Postgate, J. N.
1988 "Tribute from Tabal." *SAAB* 2/1: 31–40.

Hayes, J. M., and Miller, J. M.
1977 *Israelite and Judean History.* London.

Head, D.
1992 *The Achaemenian Persian Army.* Stockport: Montvert.

Heckel, W.
1992 *The Marshalls of Alexander's Empire.* London–New York.

Hegyi, D.
1966 "The historical background of the Ionian revolt." *AAH* 14: 285–302.
1971 "Der ionische Aufstand und die Regierungsmethoden Dareios' I." *Das Altertum* 17: 142–50.
1983 "Athens und die Achämeniden in der zweiten Hälfte des 5. Jhrdts. v.u.Z." *Oikuménè* 4: 53–59.

Heidorn, L. A.
1991 "The Saïte and Persian period forts at Dorginarti." Pp. 205–19 in *Egypt and Africa: Nubia from Prehistory to Islam* (ed. W. W. Davies). London.
1992 *The Fortress of Dorgirnarti and Lower Nubia during the Seventh to Fifth Centuries B.C.* Ph.D. University of Chicago.

Heinrichs, A.
1976 "Despoina Kybele: ein Beitrag zur religiösen Namenskunde." *HSCP* 80: 253–86.

Heinrichs, J.
1987 "'Asiens König': Die Inschriften des Kyrosgrabs und das Achämenidische Reichsverständnis." Pp. 487–540 in *FS G. Wirth*, I.
1989 *Ionien nach Salamis: Die kleinasiatischen Griechen in der Politik und politischer Reflexion des Mutterlandes.* Antiquitas 1/39. Bonn.

Heisserer, A. J.
1981 *Alexander the Great and the Greeks.* University of Oklahoma Press.

Helm, P. R.
1980 *"Greeks" in the Neo-Assyrian Levant and "Assyria" in early Greek Writers.* Ph.D. University of Pennsylvania.
1981 "Herodotus' *Medikos logos* and Median history." *Iran* 19: 85–90.

Heltzer, M.
1979 "À propos des banquets des rois achéménides et du retour d'exil sous Zorobabel." *RB* 86: 102–6.
1981 "The story of Susanna and the self-government of the Jewish community in Achaemenid Babylonia." *AION* 41/1: 35–39.
1989a "The Persepolis documents, the Lindos Chronicle and the Book of Judith." *PdP* 245: 81–101.
1989b "The social and fiscal reforms of Nehemia in Judah and the attitude of the Achaemenid Kings to the internal affairs of the autonomous provinces." *Apollinaris* 62: 333–54.
1991 "The early relations of Cyprus and Anatolia, the kypros measure and the Achaemenid land-tax." *RDAC*: 157–62.
1992a "The provincial taxation in the Achaemenian Empire and 'Forty shekel of silver (Neh. 5.15).'" *Michmanim* 6: 15–25.
1992b "A recently published Babylonian tablet and the province of Judah after 516 B.C." *Trans* 5: 57–61.
1992c "Again on some problems of the Achaemenid taxation in the province of Judah." *AMI* 25 [1994]: 173–75.
1994 "Neh. 11.24 and the provincial representation at the Persian court." *Trans* 8: 109–19.

Henkelman, W.
forthcoming "The Royal Achaemenid crown." *AMI.*

Henning, W. B.
1954 "The 'coin' with cuneiform inscriptions." *NC* 16: 327–28.

Herman, G.
1987 *Ritualised Friendship and the Greek City.* Cambridge University Press.

Hermary, A.
1984 "Un nouveau relief 'gréco-perse' en Cilicie." *RA*: 289–99.
1987 "Amathonte de Chypre et les Phéniciens." *Studia Phoenicia* 5: 357–88.

Herr, L. G.
1992 "Epigraphic finds from Tell El-ʿUmeiri during the 1989 season." *AUSS* 30/3: 187–200.

Herrenschmidt, C.
1976 "Désignations de l'Empire et concepts politiques de Darius Iᵉʳ d'après ses inscriptions en vieux-perse." *STIR* 5/1: 33–65.
1977 "Les créations d'Ahuramazda." *STIR* 6/1: 17–58.
1979a "La Perse, rien que la Perse: Essai sur la royauté d'Ariyaramnès et d'Arsamès." Pp. 5–21 in *Pad Nâm i Yazdân.* Travaux de l'Institut d'études iraniennes 9. Paris.
1979b "La première royauté de Darius avant l'invention de la notion d'Empire." Pp. 23–33 in *Pad Nâm i Yazdân.* Travaux de l'Institut d'études iraniennes 9. Paris.
1980a "La religion des Achéménides: État de la question." *STIR* 9/2: 325–39.
1980b "L'Empire perse achéménide." Pp. 69–102 in M. Duverger (ed.), *Le Concept d'Empire.* Paris.
1980c *Les Inscriptions achéménides en vieux-perse, élamite et accadien: Aspects d'une analyse formelle et tentative d'interprétation.* Third-year thesis, EPHE, Vᵉ section. Paris (type-written).
1982 "Les historiens de l'Empire achéménide et l'inscription de Bisotun." *Annales ESC* 37: 813–23.

1983a "Sur la charte de fondation *DSaa*." *RAss* 77: 177–79.
1983b "Notes sur les deux textes accadiens de Persépolis." *RAss* 77: 180.
1985 "Une lecture iranisante du poème de Symmachos dédié à Arbinas, dynaste de Xanthos." *REA* 87/1–2: 125–36.
1987a "Aspects universalistes de la religion et de l'idéologie de Darius Iᵉʳ." Pp. 617–25 in *Orientalia Iosephi Tucci memoriae dicata*. Rome.
1987b "Notes sur la parenté chez les Perses au début de l'Empire achéménide." *AchHist* 2: 53–67.
1988 "Il était une fois dans l'Est." Pp. 301–39 in *L'Impensable polythéisme* (ed. F. Schmidt). Paris.
1989a "Le tribut dans les inscriptions en vieux-perse et dans les tablettes élamites." Pp. 128–77 in Briant and Herrenschmidt (eds.).
1989b "Le paragraphe 70 de l'inscription de Bisotun." Pp. 193–208 in *Études irano-aryennes offertes à Gilbert Lazard*. Studia Iranica, Cahier 7. Paris.
1990a "Nugae antico-persianae." *AchHist* 4: 37–61.
1990b "Manipulations religieuses de Darius Iᵉʳ." Pp. 195–207 in *Mélanges Pierre Lévêque*, IV. Paris.
1991 "Vieux-perse ŠIYĀTI-." Pp. 13–21 in Kellens (ed.).
1993a "La poste achéménide." *DATA*, note 9.
1993b "*Aggareion-aggaros*." *DATA*, note 10.
1993c "Notes de vieux-perse III." *IIJ* 36/1: 45–50.
1994 "Les *xwétôdas*, ou mariages 'incestueux' en Iran ancien." Pp. 113–25 in P. Bonte (ed.), *Épouser au plus proche: Inceste, prohibitions et stratégies matrimoniales autour de la Méditerranée*. Paris.

Herrenschmidt, C., and Kellens, J.
1994 "La question du rituel dans le mazdéisme ancien et achéménide." *Arch. soc. rel.* 85: 45–67.

Herzfeld, H.
1968 *The Persian Empire: Studies in Geography and Ethnography of the Ancient Near East* (ed. G. Walser). Wiesbaden.

Hewsen, R. H.
1983 "The boundaries of Achaemenid Armenia." *REArm* 17: 123–43.
1984 "The boundaries of Orontid Armenia." *REArm* 18: 347–66.

Hiebert, F. D.
1992 "Pazyryk chronology and early horse nomads reconsidered." *BAI* 6: 117–29.

Higgins, W. E.
1980 "Aspects of Alexander's Imperial administration: some modern methods and views reviewed." *Athenaeum*: 129–52.

Hignett, C.
1963 *Xerxes' Invasion of Greece*. Oxford.

Hill, G. F.
1923 "Alexander the Great and the Persian lion-griffin." *JHS* 43: 156–61.

Hilprecht, H. V., and Clay, A. T.
1888 *Business Documents of Murašû Sons of Nippur, dated in the Reign of Artaxerxes I (464–424 B.C.)*. The Bab. Exp. of the University of Pennsylvania 9. Philadelphia.

Hinz, W.
1950 "The Elamite version of the record of Darius' Palace at Suse." *JNES* 9/1: 1–7.
1969 *Altiranische Funde und Forschungen*. Berlin.
1970 "Die elamischen Buchungstäfelchen der Darius-Zeit." *Orientalia* 39: 421–40.
1972a "Die Quellen." Pp. 5–14 in Walser (ed.).
1972b "Achämenidische Hofverwaltung." *ZA* 61: 260–311.
1973 *Neue Wege im Altpersischen*. Wiesbaden.
1975a "Darius und die Suezkanal." *AMI* 8: 115–21.
1975b *Altiranisches Sprachgut der Nebenüberlieferungen*. Wiesbaden.
1976 *Darius und die Perser*, I. Baden-Baden.
1986 "Zu den elamischen Briefen aus Ninive." Pp. 227–34 in *Fragmenta Historiae Elamicae*.
1987 "Elams Übergang ins Perserreich." Pp. 125–34 in *Transition Periods in Iranian History*. STIR Cahier 5. Paris-Louvain.
1988 "Grosskönig Darius und sein Untertan." Pp. 473–81 in *A Green Leaf (Papers Asmussen)*.

Hinz, W., and Koch, H. M.
1987 *Elamisches Wörterbuch*, 1–2. AMI suppl. 17. Berlin.

Hirsch, S.
1985a *The Friendship of the Barbarians: Xenophon and the Persian Empire*. Hanover-London.
1985b "1001 Iranian nights: history and fiction in Xenophon's Cyropaedia." Pp. 65–85 in *The Greek Historians: Literature and History: Papers presented to A. E. Raubitschek*. Saratoga.
1986 "Cyrus' parable of the fish: sea power in the early relations of Greece and Persia." *CJ* 81/3: 222–29.

Hodjache, S., and Berlev, O.
1977 "Le sceau de Cambyse." *CdE* 103: 37–39.

Hoffmann, H.
1961 "The Persian origin of Attic rhyta." *AK* 21–26.

Hoffmann, K.
1979 "Das Avesta in der Persis." Pp. 89–93 in J. Harmatta (ed.), *Prolegomena to the Sources on the History of Pre-Islamic Central Asia*. Budapest.

Hofmann, I., and Vorbichler, A.
1980 "Das Kambysebild bei Herodot." *AfO* 37: 86–105.

Hofstetter, J.
1972 "Zu den griechischen Gesandschaften nach Persien." Pp. 94–107 in Walser (ed.).
1978 *Die Griechen in Persien: Prosopographie der Griechen im Persischen Reich vor Alexander.* Berlin.

Högeman, P.
1985 *Alexander der Grosse und Arabien.* Munich.
1992 *Das alte Vorderasien und die Achämeniden: Ein Beitrag zur Herodot-Analyse.* Suppl. TAVO series B. Wiesbaden.

Hoglund, K. G.
1989 *Achaemenid Imperial Administration in Syria–Palestine and the Missions of Ezra and Nehemiah.* Ph.D. Duke University.
1991 "The Achaemenid context." Pp. 54–72 in P. R. Davies (ed.).
1992 *Achaemenid Imperial Administration in Syria–Palestine and the Missions of Ezra and Nehemiah.* SBL diss. Series 125. Atlanta.

Holladay, A. J.
1986 "The dentente of Callias?" *Historia* 35/4: 303–507.
1987 "The Hellenic disaster in Egypt." *JHS* 109: 176–82.

Holladay, J. S.
1982 *Cities of the Delta, III: Tell-el Maskhuta. Preliminary Report on the Wadi Tumilat Project, 1978–79.* Malibu, California.
1992 "Maskhuta, Tell el-." *The Anchor Bible Dictionary* 4: 588–92.

Holleaux, M.
1968 *Études d'épigraphie et d'histoire hellénistique, III: Lagides et Séleucides.* Paris.

Hölscher, T.
1973 *Griechische Historienbilder des 5. und 4. Jhrdt. v. Chr.* Würzburg.
1981/83 [1990] "Zur Deutung des Alexandermosaiks." *Anadolu* 22 (= *Mél. Akurgal*): 297–307.

Holt, F.
1988 *Alexander the Great and Bactria: The Formation of a Greek Frontier in Central Asis.* Leiden.

Hornblower, S.
1982 *Mausolus.* Oxford.
1983 *The Greek world (479–323 B.C.).* London–New York.
1990a "A reaction to Gunter's look at Hekatomnid patronage from Labraunda." *REA* 92/1–2: 137–39.
1990b Review of *AchHist* I–III in *CQ* 90/1: 89–95.
1994a "Persia." *CAH* 6²: 45–96.
1994b "Asia Minor." *CAH* 6²: 209–33.
1994c "Epilogue." *CAH* 6²: 876–81.

Houtkamp, J.
1991 "Some remarks on fire altars of the Achaemenid period." Pp. 23–48 in Kellens (ed.).

Houwink Ten Cate, H. J.
1961 *The Luwian Population Groups of Lycia and Cilicia Aspera during the Hellenistic Period.* Leiden.

How, W. W., and Wells, J.
1912 *A Commentary on Herodotus,* I–II. Oxford.

Huart, Cl., and Delaporte, L.
1943 *L'Iran antique: Elam et Perse et la civilisation iranienne.* Paris.

Hughes, G. R.
1984 "The so-called Pherendates correspondence." Pp. 75–86 in *Grammatica demotica: FS E. Lüddeckens.* Würzburg.

Hulin, P.
1954 "The signs on the Kabul silver piece." *NC* 14: 174–76.
1972 "An inscribed silver piece of Darius." *OLP* 3: 121–24.

Hurter, S.
1979 "Der Tissaphernes-Fund." Pp. 97–108 in Mørkholm-Waggoner (ed.).

Hüsing, G.
1933 *Porysatis und das achämenidische Lehenswesen.* Vienna.

Huss, W.
1994a "Der Rätselhäfte Pharao Chababasch." *SELVOA* 11: 97–112.
1994b "Das Haus des Nektanebis und das Haus des Ptolemaios." *AncSoc* 25: 111–17.

Huyse, P.
1990a "Die persische Medizin auf der Grundlage von Herodots *Historien.*" *AncSoc* 21: 141–48.
1990b *Iranische Namen in den griechischen Dokumenten Ägyptens.* Vienna.
1991 "Die Perser in Ägypten: Ein onomastischer Beitrag zu ihrer Erforschung." *AchHist* 6: 311–20.
1992 "'Analecta Iranica' aus dem demotischen Dokumentes von Nord-Saqqara." *JEA* 78: 287–99.

Imbert, J.
1889–90 "Pharnabazus and Tissaphernes mentioned on the great stela of Xanthus." *BOR* 4: 152–63.

In der Smitten, W. Th.
1972–74 "Historische Probleme zum Kyrosedikt und zum Jerusalemer Tempelbau von 515." *Persica* 6: 167–78.

Ingraham, M.
1986 *Theories of Imperialism and Archaeological Practices in the Study of the Perceptible Rise of the Achaemenid-Persian Empire.* Ph.D. University of Toronto.

Isager, J. (ed.)
1994 *Hekatomnid Caria and the Ionian Renaissance.* Odense University Press.

Isserlin, B. S. J.
1991 "The canal of Xerxes: facts and problems." *BSA* 86: 85–91.

Isserlin, B.; Jones, R.; Papamarinopoulos, S.;
and Uren, J.
1994 "The canal of Xerxes on the Mount Athos
peninsula: preliminary investigations in
1991–92." *BSA* 89: 277–84.

Jackson, A. V. W.
1894 "Herodotus VII.61 and the armours of the
Ancient Persians illustrated from Iranian
sources." Pp. 95–125 in *Classical Studies in
Honour of H. Drisler*. London.
1900 "The religion of the Achaemenid kings."
JAOS 21: 160–84.

Jacobs, B.
1987 *Griechische und persische Elemente in der
Grabkunst Lykiens zur Zeit der Achäme-
nidenherrschaft*. Studies in Mediterranean
Archaeology 78. Jonsered.
1991 "Der Sonnengott im Pantheon der Achämeniden." Pp. 49–80 in Kellens (ed.).
1992 "Der Tod des Bessos: Ein Beitrag zur Frage
der Verhältnisses der Achaimeniden zur
Lehre des Zoroasters." *Acta Preh. Arch.* 241:
177–86.
1993 "Die Stellung Lykiens innerhalb der achä-
menidisch-persischen Reichsverwaltung."
Pp. 63–69 in J. Borchhardt and G. Dobesch
(eds.), *Akten des II. Intern Lykien-Symposions*. ÖAW Denkschr. 231 Bd. Vienna.
1994a *Die Satrapienverwaltung im Perserreich zur
Zeit Darius' III*. Wiesbaden.
1994b "Drei Beiträge zu Fragen der Rüstung und
Bekleidung in Persien zur Achämenidenzeit." *IA* 19: 125–56.

Jacobsthal, P.
1927 *Ornamente griechischer Vasen*. Berlin.
1938 "A Sybarite Himation." *JHS* 58/2: 205–14.

Jacoby, F.
1922 "Ktesias." *RE* 290: 2032–73.

Jafarey, A. A.
1975 "Mithra, Lord of Lands." *Mithraic Studies*
1: 54–61.

Jamzadeh, P.
1982 "The winged ring with human bust in
Achaemenid art as a dynastic symbol." *IA*
17: 91–99.
1987 "The function of girdle on Achaemenid
costume in combat." *IA* 22: 267–73.
1991 *The Achaemenid Throne: Its Significance
and its Legacy*. Ph.D. University of California, Berkeley.
1992a "An Achaemenid epical poem hypothesized." *STIR* 20/2: 229–32.
1992b "The Apadana stairway reliefs and the
metaphor of conquest." *IA* 27: 125–47.
1995 "Darius' throne: temporal and eternal." *IA*
30: 1–21.

Japhet, S.
1982 "Sheshbazzar and Zerubbabel: Against the
background of the historical and religious
tendencies of Ezra–Nehemiah." *ZAW*
94/1: 66–98.

1991 "'History' and 'Literature' in the Persian
period: the restoration of the Temple."
Pp. 174–88 in *Ah Assyria! . . . Studies presented to H. Tadmor*. Scripta Hierosolymi-
tana 33. Jerusalem.

Jedelsohn, D.
1974 "A new coin-type with Hebrew inscription." *IEJ* 24/2: 77–78.

Jelinkova-Reymond, E.
1951 *Les Inscriptions guérisseuses de Dejd-Her le
Sauveur*. IFAO, Bib. ét. 23. Cairo.
1967 "Quelques recherches sur les réformes
d'Amasis." *ASAE* 54/2: 251–81.

Jidejian, N.
1969 *Tyre through the Ages*. Beirut.
1971 *Sidon through the Ages*. Beirut.

Joannès, F.
1982 *Textes économiques de la Babylonie récente*.
Paris.
1984 "Les archives d'une famille de notables
babyloniens du VIIᵉ au Vᵉ siècle av. J.-C."
JS: 135–50.
1987 "À propos de la tablette cunéiforme de Tell
Tawilan." *RAss* 81: 147–58.
1988 "*ig. gurki = Suse." *NABU*, note 19.
1989a *Archives de Borsippa: La famille Ea-Ilûta-
Bâni. Études d'un lot d'archives familiales
en Babylonie du VIIIᵉ au Vᵉ siècle av. J.C.*
Geneva-Paris.
1989b "La titulature de Xerxès." *NABU*, note 37.
1989c "Un quartier fantôme de Babylone."
NABU, note 78.
1989d "Médailles d'argent d'Hammurabi?"
NABU, note 108.
1990a "Pouvoirs locaux et organisation du territoire en Babylonie achéménide." *Trans* 3:
173–89.
1990b "Textes babyloniens d'époque achéménide." Pp. 173–80 in Vallat (ed.).
1990c "Cadastre et titre de propriété en Babylonie achéménide." *NABU*, note 10.
1992a "Les conséquences du retour de Nabonide." *NABU*, note 20.
1992b "Les temples de Sippar et leurs trésors à
l'époque néobabylonienne." *RAss* 86/2:
159–84.
1992c "Les archives de Ninurta-Aḫḫé-Bullit."
Pp. 87–100 in M. DeJong Ellis (ed.), *Nippur at the Centennial: Papers read at the
35th RAI (Philadelphia, 1988)*. Philadelphia: The University Museum.
1994a "Métaux précieux et moyens de paiement
en Babylonie achéménide et hellénistique." *Trans* 8: 137–44.
1994b "À propos du *zazakku* à l'époque néo-
babylonienne." *NABU*, note 103.
1995a "Lépreux fantômes?" *NABU*, note 20.
1995b "Les relations entre Babylone et les
Mèdes." *NABU*, note 21.
1995c "L'itinéraire des Dix-Mille en Mésopotamie et l'apport des sources cunéiformes."

Pp. 173–99 in P. Briant (ed.), *Dans les pas des Dix-Mille: Peuples et pays du Proche-Orient vus par un Grec* (Actes de la Table ronde, Toulouse 3–4 février 1995). Pallas 43.

Johnson, A. E. M.
1967 "The earliest preserved Greek map: a new Ionian coin type." *JHS* 87: 85–94.

Johnson, J. H.
1974 "The Demotic Chronicle as an historical source." *Enchória* 4: 1–17.
1984 "Is the Demotic Chronicle an anti-Greek tract?" Pp. 107–24 in *Grammatica demotica: FS E. Lüddeckens*. Würzburg.

Johnson, J. H. (ed.)
1992 *Life in a Multicultural Society: Egypt from Cambyses to Constantine and beyond.* SAOC 51. Chicago.
1994 "The Persians and the continuity of Egyptian culture." *AchHist* 8: 149–59.

Jones, C. E., and Stolper, M.
1986 "Two late Elamite tablets at Yale." Pp. 243–54 in *Fragmenta Historiae Elamicae (Mélanges M. J. Stève)*. Paris.

Jones, C. P., and Habicht, C.
1989 "A Hellenistic inscription from Arsinoe in Cilicia." *Phoenix* 43/4· 317–46.

Jouguet, P.
1930 "La politique intérieure du premier Ptolémée." *BIFAO* 30: 513–36.

Judeich, W.
1892 *Kleinasiatische Studien: Untersuchungen zur griechisch-persischen Geschichte des IV. Jhdt. v. Ch.* Marburg.

Julien, P.
1914 *Zur Verwaltung der Satrapien unter Alexander dem Grossen.* Weida i. Th.

Junge, P. J.
1940 "Hazarapatiš." *Klio* 33: 13–33.
1942 "Satrapie und Natio. Reichsverwaltung und Reichspolitik im Staate Dareios' I." *Klio* 34: 1–55.

Jursa, M.
1993 "Neues aus der Zeit des Bardia." *NABU,* note 19.
1995 "Zu *NABU* 1995/4." *NABU,* note 61.

Kagan, D.
1982 "The dates of the earliest coins." *AJA* 86/3: 343–60.

Kakosky, L.
1977 "The fiery aether in Egypt." *AAH* 25: 137–42.

Kamal, A. B.
1905 *Stèles ptolémaïques du Musée du Caire*, I. Cairo.

Känel, F. von
1980 "Les mésaventures du conjurateur de Serket Onophris et de son tombeau." *BSFE* 87–88: 31–45.
1984 *Les Prêtres-Ouab de Sekhmet et les conjurateurs de Serket.* Paris.

Kaptan-Bayburtluoìglu, D.
1990 "A group of seal-impressions on the bullae from Ergili/Daskyleion." *EA* 16: 15–26.

Karsten, H.
1987 "Religion und Politik in Vorderasien im Reich der Achämeniden." *Klio* 69: 317–25.

Katzenstein, H. J.
1973 *The History of Tyre.* Jerusalem.
1979 "Tyre in the early Persian period (539–486 B.C.)." *BA* 42/1: 23–34.
1989 "Gaza in the Persian period." *Trans* 1: 67–86.

Kawami, T. S.
1986 "Greek art and Persian taste: some animal sculptures from Persepolis." *AJA* 90: 259–67.
1992 "Antike persische Gärten." Pp. 81–100 in M. Carroll-Spillecke (ed.), *Der Garten von der Antike bis zum Mittelalter.* Mainz am Rhein.

Kawase, T.
1980 "Sheep and goats in the Persepolis royal economy." *Acta Sumerologica* 2: 37–51.
1984 "Female workers 'pašap' in the Persepolis royal economy." *Acta Sumerologica* 6: 19–31.
1986 "*Kapnuški* in the Persepolis fortification texts." Pp. 263–75 in *Fragmenta Historiae Elamicae: Mélanges M. J. Stève.* Paris.

Keel, O.
1990 "Siegel und Siegeln." Pp. 87–92 in O. Keel and C. Uehlinger, *Altorientalische Miniaturkunst.* Mainz.

Keen, A. G.
1992a *A Political History of Lycia and its Relations with Foreign Powers, 545–300 B.C.* Ph.D. Manchester.
1992b "The dynastic tombs of Xanthos: Who was buried where?" *AnSt* 42: 53–63.
1993a "Gateway from Aegean to the Mediterranean: the strategic value of Lycia down to the fourth Century B.C." Pp. 71–77 in J. Borchhardt and G. Dobesch (eds.), *Akten des II. Intern. Lykien-Symposions.* ÖAW, Denkschr. 231 Bd. Vienna.

Keen, T.
1993b "Athenian campaigns in Karia and Lykia during the Peloponnesian War." *JHS* 113: 152–57.
1995 "A confused passage of Philochoros (F 149A) and the peace of 392/1 B.C." *Historia* 44/1: 1–10.

Kellens, J.
1976a "L'Avesta comme source historique: la liste des Kayanides." *AAH* 24: 37–49.
1976b "Trois réflexions sur la religion des Achéménides." *SII* 2: 113–32.
1983 "Yasna 46,1 et un aspect de l'idéologie politique iranienne." *STIR* 12/2: 143–50.
1987 "DB V: un témoignage sur l'évolution de l'idéologie achéménide." Pp. 677–82 in

Orientalia, I: Tucci memoriae dicata. ISMEO 2. Rome.

1988a "Avesta." *EncIran* 3/1: 35–44.

1988b "Caractères du mazdéisme antique." Pp. 341–74 in *L'Impensable Polythéisme* (ed. Fr. Schmidt). Paris.

1989 "Ahura Mazda n'est pas un dieu créateur." Pp. 217–28 in *Études irano-aryennes offertes à G. Lazard.* Paris.

1991a "Questions préalables." Pp. 81–86 in Kellens (ed.).

1991b *Zoroastre et l'Avesta: Quatre leçons au Collège de France.* Travaux de l'Institut d'Études iraniennes de l'université de la Sorbonne nouvelle 14. Paris.

1995 "L'âme entre le cadavre et le paradis." *JA* 283: 19–56.

Kellens, J. (ed.)
1991 *La Religion iranienne à l'époque achéménide (Actes du colloque de Liège 11 décembre 1987).* Iranica Antiqua suppl. 5. Gand.

Kelly, T.
1987 "Herodotus and the chronology of the kings of Sidon." *BASOR* 268: 39–56.

Kent, R. G.
1953 *Old Persian: Grammar, Texts, Lexicon.* New Haven[2].

Kervran, M.
1972 "Une statue de Darius découverte à Suse: Le contexte archéologique." *JA* 260/3–4: 235–39.

Kessler, J.
1992 "The second year of Darius and the prophet Haggai." *Trans* 5: 63–84.

Kestemont, G.
1983 "Tyr et les Assyriens." *Studia Phoenicia* 1/2: 53–78.

1985 "Les Phéniciens en Syrie du Nord." *Studia Phoenicia* 3: 135–61.

Khatchatrian, Z.
forthcoming "The archives of sealings found at Artashat (Artaxāta)." In A. Invernizzi and M. F. Boussac (eds.), *Archives et Sceaux du monde hellénistique.* BCH suppl. Paris.

Khlopin, I.
1977 "Die Reiseroute Isidors von Charax und die oberen Satrapien Parthiens." *IA* 12: 118–65.

Kienast, D.
1973 *Philipp von Makedonien und das Reich der Achämeniden.* Marburg.

1994 "Die Auflösung der ionischen Aufstände und das Schicksal des Hestiaios." *Historia* 43/4: 387–401.

Kienitz, F. K.
1953 *Die politische Geschichte Ägyptens vom 7. bis 4. Jhrdt. v.u. Z.* Leipzig.

Kimball Armayor, O.
1978a "Herodotus' catalogues of the Persian Empire in the light of the monuments and the Greek literary tradition." *TAPA* 108: 1–9.

1978b "Herodotus' Persian vocabulary." *AJAH* 1/4: 147–56.

Kindler, A.
1974 "Silver coins bearing the name of Judea from the Early Hellenistic period." *IEJ* 24/2: 73–76.

Kingsley, P.
1995 "Meeting with Magi: Iranian themes among the Greeks, from Xanthos of Lydia to Plato's Academy." *JRAS* 3d series 5/2: 173–209.

Kinns, P.
1989 "Ionia: the pattern of coinage during the last century of the Persian Empire." *REA* 91/1–2: 183–93.

Kippenberg, H. G.
1982 *Religion und Klassenbildung in Antiken Judäa*[2]*.* Göttingen.

Kjeldsen, K., and Zahle, J.
1976 "A dynastic tomb in Central Lycia." *Acta Arch.* 47: 29–46.

Kleemann, I.
1958 *Der Satrapen-Sarkophag aus Sidon.* Berlin.

Klein, R. W.
1978 "Sanballat." Pp. 781–82 in *The Interpreter's Dictionary of the Bible,* suppl. vol. Nashville.

Kleiss, W.
1981 "Ein Abschnitt der achaemenidischen Königstrasse von Pasargadae und Persepolis nach Susa, bei Naqsh-i Rustam." *AMI* 14: 45–53.

1988 "Achaemenidische Staudämme in Fārs." *AMI* 21: 63–68.

1991 "Wasserschutzdämme und Kanalbauten in der Umgebung von Pasargadae." *AMI* 24: 23–34.

1992a "Dammbauten aus achaemenidischer und sassanidischer Zeit in der provinz Fārs." *AMI* 25 [1994]: 131–45.

1992b "Beobachtungen auf dem Burgberg von Persepolis." *AMI* 25 [1994]: 155–67.

1993a "Flächensteinbrüche und Einzelsteinbrüche in der Umgebung von Persepolis und Naqsh-i Rustam." *AMI* 26 [1995]: 91–103.

1993b "Bemerkungen zur Felsanlage Qadamgah am Kuh-i Rahmat südöstliche von Persepolis." *AMI* 26 [1995]: 161–64.

Kleiss, W., and Calmeyer, P.
1975 "Das unvollendete achaimenidische Felsgrabe bei Persepolis." *AMI* 8: 81–98 (pls. 14–24).

Knauf, E.
1990 "The Persian administration in Arabia." *Trans* 2: 201–18.

Knauth, W., and Nadjamabadi, S.
1975 *Das altiranische Fürstenideal von Xenophon bis Ferdousi.* Wiesbaden.

Koch, H.
1977 *Die religiöse Verhältnisse der Dareioszeit.* Wiesbaden.

1981 "Steuern in der achämenidischen Persis?" *ZA* 70/1: 105–37.

1982 "'Hofschatzwarte' und 'Schatzhäuser' in der Persis." *ZA* 71/2: 232–47.

1983 "Zu den Lohnverhältnissen der Dareioszeit in Persien." Pp. 19–50 in H. Koch and D. N. Mackenzie (eds.), *Kunst und Kultur der Achämenidenzeit und ihr Fortleben.* AMI suppl. 10. Berlin.

1986 "Die achämenidische Poststrasse von Persepolis nach Susa." *AMI* 19: 133–47.

1987a "Götter und ihre Verehung im achämenidischen Persien." *ZA* 77/2: 239–78.

1987b "Einige Überlegungen zur Bauplanung in Persepolis." *AMI* 20: 147–59.

1988a *Persien zur Zeit des Dareios: Das Achämenidenreich im Lichte neuer Quellen.* Marburg.

1988b "Zur Religion der Achämeniden." *ZAW* 100/3: 393–405.

1989a "Tribut und Abgaben in Persis und Elymaïs." Pp. 121–28 in Briant and Herrenschmidt (eds.).

1990 *Verwaltung und Wirtschaft im persischen Kernland zur Zeit der Achämeniden.* Suppl TAVO series B 89. Wiesbaden.

1991 "Zu Religion und Kulten im Achämenidischen Kernland." Pp. 87–109 in Kellens (ed.).

1992 *Es kundet Dareios der König: Von Leben im persischen Grossreich.* Mainz.

1993a *Achämeniden-Studien.* Wiesbaden.

1993b "Elamisches Gilgameš-Epos oder doch Verwaltungstäfelchen?" *ZA* 83/2: 219–36.

1993c "Feuertempel oder Verwaltungszentrale? Überlegungen zu den Grabungen in Takhte Sangin am Oxos." *AMI* 26 [1995]: 175–86.

1994 "Zu den Frauen im Achämenidenreich." Pp. 125–41 in P. Vavroucek (ed.), *Iranian and Indo-European Studies: Memorial Volume of O. Klima.* Prague.

Könhken, A.
1990 "Der listige Oibares: Dareios' Aufstiege zum Grosskönig." *RhM* 133/2: 115–37.

König, W. F.
1972 *Die Persika des Ktesias von Knidos.* Graz.

Konstan, D.
1987 "Persians, Greeks and Empire." *Arethusa* 20/1–2: 59–73.

Kraay, C. M.
1962 "The Celenderis hoard." *NC*: 1–15.
1976 *Archaic and Classical Greek Coins.* University of California Press.
1979 "The Isparta hoard." Pp. 131–37 in Mørkholm-Waggoner (eds.).

Kraay, C. M., and Moorey, P. R. S.
1981 "A Black sea hoard of the late fifth century B.C." *NC*: 1–19.

Kraeling, E. G.
1953 *The Brooklyn Museum Aramaic Papyri: New Documents of the Fifth Century B.C.*

from the Jewish Colony at Elephantine. New Haven.

Kraft, K.
1971 *Der "rationale" Alexander.* Kallmünz.

Krappe, A. H.
1928 "La vision de Balthassar (Dan. V)." *RHR* 97/4: 78–86.

Krasnowolska, A.
1987 "The heroes of the Iranian epic tale." *FO* 24: 173–89.

Krefter, F.
1971 *Persepolis-Rekonstruktionen.* Berlin.
1989 "Persepolis in Farbe." *AMI* 22: 131–32.

Kreissig, H.
1973 *Die sozialökonomische Situation in Juda zur Achämenidenzeit.* Schr. z. Gesch. und Kultur des Alten Orients 7. Berlin.

Krentz, P. (ed., trans., comm.)
1989 *Xenophon, Hellenika I–II.3–10.* Warminster.

Krumbholz, P.
1883 *De Asiae Minoris satrapis persicis.* Leipzig.

Kuhlmann, K. P.
1981 "Ptolemäis-Queen of Nectanebo I: Notes on the inscription of an unknown princess of the XXXth dynasty." *FS I. Habachi.* MDAIK 37: 268–79.

Kuhrt, A.
1983a "A brief guide to some recent work on the Achaemenid Empire." *LCM* 8–10: 46–53.
1983b "The Cyrus cylinder and Achaemenid imperial policy." *JSOT* 25: 83–97.
1984 "The Achaemenid concept of kingship." *Iran* 22: 156–60.
1987a "Survey of written sources available for the history of Babylonia under the later Achaemenids (concentrating on the period from Artaxerxes II to Darius III)." *AchHist* 1: 147–67.
1987b "Usurpation, conquest and ceremonial: from Babylonia to Persia." Pp. 20–55 in D. Carradine and S. Price (eds.), *Rituals of Royalty: Power and Ceremonial in Traditional Societies.* Cambridge.
1987c "Berossus' *Babyloniaka* and Seleucid rule in Babylonia." Pp. 32–56 in A. Kuhrt and S. Sherwin-White (eds.).
1988a "Earth and water." *AchHist* 3: 87–99.
1988b "Babylonia from Cyrus to Xerxes." *CAH* 4²: 112–38.
1988c "The Achaemenid Empire: a Babylonian perspective." *PCPS* 214 (n.s. 34): 60–76.
1989 "Conclusions." Pp. 217–22 in Briant and Herrenschmidt (eds.).
1990a "Achaemenid Babylonia: sources and problems." *AchHist* 4: 177–94.
1990b "Alexander in Babylon." *AchHist* 5: 121–30.
1990c "Nabonidus and the Babylonian priesthood." Pp. 119–55 in M. Beard and J. North (eds.), *Pagan Priests.* London.
1992 "The governor of Egypt under Cambyses: Strassmaeier *Camb.* 344." *DATA*, note 2.

1995 "The Assyrian Heartland in the Achaemenid period." Pp. 239–54 in P. Briant (ed.), *Dans les pas des Dix-Mille: Peuples et pays du Proche-Orient vus par un Grec* (Actes de la Table ronde, Toulouse, 3–4 février 1995). Pallas 43.

Kuhrt, A. (ed.)
1987 *Hellenism and the East: The Interaction of Greek and Non-Greek Civilizations from Syria to Central Asia after Alexander.* London.

Kuhrt, A., and Sherwin-White, S.
1987 "Xerxes' destruction of Babylonian temples." *AchHist* 2: 69–78.
1991 "Aspects of royal Seleucid ideology: the cylinder of Antiochus I from Borsippa." *JHS* 111: 71–86.
1994 "The transition from the Achaemenid to the Seleucid rule in Babylonia: revolution or evolution?" *AchHist* 8: 311–27.

Kuiper, J.
1976 "Ahura Mazda 'Lord Wisdom'?" *IIJ* 18: 25–42.

Kümmel, H. M.
1979 *Familie, Beruf und Amt im spätbabylonischen Uruk.* Berlin.

Kunkel, W., and Haas, W.
1986 "Ein orichalkeisches Minengewicht aus Trapezunt: Ein Beitrag zur Geltung der persischen Goldwärung an der pontische Küste." *AMI* 19: 151–61.

Kuyper, J. de
1979 "Les auteurs grecs et la dénomination des régions du Proche-Orient ancien." *Akkadica* 14: 16–31.
1991 "Leben und Tod assyrischen Städte nach der Berichten Xenophons." *AfO* suppl. 19: 210–14.

Laato, A.
1990 "The composition of Isaiah 40–55." *JBL* 109/2: 207–28.

Labarbe, J.
1984 "Polycrate, Amasis et l'anneau." *RBPh* 53: 15–33.

Labat, R.
1939 *Les Caractères religieux de la royauté babylonienne.* Paris.
1960 "Ordonnances médicales ou magiques." *RAss* 54/1: 169–76.

Labrousse, A., and Boucharlat, R.
1972 "La fouille du palas du Chaour à Suse." *CDAFI* 9: 61–167.

La Bua, V.
1977 "Gli Ioni e il conflitto lidio-persiano." Pp. 1–64 in *Quinta Miscellanea greca e romana.* Rome.

Lackenbacher, S.
1990 *Le Palais sans rival: Le récit de construction en Assyrie.* Paris.
1992 "Un pamphlet contre Nabonide, dernier roi de Babylone." *DHA* 18/1: 13–28.

Lalouette, C.
1984 *Textes sacrés et Textes profanes de l'ancienne Égypte.* Paris.

Lamberterie, Ch. de
1989 "Arménien ARI et ANARI." Pp. 237–46 in *Études irano-aryennes offertes à G. Lazard.* Cahiers de STIR 7. Paris.

Landucci Gattinoni, F.
1994 "I mercenari nella politica ateniese dell'età di Alessandro, I: Soldati e ufficiali mercenari ateniesi al servizio della Persia." *AncSoc* 25: 33–61.

Lane, E. N.
1975 "Two notes on Lydian topography." *AnSt* 25: 105–10.

Lanfranchi, G. B.
1990 *I Cimmeri: Emergenza delle élites militari iraniche nel Vicino Oriente (VIII–VII sec. a.C.).* Padua.

Lang, M.
1992 "Prexaspes and usurper Smerdis." *JNES* 51/3: 201–7.

Langdon, S.
1924 "The Babylonian and Persian Sacaea." *JRAS*: 65–72.

Laperrousaz, E.
1979 "À propos du 'premier mur' et du 'deuxième mur' de Jérusalem, ainsi que du rempart de Jérusalem à l'époque de Néhémie." *REJ* 138/1–2: 1–16.
1982 "Le régime théocratique juif a-t-il commencé à l'époque perse, ou seulement à l'époque hellénistique?" *Semitica* 32: 93–96.
1990 "Quelques remarques sur le tracé de l'enceinte de la ville et du temple de Jérusalem à l'époque perse." *Syria* 57/3–4: 629–31.

Laperrousaz, E., and Lemaire, A. (under the direction of)
1994 *La Palestine à l'époque perse.* Paris.

La Persia e il mondo lassico
1972 Special issue of *La Parola del Passato*, vol. 27.

Laroche, E.
1974a "Les épitaphes lyciennes." Pp. 49–127 in P. Demargne (ed.).
1974b "La stèle trilingue découverte récemment au Létôon de Xanthos: le texte lycien." *CRAI*: 115–25.
1976 "Les dieux de la Lycie classique d'après les textes lyciens." Pp. 1–6 in *Actes du colloque sur la Lycie antique.* Paris.
1979 "L'inscription lycienne." Pp. 49–127 in Metzger (ed.).
1987 "Nouveaux documents lyciens du Létôon de Xanthos." *Hethitica* 8: 237–40.

Laroche, E., and Davesne, A.
1982 "Les fouilles de Meydandjïk près de Gülnar (Turquie) et le trésor monétaire hellénistique." *CRAI*: 356–57.

Lateiner, D.
1982 "The failure of the Ionian revolt." *Historia* 31/2: 129–60.
Launey, M.
1949 *Recherches sur les armées hellénistiques*, I–II. Paris.
Lavagne, H.
1988 *Operosa antra: Recherches sur la grotte à Rome de Sylla à Hadrien*. BEFAR 272. Paris.
Lawrence, A. W.
1951 "The Acropolis and Persepolis." *JHS* 71: 111–19.
Lazenby, J. F.
1993 *The Defence of Greece, 490–479 B.C.* Warminster.
Lebram, J. C. H.
1987 "Die Traditionsgeschichte der Esragestalt und die Frage nach dem historischen Esra." *AchHist* 1: 103–38.
Leclant, J.
1930 "*Per Africa sitientia*: Témoignages des sources classiques sur les pistes menant à l'oasis d'Ammon." *BIFAO* 49: 193–253.
Lecoq, P.
1974a "Le problème de l'écriture vieux-perse." *Acta Iranica* 3: 25–107.
1974b "La langue des inscriptions achéménides." *Acta Iranica* 3: 55–62.
1984 "Un problème de religion achéménide: Ahura Mazda ou Xᵛarnah?" Pp. 301–26 in *Orientalia Duchesne-Guillemin*.
1987 "Le mot FARNAH- et les Scythes." *CRAI*: 671–82.
1990a "Observations sur le sens du mot *dahyu* dans les inscriptions achéménides." *Trans* 3: 131–40.
1990b "Paradis en vieux-perse?" Pp. 209–12 in Vallat (ed.).
Lefebvre, G.
1924 *Le Tombeau de Petosiris*, I. Paris.
Legrain, L.
1925 *The Culture of the Babylonians from their Seals in the Collections of the Museum.* PBS 14 and 14 bis. Philadelphia: University of Pennsylvania.
Legrand, P. E. (ed. and trans.)
1956–66 *Hérodote: Histoires*, I–VIII, and analytical index. Paris.
Lehmann-Haupt
1921 "Satrap (und Satrapie)." *RE* n.s., pp. 82–188.
Leith, M. J. W.
1990 *Greek and Persian Images in Pre-Alexandrine Samaria: The Wadi ed-Daliyeh Seal-Impressions.* Ph.D. Harvard University.
Lemaire, A.
1977 *Inscriptions hébraïques*, I: *Les ostraka*. Paris.
1988 "Lakish: archéologie, épigraphie et histoire." Pp. 99–118 in E. Laperroussaz (ed.), *Archéologie, art et histoire de la Palestine.* Paris.

1989 "Remarques à propos du monnayage cilicien d'époque perse et de ses légendes araméennes." *REA* 91/1–2: 141–56.
1989b "Les inscriptions palestiniennes d'époque perse: un bilan provisoire." *Trans* 1: 87–109.
1990 "Populations et territoires de la Palestine à l'époque perse." *Trans* 3: 31–74.
1991a "Recherches de topographie historique sur le pays de Qué (IXᵉ–VIIᵉ siècle av. J.-C.)." Pp. 267–75 in *De Anatolia antiqua.* Bib. Inst. Fr. Anatol. Istanbul 32. Paris.
1991b "Le monnayage phénicien." Pp. 96–101 in *A Survey of Numismatic Research 1985–1990.* Intern. Ass. Prof. Numismatics, Special Pub. 12. Brussels.
1991c "Recherches d'épigraphie araméenne en Asie Mineure et en Égypte et le problème de l'acculturation." *AchHist* 6: 119–206.
1991d "Monnaie de Mazdai avec légende araméenne: b'l dgn." *Semitica* 40: 47–51.
1991e "Le royaume de Tyr dans la seconde moitié du IVᵉ siècle." Pp. 131–50 in *Atti del II. Congresso di Studi Fenici e Punici*, I. Rome.
1992 "Sceau 'de Clercq 2505': araméen ou plutôt lydien?" *Kadmos* 31/2: 124–26.
1993 "Deux nouvelles inscriptions araméennes d'époque perse en Cilicie orientale." *EA* 21: 9–14.
1994a "Histoire et administration de la Palestine à l'époque perse." Pp. 11–53 in Laperrousaz and Lemaire (eds.).
1994b "Deux nouvelles stèles funéraires araméennes de Cilicie orientale." *EA* 23: 91–98.
1995a "La fin de la période perse en Égypte et la chronologie judéenne vers 400 av. J.C." *Trans* 9: 51–61.
1995b "Les inscriptions araméennes de Cheikh-Fadl (Égypte)." Pp. 77–132 in M. J. Geller, J.-C. Greenfield, and M. P. Weitzman (eds.), *Studia aramaica.* JSS suppl. 4. Oxford.
1995c "The Xanthos trilingual revisited." Pp. 423–32 in Z. Zevit, S. Gitin, and M. Sokoloff (eds.), *Solving Riddles and Untying Knots: Biblical, Epigraphic, and Semitic Studies in Honor of Jonas C. Greenfield.* Winona Lake, Indiana.
1995d "Épigraphie palestinienne: nouveaux documents, II: Décennies 1985–95." *Henoch* 17: 209–42.
Lemaire, A., and Joannès, F.
1994 "Premières monnaies avec signes cunéiformes: Samarie, IVᵉ s. av. n.è." *NABU*, note 95.
Lemaire, A., and Lozachmeur, H.
1987 "Birāh/Bîrtha en araméen." *Syria* 64/3–4: 261–66.
1990 "La Cilicie à l'époque perse: recherche sur les pouvoirs locaux et l'organisation du territoire." *Trans* 3: 143–55.

Lendle, O.
1986 "Xenophon in Babylonien: Die Märsche der Kyreer von Pylai bis Opis." *RhM* 129: 193–222.
1988 "Wo lag Thapsakos? (Xenophon, *Anabasis* 1.4.10ff)." Pp. 301–5 in *Bathron: Beiträge zur Architektur und Verwandten Künsten = FS H. Drupp.* Saarbrücker Beit. z. Arch. u. Alte Geschichte 3. Saarbrücken.

Lentz, W.
1975 "The 'social functions' of the old Iranian Mithra." *Mithraic Studies* 2: 245–75.

Le Rider, G.
1965 *Suse sous les Séleucides et les Parthes.* MDAFI 38. Paris.
1994a "Un trésor d'oboles de poids persique entré au musée de Silifke en 1987." Pp. 13–18 in M. Amandry and G. Le Rider (eds.), *Trésors et Circulation monétaire en Anatolie antique.* Paris.
1994b "Histoire économique et monétaire de l'Orient hellénistique." Pp. 815–21 in *Annuaire du Collège de France: Résumés des cours et travaux.* Paris.

Lerner, J.
1991 "Some so-called Achaemenid objects from Pazyryk." *Source* 10/4: 8–15.

Le Roy, C.
1981/83 "Aspects du plurilinguisme dans la Lycie antique." *Mélanges E. Akurgal 2 = Anadolu* 22 [1990]: 217–26.
1987 "La formation d'une société provinciale en Asie Mineure: l'exemple lycien." Pp. 41–47 in E. Frézouls (ed.), *Sociétés urbaines, sociétés rurales dans l'Asie Mineure romaine et la Syrie hellénistique et romaine.* Strasbourg.

Leuze, E.
1935 *Die Satrapieneinteilung in Syrien und im Zweistromlande von 520–320.* Halle.

Levante, E.
1994 "Le 'trésor de Nagidos.'" Pp. 7–11 in M. Amandry and G. Le Rider (eds.), *Trésors et circulation monétaire en Anatolie antique.* Paris.

Levi, M. A.
1938 "La spedizione scitica di Dario." *RFIC* 61: 58–59.

Levrero, R.
1992 "La géographie de l'Afrique selon Hérodote: les expéditions de Cambyse contre les Éthiopiens et les Ammoniens." Pp. 397–408 in *VI. Congresso intern. d'Egittologia,* I. Turin.

Lévy, É.
1983 "Les trois traités entre Sparte et le Grand Roi." *BCH* 107: 221–41.

Lévy, I.
1939 "L'inscription triomphale de Xerxès." *RH* 185: 105–22.
1940 "Platon et le faux Smerdis." *REA* 42: 234–41.

Lewis, B. L.
1980 *The Sargon Legend.* Cambridge, Massachusetts.

Lewis, D. M.
1958 "The Phoenician fleet in 411." *Historia* 7/4: 392–97.
1977 *Sparta and Persia.* Leiden.
1980 "Datis the Mede." *JHS* 100: 194–95.
1984 *Postscript* à Burn 1984: 587–609.
1985 "Persians in Herodotus." Pp. 101–17 in *The Greek Historians: Literature and History: Papers presented to A. E. Raubitschek.* Stanford University.
1987 "The King's dinner (Polyaenus IV.3.32)." *AchHist* 2: 89–91.
1989 "Persian gold in Greek international relations." *REA* 91/1–2: 227–34.
1990a "The Persepolis fortification texts." *AchHist* 4: 1–6.
1990b "Brissonius: *De regio Persarum principatu libri tres* (1590)." *AchHist* 5: 67–78.
1992a "The thirty years' peace." *CAH* 5²: 121–46.
1992b "The Archidamian war." *CAH* 5²: 370–432.
1994 "The Persepolis tablets: speech, seal and script." Pp. 17–32, 218–20 in A. K. Bowman and G. Woolf (eds.), *Literacy and Power in the Ancient World.* Cambridge.

Liagre Böhl, F. M. de
1962 "Die babylonische Prätendenten zur Zeit des Xerxes." *BiOr* 19/3–4: 110–14.
1968 "Die babylonische Prätendenten zur Anfangszeit des Darius (Dareios) I." *BiOr* 25/3–4: 150–53.

Lichtheim, M.
1960 *Ancient Egyptian Literature,* III. University of California Press.

Liebert, G.
1974 "Indoiranica: *v.p.* vazraka, *av.* vazra, *v. ind.* vajra." *Acta Iranica* 1: 63–90.

Lipiński, E.
1975 *Studies in Aramaic Inscriptions and Onomastics,* I. Louvain.
1977 "Western Semites in Persepolis." *AAH* 25: 101–12.
1981–84 "Un culte de XᵛAN et de HAΘYA à Éléphantine au Vᵉ siècle av. n.è." *FO* 22: 5–11.
1982a "Le culte d'Ištar en Mésopotamie du Nord à l'époque parthe." *OLP* 13: 117–24.
1982b "Egyptian aramaic coins from the fifth and fourth centuries B.C." Pp. 22–33 in *Studies P. Naster oblata,* I: *Numismatica antiqua.* OLA 12. Louvain.
1989 "'Cellériers' de la province de Juda." *Trans* 1: 109–77.
1990 "Géographie linguistique de la Transeuphratène à l'époque achéménide." *Trans* 3: 95–107.
1994 "Aramaic documents from Ancient Egypt." *OLP* 25: 61–68.

Lipiński, E. (ed.)
1977 *State and Temple in the Ancient Near East*, I–II. Louvain.

Littman, R. J.
1975 "The religious policy of Xerxes and the Book of Esther." *JQR* 65: 145–55.

Liverani, M.
1976 [Review of Oates 1978], *OA* 10: 155–59.
1979 "Dono, tributo, commercio: ideologia delle scambio nelle tarda età del Bronzo." *AIIN*: 9–28.
1988 "The growth of the Assyrian Empire in the Habur/Middle Euphrates area: a new paradigm." *SAAB* 2/2: 81–98.
1990 *Prestige and Interest: International Relations in the Near East ca. 1600–1100 B.C.* Padua.

Livingstone, R.
1989 "Arabians in Babylonia/Babylonians in Arabia: some reflections à propos new and old evidence." Pp. 97–105 in T. Fawd (ed.), *L'Arabie préislamique et son environnement historique et culturel*. Strasbourg.

Lloyd, A. B.
1972 "Triremes and the Saite navy." *JEA* 58: 268–79.
1975 *Herodotus, Book II: A Commentary*. Leiden.
1976 *Herodotus, Book II: Introduction*. Leiden.
1982a "Nationalistic propaganda in Ptolemaic Egypt." *Historia*: 33–55.
1982b "The inscription of Udjahorresnet: A collaborator's testament." *JEA* 68: 166–80.
1983 "The late period (664–323)." Pp. 279–364 in *Ancient Egypt: A Social History* (ed. B. G. Trigger et al.). Cambridge.
1988a "Herodotus on Cambyses: some thoughts on recent works." *AchHist* 3: 55–66.
1988b "Manetho and the thirty-first dynasty." Pp. 154–60 in J. Baines et al. (eds.), *Pyramid Studies and essays presented to I. E. S. Edwards*. CEES occasional publications 7. London.
1988c *Herodotus Book II: Commentary 99–162.* Leiden–New York.
1990 "Herodotus on Egyptians and Lydians." Pp. 215–44 in *Hérodote et les peuples non grecs*. Entretiens Hardt sur l'Antiquité classique 35. Geneva.
1994 "Egypt, 404–332 B.C." *CAH* 6²: 337–60.

Lombardo, M.
1974 "Per un inquadramento storico del problema delle Creseidi." *ASNP* 3d series 4/3: 687–733.
1979 "Elementi per una discussione sulle origini e funzioni della moneta coniata." *AIIM*: 75–137.
1980 "Osservazioni chronologiche e storiche sul regno di Sadiatte." *ASNP* 3d series 10/2: 307–62.
1989 "Oro lidio e oro persiano nelle *Storie* di Erodoto." *REA* 91/1–2: 197–208.

Lommel, H.
1974 "Les espions de Varuna et de Mitra et l'Œil du Roi." Pp. 91–100 in *Hommage universel à l'Iran*. Acta Iranica 2. Tehran-Liège.

Longo, O.
1981 "Liberalità, dono, gratitudine: fra medioevo cortese e grecità antica." Pp. 1043–61 in *Lettaratura comparata, problemi di metodo* (Studi in onore di E. Paratore). Bologna.

Loraux, N.
1981 *L'Invention d'Athènes*. Paris–La Haye.

Lorton, D.
1971 "The supposed expedition of Ptolemy II to Persia." *JEA*: 160–64.

Lozachmeur, H.
1975 "Sur la bilingue gréco-araméenne d'Agcakale." *Semitica* 25: 97–102.
1990 "Un ostracon araméen d'Éléphantine (collection Clermont-Ganneau no. 125?)." *Semitica* 39 (= *Hommages à M. Sznycer*, II): 30–36.

Lucas, A.
1943 "Ancient Egyptian measures." *ASAE* 42: 165–66.

Lüddeckens, E.
1965 "P. Wien D.10051: eine neue Urkunde zum ägyptischen Pfrüdenhandel in der Perserzeit." *NAWG*: 103–20.
1971 "Das demotische graffito vom Tempel der Satet auf Elephantine." *MDAIK* 27/2: 203–10.

Lukonin, V. G.
1989 "The early history and culture of the Iranian peoples of West Asia." Pp. 1–89 in M. A. Dandamaev and V. G. Lukonin (eds.), *The Culture and Social Institutions of Ancient Iran* Cambridge University Press.

Lund, J.
1990 "The Northern coastline of Syria in the Persian period: A survey of the archaeological evidence." *Trans* 2: 13–36.
1993 "The archaeological evidence for the transition from the Persian period to the Hellenistic age in Northwestern Syria." *Trans* 6: 13–26.

Luschey, H.
1968 "Studien zu dem Darius-Relief von Bisutun." *AMI* 1: 63–94.
1983 "Thrakien als ein Ort der Begegnung der Kelten mit der iranischen Metallkunst." Pp. 315–29 in *FS K. Bittel*. Mainz.

Lyonnet, B.
1990 "Les rapports entre l'Asie centrale et l'Empire achéménide d'après les données de l'archéologie." *AchHist* 4: 77–92.
1994 "L'occupation séleucide en Bactriane orientale et en Syrie du Nord-Est d'après les données archéologiques (prospections surtout)." *Topoi* 4/2: 541–46.

Maas, E.
1921   "Eunuchos und Werwandtes." *RhM* n.s.
        74: 432–76.
Macchi, J. D.
1994   *Les Samaritains: histoire et légende: Israël
        et la province de Samarie.* Geneva.
Macdonald, M. C. A.
1991   "Was the Nabatean kingdom a 'Bedouin
        State'?" *ZPDV* 107: 102–19.
Macevenue, S. C.
1981   "The political structure in Judah from
        Cyrus to Nehemiah." *CBQ* 43: 353–64.
Macginnis, J. D. A.
1986   "Herodotus' description of Babylon." *BICS*
        33: 67–86.
1987a   "Ctesias and the fall of Nineveh." *ICS*
        13/1: 37–41.
1987b   "A new Assyrian text describing a royal fu-
        neral." *SAAB* 1: 1–11.
1994   "The royal establishment at Sippar in the
        6th cent. B.C." *ZA* 84/2: 198–219.
1995   *Letter Orders from Sippar and the Adminis-
        tration of the Ebabbara in the Late Babylo-
        nian Period.* Poznan.
Machinist, P.
1994   "The first coins of Judah and Samaria: nu-
        mismatics and history in the Achaemenid
        and Early Hellenistic periods." *AchHist* 8:
        365–79.
Maclaurin, E. C. B.
1968   "Date of the foundation of the Jewish col-
        ony at Elephantine." *JNES* 27: 89–96.
Macridy, T.
1913   "Reliefs gréco-perses de la région de Dasky-
        leion." *BCH*: 340–57.
Magen, U.
1986   *Assyrische Königsdarstellungen: Aspekte der
        Herrschaft. Eine Typologie.* Mainz.
Maier, F. G.
1994   "Cyprus and Phoenicia." *CAH* 6²: 297–
        336.
Maier, F. G., and Karageorghis, V.
1984   *Paphos: History and Archaeology.* Nicosia.
Majizadeh, Y.
1992   "The Arjan bowl." *Iran* 30: 131–44.
Malaise, M.
1966   "Sésostris, pharaon de légende et d'his-
        toire." *CdE* 81/82: 244–72.
Malamat, A.
1988   "The kingdom of Judea between Egypt
        and Babylon: a small state within a great
        power confrontation." Pp. 117–29 in *Text
        and Context: Old Testament Studies for
        F. C. Fenscham.* JSOT suppl. 48. Sheffield.
Malay, H.
1983   "A royal document from Aigai in Aiolis."
        GRBS 24/4: 349–53.
Malay, H., and Schmitt, R.
1985   "An inscription recording a new Persian
        name: Mithraboges or Mithrobogos." *EA* 5:
        27–29.

Malbran-Labat, F.
1982   *L'Armée et l'organisation militaire de l'Assy-
        rie.* Geneva-Paris.
1992   "Note sur le §70 de Behistoun." *NABU*,
        note 86.
1994   *La Version akkadienne de l'inscription tri-
        lingue de Darius à Behistun.* Rome.
Malikhzade, F.
1972   "Daskyleion." *Anatolia* 17–18: 131–40.
Malinine, M.
1950   "Un prêt de céréales à l'époque de Darius."
        Kemi 11: 1–23.
Mallowan, M.
1966   *Nimrud and Its Remains,* I–II. London.
1972   "Cyrus the Great (558–529 B.C.)." *Iran* 10:
        1–17.
1984   "Cyrus the Great (558–529 B.C.)." *CHI* 2:
        392–419.
Mancini, M.
1987   *Note iraniche.* Bib. Ric. Ling. Filol. 20.
        Rome.
Manfredi, V.
1986   *La strada dei Diecimila: Topografia e geo-
        grafia dell'Oriente di Senofonte.* Milan.
1991   "Tapsaco: un problema di topografia feni-
        cia." Pp. 1019–23 in *Atti del II. Congresso
        Intern. di Studi Fenici e Punici,* III. Rome.
Manfredini, M., and Orsi, P. (eds.)
1987   *Plutarco: Le vite di Arato e di Artaserse.* Flo-
        rence.
Mannes, E. L.
1962   "Il decreto ateniese di atimia contro Art-
        mio di Zeleia (prosseno degli Ateniesi?)."
        RSA: 241–50.
Manukian, H.
forthcoming "Les empreintes des cachets d'argile
        découverts dans l'ancienne Artachat (Ar-
        taxāta)." In A. Invernizzi and M. F. Boussac
        (eds.), *Archives et Sceaux du monde hellé-
        nistique.* BCH suppl. Paris.
Manville, P. B.
1977   "Aristagoras and Histiaios: the leadership
        struggle in the Ionian revolt." *CQ* 37: 80–
        91.
Marasco, G.
1985   "La 'Profezia dinastica' e la resistenza
        babilonese alla conquista di Alessandro."
        ASNP 15/2: 529–37.
1987   "Alessandro Magno a Priene." *Sileno* 13/2:
        59–77.
1988   "Ctesia, Dinone, Eraclide di Cuma e le
        origini della storiografia 'tragica.'" *RFIC*
        81: 48–67.
1992   "Alessandro e Babilonia." Pp. 103–23 in
        G. Marasco, *Economia e storia.* Viterbo.
Marcus, R.
1937   *Josephus: Jewish Antiquities,* Books IX–XI.
        Harvard University Press.
Marinoni, E.
1976   "Talete in Erodoto: la cronologia e l'atti-
        vità politico sullo sfondo della conquista

persiana delle'Asia Minore." *Acme* 29/2: 172–231.

Marinovic, L. H.
1989 *Le Mercenariat grec au IVᵉ siècle et la crise de la polis.* Paris.

Marquart, J.
1892 *Die Assyriaka des Ktesias.* Philologus suppl. 6/1. Göttingen.
1895 "Untersuchungen zur Geschichte von Eran, I: Diodors Nachrichten über das pontische und kappadokische Fürstenhaus." *Philologus* 54: 489–512.

Martin, G. T., and Nicholls, R. V.
1978 "Hieroglyphic stelae with Carian texts and Carian stelae with egyptianizing or hellenizing motifs." Pp. 57–87 in O. Masson (ed.), *Carian Inscriptions from North Saqqâra and Buhen.* London.

Martin, R.
1978 "L'architecture d'époque classique en Asie Mineure." Pp. 403–505 in *The Proceedings of the Xth Congress of Classical Archaeology.*

Martin, T. R.
1985 *Sovereignty and Coinage in Classical Greece.* Princeton.

Martin, V.
1940 *La Vie internationale dans la Grèce des cités.* Geneva.
1963 "Quelques remarques à l'occasion d'une nouvelle édition des *Staatsverträge des Altertums.*" *MH* 20: 230–33.

Martorelli, A.
1977 "Storia persiana in Erodoto: echi di versioni ufficiali." *RIL* 111: 115–25.

Mason, K.
1920 "Notes on the canal system and Ancient sites of Babylonia in the times of Xenophon." *JRGS* 56: 466–84.

Masqueray, P.
1928 "Origine de l'expression les 'Dix-Mille.'" *CRAI*: 111–14.

Masson, O.
1950 "À propos d'un rituel hittite pour la lustration d'une armée: le rite de purification par le passage entre les deux parties d'une victime." *RHR* 137–38: 5–25.
1969 "Un nom pseudo-lydien à Sardes: Beletras." *Athen.* 47 (= *Studi P. Merigi*): 193–96.
1987a "Le sceau paléo-phrygien de Manes." *Kadmos* 26/2: 109–13.
1987b "L'inscription d'Ephèse relative aux condamnés à mort de Sardes (*I. Ephesos* 2)." *REG*: 225–39.
1991 "Anatolian languages." Pp. 666–71 in *CAH* 3/2.

Masson, O., and Sznycer, M.
1972 *Recherches sur les Phéniciens à Chypre.* Geneva-Paris.

Masson, O., and Yoyotte, J.
1988 "Une inscription ionienne mentionnant Psammétique Iᵉʳ." *EA* 11: 171–79.

Mattila, R.
1990 "Balancing the accounts of the Royal New Year's reception." *SAAB* 4/1: 7–22.

Mauss, M.
1921 "Une forme ancienne de contrat chez les Thraces." *REG* 34: 388–97.

Maxwell-Hyslop, R.
1984 "The gold jewelry." *Levant* 21: 22–23.

Mayer, R.
1960 "Das achämenidische Weltreich und seine Bedeutung in der politischen und religiösen Geschichte des antike Orients." *BZ* 12: 1–16.

Mayrhofer, M.
1972 "Alltagsleben und Verwaltung in Persepolis: Linguistisch-onomastisches Aufgaben aus neuerschlossen Profantext." *AÖW, Phil. hist. Kl.* 109: 192–202.
1973a *Onomastica Persepolitana: Das altiranische Namenbuch der Persepolis-Täfelchen.* Vienna.
1973b *Kleinasien zwischen Agonie des Perserreiches und hellenistischen Frühling.* Vienna.
1974 "Xerxès, roi des rois." *Acta Iranica* 2: 108–16.
1978 *Supplement zur Sammlung der Altpersischer Inschriften.* Vienna.
1979 "Die iranischen Elemente im aramäischen Text." Pp. 181–85 in Metzger (ed.).

Mazzarino, S.
1947 *Fra Oriente e Occidente: Ricerche di storia greca arcaica.* Florence.
1959 "L'image des parties du monde et les rapports entre l'Orient et la Grèce à l'époque classique." *AAH* 7: 85–101.
1966 "Le vie di comunicazione fra impero achemenide e mondo greco." Pp. 75–84 in *Atti del convegno.* . . .

Mazzoni, S.
1990 "La période perse à Tell Mardikh et dans sa région dans le cadre de l'âge du fer en Syrie." *Trans* 2: 187–200.
1991–92 "Lo sviluppo degli insidiamenti in Syria in età persiana." *EVO* 14/15: 55–72.

McCoy, W. J.
1989 "Memnon of Rhodes at the Granicus." *AJPh* 110: 413–33.

McDougall, I.
1990 "The Persian ships at Mycale." Pp. 143–49 in *Owls for Athens: Essays on Classical Subjects presented to Sir K. Dover.* Oxford.

McEwan, G. J. P.
1982 *The Late Babylonian Tablets in the Royal Ontario Museum.* Toronto.
1983 "Late Babylonian Kish." *Iraq* 45/1: 117–23.
1988 *Priest and Temple in Hellenistic Babylonia.* Wiesbaden.

McKeon, J. Fr. X.
1973 "Achaemenian cloisonné-inlay jewelry: an important new example." Pp. 109–17 in *Orient and Occident: Essays presented to C. H. Gordon.* Neukirchen-Vluyn.

Mecquenem, R. de
1947   "Contributions à l'étude du palais achémé-
        nide de Suse." Pp. 1–119 in R. de Mecque-
        nem, L. Le Breton, and M. Rutten (eds.),
        Archéologie susienne. MMAI 30, Mission
        de Susiane.
Medvedskaya, I.
1992   "The questions of the identification of 8th–
        7th Century Median sites and the forma-
        tion of the Iranian architectural traditions."
        AMI 25 [1994]: 73–79.
Meeks, D.
1972   Le Grande Texte des donations au temple
        d'Edfou. Bib. Et. 69. Cairo.
1979   "Les donations aux temples dans l'Égypte
        du Ier millénaire av. J.-C." Pp. 605–87 in
        E. Lipiński (ed.).
Meiggs, R.
1972   The Athenian Empire. Oxford.
Meiggs, R., and Lewis, D.
1980   A Selection of Greek Historical Inscriptions.
        Oxford.
Meillet, A.
1925   Trois conférences sur les Gâthâ de l'Avesta.
        Paris
Meillet, A. and Benveniste, É.
1931   Grammaire du vieux perse. Paris.
Meissner, B.
1896   "Pallacotas." MVAG 1/4: 1–13.
Meister, K.
1982   Die Ungeschichtlichkeit des Kalliasfriedens
        und deren historischen Fölgen. Wiesbaden.
Melchert, H. C.
1993   "A new interpretation of lines C 3–9 of the
        Xanthos stele." Pp. 31–34 in J. Borchhardt
        and G. Dobesch (eds.), Akten des II. Intern.
        Lykien-Symposions. ÖAW, Denkschr. 231
        Bd. Vienna.
[Mélèze]-Modrzejewski, J.
1966   "La règle de droit dans l'Égypte ptoléma-
        ïque." Pp. 125–73 in Essays in Honor of
        C. B. Welles. New Haven.
1981   "Sur l'antisémitisme païen." Pp. 411–39 in
        H. Poliakov (ed.), Le Racisme, mythes et
        sciences. Brussels.
1986   "'Livres sacrés' et justice lagide." Acta
        Univ. Loziensis. Fol. Jurid. 21: 11–44.
1989   "La loi des Égyptiens: le droit grec dans
        l'Égypte romaine." Pp. 97–115 in Historia
        testis: Mélanges T. Zawadzki. University of
        Fribourg.
1991   Les Juifs d'Égypte de Ramsès II à Hadrien.
        Paris.
Melikian-Chirvani, A. S.
1993   "The international Achaemenid style." BAI
        7: 111–30.
Mellink, M.
1976   "A sample problem from the painted tomb
        at Kizilbel." Pp. 15–21 in Actes du colloque
        sur la Lycie antique. Paris.

1979   "Fouilles d'Elmali en Lycie du Nord (Tur-
        quie):   Découvertes   préhistoriques   et
        tombes à fresques." CRAI: 476–95.
1988   "Anatolia." CAH 4²: 211–33.
1991   "The native kingdoms of Anatolia." CAH
        3/2: 619–55.
Meloni, P.
1951   "La grande rivoltà dei satrapi contro Arta-
        serse II (370–359 a.C.)." RSI 63: 13–27.
Melville-Jones, J. R.
1979   "Darics at Delphi." RBN 125: 25–36.
Menasce, J. de
1974   "Vieux perse Artâvan et pehlevi Ahrar." Pp.
        57–60 in Mélanges d'histoire des religions
        offerts à M. C. Puech. Paris.
Menu, B.
1994   "Le tombeau de Pétosiris: Nouvel exa-
        men." BIFAO 94: 311–27.
1995   "Les carrières des Égyptiens à l'étranger
        sous les dominations perses: les critères de
        justification, leur évaluation et leurs li-
        mites." Trans 9: 81–90.
Menu, B. (ed.)
1996   Égypte pharaonique: pouvoir, société. Mé-
        diterranées 6. Paris.
forthcoming   "Le tombeau de Pétosiris: Nouvel
        examen (suite)." BIFAO 95.
Meritt, B. D.; Wade-Gery, H. T.; and MacGregor,
    M. F.
1950   The Athenian Tribute Lists, III. Princeton.
Merkelbach, R.
1991   "Ein Orakel des Apollon für Artemis
        Koloè." ZPE 88: 70–72.
Meshorer, Y., and Qedar, S.
1991   The Coinage of Samaria in the fourth Cent.
        B.C. Jerusalem.
Metzger
1971   "Sur deux groupes de reliefs 'gréco-perses'
        d'Asie Mineure." AC 40: 505–25.
1974   "La stèle trilingue récemment découverte
        du Létôon de Xanthos: le texte grec."
        CRAI: 82–93.
1975   "Ekphora, convoi funèbre, cortège de dig-
        nitaires en Grèce et à la périphérie du
        monde grec." RA: 209–20.
Metzger (ed.)
1979a   Fouilles de Xanthos, VI: La stèle trilingue
        du Létôon. Paris.
1979b   "L'inscription grecque." Pp. 29–48 in
        Fouilles de Xanthos, VI: La stèle trilingue
        du Létôon. Paris.
1987   "Étapes de la découverte du monde lycien
        et perspectives nouvelles offertes à l'étude
        des périodes pré-hellénistiques en Lycie."
        REA 89/1–2: 3–19.
Metzger, H. (under the direction of)
1992   La Région nord du Létôon: Les sculptures.
        Les inscriptions gréco-lycienne. FdX 9/1–2.
        Paris.
Metzler, D.
1975   "Beobachtungen zum Geschichtsbild der
        frühen Achämeniden." Klio 57/2: 443–59.

Meulenaere, H. de
1938   "La famille du roi Amasis." *JEA* 24: 183–87.
1951   *Herodotos over de 26ste dynastie.* Bib. du Muséon 27. Louvain.
1963   "La famille royale des Nectanébo." *ZÄS* 90: 90–93.
1989   "Recherches chronologiques sur un groupe de monuments memphites." Pp. 567–73 in Meyer-Haerinck (eds.).

Meull, K.
1975   "Ein altpersischer Kriegsbrauch." Pp. 699–729 in *Gesammelte Schriften*, II. Basel-Stuttgart.

Meyer, E.
1879   *Geschichte des Königsreiches Pontos.* Leipzig.
1919   "Zu den aramäischen Papyri von Elephantine." *SKPAW* 47: 1026–53.
1924   "Ägyptische Dokumente aus der Perserreich." Pp. 70–100 in *Kleine Schriftren*, II. Halle.

Meyer, L. de., and Haerinck, E. (eds.)
1989   *Archeologia iranica et orientalis: Miscellanea in honorem Louis Vanden Berghe*, I–II. Gand.

Meyers, E. M
1985   "The Shelomite seal and the Judean restoration: Some additional considerations." *Eretz Israel* (Avigad volume) 16: 33–38.

Michaelidis, G.
1943   "Quelques objets inédits d'époque perse." *ASAE* 43: 91–103.

Michaelidou-Nicolaou, I.
1987   "Repercussions of the Phoenician presence in Cyprus." *Studia Phoenicia* 5: 331–38.

Milano, L.
1989   "Food and diet in pre-classical Syria." Pp. 201–71 in *Production and Consumption in the Ancient Near East* (Essays collected by C. Zaccagnini). Budapest.

Mildenberg, L.
1979   "Yehûd: a preliminary study of the provincial coinage of Judaea." Pp. 183–95 in Mørkholm-Waggoner (eds.).
1987   "Baana: Preliminary studies of the local coinage in the fifth Persian satrapy, Part 2." *Eretz-Israel* 19: 28–34.
1988   "Über das Kleingeld in der persischen Provinz Juda." Pp. 721–28, appendix, in H. Weippert.
1990   "Gaza mint authorities in Persian time: Preliminary studies of the local coinage in the fifth satrapy, Part 4." *Trans* 2: 137–46.
1990–91 "Notes on the coin issues of Mazday." *INJ* 11: 923.
1991   "Palästina in der persischen Zeit." Pp. 102–5 in *A Survey of Numismatic Research 1985–1990*. Intern. Ass. Prof. Numismatists, Special Pub. 12. Brussels.
1993   "Über das Münzwesen im Reich der Achämeniden." *AMI* 26 [1995]: 55–79.

1994   "On the money circulation in Palestine from Artaxerxes II till Ptolemy I: Preliminary studies on the local coinage in the fifth Persian satrapy, Part 5." *Trans* 7: 63–71.

Milik, J. T.
1960   "Lettre araméenne d'El-Hibeh." *Aegyptus*: 79–81.
1967   "Les papyrus araméens d'Hermoupolis et les cultes syro-phéniciens en Égypte perse." *Biblica* 48: 546–622.

Millar, F.
1987   "The problem of Hellenistic Syria." Pp. 110–33 in A. Kuhrt and S. Sherwin-White (eds.).

Miller, M. C.
1985   *Perseries: the Arts of the East in Fifth Century Athens.* Ph.D. Harvard University.
1988   "Midas as the Great King in Attic fifth century vase-painting." *AK* 31/2: 79–89.
1989   "The parasol: an oriental status-symbol in Late Archaic and Classical Athens." *JHS* 112: 91–105.
1993   "Adoption and adaptation of Achaemenid metalware forms in Attic black-gloss ware of the fifth century." *AMI* 26 [1995]: 109–46.

Milne, J. G.
1938   "The silver of Aryandes." *JEA* 2: 245–46.
1939   "Trade between Greece and Egypt before Alexander the Great." *JEA* 25: 177–83.

Miltner, F.
1952   "Der Okeanos in der persischen Weltreichsidee." *Saeculum* 3: 522–55.

Minns, E. H.
1913   *Scythians and Greeks.* London.

Miroschedji, P. de
1981a "Fouilles du chantier Ville Royale à Suse (c 1100–540)." *CFAFI* 12: 9–121.
1982   "Notes sur la glyptique de la fin d'Elam." *RAss* 76: 51–63.
1978   "Stratigraphie de la période néo-élamite à Suse." *PaléoOrient* 4: 213–21.
1981b "Observations sur les couches néo-élamites au nord-ouest du Tell de la Ville Royale à Suse." *CDAFI* 12: 143–67.
1985   "La fin du royaume d'Anšan et la naissance de l'Empire perse." *ZA* 75/2: 265–306.
1986   "La localisation de Madaktu et l'organisation politique de l'Élam à l'époque néo-élamite." Pp. 209–25 in *Fragmenta Historiae Elamicae: Mélanges offerts à M. J. Stève.* Paris.
1987   "Fouilles du chantier Ville Royale II à Suse (1975–77), II: Niveaux d'époque achéménide, séleucide, parthe et islamique." *CDAFI* 15: 11–64.
1990a "La fin de l'Élam: essai d'analyse et d'interprétation." *IA* 25: 47–95.
1990b "Note d'orfèvrerie néo-élamite." Pp. 181–94 in Vallat (ed.).

Mitchell, B. M.
1966   "Cyrene and Persia." *JHS* 86: 99–113.

Mitchell, S.
1976 "Requisitioned transport in the Roman Times: A new inscription from Pisidia." *JRS* 66: 106–31.
Mitchell, T. S.
1973 "The bronze lion weight from Abydos." *Iran* 11: 173–75.
Mithraic Studies, 1–2
1975 J. R. Hinnels (ed.). Manchester.
Mittwoch, A.
1955 "Tribute and land-tax in Seleucid Judea." *Biblica* 36: 352–61.
Moggi, M.
1972 "Autori greci di Persika, I: Dionisio di Mileto." *ASNP* 3d series 2/2: 433–68.
1973 "I furti di statue attributi a Serse e le relative restituzione." *ASNP* 3d series 3/1: 1–42.
1977 "Autori greci di Persika, II: Carone di Lampsaco." *ASNP* 3d series 7/1: 1–26.
Momigliano, A.
1929 "La spedizione ateniese in Egitto." *Aegyptus* 10: 190–206.
1933 "Dalla spedizione scitica di Filippo alla spedizione scitica di Dario." *Athenaeum* n.s. 11: 336–39.
1992 *Philippe de Macédoine*. Paris. [Italian ed., Florence, 1934]
Mooren, L.
1977 *La Hiérarchie de cour ptolémaïque: Contribution à l'étude des institutions et des classes dirigeantes à l'époque hellénistique*. Studia Hellenistica 23. Louvain.
Moorey, P. R. S.
1975 "Iranian troops at Deve Hüyük in Syria in the earlier fifth century B.C." *Levant* 7: 108–17.
1978 "The iconography of an Achaemenid stamp-seal acquired in Lebanon." *Iran* 16: 143–54.
1979 "Aspects of worship and ritual on Achaemenid seals." Pp. 218–26 in *Akten des VII. Int. Kongress für Iran: Kunst und Archäologie* (Munich, 1976). AMI suppl. 6.
1980 *Cemeteries of the First Millennium B.C. at Deve Hüyük*. BAR series 87. Oxford.
1982 "Archaeology and pre-Achaemenid metalworking in Iran: a fifteen years retrospective." *Iran* 20: 81–101.
1984 "The Iranian contribution to Achaemenid material culture." *Iran* 23: 21–37.
1985 "Metalwork and glyptic." *CHI* 2: 856–69.
1988 "The Persian Empire." *CAH* 4² (plates): 1–94.
Morgan, J. de
1905 "Tombe achéménide." *MDP* 8: 30–58.
Morgenstern, J.
1956–60 "Jerusalem, 485 B.C." *HUCA* 27: 101–79; 28: 15–37; 31: 1–29.
Mørkholm, O.
1974 "A coin of Artaxerxes III." *NC* 14: 1–4.

Mørkholm, O., and Waggoner, N. M. (eds.)
1979 *Greek Numismatics and Archaeology: Essays in Honor of Margaret Thompson*. Wetteren.
Mørkholm, O., and Zahle, J.
1972 "The coinage of Kuprlli." *Acta Arch.* 48: 57–113.
1976 "The coinages of the Lycian dynasts Kheriga, Kherei and Erbina: A numismatic and archaeological study." *Acta Arch* 47: 47–90.
Morschauser, S. N.
1988 "Using history: reflections on the Bentresh Stela." *SAK* 15: 203–23.
Moscati, S.; Tilia, A. B.; and Ciceroni, T.
1980 *Persepolis, luce e silenzi di un impero scomparso*. Milan.
Mosley, D. J.
1971 "Greeks, Barbarians, language and contact." *AncSoc* 2: 1–6.
Mostafavi, M. T.
1960 "The Achaemenid royal road post stations between Susa and Persepolis." *A Survey of Persian Art* 14: 3008–10.
Mouravieff, S. N.
1993 "Les satrapies achéménides selon Hérodote III. 89–97: la solution du casse-tête." Paper read at a conference in Paris on 31 March 1993. [Russian text, Moscow, 1990]
Mousavi, A.
1989 "The discovery of an Achaemenid station at Deh-Bozan in the Asadābad valley." *AMI* 22: 135–38.
1992 "Pārsa, a stronghold for Darius: a preliminary study of the defence system of Persepolis." *EW* 42/2–4: 203–26.
Moysey, R.
1975 *Greek Relations with the Persian Satraps (371–343 B.C.)*. Ph.D. Princeton.
1985 "Chares and Athenian foreign policy." *CQ* 80/3: 221–27.
1986 "The silver stater issues of Pharnabazos and Datames from the mint of Tarsus in Cilicia." *ANSMN* 31: 7–61.
1987 "IG II² 207 and the great satrap's revolt." *ZPE* 67: 93–100.
1989 "Observations on the numismatic evidence relating to the great satrap revolt of 362/1." *REA* 91/1: 107–39.
1991 "Diodoros, the satraps and the decline of the Persian Empire." *AHB* 5: 113–22.
1992 "Plutarch, Nepos and the Satrapal revolt of 362/1 B.C." *Historia* 41/2: 158–66.
Müller, D.
1994 "Von Kritalla nach Doriskos: Die persische Königstrasse und der Marschweg des Xerxesheeres in Kleinasien." *IM* 44: 17–38.
Mulliez, D.
1982 "Notes sur le transport du bois." *BCH* 106: 107–18.
Munson, R. V.
1988 "Artemisia in Herodotus." *CSCA* 7/1: 91–106.

1991   "The madness of Cambyses (Herodotus 3. 16–38)." *Arethusa* 24/1: 43–64.

Murray, O.
1966   "Ho archaios dasmos." *Historia* 15: 142–56.
1987   "Herodotus and oral history." *AchHist* 2: 93–115.
1988   "The Ionian revolt." *CAH* 4²: 461–90.

Muscarella, O.
1980   "Excavated and unexcavated Achaemenian art." Pp. 23–42 in Schmandt-Besserat (ed.).
1987   "Median art and Medizing scholarship." *JNES* 46/2: 109–27.
1994   "Miscellaneous Median matters." *AchHist* 8: 57–64.

Musche, B.
1989   "Das Mahabarata und die Reliefs von Persepolis." *AMI* 22: 139–49.
1992   *Vorderasiatischer Schmuck von den Anfängen bis zur Zeit der Achaemeniden.* Leiden–New York.

Musti, D.
1965   "Aspetti dell'organizzazione seleucidica in Asia Minore nel III. Sec. a.C." *PdP* 101: 153–60.
1966   "Lo Stato dei Seleucidi: Dinastia, populi, città, da Seleuco ad Antioco III." *SCO* 15: 61–197.

Mutafian, C.
1988   *La Cilicie au carrefour des Empires*, I–II. Paris.

Mysliwiec, K.
1991   "Un *naos* de Darius—roi de l'Égypte." Pp. 221–45 in *Near Eastern Studies dedicated to H. I. H. Prince T. Mikasa.* Wiesbaden.

Naʾaman, N.
1991   "Chronology and history in the Late Assyrian Empire (631–619 B.C.)." *ZA* 81/2: 243–67.

Nagel, W.
1963   "Datierte Glyptik aus Altvorderasien." *AfO* 20: 125–40.

Nagel, W., and Jacobs, B.
1989   "Königsgötter und Sonnengottheit bei altiranischen Dynastien." *Mélanges Amiet* II = *IA* 34: 338–89.

Narain, A. K.
1987   "The Saka Haumavarga and the Amyrgioi: the problem of their identity." *BAI* 1: 27–32.

Naster, P.
1931   *L'Asie Mineure et l'Assyrie aux VIIIᵉ et VIIᵉ s. av. J.-C. d'après les Annales des rois assyriens.* Bib. du Museon 8. Louvain.
1948   "Un trésor de tétradrachmes athéniens trouvé à Tell el-Maskhouta (Égypte)." *RBN* 94: 5–14.
1970a   "Were the labourers of Persepolis paid by means of coined money?" *AncSoc* 1: 129–34.
1970b   "Karsha et Sheqel dans les documents araméens d'Égypte." *RBN* 116: 31–35.

1974   "Indices de peinture de reliefs à Persépolis." *OLP* 5: 47–51.
1979   "Les monnayages satrapaux, provinciaux et régionaux dans l'Empire perse face au numéraire officiel des Achéménides." Pp. 597–604 in Ed. Lipiński (ed.), *State and Temple.*
1989   "Les statères ciliciens de Pharnabaze et de Datame à types communs." Pp. 191–201 in *Kraay-Mørkholm Essays.* Louvain.
1990   "L'or et l'argent dans les textes élamites de Persépolis." Pp. 323–35 in *Opes Atticae: Miscellanea R. Bogaert et H. Van Loon Oblata.* Sacris Erudiri 31. La Haye.

Naveh, J.
1979   "The Aramaic ostraca from Tell Beer-Sheba (Seasons 1971–76)." *Tel-Aviv* 6: 182–95.
1981   "The Aramaic ostraka from Tell-Arad." Pp. 153–76 in Y. Aharoni, *Arad Inscriptions.* Jerusalem: Israel Exploration Society.

Naveh, J., and Greenfield, J. C.
1984   "Hebrew and Aramaic in the Persian period." *CHJ* 1: 115–29.

Nemet-Nejat, K.
1982   *Late Babylonian Field-plans in the British Museum.* Rome.

Nenci, G.
1950   "Le fonti di Erodoto sull'insurrezione ionica." *RAL* ser. VIII, 5/1–2: 106–18.
1958   *Introduzione alle guerre persiane.* Pisa.
1994   *Erodoto. Le Storie. Libro IV: La rivolta della Ionia* (introduction and commentary by Nenci). Florence-Rome.

Neville, J.
1979   "Was there an Ionian revolt?" *CQ* 29: 269–75.

Nichol, M. B.
1970   "Rescue excavations near Dorudzan." *EW* 20: 245–84.

Nicolet, C. (under the direction of)
1978   *Rome et la conquête du monde méditerranéen*, II: *Genèse d'un empire.* Paris.

Nicolet-Pierre, H.
1979   "Les monnaies des deux derniers satrapes d'Égypte avant la conquête d'Alexandre." Pp. 221–30 in Mørkholm-Waggoner (ed.).
1992   "Xerxès et le trésor de l'Athos." *RN* 34: 7–22.

Nicolet-Pierre, H., and Amandry, M.
1994   "Un nouveau trésor de monnaies d'argent pseudo-athéniennes venu d'Afghanistan (1990)." *RN* 36: 34–54.

Nikoforov, V. P., and Savouk, S. A.
1992   "New data of Ancient Bactrian body-armours (in the light of finds from Kampyr-tepe)." *Iran* 30: 49–54.

Nixon, L., and Price, S.
1992   "La dimension et les resources des cités grecques." Pp. 163–200 in O. Murray and S. Price (eds.), *La Cité grecque d'Homère à Alexandre.* Paris.

Nock, A. D.
1972 "Eunuchs in Ancient religion." Pp. 7–15 in *Essays on religion and the Ancient World*, I. Oxford.

Nollé, M.
1992 *Denkmäler vom Satrapensitz Daskyleion: Studien zur graeco-persischen Kunst*. Berlin.

Nougayrol, J.
1947 "Petits textes religieux d'époque achéménide." *RAss* 41/1–4: 29–42.

Nouhaud, M.
1982 *L'Utilisation de l'histoire par les orateurs attiques*. Paris.

Nowak, T. J.
1988 *Darius' Invasion into Scythia: Geographical and Logistical Perspectives*. Ph.D. Miami University.

Nowicki, H.
1982 "Zum Herrschernamen auf dem sogennanten 'Tarkondemos' Siegel." Pp. 227–32 in *Serta Indogermanica = FS Neumann*. Innsbruck.

Nunn, A.
1988 *Die Wandmalerei und das glassierte Wandschmück in Alten Orient*. Leiden.

Nylander, C.
1966 "Clamps and chronology: Achaemenid problems, II." *IA* 6: 130–46.
1968 "*Assyria grammata*: Remarks on the 21st 'Letter of Themistokles.'" *OpRom* 14–15: 119–36.
1970 *Ionians in Pasargadae: Studies in Old Persian Architecture*. Uppsala.
1974a "Al-Beruni and Persepolis." *Acta Iranica* 1: 137–50.
1974b "Anatolians in Susa—and Persepolis(?)." *Acta Iranica* 2: 317–23.
1979 "Achaemenid imperial art." Pp. 345–59 in M. T. Larsen (ed.), *Power and Propaganda: A Symposion on Ancient Empires*. Copenhagen.
1982 "Il milite ignoto: un problema nel mosaïco di Alessandro." Pp. 689–95 in *La regione sotterata dal Vesuvio: Studie prospettive*. Naples.
1983 "The standard of the Great King: A problem in the Alexander mosaic." *OpRom* 19/2: 19–37.
1988 "Masters from Persepolis? A note on the problem of the origins of Maurya Art." Pp. 1029–38 in *Orientalia I: Tucci memoriae dicata*. ISMEO 3. Rome.
1991 "The toothed chisel." *Arch Class* 43: 1037–52.
1993 "Darius III—the coward king: Point and counterpoint." Pp. 145–59 in *Alexander the Great: Reality and Myth*. ARID suppl. 20. Rome.
1994 "Xenophon, Darius, Naram-Sin: A note on the king's 'Year.'" Pp. 57–59 in *Opus mixtum: Essays in Ancient Art and History*.

Acta Inst. Rom. Regn. Suec., ser. in 8°, 21. Stockholm.

Nylander, C., and Flemberg, J.
1981–83 "A foot-note from Persepolis." *Anadolu* 22 [1989]: 57–68.

Oates, D.
1968 *Studies in the Ancient History of Northern Iraq*. London-Oxford.

Obsomer, C.
1989 *La Campagne de Sésostris dans Hérodote: Essai d'interprétation du texte grec à la lumière des réalités égyptiennes*. Brussels.

Oded, B.
1977a "The last days of Judah and the destruction of Jerusalem (609–586 B.C.)." Pp. 469–76 in Hayes and Miller (eds.).
1977b "Judah during the exilic period." Pp. 476–80 in Hayes-Miller (eds.).
1977c "Exile and diaspora." Pp. 480–88 in Hayes-Miller (eds.).
1977d "The Persian period." Pp. 489–531 in Hayes-Miller (eds.).
1979 *Mass Deportations and Deportees in the Neo-Assyrian Empire*. Wiesbaden.

Oden, R. A.
1977 *Studies in Lucian's De Dea Syria*. HSM 15. Missoula, Montana.

Oelsner, J.
1976 "Zwischen Xerxes und Alexander: babylonische Rechtsurkunden und Wirtschaftstexte aus der späten Achämenidenzeit." *WO* 8: 310–18.
1988 "Grundbesitz/Grundeigentum im achämenidischen und seleukidischen Babylonien." Pp. 117–34 in *Das Eigentum in Mesopotamien*. JfW, Sonderband. Berlin.
1989 "Weitere Bemerkungen zu den Neirab-Urkunden." *Klio* 1989/1: 68–77.

Oestergaard, U.
1991 *Akropolis-Persepolis: Tur/Retur*. Aarhus.

Oikonomides, A. N.
1982 "Artemis Medeia: An unpublished funerary stele in the Paul-Getty Museum." *ZPE* 45: 115–18.

Olmstead, A. T.
1935 "Darius as lawgiver." *AJSL* 51: 247–49.
1939 "Persia and the Greek frontier problem." *CIPh* 34/4: 305–22.
1944 "Tattenai, governor of 'Across the river.'" *JNES* 3: 46.
1948 *History of the Persian Empire*. [Repr., Chicago: Phoenix, 1959]

Oppenheim, A. L.
1946 "A fiscal practice of the Ancient Near East." *JNES* 5: 116–20.
1958 "The eyes of the Lord." Pp. 173–80 in *Essays in Memory of E. A. Speiser*. AOS 53.
1965 "On royal gardens in Mesopotamia." *JNES*: 328–33.
1967 "Essay on Overland trade in the first millennium B.C." *JCS* 21: 236–54.

1973   "A note on *ša rēši.*" *JANES* 5 (The Gaster Festschrift): 325–34.
1985   "The Babylonian evidence of Achaemenian rule in Mesopotamia." *CHI* 2: 529–87.

Oren, E. D.
1982   "La période perse [Migdol]." *Le Monde de la Bible* 22: 15–17.
1985   "Migdol: a new fortress on the edge of the Eastern Nile Delta." *BASOR* 256: 7–44.

Orientalia J. Duchesne-Guillemin emerito oblata
1984   *Acta Iranica*, 2d series. Hommages et Opera Minora 23. Leiden.

Orlin, L. L.
1976   "Athens and Persia ca. 507 B.C.: A neglected perspective." Pp. 255–56 in *Michigan Oriental Studies in Honor of G. G. Cameron.* Ann Arbor.

Orsi, D. P.
1979–80 "Tracce di tendenza anticirea (Plutarco, *Vita di Artaserse,* capp. 1–19)." *Sileno* 5–6: 113–46.
1981   "Il daimon del re." *QS* 13: 259–69.
1988   "La rappresentazione del sovrano nella *Vita di Artaserse* plutarchea." *AncSoc* 19: 135–60.

Osborne, M. J.
1971   "Athens and Orontes." *BSA* 66: 297–321.
1973   "Orontes." *Historia*: 515–51.
1975   "The satrapy of Mysia." *Grazer Beiträge* 3: 291–309.
1981   *Naturalization in Athens, I: Decrees granting Citizenship.* Brussels.
1982   *Naturalization in Athens, II: Commentaries on the Decrees granting the Citizenship.* Brussels.
1983   *Naturalization in Athens, III–IV: The testimonia for Grants of Citizenship.* Brussels.

Özet, M. A.
1994   "The tomb of a noble woman from the Hekatomnid period." Pp. 88–96 in J. Isager (ed.), *Hekatomnid Caria and the Ionian Renaissance.* Odense.

Özyigit, O.
1994   "The city walls of Phokaia." *REA* 96/1–2: 77–110.

Pagliaro, A.
1974   "Cyrus et l'Empire perse." *Acta Iranica* 2: 3–23.

Pagliaro, A., and Bausani, A.
1968   *La letteratura persiana.* Milan.

Paice, P.
1986/97 "A preliminary analysis of the Saite and Persian pottery at Tell-el Maskhuta." *BES* 8: 95–107.
1993   "The Punt relief, the Pithom stele and the Periplus of the Erythrean Sea." Pp. 227–35 in A. Harrack (ed.), *Contacts between Cultures: West Asia and North Africa,* I. Lewiston/Queenstone/Lampeter.

Pajakowski, W.
1981   "Satrapia Skudra." *Meander* 2: 75–90.

Panaino, O.
1986   "Tištrya e la stagione delle piove." *Acmè* 39/1: 125–33.
1988   "Tištrya e Mithra." *Acmè* 41/3: 229–42.

Panaino, A.
1990   *Tištrya,* I: *The Avestan Hymn to Sirius.* ISMEO Seria oriental Roma 58/1. Rome.

Papatheophanes, M.
1985   "Heraclitus of Ephesus, the Magi and the Achaemenids." *IA* 20: 101–61.

Papers in Honor of Prof. E. Yarshater
1990   Acta Iranica 30. Leiden.

Parayre, D.
1989   "À propos d'une plaque de harnais en bronze découverte à Samos: réflexions sur le disque solaire ailé." *RAss* 83: 45–51.

Pareti, L.
1961   "Per la storia di alcuni dinaste greche dell'Asia Minore" [1911]. Repr., pp. 179–91 in *Studi minori di storia antica,* II.

Parise, N.
1983   "Fra Assiria e Greci: Dall'argento di Ištar alla moneta." *DdA* 5/2: 37–39.

Parke, H. W.
1933   *Greek Mercenary Soldiers from the Earliest Times to the Battle of Ipsos.* Oxford.
1985   "The massacre of the Branchidae." *JHS* 105: 59–68.

Parlato, S.
1981   "La cosidetta campagna scitica di Dario." *AION:* 213–50.

Parpola, S.
1970–83 *Letters from Assyrian Scholars to the Kings Esarhaddon and Assurbanipal,* I: Texts; II: Commentary and Appendices. Neukirchen-Vluyn.
1987   "Neo-assyrian treaties from the Royal archive of Nimrud." *JCS* 39: 161–86.

Parpola, S., and Watanabe, K.
1988   *Neo-Assyrian Treaties and Loyalty Oath.* SAA 2. Helsinki.

Peat, J.
1989   "Cyrus 'King of lands,' Cambyses 'King of Babylon': The disputed co-regency." *JCS* 31/2: 199–216.

Pedley, J. G.
1972   *Ancient Literary Sources on Sardis.* Cambridge, Massachusetts.
1974   "Carians in Sardis." *JHS:* 96–99.

Penella, R. J.
1974   "Scopelianus and the Eretrians in Cissia." *Athenaeum* 52: 295–300.

Perdrizet, P.
1912   "La légende du châtiment de l'Hellespont par Xerxès." *REA* 14: 357–69.
1921   "Le témoignage d'Eschyle sur le sac d'Athènes par les Perses." *REG* 34: 57–79.

Perdu, O.
1985   "Le monument de Samtoutefnakht à Naples." *RdE* 36: 89–113.
1986   "Prologue à un corpus des stèles royales de la XXVIe dynastie." *BSFE* 105: 23–38.

Perreault, J. Y.
1986 "Céramiques et échanges: les importations attiques au Proche-Orient, du VIᵉ au milieu du IVᵉ s. av. J.-C. Les données archéologiques." *BCH* 110: 145–75.

Perrin, Y.
1990 "D'Alexandre à Néron: le motif de la tente d'apparat. La salle 29 de la *Domus Aurea.*" Pp. 213–29 in J. M. Croisille (ed.), *Neronia IV. Alejandro Magno: modelo de los emperadores romanos.* Coll. Latomus 209. Brussels.

Perrot, J.
1981 "Architecture militaire et palatiale des Achéménides à Suse." Pp. 79–94 in *150 Jahre Deutsches Archäologisches Institut.* Mainz.

Perrot, J., and Ladiray, D.
1974 "La Porte de Darius à Suse." *CDAFI* 4: 43–56.

Petit, T.
1981 *Tissapherne ou les Mésaventures d'une ambition.* Ann Arbor (Univ. microfilms).
1983 "Étude d'une fonction militaire sous la dynastie perse achéménide." *LEC* 51/1: 35–35.
1984 "La réforme impériale et l'expédition européenne de Darius Iᵉʳ: Essai de datation." *RBPh* 53: 36–46.
1985 "L'intégration des cités ioniennes dans l'Empire achéménide (VIᵉ siècle)." *REA* 87/1–2: 43–52.
1987 "Notes sur la réforme impériale de Darius Iᵉʳ et de son expédition européenne: Nouvelle contribution." *LEC* 55/2: 175–79.
1988a "À propos des 'satrapies' ionienne et carienne." *BCH* 112: 307–22.
1988b "L'évolution sémantique des termes hébreux et araméens *phh* et *sgn,* et acadiens *pâḫuatu* et *šaknu.*" *JBL* 107: 53–67.
1990 *Satrapes et Satrapies dans l'Empire achéménide de Cyrus le Grand à Xerxès Iᵉʳ.* Bib. Fac. Phil. Lettres Univ. Liège, fasc. 204. Paris.
1991 "Présence et influence perses à Chypre." *AchHist* 6: 161–78.
1993 "Synchronie et diachronie chez les historiens de l'Empire achéménide: À propos de deux ouvrages de M. A. Dandamaev." *Topoi* 3/1: 39–71.

Petrie, W. M. F.
1909–10 *Meydum and Memphis,* II, III. London.

Petschow, H.
1987 "Zur Eroberung Babyloniens durch Cyrus: Die letzen vorpersischen und ersten persischen Datierung aus dem Tagen und die persische Eroberung Babyloniens." *NABU,* note 84.
1988 "Das Unterkönigtum des Cambyses als 'König von Babylon.'" *RAss* 82: 78–82.

Pfrommer, M.
1991 "Ein achämenidisches Amphorenrhyton mit Aegyptischem Dekor." *AMI* 23: 191–209.

Picard, C.
1922 *Éphèse et Claros.* Paris.
1930 "Les influences étrangères au tombeau de Pétosiris: Grèce ou Perse?" *BIFAO* 30/1: 201–27.

Picard, O.
1980 *Les Grecs devant la menace perse.* Paris.

Picirilli, L. (ed.)
1973 *Gli arbitrati interstatali greci,* I. Pisa.

Piérart, M.
1984 "Deux notes sur la politique d'Athènes en mer Égée." *BCH* 108: 162–76.
1987 "Athènes et son empire: La crise de 447/445." Pp. 297–303 in *Stemmata: Mélanges de philologie, d'histoire et d'archéologie offerts à J. Labarbe.* Liège-Louvain.
1988 "IG I³ 281–284 et le *phoros* de Thrace." Pp. 309–21 in *Comptes et Inventaires dans la cité grecque.* Univ. de Neufchâtel: Recueils et travaux publiés par la faculté des lettres, fasc. 40. Neufchâtel-Geneva.

Pinches, T. G.
1982 *Neo-Babylonian and Achaemenid Economic Texts,* ed. I. L. Finkel. London.

Pirart, E.
1995 "Les noms des Perses." *JA* 283: 57–68.

Pitard, W. T.
1987 *Ancient Damascus: A Historical Study of the Syrian City-State from Earliest Times until Its Fall to the Assyrians in 732 B.C.E.* Winona Lake, Indiana.

Pitschikjan, I. R.
1992 *Oxos-Schatz und Oxos-Tempel: Achämenidische Kunst in Mittelasien.* Berlin.

Planhol, X. de
1963 "Geographica Pontica, I–II." *JA* 251: 293–309.
1981 "La Cappadoce: formation et transformation d'un concept géographique." Pp. 25–38 in *Le aree omogenee della civiltà rupestre nell'ambito dell'impero bizantino: La Cappadocia.* Galatina.
1992 "Les galeries drainantes souterraines: Quelques problèmes généraux." Pp. 129–42 in D. Balland (ed.), *Les Eaux cachées: Études géographiques sur les galeries drainantes souterraines.* Paris.

Poebel, A.
1937–38 "Chronology of Darius' first year of reign." *AJSL* 54–55: 142–65, 285–314.

Poetto, M.
1985 "Un nuovo sigillo anatolico-persiano." *Kadmos* 24: 83–85.

Pomeroy, S. B.
1984 "The Persian king and the queen bee." *AJAH* 9/2 [1990]: 98–108.
1994 *Xenophon's Œconomicus: A Social and Historical Commentary.* Oxford.

Pons, N.
1993 "Abû Qubûr: Les objets en métal d'époque achéménide tardive." *NAPR* 8: 3–30.

Pope, A. U.
1957 "Persepolis as a ritual city." *Archaeology* 10: 123–30.

Porada, E.
1960 "Greek impressions from Ur." *Iraq* 27: 228–34.
1961 Review of Schmidt 1957, in *JNES* 20: 66–70.
1963 *Iran ancien* (coll. "L'art dans le monde"). French trans. Paris.
1979 "Achaemenid art, monumental and minute." Pp. 57–94 in R. Ettinghausen and E. Yarshater (eds.), *Highlights of Persian Art*. Boulder, Colorado.
1985 "Classic Achaemenian architecture and sculpture." *CHI* 2: 828–31.
1989 "A ram's head from Iran in the Honolulu Academy of arts." Pp. 537–42 in Meyer and Haerinck (eds.).

Porten, B.
1968 *Archives from Elephantine: The Life of an Ancient Jewish Military Colony*. Berkeley–Los Angeles.
1969 "The religion of the Jews of Elephantine in light of the Hermopolis papyri." *JNES* 28: 116–21.
1983 "Une lettre araméenne conservée à l'Académie des inscriptions et belles-lettres (AI 5–7): une nouvelle reconstruction." *Semitica* 33: 89–100.
1984 "The Jews in Egypt." *CHJ* 1: 372–400.
1985a "Hereditary leases in Aramaic letters." *BiOr* 42/3–4: 284–88.
1985b "Aramaic letters in Italian Museums." Pp. 429–53 in *Studi in onore di Edda Bresciani*. Pisa.
1986a "Une autre lettre araméenne à l'Académie des inscriptions (AI 2–4): une nouvelle reconstruction." *Semitica* 36: 71–86.
1986b *Select Aramaic Papyri from Ancient Egypt*. Jerusalem.
1987a "Royal grants in Egypt: a new interpretation of Driver 2." *JNES* 46/1: 39–48.
1987b "Cowley 7 reconsidered." *Orientalia* 56/1: 89–92.
1988a "Aramaic papyrus fragments in the Egyptian Museum of West Berlin." *Orientalia* 57/1: 14–54.
1988b "The Aramaic boat papyrus (P. Ber. 23000): a new collation." *Orientalia* 57/1: 76–81.
1990 "The calendar of Aramaic texts from Achaemenid and Ptolemaic Egypt." Pp. 13–32 in P. Shaked and A. Netzer (eds.), *Irano-Judaica* II. Jerusalem.

Porten, B., and Yardeni, A.
1986 *Textbook of Aramaic Documents from Ancient Egypt*, I: *Letters*. Jerusalem.
1992 *Textbook of Aramaic Documents from Ancient Egypt*, II: *Contracts*. Jerusalem.
1993 *Textbook of Aramaic Documents from Ancient Egypt*, III: *Literature, Accounts, Lists*. Jerusalem.

Porter, S. E.
1992 "Artemis Medeia inscription again." *ZPE* 93: 219–21.

Posener, G.
1934 "À propos de la stèle de Bentresh." *BIFAO* 34: 74–81.
1936 *La Première Domination perse en Égypte*. Cairo.
1938 "Le canal du Nil à la mer Rouge avant les Ptolémées." *CdE* 25: 259–73.
1947 "Les douanes de la Méditerranée dans l'Égypte saïte." *RPh* 21: 117–31.
1975 "L'*anachôrésis* dans l'Égypte pharaonique." Pp. 663–69 in *Le Monde grec: Hommages à Claire Préaux*. Brussels.
1986 "Du nouveau sur Kombabos." *RdE* 37: 91–96.

Postgate, N.
1993 "The land of Aššur and the yoke of Aššur." *World Archaeology* 23/3: 247–63.
1994 "In search of the first empires." *BASOR* 293: 1–13.

Pottier, E.
1903 "L'auteur du vase trouvé à Suse: Note complémentaire." *CRAI*: 216–19.

Potts, D. T.
1990a *The Arabian Gulf in Antiquity*, I: *From Prehistory to the Fall of the Achaemenid Empire*. Oxford.
1990b *The Arabian Gulf in Antiquity*, II: *From Alexander the Great to the Coming of Islam*. Oxford.

Powell, M.
1978 "A contribution to the history of money in Mesopotamia prior to the invention of coinage." Pp. 211–43 in B. Hruška and G. Komoroczy (eds.), *Festschrift für L. Matouš*, II. Budapest.

Préaux, Cl.
1954 "Sur l'origine des monopoles lagides." *CdE*: 312–27.

Preisigke, F.
1907 "Der ptolemäische Staatspost." *Klio* 7: 241–77.

Price, M. J.
1989 "Darius I and the daric." *REA* 91/1–2: 9–14.
1991 *The Coinage in the Name of Alexander the Great and Philipp Arrhidaeus* (A British Museum Catalogue), I–II. Zurich/London.

Price, M. J., and Waggoner, A.
1975 *Archaic Greek Coinage: The Asyut Hoard*. London.

Pritchett, W. K.
1969 "The transfer of the Delian Treasury." *Historia* 18/1: 17–21.
1991 *The Greek State at War*, Part V. Berkeley-Los Angeles-Oxford: University of California Press.

Purvis, J. D.
1988   "Exile and return." Pp. 151–75, 252–54 in
        H. Shanks (ed.), *Ancient Israel: A Short
        History from Abraham to the Roman De-
        struction of the Temple*. Washington, D.C.
Quaegebeur, J.
1980–81 "Sur la 'loi sacrée' dans l'Égypte gréco-
        romaine." *AncSoc* 11–12: 227–40.
1990   "Les rois saïtes amateurs de vin." *AncSoc*
        21: 241–71.
Radet, G.
1893   *La Lydie et le monde grec au temps des
        Mermnades*. Paris.
1909   "La première incorporation de l'Égypte à
        l'Empire perse." *REA* 11: 201–10.
1925   "Notes sur l'histoire d'Alexandre, IV: Les
        négociations entre Darius et Alexandre."
        REA 27: 183–208.
1930   "Alexandre en Syrie: Les offres de paix que
        lui fit Darius." Pp. 236–47 in *Mélanges
        R. Dussaud*. Paris.
Raditsa, L.
1983   "Iranians in Asia Minor." *CHI* 3: 100–15.
Radt, W.
1983   "Eine gräko-persische Grabstele im Mu-
        seum Bergama." *IM* 33: 53–68.
Rahe, P. A.
1980   "The military situation in Western Asia on
        the eve of Cunaxa." *AJPh* 101/1: 79–96.
Rahimi-Laridjani, F.
1988   *Die Entwicklung der Bewässerungsland-
        wirtschaft im Iran bis in sasanidisch-früh-
        islamische Zeit*. Wiesbaden.
Rahmani, L. Y.
1971   "Silver coins of the fifth century from Tell-
        Gamma." *IEJ* 21: 158–60.
Rainey, A. F.
1969   "The satrapy 'beyond the river.'" *AJBA* 1:
        51–78.
Rantz, B.
1989   "À propos de l'Égyptien au geste 'perse.'"
        RBPh 67/1: 103–21.
Rapin, C.
1983   "Les inscriptions économiques de la tré-
        sorerie hellénistique d'Aï-Khanoum." *BCH*
        107: 315–72.
1992a   *La Trésorerie du palais hellénistique d'Aï-
        Khanoum. Fouilles d'Aï-Khanoum 8*. Paris.
1992b   "Les sanctuaires de l'Asie centrale à l'é-
        poque hellénistique: état de la question."
        Pp. 101–24 in *Études de lettres*. Lausanne.
Rapin, C., and Isamiddinov, M.
1994   "Fortifications hellénistiques de Samar-
        cande (Samarkand-Afrasiab)." *Topoi* 4/2:
        547–65.
Rapp, A.
1865   "Die Religion und Sitte der Perser und
        übrigen Iranier nach den griechischen und
        römischen Quellen." *ZDMG* 19: 1–89.

Rappaport, U.
1969   "Gaza and Ascalon in the Persian and Hel-
        lenistic periods in relation to their coins."
        IEJ 19/4: 75–80.
1981   "The first Judean coinage." *JJS* 32/1: 1–17.
Ratté, C.
1989   "Five Lydian felines." *AJA* 93: 379–93.
1992   "The 'Pyramid tomb' at Sardis." *IM* 42:
        135–61.
Rawlinson, G.
1871   *The Five Great Monarchies of the Ancient
        World*, I–III. London.
Ray, J. D.
1986   "Psammuthis and Hakoris." *JEA* 72: 149–
        58.
1987   "Egypt: dependence and independence
        (424–343 B.C.)." *AchHist* 1: 79–96.
1988   "Egypt 525–404 B.C." *CAH* 4²: 254–86.
Reade, J.
1986   "A hoard of silver currency from Achaeme-
        nid Babylonia." *Iran* 24: 79–87.
1972   "The neo-Assyrian court and army: evi-
        dence from the sculptures." *Iraq* 34: 87–112.
1978   "Studies in Assyrian geography (suite)."
        RAss 72/2: 157–80.
Rebuffat, F.
1983   "Alexandre le Grand et les problèmes fi-
        nanciers au début de son règne (été 336–
        printemps 334)." *RN* 25: 43–52.
Reding-Hourcade, N.
1984   "Recherches sur l'iconographie de la dé-
        esse Anáhita." Pp. 199–207 in Doncel and
        Lebrun (eds.).
Redmount, C. A.
1995   "The Wadi Tumilat and the 'Canal of the
        Pharaohs.'" *JNES* 54/2: 127–35.
Rehm, E.
1992   *Achämenidisches Schmuck*. Berlin.
1993   "Inkrustation bei Achämenidischen Arm-
        reifen." *AMI* 26 [1995]: 105–7.
Reich, J.
1933   "The codification of the Egyptian laws by
        Darius and the origin of the 'Demotic
        Chronicle.'" *Mizraim* 1: 1–18.
Reich, R.
1992   "The Beth-zur, Citadel II: a Persian resi-
        dency?" *Tel-Aviv* 19/1: 113–23.
Reinach, S.
1905   "Xerxès et l'Hellespont." *RA*: 1–14.
Reinach, T.
1887   *Essai sur la numismatique des rois de Cap-
        padoce*. Paris.
1890a   *Mithridate Eupatôr, roi du Pont*. Paris.
1890b   "La dynastie de Commagène." *REG* 2:
        362–79.
1892   "Un fragment d'un nouvel historien d'A-
        lexandre." *REG* 5: 306–26.
Revere, R. B.
1975   "Les ports de commerce de la Méditer-
        ranée orientale et la neutralité des côtes."
        In K. Polanyi and C. Arensberg (eds.), *Les

Systèmes économiques dans l'histoire et la théorie. Paris. [French trans.]

Revillout, E.
1880 "Premier extrait de la Chronique démotique de Paris." *RdE* 2: 349–87.

Rey-Coquais, J. P.
1974 *Arados et sa pérée aux époques grecque, romaine et byzantine.* BAH 97. Paris.

Reyes, A. T.
1994 *Archaic Cyprus: A Study of the Textual and Archaeological Evidence.* Oxford.

Rhodes, P. J.
1985 *The Athenian Empire.* G & R New Surveys in the Classics 17. Oxford.
1992 "The Delian League to 449 B.C." *CAH* 5²: 34–61.

Ricciardi, R. V.
1980 "Archaeological survey in the upper Atrek valley (Khorassan, Iran): preliminary report." *Mesopotamia* 15: 51–72.

Richter, G. M. A.
1946 "Greeks in Persia." *AJA* 50: 15–30.
1949 "The late 'Achaemenians' or 'Graeco-Persian' gems." Pp. 291–98 in *Studies L. Shear.* Hesperia suppl. 8. Princeton.
1952 "Greek subjects on 'Graeco-persian' seal stones." Pp. 189–94 in *Archeologia orientalia in memoriam E. Herzfeld.* New York.

Ritner, R. K.
1980 "Khababash and the Satrap stela: a grammatical rejoinder." *ZÄS* 107: 135–37.

Ritter, H. W.
1965 *Diadem und Königsherrschaft.* Munich.
1987 "Die Bedeutung des Diadems." *Historia* 36/3: 291–301.

Roaf, M.
1974 "The subject peoples on the base of the statue of Darius." *CDAFI* 4: 73–160.
1979 "Texts about the sculptures and sculptors at Persepolis." *Iran*: 65–74.
1983 *Sculptures and Sculptors at Persepolis.* Iran 21. London.

Roaf, M., and Boardman, J.
1980 "A greek painting at Persepolis." *JHS* 100: 204–6.

Robert, J., and Robert, L.
1983 *Fouilles d'Amyzon en Carie, I: Exploration, histoire, monnaies et inscriptions.* Paris.

Robert, L.
1937 *Études anatoliennes.* Paris.
1945 *Le Sanctuaire de Sinuri près de Mylasa, I: Les Inscriptions grecques.* Paris.
1948a "Hyrcanis." *Hellenica* 6: 16–26. Paris.
1948b "Hiérocésarée." *Hellenica* 6: 27–56. Paris.
1948c "Le site ancien de Sariçam, Moschakômè et Maschakômè." *Hellenica* 6: 56–59.
1963 *Noms indigènes dans l'Asie Mineure gréco-romaine.* Paris.
1964 "La déesse de Hiérapolis Castabala à l'époque gréco-romaine." Pp. 17–100 in A. Dupont-Sommer and L. Robert (eds.), *La*

Déesse de Hiérapolis Castabala (Cilicie). Paris.
1967 "Sur des inscriptions d'Éphèse." *RPh* 41/1: 7–84.
1973 "Statues de héros mysiens à Délos." Pp. 478–85 in *Études déliennes.* BCH suppl. 1. Paris.
1975 "Une nouvelle inscription de Sardes: Règlement de l'autorité perse relatif à un culte de Zeus." *CRAI*: 306–30.
1976 "Monnaies grecques de l'époque impériale." *RN*: 25–56.
1978a "Une malédiction funéraire dans la plaine de Karayük." *CRAI*: 277–86.
1978b "Les conquêtes du dynaste lycien Arbinas." *JS*: 3–47.
1980 *À travers l'Asie Mineure: Poètes et prosateurs, monnaies grecques, voyageurs et géographie.* BEFAR 239. Paris.
1987 *Documents d'Asie Mineure.* BEFAR 239 bis. Paris.

Robertson, D. S.
1939 "A Sybarite Himation." *JHS* 69/1: 136.

Robertson, N.
1980 "The sequence of events in the Aegean in 408 and 407 B.C." *Historia* 29/3: 282–301.
1987 "Government and society at Miletus, 525–442 B.C." *Phoenix* 41: 356–98.

Robin, C.
1991–93 "Quelques épisodes marquants d'histoire sud-arabique." Pp. 56–70 in *L'Arabie antique de Karib'îl à Mahomet (nouvelles données sur l'histoire des Arabes grâce aux inscriptions).* Vol. 61 of *Rev. du Monde méditerranéen et musulman.*

Robins, G.
1987 88 "Proportions in Persian and Egyptian art." *BES* 9: 57–60.

Robinson, E. S. G.
1958 "The beginnings of Achaemenid coinage." *NC*: 187–93.

Roche, M. J.
1994 "Les débuts de l'implantation nabatéenne à Petra." *Trans* 8: 35–46.

Rodenwalt, G.
1933 "Griechische Reliefs in Lykien." *SB Berlin*: 1028–55.

Roebuck, C.
1988 "Trade." *CAH* 4²: 446–60.

Roller, L. E.
1987 "Hellenistic epigraphic texts from Gordion." *AnSt* 37: 103–33.
1991 "The Great Mother at Gordion: the Hellenization of an Anatolian cult." *JHS* 111: 128–43.

Rollinger, R.
1993 *Herodots babylonischen Logos: Eine kritische Untersuchung der Glaubwürdigkeitsdiskussion.* Innsbrücker Beiträge z. Kulturwissenschaft, Sonderheft 84. Innsbruck.

Romane, P.
1988 "Alexander's siege of Gaza." *AW* 18: 21–30.
1994 "Alexander's sieges of Miletus and Halicarnassus." *AW* 25/1: 77–91.
Root, M. C.
1979 *The King and Kingship in Achaemenid Art: Essays on the Creation of an Iconography of Empire.* Acta Iranica, textes et Mémoires 9. Leiden.
1980 "The Persepolis perplex: some prospects borne of retrospect." Pp. 5–63 in Schmandt-Besserat (ed.).
1985 "The Parthenon Frieze and the Apadana reliefs at Persepolis: reassessing a programmatic relationship." *AJA* 89: 103–20.
1988 "Evidence from Persepolis for the dating of Persian and Archaic Greek coinage." *NC:* 1–12.
1989 "The Persian archer at Persepolis: aspects of chronology, style and symbolism." *REA* 91/1–2: 33–50.
1990 "Circles of artistic programming: strategies for studying creative process at Persepolis." Pp. 115–39 in A. C. Gunter (ed.), *Investigating Artistic Environments in the Ancient Near East.* Washington.
1991 "From the heart: powerful persianisms in the art of the Western Empire." *AchHist* 6: 1–29.
1994 "Lifting the veil: approaches to the study of artistic transmission beyond the boundaries of historical periodization." *AchHist* 8: 9–37.
Rossi, A. V.
1981 "La varietà linguistica nell'Iran achemenide." *AION, sez. ling.* 3: 141–95.
Rostovtzeff, M.
1909 "Angariae." *Klio* 6: 249–58.
1941 *The Social and Economic History of the Hellenistic World,* I–III. Oxford.
Roueché, C., and Sherwin White, S.
1985 "Some aspects of the Seleucid Empire: the Greek inscriptions from Failaka in the Arabian Gulf." *Chiron* 15: 1–39.
Rougé, J.
1988 "La navigation en mer Érythrée dans l'Antiquité." Pp. 59–74 in J. F. Salles (ed.), *L'Arabie et ses mers bordières, I: Itinéraires et voisinages.* TMO 16.
Roy, J.
1967 "The mercenaries of Cyrus." *Historia* 16: 287–323.
Rozenberg, S.
1993 "An Achaemenian ivory vessel." *IMJ* 11: 51–58.
Ruzicka, S.
1983a "Clazomenae and Persian foreign policy, 387/6 b.c." *Phoenix* 37/2: 104–8.
1983b "Curtius 4.1.34–37 and the *magnitudo belli.*" *CJ* 79/1: 30–34.
1985a "Cyrus and Tissaphernes, 407–401 b.c." *CJ* 80/3: 204–11.

1985b "A note on Philip's Persian War." *AJAH* 10 [1990]: 84–95.
1988 "War in the Aegean, 333–331 b.c.: a reconsideration." *Phoenix* 42/2: 131–51.
1992a "Athens and the politics of the Eastern Mediterranean in the fourth cent. b.c." *AW* 23/1: 63–70.
1992b *Politics of a Persian Dynasty: the Hecatomnids in the Fourth Century b.c.* Oklahoma Series in Classical Literature 14. Norman, Oklahoma.
Sachs, A. J., and Hunger, H.
1988 *Astronomical Diaries and Related Texts from Babylonia,* I. ÖAW, Phil. Hist. Kl., Denkschriften 195. Vienna.
Sack, R. H.
1983 "The Nabonidus Legend." *RAss* 77: 59–67.
1994 *Cuneiform Documents from the Chaldean and Persian Periods.* London-Toronto.
Saggs, H. W. F.
1959 "Two administrative officials at Erech in the 6th cent. b.c." *Sumer* 15: 29–38.
Salles, J. F.
1987 "The Arab-Persian Gulf under the Seleucids." Pp. 75–109 in A. Kuhrt and S. Sherwin-White (eds.).
1988b "La circumnavigation de l'Arabie dans l'Antiquité classique." Pp. 75–102 in Salles (ed.).
1990 "Les Achéménides dans le Golfe arabo-persique." *AchHist* 4: 111–30.
1991a "Du blé, de l'huile et du vin." *AchHist* 6: 207–36.
1991b "Du bon et du mauvais usage des Phéniciens." *Topoi* 1: 48–70.
1992a "L'Arabie sans Alexandre [Review of Pots 1990b]." *Topoi* 2: 201–35.
1992b "Découvertes du Golfe arabo-persique aux époques grecque et romaine." *L'Océan et les mers lointaines dans l'Antiquité* = REA 94/1–2: 79–97.
1994 "Du blé, de l'huile et du vin: Notes sur les échanges commerciaux en Méditerranée orientale vers le milieu du Ier millénaire av. J.-C." *AchHist* 8: 191–215.
Salles, J. F. (ed.)
1988a *L'Arabie et ses mers bordières.* TMO 16. Lyon.
Salmon, P.
1961 "Charon d'Aphrodisias et la révolte égyptienne de 360 av. J.-C." *CdE* 36: 365–76.
1965 *La Politique égyptienne d'Athènes (VIᵉ–Vᵉ siècles av. J.-C.).* Brussels.
1985 "Les relations entre la Perse et l'Égypte du VIᵉ au IVᵉ s. av. J.-C." Pp. 147–68 in *The Land of Israel: Cross-Roads of Civilizations.* Louvain.
Samsaris, D.
1983 "Les Péoniens dans la vallée du bas Strymon." *Klio* 64/2: 340–77.
Sancisi-Weerdenburg, H.
1980 *Yaunā en Persai.* Groningen.

1982   *Geschiedenis van het Perzische Rijk.* Haarlem.

1983a "Exit Atossa: images of women in Greek historiography on Persia." Pp. 21–33 in A. Cameron and A. Kuhrt (eds.), *Images of Women in Antiquity.* London-Canberra.

1983b "The Zendan and the Ka^cbah." Pp. 145–51 in H. Koch and D. N. MacKenzie (eds.), *Kunst und Kultur der Achämenidenzeit und ihr Fortleben.* AMI suppl. 10. Berlin.

1985   "The death of Cyrus: Xenophon's *Cyropaedia* as a source for Iranian history." Pp. 459–71 in *Papers in Honour of Mary Boyce,* II. Hommages et Opera Minora 11. Leiden.

1987a "Decadence in the Empire or decadence in the sources? From source to synthesis: Ctesias." *AchHist* 1: 33–46.

1987b "The fifth Oriental monarchy and Hellenocentrism." *AchHist* 2: 117–31.

1988a "Was there ever a Median Empire?" *AchHist* 3: 197–212.

1988b *"Persikon de karta o stratos dôron*: a typically Persian gift (Hdt. IX.109)." *Historia* 37/3: 372–74.

1989a "The personality of Xerxes, King of Kings." Pp. 549–61 in *Archeologia iranica et orientalis: Miscellanea in honorem I. Vanden Berghe,* I. Ghent.

1989b "Gifts in the Persian Empire." Pp. 129–46 in Briant and Herrenschmidt (eds.).

1990   "'The quest for an elusive Empire." *AchHist* 4: 263–74.

1991a "Through travellers' eyes: the Persian monuments as seen by European travellers." *AchHist* 7: 1–35.

1991b "Nowruz in Persepolis." *AchHist* 7: 173–201.

1992   Review of Roaf 1983, *BiOr* 59/1–2: 245–51.

1993a "The orality of Herodotus' Medikos Logos or: the Median empire revisited." *AchHist* 8 [1994]: 39–55.

1993b "Alexander at Persepolis." Pp. 177–88 in *Alexander the Great: Myth and Reality.* ARID suppl. 21. Rome.

1993c "Found, a gazelle!" *DATA,* note 8.

1993d "The effect of cardamum." *DATA,* note 11.

1993e "Caranus' distribution of tableware." *DATA,* note 13.

1994   "Xerxes vanuit Perzische optiek." *Lampas* 27: 194–212.

1995   "Persian food: Stereotypes and political identity." Pp. 286–302 in J. Witkin, D. Harvey, and M. Dobson (eds.), *Food in Antiquity.* Exeter.

forthcoming 1 "Xerxes and the Daiva."

forthcoming 2 "Persian education and the Greeks."

Sancisi-Weerdenburg, H. (ed.)

1987c *Persepolis en Pasargadae in Wisseland Perspectief.* Groningen-Leiden.

San Nicolo, M.

1933a "Die Monstreprozess des Gimillu, eines *širku* von Eanna." *AOr* 5: 61–77.

1933b "Zur Chronologie des Bēl-šimmani und Samaš-eriba." *AOr* 6: 335–38.

Santoro, A.

1972   "A proposito del cerimoniale delle 'mani coperte' nel mondo achemenide." *RSO* 47/1–2: 37–42.

Sapin, J.

1990   "Essai sur les structures géographiques de la toponymie araméenne dans la Trouée de Homs (Liban-Syrie) et sur leur signification historique." *Trans* 2: 73–108.

1992   "La géographie, outil de recherche sur la Syrie–Palestine achéménide." *Trans* 5: 95–112.

Sarfaraz

1971   "Un pavillon de l'époque de Cyrus le Grand à Borazdjan." *Bastan Chenasi va Honar-e Iran* 7–8: 22–25.

Sartre, M.

1988   "La Syrie creuse n'existe pas." Pp. 15–40 in *Géographie historique du Proche-Orient.* Paris.

1989   "La Syrie sous la domination achéménide." Pp. 9–18 in C. R. Dentzer and W. Orthmann (eds.), *Archéologie et Histoire de la Syrie, 2: La Syrie de l'époque achéménide à l'avènement de l'Islam.* Schrift. z. Vorderas. Arch. 1. Saarbrück.

Sauneron, J., and Yoyotte, J.

1952   "La campagne nubienne de Psammétique II et sa signification historique." *BIFAO* 50: 157–207.

Savalli, I.

1987   "Les pouvoirs de Ptolémée de Telmessos." *ASNP* 3d series 17/1: 129–37.

1988   "L'idéologie dynastique des poèmes grecs de Xanthos." *AC* 57: 103–23.

Sayar, M. H.

1993   "Epigraphische Forschungen in Ostkilikien 1990." Pp. 319–27 in G. Dobesch and G. Rehrenböck (eds.), *Die epigraphische und altertumskundliche Erforschung Kleinasiens* (Hundert Jahre Kleinasiatische Kommission der Österreichischen Akademie der Wissenschaften). Suppl. to TAM 14, ÖAW Phil. Hist Kl. Denkschr. 236. Vienna.

Schachermeyr, F.

1970   *Alexander in Babylon und die Reichsordnung nach seinem Tode.* Vienna-Cologne-Graz.

1973   *Alexander der Grosse: Das Problem seiner Persönlichkeit und seine Wirken.* Vienna.

1975   "Alexander und die unterworfenen Nationen." Pp. 47–79 in *Alexandre le Grand: Image et réalité.* Entretiens Hardt 22. Geneva.

Schauenberg, K.

1975   "Eurymédôn eimi." *AthMitt* 90: 90–100.

Scheil, V.

1907   *Textes élamites-anzanites.* MDFP 9. Paris.

1914 "Le Gobryas de la Cyropédie et les textes cunéiformes." *RAss* 11: 17–27.

Schiwek, H.
1962 "Der Persische Golf als Schiffarts und Seehandelsroute im Achämenidischen Zeit und in der Zeit Alexanders des Grossen." *Bonn. Jahrb.* 162: 4–97.

Schlumberger, D.
1953 *L'Argent grec dans l'Empire achéménide.* Paris.
1971 "La coiffure du Grand Roi." *Syria* 48: 375–83.

Schmandt-Besserat (ed.)
1980 *Ancient Persia: the art of an Empire.* Malibu: Undena.

Schmidt, E. F.
1953 *Persepolis* I. OIP 68. Chicago.
1957 *Persepolis* II: *Contents of the Treasury and other Discoveries.* OIP 69. Chicago.
1970 *Persepolis* III: *The Royal Tombs and other Monuments.* OIP 70. Chicago.

Schmitt, R.
1970 "Βαρζοχαρα: ein neues Anahita-Epitheton aus Kappadokien." *ZVS* 84: 207–10.
1972 "Die achaimenidische Satrapie ΤΑΥΑΙΥ ΔΡΑΥΑΗΥΑ." *Historia* 21: 523–27.
1976a "Der Titel 'Satrap.'" Pp. 373–90 in *Studies in Greek, Italic and Indo-European Linguistics offered to L. R. Palmer.* Innsbruck.
1976b "The Medo-Persian names of Herodotus in the light of the new evidence from Persepolis." *AAH* 24: 25–35.
1977 "Achaemenid Throne-names in Babylonian astronomical texts." *AJAH*: 129–47.
1978a *Die Iranier-Namen bei Aischylos.* Iranica Graeca Vetustiora; Veröffent. Iran. Komm. 6. Vienna.
1978b "Königtum im alten Iran." *Saeculum* 28/4: 384–95.
1979 "Iranische Personennamen auf griechischen Inschriften." Pp. 137–52 in *Actes du VIIe congrès international d'épigraphie grecque et latine (Constantza, 9–15 septembre 1977).* Paris-Bucharest.
1980 "Zur babylonischen Version der Bisutun-Inschrift." *AfO* 27: 106–26.
1981 *Altpersische Siegel-Inschriften.* Vienna.
1982a "Iranische Wörter und Namen im Lykischen." Pp. 373–88 in *Serta Indogermanica = Festsch. Neumann.* Innsbruck.
1982b *Iranische Namen in den Indogermanischen Sprachen Kleinasiens (Lykisch, Lydisch, Phrygisch).* Vienna.
1982c "Achaemenid Throne-names." *AION* 42/1: 83–95.
1983a "Achaemenid dynasty." *Encyclopaedia Iranica* 1/4.
1983b "Achaimenidisches bei Thukydides." Pp. 69–86 in H. Koch and D. MacKenzie (eds.), *Kunst, Kultur und Geschichte der Achämenidenzeit und ihr Fortleben.*

1984 "Perser und Persisches in der alten Attischen Komödie." Pp. 459–72 in *Orientalia Duchesne-Guillemin.*
1987 "Der Namen des bei Issos gefallenen satrap." *AMI* 20: 247–50.
1988 "Achaimenideninschriften in griechischer literarischer Überlieferung." Pp. 17–38 in *A Green Leaf (Papers Asmussen).*
1990a "The name of Darius." Pp. 194–99 in *Papers Yarshater.*
1990b "Der erste 'Mager' Name aus Babylonien." *STIR* 19/1: 5–12.
1990c *Epigraphisch-exegetischen Noten zu Dareios' Bisutun-Inschriften.* ÖAW, Phil. Hist. Kl., Sitzber. 561. Vienna.
1991a "Name und Religion: Anthroponomastisches zur Frage der religiösen Verhältnisse des Achämenidenreiches." Pp. 111–28 in Kellens (ed.).
1991b *The Bisutun Inscriptions of Darius the Great: Old Persian Text.* CII part 1, vol. 10. London.
1991c "Zu dem 'Arischen Ahuramazda.'" *STIR* 20/2: 189–92.
1992 "Zum Schluss von Dareios' Inschrift *Susa e.*" *AMI* 25 [1994]: 147–54.

Schnabel, P.
1923 *Berossos und die babylonische-hellenistische Literatur.* Leipzig-Berlin.

Schnoll, R.
1987 "Alexander der Grosse und die Sklaverci am Hofe." *Klio* 69: 108–21.

Schottky, M.
1989 *Media Atropatene und Gross-Armenien in hellenistischer Zeit.* Bonn.

Schrader, C.
1976 *La paz de Calias: Testimonios e interpretacion* (epilogue by A. E. Raubitschek, pp. 215–17). Barcelona.

Schreiner, J. H.
1984 "Historical methods, Hellanikos, and the era of Kimon." *OpAth* 15: 163–71.

Schulman, A. R.
1981 "A 'Persian gesture' from Memphis." *BES* 3: 103–11.

Schumacher, L.
1987 "Themistokles und Pausanias: Die Katastrophe der Sieger." *Gymnasium* 94: 218–46.

Schur, N.
1989 *History of the Samaritans.*

Schur, W.
1926 "Zur Vorgeschichte des Ptolemäerreiches." *Klio* 20: 270–302.

Schwartz, D. R.
1990 "On some papyri and Josephus' sources and chronology for the Persian period." *JSJ* 21/2: 175–99.

Schwartz, J.
1949 "Les conquérants perses et la littérature égyptienne." *BIFAO* 48: 65–80.

1986 "Récits bibliques et mœurs perses." Pp. 267–77 in *Hellenica et Judaica: Hommages à V. Nikiprowetzky.* Louvain-Paris.

Schwartz, M.
1985 "The religion of Achaemenian Iran." *CHI* 2: 664–97.

Schwenk, C. J.
1985 *Athens in the Age of Alexander: The dated Laws and Decrees of the Lykourgean Era (338–323 B.C.).* Chicago.

Scialpi, F.
1984 "The ethics of Asoka and the religious inspiration of the Achaemenids." *EW* 34/1–3: 55–74.

Scurlock, J. A.
1990a "Herodotos' Median chronology again?!" *IA* 25: 149–63.
1990b "The Euphrates flood and the ashes of Nineveh (Diod. II.27.1–28.7)." *Historia* 39/3: 382–84.

Seager, R. J., and Tuplin, C.
1980 "The freedom of the Greeks of Asia." *JHS* 100: 141–54.

Sealey, R.
1966 "The origin of the Delian League." Pp. 233–55 in *Studies V. Ehrenberg.* Oxford.

Segal, B.
1956 "Notes on the iconography of Cosmic kingship." *Art Bull.* 38: 75–80.

Segal, J. B.
1983 *Aramaic Texts from North Saqqara.* London: Egypt Exploration Society.

Segre, M.
1938 "Iscrizioni di Licia, I: Tolomeo di Telmesso." *Clara Rhodos* 9: 181–208.

Seibert, J.
1972 *Alexander der Grosse.* Darmstadt.
1983 *Das Zeitalter der Diadochen.* Darmstadt.
1985 *Die Eroberung des Perserreiches durch Alexander den Grossen auf kartographischer Grundlage,* I–II. TAVO 68. Wiesbaden.
1987 "Dareios III." Pp. 437–56 in *Festsch. G. Wirth,* I.

Seibt, G.
1977 *Griechische Söldner im Achaimenidenreich.* Bonn.

Seidl, U.
1976 "Ein Relief Dareios' I. in Babylon." *AMI* 9: 125–30.
1994 "Achaimenidische Entlehnungen aus der urartäischen Kultur." *AchHist* 8: 107–29.

Sekunda, N.
1985 "Achaemenid colonization in Lydia." *REA* 87/1–2: 7–30.
1988a "Persian settlement in Hellespontine Phrygia." *AchHist* 3: 175–96.
1988b "Some notes on the life of Datames." *Iran* 26: 35–53.
1988c "Achaemenid military terminology." *AMI* 21: 69–77.
1991 "Achaemenid settlement in Caria, Lycia and Greater Phrygia." *AchHist* 6: 83–143.

1992 *The Persian Army 560–330 B.C.* London.

Seux, M. J.
1980 "Königtum." *RLA*: 140–73.

Sevoroškin, V.
1977 "Zu einigen karischen Wörtern." *MSS* 36: 117–30.

Seyrig, H.
1952 "Cachets achéménides." Pp. 195–202 in *Archeologia orientalia in memoriam E. Herzfeld.* New York.
1959 "Le roi de Perse?" *Syria* 36: 53–56 [= *Antiquités syriennes* 6 (1966): 26–30].
1966 "Aelxandre fondateur de Gerasa." *Syria* 42: 25–28 [= *Antiquités syriennes* 6: 141–44].
1970 "Séleucus I et les fondations de la monarchie syrienne." *Syria* 47: 290–311.

Shahbazi, A. S.
1971 "Le 'Farre Kiyani' sur un bas-relief représentant Cyrus le Grand à Pasargade." *Bastan Chenasi va Honar-e Iran* 7–8: 26–29.
1972a "The 'One year' of Darius reexamined." *BSOAS* 35/3: 609–14.
1972b "The Achaemenid tomb in Buzpar (Gur-i Dukhtar)." *Bastan Chenasi va Honar-e Iran* 9–10: 54–56.
1974 "An Achaemenid symbol, I: A Farewell to 'Fravahr' and 'Ahuramazda.'" *AMI* 7: 135–44.
1975 *The Irano-lycian Monuments.* Persepolis.
1976a "The Persepolis 'Treasury reliefs' once more." *AMI* 9: 151–56.
1976b *Persépolis illustré.* Persepolis-Tehran.
1978 "New aspects of Persepolitan studies." *Gymnasium* 85: 487–500.
1980a "From PARSA to TAXT-E JAMSHID." *AMI* 13: 197–207.
1980b "An Achaemenid symbol, II: Farnah ('God given fortune symbolised')." *AMI* 13: 119–47.
1982 "Darius in Scythia and Scythians in Persepolis." *AMI* 15: 190–235.
1983 "Darius' 'Haft Kishvar.'" Pp. 239–46 in *Kunst, Kultur und Geschichte der Achämenidenzeit und ihr Forleben.* AMI suppl. 10. Berlin.
1985a "Iranian notes 1–6." Pp. 495–510 in *Papers Mary Boyce.*
1985b *The Old Persian Inscriptions.* CII 1.1.1. London.
1986 "Iranian notes 7–13." *AMI* 19: 163–70.

Shaked, S.
1990 "'Do not buy anything from an Aramean': A fragment of Aramaic proverbs with a Judaeo-iranian version." Pp. 230–39 in *Papers Yarshater.*

Shaked, S., and Naveh, J.
1986 "Three Aramaic seals of the Achaemenid period." *JRAS*: 21–27.

Shea, W. H.
1977 "A date for the recently discovered canal of Egypt." *BASOR* 226: 31–38.

Shepherd, D. S.
1980   "The iconography of Anahitā." *Berytus* 28: 47–86.
Sherman, E. J.
1981   "Djehor the Savior." *JEA*: 81–102.
Sherwin-White, S.
1978   "Hand-tokens and Achaemenid practice." *Iran* 16: 183.
1982   "'Median' Artemis in an Early hellenistic funerary inscription." *ZPE* 49: 30.
1983   "Aristeas Ardibelteios: some aspects of the use of double-names in Seleucid Babylonia." *ZPE* 50: 209–24.
1985   "Ancient archives: the edict of Alexander to Priene: a Reappraisal." *JHS* 125: 69–89.
1987   "Seleucid Babylonia: a case-study for the installation and development of Greek rule." Pp. 1–31 in A. Kuhrt and S. Sherwin-White (eds.).
Sherwin-White, S., and Kuhrt, A.
1993   *From Samarkhand to Sardis*. London.
Shore, A. F.
1974   "The Demotic inscription on a coin of Artaxerxes." *NC* 14: 5–8.
1988   "Swapping property at Asyut in the Persian period." Pp. 200–206 in *Pyramids Studies and other Essays presented to I. E. S. Edwards*. London.
Shrimpton, G.
1991   "Persian strategy against Egypt and the date for the battle of Cition." *Phoenix* 45: 1–20.
Sims-Williams, N.
1981   "The final paragraph of the tomb-inscription of Darius I (DNb, 50–60): the Old Persian text in the light of an Aramaic version." *BSOAS* 44: 1–7.
1990   "Old Persian Patišuvarna 'Cup.'" Pp. 240–43 in *Papers Yarshater*.
1991   "Mithra the Baga." Pp. 200–206 in P. Bernard and F. Grenet (eds.).
Sinclair, R. K.
1978   "The King's peace and the employment of military and naval forces." *Chiron* 8: 29–54.
Skalmowski, W.
1988   "Old Persian Vazraka." Pp. 39–42 in *A Green Leaf (Papers Asmussen)*.
1992–93   "Old Persian *artācā brazmaniya* again." *FO* 29: 239–45.
Skjærvø, P. O.
1983   "Farnah: mot mède en vieux-perse." *BSL* 78: 241–59.
1994a   "Achaemenid *vispašiyātiš*—Sasanian *wispšād*." *STIR* 23/1: 79–80.
1994b   Review of Yamauchi 1990, *JAOS* 114/3: 499–504.
Slotsky, A. L.
1993   *The Bourse of Babylon: an Analysis of the Market Quotations in the Astronomical Diaries of Babylonia*, I–II. Ph.D. Yale University.

Smelik, K. A. D.
1978–79   "The *omina mortis* in the Histories of Alexander the Great: Alexander's attitude towards the Babylonian priesthood." *Talanta* 10/11: 92–111.
Smith, H. S.
1972   "Date of the obsequies of the mothers of Apis." *RdE* 24 (*Mélanges M. Malinine*): 276–87.
1988   "A Memphis miscellany." Pp. 184–92 in *Pyramids Studies and other Essays presented to I. E. S. Edwards*. London.
1992a   "The death and life of the mothers of Apis." Pp. 201–25 in *Studies in Religion and Society in Honour of J. G. Griffith* (ed. A. B. Lloyd). London.
1992b   "Foreigners in the documents from the sacred animal necropolis, Saqqara." Pp. 305–11 in J. Johnson (ed.), *Life in a Multicultural Society: Egypt from Cambyses to Constantine and beyond*. Chicago.
Smith, H. S., and Kuhrt, A.
1978   "A letter to a foreign general." *JEA* 68: 199–209.
Smith, L. L.
1991   "The politics of Ezra: sociological indicators of postexilic Judean society." Pp. 73–97 in P. R. Davies (ed.).
Smith, M.
1963   "II: Isaiah and the Persians." *JAOS* 23: 415–21.
1984   "Jewish religious life in the Persian period." *CHJ* 1: 219–78.
Smith, S.
1924   *Babylonian Historical Texts*. Chicago.
Sourdel, D.
1960   "Barid." *EncIsl²* 1: 1077–78.
Spaer, A.
1977   "Some Yehud coins." *IEJ* 27: 200–203.
1986–87   "Jaddua the High Priest?" *INJ* 9: 1–3.
Spalinger, A.
1978a   "The reign of King Chabbash: an interpretation." *ZÄS* 105: 142–54.
1978b   "The concept of monarchy in the Saite period: An essay of synthesis." *Orientalia* 47/1: 12–37.
1978c   "Psammetichus, king of Egypt." *JARCE* 15: 49–57.
Spiegelberg, W.
1914   *Die sogennante demotische Chronik*. Leipzig.
1930   "Das demotische Papyrus Loeb der Universit. München." Pp. 95–102 in *Festschrift J. Loeb*. Munich.
Spycket, A.
1980   "Women in Persian art." Pp. 43–45 in Schmandt-Besserat (ed.).
1981   *La Statuaire du Proche-Orient ancien*. Leiden-Cologne.
1991   "Abū Qūbur: Les figurines de la 'résidence achéménide.'" *NAPR* 5: 47–55.

Stamatiou, A.
1989 "A note on the Mausoleum chariot." *AK* 104: 379–85.
Starr, C. G.
1962 "Why did the Greeks defeat the Persians?" *PdP* 86: 321–32.
1976 "A sixth-century Athenian decadrachm used to seal a clay tablet from Persepolis." *NC* 26: 219–22.
1976–77 "Greeks and Persians in the fourth century B.C.: A study in cultural contacts before Alexander." *IA* 11: 39–99; 12: 49–115.
Stato, economia, lavoro nel Vicino Oriente antico
1988 Istituto Gramsci Toscano: Seminario di Orientalistica antica. Presentazione di A. Zanardo. Introduzione di G. Pugliese Carratelli. Milan.
Steiner, R. C.
1993 "Why the Aramaic script was called 'Assyrian' in Hebrew, Greek and demotic." *Orientalia* 69/2: 80–92.
Stern, E.
1971 "Seal-impressions in the Achaemenid style in the province of Judah." *IEJ* 22: 6–16.
1982a "Achaemenid clay-rhyta from Palestine." *IEJ* 32/1: 36–43.
1982b *Material Culture of the Land of the Bible in the Persian Period (538–332 B.C.).* Warminster-Jerusalem.
1984a "The Persian Empire and the political and social history of Palestine in the Persian period." *CHJ* 1: 70–87.
1984b "The archaeology of Persian Palestine." *CHJ* 1: 88–114.
1988 "The walls of Dor." *IEJ* 38/1–2: 6–14.
1990 "The Dor province in the Persian period in the light of recent excavations at Tel Dor." *Trans* 2: 147–56.
1993 "Tel Mikhmoret: Persian and Hellenistic periods." Pp. 1044–45 in *The New Encyclopaedia of Excavations in the Holy Land* 4. Jerusalem.
1994a "Assyrian and Babylonian elements in the material culture of Palestine in the Persian period." *Trans* 7: 51–62.
1994b "Dor à l'époque perse." Pp. 77–115 in A. M. Laperrousaz and A. Lemaire (eds.).
1994c *Dor, Ruler of the Seas: Twelve Years of Excavations at the Israelite-Phoenician Carmel Coast.* Jerusalem: Isr. Expl. Soc.
Stern, M.
1974–80 *Greek and Latin Authors on Jews and Judaism*, I–II. Jerusalem.
Stève, M. J.
1974 "Inscriptions des Achéménides à Suse." *STIR* 3: 6–28 et 4: 135–69.
1986 "La fin de l'Élam: à propos d'une empreinte de sceau-cylindre." *STIR* 15/1: 7–21.
1987 *Ville royale de Suse VII: Nouveaux mélanges épigraphiques. Inscriptions royales de Suse et de la Susiane.* MDAI 53. Nice.

Stevenson, D. W. W.
1992 "A proposal for the irrigation of the hanging Gardens of Babylon." *Iraq* 54: 35–55.
Stevenson, R. B.
1987 "Lies and invention in Deinon's Persica." *AchHist* 2: 27–35.
Stiehl, R.
1964 "Aramaisch als Weltsprache." Pp. 69–85 in *Neue Beiträge zur Geschichte des Alten Welt*, I. Berlin.
Stigers, H. G.
1976 "Neo- and Late Babylonian business documents from the John Frederik Lewis Collection." *JCS* 28/1: 3–59.
Stol, M.
1994 "Beer in Neo-babylonian times." Pp. 155–83 in L. Milano (ed.), *Drinking in Ancient Societies: History and Culture of Drinks in the Ancient Near East.* Padua.
Stolper, M.
1976 "The genealogy of the Murašû family." *JCS*: 189–99.
1977 "Three Iranian loan-words in Late Babylonian texts." *Bib. Mesop.* 7: 250–53.
1983 "The death of Artaxerxes I." *AMI* 16: 223–36.
1984a "The Neo-babylonian text from the Persepolis fortification." *JNES* 43/4: 299–310.
1984b *Texts from Tall-i Malyan, I: Elamite Administrative Texts (1972–1974).* Occasional Publications of the Babylonian Fund 6. Philadelphia.
1985a *Entrepreneurs and Empire: The Murašû Archive, the Murašû Firm and Persian Rule in Babylonia.* Leiden.
1985b "Empire and province: abstract of remarks on two late Achaemenid Babylonian archives." *PaléoOrient* 11/2: 63–65.
1986 "A Neo-babylonian text from the reign of Hallušu." Pp. 235–40 in *Fragmenta Historiae Elamicae (Mélanges offerts à M. J. Stève).* Paris.
1987 "Bēlšunu the satrap." Pp. 389–402 in Rochberg-Halton (ed.), *Language, Literature and History: Philological and Historical Studies presented to Erica Reiner.* AOS 67. New Haven: AOS.
1988a "Some ghost facts from Achaemenid Babylonian texts." *JHS* 108: 197–98.
1988b "The šaknu of Nippur." *JCS* 40/2: 127–55.
1989a "Registration and taxation of slaves in Achaemenid Babylonia." *ZA* 79/1: 80–101.
1989b "The governor of Babylon and Across-the-River in 486 B.C." *JNES* 48/4: 283–305.
1989c "On interpreting tributary relationships in Achaemenid Babylonia." Pp. 147–56 in Briant and Herrenschmidt (eds.).
1990a "The Kasr archive." *AchHist* 4: 195–205.
1990b "Late Achaemenid Legal texts from Uruk and Larsa." *BM* 21: 559–622.

1990c   "Tobits in reverse: more Babylonians in Ecbatana." *AMI* 23: 161–76.
1991   "A property in Bīt Paniya." *Rass* 85: 49–62.
1992a   "Babylonian evidence for the end of the reign of Darius I: A correction." *JNES* 51/1: 61–62.
1992b   "Late Achaemenid texts from Dilbat." *Iraq* 54: 119–39.
1992c   "The Murašū texts from Susa." *RAss.* 86: 69–77.
1992d   "The estate of Mardonios." *Aula orientalis* 10 [1994]: 211–21.
1993   *Late Achaemenid, Early Macedonian, and Early Seleucid Records of Deposit and related Texts.* AION suppl. 77. Naples.
1994a   "On some aspects of continuity between Achaemenid and Hellenistic legal Babylonian legal texts." *AchHist* 8: 329–51.
1994b   "Mesopotamia, 482–330 B.C." *CAH* 6²: 234–60.
1994c   "Iranians in Babylonia." *JAOS* 114/4: 617–24.
1994d   "A late Achaemenid text from the Rich collection." *JAOS* 114/4: 625–27.
1995a   "Flogging and plucking." *DATA*.
1995b   "The Babylonian enterprise of Belesys." Pp. 217–38 in P. Briant (ed.), *Dans les pas des Dix-Mille: Peuples et pays du Proche-Orient vus par un Grec* (Actes de la Table ronde de Toulouse, 3–4 février 1995). Pallas 43.

Stork, H. A.
1989   "The Lydian campaign of Cyrus the Great in classical and cuneiform sources." *AW* 19: 69–75.

Strogetsky, V. M.
1991   "The problem of Callias' peace and its significance for the evolution of the Delian League." *VDI*: 158–68. [Eng. summary, p. 168]

Stronach, D.
1967   "Urartian and Achaemenian tower-temples." *JNES* 26/4: 277–88.
1971   "Cyrus the Great." *Bastan Chenasi va Honar-e Iran* 7–8: 4–21.
1974   "La statue de Darius découverte à Suse." *CDAFI* 4: 61–72.
1977   "La découverte du premier temple mède dans la région d'Ecbatane Hamadan, Iran." *CRAI*: 668–98.
1978   *Pasargadae.* Oxford.
1981   "Notes on Median and early Achaemenian religious monuments." Pp. 123–30 in *Temples and High Places in Biblical Times.* Jerusalem.
1984   "Notes on religion in Iran in the seventh and sixth centuries B.C." Pp. 479–90 in *Orientalia Duchesne-Guillemin emerito oblata.* Hommages et Opera Minora 9. Leiden.
1985a   "On the evolution of the early Iranian fire-temple." Pp. 605–27 in *Papers in Honour of Professor Mary Boyce.* Hommages et Opera Minora 11. Leiden.

1985b   "The Apadana: a signature of two lines of Darius." Pp. 433–45 in *De l'Indus aux Balkans: Recueil J. Deshayes.* Paris.
1985c   "Tepe Nush-i Jān: the Median settlement." *CHI* 2: 832–37.
1985d   "Pasargadae." *CHI* 2: 838–55.
1989a   "The royal garden at Pasargadae: evolution and legacy." Pp. 475–502 in Meyer and Haerinck (eds.).
1989b   "Early Achaemenid coinage: perspectives from the Homeland." *Mélanges P. Amiet* II = *IA* 24: 255–79.
1990   "On the genesis of the Old-Persian cuneiform script." Pp. 195–204 in Vallat (ed.).

Strouvé, V. V.
1960   "The religion of the Achaemenids and Zoroastrianism." *CHM* 5/3: 529–45.

Stucky, R. A.
1984   *Tribune d'Echmoun: Ein griechischen Reliefzyklus des 4. Jahrdt. in Sidon.* Basel.
1985   "Achämenidische Hölzer und Elfenbeine aus Ägypten und Vorderasien im Louvre." *AK* 28/1: 7–32.
1993   "Lykien-Karien-Phönizien kulturelle Kontakte zwischen Kleinasien und der Levante während der Perserherrschaft." Pp. 261–68 in G. Dobesch (ed.), *Akten des II. Intern. Lykien-Symposions.* ÖAW, Denkschr. 231. Vienna.

Sulimirski, T.
1985   "The Scyths." *CHI* 2: 149–99.

Summers, G. D.
1993   "Archaeological evidence for the Achaemenid period in Eastern Turkey." *AnSt* 43: 85–108.

Sumner, W. H.
1972   *Cultural Development in the Kur Basin, Iran: An Archaeological Analysis of settlement Patterns.* Ph.D. University of Pennsylvania.
1986   "Achaemenid settlement in the Persepolis plain." *AJA* 90: 3–31.
1988   "Maljan, Tall-e (Anšan)." *RLA* 7/3–4: 306–20.
1994   "Archaeological measures of cultural continuity and the arrivals of Persians in Fārs." *AchHist* 8: 97–105.

Susumu, S.
1991   "Some remarks on the tax system of the Achaemenid Empire." *Kodai* 2: 45–48.

Swinnen, W.
1973   "Sur la politique religieuse de Ptolémée Iᵉʳ." Pp. 115–23 in *Les Syncrétismes dans les religions grecque et romaine.* Paris.

Syme, R.
1988   "The Cadusians in history and fiction." *JHS* 108: 137–50.
1995   *Anatolica: Studies in Strabo*, A. Birley (ed.). Oxford.

Symington, D.
1991   "Late Bronze Age writing-boards and their uses: textual evidence from Anatolia and Syria." *AnSt* 41: 111–23.

Szubin, H. Z., and Porten, B.
1988 "A life estate of usufruct: a new interpretation of Kraeling 6." *BASOR* 269: 29–45.
1992 "An Aramaic joint-venture agreement: a new interpretation of the Bauer-Meissner papyrus." *BASOR* 288: 67–84.

Tadmor, H.
1965 "The inscriptions of Nabunaid: historical arrangements." Pp. 351–63 in *Studies in Honour of B. Landsberger*. Assyr. Stud. 16. Chicago.
1982 "Treaty and oath in the Ancient Near East: A historical approach." Pp. 127–52 in G. N. Tucker and D. A. Knight (eds.), *Humanizing America's Iconic Book: Society of Biblical Literature Centennial Addresses, 1980*. SBL 6. Chico, California.
1983 "Rab-saris and Rab-shakeh in 2 Kings 18." Pp. 279–85 in *The Word of the Lord shall go forth: Essays in Honor of David Noel Freedman*. Winona Lake, Indiana.
1994 "Judah." *CAH* 6²: 262–96.

Talamo, C.
1979 *La Lidia arcaica*. Bologna.

Tallon, Ph.
1994 "Les textes prophétiques du premier millénaire en Mésopotamie." Pp. 97–125 in *Prophéties et Oracles, I: Dans le Proche-Orient ancien*. Suppl. *Cahier Évangile* 88. Paris.

Tanabe, K.
1989 "An Achaemenid silver Pegasus-rhyton." Pp. 525–36 in Meyer and Haerinck (eds.), 1989.

Tappeiner, M.
1990 "Ein Beitrag zu den Wagenzügen auf den Stelen aus Daskyleion." *FA* 81–96.

Tatum, J.
1988 *Xenophon's Imperial Fiction: on the Education of Cyrus*. Princeton University Press.

Teissier, B.
1985 *Ancient Near Eastern cylinder-seals from the Marcopoli Collection*. Berkeley-Los Angeles-London.

Teixidor, J.
1964 "Un nouveau papyrus du règne de Darius II." *Syria* 41/3–4: 285–90.
1977 *The Pagan god*. Princeton.
1978 "The Aramaic text in the trilingual stele from Xanthus." *JNES* 37: 181–85.
1985 Review of Segal 1983, *JAOS* 105/4: 731–34.
1993 "Historiographical sources and absolute chronology." Pp. 289–94 in V. Finkbeiner (ed.), *Materialen zur Archäologie des Seleukiden und Partherzeit im südlichen Babylonien und im Golfengebiet*. Tübingen.

Temerev, A. H.
1980 "The provisioning system in Achaemenid garrison *dgl'n*." *VDI*: 124–31. [Russian; Eng. summary, p. 131]

Ter-Martirossov, F.
1994 "Fouilles à Beniamin (Arménie): rapport préliminaire." *Orient-Express* 1994/3: 71–73.

Thalmann, J. P.
1990 "Tell 'Arqa à l'époque perse." *Trans* 2: 51–58.

Thillet, P.
1969 "Les *Économiques* d'Aristote." *REG* 82: 563–89.

Thomassen, L. A.
1984 *The Aegean War of Alexander the Great, 334–331 B.C.* M.A. Pennsylvania State University.

Thompson, D.
1984 "The passage of the Ten Thousand through Cilicia." *PdP* 94: 22–25.

Thompson, D. B.
1956 "Persian spoils in Athens." Pp. 281–91 in *The Aegean and the Near East: Studies presented to H. Goldman*. Locust Valley.

Thompson, D. J.
1988 *Memphis under the Ptolemies*. Princeton University Press.
1992 "Language and literacy in Early Hellenistic Egypt." Pp. 39–52 in P. Bilde, T. Engels-Pedersen, L. Hannestad, and J. Zahle (eds.), *Ethnicity in Hellenistic Egypt*. Studies in Hellenistic Civilization 3. Aarhus.

Thompson, H. O.
1987 "A Tyrian coin in Jordan." *BA*: 101–4.

Thompson, W. E.
1981 "The Carian tribute." *AnSt* 31: 95–100.

Tilia, A. B.
1972 *Studies and Restorations at Persepolis and other sites of Fārs*. Rome.
1974 "Persepolis sculptures in the light of new discoveries." Pp. 127–34 in Farkas, *Achaemenid Sculpture*.
1977 "Recent discoveries at Persepolis." *AJA* 81/1: 67–77.

Tiratsian, G. A.
1981 "Some aspects of the inner organization of the Armenian satrapy." *AAH* 29: 151–68.

Tod, M. N.
1948 *A Selection of Greek Historical Inscriptions*. Oxford.

Tollefson, K. D., and Williamson, H. G. M.
1992 "Nehemiah as cultural revitalization: an anthropological perspective." *JSOT* 56: 41–68.

Torrey, C. C.
1943 "The evolution of a financier in the Ancient Near East." *JNES* 3: 295–301.
1946 "Medes and Persians." *JAOS* 66: 1–15.

Toynbee, A.
1955 "The administrative geography of the Achaemenian Empire." *A Study of History* 7²: 580–689.

Tozzi, P.
1978a "Per la storia della politicà religiosa degli Achemenidi: Distruzioni persiane di templi greci agli inizi del V. secolo." *RSI* 31: 18–32.

1978b *La rivoltà ionica*. Pisa.
Traunecker, C.
1973–77 "Un document nouveau sur Darius Ier à Karnak." *Cahiers de Karnak* 7: 40–213. [Cairo, 1980]
1979 "Essai sur l'histoire de la XXIXe dynastie." *BIFAO* 79: 395–436.
1995 "Un portrait ignoré d'un roi perse: la tête 'Strasbourg 1604.'" *Trans* 9: 101–17.
Traunecker, C.; Le Saout, F.; and Masson, O.
1981 *La Chapelle d'Hakôris à Karnak*, II. Cairo.
Treidler, H.
1982 "Pasargadae." *RE* suppl. 9: 777–99.
Tresson, P.
1931 "La stèle de Naples." *BIFAO* 30/1: 368–91.
Trichet, J., and Vallat, F.
1990 "L'origine égyptienne de la statue de Darius." Pp. 205–8 in Vallat (ed.).
Tripodi, B.
1986 "La Macedonia, la Peonia, il carro di Serse (Herodot 8, 115–16)." *Giorn. Ital. Filol.* 38/2: 243–51.
Troxelle, H. A., and Kagan, J. H.
1989 "Cilicians and neighbours in miniature." Pp. 275–81 in *Kraay-Mørkholm Essays*. Louvain.
Trümpelmann, L.
1967 "Zur Entstehungsgeschichte des Monumentes Darius' I. von Bisutun und zur Datierung der Einführung der altpersischen Schrift." *AA* 82: 281–98.
1983 "Zu den Gebäuden von Persepolis und ihrer Funktion." Pp. 225–37 in H. Koch and D. N. MacKenzie (eds.), *Kunst und Kultur der Achämenidenzeit und ihr Fortleben*. AMI suppl. 10. Berlin.
1988 "Zur Herkunft von Medern und Persern." *AMI* 21: 79–90.
Tsetskhladze, G.
1992 "The cult of Mithra in Ancient Colchis." *RHR* 209/2: 115–24.
1993–94 "Colchis and the Persian empire: the problems of their relationships." *SRA* 3: 11–49.
1994 "Colchians, Greeks and Achaemenids in the 7th–5th centuries BC: a critical look." *Klio* 76: 78–102.
Tuplin, C.
1983 "Lysias XIX, the Cypriot war and Thrasyboulos' naval expedition." *Philologus* 127/2: 170–86.
1987a "The treaty of Boiotios." *AchHist* 2: 133–53.
1987b "The administration of the Achaemenid Empire." Pp. 109–66 in I. Carradice (ed.), *Coinage and Administration in the Athenian and Persian Empires*. BAR series 34. London.
1987c "Xenophon and the garrisons of the Persian Empire." *AMI* 20: 167–245.
1989 "The coinage of Aryandes." *REA* 91/1: 61–82.

1990 "Persian decor in Cyropaedia: some observations." *AchHist* 5: 17–29.
1991a "Darius' Suez canal and Persian imperialism." *AchHist* 6: 237–83.
1991b "Modern and Ancient travellers in the Achaemenid Empire: Byron's Road to Oxiana and Xenophon's *Anabasis*." *AchHist* 7: 37–57.
1993 *The Failings of Empire: A Reading of Xenophon Hellenica* 2.3.11–7.5.27. Historia Enzelschr. 76. Wiesbaden.
1994 "Persians as Medes." *AchHist* 8: 235–56.
Turner, E. G.
1974 "A commander-in-chief's order from Saqqâra." *JEA* 60: 239–42.
Uchitel, A.
1989 "Organization of manpower in Achaemenid Persia according to the fortification archive." *Acta Sumerol.* 1: 225–38.
1991 "Foreign workers in the fortification archive." Pp. 127–35 in *Mésopotamie et Élam* (Actes de la XXXVe RAI, 1989). Gand.
Urban, R.
1991 *Der Königsfrieden von 387/6 v. Chr.: Vorgeschichte, Zustandkommen, Ergebnis und politische Umsetzung*. Historia Einzschr. 68. Wiesbaden.
Usmanova, Z. I.
1992 "New material from Ancient Merv." *Iran* 30: 55–63.
Valbelle, D.
1989 "Recherches archéologiques récentes dans le Nord Sinaï." *CRAI*: 594–607.
1990 *Les Neuf Arcs: L'Égyptien et les étrangers de la préhistoire à la conquête d'Alexandre*. Paris.
Valbelle, D., and Defernez, C.
1995 "Les sites de la frontière égypto-palestinienne à l'époque perse." *Trans* 9: 93–99.
Valdez, R., and Tuck, R. G.
1980 "On the identification of the animals accompanying the 'Ethiopian' delegation in the bas-reliefs of the Apadana at Persepolis." *Iran* 18: 156–57.
Vallat, F.
1970 "Table élamite de Darius." *RAss* 64: 149–60.
1971 "Deux nouvelles 'Chartes de fondation' d'un palais de Darius Ier à Suse." *Syria* 48/1–2: 53–59.
1974a "Les inscriptions cunéiformes de la statue de Darius." *CDAFI* 4: 161–70.
1974b "L'inscription trilingue de Xerxès à la porte de Darius." *CDAFI* 4: 171–80.
1979 "Les inscriptions du palais d'Artaxerxès II sur la rive droite du Chaour." *CDAFI* 10: 145–54.
1980 *Suse et l'Élam*. Paris.
1984 "Kidin-Hutran et l'époque néo-élamite." *Akkadika*: 1–17.

1986 "Tablette acadienne de Darius Ier (DSaa)." Pp. 277–83 in *Fragmenta Historiae elamicae: Mélanges offerts à M. J. Stève*. Paris.
1987 "Expéditions orientales des rois assyriens." *Dossiers Histoire et Archéologie* 122: 60–62.
1988 "À propos des tablettes élamites dites 'de Ninive' conservées au British Museum." *NABU*, note 39.
1989a "Le palais d'Artaxerxès II à Babylone." *NAPR* 2: 3–6.
1989b "À propos du 'Mur de Médie.'" *NAPR* 4: 70–71.

Vallat, F. (ed.)
1990 *Contribution à l'histoire de l'Iran: Mélanges offerts à Jean Perrot*. Paris: Éditions Recherches sur les civilisations.
1993 *Les Noms géographiques des sources suso-élamites*. TAVO Beiheft series B 7/11 (RGTC 11). Wiesbaden.
1994 "Deux tablettes élamites de l'université de Fribourg." *JNES* 53/4: 273–84.
1995 "Épopée de Gilgameš ou tablette économique de Persépolis? Ni l'un ni l'autre!" *NABU*, note 46.

Van den Hout, M.
1949 "Persian royal letters in Greek traditions." *Mnem.* 2: 141–52.

Van der Kooij, G.
1987 "Tell Deir ʿAlla (East Jordan Valley) during the Achaemenid period." *AchHist* 1: 97–102.

Van der Spek, R. J.
1982 "Did Cyrus the Great introduce a new policy towards subdued nations? Cyrus in Assyrian perspective." *Persica* 10: 278–81.
1983 "Cyrus de Pers in Assyrisch perspectief." *Tijdschrift voor Geschiedenis* 96: 1–27.
1986 *Grondbezit in het Seleucidische Rijk*. Ph.D. Amsterdam.
1992 "Nippur, Sippar and Larsa in the Hellenistic period." Pp. 235–80 in M. de Jong-Ellis (ed.), *Nippur at the Centennial*. Occasional Publications of the S. N. Kramer Fund 14. Philadelphia.
1993a "The astronomical diaries as a source for Achaemenid and Seleucid history." *BiOr* 50: 91–102.
1993b "New evidence on Seleucid land policy." Pp. 61–77 in H. Sancisi-Weerdenburg et al. (eds.), *De agricultura: In memoriam P. W. De Neeve*. Amsterdam.
1994 "The Seleucid State and the economy." Pp. 15–27 in E. Lo Cascio and D. Rathbone (eds.), *Production and Public Powers in Antiquity*. Proceedings of the Eleventh International History Congress. Milan.
1995 "Land-ownership in Babylonian cuneiform documents." Pp. 173–245 in M. J. Geller, H. Maehler, and A. D. E. Lewis (eds.), *Legal Documents of the Hellenistic Period*. London.

Van der Veen, J. E.
1995 "A minute's mirth: Syloson and his cloak in Herodotus." *Mnem.* 48/2: 129–45.

Van Driel, G.
1987 "Continuity or decay in the late Achaemenid period: evidence from Southern Mesopotamia." *AchHist* 2: 159–81.
1989 "The Murašûs in context." *JESHO* 32: 203–29.
1992 "Neo-Babylonian texts from Borsippa." *BiOr* 49: 29–50.

Van Groningen, B. A.
1933 *Aristote: Le second livre de l'Économique*. Leiden.

Van Gulik, R. H.
1961 *Sexual Life in Ancient China*. Leiden: Brill.

Van Haeperen-Pourbaix, A.
1984 "Recherche sur les origines, la nature et les attributs du dieu Mên." Pp. 221–57 in Doncel and Lebrun (eds.).

Van Laere, R.
1977 "Le droit hydraulique selon la législation néo-babylonienne." *OLP* 8: 63–74.
1980 "Techniques hydrauliques en Mésopotamie ancienne." *OLP* 11: 11–53.

Van Voss, M. H.
1993 "Alexander und die ägyptische Religion: Einige ägyptologische Bemerkungen." Pp. 71–73 in *Alexander the Great: Reality and Myth*. ARID suppl. 20. Rome.

Van Wijngaarden, W. D.
1954 "Der Hibistempel in der Oase El-Chargeh." *ZÄS* 179: 387–411.

Van't Dack, E.
1962 "Postes et télécommunications ptolémaïques." *CdE* 37: 338–41.

Vanden Berghe, L.
1964 "Le tombeau achéménide de Buzpar." Pp. 243–58 in *Vorderasiatische Archäologie: Studien und Aufsätze. Festschrift für A. Moortgaat*. Berlin.
1986 "Le relief rupestre de Gardanah Galumushk (Qir)." *IA* 21: 141–55.
1987 "Les scènes d'investiture sur les reliefs de l'Iran ancien: évolution et signification." P. 15 in *Studi Tucci*, III. Rome.

Vargas, P.
forthcoming *A History of Babylonian Prices in the First Millennium B.C.*, I: *Prices of the Basic products*. Budapest.

Vaux, R. de
1937 "Les décrets de Cyrus et de Darius sur la reconstruction du temple." *RB*: 29–57.

Veenhof, K. (ed.)
1986 *Cuneiform Archives and Libraries: XXXe RAI, Leiden, 4–8 July 1983*. Istanbul-Leiden.

Vercoutter, J.
1950 "Les statues du général Hor, gouverneur d'Héracléopolis, de Busiris et d'Héliopolis." *BIFAO* 49: 85–114.

1962   *Les Stèles biographiques du Serapeum de Memphis.* Paris.

Verdin, H.
1982   "Hérodote et la politique expansionniste des Achéménides: Notes sur Hdt. VII.8." Pp. 327–36 in *Studia P. Naster oblata,* II. Louvain.

Verger, A.
1965   *Ricerche giuridiche nei papiri aramaici di Elefantina.* Rome.

Vergote, J.
1959   *Joseph en Égypte.* Louvain.

Verkinderen, F.
1987   "Les cités phéniciennes dans l'Empire d'Alexandre le Grand." *Studia Phoenicia* 5: 287–308.

Verner, M.
1989   "La tomb d'Oudjahorresnet et le cimetière saïto-perse d'Abousir." *BIFAO* 89: 283–90.

Vickers, M.
1984   "Demus' gold phiale (Lysias 19.25)." *AJAH* 9/1 [1988]: 48–53.
1989   "Persian gold in Persian inventories." *REA* 91/1–2: 249–57.
1990   "Interactions between Greeks and Persians." *AchHist* 4: 253–62.

Vidal-Naquet, P.
1983   *Le Chasseur noir.* Paris.
1989   "Retour au chasseur noir." Pp. 387–411 in *Mélanges P. Lévêque,* II. Paris.

Villenueva-Puig, M. C.
1989   "Le vase des Perses: Naples 3253 (Inv. 81947)." *REA* 91/1–2: 277–98.

Vincent, A.
1937   *La Religion des judéo-araméens d'Égypte.* Paris.

Virgilio, B.
1975   *Commento storico al quinto libro delle Storie di Erodoto.* Pisa.

Visser, E.
1975   "Griechen am Hof und die Proskynesis." Pp. 453–57 in *Festschrift z. 150 Jähringen Bestehen des Berliner Ägyptischen Museums.* Mitt. d. Ägypt. Samml. 8. Berlin.

Vittmann, G.
1991–92   "Ein altiranische Titel im demotischen Überlieferung." *AfO* 28–29: 159–60.

Vleeming, S.
1981   "The artaba and Egyptian grain-measure." In *Proceedings of the XVIth Intern. Congr. of Papyrology = Amer. Stud. in Papyr.* 23: 537–45.

Vogelsang, W.
1985   "Early historical Arachosia in South-East Afghanistan: Meeting-places between East and West." *IA* 20: 55–99.
1986   "Four short notes on the Bisutun text and monument." *IA* 21: 121–40.
1987   "Some remarks on Eastern Iran in the late Achaemenid period." *AchHist* 1: 183–90.
1988a   "Some observations on Achaemenid Hyrcania: a combination of sources." *AchHist* 3: 121–36.

1988b   "Indian antics: A reply to P. Bernard." *STIR* 17/2: 253–58.
1989a   "Gold from Dardistan: Some comparative remarks on the tribute system in the extreme Northwest of the Indian subcontinent." Pp. 157–71 in Briant and Herrenschmidt (eds.).
1989b   "Peripheral remarks on the Persian Achaemenid Empire." Pp. 543–62 in Meyer and Haerinck (eds.).
1990   "The Achaemenids and India." *AchHist* 4: 93–110.
1992   *The Rise and Organisation of the Achaemenid Empire: The Eastern Iranian Evidence.* Leiden.

Vogt, J.
1952   "Die Tochter des Grosskönigs und Pausanias, Alexander, Caracalla." Pp. 163–82 in *Satura: Früchte aus der antiken Welt.* Baden-Baden.

Von Bothmer, D.
1981   "Les trésors de l'orfèvrerie de la Grèce orientale au Metropolitan Museum de New York." *CRAI:* 194–207.

Von Gall, H.
1966   *Die paphlagonischen Felsgräber: Eine Studie zur kleinasiatischen Kunstgeschichte.* IM suppl. 1. Istanbul.
1972   "Persische und medische Stämme." *AMI* 5: 261–83.
1981–83   "Zum Bildgehalt der Graeco-Persischen Grabstelen." *Anadolu* 22 (= *Mél. Akurgal* [1990]): 143–65.
1989   "Das achämenidische Königsgrab: Neue Überlegungen und Beobachtungen." Pp. 503–23 in Meyer and Haerinck (eds.).

Von Graeve, V.
1970   *Der Alexandersarkophag und seine Werksatt.* Berlin.
1987   "Eine Miszelle zur griechische Malerei." *IM* 37: 131–44.

Von Hagen, V.
1981   *La Voie royale des Perses.* Fr. trans. Paris.

Von Voigtlander, E. N.
1963   *A Survey of Neo-Babylonian History.* Ph.D. University of Michigan.
1978   *The Bisutun Inscription of Darius the Great: Babylonian Version.* CII 1: Inscriptions of Ancient Iran, Texts 1. London.

Wacholder, B. Z.
1962   *Nicolaus of Damascus.* Berkeley–Los Angeles.

Waddel, W. G.
1966   *Manetho.* LCL. London.

Wade-Gery, H. Y.
1958   *Essays in Greek History.* Oxford.

Wagner, J.
1983   "Dynastie und Herrscherkult in Kommagene: Forschungsgeschichte und neuer Funde." *IM* 33: 177–210.

Walbank, M. B.
1982   "A correction to IG II² 65." *ZPE* 48: 261–63.

1983   "Herakleides of Klazomenai: a new rejoin-
        der at the Epigraphical Museum." *ZPE* 51:
        183–84.
1989   "Herakleides and the Great King." *EMC* 8:
        347–52.
Waldman, H.
1973   *Die Kommagenischen Kultreformen unter
        Mithridates I. Kallinikos und seinem Sohne
        Antiochos I.* EPRO 34. Leiden.
Wallace, R. W.
1989   "On the production and exchange of early
        Anatolian electrum coinage." *REA* 91/1–2:
        87–94.
Wallinga, H.
1984   "The Ionian revolt." *Mnem.* 37/3–4: 401–
        37.
1987   "The Ancient Persian navy and its prede-
        cessors." *AchHist* 1: 47–78.
1989   "Persian tribute and Delian tribute." Pp.
        173–81 in Briant and Herrenschmidt (eds.).
1991   "Naval installations in Cilicia Pedias: the
        defence of the parathalassia in Achaimenid
        times and after." Pp. 277–81 in *De Anatolia
        antiqua.* Bib. Inst. Fr. Anatol. Istanbul 32.
        Paris.
1993   *Ships and Sea-Power before the Great Per-
        sian Wars: The Ancestors of the Ancient Tri-
        reme.* London/New York/Cologne.
Walser, G.
1966   *Die Völkerschaften auf den Reliefs von Per-
        sepolis.* Berlin.
1967   "Griechen am Hofe des Grosskönigs." Pp.
        189–201 in *Festgabe Hans von Greyerz.*
        Bern.
1981   *Persépolis: La cité royale de Darius.* Fri-
        bourg.
1983   "Der Tod des Kambyses." Pp. 8–23 in *Alt-
        historischen Studien H. Bengtson.* Historia-
        Einzelschr. 40. Wiesbaden.
1984   *Hellas und Iran.* Darmstadt.
1985   "Die Route des Isidorus von Charax durch
        Iran." *AMI* 18: 145–56.
1987   "Persischer Imperialismus und Griech-
        ische Freiheit." *AchHist* 2: 155–65.
Walser, G. (ed.)
1972   *Beiträge zur Achämenidengeschichte.* Wies-
        baden.
Walsh, J. A.
1984   *Prolegomena to a Revisionist History of the
        Pentecontaetia.* Ph.D. Austin University.
Waltley, K.
1939   "On the possibility of reconstructing Mara-
        thon and other ancient battles." *JHS* 84:
        119–39.
Wanke, G.
1984   "Prophecy and psalms in the Persian pe-
        riod." *CHJ* 1: 162–88.
Ward, W. A.
1983   "Reflections on some Egyptian terms pre-
        sumed to mean "harem, harem-woman,
        concubine." *Berytus* 31: 67–74.

Watkin, H. J.
1984   "The Cypriote surrender to Persia." *JHS*
        107: 154–63.
Weidner, E. F.
1930   "Die älteste Nachricht über das persische
        Königshaus." *AfO* 7: 1–7.
1939   "Jojachin, König von Juda, in babyloni-
        schen Keilinschriften." Pp. 923–34 in *Mé-
        langes syriens R. Dussaud,* II. Paris.
1956   "Hof- und Harems-Erlasse assyrischer Kö-
        nige aus dem 2. Jahrtausend v. Chr." *AfO*
        17: 257–93.
Weinberg, J. P.
1974a   "Die Agrarverhältnisse in der Bürger-
        Temple-Gemeinde der Achämenidenzeit."
        AAH 22/1–4: 473–86.
1974b   "Der *am ha areṣ* des 6.4 Jhdt. v.u.Z." *Klio*
        56: 325–35.
1977   "Zentral- und Partikulargewalt im achäme-
        nidischen Reich." *Klio* 59/1: 25–43.
1992a   *The Citizen-Temple Community.* JSOT
        suppl. 151. Sheffield.
1992b   "Die Mentalität der Jerusalemischen
        Bürger-Tempelgemeinde des 6–4 Jh. v.u.
        Z." *Trans* 5: 133–41.
Weinfeld, M.
1976   "Loyalty oath in the Ancient Near East."
        UF 8: 379–414.
Weippert, H.
1988   *Palästina im vorhellenistischer Zeit.* Wies-
        baden.
Weisberg, D.
1980   *Texts from the Time of Nebuchadnezzar.*
        YOS 17. New Haven.
1984   "Kingship and social organization in Chal-
        dean Uruk." *JAOS* 104/4: 739–43.
Weiser, W.
1989   "Die Eulen von Kyros dem Jüngeren: Zu
        den ersten Münzporträts lebender Men-
        schen." *ZPE* 76: 267–96.
Weiskopf, M.
1982   *Achaemenid System of Governing in Anato-
        lia.* Ph.D. Berkeley.
1989   *The So-Called "Great Satraps' Revolt,"
        366–360* B.C.. Historia Einzelschr. 63.
        Wiesbaden.
Welles, C. B.
1934   *Royal Correspondence in the Hellenistic Pe-
        riod.* New Haven.
Welwei, K. W.
1979   "Abhängige Landbevölkerungen auf 'Tem-
        pelterritorien' im hellenistischen Klein-
        asien und Syrien." *AncSoc* 10: 97–118.
Wenning, R.
1990   "Attische keramik in Palästina: Ein Zwi-
        schenbericht." *Trans* 2: 157–68.
West, St.
1985   "Herodotus' epigraphical interests." *CQ*
        35/2: 278–305.
1988   "The Scythian ultimatum (Herodotus IV.
        131, 132)." *JHS* 108: 207–11.
1992   "Sesostris Stelae (Herodotus 2. 102–106)."
        Historia 41/1: 117–20.

Westlake, H. D.
1977   "Thucydides on Pausanias and Themisto-
       cles: a written source." CQ 27: 95–110.
1979   "Ionians in the Ionian war." CQ 29: 9–44.
1981   "Decline and fall of Tissaphernes." Histo-
       ria 30/3: 257–79.
1983   "Conon and Rhodes: the troubled after-
       math of synoecism." GRBS 24/4: 333–44.
1985   "Tissaphernes in Thucydides." CQ 35: 43–
       54.
1986   "Spartan intervention in Asia, 400–397
       B.C." Historia 35/4: 405–26.
1987   "Diodorus and the expedition of Cyrus."
       Phoenix 41/3: 241–54.
Wheeler, M.
1974   "The transformation of Persepolis architec-
       tural motifs into sculpture under the In-
       dian Mauryan dynasty." Acta Iranica 1:
       249–61.
Whitcomb, D. S.
1987   "Bushire and the Angali canal." Mesopota-
       mia 22: 311–36.
Whitehead, J. D.
1974   Early Aramaic Epistolography. Ph.D. Uni-
       versity of Chicago.
Widengren, G.
1959   "The sacral kingship of Iran." Pp. 242–57
       in La Regalità sacra. Leiden.
1965   "Recherches sur le féodalisme iranien."
       Orientalia Suecania: 79–152.
1966   "La légende royale de l'Iran antique." Pp.
       225–37 in Hommages G. Dumézil. Brus-
       sels.
1968a Les Religions de l'Iran (Fr. trans.). Paris.
1968b "Le symbolisme de la ceinture." IA 8: 133–
       55.
1969   Der Feudalismus im alten Iran. Cologne-
       Opladen.
1973   "The Persians." Pp. 312–57 in D. J. Wise-
       man (ed.), The Peoples of Old Testament
       Times. Oxford.
Wiesehöfer, J.
1978   Der Aufstand Gaumatas und die Anfänge
       Dareios' I. Bonn.
1980   "Die 'Freunde' und die 'Wohltäter' des
       Grosskönigs." STIR 9/1: 7–21.
1982   "Beobachtungen zum Handel des Achä-
       menidenreich." MBH 1/1: 5–15.
1987a "Kyros und die unterworfenen Völker: ein
       Beitrag zur Entstehung von Geschichts-
       bewustein." QS 26: 107–26.
1987b "Zur Frage der Echtheit des Dareios-Briefes
       an Gadatas." RhM 130/3–4: 396–98.
1989   "Tauta gar en atelea: Beobachtungen zur
       Abgabenfreiheit im Achaimenidenreich."
       Pp. 183–91 in Briant and Herrenschmidt
       (eds.).
1990   "Zypern unter persischer Herrschaft." Ach-
       Hist 4: 239–52.
1991a "Beobachtungen zu den religiösen Verhält-
       nisse in der Persis in frühhellenistischer
       Zeit." Pp. 129–35 in J. Kellens (ed.).

1991b "PRTRK, RB HYL', SGN und MR.'" Ach-
       Hist 6: 305–9.
1993   Das antike Persien von 550 v. Chr. vis 650 n.
       Chr. Zurich.
1994   Die "dunklen Jahrhunderte" der Persis: Un-
       tersuchungen zu Geschichte und Kultur von
       Fārs in frühkellenistischer Zeit (330–140
       v. Ch.). Munich.
Wikander, C.
1992   "Pompe and circumstances: the procession
       of Ptolemaios II." OpA 19: 143–50.
Wikander, S.
1946   Feuerpriester in Kleinasien und Iran. Lund.
1972   "BARZOKAPA." FO 34: 13–15.
Wilber, D. N.
1969   Persepolis: The Archaeology of Parsa, Seat of
       the Persian Kings. London.
Wilcken, U.
1897   "Zur Satrapenstele." ZÄS 35: 81–87.
Wilhelm, G.
1973   "La première tablette cunéiforme trouvée à
       Tyr." BMB 26: 35–39.
Wilkinson, R. H.
1991   "The representation of the bow in the art
       of Egypt and the Ancient Near East."
       JANES 20: 83–89.
Will, Édouard
1960   "Chabrias et les finances de Tachos." REA
       62: 254–75.
1964   "Deux livres sur les guerres Médiques et
       leur tempts." RPh 38: 70–88.
1972   Le Monde grec et l'Orient, I. Paris.
Will, Ernest
1967   "Hérodote et la jeune Péonienne." REG
       80: 176–81.
1976   "Un nouveau monument de l'art grec en
       Phénicie: la 'tribune' du sanctuaire d'Ech-
       moun à Sidon." BCH 100: 565–74.
Will, Ernest; Larché, F.; et al.
1991   Iraq al Amir: Le château du Tobiade Hyr-
       can, I–II. BAH 132. Paris.
Will, W., and Heinrichs, J. (eds.)
1987   Zu Alexander der Grosse: Festschrift G.
       Wirth, I. Amsterdam.
Williamson, H. G. M.
1987   Ezra and Nehemiah. Old Testament
       Guides. Sheffield.
1988   "The governors of Judah under the Per-
       sians." TB 39: 59–82.
1990   "Eben gelal" (Ezra 5:8; 6:4) again." BASOR
       280: 83–88.
1991   "Ezra and Nehemiah in the light of the
       texts from Persepolis." BBR 1: 41–62.
Wilson, J. V. Kinnier
1972   The Nimrud Wine Lists: A Study of Men
       and Administration at the Assyrian Capital
       in the Eighth Cent. B.C. London.
Winlock, H. E., et al.
1941   The Temple of Hibis in El-Khargeh Oasis, I.
       New York.

Winnicki, K.
1977   "Die Kalasirier der spätdynastischen Zeit und der ptolemaïschen Zeit." *Historia* 26: 257–68.
1989   "Militäroperationen von Ptolemaios I. und Seleukos I. in Syrien in der Jahren 312–311 v. Chr. I." *AncSoc* 20: 55–92.
1990   "Bericht von einem Feldzug des Ptolemaios I Philadelphos in der Pithom-Stele." *JJP* 20: 157–67.
1991   "Militäroperationen von Ptolemaios I. und Seleukos I. in Syrien in den Jahren 312–311 v. Chr. II." *AncSoc* 22: 147–201.
forthcoming   "Die von Persern entführten Götterbilder."
Wirth, G.
1971a   "Dareios und Alexander." *Chiron* 1: 133–52.
1971b   "Alexander zwischen Gaugamela und Persepolis." *Historia* 20/4: 617–32.
1972   "Die *syntaxeis* von Kleinasien 334 v. Chr." *Chiron* 2: 91–98.
1980   "Zwei Lager bei Gaugamela: Zur grossen Konfrontation 331 B.C." *QCSC* 2/3: 51–100; 2/4: 5–61.
Wiseman, D. J.
1952   "A new stela of Aššur-naṣir-pal II." *Iraq* 24: 24–37.
1953   "Mesopotamian gardens." *AnSt* 33: 137–44.
1956   *Chronicles of Chaldean Kings (626–556 B.C.) in the British Museum.* London.
1983   *Nebuchadrezzar and Babylon.* Oxford.
Wooley, L.
1962   *Ur Excavations,* IX.
Wörrle, M.
1976   "Telmessos in hellenistischer Zeit." Pp. 63–72 in *Actes du colloque sur la Lycie antique.* Paris.
1977   "Epigraphische Forschungen zur Geschichte Lykiens I." *Chiron* 7: 43–66.
1978   "Epigraphische Forschungen zur Geschichte Lykiens II: Ptolemaios II und Telmessos." *Chiron* 8: 203–46.
1979   "Epigraphische Forschungen zur Geschichte Lykiens III: Ein hellenistischen Königsbrief am Telmessos." *Chiron* 9: 83–111.
1988   "Inschriften von Herakleia am Latmos I: Antiochos III, Zeuxis und Kerakleia." *Chiron* 18: 421–70.
1991   "Epigraphische Forschungen zur Geschichte Lykiens IV: Drei griechische Inschriften aus Limyra." *Chiron* 21: 203–35.
1993   "Perikles von Limyra: endlich etwas mehr griechisches." Pp. 187–89 in J. Borchhardt and G. Dobesch (eds.), *Akten des II. Internationalen Lykien-Symposions.* ÖAW, Denkschr. 231. Vienna.
Wunsch, C.
1993   *Die Urkunden des babylonischen Geschäftsmannes Iddin-Marduk: Zum Handel mit*

Naturalien im 6. Jahrhundert v. Chr., I–II. Groningen.
Wylie, D.
1992   "Agesilaus and the battle of Sardis." *Klio* 74: 115–30.
Wylie, G.
1992   "Cunaxa and Xenophon." *AC* 61: 119–31.
Yamauchi, E. M.
1980a   "Two reformers compared: Solon of Athens and Nehemiah of Jerusalem." Pp. 269–92 in *The Bible World: Essays in Honour of C. H. Gordon.* New York.
1980b   "Was Nehemiah the cupbearer a eunuch?" *ZAW* 92: 132–42.
1990   *Persia and the Bible.* Grand Rapids, Michigan.
Yardeni, A.
1994   "Maritime trade and royal accountancy in an erased customs account from 475 B.C.E. on the Ahiqar scroll from Elephantine." *BASOR* 293: 67–78.
Yoffee, N.
1988   "The collapse of Ancient Mesopotamian states and civilization." Pp. 44–68 in N. Yoffee and G. L. Cowgill (eds.), *The Collapse of Ancient States and Civilizations.* Tucson.
Yon, M., and Caubet, A.
1993   "Arouad et Amrit: VIIIᵉ–Iᵉʳ siècles av. J.-C. Documents." *Trans* 6: 47–67.
Yon, M., and Snyczer, M.
1991   "Une inscription phénicienne royale de Kition (Chypre)." *CRAI*: 791–821.
1992   "A Phoenician victory trophy at Kition." *RDAC*: 157–65.
Young, R. S.
1953   "Making history at Gordion." *Archaeology*: 159–66.
Yoyotte, J.
1952   "la provenance du cylindre de Darius [B.M. 89.132]." *RAss* 46/3: 165–67.
1961   "Les principautés du delta au temps de l'anarchie libyenne (Études d'histoire politique)." Pp. 121–79 in *Mélanges Maspero, I: Orient ancien.* MIFAO 66. Cairo.
1962   "L'Égypte ancienne et les origines de l'antisémitisme." *Bull. Soc. E. Renan* 11: 133–43.
1972a   "Les inscriptions hiéroglyphique:. Darius et l'Égypte." *JA* 260/3–4: 253–56.
1972b   "Petoubastis III." *RdE* 24: 216–23.
1974   "Les inscriptions de Darius découvertes à Suse." *CDAFI* 4: 181–83.
1989   "Le nom égyptien du 'Ministre de l'Économie': de Saïs à Méroè." *CRAI*: 73–88.
1992   *Leçon inaugurale au Collège de France.* Chaire d'égyptologie. Paris.
1993   "1. Recherches de géographie historique et religieuse: sources et méthodes; 2. Naucratis égyptienne." Pp. 625–44 in *Annuaire du Collège de France* (Résumé des cours et travaux). Paris.

1994   "Le soubassement de Ptolémée Sôter." Pp.
        684–89 in *Annuaire du Collège de France*
        (Résumé des cours et travaux). Paris.
Zaccagnini, C.
1973   *Lo scambio dei doni nel Vicino Oriente du-*
        rante i secoli XV–XII. OAC 11. Rome.
1981   "Modo di produzione asiatico e Vicino
        Oriente antico: Appunti per une discus-
        sione." *DdA* 3: 3–65.
1983   "Patterns of mobility among Ancient Near
        Eastern craftsmen." *JNES* 42/4: 245–64.
1989   "Prehistory of the Achaemenid tributary
        system." Pp. 193–215 in Briant and Herren-
        schmidt (eds.).
1990   "The forms of alliance and subjugation in
        the Near East of the Late Bronze age." Pp.
        37–79 in *I trattati nel mondo antico:*
        Forma, ideologia, funzione (ed. L. Canfora,
        M. Liverani, and C. Zaccagnini). Rome.
Zadok, R.
1976   "On the connections between Iran and
        Babylonia in the sixth century B.C." *Iran*
        14: 61–78.
1977   "Iranians and individuals bearing Iranian
        names in Achaemenian Babylonia." *IOS* 7:
        89–138.
1978   "The Nippur region during the late Assyr-
        ian, Chaldean and Achaemenian periods
        chiefly according to written sources." *IOS*
        8 [1983]: 266–332.
1979   "'Arab' in Babylonia in the 6th cent. B.C."
        JAOS 94: 108–15.
1984   "Assyrians in Chaldean and Achaemenian
        Babylonia." *Assur* 4/3: 3–28.
1986   "Archives from Nippur in the first millen-
        nium B.C." Pp. 278–88 in Veenhof (ed.).
Zahle, J.
1976   "Lycian tombs and Lycian cities." Pp. 37–
        49 in *Actes du colloque sur la Lycie antique.*
        Paris.
1982   "Persian satraps and Lycian dynasts: The
        evidence of the diadems." Pp. 101–12 in
        Actes du 9ᵉ congrès international de numis-
        matique (Berne, septembre 1979). Louvain-
        Luxembourg.
1988   "Power and portrait: in the eldest coin-
        portraits in the world." *Nationalmuseets Ar-*
        bejdsmark: 155–66.
1989   "Politics and economy in Lycia during the
        Persian period." *REA* 91/1–2: 169–82.
1991   "Achaemenid influences in Lycia (coinage,
        sculpture, architecture): Evidence for po-
        litical changes during the 5th cent. B.C."
        AchHist 6: 145–60.
Zahrnt, M.
1992   "Der Mardonioszug des Jahres 492 v. Chr.
        und seine historische Einordnung." *Chiron*
        22: 237–79.
Zauzich, K. Th.
1983   "Die demotischen Papyri von der Insel El-
        ephantine." Pp. 421–35 in *Egypt and the*

Hellenistic World. Studia Hellenistica 27.
        Louvain.
1984   "Von Elephantine bis Sambehdet." *En-*
        chôria 12: 193–94.
Zawadski, S.
1986   "New data concerning *qīpu* and *sangû* of
        Ebabbar temple in Sippar in the Neo-
        Babylonian and Early Persian periods." *Eos*
        74: 85–89.
1988a   *The Fall of Assyria and Median-Babylonian*
        Relations in Light of the Nabopolassar
        Chronicle. Poznan-Delft.
1988b   "Umman-Manda: Bedeutung des terminus
        und Gründe seiner Anwendung in der
        Chronik von Nabopolassar." Pp. 379–87 in
        Šulmu (ed. P. Vavroušek and V. Souiek).
        Prague.
1990   "Great families of Sippar during the
        Chaldean and early Persian periods." *RAss*
        84: 2–25.
1992   "The date of the death of Darius I and the
        recognition of Xerxes in Babylonia."
        NABU, note 49.
1995a   "Is there a document dated to the reign of
        Bardiya II (Vahyazdāta)?" *NABU*, note 54.
1995b   "Chronology of the reigns of Nebuchad-
        nezzar III and Nebuchadnezzar IV."
        NABU, note 55.
1995c   "BM 63282: The earliest Babylonian text
        dated to the reign of Nebuchadnezzar IV."
        NABU, note 55.
Zecchini, G.
1989   "Entimo di Gortina (Athen. II.48d) e le
        relazioni greco-persiane durante la Pente-
        contaetia." *AncSoc* 20: 5–13.
1989   *La cultura storica di Ateneo.* Milan.
Zertal, A.
1990   "The Pahwah of Samaria (Northern Israel)
        during the Persian period: Types of settle-
        ment, economy, history and new discover-
        ies." *Trans* 3: 9–30.
Zervos, O. H.
1979   "Near Eastern elements in the tetra-
        drachms of Alexander the Great: The East-
        ern mints." Pp. 295–305 in Mørkholm-
        Waggoner (ed.).
Zettler, R. L.
1979   "On the chronological range of the Neo-
        Babylonian and Achaemenid seals." *JNES*
        38/4: 257–60.
Zimansky, P.
1995   "Xenophon and the Urartian legacy." Pp.
        255–58 in P. Briant (ed.), *Dans les pas des*
        Dix-Mille: Peuples et pays du Proche-Orient
        vus par un Grec (Actes de la Table ronde de
        Toulouse, 3–4 février 1995). Pallas 43.
Zimmermann, P.
1992   "Die lykischen Häfen und die Handels-
        wege im östlichen Mittelmeer." *ZPE* 92:
        201–17.

Index of Sources

Page numbers printed in bold type mark pages with a citation given *in extenso*.

Classical Sources

Aelian
   De natura animalium
      I.14   283–284
      II.11   291
      III.2   539
      III.13   186
      IV.21   396
      IV.41   263, 396
      IV.46   396, 520
      VI.25   798, 922
      VI.39   986
      VI.48   228
      VII.1   201, 911
      X.16   186
      XII.21   111
      XII.23   254
      XIII.17   201
      XIII.18   970
      XIII.21   330
      XV.26   189, 334, 361,
         402, 933
      XVI.25   253, 539
   Varia historia
      I.21   222, 511
      I.22   **307**, 312, 349, 669,
         934
      I.25   319, 856
      I.26.28   289
      I.27   291
      I.31–32   442, 511
      I.31–33   621
      I.31   **192, 223**, 317, **398**,
         442, 470, 942, 957
      I.32   192, 307, 317, 332–
         333, 398, 442–443,
         931
      I.33   192, 251, 289–291,
         676, 918, 935
      I.34   129, 333, **338**, 442,
         468, 508, 729
      II.14   **234**, 970
      II.17   96, 273, 290

Aelian, *Varia historia (cont.)*
      II.25   1050
      V.1   288, 291, 665
      VI.8   **270**, 688
      VI.14   231, 274, 298–
         299, **323**, 324, 352,
         751, 893
      VI.25   276
      VII.1   958
      VII.2   202, 672
      VII.8   1023
      VIII.8   305
      IX.3   256, 261
      IX.4   83
      IX.39   235
      IX.42   681
      X.14   894
      XII.1   257, 269, 278,
         279, 292, 314, 347,
         502, 522, 809, 890,
         917
      XII.39   **231**
      XII.40   317, 333, 847
      XII.43   82, 110, 112,
         310, 770–771, 1033
      XII.62   **317**, 511, 923
      XII.64   129, 522
      XIII.3   516, 542, 563,
         962
      XIII.7   1022
      XIV.12   423
      XIV.14   **188**
      XIV.46   922
      XIX.41   910
Aeschines
      III.164   826
      III.238   690
Aeschylus
   Persians
      2   324
      13–14   370
      74   527

Aeschylus, *Persians (cont.)*
      90   527
      249–56   370
      303–30   540
      327   498
      353–64   517
      441–44   517
      465–67   227
      469–70   517
      480–515   530
      510   517
      550   517
      555–56   517
      585–95   **517**
      596   517
      650   517
      665–70   517
      715–25   517
      728–31   517
      740ff.   517
      763   415
      765ff.   517
      770–75   98
      773–75   106
      776–77   898
      829–31   517
      853–55   517
      908–15   517
      934ff.   517
      956–960   901
      1000   361
   Alexander Romance
      II.15.8   912
      III.28.10   206
Ammianus Marcellinus
      XXIV.6.1   **207**
      XXIV.6.1–2   1019
      XXX.8.4   572, 959
Andocides
   Pace
      29   591
   Anth. Pal.   see Palatine Anth.

Appian
   Mithradatic Wars
      2.8   1025
      2.9   899
      9   134
      10   640
      12.66   **243**
Aristophanes
   Acharnians
      50ff.   312
   Frogs
      937   205
Aristotle
   Athenain Politeia
      22.1   160
   Historia Animalium
      VI.26.580b   201
      VIII.9   426
   Politica
      V.10.1311b   564–565
      VII.6   302
      VII.7   302
   Rhetorica
      II.20.3   907
[Aristotle]
   De Inund. Nili
      §6   1004
   De Mirabilibus Auscult.
      39a.15–26   208
   De Mundo
      398a   185, 205, 223,
         258, **259**, 298,
         327, 377, 396, 410,
         772
      398a 20–30   255
      398a 25   179
Pseudo-Aristotle
   Oeconomica
      I.6.1–3   389
      II.1.1–8   389
      II.1.2   452, 912
      II.1.3   419, 452, 455

1125

Biblical Sources

Elamite Tablets

Royal Inscriptions

Hieroglyphic Inscriptions

Aramaic Texts

Other Sources

Index of Personal Names

Demos 313
Demosthenes 657–658, 662, 689–690, 787–789, 792
Derbices 893
Dercyllidas 635, 637, 644–645
Derketo 917
Dibictus 790
Dion 668, 709
Dionysius (Greek commander) 155
Dionysius of Heraclea 699, 768
Dionysius of Syracuse 763
Dionysius the Elder 208, 906
Diophantus 786
Diotimus 382, 582
Diphridas 645–646
Djedherbes 1031
Djethotefankh (grandson of Djethotefankh the Elder) 861
Djethotefankh the Elder 861
Doloaspis 718
Dorates 678
Dorkis 555
Droaphernes 678, 704, 972, 1000–1001, 1009
Droysen, H. (historian) 2, 801, 1038
Drypetis 1044

Ea-bulliṭsu 461
Ea-iddin 601–602
Egibi 33, 72, 88, 381, 485–486, 882, 891, 933
Elli-šum-iddin 598
Elnap 502
Elnathan 488, 951
Engels, F. 802
Enlil-itannu 461
Entimus 297, 308, 310, 312, 315, 349
Ephialtes 557, 790
Ephorus 531, 557–558, 612, 618–619, 626, 775, 779, 784–788, 790, 792, 985, 1005, 1034–1035
Epilycus 591
Epixyes 368
Epyaxa 198, 360, 498, 610, 1013
Eratosthenes 382
Erbbina 670, 1012
    see also Arbinas
Erigyius 229, 732
Erttimeli 707
Erythras 758, 1028
Esarhaddon 271, 360, 372, 678, 685, 927, 954
Esemteu 81
Eškuš 431
Ešmunazar II 419, 490, 608, 713, 936, 952, 1015
Espemet 448–449, 456
Esther 129, 279, 282
Eteocles 230
Eudamus 756

Euelthon 489
Eumanes 703
Eumenes of Cardia 2, 133, 247, 371–372, 447, 452, 696, 711, 743, 746, 876, 943, 1025
Euphorbus 159
Eurybates 36, 882
Eurybiades 529
Eurysthenes 562
Evagoras 314, 321, 455, 611, 636, 647–653, 716, 985, 990–992, 1015
Ezekiel 46
Ezra 368, 511, 570, 578, 583–586, 928, 976, 992

Frāda 116–117, 120–121, 123, 125
Frādafarna 364
Fravartipāta 607
Fravartiš 116–121, 123, 125, 738

Gadal-lāma 598, 979
Gadatas (*Cyropaedia*) 259, 271, 276, 314
Gadatas (ML 12) 8, 201, 292, 303, 324, 401–402, 418, 459, 463, 491–493, 508, 605, 837, 856, 903, 906, 952
Gašmū 587, 977
Gastron 786
Gaubaruva 108
    see also Gobryas (one of the Seven)
Gaulites 626
Gaumata 91, 93, 96, 99–100, 103–105, 107–109, 113–116, 120–121, 125, 130, 137, 213, 770, 772, 895–896, 899
Gawzīna 364
Gergis 609, 670, 984, 996, 1012
Gilgamesh 938, 1025
Gillus 139
Gimillu 73, 75, 484, 892
Glaucippus 857
Glaucus 798
Glus 338, 361, 455, 626, 631–632, 652–653, 987–988
Gobares (= Gobryas [one of the Seven] or Gobryas [governor under Darius II and Artaxerxes II]) 467, 736, 850
Gobares (=Gobryas (one of the Seven or Gobryas (governor under Darius II and Artaxerxes II)) 892
Gobares (=Gobryas [one of the Seven] or Gobryas [governor under Darius II and Artaxerxes II]) 892, 988
Gobryas (compatriot of Cyrus II) 42, 881, 884
Gobryas (governor under Darius II and Artaxerxes II) 271, 601, 627, 629, 988

Gobryas (one of the Seven) 101, 107–108, 112–113, 121, 127–128, 131–132, 135–137, 142, 156, 170, 211, 214, 309–310, 331, 351–352, 518, 520, 557, 898, 902, 988
    see also Gaubaruva; Gubāru (satrap under Cyrus and Cambyses)
Gongylus 348, 561–562, 643, 969
Gorgion 561
Gorgus 151, 488–489
Gūbaru (governor of Gutium = Ugbaru) 41
Gūbaru (governor under Darius II) 392, 468, 601, 892, 988
    see also Gobares
Gubāru (satrap under Cyrus and Cambyses) 902
Gūbaru (satrap under Cyrus and Cambyses) 64, 66, 71–75, 82, 351, 810–811, 889–893, 898, 988
    see also Gaubaruva; Gobares
Guzānu 342–343, 485, 925
Gygaea 145, 350
Gyges 65, 80, 502, 892

Haephestion 225, 522, 729, 931, 1023–1024
Hakoris 634, 648, 650–653, 655, 675, 786, 982, 987, 992
Halpa 333, 466
Haman 303
Hammurabi 923, 934, 956–957
Hananī 448, 456, 586, 603, 714
Hanani (Nehemiah's brother) 584, 586, 604, 714
Hananiah 584
Hannibal 841
Haradduma 431
Harbamišša 351, 392
    see also Arbamisa
Harina (Aryaina) 21
Harišānu 485
Harmamithras 352
Harpagus 15, 31–32, 38, 64, 81, 155, 369, 501, 505, 583, 609, 670, 881, 883, 890, 893, 955, 968
Harpalus 202, 290, 760
Harrena 426, 439–440, 446, 465, 470, 940
Hatūbašti 462
Hecataeus of Miletus 148, 153, 155, 494, 817
Hecatomnids 668, 707, 714, 783, 991, 1011
Hecatomnus 646, 648, 650–651, 667, 669, 707, 991
Hecatonymus 378
Hegai 273, 282, 284
Hegelochus 825, 828–829, 832
Hegesistratus 547–548, 843, 847, 855

Index of Divine Names

Index of Geographical Names

Index of Ancient Words

Index of Topics